Handbook
for Reading
Social Studies

One of the most important things you will do in your study of Social Studies this year is read this textbook. In order to understand important facts and ideas in any subject area—Social Studies, or Science, or even Mathematics—it is necessary to read in a certain way. This Reading Handbook will show you a few strategies for effectively reading social studies.

Main Idea and Supporting Details

As you read, remember to look for the **main idea** and **supporting details**. The main idea is what a paragraph or section is mostly about. The details support or expand the main idea. Keeping track of the main idea and supporting details will help you remember what you read.

- The first sentence or two of a paragraph often—but not always—contains the main idea.

- Use the titles and subheads as a guide in identifying the main idea.

- Make an outline of the main idea and supporting details of a lesson to help you review.

To Find the Main Idea
Ask yourself:

- What is this paragraph or section mostly about?

To Find the Supporting Details
Ask yourself:

- What words give more information about the main idea?

In your book you will read about the agriculture and climate of Greece. Climate is the pattern of weather in a place over many years. Read this paragraph to find the main idea and supporting details.

> Besides having little fertile land, Greece has a climate that presents special challenges for farmers. Summers are hot and dry. Winters can be wet and fiercely windy. Fields can become parched in the summer but soaked with rain in the winter.
>
> *from page 194*

The *main idea* is how climate affects farming in Greece.

The *supporting details* include information about each season.

TRY IT!

Read this paragraph about farming in ancient Greece. Copy and complete the main idea and supporting details chart below.

> Ancient Greek farmers raised crops and animals that were well suited to this environment. They grew some wheat and barley to make bread, which was important to the Greek diet. Olives and grapes became Greece's other major crops. Both grew well in rocky and hilly areas. Shrubs on Greece's many hills and mountains provided food for herds of sheep, goats, and cattle.
>
> *from page 194*

Main Idea | Ancient Greek farmers raised crops and animals suited to the environment.

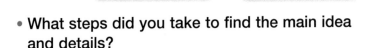

Details | Olives and grapes grew well in rocky, hilly areas. |

- What steps did you take to find the main idea and details?

Practice Activities

1 **READ** Read the first paragraph under the heading "A New Government" on page 237. Copy the chart above and record the main idea and supporting details of this paragraph.

2 **WRITE** Write a paragraph describing one aspect of your local environment. Be sure to use a main idea sentence and supporting details.

Keep in Mind...

For more help in reading social studies, try these strategies:

☑ **Reread**
Review each sentence carefully. Make sure you understand what each sentence means before you read further.

☑ **Look up unknown words**
Use a dictionary or the glossary in your book to find the meaning of any unfamiliar words or terms.

☑ **Form a mental picture**
As you read, think about what your reading would look like.

Context Clues

As you read a sentence or paragraph in your book, you may find a word or term that you do not know. One way to find the meaning of a new word is to look for **context clues.** Context clues are the words and sentences around the unfamiliar term. Using context clues helps you become a better reader.

To Use Context Clues
Ask yourself:

• What word is unfamiliar to me?

• What might the word mean?

• What other words, phrases, and sentences help me figure out the meaning of the new word?

• What information do these other words, phrases, and sentences provide?

In your book you will read about the climate of Arabia. Read the following paragraph and see how context clues can help you learn the meaning of the word *cloudbursts*.

TIP!

■ Have you heard this word before? How was it used?

■ Write down the context clues you used to find the meaning of the new word.

■ Use the new word in a sentence of your own to help you remember it.

Some of Arabia's deserts contain stone cliffs. Others have huge hills of sand. The world's largest continuous body of sand is on the Arabian peninsula. This region, called the Empty Quarter, is uninhabitable. Some parts have no rain for 10 years or more. Other parts enjoy winter cloudbursts that allow desert plants to grow. All of Arabia's deserts have a lack of water and oven-like summer heat.

from page 263

Clue:
Some parts don't have rain for 10 years.

Clue:
Cloudbursts allow desert plants to grow.

Word:
cloudbursts

TRY IT!

Read this paragraph from your book. Copy and complete the chart below to list context clues for the term *treaty*.

The world had come dangerously close to a nuclear war. In the following year, 1963, the two superpowers signed a treaty banning most kinds of nuclear weapons testing. World leaders hoped that the treaty would reduce the chance that nuclear weapons would ever be used in war.

from page 561

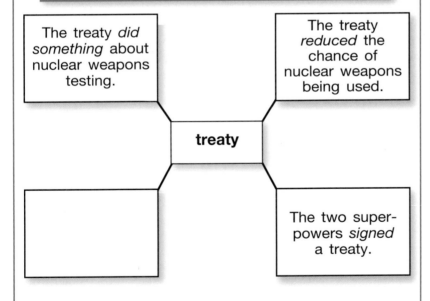

The treaty *did something* about nuclear weapons testing.

The treaty *reduced* the chance of nuclear weapons being used.

treaty

The two superpowers *signed* a treaty.

• How did you find the meaning of *treaty*?

Keep in Mind...

For more help in reading social studies, try these strategies:

☑ **Reread**
Review each sentence carefully. Make sure you understand what each sentence means before you read further.

☑ **Form the big picture**
As you read, think about the topic and the most important information in each paragraph section.

☑ **Make predictions**
As you read, think about what might happen next in your reading.

Practice Activities

1 **READ** Read the section of your book titled "Cultural Expansion" on page 404 of your book. Tell how you understood the word *expeditions*.

2 **WRITE** Write a short paragraph about an expedition you have made.

Sequencing

As you read, look for the order in which things happen. **Sequencing** events is listing them in the order in which they happen. Sequencing events helps you understand and remember what you read.

■ Look for dates—years, months, or centuries—that tell when events happened.

■ Look for words like *first*, *next*, *then*, *followed*, *finally*, *last*, *before*, and *later* to identify the order of events.

■ Use chapter time lines to help you remember the sequence of events.

To Use Sequencing

Ask yourself:

• **Which event happened first?**

• **Which event happened next?**

• **Which order of events makes sense?**

Read the following paragraph about archaeologists. Archaeologists study *artifacts*, or objects left by past groups of people. Pay attention to the sequence of events.

The archaeologists' first task was to make a detailed map of the location. They also took photographs showing where each artifact was found. Next, they used steam blowers and even hair dryers to melt snow and ice around the artifacts. The melted water was filtered three times. Archaeologists wanted to make sure that even the tiniest specks of evidence were not lost.

from page 34

First Event:
Make a map.

Second Event:
Take photographs.

Third Event:
Melt snow and ice.

Fourth Event:
Filter the melted water.

TRY IT!

Read this paragraph from your book about the Mogul Empire. Copy and complete the chart below to record the sequence of events.

> The Moguls were originally from Central Asia and may have been related to the Turks. In 1526 Moguls invaded the Indus plain. Within three years the Moguls controlled much of northern India . . . India's Mogul Empire would grow even bigger during its 235-year rule. At one time it would cover most of the Indian subcontinent. Much of that growth would take place under Akbar, the ruler whose name meant "Great" in Arabic.
>
> *from page 393*

1526 Moguls invaded Indus plain

▼

1529 they controlled northern India

▼

- **What steps did you take to determine the sequence of events?**

Keep in Mind...

For more help in reading social studies, try these strategies:

☑ **Look up unknown words**
Use a dictionary or the glossary in your book to find the meanings of any words you do not know.

☑ **Reread**
Review each sentence carefully. Make sure you understand what each sentence means before you read further.

☑ **Summarize**
In your own words, briefly describe what your reading is about. Look for topic sentences that contain the main ideas.

Practice Activities

1 READ Read the second and third paragraphs under "Hatshepsut's Trading Journey" on page 87 of your book. List the key events in sequence.

2 WRITE Write what steps you take to prepare for a vacation. Include the words *first*, *then*, *next*, and *finally*.

Make Predictions

As you read a paragraph or section in your book, think about what might come next. What you think will happen is your **prediction.** A prediction does not have a correct or incorrect answer. Making predictions helps you to carefully consider what you are reading.

- Think about other things you know that will help you make an "educated guess."

- Test your prediction: read further to see if you were correct.

- Revise your prediction: read further to see if more information changes your prediction.

To Make a Prediction

Ask yourself:

- What happened in this paragraph or section?

- What prior knowledge do I have about the events in the text?

- What similar situations do I know of?

- What do I think might happen next?

The lessons in this book begin with a Read Aloud. These sections are sometimes poems or quotations that give you an idea of the lesson subject. Read this Read Aloud to make a prediction about the following lesson.

Text Information:
The Ojibwa moved each season. They used the resources in different environments.

Background Information:
I know that European settlers changed Native Americans' way of life.

In the summer the Ojibwa lived by the waters of Lake Superior. When summer changed to autumn, they moved to the marshes where wild rice grew. They left the marshes before the heavy snows fell, living now near the herds that could be hunted. In spring sap flowed in the maple trees, and the Ojibwa came to collect it.

Like many of the peoples of North America, the Ojibwa moved their villages each season. This way of living allowed them to use many of the resources of their environment.

from page 440

Prediction:
The Ojibwa way of life will be changed because of the arrival of European settlers.

TRY IT!

Read this paragraph about a struggle for independence. On a separate sheet of paper, copy and complete the prediction chart below.

> "The force generated by nonviolence is infinitely greater than the force of all the arms invented by man's ingenuity."
>
> Mohandas Gandhi wrote these words during a period when Britain ruled his nation, India. His words describe a way of working toward independence without fighting battles that would harm and kill people. For many years Gandhi led the people of India in a largely nonviolent struggle against Britain.
>
> *from page 580*

Text Information

Gandhi said nonviolence was stronger than weapons.

Background Information

My Prediction

The nonviolent struggle will make the British leave India.

- On what did you base your prediction?

Keep in Mind...

For more help in reading social studies, try these strategies:

☑ **Sequencing**
As you read, think about the order in which things happened.

☑ **Form the big picture**
As you read, find the most important information about the topic in the paragraph or section.

☑ **Relate to personal experience**
Think about how what you are reading about relates to your own life.

Practice Activities

1 READ Read the paragraphs under the title "Working for Change" on page 608 of your book. Predict whether the sanctions will affect apartheid.

2 WRITE Write a short paragraph that predicts what high school might be like. Interview someone in high school to test your prediction.

Compare and Contrast

This book often **compares** and **contrasts** people or events. To compare things is to see how they are alike. To contrast things is to see how they are different. Comparing and contrasting helps you understand the relationships between things.

To Compare

Ask yourself:

• What are the things being compared?

• How are they alike?

To Contrast

Ask yourself:

• What are the things being contrasted?

• How are they different?

■ To compare, look for clue words such as *like*, *similar*, *in common*, *same*, and *resemble*.

■ To contrast, look for clue works such as *before*, *after*, *different from*, *unlike*, and *by contrast*.

In your book you will read about different parts of North and South America. Read this paragraph to compare and contrast parts of these continents.

The Western Hemisphere includes two cultural regions. The United States and Canada make up Anglo-America. This region was influenced strongly by British culture. Latin America includes Mexico, Central America, the Caribbean Islands, and South America. It was influenced by Spain, Portugal, and France.

from page 623

> **Contrast:**
> *The U.S. and Canada drew from British culture.*

> **Compare:**
> *Anglo America and Latin America are both cultural regions.*

> **Compare:**
> *Both regions were influenced by European countries.*

> **Contrast:**
> *Latin American countries drew from Spain, Portugal and France.*

TRY IT!

Read this paragraph about Europe in the early 1900s. Copy and complete the Venn diagram below, comparing and contrasting some European nations.

> In the early 1900s Europe was like a huge jigsaw puzzle. The "pieces" were nations. Some, such as Britain and France, had existed for centuries. Others, such as Italy and Germany, had been unified only in the 1800s.
>
> *from page 527*

Older Countries:

Alike: European countries

Newer Countries: Germany and Italy became unified countries in 1800s

• What steps did you take to compare and contrast?

Practice Activities

1 **READ** Read the first paragraph on page 577 of your book. Compare and contrast the two groups living in Palestine after World War II.

2 **WRITE** Write a paragraph in which you compare and contrast the activities on two recent weekends.

Keep in Mind...

For more help in reading social studies, try these strategies:

☑ **Look up unknown words**
Use a dictionary or the glossary in your book to find the meaning of any unfamiliar words.

☑ **Form the big picture**
As you read, think about the most important information of the paragraph or section.

☑ **Summarize**
In your own words, briefly describe what your reading is about.

Summarize

After you read a paragraph or section of this book, you can **summarize** what you have read. In a **summary**, you briefly tell in your own words about the most important information in the section. Summarizing is a way to help you understand what you read.

- Look for titles, headings, and key words that identify important information.

- Keep your summary brief, and organize the information in a clear way.

- Don't include information and facts that are not the most important.

To Summarize
Ask yourself:

- What is this paragraph or section about?

- What information is most important?

- How can I say this in my own words?

In your book you will read about the ancient civilization of the Maya. Read this paragraph and sample summary about life in a Maya city.

Boys and girls lived very differently in Copán. <u>When boys were in their teens, they moved out of their family homes into large group homes</u>. There <u>they learned to play the ball game</u>. <u>Boys also learned to become soldiers</u>. <u>Girls stayed at home</u>, where they were strictly raised by their mothers. <u>They learned how to cook maize and other food and how to run a household</u>.

from page 301

Summary:
Mayan teenage boys and girls lived in different homes. They learned different skills.

The important information is underlined.

TRY IT!

Read the following paragraph about an ancient Maya ball game. Copy and complete the diagram below to organize a summary of the paragraph.

Among the impressive structures at Copán is the ball court. Here a fierce Maya ball game, called *pokta-pok* (POHK tuh POHK), was played. Players wore helmets and padding on their arms and legs, for the game was rough. They were not allowed to touch the five-pound rubber ball with their hands. The two teams rushed up and down the court trying to get the ball through a stone hoop. If they succeeded, they won the game. Excited spectators filled the stands and gave clothing to the winning team.

from page 299

Important Information

| Players wore helmets and padding. |

My Summary

Pokta-pok was a fierce, exciting ball game. Fans rewarded the winners.

• How did you choose what to include in your summary?

Keep in Mind...

For more help in reading social studies, try these strategies:

☑ **Reread**
Review each sentence. Make sure you understand what each sentence means before you read further.

☑ **Form the big picture**
As you read, think about the topic and the main ideas of the paragraph or section.

☑ **Make an outline**
As you read, write an outline of the topic and the main ideas of the reading.

Practice Activities

1 READ Read and summarize the Legacy feature on page 304.

2 WRITE Think about a recent time when you went shopping. Write a summary of what happened.

Use Visuals

One way to learn from your reading is to use **visuals.** Visuals are the graphs, charts, pictures, and maps in your book. Visuals provide useful information in a clear, easy-to-study form.

- Read the caption and labels for information they provide.

- Look for objects in the picture that might give additional information.

- When looking at graphs, maps, or charts, be sure to read the legend or key to find the meanings of special symbols.

To Use Visuals

Look closely at the visual. Ask yourself:

- What does the graph, chart, picture, or map show?

- How does it help me to understand what I have read?

- How does it add to the information I have read?

- What information does the caption or labels provide?

You will read about the development of writing. Study this diagram showing the development of the Roman alphabet, which we use today.

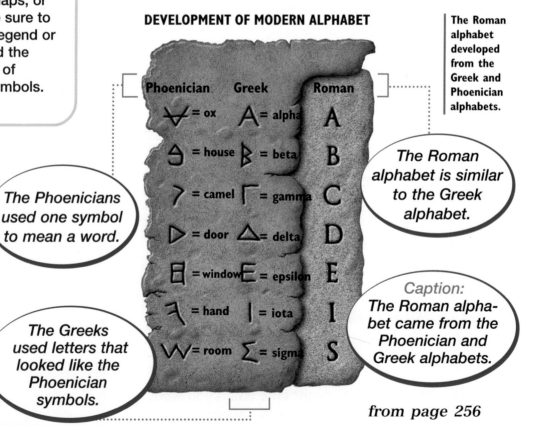

DEVELOPMENT OF MODERN ALPHABET

The Roman alphabet developed from the Greek and Phoenician alphabets.

Phoenician   Greek   Roman

= ox   = alpha   A
= house   = beta   B
= camel   = gamma   C
= door   = delta   D
= window   = epsilon E
= hand   = iota   I
= room   = sigma   S

The Phoenicians used one symbol to mean a word.

The Roman alphabet is similar to the Greek alphabet.

The Greeks used letters that looked like the Phoenician symbols.

Caption:
The Roman alphabet came from the Phoenician and Greek alphabets.

from page 256

TRY IT!

Study this picture of a crowd of people. On a sheet of paper, copy the chart below. Think about the information in the picture and complete the chart.

In the early days of television, not everyone was lucky enough to own their own set. Often, people would crowd sidewalks to watch.

from page 26

Caption Information:
Not everyone had a set so they watched where they could.

Visuals:

Visual Information:
People's clothes suggest late 1940s or early 1950s.

Visual Information:

Keep in Mind...

For more help in reading social studies, try these strategies:

☑ **Use Visuals**
Photographs and drawings of people and places will help you understand the reading.

☑ **Study the charts and graphs**
Charts and graphs provide information in an easy-to-understand form.

☑ **Study the unit and chapter openers**
The first page of a unit or chapter often summarizes what you will read about. It also may contain useful maps and pictures.

Practice Activities

1 **READ** Study the photo on page 494 in your book. What information do the caption and the visual provide?

2 **WRITE** Copy the chart above, and write what you learn from the pictures and caption on page 505 of your book.

World

ADVENTURES IN TIME AND PLACE

James A. Banks

Barry K. Beyer

Gloria Contreras

Jean Craven

Gloria Ladson-Billings

Mary A. McFarland

Walter C. Parker

NATIONAL
GEOGRAPHIC
SOCIETY

THIS IMAGE WAS CARVED ON THE
THRONE OF TUTANKHAMUN, WHO
RULED ANCIENT EGYPT MORE
THAN 3,000 YEARS AGO. THIS IS
ONE OF THE MANY IMAGES THAT
HELP TELL THE STORY OF OUR
WORLD'S HISTORY.

THE
PRINCETON
REVIEW

 **McGraw-Hill
School Division**

New York   Farmington

PROGRAM AUTHORS

Dr. James A. Banks
Professor of Education and
Director of the Center for
Multicultural Education
University of Washington
Seattle, Washington

Dr. Barry K. Beyer
Professor Emeritus, Graduate
School of Education
George Mason University
Fairfax, Virginia

Dr. Gloria Contreras
Professor of Education
University of North Texas
Denton, Texas

Jean Craven
District Coordinator of
Curriculum Development
Albuquerque Public Schools
Albuquerque, New Mexico

Dr. Gloria Ladson-Billings
Professor of Education
University of Wisconsin
Madison, Wisconsin

Dr. Mary A. McFarland
Instructional Coordinator of
Social Studies, K–12, and
Director of Staff Development
Parkway School District
Chesterfield, Missouri

Dr. Walter C. Parker
Professor and Program Chair for
Social Studies Education
University of Washington
Seattle, Washington

NATIONAL
GEOGRAPHIC
SOCIETY
Washington, D.C.

PROGRAM CONSULTANTS

Daniel Berman
Asian Studies Specialist
Coordinator of Social Studies
Bedford Central Schools
Bedford, New York

Dr. Khalid Y. Blankinship
Affiliated Scholar, Council on Islamic
Education
Fountain Valley, California
Assistant Professor of Religion
Temple University
Philadelphia, Pennsylvania

Dr. John Bodnar
Professor of History
Indiana University
Bloomington, Indiana

Dr. Roberto R. Calderón
Department of Ethnic Studies
University of California at Riverside
Riverside, California

Dr. Sheilah Clarke-Ekong
Asst. Professor, Department of
Anthropology and Research Associate,
Center for International Studies
University of Missouri, St. Louis
St. Louis, Missouri

Dr. John L. Esposito
Professor of Religion and International
Affairs
Georgetown University
Washington, D.C.

Dr. Darlene Clark Hine
John A. Hannah Professor of History
Michigan State University
East Lansing, Michigan

Paulla Dove Jennings
Project Director
The Rhode Island Indian Council, Inc.
Providence, Rhode Island

Dr. Henrietta Mann
Professor of Native American Studies
University of Montana, Missoula
Missoula, Montana

Dr. Gary Manson
Professor, Department of Geography
Michigan State University
East Lansing, Michigan

Dr. Juan Mora-Torrés
Professor of Latin American History
University of Texas at San Antonio
San Antonio, Texas

Dr. Valerie Ooka Pang
Professor, School of Teacher Education
San Diego State University
San Diego, California

Dr. Joseph R. Rosenbloom
Professor, Classics Department
Washington University
St. Louis, Missouri

Dr. Joseph B. Rubin
Director of Reading
Fort Worth Independent School District
Fort Worth, Texas

Dr. Robert M. Seltzer
Professor of Jewish History
Hunter College of The City University
of New York
New York, New York

Dr. Peter N. Stearns
Dean, College of Humanities and
Social Studies
Carnegie Mellon University
Pittsburgh, Pennsylvania

CONSULTING AUTHORS

Dr. James Flood
Professor of Teacher Education,
Reading and Language Development
San Diego State University
San Diego, California

Dr. Diane Lapp
Professor of Teacher Education,
Reading and Language Development
San Diego State University
San Diego, California

GRADE-LEVEL CONSULTANTS

Dianne C. Baker
Sixth Grade Teacher
Ingleside Middle School
Phoenix, Arizona

Maureen F. Barber
Sixth and Seventh Grade
Social Studies Teacher
Center Based Gifted Program
Manchester Middle School
Chesterfield, Virginia

David H. Delgado
Sixth Grade Social Studies Teacher
Rogers Middle School
San Antonio, Texas

Martha Doster
Sixth Grade Teacher
Northwest Rankin Attendance Center
Brandon, Mississippi

Joyce Garbe Orland
Sixth–Eighth Grade Teacher and Chair-
person, Social Studies Department
Pershing School
Berwyn, Illinois

CONTRIBUTING WRITERS

Ruth Akamine Wassynger
Winston-Salem, North Carolina

Spencer Finch
Brooklyn, New York

Linda Scher
Raleigh, North Carolina

CONSULTANTS FOR TEST PREPARATION

THE
PRINCETON
REVIEW
The Princeton Review is not affiliated
with Princeton University or ETS.

Acknowledgments

The publisher gratefully acknowledges permission to reprint the following copyrighted material:

From **Lost Civilizations: Sumer: Cities of Eden** by the editors of Time-Life Books. Copyright 1993 Time-Life Books, Inc. Reprinted by permission.
From **Tropical Rainforests** by Arnold Newman. Text copyright 1990 Arnold Newman. Reprinted with permission of Facts On File, Inc., New York.
From **The Iliad of Homer: The Wrath of Achilles**, translated by I.A. Richards, Translation copyright 1950 by W.W. Norton & Company, Inc.,
renewed 1978 by I.A. Richards. Reprinted with permission of W.W. Norton & Company, Inc.
Excerpts from **Corpus of Early Arabic Sources for West African History.** Copyright University of Ghana, International Academic Union,
Cambridge University Press 1981. Reprinted with the permission of Cambridge University Press.

(continued on page R79)

McGraw-Hill School Division ✂

A Division of The **McGraw-Hill** *Companies*

McGraw-Hill School Division
Two Penn Plaza
New York, New York 10121

Printed in the United States of America

ISBN 0-02-149138-0

9 027/046 04 03 02

CONTENTS

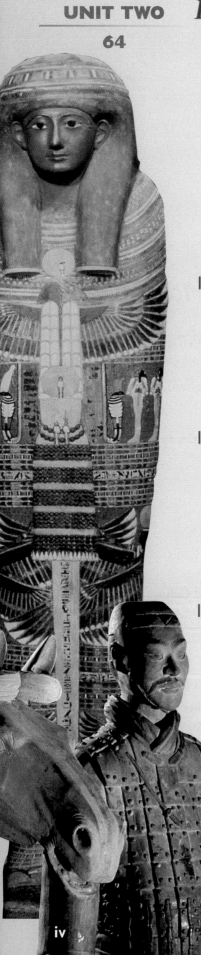

UNIT TWO *River Valley Civilizations*

64

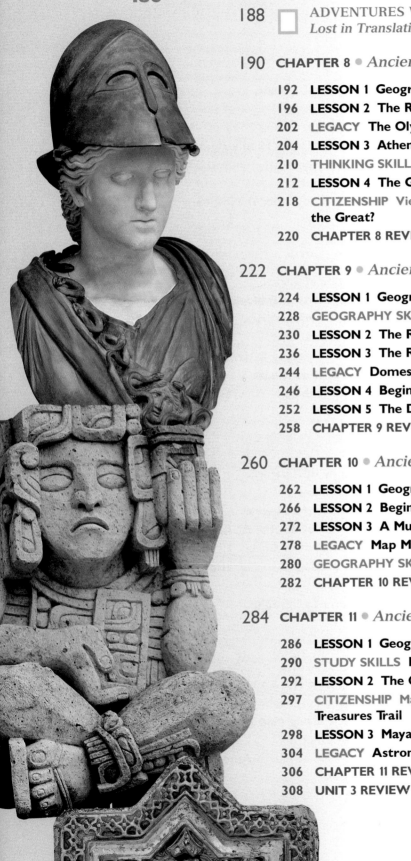

UNIT THREE New Ideas and New Empires
186

UNIT FOUR
310

World Regions in Transition

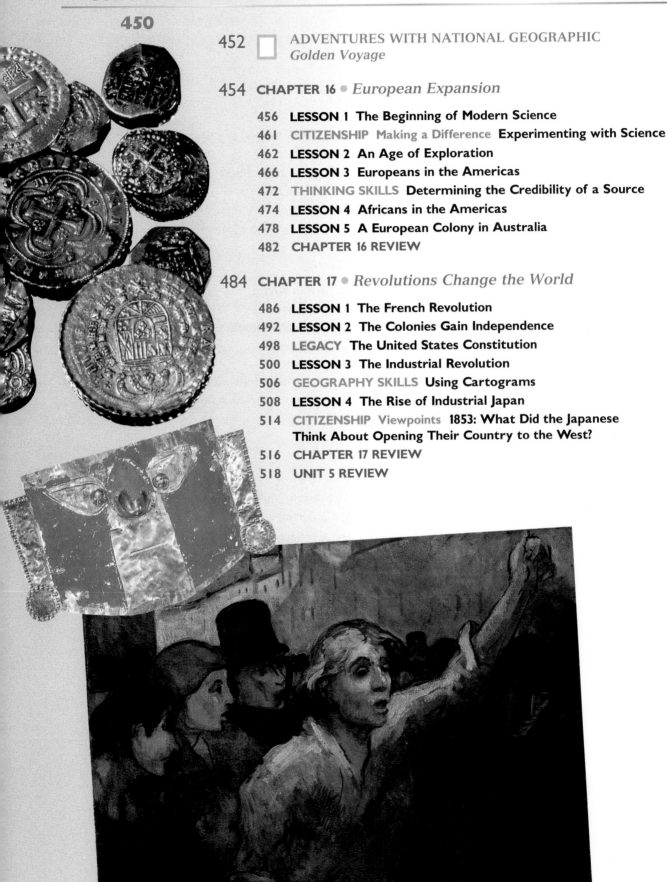

UNIT FIVE *Dawn of the Modern World*

450

UNIT SIX *A Century of Conflict*

520

REFERENCE

STANDARDIZED TEST SUPPORT

THE PRINCETON REVIEW

FEATURES

CHARTS, GRAPHS, & DIAGRAMS

TIME LINES

MAPS

YOUR TEXTBOOK at a glance

Your textbook is called *World: Adventures in Time and Place*. It has 20 chapters, each with two or more lessons. There are also many special features for you to study and enjoy.

NATIONAL GEOGRAPHIC

Five Themes of Geography

Location
How do these bicyclists know they are entering another country?

Place
What makes the Netherlands different from other places?

▲ **Special pages right after these two pages and before each unit bring you ideas and Adventures in geography with National Geographic.**

hes the forest floor. In the cooler forests of tierra templada, clouds etimes blanket the entire forest.

ople in Middle America
The first people in Middle America obably arrived about 11,000 years o. Small knives and arrow points ve been found in the Central Plateau. ese stone tools were left in caves by rly hunter-gatherers. Early athered onions, squash, an nd hunted rabbits and deer eople in other parts of the noved around in search of

WHY IT MATT
After the first people came i Beringia to North America, moved southward to Middle The diverse lands of this reg ed a warm climate and abur These resources made Midd ideal for human settlement. lesson you will read about c many groups of people who civilization on this land.

Reviewing Facts a

MAIN IDEAS
• The first people in the An have come from Asia acr Beringia land bridge abou 25,000 years ago.

DID YOU KNOW?

How hot WAS it?
To learn about recent changes in climate, scientists often look at written records. By studying records, such as the dates of cherry blossom festivals in Japan or harvest records in France,

WHY IT MATTERS
The region called Mesopotamia is not naturally an inviting place to live. Yet it was here that one of the world's earliest civilizations developed. Water and soil brought by the Tigris and the Euphrates helped to make this civilization possible. Even more important were the farmers of ancient Mesopotamia. These early farmers figured out how to use the two rivers to make the land more fertile.

As in some other early cultures, the farmers of Mesopotamia produced surplus crops. These surpluses allowed for specialization, which in turn led to the growth of towns and cities. The early cities formed a great civilization. As you will see, the legacy of early Mesopotamian civilization reaches even into our own times.

Links to CURRENT EVENTS

High Water!
Do floods still destroy people's homes and property today?

Unfortunately, despite the existence of modern dams, the answer is yes. In 1997, after an unusually harsh winter, melting snow caused severe spring flooding of the Red River in North Dakota. Volunteers worked together to build dikes, sometimes in the middle of town, to stop the river from overflowing further into their neighborhoods. The federal government committed over $150 million to help North Dakotans rebuild their lives.

Find another example of a flood in modern times. When and where did this flood occur? Your teacher can show you how to research recent newspapers to learn more about current events.

FLOODS!

Reviewing Facts and Ideas

MAIN IDEAS
• Mesopotamia is the region between the Tigris and Euphrates rivers. It is divided into a rugged plateau to the north and fertile plains to the south.
• Like the Nile River, the Tigris and the

THINK ABOUT IT
1. What were the main crops grown in ancient Mesopotamia? What other foods were grown there?
2. Why was the timing of spring floods so important to farmers in ancient Mesopotamia? What could happen to crops if the floods came a little earlier

---

LESSON 2

509 B.C.	100 B.C.	A.D. 1	A.D. 250	A.D. 500

The Rise of the Roman Republic

Read Aloud
The Roman leader Cicero declared that Rome should be governed by its "best" citizens. But just who were Rome's "best" citizens? Were they the city's small circle of nobles? Or did they also include the many other citizens, poor and rich, who contributed to life in Rome? The way Romans answered this question would shape their lives and ours.

Focus Activity

READ TO LEARN
What kind of government did the Romans establish?

VOCABULARY
• plebeian
• patrician
• republic
• representative
• Senate
• tribune
• consul
• Twelve Tables
• Punic Wars

PEOPLE
• Livy
• Hannibal
• Scipio

PLACES
• Forum
• Carthage
• Zama

230

THE BIG PICTURE

Almost 3,000 years ago, when the city of Anyang in China was losing power, Rome was only a cluster of mud huts on the hills overlooking the Tiber River. From the hilltops, farmers could enjoy a view of two small lakes that rippled in the valley below. The sound of lowing cattle drifted across the marshland at the river's edge.

By 509 B.C. Romans had overthrown their king, Tarquinius. They began setting up a new government in which citizens played a larger part. Their community became a city. A wooden bridge now crossed the Tiber River. The valley's marshland was drained and served as a busy market and meeting place.

High atop one of Rome's hills stood a stone temple as big as any in Greece. On other hilltops, fine brick homes housed Rome's wealthy. Some Romans clearly had become richer than others. The division between rich and poor, powerful and not so powerful, would affect the shape of the new government Romans were creating for themselves.

◀ **Some lessons have features called Links or Did You Know—activities to try and interesting information to share.**

Look for a variety of lessons and features. **Infographics** bring you information with pictures, charts, graphs, and maps. You will build your **Skills**, learn about **Legacies** that connect us to the past, and meet people who show what **Citizenship** is. ▶

THE CITIZENS OF ROME

As in Greece, society in Rome was divided into two groups: those who were citizens and those who were not. At first, Rome had few slaves. The city did have many women, but none of them were citizens.

The body of citizens included two groups. Most Roman citizens were plebeians (plih BEE unz). Plebeians were men who farmed, traded, and made things for a living. The second group was made up of Rome's handful of patricians (puh TRISH unz). Patricians were members of Rome's noble families. They owned large farms and had plebeians work the land for them.

Plebeians Protest

After Rome's last king was overthrown in 509 B.C., the patricians took power. As they did this they remade the city's government. Only patricians could belong to a ruling assembly or become government leaders.

Rome's many plebeians reacted to the patricians' rules with protest. According to the Roman historian Livy,

---

A patrician woman had no voice in Rome's government.

---

plebeians rebelled in 494 B.C., demanding changes in the government. To calm them down, Livy wrote, the patricians sent a popular leader to speak with the plebeians. He told them this story. How do you suppose the plebeians reacted?

MANY VOICES
PRIMARY SOURCE

Excerpt from
Stories of Rome, Livy, c. 20 B.C.

*Once upon a time, the different parts of the human body were not all in agreement. . . . And it seemed very unfair to the other parts of the body that they should worry and sweat away to look after the belly. After all, the belly just sat there . . . doing nothing, enjoying all the nice things that came along. So they hatched a plot. The hands weren't going to take food to the mouth; even if they did, the mouth wasn't going to accept it. . . . They went into a **sulk** and waited for the belly to cry for help. But while they waited, one by one all the parts of the body got weaker and weaker. The moral of this story? The belly too has its job to do. It has to be fed, but it also does feeding of its own.*

sulk: to be in a bad mood and stay silent

A New Government

According to Livy both sides in time agreed to work together to improve Rome's government. The new government was called a republic, which means "public things" in Latin. Latin was the language of ancient Rome. In a republic citizens choose their leaders.

231

Use the **Reference Section** at the end of your book to look up words, people, and places. This section includes the **World History Time Lines** and a table of **Countries of Our World.** ▼

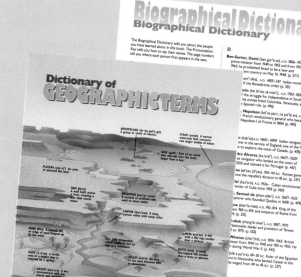

▲ Lessons begin with a **Read Aloud** selection and **The Big Picture.** Study the **Read to Learn** question and list of words, people, and places. Enjoy **Many Voices**—writings, songs, and art by various people.

NATIONAL GEOGRAPHIC

Five Themes of Geography

Location
How do these bicyclists know they are entering another country?

Stop
Border Open
7 A.M. To 10 P.M.

Place
What makes the Netherlands different from other places?

Human/Environment Interactions
How have people changed this landscape in Indonesia?

Region
What are some things that help make the Middle East a special region?

Movement
How do goods travel from place to place?

Reviewing
GEOGRAPHY SKILLS

PART 1
Using Globes

VOCABULARY

continent	meridian
hemisphere	prime meridian
equator	latitude
longitude	parallel

What do globes show?

- A globe is a model that shows Earth as it looks when seen from outer space.

- A globe shows Earth's seven continents, or large bodies of land. They are Africa, Antarctica, Asia, Australia, Europe, North America, and South America. Which continents are shown on this globe?

- Much of Earth is covered by four oceans, or large bodies of salt water. They are the Atlantic, Arctic, Indian, and Pacific oceans. Which oceans do you see on the globe? Which continents and oceans are not shown?

What is a hemisphere?

- A globe, much like Earth, is in the shape of a ball or sphere. Looking at a globe from any direction, you can see only half of it. *Hemi* is a Greek word for "half." Hemisphere means "half a sphere."

- Geographers divide Earth into the four hemispheres shown at the top of the next page.

- An imaginary line dividing the world into the Northern Hemisphere and Southern Hemisphere is called the equator. It lies halfway between the North Pole and South Pole. Which continents are in the Northern Hemisphere? In the Southern Hemisphere?

- Geographers divide Earth into the Eastern and Western hemispheres. Which hemi-

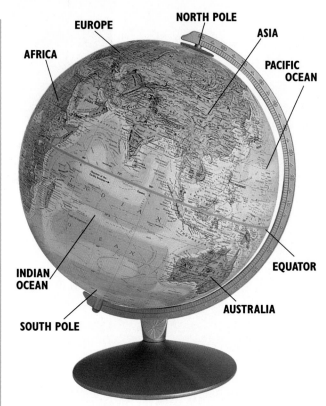

sphere includes all of Africa? Which hemisphere does not include Antarctica?

How are longitude and latitude useful?

- You can locate places on a map or globe by using a grid of imaginary lines.

- Running north to south are longitude lines, or meridians. These imaginary lines measure the distance east and west of the prime meridian. The unit of measurement is degrees. Look at the map at the bottom of the next page. What is the longitude of Cape Town?

- Running east to west are latitude lines, or parallels. These show distance in degrees north and south of the equator. What are the latitude and longitude of Mexico City?

More Practice

You can find longitude and latitude lines on many maps in this book. For examples, see pages 9, 12, and 13.

THE HEMISPHERES

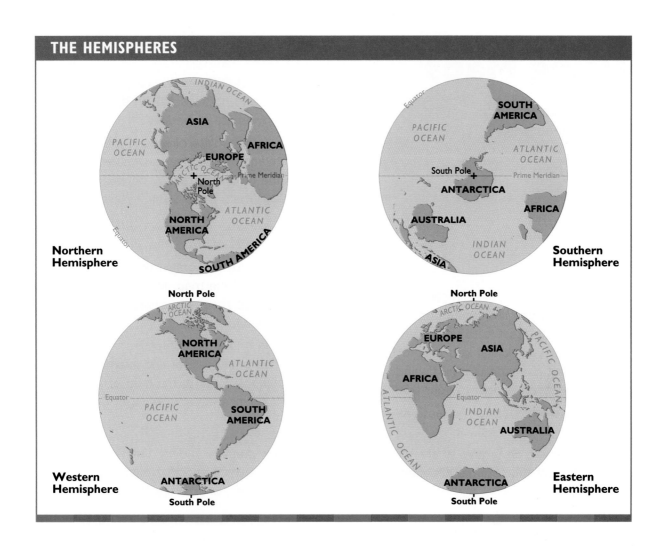

Northern Hemisphere

Southern Hemisphere

Western Hemisphere

Eastern Hemisphere

GLOBAL GRID

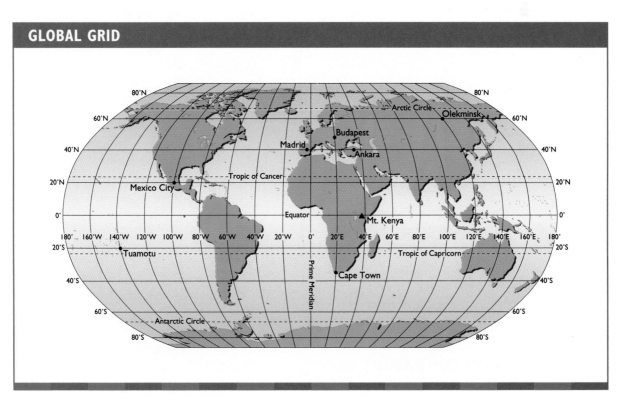

PART 2

Using Maps

VOCABULARY
cardinal directions
intermediate directions
compass rose
scale
symbol
map key
locator

What are cardinal directions?

- When you face in the direction of the North Pole, you are facing north. Behind you is south. East is to your right and west is to your left. If you turn to face east, what direction is now behind you? What direction is now to your left?

- There are four cardinal directions–north, south, east, and west.

- The letters **N**, **S**, **E**, and **W** are often used to represent the cardinal directions. What does **W** stand for?

How can you determine intermediate directions?

- Northeast (**NE**), southeast (**SE**), southwest (**SW**), and northwest (**NW**) are called intermediate directions.

- The intermediate directions are halfway between the cardinal directions. Northeast is the direction halfway between north and east. Where does **SE** lie?

How can you find directions on maps that do not include the North Pole?

- Most maps are drawn with north toward the top of the map. Many also include a compass rose, a drawing that shows directions.

- In this book, the compass rose usually shows both cardinal and intermediate directions. Look at the map of Australia. Which cities are southwest of Canberra?

More Practice
You can practice finding directions and using a compass rose on most maps in this book. For examples, see pages 105, 225, and 355.

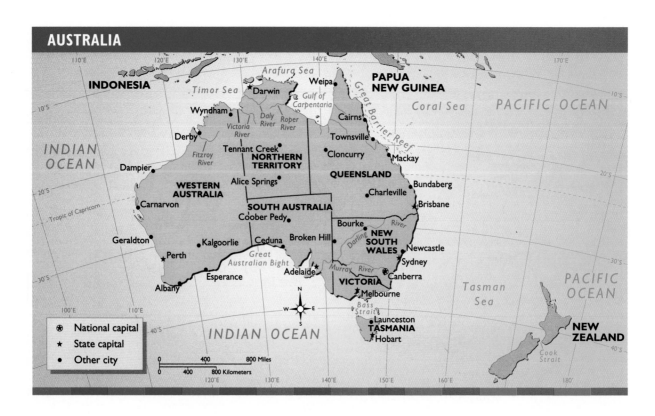

MAP A: TRINIDAD AND TOBAGO

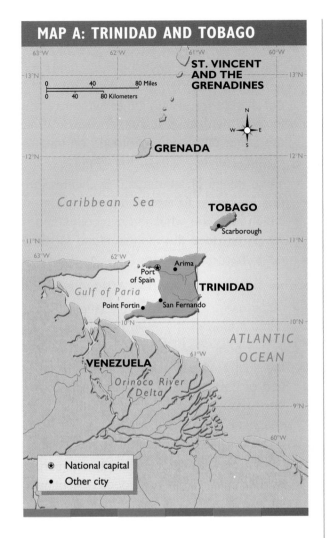

MAP B: TRINIDAD AND TOBAGO

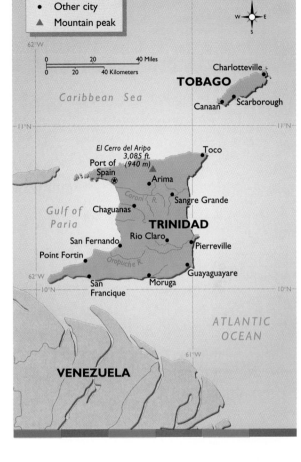

What is a map scale?

- Maps are always smaller than the actual places they show. The scale tells you how much smaller the distance on a map is compared with the actual distance.

- Map scales in this book include two lines for measuring distances. Which unit of measurement does each line show?

How do you use a scale? Why are map scales sometimes different?

- You can use a ruler to measure distances on a map.

- To determine the distance in miles between San Fernando and Scarborough, measure the length on the scale that represents 80 miles on Map A. The length is one inch. Now measure the distance between San Fernando and Scarborough

in inches. Multiply the result by 80 to determine the distance. What is the distance between the two cities?

- Different maps often show the same area using different scales. Map A and Map B both show the Caribbean country of Trinidad and Tobago. However, the islands look larger on Map B. They look larger because one inch stands for fewer miles on the Map B scale than on the A scale. The larger scale allows more details to be shown. What kinds of details are shown on Map B that are not on Map A?

More Practice

Most of the maps in the book show map scales. For example, see pages 76, 135, and 403.

ARGENTINA: Resources

Key:
- ✳ National capital
- • Other city
- ▲ Oil
- 🜂 Natural gas
- PbZn Lead and Zinc

0 200 400 Miles
0 200 400 Kilometers

What information does a map key give?

- Maps often use symbols to give information. A symbol is anything that stands for something else. On many maps a black dot stands for a city. Other symbols include triangles, squares, and lines. What are some other symbols found on maps?

- Symbols do not always stand for the same things on all maps. For this reason it is important to read the map key, which tells you what the symbols stand for. What does the triangle stand for on each map on this page?

How do locators help in studying maps?

- Maps use locators to show where the subject area of the main map is located.

- In this book the locator is a small map in the shape of a globe or a rectangular portion of Earth's surface. The area of the main map is shown in red. What is the shape of Switzerland's locator?

- Some locators show a hemisphere. Others may show a continent, a region, or a country. What area does Argentina's locator show?

More Practice

You will see many keys and locators. For examples of map keys, see pages 172, 280, and 281. For examples of locators, see pages 287, 385, and 601.

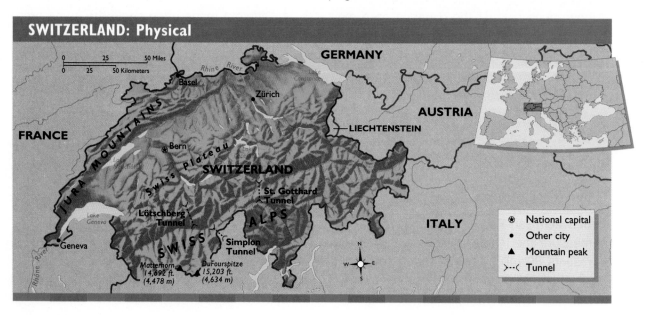

SWITZERLAND: Physical

0 25 50 Miles
0 25 50 Kilometers

Key:
- ✳ National capital
- • Other city
- ▲ Mountain peak
- ⟩··⟨ Tunnel

PART 3

Different Kinds of Maps

VOCABULARY

political map   relief map
physical map   historical map
elevation map   distribution map

Why are there different kinds of maps?

- Maps differ in the kinds of information they give. This section will cover four kinds of maps.

- When studying a map, first look at the map title. It will tell you the subject area and the type of information provided. What subject area does the map below show?

- A map may include areas that are not part of its subject area. In this book such areas are shown in gray. What countries are not in the subject area of the map below?

What is a political map?

- A political map shows information such as countries, states, cities, and other important political features. Although many maps include national or state boundaries, a political map may also use colors to highlight countries or states.

- Look at the map below. What color is used to show Nepal? How many different colors are used to show countries? What countries have disputed borders? What are the capital cities of those countries?

More Practice

You can find other political maps in this book. For examples, see pages 528, 576, and 623.

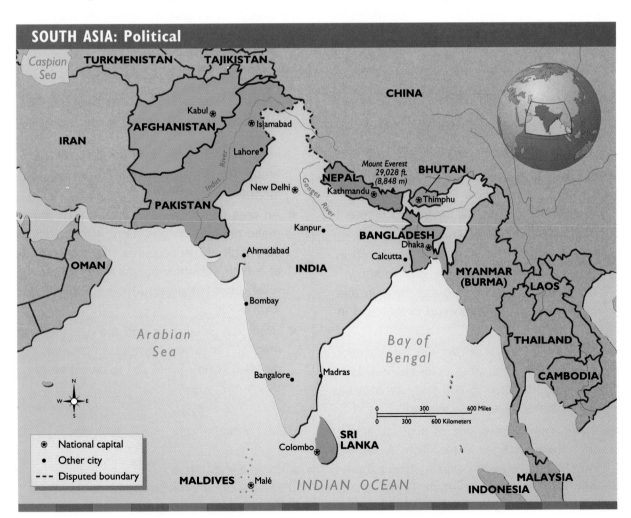

SOUTH ASIA: Political

- ⊛ National capital
- • Other city
- --- Disputed boundary

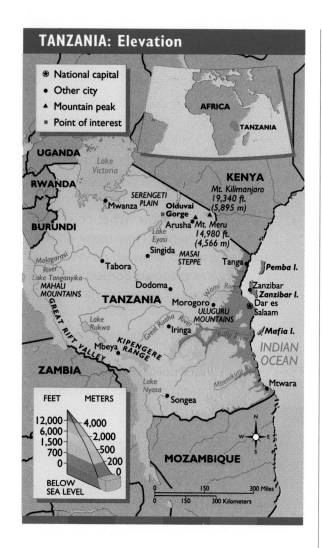

TANZANIA: Elevation

- ⊛ National capital
- • Other city
- ▲ Mountain peak
- ▪ Point of interest

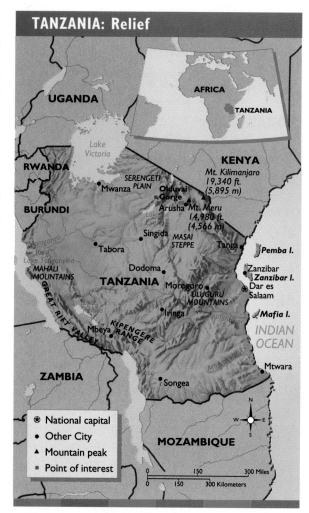

TANZANIA: Relief

- ⊛ National capital
- • Other City
- ▲ Mountain peak
- ▪ Point of interest

What do different kinds of physical maps show?

- **Physical maps** show Earth's natural features. This section will cover two different kinds of physical maps.

- One type of physical map is an **elevation map**. Elevation maps use color to show the height of land above sea level. In this book elevation is measured in feet and in meters.

- Look at the maps above. On the elevation map of Tanzania, what color represents the elevation of 0 to 700 feet? What areas of Tanzania have this elevation?

- **Relief maps** are a kind of physical map that show changes in elevation. Areas with no shading represent places where there are no changes in elevation. Lightly shaded areas show places where changes are

very gradual. Dark shading represents areas with sharp changes in elevation, such as a steep hill.

- An area can show a lot of relief, or dramatic changes in elevation, without being very high above sea level. An area can be at a high elevation but have very little relief, as a flat plateau high above sea level does.

- Study the relief map and the elevation map of Tanzania. What area has the greatest relief? What is the elevation of this area?

More Practice

There are other physical maps in this book. For examples, see pages 71, 131, and 317.

What is an historical map?

- Maps that show information about the past or where past events took place are called historical maps.

- The map title tells you the subject of the map. Many of the historical maps in this book include dates in the title or in the key. Study the map of the United States' expansion below, in the middle of the page. Between what dates did the expansion shown in this map occur? By what year did the United States own land west of the Mississippi River?

What is a distribution map?

- Distribution maps show how things such as language, religion, population, and rainfall are distributed throughout an area.

- The map key on the distribution map below shows colors that represent kinds of plants found in Russia. What kind of plants cover the largest area of land?

More Practice

You can find many different kinds of maps in this book. For historical maps, see pages 280, 281, and 464. For distribution maps, see pages 345, 370, and 371.

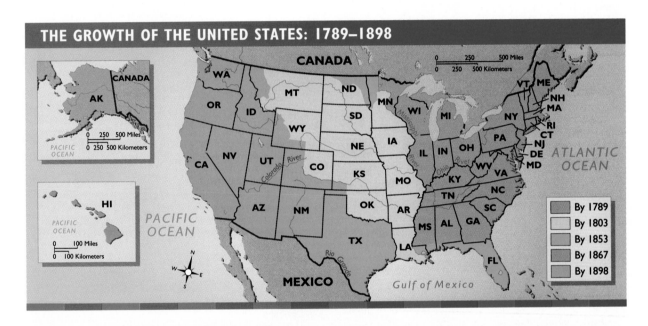

THE GROWTH OF THE UNITED STATES: 1789–1898

By 1789
By 1803
By 1853
By 1867
By 1898

RUSSIA: Vegetation

Deciduous Forest
Evergreen Forest
Grassland
Desert Vegetation
High Mountain Vegetation
Tundra

NEAR LIFE-SIZED CHESS PIECES, INDIA;
PYRAMID AND SPHINX, EGYPT

Understanding the World

"My imagination was caught by the great age of the world."

from Self Made Man by Jonathan Kingdon
See page 44.

Why Does It Matter?

These are the words of scientist Jonathan Kingdon, who was born and grew up in East Africa. They could also be the thoughts of anyone who has imagined what life was like hundreds or even thousands of years ago. How did people live? What did they eat? What was their land like? People have always wanted to know what things were like for those who lived before them.

Thanks to historians and other scholars, answers to many of these questions are being discovered. Objects made by ancient people have been uncovered all over the world. These objects reveal mysteries of the distant past. They also help us to better understand who we are.

INDIA OLMEC SCULPTURE, MEXICO

FIND OUT MORE!
Visit our website:
www.mhschool.com

inter**NET**
CONNECTION

Adventures with
with
NATIONAL
GEOGRAPHIC

Stony Silence

Some of the stones have toppled. But others still stand, tall and mysterious, on this plain in southern England—just as they have for thousands of years. Who built Stonehenge? How were the 50-ton stones transported to this place and raised up by prehistoric people using only simple tools? And, perhaps more mysterious, why? Some archaeologists suggest that Stonehenge may have been a temple that marked the movements of the sun. But we may never know for sure.

GEO JOURNAL

If you could talk to one of the workers who helped build Stonehenge long ago, what questions would you ask?

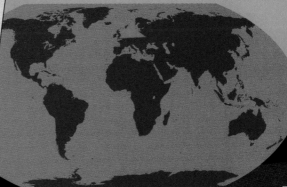

CHAPTER 1

Regions of the World

THINKING ABOUT GEOGRAPHY AND CULTURE

What do you think of when you see a photo of Earth from outer space? Try imagining a world of over 6 billion people, living in thousands of places. Some may have lives much like yours. People's lives may be as different as night and day. These differences, as well as the similarities, tell the great story of the world's regions and cultures.

China
ASIA

Farmers in China have long used terraces like these in Guangxi to farm in hilly areas. The rice grown in these southern terraces feeds millions of people.

Namibia
AFRICA

Southern Africa has many busy harbors like this one at Lüderitz. People along Africa's coasts have traveled and traded by sea for hundreds of years.

Austria
EUROPE

The town of Sankt Gallen lies high in the southern Alps. The people who settled these fertile mountain valleys have long been famous for their herding and dairy farms.

Canada
THE AMERICAS

This icy plain in the Arctic is part of a vast area of awesome beauty. Plants and animals like this polar bear have had to adapt to the Arctic's unique environment.

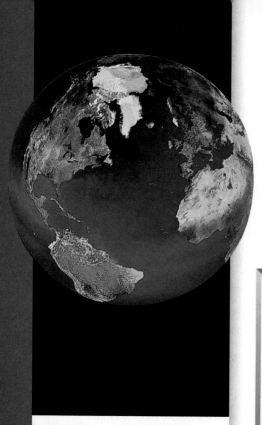

World Regions

Read Aloud

How many different living areas do you pass through each day? Bedroom, bathroom, kitchen, classroom, gym, lunchroom . . . all of these areas serve different purposes in your life. When you stop and think about them, these areas, or regions, also reveal a great deal about who you are. The world, too, is divided into many different regions. They can tell us much about what life is like all across planet Earth.

Focus Activity

READ TO LEARN

What does studying regions tell us about the world?

VOCABULARY

- geography
- region
- landform
- climate
- culture

THE BIG PICTURE

Learning about life on planet Earth—that's what **geography** is all about. Geography is the study of Earth, how it shapes people's lives and is shaped in turn by people's activities. In fact, the word *geography* comes from a Greek word that means "Earth writing," or "writing about Earth."

You don't have to be in a classroom to learn about geography. Geography is a part of almost everything you do. When you coast down a hill on your bike, splash in a pool on a hot summer day, or wipe frost from a window in winter, you are experiencing part of geography. Each time you read a road sign on a highway or listen to the weather report on the radio, you become, for a moment, a geographer. You are using the tools of geography to study planet Earth.

WHAT IS A REGION?

Geographers divide Earth's surface into different kinds of regions. A region is an area with common features that set it apart from other areas. By studying different regions we can learn more about the world, more about ourselves, and more about people in other parts of the world.

Regions can be huge. Some are as big as half of Earth's surface. You have learned about these kinds of regions, called hemispheres, on pages G4–G5. Regions can also be very small. Your school's playground, for example, is an "exercise region" of your school.

Physical Regions

Regions that are defined by Earth's natural environment are called physical regions. Physical regions often have common landforms, such as mountains or plains.

As you can see from the map on this page, continents are the biggest kind of physical region. Continents can be divided into many smaller physical regions. In the region of South America, for example, the Andes Mountains make up a physical region.

Climate Regions

Physical regions can also be organized by climate, or the weather pattern that an area has over a long period of time. For example, the climate around Earth's central part, near the equator, is hot and humid. This is the world's tropical region. Around the North Pole, by contrast, the average winter temperature is -30°F. The North Pole is located in one of the two polar regions of the world.

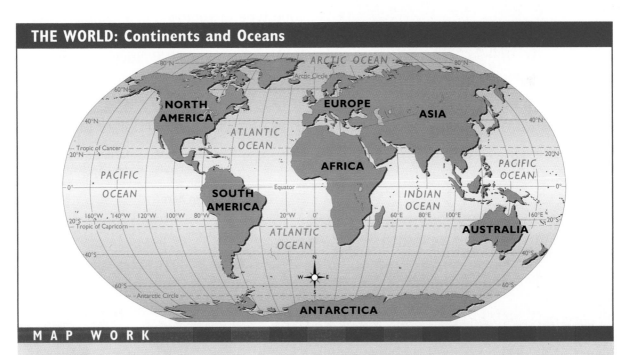

THE WORLD: Continents and Oceans

M A P   W O R K

Continents are the largest land regions.

1. How many continents are there?

2. What is the largest continent?

3. On which continent do you live?

4. Is most of Earth's land mass north or south of the equator?

LOOKING AT REGIONS

If you were to fly in an airplane, you would see many landforms that make up the world's physical regions. Another type of region, however, is invisible from an airplane. These regions are based on culture. Culture is the way of life of a group of people, including their daily habits, beliefs, and arts.

Cultural Regions

To learn about cultural regions, you must come down to Earth and meet the people who live in a place. Language, religion, and ethnic heritage are some of the parts of culture that make up cultural regions. For example, South America, Central America, and most of the Caribbean Islands form the cultural region of Latin America. Most people there speak Spanish, Portuguese, or French—all offshoots of an old language called Latin. Religion also ties Latin America together, since many Latin Americans are Roman Catholics.

Within Latin America are many smaller cultural regions, such as the region of Chiapas (chee AH pus) in the southeastern corner of Mexico. In Chiapas, unlike in the rest of Mexico, most people are Indians. Many speak a Mayan Indian language rather than Spanish. They eat traditional foods such as *tamales de frijol* (tuh MAH leez duh FREE hohl), a dish made of corn, black beans, and hot peppers.

Other Regions

Most places are part of more than one type of region. For example, Chiapas is a cultural region, but it is a political region as well. Political regions are

Many people in Chiapas follow traditions of their culture. These include clothing, farming methods, and festivals. In some festivals, people wear masks like the ones shown here.

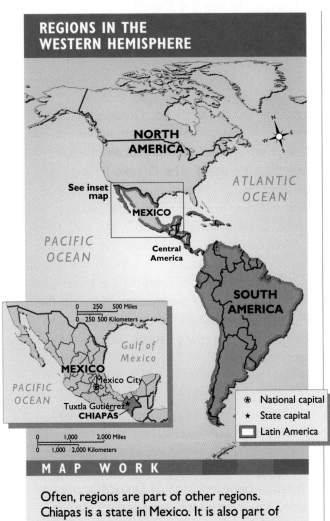

REGIONS IN THE WESTERN HEMISPHERE

NORTH AMERICA

ATLANTIC OCEAN

See inset map

MEXICO

PACIFIC OCEAN

Central America

SOUTH AMERICA

0 250 500 Miles
0 250 500 Kilometers

Gulf of Mexico

MEXICO

Mexico City

PACIFIC OCEAN

Tuxtla Gutiérrez
CHIAPAS

⊛ National capital
★ State capital
☐ Latin America

0 1,000 2,000 Miles
0 1,000 2,000 Kilometers

M A P   W O R K

Often, regions are part of other regions. Chiapas is a state in Mexico. It is also part of North America, which in turn is part of the Western Hemisphere.

Is Chiapas a physical or cultural region?

set up by governments. Just as Texas is one state of the 50 United States, Chiapas is one of the 31 states in Mexico.

Many of the people in Chiapas work as farmers. They live in the state's rugged countryside, in rural regions. Their lives are very different from the 20 million Mexicans who live 500 miles away in one of the world's largest urban regions—Mexico City.

By looking at Chiapas you can see that different kinds of regions often overlap. Look at the map on this page. How many different regions is Chiapas a part of?

WHY IT MATTERS

Throughout this book you will be learning about life in different regions. You will discover how the environment has shaped life in each region. You will explore the physical and cultural features that make regions similar to and different from each other. You will study how these regions have interacted over time. Finally, you will learn how certain cultural forces have, over time, tied all of Earth's regions into one interdependent world.

✓ Reviewing Facts and Ideas

MAIN IDEAS

- Geographers use regions to help them understand planet Earth.
- Physical regions are often defined by landforms and climate.
- Cultural regions are often defined by language and religion.
- There are many different kinds of regions, and they often overlap.

THINK ABOUT IT

1. What is geography? How is riding downhill on a bike an example of geography in action?

2. Why is it helpful to meet the people in a place when learning about their region?

3. **FOCUS** Why do geographers divide the world into regions?

4. **THINKING SKILL** List different regions of your community and then _classify_ them as physical or cultural regions.

5. **WRITE** Suppose that you are flying around the earth in an airplane. Describe the large bodies of water and landforms you see.

Geography Skills

Working with Latitude and Longitude

VOCABULARY

latitude   parallel
longitude   meridian
degree   global grid

WHY THE SKILL MATTERS

The people of the world are separated by many differences in language, religion, and customs. One skill that most of us share today, however, is the ability to read maps.

People around the world have long made maps. Yet not all maps were the same. Some people drew their maps so that east, rather than north, was at the top of the map. Others made their own region huge and out-lying areas tiny. It was not always easy for people to understand each other's maps.

Over 2,000 years ago, Greek scientists developed a way to divide the world into an imaginary grid so that all places could be exactly pinpointed. The Greeks based their system on two sets of lines called latitude and longitude. Lines of latitude run east and west. Lines of longitude run north and south.

Today mapmakers all over the world use this system. All places have their own unique address and can be located by anyone who knows how to use the system. Refer to the Helping Yourself box on the next page for help in locating places using latitude and longitude.

USING THE SKILL

Although lines of latitude run east and west, they measure distance in degrees north and south of the equator. A degree is a unit of measurement that describes the distance between lines of latitude and longi-tude. The symbol for degrees is °. As you can see on Map A, the equator is the start-ing line for measuring latitude.

LINES OF LATITUDE

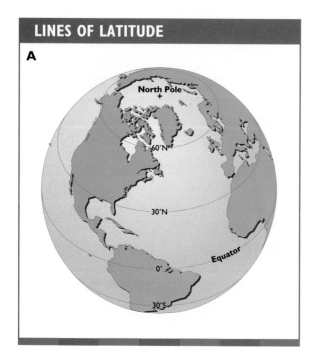

LINES OF LONGITUDE

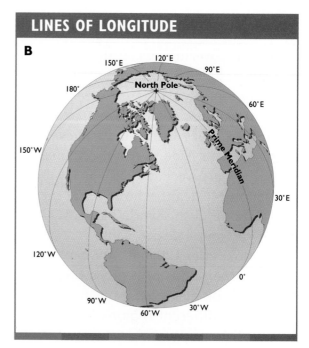

Lines of latitude are also known as parallels. Parallels are lines that run in the same direction and are always the same distance apart.

If you imagine that Earth is an apple, lines of latitude would cut the apple into a stack of rings. Lines of longitude, by contrast, would cut the apple into equal wedges. Lines of longitude run north and south, and measure distance in degrees east and west of the prime meridian.

Look at Map B on page 12. The prime meridian is marked 0°, meaning zero degrees longitude, and it separates east from west. All lines east and west of the prime meridian are called meridians.

Helping yourself

- Lines of **latitude** measure the distance north and south of the equator.
- Lines of **longitude** measure the distance east and west of the prime meridian.
- Lines of longitude and latitude cross to form a grid that can be used to locate any place.

TRYING THE SKILL

On Map C the parallels and meridians cross each other to form a global grid. This grid makes it possible to pinpoint exact locations. Which line of latitude is New Delhi, India, closest to? Which line of longitude is it closest to?

REVIEWING THE SKILL

Now find the correct latitude and longitude of Oslo, Norway, on Map C.

1. Starting from the equator, in which direction do you travel to get to Oslo?

2. Which line of latitude does Oslo lie on?

3. How might latitude and longitude be helpful to travelers?

GLOBAL GRID

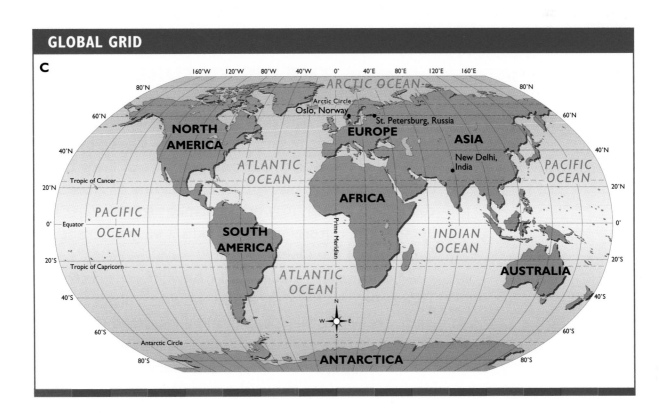

Regions and Culture

Focus Activity

READ TO LEARN

What is daily life like for a boy in India?

VOCABULARY

- custom
- values
- interaction

PLACES

- New Delhi

Read Aloud

Azeez Narain (uh ZHEEZ nuh RAHN) is an eleven-year old boy who lives in New Delhi, India. Azeez begins each day with prayers in his family's temple room and then heads to the kitchen for breakfast. Sometimes he eats toast and cereal. More often he eats poha, which is puffed rice with nuts and coconut roasted in butter and spices. Then Azeez rides a bus to school, where he studies 11 subjects six days a week. Four of those subjects are different languages.

THE BIG PICTURE

Do parts of Azeez's life sound familiar to you? Some probably do, like eating cereal for breakfast and riding a bus to school. Many such customs are shared by people around the world. Customs are ways of living that people practice regularly over time. Some of Azeez's customs, however, may not be familiar to you. That is because the cultural region of India is very different from that of the United States.

All cultures are made up of many different customs. Those customs determine how we dress, play, eat, learn, live with other people, and understand the world. Customs can reveal a great deal about what we believe is important in life. In fact, every detail of our life says something about the culture in which we live.

14

LIVING IN INDIA

Azeez Narain lives with his parents and six-year-old brother in New Delhi, India. The Narains share many customs with people in other parts of the world. Both parents work, for example. Azeez's mother teaches at a university and his father works as a journalist. Azeez and his friends like to ride their bikes and play computer games.

Many of the Narains' other customs are unique to the culture of India. Before you can understand these customs, however, you need to know a bit about India's past.

Culture and History

Throughout history people have brought new customs and ideas to India. Thousands of years ago the religion of Hinduism began shaping Indian culture. It remains a very important influence on Indian culture.

About 1,000 years ago Muslims began to settle in India. Muslims are people who follow the religion of Islam. Hinduism and Islam call for different ways of thinking and living. These differences in culture have caused conflicts between these groups in India.

About 250 years ago British traders arrived in India and brought their own customs with them. Britain took over

INDIA: Political

MAP WORK

The country of India is located in the southern part of Asia.

1. What bodies of water surround India on three sides?
2. Which countries border India?
3. Why would it be difficult for the people of Hyderabad to reach the ocean?

India's government in 1858 and ruled India for nearly 100 years. Today, some Indians still speak English.

The lives of Azeez and his family reflect the different cultures that are part of India's rich past. The Narains speak both Hindi and English. Azeez loves to play cricket, a game invented in Britain that is a bit like baseball. The Narains are Hindu, as are most Indians. However, the name *Azeez* is a combination of Muslim and Hindu words that means "community-harmony."

15

CULTURE HAS MANY PARTS

As you can see, a culture is made up of customs that are passed down through time. Azeez's life shows that the ways we speak, play, and view others can reveal clues about our culture.

Values and Beliefs

One of the most important parts of any culture is its values, or the things people believe are most important in life. Many people's values are shaped by their religious beliefs.

As a Hindu, for example, Azeez believes that all living things have souls and are "a fraction of God." Azeez's parents and grandparents have passed many other Hindu values down to him.

The most important lessons which my grandparents have taught me are that we should live a simple life and that we should not be attracted by money. We should not hurt anyone, including the animals. That's why we are strict vegetarians and don't even eat eggs.

Think about how the values or religious beliefs that you have been taught affect the way you live from day to day.

Culture at Home

You can get many hints about what a culture is like by seeing how people live at home. The Narains live in a six-room apartment. Their living room is filled with books, sofas, a television with 15 channels, and carvings and pictures of Indian leaders and Hindu gods. Mainly traditional Indian food is cooked in the kitchen, including Azeez's favorite dish—*uttapam* (OOT uh pam). Azeez describes this as "a sort of south Indian pizza made of rice with vegetables, coconut, and dried fruit."

A temple room honors the Hindu god Krishna. Each morning and evening Azeez goes there to offer his prayers. On Sundays the Narains travel to the local temple to worship.

Think about how the way you live at home reflects your family's beliefs and customs.

Cultures Change

Cultures do not stay the same forever. They constantly change through their interaction with other cultures. Interaction is the exchange of ideas and customs.

The Narains, for example, do not cook only Indian food. Sometimes they make Chinese or American food as well. Once in a while Azeez plays chess, a game probably invented in India

over 1,000 years ago. The style of chess Azeez plays today, though, was created through interaction between Asian and European cultures.

Another part of Indian culture that has changed is the role of women. Today women in India, especially in cities, have much more freedom and many more rights than in the past. In fact, Indians elected a woman, Indira Gandhi, as head of their government in 1966. Azeez's 11-year-old cousin Kalayani (ka luh YAH nee) says of her future, "I can do anything I want to do."

Azeez at School

Just as home life reveals much about a culture, so does life at school. Azeez attends school six days a week and must wear a uniform. Because so many different languages are spoken in India, Azeez studies four different languages: Hindi, English, Bengali, and Sanskrit, which is an ancient written language. Classes are taught in Hindi and English. Besides languages, Azeez also studies history, geography, math, science, government, and music.

Azeez enjoys playing chess and making music with friends. Here, he is playing the mridanga, a traditional Indian two-headed drum.

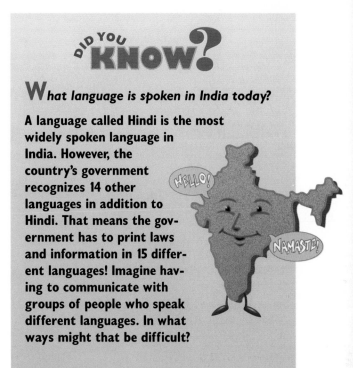

Other Parts of Culture at School

One instrument Azeez plays in music class at school is the *mridanga* (mri DAHNG guh), a two-headed drum used in Indian music. Every day Azeez eats in the school lunchroom with his friends. No meat or egg dishes are served. Instead, the students have spicy vegetables and lentils with rice, and flat breads fried in butter.

Government

New Delhi, where Azeez lives, is the capital of India. India's government is similar to that of the United States. Indians vote for leaders to represent them in government. This form of government, called a representative democracy, is an important part of India's culture. It gives all Indians a say in how they are ruled. When Azeez turns 18, he, too, will be able to vote for the leaders of his government. How old will you have to be to vote in elections in the United States?

Infographic

inter**NET**
CONNECTION
Visit our website:
www.mhschool.com

Cultures Around the World

You have met Azeez Narain in this lesson. Now meet five more young people in this Infographic. What do they have in common? What are some differences in their lives?

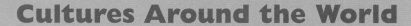

Rachel Dennis, age 11
Halifax, Nova Scotia, Canada

HOME: Lives in a house on the Atlantic coast with her parents, brother, and dog
LANGUAGE: English
SCHOOL SUBJECTS: Social studies, science, English, math, art, health, music, physical education
HOBBIES: Gymnastics, horseback riding
FAVORITE FOOD: Waffles

Anna Patricia de Martinez, age 12
Lima, Peru

HOME: Lives in a brick house with her mother, brother, and grandparents
LANGUAGE: Spanish
SCHOOL SUBJECTS: Science, math, Spanish, social studies, English, physical education, music, gardening
HOBBIES: Swimming, volleyball, aerobics
FAVORITE FOOD: Pastelle de Manzanas (pie)

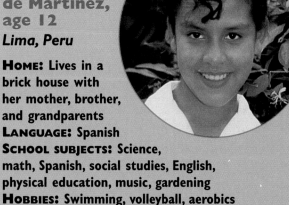

Olanike Olakunri, age 10
Lagos, Nigeria

HOME: Lives in a cinder block house with her parents
LANGUAGES: Yoruba, English
SCHOOL SUBJECTS: Math, English, Citizenship, music
HOBBIES: Board games, mystery books, school running team
FAVORITE FOOD: Eba (a porridge made of cassava flour and okra)

Brian Lawlor, age 11
County Tipperary, Ireland

HOME: Lives in a farm cottage with his parents and sister
LANGUAGE: English
SCHOOL SUBJECTS: Math, English, geography, music, science, Gaelic studies, physical education
HOBBIES: Hurling (like field hockey), and playing the accordion
FAVORITE FOOD: Apple tart

Harry Tan, age 10
Singapore

HOME: Lives in an apartment with his parents, brother, sister, and dog
LANGUAGE: Mandarin Chinese
SCHOOL SUBJECTS: English, Chinese, social studies, math, science, art, physical education
HOBBIES: Video games, skateboarding, baseball
FAVORITE FOOD: Rice with chicken in curry gravy

WHY IT MATTERS

Whenever and wherever people have lived, their lives have been shaped by the culture around them. A culture's language, government, values, foods, and entertainment make people who they are. Cultures also change as they interact with others over time.

This process of interaction is a big part of the story you will read in this book. In the chapters to come you will read about the world's many different cultures. Interaction between these cultures over the years has created the fascinating and complex world that we live in today.

✓/// Reviewing Facts and Ideas

MAIN IDEAS

- All cultures are made up of similar parts, such as religion, government, and education.

- Values affect not only what people believe, but also how they live.

- Cultures change as people of different cultures interact with one another.

THINK ABOUT IT

1. What are some clues you can study to learn about a culture?

2. How has religion shaped life for people in India?

3. **FOCUS** What has Azeez Narain's life taught you about the many parts of Indian culture?

4. **THINKING SKILL** What are two *generalizations* that you could make about Azeez's family?

5. **WRITE** Write an article for visitors from other countries. Describe how culture in the United States has been shaped by interaction with other cultures.

CHAPTER 1 REVIEW

THINKING ABOUT VOCABULARY

Number a sheet of paper from 1 to 10. Beside each number write the word from the list below that best matches the statement.

climate   landform
culture   latitude
custom   longitude
degree   region
geography   values

1. The things that people believe are most important in life

2. The distance east or west of the prime meridian measured by imaginary lines that run north and south on a map or globe

3. An area with common features that set it apart from other areas

4. The way of life of a group of people at a particular time that includes their daily habits, beliefs, and arts

5. The distance north or south of the equator measured by imaginary lines that run east and west on a map or a globe

6. The study of Earth

7. A weather pattern of an area over a long period of time

8. A physical feature such as a mountain range, plain, or plateau

9. A unit of measurement describing the distance between lines of latitude and longitude

10. A way of living that people practice regularly over time

THINKING ABOUT FACTS

1. What is geography and what can we learn by studying it?

2. Why do geographers use the concept of regions?

3. What are three types of regions?

4. What defines a physical region?

5. What do the equator and the prime meridian have in common?

6. How does a global grid make it possible to find locations?

7. What makes up a culture?

8. Explain one way in which culture influences a country.

9. What is the role that religion plays in a culture?

10. How is India's government an example of cultural interaction?

THINK AND WRITE ◄═►

WRITING A PARAGRAPH OF DESCRIPTION

Write a paragraph about the region where you live. In it describe the region's major landforms, its climate, and some important features of its culture.

WRITING A LETTER

Write a letter to Azeez Narain in India. Tell him about the culture and values of the community in which you live. Also tell him about some of the ways you think your life is similar to or different from his.

WRITING A TRAVEL PAMPHLET

Write a brief pamphlet about an interesting place you have visited. Suppose you are writing it for people from another country who will be visiting the place you describe.

APPLYING GEOGRAPHY SKILLS

LONGITUDE

Use the map on this page to answer the following questions.

1. What are lines of longitude?

2. What is the prime meridian?

3. What is the first line of longitude shown west of the prime meridian? What is the first line of longitude shown east of the prime meridian?

4. How far apart are the lines of longitude shown on the globe?

5. What is useful about having lines of longitude on a map?

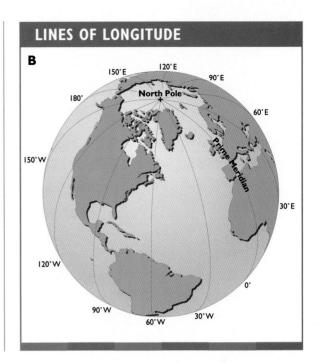

LINES OF LONGITUDE

Summing Up the Chapter

Copy the main idea table below on a separate sheet of paper. Then place each item in the feature list in the correct category below. Think of other features you might want to add. When you have completed the table, write a paragraph answering the question "How might the land, water, and climate of a region help shape the culture of the people who live there?"

MAIN IDEA	The geographical features of a region—land, water, climate—help shape the culture of the people who live there.	
Features	landforms, temperature, religion, education, bodies of water, vegetation, humidity, rainfall, music, natural resources, air currents, government, soil, latitude, values, altitude	
PHYSICAL	**CLIMATE**	**CULTURAL**
landforms	rainfall	religion

A Look Into the Past

THINKING ABOUT GEOGRAPHY AND CULTURE

These photographs show places built by people many centuries ago. While the places or their ruins remain, the people who built them are gone. Read Chapter 2 to begin your journey into the mystery of the very distant past.

India
ASIA

The Taj Mahal in Agra, India, is among the world's most beautiful buildings. A ruler had it built to honor his wife.

Mesa Verde
THE AMERICAS

In what is now southwestern Colorado, Native Americans began building their homes right into the area's cliffs about 1,400 years ago.

Athens
EUROPE

Ruins at the Acropolis hint at the glory of Ancient Greece. Its people developed a great civilization and formed the first democratic government.

Egypt
AFRICA

Thousands of years ago traders made their way across the dry lands of northern Africa. Their journey was made easier by camels.

Understanding History

Read Aloud

How has your life changed from the way it was five years ago? You're probably playing different games and have long outgrown your old clothes. Your family may have moved into a new home. Your life will continue to change as you grow older. Look around carefully. Ten years from now, everything around you—every object you use, every song you enjoy listening to—will help tell the story of what your life was like today.

Focus Activity

READ TO LEARN

What do historians do to look into the past?

VOCABULARY

- history
- oral tradition
- artifact
- primary source
- secondary source

THE BIG PICTURE

As the story of your life unfolds, it becomes part of an even bigger story of human **history**. History is the story of the past. People who study what has happened in the past are called historians. They may study details of daily life, or they may examine events that have changed the world. Historians have learned, for example, that people in Central America first enjoyed what we now call bubble gum hundreds of years ago. Historians have also learned how terrible wars brought huge changes for these same people in Central America.

Whether they study life-changing events or interesting details, historians use different kinds of sources, from books to bones, to discover what life was like in the past. Sources are an historian's most important tools. Like all tools, they need to be used carefully and skillfully.

HISTORY ALL AROUND

Nina was so excited that she forgot to say hello as she burst through her grandfather's front door.

"Grandpa, guess what? We're getting a new computer tonight!"

"Why, hello Nina," Grandpa Joe replied, putting down his magazine. "What is all this I hear about a new computer?"

An attic or storeroom (above) can be an excellent place to find artifacts from the past. An old camera is an example of an artifact.

"It's a lot more powerful, so my friends and I can play CD-ROMs on it."

"Whoa, Nina," laughed Grandpa Joe. "I still don't understand that much about computers. See, back when I was your age, we didn't even have television. Most people didn't."

"What?" gasped Nina.

"It's true," her grandfather continued. "Back in 1950 our family was the first in our neighborhood to get a TV. That was a big deal! I'll never forget how our neighbors crowded around that TV wanting to see all the new shows. . . ."

Grandpa Joe was describing the past using oral tradition—passing on history by word of mouth. Oral tradition is an important way that people remember the past. This was how history was kept alive before writing was invented.

"You know," mused Grandpa Joe, "I kept that old TV set. It's up in the attic. You should see it! It's nothing like what we have today."

"Hmmm . . . OK," answered Nina, her curiosity getting the better of her.

Learning from Artifacts

The old TV was definitely an artifact (AHR tuh fakt) from another time. An artifact is an object made by someone in the past. The TV's small screen was housed in a big, bulky, wooden cabinet. It was hard to imagine that such a homely machine had once been the center of so much attention. Propped up against the TV was another artifact—a large plastic ring that rattled when Nina picked it up. What did it do? Nina shook it, rolled it, then looped it around her shoulder. She decided to take it with her and figure it out later.

DIFFERENT SOURCES

On the shelf next to the TV lay other interesting artifacts: a dusty model of an old car, a big scrapbook filled with newspaper clippings, and a yellowing stack of magazines.

Nina scooped up as many items as she could, along with a newer-looking book called *God's Country: America in the Fifties*. Then she headed back downstairs to examine her finds.

Using Primary Sources

Except for the book, all of the items that Nina picked up in the attic were primary sources from the 1950s. Primary sources are materials that were created during the time under study. They can be written things, such as magazine articles or advertisements. They can also be nonwritten things, such as toys or tools or pictures.

Read the following excerpt from one of Nina's written sources. It describes a time in America's past when televisions were a novelty. What clues in the text tell you this is a primary source?

MANY VOICES
PRIMARY SOURCE

Excerpt from
an interview published in *Television*,
by Michael Winship, 1988.

I first saw television when I was a kid growing up in Brooklyn. . . . We didn't own a television set—most people didn't. But the Texaco Star Theater with Milton Berle was on Tuesday nights. So we all stood on the street, and the people who had a television set on my block would put it in the window facing the street. Half the block would gather —maybe 50 people would watch the show.

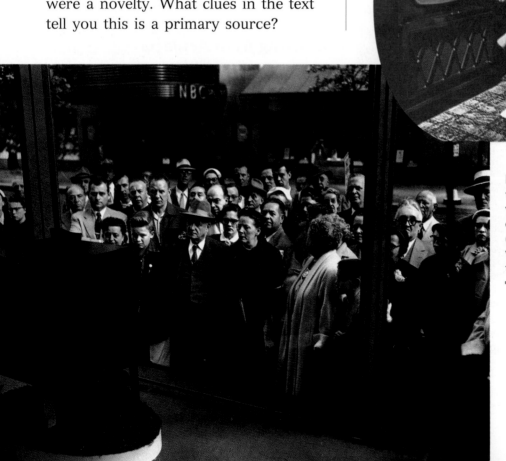

In the early days of television, not everyone was lucky enough to own their own set (above). Often, people would crowd sidewalks to watch (left).

A Secondary Source

Secondary sources are records of the past that are based on studies of primary sources. Nina's secondary source was the book *God's Country: America in the Fifties*. This is a study of life in the 1950s written by J. Ronald Oakley in 1986. Read the following excerpt from *America in the Fifties*.

> *In the America of 1950, almost 90 percent of all families did not have a television set. . . . By the early 1960s, 90 percent of all American homes had at least one television set. Never had a new product expanded so rapidly or so quickly become an essential part of American life.*

How does the information given in this secondary source differ from the information given in the primary source on the previous page?

Different Viewpoints

Nina could appreciate the old TV in the attic much more now that she knew how rare TVs were in 1950. But what could she make of the cars from the 1950s?

"They were so *huge,* so different from the cars we have today," Nina marveled as she picked up the old car model. "They couldn't have been very practical—and they must have been real gas guzzlers, too."

"But people didn't *care* that much about being practical back then," Grandpa Joe answered. "We wanted comfort and grandness, and those cars delivered!" To support his opinion, Grandpa Joe turned to an old car advertisement in his scrapbook. Look at the advertisement on this page.

Nina and her grandfather looked at the model car from different viewpoints. Nina noticed how the car contrasted

An advertisement in a scrapbook can show what was important to car buyers in the 1950s.

with today's cars. On the other hand, Grandpa Joe was reminded of people's attitudes about cars during the 1950s. These different viewpoints brought them to different conclusions.

Historians often disagree about how sources should be interpreted, or how life in a past time should be remembered. Since their own viewpoints shape the way they view the past, historians can end up constructing different pictures of the same historical period.

Historians also have trouble reconstructing the past. The further back in time something happened, the harder their job becomes. In addition, many important sources from the past have been destroyed or lost. This makes it impossible to understand certain past cultures and events.

PUTTING IT ALL TOGETHER

Based on the sources she had to work with, Nina was beginning to put together a picture of what life was like in the 1950s. In some ways the 1950s were similar to the 1990s. People worked hard and enjoyed relaxing with their families and friends. There were major differences, too. Television was still a new invention, so it was just starting to become the basic part of American life it is today. Cars were larger and used more gasoline. Conserving natural resources such as oil was not as much of a concern then as it is now.

Looking at an Artifact

But what purpose did the big plastic ring serve? The answer came as Nina flipped through a 1958 issue of *Life* magazine. A photograph in an article caught her eye. It showed teenagers swinging the rings around their waists.

A library is a good place to find primary and secondary sources. **Your local library probably has sections for books and magazines from the past. Many modern libraries now also have computers and CD-ROMs.**

The article called the rings "hula hoops" and said they were "the newest national craze. . . bigger than anything that ever hit the toy business." You can see a page from that article on page 28.

Combining Sources

Nina's article shows why written sources can be so valuable to historians. They can speak for people and things from another time. The article, a written source, helped explain the hula hoop, an artifact.

Without realizing it Nina had done work similar to that of a true historian. She used primary and secondary sources to shed light on her topic, life in the United States in the 1950s. She also examined artifacts to learn their purpose and importance in a culture. Lastly, she used and interpreted written sources to try to understand one of a culture's customs.

WHY IT MATTERS

The work of an historian is like that of a detective. Clues to an historical period or event may be deeply buried. So historians have to rebuild the past as accurately as possible, using the evidence that is available to them. Sometimes key evidence has been lost or destroyed, making the job even harder.

Historians are not alone in their task, however. They have skilled partners—scientists—who help them uncover written and unwritten sources from the past. You will read about these scientists and the work they do in the next lesson.

Reviewing Facts and Ideas

MAIN IDEAS

- History is the study of what happened in the past.
- Before writing was invented, history was passed down through oral tradition, or word of mouth.
- Artifacts, or objects made in the past, can also tell how people lived.
- Historians use primary and secondary sources to interpret what life was like in the past.
- The sources that historians use, the way they use these sources, and their points of view, shape the way the past is remembered.

THINK ABOUT IT

1. How does oral tradition differ from a written source? How can both help to preserve history?

2. What is a secondary source? Give an example of a secondary source you use at school.

3. **FOCUS** How do sources help us to learn about the past?

4. **THINKING SKILL** What *effects* do the sources available to a historian have on the ways she or he understands the past? How might a historian's point of view affect the way she or he understands history?

5. **WRITE** Use your imagination to write about how the artifacts in your classroom might be viewed by an historian 100 years from now. What are three conclusions the historian could make from these artifacts about life in the 1990s?

29

Decision Making

VOCABULARY
decision
evaluate

WHY THE SKILL MATTERS

One of the most important parts of an historian's job is making choices. Every historian chooses which sources to study and how to interpret those sources. When historians make these choices, they are making **decisions**. To make a decision is to choose from a number of alternatives.

USING THE SKILL

One of the most thrilling historical studies ever made involved the search for the ancient city of Troy by Heinrich Schliemann (HĪN rihk SHLEE mahn) in 1870. Many legends told of a great walled city called Troy, where heroic warriors long ago had fought fierce and bloody battles. You will

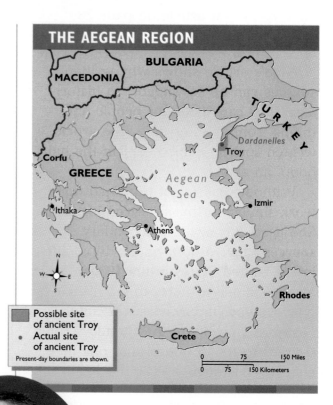

THE AEGEAN REGION

MACEDONIA
BULGARIA
TURKEY
Corfu
Dardanelles
Troy
GREECE
Aegean Sea
Ithaka
Izmir
Athens
Rhodes
Crete

N W S E

Possible site
of ancient Troy
• Actual site
of ancient Troy
Present-day boundaries are shown.

0   75   150 Miles
0   75   150 Kilometers

Heinrich Schliemann located the site of ancient Troy (left and above).

learn more about these legends when you study Ancient Greece in Chapter 8.

No one knew for sure whether Troy had been a real city or whether it had been created in the imaginations of ancient poets. Schliemann was fascinated by the stories of this old city, and he was determined to find it's location and learn it's secrets.

Now that Schliemann had set his goal, he identified the different alternatives for the possible location of ancient Troy. Some historians thought that Troy could be found on the island of Corfu, northwest of mainland Greece. Others believe that the city was located on the west coast of Turkey. Schliemann himself thought that Troy might be buried under a mound near the Dardanelles Strait in Turkey.

He was then ready to evaluate the different alternatives to choose the most promising location. To evaluate something is to judge it's worth. In order to evaluate the possible locations of Troy, Schliemann examined many different sources of information. among these sources were descriptions of Troy in a book called *The Iliad*, by Greek poet Homer. Schliemann believed that this book was the most accurate source because it was the oldest one, written about 2,800 years ago. Schliemann also studied the landforms of Greece and Turkey in hopes of finding more clued about Troy.

From his research, Schliemann decided that the mound in Turkey he had seen was the best choice from among the different alternatives. This mound was called Hissarlik (hih sur LIK), and it was there that he began his search. In 1870 Schliemann and his wife Sophia began a large project at Hissarlik to

Helping yourself

- **A decision** is a choice between alternatives.
- **Identify the goal you want to reach.**
- **Identify the different alternatives for reaching your goal.**
- **Evaluate each alternative.**
- **Choose the best alternative.**

unearth the long-lost city of Troy. Soon they found the stone walls of an ancient city. As they dug deeper and deeper they found gold and silver artifacts and other evidence of the magnificent city that had once been Troy. Eventually, the remains of nine cities, newer ones built upon the ruins of older ones, were uncovered. Today historians believe that the sixth city was the one that Homer wrote about in *The Iliad* many years ago.

TRYING THE SKILL

Refer to the Helping Yourself box for help in making a decision. Imagine that you are trying to learn about the history of your hometown. Your goal is to find the best historical source about the first people who lived there. What are three sources that you could choose to find out more about the first people in your hometown? Decide which of these sources is the best one. Why?

REVIEWING THE SKILL

1. What are the main steps in making a good decision?
2. Why is it important to set a goal when making decisions?
3. Why is it important to identify alternatives for reaching a goal?
4. When might it be useful to be able to make good decisions?

Iceman of the Alps

Focus Activity

READ TO LEARN

What can artifacts tell us about the ancient past?

VOCABULARY

- archaeology
- excavate
- prehistory

PEOPLE

- Konrad Spindler

PLACES

- Alps

Read Aloud

It was warm and sunny in the Alps on September 19, 1991—a perfect day for hiking. As Erika and Helmut Simon moved along a mountain ridge, they spotted something in the melting ice. At first they thought it was trash, or maybe a doll. When they got closer Erika cried out, "It's a man!" The leathery-brown body was indeed human, lying half-buried in the snow. Shocked, the Simons hurried down the mountain to tell the police. They would not learn until several days later that the body they stumbled upon was over 5,000 years old.

THE BIG PICTURE

History is full of mysteries. It is the job of historians to do the detective work needed to solve these mysteries. As you learned in the last lesson, written sources can be a big help to historians trying to interpret past events. Artifacts are helpful clues, too.

The science of **archaeology** (ahr kee AHL uh jee) is the study of the remains of past cultures. Archaeologists carefully dig up, or **excavate**, historical sites. They use instruments to discover, identify, and save these remains. They take X rays to see what is inside an object and how it was made. They do tests to determine the age of artifacts. Above all, archaeologists must link different clues to figure out what artifacts and remains might say about how people lived in past cultures.

A DISCOVERY IN THE ALPS

The Alps are Europe's highest mountain range. They contain dozens of snow-covered peaks and massive slabs of ice called glaciers. On some days the Alps are a beautiful and safe place to hike. On other days the Alps can be deadly. In fact, each year more than 100 people die in sudden snowstorms there.

Thus police and local reporters were not too surprised when the Simons found a body in the Alps. Two days after the discovery, a local newspaper reported:

> Judging by the dead man's equipment, he was a mountaineer. It seems that the accident occurred some decades ago. The body has not yet been identified.

The article was accurate in many ways, but very wrong in one. Soon it would become clear that this "mountaineer" had been frozen for far more than 40 or 50 years.

A Mystery in the Ice

A few days after the Simons made their discovery, the police set out to recover the body. Look at the map on this page to see where the body was found. The police also saved some items scattered around the area. These included a knife, some bits of rope and leather, and an ax. After a closer look they realized that this ax was no ordinary hiking tool. Its metal blade was lashed to a wooden handle with strips of leather. The ax looked hundreds of years old!

The story of the "Iceman" now became big news, especially to archaeologists. Five days after the Iceman was found, German archaeologist Konrad Spindler came to investigate. When he saw the Iceman's belongings, Spindler's eyes widened. "This [was] something any first-year archaeology student could identify," he later wrote. Spindler estimated the Iceman's age by observing that his ax was made of copper and his knife-blade of chipped stone. Looking up, Spindler announced his conclusion: "Roughly 4,000 years old!"

Later on, detailed testing would prove that the Iceman was actually about 5,300 years old. From these results, archaeologists realized that the Iceman had lived in Europe in the age of prehistory, or the time before writing was developed there. "A fully equipped prehistoric man—nothing like it had ever been seen by an archaeologist," Spindler wrote.

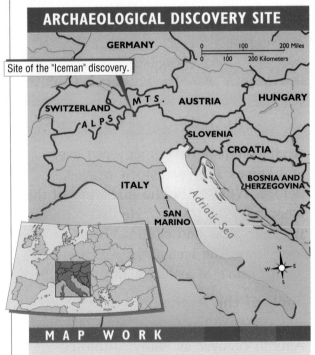

ARCHAEOLOGICAL DISCOVERY SITE

Site of the "Iceman" discovery.

GERMANY
SWITZERLAND
MTS.
ALPS
AUSTRIA
HUNGARY
SLOVENIA
CROATIA
ITALY
BOSNIA AND HERZEGOVINA
SAN MARINO
Adriatic Sea

0 100 200 Miles
0 100 200 Kilometers

MAP WORK

The site of the Iceman discovery lies high in Europe's Alps mountains.

1. The Iceman was found very near the border of which two countries?

2. In what direction did archaeologist Konrad Spindler travel to get from Germany to the site?

When hikers in the Alps stumbled upon his body, the "Iceman" (left and above) had been frozen for over 5,000 years!

AN AMAZING FIND

Archaeologists have uncovered axes and knives and prehistoric graves before. What made the discovery of the Iceman so interesting? He was found with the tools and clothes he used every day. The Iceman brought a priceless treasure of artifacts into the 1990s.

Tools of the Archaeologist

Several archaeologists rushed to the Alps to recover as many of the Iceman's belongings as possible. They were able to work only a few days, however, before the first winter snows buried the site. The following summer, these archaeologists shoveled away over 600 tons of snow before they could pick up where they had left off.

The archaeologists' first task was to make a detailed map of the location. They also took photographs showing where each artifact was found. Next, they used steam blowers and even hair dryers to melt snow and ice around the artifacts. The melted water was filtered three times. Archaeologists wanted to make sure that even the tiniest specks of evidence were not lost.

The archaeologists found flecks of wheat. This proved that the Iceman must have had contact with a village where grain was grown. Archaeologists also recovered over 2,000 grains of pollen, or plant dust. Study of the pollen with a microscope showed that most of the grains came from alder and pine trees. Scientists reasoned that the

Iceman probably died in autumn, the season when pine and alder trees give off the most pollen.

Equipped for Survival

Near the Iceman, archaeologists found all sorts of survival gear, such as knife-blades, rope, and hunting arrows. They also recovered a small net. Was the net used to carry things? Was it a fishing net? The wide spaces in the mesh seemed to rule out both of these possibilities. Then Konrad Spindler compared the net to modern nets used by European farmers to catch birds. They matched exactly. The question of the net's purpose seemed to be answered.

In a leather belt-pouch the Iceman carried needed tools, such as small flint blades and a bone needle probably used to repair equipment. There was also a handful of a black fungus. Chemical study showed that tiny crystals of sulfur and iron were attached to the fungus. These are ingredients in today's match-es. Archaeologists concluded that the Iceman used the fungus as a kind of fire-starter.

The Iceman also carried two small beads of a different kind of fungus on a leather strap. Close comparison of samples with those in a huge fungus collection showed that the Ice-man's beads were made from birch fungus. Birch fungus contains an ingre-dient that helps fight disease. Therefore, archaeologists believe that this was the Iceman's "medicine chest."

Artifacts found near the Iceman tell archaeologists much about life in pre-historic Europe. It seems that people then had survival skills possessed by few people today.

Examining the Evidence

The Iceman was moved from the Alps to a special refrigerated room in Innsbruck, Austria. There scientists determined that he was about 5 feet 2 inches tall. From the amount of wear on his teeth, they reasoned that he was 35 to 40 years old when he died. Pieces of his hair showed that he had wavy dark-brown hair and a beard.

X rays indicated that the Iceman had some broken ribs on his right side. Some archaeologists believe that the Iceman was somehow injured before he died, because he was found lying on his left side. Shortly after his death, he was covered by snowfall. Glacier ice gradu-ally encased him. It would imprison—and preserve—him for 5,000 years.

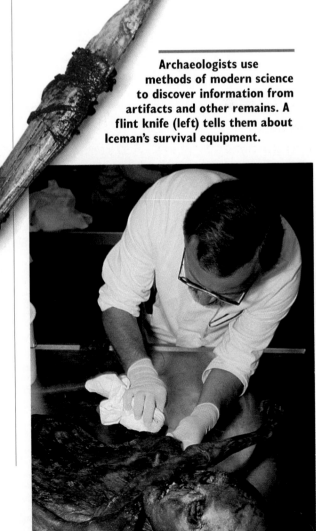

Archaeologists use methods of modern science to discover information from artifacts and other remains. A flint knife (left) tells them about Iceman's survival equipment.

WHO WAS THE ICEMAN?

From the body of one man and a few of his belongings, archaeologists have learned much about what life was like in the Alps during prehistoric times. Many mysteries have been solved, but some still remain.

Living 5,000 Years Ago

We now know at least the following about the Iceman's world. The people of the Iceman's time were experts at interacting with their environment. Archaeologists concluded this because as many as 17 different kinds of trees and 8 different kinds of animals were used to make the Iceman's belongings. These prehistoric people were also skilled metalworkers. They were able to shape copper into tools. And the Iceman must have had contact with farmers. We know this because traces of grain were found in his belongings.

The Mystery Remains

What about the Iceman himself? Who was he and what did he do for a living? Why did he hike up into the high mountains of the Alps just before

THE ICEMAN OF THE ALPS

The Iceman's clothes and tools help archaeologists to figure out what his life may have been like.

BOW
Six-foot bow for hunting game

AX
Copper ax for chopping firewood

CAPE
Woven grass cape for extra warmth

COAT
Deerskin coat for protection from the cold

LEGGINGS
Leather pants of animal skins

SHOES
Leather boots insulated with grass

NET
Net similar to modern European bird nets

KNIFE
Flint knife with leather case

winter set in? Spindler believes that the Iceman may have been a shepherd who spent long periods of time in the mountains, away from his village below. We may never know for certain what he was doing high in the mountains that long-ago autumn day. Whatever the reason, the Iceman's misfortune has proven to be history's great gain.

WHY IT MATTERS

We can sometimes learn facts about an entire culture by focusing on one individual, such as the Iceman. Archaeologists looked carefully at artifacts that the Iceman used every day. They discovered much about how people lived in the highlands of prehistoric Europe.

In chapters to come, you can use some of the same methods you learned about in this lesson. You will read about great ideas and events that changed the world. But you will also have the opportunity to think about individuals like the Iceman. These individuals add fullness and detail to the big picture of history.

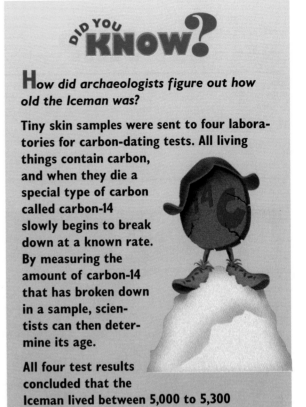

DID YOU KNOW?

How did archaeologists figure out how old the Iceman was?

Tiny skin samples were sent to four laboratories for carbon-dating tests. All living things contain carbon, and when they die a special type of carbon called carbon-14 slowly begins to break down at a known rate. By measuring the amount of carbon-14 that has broken down in a sample, scientists can then determine its age.

All four test results concluded that the Iceman lived between 5,000 to 5,300 years ago.

✓✓ Reviewing Facts and Ideas

MAIN IDEAS

- Archaeologists use science to study and interpret the remains of past cultures.

- Our understanding of prehistory, or the time before writing was invented, is often based on the work done by archaeologists.

- Archaeologists and historians can sometimes make conclusions about life in past cultures. One of the ways they do this is by looking closely at information about one or two individuals.

THINK ABOUT IT

1. What made Spindler realize that the Iceman was actually very old?

2. What was the Iceman's net probably used for? How did Spindler find out?

3. **FOCUS** How do archaeologists help to uncover secrets of the past?

4. **THINKING SKILL** What are two _facts_ and two _opinions_ presented about the Iceman in this lesson?

5. **GEOGRAPHY** Describe how the Iceman's belongings tell the different ways in which he interacted with his environment.

CITIZENSHIP
VIEWPOINTS

Rather than let them be flooded, workers took apart and moved the temples at Abu Simbel, in Egypt.

When should cultural sites around the world be protected?

Many places have ruins of ancient temples and palaces. These ruins provide clues to ancient cultures. Both in the past and today, people have not always protected such places. Wars and pollution damaged some. Other sites became overgrown. Still others have been destroyed to make room for new buildings.

Serious efforts to protect archaeological sites began in 1959. Archaeologists learned that a huge dam being built at Aswan in Egypt would flood temples thousands of years old. The United Nations Educational, Scientific, and Cultural Organization (UNESCO) worked with the Egyptian government to save these temples.

Along with archaeologists and officials from many nations, UNESCO has drawn up a list of almost 400 "World Heritage sites" to be preserved. The list includes Southeast Asian temples, Mexican pyramids, European cathedrals, and ancient African cities. Sites in the United States are in danger of being destroyed as well. Some people think such sites should be preserved. Nancy Marzulla explains other factors that should be considered, such as the use and value of property. Consider the viewpoints on this issue and answer the questions that follow.

Three DIFFERENT Viewpoints

1 GUSTAVO ARAOZ
Architect, Washington, D.C.
Excerpt from Interview, 1995

We need to protect our global cultural heritage, because if such places are not properly kept up, they can be changed beyond recognition or destroyed. Once you lose a cultural site, you can never get it back. It's like losing a book and all the information in it. It's gone forever. When the tombs of ancient Egypt were looted and the artifacts stolen, the world lost a significant source of information about the past.

"It's gone forever."

2 NANCY MARZULLA
Lawyer, Washington, D.C.
Excerpt from Interview, 1995

Historic preservation is fine as long as we also protect the rights of property owners. In the United States the Constitution guarantees these rights. The owner of a house or building has the right to be paid a fair amount for any property to be preserved if it results in the destruction of private property rights. Preservation laws may require the owner to keep a site or building exactly as it is, which could destroy the value of the property.

". . . protect the rights of property owners."

3 BREDA PAVLIC
International Relations Specialist, Paris, France
Excerpt from Interview, 1995

Today our global cultural resources are threatened in many ways. Among these threats are industrial pollution, urban growth, war, natural disasters such as earthquakes, floods, hurricanes, and too much tourism. The loss of any one of these unique sites is irreplaceable. These sites are a link between the past and the present, and, if we manage to preserve them, a link with the future. They give us a feeling of belonging to the world as a whole.

". . . a link between the past and the present . . ."

BUILDING CITIZENSHIP

1. Explain how each person supports her or his view.
2. In what ways are some of the viewpoints alike? In what ways are they different?
3. What other viewpoints might people have on this issue? How could you find out about historical sites in your community?

SHARING VIEWPOINTS

Discuss what you agree with or disagree with about these and other viewpoints. Discuss why you think the speakers might feel as they do. Then, as a class, write two statements that all of you can agree with about preserving historical sites.

CHAPTER 2 REVIEW

THINKING ABOUT VOCABULARY

Number a sheet of paper from 1 to 10. Beside each number write the word or term from the list below that best completes the sentence. You will need to use some words more than once.

archaeology
artifact
excavate
history
oral tradition
prehistory
primary source
secondary source

1. Before written records were kept, people passed on their history by word of mouth or _____.

2. A written study of the past that is based on a primary source is called a _____.

3. An object made by someone in the past is an _____.

4. The scrapbook that Nina found in her grandfather's attic is an example of a _____.

5. _____ is the study of the remains of past cultures.

6. Archaelogists often dig up, or _____, historical sites.

7. _____ can be identified as the story of the past.

8. The time before the development of writing is called _____.

9. _____ often involves the search for artifacts.

10. Stories and legends were passed on during prehistory through _____.

THINKING ABOUT FACTS

1. What sources do historians use to study the past?

2. What is the difference between primary and secondary sources?

3. How is an historian like a detective?

4. What do artifacts show about the past?

5. How is history different from prehistory?

6. What do archaeologists study?

7. What conclusions did the archaeologist Konrad Spindler make about the frozen man found in the Alps?

8. What belongings of the Iceman were discovered, and what did archaeologists learn from examining them?

9. Name at least one method the archaeologists used to find information about the Iceman.

10. What mysteries still remain to be solved about the Iceman?

THINK AND WRITE

WRITING A SUMMARY
Write a paragraph summarizing what you know about the history of your community.

WRITING AN ARTICLE
Suppose you are writing an article for your school newspaper about "The Iceman of the Alps." Describe the discovery and what archaeologists learned from it.

WRITING AN INTERVIEW
Suppose you were able to interview the Iceman. Write at least three questions you would ask him, and provide the answers you think he might give.

APPLYING THINKING SKILLS

DECISION MAKING

Suppose you are Heinrich Schliemann in 1870. You are fascinated by stories of an ancient city called Troy. No one knows for sure if the city is real or imaginary. You decide to find out.

1. What goal do you set for yourself?

2. What alternatives do you consider to reach your goal?

3. What are the possible consequences of each alternative?

4. Will a map like this one help you to set your goal?

5. Do you think you made a good decision?

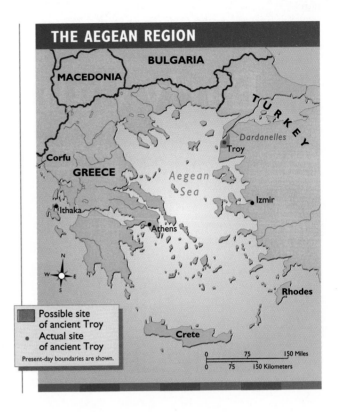

THE AEGEAN REGION

Possible site of ancient Troy

• Actual site of ancient Troy

Present-day boundaries are shown.

0   75   150 Miles
0   75   150 Kilometers

Summing Up the Chapter

Copy the main-idea diagram below on a separate sheet of paper. Then review the chapter to find at least two details that support the main ideas. When you have filled in the diagram, answer the question "How do we learn about past cultures?"

Sources

MAIN IDEA Archaeologists and historians use a variety of methods and sources to learn about the past.

Methods

41

CHAPTER 3

Early Cultures

THINKING ABOUT HISTORY AND GEOGRAPHY

Most scientists believe humans have walked on Earth for many thousands of years. Follow the story of these early people by linking the colored squares on the map to the colored panels of the time line. You will read more of this story as you study Chapter 3.

ATLANTIC OCEAN

30,000 YEARS AGO

AVIGNON, FRANCE
People create paintings on the walls of caves

45,000 YEARS AGO

OLDUVAI GORGE, TANZANIA
Early people hunt and gather their food

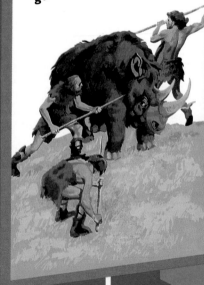

40,000 YEARS AGO

BORDER CAVE, SOUTH AFRICA
People make tools from stone

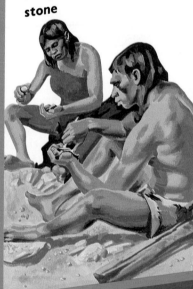

50,000 B.C.   40,000 B.C.   30,000 B.C.

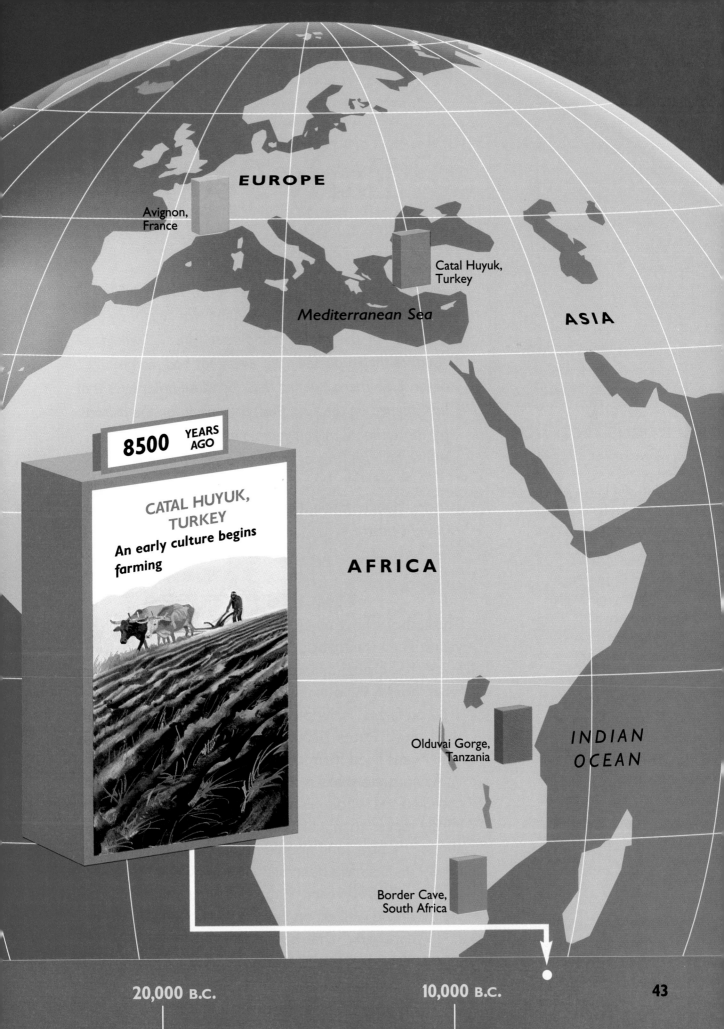

EUROPE

Avignon,
France

Catal Huyuk,
Turkey

Mediterranean Sea

ASIA

8500 YEARS
AGO

CATAL HUYUK,
TURKEY

**An early culture begins
farming**

AFRICA

Olduvai Gorge,
Tanzania

*INDIAN
OCEAN*

Border Cave,
South Africa

20,000 B.C.

10,000 B.C.

50,000 B.C.   40,000 B.C.   10,000 B.C.

Early People

Focus Activity

READ TO LEARN

What did early people do to survive?

VOCABULARY

- technology
- Old Stone Age
- hunter-gatherer

PLACES

- Border Cave

Read Aloud

"I was born and grew up in East Africa where, while I was still very young, my imagination was caught by the great age of the world I found myself in. . . . I would visualize the [procession] of lives that had [come before] me there. I would think of those other eyes that had opened on the first flush of sunlight on the hilltops for more than 2 million years, noses that whiffed the smoke of bush fires or scent of acacia blossom."

Archaeologist Jonathan Kingdon wrote these words to describe his fascination with the people of the ancient past.

THE BIG PICTURE

Think about how much your life has changed in ten years. Then think about how much life in the United States has changed from 100 years ago. That was a time when horses far outnumbered cars and most people lived on farms. Now picture in your mind the land of the United States 1,000 years ago. At this time Native Americans lived from coast to coast.

A thousand years is a very long time. When compared to the whole history of the world, however, it is hardly longer than a blink of the eye. Scientists disagree about just how long people have been around. Many think humans have been around for over 40 times 1,000 years, or 40,000 years. Some scientists think that people may have walked on Earth as long as *2,000* times 1,000 years ago—that is, 2 *million* years ago!

LIFE LONG AGO

When did human life begin, and what was life like for the world's early people? These are big questions for historians and archaeologists. Many different answers have been given over time.

Discoveries in Africa

Scientists do not agree about where or when human life began. Some scientists today think that human life may have begun in Africa over 2 million years ago and then spread throughout the rest of the world. This conclusion is based on remains found by archaeologists in East Africa. Ancient remains uncovered there are the oldest of their kind ever found.

At one site in the country of Tanzania, a long canyon cuts deeply through the surrounding plains. In this canyon are dry beds of big prehistoric lakes. In those ancient lakebeds archaeologists have found remains that some think may be about 2 million years old.

Tools from Long Ago

Along with these remains, archaeologists have found what may have been the world's first tools. Viewed under a microscope, stones like the ones on this page reveal edges that were pounded to create a knife-like sharpness. They may not look like much to us, but the stones could cut through the hides of animals and chop through wood. These simple but useful tools mark the start of technology in culture. Technology is the use of skills and tools to meet practical needs. Stone tools were the most common technology until about 12,000 years ago. That period of time is called the Old Stone Age.

Remains of ancient animal bones found with the stone tools suggest that the early people hunted for survival. During the Old Stone Age, people learned another skill besides hunting and tool-making. This new skill was using fire, and it changed their lives. The technology of fire-building made it possible to cook food for the first time. It also meant people could move into colder climates. Warmth from fires helped people survive through the long winter months.

Early people in Peru made this firestarter (above right). Many stone tools (above) have been found in the Great Rift Valley, Tanzania (right).

Archaeologists probe the darkness of the Border Cave. History's treasures, in the form of artifacts, await.

LIFE IN THE OLD STONE AGE

Many scientists believe that before 40,000 years ago, stone-age technology gradually became more complex. Smaller, finer blades were crafted, for example. Some blades were tied to wooden handles to make small axes. From about 40,000 years ago, changes came more rapidly. This also marked the time when people began to work more closely together and to develop cultures.

Hunting and Gathering

What was it like to live on Earth about 40,000 years ago? Families that once lived in a cave in South Africa have left behind enough clues to give us an idea.

Border Cave is located in Zululand, the northeastern tip of South Africa. Look at the map on the following page to see where Border Cave is. Back then, much like now, the cave nestled in the side of a cliff. It overlooked a grassy river valley dotted with buffalo-thorn trees and other shrubs. Herds of eland (EE lund), a type of antelope, moved into the valley each year. There they ate grass and drank from the river. Border Cave was an excellent base for people who followed the herds and hunted them for survival.

Remains show that the people of Border Cave made their home as comfortable as possible. They lined its cool dirt floor with grass for bedding. They made campfires to cook on and to light the cave's darkness.

From the opening of the cave high on the cliff, the people of the Border Cave could keep watch over the animals' movement. These people probably traveled many miles to hunt the eland herds. Small, arrowhead-like blades suggest that these people may have used bows and arrows to kill animals for food.

The people of Border Cave were not just hunters, though. They knew a great deal about the plants around them. They knew which ones were tasty, useful as medicine, or filled with dangerous poisons. Ancient remains of seeds and leaves show that they gathered wild plums, oranges, and starchy plants for food. They also may have used seeds from nearby trees to help soothe coughs and upset stomachs. Since these people met their needs by hunting and by gathering plants, they are known as hunter-gatherers

A Changing Culture

At some point many thousands of years ago, a small baby was buried along with a seashell bead towards the back of the cave. This act reveals several important things about life among the people of Border Cave.

It suggests that the baby was deeply cared for. Otherwise people would not have bothered to bury it. It also suggests that the people believed the child would somehow live on after death, or it would not have mattered that the child be buried with the bead. Many archaeologists think that such thoughts about life and death marked the beginning of religious belief in the world.

The seashell bead says other things about the everyday lives of the people of Border Cave. At times they must have traveled to the shores of the Indian Ocean, some 50 miles away. Additionally, the bead shows that these early people valued beauty. Why else would they take the time to make something otherwise "useless" out of the shell?

The earliest signs of art in human culture date back about 40,000 years. Amazing rock paintings in France and Spain date back to about 30,000 years ago. Many other breathtaking rock paintings and carvings dating back

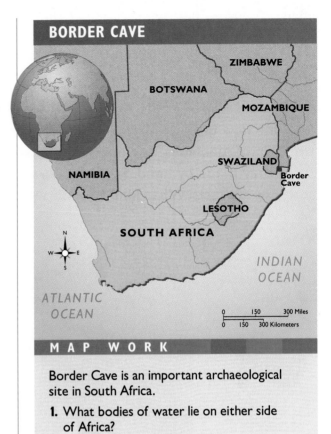

BORDER CAVE

ZIMBABWE

BOTSWANA

MOZAMBIQUE

SWAZILAND

NAMIBIA

Border Cave

LESOTHO

SOUTH AFRICA

INDIAN OCEAN

ATLANTIC OCEAN

| 0 | 150 | 300 Miles |
| 0 | 150 | 300 Kilometers |

M A P   W O R K

Border Cave is an important archaeological site in South Africa.

1. What bodies of water lie on either side of Africa?

2. Which of them is Border Cave closer to?

10,000 years have been found on every continent inhabited by humans. The exact purpose of these pieces of artwork is not known. It is clear, however, that the makers of each had something they wanted to say. The ancient artists found a way to express themselves through their artwork.

Early hunters made these rock paintings (left) showing great herds of eland in South Africa.

Infographic

Old Stone Age Technology Around the World

Imagine how difficult it would be for people to build things without the help of machines. As you read in Lesson 1, Stone Age people used tools they made by hand. Some of the things they created still survive today as artifacts. What kind of skills were needed to create these objects?

●NORTH AMERICA

Arrowheads, United States, about 12,000 years ago

●SOUTH AMERICA

Firestarter, Peru, about 11,000 years ago

●AFRICA

Fishing sinkers, South Africa, 40,000 years ago

EUROPE
Spearthrower, France,
about 14,000 years ago

ASIA
Bead necklace,
China, about
30,000 years ago

AUSTRALIA
Rock art, Australia, about
20,000 years ago

WHY IT MATTERS

From about 40,000 years ago until the end of the Old Stone Age roughly 12,000 years ago, human beings spread throughout the world.

During the next 6,000 years, life would change rapidly. For the first time in the long history of the world, some people would live in small cities. Their homes would not be caves, but apartment-like buildings packed side by side. In the next lesson you will read about the changes that made such developments possible.

✓ Reviewing Facts and Ideas

MAIN IDEAS

- Early people survived by hunting animals and gathering plants.
- Technology began with the creation of tools out of stone.
- At the end of the Old Stone Age, art and religious beliefs were a part of human life.

THINK ABOUT IT

1. How did the Old Stone Age get its name?

2. How did life on Earth change during the Old Stone Age, beginning around 40,000 years ago?

3. **FOCUS** What kinds of technology did the people of Border Cave use in order to survive?

4. **THINKING SKILL** Based on what evidence can we make the *conclusion* that human life became more complex at the close of the Old Stone Age?

5. **WRITE** Write a paragraph that compares your life today with what it might have been like to live in Border Cave in the Old Stone Age.

ARTISTS
AND THEIR ENVIRONMENTS

Try to picture a world without art—no paintings, no sculpture, no photographs, or music. It would be a less interesting world!

Art has been here from very early times. Although art has changed much since then, there are many similarities between ancient and modern artists.

Artists from ancient times drew their world as they saw it. They painted objects and events that were important to them and their cultures. Modern artists also respond to their environments. They create art that reflects today's concerns.

Art from ancient times becomes especially important when there are no written records. Often historians study this art to discover early people's concerns and beliefs.

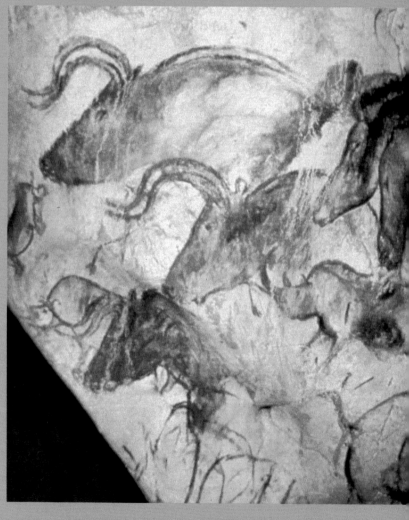

In 1994 hikers discovered cave paintings near Avignon (a vee NYAWN), France. These paintings are believed to be 20,000 years old. The artists used iron dust, sand, and clay to paint these images. Looking at art tells us some of what was important to the people who created it. What do you think was important to the artist who painted the animals here?

This Chinese painting was created around A.D. 1000. The artist painted this scene on silk cloth.

Dutch painter Pieter Brueghel (BROY gul) painted this agricultural scene in the mid-1500s. What does this painting show about life in Europe in the 1500s?

Similar to artists in ancient France, modern artists use materials available to them to give their impressions of the world. American artist Hima Pamoedjo used a computer to create the image shown here.

50,000 B.C.	40,000 B.C.	30,000 B.C.	20,000 B.C.	10,000 B.C.	4,000 B.C.

Agriculture Changes the World

Read Aloud

What would you do if there were no markets or restaurants from which to buy food? How would you find something to eat? You learned in the last lesson that early people faced this challenge by hunting and gathering their food from the wild. However, you can probably think of another way people get food from Earth.

Focus Activity

READ TO LEARN

What was life like in an early farming community?

VOCABULARY

- agriculture
- New Stone Age
- domesticate
- surplus
- specialization
- civilization
- trade

THE BIG PICTURE

About 12,000 years ago Earth's cool climate began to warm. This change caused the number of plants and animals on Earth to soar. The number of people grew as well, as hunters and gatherers around the world took advantage of Earth's new bounty.

Many archaeologists think that some hunters and gatherers began building permanent homes in places rich with wild grains and animals. In time, these early people started to experiment with agriculture. Agriculture is the raising of crops and animals for human use. These experiments changed life on Earth forever.

The period beginning about 12,000 years ago and ending roughly 6,000 years ago is called the New Stone Age. During this time people all around the world still depended on stone tools, but began experimenting with agriculture. Agriculture continues to shape the ways we live today. It is the reason you can go to a supermarket. It is also the reason you may live on a farm—or in a town or city.

52

CATAL HUYUK

On the grassy banks of the Carsamba (chahr SHAHM bah) River in southern Turkey sits a large mound. The mound covers over 32 acres, an area the size of 21 football fields. Underneath this big but ordinary-looking hill rests one of the world's first cities: Catal Huyuk (CHAH tul HOO yook). Parts of this city on the Carsamba River plain existed over 8,500 years ago.

Catal Huyuk is the largest city this old ever uncovered by archaeologists. The city once housed about 5,000 people. How could so many people live close together at a time when most still lived as hunters and gatherers? The answer is agriculture.

Agriculture Brings Change

Agriculture provided a way for people to live in large groups without the need to travel great distances to gather food. To use agriculture, people first had to domesticate (duh MES tih kayt) plants and animals. To domesticate means to train something to be useful to people. For example, people at Catal Huyuk learned to plant seeds and care for edible plants like wheat, barley, peas, and lentils.

The world's first farmers also learned to domesticate animals such as wild goats, cattle, and sheep. Domestica-

CATAL HUYUK

MAP WORK

Catal Huyuk, the site of one of the world's first farming communities, lies in present-day Turkey.

What countries border Turkey?

tion involved more than taming the animals. It meant breeding them to be most useful to humans. Wild sheep, for example, have very little wool. In contrast, domestic sheep have been bred to grow thick layers of the useful material.

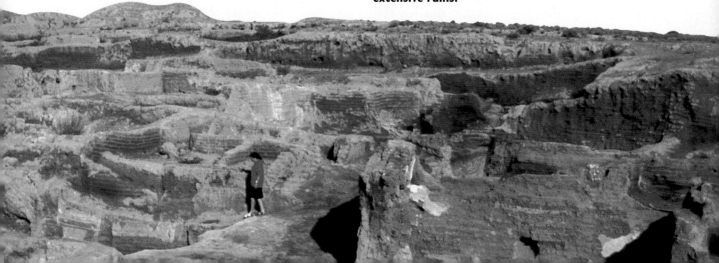

The ruins of Catal Huyuk were not discovered until 1958. Today many tourists visit these extensive ruins.

LIVING IN CATAL HUYUK

In some ways living in Catal Huyuk was like living in a city today. In other ways it was very different. The similarities and differences begin with the kinds of houses people lived in.

A New Kind of Home

The homes of Catal Huyuk were built to last. Houses had brick walls coated with white plaster. The large, flat reed roofs were supported by wooden beams. Houses were built right against each other, perhaps to defend the city from attack. There were no streets in Catal Huyuk and no doors on the houses. People entered their homes from the roof, by climbing down ladders!

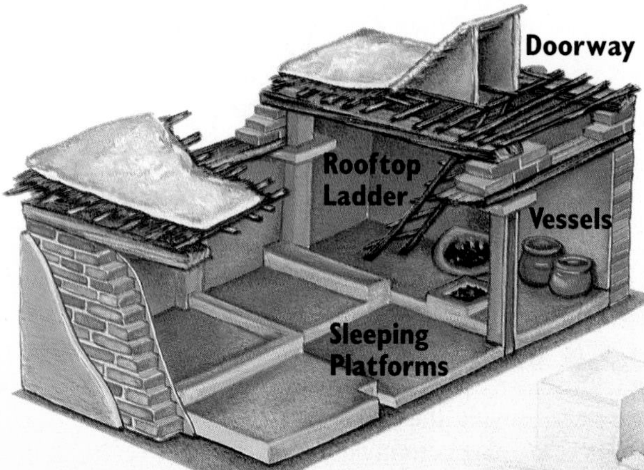

Doorway

Rooftop Ladder

Vessels

Sleeping Platforms

ROOFTOP LIVING IN CATAL HUYUK

What jobs shown in the diagram required special skills?

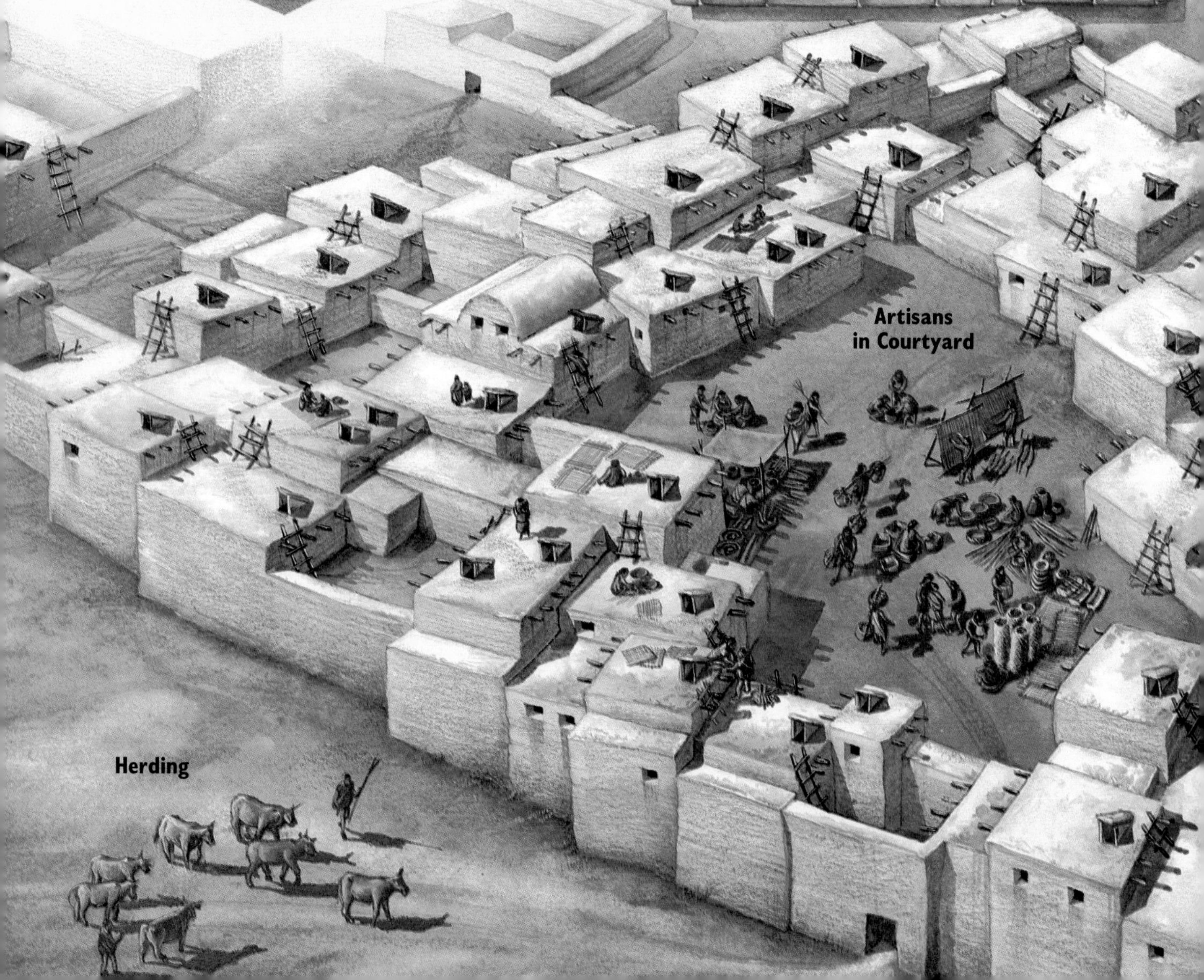

Artisans in Courtyard

Herding

About one out of every three buildings in the city was probably a temple. Therefore, archaeologists think that religion played a big role in daily life. And what may have been the world's first wall paintings—of cattle, leopards, and other things—filled these rooms. This fact suggests that religion in Catal Huyuk may have focused on the success of domestic crops and animals. These were important to the survival of people of the city.

Like many apartment buildings today, homes in Catal Huyuk were all about the same size and shape. Coming down from the roof, people entered a home's main living room. Near the base of the ladder were a fireplace and an oven for heating and cooking. Built into the walls were raised platforms covered with reed mats. These platforms served as all-purpose sofas and beds. A tiny doorway led to the family's storage room. There, large clay pots held stores of wheat and barley.

New Ways of Life

People in Catal Huyuk depended on the grain stores kept in these pots. Agriculture created a new food surplus that hunters and gatherers never had. A surplus is an extra supply of something. Enough crops could be harvested to provide food for the whole year. Cattle provided a steady supply of milk and meat.

The people who worked as farmers were able to provide food for all of the people of Catal Huyuk. There was even some left over for winter. But farming for a whole community was a demanding job. It left little time for other tasks.

The demands on farmers' time led to specialization, or people training to do particular kinds of work. Thus, while some people farmed, other people made wheat into bread flour. Others specialized in making things like tools, bricks, and pots. Since farmers could produce more food than their families needed, they could exchange their surplus food with workers who made other products.

Agriculture changed everyday chores in the city as well. Taking out the trash, for example, was not as simple as burying it in a nearby field. People had to carry it up to the roof, across other people's roofs, and over to the nearest empty courtyard. Courtyards, spaces often left by broken-down homes, served as local garbage dumps.

These changes in community life sparked the growth of a complex new civilization (sihv uh luh ZAY shun) at Catal Huyuk. A civilization is a culture that has developed systems of specialization, religion, learning, and government. The busy town grew until it had about 1,000 homes.

Links to MATHEMATICS

That's a Lot of Wheat!

How much more wheat can we produce now than people could during the New Stone Age?

It's impossible to know exactly how much wheat people were able to grow in Catal Huyuk. But one thing is certain. Agriculture has come a long way since the New Stone Age. In the United States today, modern farming methods help to provide wheat for everyone in America—with surplus to sell to other countries.

In the modern United States, each acre of farmland yields about 35 bushels of wheat per year. If each bushel weighs 60 pounds, how many pounds of wheat are produced on each acre of farmland?

A BUSY CITY

In its time, Catal Huyuk was probably widely known for its arts, crafts, and tools. The city's workers used new kinds of technology to make wonderful assortments of clay pots, woven cloth, and copper jewelry. These were among the first of their kind in the world. By about age 12, girls and boys probably helped to make these products, since they were taught the skills of their mothers and fathers.

Although people in Catal Huyuk depended on stone tools, they began to work with a new material: copper. After gathering pieces of copper, craftworkers made their fires burn hot enough to soften the metal. Once softened, the copper was hammered into the shapes of rings, beads, or pins.

It also took several steps to produce fine wool cloth. First, wool was sheared from domestic sheep. Next, the material was separated and twisted into thread. Finally, the thread was carefully woven into cloth on wooden looms.

Artifacts from Catal Huyuk include necklaces and artwork of a hunt dance.

Signs of Movement

Catal Huyuk's crafts attracted many people to the city. They wanted to own some of the useful and beautiful new products. People in Catal Huyuk wanted to see the things others had to offer. Trade, or the exchange of goods, boomed between city residents and visitors to the city.

One thing that people in Catal Huyuk traded was obsidian (ub SIHD ee un). Obsidian is a glassy, black rock used to make beautiful mirrors and razor-sharp knives. City residents probably traveled to a nearby volcano to gather the black stones. Cattle were used to carry back the heavy loads. Craftworkers then made the obsidian into goods to trade with people from all around the region.

People from Near and Far

The people of Catal Huyuk probably traded obsidian knives and arrowheads with people who lived in forests miles away. In return, they received oak wood needed for house-building, along with such treats as apples and nuts.

Traders from nearby areas probably brought many other popular goods to Catal Huyuk. These goods included red paint used in temples and raw copper to be made into tools and jewelry.

Traders also came to Catal Huyuk from faraway places. Archaeologists have found remains of the city's special obsidian goods in ancient settlements as far away as modern Syria. They have also found pieces of Syrian pottery in Catal Huyuk, along with shells from the Red Sea.

People, as well as goods, were on the move, both to and from Catal Huyuk. Archaeologists have found evidence that people from far and wide

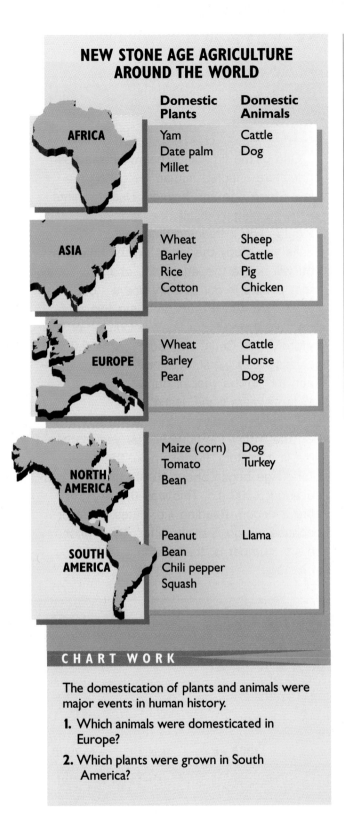

NEW STONE AGE AGRICULTURE AROUND THE WORLD

	Domestic Plants	Domestic Animals
AFRICA	Yam Date palm Millet	Cattle Dog
ASIA	Wheat Barley Rice Cotton	Sheep Cattle Pig Chicken
EUROPE	Wheat Barley Pear	Cattle Horse Dog
NORTH AMERICA	Maize (corn) Tomato Bean	Dog Turkey
SOUTH AMERICA	Peanut Bean Chili pepper Squash	Llama

CHART WORK

The domestication of plants and animals were major events in human history.

1. Which animals were domesticated in Europe?

2. Which plants were grown in South America?

moved to and lived in the city. They brought with them their own skills and traditions. This may be part of the reason for the growth of this rich and complex civilization.

WHY IT MATTERS

As the chart on this page shows, many groups began to develop agriculture during the New Stone Age. The relatively complex civilization of Catal Huyuk showed just how much agriculture could change life. Even bigger changes were yet to come. In the next chapter you will read about another civilization based on agriculture. It, too, rose up along the banks of a river. Unlike the people of Catal Huyuk, the people there developed ways to tell their secrets to others through the ages.

✓ Reviewing Facts and Ideas

MAIN IDEAS

● Agriculture made it possible for a few people to raise food for an entire group. Others could specialize, or concentrate on other tasks.

● People of Catal Huyuk were among the first to make pottery and obsidian and metal products. They also traded.

THINK ABOUT IT

1. What is involved in domesticating plants and animals?

2. How did trade help people, both outside and within Catal Huyuk? How did trade help the city to grow?

3. **FOCUS** How did the development of agriculture change the way people lived?

4. **THINKING SKILL** Suppose that you are a visitor to Catal Huyuk. _Decide_ whether you want to become a farmer or craftworker for the city, or to remain a hunter and gatherer in the forests nearby.

5. **GEOGRAPHY** Explain how agriculture changed the way people interacted with their environments.

Reading Time Lines

VOCABULARY

time line
circa

WHY THE SKILL MATTERS

During the New Stone Age, agriculture became a worldwide development. People in North Africa began domesticating cattle and barley, while people in Central and South America raised corn, beans, and animals called llamas. Farmers in other regions domesticated other plants and animals.

One of the easiest ways to keep track of when events happened is to use a time line. A time line is a diagram that shows when things took place in a given period of time. Its words tell what happened and when. The spaces between descriptions indicate how much time passed between events.

USING THE SKILL

One of the time lines below shows how agriculture affected human life during the New Stone Age and beyond. Use the hints in the Helping Yourself box on the next page to guide you in reading time lines.

As you study the labels on the time lines, you will notice the letters B.C. and A.D. Today most people in our country use a 1,500-year-old system that divides time into two periods. "B.C." stands for "before Christ," or before Jesus Christ was born (about 2,000 years ago). "A.D." stands for "anno Domini"—Latin for "in the year of our Lord"—and refers to years since Jesus' birth.

To read B.C. dates you need to remember: the *higher* the number, the *earlier* that time is in history. For example, the New Stone Age began about 10,000 B.C. and ended about 4000 B.C. This was 6,000 years after it began. Reading A.D. dates is easier because we do it all the time. The *higher* an A.D. number is, the *later* that time is in history.

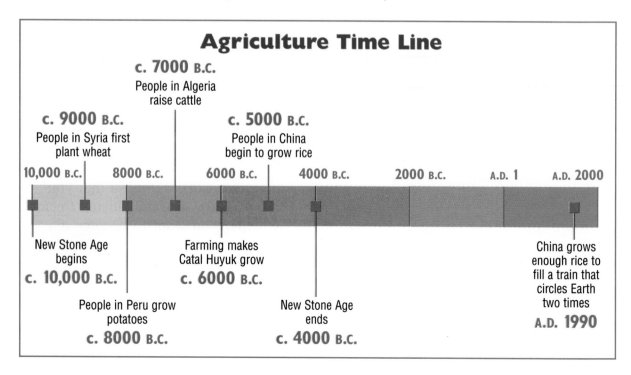

Agriculture Time Line

c. 7000 B.C.
People in Algeria raise cattle

c. 9000 B.C.
People in Syria first plant wheat

c. 5000 B.C.
People in China begin to grow rice

10,000 B.C.   8000 B.C.   6000 B.C.   4000 B.C.   2000 B.C.   A.D. 1   A.D. 2000

New Stone Age begins
c. 10,000 B.C.

Farming makes Catal Huyuk grow
c. 6000 B.C.

China grows enough rice to fill a train that circles Earth two times
A.D. 1990

People in Peru grow potatoes
c. 8000 B.C.

New Stone Age ends
c. 4000 B.C.

You will also notice that some dates on the time lines have the letter *c.* before them. The lowercase *c.* stands for **circa**, another Latin word. Circa means "about" or "around." If historians are not sure exactly when something happened, they use the term *circa*.

Study the agriculture time line on the opposite page. On what period of time does it focus? Is most of that time A.D. or B.C.? About how many years passed between the time people in China began to grow rice and the end of the New Stone Age?

TRYING THE SKILL

After you have practiced reading the agriculture time line, try studying the time line about the growth of technology. Each entry describes how people used materials from

their environments to make useful tools or crafts. With what material did people in Peru make nets and baskets in 8000 B.C.? What sorts of materials are people using in A.D. 1997?

REVIEWING THE SKILL

Use the technology time line on this page to answer the following questions:

1. What sort of information do time lines show?

2. About how many years does the time line below cover?

3. How many years passed between the time Japanese people first began making clay pots and the time people in Iraq began painting pottery?

4. How does using the time line help you to understand the development of agriculture?

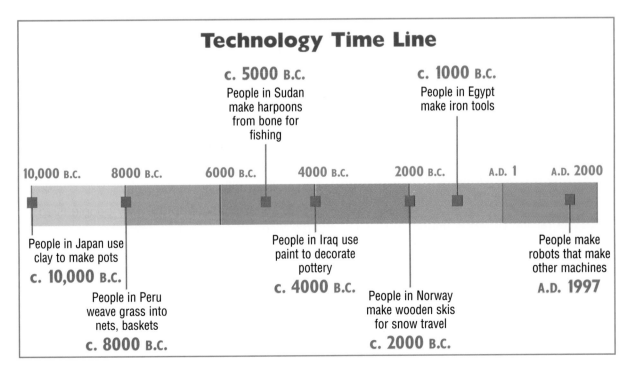

Technology Time Line

c. 5000 B.C.
People in Sudan make harpoons from bone for fishing

c. 1000 B.C.
People in Egypt make iron tools

| 10,000 B.C. | 8000 B.C. | 6000 B.C. | 4000 B.C. | 2000 B.C. | A.D. 1 | A.D. 2000 |

People in Japan use clay to make pots
c. 10,000 B.C.

People in Peru weave grass into nets, baskets
c. 8000 B.C.

People in Iraq use paint to decorate pottery
c. 4000 B.C.

People in Norway make wooden skis for snow travel
c. 2000 B.C.

People make robots that make other machines
A.D. 1997

CHAPTER 3 REVIEW

Major Events

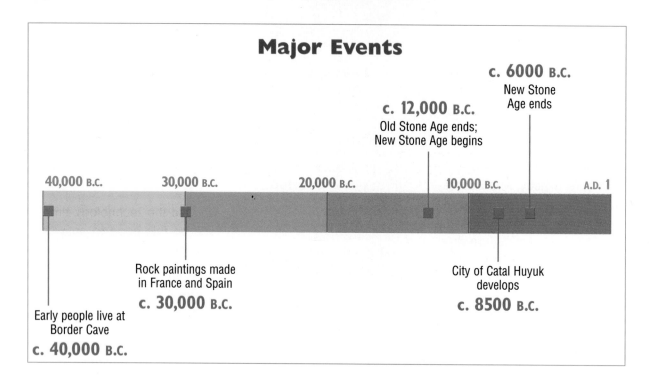

c. 6000 B.C.
New Stone Age ends

c. 12,000 B.C.
Old Stone Age ends;
New Stone Age begins

40,000 B.C.   30,000 B.C.   20,000 B.C.   10,000 B.C.   A.D. 1

Rock paintings made
in France and Spain
c. 30,000 B.C.

City of Catal Huyuk
develops
c. 8500 B.C.

Early people live at
Border Cave
c. 40,000 B.C.

THINKING ABOUT VOCABULARY

Number a sheet of paper from 1 to 10. Beside each number write the word or term from the list below that best matches the definition.

agriculture   Old Stone Age
circa   specialization
civilization   surplus
domesticate   time line
New Stone Age   trade

1. An exchange of goods
2. The period until about 12,000 years ago when the use of stone tools was widespread
3. The raising of crops and animals for human use
4. To train plants or animals to be useful to people
5. An extra supply of something
6. The doing of particular kinds of work

7. The period from 12,000 to 6,000 years ago when people developed agriculture and used stone tools
8. A Latin word that means "about" or "around"
9. A diagram that shows when things took place in a certain period of time
10. A culture with developed systems of religion, learning, and government

THINKING ABOUT FACTS

1. What are the earliest signs of human life that scientists have found?
2. How was the New Stone Age different from the Old Stone Age?
3. What changes in the way people lived did agriculture make possible?
4. What is Catal Huyuk, and where is it located? What did archaeologists learn after they uncovered it?
5. What is obsidian? Why was it important to the people of Catal Huyuk?

THINK AND WRITE ◄▬▬►

WRITING A PARAGRAPH OF CONTRAST
Write a paragraph about the differences between the Old Stone Age and the New Stone Age. Discuss methods of obtaining food, types of shelter, and tools.

WRITING A JOURNAL ENTRY
Suppose that you have gone back in time to live in the New Stone Age. Using the diagram of Catal Huyuk on page 54, write a journal entry about your life there. Include details about the way you live, the work you do, and the people you see.

WRITING ABOUT PERSPECTIVES
We are different in many ways from people who lived in the Old Stone Age. However, we also have much in common. Describe three ways you think you are like a person of your age who lived near Border Cave about 40,000 years ago.

APPLYING STUDY SKILLS

READING TIME LINES
1. What is a time line?
2. Look at the time line on page 60. Add the following event in its correct place on the time line: People in Peru weave grass into nets and baskets.
3. Look at the time line on page 60. Add the following event in its correct place: People in China begin to grow rice.
4. On the time line on page 60, add the following event in its correct place: Earth's cool climate began to warm.
5. In what ways are time lines useful?

Summing Up the Chapter

Copy the compare-and-contrast chart below on a separate piece of paper. Then review the chapter to find some of the things that changed during the Old and the New Stone Ages. When you have filled in the chart, use the information to write a paragraph that answers the question "How did early people use their environment to improve their lives?"

MAIN IDEA Early people developed innovative ways of adapting to their environment in order to meet their basic survival needs.	
Old Stone Age	**New Stone Age**
....	....
....	....
....	....

UNIT 1 REVIEW

THINKING ABOUT VOCABULARY

archaeology
artifact
civilization
climate
degree

geography
Old Stone Age
oral tradition
time line
values

Number a sheet of paper from 1 to 10. Beside each number write the word or term from the list above that best matches the definition.

1. A culture with developed systems of religion, learning, and government

2. The study of Earth, including its land, water, weather, and plants

3. The study of the remains of past cultures

4. The things people believe in and think are important

5. The passing on by word of mouth of stories, history, and information

6. The weather pattern over a long period of time

7. The period from 2 million to about 12,000 years ago when people used mostly stone tools

8. A diagram that shows when things happened during a certain period of time

9. A unit of map measurement that describes distance between lines of latitude and longitude

10. An object made by somebody in the past

THINK AND WRITE

WRITING A LETTER
Write to somebody who lives far away. Describe the climate and two or three interesting geographical features of your area. Also tell about some of the customs of the people who live in your community.

WRITING ABOUT PERSPECTIVES
Suppose that you are asked to bury three things that belong to you. These objects should help some future historian learn about the way you lived. Write a paragraph about what you would choose and why.

WRITING AN INTERVIEW
Suppose you could interview one person from the Old Stone Age and one person from the New Stone Age. Write a set of questions you would ask each person and the answers you think they would give.

BUILDING SKILLS

1. **Latitude and longitude** Look at the map on page 15. What is the approximate latitude and longitude of Sri Lanka?

2. **Latitude and longitude** Look at an atlas of the United States and find a map that shows your area. What is the latitude and longitude of your community? Find a community on the other side of the world that has the same latitude. What is the longitude of that community?

3. **Decision making** What is a good first step in making a decision?

4. **Decision making** How would you go about deciding what book to read for an end-of-unit book report? What are the steps you would take?

5. **Time lines** Using events from Unit 1, make a civilizations time line. Put the events in their correct places. Keep this time line so you can add more events.

YESTERDAY, TODAY &
TOMORROW

Historians learn about past civilizations from the artifacts and records that have been left behind. Our civilization will leave large numbers of artifacts and records. Which ones do you think will be most valuable for future historians? Explain your choices.

READING ON YOUR OWN

Here are some books you might find at the library to help you learn more.

THE ICEMAN
by Don Lessem

This book tells of the discovery – found between Austria and Italy – of the remains of a man estimated to have lived over 5,000 years ago.

DIG THIS!
by Michael Avi-Yonah

This discussion highlights archaeological excavations of ancient cities.

STORIES ON STONE
by Jennifer Owings Dewey

Read this story to find out who drew pictures on stone long ago in the southwestern United States.

UNIT PROJECT

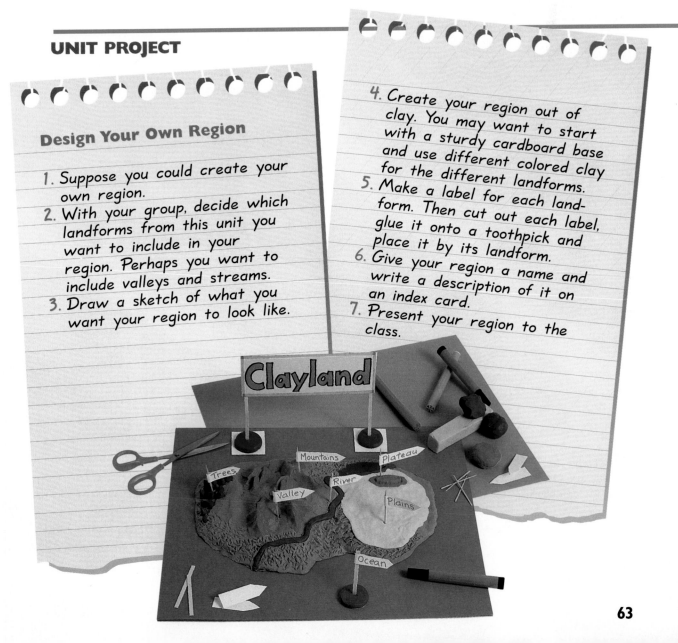

Design Your Own Region

1. Suppose you could create your own region.
2. With your group, decide which landforms from this unit you want to include in your region. Perhaps you want to include valleys and streams.
3. Draw a sketch of what you want your region to look like.
4. Create your region out of clay. You may want to start with a sturdy cardboard base and use different colored clay for the different landforms.
5. Make a label for each landform. Then cut out each label, glue it onto a toothpick and place it by its landform.
6. Give your region a name and write a description of it on an index card.
7. Present your region to the class.

Clayland

Mountains
Plateau
Trees
River
Valley
Plains
Ocean

SEDER PLATE, SPAIN

ANCIENT COFFIN, EGYPT

LIFE-SIZED HORSEMAN, CHINA

River Valley Civilizations

"I have inscribed my precious words."

from the Code of Hammurabi
See page 113.

Why Does It Matter?

Hammurabi, the king of the ancient empire of Babylonia, had these words inscribed in stone about 4,000 years ago. His words introduced the laws he had created for the people of his empire. This is one of the earliest recorded examples of written laws. Even before Hammurabi lived, people in that part of the world had developed systems of writing. They recorded important information about their lives. By studying texts like this, historians have learned about languages, laws, and customs of ancient civilizations. Babylonia was a powerful civilization that grew in the fertile river valleys of Mesopotamia, in western Asia. Other river valley civilizations developed in Egypt, India, and China. In this unit you will read about legacies left by these ancient peoples that continue to influence the world today.

FIND OUT MORE!
Visit our website:
www.mhschool.com

inter**NET**
CONNECTION

Adventures
with
NATIONAL
GEOGRAPHIC

HIGH AND DRY

Around 1270 B.C., an Egyptian pharaoh named Ramses II had two temples built along the banks of the Nile. Four colossal statues of Ramses himself—each more than 60 feet high—marked the entrance to the larger temple. For 3,000 years, the statues sat on their enormous stone thrones. Then, in the 1960s, the Egyptians built a dam on the Nile, and water started rising behind the dam. Soon, the water would cover the temples! Many nations got together for a massive rescue effort. Workers cut the temples into more than a thousand pieces, lifted them to a place above the level of the water, and put the pieces together again. Now the statues again sit high and dry.

GEO JOURNAL

You're an Egyptian official in the 1960s. Write a letter to the United Nations, explaining why the world should help save the temples of Ramses II.

Ancient Egypt

THINKING ABOUT
HISTORY AND GEOGRAPHY

The story of ancient Egypt begins with farmers along the Nile River. They formed communities that grew into cities. In 3100 B.C. Menes united Egypt. Rulers who came after him ordered the building of large, stone monuments such as the pyramids. They also led trading expeditions south and east and increased their land. By 1200 B.C. goods and ideas spread from Egypt's capital city, Thebes, to three continents.

2600 B.C.

5000 B.C.

3100 B.C.

GIZA
Khufu orders the building of the Great Pyramid

NILE RIVER DELTA
Egyptians begin to farm

MEMPHIS
Menes unites Egypt

5000 B.C.   4000 B.C.   3000 B.C.

EUROPE

Mediterranean Sea

Nile River delta

ASIA

Giza

Memphis

EGYPT

Thebes

AFRICA

RED SEA

1500 B.C.

1200 B.C.

Punt

PUNT

Hatshepsut expands Egypt's trade to other parts of Africa

THEBES

Goods produced in Thebes are traded across the Egyptian empire

INDIAN OCEAN

2000 B.C.   1000 B.C.

National Geographic Society

Focus Activity

READ TO LEARN

In what ways did the ancient Egyptians depend upon the Nile River?

VOCABULARY

- silt
- delta
- irrigation

PLACES

- Nile River
- Lower Egypt
- Upper Egypt

Geography of Ancient Egypt

Read Aloud

"Hail O Nile, who comes to give life to the people of Egypt. Created by the sun-god to give life to all who thirst. Who lets the desert drink with streams descending from heaven. Who makes barley and creates wheat so that temples celebrate. When the Nile overflows, offerings are made to you, cattle are [killed] for you, that your goodness be repaid."

These words are from a 3,000-year-old Egyptian song, "Hymn to the Nile."

THE BIG PICTURE

Around 5000 B.C. people began building farming villages in a river valley in Africa, several hundred miles south of Catal Huyuk. The area around Egypt's **Nile River** valley probably did not look like a very good place to start farming.

The river wound its way through a vast desert with few signs of life. Yet every year the Nile flooded its banks. The river swamped everything in its path with water and mud for four solid months—from July through October.

This yearly flood made the Nile Valley lush and green. It also allowed people to make use of the land. With the help of water from the Nile River, ancient farmers turned the Nile Valley into a productive agricultural region.

THE GIFT OF THE NILE

In many ways, Egyptian civilization owes its life to the Nile River. The Nile provided water and food in the desert. This seemed like a blessing from the gods of the ancient people. For that reason, Egypt has often been called the "Gift of the Nile."

A Mighty River

The Nile is the world's longest river. It flows over 4,000 miles north from the snowcapped mountains of East Africa. It passes through the present-day countries of Uganda, Ethiopia, Sudan, and Egypt. Then the Nile empties into the warm Mediterranean Sea.

Much of East Africa has a rainy season that lasts from May until September. During that time the Nile swells with rainwater and rushes northward with extra power. The river carries off silt as it goes. Silt is a mixture of tiny bits of soil and rock.

Over time, much of the silt has been deposited where the Nile empties into the Mediterranean. There the river divides into several branches, forming a vast, fan-shaped delta. A delta is very fertile, flat land made of silt left behind as a river drains into a larger body of water. Look at the map on this page. Use the map scale to find the width of the Nile Delta at its widest point.

The Nile Delta region is in northern Egypt, and appears nearer the top on maps that have north at the top. This makes the delta seem to be "higher." The delta, however, is called Lower Egypt, because it is the lower, or downstream, part of the Nile.

In Upper Egypt, to the south, the Nile cuts through stone cliffs and desert sands. This landscape is very different from the mild, fertile delta.

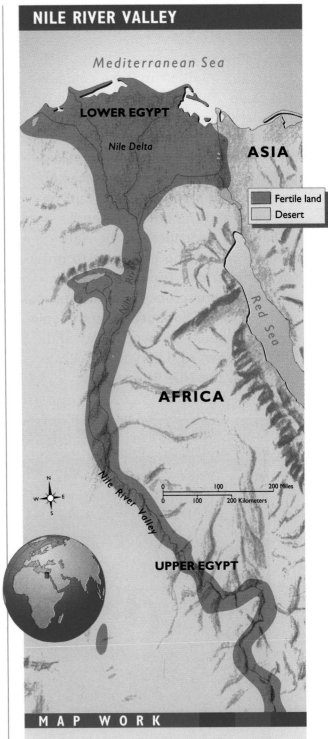

NILE RIVER VALLEY

Mediterranean Sea

LOWER EGYPT

Nile Delta

ASIA

Fertile land
Desert

Nile River

Red Sea

AFRICA

Nile River Valley

UPPER EGYPT

M A P   W O R K

The mighty Nile River winds its way through the northeastern part of Africa.

1. In which direction would you travel to get from the Nile River to the Red Sea?

2. The Nile Delta is near the division between which two continents?

3. Where is the largest fertile region along the Nile?

A LAND OF DROUGHT AND FLOOD

Egyptian farmers almost always welcomed the mud left by each summer's Nile flood. This silt-filled mud was rich in minerals needed by plants. The black soil brought by the Nile contrasted sharply with the dry, yellow sand of Egypt's desert. In many places a farmer could stand with one foot on farmland and the other on sand!

Farmers depended on the right amount of flooding each year to grow successful crops. Too little flooding meant farmers' crops failed and people went hungry. Too much meant people and cattle could be swept away and homes destroyed. Life was a delicate balance in the Nile River valley.

A System of Agriculture

In October the flooded land began to dry. Then farmers planted wheat and barley. They also planted garden vegetables such as cucumbers, lettuce, onions, and beans. Farmers also grew flax, a plant used to make cloth.

To water their newly planted crops, Egypt's farmers used a form of technology called irrigation. Irrigation is the watering of land by means of canals or pipes. At first, farmers simply built dirt walls around their farmland to hold the Nile floodwaters in the fields. Later, they dug small channels, or canals, to bring water from the Nile directly to their farmland. Farmers scooped water from the canals and poured it into the fields, using a bucket-lifter called a shadouf (shah DOOF). The photograph on this page shows how this tool is still used today.

By March the crops were ready for harvesting. In good years the fields were filled with ripe vegetables and grains. Then farm families had more food than they needed. Their surplus, or extra supply of goods, was then gathered up and carried off to storehouses. As in Catal Huyuk, these grain stores made specialization and community life possible.

Travel Along the Nile

Harvest-time ended in late June, before the Nile once again began to flood. During the four-month flood

Ancient Egyptians found ways to make farming easier and more productive. A shadouf, shown in the picture (above), helped distribute water to the fields. Farmers also built plows, like the one in the model (left), which animals pulled through the fields.

The British Museum

season, farmers could not work in their fields. Instead, many used the time to visit neighboring villages.

Flood season was one of the busiest times for travel on the Nile. Yet river traffic was heavy all year. The Nile was the main way that people and goods moved from place to place. The 600-mile journey between Upper and Lower Egypt would take over a month to walk. In a reed boat it took only about half that time.

WHY IT MATTERS

By 5000 B.C. life in the early farming communities of ancient Egypt centered around the Nile River. The river provided the Egyptian people with fertile soil, water for irrigation, and a means of transportation.

Throughout Egypt's long history, the world's longest river has played a key role. In time, the ancient Egyptians would use the Nile to build the largest civilization the world had ever seen. The following lessons will introduce you to this rich civilization.

Links to MATHEMATICS

The Trusty Nilometer!

How did Egyptians measure the yearly level of the Nile flood?

Ancient Egyptians built special staircases along the river to measure the height of the Nile as it rose. Each step was one "cubit" high—the distance from a person's elbow to the tip of the thumb. One cubit is about 20 inches.

In a good flood year, the Nile rose 16 steps on the Nilometers. How many feet does this equal? In a bad flood year, the Nile rose only 7 steps or less. How many feet is this?

 Reviewing Facts and Ideas

MAIN IDEAS

- The Nile is the world's longest river. It is more than 4,000 miles long.
- Farmers' understanding of the yearly Nile floods made community life in Egypt possible.
- Mineral-rich silt deposits and irrigation technology made farming in ancient Egypt very productive.
- People used boats to get from place to place along the Nile.

THINK ABOUT IT

1. Describe the irrigation methods used by the ancient Egyptians.

2. How did the Nile's yearly floods help ancient Egyptian farmers?

3. **FOCUS** Name three ways the people of ancient Egypt used the Nile River.

4. **THINKING SKILL** As an ancient farmer, *decide* whether Upper Egypt or Lower Egypt is a better place for farming.

5. **GEOGRAPHY** Look at the map on page 71. Describe three different types of physical regions that the Nile flows through.

Land of the Pharaohs

Focus Activity

READ TO LEARN

What role did the pharaohs play in ancient Egypt?

VOCABULARY

- unification
- pharaoh
- economy
- hieroglyphics
- scribe
- papyrus

PEOPLE

- Menes
- Khufu

PLACES

- Memphis
- Thebes

Read Aloud

About 3100 B.C. two mighty kings met in battle. One king wore a white crown and ruled over a long stretch of the Nile River in Upper Egypt. The other king had a red crown and controlled a large area in Lower Egypt. The outcome of the battle was of enormous importance. Whoever won it would control the biggest kingdom in the world.

THE BIG PICTURE

You have already read that farming towns began appearing in different parts of the world during the New Stone Age. Some towns grew into small cities, as people specialized and developed trade with neighboring towns.

These communities created rules to promote peace and fairness among neighbors. Village leaders were usually in charge of creating these rules and making sure that the rules were followed. As the communities grew larger, their governments changed to meet their many new needs.

Along the Nile River in Egypt, groups of villages joined together under the leadership of kings. These larger communities developed complex systems of government. Soon the people of the Nile River valley would see even greater changes in the way their communities were run.

74

UNION OF TWO CROWNS

Along the Nile River 5,000 years ago, Egypt's villages were thriving. Farmers were learning how to produce more surplus crops. Craftworkers in villages were using new technology to make tools, pottery, and jewelry. How do you think this affected trade? As you may have guessed, the Nile River became crowded with boats as trade increased between towns.

Egyptians Join Together

In the midst of all this activity, there were also terror and fear. Ruins of walls around early towns and paintings of bloody battle scenes suggest that there were many wars between villages. To better protect themselves and their belongings, the people along the Nile banded together into two separate kingdoms. Towns in Upper Egypt supported a king who wore a white crown. Towns in Lower Egypt followed a king who wore a red crown.

Then, about 3100 B.C., this changed. Forces led by **Menes** (MEE nees), the king of Upper Egypt, swept north into the Nile Delta. Menes's army overthrew the king of Lower Egypt. To show his victory, Menes wore a double crown. It combined his white crown with the red crown of Lower Egypt. This change stood for the **unification** of Egypt. Unification is the joining of separate parts into one.

Following this unification of the two kingdoms, Menes became the first **pharaoh** (FAY roh) of Egypt. The word *pharaoh* actually refers to the "great palace" in which the rulers lived. Later it became the name given to all the rulers of Egypt. The time when Egypt's early pharaohs worked to build unity within the country is called the Old Kingdom. It lasted from about 2686 B.C. until 2181 B.C. Two other major periods in ancient Egypt's history, the Middle Kingdom and the New Kingdom, would follow.

These Egyptian carvings show rulers and the crowns they wore. The middle crown represents a unification of the other two.

Red Crown   Double Crown   White Crown

LIFE IN THE OLD KINGDOM

At first, Egypt's pharaohs did not greatly change the civilization that they ruled. They mainly added to the practices of local government, trade, and religion that had existed for hundreds of years along the Nile.

In time, though, the pharaoh became the center of the civilization. His or her actions shaped the fate of all Egypt.

Government Under the Pharaohs

After unification, the most powerful local leaders in Egypt were made area governors for the new government. They performed some of the same services as your local leaders. They were in charge of collecting taxes in their areas and served as local judges. They had different duties as well. Ancient Egyptian governors made sure that precious flood waters were shared fairly among farmers through the use of canals and storage pools.

The area governors reported to the pharaoh's headquarters in Memphis, Egypt's capital city. Memphis was located between Upper and Lower Egypt, near present-day Cairo. From the palace in Memphis, the pharaoh decided how Egypt's affairs should be run, from the highest to the lowest levels.

Religion in Egypt

The pharaoh had great political power in Egypt. He or she had great religious powers as well. In fact, Egyptians believed that the pharaoh was a child of their sun god Ra (RAH). Just as Egyptians believed that Ra gave life to Earth, so they believed that the pharaoh gave life to Egypt and its people. Just as Ra deserved to be worshiped, so, too, did the pharaoh.

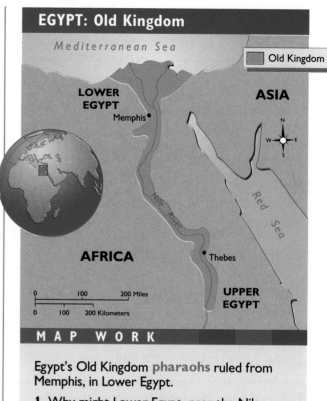

EGYPT: Old Kingdom

□ Old Kingdom

Mediterranean Sea
LOWER EGYPT
Memphis
ASIA
AFRICA
Thebes
Nile River
Red Sea
UPPER EGYPT

0   100   200 Miles
0   100   200 Kilometers

MAP WORK

Egypt's Old Kingdom pharaohs ruled from Memphis, in Lower Egypt.

1. Why might Lower Egypt, near the Nile Delta, be a good place for a rich capital city?

2. Suppose you lived in Upper Egypt and were invited to Memphis. Would you travel with the flow of the Nile, or against it?

Ra was the most important of the many gods whom ancient Egyptians worshiped. Egyptians believed different gods had different roles. For example, one god caused the flooding of the Nile. Another gave potters and metalworkers their creativity. Other gods took the form of snakes or crocodiles. The god Isis protected people from sickness and harm. Her husband Osiris represented the dead who awaited rebirth.

Osiris was important because belief in the afterlife was central to the religion of Egypt. Egyptians believed that after a person died, he or she would go on to the "Next World." Egyptians believed that the dead could take food and objects into the "Next World." Thus, food and belongings were buried with the dead.

Ancient Egyptians preserved the bodies of dead royalty with a process called *mummification*. The bodies were dried and wrapped in strips of cloth. Sometimes pets such as cats were also mummified to accompany their owners into the afterlife.

Egypt's Economy

Since the pharaoh was considered a god, all things in Egypt belonged to him or her. This put the pharaoh at the center of Egypt's economy. The economy of a country is the way its people manage money and resources for the production of goods and services.

Egypt's economy was based on agriculture. Farmers produced a surplus of food, which fed the whole country. How was that surplus divided? The main way was through taxes. The pharaoh collected a large part of every farmer's crops each year as taxes. The grain, eggs, meat, fruits, and olive oil were then used to feed

the pharaoh's family and servants. The goods were also used to pay for any other items the pharaoh wanted.

The pharaoh also took taxes on everything else made in Egypt, such as leather goods, linen cloth, and baskets. The pharaoh even taxed people's time. During flood season, for example, Egyptians from priests to potters to farmers were called upon to build canals or buildings for the government.

Egypt's craftworkers and artists depended on the pharaohs for their jobs. These people spent most of their time working to keep Egypt's many temples supplied. For example, temples needed golden bowls and stone statues.

Since the pharaoh owned all of Egypt's temples, it was the government's job to pay for all the supplies they used. No money changed hands, since money did not exist in Egypt at that time. Rather, goods of equal value were traded. For their efforts, craftworkers received clothes and food.

Mummies were wrapped in cloth and covered with masks before being put in coffins. Portraits and scenes of daily life were painted on the tomb walls.

The British Museum

The Granger Collection

A SYSTEM OF WRITING

How was it possible for the pharaoh's government to keep track of all of its business details? How could it make sure, for example, that a farmer in Upper Egypt was paying taxes or that a temple in the Delta had enough linen?

The pharaoh's local governors helped by communicating with the pharaoh's government in Memphis. What made this communication possible was a system of writing.

Ancient Egyptians developed a system of writing sometime before unification. This system, called hieroglyphics (hi roh GLIF ix), was made up of about 800 picture-signs. These individual picture-signs, or symbols, were called *hieroglyphs*. Hieroglyphs could stand for objects, such as bread, or for sounds, such as *s*. Hieroglyphics are the reason why we now know so much about the lives of ancient Egyptians.

The Life of a Scribe

Pharaohs depended on written records to keep their government in order. A number of writers called scribes traveled throughout Egypt to keep records of details great and small. They went out into the fields with local leaders to record how much grain farmers harvested. Scribes also determined how much farmers owed to the government. Scribes drafted letters and marriage contracts for townspeople. Because writing was taught to only a few, scribes were highly respected in Egyptian culture. It was a great honor to become a scribe.

Only boys could become scribes, and they began training when they were about 10 years old. Each day in school they chanted passages aloud to improve their reading skills. Then they spent hours writing out lessons and

This statue shows Imhotep, a doctor who later was worshiped as the god of medicine. The hieroglyphics are from a king's tomb.

stories over and over. If their attention wandered, they ran the risk of being beaten. Junior scribes used broken pottery as their "scrap paper."

Writing on Paper

After the boys mastered a simple type of hieroglyphics used for record keeping, they graduated to writing on papyrus (puh PĪ rus). Papyrus is a reed plant that grows along the Nile. Ancient Egyptians used these reeds to make a kind of paper, also called papyrus. Papyrus paper was not very different from the paper we use today. Did you notice how similar the words *papyrus* and *paper* are? Our modern word comes from the ancient one!

Scribes used sharpened reeds as pens. They dipped the reeds into small disks of red or black ink. Then the scribes carefully wrote the information they needed to record on their rolls of papyrus paper.

Scribes had to have good penmanship. They also needed to be good at math. After all, they had to keep correct records of the pharaoh's many goods. Scribes also figured out the number of workers and the amount of materials needed to complete building projects.

The Key to a Lost Language

By about A.D. 400, hieroglyphics fell out of use and their meaning was lost. The ancient symbols found on Egyptian tombs and walls were a mystery to people who came upon them many centuries later.

In 1799 a French soldier was digging in the Nile Delta town of Rosetta. There, he found a large, black stone with writing on it. This stone was later called the Rosetta Stone, after the place where it was found. It contained a pas-sage written three times, in hieroglyphics, Greek, and another type of Egyptian writing called *demotic*. By comparing the three languages, a French scholar named Jean François Champollion (shahm pohl YON) worked to solve the mystery of hieroglyphics. By 1822 he had succeeded. Look at the photograph of the Rosetta Stone. How has its writing helped historians?

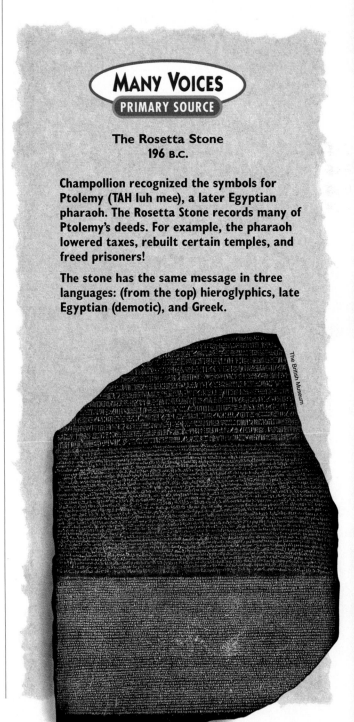

MANY VOICES
PRIMARY SOURCE

The Rosetta Stone
196 B.C.

Champollion recognized the symbols for Ptolemy (TAH luh mee), a later Egyptian pharaoh. The Rosetta Stone records many of Ptolemy's deeds. For example, the pharaoh lowered taxes, rebuilt certain temples, and freed prisoners!

The stone has the same message in three languages: (from the top) hieroglyphics, late Egyptian (demotic), and Greek.

The British Museum

BUILDING THE GREAT PYRAMID

GREAT PYRAMID OF KHUFU
Average weight of blocks: 2.5 tons
Total number of blocks: 2,300,000
Number of blocks added each day: 285

Air Shaft

King's chamber

Air Shaft

Queen's chamber

Underground Room

BUILDING THE PYRAMIDS

No project could have been more challenging to scribes than keeping track of the building of the pyramids. These huge stone structures were built as tombs, or burial places, for pharaohs.

The Great Pyramid is the Old Kingdom's most spectacular monument. It is by far the biggest of all pyramids built in Egypt's history. Pharaoh Khufu (KOO foo) ordered construction to begin about 2600 B.C. This mountain of stone was to be his tomb. It would bring glory not only to himself but to all of Egypt. He would be buried inside with many belongings that he would take into the afterlife.

The 20-year project involved as many as 100,000 people and took a huge amount of Egypt's resources. Few families escaped the call to work at the site. Large amounts of Egyptian taxes went to feed and clothe the project's workers. Even the Nile River landscape changed. Entire cliffs of stone were cut into blocks to make up the pharaoh's great stone monument! Look at the diagram on page 80 to see the construction of the Great Pyramid.

WHY IT MATTERS

Khufu was not the only pharaoh who demanded such massive building projects. Other rulers during the Old Kingdom called for similar, if smaller, monuments. The huge projects took their toll on Egypt's economy and people. Anger against the pharaohs probably began to grow.

Egypt's hard-won unity started breaking down. Local governments began resisting the orders of the pharaohs. In about 2000 B.C. leaders in Upper Egypt revolted and eventually set up a new pharaoh. They based their new capital in the southern town of Thebes. With this division of the country, the Old Kingdom came to an end.

The breakdown of the Old Kingdom, however, led to the rise of an even greater civilization in ancient Egypt. The next lesson tells how the pharaohs learned from their mistakes. They stopped building pyramids. Instead, they built the richest and most powerful civilization the world had ever known.

✓// Reviewing Facts and Ideas

MAIN IDEAS

- Menes united the kingdoms of Upper and Lower Egypt to form the largest government in the world at that time.

- The pharaoh was central to Egypt's government, economy, and religion.

- The writing system of Egypt, called *hieroglyphics,* provided a way for government workers to communicate over long distances.

- Ordinary people worked to build huge, government building projects like the Great Pyramid. This strained both Egypt's economy and its people.

THINK ABOUT IT

1. How did local governors help the pharaoh to rule all of Egypt?

2. Why was Memphis a good place to build Egypt's capital city?

3. **FOCUS** How did the pharaohs' government affect the lives of Egyptians?

4. **THINKING SKILL** What *effects* did hieroglyphic writing have on Egypt? Explain why these were effects.

5. **WRITE** Create your own hieroglyph symbols that represent objects or sounds. See if a partner can read your message.

EGYPTIAN BOATS

People have been living along the Nile, the first "superhighway of Egypt," for thousands of years. We may never know when they first tied together bundles of papyrus plant stems to build boats. We do know that boat-building technology was developed very early in ancient Egypt. Egyptians today still sail the Nile, and they see some of the same sights their ancestors saw over 5,000 years ago. As you look at the photos and art on these pages, think about why advances in boat building have played an important part in history.

The British Museum

Models like this were put in Egyptian tombs. Ancient Egyptians believed they would use them in the afterlife. Note the jobs performed by the crew as the boat's owner rests under a canopy. The man on the bow is measuring the water's depth with a plumb line.

River travel was so important to the ancient Egyptians, even their written language showed it. The hieroglyphic sign for "traveling south" was a boat with sails, because the winds in Egypt usually blow from the north. The sign for "traveling north" was a boat with oars. These signs were used even when the travel was by land!

This boat is made of papyrus stalks tied together. It is similar to boats built by the ancient Egyptians. In 1970 explorer Thor Heyerdahl (HAY air dahl) sailed this papyrus boat from Africa to America. Heyerdahl proved that ancient Egyptians could have made this trip!

This modern Egyptian sailboat, or felucca (fuh LUK uh), is not that different from boats used on the Nile thousands of years ago. Many historians believe that ancient Egyptians invented the sail. Most boats on the Nile today, however, use diesel engines.

3000 B.C.	2500 B.C.	2100 B.C.	1300 B.C.	1000 B.C.

Ancient Egyptian Civilization

Read Aloud

If you took ancient Egypt's two major trade routes and put them in the United States, one would stretch from Washington, D.C., to Chicago and the other from Washington, D.C., to the northern tip of Maine. These were large distances to travel by boat and caravan. But those distances did not keep Egypt from bringing in a fortune along those roads, as you will see.

Focus Activity

READ TO LEARN

What made Egypt's civilization a rich one?

VOCABULARY

- empire
- expedition

PEOPLE

- Ahmose
- Hatshepsut
- Tutankhamun

PLACES

- Nubia
- Kush
- Punt
- Valley of Kings

THE BIG PICTURE

While Egyptian civilization was spreading along the Nile, neighboring cultures were also growing. To the north, people in Europe were developing the islands and peninsulas across the Mediterranean Sea. To the west, other Africans were finding ways to survive in the harsh desert environment of the Sahara. To the south, the kingdoms of Nubia were thriving, due to gold mines and trade networks. To the east, Asian communities large and small were forming in what are today Israel, Jordan, Lebanon, Syria, and Iraq.

Trade and movement of people and ideas helped to shape development in all of these cultures. Each culture had different resources, products, and ideas to exchange. Egyptian civilization affected neighboring areas. Other cultures had their effects on Egypt as well.

NEW RULERS IN EGYPT

Following the collapse of the Old Kingdom, a new era began in Egyptian history. Historians call this period, from about 2100 B.C. until about 1700 B.C., Egypt's Middle Kingdom.

During this time Egypt's contact with other parts of the world increased. For example, the pharaoh's armies conquered kingdoms in Nubia and made use of the area's gold mines. The name *Nubia,* in fact, may come from the Egyptian word *nub,* for gold. Find Nubia on the map on page 86.

Meanwhile Egyptian traders increased their business with cities in western Asia. As trade grew, people also began moving. People from Asia came to live in Egypt's delta region. By 1650 B.C. these new settlers from the hills of western Asia, called Hyksos (HIK sohs), were powerful enough to challenge the pharaoh.

War with the Hyksos

For the next 100 years, the Hyksos—Greek for "rulers of hill-lands"—ruled Lower Egypt. The Hyksos people used horses, chariots, strong bronze weapons, and bows and arrows to defeat Egyptian armies in battle. Egyptian leaders at Thebes, however, continued to control Upper Egypt.

Although they lost Lower Egypt, the Egyptians learned from their war with the Hyksos. In 1550 B.C., about 100 years after the Hyksos gained control of the delta, Egypt rallied behind Pharaoh Ahmose (AH mohs). This time, with the help of weapons and chariots copied from the Hyksos, the Egyptians succeeded in taking back the delta.

The defeat of the Hyksos began the period in Egyptian history called the New Kingdom. Pharaoh Ahmose vowed that outsiders would never again control any part of Egypt. Ahmose and later pharaohs set out to make Egypt the strongest military power in its part of the world.

Tomb walls often had paintings like this scene of the Egyptians fighting the Hyksos. At right is a model Egyptian army.

EXPANSION AND TRADE

During the New Kingdom period, Egypt's leaders worked to win back the lands lost in war. Nubia had gained its independence, but now the armies of the New Kingdom conquered the valuable territory once more.

Egyptian armies also marched northeast, into what is today Israel, and took over that territory. They even pushed as far as the Euphrates River, the edge of another powerful civilization that you will read about in Chapter 5.

During the New Kingdom period, Egypt became an empire. An empire is a group of lands and peoples ruled by one government. Egypt's economy no longer revolved around farming along the Nile. The Egyptian empire now had other valuable resources from conquered lands.

Across Land and Sea

Egypt's New Kingdom traders spread far and wide. Egyptian ships loaded with golden jewelry, linen cloth, and papyrus sailed to what are today Lebanon and Syria. The ships returned carrying silver, timber, and wine—rare treasures in the land of the pharaoh. Remains of oil jars and paintings from what is now Greece have been found in Lower Egypt. These artifacts suggest that Egypt also traded with its neighbors across the Mediterranean Sea.

Egypt's most important trading partner, however, lay to the south. When the pharaoh's armies conquered Nubia, they also gained control of the ancient and wealthy kingdom of Kush (KUSH). Kush controlled rich trade routes to other African kingdoms. Trade goods came from parts of Africa even farther south. The kingdom of Kush traded ebony, leopard skins, and elephant

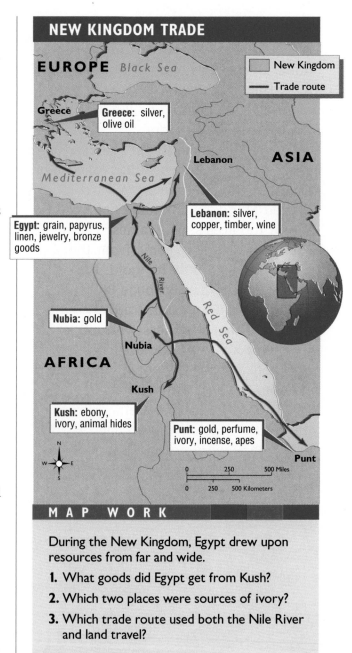

NEW KINGDOM TRADE

Greece: silver, olive oil

Lebanon: silver, copper, timber, wine

Egypt: grain, papyrus, linen, jewelry, bronze goods

Nubia: gold

Kush: ebony, ivory, animal hides

Punt: gold, perfume, ivory, incense, apes

New Kingdom

Trade route

MAP WORK

During the New Kingdom, Egypt drew upon resources from far and wide.

1. What goods did Egypt get from Kush?
2. Which two places were sources of ivory?
3. Which trade route used both the Nile River and land travel?

ivory. Elephant ivory is ivory from elephant tusks. Kush also owned reserves of gold, copper, and precious stones.

Caravans of men and pack animals brought these treasures out of Kush and back to Egypt. On some trading trips, it took 150 men just to carry all of the gold bars that were being sent to Egypt. Soldiers traveled with trading caravans to keep the pharaoh's treasures safe from bandits. Large, castle-like forts were also built along the Upper Nile to scare away robbers.

Back in Egypt, craftworkers made raw materials into beautiful objects. These included furniture, jewelry, and other fine goods for the pharaoh and Egypt's wealthy families.

Hatshepsut

One pharaoh expanded Egyptian trade well beyond the boundaries of the Egyptian empire. That pharaoh was one of Egypt's few female rulers. Her name was **Hatshepsut** (hat SHEP soot), "Foremost [first] of the Noble Ladies."

Hatshepsut was a princess and the wife of a pharaoh. She seized the chance to become pharaoh herself when her husband died. Her young stepson was supposed to become the new pharaoh of Egypt. Hatshepsut proclaimed, however, that the ten-year-old boy was too young to rule on his own. In this way she succeeded in being named co-ruler.

Hatshepsut's Trading Journey

In the eighth year of her reign, Hatshepsut organized the biggest trading **expedition** of her career. An expedition is a group of people who go on a trip for a set reason. The goal of Hatshepsut's expedition was to trade with Egypt's neighbors to the south in **Punt**. Historians think Punt may have been in what is today Ethiopia or Somalia. Look at the map on page 86. Find the place where the kingdom of Punt is believed to have been located.

The huge caravan of scribes, soldiers, artists, and attendants set off along a dusty road that led east to the Red Sea. There they loaded their cargo onto five sleek ships for the long journey south.

When they finally arrived in Punt, the ships were welcomed by the king and queen. Hatshepsut's scribes then displayed the jewelry, papyrus, and bronze weapons the Egyptians had brought to trade. In exchange the pharaoh received gold, perfume, ivory, leopard skins, and even live apes. Hatshepsut's traders also received rare incense trees. Incense trees produce a perfumelike smell.

After touring the kingdom of Punt, the Egyptians began to prepare for their return home. Scribes carefully recorded the exact numbers of goods loaded aboard the ships. Then the members of the expedition climbed aboard. They also brought with them several leaders from Punt who wanted to visit Egypt, which they knew as Khmet, to meet Pharaoh Hatshepsut. The expedition had lasted two years.

Craftworkers made beautiful jewelry (above) and other items. Hatshepsut (right) organized trade of such objects.

interNET CONNECTION Visit our website: www.mhschool.com

Treasures of an Ancient Tomb

West of ancient Thebes, under the piercing blue sky and scorching sun of the Egyptian desert, steep cliffs plunge into a rocky valley. This is the **Valley of the Kings**, resting place of 30 New Kingdom pharaohs.

One of the pharaohs buried in the valley was a very young man. He ruled Egypt from the time he was about 9 years old until he died at about age 19. This pharaoh, **Tutankhamun** (too tahng KAH mun), is best-known today for his magnificent tomb.

Tutankhamun's tomb remained untouched for over 3,000 years. It was finally found in 1922 by two British archaeologists, Howard Carter and Lord Carnarvon. Fabulous treasures from the tomb tell a great deal about ancient Egyptian trade and values. The beautiful materials and crafting of the artifacts also show just how rich Egypt had become in the New Kingdom.

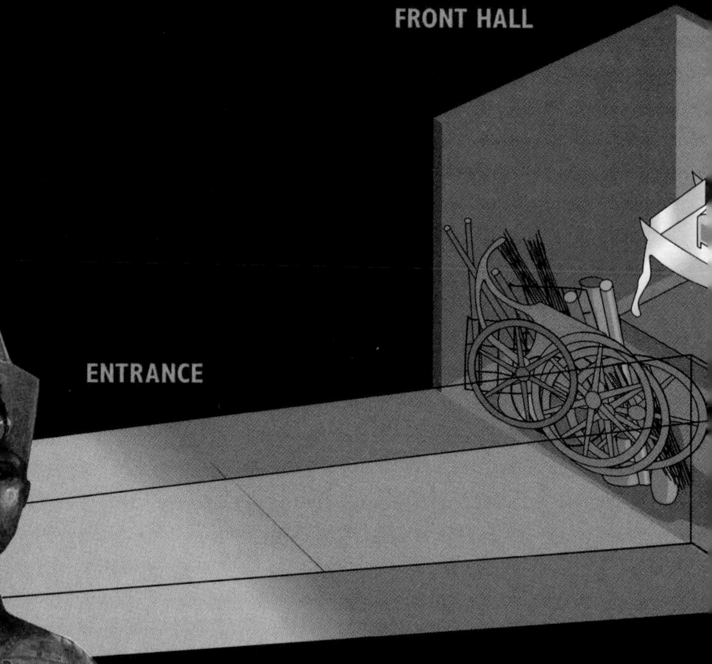

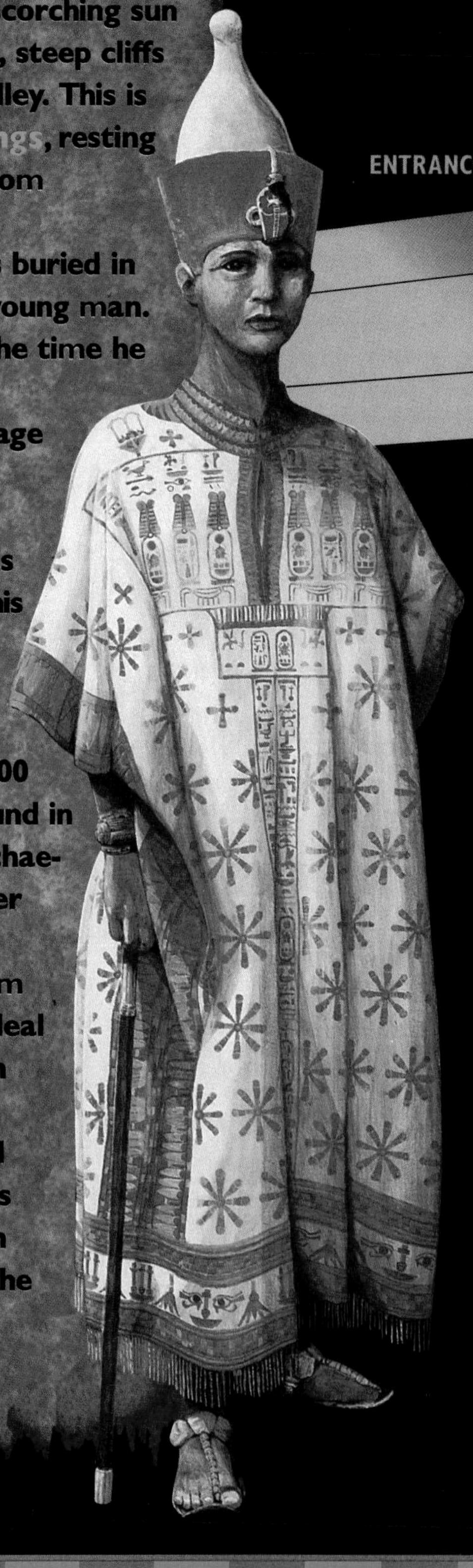

FRONT HALL
ENTRANCE

Among the artifacts found in the tomb were more than 300 articles of Tutankhamun's clothing. The clothes are teaching archaeologists much about how ancient Egyptians really looked. For example, ancient Egyptian "underwear" was a triangle-shaped piece of cloth tied around the waist. Since the only fasteners used in ancient Egypt were string ties, the young king probably had to adjust his clothing constantly.

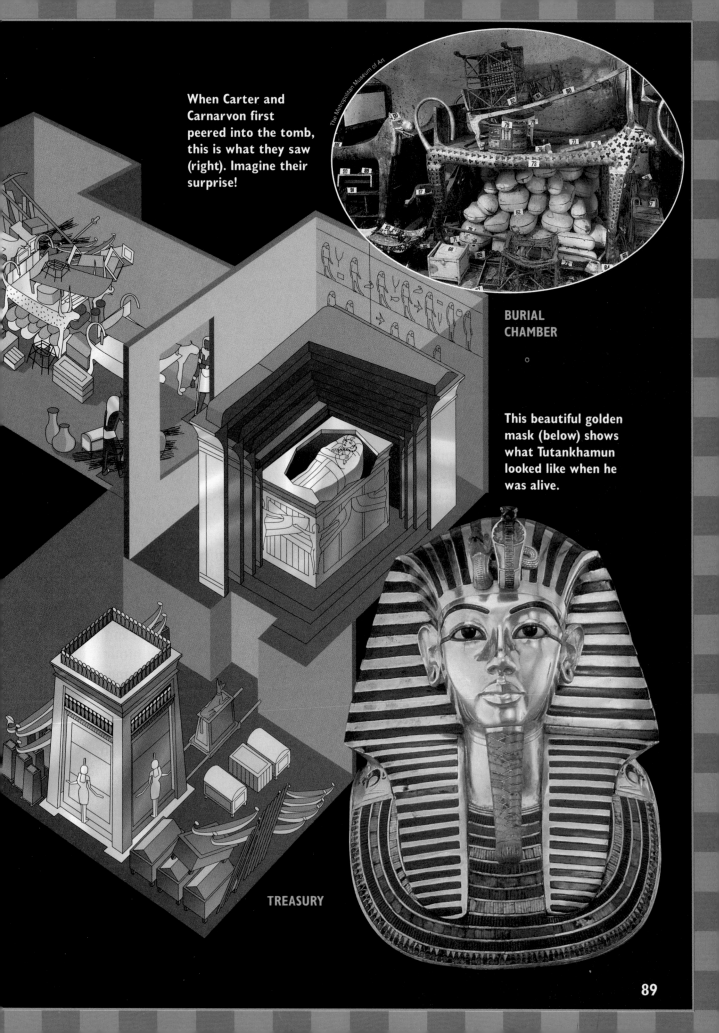

When Carter and Carnarvon first peered into the tomb, this is what they saw (right). Imagine their surprise!

The Metropolitan Museum of Art

BURIAL CHAMBER

This beautiful golden mask (below) shows what Tutankhamun looked like when he was alive.

TREASURY

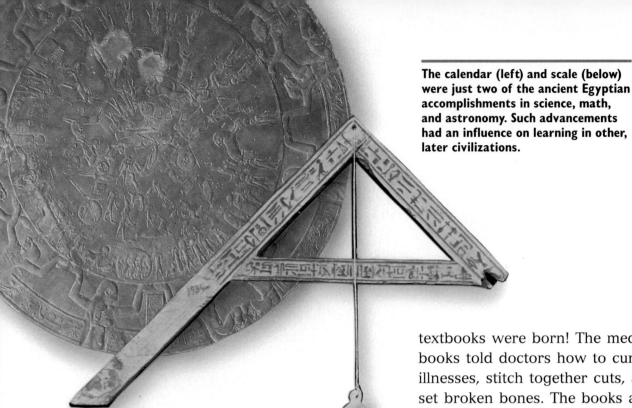

The calendar (left) and scale (below) were just two of the ancient Egyptian accomplishments in science, math, and astronomy. Such advancements had an influence on learning in other, later civilizations.

MOVING IDEAS

In the time of the Egyptian empire, trade goods were not the only things that moved from place to place. Ideas and skills spread too.

You have already read how the Egyptians learned about new weapons from their old enemy, the Hyksos. Other cultures, in turn, learned from Egypt. Egyptian understanding of medicine, mathematics, and astronomy became famous in other countries. Records tell of a king in Lebanon who became sick. He insisted on being treated only by an Egyptian doctor.

Medicine in Egypt

Most Egyptian doctors were actually priests who learned their skills in temple schools. The storehouse of medical knowledge in temple schools was vast and old. For thousands of years priests had noted different kinds of illnesses and injuries and what worked best in treating them. When writing was invented, scribes wrote down this knowledge. The world's first medical textbooks were born! The medical books told doctors how to cure illnesses, stitch together cuts, and set broken bones. The books also explained how to "measure the heart" to see if it was beating too quickly or slowly. Do you know how to measure your own pulse?

Many ancient Egyptian cures centered around treatments that are no longer used. Many other cures, however, introduced ingredients that we still use today. Chamomile, an herb used to make tea, was used to calm upset stomachs. Moldy bread was often placed on wounds. This sounds terrible until we remember that modern antibiotics, or germ-killing drugs, are often made from certain kinds of molds!

Math and Science

Along with medicine, Egyptian priests knew a great deal about mathematics. They developed the mathematical rules needed in building the pyramids, for example.

The priest-scientists also used their knowledge of math to understand the stars. Without telescopes, Egyptians identified five of the solar system's planets, which they called the "stars that know no rest." The mysterious darkness of eclipses did not scare priests. They had figured out that such events were just "meetings of the Sun and Moon."

WHY IT MATTERS

These ideas and others spread throughout the Egyptian empire. In chapters to come you will learn how Egyptian culture influenced other civilizations.

The creation of an empire made Egypt one of the largest civilizations the world had ever known. With resources gained through new territories and trade, Egypt also became incredibly rich. Pharaoh Tutankhamun's tomb has taught archaeologists much about the empire's riches. In the next lesson you will learn how the growth of the empire affected everyday life.

How did ancient Egyptians invent a 365-day calendar?

They based the calendar on the yearly rising and setting of a star named Sirius. Each year Sirius shines in the sky for about 295 nights. Then the star disappears for 70 days. On the day it reappeared in the sky—just before the Nile began flooding—the Egyptians celebrated the start of a new year.

The Egyptian calendar was broken into 12 months of 30 days each. How many "left-over" days did Egyptians have as holidays each year?

Reviewing Facts and Ideas

MAIN IDEAS

- Trade and war helped to link Egypt with its neighbors in the Sahara, Nubia, western Asia, and the Mediterranean.

- Egypt became an empire when it conquered Nubia, Syria, and Lebanon. These new lands gave Egypt a wealth of new resources upon which to draw.

- Pharaoh Hatshepsut expanded trade to a region of eastern Africa called Punt.

- The discovery of Tutankhamun's tomb in 1922 yielded hundreds of New Kingdom artifacts.

- The Egyptians' knowledge of medicine, math, and science became famous among their neighbors. Hyksos skills in metalworking became part of life in Egypt.

THINK ABOUT IT

1. Why were Egypt's leaders interested in conquering Nubia?

2. When was Tutankhamun's tomb discovered? What did archaeologists find there?

3. **FOCUS** In what ways was ancient Egypt a rich civilization?

4. **THINKING SKILL** Think about the different ways Egypt "grew" during the New Kingdom. What _effects_ did this growth have on Egypt? How did Egypt affect its neighbors?

5. **GEOGRAPHY** Use the map on page 86 to trace an outline of Egypt and its trading partners during the New Kingdom. Then write in the resources of each territory.

Geography Skills

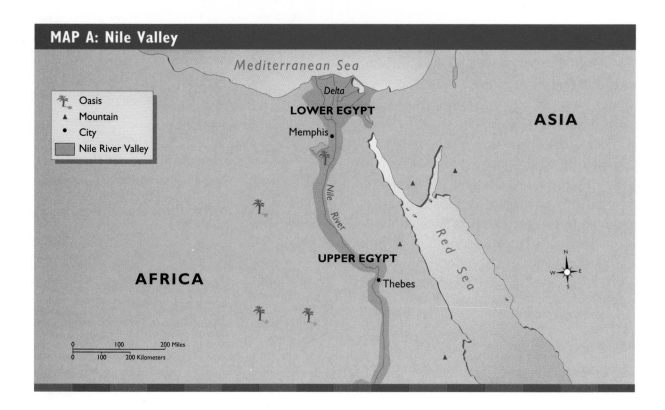

MAP A: Nile Valley

Mediterranean Sea

Delta

LOWER EGYPT

Memphis

ASIA

Nile River

Red Sea

UPPER EGYPT

AFRICA

Thebes

Oasis
Mountain
City
Nile River Valley

0   100   200 Miles
0   100   200 Kilometers

Using Maps at Different Scales

VOCABULARY
scale
small-scale map
large-scale map

WHY THE SKILL MATTERS

As the Egyptian empire grew during the New Kingdom, so did the new capital city at Thebes. Beautiful palaces sprang up along the banks of the Nile. More than a dozen massive temples were built in the surrounding desert to honor gods and pharaohs. Throughout the New Kingdom, Thebes was a symbol of the power of the pharaohs.

Mapmakers can show Thebes up close or in relation to the rest of Egypt. Mapmakers can do this with any other place on Earth by using different map **scales**. A map scale is a unit of measure, such as an inch, used to represent a distance on Earth.

USING THE SKILL

Map scales can be large or small. Mapmakers use **small-scale maps** to give viewers the "big picture" of a place. **Large-scale maps** provide more details about smaller areas. Of course, the real distances on Earth stay the same! Both types of maps are useful, however. Depending on the kind of information needed, you might use one or both types.

Look at Map A. On this small-scale map, one inch stands for 200 miles. Compare this map with Map B, on the next page. Map B shows a smaller area and more details than Map A. Because one inch represents different distances on the two maps, they have different scales. What distance does one inch stand for on Map B?

Suppose you wanted to figure out how to get from Tutankhamun's tomb to Hatshepsut's temple. First, you need to decide which map to use. Which map shows the detail you need? As you can see, Map B, a large-scale map, better shows the detailed information of a small area. Now measure the distance using the map's scale.

Helping yourself

- **A map's scale is a unit of measure that relates distance on the map to distance on Earth.**
- **Maps use different scales to show places up close or at great distances from each other.**
- **Remember that large-scale maps measure distance in *smaller* units. Small-scale maps measure distance in *larger* units.**

TRYING THE SKILL

Suppose that you are writing a book about places near Thebes. Use the Helping Yourself box to answer these questions. Which map would you use to find the oasis, or watered area within a desert, nearest to Thebes? Find the Red Sea. How far is ancient Egypt's capital, Thebes, from the Red Sea? Which type of map gives a "big picture" of this place?

REVIEWING THE SKILL

1. What are the differences between small-scale and large-scale maps?
2. From which map could you find the width of the Nile Delta region?
3. About how wide did the Nile River become near Thebes? Which map gave you the answer to that question?
4. How might using large- and small-scale maps help you in planning a trip?

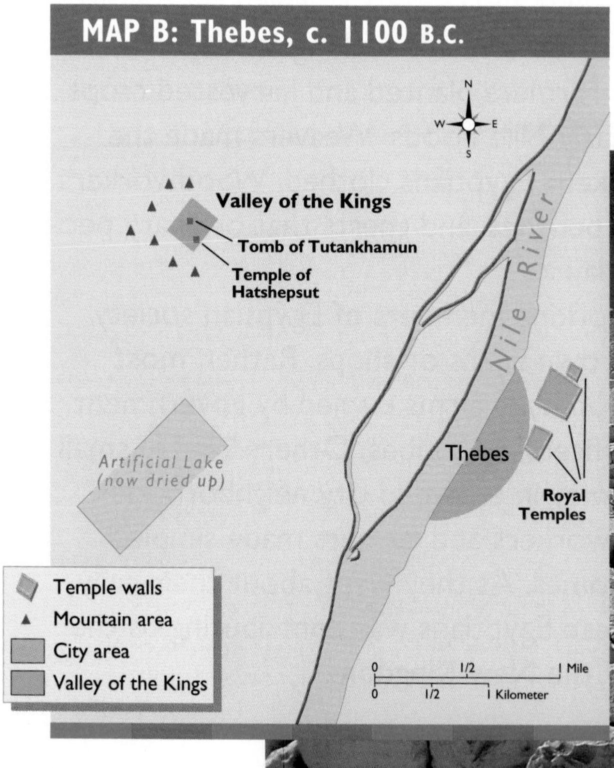

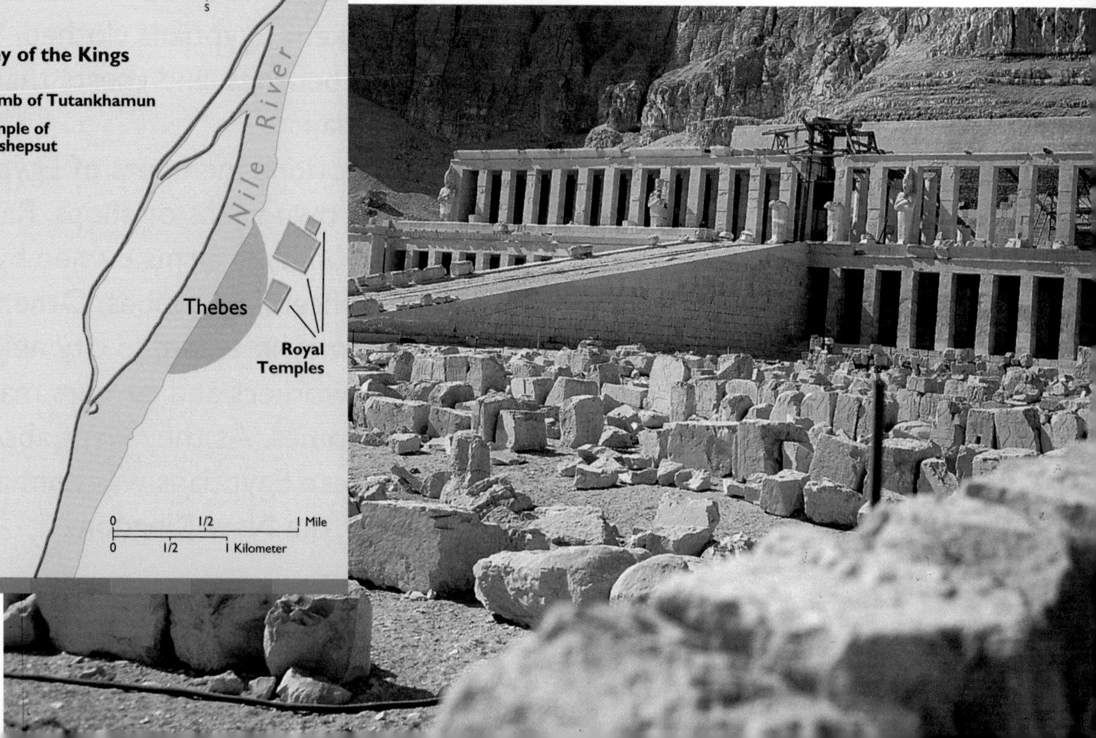

MAP B: Thebes, c. 1100 B.C.
N
W
E
S
Valley of the Kings
Tomb of Tutankhamun
Temple of Hatshepsut
Nile River
Thebes
Royal Temples
Artificial Lake (now dried up)
Temple walls
Mountain area
City area
Valley of the Kings
0
1/2
1 Mile
0
1/2
1 Kilometer

Huge temples, like this one for Hatshepsut, were built to honor Egyptian gods and pharaohs.

3000 B.C.　　2500 B.C.　　2000 B.C.　　1550 B.C.　　1100 B.C.

Daily Life in Ancient Egypt

Focus Activity

How did people of the New Kingdom live and work?

- social pyramid
- slavery

Read Aloud

Under the pharaohs of the New Kingdom, Egypt became the largest and most powerful empire in the world. As you have read, the empire spread eastward into western Asia. Egypt also conquered Nubia, to the south. You have also read how Egyptian goods and ideas spread far from the Nile Valley. How did this growing wealth and power affect the ordinary people who lived in the Egyptian empire?

THE BIG PICTURE

While Egypt's armies and traders traveled far and wide, Egyptians at home continued working to make their country strong. Farmers planted and harvested crops between the yearly Nile floods. Weavers made the linen cloth that kept Egyptians clothed. Woodworkers built the plows, benches, and chests that ordinary people used every day.

These hardworking members of Egyptian society rarely had their own farms or shops. Rather, most people worked on huge farms owned by government leaders, army officers, or scribes. Others lived in small houses tucked away in crowded city neighborhoods. There the craftworkers and farmers made simple goods in their homes. As they went about their daily lives, each of these Egyptians was contributing to the great success of the New Kingdom.

A SOCIAL PYRAMID

From the earliest days of Egypt's history, a person's position in society depended on what he or she did for a living. As a result the shape of Egyptian society was similar to that of a pyramid. The most powerful person, the pharaoh, was at the top of this social pyramid. Below the pharaoh ranked government officials, and below them, craftworkers. At the pyramid's base were farmers and captured people who made up the largest part of society.

Egyptians were not the only people who filled the empire's social pyramid. Nubian soldiers made up a large part of the pharaoh's army and police force. Syrian princes joined the ranks of Egypt's government officials. Syrian and Nubian craftworkers worked side by side with Egyptian craftworkers.

Slavery in Egypt

The people at the lowest level of this social pyramid were those who lived under slavery. Slavery is the practice of one person owning another person. When Egypt conquered Nubia and part of western Asia, Egyptians captured prisoners of war and enslaved them. Most of these people were Syrians, though many were Nubians.

Slaves did some of the hardest work that had to be done in Egypt. They worked in the heat of the desert to mine gold in Nubia. They worked alongside free farmers in the floodwaters of the Nile. They dug canals and prepared land for planting. Enslaved people also worked as house servants to wealthy Egyptians.

Egyptians bought enslaved Syrians and Nubians like they did cattle or cloth. One Syrian girl, for example, was sold for the price of four big sacks of grain and a piece of silver. However, enslaved people did have some basic rights in Egypt. They had the right to be treated fairly under the law and even to own property.

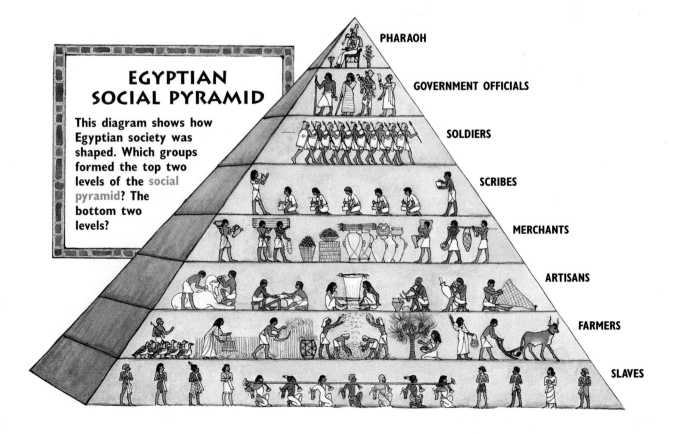

EGYPTIAN SOCIAL PYRAMID

This diagram shows how Egyptian society was shaped. Which groups formed the top two levels of the social pyramid? The bottom two levels?

PHARAOH

GOVERNMENT OFFICIALS

SOLDIERS

SCRIBES

MERCHANTS

ARTISANS

FARMERS

SLAVES

FARMS AND CITIES

During the New Kingdom huge farms and busy cities dotted the shores of the Nile River. Life was very different in the two settings, but some things were similar. In both places ordinary people worked long hours for few rewards. Both in cities and on farms, people also enjoyed simple pleasures, such as celebrating holidays and playing games.

Farm Life

As you have read, most Egyptians lived on big farms owned by powerful people from the top of the social pyramid. These farms were run by loyal scribes. Farmers, craftworkers, and slaves did most of the work. Farms were like small worlds of their own. They produced most of the goods the people living there needed.

Farms bustled with many different kinds of activities. Farmers grew and harvested crops. Herders tended cattle and goats. Bakers ground wheat from the fields and baked bread. Brewers made beer from wheat and barley, and fishers caught fish in the Nile. Brickmakers shaped bricks from river mud for workers' houses.

As many as half of these products went to the pharaoh as taxes. Most of what remained went to the owner of the farm. Workers and slaves divided the little that was left.

Planting and Harvesting

None of the jobs were easy, but farming was perhaps the hardest of all. To prepare the soil for planting, farmers dug up large fields with cattle-drawn wooden plows and hoes. To

This figure was made from carved limestone over 4,000 years ago. It shows an Egyptian brewer at work.

The Granger Collection

bring water to the fields, farmers dug irrigation canals and hauled water using shadoufs. In addition farmers were often called upon by the government to help build canals, temples, or tombs for the pharaoh. It seemed like a farmer's work never ended!

At harvesttime women, men, and children headed out to the fields to cut, stack, and carry grain. As they worked in the blazing sun, a song leader chanted out songs and everyone sang along. Singing helped to make the time pass more quickly.

Farmers loaded the cut stalks into baskets and took them to threshing, or separating, areas. There, oxen or donkeys were walked over the stalks to separate the grain from the straw. Once again people sang songs, like this one, to make the hard work more fun:

Strike [sort grain] for yourselves,
Strike for yourselves, oxen!
Straw to eat for yourselves
  and barley for your masters.
Don't let your hearts grow weary!

Once the grain was separated, girls tossed it into the air using wooden shovels so the wind would blow the remaining straw away. Scribes measured and took away the shares claimed by the pharaoh and the farm owner. Despite the hard work harvest was a time for celebration. During this time special offerings were made to Ra and Rennunet, the gods of the harvest.

Cities in Egypt

In Egypt's cities craftworkers and artists worked under similar conditions. Most lived in small, mud-brick homes crowded along narrow, winding streets. Archaeologists have uncovered the home of one family that lived in Memphis during Tutankhamun's rule. This house tells us much about life in Egypt's cities during the New Kingdom.

A Busy Neighborhood

The house in which this family lived opened onto a busy, noisy alley. The entrance room served as a workshop where the parents made baskets or leather products. Behind the workshop were a small living room with a fireplace and two tiny rooms that may have been bedrooms. A stairway led up to the flat roof—a cool place to sleep on hot summer nights.

The family also had "everyday" chores to do. Every morning the women of the house went down to the local canal to get water. As the sun rose they chatted with friends who also were getting water. They returned home with clay water pots balanced on their heads. Women also had to bake bread. Bread was an important part of the ancient Egyptians' diet.

Each day the family probably went to market to sell their wares. At local markets the family could buy wheat, grapes, olives, fresh fish, beef, pork, and chicken. They may have bought linen cloth from the woman next door. Archaeologists think she made her living as a weaver. A toolmaker also lived nearby. Imagine the clang of his hammer above the sounds of the city.

Townspeople worked hard at their jobs, but they liked to have fun too. Among the artifacts found in the house in Memphis were board games, for moments of free time.

These statues and walls are the remains of a temple in Luxor, Egypt. Note the size of the statues compared to the people standing nearby.

Tomb paintings show many animals living along the Nile River. Tombs also contained mummies of pets, such as dogs and cats.

CHILDREN IN EGYPT

Adults were not the only Egyptians who played games. Children rich and poor loved to spin tops, make cloth dolls, wrestle, run, and play games. Favorite pets included dogs, cats, and monkeys. Young boys and girls often played in the canals that flowed through the farms and villages. The children of pharaohs swam in their own swimming pools!

The amount of time children had to play depended on what their family did for work. Farmers' children had little time to play since they were often needed to help in the fields. Besides working at harvest time, farm children helped scatter seeds during planting time. Farm children also did daily chores, such as carrying water or feeding the family's many farm animals.

From about age five the children of craftworkers began working alongside their parents. In this way children learned the trade they would work at as adults. At an early age potters' children helped their parents put a smooth finish on their pots. At about age 12 girls studying to become weavers started training. This training could sometimes last up to five years.

Sons of government leaders became assistants to their fathers. They, too, would become leaders one day. Sons of scribes knew that from age ten they would be going to scribe school. That was a skill usually passed down from father to son as well.

WHY IT MATTERS

The Egyptian empire went through great changes around the end of the New Kingdom. New armies from the west and northeast challenged the pharaoh's hold on the empire. The Egyptian army began to lose its firm control over the region. Finally, around 1100 B.C., united Egypt collapsed. The fall of the New Kingdom ended one of the richest civilizations in history.

Still, the "Gift of the Nile" would live on and affect people everywhere for centuries to come. Ancient Egypt's legacy extends even to our own time. Think about this legacy the next time you see a sailor harnessing the wind. You may think of another Egyptian legacy as you answer the Think About It questions on a sheet of *paper!*

✔️ Reviewing Facts and Ideas

MAIN IDEAS

- While Egypt became a mighty empire, ordinary people continued to work in much the same ways as they had for thousands of years.
- Enslaved Syrians and Nubians became key workers in Egypt's empire. They worked alongside farmers and craftworkers to produce needed crops and goods.
- Most farmers worked on large farms owned by powerful families.
- Most people in Egypt's towns and cities lived in crowded neighborhoods and crafted goods for a living.

THINK ABOUT IT

1. How did Egypt's social pyramid shape life in the New Kingdom?

2. How did the growth of Egypt's empire play a role in the growth of slavery along the Nile? How did enslaved people add to the empire's economy?

3. **FOCUS** What was everyday life like for ancient Egyptians of the New Kingdom?

4. **THINKING SKILL** Make a *conclusion* about the variety of goods available in ancient Egyptian cities. What evidence can you find in the lesson to support your conclusion?

5. **WRITE** Suppose you are a scribe in ancient Thebes. Write a letter to the owner of a large farm. Tell him or her what goods to send to your city.

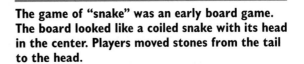

The game of "snake" was an early board game. The board looked like a coiled snake with its head in the center. Players moved stones from the tail to the head.

CHAPTER 4 REVIEW

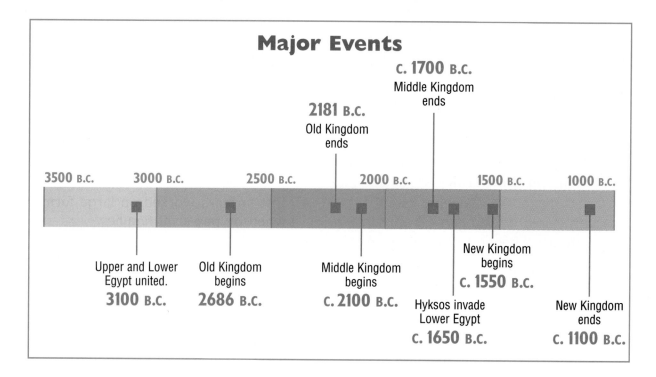

Major Events

c. 1700 B.C.
Middle Kingdom ends

2181 B.C.
Old Kingdom ends

| 3500 B.C. | 3000 B.C. | 2500 B.C. | 2000 B.C. | 1500 B.C. | 1000 B.C. |

Upper and Lower Egypt united.
3100 B.C.

Old Kingdom begins
2686 B.C.

Middle Kingdom begins
c. 2100 B.C.

Hyksos invade Lower Egypt
c. 1650 B.C.

New Kingdom begins
c. 1550 B.C.

New Kingdom ends
c. 1100 B.C.

THINKING ABOUT VOCABULARY

Number a sheet of paper from 1 to 10. Decide whether the underlined word in each of the following statements correctly completes the sentence. If the word is correct, write **C** beside the number. If the word is incorrect, write **I** and then write the word that completes the sentence.

delta   hieroglyphics   slavery
economy   irrigation   unification
empire   scale
expedition   scribe

1. Irrigation is the joining of parts into one.
2. Slavery is the owning of one person by another.
3. A scribe is a writer of records, letters, and contracts.
4. An empire is the flat, fertile land made of silt left behind as a river drains into a larger body of water.
5. The watering of land by means of canals or pipes is called scale.
6. An economy is the way people manage money and resources.
7. Delta is the ancient Egyptian system of writing.
8. A group of lands or peoples ruled by one government is called an expedition.
9. Hieroglyphics is a unit of measure used on a map to represent a distance.
10. A group of people who go on a trip for a set reason is called a unification.

THINKING ABOUT FACTS

1. What was the role of the Nile River in the development of Egyptian civilization?
2. How did its first pharaoh unify Egypt?
3. How has the Rosetta Stone helped historians to understand Egypt's past?
4. Where did Egypt get its slaves? Who were above slaves on the Egyptian social pyramid?
5. Look at the time line above. How many years after Egypt was united did the Middle Kingdom begin?

THINK AND WRITE ◄ ▄▄▄

WRITING A LIST
Make a list of three things about ancient Egypt that you think mark it as an important civilization.

WRITING AN EXPLANATION
Explain how the shape of Egyptian society was similar to that of a pyramid. Then describe the groups that made up the Egyptian social pyramid.

WRITING A PARAGRAPH OF ANALYSIS
Write a paragraph about the effect of the Nile River on ancient Egyptian civilization. Tell about the problems the Nile caused and what people did to solve them.

APPLYING GEOGRAPHY SKILLS

USING MAPS AT DIFFERENT SCALES
1. What is meant by the term *scale*?
2. What does a small-scale map show?
3. What does a large-scale map show?
4. Which kind of map can show the most information? How is that possible? Explain.
5. What are the advantages of knowing how to use maps at different scales?

Summing Up the Chapter

Copy the main-idea pyramid below on a separate piece of paper. Then review the chapter to find at least two pieces of information that support each part of the main idea. Add these to the bottom of the pyramid. When you have filled in the pyramid, use it to write a paragraph titled "How did the ancient Egyptians create their complex civilization?"

Ancient Egypt

Ancient Egyptians used their environment.

Organization helped the Egyptians to unite.

Ancient Mesopotamia

THINKING ABOUT
HISTORY AND GEOGRAPHY

Around 4000 B.C. farmers living between the Tigris and Euphrates rivers built canals to try to control flooding. They also built cities and developed a system of writing. Eventually, a strong ruler, Sargon, united the region into a kingdom called Sumer. Much later Hammurabi conquered Sumer and wrote a code of laws. The movement of the Hebrews into Canaan led to the development of Judaism.

AFRICA

2300 B.C.

KISH
Sargon unites Sumer

4000 B.C.

MESOPOTAMIA
Farmers build irrigation ditches to control river floods

3000 B.C.

UR
Schools are built in Sumer to teach writing

4000 B.C.   3000 B.C.   2000 B.C.

EUROPE

ASIA

Tigris
River

Euphrates
River

Kish

Mediterranean
Sea

Canaan   Babylon

Ur

Mesopotamia

Red Sea

Persian Gulf

1800 B.C.

BABYLON
**Hammurabi creates a
code of laws**

1250 B.C.

CANAAN
**Moses leads the Hebrews
to Canaan**

INDIAN
OCEAN

1000 B.C.

A.D. 1

Geography of the Fertile Crescent

Focus Activity

READ TO LEARN

In what ways did two great rivers affect life in this region?

VOCABULARY

- plateau
- drought

PLACES

- Fertile Crescent
- Tigris River
- Euphrates River
- Mesopotamia

Read Aloud

"For six days and seven nights the wind blew, flood and tempest [storm] overwhelmed the land; when the seventh day arrived, the tempest [and] flood . . . blew themselves out. The sea became calm, the . . . wind grew quiet, the flood held back. . . . Silence reigned, for all mankind had returned to clay."

These words come from an ancient western Asian story about a flood that destroyed most of humanity. Ancient stories like this one later influenced people all around the world.

THE BIG PICTURE

Around 4000 B.C. Egyptian farm communities were growing along the Nile River in Africa. Another civilization was also developing in a vast region to the northeast. This region, in western Asia, was later called the Fertile Crescent. A crescent shape looks like a quarter moon. Find the Fertile Crescent on the map on the next page. It covers the present-day countries of Iraq, Syria, Lebanon, and Israel.

Much of this land was either rocky mountains or desert. Parts of the Fertile Crescent, however, were lush and green. Two rivers, the Tigris (TĪ grihs) and the Euphrates (yoo FRAY teez), made life in these areas possible. Like the Nile in Egypt, these rivers affected the people living along the banks. As you can see from the story above, the rivers' effects were not always positive.

BETWEEN TWO RIVERS

The region between the Tigris and the Euphrates is known as Mesopotamia (mes uh puh TAY mee uh). In Greek, *Mesopotamia* means "Land Between Two Rivers." This area is now known as Iraq. Mesopotamia included several types of physical regions. Follow the course of the two rivers on the map. Let's see how Mesopotamia's northern and southern regions differ.

From Mountains to the Sea

Both the Tigris and Euphrates rivers begin in the snow-capped Taurus Mountains of what is today Turkey. The rivers rush down narrow canyons to the valleys below. Then the Tigris and Euphrates reach the plateau (pla TOH) of present-day northern Iraq. A plateau is an area of elevated flatland. In southern Iraq the rivers continue to flow to lower land. Here they make their way to the Persian Gulf.

Flood!

As in Egypt, early communities in Mesopotamia depended on river deposits of silt. Silt made the region a good place for farming. Early farmers had to meet several challenges, though.

Mesopotamia's yearly floods did not come as regularly as those in Egypt. In fact, they often came at just the wrong time for farmers. The Tigris and the Euphrates did not flood during planting season, when dry fields needed to be softened and prepared for new growth. Instead, the floods often burst through fields just as crops were about to be harvested. Such deadly floods cost not only crops, but lives and homes as well.

Farmers had to protect their fields from flood damage. They also had to keep their crops watered in the hot, dry climate. Southern Mesopotamia rarely received more than a few sprinkles of rain each year. Droughts, or long periods of dry weather, were a constant threat to farmers and their crops in southern Mesopotamia.

Northern Mesopotamia, in contrast, usually had enough rain to make some farming possible. Yet the rocky earth of the northern plateau had only pockets of fertile soil. The flooding rivers did not leave behind as much silt here in the north as to the south. For this reason southern Mesopotamia became better known for its fertile fields than northern Mesopotamia.

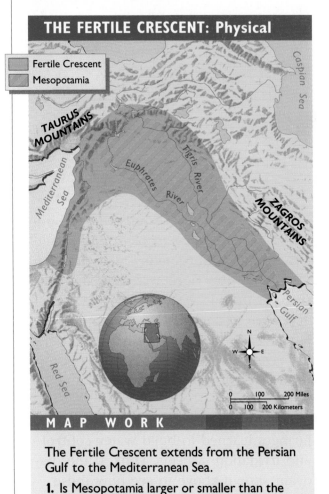

THE FERTILE CRESCENT: Physical

Fertile Crescent
Mesopotamia

MAP WORK

The Fertile Crescent extends from the Persian Gulf to the Mediterranean Sea.

1. Is Mesopotamia larger or smaller than the Fertile Crescent?

2. What mountain range lies east of the Fertile Crescent?

WATER CONTROL IN MESOPOTAMIA

Like the ancient Egyptians, Mesopotamians also adapted rivers for farming.

Artificial Lake

Gate

Tigris River

Irrigation Canal

Gate

FROM RIVER TO FIELD

In the fall farmers in southern Mesopotamia needed water to plant and raise new crops. Unfortunately, fall was the time when the Tigris and the Euphrates were at their lowest. Spring was harvest time in ancient Mesopotamia. However, it was also the time when the rivers flooded their banks. Then farmers often got more water than they wanted.

To solve these difficulties, ancient farmers learned to build water-control and irrigation systems. Look at the diagram shown above to see how these systems worked.

Farming in Ancient Mesopotamia

Early Mesopotamian farmers grew many different crops. If you were able to go back there in time, you would see fields of wheat and barley. These were the region's most important crops. You would also see gardens of beans, onions, lettuce, cucumbers, and spice plants. Ancient farmers also grew date palm, apple, and pomegranate trees. Because crops and trees need plenty of water, Mesopotamian farmers often planted them along canal banks.

In the distance, on the edges of village farmland, you might see shepherds caring for sheep and goats. Shepherds also had to ward off attacks from wild animals such as lions and jackals. Sheep were especially prized in Mesopotamia for their milk and wool. Ancient Mesopotamians also valued cattle. Cattle were good work-animals, besides being used for milk, leather, and meat.

WHY IT MATTERS

The region called Mesopotamia is not naturally an inviting place to live. Yet it was here that one of the world's earliest civilizations developed. Water and soil brought by the Tigris and the Euphrates helped to make this civilization possible. Even more important were the farmers of ancient Mesopotamia. These early farmers figured out how to use the two rivers to make the land more fertile.

As in some other early cultures, the farmers of Mesopotamia produced surplus crops. These surpluses allowed for specialization, which in turn led to the growth of towns and cities. The early cities formed a great civilization. As you will see, the legacy of early Mesopotamian civilization reaches even into our own times.

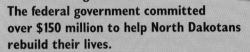
✓✓ Reviewing Facts and Ideas

MAIN IDEAS

- Mesopotamia is the region between the Tigris and Euphrates rivers. It is divided into a rugged plateau to the north and fertile plains to the south.

- Like the Nile River, the Tigris and the Euphrates flooded each year. These floods brought water and silt to Mesopotamia.

- Unlike those in Egypt, floods in Mesopotamia were often destructive and badly timed for farmers.

- Mesopotamian farmers used canal systems to control dangerous flooding, making their land productive.

THINK ABOUT IT

1. What were the main crops grown in ancient Mesopotamia? What other foods were grown there?

2. Why was the timing of spring floods so important to farmers in ancient Mesopotamia? What could happen to crops if the floods came a little earlier than expected?

3. **FOCUS** In what ways did Mesopotamian farmers adapt to and change their environment?

4. **THINKING SKILL** Suppose you lived in ancient Mesopotamia. Write a poem about the Tigris and Euphrates rivers from a farmer's _point of view_.

5. **GEOGRAPHY** Where is the Fertile Crescent located?

The British Museum

| 4000 B.C. | 3500 B.C. | | | 689 B.C. | A.D. 1 |

Sumer and Babylon

Read Aloud

This is an ancient Mesopotamian riddle. See if you can solve it.

"He whose eyes are not open enters it.
He whose eyes are wide open comes out of it.
What is it?
The solution is: It's a school."

How might school "open your eyes"?

Focus Activity

READ TO LEARN

What changes did the development of writing bring to ancient Mesopotamia?

VOCABULARY

- cuneiform
- city-state
- ziggurat
- polytheism
- code of law

PEOPLE

- Sargon
- Hammurabi

PLACES

- Sumer
- Babylonia

THE BIG PICTURE

You have read about southern Mesopotamia's large surpluses. These allowed an increasing number of people to live as skilled workers in cities. By 3000 B.C.— around the time that Menes unified Egypt—about a dozen small cities dotted southern Mesopotamia. This region was also known as **Sumer** (SOO mur).

The people of Sumer's cities valued their independence highly. They often fought against being ruled by other cities. However, all Sumerians shared a rich cultural heritage. They worked hard to control the Tigris and Euphrates rivers to produce food crops. They worshiped similar gods. The Sumerians made some of the world's first wheeled vehicles and sailboats. They also made simple machines, such as pottery wheels. In addition, early Sumerians explored new ideas in math and science.

The invention of writing helped to bring the ancient cities together. Laws, letters, records, stories, instructions, riddles, and proverbs could all be widely shared, thanks to **cuneiform** (kyoo NEE uh fawrm). Cuneiform was the system of writing invented in Sumer.

A SYSTEM OF WRITING

Some historians believe that cuneiform was first developed to record farm surpluses. Ancient Sumerians used sharp reeds to scratch the records into wet clay tablets. The dried tablets became permanent records.

In 3500 B.C.—the time of the oldest tablets that have been found—cuneiform symbols looked like the things they described. Over time, however, Sumerian scribes developed faster ways to write. They simplified their figures so they could be formed more quickly. Look at the chart on this page for examples.

About 500 signs were regularly used! These signs could also be combined to form more complex words. Like Egyptian hieroglyphs, cuneiform signs represented sounds and ideas as well as objects. The sign for "arrow," called *ti* (TEE), looked like this: ⤙. Since *ti* also meant "life," the symbol could stand for this word too.

School in Sumer

As in ancient Egypt few people could write. Even kings usually could not. It was an honor to be able to go to school and learn to be a scribe. Boys and, very rarely, girls spent years studying in local schools. First they learned how to make clay tablets and reed "pens." Then students practiced over and over how to write the basic signs of cuneiform. Scribes in Sumer also had to study mathematics so they would be able to keep accurate records.

Trained scribes could and did write almost anything. They even wrote love letters for people and sealed them in clay "envelopes"! Scribes also recorded stories, laws, and songs.

The sturdy ancient tablets have survived thousands of years. They have helped historians to piece together a detailed picture of early Mesopotamia.

Scribes (left) filled an important role in ancient Sumer. They were record keepers, since most people could not write.

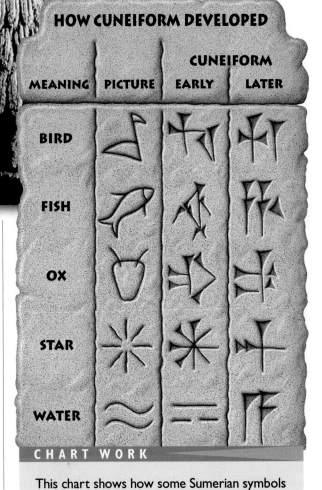

HOW CUNEIFORM DEVELOPED

MEANING	PICTURE	CUNEIFORM	
		EARLY	LATER
BIRD			
FISH			
OX			
STAR			
WATER			

CHART WORK

This chart shows how some Sumerian symbols changed over time.

The photo on page 108 shows a cuneiform symbol found on this chart. What is this symbol? Is it early or later cuneiform?

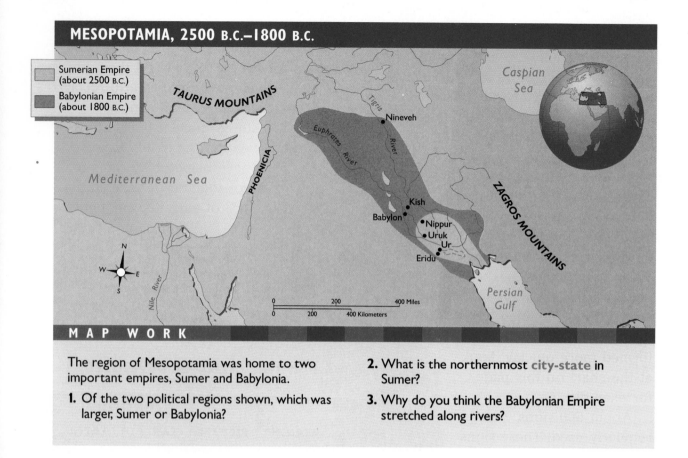

Sumerian Empire (about 2500 B.C.)

Babylonian Empire (about 1800 B.C.)

TAURUS MOUNTAINS

Caspian Sea

Nineveh

Euphrates River

Tigris River

Mediterranean Sea

PHOENICIA

ZAGROS MOUNTAINS

Kish

Babylon

Nippur

Uruk

Ur

Eridu

Nile River

N W E S

Persian Gulf

0   200   400 Miles
0   200   400 Kilometers

MAP WORK

The region of Mesopotamia was home to two important empires, Sumer and Babylonia.

1. Of the two political regions shown, which was larger, Sumer or Babylonia?

2. What is the northernmost **city-state** in Sumer?

3. Why do you think the Babylonian Empire stretched along rivers?

CITY-STATES OF SUMER

Cuneiform writing first appeared in about 3500 B.C. Over the next thousand years, Sumerian life centered around the city-states of southern Mesopotamia. A city-state is a self-governing city that also governs surrounding villages. Find the city-states Ur, Uruk, and Eridu on the map.

Through cuneiform we know about an early Sumerian mythical hero named Gilgamesh (GIHL guh mesh). Read the following passage about Gilgamesh. Think about what made him a hero to the ancient Sumerians.

The great Gilgamesh was one who knew everything. He had seen all there was to see and done all there was to do. He had built the walls of the city, Uruk. Look at its brickwork! Nobody could build a better wall. It was made of copper and burnt brick, and was wide enough to walk upon.

Gilgamesh was part god and part [man], and as strong as an ox. He was the strongest in the land, and the best fighter.

Living in a Sumerian City

City-states often went to war to gain control of precious river water. For this reason strong walls were built to protect against attack. Large gateways in city walls allowed people and goods to get into and out of cities. City gates were also where people gathered to buy fresh vegetables and other goods. Goods were brought to the cities by farmers and traders.

The king's palace could be seen from almost everywhere in a city. The palace was where a city-state's planning and

110

decision making took place. Kings served as generals, judges, and canal overseers. Unlike Egyptian pharaohs, though, Sumerian kings were not considered to be gods.

Religion in Ancient Sumer

In the center of most ancient Sumerian cities stood a towering mud-brick building. That building was a ziggurat (ZIHG oo rat). A ziggurat was a large building with a temple on its peak.

Since these temples were located in the center of cities, historians believe that religion was very important in Sumer. Like the Egyptians, Sumerians' religious beliefs involved polytheism. Polytheism is a belief in many gods and goddesses. Each city-state had a special god or goddess. That god or goddess was worshiped at the city's ziggurat. People also worshiped other gods and goddesses at home. One favorite was Ishtar, the goddess of love and war. Another was Enki, the god of water.

Uniting the City-States

In time the city-states were united under one ruler—Sargon, king of the city-state Kish. Sargon rose to power about 2300 B.C. His rule began a new period in Mesopotamia's history. Sargon expanded his empire to the northern end of the Fertile Crescent, in what is present-day Syria.

Along the Mediterranean Sea, Sumerians traded with the ancient seafaring people called Phoenicians (fih NEE shunz). The Phoenicians also traded with merchants from Egypt. Phoenicians sent wine and timber to Sargon's city-states. In return they received Mesopotamian farm products and other goods.

Cuneiform writing spread through the Fertile Crescent along with trade goods. Other cultures began using cuneiform to write out their own languages. Because cuneiform was used throughout his empire, Sargon could send instructions and govern over great distances.

Sargon, king of Kish, led the world's first empire. Ziggurats (below) dominated most Sumerian cities around 2000 B.C.

THE RISE OF BABYLON

Sargon's rule lasted about 56 years, until about 2279 B.C. Then the city-states rebelled against the empire. Almost 500 years would pass before another empire controlled Mesopotamia.

During those years a group of people from the Syrian desert moved into northern Mesopotamia. They created a small kingdom centered around a city-state called Babylon.

A Northern Empire

About 1800 B.C. Babylon's king, Hammurabi (hah moo RAH bee), began a drive to gain control over the old city-states of Sumer. Hammurabi and the Babylonians dammed key parts of the Euphrates. This gave them the power to cut off the flow of water or cause terrible floods downstream. Next, Hammurabi's armies attacked the weakened Sumerians. Hammurabi also won control of the city-states around Babylon. He created a huge empire. Find Babylon and the Babylonian empire on the map on page 110.

The empire of Babylonia under Hammurabi became rich and powerful. Shipments of silver, copper, timber, and wine poured into Babylonia. These goods came from people in what are today Turkey, Iran, and Syria. In exchange people in Babylonia sent grain and fruits. Servants even floated ice from distant mountains down rivers to refrigerate food and drink.

Under Hammurabi Mesopotamia's center of power shifted north to Babylon. Yet many Sumerian traditions remained. Babylonians used cuneiform to communicate in writing. In fact the world's first dictionaries were created so Babylonians could adopt Sumerian culture and language.

This dagger and sheath are typical of the weapons used by soldiers in Mesopotamia. The mosaic (below), known as the Standard of Ur, was found in a king's grave in the city of Ur.

The British Museum

A CODE OF LAW

When Hammurabi gained control of Sumer, he set out to act as the Sumerian kings had done. He oversaw projects to build and repair canals. Hammurabi also acted as a judge. He used some of the laws that Sumerians had written down hundreds of years before him.

In 1901 archaeologists found a large stone pillar from ancient Babylon. The pillar was inscribed with over 200 laws written in cuneiform. Imagine historians' excitement when they realized that the laws had actually been formed by Hammurabi himself. They had been written almost 4,000 years before they were discovered!

The Code of Hammurabi is one of the world's oldest codes of law. A code of law is a written set of laws that apply to everyone under a government.

The pillar shows that slavery existed in Babylonia and that not everyone was treated equally under the law. Copies of the pillar were also found outside of Babylon. This suggests that Hammurabi meant for his laws to be followed throughout the empire. Cuneiform made this possible. How important is writing in our own civilization? What other ways do we have to communicate over long distances?

Read the following excerpt from the Code of Hammurabi. What does it tell you about what justice meant to Hammurabi and other Babylonians?

MANY VOICES
PRIMARY SOURCE

Excerpt from
The Code of Hammurabi, c. 1800 B.C.

[So] that the strong may not [abuse] the weak, to give justice to the orphan and the widow, I have inscribed my precious words. . . .

If a Freeman has put out the eye of another Freeman, they shall put out his eye.

If he breaks the bone of another Freeman, they shall break his bone.

If he puts out the eye of a Poor Man, or breaks the bone of a Poor Man, he shall pay 1 mina [17.5 ounces] of silver. If he puts out the eye of the Slave of another Freeman . . . , he shall pay half his price.

THE "NEW" BABYLONIA

After Hammurabi died, about 1750 B.C., Babylonia began to fall apart. The city-states in the south rebelled again, much as they had against Sargon. Powerful armies from the mountains to the north and east began taking the empire's territory. Throughout western Asia new powers overthrew old ones.

During this time of change, however, Babylon remained one of the most powerful cities in the Fertile Crescent. Just as Hammurabi had used Sumerian ideas, new rulers respected the history of "Old Babylonia." They worshiped its gods and passed down its legends— many of which had begun in Sumer.

In 689 B.C. Babylon was destroyed by powerful rulers from a northern Mesopotamian city called Nineveh. About 60 years later the Babylonians were able to rebuild Babylon and make it the capital of an even stronger empire.

Links to LANGUAGE ARTS

What Did You Call Me?!

Words are often "borrowed" when different cultures come into contact. Some historians think modern English may have been affected by ancient Mesopotamian languages! On an ancient cuneiform tablet, one student insults another, calling him a "clever fool." Ancient Greeks probably borrowed the phrase for their compound word *sophos-moros*—clever fool. Modern English takes the word from the Greeks. When you reach your second year of high school, you will be known as a *sophomore*!

Most dictionaries show how some English words came from other languages. Look up the English meaning of *sophomore*. What are the meanings and origin of *cuneiform*?

The "New" Babylon

The new Babylon soon became the world's largest city. It grew famous for its great beauty and technology. Two massive walls and a moat now protected Babylon. The city was split in two by the Euphrates River but was connected by a movable bridge and an underwater tunnel! At the center of the city stood a huge ziggurat. It was 200 yards wide and rose 100 yards into the sky. Elsewhere were grid-style streets, sewer and water systems, and three- and four-story homes. Babylon was also known for its marvelous "hanging gardens." Unfortunately, we do not know exactly what they looked like.

Sorrow in Babylon

Not everyone thought of Babylon as a wonderful place. To some who were brought to the great city, Babylon was anything but beautiful and certainly not home. One poet wrote:

By the rivers of Babylon,
there we sat,
sat and wept,
when we thought of [home].

These newcomers were prisoners. They were brought from what is today Israel.

The carving shows a Sumerian husband and wife. The ruins (above) are all that remain of the ziggurat of Ur. It was dedicated to the storm god, Enlil.

Oriental Institute of Chicago

WHY IT MATTERS

One cuneiform tablet reads:

The gods alone live forever under the divine sun. But as for [humans], their days are numbered. All their activities will be nothing but wind.

It is hard to believe that the ruins of an ancient Mesopotamian city-state were once home to thousands of people. Yet this land was covered with green fields and bustling cities. The people who lived here shared many of the same concerns that we have today.

The ancient Sumerians and Babylonians left records of their civilizations in cuneiform writing. Ideas formed in ancient times—about schools, literature, science, and law—echo into our own time. Despite the ancient scribe's prediction, the legacy of Mesopotamia has not been lost.

The modern countries of the Fertile Crescent are Iraq, Syria, Lebanon, and Israel. Like the ancient empires, these countries are also covered with farms and cities.

✔️ Reviewing Facts and Ideas

MAIN IDEAS

- Cuneiform probably developed as a way to keep track of farm supplies and surplus. The system was later expanded to communicate more complex ideas as well.

- Mesopotamia was not always unified into a single empire. Both government and religion greatly shaped life on a local level.

- Cuneiform writing helped Sargon, king of Kish, to rule over great distances.

- The rise to power of Hammurabi made Babylon one of the world's richest and most powerful cities in ancient times.

THINK ABOUT IT

1. Why was it an honor to become a scribe in Mesopotamia?

2. How was Egyptian culture similar to the culture of Mesopotamia? How was it different?

3. **FOCUS** How did cuneiform help Sargon to create and rule an empire in Mesopotamia?

4. **THINKING SKILL** Look at the excerpt from the story of Gilgamesh on page 110. *Make conclusions* about what was important in ancient Sumer.

5. **WRITE** Write a one-paragraph response to the laws found in the Code of Hammurabi. How did they protect the people of Babylon?

115

THE WHEEL

How did you get to school this morning? If you did not walk, you probably used a vehicle with wheels. Can you imagine what life would be like if the wheel had never been invented?

Most archaeologists believe that ancient Mesopotamians invented the wheel. Some of the first wheels were used on farm carts and war chariots. Over time, people found other uses for the wheel.

The wheel still plays an important role in transportation. There are wheels turning in machines in our homes and factories, too. You can find them winding the film on a movie projector or spinning a compact disc. The wheel has proven to be one of the most important inventions in human history!

Some of the earliest wheels found were used on Sumerian war chariots like this one. This 6,000-year-old chariot was pulled by a donkey. The solid wood wheels made it very heavy and difficult to steer.

The turning motion of inter-locking wheels, or *gears,* is a key part of many machines. The gears in this watch turn at just the right speeds to keep accurate time. What other machines can you think of that use gears?

The wheel can be put to practical use or it can be used for fun. Originally called a *pleasure wheel,* this ride is named after the man who built the largest one ever for the Chicago World's Fair in 1893: George Ferris.

Countries all over the world have built vast networks of roads and highways. Millions of people travel these roads each day. Bicycles and cars share this street in Beijing, China.

Thinking Skills

Identifying Cause and Effect

VOCABULARY
cause
effect

WHY THE SKILL MATTERS

By about 3000 B.C. Sumerians had built their first city-states on the plains of southern Mesopotamia. At about the same time, craftworkers in what is today Syria learned how to make a useful and beautiful new material. They mixed together and then heated sand and a certain kind of plant ash. In this way they created the world's first known glass.

The development of glass brought many changes in the ways people lived. These changes interest historians, who analyze cause and effect connections. A cause is something that makes something else happen. What happens as a result of a cause is called an effect. Historians study causes and their effects to understand why events happened the way they did.

USING THE SKILL

Now practice tracing a cause, such as the invention of glassmaking, to its effects.

By Hammurabi's time glassmaking was just being introduced in Mesopotamia. As time passed, craftworkers figured out how to make elegant vases and other containers from glass. These beautiful glass products attracted the eyes of the empire's rich people. Remember, up until now they had seen only clay and metal containers.

People began buying the new glass goods and using them. The glass items also became popular outside the empire. They

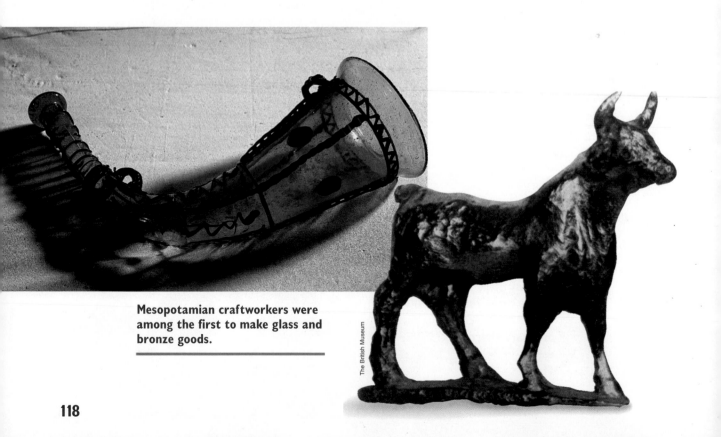

Mesopotamian craftworkers were among the first to make glass and bronze goods.

The British Museum

were traded in such faraway places as what are today Iran and Greece. Some historians also think that glassmakers from the Fertile Crescent may have gone to work in Egyptian workshops. There they introduced their skill to Egyptian craftworkers. It is thought that the art of glassmaking spread from Egypt and Mesopotamia to areas in India, Russia, Spain, and China.

Do you see a cause in the above paragraphs? It is the invention of glass in Mesopotamia. One effect, in this case, was the development of different uses for the new material. Another effect was the spread of glassmaking technology to other parts of the world. As you can see, one cause can have more than one effect. It works the other way around too—an effect can have more than one cause.

Can you trace a cause to all of its effects in this example? Try numbering the events in the order in which they happened. The invention of glass happened first—it is a cause. Related events that happened later are effects of that cause.

TRYING THE SKILL

As you read the following passage, look for cause-and-effect connections. Refer to the Helping Yourself box for help in finding the connections between events.

Glass was not the only material that craftworkers in ancient Mesopotamia experimented with. Around 2000 B.C. Mesopotamians were among the first in the world to blend copper and tin to make bronze.

Bronze brought many changes to life in Mesopotamia. For one thing, bronze was much harder than the copper products that were used until that time. Because it was harder, bronze made better tools and sharper weapons. This improvement in technology was a help to farmers, craftworkers, and soldiers alike.

Molten [melted] bronze was also easier to pour than the metals used earlier. Craftworkers could pour the hot liquid metal into more varied and detailed molds. As a result, these craftworkers were able to make finer arrows, ax-heads, statues, bowls, and other objects.

More and more tin was needed as the demand for products made from bronze increased. Historians believe that traders brought the tin needed to make bronze from distant regions.

In what ways did the invention of bronze affect trade between Mesopotamia and its neighbors?

REVIEWING THE SKILL

1. What are some ways to go about identifying cause-and-effect connections?
2. In the passage on the invention of bronze, what were some different causes and effects?
3. How does finding cause-and-effect connections help you to understand historical events?

4000 B.C.	3000 B.C.	2000 B.C.	1700 BC.	586 B.C.	A.D. 1

The Beginnings of Judaism

Read Aloud

"Hear, O Israel! The Lord is our God, the Lord alone." This short passage from the Bible expresses the basis of Jewish religious belief. In this lesson you will read about the great meaning it would have for the ancestors of the Jewish people in the changing world of the Fertile Crescent.

Focus Activity

READ TO LEARN

How did the writings in the Torah shape Judaism?

VOCABULARY

- Judaism
- Torah
- monotheism
- Ten Commandments
- Sabbath
- Diaspora

PEOPLE

- Abraham
- Moses

PLACES

- Jerusalem

THE BIG PICTURE

Hammurabi ruled the Babylonian empire in the late 1700s B.C. Meanwhile people were on the move throughout the Fertile Crescent. Phoenician port cities along the Mediterranean Sea were expanding their trade with Egypt and cities across the sea. Merchants were traveling along the dusty roads that connected Egypt and Mesopotamia.

Some information about this exciting time comes from a source that millions of people continue to read today. That source is the collection of books known as the Hebrew Bible. Its original language was Hebrew. It has been translated into almost every language on Earth. Its writings are sacred to more than 17 million Jews today. Christians and Muslims also read and honor the Hebrew Bible.

The Hebrew Bible is the Jewish people's record of their history and their religion, which is called Judaism. In this lesson you will follow the Bible's account of Judaism's beginnings.

ABRAHAM OF UR

The first book of the Bible tells of a family that lived in Mesopotamia. This family came from the city-state of Ur. In this city people worshiped the Sumerian moon goddess. However, this family worshiped a different god. The Bible tells about a man named **Abraham** and his wife Sarah:

> The Lord said to Abraham: "Go forth from your native land and from your father's house to the land that I will show you. I will make of you a great nation, and I will bless you. . . ." [So] Abraham took his wife, Sarah . . . and they set out for the land of Canaan.

The Covenant

To reach the land of Canaan from Mesopotamia, the travelers would have set out on the trade routes that linked major cities of the Fertile Crescent. Look at the map on this page to see their route. The journey would have taken months, and it would have been hard to be a stranger in a new place. When Abraham arrived in Canaan, the Bible says that God made a covenant, or special agreement, with him.

> I am God Almighty. Walk in My ways and be blameless. I will establish My covenant with you, and I will make you exceedingly numerous. . . . I assign the land you sojourn [rest] in to you and your offspring to come . . . I will be their God.

This covenant is considered by the Jewish people to be the beginning of their history. Later, their descendants would become known as people of Israel, or Israelites, after Abraham's grandson Israel. They also came to be known as Jews.

Going to Egypt

As time passed, the Bible says, Abraham's children and grandchildren prospered as shepherds in Canaan. Then came a time of poor crops and terrible hunger. The people of Israel went to Egypt, where food could be found.

Here the people of Israel were welcomed. As time passed, things changed. "A new king arose over Egypt," the Bible says. This pharaoh "set taskmasters over [the people of Israel] to oppress them with forced labor." Like others in ancient Egypt, the people of Israel had become slaves.

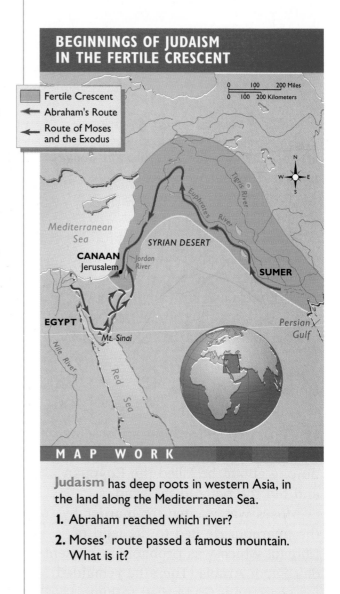

BEGINNINGS OF JUDAISM IN THE FERTILE CRESCENT

- Fertile Crescent
- Abraham's Route
- Route of Moses and the Exodus

0 100 200 Miles
0 100 200 Kilometers

Mediterranean Sea · SYRIAN DESERT · Tigris River · Euphrates River · CANAAN · Jerusalem · Jordan River · SUMER · EGYPT · Mt. Sinai · Nile River · Red Sea · Persian Gulf

M A P   W O R K

Judaism has deep roots in western Asia, in the land along the Mediterranean Sea.

1. Abraham reached which river?
2. Moses' route passed a famous mountain. What is it?

MOSES IN EGYPT

Fortunately for the Israelites, a man named Moses rose to leadership. According to the Bible, Moses was born to Israelite parents but was adopted as a baby by the pharaoh's daughter. Raised in the royal household, Moses experienced all the wealth and power of Egypt. Yet he would someday become leader and teacher to enslaved Israelites who lived all around him.

Becoming a Prophet

One day, the Bible says, Moses saw an Egyptian beating an Israelite slave. Moses looked around, and seeing no one about, he killed the Egyptian and hid the body in the sand.

Moses was wanted for murder by the pharaoh. He fled to the land of Midian, which was probably in present-day Saudi Arabia. There he remained for years until God called to him,

This family celebrates Passover by praying and sharing a traditional meal. The foods on the plate are symbolic of an ancient story.

"Come . . . I will send you to Pharaoh, and you shall free My people, the Israelites, from Egypt."

At first Moses protested, saying, "Please, O Lord, I have never been a man of words. . . . I am slow of speech and slow of tongue." In the end, however, the Bible says, he obeyed God and made the long trek back to Egypt. Moses was now seen as a *prophet,* or a person who speaks for God. Moses walked the halls of the pharaoh's court once again. There he tried to convince the pharaoh to free the Israelite slaves. Moses wanted to lead them to safety.

The Bible describes how Moses, with the help of God, led the Israelite captives from Egypt. To this day Jews celebrate the Passover festival each year to remember their freedom from slavery.

The Torah

According to the Bible, Moses led the Israelites into the wilderness of eastern Egypt. There they wandered for 40 difficult years. Early in their journey the Israelites traveled to a mountain called Mount Sinai. There, the Bible says, God gave Moses five books of laws and teachings. These five books are the first books of the Bible. In Hebrew they are known as the Torah, which comes from the word meaning "to teach."

Some of these laws are very similar to laws that were common in Babylonia. Like the Code of Hammurabi, for example, the Torah also had laws that forbade stealing and hurting others. In one very important way, however, the Torah was different. The God of the Hebrews forbade them to worship any other gods. This belief in only one God became known as monotheism. It set the Israelites apart from the other peoples living in the Fertile Crescent.

Among the laws that God gave to Moses at Mount Sinai were the Ten Commandments. These commandments became the core of the Jewish religion and teachings. In what ways do the Ten Commandments differ from Hammurabi's laws?

MANY VOICES
PRIMARY SOURCE

The Ten Commandments (Exodus 20:1–14).

I the Lord am your God. . . . You shall have no other gods besides Me.

You shall not make for yourself a sculptured image, or any likeness of what is in the heavens above, or on the earth below. . . . You shall not bow down to them or serve them.

You shall not swear falsely by the name of the Lord your God.

Remember the Sabbath [day of rest] and keep it holy.

Honor your father and your mother.

You shall not murder.

You shall not commit adultery.

You shall not steal.

You shall not bear false witness against your neighbor.

You shall not covet [desire] . . . anything that is your neighbor's.

The Jewish Museum, NYC

Many of the scrolls that hold the Torah are beautifully decorated. The Torah shown here is written in Hebrew.

123

Jerusalem is the capital of Israel and a religious center. Jews gather at the Western Wall to pray.

THE KINGDOM OF ISRAEL

After 40 years in the wilderness, the Israelites prepared to enter Canaan. The Bible says that Moses spoke to his people one last time before he died.

This is the Instruction—the laws and the rule—that the Lord your God has commanded me to impart to you . . . so that you, your children, and your children's children may revere [worship] the Lord your God . . . to the end that you may long endure [survive].

The Bible says that after hearing Moses' final words, the Israelites crossed the Jordan River into the land of Canaan. There they defeated several kings and set up a nation of their own, called Israel. Now the Israelites were not only a people defined by their religious beliefs. They were a nation with a land, as well.

A Nation of Israel

For the people of Israel, the Torah was the basis of life and faith. It commanded people, for example, to "remember the Sabbath, and keep it holy." The Sabbath is the weekly day of rest, prayer, and study. It falls on Saturday. The instructions of the Torah reminded Israelites of their closeness to God. They continue to do so today.

According to the Bible, Israel became a powerful kingdom under the leadership of King David. He made the city of Jerusalem his capital about 1000 b.c. Jerusalem became even more important to Israel when David's son Solomon built a great temple there. Jerusalem became a center of both religious and political life.

Exile to Babylonia

After Solomon's death, about 928 B.C., the kingdom of Israel split into two kingdoms. The northern kingdom, Israel, was conquered by the Assyrians in 721 B.C. The southern kingdom was called Judah. This is where the name Jews comes from. The kingdom of Judah survived until 586 B.C. When Babylonian armies destroyed Jerusalem and Solomon's temple, many Jews were led away to Babylon. This would not be the last time the Jews were exiled, or forced to leave their homeland. The scattering of the Jews to many parts of the world is called the Diaspora (di AS pur uh).

WHY IT MATTERS

Alas!
Lonely sits the city
Once great with people! . . .
Take us back, O Lord, to Yourself,
And let us come back;
Renew our days as of old!

These words from the Bible record the despair felt by the Jews. However, even in the Diaspora, many Jews would continue to live by the Torah. They would also remember the covenant described in the Bible so many lifetimes earlier.

A Jewish boy studies the Torah in preparation for his bar mitzvah. After this ceremony he will be recognized as an adult.

MAIN IDEAS

- Trade and movement of people in the 1700s B.C. helped link major cities of the Fertile Crescent and Egypt.
- The Bible says Moses led the Israelites out of slavery in Egypt and passed on laws from God regarding how they should live.
- Monotheism—the belief in one God—set the Hebrews apart from other groups around them.
- Sacred writings, called the Torah, form the heart of Judaism.

THINK ABOUT IT

1. What role did Abraham play in the history of Judaism?
2. Why do Jews still celebrate Passover?
3. **FOCUS** How were Moses and the teachings of the Torah important to the beginnings of Judaism?
4. **THINKING SKILL** According to the Bible, what was the *cause* of the Israelites' move to Egypt?
5. **WRITE** Briefly compare and contrast polytheism and monotheism.

CHAPTER 5 REVIEW

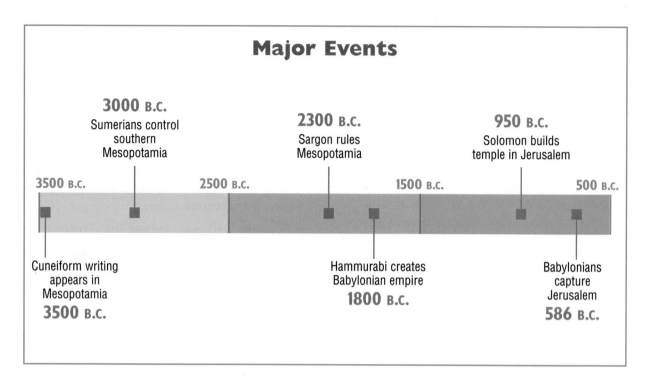

Major Events

3000 B.C.
Sumerians control southern Mesopotamia

2300 B.C.
Sargon rules Mesopotamia

950 B.C.
Solomon builds temple in Jerusalem

3500 B.C.   2500 B.C.   1500 B.C.   500 B.C.

Cuneiform writing appears in Mesopotamia
3500 B.C.

Hammurabi creates Babylonian empire
1800 B.C.

Babylonians capture Jerusalem
586 B.C.

THINKING ABOUT VOCABULARY

Each of the following statements contains an underlined vocabulary word. Number a sheet of paper from 1 to 5. Beside each number write **T** if the statement is true and **F** if the statement is false. If the statement is false, rewrite the sentence using the vocabulary word correctly.

1. <u>Monotheism</u> is a belief in many gods.

2. A <u>ziggurat</u> is a long, pointed weapon used by Sumerian warriors.

3. The system of writing invented in Sumer is <u>cuneiform.</u>

4. The <u>Diaspora</u> is the trip Jews made to live in Israel.

5. An area of fertile land near the coast that is good for farming is called a <u>plateau.</u>

THINKING ABOUT FACTS

1. What is the Fertile Crescent?

2. Who were two of the Sumerian gods?

3. How did Hammurabi create his powerful empire?

4. Where was Nineveh? Why was it famous?

5. According to the Bible, what was the covenant with Abraham? Why is it important in Jewish history?

6. Who invented the wheel? How was it used?

7. What did early Mesopotamian farmers grow?

8. What is the Hebrew Bible? Why is it important?

9. Who was Sargon and what did he accomplish?

10. According to the time line above, about how many centuries before Solomon did Hammurabi live? How many centuries before Hammurabi did Sargon live?

THINK AND WRITE

WRITING COMPARISONS
Write a comparison of the governments and rulers of ancient Egypt and Sumer. How were they similar? How were they different?

WRITING AN EXPLANATION
Write two or three paragraphs about the Code of Hammurabi and the Ten Commandments. Explain why they are regarded as important steps forward in civilization.

WRITING BIOGRAPHICAL PARAGRAPHS
Write one paragraph about two of the following people: (1) Sargon, (2) Hammurabi, (3) Abraham, and (4) Moses.

APPLYING THINKING SKILLS

IDENTIFYING CAUSE AND EFFECT

1. What is a cause? What is an effect?
2. Can you think of an example from the chapter of an effect having two or more causes?
3. Name as many causes as you can for the rise of civilization in Mesopotamia.
4. Name two or more effects of the invention of the wheel. Can you think of another example from the chapter of a cause having more than one effect?
5. How do cause-and-effect connections help historians understand the past?

Summing Up the Chapter

Copy the main idea chart below on a separate piece of paper. Then review the chapter to find information for each category on the chart. When you have filled in the chart, use the information to answer the question "What contributions did the peoples of the Fertile Crescent make to civilization?"

MAIN IDEA	People of the Fertile Crescent made many contributions to civilization.		
People	**Writing Systems**	**Government/Law**	**Type of Religion**
Sumerians	cuneiform records		
Babylonians			polytheism
Israelites		Torah Ten Commandments	

Ancient India

THINKING ABOUT
HISTORY AND GEOGRAPHY

Indian civilization begins around 6000 B.C. in the
Indus River valley, in what is today Pakistan. Mohenjo-
Daro and Harappa were the most powerful cities in the
valley until the arrival of horse-riding herders from the
north. Their meeting changed both cultures and led to
the development of a religion called Hinduism. India
later became the birthplace of Buddhism as well.

6000 B.C.

INDUS RIVER VALLEY
People begin growing rice

2500 B.C.

MOHENJO-DARO
Craftworkers have the
time and skill to make
beautiful pottery

1900 B.C.

KHYBER PASS
After crossing the Hindu
Kush, Aryans win control
of the Indus Valley

6000 B.C.   3000 B.C.   2000 B.C.

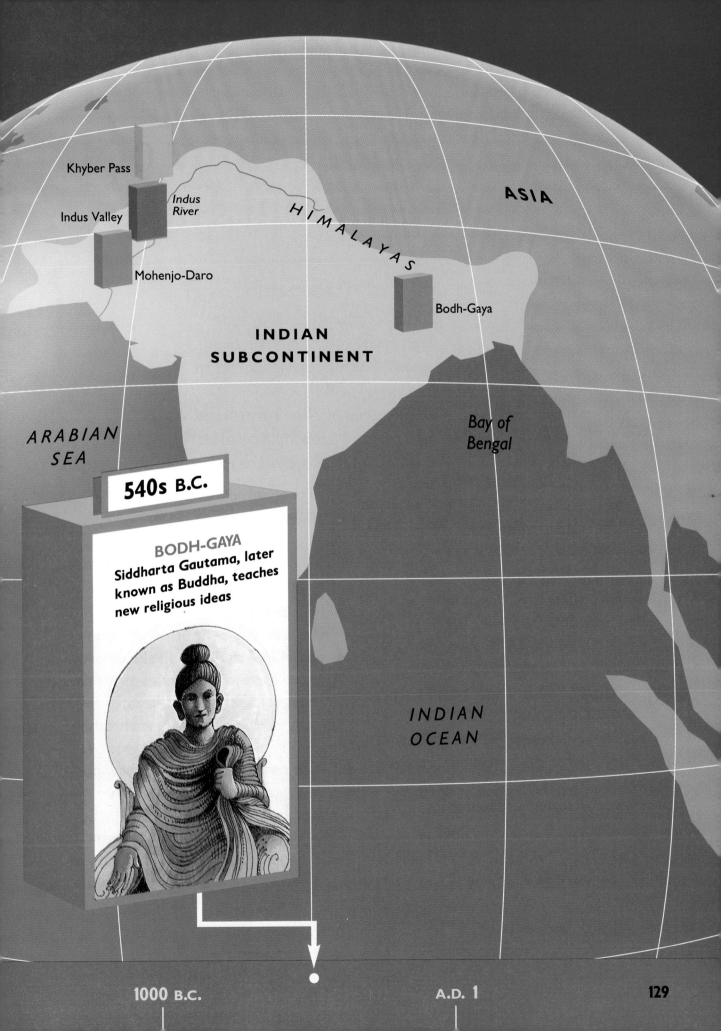

Khyber Pass

Indus River

Indus Valley

Mohenjo-Daro

H I M A L A Y A S

ASIA

Bodh-Gaya

INDIAN
SUBCONTINENT

ARABIAN
SEA

Bay of
Bengal

540s B.C.

BODH-GAYA
Siddharta Gautama, later known as Buddha, teaches new religious ideas

INDIAN
OCEAN

1000 B.C.

A.D. 1

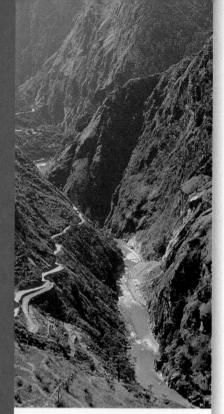

Geography of Ancient India

Read Aloud

Boulders [ground] to silt by water . . .
deep, round valleys, robed in cloud
against the crag-carving sunlight on
[mountain] peaks . . .
And centuries of cloud have melted, valleys
have sweated froth-white cascades
to draw that long, brown line down to the sea.

This is how Pakistani poet Salman Tarik Kureshi
describes the Indus River.

Focus Activity

READ TO LEARN

*What did the Indus River
contribute to a new
civilization?*

VOCABULARY

• subcontinent

PLACES

• Indus River
• Himalayas
• Indus Plain

THE BIG PICTURE

As the poem above describes, the Indus River begins in the snow-covered mountains of South Asia. It flows through what are today China, India, and Pakistan. In India and Pakistan other rivers join the Indus as it flows south. The silt it carries makes the river the color of cocoa. During spring floods this silt is spread throughout the Indus Valley.

The silt deposits and river water make farming possible in the otherwise dry environment of western South Asia. For this reason the Indus is similar to the Nile, Tigris, and Euphrates rivers. They have all been great givers of life to people for thousands of years. In fact, the Indus Valley was one of the first places in the world where farming developed. Archaeologists have found evidence of farming communities there that have been dated to around 6000 B.C.

A GREAT RIVER IS BORN

The Indus River begins as an icy stream high in the world's tallest mountains. These mountains are the Himalayas (hihm uh LAY uz). You have probably heard of their highest peak, Mount Everest. It stands 29,028 feet tall. The towering Himalayas separate the Indian subcontinent from much of Asia. A subcontinent is a large landmass that is geographically separated from the rest of a continent. Find the Indian subcontinent, the Himalayas, and the Indus River on the map on this page.

Long Journey of the Indus

In the spring the Indus swells with melting snow. It flows south to the Arabian Sea on an 1,800-mile journey through what is today mainly Pakistan. As the river passes through the Himalayas, it rushes through vast canyons. Some of these canyons are three miles deep! Imagine dropping a coin straight from the top of one canyon. It would take about 90 seconds for it to hit the river below. That same coin would hit the floor of America's Grand Canyon in 30 seconds.

The Indus flows swiftly down the mountains until it is joined by other rivers. Locate these on the map. These rivers join the Indus in the northern part of the dry, desert-like

This palace at Stok, in Northern India, nestles in the Himalayas.

Indus Plain. During the spring flood season, the enlarged river spills across the plain, spreading fertile silt.

The Indus actually carries twice as much silt as the mighty Nile in Egypt. Like the Nile, the Indus branches into a huge delta before it reaches the sea.

Think about what you have learned about other river valleys. How do you think the river might have affected people centuries ago in the Indus Valley?

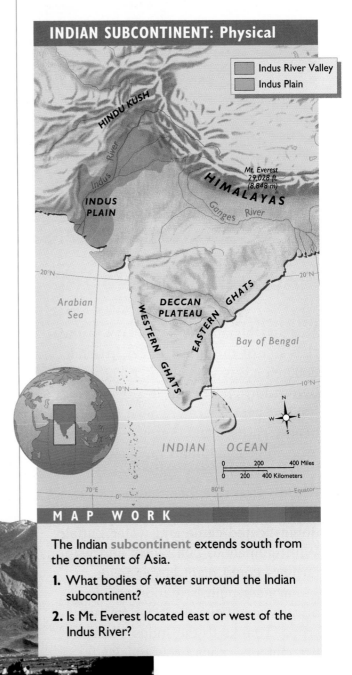

INDIAN SUBCONTINENT: Physical

Indus River Valley
Indus Plain

HINDU KUSH
Indus River
Mt. Everest 29,028 ft (8,848 m)
HIMALAYAS
INDUS PLAIN
Ganges River
20°N
Arabian Sea
DECCAN PLATEAU
WESTERN GHATS
EASTERN GHATS
Bay of Bengal
20°N
10°N
10°N
INDIAN OCEAN
200   400 Miles
0   200   400 Kilometers
70°E
80°E
Equator
0°

MAP WORK

The Indian subcontinent extends south from the continent of Asia.

1. What bodies of water surround the Indian subcontinent?

2. Is Mt. Everest located east or west of the Indus River?

The Indus is still an important source of water for agriculture. These children (left) are washing domestic water buffaloes. A woman in the Indus Valley harvests vegetables (above).

AGRICULTURE AND THE INDUS RIVER

Farmers began planting crops in the rich soil of the Indus Valley around 6000 B.C. This was about 1,000 years before farming began in Egypt. Indus Valley farmers grew wheat, barley, beans, and sesame. Sesame is a seed used for cooking and for making oil. These farmers also grew some of the world's first rice, banana, black pepper, mustard, and cotton crops. In time they domesticated cattle and water buffalo. With animals to pull plows and wagons, farmers could plant larger fields.

Farmers built irrigation canals to bring water from the river to their crops. Thanks to the Indus Valley's hot climate, crops grew quickly. Archaeologists believe that this made it possible for farmers to plant and harvest twice a year.

In the fall, farmers planted wheat and barley. They harvested just before the melting snow caused spring floods. Then farmers quickly planted fields of cotton and sesame. Dirt walls were constructed to protect these crops from the Indus flood. By the next fall, crops were ready for another harvest.

Working with the Environment

Successful harvests did not always come easily in the Indus River valley. Earth and rock walls could not always hold back the floodwaters. Fields and entire villages could sometimes be swept away.

Wildlife in the valley also brought problems. Tigers, jackals, and wild pigs could threaten lives. Deer and such birds as wild parakeets often ate farmers' crops. Archaeologists think that ancient Indus farmers used slings and clay balls to scare birds from fields and fruit trees. Farm children in India and Pakistan today often have the chore of scaring away birds. Perhaps children in ancient times had this job too.

WHY IT MATTERS

As in ancient Egypt and Mesopotamia, civilization in the Indus River valley developed along a river. The civilization could not have survived without the crops that farmers grew in the fertile valley soil. By about 3000 B.C. villages and small towns had grown throughout the valley. Within 300 years cities would develop along the mighty river. In the next lesson you will read about life in one of those cities.

MAIN IDEAS

- The Indus River brings water and silt that make farming possible.
- The Indus begins in the Himalayas and crosses desert-like plains before reaching the Arabian Sea.
- Ancient Indus Valley farmers irrigated their fields and built dirt walls to protect their crops and homes from terrible floods.

THINK ABOUT IT

1. Compare the Indus and the Nile rivers. How are they similar?

2. What made it possible for Indus Valley farmers to harvest crops two times a year?

3. **FOCUS** In what ways did the Indus River help farmers? In what ways could it hurt them?

4. **THINKING SKILL** You have now learned about three early river-valley civilizations. Based on what you have read, make a *generalization* about how rivers shaped the lives of early people. On what facts did you base your generalization?

5. **GEOGRAPHY** Draw a map of the Indian subcontinent and the Himalayas. Trace the routes of the Indus and Ganges rivers.

Chili peppers are an important crop in India. Millions are bought and sold in markets like this one.

Karachi Museum, Pakistan

| 2500 B.C. | 1500 B.C. | 1000 B.C. | 500 B.C. |

Early Indian Civilization

Read Aloud

In 1921 archaeologists gathered around a huge dirt mound on the southern plains of the Indus Valley. They knew remains of the past lay hidden beneath the mound. Earlier visitors had found artifacts there. But how old were the remains? What would they reveal about how Indian people lived long ago?

As the archaeologists dug down, the ruins of a great city began to appear. A new understanding about India's ancient past had begun.

Focus Activity

READ TO LEARN

What was life like in the ancient cities of the Indus River valley?

VOCABULARY

- citadel
- migrate

PLACES

- Harappa
- Mohenjo-Daro

THE BIG PICTURE

Over 1,000 miles separate the Indus River valley from Iraq, the region once known as Mesopotamia. This distance did not keep people from traveling between the two regions over 4,000 years ago, though. Like merchants from Egypt, Indian merchants traded goods in Mesopotamian cities.

Of these three ancient civilizations—Mesopotamia, Egypt, and the Indus River valley—the least is known about the Indus River valley civilization. One reason that historians know less about this culture is that experts have not been able to figure out how to read ancient Indian writing. Another reason is that few Indus artifacts and remains have been found. Despite these limits, historians have pieced together a picture of what ancient life may have been like for the people along the Indus River.

134

A CIVILIZATION IN THE INDUS VALLEY

The city described in the Read Aloud is called Harappa (huh RAH puh). The people who lived nearby named the ruins after an Indian god. Archaeologists have no way of knowing what early people living along the Indus called themselves. Therefore, the entire ancient Indus Valley civilization is called Harappan civilization. It lasted from about 2500 B.C. until about 1600 B.C.

One year after the city of Harappa was uncovered, archaeologists found a city almost exactly like it about 400 miles to the south. The local name for it was Mohenjo-Daro (moh HEN joh DAH roh), which means "Mound of the Dead" in Sanskrit. Sanskrit is an ancient Indian language. Locate the ancient cities of Harappa and Mohenjo-Daro on the map on this page.

A City Along the Indus

The city of Mohenjo-Daro was not small. Archaeologists believe that as many as 40,000 people once lived there! Dozens of streets crisscrossed each other. Larger avenues were paved with tan-colored bricks. The streets that crossed them were narrower and were usually left unpaved.

Hundreds of sturdy brick houses lined the streets of Mohenjo-Daro. Most homes were small, one-room buildings. Others were several stories high. Some even had such luxuries as airy courtyards or balconies.

At the west end of the city stood a massive fort, or citadel (SIT uh dul). Surrounding this citadel were thick walls that protected against both floods and enemy attacks. Next to the citadel was an enormous grain warehouse. Judging from its size, farmers around Mohenjo-Daro must have been very successful at growing barley and wheat.

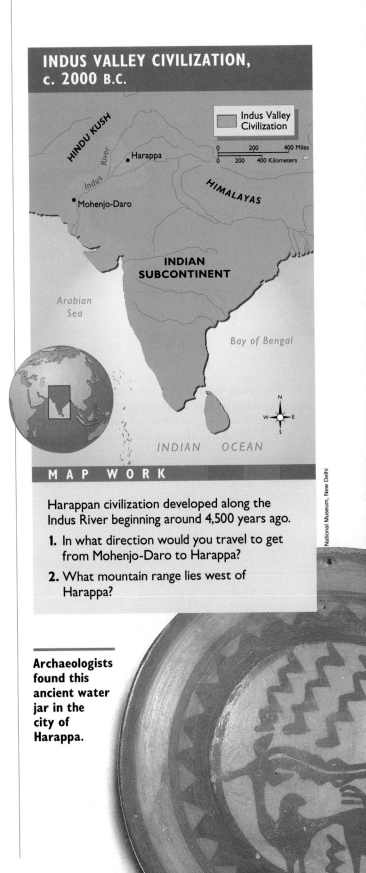

INDUS VALLEY CIVILIZATION, c. 2000 B.C.

HINDU KUSH
Indus River
• Harappa
Indus
• Mohenjo-Daro
HIMALAYAS

Indus Valley Civilization

0   200   400 Miles
0   200   400 Kilometers

INDIAN SUBCONTINENT

Arabian Sea

Bay of Bengal

INDIAN   OCEAN

National Museum, New Delhi

MAP WORK

Harappan civilization developed along the Indus River beginning around 4,500 years ago.

1. In what direction would you travel to get from Mohenjo-Daro to Harappa?

2. What mountain range lies west of Harappa?

Archaeologists found this ancient water jar in the city of Harappa.

LIFE IN MOHENJO-DARO

Suppose that you are an archaeologist living 4,000 years in the future. You have just stumbled upon the ruins of a small North American city dating back to the A.D. 1990s. You uncover buildings and dusty artifacts. You find machines and bits of plastic labels. You cannot read the city's languages, though. How much will you be able to understand about everyday life in this city? How many conclusions will you be able to make about the culture of the North American civilization?

Archaeologists studying ancient Harappan civilization have faced these kinds of challenges since the early 1900s. Yet they have succeeded in making some conclusions about what life was like for ancient Harappans. Many of their conclusions are based on remains found in Mohenjo-Daro.

City Planning

One of the most striking things about Mohenjo-Daro is the exactness of the measurements used in making and building things. Bricklayers used thousands of same-sized bricks to pave streets and build homes. City engineers dug wells throughout the city. They also created a sewer system, complete with "manholes," to keep the city clean.

Projects like this need much planning. Therefore, historians believe

Stone seals (right) and other artifacts have taught archaeologists about Mohenjo-Daro. An artist depicted daily life in the city (below).

Mohenjo-Daro must have had a strong government. Harappa had almost the same layout as Mohenjo-Daro. Therefore, historians conclude that the Indus River valley also must have had a strong central government.

On top of Mohenjo-Daro's citadel are the remains of a large, pillar-supported building. Archaeologists think it may have served as a "city hall," because it overlooked the city. Next door was a building that housed a pool-sized bath. The bath may have had religious importance. Cleansing practices later became a key part of Indian religions. The artwork at left shows what Mohenjo-Daro may have looked like in 2000 B.C.

Working in Mohenjo-Daro

Harappan builders, engineers, and craftworkers were highly skilled. Archaeologists have found remains of their work in the workshops that lined city avenues.

Skilled workers carved beautiful figures into small squares of stone. These stone squares were probably used as seals for marking belongings. Potters made water jars, cooking bowls, and other containers. These were covered with colorful paintings. Metalworkers made everything from copper fish hooks to razors. They also made fine statues of people cast in bronze. Perhaps for the first time anywhere, weavers made cloth from cotton.

As in other ancient cities, such specialization meant that Harappan farmers produced surplus food. Surplus grain was stored in a great warehouse. Perhaps, as in ancient Egypt, government workers collected grain from farmers as taxes. The stored grain could later be measured out again, possibly as payment to city workers.

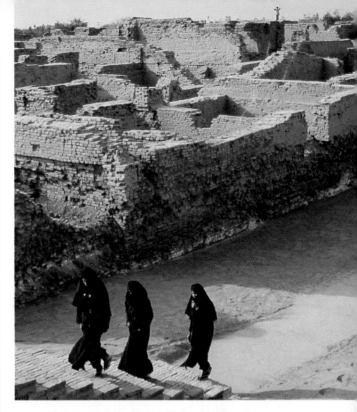

The once-busy city of Mohenjo-Daro is empty today. These women climb steps that are thousands of years old.

Harappan Trade

Historians are not sure of the exact trade routes used by ancient Harappans. However, historians do know that Harappan merchants traded with neighbors both near and far.

From artifacts, archaeologists know that Harappans sold stone seals in what is today Iran. They brought home blue stones called lapis lazuli from what is today Afghanistan. Beadmakers made necklaces from stones brought from what is today India. These and other goods were then traded in faraway Mesopotamia.

The long journey to Mesopotamia was probably made in small sailboats. From the Indus River delta, the boats headed west along the southern coast of Asia. The sailors may have taken along field birds such as crows and swallows. When set free, the birds would fly toward land.

NEWCOMERS

Sometime around 1600 B.C. the city of Mohenjo-Daro was totally abandoned. So was the city of Harappa. Why?

Unfortunately we may never know for sure why these ancient cities were abandoned. One possible answer, archaeologists say, is that an earthquake caused the Indus to change its course. Without river water, farming would have become very difficult in this area. This earthquake may also have created massive floods. Floods may have destroyed the region's two largest cities. Life went on in the Indus Valley after the disaster. Harappan civilization, however, was never the same again.

Life in the Indus Valley changed even more, beginning around 1500 B.C. At that time newcomers began crossing the icy passes of the Hindu Kush Mountains. The Aryan (AYR ee un) people, originally from central Asia, herded cattle and sheep on horseback. Perhaps due to natural disasters or wars at home, they migrated (MĪ gray tud). To migrate means to move from one place to another to live. The Aryans migrated both to Europe and India. Follow their routes to India on the map.

Aryans means "noble ones" in Sanskrit. The Aryan people brought this language to the Indus Valley and the rest of the subcontinent. They also

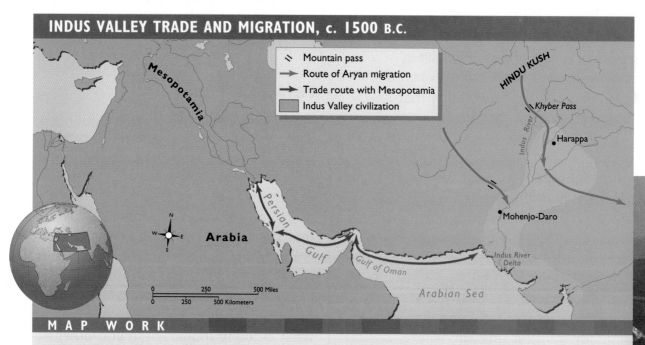

INDUS VALLEY TRADE AND MIGRATION, c. 1500 B.C.

Mountain pass
Route of Aryan migration
Trade route with Mesopotamia
Indus Valley civilization

Mesopotamia
HINDU KUSH
Khyber Pass
Indus River
Harappa
Persian Gulf
Arabia
Gulf of Oman
Mohenjo-Daro
Indus River Delta
Arabian Sea

0   250   500 Miles
0   250   500 Kilometers

MAP WORK

Aryan peoples migrated to the Indian subcontinent through mountain passes.

1. What is the name of a mountain pass through which Aryans probably migrated?

2. About how far is Mesopotamia from the city of Mohenjo-Daro?

3. Why would a boat trip from Harappa to Mohenjo-Daro be faster than a return trip by boat?

Narrow passes through the Hindu Kush Mountains continue to be useful in modern transportation of goods.

brought new religious ideas, which you will read about in the next lesson.

WHY IT MATTERS

Harappan civilization existed in the Indus River valley for almost 1,000 years. During that time farmers produced a large surplus of food. This surplus fed the populations of the great cities that developed along the fertile plains. Workers in cities like Mohenjo-Daro created items unknown in other parts of the world at that time. These included cotton cloth, stone seals, and citywide drainage systems.

In the end, Harappan civilization may have been destroyed by the very thing that made it possible—the Indus River. Yet parts of that civilization would continue in new forms. New peoples would come to control the Indian subcontinent. In time their cultures would blend with the culture of the Harappans to create a new, rich culture.

Reviewing Facts and Ideas

MAIN IDEAS

- Little is known about Harappan civilization because its writing system has not yet been figured out.

- The city of Mohenjo-Daro included many brick buildings and a huge citadel. The city also had a sewer system more advanced than any other of its time.

- The orderly layout of the city and its large grain warehouse suggest that Mohenjo-Daro was ruled by a strong local government.

- Harappan merchants traded goods in many places, some of which were as far away as Mesopotamia.

- In about 1500 B.C. people called Aryans migrated to the Indian subcontinent. They brought new ideas to the region.

THINK ABOUT IT

1. Why is ancient Indus Valley civilization called Harappan civilization?

2. What have historians learned about Harappan civilization from written sources? What have they learned from building remains in cities like Mohenjo-Daro?

3. **FOCUS** What do we know about the early culture of Mohenjo-Daro?

4. **THINKING SKILL** Based on the information in this lesson, what _conclusions_ can you make about the people who lived in Mohenjo-Daro? What evidence supports your conclusions?

5. **GEOGRAPHY** Sketch a map of southern and western Asia. Draw the routes of the Aryan migration and the trade route between Harappa and Mesopotamia. Be sure to include physical features like mountains, rivers, and seas in your sketch.

Geography Skills

Comparing Different Kinds of Maps

WHY THE SKILL MATTERS

In Lesson 1 you read that yearly floods and deposits of silt made farming possible in the ancient Indus River valley. Farming, in turn, led to the development of city life in the valley.

Today farming is still an important part of life in the Indus River valley. This area is now a part of Pakistan. The success of present-day farmers there still depends on the Indus River.

To better understand the ties between land and human life in the Indus River valley, it helps to compare different kinds of maps.

Comparing maps showing the same area allows you to discover new information that you would not be able to get by looking at maps separately. Different types of maps show different information. For example, look at Map A and Map B, both on this page.

USING THE SKILL

As you can see from the map titles, Map A shows Pakistan's borders and major cities, while Map B shows Pakistan's physical features. What kinds of features does Map B highlight?

When you compare the information on both maps, you can learn different things about Pakistan. For example, you can see that there are no large cities in most of the southwestern part of Pakistan. What are the physical features of that region? How do you think they affect the way in which people settled there?

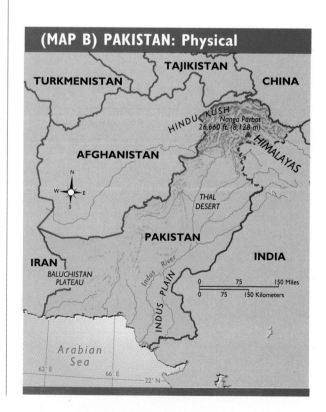

(MAP A) PAKISTAN: Political

(MAP B) PAKISTAN: Physical

TRYING THE SKILL

In the first lesson you also learned that ancient Indus farmers planted wheat as well as some of the world's first crops of rice. As you can see from Map C on this page, those two crops are still important in the Indus Valley area today.

Use the Helping Yourself box on this page to compare Maps B and C. This study will help you to gain more information about modern farming in Pakistan. What kind of physical features does the land have where most wheat and rice farming are done?

REVIEWING THE SKILL

1. How can comparing maps help you to better understand a place?
2. Look at maps B and C. Which natural features are needed to support agriculture for a large population? How did you reach your conclusion?
3. What might you learn about where you live by studying and comparing different kinds of maps?

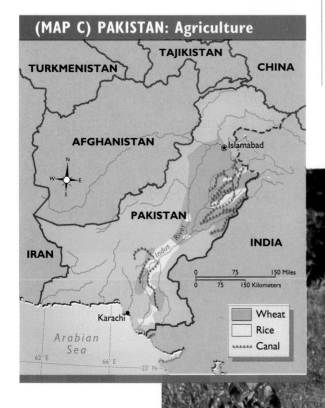

(MAP C) PAKISTAN: Agriculture

TAJIKISTAN
TURKMENISTAN
CHINA
AFGHANISTAN
Islamabad
PAKISTAN
Indus River
INDIA
IRAN

0   75   150 Miles
0   75   150 Kilometers

Karachi

Arabian Sea

62° E   66° E   22° N

Wheat
Rice
Canal

In Pakistan today, oxen are sometimes used to draw well water. The water irrigates crops.

LESSON 3

Beginnings of Hinduism

Focus Activity

READ TO LEARN

How did the Vedas shape Indian culture?

VOCABULARY

- Hinduism
- Vedas
- caste system
- reincarnation
- dharma

Read Aloud

Ancient Hindu writings tell the story of a father who used simple examples to teach his son about the meaning of life. One day he told his son to bring him a fig from a fig tree. The boy did so, and his father told him to split the fruit open.

"What do you see?"

"These fine [tiny] seeds," replied the son.

"Break one open! What do you see?"

"Nothing at all, sir!"

His father said, "This finest element, which you cannot see—out of this finest element comes this big fig tree!" The boy was similar to the tree, he said. The father was teaching his son the Hindu belief that all life is connected by an invisible force.

THE BIG PICTURE

This belief in a link between a powerful, invisible force and everything in the world is a key part of Hinduism (HIHN doo ihz um). Hinduism, one of the world's oldest religions, grew out of the beliefs of the Aryans, whom you read about in the last lesson. Today it has nearly 800 million followers. As is the case with most religions, Hinduism is practiced in many different ways. Yet all Hindus share some basic beliefs. Hindus also share a history that stretches back to the ancient past of the Indian subcontinent.

WRITINGS OF A NEW RELIGION

When Aryans migrated to the Indian subcontinent around 1500 B.C., they had little in common with Harappans. The two peoples spoke different languages and had different cultures. Many Harappans lived in great cities like Mohenjo-Daro. As herders, the Aryan people were used to moving around more. They lived in smaller villages and moved often.

As time passed, the two cultural groups began to learn from each other. Aryans began farming and specializing in crafts like their Harappan neighbors.

Harappans, meanwhile, learned ancient Aryan songs about how the world works. These songs, believed to be holy, were passed down by oral tradition. Around 600 B.C. the sacred songs were finally collected. The books containing them were called the Vedas (VAY duz), or "Books of Knowledge."

The Vedas

The Vedas were the first building blocks of Hinduism. They told Hindus how they should live, and explained life. The oldest Veda has more than 1,000 hymns. It says that the world is run by many gods and goddesses. Which Hindu goddess does this hymn praise? What are her "twinkling eyes"?

Victoria and Albert Museum

MANY VOICES
PRIMARY SOURCE

Song from the *Rig Veda*, first written down in about 1000 B.C.

Goddess Night, with all her
    twinkling eyes,
To different points in splendor she
    comes.
Immortal, she **broods over** the
    high and low;
The Goddess, with her gaze, lightens
    the dark.

In her trail, her sister Dawn follows,
And with her the darkness
    vanishes. . . .
The villagers, all that flies and walks
Are closed in their homes. Even
    vultures ignore their **prey**.

O [Night], fence off the wolf and its
    mate;
Fence off the thief. Be easy for us to
    pass.

Bright, she has come near me, the
    darkness **subdued**
With light's promise. Dawn, cancel
    darkness.

---

immortal: never dying
broods over: thinks about
prey: animal hunted for food
subdued: conquered

Many Hindu temples are decorated with statues of gods and goddesses.

HINDUISM AND CULTURE

The Vedas explain how Hindus believe people were created and what is the proper way to live. The following hymn explains the Hindu belief that four different kinds, or classes, of people were created. These first humans were said to be born from the different parts of a god's body.

The Priest was his mouth;
The Princes became his arms;
His [legs] produced the
Professionals and Merchants;
His feet gave birth to the [Servant].

The Caste System

These four classes of people developed into India's caste system (KAST SIHS tum). The caste system is a way of organizing people into hundreds of different levels.

In a Hindu caste system a person's place in society is determined by the rank of the family she or he is born into. People born into the priestly caste of India have the highest rank and respect. Their main job is to study and

Bathing in the Ganges is an important Hindu ceremony. Caste is often shown with a mark on the forehead. There are as many as 3,000 castes in India.

teach people about the Vedas. People of the servant caste are said to be born to serve the other castes.

According to the Vedas, people do have some control over the caste they are born into. The Vedas state that people move in a constant circle of birth, death, and rebirth. This cycle is called reincarnation (ree ihn kahr NAY shun).

Hindus believe that bad deeds done in one lifetime must be paid for in a person's next life. According to this belief, people born as servants, then, are paying for wrongs done in the past. Priests, on the other hand, have done many good things in past lives.

The Importance of Duty

How did Hindus know what was right and good? They followed the **dharma** (DAHR muh) of their caste, described in the Vedas. Dharma means laws and duties. It includes hundreds of rules that instruct Hindus how to live.

For example, part of the dharma of servants was to do their jobs cheerfully. Professionals and merchants were responsible for producing and selling goods and services. Priests also had to spend some of their time working to support their families. The Vedas told which jobs people in each caste could and could not do.

Following dharma helped to keep Hindu society running in an orderly fashion. When people broke the rules of dharma, the Vedas warned, disorder would be the result. One of the sacred writings said:

> If a person is engaged in doing his proper work, he reaches the highest end.

People who married against the rules of their caste, or who did a job their caste was not allowed to do, were forced to live outside all castes. These "outcastes" were looked down upon by others and said to be "impure." Some Hindu priests performed a "cleansing" ceremony if they were touched by even the shadow of an outcaste.

Outcastes had few rights. Because their children were born outside all castes, they too, had to live their lives as "untouchables."

Many Paths to Truth

Over time, Hinduism developed hundreds of different forms. Some Hindus believed their dharma called them to become priests or to perform special exercises. Others felt it was important to eat no meat, eggs, or fish. Still others explored non-Hindu beliefs in their search to understand the meaning of life and the proper way to live.

These different approaches did not upset Hindu priests. Hinduism allows for the existence of more than one god and more than one way to truth. In a very popular Hindu book—called the *Bhagavad Gita* (BUG uh vud GEE tah)—the god Vishnu says:

> Howsoever people approach me, even so do I accept them; for on all sides, whatever path they may choose is mine.

Today Hindu priests read from the sacred Vedas, just as their ancestors have for hundreds of years.

145

HINDUISM TODAY

As in ancient times, Hindus of today worship many different gods and goddesses. Some gods, however, have become special favorites. The god Vishnu is worshiped as "The One that is the All" by millions of Hindus. Millions more honor Shiva, "The God of Time and Destruction." Still other believers prefer the goddess Devi, "The Mother of All Creation."

Most Hindu families today worship their favorite gods at home, at temples, and at special festivals.

A Changing Religion

Many Hindus still consider the Vedas the most holy books of their religion. Other books of adventure-filled stories, or *epics*, are also considered to be holy guides to living. Some of these stories have even been made into films.

Although Hinduism has roots in the ancient past, it has changed over the years. Some important changes have had to do with the caste system. In 1950, for example, the Indian government made it illegal to mistreat or to show disrespect for Hindu "outcastes."

Karachi Museum, Pakistan

Art of Hindu gods and goddesses shows (clockwise from left) Krishna and his wife Radha, Vishnu, and Ganesh.

Many Hindus observe traditional customs for important occasions, such as weddings. At this wedding ceremony in India, garlands of flowers surround a happy couple.

WHY IT MATTERS

Hinduism, one of the world's oldest religions, is followed by hundreds of millions of people today. Hinduism began in the blending of two cultures and honors many gods and goddesses. Today Hinduism continues to combine beliefs from different cultures. Most modern Hindus live in present-day India and Pakistan.

The legacy of Hinduism has influenced the arts, science, and society for great numbers of Hindus. As you will read in the next lesson, it also affected millions of others. Hinduism became the starting point for another world religion.

MAIN IDEAS

- Hinduism is practiced in many different ways. It is one of the world's oldest religions and has nearly 800 million followers today.

- Aryan newcomers to the Indian subcontinent introduced sacred songs written in the Vedas. They became the foundation of Hinduism.

- The Vedas supported a way of dividing Hindu society into four major classes of people. These four classes developed into the caste system.

- An important theme in Hinduism is reincarnation. This is the idea that people live in a constant circle of birth, death, and rebirth.

- By following the dharma, or instruction, of their caste, Hindus believe that people can break free of the cycle of reincarnation.

THINK ABOUT IT

1. What is dharma? Is it the same for all Hindus?

2. Why was it important for Hindus to do the duties expected of their caste?

3. **FOCUS** What are the Vedas? What role did they play in the shaping of Indian culture?

4. **THINKING SKILL** Make three _generalizations_ about what can happen when different cultures come into contact. Base your generalizations on what you have learned about each of the ancient river-valley civilizations.

5. **WRITING** Suppose you are interviewing a Hindu for a newspaper article. On a sheet of paper, write a list of questions you would ask.

INDIAN DANCE

The ancient Hindus believed that dance was given to them by the gods and goddesses. From the earliest times dance has been an important part of Indian life.

Indian dances vary greatly. Some of them tell a story without words. Other dances were created for their own sakes. In fact the people of ancient India used the same word, *natya* (NAH tyah), for both dance and drama. Both art forms told stories of Hindu gods and heroes.

Many Indian dances require great skill. Today dancers learn rules taught by Bharata (BAH ruh tuh), a teacher who lived some 1500 years ago. He even told dancers how to move their eyelashes!

In Hindu legend the god Shiva created the world by destroying his monster enemies. From then on the gods and goddesses danced. This sculpture shows Shiva performing his dance of destruction.

Dance is still an important part of life in India. These dancers are acting out a Hindu story. This ancient sculpture shows that if you had lived in India 1,000 years ago, you might have seen the very same dance performed in a temple.

Museum of Oriental Art, Rome

Bharata natyam is the oldest dance in the world that is still performed today. Hand gestures, or mudras (MOO drus), are an important part of this solo dance. Mudras often stand for animals, plants, or feelings.

2500 B.C.	2000 B.C.	1500 B.C.	1000 B.C.	563 B.C.	100 B.C.

Beginnings of Buddhism

Read Aloud

According to its followers, the founder of one of the world's major religions began his life as a prince in a mountain kingdom of northern India. He enjoyed all the best the world had to offer him—the finest clothes, many servants, and a beautiful palace for each season of the year. As a young man, though, the prince gave up his fame and fortune to seek the true meaning of life. His followers believe he found the answer. The man would become known as "the Buddha."

Focus Activity

READ TO LEARN

What did the Buddha teach?

VOCABULARY

- **Buddhism**
- **monk**
- **karma**
- **Four Noble Truths**
- **Eightfold Path**
- **Middle Way**

PEOPLE

- **Siddhartha Gautama**

PLACES

- **Kosala**

THE BIG PICTURE

Between about 1500 B.C. and 500 B.C., Aryan settlers spread eastward across the Indian subcontinent. They conquered many towns and cities as they went. By around 500 B.C. Aryan princes were in control of much of the Indian subcontinent.

In the far north, at the base of the Himalayas, some kingdoms held onto their independence. To keep their freedom, however, they had to make yearly payments to Aryan rulers to the south. In spite of this, conflict and struggle remained a part of their lives. Some Indians began to look for answers to life's problems beyond the Vedas. One was the prince described in the Read Aloud. His name was **Siddhartha Gautama** (sih DAHR tuh GOW tah muh). The answers he found would become **Buddhism** (BOOD ihz um), a religion that continues to attract followers. Today there are more than 330 million Buddhists.

LIFE OF THE BUDDHA

Siddhartha Gautama is traditionally said to have been born around 563 B.C. His parents were the king and queen of Kosala, a northern kingdom near the Himalayas. Siddhartha means "He Who Has Reached His Goal" in Sanskrit.

The Young Prince

Ancient Buddhist writings say that Siddhartha's mother dreamed about her son's future. The dreams predicted that if Siddhartha stayed at home, he would rule a great kingdom. If he left home, he would become a wise teacher and monk. A monk is a man who devotes his life to a religious group. Monks often give up all they own and live only a religious way of life.

Siddhartha's father wanted the boy to be a king. From that point on, Buddhist texts state, the king did all he could to keep his son happy at home. He had the best singing groups entertain his son and arranged for the prince to marry the woman of his dreams. He built stunning gardens around the royal palace so Siddhartha would be surrounded by beauty.

Discovery in the Garden

Even in his own garden, though, the king could not shelter Siddhartha from sorrow forever. One day the prince went for a ride in the royal gardens. There he spotted an elderly man hobbling painfully along with a cane. Siddhartha asked his chariot driver what was wrong with the man. He learned that all people grow old someday and said, "Shame on birth, since to everyone that is born, old age must come!"

During another ride through the gardens, Siddhartha saw someone

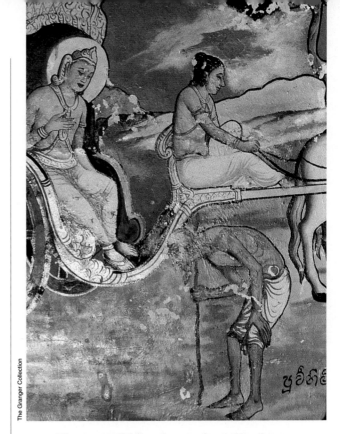

The Granger Collection

The young Siddhartha was introduced to sickness, old age, and death in his daily rides through his father's gardens.

who was very ill. It troubled him to find out that sickness was part of life. On yet another day the prince came upon a funeral procession. He learned that death was a part of life.

Finally Siddhartha spotted a man in the park who seemed to be at peace with the world. The man was calm even though he was asking people for help in getting his next meal. Siddhartha asked his driver who the man was and learned that the man was a monk. The prince was amazed that someone could be so at peace in a world filled with sorrow and suffering.

That day, Buddhist texts state, the prince made a difficult decision. He chose to give up all he had and become a monk. After saying good-bye to his wife and newborn son, he left the palace. His journey to find the meaning of life had begun.

THE TRAVELS OF THE BUDDHA

For the next six years, Siddhartha traveled throughout northern India as a monk. In his search for wisdom, he talked at length with Hindu priests, but felt their answers were not enough. To clear his mind, he stopped eating, but began again when he nearly starved himself to death.

At last, Buddhist texts say, an understanding came to the former prince one day as he sat under a fig tree. The wisdom it is said he received that day would later earn him the title *the Buddha,* which means "Awakened One."

The Teachings of Buddhism

Some of the Buddha's ideas were not new to India. He used some Hindu ideas and changed others. Like Hindus, the Buddha believed that all people went through a circle of birth, death, and rebirth, or reincarnation. Also like Hindus, he believed in karma. Karma is described by both Hindus and Buddhists as a force caused by a person's good and bad acts. Karma is said to affect future lives.

Buddhist prayer flags (top) float in the breeze near Kanchenjunga, India, the world's third-highest mountain. Buddhist monks (above) in Thailand wear traditional robes.

Unlike Hindus, the Buddha did not search for the one powerful force believed to connect all of life. Instead, the Buddha believed that the most important thing in life was to reach peace by ending suffering. How did he reach his conclusion, and how did he hope to reach this end?

152

The Way to End Suffering

Buddhist texts say that as he sat under the tree that day, the Buddha concluded that life is ruled by **Four Noble Truths**.

1. Life is filled with suffering.
2. Suffering is caused by people's wants. People may want more pleasure, more power, or a longer life.
3. Suffering can be ended if people stop wanting things.
4. To stop wanting things, people must follow eight basic laws.

The Buddha explained these Four Noble Truths to his followers, but they were not written down until later. He called the way to end suffering the **Eightfold Path**. The Eightfold Path is a set of instructions on the proper way to live. By following the Eightfold Path, the Buddha taught, people could end the suffering in their lives.

The Middle Way

The laws of the Eightfold Path were meant to represent a **Middle Way** of living for Buddhists. This way of life was meant to be neither too strict nor too easy. The Buddha compared the Middle Way to playing a stringed instrument. If the strings are kept too loose, they will not make a sound. On the other hand, if they are too tight, they will break when they are played. Only those strings that are kept at just the right amount of tightness will make beautiful sounds. Life works the same way, the Buddha concluded.

The Buddha's Final Journeys

The Buddha spent the rest of his life traveling around India and sharing his message with people of all castes. One of the first places he went to was his father's palace.

At first the elderly king was shocked. His son looked no different from any other humble monk he had met. But after listening to his son's message, Buddhists believe that the king, too, became a follower of the Buddha. So did the Buddha's wife and son.

By the time the Buddha died at age 80, there were thousands of Buddhists in northern India. They lived according to his Four Noble Truths. Like the Buddha, Buddhist monks gave up all they owned and depended on other Buddhist followers to give them food each day. They worked to live peacefully among all living things and to love others.

Special prayers are written in Sanskrit on "Mani" stones (below). The stones are left along roadsides. Scenes from the Buddha's life are painted in the Ajanta caves in India (right).

THE GROWTH OF BUDDHISM

After the Buddha's death in 483 B.C., Buddhism spread throughout southern and eastern Asia. Traveling monks introduced the Buddha's teachings in other places. These included what are today China, Tibet, Sri Lanka, Japan, Korea, Thailand, and Vietnam.

Buddhists everywhere lived by the Buddha's teachings, which were written down as proverbs. According to the proverbs that follow, what qualities do Buddhists value and believe to be the most important in life?

MANY VOICES
PRIMARY SOURCE

**Verses on the Law,
an ancient Buddhist text,
written down around 100 B.C.**

*Hatreds never **cease** by hatred in this world; by love alone they cease. This is an ancient law.*

*The reputation of him who is energetic, mindful, pure in deed, considerate, self-controlled, right-living, and **heedful** steadily increases.*

Calm is his mind, calm is his speech, calm is his action, who, rightly knowing, is wholly freed, perfectly peaceful, and self-controlled.

Irrigators lead the waters; carpenters bend the wood; the wise control themselves.

As a solid rock is not shaken by the wind, even so the wise are not ruffled by praise or blame.

cease: stop
heedful: aware

Changing Buddhism

As in Hinduism, many different schools of thought developed in Buddhism over the years. Some suggested that the Buddha was a god. Others thought that the Buddha was an ordinary person who discovered a way to end suffering. Buddhists differed with each other on what it meant to live according to the Middle Way. Buddhists also disagreed about how people reached peace and truth and freedom from suffering.

These differences of opinion continue today among Buddhists around the world. Yet some basic teachings continue to be shared by all Buddhists. These include honoring the Buddha and his teachings and helping others to end suffering.

WHY IT MATTERS

Buddhism developed in ancient India. From the beginning, it centered around the life and thoughts of Siddhartha Gautama. This man had much wealth as a prince, but left it all behind when he chose to become a penniless monk.

The teachings of the Buddha would have a big impact on Indian civilization for a time. However, Buddhism gained even greater influence in other parts of Asia. You will read about more of this story in chapters to come.

✔ Reviewing Facts and Ideas

MAIN IDEAS

- Between about 1500 and 500 B.C., Aryan rulers gained control over much of India and spread Hinduism.

- Siddhartha Gautama founded Buddhism. He gave up all he owned to search for a way to end suffering.

- The Buddha borrowed beliefs from Hinduism. He also taught the Four Noble Truths, the Eightfold Path, and the Middle Way.

- Buddhism spread after the Buddha's death. This religion has 330 million followers today.

THINK ABOUT IT

1. What were the two ways of life that the young prince Siddhartha was said to have to choose between?

2. What might a Buddhist hope to achieve by following the Buddha's Eightfold Path?

3. **FOCUS** How did the Buddha say people should live? What guidelines did he offer?

4. **THINKING SKILL** What _caused_ Siddhartha Gautama to become a monk? What _effects_ did his becoming the Buddha have on life in India?

5. **WRITE** Write a paragraph comparing and contrasting Hindu and Buddhist beliefs. What do they share?

CHAPTER 6 REVIEW

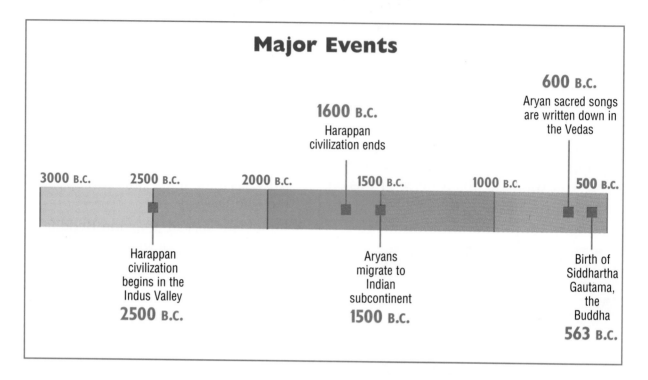

Major Events

600 B.C.
Aryan sacred songs are written down in the Vedas

1600 B.C.
Harappan civilization ends

3000 B.C.   2500 B.C.   2000 B.C.   1500 B.C.   1000 B.C.   500 B.C.

Harappan civilization begins in the Indus Valley
2500 B.C.

Aryans migrate to Indian subcontinent
1500 B.C.

Birth of Siddhartha Gautama, the Buddha
563 B.C.

THINKING ABOUT VOCABULARY

Number a sheet of paper from 1 to 5. Beside each number write the word or term from the list below that best completes each sentence.

karma   subcontinent
Middle Way   Vedas
reincarnation

1. The constant cycle of life, death, and rebirth is called _____.

2. A _____ is a large landmass that is geographically separated from the rest of a continent.

3. The sacred songs of the ancient Aryans were written down about 600 B.C. in books called the _____.

4. According to Hindu belief, _____ is the force created by a person's good and bad deeds that affects his or her future life.

5. According to Buddhist belief, the laws of the Eightfold Path lead to the _____.

THINKING ABOUT FACTS

1. What made Siddhartha Gautama give up all he had and become a monk?

2. How did Siddhartha Gautama become the Buddha?

3. How has Hinduism changed recently?

4. What are the Four Noble Truths?

5. What four groups of people make up the Indian caste system?

6. How does the caste system shape the lives of Indians?

7. What was the role of the Indus River in the creation of Indian civilization?

8. Why do historians know less about the Indus River valley civilization than about ancient Egypt and Mesopotamia?

9. What did Harappan workers create that was unknown to other cultures?

10. According to the time line above, how long after the Aryans migrated to the Indian subcontinent were their sacred songs written down?

THINK AND WRITE

WRITING A LETTER

Suppose that you are one of the archaeologists who had uncovered the remains of Mohenjo-Daro. In a letter to a friend, describe the most interesting artifacts you found and what they reveal about the lives of the people who lived there.

WRITING A REPORT

Write a class report about the Hindu belief that people live in a constant cycle of birth, death, and rebirth. Explain this cycle and how it affects the way Hindus live.

WRITING AN ESSAY

Write a short essay about India's caste system. Describe what it is and discuss the beliefs that created it. Finally describe how the caste system is changing.

APPLYING GEOGRAPHY SKILLS

COMPARING DIFFERENT KINDS OF MAPS

1. Look back at "Using the Skill" on page 140. What did you learn by comparing Maps A and B?

2. What do you learn about Islamabad by comparing the three maps in the skill?

3. What conclusions can you make by comparing the maps on page 131 and page 135?

4. Look at the map on page 138. Can you learn anything by comparing it with the maps on pages 131 and 135?

5. What kind of information might one map show that another might not?

Summing Up the Chapter

Copy the word map below on a separate piece of paper. Then review the chapter and fill in details that support the main idea. After you have filled in the details, use the word map to write a paragraph that answers the question "How did civilization develop in India?"

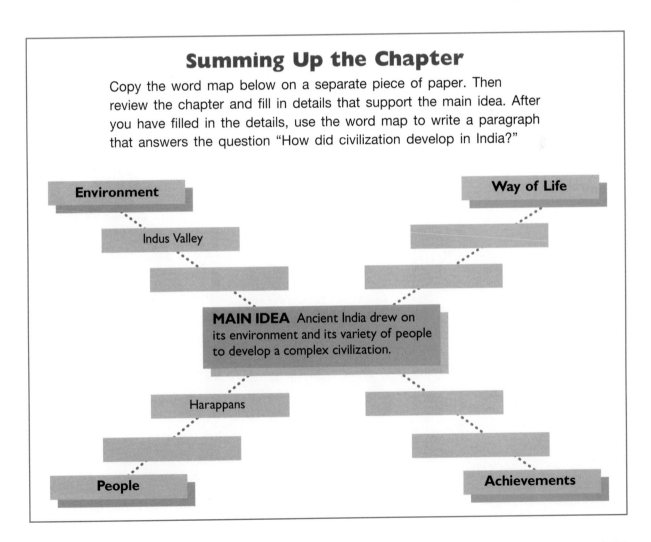

Environment

Indus Valley

MAIN IDEA Ancient India drew on its environment and its variety of people to develop a complex civilization.

Harappans

People

Way of Life

Achievements

CHAPTER 7

Ancient China

THINKING ABOUT
HISTORY AND GEOGRAPHY

Around 3000 B.C. farmers in the Huang River valley learned to control the river's floods in order to grow food. A group that ruled over a large area of the valley developed a written language around 1100 B.C. This was the beginning of modern Chinese writing. China grew into a large area. Within it, the teachings of a great scholar shaped life from about 500 B.C. to the present.

3000 B.C.

HUANG RIVER VALLEY
Farmers use levees to control floods

1100 B.C.

ANYANG
Priests use a writing system to record events and make predictions

221 B.C.

XIANYANG
A powerful leader creates the first Chinese empire

3000 B.C.   1000 B.C.   500 B.C.

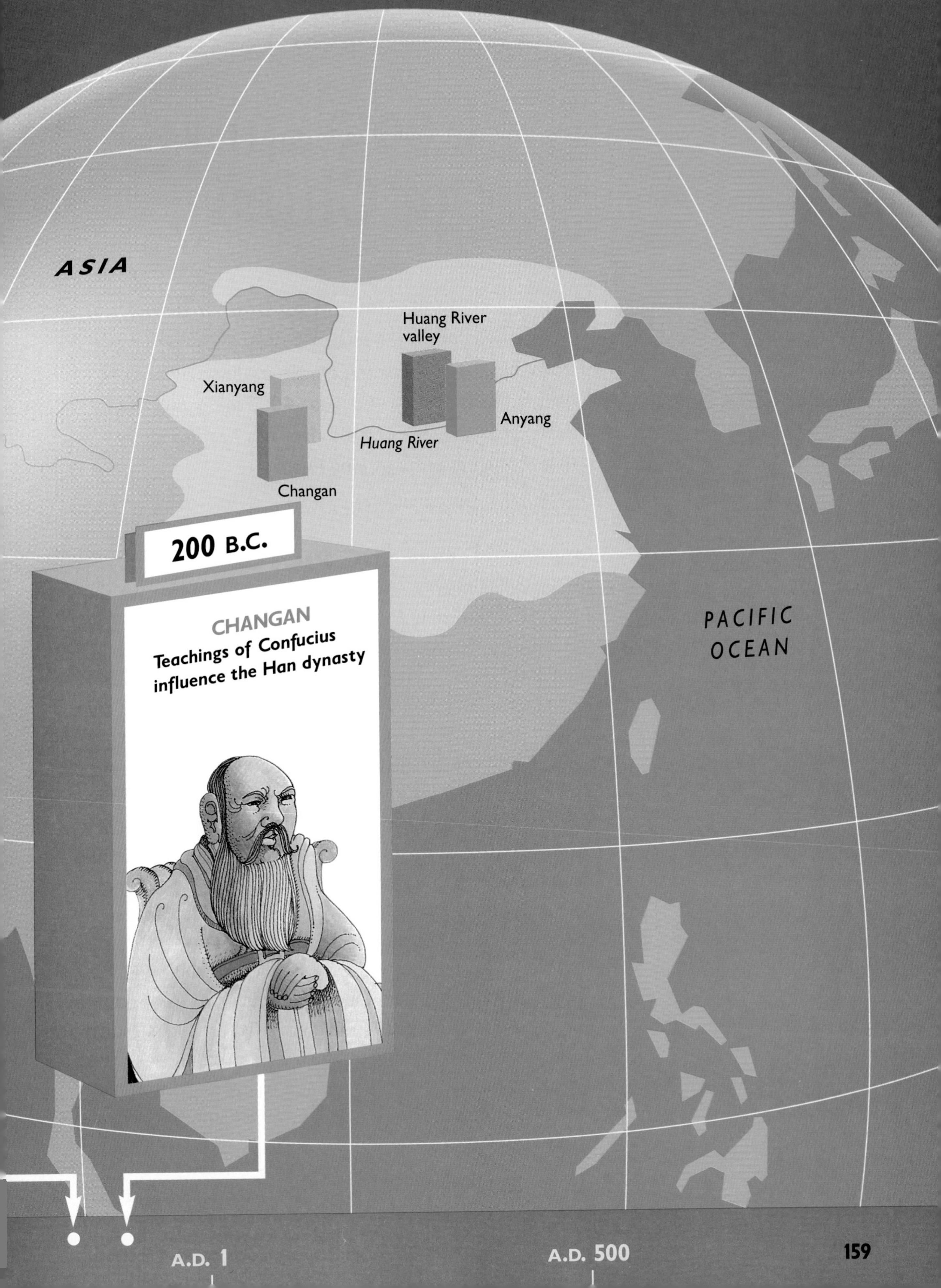
ASIA
Huang River valley
Xianyang
Anyang
Huang River
Changan
200 B.C.
CHANGAN
Teachings of Confucius influence the Han dynasty
PACIFIC OCEAN
A.D. 1
A.D. 500

Geography of China

Read Aloud

"Whoever controls the Huang (HWAHNG) River controls China." According to Chinese tradition a powerful ruler spoke these words almost 4,000 years ago. In this lesson you will learn why the river has been so important throughout China's long history.

Focus Activity

READ TO LEARN

How did the Huang River affect ancient Chinese civilization?

VOCABULARY

- loess
- levee
- erosion
- famine
- steppe

PLACES

- Huang River
- North China Plain

THE BIG PICTURE

In Chapter 6 you read that the Himalayas separate the Indian subcontinent from the rest of Asia. Within those mountains is "The Roof of the World"—the huge plateau, or raised plain, that forms most of Tibet. This plateau sits higher than most mountaintops in the United States. The Indus and many of Asia's largest rivers begin on this plateau. It is here that the **Huang River** begins its 3,000-mile trip across northern China.

The Huang has been a major force in China's history. Like the Indus, it starts as a clear stream but grows and picks up silt along its winding journey. During summer floods the Huang spreads enough silt on the **North China Plain** to create one of the world's largest deltas. The river also creates miles of fertile marshland.

About 4000 B.C. farming communities developed along the lower part of the Huang River. China's oldest civilization grew from these farming communities. This civilization later spread to include many regions and groups of people. Find the Huang River and the North China Plain on the map on the next page.

Loess washes into the Huang River, giving it a yellow color. The word *Huang* means "yellow" in Chinese.

THE HUANG RIVER VALLEY

At one point along its journey, the Huang makes a giant curve around the edge of the Ordos Desert. Find this curve on the map below. As it turns, the Huang cuts through a hilly region. The hills are made almost entirely out of **loess** (LES). Loess is a dusty, yellow soil that has been deposited in this region by wind.

Working with the Environment

Loess has been a blessing and a curse to Chinese farmers. During summer rains, huge amounts of it are washed into the Huang. In fact, the Huang is the world's muddiest river.

When the Huang floods the North China Plain, the silt deposits create a unique environment. This loess-silt helps farmers because it is fine, rock-free, and very fertile. Because it is so light and fluffy, however, loess is easily carried away by storms. When this happens farmers are left with poor soil.

Like farmers in the Indus Valley, ancient farmers made use of the Huang Valley's fertile soil. They also fought to control river floods. This battle with nature has been going on since China's earliest days. It continues to this day.

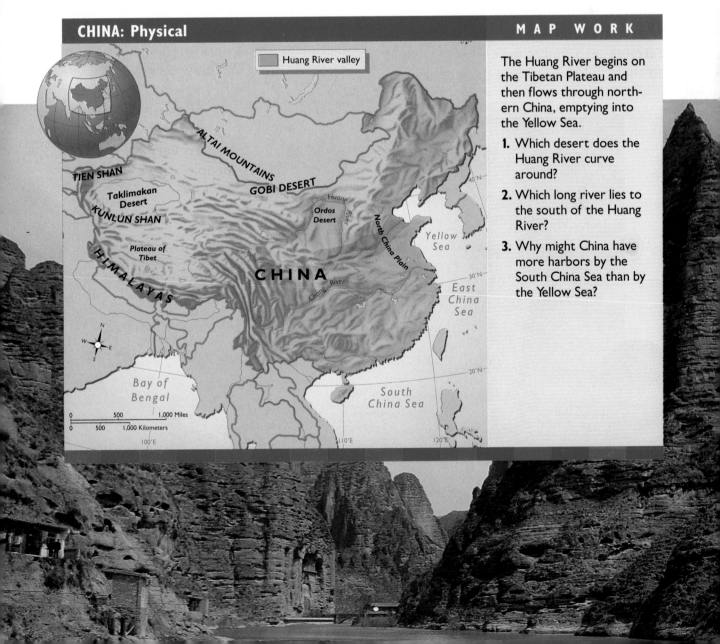

CHINA: Physical

Huang River valley

ALTAI MOUNTAINS
TIEN SHAN
Taklimakan Desert
KUNLUN SHAN
GOBI DESERT
Huang River
Ordos Desert
North China Plain
Plateau of Tibet
HIMALAYAS
CHINA
Chang River
Yellow Sea
East China Sea
Bay of Bengal
South China Sea

0 500 1,000 Miles
0 500 1,000 Kilometers
100°E   110°E   120°E
40°N
30°N
20°N

M A P   W O R K

The Huang River begins on the Tibetan Plateau and then flows through northern China, emptying into the Yellow Sea.

1. Which desert does the Huang River curve around?

2. Which long river lies to the south of the Huang River?

3. Why might China have more harbors by the South China Sea than by the Yellow Sea?

AGRICULTURE ALONG THE HUANG

Do you remember how Egypt's farmers usually welcomed the Nile's summer floods? China's farmers could not afford to let the Huang overflow freely. Their fields could be washed away. Huang Valley farmers needed to control floods.

Controlling the River

About 3,000 years ago, farmers began building earth levees (LEV eez) to hold back the Huang. A levee is a wall that keeps a river within its banks. Over time, though, a thick layer of mud built up along the riverbed. As the mud deposits grew, the river eventually spilled over the farmers' levees.

Like the Sumerians, ancient Chinese farmers also built canals to bring water to their fields. Yet loess once again caused problems. It constantly clogged the canals and had to be cleared away.

Crops Grow in Loess Soil

In spite of the problems it caused, loess also provided a rich soil. Many kinds of plants could grow in it. Huang farmers grew rice, millet (a type of grain), wheat, green onions, and ginger. They harvested grapes, peaches, plums, and wild chestnuts.

Because Huang Valley farmers were successful, the area's population grew. More farmable land became needed to feed people. Farmers had to clear trees from rich loess-lands to plant crops. One result was erosion. Erosion is the wearing away of soil by wind or water. This loss of soil occurs in areas where trees and shrubs are removed. Erosion of fertile soil sometimes makes it difficult for farmers to grow successful crops. If too much soil washes away and crops fail, a famine can happen. Famine is a time when very little food is available and people starve.

Other Regions in Ancient China

Not all of China was as suitable for farming as the Huang River valley. Growing crops is very difficult or impossible in many parts of China. To the north of the Huang Valley are windswept **steppes** (STEPS). A steppe is a dry, treeless plain. In this region people used another type of agriculture. Here, instead of planting crops, they herded sheep and cattle on horseback.

Lifestyles were very different along the Huang and on the steppes. How might a typical daily meal on the steppes differ from a meal in the river valley?

WHY IT MATTERS

The hard work of China's ancient farmers paved the way for powerful kingdoms to develop throughout China. Many of those kingdoms grew along the Huang River. You will read about one of the earliest and most powerful of these kingdoms in the next lesson.

DID YOU KNOW?

Why is the Huang River often called "China's Sorrow"?

The flooding of the Huang has cost millions of lives throughout China's history. Famine, as much as drowning, has been a cause of these deaths. When the river washes away crops, it leaves people with little or nothing to eat.

Chinese generals have also used the power of the river as a deadly weapon. In World War II, for example, one general blew up key levees during flood season to stop the Japanese army. His plan worked—but it also took the lives of almost one million farmers. Many more died during the famine that followed.

Reviewing Facts and Ideas

MAIN IDEAS

- Loess has made the Huang River valley extremely fertile, but it causes many problems too.

- Ancient Chinese farmers built dirt levees along the Huang to try to keep the river on its course.

- Like people in other river valleys, farmers along the Huang raised crops. On China's northern steppes, people herded animals.

The farmer (far left) is harvesting rice. China produces about 35 percent of the world's rice each year. Herders who live on China's **steppes** often live in tents (left). The herders move to new grazing land each season.

THINK ABOUT IT

1. What does the Huang River share in common with the Indus River?

2. How has loess helped China's farmers? How has it caused problems?

3. **FOCUS** Why was it important for ancient farmers to control the Huang River? What made it hard for them to achieve their goal?

4. **THINKING SKILL** What _caused_ ancient farmers to strip loess-lands of their trees and shrubs? What _effects_ did this have on life along the Huang?

5. **GEOGRAPHY** Why is the big curve of the Huang an important part of the river? What happens here?

163

2000 B.C. 1700 B.C. 1100 B.C. 500 B.C. A.D. 1

The First Dynasty

Read Aloud

In 1899 a Chinese scholar became ill and asked his doctor for help. He was given a packet of animal bones that, when ground up, would make a popular medicine. When the scholar looked closely at the bones, he noticed that they were covered with mysterious ancient writing. He became determined to find out where the bones came from and what they meant. Later the scholar led archaeologists to a site along the Huang River. What they found would change history books about ancient China.

Focus Activity

READ TO LEARN

What do the remains at Anyang tell us about life in early China?

VOCABULARY

- dynasty
- nobles
- oracle bones

PEOPLE

- Fu Hao

PLACES

- Anyang

THE BIG PICTURE

By 3000 B.C. Egypt was being united and city-states and towns were expanding in the Fertile Crescent and the Indus Valley. At the same time farms along China's Huang River were growing larger and more productive. Towns grew too, and the largest of these became capitals of states.

By about 1700 B.C. one kingdom had won control over the large Huang River delta. One of its earliest capitals was a city called Shang. That name also became the state's name. Since it was ruled by one family for a long period of time, the government became known as the Shang **dynasty**. A dynasty is a line of rulers who belong to the same family. Control is passed from one generation to the next. For 600 years the Shang dynasty would shape the lives of people along the Huang River.

TOWNS ALONG THE HUANG RIVER

The Shang state spread along the Huang River until it ruled hundreds of towns. The Shang kings created new towns by giving land to their relatives, or **nobles**. These nobles oversaw the construction of the new towns and became their rulers.

Think of what it might have been like to rule a town during the Shang dynasty. You would have been very busy. The towns were important centers of production. They supplied food, clothing, and other products for the king and the nobles. These towns also helped to keep enemy states from invading the vast Shang lands. People from the towns often were part-time soldiers. They were sent to war whenever they were needed.

An Ancient City

Near the end of the Shang dynasty's 600-year rule, the capital was moved. Its new site was near the town that is today Anyang (AHN YAHNG). Find Anyang on the map on this page. The writing on the bones described

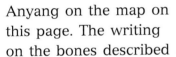

This Shang dynasty mask was found in a tomb in Anyang.

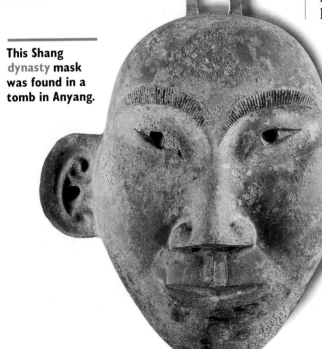

LANDS OF THE SHANG DYNASTY, 1200 B.C.

MAP WORK

The Shang dynasty controlled lands along the Huang River.

1. How far from the Yellow Sea is Anyang?
2. Where was the city of Anyang located— north or south of the Huang River?

in the lesson introduction led archaeologists to the ancient city. Its ruins have taught much about life in Shang China.

Shang society was organized like a pyramid. At the top were the king and his family. Below them were nobles, then craftworkers, then farmers. Prisoners of war were at the bottom.

Archaeologists at Anyang have uncovered many huts. Dug halfway into the ground, these "pithouses" served as homes and workshops for metalworkers, potters, and servants. Remains of what seem to be palaces lie in the city's center. Bronze cups, stone carvings, and magnificent chariots were found in nearby royal tombs.

BURIED TREASURES

The finds at Anyang are a treasure for archaeologists and historians. One royal tomb found at Anyang contained more artifacts than any other. Hundreds of bronze containers, ivory statues, and other valuable objects were in the grave. Artifacts from this tomb tell how rich Shang rulers were. For whom were all of these riches made?

Archaeologists have determined that this grave belonged to a king's wife. Her name was Fu Hao (FOO HOW), or "Lady Hao." Fu Hao succeeded at many things during her life. She led troops to war. She ruled her own town. Unlike most other Shang leaders, she succeeded at being remembered in history. That is because records about her life have been preserved in her tomb.

A Written Record

A writing system had developed along parts of the Huang River before the Shang dynasty. Like early cuneiform, the earliest Chinese signs looked like pictures of objects. By the time of the Shang dynasty, though, characters were simpler. Symbols could stand for objects or ideas. Look at the diagram on this page to see one way this writing system developed over time.

One ancient Chinese historian mentioned that many records of the Shang were "written on bamboo and silk." Unfortunately, no bamboo tablets or silk cloth have survived from Shang times. However, writing has been found on bronze pots and stone.

More writing has been discovered on the thousands of "dragon bones" found

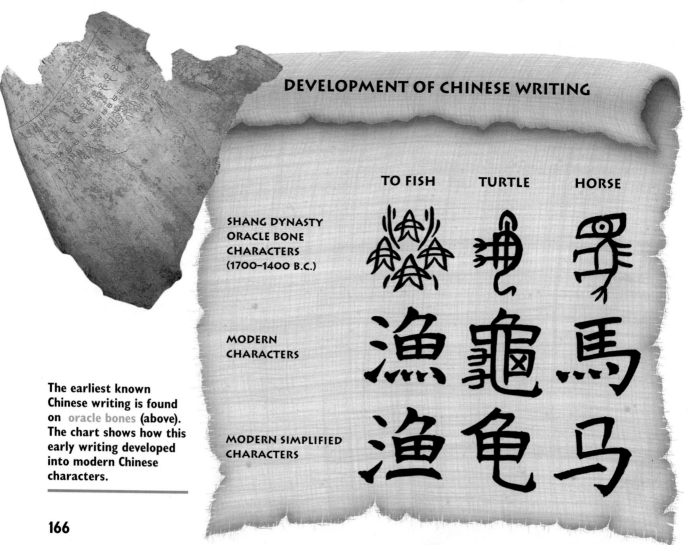

The earliest known Chinese writing is found on oracle bones (above). The chart shows how this early writing developed into modern Chinese characters.

DEVELOPMENT OF CHINESE WRITING

	TO FISH	TURTLE	HORSE
SHANG DYNASTY ORACLE BONE CHARACTERS (1700–1400 B.C.)			
MODERN CHARACTERS	漁	龜	馬
MODERN SIMPLIFIED CHARACTERS	渔	龟	马

This container, found in Fu Hao's tomb, shows the skill of Shang craftworkers.

at Anyang. Most of these bones came from cattle or sheep. They were used by special priests who the Shang believed were oracles (AWR uh kulz), or people who could predict the future. The bones became known as "oracle bones." Priests heated the oracle bones over a fire until they cracked. The pattern of cracks was used to answer questions about the future.

Like most Shang kings, Fu Hao's husband, Wu Ding, depended on priests to read oracle bones and predict the future. Would Fu Hao recover from an illness? Would farmers have a good harvest? Should Wu Ding go to war? It was believed that the pattern of cracks in the oracle bones gave the answers to his questions.

Religion of the Shang

Shang Chinese believed that their ancestors lived in another world and controlled human life. If an oracle's prediction came true, they believed that the king was being helped by his ancestors. This, they believed, proved that he was the right person to be king.

The people of the Shang dynasty worshiped many different gods. They believed these gods controlled nature. The ancient people also believed that when they died, they would join their ancestors and the gods.

WHY IT MATTERS

The Shang dynasty of the Huang River valley created a legacy that would shape life in China for centuries. Shang religious beliefs and style of government would live on for hundreds of years. The writing system developed during this time is similar to the system that is still used in China today. In the next lesson you will read about a man who spread many Shang ideas about religion and government throughout China.

✓ Reviewing Facts and Ideas

MAIN IDEAS

- Around 1700 B.C. the Shang state won control over the Huang Valley region. This area was ruled by the Shang dynasty until about 1100 B.C.
- The Shang used writing to record and predict important events.

THINK ABOUT IT

1. Describe the social pyramid of China during the Shang dynasty.

2. What were oracle bones? How were they used in ancient China?

3. **FOCUS** What were three artifacts found at Anyang? What do they tell us about the people who lived there?

4. **THINKING SKILL** *Compare* the Shang system of government with that of the pharaohs' government in Egypt.

5. **GEOGRAPHY** Imagine you are a noble who is building a town in Shang China. Where would you decide to build? What would you consider in making your decision?

2000 B.C. 1500 B.C. 1000 B.C. 500 B.C. 221 B.C. 206 B.C. A.D. 1

The Emperor's Clay Army

Focus Activity

READ TO LEARN

How did Shihuangdi build an empire in China?

VOCABULARY

- emperor
- province

PEOPLE

- Shihuangdi

PLACES

- Qin
- Qinling Mountains
- Xianyang
- Great Wall of China

Read Aloud

In 1974 farmers living near the southern curve in the Huang River began digging a new well. Imagine their surprise when they began to uncover life-sized clay soldiers! Archaeologists were called to the site. Since that day an entire clay army—more than 8,000 soldiers, horses, and chariots—has been unearthed. No two of the soldiers look alike. Each one once held a real weapon to fight off some unknown enemy. Who built this amazing clay army and why? Following is the story of China's Qin (CHIN) dynasty.

THE BIG PICTURE

The Shang dynasty came to an end around 1100 B.C. For many years afterward the Huang River valley was a place of conflict and turmoil. Slowly one region, called Qin, built up its strength. Qin's ruler was a general who would one day order the making of the great clay army described above. In 221 B.C. this general led a real army in a bold drive to take control of the Huang River delta. He and his army won battle after battle, eventually conquering all of northern China.

When his victory was complete, the Qin general declared himself China's emperor. An emperor is the supreme ruler of an empire. He celebrated his new role by taking the name Shihuangdi (SHEE hwahng dee), or "First Grand Emperor." Shihuangdi boasted that his Qin dynasty would last for 10,000 generations.

THE RISE OF AN EMPIRE

What made it possible for Shihuangdi and the Qin armies to win control and hold an empire together? Geography played a part in their victory. The original Qin region was protected by the Qinling (CHIN LING) Mountains on one side and by the Huang River on the other. From this central point, soldiers were able to march out and expand the Qin empire.

A New Kind of Government

Shihuangdi had new ideas about how a government should be run. These ideas were even more important than his armies in strengthening Qin's power. Shihuangdi split the empire into 36 provinces (PRAHV in sez), or political divisions of land.

The emperor also let farmers own land. This weakened the power of the nobles. Shihuangdi also forced many nobles to move to the capital city, Xianyang (shee AHN yang). There he took away their bronze weapons.

As in ancient Egypt, new ideas about communication helped to unify China. Shihuangdi set up a single system of writing throughout the empire. Local leaders used this writing system to report to the capital. Written language also helped the government to record and collect taxes.

Shihuangdi also created a single system of money to be used throughout the empire. Craftworkers made coins out of bronze. Holes in the coins allowed people to keep their money on a string. These changes were strictly enforced by the emperor's soldiers.

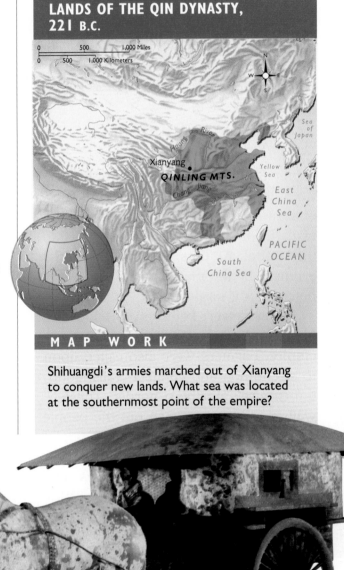

LANDS OF THE QIN DYNASTY, 221 B.C.

0 500 1,000 Miles
0 500 1,000 Kilometers

Hoang River

Xianyang
QINLING MTS.

Chang Jiang

Sea of Japan

Yellow Sea

East China Sea

PACIFIC OCEAN

South China Sea

MAP WORK

Shihuangdi's armies marched out of Xianyang to conquer new lands. What sea was located at the southernmost point of the empire?

A bronze chariot and horses were in Shihuangdi's tomb.

FARMERS BUILD THE EMPIRE

Under Shihuangdi's leadership, unified China grew bigger and stronger. The empire also became increasingly rich as taxes from China's farmers flowed into the capital. As time went by, the government began making ever greater demands on its people.

Farmers were required to build the highways that linked the cities of the empire. Farmers were also called upon to strengthen and connect walls along the empire's northern border. These walls were built to keep out the people of the northern steppes. Much later, similar walls would be built across these same mountains and valleys. The later walls made up the Great Wall of China that we can see today. The Great Wall of China eventually grew to be more than 1,500 miles long!

Farmers were the backbone of the Qin empire. Their hard work as farmers, soldiers, and builders kept the empire strong. Still, their lives mostly

centered around the seasonal floods of the Huang. As before, they continued to grow the wheat, rice, and other crops needed to feed an empire.

Building the Emperor's Tomb

One of the greatest building projects in the Qin empire was the construction of a tomb for Shihuangdi. The emperor wanted his tomb to be a spectacular mirror of the real world. The clay army, which you read about in the lesson introduction, was just one part of this "mirror world." Its many soldiers and

Shihuangdi ordered that these clay soldiers be set up in formation. They stood with their backs to the emperor in order to protect him from attack.

horses stood guard, ready to protect the emperor from attack.

Shihuangdi's burial place lies under a giant mound near the clay army. Archaeologists have not yet uncovered the contents of the tomb. However, an ancient Chinese historian once told what lay inside.

The treasure-filled tomb, the historian wrote, was laid out like a giant map of the empire. Models of the Huang and other rivers, he said, flowed with mercury pumped by machines. On the ceiling sparkled bright stars. To keep out robbers, crossbows were set up that would shoot arrows if the tomb's entrance was disturbed. One day archaeologists may be able to compare the ancient historian's description with the actual remains in the tomb.

WHY IT MATTERS

In 221 B.C. Shihuangdi had boasted that the Qin dynasty would rule China for 10,000 generations. It actually lasted only 15 years. After Shihuangdi's death in 210 B.C., farmers and nobles alike revolted against his dynasty's harsh rule. However, China's first emperor would leave a lasting legacy. The centralized systems of writing, government, and money that he created would live on for centuries.

Reviewing Facts and Ideas

MAIN IDEAS

- Around 221 B.C. Shihuangdi unified China with his powerful armies and by strengthening government. He created standard writing and money systems across the empire.

- Farmers were the backbone of the Qin economy. They also served as part-time soldiers and builders.

THINK ABOUT IT

1. How did farmers help make Shihuangdi's empire strong?

2. What qualities might have been admired in the first emperor? What qualities were probably feared?

3. **FOCUS** How was Shihuangdi able to gain control over China?

4. **THINKING SKILL** Suppose you are a noble governing your own town in Qin China. Emperor Shihuangdi has just called you to his capital at Xianyang. Write a letter in response to the emperor's request from the noble's _point of view_.

5. **GEOGRAPHY** Look at the map on page 169. How did geographical features help Shihuangdi's army to conquer northern China?

171

Writing a Summary

VOCABULARY
summary
topic sentence

WHY THE SKILL MATTERS

Soon after Shihuangdi became China's first emperor in 221 B.C., he sent his army to strengthen the northern border of his empire. The story of how and why he did this is complicated, but it is an important part of China's early history. Many stories from history are long and complicated. They usually contain much information. However, people can present the important information in a story by creating a summary. A summary briefly states the main ideas contained in a piece of writing or group of ideas.

USING THE SKILL

Read the following paragraph about Shihuangdi and the herders of northern China.

After Shihuangdi won the battle for control over China in 221 B.C., one challenge remained. Herders who lived on the steppes of northern China had crossed the Huang River and set up their tents on the plains near the river's big curve. This narrowed the distance between these two very different cultures. Because they were expert riders and hunters, the herders were a threat to the empire. Shihuangdi feared that the herders would decide to invade China, taking its land and crops. He ordered his army to push the herders back beyond the Huang.

To prepare for writing a summary, find the topic sentences, or the sentences that contain the main ideas. Often a topic sentence is the first sentence of the paragraph. However, it may also be at the end of the paragraph. The topic sentences in the previous paragraph tell that the people of the steppes became a threat to Shihuangdi. How he responded is also important.

Other sentences give supporting details, such as information about the herders being expert riders and hunters.

After you identify the main ideas and supporting details, you can write a short summary. What main ideas are expressed in the paragraph on Shihuangdi and the herders? What are some supporting details?

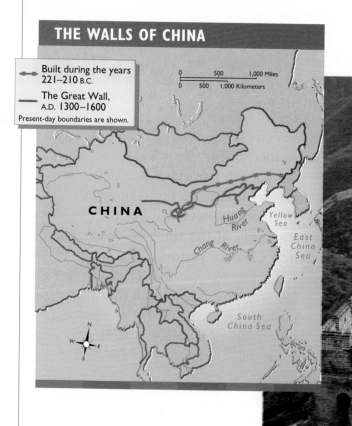

THE WALLS OF CHINA

Built during the years 221–210 B.C.

The Great Wall, A.D. 1300–1600

Present-day boundaries are shown.

0   500   1,000 Miles
0   500   1,000 Kilometers

CHINA

Huang River

Chang River

Yellow Sea

East China Sea

South China Sea

N W E S

Little remains of Shihuangdi's wall (far right). The Great Wall (right) is about 1,500 miles in length.

TRYING THE SKILL

Now read the story below and use the Helping Yourself box to write a summary.

In about 215 B.C. Shihuang-di's army succeeded in driving the herders out. To help keep them out, more than 300,000 workers strengthened a 100-year-old wall along China's northern border. It was just rock-hard mounds of earth. Lookouts posted on the wall would signal an invasion by waving flags or by lighting fires. The army would then come to chase the herders away. China's leaders carried on this idea of

wall building. Most famous of all was the Great Wall. This wall was mostly built between A.D. 1300 and 1600. It was much larger than the previous earthen walls and was made of bricks. Even the Great Wall was not a very effective barrier. Invaders continued to make their way over or around the wall.

What is the main idea that runs through this entire paragraph? What are the supporting details?

REVIEWING THE SKILL

1. How does writing a summary differ from simply rewriting an entire piece in your own words?

2. If you had to write a single summary of both paragraphs about Shihuangdi in this lesson, what would that summary include?

3. How did you choose what would go into your summary? Could you use the map?

4. When might writing a summary be a helpful skill?

173

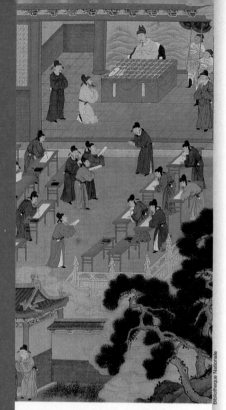
Bibliotheque Nationale

| 2000 B.C. | 1500 B.C. | 1000 B.C. | 500 B.C. | 206 B.C. | A.D. 220 |

Confucius Changes China

Read Aloud

"When a prince's personal conduct is correct, his government is effective without the issuing of orders. If his personal conduct is not correct, he may issue orders, but they will not be followed."

These words were spoken by Confucius, an important Chinese philosopher, teacher, and scholar.

Focus Activity

READ TO LEARN

What effects did the teachings of Confucius have on China?

VOCABULARY

- Confucianism
- Mandate of Heaven
- Grand School
- seismograph

PEOPLE

- Han Gaozu
- Confucius
- Wudi

THE BIG PICTURE

In 206 B.C. Shihuangdi's Qin dynasty was overthrown by rebel armies. These armies were led by a farmer-turned-general called **Han Gaozu** (HAHN GOW ZOO). His family began the mighty Han dynasty, which would rule China for over 400 years. During the Han dynasty, China expanded north to what are today North and South Korea and south to the country of Vietnam.

Shihuangdi had lived by the idea that a ruler should be able to do whatever he chooses. Later, Han rulers developed different ideas about government. Their thoughts were based on the teachings of a man named **Confucius**, who lived between 551 B.C. and 479 B.C.

Like the Buddha, who was teaching in India during this time, Confucius lived through an age of warfare and conflict. In this time of conflict, Confucius suggested a different, more peaceful way of living. Also like the Buddha, he won many followers during and after his lifetime. Unlike the Buddha, Confucius's ideas would not start a new religion. However, Confucius's ideas would reshape entire civilizations.

CONFUCIUS

Both of his parents died when he was young, so Confucius had to make his own way in life. He had a passion for learning. He mastered subjects such as writing, mathematics, history, and archery. This helped Confucius to get a job in government. In later years, though, he devoted his life to teaching.

The Followers of Confucius

Confucius's ideas, later called Confucianism, taught that Chinese culture had lost its traditions. According to Confucius, ancient traditions had once made society just and good. Through education, Confucius said, people from rulers to farmers could learn how to become good people once again. Good people would make a good civilization.

A central idea of Confucianism was to have respect within the family. This idea also applied to government. Just as a child must respect a parent, a subject must respect the ruler. However, the ruler had a duty to be wise and good. Some followers of Confucius said that emperors did not have the right to rule just because they came from a certain family. Rather, each emperor received a right to rule from the gods, called the Mandate of Heaven. This mandate, or command, echoed the Shang belief that the gods spoke to kings through oracle bones.

Confucius's thoughts were recorded by his students in a book called *The Analects*. Analects are selected writings. What does a good person do, according to Confucius?

MANY VOICES

PRIMARY SOURCE

Excerpt from
The Analects of Confucius,
c. 400 B.C.

Do not do unto others what you would not want others to do to you.

If you make a mistake and do not correct it, this is called a mistake.

Be dutiful at home, brotherly in public; be discreet and trustworthy, love all people, and draw near to humanity. If you have extra energy as you do that, then study literature.

If leaders are courteous, their people will not dare to be disrespectful. If leaders are just, people will not dare to be [ungovernable]. If leaders are trustworthy, people will not dare to be dishonest.

A certain pupil asked Confucius about government: "What qualifies one to participate in government?"

Confucius said, "Honor five **refinements**. . . . Then you can **participate** in government."

The pupil asked, "What are the five refinements?"

Confucius said, "Good people are generous without being wasteful; they are hard-working without being resentful; they desire without being greedy; they are at ease without being [proud]; they are dignified without being fierce."

---

refinements: improvements
participate: take part in

175

This man is participating in a ceremony to honor Confucius. The ceremony is taking place at a temple in Qufu, located in China's Shandong province.

LANDS OF THE HAN DYNASTY, A.D. 100

RISE OF THE HAN DYNASTY

The powerful Han army expanded the borders of the empire. Look at the Han dynasty lands on the map on this page. Controlling the huge empire was a difficult job. During the Qin dynasty Shi-huangdi had many people who disagreed with him killed. Some of them were Confucianists. He did not want anyone to question his right to rule. During the Han dynasty, however, Confucianism became accepted again. Han emperors wanted to find ways to rule more fairly. They also wanted to lessen the power of the nobles.

Han rulers kept the Qin dynasty's system of government. However, they gave government jobs to educated people, rather than just to nobles. Wudi (WOO DEE), was the first strong emperor of the Han dynasty. His rule

MAP WORK

Han rulers expanded their empire into central China.

1. What two cities were located on the Huang River?
2. Which city was farther west?

lasted from 140 B.C. to 87 B.C. Wudi created schools to prepare students for government service. These schools were run by Confucian teachers.

The Grand School

Under Wudi's government, schools were set up in each province, or state. The schools taught Chinese literature to students who would serve in local government. Very good students sometimes were sent to the empire's best school, the Grand School.

During Wudi's rule only 50 students were allowed to study at the Grand School. By A.D. 200 it had more than 30,000 students. For one year they learned about ancient China's poetry, history, proper behavior, and folk songs. These had all been preserved by Confucius. The teachers were China's most brilliant Confucian scholars. At the end of the year, students at the Grand School took a long test. If they passed, they earned jobs as government workers or as teachers in province schools. They also won great respect in society because they were so well educated.

During the Han dynasty, learning of many different kinds blossomed throughout the empire. Like the ancient Egyptians, Chinese scientists and mathematicians learned to predict eclipses of the sun. Doctors discovered new kinds of medicines, and poets wrote about the beauty of the land. In fact, during the course of the Han dynasty, the Chinese language grew from 3,000 to 9,000 characters. In A.D. 100 scholars wrote the first Chinese dictionary.

The Invention of Paper

Confucian emphasis on education brought increased knowledge and discovery in the Han dynasty. This can be seen in the many inventions that appeared during this time. For example, Han craftworkers invented paper. Like Egyptian papyrus, paper provided a way to keep written records. The Chinese made paper by pounding bark of mulberry trees. These are the same trees that feed China's silkworms.

An Amazing Instrument

One of the most remarkable achievements of Han inventors was the seismograph (SĪZ muh graf). This is a machine used to detect earthquakes. Although this ancient seismograph looks like a bronze vase covered with dragons and toads, it is actually a complicated scientific instrument.

Inside the vase swung a long metal pendulum. When the ground shook ever so slightly, the pendulum would swing in the direction in which the earthquake occurred. The pendulum would hit a rod inside the vase. This rod, in turn, would knock a ball out of a dragon's mouth. The ball came out in the direction in which the earthquake had occurred.

In this way Han rulers could learn about an earthquake as soon as it happened. They could immediately send food and supplies to the damaged area.

This is a model of the seismograph invented by Zhang Heng. The original detected an earthquake hundreds of miles away.

LIFE DURING THE HAN DYNASTY

As you have read, the Han empire stretched across thousands of miles and achieved many things. Still, farming continued to be the center of China's economy and society. Most people lived on farms and in small villages. China's farmers grew food for the entire empire. The economy was based on customs handed down over generations. This is an example of a traditional economic system.

The lives of farmers during the Han dynasty centered around their families and the endless work in the fields. This has remained relatively unchanged through much of China's long history.

WHY IT MATTERS

Confucius wanted China to become a civilization of good and dutiful people. He believed it had once been that way. During the Han dynasty China's government adopted some of Confucius's

ideas. Despite this, however, conflict and hardship remained part of life in ancient China. The Han dynasty ended around A.D. 220. It broke down under the strain of failed military campaigns beyond China and fights among its leaders. In the centuries to come, many Chinese looked to the teachings of Confucius to renew their civilization. The legacy of Confucian ideas of fairness and learning continues in China today.

✓/// Reviewing Facts and Ideas

MAIN IDEAS

- Confucian ideas about duty and education influenced life during the Han dynasty.
- The Han emperor Wudi started Confucian schools in order to educate government workers.
- The Han dynasty produced many great achievements in science, mathematics, the arts, and trade.
- As in earlier dynasties, farmers during the Han dynasty produced the food and goods that brought China great wealth.

THINK ABOUT IT

1. What did Confucius believe was the duty of a ruler?

2. What are three ways Confucius defined goodness in people?

3. **FOCUS** How did Confucianism affect life during the Han dynasty?

4. **THINKING SKILL** Imagine that you are Emperor Wudi. _Decide_ which aspects of Confucianism you can use to help you govern the empire. Explain how you made your choices.

5. **GEOGRAPHY** Compare the maps on pages 165, 169, and 176. How did China's empire change in the Shang, the Qin, and the Han dynasties?

This model of a house came from a Han dynasty tomb.

MAKING A DIFFERENCE

Working for Education

GUIZHOU (GWEE JOH), CHINA—In this small village in rural China, a group of six women come together once a week. They sit in a circle listening intently to a seventh woman. She reads slowly and clearly from a small magazine. Sometimes she stops and points to pictures on the page.

Except for the woman holding the magazine, none of these women can read. Yet they would like to learn. The magazine, called in English "Rural Women Knowing All," is helping these six women and many thousands more all over China to do just that. The magazine has articles that teach reading and writing. It also has articles about women who have become leaders in their villages and towns.

Ever since the days of the Han dynasty, education has been an important part of Chinese culture. Unfortunately it has not always been easy for girls to receive an education. For much of Chinese history, it was considered more important for boys to go to school. Girls often stayed at home. It is now the law in China that all children, boys and girls, must attend school for at least six years.

Wu Qing (WOO CHING), who teaches at Beijing Foreign Studies University, helped start this magazine in 1993. She is its chief adviser and fundraiser. "The need to educate rural women is great," she says, "because girls, especially in rural areas, have had fewer chances than boys to go to school. If a poor family could only afford to educate one child, the boy almost always would be chosen."

The magazine, which in American money costs about 12¢ a copy, is growing rapidly. It has over 200,000 subscribers and many thousands more readers. As a fundraiser, Wu convinced several large companies to donate cars, televisions, and other prizes for those women's groups that sell large numbers of subscriptions.

Wu believes in educating rural women because "Once rural women know how to read and write, . . . it will make a lot of difference for China." Helping others comes naturally to Wu. "I feel it is up to me to help change China," she says. "That is why I have the energy to work hard."

"I feel it is up to me to help change China."

Wu Qing

SILK MAKING

Bibliothèque Municipale, Poitiers

Have you ever watched a caterpillar spin a cocoon? One kind of caterpillar, the silkworm, spins a cocoon that can be used to create a special cloth. This cloth is called silk. Ancient Chinese farmers discovered how to make silk around 2700 B.C.

In the spring women cut leaves from mulberry trees to feed the silkworms. After several weeks of noisy eating, the silkworms spun their cocoons. Women unwound the cocoons and twisted the strands into threads. These threads were then woven to make cloth. In China today silk is made the same way, except for the added help of machines.

Silk is a strong, beautiful, smooth fabric. It stretches easily and is light and warm. The legacy of making silk enables people all over the world to enjoy the special qualities of this cloth.

This Chinese painting from the 1800s shows a farm family making silk. Women and girls made most of the silk.

Chinese emperors decided to keep silk making a secret from other civilizations. Rulers threatened people with death if they told the secret. This threat worked for over 3,000 years!

Modern factories produce millions of yards of silk cloth. The source of the silk, however, is the same as ever: the cocoon of the silkworm. Today people around the world wear silk to work and to school. It is often used to make suits, shirts, ties, and dresses.

CHAPTER 7 REVIEW

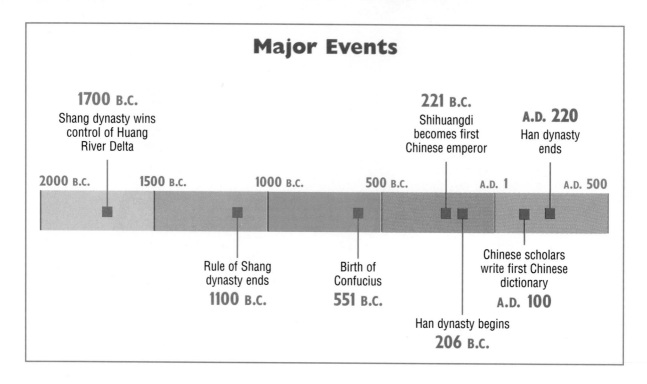

Major Events

1700 B.C.
Shang dynasty wins control of Huang River Delta

221 B.C.
Shihuangdi becomes first Chinese emperor

A.D. 220
Han dynasty ends

2000 B.C.   1500 B.C.   1000 B.C.   500 B.C.   A.D. 1   A.D. 500

Rule of Shang dynasty ends
1100 B.C.

Birth of Confucius
551 B.C.

Chinese scholars write first Chinese dictionary
A.D. 100

Han dynasty begins
206 B.C.

THINKING ABOUT VOCABULARY

Number a sheet of paper from 1 to 10. Beside each number write the word or term from the list below that matches the definition.

dynasty   Mandate of Heaven
emperor   province
erosion   seismograph
famine   steppe
levee   topic sentence

1. A dry, treeless plain
2. A wall that keeps a river within its banks
3. A special machine used to detect earthquakes
4. The wearing away of soil by wind or water
5. A time when food is scarce and people starve
6. A line of rulers who belong to the same family
7. A sentence that contains the main idea
8. The supreme ruler of an empire
9. A division of land
10. A special right to rule that the emperor is thought to receive from the gods

THINKING ABOUT FACTS

1. In what ways did the Huang River help early Chinese farmers?
2. How have discoveries made at Anyang helped historians to understand ancient China?
3. Who was China's first emperor? What did he do to unify China?
4. What is Confucianism?
5. Look at the time line above. How long were the reigns of the Shang and Han dynasties?

THINK AND WRITE

WRITING A JOURNAL

Suppose you live in the time of the Han Dynasty and are a student in the Grand School. Write an entry in your journal describing your thoughts about your studies and the long test you have to take at the end of the year.

WRITING AN ARTICLE

Write a short article for your school newspaper about ancient Chinese civilization. Describe the contributions it has made to world history.

WRITING ABOUT PERSPECTIVES

Suppose you live in ancient China and your teacher asks you to write about what you learned about the Huang River from books and from your parents' experiences. Write three paragraphs about your impressions.

APPLYING STUDY SKILLS

WRITING A SUMMARY

1. What is a summary?
2. How is writing a summary different from rewriting something entirely?
3. What are topic sentences? How can they be useful in writing a summary?
4. After rereading "Silk Making" on page 180, write a three-sentence summary of what you read.
5. How are summaries useful?

Summing Up the Chapter

Copy the main-idea diagram below on a separate piece of paper. Then review the chapter to find at least two pieces of information that support each part of the main idea. After you have filled in the information, use it to write a paragraph that answers the question "What developments of China's Huang River civilization continue to affect China today?"

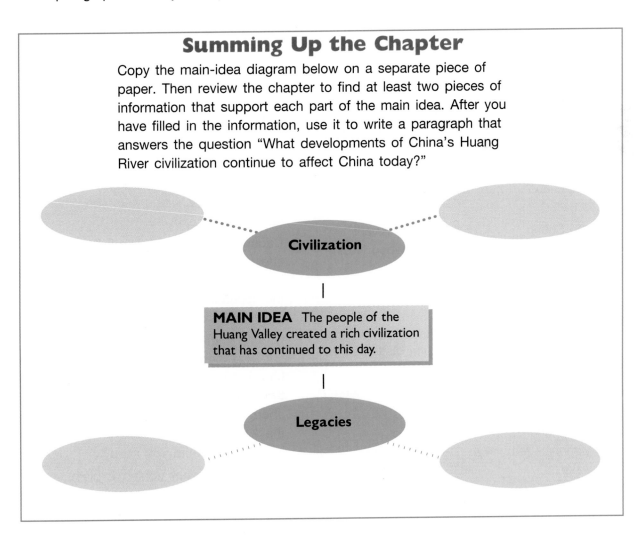

Civilization

MAIN IDEA The people of the Huang Valley created a rich civilization that has continued to this day.

Legacies

UNIT 2 REVIEW

THINKING ABOUT VOCABULARY

dynasty	Sanskrit
empire	summary
hieroglyphics	Torah
polytheism	Vedas
reincarnation	ziggurat

Number a sheet of paper from 1 to 10. Beside each number write the word from the list above that best completes each sentence.

1. A large religious building with a temple on its peak that stood at the center of most ancient Sumerian cities is called a _____.

2. A brief statement of the main ideas in a piece of writing or group of ideas is a _____.

3. Egypt became an _____ during the New Kingdom period.

4. The books that contain the ancient Aryan sacred songs are called the _____.

5. The belief of the ancient Egyptians and Sumerians in many gods and goddesses is called _____.

6. The Shang _____ of the Huang River valley created a legacy that shaped life in China for centuries.

7. The first five books of the Hebrew Bible are called the _____.

8. Government workers in ancient Egypt could communicate over long distances using a writing system called _____.

9. _____ is what Hindus call a cycle of life, death, and rebirth.

10. In the ancient Indian language of _____, *Mohenjo-Daro* means "Mound of the Dead."

THINK AND WRITE

WRITING ABOUT PERSPECTIVES
Write a comparison of the ancient civilizations of Egypt, Sumer, and China. What were their main features? How were they similar? How were they different?

WRITING A TRAVEL PAMPHLET
Suppose you lived in Han China. Write a pamphlet describing some of the things visitors might see there. Describe the geography as well as the people.

WRITING AN INTERVIEW
Interview a person from this unit—for example, Hammurabi, Shihuangdi, or Siddhartha Gautama. Write down your questions and the answers you receive.

BUILDING SKILLS

1. **Summarizing** Reread the section "Children in Egypt" on page 98. Then write four sentences that summarize the section.

2. **Summarizing** Do you think that having summaries of the material you need to know for a test would help you prepare for it or not? Explain.

3. **Cause and effect** Explain the causes and effects of Moses' leading the Hebrews out of Egypt. Tell about the events leading to the departure of the Hebrews from Egypt. What resulted from it?

4. **Different kinds of maps** Look at the map showing the Alps on page 33. Why would knowing only the latitude and longitude of the Alps not be enough to inform you about the temperature and precipitation in the Alps? What other kind of map or information would you need?

5. **Maps at different scales** Explain why it would be helpful to have maps of different scales for a car trip across the country.

YESTERDAY, TODAY & *TOMORROW*

Writing helped in the development of ancient civilizations. Writing is also important to us today. Do you think writing will continue to be as important in the future? Will there be as many books and magazines? Do you think something else will take their place? Explain your answers.

READING ON YOUR OWN

Here are some books you might find at the library to help you learn more.

THE TERRA COTTA ARMY OF EMPEROR QIN
by Caroline Lazo
This book tells how a clay army was uncovered near the tomb of China's first emperor.

THE GREAT PYRAMID
by Elizabeth Mann
This illustrated book describes how the Great Pyramid in ancient Egypt was built.

GODS AND PHARAOHS FROM EGYPTIAN MYTHOLOGY
by Geraldine Harris
These imaginative stories tell much about ancient Egypt.

UNIT PROJECT

Comparing Then and Now

1. Choose a river that was important to an ancient civilization.

2. Research that river to see how it affects the people who live there today.

3. Write a paragraph explaining your findings. Include items such as how the river affects the jobs people have and the foods they eat.

4. Create a poster comparing the civilization and its river then and now. You can use a sheet of large oaktag, colorful markers, and paints.

5. Be sure to include a label and a description for each picture.

6. Present your poster to the class.

ISLAMIC TILE, SPAIN;
STATUE OF MAYA
GODDESS, HONDURAS

STATUE OF GODDESS OF
WISDOM, ROME;
THE COLOSSEUM, ROME

New Ideas and New Empires

"The armor upon their bodies flashed in the sun."

from the Iliad, by Homer
See page 200.

Why Does It Matter?

A poet in ancient Greece wrote these words to describe a great battle. Today people around the world are familiar with Homer's words as well as many other achievements of his time. People of the world today owe much to the early peoples of Greece, Rome, Arabia, and the Americas. Their ideas about government, law, beauty, education, science, and religion continue to influence us today. Such accomplishments are only a few of the reasons for calling certain periods "Classic."

VASE WITH BATTLE SCENE, GREECE

FIND OUT MORE!
Visit our website:
www.mhschool.com

187

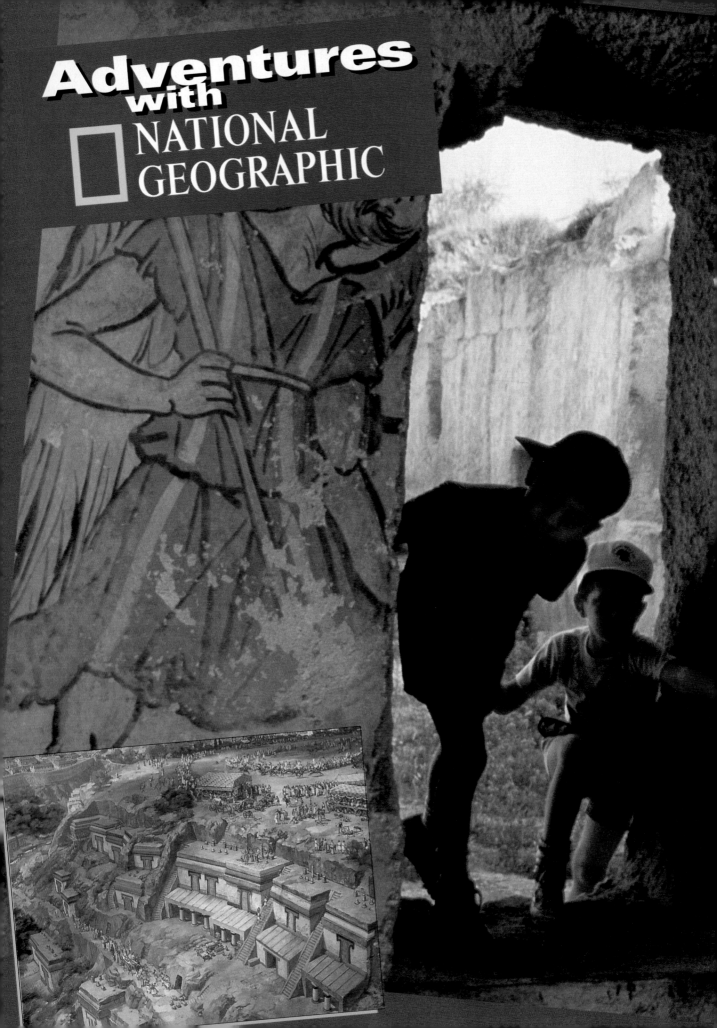

Adventures
with
NATIONAL
GEOGRAPHIC

LOST IN TRANSLATION

You poke your head into the doorway of a ruined tomb, and you wonder about the people who painted the walls more than 2,000 years ago. You're not alone. Archaeologists also wonder about the Etruscans, who lived in Italy about the same time that the ancient Greeks were flourishing nearby. The Etruscans built great cities and elaborate tombs. But unlike the Greeks, they left few written records. And the records they *did* leave—well, no one can read them now, for no one knows the language. So archaeologists hunt through the ruins, looking for other clues about the mystery people of the ancient world.

GEO JOURNAL

List some ways you might find out about a culture even if you couldn't read its language.

Ancient Greece

THINKING ABOUT
HISTORY AND GEOGRAPHY

In this chapter you will read about a civilization that developed in the rocky landscape by the Aegean Sea more than 3,000 years ago. Following the time line, you see how the ancient Greeks built cities with unique ways of life. In time, interaction and conflict among the cities and peoples of the region led to a period of tremendous creativity. Greek civilization eventually spread to areas around the Mediterranean Sea.

450 B.C.

ATHENS
Pericles encourages poor and rich citizens to take part in government

1400 B.C.

AEGEAN SEA
Seagoing people trade among the islands of Greece

800 B.C.

SPARTA
Boys and girls train to build a strong city

1400 B.C.   600 B.C.   500 B.C.

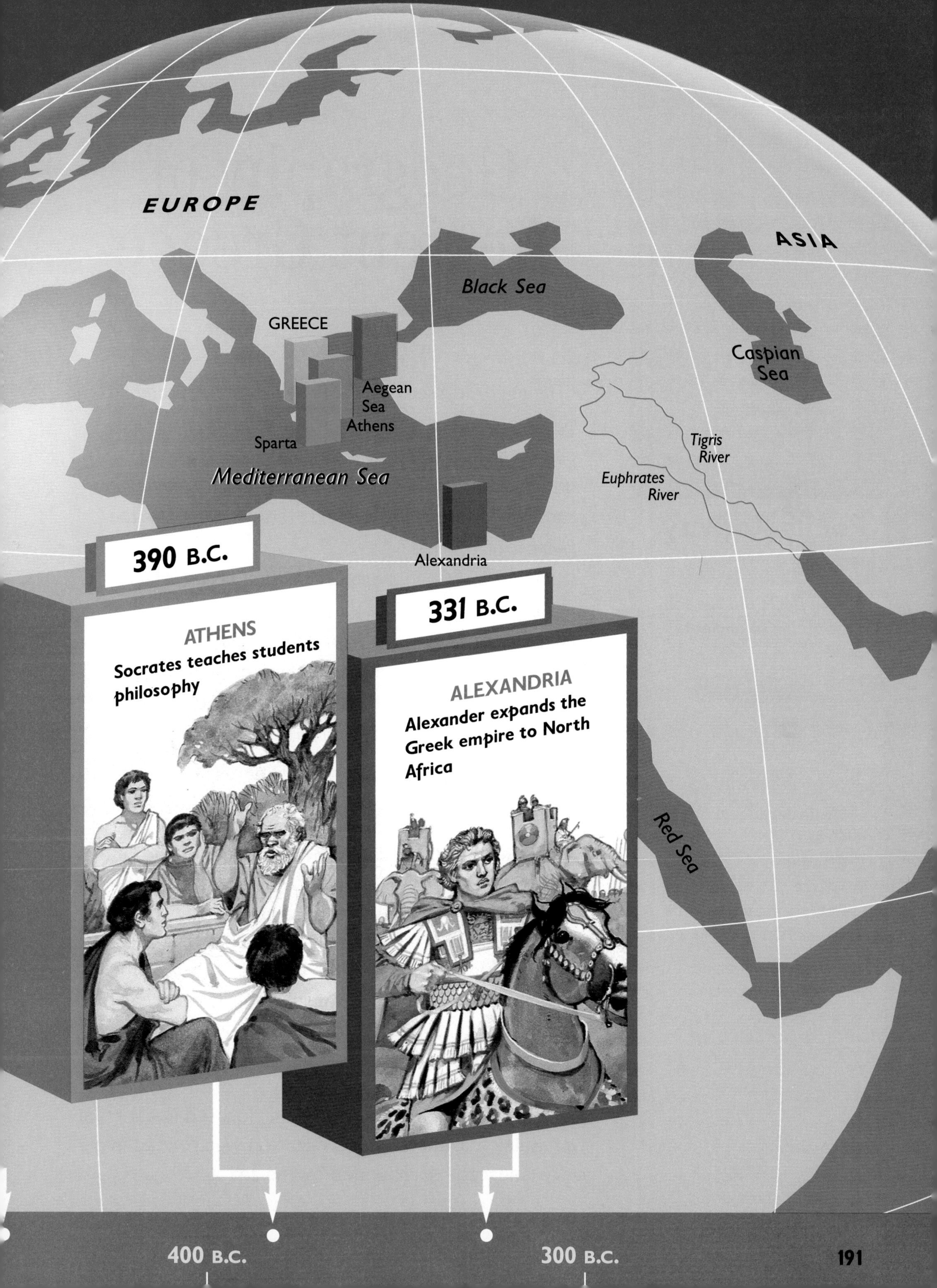
EUROPE
ASIA
Black Sea
GREECE
Caspian Sea
Aegean Sea
Athens
Sparta
Mediterranean Sea
Tigris River
Euphrates River
Alexandria
390 B.C.
ATHENS
Socrates teaches students philosophy
331 B.C.
ALEXANDRIA
Alexander expands the Greek empire to North Africa
Red Sea
400 B.C.
300 B.C.

Geography of Ancient Greece

Focus Activity

What effects did the sea have on life in ancient Greece?

- peninsula
- harbor

- Mediterranean Sea
- Crete
- Rhodes
- Attica
- Peloponnesus
- Phoenicia

Read Aloud

"The good Odysseus (oh DIHS ee us) gladly spread his sail: seated, he steered. . . . Seventeen days he sailed across the sea; on the eighteenth he saw that he'd drawn close to shadowed peaks: he now was near the coast of [an] island; in the mist that land took on the likeness of a shield."

About 2,700 years ago Greeks first began listening to the exciting tales, like the one above, of a poet named Homer. Homer's stories about Odysseus helped the ancient Greeks imagine a distant age much different from their own. They also expressed the strong connection the people of ancient Greece felt with the sea.

THE BIG PICTURE

In 1500 B.C. the Shang dynasty ruled much of the land along the Huang River. In Egypt the pharaohs of the New Kingdom were building an empire along the southeastern shores of the Mediterranean Sea. Along the Mediterranean's northeastern shores, meanwhile, another civilization was growing. It was that of ancient Greece, a civilization that had been developing for more than 1,000 years.

No great river carrying thick layers of silt flowed through this land. Rather than being located in a fertile river valley, ancient Greek civilization was rooted in a rocky landscape surrounded by the sea.

MOUNTAINS AND SEA

The land of ancient Greece was made up of a part of the southern European mainland along with over 400 islands. This is the same area that makes up Greece today. As you can see on the map, the biggest of the islands is Crete. Crete lies about one day's sail south of the Greek mainland. East of Crete lies Rhodes, an island near what is today Turkey. Rhodes provides an ideal rest stop for ships sailing between Greece and western Asia.

Mountains and hills cover about nine out of every ten acres in Greece. The most mountainous region, however, is located in western Greece. There, travel by land is difficult, and little farmable land exists. Herds of sheep and goats live on wild plants that grow on the rugged hillsides.

Land Along the Coast

Larger plains suitable for farming lie in eastern Greece, near the coast. A few of these plains are on Attica, a wedge-shaped peninsula that juts into the Mediterranean Sea. A peninsula is an area of land nearly surrounded by water. Attica also contains excellent natural harbors for ships. A harbor is a sheltered place along a coast.

A large peninsula called the Peloponnesus (pel uh puh NEE sus) lies to the southwest of Attica. Shaped like a giant hand reaching toward Crete, the Peloponnesus is a mountainous region ringed by a thin band of fertile land. Like the rest of Greece, the Peloponnesus contains several rivers. Many of the region's rivers, however, dry up in the summertime, unlike rivers in Egypt or Mesopotamia.

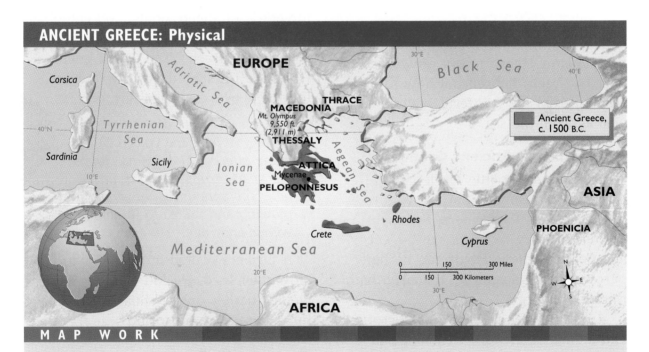

ANCIENT GREECE: Physical

Ancient Greece, c. 1500 B.C.

MAP WORK

For its size, the land of ancient Greece had a very long coastline. Much of the land is also mountainous. This geography had a great impact on life in the region.

1. What method of transportation do you suppose was quickest in ancient Greece?

2. About how long is the island of Crete? Use the map scale to find this answer.

3. What body of water lies east of Attica?

4. In which direction would you travel to get from Crete to Rhodes?

Like their ancestors in ancient times, many farmers in Greece today herd sheep (left) and raise olives (above).

EARLY ECONOMY IN GREECE

Greece is not as fertile as the valleys of the Indus or Huang rivers. However, ancient Greeks figured out how to make a living from the few fertile valleys as well as from the sea.

Agriculture in Ancient Greece

Besides having little fertile land, Greece has a climate that presents special challenges for farmers. Summers are hot and dry. Winters can be wet and fiercely windy. Fields can become parched in the summer but soaked with rain in the winter.

Ancient Greek farmers raised crops and animals that were well suited to this environment. They grew some wheat and barley to make bread, which was important to the Greek diet. Olives and grapes became Greece's other major crops. Both grew well in rocky and hilly areas. Shrubs on Greece's many hills and mountains provided food for herds of sheep, goats, and cattle.

Timing was important to successful farming in Greece. The Greek poet Hesiod (HEE see ud), who wrote during the 700s B.C., urged farmers:

Take careful note of the time when you hear the voice of the crane uttering high in the clouds her yearly trumpeting cry [in the fall]. She announces the signal for plowing and points to the time of winter and rain.

If farmers waited until winter to plow their land, Hesiod warned, they would "gather only a small little handful" of grain in the spring.

Crossing the Seas

Because farmers could not produce huge grain surpluses, and because travel on the hilly land was difficult, sailing became an important part of life in Greece. Sailors traveled as far as

194

ancient Egypt to trade. Greek merchants competed with traders from Phoenicia (fuh NEE shuh), in what is today Lebanon. Phoenician sailors were as skilled as the Greeks and traveled to ports all across the Mediterranean Sea.

For many years olive oil was one of the most prized of Greek exports. People loved the flavor it gave food as well as its usefulness as lamp fuel and body lotion. The sale of olive oil made it possible for Greeks to buy much-needed grain for their markets at home.

WHY IT MATTERS

In the lessons to come, you will read the story of Greek civilization. Beginning around 800 B.C., great changes would take place on these rocky islands and peninsulas. Some things, however, would never change. Farming and sailing would always be lifelines for the people of ancient Greece.

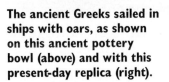

The ancient Greeks sailed in ships with oars, as shown on this ancient pottery bowl (above) and with this present-day replica (right).

✔ Reviewing Facts and Ideas

MAIN IDEAS

- Unlike the Nile or Huang River valleys, Greece has land that is hilly and rocky, making farming difficult in most areas.
- Ancient Greeks used the Mediterranean Sea as a "highway" to trade for goods they could not produce themselves.
- Olive oil—a product of a crop that grows well in Greece's rocky soil—became valuable to trade for grain.

THINK ABOUT IT

1. Why was farming a challenge in Greece? Why was timing important?

2. Contrast the geography of Greece with that of an ancient river valley civilization such as Mesopotamia or the Indus Valley.

3. **FOCUS** How did ancient Greeks use the sea to spread their products and culture to other regions?

4. **THINKING SKILL** What *effects* did geography have on the ways ancient Greeks met their needs?

5. **GEOGRAPHY** Draw a map of the Mediterranean Sea region. Draw in arrows to show where ancient Greeks sailed.

| 700 B.C. | | 600 B.C. | 500 B.C. | | 400 B.C. | 300 B.C. |

The Rise of Greek Cities

Read Aloud

"Shared blood, shared language, shared religion, and shared customs." Long ago a Greek historian named Herodotus (hih RAHD uh tus) used these words to describe what it meant to be Greek. Greeks were very proud of what they shared. However, they prized just as highly those things that made them different from one another. Those differences began in the many city-states that dotted the mainland and islands of ancient Greece.

Focus Activity

READ TO LEARN

What was life like in the ancient Greek cities of Sparta and Athens?

VOCABULARY

- polis
- acropolis
- agora
- citizen
- oligarchy
- monarchy
- democracy
- colony

PEOPLE

- Homer

PLACES

- Athens
- Sparta
- Mount Olympus

THE BIG PICTURE

By 1100 B.C. both Egypt's New Kingdom empire and China's Shang dynasty had lost their power. Historians know little about how people in Greece lived during this period or during the next 400 years. Very few artifacts from Greece at this time have been found. However, many artifacts dating from about 700 B.C. onward have been found. They show that life had changed greatly since the earliest days of ancient Greece. In many cities, groups of powerful men worked together to make decisions for their communities. Each community usually revolved around one city. The Greek word for this kind of city-state was **polis** (POH lihs).

A GREEK POLIS

Most city-states were laid out according to a similar plan. Most were built around an acropolis (uh KROP uh lihs). An acropolis was a large hill where city residents could seek shelter and safety in times of war. In a nearby clearing farmers would gather to trade with each other and with craftworkers. The clearing, called an agora (AG ur uh), often served both as a marketplace and as a meeting place.

Developing Governments

Although city-states often looked similar, each one had a different type of government. In each type, however, leaders had to be citizens of their polis. Today a citizen is a person who has certain rights and responsibilities in his or her country or community. In ancient Greece, though, only men could be citizens. Women and slaves were not allowed to be citizens and had few rights. Slaves, or *helots* (HEL uts), in ancient Greece were usually conquered neighbors. Slavery was common throughout ancient Greece.

Being a citizen did not automatically give men a role in their government. In many city-states a small group of the richest, most powerful citizens controlled decision making. This type of government is called an oligarchy (OL ih gahr kee). By 600 B.C. the Greek city-state of Athens was governed by an oligarchy. One Athenian said:

Oligarchy is a government resting on the value of property, in which the rich have power and the poor have none.

Before the oligarchy Athens had another form of government. Like other Greek city-states, it was ruled by one ruler, or king. This type of government is called a monarchy. In fact the word *monarchy* comes from two Greek words meaning "rule by one."

The Acropolis in Athens is the best known of the many acropolises built in Greece.

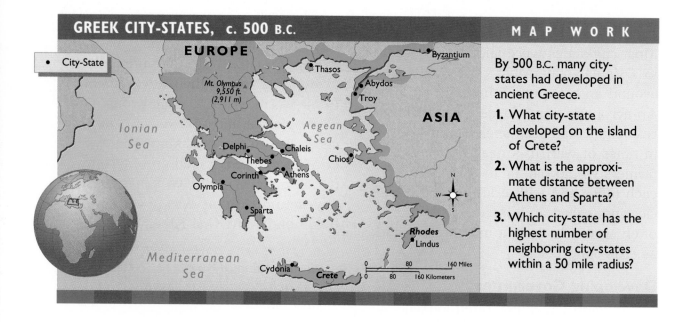

EUROPE

• City-State

Byzantium

Thasos

Mt. Olympus
9,550 ft.
(2,911 m)

Abydos

Troy

ASIA

Ionian
Sea

Aegean
Sea

Delphi
Chaleis
Thebes
Chios
Corinth
Athens
Olympia

Sparta

Rhodes
Lindus

Mediterranean
Sea

Cydonia
Crete

0   80   160 Miles
0   80   160 Kilometers

By 500 B.C. many city-states had developed in ancient Greece.

1. What city-state developed on the island of Crete?

2. What is the approximate distance between Athens and Sparta?

3. Which city-state has the highest number of neighboring city-states within a 50 mile radius?

TWO GREEK CITIES

Of Greece's many city-states, historians know most about Athens and Sparta. Many documents and artifacts from those cities have been preserved. Like all Greek city-states, they had much in common. The way people lived in the two powerful city-states from day to day, however, differed a great deal.

Sparta

In 700 B.C. Sparta covered much of the southern Peloponnesus and was Greece's largest city-state. Dozens of villages belonged to this polis. Sparta's central "city" was a cluster of villages that lay almost 30 miles from the Mediterranean Sea. A low mountain nearby formed Sparta's acropolis. Near its base lay the polis agora, or meeting place. Here Sparta's leaders made the decisions that shaped life in this polis.

As in other city-states, farmers gathered at Sparta's agora to do business. Most of Sparta's farm workers, however, were slaves. Sparta had many more slaves than other city-states. At some times, there were as many as seven slaves for every one Spartan.

The Spartan Military

Around 600 B.C. Sparta's slaves revolted. The Spartans, however, managed to overpower their slaves. Polis leaders then set out to make Sparta the strongest military power in Greece. They wanted to make sure that neither slaves nor another polis could ever gain control of Sparta.

Sparta's people dedicated much of their lives to making their polis strong. Spartan children, too, were expected to do their part for the polis. At about age seven, boys and girls began training. Although they spent some time learning to read and write, boys spent even more time training to be soldiers. Girls practiced running, throwing spears called javelins, and playing ball games. In Sparta, girls trained not to become soldiers but rather to be strong mothers of strong children.

Athens

Life for girls and boys was very different in the city of Athens. Athens lay on the peninsula of Attica, northeast of Sparta. Athenian girls did not practice sports. Rather, they were told to "see little, hear little, and ask no more questions than are absolutely necessary." Girls stayed at home to help their mothers. They carried out such duties as weaving cloth from sheep's wool. Girls who lived on farms helped in the fields at harvesttime.

Many Athenian boys worked each day with their fathers in the fields, or in pottery or stoneworking shops. If their parents could afford to send them to school, boys studied reading and writing. After classes they would practice wrestling or boxing at a local gymnasium before returning home.

Government in Athens

Life in Athens was different from that in Sparta. Athenians did not spend as much time and energy building a strong army. Yet Athens had challenges of its own.

Remember, Athens' government around 600 B.C. was an oligarchy. Most of Athens' early leaders belonged to noble families that were both rich and powerful. In time the poorer citizens of Athens demanded to have more say in how their government was run. The nobles were forced to share some of their power with other citizens.

Power to the People

The developing new government featured large meetings where all the citizens could take part in making decisions for the polis. This form of government is today called a democracy. The word *democracy* combines two Greek words meaning "rule by the people." It means that citizens vote to make government decisions.

The beginnings of democracy marked an important time in world history. Some historians, in fact, trace our own ideas of democracy back to ancient Greece. In the next lesson you will read about further developments in Greece's new democratic system.

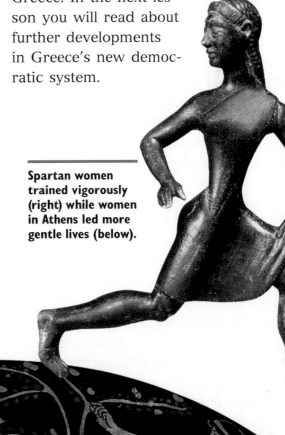

Spartan women trained vigorously (right) while women in Athens led more gentle lives (below).

SHARED CULTURE

The citizens of Athens did not meet to discuss government policies every day. Like the people of the other Greek cities, Athenians reserved a few days of every month for religious celebrations to honor gods and goddesses.

Ancient Greeks believed that many gods and goddesses ruled the world. The most powerful were said to live on Mount Olympus. Mount Olympus is a mountain in northern Greece.

Special Festivals

Each polis honored at least one god or goddess as its special protector and provider. In Athens people worshiped *Athena*, the goddess of wisdom. Every summer they held a huge festival in her honor. After singing and dancing all night, Athenians walked to the top of the city's acropolis. There, as the sun rose in the sky, priests killed cattle in honor of Athena.

People from all over Greece also gathered at temples to worship Zeus (ZOOS), the most powerful god in the ancient Greek religion. The city-states also came together to compete in athletic competitions. You will read more about the most well known of these games, the Olympics, in this chapter's Legacy on pages 202–203. At the Olympic Games crowds cheered athletes from many city-states.

A Greek Poet

People in all city-states loved to hear the stories of the poet Homer. Many of these stories described Greece's past. Homer is thought to have lived sometime between 800 and 700 B.C. His most famous epic poems, the *Iliad* and the *Odyssey*, tell stories of war and adventure. The *Iliad* describes what happened when a prince from Troy, an ancient city in what is today Turkey, kidnapped Helen, a Greek queen. The poem also describes how the gods created Greek cities. How does Homer describe the Greek army?

MANY VOICES
PRIMARY SOURCE

Excerpt from the *Iliad*, by Homer, c. 700 B.C.

As when, at the edge of the sounding sea, wave after wave comes up under the driving of the West Wind—out on the deep it lifts its crest and is broken on the land with a noise like thunder, and far over the headlands shoots its salt foam—so did the Greek lines then go into battle. Each chief gave his men their orders, but the rest said not a word. You would not have thought that all that great army had a voice among them, in such silence they all went through fear of their chiefs. And as they moved, the armor upon their bodies flashed in the sun.

Beyond Greece

Not long after the Greek festivals and Olympics were begun, athletes from faraway Greek colonies came to participate. The colonies were made up of groups of people who lived apart from, but kept ties with, Greece. Colonies were founded by Greeks in the 700s B.C. Many colonies became important trading partners because they grew grains that were much in demand in Greece. Greek ships also traveled south to Egypt's Nile Delta.

By 500 B.C. Greek city-states ringed the Mediterranean "like frogs around a pond," as a teacher named Plato put it. Some of Greece's eastern territories, however, were being taken over by a growing empire that was already vastly larger than Greece. At its height this empire of Persia—based in what is today Iran—was bigger than any that had yet existed in the world. It included all lands from Egypt and the western edge of the Mediterranean Sea to the Indus Valley.

Ancient Greeks worshiped Apollo, their god of the sun.

WHY IT MATTERS

The city-states of ancient Greece had their differences and valued their independence. Many of the Greek cities even had different types of government. One of these cities, Athens, began to develop a new kind of government called democracy. The idea of democracy is important in the United States.

Despite their differences, the cities of ancient Greece shared many cultural ties. In 499 B.C. a Greek colony on the edge of what is today Turkey wanted to break free from Persian control. People of the colony asked the Greek city-states for help. Athens, Sparta, and other city-states joined together to fight Persia. The war that followed would change Greece forever.

Reviewing Facts and Ideas

MAIN IDEAS

- Life in most of the Greek city-states revolved around an agora and an acropolis.

- Spartans spent much of their time working to strengthen their bodies and their army. In Athens free women and girls worked at home. Boys and men worked, went to school, or took part in government.

THINK ABOUT IT

1. What did city-states have in common? What made them different?

2. Who was allowed to vote in the developing democracy of Athens?

3. **FOCUS** Why was life in Sparta so different from life in Athens?

4. **THINKING SKILL** What *effects* did slavery have on life in Sparta?

5. **GEOGRAPHY** What made the agora a center for cultural interaction?

201

THE OLYMPICS

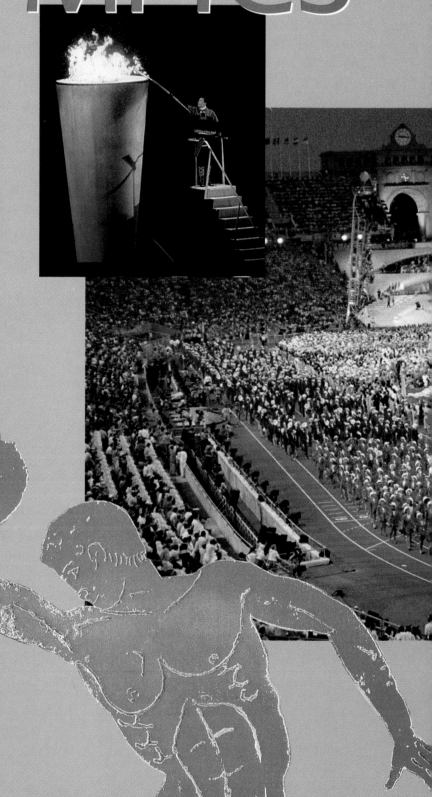

Have you ever dreamed of competing in the Olympic Games? You may have imagined yourself crossing the finish line at the end of a race. Perhaps you simply enjoy watching the events on television.

The Olympic Games were first held nearly 3,000 years ago in ancient Greece. City-states cooperated to make the games an important part of Greek culture.

By about A.D. 400 the ancient Olympics had faded away. The tradition was revived in 1896. Today the international games take place every two years. Most nations of the world send their best athletes to take part in the Summer and the Winter Olympic Games.

Look at the pictures on these pages. Think about how the modern Olympic Games help people to remember an important legacy of the past.

Disabled athletes compete in Special Olympic Games. The first Special Olympic Games were held in Chicago in 1968. Today athletes from more than 100 different countries participate in these events.

Unlike ancient Olympic Games, women now compete in most sports. American speed skater Bonnie Blair won two gold medals during the 1994 Winter Olympics. Other sports in the Winter Olympics are cold-weather sports, such as skiing, ice hockey, and bobsledding. Those events became part of Olympic competition in 1924.

The modern games begin with a parade of Olympic athletes from every participating nation. Today many of the athletes take part in team competitions. Such team events were not part of ancient Olympic Games.

| 700 B.C. | 600 B.C. | 500 B.C. | 460 B.C. | 399 B.C. | 300 B.C. |

Athens' Age of Glory

Read Aloud

If Athenians living in 500 B.C. could somehow have traveled 65 years into the future, they would have been amazed by what they saw. In the city's harbor many ships would be tied at a long dock leading straight to a huge trading area. People could buy a wide range of goods, from Egyptian papyrus to Italian cheese, with coins from Athens or Persia. Walking up the road to the city—now surrounded by walls—they would have seen grand stone temples where far simpler ones had once stood. Athens, clearly, was flourishing.

Focus Activity

READ TO LEARN

What did the Athenians achieve during Athens' "Golden Age"?

VOCABULARY

- assembly
- jury
- philosophy
- Peloponnesian Wars

PEOPLE

- Pericles
- Socrates
- Plato

PLACES

- Acropolis
- Parthenon

THE BIG PICTURE

What happened to bring about the success of Athens? As you read in the last lesson, the city-states of Greece went to war against the empire of Persia in 499 B.C. Understanding the importance of sea power, the Athenians built a mighty naval fleet. Over the next 20 years they joined forces with the armies of Sparta and other city-states. Together they defeated the Persians.

Many Greek colonies were still in danger of Persian attack, however. Some of them began paying money for protection by the Athenian navy. Athens became rich from these payments. Some of that money went toward building an even more powerful navy. Much of the rest went to improve life in the city itself.

Around 460 B.C. Athens entered a period of rich culture. Some historians call the next 30 years the "Golden Age" of Athens. It was a time of great achievement.

GOLDEN AGE OF ATHENS

In the middle 400s B.C. Athens was the same in many ways as it had been 65 years earlier. Life still revolved around the agora and the acropolis. Citizens still voted on issues that shaped life in the city. Festivals honoring Athena were still held every summer. Much, however, had changed.

A Walk Through Athens

The Acropolis, high above the city, was the religious center of Athens. Many Greek cities had their own acropolises. The one at Athens, however, was larger than others—that is why it is generally spelled with a capital *A*. Here a group of buildings displayed the city's new wealth and power. At their center rose a temple to Athena made of marble cut from a nearby mountain. This stunning temple was the Parthenon (PAHR thuh nahn). It still sits on the highest point of the Acropolis and can be seen from all over the city.

Beautifully made vases (left) and the Parthenon (below) were among the many achievements of the ancient Greeks.

Looking down from the Acropolis, one could see many buildings. About 100,000 people lived in Athens, making it the largest city in Greece.

Activity in the Agora

Following the winding road down from the Acropolis, one might see crowds of people. Many had come to do business at the agora. There were shopkeepers, students, and lawyers heading for the market or government buildings. In one corner of the agora, citizens gathered at a monument that served as the city's "bulletin board." Here people could leave messages or read postings about upcoming matters to be voted on.

Merchants sold perfume, vegetables, and clothing or offered haircuts. In nearby workshops, potters crafted vases and bowls. The diagram on page 207 shows what Athens may have looked like.

ATHENIAN GOVERNMENT

In the early 400s B.C. a small council of powerful citizens made all of the city's important decisions. Later in the century, though, the council's powers had been taken over by an **assembly** of citizens. An assembly is a lawmaking body of a government. The assembly voted on issues that helped to shape the future of the city.

Do you remember from the last lesson who were considered citizens in Athens and who were not? No women and no enslaved men had a voice in Athens' government. In fact they did not enjoy any of the rights of citizenship, such as land ownership. However, the people of ancient Athens took a big step toward creating a government that represented the people.

DID YOU KNOW?

What did ancient Greeks do for entertainment?

Famous people such as Socrates and Pericles were made fun of by writers such as Aristophanes (ar uh STOHF uh neez). He wrote funny plays called comedies. Comedies, along with serious plays called tragedies, were performed at festivals. Another playwright, Aeschylus (ES kuh lus), wrote tragedies about events in Greek history.

Over 13,000 people crowded into outdoor theaters to watch the popular plays. Actors played their parts with the help of big masks. A group called the "chorus" sang, danced, and acted in the plays.

A Great Statesman

Pericles (PER ih kleez), an Athenian leader around 450 B.C., explained his city's government this way:

> *Our city is called a democracy because it is governed by the many, not the few. . . . No one, moreover, if he has it in him to do some good for the city, is barred because of poverty or humble origins.*

Pericles made sure poor as well as rich citizens could take part in government.

Citizens served on the assembly and sat on **juries**. A jury is a group of citizens chosen to hear evidence and make decisions in a court of law. Pericles arranged for citizens to be paid when they held office or served on a jury. This meant that farmers and other poor citizens could afford to take the time to become involved in government.

Philosophy in Athens

While citizens debated government issues, famous teachers like **Socrates** (SAHK ruh teez) led discussions about the right way to live. Socrates lived around the middle 400s B.C. He taught his students **philosophy**, or the search for wisdom and the right way to live. They discussed what makes the best kind of government or what it means to love or to be a good citizen.

Shortly before 400 B.C. Socrates began questioning Athenian values, such as laws, customs—even religion. It made some Athenians angry that he would doubt anything about the polis. In 399 B.C. Socrates was brought to trial for "urging Athens' young people to revolt." The jury decided he was guilty and sentenced him to death. His teachings, however, were written down by a student, **Plato** (PLAY toh), who also became a famous philosopher.

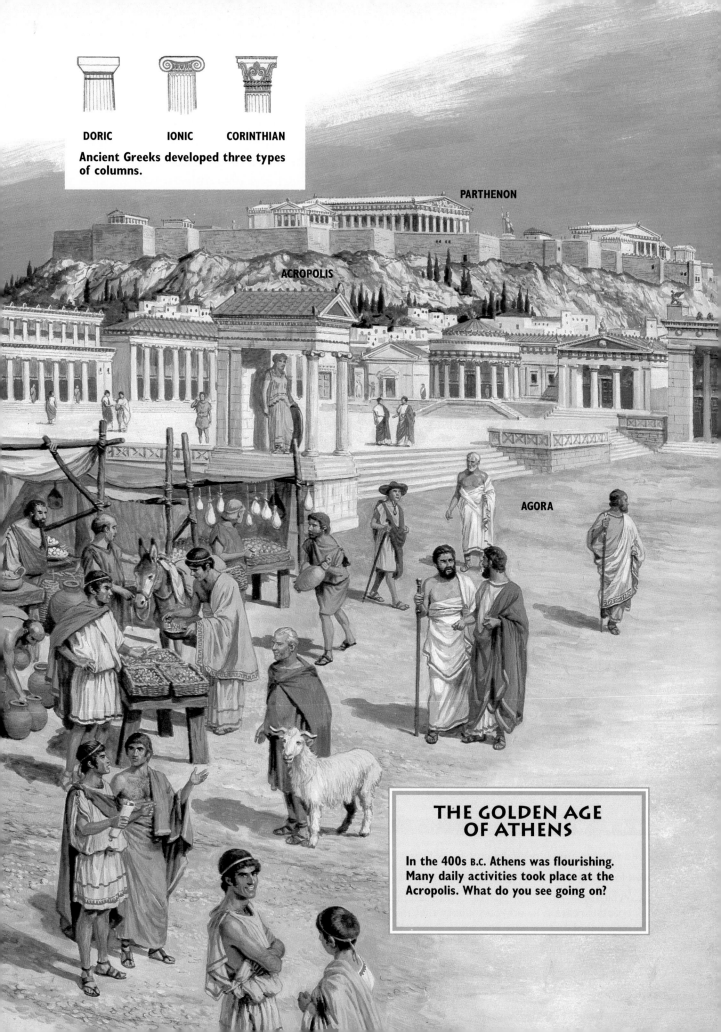

DORIC   IONIC   CORINTHIAN
Ancient Greeks developed three types of columns.

PARTHENON

ACROPOLIS

AGORA

THE GOLDEN AGE OF ATHENS

In the 400s B.C. Athens was flourishing. Many daily activities took place at the Acropolis. What do you see going on?

WAR AND CONFLICT

The Golden Age of Athens did not last, however. Sparta and other Greek city-states were jealous of the power and wealth of Athens. They formed what they called the Peloponnesian League. You can see where the allies of Sparta and the allies of Athens were located on the map on this page. In 431 B.C. the two sides began what became known as the Peloponnesian (pel uh puh NEEZH un) Wars.

Battles on Land and Sea

The wars began with an attack by the Spartan army. Pericles knew that his army was no match for Sparta's. He called for Athenians living outside the city to move inside the city walls. The walls protected the city, but Sparta's army destroyed the farmland around Athens. The Athenians did not starve, however, because their navy controlled the Aegean Sea. Ships were able to bring in grain from other areas.

In fact the powerful Athenian navy kept the wars in a deadlock for many years. Athens was able to win most of the battles at sea while Sparta won more often on land. However, the course of the wars worsened for Athens. A terrible disease swept through the crowded city. At least one third of the population died from it. One of its victims was Pericles. Meanwhile the wars continued, taking many more lives.

A Final Blow

In 404 B.C. Sparta was able to cut off the Athenian grain supply from the Black Sea. The starving Athenians had to surrender. All of Greece had suffered great losses from the Peloponnesian

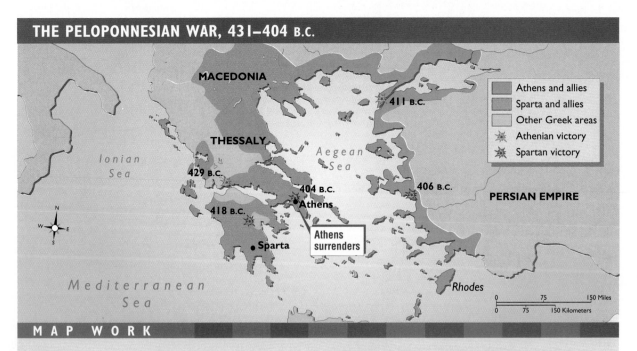

THE PELOPONNESIAN WAR, 431–404 B.C.

MACEDONIA

411 B.C.

THESSALY

Ionian Sea

429 B.C.

Aegean Sea

404 B.C.
Athens

406 B.C.

418 B.C.

• Sparta

Athens surrenders

PERSIAN EMPIRE

Rhodes

Mediterranean Sea

Legend:
- Athens and allies
- Sparta and allies
- Other Greek areas
- ✴ Athenian victory
- ✴ Spartan victory

0   75   150 Miles
0   75   150 Kilometers

MAP WORK

The Peloponnesian Wars cost many lives.

1. How long did the Peloponnesian Wars last?

2. Which side, Athens or Sparta, controlled more coastal areas? Why do you suppose that might have been?

3. What northern region did Sparta control?

4. How does this map show that Athens and its allies were mainly on the defensive during the Peloponnesian War?

Ancient Greek soldiers went into battle protected by bronze helmets and chest plates.

Between 500 B.C. and 400 B.C. Athens gave the world some of ancient Greece's most enduring legacies. Athenians improved their democracy and built splendid temples. They searched for wisdom through philosophy and created new dramatic forms. After 400 B.C. a young warrior-king from another land would spread those legacies far and wide. His name was Alexander. You will read about him in the following lesson.

✓ Reviewing Facts and Ideas

MAIN IDEA

- In the 400s B.C., during their "Golden Age," Athenians discussed philosophy, wrote plays, and built many grand buildings.

- Though democracy was still limited to male citizens, Pericles worked to give poorer citizens a voice in Athenian government.

- The Peloponnesian Wars ended the "Golden Age" of Athens. Afterward no single polis dominated Greece.

THINK ABOUT IT

1. How did the war against Persia bring new wealth and power to Athens?

2. What changes did Pericles introduce in Athens?

3. **FOCUS** List three things that reflect how the century before 400 B.C. was a "golden age" for Athens.

4. **THINKING SKILL** Make a _generalization_ about the changes that occurred in Athenian government between 500 B.C. and 400 B.C.

5. **WRITE** Write a paragraph comparing democracy in Athens with democracy in the United States.

Wars. The Greek historian Thucydides (thoo SIHD ih deez), who lived during the time, concluded that war "is a violent teacher."

The End of a Golden Age

Following the Peloponnesian Wars, Sparta was once again the leading polis in Greece. Yet its victory was short-lived. For the next 50 years no city-state was able to maintain control for long before others challenged it. These unsettled times would leave Greece open to threats from a new power to the north.

The painting *School of Athens* by Raphael shows Socrates with other philosophers. Plato (left), shown in another part of the painting, takes notes.

Making Conclusions

VOCABULARY

conclusion

WHY THE SKILL MATTERS

In the last lesson you read about a type of government that developed in Athens. While you read, you may have made certain conclusions about democracy. A conclusion is a final statement about the meaning of many facts. The skill of making conclusions is especially important to students of history because it helps them to see events within the "big picture."

Making a conclusion also helps you to make sense of specific facts because you can see how they fit into the big picture. Use the Helping Yourself box for some hints on "adding up" facts to make conclusions.

USING THE SKILL

Read the paragraph on the next page. Look for a common idea suggested by all of the facts. Then, make a conclusion based upon this idea.

In the 400s B.C. more schools were created in Athens than ever before—though none were for girls or slaves. Families who could afford the cost began sending their boys to school at age seven. There they learned to read, write, and memorize the poems of Homer. Math and science were rarely taught. Most students left school after learning basic skills. The sons of wealthy families kept studying until they were teenagers. Their teachers worked to make them good thinkers and speakers so they would be respected in the city's assembly.

Helping yourself

- Making a **conclusion** involves finding a statement about the meaning of many facts.

- Start by identifying a topic that is related to all the facts.

- Find an idea about the topic that is supported by all the facts.

- State this common idea as your conclusion.

The paragraph provides information about education in Athens. Because many schools were created and some students attended until they were teenagers, you might conclude that education became more important in Athens during the 400s B.C. You might also conclude that the sons of wealthy families were given more opportunities to learn. You can often make more than one conclusion from the same information.

TRYING THE SKILL

Read the following paragraph. What conclusion can be made from it?

Most teachers of wealthy students in Athens charged fees to teach public speaking. A few philosophers like Socrates, though, taught students for free. To those thinkers, understanding the proper way to live was more important than money or the skills that made money. Thanks to Socrates and his fellow philosophers, the search for knowledge and truth would become an important part of life in Athens for years to come.

REVIEWING THE SKILL

1. What is a conclusion?

2. What steps are involved in making a conclusion?

3. How does making conclusions help you to better understand many specific facts?

This sculpture shows Aristotle, a student of Plato, thinking. Aristotle is considered to be one of the greatest Greek philosophers.

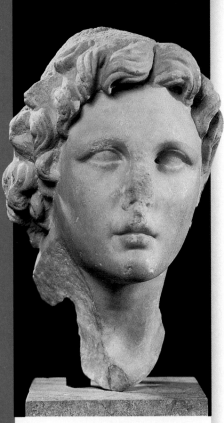

| 700 B.C. | 600 B.C. | 500 B.C. | 400 B.C. | 336 B.C. | 300 B.C. |

The Greek Empire

Read Aloud

Stadium. Gymnasium. Museum. Democracy. *These words represent things that are important in our lives today. All of them had beginnings in ancient Greece. The story of Greek civilization continues with a young man named Alexander.*

Focus Activity

READ TO LEARN

What did Alexander the Great do to spread legacies of Greek civilization?

PEOPLE

- Alexander
- Aristotle

PLACES

- Macedonia
- Alexandria

THE BIG PICTURE

In the late 400s B.C. the Peloponnesian Wars raged in Greece. During this time the Persian empire, which you read about in the last lesson, still controlled a huge part of the world. Egyptians, Phoenicians, Jews, Babylonians, and Indians all lived under the rule of Persian kings. Connecting this empire was a network of roads and messenger services.

The Greek historian Herodotus may have traveled those roads around 450 B.C. He once made a 1,500-mile journey in about 90 days. He was amazed by the relay of royal messengers who traveled the same roads in just nine days! "Neither snow nor rain nor heat nor night holds back [the messenger from] the accomplishment of the course that has been assigned him," he marveled. Today the United States Postal Service uses similar words to describe the task of letter carriers as they transport mail across the country and around the world.

A man named Alexander traveled the roads of the Persian empire between 334 and 323 B.C., a little over 100 years after Herodotus. He conquered many areas and eventually became known as "Alexander the Great." As a result of his victories, Greek language and traditions spread as far as Egypt in Africa and the Indus Valley in Asia.

ALEXANDER OF MACEDONIA

Although the Peloponnesian Wars ended in 404 B.C., conflict continued to weaken the Greek city-states. This left them open to attack from Macedonia (mas ih DAHN nee uh), a powerful kingdom to the north. By 336 B.C. Macedonia's army had conquered most of Greece.

Macedonia's king at this time was a 20-year-old man named Alexander. He had already proven that he was a bold commander. He was also well educated. Aristotle (AR uh staht ul), one of the most famous philosophers in Athens, had been his private teacher. Because of Aristotle's teachings, Alexander developed a deep respect for Greek culture and traditions.

Expanding the Empire

In 334 B.C. Alexander and his armies set out to conquer Persia. Find their route on the map on the next page. For three years they fought their way along the eastern coast of the Mediterranean. Everywhere they went, they seized food and whatever else they needed to continue their journey.

The powerful Macedonian army never lost a battle. In 331 B.C. Alexander proclaimed, or publicly declared, himself ruler of Persia's vast empire as well as of Greece. To secure his power, Alexander pushed his army farther east.

In a few more years his troops had entered the Indus River valley. There they defeated an army that used elephants. Many of Alexander's soldiers had never seen such animals before. After his victory, though, the young emperor became sick. Unable to complete the journey, he died in June 323 B.C., in Babylon.

Alexander the Great was a brilliant military leader. These works of art show Alexander in battle.

A CITY IN THE EMPIRE

About nine years before he died, Alexander planned the creation of a city in Egypt, on the western edge of the Nile Delta. Alexandria, named after the emperor, soon became one of the most important cities in the Greek empire. The city of Alexandria was an example of how Greek civilization and ideas were carried far beyond Greece.

A Blending of Cultures

Like the many cities that Alexander had built, Alexandria's basic layout mirrored a Greek polis. It had an agora, a theater, several temples, a stadium, and a gymnasium. Alexandria's harbor became a major hub of Mediterranean trade. At the mouth of the harbor stood a gigantic lighthouse. This was one of the first lighthouses in the world. Its beam was a guide for sailors many miles away at sea.

The mixture of peoples and cultures in Alexandria created an unusual community. Besides building temples to Greek gods, Alexander planned a temple to the Egyptian goddess Isis. The Greek and Macedonian citizens of Alexandria took part in democratic assemblies. Egyptians in Alexandria had courts of their own. So did the city's Jews, who lived in their own section of the city. Craftworkers made Greek-style pottery. Papermakers continued to practice their ancient craft.

A Legacy of Learning

Not far from Alexandria's busy agora stood the city's museum. At the museum, scholars studied the world and how it worked. To help with their research,

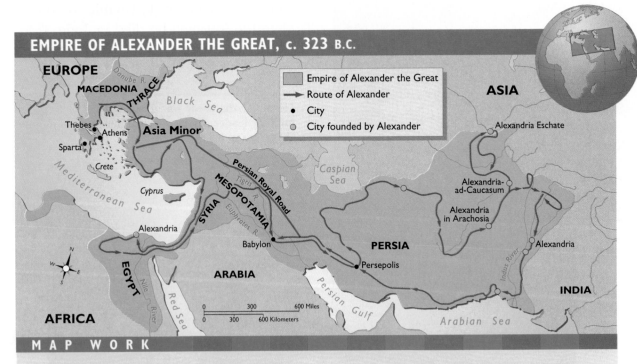

EMPIRE OF ALEXANDER THE GREAT, c. 323 B.C.

Empire of Alexander the Great
→ Route of Alexander
• City
○ City founded by Alexander

EUROPE
MACEDONIA
THRACE
Black Sea
Thebes
Athens
Sparta
Crete
Asia Minor
Mediterranean Sea
Cyprus
SYRIA
MESOPOTAMIA
Tigris R.
Euphrates R.
Persian Royal Road
Caspian Sea
ASIA
Alexandria Eschate
Alexandria-ad-Caucasus
Alexandria in Arachosia
Alexandria
Alexandria
Babylon
PERSIA
Persepolis
Indus River
EGYPT
ARABIA
Nile River
Red Sea
Persian Gulf
INDIA
AFRICA
Arabian Sea

0   300   600 Miles
0   300   600 Kilometers

MAP WORK

Alexander the Great controlled enormous territories with the help of a very powerful army.

1. Alexander's vast empire included land on three continents. What are they?

2. What region south of Mesopotamia did Alexander not gain control of?

3. What is the easternmost river within Alexander's empire?

4. What river marks the northernmost border of Alexander's empire?

5. In which direction did Alexander travel along the coast of the Arabian Sea?

they used the books in the library nearby. Alexandria's library had almost 500,000 books written on papyrus rolls, and librarians were always searching for more! Inspectors at the harbor searched newly arrived ships to see if they carried any books. They kept whatever they found until copies could be made for the city's library.

Alexander (left) founded Alexandria, one of the most important cities in the Greek empire. Today it is the second largest city in Egypt.

An Alphabet

Scholars from many countries visited the library in Alexandria to study the books there. The skills of reading and writing had become important for preserving information. Unlike Egyptian hieroglyphics, Mesopotamian cuneiform, and Chinese characters, written Greek used a simple alphabet. Each symbol represented a sound. Learning to read required mastering less than 30 letters, rather than hundreds of symbols. The alphabet made it easier for more people to learn to read and write.

Math and Science

The library in Alexandria contained many books on mathematics. Ancient Greece produced brilliant mathematicians. They had learned a great deal from earlier Egyptian scholars, whose achievements in math and science you learned about in Chapter 4. Today many of the things you do in math class are legacies of their work. *Arithmetic, geometry,* and *mathematics* are all words that have Greek origins.

Infographic

Seven Wonders of the World

Around the time of Alexander, travelers told of the "Seven Wonders of the World." They were called wonders because of their size, beauty, craftwork, or all three. Today only the pyramids still stand, but many people try to imagine the other ancient wonders. This is an artist's idea of what they may have looked like.

Are there Seven Wonders of the modern world? What list would you give a traveler today?

216

1 Statue of Zeus at Olympia
about 435 B.C.

The statue of Zeus showed the god on his throne. It is said to have been about 40 feet high. Historians say it was probably the most famous statue in the ancient world.

2 Temple of Artemis at Ephesus
about 550 B.C.

This temple is said to have been more than 40 feet high. It was made almost entirely of marble and was dedicated to the Greek god Artemis.

3 Mausoleum at Halicarnassus
about 353 B.C.

This tomb was built for a Persian ruler called Mausolus. It was decorated with a pyramid. The tomb was so famous that all large tombs are now called *mausoleums*.

4 Colossus of Rhodes
about 200 B.C.

The Colossus was a bronze statue built to honor the sun god Helios. A Greek sculptor is said to have worked for 12 years to create the statue.

5 Lighthouse of Alexandria
about 283-246 B.C.

This lighthouse stood over 400 feet high. A fire that burned at the top of it guided ships into the harbor of Alexandria for about 1,500 years.

6 Pyramids of Egypt at Giza
about 2600-2500 B.C.

The pyramids were built as tombs for Egyptian kings. The largest one, called the Great Pyramid, stands about 450 feet high.

7 Hanging Gardens of Babylon
about 605-562 B.C.

These gardens were probably laid out on a large terrace about 75 feet above the ground. They were watered by the Euphrates River.

WHY IT MATTERS

After Alexander died, no one person was able to control the vast empire. By 300 B.C. Alexander's generals had divided it up.

Although Alexander's empire did not last, his short rule had far-reaching effects. One of the most important was the mixing of cultures throughout North Africa and western and central Asia.

Many legacies of ancient Greece continue to influence cultures today. You can see Greek influence in classes on such subjects as math, philosophy, and science. Perhaps most important, Greek ideas live on in the way our government operates—as a democracy.

✓ Reviewing Facts and Ideas

MAIN IDEAS

- When Alexander the Great conquered the Persian empire, he spread Greek culture from Egypt to India.

- Alexandria, one of the empire's most powerful cities, reflected the great mix of cultures within the empire.

- Legacies from ancient Greece influence today's education, government, philosophy, sports, and drama.

THINK ABOUT IT

1. How was Alexander influenced by Greek culture?

2. What did Alexandria have in common with a polis? How was it influenced by a variety of cultures?

3. **FOCUS** How did Alexander change life around the Mediterranean region?

4. **THINKING SKILL** What *conclusions* can you *make* about Greece's importance to history?

5. **WRITE** In one paragraph describe how a Greek legacy affects your life.

CITIZENSHIP
VIEWPOINTS

Historians often have very different viewpoints on historical figures such as Alexander the Great.

How Great was Alexander the Great?

Over the centuries, historians have had different opinions of Alexander the Great, some good and some not. One historian has called him the "greatest general of all times." Others, however, have labeled him a "ruthless murderer" and a "cruel dictator."

One ancient Greek historian, Plutarch, believed that Alexander was a man of vision who tried to bring people of different areas into a great world state. Plutarch lived around the first century A.D., over 300 years after the death of Alexander. Arrian, a Greek historian from the second century A.D., also praised Alexander. Arrian wrote a biography of Alexander, saying that he was very heroic and inspired great confidence in his men. Arrian based the biography on the accounts of two of Alexander's generals.

A modern historian, Eugene Borza, offers a different view. He feels that Alexander needlessly killed many people and that he was considered ruthless by those he conquered. He also believes that Alexander was more interested in gaining a large empire than in spreading civilization. Consider three viewpoints on this issue and answer the questions that follow.

Three DIFFERENT Viewpoints

1 PLUTARCH
Historian, Ancient Greece
Excerpt from writings, A.D. 90

Alexander, by founding more than seventy cities among the barbarian tribes, . . . suppressed their savage and uncivilized customs. . . . Those whom Alexander conquered were more fortunate than those who escaped. . . . [He] conducted himself . . . out of a desire to [give] all the races in the world . . . one rule and one form of government, making all mankind a single people.

". . . making all mankind a single people."

2 ARRIAN
Historian, Ancient Greece
Excerpt from The Age of Alexander, A.D. 171

[Alexander] was . . . very [famous] for rousing the courage of his soldiers, filling them with hopes of success and dispelling their fear in the midst of danger by his own freedom from fear. . . . I think there was at that time no race of men, no city . . . to whom Alexander's name and fame had not [reached]. For this reason it seems to me that a hero [like him] could not have been born without the [help of the gods].

". . . filling them with hopes of success and dispelling their fear . . ."

3 EUGENE N. BORZA
Historian and professor of ancient history, North Dakota
Excerpt from interview, 1997

[Alexander] slaughtered hundreds of thousands of innocent civilians in his conquests. . . . He ended the Persian empire, but he was not a good organizer and his empire fell apart as soon as he died. He was ill-tempered and had a strange personality. . . . In Central Asia he is remembered as a ruthless conqueror. He did not intend to spread the civilization of the Greeks to the East. It happened as a by-product of his wars, but it was not his intent.

"He did not intend to spread the civilization of the Greeks . . ."

BUILDING CITIZENSHIP

1. What is the viewpoint of each person?
2. In what ways are some of the viewpoints alike? In what ways are they different? How might the time period in which a person lived affect his or her viewpoint?
3. What resources could you use to form your own opinion of Alexander the Great?

SHARING VIEWPOINTS

Discuss what you agree with or disagree with about these and other viewpoints. Discuss what makes an historical figure truly "great." Then as a class, write three statements that all of you can agree with about Alexander the Great.

CHAPTER 8 REVIEW

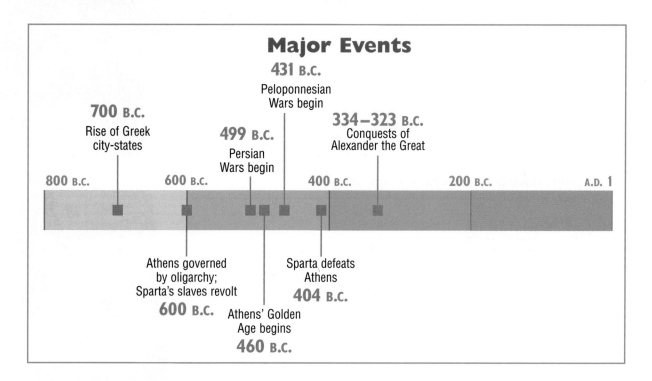

Major Events

431 B.C.
Peloponnesian
Wars begin

700 B.C.
Rise of Greek
city-states

499 B.C.
Persian
Wars begin

334–323 B.C.
Conquests of
Alexander the Great

800 B.C.   600 B.C.   400 B.C.   200 B.C.   A.D. 1

Athens governed
by oligarchy;
Sparta's slaves revolt
600 B.C.

Athens' Golden
Age begins
460 B.C.

Sparta defeats
Athens
404 B.C.

THINKING ABOUT VOCABULARY

Number a sheet of paper from 1 to 10. Beside each number write the word from the list below that matches the statement.

acropolis	monarchy
assembly	oligarchy
democracy	peninsula
harbor	philosophy
jury	polis

1. A government of one ruler
2. A law-making body of government
3. Rule by the people
4. A group of citizens chosen to decide in court cases
5. A large hill where city residents went for safety
6. An area of land nearly surrounded by water
7. A sheltered place along a coast
8. A Greek city-state
9. The search for wisdom and the right way to live
10. Rule by a small, rich group

THINKING ABOUT FACTS

1. What were two main crops of the ancient Greeks?
2. What was the largest city-state in Greece in 700 B.C.? What made this city-state strong?
3. What did Socrates teach? Why was he put to death?
4. How did Alexander the Great affect the history of his time?
5. Look at the time line above. What important events happened between 500 and 400 B.C? Why was the century such an important one for Athens?

THINK AND WRITE

WRITING ABOUT CONTRASTS
Reread pages 198–199. Then write a paragraph describing the main differences between Athens and Sparta.

WRITING ABOUT PERSPECTIVES
Suppose you live in ancient Athens. Write a paragraph about why you think women should or should not participate fully in Athenian democracy.

WRITING BIOGRAPHIES
Write one paragraph about two of the following people: (1) Homer, (2) Socrates, (3) Pericles, and (4) Alexander the Great.

APPLYING THINKING SKILLS

MAKING CONCLUSIONS
1. What is a conclusion?
2. Reread "Did You Know?" on page 206 and make a conclusion about why the Greeks liked drama. What information did you use to come to your conclusion?
3. If you were asked to make a conclusion about how successful drama is today in America, what facts would you need to know?
4. When in your life have you made a conclusion about something but later made a different conclusion about the same thing?
5. Why is the ability to make conclusions important for studying history?

Summing Up the Chapter

Review the chapter, then copy the word map below on a separate sheet of paper. Next, fill in each box with at least two related details. After you have filled in the details, use the word map to write a paragraph that answers the question "What did the ancient Greeks contribute to world civilization?"

Geography
....
peninsula

Sparta
....

Athens
....

ANCIENT GREECE

Wars
....

Legacy
....

Greek Empire
....
Spread of Greek learning

Ancient Rome

THINKING ABOUT
HISTORY AND GEOGRAPHY

About 700 B.C. people of the Italian peninsula founded a city called Rome. Within 200 years, Rome would develop a government ruled by its citizens. Under later rulers, Rome grew into a vast empire that stretched across Europe, touching Africa and western Asia. The influence of this great empire, including its laws, language, technology, and religion, spread far and wide and has lasted into modern times.

509 B.C.

ROME
Roman citizens start a republic

48 B.C.

ALEXANDRIA
Julius Caesar and Cleopatra join forces

27 B.C.

ROME
Augustus becomes the first Roman emperor and continues expansion of the empire

500 B.C.   250 B.C.   A.D. 1

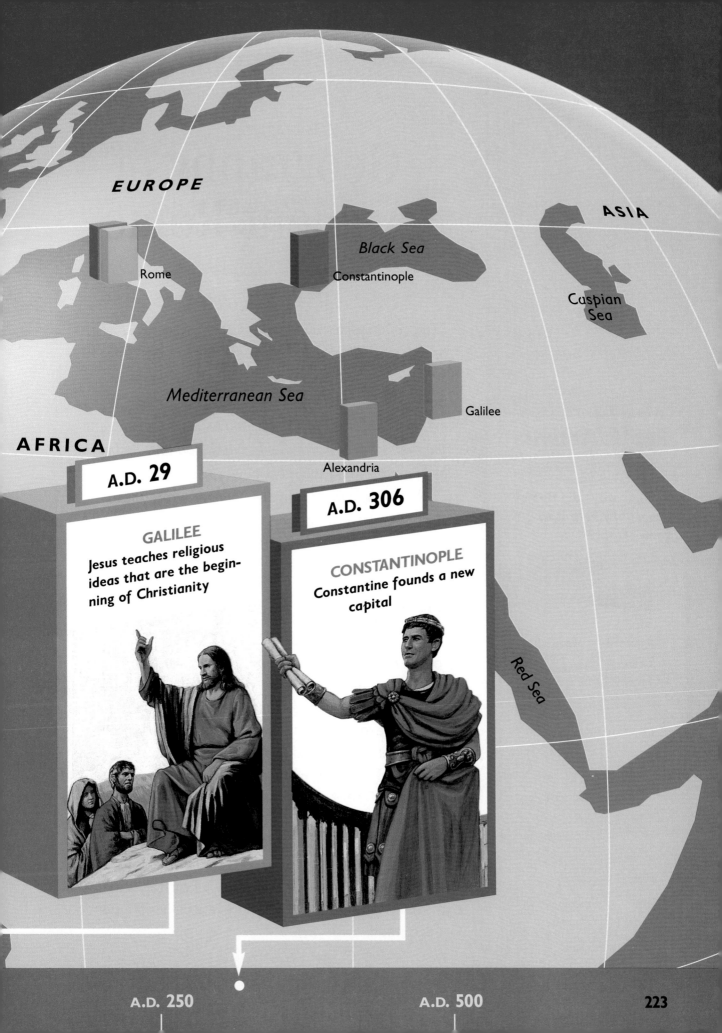

EUROPE

ASIA

Black Sea

Rome

Constantinople

Caspian
Sea

Mediterranean Sea

Galilee

AFRICA

Alexandria

A.D. 29

A.D. 306

GALILEE
Jesus teaches religious ideas that are the beginning of Christianity

CONSTANTINOPLE
Constantine founds a new capital

Red Sea

Geography of Ancient Rome

Read Aloud

"The countryside round here is very beautiful. . . . The broad, spreading plain is ringed by mountains, their summits topped by ancient woods of tall timber. . . . Below these the vineyards extend on every side, weaving their uniform pattern far and wide. . . . Then come the meadows and grainfields, which can only be broken by huge oxen and the most powerful plows."

A Roman named Pliny the Younger wrote these words in a letter to a friend almost 2,000 years ago. As you will see, they describe the land around ancient Rome well.

Focus Activity

READ TO LEARN

In what ways did Rome's geography help it to grow strong?

PLACES

- **Rome**
- **Sicily**
- **Alps**
- **Apennine Mountains**
- **Latium**
- **Tiber River**

THE BIG PICTURE

Around 700 B.C. people from Sparta and other city-states began leaving Greece to start new colonies in other parts of the Mediterranean region. Many sailed west to present-day Italy, where the land was rich and fertile. There the Greek colonists settled among several groups of peoples who spoke different languages and followed different customs. The communities shared in common their ways of making a living from the land.

While Sparta and Athens rose to power in Greece, another city was growing strong in Italy. That city was Rome. In time, Rome would unify all of Italy's many communities under its rule and eventually conquer Greece itself.

A BOOT INTO THE SEA

The Italian peninsula is part of the European continent. It juts out into the Mediterranean Sea like a kicking boot. Find the "toe" of the boot on the map on this page. The island to the west of the toe is called Sicily. It was a popular destination for ancient Greek colonists because of its rich farmland.

Mountains of Italy

At the northern border of present-day Italy stand the craggy Alps. The Alps are Europe's highest mountain range. Do you remember how the Himalayas separate the Indian subcontinent from the rest of Asia? The Alps wall off the Italian peninsula from the rest of Europe in a similar way.

Another mountain range has had an even greater effect on life in Italy. The Apennine (AP uh nin) Mountains form a giant "backbone" through the Italian peninsula. Their towering height makes it difficult to travel across the peninsula. The Apennines also lack rich soil, so there is more sheep herding than farming on the mountainsides.

Fertile Plains

Italy, like Greece, has much mountainous land. Also like Greece, Italy has a number of fertile plains. One important plain, Latium (LAY shee um), is located on the west coast of central Italy. The Tiber River runs through the center of this plain. Archaeologists have found remains of ancient communities on the Latium plain that date back about 3,000 years. Eventually, a great city called Rome would also arise on the plain along the Tiber River.

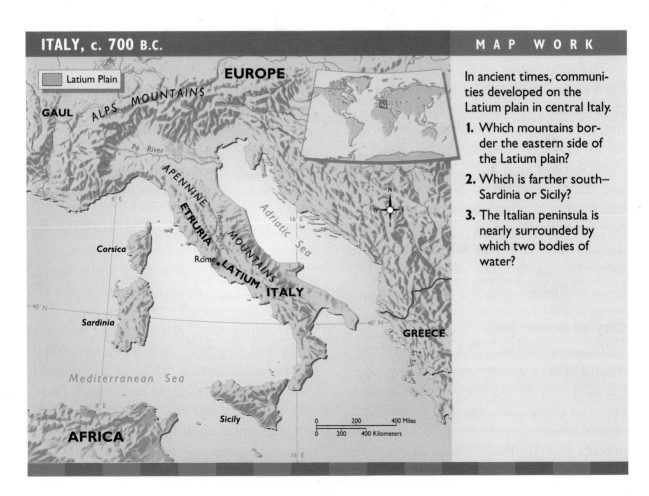

ITALY, c. 700 B.C.

Latium Plain

EUROPE

GAUL — ALPS MOUNTAINS

Po River

APENNINE

ETRURIA

Corsica

Rome — LATIUM

ITALY

Tiber River

Adriatic Sea

MOUNTAINS

Sardinia

GREECE

Mediterranean Sea

Sicily

AFRICA

0 200 400 Miles
0 200 400 Kilometers

MAP WORK

In ancient times, communities developed on the Latium plain in central Italy.

1. Which mountains border the eastern side of the Latium plain?

2. Which is farther south—Sardinia or Sicily?

3. The Italian peninsula is nearly surrounded by which two bodies of water?

A CITY ALONG THE TIBER

Today Rome is a large, modern city beside the Tiber River, on the northern edge of the Latium plain. Rome was also a great city over 2,000 years ago. How did this city come into being?

The Legend of Romulus and Remus

According to Roman legend, a king ruled a small city near the Tiber River over 2,700 years ago. His younger brother overthrew him and drove away the rest of the royal family. Later the older brother's daughter gave birth to twin boys, Romulus and Remus. The new king was afraid these boys would try to claim the throne. He gave orders to throw the twins into the flooded Tiber River. This was done—but miraculously the boys did not drown. They were both washed up on a hilltop where a wolf happened along and rescued them.

The story goes on to say that a shepherd came upon the wolf's den and took the boys home. Romulus and Remus grew up to be strong and brave. In the end they helped their grandfather become king again. Then Romulus and Remus founded a new city on the hill where they had been rescued. The two brothers fought over the naming of the city, and Romulus killed Remus. The city was named Rome after its first king, Romulus.

City of Seven Hills

The story of Romulus and Remus is a legend. There are, however, many good reasons why Rome grew where it did. First, as Rome developed, it expanded across seven hills. These hills helped to protect the city from attack. Second, the Tiber River made a fine "highway" for

An ancient Roman bridge spans the Tiber River (above). Grapes remain a major crop in Italy (right).

travel between the mountains and the Mediterranean coast. Boats brought goods from faraway seaports as well as news from communities upriver. Last but not least, the Latium plain was surrounded by inactive volcanoes. Ash from earlier eruptions had created a thin but rich soil. As a result, farmers were able to produce large surpluses on the Latium plain.

Latium farmers grew wheat to make bread. They also grew beans, cabbage, and lettuce, as well as figs and other fruits. Perhaps most important were the grapes they raised to make wine. Grapevines grow best in rocky soil, and Italy had plenty of that. Wine sold well in the marketplace. Most people drank watered-down wine at mealtimes. People poured wine into cuts and wounds to help them heal. In time, Italy's fine wines became one of the peninsula's most valued trade goods.

Peoples of the Peninsula

Before the founding of Rome, there were other peoples who developed civilizations in Italy. One group, called the Etruscans, settled on the plain northwest of the Tiber River. Find this plain, called Etruria (ih TRUR ee uh), on the map on page 225.

Around 575 B.C. the Etruscan army conquered much of the Italian peninsula, including Rome. Etruscan kings led the city to victory over many of its neighbors in Latium. However, in about 509 B.C., the leading families of Rome overthrew their Etruscan king.

WHY IT MATTERS

During the period of Etruscan rule, Rome continued to grow and develop. However, the people of the small city on the Tiber River could not have known what the future would hold. As you will soon see, Rome would one day become the center of a mighty empire. Roman laws, language, and achievements would affect not only all of Italy, but in time, much of the world.

✓ Reviewing Facts and Ideas

MAIN IDEAS

- At the base of Italy's two mountain ranges—the Alps and the Apennines—lie fertile regions, such as the Latium plain.

- Italy's fertile plains were well used by local farmers as well as colonists from ancient Greece.

- The city of Rome was founded on seven hills. They helped to protect it from attack. The nearby Latium plain provided fertile farmland.

- Etruscan kings ruled Rome and other regions of Italy before being overthrown by Romans in 509 B.C.

THINK ABOUT IT

1. Why did grapes become an important crop in ancient Italy?

2. How did Rome come to be founded, according to legend? What role does geography play in this story?

3. **FOCUS** Why was the location of Rome a good place for a city?

4. **THINKING SKILL** What were the *causes* of farmers' success at growing grapevines in Italy?

5. **GEOGRAPHY** How did the mountains of Italy affect communication and transportation?

227

Geography Skills

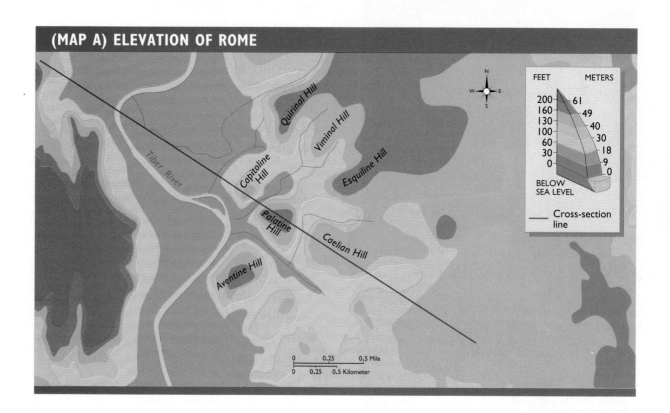

(MAP A) ELEVATION OF ROME

FEET | METERS
200 — 61
160 — 49
130 — 40
100 — 30
60 — 18
30 — 9
0 — 0
BELOW SEA LEVEL

—— Cross-section line

Quirinal Hill
Viminal Hill
Esquiline Hill
Tiber River
Capitoline Hill
Palatine Hill
Caelian Hill
Aventine Hill

0   0.25   0.5 Mile
0   0.25   0.5 Kilometer

Reading Elevation Maps and Profiles

VOCABULARY

elevation

profile

WHY THE SKILL MATTERS

The geography of the region around Rome includes a variety of landforms, ranging from jutting hills to flat plains. You can see the height of such landforms on maps. Mapmakers show differences in the height of land in several ways. For example, the varying heights of Rome can be shown using an elevation map. **Elevation** means height above sea level. Elevation can also be shown in another way. Mapmakers can take an imaginary slice of the land through a place such as Rome and make a profile map of the area. **Profile** means to view something from the side. Another term for *profile* is "cross section."

USING AN ELEVATION MAP

Study Map A. This is an elevation map of Rome and the region around it. According to the map key, elevation is measured in feet and in meters on the map. What color shows the highest elevation? What color shows the lowest elevation? Look for the part of the city with the lowest elevation. Notice that it is the area around the Tiber River, shown on the left of the map. According to the map key, the elevation here is almost at sea level. Notice that the seven hills of Rome are east of the river. One of the purposes of elevation maps is to show relative location—or, how one place in a region relates to another.

USING A PROFILE MAP

Now study Map B. This is a profile map of the same region. Find the Palatine hill on the map. This hill was where the richest people in ancient Rome lived. Based on the map key, how many feet high is this hill? Look at the height of the Palatine Hill as compared to the height of the Caelian (SEE lee un) Hill. You might find that it is often easier to see differences in elevation using a profile map like Map B. Because profile maps show only a "slice" of land, however, they do not show an area's relative location as well as elevation maps do.

TRYING THE SKILL

Now try to find other information using the elevation map and the profile map. Refer to the Helping Yourself box if you need help answering questions.

In the last lesson you read that, according to the story about the founding of Rome,

the twins Romulus and Remus were thrown into the flooded Tiber River. They were saved when they washed up on a hill. The story says the twins built the city of Rome on the spot where they were saved. Assuming that the twins washed up on the highest hill in Rome, which hill was it? How many meters higher is it than the land along the Tiber River? You can see this well on the profile map below. Find that same hill on the elevation map of Rome.

REVIEWING THE SKILL

1. What facts about these maps let you know that they are elevation and profile maps?

2. What is the difference in elevation between the Aventine Hill and the Latium plain? How did you arrive at this answer?

3. When might it be helpful to be able to read elevation and profile maps?

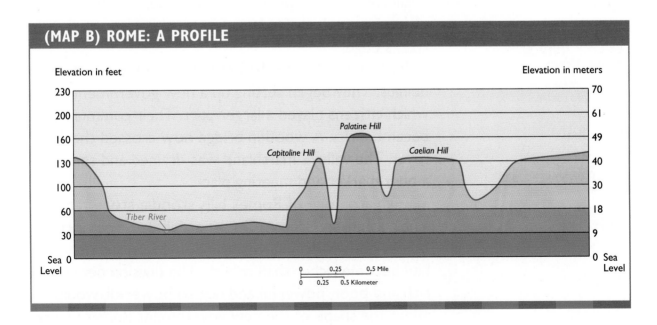

(MAP B) ROME: A PROFILE

Elevation in feet

Elevation in meters

Feet	Meters
230	70
200	61
160	49
130	40
100	30
60	18
30	9
Sea Level 0	0 Sea Level

Capitoline Hill

Palatine Hill

Caelian Hill

Tiber River

0   0.25   0.5 Mile
0   0.25   0.5 Kilometer

509 B.C.	100 B.C.	A.D. 1	A.D. 250	A.D. 500

The Rise of the Roman Republic

Focus Activity

READ TO LEARN

What kind of government did the Romans establish?

VOCABULARY

- plebeian
- patrician
- republic
- representative
- Senate
- tribune
- consul
- Twelve Tables
- Punic Wars

PEOPLE

- Livy
- Hannibal
- Scipio

PLACES

- Forum
- Carthage
- Zama

Read Aloud

The Roman leader Cicero declared that Rome should be governed by its "best" citizens. But just who were Rome's "best" citizens? Were they the city's small circle of nobles? Or did they also include the many other citizens, poor and rich, who contributed to life in Rome? The way Romans answered this question would shape their lives and ours.

THE BIG PICTURE

Almost 3,000 years ago, when the city of Anyang in China was losing power, Rome was only a cluster of mud huts on the hills overlooking the Tiber River. From the hilltops, farmers could enjoy a view of two small lakes that rippled in the valley below. The sound of lowing cattle drifted across the marshland at the river's edge.

By 509 B.C. Romans had overthrown their king, Tarquinius. They began setting up a new government in which citizens played a larger part. Their community became a city. A wooden bridge now crossed the Tiber River. The valley's marshland was drained and served as a busy market and meeting place.

High atop one of Rome's hills stood a stone temple as big as any in Greece. On other hilltops, fine brick homes housed Rome's wealthy. Some Romans clearly had become richer than others. The division between rich and poor, powerful and not so powerful, would affect the shape of the new government Romans were creating for themselves.

THE CITIZENS OF ROME

As in Greece, society in Rome was divided into two groups: those who were citizens and those who were not. At first, Rome had few slaves. The city did have many women, but none of them were citizens.

The body of citizens included two groups. Most Roman citizens were **plebeians** (plih BEE unz). Plebeians were men who farmed, traded, and made things for a living. The second group was made up of Rome's handful of **patricians** (puh TRISH unz). Patricians were members of Rome's noble families. They owned large farms and had plebeians work the land for them.

Plebeians Protest

After Rome's last king was overthrown in 509 B.C., the patricians took power. As they did this they remade the city's government. Only patricians could belong to a ruling assembly or become government leaders.

Rome's many plebeians reacted to the patricians' rules with protest. According to the Roman historian **Livy**,

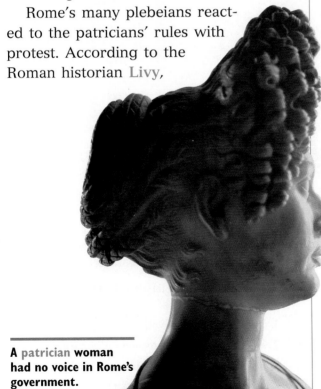

A **patrician** woman had no voice in Rome's government.

plebeians rebelled in 494 B.C., demanding changes in the government. To calm them down, Livy wrote, the patricians sent a popular leader to speak with the plebeians. He told them this story. How do you suppose the plebeians reacted?

MANY VOICES
PRIMARY SOURCE

Excerpt from
Stories of Rome, Livy, c. 20 B.C.

*Once upon a time, the different parts of the human body were not all in agreement. . . . And it seemed very unfair to the other parts of the body that they should worry and sweat away to look after the belly. After all, the belly just sat there . . . doing nothing, enjoying all the nice things that came along. So they hatched a plot. The hands weren't going to take food to the mouth; even if they did, the mouth wasn't going to accept it. . . . They went into a **sulk** and waited for the belly to cry for help. But while they waited, one by one all the parts of the body got weaker and weaker. The moral of this story? The belly too has its job to do. It has to be fed, but it also does feeding of its own.*

---

sulk: to be in a bad mood and stay silent

A New Government

According to Livy both sides in time agreed to work together to improve Rome's government. The new government was called a **republic**, which means "public things" in Latin. Latin was the language of ancient Rome. In a republic citizens choose their leaders.

GOVERNING THE REPUBLIC

Unlike in the democracy of Athens, not all Roman citizens participated in the assembly that ran their city. Instead, they elected representatives, people who acted for them.

Does this sound familiar? The government of the United States is often called a republic. Citizens elect representatives who serve in Congress or in state legislatures. Unlike in the United States, however, not all the votes of Roman citizens were equal. In Rome the more powerful a man was, the greater influence his vote had.

Rome's republic lasted for nearly 500 years. During that time, three different government branches ran the city's affairs. Each of these branches had decision-making powers that allowed it to have some control over the actions of the other branches. What were the three branches?

The oldest and most powerful branch of the republic was the Senate. The Senate was controlled by Rome's patricians. Like the Senate of the United States, the Roman Senate determined how Rome would act toward other governments. It also had control of all the money collected and spent by the Roman Republic.

Power for the Plebeians

To make their voices heard in Rome, plebeians formed a citizen assembly. Beginning in 494 B.C., the citizen assembly elected tribunes (trih BYOONZ) who worked to gain rights for the plebeians of Rome. The tribunes were the leaders of the large citizen assembly.

The Consuls

Early tribunes worked to make sure plebeians got fair trials. They brought plebeian complaints before the Senate and the consuls. The consuls were the third branch of Rome's republic.

Each year the citizen assembly elected two men to become consuls. Consuls served as Rome's army commanders and the city's most powerful judges. They could order anyone to be arrested. The consuls could also propose new laws for Rome. The citizen assembly, however, could veto, or stop, any of the consuls' actions.

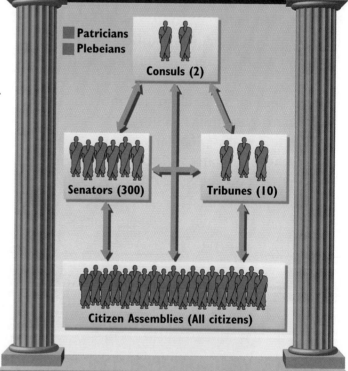

ROMAN GOVERNMENT ABOUT 287 B.C.

- Patricians
- Plebeians

Consuls (2)

Senators (300) Tribunes (10)

Citizen Assemblies (All citizens)

CHART WORK

Both patricians and plebeians had a role in the government of Rome.

1. Which citizens served as Rome's consuls?
2. How many citizens served as Senators?
3. In which parts of government could plebeians participate?

Power in Rome was shared, if very unevenly, among the different branches of the republic. Study the chart to see how power was divided.

Plebeian Influence Grows

The citizens in the assembly often met to vote in a large field along the Tiber River. The field was also the headquarters of Rome's mostly plebeian army. Rome's patricians depended heavily on the army. In its early years Rome was constantly at war.

The plebeian army protected both the city of Rome and its patrician leaders. This role gave plebeians added power to change Rome's government in an important way.

For many years patrician leaders had ruled Rome according to laws that were unwritten. Only the patrician leaders had knowledge of those laws. As a result, plebeians had no way of knowing just what was and was not against the law. If brought to court, plebeians could only hope that the patrician judges would give them a fair trial.

About 450 B.C. the plebeians protested the unfairness of Rome's unwritten laws. Finally the patricians agreed to write a collection of laws on twelve wooden tablets, or tables. These became known as the Twelve Tables.

The Laws of the Republic

Historians today know little about what the Twelve Tables actually said. They do know, though, that the laws governed everything from marriage to slavery. Plebeians could not marry patricians. People who did not pay their debts could be made slaves. Like Hammurabi's Code in Babylon, the Twelve Tables were an important step in the development of written laws.

The Twelve Tables were posted in the city's crowded Forum. In the late 400s B.C. the Forum was a gravel clearing not much bigger than a soccer field. This clearing was the center of life in Rome. Here senators met and citizens pleaded their cases before judges. Women sometimes joined in the debates that took place there, hoping to influence those who could vote.

This painting shows a Roman trial by law. The Twelve Tables developed into a code of laws that influenced the laws of many future governments.

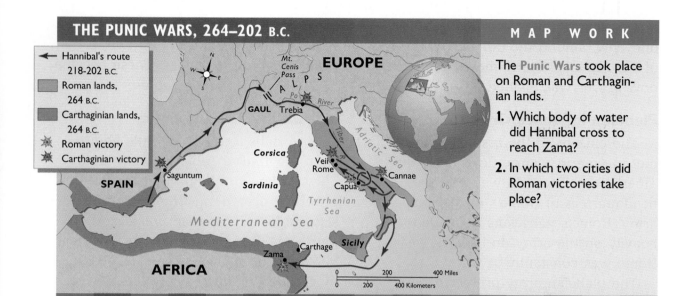

Legend:
- Hannibal's route 218-202 B.C.
- Roman lands, 264 B.C.
- Carthaginian lands, 264 B.C.
- Roman victory
- Carthaginian victory

EUROPE

Mt. Cenis Pass

ALPS

GAUL — Po River — Trebia

Corsica

Adriatic Sea

Veii — Rome

Saguntum

Sardinia

Capua — Cannae

SPAIN

Tyrrhenian Sea

Mediterranean Sea

Zama — Carthage — Sicily

AFRICA

0 200 400 Miles
0 200 400 Kilometers

The Punic Wars took place on Roman and Carthaginian lands.

1. Which body of water did Hannibal cross to reach Zama?
2. In which two cities did Roman victories take place?

THE REPUBLIC EXPANDS

The Roman army moved out across the peninsula to conquer other areas. By 265 B.C. Rome controlled all of the Italian peninsula.

A Rival Across the Sea

In 264 B.C. Roman soldiers landed on the island of Sicily. Their arrival sparked a long conflict with the powerful empire of Carthage. Carthage was a city based in present-day Tunisia, on the northern coast of Africa. This city controlled much of the land around the western Mediterranean, including Sicily. Since Carthage had once been a colony of Phoenicia, Romans named their conflicts with that city the Punic Wars. *Punic* comes from the Latin word for Phoenicia.

In 241 B.C., after more than 20 years of fighting, Carthage surrendered control of Sicily to Rome. Rome then seized even more of the lands controlled by Carthage. The leaders of Carthage were outraged! One general asked his son Hannibal to seek revenge. In 218 B.C., when he was 29 years old, Hannibal led an army against the forces of Rome.

Hannibal's Plan

Hannibal came up with a daring plan. Since Rome's navy controlled the waters around Italy, he decided to attack by land. Hannibal marched from Spain to Rome with an army of about 90,000 men. He also brought elephants, which scared the Romans. In front of Hannibal, though, lay 1,000 miles of enemy territory.

More than 15 soldiers could ride atop one of Hannibal's elephants.

The Granger Collection

The army from Carthage actually carried out much of this plan, though thousands died along the way. Hannibal won major battles in Italy and caused great destruction there. Hannibal's success, however, did not win victory for Carthage. In Rome a 25-year-old general, Scipio (SIHP ee oh), was elected as consul. Scipio's large army defeated Hannibal outside Carthage in the Battle of Zama in 202 B.C. The defeat of Hannibal gave Rome control over Carthage's vast territory. Rome became the most powerful nation in the Mediterranean region.

The Changing Republic

All of these changes upset the workings of the republic. Patricians and plebeians struggled for government control. Slaves and conquered peoples revolted against their Roman leaders. Roman generals used their troops to take control of the government. By about 100 B.C. the republican government of Rome was fighting for its life.

WHY IT MATTERS

When the Roman republic was first set up, participation was limited to those who lived in and around the city. By 100 B.C., though, the republic was huge. It extended around the Mediterranean Sea and included millions of people.

The republic would not long survive. However, the ideas about how people could govern themselves—using a Senate, a people's assembly, and elected officials—would inspire the creators of the United States government over 2,000 years later.

✓ Reviewing Facts and Ideas

MAIN IDEAS

- After about 509 B.C. Rome's citizens created a republic in which citizens elected leaders to run the government. Wealthy patrician citizens had more power than plebeian citizens.

- The republic of Rome was divided into three main branches—the Senate, the citizen assembly, and the consuls.

- Defeating Carthage in the Punic Wars made Rome the leading power in the Mediterranean region by 202 B.C.

THINK ABOUT IT

1. Describe the differences between patricians and plebeians.

2. Why was it important for Rome's laws to be written down?

3. **FOCUS** How did the struggle between the plebeians and patricians affect Roman government?

4. **THINKING SKILL** *Make conclusions* about the importance of the Punic Wars to Rome's history.

5. **WRITE** In a paragraph, explain the branches of Rome's republic.

500 B.C.   250 B.C.   100 B.C.   A.D. 14   A.D. 250   A.D. 500

The Roman Empire

Read Aloud

"He found Rome built of brick and left it in marble." About 2,000 years ago, the biographer Suetonius (swih TOH nee us) wrote these words to describe how greatly Rome had changed under the leadership of one man. That leader was Augustus (aw GUS tus), the first Roman emperor.

Focus Activity

READ TO LEARN

What events led to the Pax Romana?

VOCABULARY

- Pax Romana
- civil war
- dictator
- aqueduct
- census
- gladiator

PEOPLE

- Julius Caesar
- Cleopatra
- Augustus

PLACES

- Gaul
- Colosseum
- Pantheon
- Pompeii

THE BIG PICTURE

About 100 B.C. the leaders of the Han dynasty were ruling a unified China. Around the Mediterranean, meanwhile, the struggle for power in Rome grew. Patricians and plebeians each tried to win control for themselves. As problems in Rome increased, conquered peoples rebelled against their Roman governors.

By the century's end, though, a period known as the Pax Romana began. *Pax Romana* is Latin for "Roman peace." During the Pax Romana, which lasted about 200 years, goods moved freely within Rome's far-reaching borders. In Rome the people had bread to eat each day, thanks to shipments of North African wheat. They could cook in pots made from Spanish copper. Wealthy Romans ordered clothes made from Greek wool, Egyptian linen, or even Chinese silk! These goods were bought, along with pepper and pearls, by traders at markets in Asia. The Pax Romana benefited other nations, too, as Roman money and goods flowed in.

How did peace replace war in Rome? The story is a complex one. The story of Augustus and the building of a Roman empire actually begins with a leader who ruled before him.

THE RULE OF CAESAR

Julius Caesar (JOOL yus SEE zur) was born into a patrician family in 100 B.C. As a boy, he dreamed of becoming a Senate leader, which he did. He also served as a commander in the army.

By 59 B.C. Caesar was elected consul of Rome. The following year he became the military governor of Gaul—which today is France. There he won fame, riches, and the loyalty of a great army. Caesar could now try for his biggest goal—total control of Rome.

Civil War

In 49 B.C. Caesar and his rebel army marched into Italy. Civil war, or war between groups within one country, began. This war spilled into Egypt. There Caesar joined forces with Cleopatra (klee uh PA truh). She was the 21-year-old ruler of the Egyptian government based in Alexandria. In Chapter 8 you read about this Greek city-state on the Nile Delta.

Caesar helped Cleopatra defeat her brother, the pharaoh of Egypt. She gave Caesar money he needed to continue fighting for control of Rome. In 45 B.C. Caesar returned in triumph to Rome and made himself dictator. A dictator is someone who rules with absolute power. Government under a dictator is called a dictatorship.

A New Government

As dictator, Julius Caesar made important changes to life in Rome. He changed the way people measured time—creating the basis for the calendar we still use today. In Julius's honor the month of his birth was named "July." Caesar also gave land to his soldiers and free grain to poor citizens. He increased the number of people who could serve in the Senate. Also, he granted Roman citizenship to many people not born in Rome.

Some senators hated Caesar for ruling as a dictator. They felt he was destroying the traditions of Rome's republican government. Some began plotting to kill him. According to legend, a friend warned Caesar to "Beware the Ides (ĪDZ) of March," which is March 15. Caesar ignored the warning. On that day in 44 B.C. he arrived at the Senate, as usual without a bodyguard. There he was stabbed to death by enemies. The senators who killed Caesar believed they had saved the republic from dictatorship.

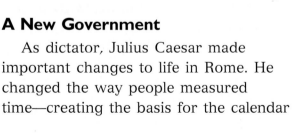

Cleopatra (coin, above) supported Caesar before his murder (right).

EMPEROR AUGUSTUS

After Caesar's death, civil war broke out once more as different groups fought for control. After 14 long years of fighting, the winner was Julius Caesar's grand-nephew and adopted son Octavian. He was just 18 years old when the fighting began. By 27 B.C. Octavian had defeated some of Rome's most experienced generals. These victories cleared the way for him to become dictator in all but name. As a sign of his new power, Octavian took the name Augustus, or "honored one." The month of August is named after this powerful ruler and general who helped to build Rome into a huge empire.

Pax Romana

Under Augustus, life throughout the Roman empire underwent great changes. Most important, his rule began the Pax Romana. During this period of peace Augustus ordered the building of new roads, buildings, and water systems. Like the emperors of China, Augustus also worked to create a single system of government and money throughout the empire.

Both the empire itself and the city of Rome now were bigger than ever. About one million people lived in the city of Rome. In the city's center the Forum now included large marble temples and government buildings. Nearby stood new theaters and public baths. New waterways called aqueducts (AK wuh duktz) were built to bring streams of fresh water into the city.

Thanks to Augustus, Romans now enjoyed police and fire protection. Even so, daily life had its unexpected dangers. Read this amusing description of Roman life. How did Rome's cramped quarters affect the way people lived?

MANY VOICES
PRIMARY SOURCE

Excerpt from
Satires, by Juvenal, c. A.D. 100.

*To get to an urgent business call, the rich man travels by **litter** and the crowd has to give way as the huge contraption is hurried along over their heads—while inside he reads, or writes, or just sleeps. . . . We might get a move on but for the people in front blocking our way. . . . Someone digs me in the ribs with his elbow; someone else hits me with a **sedan-chair** pole. A **beam** catches me full in the face; someone else drops a barrel on my head. My legs are caked with mud and I'm trampled to death by huge feet and my toes are flattened by a soldier's hobnailed boot.*

---

litter: a covered couch used for carrying a single passenger
sedan-chair: a chair carried on poles by two people
beam: a long piece of heavy wood

Roman **aqueducts** (left) brought millions of gallons of water each day to Roman cities. Modern travelers still find Roman roads in use in Europe (below).

Running an Empire

From Spain to Sparta, Alexandria to Jerusalem, people felt the pull of Rome through its laws. Laws were upheld by governors who also acted as judges.

The pull of Rome was even stronger through its taxes. Taxes paid by craft-workers and merchants helped to pay for the upkeep of the empire. Few people escaped paying. Every five years Rome took a **census**, or count, of people living in the empire.

Army units were posted far and wide to enforce Roman law, as well as to help build the empire's roads. Unlike the soldiers of the old Roman Republic, most soldiers of the Roman empire were not citizens. They were paid to serve in the army full-time. For many poor men, the army offered the best chance to earn a decent living.

Travel and Trade

One sign of the strength of the Roman government was safe travel. In the empire, the army made sure that bandits could not threaten citizens on land or sea. On the empire's roads, soldiers passed messengers carrying letters written on papyrus sheets. The Roman empire had a mail system similar to America's pony express. Every 8 miles riders would exchange their tired horses for fresh ones.

Merchants clattered along on ox-drawn carts, bringing goods like wine or dried fish to market. If their paths overlooked the sea, travelers probably saw merchant sailboats cutting through the blue waters. The cargoes might have included anything from Spanish silver to Egyptian linen.

"All Roads Lead to Rome"

Amid the crowds of people who filled the Forum each day stood a tall stone marker. Its size reflected its importance. It marked the start of all major roads leading out of Rome.

The Roman empire at its peak was crisscrossed by more than 50,000 miles of roads! Those roads—along with boats—helped to make communication, trade, and travel throughout the empire possible. Not all the roads led to Rome, of course. Many of the people and goods traveling along the stone pathways, however, either began or finished there. Rome acted like a giant magnet. Everyone in the empire felt its pull on their lives in one way or another.

VAST PROJECTS

The sheer size of the Roman empire united some of the world's most skilled craftworkers and engineers. They built beautiful—as well as useful—structures that reflected the empire's great wealth and power.

Throughout the empire Roman engineers built long aqueducts to bring fresh water to cities. Engineers spanned rivers with stone bridges to speed up the movement of soldiers and merchants. For cleanliness, engineers built public baths complete with heated floors. For entertainment, they created huge stadiums where gladiators fought animals, such as lions or bears, or each other—often

Crowds of Romans often filled the Colosseum seats (right) to watch the popular sport of chariot racing (below).

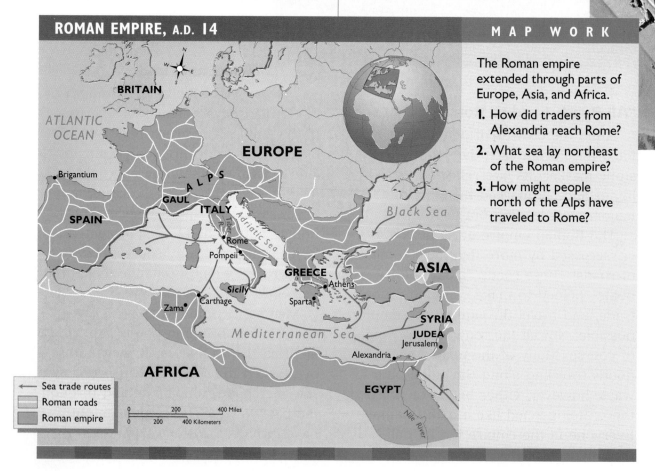

ROMAN EMPIRE, A.D. 14

BRITAIN
ATLANTIC OCEAN
EUROPE
Brigantium
ALPS
GAUL
ITALY
SPAIN
Adriatic Sea
Rome
Pompeii
Black Sea
GREECE
Athens
ASIA
Sicily
Carthage
Sparta
Zama
SYRIA
JUDEA
Mediterranean Sea
Jerusalem
AFRICA
Alexandria
EGYPT
Nile River

Sea trade routes
Roman roads
Roman empire

0   200   400 Miles
0   200   400 Kilometers

MAP WORK

The Roman empire extended through parts of Europe, Asia, and Africa.

1. How did traders from Alexandria reach Rome?

2. What sea lay northeast of the Roman empire?

3. How might people north of the Alps have traveled to Rome?

A Fabulous Temple

About a mile west of the Colosseum stood another Roman monument—the Pantheon. The Pantheon was just one of many temples in the city. It honored all the gods and goddesses of the Roman world.

By the time of the empire, Romans honored gods and goddesses from many parts of the world. They believed that these gods and goddesses had helped Rome to grow. For example, the Romans worshiped the major gods and goddesses of Greece, although they gave them Latin names. Many Romans also made sacrifices to Isis, the powerful goddess of Egypt, and Mithra, a Persian sun-god.

Large temples were also built to honor emperors like Augustus. Emperors of Rome were thought to become gods when they died.

to the death. Most of the gladiators were slaves. Some, however, were condemned criminals or prisoners of war. All were forced to fight in bloody contests of strength.

Many of these contests were held in the largest and most famous stadium in Rome, the Colosseum (kol uh SEE um), completed in 80 A.D. It held about 50,000 people. The Colosseum was so vast that fake sea battles were staged in it! Among the other contests that ancient Romans held in their stadiums were chariot races.

DID YOU KNOW?

How were Roman architects able to build large, lasting structures?

Roman architects mixed sand, lime, and pieces of stone and brick to make the very first cement. They used this material to bind stones and bricks into walls and foundations. Using its strength, the Romans built temples, bridges, and baths that still stand today.

Modern builders make cement in much the same way. They use it to build sidewalks, swimming pools, apartment buildings, and bridges. Perhaps some of these structures will last 2,000 years too.

Daily Life in Pompeii

You have read about many aspects of life in the Roman empire. How did ordinary people live during the days of Augustus and later emperors? Here are a few things archaeologists have found in the Roman city of Pompeii (pahm PAY). You can find this city on the map on page 240. Pompeii was destroyed by the eruption of Mount Vesuvius in A.D. 79. Many artifacts have been preserved in the volcanic ash that fell on the city. What similarities can you find between items shown here and things you see every day?

Makeup Kit

Makeup kits (right) included white powdered chalk, red ocher (iron dust), and ash. Perfume was another popular item among the women of Rome.

Mosaic of Wealthy Woman

Wealthy Roman women wore different kinds of jewelry. Some also had their ears pierced for earrings.

Carbonized Bodies

Up to 13 feet of volcanic ash suddenly rained down on the city, trapping people beneath it. The ash quickly hardened, preserving the bodies.

Serving Bowls

Partly eaten meals—here eggs and hazelnuts (left and below)—were among the items in Pompeii preserved in volcanic ash.

"Beware of Dog"

Guard dogs were sometimes kept chained to a door. Signs (above) warned would-be thieves not to enter.

WHY IT MATTERS

Under Julius Caesar, and later, Augustus, Roman citizens lost some of the political rights they had once enjoyed. Yet under Augustus, Rome was also more peaceful than it had been for many years. Before his death in A.D. 14, Augustus also had made many improvements in daily life.

Around this time in a dusty town not far from Jerusalem another important development began that would affect the entire world. You will read about it in the next lesson.

✓ Reviewing Facts and Ideas

MAIN IDEAS

- Julius Caesar became dictator of Rome in 45 B.C. He was killed by senators opposed to his rule on the Ides of March in 44 B.C.

- Under Augustus, around 27 B.C., the Roman empire began a 200-year period of peace and active trade called the Pax Romana.

- Roman religion shared many similarities with that of ancient Greece. Romans also worshiped Egyptian and Persian gods and goddesses.

THINK ABOUT IT

1. What happened to the republican government of Rome when Julius Caesar took control?

2. What did Roman religion have in common with that of ancient Greece?

3. **FOCUS** How did life in Rome change during the Pax Romana?

4. **THINKING SKILL** What *effects* did Augustus's rule have on life throughout the Mediterranean?

5. **GEOGRAPHY** Why were roads a major lifeline for the Roman empire?

DOMES & ARCHES

How would you begin to build something? You might first look at how similar things have been built by others. That is how the ancient Romans began when they built houses, temples, and public buildings. They learned the building techniques used by other civilizations, such as the Egyptian and the Greek. Then they developed some new techniques.

Romans used arches in many of their building projects. An arch is a curved structure used as a building support.

Learning how to use arches helped Roman engineers develop a new structure. This was the dome. A dome is a curved roof that looks like a bowl turned upside down. A dome can cover a huge space without any supports.

Roman engineering is a legacy that can be seen throughout the world. Look around you to see domes and arches.

You have already read that ancient Romans worshiped the gods and goddesses represented at the Pantheon. The Pantheon is a temple with one of the largest domes ever built.

This aqueduct in Spain was built by Romans. Arches help support it. The structure was once used as an aqueduct. Water flowed through a channel along the top which gradually sloped downward.

The large area covered by the Houston Astrodome (above) can seat 70,000 people—with no supports other than itself! The United States Capitol (left) has both arches and a dome.

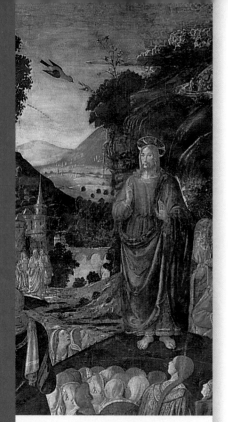

500
B.C.

250
B.C.

A.D.
1

A.D.
100

A.D.
250

A.D.
500

Beginnings of Christianity

Read Aloud

"Fear not; for, behold, I bring you good news of great joy . . . for to you is born in the city of David a Savior, who is Christ the Lord. And this will be a sign for you; you will find the babe wrapped in swaddling clothes, lying in a manger."

These words, taken from the writings of an important new religion, announce the birth of a child in the Roman empire. Despite his humble birth, this child grew up to change the world.

Focus Activity

READ TO LEARN

What did Jesus teach?

VOCABULARY

- Christianity
- New Testament
- Messiah
- parable
- apostle
- bishop
- pope

PEOPLE

- Jesus
- Peter
- Paul

PLACES

- Judea
- Bethlehem
- Nazareth

THE BIG PICTURE

During the rule of Augustus, Rome increased its control over Judea, the region that once had been known as Canaan. You read in Chapter 5 that many Jews had been exiled from this land and brought to ancient Babylon. Many descendants had by now returned from their exile to rebuild their towns and cities. In Jerusalem they built a new temple that stood on the remains of the one that had been destroyed long ago. Elsewhere, towering aqueducts stood as reminders of the newer, Roman rule.

Into this world a new religion, Christianity, was born. The story of its birth is told in a collection of books called the New Testament. The Hebrew Bible, which you read about in Chapter 5, came to be called the Old Testament by followers of Christianity. Together, the Old and New Testaments formed their Bible. Its words are sacred to nearly 2 billion Christians living in the world today.

THE LIFE OF JESUS

One book of the New Testament begins with an important order from Emperor Augustus that a census be taken throughout the entire empire. Augustus's order meant that all the people in the empire had to return to the towns where they were born so that they could be counted. So a Jewish carpenter named Joseph and his wife Mary set out for Bethlehem (BETH luh hem), a small town south of Jerusalem. Find Bethlehem on the map on this page. While there, the Bible says, Mary gave birth to a son, Jesus.

Jesus' Childhood

The New Testament says little about Jesus' childhood. Jesus and his family lived in Nazareth (NAZ ur uth), a tiny village in the northern hills of Judea. The New Testament does say, though, that as a boy Jesus learned a great deal about the teachings of Judaism. According to the Bible, that became clear when Jesus was 12 years old and he went to Jerusalem with his parents. They went to celebrate the Passover festival there.

> When the festival was ended and they started to return, the boy Jesus stayed behind in Jerusalem, but his parents did not know it. . . . When they did not find him, they returned to Jerusalem to search for him. After three days they found him in the temple, sitting among the teachers, listening to them and asking them questions. And all who heard him were amazed at his understanding and his answers.

This passage would by no means be the last one in which the New Testament describes how Jesus amazed those around him.

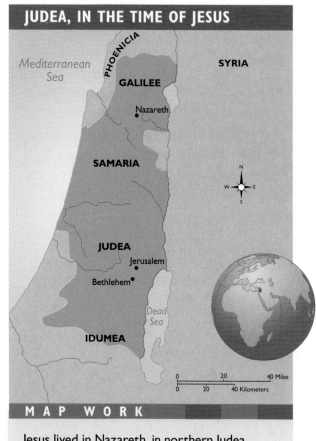

JUDEA, IN THE TIME OF JESUS

PHOENICIA · Mediterranean Sea · SYRIA · GALILEE · Nazareth · SAMARIA · JUDEA · Jerusalem · Bethlehem · Dead Sea · IDUMEA

0 — 20 — 40 Miles
0 — 20 — 40 Kilometers

M A P   W O R K

Jesus lived in Nazareth, in northern Judea.

1. Which is farther east—Jerusalem or Bethlehem?
2. About how many miles from Jerusalem is Nazareth?

From the age of 30 on, the Bible says, Jesus spent much of his time teaching crowds of people. Many came to hear him, the Bible says, because he healed sick people and performed many other miracles.

According to Jewish belief, the Messiah is a special leader to be sent by God in order to guide the Jewish people and to set up God's rule on Earth. The word *Messiah* in Greek is *Christos.* In time the followers of Jesus came to believe that he was the Messiah, or Christos. The people who followed Jesus became known as Christians. Their religion soon became known as Christianity.

THE TEACHINGS OF JESUS

The New Testament states that Jesus often used parables, or simple stories that contain a message or truth. Some of these stories taught the value of seeking the right path in life. Others described the greatness of God's love for all people. Still others stressed the importance of loving other people. Many of Jesus' parables are recorded in the New Testament. How does Jesus describe love in this passage?

MANY VOICES
PRIMARY SOURCE

Excerpt from the Gospel of Luke, New Testament, c. A.D. 90

I say to you that listen, love your enemies, do good to those who hate you, bless those who curse you, pray for those who abuse you. If anyone strikes you on the cheek, offer the other also; and from anyone who takes away your coat do not withhold even your shirt. Give to everyone who begs from you; and if anyone takes away your goods, do not ask for them again. Do to others as you would have them do to you.

In the Sermon on the Mount, Jesus revealed many of his most important teachings.

Twelve Apostles

Jesus' closest followers were called apostles (uh PAHS ulz). The apostles were 12 men Jesus had chosen to help him in his teaching. The Bible says they came from all walks of life. One of the apostles, Peter, had fished for a living before joining Jesus. Another, Levi, had been a tax collector for Rome. The Bible tells us that the apostles had little in common before they met Jesus. It goes on to say, however, that they became united through Jesus' teachings. The apostles helped to spread Jesus' teachings after he died.

A Growing Following

The New Testament says that while he taught, Jesus also cured many people of illnesses. Both Jews and non-Jews benefited from these miracles, the Bible says. As a result, the number of Jesus' followers grew. The New Testament states that a prophet called John the Baptist sent people to ask Jesus if he was the Messiah the Jews were

Christian church services (left) honor Jesus' life and teachings. Leonardo da Vinci's *The Last Supper* (above) shows Jesus' final meal with the twelve apostles.

waiting for. The Bible says Jesus answered:

> Go and tell John what you hear and see: the blind receive their sight, the lame walk . . . , the deaf hear, the dead are raised, and the poor have good news brought to them.

Jesus' answer was made up of quotes from the Hebrew Bible.

Trouble with Rome

Jesus' growing popularity troubled many people. Some of them were afraid that he wanted to be a king and was going to set up a new kingdom in Judez. These beliefs added to the fears of the Roman governors that talk of revolt was spreading throughout Judea.

When crowds jammed the streets of Jerusalem to celebrate the Passover festival, soldiers moved in on Jesus to arrest him. After questioning Jesus, a Roman governor sentenced him to die by crucifixion (kroo suh FIK shun). The word *crucifixion* means "putting to death by hanging from a cross." Roman leaders throughout the empire commonly used crucifixion to punish slaves, rebel leaders, and others regarded as criminals.

According to the New Testament, Jesus may have been in his thirties when he died. The Bible also tells us that Jesus rose from the dead three days after he was crucified. Then he rejoined his apostles and told them again about the coming kingdom of God. Afterwards, the Bible says, Jesus rose to heaven. Today Christians try to follow Jesus' teachings and to celebrate his renewed life and message of hope on Easter Sunday.

THE SPREAD OF CHRISTIANITY

The New Testament does not end with the story of Jesus' ascent, or rise, into heaven. It goes on to tell how Christianity spread throughout the Roman world. Leading the growth of Christianity were the apostles of Jesus.

A Christian Church

The New Testament says that after the death of Jesus, Christians scattered to cities throughout the Roman empire. There they set up dozens of Christian churches. Soon these churches drew the attention of Roman leaders. Some Roman rulers were angry at the Christians for refusing to worship the emperor. Still, the new religion continued to grow and attract followers.

According to the New Testament, the new churches included people from all ranks in life. These included the Roman commander Cornelius, the cloth merchant Lydia, and the slave Onesimus.

A church leader named Paul reminded them that

There is no longer Jew or Greek, . . . slave or free, . . . male or female; for all of you are one in Christ Jesus.

Paul was not one of the first 12 apostles. Unlike the earliest followers of Jesus, Paul grew up in a big city, Tarsus, in what is today Turkey. Paul was well educated in both the Hebrew Bible and Greek classics. At first he was against Christianity, but later he became a Christian himself. Paul spoke in many different cities about Christianity. The New Testament says he debated with Jewish teachers in Jerusalem and with philosophers in the streets of Athens. Paul, together with other Christians, spread Christianity throughout the Roman world.

The Christians above are praying in a church in the United States. The Pope (right) blesses Christians in Rome.

Christianity in Rome

Early church historians wrote that the apostle Peter helped bring Christianity to Rome's crowded neighborhoods. Before they died, Peter and Paul helped build the framework that would make Rome's Christian community the largest in the empire. Christians call Peter the first bishop, or regional church leader, of Rome. Later, Christians would give the bishop of Rome the title pope—from the Latin word for "father." The pope today is the leader of a branch of Christianity known as Roman Catholicism.

As time passed, Christians were tortured and killed by the Roman government. Despite increasing violence against Christians, Christianity continued to flourish in Rome and elsewhere. Both rich and poor continued to be drawn to Jesus' message of love and hope.

WHY IT MATTERS

One of the most powerful supporters of Christianity was a man who became emperor of Rome. You will read about this man and the effects of his actions in the next lesson.

Since its beginnings in the hills of Judea and its spread throughout the Roman empire, Christianity has become one of the world's major religions. In chapters to come you will read about how Christianity has affected life on every continent on Earth.

✓✓ Reviewing Facts and Ideas

MAIN IDEAS

- Christianity developed in Roman-occupied Judea during the Pax Romana.

- The life and teachings of Jesus are recorded in the New Testament of the Christian Bible.

- The New Testament says that the followers of Jesus believed that he was the Messiah.

- Two of Jesus' followers, Peter and Paul, helped to spread Christianity throughout the Roman world.

THINK ABOUT IT

1. Why, according to the New Testament, was Jesus born in Bethlehem?

2. Why were the followers of Jesus called *Christians?*

3. **FOCUS** How were Jesus' teachings rooted in Judaism?

4. **THINKING SKILL** *Make a conclusion* about the importance of the Apostles to the spread of Christianity.

5. **GEOGRAPHY** What role did the Roman empire play in the movement of Christianity throughout the ancient Mediterranean world?

| 500 B.C. | 250 B.C. | A.D. 1 | A.D. 180 | A.D. 500 |

The Decline of the Roman Empire

Focus Activity

READ TO LEARN

What contributed to the decline of Rome?

VOCABULARY

- **Eastern Orthodox Christianity**
- **architecture**
- **Roman Catholicism**

PEOPLE

- **Diocletian**
- **Constantine**

PLACES

- **Palestine**
- **Constantinople**
- **Byzantine empire**

Read Aloud

About A.D. 400 Rome's emperor passed a law banning people from wearing pants or certain kinds of boots. People who broke the law faced losing all of their belongings and being thrown out of the city. Why did the emperor pass such laws about fashion? Pants were the everyday clothes of foreign soldiers whom the Romans called "barbarians." By A.D. 400 these peoples had the power to take over the once-mighty city of Rome.

THE BIG PICTURE

During the Pax Romana from 27 B.C. to A.D. 180, the Roman empire was by no means the only power in its area of the world. On Rome's eastern border, a new Persian empire was developing and growing. North of Rome, different groups were beginning to outgrow the heavily forested lands of northern Europe. After a while some of these people began looking toward the fertile lands within Rome's borders. Like the hunters of China's northern steppes, Europe's northern peoples began raiding the wealthy lands to their south.

Invasions from the north would eventually bring many changes to the Roman empire. The Pax Romana came to an end while new groups moved through the lands of the empire. Many Romans tried to protect themselves and their property. As fear spread, a Roman emperor made a decision that would have a tremendous impact on the Roman empire.

THE DECLINE OF AN EMPIRE

Despite its name, the Pax Romana was not a completely peaceful time in Rome's history. Revolts and border wars flared up often, but the Roman army had always managed to regain control. The Pax Romana ended when large armies from northern Europe began to invade the empire in the late A.D. 100s.

The Empire Under Attack

The northern invaders were German-speaking peoples. They were attacking a Roman empire that had become too big to control. There were increasing difficulties with communicating and collecting taxes. The army weakened, and the empire became poorer.

The raids from the north destroyed cities and farmlands. They made the empire's roads and coasts unsafe. Thieves held up travelers, and pirates hijacked ships. Trade suffered.

As time passed the raids caused life in the empire to change in almost every way. Many cities in the western empire isolated themselves behind thick new walls. In the countryside, wealthy landowners withdrew into their well-protected villas. In the west, where most invasions took place, the Roman empire was rapidly falling apart.

The Empire Is Divided

In A.D. 284 an emperor who was named **Diocletian** (di uh KLEE shun) came to power. Like other emperors who ruled during this time of war, Diocletian was a powerful general. He realized that the empire was simply too big to be ruled by one man, so he divided it into two main parts.

Three assistants took charge of affairs in the troubled western empire. Diocletian became head of the eastern empire. This region included the wealthy cities of Egypt, Greece, and Palestine—the Roman name for Judea. By choosing to oversee the eastern empire, Diocletian created a major turning point in Roman history. For the first time, Rome was no longer the most important city in the empire. Power was shifting from west to east.

This painting shows the northern invaders who began to attack the Roman empire in the late A.D. 100s.

A CAPITAL IN THE EAST

In 306 Constantine became emperor. He reunited the Roman empire under his rule. Like Diocletian, Constantine focused on the eastern half of the empire. He based the empire in a new city on the site of an ancient Greek colony named Byzantium (bih ZAN tee um). Renamed Constantinople (kahn stan tuh NOH pul) in his honor, it became the capital of a huge empire. The city still exists today, as Istanbul, Turkey.

The location of the new capital was perfect for many reasons. Surrounded on three sides by water, Constantinople was easy to protect. It was on major trade routes between the eastern empire and Asia. Finally, the city was far away from Rome and all its traditions of government and religion. This distance made changing the government easier.

Constantinople had an elegant marble forum and aqueducts that flowed with clear water. Thousands of fans attended events in the city stadium. Constantinople, however, not only had temples to many gods but numerous Christian churches as well.

Freedom for Christians

Earlier emperors had Christians killed for refusing to honor Rome's gods and goddesses. Constantine, however, became a supporter of Christianity.

In a dream Constantine was said to have had the night before a major battle in 312, he was told to mark the sign of the cross on his soldiers' shields. He had this done and won the battle. The cross is a religious symbol of Christians.

As a result, Constantine granted freedom to Christians. He donated

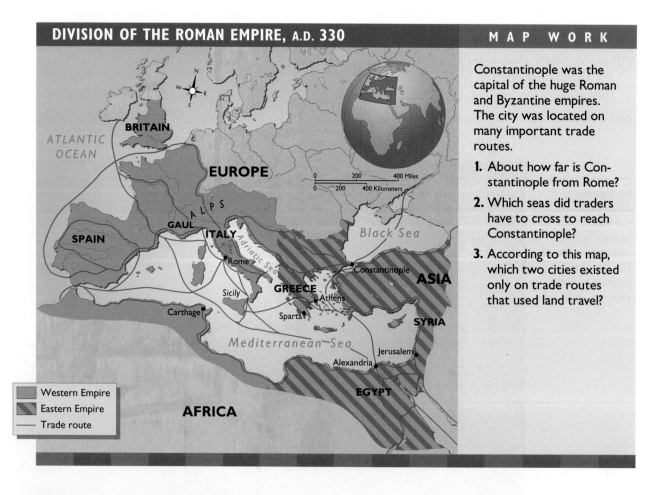

DIVISION OF THE ROMAN EMPIRE, A.D. 330

MAP WORK

Constantinople was the capital of the huge Roman and Byzantine empires. The city was located on many important trade routes.

1. About how far is Constantinople from Rome?

2. Which seas did traders have to cross to reach Constantinople?

3. According to this map, which two cities existed only on trade routes that used land travel?

Legend:
- Western Empire
- Eastern Empire
- Trade route

Istanbul, Turkey (above), was founded by Constantine (below) as Constantinople. It lies partly in Europe and partly in Asia.

money to build Christian churches throughout the empire. He also appointed Christians to important government posts. Constantine became the first of many future rulers in Europe who saw themselves as protectors of Christianity.

End of the Roman Empire

Meanwhile the western empire continued to weaken. Northern peoples settled into more parts of the empire. In 410 their soldiers took Rome itself. In 476, Rome's last emperor was removed from the throne. The city of Rome—once all-powerful in the western Mediterranean—no longer had much influence.

The Eastern Empire Lives On

After the fall of the western Roman empire, the eastern half lived on for another 1,000 years. It became known as the Byzantine empire, in honor of its roots in the Greek city of Byzantium.

Greek culture had a large role in Byzantine life. People spoke Greek rather than the Latin of Rome. Greek as well as western Asian cultures also influenced Byzantine art and building styles. Christianity spread through the empire and influenced the life and arts as well.

Christianity in the Byzantine empire was influenced by Greek culture. As a result, Christianity developed differently than in the west. Western Christians regarded the pope as the only leader who could speak for the church. Eastern Christians did not agree. Their religion, Eastern Orthodox Christianity, would also have a deep influence on people's lives in eastern Europe and western Asia.

Even though there were differences, Byzantine civilization preserved the strong traditions of the Roman empire. Many years later, Roman laws would revive in western Europe thanks to their survival in the Byzantine empire.

THE LEGACY OF ROME

Though the western Roman empire collapsed in the 400s, many important legacies live on. You read about Roman engineering earlier. There were many others too.

Law and Government

Even before the empire was born, Romans crafted the foundations of their laws and government. That was to be their most important legacy. The basic framework of the Roman republic has often been copied. Founders of the United States were inspired by the republic's idea of having leaders serve in three branches of government. They also used the word *senate* and the idea of *veto* power.

New Languages

As the Roman empire spread, the Latin language spread as well. Long after the western empire died, many new languages grew out of Latin. Today these "Romance" languages are still spoken in western Europe and the rest of the world. They include Italian, Spanish, French, Portuguese, and Romanian.

Today even more people use the Roman alphabet. Look carefully at the chart. The Roman alphabet owed much to the Greek alphabet, which in turn grew out of the Phoenician alphabet. The Roman style of letters, though, became the base for the ones we use today. English is just one of many languages that are written with the Roman alphabet.

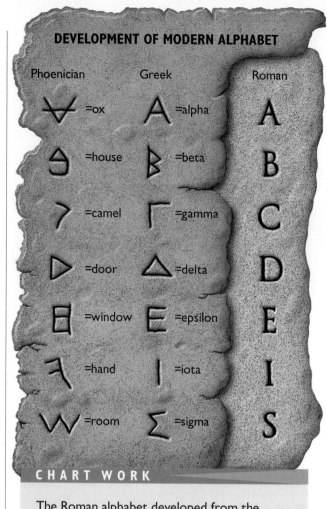

DEVELOPMENT OF MODERN ALPHABET

Phoenician	Greek	Roman
=ox	=alpha	A
=house	=beta	B
=camel	=gamma	C
=door	=delta	D
=window	=epsilon	E
=hand	=iota	I
=room	=sigma	S

CHART WORK

The Roman alphabet developed from the Greek and Phoenician alphabets.

1. In what way is the Roman "A" different from the Phoenician symbol for ox?
2. Which Greek letter is similar to the Roman "E"?

Roman Buildings

As you read earlier, architecture, or the science of planning and constructing buildings, was a major legacy of ancient Rome. Roman architecture borrowed heavily from other cultures. Greek columns and Etruscan arches were parts of many Roman buildings. Yet Roman engineers developed new ideas from these old forms.

Christianity in the West

Roman language and architecture enriched the development of Christianity. Church ceremonies and writings were in Latin. Many huge churches all over Europe were built in the Roman style. Some of the grandest were built in Rome itself. Rome would be the city that would later become the leader of Christianity in western Europe. This western Christianity was later known as Roman Catholicism. Like Eastern Orthodox Christianity, Roman Catholicism has many followers today.

The remains of the Roman Forum (below), mark the site where the senate met in 27 B.C. to name Augustus emperor.

WHY IT MATTERS

The civilization of ancient Rome influenced life in the eastern Mediterranean and western Europe for centuries. As the peoples of western Europe developed a new civilization, they would carry Roman ideas with them. Eventually these ideas influenced peoples throughout the world. The story of this influence will be told in chapters to come.

Reviewing Facts and Ideas

MAIN IDEAS

- Invasions, tax collection problems, and other factors weakened the Roman empire in the A.D. 200s.
- In about 284 Diocletian divided the Roman empire into two parts, making it easier to rule.
- Constantine established the Byzantine empire in the east, where Christianity also became a powerful force.
- While the eastern empire continued to live on, the western empire collapsed in the 400s.
- Rome has left legacies of government, language, and architecture.

THINK ABOUT IT

1. What brought about the end of the Pax Romana?

2. How did Romans use the legacies of other civilizations? What Roman legacies affect our lives today?

3. **FOCUS** Why did the western empire finally collapse?

4. **THINKING SKILL** What _conclusions_ can you make about the changes that occurred in the Eastern Roman empire under Constantine?

5. **WRITE** Why was Constantinople a good location for the new capital?

CHAPTER 9 REVIEW

Major Events

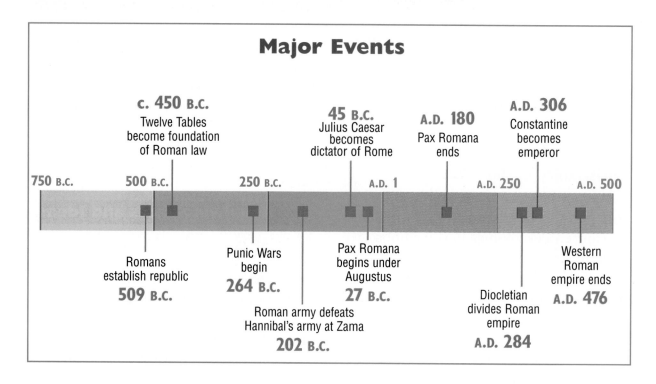

c. 450 B.C.
Twelve Tables
become foundation
of Roman law

45 B.C.
Julius Caesar
becomes
dictator of Rome

A.D. 180
Pax Romana
ends

A.D. 306
Constantine
becomes
emperor

750 B.C.   500 B.C.   250 B.C.   A.D. 1   A.D. 250   A.D. 500

Romans
establish republic
509 B.C.

Punic Wars
begin
264 B.C.

Pax Romana
begins under
Augustus
27 B.C.

Roman army defeats
Hannibal's army at Zama
202 B.C.

Diocletian
divides Roman
empire
A.D. 284

Western
Roman
empire ends
A.D. 476

THINKING ABOUT VOCABULARY

Number a sheet of paper from 1 to 10. Beside each number write the word or phrase from the list below that best completes the sentence.

architecture   Messiah
civil war   patrician
consul   profile
dictator   representative
elevation   republic

1. Height above sea level is called _____.
2. A _____ is a war between groups inside a country.
3. A _____ is a member of a noble family.
4. In a _____ people get to choose their own government leaders.
5. A person elected to act for others is called a _____.
6. A _____ was one of the Roman leaders elected by the citizen assembly.
7. The _____ is believed by his followers to have been a special leader sent by God to lead the Jewish people.
8. A _____ is a view of something from the side or a cross section.
9. A _____ is somebody who rules with absolute power.
10. _____ is the science of planning and constructing buildings.

THINKING ABOUT FACTS

1. How did the Alps and the Apennine Mountains cause difficulty for travelers in Italy?
2. What role did Hannibal play in Roman history?
3. Why was Julius Caesar assassinated?
4. What is the New Testament? Why is it important to Christianity?
5. According to the time line above, for about how long had Rome been a republic before Julius Caesar became a dictator?

THINK AND WRITE ◄▤▤▷

WRITING AN EXPLANATION
Write two paragraphs about Rome's republican government. First explain how it worked. Then compare and contrast it with Athenian democracy.

WRITING A TV REPORT
Suppose you are a television reporter sent back in time to ancient Rome to cover the assassination of Julius Caesar. Write a report that you will give on the evening news.

WRITING A COMPARISON
Write a paragraph about the decline of the Roman empire. Compare the problems of the western empire with the successes of the Byzantine empire in the east.

APPLYING GEOGRAPHY SKILLS

READING ELEVATION PROFILES AND MAPS

1. What is an elevation map? What is a profile map?

2. Look at the elevation map of Rome (Map A) on page 228 to find the elevations of the seven hills. Which hills are the highest? Which is the lowest? List the hills of Rome in order of elevation from highest to lowest.

3. Look at the profile map of Rome (Map B) on page 229. How much higher is the Palatine Hill than the Caelian Hill? How much higher is the Caelian Hill than the Tiber River?

4. Why can an elevation map show the locations of places in an area better than a profile map can? What is the advantage of a profile map?

5. Why are elevation and profile maps useful? When may they be too limiting?

Summing Up the Chapter

Copy the cause-and-effect chart below on a separate piece of paper. Then review the chapter to find at least three causes for each effect listed. After you have filled in the causes, use the chart to write a paragraph that answers the question "How did Rome grow into a great empire?"

CAUSE	EFFECT
	Rome becomes a powerful empire.
	The Western Roman empire declines.

CHAPTER 10

Ancient Arabia

THINKING ABOUT
HISTORY AND GEOGRAPHY

In this chapter you will read how early peoples lived in the deserts and mountains of Arabia. Farming, herding, and trade developed in this region. The religion of Islam spread rapidly to unite many Arabs in one belief. The civilization that followed built a glorious capital city and created many legacies that still influence people today.

A.D. 762

300 B.C.

A.D. 622

BAGHDAD
Caliph Al-Mansur founds a capital city

PETRA
Petra becomes a caravan stop for Arab traders

MEDINA
Muhammad moves to Medina; Islamic calendar begins

400 B.C.

A.D. 600

A.D. 800

EUROPE

Mediterranean Sea

Euphrates
River   Baghdad   Isfahan

Petra

Red Sea

Medina

AFRICA

ASIA

Persian Gulf

ARABIAN
PENINSULA

A.D. 1000

ISFAHAN
Avicenna's medical book
helps doctors prevent the
spread of disease

INDIAN
OCEAN

Geography of Arabia

Read Aloud

*The summer wind picked up, its passing
    gusts and fiery blasts.
Back and forth they tugged a flowing train
    of stirred-up dust
Whose cloud flies up like smoke when the
    kindling is lit.*

This 1,400-year-old Arabic poem describes
parts of Arabia in the summertime.

Focus Activity

READ TO LEARN

*How did the people of the
Arabian peninsula adapt
to the region's geography?*

VOCABULARY

- oasis
- caravan

PLACES

- Arabia
- Persian Gulf
- Arabian Sea
- Red Sea
- Yemen
- Petra

THE BIG PICTURE

Arabia is a huge peninsula in southwestern Asia. It lies south of the Fertile Crescent and east of Egypt. By the time Constantine rose to power in Europe around A.D. 300, Arabia had a number of flourishing civilizations.

Arabian traders had long been traveling to cities in Egypt, Mesopotamia, India, and Palestine. In the busy cities of Palestine, for example, merchants sold luxury items such as frankincense (FRANG kihn sens). This costly, perfume-like ingredient is made from the frankincense tree, which grows in few places outside of southern Arabia.

Today the region of Arabia contains several nations, including Yemen, Kuwait, and Saudi Arabia. In this lesson you will read about the ways in which early people of these areas used their environment to develop thriving civilizations.

**Dates are an important crop
of the Arabian peninsula.**

THE ARABIAN PENINSULA

The Arabian peninsula is bounded by the Persian Gulf to the east. To the south is the Arabian Sea. To the west, the Red Sea almost completely separates Arabia from Africa. Find these places on the map below.

Arabia can be divided into three environmental areas. Find them on the map. The Jabal al-Hijaz (JAB al al hihj AZ) mountains rise along Arabia's west coast to its southernmost tip. The rainfall here makes agriculture possible.

Arabia's east coast is the second environmental area. It is also fertile enough for farming.

The third area covers the inner part of the Arabian peninsula. It is mostly desert. About one quarter of Arabia gets fewer than 10 inches of rain each year, and there are few rivers.

The Desert Environments

Some of Arabia's deserts contain stone cliffs. Others have huge hills of sand. The world's largest continuous body of sand is on the Arabian peninsula. This region, called the Empty Quarter, is uninhabitable. Some parts have no rain for 10 years or more. Other parts enjoy winter cloudbursts that allow desert plants to grow. All of Arabia's deserts have a lack of water and an oven-like summer heat.

Some parts of a desert are not dry. Such an area is an oasis (oh AY sis). Oases are watered by underground springs. People can grow crops in the soil of these areas. Some oases are even large enough to support towns. However, there are few oases in Arabia, and few people live in any part of the peninsula's deserts.

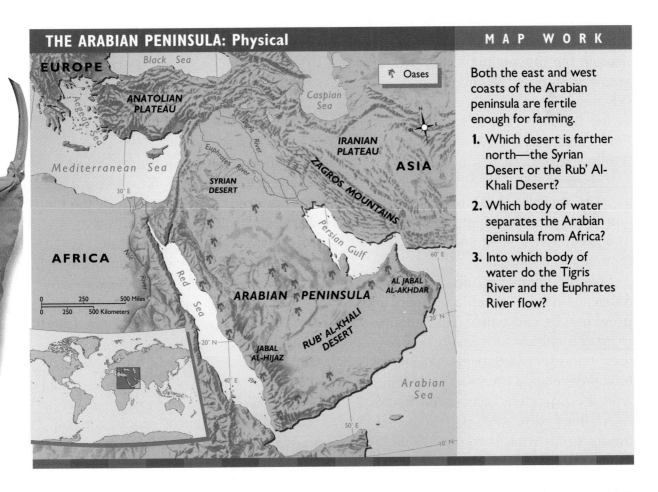

THE ARABIAN PENINSULA: Physical

EUROPE · Black Sea · ANATOLIAN PLATEAU · Aegean Sea · Mediterranean Sea · Caspian Sea · IRANIAN PLATEAU · ASIA · Tigris River · Euphrates River · ZAGROS MOUNTAINS · 30° E · SYRIAN DESERT · Oases · AFRICA · Nile River · Red Sea · Persian Gulf · 60° E · ARABIAN PENINSULA · AL JABAL AL-AKHDAR · 20° N · JABAL AL-HIJAZ · RUB' AL-KHALI DESERT · 40° E · 50° E · Arabian Sea · 10° N

0 250 500 Miles
0 250 500 Kilometers

MAP WORK

Both the east and west coasts of the Arabian peninsula are fertile enough for farming.

1. Which desert is farther north—the Syrian Desert or the Rub' Al-Khali Desert?

2. Which body of water separates the Arabian peninsula from Africa?

3. Into which body of water do the Tigris River and the Euphrates River flow?

PEOPLES OF ARABIA

The Arabian peninsula is named for the Arabs, the people who have lived there for over 3,000 years. The word "Arab" was first recorded around 800 B.C. It referred to the people living in northern Arabia who had domesticated the camel. Early Arabs used these animals to travel around the peninsula.

Arabia's Fertile Regions

Most of the early people of Arabia lived in fertile regions. Some Arabians lived in the mountainous southwestern area that is now the country of **Yemen** (YE mun). These people became known as the Sabaean (suh BEE un) civilization. Find Yemen on the Atlas map on page R10 in the back of this book.

This area receives enough rainfall to support agriculture. Think about what you read in earlier chapters. What type of agriculture is most successful in mountainous regions?

Like the people in Italy and Greece, Sabaeans herded sheep and goats and grew grapes and wheat. By building irrigation canals, farmers improved their harvests. As Sabaean coastal towns developed, they began trading with the Egyptians, across the Red Sea.

Another early Arab people lived to the north, in what is today Jordan, around 300 B.C. Their kingdom was

Trade caravans like the one above stopped in Petra (right), the capital of the Nabataean civilization. This temple was carved out of rock there.

called Nabataea (nab uh TEE uh). They built their capital, **Petra** (PEH truh), in a place that had a large supply of water brought by aqueducts. Find Petra on the map on page 267.

Trade Across Desert and Sea

It is easy to see why Petra became an important stop on a trade route. There are no other well-watered places for hundreds of miles south of the city. Through trade with Asia and the Mediterranean, the Nabataean (nah buh TEE un) civilization grew rich. It flourished for about 400 years.

Ancient Arabs domesticated camels because they are very useful for desert travel. Camels can carry heavy loads, and go for days without water. They also provide milk to drink. Arab traders often traveled in camel **caravans**. A caravan is a group of people and animals traveling together. Caravans traveled along routes well known to desert

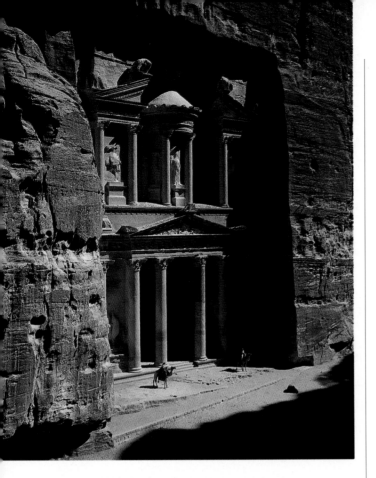

experts. Arab traders journeyed throughout the Arabian peninsula. They traded in cities of the Fertile Crescent and across the Red Sea in Egypt.

Peoples on the Move

One of the groups of people who traded in Arabia were called Bedouins (BED uh wunz). The word *Bedouins* means "people of the desert." They were family groups who lived mostly in the desert, traveling in caravans and sleeping in tents. Many Bedouin traders became wealthy and powerful, sometimes because they raided towns and other caravans.

Other peoples who often moved about were mountain herders. Like the herders of northern China, they moved to new grazing lands at different times of the year. Some went as far as the Fertile Crescent. As in China, the differences in lifestyle between herders and farmers sometimes caused conflict.

WHY IT MATTERS

The geography of Arabia presented unique challenges to the people who built civilizations in this region. The rugged mountains and water-rich oases of the Arabian peninsula received enough moisture to make farming, herding, and some city-building possible. The people who lived in Arabia's vast stretches of desert had to adapt to very harsh conditions.

Ancient Arabia was divided by geography. However, in the A.D. 600s its people would become unified under a new religion. You will read about this religion in the next lesson.

Reviewing Facts and Ideas

MAIN IDEAS

- While some of Arabia is desert, the coastal areas receive enough rain to support agriculture.
- Towns and trade developed in fertile regions, at desert edges, and at oases.
- Trade linked ancient Arabia with Egypt and the Fertile Crescent.

THINK ABOUT IT

1. In what ways do environments differ in various parts of Arabia?

2. How did people live in the mountainous environment of Yemen?

3. **FOCUS** How did varied geography influence the development of different cultures in Arabia?

4. **THINKING SKILL** Explain why the following statement is a *fact* or why it is an *opinion:* "The best Arabian trade routes were found in the western part of the peninsula."

5. **GEOGRAPHY** Study the map of Arabia. Which coast has more areas of high elevation?

265

400   500   750 800   1000   1200

Beginnings of Islam

Read Aloud

"Allah—there is no god but He . . . Muhammad is the Messenger of Allah." These words are from the Quran (kur AHN), the most holy book of the religion called Islam. It contains the most basic teachings of Islam. In this lesson you will read about how this religion came to hold great influence on the Arabian peninsula. In time Islam would spread throughout many areas of the world.

Focus Activity

READ TO LEARN

What are some of the major teachings of Islam?

VOCABULARY

- Islam
- Quran
- Kaaba
- hijra
- Five Pillars
- pilgrimage

PEOPLE

- Muhammad
- Khadija

PLACES

- Mecca
- Medina

THE BIG PICTURE

By A.D. 500 Hinduism had deep roots in the Indian sub-continent. Buddhism had spread to Southeast Asia and China. In China, Buddhism mixed with Confucian ideas. Christianity had grown around the Roman empire and spread into North Africa and Mesopotamia. Judaism, which had also grown in the eastern Mediterranean, reached as far as the oasis towns of western Arabia.

In the same region of Arabia, a new religion called Islam (is LAHM) was born. *Islam* means "submit to the will of God" in Arabic, the Arab language. Followers of Islam are called Muslims—which translates "ones who submit to God." The story and teachings of Islam have been written down in the Quran, the most important book of Islam. Its words are sacred to the more than 1 billion Muslims in the world today.

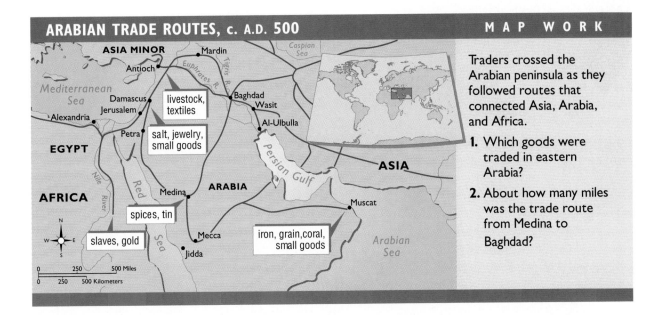

ARABIAN TRADE ROUTES, c. A.D. 500

Traders crossed the Arabian peninsula as they followed routes that connected Asia, Arabia, and Africa.

1. Which goods were traded in eastern Arabia?
2. About how many miles was the trade route from Medina to Baghdad?

THE BIRTH OF MUHAMMAD

In the last lesson you read that traders had been crisscrossing the Arabian peninsula for hundreds of years. Find some of the caravan trade routes on the map on this page. By A.D. 500 traders carried goods and ideas to and from many different communities. In some towns Arab traders could buy iron tools from a Jewish craftworker or have a tooth pulled by a Christian dentist. Religious beliefs differed from place to place, as did languages and writing systems. The people in western Arabia had developed a written language, Arabic, sometime before 800 B.C. An example of Arabic writing is shown below.

According to Muslim tradition, a boy named Muhammad (mu HAM ud) was born in the oasis city of Mecca about A.D. 570. His father died before he was born. Because Muhammad's mother died not long after his birth, he was raised by an uncle who was a trader. In time Muhammad mastered the skill of leading caravans.

The writings that trace Muhammad's life say that his skills caught the eye of a wealthy widow and merchant, Khadija (ka DEE jah). On her behalf Muhammad traveled to the Fertile Crescent to trade goods. When he returned from his journey, they were married.

The City of Mecca

Muhammad's marriage to Khadija is said to have given him wealth and respect in busy Mecca, where they lived. Mecca lay on the main trading route through western Arabia. Therefore, many merchants came to do business there.

The city also attracted other visitors because of the Kaaba (KAH buh), Mecca's temple. At this time the Kaaba was like the Pantheon of Rome. It honored gods and goddesses worshiped by the people of Mecca.

A young Bedouin reads from the Quran (left). Thousands of Muslims face the Kaaba as they pray (below).

TEACHINGS OF ISLAM

According to Muslim belief Muhammad often went to a mountain cave near Mecca to pray. The writings say that one night, when Muhammad was about 40 years old, something happened that would change the history of Arabia.

Muslims believe that Muhammad received a message from Allah (ahl LAH). *Allah* is the Arabic word for God. Muhammad was told, "O Muhammad, you are the Prophet of Allah." As you learned in Chapter 5, a prophet is believed by followers to speak for God. Over many years, Allah is said to have given other messages to Muhammad.

The Prophet Muhammad

Muslim writings say that Muhammad's wife Khadija helped him greatly. With her encouragement and support, he set out to teach people in Mecca about Allah. Over the next three years, his group of followers slowly grew.

According to tradition Muhammad aroused the anger of city leaders. They were upset because he criticized the Meccans' way of life and their belief in many gods. His disagreement with city leaders is said to have caused him and his followers to leave Mecca in 622.

Muhammad's Migration

The writings about Muhammad say that he moved over 200 miles from Mecca to another oasis town, Medina (muh DEE nuh). He gained many supporters there. Muhammad's hijra (HIHJ ruh)—Arabic for "migration"— marked a major turning point in Islamic history. The year of the hijra, 622, marks the starting point of the Islamic calendar.

Return to Mecca

Muslim scholars say that in 624 Muhammad led attacks on Meccan caravans, cutting off Mecca's source of riches. Later, with peace agreements, he is said to have won Mecca's surrender. After his victory in 630, Muhammad destroyed the statues of the gods and goddesses in the Kaaba and proclaimed Mecca a Muslim city. It is holy to Muslims to this day.

Writings state that Muhammad won the support of many Arabian communities. In 632 he is said to have spoken to his followers at Mecca. His words, taken from the Quran, were "[Muslim] believers are brothers one of another." Later that year Muhammad died.

The Sacred Book of Islam

In Islamic belief the Quran contains Allah's teachings to Muhammad. Muslims believe these words were written down soon after Muhammad's death. The most important teaching was that there was only one God in the universe—Allah. The Quran says that Allah is the God worshiped both by Christians and Jews.

> We believe in God, and in that which has been sent down on Abraham . . . and that which was given to Moses and Jesus.

The Quran serves as a guide for living for Muslims, as the Bible does for Jews and Christians. Through its words, Muslims learn about Allah's teachings.

The Five Pillars of Islam

The Quran outlines five basic duties of all Muslims. The purpose of these duties—the Five Pillars of Islam—is to strengthen Muslims' ties to Allah and to other people. The first pillar is the belief in one God, Allah, and that Muhammad is Allah's prophet. The second describes the prayers Muslims offer Allah five times each day. Wherever they are in the world, as they pray, Muslims look toward Mecca, their holy city. The third pillar speaks of giving to those in need, especially the poor. The fourth instructs Muslims to fast during the holy month of Ramadan (rahm uh DAHN). From sunrise to sunset Muslims neither eat nor drink. They spend time in worship. The final pillar instructs Muslims who can afford it to visit Mecca at least once in their lives. A journey for religious purposes is called a pilgrimage.

The Quran's first chapter has important instructions. What do these words say about Islam?

MANY VOICES
PRIMARY SOURCE

**Excerpt from
The Quran, about A.D. 650
Chapter One, Verses 2–7.**

Praise be to [Allah], The Cherisher and Sustainer of the worlds;

Most Gracious, Most Merciful

Master of the Day of Judgment.

Thee do we worship and Thine aid we seek.

Show us the straight way,

The way of those on whom Thou hast bestowed Thy Grace.

MUSLIMS AROUND THE WORLD

Muhammad's death must have caused his followers great sorrow. One said, "O men, if you worship Muhammad, Muhammad is dead; if you worship Allah, Allah is alive." Muslims then joined together to spread the message of Islam.

During the 100 years after the death of Muhammad, the Islamic community grew steadily. It spread and flourished, and by A.D. 750, followers of Islam could be found from Spain all the way to the Indus valley.

Gradually, over a period of time, nonreligious legacies spread throughout this vast region, as well. Just as the Latin language spread through the Roman empire, for example, Arabic became the common language in many Islamic lands. The different peoples who came under Islamic rule also made many important contributions to the heritage of Islam. You will read about some of these contributions in the next lesson.

Islam Today

Of the great number of Muslims in the world today, around 5 million live in the United States. The customs of Muslims often vary from one country to another. However, nearly all Muslims honor the end of Ramadan with a joyful feast. People wear new clothes to celebrate the beginning of the month following the long fast.

Millions of Muslims from all around the world still make the pilgrimage to the holy city of Mecca every year. Muslims everywhere view the pilgrimage as one of the most important events in their lives.

Muslims gather for worship in Cordoba, Spain (top). The end of Ramadan is celebrated by many with music and dance (right).

At home Muslim women take time to teach their children about the Quran. Muslim families have celebrations when sons or daughters memorize large parts of the Quran. Some young people go on to study Islam and other subjects at Muslim schools and colleges.

WHY IT MATTERS

The modern city of Mecca, in Saudi Arabia, is the center of a world-wide Muslim community. No matter where they may be in the world, when they pray, Muslims always position themselves to face this holy city.

For almost 1,400 years Islam has been anchored in both the life of Muhammad and the teachings of the Quran. Throughout that long stretch of time, the religion of Islam has shaped civilizations and human achievements. You will read about some of those achievements in the next lesson.

✔✔ **Reviewing Facts and Ideas**

MAIN IDEAS

- According to Muslim belief Muhammad, the founder of Islam, lived from A.D. 570 to 632. Muhammad preached that there was only one God—Allah.

- Muhammad journeyed from Mecca to Medina in 622. This event is called the hijra. Muhammad went on to become a powerful leader in Medina. Later he returned and proclaimed Mecca a holy city.

- Muslims believe that the sacred book of Islam, the Quran, contains holy teachings that Muhammad received from Allah.

- The Five Pillars of Islam from the Quran instruct Muslims about how they should honor Allah in their lives.

THINK ABOUT IT

1. Why was Mecca an important religious center even before Islam was founded? Why was it an important trading city?

2. What is the most important teaching of Islam?

3. **FOCUS** How do the teachings of Islam affect the daily lives of Muslims?

4. **THINKING SKILL** According to Islamic writings, what was the main *cause* of Muhammad's *hijra*, or migration? What were some of its *effects*?

5. **GEOGRAPHY** Find the holy city of Mecca on the map on page 267. In what direction would a Muslim living in Mardin face during prayer? Estimate the distance that he or she would need to journey in making a pilgrimage to Mecca.

400   600   750   1200

A Muslim Caliphate

Focus Activity

READ TO LEARN

What did Muslims achieve in the city of Baghdad?

VOCABULARY

- caliph
- mosque
- algebra
- astrolabe

PEOPLE

- Avicenna

PLACES

- Baghdad

Read Aloud

Lining the docks, ships filled with Egyptian rice, Chinese dishware, Syrian glass, and Arabian pearls could be seen bobbing on the river. The roads leading to the city were crowded with farmers bringing oranges and cucumbers, and with traders carrying elegant carpets. Occasionally the government's "air-mail" service flew overhead. The service was actually pigeons that had been trained to carry letters! Even more wonders lay within the incredible city of Baghdad (BAG dad).

THE BIG PICTURE

Centuries before the founding of **Baghdad**, Persian rulers controlled lands north of the Arabian peninsula, from Egypt to India. By the A.D. 600s the Persian empire was in decline. As Islam developed in Mecca, Muhammad gained power on the Arabian peninsula. Leaders who ruled after Muhammad extended Islam to Persian lands and other areas. By 700 Muslim rulers controlled the Mediterranean region.

In 762 the Muslim ruler al-Mansur (al man SUR) decided to build a capital city along the Tigris River in present-day Iraq. He reportedly declared, "This is the site on which I shall build. Goods can arrive here by way of the Euphrates, Tigris, and a network of canals. Only a place like this will support the army and the general population." Not long afterwards the city of Baghdad began to take shape. The city along the Tigris quickly became the center of the Muslim civilization's greatest achievements in science, art, and architecture.

272

MUSLIM RULE

In the 760s Islam was just over 100 years old. Much had changed in this time. Caliphs (KAY lihfs) had been chosen to govern the land and religion of Islam. *Caliph* means "successor [to the Prophet]." The lands ruled by the caliph were called the caliphate (KAY luh fayt). As the map below shows, the caliphate expanded to western Asia and North Africa. In many places people welcomed the Muslims, who overthrew hated rulers of old. Many people became Muslims. Others did not, but they learned Arabic. An Islamic civilization united by Muslim leadership developed.

Baghdad

From the late 700s until the 1200s, Baghdad was the capital of the Muslim caliphate. One of the world's largest cities, it had about 1 million residents.

Baghdad's layout reflected the grandness of the Muslim caliphate. At the center of the city stood the caliph's huge, domed palace. Next to it rose a great mosque (MAHSK). A mosque is a place of worship where Muslims go for daily prayers.

From the center of Baghdad, four main roads went to all parts of the caliphate. Traders used these roads to bring riches from all over the caliphate and beyond.

Baghdad had an international flavor. Shoppers packed the streets where Arabian perfume, Indian pepper, African ivory, and Russian furs were among the items sold. Some shops sold only Chinese dishware, while others sold only books. Merchants had learned papermaking from the Chinese, and Baghdad's new paper mill made it possible to create many books.

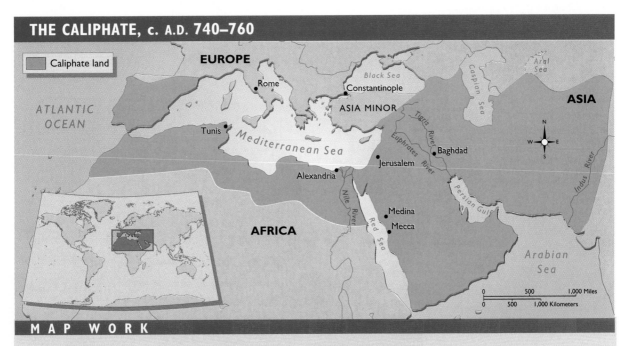

THE CALIPHATE, c. A.D. 740–760

Caliphate land

EUROPE · ATLANTIC OCEAN · Rome · Black Sea · Constantinople · ASIA MINOR · Aral Sea · Caspian Sea · ASIA · Tunis · Mediterranean Sea · Tigris River · Euphrates River · Baghdad · Jerusalem · Alexandria · Nile River · Red Sea · Medina · Mecca · Persian Gulf · Indus River · AFRICA · Arabian Sea

0 500 1,000 Miles
0 500 1,000 Kilometers

MAP WORK

Under the rule of the caliphs, an Islamic civilization spread throughout Arabia, North Africa, and western Asia.

1. Which rivers flowed near Baghdad?

2. Which city is closest to the Persian Gulf—Constantinople, Baghdad, or Mecca?

3. About how far is Baghdad from Mecca?

ACHIEVEMENTS OF THE CALIPHATE

Baghdad's caliphs valued education and learning. Muhammad was said to have declared, "He who travels in search of knowledge, travels along Allah's path of Paradise." As a result, the caliphs preserved works from all over the caliphate in a huge library, the House of Wisdom. There, Greek, Roman, and Indian works were translated into Arabic. Over time these works spread throughout the caliphate and the world. Arab scholars read these books on history, science, law, and mathematics. Many later developed and improved these fields of study.

Advances in Medicine

Muslim doctors studied translations of Greek medical texts and a work by a famous Muslim doctor who lived in Persia in the early 1000s. His name was Ibn Sina (IHB un SEE nuh), or Avicenna (av ih SEN uh) in Latin. Avicenna described how some diseases spread through air and water. He wrote that stress could cause stomach problems and that cancer could be fought with surgery. In time Avicenna's book became a standard medical text in many parts of North Africa, western Asia, and Europe.

The caliphate had many doctors. Some of them treated patients in Baghdad's large hospitals. Others oversaw the government's "moving hospitals." These doctors and their assistants gave free treatment to patients who lived far from Baghdad. Such traveling medical teams carried beds, medicines, and other supplies by camel.

Math and Science

When calculating doses of medicine, doctors used a simpler number system

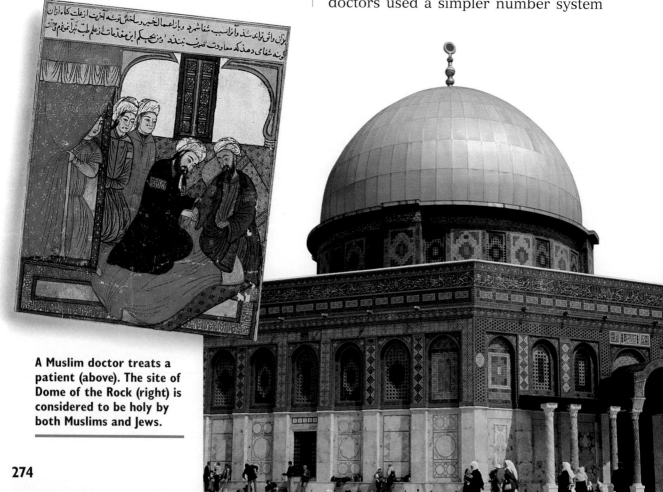

A Muslim doctor treats a patient (above). The site of Dome of the Rock (right) is considered to be holy by both Muslims and Jews.

than that of the Romans. In the Roman system, "XVIII" was "18"—its equal in Arabic numbers. You know the Arabic number system because we use it today.

Muslim mathematicians built on the work of Hindu scholars in India. For example, they helped improve earlier mathematics methods and notation. Muslims also added greatly to the field of *al-jabr* (al JAHB ur). In English, it's algebra, a type of mathematics.

In its vast collections, the House of Wisdom had many Arabic volumes on astronomy. Astronomy, the study of the stars and planets, was of great interest to Muslims. The Islamic calendar was based on the moon's movement. Stars also helped people determine directions. Muslims used a Greek instrument, the astrolabe (AS truh layb), which they improved, to figure out position from the stars.

Places of Worship

Throughout the caliphate, mosque builders took care to follow certain standards. They had to make sure the mosque faced Mecca. Special nooks in the walls showed people the direction of Mecca. From tall towers, religious leaders could call Muslims to prayer. Walled-in courtyards held hundreds of worshipers. Beyond these basic features, builders used their imaginations to make each mosque as beautiful as possible. Many remain standing today.

The oldest Muslim monument still standing is the Dome of the Rock in Jerusalem. Built in 691, this building is not a mosque. Instead it honors the place where Muslims believe Muhammad ascended into heaven. Its Roman-style dome and Greek columns show how Muslims combined old and new ideas to create a unique style of architecture.

Literature and Music

Long before Islam was born in Arabia, literature and music had been popular there. You read an excerpt from a pre-Islamic poem in the introduction to Lesson 1. Poetry remained well loved among the people of Baghdad, and its appreciation spread throughout the region at this time.

Folktales were also very popular among the citizens of Baghdad and the rest of the caliphate. Over time, favorites from Persia, India, Arabia, and other places were collected into a book called *The Arabian Nights*. The book's main story is of a wise princess named Scheherazade (she HAIR ah zahd). She is married to a cruel king who threatens to kill her after their wedding. She saves herself by distracting him with tales of Aladdin, Ali Baba and the 40 thieves, and other exciting stories.

infographic

inter**NET** CONNECTION

Visit our website:
www.mhschool.com

Life in the Caliphate

During the time of the Baghdad Caliphate, Muslim control spread to parts of Europe, North Africa, and western Asia. Important cultural and scientific achievements spread as well. The stunning architecture of the Alhambra (left), a palace in Spain, is an example. What were some other achievements found in the Caliphate?

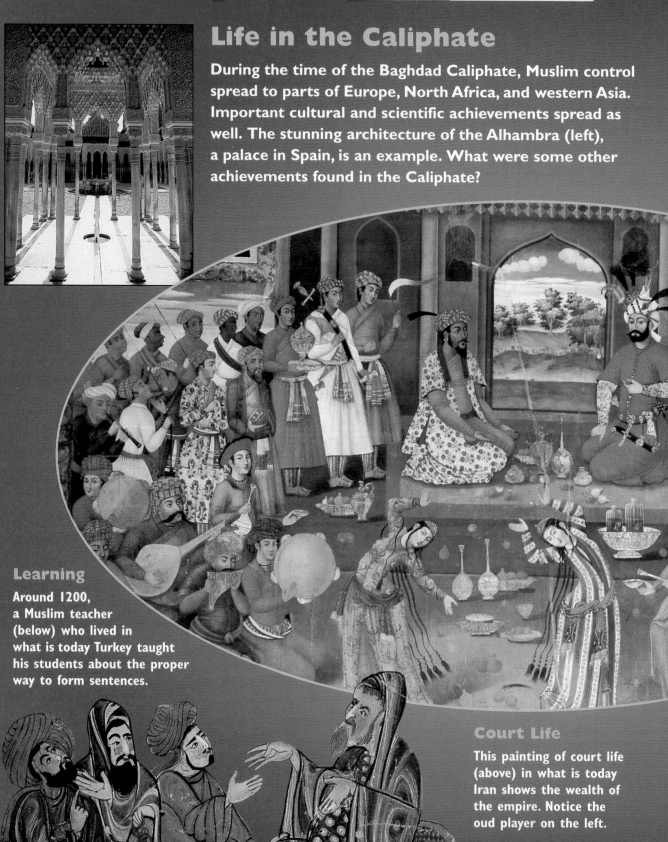

Learning

Around 1200, a Muslim teacher (below) who lived in what is today Turkey taught his students about the proper way to form sentences.

Court Life

This painting of court life (above) in what is today Iran shows the wealth of the empire. Notice the oud player on the left.

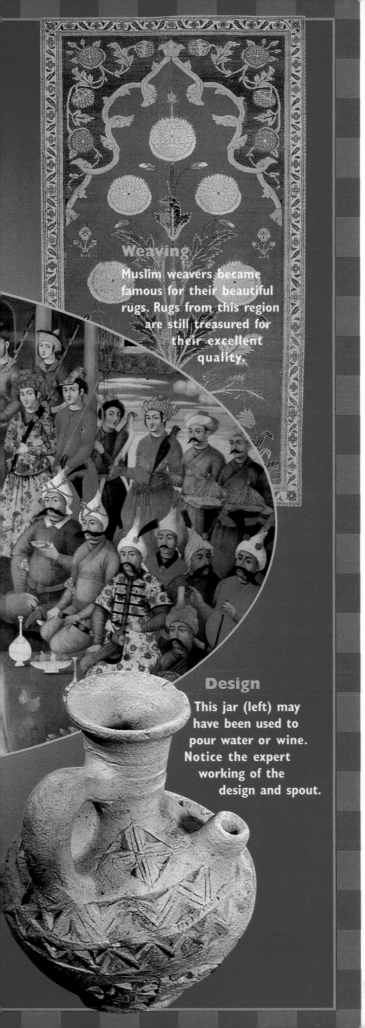

Weaving
Muslim weavers became famous for their beautiful rugs. Rugs from this region are still treasured for their excellent quality.

Design
This jar (left) may have been used to pour water or wine. Notice the expert working of the design and spout.

WHY IT MATTERS

Baghdad's caliphs ruled lands that stretched from Morocco to India. Islam established deep roots in that area. So did a rich heritage that included major achievements in the arts and sciences.

As you have read, the Arabic language developed on the Arabian peninsula. It is now the common language of most of northern Africa and of parts of western Asia. Today Muslims in many different nations are united by the legacy of Islam. People around the world share other Arabian legacies.

✓// Reviewing Facts and Ideas

MAIN IDEAS

- Under the caliphs who came after Muhammad, Islam spread into Asia, Africa, and Europe. For centuries the caliphs ruled from Baghdad.
- The caliphate furthered learning in medicine, math, and astronomy.
- Mosques were centers of Muslim worship throughout the caliphate and remain religious centers today.

THINK ABOUT IT

1. Which of Baghdad's trade goods came from other regions?

2. What were some of the achievements of the Muslim caliphate in medicine?

3. **FOCUS** In what ways did Islam influence life in the city of Baghdad?

4. **THINKING SKILL** Based on your study of the geography of Mesopotamia, _make a conclusion_ about the dangers of building Baghdad on the Tigris.

5. **WRITE** Write an article for a science journal describing Baghdad's House of Wisdom. How might it have helped scientists and mathematicians develop new ideas?

Legacy

map making

As the Muslim caliphate expanded, the mapping of new lands became important to the caliphs. The science of making maps is called cartography (cahr TOG ruh fee). To improve their skills, Muslim cartographers, or mapmakers, learned techniques used in earlier civilizations, such as ancient Greece. They also used their mathematical skills to develop new methods that helped make maps more accurate than earlier versions.

One technique that Muslim cartographers used was to draw lines dividing the world into different climate zones. These lines, shown on the map at right, were similar to today's lines of latitude.

Cartography is an important legacy that helps us to understand the world around us. Today, different mapping techniques can be used to show us every part of the world, from the ocean floor to the skies above us.

Muslim cartographer al-Idrisi (al IHD rih see) made this circular map of the world around 1150. The Arabian Peninsula looks different from the way you usually see it, because on this map, north points *down*!

In the 1700s sailors relied on maps similar to this one (left) during ocean voyages. Several centuries earlier, Muslim cartographers used the astrolabe (below) to estimate their position on Earth.

This colorful map is made up of photographs taken by satellites in orbit around our planet. The map shows how Earth might look from space if it were not covered by clouds! The cartographer used only photographs that contained no clouds.

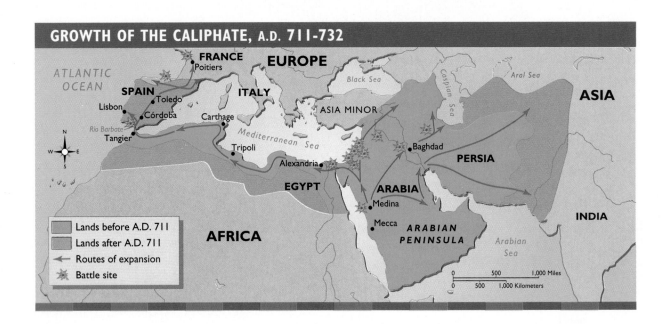

GROWTH OF THE CALIPHATE, A.D. 711-732

Lands before A.D. 711
Lands after A.D. 711
Routes of expansion
Battle site

Reading Historical Maps

VOCABULARY
historical map

WHY THE SKILL MATTERS

In A.D. 711, while the caliph extended his power throughout western Asia, he also sent an army into Europe. Before very long the caliphate controlled all the land in present-day Spain and Portugal.

One way to get a quick overview of such events is to study historical maps. Historical maps show information about the past. Use the Helping Yourself box on the next page to guide you in reading historical maps.

USING THE SKILL

Study the map of the caliphate's expansion into Europe on this page. Read the map title. It is an historical map because it shows places and events from the past. Notice that the map shows the names of several countries. These are included to help you locate areas and events.

In 711 the caliph's forces crossed from North Africa to Spain and defeated the army of Roderick, a Spanish king. Now read the map key. It explains a symbol that stands for caliphate battles. As you can see, the Muslim army passed Toledo (tuh LEE doh). Actually, the people of Toledo surrendered without a battle. The next year, more Muslim armies arrived. Find Poitiers (pwah TYAY) in France. Did the caliphate army fight a battle in this city?

Although the caliphate did not conquer France, Muslims ruled parts of Spain for 700 years. In that time Spanish caliphs had magnificent mosques and libraries built. The most stunning mosque, in Córdoba, still stands.

TRYING THE SKILL

The map on page 281 shows events that happened over 600 years after the caliphate victories in Spain. Refer to the Helping Yourself box as you answer questions.

At the time shown here, a Muslim, Ibn Battuta (IHB un bat TOO tuh), set out on a pilgrimage to Mecca from Tangier in present-day Morocco. Little did he know that he would travel 75,000 miles, exploring Africa, Asia, and Europe before returning home. When did Ibn Battuta travel?

Ibn Battuta saw the lighthouse at Alexandria and Jerusalem's Dome of the Rock before visiting Mecca. Baghdad followed. When did he visit Jerusalem?

After he returned to Mecca, Ibn Battuta heard tales about India. Instead of taking the shorter but riskier sea route, he went by land. Constantinople was one stop on this long journey. What city did he visit north of Constantinople? Between what years did

Helping yourself

- An **historical map** shows places or events from the past.
- Study the map title and map key.
- Find the symbols on the map, and examine any other information given on it.

Ibn Battuta visit the Maldive Islands?

Later Ibn Battuta explored Muslim Spain and went by caravan far into Africa. Before Battuta died in about 1377, he recounted his travels to a scribe. As far as we know, he was the only person who had explored the world so thoroughly up to that time.

REVIEWING THE SKILL

Use the map on this page to answer the following questions.

1. What makes this is a historical map?
2. Between what years did Ibn Battuta visit the east coast of Africa?
3. Did he visit Delhi before or after Mecca? How do you know?
4. When is a historical map helpful?

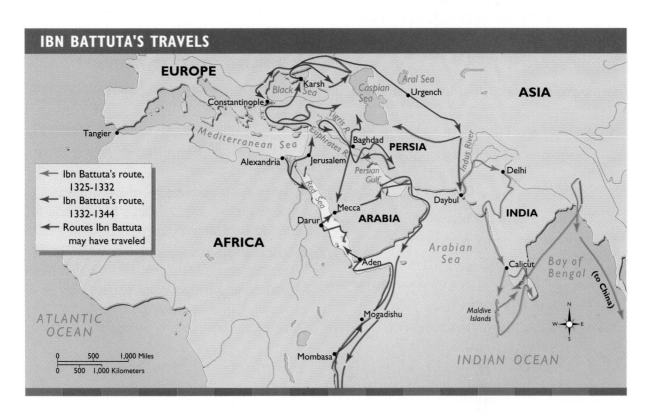

IBN BATTUTA'S TRAVELS

← Ibn Battuta's route, 1325-1332
← Ibn Battuta's route, 1332-1344
← Routes Ibn Battuta may have traveled

CHAPTER 10 REVIEW

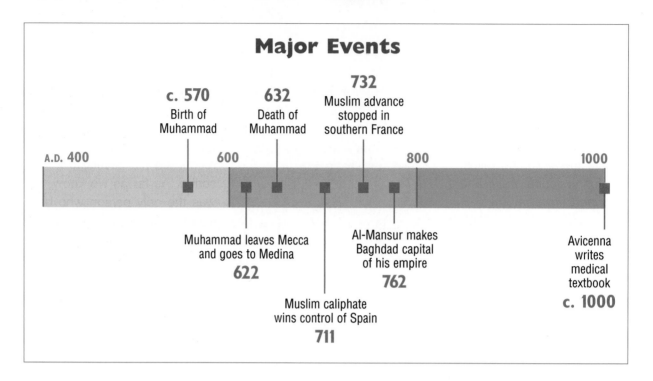

Major Events

732
Muslim advance stopped in southern France

c. 570
Birth of Muhammad

632
Death of Muhammad

A.D. 400   600   800   1000

Muhammad leaves Mecca and goes to Medina
622

Al-Mansur makes Baghdad capital of his empire
762

Avicenna writes medical textbook
c. 1000

Muslim caliphate wins control of Spain
711

THINKING ABOUT VOCABULARY

Each of the following statements contains an underlined vocabulary word. Number a sheet of paper from 1 to 10. Beside each number write **T** if the statement is true and **F** if the statement is false. If the statement is false, rewrite the sentence using the vocabulary word correctly.

1. A caliph is a Muslim ruler.
2. An oasis is a Muslim place of worship.
3. The Kaaba is a temple in Mecca that was used to honor gods and goddesses.
4. The Five Pillars are part of the Kaaba.
5. A journey made for religious reasons is called a pilgrimage.
6. The Quran is a famous mosque in Cairo.
7. A caravan is a desert tent.
8. Algebra is a type of mathematics.

9. Muslims used an astrolabe to help them illustrate books.
10. Muhammad's migration from Mecca to Medina, which marks the beginning of the Islamic calendar, is called the hijra.

THINKING ABOUT FACTS

1. Who are the Bedouins? How did some of them become wealthy and powerful?
2. Why is the Quran important to Muslims?
3. What are the Five Pillars of Islam? What is their purpose?
4. What have been some of the important contributions that Muslims have made to world civilization?
5. Look at the time line above. What information do you find there that would make you conclude that Islam spread very rapidly? In what year did the Muslim caliphate gain control of Spain?

THINK AND WRITE

WRITING A DESCRIPTION

Write a paragraph about the geography and climate of the Arabian peninsula. Describe both the fertile and desert parts of the peninsula. Provide information about the climate of the Empty Quarter.

WRITING AN ARTICLE

Write a short article for your school newspaper about Islam. Describe its main beliefs and practices.

WRITING A LETTER

Suppose you are on a pilgrimage to Mecca. Write a letter home describing what you are doing and what you see. Describe the things that impress you the most. Provide descriptions of the art and architecture you see in Mecca.

APPLYING GEOGRAPHY SKILLS

READING HISTORICAL MAPS

1. What is an historical map?

2. Look at the historical map on page 280. What historical information does it provide?

3. What does the map on page 280 tell you about the speed and direction of Muslim expansion?

4. Look at the historical map on page 281. What type of information does it provide? How does the map show different routes of travel?

5. How are historical maps helpful?

Summing Up the Chapter

Review the chapter. Then copy the main-idea chart below on a separate piece of paper. Fill in details in each column that are connected to the main idea. After completing the chart, use it to help you write a paragraph that answers the question "What are the greatest contributions of Muslims to world civilization?"

MAIN IDEA: Islam Spread Throughout Muslim Caliphate

Geographic Setting	Teachings	Achievements

Ancient America

THINKING ABOUT HISTORY AND GEOGRAPHY

Some scientists believe that early peoples crossed a land bridge from Asia to North America about 30,000 years ago. From there they moved through North and South America. Some settled on the rich lands of Mexico and Central America. The time line shows that these early peoples developed agriculture and built civilizations there. One group, the powerful Maya, built many large cities, which they suddenly and mysteriously abandoned.

30,000 YEARS AGO

BERINGIA
Hunters and gatherers cross a land bridge in search of food

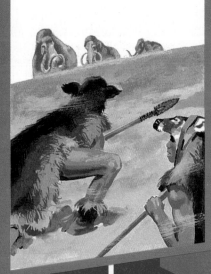

5000 B.C.

VALLEY OF MEXICO
Early people in Mexico cultivate corn

1000 B.C.

LA VENTA
The Olmec use waterways to transport goods

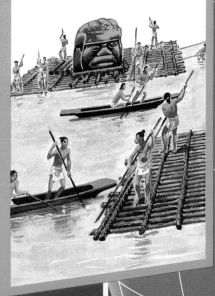

30,000 B.C.   5000 B.C.   1000 B.C.

Site of Beringia

PACIFIC OCEAN

NORTH AMERICA

Gulf of Mexico

Chichén Itzá

Valley of Mexico

La Venta

Copán

A.D. 600s

COPÁN
The Maya build a city and stone monuments

A.D. 800s

CHICHÉN ITZÁ
Maya astronomers observe the stars and planets

A.D. 1

A.D. 1000

Geography of Middle America

Focus Activity

What is unique about the geography of Middle America?

- Ice Age
- glacier
- tropical
- rain forest

- Beringia
- Middle America
- Central Plateau

Read Aloud

The land of Middle America is one of great variety— from the lush green forests, dripping with rain, to the dry brown plateaus, scorched by the sun. Within this diverse region, with its icy mountain peaks and wandering river valleys, early people forged a series of remarkable civilizations.

THE BIG PICTURE

About 40,000 years ago, Earth's climate was much colder than it is today. This period of time is called the Ice Age, because ice covered nearly half of Earth's land mass. Ice formed in great sheets called glaciers that slowly spread south from the North Pole. As more water turned to ice, the level of the oceans began to drop. When the oceans sank, more land became visible. A "land bridge" we call Beringia (buh RIN jee uh) formed between Asia and North America.

Beringia was located where the Bering Strait is today. Find this area on the map on page R11. Many scientists believe that it was across Beringia that people first came to the Americas. Asian hunters probably followed herds of reindeer across the land bridge and onto the unknown continent. By 15,000 years ago, hunters and gatherers had spread throughout the Americas. In this chapter you will read about the region where the first American civilizations developed. It is called Mesoamerica, or Middle America. *Meso* is from the Latin word meaning "middle."

ENVIRONMENTS OF MIDDLE AMERICA

The early people who traveled south from what is now the United States found warmer lands of great variety. There were towering mountains, lush coastal plains, and dry plateaus. These lands also had large animal populations to hunt and ideal climates for growing food. Many early people settled in Middle America. Look at the map on this page to find this region. It included parts of what are now Mexico and Central America. Here, thousands of years ago, people developed unique cultures that included traditions of farming, religion, government, and art.

The Land of Middle America

Much of Middle America is covered by steep mountains. A large area of rolling hills, called the Central Plateau, is located in the northern part of the region. Ancient volcanoes are found in the valleys of the Central Plateau. As Earth warmed after the Ice Age, this region became home to many different kinds of animals and plants. Not surprisingly, archaeologists have also found bones of early people here. Today the Central Plateau is the location of one of the world's most populous cities, Mexico City.

The Climate of Middle America

Most of Middle America is in the tropical zone. *Tropical* refers to the area of Earth that is near the equator, between the Tropic of Cancer and the Tropic of Capricorn. Middle America has many mountains, so the climate changes with elevation.

The hottest regions, from sea level to 3,000 feet, are called *tierra caliente* (tee AIR ruh cahl YEN tay), which in English means "hot land." These regions are found mostly in the low coastal plains. Here the temperature is over 80°F most of the time. The next level of elevation in Middle America, which includes the Central Plateau, is called *tierra templada* (tee AIR ruh tem PLAH dah), or "temperate land." At this elevation the climate is generally mild. The highest mountain elevations, above 6,000 feet, are known as *tierra fría* (tee AIR ruh FREE ah), or "cold land." The weather there is usually cooler than that of the other two regions.

These varying climate regions all have one thing in common—the rainy season. Almost all the rain that falls in Middle America comes between the months of May and October. Between the months of November and April, the skies are usually clear.

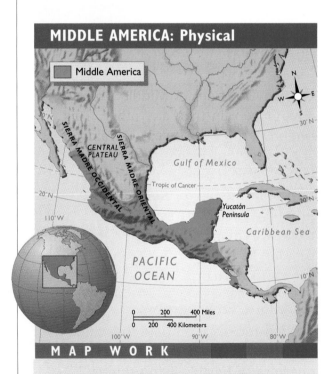

MIDDLE AMERICA: Physical

Middle America

SIERRA MADRE OCCIDENTAL

SIERRA MADRE ORIENTAL

CENTRAL PLATEAU

Gulf of Mexico

Tropic of Cancer

Yucatán Peninsula

Caribbean Sea

PACIFIC OCEAN

30° N
20° N
110° W
20° N
10° N
100° W
90° W
80° W

0   200   400 Miles
0   200   400 Kilometers

MAP WORK

Middle America has a variety of landforms.

1. Where are the highest lands found?
2. The Yucatán Peninsula is bordered by which two bodies of water?

Monkeys like these (below) are found in Middle America's rain forests. Abundant plant and animal life have provided food for the Olmec and modern peoples.

THE RAIN FOREST

One environment of Middle America gets more rain than any other. This region is the rain forest. A rain forest is a forest that receives more than 80 inches of rain per year. That's more rain than the city of San Francisco gets in four years! Most rain forests are in tropical regions. The world's tropical regions lie between the Tropics of Cancer and Capricorn.

A Unique Environment

Rain forests are home to a huge variety of plants and animals. Three-quarters of Earth's living things are found in rain forests. Writer Arnold Newman describes this unique environment:

The forest interior is a magical and mercurial [changing] place—an enchanted realm where anything is possible. . . . There are "roses" with 145-foot trunks; daisies and violets as big as apple trees . . . 18 foot cobras . . . [and] frogs so big they eat rats. . . . The forest's climate is the key to all this.

The rain forests of Middle America are in the tierra caliente and in the tierra templada. The trees in the tropical rain forests near the Gulf of Mexico can grow 200 feet tall—about as high as a stack of 20 school buses. Here thousands of kinds of plants and animals live under the canopy, or roof, of trees.

The canopy is so thick that little sun

reaches the forest floor. In the cooler rain forests of tierra templada, clouds sometimes blanket the entire forest.

People in Middle America

The first people in Middle America probably arrived about 11,000 years ago. Small knives and arrow points have been found in the Central Plateau. These stone tools were left in caves by early hunter-gatherers. Early Americans gathered onions, squash, and avocados, and hunted rabbits and deer. Like early people in other parts of the world, they moved around in search of food.

WHY IT MATTERS

After the first people came across Beringia to North America, some moved southward to Middle America. The diverse lands of this region provided a warm climate and abundant food. These resources made Middle America ideal for human settlement. In the next lesson you will read about one of the many groups of people who created a civilization on this land.

How hot WAS it?

To learn about recent changes in climate, scientists often look at written records. By studying records, such as the dates of cherry blossom festivals in Japan or harvest records in France, they can learn if a region's climate has become hotter or colder, wetter or drier, over time. The study of climate is called climatology.

The study of climates in past ages is called paleoclimatology (pay lee oh kli muh TAHL uh jee). To learn about ice ages and other big changes in climate, scientists study clues such as pollen, seeds, or soil found in rocks, fossils, and glaciers.

 Reviewing Facts and Ideas

MAIN IDEAS

- The first people in the Americas may have come from Asia across the Beringia land bridge about 40,000 to 25,000 years ago.

- Middle America has mountains, rolling hills, and coastal plains. It also has three main climate regions defined by elevation.

- The rain forests of Middle America are unique environments with a huge variety of plant and animal life.

- The first settlers of Middle America were hunters and gatherers who lived in the Central Plateau region.

THINK ABOUT IT

1. How did a land bridge form between Asia and the Americas thousands of years ago?

2. What are the three major climate regions found in Middle America?

3. **FOCUS** What are three kinds of land areas found in Middle America?

4. **THINKING SKILL** What are three _conclusions_ that you can make about the rain forest environment?

5. **GEOGRAPHY** How might a rainy season affect the pattern of agriculture in an area?

Reading Climographs

VOCABULARY

climograph

WHY THE SKILL MATTERS

In the last lesson you read about the three different climate zones that are found in Middle America. They are tierra caliente, tierra templada, and tierra fría. Climate in these zones is largely determined by elevation, or the height of the land above sea level. Other factors that can affect the climate of a place are its distance from the equator and its distance from oceans or mountains.

Since there are many things that influence climate, the climate within a large region can vary greatly. Remember that the two most important parts of climate are temperature and precipitation. In Middle America, for example, temperatures of 90°F are common in some low-lying areas. In high mountain areas, however, the temperature is usually lower, around 40°F. Also, some areas in the region receive more than 80 inches of rain each year while other areas receive less than 15 inches.

The rain does not fall evenly throughout the year in this region. As you have read, Middle America has a rainy season. This means that for part of the year the climate here is very wet and for part of the year it is very dry.

One way to learn about the climate of a place is to study a climograph of that place. A climograph is a graph that shows the temperature and precipitation in a place over a period of months.

USING THE SKILL

Look at Climograph A. Notice that it includes two graphs—a bar graph and a line graph. The bar graph shows the average monthly precipitation. The line graph shows the average monthly temperature.

Read a climograph the same way you would read other kinds of graphs. First read the title. Then read the other information below the title. This useful information will help you to compare the climates of three cities in Mexico. Next read the labels on the sides and bottom of the climograph. The left side lists precipitation and is the key for reading the bar graph. The right side lists the temperature and is the key for reading the line graph. The labels along the bottom show that time is measured in months.

Having temperature and precipitation together on the same graph can be useful. Suppose you wanted to find out in which

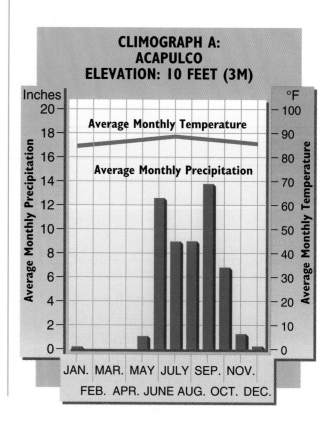

**CLIMOGRAPH A:
ACAPULCO
ELEVATION: 10 FEET (3M)**

month the rainy season begins in Acapulco. By looking for a sharp increase in precipitation on the bar graph, you can tell that the rainy season begins in June. You can also see on the line graph that the average temperature in Acapulco during April, May, and June rises to about 87°F.

TRYING THE SKILL

Climographs are useful for comparing the climate of two different places. Study Climographs B and C on this page. Notice that the elevation of Mexico City and Veracruz are very different. Mexico City is in tierra templada and Veracruz is in tierra caliente. Which city would you expect to have a warmer climate? Why?

In which month does Veracruz receive the most rain? In which month does Mexico City receive the most rain? Which city receives the most rain during the month of October? How did you find this answer?

REVIEWING THE SKILL

1. What is a climograph? How can climographs be useful?

2. Which of the three Mexican cities shown has the most rainfall in August? The least rainfall during June?

3. Which city has hotter temperatures in June, Veracruz or Mexico City?

4. Suppose you were planning a vacation to Acapulco. How would using a climograph help you to plan your trip?

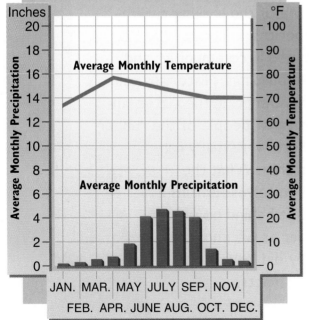

CLIMOGRAPH B:
MEXICO CITY
ELEVATION: 7,340 FEET (2,237M)

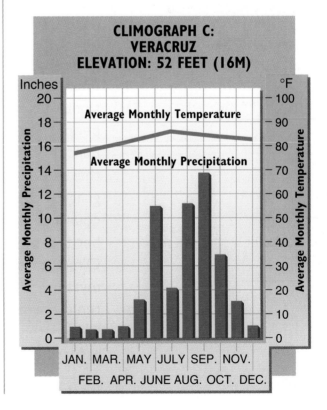

CLIMOGRAPH C:
VERACRUZ
ELEVATION: 52 FEET (16M)

1400 B.C.	1200 B.C.	400 B.C.	200 B.C.	A.D. 400	A.D. 1000

The Olmec Civilization

Focus Activity

Read Aloud

In the 1860s a farmer in the Mexican state of Veracruz was clearing dense forest to build a new field for sugar-cane. He came upon a large dome-shaped object which he thought was a big, upside-down pot. He called for help to uncover the mysterious object. When the "pot" was finally unearthed, it turned out to be a giant stone head nearly 5 feet high! The uncovering of this sculpture led to more excavations in the area. Slowly the story of an ancient people of Middle America began to unfold. We call these people the Olmec (OHL mek).

THE BIG PICTURE

In the lush rain forest along the Gulf of Mexico arose one of the earliest civilizations of the Americas. In about 1200 B.C. people here settled in communities and built remarkable buildings. Historians call these people the Olmec. In the Aztec language, Olmec means "people of the rubber country," for there were many rubber trees in the area. What the Olmec called themselves remains a mystery. They left behind no written records as far as we know. Fortunately, they did leave a rich assortment of artifacts.

This stone carving was found at La Venta.

Beneath a blanket of forest and greenery at Laguna de los Cerros (right), the remains of an ancient city may hold answers to mysteries of the Olmec.

THE OLMEC

Archaeologists believe the Olmec flourished along the Gulf of Mexico from about 1200 B.C. to 400 B.C. The area is still made up almost entirely of rain forest. Rivers cut through the forest on their way to the Gulf of Mexico. This lush environment was rich in food. Fish, turtles, ducks, wild turkeys, boars, and deer were plentiful. The forest also provided fruits, such as guava. The Olmec probably hunted and gathered, as earlier people in the region had done.

It was their success in agriculture, however, that allowed the Olmec to build a stable culture. They used a farming method known as slash and burn. In this method, farmers first cleared, or slashed, the dense jungle growth with stone axes. Then during the dry season, they burned what remained. The left-over ashes helped enrich the soil.

MIDDLE AMERICA, 500 B.C.

SIERRA MADRE OCCIDENTAL

CENTRAL PLATEAU

SIERRA MADRE ORIENTAL

Gulf of Mexico

Tropic of Cancer

20°N

Yucatán Peninsula

20°N

MEXICO ● La Venta

0 150 300 Miles
0 150 300 Kilometers

PACIFIC OCEAN

10°N

10°N

Olmec lands

100°W   90°W

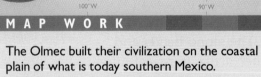

M A P   W O R K

The Olmec built their civilization on the coastal plain of what is today southern Mexico.

1. To what degree of latitude is La Venta closest?

2. What landform lies to the northeast of the Olmec lands?

Like early farmers in Egypt and China, the Olmec made use of the flooding rivers to grow crops. After the summer floods deposited new soil, the Olmec planted the fertile river banks with crops. Three main crops were corn, beans, and squash.

293

LIFE IN AN OLMEC TOWN

Archaeologists have uncovered four important Olmec settlements. By about 1000 B.C. the town of La Venta had become the major center of Olmec culture. La Venta is located on a large island, surrounded by swamps and rivers, near the northern coast of what is now southern Mexico. Look at the map on page 293 to find La Venta.

The People of La Venta

In the center of what was La Venta sits a huge earthen mound, 82 feet high. This was probably the base of an Olmec pyramid. Beyond this mound are smaller mounds and a large plaza surrounded by stone pillars. In the plaza are four enormous stone heads. The largest weighs 24 tons! These heads are probably statues of Olmec rulers. Each stone head wears a hat that looks like a football helmet. Each helmet has its own symbol, which may stand for the name of a ruler.

The stone heads and other artifacts reveal interesting clues about the Olmec people. We know, for example, that the people who lived in La Venta did specialized work. Some people worked as stone carvers. They carved the gray basalt, a hard volcanic rock, into statues or into tools for grinding corn. Others carved more delicate items out of jade and obsidian, another kind of volcanic rock. These small objects probably had religious uses. Most of the Olmec, however, were farmers, and growing food was the central activity at La Venta.

The Olmec made this rubber ball (left) over 3,000 years ago. Similar balls were used in games by later cultures in Middle America.

The leaders of La Venta controlled most of the land that was used for farming. They also built stone monuments with carvings. The monuments also reminded the people of the authority of their leaders.

Olmec Religion

Artifacts and ruins in La Venta also provide us with some hints about the religious beliefs of the Olmec. Like the other people of Middle America, the Olmec practiced polytheism. They

Crafts of the Olmec

Since they lived in a warm climate, the Olmec probably wore simple, light articles of clothing. The many beads and small carvings that have been found indicate that the Olmec liked to wear jewelry. Both men and women wore bracelets, necklaces, and earrings made of jade and other beautiful stones. Some people, perhaps town leaders, wore headdresses decorated with colorful feathers and beads. These creations may have been worn for special religious ceremonies.

The Olmec collected sap from rubber trees to make rubber balls. They used these balls to play special games in open fields. For musical entertainment, the Olmec made flutes and other musical instruments out of clay and wood.

believed in more than one god, such as gods of fire, rain, and sun. Throughout La Venta archaeologists have found special altars that were used to make sacrifices to the gods. To sacrifice means to give up or destroy something for the sake of something else.

The Olmec also believed that certain animals had special powers. No animal, they believed, was as powerful as the jaguar. This rain forest cat played a central role in Olmec beliefs that remains a mystery to us. Perhaps the Olmec believed that the jaguar helped bring fertile crops. Many carvings and statues of jaguars have been found in Olmec settlements. Near the plaza at La Venta, archaeologists have discovered a large mosaic, or pattern of stones, in the image of a jaguar.

Beautiful jade carvings, like this jaguar-headed figure, have been found at La Venta and other Olmec sites.

295

The figure (above) is typical of the stone monuments carved by the Olmec.

Olmec Traders

Archaeologists believe that the Olmec traded with other groups of people in Middle America. Clay goods and figures made in the Olmec style have been found in places as distant from Olmec lands as central Mexico, more than 300 miles to the north. Perhaps the Olmec traded these objects for food, feathers, and animal skins. Traders would have traveled to distant settlements by foot on narrow forest paths.

WHY IT MATTERS

Around 400 B.C. Olmec civilization was gradually beginning to disappear. Historians are not certain why the culture faded. Some think that the system of agriculture began to break down from overuse of the land. La Venta and the other Olmec settlements were abandoned. Eventually thick rain forest grew up around the Olmec towns. The achievements of this early Middle American civilization lived on, however, in artifacts left behind. You are about to read of a huge civilization that developed in Middle America and built on the achievements of the Olmec.

✓ Reviewing Facts and Ideas

MAIN IDEAS

- The Olmec built one of the earliest civilizations in the Americas, starting around 1200 B.C.

- The Olmec developed a system of slash and burn agriculture in the dense rain forest environment.

- The Olmec were craftworkers who designed objects such as earrings, beads, and necklaces. They probably traded these objects with people in other parts of Middle America.

THINK ABOUT IT

1. In which part of Middle America did the centers of Olmec culture grow?

2. How did the Olmec create fields for growing crops?

3. **FOCUS** What clues have helped archaeologists to gain knowledge about Olmec culture?

4. **THINKING SKILL** What _effects_ did the environment of the Olmec have on their system of farming? How in turn might the Olmec have affected their environment?

5. **WRITE** Suppose you were a trader who lived in Olmec times. Write a description of some of the Olmec objects that you would like to trade with other people.

MAKING A DIFFERENCE

The Rain Forest Treasures Trail

SYLVESTER VILLAGE, BELIZE—The Gallon Jug Community School is located in the middle of a vast rain forest in Belize.

Near the Gallon Jug school, a trail extends into the forest. The school's 75 students helped create the trail. They call it the Rain Forest Treasures Trail, and they use it to teach visitors about the special plants and animals found in the tropical rain forest.

Tropical rain forests cover only about 7 percent of Earth's land. Yet they are home to fully half of Earth's plant species. Many rain forest plants provide medicines that have been used for centuries to treat everything from colds to deadly diseases.

Teacher Nancy Zuniga directs the school along with her husband, Julio. She explains that the trail came about because "the kids were always teaching me about this plant or that plant. They knew from their parents which plants helped soothe a burn or bring down a fever."

Dr. Rosita Arvigo, from Belize's Ix Chel tropical research center, taught students to recognize medicinal plants. Older villagers also helped the students learn the uses of many plants.

After the children and their parents cleared the trail, they located and labeled plants along the path. "Now," says student Adolio Bolaños, "we are tour guides. We take visitors on a half-hour walk on the trail. Along the way we teach them about the different plants and their uses."

Tourists and school groups from other parts of Belize come to walk the Rain Forest Treasures Trail. Adolio tells visitors that rain forests around the world are disappearing. Loggers cut down trees and ranchers clear land for cattle grazing. Now the children of the Gallon Jug school are working to protect rain forest plants and to replace trees. Adolio worries that "if people clear away the rain forest, we will not have medicinal plants. If we keep the forests, someday doctors may find new ways to use these plants to cure sicknesses. I read that somewhere in the forest there is a plant for every sickness. I hope it's true."

"The kids were always teaching me about this plant or that plant."

Nancy Hinchler Zuniga

1400
B.C

800
B.C

200
B.C

A.D.
250

A.D.
900

A.D.
1000

Maya Civilization

Read Aloud

Throughout Middle America archaeologists have uncovered ruins of huge stone cities. They were built by a civilization of great builders, astronomers, and craft-workers. By studying the spectacular ruins of the ancient Maya (MAH yuh), archaeologists have developed a picture of a culture that dominated Middle America for almost 1,000 years.

Focus Activity

READ TO LEARN

What were some of the achievements of the Maya civilization?

VOCABULARY

- Classic Period
- maize
- glyph
- stela

PLACES

- Copán

THE BIG PICTURE

The Maya developed their civilization about 600 years after Olmec culture declined. Because most Maya books were lost or destroyed, many details of their lives remain a mystery. Stone pyramids and plazas, however, hint at the complex culture that thrived on the plains and in the valleys of Middle America. The Maya created a written language and achieved a remarkable understanding of the stars and planets. They also kept records of their work in stone carvings. This civilization developed in a region close to where the Olmec had lived.

THE RISE OF THE MAYA

The Maya had lived in the southern part of Middle America as early as 1000 B.C. From the lowlands of the Yucatán (yoo kuh TAN) peninsula to the highlands of present-day Guatemala, they developed a culture based on agriculture and hunting. They had contact, no doubt, with the Olmec and other nearby groups.

Between about A.D. 250 and A.D. 900, the Maya built the richest civilization yet seen in the Americas. Historians call this period of Maya history the Classic Period. A classic period is an important time of cultural achievement for a civilization. Other classic periods often discussed by historians include those of Greece and Rome.

A Maya City

One of the great centers of classic Maya culture was Copán (ko PAHN), a city in present-day Honduras. Even today the ruins at Copán are impressive.

Among the impressive structures at Copán is the ball court. Here a fierce Maya ball game, called *pokta-pok* (POHK tuh POHK), was played. Players wore helmets and padding on their arms and legs, for the game was rough. They were not allowed to touch the five-pound rubber ball with their hands. The two teams rushed up and down the court trying to get the ball through a stone hoop. If they succeeded, they won the game. Excited spectators filled the stands and gave clothing to the winning team.

This game was part of Maya religion. You can see an illustration of a game on page 294. Those who lost were sometimes killed as a sacrifice to Maya gods. The Maya believed their gods would help them if they sacrificed something as important as a human life.

Other buildings in Copán included the tall temple-pyramids and palaces around the main plaza. These structures were built out of huge stone blocks. Since the Maya did not have wheels or work animals, all the moving and lifting was done by humans. Sometimes this work was done by enslaved people who had been captured during wars.

THE MAYA, A.D. 250–900

Maya lands

NORTH AMERICA

ATLANTIC OCEAN

Gulf of Mexico

Yucatán Peninsula

Chichén Itzá Tulum

Tikal

Copán

Caribbean Sea

PACIFIC OCEAN

SOUTH AMERICA

0   300   600 Miles
0   300   600 Kilometers

M A P   W O R K

The Yucatán Peninsula covers an area of about 70,000 square miles in Mexico.
1. Into what body of water does the Yucatán Peninsula extend?
2. About how far is Copán from Chichén Itza?

This building at Chichén Itza is the Temple of the Feathered Serpent.

LIFE IN COPÁN

At its peak between about A.D. 600 to 800, Copán was home to about 20,000 people. The region of Copán was crowded with hundreds of buildings, yet a person could have walked from one side of the city center to the other in less than ten minutes. The buildings ranged from small plaster-and-thatch houses to the huge stone pyramids that still stand today.

Copán had many visitors from nearby villages. Traders came from other Maya cities many miles away. In some ways, however, life in Copán was not so different from life for earlier Middle Americans. For example, most of the people in Copán worked as farmers.

The Most Important Crop

Agriculture was the heart of the Maya economy. Maize (MAYZ), or corn, was the heart of Maya agriculture. Maize was first grown in Middle America in about 5000 B.C. The cob of this early maize was tiny, about the size of a shelled peanut. When it was heated, maize exploded like modern popcorn.

Over the years Middle American farmers improved their crops of maize. It was the most important part of the Maya diet. Yum Kax, the maize god, became a significant part of the Maya religion. According to one belief, the gods created the Maya people from maize dough. The Maya performed special ceremonies for the planting and harvesting of maize.

The farmers of Copán planted other crops, too, such as beans, squash, and peppers. They also grew cacao trees, which provided chocolate—the favorite

In this painting by Diego Rivera, Maya women sort their most important crop, maize.

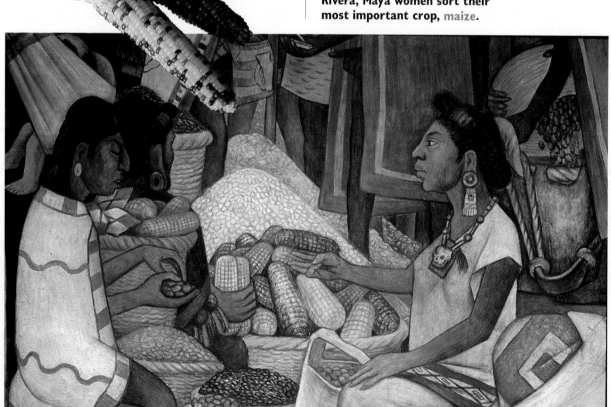

drink of Maya rulers. Most Maya grew avocado and papaya trees near home. They hunted for animals such as deer. Farmers and hunters sold many of their crops and products in city marketplaces.

Growing Up in Copán

Boys and girls lived very differently in Copán. When boys were in their teens, they moved out of their family homes into large group homes. There they learned to play the ball game. Boys also learned to become soldiers. Girls stayed at home, where they were strictly raised by their mothers. They learned how to cook maize and other food and how to run a household.

Maya Society

At the top of society in Copán was the king. Below the king were warriors, wealthy farmers, and merchants. As in the societies of Egypt and Mesopotamia, farmers made up the largest group. Below the farmers were slaves, who were usually prisoners taken during wars with neighboring cities.

The Religion of the Maya

Religion was very important to the Maya. They believed that the universe was made up of three levels—the upperworld of the heavens, the middleworld of humans, and the underworld of the dead. The Maya believed that their king could communicate with the upperworld. He also could bring spirits into the middleworld.

The Maya worshiped hundreds of gods. In addition to important gods such as Yum Kax, god of maize, they also believed in lesser gods. For example, hunters, poets, and beekeepers each worshiped different gods. The king and other nobles led many of the ceremonies for worshiping these gods. The Maya believed that their ancestors lived on in the upperworld.

As part of their religion, the Maya closely studied the stars and planets. The planet Venus was considered especially important. Its movement was used to make decisions about when to attack other cities. By studying the night sky, the Maya also developed an accurate calendar. This allowed them to record the exact dates of events.

The Maya, like the Olmec, carved stone figures of their gods and leaders.

MAYA WRITING

The Maya were the first people of Middle America to use a written language widely. Although almost all of their books were lost or burned by the Spanish in the 1500s, the Maya left behind a written record in stone. It is from these records as well as from other artifacts that archaeologists have been able to form a picture of what life was like for the Maya.

Unlocking Written Mysteries

Only in the last 50 years have archaeologists begun to understand the writing of the Maya. These symbols, called glyphs (GLIFS), are carved into the stones of Maya cities and towns. Some glyphs are like the pictures of Chinese writing and stand for objects. Others stand for sounds, as in the Roman alphabet.

At Copán the Maya built a magnificent 72-step "hieroglyphic stairway," with over 2,200 glyphs. These symbols tell the story of Copán from its beginnings until A.D. 755, when the stairway was built. Not unlike the epics of Homer in ancient Greece, this stairway recounts the heroic deeds and deaths of Maya leaders.

Maya leaders also had tall, flat stones, called stelae (STEE lee), carved with glyphs. These stones were put on display in the city. A stela was often used to mark an important historical event in the life of the leader. On this page you can see a stela from Copán that told about the life of the king Yax-Pac (YAKS PAK). How are these glyphs similar to Egyptian hieroglyphics?

Copán Stela A
c. A.D. 700
Stelae like this one found at Copán were carved to record important dates and events in Maya history. The Maya must have felt that stelae looked like trees, for they called them *te-tun*, or "tree-stones." Maya stelae focus only on the lives of rulers. Information about other people of the valley is more difficult to find.

Maya Math

The Maya also created a mathematical system that helped merchants keep track of goods and scribes keep track of history. This system used glyphs that the Maya developed to represent numbers. It helped the Maya to make very exact calculations.

WHY IT MATTERS

Many of the great Maya cities were abandoned in the A.D. 900s. No one knows why for sure. Some scientists believe that, like the Olmec, the Maya may have suffered crop failures. Others think that the many wars the Maya waged contributed to the decline of the civilization. Although they abandoned the cities, however, Maya people continued to live in the area.

Today the descendants of the Maya live in the highlands and lowlands of central and southern Middle America. There 4 million Maya continue many of the traditions that began hundreds of years ago. Many speak a version of the Maya language and follow ancient ceremonies of agriculture, marriage, and healing. They also grow maize and other traditional crops. Some Maya raise crops, such as coffee, that are sold around the world. Such products link the rich Maya past with the realities of today's economy.

Descendants of the Maya, like these women in Central America, continue to follow many traditional ways.

Reviewing Facts and Ideas

MAIN IDEAS

- The Maya built a complex civilization in Middle America from about A.D. 250 until A.D. 900.

- The Maya created large cities throughout Middle America. The cities contained temples, ball courts, and other buildings.

- Religion was an important part of life for the Maya. The Maya practiced polytheism.

- The Maya developed systems of writing and mathematics that allowed them to record important events in their history.

THINK ABOUT IT

1. What was the most important crop to the Maya?

2. What was one kind of god that the Maya worshiped?

3. **FOCUS** What are three achievements that set the Maya apart from earlier Middle American civilizations? What made Maya civilization "classic"?

4. **THINKING SKILL** _Compare_ the systems of learning of the Maya with those of ancient Greece.

5. **WRITE** Suppose you are an archaeologist exploring Maya ruins. Write a description of Copán for a magazine for sixth graders.

ASTRONOMY

Have you ever looked up into the sky on a clear night and wondered about the stars and planets? The ancient Maya must have wondered too.

Scientists have discovered that the Maya had a great interest in astronomy, or the study of stars and planets. The Maya spent much time observing the sun, moon, and the planet Venus. Using these observations the Maya were able to design a complex and accurate calendar. Like ancient Egyptians, they also predicted eclipses of the sun and moon.

People have always wanted to know what is in the sky. Astronomy continues to be an important part of scientific life. Through modern high-powered telescopes, satellites, and space shuttle missions, we continue to learn about the universe.

The United States launched the Hubble Space Telescope (right) in 1990. In 1995 it took this photo of a star being "born." The star is so far away, that the light captured in this picture began its journey across space 7,000 years ago—about the time ancient Egyptians were beginning to farm along the Nile.

The Maya built this observatory (left) at Chichén Itza. Based on their studies of planets, they created a calendar. Centuries later another people, the Aztec, developed a similar calendar (above left).

CHAPTER 11 REVIEW

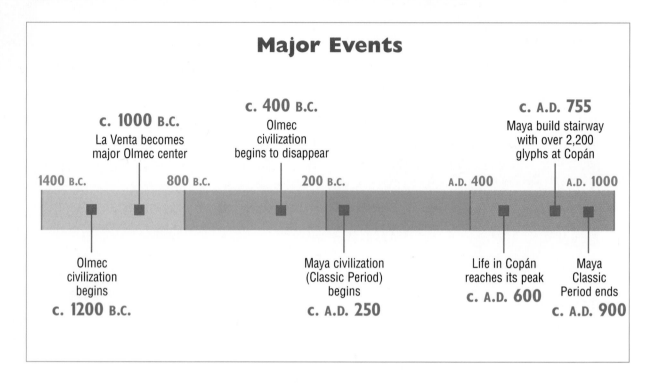

Major Events

c. 1000 B.C.
La Venta becomes major Olmec center

c. 400 B.C.
Olmec civilization begins to disappear

c. A.D. 755
Maya build stairway with over 2,200 glyphs at Copán

1400 B.C.   800 B.C.   200 B.C.   A.D. 400   A.D. 1000

Olmec civilization begins
c. 1200 B.C.

Maya civilization (Classic Period) begins
c. A.D. 250

Life in Copán reaches its peak
c. A.D. 600

Maya Classic Period ends
c. A.D. 900

THINKING ABOUT VOCABULARY

Number a sheet of paper from 1 to 10. Beside each number write the word or term from the list below that best completes each sentence.

Classic Period   maize
climograph   rain forest
glacier   slash and burn
glyph   stela
Ice Age   tropical

1. A tall, flat stone carved with glyphs is a _____.

2. The Maya civilization was at the height of achievement during its _____.

3. A body of ice that inches along the land is a _____.

4. A _____ measures temperature and precipitation over a period of months.

5. The main food of the Maya was _____.

6. A _____ receives more than 80 inches of rain per year.

7. One way to clear jungle areas for farming is to _____.

8. _____ refers to the climate area near the equator where it is very warm.

9. The _____ was a period when nearly half of Earth's land surface was covered by ice.

10. A symbol called the _____ is the basis of Maya writing.

THINKING ABOUT FACTS

1. How did the Ice Age affect the history of the Americas?

2. What makes rain forests unique?

3. How did the Olmec get food? What types of food did they eat?

4. What was pokta-pok?

5. Look at the time line above. How long did the Olmec and Maya civilizations last? What may have brought them to an end?

THINK AND WRITE

WRITING ABOUT PERSPECTIVES

Write about the people who traveled between Asia and North America during the Ice Age. Describe why there was a land bridge and the reasons why people may have crossed it.

WRITING A JOURNAL ENTRY

Suppose that you have gone back about 3,000 years to live in the Olmec center of La Venta. Write a journal entry about your life there. Include details about the way you live, the work you do, and some of the interesting features of the town.

WRITING A REPORT

Write a report about the civilization the Maya built in Middle America. Describe their main achievements and the way people lived in the city of Copán.

APPLYING STUDY SKILLS

READING CLIMOGRAPHS

1. What does a climograph measure?

2. Look at the climographs on pages 290–291. Which of the three Mexican cities shown has the highest average annual precipitation? Which has the highest average annual temperature?

3. Is the rainy season the same for all three cities? If not, how is it different?

4. What can you tell about the climate of the three cities by reading the climographs?

5. How are climographs helpful?

Summing Up the Chapter

Review the chapter and copy the main idea table below on a separate piece of paper. Then place each feature listed in the correct column. Add any additional features you find when you review the chapter. After filling in the table, use it to help write a paragraph that answers the question "What were some achievements of the early peoples in Middle America?"

MAIN IDEA: Civilizations developed in Middle America.

Features: Central Plateau; Classic Period; Copán; crafts; glyphs; La Venta; worship for Jaguar; rain forests; slash and burn; tropical climate; Yum Kax, god of maize

Geography	Olmec	Maya
Central Plateau	La Venta	Copán

UNIT 3 REVIEW

THINKING ABOUT VOCABULARY

Number a sheet of paper from 1 to 10. Beside each number write the word or term from the list below that best matches the statement.

algebra New Testament
dictator peninsula
glyph philosophy
maize pilgrimage
monarchy republic

1. Area of land mostly surrounded by water
2. Government in which people choose their own leaders
3. Corn
4. Collection of books that describes the beginnings of Christianity
5. Branch of mathematics developed by the Arabs
6. Someone who rules with absolute power
7. Search for wisdom and the right way to live
8. Journey made for religious reasons
9. Government ruled by one person, often a king or queen
10. Mayan symbol carved into stones

THINK AND WRITE

WRITING ABOUT PERSPECTIVES

Write a paragraph comparing the perspectives of a woman from ancient Sparta and a woman from ancient Athens. How would they have viewed city laws and government? What might they have wanted to change? How were their perspectives alike? How were they different? Explain your answers.

WRITING AN ESSAY

Write a short essay about Islam as one of the world's major religions. What are its main beliefs and practices?

WRITING ABOUT CONTRASTS

Write a paragraph describing the differences between the environments of the Arabian Peninsula and Middle America. Include information about landforms and climate. Explain the challenges faced by people who have lived in these two regions. Describe how they have adapted to the environments around them.

BUILDING SKILLS

1. **Making conclusions** What is a good conclusion? Why is a conclusion stronger with more evidence to back it up?

2. **Making conclusions** Suppose you visit a distant city for a weekend. Based on what you see during the short time, give an example of a conclusion you might make about the city.

3. **Elevation maps and profiles** What are ways you could use both an elevation map and a profile map of the Alps? Explain your answer.

4. **Historical maps** Look at the historical map on page 280. Explain the information the map provides and how you found the information by using the map.

5. **Climographs** Construct a climograph that shows the monthly temperature and precipitation in your area. Compare it with the climographs of the Mexican cities on pages 290–291. Make a conclusion about how the climate where you live differs from that of Mexico.

YESTERDAY, TODAY &
TOMORROW

You have read about the achievements of great civilizations of the past. Someday future students will read about us. What do you think future historians will say our greatest achievements were? Explain your choices. How are our achievements different from those of the past?

READING ON YOUR OWN

Here are some books you might find at the library to help you learn more.

SPIRIT OF THE MAYA: A BOY EXPLORES HIS PEOPLE'S MYSTERIOUS PAST
by Guy Garcia

Kin, a twelve-year-old descendant of the ancient Maya, gains pride in his ancestry when he discovers clues to the secrets of his society.

THE ROMAN NEWS
by Andrew Langley and Philip De Souza

Life in ancient Rome as it would appear in today's newspapers; done with headlines and features on everyday life.

BLACK SHIPS BEFORE TROY: THE STORY OF THE ILLIAD
by Rosemary Sutcliff

This thrilling story tells the tale of the Trojan War.

UNIT 3 REVIEW PROJECT

Perform a Scene About Life in Ancient Times

1. With your group, choose an ancient civilization from this unit.
2. Research some additional information about the civilization. Your school or local library can provide the information you will need.
3. Then write a scene that includes a character for each group member. You might tell what daily life was like in the civilization or about an event that affected the civilization.
4. Make sure each group member has several lines.
5. Next make costumes out of paper or material. Create scenery using paints and oaktag.
6. Finally, perform the scene for your class.

INCA KNIFE, PERU

ROSE WINDOW,
THE CATHEDRAL
OF NOTRE DAME, FRANCE;
GOLD MASK, BENIN

MODEL OF MING
DYNASTY SHIP, CHINA

World Regions in Transition

"To no one will we deny, or delay, rights or justice."

from the Magna Carta
See page 327.

Why Does It Matter?

The idea of protecting people's rights was just beginning to develop in the period covered in this unit. Many of the ways of life that we think of as "modern" began in the years between about a.d. 600 and a.d. 1600. In fact, many historians call this period the Middle Ages because they think of it as being between ancient and modern times. During these years, religious ideas spread and developed in Europe, Africa, Asia, and the Americas. These ideas affected the arts, science, and the ways people viewed the world and their place in it.

PORTRAIT OF
QUEEN ELIZABETH I,
ENGLAND

FIND OUT MORE!
Visit our website:
www.mhschool.com

*inter*NET
CONNECTION

Adventures with

City in the Sky

High in the Andes mountains, the Inca built a spectacular city. It had houses and stairways of stone, and terraced fields for growing crops on the steep slopes. But war came. The city was abandoned. The houses sat empty for four centuries. Forest plants engulfed the buildings. Then, in 1911, local people led American explorer Hiram Bingham to the site. After struggling through gorges and up mountainsides, he reached the ruins. "The sight held me spellbound," he declared. Later, he returned to Peru to begin clearing and excavating the city. Archaeologists are still exploring Machu Picchu today.

GEO JOURNAL

You stumble upon an empty city hidden in the mountains. Write a telegram announcing your discovery.

Cultures of Medieval Europe

THINKING ABOUT HISTORY AND GEOGRAPHY

In the period called the Middle Ages, most Europeans lived, worked, and worshiped in farming communities. During this "Age of Faith," Christianity spread throughout Europe. At the same time, rulers and nobles struggled for power. At the end of the Middle Ages came a time of great creativity in the arts, sciences, and religion.

ATLANTIC OCEAN

1095

ROME
Pope Urban II calls for Crusades to Jerusalem

about 1200

CHARTRES
Craftworkers build a magnificent cathedral

1215

ENGLAND
King John signs the Magna Carta

1100

1200

1400

ENGLAND

Wittenberg

Chartres

EUROPE

Florence

Rome

ASIA

1503

Mediterranean Sea

1517

FLORENCE
Leonardo da Vinci paints the Mona Lisa

WITTENBERG
Martin Luther posts his 95 Theses

Red Sea

AFRICA

1500

1600

Geography of Europe

Focus Activity

READ TO LEARN

What effects did the waterways of Europe have on the development of civilizations there?

VOCABULARY

* temperate
* deforestation
* navigable

PLACES

* Eurasia
* North Sea
* North European Plain
* Seine River

Read Aloud

"The great rivers and the strange number of canals . . . do not only lead to every great town, but almost to every village, and every farm-house in the country; and the [countless number] of sails are seen everywhere coursing up and down upon them."

These words were written by an English man named William Temple, after he visited the Netherlands 300 years ago. Like others before and after him, he was fascinated by the many rivers and canals throughout Europe.

THE BIG PICTURE

You have already studied the geography of two parts of Europe—Greece and Italy. The Netherlands, often called Holland, is a small present-day country in northern Europe. In this chapter you will learn more about the European continent and its history.

Next to Australia, Europe is the world's smallest continent. Europe, however, connects with Asia to create the world's largest landmass, called Eurasia. Find the Ural (YUR ul) and Caucasus (KAW kuh sus) mountains on the map on the next page. They are considered to be the border between Europe and Asia.

In Europe you can find some of the most unusual features of geography—from spouting geysers in Iceland to huge glaciers in the Alps. Waterways are an important part of Europe's geography. Much human activity here has been shaped by rivers and canals, seas and bays, and harbors and channels.

EUROPE

Europe is shaped like a big peninsula jutting westward off Eurasia. The continent has many peninsulas and islands. Europe also has a long, jagged coastline. It is surrounded by the Atlantic Ocean, the Mediterranean Sea, the North Sea, and the Baltic Sea. The Scandinavian peninsula, located in the north, has narrow inlets called fjords (FYORDZ) where the sea surges in between cliffs.

The climate of Europe is temperate, or mild, because of the winds that blow over the warm currents of the ocean. Even some lands near the Arctic Circle are relatively temperate. Extreme temperatures are found mostly along the border with Asia and on the peaks of the Alps.

EUROPE: Physical

MAP WORK

The geography of Europe is varied. The continent has mountainous areas, plains, and rivers.

1. Which mountains separate the Iberian Peninsula from the rest of Europe?

2. Which is farthest north—the Aegean Sea, the Baltic Sea, or the Black Sea?

3. Which is the highest mountain in Europe?

LAND AND WATER

The land and water of Europe are rich in natural resources. These resources have helped to make Europe a wealthy and productive region.

From Forests to Farmland

Two thousand years ago most of Europe lay under a blanket of dense forest. One group of Roman explorers is said to have walked through forests from Poland to France without ever seeing sunlight! Europeans began to clear forests to make room for farms and cities, especially after about A.D. 1100. The process of clearing forests is called deforestation. It has happened in many places around the world throughout history.

After forests were cleared, Europeans could farm more land. The most fertile farmland in Europe is found in a region called the North European Plain. Look at the map on page 317 to see this region. A long growing season helps farmers to grow crops like wheat in the plain's rich soil. In southern countries, like Greece and Spain, oranges and olives are grown.

Bounty from Rivers and Seas

Much of the European continent is within 300 miles of the sea. The jagged coastline creates natural harbors that help to protect boats. For these reasons, it is no surprise that fishing has always been important to the European economy. Fish are especially plentiful in the North Atlantic. Today nearly a third of all fish caught in the world come from waters around Europe.

Europe's rivers are also important to the economy. Over 2,000 years ago, Europeans began using river power to turn waterwheels that ground wheat. Traders transported goods on Europe's many long, navigable (NAV ih guh bul) rivers. Navigable rivers are deep

Today people still fish the waters near Iceland and herd cattle in mountainous Switzerland.

EUROPE AT A GLANCE

	Total Land Area	4,032,000 sq. miles 10,443,000 sq. km
	Highest Mountain	Mt. Elbrus, Russia 18,510 feet (5,642 m)
	Longest River	Volga River, Russia 2,194 miles 3,531 km
	Largest City	Moscow, Russia Population 8,769,000
	Current Population Percent of World Population	707,000,000 13%

GEO FACT

Though many of Europe's forests have been cleared, there are still large forests in Northern Europe. One of them is the Black Forest of Germany. This region gets its name from the dark fir and spruce trees covering its mountainsides. Many German fairy tales tell of the creatures of the Black Forest.

CHART WORK

The chart provides information about the size and geography of Europe.

1. What is the largest city in Europe? What is its population?
2. How did the Black Forest get its name?

---

enough for boat travel. One important navigable river is the Seine River. Paris, France, one of Europe's largest cities, grew alongside the Seine River. Europeans have developed thriving economies by using rivers for power and transportation.

European engineers created more waterways by building canals. In fact, it is possible to travel by boat from the English Channel in the west to the Ural Mountains in the east. Locate these features on the map on page 317.

WHY IT MATTERS

Rivers and coasts were very important in the growth of European cultures. Waterways provided power and helped to make transportation and trade possible. Remember, though, that Europeans added to their natural river system.

Europe's rivers and coasts still affect the way people live. They are used for transport. The fishing trade helps feed millions of Europeans.

In upcoming lessons, you will read how Europeans used their continent's resources to build civilizations.

✓✓ Reviewing Facts and Ideas

MAIN IDEAS

- Europe, Earth's second-smallest continent, has a long, jagged coastline.
- Closeness to the sea has had important effects on Europe's climate and economy.
- Europe's rivers and seas are great sources of fish. Waterways are also used for transportation and power.

THINK ABOUT IT

1. What makes the climate of Europe temperate?
2. Name a trade that has always been important to the European economy.
3. **FOCUS** How did the waterways of Europe affect life there?
4. **THINK** Explain why the following statement is a _fact_ or why it is an _opinion_: "Europe's navigable rivers help in the transport of goods."
5. **GEOGRAPHY** Find the island of Corsica and the English Channel on the map on page 317. Trace two possible sailing routes between these places—one by sea and one by river. Which route is longer? How much longer?

(removed)

400 500   1250 1300   1600

The Middle Ages

Read Aloud

"Woe to thee, Rome, that thou art crushed and trodden down by so many peoples; who has been seized by a northern king, and thy folk slaughtered and thy strength brought to nothing."

These words were written around A.D. 900 by a monk after an attack on Rome. The invaders were from England.

Focus Activity

READ TO LEARN

What was life like in Europe during the Middle Ages?

VOCABULARY

- Middle Ages
- manor
- serf
- feudalism
- lord
- vassal
- fief
- guild
- Magna Carta

PEOPLE

- Charlemagne
- William the Conqueror
- King John I

PLACES

- Aachen
- Normandy
- England

THE BIG PICTURE

Following the end of the western Roman empire around A.D. 500, Europe entered a new era of history. This period became known as the Middle Ages. It lies between the Roman period and about the 1400s.

The Roman empire left behind many legacies, including the Latin language and a large network of roads. The Christian religion also continued to grow and spread. However, the breakdown of Roman rule brought great changes for the people of Europe. Many small kingdoms developed.

Along with changes in government, the end of the Roman empire also brought about economic changes in Europe. Trade declined, after which ownership of land came to mean wealth and power. Large estates owned by wealthy nobles were called manors. Workers, called serfs, became bound to work on the manors. Serfs had little more freedom than slaves. Unlike slaves, however, serfs could not be bought or sold.

THE FRANKISH EMPIRE

Of the many small kingdoms in western Europe, one rose to great power in the 700s. This kingdom, ruled by a people called the Franks, was based in present-day France. You may remember from Chapter 9 that this region was the place the Romans called Gaul. The Franks built an empire that was the largest and richest in Europe since Roman times. Find it on the map.

A Powerful Ruler

The greatest leader of the Franks was called Charles the Great, or Charlemagne (SHAHR luh mayn). He conquered lands in southwestern parts of what is now France and in Italy and Germany. Charlemagne was a Christian. As his armies spread across Europe, they also spread Christianity.

Charlemagne's biggest achievement came in 800, when he arrived with his army in Rome. The leader of the Roman Church, Pope Leo III, placed a golden crown on Charlemagne's head and declared him Emperor. For a while, it appeared to western Europeans that the old Roman empire had risen again.

Charlemagne's Court

Charlemagne set up his capital in the city of Aachen (AH khun) in what is today Germany. His court became a lively political and cultural center.

Charlemagne was very tall for his time—over 6 feet. He loved to ride horses and swim in a pool he had built at Aachen. Perhaps most remarkably for his time, he also loved learning.

During the Middle Ages books were scarce and very few people could read. Charlemagne filled his court with scholars, poets, and musicians. One scholar at Charlemagne's court wrote this about the emperor:

You know very well how sweet is arithmetic in its reasoning, and how pleasant is a knowledge of the heavenly stars in their courses. And yet how rare it is to find a man who takes the trouble to know these things!

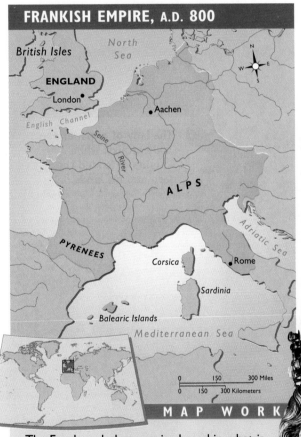

FRANKISH EMPIRE, A.D. 800

British Isles
North Sea
ENGLAND
London
Aachen
English Channel
Seine River
ALPS
PYRENEES
Corsica
Rome
Adriatic Sea
Sardinia
Balearic Islands
Mediterranean Sea

0   150   300 Miles
0   150   300 Kilometers

MAP WORK

The Franks ruled an empire based in what is today France.

1. Which Mediterranean islands were part of the Frankish empire?

2. About how many miles was the city of Aachen from Rome?

Charlemagne established a school at his palace where scholars collected and copied Roman works.

LIFE IN THE MIDDLE AGES

During the Middle Ages, the manor was almost a world within itself. Some manors were so large that they included several villages as well as many acres of farmland. Often things that were needed were grown or made right on the manor. This meant that money was not needed to buy goods. It also meant that most people seldom left the manor during their entire lives.

Starting around A.D. 800 a system called feudalism developed in Europe. Feudalism is a way of organizing and governing society, based on land and service. Like the laws of ancient Rome, feudalism required that people behave in certain ways.

Lords and Ladies

At the top of feudal society was the noble, called the lord, who owned the manor. The lord had total control over his manor. In some parts of Europe, the lord also had to serve a king.

The lord's wife was the lady of the manor and was in charge of castle affairs. When the lord was away, she often led the defense of the castle if it was attacked.

As you can see on the diagram, the lord's castle was the center of all activity on the manor. The castle served both as a house for the lord's family and as a fort to protect the manor in case of attack.

The Lord's Vassals

Manor lords chose nobles who did not own land to serve as vassals. Vassals took an oath of loyalty to the lord, pledging to serve him. In return, the lord gave each vassal a fief (FEEF). A fief was usually a separate manor. The vassal often did not own his fief, but he had authority over its serfs. Next to the lord, vassals were the most powerful people in feudal society.

The lady of a manor ran daily affairs, while knights defended the lord and his lands.

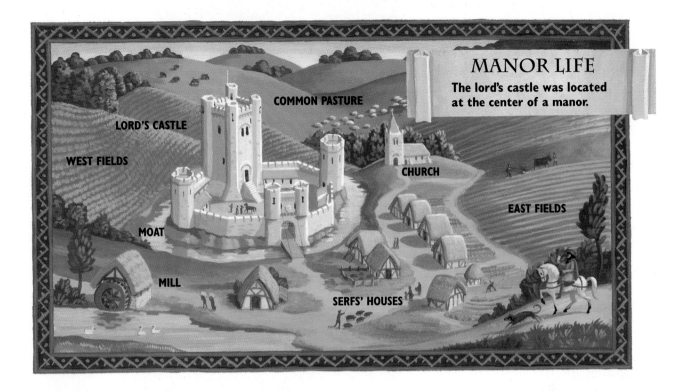

MANOR LIFE

The lord's castle was located at the center of a manor.

Labels on image: COMMON PASTURE, LORD'S CASTLE, WEST FIELDS, MOAT, MILL, CHURCH, EAST FIELDS, SERFS' HOUSES

The most important duty of a vassal was to serve as the lord's knight. Knights were soldiers who protected the manor. Sometimes they traveled with their lords to fight in distant lands.

A Knight's Training

The son of a noble began preparing for knighthood when he was young. First he learned to ride and care for horses. At the age of seven he left home to live and train in a knight's household. There he learned to behave with courtesy and to handle small weapons.

From the ages of 15 to 20, the young noble began to ride into battle alongside the knight. After this experience he was ready to become a knight himself. In a special ceremony he knelt before a lord and was declared a knight.

Life of a Serf

In Europe during the Middle Ages, only about one person in a hundred was a noble. Most Europeans were serfs or village craftworkers. Craftworkers were free, but they had to follow the rules of the nobles.

Serfs were given some land to farm for themselves, but they had to work the lord's land too. Serfs also had to pay rents and taxes to the lord. They even had to ask the lord's permission to get married.

Serfs usually lived in small one-room houses with a fire in the center for cooking and warmth. The whole family slept in one large, straw bed. Most shared their houses with animals. One observer said, "The livestock use the same entrances as the people, and they are not far from sleeping together."

Life was short and difficult—few serfs lived past the age of 40. Most people married while they were in their early teens. Serfs' lives revolved around work in the manor fields. Everyone, including young children, gathered wheat and picked vegetables. The village church bell rang every hour and signaled breaks for meals.

GROWTH OF TOWNS

Around A.D. 1000 Europe's economy began to change. The nobles began to spend less time in battle and more time on the manors. Nobles increased their farmlands, clearing forests and draining swamps. This created crop surpluses for the manor lords. Towns developed to provide a marketplace for the surpluses.

European traders exchanged goods like grains, wool cloth, and wine for spices and silk from Asia and Africa. They also used coin money for the first time since the days of ancient Rome.

With more to eat, people lived longer and the population grew. So did the towns. By the 1200s many towns had become crowded and dirty. Houses were so close that upstairs neighbors could shake hands across the street. Many serfs saw towns as places where they could escape from the manors. They came to the towns because they said the "air was freer." In fact, serfs could win their freedom if they remained in a town without being caught for a year and a day.

Much trading took place in towns like Rothenburg, Germany (left). Food brought to town from manors was sold in busy markets (below).

Town Craftworkers

The narrow town streets were lined with shoemaking, saddle making, and other craft shops. Most shops were family-owned businesses on the ground floor of a house. The father might have been an expert craftsman, or master. He ran the business while his wife and children helped. If her husband died, the wife often took over the business.

Traders and craftworkers organized themselves into groups called **guilds** (GILDZ). Each craft, such as carpentry, had its own guild that made rules about quality and prices. The guild also set the path by which an apprentice, or a beginner craftworker, became a master.

Europe's Cities

Some towns, such as London, grew into cities. In 1175 one London resident, William fitz Stephen, wrote:

Among the noble and celebrated cities of the world, London, the capital of the kingdom of the English, extends its glory farther than all others and sends its wealth and [goods] more widely.

Not everyone agreed that London was a glorious city. Some people thought that London was very dangerous. One trader from France who visited there said,

If you go to London pass through it quickly ... Every evil or [vicious] thing that can be found anywhere on earth you will find in that one city.

Carcassonne, a town in southern France, was protected by three rows of stone walls. The French restored the town beginning in the 1800s.

Popular Songs

Some of the people passing through Europe's towns and cities during this time were traveling musicians. These people of the 1100s and 1200s were called troubadours (TROO buh dawrz) and minstrels (MIN strulz). Troubadours and minstrels wrote and performed songs about love and life for Europe's nobles. These traveling musicians usually accompanied themselves on the guitar or lute. You may remember that both instruments had been introduced to Europe by Arab musicians in the 700s.

Although many troubadour songs praised the idea of love, some of them were funny. This song, by a woman troubadour named Isabella, tells about a man she once loved.

*Elias Cairel, you're a phony
if I ever saw one,
like a man who says he's sick
when he hasn't the slightest pain.
If you'd listen I'd give you good
   advice:
go back to your [home] and don't
dare pronounce my name again.*

Minstrels often had to wander from court to court looking for work.

CONQUERORS AND KINGS

The growth of towns and trade had greatly changed the economy and social life of Europe by the 1200s. At the same time, western Europe's political life was also undergoing developments.

Invasions from the North

At the end of Charlemagne's reign, in the early 800s, mainland Europe had come under attack by people from the north. These invaders were called Vikings, or Norsemen. The name Norsemen means "Northmen." The Norsemen sailed from Scandinavia in search of riches and land. For hundreds of years they made surprise attacks across Europe. Their invasions were part of the reason that the Frankish empire fell apart after Charlemagne's death.

By 900 some Norsemen began setting up villages around the mouth of the Seine River. Find this region on the map on page 321. These Norsemen became known as Normans. The region in which the Normans settled was called Normandy. The Normans adopted Christianity, the French language, and many Frankish customs.

Normans Invade England

In 1066 Norman forces crossed the English Channel and conquered the Anglo-Saxon people of England. The Norman leader became known as William the Conqueror.

William, the first Norman king of England, established a strong and well-organized rule in England. As a result, Norman and English cultures blended. In fact, the English language we speak today comes from a mix of French and the language of the Anglo-Saxons.

These Viking chess pieces were carved from walrus ivory.

The Power of English Kings

One of the kings who ruled England after William was King John I. King John was crowned in 1199. Like other kings before him, he tried to increase his power over England's lords. John demanded money from the lords to pay for wars. He also claimed the power to imprison a person without a trial.

In 1215 a group of lords took action to limit the king's power. They wrote a charter, or legal document, which stated that they had certain rights, such as the right to a fair trial. This charter was called the Magna Carta, which means "great charter" in Latin.

With the support of their knights, the lords forced the king to sign the Magna Carta. Some of the laws are shown on the next page. Which one guarantees that even the king would have to follow the laws?

MANY VOICES
PRIMARY SOURCE

**Excerpts from
the Magna Carta,
by the lords of England, 1215.**

We have granted to all free men of our kingdom for us and our heirs forever, all the liberties written below.

No widow shall be forced to marry so long as she wishes to live without a husband.

A free man shall not be fined for a small offense.

No sheriff, or anyone else, shall take horses or wagons of anyone without permission.

No freeman shall be taken, or imprisoned, or banished, or in anyway injured, except by the law of the land.

To no one will we sell, to no one will we deny or delay, rights or justice.

All merchants shall be safe and secure in leaving and entering England . . . both by land and by water, for buying and selling.

All these customs and liberties . . . shall be observed by all men of our kingdom.

The Magna Carta (left) contains 63 articles, or parts. The charter has influenced many political leaders.

WHY IT MATTERS

The Magna Carta was a beginning toward limiting the power of a ruler by law. It gave rights mainly to nobles. Eventually, it would serve as an example of rights for all people. As you will read in the next lesson, the Christian Church also had great effects on the lives of Europeans during the Middle Ages.

✓ Reviewing Facts and Ideas

MAIN IDEAS

- Charlemagne, a king of the Franks, built an empire in Europe in the 800s.
- The manor was the center of life for most Europeans in the Middle Ages.
- In the late Middle Ages towns grew and trade expanded.
- Normans, a people from Scandinavia, invaded many parts of Europe and eventually conquered England.
- King John I was forced to sign the Magna Carta in 1215, protecting certain rights of England's nobles.

THINK ABOUT IT

1. What did vassals promise to a lord under feudalism? What did the lord give in return?

2. What was the purpose of guilds in European towns?

3. **FOCUS** How was life different for serfs and town residents during the Middle Ages?

4. **THINKING SKILL** What *effects* did the Magna Carta have on the relationship between England's lords and kings?

5. **WRITE** Suppose you are a visitor to a manor during the Middle Ages. Write three daily journal entries about what you see at the manor.

Determining Point of View

VOCABULARY
point of view

WHY THE SKILL MATTERS

In the last lesson you read about some of the different people who made up European society in the Middle Ages—lords and ladies, serfs and craftworkers, troubadours and minstrels. All these people had different roles in society, with different jobs, rights, and duties. They also had different points of view.

A point of view is the position from which someone looks at the world. It is shaped by his or her background, concerns, likes and dislikes, interests, and fears. A person's point of view helps shape his or her opinion on many things. Different people have different points of view about the same subject. No one point of view presents that subject completely and accurately. In a classroom, for example, a teacher's point of view is usually different from a student's point of view. Determining a person's point of view helps us to understand how that person sees things. To understand something completely and accurately, you must look at it from a variety of points of view.

USING THE SKILL

One way to determine a person's point of view is to look carefully at a statement that he or she has made. The person's focus, the words he or she uses, and the opinions expressed often reveal his or her point of view.

The poem you will read was written during the Middle Ages. First identify the subject. The first line tells you that the writer was writing about his lord. Apparently, his relationship to the lord was very important. As you read the poem, try to find clues that tell how the writer felt about his lord. These clues will help you to determine his point of view and who he was.

> If my dear lord is slain, his fate I'll
>   share.
> If he is hanged, then hang me by his
>   side.
> If to the stake he goes, with him I'll
>   burn;
> And if he's drowned, then let me
>   drown with him.

One clue that you might notice right away is the word *dear*. This word shows you the writer's opinion about his lord, which was that he cared for him very much. Other phrases also show that the writer felt that the lord was very important. In fact, the writer was willing to die with him. What kind of person wrote this poem? A knight? Remember that a knight was a lord's vassal. He pledged to serve his lord. This poem

The Bayeaux Tapestry, embroidered in the 1100s, is a Norman record of their invasion of England in 1066.

shows *loyalty*, one of the most important qualities for a knight to have. Can you think of another word that might describe this knight's point of view?

TRYING THE SKILL

Now read the following announcement that Charlemagne sent to all the lords in his empire. Remember that Charlemagne was a ruler of the Franks during the Middle Ages. As you read this announcement, use the Helping Yourself box to help you determine Charlemagne's point of view.

You must arrive at Strassfurt with your men on June 18, complete with supplies, so that you will be able to proceed from there in any direction in which you may be ordered to go.

What are some key words or phrases in this announcement that tell how Charlemagne felt about the lords? Compare this announcement with the earlier example. How was Charlemagne's point of view about the lords different from the knight's? How can you tell?

REVIEWING THE SKILL

1. What is a point of view?

2. What shapes people's points of view? Explain your answer.

3. How does one's point of view influence how he or she sees things?

4. Why might learning about various points of view be important in a democracy?

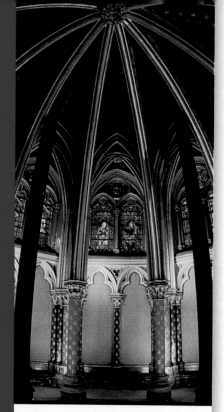

400   500   1350   1600

The Church in the Middle Ages

Read Aloud

The overwhelming majority of people in Europe in the Middle Ages were Christian. In fact, Europe was a large part of what the Christians called Christendom—or "kingdom of the Christians." At the center of this "kingdom" was the Christian Church based in Rome. The Church leader was the Pope, who was as powerful as any king or lord.

Focus Activity

READ TO LEARN

How did Christianity affect life in Europe?

VOCABULARY

- **monastery**
- **nun**
- **convent**
- **cathedral**
- **saint**
- **Crusade**
- **plague**

PEOPLE

- **Benedict**
- **Francis of Assisi**
- **Pope Urban II**

PLACES

- **Chartres**

THE BIG PICTURE

During the Middle Ages Christianity spread throughout the entire continent of Europe. Kings, such as Charlemagne, brought Christianity to conquered lands. In other places, such as Ireland, priests brought the new religion. Eventually Christianity became central to life for almost everyone in Europe. People even measured a simple act like boiling an egg by the length of time it took to say a certain prayer.

Not all Europeans were Christian, however. Jews had lived in villages and towns throughout Europe since the early days of the Roman Empire. Muslims had come to Spain around A.D. 700. In this lesson you will read how the Christian Church in Rome affected Europe during the Middle Ages.

AN "AGE OF FAITH"

The growth of Christianity in Europe happened gradually. Over time most people of other religions began to accept the Christian faith. Eventually Christian belief grew so strong that the later Middle Ages became known as the "Age of Faith."

Life in Monasteries and Convents

For several centuries, life in Europe revolved around religion. Some men, called monks, devoted their lives to religion. They lived in communities called monasteries. Women who vowed to devote their lives to religion were called nuns. Their communities were called convents. Many people entered convents and monastaries at a young age and stayed until death. In no place was faith stronger.

An Italian monk named Benedict wrote the first plan for monasteries in the A.D. 500s. Monks had to obey the head monk, who was called the abbot. Here are some of Benedict's rules:

No one, without permission of the abbot, shall presume to give, or receive, or keep as his own, anything whatever: neither book nor tablets, nor pen: nothing at all.... All things are to be common to all.

Monasteries and convents, like manors, were churches, farms, homes, and schools all rolled into one. Most monks and nuns spent much of the day in prayer. They also farmed and studied, and made wine, medicines, and craft goods.

Monasteries served as centers of learning in the Middle Ages. Most monasteries had a scriptorium, or a room for making books. Since no printing press existed, all books were carefully copied by hand. Monks wrote books of prayer and poetry. They also copied old Greek and Roman texts. These beautifully decorated books are called manuscripts. Some had such value that they were chained to desks. Today they are important records of ancient life and the Middle Ages.

In addition to praying, monks often spent time making illustrated books.

THE ROMAN CHURCH

For years there had been tension between the Pope in Rome and other Christian leaders in Constantinople. In 1054 these tensions led to a split in the Christian Church. The Church based in Constantinople was called the Eastern Orthodox Church. The Church based in Rome later became known as the Roman Catholic Church.

At around the same time as the split in the Christian Church, towns began to grow in size and wealth. Townspeople expressed their religious beliefs by building grand churches, or cathedrals. Skilled craftworkers created windows for the cathedrals out of pieces of colored glass. These stained-glass windows often showed scenes from Christian writings.

A Magnificent Cathedral

Suppose you are a traveler to Chartres (SHAHRT), France, in 1260. The road is narrow and muddy. As you emerge from the thick forest, you see the spires of the town's magnificent cathedral rising high into the sky.

Chartres Cathedral took about 36 years to build. Many workers never saw their cathedrals completed. Some took more than 400 years to build. Many cathedrals still stand as one of the great legacies of the Middle Ages.

Saints and Pilgrimages

Another way that Christians showed their devotion was through pilgrimages. Europe's Christian pilgrims traveled great distances to Rome or Jerusalem. Jerusalem was and is a holy city to Jews, Muslims, and Christians.

During the Middle Ages, pilgrims also traveled to shrines, or special buildings that had been built for saints.

The Cathedral of Notre Dame in Paris is known for its tall spires and many stained-glass windows (right). Sometimes knights on pilgrimage were women (below).

Saints are women and men considered to be especially holy.

One of the most honored saints of the Middle Ages was Francis of Assisi. He lived from about 1181 to 1226. Francis devoted his life to serving the poor and sick in Italy. His followers came to be called Franciscans.

The First Crusade

In 1095 Pope Urban II called for Christians throughout western Europe to make a pilgrimage to Jerusalem. He also urged the pilgrims to capture Jerusalem from the Seljuk Turks, who were Muslim. Thousands of Europeans responded to the Pope's call. This journey to gain control of Jerusalem was the first Crusade. Those who went were called Crusaders.

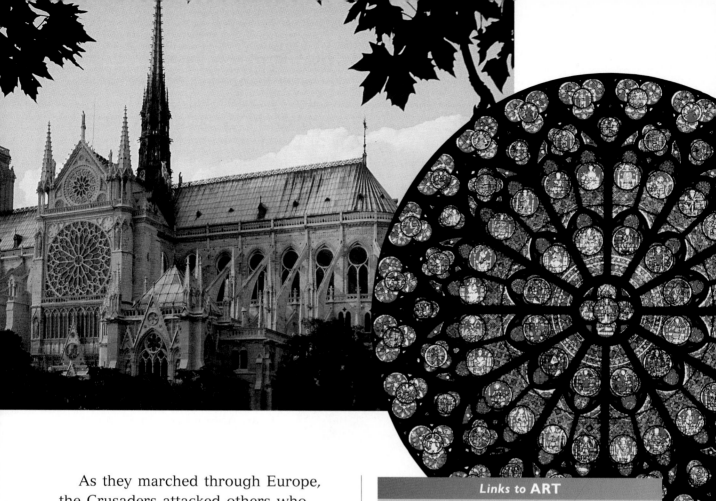

As they marched through Europe, the Crusaders attacked others who were not Christian. They raided Jewish communities in France and Germany. One shocked Christian wrote:

> They should have traveled their road for Christ. Instead they turned to madness and shamefully, cruelly cut down the Jewish people in the cities and towns through which they passed.

About 100,000 knights, priests, and other pilgrims left for the "Holy Land," as the Crusaders called the land around Jerusalem. The Crusaders battled against Turkish armies even before they reached Jerusalem. The Crusaders suffered such great hunger and sickness that half died before they reached Jerusalem in 1099.

For two days the Crusaders attacked Jerusalem, killing many Muslims and Jews. The Crusaders captured Jerusalem, which would remain in Christian hands for about 100 years.

Links to ART

Design a Stained-Glass Window

The art of making stained-glass windows developed in western Europe during the Middle Ages. These windows are made of pieces of glass joined by strips of lead. At first the windows were small. By the 1200s, though, stained-glass windows were larger and had different shapes.

Many stained-glass windows in churches and cathedrals tell stories. Such windows helped people who did not know how to read to learn Bible stories.

Draw a design for a stained-glass window that you would like to see at the entrance of your school. As examples, look at stained-glass windows in churches and other buildings in your community. Then draw a sketch of the design and pieces of colored glass.

END OF THE MIDDLE AGES

Other Crusades took place over the next 200 years, but most of these failed. Despite their failure the effects of the Crusades were felt far beyond the Holy Land. Find the Crusade routes on the map on this page. As you can see, the Crusaders often passed through the Italian port cities on their way to the Holy Land. With more people passing through, trade began to grow in these cities. The Crusaders also returned to Europe, bringing products and new knowledge from Asia and Africa.

By the end of the Crusades in 1291, Europe had changed in many ways. With changes in Europe's economy, the system of feudalism was gradually breaking down.

"Most Terrible of Terrors"

One of Europe's cities bustling with activity was Siena, Italy. Here trade flourished and the people had been building a great cathedral since the 1100s. This cathedral remains unfinished to this day, however. Its construction was halted in 1348, when a **plague** struck Western Europe. A plague is a terrible disease that spreads quickly. This plague was caused by bacteria that was spread by rats and fleas. At that time, however, no one knew what caused the sickness. They just knew terrible misery and sadness. This plague, which was later called the Black Death, wiped out one third of the western European population. In Siena, two thirds of the people died. One man from that city described the horrible effects that the Black Death

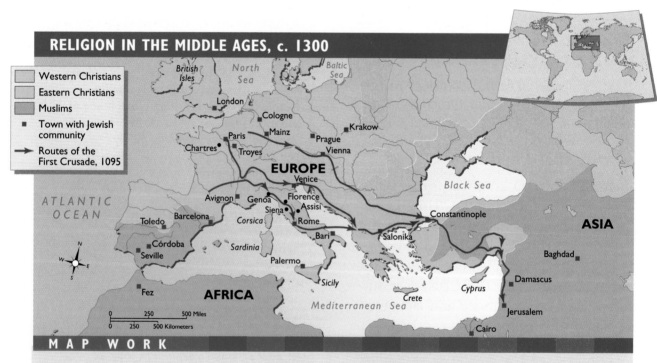

RELIGION IN THE MIDDLE AGES, c. 1300

- Western Christians
- Eastern Christians
- Muslims
- ■ Town with Jewish community
- → Routes of the First Crusade, 1095

British Isles • North Sea • Baltic Sea • London • Cologne • Krakow • Paris • Mainz • Prague • Chartres • Troyes • Vienna • **EUROPE** • Venice • ATLANTIC OCEAN • Avignon • Genoa • Florence • Assisi • Black Sea • Barcelona • Siena • Rome • Constantinople • **ASIA** • Toledo • Corsica • Bari • Salonika • Córdoba • Sardinia • Baghdad • Seville • Palermo • Sicily • Cyprus • Damascus • Fez • **AFRICA** • Mediterranean Sea • Crete • Jerusalem • Cairo

0 250 500 Miles
0 250 500 Kilometers

MAP WORK

Crusaders traveled throughout Europe on their way to Jerusalem.

1. Which towns east of Constantinople had a Jewish community?

2. Where did more Muslims live—in Europe or in northern Africa?

3. Between which two cities did Crusaders need to cross a large body of water?

These Crusaders are preparing to sail from Italy to Jerusalem.

had on people who became infected with the disease:

> The plague began in Siena in May, a horrible and cruel event. They died almost immediately . . . they would swell up under the armpits and drop dead while talking. People brought members of their own household to the ditches as best they could, without priest or holy ceremony or ringing of bells. Nobody wept for the dead, since each was awaiting death; and so many died that everyone thought the end of the world had come.

Towns in France flew black flags from church towers to warn travelers of the plague. Nearly 130 years would pass before the plague was completely gone from Europe.

WHY IT MATTERS

Today the Roman Catholic Church and the Eastern Orthodox Church continue to be important to the lives of many Christians around the world. Some men and women still live in monasteries and convents. The splendid cathedrals of the Middle Ages remain as well. These creations of technology, imagination, and faith stand as stunning reminders of the achievements of the Middle Ages.

Reviewing Facts and Ideas

MAIN IDEAS

- The Christian Church had a great influence on the lives of Europeans during the Middle Ages.
- Christians in Europe built magnificent cathedrals for worship.
- Monasteries across Europe served as centers of faith and learning.
- During the first Crusade, beginning in 1095, Christians conquered Jerusalem.
- In 1348 a plague struck Europe, killing one out of three people.

THINK ABOUT IT

1. What rule did Benedict give about property for monks?

2. For Pope Urban II, what was the main purpose of the Crusades?

3. **FOCUS** Why are the Middle Ages known as the "Age of Faith"?

4. **THINKING SKILL** Read the quote by the Christian writer on page 333. What shaped this person's _point of view_? What might have been the point of view of a Crusader?

5. **GEOGRAPHY** Study the map on page 334. What city was a stop along all Crusade routes shown? What empire ruled this city?

400　700　1000　1300　1350　1550　1600

The Renaissance

Focus Activity

READ TO LEARN

What were some major achievements of the Renaissance?

VOCABULARY

- Renaissance
- humanism
- patron

PEOPLE

- Lorenzo Medici
- Petrarch
- Michelangelo
- Leonardo da Vinci
- Nicolaus Copernicus

PLACES

- Florence

Read Aloud

"This is the supreme, marvelous truth of man. He can be that which he wills to be. God the Father endowed man, from birth, with the seeds of every possibility and every life."

These words are by Pico della Mirandola (PEE koh DAYL luh mee RAHN doh lah), an Italian scholar of the 1400s. He expressed a powerful new way of thinking that arose in Europe as the Middle Ages came to an end.

THE BIG PICTURE

Out of the misery of the Black Death came new ideas that stirred Europe. Starting around 1350 enthusiasm for art, literature, and trade increased throughout northern Italy. This was the beginning of a period called the Renaissance (REN uh sahns), from the French word meaning "rebirth." Many Europeans saw this time as a rebirth of the classical periods of Greece and Rome. Although the Renaissance began in Italy, within a century it had spread to the rest of Europe.

The Renaissance was a time of great creativity. Central to the ideas of the Renaissance was a powerful interest in humanism (HYOO muh niz um). Humanism meant concern with human interests and values. People in the Middle Ages had often turned their thoughts toward the "next world," or heaven. People of the Renaissance were still usually very religious. However, they began to focus more on what people could achieve in this world.

RENAISSANCE IN ITALY

Of course, the Renaissance did not happen overnight. Europeans did not wake up one morning and start a new era. Change came first to the city of Florence, in northern Italy. Why did the Renaissance begin in Florence?

The Glory of Florence

As you read in the last lesson, growth in trade, partly caused by the Crusades, benefited Italian cities. By 1400 Florence had become one of the richest cities in Europe. Find this city on the map on page 334. Traders from Florence journeyed to the towns of France and to the port cities of the Black Sea. They also traveled to Asia and Africa, returning with spices and silks. Florence was a busy craft-producing city. People worked in about 200 shops, turning out enormous amounts of woolen cloth.

Lorenzo the Magnificent

One of the wealthiest families in Florence was the Medici (MED ih chee) family. The Medicis gained great wealth through banking and trading. Although Florence had become a republic around 1300, by the 1400s the Medicis had gained control. The most famous member of the family was Lorenzo Medici. He came to power in 1469. Some considered him a tyrant—an all-powerful and often unjust ruler. One Florentine, however, said, "If Florence was to have a tyrant, she could never have a better or more delightful one."

Lorenzo Medici was a patron, or supporter, of the arts. He loved poetry and painting. Before long, scholars and artists flocked to Florence, where they were paid by Lorenzo to pursue their work. The city was soon bursting with art and learning, and its leader became known as "Lorenzo the Magnificent."

Lorenzo Medici (right) made Florence a powerful city in the late 1400s.

ARTS AND IDEAS

As you have read, the Renaissance was a time of looking back to achievements of earlier civilizations. During the 1300s humanists began to search the Italian countryside for Greek and Roman artifacts. They found examples of classical cultures such as manuscripts, coins, and statues to study for ideas.

European scholars, especially scientists, also learned from Arab scholars. As you read in Chapter 10, scholars in Baghdad preserved and developed Greek, Roman, and Indian scientific knowledge. As trade between Europe, Asia, and Africa grew during the Crusades, goods and knowledge spread.

The Power of Words

One of the earliest Italian humanists to study classics—works of literature from ancient Greece, Rome, and Arabia—was Petrarch (PEE trahrk). Petrarch was a poet who lived from 1304 to 1374. He loved learning, and he read every book he could find. Petrarch believed the classics were better than any works written later.

Petrarch became the most celebrated poet in all of Europe. He once described his love of writing as follows:

There is no lighter burden, nor more agreeable, than a pen.... As there is none among earthly delights more noble than literature, so there was none more lasting, none gentler or more faithful.

Renaissance Artists

Artists as well as poets learned from ancient Romans and Greeks. One of the greatest Renaissance artists was Michelangelo. He used many classical ideas—such as balance of form—in his paintings, sculptures, and architecture.

You can see his *David* at the beginning of this lesson.

A very famous painter of Italy was the humanist Leonardo da Vinci (lee uh NAHR doh duh VIHN chee). He lived from 1452 to 1519. Like Michelangelo, Leonardo da Vinci was a painter, sculptor, and architect. However, Leonardo da Vinci was a scientist, engineer, and musician as well. Da Vinci's interests and talents were as broad as the Renaissance itself.

Leonardo da Vinci, the Painter

As a child, Leonardo da Vinci showed great ability in drawing. When he turned 15, his father took him to study with the greatest painter in

Mona Lisa, by Leonardo da Vinci, is one of the most famous paintings in the world.

Florence. Leonardo painted with such skill that his teacher put down his own paintbrushes and never picked them up again. Before long, Leonardo was invited to set up his studio in the garden of his patron, Lorenzo Medici.

Da Vinci loved the world of Florence. He would sometimes follow interesting townspeople for a whole day and then paint them from memory. Leonardo da Vinci's careful observation helped him create paintings that were so realistic they surprised viewers.

Da Vinci drew this portrait of himself. He also made many sketches of his inventions such as a flying machine (below).

Leonardo da Vinci, the Inventor

Besides painting, da Vinci also kept hundreds of notebooks in which he wrote down all kinds of new ideas. Da Vinci always wrote backward to keep his ideas secret. He made plans for a submarine and a machine gun. He wrote this plan for a parachute:

If a man has a tent made of linen, of which the holes have all been stopped up, and it is 20 feet across and 20 in depth, he will be able to throw himself down from any great height without sustaining any injury.

Leonardo da Vinci studied carefully the flight of birds. His close observation helped him to design a flying machine. Four hundred years would pass before a human actually flew. Leonardo da Vinci's love of knowledge inspired future artists and inventors.

Earth, Sun, and Stars

In a small town in Poland, a young man named Nicolaus Copernicus (kuh PUR nih kus) studied books of Greek and Arab astronomy. He observed the night sky with a simple telescope and carefully recorded the positions of the stars he saw.

In 1514 Copernicus made a startling discovery. Earth seemed to orbit around the sun, once each year. This was a new idea. Since people first tracked the stars and moon, they believed that Earth was the center of the universe. Many European leaders, including officials of the Church in Rome, found this new theory unacceptable. They felt it went against Church teachings, which put Earth at the center of the universe. It was not until after Copernicus died that his book was published. It was called *On the Revolutions of the Heavenly Spheres*. Copernicus's ideas about the universe greatly changed our knowledge of astronomy.

interNET CONNECTION

Visit our website: www.mhschool.com

Spread of the Renaissance

As you have read, the Renaissance began in Florence, Italy, around 1350 and later spread throughout Europe. Artists, writers, and scientists often traveled to different Europeans cities to study and work. How might exchanging ideas have led to achievements?

"All the world's a stage, And all the men and women merely players."

by William Shakespeare

Clock

This clock and its decorated cover were made in France around 1540. Powered by a coiled spring, the clock was portable.

El Greco "A View of Toledo"

El Greco was a Greek who studied art in Venice. He settled in Toledo, Spain, and painted many scenes of life in that city.

Tempietto

Donato Bramante designed Tempietto, a temple in Rome. Completed in 1502, the temple has features of classical architecture such as columns.

Caterina Van Hemmessen

Painters in Europe often painted themselves, as in this self-portrait by a German woman.

WHY IT MATTERS

The Renaissance was a time of looking back to the classical achievements of Greece, Rome, and Arabia. It was also a time of looking forward, for much remained to be discovered.

Though the Renaissance began in Italy, it soon spread to the rest of Europe. The Renaissance brought about changes to many old ways of thinking. For this reason, historians often call it the beginning of the modern age.

In the next lesson you will read about the spread of new ideas into the Roman Catholic Church.

✔ Reviewing Facts and Ideas

MAIN IDEAS

- The Renaissance began in Italy, where an interest in humanism first developed.

- In Florence wealthy patrons like Lorenzo Medici supported artists and scholars.

- Renaissance scientists studied Greek, Roman, and Arab texts, and made new discoveries about the world.

THINK ABOUT IT

1. What did the people of the Renaissance mean by *humanism*?

2. How did Florence become one of the richest cities in Europe?

3. **FOCUS** How did Renaissance achievements reflect both the past and their own time?

4. **THINKING SKILL** Make and explain at least two *generalizations* about Renaissance thinkers.

5. **WRITE** Look at one of the Renaissance artworks in this lesson. Write a paragraph explaining what you like or dislike about the art.

400   700   1000   1300   1450   1600

The Reformation

Read Aloud

"Here I stand; I can do no other. God help me. Amen."

These words were spoken in the 1500s by a German monk named Martin Luther. Luther had spoken out against the Church in Rome. Church leaders had called upon Luther to take back his criticisms. Luther's beliefs were too strong, however. He refused to back down.

Focus Activity

READ TO LEARN

What changes did the Reformation bring to Europe?

VOCABULARY

- indulgence
- reform
- Reformation
- Protestantism
- armada

PEOPLE

- Erasmus
- Martin Luther
- Johannes Gutenberg
- King Henry VIII
- Queen Elizabeth I
- William Shakespeare

THE BIG PICTURE

As humanism gained popularity among Europe's artists and scholars, people began to question everything around them. They studied books and started schools in an effort to find answers to their questions. Nicolaus Copernicus, you may recall, questioned the old belief that Earth was the center of the universe. The Renaissance had shaken many of Europe's established traditions and beliefs.

At the same time some Christians began to be concerned. They thought that some Renaissance artists and scientists had gotten too far away from their religious teachings. These Christians said that many artists and scientists were too worldly, or concerned about this world. Many also felt that the Church in Rome had become too worldly and rich. A few Christians began to question the authority of the Pope.

THE CHURCH OF ROME

By 1500 the Roman Church had become the most powerful institution in Europe. The Pope claimed authority over all of Europe's rulers. The Pope's power also brought great wealth to the Roman Church. Like the government of the Roman empire, the Roman Church taxed the people of Europe. Some of this money was spent on works of art.

Questions of Faith

Starting around 1500, humanists such as **Erasmus** (ih RAZ mus) began to criticize the Roman Church. He especially questioned the Church policy concerning **indulgences** (ihn DUL juns ez). An indulgence is a pardon, or forgiveness, from the Church. During the Middle Ages, some people began to pay to be forgiven by the priest for acting against Christian teachings. Erasmus believed that the indulgences were wrong. He hoped to **reform**, or change, the Roman Church.

In Wittenberg, Germany, the sale of indulgences also made a monk, **Martin Luther**, angry. He felt that the money, often given by people who were poor, should not be spent on the building of Saint Peter's, a great cathedral in Rome.

In 1517 Luther wrote 95 Theses (THEE seez), or statements, of protest. He placed this list on a Wittenberg church door. Luther had no idea that this simple act would soon shake beliefs across the entire continent.

Read the excerpts from Luther's Theses. How did he suggest that the Church pay for building Saint Peter's?

MANY VOICES
PRIMARY SOURCE

Excerpt from
the 95 Theses, written by
Martin Luther in 1517.

*O*ut of love and **zeal** for truth and the desire to bring it to light, the following theses will be publicly discussed at Wittenberg under the chairmanship of the Reverend Martin Luther.

Before long all the churches, palaces, walls, and bridges of Rome will be built out of our [indulgence] money.... We Germans can not attend Saint Peter's. Better it should never be built than that our **parochial** *churches should be* **despoiled**.... *Why doesn't the pope build the* **basilica** *out of his own money?*

---

zeal: eagerness
parochial: local
despoiled: robbed
basilica: cathedral

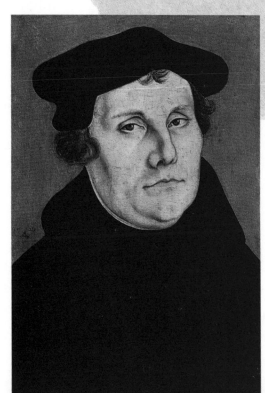

Martin Luther studied law before he became a monk in 1505.

A CALL FOR REFORM

Martin Luther's 95 Theses in Wittenberg started a movement called the Reformation (ref ur MAY shun). This movement brought reform to the Church in Rome. It would also lead to another division of Christianity.

Spreading the Word

News of Luther's bold action in Wittenberg spread with the help of a recent invention. In 1448 a man named Johannes Gutenberg (yoh HAHN uhs GOO tun burg) had built a printing press. It used metal letters called movable type to spell out words on a page.

Before 1448, each page had to be hand-carved. Now that letters could be

Johannes Gutenberg built the first printing press out of a device used to press grapes and cheese.

moved around, printing was cheaper and easier as well as faster. Gutenberg's press could print 300 pages a day. By 1500 several million books had been printed in Europe!

The new invention helped spread Luther's criticisms of the Roman Church and a translation of the Bible. In those days almost everything was printed in Latin. Luther wrote in German, which helped to unite many German-speaking people on his side.

Division of the Roman Church

In 1520 Pope Leo X (the Tenth) ordered that Luther's books be burned, but Luther did not stop his protest. A visitor from Rome reported: "All Germany is up in arms against Rome."

Although the leaders of the Roman Church in Rome wanted Luther punished, German rulers protected him. By this time their loyalty to their homeland had become stronger than their loyalty to the Pope. These rulers also hoped to keep taxes intended for Rome.

In 1529 the break in the Roman Church became permanent. Luther's followers were now called Protestants, because they protested against the Roman Church. Western Christianity was divided in two—Protestantism (PROT uh stun tiz um) and Roman Catholicism.

The Protestant Church

The indulgence issue was not the only Church policy with which Protestant leaders disagreed. These leaders taught that monasteries and convents were unnecessary. Protestants also thought that church decorations and services should be simpler. They worked to spread translated Bibles and have church services in local languages.

In time, new Protestant leaders arose, such as John Calvin in Switzerland. Calvin founded a separate Protestant group called the Calvinists. The new Protestant groups did not agree on every issue, but they were united in their refusal to follow the Pope.

Roman Catholic Reform

Even before the Protestants split from the Roman Church, Catholic leaders had begun making reforms. Between 1545 and 1563 a group of Catholic leaders met in the city of Trent, Italy. They ordered that parts of church services should be in the language of the people of a country, not just in Latin. They also tried to see that the Church's money was spent more carefully. These reforms helped to strengthen the Roman Catholic religion. Some critics, such as Erasmus, decided not to leave the Catholic Church.

During the 1500s most people in Germany, Scandinavia, Holland, and Switzerland became Protestant. As you can see on the map on this page, most of Spain, Italy, and France remained Catholic. Tensions between Protestants and Roman Catholics increased.

England's Break With Rome

At this time of religious conflict, a new ruler brought religious change to England. This ruler was King Henry VIII. Henry was building a strong monarchy, or a government ruled by a king or a queen.

At the beginning of his rule in 1509, Henry supported the Roman Church. His view, however, changed in 1527. Henry, who had one daughter, wanted a son to inherit his throne. His wife, Queen Catherine, was unable to have more children. So the king asked the

CHRISTIANITY IN WESTERN EUROPE, c. 1560

Roman Catholics
Lutherans
Calvinists
Anglicans
Eastern Christians
Mixture of Catholics, Lutherans & Calvinists
— Present-day boundaries

MAP WORK

By 1560 many different Christian groups had formed. Followers of these groups were spread throughout western Europe.

1. In which country was the Anglican religion common?

2. Which religion was most widespread?

Pope to give him permission to divorce the Queen. The Pope refused.

Henry VIII stated that the Pope did not have authority over the English monarchy. He then took control of Church land and cut off payments to Rome. Henry started a new Protestant church, the Church of England, also called the Anglican Church. With control over England's church, Henry's monarchy became more powerful.

England's Queen Elizabeth I (below) stands on a map of her empire. England defeated the Spanish Armada (right).

QUEEN ELIZABETH I

In the years following the split with the Catholic Church, England was torn by religious differences. During this troubled time, Henry VIII's daughter, Elizabeth, came to the throne. In 1558 she became Queen Elizabeth I. Not only did the queen face conflict at home, but also there were threats of invasion from mainland Europe. Despite these problems, Elizabeth became one of the most powerful and popular monarchs England has ever known.

The Elizabethan Age

Under Elizabeth the anger between England's Protestants and Catholics cooled. London bustled with business and trade. Also during this time, the Renaissance arrived in England. Elizabeth enjoyed poetry and plays. Some-times she watched the performances of a young writer and actor named William Shakespeare. Shakespeare was one of the greatest writers in the English language. You will learn more about him in the Legacy on page 348.

The Spanish Armada

Elizabeth hated war and worked hard to keep her country at peace. In 1588, however, Elizabeth faced the threat of a war with Spain.

The Spanish hoped to gain control of Atlantic trade routes. They also hoped to return England to the Catholic faith. Under King Philip II, Spain had gathered a huge and powerful fleet, called an armada, of 130 warships. They prepared to attack England.

Queen Elizabeth assembled her troops and delivered a stirring speech. How do you think the troops reacted?

MANY VOICES
PRIMARY SOURCE

Excerpt from Queen Elizabeth's speech to her troops during the battle with the Spanish Armada, 1588.

*Let tyrants fear. I have always so behaved myself that, under God, I have placed my **chiefest** strength and **safeguard** in the loyal hearts and good will of my **subjects**; and therefore I am come.... to live or die amongst you all, and to lay down for my God and for my kingdom and for my people, my honor and my blood, even in the dust. I know I have the body of a weak and feeble woman, but I have the heart and stomach of a king, and a king of England too, and think **foul scorn** that ... Spain, or any prince of Europe should dare to invade the borders of my **realm**.*

chiefest: greatest
safeguard: protection
subjects: people of the kingdom
foul scorn: badly
realm: kingdom

Battle at Sea

With only 90 ships, England's fleet was smaller than the Spanish Armada. However, the English ships were faster and had better guns. This battle for the seas took place in the English Channel. After nine days the Spanish Armada was badly beaten. Not one English ship was sunk. Many Spanish ships escaped, only to be wrecked in a violent storm. Only half of the Spanish Armada made it back to Spain. England continued to build its fleet. The country would soon become the greatest naval power in the entire world.

WHY IT MATTERS

By 1600 the unity that had brought Europe together under the Roman Church had broken apart. The Pope was no longer the most powerful leader in Europe. Kings and queens began to act in the interest of their own countries. In coming years, these kingdoms would extend their power to places beyond Europe—to Africa, the Americas, and Asia.

The Christian Church remained split. Of the almost 2 billion Christians in the world today, over 1 billion are Roman Catholics. Almost 400 million are Protestants. In the United States alone, there are 59 million Roman Catholics and 90 million Protestants.

✓ Reviewing Facts and Ideas

MAIN IDEAS

- In 1517 Martin Luther put the 95 Theses on a church door in Germany.
- Luther's actions led to the Reformation. The Western Christian Church soon split into the Protestant and Roman Catholic Churches.
- Under Elizabeth I, England's culture and power flourished.

THINK ABOUT IT

1. What were indulgences? What did Martin Luther think about them?
2. What reforms did the Protestant and Catholic Churches make in the 1500s?
3. **FOCUS** How did the Reformation affect the unity of Europe?
4. **THINKING SKILL** What was the *point of view* of Queen Elizabeth toward Spain in her speech to her troops?
5. **GEOGRAPHY** Study the location of England and Spain on the map on page 345. Why did both countries need a powerful navy?

THE ART OF LANGUAGE: SHAKESPEARE

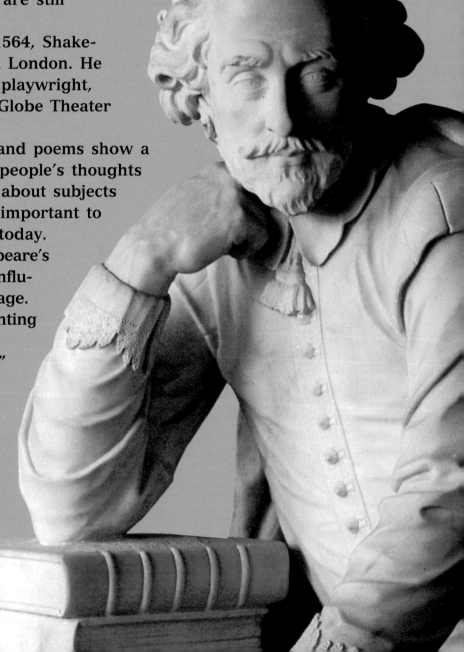

The Granger Collection

Many people today take a break from their routines to see a movie or a play. If you lived in London during the Elizabethan Age, you might have gone to a play by one of the greatest writers of all time, William Shakespeare. His plays are still performed today.

Born in England in 1564, Shakespeare went to work in London. He became an actor, poet, playwright, and part-owner of the Globe Theater in London.

Shakespeare's plays and poems show a deep understanding of people's thoughts and feelings. He wrote about subjects and ideas that are still important to audiences and readers today.

The genius of Shakespeare's works has also greatly influenced the English language. He is credited with inventing familiar phrases such as "catch cold" and "bump."

Before his death in 1616, Shakespeare had a successful career. However, his audiences could not have guessed how lasting his legacy would be.

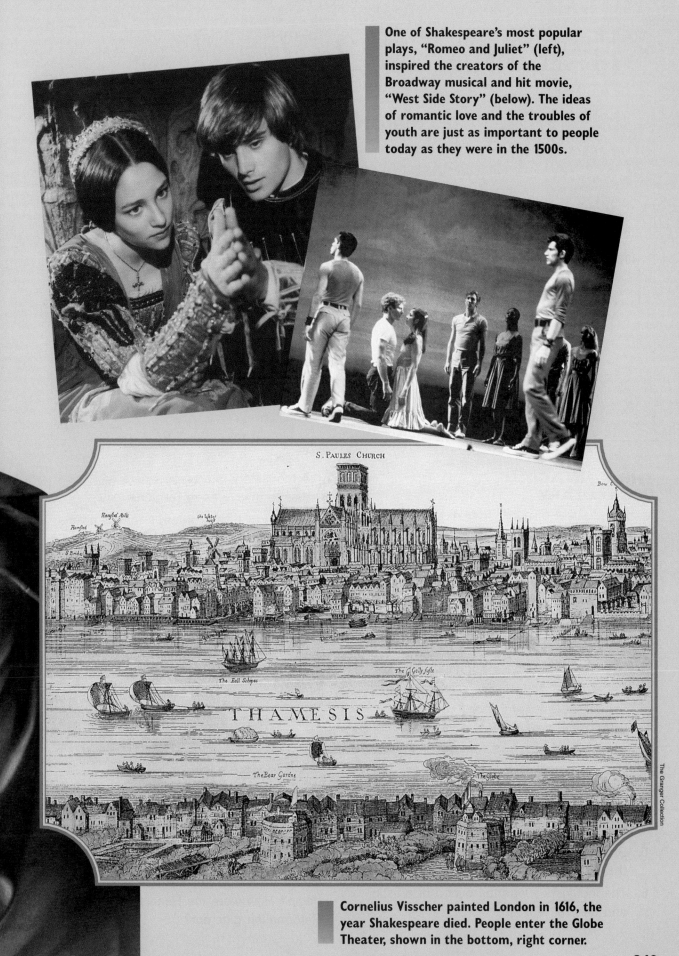

One of Shakespeare's most popular plays, "Romeo and Juliet" (left), inspired the creators of the Broadway musical and hit movie, "West Side Story" (below). The ideas of romantic love and the troubles of youth are just as important to people today as they were in the 1500s.

S. PAULES CHURCH

THAMESIS

The Bear Gardine

The Globe

Cornelius Visscher painted London in 1616, the year Shakespeare died. People enter the Globe Theater, shown in the bottom, right corner.

CHAPTER 12 REVIEW

Major Events

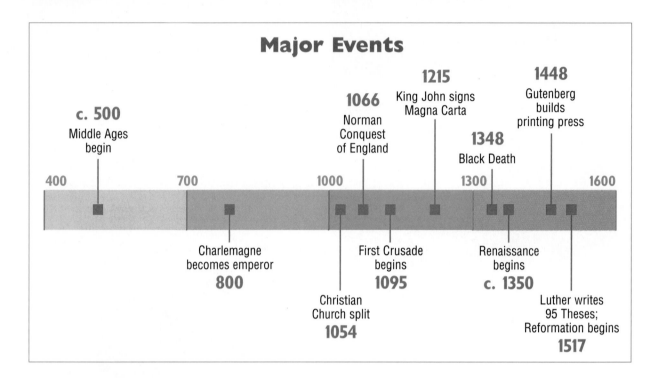

c. 500
Middle Ages begin

800
Charlemagne becomes emperor

1066
Norman Conquest of England

1054
Christian Church split

1095
First Crusade begins

1215
King John signs Magna Carta

1348
Black Death

c. 1350
Renaissance begins

1448
Gutenberg builds printing press

1517
Luther writes 95 Theses; Reformation begins

Timeline: 400 700 1000 1300 1600

THINKING ABOUT VOCABULARY

Number a sheet of paper from 1 to 10. Decide whether the underlined word or term in each of the following statements correctly completes the sentence. If the word or term is correct, write **C** beside the number. If the word or term is incorrect, write **I** and then write the word or term that correctly completes the sentence.

1. A <u>patron</u> is a wealthy or influential supporter of art and artists.

2. <u>Feudalism</u> is a pardon or forgiveness from the Pope.

3. <u>Renaissance</u> is a way of organizing and governing society based on land and service.

4. A <u>guild</u> was a group of traders or craftworkers in a medieval town.

5. Protestantism was an attempt to <u>reform</u> the Roman Catholic Church.

6. The <u>indulgence</u> was the period of artistic and cultural rebirth.

7. A <u>monastery</u> is a place where monks devote their lives to religion.

8. A <u>fief</u> was part of a lord's manor given to a vassal to manage.

9. The period when many people lived on manors owned by lords is called the <u>Middle Ages</u>.

10. <u>Deforestation</u> is the clearing of forests to make room for farms and cities.

THINKING ABOUT FACTS

1. How did serfs live?

2. What was the Black Death?

3. What did Copernicus learn from observing the sky?

4. What major changes in the Christian Church did you read about in this chapter?

5. According to the time line above, how long after the beginning of the Renaissance did the Protestant Reformation begin? How were the Renaissance and Reformation different?

THINK AND WRITE

WRITING AN EXPLANATION
Write a paragraph about feudalism. Identify lords, ladies, vassals, and serfs and explain their roles in feudal society.

WRITING AN INTERVIEW
Suppose you could go back into the Middle Ages and interview a monk or a nun. Write at least three questions you would ask the person and the answers you think he or she might give.

WRITING A LIST
Make a list of three complaints some people had about the Roman church that led to the Protestant Reformation.

APPLYING THINKING SKILLS

DETERMINING POINT OF VIEW

1. What is a point of view?
2. What point of view do you think the lord of a manor might have toward his serfs? What point of view might a serf have toward the lord?
3. Reread the words of Petrarch on page 338. What is his point of view about writing? Why do you think he had that point of view?
4. How did the points of view of Protestant and Catholic leaders differ during the Reformation?
5. Why is it important to the study of history to be able to understand different points of view?

Summing Up the Chapter

Review the chapter. Then copy on a separate piece of paper the flow chart shown below. Using what you learned in the chapter, fill in the remaining events. Then use the chart to write a paragraph that answers the question "What led to the decline of the feudal system?"

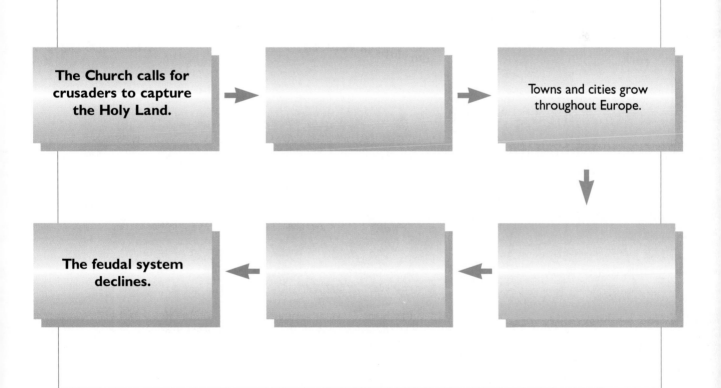

The Church calls for crusaders to capture the Holy Land. → → Towns and cities grow throughout Europe.

The feudal system declines. ← ←

Empires and Cultures of Africa

THINKING ABOUT HISTORY AND GEOGRAPHY

The stories of Africa's cultures often take place on the continent's fertile grasslands. Following the time line, see how civilizations developed in different parts of the continent. The great amounts of gold and other trade goods in Africa made these civilizations wealthy. As different peoples came into contact, new religious and cultural traditions were born.

ATLANTIC OCEAN

1324

MALI
King Mansa Musa makes a pilgrimage to Mecca

1200

LALIBELA
Ethiopians carve magnificent churches out of solid rock

1300

TIMBUKTU
An important trade center develops in West Africa

1200

1250

1300

EUROPE

AFRICA

Mali

Timbuktu

Lalibela

Red Sea

1350

ZANZIBAR
Swahili cultures develop
along Africa's east coast

1400

GREAT ZIMBABWE
A civilization in South
Africa develops an
important gold trade

Zanzibar

Great
Zimbabwe

1350

1400

Geography of Africa

Focus Activity

READ TO LEARN

How did the savanna of Africa affect the people that lived there long ago?

VOCABULARY

- savanna

PLACES

- Mount Kilimanjaro
- Sahara Desert
- Sahel
- Niger River
- Zambezi River
- Great Rift Valley
- Red Sea

Read Aloud

"The last rays of the sun filtered through a shredded lacework of clouds . . . the group of mud-walled houses and the dry grass, still scorched by the heat of noon, now swam in the red waters of the setting sun. . . . It was an afternoon in mid-October, at the end of the season of rains."

West African author Ousmane Sembene (oos MAH nee sem BAY nee), from the country of Senegal, wrote these words describing the end of one day in Africa. Throughout this huge continent, and throughout history, the sun—along with rain and vast stretches of grassland—has shaped the pattern of millions of lives.

THE BIG PICTURE

Africa is larger than the United States and all of the countries of Europe put together. The history of this enormous continent is long and varied. In Chapter 3 you read about the early people who lived in places like Border Cave. Then in Chapter 4, you read about one of the most powerful civilizations of the ancient world, ancient Egypt.

Civilization in Egypt, you may recall, was made possible by the "gift of the Nile." The Nile River provided both water and fertile soil in a dry environment. Several other life-giving rivers flow through Africa. Africa also has deserts, rain forests, and vast plains. This great variety has presented special challenges and opportunities for the many peoples of the continent.

AFRICA

As you can see on the map, the equator runs through the middle of Africa. Mountains rise along Africa's eastern and northern edges. Snow lingers year round on Mount Kilimanjaro. In the Sahara Desert, though, temperatures can reach a sizzling 136°F! This is the world's largest desert. Dry grasslands of the Sahel (SA hihl) form a narrow belt along the Sahara's southern edge. *Sahel* is an Arabic word that means "shore." Find the Sahel on the map.

The Niger River and the Zambezi (zam BEE zee) River water thirsty lands. The Great Rift Valley extends nearly 3,000 miles, from the Mozambique Channel to the Red Sea.

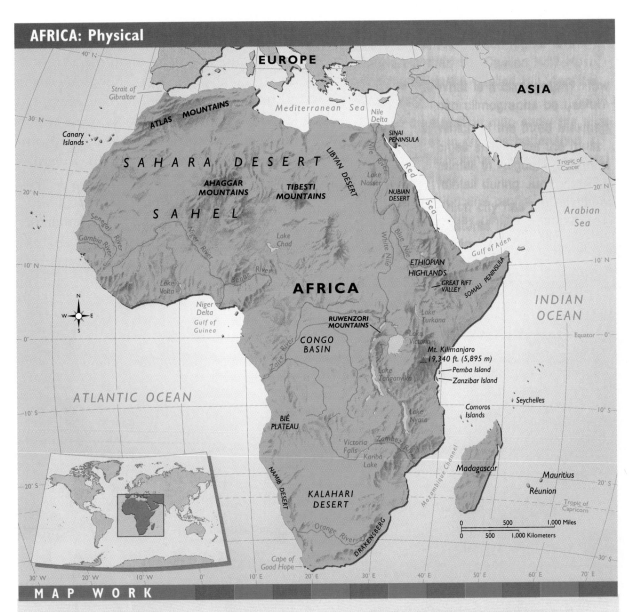

AFRICA: Physical

MAP WORK

The varied geography of Africa includes dense rain forests and empty deserts where rain may not fall for years at a time.

1. Which desert is found on the southwestern coast of Africa?

2. In which direction would you travel to go from the Tibesti Mountains to Lake Victoria?

3. How is it possible to reach Kariba Lake from Lake Victoria without land travel?

THE GRASSY PLAINS

Grassy, tree-dotted plains called savannas cover a large area of Africa. This area is about the size of the entire United States. Savannas cover most of southern Africa and the region between Ethiopia and Senegal.

The savannas have a dry season and a rainy season. During the dry season, savanna grasses turn brown and the ground dries and cracks. This quickly changes, though, when the rainy season arrives. Author Bessie Head describes the effect of rain on the savanna of Botswana, in southern Africa.

Before the first rains fall, it gets so hot that you cannot breathe. Then one day the sky just empties itself in a terrible downpour. After this, the earth and sky [come] alive and there is magic everywhere. . . . With just a little rain everything comes alive all at once; over-eager and hungry. . . . Crickets and frogs appear overnight in the pools around the village: there is a heavy, rich smell of breathing earth everywhere.

New grass and leaves sprout up across the savanna, providing a welcome feast for antelopes, zebras, and giraffes. The rains also bring needed water for crops and domestic animals.

Early Farmers

Africans began farming the savanna about 4,000 years ago. They domesticated grains called millet and sorghum (SAWR gum). These grains grew well in the thin, dry soil of the savannas. Both crops grew so quickly that they were ready for harvest before the dry season set in. Best of all, millet and sorghum contain vitamins, protein, and other nutrients needed for a healthy diet.

Modern equipment is used to harvest wheat on Kenya's savanna. Zambian women grind grain traditionally.

AFRICA AT A GLANCE

	Total Land Area	11,704,000 sq. miles 30,312,999 sq. km
	Highest Mountain	Mt. Kilimanjaro, Tanzania 19,340 feet (5,895 m)
	Longest River	Nile River 4,160 miles 6,671 km
	Largest City	Cairo, Egypt Population 6,052,832
	Current Population	706,000,000
	Percent of World Population	13%

 GEO FACT
More than half of Africa receives less than 20 inches (51 cm) of rain each year. In parts of the Sahara and Namib deserts, rain may not fall for six or seven years in a row. On the other hand, the rain forests of the Congo River Basin and the coastal region of western Africa receive more than 80 inches (203 cm) of rain each year.

CHART WORK

Africa is a continent of contrasts.

1. What, according to the chart, is one of Africa's greatest contrasts?

2. Which is Africa's longest river? How long is it?

These crops—along with okra, peas, and other vegetables—became the fuel for growing civilizations throughout Africa. The crops remain important today.

People and the Environment

In ancient times farmers set fire to the savannas and nearby areas to clear the land for farming or to make room for the growth of new grass for the herds. New grasses caused savannas to spread. Many historians believe that grasslands now ripple where forests once stood.

WHY IT MATTERS

The landforms of Africa are vast and varied. So are the continent's climate and bodies of water. All of these factors have affected the way Africans have lived. Ancient Africans farmed on the savannas. So do many Africans today.

Many people have worked to preserve and protect these important regions. Some savannas have become protected areas on which thousands of wild animals roam and feed.

You have learned how farming traditions shaped Africa's environment. In the next lesson you will read about a civilization that created unique religious legacies in a rocky environment.

Reviewing Facts and Ideas

MAIN IDEAS

● Africa's many climate regions range from the snow-covered top of Mount Kilimanjaro to the Sahara, the world's largest desert.

● Savannas cover much of southern Africa and are home to wildlife.

● Farmers began growing millet and sorghum about 4,000 years ago.

THINK ABOUT IT

1. What parts of Africa have hills and mountains?

2. What is the Sahel? Where is this region located?

3. **FOCUS** How have Africa's savannas shaped the lives of the people who have lived on them? How have people affected the savannas?

4. **THINKING SKILL** What are some *effects* of rainfall on the savanna?

5. **GEOGRAPHY** In what ways do people interact with the savanna environment in Africa?

600　700　1225　1350　1600

The Kingdoms of Ethiopia

Read Aloud

It began with a cliff some four stories high. From the hard red stone, workers carved out a massive block. The carvers then hollowed out the block and gave it windows and doors. They carved elegant arches, columns, and designs into the rock. The stone cliff slowly turned into a beautiful church. Such carving took place in the 1200s, in the highlands of Ethiopia.

Focus Activity

READ TO LEARN

How did kingdoms develop in what is today Ethiopia?

VOCABULARY

- **Queen Amanishakhete**
- **Lalibela**

PLACES

- **Ethiopia**
- **Kush**
- **Aksum**

THE BIG PICTURE

While castles and churches were being built in Europe during its Middle Ages, communities and kingdoms in Africa flourished as well. One of them developed a rich culture in northeastern Africa, near the tip of the Arabian peninsula.

In Chapter 4 you read that the Egyptian pharaoh Hatshepsut sent trading ships to the wealthy kingdom of Punt. Punt may have been located in the present-day country of **Ethiopia**. You also read that ancient Egypt's army conquered **Kush**, located in what is now Sudan. Egypt, Punt, and Kush were just three of the early civilizations of northeastern Africa. In this lesson you will read about other kingdoms that developed there.

This painting of apostles is in a stone church in Ethiopia.

CIVILIZATIONS IN NORTHEASTERN AFRICA

When Egyptian civilization declined, Kush became an independent kingdom. Kushite kings based their government at Meroe (MER oo ee), a city along the banks of the Nile.

The Kingdom of Kush

From about 500 B.C. to A.D. 150, Kush's rulers controlled a large trade network. This network stretched east to Arabia, north to the Mediterranean, and southwest toward the center of Africa.

Meroe's ruins give some clues to what life in Kush was like. There are remains of grand palaces, temples, and pyramid-shaped tombs. These remains show Kush's rulers had great wealth. Some of that wealth was found inside the tomb of Queen Amanishakhete (ah mahn uh SHAHK huh tee).

Queen Amanishakhete ruled Kush around 27 B.C. Archaeologists found gold bracelets, chains, rings, and statues within her tomb. The large amount of gold found in the tomb shows the richness of the Kush kingdom. The jewelry's beauty shows the skill of Kush's craftworkers.

The Kingdom of Aksum

By A.D. 350 the kingdom of Kush and its capital city had weakened. Historians are uncertain about the events that led to the decline of Kush. They know that Kush was conquered in 350 by Aksum, a powerful kingdom to the southeast.

Aksum was located high in the hills and mountains of what are today Eritrea and Ethiopia. Find Aksum on the map. Like Meroe, Aksum gained power and wealth by controlling important cities and trade routes. Traders traveled to the port city of Adula on the Red Sea.

There ships unloaded treasures from Arabia, Egypt, and India. People bought goods with gold coins or ivory.

Christianity in Africa

Many of Aksum's coins were stamped with signs of the Christian cross. Aksum's rulers became supporters of Christianity around A.D. 300. This early date makes ancient Ethiopia's Christian Church among the oldest in the world.

Christians in Ethiopia developed some beliefs that differed from those of Christians in Rome. For example, Ethiopians did not look to the Pope as their religious leader. Instead, Christians in Ethiopia follow a leader called a patriarch (PAY tree ark). Today nearly half of all Ethiopians are Christians.

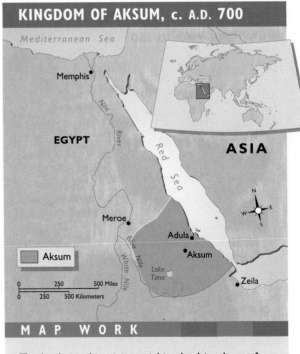

KINGDOM OF AKSUM, c. A.D. 700

MAP WORK

Trade thrived in cities within the kingdom of Aksum. Many traders crossed the Red Sea.

1. In which direction did Aksum's traders travel to reach the Red Sea?

2. About how far was Meroe from Adula?

3. Which rivers flowed along the western edge of Aksum?

A NEW KINGDOM

Aksum's trading success came to an end around A.D. 700. The kingdom suffered when the growing Baghdad caliphate took control of all shipping on the Red Sea. The loss of this important source of trade and wealth caused Aksum's economy to weaken. Bronze coins began to replace the more valuable gold coins. Around A.D. 900 Aksum stopped making coins altogether. By that time, the capital of the kingdom had been moved to more fertile lands farther south. Then Aksum's rulers were overthrown by local nobles called the Zagwe (ZAHG we).

Churches Carved in Rock

The Zagwe nobles, like the rulers of Aksum, supported Christianity. The most powerful Zagwe king, Lalibela (LAH lee be lah), ruled Ethiopia from about 1185 to 1225. During his rule, workers carved 11 stone churches in Ethiopia's new capital city. The city was named Lalibela to honor the king.

Day after day, year after year, people of the city probably heard sounds of clanging and chipping. Stoneworkers from as far away as Palestine and Egypt came to work on the projects. Their different languages must have been heard throughout the city.

Rock churches carved from huge pieces of stone still stand in Lalibela (left, below). Some of the services (far left) in Christian churches there and in other parts of Ethiopia follow traditions that developed under the Zagwe rulers.

Historians believe that each church in Lalibela was designed to look like a famous earlier church in Aksum. Some of the churches in Aksum had wooden beams jutting from the buildings. Lalibela's stonecutters carved out similar structures in stone. Since many of the churches were carved out of a single piece of stone, the stoneworkers had to be very careful. One slip of the chisel could result in a mistake that could not be corrected!

WHY IT MATTERS

The churches of Lalibela show the importance of Christianity in ancient Ethiopia. They also brought fame and honor to their builder, Lalibela. While little is known about the Zagwe kingdom, the stone churches have provided clues about the people of Zagwe.

The Zagwe kingdom of Ethiopia was only one of many that developed in Africa. In the next lesson you will read about a rich and powerful empire in western Africa. It grew at about the same time as the Zagwe kingdom.

✓ Reviewing Facts and Ideas

MAIN IDEAS

- Between 500 B.C. and A.D. 150, Kush grew wealthy from trade across the Mediterranean, in Arabia, and farther south in Africa.

- In A.D. 350 Kush was conquered by Aksum, a powerful trading state to the south. Christianity took root in Africa around this time.

- After 1100, Zagwe kings such as Lalibela created stone churches.

THINK ABOUT IT

1. How were Kush and Aksum similar? Describe one way in which the kingdoms were different.

2. Why were the churches of Lalibela so unusual and difficult to build?

3. **FOCUS** How was trade important to civilizations in ancient Ethiopia?

4. **THINKING SKILL** What _effects_ did the loss of Red Sea trade have on the kingdom of Aksum?

5. **WRITE** Write a short paragraph explaining what the artifacts in the tomb of Queen Amanishakhete reveal about Kush civilization.

600   750   1591   1600

Empires of West Africa

Read Aloud

What did jewelry and coins from such places as Morocco, Spain, and the storage rooms of the Medici family in Florence have in common? The answer is African gold. From 900 to 1500 most gold in western Asia and Europe came from the rich mines of West Africa. The resources from these mines would shape life throughout the Eastern Hemisphere—most of all in Africa—for hundreds of years.

Focus Activity

READ TO LEARN

What resources helped the empires of West Africa to grow wealthy and powerful?

VOCABULARY

- supply
- demand
- griot

PEOPLE

- **Sunjata**
- **Mansa Musa**

PLACES

- **Ghana**
- **Mali**
- **Timbuktu**
- **Songhai**
- **Morocco**

THE BIG PICTURE

As new kingdoms grew in northeastern Africa, other civilizations developed on the savannas of western Africa. These civilizations flourished while Baghdad's caliphs ruled a vast area in western Asia and northern Africa. At the same time, the Renaissance and Reformation swept through Europe.

As you read in Lesson 1 of this chapter, the savannas were a challenging environment for raising crops. Farmers could usually raise the sorghum, millet, and other crops that people needed for food. They could not, however, grow a very important item—salt. Salt was important because it could be used to prevent food from spoiling in warm climates. In parts of western Africa, salt actually became worth its weight in gold! Gold was another important item in West Africa. Much gold was bought and sold in the region's trade centers. Trade routes grew because of the need for salt and gold. These trade routes linked the empires of West Africa with the rest of Africa, Asia, and Europe.

In the Ghana empire, people sold salt in solid blocks. In some African towns, salt is still sold in the same way (left). Other trade goods included spoons, boxes to hold gold dust, and shells (below).

GHANA: AN EARLY EMPIRE

By the 700s the empire of Ghana was already a major power in Africa. Ghana was located at the southwestern edge of the Sahara, between the Senegal and Niger rivers.

The "Land of Gold"

In the 700s Muslim traders from northern Africa first began arriving in Ghana. What they saw amazed them. One trader, named al-Bakri, described the king's court in Ghana's capital city, Kumbi Salei (KOOM bee sah LEH).

> Behind the king stand ten helpers holding shields and swords decorated with gold; and on his right are the sons of his vassal kings, wearing splendid garments and with gold woven in their hair. At the door of the pavilion are dogs guarding him. Round their necks they wear collars of gold and silver.

Ghana's merchants were allowed to handle only gold dust. Nuggets of gold were kept by the king. Al-Bakri explained the reason for this practice. If all of Ghana's gold was allowed into the marketplace, he wrote, "the people would [collect] gold until it lost its value."

By keeping gold scarce, Ghana's kings followed an important rule of economics called supply and demand. Supply is a quantity of some good, product, or resource. Demand is people's desire for that particular item. According to the rule of supply and demand, items that are plentiful in supply do not have high value—because they are easy to get. Items that are scarce, however, are high in value—because they are *not* easy to get. By keeping gold scarce, Ghana's kings kept its demand—and price—high.

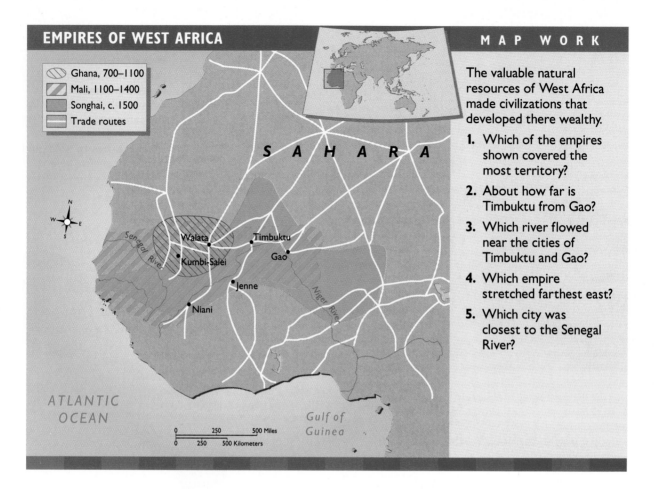

Ghana, 700–1100
Mali, 1100–1400
Songhai, c. 1500
Trade routes

SAHARA

Senegal River

Walata
Kumbi-Salei
Timbuktu
Gao
Jenne
Niani

Niger River

N
W E
S

ATLANTIC OCEAN

Gulf of Guinea

0   250   500 Miles
0   250   500 Kilometers

The valuable natural resources of West Africa made civilizations that developed there wealthy.

1. Which of the empires shown covered the most territory?

2. About how far is Timbuktu from Gao?

3. Which river flowed near the cities of Timbuktu and Gao?

4. Which empire stretched farthest east?

5. Which city was closest to the Senegal River?

THE RISE OF MALI

Ghana's kings controlled western Africa's gold supply for over 500 years. Eventually, though, other empires began challenging Ghana's power. According to traditional African stories, all but one prince in an empire called Mali (MAH lee) were killed.

Sunjata (sahn JAH tah) was spared because he was disabled and seemed harmless. The stories say that Mali's enemies, including Ghana, made a deadly mistake by misjudging Sunjata. He conquered his old enemies and all of Ghana as well. Sunjata died in 1255, but Mali continued to grow after his death. Look at the map to see how large Mali was at its peak in the 1300s.

From Mine to Market

Like Ghana, Mali grew very rich by controlling the gold trade. In the 1300s gold became more valuable than ever. Gold was mined in tunnels and pits throughout western Africa. Miners dug dirt and rock out of the ground.

Women sifted the gold dust. Grains they found were then poured into hollow feather quills or other containers and transported to Mali's market cities.

One of these cities was Timbuktu (tim buk TOO). It was located at a crossroads of major trade routes, near the Niger River. Timbuktu also bordered the Sahara and was a final stop for caravan routes that crossed the desert.

In Timbuktu's busy markets, farmers sold vegetables and grains. Some bargained over the price of gold, salt, and North African horses. Other traders settled the price of enslaved prisoners. Most of the enslaved people would be taken to Europe and Northern Africa.

Timbuktu

Timbuktu grew as a trading center near the great bend of the Niger River. Located at the end of Arab trade routes that crossed the Sahara, Timbuktu was the site of much cultural exchange during the Mali and Songhai empires. How did cultural influences combine in Timbuktu?

Religion

Arab Muslims brought Islam to West Africa. The Sankore Mosque was built in 1325 while Mansa Musa ruled Mali.

Trade

The trade that flourished between Africans and Arabs continues in Timbuktu today. While salt remains a popular item, many other goods are also bought and sold.

Architecture

This 1830 watercolor shows how both Arab and African building styles were used in Timbuktu. Traditional African buildings are rounded and Arab-style structures are square.

LIFE IN THE EMPIRES

In the early 1300s the best horses and goods were bought by a Mali king called Mansa Musa. During Mansa Musa's reign, from 1312 to 1337, Mali was at its peak of wealth and power. Mansa Musa ruled with great authority. Nevertheless, he recognized at least one power as being greater than himself: Allah. The religion of Islam had been spreading throughout western Africa ever since the first Muslim traders arrived there in the 700s.

In 1324 Mansa Musa fulfilled one of the Five Pillars of Islam. He made a pilgrimage to Mecca. During the year-long journey, the king gave away gifts of gold to rich and poor people alike. How does the following excerpt, by a northern African writer, reflect Mansa Musa's power?

MANY VOICES
PRIMARY SOURCE

From the writings of Al-'Umari, about 1337-1338.

*W*hen the king of this kingdom comes in from a journey an [umbrella] and a **standard** are held over his head as he rides, and drums are beaten and guitars and trumpets well made of horn are played in front of him.... When one whom the king has charged with a task or assignment returns to him he questions him in detail about everything which has happened to him from the moment of his departure until his return. Complaints and appeals against **administrative oppression** are placed before this king and he delivers judgment on them himself. As a rule nothing is written down; his commands are given **verbally**.

standard: flag
administrative: governmental
oppression: unjust power
verbally: by speaking

The Granger Collection

This map made in 1375 shows West African trade routes. Find Mansa Musa in the bottom right-hand corner.

This figure of an archer from Mali was found near the Niger River.

The Songhai Empire

As Mansa Musa ruled Mali, a small eastern territory called Songhai (SOHNG hi) was growing strong. In the next 150 years, Songhai rose to take Mali's place as the most powerful empire in western Africa. The empire of Songhai lasted from about 1490 until 1590.

Like the kings of Ghana and Mali, Songhai kings were all-powerful rulers. Among the most important assistants to the kings were griots (GREE ohs). Griots are people who tell stories that describe historical events. Such stories are told again and again so people can learn about the past. Kings also made use of scribes. Scribes wrote official documents in Arabic.

WHY IT MATTERS

In 1591 the Songhai empire collapsed when it was attacked by an army from the north. This army used guns against the arrows and spears of the Songhai empire. The army came from the African country of Morocco. Morocco had long had trading ties with West Africa. Its leader wanted to gain complete control of this trade and perhaps of the gold mines as well.

The great demand for gold affected life for many people in West Africa. Gold played a part in the lives of the miners who recovered it, the traders who brought it to market, and the kings who used it to bring glory to their rule. Africa's gold was also in demand in Europe. Gold coins in Venice and Florence helped pay for the great art projects of the European Renaissance.

The empires of western Africa were not the only civilizations to spread African wealth to far-off places. In the next lesson you will read about busy port cities on the continent's east coast. Those cities had contact with places as far away as China.

Reviewing Facts and Ideas

MAIN IDEAS

- The empire of Ghana lasted from before 700 until around 1200. It was nicknamed the "land of gold."
  - The empire of Mali ruled from about 1240 to 1400. Timbuktu became a major center of trade.
- Mansa Musa ruled Mali between 1312 and 1337. Islam spread in West Africa during this time.
- The empire of Songhai lasted from about 1490 to 1590. Oral historians, or griots, and scribes kept records of events in the empire.

THINK ABOUT IT

1. What did Sunjata do to build the empire of Mali?

2. How were griots and scribes important to rulers of the Songhai empire?

3. **FOCUS** What role did the gold trade play in West Africa's empires?

4. **THINKING SKILL** Explain the *effects* produced when Ghana's kings kept gold scarce in the marketplace.

5. **GEOGRAPHY** How might the Niger River have been important for trade in West Africa?

GRIOTS
AND ORAL HISTORY

During the time when empires ruled West Africa, griots told stories and sang songs for traders, villagers, and kings alike. These special stories and songs described the history, beliefs, and traditions of African families and of the land. They became the oral history, or spoken record of events, of Africa.

Because many people could not read a written language, they depended upon the spoken words of the griots. African kings depended on griots to help keep people informed about happenings in the empire. In time the singing and speaking skills of the griots became an important West African legacy.

That legacy continues today. Modern griots tell African history and traditions to people around the world. Some have become teachers and historians. Others perform before audiences in order to entertain as well as educate.

Griots in ancient Africa told stories that taught people their history. Griots often know hundreds of events by heart.

Some griots travel around the world telling the stories of their cultures. Many wear traditional clothing styles that griots have worn in Africa for more than 700 years.

The griot uses a *kora* during his performance. A kora is a hand-crafted instrument that is traditionally used by griots. Each year thousands of people attend performances in which griots tell stories about history, cultural traditions, and current events.

Reading Distribution Maps

VOCABULARY
distribution map
population density

WHY THE SKILL MATTERS

In the last lesson you learned that West Africa's earliest known empires developed between the Senegal and Niger rivers. Some 25,000 people lived in Timbuktu, making it one of the region's biggest cities. Thousands more lived in the towns and villages that developed on the nearby savannas and in forests.

Today much has changed in western Africa. The region's population as a whole has grown. So has the Sahara Desert, partly as a result of human interaction with the environment. The once-productive heartland of Ghana's empire, for example, is now part of the desert.

Looking at a distribution map can help you see how such changes have affected where people live in Africa today. A distribution map is a special purpose map. It shows how one particular feature is spread over an area. The maps on these pages show current population density in Africa. Population density is the number of people living in a given amount of space. Distribution maps can also show such features as climate, land use, products, and languages spoken in an area.

Traders bargain at a busy market in Burundi.

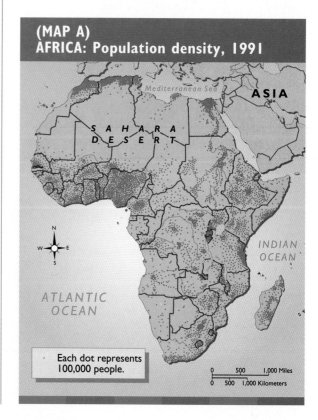

(MAP A)
AFRICA: Population density, 1991

Each dot represents 100,000 people.

USING THE SKILL

Study Map A. The title tells you that the map provides information about population density in Africa. The map key shows that each dot on the map represents 100,000 people. The closer together the dots, the more dense is the population. The more spread out and fewer the dots, the less dense is the population. The great bend of the Niger River is one of the most populated areas in West Africa. This is shown by the large number of dots in that area.

TRYING THE SKILL

Distribution Map B on this page shows the population density of the continent of Africa in another way. How many people per square mile live near the coast of present-

Helping yourself

- A **distribution map** shows how one kind of feature, such as **population density**, is spread over an area.
- Study the map title and key.

day Ghana? How many people per square mile live near the Nile River delta?

REVIEWING THE SKILL

Use the map on this page to answer the following questions:

1. How do you know this is a distribution map?

2. Which city has more people, Nairobi or the western coastal city of Abidjan?

3. Which region has a higher population density today, the Sahara Desert or eastern lands along the coast of the Indian Ocean? How do you know?

4. What kind of distribution map could help you to better understand life in your own community?

(MAP B) AFRICA: Population density, 1991

Casablanca • Algiers •
Mediterranean Sea
ASIA
Cairo •
S A H A R A
D E S E R T
Lagos •
Abidjan •
GHANA
Addis Ababa •
ATLANTIC OCEAN
Kinshasa •
Nairobi •
INDIAN OCEAN
Johannesburg •
Cape Town •

People per square mile	People per square kilometer
0–25	0–10
25–250	10–100
250–500	100–200
over 500	over 200

• Major city

0   500   1,000 Miles
0   500   1,000 Kilometers

About 1.2 million people live in Harare, Zimbabwe's capital.

600   850   1100   1300   1600

Africa's Eastern Coast

Focus Activity

READ TO LEARN

What was life like in the trading cities along the coast of the Indian Ocean?

PLACES

• Mombasa
• Zanzibar
• Mogadishu

Read Aloud

The king of the city of Kilwa had a palace with over 100 rooms and a maze of courtyards. He even had an eight-sided pool built into a cliff overlooking the blue waters of the Indian Ocean. The immense palace was just a small part of the great wealth in eastern Africa during the 1300s. That wealth was the result of trade.

THE BIG PICTURE

Before A.D. 1100 the kingdom of Ghana was at its peak. Another powerful African civilization was growing some 2,500 miles to the east of Ghana. Actually, this civilization's villages, towns, and cities were closer to the Indus River valley of Asia than they were to the Niger River of western Africa. Yet the African civilizations had important things in common. For example, their many languages were rooted in an ancient language called Bantu. Both civilizations also profited from trade within Africa and with other continents.

In the last lesson you read that West African gold was transported to northern Africa and Europe. There it was made into coins. In eastern Africa, gold was shipped to cities in Arabia, India, and China. So were elephant tusks, which are the material called ivory.

Ivory from East Africa was used to make this jeweled lion. It was worn on the arm.

ASIA

AFRICA

Zeila

Berbera

Ras Hafun

Somali Peninsula

City

Swahili civilization

Lake Victoria

Mogadishu

N
W — E
S

Lamu

Malindi

Mombasa

Pemba I.

Zanzibar

Lake Tanganyika

INDIAN OCEAN

Kilwa Kisiwani

0   500   1,000 Miles
0   500   1,000 Kilometers

Cities that developed along the east coast of Africa linked the continent with Asian traders.

1. Which ocean bounded the east coast of Africa?

2. Which was the southernmost Swahili city?

3. What peninsula lies north of Mogadishu?

4. About how far is Mombasa from Mogadishu?

5. Which lake is farther west—Lake Tanganyika or Lake Victoria?

TRADE ALONG THE INDIAN OCEAN

The coastal cities of eastern Africa linked Africa to Asia. For hundreds of years, boats loaded with trade goods sailed the Indian Ocean. In the coastal cities, merchant-sailors from Asia eagerly bought African goods.

Many of the goods were brought from further inland. These goods included gold, leopard skins, rhinoceros horns, and ivory. Demand for East African ivory in Asia was high. This ivory was softer and easier to carve than West African ivory. Arabian craftworkers made chess pieces from ivory. Chinese used it to make beautiful artwork and containers.

In the coastal markets, African merchants were able to buy goods from Asia and other places. Metal tools, fine pottery, cloth, glass containers, and wheat were in great demand in the coastal cities of Africa.

The "People of the Shore"

Over time, some of the foreign merchants settled in Africa's eastern coastal cities. Many were Arab Muslims. They made important contributions to the civilization that became known as Swahili. *Swahili* means "people of the shore" in Arabic. Many Arabic words also became part of the Swahili language. Settlers from Arabia also shared the traditions of Islam with the Swahili people. Islam became an important religious heritage for many Africans in the busy port cities that developed on the east coast.

373

LIFE ALONG THE COAST

Between 1000 and 1500, Swahili cities grew in size and strength. Like the trading cities of West Africa, Swahili cities grew when they controlled important trade routes. Cities often declined when that control slipped away. Unlike the empires to the northwest, Swahili cities and villages were each ruled by their own leaders.

Swahili Cities

Mombasa (mom BAH suh), located on an island of present-day Kenya, was one important trading center. The city had a port and crowded markets. Many ships were attracted to Mombasa each season. Another main Swahili city, Zanzibar (ZAN zuh bar), was located on a much bigger island about 100 miles to the south, in what is today the country of Tanzania (tan zuh NEE uh).

Mogadishu (mohg uh DISH oo), in present-day Somalia, was one of the largest of the coastal cities. Find Mogadishu on the map on page 373.

The people of Mogadishu lived by farming and fishing. Some used sailboats to transport gold to other trading centers. Mogadishu controlled much of Africa's gold trade from about 1000 to 1300. On days when the wind was still, the sailors sang songs. They often sang this one as they worked.

Plunge in the paddles,
Plunge in the paddles,
If the sail is against the mast,
Plunge in the paddles.

For much of the year Mogadishu's sailors shared their port with the larger sailboats that brought cargo and merchants from Asia. In the city's marketplaces, foreign merchants bought load after load of ivory, gold, and leopard

Sculpted elephant tusks arch over a main street in Mombasa, Kenya (above). The illustration (left) shows Mombasa during the 1300s.

skins. They also purchased tortoise shells, tools, and glass.

WHY IT MATTERS

Today some important legacies of early Swahili civilization remain in the countries of East Africa. Swahili has become the common language of Tanzania, Kenya, Zaire, and Uganda. Old Swahili ports such as Mombasa and Zanzibar still ship goods around the globe.

Once-powerful cities like Mombasa, however, are not as strong as they were long ago. The decline of these cities was a result of conflicts that broke out in the 1500s. These conflicts took place between Swahilis and newcomers to eastern Africa. You will read in Chapter 16 about how those newcomers came to explore Africa's east coast.

What trade good from Zanzibar is commonly in demand today?

In the 1400s Zanzibar was known for its ivory, tortoise shells, and other goods. Today Zanzibar is the world's largest producer of tiny flowers from a special kind of evergreen tree. The unopened buds of these flowers are dried, then sold to buyers across the world. After being shipped and packaged, some of these buds eventually make their way into the spice sections of your local grocery stores. You will find them under the name "cloves." Cloves are used as spice in cooking.

 Reviewing Facts and Ideas

MAIN IDEAS

- Many eastern African coastal cities grew as a result of trade with Asian countries across the Indian Ocean.

- The coastal cities of Mogadishu, Mombasa, and Zanzibar were enriched by trade in ivory and gold.

- Eastern Africa's earliest Arab settlers contributed to Swahili civilization in the areas of language and religion.

- Swahili cities flourished mainly between 1000 and 1500, when a period of conflict began.

THINK ABOUT IT

1. Why was eastern African ivory a valuable trade item? What other items were traded in the coastal cities?

2. In what ways did Muslim Arabs who settled on Africa's eastern coast contribute to Swahili culture? Describe an important legacy of the Swahili civilization.

3. **FOCUS** How did life in Mogadishu reflect the importance of trade in Swahili cities?

4. **THINKING SKILL** Name one major *cause* for the settlement of Arabs in eastern Africa. Describe two *effects* of their settlement there.

5. **GEOGRAPHY** In what ways did the people of Africa's coastal cities interact with their environment?

600   850   1100   1350   1400   1500

Great Zimbabwe

Read Aloud

Around 1400 a powerful city surrounded by stone walls was located in a hilly region south of the Zambezi River. The city had covered passages that led through different sections within the walls.

One section of the city was once known as "the house of the great woman" by later neighbors. Who was that woman? What role did she play in the city? So far, the answers to those questions have remained unknown. They are just a few of the unsolved mysteries that surround the southern African civilization known as Great Zimbabwe.

Focus Activity

READ TO LEARN

What effects did the growth of Great Zimbabwe have on southern Africa?

PLACES

• Great Zimbabwe
• Sofala

THE BIG PICTURE

In the last lesson you read about wealthy cities that developed along the eastern African coast. These cities grew rich from trade in ivory, gold, and other goods. Much of the gold came from inland mines to the west, in present-day Zimbabwe.

Farming and herding villages had existed here for hundreds of years. Over time historians believe one village won control over the region's gold trade. During the 1300s this community grew in power.

Historians know very little about this community. Its people left behind no oral traditions or written documents. Historians are even unsure about the meaning of its name: **Great Zimbabwe**. In the Shona language, *Zimbabwe* can mean either "houses of stone" or "honored houses." By closely examining artifacts left by the peoples of Great Zimbabwe, however, archaeologists and historians have learned something about this community.

THE PEOPLE OF GREAT ZIMBABWE

Between bare granite hills and rolling, tree-filled savannas are the ruins of Great Zimbabwe. Early farmers and herders made use of the region's fertile areas. Farmers raised crops year after year. Herds of cattle, sheep, and goats lived on nearby savannas.

People built their villages and cities near these areas. Craftworkers made jugs and other containers from clay. These pieces of pottery helped people cook, carry water, and collect grains. Pottery fragments in the area show that the community of Great Zimbabwe grew between about 1000 and 1500. During that time people built houses with walls that were made of mud. Archaeologists have found holes that held the main poles of the houses. They have also found the remains of thick stone walls. The walls, they say, were built around the city in the 1300s. What life was like within those walls, though, is a mystery.

Walls of Stone

For the people of Great Zimbabwe, of course, the stone walls and buildings of their city were not new and different. In fact, in southern Africa at the time, over 100 other stone towns are known to have existed. The walls of Great Zimbabwe, however, were by far the biggest. Many historians believe that trade helped make the construction of these walls possible. Who was responsible for building the walls around the growing city?

Great Zimbabwe's kings probably ordered workers to make the city's walls. To do this, stoneworkers used a material that was very close at hand. They used huge granite rocks that lay in and around the city to build the walls. Many of these rocks were larger than several homes put together. Workers heated sheets of the stone, then cracked them into pieces that had straight edges. Next they cut the stones into brick-sized pieces. The work was hard. Workers stacked the granite bricks to form walls as high as 30 feet. The heavy weight of the stones held the walls in place.

This carved bird was found in an area used for ceremonies.

GREAT ZIMBABWE, c. 1400

Great Zimbabwe

AFRICA

Lake Nyasa

Zambezi River

Sofala

Madagascar

KALAHARI DESERT

Phalaborwa

INDIAN OCEAN

0   300   600 Miles
0   300   600 Kilometers

MAP WORK

Great Zimbabwe was located in a fertile area that was rich in natural building materials.

1. Great Zimbabwe was located east of which desert?

2. Which river flowed to the north of Great Zimbabwe?

3. About how many miles did traders from Great Zimbabwe have to travel to reach the Indian Ocean?

THE CITY ON A HILL

Historians believe that most of the stone walls of Great Zimbabwe surrounded the large homes of the ruling families. Were the walls meant to keep something in—or out? The walls may have been built to keep the city safe from attack by other cities and villages. Or they may have given extra privacy to the lives of Great Zimbabwe's leaders. Maybe the walls reflected their great power in the community. There is no way to know for certain. Historians can only guess at what their lives may have been like. It is likely, however, that many of these ruling families became powerful by trading gold.

Controlling the Gold Trade

Some of southern Africa's richest gold fields are located around Great Zimbabwe. Sometime in the 1300s Great Zimbabwe began to trade with an important Swahili coastal city called Sofala. Miners probably worked hard to increase the gold supply that was brought to Sofala. They probably brought gold from the mines back to Great Zimbabwe. There, workers used a special furnace to melt the gold. Melted gold then was reshaped for shipment.

Great Zimbabwe's powerful families grew wealthy from the increase in the flow of gold among the mines, the city, and Sofala. Artifacts show that they used some of their new wealth to buy loads of glass beads, cloth, and pottery from China and Persia.

Most people, however, still used locally made pottery to carry water or for cooking. Metalworkers in the city coiled gold wire into bracelets for their customers. The people who lived in Great Zimbabwe liked to wear the gold and beaded jewelry they created. The city's metalworkers also made iron hoes and axes for farmers. Farmers used those tools to raise millet and sorghum at the edges of Great Zimbabwe. Those grains, along with milk and meat, were important items in the daily diet of the city's residents. During the period in which Great Zimbabwe thrived in the

Great Zimbabwe (above) was a main trading center for 400 years. Today Harare (left) is the business center in the country of Zimbabwe.

early 1400s, about 18,000 people lived in the community. This meant that farmers and herders worked hard to provide food for the people of the walled city.

For reasons unknown to historians, Great Zimbabwe began to decline in the late 1400s. Most of its residents left and moved to other regions. Did too much farming wear out the land around the city and create hardship? Did some natural catastrophe happen? Archaeologists and historians are working to learn more about Great Zimbabwe. Even so, they may never be able to answer these questions.

WHY IT MATTERS

Events after Great Zimbabwe was abandoned are not such a mystery. In the late 1490s a small European ship sailed past Sofala. It was the first one ever to do so. In its wake would come many changes for all of Africa.

Meanwhile, a new group of peoples began to farm and trade in southern Africa. Today these distant relatives of the people of Great Zimbabwe continue to live in Zimbabwe, the country that is named after the ancient city.

✓✓ Reviewing Facts and Ideas

MAIN IDEAS

- Information about Great Zimbabwe is limited due to a lack of oral traditions and written documents.
- The city thrived in the 1300s and 1400s, due in part to its control of local gold trade routes.
- Great Zimbabwe's trade in gold tied it to Swahili cities and to Asia.

THINK ABOUT IT

1. What purposes might the walls of Great Zimbabwe have served?

2. Why was the coastal city of Sofala important to the growth and strength of Great Zimbabwe?

3. **FOCUS** How did Great Zimbabwe's involvement in the gold trade affect life in the city?

4. **THINKING SKILL** Based on your reading, make a _conclusion_ about why Great Zimbabwe's wealthy families may have needed the protection of the stone walls. Explain how you made your conclusion.

5. **GEOGRAPHY** How did the people of Great Zimbabwe make use of raw materials when they built their city?

CHAPTER 13 REVIEW

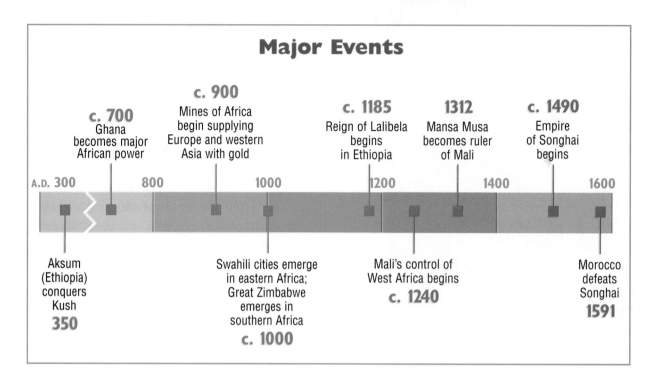

Major Events

c. 700
Ghana becomes major African power

c. 900
Mines of Africa begin supplying Europe and western Asia with gold

c. 1185
Reign of Lalibela begins in Ethiopia

1312
Mansa Musa becomes ruler of Mali

c. 1490
Empire of Songhai begins

A.D. 300   800   1000   1200   1400   1600

Aksum (Ethiopia) conquers Kush
350

Swahili cities emerge in eastern Africa; Great Zimbabwe emerges in southern Africa
c. 1000

Mali's control of West Africa begins
c. 1240

Morocco defeats Songhai
1591

THINKING ABOUT VOCABULARY

Number a sheet of paper from 1 to 5. Beside each number write the word that best matches the statement.

demand   savanna
griot   supply
Sahel

1. A grassy plain dotted with trees
2. The people's desire for an item or service
3. A quantity of available goods, products, or resources
4. The dry southern edge of the Sahara
5. A person who tells stories that describe historical events

THINKING ABOUT FACTS

1. What is the world's largest desert?
2. How long is the Great Rift Valley?
3. How much of Africa is covered by savannas? What is the weather like on the savannas?
4. What grains have Africans been growing on the savannas for 4,000 years?
5. How did the ancient kingdom of Kush become wealthy?
6. How long did the empire of Ghana last? What did Ghana's kings do to keep the value of gold high?
7. According to the time line above, when did Mansa Musa become ruler of Mali? What important change took place in West Africa about that time?
8. Name three important Swahili cities. What two important products did they trade with Asia?
9. What was Great Zimbabwe? Why don't we know more about it?
10. According to the time line above, how many years were there between Aksum's conquest of Kush and the beginning of the Songhai empire? Name three African states that arose during that time.

WRITING A DIARY

Suppose you are Queen Amanishakhete of Kush. Write a diary entry about some of the things you did today.

WRITING A TRAVEL BROCHURE

Imagine you are a travel agent who wants to interest people in Timbuktu. Write a brief brochure about the city's history so people will want to visit it.

WRITING A DESCRIPTION

Write a paragraph describing the Swahili civilization of eastern Africa. Include information about Swahili cities and about trade on the Indian Ocean.

APPLYING GEOGRAPHY SKILLS

READING DISTRIBUTION MAPS

1. What is a distribution map?
2. What information do the two distribution maps on pages 370 and 371 provide?
3. What other features might distribution maps of Africa and West Africa show?
4. Look at Map B on page 371. Which is more densely populated, Cairo or Casablanca?
5. Why is a distribution map useful?

Summing Up the Chapter

Copy the main idea map below on a separate sheet of paper. Then review the chapter and fill in information for each region. After you complete the diagram, write a paragraph that answers the question "What helped to make ancient Africa diverse?"

Ethiopian Kingdoms

Kush
Aksum
Zagwe

Swahili Cities in East Africa

Mombasa
Zanzibar
Mogadishu

Civilization and Cultures Flourished in Sub-Saharan Africa

West African Empires

Ghana
Mali
Songhai

Southern Africa

Great Zimbabwe

Empires and Cultures of Asia

THINKING ABOUT
HISTORY AND GEOGRAPHY

For centuries, Asia has been home to many civilizations. The time line and map show where some of them developed. Asian peoples between A.D. 1100 and A.D. 1650 used trade and military power to increase their influence. Many also constructed buildings that remain among the world's finest architectural achievements.

Constantinople

AFRICA

1100s

ANGKOR
Suryavarman II builds Angkor Wat

1279

BEIJING
Kublai Khan conquers and unites China

1453

CONSTANTINOPLE
Turks conquer the Byzantine empire

1100

1250

1400

ASIA

Beijing

Edo

Agra

PACIFIC
OCEAN

1603

EDO

**The reign of the
Tokugawa Shogun begins
in Japan**

Angkor

1631

AGRA

**Shah Jahan begins con-
struction of the Taj Mahal**

INDIAN
OCEAN

1550

1700

Geography of Asia

Read Aloud

"The summer sun, who robbed the pleasant nights, and plundered [stole] all the water of the rivers, and burned the earth, and scorched the forest trees, is now in hiding; and the autumn clouds, spread thick across the sky to track him down, hunt for the criminal with lightning flashes."

Indian poet Amaru, writing in Sanskrit, described India's yearly change of seasons over 1,000 years ago. This change is a big event for many people across Asia. Many, in fact, depend on it for their lives.

Focus Activity

READ TO LEARN

How do the Himalayas affect the geography of Asia?

VOCABULARY

- archipelago
- monsoon

PLACES

- Himalayas
- Mount Everest
- Tibetan Plateau
- Gobi Desert

THE BIG PICTURE

Asia is the world's largest continent. It stretches from Saudi Arabia and Turkey in the west to the eastern parts of China and Japan. Asia has many regions. The continent is made up of areas called North, West, Central, South, Southeast, and East Asia. Each of these regions has a great variety of people and environments.

Asia includes many climates, landforms, peoples, and histories. Some of the ancient Asian civilizations you have already read about include Harappa, Mesopotamia, and Shang China.

A thin strip of land in northeastern Egypt is considered Asia's border with Africa. The Ural mountains separate North Asia from Europe. Asia has more mountains than any other continent. It also has the highest mountains. Not surprisingly, mountains greatly affect life on the continent. You will read about the world's highest mountain range in this lesson.

ASIA

The Himalayas (him uh LAY uz) and neighboring mountains make up the heart of Asia. Many of the world's highest peaks are here, including the tallest of all—Mount Everest. The Himalayas form the southern border of the vast Tibetan Plateau. This plateau is a high mountain plain where more than a half dozen of the continent's powerful rivers begin. Locate the Tibetan Plateau and the Himalayas on the map below.

Asia has several island chains off its shores. One of these chains is Japan. Find it on the map. Japan forms an archipelago (ahr kuh PEL ih goh). *Archipelago* is the word for such a group or chain of islands.

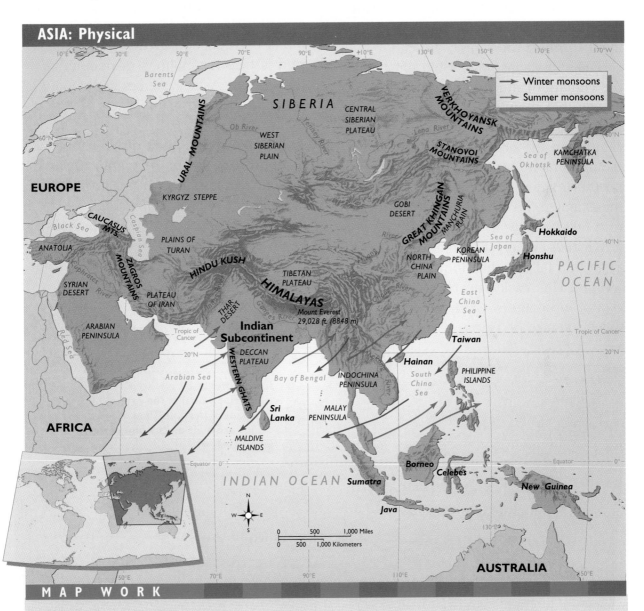

ASIA: Physical

| Winter monsoons |
| Summer monsoons |

MAP WORK

Asia is a land of extreme contrasts in geography. In addition to the highest mountains in the world, it has vast plains and deserts.

1. What mountain ranges border the Gobi Desert to the east and northeast?

2. What other deserts are in Asia?

3. Which coast of the Indian Subcontinent, the east or west, would be more likely to encounter flooding in the summer?

385

A WALL OF MOUNTAINS

Himalaya means "snowy range" in Sanskrit. This vast range stretches across central Asia for 1,500 miles. Many of the peaks are over 25,000 feet high. Their immense heights form the world's highest natural wall.

The Himalayas and neighboring mountain ranges form a towering wall that divides India and Nepal from Tibet and China. The barrier makes movement through the region difficult.

The Himalayas have a big effect on the climate of much of Asia. They block clouds that blow north from the Indian Ocean. This causes large amounts of rainfall on the ocean-facing sides of the mountains and small amounts on their northern sides. In Cherrapunji, India, for example, an average of 38 feet of rain falls each year! By contrast, only a few inches fall on the other side, Tibet. Even less falls in the Gobi (GOH bee) Desert. This rocky, nearly treeless region in northern China is almost twice the size of Texas.

Monsoons

Plenty of rain is usually good news for Asia's many farmers. Throughout much of South Asia, though, most rain falls during only one season. The rest of the year remains dry. Rain clouds are brought to the region by seasonal winds called monsoons.

An Indian leader named Indira Gandhi once remarked, "for us in India scarcity [shortage of resources] is only a missed monsoon away." What she said is true for millions of people throughout Asia. Farmers count on the monsoons to bring water for their crops.

In India the months of November through May remain dry and, toward the end, intensely hot. During these months dry winter monsoons blow across South Asia from the northeast. From about June through October, however, moisture-bearing winds from the southeast and southwest sweep across the continent. These winds are the summer monsoons. Farmers joyfully

Rains brought by monsoon winds flood Dhaka, the capital of Bangladesh (left). In Tibet camps are built on the high, drier plains (below).

ASIA AT A GLANCE

	Total Land Area	16,992,000 sq. miles 44,009,000 sq. km

	Highest Mountain	Mt. Everest, Nepal 29,028 feet (8,848 m)

	Longest River	Chang River, China 3,915 miles 6,300 km

	Largest City	Tokyo, Japan Population 8,112,000

	Current Population	3,389,000,000
	Percent of World Population	61%

GEO FACT

Giant pandas live in bamboo forests in the high elevations of southwestern China. The bearlike animals eat bamboo shoots. Because there is often a shortage of bamboo for the pandas to eat, panda numbers are limited. In the late 1980s scientists estimated that only about 600 pandas were left in the wild.

CHART WORK

The chart provides information about the size and geography of Asia.

1. What is one condition that contributes to the limited population of the giant panda?

2. What percentage of the world's population lives in Asia?

greet the huge sheets of rain brought by summer monsoons that water their rice, sorghum, millet, and chickpeas, among other crops.

As long as the rain-bearing monsoon runs its normal course, farmers can count on successful harvests. An Indian proverb, however, warns "if the sky fails, the earth will fail." If too much rain falls, as often happens in some regions, flooding may result in loss of life and property.

WHY IT MATTERS

From the chart on this page you can see that Asia has a large population. People in the many regions of Asia have adapted to the great variety of geographical features on the continent.

Some of these features—mountains, river valleys, and monsoons—helped create rich farmland on which people could live. In the following lessons you will read about some of the people who lived in these different environments.

✔ Reviewing Facts and Ideas

MAIN IDEAS

- Asia, the world's largest continent, has more mountains than any other. These mountain ranges include the awesome Himalayas.

- The Himalayas block clouds blowing north from the Indian Ocean. As a result, large amounts of rain fall south of the mountains while little falls to the north.

- Seasonal winds called monsoons affect many Asians' lives. Important crops depend on rain the summer monsoons bring each year.

THINK ABOUT IT

1. Why are monsoons important to farmers in South Asia?

2. How does the Tibetan plateau affect other regions of Asia?

3. **FOCUS** How is life in Asia affected by the Himalayas?

4. **THINKING SKILL** What _conclusions_ can you make about life in Asia from the information in this lesson? On what facts did you base your conclusions?

5. **GEOGRAPHY** Look at the map on page 385. What major rivers begin on the Tibetan Plateau?

800   1050   1300   1566   1800

The Ottomans

Read Aloud

"In Baghdad I am the shah [king], in Byzantine realms the caesar, and in Egypt the sultan; who sends his fleets to the seas of Europe, North Africa, and India."

These words were written by a leader named Süleyman, who headed one of the world's biggest empires in the early 1500s. His capital was not Baghdad, nor was it a new city. Rather it was a city that had once been the capital of the Eastern Roman empire. That city was Constantinople.

Focus Activity

READ TO LEARN

What was life like in the Ottoman empire?

VOCABULARY

- sultan
- grand mufti

PEOPLE

- Osman
- Süleyman
- Sinan

PLACES

- Istanbul
- Anatolia

THE BIG PICTURE

The city once known as Constantinople is located in present-day Turkey. Now called Istanbul, the city crosses two continents. It extends across both sides of the Bosporus Strait, which separates Asia from eastern Europe. Anatolia, as Turkey was known during the Byzantine empire, has been home to some of the world's oldest civilizations. In Chapter 3 you read about the prehistoric city of Catal Huyuk, which thrived there over 8,000 years ago. In Chapter 9 you learned about the Roman emperor Constantine. He built Constantinople and its many Christian churches around A.D. 330.

For 1,000 years after Constantine built this city, the Byzantine empire remained a center of Christianity. In the 1300s, though, Anatolia was settled by a people called Turks. The Turks were Muslims from Central Asia. Within 150 years the Turks had made the city of Constantinople the capital of a new Turkish-led empire.

AN EXPANDING EMPIRE

In 1301 Turkish warriors rallied behind a leader named Osman (OHZ mahn). He led them to their first major victory against the Byzantine empire. In honor of Osman's great skill as a leader, his followers called themselves "Osmanlis." In the next 150 years the "Osmanlis" became known as Ottomans. Their growing empire eventually surrounded the city of Constantinople.

The Battle for Constantinople

In 1453 Constantinople had the strongest defense of any city in Europe. It was surrounded on three sides by the sea. Attackers had to break through massive stone walls to get inside the city. Moats and ditches were built between the walls. Defenders could shoot from the tops of these walls.

The Ottoman empire also had strengths, though. Ottoman soldiers had the newest and largest cannons in Europe. These cannons hurled half-ton cannonballs more than a mile.

In the pre-dawn hours of May 29, 1453, the Ottomans fired heavily on the walls of Constantinople. Before the morning was over, Constantinople had fallen into Ottoman hands. After more than 1,000 years, the Byzantine empire was no more.

The Christian rulers of Europe, who once waged crusades against Islam, now had Muslim neighbors to the east. Those neighbors would be a powerful force in Europe for years to come.

Leadership of the Empire

When Constantinople became the new capital of the Ottoman empire in 1453, the Turks called the city Istanbul. This name comes from a Greek word meaning "in the city." Istanbul remained the empire's center until 1918. Today it is the largest city in Turkey.

During the 500 years of Ottoman rule, sultans, or supreme rulers, governed the empire. They passed control to their oldest or favorite sons. Religious leaders called grand muftis interpreted the laws of Islam and applied them to life in the Ottoman empire.

The Mosque of Süleyman is a striking sight in the landscape of Istanbul.

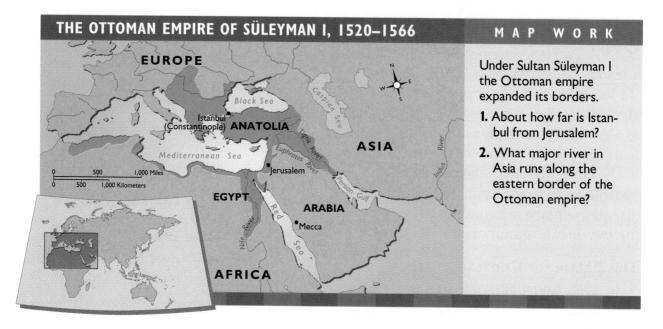

Under Sultan Süleyman I the Ottoman empire expanded its borders.

1. About how far is Istanbul from Jerusalem?

2. What major river in Asia runs along the eastern border of the Ottoman empire?

THE AGE OF SÜLEYMAN

Between 1520 and 1566 the Ottoman empire reached its peak under Sultan Süleyman (SOO lay mahn). As you can see from the map, Süleyman's empire sprawled over three continents. It included Jerusalem.

Life in Istanbul

If "all roads led to Rome" during the Roman empire, all routes in the Ottoman empire—whether on sea or land—led to Istanbul. Coffee flowed into the city's coffeehouses from southern Arabia. Ships from Egypt brought rice and African gold. Butter, cheese, grain, and wheat, which helped feed the Ottoman army, were shipped across the Black Sea from present-day Ukraine, along with Russian furs.

Jews who had fled persecution in Spain now lived and worked in the city. So did Christians from all over Europe. Jews, Christians, and other non-Muslims worshiped freely in Istanbul.

At times Istanbul's non-Muslim merchants did business in the vast outer courtyard of Süleyman's palace. There they blended with the thousands of guards, weavers, armor-makers, horse-tenders, and gardeners who worked for the sultan. Few, however, could enter the beautiful, walled-off garden and palace beyond the courtyard. The sultan lived and worked within these walls, along with his grand mufti and advisors, court musicians, painters, and poets. Almost all of Süleyman's assistants, soldiers, and closest advisers were slaves.

Government workers chose boys who were 8 or older to be slaves at the palace. The boys were trained to do many jobs. Some became craftworkers, surgeons, and architects.

One of the boys drafted into service, Sinan (suh NAHN), was the son of an Anatolian stoneworker. After years of training he became Süleyman's chief architect. He designed dozens of libraries, hospitals, and colleges for the sultan. Sinan also built buildings for Süleyman's wife, Hürrem Sultan. Among these buildings were a school for orphans and a soup kitchen for the poor. Sinan's greatest achievement was the mosque he designed for Süleyman. It still stands in the center of Istanbul.

WHY IT MATTERS

The battle for Constantinople in 1453 marked an important turning point in world history. It brought to an end the Byzantine empire and its 1,000-year-old link with ancient Rome. That battle also caused the center of Eastern Orthodox Christianity to give way to the Islam of the Ottoman empire.

Under Süleyman, the Ottoman empire grew and prospered on three continents—Europe, Asia, and Africa. A large mix of goods came to Istanbul from the empire's vast lands. Many different peoples came to Süleyman's capital as well. Enslaved youths from all over the empire rose through the ranks to carry out the sultans' laws.

The Ottoman empire lasted until 1922. Soon after the empire dissolved, the Turkish Republic was formed. Today the legacy of the Ottoman empire lives on. It can be found in the people and the grand mosques of southeastern Europe and Istanbul.

✓/ Reviewing Facts and Ideas

MAIN IDEAS

- The Ottoman victory at Constantinople in 1453 ended the Byzantine empire and began a new era of Muslim rule in part of Europe.

- The Ottomans renamed the city of Constantinople, calling it Istanbul.

- The Ottoman empire was governed by leaders called sultans.

- During Süleyman's rule Istanbul drew products and peoples from across the empire. Non-Muslims were allowed to worship freely.

THINK ABOUT IT

1. Who was Sinan? What were some of the buildings he designed?

2. Why was Constantinople a difficult city to conquer? What role did technology play in its defeat in 1453?

3. **FOCUS** How did Süleyman's palace in Istanbul affect life in the city?

4. **THINKING SKILL** Why was the battle for Constantinople a disaster from the _point of view_ of the Byzantines? Why was it a triumph in the eyes of the Ottomans?

5. **WRITE** Write a paragraph explaining why the fall of Constantinople was an important event in history.

800   1050   1300   1526   1658   1800

India Under the Moguls

Read Aloud

In 1543 a prince was born in a desert near the Indus River, where his parents were on the run from enemy leaders. In his youth he became an expert hunter. He also battled what may have been seizures and a reading disorder. At the age of 13 he became ruler of his father's battered territory in India. This prince, whose name meant "Great" in Arabic, would build a powerful empire.

Focus Activity

READ TO LEARN

Who were the Moguls and what did they achieve?

PEOPLE

- Akbar
- Shah Jahan
- Mumtaz Mahal

PLACES

- Agra
- Taj Mahal

THE BIG PICTURE

A powerful new empire began when Muslims from Central Asia began moving onto the Indian subcontinent. In Chapter 6 you read that Aryan princes gained control over much of the Indian subcontinent around 500 B.C. In the thousand years that followed, Hindu traditions became deeply rooted in India. Hindu rulers were challenged, however, by Muslim conquerors. By A.D. 1200 the fertile lands of the Indus plain had come under Muslim control.

The new sultans of the plain made Islam the law of the land. Hindus were called upon to pay a special tax, which cost ordinary workers as much as a month's wages. By law Hindus could no longer build any new temples. These and other rules caused anger among the large Hindu population. The result was more war, rather than peace. However, a new prince was about to bring big changes to the Indian subcontinent.

THE MOGUL EMPIRE

The conquerors you read about in the Big Picture were called Moguls. The Moguls were originally from Central Asia and may have been related to the Turks. In 1526 Moguls invaded the Indus plain. Within three years the Moguls controlled much of northern India. The map on this page shows you the region where the Moguls ruled. India's Mogul empire would grow even bigger during its 235-year rule. At one time it would cover most of the Indian subcontinent. Much of that growth would take place under Akbar, the ruler whose name meant "Great" in Arabic.

Akbar's Achievements

As you read in the Read Aloud, Akbar was made ruler of the Mogul empire when he was just 13. The year was 1556—when workers were completing Süleyman's mosque in Istanbul and shortly before Elizabeth I became queen of England.

At the age of 19, Akbar led an army into battle for the first time. Over the next 43 years he and his army fought many wars to expand the Mogul empire. During that time Akbar almost never lost a battle, and his fame as a brilliant commander grew.

Akbar offered no mercy to those who opposed him. At the same time he worked hard to improve life for those under his rule. He created a unified money system so that business would run smoothly throughout the empire. He varied the amount that farmers had to pay in taxes, based on how

fertile their land was. Akbar also ordered government workers to build new canals and wells to help farmers.

Akbar's major changes, though, affected Hindus, the majority of people in India at that time. The changes helped to create a remarkable period of unity and power in Indian history.

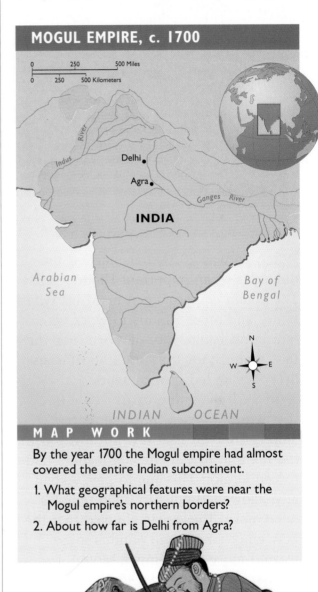

MOGUL EMPIRE, c. 1700

0   250   500 Miles
0   250   500 Kilometers

Indus River

Delhi

Agra

Ganges River

INDIA

Arabian Sea

Bay of Bengal

N
W   E
S

INDIAN OCEAN

MAP WORK

By the year 1700 the Mogul empire had almost covered the entire Indian subcontinent.

1. What geographical features were near the Mogul empire's northern borders?

2. About how far is Delhi from Agra?

Tiger hunting was a favorite sport of Akbar.

Today only official buildings like the Hall of Public Audience (left) remain in Fatehpur Sikri. Akbar had the city built in 1570.

AN ERA OF HARMONY

When he was 20, Akbar married the daughter of an important Hindu leader. The young emperor then hired his wife's father and other Hindus to work with him in his capital city of Agra. For the first time, Hindus became top officials in a Muslim-led government.

In 1579 the emperor passed a law that won him even more support among Hindus. That law did away with the tax that earlier Muslim leaders had forced all non-Muslims to pay. Akbar also allowed Hindus to build temples once more. These acts showed that the new emperor wanted Hindus to be treated more fairly under Mogul law.

Akbar himself had a strong interest in other religions. He had a special building constructed at his palace where Muslims, Hindus, Christians, and other religious leaders could meet and explain their beliefs. It is said that Akbar would pace back and forth on walkways above the building floor, listening to those sitting below. At times he would toss out questions that sparked heated debates.

The Leader's Interests

In addition to learning from such debates, Akbar learned from books in his library. The library included custom-made translations of Hindu, Persian, Arabic, and Greek classics. Since he could not read, Akbar had someone read to him every day. His legendary memory helped him to remember most of what he heard.

Akbar also loved the beauty of arts and crafts. He paid fortunes to bring Asia's best painters, poets, musicians, and craftworkers to his palace. During the day he often visited the palace's 100 workshops. There experts made carpets, curtains, weapons, jewelry, and paintings, among other things. It was not uncommon to see the emperor hammering iron, shaving camel hair, or discussing painting. At night musicians played for him and sometimes he joined in on drums.

Akbar oversaw the creation of many new buildings. Under his direction workers built several huge forts and new palaces.

In this painting an artist captured the creation of one of Akbar's palaces in Fatehpur Sikri. What does the painting tell you about how buildings were made in Akbar's time?

MANY VOICES
PRIMARY SOURCE

**Painting from
Mogul India depicting the building of
Fatehpur Sikri, 1570**

This painting is one of a series illustrating a biography of Akbar by his closest assistant. It shows ordinary people working together to create a lasting legacy of the Mogul empire.

Stone workers shape the stones used in construction.

Workers carry piles of bricks up to the bricklayers.

Lime is used to produce mortar.

Akbar inspects the soundness of the stonework.

Workers split beams to use for reinforcing stonework.

Victoria & Albert Museum

395

SHAH JAHAN

In 1605 Akbar died at the age of 63. As his legacy, he left behind one of the wealthiest and most powerful empires in the world at that time.

Akbar's grandson, Shah Jahan (SHAH juh HAHN) ruled the Mogul empire from 1628 to 1658. His name meant "Emperor of the World" in Arabic. In addition to expanding the empire, Shah Jahan spent immense fortunes constructing spectacular objects and buildings. His throne alone cost twice as much to make as the palace of Akbar in which it sat! The throne took seven years to build and was made of diamonds, pearls, rubies, and other jewels set in gold.

The Taj Mahal

The tomb Shah Jahan had made for his wife, Mumtaz Mahal (mum TAHZ mah HAHL), or "Chosen One of the Palace," was even more amazing. Mumtaz Mahal died during childbirth in 1631. The grief-stricken emperor ordered his chief architect and thousands of workers to build a special tomb for her in Agra. No expense was spared. When it was completed nearly 20 years later, the Taj Mahal stood as one of the most beautiful buildings ever made.

The white marble dome of the Taj Mahal rises some 20 stories from the ground. Passages from the Koran elegantly carved over each gateway

describe the paradise said to await all Muslims upon death. In this way the Taj Mahal honors not only the life of Mumtaz Mahal and her husband, but also the beliefs of Islam.

Trading With Europe

The Taj Mahal was one of the costliest buildings ever built under Mogul rule. One reason Shah Jahan could afford to spend so much on it was because trade in India was booming as never before. India's cotton fabric now clothed many people in Asia and even Africa and Europe. For the first time, spices and silks were sold directly to eager merchants from Portugal, England, and the Netherlands. In Chapter 19 you will read about how Europeans took part in Indian life.

The Mogul empire is known for its beautiful jewelry and the Taj Mahal (left), built by Shah Jahan in honor of his wife (far left).

WHY IT MATTERS

During the 1500s and 1600s, the rulers of the Mogul empire united most of the Indian subcontinent under one government. That government in turn benefited from India's growing trade with the rest of the world. Akbar also changed life in India by passing laws that promoted harmony between the Hindu majority and India's small but powerful Muslim population. By this time, Hinduism had spread to other regions of Asia, especially Southeast Asia. You will read about its influence there in the next lesson.

Reviewing Facts and Ideas

MAIN IDEAS

- By 1200 India's Indus plain was controlled by Muslims who had arrived from central Asia.

- Akbar expanded the large and wealthy Mogul empire. He gave Hindus rights which had been denied them by other Mogul leaders.

- Akbar's grandson Shah Jahan built the Taj Mahal in honor of his wife and the religion of Islam.

THINK ABOUT IT

1. What was the Mogul empire?

2. Why was it helpful to the Mogul empire that Akbar was a strong military commander?

3. **FOCUS** How did Akbar's rule affect Hindus in the Mogul empire?

4. **THINKING SKILL** Describe the main *cause* that led Akbar to construct a special building for religious meetings. What is one *effect* this building might have had on life in India?

5. **WRITE** Write a paragraph describing the Taj Mahal.

800   1450 1550   1800

The Khmer of Southeast Asia

Focus Activity

READ TO LEARN

What cultures influenced the Khmer of Southeast Asia?

PEOPLE

- Jayavarman II
- Suryavarman II

PLACES

- Mekong River
- Tonle Sap
- Angkor
- Phnom Penh

Read Aloud

The stone temple enclosed an area the size of 370 football fields. Its walls were covered with carvings of famous Hindu stories. At its center rose five towers shaped like the buds of water lilies. On the first day of spring, visitors standing at the temple's west gate could see the sun rise directly over the highest tower. This was fitting since the name of the temple's patron meant "one protected by the sun."

THE BIG PICTURE

The temple described above is called Angkor Wat (ANG kawr WAHT). Today it is a tourist attraction in the country of Cambodia. Some 700 years ago, however, it was the center of a great kingdom in Southeast Asia.

About 2,000 years ago, Indian merchants stopped at various places in Southeast Asia. The peninsula region of Southeast Asia includes what are now Vietnam, Cambodia, Thailand, Myanmar, and Laos. Some stopped at the mouth of the **Mekong** (MAY KAHNG) **River**, a highway of ships and goods since ancient times. Chinese merchants and diplomats also came, bringing their own traditions. As a result, Indian traditions of Hinduism and Buddhism began to take root in Southeast Asia.

Many civilizations were enriched by Chinese and Indian traditions. One of those, along the Mekong, was the Khmer (kuh MER) Kingdom. It occupied present-day Cambodia. Angkor Wat, built in the 1100s, was one of many amazing structures in the Khmer kingdom.

LIFE ALONG THE MEKONG

The Mekong, like many of the world's great rivers, provides needed water and silt to farmers of Southeast Asia. During the monsoon rains, torrents of rainwater fill the Mekong to overflowing. In fact, so much water pours into the river that a branch of it starts to flow *backward* into **Tonle Sap** (tahn LAY SAP) or "Great Lake." When the rains end, that branch of the Mekong flows forward again and the Tonle Sap returns to its normal size. Locate the Mekong and Tonle Sap on the map.

About 2,000 years ago, Khmer farmers were already using floods along the Mekong and Tonle Sap. Plentiful silt and water allowed them to grow large rice crops. Along with fish, rice became a mainstay of Khmer meals.

Farmers and God-Kings

A food surplus made it possible for a complex civilization to grow in Cambodia. Like their counterparts in ancient Egypt and medieval Europe, Khmer farmers often worked on land owned by religious or government officials. The rice, fruits, vegetables, and livestock that farmers raised fed temple workers, craftworkers, and nobles as well.

Much of the surplus supported the head of Khmer society, the king. The Khmer believed that their king was not only all-powerful, but a living god as well. One of Cambodia's first kings, **Jayavarman II** (jah yah VAHR mahn), ruled in the 800s. He, like many Khmer kings to come, observed Hindu traditions and claimed to be a human form of the god Shiva.

Khmer, whether farmers or nobles, were expected to do their part to support their god-king. In local markets women sold rice, fish, and fruits like bananas. Like other workers, they gave some of their goods to the king as taxes. Military leaders promised:

> We will not revere another king. . . .
> If there is a war, we will strive to
> fight and disregard life, with all our
> soul, in devotion to the king. . . . The
> reward of those who are devoted to
> their masters, may we obtain it from
> this world into the next.

Kings, in return, built canals and roads in the kingdom. Canals watered the fields, producing better crops. Roads provided better means of transportation. Kings also led troops in war and judged disputes.

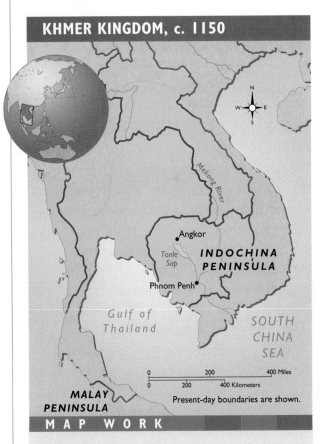

KHMER KINGDOM, c. 1150

Mekong River

Angkor

Tonle Sap

INDOCHINA PENINSULA

Phnom Penh

Gulf of Thailand

SOUTH CHINA SEA

MALAY PENINSULA

0   200   400 Miles
0   200   400 Kilometers
Present-day boundaries are shown.

M A P   W O R K

Trade and travel routes helped the cultures of southeast Asia to grow.

1. The Mekong River empties into which body of water?

2. On which peninsula is Phnom Penh located?

A CAPITAL CITY

Between 800 and 1200, Khmer forces expanded the borders of their kingdom into present-day Vietnam, Laos, and Thailand. The map on page 399 shows the territory of the Khmer. This expansion made the kingdom rich. In the early 1100s the king was Suryavarman II (sur yuh VAHR mun). He used a large part of this wealth to build a temple in the capital city of Angkor, on the north shore of Tonle Sap. You read about this temple, Angkor Wat, at the lesson's beginning. *Angkor* means "holy city" in the Khmer language.

Angkor Wat was the biggest temple built by the Khmer up to that time. Like the pyramids of ancient Egypt, it was built with thousands of stones from distant sources. Farmers working as laborers loaded the heavy stones onto boats. Stones were transported about 20 miles on canals. Architects designed the temple so that, in the spring, the sun shone on the walls, which told Hindu stories about the world's creation. At year's end, by contrast, the sun highlighted scenes that described death.

The Walls of Angkor Thom

One of the boys who watched Angkor Wat being built was the king's great-grandson, the future Jayavarman VII. When he became king in 1181, Jayavarman VII set out to create an even grander complex than his great-grandfather's. His Angkor Thom (ANG kawr TAWM) became just that. In 1296 a Chinese diplomat named Zhou Daguan visited the city. He wrote this description:

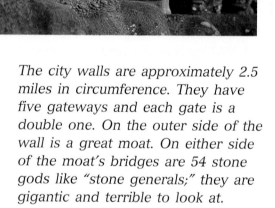

The city walls are approximately 2.5 miles in circumference. They have five gateways and each gate is a double one. On the outer side of the wall is a great moat. On either side of the moat's bridges are 54 stone gods like "stone generals;" they are gigantic and terrible to look at.

At the center of the city stood a large temple. This one honored Buddhist, rather than Hindu, beliefs. In this respect Jayavarman VII differed greatly from his forefathers. Over time many Khmer would adopt Buddhism as their religious belief. Today, as a sign of this change, Angkor Wat itself contains Buddhist as well as Hindu statues, and the people of Cambodia are mostly followers of Buddhism.

Angkor Wat (above) was built by the Khmer in the 1100s. Many of the statues at the temple (left) represent both Hindu and Buddhist figures.

The Decline of Angkor

The great building projects of Angkor drained Khmer resources. So did the constant wars that Khmer kings waged against neighboring kingdoms. Their strongest enemies were kingdoms that were in what are today Vietnam and Thailand. Jayavarman VII won control over both kingdoms, but they broke free of Khmer rule after his death. In the 1430s Thai soldiers attacked Angkor itself. The city was abandoned shortly thereafter. Khmer rulers moved their capital to a site farther south along the Mekong. Later the kingdom would become known as Kampuja and its capital as Phnom Penh (puh NOM PEN). It remains Cambodia's capital city today.

WHY IT MATTERS

The Khmer are just one of the many peoples who built a lasting civilization in the monsoon environment of Southeast Asia. As a reminder of their ancient heritage, today's Cambodians have put an image of Angkor Wat at the center of their flag. Each time they salute their flag, Cambodians honor the special blend of traditions that makes their country unique.

✓ Reviewing Facts and Ideas

MAIN IDEAS

- The Khmer kingdom of Southeast Asia was located along major shipping routes between India and China. For this reason, Indian and Chinese traditions became part of life in the Khmer kingdom.

- Khmer kings were considered to be living gods who deserved great power and respect.

- In the 1100s and 1200s, Khmer kings ordered the construction of great buildings and temples in the capital city of Angkor.

THINK ABOUT IT

1. Why was the Mekong River important to life in early Cambodia?

2. Explain why an advanced civilization was needed to build a place like Angkor Wat.

3. **FOCUS** How did Angkor Wat reflect what—or who—was most important to the Khmer?

4. **THINKING SKILL** What would you do to determine the _credibility_ of the description of Angkor Thom quoted on page 400?

5. **GEOGRAPHY** How did monsoons affect life in early Cambodia?

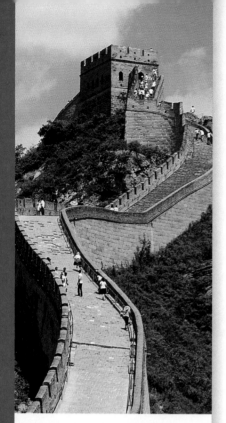

800　　1050　　1209　　1525　　1800

Great Empires of China

Focus Activity

READ TO LEARN

How did the Mongols affect life in China?

VOCABULARY

• **Grand Canal**

PEOPLE

• **Genghis Khan**
• **Kublai Khan**
• **Marco Polo**

PLACES

• **Beijing**
• **Forbidden City**

THE BIG PICTURE

In the 1100s—while the Khmer were building Angkor and Europeans were fighting the Crusades—China was prospering as never before. Chinese farmers began to grow a new kind of rice developed by the Khmer and their neighbors. They were able to grow more of this rice in less time, especially in southern China's warm and wet climate. Huge surpluses were shipped to faraway cities using a system of canals that kept water flowing for hundreds of miles.

Port cities such as Guangzhou (GWAHNG JOO)—later known as Canton—linked China to international trade. In those busy cities people made new kinds of printed books, paintings, compasses, and large ships that could carry as many as 500 people.

All of this was threatened in the 1200s, when invaders from the north set out to take over China. China's ancient border walls could not stop them. These invaders were called Mongols. They were herders and horse-riding experts from the grassy steppes north of China. Sheep provided much of what they needed. The Mongols also depended on trade for goods such as cloth and weapons.

NORTHERN INVADERS

In 1209, Mongol leader Genghis Khan (JENG gihs KAHN) united Mongol communities to conquer China, their main source of supplies. The Mongols rode south into China. They were helped by Chinese military leaders who joined their side after being defeated. When Genghis Khan died in 1227 he controlled almost all of northern China.

Kublai Khan

In 1252 Genghis Khan's grandson Kublai Khan (KOO bli KAHN) invaded southern China. After 27 years, all of China yielded to Kublai Khan's rule. China's Mongol rulers were called the Yüan dynasty. How would Mongols, who lived neither on farms nor in cities, govern a land of both?

Kublai Khan's answer was to have Mongols oversee China's already vast government. Kublai Khan made tax collection easier, though, by establishing paper money. The world's first all-paper money system made things easier on people's pockets. One note replaced about 8 pounds of coins!

Kublai Khan also oversaw the expansion of the Grand Canal. This canal had been built many years earlier to connect the Huang and Chang rivers. With Kublai Khan's expansion, it connected the new capital city, Beijing (BAY JING), with cities over 1,000 miles to the south. The Grand Canal is still used for shipping today.

Kublai Khan assigned soldiers to protect merchants traveling on the ancient Silk Road that connected Asia with Europe. You will read more about the Silk Road and one man who traveled on it, Marco Polo, in the Infographic on page 406.

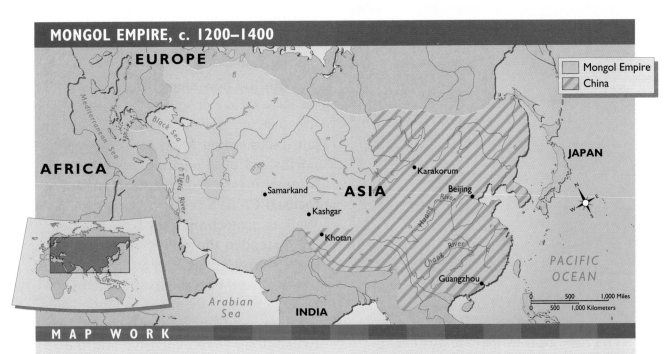

MONGOL EMPIRE, c. 1200–1400

Mongol Empire
China

EUROPE
AFRICA
ASIA
JAPAN
INDIA

Mediterranean Sea
Black Sea
Tigris River
Samarkand
Kashgar
Khotan
Karakorum
Beijing
Huang River
Chang River
Guangzhou
Arabian Sea
PACIFIC OCEAN

0   500   1,000 Miles
0   500   1,000 Kilometers

MAP WORK

In the 1200s the Mongol empire extended west into eastern Europe.

1. Which river flowed near the westernmost Asian boundary of Mongol lands?

2. About how far from Beijing is the mouth of the Tigris River?

3. Which cities in the empire were *not* in China?

THE MING DYNASTY

After Kublai Khan's death in 1294, Mongol control over China began to weaken. Terrible floods along the Huang River, famine, and disease added to the country's distress. In 1368 the Mongols were driven out by rebel Chinese forces. Chinese rulers once again came to control China. The Ming Dynasty had begun.

Cultural Expansion

During the Ming dynasty's 276-year history, China prospered. Between 1417 and 1420 almost one million people worked to build the Forbidden City in Beijing. Stoneworkers and carpenters built almost 1,000 stately palaces, libraries, temples, and gardens. Ming emperors lived and ruled from within the walls of this city. Outside the poor sang to passersby, asking for money. You can see one of their songs on the next page.

When the Forbidden City was completed, China's best porcelain, silk, and paintings were sent to fill its palaces and kitchens. The Ming government controlled thousands of porcelain workshops. They produced blue-and-white dishes that became world-famous. The government also controlled silk workshops. In those shops women and children over the age of 10 worked to produce China's valuable silk cloth.

Many of these luxury products went to the emperor's palace. Still more were bought by foreign merchants. Some merchants brought goods home along the Silk Road. Others shipped their goods from port cities like Guangzhou.

In 1405 large ships were built to take Ming officials on trading expeditions. The largest ship was about 400 feet long! Ming ships reached East Africa.

Looking Inward

With the new ships, China was well on its way to becoming the world's greatest sea power. That changed in the late 1400s, when Ming concerns shifted northward once again. Fears of another Mongol invasion grew. Ming emperors focused China's resources on the Great Wall as protection. They strengthened and extended the walls Shihuangdi had built almost 2,000 years earlier.

Because their resources were being used to protect their borders, the Ming abandoned efforts in shipbuilding. Expeditions were expensive and the Ming government was not interested in expansion. By the year 1525 it had given up all efforts in sea travel. China's interests turned inward for the next several centuries.

MING CHINA, 1368–1644

- Ming China
- Great Wall
- Grand Canal

0   400   800 Miles
0   400   800 Kilometers

Huang River
Beijing
Yellow Sea
Chang Jiang
Hangchow
East China Sea
Guangzhou
PACIFIC OCEAN
South China Sea

MAP WORK

Ming rulers expanded the canal system to increase trade.

1. To which sea did the Grand Canal link Beijing?
2. The Great Wall extended along which of China's borders?

Fung Yang Song

Chinese Folk Song
Arranged by Marilyn Davidson

Pronunciation: jooaw shohoo looaw yoo shohoo goo
English: **Sing the Fung Yang song. Sing it loud and long.**

shohoo nah looaw goo lahee chahng guh
With drums and cym-bals we sing the Fung Yang song.

biheh dee guh ur waw yeh boo hway chahng
This is a song we can sing the whole day long.

juh hway chahng guh fung yahng guh
We strike the gong to the Fung Yang song.

Trade on the Silk Road

In the 13th century a Venetian explorer named Marco Polo traveled the entire route of the Silk Road, from Constantinople to Khanbalik, China. As he traveled, he kept records of the places he visited and the things he saw. The Silk Road provided a route for merchants and traders to transport goods. What are some of the items Marco Polo saw and described in his travels along the Silk Road?

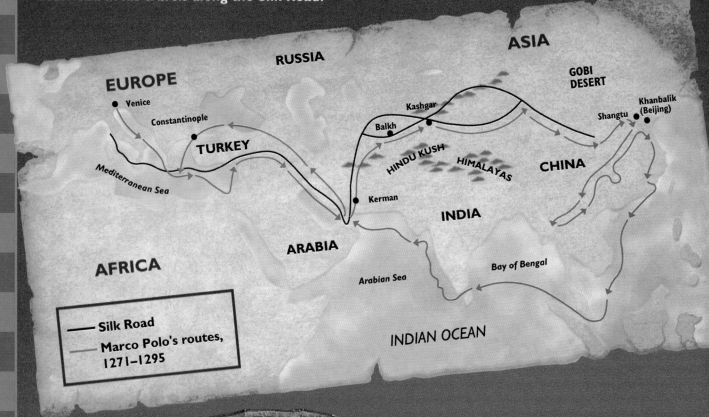

EUROPE · Venice · Constantinople · TURKEY · Mediterranean Sea · RUSSIA · ASIA · GOBI DESERT · Kashgar · Balkh · HINDU KUSH · HIMALAYAS · CHINA · Shangtu · Khanbalik (Beijing) · Kerman · INDIA · ARABIA · Arabian Sea · Bay of Bengal · AFRICA · INDIAN OCEAN

Legend:
—— Silk Road
—— Marco Polo's routes, 1271–1295

Beautiful items like this porcelain jar (far left) and Chinese silk fan were traded along the Silk Road.

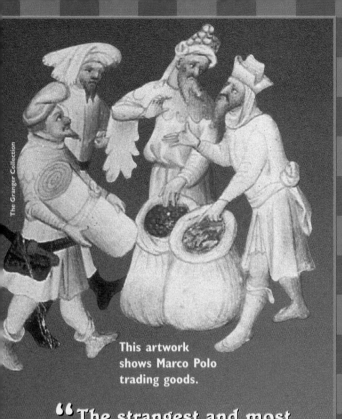

This artwork shows Marco Polo trading goods.

66 **The strangest and most valuable things come from [China] and other provinces.... At least 1,000 cartloads of silk are sent [here] every day.** 99

66 **The Great Khan's subjects are perfectly willing to be paid in paper money since with it they can buy anything, including pearls, precious stones, gold, and silver.** 99

WHY IT MATTERS

Between the 1200s and 1500s, China underwent many changes. The Mongol invasions hurt once-bustling cities. Under Kublai Khan, though, China's cities and trade grew once again. In the Ming dynasty that followed, China became even stronger.

Wherever its trade goods went, China's ideas and traditions soon followed. China's influence was especially strong in the chain of islands that lay to the east. Those were the islands of Japan, which will be the focus of the next lesson.

✔// Reviewing Facts and Ideas

MAIN IDEAS

- Genghis Khan began the Mongol invasion of China in the 1200s.

- Kublai Khan ruled by using China's ancient government system. He also started the world's first all-paper money system and made the Silk Road safer for travel.

- Trade, cities, and sea travel grew under the early Ming dynasty. With the threat of foreign invasion, Ming emperors focused on defense projects such as the Great Wall.

THINK ABOUT IT

1. Why did Mongols invade China?

2. What did Kublai Khan do to govern China? Why might he have wanted to protect travelers?

3. **FOCUS** How did Kublai Khan improve life in China?

4. **THINKING SKILL** Make at least two *conclusions* about the importance of trade in Ming China. On what facts did you base each conclusion?

5. **GEOGRAPHY** How did the Grand Canal affect movement in China?

407

Queen Elizabeth I (left) and Ghengis Khan were powerful leaders who ruled vast empires.

National Portrait Gallery, London

The Granger Collection

Making Generalizations

VOCABULARY

generalization

WHY THE SKILL MATTERS

In the last lesson you read about Ghengis Khan and the Mongols' rise to power in China. You have also read about other leaders and how they came to rule—Alexander the Great, Sunjata, and Elizabeth I, to name a few. If you compare their histories, you might notice certain similarities. As a result, you might make a general statement about what things are necessary for people to become powerful leaders.

If you did so, you would be making a generalization. A generalization is a statement that points out a common feature shared among different things. A generalization shows how some things that might seem very different on the surface can actually be similar underneath.

Why are generalizations useful? Generalizations allow you to draw conclusions from specific examples. Once you make a generalization, you can better understand how things fit within a larger framework. You can see new relationships between separate things. This is very useful in the study of history. Use the Helping Yourself box to guide you in making generalizations.

USING THE SKILL

Suppose you wanted to make a generalization about how people become powerful leaders. To start, you might choose three leaders to serve as your examples. Say that you chose Ghengis Khan, Sunjata, and Alexander the Great.

Your next step would be to examine these different examples, looking for similarities. Ghengis Khan's great armies of soldiers and expert horsemen brought almost all of Northern China under his control in the 1200s. At roughly the same time in West Africa, the swift armies of the underestimated Sunjata helped him to rule the huge empire of Mali. Over 1,000 years earlier, Alexander the Great led his undefeated army to conquer vast lands from Asia Minor to Persia.

In order to make a generalization, think about what features or qualities these leaders may have shared. Recall that, by making the most of their powerful armies, all won control over vast stretches of land. The use of a strong military is therefore a feature that was common to all of these leaders.

More than one generalization might be made about this topic. Based on these facts, though, one possible generalization might be: Many leaders gain power as a result of control they have over a strong military force.

Helping yourself

- A generalization states a feature shared by a group of examples.
- Select a topic to make a generalization about.
- Identify a feature that relates to the topic and is common to all of the examples.
- Based on this common feature, make a generalization.

TRYING THE SKILL

You just made a generalization about leaders' rise to power. Now try making a generalization about how leaders can use their power to develop strong governments. Remember to look for common features with which to make a generalization.

Use as your examples the rules of Akbar, Elizabeth I, and Caesar Augustus. You may recall that Akbar faced religious conflict. Elizabeth I and Augustus were challenged by threats of war when they came to power. Akbar used his power to bring peace and religious tolerance to India. Elizabeth I faced down the Spanish Armada while England enjoyed the Renaissance. Augustus brought the Pax Romana to ancient Rome. How did their actions win these rulers special popularity, thereby strengthening their governments? What generalization can you make from these three examples?

REVIEWING THE SKILL

1. What is a generalization?

2. How can generalizations help us to better understand history?

3. Consider whether or not generalizations are always true. Suppose you made the following statement: "Strong government results only when leaders address the greatest needs of their citizens." Do you think this generalization is always true? Explain.

4. What generalization can you make about leaders today? What facts did you use to make your generalization?

409

800   1050   1192   1867

Feudal Japan

Read Aloud

"Nothing is more important than duty. Second in importance comes life, and then money." To writer Muro Kyuso, who lived almost 300 years ago, these words described life for a certain group of people in Japan. They were Japan's soldiers.

Focus Activity

READ TO LEARN

What changes did the shoguns make in feudal Japan?

VOCABULARY

- Shinto
- shogun
- samurai

PEOPLE

- Yoritomo
- Tokugawa Ieyasu
- Lady Murasaki Shikibu

PLACES

- Edo
- Tokyo
- Kyoto

THE BIG PICTURE

As you read in Lesson 1, Japan is located in the Pacific Ocean east of mainland Asia. Its four main islands form a 2,000-mile-long archipelago. This arc stretches from Russia in the north toward the Korean Peninsula in the south. From ancient times Chinese and Korean people moved to the islands of Japan. They brought Confucian teachings with them. Immigrants from Korea also introduced Buddhism to Japan around A.D. 550, along with China's writing system and new forms of art.

These immigrants arrived in a region that already had ancient traditions of its own. Most important was the Japanese religion called Shinto (SHIN toh), or "the way of the gods." According to Shinto belief, everything on Earth has a spirit of its own, including the land and such crops as rice. As in ancient Greece, Japan's farmers tried to ensure good harvests by offering prayers before planting or harvesting. The most important prayers, though, were offered by Japan's emperor. The emperor's family was believed to be descended from the Shinto sun goddess.

In time Shinto, Buddhism, and Confucianism blended together in Japan to form a unique way of life. All Japanese were believed to be part of one big family, whose head was the emperor. As in all families, each member had duties to fulfill. Not all duties were the same, and not everyone had equal rank, as you will see.

410

A FEUDAL SYSTEM

The ruler of Japan was the emperor. However, powerful families fought for control over Japan's mountains and plains. One family won the long, fierce struggle for power in 1192. The emperor made the leader of this struggle, Yoritomo (yawr ee TOH moh), Japan's first shogun, or military commander. Yoritomo changed the way Japan was governed. While the emperor headed Japan in name, the shogun ruled the country as military dictator.

Samurai Warriors

Life in Japan, like life in Europe at this time, was shaped by a type of feudalism. Lords controlled large pieces of land, which were worked by farmers. Protecting the lords and their lands were soldiers called samurai. They believed their main duty was to remain loyal to their lord. "Nothing is so important in a warrior as loyalty," wrote one samurai in the 1400s.

Although lords held great power in their regions, they were considered vassals of the shogun. Lords had to serve the shogun. This service could mean providing rice or samurai for war. In return the shogun granted new lands or privileges to lords.

The shogun, his lords, and their samurai formed the upper part of Japan's social pyramid. Below them were farmers, craftworkers, and merchants. These commoners—non-nobles—had to show utmost respect to those above them in society. Whenever a lord and his samurai passed through a village, servants shouted "Down! Down!" This signal prompted commoners to fall face-down on the ground in respect. Those who did not do so risked death.

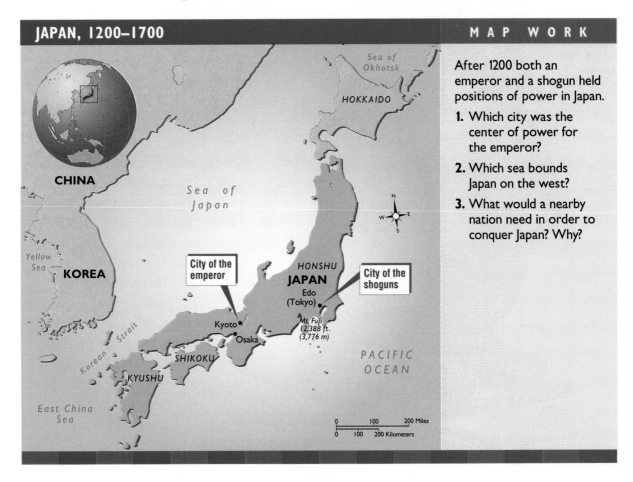

JAPAN, 1200–1700

Sea of Okhotsk

HOKKAIDO

CHINA

Sea of Japan

Yellow Sea

KOREA

Korean Strait

SHIKOKU

KYUSHU

East China Sea

City of the emperor

HONSHU

JAPAN

Kyoto

Osaka

Edo (Tokyo)

Mt. Fuji 12,388 ft. (3,776 m)

City of the shoguns

PACIFIC OCEAN

0   100   200 Miles
0   100   200 Kilometers

MAP WORK

After 1200 both an emperor and a shogun held positions of power in Japan.

1. Which city was the center of power for the emperor?

2. Which sea bounds Japan on the west?

3. What would a nearby nation need in order to conquer Japan? Why?

TOKUGAWA SHOGUN

Shoguns like Yoritomo were very powerful. However, they were not always strong enough to keep lords from rebelling and seizing more land for themselves. Remember, Japan is a very long archipelago. For this reason, keeping control over Japan's dozens of powerful lords proved almost impossible. By the early 1500s the shoguns had lost much of their power.

In 1603, though, the emperor made Tokugawa Ieyasu (toh koo GAH wah ee yeh YAH soo) Japan's ruler. Under the Tokugawa, Japan became not only unified but remained at peace for over 200 years. How did the Tokugawa leaders achieve what no one else had been able to do?

A samurai wore the decorated headdress and cloak shown. Samurai also carried two swords.

Ruling Japan

The Tokugawas became the unchallenged masters of Japan by ordering massive changes in society. To prevent rebellion, only samurai could own weapons. Lords who opposed the Tokugawa leaders were stripped of their lands. Those lands amounted to half the farmable land in Japan. These lands were given to loyal vassals.

Most importantly, all lords had to live in the Tokugawa capital city of Edo (ED oh), or what is today Tokyo. There the shogun's assistants could keep a close watch on the lords, making sure no rebellions were planned. Every two years the lords could return to their towns. Their wives and children, however, had to stay in Edo to insure that the lords would return.

Lords oversaw most everyday affairs in Japan, including collecting taxes from commoners. The lords were not taxed, but were expected to contribute whenever a new national road or castle was built. Lords had to prove their loyalty to the shoguns by giving them many gifts. Lords who did not risked the chance of losing land or privileges. The lords also had to obey strict rules about everything, from what kind of silk they wore to how many servants they had. These rules forced the lords to spend lots of money. Without plenty of money, no lord would have the resources to wage a war against the shoguns.

Life in Villages and Cities

One road that Japan's lords helped pay for connected Edo with the emperor's capital city of Kyoto (KYOH toh). In time its 300-mile length became crowded with the shogun's servants carrying messages from the shogun to the emperor. Merchants also used the road on their way to market, as did lords traveling to and from Edo.

As the lords traveled with their servants and samurai, they passed through a Japan that was steadily changing. Peace had brought boom times. In farming villages, people leveled forests to clear new farmland. With improved irrigation more rice, cotton, and other crops could be grown. Village shrines and temples were also being expanded. Many of them started schools where children could study reading, writing, arithmetic, and religion.

More and more, older children of farmers were leaving their villages. They left to live in Japan's growing towns and cities. Some found work as servants or laborers on building projects. Others became maids in the homes of samurai families.

Development of Edo

No other city grew as big or as fast as Edo. After 1603 more than 200 lords and their families moved into stately city homes. These households required the services of thousands of maids, cooks, and other servants. Etsu Sugimoto described the maids who worked in her family's kitchen:

> Here the air was filled with the buzz of work mingled with chatter and laughter. In one corner, a maid was grinding rice for tomorrow's dumplings; another was making padded scrub-cloths out of an old kimono; . . . and a little apart from the others sat another whirling her spinning wheel.

Servants searched the city's markets each day for fresh goods. While the lords and samurai spent money to satisfy the shogun, merchants became rich. Some became far richer than many lords.

413

A FLOURISHING CULTURE

New traditions were being born in the heart of Edo. Actors playing in a new form of drama called Kabuki packed Edo's theaters each night. Their plays dealt with samurai heroes and ordinary people, often torn by love or by struggles between duty and freedom.

New technology also made book printing easier than ever before. Merchants carried huge stacks of books on their backs. Books were rented for next to nothing. Some people read adventure stories about the golden age of the samurai. Others read love stories or classics like Lady Murasaki Shikibu's *The Tale of Genji* (GEN JEE), from around the year 1000. It is thought to be the world's first novel. In this excerpt, the main character decides on a way to solve his problems.

For Genji life had become an unbroken string of problems. He must consider what to do next. If he went on pretending that all was well, then even worse things might lie ahead.

Genji thought of the Suma coast [near present-day Kobe]. People of great value had once lived there, he was told, but now it was deserted, save for the huts of fishermen. According to his attendants, however, Suma was known to be the home of one mysterious resident: a puppet. And the puppet had powers to make human beings a joyful lot.

Genji thought to himself, "Soon, I shall make the journey to Suma. Soon, a wonderful puppet shall rest on my arm. Soon, I shall turn to a puppet and gain the gifts of friendship and joyfulness."

This painting (right) shows a scene from *The Tale of Genji*. Today actors continue to perform Kabuki drama.

The Closing of Japan

The Tokugawa shoguns kept an iron-handed grip over life in Japan for over 200 years, between 1603 and 1867. During this time Japan had almost no contact with other countries. Like the emperors of Ming China, the shoguns of Tokugawa Japan saw outside influences as threats to their rule. Their response was to seal off their borders. Lords were forbidden to have any foreign contact or to build ships. Throughout most of its history, Japan had grown from contacts with the outside world; now it remained isolated.

WHY IT MATTERS

Japan was one of the few countries in Asia to remain largely untouched by outside forces in the 1600s and 1700s. Even without the benefits of international trade and movement, though, life in Japan continued to grow and change. Most importantly, feudal society changed as lords moved to Edo.

Samurai no longer fought wars but instead often held desk jobs. Drawn to new economic and cultural opportunities, farmers set off for growing towns and cities. A new age had begun in Japan. That age, however, would be jolted in the 1800s, as foreign ships came to challenge Japan's closed borders. You will read about where the ships came from and why in Chapter 17.

✔️ Reviewing Facts and Ideas

MAIN IDEAS

- The Japanese religion of Shinto was changed by the arrival of Buddhism and Confucianism. Together they formed the belief that Japan was like a family, with the emperor as head.

- Feudal society in Japan was run by a military leader called a shogun.

- The Tokugawa shoguns held power for over 200 years. They forced lords to live in Edo and also shut off Japan to outside influence.

THINK ABOUT IT

1. Describe Japan's social pyramid during feudal times.

2. Why was the order for lords to move their families to Edo so important to Tokugawa rule?

3. **FOCUS** How did life change for people in Japan under shogun rule?

4. **THINKING SKILL** How might Tokugawa history support this *generalization*: "Strict rule can bring positive results."

5. **GEOGRAPHY** How did Japan's sheer length affect the early shoguns' ability to keep order in the country?

PRINTING AND Calligraphy

Do you remember how difficult writing seemed when you first learned to do it? You probably practiced drawing letters over and over. Then you began to learn to write words and sentences.

Japanese of feudal times also worked hard at their writing. They used brush strokes similar to painting. They developed their written language, which they borrowed from the Chinese, into an art form called calligraphy (kuh LIHG ruh fee).

Advances in printing technology brought this art to many people. Printing made it possible for many people to own beautifully written works of art.

Calligraphy is still an important part of education for many Asian students. This Chinese girl practices her writing at school.

416

The woman in this Japanese print (above) is writing a letter using a calligraphy brush. The scroll (left) shows the following Japanese poem, titled "Waiting for the Cuckoo." The calligraphy, handwritten by the poet Yoshimasa, is still admired for its beauty.

Oh, cuckoo, crying for thy mate
Up in the sky, on mine own part,
I wait for thee tonight
With my whole heart.

417

CHAPTER 14 REVIEW

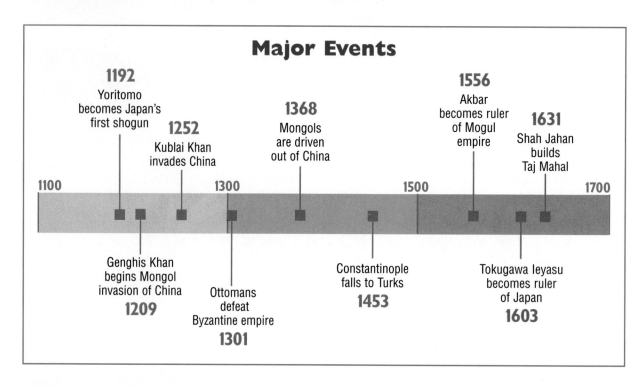

Major Events

1192 Yoritomo becomes Japan's first shogun

1252 Kublai Khan invades China

1368 Mongols are driven out of China

1556 Akbar becomes ruler of Mogul empire

1631 Shah Jahan builds Taj Mahal

1100 — 1300 — 1500 — 1700

Genghis Khan begins Mongol invasion of China **1209**

Ottomans defeat Byzantine empire **1301**

Constantinople falls to Turks **1453**

Tokugawa Ieyasu becomes ruler of Japan **1603**

THINKING ABOUT VOCABULARY

Number a sheet of paper from 1 to 5. Beside each number write the word or term from the list below that best completes each sentence.

archipelago
Grand Canal
samurai
shogun
sultan

1. _____ were soldiers used by Japanese lords.

2. A _____ is a supreme ruler of a Muslim state.

3. _____ is a word meaning "a chain of islands."

4. The name of the human-made waterway in China that connects the Huang and Chang rivers is the _____.

5. A _____ was a military commander who governed Japan.

THINKING ABOUT FACTS

1. What Asian rivers begin on the Tibetan Plateau?

2. Who was Sinan and what were his accomplishments?

3. What did Akbar do to strengthen the Mogul empire in India?

4. Why was the Taj Mahal built?

5. What is Angkor Wat?

6. Why did the Mongols invade China?

7. Who was Kublai Khan? How did he govern China?

8. What was the effect of the Tokugawa dynasty on Japanese history?

9. What was the most significant achievement of Lady Murasaki Shikibu?

10. According to the time line above, how long after Ghengis Khan invaded China were the Mongols driven out?

Empires and Cultures of the Americas

THINKING ABOUT
HISTORY AND GEOGRAPHY

In this chapter you will read about civilizations that developed in North America and South America. Follow the time line to see how empires developed in what are today Mexico and Peru. The peoples of these empires built unique and powerful civilizations. Near the Great Lakes of North America, Native Americans became skilled farmers who traded across a wide area.

1400

1325

1350

ANDES MOUNTAINS
The Inca fertilize crops to feed an expanding empire

TENOCHTITLÁN
The Aztec build a city in the Valley of Mexico

CUZCO
The Inca develop a wealthy and productive civilization in Peru

1300

1350

1400

THINK AND WRITE

WRITING A NEWS ARTICLE

Suppose you are a newspaper reporter sent back in time to cover the fall of Constantinople. Reread page 389. Then use the information to write an on-the-scene report about what happened.

WRITING A COMPARISON

Write a comparison of the Mogul empire in India and the Mongol empire in China. How were they similar? How were they different? Include the contributions made by Akbar and Kublai Khan.

WRITING DESCRIPTIONS

Write one paragraph each about two of the following places: (1) Taj Mahal, (2) Angkor Wat, and (3) the Forbidden City.

APPLYING THINKING SKILLS

MAKING GENERALIZATIONS

1. What is a generalization?

2. Review Lesson 2. Explain how using the example of the Mogul emperor Akbar helps to support this generalization: "Effective rulers make the people they govern feel they are being treated fairly."

3. Make a generalization about what is required to become ruler of a large area. Use information from this and other chapters you have read.

4. What generalization can you make about the ways rulers of the past governed? Use as examples the rulers you chose for number 3.

5. Why are generalizations useful?

Summing Up the Chapter

Copy the main-idea chart below on a separate sheet of paper. Then fill in each column with information from the chapter. When you have completed the chart, use the information to write a paragraph that answers the question "What contributions did peoples of Asia make to civilization?"

MAIN IDEA: Powerful civilizations were built in Turkey, India, Cambodia, China, and Japan.

Country	Dynasty	Rulers	Capital Cities	Achievements
Turkey				
India				
Cambodia				
China				
Japan				

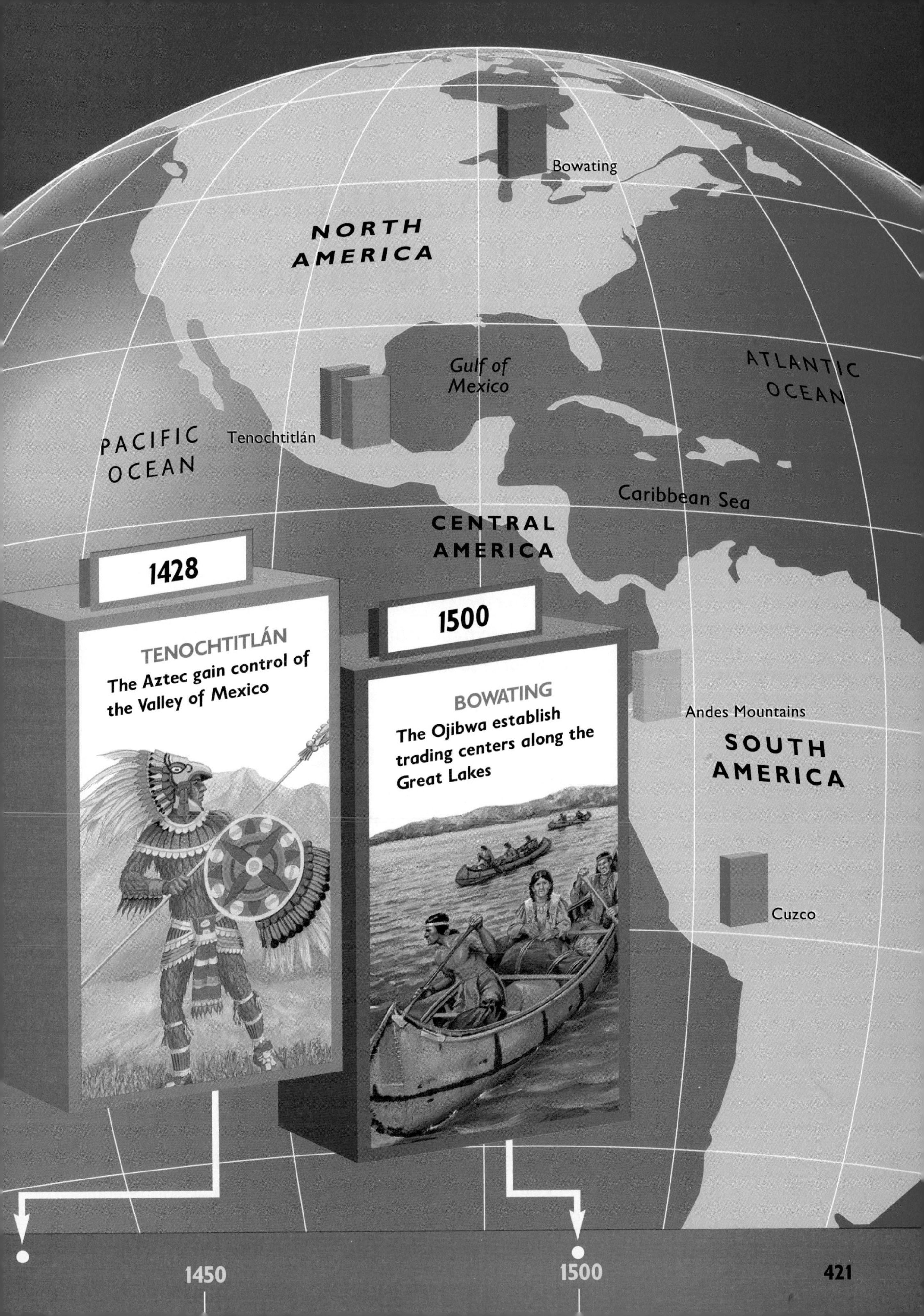
Bowating
NORTH AMERICA
Gulf of Mexico
ATLANTIC OCEAN
PACIFIC OCEAN
Tenochtitlán
Caribbean Sea
CENTRAL AMERICA
1428
TENOCHTITLÁN
The Aztec gain control of the Valley of Mexico
1500
BOWATING
The Ojibwa establish trading centers along the Great Lakes
Andes Mountains
SOUTH AMERICA
Cuzco
1450
1500

Geography of the Americas

Read Aloud

"Here at the top of the continent, I felt that the Americas 'belonged' to me in a way that they belonged to no one else. . . . The fog's curtain slowly lifted. . . . This was the end. Great sobs shook my frame, and my tears mingled with frozen dust."

These words were written in 1976 by the Englishman George Meegan. Over a period of seven years, he walked from the southern tip of South America all the way north to the Arctic Ocean.

Focus Activity

READ TO LEARN

How have mountains affected the growth of civilizations in the Americas?

VOCABULARY

- tundra
- isthmus
- timberline

PLACES

- Andes Mountains
- Great Lakes
- Rocky Mountains
- Canadian Shield

THE BIG PICTURE

Pulling his belongings in a cart, Meegan climbed up the **Andes Mountains** and down to the steamy rain forests of Central America. He also traveled across Mexico's dry deserts and through the Great Plains of North America. He walked along the shores of the **Great Lakes**, up and over the **Rocky Mountains**, and across the **tundra**, or treeless plain, of Alaska. After 19,000 miles, Meegan had crossed both North and South America—the two continents that form the Western Hemisphere.

Many civilizations have developed in the Americas during the past 10,000 years. Among the earliest of them, as you may recall, were the Olmec and the Maya of Middle America. In this lesson you will read about the geography of the Americas and the ways in which some people adapted to it.

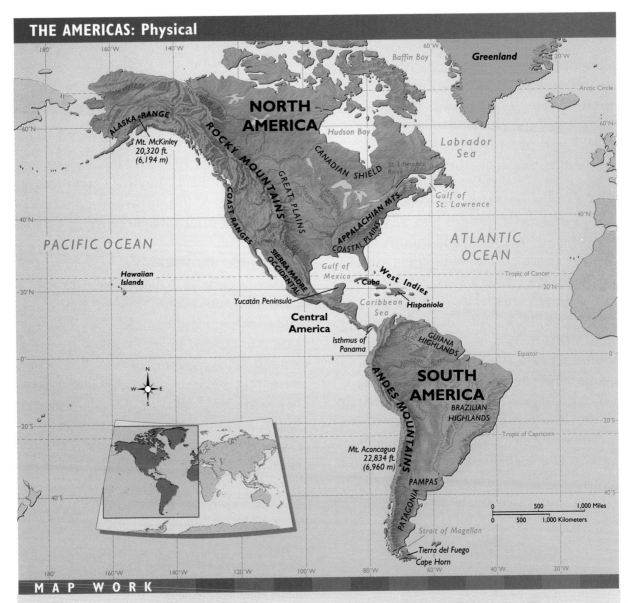

THE AMERICAS: Physical

MAP WORK

The Americas have many physical features.

1. Which mountain range extends along the western part of South America?

2. Which oceans bound the Americas?

3. Which are the two largest gulfs in the Americas?

4. Where are the Great Plains located?

5. In which mountain range is Mt. McKinley located?

THE AMERICAS

Many physical features in the Americas were shaped by glaciers during the Ice Age. The Canadian Shield is a huge rocky region in northern Canada where soil was removed by glaciers. Their crushing weight also carved the basins of the Great Lakes. When the Ice Age ended about 15,000 years ago, glaciers melted and filled the basins with water.

Melting glaciers also caused the ocean levels to rise. At the southern tip of Central America, rising waters covered land, leaving only an isthmus (IHS mus) between the continents. An isthmus is a narrow strip of land that connects two larger land masses.

423

MOUNTAINS OF THE AMERICAS

Climbing the tall mountains of the Americas was an exhausting part of George Meegan's journey. The mountains are some of the spectacular features—and great resources—of the continents that make up the Americas.

The Andes and the Rockies

North America and South America are similar in at least one important way. A great wall of mountains stretches along the western side of each continent. Huge plains extend to the east of these mountains. The Andes Mountains in South America make up the longest mountain range in the world. The range spans 4,500 miles. Mount Aconcagua (ak un KAH gwuh), the tallest mountain in the Americas, towers to 22,834 feet.

North America's Rocky Mountains extend over 3,000 miles, from Texas to Alaska. They are not quite as tall as the Andes. Mountain goats and bighorn sheep live on the steepest peaks above the timberline. Above this imaginary line on a mountain, trees cannot grow. Below the timberline, mountain lions and bears can be found living in forests of fir and spruce trees.

Like the Himalayas in Asia, the Andes and the Rockies have a great effect on climate. They have also influenced ways of life, transportation, and the history of civilizations.

Life in the Mountains

Many peoples have adapted to mountain life. In fact, one of South America's most advanced early civilizations developed in the highlands of the Andes. Early peoples of this region built irrigation systems and developed effective ways of fertilizing the soil. They found ways to farm crops such as maize, peppers, and potatoes on the slopes of the Andes. They also built rope bridges to make travel possible between some of the mountain peaks.

Hiking is a popular activity in the Rocky Mountains (left). Reed boats are used on Lake Titicaca in the Andes Mountains (below).

THE AMERICAS AT A GLANCE

	Total Land Area	16,236,000 sq. miles 42,051,000 sq. km
	Highest Mountain	Mt. Aconcagua, Argentina 22,834 feet (6,960 m)
	Longest River	Amazon River 4,000 miles 6,437 km
	Largest City	Mexico City, Mexico Population 10,263,275
	Current Population	757,000,000
	Percent of World Population	14%

GEO FACT

Northern Canada and Alaska make up part of the Arctic tundra. The climate of the tundra is so cold that the ground from 1 to 5 feet below the surface stays frozen all year. During the summer, the surface of the tundra thaws and moss and wildflowers grow.

CHART WORK

The Americas are rich not only in resources, but also in plants and minerals.

1. What is the longest river in the Americas?
2. How does the climate of the Arctic tunda affect the ground?

In North America's Rocky Mountains, early peoples had more difficult lives. Longer winters than those in the Andes, and less fertile soil, made farming a greater challenge.

WHY IT MATTERS

From the windy tip of South America to the icy rivers of Alaska, the Americas provide a 10,000-mile span of varied geography. Every possible climate zone can be found here, including polar, temperate, and tropical. Many physical features, such as North America's Grand Canyon and South America's Amazon River, which flows through the world's largest rain forest region, make these continents unique.

A study of this great land is incomplete, however, without meeting the people who live here. You have already read about the ancient civilizations of the Olmec and the Maya. Soon you will read about later peoples who lived in other parts of the Western Hemisphere.

✓/// Reviewing Facts and Ideas

MAIN IDEAS

- Glaciers shaped much of the land of North America.
- The Isthmus of Panama connects North America and South America.
- The Andes Mountains and the Rocky Mountains are the two major mountain ranges of this region.
- North and South America contain a variety of landforms and climates.
- Early peoples of the Andes region built irrigation systems and developed ways of growing maize, peppers, and potatoes on the mountain slopes.

THINK ABOUT IT

1. How were the Great Lakes formed?
2. What is the timberline?
3. **FOCUS** How have mountains affected the growth of civilization in the Americas?
4. **THINKING SKILL** How might mountains such as the Andes and Rockies have *effects* on trade?
5. **GEOGRAPHY** Use the map on page 423 to determine at what degrees of latitude and longitude Lake Superior is located. At about what latitude is the Amazon River located?

1200 1325 1521 1600

The Aztec Empire

Focus Activity

READ TO LEARN

How did the Aztec build an empire?

VOCABULARY

- chinampas
- tribute
- Triple Alliance
- codex

PLACES

- Tenochtitlán
- Valley of Mexico
- Lake Texcoco

THE BIG PICTURE

As you have read, Middle America was the scene for the development of two great ancient civilizations— the Olmec and the Maya. As time passed, these civilizations lost their power. Other peoples carried on their traditions of farming and building. In the 1400s the Aztec built an empire that rivaled the achievements of the Maya hundreds of years earlier. The center of Aztec culture and power was the great capital city called **Tenochtitlán** (te noch tee TLAHN).

At the time the Spanish soldier observed it, Tenochtitlán was probably larger than any other city in the world. Today one of the world's largest cities, Mexico City, is located in the same area. That area is a fertile valley where the great drama of the Aztec unfolded.

THE AZTEC SETTLE IN MIDDLE AMERICA

According to legend, the Aztec, who called themselves *Mexica*, journeyed for years in Middle America, searching for a place to settle. In the 1100s the Aztec came to the Valley of Mexico. They were among many newcomers there seeking a home. In this high valley surrounded by mountains are several lakes. About 1325 the Aztec arrived at the shores of Lake Texcoco (tay SKOH koh).

The Aztec saw an island in the center of the lake. On that island, their historical accounts state, they received a sign. An eagle flew from the sky, perched atop a cactus, and began eating a snake. The Aztec took this to mean that they should build a city on the island. The Aztec named the city Tenochtitlán. *Tenochtitlán* means "place of the prickly pear cactus" in the Aztec language, Nahuatl (NAH wah tul).

Creating Farmland

At first Tenochtitlán was no more than a collection of reed huts surrounding a temple. Although their land was poor, the Aztec soon developed a system of agriculture similar to the ones used by other peoples of the area. They carved canals through the marshland. In the lake they piled up the lake's soil to make smaller islands. Most of these islands were about the size of a football field. These human-made islands, were known as chinampas (chin AHM pahz). Chinampas were held in place by wooden stakes and the roots of willow trees. Some chinampas actually floated. They could be moved from one part of the lake to another!

By carefully planting different crops year round, Aztec farmers created a constant supply of squash, tomatoes, chili peppers, and flowers. The most important crop, maize, was grown mostly in fields on the lake shore.

Building a City

Although three out of four Aztec worked as farmers, many worked at other jobs in Tenochtitlán. Some people worked to make stone buildings that gradually replaced the reed huts. Others built three long bridges, or causeways, that connected the island to the lake shore. Although most people lived in one-room stone or mud houses, Aztec rulers lived in grand palaces surrounded by luxurious gardens. A Spanish soldier described one of these palaces: "I walked until I was tired and never saw the whole of it." That palace even had its own zoo!

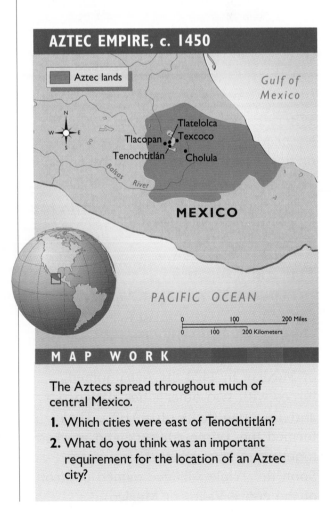

AZTEC EMPIRE, c. 1450

Aztec lands

Gulf of Mexico

Tlatelolca
Texcoco
Tlacopan
Tenochtitlán
Cholula

MEXICO

Bolsas River

PACIFIC OCEAN

| 0 | 100 | 200 Miles |
| 0 | 100 | 200 Kilometers |

MAP WORK

The Aztecs spread throughout much of central Mexico.

1. Which cities were east of Tenochtitlán?

2. What do you think was an important requirement for the location of an Aztec city?

GROWTH OF AN EMPIRE

When the Aztec first arrived in the Valley of Mexico, they had to pay tribute, or taxes, to the rulers of nearby cities. This tribute was usually a part of their crops, which people carried by boat and on foot from Tenochtitlán to the other cities.

The Triple Alliance

Before long, though, tribute was pouring into Tenochtitlán instead of pouring out. The Aztec became one of the most powerful groups in the Valley of Mexico. In 1428 the Aztec joined forces with two other cities, Texcoco and Tlacopan (tlahk oh PAHN). They formed the Triple Alliance and worked together to strengthen their power. Soon the Triple Alliance gained control of the entire Valley of Mexico.

By 1450 Aztec power spread beyond the mountains surrounding the Valley of Mexico. Under the leadership of the Aztec ruler Ahuítzotl (ah WEE soht ul), the armies of the Triple Alliance conquered areas west to the Pacific Ocean and south to what is today Guatemala. Equipped with wooden shields and sharp stone spears, the Aztec army caused great fear among the peoples of Mexico.

One Aztec poet described the great respect paid to soldiers who died in battle, writing "There is nothing like death in war." Soldiers preferred, however, to capture enemies as prisoners. These prisoners were sacrificed to honor the Aztec god of the sun, Huitzilopochtli (weet si loh POHCH tlee). To sacrifice means to kill in a religious ceremony. The Aztec believed that only human blood could nourish the sun god.

The tribute the conquered cities paid brought the Aztec great wealth. Workers brought more than one million loads of food for tribute to the Aztec capital each year. Tenochtitlán grew until it reached a population of about 150,000 people.

Governing the Empire

Like those of many other cultures you have read about, the Aztec social pyramid was made up of several levels. At the top was the emperor, who held great political and religious power. He was the richest person in Tenochtitlán. He also led the Aztec army. The emperor was worshiped by the Aztec people, who believed he had godlike powers. The emperor even had a special color—turquoise. No one else was allowed to wear clothing of this color.

Below the emperor were nobles and government workers. Nobles were in charge of running the Aztec empire. They made sure tributes were paid, temples were built, and streets were swept. Nobles also planned wars.

The majority of the population made up the family groups called *calpulli* (kahl POOL lee). *Calpulli* means "groups of houses" in Nahuatl. In Tenochtitlán there were 20 different calpulli. Each had its own leaders and was settled in a different part of the city. Each also had its own temple, school, and farmland. Members worked as farmers, craftworkers, merchants, and soldiers.

Near the base of Aztec society were poor farmers. They were among the poorest members of society, since they owned no land and had to work for others. Below the farmers were slaves. Only about 2 percent of the people in Tenochtitlán were enslaved. Most slaves were captured outside Aztec lands and brought to the capital by merchants. Slaves had no freedom and had to do whatever work their owners told them to do. Unlike those in most other cultures that practiced slavery, the children of Aztec slaves were free and could make choices about their lives.

This mosaic serpent was made to be worn on the chest. The serpent was a god to the Aztec.

AZTEC CIVILIZATION

By 1500 the city of Tenochtitlán bustled with trade and learning. Aztec doctors made more than 1,000 medicines from plants. Plants were used to heal wounds, reduce fevers, and cure stomachaches. Predicting eclipses and the movements of planets, Aztec astronomers built on Maya knowledge of the heavens. Craftworkers created beautiful feather headdresses, gold and copper jewelry, ceramic storage jars, and woven cloth.

The Great Temple

From birth until death, from morning until night, religion played a central role in the lives of the Aztec. The center of religious life in Tenochtitlán was the temple district. This district was located where three main streets came together. Here stood temples to

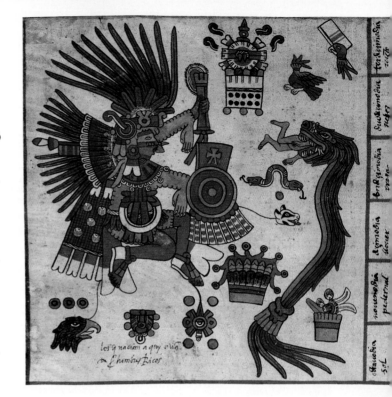

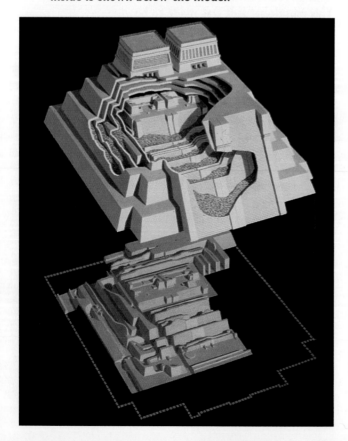

This model shows the outside of the Great Temple at Tenochtitlán. The inside is shown below the model.

different gods, homes for men and women priests, schools for young priests, and ball courts. Rising as high as an eight-story building was the Great Temple. Aztec built this temple to honor Huitzilopochtli, their sun god, and Tlaloc (TLAH lohk), their rain god.

Two staircases, decorated with carved and painted sculptures, led up to the top of the temple platform. It was here, on two massive stone blocks, that special priests sacrificed thousands of war prisoners every year.

Aztec Writing

In addition to performing temple ceremonies, priests kept a calendar that was used to predict the future. Some kept records using a special Aztec system of writing. Colorful pictures and symbols were drawn on a long folded sheet of paper. Each of these folded sheets was called a codex (KOH deks). Two or more of these sheets were called codices (KOH dih seez). Codices contained information about the history, religion, government, and science of the Aztec. Few

The **codex** (far left) shows the god of spring. A statue of the god of flowers and song is at left.

remain because the Spanish destroyed most Aztec records in the 1500s.

The Aztec also had a strong oral tradition. People memorized many poems, songs, and speeches. Poems were often recited on special occasions, accompanied by drums and flutes. This is an Aztec poem:

An emerald fell to the ground,
and a flower was born; this is your
song!
Whenever you sing your songs here
in Mexico
the sun shines eternally [forever].

WHY IT MATTERS

Within only a hundred years, the Aztec built one of the most powerful empires in the Americas. Farming techniques and efficient government helped the empire to grow and run smoothly. Constant warfare brought many enemies under Aztec rule. In 1521 the Aztec fell to the European kingdom of Spain.

Aztec people and many of their traditions survived. Food such as maize, Aztec crafts, and even the Nahuatl language are all part of Mexican culture today. The name *Mexico* comes from the name the Aztec called themselves. Even the flag of Mexico celebrates the Aztec legacy. At its center the flag shows the Aztec symbol of an eagle with a snake in its beak.

✓// Reviewing Facts and Ideas

MAIN IDEAS

- The Aztec first settled in the Valley of Mexico in about 1325.
- The Aztec built a powerful empire centered at Tenochtitlán.
- The Aztec gained much knowledge in medicine and astronomy and created beautiful buildings and works of art.

THINK ABOUT IT

1. Why did the Aztec settle in the Valley of Mexico?

2. How did the people of nearby cities help make Tenochtitlán wealthy?

3. **FOCUS** How did the Aztec expand their empire to areas beyond the Valley of Mexico?

4. **THINKING SKILL** Make a *conclusion* about how the people of conquered villages were treated in the Aztec empire. Explain how you reached your conclusion.

5. **WRITE** Write a paragraph describing one major achievement of the Aztec. Explain why that achievement was important for the Aztec civilization.

431

Geography Skills

MAP A: EQUAL-AREA PROJECTION

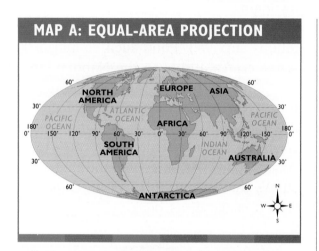

MAP B: EQUAL-AREA PROJECTION

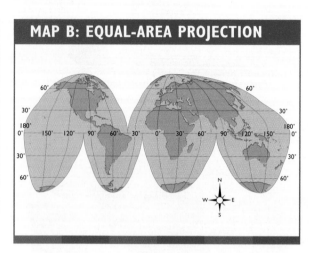

Using Map Projections

VOCABULARY

distortion
projection
equal-area projection
mercator projection
polar projection

WHY THE SKILL MATTERS

Only one tiny map fragment remains from Aztec times, but most historians believe that the Aztec commonly used maps. Maps would have been an important tool for keeping track of the widespread Aztec empire.

Today some maps are more accurate than others. Maps that show the entire world vary greatly in accuracy. Since Earth is a sphere, cartographers must stretch or cut parts of the globe, making it fit onto a flat map. This stretching and cutting causes distortion—errors that make the map less accurate.

When cartographers create a map of Earth's entire surface, they must use a projection. A projection is a way of showing parts of Earth on a flat map.

USING MAP PROJECTIONS

One of the most common types of map projections is the equal-area projection. An example of this projection is shown on Map A. This map is especially useful for comparing sizes of land masses. However, it distorts the shapes of land. Distances between places at the edges of this map are distorted. It is also difficult to find north and south on this map, because these directions curve along meridians.

Map B is another kind of equal-area projection. The shapes on Map B are more accurate than the shapes on Map A. However, the cuts in this map make it very difficult to tell the distances between places.

Another kind of world map, the mercator projection, is shown on Map C. This projection was invented by a Flemish mapmaker in the 1500s. Near the equator there is little distortion and sizes are accurate, too. However, as you move farther from the equator, sizes become more distorted.

Polar projections are used to show the area around the North Pole or the South

Pole. Most polar projections show only half the globe or less. Map D shows a polar projection of the North Pole. Sizes and shapes near the center are accurate. Near the edges, however, there is distortion.

Polar projections like Map D are used by pilots flying over the North Pole. The shortest distance between two points on a polar projection is a straight line.

TRYING THE SKILL

Suppose you are traveling on a long trip through the Americas. You want to use a map that will accurately show the distances you have traveled and how far you still have to go. Which kind of projection

would you select? Would you have any use for a polar projection on this trip?

REVIEWING THE SKILL

1. Why do all flat maps of the world have some distortion?

2. Where does distortion occur on a mercator projection map?

3. Look at the Atlas map of the world on page R18. Which type of projection is used for this map?

4. In what ways is a flat map better than a globe? In what ways is a globe better?

5. Why are there many different kinds of map projections?

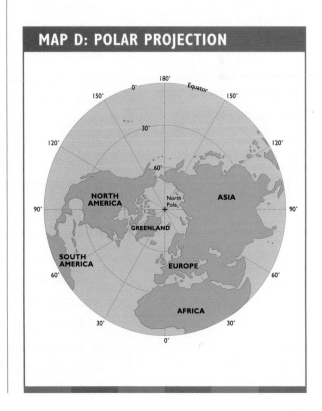

MAP C: MERCATOR PROJECTION

MAP D: POLAR PROJECTION

1200   1531   1600

The Inca Empire

Read Aloud

I am rich in silver

I am rich in gold.

These words come from an Inca poem. They celebrate the wealth of the Inca civilization, which developed in the Andes Mountains of South America. In these mountains the Inca found the large amounts of metal and minerals that made their empire rich. They also found a place to develop traditions that made their culture rich as well.

Focus Activity

READ TO LEARN

What were some of the major achievements of the Inca?

VOCABULARY

- terrace
- quipu

PEOPLE

- Pachakuti Inca

PLACES

- Cuzco
- Machu Picchu

THE BIG PICTURE

While the Aztec were extending their rule beyond the Valley of Mexico, another culture was expanding in the mountains of South America. This people, known as the Inca, built an empire along the Andes Mountains. The empire stretched from what is today Ecuador to central Chile. This distance is about equal to the distance from New York City to the Panama Canal. At its peak the Inca empire had about 12 million people. Although they had little contact with the Aztec, the Inca, too, worshiped the sun, depended on maize as a major crop, and organized a strong army. Like the Aztec to the north, the Inca also created a system of government in their empire. In many other ways, however, the Inca were unique in the Americas and in the world.

THE RISE OF THE INCA

The Inca empire rose out of a small village called Cuzco (KOOS koh) in a fertile valley in what is today Peru. About 1200 the Inca settled at Cuzco to grow maize and other crops. At first the word *Inca* was the name for the ruler. Later the word applied to all of the people. When drought reduced the amount of fertile farmland, the Inca took over their neighbors' land. During the 1300s the Inca ruled most of the Cuzco Valley and demanded tributes from the other people living there.

Building an Empire

In 1438 a ruler called Pachakuti (pah chah KOO tee) Inca greatly extended the Inca borders. Soon the Inca controlled land west to the Pacific Ocean and south to the area of Lake Titicaca. Find the Inca lands on the map on this page. The Inca army seemed unstoppable in its quest to conquer new areas. In the Inca language, the word *Quechua* (KECH oo uh) means "to fight" and "to enjoy oneself."

Pachakuti became known as Sapa Inca, or Supreme Inca. As emperor, Pachakuti set about organizing the new land he controlled. He forced conquered people off their land. Then he allowed people who

This poncho was made of feathers by an Inca craftworker. It was worn during Inca ceremonies.

were loyal to the Inca to settle there. Pachakuti appointed governors in each region. People from all corners of the empire were required to do jobs for the government. Men built roads and raised crops; women made cloth.

Pachakuti also spread the Inca religion throughout the empire. Their religion was based on the worship of an ancient Inca god called Viracocha. According to Inca beliefs, this god had appeared in the emperor's dream during a war. Conquered people were forced to worship Viracocha and provide offerings of food. However, the Inca also let people continue to worship their own gods, as well.

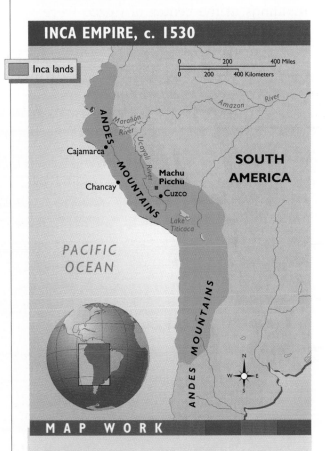

INCA EMPIRE, c. 1530

Inca lands

0   200   400 Miles
0   200   400 Kilometers

Amazon River
Marañón River
Ucayali River
ANDES MOUNTAINS
Cajamarca
Chancay
Machu Picchu
Cuzco
Lake Titicaca
PACIFIC OCEAN
SOUTH AMERICA
ANDES MOUNTAINS

MAP WORK

The Inca empire stretched along the western edge of South America.

1. Which city was located along the Ucayali River?

2. About how far is Lake Titicaca from Machu Picchu?

CHILDREN OF THE SUN

After his victory Pachakuti built a temple with a gold sculpture of the god Viracocha. This temple was located in the city of Cuzco. The most important temple in Cuzco, though, honored Inti, the sun god. In the center of this temple was a huge golden sculpture of the sun, decorated with precious stones. The Inca considered Inti to be their parent and often called themselves "Children of the Sun."

Life in Cuzco

Cuzco served as the center of government, religion, and trade in the Inca empire. The temples and government buildings at the center of Cuzco were constructed of stone blocks. These blocks fit together so well that it is impossible to put a knife between them!

Beyond the main plaza lived the emperor and wealthy nobles. These people were easy to recognize by the special headbands and earrings they wore. One of the first Spanish soldiers to visit the city was impressed by Inca building skill. He wrote the following description in the 1500s:

Cuzco is large enough and handsome enough to compare to any Spanish city. Most of the houses are of stone; others have stonework only halfway up; many are of adobe [clay bricks] and all are regularly built. The streets, all stone-paved and straight, cross each other at right angles, and have each a stone-lined water channel running down the middle. The city is placed on high ground, and many houses cling to the slopes above and many can be seen on the flat lands below.

The Inca were skilled at building with stone (left) and at farming, as the codex (below) shows.

Outside Cuzco, workers and farmers lived in small mud huts with high windows. Also outside the city were many government storage buildings. Some contained food, such as maize, dried fruit, or salt. Others contained neat piles of beautiful wool and cotton cloth. There was even a building just to hold the feathers of hummingbirds, which were used as decoration for clothing.

Inca Agriculture

Every year the Inca emperor, followed by a group of nobles, traveled to a field outside Cuzco and dug up the ground with a plow made of pure gold. This act signaled the importance of agriculture to all of Inca society.

Inca farmers grew potatoes, maize, and peppers. They adapted their farming methods to the geography of different parts of the empire. In hilly areas they built terraces, level platforms of earth that climbed each hill like a staircase. In rocky areas Inca farmers dug huge pits 20 feet deep. Farmers enriched the soil by placing fish in the pits. In dry areas the Inca brought water through a system of canals and aqueducts. One stone aqueduct crossed nearly 500 miles to bring water from a faraway mountain lake.

Although all farming was done by human labor, the Inca did raise animals for other uses. They used llamas as pack animals to carry many trade items through the empire. The best wool came from wild sheep. Only the nobles were allowed to wear the fine wool from these sheep. The Inca also hunted deer for food and clothing.

As in the past, llamas are still used to carry goods in the Andes Mountains.

437

TRAVELING THROUGH THE EMPIRE

Nothing was more important to keeping the empire together than the huge network of roads. The Inca built more than 19,000 miles of roads—over some of the most rugged landscape in the world. One Spanish visitor wrote this report in the 1500s:

> I believe there is no account of a road as great as this, running through deep valleys, high mountains, banks of snow, torrents of water, living rock, and wild rivers. Through some places it went flat and paved; it was dug out of steep rock in the mountains; it passed with walls along rivers, and had steps and resting spots in the snow.

Important quipu messages were carried through the empire by runners. Messengers stopped every few miles to pass on messages to the next runner. Huge armies and long trade caravans made up of hundreds of llamas also traveled along the useful stone highways.

A City in the Clouds

Roads connected all corners of the empire, but some places were still difficult to reach. One road wound high into the mountains north of Cuzco, through stone tunnels and along steep cliffs. The road ended on a mountaintop, at a town called Machu Picchu (MAHCH oo PEEK choo). Machu Picchu is so far from other towns that it was forgotten until an American

438

This girl from Peru wears traditional clothing suited to the cool climate of the Andes.

The few gold artifacts that remain show the skill of Inca craftworkers. Stone roads and city walls are evidence of great building knowledge. The songs and poems recorded by Spanish conquerors give a hint of the Inca's rich oral tradition. The language of the Inca is kept alive by millions of people today. People who speak Quechua still live in the Andes region of Peru. Through these sources historians can still get a sense of the brilliant culture created by the "Children of the Sun."

Reviewing Facts and Ideas

MAIN IDEAS

- The Inca built a huge empire in the Andes Mountains in western South America.

- The Inca capital of Cuzco was the center of government, religion, and trade in the empire.

- Inca farmers used terraces and irrigation to grow crops.

- The vast Inca road system helped unite the empire. Roads allowed easy travel for armies, merchants, and messengers.

THINK ABOUT IT

1. Why did the Inca call themselves "Children of the Sun"?

2. How did terraces help the Inca expand their agriculture?

3. **FOCUS** List three major achievements of the Inca.

4. **THINKING SKILL** _Compare_ the Inca empire with the Aztec empire. How were they similar? How were they different?

5. **GEOGRAPHY** Describe two ways in which the Inca interacted with their environment.

explorer named Hiram Bingham came across it in 1911.

Bingham found stone ruins of buildings, walls, and terraces at the mountaintop location. No one is sure why Machu Picchu was built or why it was forgotten. Some historians think that it may have been a special religious town, similar to a European monastery. There Inca may have worshiped at shrines. Many historians believe the town was built around 1438 by the Inca ruler Pachakuti, who wanted a place to worship. Another possibility is that the town was used as a fortress during war.

WHY IT MATTERS

The lost city of Machu Picchu is just one of many mysteries that surround the Inca. When Spanish soldiers conquered the Inca empire in the 1500s, they destroyed many Inca treasures. Fortunately, many quipu records remain, and some Spanish soldiers wrote down their thoughts about this civilization.

Early People of North America

Read Aloud

In summer the Ojibwa (oh JIHB wah) lived by the waters of Lake Superior. When summer changed to autumn, they moved to the marshes where wild rice grew. They left the marshes before the heavy snows fell, living now near the herds that could be hunted. In spring sap flowed in the maple trees, and the Ojibwa came to collect it.

Like many of the peoples of North America, the Ojibwa moved their villages each season. This way of living allowed them to use many of the resources of their environment.

Focus Activity

READ TO LEARN

How did the Ojibwa make use of their northern forest environment?

VOCABULARY

- diversity
- Three Fires Council
- wigwam

PLACES

- Bowating

THE BIG PICTURE

As you have read, North America and South America were home to many peoples before the arrival of Europeans. These peoples and their descendants are called Indians. Tremendous **diversity** has always existed among these peoples. Diversity refers to differences. Peoples who lived in what is now the United States, and their descendants, are also called Native Americans. All of these peoples had many things in common, but each group adapted to its environment in unique ways.

Around 1400, in the Great Lakes region of North America, a group of Native Americans called the Ojibwa learned to make use of the forest environment. The Ojibwa harvested wild rice, collected maple sap in the forest, and developed many cultural traditions based on the changing seasons of their region.

PEOPLE OF THE WOODLANDS

About 500 years ago nearly all the land east of the Mississippi River was thick forest. The Native Americans who lived here used the forest as a source of fuel, tools, shelter, and food. The forest provided such things as wood and maple syrup. One group of Native Americans, the Seneca, praised the forest in this poem about the sugar maple tree:

> To The Tree:
> O we share your scents,
> You the forests!
> We beg you
> To continue as before,
> The flowing waters of the maple.

The Ojibwa

Among the other woodland groups living in the eastern part of North America was the Ojibwa. The Ojibwa lived in the Great Lakes area of what are today Canada and the United States. The Ojibwa called themselves *Anishinabe* (ahn ish uh NAH bee), which means "original people."

According to their traditions, the Ojibwa once lived near the mouth of the St. Lawrence River, near the Atlantic Ocean. They migrated to the Great Lakes region about 500 years ago. There the Ojibwa settled along the eastern end of Lake Superior, which they called Kitchigami. A tremendous lake, with cold, deep waters, Kitchigami was an object of wonder and worship for the Ojibwa.

Villages at the Shore

The Ojibwa lived in villages of a few hundred people each. Many of these villages were scattered along the shores of Kitchigami and on the north shore of the peninsula between Lakes Huron and

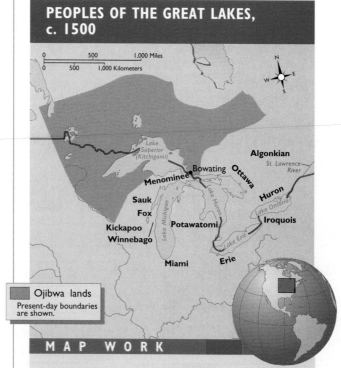

PEOPLES OF THE GREAT LAKES, c. 1500

Ojibwa lands
Present-day boundaries are shown.

MAP WORK

The Ojibwa were one of many groups who lived near the Great Lakes.

1. On which side of Lake Superior was the village of Bowating located?

2. Near which lake did the Winnebago and Miami groups live?

Michigan. Some of the larger villages served as trading centers. One trading center was the village of **Bowating** (BOH ah tihng). *Bowating* means "place at the falls." This village was located on an island in the river that connects Lake Superior and Lake Huron. As you can see on the map on this page, Bowating was centrally located for people who depended on boat travel.

Two neighboring Native American communities—the Potawatomi and the Ottawa—joined the Ojibwa to form the **Three Fires Council**. This council was a league, or cooperative group. Its main purpose was trade. People traveled among communities, bringing their trade goods in bark canoes. At what time of day does canoe travel take place in the song on the next page?

441

MY BARK CANOE

Ojibwa Song

Pronunciation: Che - kah - bay   te - bick   on   dan - dey - an
English: In   the   dark___   night,   the   long night through,

Che - kah   bay   te - bick   on   dan - dey - an
I___   guide___   my   bark   ca - noe,

Ah   gah - mah - si - bi   on - dan - dey - an.
My   bark   ca - noe___   the   long   night through.

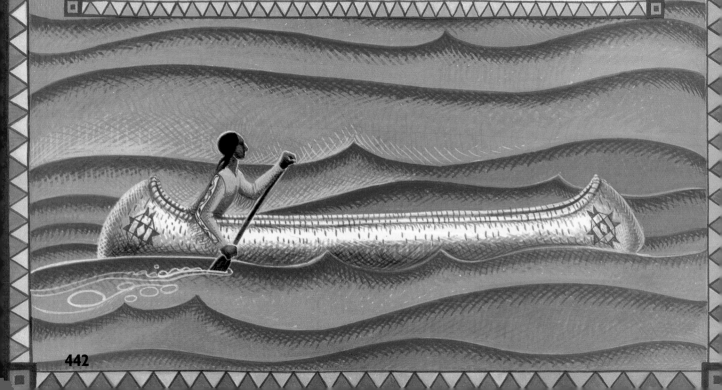

CYCLE OF THE SEASONS

To make the best use of their environment, the Ojibwa followed the cycle of the seasons. This meant that the Ojibwa moved with the change of seasons during the year. In each village families built dome-shaped houses they called wigwams. The Ojibwa made these houses by placing sheets of birch bark and cattail reeds over a frame of wooden poles. Families could roll up the birch bark sheets, leaving the wood frame behind.

Summer and Fall

The Ojibwa settled near a lake during the summer months. However, they often traveled as far as 50 miles away to find food. Men fished in the lakes and rivers and hunted in the surrounding forests. Women and children gathered nuts and berries. They also grew corn, beans, and squash.

To relax, the Ojibwa sometimes played a game called *baggataway*. Villages competed against each other to drive a ball over a goal line, using sticks with nets attached. Today a modern version of this game, lacrosse, is still played in many parts of the United States and in Canada.

When fall came, the Ojibwa moved near the marshes and ponds where wild rice grew. There women and men worked together to harvest the rice. Men used poles to push birch bark canoes through the shallow lakes and streams. Women used special sticks to knock rice grains into the canoes. The Ojibwa also worked to spread wild rice to new areas.

Winter and Spring

During winter the Ojibwa moved to areas where they could hunt. To travel through the deep snow of their long winter season, they wore snowshoes and used toboggans, or sleds. The Ojibwa hunted deer, moose, bear, and fox. They used bows and arrows, spears, and special traps that dropped logs or other heavy weights on animals. Meat was roasted or boiled and then smoked so that it could be stored. The skins from animals were tanned and then sewn into clothing and moccasins.

In spring the Ojibwa moved to an area where many sugar maple trees grew. The Ojibwa collected the maple sap in birch bark buckets and then boiled it down to make maple sugar. This sugar was used to flavor rice, fish, and other food. The Ojibwa moved on to their summer villages after maple sugar season ended. They carried the maple sugar with them in containers decorated with pictographs. Pictographs are drawings of symbols that are used as a writing system. In fact, the name *Ojibwa* comes from a term that means "those who make pictographs."

People of the Great Lakes region still make products from maple sap.

infographic

interNET CONNECTION

Visit our website:
www.mhschool.com

Cultural Regions of North America, c. 1500

- ☐ Arctic
- ☐ Subarctic
- ☐ Eastern Woodlands
- ☐ Southeast
- ☐ Plains
- ☐ Northwest Coast
- ☐ California
- ☐ Basin and Plateau
- ☐ Southwest
- ☐ Northern Mexico
- ☐ Central America
- ☐ Middle America
- ☐ Caribbean

Inuit

Inuit

Inuit

Haida

Cree

Micmac

Ojibwa

Ottawa

Penobscot

Walla-Walla

Nez Percé

Crow

Menominee

Huron

Iroquois

Winnebago

Mohawk

Hupa

Lakota

Kickapoo

Mohegan

Pomo

Cheyenne

Powhatan

Chumash

Hopi

Shawnee

Navajo

Pueblo

Cherokee

Zuni

Comanche

Cochimi

Choctaw

Seminole

Huichol

Taino

Toltec

Aztec

Maya

Zapotec

Hupa girls and women used shells and feathers to decorate their clothing. They wore necklaces like this one made of abalone and clam shells.

Native North Americans

Native North Americans lived in all parts of the continent. Many different groups lived in each of the cultural regions shown on the map. They made distinctive types of jewelry and clothing. Why might these items have been important to the different groups?

Young Menominees wore beaded bags (above right) that were sometimes called Friendship Bags because they were given as gifts. The Aztec wore jewelry like this gold pendant (right). Other Aztec items were made of beautiful stones or crystals.

WHY IT MATTERS

The arrival of Europeans in North America in the 1600s brought great change for the Ojibwa and other Native American groups. Wars, disease, and European settlement all took a tremendous toll on the Ojibwa and their way of life. Still, the Ojibwa survived, and they continued many of the traditions of their people.

Today nearly 200,000 Ojibwa live in the Great Lakes region of the United States and Canada. Gerald Vizenor, an Ojibwa writer, recently described his feelings about his homeland:

> The land is everything to me. The land is part of my language, part of the way I perceive [become aware of] the world. The water, the trees, the smell of pine, the smell of autumn, the smell of wet leaves in the spring. It is all part of my imagination, part of my dreams.

Today the Ojibwa continue to follow important cultural traditions. This Ojibwa dance group is performing at a Native American harvest festival in Wisconsin.

Reviewing Facts and Ideas

MAIN IDEAS

- The woodlands of North America provided many resources for the Native Americans who lived there.

- The Ojibwa settled around the area of Lake Superior about 500 years ago.

- The Ojibwa moved with the seasons to hunt, fish, farm, and harvest food in different places.

- Many Ojibwa continue to live in the Great Lakes region and carry on their cultural traditions.

THINK ABOUT IT

1. According to tradition, from where did the Ojibwa migrate when they settled near Lake Superior about 500 years ago?

2. Why did the Ojibwa travel to different areas throughout the year?

3. **FOCUS** How did the Ojibwa use forest resources to make their homes?

4. **THINKING SKILL** What _conclusions_ can you make from the fact that wigwams were easily taken apart?

5. **WRITE** Create a calendar that describes what the Ojibwa did during each season of the year.

445

CHAPTER 15 REVIEW

Major Events

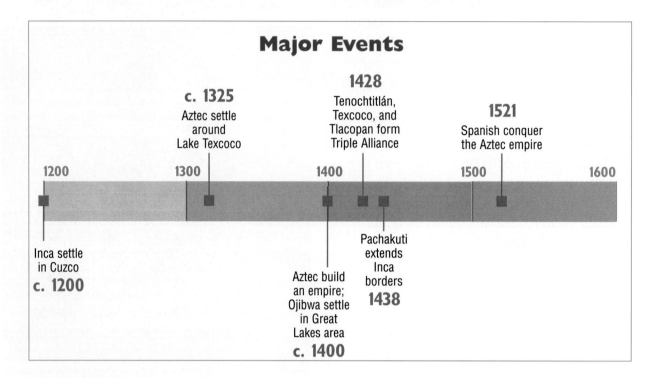

c. 1325
Aztec settle around Lake Texcoco

1428
Tenochtitlán, Texcoco, and Tlacopan form Triple Alliance

1521
Spanish conquer the Aztec empire

1200   1300   1400   1500   1600

Inca settle in Cuzco
c. 1200

Aztec build an empire; Ojibwa settle in Great Lakes area
c. 1400

Pachakuti extends Inca borders
1438

THINKING ABOUT VOCABULARY

Each of the following statements contains an underlined vocabulary word or term. Number a sheet of paper from 1 to 10. Beside each number write **T** if the statement is true and **F** if the statement is false. If the statement is false, rewrite the sentence using the vocabulary word or term correctly.

1. Great <u>diversity</u> existed among various Native American peoples.

2. <u>Wigwams</u> were made by placing sheets of birch bark and cattail reeds over a frame of wooden poles.

3. The islands the Aztec made in a lake for farming were called <u>quipus</u>.

4. The Aztec had to pay <u>tribute</u> to the rulers of nearby cities when they arrived in the Valley of Mexico.

5. A <u>codex</u> is a weapon used by Ojibwa warriors.

6. Inca farmers planted crops on <u>terraces</u> that climbed up hills like stairs.

7. <u>Chinampas</u> was the name of the corn eaten by the Ojibwa people, who lived in the Great Lakes region.

8. During the last part of his seven-year walk from the southern tip of South America to the Arctic Ocean, George Meegan walked across the warm, swampy <u>tundra</u> of Florida.

9. North America and South America are connected by an <u>isthmus</u>.

10. A <u>timberline</u> separates Native American villages.

THINKING ABOUT FACTS

1. How did the Ice Age glaciers affect physical features of North America?

2. Describe the Aztec system of writing.

3. What role did Pachakuti play in Inca history?

4. What was the Three Fires Council? Why was it formed?

5. According to the time line above, how long did the Aztec empire last?

THINK AND WRITE

WRITING A LETTER

Suppose you are George Meegan in 1976 and you have just finished your seven-year walk across the length of the Americas. Write a letter to a friend about your journey.

WRITING A SUMMARY

Write a paragraph summarizing the achievements of the Aztec civilization.

WRITING A DESCRIPTION

Write a paragraph describing how the Ojibwa of the Great Lakes region adapted to their forest environment.

APPLYING GEOGRAPHY SKILLS

USING MAP PROJECTIONS

1. What is a map projection?

2. Maps A and B on page 432 both show equal-area projections. What are some of the advantages and disadvantages of each map?

3. Place a ruler between North America and South America on Map C. Then find a globe and use a string to measure the same straight-line distance. Explain why that line would look curved on Map C.

4. Compare Maps A and D on pages 432–433. If you were exploring the North Pole, which map would you bring with you? Why?

5. Why are map projections useful?

Summing Up the Chapter

Copy the word map below on a separate sheet of paper. Review the chapter to find at least two pieces of information to support each topic in the word map. When you have filled in the map, write a paragraph that answers the question "What made the Aztec, Inca, and Ojibwa civilizations similar and what made them different?"

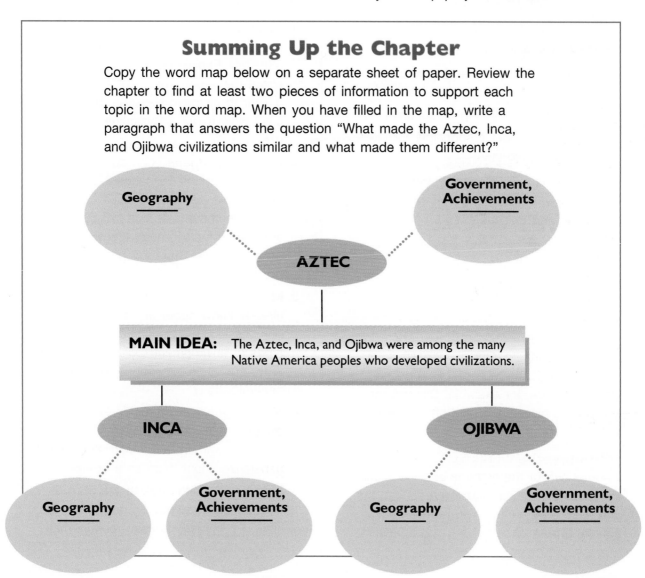

Geography

Government, Achievements

AZTEC

MAIN IDEA: The Aztec, Inca, and Ojibwa were among the many Native America peoples who developed civilizations.

INCA

OJIBWA

Geography

Government, Achievements

Geography

Government, Achievements

UNIT 4 REVIEW

THINKING ABOUT VOCABULARY

Number a sheet of paper from 1 to 10. Beside each number write the word or term from the list below that best matches the definition.

diversity	monarchy
feudalism	monsoon
grand mufti	navigable
griot	savanna
isthmus	shogun

1. A grassy, tree-dotted plain

2. A seasonal wind

3. A military ruler of Japan

4. Can be traveled by ships

5. A way of organizing and governing society based on land and service

6. A government by king or queen

7. A religious leader responsible for interpreting Islamic law

8. Made up of or showing different kinds

9. A narrow strip of land that connects two larger land masses

10. A special African storyteller and oral historian

THINK AND WRITE

WRITING ABOUT PEOPLE

Write about somebody you read about in the unit—Michelangelo, Queen Amanishakhete, Kublai Khan, Lady Murasaki Shikibu, or Pachakuti Inca, for example. Discuss the person's achievements and his or her importance in history.

WRITING ABOUT PERSPECTIVES

Choose two of the empires or civilizations in Europe, Africa, Asia, and the Americas that you have read about. Write about what someone from each culture would have thought about war. What might they consider to be important reasons for going to war? Explain why there might be differences in their perspectives.

WRITING AN EXPLANATION

Write two paragraphs about the rise of empires in West Africa. Explain how the area's natural resources played a role in the development of trade. Describe the effects of this trade on the people living in the area. Include facts about powerful rulers who led the empires.

BUILDING SKILLS

1. **Point of view** Reread the section about the fall of Constantinople on pages 388–389. Explain different points of view about the event. For example, how might a Turkish historian describe the fall of the city? How might a Byzantine historian describe it?

2. **Distribution maps** Look again at the population maps on pages 370–371 to review how distribution maps can show how something is spread out over an area. Then look through the book for at least two other distribution maps. What do they show?

3. **Making generalizations** From what you already know about the growth of civilizations, make a generalization about the types of environment civilizations require. What are some exceptions to your generalization?

4. **Making generalizations** Make a generalization about students. What do they have in common that would allow you to generalize about them as a group?

5. **Map projections** Look at the map of Marco Polo's journey on page 406. What kind of projection is used for this map?

YESTERDAY, TODAY &
TOMORROW

Civilizations in Europe, Africa, Asia, and the Americas had very different cultures and languages. Today mass communication is helping people around the world understand each other better. Do you think people in different civilizations will be more similar in the future? Do you think someday everybody will speak the same language? Explain your answers.

READING ON YOUR OWN

Here are some books you might find at the library to help you learn more.

LEONARDO DA VINCI
by Diane Stanley
A beautifully illustrated picture book of this famous painter's life and art techniques.

KNIGHTS IN ARMOR
Edited by John D. Clare
A well-illustrated overview of the lifestyle and role of the knight during the Middle Ages.

ALL OF YOU WAS SINGING
by Richard Lewis
This is a retelling of an Aztec myth.

UNIT 4 REVIEW PROJECT

Make a Building

1. Choose a culture you learned about in this unit such as the Aztec.
2. Research the building styles of that culture in your school or local library.
3. Write a report about the building styles. Be sure to include the types of materials and tools they used and who the builders were in the society.
4. Create a model building for the culture. You can use such materials as clay, toothpicks, paper, cartons, or popsicle sticks.
5. Share your building and report with the class.

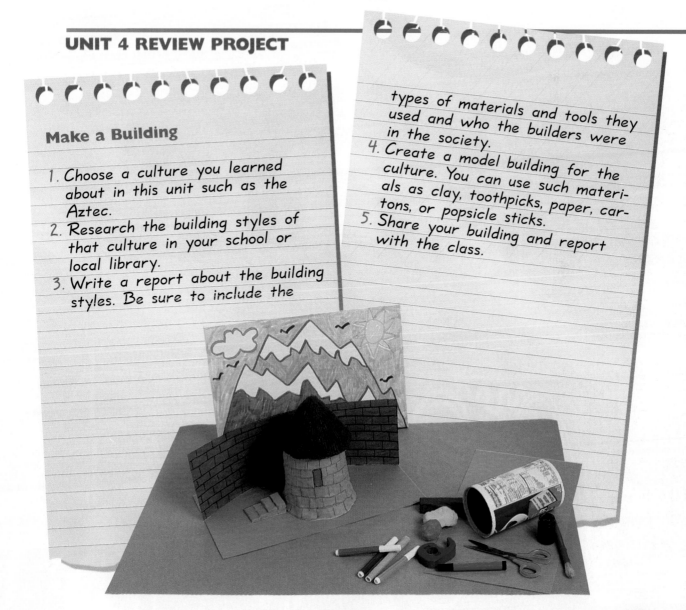

EXPLORER'S
COMPASS, EUROPE;
GOLD AND SILVER
COINS, SPAIN

STEAM
LOCOMOTIVE,
UNITED STATES

Dawn of the Modern World

*"Knowledge shall be sought
throughout the world."*

from the Charter Oath
See page 511.

Why Does It Matter?

These words, from a Japanese document
of 1889, express a yearning for new ideas and
knowledge. During the period you will read
about—when our modern world was just
beginning to take shape—new ways of thinking spread among many peoples.

People began to learn more about the
world around them. European explorers
sailed to the Western Hemisphere, charting new courses
and coming into contact with peoples of the Americas.
Scientists learned about Earth and its position in the
solar system. They invented new technologies. The
changes that resulted created a world of new ideas
and challenges.

GALILEO'S ROOM,
ITALY

FIND OUT MORE!
Visit our website:
www.mhschool.com

*inter***NET**
CONNECTION

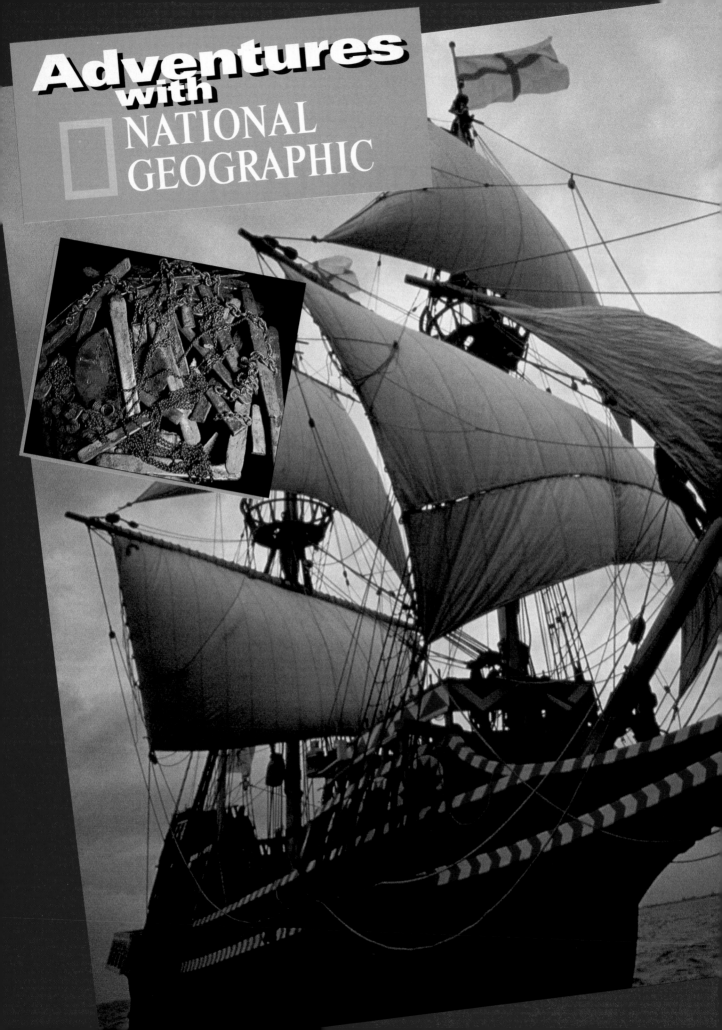

Adventures
with
NATIONAL GEOGRAPHIC

Golden VOYAGE

Today, a reproduction of the *Golden Hind* sails off the coast of England. Four hundred years ago, the real *Golden Hind* carried explorer Francis Drake from England around the world. Surviving violent storms, Drake rounded South America and headed up its western coast. Along the way, he picked up a fortune in treasure—by raiding Spain's South American ports. Three years after his departure, Drake returned to England. Queen Elizabeth was so pleased by his feat—and by the treasure he brought home—that she knighted him right on the deck of the *Golden Hind*.

GEO JOURNAL

You're Queen Elizabeth's speechwriter. Compose a speech to welcome Drake home.

European Expansion

THINKING ABOUT
HISTORY AND GEOGRAPHY

The story of European movement around the World begins in the late 1400s. Explorers were able to sail to distant lands as a result of new technology. Following the time line, you can see how the explorers encountered civilizations that were thousands of years old. This meeting began an exchange of goods, ideas, and people that changed the shape of history.

Valley of Mexico

Santo Domingo

Lima

SOUTH AMERICA

Strait of Magellan

1519

VALLEY OF MEXICO
Moctezuma watches the Spanish approach the Aztec capital

1520

STRAIT OF MAGELLAN
Ferdinand Magellan sails around the southern tip of South America

1535

LIMA
Francisco Pizarro founds the city of Lima as the capital of Peru

1500

1525

1550

NORTH
AMERICA

ARCTIC
OCEAN

ASIA

PACIFIC
OCEAN

ATLANTIC
OCEAN

EUROPE

New South
Wales

AFRICA

AUSTRALIA

1600

SANTO DOMINGO
Enslaved Africans work on
sugarcane plantations

1778

NEW SOUTH WALES
The English establish a
colony on the east coast
of Australia

INDIAN
OCEAN

1575

1600

1778

TVBVM OPTICVM VIDES GALILAEI INVENTVM ET OPVS QVO SOLIS MACVLAS
ET EXTIMOS LVNAE MONTES, ET IOVIS SATELLITES, ET NOVAM QVASI
RERVM VNIVERSITATE PRIMVS DISPEXIT A. MDCIX.

1400   1490   1700   1800

The Beginning of Modern Science

Read Aloud

In the early 1600s Galileo Galilei (gal uh LAY oh gah lee LE ee) used a new invention, the telescope, to look into space for the first time. He saw more stars than he could count. He wrote:

"Upon whatever part of the galaxy the telescope is directed, a crowd of stars is immediately presented to view. Many of them are rather large and quite bright, while the number of smaller ones is quite beyond calculation."

Focus Activity

READ TO LEARN

What were the achievements of Galileo Galilei and Isaac Newton?

VOCABULARY

- geocentric
- heliocentric
- telescope
- gravity
- scientific method

PEOPLE

- Galileo Galilei
- Isaac Newton

THE BIG PICTURE

Around 1500 Europeans were expanding their influence in other parts of the world. Explorers were making new connections between Europe and other continents. In the cities of Renaissance Italy, artists such as Leonardo da Vinci were painting the world around them in exciting new ways. As you read in Chapter 12, the Christian world was changing as well.

Scientists, too, began to take a fresh look at the world around them. Until this time most Europeans' understanding of the universe and how it worked came from ancient times. Most people believed that the universe was **geocentric** (jee oh SEN trihk), or centered around Earth. This view seemed to make sense. After all, it was the sun that seemed to "rise" and "set" each day, while Earth seemed not to move. In the early 1500s, however, a challenge to this belief would excite and disturb many Europeans.

NEW VIEWS

At this time scientists were talking about the ideas of Polish scientist Nicolaus Copernicus. In Chapter 12 you read that Copernicus suggested that Earth is not located at the center of the universe. He put forth a heliocentric (hee lee oh SEN trihk), or sun-centered, view. In this view, Earth and other planets move in orbits, or paths, around the sun. The heliocentric view caused a great stir. Was it really possible that Earth—and the people who lived on it— were not at the center of all things?

Copernicus spent much time studying the night sky. He also spent a great deal of time doing mathematics. Copernicus and many other scientists saw astronomy as a kind of mathematics. Astronomy is the science that deals with the sun, moon, stars, and planets. Scientists' ideas began to change when a new way of actually *seeing* the stars was invented. That invention was the telescope, which made faraway things appear close. As you will read, the telescope first became a useful scientific tool in the hands of Galileo Galilei.

Observing the World

Galileo was born in 1564 in the Italian city of Pisa, famous for its Leaning Tower. Like Copernicus, Galileo became interested in mathematics. Everywhere he looked, Galileo saw mathematics as part of daily life. A hailstorm made him wonder, do large hailstones fall faster than smaller ones? Ancient Greek thinkers such as Aristotle said that they do, because large hailstones are heavier than smaller ones. Yet when Galileo carefully watched hail falling from the sky, he thought Aristotle might have been wrong. A new age of testing ideas through observation had begun.

Galileo learned a great deal by looking closely at the world around him. In a cathedral one day, he saw an oil lamp swinging in a draft. Galileo made careful notes about the swinging lamp. Other inventors used Galileo's ideas to create clock pendulums. A pendulum is a weight hung so that it can swing back and forth—much like the oil lamp Galileo noticed!

Copernicus (right) studied the sky and made drawings of planets orbiting the sun (below).

The Granger Collection

Galileo (below) often worked on his telescope and other instruments in his room in Florence, Italy (left).

The Granger Collection

EXPERIMENTS AND INVENTIONS

Not long after he observed the swinging lamp, Galileo went on to study and to teach. Though he loved his new work as a teacher, he did not earn much money. So Galileo tried to come up with ideas for useful items that he could sell. He created the world's first thermometer. A thermometer measures temperature. It was 22 inches long and filled with water. No one had much use for the thermometer in the late 1500s, so it did not seem important then.

Galileo came up with a very successful device, however, in 1609. He learned that a maker of eyeglasses had invented an instrument that made distant things seem close. Galileo quickly made some changes and created his own model of a telescope. He gained wealth and success when he gave a telescope to the ruler of Venice. Commanders of the ruler's navy used the telescope for looking at far-off ships.

A Look into Space

The telescope brought changes to Galileo's life—and to the world—in another way. One night Galileo looked at the moon through the telescope. He expected to see the smooth surface that the ancient Greeks and many others had described. Instead, he saw that the moon was "rough and uneven, covered everywhere, just like Earth's surface, with huge mountains and deep valleys."

Galileo now began to study the sky carefully, night after night. He realized that it was far more complex than most people had ever realized. Far more stars existed than anyone had ever dreamed! Galileo discovered that another planet, Jupiter, also had moons orbiting it—just as the moon orbits Earth. Earth itself appeared to be slowly spinning, and moving around the sun.

Galileo began to think that the long-held belief that Earth was at the center of the universe was wrong. His studies supported Copernicus' heliocentric idea.

Galileo made his findings public in 1610. At the time, it was as if a "new" universe had been discovered. Anyone could see it simply by looking through a telescope. Some people were shocked and surprised. Others, especially Church leaders, were angry.

Science and the Church

Leaders of the Catholic Church prepared to put Galileo on trial. They said that his views went against the Church's teachings. Earlier scientists had been sentenced to death because they wrote about heliocentric ideas.

Galileo, who was Roman Catholic, faced great danger. In 1633 the 69-year-old scientist was arrested and brought to Rome for trial. There Galileo was strongly advised to take back what he had said about the place of the sun in the universe.

Threatened with torture, Galileo finally stated, "I do not hold this opinion of Copernicus." Galileo was then taken back to his home in northern Italy. For the rest of his life, he was not allowed to leave his home. Galileo never publicly upheld the heliocentric view again. Before he died in 1642, though, he wrote:

> *I have two sources of comfort—first, that in my writings there cannot be found the faintest shadow of disobedience towards the Holy Church; and second, the truth of my own conscience, which only I and God in Heaven thoroughly know. And He knows that in this cause for which I suffer, none have spoken with more religious devotion or with greater enthusiasm for the Church than I.*

DID YOU KNOW?

How have telescopes changed since Galileo's time?

Galileo's first telescope was about as long as his arm. It was made only of a tube and two-inch lenses.

By contrast, the Hubble Space Telescope, launched in 1990, is over 43 feet long. It uses mirrors over 7 feet wide and has a tangle of wires 26,000 miles long! The Hubble Telescope travels around Earth at a distance of 380 miles above the planet's surface. From there, the Hubble Telescope can spot stars *trillions* of miles away. Here's another way to put it: The Hubble could spot the punctuation mark at the end of this sentence from a mile away, or a dime from 20 miles away!

The Work of Isaac Newton

In the same year that Galileo died, Isaac Newton was born in the country-side of England. Newton grew up to become one of the world's giants in science. In fact, he built on Galileo's scientific legacy.

According to one story, the young Newton found a key to unlock these mysteries one day in 1675, when an apple fell on his head. The apple's fall from a tree led him to study the force of gravity. Gravity is the force that pulls things toward Earth. Newton calculated that the same force that pulls a falling apple toward Earth also pulls at the moon. Instead of falling to Earth's surface, the moon is kept moving in a circular path around the planet. Newton's study of gravity helped scientists in the late 1600s understand how a heliocentric universe actually worked.

WHY IT MATTERS

European discoveries in science had many results. They led to a new under-standing of humanity's place in the uni-verse and how that universe worked. Improvements in technology came about as well. For example, ship cap-tains could now use telescopes to see faraway land, or to quickly spot enemy ships on the way. The pendulum clock helped people to measure time accurately.

European interest in learning about the natural world had another impor-tant result. It led to the development of what is called the scientific method. The scientific method is a way of ques-tioning and studying things that occur in nature. With this method, an idea must be thoroughly tested before it is accepted as true. This is what Galileo did when he carefully studied the motions of the stars and planets. His experiments, and the work of other sci-entists, led Europe and the rest of the world into a new age of science. Scien-tific advances in astronomy, medicine, and other fields continue to have great effects on the way we live and view the world.

This is a reconstruction of a clock part invented by Galileo. The swinging pendulum causes the gears to move.

✓// Reviewing Facts and Ideas

MAIN IDEAS

- Most Europeans in the Middle Ages shared the ancient Greeks' belief that the universe was geocentric, or cen-tered around Earth.
- In the early 1600s, Galileo Galilei built on the heliocentric, or sun-centered, ideas of Copernicus.
- Galileo's findings clashed with Catholic teachings. The Church sup-ported geocentric ideas.
- Isaac Newton's studies of gravity in the late 1600s helped scientists to learn how a heliocentric system might work.

THINK ABOUT IT

1. How did the scientific method help both Galileo and Newton in their work?

2. Why was Newton's work with gravity important?

3. **FOCUS** How did scientists like Galileo and Newton change the way people thought about the world?

4. **THINKING SKILL** Explain some differ-ent *points of view* people held about the universe in the 1500s. What might account for each of these?

5. **WRITE** Write a paragraph explaining how science affects the way we live today.

MAKING A DIFFERENCE

Experimenting with Science

NEW YORK CITY, NEW YORK—Ever since Adam Exra Cohen was a small child, he's had the mind of an inventor. In third grade he would take home broken computers and televisions. He enjoyed taking them apart and figuring out how they worked. Adam also liked doing science experiments. "Sometimes," he explains, "my mother would bring home a whole fish for dinner. She would let me dissect it in the kitchen sink." His mother had only two rules. His experiments could not be dangerous and he had to clean up afterwards.

By the time Adam was in the fifth grade, he started keeping a notebook of his ideas for inventions. "I drew sketches and made written descriptions of each idea." Now he's up to 160 ideas.

Today, at age 18, this teenage science whiz has invented an amazing new way to build a type of electron microscope called a scanning tunneling microscope. Adam says that a person using this microscope can "scratch as many as 50 words in a space the width of a human hair." It can also be used in making computer chips.

Adam built his award-winning microscope in his bedroom using modeling clay, Legos, and bungee cord. "I used the cord," he explains, "to hang the microscope from the ceiling of my bedroom. This kept the microscope from jiggling around. Vibrations from the air make it harder for the machine to do its work." His microscope also contains some very high-powered electronic parts, but the entire microscope only cost Adam about $100 for parts. Most scanning tunneling microscopes cost many thousands of dollars.

Not all of Adam's inventions work as well as his microscope. In fact, it wasn't until his third science fair that an invention of his was really successful. "I'm always doing lots and lots of experiments," he says. "Most of them don't work. This one did." Adam hopes some day to invent something that he says "will help other people lead easier lives." In the meantime, he has come advice for other young inventors. "Young kids have just as good ideas as grownups. Write down every idea and don't be discouraged. It could be very valuable some day."

"Young kids have just as good ideas as grownups."

1394   1522   1600   1700   1800

An Age of Exploration

Read Aloud

"They sent out a small boat in order to find the cape of the other sea, and they came back at the end of the third day and told how they had seen the cape of the great sea. And the Captain General wept with joy. And they named that cape Cape Desire because they had desired it for so long."

This description was written by a passenger on a ship captained by Ferdinand Magellan (muh JEL un). In the middle 1400s few Europeans had traveled far into the Atlantic Ocean. By 1520, though, European sailors were regularly crossing the Atlantic. One sailor, Magellan, was about to sail into the great Pacific Ocean. His goal was to sail around the world.

Focus Activity

READ TO LEARN

How did European explorers bring distant parts of the world into contact with each other?

VOCABULARY

- caravel
- strait

PEOPLE

- **Prince Henry**
- **Bartholomeu Dias**
- **Vasco da Gama**
- **Christopher Columbus**
- **Ferdinand Magellan**

PLACES

- **Strait of Magellan**

THE BIG PICTURE

In the middle 1400s the Aztec empire and its capital city, Tenochtitlán, were at the height of power and influence in Mexico. Across the Atlantic Ocean in western Africa, meanwhile, gold was flowing north from Mali to the coastal cities of North Africa. Cities in Italy were becoming rich from trade with Asia.

Soon trade would link these different parts of the world more closely. Already goods were moving between Asia, Africa, and Europe. However, the route to Asia was very long and expensive. In order to buy spices and other goods, European merchants would have to find another way to reach Asia. That search would bring the two hemispheres—East and West—into contact.

TRAVEL FOR TRADE

European trade with Asia started to grow thanks largely to Marco Polo's travels on the Silk Road. In 1295 Polo returned to Venice from China. Not long after, his tales of the Silk Road and China became widely known. Polo's accounts made many Europeans want to take part in trade with Asia. Trade along the Silk Road thrived for more than 100 years afterward.

One of the most profitable goods to bring home was pepper. Since people did not have refrigerators, meat quickly spoiled unless it was preserved with salt. The salt, however, gave the meat a flavor that many people did not like. Europeans found that adding pepper made meat taste much better. Pepper became a very popular item.

A journey along the Silk Road sometimes took years to complete and was expensive. Yet those who returned could make as much as 60 times the amount they had spent making the journey. For this reason, some European leaders spent huge sums of money on the search for quicker, cheaper routes to Asia.

The Search for a Shorter Route

Prince Henry of Portugal was one leader who supported the search for such routes. He became known as Henry the Navigator. Henry lived between 1394 and 1460. He wanted to find a sea route to the gold mines of western Africa. He provided money and help to Europe's finest sailors, mapmakers, and shipbuilders. These people improved the compass, updated maps, and simplified the astrolabe, which you read about in Chapter 10.

Most important, the people working with Prince Henry designed a new kind of boat called a caravel (KAR uh vel). Caravels combined the smooth bodies of European sailing ships and the three-sided sails of Arab boats. These sails allowed boats to sail into the wind. Earlier captains usually had to direct their ships wherever the wind was blowing. Now, for the first time, European ships could go in almost any direction their captain wished. You can see a type of caravel on page 462.

Prince Henry helped navigators improve the compass. Italian sailors used this compass (right) around 1580.

1400 1500 1700 1800

Europeans in the Americas

Read Aloud

The commander of the exhausted men drew a line in the sand and challenged, "Here, you return to Panama to be poor; there, you may go on to Peru to be rich. Choose which best becomes you as good Spaniards!"

All but one man crossed the line in the sand with the commander, Francisco Pizarro (frahn SEES koh pih ZAHR oh). They went on to gain great fortunes at the expense of one of the world's largest empires—the Inca empire.

Focus Activity

READ TO LEARN

How did the empires of the Americas fall to Spain?

VOCABULARY

- Line of Demarcation
- conquistador
- missionary
- convert
- hacienda

PEOPLE

- Pedro Álvarez Cabral
- Hernando Cortés
- Moctezuma
- Francisco Pizarro
- Atahualpa

PLACES

- Hispaniola
- Cuzco
- New Spain
- Peru
- Mexico City
- Lima

THE BIG PICTURE

Growth and change were taking place all around the world in the late 1400s. In western Africa the markets of Timbuktu were growing within the Songhai empire. China's Ming rulers were adding to the Great Wall, as Chinese workers produced more and more porcelain, a fine hand pottery, and silk. In the Americas, meanwhile, both the Aztec and Inca empires were growing larger than any civilizations that had yet developed in the Western Hemisphere.

In 1492, Christopher Columbus crossed the Atlantic Ocean, opening up the Americas to European exploration. Within 40 years the Atlantic Ocean had become a vast highway crisscrossed by ships filled with people, trade goods, and treasure. Most of this traffic was controlled by just two European countries—Spain and Portugal. Though these countries were small in size, their power stretched across the globe.

EUROPEAN CLAIMS

In Lesson 2 you read that, in the late 1400s, Europe's race for new routes and territories was on. Portugal and Spain were in the lead. Their leaders believed that they had the right to claim whatever lands they explored. In 1494 the leaders of Spain and Portugal met to divide the lands of the Americas. They agreed upon an imaginary line, called the Line of Demarcation, across a map. Look at the map to see how this line affected claims in the Americas.

In 1493, Columbus had crossed the Atlantic for a second time. He brought more than 1,000 people with him to the island he called Hispaniola (his pun YOH luh). The Spanish were not coming simply to trade or explore—they meant to stay and colonize.

Portugal soon made its own claim in the Americas. Pedro Álvarez Cabral (PE droh AHL vah res kah BRAHL) set sail for India in 1500. A storm blew his ships west. So began a 300-year period of Portuguese rule in Brazil.

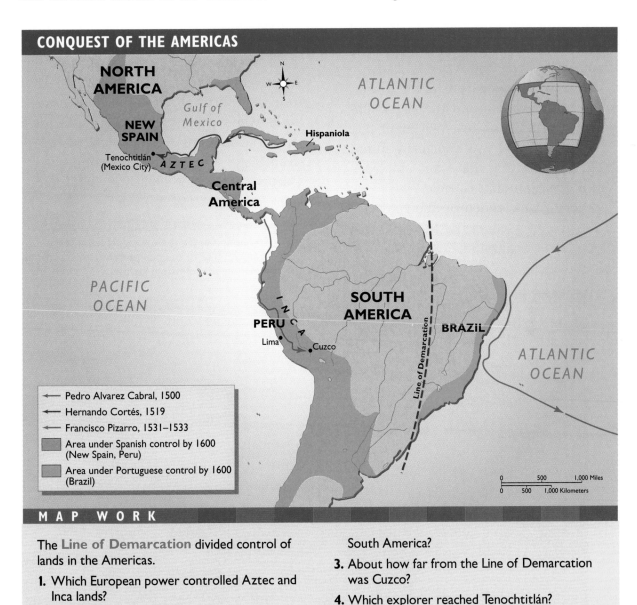

CONQUEST OF THE AMERICAS

NORTH AMERICA

NEW SPAIN

Gulf of Mexico

ATLANTIC OCEAN

Hispaniola

Tenochtitlán (Mexico City)

AZTEC

Central America

PACIFIC OCEAN

SOUTH AMERICA

PERU

Lima

Cuzco

INCA

BRAZIL

Line of Demarcation

ATLANTIC OCEAN

← Pedro Alvarez Cabral, 1500
← Hernando Cortés, 1519
← Francisco Pizarro, 1531–1533
Area under Spanish control by 1600 (New Spain, Peru)
Area under Portuguese control by 1600 (Brazil)

0   500   1,000 Miles
0   500   1,000 Kilometers

M A P   W O R K

The Line of Demarcation divided control of lands in the Americas.

1. Which European power controlled Aztec and Inca lands?

2. Which explorer sailed to the east coast of South America?

3. About how far from the Line of Demarcation was Cuzco?

4. Which explorer reached Tenochtitlán?

THE CONQUISTADORS

Beginning in the early 1500s, Spain sent more men to explore and make claims in the Americas. These conquistadors (kon KEES tuh dawrz), or "conquerors," soon defeated the Aztec and Inca empires and took control of their lands and resources.

Cortés and the Aztec

Conquistador Hernando Cortés (er NAHN doh kor TES) and over 500 soldiers arrived in 1519 in the area that is now Mexico. Cortés had already lived in Spain's Caribbean colonies. He had heard stories of a powerful inland empire. This was the Aztec empire.

With the help of translators who knew both Spanish and the Aztec language, Cortés soon learned about the Aztec people. He was especially interested to learn that the Aztec empire had a great amount of gold.

After Cortés landed on the coast of Mexico, messengers of the Aztec ruler, Moctezuma (mahk tuh ZOO muh), watched his movements. These messengers told the emperor that Cortés and his men were coming to the capital of the empire, Tenochtitlán.

When the Spaniards arrived in the city, Moctezuma welcomed them as guests. That welcome eventually proved the downfall of both Moctezuma and the Aztec empire. With the help of Indians who turned against the Aztec, the conquistadors kidnapped and killed Moctezuma. After a war that ended in 1521, Cortés destroyed Tenochtitlán and conquered the Aztec empire.

Pizarro and the Incas

Ten years after Cortés conquered the Aztec, another conquistador prepared to invade Inca lands. Recall that these lands were located to the south, in the Andes Mountains. Francisco Pizarro (fran SEES koh pee SAHR roh), like Cortés, was a military leader who had

Hernando Cortés (below right) led a large Spanish force in the conquest of Tenochtitlán, shown in the painting (below).

spent some time in the Americas. He too had heard stories of a kingdom filled with treasure.

Pizarro began his conquest of the Inca empire in 1531. The Inca were just ending a civil war that left Atahualpa (ah tah WAHL pah) emperor. As Atahualpa and his army traveled to the Inca capital of Cuzco (KOOZ koh), they heard news of some 160 strangers marching along a nearby coastal road. Meanwhile, Pizarro learned that Atahualpa was nearby. The conquistadors made their way to Atahualpa's camp. There, they were amazed to see the large number of tents that housed the new emperor's army.

This Inca codex, created in 1565, shows a battle between the Spanish and the Inca.

The Death of Atahualpa

That night, Pizarro and his men talked about what they should do when they met with Atahualpa the next day. One soldier later wrote:

> *Few slept, and we kept watch in the square, from which the camp fires of the Indian army could be seen. It was a fearful sight. Most of them were on a hillside and close to one another: it looked like a brilliantly star-studded sky.*

Pizarro chose to set a trap for the emperor and the thousands of Inca who would come with him to the meeting. During the meeting, the conquistadors captured Atahualpa. In exchange for his freedom, the emperor offered to fill the room in which he was held prisoner once with gold and twice with silver. The Inca honored Atahualpa's part of the bargain. Pizarro, nevertheless, ordered the emperor's death. Many bloody battles between the Spanish and the Inca followed. By 1535 much of the 3,000 mile-long Inca empire had fallen to the conquistadors.

The Spread of Spanish Control

By the 1540s conquistadors had claimed land for Spain from what is today Kansas almost to the tip of South America. Spain's rulers divided this enormous area into two colonies, called New Spain and Peru.

New Spain stretched from southern Central America northward into what is now the southwestern United States. Its capital, Mexico City, was built over Tenochtitlán. The colony of Peru—today the name of a country—included most of South America except present-day Brazil. Peru's capital was the coastal city of Lima, built by Pizarro in 1535.

The street plan of Lima showed what life was like in the Americas under Spanish rule. Lima boasted majestic churches and a university. At the center of town stood the homes of Peru's most powerful citizens. Many of these people had been conquistadors like Pizarro. Top government jobs were held by men who were from Europe or had only European heritage. Neither Indians nor *mestizos*, people of both Indian and Spanish heritage, could get such jobs.

This cathedral (left) in Lima is on the site of a church built by the Spanish in 1535. Churches are also found in Peru's rural areas.

LIFE IN SPANISH AMERICA

By the late 1500s it seemed nothing in Spanish America was as powerful as the Catholic Church. Most people who came to the Americas from Spain, whether conquistadors or craftworkers, were Catholic. Among them were missionaries, or people who worked to make others see the truth of their religion. Their main goal was to convert, or win over to Catholicism, the millions of Indians in the Americas.

Missionaries often achieved their goal through teaching. They built churches and schools throughout the colonies. Missionaries educated many Indians in the subjects that Europeans learned about. All schools in New Spain and Peru—including the university— were run by priests and nuns. At times though, the goal to convert Indians was achieved by force.

Indians at Work

Almost half of all Spaniards in the Americas lived in major cities like Lima or Mexico City. Most of the Indians, however, continued to live in the coun-tryside. Many were forced to work on haciendas (ah see EN dahs) owned by Spaniards or the Catholic Church. *Hacienda* is Spanish for a large area of land used for agriculture.

Like the feudal manors of Europe, haciendas were like small towns. Indian families lived and worked there to raise wheat, grapes for wine, cattle, and other products that were sold in colonial cities. Although such products brought large profits to hacienda owners, Indians received low wages. To feed themselves, Indian workers raised corn and beans on small plots of land set aside for their use.

Indians also provided another source of wealth in Spanish America—silver. By law all Indian men had to spend some time working in the silver mines of Peru and New Spain. Men who had to carry the precious metal had the worst job of all. They worked in darkness, with candles tied to their fore-heads or little fingers for light. Carriers hauled as much as 300 pounds of silver at a time. Accidents often happened on what was sometimes a 60-story climb to the mine entrance.

Illness Strikes the Indians

Accidents and overwork caused many Indian deaths. Disease, however, caused an even greater number. Indians had no resistance to, or ability to over-come the effects of, several of the germs that caused diseases in Europe. Historians believe that in the 50 years following conquest, smallpox and measles were among the diseases that caused the most deaths. In those 50 years New Spain's Indian population may have fallen from about 25 million people to under three million. Peru's decreased from perhaps nine million people to under two million.

Hacienda owners, and those who ran the mines, saw a rapid drop in the number of available workers. They soon came up with a new source for cheap workers—enslaved Africans. You will read more about slavery in the Americ-as in the next lesson.

These children are a few of the more than five million people who live and work in Lima today.

WHY IT MATTERS

In 1519, on the eve of Hernando Cortés' journey into Mexico, the Aztec and Inca empires controlled vast stretches of land in the Americas. By the century's end, their lands had been conquered and many monuments destroyed. Many Indians died of disease or overwork.

In the place of the Indian empires, Spanish conquistadors created a new civilization with ties to Spain and Portugal. Many European legacies exist today in the Americas, including languages and the Catholic religion. Legacies of the Aztec and Inca continue, as well. These can be seen in customs, language and, most importantly, people.

Reviewing Facts and Ideas

MAIN IDEAS
- In 1521 Hernando Cortés conquered the Aztec empire for Spain. Francisco Pizarro brought Spanish rule to the people of the Inca empire after 1531.
- Life for Indians in Spanish America was shaped by missionaries, mining, and farm work. Millions died from disease and overwork.

THINK ABOUT IT
1. What is a conquistador?
2. How did Pizarro gain control of the Inca empire?
3. **FOCUS** How did Spain's conquest of the Americas affect Indians there?
4. **THINKING SKILL** Support or deny the *generalization:* "One person can change the world." Use evidence in the lesson.
5. **WRITE** Write a paragraph describing some ways in which Spain might have had trouble controlling its colonies in the faraway Americas.

Determining the Credibility of a Source

VOCABULARY

credibility

WHY THE SKILL MATTERS

In the 1500s news of conquistadors in the Americas spread throughout Spain. Many Europeans learned about the Americas from sources such as books, reports, and letters. Did such sources give them honest and accurate information?

Being able to determine the credibility, or believability, of a source is an important skill. People use many types of sources to learn about unfamiliar things. How can we know which we can believe, and which, perhaps, are less believable?

The most important task in determining the believability of a source is learning as much as possible about its author. Does he or she have a reputation for being accurate? Does he or she have firsthand knowledge of the subject. Does he or she have something to gain by giving false or distorted information?

USING THE SKILL

Suppppose that you came across a letter written in the 1500s by a well-respected traveler. The letter was written to a relative and contained this excerpt about the early Spanish settlement of Mexico City:

Upon my arrival, it was obvious that life is hard in this rough, new city. Furthermore, I soon saw the difficulty of adaptinf our farming techniques to the surrounding area.

Is this a credible source about life in Mexico City? To find out, apply the steps in the

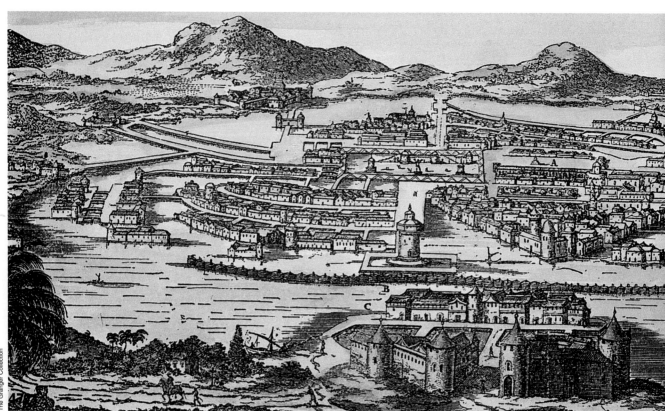

The Granger Collection

Helping Yourself box. The author was a well-respected traveler. We can assume from this that he had a reputation for accuracy. The author visited Mexico City and therefore had firsthand knowledge of the subject. Since the author was writing to a relative, he doesn't appear to have had a reason to portray information inaccurately. From this we can conclude that the source is probably credible.

TRYING THE SKILL

Now consider a second example. Suppose a ship merchant from the 1500s who had never been to the Americas was planning to sail to Mexico City. He was hoping to pay for the passage by carrying passengers. He posted this

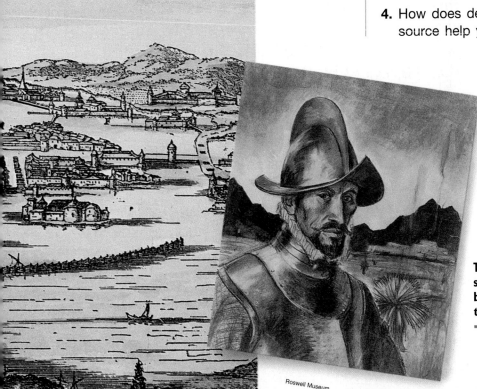

Helping yourself

- Determining the credibility of a source helps you to tell whether the information can be trusted.
- Determine if the source has a reputation for being accurate.
- Determine whether the author has firsthand or expert knowledge of the subject.
- Determine whether the author would have a reason to portray information inaccurately.

notice in the center of a Spanish town.

If you can afford the meager fare, you can join my expedition for Mexico City, where gold and silver glitter from the hills. The land is so fertile that farming is little work at all.

Is this a more or less credible source on Mexico City than the first? Why?

REVIEWING THE SKILL

Use the Helping Yourself box to help you answer the questions below.

1. What are some factors in determining whether a source is credible?

2. How would firsthand knowledge of the author on a subject affect the credibility of his or her information?

3. What are some factors that might make a source less than credible?

4. How does determining the credibility of a source help you in the study of history?

Roswell Museum

This artwork (far left) shows Mexico City, built by the conquistadors on the site of Tenochtitlán.

The Granger Collection

Focus Activity

How did slavery develop in the Americas?

VOCABULARY

- sugarcane
- plantation
- Middle Passage
- triangular trade

PEOPLE

- Olaudah Equiano

PLACES

- West Indies
- Caribbean Sea
- Santo Domingo

1400   1505   1789

Africans in The Americas

Read Aloud

"Among the poor chained men, I found some from my own nation, which in a small way eased my mind. I asked what was to be done with us? They told me we were to be carried to the white people's country to work for them."

An African named Olaudah Equiano (AHL uh duh ih kwee AH nah) (left) wrote about his experiences in 1789. He was a captive on a slave ship bound for the Americas.

THE BIG PICTURE

The islands known as the **West Indies** were explored by Christopher Columbus in 1492. Later, ships loaded with silver from Lima and Mexico City sailed among these islands in the **Caribbean Sea** on their way back to Spain. In the early 1500s, Europeans began to establish colonies in the West Indies. The colonists learned that the region's tropical climate was ideal for growing sugar-producing plants. Enslaved persons were used to produce sugar for European markets.

You have read about slavery many times in this book. Nearly all the ancient empires in every part of the world kept people as property and forced them to work without pay. In the 1500s, however, a new form of slavery, based on an enormous demand for labor, took hold in the Americas. Millions of Africans were forced to lead harsh and difficult lives as slaves. Slavery in the Americas also had far-reaching effects on trade. This new form of slavery would create suffering as well as wealth for people on both sides of the Atlantic Ocean.

WEST INDIAN COLONIES

The first West African slaves were brought to Spanish colonies in the Caribbean about 1505. Many were brought to Santo Domingo, a settlement in what is today the Dominican Republic. Santo Domingo had been established by the Spanish just nine years earlier, in 1496. You can see other European colonies on the map.

The islands' warm climate was perfect for growing sugarcane. Sugarcane is a tall grass with a thick, woody stem. It is a source of sugar. Many Europeans in the West Indies set up sugarcane plantations, or large farms. The region's Arawak Indians worked the plantations. However, like the Inca of South America, many Arawak soon died from diseases brought by the Europeans. Many were also killed in conflicts with the Spaniards.

Slavery in the Colonies

To take the place of the Arawak workers, enslaved people were brought from Africa to the colonies. Between 1500 and the middle 1800s, more than nine million Africans were shipped to the Americas.

Most West Africans who became slaves were kidnapped during surprise attacks led by European, Arab, and African traders. Captives were sold to other traders who would send them across the Atlantic Ocean to the West Indies. During the voyage across the Atlantic, captured Africans experienced many hardships. This part of the journey to the Americas became known as the Middle Passage. Captives were chained in crowded sections of ships. They were often given spoiled food and unclean water. Large numbers did not survive the voyage.

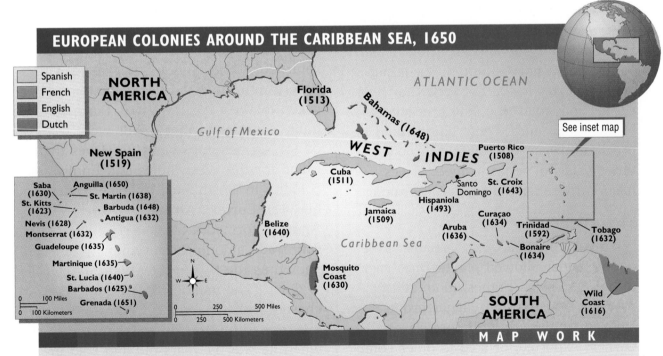

EUROPEAN COLONIES AROUND THE CARIBBEAN SEA, 1650

Legend:
- Spanish
- French
- English
- Dutch

NORTH AMERICA

Florida (1513)

ATLANTIC OCEAN

Bahamas (1648)

Gulf of Mexico

See inset map

WEST INDIES

Puerto Rico (1508)

New Spain (1519)

Cuba (1511)

Santo Domingo

St. Croix (1643)

Saba (1630)
Anguilla (1650)
St. Martin (1638)
St. Kitts (1623)
Barbuda (1648)
Nevis (1628)
Antigua (1632)
Montserrat (1632)
Guadeloupe (1635)
Martinique (1635)
St. Lucia (1640)
Barbados (1625)
Grenada (1651)

Hispaniola (1493)

Jamaica (1509)

Curaçao (1634)

Aruba (1636)

Trinidad (1592)

Tobago (1632)

Belize (1640)

Caribbean Sea

Bonaire (1634)

Mosquito Coast (1630)

0   100 Miles
0   100 Kilometers

N W E S

0   250   500 Miles
0   250   500 Kilometers

SOUTH AMERICA

Wild Coast (1616)

MAP WORK

By 1650 most of the islands of the Caribbean Sea had been claimed as colonies by European powers.

1. Which power claimed the largest land area in the Americas?

2. Which European power claimed Nevis?

3. Which European power was best positioned to challenge Spain's Carribbean lands? Why?

PLANTATIONS AND THE SUGAR TRADE

Plantation owners depended on the hard work of enslaved Africans for success. Slaves cleared forests for planting. They hoed the soil and kept fields clear of weeds. At harvesttime they cut sugarcane all day in the hot sun. They also rushed the sugarcane stalks, or stems, to plantation mills. There liquid could be pressed out and boiled. During boiling, tiny crystals of sugar formed. Slaves filled barrel after barrel with the sugar.

The Atlantic Routes

Barrels of sugar were valuable trade goods. Sugar allowed plantation owners to buy expensive clothes, food, and furniture. Most important, sugar profits enabled planters to buy more slaves. Owners exported, or sold to other countries, sugar. Enslaved Africans were imported, or brought from other lands. This exporting and importing of sugar and slaves tightly linked plantations to the rest of the world.

Ships loaded with sugar traveled from the West Indies to Europe. Some returned to the West Indies loaded with fine furniture or cloth. Many, though, sailed to West Africa. There, European guns, cloth, and other goods were traded for slaves. Ships carrying slaves then sailed for the West Indies and English colonies in North America. The routes between Europe, Africa, and North America formed a triangle. For this reason, trade among these regions was known as the triangular trade.

One of the millions of Africans purchased in the triangular trade was Olaudah Equiano. He was kidnapped when he was 11 years old and sold in 1756. Read the following short piece from his autobiography, the story of his life. How was Equiano treated on the slave ship? How does he describe the way Africans lived in Jamaica?

Excerpt from
The Life of Olaudah Equiano,
written by himself, 1789.

*The first object which saluted my eyes when I arrived on the [African] coast, was the sea, and a slave ship, which was then riding at anchor, and waiting for its cargo. . . . I was soon put down under the decks, and there . . . , with the **loathsomeness** of the **stench**, and crying together, I . . . wished for the last friend, death, to relieve me. . . .*

*I found Jamaica to be a very fine, large island. . . . There (were) a vast number of Negroes here, whom I found as usual, **exceedingly imposed** upon by the white people, and the slaves punished as in the other islands. . . . When I came to **Kingston**, I was surprised to see the number of Africans who were assembled together on Sundays. . . . Here each different nation of Africa meet and dance after the manner of their own country.*

loathsomeness: quality of being hateful or disgusting
stench: odor
exceedingly: to a large degree
imposed: to have had unfair demands made upon one
Kingston: a large town in Jamaica

WHY IT MATTERS

The civilization developed by Europeans in the West Indies affected not only that region but also the whole world. The demands of working on a sugarcane plantation cost the lives of thousands of Arawak Indians. Those Indian workers were replaced by enslaved people taken from their homes in Africa. Sugar from the plantations, and slaves themselves, became valuable and important goods in a triangle of trade that involved the West Indies, Europe, and Africa. By the 1800s the fortunes made in the sugar trade helped to make islands in the West Indies among the wealthiest and most powerful in the world. In time, as you will read in Chapter 17, those enslaved persons who made sugar plantations successful would fight for their own freedom.

✓ Reviewing Facts and Ideas

MAIN IDEAS

- The warm climate of islands in the West Indies was perfect for growing sugarcane.

- Sugarcane plantations in the West Indies depended on enslaved Africans for success.

- Between 1500 and the middle 1800s, more than nine million Africans were shipped to the Americas as slaves. They had been kidnapped from their homes and brought to slave ships.

- Trade of sugar, European goods, and slaves linked the West Indies, Africa, and Europe in the triangular trade.

THINK ABOUT IT

1. How did trade link the West Indies with other parts of the world?

2. How did many Africans become slaves?

3. **FOCUS** Why did slavery develop on sugarcane plantations in the West Indies?

4. **THINKING SKILL** Analyze the *credibility* of Olaudah Equiano as a source of information about slavery. What steps will you follow?

5. **GEOGRAPHY** Why was sugarcane a successful crop in the West Indies?

1400   1500   1606   1894

A European Colony in Australia

Read Aloud

"All the bondage I am under is to answer my name every Sunday before I goes to church, so you must not think that I am made a slave of. . . . I have got plenty to eat and drink as good as ever a gentleman in this country [has] . . . "

This letter was written in 1883 by a political prisoner serving his sentence in Australia. While some prisoners sent there were treated harshly, others saw Australia as a land of opportunity.

Focus Activity

READ TO LEARN

How did democracy develop in Australia?

VOCABULARY

- aborigine
- convict
- emancipee

PEOPLE

- James Cook
- Elizabeth Veale
- Lachlan Macquarie

PLACES

- New South Wales

THE BIG PICTURE

As you read in Lesson 2, Europeans set out in the 1400s to find new trade routes to the East. In the 1500s, explorers also began to search for a legendary southern continent that had been rumored to exist for centuries. It was called the "terra australis incognita," which means "unknown southern land" in Latin.

Would the continent turn out to be as rich as the Americas? When explorers reached Australia, they were disappointed. To their eyes, much of the land was very dry and did not look promising.

In 1788, the English founded **New South Wales**, the first European settlement in Australia. At first, New South Wales was a prison colony. In time, the colony would become a thriving democracy in which both ex-prisoners and free settlers would have the right to vote. For Australia's original inhabitants, however, the coming of the English meant disaster.

A DIFFICULT LAND

Australia's first inhabitants were aborigines (ab or IH jin eez). The term aborigine means that they were the original people to live in this land. Historians believe that they arrived in Australia between 40,000 and 100,000 years ago from Indonesia and Asia.

The aborigines believed that the land was created by great spirits during a period called the "dreamtime." They also believed that the spirits created the "dream trails" across earth that connected important places for food and water. The aborigines' survival often depended on these trails, which could stretch over a thousand miles. They believed that land was a sacred gift and could not be owned.

This aboriginal art (above) was created with tree bark, ochre, and natural pigments.

In 1606, the Dutch landed on Australia—although historians think that Asian and Portuguese ships had probably visited Australia before this. The Dutch did not see any gold, only flat and dry land. Disappointed, they soon lost interest in Australia.

New South Wales

In 1768, England sent James Cook, a respected navigator, to explore the southern continent. In 1770, Cook claimed land for England on the East Coast of Australia, naming it New South Wales after a region of Great Britain.

Traveling with Cook was a young scientist named Joseph Banks. Banks sketched and labeled 1,600 species of Australian plants that were previously unknown to Europeans. He reported that the land was rich and fertile.

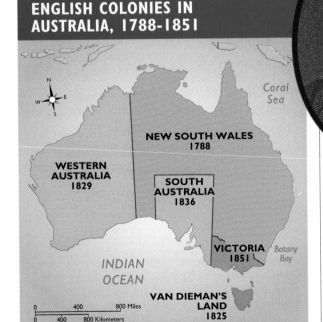

ENGLISH COLONIES IN AUSTRALIA, 1788-1851

Coral Sea

NEW SOUTH WALES
1788

WESTERN AUSTRALIA
1829

SOUTH AUSTRALIA
1836

VICTORIA 1851   Botany Bay

INDIAN OCEAN

VAN DIEMAN'S LAND
1825

0   400   800 Miles
0   400   800 Kilometers

M A P   W O R K

James Cook, right, landed in Botany Bay during his exploration of Australia.

1. What was the second colony to be founded, after New South Wales?

2. What was the second smallest colony in 1836?

CONVICTS IN THE NEW COLONY

For decades, England's jails had been overcrowded. Following a policy called "transportation," some prisoners had been sent to work in the American colonies. After the American Revolution, the English needed a new place to send its prison convicts. A convict is a person who has been found guilty by the government of committing a crime and has received a sentence for it. The English government decided to send many of its convicts to New South Wales.

The first ships carrying convicts arrived in Australia in January 1788 with 736 convicts and about 200 soldiers. The oldest convict was eighty-two years old. The youngest was nine. Some convicts had committed serious crimes such as violent robbery. Others were in chains for their political beliefs or for pickpocketing. One man was sentenced for destroying 12 cucumber plants. All convicts were sentenced to work for the new colony's government for at least seven years.

At first, soldiers and convicts struggled side by side to survive in New South Wales. They had few tools to build housing. Droughts and unfamiliar soil ruined crops. Many convicts and soldiers suffered from near-starvation.

During the 1790s, as the colony became more successful, the promise of land and a fresh start attracted free settlers to Australia. The convicts soon filled the important role of providing labor to the free settlers. Like slaves, the convicts' fates depended on the kindness or cruelty of their masters. Unlike slaves, convicts were never considered property. Some convicts who behaved well could return to England. Many, however, stayed in Australia to work for themselves or as laborers. Convicts were often given land when their sentences ended.

Many women, convict and free, helped build the colony's future. One such woman was Elizabeth Veale, who was married to a successful sheep owner named John Macarthur. Her husband spent much of his time outside the colony. As a result, she was often responsible for running their estate in Australia. She did this very successfully, and helped establish the production of wool as an important industry in Australia.

Convict laborers in New South Wales had rights often denied to slaves, such as the right to bring their master to court for ill-treatment.

Lachlan Macquarie created a public works program and established a currency for New South Wales.

Conflict and Opportunity

As colonists settled new land, they clashed with the aborigines who had only simple weapons with which to defend themselves. Eventually, European diseases and guns would almost wipe out the aborigines.

Conflict also developed between groups of English settlers. One such group of settlers were emancipees (e MAN sih peez). Emancipees were convicts who had been freed from their sentence. Many landowners who had never been convicts did not want emancipees to have the rights they had.

Lachlan Macquarie (LAHK lan mak WAR ee), who favored the rights of emancipees, became governor of New South Wales in 1810. Once he invited some of the emancipees to dinner to show his support for them. Many of the non-convicted settlers were outraged. Macquarie also showed support by choosing Francis Greenaway, an ex-convict, as his architect when he built a hospital for the new colony.

As the colony grew, new British laws allowed the passage of the New South Wales Act of 1823. This enabled the colony to create a legislative body. In 1842 free settlers, including emancipees, won the right to vote for its members. Similar changes took place in other colonies, which were founded as British colonists settled more land in Australia.

Although unable to vote at this time, women would win the vote in the colony of South Australia in 1894. Australia was becoming one of the important democratic nations of the world.

WHY IT MATTERS

Convicts and soldiers struggled together to build a colony 15,000 miles across the ocean from their homes in England. Convicts arrived in chains, but they were not slaves. When their sentences ended, they were often granted land and the chance to participate in a democratic government.

As in the Americas, the original inhabitants of Australia did not fare well when the Europeans arrived. Currently, however, the Australian government is seeking to better recognize the aborigines' claims to their lands.

Reviewing Facts and Ideas

MAIN IDEAS

- Australia's first inhabitants were aborigines. The arrival of the colonists almost destroyed their way of life.

- After the American Revolution, England chose Australia as a new place to send its convicts.

- Australia's English settlers developed a democratic system of government.

THINK ABOUT IT

1. Why did European explorers begin to search for a southern continent?

2. Why was there conflict between the emancipees and the free settlers?

3. **FOCUS** What were the stages in Australia's development of democracy?

4. **THINKING SKILL** How might the different ideas of land ownership between colonists and aborigines have been a _cause_ of their conflict?

5. **GEOGRAPHY** Where in Australia did the English discover fertile land?

CHAPTER 16 REVIEW

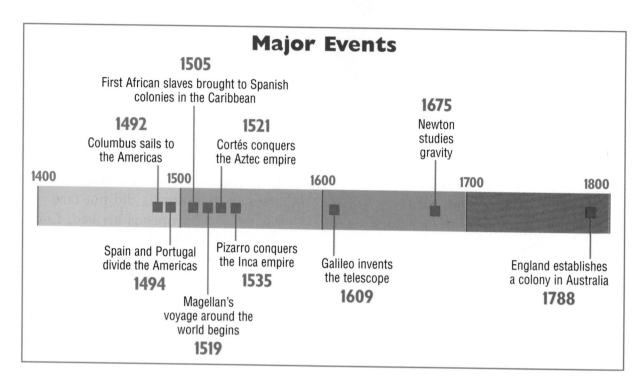

Major Events

1505
First African slaves brought to Spanish colonies in the Caribbean

1492
Columbus sails to the Americas

1521
Cortés conquers the Aztec empire

1675
Newton studies gravity

1400   1500   1600   1700   1800

Spain and Portugal divide the Americas
1494

Pizarro conquers the Inca empire
1535

Galileo invents the telescope
1609

England establishes a colony in Australia
1788

Magellan's voyage around the world begins
1519

THINKING ABOUT VOCABULARY

Number a sheet of paper from 1 to 10. Beside each number write the word or term from the list below that best completes the sentence.

caravel
conquistador
credibility
geocentric
Line of Demarcation

Middle Passage
plantations
scientific method
strait
telescope

1. The _____ was a voyage that captured Africans were forced to make.

2. Galileo's invention of the _____ allowed him to study the sky more closely.

3. A _____ is a narrow waterway that connects two larger bodies of water.

4. The Portuguese ship that allowed explorers to sail into the wind was the _____.

5. Thoroughly testing an idea before accepting it as true is the _____.

6. Large farms in the West Indies where sugarcane was grown were called _____.

7. Somebody who can not be believed has lost his or her _____.

8. A _____ was a military person sent to the Americas to explore and gain land for Spain.

9. In 1494 Spain and Portugal drew the _____ to divide lands in the New World between them.

10. _____ means "centered around Earth."

THINKING ABOUT FACTS

1. What was Isaac Newton's main contribution to science?

2. What did Portuguese explorers accomplish in the New World?

3. How did colonial trade link the West Indies to other parts of the world?

4. What was one important result of England's system of transportation for convicts?

5. According to the time line above, which were the first two European countries to colonize the Americas?

THINK AND WRITE

WRITING AN ESSAY

Write a short essay about differences between Spanish and English colonies that are discussed in this chapter. Mention what each country gained from its settlements. Also describe the way the colonists interacted with the original inhabitants of the land they settled.

WRITING BIOGRAPHICAL PARAGRAPHS

Write a paragraph about two of the following people: (1) Galileo (2) Henry the Navigator (3) Magellan (4) Cortés.

WRITING ABOUT PERSPECTIVES

Write about the different perspectives Native Americans and Europeans had toward each other in the 1500s. What do you think each thought of the other one? What do you think they might have found strange? What do you think they might have found appealing?

APPLYING THINKING SKILLS

EVALUATING THE CREDIBILITY OF A SOURCE

1. What is a credible source?

2. To evaluate the credibility of a source, what three things should you find out?

3. Reread the account of Olaudah Equiano on page 474. Do you find it credible? Why or why not?

4. Give an example of an account of the trip slaves were forced to make from Africa that would be less credible than Equiano's.

5. In what ways will this skill be helpful to you as a student?

Summing Up the Chapter

Copy the main-idea pyramid below on a separate sheet of paper. Then review the chapter to find information to finish filling in the pyramid. When you have filled in the pyramid, use the information to answer the question "What were the main accomplishments of European scientists and explorers from the 1400s to the 1700s?"

Europeans from the 1400s to the 1700s made important discoveries in science and exploration.

Europeans explore the world and establish colonies

European scientists make important discoveries

Cortés - Mexico

Revolutions Change the World

THINKING ABOUT HISTORY AND GEOGRAPHY

In this chapter you will read about revolutions that changed the lives of people around the world. Follow the time line and the map to find out when and where these changes occurred. Some happened very quickly while others took longer. In each case, people's lives were changed, with effects that are still felt today.

PACIFIC OCEAN

1821

CARABOBO, VENEZUELA
Simon Bolívar defeats the Spanish army

1789

PARIS, FRANCE
French citizens storm the Bastille

1810

DOLORES, MEXICO
Miguel Hidalgo calls on Mexicans to fight for freedom

1775

1800

1825

NORTH
AMERICA

Dolores

Gulf of
Mexico

ATLANTIC OCEAN

Carabobo

Manchester

Paris

EUROPE

ASIA

Tokyo

AFRICA

INDIAN
OCEAN

1824

**MANCHESTER,
ENGLAND**

Workers form unions to
demand shorter hours and
better pay

1868

TOKYO, JAPAN

The Meiji era begins

1850

1875

1700   1750   1789   1815   1850   1900

The French Revolution

Read Aloud

Can you not hear in your hearts the voices of the citizens who died? Can you not see all the nations of the world, all the generations present and future, waiting until you show them whether the King has the right to murder citizens and groups without punishment; whether a monarch is a god whose actions must be blessed or a man whose crimes must be punished."

The words above were spoken by Jean Mailhe (MAY yuh) in France in 1792. As a member of the newly elected National Assembly, Mailhe was calling for the execution, or killing, of the king.

Focus Activity

READ TO LEARN

What conditions led to the French Revolution?

VOCABULARY

- absolute monarchy
- divine right
- revolution
- estates
- aristocracy
- peasants
- Declaration of the Rights of Man and of the Citizen
- Reign of Terror

PEOPLE

- Louis XVI
- Marie Antoinette
- Maximilien Robespierre
- Napoleon Bonaparte

PLACES

- Versailles
- Paris
- Bastille

THE BIG PICTURE

Just four years earlier King Louis XVI held firm control over his kingdom. France was an **absolute monarchy**. This means that the king had complete power to govern. His title, "Louis, by the Grace of God, King of France," showed the belief in his **divine right**. Divine right was a belief that a monarch's authority came from God. Now, in a sudden turn of events, the king faced the judgment of people he once ruled.

Throughout the continent, a system of rule based on the power of monarchs, nobles, and church leaders had been in place for centuries. Unhappiness with this system, however, was leading the people of France closer to a **revolution**. A revolution is a sudden or great change. The revolution in France would upset the old system of government and change Europe.

AN AGE OF DISCONTENT

In many ways France in 1789 was not much different from France in the Middle Ages. Although feudalism no longer existed, most people still worked the land. By 1789, however, the population had been divided into three estates, or social classes. The chart on this page shows France's three estates.

The Three Estates

The First Estate was made up of the Catholic clergy. The clergy consists of people who perform religious services. About 130,000 of France's 26 million people belonged to the clergy. The wealthy Catholic Church owned nearly 15 percent of France's land and paid no regular taxes.

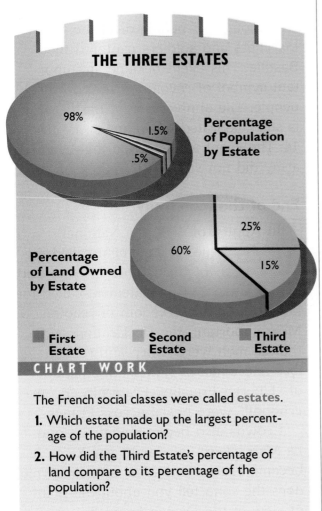

THE THREE ESTATES

98%
1.5%
.5%
Percentage of Population by Estate

25%
60%
15%
Percentage of Land Owned by Estate

■ First Estate ■ Second Estate ■ Third Estate

CHART WORK

The French social classes were called estates.

1. Which estate made up the largest percentage of the population?

2. How did the Third Estate's percentage of land compare to its percentage of the population?

Aristocracy (ar uh STOHK ruh see) made up the Second Estate. The aristocracy included members of noble families. In the late 1700s nobles owned about 25 percent of the land in France. Most of them did not pay taxes. Although most nobles were rich, they had little power in government. In fact they were unhappy that the king held all political power in France. Even the richest nobles could not make laws.

The vast majority of people, nearly 98 percent, belonged to the Third Estate. This group included merchants and lawyers as well as craftworkers and peasants. Peasants are farm workers. A few members of the Third Estate were rich. Most, however, were poor.

Although many peasants owned land, they often did not have enough to support themselves and their families. One traveler described a seven-year-old peasant girl as "terribly ragged, if possible worse clad than if with no clothes at all." The different members of the Third Estate had two things in common. They paid taxes and had no say in how they were governed.

This cartoon from 1789 shows the First and Second estates riding on the back of the Third Estate.

A STRUGGLE FOR LIBERTY

By the late 1770s the French had been greatly influenced by the American Revolution. One French noblewoman said,

The American cause seemed our own; we were proud of their victories, we cried at their defeats, we tore down bulletins and read them in our houses. None of us reflected on the danger that the New World could give to the Old.

France had given millions of dollars to support the American colonies in their war against the British. This expense, as well as the cost of the king's lifestyle, drained money from the French government. By 1789 there was no money left.

The Revolution Begins

King Louis XVI hoped to raise more money by taxing the nobles, or the Second Estate. The nobles refused. They demanded a meeting of the Estates General. The Estates General was a group made up of representatives from each of the three estates.

The Estates General met near the king's palace in Versailles (vair SIGH) in May of 1789. Members of the Third Estate wanted equal rights. They did not like being the least powerful group in France. A priest described the dissatisfaction of the Third Estate:

What is the Third Estate? Everything. What has it been up 'til now in the political order? Nothing. What does it desire to be? Something.

Soon the members of the Third Estate began meeting to write a constitution. They formed a new law making body, called the National Assembly. The French Revolution had begun.

Storming the Bastille

Struggle for power between the estates and the king developed so quickly that rumors began to fly. One rumor was that the king was sending troops to break up the National Assembly. On July 14, 1789, about 800 people gathered in Paris, the capital of France. They marched to the big stone prison fortress called the Bastille (bas TEEL). They hoped to get weapons there to defend themselves. As people surrounded the prison, someone fired a cannon into the crowd.

Nearby, a citizen named Pierre Hulin convinced a group of 60 soldiers to help the crowd. "Do you not hear the cannons? Parisians are being slaughtered like sheep. Will you not march on the Bastille?" he said.

Although 98 people died, the marchers and soldiers captured the Bastille. This event became an important symbol of revolution to the French people. The anniversary of Bastille Day is still celebrated in France every July 14. The event also showed that even the army did not support the king.

End of the Monarchy

In August of 1789 the National Assembly issued a statement called the Declaration of the Rights of Man and of the Citizen. This statement called for fair taxation and freedom of religion. Most important, the Declaration said that all men were "born and remain free and equal in rights." Soon shouts of "Liberty! Equality! Fraternity [brotherhood]!" were heard across France.

Crowds also began singing a song, *La Marseillaise* (lah mahr say YEZ). It became France's national anthem. What does the song tell you about the point of view of the French people?

NEW RULERS IN FRANCE

The old France was gone. A new democratic government was rising in its place. The king was still leader of the government, but the National Assembly now had most of the power. In 1791 King Louis XVI was forced to approve the Declaration of the Rights of Man and of the Citizen.

After approving the Declaration, King Louis, Queen Marie Antoinette (muh REE an twuh NET), and their family tried to escape. They left Paris disguised as a family of tourists. They had not gone far, however, before someone recognized the king from his picture on money. The man tipped over a cart of furniture on a bridge to block the family's escape. Soldiers soon arrived and returned the royal family to Paris. In 1792 the monarchy was abolished and France became a republic.

The Reign of Terror

The change from a monarchy to a republic was not smooth for France. The Assembly angered many people by taking all land away from the Catholic Church. Priests who did not support the revolution lost their churches.

Maximilien Robespierre (MAX ih mihl yen ROHBZ pee air), a Revolution leader, became the most powerful man in the new government. He waged a war against enemies of the revolution by executing suspects. This period of cruelty became known as the Reign of Terror.

Robespierre's weapon was a machine, the guillotine (GEE oh teen),

Marie Antoinette (above), Queen of France and wife of Louis XVI, was beheaded in 1793. The guillotine (below) killed thousands during the revolution.

with a steel blade that chopped off people's heads. In January 1793 King Louis XVI was tried and executed by guillotine in a public square in Paris. Queen Marie Antoinette's execution by guillotine followed in October.

Aristocrats and nobles were targeted for death. However, it seemed no one was safe from the threat of execution. People feared execution for such "crimes" as giving sour wine to soldiers or weeping at the murder of a family member. When the Reign of Terror came to an end in 1794, about 40,000 French citizens had been killed. One of them was Robespierre himself.

The Revolution Ends

The time has come when people would ask for bread and be given corpses.

The woman who wrote this statement lived during the Reign of Terror.

She summed up the disappointment that many people felt. Five years of revolution and bloodshed left many people hoping for peace and stability.

In this environment, the army gained more and more power. A 26-year-old general named Napoleon Bonaparte (nuh POH lee un BOH nuh pahrt), from the island of Corsica, became extremely popular. His success in a French war against Italy won him great support. When he returned to Paris in 1799, one newspaper reported: "Everyone is thrilled" by his victory.

Five years later, the young general had gained control of the new French Republic and crowned himself Emperor Napoleon I. Barely 10 years after the execution of Louis XVI, France had another absolute ruler. The French Republic was over.

After making himself emperor of France in 1804, Napoleon set out to conquer lands across Europe.

WHY IT MATTERS

Napoleon expanded French power across Europe. His armies conquered Holland, Germany, Italy, and Belgium, bringing new riches to the French.

Although France once again had a monarch, many of the changes that had come with the Revolution remained. For example, the old system of three estates was gone forever.

Napoleon's vast empire collapsed in 1815. The French began again to build a republic. They picked up many of the ideas that had fueled the revolution 25 years earlier. After the fateful events in France in 1789, the world would never be the same again. From India to Turkey to South America, the ideas of "Liberty, Equality, Fraternity" sparked national freedom movements around the world.

✓✓ Reviewing Facts and Ideas

MAIN IDEAS

- Before the Revolution French society was divided into three "estates."
- The French Revolution began in 1789.
- Robespierre's Reign of Terror brought fear and disorder to France.
- Napoleon Bonaparte created a huge European empire.

THINK ABOUT IT

1. Who made up the Three Estates?
2. Why was a meeting of the Estates General called in 1789?
3. **FOCUS** List three reasons for the discontent among many French people before the Revolution.
4. **THINKING SKILL** What *effects* did the American Revolution have on France?
5. **WRITE** As a member of the Third Estate, write a paragraph describing changes you would like to see.

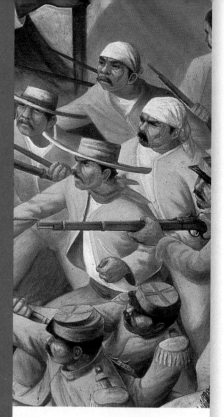

1700 1750 1791 1867 1900

The Colonies Gain Independence

Read Aloud

"We are threatened with the fear of death, dishonor, and every harm; there is nothing we have not suffered at the hands of . . . Spain."

Simón Bolívar (see MOHN boh LEE vahr) wrote these words in a letter in 1815. He went on to free his native Venezuela and several other South American nations from Spanish rule. Freedom was a goal that inspired many people in colonies around the world.

Focus Activity

READ TO LEARN

How did European colonies gain independence?

VOCABULARY

- Latin America
- mestizo
- confederation

PEOPLE

- Toussaint L'Ouverture
- Miguel Hidalgo
- José María Morelos
- Agustín de Iturbide
- Simón Bolívar
- José de San Martín

PLACES

- Hispaniola
- Dolores
- Venezuela

THE BIG PICTURE

In the year 1800 the United States was the only independent country in the Americas. Yet the desire for independence was felt in colonies throughout the world. The American and French Revolutions caused others in the Americas to think about gaining their own rights. Many Spanish colonists said, "I am not a Spaniard, I am American." These feelings spread throughout **Latin America**. Latin America is a cultural region south of the United States that was strongly influenced by Spain, Portugal, and France.

Europe's costly wars with Napoleon made it possible for colonies to take control of their own governments. A period of 300 years of European rule in the Americas was ending. By 1830 North and South America were made up almost entirely of independent nations. Eventually, Australia would also begin the journey towards independence.

A SPIRIT OF FREEDOM

Although each colony in Latin America was unique, all had some things in common. For one, they felt that European nations were taking advantage of them. Europeans took minerals and crops, but gave little in return.

People born in the Latin American colonies struggled to grow crops or to work in mines for other people. Like the English colonists of North America, Latin Americans also had to pay taxes without having a voice in their government. One popular song expressed the Latin American colonists' viewpoint:

If anyone wants to know
Why I go shirtless
It's because of the taxes
Of the king.

Revolution in the Caribbean

The first rumblings of independence began on the large Caribbean island of Hispaniola (hihs pun YOH luh). Although Columbus had claimed Hispaniola for Spain in 1492, France controlled the western part of the island. In the French colony, called Saint Domingue (san duh MANG), enslaved Africans grew coffee and sugar on plantations.

When the French Revolution broke out across the Atlantic, distant cries of "Liberty, Equality, Fraternity" echoed in Saint Domingue. In 1791 a group of about 100,000 slaves rose up against plantation owners. This group was led by Toussaint L'Ouverture (too SAN loo ver TYUR). L'Ouverture believed that slavery was wrong. He and other former slaves forced the French to abolish it throughout Saint Domingue. In 1796 L'Ouverture took control of the colony's government.

In 1802 Napoleon Bonaparte tried to regain control of Saint Domingue. He sent a huge army to restart the practice of slavery on the island. This time L'Ouverture began a revolution to drive the French out completely.

Although L'Ouverture was captured and taken to France, the revolution became the first successful slave revolution in history. From it, the independent country of Haiti was born on Hispaniola in 1804.

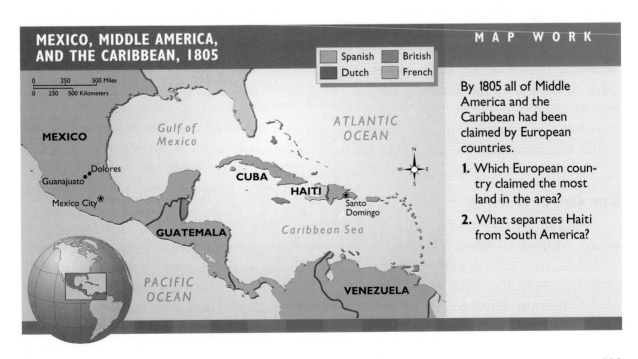

MEXICO, MIDDLE AMERICA, AND THE CARIBBEAN, 1805

Spanish | British
Dutch | French

0 250 500 Miles
0 250 500 Kilometers

MEXICO
Gulf of Mexico
ATLANTIC OCEAN
Dolores
Guanajuato
Mexico City
CUBA
HAITI
Santo Domingo
GUATEMALA
Caribbean Sea
PACIFIC OCEAN
VENEZUELA
N W E S

MAP WORK

By 1805 all of Middle America and the Caribbean had been claimed by European countries.

1. Which European country claimed the most land in the area?

2. What separates Haiti from South America?

493

This painting by Mexican artist José Orozco shows Miguel Hidalgo rallying Mexicans to fight for independence from Spain.

REVOLUTION IN MEXICO

Six years after independence in Haiti, the bells of freedom began ringing in Mexico as well. The Spanish grip on New Spain, or Mexico, weakened when Napoleon conquered Spain in 1808.

Mexico was the richest of Spain's colonies. Remember that the colony's economy depended on silver mines and large farms called haciendas. Nearly half of the money made here went to the king's treasury in Spain. As a result, a few Mexicans became very rich. Most, though, were very poor.

The Call of Dolores

One Sunday morning in 1810, a priest, Miguel Hidalgo (mee GEL ee DAHL goh) was speaking to the poor people in the town of Dolores (doh LOHR es). Hidalgo felt a duty to improve life for Mexicans. He called upon his listeners to sweep the Europeans from office and create a better government. In this stirring speech, now known as *The Call of Dolores,* Hidalgo encouraged the local people to "recover from the hated Spaniards the land stolen from your forefathers."

The response to Hidalgo's speech was explosive. His words fueled a revolution that called for freedom from Spain and equality for all people. Most of Hidalgo's supporters were poor Native Americans and mestizos (me STEE sohs). Mestizos are people of mixed Native American and European ancestry. People of African descent also joined the cause.

Combined, the poor mestizos and Mexicans of African descent made up about 80 percent of Mexico's population. Some Mexicans of European descent also supported the movement for independence.

494

A Setback

The angry crowd in Dolores arrested Spanish officials and destroyed Spanish haciendas. The number of revolutionaries swelled to 25,000, and Hidalgo's army captured the nearby city of Guanajuato (gwah nah HWAH toh). As they moved on toward Mexico City, another 60,000 people joined in the march. Hidalgo called for equality for all groups. He also declared the end of slavery and the unfair taxes that the people had to pay the Spanish government.

Hidalgo's army never reached Mexico City. The Spanish army pursued the rebels, captured Hidalgo, and executed him in 1811. All hope for the Mexican war of independence seemed lost.

After Hidalgo's death, another priest, named José María Morelos (ho SE mah REE ah moh RE lohs), carried on the revolution. Morelos led a small army in central Mexico. He fought strong Spanish forces for several years. In 1813 Morelos called Mexico's first national congress and declared the colony's independence from Spain. In 1815, like Hidalgo before him, Morelos was captured and killed by Spanish soldiers.

An Independent Mexico

One of the soldiers who had fought against both Hidalgo and Morelos soon came to power. Agustín de Iturbide was an officer in the Spanish army. In 1821 Iturbide issued the *Plan de Iguala* (PLAHN DE ee GWAH lah). It described his own ideas about Mexico.

All inhabitants of New Spain, without any distinction between Europeans, Africans, and Indians, are citizens of this monarchy. . . . Behold the sweet chain that unites us; consider the bonds of friendship, interdependence of interest, education, language, and harmony of feelings. . . . The time has arrived . . . that our union should emancipate [free] America without need of foreign help. At the head of a brave and determined army, I [declare] the Independence of Northern America.

Finally, 11 years after Miguel Hidalgo rang the bell at his church in Dolores, Mexico was independent. However, Hidalgo's dream of liberty and equality for all Mexicans was lost. In 1822 Iturbide declared himself Emperor of Mexico. Five months later he dismissed the congress Morelos had started. Many years would pass before all Mexicans were given a say in their government.

This huge monument was built in honor of José Morelos.

INDEPENDENCE MOVES

The forces of liberty soon pressed upon other parts of the world. Beginning in 1810 the Spanish-speaking colonies of South America began to revolt. Brazil, ruled by Portugal, was not far behind. On the other side of the world, Australia was also headed for change.

The Liberator of South America

The driving force behind independence in South America was Simón Bolívar. Bolívar was born into one of the richest families in Venezuela. He had read books by French writers explaining ideas of freedom. Liberty and equality served as the main goals of his struggle. Bolívar offered the hope of freedom from colonial rule to all people who joined his cause.

Bolívar spent ten years struggling to free his homeland from Spain. In 1821 a decade of leading armies through the rain forests and mountains of South America finally paid off. Bolívar's forces defeated the Spanish army in Venezuela. In a speech to his troops, Bolívar said:

> But we cannot rest. Other obligations await us. And when our native land is entirely free, we shall go to fight the Spaniards in any part of America where they are in control, and we shall throw them into the sea. Freedom shall live protected by our swords!

Bolívar carried the revolution further into South America, freeing the areas now known as Colombia, Bolivia, Panama, Ecuador, and Peru from Spanish rule. His actions won him the nick-

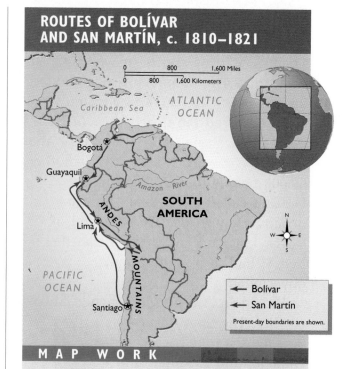

ROUTES OF BOLÍVAR AND SAN MARTÍN, c. 1810–1821

→ Bolívar
→ San Martín
Present-day boundaries are shown.

MAP WORK

Bolívar and San Martín won independence for many of the lands of South America.

1. Which of these two liberators traveled farther south in South America?

2. How far is Santiago from Lima?

Simón Bolívar, a Venezuelan soldier, liberated much of northern South America.

name "Liberator of South America."

From the southern part of the continent came another liberator. His name was José de San Martín (ho SE DE sahn mahr TEEN). San Martín led revolutions in Argentina and Chile. Find his route on the map on this page.

Changes in Australia

Remember that in 1788 the English founded the colony of New South Wales in Australia. Eventually, other colonies such as Van Diemen's Land, South Australia, and Western Australia were also established.

496

The Parliament House in Canberra is the center of Australia's government.

It was difficult for England to govern these colonies from so far away. As a result, the Australian Colonies Government Act was passed in 1850. This allowed the colonies to create constitutions and legislative bodies.

Years later, as France and Germany became interested in lands near Australia, Australians began to see a need for a confederation that would help protect the colonies by unifying them. A confederation is a group of provinces or states under a central government. The Commonwealth of Australia came into existence on January 1, 1901. Although this new commonwealth kept the British monarch as its highest ruler, it was united and free to govern itself.

WHY IT MATTERS

The 1800s brought many freedoms to European colonists throughout the world. Sometimes the change came peacefully, as it did in Australia. Often, however, people had to fight for their freedom.

With liberty came responsibility. The young countries were now able to make decisions for themselves. Faraway kings and queens no longer took a large share of wealth. However, it was still difficult for the new nations to build strong economies. Often a few rich families controlled the country's land and money.

The peasants of Mexico often said their revolution "placed the same rider on a new mule." They meant that one group of rulers usually just replaced another. Although the colonies were free, freedom and equality for all people remained a distant promise.

Reviewing Facts and Ideas

MAIN IDEAS

- In 1804 Haiti became the second independent country in the Americas, after the United States.

- Miguel Hidalgo led Mexicans in a revolt against Spain in 1810. Mexico became independent in 1821.

- Simón Bolívar and José de San Martín liberated much of South America from Spanish rule.

- An act passed in 1850 began self-rule in Australian colonies.

THINK ABOUT IT

1. How did Haiti gain independence?

2. From which social classes did Hidalgo gain most of his support?

3. **FOCUS** How did events in Europe influence the fight for independence in American colonies?

4. **THINKING SKILL** What steps would you take to *determine the credibility* of the quote by Iturbide on page 495?

5. **WRITE** Suppose you are a reporter recording the early events of the war of Mexican independence. Write a list of questions you could ask Miguel Hidalgo about his actions and his hopes for the future.

497

THE UNITED STATES
CONSTITUTION

As you know from studying United States history, people in our country fought a revolution earlier than the ones in France and Latin America that you have read about. When the founders of our country wrote the Constitution in 1787, they made sure to protect the freedoms they had just won.

Because the United States had the first written constitution in the world, other countries used it as a model for their own constitutions. Many Latin American countries were especially influenced by the United States Constitution. In Costa Rica all citizens are considered equal before the law and can state political opinions freely.

In another part of the world, India's constitution protects freedom of religion, the right to assemble peaceably, and other rights. These freedoms have been guaranteed in the United States for over 200 years.

The first part of the United States Constitution states the goals and freedoms that the colonists sought. These students are looking at the Constitution in Washington, D.C.

498

A woman in India votes in elections that are protected by the nation's constitution. A politician (below) speaks openly to the press in Costa Rica. Free press is guaranteed in both of these countries.

Like the constitutions of India and Costa Rica, the Japanese constitution protects freedom of the press. Here a reporter prepares a news broadcast.

499

The Granger Collection

1700   1888 1900

The Industrial Revolution

Read Aloud

"From this foul drain the greatest stream of human industry flows out to fertilize the whole world. From this filthy sewer pure gold flows."

This is how French writer and historian Alexis de Tocqueville (a LEKS ihs dih tawk VEEL) described Manchester, England, in 1835. A revolution was taking place in Manchester and other European cities. This revolution did not cause the bloodshed that had taken place in France and Latin America. It did, however, permanently change the lives of people around the world.

Focus Activity

READ TO LEARN

What changes were brought about by the Industrial Revolution?

VOCABULARY

- Industrial Revolution
- textile
- factory
- middle class
- working class
- socialism

PEOPLE

- John Kay
- James Hargreaves
- Richard Arkwright
- Edmund Cartwright
- James Watt
- Karl Marx

THE BIG PICTURE

Before 1700 the most important event across Europe every year was the harvest. Most people lived and worked the land in rural areas. Many never traveled more than ten miles from their villages.

From 1700 to 1800, however, rural life throughout Europe began to change. New farming methods and technology—such as iron plows, crop rotation, and fertilizers—made farms much more productive. Europe's population exploded, nearly doubling to 190 million by 1800. No change, however, had as many effects as the one that began in England in the 1700s. The Industrial Revolution was a period of time when great technological advances changed the way goods were made and the ways people lived. Industry became the focus of economic activity. Unlike national revolutions, this revolution was felt around the world.

THE GROWTH OF INDUSTRY

The Industrial Revolution started in Britain, spread across Europe, and reached the United States. It began in Britain for a number of reasons. British laws allowed people to start businesses, protect their property, and earn money. Britain also had a stable government and a rich supply of the raw materials coal and iron.

Work in the Country

The Industrial Revolution did not happen all at once. Industry first appeared in the countryside. Peasants produced thread and cloth on spinning wheels and looms in their homes. Peasants worked the fields in the summer. Then in the winter they spun yarn and made textiles. A textile is a cloth fabric that is either woven or knitted.

This type of work soon became an important source of income for rural families. As one Irish traveler observed:

The poor people spin a good deal of wool, and weave it into flannel for their own wear.

The Textile Boom

By the middle 1700s a growing population created more demand for textiles. New machines were invented that could make textiles more quickly and cheaply. Some of these machines are shown in the Infographic on

page 503. They were expensive and too big to fit in a farmer's two-room cottage. Merchants built large buildings, called factories, to house new machines.

Most of these new machines were made for weaving cotton. Cotton does not grow well in the cold, wet climate of Britain. However, it is cheaper than wool and has many uses. In the 1700s Britain became part of the triangular trade you read about in Chapter 16. The British found a vast source of cotton in the colonies of North America.

Soon a brisk trade developed. Raw cotton was shipped from America to the mills of Britain. Finished textiles were then shipped to Africa and traded for enslaved persons. Captured Africans were sent to work as slaves on cotton plantations in British colonies in America. British cities such as Liverpool soon became centers of textile manufacturing and shipping.

Before factories started, families made textiles at home (right). A hand-operated spinning wheel (above) was used to make thread.

Victoria & Albert Museum

501

Ironworks produced large amounts of iron needed for railroads and other new inventions.

THE SPREAD OF INDUSTRY

The Industrial Revolution began mostly with cotton textiles. It soon included many textiles. The Industrial Revolution widened to cover other goods as well. In Britain coal and iron mines provided raw materials used to build machines and power factories.

The Iron Horse

No new machine created as much interest as the locomotive. These steam-powered railway engines hissed, belched, and squeaked along Britain's iron rails. The first passenger railroad, between Stockton and Darlington, opened in 1825. Within 15 years, more than 1,000 miles of track crisscrossed Europe. By 1870 the railroad had cut the travel time from London, England, to Edinburgh, Scotland, from 4 days to 12 hours! In 1888 the railroad, nicknamed the "iron horse," linked Europe from Calais, in France, to Istanbul. Passengers and goods could reach more distant places in less time than ever before.

More Products for Sale

As factories hummed and railroads chugged, the number of products people could buy increased. A pamphlet called *The Results of Machinery* gave one example in 1831:

> *Two centuries ago not one person in a thousand wore stockings; one century ago not one person in five hundred wore them; now not one person in a thousand is without them.*

This description was an exaggeration, since many workers could not even afford shoes. However, it shows an important change in the economy. Before the Industrial Revolution began, most people lived on farms that provided them with food and clothing. By 1800 about 20 percent of the population lived in cities.

The people who did move from farms to cities now worked in factories and were paid wages. New factory workers used this money to buy food, cotton clothing, and other goods.

Inventions of the Industrial Revolution

New machines and new sources of power drove the Industrial Revolution forward. Each of the machines shown here was invented in Britain. The effects of these inventions on industry and on people's lives soon spread throughout Europe and the Americas. How did each invention make a later one possible?

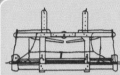

Flying Shuttle

John Kay invented the flying shuttle in 1733. This simple wooden device had yarn attached. It replaced the hand loom, allowing weavers to work twice as fast.

Spinning Jenny

Because weaving was so much faster, the demand for yarn increased. In 1765 James Hargreaves invented the spinning jenny, a machine that allowed workers to spin 16 spindles of yarn at once.

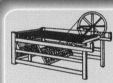

Water Frame

Richard Arkwright invented the water frame in 1769. This waterpowered device made even better thread for fabrics than the spinning jenny did.

Power Loom

An invention that made use of the yarn and thread that were being produced so quickly was Edmund Cartwright's power loom. Although this machine only became common in factories in the early 1800s, it speeded up the production of textiles tremendously.

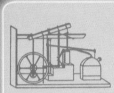

Steam Engine

James Watt perfected a steam engine in 1769. This machine, more than any other, gave a boost to the Industrial Revolution. By using coal as fuel, the steam engine provided a steady and unlimited source of power to run factory machines and later inventions like the steam locomotive.

A NEW SOCIAL PYRAMID

As the economy of Britain shifted from farms to factories, British society changed too. The middle class became more important as cities grew larger. The middle class was made up of business people, including merchants, lawyers, factory owners, and bankers. Although they did not have land or political power, the middle class increased trade and manufacturing. Some members of the middle class became rich.

The biggest group in British society was the working class. These men and women were mostly farmers who left farms to work in towns and cities. The rural lives they left behind were often difficult. However, many workers found life in the cities was sometimes worse.

Working Conditions

Working hours in the textile factories and mines were long and the conditions dangerous. Unlike farming or traditional craft work, factory work was boring and repetitive. One writer described what it was like:

They work fourteen hours per day, including the hour for dinner; the door is locked in working hours, except half an hour at tea time; the workpeople are not allowed to send for water to drink in the hot factory: and even the rain water is locked up, by the master's order, otherwise they would be happy to drink even that.

Many children worked in the narrow, wet, underground tunnels of the mines. Children as young as four years of age also worked in factories. Although children had always worked on farms, the conditions of the factories were severe. A French writer described a group of people leaving work, including

. . . young children, in greater numbers than the women, just as dirty, just as haggard, covered with rags which are thick with oil splashed over them as they toiled at the loom.

This painting (left) contrasts the middle class and the working class. Children often pulled carts through the narrow tunnels of coal mines (above).

Karl Marx believed there had always been conflict between economic classes.

An Idea for Change

Conditions in factories led many workers to organize. They formed organizations called unions. Weak at first, these organizations were outlawed by the government until 1824.

Karl Marx, a German philosopher living in England, wrote about the workers. In *Das Kapital* he wrote, "The [workers] have nothing to lose but their chains; they have the world to gain." Marx believed that those who owned property became rich while those who did not remained poor. The solution, he felt, was for workers to own the factories.

Marx believed that the world was entering a new economic period when workers would rise up and take control. In time, Marx wrote, there would be no social classes, and government would disappear. Many people in Europe became interested in some of his ideas, which became known as socialism. Much later, in Russia, these ideas would form the basis of a new type of government.

WHY IT MATTERS

Thousands of years ago people experienced an economic revolution—agriculture. Farming meant that people no longer had to hunt and gather to meet their needs. The Industrial Revolution was another revolution that changed the way people met their needs.

The Industrial Revolution did not bring sudden change, as the French Revolution did. The term "Industrial Revolution" was not even used by the people who lived through it. Still, industry created new cities, bustling with activity and spewing clouds of smoke.

The Industrial Revolution spread from its birthplace in Britain throughout Europe and the Western Hemisphere. It would eventually change most of the planet. As these incredible changes took place, there would be no going back.

✔ Reviewing Facts and Ideas

MAIN IDEAS

- The Industrial Revolution began in Britain in the middle 1700s.
- New inventions in textile manufacturing led to the building of factories.
- The middle class gained much money and power during this period.
- Life for the working class was frequently difficult, with low wages and poor working conditions.
- The Industrial Revolution spread from Britain to Europe and the Americas.

THINK ABOUT IT

1. What work did peasants do in their homes before factories were built?
2. What was the first product of the Industrial Revolution?
3. **FOCUS** List some good and bad effects of the Industrial Revolution.
4. **THINKING SKILL** How might the *point of view* of a working class person differ from that of a middle class person?
5. **GEOGRAPHY** How might the invention of the steam engine allow factories to be built anywhere?

Geography Skills

Using Cartograms

VOCABULARY
gross domestic product
cartogram

WHY THE SKILL MATTERS

The Industrial Revolution had a great impact on the economy of Great Britain and eventually on the entire world. As more countries built factories and trade increased, the economies of the world became connected. A price increase on cotton in the Americas, for example, affected textile factories and buyers of textiles throughout the world.

To understand these effects it is important to be able to measure and compare economic information. Suppose that you want to learn about a country's gross domestic product, or GDP. GDP is the total value of goods and services produced by a country during a certain period, usually one year. You might look up a country's GDP on an economic table.

Suppose you want to compare the GDPs of different countries. You could use a cartogram. A cartogram is a special kind of map used to present economic and other kinds of information. Cartograms are especially useful for comparing information about many countries.

USING THE SKILL

Most maps show the shapes of land as they look from above. You read about the different ways map makers project these shapes onto flat surfaces in the Using Map Projections Skills Lesson, on page 432. Physical maps, political maps, and historical maps all show countries or continents in relation to their actual size. On a cartogram, however, the size of a country is not related to the country's physical size, but rather to the information that is being compared. For example, on a cartogram showing populations of countries, China would appear as the biggest country on the map. This is because China has the largest population in the world.

The cartogram on this page shows the GDP of all of the countries in the world. The larger a country appears on this map, the greater is the value of all the goods and services produced by its economy. We see on political maps that Russia is the largest country in physical size. Does Russia also have the greatest GDP?

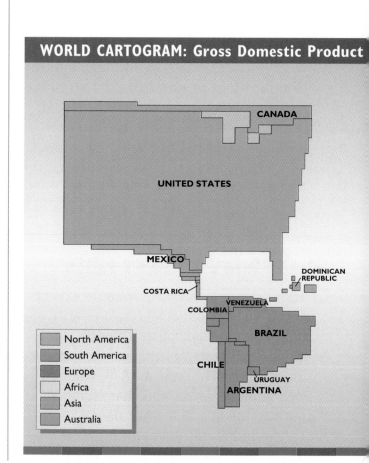

WORLD CARTOGRAM: Gross Domestic Product

CANADA
UNITED STATES
MEXICO
COSTA RICA
COLOMBIA
VENEZUELA
DOMINICAN REPUBLIC
BRAZIL
CHILE
URUGUAY
ARGENTINA

- North America
- South America
- Europe
- Africa
- Asia
- Australia

TRYING THE SKILL

In the last lesson you read that the Industrial Revolution began in Great Britain and then spread throughout Europe and to the Americas. You will read in the next lesson that it also spread to Japan. The influence of the Industrial Revolution is still felt today. For example, many of the countries with the greatest GDPs were among the first to build factories over 100 years ago. Which country has the largest GDP in the world? Which regions have countries with smaller GDPs? Why do you think this is so?

REVIEWING THE SKILL

1. How are cartograms different from other kinds of maps?

2. How are cartograms useful for comparing countries?

3. Look at the cartogram on this page. Which country has the second-largest GDP?

4. Britain was the birthplace of the Industrial Revolution. Does this country still have the world's biggest GDP? Is its GDP greater or smaller than Germany's?

5. What other kinds of information could be presented in a cartogram?

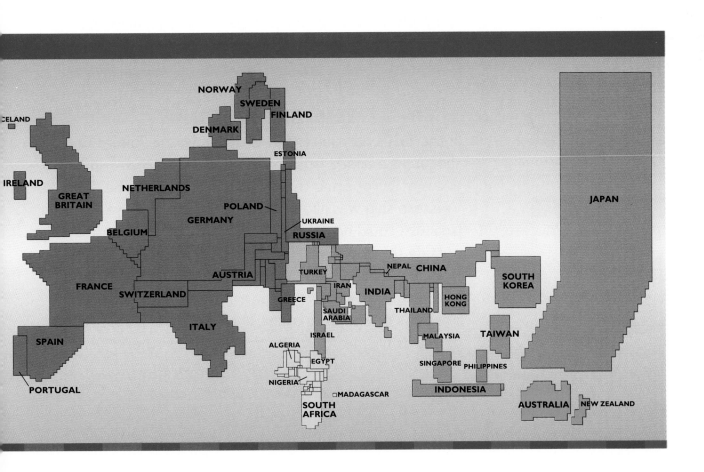

1700   1750   1800   1854   1912

The Rise of Industrial Japan

Focus Activity

READ TO LEARN

How did Japan change during the Meiji Restoration?

VOCABULARY

- imperialism
  Meiji Restoration
- bureaucracy

PEOPLE

- Matthew C. Perry
- Meiji

PLACES

- Tokyo

Read Aloud

"We recognize the excellence of Western civilization. We value the Western theories of rights, liberty, and equality; and we respect Western philosophy and morals. . . . Above all, we esteem Western science, economics, and industry. These, however, ought not to be adopted simply because they are Western; they ought to be adopted only if they can contribute to Japan's welfare."

This statement was written in a Japanese newspaper in 1889. It expressed the feelings of many Japanese citizens at that time.

THE BIG PICTURE

In the 1630s, as you read in Chapter 14, the Tokugawa shogun had closed Japan to Western influences—influences of Europe and the United States. Only one Western ship was allowed to enter Japan each year. Japanese could not, under punishment of death, travel outside the country.

By the middle 1800s Western nations had adopted a policy of **imperialism**. Imperialism is the extension of a nation's power over other lands by military, political, or economic means. It was at this time, in the 1850s, that Japan was forced to reopen its borders.

OPENING A CLOSED COUNTRY

After the 1630s almost every foreign ship that sailed to Japan for any reason was turned away. Although many ships from Europe and the United States sailed near Japan, few made contact with the Japanese.

Arrival of the Western Fleet

By the 1850s, however, the foreign pressure on Japan to reopen its borders increased. Many Western nations were seeking markets for new, factory-made goods. The United States, especially, wanted to sail its ships to Japan. During this time many American ships crossed the Pacific to hunt whales for oil. Japan would provide a perfect resting stop for these ships. The United States was also expanding its trade with China. Japan was located along the sea routes from California to China's ports.

In 1853 the United States government sent four warships to Japan. They were commanded by Commodore Matthew C. Perry. Perry carried a letter from President Millard Fillmore. The letter said that the United States wanted to be friends with Japan. "But no friendship can long exist," warned the letter, "unless Japan ceases to act toward Americans as if they were her enemies." Perry said he would return the next year for a response. Perry returned to Japan in 1854. This time he sailed eight warships into Edo Bay. The Japanese realized they could not match the firepower of these ships and agreed to meet with Commodore Perry.

Japanese leaders agreed to open two ports to American ships. The ships could stop at these ports to pick up supplies as they crossed the Pacific. Britain, France, Russia, and Holland also made trade agreements with the Japanese after Perry opened the door to trade with Japan.

The Granger Collection

The arrival of Matthew Perry (left) pushed Japan to negotiate a trade agreement with the United States.

The emperor Meiji (above) moved to the imperial palace (left) in Tokyo after the shogun was overthrown in 1868.

THE MEIJI RESTORATION

The opening of Japan to foreign trade shook Japanese society. Many leaders opposed the shogun's agreements with Western countries. They believed Japan was giving too much away. A few Europeans and Americans living in Japan were attacked and killed.

A New Government

In 1868 the disagreement with the shogun grew into a revolt. Leaders of several samurai groups took over the shogun's palace in Kyoto. They returned control of Japan to the emperor, who had long been powerless in the Tokugawa government. Since the emperor's name was Meiji (MAY JEE), this event is known as the Meiji Restoration. While the uprising was really a revolution against the shogun, it was called a restoration because power was restored to the emperor.

The new Japanese government began to adopt foreign ways of governing. The feudal system was abolished. Lords became regional governors for the new central government. Lords also had to give all of their land to the emperor in exchange for money.

A modern army was created, and the samurai lost their special right to carry swords. Many samurai had to look for jobs as farmers or merchants. The emperor moved from Kyoto to what had been the shogun's palace in Edo. Edo was renamed Tokyo, which means "eastern capital" in Japanese.

Although the emperor was now the official head of Japanese government, leaders called ministers made most decisions. They controlled a large bureaucracy. A bureaucracy is a large organization that runs the daily business of government. The new central government issued a declaration called the Charter Oath. This document declared that all Japanese would be given a say in their government. It also stated that old customs would be abandoned and "knowledge shall be sought throughout the world." In 1889 Japan had a new constitution and a parliament called the Diet (DIE et). The island nation was entering a new era.

Changes in Japan

This was not the first time that Japan looked to the outside for new ideas. Buddhism from China and Korea, and Confucianism from China, had been important parts of Japanese culture for centuries. Now, to learn about Western cultures, the Japanese government sent hundreds of students to the United States and Europe. Most studied such subjects as shipbuilding and navigation that would make Japan stronger. Some studied medicine and other subjects that would help Japanese people.

The Japanese government paid foreigners for expert advice on building railways, running factories, and sailing steamships. By 1889 telegraph lines and railroads linked all major cities. On steamships built in new shipyards, Japan began to export silk and tea to Europe and the United States. The first factories made silk textiles, but soon cotton mills were also built.

As contact with other cultures continued, styles of dress changed too. People began to wear suits or dresses instead of Japanese-style kimonos. In 1873 one person reported that he had seen a man wearing a samurai outfit in Tokyo. The man was stared at because his clothes seemed so strange. The samurai hairstyle, with hair pulled up on top, quickly went out of style. The new government built buildings in Western styles of architecture. Some people even began to eat beef and other Western foods.

These changes broke down many Japanese feudal customs. For example, the strict separation between social classes became blurred. A foreign visitor described the attitude of many farmers:

In the old days the farmer did not complain; he thought his lot could not be changed. He was forbidden to adopt a new calling and he was restricted by law to a frugal way of living. Now farmers can be soldiers, merchants, or officials, and can live as they please. They begin to compare their standard of living with that of other callings.

Links to ART

From East to West

The flow of information between Japan and the West ran in both directions. Many artists in Europe and the United States became interested in Japanese art, particularly the colorful prints called Ukiyo-e. Artists such as Vincent van Gogh, Claude Monet, and James Whistler adapted many of the colors and styles of these prints. In fact, the French coined a term— *japonisme* (jap oh NEEZ mah)— to describe this use of Japanese artistic styles.

You can find art books in your library showing paintings by the artists listed above. Find also Japanese woodblock prints, such as the one by Hiroshige on page 514. How were European and Japanese styles similar and how were they different?

EXPANSION OF JAPAN

Japan changed quickly because of the Meiji Restoration. The country soon became a military and economic power. Between 1883 and 1912 an increase in Japanese exports more than doubled world trade. In the 1890s Japanese leaders began to change unequal trade treaties they had signed years before.

Through all these changes Japan grew stronger and kept its own identity.

Military Activity Overseas

Japan soon began to show its power overseas. In 1894 Japan invaded Korea, which had long been occupied by China. China demanded that Japan remove its troops. Japan refused. Soon, Japan controlled most of the Korean Peninsula and the surrounding seas. Japan continued its push into Asia, attacking the Chinese mainland. In 1895 a treaty gave Japan control of Korea as well as the island of Taiwan.

In 1904 Japan entered into war against another neighbor—Russia. The most important battle of this war was in the stormy seas of the Tsushima (tsoo SHEE muh) Straits, which are part of the Korean Strait. There, Japan's navy destroyed the powerful Russian

GROWTH OF JAPAN, 1870-1905

Legend:
- 1870
- 1874-1875
- 1905

0   250   500 Miles
0   250   500 Kilometers

RUSSIA

SAKHALIN ISLAND

KURIL ISLANDS

HOKKAIDO

Sea of Japan

JAPAN

HONSHU

KOREA
CHINA

Korea Strait

Tokyo

Kyoto

PACIFIC OCEAN

KYUSHU   SHIKOKU

RYUKYU IS.

TAIWAN

N E S W

M A P   W O R K

Japanese wealth and military power led to expansion into neighboring territories.

1. In which direction did Japan expand?
2. What body of water separates Japan from Korea?

Today bullet trains (right) run the length of the main Japanese island, Honshu.

navy. The war was costly for both sides, but the Japanese victory caused the rest of the world to notice Japan's new strength. When the two countries signed a peace treaty in 1905, Japan gained land from Russia on the Asian mainland as well as half of Sakhalin Island. Look at the map on page 512 to see new lands controlled by Japan.

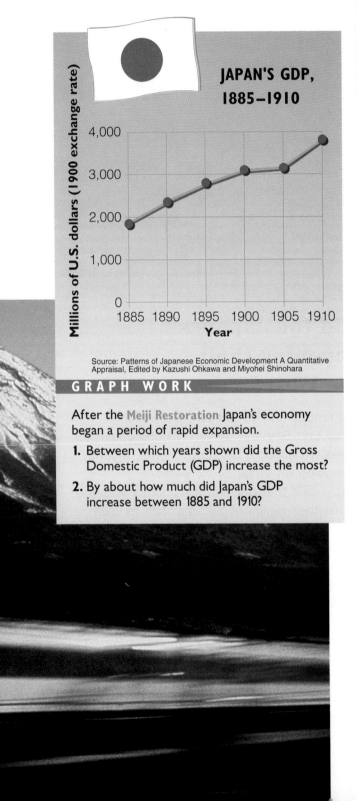

JAPAN'S GDP, 1885–1910

Source: Patterns of Japanese Economic Development A Quantitative Appraisal, Edited by Kazushi Ohkawa and Miyohei Shinohara

GRAPH WORK

After the Meiji Restoration Japan's economy began a period of rapid expansion.

1. Between which years shown did the Gross Domestic Product (GDP) increase the most?

2. By about how much did Japan's GDP increase between 1885 and 1910?

WHY IT MATTERS

The Emperor Meiji died in 1912, bringing to an end a remarkable era in Japanese history. During his nearly 50-year reign, Japan emerged from two centuries of isolation and feudal rule. It grew to become the most powerful military and economic force in Asia.

Japan's expansion did not end with the Meiji era. The small island nation grew even more powerful. When most of the world went to war in the 1940s, as you will read in Chapter 18, Japan played a major part in the conflict.

Reviewing Facts and Ideas

MAIN IDEAS

- In 1854 the United States forced Japan to reopen to outside trade.

- In 1868 the Meiji Restoration created a new central government, with the Emperor as its head.

- Japan rapidly modernized, borrowing many ideas from other cultures.

- By the 1890s Japan had become a powerful industrial country and began to expand into mainland Asia.

THINK ABOUT IT

1. Why did Japan have so little contact with the outside world under the Tokugawa Shogun?

2. How did Commodore Perry force Japan to begin trade with the West?

3. **FOCUS** What did Japan do to interact with the countries of the West?

4. **THINKING SKILL** In what ways did the establishment of a new government in 1868 *affect* Japan's relationship with other countries?

5. **GEOGRAPHY** How did Japan's island location help it first become isolated and later become industrialized?

CITIZENSHIP
VIEWPOINTS

This woodblock drawing of Perry arriving in Shimoda, Japan, was made by Hiroshige in 1855.

1853: What did the Japanese think about opening their country to the West?

In July 1853, as you read in the last lesson, Commodore Matthew Perry sailed into Edo Bay and demanded that Japan be opened to trade with western nations. His arrival added urgency to a debate that had been going on in Japan for years.

Many Japanese people said that opening the country was too great a risk. They felt that their nation should maintain its own culture, without Western influences. A scholar named Fujita Toko wrote that once foreign ideas took hold there would be no way to restore Japanese traditions.

Japanese Lord Ii Naosuke believed that Japan should strengthen and protect itself by setting aside some of its feudal customs and learning from the West. He explained that the technology of Western nations made them strong enough to overpower Japan.

A Japanese writer stated that Japan should remain isolated. As you will read in the second viewpoint, he favored attacking Westerners who were in Japan.

Read and consider three viewpoints on this issue.

Three DIFFERENT Viewpoints

1 **LORD II NAOSUKE**
Feudal lord, Excerpt from a letter, 1847

The condition of foreign states is not what it once was: they have invented the steamship and introduced radical changes in the art of navigation. They have also built up their armies to a state of great efficiency and are possessed of war implements of great power and precision; in short, they have risen to be imposing powers. If we cling to our outdated systems, heaven only knows what mighty calamity may befall our empire.

". . . our outdated systems . . ."

2 **AIZAWA SEISHISAI**
Writer, Excerpt from New Proposals, 1825

Second-rate leaders, thinking only of easy peace, let the foreigners go unchecked. . . . They make the situation worse through half-hearted inaction. If, instead, the government issues orders to the entire nation to smash the foreigners whenever they come into sight and to treat them openly as our nation's foes, everyone high and low will push forward to enforce the order. This is a great opportunity. It must not be lost.

". . . treat them openly as our nation's foes . ."

3 **FUJITA TOKO**
Scholar, 1849

Why should we not be able to defend our land against the invaders, though our defenses are not quite what we wish them to be? If once permitted, foreigners will soon try to win the hearts of the common people. If we suddenly find ourselves with the minds of our people loosened, our defenses neglected, the foreign religion (*Christianity*) gaining ground, what remedy would there be to reverse this awful state of things?

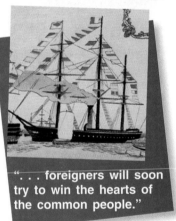

". . . foreigners will soon try to win the hearts of the common people."

BUILDING CITIZENSHIP

1. What was the viewpoint of each person?
2. In what ways were some of the viewpoints alike? In what ways were they different?
3. What viewpoints might people have on this issue today?

SHARING VIEWPOINTS

Discuss what you agree with or disagree with about these viewpoints. Discuss why you think each speaker might feel as he did. Then as a class, write a statement that all three of the speakers might have agreed with in the Japanese debate over the opening of their country.

CHAPTER 17 REVIEW

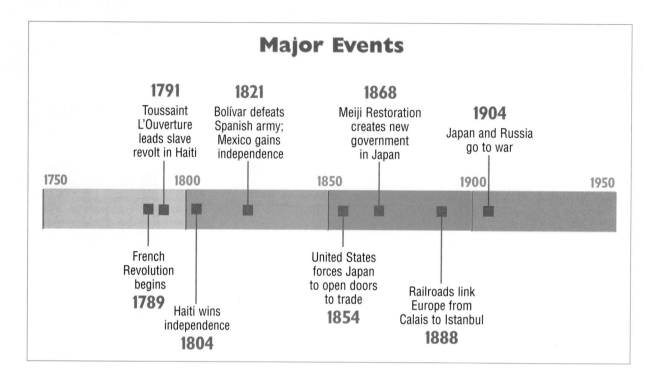

Major Events

1791
Toussaint L'Ouverture leads slave revolt in Haiti

1821
Bolívar defeats Spanish army; Mexico gains independence

1868
Meiji Restoration creates new government in Japan

1904
Japan and Russia go to war

1750   1800   1850   1900   1950

French Revolution begins
1789

Haiti wins independence
1804

United States forces Japan to open doors to trade
1854

Railroads link Europe from Calais to Istanbul
1888

THINKING ABOUT VOCABULARY

Number a sheet of paper from 1 to 10. Beside each number write the term from the list below that matches the statement.

absolute monarchy	Latin America
aristocracy	mestizo
bureaucracy	middle class
cartogram	revolution
Industrial Revolution	socialism

1. A large organization that runs the daily business of government

2. The period of rapid industrial and technological growth that began in England in the 1700s

3. The region south of the United States influenced by Spanish and Portuguese culture

4. A form of government in which a king or queen has complete power

5. A special map used to present economic and other kinds of information

6. A system of society based on ideas of Marx in which workers would own and control all property

7. A social class that includes merchants, lawyers, bankers, and business owners

8. A person of mixed Native American and European ancestry

9. A social class made up of nobles and their families

10. A sudden or great change

THINKING ABOUT FACTS

1. What role did the Estates General play in triggering the French Revolution?

2. What effect did Simón Bolívar have on South American history?

3. What were the main ideas of Karl Marx?

4. What part did Commodore Perry play in opening Japan to trade?

5. What does the time line above suggest about the possible influence of the French Revolution on events in Haiti and Latin America?

THINK AND WRITE ◄ ▤▤▶

WRITING AN ANALYSIS
Write a paragraph about the Industrial Revolution. Describe both the progress it brought and the social problems it created.

WRITING A JOURNAL ENTRY
Suppose you were alive during the French Revolution. Choose one event: (1) the meeting of the National Assembly (2) the storming of the Bastille or (3) the execution of the king and queen. Write a journal entry about what you saw or know happened.

WRITING AN EXPLANATION
Describe the changes that took place in Japan during the 45-year reign of the Emperor Meiji. Reread pages 510–511. Then write a short essay about the reasons behind the emergence of Japan from two centuries of isolation and feudal rule.

APPLYING GEOGRAPHY SKILLS

USING CARTOGRAMS
1. What is a cartogram?
2. Look at the cartogram on pages 506–507. Name in order the ten countries with highest GDPs. On which continents are they located?
3. According to the cartogram, which five countries in Africa have the highest GDPs? Is Algeria's GDP greater or less than Singapore's?
4. Is India's GDP greater or less than Argentina's? Than Great Britian? Than South Africa's?
5. Why are cartograms useful?

Summing Up the Chapter

Copy the cause-and-effect chart below on a separate sheet of paper. Review the chapter and fill in at least two effects for each cause listed. When you have filled in the information, use it to answer the question "What important changes came about because of revolutions in Europe, the Americas, and Japan?"

CAUSE		EFFECTS
French Revolution	As a Result ▶	
Latin American Revolutions	As a Result ▶	
Industrial Revolution	As a Result ▶	
Meiji Restoration	As a Result ▶	

UNIT 5 REVIEW

THINKING ABOUT VOCABULARY

Number a sheet of paper from 1 to 10. Decide whether the underlined word in each of the following statements correctly completes the sentence. If the word is correct, write **C** beside the number. If the word is incorrect, write **I** and then write the correct word to complete the sentence.

confederation missionary
convert Reign of Terror
divine right sugarcane
heliocentric textile
Meiji Restoration Triangular Trade

1. The belief that a monarch's authority came from God was called <u>divine right</u>.

2. <u>Reign of Terror</u> is the name of the trade that developed between England, Africa, and North America in the 1600s.

3. To <u>convert</u> people is to win them over to one's point of view or beliefs.

4. The <u>Meiji Restoration</u> was the return to the throne of a Japanese emperor during a revolt against the shogun.

5. Enemies of the French Revolution were executed during a period called the <u>Triangular trade</u>.

6. <u>Sugarcane</u> is a tall grass with a thick, woody stem that contains the liquid source of sugar.

7. The <u>missionary</u> view, developed by Copernicus, Galileo, and Newton, states that the sun is the center of the universe.

8. A <u>textile</u> is a group of states that join together under a central government.

9. A <u>heliocentric</u> is a cloth that is woven or knitted.

10. A <u>confederation</u> tries to make other people see the truth of his or her religion.

THINK AND WRITE

WRITING ABOUT PERSPECTIVES
Suppose you were an African who crossed the Atlantic on a slave ship. Describe how your perspective would be different from an African who had never left home.

WRITING AN INTERVIEW
Suppose you could interview one person you read about in this unit. Write down your questions and his or her answers.

WRITING A PAMPHLET
Write a pamphlet explaining the reasons for the French revolution.

BUILDING SKILLS

1. **Analyzing credibility** How would you determine the credibility of the statement made by the woman who lived during the Reign of Terror? Look back at page 490.

2. **Analyzing credibility** Reread the excerpt on page 502. What does the point of view expressed suggest about the author?

3. **Analyzing credibility** Reread the two quotations on page 504. What is the point of view of these writers and how does it differ from the quote on page 502?

4. **Using cartograms** Look at the cartogram on page 506. Find three places in the world where rich and poor countries are located near each other.

4. **Using cartograms** The cartogram on page 506 shows the GDP of countries but *not* the average wealth of people in each country. Explain how people in a country with a relatively high GDP, like China, might actually be poorer than people in countries with lower GDPs but also fewer people. What kind of cartogram would give an accurate picture of the relative wealth of people in each country?

YESTERDAY, TODAY & TOMORROW

History has shown that some changes are brought about rapidly through revolution. Others are more gradual. What important changes do you think are taking place today? What changes do you think will take place in the future? What do you think the world will be like centuries from now? Explain your answers.

READING ON YOUR OWN

These are some books you might find at the library to help you learn more.

EXPLORER
by Rupert Matthews
This visual history with background information takes you from ancient to modern times through land, sea, air, and space.

THE INDUSTRIAL REVOLUTION
edited by John D. Clare
This illustrated book helps trace the technology that grew out of the Industrial Revolution.

MAGELLAN
by Jim Hargrove
Read the biography of the explorer who launched the first voyage around the world.

UNIT PROJECT

Make a Famous People Game

1. First each partner will choose six names from the unit. Then each player will write each name on a separate index card. Choose the people together to avoid repeating names.
2. Next each partner will write a fact about each of the people named on six additional cards. For example, if you choose Marie Antoinette, your fact might be that she was the queen of France until the French Revolution.
3. To play, mix the 24 cards and lay them face-down. Take turns turning over two cards. Your goal is to match each person with his or her correct fact. If you don't turn up a name with a matching fact, turn the cards face down again. If you turn up two matching cards, keep them and take another turn. The player with the most cards at the end wins.

WAR POSTER,
GREAT BRITAIN;
WAR PLANE, WWI

ANNE FRANK;
F. W. DE KLERK AND
NELSON MANDELA,
SOUTH AFRICA

A Century of Conflict

"This cruelty too will end."

from The Diary of Anne Frank
See page 546.

Why Does It Matter?

A young girl, Anne Frank, wrote these words during a war that affected the entire world. In this, the second World War, as well as in the first World War, new weapons and fighting techniques caused tremendous loss of life.

Other struggles affected nations in the 1900s. Democratic beliefs and human rights were challenged. Colonies around the world struggled to gain independence.

As Anne Frank hoped, and as millions around the world continue to hope, conflicts have been giving way to greater peace, freedom, and cooperation. The technology that caused destruction has also been a source of life. New medicines and techniques have enabled people to live longer, more healthful lives. New ways of sharing information have also linked the whole world. People today share ideas that will shape the present and the future.

FIND OUT MORE!
Visit our website:
www.mhschool.com

*inter*NET
CONNECTION

Adventures
with
NATIONAL
GEOGRAPHIC

The Last Unknown Place

A human being's foot leaves an imprint on the moon. A blue and white planet—our Earth—appears over the horizon of a gray lunar surface. The space shuttle blasts away from Earth, carrying astronauts who will live and work in space for days at a time. Throughout history, people have experienced the urge to explore. In this century, that urge takes us far beyond our own atmosphere. But the courage and imagination needed for exploration today are the same as they were for the first human beings who set their eyes on the horizon and started out for unknown places.

GEO JOURNAL

Write an application to become an astronaut. What qualities do you have that would make you a good one?

A World at War

THINKING ABOUT HISTORY AND GEOGRAPHY

The twentieth century has been a time of great change and conflict. Old ways of governing were overthrown in many parts of the world. Two world wars were fought with weapons of great destruction. When the fighting ended, two superpowers with opposing goals sought to influence other nations. Follow these events on the map and on the time line.

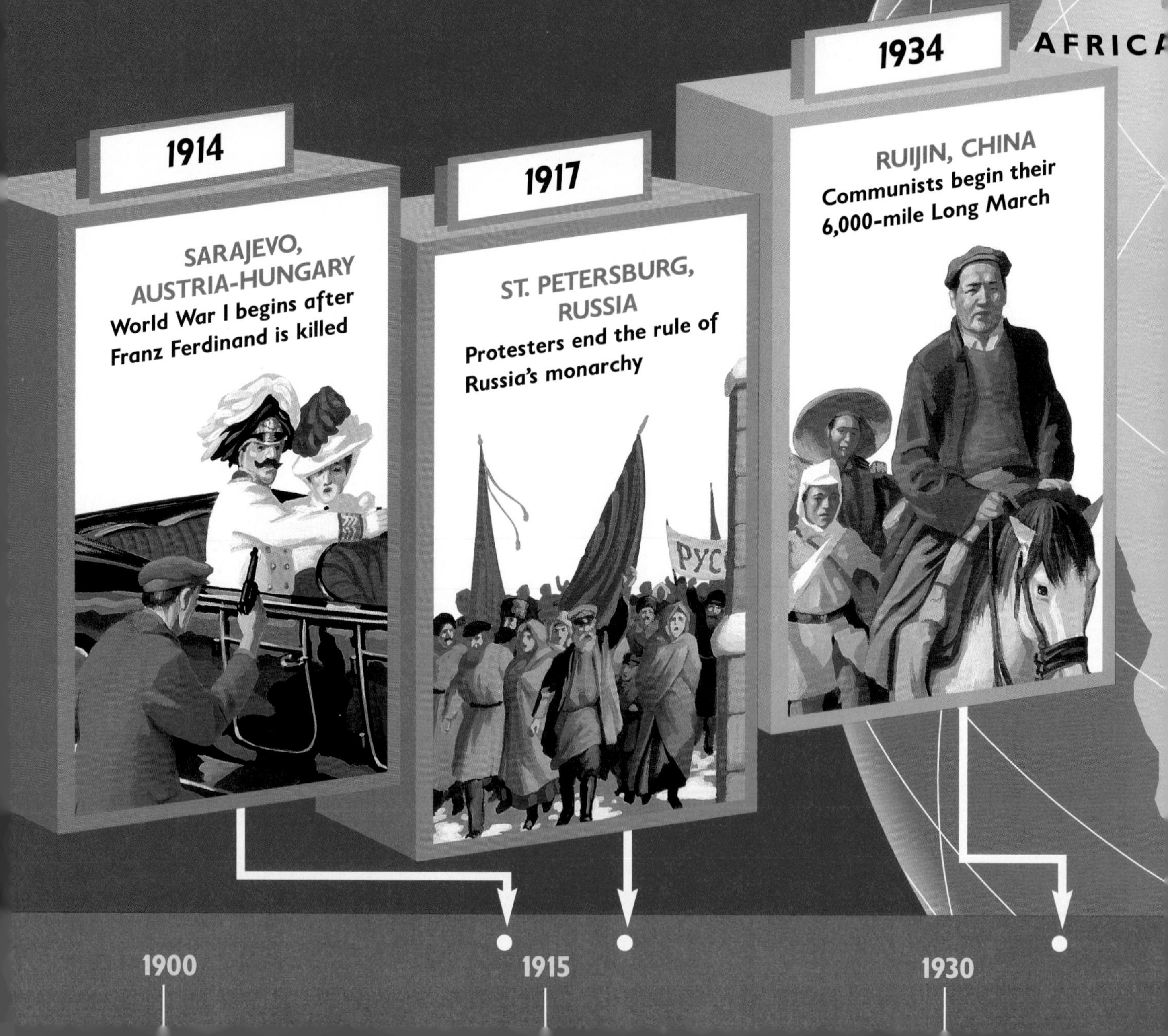

AFRICA

1934

RUIJIN, CHINA
Communists begin their 6,000-mile Long March

1914

SARAJEVO, AUSTRIA-HUNGARY
World War I begins after Franz Ferdinand is killed

1917

ST. PETERSBURG, RUSSIA

Protesters end the rule of Russia's monarchy

РУС

1900

1915

1930

ARCTIC
OCEAN

Normandy

Berlin

St. Petersburg

EUROPE

Sarajevo

ASIA

Ruijin

1944

NORMANDY, FRANCE
Allied forces successfully invade Europe during World War II

1961

BERLIN, EAST GERMANY
East German police build a wall between East and West Berlin

INDIAN
OCEAN

1945

1960

1890   1900   1918   1940   1965   1990

The "Great War"

Read Aloud

"I saw the ship go down. There was this huge lovely liner, and as I watched one [smokestack] went [under] and then the other and the other until the ship was gone and the sea was calm, and all you could see was bodies, and wreckage of furniture and everything that had been in the ship floating in the water."

This was how Alice Lines remembered the 1915 German submarine attack on the Lusitania, a ship crossing the Atlantic. The ship carried many American passengers. Lines was one of the few survivors. The 1,198 people who died were victims of an international conflict, the "Great War."

Focus Activity

READ TO LEARN

In what ways did nationalism affect the events leading to World War I?

VOCABULARY

- nationalism
- alliance
- Central Powers
- Allied Powers
- armistice
- League of Nations
- Treaty of Versailles
- World War I

PEOPLE

- Franz Ferdinand

PLACES

- Sarajevo
- Serbia

THE BIG PICTURE

The sinking of the *Lusitania* angered many people in the United States. Two years after that event, the country entered a war that had already involved many nations of the world. What forces and events led to the war?

In Chapter 17 you read about vast changes that swept through the world in the late 1700s and 1800s. Factories were built during the Industrial Revolution. Overland travel sped along with the help of railroads. Steamships crossed the Atlantic Ocean in just six days.

Countries such as Britain, Germany, and France grew economically because of the Industrial Revolution. The populations and military strength of many European countries also increased. This growth brought with it many new problems. European leaders wondered which countries would continue to strengthen. Which ones would eventually become the most powerful nations?

EUROPE AT THE TURN OF THE CENTURY

In the early 1900s Europe was like a huge jigsaw puzzle. The "pieces" were nations. Some, such as Britain and France, had existed for centuries. Others, such as Italy and Germany, had been unified only in the 1800s.

In many of these European nations, a feeling of unity had grown among peoples who spoke the same language and shared a common history and culture. These feelings developed into the force that is known as nationalism (NASH uh nuh lihz um). Nationalism is a strong loyalty to one's own country and culture. Those who are influenced by nationalism want their countries to be more powerful than any others.

By the early 1900s nationalism had grown stronger in Europe. So had tensions between neighboring countries. To prepare for the possibility of war, countries trained large armies and formed alliances (uh LI un sez). An alliance is an agreement between countries that ties their interests together. Members of an alliance, called allies, pledge to defend each other if any of them are attacked.

Two Shots that Started a War

On June 28, 1914, Archduke Franz Ferdinand, the heir to the throne of Austria-Hungary, visited Sarajevo (sar uh YAY voh). This city had come under his empire's control. Sarajevo, capital of a region called Bosnia, shared ties with Serbia, a nearby kingdom. Many Serbian nationalists thought that Sarajevo and Bosnia should be part of Serbia. Some of them decided to send a message to the archduke's government.

As Ferdinand and his wife Sophie drove through Sarajevo, someone threw a bomb at them. The archduke knocked it away and the bomb exploded behind them. A wrong turn, however, took them in front of another Serbian nationalist. This man used a gun. He fired twice, killing them both.

Austria-Hungary, backed by Germany, declared war on Serbia in July. Serbia was aided by its ally, Russia. Russia's allies, France and Britain, also came to Serbia's aid. A British leader described Europe on the brink of war: "The lights are going out all over Europe. We shall not see them lit again in our lifetime." By August 1914 the "Great War" had begun.

Archduke Franz Ferdinand and his wife Sophie were killed by a Serbian nationalist as they rode through Sarajevo. This photo shows them preparing for the ride.

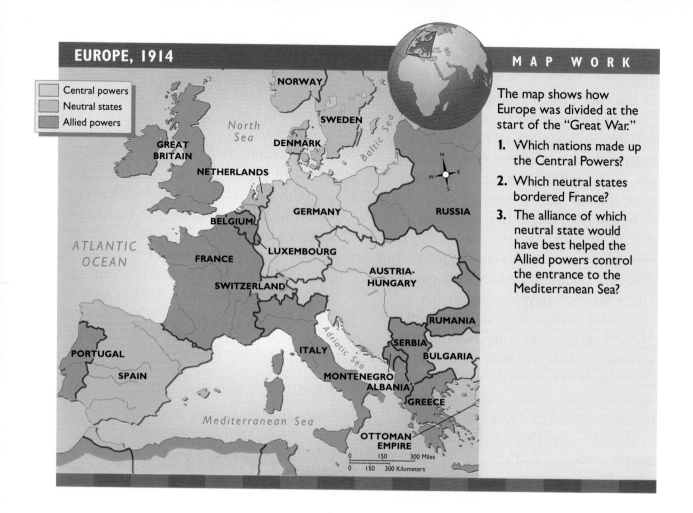

Central powers
Neutral states
Allied powers

NORWAY

SWEDEN

North
Sea

Baltic Sea

DENMARK

GREAT
BRITAIN

NETHERLANDS

GERMANY

RUSSIA

BELGIUM

ATLANTIC
OCEAN

LUXEMBOURG

FRANCE

AUSTRIA-
HUNGARY

SWITZERLAND

Adriatic Sea

RUMANIA

PORTUGAL

ITALY

SERBIA

BULGARIA

SPAIN

MONTENEGRO
ALBANIA

GREECE

Mediterranean Sea

OTTOMAN
EMPIRE

0   150   300 Miles
0   150   300 Kilometers

The map shows how
Europe was divided at the
start of the "Great War."

1. Which nations made up
the Central Powers?

2. Which neutral states
bordered France?

3. The alliance of which
neutral state would
have best helped the
Allied powers control
the entrance to the
Mediterranean Sea?

NATIONS AT WAR

As you can see on the map, Austria-Hungary, Germany, and their allies became known as the Central Powers. Serbia, Russia, France, Britain, and others were called the Allied Powers.

The Central Powers had some military success in the fall of 1914. Their armies forced their way deep into France and Russia. The Allied Powers, however, had a greater number of soldiers and more supplies. They were better equipped to survive a long war.

The Battlefront

Over the next four years the battlefront in France hardly changed. The battlefront, or front, is the place where opposing armies fight. Millions of soldiers died trying to push the front east or west. During many battles at the front, generals stuck to old-style war techniques. These ways of fighting were no match for the deadly technology now being used in war. Machine guns and poison gas could kill hundreds of enemy soldiers in a short time.

All across France, soldiers on both sides dug maze-like dirt trenches, or ditches, for protection. Soldiers camped in the trenches while waiting for orders. Bombs exploded nearby and bullets whizzed overhead. In winter, rain filled the trenches with puddles and mud. In summer, the heat and dust were almost unbearable. The worst times, though, were when the soldiers were ordered to go "over the top." This phrase meant climbing out of the trenches and into enemy machine-gun fire. How did one British soldier describe fighting at the front?

Excerpt from an interview with British soldier, Charles Quinnell, about the Battle of the Somme in 1916.

I gave the order "advance—up the ladders—over the top.". . . We went through, we got halfway across and then the two machine guns found us . . . they played on us like spraying with a hose. At the finish I was the only man standing but I'm not one of those heroes who want to take on the German Army on my own and so I went to earth, I got down behind the lip of a big shell-hole. . . . The machine gun crew spotted me and they opened up on me. I ducked my head down . . . and the dirt was just spraying down the back of my neck.

---

shell-hole: hole caused by an explosion

The Home Front

While millions of troops served in the war, people at home did what they could to help. People who worked to support the troops were said to be fighting on the "home front." Women and men worked in factories to make bullets, bombs, and airplanes. Others volunteered to serve as nurses or ambulance drivers at the war front.

In order to save food for the soldiers, governments controlled the amount of food people could buy. In Britain, laws for restaurants stated:

Two meatless days are to be observed. No milk may be served or consumed (drunk), except by children under 10 years of age.

In Germany and eastern European countries, food prices soared. Many people ate potato peels and watery soup given out by their government.

The United States Enters the War

Conditions were better for the Allied Powers because they received supplies from the United States. These supplies were sent on ships. In 1915 German submarines sank the *Lusitania*, which was carrying war supplies. The ship's passengers included 128 United States citizens. Many died in the attack. Attacks on ships outraged leaders and citizens of the United States. So did a secret message sent by Germany to Mexico that plotted an alliance against the United States.

In April 1917 the United States declared war on Germany and the other Central Powers. Large numbers of American soldiers, as well as vast amounts of money and supplies, greatly helped the Allied Powers. As you will read on page 531, the United States used posters and slogans to help send more than 2 million troops to Europe.

Out of their trenches, soldiers near the front went fully prepared for enemy attacks.

Weapons of World War I

Nations have always made use of the latest developments in technology to produce new weapons. Some of the weapons used during World War I were not only capable of tremendous destruction, but also changed the way wars were fought. How did the weapons shown change modern war?

TANKS were armored vehicles invented by the British to cross trenches. Soldiers inside fired guns.

AIRPLANES were used to drop bombs on enemy territory. Bombs were often carried under the wings.

GAS MASKS were worn by soldiers fighting at the front for protection from poison gas.

AN END TO THE WAR

On November 11, 1918, Germany and the Allies signed an armistice (AHR muh stihs), or agreement to stop fighting. In January 1919, Allied leaders worked out terms for peace. As part of their treaty, they created the League of Nations, an international council that would work to prevent future wars. German leaders were forced to sign the Treaty of Versailles (vair SĪ) on June 28, 1919.

WHY IT MATTERS

The Treaty of Versailles caused great anger in Germany because it blamed that nation for the war. It also called for the payment of enormous fines to repair war damages. Even Ferdinand Foch, the commander of the Allied armies exclaimed, "This isn't peace! This is an armistice for 20 years!" Three months after those 20 years had passed, the nations of the world would again go to war. When that happened, the war that had been called the "Great War" became known as World War I.

✓ Reviewing Facts and Ideas

MAIN IDEAS

- Nationalism was a factor that led to World War I, which was fought from 1914 to 1918.

- Modern technology played a deadly new role in the trench, sea, and air battles of World War I.

- On the "home front" women and men worked in factories, and governments controlled food supplies to make sure troops were fed.

- United States supplies and troops played an important role in helping the Allied Powers win World War I.

THINK ABOUT IT

1. What role did technology play in World War I?

2. How did people on the "home front" contribute to the war effort?

3. **FOCUS** How did nationalism play a role in the start of World War I?

4. **THINKING SKILL** Make a _conclusion_ about the impact alliances had on Europe in the early 1900s.

5. **WRITE** Read the excerpt from the interview with the soldier again. Write a letter to that soldier describing your reaction to his description of the front.

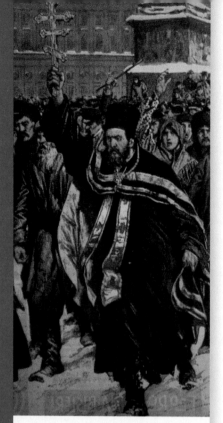

1890   1900   1940   1965   1990

The Russian Revolution

Read Aloud

"Peace! Land! Bread!"

This slogan summed up what ordinary Russians wanted most in the bloody, food-starved days of World War I. One group promised to give them all these things and more. Once in power, this group would transform Russia and affect the whole world.

Focus Activity

READ TO LEARN

What were the causes and effects of the Russian Revolution?

VOCABULARY

- Russian Revolution
- tsar
- strike
- communism
- totalitarian

PEOPLE

- Alexander II
- Nicholas II
- Vladimir Ilyich Lenin
- Josef Stalin

PLACES

- Russia
- St. Petersburg
- Moscow
- Soviet Union

THE BIG PICTURE

World War I was the peak of a long era of conflict and revolution. You have already read about political and industrial revolutions that rocked the world in the 1700s and 1800s. In the early 1900s, while the "Great War" still raged, yet another revolution broke out—in **Russia**. The **Russian Revolution** was an extremely important event in modern world history.

In 1900 the Russian empire stretched across parts of Europe and Asia. It included people of many different cultures. Most, though, lived in western Russia, where the land was better suited for the empire's main activity— farming. Most Russians were Christians. Muslims also lived in the empire, however, as well as many Jews.

World leaders took notice when revolutionaries overthrew Russia's leaders in 1917. Revolutionary leaders began to build a government around the ideas of Karl Marx, whom you read about in Chapter 17. The world watched and waited. What would happen in Russia? Would Russia continue to fight in World War I? How would the revolution affect other nations?

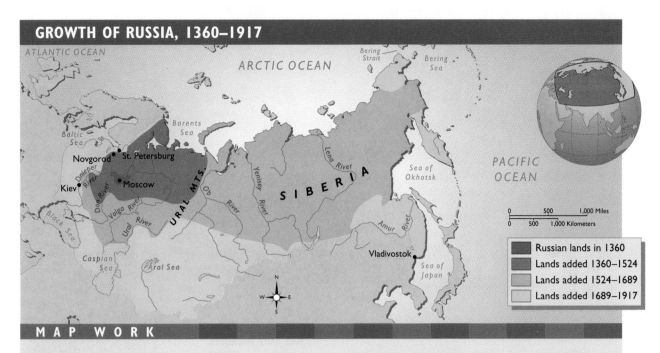

GROWTH OF RUSSIA, 1360–1917

Russian lands in 1360
Lands added 1360–1524
Lands added 1524–1689
Lands added 1689–1917

MAP WORK

Russian tsars greatly expanded their nation's lands.

1. Which city was the center of Russia in 1360?

2. In which direction is St. Petersburg from Moscow?

3. During which years did Russian lands first reach the Caspian Sea?

4. What was the eastern boundary of Russia in 1524? In 1689?

5. After what year did Russian lands extend past the Ural Mountains?

RUSSIA UNDER THE TSARS

In the middle 1800s Russia was far from being a world power. While industry changed many parts of Europe, most Russians lived much as they had during the Middle Ages.

At the top of Russia's social pyramid was the **tsar** (ZAHR), or emperor. The tsar ruled with an iron hand. Anyone who displeased the tsar might be killed or sent to prison in Siberia. Find this frozen steppe region on the map.

Beneath the tsar were a handful of rich noble families. At the bottom of Russia's social pyramid were millions of poor farmers. Their crops fed the empire.

Russian Serfs

By the late 1700s France and other European countries no longer had serfs, or farmers, bound to the land. In the early 1800s, however, most Russians were still serfs. Russian law said serfs were the property of their owners, although serfs could not be sold.

By the middle 1800s serf revolts in Russia were increasing in number. Tsar **Alexander II** began to fear a revolution. He also wanted to shift Russia's work force away from farming and toward industry. Alexander decided to abolish serfdom in 1861. To abolish means to end a practice. The Tsar said: "It is better to abolish serfdom from above than to wait until the serfs begin to free themselves from below."

In exchange for freedom and small plots of land, the freed serfs had to pay heavy taxes. Paying the taxes was difficult, since many families were given small areas to farm.

533

WORLDS IN CONFLICT

By the late 1800s Russian cities were growing. Hard times in rural areas forced many former serfs to move to the cities in search of work. By the 1890s factories and mills of the Industrial Revolution were springing up in Russia's capital, St. Petersburg.

Two Sides of a City

To poor farmers St. Petersburg was a new world. They stared in wonder at the grand winter palace of Tsar Nicholas II, who began his rule in 1894. Dozens of mansions, churches, theaters, schools, and universities lined the streets of the city. More than one million people lived in St. Petersburg.

The city also had a less spectacular side. Away from the palace and other beautiful mansions, mills and factories clustered together. Smoke from their chimneys filled the air above the over-crowded apartment buildings where workers lived.

Workers Protest

Inside the factories and mills, conditions were often grim and workers

Wealthy Russians like Tsar Nicholas and army officials owned expensive items like this egg by Fabergé (right).

were angry. A protest in 1897 won them a shortened work day—to $11\frac{1}{2}$ hours. Factory workers protested again in 1905, shutting down the city with their strikes. A strike is a refusal to work in protest of unfair treatment.

On Sunday, January 22, 1905, thousands of striking workers marched toward the Winter Palace to speak with the tsar himself. The tsar's soldiers responded by shooting into the crowd. More than 100 people were killed. Many others were injured. The day became known as "Bloody Sunday."

A storm of revolts and strikes swept through the country after "Bloody Sunday." Tsar Nicholas II agreed to share some of his power with a new elected parliament, called the Duma. The Duma called for changes that would advance democracy and help the poor. The tsar refused. During the next nine years, Nicholas and the Duma were in constant conflict.

War and Hunger

In the years following "Bloody Sunday," unrest deepened in Russia. Things became even worse during World War I. More than a million Russian troops died on the battlefront. Some never even had guns or bullets to protect themselves, since weapons were in short supply. Most of the nation's railroads carried supplies to battle. Only a few trains were available to bring food and fuel to cities. As a result, factories and stores often closed. Many people were left without work. Goods that were already hard to get became even more scarce.

March of 1917 began as one of the coldest, snowiest months that many people in St. Petersburg could remember. The weather kept farmers and their food carts away from city markets. Within the city hungry workers lined up in the cold for hours. They hoped to spend what little money they had on small loaves of bread.

This photo from around 1900 shows workers on a farm in Russia. The lives of many Russian farmers were filled with hard work and hunger.

Revolution Begins

The skies cleared and the weather changed in time for a protest held by thousands of unhappy people. For four days, demonstrators jammed the streets of St. Petersburg. Shouts of "Down with the war!" and "Down with the government!" soon drowned out the simple cry for "Bread!"

The tsar's police called for help from soldiers who were staying in the city. Most of the soldiers, however, joined in the protest and turned on the police. With the soldiers' help the protest became a full-scale revolution against the government.

Tsar Nicholas, who was away meeting with his generals, had no idea of what was happening in his capital. By the time he set out to return home, the spirit of revolution had spread. Angry railroad workers forced his train to a standstill. On March 15, 1917, Nicholas II was forced to give up his role as tsar. Sixteen months later he, his wife Alexandra, and their children were executed. The rule of Russian tsars had come to an end. Who would rule the giant nation now?

In November 1917 soldiers marched to the Duma, where they helped the Bolsheviks gain control of government.

A NEW GOVERNMENT

After the revolution in March, the Duma chose leaders to run the country. Russia's many problems, however, continued. World War I was still underway and Russian military leaders demanded that their troops be withdrawn from the front. City workers went on striking in protest of even longer bread lines and lower wages. Many farmers, hungry and impatient for change, began seizing land for themselves.

Meanwhile a political group called the Bolsheviks was gaining strength. The Bolsheviks were led by a Russian lawyer named Vladimir Ilyich Lenin (VLAD uh meer IHL yitch LEN in). He believed that a different kind of revolution was necessary to change the government. The Bolsheviks planned a socialist revolution based on the ideas of Karl Marx whom you read about in Chapter 17. They wanted workers to control the government and own all property. Lenin promised Russians "Peace, Land, and Bread."

The Bolsheviks Take Control

With the support of the soldiers in St. Petersburg, Lenin and the Bolsheviks overthrew the Duma in November 1917. Soon after this second revolution they pulled Russian troops out of the Allied war effort. Russia began peace talks with Germany. The Bolsheviks allowed workers to control factories and farmers to use the farmland of wealthy nobles. The Bolsheviks also moved the capital of Russia south to the ancient city of Moscow.

The new Bolshevik government had many opponents. Landowners, factory owners, and nobles were losing their rights, as well as their wealth and power. Christians and different ethnic

groups also opposed the government. These people led a civil war against Lenin and the Bolsheviks.

The Russian people were already battered from world war and revolution. Their suffering became even greater, however, during this new civil war. Between 1918 and 1920, millions died from disease and starvation, as well as in violent battles.

Communism

Lenin wanted to create communism in Russia. Communism is a political and economic system in which all land and all businesses are controlled by the government.

In the months before the outbreak of the civil war, Lenin wrote, the Bolsheviks had left "one foot in socialism." In other words, they had been moving slowly toward a society controlled by workers. Now, though, Bolshevik leaders took harsh steps to achieve communism in Russia.

The Bolsheviks outlawed all private property, including farms. Farmers were forced to give all of their grain to the government. Lenin replaced factory workers' committees with new managers who were controlled by the Communist Party. Citizens were called upon to serve in the military. To break people's loyalty to religion, the Bolsheviks closed churches and arrested religious leaders. Lenin insisted that all loyalty be focused on the government.

Union of Soviet Socialist Republics

By 1920 the Bolsheviks had defeated their enemies. Two years later they renamed the old Russian empire. The new nation became known as the Union of Soviet Socialist Republics, or the Soviet Union. The soviets were councils of workers and soldiers formed during the revolution.

In 1922 Lenin became ill. He struggled to return to work, but another leader in the Soviet government was growing more powerful. His name was Josef Stalin.

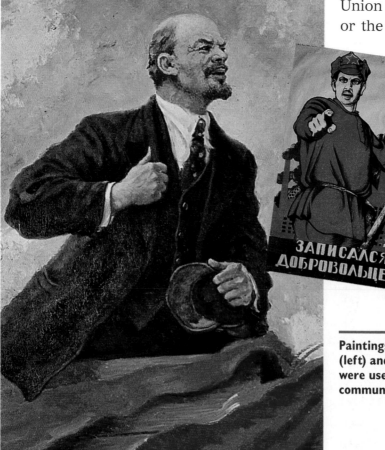

Paintings such as this one of Lenin (left) and political posters (above) were used to urge people to support communism and join the military.

STALIN'S RULE OF TERROR

Lenin died in 1924. Soon after, Josef Stalin became the new leader of the Soviet Union. In 1928 Stalin began working to make the Soviet Union stronger. He drew all power into the government. Stalin also created huge collective farms. Collective farms were run by the government and worked by many families. People not needed on farms were sent to work in mines and factories springing up across the nation. An economy completely controlled by government is called a command economy.

Within just 20 years the Soviet Union became one of the world's strongest industrial nations. Thousands of railroad lines crisscrossed the country, linking towns and cities that had never been connected before. Around 1900 many Russian farmers had never seen a tractor. By the 1940s Soviet factories were making more tractors than any other factories in the world.

Totalitarian Rule

People paid a huge price, however, for growth and change in the Soviet Union. Stalin used totalitarian (toh tal ih TAIR ee un) methods to rule the nation. In a totalitarian society, a dictator, often representing a single political party, controls all aspects of people's lives. Stalin and the Communist Party controlled the Soviet Union through fear and terror. For many, life was more difficult than it had been under the tsars. People were arrested for speaking their minds freely or for writing to friends in other countries. Many managers were killed because their factories or farms did not produce an expected amount. Stalin also ordered his secret police to arrest anyone who he thought challenged him in any way.

Many of those arrested were religious leaders. Their followers were forced to worship secretly or face arrest themselves. Stalin had more than 15 million people killed or sent to prison camps in Siberia. Almost half of them were Ukrainians. Many starved because the collective farms failed to produce enough food. Large numbers of people were sent to camps where religious

---

Stalin (below left) forced thousands of people to work on collective farms (below). Despite much hard work, many collective farms failed.

leaders, teachers, workers, and others Stalin considered "enemies of the people" were imprisoned.

Oil, iron, timber—all the resources of the Soviet Union's new industry—were in great supply in Siberia. Since few people lived there, Stalin used political prisoners to help collect the resources.

One women's camp had the job of cutting down trees. One of the prisoners, a teacher, described the camp this way:

The cold and the hunger; the hunger and the cold. This must have been the blackest, the most [deadly], the most evil of all my winters in the camps.

WHY IT MATTERS

In the early 1900s life changed dramatically in Russia during a period of revolution. Many of the changes that took place became the foundation of a communist system of government. For this reason, the Russian Revolution is also known as a communist revolution. One of the revolution's many effects was the formation of the Soviet Union.

Revolutionary leaders had promised "peace, land, and bread." Under the communist government, however, most people in the Soviet Union had none of these things. Millions were killed and sent to prison camps in Siberia by Josef Stalin. Stalin used totalitarian methods to rule the nation.

For many, suffering worsened when the Soviet Union and many other countries became involved in another world conflict. To the west of the Soviet Union, a dictator in Germany was making plans that would lead to war.

✓ Reviewing Facts and Ideas

MAIN IDEAS

- Millions of serfs under Russia's tsars lived in poverty. The abolition of serfdom in 1861 gave farmers a limited amount of freedom.

- The Russian Revolution began in 1917 as a revolt against World War I, the tsar, and poor working and living conditions. Seven months later Lenin and the Bolsheviks seized control, bringing communism to the country they later renamed the Soviet Union.

- Under Stalin, the Communist Party controlled the Soviet Union using totalitarian methods.

THINK ABOUT IT

1. What were the policies of the Soviet Union regarding religious beliefs and practices?

2. Define the term *communism*.

3. **FOCUS** How were the governments led by Tsar Nicholas II and Josef Stalin similar? How were they different?

4. **THINKING SKILL** Describe Josef Stalin's *point of view* about the need to totally control the economy of the Soviet Union.

5. **GEOGRAPHY** Why might Stalin have chosen Siberia as a site for prisons?

1890 1915 1929 1945 1965 1990

World War II

Read Aloud

"I pray to Almighty God that He shall spare the nations the terrible sufferings that have just been [forced] on my people. . . . Are [you] going to set up the terrible precedent of bowing before force?"

In 1936 Ethiopian emperor Haile Selassie (HĪ lee suh LAS ee) appeared before the League of Nations to protest Italy's invasion of his African country. The League, however, did not come to Selassie's aid. Ethiopia would not regain its independence for nearly five years. During much of that time, the world was once again plunged into war.

Focus Activity

READ TO LEARN

What conditions led to the outbreak of World War II?

VOCABULARY

- fascism
- inflation
- depression
- propaganda
- World War II
- Axis
- Allies
- concentration camp
- Holocaust

PEOPLE

- Adolf Hitler
- Winston Churchill
- Franklin Roosevelt
- Anne Frank

PLACES

- Pearl Harbor
- Normandy

THE BIG PICTURE

After the signing of the Treaty of Versailles, the countries that had fought in World War I turned to their own affairs. In the last lesson you read about the communist revolution in Russia. In 1922, the dictator Benito Mussolini and his Fascist (FASH ihst) party rose to power in Italy.

The Fascists believed in a powerful leader, totalitarian government, and an extreme form of nationalism. They supported a government whose goals they thought to be more important than those of individual people. This type of government came to be known as fascism. In some places fascism also came to mean hatred of certain ethnic groups.

After Italy took control of Ethiopia in 1936, Mussolini joined forces with another fascist dictator, Adolf Hitler of Germany. The people of nearby nations began to see that fascism was a serious threat to peace.

540

GERMANY AFTER WORLD WAR I

In 1919 Germany began to live by the conditions of the Treaty of Versailles. The treaty stripped Germany of land and forced it to pay huge fines.

To meet these expenses the German government began printing large amounts of paper money. Before long Germany had printed so much money that it began to lose its value. The result was a period of inflation, or rising prices. Huge amounts of money were needed even to buy necessities such as food. By 1923 inflation had made German money practically worthless, and people's savings were gone.

In that year a bitter ex-soldier named Adolf Hitler led an attack against the German government in the state of Bavaria. Although the attack failed and Hitler was jailed, many Germans supported his actions. His followers were known as the Nazi (NAHT see) party.

Fascism in Germany

By the early 1930s, Germany and much of the world suffered a depression (di PRESH un). During a depression, fewer goods are produced, prices drop, many people lose their jobs, and money is hard to get.

During these hard times Hitler used propaganda (prahp uh GAN duh) to convince Germans that their nation could once again become powerful. Propaganda is the spreading of certain ideas or attitudes that have been exaggerated or falsified to advance a particular cause.

Hitler's propaganda spread the false idea that the Germans were a "master race," meant to rule the world. The Nazis wrongfully blamed Germany's Jews, along with the Treaty of Versailles, for the depression that was devastating the country. Promising to raise Germany back to glory, Hitler once again tried to gain control in 1933. This time he succeeded.

Hitler ruled as a fascist dictator, forming an alliance with Mussolini in Italy. He and the Nazis stirred up hatred against Jews. In five years the Nazis' plans would lead to the largest war in history.

Hitler (left) used propaganda methods to convince Germans that Germany would become powerful. His followers raised their arms and shouted "Hail Victory!"

A SECOND WORLD WAR

In 1938 Hitler ordered Nazi troops to occupy neighboring Austria. With this command, Hitler knowingly broke the rules of the Treaty of Versailles. Then, in March 1939, Hitler seized control of Czechoslovakia. After years of trying to avoid war with Germany, the leaders of Britain and France promised to defend Hitler's next target—Poland. Europe was on the brink of war once again.

The German Advance

World War II began in Europe on September 1, 1939. On that day German tanks began a *blitzkrieg* (BLIHTZ kreeg), or "lightning war," in Poland. Hitler and Josef Stalin, whom you read about in Lesson 2, had recently signed a friendship treaty. With the help of the Soviet Union, Germany defeated Poland within weeks. Britain and France declared war on Germany but had not been able to defend their ally, Poland.

Eight months later German forces turned west. Hitler's armies quickly overran Belgium. They went on to seize Paris by June 1940. Hitler's fighting method of blitzkrieg was proving very effective. Germany had beaten France—a major world power—in only six weeks! With much of France under German control, Hitler made Britain the next Nazi target.

Many areas in London (left) were destroyed during the Battle of Britain. People often found their homes reduced to rubble by nightly bombings (above).

The Battle of Britain

The British people prepared for the worst. The country's leader, Prime Minister Winston Churchill, declared:

We shall fight on the seas and oceans, we shall fight with growing confidence and growing strength in the air, we shall defend our island, whatever the cost may be. . . . We shall never surrender.

Two months later, in August 1940, the Battle of Britain began. For almost a year German planes bombed the island nation every night. The British air force fought back. Although many sought safety in underground shelters, more than 12,000 British people were killed in the fighting. Despite the cost Britain did not surrender. The nation stood firm, as Churchill had predicted.

Weather Plays a Part

In June 1941 Hitler ended the bombing of Britain. Germany had lost more than 2,000 planes, along with their crews. Having failed in Britain, Hitler decided to break his treaty with Stalin. He ordered his armies to turn east and invade the Soviet Union. The Germans began what was to become a three-year struggle for control of major Soviet cities and supply centers. Millions of Soviet soldiers and civilians died during the struggle.

The Soviet Union now became an ally of Britain. In spite of their political differences, the British welcomed the Soviets in the fight against their common enemy, the Nazis. By November 1941 German troops were very close to one of their goals: the Soviet capital, Moscow. Soviet armies fought to defend their capital and their country. The German troops were finally stopped, however, by a deadly northern winter. On December 6, the near-frozen Germans began to retreat. It would not be the last time nature played a part in the outcome of the war.

An Attack on the United States

War had begun earlier in Asia than it had in Europe. Japan had hoped to create an empire with an endless supply of raw materials and labor for industry. By 1931 Japanese forces had invaded northern China. Later Japan conquered about one quarter of China and some islands off the coast of South Asia. Find the region of Japanese expansion on the map on pages 544–545.

In 1940 Japan formed an alliance with Germany. The conquests and the alliance created tension between Japan and the United States, which was against Japan's continuing expansionist policy. Japan was determined to stop the United States from involvement in its expansionist plans.

On December 7, 1941, Japan launched an attack without any warning or declaration of war. The target was the United States naval base at Pearl Harbor, Hawaii. More than 2,000 people died in the attack. The United States was now involved in World War II.

President Franklin Roosevelt declared war on Japan on December 8, 1941. Three days later, on December 11, Germany and Italy declared war on the United States. Japan, Germany, Italy, and their other allies were known as the Axis. The Allies included Britain, France, the Soviet Union, the United States, and China, among others. The United States had to fight Japan in Asia and Germany and Italy in Europe and Africa. As in World War I, United States forces would be very important to the Allied war effort.

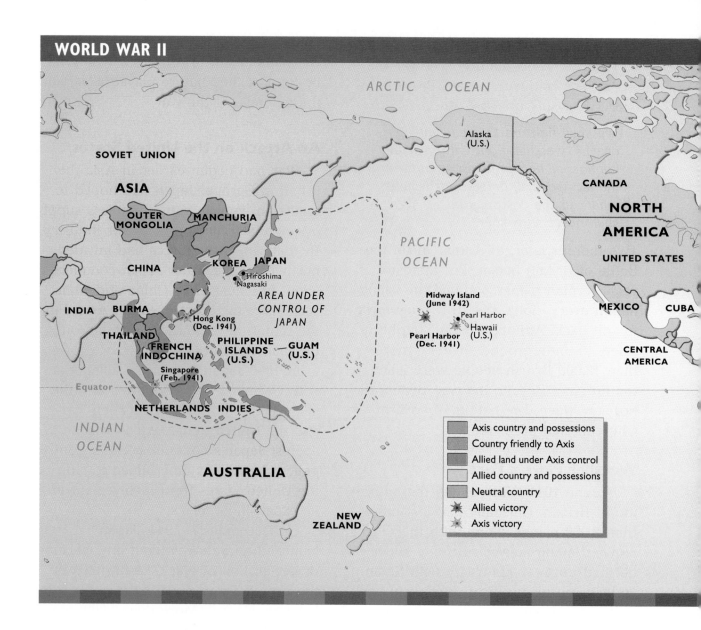

Map legend:
- Axis country and possessions
- Country friendly to Axis
- Allied land under Axis control
- Allied country and possessions
- Neutral country
- Allied victory
- Axis victory

"THE LONGEST DAY"

For three years the United States, Britain, and other Allies fought the Nazis in Europe and North Africa. In that time, the Soviet Union struggled to push back and destroy the German invaders on its soil. Finally, Allied leaders prepared to put a risky plan into action. On the night of June 5, 1944, the Allies would begin a surprise invasion of Axis-held France. If they succeeded, Germany would be surrounded on three sides—west, east, and south. The Allies' code name for this operation was D-Day.

Allied leaders prepared their forces to land on the beaches of Normandy, France, at dawn on June 6. They would reach shore while the tide was low so that German weapons on the beach would be open to attack. Months earlier, weather experts had concluded that the best conditions for an attack would exist between June 5 and 7. On June 4, though, a terrible storm raged across the English Channel. Would nature stop the biggest sea invasion in history?

The storm actually helped the Allies. German commander Erwin Rommel believed that the Allies would not

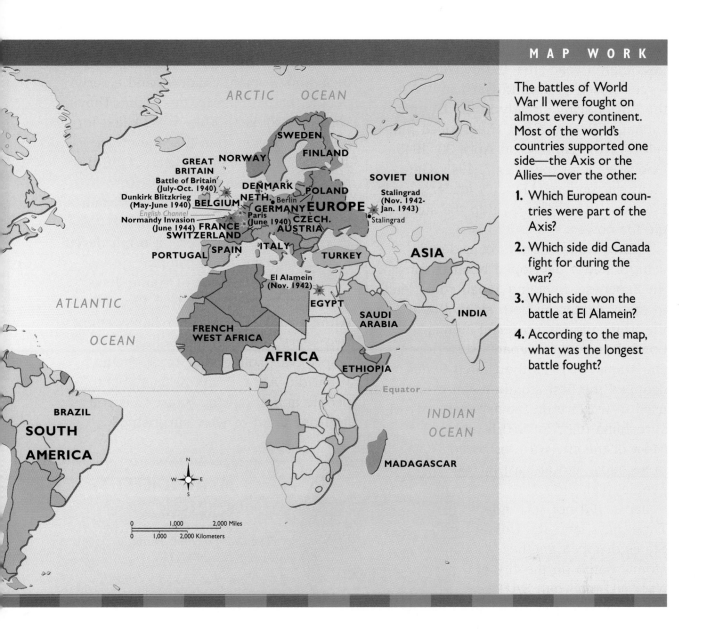

ARCTIC OCEAN

SWEDEN
NORWAY
FINLAND
GREAT
BRITAIN
Battle of Britain
(July-Oct. 1940)
Dunkirk Blitzkrieg
(May-June 1940) BELGIUM
DENMARK
NETH.
Berlin
POLAND
GERMANY EUROPE
SOVIET UNION
Stalingrad
(Nov. 1942-
Jan. 1943)
English Channel
Normandy Invasion
(June 1944) FRANCE
Paris
(June 1940)
CZECH.
AUSTRIA
Stalingrad
SWITZERLAND
PORTUGAL SPAIN ITALY
TURKEY
ASIA
El Alamein
(Nov. 1942)
EGYPT
SAUDI
ARABIA
INDIA
FRENCH
WEST AFRICA
AFRICA
ETHIOPIA
ATLANTIC
OCEAN
Equator
BRAZIL
SOUTH
AMERICA
INDIAN
OCEAN
MADAGASCAR

N
W E
S

0   1,000   2,000 Miles
0   1,000   2,000 Kilometers

The battles of World War II were fought on almost every continent. Most of the world's countries supported one side—the Axis or the Allies—over the other.

1. Which European countries were part of the Axis?

2. Which side did Canada fight for during the war?

3. Which side won the battle at El Alamein?

4. According to the map, what was the longest battle fought?

invade during such weather. He traveled home to Germany for a few days, just when D-Day arrived. The Allies attacked. Over 11,000 Allied planes dropped bombs and over 2,700 ships unloaded almost 200,000 men onto the beaches of Normandy. Find Normandy on the map.

Afterwards, an Allied soldier said D-Day seemed like "the longest day" of his life. At the end of that day, allied forces held the beaches. The Allies would now begin to push the Axis powers east across Europe and west from the Soviet Union.

On D-Day Allied soldiers gained control of the German-held beaches in Normandy, France, then moved inland to free Paris.

THE END OF THE WAR

Less than a year after D-Day, Allied forces closed in around Germany. With the Soviet army already in the German capital of Berlin, Adolf Hitler killed himself to avoid capture on April 30, 1945. One week later, on May 7, 1945, Germany surrendered. Japan's leaders, however, refused to give up the struggle for power.

United States leaders considered using a newly developed bomb against the Japanese. Invading Japan could lead to many deaths on both sides. Could the tremendously powerful atomic bomb bring about Japan's surrender? On August 6, 1945, the United States dropped the first atomic bomb ever used in warfare on the Japanese city of Hiroshima (hihr uh SHEE muh). Most of the city was destroyed in seconds, and at least 80,000 people died.

Japan did not surrender. Three days later the United States dropped another atomic bomb on the city of Nagasaki (nah guh SAH kee). Japan surrendered on August 14, 1945. The most terrible war in history was finally over.

The Terrible Effects of Fascism

In the days before their defeat, German and Japanese commanders rushed to hide evidence of their concentration camps. Concentration camps are places where people are imprisoned because of their heritage, religious beliefs, or political views. Prisoners in Japanese and Nazi concentration camps were tortured and often killed. Millions of others were murdered as well.

The Nazis murdered about 6 million Jews, or two-thirds of Europe's Jewish population, in concentration camps or by execution squads. These people, including women, children, and elderly people, had committed no crime. They were not soldiers. They were killed for no other reason than that they were Jewish. This deliberate destruction of human life is called the Holocaust (HOL uh kawst). About another 6 million people, among them Gypsies, Poles, Russians, and Slavs were also murdered in Nazi concentration camps.

One of the millions of young Jews who died in the camps was 15-year-old Anne Frank. She and her family spent two years hiding in the Netherlands before Nazi soldiers captured them. What did Anne Frank believe about people and about the future? Do you find her point of view surprising?

MANY VOICES
PRIMARY SOURCE

Excerpt from
The Diary of Anne Frank,
July 1944.

It's really a wonder that I haven't dropped all my ideals, because they seem so absurd and impossible to carry out. Yet I keep them, because in spite of everything I still believe that people are really good at heart. I simply can't build up my hopes on a foundation consisting of confusion, misery, and death. I see the world gradually being turned into a wilderness, I hear the ever approaching thunder, which will destroy us too, I can feel the sufferings of millions and yet, if I look up into the heavens, I think that it will all come [out] right, that this cruelty too will end, and that peace and tranquility will return again.

Children like these brothers at the Auschwitz concentration camp were imprisoned by the Nazis. Prisoners in the camps were often tortured and killed.

WHY IT MATTERS

World War II was the largest war in history. Unlike World War I, which had been fought mostly in Europe, World War II took place in Europe, Asia, Africa, and the islands of the Pacific. While many battles took place on land, there were sea battles on the world's oceans, as well. The war left as many as 50 million people dead. Many millions more would be affected by its horrors throughout their lives.

People once again began to adjust to peace after a world war. It was not always easy. Destroyed roads, bridges, homes, and cities around the world had to be rebuilt. There were other serious problems, too.

Leaders of the United States and Western Europe feared the communist government of the Soviet Union. Soon the two most powerful Allies, the United States and the Soviet Union, would become bitter enemies. You will read about their conflict later in the chapter.

Reviewing Facts and Ideas

MAIN IDEAS

- In the 1930s Nazi leader Adolf Hitler used propaganda to convince many Germans that their nation could return to its former power.

- A world depression in the 1930s caused suffering in many nations and helped to bring about the rise of fascist dictators, such as Hitler.

- The Nazis murdered about 6 million Jews in concentration camps. This became known as the Holocaust. There were also some 6 million other victims of the Holocaust, including Gypsies, Poles, Russians, and Slavs.

- Japan attacked and conquered parts of Southeast Asia and the Pacific. After Japan attacked Pearl Harbor, the United States entered World War II. The war came to an end after the United States used two atomic bombs on Japanese cities.

THINK ABOUT IT

1. How did the United States help the Allied war effort?

2. Why was D-Day an important battle?

3. **FOCUS** How did Hitler use the problems created by inflation, the depression, and unemployment to make himself dictator of Germany? How did he use this power to bring about World War II?

4. **THINKING SKILL** List three *facts* and one *opinion* about fascism.

5. **GEOGRAPHY** What role did the weather and time of attack play in the planning and outcome of D-Day?

Geography Skills

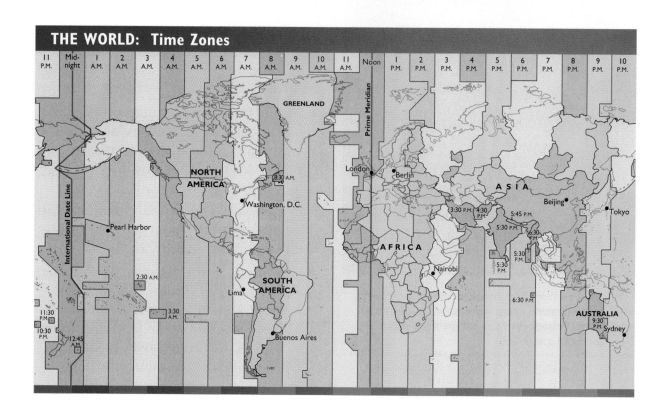

THE WORLD: Time Zones

| 11 P.M. | Midnight | 1 A.M. | 2 A.M. | 3 A.M. | 4 A.M. | 5 A.M. | 6 A.M. | 7 A.M. | 8 A.M. | 9 A.M. | 10 A.M. | 11 A.M. | Noon | 1 P.M. | 2 P.M. | 3 P.M. | 4 P.M. | 5 P.M. | 6 P.M. | 7 P.M. | 8 P.M. | 9 P.M. | 10 P.M. |

GREENLAND

Prime Meridian

International Date Line

NORTH AMERICA

London • Berlin

ASIA

8:30 A.M.

Washington, D.C.

Beijing • Tokyo

Pearl Harbor

3:30 P.M. 4:30 P.M. 5:45 P.M.

AFRICA

5:30 P.M. 6:30 P.M.

2:30 A.M.

Nairobi

5:30 P.M.

Lima • SOUTH AMERICA

11:30 P.M.

3:30 A.M.

6:30 P.M.

AUSTRALIA

10:30 P.M.

9:30 P.M. Sydney

12:45 A.M.

Buenos Aires

Time Zone Maps

VOCABULARY

time zone
International Date Line

WHY THE SKILL MATTERS

Just before 8 A.M. on December 7, 1941, Japanese warplanes began bombing the United States naval base at Pearl Harbor, Hawaii. What time was it in Washington, D.C.? You can figure out the answer by reading a time-zone map.

Not everyone in the world is on the same time schedule. In fact, the world is divided into 24 **time zones**. Time zones were created by scientists in the 1800s to standardize timekeeping throughout the world. They based their work on the fact that Earth rotates 360° each day and that it always moves from west to east while rotating. Since Earth completes one rotation every 24 hours, the scientists divided 360° by 24. The result, 15°, is the amount that Earth rotates in one hour. Each time zone is a strip on a map about 15 degrees of longitude wide. As you can see from this time-zone map, though, some zones have been divided differently to make timekeeping easier for people living in certain regions.

USING THE SKILL

You can see Earth's 24 time zones marked in different colors on this map. As a line of reference, find the line of longitude called the prime meridian. The top of each zone tells what time it is when the time at the prime meridian is noon. Because Earth

548

rotates eastward, zones east of the prime meridian have times that are later in the day. Zones to its west have times that are earlier in the day.

Find the zone in which Hawaii is located. Now find the zone in which Washington, D.C., is located. How many zones east of Pearl Harbor is Washington, D.C.? Since Washington, D.C., is 5 zones east, it is 5 hours ahead in time. The bombing of Pearl Harbor began at 7:55 A.M., Hawaii time, or 12:55 P.M. in Washington, D.C. President Franklin Roosevelt first received word of the bombing at 1:50 P.M., Washington, D.C., time. What time was that in Hawaii? Count west 5 zones and you know that it was 8:50 A.M., Hawaii time.

The tricky part begins when crossing the International Date Line. This is an imaginary line in the Pacific Ocean. The line marks the boundary between one day and the next. Whenever the International Date Line is crossed heading *east*, today becomes *yesterday!* Take the time difference between Japan and Hawaii, for example. Travelers from Japan add 5 hours to their watches when heading east to Hawaii. They also set back their calendars by one day! Imagine that it's 9:00 A.M. on Wednesday in Tokyo. What time and day would it be in Hawaii? It would be 2:00 P.M. on Tuesday.

What happens when travelers head west across the International Date Line? They count *backward* in the time of day, but *forward* one day. Travelers heading from Lima to Beijing, for example, would set their clocks back 11 hours, but move their calendars up one day.

Helping yourself

- A time-zone map shows how Earth's 24 **time zones** are divided.

- When traveling east, add hours to count time. When traveling west, subtract hours.

- When crossing the **International Date Line**, you subtract a day going east and add a day going west.

TRYING THE SKILL

At 2:41 A.M. on May 7, 1945, German leaders surrendered to Allied leaders in Berlin. Thus began V-E (Victory-in-Europe) Day. What time and date was it in London when V-E Day officially began? In Tokyo?

REVIEWING THE SKILL

Use the Helping Yourself box to help determine the answers to the following questions.

1. What are time zone maps?

2. Why are time zones east of the prime meridian later than those to its west?

3. Why can crossing the International Date Line be tricky? What do travelers have to remember as they cross it heading east? Heading west?

4. What were your answers for the section above? How did you figure them out?

5. When might you need to read a time-zone map in your own life?

Airplanes like the Concorde can travel quickly through many time zones.

1890 1900   1976 1990

Communism In China

Read Aloud

"Many times my husband told me that it was in those early days, as a poor son of a poor peasant family, that he became a revolutionary. He was determined that the [life] of the Chinese peasant should not continue to be so wretched, that little boys in China should have shoes to wear and rice to eat."

Soong Chingling (SOONG CHING LING) wrote these words about her husband, Sun Yat-sen (SUN YAHT SEN), known also as the "father of modern China." He would help start an age of revolution in China.

Focus Activity

READ TO LEARN

What were the causes and effects of revolution in China?

VOCABULARY

- warlord
- Long March
- commune
- Cultural Revolution

PEOPLE

- Sun Yat-sen
- Chiang Kai-shek
- Mao Zedong

THE BIG PICTURE

In the early 1900s Russia was not the only country on the edge of revolution. Like Russia, China had not kept pace with the technological and economic changes that were changing western societies. Most Chinese worked as farmers, just as they had since the Han dynasty. For poor farmers, survival was a daily struggle that could be lost when a flood, drought, or big tax bill hit.

By the early 1900s, however, change had come to China. Britain had seized control of Hong Kong, and forced China to open its markets to trade. Japan had taken over the island of Taiwan. Britain and other nations also set up zones within China that were subject to their laws, rather than China's. Many Chinese disliked the way their country was being treated by European nations. Some of these people believed the time had come for another change.

THE END OF DYNASTIES

During this time of unrest, the Qing (CHING) dynasty ruled China. The Qing were Manchus. They had come from the region of Manchuria, located northeast of China. During their 267-year reign, the Manchus saw several challenges to their rule. In the late 1800s, however, unhappiness with the Manchus was perhaps greater than in the past. Many people in China called for the government to be more democratic and less influenced by other nations. Strong leaders began to call for China to change. You read about one such leader in the Read Aloud.

A Voice of the People

Sun Yat-sen was born in 1866, near the southern city of Guangzhou (GWAHNG JO). However, he lived and studied in the Hawaiian Islands when he was young. That time spent away from China helped to shape Sun's views of how life could be improved in his own country.

After returning to China, Sun devoted much of his time to trying to change the government. Sun believed that his country needed to free itself of foreign rule in order to become great again. He said society would be fairer if ordinary citizens had a voice in their government. Finally, Sun told his audiences, China needed to focus on improving agriculture and industry. Many people agreed with his message. Sun once described his goal in this way:

> The real trouble is that China is not an independent country. She is the victim of foreign countries. . . . I set myself the object of the overthrow of the Qing dynasty and the establishment of a Chinese republic in its ruins.

The End of Imperial Rule

Sun and his supporters began a revolt against the Manchus in 1905. Six years later the Qing dynasty fell. It was the last of a series of dynasties that had begun ruling China more than 2,000 years earlier. On January 1, 1912, Sun Yat-sen and his Nationalist party took control of the government. They formed the new Republic of China.

Keeping the republic united turned out to be difficult. Strong local military leaders, called warlords, took advantage of China's unrest to seize power in their own areas. Nationalist forces struggled until 1927 to defeat many of the warlords. Even then it was only with the help of Chinese and Soviet communist allies that they succeeded. While Nationalist forces fought against the warlords, Sun Yat-sen died. Who would be the next leader of China?

Sun Yat-sen and Soong Chingling, his wife, helped China become a republic in 1912.

DIVIDED NATION

A Nationalist general became the next leader of the Republic of China. He was Sun's brother-in-law, Chiang Kai-shek (CHANG ki SHEK). Chiang did not want to keep lasting ties to the communist allies who had helped to defeat the warlords. Neither he nor his supporters wanted China to become communist, as the Soviet Union had. However, Communists were becoming a large political group in China. In 1927 Chiang turned on the Communists with force. A new period of civil war began in China.

The Long March

In 1934 Chiang ordered his troops to surround the Communists in southern China. The troops stopped food and supplies from getting through. Chiang hoped this plan would end the communist movement once and for all.

An army of 80,000 Communists, led by Mao Zedong (MOU DZE DUNG), broke past the Nationalist troops, however. This army began a long flight to safety in the north. The journey came to be known as the Long March. Men and women hiked and climbed almost 6,000 miles in about a year. On the map you can see the route the communists traveled in that time.

The Long March was equal to almost the entire length of a round trip across the mainland United States! During their flight the communists faced many Nationalist air attacks and battles. Also they traveled across harsh land. The marchers found it hard to cross the steep mountains. They were hungry and had little more than straw sandals for shoes. One man recalled:

As we climbed higher, we were caught in a terrible hailstorm and the air became so thin we could hardly breathe. . . . Our breath froze and hands and lips turned blue. . . .

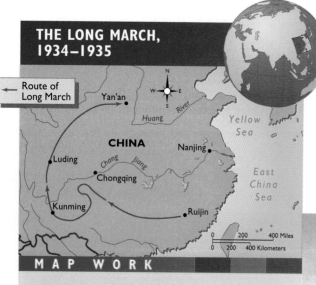

THE LONG MARCH, 1934–1935

Route of Long March

Yan'an · Huang He River · Yellow Sea · CHINA · Luding · Chang Jiang · Nanjing · Chongqing · East China Sea · Kunming · Ruijin

0 200 400 Miles
0 200 400 Kilometers

MAP WORK

Mao Zedong led the Communists on a 6,000-mile march, trying to avoid Nationalist forces.

1. Where did the Long March start? Where did it end?

2. What major river did the Communists cross?

This poster shows Mao Zedong many years after the communists took control of China.

*Those who sat down to rest . . .
froze to death on the spot.*

Those who survived the mountains faced more hardships in the rainy marshes of northern China. There, quicksand could suck people down in minutes. Finding food and clean water was very difficult.

Only about one out of ten people who began the Long March arrived at the great bend of the Huang River. There, the survivors recovered from their journey and began to spread the ideas of communism.

Enemies Cooperate—Briefly

In 1937, two years before World War II began in Europe, Japan launched a full-scale invasion of China. The Communists and the Nationalists agreed to work together to fight the Japanese. In 1945, when Japan was defeated at the end of World War II, the two parties prepared to fight each other once again.

This time the Communists had an advantage. The Nationalist government had done most of the heavy fighting against the Japanese. They were also being blamed for inflation. Remember that inflation was a problem in Germany before Hitler took power.

The Communists, meanwhile, had become very popular in rural areas. Mao and his followers talked with thousands of people. The Communists also worked with farmers, showing them ways to produce more crops.

After two years of fighting, the Communists succeeded in driving the Nationalists from mainland China. Chiang and his

On Taiwan, Chiang Kai-shek (above) and the Nationalists established a government in exile.

followers retreated to the island of Taiwan. There they continued the Republic of China in exile from the mainland. In 1949 Mao and his followers created the People's Republic of China on the mainland. It was now the Communists' turn to try to lead China.

Recovering from Civil War

In October 1949 Mao proclaimed before cheering crowds, "China has stood up!" Gone were the warlords and Nationalist leaders. Many people believed that China's new Communist leaders would bring good government and good jobs to people everywhere.

The Communists quickly set out to rebuild their war-torn nation. They provided housing, medical care, and food supplies for city workers. They supported education for all, along with equal rights for women.

The changes brought by Mao and the Communists, however, had a great price. Between 1949 and 1952, the new government took over all businesses. As in the Soviet Union, landlords had all of their property taken away. As many as one million people were killed by the Communists during the takeover.

CHINA UNDER MAO

In the early 1950s the Chinese economy was growing, but not at a pace that pleased Mao. In 1957 he announced that it was time for China to take a "Great Leap Forward." There was no telling what China could do, he said, if people pitched in and worked harder. "More, faster, better, cheaper" became the slogan of the day. Factories worked around the clock to produce more steel, the building block of industry. Families tried to help by setting up tiny steel-making furnaces in their backyards.

Commune Life

Many farmers and their families were forced to join large **communes** (KAHM yoonz). A commune is an organized community in which all members share work and resources. Mao told people that by working together they would make the land more productive. Villages were combined to form single communes of up to 20,000 people. They could not choose the crops they wanted to farm. Instead the government assigned each commune a crop to produce. People in communes were also forced to build bridges, dams, and work on other projects for the government.

Family life in the commune was very different than it had been on small farms. People were expected to put loyalty to the government and commune ahead of loyalty to their families. At first, men, women, and children each slept in separate buildings. All residents of the commune ate together in large dining halls. Commune workers were divided into teams. Each team was responsible for a particular job such as cooking the meals, hoeing the fields, or schooling the children who lived on the commune.

Instead of producing more grain, communes produced less. This happened partly because farmers were so busy doing other things, such as making steel. China, however, lacked the resources to produce the steel it needed. Also, much of the steel produced could not be used because it was made incorrectly. Few Chinese workers had been trained in the modern ways of making steel.

In time Mao's plan for China failed. As many as 20 million people may have starved to death during a famine that followed the Great Leap Forward.

A New Revolution

Some regional leaders tried to help the situation by allowing farmers to once again own and control small pieces of land. Mao accused those leaders of "copying the West." In 1966 he removed them from power and put a new plan into action.

Mao began a ten-year period called the **Cultural Revolution**. He called for the destruction of all non-communist beliefs. These included many long-held religious and cultural beliefs. Any leaders critical of Mao were punished. With

Mao Zedong's supporters wave his Little Red Book of teachings. Their banner says that they are building a new world.

government support, groups of students broke into people's homes. They destroyed Confucian books and ancient Chinese classics, as well as non-Chinese writings. Anyone with western-made clothing or a European-style haircut faced attack. Many innocent people were accused of being American spies. They were harshly punished.

One schoolgirl, Anchee Min, was forced to say her teacher was a spy. Anchee Min could not believe that her teacher, Autumn Leaves, was an enemy of China. But government leaders said that any teacher who asked students to read foreign literature was a traitor. Min later described how her teacher was treated by government officials.

Two strong men escorted Autumn Leaves onto the stage facing the crowd of 2,000 people. . . . Her arms were twisted behind her. . . . A rectangular board reading "Down with American Spy" hung from her neck. . . . Autumn Leaves kept silent. When kicked hard, she said that she had nothing to confess.

The dream of a China transformed by communism had turned into a nightmare.

WHY IT MATTERS

The Cultural Revolution ended in 1976 with the death of Mao Zedong. During Mao's 27-year rule, major changes had taken place in China. China had closed its doors to the United States and some other democratic nations until 1971. After Mao's death, though, some leaders who had been punished during the Cultural Revolution returned to power. They had new ideas for China. You will read about them in Chapter 20.

✓ Reviewing Facts and Ideas

MAIN IDEAS

- In the early 1900s many Chinese felt China should be free of foreign rule and should become more democratic.

- Sun Yat-sen led a revolt that overthrew the Qing dynasty in 1911. His Nationalist Party later fought the Communists for power.

- In 1949 the Nationalists retreated to Taiwan and the Communists created the People's Republic of China.

- Mao Zedong's Great Leap Forward and Cultural Revolution brought great unrest to China.

THINK ABOUT IT

1. Why was anti-foreign feeling so strong in China in the early 1900s?

2. What were the effects of the Cultural Revolution?

3. **FOCUS** List <u>causes</u> and <u>effects</u> of the communist victory in China.

4. **THINKING SKILL** *Determine the credibility of the source* on page 552. How did you reach your conclusion?

5. **GEOGRAPHY** How might geography have played a role in helping Mao and his followers escape Nationalist forces during the Long March?

1890   1915   1940   1945   1989

Cold War

Read Aloud

"An iron curtain has descended across the Continent [of Europe]. Behind that line lie all the capitals of the ancient states of central and eastern Europe."

Winston Churchill, Prime Minister of Great Britain, said these words in 1946. He imagined an "iron curtain" that formed a dividing line between communist Europe in the East, and democratic Europe in the West. The idea of that "iron curtain" became a symbol of a new kind of war—one that would dominate world events for over 40 years.

Focus Activity

READ TO LEARN

How did the Cold War develop after World War II?

VOCABULARY

- superpower
- free enterprise
- Cold War
- United Nations
- NATO
- Warsaw Pact
- Korean War
- nuclear arms race

PEOPLE

- Fidel Castro
- Nikita Khrushchev
- John F. Kennedy

PLACES

- Yalta
- Berlin

THE BIG PICTURE

After World War II, several European countries had lost millions of people, had tremendous debts, and were in ruins. Although the Soviet Union had lost nearly 20 million people, its armies held most of Eastern Europe. Only the United States was stronger and richer than before the war. Yet about 300,000 Americans had died.

Because of their strength, the United States and the Soviet Union became known as **superpowers**. As you have read, the Soviet Union had a communist government. The United States supported **free enterprise** and democracy. A free enterprise economy, also called a market economy, is based on private ownership of land and businesses.

Tensions between the superpowers and their supporters developed into what became known as the **Cold War**. The Cold War was a struggle between the United States and the Soviet Union without the two nations fighting a full-scale war against each other.

NEW TENSIONS

In February 1945 the end of World War II in Europe was still three months away. Allied leaders met in the town of Yalta in the Soviet Union to discuss their plans. They agreed to create a United Nations organization. This world organization would be stronger than the League of Nations. It would work to prevent future conflicts.

The Allies also agreed to divide Germany into zones that the Allies would control for a period of time. Lastly, they agreed that the Eastern European nations taken over by Soviet troops when they defeated the Nazis there should be given the right to choose their own governments.

New Alliances

The Soviet Union's leader, Josef Stalin, quickly broke the agreement at Yalta. He refused to remove his troops from neighboring countries, including Poland, Czechoslovakia, and Romania. Soviet troops forced those nations to accept communist governments.

Fearful of further Soviet expansion, nations in western Europe and North America formed NATO, or the North Atlantic Treaty Organization, in 1949.

They pledged to defend each other if attacked. The Soviet Union and the communist countries of Eastern Europe signed a similar agreement called the Warsaw Pact in 1955.

War in Korea

A year after the creation of NATO, the Cold War heated up when a conflict with weapons took place in Asia. This conflict was the Korean War. After World War II, Korea had been freed from Japanese control. The Korean peninsula was then divided into two nations. The northern nation was communist and the southern nation was democratic.

In 1950 communist North Korea invaded democratic South Korea. To prevent the spread of communism, the United States sent thousands of troops to help United Nations troops fight North Koreans. The North Koreans were aided by the Chinese. The war lasted three years without a clear victory for either side. However, North Korean troops had been forced to withdraw from South Korea. At the war's conclusion, much of the Korean landscape was devastated and four million people were dead.

Allied leaders Winston Chuchill, Franklin Roosevelt, and Josef Stalin met in Yalta in 1945 to discuss the ending of World War II.

TENSIONS BUILD UP

Korea was not the only country to be damaged by the Cold War. When World War II ended, Germany had been split. The Soviet Union was left in control of eastern Germany including the eastern part of Berlin, the capital city. Britain, France, and the United States controlled western Germany and the western part of Berlin.

By 1948 it was clear that the Soviet Union was not going to withdraw its troops from Germany. Soviet leaders established a communist government in the areas occupied by their troops. The communist part of Germany became the country of East Germany. The western part of Germany became the country of West Germany. The city of Berlin was split in the same way.

In the years that followed, thousands of East Germans who did not want to live in a communist nation moved to West Berlin. Such movement ended, however, in the early morning hours of August 13, 1961. While the people of Berlin slept, East German police built a barbed-wire fence between East and West Berlin. Over the next few days that fence became a concrete wall.

EUROPE, 1948–1989

- Communist countries
- Non-communist countries
- "Iron Curtain"

MAP WORK

After World War II Europe was divided between the mostly communist eastern countries and the mostly democratic western ones.

1. Which communist countries were east of the Iron Curtain?

2. What country bordered the Iron Curtain on the southeast?

The Berlin Wall was built in 1961 to stop the flow of East Germans crossing the border into democratic West Germany.

A Divided City

The Berlin Wall divided backyards, streets, and even houses and churches. It was guarded by East German soldiers with machine guns. Escape became very difficult. Yet many people did make their way west. Some traveled in tiny tunnels or hot-air balloons. Others crossed the border hidden in coffins or secret car trunks. For every one person who made it, however, many more failed. At least 80 people were killed and hundreds more arrested while trying to leave East Berlin.

The Race to Build Nuclear Arms

A new competition between the superpowers began as Cold War tensions in Germany continued. In 1945 the United States had been the only nation with the ability to make atomic bombs. Remember the United States had used atomic bombs against Japan during World War II. By 1949, though, the Soviet Union also had these destructive weapons.

American scientists then developed the far more deadly hydrogen bomb. The Soviets matched this development a year later. The power for these weapons comes from nuclear energy. For this reason, the competition between the superpowers became known as the nuclear arms race.

In 1957 the Soviet Union's next development amazed the world. They launched *Sputnik*, a human-made satellite that orbited Earth. Scientists had come a long way since Isaac Newton first discovered how gravity held the planets in orbit. Western leaders became concerned. They were worried that *Sputnik*—and other satellites like it—could be used to launch nuclear weapons toward the West.

The Soviet Union often held military rallies like this one in Moscow's Red Square in 1988.

Preparing for Disaster

Many Americans feared that a Soviet nuclear attack could begin at any time. Students practiced what to do if a bomb exploded while they were at school. Some school principals handed out metal tags for children to wear. The tags would help them to be identified after an explosion. Thousands of families built small bomb shelters in their backyards. They stocked them with goods needed for survival.

CUBAN MISSILE CRISIS

In 1959, Cuba's Fidel Castro succeeded in establishing the first communist government in the Americas. He won the support of Nikita Khrushchev, the Soviet leader who had come to power after Josef Stalin's death in 1953. The President of the United States, John F. Kennedy, tried—unsuccessfully—to end Castro's government in 1961. In 1962 a crisis arose over this island nation.

A Nuclear Target

Khrushchev sent nuclear weapons to Cuba in the summer of 1962. By October the weapons in Cuba were ready for use. Missiles far more powerful than the atom bombs used in Japan were now just a 20-minute flight away from the capital of the United States. Millions would die if the missiles were fired.

On October 22 Kennedy told Americans of the great danger. He warned that the United States would respond to the fire of any Cuban missile with an attack upon the Soviet Union. He also ordered Soviet ships to stay out of Cuban waters or risk the start of war.

On Saturday, October 27, the crisis reached a peak. American forces around the world were on full alert. In Cuba, over 40,000 Soviet and Cuban troops checked their weapons and missiles. In Washington, D.C., hundreds of people stood outside the White House—some shouting for peace, others for war. A single Soviet ship continued on a course toward Cuba.

To many, the end of the world seemed just around the corner. An adviser to the President of the United States later recalled,

It was a beautiful fall evening . . . and I went up into the open air to look and to smell it, because I thought it was the last Saturday I would ever see.

An adviser to Khrushchev remembered,

I went and telephoned my wife and told her to drop everything and get out of Moscow. I thought [United States] bombers were on the way.

Kennedy and Khrushchev met in 1962 (above) after Castro (above right) allowed Soviet missiles into Cuba.

THE COLD WAR: GOVERNMENTS AND ECONOMIES

	Government	Economy
United States and Allies	**Democracy** Citizens elect their leaders and can influence government decisions. Rights are protected.	**Free Enterprise** Resources, property, and production are controlled by individuals and companies and the laws of supply and demand.
Soviet Union and Allies	**Communism** Totalitarian government controls nearly every aspect of people's lives.	**Command Economy** Government controls all resources and production. Citizens have little control over which goods and services are produced.

CHART WORK

The two superpowers had very different economies and ways of governing.

1. Which form of government gives citizens more rights?

2. Who controls resources and production in a command economy?

The Crisis Ends

As world leaders nervously watched and waited, Kennedy and Khrushchev reached an agreement. The United States promised not to invade Cuba. The Soviet Union's ships agreed to return home. The Soviet Union also removed its missiles from Cuba. In return the United States removed missiles based in Turkey.

The world had come dangerously close to a nuclear war. In the following year, 1963, the two superpowers signed a treaty banning most kinds of nuclear weapons testing. World leaders hoped that the treaty would reduce the chance that nuclear weapons would ever be used in war.

WHY IT MATTERS

For the next 25 years the United States and the Soviet Union continued their struggle. No part of the world was untouched by the Cold War. Conflicts between the ideas and values of communism and democracy took place around the globe. Look at the chart to compare the different systems that clashed in the Cold War. In the next chapter you will read about one such conflict in Vietnam. In the 1980s, however, Cold War tensions began to ease. You will read about that in Chapter 20.

✓ Reviewing Facts and Ideas

MAIN IDEAS

- The Cold War was a struggle between the United States and the Soviet Union without the nations fighting a real war with each other.

- Josef Stalin forced some nations of Eastern Europe to accept communism.

- Communist attempts at expansion resulted in the division of Korea and Germany into separate communist and democratic nations.

- The nuclear arms race increased Cold War tensions. Nuclear war almost began after the Soviet Union placed missiles in Cuba in 1962.

THINK ABOUT IT

1. What factors led to the Cold War?

2. What was the Berlin Wall? Why was the wall such a powerful symbol of the Cold War?

3. **FOCUS** How did Cold War tensions affect the relationships between Eastern and Western nations?

4. **THINKING SKILL** What were some _causes_ of the Cuban Missile Crisis? What were some of its _effects_ on the United States and Soviet Union?

5. **WRITE** Suppose you are a journalist in Berlin at the end of World War II. Write an article describing the changes taking place in the city.

CHAPTER 18 REVIEW

Major Events

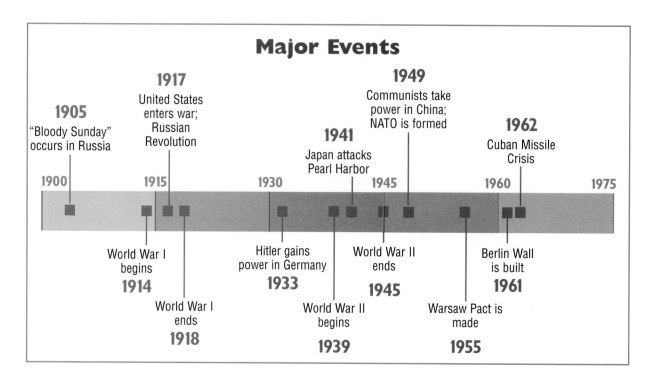

1905
"Bloody Sunday" occurs in Russia

1917
United States enters war; Russian Revolution

1941
Japan attacks Pearl Harbor

1949
Communists take power in China; NATO is formed

1962
Cuban Missile Crisis

1900 1915 1930 1945 1960 1975

World War I begins
1914

World War I ends
1918

Hitler gains power in Germany
1933

World War II begins
1939

World War II ends
1945

Warsaw Pact is made
1955

Berlin Wall is built
1961

THINKING ABOUT VOCABULARY

Number a sheet of paper from 1 to 10. Beside each number write the word or term from the list below that matches the statement.

alliance   nuclear arms race
commune   propaganda
depression   superpower
fascism   totalitarian
nationalism   tsar

1. Strong loyalty to one's country and culture

2. A much stronger country than other countries

3. Exaggerated or false information used to persuade people to help advance a cause

4. Title of an emperor of Russia before the revolution

5. An agreement between countries to defend each other if attacked

6. A form of government in which a dictator controls all aspects of people's lives

7. A form of government in which the goals of a nation are more important than its individuals

8. An organized community where members share work and resources

9. The build-up of nuclear weapons by superpowers

10. An extended period of economic difficulties in a nation

THINKING ABOUT FACTS

1. How did World War I begin?

2. What was the Russian Revolution?

3. Why did Hitler gain power in Germany after World War I?

4. What was the Cultural Revolution? Why did Mao Zedong launch it? What were its consequences?

5. Look at the time line above. Which events listed after the end of World War II have to do with the Cold War? Explain.

WRITING AN EXPLANATION
Briefly describe the conflicts that started World War I. Then explain why the United States entered it. What factors went into changing the American policy of neutrality. How did the United States help the Allied Powers to win the war?

WRITING A COMPARISON
Write two paragraphs in which you compare Hitler and Stalin. How were they alike? How were they different?

WRITING A REPORT
Write a report about the Cold War. Describe the nuclear arms race and several of the crises and conflicts that took place during this time.

APPLYING GEOGRAPHY SKILLS

TIME ZONE MAPS

1. What is a time zone map?
2. What is the International Date Line?
3. Look at the time zone map on page 548. As you can see, Africa is larger than the United States. How many time zones cross Africa?
4. What is the time difference between the East Coast and West Coast of the United States? If you lived in San Francisco and wanted to call somebody in Boston at noon, Boston time, what time would you make your call?
5. How are time zone maps useful?

Summing Up the Chapter

Copy the sequence chains below on a separate sheet of paper. Review the chapter to find a chain of two events that led to the main event listed. When you have filled in the blanks, use the chains to answer the question "What are some of the conditions that led to the main conflicts of the twentieth century?"

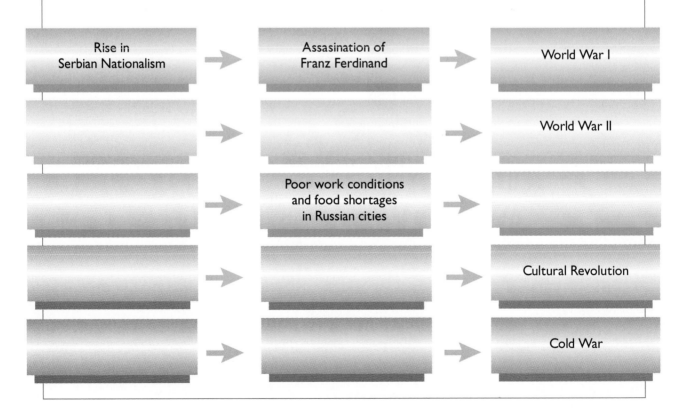

Rise in Serbian Nationalism →	Assasination of Franz Ferdinand →	World War I
→	→	World War II
→	Poor work conditions and food shortages in Russian cities →	
→	→	Cultural Revolution
→	→	Cold War

New Nations

THINKING ABOUT
HISTORY AND GEOGRAPHY

In this chapter you will read how nations in many parts of the world gained independence from colonial powers in the 1900s. In places such as Ghana and India, strong leaders led the nationalist movements that broke colonial ties. For many, though, independence brought more war.

AFRICA

Accra

1869

EGYPT
The Suez Canal is built

1940s

DELHI, INDIA
Mohandas Gandhi leads protests against the rule of Britain

1850

1930

1950

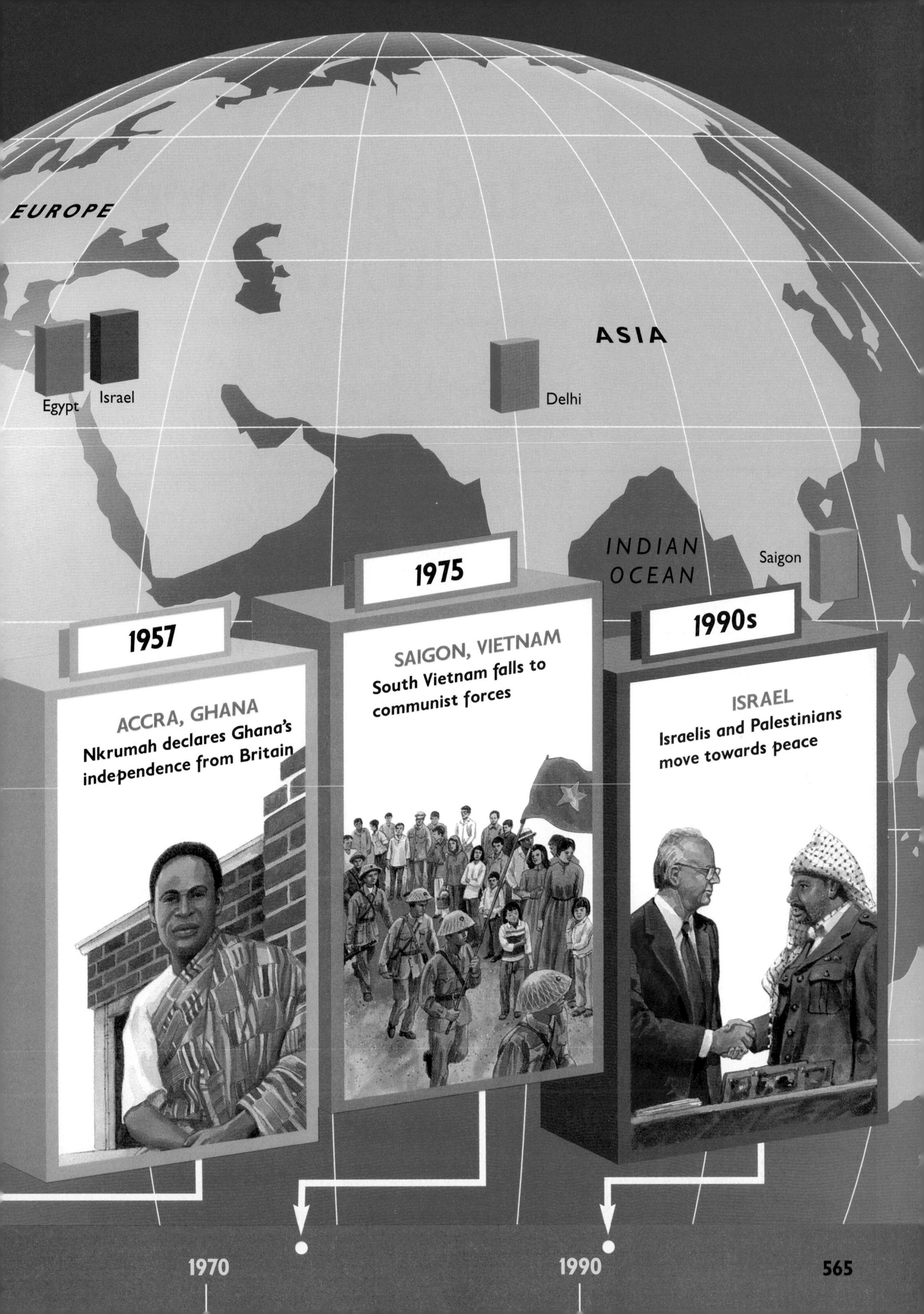
EUROPE
ASIA
Egypt
Israel
Delhi
INDIAN OCEAN
Saigon
1957
ACCRA, GHANA
Nkrumah declares Ghana's independence from Britain
1975
SAIGON, VIETNAM
South Vietnam falls to communist forces
1990s
ISRAEL
Israelis and Palestinians move towards peace
1970
1990

1800   1850 1874   1995 2000

Independence in Africa

Focus Activity

READ TO LEARN

How did countries in Africa gain independence from European rule?

VOCABULARY

• boycott

PEOPLE

• Kwame Nkrumah
• Gamal Abdel Nasser

PLACES

• Accra
• Ghana
• Egypt
• Suez Canal
• Cairo

Read Aloud

"You ask what the difference between colonialism and independence means to me. . . . Before white and black did not talk. But now at this moment I have the pleasure of sitting with you, a white, and I speak to you like a man. That is all we fought for, the right to respect."

Carlos Miranda spoke these words to a writer after his country, Guinea-Bissau (GIHN ee bihs OW), gained independence from Portugal in 1974. Millions of other Africans shared his feelings about the long period of European rule in Africa.

THE BIG PICTURE

The Portuguese were the first Europeans to set up colonies in Africa. They built stone forts along the West African coast in 1482. By 1900, millions of Africans had come to be ruled by Europeans. Look at the map on page 570 to see how England, France, Portugal, Belgium, Germany, and Spain carved Africa into colonies. In 1914 Ethiopia and Liberia were the only independent nations south of the Sahara Desert. In some areas European colonists set up European-style communities and profited from the continent's natural resources.

During the 1900s many Africans spoke out against the European nations that had controlled their continent. In the decades that followed World War II, Africans once again began to control their own lands and lives. In this lesson you will read about two examples of nations struggling to gain independence.

THE GOLD COAST

In 1874 the British established the colony they called the Gold Coast on Africa's west coast. The British named the colony after the gold that was plentiful in West Africa at the time. The Gold Coast is the area where the ancient African kingdoms of Ghana and Mali, which you read about in Chapter 13, were located.

As you read in Chapter 16, from the early 1500s to the middle 1800s, the Gold Coast had been a center of the slave trade. Both African and European slave traders raided villages of the region. Traders sold their captives for guns, cloth, and other goods.

Profits from Trade

Even after the British government outlawed slave trade, the Gold Coast continued to grow as an important center for British trade. By 1874, other European colonies in Africa and North America were already settled by British citizens. The Gold Coast, however, was run by fewer than 4,000 British soldiers and government officials. Profits gained in the Gold Coast were sent to Britain.

The supply of gold available in West Africa dwindled over time. The British colonists soon found a new source of income, though. The British planted cacao (kuh KAH oh) throughout large areas of the Gold Coast. The cacao tree produces seeds that are used to make chocolate. By 1920 half of the world's supply of cacao was grown in the Gold Coast.

Colonial Conflict

Many Africans in the Gold Coast had long resented British control of their land. Earlier, the British government of

Cacao beans (right) are used to make chocolate. This man in Ghana (above) is gathering dried beans.

the Gold Coast had also faced resistance from the Asante. These Africans, who lived in an independent kingdom to the north, had taken part in the slave trade along with the British and the Dutch in the 1700s. As the Asante gained wealth and power, they expanded the borders of their land. They resisted British rule until 1902.

Later, still others began to oppose British rule. Among them was a young man who studied philosophy in the United States. His name was Kwame Nkrumah (KWAHM ee en KROO muh). After leaving the United States in 1945 he wrote:

I saw the Statue of Liberty with her arm raised as if in personal farewell to me. [I said silently] "You have opened my eyes to the true meaning of liberty. I shall never rest until I have carried your message to Africa."

THE RISE OF AFRICAN NATIONALISM

When Kwame Nkrumah returned home, he found a nationalist spirit already growing in the Gold Coast. Africa's nationalist leaders wrote for newspapers and talked with people in the colonies. In response the British gave some positions in the colonial government to Africans. Nearby French colonies did the same, giving Africans control of agriculture and education.

Economic Protest

Some African leaders were happy with the way change began to take root in the colonies. Others, like Nkrumah, wanted full independence right away. Nkrumah's slogan was "Self-Government Now." He began to organize boycotts of British goods. A boycott is a form of protest in which people join together and refuse to buy goods unless their demands are met. Nkrumah also led strikes against British companies in the Gold Coast.

DID YOU KNOW?

What is the origin of the word boycott?

The word *boycott* was first used in the 1880s in Ireland. Ireland was then a colony of Great Britain. Captain Charles Cunningham Boycott managed a large farm for the Earl of Erne in County Mayo. He was a cruel and demanding landlord who forced the farmers living on the earl's lands to pay high rents. In 1880 many farmers refused to pay the rent that Captain Boycott demanded. Soon the word *boycott* began to be used to describe this and other kinds of economic protest. The word and the protest were later used around the globe.

A Big Step

In time the British governor agreed to let the people of the Gold Coast elect a prime minister. In the 1951 election, Nkrumah's party won almost all the votes in the center of Accra, the capital city. The British governor asked Nkrumah to form a government. The governor did not, however, give the government full power immediately. Control of the colony remained in British hands for six more years.

Independence at Last

On March 6, 1957, the Gold Coast became a new African nation called Ghana. The new nation was named after the ancient kingdom of Ghana, which, as you have read, ruled part of West Africa from the 700s to the 1200s.

Africans living under colonial rule in Africa were inspired by the new nation. Kwame Nkrumah, now the new nation's prime minister, said:

> *If we are to remain free, if we are to enjoy the full benefits of Africa's enormous wealth, we must unite to plan for the full [use] of our human and material resources in the interest of all our people.*

Over the next 30 years, Africans in other nations gained control of their governments, ending European rule on most of the continent. Independence was not always won peacefully, though. Also, as in Ghana, independence did not always bring full democracy. The map on page 570 shows when each African nation gained independence from a European power.

Fight for Control of Egypt

Across the Sahara Desert, 2,500 miles northeast of Ghana, a struggle for independence was taking place in

Kwame Nkrumah, center, is shown in 1957, just after Ghana gained independence from Britain.

Egypt. The British had controlled this land since the 1880s. Britain ruled Egypt less directly than it did Ghana. Even so, the Egyptian leader had little power to govern.

British colonists in Egypt developed an economic system based on cotton. The cotton was used to supply British textile factories. More important than cotton, however, was the location of Egypt. The point where Asia and Africa meet is in the northeast corner of Egypt. There the Suez Canal Company, owned mostly by French and Egyptians, built the **Suez Canal**. Later the British became part of the company, and, along with the French, controlled the canal.

The Suez Canal connected the Mediterranean Sea and the Red Sea, providing a shortcut for ships sailing between Europe and Asia. British ships sailing to the British colony of India could now pass through the Suez Canal instead of traveling around Africa. The canal cut 6,000 miles from the trip.

During World War I nationalist spirit in Egypt grew. Many Egyptians were angry over British demands for men and supplies. Continued unrest led Britain to give Egyptians limited power in their government in 1922. Although Egyptians elected a parliament, Britain appointed the king, Fuad (foo AHD) I. Fuad I ruled according to the wishes of the British. Europeans continued to control the Suez Canal.

A Republic is Born

Many Egyptians were angry that they had not truly been given a voice in their government. In 1952 a group of Egyptian officers in the British army seized control of the government. The group was led by Gamal Abdel Nasser (guh MAHL ahb DEL NAHS ur). The officers forced the king to leave Egypt. People celebrated in the streets of the capital city, Cairo, singing "Raise up your head my brother, the days of humiliation have passed."

In 1956 Nasser gained control of the Suez Canal.

Today I seize the canal in the name of the people. . . . This night our canal shall be Egyptian, controlled by Egyptians!

The British and their allies sent an army to try to prevent Egypt from taking over the canal. However, governments around the world supported the Egyptians, and the British were forced to give up their claim to the canal. Finally British rule and political influence had come to an end in Egypt.

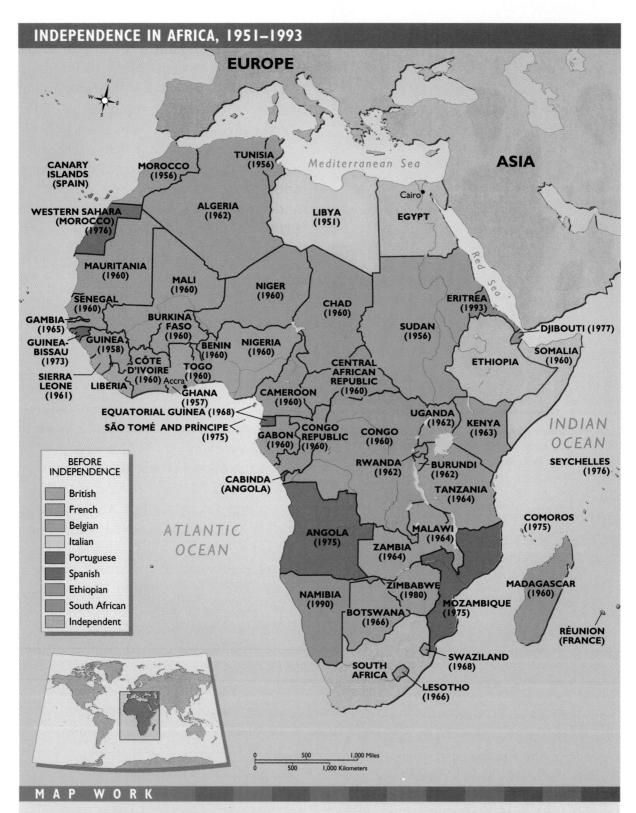

INDEPENDENCE IN AFRICA, 1951–1993

EUROPE

ASIA

Mediterranean Sea

Cairo

Red Sea

CANARY ISLANDS (SPAIN)

MOROCCO (1956)

TUNISIA (1956)

ALGERIA (1962)

LIBYA (1951)

EGYPT

WESTERN SAHARA (MOROCCO) (1976)

MAURITANIA (1960)

MALI (1960)

NIGER (1960)

CHAD (1960)

SUDAN (1956)

ERITREA (1993)

DJIBOUTI (1977)

SENEGAL (1960)

BURKINA FASO (1960)

GAMBIA (1965)

GUINEA (1958)

GUINEA-BISSAU (1973)

BENIN (1960)

NIGERIA (1960)

SIERRA LEONE (1961)

CÔTE D'IVOIRE (1960)

LIBERIA

TOGO (1960)

Accra

GHANA (1957)

EQUATORIAL GUINEA (1968)

SÃO TOMÉ AND PRÍNCIPE (1975)

CAMEROON (1960)

CENTRAL AFRICAN REPUBLIC (1960)

SOMALIA (1960)

ETHIOPIA

GABON (1960)

CONGO REPUBLIC (1960)

CONGO (1960)

UGANDA (1962)

KENYA (1963)

INDIAN OCEAN

CABINDA (ANGOLA)

RWANDA (1962)

BURUNDI (1962)

TANZANIA (1964)

SEYCHELLES (1976)

BEFORE INDEPENDENCE

- British
- French
- Belgian
- Italian
- Portuguese
- Spanish
- Ethiopian
- South African
- Independent

ATLANTIC OCEAN

ANGOLA (1975)

ZAMBIA (1964)

MALAWI (1964)

COMOROS (1975)

NAMIBIA (1990)

ZIMBABWE (1980)

BOTSWANA (1966)

MOZAMBIQUE (1975)

MADAGASCAR (1960)

RÉUNION (FRANCE)

SWAZILAND (1968)

SOUTH AFRICA

LESOTHO (1966)

0   500   1,000 Miles
0   500   1,000 Kilometers

Colonies in Africa gained independence from European rule beginning in 1951. Over a period of more than 40 years, many new nations emerged.

1. In what year did Tanzania gain independence?

2. Which country gained independence in 1951?

3. Which countries were formerly ruled by the Portuguese?

4. Which two European powers ruled the most land in Africa?

WHY IT MATTERS

European colonies in Africa were used to produce wealth for Europeans, rather than building the economy for the benefit of Africans. Europeans also created boundaries in Africa without considering that the continent's 2,000 different peoples had lived in certain areas for centuries. Often a new boundary divided an area where a group lived. When nations became independent, the borders were often the European boundaries. Many conflicts developed as people fought for land that had historically belonged to them but was now part of another nation.

By 1995 all of Africa had thrown off European rule and gained independence. However, many problems remained for its nations—the result of years of foreign rule. In recent years, several African nations have taken steps to solve those problems. In the next chapter you will read about one large African nation and how it achieved democracy and human rights.

President Abdel Nasser of Egypt addresses a crowd in 1958. In 1952 he had won control of the Egyptian government.

✓ Reviewing Facts and Ideas

MAIN IDEAS

- Beginning in the 1500s several European nations established colonies in Africa.

- In 1957 the Gold Coast became the first colony south of the Sahara to gain independence. The new nation was named Ghana.

- Following several steps towards independence, Egyptians gained control of their government in 1952.

- By 1995 all European colonies in Africa had become independent.

THINK ABOUT IT

1. How did European countries gain wealth from their African colonies?

2. How did the British respond to the activities of nationalist leaders in western Africa?

3. **FOCUS** How did the country of Ghana gain its independence from Britain?

4. **THINKING SKILL** Explain two _effects_ of European colonialism on Africa.

5. **GEOGRAPHY** How did the Suez Canal affect the movement of people and goods between continents?

Political Cartoons

VOCABULARY
political cartoon
symbol

WHY THE SKILL MATTERS

During the 1800s powerful European countries established colonies all over the world. Very often colonial powers had disagreements. People who lived in such countries as Britain and France also disagreed at times about whether their countries should establish colonies. Writers discussed these topics in magazines and newspapers.

Also during this time political cartoons began to appear more frequently in European magazines. Political cartoons are pictures that show an opinion about a political matter, such as a government action or an election. Political cartoons are useful historical sources. They tell the modern reader many things about cartoonists and people from the past for whom the cartoons were drawn.

USING THE SKILL

Cartoonists often use symbols in their cartoons to convey information. A symbol is a sign that stands for something else. For example, the character Uncle Sam is a symbol for the United States. The Statue of Liberty and the bald eagle are also symbols for the United States. Symbols provide an easy way for cartoonists to refer to a country such as the United States in a cartoon.

When you look at a political cartoon, study the symbols and try to figure out what they stand for. For example, look at Cartoon A on this page. This cartoon was published in a French magazine. The large figure is

This cartoon expresses the political viewpoint of many French who were angered by Britain's control of the canal.

John Bull, a symbol that stands for Great Britain. The smaller figures standing around John Bull are symbols that stand for other European countries.

It is also important to read any signs or captions that appear in the cartoon. In Cartoon A the words *Canal de Suez* are very important. These are the French words for Suez Canal. Remember what you read about Britain and the Suez Canal in Lesson 1.

Finally, think about the story or opinion that the cartoonist is trying to communicate. Cartoonists often use exaggeration to make their point. In Cartoon A, John Bull is much bigger than the other people. The cartoonist seems to be saying that Britain is over-exerting control of the canal.

TRYING THE SKILL

Cartoon B is from a United States newspaper. The title of this cartoon is "To France! 1917." It shows the Statue of Liberty marching with a number of soldiers. Look carefully at all of the information in the cartoon. What do you think the Statue of Liberty is a symbol for? What do you think she and the soldiers are headed off to do?

Remember what you read earlier about World War I and the role of the United States in the war. How does the title of Cartoon B help you understand its meaning? What do you think the cartoon "says" about the cartoonist's feelings about Americans fighting at the battlefront in France? How can you tell?

REVIEWING THE SKILL

1. Why are political cartoons a useful source for studying history?

2. Why do cartoonists often use symbols?

3. Look at Cartoon A. How do you think an Egyptian would feel about this cartoon?

4. Look at Cartoon B. Do you think that people who lived in France would agree with the opinion of this cartoonist? Why or why not?

5. Find a political cartoon in your local newspaper. What does it tell you about how the cartoonist feels about the topic?

B

Political cartoons often rely on exaggerated representations or humor to express their viewpoints.

1800   1850 1874   1995 2000

New Nations in The Middle East

Read Aloud

"The Government of the State of Israel and the . . . Palestinian people agree that it is time to put an end to decades of . . . conflict."

This is the opening of the Declaration of Principles, a special treaty written in 1993. After half a century of fighting, two peoples came to an agreement: the killing must stop. What caused their conflict?

Focus Activity

READ TO LEARN

What events led to the Israeli-Palestinian conflict?

VOCABULARY

- Zionism
- anti-semitism
- refugee
- Intifada

PEOPLE

- David Ben Gurion
- Yasir Arafat
- Anwar Sadat
- Yitzak Rabin

PLACES

- Middle East
- Palestine
- Turkey
- Iraq
- Israel
- Gaza
- Golan Heights
- West Bank

THE BIG PICTURE

Between the Mediterranean Sea and the western borders of Pakistan and Afghanistan is a region known as the Middle East. It spans all of western Asia and a small part of southeastern Europe. Find the 14 countries of the region on the map on page 576.

This region was the heart of the Baghdad Caliphate from the late 700s to the 1200s. From the 1500s until the end of World War I, the Middle East was ruled by the Ottoman empire. After 1918 Britain and France took control of most of the Middle East.

Along the western edge of the Middle East is a narrow wedge of land lying along the Mediterranean Sea. This land has had great impact on world events, and you have read about it more than once in this book. It has had many names: Canaan, Judea, Palestine, the Holy Land, Israel. Throughout history, it has been home to many peoples and cultures. In this lesson you will read about the struggle that developed between two of these peoples over a land that both claimed as their own.

A JEWISH HOMELAND

How did this struggle over the area that is today Israel develop? Part of the answer lies in the history of Zionism (ZI uh niz um). Zionism is a movement to establish a Jewish homeland, or nation. The word comes from Mount Zion, a mountain in Jerusalem.

An Ancient and Modern Hope

Modern Zionism began in the late 1800s. Its goal, in the words of a Hebrew song, was to make the Jews "a free people in our own land." Actually, the idea of a homeland for the Jewish people began much earlier. This idea began, in fact, in the time of the Diaspora. Remember from Chapter 5 that *Diaspora* means the "scattering" of the Jews from the land of Israel. This scattering began around 600 B.C., when the Babylonians conquered Judah. The Diaspora continued, but some Jews remained in the area. The Romans called it Palestine.

By the late 1800s, when modern Zionism began, Palestine was home to about 450,000 people. Most of them were Arabs. About 25,000 Jews also lived here. Most of the world's Jewish population lived outside of Palestine, in Europe and the rest of the world. However, they had never forgotten their ancient homeland. The yearly Passover seder always ends with the words: "Next year in Jerusalem!"

Troubles in Europe

The desire to return to Jerusalem grew stronger among many Jews in Europe. Feelings of nationalism had spread throughout the world since the French Revolution. Some European Jews, too, began hoping to have their own nation.

Also during this time anti-semitism grew stronger in Europe. Anti-semitism is discrimination against Jews. In Eastern European countries such as Russia and Poland where many Jews lived, Jews were often subjected to sudden, violent attacks. Many Jews left Europe for the United States and other regions, including Palestine.

These Jewish immigrants at a dock in Haifa reflect the desire of many Jews to return to the Jewish homeland and form their own nation.

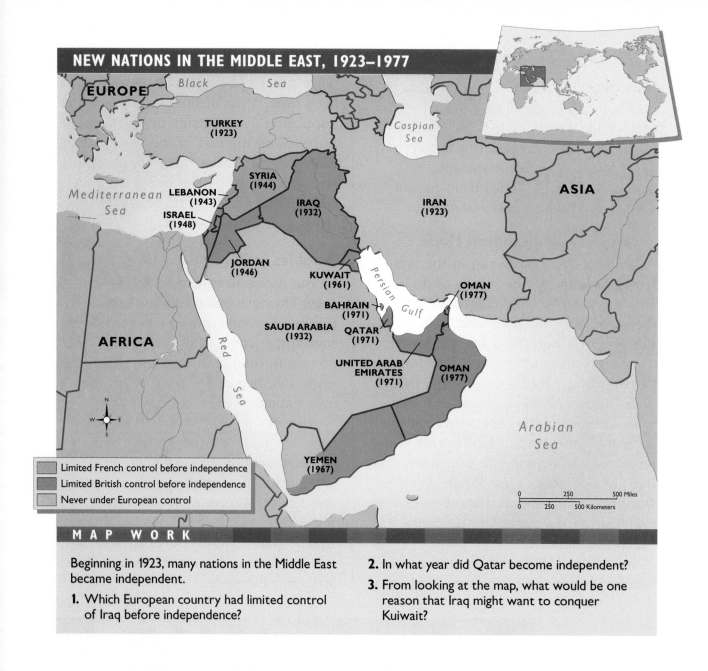

NEW NATIONS IN THE MIDDLE EAST, 1923–1977

EUROPE

Black Sea

TURKEY
(1923)

Caspian
Sea

SYRIA
(1944)

LEBANON
(1943)

ISRAEL
(1948)

IRAQ
(1932)

IRAN
(1923)

ASIA

Mediterranean
Sea

JORDAN
(1946)

KUWAIT
(1961)

Persian Gulf

OMAN
(1977)

BAHRAIN
(1971)

SAUDI ARABIA
(1932)

QATAR
(1971)

UNITED ARAB
EMIRATES
(1971)

OMAN
(1977)

AFRICA

Red Sea

Arabian
Sea

YEMEN
(1967)

Limited French control before independence

Limited British control before independence

Never under European control

0   250   500 Miles
0   250   500 Kilometers

MAP WORK

Beginning in 1923, many nations in the Middle East became independent.

1. Which European country had limited control of Iraq before independence?

2. In what year did Qatar become independent?

3. From looking at the map, what would be one reason that Iraq might want to conquer Kuiwait?

CHANGES IN THE MIDDLE EAST

After the defeat of the Ottoman empire in World War I, Britain and France took over much of the Middle East. By this time, however, nationalist movements were beginning to form in the region.

In 1923 nationalists in what was left of the Ottoman empire established an independent Republic of **Turkey**. It was only the first of several new nations in the Middle East. In 1932, after a period of British rule, the people of **Iraq**

gained independence. Find these and other new nations on the map.

A Growing Population

Feelings of nationalism had been developing among both Arabs and Jews in British-controlled Palestine.

Growing numbers of Jews created tensions with Arabs who were already living in Palestine. Many Palestinian Arabs hoped to build new lives in an independent nation of Palestine. They feared that their own nationalist dreams would be lost.

World War II brought great changes to British Palestine. Many European Jews managed to escape Nazi oppression by immigrating to Palestine. After the war many survivors of Nazi concentration camps arrived in Palestine. By 1947 the number of Jews living in Palestine reached about 650,000, or about one-third of the population. The remaining two-thirds were Palestinian Arabs, most of whom were Muslims.

The Founding of Israel

After World War II the United Nations agreed to divide Palestine between Arabs and Jews. The Jews there accepted the plan. On May 14, 1948, they declared independence as the country of Israel. David Ben Gurion, a leader of the Jewish independence movement, became Israel's first prime minister.

War and Refugees

The day after Israel became an independent nation, armies from five Arab countries attacked the new nation. Jews fought to defend their new country. After more than six months of fighting, the Jews came out as victors. This war, however, was only the first of several wars that would be fought between Israel and Arab countries.

As the result of the Arab-Israeli conflict, as many as 750,000 Palestinian Arabs left Israel. Some fled out of fear. Some were forced to leave. Many settled in refugee camps in Jordan, Syria, and Lebanon. Refugees are people who have to flee their country for safety. About 600,000 Palestinians remained. Mahmoud Darwish, a Palestinian poet described his feelings about living in a homeland controlled by others:

You are my grief and my joy,
my wound and my rainbow,
my prison and my freedom.

In June 1967 war broke out again. In this conflict, the Six-Day War, Israel gained more land, including Gaza, the Golan Heights, and the West Bank. Find these areas on the map on page 578.

To gain back the land for Arabs, the Palestine Liberation Organization, or PLO, was formed in 1964. In 1968, under the leadership of Yasir Arafat, the PLO began to fight to get the land back from Israel.

The First Sign of Peace

Fighting between Arabs and Israelis continued on and off for years. Then in 1977 Egypt's President Anwar Sadat took a daring trip to Israel. For the first time an Arab leader publicly met with leaders of the Jewish nation. The Camp David agreement, signed by Egypt and Israel in 1978, established peaceful relations between those nations.

Golda Meir, Israeli prime minister from 1969 to 1974, greets Egyptian president Anwar Sadat in November 1977.

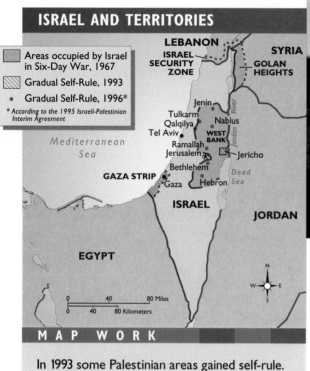

ISRAEL AND TERRITORIES

Areas occupied by Israel in Six-Day War, 1967

Gradual Self-Rule, 1993

• Gradual Self-Rule, 1996*

*According to the 1995 Israeli-Palestinian Interim Agreement

LEBANON

ISRAEL SECURITY ZONE

SYRIA

GOLAN HEIGHTS

Jenin

Tulkarm

Qalqilya

Tel Aviv

Nablus

WEST BANK

Jordan River

Ramallah

Jerusalem

Jericho

Bethlehem

Dead Sea

GAZA STRIP

Gaza

Hebron

Mediterranean Sea

ISRAEL

JORDAN

EGYPT

0   40   80 Miles
0 40   80 Kilometers

N W E S

MAP WORK

In 1993 some Palestinian areas gained self-rule.

1. Which areas were the first to gain self-rule?
2. When did Jenin gain self-rule?

Palestinians show support for their leader Yasir Arafat in September 1988.

WHY IT MATTERS

The Camp David agreement did not end the struggle between Israel and the Palestinians. In 1987 Palestinians in Gaza and the West Bank began a revolt called the Intifada (ihn te FAH duh). *Intifada* means "shaking" in Arabic. Palestinians tried to "shake off" the rule of the Israelis.

Slowly, however, hopes for peace returned to this war-torn land. PLO leader Yasir Arafat and Yitzhak Rabin (YIHT zak rah BEEN), Prime Minister of Israel, signed agreements in 1993 and 1995. You read part of the 1993 agreement in this lesson's Read Aloud. They agreed that a Palestinian homeland would be established in Gaza and the West Bank.

Peace remains a difficult goal. In 1995 an Israeli opposed to the peace process *assassinated* Yitzhak Rabin. To assassinate means to kill for political reasons. Still, hope for peace remains, as Israelis and Palestinians continue to work together to solve their decades-old conflict.

✓ Reviewing Facts and Ideas

MAIN IDEAS

● In the 1900s Zionist immigration to Palestine concerned Palestinians, who desired a country of their own.

● In 1948 Arab armies attacked in an unsuccessful effort to destroy the new Jewish country of Israel. Palestinian refugees fled to other Arab lands.

● An uneasy peace began in the 1990s.

THINK ABOUT IT

1. What were two reasons for the creation of the Zionist movement?

2. Why was the PLO formed?

3. **FOCUS** How did modern Israel begin?

4. **THINKING SKILL** What were two *causes* for the Israeli-Palestinian conflict?

5. **GEOGRAPHY** Why might Israel's shape make it difficult to defend?

MAKING A DIFFERENCE

Building Bridges to Friendship

HERZLIYA, ISRAEL—In Hebrew, the word *shalom* means both "hello" and "peace." In Arabic the word *salaam* has a similar sound and meaning. The group Interns for Peace, led by Rabbi Bruce Cohen, is helping Jews and Arabs in Israel greet each other with these words and build peaceful friendships.

Since 1976, Interns for Peace has trained over 200 Arab and Jewish volunteers to work with Arabs and Jews in schools, homes, community centers, and summer camps in Israel. The volunteers, called interns, organize projects such as building parks or planting trees.

Two 15-year-old girls, Arab Israeli Rola Gbaly (gi BALLY) and Jewish Israeli Sivan Harel participated in a project called Education for Democracy. This project pairs Jewish and Arab schools for monthly get-togethers. Sivan's and Rola's eighth-grade classes met first at Sivan's all-Jewish school in Herzliya. "The most difficult part," says Sivan, "was when we first came together. We were nervous. It wasn't just that we were meeting with new kids. It was that we were meeting with new Arab kids. We thought there would be disagreements. Then we got to know them a little and saw that they are different from us but not very different. They are children just like us."

On the second visit, Sivan's class visited Rola's school in Taibeh, Israel. There, Rola says, "we painted a peace wall." Both girls agreed that the third meeting was the best, because, says Sivan, "The conversations were like with normal friends. We didn't talk about really important things, just about daily life." Rola adds, "I tell people my age that this is a way for us to understand each other." According to Rabbi Cohen, building understanding between Arabs and Jews is the goal of all the projects. "We do not teach people to love one another, we teach understanding and tolerance."

" . . . this is a way for us to understand each other."

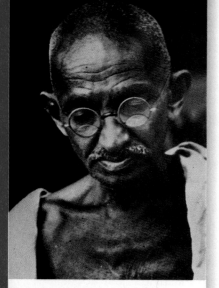

1800   1850   1885   1971   2000

India's Struggle For Independence

Read Aloud

"The force generated by nonviolence is infinitely greater than the force of all the arms invented by man's ingenuity."

   Mohandas Gandhi (moh han DAHS GAN dee) wrote these words during a period when Britain ruled his nation, India. His words describe a way of working toward independence without fighting battles that would harm and kill people. For many years Gandhi led the people of India in a largely nonviolent struggle against Britain.

Focus Activity

READ TO LEARN

How did the nation of India gain independence?

VOCABULARY

- **Raj**
- **civil disobedience**
- **Green Revolution**

PEOPLE

- **Mohandas Gandhi**
- **Mohammed Ali Jinnah**
- **Jawaharlal Nehru**
- **Indira Gandhi**

PLACES

- **India**
- **Pakistan**
- **Bangladesh**

THE BIG PICTURE

By the end of the 1800s Britain's empire stretched around the globe. You have already read about British colonies in the Americas, Africa, and the Middle East. Britain also controlled Hong Kong in East Asia and the island-continent of Australia. However, many British people thought one colony in particular to be "the brightest jewel in the imperial crown."

This "jewel" was India. It was exactly what Britain wanted a colony to be. The Indian subcontinent provided the British with raw materials for industry. The British introduced their way of organizing government and parts of their culture. British technologies such as the railroad helped build industry in India. Even so, as time passed, more and more Indians believed that their nation should gain independence from British rule.

COLONIAL INDIA

The story of British rule in India begins in 1600. In that year Britain's Queen Elizabeth I granted a charter to a group of English merchants. The charter gave the merchants the right to develop trade in Asia for the British government. These merchants hoped to take part in the spice trade that was controlled mostly by Dutch and Portuguese traders. Remember Europeans bought these spices to preserve meat and flavor food. In 1601 the first five English ships set sail for India. You can see India on the map on page 583.

A Powerful Trade Company

The company of merchants became known as the British East India Company. By 1700 the merchants had set up trading centers, which they called "factories," in such cities as Bombay, Madras, and Calcutta.

At the same time as the East India Company pushed farther into India, the Mogul rulers of India were losing power. The British then took part in wars that broke out between local rulers. In the 1850s, after more than ten wars within India, the Company controlled two thirds of the subcontinent. Indian princes ruled the rest of India. They were loyal to the British government. The East India Company became known as the Raj, which comes from a Sanskrit word meaning "king." The Raj set up telegraph lines, organized a postal service, and built railroads between the major cities.

Most Indians were not satisfied with life under the Raj. They resented foreign rule. In 1857 thousands of Indian soldiers in the British army revolted. Soon, the Great Mutiny, as it was called by the British, or the first war of independence as it was called by the Indians, spread across north and central India. Thousands of Indians and British died before Britain put down the revolt. After the war the British government took control of India from the East India Company.

This photo from the late 19th century shows British citizens in India being served by Indian servants. Many Indians resented the British rule of India.

STRUGGLE FOR INDEPENDENCE

The desire for Indian independence grew. In 1885 a group of 73 Indians attended the first Indian National Congress in Bombay. Many of the members had been educated in England. They asked that the Raj spend less of India's tax money on the army and that Indians be given important positions in the government. A few began to talk about gaining independence from Britain.

By 1905 Indian nationalism had become widespread. In that year people began to boycott British cloth. Cloth made in British textile mills and imported to India was sold cheaply. However, the British had placed a tax on Indian cloth that was sent to Britain. The tax hurt India's textile industry. Many people began wearing Indian-made cloth as a sign of national pride.

Mohandas Gandhi

Among the leaders who planned later boycotts and strikes was a young lawyer named Mohandas Gandhi. Gandhi studied law in London and then worked in South Africa to gain rights for Indians who went to live there. When he returned to India in 1915, Gandhi became an important leader in India's fight for independence.

Gandhi had three goals for India. He hoped to see the end of British rule, peace between Muslims and Hindus, and an end to poor treatment of the untouchable caste. Remember untouchables were the people at the lowest level of Hindu society.

Gandhi wore only the simplest handmade cloth and began spinning yarn in his spare time. Soon, the Indian spinning wheel became a symbol of nationalism. Because of his simple life and religious ways, Gandhi became known by the Hindi word *Mahatma*, which means "great soul."

To achieve independence in India, Gandhi believed people should practice civil disobedience. Civil disobedience is a means of protest without violence. One example was the boycott. Another was refusing to obey laws that they believed to be unjust. Gandhi said, "Mass civil disobedience is like an earthquake" and Gandhi's followers were soon shaking the foundations of British rule. Indians joined this movement by refusing to pay taxes or to buy British goods. Thousands, including Gandhi, were jailed. Even the fact that Gandhi was in prison did not stop the protest. Soon nearly all of India followed Gandhi's lead. How did Gandhi describe his work in leading India's struggle for independence?

MANY VOICES
PRIMARY SOURCE

Excerpt from
The Words of Gandhi, c. 1947.

I *have nothing new to teach the world. Truth and nonviolence are as old as the hills. All I have done is to try experiments in both on as vast a scale as I could. In doing so, I have sometimes erred and learnt by my errors. Life and its problems have thus become to me so many experiments in the practice of truth and nonviolence. . . . I have not the shadow of a doubt that any man or woman can achieve what I have, if he or she would make the same effort and* ***cultivate*** *the same hope and faith.*

---

cultivate: to help the growth of

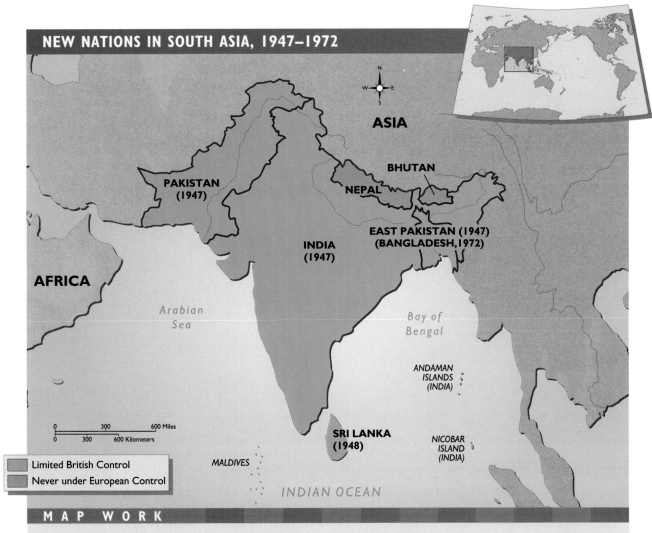

NEW NATIONS IN SOUTH ASIA, 1947–1972

ASIA

PAKISTAN (1947)

BHUTAN

NEPAL

EAST PAKISTAN (1947) (BANGLADESH,1972)

INDIA (1947)

AFRICA

Arabian Sea

Bay of Bengal

ANDAMAN ISLANDS (INDIA)

SRI LANKA (1948)

NICOBAR ISLAND (INDIA)

MALDIVES

Limited British Control
Never under European Control

INDIAN OCEAN

MAP WORK

Some nations in South Asia gained independence from European rule beginning in 1947. Others had never come under Euopean control.

1. Which nations were under British control?

2. In what year did Sri Lanka gain independence?

3. Which country became independent in 1972?

The Brink of Independence

In 1942 the Indian National Congress planned a new campaign to convince the British to leave. People shouted "Quit India" at British soldiers in India's cities. By 1947 the British were ready to give up control of India. Muslims feared that they would be treated poorly by a Hindu-led government. They demanded a separate country. On August 15, India and Pakistan gained independence.

Pakistan was made up of two separate areas in the northern corners of India. Many Muslims lived in these areas known as West and East Pakistan. The prime minister of Pakistan was Mohammad Ali Jinnah (muh HAM ud ah LEE JIHN ah). Jawaharlal Nehru (juh WAH hur ah NAY roo) was prime minister of India.

About ten million people moved across the border to be with people of their own faith. Nearly one million people died in violent conflicts between Hindus and Muslims. Gandhi was shot and killed in such a conflict in January 1948.

THE NEW NATIONS

Although conflicts continued between India and Pakistan, the governments of both countries set about moving their countries forward. Achieving independence had been a huge challenge, but it was only the first of many.

India's Early Years

One of the many problems faced by independent India was raising enough food to feed the country's huge population. The government worked to make agriculture more productive. New types of wheat and rice crops were developed. The new focus on agriculture throughout the nation became known as the Green Revolution.

Other changes fulfilled many of the goals of Mahatma Gandhi. The untouchable caste was officially abolished, although discrimination against untouchables continued. Also, women gained new rights. In the 1940s and 1950s women were granted the right to own property and the right to vote.

In 1966 a woman, Indira Gandhi (ihn DEE rah GAHN dee), became India's prime minister. She was the daughter of Jawaharlal Nehru. Indira Gandhi continued many of her father's plans and policies. However, she also led India in a war against Pakistan. Trouble between East and West Pakistan led to civil war in 1971. In that year the Indian army helped East Pakistan. Soon after, the leaders of East Pakistan established the new independent country called Bangladesh. The Indian subcontinent, once the "jewel in the British crown," now contained three independent nations.

Among the several programs that Indira Gandhi (left) started after she became India's prime minister in 1966, was one to make farming more productive (below).

WHY IT MATTERS

The Ganges, especially, is the river of India. . . . [It is] a symbol of India's age-long culture and civilizations, ever-changing, ever-flowing, and yet ever the same.

With these words, Jawaharlal Nehru summed up his feelings for India. He believed the flow of the Ganges River was as constant and lasting as the nation itself. Today India is the largest democracy in the world with a population of more than 900 million. Its history is long and varied. Great changes occurred in the subcontinent over the centuries. British colonialism had great effects on India in the 1800s and 1900s.

Change in India also influenced other parts of the world. As India struggled to free itself from British rule, other colonies around the world began to work toward independence, as well. Many people have been influenced by Gandhi's method of civil disobedience. In the United States, Martin Luther King, Jr., followed some of the teachings of Gandhi in the fight for civil rights. King described Gandhi with these words: "He lived, thought, and acted, inspired by the vision of humanity evolving toward a world of peace and harmony."

Reviewing Facts and Ideas

MAIN IDEAS

- The British East India Company began to establish trade with India in the 1600s.
- By the middle 1800s the British government had gained control of most of the Indian subcontinent.
- Mohandas Gandhi's civil disobedience program led India to independence.
- In 1947 British rule ended and the independent nations of India and Pakistan were formed.

THINK ABOUT IT

1. Describe three changes that the British East India Company brought to the Indian subcontinent.

2. Why did Indians boycott British-made cloth in 1905?

3. **FOCUS** How did India become an independent nation?

4. **THINKING SKILL** *Compare* India's struggle for independence with the struggle of a country in Africa or the Americas. How was it similar? How was it different?

5. **WRITE** Write an editorial describing how Gandhi's teachings might or might not be useful in solving problems in the world today.

1800   1858   1995 2000

New Nations in Southeast Asia

Read Aloud

In 1949 a leader named Ho Chi Minh declared the independence of his nation, Vietnam. This act followed over 100 years of colonial rule by the French. During those years many Vietnamese struggled to survive. Yet independence did not bring safety and peace to the new nation. Instead the Vietnamese continued to struggle through conflicts and war that divided the nation in many ways.

Focus Activity

READ TO LEARN

How did nations in Southeast Asia gain independence?

VOCABULARY

• Vietnam War

PEOPLE

• Ho Chi Minh

PLACES

• Vietnam
• Southeast Asia
• Laos
• Cambodia
• Burma
• Thailand

THE BIG PICTURE

Vietnam is located in Southeast Asia. In chapter 14 you read about the Khmer who lived in this region around A.D. 1000. For centuries Vietnam was invaded by neighbors such as the Khmer and the Ming of China.

In the middle 1800s, French ships began sailing into the port city of Da Nang. France established colonies in Vietnam and the neighboring countries of Laos and Cambodia. Around the same time, Britain took over parts of Burma, the westernmost kingdom in the region. Nearby Thailand remained one of the few independent areas in Southeast Asia. For about 100 years European powers would shape life for many people in the region. However, desire for the independence of the past grew very strong in Vietnam. This led to conflicts with other countries and within Vietnam.

A COLONY OF FRANCE

In 1858 the French took control of Vietnam's coast. As French soldiers moved inland, local armies slowed their progress. By 1887 France succeeded in occupying Vietnam, Laos, and Cambodia, all of which they called Indochina.

The Colonists Prosper

Vietnam was an important source of raw materials. French colonists sent tons of rice, coal, and tin to France. While the French gained wealth, many of the people of Vietnam suffered. Before the French arrived, almost every family owned some land. By 1920, however, only French colonists and wealthy Vietnamese owned land. Many people were forced to work for others. One worker wrote:

> The larger parts of our wages are taken by the supervisors and foremen . . . [and] our salaries are already too low. . . . Food prices increase every day and we have become hungrier and hungrier.

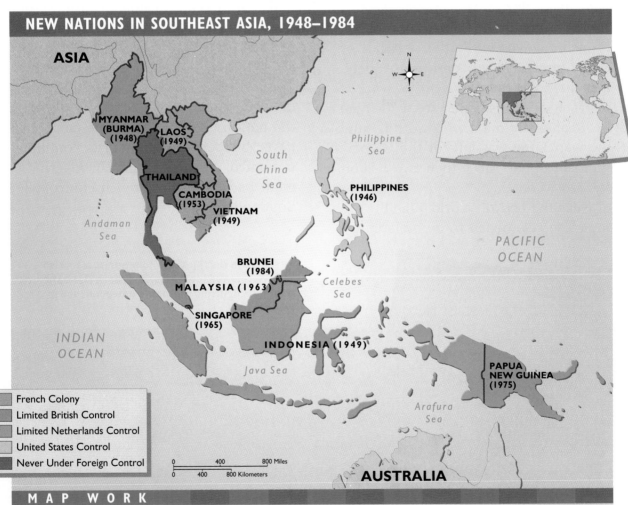

NEW NATIONS IN SOUTHEAST ASIA, 1948–1984

ASIA

MYANMAR (BURMA) (1948)
LAOS (1949)
THAILAND
CAMBODIA (1953)
VIETNAM (1949)
PHILIPPINES (1946)
BRUNEI (1984)
MALAYSIA (1963)
SINGAPORE (1965)
INDONESIA (1949)
PAPUA NEW GUINEA (1975)

Philippine Sea
South China Sea
Andaman Sea
Celebes Sea
PACIFIC OCEAN
INDIAN OCEAN
Java Sea
Arafura Sea

AUSTRALIA

French Colony
Limited British Control
Limited Netherlands Control
United States Control
Never Under Foreign Control

0   400   800 Miles
0 400 800 Kilometers

MAP WORK

Nations in Southeast Asia struggled for freedom from foreign rule. All succeeded in becoming independent.

1. Which nations became independent after 1950?

2. Which foreign power had control in the Philippines?

3. In what year did Malaysia gain independence?

FIGHTING COLONIAL RULE

In the 1920s anti-French feeling began to take shape. Many Vietnamese people formed organizations that opposed French rule. One group, the Vietnamese communists, was led by Ho Chi Minh (HOH CHEE MIHN). His goal was to create an independent Vietnam. The Vietnamese communists worked toward that goal by planning protest marches and labor strikes against the French.

Independence Is Declared

In 1940, during World War II, the Japanese captured Vietnam and other French colonies in Southeast Asia. Japan immediately began to use Vietnam's resources to support its war effort. Rice was shipped from Vietnam to Japanese soldiers who were fighting the war. Little was left for the people of Vietnam to eat. More than two million starved to death.

Near the end of World War II, Japanese rule began to crumble in Southeast Asia. In 1945 an army of Vietnamese communists, called the Viet Minh (VEE et MIHN), took action. The Viet Minh gained control of many areas of the country, especially in the northern region. By September 1945 the communists controlled nearly all of Vietnam. Ho Chi Minh declared the nation's independence and became the head of a new communist government.

The French, however, were not ready to give up their claims to Vietnam. In 1946 the French, aided by the British, went to war against the communists. After eight years of fighting, the French lost an important struggle at the town of Dien Bien Phu (dyen byen FOO). In 1954 the two sides signed an armistice. The armistice called for Vietnam to be divided in half until elections to unify the nation could be held. The elections never happened. Communists continued to control North Vietnam. A government backed by the French controlled South Vietnam.

Ho Chi Minh (left) led the communist effort to gain Vietnam's independence. France signs the treaty recognizing Vietnam's independence in 1954 (below).

From 1965 to 1973, American troops fought to try to prevent communist North Vietnam from taking over South Vietnam.

The United States in Vietnam

The armistice failed to bring peace to Vietnam. The communists wanted to unite South Vietnam with North Vietnam under their leadership. The leaders of South Vietnam, however, wanted to remain independent.

Many leaders in the United States were worried about the spread of communism from North Vietnam. By speaking out in favor of the government of South Vietnam, the United States stood firm against communism in the Cold War. American leaders wanted to keep communism from threatening democratic governments in other parts of Southeast Asia. This led the United States to take action in Vietnam. United States Secretary of State John Foster Dulles said that:

[T]he United States should not stand passively by and see the extension of communism by any means into Southeast Asia.

War Breaks Out

South Vietnamese rebels, supported by North Vietnam, began a war against the government of South Vietnam. Later, North Vietnamese forces also moved into South Vietnam as they tried to spread communism and unite the nations.

The United States had begun to help the government of South Vietnam in 1954. The United States provided the country with money, weapons, and advisers. Then, in 1965, the United States sent troops and planes to help in the fighting. A war that became known as the Vietnam War was now raging. A million tons of United States supplies arrived in South Vietnam every month. By 1968, about half a million troops were stationed in Vietnam.

As American troops suffered losses in Vietnam, public opinion in the United States became divided. Some people believed the United States should be involved in the Vietnam War. Others, however, did not agree. In 1973 the United States began pulling its troops out of Vietnam. Two years later South Vietnam surrendered to North Vietnam. More than 58,000 Americans had died in the war. Nearly two million Vietnamese people had died.

After the Vietnam War, Vietnamese refugees (left) crowded into boats on a voyage to Hong Kong, where they sought freedom from communism.

FACING THE FUTURE

Vietnam faced serious problems after the war. Much of the country had been damaged by bombing and ground fighting. The communist government took control of property and businesses throughout the country after the war. Droughts and floods caused shortages of food. Planting new crops was dangerous because fields contained many unexploded bombs left from the war. Many Vietnamese were unhappy with communist government.

More than one million South Vietnamese people left their nation in overcrowded boats. They decided to risk their lives at sea to settle in free countries rather than live under a communist government. These Vietnamese eventually settled in countries throughout the world. More than 600,000 moved to the United States.

Change in Southeast Asia

Vietnam also had trouble with its neighbor Cambodia. Cambodia's communist leader, Pol Pot, had come to power in 1975 after leading a commu-nist group against the government. During Pol Pot's rule there was a reign of terror. People were forced to leave the cities to live and work in rural camps. Educated Cambodians were considered enemies, and many of them were murdered. There was little food

and no freedom. More than one million people were killed. Many others fled the country. In 1978 Vietnamese soldiers invaded Cambodia, forcing Pol Pot and his supporters to flee. After the United Nations supervised elections in 1993, Vietnamese troops left Cambodia, and a government including different political groups took power.

WHY IT MATTERS

When Vietnam gained independence, it became one of more than 100 new nations formed since 1943. Like many of the other new nations of the world, those in Southeast Asia faced difficult problems. Over 100 years of colonial rule and 30 years of war had harsh effects on Vietnam and on the other nations in Southeast Asia.

Today Hanoi (below), Vietnam's capital, is a busy industrial center, producing textiles, chemicals, and food products.

Since the end of the war in 1975, changes have begun to occur in Vietnam. For years Vietnam depended on the Soviet Union for aid. After the Soviet Union broke up, the leaders of Vietnam, as well as other Southeast Asian leaders, began to work toward an economy that allowed more free enterprise. Foreign companies have built factories in Vietnam. In 1995 Vietnam and the United States once again began to trade and have diplomatic relations.

✓/// Reviewing Facts and Ideas

MAIN IDEAS

- In the middle 1800s the French began to establish a colony in Vietnam. By 1887 they had influence in much of Southeast Asia.

- The colony of Vietnam provided France with many raw materials.

- After World War II the Viet Minh, led by Ho Chi Minh and others, fought for independence from France.

- The United States fought with South Vietnam against communist forces of North Vietnam until 1973.

- In 1975 Vietnam became unified, but faced economic and social problems.

THINK ABOUT IT

1. Why were many Vietnamese people unhappy under French colonial rule?

2. How did World War II change colonial rule in Vietnam?

3. **FOCUS** How did the people of Vietnam finally gain independence?

4. **THINKING SKILL** Describe the *point of view* of United States official John Foster Dulles, quoted on page 589.

5. **WRITE** Write five questions that you might ask a United States soldier who served in Vietnam.

CHAPTER 19 REVIEW

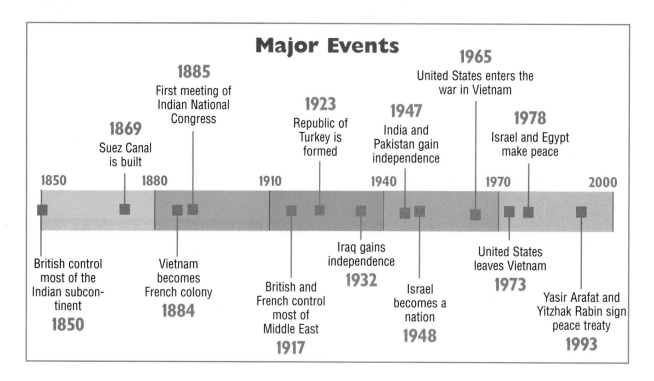

Major Events

1965
United States enters the war in Vietnam

1885
First meeting of Indian National Congress

1923
Republic of Turkey is formed

1947
India and Pakistan gain independence

1978
Israel and Egypt make peace

1869
Suez Canal is built

1850   1880   1910   1940   1970   2000

British control most of the Indian subcontinent
1850

Vietnam becomes French colony
1884

British and French control most of Middle East
1917

Iraq gains independence
1932

Israel becomes a nation
1948

United States leaves Vietnam
1973

Yasir Arafat and Yitzhak Rabin sign peace treaty
1993

THINKING ABOUT VOCABULARY

Number a sheet of paper from 1 to 5. Beside each number write the word or term from the list below that best completes the sentence.

anti-semitism
boycott
civil disobedience
refugee
Vietnam War

1. A _____ is a person who flees his or her country for safety.

2. A nonviolent breaking of the law to protest something is called _____.

3. The _____ in Southeast Asia divided Americans against each other in the 1960s and early 1970s.

4. A _____ is the refusal to buy goods to protest something.

5. Discrimination against Jewish people is called _____.

THINKING ABOUT FACTS

1. Who was Kwame Nkrumah?

2. What role did Gamal Abdel Nasser play in Egyptian history?

3. Where did the Jews who left Russia and eastern Europe go to avoid persecution in the early 1900s?

4. How was Israel created?

5. What was the Camp David agreement? Why was it significant?

6. What was the British East India Company called? Why did most Indians dislike it?

7. Who was Mohandas Gandhi and what were his goals?

8. Why did the French colonize Vietnam, Laos, and Cambodia?

9. Who fought in the Vietnam War? What did each side hope to achieve?

10. Many new nations were created during the twentieth century. Look at the time line above and name as many newly formed nations as you can.

WRITING AN INTERVIEW

Suppose you are going to interview Mohandas Gandhi. Write at least three questions you would ask him. Then list the answers you think he might give.

WRITING A REPORT

Write a report about the Vietnam War and the disagreements it caused in the United States. Explain arguments made by opponents and supporters of the war.

WRITING ABOUT PERSPECTIVES

Write about how Zionists and Palestinian nationalists have seen the situation in the Middle East during the past 40 years.

APPLYING STUDY SKILLS

POLITICAL CARTOONS

1. What is a political cartoon?

2. Look at Cartoon B on page 573. It shows in a positive light the American decision to send troops to fight against Germans during World War I. If a cartoon on the same subject had appeared in a German newspaper, what might it have shown?

3. Review Lesson 3. Describe what political cartoons about British control of India might show. How might the British show their presence in India? How might the Indians illustrate it?

4. How might American cartoonists who supported the Vietnam War have shown it? How might cartoonists who opposed the war have pictured it?

5. Look at Cartoon B in the skills lesson again. Why are the Statue of Liberty and the American flag important to the message of this cartoon?

Summing Up the Chapter

Copy the main-idea chart below on a separate sheet of paper. Then fill in the blanks in each column with information from the chapter. When you have filled in the blanks, write a paragraph that answers the question "What are some of the new countries in this century and how were they formed?"

MAIN IDEA In this century many new countries have emerged in Africa and Asia.		
Region	**New Countries**	**Leaders**
Africa		
Middle East		
South Asia		
Southeast Asia		

A Changing World

THINKING ABOUT
HISTORY AND GEOGRAPHY

Today communication and travel around the world are easier than at any other time in history. In this chapter you will read about some of the changes that have taken place in this shrinking world. Many of the changes have resulted in more freedom and opportunities. Others have left people struggling to meet challenges.

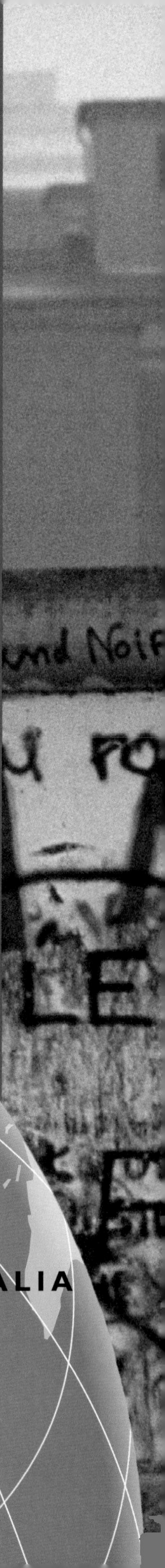

PACIFIC
OCEAN

NORTH
AMERICA

ARCTIC
OCEAN

ASIA

ATLANTIC
OCEAN

EUROPE

SOUTH
AMERICA

AUSTRALIA

AFRICA

INDIAN
OCEAN

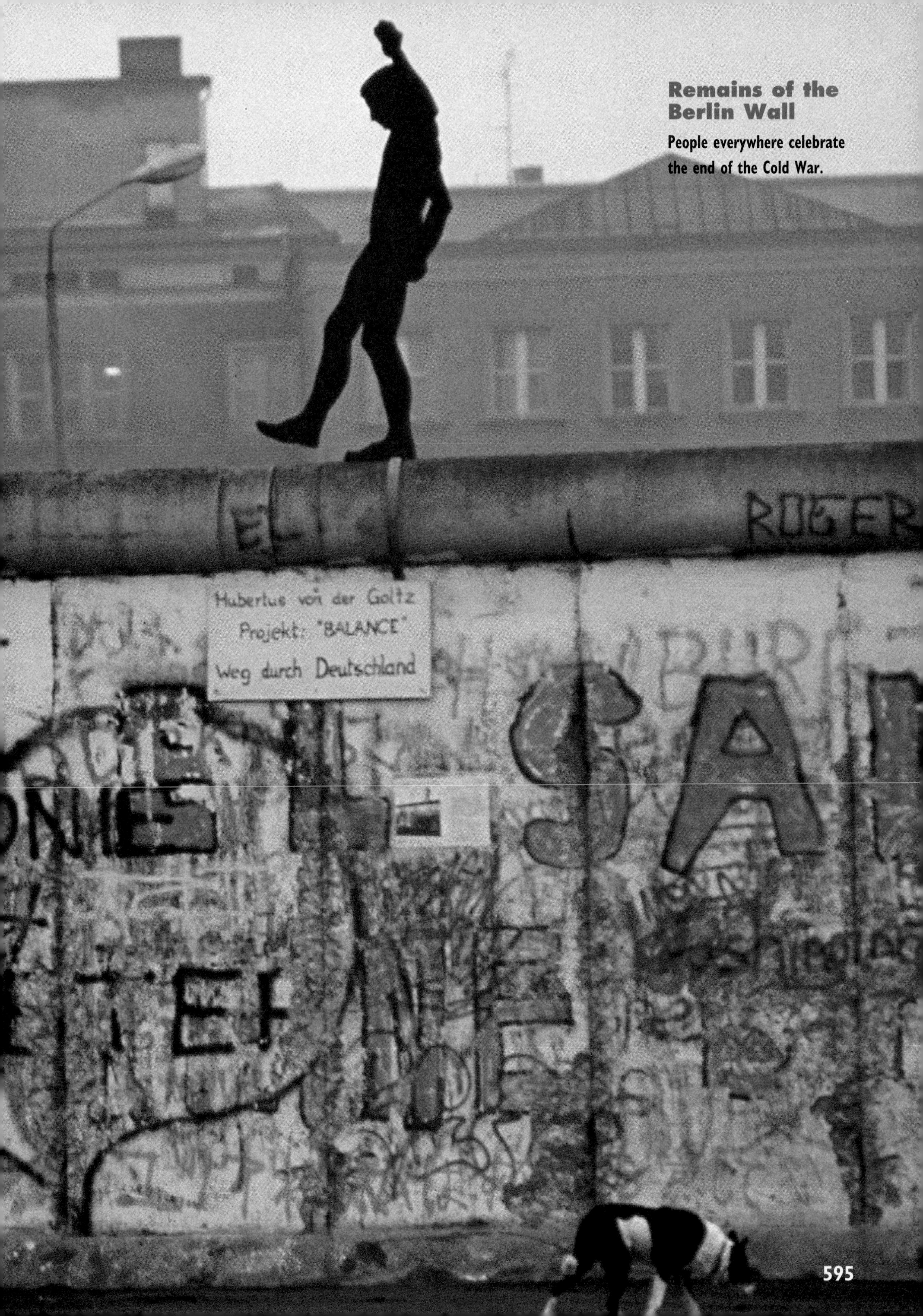

ROGER

Hubertus von der Goltz
Projekt: "BALANCE"
Weg durch Deutschland

A Changing Europe

Read Aloud

In February 1989 an East German man was shot and killed trying to escape over the Berlin Wall. Just nine months later, hundreds of East Germans gathered on and around the wall. They were there to celebrate one of the most memorable days in the twentieth century. The Berlin Wall was about to come tumbling down.

Focus Activity

READ TO LEARN

How has Europe changed with the fall of communism?

VOCABULARY

- ethnic group
- per capita income
- European Union

PEOPLE

- Mikhail Gorbachev
- Ronald Reagan
- Lech Walesa
- Boris Yeltsin

PLACES

- Yugoslavia
- Balkan Peninsula

THE BIG PICTURE

By the middle 1980s the Cold War had been going on for about 40 years. During that time the United States and the Soviet Union spent huge amounts of money to develop nuclear weapons.

Each country also spent vast amounts on military struggles. In Chapter 19 you read about United States' efforts to stop the spread of communism in Vietnam. In the 1950s and 1960s, the Soviet Union used its army to crush movements for democracy in Hungary and Czechoslovakia. In the 1970s the Soviet Union invaded the South Asian nation of Afghanistan. The fighting in Afghanistan took its toll in many Soviet and Afghan lives and resources.

Problems were also growing within the Soviet Union and other Warsaw Pact countries. Government-run businesses could not provide enough food and other goods to meet people's needs. People could not discuss these problems without risking arrest. The communist system was not working well.

CHANGES IN THE SOVIET UNION

President Mikhail Gorbachev (MIHK el GAWR buh chawf) was the first top Soviet leader born and raised in Soviet society. Earlier leaders had been born before the Russian Revolution. Gorbachev's grandfather had been imprisoned as an "enemy of the people." As you read in Chapter 18, Josef Stalin jailed and killed millions in the 1930s.

As a young man Gorbachev studied law in Moscow and gained a position in the Communist party. By 1985 he had become the leader of the Soviet Union. One of his early actions was to point out the country's need for *perestroika* (per es TROY kuh), or rebuilding the failing Soviet economy. Gorbachev soon concluded however, that perestroika could not succeed without *glasnost* (GLAS nohst). Glasnost was his new policy of permission to speak freely.

The communist economy was controlled by the government. Workers had almost no voice in planning. There was little reason for them to work hard or carefully. Wages stayed much the same no matter how hard people worked. Some workers joked, "They pretend to pay us and we pretend to work."

Greater Freedom

Gorbachev believed that workers' views would change only when people had the freedom to speak up. He thought they should have some say in their government. Gorbachev said:

> Wide, prompt, and frank information is evidence of [the government's] confidence in the people. . . . It enhances the resourcefulness of the working people.

In the new era of glasnost, political prisoners were released. Some religious freedom was also allowed.

Soviet relations with the United States also began to improve. In 1987 Gorbachev signed a treaty with United States President Ronald Reagan. Both countries agreed to reduce nuclear weapons stockpiles. The Soviet Union also agreed to begin pulling troops out of its unpopular war with Afghanistan.

Food shortages in the Soviet Union led to long lines for food (left). Such problems caused Mikhail Gorbachev (above) to begin his policy of perestroika.

A "YEAR OF MIRACLES"

The ideas of glasnost and perestroika soon spread to neighboring eastern European nations controlled by the Soviet Union. In just one year—1989—these movements helped overturn more than 40 years of Communist rule.

Spring Thaw

In January 1989 Hungary planned its own elections. In 1956 a Hungarian revolt for more democracy had resulted in a fierce Soviet crackdown. Now Soviet troops stood by as Hungarians moved towards democracy. In May Hungarians tore down an electric fence separating Hungary from democratic Austria. In the months to come, many eastern Europeans used this hole in the "Iron Curtain" to escape to western Europe.

In Poland a workers' group called Solidarity won recognition from the government in March 1989. Eight years earlier shipworker Lech Walesa (LEK wuh LEN suh) and other Solidarity leaders had been jailed for protesting poor living conditions. Their group had been outlawed and almost disappeared under government pressure. In June 1989, however, the Solidarity party won many seats in both houses of Poland's Parliament.

Season of Fall

Still more changes took place in East Germany in the fall. Thousands of East Germans jammed city squares to demand changes in their government. East Germany's leader, Erich Honecker, ordered the army to break up the crowds. His command, however, was not followed. On October 15 Honecker stepped down. Twenty one days later East Berlin opened its gates to West Berlin.

Winter's Discontent

The "Year of Miracles," as 1989 has been called, did not end without bloodshed. In November students in Czechoslovakia protested for democracy. When they sang the American civil-rights song, "We Shall Overcome," police beat hundreds of the students. By December, however, the communist government had been overthrown. Citizens elected two new leaders. Both had served time in prison for speaking against the communist government. One year later, nearly all of eastern Europe had freed itself of communism.

Lech Walesa (right) helped end communist rule by defending workers' rights. Boris Yeltsin (below) spoke out against the actions of communists in Russia.

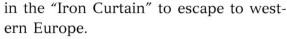

The Soviet Collapse

After the "Year of Miracles," the Soviet Union also began to change. You read in Chapter 18 that the Soviet Union's full name was the Union of Soviet Socialist Republics. Many different ethnic groups lived in its 15 republics. An ethnic group is a group of people who share a heritage of common customs, values, and language.

In 1990 and 1991, many republics broke away from Soviet control. This began with the republics of Latvia, Lithuania, and Estonia. In 1991 Russia, the biggest republic of all, held a democratic election. The Russians elected Boris Yeltsin to be their president.

These changes angered some Communist leaders. In August 1991 they tried to overthrow Gorbachev and take power themselves, moving tanks into Moscow. Before glasnost, these actions would have terrified citizens. Now, however, the Soviet people rallied behind Yeltsin, who, standing on top of a tank in Moscow, called these acts illegal. Soldiers refused to follow Communist orders. Without force to back them up, the communists had no chance of success. Yeltsin warned them:

> *You can build a throne of bayonets but you cannot sit on it for very long. There is no return to the past, nor will there be.*

Three days after it began, the revolt came to an end. Just as Yeltsin had predicted, there was no returning to the past. One by one Soviet republics declared their independence. In December 1991, Gorbachev stepped down and the Soviet Union ceased to exist. In its place stood 15 independent republics. Find these new nations on the map.

COUNTRIES OF THE FORMER SOVIET UNION

MAP WORK

Many of the republics that once made up the Soviet Union are now independent nations.

1. Which is the largest of these nations?

2. What is the capital of Ukraine?

3. Of which nation is Minsk the capital?

4. Which countries shown only have access to the Black Sea?

AFTER THE FALL

There was much to cheer about as the Soviet Union broke apart. The Cold War had ended and the countries of the Warsaw Pact were turning toward democracy. Democracy and free enterprise had won the conflict with communism. Yet now there was much to worry about. Conflicts over nationalism and ethnic differences had replaced Cold War tensions.

Local Wars

One conflict resulting from these differences has involved the former Soviet republics of Armenia and Azerbaijan (ah zur bi JAHN). Armenia, mostly Christian, and Azerbaijan, mostly Muslim, fought a war over territory in 1993. Thousands of people left their homes as the borders shifted during the fighting.

Another place torn apart by war is the area that made up Yugoslavia until 1991. The area is part of the Balkan Peninsula, which has had a long history of ethnic and religious conflict. In 1991 Yugoslavia began to break apart. By 1992, the country had split into five separate republics. One of these republics is still called Yugoslavia. It includes Serbia and Montenegro. The other republics are Bosnia and Herzegovina, Croatia, Macedonia, and Slovenia. Find the republics on the map.

Since this breakup, many ethnic conflicts have flared in the republics. A civil war began in 1991 in Croatia between two ethnic groups, Croats and Serbs. Some of the worst fighting began in 1992 in the tiny country of Bosnia. There Bosnian Serbs, who are Orthodox Christians, and the mostly Muslim government battled for control. The fighting has had terrible effects for every group involved. Cities and towns have been destroyed. Thousands of people have been killed or forced to flee. In 1995, however, the region's leaders signed a peace agreement. Today this agreement helps to maintain some peace in the area.

The war in Bosnia has left thousands of people homeless and hungry. Many refugees have fled areas of heavy fighting.

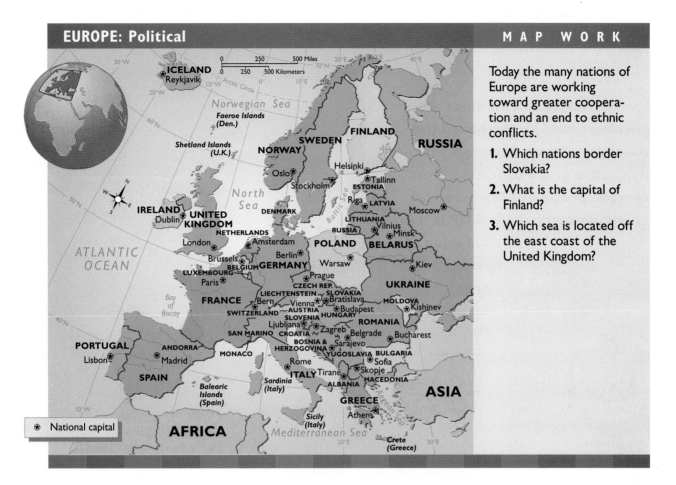

Today the many nations of Europe are working toward greater cooperation and an end to ethnic conflicts.

1. Which nations border Slovakia?

2. What is the capital of Finland?

3. Which sea is located off the east coast of the United Kingdom?

⊛ National capital

Life after Communism

Conflicts such as the one in Bosnia are among the toughest that European leaders face today. How far should nations go to help their neighbors? Ethnic conflicts in Europe and the debate over how to deal with them threaten to continue in the future. The issue is made more complicated by the reality of nuclear weapons. How can leaders be kept from using these weapons, left from the Cold War, if war breaks out?

Another concern for Europe is the continued struggle of eastern European economies. Years of communist rule left many old factories in need of complete rebuilding. Pollution from uncontrolled industry needs to be cleaned up. Costly rebuilding and repair efforts are moving along slowly, though. Today there is still a huge gap between the nations

of western and eastern Europe in per capita income. Per capita income is the amount of money each person of a country would have if that country's total income were divided equally among its people. Look at the Infographic on page 602 to learn more about economies in Europe.

In 1995 the most powerful organization in Europe, the European Union (EU), agreed to consider allowing eastern European nations to join. The EU is a group of western European nations working to build a common economy throughout Europe. The EU has already broken down many barriers to trade and movement in western Europe. For example, cars and trucks can now travel freely between the nations of western Europe. German students can apply to British or French universities as easily as to colleges in their hometowns.

infographic

*inter*NET
CONNECTION
Visit our website:
www.mhschool.com

Economy of Europe

New businesses and methods of agriculture have strengthened the economies of many nations in Europe. Look at the graph to see the gross domestic product of five European nations. Remember the GDP is the total value of goods and services produced in one year. Which is highest?

With 8.8 million people, Moscow is Europe's largest city and an important Russian economic center.

ZEHN DEUTSCHE MARK
1777–1855 Carl Friedr. Gauß
DD6248255N6

Rural-Urban Population

Rural 27 %

Urban 73 %

German marks

GDP: Largest Five Economies

GERMANY
2,416

FRANCE
1,536

UNITED KINGDOM
1,106

ITALY
1,087

SPAIN
559

GDP in billions of United States dollars (1995)

2,000

1,500

1,000

500

0

Coal (above) is an important natural resource for many European countries. It is used for heating and by industries. Cheese from Switzerland (below) is among many products of Europe's vast and profitable agriculture industry.

Source: World Development Indicators 1997 CD-ROM, World Bank

WHY IT MATTERS

The EU's pledge to help its eastern neighbors has led many to believe that all of Europe might someday be united. Supporters see much to be gained from strong bonds between European countries. Former enemies like France and Germany have become close partners through the EU. An economic alliance with Western Europe could help the countries of Eastern Europe solve some of their economic problems.

Peace and prosperity in Eastern Europe also depends on its relationship with the rest of the world. In March of 1997 Yeltsin met with United States' President Bill Clinton in Helsinki, Finland. There they signed an agreement aimed at improving Russian economic growth and helping Russia join the global economy. Many people feel that agreements such as this are a positive step into the twenty-first century.

Links to **CURRENT EVENTS**

The European Union

What does the European Union do?

The European Union distributes funds collected from its member states to improve the economies of Europe. In 1996 the European Union committed 48% of its budget, amounting to $52 billion, to various agriculture programs. The European Union also helps develop poor areas of Europe, funds research and environmental programs, and assists the restructuring of Eastern European countries.

Find out how EU programs are helping the development of Europe today. Use current newspapers or the Internet in your research. Write a paragraph describing the effects of these programs.

✓ Reviewing Facts and Ideas

MAIN IDEAS

- Mikhail Gorbachev's program of glasnost sparked pro-democracy movements in the Soviet Union and eastern Europe in the late 1980s.

- Communist governments throughout eastern Europe fell in 1989, called the "Year of Miracles."

- The Cold War ended when the Soviet Union ceased to exist in 1991. However, new conflicts rooted in national, ethnic, and religious differences arose in Europe.

- The European Union has created a strong partnership between many European nations.

THINK ABOUT IT

1. Why has 1989 been called a "Year of Miracles" in Europe?

2. What problems and conflicts have arisen in the Soviet Union and the nations of eastern Europe since the fall of communism?

3. **FOCUS** What are some of the challenges that Europe faces since the Cold War has ended?

4. **THINKING SKILL** *Make Conclusions* about how ordinary people brought about the end of the Cold War.

5. **WRITE** Use what you have learned about European history this year to explain why the European Union can be called a bold experiment in the continent's history.

Thinking Skills

Evaluating Information for Accuracy

VOCABULARY

evaluate

accuracy

WHY THE SKILL MATTERS

In the last lesson you read about the civil war that is raging in Bosnia. Like most historical events, this conflict is complicated and difficult to understand. Many people have said many different things about this war. How will you know which information regarding this issue is accurate?

Being able to evaluate the accuracy of information is crucial to understanding history. To *evaluate* means to judge something. *Accuracy* refers to the truth of a statement. When we evaluate information for accuracy, we make a judgment about whether the information is true.

Historians constantly evaluate information for accuracy. "History," in fact, is always an interpretation based on the most accurate information available.

The skill of evaluating information for accuracy combines some of the Thinking Skills presented in this book. For example, you must determine the credibility of the source. To do this, you must also determine the author's point of view. Other Thinking Skills are called on as well, such as comparing information between different sources and distinguishing facts from opinions. You might want to review these skills before going on.

USING THE SKILL

Read these excerpts regarding Bosnia's civil war. Bosnia used to be part of Yugoslavia, but became a republic when Yugoslavia split apart in 1992. Since the Cold War had ended, ethnic differences had caused much tension in the area. The civil war in Bosnia resulted mainly from tensions between two groups, the Bosnian Serbs and the primarily Muslim government. As you read, consider the following questions: What are the points of view of the authors? Does the author have a reason to portray information inaccurately? Does the source have a reputation for being accurate? Does the information agree with information from other sources? Is the information fact or opinion?

Hundreds of thousands of Serbs have been killed for no reason.

from a Serbian Soldier

More than 17,000 have been killed and 110,000 wounded [in Sarajevo].

Time

About 130,000 people in Sarajevo have been killed or injured, including children and women.

from an international news bulletin

How can you determine the accuracy of each piece of information? First, determine the points of view of the authors. The first excerpt is from someone directly involved in the fighting. As a result, he might tend to give less than accurate information so that others would favor his side of the conflict.

Next, determine if the source has a reputation for being accurate and if the information agrees with other credible sources. Only the last two excerpts are from sources that would seem to have a reputation for accuracy. Furthermore, only these two sources agree on the number of people killed and injured in Sarajevo.

Finally, determine if the information presented is fact or opinion. The last two excerpts present only solid facts that can be proven. The first excerpt is mainly an opinion.

Considering all these factors, we can conclude that the second and third excerpts probably contain more accurate information than the first.

Helping yourself

- **Evaluating for accuracy** determines which statements can be considered true.
- **Determine the author's point of view.**
- **Analyze the credibility of the source.**
- **Compare the source to other credible sources.**
- **Identify facts and opinions.**
- **Evaluate for accuracy.**

TRYING THE SKILL

Now evaluate the accuracy of this information. Its teenage author, Zlata Filipovic, lived her whole life in Sarajevo until the war forced her and her family to leave. In May 1993 she wrote in her diary:

I have another sad piece of news for you. A boy in my drama club got killed! . . . A shell fell in front of the community center and a horrible piece of shrapnel [metal] killed him. His name was Eldin and he was a refugee from Grbavica.

Another innocent victim of this disgusting war, another child among thousands of other children killed in Sarajevo. I feel so sorry, he was a sweet, good boy.

Does the author have a reason to give inaccurate information? Does she provide information that agrees with excerpts from the previous page? What information does she give that is fact? What is opinion? How accurate do think this information is?

REVIEWING THE SKILL

1. Why is it important to evaluate information for accuracy? How can you do so?
2. How did you determine the accuracy of the information in Zlata Filipovic's statement?
3. How does this skill combine other Thinking Skills you learned about earlier in the book?
4. How can the ability to evaluate information for accuracy help you in your own life?

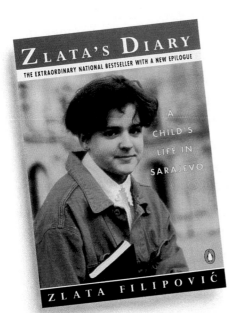

ZLATA'S DIARY
THE EXTRAORDINARY NATIONAL BESTSELLER WITH A NEW EPILOGUE
A CHILD'S LIFE IN SARAJEVO
ZLATA FILIPOVIĆ

A Changing Africa

Focus Activity

READ TO LEARN

What did South Africans do to achieve democracy?

VOCABULARY

- apartheid
- township
- sanction

PEOPLE

- Nelson Mandela
- Frederik Willem de Klerk

PLACES

- Cape Town
- Soweto
- Johannesburg

Read Aloud

"When I walked to the voting station, my mind dwelt on the heroes who had fallen so that I might be where I was that day, the men and women who had made the ultimate sacrifice for a cause that was now finally succeeding. . . . I did not go into that voting station alone on April 27 [1994]; I was casting my vote with all of them."

Nelson Mandela wrote these words in his auto-biography. Mandela and millions of other South Africans had finally voted in their nation's first democratic election.

THE BIG PICTURE

Democracy once seemed like a dream in South Africa. Europeans had ruled much of South Africa since the 1700s. Dutch settlers formed a colony at Cape Town. Find Cape Town on the map on page 607. Their descendants are called Afrikaners. Afrikaners make up 60 percent of South Africa's white population today. However, whites are only about 19 percent of the population. Most of the people are black.

The British took control from the Dutch in 1814. By 1900 Britain had established rule over all of South Africa. A large European population lived in the colony. When South Africa won full independence from Britain in 1961, the white minority continued to rule. Blacks like Nelson Mandela faced a future without freedom or a voice in government.

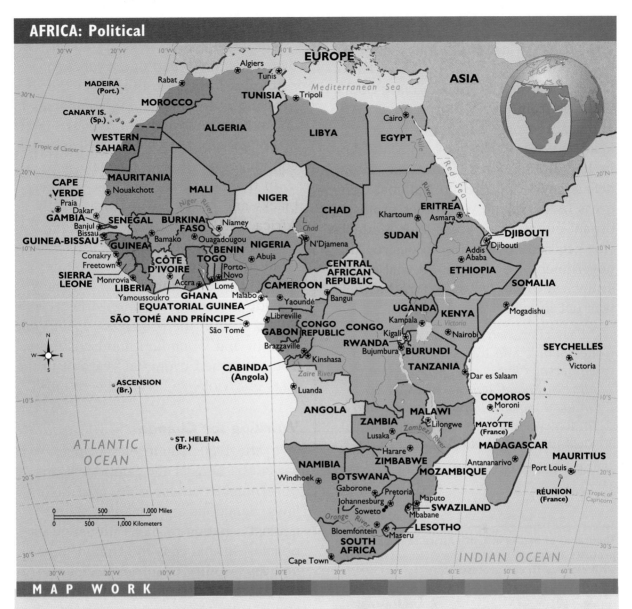

AFRICA: Political

EUROPE

ASIA

Mediterranean Sea

MADEIRA (Port.)

Algiers
Rabat
Tunis
TUNISIA
Tripoli

MOROCCO

CANARY IS. (Sp.)

Cairo

WESTERN SAHARA

ALGERIA

LIBYA

EGYPT

Tropic of Cancer

MAURITANIA

Nouakchott

MALI

NIGER

CHAD

Khartoum
ERITREA
Asmara

DJIBOUTI

CAPE VERDE

Praia
Dakar

GAMBIA
Banjul
Bissau
GUINEA-BISSAU

SENEGAL

Niamey

Niger River

N'Djamena

SUDAN

Addis Ababa

Djibouti

BURKINA FASO

Bamako
Ouagadougou

NIGERIA

L. Chad

CENTRAL AFRICAN REPUBLIC

ETHIOPIA

SOMALIA

GUINEA
Conakry
Freetown

BENIN
TOGO

Abuja

SIERRA LEONE
Monrovia

CÔTE D'IVOIRE

Accra

Porto-Novo
Lomé

CAMEROON

Bangui

UGANDA
Kampala

KENYA

Mogadishu

LIBERIA
Yamoussoukro

GHANA

Malabo

Yaoundé

Nairobi

EQUATORIAL GUINEA

Libreville

CONGO REPUBLIC

CONGO

RWANDA
Kigali

L. Victoria

SÃO TOMÉ AND PRÍNCIPE

São Tomé

GABON

Brazzaville

BURUNDI
Bujumbura

SEYCHELLES

Victoria

ASCENSION (Br.)

CABINDA (Angola)

Kinshasa

Zaire River

TANZANIA

Dar es Salaam

Luanda

COMOROS
Moroni

ATLANTIC OCEAN

ST. HELENA (Br.)

ANGOLA

ZAMBIA
Lusaka

MALAWI
Lilongwe

Zambezi River

MAYOTTE (France)

MADAGASCAR

MAURITIUS

NAMIBIA

Windhoek

BOTSWANA
Gaborone

ZIMBABWE
Harare

MOZAMBIQUE

Antananarivo

Port Louis

RÉUNION (France)

Tropic of Capricorn

Pretoria
Johannesburg
Soweto

Maputo

SWAZILAND
Mbabane

Orange River

Bloemfontein

LESOTHO
Maseru

INDIAN OCEAN

SOUTH AFRICA

Cape Town

N W E S

| 0 | 500 | 1,000 Miles |
| 0 | 500 | 1,000 Kilometers |

MAP WORK

More than 50 nations are found on the continent of Africa today.

1. What is the capital of Gabon?

2. Which nations border Sudan to the east?

3. Which country has access to two seas shown on the map?

SOUTH AFRICA DIVIDED

Even after independence, blacks did not gain many rights or freedoms. They could not vote, own land, or move freely in the country. In 1948 white leaders created a system of laws called apartheid (uh PAHR tid). In the Afrikaans (af ri KAHNZ) language spoken by Afrikaners, *apartheid* means "apartness."

Under apartheid, millions of blacks were forced to give up their land to whites and live in townships, crowded areas for blacks in or near cities. Blacks and other nonwhites could not live or go to school in white neighborhoods. Township schools and services were of poor quality. In some cases, these services did not exist.

PROTEST AND STRUGGLE

The South African police often used force to uphold apartheid. The threat of violence did not stop many black South Africans from protesting, however. An important leader in the fight to end apartheid was lawyer Nelson Mandela. In 1960 the government banned Mandela's group, the African National Congress (ANC), along with other protest organizations. Four years later Mandela was accused of planning to destroy the government. He was put on trial and sentenced to life in jail. Before Mandela was put in jail he declared:

> I have cherished the ideal of a democratic and free society in which all persons live together in harmony and with equal opportunities. It is an ideal which I hope to live for and to achieve. But if needs be, it is an ideal for which I am prepared to die.

Nelson Mandela was kept in prison for 27 years.

Thousands of blacks in South Africa took part in protests against apartheid. The police often acted with violence to end protests.

Growing Tensions

During the 1960s and 1970s, sales of diamonds, gold, and other valuable resources increased. In spite of the growing economy, mining companies and other employers kept wages for black workers low. South African police continued to enforce apartheid.

In the late 1970s, tensions between blacks and police increased in South Africa. In 1976 thousands of young black students led a protest for better education in Soweto. Soweto is the name for the "South-West Townships" outside the city of Johannesburg. Police fired at the protesters, killing one student and wounding hundreds more. The bloodshed triggered years of protests and violence across the country.

Working for Change

In the 1980s countries set up sanctions against the South African government because of its apartheid laws. Sanctions are penalties placed against a nation to make it change its policies. In this case the United States and many other countries decided to boycott South African goods. In addition, South African athletes were banned from international sports events like the Olympics. World leaders hoped that these sanctions would convince the South African government to end its policy of apartheid.

The struggle for freedom continued in South Africa. Blacks often sang a song called *N'kosi Sikelel'i Afrika* (n KAW see see keh LEH lee AH free kah), or "Prayer for Africa." Groups such as the African National Congress adopted it as an anthem. What similarities can you find in the words of *N'kosi Sikelel'i Afrika* and the United States' national anthem?

N'KOSI SIKELEL'I AFRIKA
PRAYER FOR AFRICA

Words and Music by
Enoch Sontonga

Moderate

Zulu: Nkaw-see see-keh-leh lee Ah-free-kah, Mah-loo-pah-kah-nyee-soo-

English: Bless, O Lord, our coun-try Af-ri-ca, So that all may see her

pawn-daw lwah-yoh; Yeez-wah eem-ee-tahn-dah-zoh yeh-too.

glo-ry held high; Lis-ten and pro-tect us, be our guide.

1.

Nkaw-see see-keh-leh-lah, Nkaw-see see-keh-leh-lah.

Bless our moth-er Afri-ca. Bless our moth-er Afri-ca.

2.

Tee-nah loo-sah-paw lwah-yoh, Waw-zah maw-yah,

Bless our moth-er Afri-ca. Spir-it de-scend,

Waw-zah maw-yah, Waw-zah maw-yah, aw-yeeng, chweh-leh.

Spir-it de-scend, Spir-it de-scend, Spir-it de-scend, Spirit di-vine.

Oo-see-see-keh-leh-lah. Tee-nah loo-sah-paw lwah-yoh.

Bless our moth-er Afri-ca. Bless our moth-er Afri-ca.

Nelson Mandela and F. W. de Klerk greeted a crowd of South Africans after Mandela became president of the nation.

AFRICA TODAY

In 1989 Frederik Willem de Klerk became the president of South Africa. De Klerk thought that the time had come for change in South Africa. In 1990 he released Nelson Mandela, then 72 years old, from prison. In 1991 De Klerk abolished most apartheid laws. As a result international sanctions against South Africa were stopped.

Even bigger changes followed in 1993. De Klerk, Mandela, and other leaders agreed that national elections should be held the following year. They would be the first in the nation's history in which all South Africans, black and white, would have the right to vote.

Despite threats of violence by extreme groups opposed to democracy, the elections were held peacefully in April 1994. Black citizens, who made up 72 percent of the total population, lined up and cast the first votes of their lives. Nelson Mandela was elected president. Members of the African National Congress won many other positions in government as well.

Life in South Africa

Democracy has put down strong new roots in South Africa. The nation, however, still faces many challenges. The challenge of overcoming the effects of apartheid will be a difficult one and will likely take years. The government is now building thousands of new homes for poor people. Many more are needed. Formerly all-white schools have been opened to students of all races. However, most black students in South Africa still attend overcrowded, poorly equipped schools.

Facing the Future in Africa

South Africa is not alone in facing such great challenges. Other African nations are also working for change. Many hope to move toward democracy after years of dictatorships and government corruption.

The greatest problem facing most African nations is poverty. As you read in Chapter 19, the economies of colonies in Africa were built to create wealth for Europe. The end of colonialism left many African nations economically weak. Now these nations are struggling to build strong businesses and develop industry. As their economies grow, African nations continue to strengthen through international trade.

One advantage for many African countries is a wealth of natural resources. Botswana produces even more diamonds each year than its neighbor, South Africa. Nigeria pumps thousands of gallons of oil each day and Algeria is rich in natural gas.

Infographic

Economy of Africa

Many African nations have gradually developed strong businesses. Because much of the continent's population is rural, agriculture has long played an important role in the economies of many of its nations. Today the gross domestic products of several nations are growing steadily. Which one has the largest GDP?

With a population of 6.6 million, Cairo is the largest city in Africa. Cairo is the center of Egypt's government as well as of its manufacturing and tourist industries.

Rural-Urban Population

Urban 31%

Rural 69%

South African rand

When rich deposits of gold were found in South Africa in the 1800's, mining became the center of the nation's economy. Cattle herding has long been an important economic activity in Africa. For many cultures the cattle symbolize wealth.

GDP: Largest Five Economies

GDP in billions of United States dollars (1995)

- SOUTH AFRICA 136
- EGYPT 47
- ALGERIA 41
- NIGERIA 40
- MOROCCO 32

Source: World Development Indicators 1997 CD-ROM, World Bank

After years of unequal schooling for blacks, children of all races now attend classes together in South African cities.

LOOKING TO THE FUTURE

Just as Europeans formed the European Union (EU), in 1980 many southern African nations formed the Southern African Development Community (SADC). Economies of the SADC member nations are not yet as closely linked as those in the European Union. Many experts, however, believe that southern Africa's natural resources and growing democratic movements hold great promise for the economies of individual nations and for the region as a whole.

WHY IT MATTERS

It may take many years for Africans to overcome their histories of colonialism and economic problems. Yet events such as the end of apartheid and the election of a democratic government in South Africa have given many people hope. Throughout the coming years many of the peoples of Africa's diverse nations hope to continue the development of democratic governments. By gaining, protecting, and practicing new rights and freedoms, people in Africa will shape their own futures.

✓ Reviewing Facts and Ideas

MAIN IDEAS

- After gaining independence from British rule, South Africa was ruled by a white minority.

- In 1994 South African apartheid ended. Black and other nonwhite citizens voted in a national election for the first time, electing Nelson Mandela president.

- Many African nations are moving to overcome years of colonialism and economic problems.

THINK ABOUT IT

1. What was apartheid?

2. Why are natural resources so important to Africa's future?

3. **FOCUS** How did South Africans succeed in ending apartheid? What did their success mean to the nation?

4. **THINKING SKILL** What was the _cause_ of the Soweto students' uprising of 1976? What were some of its _effects_?

5. **GEOGRAPHY** Locate Cape Town, South Africa, on a globe. Write a paragraph explaining why Dutch settlers may have chosen this spot for a colony.

MAKING A DIFFERENCE

Preparing for a New South Africa

CAPE TOWN, SOUTH AFRICA— Peter Volmink (VOHL mihnk) grew up under apartheid in South Africa. Opportunities for his parents were limited. "My dad worked for the township government. He dug holes and worked in the department of sewers. My mom was a tea lady, she made tea for the bosses in an oil company." In the 1970s, as a student, Volmink protested apartheid and studied law. Once Peter became a lawyer in the 1980s, he continued protesting apartheid and worked on human right cases.

In 1989, Volmink began teaching young people about human rights. "For me," says Volmink, "human rights is respect for the dignity of all people of all races." He taught human rights to teenagers using theater, music, art and dance. He also helped prisoners in South African jails learn about their legal rights and started education projects in remote areas of South Africa.

Now he is taking his message to teachers and young children, ages 7–10, in South Africa's elementary schools. "My materials for young children," says Volmink, "reflect core values of the African experience: compassion for the less fortunate, working together, and mutual respect." When teaching in the classroom, Volmink uses the traditional African teaching tool of storytelling. One of the stories he uses, *Jubalani and the Lion*, shows the importance of treating everyone fairly and not returning good with evil. Volmink also encourages the students to make songs, dances, and plays from the ideas that he presents.

Volmink believes human rights should be an important part of the school curriculum in the new South Africa. "A truly great nation," he says, "is one in which the majority of its citizens believe in the dignity and worth of all people regardless of any differences. Young children must learn the values of fairness and respect for human life at a very early age if our democracy is to succeed."

"... human rights is respect for the dignity of all people of all races."

Peter Volmink

A Changing Pacific Rim

Focus Activity

READ TO LEARN

How has economic growth affected the peoples of eastern Asia?

VOCABULARY

- **Pacific Rim**

PEOPLE

- **Deng Xiaoping**

PLACES

- **Japan**
- **South Korea**
- **Singapore**
- **Tiananmen Square**
- **Hong Kong**

Read Aloud

World War II left big stretches of Asia in ruins. China, Hong Kong, and other areas conquered by Japanese forces lay in shambles. Much of Japan had also been destroyed. Most buildings in its major cities had been turned to ashes by Allied bombs. People wearing rags hunted for scraps to eat. In 1946 few would have guessed that Japan and other countries of Asia would become economic giants within a few decades.

THE BIG PICTURE

In Chapter 18 you read that the Cold War began in Europe in the middle 1940s. Before long the conflict between communist and democratic governments deeply divided Asia as well. Communists took control of North Korea in 1948, mainland China in 1949, and North Vietnam in 1954. Both communist and non-communist nations throughout Asia faced similar challenges. How could they build strong governments and economies after years of war?

You have already read about Mao Zedong's attempts to meet such challenges in China. His programs, known as the Great Leap Forward and Cultural Revolution, led to some disastrous results for the Chinese people. Meanwhile, other nations in East Asia tried different methods to build stable governments and industries. Perhaps most successful of all in its efforts to rebuild after war was Japan.

THE REBUILDING OF JAPAN

Between 1945 and 1952 the United States, which occupied Japan after World War II, oversaw the rebuilding of Japan. Under United States direction, a new Japanese constitution was written. The new constitution gave Japanese women equal rights as citizens for the first time. The new constitution also stated that Japan could not go to war. United States supervision of Japan ended in 1952.

Building Japan's Economy

In Chapter 18 you read that the United States sent thousands of troops to fight in Korea between 1950 and 1953. Japan became the main United States base. At its closest point Japan is only 100 miles away from Korea. Thanks partly to the huge American military demand for everything from trucks to sleeping bags, bandages, and bootlaces, Japan's economy boomed.

After the Korean war ended, the Japanese government took steps to keep businesses growing. Schools taught business and technical skills so students would become good industrial workers. The government encouraged companies to produce goods for export. As more cash came in from trade, money was invested in new factories. More cash and new factories led to an increase in Japanese exports.

By the 1960s Japan's economy was expanding at a very fast rate. In 1950 Japan's Gross Domestic Product had been smaller than the GDP of any western country. By 1965 it had grown larger than those of Britain and France. Today the United States' GDP is still the world's largest, followed by that of Japan.

Manufacturing and shipping contributed greatly to Japan's economic expansion.

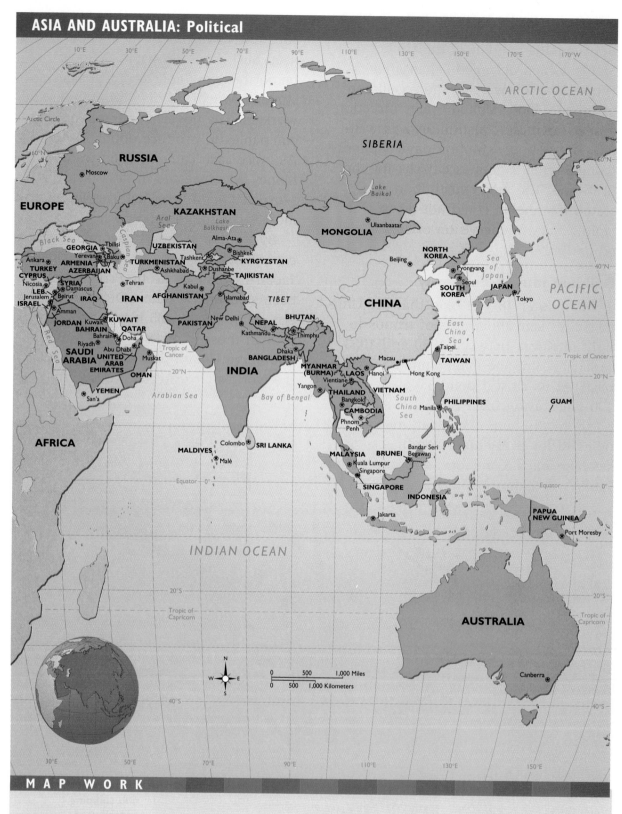

10°E 30°E 50°E 70°E 90°E 110°E 130°E 150°E 170°E 170°W

ARCTIC OCEAN

Arctic Circle

SIBERIA

60°N 60°N

RUSSIA

⊛ Moscow

EUROPE

KAZAKHSTAN

Aral Sea

Lake Balkhash

MONGOLIA

⊛ Ulaanbaatar

Lake Baikal

Black Sea

GEORGIA ⊛ Tbilisi UZBEKISTAN Alma-Ata ⊛ NORTH KOREA

Ankara ⊛ ARMENIA Yerevan ⊛ ⊛ Baku TASHKENT Bishkek ⊛ Beijing ⊛ Sea of Japan

TURKEY AZERBAIJAN TURKMENISTAN Tashkent KYRGYZSTAN ⊛ Pyongyang 40°N

CYPRUS ⊛ Ashkhabad ⊛ Dushanbe TAJIKISTAN Seoul ⊛ JAPAN PACIFIC

Nicosia ⊛ SYRIA ⊛ Tehran SOUTH KOREA OCEAN

LEB. ⊛ Damascus Kabul ⊛ ⊛ Tokyo

Jerusalem ⊛ Beirut IRAQ IRAN AFGHANISTAN ⊛ Islamabad TIBET CHINA

ISRAEL ⊛ Amman

JORDAN Kuwait ⊛ KUWAIT PAKISTAN New Delhi ⊛ NEPAL BHUTAN East China Sea

BAHRAIN QATAR Kathmandu ⊛ ⊛ Thimphu

Bahrain ⊛ Doha Dhaka ⊛ Macau Taipei ⊛

Riyadh ⊛ Abu Dhabi Tropic of Cancer BANGLADESH TAIWAN Tropic of Cancer

SAUDI ⊛ Muskat MYANMAR Hanoi ⊛ Hong Kong 20°N

ARABIA UNITED ARAB EMIRATES 20°N INDIA (BURMA) LAOS

OMAN Yangon Vientiane ⊛ VIETNAM

YEMEN Arabian Sea THAILAND South China Sea PHILIPPINES GUAM

San'a ⊛ Bay of Bengal Bangkok ⊛ Manila ⊛

CAMBODIA Phnom Penh

AFRICA Colombo ⊛ SRI LANKA

MALDIVES MALAYSIA BRUNEI Bandar Seri Begawan

⊛ Malé ⊛ Kuala Lumpur

Singapore

Equator 0° SINGAPORE

INDONESIA

Jakarta ⊛ PAPUA NEW GUINEA

INDIAN OCEAN Port Moresby

20°S 20°S

Tropic of Capricorn Tropic of Capricorn

AUSTRALIA

N W E S

0 500 1,000 Miles
0 500 1,000 Kilometers

Canberra ⊛

30°E 50°E 70°E 90°E 110°E 130°E 150°E

40°S 40°S

MAP WORK

Many Asian nations have developed strong economies based on industry. Several nations support large populations.

1. Which nations border Pakistan to the north?

2. Of which nation is Port Moresby the capital?

3. Which country shown is furthest from a sea or an ocean?

The modern buildings of downtown Singapore (right) reflect the wealth of the city and its businesses.

JAPAN AND THE PACIFIC RIM

The big push to industrialize made Japan wealthy. Though Japan is poor in natural resources, its workers turned imported raw materials into expensive goods such as cars, computer parts, televisions, and cameras.

Today other nations along the Pacific Rim—the ring of countries surrounding the Pacific Ocean—have grown economically as well. Among them are South Korea, Taiwan, Hong Kong, Singapore, and Thailand. South Korea, in particular, quickly and successfully rebuilt its economy after the Korean War of the early 1950s. Look at the map on page 616 to locate these countries.

The Rise of the Pacific Rim

The economic growth in the Pacific Rim has led to a shift in the power of the world's regions. For hundreds of years much of world trade and power centered around the Atlantic Ocean. With the growth of Pacific Rim nations, however, a new region of wealth and power has emerged whose economies compete with those of the West.

The tiny republic of Singapore is a Pacific Rim country that has become a giant in world trade. The electronics industry provides many high-paying jobs. Many homes have televisions and other appliances that are considered luxuries throughout much of Asia.

Growth in Australia

Another member of the Pacific Rim, Australia, has been gaining increasing prominence in the world. In 1951 it formed an economic and political partnership with the United States. It has been actively involved with international peacekeeping missions and has supported economic advancement in Asia.

With ideal land for grazing sheep, Australia is the world leader in wool production. It also has a strong economy in mineral exports. In recent years Australia has moved toward other areas of production as well. It exports large amounts of computer parts to Japan, Hong Kong, and South Korea. It is also a pioneer in solar research.

CHANGE COMES TO CHINA

Should jobs and the economy be more important in society than citizens' rights and freedoms? What is too high a price to pay for economic growth? People in the wealthy, capitalist nation of Singapore are not the only ones debating such questions. People in China have also been facing this complex issue.

According to legend the French leader Napoleon Bonaparte declared in the 1800s, "when China wakes, it will shake the world." Today about one out of every five people on Earth lives in China. To business leaders in other countries, China's huge population means a huge number of customers. To military planners, it means a possibly massive army. To world leaders, this population means that China's decisions could have huge effects on the rest of the world.

A Changing Economy

After the death of Mao Zedong in 1976, a power struggle began among China's top leaders. It ended when Deng Xiaoping (DUNG SHOW PING) won control of the government in 1978. Deng was a veteran of the Long March

In 1989, thousands of students (above) gathered in Beijing to demonstrate for democracy. About one month after they began, the Chinese government brought in tanks (right) to end the protests.

and a victim of the Cultural Revolution. When Deng gained power, his government moved away from Mao's strict style of communism.

Farmers were given more control over their work. They were allowed to sell surplus crops for profit. Mao had tried to root out everything foreign in China. Deng, on the other hand, encouraged students to study abroad. He hoped they would learn new science skills that could help China. Foreign companies began to do business in China, selling everything from airplanes to hamburgers.

A Movement For Democracy

Deng's changes led to strong economic growth. By the spring of 1989—the "Year of Miracles" in Europe—many Chinese hoped that glasnost would spread to China. In May 1989 about one million students gathered to protest for democracy in an immense square in Beijing. Tiananmen (TYEN AHN MEN) Square is at the heart of the Chinese central government area. It leads into the Forbidden City, which you read was built for China's emperors during the Ming dynasty.

Deng refused to let supporters of glasnost and democracy take over Tiananmen Square. That June the government ordered dozens of tanks into the square to destroy the democracy movement. Hundreds of student protesters were killed. Many more were wounded, and their leaders were thrown in prison. Deng succeeded in ending the democracy movement in China for the time being.

In February of 1997, Deng passed away. Many people wondered if his successor, Jiang Zemin [JAHNG ZU min], would be able to continue Deng's

Deng Xiaoping (above) encouraged free enterprise in China even after crushing the 1989 democracy movement.

methods of modernizing China. Other countries had imposed trade sanctions, or penalties, against China for its actions in Tiananmen Square. Would the communist party be able to maintain control while encouraging interaction with the rest of the world?

Uncertainty in Hong Kong

One place where people are especially interested in the changes in China is Hong Kong. This thriving city, a center for international trade, had been a British colony since the 1800s. In 1984 Britain agreed to return Hong Kong to Chinese control in 1997. On July 1, 1997, Hong Kong officially became reunited with China.

Many people in Hong Kong are concerned that the Chinese government will restrict their freedoms. China's actions in Tiananmen Square raised many of these concerns. Some of these people left Hong Kong before July of 1997 to settle in Canada and the United States. Others have stayed to see what changes will take place under China's control.

Economy of Asia

Growing economies in Asia are strengthening the political power of the countries in the region. Japan dominates the region in GDP. However, wealth in natural resources and changes toward free markets are helping to bring strong economies to other countries. Which country is second to Japan in GDP?

Tokyo (above) is Asia's largest city, with 8.1 million people. It is the center of economic activity in Japan and has over 80,000 factories and company headquarters.

Rural-Urban Population

Urban 72 %

Rural 28 %

Japanese yen

GDP: Largest Five Economies

GDP in billions of United States dollars (1995)

JAPAN 5,109

CHINA 698

SOUTH KOREA 455

INDIA 324

INDONESIA 198

700
600
500
400
300
200
100
0

Rice (above) is a major crop in much of Asia. In India more employees work in textiles than any other industry.

Source: World Development Indicators 1997 CD-ROM, World Bank

WHY IT MATTERS

In only about 50 years, the nations around Asia's Pacific Rim have grown from areas devastated by war to major economic powers. The rapid economic growth of the nations in this region is likely to continue well into the twenty-first century. Such growth assures that the power of that part of Asia will continue to increase.

As economies develop and become more connected, whatever happens in one nation or continent will have great impact in other parts of the world. Because of this, observers around the world watch carefully to detect signs of what is in store for the most populous continent.

DID YOU KNOW?

When did European explorers arrive in Australia?

Before it was named, the Dutch landed on Australia's West Coast in 1616. The British explored and colonized the East Coast in 1788.

It wasn't until the early 1800s, however, that explorers knew that the East and West Coasts did, in fact, belong to the same body of land. From 1801 to 1803 two British navigators, George Bass and Matthew Flinders, sailed around the entire continent and mapped the southern coastline. This proved that the Dutch and English had landed on the same land mass. Matthew Flinders suggested calling this land Australia, and by the 1820s this had become the accepted name.

✓ Reviewing Facts and Ideas

MAIN IDEAS

- The growing nations of the Pacific Rim make up an important new region of economic power.

- Japan's industrialization was helped by United States involvement and the Korean War. Growth was also dependent on Japanese government policies and education.

- For many Pacific Rim countries, such as Singapore, economic growth has been stressed over democracy.

THINK ABOUT IT

1. How did the Korean War affect the Japanese economy?

2. What is the Pacific Rim? Why can its growth be described as a major shift in world history?

3. **FOCUS** How has economic growth changed life for Asians since the end of World War II?

4. **THINKING SKILL** What steps would you take to *evaluate the accuracy* of the GDP graph on page 620?

5. **WRITE** Should concern about jobs and the economy have priority over the protection of individual rights? Write a paragraph describing your view of this issue.

The Changing Americas

Read Aloud

The future is the great common thread tying together Americans." To Mexican poet Octavio Paz, the "thread" that will tie people of the Americas together is not just the trade of exports and imports. It is also the free trade of ideas and cultural traditions.

Focus Activity

READ TO LEARN

In what ways are the nations of the Americas working together on common problems?

VOCABULARY

- interdependent
- urbanization
- NAFTA
- bilingual
- Internet

PEOPLE

- Jean-Bertrand Aristide

PLACES

- Brazil
- Canada
- United States
- Haiti
- Dominican Republic
- Mexico
- Mexico City
- Nunavut

THE BIG PICTURE

Earlier in this chapter you read about the great changes sweeping through Europe, Africa, and Asia in the second half of the 1900s. These include political revolutions, industrial revolutions, and a movement toward greater unity among nations. It should not surprise you to learn that change has been transforming the nations of the Americas as well.

Before World War II, the United States and Canada were the only major industrial nations in the Americas. The other nations were mainly rural. In the past Brazil imported most of its manufactured goods such as clothes and cars. Today, however, Brazilian factory workers make everything from blue jeans to armored cars. Some of their most important buyers are other nations of the Americas such as Canada and the United States.

Trade has made the nations of the Americas increasingly interdependent. This means that they count on each other to meet the needs and wants of their peoples. Agreements about trade and politics have made countries like the United States, Mexico, and Canada closer neighbors.

NATIONS OF THE AMERICAS

The Western Hemisphere includes two cultural regions. The United States and Canada make up Anglo-America. This region was influenced strongly by British culture. Latin America includes Mexico, Central America, the Caribbean islands, and South America. It was influenced by Spain, Portugal, and France.

Many Caribbean islands have gained independence from European control since the 1800s. Haiti in 1804 and the Dominican Republic in 1844 were the first. As you can see on the map, these nations are both located on one island—Hispaniola. Most Caribbean nations became independent after World War II.

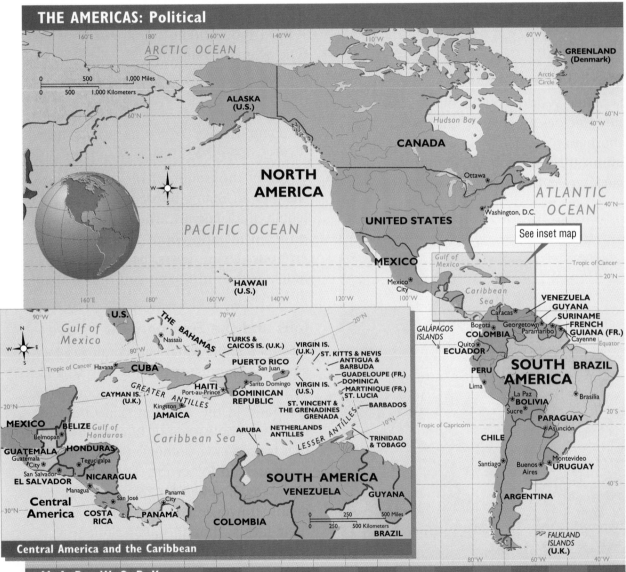

THE AMERICAS: Political

Central America and the Caribbean

MAP WORK

The two cultural regions of the Americas have been shaped by European influences. Today the many nations of these regions continue to develop new and unique traditions.

1. Of which nation is Montevideo the capital? In which of the Americas is this city located?

2. Which is farther west—Mexico City or Washington, D.C.?

3. What is the capital of Jamaica?

LATIN AMERICA TODAY

Mexico, a country of 92 million people, has become one of the world's major industrial powers. It is an important producer of such items as oil, electronic goods, and cars.

Mexico's industrial revolution began during World War II. A decline in world trade left Mexico with a shortage of manufactured goods. Because of this shortage and the need for more money, Mexican leaders decided to industrialize their nation.

Mexico City

After World War II, hundreds of new factories began to fill Mexico City, the nation's capital. New jobs brought about three million people there from rural areas between 1940 and 1970.

Oil drilling (above) became important in Mexico when vast oil reserves were found.

During the 1970s oil was discovered in southern Mexico. This "black gold" helped pay for more businesses in Mexico City and other cities. By the early 1990s Mexico City had become the world's second-largest urban area—behind Tokyo, Japan.

Need for Jobs

Mexico's economic growth has created riches for a few, but has not helped all Mexicans. Many in Mexico City have a hard time finding work and housing. One woman remembered:

> When we arrived in Mexico City, we lived in cardboard boxes and [searched] for food from the garbage dump. I cried. This is not what I had dreamed of.

Many thousands of Mexicans cross the United States border each year, legally and illegally. These Mexicans can go from making about $4 a day to $4 an hour. Living costs, however, are much higher in the United States than in Mexico.

Jobs and the Environment

Other Latin American countries face similar economic problems. In the 1980s Brazil's government offered poor people free land in the Amazon rain forest for farming. Thousands of families moved to this fragile environment. People set fires to clear land for crops. The rain forest land was ill-suited for growing rice or beans, however. Many people soon left their farms, though much damage had already been done to the land, the animals, and the Indians who had long lived there. This damage was then made worse by the arrival of new logging, mining, and ranching businesses.

One Brazilian scientist, Jacques Marcovitch, called for a new approach to this difficult problem:

We need strategies that are both economically productive and environmentally sound. . . .You cannot talk about ecology to people who are struggling to survive.

Today Brazil's government is working with other nations in the Americas to preserve the rain forests. Some United States companies are trying to build a demand for rain forest products such as nuts and oils. This demand helps to create jobs in the Amazon that are friendly to the environment.

Fighting the Drug Problem

Another difficult problem facing nations of the Americas is the drug trade. Farmers in Colombia, Peru, and Bolivia raise coca plants, which are used to make cocaine. This illegal and dangerous drug brings little money to farmers. Most profits go to crime organizations that sell the drugs around the world. The United States has joined other nations to try to stamp out the drug trade. Their efforts include destroying coca fields and helping farmers to raise other crops.

Growth of Democracy

During much of the 1900s most Latin American countries were ruled by dictators. In the 1980s democratic movements swept through the Americas, overturning most of the dictatorships. The people of Chile, for example, elected a democratic government in 1988.

Two years later, Haitians elected Jean-Bertrand Aristide (JAHN BAIR trahnd AH rihs teed) to be their president. Military leaders overthrew him the following year. With the help of the United States, Aristide regained his office in 1994.

In 1997, democratic elections in Mexico resulted in the defeat of a political party that had dominated the Mexican government for nearly 70 years. As a result, other political parties and views gained a greater opportunity to shape Mexico's future.

Growing Cities

Just as in Mexico City, millions of job-seekers have moved to cities throughout Latin America. In the 1970s in Brazil, 30 million people moved from the countryside to urban areas. Find the percentage of people now living in rural and urban areas in the Americas on the Infographic on page 628.

Urbanization, or growth of cities, has brought other challenges. As you can see on the chart on this page, two out of the five largest cities in the world are in Latin America.

THE WORLD'S FIVE LARGEST CITIES

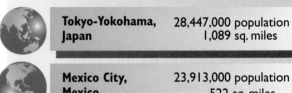

Tokyo-Yokohama, Japan — 28,447,000 population — 1,089 sq. miles

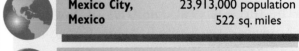

Mexico City, Mexico — 23,913,000 population — 522 sq. miles

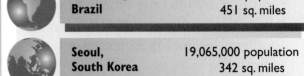

São Paulo, Brazil — 21,539,000 population — 451 sq. miles

Seoul, South Korea — 19,065,000 population — 342 sq. miles

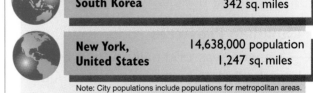

New York, United States — 14,638,000 population — 1,247 sq. miles

Note: City populations include populations for metropolitan areas.
Source: 1997 Information Please Almanac

CHART WORK

The world's five largest cities are located in Asia and the Americas.

1. What is the population of Tokyo-Yokohama?
2. Which city is located in Brazil?

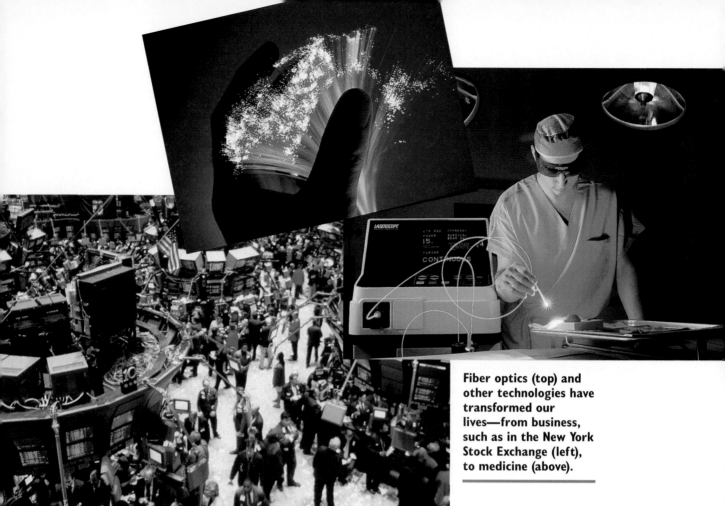

Fiber optics (top) and other technologies have transformed our lives—from business, such as in the New York Stock Exchange (left), to medicine (above).

INTO THE FUTURE

The three largest countries of North America—the United States, Canada, and Mexico, are working to develop strong ties. In 1993 the North American Free Trade Agreement, NAFTA, went into effect. Its goal is to increase trade among these nations.

Canadian Provinces

Canada was originally settled by the French. Today, in the province of Quebec, most people are bilingual—able to speak two languages. The French Canadians speak both French and English, but follow French customs.

Canada's other provinces are mainly rooted in the English language and British traditions. Many French Canadians tried to make Quebec

a separate country in 1995. But after a close vote, Quebec has remained part of Canada.

Many people in Canada have ancestors who were here long before the Europeans. In 1999 the Canadian government plans to create a vast new territory to be known as Nunavut (NUH nuh vut). This territory is for the Inuit, who are native to northern Canada.

World Role for the United States

As the remaining superpower, the United States continues to play an active role in world affairs. In 1991 the United States led an alliance of nations that sent troops to the Persian Gulf region. They forced Iraq to withdraw its troops from neighboring Kuwait. Iraq had invaded Kuwait and wanted to make it part of Iraq.

In the 1990s the United States assisted the United Nations in efforts to bring food to starving citizens in the African country of Somalia. In the last lesson you read about the civil war in Bosnia in the Balkan Peninsula. This war also brought calls for world response. Within the United States these world crises have led to heated debate. Many disagree over what the country's role in world politics should be in the future. Should it continue to act as protector of democracy and human rights as it often did during the Cold War?

New Technologies

As the United States considers its world role, it is undergoing great changes in technology at home. Scientific advances in medicine enable people to live longer, healthier lives. The average person born in the United States in 1900 lived to be only 42 years old. The average person born in this country in 1996 can expect to live more than thirty years longer, reaching 76 years of age.

Space satellites now send information back to Earth. This relay has helped scientists update their knowledge about climate and the environment. Other technological improvements have made it possible for people to communicate instantly. Fax machines and cellular phones bring the world closer together than ever before.

All of these developments are part of an "information revolution" that has changed the way we work, learn, and communicate. A big part of this revolution is the Internet. The Internet is a constantly growing group of interconnected computers around the world.

They are part of an "information superhighway"—new ways for people to share ideas.

The Internet had its start during the Cold War. United States technology experts began connecting government and research computers. They hoped that this link would allow the government to keep running in case of a nuclear attack. The network, which later grew into the Internet, has become one of the most important legacies of the Cold War. Instead of being used in war, it has united people around the world.

Today more than 40 million people from over 160 nations use the Internet. People are able to read the latest news without opening a newspaper. They can "talk" to each other without telephones or shop without going to a store. With access to the Internet, much of the world is no farther than a computer screen away.

Links to CURRENT EVENTS

What's happening now?

With today's computer technology and the help of the Internet, you can find out what is happening around the world right now. You do not need to wait for this evening's news or tomorrow's newspaper. The Internet allows you to read about things right after they happen. You might also have conversations with people from other countries about an event while it is taking place.

Ask your teacher or librarian for help using the Internet to find a news article about something that happened today. Why might it be useful to learn about events while they are happening, rather than after they are over?

Economy of Americas

As you read, nations in the Americas are becoming increasingly interdependent. As Latin America continues to industrialize, more goods are produced that can be traded in other parts of the Americas. What importance do you think agreements like NAFTA have for North American nations?

Mexico City (above), with a population of 20 million, is the largest city in the Americas. Oil is a valuable resource for Mexico, Venezuela, and Colombia. Brazil grows about 30% of the world's coffee. In the United States, the world's largest coffee consumer, we drink about 400 million cups a day.

Canadian dollars

Rural-Urban Population

Urban 72 %

Rural 28 %

GDP: LARGEST FIVE ECONOMIES

GDP in billions of United States dollars (1993)

UNITED STATES 6,260

CANADA 477

BRAZIL 444

MEXICO 343

ARGENTINA 256

500
400
300
200
100
0

Source: The World Bank World Development Report

WHY IT MATTERS

Throughout history the world has been shaped by technological, governmental, social, and cultural change. The first agricultural revolution began over 8,000 years ago. People began to build cities and specialize in the work they did. Improvements in agriculture have continued to this day. Crops like wheat, rice, corn, and potatoes were once grown in only small parts of the world. Today these crops are grown around the globe, helping to feed millions of people.

The world's urban revolution began in places like ancient Catal Huyuk. It eventually led to the creation of large, modern cities like New York City and Buenos Aires. Political revolutions of the past few centuries brought greater democracy and sometimes, losses of freedom. The Industrial Revolution began in Britain in the 1700s. It is continuing today, reaching some parts of the world for the first time.

New technological advances continue to change the ways people live. Today the world has only just begun a new "information revolution." These advances build on earlier inventions of paper and printed books. Many everyday objects in our lives may become old-fashioned in the twenty-first century. Some people believe books and newspapers could be replaced by computers. What do you think?

It is possible that you—as a future inventor, teacher, or leader in business or government—will help influence future change. In doing so you can change history and the world.

Many students of today will become the leaders of tomorrow.

MAIN IDEAS

- Industrial growth after World War II resulted in job opportunities and overcrowded cities in Latin America.
- Democratic governments have replaced dictators throughout much of Latin America.
- The North American Free Trade Agreement (NAFTA) went into effect in 1993.
- A powerful "information revolution" now links people around the world.

THINK ABOUT IT

1. What was one way the Brazilian government tried to solve the problems of urbanization? What problems have resulted?

2. What has been the United States' role in recent world events?

3. **FOCUS** In what ways are nations of the Americas interdependent?

4. **THINKING SKILL** Make and support at least two *conclusions* about how life in the Americas has changed since World War II.

5. **GEOGRAPHY** How has the Internet affected the movement of ideas in the world?

CITIZENSHIP
VIEWPOINTS

In 1997, at the Earth Summit II in New York, delegates from around the world met to discuss important environmental issues.

How should nations work together to protect the environment?

Today, the nations of the world face many threats to the environment. Some nations are trying to clean up pollution and protect endangered species. Others are working to reduce soil erosion and flooding due to the loss of forests. Many nations consider global warming, the buildup of gases that is causing Earth's climate to slowly change, to be a serious issue worldwide.

At the 1992 Earth Summit in Rio de Janeiro, Brazil, delegates from all over the world met to discuss these and other environmental issues. Then, in 1997, Earth Summit II was held at the United Nations in New York City. They agreed that international cooperation is needed to solve many of these problems. However, finding a way to cooperate is difficult because nations often blame each other for the pollution. Also, the leaders of some nations see cleaning up the environment as a luxury they cannot afford. They say finding jobs for their citizens must come first. Many poorer nations need the help of industrialized countries in developing technology that can reduce pollution. Consider these viewpoints on this issue and answer the questions that follow.

Three DIFFERENT Viewpoints

1 **SMRUTI KOPPIKAR**
Journalist, India
Excerpt from interview, 1997

Right now nations are blaming each other for our environmental problems. This finger-pointing has to stop. Each nation has its own needs and priorities. If your stomach is full and your economy is growing, you look at problems in one way. In my country, India, environment is an issue of livelihood. . . . We have to find common ground.

"Each nation has its own needs . . ."

2 **ADAM RIVAS WYZYKOWSKI**
Teacher, Venezuela
Excerpt from interview, 1997

We must first change the way Venezuelans think about the environment. Cleaning up the environment must become a high priority, because right now we have other problems we consider more important such as jobs and education. We must get people to think of the environment as a serious problem equal in importance to other problems.

"Cleaning up the environment must become a high priority . . ."

3 **EVELYN TENG**
Government worker, Malaysia
Excerpt from interview, 1997

Countries like Malaysia don't have the money to develop the clean and green technologies that industrial nations already have. We need cooperation between richer and poorer nations to exchange information and share technologies that will help us run our factories without hurting our environment. Without cooperation, it's a lose-lose situation for all nations. . . . Everyone has to work together.

"We need cooperation between richer and poorer nations . . ."

BUILDING CITIZENSHIP

1. What is the viewpoint of each person?
2. In what ways are some of the viewpoints alike? In what ways are they different? What might be the reasons each person has his or her viewpoint on this issue?
3. What other viewpoints might people have on global cooperation concerning the environment?

SHARING VIEWPOINTS

Discuss what you agree with or disagree with about these viewpoints. Discuss why you think the speakers might feel as they do. Then as a class, write two statements that all of you can agree with about global cooperation on environmental issues.

CHAPTER 20 REVIEW

THINKING ABOUT VOCABULARY

Each of the following statements contains an underlined vocabulary word. Number a sheet of paper from 1 to 10. Beside each number write **T** if the statement is true and **F** if the statement is false. If the statement is false, rewrite the sentence using the vocabulary word correctly.

1. The <u>Pacific Rim</u> is the ring of countries that surrounds the Pacific Ocean.

2. <u>NAFTA</u> is a military alliance that involves European nations.

3. The crowded areas inside or near cities in South Africa where many blacks live are called <u>townships</u>.

4. A person unable to speak more than one language is <u>bilingual</u>.

5. <u>Ethnic groups</u> have a language, customs, and a heritage in common.

6. The <u>Internet</u> is a constantly expanding network of interconnected computers around the world.

7. The system of laws once used to keep the races separate in South Africa was called <u>apartheid</u>.

8. <u>Sanctions</u> are trade agreements that countries make with each other.

9. <u>Interdependent</u> means having the ability to stand alone without getting help from other countries.

10. The amount of money each person would have if a country's total income was divided evenly among its people is called <u>per capita income</u>.

THINKING ABOUT FACTS

1. Why was 1989 considered a "Year of Miracles" in Europe?

2. How did Nelson Mandela and F.W. de Klerk transform South Africa in the first half of the 1990s?

3. What events took place at Tiananmen Square in June of 1989?

4. Who is Jean-Bertrand Aristide? What has his role been in Haiti since 1990?

5. When did the Cold War end? What helped to bring about the end? How did Europe change as a result?

6. Why did Gorbachev feel that glasnost would be an important part of rebuilding the Soviet Union's economy?

7. What are some of the economic and political problems that South Africans face now that apartheid has been abolished?

8. What changes have taken place in China under the leadership of Deng Xiaoping?

9. What did people in Hong Kong fear would happen when China took control in 1997?

10. How does NAFTA affect North American trade? How does it affect the ties between the United States, Mexico, and Canada?

THINK AND WRITE

WRITING A JOURNAL ENTRY

Suppose you were a Russian living in Moscow in 1990. Write a journal entry about the changes taking place as the Soviet Union collapses and moves toward democracy.

WRITING A PAMPHLET

Write a pamphlet about Nelson Mandela. Describe his early work for the African National Congress. Tell about his arrest, imprisonment, and release. Then describe his election as president of South Africa.

WRITING ON THE INTERNET

Suppose you could send a message on the Internet to thousands of students around the world. Write a message and two answers you might receive from South America, Africa, the Middle East, or East Asia.

APPLYING THINKING SKILLS

EVALUATING INFORMATION FOR ACCURACY

1. What does evaluating information for accuracy mean?

2. Compare this skill with the skill of analyzing the credibility of a source you learned in Chapter 16 on pages 472–473. How are they similar? How are they different?

3. Choose an article from a national news magazine or newspaper. What are some of the things that had to be evaluated before the information was printed?

4. Review the account of the Vietnamese worker's conditions under the French, quoted on page 587. How would you go about evaluating this source for accuracy?

5. Why is evaluating information for accuracy important for the study of history?

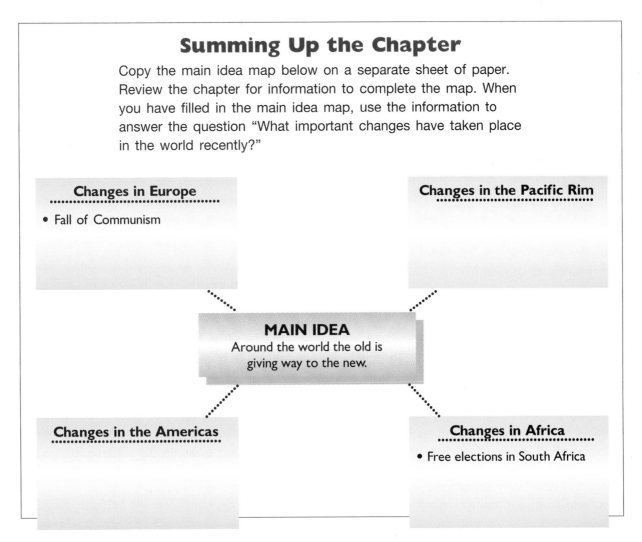

Summing Up the Chapter

Copy the main idea map below on a separate sheet of paper. Review the chapter for information to complete the map. When you have filled in the main idea map, use the information to answer the question "What important changes have taken place in the world recently?"

Changes in Europe
- Fall of Communism

Changes in the Pacific Rim

MAIN IDEA
Around the world the old is giving way to the new.

Changes in the Americas

Changes in Africa
- Free elections in South Africa

UNIT 6 REVIEW

THINKING ABOUT VOCABULARY

Number a sheet of paper from 1 to 10. Beside each number write the word or term from the list below that matches the statement.

armistice	sanctions
communism	strike
concentration camp	urbanization
European Union	warlords
Middle East	Zionism

1. The growth of cities

2. An organization of western European nations working to build a common economy in Europe

3. Local military leaders in China who took advantage of political unrest in the early 1900s to seize power in their regions

4. The region between the Mediterranean Sea and the western borders of Pakistan and Afghanistan

5. Penalties placed on a nation to make it change its behavior

6. A camp where people are imprisoned because of their heritage, religious beliefs, or political views

7. An agreement to stop fighting

8. The movement to establish a Jewish homeland or nation

9. A political system in which the government owns everything in name of the workers

10. The refusal to work in protest of unfair treatment

THINK AND WRITE

WRITING AN ESSAY

Write a short essay about two or three people in the twentieth century you most admire. Describe what they accomplished and what you admire about them.

WRITING ABOUT PERSPECTIVES

The Bosnian city of Sarajevo has been at the center of conflict more than once in this century. In 1914 the assassination there of the Austrian archduke Franz Ferdinand was the spark that ignited World War I. In the 1990s the war raging between ethnic groups in the nation hit the city particularly hard. Write about the two conflicts and the links, if any, between them.

WRITING AN INTERVIEW

Choose two leaders from wars in the twentieth century. Write questions you would ask them if you could interview them. Then write the responses they might have given.

BUILDING SKILLS

1. **Time zone maps** Look at the time zone map on page 548. When it is noon where you live, what time is it in Honolulu? Montreal? Rome? Bombay? Hong Kong?

2. **Time zone maps** Explain why it is possible for somebody to fly from Tokyo on May 2 and arrive in the United States on May 1?

3. **Political cartoons** Find a political cartoon in a newspaper or news magazine. Explain what it means. How does the cartoon make its point?

4. **Political cartoons** Choose a political event that you read about in this book. Then make a political cartoon about the event. Draw simple stick figures if you like and use words to fill out the meaning of the cartoon.

5. **Evaluating information** Choose an article from a newspaper, magazine, or newsletter or take a passage from a book. How would you evaluate the information you find there for its accuracy?

634

YESTERDAY, TODAY &
TOMORROW

The United Nations was created at the end of World War II to promote peace and help countries develop. In 1995 the UN celebrated its 50th anniversary. What role do you think the United Nations will play in the next 50 years? Do you think the United Nations should be doing more? If so, what?

READING ON YOUR OWN

These are some books you might find at the library to help you learn more.

BEHIND THE SECRET WINDOW
by Nelly Toll
This book reveals the memories and paintings of a young Jewish girl in hiding during World War.

GANDHI
by Nigel Hunter
This brief biography of Ghandi is accompanied by colorful photos.

NELSON MANDELA: DETERMINED TO BE FREE
by Jack L. Roberts
This biography describes the man who struggled against apartheid and became South Africa's first black president.

UNIT 6 REVIEW PROJECT

Make a Venn Diagram

1. With a partner, choose two events from the unit such as World War I and World War II.
2. List causes for each event.
3. On a large piece of oaktag, make a Venn diagram by drawing two circles that overlap in the middle.
4. Write the causes for one event on one side of the diagram. On the other side of the diagram, write the causes for the other event. Place common causes in the center of the diagram.
5. You may want to illustrate your diagram with copies of newspaper clippings from the library or your own drawings.
6. On the bottom of the oaktag, write a paragraph describing the diagram. What are the common causes? How do the events differ?
7. Share your conclusions with the rest of the class.

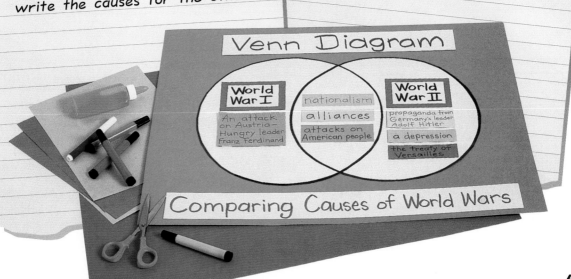

Venn Diagram

World War I	nationalism	World War II
An attack on Austria–Hungry leader Franz Ferdinand	alliances / attacks on American people	propaganda from Germany's leader Adolf Hitler / a depression / the treaty of Versailles

Comparing Causes of World Wars

REFERENCE SECTION

The Reference Section has many parts,

each with a different type of information.

Use this section to look up people,

places, and events as you study.

Atlas

An atlas is a collection of maps. An atlas

can be a book or a separate section

within a book. This Atlas is a separate

section with maps to help you study

the history and geography

presented in this book.

MAP BUILDER
The World: Climate and Population

The map on the facing page is a special kind of map. Each transparent overlay shows a different aspect of the world's climate and population. You can see where in the world similar climates exist and how climates relate to latitude. You can also compare population density around the world and see in which climates people live. Start by lifting all of the transparent overlays and observe the base map of the continents and oceans of the world. Then cover the base map with the first overlay and study the climates shown. In which climate do you live?

Allow the second overlay to cover the first and consider how climates are related to latitude. What latitude lines divide the zones shown? What kinds of climates are generally found nearest the equator? Finally, let down the third overlay and compare population densities around the world. Which areas of North America are the most densely populated? In which climates do the fewest people live?

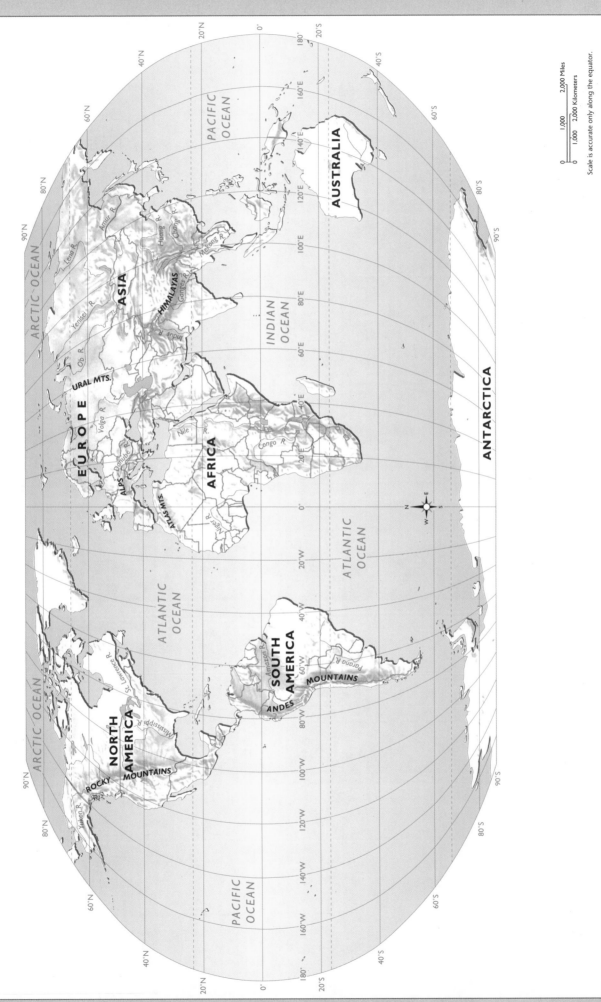

ARCTIC OCEAN

90°N

80°N

60°N

ASIA

EUROPE

URAL MTS.

Lena R.
Amur R.
Yenisei R.
Ob R.
Volga R.
ALPS
Danube R.

HIMALAYAS
Ganges R.
Indus R.
Mekong R.
Huang R.
Chang R.

ATLAS MTS.
Niger R.
Nile R.
Congo R.
AFRICA

INDIAN OCEAN

AUSTRALIA

ANTARCTICA

N
W E
S

ATLANTIC OCEAN

20°W
0°
20°E
40°E
60°E
80°E
100°E
120°E
140°E
160°E
180°

20°N
0°
20°S
40°S
60°S
80°S
90°S

ARCTIC OCEAN

NORTH AMERICA

ROCKY MOUNTAINS
Yukon R.
Mississippi R.
St. Lawrence R.

SOUTH AMERICA
Amazon R.
Paraná R.
ANDES MOUNTAINS

ATLANTIC OCEAN

PACIFIC OCEAN

180°
160°W
140°W
120°W
100°W
80°W
60°W
40°W

80°N
60°N
40°N
20°N

0
1,000
2,000 Miles

0
1,000
2,000 Kilometers

Scale is accurate only along the equator.

EUROPE: Physical

ASIA

URAL MOUNTAINS

Ural River

Volga River

Northern Dvina River

Don River

CAUCASUS MTS.

Mt. Elbrus
18,510 ft.
(5,642 m)

Caspian Sea

Sea of Azov

Black Sea

KOLA PENINSULA

White Sea

Barents Sea

LAPLAND

BALTIC PLAINS

EUROPEAN PLAIN

W. Dvina River

Dnieper River

Dniester River

Gulf of Finland

Gulf of Bothnia

SCANDINAVIAN PENINSULA

Baltic Sea

Vistula River

Oder River

CARPATHIAN MTS.

Danube River

Danube

BALKAN PENINSULA

Aegean Sea

Crete

Rhodes

30°E

ARCTIC OCEAN

40°E

30°E

20°E

10°E

Lofoten Islands

Norwegian Sea

Elbe River

Jutland Peninsula

NORTH

North Sea

ALPS

Danube River

Po River

Adriatic Sea

APENNINES

ITALIAN PENINSULA

Tyrrhenian Sea

Ionian Sea

Mediterranean Sea

Sicily

Maltese Islands

Faeroe Islands

Shetland Islands

British Isles

English Channel

Seine River

Loire River

JURA MTS.
Rhine R.

Mt. Blanc
15,771 ft. (4,807 m)

Rhône River

Garonne River

PYRENEES

Corsica

Sardinia

Balearic Islands

Iceland

20°W

Arctic Circle

70°N

0°

10°W

Bay of Biscay

Ebro River

IBERIAN PENINSULA

Tagus River

Strait of Gibraltar

AFRICA

ATLANTIC OCEAN

60°N

50°N

40°N

40°W

30°W

20°W

N
W   E
S

0   250   500 Miles
0   250   500 Kilometers

R7

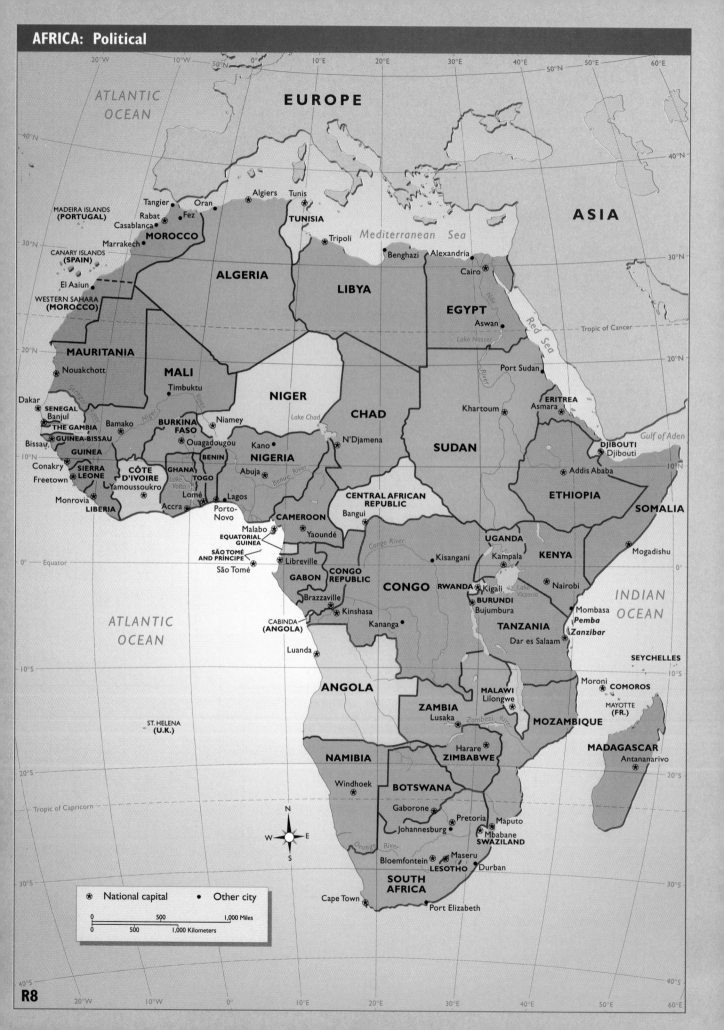

AFRICA: Political

ATLANTIC OCEAN

EUROPE

ASIA

MADEIRA ISLANDS (PORTUGAL)

Tangier ⊛ Oran
Rabat Fez
Casablanca
MOROCCO
Marrakech

CANARY ISLANDS (SPAIN)

El Aaiun

WESTERN SAHARA (MOROCCO)

Algiers Tunis
TUNISIA
⊛ Tripoli

Mediterranean Sea

Benghazi Alexandria
Cairo ⊛

ALGERIA

LIBYA

EGYPT

Aswan

Tropic of Cancer

Lake Nasser

MAURITANIA

Nouakchott ⊛

MALI
Timbuktu

Dakar
SENEGAL
Banjul
THE GAMBIA
GUINEA-BISSAU
Bissau
GUINEA
Conakry
Freetown
SIERRA LEONE
Monrovia
LIBERIA

Bamako ⊛

Senegal River

Niger River

NIGER

Niamey ⊛

Lake Chad

CHAD

N'Djamena

SUDAN

Khartoum ⊛

Port Sudan

Nile River

Red Sea

ERITREA
Asmara

Gulf of Aden

DJIBOUTI
Djibouti

BURKINA FASO
Ouagadougou ⊛

Kano
NIGERIA
Abuja ⊛

CÔTE D'IVOIRE
GHANA
Yamoussoukro
TOGO
Accra
Lomé
Porto-Novo
BENIN
Lagos

Addis Ababa ⊛

ETHIOPIA

SOMALIA

Lake Volta

Benue River

CENTRAL AFRICAN REPUBLIC
Bangui ⊛

Malabo
EQUATORIAL GUINEA
SÃO TOMÉ AND PRÍNCIPE
São Tomé

CAMEROON
Yaoundé ⊛

Libreville ⊛

GABON
CONGO REPUBLIC
Brazzaville ⊛

CONGO

Kisangani

UGANDA
Kampala ⊛

RWANDA
Kigali ⊛
BURUNDI
Bujumbura

Congo River

Kinshasa ⊛

Kananga

Mogadishu

KENYA
Nairobi ⊛

Lake Victoria

Mombasa
Pemba
Zanzibar

INDIAN OCEAN

ATLANTIC OCEAN

CABINDA (ANGOLA)

Luanda ⊛

TANZANIA
Dar es Salaam

SEYCHELLES

ANGOLA

ST. HELENA (U.K.)

Equator

ZAMBIA
Lusaka ⊛

Zambezi River

MALAWI
Lilongwe ⊛

Moroni ⊛
COMOROS

MAYOTTE (FR.)

MOZAMBIQUE

MADAGASCAR
Antananarivo ⊛

NAMIBIA
Windhoek ⊛

Harare ⊛
ZIMBABWE

Tropic of Capricorn

BOTSWANA
Gaborone ⊛

Pretoria ⊛
Maputo

Johannesburg

Mbabane ⊛
SWAZILAND
Maseru ⊛
LESOTHO
Durban

Orange River

Bloemfontein ⊛

SOUTH AFRICA

Cape Town ⊛
Port Elizabeth

N
W E
S

⊛ National capital	• Other city

0   500   1,000 Miles
0 500 1,000 Kilometers

R8

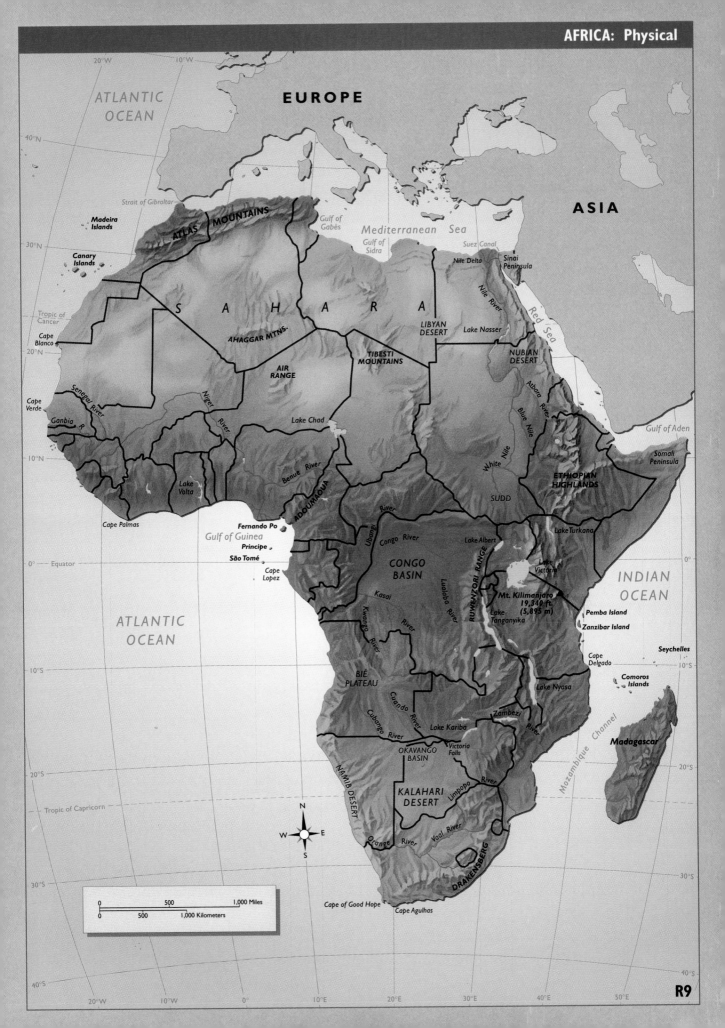

RIO

Map Legend
⊛ National capital
• Other city

0   500   1,000 Miles
0   500   1,000 Kilometers

Oceans and Seas
ARCTIC OCEAN
PACIFIC OCEAN
INDIAN OCEAN
Bering Sea
Sea of Okhotsk
Sea of Japan
East China Sea
South China Sea
Yellow Sea
Bay of Bengal
Arabian Sea
Caspian Sea
Aral Sea
Black Sea
Red Sea
Arafura Sea
Tropic of Cancer
Arctic Circle
Equator

Continents / Regions
EUROPE
AFRICA
Siberia
Manchuria
Inner Mongolia
Mongolia
Tibet
Sinkiang

Countries
RUSSIA
KAZAKHSTAN
MONGOLIA
CHINA
JAPAN
NORTH KOREA
SOUTH KOREA
TAIWAN
PHILIPPINES
INDONESIA
PAPUA NEW GUINEA
VIETNAM
LAOS
CAMBODIA
THAILAND
MYANMAR (BURMA)
MALAYSIA
SINGAPORE
BRUNEI
BANGLADESH
BHUTAN
NEPAL
INDIA
SRI LANKA
MALDIVES
PAKISTAN
AFGHANISTAN
IRAN
IRAQ
KUWAIT
BAHRAIN
QATAR
UNITED ARAB EMIRATES
OMAN
YEMEN
SAUDI ARABIA
JORDAN
ISRAEL
LEBANON
SYRIA
CYPRUS
TURKEY
GEORGIA
ARMENIA
AZERBAIJAN
TURKMENISTAN
UZBEKISTAN
TAJIKISTAN
KYRGYZSTAN

Cities
Moscow
Yekaterinburg
Chelyabinsk
Omsk
Novosibirsk
Krasnoyarsk
Irkutsk
Ulan Ude
Chita
Yakutsk
Khabarovsk
Vladivostok
Magadan
Sapporo
Tokyo
Nagoya
Kyoto
Nagasaki
Seoul
Pyongyang
Changchun
Shenyang
Harbin
Beijing
Tianjin
Jinan
Nanjing
Shanghai
Wuhan
Changsha
Chongqing
Chengdu
Lanzhou
Xi'an
Guangzhou
HONG KONG
MACAO (PORT.)
Taipei
Kunming
Hanoi
Hue
Ho Chi Minh City
Phnom Penh
Vientiane
Bangkok
Moulmein
Yangon
Mandalay
Thimphu
Dacca
Kathmandu
Lhasa
Patna
Calcutta
Nagpur
Hyderabad
Madras
Bangalore
Colombo
Bombay
Ahmadabad
Jabalpur
Agra
New Delhi
Lahore
Islamabad
Karachi
Hyderabad
Kandahar
Kabul
Herat
Mashhad
Tehran
Isfahan
Tabriz
Baku
Yerevan
Tbilisi
Ashgabat
Samarkand
Tashkent
Dushanbe
Bishkek
Almaty
Semipalatinsk
Karaganda
Ankara
Istanbul
Izmir
Bursa
Nicosia
Beirut
Damascus
Amman
Jerusalem
Baghdad
Basra
Kuwait
Manama
Doha
Abu Dhabi
Muscat
Riyadh
Medina
Mecca
San'a
Ulaanbaatar
Urumqi
Jayapura
Port Moresby
Lae
Manado
Davao
Quezon City
Manila
Kuala Lumpur
Singapore
Bandar Seri Begawan
Jakarta
Surabaya
Yogyakarta
Palembang
Padang
Malé

Islands / Regions
Kuril Islands
Sakhalin
RYUKYU ISLANDS (JAPAN)
ANDAMAN ISLANDS (INDIA)
NICOBAR ISLANDS (INDIA)
LACCADIVE ISLANDS (INDIA)
Socotra
Irian Jaya
New Ireland
New Britain
Sulawesi (Celebes)
Borneo
Sumatra
Java
Timor

Rivers / Lakes
Lena River
Amur River
Yenisey River
Ob River
Huang River
Chang River
Mekong River
Ganges River
Indus River
Tigris River
Euphrates River
Brahmaputra River
Amu Darya
Syr Darya
Ural River
Lake Baikal
Lake Balkash

ASIA: Physical

EUROPE

AFRICA

ARCTIC OCEAN

Arctic Circle

Bering Strait

Wrangel Island

New Siberian Islands

East Siberian Sea

Laptev Sea

ANADYR RANGE

KOLYMA RANGE

Kamchatka Peninsula

Bering Sea

PACIFIC OCEAN

Tropic of Cancer

CHERSKIY MOUNTAINS

VERKHOYANSK MOUNTAINS

STANOVOY MOUNTAINS

Lena River

Amur River

Kuril Islands

Sakhalin

Sea of Okhotsk

Hokkaido

Honshu

SIKHOTE-ALIN MOUNTAINS

Sea of Japan

Shikoku

Kyushu

Korean Peninsula

Yellow Sea

East China Sea

Taiwan (Formosa)

Philippine Sea

Philippine Islands

CENTRAL SIBERIAN PLATEAU

Taymyr Peninsula

Angara River

Yenisey River

STANOVOY MOUNTAINS

YABLONOVY MOUNTAINS

GREAT KHINGAN MOUNTAINS

MANCHURIAN PLAIN

MONGOLIAN PLATEAU

GOBI

INNER MONGOLIA

Huang River

NORTH CHINA PLAIN

QINLING MTS.

Chang River

Xi River

Gulf of Tonkin

Hainan

South China Sea

Celebes Sea

Sulawesi (Celebes)

Borneo

Kara Sea

Yamal Peninsula

Ob River

Irtysh River

WEST SIBERIAN PLAIN

KAZAKH UPLANDS

Lake Balkash

ALTAI MOUNTAINS

Turfan Depression −505 ft. (−154 m)

TIAN SHAN

TARIM BASIN

Tarim River

TAKLA MAKAN

ALTUN TAGH

KUNLUN MOUNTAINS

PLATEAU OF TIBET

Mekong River

Indochina Peninsula

Gulf of Siam

Malay Peninsula

Sumatra

Strait of Malacca

Java Sea

Java

URAL MOUNTAINS

KIRGHIZ STEPPE

Aral Sea

Syr Darya

Amu Darya

UST-URT PLATEAU

HINDU KUSH

KARAKORAM RANGE

HIMALAYAS

Mt. Everest 29,028 ft. (8,848 m)

Brahmaputra River

Ganges River

Godavari R.

DECCAN PLATEAU

Indian Subcontinent

EASTERN GHATS

WESTERN GHATS

Bay of Bengal

Andaman Sea

Andaman Islands

Nicobar Islands

Sri Lanka (Ceylon)

INDIAN OCEAN

Laccadive Islands

Maldive Islands

Arabian Sea

THAR DESERT

Indus River

CASPIAN Sea

PLATEAU OF IRAN

ZAGROS MOUNTAINS

Persian Gulf

Gulf of Oman

Tigris River

Euphrates River

MESOPOTAMIA

SYRIAN DESERT

NAFUD

Arabian Peninsula

RUB AL-KHALI

Socotra

Gulf of Aden

Red Sea

Mediterranean Sea

ANATOLIA (ASIA MINOR)

Bosporus

Black Sea

Sea of Azov

Ural River

New Guinea

Arafura Sea

Timor

Equator

N
E
S
W

0   500   1,000 Miles

0   500   1,000 Kilometers

R11

THE AMERICAS: Political

ARCTIC OCEAN

Beaufort Sea

GREENLAND
(DENMARK)

Baffin
Bay

ALASKA
(U.S.)

Arctic Circle

Yukon River
Fairbanks

Mackenzie River

Anchorage

Yellowknife

Iqaluit

Nuuk

Arctic Circle

60°N

60°N

NORTH AMERICA

Hudson Bay

Labrador
Sea

CANADA

Edmonton

Vancouver

Winnipeg

Great
Lakes

Quebec

Ottawa

Gulf of St. Lawrence

Seattle

Missouri River

Portland

Minneapolis

Detroit

Toronto

Boston

Salt Lake
City

UNITED

Chicago

New York City

Great
Salt
Lake

Denver

St. Louis

Washington, D.C.

ATLANTIC
OCEAN

San Francisco

Colorado River

STATES

Los Angeles

Phoenix

Atlanta

BERMUDA
(U.K.)

30°N

Rio Grande

Houston

New
Orleans

Mississippi River

30°N

Gulf of California

MEXICO

Gulf of Mexico

Miami

THE BAHAMAS

Monterrey

Nassau

Tropic of Cancer

HAWAII
(U.S.)

Havana

CUBA

HAITI

DOMINICAN REPUBLIC

Guadalajara

Port-au-Prince

Santo Domingo

BELIZE

Mexico City

Belmopan

JAMAICA

Kingston

San Juan

ST. KITTS AND NEVIS

PUERTO
RICO
(U.S.)

ANTIGUA AND BARBUDA

PACIFIC

Guatemala City

HONDURAS

DOMINICA

OCEAN

GUATEMALA

Tegucigalpa

Caribbean

ST. LUCIA

San Salvador

NICARAGUA

BARBADOS

EL SALVADOR

Managua

Sea

GRENADA

ST. VINCENT AND THE GRENADINES

San José

Panamá

Maracaibo

TRINIDAD AND TOBAGO

COSTA RICA

City

Caracas

PANAMA

VENEZUELA

SURINAME

Bogotá

Georgetown

Paramaribo

Cayenne

COLOMBIA

GUYANA

FRENCH GUIANA
(FRANCE)

0°

Equator

Quito

0°

GALAPAGOS
ISLANDS
(ECUADOR)

ECUADOR

Manaus

Belém

Guayaquil

Amazon River

SOUTH AMERICA

Recife

PERU

BRAZIL

Callao

Lima

BOLIVIA

Brasília

Bahia

La Paz

Santa Cruz

Sucre

PARAGUAY

São Paulo

Rio de
Janeiro

Tropic of Capricorn

Antofagasta

Asunción

Tucumán

30°S

CHILE

Porto Alegre

30°S

Valparaíso

Rosario

URUGUAY

Santiago

Buenos
Aires

Montevideo

La Plata

Concepción

Mar del Plata

ARGENTINA

National capital   Other city

Comodoro
Rivadavia

0   1,000   2,000 Miles

0   1,000   2,000 Kilometers

FALKLAND ISLANDS
(U.K.)

Punta Arenas

Strait of
Magellan

SOUTH
GEORGIA
(U.K.)

150°W   120°W   90°W   60°W

ARCTIC OCEAN

Queen Elizabeth Islands

Greenland

Baffin Bay

Banks Island

Victoria Island

Baffin Island

Point Barrow

Beaufort Sea

BROOKS RANGE

Mt. McKinley 20,320 ft. (6,194 m)

Yukon River

Arctic Circle

Davis Strait

ALASKA RANGE

Mackenzie River

Great Bear Lake

Great Slave Lake

Cape Farewell

60°N

Alaska Peninsula

Gulf of Alaska

COAST MOUNTAINS

NORTH AMERICA

Hudson Bay

Labrador Sea

Labrador

Vancouver Island

ROCKY MOUNTAINS

Saskatchewan River

Lake Winnipeg

CANADIAN SHIELD

Newfoundland

Gulf of St. Lawrence

CASCADE RANGE

GREAT PLAINS

Snake River

Missouri River

Great Lakes

St. Lawrence River

APPALACHIAN MOUNTAINS

Nova Scotia

Cape Mendocino

COAST RANGES

SIERRA NEVADA

GREAT BASIN

Great Salt Lake

Colorado River

Mississippi River

Ohio River

COASTAL PLAINS

Cape Cod

Long Island

ATLANTIC OCEAN

30°N

Baja California

SIERRA MADRE OCCIDENTAL

SIERRA MADRE ORIENTAL

Rio Grande

Gulf of Mexico

Florida Peninsula

30°N

Tropic of Cancer

Gulf of California

Straits of Florida

Hawaiian Islands

Yucatán Peninsula

Gulf of Honduras

Greater

Cuba

Hispaniola

Antilles

WEST

INDIES

Lesser Antilles

PACIFIC OCEAN

Caribbean Sea

CENTRAL

Lake Nicaragua

Isthmus of Panama

Gulf of Panama

Lake Maracaibo

LLANOS

Orinoco River

GUIANA HIGHLANDS

AMERICA

Magdalena River

Rio Negro

Amazon River

Galápagos Islands

AMAZON BASIN

Madeira River

SOUTH AMERICA

Cape São Roque

0°

Equator

0°

ANDES

Lake Titicaca

MATO GROSSO PLATEAU

Tocantins River

São Francisco River

BRAZILIAN HIGHLANDS

GRAN CHACO

Paraguay River

Paraná River

Uruguay River

Mt. Aconcagua 22,834 ft. (6,960 m)

Tropic of Capricorn

30°S

PAMPAS

30°S

MOUNTAINS

PATAGONIA

0   1,000   2,000 Miles

0   1,000   2,000 Kilometers

Strait of Magellan

Falkland Islands

Tierra del Fuego

South Georgia

Cape Horn

N
W   E
S

150°W   120°W   90°W   60°W

RUSSIA

ARCTIC OCEAN

ALASKA

CANADA

Nome

Yukon

Fairbanks

River

Anchorage

Juneau

PACIFIC
OCEAN

70°N

Arctic Circle

180°

60°N

170°W   160°W   150°W   140°W

0   250   500 Miles
0   250   500 Kilometers

CANADA

River

Seattle
Spokane
WASHINGTON
Olympia

Great Falls
Missouri River
Helena
MONTANA
Billings

Columbia

Portland
Salem
Eugene

OREGON

IDAHO

Boise

Snake River
Pocatello

WYOMING

Casper
Cheyenne

40°N

NEVADA

Great
Salt
Lake

Ogden
Salt Lake City
Provo

COLORADO

Reno
Carson City

Sacramento
San Francisco
Oakland
San Jose

UTAH

Denver
Colorado
Springs
Pueblo

PACIFIC OCEAN

CALIFORNIA

Las
Vegas

River

Colorado

Los Angeles
Long Beach

San Diego

30°N

ARIZONA

Phoenix

Tucson

Albuquerque

Santa
Fe

NEW MEXICO

El Paso

130°W

Rio Grande

N
W   E
S

MEXICO

160°W   PACIFIC   155°W
OCEAN
Kauai
N
Niihau   Oahu   W   E
Honolulu   Molokai   S
Lanai   Maui
HAWAII   Kahoolawe
20°N
Hawaii   Hilo

0   100   200 Miles
0   100   200 Kilometers

20°N

120°W   110°W

CANADA

NORTH DAKOTA
Grand Forks •
★ Bismarck • Fargo

MINNESOTA
Duluth •
Minneapolis • ★ St. Paul

SOUTH DAKOTA
★ Pierre

Lake Superior

WISCONSIN
Green Bay •
Madison ★ • Milwaukee

MICHIGAN
Grand Rapids •
★ Lansing
Detroit •

Lake Michigan

Lake Huron

Lake Ontario

Lake Erie

MAINE
★ Augusta

Burlington • • Montpelier
VERMONT **NEW HAMPSHIRE** • Portland
★ Concord

NEW YORK
Buffalo •
Albany ★
Hartford ★
CONNECTICUT

MASSACHUSETTS
★ Boston
Providence ★
RHODE ISLAND

PENNSYLVANIA
Pittsburgh •
Harrisburg ★
Cleveland •
Wheeling •

Newark • • New York
Trenton ★
NEW JERSEY
• Philadelphia
Dover ★
DELAWARE

IOWA
Sioux Falls •
Cedar Rapids •
Davenport •
★ Des Moines

Missouri River

NEBRASKA
Omaha •
Lincoln ★

Platte River

Rockford •
Chicago •
Peoria •

ILLINOIS
★ Springfield

Gary •
Fort Wayne •
INDIANA
★ Indianapolis

Toledo •

OHIO
Columbus ★
Cincinnati •

Ohio River

WEST VIRGINIA
Charleston ★
Wheeling •

Washington, D.C. ✪
Baltimore •
Annapolis ★
MARYLAND

VIRGINIA
Richmond ★
Norfolk •

KANSAS
Kansas City •
Topeka ★
Wichita •

Arkansas River

Kansas City •
Jefferson City ★
St. Louis •
Evansville •

MISSOURI

Mississippi River

Louisville •
Frankfort ★
KENTUCKY

Nashville ★
Knoxville •
TENNESSEE

Tennessee River

NORTH CAROLINA
★ Raleigh
• Charlotte

OKLAHOMA
Tulsa •
Oklahoma City ★

Arkansas River

ARKANSAS
Fort Smith •
Little Rock ★

Memphis •

Red River

TEXAS
Fort Worth ★ • Dallas
★ Austin
• San Antonio
• Laredo
Corpus Christi •
Houston •

MISSISSIPPI
Birmingham •
★ Jackson

ALABAMA
Montgomery ★
Columbus •

GEORGIA
★ Atlanta
Savannah •

SOUTH CAROLINA
★ Columbia
Charleston •

LOUISIANA
Shreveport •
Baton Rouge ★
New Orleans •
Biloxi •
Mobile •

★ Tallahassee
Jacksonville •

FLORIDA
Tampa •
Miami •

ATLANTIC OCEAN

Gulf of Mexico

THE BAHAMAS

CUBA

50°N
40°N
70°W
30°N
80°W
90°W
100°W

✪ National capital   ★ State capital   • Other city

0 — 150 — 300 Miles
0 — 150 — 300 Kilometers

R15

THE WORLD: Political

ARCTIC OCEAN

160°W 140°W 120°W 100°W 80°W 60°W

80°N

GREENLAND
(DENMARK)

Arctic Circle

ALASKA (U.S.)

60°N

CANADA

NORTH
AMERICA

40°N

UNITED STATES

ATLANTIC
OCEAN

BERMUDA
(U.K.)

MEXICO

See inset below

MIDWAY ISLANDS
(U.S.)

Tropic of Cancer

HAWAII (U.S.)

20°N

Caribbean Sea

PACIFIC OCEAN

VENEZUELA

GUYANA
SURINAME

FRENCH GUIANA
(FRANCE)

COLOMBIA

0° Equator

GALÁPAGOS ISLANDS
(ECUADOR)

ECUADOR

SOUTH
AMERICA

SAMOA

AMERICAN SAMOA
(U.S.)

FRENCH POLYNESIA
(FRANCE)

PERU

BRAZIL

TONGA

BOLIVIA

20°S

PARAGUAY

Tropic of Capricorn

URUGUAY

CHILE ARGENTINA

40°S

FALKLAND ISLANDS
(U.K.)

SOUTH
GEORGIA
(U.K.)

Antarctic Circle

60°S

80°S

ANTARCTICA

160°W 140°W 120°W 100°W 80°W 60°W

Central America
and West Indies

90°W

FLORIDA
(U.S.)

Gulf of Mexico

80°W

THE
BAHAMAS

70°W

Tropic of Cancer

TURKS AND
CAICOS IS. (U.K.)

ATLANTIC OCEAN

60°W

20°N

CUBA

20°N

CAYMAN ISLANDS
(U.K.)

JAMAICA

HAITI

DOMINICAN
REPUBLIC

VIRGIN ISLANDS
(U.K.)

ST. KITTS
AND NEVIS

MEXICO

BELIZE

PUERTO RICO
(U.S.)

VIRGIN ISLANDS
(U.S.)

ANTIGUA AND
BARBUDA

GUADELOUPE
(FRANCE)

GUATEMALA

HONDURAS

Caribbean Sea

DOMINICA

MARTINIQUE
(FRANCE)

ST. LUCIA

EL SALVADOR

PACIFIC
OCEAN

NICARAGUA

N
W E
S

ARUBA
(NETHERLANDS)

NETHERLANDS
ANTILLES
(NETHERLANDS)

ST. VINCENT AND
THE GRENADINES

BARBADOS

GRENADA

TRINIDAD AND
TOBAGO

10°N

COSTA
RICA

PANAMA

VENEZUELA

10°N

0 250 500 Miles
0 250 500 Kilometers

COLOMBIA

90°W

80°W

70°W

GUYANA

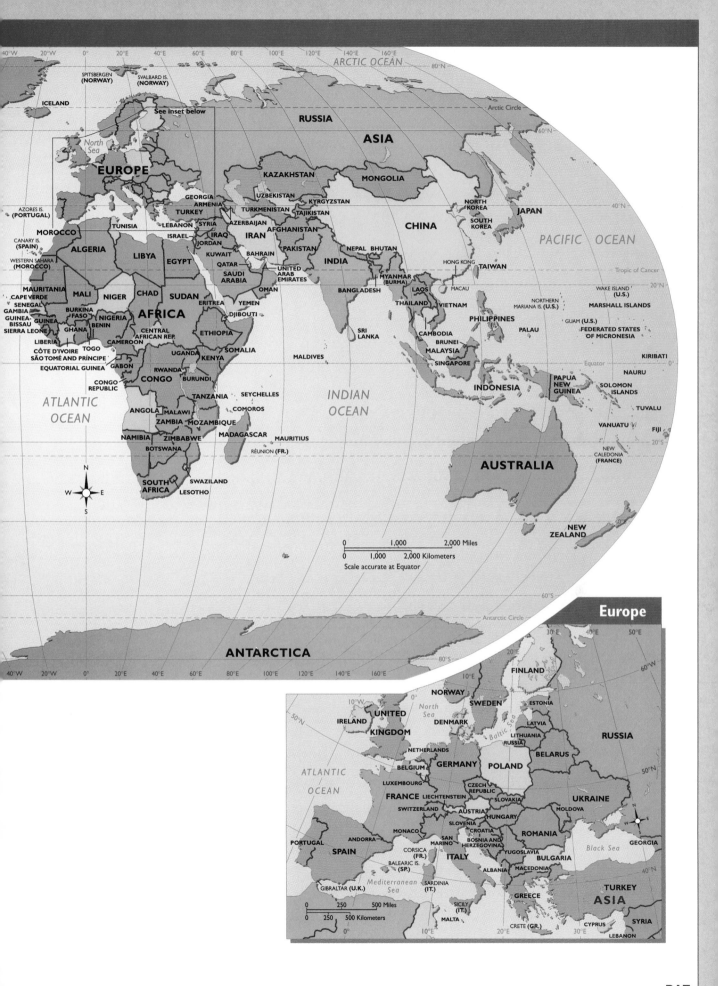

ARCTIC OCEAN

RUSSIA

ASIA

SPITSBERGEN (NORWAY)

SVALBARD IS. (NORWAY)

ICELAND

See inset below

North Sea

EUROPE

KAZAKHSTAN

MONGOLIA

AZORES IS. (PORTUGAL)

GEORGIA
ARMENIA
TURKEY
TURKMENISTAN
UZBEKISTAN
KYRGYZSTAN
TAJIKISTAN

NORTH KOREA
SOUTH KOREA

JAPAN

PACIFIC OCEAN

MOROCCO

TUNISIA
LEBANON
ISRAEL

SYRIA
IRAQ
JORDAN

AZERBAIJAN
AFGHANISTAN

IRAN

CHINA

CANARY IS. (SPAIN)

ALGERIA

LIBYA

EGYPT

KUWAIT
BAHRAIN
QATAR

PAKISTAN

NEPAL BHUTAN

HONG KONG

TAIWAN

Tropic of Cancer

WESTERN SAHARA (MOROCCO)

SAUDI ARABIA

UNITED ARAB EMIRATES

INDIA

MYANMAR (BURMA)

MACAU

WAKE ISLAND (U.S.)

MAURITANIA

MALI

NIGER

CHAD

SUDAN

OMAN
YEMEN

ERITREA

BANGLADESH

LAOS

THAILAND

VIETNAM

NORTHERN MARIANA IS. (U.S.)

20°N

MARSHALL ISLANDS

CAPE VERDE
SENEGAL
GAMBIA
GUINEA-BISSAU
SIERRA LEONE

BURKINA FASO
GUINEA

NIGERIA
BENIN

AFRICA

DJIBOUTI

PHILIPPINES

PALAU

GUAM (U.S.)

FEDERATED STATES OF MICRONESIA

GHANA

LIBERIA
CÔTE D'IVOIRE
SÃO TOMÉ AND PRÍNCIPE

TOGO

CAMEROON

CENTRAL AFRICAN REP.

ETHIOPIA

SOMALIA

CAMBODIA
BRUNEI
MALAYSIA

SINGAPORE

KIRIBATI

EQUATORIAL GUINEA

GABON

UGANDA
RWANDA
BURUNDI

KENYA

MALDIVES

Equator

NAURU

CONGO REPUBLIC

CONGO

TANZANIA

SRI LANKA

SEYCHELLES

INDONESIA

PAPUA NEW GUINEA

SOLOMON ISLANDS

ATLANTIC OCEAN

ANGOLA

MALAWI

ZAMBIA

COMOROS

MOZAMBIQUE

INDIAN OCEAN

TUVALU

NAMIBIA

ZIMBABWE

MADAGASCAR

MAURITIUS

VANUATU

FIJI

20°S

BOTSWANA

RÉUNION (FR.)

NEW CALEDONIA (FRANCE)

N
W E
S

SOUTH AFRICA

SWAZILAND

LESOTHO

AUSTRALIA

NEW ZEALAND

0   1,000   2,000 Miles
0   1,000   2,000 Kilometers
Scale accurate at Equator

60°S

Antarctic Circle

80°S

ANTARCTICA

40°W 20°W 0° 20°E 40°E 60°E 80°E 100°E 120°E 140°E 160°E

30°E 40°E 50°E

FINLAND

10°W
0°

NORWAY

SWEDEN

ESTONIA

60°W

50°N

IRELAND

UNITED KINGDOM

North Sea

DENMARK

Baltic Sea

LATVIA

LITHUANIA

RUSSIA

RUSSIA

NETHERLANDS

BELARUS

BELGIUM

GERMANY

POLAND

ATLANTIC OCEAN

LUXEMBOURG

CZECH REPUBLIC

UKRAINE

50°N

FRANCE

LIECHTENSTEIN

SLOVAKIA

MOLDOVA

SWITZERLAND

AUSTRIA

HUNGARY

N
W   E
S

SLOVENIA

ROMANIA

GEORGIA

PORTUGAL

ANDORRA

MONACO

SAN MARINO

CROATIA
BOSNIA AND HERZEGOVINA

YUGOSLAVIA

Black Sea

SPAIN

CORSICA (FR.)

ITALY

BULGARIA

40°N

BALEARIC IS. (SP.)

SARDINIA (IT.)

ALBANIA

MACEDONIA

TURKEY

GIBRALTAR (U.K.)

Mediterranean Sea

GREECE

ASIA

SICILY (IT.)

SYRIA

0   250   500 Miles
0   250   500 Kilometers

MALTA

CRETE (GR.)

CYPRUS

LEBANON

0° 10°E 20°E 30°E

R17

20°W 0° 20°E 40°E 60°E 80°E 100°E 120°E 140°E 160°E 180°

ARCTIC OCEAN 80°N

Arctic Circle

60°N

EUROPE

Volga River

URAL MTS.

Ob River

ASIA

GOBI

Mont Blanc
15,771 ft. (4,807 m)
ALPS

Mt. Elbrus
18,510 ft. (5,642 m)

40°N

HINDU KUSH

HIMALAYAS

Nile River

SYRIAN
DESERT

SAHARA

Indus R.

Ganges R.

Mt. Everest
29,028 ft.
(8,848 m)

Tropic of Cancer

AFRICA

DECCAN
PLATEAU

20°N

PACIFIC OCEAN

Equator 0°

Mt. Kilimanjaro
19,340 ft. (5,895 m)

INDIAN OCEAN

NAMIB DESERT

KALAHARI
DESERT

GREAT
SANDY
DESERT

20°S

**ATLANTIC
OCEAN**

AUSTRALIA

Tropic of Capricorn

Cape of
Good Hope

Mt. Kosciusko
7,310 ft. (2,228 m)

N

W ✦ E

S

0   1,000   2,000 Miles
0   1,000   2,000 Kilometers
Scale accurate at Equator

60°S

Antarctic Circle

80°S

ANTARCTICA

180°

COUNTRIES of the WORLD

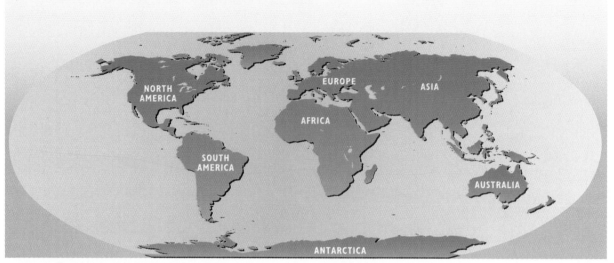

AFGHANISTAN

CAPITAL ★ Kabul

POPULATION: 22.7 million

MAJOR LANGUAGES: Pashtu and Afghan Persian

AREA: 250,000 sq mi; 647,500 sq km

LEADING EXPORTS: fruit, natural gas, and carpets

CONTINENT: Asia

ALBANIA

CAPITAL ★ Tiranë

POPULATION: 3.2 million

MAJOR LANGUAGES: Albanian and Greek

AREA: 11,100 sq mi; 28,748 sq km

LEADING EXPORTS: asphalt, petroleum products, and minerals

CONTINENT: Europe

ALGERIA

CAPITAL ★ Algiers

POPULATION: 29.2 million

MAJOR LANGUAGES: Arabic, Berber, and French

AREA: 919,595 sq mi; 2,381,751 sq km

LEADING EXPORTS: oil and natural gas

CONTINENT: Africa

ANDORRA

CAPITAL ★ Andorra la Vella

POPULATION: 68,000

MAJOR LANGUAGES: Catalan, French, and Castilian Spanish

AREA: 175 sq mi; 453 sq km

LEADING EXPORTS: electricity, tobacco products, and furniture

CONTINENT: Europe

ANGOLA

CAPITAL ★ Luanda

POPULATION: 10.3 million

MAJOR LANGUAGES: Portuguese and Bantu

AREA: 481,350 sq mi; 1,246,700 sq km

LEADING EXPORTS: oil, coffee, diamonds, and fish

CONTINENT: Africa

ANTIGUA AND BARBUDA

CAPITAL ★ St. John's

POPULATION: 66,000

MAJOR LANGUAGE: English

AREA: 171 sq mi; 442 sq km

LEADING EXPORTS: petroleum products and machinery

CONTINENT: North America

ARGENTINA

CAPITAL ★ Buenos Aires

POPULATION: 34.7 million

MAJOR LANGUAGES: Spanish, English, and Italian

AREA: 1,072,067 sq mi; 2,766,654 sq km

LEADING EXPORTS: meat, grain, hides, and wool

CONTINENT: South America

ARMENIA

CAPITAL ★ Yerevan

POPULATION: 3.5 million

MAJOR LANGUAGE: Armenian

AREA: 11,500 sq mi; 29,800 sq km

LEADING EXPORTS: machinery and processed food items

CONTINENT: Asia

AUSTRALIA

CAPITAL ★ Canberra

POPULATION: 18.2 million

MAJOR LANGUAGES: English and aboriginal languages

AREA: 2,966,150 sq mi; 7,682,300 sq km

LEADING EXPORTS: coal, gold, wool, and alumina

CONTINENT: Australia

AUSTRIA

CAPITAL ★ Vienna

POPULATION: 8.0 million

MAJOR LANGUAGE: German

AREA: 32,375 sq mi; 83,851 sq km

LEADING EXPORTS: iron and steel products, and timber

CONTINENT: Europe

AZERBAIJAN

CAPITAL ★ Baku

POPULATION: 7.7 million

MAJOR LANGUAGES: Azeri, Russian, and Armenian

AREA: 33,430 sq mi; 86,600 sq km

LEADING EXPORTS: oil and chemicals

CONTINENT: Asia

THE BAHAMAS

CAPITAL ★ Nassau

POPULATION: 0.3 million

MAJOR LANGUAGES: English and Creole

AREA: 5,380 sq mi; 13,939 sq km

LEADING EXPORTS: crawfish, medicine, and cement

CONTINENT: North America

BAHRAIN

CAPITAL ★ Manama

POPULATION: 0.6 million

MAJOR LANGUAGES: Arabic, English, Farsi, and Urdu

AREA: 240 sq mi; 620 sq km

LEADING EXPORTS: oil, petroleum products, and aluminum

CONTINENT: Asia

BANGLADESH

CAPITAL ★ Dhaka

POPULATION: 123.1 million

MAJOR LANGUAGES: Bangla and English

AREA: 55,598 sq mi; 143,998 sq km

LEADING EXPORTS: textiles, jute, leather, and seafood

CONTINENT: Asia

BARBADOS

CAPITAL ★ Bridgetown

POPULATION: 0.3 million

MAJOR LANGUAGE: English

AREA: 166 sq mi; 431 sq km

LEADING EXPORTS: sugar, molasses, and electrical components

CONTINENT: North America

BELARUS

CAPITAL ★ Minsk

POPULATION: 10.4 million

MAJOR LANGUAGES: Byelorussian and Russian

AREA: 80,200 sq mi; 207,600 sq km

LEADING EXPORTS: machinery and chemicals

CONTINENT: Europe

BELGIUM

CAPITAL ★ Brussels

POPULATION: 10.1 million

MAJOR LANGUAGES: Flemish and French

AREA: 11,781 sq mi; 30,518 sq km

LEADING EXPORTS: machinery, iron, steel, and diamonds

CONTINENT: Europe

BELIZE

CAPITAL ★ Belmopan

POPULATION: 0.2 million

MAJOR LANGUAGES: English and Spanish

AREA: 8,867 sq mi; 22,965 sq km

LEADING EXPORTS: sugar, molasses, clothing, and lumber

CONTINENT: North America

BENIN

CAPITAL ★ Porto-Novo

POPULATION: 5.7 million

MAJOR LANGUAGES: French and Fon

AREA: 43,483 sq mi; 12,622 sq km

LEADING EXPORTS: crude oil, cotton, palm products, and cocoa

CONTINENT: Africa

BHUTAN

CAPITAL ★ Thimphu

POPULATION: 1.8 million

MAJOR LANGUAGES: Dzongkha and Nepali

AREA: 18,000 sq mi; 46,620 sq km

LEADING EXPORTS: cardamom, gypsum, timber, and handicrafts

CONTINENT: Asia

BOLIVIA

CAPITALS ★ Sucre (judicial) and La Paz (administrative)

POPULATION: 7.2 million

MAJOR LANGUAGES: Spanish, Quechua, and Aymará

AREA: 424,162 sq mi; 1,098,581 sq km

LEADING EXPORTS: metals, natural gas, soybeans, and timber

CONTINENT: South America

BOSNIA AND HERZEGOVINA

CAPITAL ★ Sarajevo
POPULATION: 2.7 million
MAJOR LANGUAGE: Serbo-Croatian
AREA: 19,741 sq mi; 51,129 sq km
LEADING EXPORTS: (not available)
CONTINENT: Europe

BOTSWANA

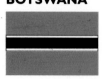

CAPITAL ★ Gaborone
POPULATION: 1.5 million
MAJOR LANGUAGES: English and Setswana
AREA: 231,800 sq mi; 600,360 sq km
LEADING EXPORTS: diamonds, copper, and nickel
CONTINENT: Africa

BRAZIL

CAPITAL ★ Brasília
POPULATION: 162.7 million
MAJOR LANGUAGES: Portuguese, Spanish, French, and English
AREA: 3,286,470 sq mi; 8,511,957 sq km
LEADING EXPORTS: coffee, iron ore, and soybeans
CONTINENT: South America

BRUNEI

CAPITAL ★ Bandar Seri Begawan
POPULATION: 0.3 million
MAJOR LANGUAGES: Malay, English, and Chinese
AREA: 2,226 sq mi; 5,765 sq km
LEADING EXPORT: oil
CONTINENT: Asia

BULGARIA

CAPITAL ★ Sofia
POPULATION: 8.6 million
MAJOR LANGUAGE: Bulgarian
AREA: 42,823 sq mi; 110,912 sq km
LEADING EXPORTS: machinery, minerals, and agricultural products
CONTINENT: Europe

BURKINA FASO

CAPITAL ★ Ouagadougou
POPULATION: 10.6 million
MAJOR LANGUAGES: French and Sudanic languages
AREA: 105,870 sq mi; 274,200 sq km
LEADING EXPORTS: oilseeds and cotton
CONTINENT: Africa

BURUNDI

CAPITAL ★ Bujumbura
POPULATION: 5.9 million
MAJOR LANGUAGES: Kirundi, French, and Swahili
AREA: 10,747 sq mi; 27,834 sq km
LEADING EXPORTS: coffee, tea, cotton, and hides
CONTINENT: Africa

CAMBODIA

CAPITAL ★ Phnom Penh
POPULATION: 10.6 million
MAJOR LANGUAGES: Khmer and French
AREA: 69,884 sq mi; 181,035 sq km
LEADING EXPORTS: rubber, rice, pepper, and raw timber
CONTINENT: Asia

CAMEROON

CAPITAL ★ Yaoundé
POPULATION: 14.3 million
MAJOR LANGUAGES: English and French
AREA: 183,569 sq mi; 475,442 sq km
LEADING EXPORTS: coffee, cocoa, timber, and petroleum products
CONTINENT: Africa

CANADA

CAPITAL ★ Ottawa
POPULATION: 29.9 million
MAJOR LANGUAGES: English and French
AREA: 3,851,809 sq mi; 9,976,186 sq km
LEADING EXPORTS: newsprint, wood pulp, and timber
CONTINENT: North America

CAPE VERDE

CAPITAL ★ Praia
POPULATION: 0.4 million
MAJOR LANGUAGES: Portuguese and Crioulo
AREA: 1,557 sq mi; 4,033 sq km
LEADING EXPORTS: fish, bananas, and salt
CONTINENT: Africa

CENTRAL AFRICAN REPUBLIC

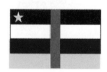

CAPITAL ★ Bangui
POPULATION: 3.3 million
MAJOR LANGUAGES: French and Sango
AREA: 241,313 sq mi; 625,000 sq km
LEADING EXPORTS: diamonds, cotton, timber, coffee, and tobacco
CONTINENT: Africa

CHAD

CAPITAL ★ N'Djamena

POPULATION: 7.0 million

MAJOR LANGUAGES: French and Arabic

AREA: 495,752 sq mi; 1,284,000 sq km

LEADING EXPORTS: cotton, cattle, fish, and textiles

CONTINENT: Africa

CHILE

CAPITAL ★ Santiago

POPULATION: 14.3 million

MAJOR LANGUAGE: Spanish

AREA: 292,132 sq mi; 756,622 sq km

LEADING EXPORTS: copper, fish, metals, and minerals

CONTINENT: South America

CHINA

CAPITAL ★ Beijing

POPULATION: 1,210 million

MAJOR LANGUAGES: Mandarin and local Chinese dialects

AREA: 3,691,521 sq mi; 9,561,000 sq km

LEADING EXPORTS: manufactured goods, footwear, and toys

CONTINENT: Asia

COLOMBIA

CAPITAL ★ Bogotá

POPULATION: 36.8 million

MAJOR LANGUAGE: Spanish

AREA: 439,735 sq mi; 1,138,910 sq km

LEADING EXPORTS: coffee, petroleum, coal, and bananas

CONTINENT: South America

COMOROS

CAPITAL ★ Moroni

POPULATION: 0.6 million

MAJOR LANGUAGES: French, Arabic, and Comoran

AREA: 690 sq mi; 1,787 sq km

LEADING EXPORTS: vanilla, cloves, perfume oil, and copra

CONTINENT: Africa

CONGO REPUBLIC

CAPITAL ★ Brazzaville

POPULATION: 2.5 million

MAJOR LANGUAGES: French, Kikongo, Lingala, and other African languages

AREA: 132,046 sq mi; 342,000 sq km

LEADING EXPORTS: crude oil, lumber, coffee, and cocoa

CONTINENT: Africa

COSTA RICA

CAPITAL ★ San José

POPULATION: 3.5 million

MAJOR LANGUAGES: Spanish and English

AREA: 19,652 sq mi; 50,898 sq km

LEADING EXPORTS: coffee, bananas, textiles, and sugar

CONTINENT: North America

CÔTE D'IVOIRE (Ivory Coast)

CAPITAL ★ Yamoussoukro

POPULATION: 14.8 million

MAJOR LANGUAGES: French and many African languages

AREA: 124,502 sq mi; 322,462 sq km

LEADING EXPORTS: cocoa, coffee, tropical woods, and petroleum

CONTINENT: Africa

CROATIA

CAPITAL ★ Zagreb

POPULATION: 5 million

MAJOR LANGUAGE: Serbo-Croatian

AREA: 21,829 sq mi; 56,537 sq km

LEADING EXPORTS: machinery, transport equipment, and other manufactures

CONTINENT: Europe

CUBA

CAPITAL ★ Havana

POPULATION: 11 million

MAJOR LANGUAGE: Spanish

AREA: 44,218 sq mi; 114,524 sq km

LEADING EXPORTS: coffee, sugar, nickel, shellfish, and tobacco

CONTINENT: North America

CYPRUS

CAPITAL ★ Nicosia

POPULATION: 0.7 million

MAJOR LANGUAGES: Greek, Turkish, and English

AREA: 3,572 sq mi; 9,251 sq km

LEADING EXPORTS: fruit, cement, and clothing

CONTINENT: Asia

CZECH REPUBLIC

CAPITAL ★ Prague

POPULATION: 10.3 million

MAJOR LANGUAGES: Czech and Slovak

AREA: 30,464 sq mi; 78,902 sq km

LEADING EXPORTS: manufactured goods and machinery

CONTINENT: Europe

COUNTRIES of the WORLD

DEMOCRATIC REPUBLIC OF CONGO

CAPITAL ★ Kinshasa

POPULATION: 46.5 million

MAJOR LANGUAGES: French, English, Swahili, Lingala and other Bantu dialects

AREA: 905,365 sq mi; 2,344,885 sq km

LEADING EXPORTS: copper, cobalt, diamonds, oil, and coffee

CONTINENT: Africa

DENMARK

CAPITAL ★ Copenhagen

POPULATION: 5.2 million

MAJOR LANGUAGES: Danish and Faroese

AREA: 16,631 sq mi; 43,075 sq mi

LEADING EXPORTS: food, machinery, and chemicals

CONTINENT: Europe

DJIBOUTI

CAPITAL ★ Djibouti

POPULATION: 0.4 million

MAJOR LANGUAGES: Arabic and French

AREA: 8,490 sq mi; 22,000 sq km

LEADING EXPORTS: hides and skins

CONTINENT: Africa

DOMINICA

CAPITAL ★ Roseau

POPULATION: 0.1 million

MAJOR LANGUAGES: English and Creole

AREA: 290 sq mi; 751 sq km

LEADING EXPORTS: bananas, coconuts, soap, and vegetables

CONTINENT: North America

DOMINICAN REPUBLIC

CAPITAL ★ Santo Domingo

POPULATION: 8.1 million

MAJOR LANGUAGES: Spanish

AREA: 18,704 sq mi; 48,442 sq km

LEADING EXPORTS: sugar, coffee, cocoa, gold, and ferronickel

CONTINENT: North America

ECUADOR

CAPITAL ★ Quito

POPULATION: 10.7 million

MAJOR LANGUAGES: Spanish and Quechua

AREA: 106,822 sq mi; 276,670 sq km

LEADING EXPORTS: oil, coffee, bananas, and cocoa

CONTINENT: South America

EGYPT

CAPITAL ★ Cairo

POPULATION: 63.6 million

MAJOR LANGUAGES: Arabic, English, and French

AREA: 386,900 sq mi; 1,002,000 sq km

LEADING EXPORTS: cotton, oil, and textiles

CONTINENT: Africa

EL SALVADOR

CAPITAL ★ San Salvador

POPULATION: 5.8 million

MAJOR LANGUAGES: Spanish and Nahua

AREA: 8,260 sq mi; 21,393 sq km

LEADING EXPORTS: coffee, cotton, sugarcane, and shrimp

CONTINENT: North America

EQUATORIAL GUINEA

CAPITAL ★ Malabo

POPULATION: 0.4 million

MAJOR LANGUAGES: Spanish, Fang, and Bubi

AREA: 10,830 sq mi; 28,051 sq km

LEADING EXPORTS: cocoa, timber, and coffee

CONTINENT: Africa

ERITREA

CAPITAL ★ Asmara

POPULATION: 3.9 million

MAJOR LANGUAGES: Tigrinya and Arabic

AREA: 45,754 sq mi; 121,300 sq km

LEADING EXPORTS: (not available)

CONTINENT: Africa

ESTONIA

CAPITAL ★ Tallinn

POPULATION: 1.5 million

MAJOR LANGUAGES: Estonian, Latvian, Lithuanian, and Russian

AREA: 18,370 sq mi; 47,549 sq km

LEADING EXPORTS: food products, textiles, vehicles, and metals

CONTINENT: Europe

ETHIOPIA

CAPITAL ★ Addis Ababa

POPULATION: 57.2 million

MAJOR LANGUAGES: Amharic, English, and local languages

AREA: 446,952 sq mi; 1,157,585 sq km

LEADING EXPORTS: coffee, leather products, gold, and petroleum products

CONTINENT: Africa

FIJI

CAPITAL ★ Suva

POPULATION: 0.8 million

MAJOR LANGUAGES: Fijian, Hindi, and English

AREA: 7,078 sq mi; 18,333 sq km

LEADING EXPORTS: sugar, copra, fish, lumber, and gold

CONTINENT: Islands in the Pacific Ocean

FINLAND

CAPITAL ★ Helsinki

POPULATION: 5.1 million

MAJOR LANGUAGES: Finnish and Swedish

AREA: 130,558 sq mi; 338,145 sq km

LEADING EXPORTS: paper and wood

CONTINENT: Europe

FRANCE

CAPITAL ★ Paris

POPULATION: 58.3 million

MAJOR LANGUAGE: French

AREA: 211,208 sq mi; 547,030 sq km

LEADING EXPORTS: manufactured goods and machinery

CONTINENT: Europe

GABON

CAPITAL ★ Libreville

POPULATION: 1.2 million

MAJOR LANGUAGES: French, Fang, and Bantu dialects

AREA: 103,346 sq mi; 267,667 sq km

LEADING EXPORTS: crude oil, manganese, and timber

CONTINENT: Africa

THE GAMBIA

CAPITAL ★ Banjul

POPULATION: 1.0 million

MAJOR LANGUAGES: English and Mandinka

AREA: 4,093 sq mi; 10,600 sq km

LEADING EXPORTS: peanut products, fish, and cotton lint

CONTINENT: Africa

GEORGIA

CAPITAL ★ Tbilisi

POPULATION: 5.2 million

MAJOR LANGUAGES: Georgian and Russian

AREA: 26,900 sq mi; 69,700 sq km

LEADING EXPORTS: agricultural products and machinery

CONTINENT: Asia

GERMANY

CAPITAL ★ Berlin

POPULATION: 83.5 million

MAJOR LANGUAGE: German

AREA: 137,826 sq mi; 356,970 sq km

LEADING EXPORTS: machinery and manufactured goods

CONTINENT: Europe

GHANA

CAPITAL ★ Accra

POPULATION: 17.7 million

MAJOR LANGUAGES: English and African languages

AREA: 92,100 sq mi; 238,537 sq km

LEADING EXPORTS: cocoa, gold, timber, and tuna

CONTINENT: Africa

GREECE

CAPITAL ★ Athens

POPULATION: 10.7 million

MAJOR LANGUAGES: Greek, English, and French

AREA: 50,961 sq mi; 131,990 sq km

LEADING EXPORTS: manufactured goods and food products

CONTINENT: Europe

GRENADA

CAPITAL ★ St. George's

POPULATION: 0.1 million

MAJOR LANGUAGES: English and French patois

AREA: 133 sq mi; 344 sq km

LEADING EXPORTS: nutmeg, cocoa, bananas, and mace

CONTINENT: North America

GUATEMALA

CAPITAL ★ Guatemala City

POPULATION: 11.3 million

MAJOR LANGUAGES: Spanish and Mayan dialects

AREA: 42,042 sq mi; 108,889 sq km

LEADING EXPORTS: coffee, sugar, and bananas

CONTINENT: North America

GUINEA

CAPITAL ★ Conakry

POPULATION: 7.4 million

MAJOR LANGUAGES: French, Soussou, and Manika

AREA: 94,925 sq mi; 245,857 sq km

LEADING EXPORTS: bauxite, alumina, diamonds, and food products

CONTINENT: Africa

GUINEA-BISSAU

CAPITAL ★ Bissau

POPULATION: 1.2 million

MAJOR LANGUAGES: Portuguese and Crioulo

AREA: 13,948 sq mi; 36,125 sq km

LEADING EXPORTS: peanut products, fish, and palm kernels

CONTINENT: Africa

GUYANA

CAPITAL ★ Georgetown

POPULATION: 0.7 million

MAJOR LANGUAGES: English, Hindi, and Urdu

AREA: 83,000 sq mi; 214,969 sq km

LEADING EXPORTS: sugar, bauxite, rice, timber, and shrimp

CONTINENT: South America

HAITI

CAPITAL ★ Port-au-Prince
POPULATION: 6.7 million
MAJOR LANGUAGES: French and French Creole
AREA: 10,714 sq mi; 27,750 sq km
LEADING EXPORTS: coffee and assembled lighting products
CONTINENT: North America

HONDURAS

CAPITAL ★ Tegucigalpa
POPULATION: 5.6 million
MAJOR LANGUAGE: Spanish
AREA: 43,872 sq mi; 112,492 sq km
LEADING EXPORTS: coffee, lumber, bananas, shrimp, and lobster
CONTINENT: North America

HUNGARY

CAPITAL ★ Budapest
POPULATION: 10.0 million
MAJOR LANGUAGE: Hungarian
AREA: 35,919 sq mi; 93,030 sq km
LEADING EXPORTS: raw materials, chemicals, and consumer goods
CONTINENT: Europe

ICELAND

CAPITAL ★ Reykjavik
POPULATION: 0.3 million
MAJOR LANGUAGE: Icelandic
AREA: 39,709 sq mi; 102,846 sq km
LEADING EXPORTS: fish, animal products, and aluminum
CONTINENT: Europe

INDIA

CAPITAL ★ New Delhi
POPULATION: 952.1 million
MAJOR LANGUAGES: Hindi, English, and 14 other official languages
AREA: 1,229,737 sq mi; 3,185,019 sq km
LEADING EXPORTS: gems and jewelry, clothing, engineering goods, and fabric
CONTINENT: Asia

INDONESIA

CAPITAL ★ Jakarta
POPULATION: 206.6 million
MAJOR LANGUAGES: Bahasa Indonesian, English, Dutch, and Javanese
AREA: 735,268 sq mi; 1,904,344 sq km
LEADING EXPORTS: oil, gas, timber, rubber, and coffee
CONTINENT: Asia

IRAN

CAPITAL ★ Tehran
POPULATION: 66.1 million
MAJOR LANGUAGES: Farsi, Turkic, and Kurdish
AREA: 636,293 sq mi; 1,648,000 sq km
LEADING EXPORTS: oil, carpets, and fruits
CONTINENT: Asia

IRAQ

CAPITAL ★ Baghdad
POPULATION: 21.4 million
MAJOR LANGUAGES: Arabic and Kurdish
AREA: 168,920 sq mi; 434,913 sq km
LEADING EXPORT: oil and chemicals
CONTINENT: Asia

IRELAND

CAPITAL ★ Dublin
POPULATION: 3.6 million
MAJOR LANGUAGES: English and Irish
AREA: 27,136 sq mi; 70,282 sq km
LEADING EXPORTS: live animals, dairy products, and machinery
CONTINENT: Europe

ISRAEL

CAPITAL ★ Jerusalem
POPULATION: 5.2 million
MAJOR LANGUAGES: Hebrew and Arabic
AREA: 8,020 sq mi; 20,772 sq km*
LEADING EXPORTS: diamonds, fruits, and textiles
CONTINENT: Asia
*does not include the 2,402 sq mi of the Gaza Strip and the West Bank

ITALY

CAPITAL ★ Rome
POPULATION: 57.5 million
MAJOR LANGUAGE: Italian
AREA: 116,500 sq mi; 301,278 sq km
LEADING EXPORTS: clothing, metals, machinery, and chemicals
CONTINENT: Europe

JAMAICA

CAPITAL ★ Kingston
POPULATION: 2.6 million
MAJOR LANGUAGES: English and Jamaican Creole
AREA: 4,411 sq mi; 11,424 sq km
LEADING EXPORTS: alumina, bauxite, sugar, and bananas
CONTINENT: North America

JAPAN

CAPITAL ★ Tokyo
POPULATION: 125.6 million
MAJOR LANGUAGE: Japanese
AREA: 145,874 sq mi; 377,815 sq km
LEADING EXPORT: machinery
CONTINENT: Asia

JORDAN

CAPITAL ★ Amman
POPULATION: 4.2 million
MAJOR LANGUAGE: Arabic
AREA: 34,573 sq mi; 89,544 sq km
LEADING EXPORTS: phosphates and agricultural products
CONTINENT: Asia

KAZAKHSTAN

CAPITAL ★ Almaty
POPULATION: 16.9 million
MAJOR LANGUAGES: Kazakh and Russian
AREA: 1,049,000 sq mi; 2,717,300 sq km
LEADING EXPORTS: oil, metals, chemicals, wool, and grain
CONTINENT: Asia

KENYA

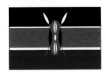

CAPITAL ★ Nairobi
POPULATION: 28.2 million
MAJOR LANGUAGES: English and Swahili
AREA: 224,960 sq mi; 582,646 sq km
LEADING EXPORTS: tea, coffee, and petroleum products
CONTINENT: Africa

KIRIBATI

CAPITAL ★ Tarawa
POPULATION: 80,900
MAJOR LANGUAGES: Gilbertese and English
AREA: 280 sq mi; 726 sq km
LEADING EXPORTS: fish and copra
CONTINENT: Islands in the Pacific Ocean

KOREA, NORTH

CAPITAL ★ Pyongyang
POPULATION: 23.9 million
MAJOR LANGUAGE: Korean
AREA: 46,768 sq mi; 121,129 sq km
LEADING EXPORTS: minerals and agricultural products
CONTINENT: Asia

KOREA, SOUTH

CAPITAL ★ Seoul
POPULATION: 45.5 million
MAJOR LANGUAGE: Korean
AREA: 38,031 sq mi; 98,392 sq km
LEADING EXPORTS: agricultural products, electronics, machinery, and clothing
CONTINENT: Asia

KUWAIT

CAPITAL ★ Kuwait
POPULATION: 2.0 million
MAJOR LANGUAGE: Arabic
AREA: 6,880 sq mi; 17,820 sq km
LEADING EXPORT: oil
CONTINENT: Asia

KYRGYZSTAN

CAPITAL ★ Bishkek
POPULATION: 4.5 million
MAJOR LANGUAGES: Kyrgyz and Russian
AREA: 76,000 sq mi; 198,500 sq km
LEADING EXPORTS: wool, chemicals, cotton, metals, and shoes
CONTINENT: Asia

LAOS

CAPITAL ★ Vientiane
POPULATION: 4.9 million
MAJOR LANGUAGES: Lao, French, and English
AREA: 91,429 sq mi; 236,800 sq km
LEADING EXPORTS: electricity, timber, tin, and coffee
CONTINENT: Asia

LATVIA

CAPITAL ★ Riga
POPULATION: 2.5 million
MAJOR LANGUAGES: Latvian and Russian
AREA: 25,400 sq mi; 65,786 sq km
LEADING EXPORTS: timber, metals, machinery, and fish
CONTINENT: Europe

LEBANON

CAPITAL ★ Beirut
POPULATION: 3.8 million
MAJOR LANGUAGES: Arabic and French
AREA: 4,015 sq mi; 10,400 sq km
LEADING EXPORTS: fruits, textiles, and chemicals
CONTINENT: Asia

LESOTHO

CAPITAL ★ Maseru
POPULATION: 2.0 million
MAJOR LANGUAGES: Sesotho and English
AREA: 11,720 sq mi; 30,355 sq km
LEADING EXPORTS: wool, mohair, wheat, cattle, peas, and beans
CONTINENT: Africa

COUNTRIES of the WORLD

LIBERIA

CAPITAL ★ Monrovia

POPULATION: 2.1 million

MAJOR LANGUAGES: English and Niger-Congo languages

AREA: 43,000 sq mi; 111,370 sq km

LEADING EXPORTS: iron ore, rubber, timber, and coffee

CONTINENT: Africa

LIBYA

CAPITAL ★ Tripoli

POPULATION: 5.4 million

MAJOR LANGUAGES: Arabic, Italian, and English

AREA: 679,536 sq mi; 1,759,998 sq km

LEADING EXPORTS: oil, peanuts, and natural gas

CONTINENT: Africa

LIECHTENSTEIN

CAPITAL ★ Vaduz

POPULATION: 31,000

MAJOR LANGUAGE: German

AREA: 61 sq mi; 157 sq km

LEADING EXPORTS: machinery, dental products, stamps, and hardware

CONTINENT: Europe

LITHUANIA

CAPITAL ★ Vilnius

POPULATION: 3.7 million

MAJOR LANGUAGES: Lithuanian, Russian, and Polish

AREA: 25,212 sq mi; 65,300 sq km

LEADING EXPORTS: textiles, chemicals, and mineral products

CONTINENT: Europe

LUXEMBOURG

CAPITAL ★ Luxembourg

POPULATION: 0.4 million

MAJOR LANGUAGES: Luxembourgisch, German, French, and English

AREA: 999 sq mi; 2,586 sq km

LEADING EXPORTS: steel products, chemicals, rubber products, and glass

CONTINENT: Europe

MACEDONIA

CAPITAL ★ Skopje

POPULATION: 2.1 million

MAJOR LANGUAGES: Macedonian and Albanian

AREA: 9,928 sq mi; 25,713 sq km

LEADING EXPORTS: manufactured goods, machinery, and transport equipment

CONTINENT: Europe

MADAGASCAR

CAPITAL ★ Antananarivo

POPULATION: 13.7 million

MAJOR LANGUAGES: French and Malagasy

AREA: 226,660 sq mi; 587,050 sq km

LEADING EXPORTS: coffee, cloves, vanilla, and sugar

CONTINENT: Africa

MALAWI

CAPITAL ★ Lilongwe

POPULATION: 9.5 million

MAJOR LANGUAGES: English and Chichewa

AREA: 45,747 sq mi; 118,484 sq km

LEADING EXPORTS: tobacco, sugar, tea, coffee, and peanuts

CONTINENT: Africa

MALAYSIA

CAPITAL ★ Kuala Lumpur

POPULATION: 20.0 million

MAJOR LANGUAGES: Malay, English, and Chinese dialects

AREA: 128,328 sq mi; 332,370 sq km

LEADING EXPORTS: rubber, palm oil, tin, and timber

CONTINENT: Asia

MALDIVES

CAPITAL ★ Malé

POPULATION: 0.3 million

MAJOR LANGUAGE: Divehi

AREA: 115 sq mi; 298 sq km

LEADING EXPORTS: fish and clothing

CONTINENT: Asia

MALI

CAPITAL ★ Bamako

POPULATION: 9.7 million

MAJOR LANGUAGES: Bambara and French

AREA: 478,819 sq mi; 1,240,142 sq km

LEADING EXPORTS: cotton, livestock, and gold

CONTINENT: Africa

MALTA

CAPITAL ★ Valletta

POPULATION: 0.4 million

MAJOR LANGUAGES: Maltese and English

AREA: 122 sq mi; 316 sq km

LEADING EXPORTS: clothing, textiles, and footwear

CONTINENT: Europe

MARSHALL ISLANDS

CAPITAL ★ Majuro
POPULATION: 58,000
MAJOR LANGUAGES: English, Marshallese dialects, and Japanese
AREA: 70 sq mi; 181 sq km
LEADING EXPORTS: coconut oil, fish, live animals, and trichus shells
CONTINENT: Islands in the Pacific Ocean

MAURITANIA

CAPITAL ★ Nouakchott
POPULATION: 2.3 million
MAJOR LANGUAGES: Arabic and Wolof
AREA: 397,953 sq mi; 1,030,700 sq km
LEADING EXPORTS: iron ore and fish
CONTINENT: Africa

MAURITIUS

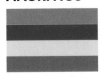

CAPITAL ★ Port Louis
POPULATION: 1.1 million
MAJOR LANGUAGES: English, Creole, and French
AREA: 787 sq mi; 2,040 sq km
LEADING EXPORTS: sugar, light manufactures, and textiles
CONTINENT: Africa

MEXICO

CAPITAL ★ Mexico City
POPULATION: 95.8 million
MAJOR LANGUAGE: Spanish
AREA: 761,600 sq mi; 1,972,547 sq km
LEADING EXPORTS: motor vehicles, consumer electronics, cotton, and shrimp
CONTINENT: North America

MICRONESIA

CAPITAL ★ Palikir
POPULATION: 125,000
MAJOR LANGUAGES: English, Trukese, Yapese, and Kosrean
AREA: 271 sq mi; 703 sq km
LEADING EXPORT: copra
CONTINENT: Islands in the Pacific Ocean

MOLDOVA

CAPITAL ★ Kishinev
POPULATION: 4.5 million
MAJOR LANGUAGES: Moldovan, Russian, and Gagauz
AREA: 13,000 sq mi; 33,700 sq km
LEADING EXPORTS: food, wine, tobacco, and textiles
CONTINENT: Europe

MONACO

CAPITAL ★ Monaco
POPULATION: 31,000
MAJOR LANGUAGES: French, Monégasque, and English
AREA: 0.7 sq mi; 1.9 sq km
LEADING EXPORTS: (not available)
CONTINENT: Europe

MONGOLIA

CAPITAL ★ Ulaanbaatar
POPULATION: 2.5 million
MAJOR LANGUAGES: Khalkha Mongolian, Turkic, Russian, and Chinese
AREA: 604,250 sq mi; 1,565,000 sq km
LEADING EXPORTS: copper, cashmere, and livestock
CONTINENT: Asia

MOROCCO

CAPITAL ★ Rabat
POPULATION: 29.8 million
MAJOR LANGUAGES: Arabic, Berber, and French
AREA: 172,413 sq mi; 446,550 sq km
LEADING EXPORTS: food, beverages, consumer goods, and phosphates
CONTINENT: Africa

MOZAMBIQUE

CAPITAL ★ Maputo
POPULATION: 17.9 million
MAJOR LANGUAGES: Portuguese and African languages
AREA: 303,073 sq mi; 799,380 sq km
LEADING EXPORTS: cashew nuts, sugar, and shrimp
CONTINENT: Africa

MYANMAR (Burma)

CAPITAL ★ Yangon
POPULATION: 50.0 million
MAJOR LANGUAGE: Burmese
AREA: 261,220 sq mi; 678,560 sq km
LEADING EXPORTS: rice, teak, oilseeds, and metals
CONTINENT: Asia

NAMIBIA

CAPITAL ★ Windhoek
POPULATION: 1.7 million
MAJOR LANGUAGES: English, Afrikaans, and German
AREA: 318,261 sq mi; 824,296 sq km
LEADING EXPORTS: diamonds, metals, and livestock
CONTINENT: Africa

NAURU

CAPITAL ★ Yaren
POPULATION: 10,000
MAJOR LANGUAGES: Nauruan and English
AREA: 8 sq mi; 21 sq km
LEADING EXPORT: phosphates
CONTINENT: Islands in the Pacific Ocean

NEPAL

CAPITAL ★ Kathmandu
POPULATION: 22.1 million
MAJOR LANGUAGE: Nepali
AREA: 54,463 sq mi; 141,059 sq km
LEADING EXPORTS: clothing, carpets, leather goods, and grain
CONTINENT: Asia

NETHERLANDS

CAPITAL ★ Amsterdam
POPULATION: 15.5 million
MAJOR LANGUAGE: Dutch
AREA: 16,033 sq mi; 41,526 sq km
LEADING EXPORTS: foodstuffs, natural gas, and chemicals
CONTINENT: Europe

NEW ZEALAND

CAPITAL ★ Wellington
POPULATION: 3.5 million
MAJOR LANGUAGES: English and Maori
AREA: 103,884 sq mi; 270,534 sq km
LEADING EXPORTS: meat, dairy products, and wool
CONTINENT: Islands in the Pacific Ocean

NICARAGUA

CAPITAL ★ Managua
POPULATION: 4.3 million
MAJOR LANGUAGE: Spanish
AREA: 50,180 sq mi; 130,000 sq km
LEADING EXPORTS: coffee, cotton, and foodstuffs
CONTINENT: North America

NIGER

CAPITAL ★ Niamey
POPULATION: 9.1 million
MAJOR LANGUAGES: French, Hausa, and Djerma
AREA: 489,206 sq mi; 1,267,044 sq km
LEADING EXPORTS: uranium ore, cowpeas, and livestock products
CONTINENT: Africa

NIGERIA

CAPITAL ★ Abuja
POPULATION: 103.9 million
MAJOR LANGUAGES: English, Hausa, Yoruba, Ibo, and Fulani
AREA: 356,700 sq mi; 923,853 sq km
LEADING EXPORTS: oil and cocoa
CONTINENT: Africa

NORWAY

CAPITAL ★ Oslo
POPULATION: 4.3 million
MAJOR LANGUAGE: Norwegian
AREA: 125,049 sq mi; 323,877 sq km
LEADING EXPORTS: oil, natural gas, fish, and ships
CONTINENT: Europe

OMAN

CAPITAL ★ Muscat
POPULATION: 2.2 million
MAJOR LANGUAGE: Arabic
AREA: 82,030 sq mi; 212,458 sq km
LEADING EXPORTS: oil and fish
CONTINENT: Asia

PAKISTAN

CAPITAL ★ Islamabad
POPULATION: 129.3 million
MAJOR LANGUAGES: Urdu, Punjabi, and English
AREA: 310,400 sq mi; 803,936 sq km
LEADING EXPORTS: cotton, rice, and textiles
CONTINENT: Asia

PALAU

CAPITAL ★ Koror
POPULATION: 16,952
MAJOR LANGUAGES: Palauan and English
AREA: 196 sq mi; 508 sq km
LEADING EXPORTS: trochus, tuna, and copra
CONTINENT: Islands in the Pacific Ocean

PANAMA

CAPITAL ★ Panama City
POPULATION: 2.7 million
MAJOR LANGUAGES: Spanish and English
AREA: 29,761 sq mi; 77,082 sq km
LEADING EXPORTS: bananas, sugar, shrimp, and coffee
CONTINENT: North America

PAPUA NEW GUINEA

CAPITAL ★ Port Moresby
POPULATION: 4.2 million
MAJOR LANGUAGES: Pidgin English, English, and Motu
AREA: 178,704 sq mi; 462,840 sq km
LEADING EXPORTS: gold, copper, coffee, palm oil, and copra
CONTINENT: Islands in the Pacific Ocean

PARAGUAY

CAPITAL ★ Asunción
POPULATION: 5.5 million
MAJOR LANGUAGES: Spanish and Guarani
AREA: 157,047 sq mi; 406,752 sq km
LEADING EXPORTS: cotton, soybeans, and meat products
CONTINENT: South America

PERU

CAPITAL ★ Lima
POPULATION: 24.5 million
MAJOR LANGUAGES: Spanish, Quechua, and Aymará
AREA: 496,222 sq mi; 1,285,216 sq km
LEADING EXPORTS: copper, fish products, and cotton
CONTINENT: South America

PHILIPPINES

CAPITAL ★ Manila
POPULATION: 74.5 million
MAJOR LANGUAGES: Filipino, Tagalog, and English
AREA: 115,830 sq mi; 300,000 sq km
LEADING EXPORTS: electronics, coconut products, and chemicals
CONTINENT: Asia

POLAND

CAPITAL ★ Warsaw
POPULATION: 38.6 million
MAJOR LANGUAGE: Polish
AREA: 120,727 sq mi; 312,683 sq km
LEADING EXPORTS: coal, machinery, chemicals, and metals
CONTINENT: Europe

PORTUGAL

CAPITAL ★ Lisbon
POPULATION: 9.9 million
MAJOR LANGUAGE: Portuguese
AREA: 35,550 sq mi; 92,075 sq km
LEADING EXPORTS: cotton, textiles, and cork
CONTINENT: Europe

QATAR

CAPITAL ★ Doha
POPULATION: 0.5 million
MAJOR LANGUAGES: Arabic and English
AREA: 4,000 sq mi; 11,437 sq km
LEADING EXPORTS: oil, steel, and fertilizers
CONTINENT: Asia

ROMANIA

CAPITAL ★ Bucharest
POPULATION: 21.7 million
MAJOR LANGUAGES: Romanian, Hungarian, and German
AREA: 91,700 sq mi; 237,500 sq km
LEADING EXPORTS: machinery, metals, chemicals, and timber
CONTINENT: Europe

RUSSIA

CAPITAL ★ Moscow
POPULATION: 148.2 million
MAJOR LANGUAGE: Russian
AREA: 6,592,800 sq mi; 17,075,400 sq km
LEADING EXPORTS: petroleum, natural gas, wood, and coal
CONTINENTS: Europe and Asia

RWANDA

CAPITAL ★ Kigali
POPULATION: 6.9 million
MAJOR LANGUAGES: Kinyarwanda, French, and Kiswahili
AREA: 10,169 sq mi; 26,338 sq km
LEADING EXPORTS: coffee and tea
CONTINENT: Africa

ST. KITTS AND NEVIS

CAPITAL ★ Basseterre
POPULATION: 41,000
MAJOR LANGUAGE: English
AREA: 65 sq mi; 169 sq km
LEADING EXPORTS: sugar, electronics, and stamps
CONTINENT: North America

ST. LUCIA

CAPITAL ★ Castries
POPULATION: 158,000
MAJOR LANGUAGES: English and French patois
AREA: 238 sq mi; 616 sq km
LEADING EXPORTS: bananas, cocoa, clothing, and vegetables
CONTINENT: North America

ST. VINCENT AND THE GRENADINES

CAPITAL ★ Kingstown
POPULATION: 118,000
MAJOR LANGUAGE: English
AREA: 150 sq mi; 389 sq km
LEADING EXPORTS: bananas, arrowroot starch, taro, and tennis racquets
CONTINENT: North America

SAMOA

CAPITAL ★ Apia
POPULATION: 214,000
MAJOR LANGUAGES: Samoan and English
AREA: 1,093 sq mi; 2,831 sq km
LEADING EXPORTS: copra, cocoa, coconut oil, and cream
CONTINENT: Islands in the Pacific Ocean

SAN MARINO

CAPITAL ★ San Marino
POPULATION: 25,000
MAJOR LANGUAGE: Italian
AREA: 23 sq mi; 62 sq km
LEADING EXPORTS: lime, chestnuts, and wheat
CONTINENT: Europe

SÃO TOMÉ AND PRÍNCIPE

CAPITAL ★ São Tomé
POPULATION: 144,000
MAJOR LANGUAGE: Portuguese
AREA: 370 sq mi; 958 sq km
LEADING EXPORTS: cocoa, coffee, copra, and palm oil
CONTINENT: Africa

SAUDI ARABIA

CAPITAL ★ Riyadh
POPULATION: 19.4 million
MAJOR LANGUAGE: Arabic
AREA: 865,000 sq mi; 2,250,070 sq km
LEADING EXPORT: oil
CONTINENT: Asia

SENEGAL

CAPITAL ★ Dakar
POPULATION: 9.1 million
MAJOR LANGUAGES: French and Wolof
AREA: 75,954 sq mi; 196,722 sq km
LEADING EXPORTS: peanuts, phosphates, and canned fish
CONTINENT: Africa

SEYCHELLES

CAPITAL ★ Victoria
POPULATION: 78,000
MAJOR LANGUAGES: Creole, English, and French
AREA: 175 sq mi; 453 sq km
LEADING EXPORTS: fish, canned tuna, copra, and cinnamon bark
CONTINENT: Africa

SIERRA LEONE

CAPITAL ★ Freetown
POPULATION: 4.8 million
MAJOR LANGUAGES: English, Mende, Temne, and Krio
AREA: 27,925 sq mi; 73,326 sq km
LEADING EXPORTS: diamonds, rutile, bauxite, and cocoa
CONTINENT: Africa

SINGAPORE

CAPITAL ★ Singapore
POPULATION: 3.4 million
MAJOR LANGUAGES: Chinese, English, Malay, and Tamil
AREA: 247 sq mi; 639 sq km
LEADING EXPORTS: petroleum products, rubber, and computer equipment
CONTINENT: Asia

SLOVAKIA

CAPITAL ★ Bratislava
POPULATION: 5.4 million
MAJOR LANGUAGES: Slovak and Hungarian
AREA: 18,917 sq mi; 48,995 sq km
LEADING EXPORTS: machinery, chemicals, fuels, and minerals
CONTINENT: Europe

SLOVENIA

CAPITAL ★ Ljubljana
POPULATION: 2.0 million
MAJOR LANGUAGE: Slovenian
AREA: 7,819 sq mi; 20,251 sq km
LEADING EXPORTS: manufactured goods and chemicals
CONTINENT: Europe

SOLOMON ISLANDS

CAPITAL ★ Honiara
POPULATION: 0.4 million
MAJOR LANGUAGES: English, Pidgin English, and Melanesian
AREA: 11,500 sq mi; 29,785 sq km
LEADING EXPORTS: fish, timber, copra, and palm oil
CONTINENT: Islands in the Pacific Ocean

SOMALIA

CAPITAL ★ Mogadishu
POPULATION: 9.6 million
MAJOR LANGUAGES: Somali and Arabic
AREA: 246,199 sq mi; 637,655 sq km
LEADING EXPORTS: live animals, hides, and bananas
CONTINENT: Africa

SOUTH AFRICA

CAPITALS ★ Pretoria, Cape Town, and Bloemfontein
POPULATION: 41.7 million
MAJOR LANGUAGES: Afrikaans, English, Zulu and other African languages
AREA: 471,440 sq mi; 1,221,030 sq km
LEADING EXPORTS: gold, other minerals, and metals
CONTINENT: Africa

SPAIN

CAPITAL ★ Madrid

POPULATION: 38.8 million

MAJOR LANGUAGES: Spanish and Catalan

AREA: 199,365 sq mi; 505,992 sq km

LEADING EXPORTS: cars and trucks, machinery

CONTINENT: Europe

SRI LANKA

CAPITAL ★ Colombo

POPULATION: 18.5 million

MAJOR LANGUAGES: Sinhala, Tamil, and English

AREA: 25,332 sq mi; 65,610 sq km

LEADING EXPORTS: textiles, tea, rubber, and petroleum products

CONTINENT: Asia

SUDAN

CAPITAL ★ Khartoum

POPULATION: 31.1 million

MAJOR LANGUAGES: Arabic, Nubian and Sudanic languages

AREA: 967,491 sq mi; 2,505,802 sq km

LEADING EXPORTS: cotton, peanuts, gum arabic, and sesame

CONTINENT: Africa

SURINAME

CAPITAL ★ Paramaribo

POPULATION: 0.4 million

MAJOR LANGUAGES: Dutch, English, and Hindi

AREA: 63,251 sq mi; 163,820 sq km

LEADING EXPORTS: bauxite, alumina, rice, and shrimp

CONTINENT: South America

SWAZILAND

CAPITAL ★ Mbabane

POPULATION: 1.0 million

MAJOR LANGUAGES: Siswati and English

AREA: 6,704 sq mi; 17,363 sq km

LEADING EXPORTS: sugar, wood products, asbestos, and citrus

CONTINENT: Africa

SWEDEN

CAPITAL ★ Stockholm

POPULATION: 8.9 million

MAJOR LANGUAGE: Swedish

AREA: 173,800 sq mi; 449,964 sq km

LEADING EXPORTS: machinery, motor vehicles, and wood products

CONTINENT: Europe

SWITZERLAND

CAPITAL ★ Bern

POPULATION: 7.0 million

MAJOR LANGUAGES: German, French, Italian, and Romansch

AREA: 15,941 sq mi; 41,288 sq km

LEADING EXPORTS: machinery, metal products, and textiles

CONTINENT: Europe

SYRIA

CAPITAL ★ Damascus

POPULATION: 15.6 million

MAJOR LANGUAGES: Arabic and Kurdish

AREA: 71,498 sq mi; 185,180 sq km

LEADING EXPORTS: oil, textiles, cotton, fruits, and vegetables

CONTINENT: Asia

TAIWAN

CAPITAL ★ Taipei

POPULATION: 21.3 million

MAJOR LANGUAGES: Mandarin, Taiwanese, and Hakka dialects

AREA: 13,895 sq mi; 35,988 sq km

LEADING EXPORTS: textiles, electronic products, and information products

CONTINENT: Asia

TAJIKISTAN

CAPITAL ★ Dushanbe

POPULATION: 5.9 million

MAJOR LANGUAGES: Tajik and Russian

AREA: 55,300 sq mi; 143,100 sq km

LEADING EXPORTS: aluminum, cotton, and fruit

CONTINENT: Asia

TANZANIA

CAPITAL ★ Dar es Salaam

POPULATION: 29.1 million

MAJOR LANGUAGES: Swahili and English

AREA: 364,879 sq mi; 945,037 sq km

LEADING EXPORTS: coffee, cotton, sisal, and cloves

CONTINENT: Africa

THAILAND

CAPITAL ★ Bangkok

POPULATION: 58.9 million

MAJOR LANGUAGES: Thai and English

AREA: 198,455 sq mi; 514,000 sq km

LEADING EXPORTS: machinery and food

CONTINENT: Asia

COUNTRIES of the WORLD

TOGO

CAPITAL ★ Lomé
POPULATION: 4.6 million
MAJOR LANGUAGES: French, Kabye, Ewe, Mina, and Dagomba
AREA: 21,925 sq mi; 56,785 sq km
LEADING EXPORTS: phosphates, cocoa, coffee, and cotton
CONTINENT: Africa

TONGA

CAPITAL ★ Nuku'alofa
POPULATION: 106,000
MAJOR LANGUAGES: Tongan and English
AREA: 290 sq mi; 751 sq km
LEADING EXPORTS: copra, coconut oil, bananas, and fruits
CONTINENT: Islands in the Pacific Ocean

TRINIDAD AND TOBAGO

CAPITAL ★ Port-of-Spain
POPULATION: 1.3 million
MAJOR LANGUAGES: English, Hindi, and French
AREA: 1,980 sq mi; 5,128 sq km
LEADING EXPORTS: oil and steel products
CONTINENT: North America

TUNISIA

CAPITAL ★ Tunis
POPULATION: 9.0 million
MAJOR LANGUAGES: Arabic and French
AREA: 63,170 sq mi; 163,610 sq km
LEADING EXPORTS: textiles, agricultural products, and chemicals
CONTINENT: Africa

TURKEY

CAPITAL ★ Ankara
POPULATION: 62.5 million
MAJOR LANGUAGES: Turkish, Kurdish, and Arabic
AREA: 300,947 sq mi; 779,452 sq km
LEADING EXPORTS: agricultural products and textiles
CONTINENTS: Asia and Europe

TURKMENISTAN

CAPITAL ★ Ashgabat
POPULATION: 4.1 million
MAJOR LANGUAGES: Turkmen, Russian, and Uzbek
AREA: 188,500 sq mi; 488,100 sq km
LEADING EXPORTS: gas, oil, chemicals, and cotton
CONTINENT: Asia

TUVALU

CAPITAL ★ Funafuti
POPULATION: 10,000
MAJOR LANGUAGES: Tuvaluan and English
AREA: 10 sq mi; 26 sq km
LEADING EXPORT: copra
CONTINENT: Islands in the Pacific Ocean

UGANDA

CAPITAL ★ Kampala
POPULATION: 20.2 million
MAJOR LANGUAGES: English, Luganda, Swahili, and Bantu languages
AREA: 91,459 sq mi; 236,880 sq km
LEADING EXPORTS: coffee, cotton, and tea
CONTINENT: Africa

UKRAINE

CAPITAL ★ Kiev
POPULATION: 50.9 million
MAJOR LANGUAGES: Ukrainian, Russian, Romanian, and Polish
AREA: 233,000 sq mi; 603,700 sq km
LEADING EXPORTS: coal, electric power, and metals
CONTINENT: Europe

UNITED ARAB EMIRATES

CAPITAL ★ Abu Dhabi
POPULATION: 3.1 million
MAJOR LANGUAGES: Arabic, Persian, English, Hindi, and Urdu
AREA: 32,000 sq mi; 82,880 sq km
LEADING EXPORTS: oil and natural gas
CONTINENT: Asia

UNITED KINGDOM

CAPITAL ★ London
POPULATION: 58.5 million
MAJOR LANGUAGES: English, Welsh, and Scottish Gaelic
AREA: 94, 247 sq mi; 244, 100 sq km
LEADING EXPORTS: machinery and chemicals
CONTINENT: Europe

UNITED STATES

CAPITAL ★ Washington, D.C.
POPULATION: 265.1 million
MAJOR LANGUAGES: English and Spanish
AREA: 3,536,341 sq mi; 9,159,123 sq km
LEADING EXPORTS: machinery, chemicals, aircraft, and military equipment
CONTINENT: North America

URUGUAY

CAPITAL ★ Montevideo
POPULATION: 3.2 million
MAJOR LANGUAGES: Spanish and Brazilero
AREA: 68,040 sq mi; 176,224 sq km
LEADING EXPORTS: meat and wool
CONTINENT: South America

UZBEKISTAN

CAPITAL ★ Tashkent
POPULATION: 23.4 million
MAJOR LANGUAGES: Uzbek, Russian, and Tajik
AREA: 172,700 sq mi; 447,400 sq km
LEADING EXPORTS: cotton, gold, textiles, and chemicals
CONTINENT: Asia

VANUATU

CAPITAL ★ Port-Vila
POPULATION: 178,000
MAJOR LANGUAGES: Bislama, English, and French
AREA: 5,700 sq mi; 14,763 sq km
LEADING EXPORTS: copra, cocoa, coffee, and fish
CONTINENT: Islands in the Pacific Ocean

VATICAN CITY (The Holy See)

CAPITAL ★ Vatican City
POPULATION: 830
MAJOR LANGUAGES: Italian and Latin
AREA: 0.17 sq mi; 0.44 sq km
LEADING EXPORTS: (not available)
CONTINENT: Europe

VENEZUELA

CAPITAL ★ Caracas
POPULATION: 22.0 million
MAJOR LANGUAGES: Spanish and Indian dialects
AREA: 352,143 sq mi; 912,050 sq km
LEADING EXPORTS: oil, iron ore, and bauxite
CONTINENT: South America

VIETNAM

CAPITAL ★ Hanoi
POPULATION: 74.0 million
MAJOR LANGUAGES: Vietnamese, French, Chinese, English, and Khmer
AREA: 127,246 sq mi; 329,566 sq km
LEADING EXPORTS: agricultural products, minerals, and marine products
CONTINENT: Asia

YEMEN

CAPITAL ★ San'a
POPULATION: 13.5 million
MAJOR LANGUAGE: Arabic
AREA: 203, 850 sq mi; 527,970 sq km
LEADING EXPORTS: cotton, coffee, hides, and vegetables
CONTINENT: Asia

YUGOSLAVIA

CAPITAL ★ Belgrade
POPULATION: 10.6 million
MAJOR LANGUAGES: Serbo-Croatian and Albanian
AREA: 39,449 sq mi; 102,169 sq km
LEADING EXPORTS: machinery and transport equipment
CONTINENT: Europe

ZAMBIA

CAPITAL ★ Lusaka
POPULATION: 9.2 million
MAJOR LANGUAGES: English and about 70 Bantu dialects
AREA: 290,586 sq mi; 752,618 sq km
LEADING EXPORTS: copper, zinc, lead, cobalt, and tobacco
CONTINENT: Africa

ZIMBABWE

CAPITAL ★ Harare
POPULATION: 11.3 million
MAJOR LANGUAGES: English, Shona, and Sindebele
AREA: 150,698 sq mi; 390,308 sq km
LEADING EXPORTS: gold, tobacco, and asbestos
CONTINENT: Africa

SOURCE: population, languages, area, exports—*Information Please Almanac*, 1997; additional information on languages—*The World Almanac and Book of Facts*, 1997

WORLD HISTORY TIME LINE

	BEFORE 6000 B.C.		6000–5000 B.C.		5000–4000 B.C.	
EUROPE	20,000 years ago	Hunter-gatherers paint the walls of caves near Avignon, France	6000 B.C.	Farming spreads to other parts of the continent	5000 B.C.	Farming villages appear in southern France
	10,000 B.C.	Early Europeans make tiny blades, called *microliths*, out of flint	5500 B.C.	Early pottery decorated with patterned lines is made through much of the continent	4500 B.C.	Stone axes are traded and used to clear forest land for farming
	7000 B.C.	Farming begins in southern Europe, as Greek farmers raise wheat and herd sheep and goats				
AFRICA	10,000 B.C.	People begin to build villages along the Nile River	6000 B.C.	Farmers build irrigation ditches along the Nile River	5000 B.C.	Farmers grow wheat and barley in Egypt
	8000 B.C.	People along the Nile use reed nets to catch fish	6000 B.C.	People use barbed harpoons to catch fish in Africa's rivers and lakes	4500 B.C.	Nubian artisans make pottery in what is now Sudan
	6500 B.C.	Rock paintings in the Sahara Desert show animals long gone from the region, such as buffalo, giraffes and elephants				
ASIA AND AUSTRALIA	40,000 years ago	Aborigines settle in Australia after arriving from Indonesia and Asia	6000 B.C.	Early agriculture begins at Catal Huyuk, in what is today Turkey	5000 B.C.	First towns settled in Sumer
	8000 B.C.	Hunter-gatherers use wild rice in East and Southeast Asia			5000 B.C.	Early settlements emerge in China
	7000 B.C.	Before the development of pottery, early people in western Asia make "white ware" from lime and ash			5000 B.C.	Copper used in Mesopotamia
THE AMERICAS	40,000 years ago	Asian hunters begin to cross the Beringia land bridge	5000 B.C.	Cochise and Chumash cultures develop in southwestern North America	5000 B.C.	Early maize farming begins in what is today Mexico
	15,000 years ago	People have spread throughout the Americas	5000 B.C.	Chinchorros people build settlements in what is today northern Chile	4500 B.C.	Indians use weighted nets to fish the waters of the American northwest
	7000 B.C.	Native American craftworkers use stone tools for woodworking				

4000-3000 B.C.		3000-2000 B.C.		2000-1000 B.C.	
4000 B.C.	Farmers cultivate crops in the British Isles	3000 B.C.	Artisans on Crete use bronze and gold	2000 B.C.	Minoan palace civilization begins to flourish in Crete
3500 B.C.	New Stone Age period begins in western Europe	3000 B.C.	Loom weaving begins in Europe	1600 B.C.	Mycenaeans gain power in Aegean region
3300 B.C.	"Iceman" takes his last hike into the Alps	3000 B.C.	Huge stone structures built at Stonehenge, England	1500 B.C.	Minoan culture ends in Crete
		2200 B.C.	Bronze Age begins in Ireland	1400 B.C.	Mycenaean culture spreads to Greece
4000 B.C.	The sail is first used on boats on the Nile River	2772 B.C.	Egyptians create a calendar of 365 days	2000 B.C.	Kushite culture develops along the Upper Nile
4000 B.C.	Artisans make pottery in Ghana, West Africa	2600 B.C.	Pharaoh Khufu orders construction of the Great Pyramid	1550 B.C.	Egyptians defeat the Hyksos and begin the New Kingdom period
3200 B.C.	Egyptians begin to develop hieroglyphic writing	2500 B.C.	Egyptians build the Great Sphinx at Giza	1500 B.C.	Queen Hatshepsut is pharaoh
3100 B.C.	Menes unites Upper and Lower Egypt	2500 B.C.	First libraries are built in Egypt	1362–1352 B.C.	Tutankhamun is pharaoh
				1250 B.C.	Possible date of Moses' Exodus
4000 B.C.	Sumerians begin to settle in the Fertile Crescent	3000 B.C.	City-states begin in Sumer	1800 B.C.	Code of Hammurabi recorded
3500 B.C.	City of Ur founded in Mesopotamia	3000 B.C.	Plow first used in China	1700 B.C.	Babylonians conquer Sumer and more of Mesopotamia
3500 B.C.	Cuneiform writing appears in Sumer	2500 B.C.	Writing and trade begin in Indus Valley	1700 B.C.	Possible date of Abraham's journey to Canaan
3100 B.C.	Bronzework begins in Mesopotamia	2300 B.C.	Mohenjo-Daro and Harappa flourish in Indus River Valley	1700 B.C.	The Shang gain control of the Huang Valley
		2250 B.C.	Ziggurat built at Ur	1500 B.C.	Aryans migrate into Indus River Valley
3500 B.C.	Villagers in what is now Peru use the llama as a pack animal	2000 B.C.	Inuit people hunt caribou and seals in the Arctic	2000 B.C.	Andean settlements thrive in Peru
3500 B.C.	Cotton becomes an important crop in what is now Peru			1400 B.C.	Farming villages develop in Central America and southwestern North America
3500 B.C.	Haida culture begins on northwest coast of what is now Canada			1200 B.C.	Olmec civilization begins in Mexico

WORLD HISTORY TIME LINE

	1000–750 B.C.	750–500 B.C.	500–250 B.C.
EUROPE	**900 B.C.** Etruscans settle north of the Tiber River, in what is now Italy **900 B.C.** Greek city-state of Sparta is founded **776 B.C.** First Olympic Games are held in Greece	**700 B.C.** According to Roman legend, Romulus and Remus found the city on seven hills **700 B.C.** Homer creates the first Greek epics **600–560 B.C.** Aesop tells fables in ancient Greece **509 B.C.** Patricians take power in Rome **500 B.C.** Greeks build the Parthenon to house statues of gods and goddesses	**499 B.C.** Persian Wars begin **450 B.C.** Twelve Tables become basis of Roman Law **431 B.C.** Peloponnesian Wars begin **399 B.C.** Socrates is on trial **336 B.C.** Alexander the Great spreads Greek culture
AFRICA	**900 B.C.** Nok people of Nigeria use terra cotta **900 B.C.** Kushite kingdom in Sudan thrives **814 B.C.** Phoenician traders found colony at Carthage	**700 B.C.** Iron tools made in Egypt **671 B.C.** Assyrians overrun Egypt **600 B.C.** Nok people of Nigeria mine iron **600 B.C.** Carthaginian explorers sail southward from North Africa	**305 B.C.** Ptolemy II founds library in Alexandria **300 B.C.** Kushite kingdom expands and develops extensive trade networks
ASIA AND AUSTRALIA	**950(?)–928 B.C.** King Solomon rules Israel **911 B.C.** Rise of Assyrian power in Mesopotamia	**689 B.C.** Assyrians invade Babylonia and sack Babylon **586 B.C.** Armies of New Babylonia conquer Judah and exile Jews **539 B.C.** Persia's Cyrus the Great conquers Babylon and frees exiled Jews **528 B.C.** Possible date that Siddhartha Gautama, founder of Buddhism, begins teaching in India	**500 B.C.** Indian traders bring Hindu ideas to Southeast Asia **400 B.C.** Buddhism spreads through Asia **400 B.C.** Confucius teaches about duty in China **322 B.C.** Chandragupta founds Mauryan empire in India **273 B.C.** Asoka spreads Buddhist teaching and religious tolerance in India
THE AMERICAS	**1000 B.C.** La Venta becomes center of Olmec culture in Mexico **850 B.C.** Peruvians build temple at Chavín de Huantar in Andes	**600 B.C.** Oaxaca culture begins to dominate Olmec civilization in Mexico	**500 B.C.** Farmers in Ohio Valley construct burial mounds **300–100 B.C.** City of Teotihuacán develops in Mexico

250 B.C.–A.D. 1		A.D. 1–250		A.D. 250–500	
73–71 B.C.	Spartacus leads slave revolt in Rome	A.D. 29	Jesus' religious teachings become the foundation for Christianity	A.D. 306	Constantine rules Roman empire
45 B.C.	Julius Caesar becomes dictator of Rome	A.D. 80	Roman Colosseum is completed	A.D. 312	Christianity tolerated in Roman empire
27 B.C.	Augustus Caesar begins Pax Romana in Roman empire	A.D. 100	Network of Roman roads increases trade and travel through the empire	A.D. 445	Attila the Hun attacks western Europe
				A.D. 476	Rome falls to Germanic invaders
250 B.C.	Kush begins Golden Age, which lasts for about 300 years	A.D. 238	North Africans revolt against Roman empire	A.D. 300	Ptolemy describes Earth-centered universe
202 B.C.	Roman army defeats Hannibal's army at Zama			A.D. 300	Gold-salt trade develops in Ghana
30 B.C.	Egypt becomes Roman province			A.D. 324	King Ezana of Ethiopia becomes a Christian
				A.D. 350	Defeated by Aksum, Kushite civilization at Meroe ends
				A.D. 400	St. Augustine spreads Christianity in North Africa
250 B.C.	Kingdom of Parthia emerges in eastern Persia	A.D. 50	St. Paul spreads Christianity	A.D. 320	Gupta empire emerges in Ganges Valley, India
215 B.C.	Shihuangdi's Qin dynasty begins construction of the Great Wall of China	A.D. 70	Romans destroy Jerusalem, beginning Jewish diaspora	A.D. 330	Constantinople becomes new capital of Roman empire
206 B.C.	Han Dynasty begins in China, adopting many Confucian ideas	A.D. 101	Chinese invent paper	A.D. 400	Chinese manufacture steel
		A.D. 120	Chinese invent seismograph		
		A.D. 220	Fall of Han Dynasty in China		
200 B.C.	Maya culture begins to develop in Central America	A.D. 100	Hopewell culture flourishes on upper Mississippi	A.D. 250	Classic period of Maya civilization in Guatemala, Honduras, and eastern Mexico
200 B.C.	Nazca culture begins in southern Peru	A.D. 100–200	Oaxaca culture reaches height	A.D. 500	Hopewell culture builds burial mounds and makes pottery and iron weapons
100 B.C.	Anasazi culture emerges in southwestern United States				

WORLD HISTORY TIME LINE

A.D. 500–750

EUROPE

A.D. 500	Middle Ages usually said to begin around this time
A.D. 529–534	Byzantine Emperor Justinian issues Codes of Law
A.D. 670	Bulgars from Russia settle near Danube River
A.D. 715	Muslims conquer most of Spain
A.D. 732	Charles Martel, king of Franks, stops Muslim advance into France

AFRICA

A.D. 500	Kingdom of Ghana rises to power in West Africa
A.D. 640–641	Islamic leader Caliph Omar conquers Egypt
A.D. 642	Arabs build first mosque in al-Fustat, new capital of Muslim Egypt
A.D. 711	Arab empire conquers North Africa

ASIA AND AUSTRALIA

A.D. 552	Buddhism spreads to Japan from China and Korea
A.D. 595	Indian mathematicians use decimal system
A.D. 605–610	Sui emperors build Grand Canal in China
A.D. 610	According to Muslim sources, the date that Muhammad founds Islam in Arabia
A.D. 622	According to Muslim sources, Muhammad makes the migration, or hijra, from Mecca to Medina

THE AMERICAS

A.D. 500	Polynesians from Southeast Asia settle in Hawaiian Islands
A.D. 600	Height of Maya civilization
A.D. 650	Teotihuacán thrives as trade center in Mexico

A.D. 750–1000

EUROPE

A.D. 800	Charlemagne becomes emperor
A.D. 800	First castles built in western Europe
A.D. 843	Charlemagne's Frankish empire breaks up
A.D. 885–886	Vikings raid Paris, France
A.D. 900	Feudalism is widespread social and economic system
A.D. 986	Viking explorer Eric the Red founds colony in Greenland

AFRICA

A.D. 800	Arabs and Persians explore East African coast and set up trading stations
A.D. 800–950	Christianity continues in Ethiopia after decline of Aksum
A.D. 950–1050	Igbo-Ukwu culture thrives in eastern Nigeria
A.D. 969	Fatimid dynasty conquers Egypt and builds Cairo
A.D. 970	Fatimids build one of the world's first universities in Cairo
A.D. 970	Ghana empire flourishes in West Africa

ASIA AND AUSTRALIA

A.D. 700–1100	Baghdad is capital of Arab empire
A.D. 794–1184	Heian period in Japan
A.D. 802	Jayavarman II rules the Khmer throne
A.D. 868	Chinese use wood blocks to print books
A.D. 889	Khmers build capital at Angkor, in what is today Cambodia
A.D. 907–26	Mongols conquer inner Mongolia and northern China
A.D. 970	Chinese introduce paper money

THE AMERICAS

A.D. 900	Maya civilization in southern Mexico mysteriously collapses
A.D. 900–1000	Pueblo settlements thrive in North America
A.D. 990	Toltec people take over Maya city of Chichén Itzá in Mexico

World Regions in Transition

A.D. 1054	Church in Constantinople breaks with Church of Rome
A.D. 1066	Normans defeat English at Battle of Hastings
A.D. 1095	Pope Urban calls for the First Crusade
A.D. 1150	Chartres cathedral built
A.D. 1209	St. Francis of Assisi founds Franciscan religious order
A.D. 1215	King John of England signs Magna Carta

A.D. 1348–1352	Bubonic plague (Black Death) devastates Europe
A.D. 1350	Renaissance begins in Italy
A.D. 1429	Joan of Arc leads French against the English at Orléans
A.D. 1448	John Gutenberg develops the printing press
A.D. 1453	Ottomans capture Constantinople; end of Byzantine empire
A.D. 1478–1492	Renaissance art patron Lorenzo de Medici rules Italy
A.D. 1492	Columbus sails from Spain to America
A.D. 1497–1499	Portuguese explorer Vasco da Gama sails around Africa to India

A.D. 1000	Bantu-speaking kingdoms emerge in southern Africa
A.D. 1000	Kingdoms in West Africa flourish from gold trade
A.D. 1100	Swahili city-states develop trade with Arabia and India
A.D. 1200	City-state of Kilwa prospers
A.D. 1235	Sunjata founds Mali empire in West Africa

A.D. 1300	Timbuktu is a major trading center
A.D. 1324	Mansa Musa, emperor of Mali, goes on pilgrimage to Mecca, Arabia
A.D. 1350	Kingdom of Great Zimbabwe thrives on gold trade
A.D. 1352–1353	Ibn Batuta writes an account of his travels across Africa
A.D. 1420	Portuguese sailors begin to explore west coast of Africa
A.D. 1488	Bartholomeu Dias sails around tip of Africa
A.D. 1490	Songhai empire begins in West Africa

A.D. 1000	Chinese perfect gunpowder
A.D. 1000	Murasaki Shikibu writes *Tale of Genji*
A.D. 1076	Muslim Seljuk Turks capture Jerusalem
A.D. 1099	Crusaders from Europe recapture Jerusalem
A.D. 1100	Samurai dominate Japan
A.D. 1100	Angkor Wat is built in what is now Cambodia
A.D. 1192	Yoritomo becomes first shogun in Japan
A.D. 1209	Genghis Khan leads Mongols to conquer China

A.D. 1271	Marco Polo sets out for China
A.D. 1279	Kublai Khan founds Yuan Dynasty
A.D. 1301	Osman I founds Ottoman dynasty in Turkey
A.D. 1368	Mongols are driven from China; Ming dynasty begins
A.D. 1453	Ottoman Turks conquer Constantinople, renaming the city *Istanbul*

A.D. 1000	Viking explorer Leif Erickson reaches America
A.D. 1100	Anasazi people in North America build cliff dwellings at Mesa Verde
A.D. 1200	Incas in Peru settle at Cuzco

A.D. 1300	Incas expand their empire throughout the central Andes
A.D. 1325	Aztecs found city of Tenochtitlán in what is today Mexico City
A.D. 1450	Inca city of Machu Picchu built in Peru
A.D. 1486–1521	Aztec empire at its height
A.D. 1497	John Cabot claims land in North America for England

WORLD HISTORY TIME LINE

A.D. 1500–1600

EUROPE

A.D. 1503	Leonardo da Vinci paints the *Mona Lisa*
A.D. 1517	Martin Luther nails the 95 Theses on a church door in Germany
A.D. 1519–1522	Ferdinand Magellan's crew completes sailing voyage around the world
A.D. 1534	Henry VIII of England makes himself head of English church
A.D. 1541–1564	John Calvin leads church reforms in Switzerland
A.D. 1550	Reformation spreads throughout Europe
A.D. 1558–1603	Elizabeth I reigns in England
A.D. 1588	English warships fight the Spanish Armada
A.D. 1595	William Shakespeare writes *Romeo and Juliet*

AFRICA

A.D. 1500	Songhai empire reaches height
A.D. 1575	Portugese begin colonization of Angola
A.D. 1590–591	Moroccan army overthrows Songhai empire
A.D. 1598	Dutch set up trading posts in western Africa

ASIA AND AUSTRALIA

| A.D. 1520–1566 | Ottoman empire reaches height under Süleyman |
| A.D. 1556–1605 | Mogul emperor Akbar reforms government in India |

THE AMERICAS

A.D. 1500	Pedro Cabral claims Brazil for Portugal
A.D. 1521	Hernando Cortés conquers Aztecs
A.D. 1531–1535	Francisco Pizarro conquers Inca empire
A.D. 1534	Jacques Cartier claims what is now Canada for France
A.D. 1549	Coronado conquers Zuñi pueblos
A.D. 1580	Iroquois League unites Five Nations
A.D. late 1500s	Powhatan confederacy organized

A.D. 1600–1700

EUROPE

A.D. 1609	Galileo proves the heliocentric theory
A.D. 1643–1715	Louis XIV rules France
A.D. 1653–1658	Oliver Cromwell is Lord Protector of Britain, replacing monarchy with parliamentary rule
A.D. 1682–1725	Peter the Great rules Russia
A.D. 1687	Isaac Newton publishes his "laws of gravity"
A.D. 1689	England's Parliament drafts a Bill of Rights, limiting the power of the monarchy

AFRICA

| A.D. 1652 | Dutch found Cape Town |
| A.D. 1680 | Asante kingdom begins in West Africa |

ASIA AND AUSTRALIA

A.D. 1600–1614	English, Dutch, Danish, and French East India Companies founded
A.D. 1603	Tokugawa period begins in Japan
A.D. 1603	Japan begins to restrict foreign contacts
A.D. 1616	Dutch explorer Dirk Hartog lands on the West Coast of Australia
A.D. 1627	Manchus conquer Korea
A.D. 1632–1648	Shah Jahan builds the Taj Mahal
A.D. 1644	Manchus conquer Beijing and found the Qing dynasty
A.D. 1683	Chinese control Formosa, what is today called Taiwan

THE AMERICAS

A.D. 1607	The English establish the Jamestown settlement in Virginia
A.D. 1608	French settlers found Quebec
A.D. 1610	Henry Hudson explores Hudson Bay
A.D. 1620	Pilgrims sail to Plymouth in the *Mayflower*
A.D. 1636	Puritans found Harvard University
A.D. 1664	English capture Dutch colony of New Amsterdam and rename it New York
A.D. 1681	Quaker William Penn founds Pennsylvania

Dawn of the Modern World

A.D. **1700**	Industrial Revolution begins
A.D. **1769**	James Watt perfects the steam engine
A.D. **1776**	Adam Smith writes *The Wealth of Nations*
A.D. **1789**	French Revolution begins
A.D. **1793**	Louis XVI is executed
A.D. **1799**	Napoleon overthrows the French government

A.D. **1720**	Yoruba kingdom of Oyo prospers
A.D. **1730**	More than 50,000 Africans are shipped each year to the Americas as slaves, in the Triangular Trade
A.D. **1795**	British seize Cape Colony from the Dutch
A.D. **1800**	Benin City becomes a center for West African slave trade

A.D. **1750**	Japanese arts and commerce flourish under Tokugawa shogunate
A.D. **1750**	Rice production in China increases greatly
A.D. **1770**	England's Captain Cook explores eastern coast of Australia
A.D. **1784**	United States begins to trade with China
A.D. **1788**	The first fleet of ships carrying convicts from England arrives in Australia; the English colony of New South Wales is founded in Australia

A.D. **1700**	Sugar plantations flourish in Caribbean
A.D. **1754–1763**	French and Indian War is fought
A.D. **1775**	American Revolution begins at Lexington
A.D. **1776**	Declaration of Independence signed
A.D. **1781**	British surrender to Americans at Yorktown
A.D. **1789**	George Washington becomes first President of the United States
A.D. **1791**	Toussaint L'Ouverture leads revolt against French in Haiti

A.D. **1804**	Napoleon crowns himself emperor
A.D. **1815**	Napoleon defeated at Waterloo
A.D. **1825**	The Industrial Revolution spreads to Germany, Belgium, and France
A.D. **1827**	First photograph taken
A.D. **1848**	Karl Marx publishes *Communist Manifesto*
A.D. **1861**	Serfdom is abolished in Russia
A.D. **1895**	Lumière brothers invent the film projector
A.D. **1895**	Marconi invents radio

A.D. **1822**	Liberia is founded as home for freed United States slaves
A.D. **1840**	Zanzibar becomes a commercial center, exporting cloves and other spices
A.D. **1850**	Slave trading is abolished in most countries
A.D. **1853–1856**	British explorer Dr. Livingstone crosses Africa
A.D. **1867**	Diamonds discovered in South Africa
A.D. **1869**	The Suez Canal is opened in Egypt
A.D. **1872**	Britain grants Cape Colony self-government

A.D. **1823**	The New South Wales Act allows the New South Wales colony in Australia to create a legislative body
A.D. **1842**	After a war with Britain, China is forced to open its ports to Western traders
A.D. **1853**	Matthew C. Perry enters Edo Bay
A.D. **1854**	United States opens Japan to trade
A.D. **1868–1912**	Meiji restoration in Japan brings industrialization; capital moves to Edo, present-day Tokyo
A.D. **1894**	Women win the right to vote in the Australian colony of South Australia

A.D. **1804–1806**	Louis and Clark explore Louisiana Territory
A.D. **1821**	Bolívar frees northern South America
A.D. **1821**	San Martín wins independence for Peru
A.D. **1821**	Mexico wins independence from Spain
A.D. **1823**	Monroe Doctrine opposes European interference in the Western Hemisphere
A.D. **1836**	Texas gains independence from Mexico
A.D. **1861–1865**	United States Civil War is fought
A.D. **1867**	Canada's provinces unite
A.D. **1869**	Transcontinental Railroad completed
A.D. **1876**	Alexander Graham Bell invents telephone
A.D. **1883**	Thomas Edison invents lightbulb

WORLD HISTORY TIME LINE

A.D. 1900–1925	A.D. 1925–1950

EUROPE

A.D. 1905	Einstein publishes his theory of relativity
A.D. 1914	World War I begins
A.D. 1917	Russian Revolution ends Tsarist rule and brings Communist Party to power
A.D. 1919	Treaty of Versailles ends World War I
A.D. 1920	League of Nations founded
A.D. 1924	Joseph Stalin becomes dictator of Soviet Union

A.D. 1926	Scotland's John Logie Baird invents the television
A.D. 1933	Adolf Hitler rises to power in Germany
A.D. 1933–1945	About 6 million European Jews are killed during the Holocaust
A.D. 1939	Germany invades Poland; World War II begins
A.D. 1944	Allies land at Normandy, France on D-Day to free Europe from Hitler's advance
A.D. 1945	World War II ends
A.D. 1945	The United Nations is created
A.D. 1949	As Cold War intensifies, Western nations organize NATO

AFRICA

A.D. 1912	The African National Congress is founded in the Union of South Africa
A.D. 1914	European powers control nearly all of Africa
A.D. 1922	Howard Carter discovers King Tut's tomb
A.D. 1923	Ethiopia joins League of Nations

A.D. 1931	South Africa gains independence from Britain
A.D. 1931	First trans-African railway completed
A.D. 1942	Battle of El Alamein fought in Egypt during World War II
A.D. 1948	Apartheid system begins in South Africa

ASIA AND AUSTRALIA

A.D. 1901	The Commonwealth of Australia comes into existence as a new nation
A.D. 1910	Japan invades Korea
A.D. 1911–1912	Manchu dynasty ends in China; Sun Yat-Sen establishes a republic
A.D. 1913	Indian poet Rabindranath Tagore receives Nobel Prize for Literature
A.D. 1920	Mohandas Gandhi begins nonviolent protest against British rule in India

A.D. 1931	Japanese occupy Chinese province of Manchuria
A.D. 1932	Abd al-Aziz ibn Saud unifies a new kingdom called Saudi Arabia
A.D. 1934	Mao Zedong leads Chinese Communists on the Long March
A.D. 1937–1945	War breaks out between China and Japan
A.D. 1945	United States drops first atomic bombs on Hiroshima and Nagasaki
A.D. 1947	India and Pakistan gain independence from Britain
A.D. 1948	Israel gains independence
A.D. 1949	Mao Zedong establishes communist rule in China

THE AMERICAS

A.D. 1903	Wright Brothers make first successful airplane flight
A.D. 1908	Henry Ford produces first Model T car
A.D. 1914	Panama Canal opens
A.D. 1918	President Wilson proposes "Fourteen Points" as a plan for lasting world peace
A.D. 1920	Women gain voting rights in the United States

A.D. 1929	Great Depression begins with the New York stock market crash
A.D. 1933	Franklin Roosevelt launches the New Deal to help end the Great Depression
A.D. 1941	Japanese bomb Pearl Harbor; United States enters World War II
A.D. 1945	United States scientists build first atomic bomb
A.D. 1948–1951	The United States' Marshall Plan helps Europe recover from the war

A Century of Conflict

A.D. **1955**	Communist countries sign the Warsaw Pact
A.D. **1956**	Eastern European countries revolt against communism
A.D. **1957**	Russians launch *Sputnik* space mission
A.D. **1961**	Berlin Wall is built

A.D. **1979**	Margaret Thatcher becomes first female prime minister of Britain
A.D. **1980**	Lech Walesa leads a strike by Polish workers and starts the Solidarity movement
A.D. **1985**	Soviet leader Mikhail Gorbachev introduces *glasnost*
A.D. **1989**	Berlin Wall is torn down
A.D. **1991**	Cold War ends as the Soviet Union collapses
A.D. **1991**	Yugoslavia breaks up; civil war begins
A.D. **1997**	President Bill Clinton and Soviet leader Boris Yeltsin sign an agreement in Finland aimed at helping Russia join the global economy

A.D. **1952**	Egypt gains independence from Britain
A.D. **1956**	Egypt takes control of the Suez Canal
A.D. **1957**	Ghana gains independence from Britain
A.D. **1958**	Sékou Touré used boycotts to help Guinea gain independence from France
A.D. **1963–1990**	Nelson Mandela imprisoned in South Africa
A.D. **1974**	Nigeria becomes leading oil producer in Africa

A.D. **1986**	Severe droughts hit Africa, especially Ethiopia
A.D. **1986**	Western nations put pressure on South Africa to abolish apartheid
A.D. **1992**	Foreign troops bring aid to Somalia
A.D. **1993**	Apartheid ends in South Africa
A.D. **1994**	Nelson Mandela is elected president of South Africa

A.D. **1950–1953**	Korean War is fought
A.D. **1951**	Australia forms an economic and political partnership with the United States
A.D. **1960**	Arab nations form the Organization of Petroleum Exporting Countries, or OPEC
A.D. **1964**	Palestinians found the Palestine Liberation Organization, or PLO
A.D. **1966**	Indira Gandhi becomes prime minister of India
A.D. **1965–1975**	Vietnam War is fought
A.D. **1966–1969**	Mao Zedong begins Cultural Revolution in China
A.D. **1970**	Japan becomes second-largest economic power in the world

A.D. **1978**	Israel and Egypt hold peace-talks at Camp David in the United States
A.D. **1980**	Iran-Iraq war begins
A.D. **1989**	Chinese students protest for democracy in Beijing's Tiananmen Square
A.D. **1990–1991**	Persian Gulf War is fought
A.D. **1993**	Palestinian and Israeli leaders sign agreement in United States for Palestinian self-rule
A.D. **1997**	Jiang Zemin becomes the leader of China after the death of Deng Xiaoping
A.D. **1997**	Hong Kong becomes reunited with China after being a British colony since the 1800s

A.D. **1960–1965**	Martin Luther King, Jr., leads civil rights movement in the United States
A.D. **1962**	The United States faces down the Soviet Union in the Cuban Missile Crisis, a tense moment of the Cold War
A.D. **1962**	Jamaica gains independence from Britain
A.D. **1969**	American Neil Armstrong becomes the first person on the moon

A.D. **1980–1992**	Civil war breaks out in El Salvador
A.D. **1987**	Oscar Arias Sánchez is first Latin American to win Nobel Peace Prize
A.D. **1990–1991**	United States leads fight against Iraq in Persian Gulf War
A.D. **1993**	Floods in Mississippi River basin destroy homes and crops
A.D. **1995**	Canadians in Quebec narrowly vote to remain a part of Canada

Dictionary of GEOGRAPHIC TERMS

ARCHIPELAGO (är kə pel'ə gō) A group or chain of islands.

STRAIT (strāt) A narrow waterway that connects two larger bodies of water.

GULF (gulf) Part of an ocean that extends into the land; larger than a bay.

PLATEAU (pla tō') An area of elevated flat land.

DAM (dam) A wall built across a river, creating a lake that stores water.

RESERVOIR (rez'ər vwär) A natural or artificial lake used to store water.

CANYON (kan'yən) A deep, narrow valley with steep sides.

MESA (mā'sə) A hill with a flat top; smaller than a plateau.

DUNE (dün) A mound, hill, or ridge of sand heaped up by the wind.

HILL (hil) A rounded, raised landform; not as high as a mountain.

BUTTE (būt) A small, flat-topped hill; smaller than a mesa or plateau.

VALLEY (val'ē) An area of low land between hills or mountains.

OASIS (ō ā'sis) A fertile area in a desert that is watered by a spring.

COAST (cōst) The land along an ocean.

DESERT (dez'ərt) A dry environment with few plants and animals.

BAY (bā) Part of an ocean or lake that extends deeply into the land.

ISTHMUS (is'məs) A narrow strip of land that connects two larger bodies of land.

ISLAND (ī'lənd) A body of land completely surrounded by water.

PENINSULA (pə nin'sə lə) A body of land nearly surrounded by water.

VOLCANO (vol kā'nō) An opening in Earth's surface through which hot rock and ash are forced out.

MOUNTAIN (moun'tən) A high landform with steep sides; higher than a hill.

PEAK (pēk) The top of a mountain.

HARBOR (här'bər) A sheltered place along a coast where boats dock safely.

GLACIER (glā'shər) A huge sheet of ice that moves slowly across the land.

CANAL (kə nal') A channel built to carry water for irrigation or navigation.

LAKE (lāk) A body of water completely surrounded by land.

PORT (pôrt) A place where ships load and unload their goods.

TRIBUTARY (trib'yə ter ē) A smaller river that flows into a larger river.

SOURCE (sôrs) The starting point of a river.

TIMBERLINE (tim'bər līn) A line beyond which trees do not grow.

RIVER BASIN (riv'ər bā'sin) All the land that is drained by a river and its tributaries.

WATERFALL (wô'tər fôl) A flow of water falling vertically.

MOUNTAIN RANGE (moun'tən rānj) A row or chain of mountains.

PLAIN (plān) A large area of nearly flat land.

RIVER (riv'ər) A stream of water that flows across the land and empties into another body of water.

BASIN (bā'sin) A bowl-shaped landform surrounded by higher land.

DELTA (del'tə) Land made of silt left behind as a river drains into a larger body of water.

MOUNTAIN PASS (moun'tən pas) A narrow gap through a mountain range.

MOUTH (mouth) The place where a river empties into a larger body of water.

OCEAN (ō'shən) A large body of salt water; oceans cover much of Earth's surface.

FJORD (fyôrd) A deep, narrow inlet of an ocean between high, steep cliffs.

R47

Gazetteer

This Gazetteer is a geographical dictionary that will help you to pronounce and locate the places discussed in this book. Latitude and longitude are given for cities and some other places. The page numbers tell you where each place appears on a map or in the text.

A

Aachen (ä′khən) Capital of Charlemagne's empire, c. 800; a city in present-day Germany; 51°N, 6°E. (m. 321, t. 321)

Accra (ə krä′) The capital and largest city of Ghana; 6°N, 0°. (m. 570, t. 568)

Acropolis (ə krop′ə lis) A hill in ancient Athens that became a religious center and meeting place; site of the Parthenon. (t. 205)

Africa (af′ri kə) The world's second-largest continent, lying south of Europe between the Atlantic and Indian oceans. (m. 607, t. 354)

Agra (ä′grə) A city in north-central India; capital of the Mogul empire around 1564–1658; 27°N, 78°E. (m. 393, t. 394)

Aksum (äk′süm) A powerful African kingdom and trading center, about 350–900, located in what is today Ethiopia. (m. 359, t. 359)

Alexandria (al ig zan′drē ə) A city in Egypt founded c. 332 B.C. by Alexander the Great; 31°N, 30°E. (m. 214, t. 214)

Alps (alps) Europe's highest mountains, extending in an arc from the Mediterranean coast to the Balkan peninsula. (m. 33, t. 33)

Anatolia (an ə tō′lē ə) Asia Minor; a peninsula in western Asia. (m. 390, t. 388)

Andes Mountains (an′dēz moun′tənz) The world's longest mountain chain, stretching along the west coast of South America. (m. 423, t. 422)

Angkor (ang′kôr) Ruined city in Cambodia; capital of the Khmer around 850–1430; 14°N, 104°E. (m. 399, t. 400)

Antarctica (ant ärk′ti kə) An ice-covered continent surrounding the South Pole. (m. G5)

Anyang (än′yäng) The ancient Chinese capital of the Shang dynasty; 36°N, 114°E. (m. 165, t. 165)

Apennine Mountains (ap′ə nin moun′tənz) A mountain range on the Italian peninsula. (m. 225, t. 225)

Arabia (ə rā′bē ə) A large peninsula in southwestern Asia. (m. 263, t. 262)

Arabian Sea (ə rā′bē ən sē) A body of water that lies between Arabia and India; the northwestern part of the Indian Ocean. (m. 263, t. 263)

Arctic Ocean (ärk′tik ō′shən) The body of water north of the Arctic Circle and surrounding the North Pole. (m. G5)

Asia (ā′zhə) The largest continent, bounded on the west by Europe and Africa, on the south by the Indian Ocean, and on the east by the Pacific. (m. 616, t. 586)

Athens (ath′ənz) For many centuries the most powerful of all ancient Greek city-states; capital of present-day Greece; 38°N, 23°E. (m. 198, t. 197)

Atlantic Ocean (at lan′tik ō′shən) The body of water separating Europe and Africa from North and South America. (m. G5, t. 317)

Attica (at′i kə) A peninsula in east-central Greece on the Aegean Sea on which Athens was built. (m. 193, t. 193)

Australia (ôs trāl′yə) The world's smallest continent, bounded by the Indian and Pacific oceans; also a country. (m. 616, t. 478)

B

Babylonia (bab ə lō′nē ə) An ancient Mesopotamian empire that extended throughout the Fertile Crescent in the 1700s B.C. (m. 110, t. 112)

Baghdad (bag′dad) Capital and cultural center of the Muslim caliphate from A.D. 762 to 1100; present-day capital of Iraq; 33°N, 44°E. (m. 273, t. 272)

Balkan Peninsula (bôl′kən pə nin′sə lə) A peninsula in southern Europe, bounded by the Black, Aegean, and Adriatic seas. (m. 601, t. 600)

pronunciation key

a	at	ī	ice	u	up	th	thin
ā	ape	îr	pierce	ū	use	th	this
ä	far	o	hot	ü	rule	zh	measure
âr	care	ō	old	ù	pull	ə	about, taken,
e	end	ô	fork	ûr	turn		pencil, lemon,
ē	me	oi	oil	hw	white		circus
i	it	ou	out	ng	song		

Bangladesh (bän glə desh´) A nation established in 1971 on the Indian subcontinent, and mostly surrounded by India; formerly known as East Pakistan. (m. 583, t. 584)

Bastille (bas tēl´) A prison fortress in Paris that was attacked and destroyed on July 14, 1789, at the start of the French Revolution. (t. 488)

Beijing (bā´jing´) The capital of the People's Republic of China; first became China's capital during the reign of Kublai Khan in the 1200s; 40°N, 116°E. (m. 403, t. 403)

Beringia (bə rin´jē ə) A land bridge that connected North America and Asia during the Ice Age; located where the Bering Strait is today. (m. 285, t. 286)

Berlin (bər lin´) The capital of Germany, divided from 1945 to 1990 into West Berlin and East Berlin; 53°N, 13°E. (m. 601, t. 558)

Bethlehem (beth´lə hem) A small town south of Jerusalem where Jesus is said to have been born; 31°N, 35°E. (m. 247, t. 247)

Border Cave (bôr´dər kāv) A major archaeological site in Zululand, South Africa and home of Old Stone Age hunters and gatherers; 27°S, 32°E. (m. 47, t. 46)

Bowating (bō´ä ting) An Ojibwa village that was located on an island in the river connecting lakes Superior and Huron; 46°N, 83°W. (m. 441, t. 441)

Brazil (brə zil´) The largest nation in South America, on the northeastern part of the continent. (m. 623, t. 622)

Burma (bər´mə) A nation in Southeast Asia on the Bay of Bengal; now known as Myanmar. (m. 587, t. 586)

Byzantine empire (bi´zən tēn em´pīr) The name by which the eastern half of the Roman empire became known some time after A.D. 400. (m. 254, t. 255)

C

Cairo (kī´rō) The capital of modern Egypt and the largest city in Africa; 30°N, 31°E. (m. 570, t. 569)

Cambodia (kam bō´dē ə) A nation in Southeast Asia. (m. 587, t. 586)

Canada (kan´ə də) A country in North America bordering the United States. (m. 623, t. 622)

Canadian Shield (kə nā´dē ən shēld) A large rocky plain in northern Canada that was formed by glaciers during the Ice Age. (m. 423, t. 423)

Cape Town (kāp toun) Seaport city in South Africa, settled by the Dutch in the late 1600s; 34°S, 18°E. (m. 607, t. 606)

Caribbean Sea (kar ə bē´ən sē) A sea bounded on the north and east by the West Indies, and by Central and South America on the west and south. (m. 475, t. 474)

Carthage (kär´thij) An ancient city on the north coast of Africa; 37°N, 10°E. (m. 234, t. 234)

Central Plateau (sen´trəl pla tō´) A high plateau extending throughout central Mexico and bounded by high mountain ranges. (m. 287, t. 287)

Chartres (shärt) A city in northwestern France, noted for its cathedral; 48°N, 1°E. (m. 334, t. 332)

China (chī´nə) A nation in East Asia, and the most populous country in the world. (m. 616, t. 618)

Colosseum (kä lə sē´əm) A large stadium in ancient Rome where athletic events took place. (t. 241)

Constantinople (kon stan tə nō´pəl) A city established as the new eastern capital of the Roman empire by the emperor Constantine in A.D. 330, now called Istanbul; 41°N, 29°E. (m. 254, t. 254)

Copán (kō pän´) An ancient city of Middle America, in what is now Honduras, that was a center of classic Maya culture; 15°N, 89°W. (m. 299, t. 299)

Crete (krēt) A Greek island in the Mediterranean Sea, southeast of Greece. (m. 193, t. 193)

Cuzco (küs´kō) A city in southern Peru; capital of the Inca empire from the 1200s to the 1500s; 14°S, 72°W. (m. 435, t. 435)

D

Dolores (də lôr´əs) A city in central Mexico where Miguel Hidalgo began Mexico's independence movement in 1810; 29°N, 108°W. (m. 493, t. 494)

Dominican Republic (də min´i kən ri pub´lik) A Caribbean nation, on the eastern part of Hispaniola, that gained independence in 1844. (m. 623, t. 623)

E

Edo (ed´ō) The former name of Tokyo, Japan; became capital under the rule of the Tokugawa shoguns in the 1600s; 36°N, 140°E. (m. 411, t. 412)

Egypt (ē´jipt) A country in northeast Africa; birthplace of ancient Egyptian civilization. (m. 570, t. 569)

England (ing´glənd) Part of the United Kingdom, on the island of Great Britain. (m. 321, t. 326)

Ethiopia (ē thē ō´pē ə) A country in eastern Africa. (m. 607, t. 358)

Euphrates River (ū frā´tēz riv´ər) A river in southwestern Asia that flows through the southern part of the Fertile Crescent. (m. 105, t. 104)

Eurasia (yü rā´zhə) A large land mass that includes the continents of Europe and Asia. (t. 316)

Europe (yür´əp) The continent north of Africa between Asia and the Atlantic Ocean. (m. 601, t. 316)

Gazetteer

F

Fertile Crescent (fûrt′əl kres′ənt) A fertile region in southwestern Asia that includes the region of Mesopotamia. (m. 105, t. 104)

Florence (flôr′əns) A city in present-day Italy; one of the great centers of Renaissance art; 44°N, 11°E. (m. 334, t. 337)

Forbidden City (fər bid′ən sit′ē) A walled area in Beijing built 1417–1420, during the Ming dynasty, that contained the palaces of the emperors. (t. 404)

Forum (for′əm) The city market and meeting place in the center of ancient Rome. (t. 233)

G

Gaul (gôl) An ancient region and Roman province that included most of present-day France. (m. 240, t. 237)

Gaza (gä′zə) A territory between Egypt and Israel on the southeastern coast of the Mediterranean Sea. Controlled by Israel from 1967 to 1994, after which it began to return to Palestinian control. (m. 578, t. 577)

Ghana (gä′nə) An empire, about 400–1235, located at the southwestern edge of the Sahara Desert; a present-day country in western Africa on the Gulf of Guinea. (m. 364, t. 363)

Gobi Desert (gō′bē dez′ərt) A large desert in east-central Asia. (m. 385, t. 386)

Golan Heights (gō′län hīts) Land occupied by Israel after the Six-Day War. 1967 (m. 578, t. 577)

Great Lakes (grāt lāks) A group of five large freshwater lakes on the border between the United States and Canada. (m. 423, t. 422)

Great Rift Valley (grāt rift val′ē) A series of cliffs and canyons caused by powerful prehistoric earthquakes that extends from Mozambique in southeastern Africa north to the Red Sea. (m. 355, t. 355)

Great Wall of China (grāt wôl əv chī′nə) A long defensive wall extending 1,500 miles (2,415 km) through northern China; built between 1300 and 1600. (m. 172, t. 170)

Great Zimbabwe (grāt zim bäb′wä) A city in southern Africa that rose to power in the 1300s through gold mining and trading; 20°S, 30°E. (m. 377, t. 376)

H

Haiti (hā′tē) A Caribbean nation, on the western part of Hispaniola, that gained independence from France in 1804. (m. 623, t. 623)

Harappa (hə ra′pə) A city of the ancient Harappan civilization, c. 2500–1600 B.C., located in the Indus Valley of South Asia; 31°N, 73°E. (m. 135, t. 135)

Himalayas (him ə lā′əz) The world's highest mountain range, forming the northern border of the Indian subcontinent. (m. 131, t. 131)

Hispaniola (his pən yō′lə) A Caribbean island settled by Spaniards in 1493; a present-day island that is divided into the Dominican Republic and Haiti. (m. 467, t. 467)

Hong Kong (häng käng) A large city and center of international trade developed as a British colony in mainland China; 22°N, 114°E. (m. 616, t. 619)

Huang River (hwäng riv′ər) [Yellow River] A river that flows from the Tibetan plateau, across northern China, and into the Yellow Sea. (m. 161, t. 160)

I

India (in′dē ə) The largest nation of the Indian subcontinent; became independent from British rule in 1947. (m. 583, t. 580)

Indian Ocean (in′dē ən ō′shən) The body of water south of Asia, between Africa and Australia. (m. G5, t. 372)

Indus Plain (in′dəs plān) A vast, dry region south of the Himalayas that is made fertile by deposits of silt from the Indus River; birthplace of the ancient Harappan civilization. (m. 131, t. 131)

Indus River (in′dəs riv′ər) A river that flows from Tibet, through the Himalayas and Hindu Kush into the Arabian Sea. (m. 131, t. 130)

Iraq (i rak′) A nation of western Asia that became independent in 1932. (m. 576, t. 576)

Israel (iz′rē əl) A country in western Asia, created in 1948 as a home for the Jews; ancient kingdom of Israelites. (m. 576, t. 577)

Istanbul (is tan bül′) Largest city in present-day Turkey; formerly the ancient city of Constantinople and later the capital of the Ottoman empire; 41°N, 29°E. (m. 390, t. 388)

J

Japan (jə pan′) An island nation off the eastern Asia mainland. (m. 616, t. 614)

Jerusalem (jə rü′sə ləm) An ancient city in western Asia; capital of present-day Israel; 31°N, 35°E. (m. 121, t. 124)

Johannesburg (jō han′əs bərg) The largest city in South Africa; 26°S, 28°E. (m. 607, t. 608)

Judea (jü dē′ə) The land in the eastern Mediterranean region populated by Jews at the time of the Roman empire. (m. 247, t. 246)

K

Kosala (kō sa′lə) An ancient kingdom in northern India where Siddhartha Gautama is said to have been born. (t. 151)

Kush (kŭsh) An ancient kingdom in northeastern Africa, conquered by Egypt. It later regained independence and flourished through trade between c. 500 B.C. and A.D. 150. (m. 86, t. 86)

Kyoto (kyō′tō) A city in Japan; formerly the emperor's capital during the rule of the shoguns; 35°N, 136°E. (m. 411, t. 413)

L

La Venta (lə vent′ə) An ancient island town of Middle America on the east coast of what is now Mexico; center of Olmec culture in 1000 B.C.; 18°N, 94°W. (m. 293, t. 294)

Lake Texcoco (lāk tā skō′kō) A lake in what is now Central Mexico on which the Aztec built Tenochtitlán. (t. 427)

Laos (lä′ōs) A nation in Southeast Asia, between northern Thailand and northern Vietnam. (m. 587, t. 586)

Latium (lā′shē əm) A plain on the west coast of Italy on which the city of Rome was built. (m. 225, t. 225)

Lima (lē′mə) The capital of Peru, founded by Francisco Pizarro in 1535; 12°S, 77°W. (m. 467, t. 469)

Lower Egypt (lō′ər ē′jipt) The northern part of ancient Egypt. (m. 71, t. 71)

M

Macedonia (mas i dō′nē ə) An ancient kingdom ruled by Alexander the Great that conquered Greece and the Persian empire in the 300s B.C. (m. 214, t. 213)

Machu Picchu (mäch′ü pēk′chü) The site of a ruined Inca city on a mountain in the Andes northwest of Cuzco, Peru; 13°S, 72°W. (m. 435, t. 438)

Mali (mä′lē) African empire that flourished between the 1200s and 1400s; a present-day country in West Africa. (m. 364, t. 364)

Mecca (mek′ə) An Arabian oasis city believed to be the birthplace of Muhammad; 21°N, 40°E. (m. 267, t. 267)

Medina (mə dē′nə) An Arabian oasis town to which, according to Muslim writings, Muhammad migrated in A.D. 622; 24°N, 40°E. (m. 267, t. 268)

Mediterranean Sea (med i tə rā′nē ən sē) A large, almost landlocked arm of the Atlantic Ocean touching Europe, Asia, and Africa. (m. 193, t. 192)

Mekong River (mā′kong′ riv′ər) A river in Southeast Asia that flows from Tibet to the South China Sea. (m. 399, t. 398)

Memphis (mem′fis) Capital of Egypt's Old Kingdom, located on the Nile near present-day Cairo; 29°N, 31°E. (m. 76, t. 76)

Mesopotamia (mes ə pə tā′mē ə) The region between the Tigris and Euphrates rivers; birthplace of the Sumerian and Babylonian civilizations. (m. 105, t. 105)

Mexico (mek′si kō) A nation in North America, south of the United States. (m. 623, t. 624)

Mexico City (mek′si kō sit′ē) The capital and largest city of Mexico; formerly Tenochtitlán, it became the capital of New Spain after the Spanish conquered the Aztec in the 1500s; 19°N, 99°W. (m. 467, t. 469)

Middle America (mid′əl ə mer′i kə) An ancient region of North America that included southern Mexico and much of Central America. It was the birthplace of the ancient Olmec and Maya civilizations. (m. 287, t. 286)

Middle East (mid′əl ēst) A region of southwestern Asia that stretches from Turkey to Iran. (m. 576, t. 574)

Mogadishu (mōg ə dish′ü) A coastal city that dominated African gold trade between about 1000 and 1300; the present-day capital of Somalia; 2°N, 45°E. (m. 373, t. 374)

Mohenjo-Daro (mō hen′jō där′ō) A city of the ancient Harappan civilization, located in the Indus Valley; 27°N, 68°E. (m. 135, t. 135)

Mombasa (mom bä′sä) An important Swahili city-state and trading center between 1100 and 1500; the main port of Kenya on the Indian Ocean; 4°N, 40°E. (m. 373, t. 374)

Morocco (mə rok′ō) A country in northwestern Africa on the Atlantic Ocean and Mediterranean Sea. (m. 570, t. 367)

Moscow (mäs′kou) The capital and largest city of Russia; 56°N, 38°E. (m. 533, t. 536)

Mount Everest (mount ev′ər əst) The tallest mountain in the world, located in the Himalayas on the border between Nepal and Tibet; 28°N, 87°E. (m. 385, t. 385)

Mount Kilimanjaro (mount kil ə mən jär′ō) The tallest mountain in Africa, located in northeastern Tanzania; 3°S, 37°E. (m. 355, t. 355)

pronunciation key

a **at**; ā **ape**; ä **far**; âr **care**; e **end**; ē **me**; i **it**; ī **ice**; îr **pierce**; o **hot**; ō **old**; ô **fork**; oi **oil**; ou **out**; u **up**; ū **use**; ü **rule**, ů **pull**; ûr **turn**; hw **white**; ng **song**; th **thin**; <u>th</u> **this**; zh **measure**; ə **about**, **taken**, **pencil**, **lemon**, **circus**

Mount Olympus (mount ə lim′pəs) The highest mountain in Greece, where the ancient Greeks believed many of their gods and goddesses lived; 40°N, 22°E. (m. 198, t. 200)

N

Nazareth (na′ zə rəth) A small town in northern Judea where, according to the New Testament, Jesus grew up; 32°N, 35°E. (m. 247, t. 247)

New Delhi (nü del′ē) The capital of India and one of the most populous cities in the world; 29°N, 77°E. (m. 15, t. 15)

New South Wales (nü south wālz) English Colony founded on the East Coast of Australia in 1788; currently a state of Australia. (m. 479, t. 478)

New Spain (nü spān) Spanish colony in North America including Mexico, Central America, the southwest United States, and many of the Caribbean Islands from the 1500s to the 1800s. (m. 467, t. 469)

Niger River (ni′jər riv′ər) A river flowing from western Africa into the Gulf of Guinea. (m. 355, t. 355)

Nile River (nil riv′ər) The world's longest river, which flows northward through East Africa into the Mediterranean Sea. (m. 71, t. 70)

Normandy (nôr′mən dē) A region in northwestern France on the English Channel. (m. 545, t. 326)

North America (nôrth ə mâr′i kə) The third-largest continent, located in the Western Hemisphere. (m. 623, t. 440)

North China Plain (nôrth chī′nə plān) A large, lowland region of eastern China that is watered by the Huang River; birthplace of Chinese civilization. (m. 161, t. 160)

North European Plain (nôrth yür ə pē′ən plān) A large, fertile area that extends from the Atlantic Ocean to the Ural Mountains. (m. 317, t. 318)

North Sea (nôrth sē) A large arm of the Atlantic Ocean, between Great Britain and continental Europe. (m. 317, t. 317)

Nubia (nü′bē ə) An ancient kingdom south of Egypt. (m. 86, t. 84)

Nunavut (nü′ nü vüt) A territory in Canada that is to be created for the Inuit in 1999. (t. 626)

P

Pacific Ocean (pə sif′ik ō′shən) The world's largest body of water, bounded by the Americas on the east and Asia and Australia on the west. (m. G5, t. 410)

Pakistan (pak′i stan) One of two independent nations formed in 1947 on the Indian subcontinent. (m. 583, t. 583)

Palestine (pal′ə stīn) Region in southwestern Asia that became the ancient home of the Jews; the ancient Roman name for Judea; in recent times, the British protectorate that became Israel in 1947. (m. 254, t. 253)

Pantheon (pan′thē on) A large, domed temple built in ancient Rome to honor many gods and goddesses. (t. 241)

Paris (par′is) Capital and largest city of France; 49°N, 2°E. (m. 601, t. 488)

Parthenon (pär′thə non) A temple to the goddess Athena, built 447–432 B.C. on the Acropolis in Athens. (t. 205)

Pearl Harbor (pûrl här′bər) A United States naval base in Hawaii that was bombed by the Japanese in 1941, causing the United States to enter World War II; 21°N, 158°W. (m. 544, t. 543)

Peloponnesus (pel ə pə nē′səs) A mountainous peninsula in southern Greece, between the Ionian and Aegean seas. (m. 193, t. 193)

Persian Gulf (pûr′zhən gulf) A body of water east of the Arabian peninsula that separates Arabia from Iran. (m. 263, t. 263)

Peru (pə rü′) Colonial lands held by Spain in South America from the 1500s to the 1800s; present-day country in western South America. (m. 467, t. 469)

Petra (pē′trə) The ancient Arabian capital of Nabataea, in what is today Jordan; 30°N, 35°E. (t. 264)

Phnom Penh (pə nom′ pen′) The capital of Cambodia; first became capital during the Khmer rule in the 1400s; 12°N, 105°E. (m. 399, t. 401)

Phoenicia (fə nē′shə) An ancient seafaring civilization located on the eastern shore of the Mediterranean Sea. (m. 193, t. 195)

Pompeii (pom pā′) An ancient city in southwestern Italy that was buried by the eruption of Mount Vesuvius in A.D. 79; 41°N, 14°E. (m. 240, t. 242)

Punt (pûnt) An ancient Egyptian name for an area of Africa south of Egypt. (m. 86, t. 87)

Q

Qin (chin) An ancient province in northern China that rose to power under Emperor Shihuangdi in 221 B.C. (m. 169, t. 168)

Qinling Mountains (chin′ling′ moun′tənz) A mountain range in north-central China. (m. 169, t. 169)

R

Red Sea (red sē) A narrow sea between Arabia and northeastern Africa. (m. 263, t. 263)

Rhodes (rōdz) A Greek island, lying east of Crete in the Aegean Sea. (m. 193, t. 193)

Rocky Mountains (rok′ē moun′tənz) A mountain range in North America that stretches from Alaska into Mexico. (m. 423, t. 422)

Rome (rōm) The former center of both the ancient Roman Republic and the Roman empire; capital of present-day Italy; 42°N, 12°E. (m. 225, t. 224)

Russia (rush′ə) A country in eastern Europe and northern Asia; the largest country in the world; a republic of the Soviet Union from 1922 to 1991. (m. 533, t. 532)

S

Sahara Desert (sə har′ə dez′ərt) The largest desert in the world, covering most of northern Africa. (m. 355, t. 355)

Sahel (sə hel′) The dry, grassy region south of the Sahara Desert, extending from Senegal to the Sudan. (m. 355, t. 355)

Santo Domingo (san′tō də ming′gō) A Spanish colony established on Hispaniola in 1496; the capital of the Dominican Republic; 19°N, 70°W. (m. 475, t. 475)

Sarajevo (sar ə yā′vō) The site of assassination that led to World War I; present-day capital of Bosnia; 44°N, 18°E. (m. 601, t. 527)

Seine River (sān riv′ər) A river that flows from eastern France northward into the English Channel. (m. 317, t. 319)

Serbia (sûr′bē ə) A country in eastern Europe. (m. 528, t. 527)

Sicily (sis′ə lē) An island in the Mediterranean Sea off the southwest tip of the Italian peninsula. (m. 225, t. 225)

Singapore (sing′ə pôr) A city and independent republic in Southeast Asia; 1°N, 104°E. (m. 616, t. 617)

Sofala (sō fäl′ə) A seaport village in eastern Mozambique; in the 1300s, an important trading center for the gold miners of Great Zimbabwe; 19°S, 35°E. (m. 377, t. 378)

Songhai (sông′hī) The most powerful empire in West Africa from about 1490 to 1590. (m. 364, t. 367)

South America (south ə mâr′i kə) The fourth-largest continent, located in the Western Hemisphere. (m. 623, t. 491)

South Korea (south kə rē′ə) A country in East Asia on the southern part of the Korean Peninsula; also a Pacific Rim nation. (m. 616, t. 617)

Southeast Asia (south ēst′ ā′zhə) A region of southern Asia bounded by the Indian and Pacific Oceans. (m. 587, t. 586)

Soviet Union (sō′vē et ūn′yən) The name commonly used for the Union of Soviet Socialist Republics, which was a country in eastern Europe and northern Asia; the largest country in the world from 1922–1991. (m. 544, t. 537)

Soweto (sə wē′tō) A black African township just outside Johannesburg, South Africa; 26°S, 28°E. (m. 607, t. 608)

Sparta (spär′tə) The largest ancient Greek city-state, located on the southern Peloponnesus; 37°N, 22°E. (m. 198, t. 198)

St. Petersburg (sānt pē′tərz bûrg) A Russian port city on the Baltic Sea; formerly the capital of Russia, it was called Leningrad when Russia was part of the Soviet Union; 60°N, 30°E. (m. 533, t. 534)

Strait of Magellan (strāt əv mə jel′ən) A narrow waterway at the southern tip of South America, linking the Atlantic and Pacific oceans. (m. 464, t. 465)

Suez Canal (sü ez′ kə nal′) A canal in northeastern Egypt connecting the Mediterranean and Red seas. (t. 569)

Sumer (sü′mər) A group of ancient city-states in southern Mesopotamia; the earliest civilization in Mesopotamia. (m. 110, t. 108)

T

Taj Mahal (täzh mə häl′) A grand tomb in Agra, India, built by Mogul emperor Shah Jahan to honor his wife. (t. 396)

Tenochtitlán (te noch tēt län′) The capital of the Aztec empire, founded around 1325 on the site of present-day Mexico City; 19°N, 99°W. (m. 427, t. 426)

Thailand (tī′land) A nation in Southeast Asia, formerly called Siam. (m. 587, t. 586)

Thebes (thēbz) An ancient city in Upper Egypt that became the capital of the New Kingdom; 26°N, 33°E. (m. 76, t. 81)

Tiananmen Square (tyen′än men skwâr) A square in Beijing, China where government troops killed hundreds of people who were demonstrating for democratic reform in 1989. (t. 619)

pronunciation key

a **at**; ā **ape**; ä **far**; âr **care**; e **end**; ē **me**; i **it**; ī **ice**; îr **pierce**; o **hot**; ō **old**; ô **fork**; oi **oil**; ou **out**; u **up**; ū **use**; ü **rule**; u̇ **pull**; ûr **turn**; hw **white**; ng **song**; th **thin**; <u>th</u> **this**; zh mea**s**ure; ə **a**bout, tak**e**n, penc**i**l, lem**o**n, circ**u**s

Tiber River (ti′bər riv′ər) A river flowing southward from north-central Italy across the Latium plain, and into the Tyrrhenian Sea. (m. 225, t. 225)

Tibetan Plateau (ti bet′ən pla tō′) A high mountain plateau in Asia. (m. 385, t. 385)

Tigris River (ti′gris riv′ər) A river in southwestern Asia that flows through the eastern part of the Fertile Crescent. (m. 105, t. 104)

Timbuktu (tim buk tü′) A trade and cultural center of the Songhai empire in the 1400s; a present-day town in the West African country of Mali; 16°N, 3°W. (m. 364, t. 364)

Tokyo (tō′kyō) The capital and largest city in Japan; formerly called Edo; 36°N, 140°W. (m. 411, t. 412)

Tonle Sap (tän lā′ sap′) A lake in western Cambodia. (m. 399, t. 399)

Turkey (tür′kē) A nation established in 1923 in western Asia and southeastern Europe. (m. 576, t. 576)

U

United States (ū ni′tid stāts) A nation mainly in North America consisting of fifty states, the District of Columbia, and several territories. (m. 623, t. 622)

Upper Egypt (up′ər ē′jipt) The southern part of ancient Egypt. (m. 71, t. 71)

V

Valley of Mexico (val′ē əv mek′si kō) A fertile valley between two mountain chains in central Mexico. (t. 427)

Valley of the Kings (val′ē əv thə kingz) West of Thebes in ancient Egypt, the burial place of 30 New Kingdom pharaohs; 26°N, 33°E. (m. 93, t. 88)

Venezuela (ven ə zwā′lə) A country in northern South America on the Caribbean Sea. (m. 493, t. 496)

Versailles (vâr sī′) A historic city in north-central France that contains the grand palace of Louis XIV; 49°N, 2°E. (t. 488)

Vietnam (vē et näm′) A nation in Southeast Asia that was divided from 1954 until 1975 into North Vietnam and South Vietnam. (m. 581, t. 586)

W

West Bank (west bangk) An area in western Asia west of the Jordan River; controlled by Israel from 1967 to 1995, after which Palestinians gained partial control. (m. 578, t. 577)

West Indies (west in′dēz) An archipelago stretching from Florida to Venezuela, separating the Caribbean Sea from the Atlantic Ocean. (m. 475, t. 474)

X

Xianyang (shē än′yang) Capital city of the Qin dynasty during the rule of the emperor Shihuangdi; 34°N, 109°E. (m. 169, t. 169)

Y

Yalta (yôl′tə) A resort city in Ukraine; site of meeting between Franklin Roosevelt, Winston Churchill, and Joseph Stalin in 1945; 44°N, 34°E. (t. 557)

Yemen (yem′ən) A present-day country in the mountainous southwestern area of Arabia; location of the ancient Sabaean civilization. (m. R10, t. 264)

Yugoslavia (yū gō slä′ vē ə) A nation that also included the republics of Bosnia and Herzegovina, Croatia, Macedonia, and Slovenia until 1991. (m. 601, t. 600)

Z

Zama (zä′mə) Site in northern Africa where the Roman army defeated the Carthaginian army in 202 B.C.; 36°N, 8°E. (m. 234, t. 235)

Zambezi River (zam bē′zē riv′ər) A river in southern Africa, flowing east through Zimbabwe and Mozambique into the Indian Ocean. (m. 355, t. 355)

Zanzibar (zan′zə bär) An important Swahili city-state and trading center between 1100 and 1500; an island port in Tanzania in the Indian Ocean; 6°S, 39°E. (m. 373, t. 374)

Biographical Dictionary

The Biographical Dictionary tells you about the people you have learned about in this book. The Pronunciation Key tells you how to say their names. The page numbers tell you where each person first appears in the text.

A

Abraham (ā′brə ham), 1700s B.C. Founder of Judaism who, according to the Bible, led his family from Ur to Canaan in obedience to God's command. (p. 121)

Ahmose (äm′ōs), d. 1546 B.C. New Kingdom pharaoh who drove the Hyksos out of the Nile Delta and reunited Egypt. (p. 85)

Akbar (ak′bär), A.D. 1542–1605 Ruler of the Mogul empire in India from A.D. 1556 to 1605. (p. 392)

Alexander II (al ig zan′dər), A.D. 1818–1881 Russian tsar who abolished serfdom in 1861. (p. 533)

Alexander the Great (al ig zan′dər), 356–323 B.C. King of Macedonia who conquered Greece, Persia, Egypt, and the Indus Valley; his conquests spread Greek culture throughout parts of three continents. (p. 212)

Amanishakhete (ä män ə shäk′hə tē), 100s B.C. Queen of Kush whose lavish tomb at Meroe reflects the richness of the Kingdom of Kush. (p. 359)

Arafat, Yasir (ar′ə fat), A.D. 1929– Leader of the Palestine Liberation Organization. (p. 577)

Aristide, Jean Bertrand (är′is tēd), A.D. 1953– Elected president of Haiti in 1990. (p. 625)

Aristotle (ar′ə stot əl), 384–322 B.C. Greek philosopher who was the private teacher of Alexander the Great. (p. 211)

Atahualpa (ä tə wäl′pə), A.D. 1502?–1533 The last Inca emperor, captured and killed by Francisco Pizarro. (p. 469)

Augustus (ô gus′təs), 63 B.C.–A.D. 14 First Roman emperor; won the civil war following Julius Caesar's assassination and went on to unify the empire and establish the Pax Romana. (p. 236)

Avicenna (av ə sen′ə), A.D. 980–1037 Persian philosopher and physician; wrote a medical encyclopedia that became a standard text in North Africa, western Asia, and Europe. (p. 274)

B

Ben-Gurion, David (ben gùr′ē ən), A.D. 1886–1973 Israeli prime minister from 1949 to 1953 and from 1955 to 1963; he proclaimed Israel to be a new and independent country on May 14, 1948. (p. 577)

Benedict (ben′i dikt), A.D. 480?–547 Italian monk; founder of the Benedictine order. (p. 331)

Bolívar, Simón (bō lē′vär, sē mōn′), A.D. 1783–1830 Leader of the struggle for independence in South America; his armies freed Colombia, Venezuela, and Peru from Spanish rule. (p. 492)

C

Cabral, Pedro Álvarez (kə bräl′), A.D. 1467?–1520? Portuguese navigator who landed on the coast of Brazil in 1500 and claimed it for Portugal. (p. 467)

Caesar, Julius (sē′zər, jül′yəs), 100–44 B.C. Roman general who became the republic's dictator in 45 B.C. (p. 237)

Castro, Fidel (kas′trō), A.D. 1926– Cuban revolutionary leader; premier of Cuba since 1959. (p. 560)

Charlemagne (shär′lə män), A.D. 742–814 King of the Franks from 768 to 814, and emperor of Rome from 800 to 814. (p. 321)

Chiang Kai-shek (chang′kī shek′), A.D. 1887–1975 Chinese Nationalist leader and president of Taiwan from 1950 to 1975. (p. 552)

Churchill, Winston (chûr′chil), A.D. 1874–1965 British prime minister from 1940 to 1945 and 1951 to 1955. He led Britain during World War II. (p. 543)

Cleopatra (klē ə pa′trə), 69–30 B.C. Ruler of the Egyptian government in Alexandria who backed Caesar in the civil war he waged from 49 to 45 B.C. (p. 237)

Columbus, Christopher (kə lum′ bəs), A.D. 1451?–1506 Italian explorer in the service of Spain who arrived in the Americas in 1492. (p. 464)

Confucius (kən fū′shəs), 551–479 B.C. Chinese philosopher who stressed the need to respect tradition; his teachings discussed the right and wrong uses of power. (p. 174)

Constantine (kon′stən tēn), A.D. 280–337 Roman emperor who founded Constantinople as the new eastern capital of the Roman empire. (p. 254)

pronunciation key

a	**at**	ī	**ice**	u	**up**	th	**thin**
ā	**ape**	îr	**pierce**	ū	**use**	th	**this**
ä	**far**	o	**hot**	ü	**rule**	zh	**measure**
âr	**care**	ō	**old**	ù	**pull**	ə	**about, taken,**
e	**end**	ô	**fork**	ûr	**turn**		**pencil, lemon,**
ē	**me**	oi	**oil**	hw	**white**		**circus**
i	**it**	ou	**out**	ng	**song**		

Cook, James (kŭk, jāmz), A.D. 1728–1779 A navigator and ship captain who explored and claimed land in Australia for England in 1770. (p. 479)

Copernicus, Nicolaus (kə pûr′ni kəs), A.D. 1473–1543 Polish astronomer; in 1514 he discovered that Earth and the other planets revolve around the sun. (p. 339)

Cortés, Hernando (kôr tes′, er nän′dō), A.D. 1485–1547 Spanish conquistador who defeated the Aztec in 1521. (p. 468)

D

Da Gama, Vasco (də gä′mə, väs′cō), A.D. 1460?–1524 Portuguese navigator who in 1498 sailed from Europe around Africa to Asia. (p. 464)

Da Vinci, Leonardo (də vin′chē, lē ə när′dō), A.D. 1452–1519 Italian Renaissance artist, inventor, and scientist. (p. 338)

De Klerk, F.W. (də klerk′), A.D. 1936– South African president from 1989 to 1994. He worked for a peaceful transition from the policy of apartheid to majority rule in South Africa. (p. 610)

Deng Xiaoping (dung′ shou′ping′), A.D. 1904–1997 Chairman of the Chinese Communist Party and of the People's Republic of China. (p. 618)

Dias, Bartholomeu (dē′ash, bâr tù lù mā′ù), A.D. 1450?–1500 Portuguese ship captain whose voyage around the southern tip of Africa in 1487 led to the opening of a sea route between Europe and Asia. (p. 464)

Diocletian (dī ə klē′shən), A.D. 245–313 Roman emperor who divided the empire in two and oversaw the eastern part. (p. 253)

E

Elizabeth I (i liz′ə bəth), A.D. 1533–1603 Queen of England from 1558 to 1603; the English Renaissance flourished during her reign. (p. 346)

Equiano, Olaudah (i kwē ä′nō, ōl′ə dä), A.D. 1750–1797 Enslaved African writer. In 1789 he wrote an autobiography describing his life in slavery. (p. 476)

Erasmus (i raz′məs), A.D. 1466?–1536 Dutch writer and humanist; he favored reform of the Catholic Church but came to oppose the Protestant Reformation. (p. 343)

F

Francis of Assisi (fran′sis əv ə sē′zē), A.D. 1181–1226 Italian monk who founded the Franciscan order; he devoted his life to serving the poor and sick. (p. 332)

Frank, Anne (frangk), A.D. 1929–1945 Dutch-Jewish girl who, with other Jews, hid from the Nazis from 1942 to 1944; she was found and sent to a concentration camp where she died. (p. 546)

Franz Ferdinand (franz fur′də nand), A.D. 1863–1914 Archduke of Austria whose assassination led to the outbreak of World War I. (p. 527)

Fu Hao (fü′hou′), 1100s B.C. A Chinese king's wife who led troops to war. Her tomb contained records of her life and times. (p. 166)

G

Galilei, Galileo (gal ə lā′ē, gal ə lā′ō), A.D. 1564–1642 Italian astronomer, mathematician, and physicist. His telescopes proved the sun is the center of the solar system. (p. 456)

Gandhi, Indira (gän′dē), A.D. 1917–1984 Prime minister of India from 1966 to 1977 and from 1980 to 1984. (p. 17)

Gandhi, Mohandas (gän′dē), A.D. 1869–1948 Indian political and religious leader; he supported the use of nonviolent methods to bring about change. (p. 580)

Genghis Khan (geng′gəs kän′), A.D. 1162?–1227 Mongol conqueror. At its peak, his empire included China, western Asia, and parts of eastern Europe. (p. 403)

Gorbachev, Mikhail (gôr′bə chəf), A.D. 1931– Soviet secretary general of the Communist Party from 1985 to 1990, and last president of the Soviet Union, 1990–1991. (p. 597)

Gutenberg, Johannes (gü′tən bûrg), A.D. 1400?–1468 German printer; in 1448 he invented a printing press that used movable type. (p. 344)

H

Hammurabi (hä mù rä′bē), 1800?–1750? B.C. King of the Babylonian empire; creator of the Code of Hammurabi, one of the world's oldest codes of law. (p. 112)

Han Gaozu (hän′gou′zü′), 200s B.C. A farmer-turned-general who, in 206 B.C., overthrew the Qin dynasty; he founded the Han dynasty. (p. 174)

Hannibal (han′ə bəl), 247?–183? B.C. General of Carthage who marched his army from Spain to Rome in the Second Punic War. (p. 234)

Hargreaves, James (här′grēvz), A.D. 1720–1778 English inventor of the spinning jenny. (p. 503)

Hatshepsut (hat shep′süt), 1520?–1482 B.C. One of the few women Egyptian pharaohs; organized a trade expedition to Egypt's southern neighbor, Punt. (p. 87)

Henry VIII (hen′rē), A.D. 1491–1547 King of England from 1509 to 1547 and founder of the Church of England; he broke with the Catholic Church because the pope would not grant him a divorce. (p. 345)

Henry, Prince (hen′rē), A.D. 1394–1460 Portuguese prince who directed the search for a sea route to the gold mines of western Africa. He also designed a fast, steerable ship known as a caravel. (p. 463)

Hidalgo, Miguel (ē däl′gō), A.D. 1753–1811 Mexican priest and revolutionary who led a revolt that started the Mexican war of independence. (p. 494)

Hitler, Adolf (hit′lər), A.D. 1889–1945 German dictator. He founded the National Socialist (Nazi) Party, which led Germany during World War II. (p. 540)

Ho Chi Minh (hō′chē′min′), A.D. 1890–1969 Communist leader in Vietnam who became head of the communist government in 1945. (p. 586)

Homer (hō′mûr), 700s B.C. Ancient Greek poet. (p. 200)

I

Iturbide, Agustin de (ē tür bē′de), A.D. 1783–1824 Mexican soldier and leader; he won Mexican independence from Spain and became ruler of Mexico from 1822 to 1823. (p. 495)

J

Jayavarman II (jä yä vär′män), A.D. 800s One of the first Khmer kings of Cambodia. (p. 399)

Jesus (jē′zəs), 4? B.C.–A.D. 29? Religious leader and founder of Christianity. (p. 247)

Jinnah, Mohammad Ali (jin′ə), A.D. 1876–1948 First president of Pakistan from 1947 to 1948. (p. 583)

John I (jon), A.D. 1167?–1216 King of England from A.D. 1199 to 1216; in 1215 he signed the Magna Carta, giving more rights to British nobles. (p. 326)

K

Kay, John (kā), A.D. 1704–1764 English watchmaker who invented the flying shuttle used in weaving. (p. 503)

Kennedy, John F. (ken′i dē), A.D. 1917–1963 The 35th President of the United States from 1961 to 1963. He successfully negotiated the removal of Soviet nuclear missiles from Cuba. (p. 560)

Khadija (ka dē′jä), d. A.D. 619 A wealthy merchant who became the first wife of Muhammad. (p. 267)

Khrushchev, Nikita (krüsh′chef), A.D. 1894–1971

Secretary general of the Soviet Communist Party from 1958 to 1964. (p. 560)

Khufu (kü fü′), 2650?–2600? B.C. Egyptian pharaoh who built the Great Pyramid. (p. 81)

Kublai Khan (kü′blə kän′), A.D. 1215–1294 Grandson of Genghis Khan, founder of China's Yuan Dynasty. (p. 403)

L

Lady Murasaki Shikibu (mūr ä säk′ē shē kē′bū), A.D. 978?–1026? Japanese author who wrote *The Tale of Genji*, which is thought to be the world's first novel. (p. 414)

Lalibela (lä′lē be lä), b. A.D. 1100s Zagwe king who ruled Ethiopia from about A.D. 1185 to 1225. (p. 360)

Lenin, Vladimir Ilyich (len′in), A.D. 1870–1924 Bolshevik leader and founder of the Soviet Union. (p. 536)

Livy (liv′ē), 59 B.C.–A.D. 17 Historian of the Roman Republic who wrote about the struggle between plebeians and patricians of Rome. (p. 231)

Louis XVI (lü′ē), A.D. 1754–1793 King of France from 1774 to 1792; executed during the French Revolution. (p. 486)

Luther, Martin (lüth′ər), A.D. 1483–1546 German monk and leader of the Protestant Reformation. (p. 342)

M

Macquarie, Lachlan (mak wôr′ ē, läk län), A.D. 1761–1824 Governor of the English colony of New South Wales in Australia from 1810 to 1821. He supported the rights of the emancipees in New South Wales. (p. 481)

Magellan, Ferdinand (mə jel′ən), A.D. 1480?–1521 Portuguese explorer in the service of Spain; he set out to find a route to Asia by sailing around the southern tip of South America. (p. 462)

Mandela, Nelson (man del′ə), A.D. 1918– South African civil rights leader who became president of South Africa in 1994. (p. 606)

Mansa Musa (män′sä mü′sä), A.D. 1297?–1337? Emperor of Mali from 1312 to 1337, when the kingdom was at its peak of wealth and power. (p. 366)

Mao Zedong (mou′dze′dùng′), A.D. 1893–1976 Chinese communist leader and founder of the People's Republic of China. (p. 552)

Marie Antoinette (mə rē′ an twə net′), A.D. 1755–1793 Queen of France from 1774 to 1792, who was executed during the French Revolution. (p. 490)

Marx, Karl (märks), A.D. 1818–1883 German philosopher and economist. His ideas, called Marxism, formed the basis of communism. (p. 505)

Medici, Lorenzo (med′i chē), A.D. 1449–1492 Ruler of Florence during the Renaissance and patron of artists such as Michelangelo. (p. 337)

Meiji (mā′jē′), A.D. 1852–1912 Japanese emperor from 1867 to 1912 who led Japan into a period of rapid modernization. (p. 510)

Menes (mē′nēz), 3100? B.C. King of Upper Egypt who united Upper and Lower Egypt. (p. 75)

Michelangelo (mī kəl an′jə lō), A.D. 1475–1564 Italian Renaissance sculptor, painter, architect, and poet. (p. 338)

Moctezuma (mäk tə zü′mə), A.D. 1468?–1520 Aztec emperor defeated and killed by the Spanish conquistador Hernando Cortés in 1520. (p. 468)

Morelos, José María (mō re′lōs), A.D. 1765–1815 Mexican priest and revolutionary who succeeded Miguel Hidalgo as rebel leader and issued a declaration of independence from Spain in 1813. He was captured and killed by Spanish soldiers in 1815. (p. 495)

Moses (mō′ziz), 1200s B.C. Prophet who led the Israelites out of slavery in Egypt. (p. 122)

Muhammad (mú ham′əd), A.D. 570?–632? Founder of Islam whose words are recorded in the Quran. (p. 267)

Mumtaz Mahal (mùm täz′ mä häl′), A.D. 1592–1631 Wife of Shah Jahan, emperor of India; the Taj Mahal in Agra, India, was built in her memory. (p. 396)

N

Napoleon Bonaparte (nə pō′lē ən bō′nə pärt), A.D. 1769–1821 French revolutionary general who became Emperor Napoleon I of France in 1804. (p. 491)

Nasser, Gamal Abdel (nas′ər), A.D. 1918–1970 First President of Egypt from 1956 to 1958, and of the United Arab Republic from 1958 to 1970. (p. 569)

Nehru, Jawaharlal (nā′rü), A.D. 1889–1964 Prime minister of India from 1947 to 1964 and father of Indira Gandhi; close associate of Mohandas Gandhi. (p. 583)

Newton, Isaac (nü′tən), A.D. 1642–1727 English scientist who studied gravity. (p. 459)

Nicholas II (nik′ə ləs), A.D. 1868–1918 Last Russian tsar from 1894 to 1917. Discontent with his policies led to the Russian Revolution of 1917. (p. 534)

Nkrumah, Kwame (en krü′mə), A.D. 1909–1972 Leader in the liberation of the Gold Coast from British rule and first president of Ghana from 1960 to 1966. (p. 567)

O

Osman (äs män′), A.D. 1258–1326? Founder of the Ottoman empire. (p. 389)

P

Pachakuti Inca (pä chä kü′tē), d. A.D. 1471 Inca emperor from 1438 to 1471; he greatly extended Inca borders in 1438 and became known as Sapa Inca, or Supreme Inca. (p. 435)

Paul (pôl), A.D. 11?–67? Follower of Jesus who helped spread Christianity throughout the Roman world. (p. 250)

Pericles (per′i klēz), 495?–429 B.C. Athenian general who led Athens during the war with Sparta; he made sure that poor as well as rich citizens could take part in government. (p. 206)

Perry, Matthew (per′ē), A.D. 1794–1858 U.S. naval officer who sailed to Japan in 1853 with a demand that Japanese ports be opened to U.S. trade. (p. 509)

Peter (pē′tər), A.D. 5?–67? One of the 12 apostles of Jesus; Roman Catholics consider him to be the first pope, or bishop of Rome. (p. 248)

Petrarch (pē′trärk), A.D. 1304–1374 Italian Renaissance poet and humanist. (p. 338)

Pizarro, Francisco (pē sär′rō), A.D. 1471?–1541 Spanish conquistador who in 1532 defeated the Inca emperor Atahualpa. (p. 468)

Plato (plā′tō), 428?–347? B.C. Greek philosopher and student of Socrates. (p. 201)

Polo, Marco (pō′lō), A.D. 1254–1324 Italian merchant who traveled to China, where he lived for 17 years, at times serving as diplomat for Kublai Khan. (p. 403)

Pope Urban II (ur′bən), A.D. 1042–1099 Pope who called for the First Crusade to reclaim Jerusalem from the Muslims. (p. 332)

R

Rabin, Yitzhak (rä bēn′), A.D. 1922–1995 Prime minister of Israel who negotiated a peace plan with Palestinians in the West Bank and Gaza. (p. 578)

Robespierre, Maximilien (rōbz′pē âr), A.D. 1758–1794 French revolutionary. He sent suspected traitors to the guillotine during the Reign of Terror from 1793 until his own death by guillotine in 1794. (p. 490)

Roosevelt, Franklin Delano (rō′zə velt), A.D. 1882–1945 The 32nd President of the United States. He led the nation against the Axis powers in World War II. (p. 543)

S

Sadat, Anwar (sə dat′), A.D. 1918–1981 Egyptian president who established peaceful relations with Israel in 1978. (p. 577)

San Martín, José de (sän mär tēn′), A.D. 1778–1850 Argentine soldier who led revolutions that freed Argentina and Chile from Spanish rule. (p. 496)

Sargon (sär′gon), died 2279? B.C. King of the city-state Kish; united the city-states of Sumer to create an empire. (p. 111)

Schliemann, Heinrich (shlē′män, hīn′rikh), A.D. 1822–1890 German archaeologist and discoverer of the remains of Troy. (p. 30)

Scipio (sip′ē`ō), 234?–183? B.C. Roman general who defeated Hannibal in the Battle of Zama outside Carthage, North Africa, in 202 B.C. (p. 235)

Shah Jahan (shä jə hän′), A.D. 1592–1666 Mogul emperor of India; he built the Taj Mahal in Agra, India, in memory of his wife Mumtaz Mahal. (p. 396)

Shakespeare, William (shāk′spēr), A.D. 1564–1616 English dramatist and poet; considered one of the greatest writers in the English language. (p. 346)

Shihuangdi (shē′hwäng dē), 259?–210 B.C. Chinese emperor who founded the Qin dynasty and unified China with a standardized system of writing and money; his tomb contained the famous "clay army." (p. 168)

Siddhartha Gautama (sid där′tə gô′tə mə), 563?– 483? B.C. Ancient Indian religious leader known as the Buddha, or Enlightened One, who founded Buddhism. (p. 150)

Sinan (sə nän′), A.D. 1489–1588 Süleyman's chief architect; he designed more than 300 buildings, including the mosque in Istanbul. (p. 390)

Socrates (sok′rə tēz), 470?–399 B.C. Greek philosopher who discussed laws, customs, values, and religion with students; accused of urging young people to revolt, he was sentenced to death. (p. 206)

Spindler, Konrad (shpin′dlər), A.D. 1939– German archaeologist who analyzed the 5,000–year–old "Iceman" body found in the Alps in 1991. (p. 33)

Stalin, Josef (stä′lin), A.D. 1879–1953 Soviet revolutionary and dictator who ruled the Soviet Union from 1924 to 1953. (p. 537)

Süleyman (sü′lā män), A.D. 1495?–1566 Sultan of the Ottoman empire during its peak from 1520 to 1566. (p. 389)

Sun Yat-sen (sün′ yät sen′), A.D. 1866–1925 Leader of the Chinese Nationalists and founder of the Republic of China in 1912. (p. 550)

Sunjata (sän jä′tä), d. A.D. 1255 King of Mali who conquered all of Ghana. (p. 364)

Suryavarman II (sur yə vär′mən), A.D. 1100s Khmer king who filled his capital city of Angkor with magnificent Hindu temples. (p. 400)

T

Tokugawa Ieyasu (tō kù gä′wä ē yä′sü), A.D. 1543–1616 Shogun, or military commander, of the Tokugawa dynasty from 1603 to 1605; his family's shogunate kept Japan peaceful for more than 200 years. (p. 412)

Toussaint L'Ouverture (tü san′ lü vər tyùr′), A.D. 1743?–1803 Haitian general; in 1802 he led a successful slave revolution, leading to the independence of Haiti in 1804. (p. 493)

Tutankhamun (tü täng kä′mən), 1371?–1352 B.C. Egyptian pharaoh who ruled from about the ages of 7 to 17; his tomb remained nearly untouched until its discovery in 1922. (p. 88)

V

Veale, Elizabeth (vēl, i liz′ ə bəth), A.D. 1767–1850 Early colonist of the English colony of New South Wales in Australia who helped establish the production of wool as an important Australian industry. (p. 480)

W

Walesa, Lech (wə len′sə), A.D. 1943– Polish labor leader who became the first president of democratic Poland in 1990. (p. 598)

Watt, James (wot), A.D. 1736–1819 Scottish engineer and inventor who developed a steam engine that burned coal in 1765. (p. 503)

William the Conqueror (wil′yəm), A.D. 1027–1087 Norman king; in 1066 he defeated Harold, the Anglo-Saxon king, to become the first Norman king of England. (p. 326)

Wudi (wü′dē′), 100s B.C. Han emperor who ruled China from 140 B.C. to 87 B.C.; he set up a system of schools that prepared students for government jobs. (p. 176)

Y

Yeltsin, Boris (yel′tsin), A.D. 1931– Russian politician; in 1991 he became the first president of post-Soviet Russia. (p. 599)

Yoritomo (yōr ē tō′mō), A.D. 1147–1199 Japanese shogun, or military commander; in 1192 he attained supreme power from the emperor and ruled the country as a military dictator. (p. 411)

pronunciation key

a **at**; ā **ape**; ä **far**; âr **care**; e **end**; ē **me**; i **it**; ī **ice**; îr **pierce**; o **hot**; ō **old**; ô **fork**; oi **oil**; ou **out**; u **up**; ū **use**; ü **rule**; ù **pull**; ûr **turn**; hw **white**; ng **song**; th **thin**; <u>th</u> **this**; zh **measure**; ə **about, taken, pencil, lemon, circus**

Glossary

This Glossary will help you to pronounce and understand the meanings of the vocabulary in this book. The page number at the end of the definition tells where the word first appears.

A

aborigine (ab′ ə rij′ ə nē) A person belonging to, or descending from, the group of people who first inhabited Australia. (p. 479)

absolute monarchy (ab′sə lüt mon′ər kē) A form of government headed by a ruler, or monarch, with unlimited power. *See* **divine right.** (p. 486)

accuracy (ak′yər ə sē) Being true or correct. (p. 604)

acropolis (ə krop′ə lis) A large hill in ancient Greece where city residents sought shelter and safety in times of war and met to discuss community affairs. (p. 197)

agora (ag′ər ə) A central area in Greek cities used both as a marketplace and as a meeting place. (p. 197)

agriculture (ag′ri kul chər) The raising of crops and animals for human use. (p. 52)

algebra (al′je brə) A type of mathematics to which Muslims made great contributions. (p. 275)

alliance (ə li′əns) An agreement between countries to work together in war or trade. (p. 527)

Allied Powers (al′id pou′ərz) In World War I, the nations allied against the Central Powers; included Serbia, Russia, France, Britain, and the United States. (p. 528)

Allies (al′īz) In World War II, the nations allied against the Axis powers, including Britain, France, the Soviet Union, the United States, and China. (p. 543)

anti-semitism (an tē sem′i tiz əm) Discrimination against and hatred of Jews. (p. 575)

apartheid (ə pär′tīd) The government policy of strict and unequal segregation of the races as practiced in South Africa from 1948 to the early 1990s. (p. 607)

apostle (ə pos′əl) One of the 12 closest followers of Jesus, chosen by him to help him teach. (p. 248)

aqueduct (ak′wə dukt) A high, arched structure built to carry water over long distances. (p. 238)

archaeology (är kē ol′ə jē) The study of the remains of past cultures. (p. 32)

archipelago (är kə pel′ə gō) A large group of islands. (p. 385)

architecture (är′ki tek chər) The science of planning and constructing buildings. (p. 257)

aristocracy (ar ə stok′rə sē) The class of a society made up of members of noble families, usually the most powerful group. (p. 487)

armada (är mä′də) A fleet of warships. (p. 346)

armistice (är′mə stis) An agreement to stop fighting; a truce. (p. 531)

artifact (är′tə fakt) An object made by someone in the past. (p. 25)

assembly (ə sem′blē) A lawmaking body of government made up of a group of citizens. (p. 206)

astrolabe (as′trə lāb) An instrument invented by Muslims that is used to determine direction by figuring out the position of the stars. (p. 275)

Axis (ak′sis) In World War II, the nations who fought the Allies, including Japan, Germany, and Italy. (p. 543)

B

bilingual (bī ling′gwəl) Able to speak two languages. (p. 626)

bishop (bish′ əp) A church official who leads a large group of Christians in a particular region. (p. 251)

boycott (boi′kot) A form of protest in which people join together to refuse to buy goods. (p. 568)

Buddhism (bůd′iz əm) A religion founded in India by Siddhartha Gautama which teaches that the most important thing in life is to reach peace by ending suffering. (p. 150)

bureaucracy (byů rok′rə sē) The large organization that runs the daily business of government. (p. 511)

pronunciation key

a	at	ī	ice	u	up	th	thin
ā	ape	îr	pierce	ū	use	th	this
ä	far	o	hot	ü	rule	zh	measure
âr	care	ō	old	ů	pull	ə	about, taken,
e	end	ô	fork	ûr	turn		pencil, lemon,
ē	me	oi	oil	hw	white		circus
i	it	ou	out	ng	song		

c

caliph (kā′lif) A Muslim leader who had both political and religious authority. (p. 273)

caravan (kar′ə van) A group of people and animals traveling together for safety, especially through a desert. (p. 264)

caravel (kar′ə vel) A sailing ship developed in Portugal in the 1400s that had greater directional control than earlier ships and could sail great distances more safely. (p. 463)

cardinal directions (kärd′ən əl di rek′shənz) The directions north, south, east, and west. (p. G6)

cartogram (kär′tə gram) A special kind of map that distorts the shapes and sizes of countries or other political regions to present economic or other kinds of data for comparison. (p. 506)

caste system (kast sis′təm) The social system in Hindu society in which a person's place is determined by the rank of the family into which he or she is born. (p. 144)

cathedral (kə thē′drəl) A large or important Christian church. (p. 332)

cause (kôz) Something that makes something else happen. *See* **effect**. (p. 118)

census (sen′səs) A periodic count of all the people living in a country, city, or other region. (p. 239)

Central Powers (sen′trəl pou′ərz) In World War I, the nations who fought against the Allied Powers, including Austria-Hungary and Germany. (p. 528)

chinampas (chin äm′paz) One of the floating islands made by the Aztec around Tenochtitlán for growing crops. (p. 427)

Christianity (kris chē an′i tē) A religion based on the teachings of Jesus, as recorded in the New Testament. (p. 246)

circa (sûr′kə) A Latin word, often abbreviated "c." that means "about" or "around." (p. 59)

citadel (sit′ə dəl) A walled fort that protects a city. (p. 135)

citizen (sit′ə zən) A person with certain rights and responsibilities in his or her country or community. (p. 197)

city-state (sit′ē stāt) A self-governing city, often with surrounding lands and villages. (p. 110)

civil disobedience (siv′əl dis ə bē′dēəns) A means of protest by refusing to obey a law that is considered to be unjust. (p. 582)

civil war (siv′əl wôr) An armed conflict between groups within one country. (p. 237)

civilization (siv ə lə zā′shən) A culture that has developed systems of specialization, religion, learning, and government. (p. 55)

Classic Period (klas′ik pêr′ē əd) A time of great cultural achievement for a civilization. (p. 299)

climate (klī′ mit) The weather pattern of an area over a long period of time. (p. 9)

climograph (klī′mə graf) A graph that shows the temperature and precipitation in a place over a period of months. (p. 290)

code of law (kōd uv lô) A written set of laws that apply to everyone under a government. (p. 113)

codex (kō′deks) A manuscript page such as the kind used by the Aztec to record historical, religious, governmental and scientific knowledge. (p. 430)

Cold War (kōld wôr) A term used for the battle of words and ideas that developed between the democratic nations of the West and the Soviet Union and Eastern Europe from about 1945 to 1990. (p. 556)

colony (kol′ ə nē) A territory or community that is under the control of another country. (p. 201)

commune (kom′ūn) A community in which resources, work, and living space are shared by all members of the group. (p. 554)

communism (kom′yə niz əm) A system in which the government owns all property and makes nearly all decisions for its citizens. (p. 537)

compass rose (kum′pəs rōz) A drawing on a map that shows directions. (p. G6)

concentration camp (kon sən trā′shən kamp) A place where people are imprisoned because of their heritage, religious beliefs, or political views. (p. 546)

conclusion (kən klü′zhən) A final statement or opinion reached by putting together information about a subject. (p. 210)

confederation (kən fed ə rā′shən) A group of states or provinces under a central government. (p. 497)

Confucianism (kən fū′shə niz əm) In China, a system of beliefs and behavior based on the teachings of Confucius, who said that people should lead good lives by studying ancient traditions; stressed the importance of respecting one's family and ancestors. (p. 175)

conquistador (kon kēs′tə dôr) A Spanish conqueror who came to the Americas to search for gold, land, and glory. (p. 468)

consul (kon′səl) One of two elected officials of the Roman Republic who commanded the army and were supreme judges. (p. 232)

continent (kon′tə nənt) One of Earth's seven large bodies of land. (p. G4)

convent (kon'vent) A religious community in which women, or nuns, live and pray. *See* **nun.** (p. 331)

convert (kən vūrt') To adopt or cause someone to adopt a new religion. (p. 470)

convict (kon' vikt) A person who has been found guilty by the government of committing a crime and receives a sentence of punishment. (p. 480)

credibility (kre də bi'lə tē) Believability. (p. 472)

Crusade (krü sād') Any of the journeys and battles undertaken by European Christians between 1095 and 1270, to win control of the Holy Land (Palestine) from the Muslims. (p. 332)

Cultural Revolution (kul'chər əl rev ə lü'shən) A campaign in China, 1966–1976, when the Communist Party under Mao Zedong called for the destruction of all noncommunist beliefs. (p. 554)

culture (kul' chər) The way of life of a group of people at a particular time, including their daily habits, beliefs, and arts. (p. 10)

cuneiform (kū nē' ə fōrm) A system of writing that used wedge-shaped symbols to represent sounds, ideas, and objects; developed in ancient Sumer. (p. 108)

custom (kus'təm) A way of living that people of the same culture practice regularly over time. (p. 14)

D

decision (di sizh'ən) a choice made from a number of alternatives. *See* **conclusion.** (p. 30)

Declaration of the Rights of Man and of the Citizen (dek lə rā'shən) A statement issued by the French National Assembly in August 1789 that all men were "born and remain free and equal in rights." (p. 488)

deforestation (dē for ə stā'shən) The process of clearing the land of forests, often to make space for farms and cities. (p. 318)

degree (di grē') In geography, a unit of measurement that indicates the distance between lines of latitude and longitude; a unit of measurement for temperature. (p. 12)

delta (del'tə) The flat, fan-shaped land made of silt deposited at the mouth of a river. (p. 71)

demand (di mand') In economics, people's desire for a particular item. *See* **supply.** (p. 363)

democracy (di mok'rə sē) A system of government in which citizens vote to make governmental decisions. (p. 199)

depression (di presh'ən) A severe slowdown in business characterized by high unemployment and falling prices. (p. 541)

dharma (där'me) In Hinduism, the laws and duties that guide the behavior of each caste member. (p. 145)

Diaspora (dī as'pər ə) The scattering of Jews to many parts of the world. (p. 125)

dictator (dik'tā tər) A ruler who has absolute power. (p. 237)

distortion (di stôr'shən) In cartography, or map-making, the unavoidable inaccuracy caused by stretching or cutting parts of the globe to fit them onto a flat map. (p. 432)

distribution map (dis trə bū'shən map) A special purpose map that shows how a particular feature such as population density is spread over an area. (p. G11)

diversity (di vûr'si tê) Differences; variety. (p. 440)

divine right (di vīn' rīt) The belief that a monarch received authority to rule from God and therefore could not be questioned. *See* **absolute monarchy.** (p. 486)

domesticate (də mes'ti kāt) To train plants or animals to be useful to people. (p. 53)

drought (drout) A long period of dry weather. (p. 105)

dynasty (dī'nə stê) A line of rulers who belong to the same family. (p. 164)

E

Eastern Orthodox Christianity (ēs'tərn ôr'thə doks kris chē an'i tē) A branch of Christianity that developed in the Byzantine Empire and that did not recognize the pope as its supreme leader. (p. 255)

economy (i kon'ə mē) The way people manage money and resources for the production of goods and services. (p. 77)

effect (i fekt') Something that happens as a result of a cause. *See* **cause.** (p. 118)

Eightfold Path (āt'fōld path) In Buddhism, the basic rules of behavior and belief leading to an end of suffering. *See* **Four Noble Truths.** (p. 153)

elevation (el ə vā'shən) Height above sea level. (p. 228)

elevation map (el ə vā'shən map) A map that shows the height of land above sea level. (p. G10)

emancipee (i man' sə pē) A person who has been freed, or emancipated, from a sentence of punishment given to him or her by the government. (p. 481)

emperor (em'pər ər) The supreme ruler of an empire. (p. 168)

empire (em'pīr) A group of lands and peoples ruled by one government. (p. 86)

Glossary

equal-area projection (ē'kwəl ār'ē ə prə jek'shən) A map that is useful for comparing sizes of land masses, on which shapes at the center are fairly accurate but are very distorted at the edges of the map. (p. 432)

equator (i kwā'tər) An imaginary line circling Earth halfway between the North and South poles and dividing Earth into Northern and Southern Hemispheres. (p. G4)

erosion (i rō'zhən) The gradual wearing away of soil and rock by wind, glaciers, or water. (p. 162)

estates (e stāts') The three social classes into which France was divided before the French Revolution, including the clergy, the aristocracy, and the common people. (p. 487)

ethnic group (eth'nik grüp) A people who share a heritage of common customs, values, and language. (p. 599)

European Union (EU) (yür ə pē'ən ūn'yən) A group of European nations working to build a common economy and create cultural ties throughout Europe. (p. 601)

evaluate (i val'ū āt) To judge. (p. 31)

excavate (eks' kə vāt') To dig or to scoop out earth. (p. 32)

expedition (ek spi dish'ən) A group of people who go on a trip for a specific reason. (p. 87)

F

factory (fak'tə rē) A building in which machines used to manufacture goods are located. (p. 501)

famine (fam'in) A widespread lack of food resulting in hunger and starvation. (p. 162)

fascism (fash'iz əm) A totalitarian government that promotes a form of nationalism in which the goals of the nation are more important than those of the individual. (p. 540)

feudalism (fū'də liz əm) Starting in Europe around A.D. 800, a system for organizing and governing society, based on land and service. See **fief, lord, vassal.** (p. 322)

fief (fēf) In the Middle Ages, a property given to a vassal in exchange for his loyalty. (p. 322)

Five Pillars (fīv pil'ərz) The five basic duties of all Muslims. (p. 269)

Four Noble Truths (fôr nō'bəl trüthz) In Buddhism, the principles that rule life and promise an end to suffering. See **Eightfold Path.** (p. 153)

free enterprise (frē en'tər prīz) The economic system of private ownership of land and businesses that allows people to make their own economic decisions and profit from their own work. (p. 556)

G

generalization (jen ər ə lə zā'shən) A broad statement that points out a common feature shared by different kinds of examples. (p. 408)

geocentric (jē ō sen'trik) Based on the idea that Earth is the center of the universe and that the sun, stars, and planets revolve around Earth. (p. 456)

geography (jē og'rə fē) The study of Earth's environment and how it shapes people's lives and how Earth is shaped in turn by people's activities. (p. 8)

glacier (glā'shər) A great sheet of ice that moves slowly over a land surface. See **Ice Age.** (p. 286)

gladiator (glad'ē ā tər) A Roman athlete, usually a slave, criminal, or prisoner of war, who was forced to fight for the entertainment of the public. (p. 240)

global grid (glō'bəl grid) Pattern formed on a map or globe by the crossing of parallels and meridians. This pattern makes it possible to pinpoint exact locations. (p. 13)

glyph (glif) A writing symbol, often carved into stone, that stands for an object or a sound. See **stela.** (p. 302)

Grand Canal (grand kə nal') A waterway in China connecting Beijing with cities to the south. (p. 403)

Grand School (grand skül) A school begun by Confucian scholars in China that trained students for government jobs. (p. 176)

grand mufti (grand muf'tē) A religious leader of the Ottoman empire responsible for interpreting the laws of Islam. (p. 389)

gravity (grav'i tē) The force that pulls objects toward Earth and that draws planets into orbits around the sun. (p. 459)

Green Revolution (grēn rev ə lü'shən) A campaign by the government of India in the 1950s to increase agricultural productivity. (p. 584)

griot (grē'ō) An oral historian and musician who became important in western Africa in the 1500s and still carries on oral traditions today. (p. 367)

gross domestic product (grōs də mes'tik prod'ukt) The total value of goods and services produced by a country during a year. (p. 506)

pronunciation key

a **at**; ā **ape**; ä **far**; âr **care**; e **end**; ē **me**; i **it**; ī **ice**; îr **pierce**; o **hot**; ō **old**; ô **fork**; oi **oil**; ou **out**; u **up**; ū **use**; ü **rule**, ù **pull**; ûr **turn**; hw **white**; ng **song**; th **thin**; <u>th</u> **this**; zh **measure**; ə **about**, tak**e**n, penc**i**l, lem**o**n, circ**u**s

Glossary

guild (gild) In the Middle Ages, an organization of workers in a trade or craft that set standards and protected the interests of its members. (p. 324)

H

hacienda (hä sē en′də) A large agricultural estate owned by Spaniards or the church in Spain's American colonies. (p. 470)

harbor (här′bər) A sheltered place along a coast used to protect boats and ships. (p. 193)

heliocentric (hē lē ō sen′trik) Based on Copernicus's idea that the Earth and the other planets revolve around the sun. (p. 457)

hemisphere (hem′is fîr) One of the halves of Earth. (p. G4)

hieroglyphics (hī ər ə glif′iks) The ancient Egyptian system of writing that used symbols to stand for objects, ideas, or sounds. (p. 78)

hijra (hij′rə) The migration of Muhammad from Mecca to Medina in A.D. 622, marking the founding of Islam. (p. 268)

Hinduism (hin′dü iz əm) The religion of India that grew out of the beliefs of the ancient Aryan peoples; it stresses that one main force connects all of life. (p. 142)

historical map (hi stôr′i kəl map) A map that shows information about the past. (p. 280)

history (his′tə rē) The story or record of what has happened in the past. (p. 24)

Holocaust (hol′ə kôst) The deliberate killing of 6 million Jews solely because they were Jewish by the Nazis during World War II. (p. 546)

humanism (hū′mə niz əm) An idea important to the Renaissance that focused on human values and what people can achieve in this world. (p. 336)

hunter-gatherer (hun′tər gath′ər ər) A person of the Old Stone Age who met needs by hunting animals and gathering plants. (p. 46)

I

Ice Age (īs āj) Any of the periods of time in the past lasting for millions of years when glaciers spread to cover nearly half of Earth's land. (p. 286)

imperialism (im pîr′ē ə liz əm) The extension of a nation's power over other lands by military, political, or economic means. (p. 508)

indulgence (in dul′jəns) A pardon or forgiveness given by the Roman Catholic Church to people who act against Christian teachings. (p. 343)

Industrial Revolution (in dus′ trē əl rev ə lü′ shən) A time when great technological advances changed the way goods were made and the ways people lived; it began in England in the 1700s and then spread throughout Europe and the United States. (p. 500)

inflation (in flā′shən) A period of rising prices. (p. 541)

interaction (in tər ak′shən) The exchange of ideas and customs among cultures. (p. 16)

interdependent (in tər di pen′dənt) Depending upon one another to meet needs and wants. (p. 622)

intermediate directions (in tər mē′dē it di rek′shənz) The directions halfway between the cardinal directions; northeast, southeast, southwest, and northwest. (p. G6)

International Date Line (in tər nash′ə nəl dāt līn) An imaginary line in the Pacific Ocean marking the boundary between one day and the next. (p. 549)

Internet (in′ tər net) A constantly growing international group of interconnected computers. (p. 627)

Intifada (in tə fä′də) The Palestinian uprising against Israeli rule that began in 1987. (p. 578)

irrigation (ir i gā′shən) The watering of dry land by means of canals or pipes. (p. 72)

Islam (is läm′) The religion of Muslims based on the teachings of the prophet Muhammad in the A.D. 600s. (p. 266)

isthmus (is′məs) A narrow strip of land that connects two larger land masses. (p. 423)

J

Judaism (jü′dē iz əm) The religion of the Jewish people. (p. 120)

jury (jùr′ē) A group of citizens chosen to hear evidence and make a decision in a court of law. (p. 206)

K

Kaaba (kä′bə) A religious temple in Mecca that became sacred to Muslims. (p. 267)

karma (kär′mə) In Hinduism and Buddhism, the end result of all of a person's good and bad acts, which determines his or her rebirth. (p. 152)

Korean War (kə rē′ən wôr) A war fought between communist North Korea, aided by China, and South Korea, aided by United Nations members, during 1950–1953. (p. 557)

L

landform (land′fôrm) A feature of Earth's surface, such as a mountain range, plain, or plateau. (p. 9)

large-scale map (lärj skāl map) A map that provides many details about a small area by measuring lesser distances in small units. (p. 92)

Latin America (lat′in ə mer′i kə) The cultural region including Mexico, the Caribbean, and South America that has been strongly influenced by Spain and Portugal. (p. 492)

latitude (lat'i tüd) Distance north or south of the equator, measured by a set of imaginary lines, or parallels, that run east and west around Earth. *See* **parallel.** (p. G4, 12)

League of Nations (lēg əv nā'shənz) An international council created in 1920 by the Allied Powers to try to prevent future wars. (p. 531)

levee (lev'ē) A wall built along a river bank to prevent flooding. (p. 162)

Line of Demarcation (līn əv dē mär kā'shən) An imaginary line drawn across North and South America in 1494 to divide the claims of Spain and Portugal. (p. 467)

locator (lō'kāt ər) A small map that shows where the subject area of a main map is located. (p. G8)

loess (les) A fine, yellow soil that is easily carried by wind and rain, found in China. (p. 161)

longitude (lon'ji tüd) Distance east or west of the prime meridian measured by a set of imaginary lines, or meridians, that run north and south from Earth's poles. *See* **meridian.** (p. G4)

lord (lôrd) In the Middle Ages, a noble who owned and controlled all activities on his manor. *See* **vassal.** (p. 322)

M

Magna Carta (mag'nə kär'tə) A legal document written by English lords in 1215 that stated certain rights and limited the power of the king. (p. 326)

maize (māz) Corn; a crop first grown in Middle America about 5,000 B.C. (p. 300)

Mandate of Heaven (man'dāt uv hev'ən) The belief that the Chinese emperor's right to rule came from the gods. (p. 175)

manor (man'ər) In the Middle Ages, a large self-sufficient estate granted to a lord and worked by serfs. (p. 320)

map key (map kē) A list of map symbols that tells what each symbol stands for. (p. G8)

Meiji Restoration (mā' jē' res tə rā' shən) The overthrow of Japan's shogun in 1868 and restoration of power to the emperor Meiji. (p. 510)

mercator projection (mər kā'tər prə jek'shən) A map that shows accurate shapes of land masses and correct straight-line directions, but which is distorted for areas near the poles. (p. 432)

meridian (mə rid'ē ən) Any line of longitude east or west of Earth's prime meridian. *See* **parallel.** (p. G4)

Messiah (mə sī'ə) A special leader the Jewish people believe will be sent by God to guide them and set up God's rule on Earth. Christians believe Jesus to be the Messiah. (p. 247)

mestizo (me stē'zō) A person of mixed Native American and Spanish ancestry. (p. 494)

Middle Ages (mid'əl āj'əz) A period in European history between A.D. 500 and about the 1500s. (p. 320)

Middle Passage (mid'əl pas'ij) The difficult voyage made by enslaved Africans across the Atlantic Ocean to the West Indies where they were sold. (p. 475)

Middle Way (mid'əl wā) In Buddhism, a way of life, neither too strict nor too easy, that results from following the Eightfold Path. (p. 153)

middle class (mid'əl klas) During the Industrial Revolution, the new class of business people. (p. 504)

migrate (mī'grāt) To move from one place to another to live, especially a large group of people. (p. 138)

missionary (mish'ə ner ē) A person who teaches his or her religion to people with different beliefs. (p. 470)

monarchy (mon'ər kē) A government ruled by a king or queen. (p. 197)

monastery (mon'ə ster ē) A community in which monks lead lives devoted to religion. *See* **convent.** (p. 331)

monk (mungk) A man who devotes his life to a religious group, often giving up all he owns. *See* **monastery.** (p. 151)

monotheism (mon'ə thē iz əm) A belief in one God. *See* **polytheism.** (p. 123)

monsoon (mon sün') A seasonal wind that blows across South Asia bringing dry weather in the winter and heavy rains in the summer. (p. 386)

mosque (mosk) A Muslim place of worship. (p. 273)

N

NAFTA (naf'tə) The North American Free Trade Agreement, which went into effect in 1993, allowing free trade for many goods traded between Canada, Mexico, and the United States. (p. 626)

nationalism (nash'ə nə liz əm) A strong loyalty to one's own country and culture. (p. 527)

pronunciation key

a **a**t; ā **a**pe; ä f**a**r; âr c**a**re; e **e**nd; ē m**e**; i **i**t; ī **i**ce; îr p**ie**rce; o h**o**t; ō **o**ld; ô f**o**rk; oi **oi**l; ou **ou**t; u **u**p; ū **u**se; ü r**u**le, u̇ p**u**ll; ûr t**ur**n; hw **wh**ite; ng so**ng**; th **th**in; <u>th</u> <u>th</u>is; zh mea**s**ure; ə **a**bout, tak**e**n, penc**i**l, lem**o**n, circ**u**s

NATO (nā′tō) The North Atlantic Treaty Organization, a military alliance formed in 1949 by nations in western Europe and North America. (p. 557)

navigable (nav′i gə bəl) Able to be traveled by boats or ships. (p. 318)

New Stone Age (nü stōn āj) The period of human prehistory that lasted from 12,000 years ago to about 6,000 years ago, during which people still depended mainly on stone tools and began experimenting with agriculture. (p. 52)

New Testament (nü tes′tə mənt) The second part of the Christian Bible, containing descriptions of the life and teachings of Jesus and of his early followers. (p. 246)

noble (nō′bəl) A member of a ruling family or one of high rank. See **aristocracy**. (p. 165)

nuclear arms race (nü′klē ər ärmz rās) The Cold War competition between superpowers to develop more powerful and greater numbers of nuclear weapons. (p. 559)

nun (nun) A woman who devotes her life to religion, often living in a convent. See **convent**. (p. 331)

oasis (ō ā′sis) A well-watered area in a desert. (p. 263)

Old Stone Age (ōld stōn āj) The period of human prehistory that lasted until about 12,000 years ago, during which stone tools were the most common technology used by humans. (p. 45)

oligarchy (ol′i gär kē) A type of government in which a small group of citizens control decision-making. (p. 197)

oracle bone (ôr′ə kəl bōn) In ancient China, a cattle or sheep bone used to predict the future. (p. 167)

oral tradition (ôr′əl trə dish′ən) The passing on of history, beliefs, or customs by word of mouth. (p. 25)

Pacific Rim (pə sif′ik rim) The ring of countries surrounding the Pacific Ocean. (p. 616)

papyrus (pə pī′rəs) A kind of paper made from papyrus, a reed plant growing along the Nile, that the ancient Egyptians used for writing. (p. 79)

parable (par′ə bəl) A simple story that contains a message or truth. (p. 248)

parallel (par′ə lel) In geography, any line of latitude north or south of the equator; parallels never cross or meet. See **meridian**. (p. G4)

patrician (pə trish′ən) A member of the noble families who controlled all power in the early years of the Roman Republic. (p. 231)

patron (pā′trən) A supporter of the arts. (p. 337)

Pax Romana (paks rō mä′nə) A period of peace for the Roman Empire that began with the rule of Augustus in about 27 B.C. and lasted around 200 years. (p. 236)

peasant (pez′sənt) A small farm owner or farm worker. (p. 487)

Peloponnesian War (pel ə pə nē′zhən wôr) A war fought between Athens and Sparta in the 400s B.C., ending in a victory for Sparta. (p. 208)

peninsula (pə nin′sə lə) An area of land almost entirely surrounded by water. (p. 193)

per capita income (pūr kap′i tə in′kum) The amount of money each person would have if his or her country's total income were divided equally among its people. (p. 601)

pharaoh (fâ′rō) The title used by the rulers of ancient Egypt. (p. 75)

philosophy (fə los′ə fē) The study of or search for truth, wisdom, and the right way to live. (p. 206)

physical map (fiz′i kəl map) A map that primarily shows natural features of Earth, such as lakes, rivers, mountains, and deserts. (p. G10)

pilgrimage (pil′grə mij) A journey for religious purposes. (p. 269)

plague (plāg) A terrible disease that spreads quickly and kills many people. (p. 334)

plantation (plan tā′shən) A large farming estate where mainly a single crop is grown; until the mid-1800s slaves often worked on plantations. (p. 475)

plateau (pla tō′) An area of flat land that rises above the surrounding land. (p. 105)

plebeian (pli bē′ən) A common farmer, trader, or craftworker in ancient Rome. (p. 231)

point of view (point əv vū) The position of someone toward the world or a subject, shaped by his or her thinking, attitudes, and feelings. (p. 328)

polar projection (pō′lər prə jek′shən) A map projection that shows the area around the North or South Pole. (p. 432)

polis (pō′lis) A city-state in ancient Greece. (p. 196)

political cartoon (pə lit′i kəl kär tün′) A drawing that states an opinion about a political matter. (p. 572)

political map (pə lit′i kəl map) A map mainly showing political divisions, such as national or state boundaries, cities, and capitals. (p. G9)

polytheism (pol′ē thē iz əm) The belief in many gods and goddesses. See **monotheism**. (p. 111)

pope (pōp) The bishop, or church leader, of Rome and head of the Roman Catholic Church. (p. 251)

population density (pop yə lā'shən den'si tê) The number of people living in a given space. (p. 370)

prehistory (prē his'tə rē) The period before events were recorded in writing. (p. 33)

prime meridian (prīm mə rid'ē ən) The line of longitude marked 0° on the world map, from which longitude east and west are measured. (p. G4)

primary source (prī'mer ē sôrs) A first-hand account of an event or an artifact created during the period of history being studied. *See* **secondary source**. (p. 26)

profile (prō'fil) In geography, a map showing a cross-section of a land surface. (p. 228)

projection (prə jek'shən) A way of placing parts of Earth onto a flat map. (p. 432)

propaganda (prop ə gan'də) The spreading of persuasive ideas or attitudes that are often exaggerated or falsified in order to help or hurt a particular cause or group. (p. 541)

Protestantism (prot'ə stən tiz əm) The beliefs of Christians who opposed, or protested against, the Roman Catholic Church in the 1500s; the beliefs of people who follow a Protestant religion today. (p. 344)

province (prov'ins) A division of land within an empire or country. (p. 169)

Punic Wars (pū'nik wôrz) A series of conflicts between Rome and Carthage in the 200s B.C., ending in a victory for Rome. (p. 234)

Q

quipu (kē'pü) A knotted cord used for record-keeping by the Inca. (p. 437)

Quran (kù rän') The most holy book of Islam, believed to contain the teachings of Allah, or God, to Muhammad. (p. 266)

R

rain forest (rān fōr'ist) A warm, wet forest that receives more than 80 inches of rain per year. (p. 288)

Raj (räj) The period in India from the 1850s to 1947 when it was ruled by the British. (p. 581)

reform (ri fôrm') To change. (p. 343)

Reformation (ref ər mā'shən) A movement beginning in Europe in the 1500s, to bring reform to the Roman Catholic Church, and leading to Protestantism. (p. 344)

refugee (ref yù jē') A person who flees his or her country for safety. (p. 577)

region (rē'jən) An area with common features that set it apart from other areas. (p. 9)

Reign of Terror (rān əv ter'ər) The period 1793–1794 in revolutionary France when suspected traitors were beheaded in great numbers. (p. 490)

reincarnation (rē in kär na'shən) A Hindu belief that people move in a constant cycle of life, death, and rebirth. (p. 144)

relief map (ri lēf' map) A map that shows changes in elevation. (p. G10)

Renaissance (ren ə säns') A period of great cultural and artistic change that began in Italy around 1350 and spread throughout Europe. (p. 336)

representative (rep ri zen'tə tiv) A person who is elected by citizens to speak or act for them. *See* **Republic**. (p. 232)

republic (ri pub'lik) A form of government in which citizens elect representatives to speak or act for them. (p. 231)

revolution (rev ə lü'shən) The overthrow of an existing government and its replacement with another; any sudden or very great change. (p. 486)

Roman Catholicism (rō'mən kə thol'ə siz əm) A branch of Christianity that developed in the western Roman empire and that recognized the Pope as its supreme head. (p. 257)

Russian Revolution (rush'ən rev ə lü'shən) Beginning in 1917, the events leading up to the overthrow of tsarist rule and the eventual establishment of the Soviet government led by Vladimir Ilyich Lenin and the Bolsheviks. (p. 532)

S

Sabbath (sab'əth) A weekly day of rest, prayer, and study. (p. 124)

saint (sānt) A woman or man considered by a religious group to be especially holy. (p. 332)

samurai (sam'ù rī) A class of soldiers in fuedal Japan who were loyal only to their lords. (p. 411)

sanction (sangk'shən) A penalty placed against a nation to make it change its behavior, such as a refusal to buy its goods or sell it products. (p. 608)

savanna (sə van'ə) A broad, grassy, plain with few trees, found especially in large parts of Africa. (p. 356)

pronunciation key

a **at**; ā **ape**; ä **far**; âr **care**; e **end**; ē **me**; i **it**; ī **ice**; îr **pierce**; o **hot**; ō **old**; ô **fork**; oi **oil**; ou **out**; u **up**; ū **use**; ü **rule**, ù **pull**; ûr **turn**; hw **white**; ng **song**; th **thin**; <u>th</u> **this**; zh **measure**; ə **about**, tak**e**n, penc**i**l, lem**o**n, circ**u**s

scale (skāl) A unit of measure on a map, such as an inch, that is used to represent a distance on Earth. (p. G7)

scientific method (sī ən tif′ik meth′əd) A way of studying things through questioning and thorough testing. (p. 460)

scribe (skrīb) A professional writer who kept records and copied letters and official documents. (p. 78)

secondary source (sek′ən der ē sôrs) A record of the past, based on information from primary sources. (p. 27)

seismograph (sīz′mə graf) A scientific instrument that could detect earthquakes hundreds of miles away, invented during the Han dynasty. (p. 177)

Senate (sen′it) The lawmaking body and most powerful branch of government in ancient Rome's Republic. (p. 232)

serf (sûrf) In the Middle Ages, a person who was bound to work on a noble's manor. (p. 320)

Shinto (shin′tō) A Japanese religion marked by the belief in the spirits of nature. (p. 410)

shogun (shō′gən) The ruler of feudal Japan from the 1100s to the 1800s who, although appointed by the emperor, ruled the country as a military dictator. (p. 411)

silt (silt) A mixture of tiny bits of soil and rock carried and deposited by a river. (p. 71)

slash and burn (slash and bûrn) A farming method involving the cutting of trees, then the burning of them to provide ash-enriched soil for the planting of crops. (p. 293)

slavery (slā′və rē) The practice of one person owning another person. (p. 95)

small-scale map (smôl skāl map) A map that shows a big area in less detail by measuring its greater distance in large units. (p. 92)

social pyramid (sō′shəl pir′ə mid) A diagram illustrating the divisions within a culture; usually showing the most powerful person or group at the peak and the least powerful groups at the bottom. (p. 95)

socialism (sō′shə liz əm) An economic and political system based on collective or government ownership and control of all resources and industry; also a political philosophy based on the writings of Karl Marx. (p. 505)

specialization (spesh ə lə zā′shən) Training to do a particular kind of work. (p. 55)

stela (stē′lə) A tall, flat stone, often carved with writing, used to mark an important historical event. (p. 302)

steppe (step) A dry, grassy, treeless plain found in Asia and eastern Europe. (p. 163)

strait (strāt) A narrow channel, or body of water, connecting two larger bodies of water. (p. 464)

strike (strīk) A refusal to work as a protest against unfair treatment. (p. 534)

subcontinent (sub kon′tə nənt) A large landmass that is connected to the rest of a continent. (p. 131)

sugarcane (shug′ər kān) A tall grass with a thick, woody stem containing a liquid that is a source of sugar. (p. 475)

sultan (sult′ ən) Supreme ruler of the Ottoman empire. (p. 389)

summary (sum′ə rē) A brief statement of main ideas. (p. 172)

superpower (sü′pər pou ər) A term used for the world's strongest nations—the United States, China, and the Soviet Union—during the Cold War. (p. 556)

supply (sə plī′) In economics, the available quantity of a good, product, or resource. *See* **demand.** (p. 363)

surplus (sûr′plus) An extra supply of something, such as crops that are not needed immediately for food. (p. 55)

symbol (sim′bəl) Anything that stands for something else. (p. G8)

T

technology (tek nol′ə jē) The use of skills and tools to meet practical human needs. (p. 45)

telescope (tel′ə skōp) An optical instrument for making distant objects, such as planets and stars, appear nearer and larger. (p. 457)

temperate (tem′pər it) Mild; moderate in temperature. (p. 317)

Ten Commandments (ten kə mand′mənts) According to the Hebrew Bible, the laws God gave to Moses on Mount Sinai. (p. 123)

terrace (ter′is) A level platform of earth built into a hillside, usually used for farming. (p. 437)

textile (teks′tīl) A cloth fabric that is either woven or knitted. (p. 501)

Three Fires Council (thrē fīrz koun′səl) A league or cooperative group formed by the Ojibwa and the neighboring Potawatomi and Ottawa to promote trade. (p. 441)

timberline (tim′bər līn) An imaginary line on high mountains or in the arctic; above or beyond it trees cannot grow. (p. 424)

time line (tīm līn) A diagram that shows when events took place during a given period of time. (p. 58)

time zone (tīm zōn) A geographic region where the same standard time is used. (p. 548)

topic sentence (top′ik sen′təns) A sentence that contains the main idea of a paragraph, often the first sentence in that paragraph. (p. 172)

Torah (tôr′ə) The first five books of the Hebrew Bible containing the laws and teachings of Judaism. (p. 123)

totalitarian (tō tal i târ′ē ən) A government in which a dictator or a small group of leaders control all aspects of people's lives. (p. 538)

township (toun′ship) A segregated area where blacks in South Africa were forced to live under apartheid. (p. 607)

trade (trād) The exchange of goods between peoples. (p. 56)

Treaty of Versailles (trē′tē əv vâr sī′) The treaty that the Allied Powers forced Germany to sign at the end of World War I. (p. 531)

Triangular Trade (trī ang′gyə lər trād) From the 1500s to the mid-1800s, the triangular-shaped trade routes between the Americas, England, and Africa, which involved the buying and selling of captive Africans as well as guns, sugar, and iron goods. (p. 476)

tribune (trib′ūn) An elected leader of ancient Rome who represented the interests of the plebeians. (p. 232)

tribute (trib′ūt) A tax, often in the form of crops, paid by one ruler to another, usually to ensure peace or protection. (p. 428)

Triple Alliance (trip′əl ə lī′əns) The pact that the army of the Aztec made with the forces of Texcoco and Tlacopan in 1428 in order to gain control of the Valley of Mexico. (p. 428)

tropical (trop′i kəl) Of or relating to the area of Earth between the Tropic of Cancer (23.5°N) and the Tropic of Capricorn (23.5°S). (p. 287)

tsar (zär) In pre-revolution Russia, the emperor. (p. 533)

tundra (tun′drə) A vast, treeless plain in arctic or subarctic places such as Alaska and northern Canada. (p. 422)

Twelve Tables (twelv tā′bəlz) The earliest written collection of Roman laws, drawn up by patricians about 450 B.C., that became the foundation of Roman law. (p. 233)

unification (ū nə fi kā′shən) The joining of separate parts, such as kingdoms, into one. (p. 75)

United Nations (ū nī′tid nā′shənz) An organization founded in 1945 whose members include most of the world's nations. It works to preserve world peace, settle disputes, and aid international cooperation. (p. 557)

urbanization (ur bən ə zā′shən) The growth of cities. (p. 625)

values (val′ūz) Ideals or beliefs that guide the way people live. (p. 16)

vassal (vas′əl) In the Middle Ages, a noble who usually was given a fief by his lord in exchange for loyalty. (p. 322)

Vedas (vā′dəz) In Hinduism, the ancient books of sacred songs on which much of its religious beliefs are based. (p. 143)

Vietnam War (vē et näm′ wôr) A civil war fought between South Vietnam, aided by the United States, and communist North Vietnam during 1954–1975. (p. 589)

warlord (wôr′lôrd) In China, 1912–1927, a strong local military leader who took advantage of political unrest to seize power in the area. (p. 551)

Warsaw Pact (wôr′sô pakt) A military alliance formed in 1955 by the Soviet Union and seven eastern European nations. (p. 557)

wigwam (wig′wom) A dome-shaped dwelling built by the Ojibwa and other Native Americans made of birch bark, cattail reeds, and wooden poles. (p. 443)

working class (wûrk′ing klas) People who work for wages, such as factory workers. (p. 504)

World War I (wûrld wôr) Called the "Great War" at the time, the war of 1914–1918 in which the Allied Powers defeated the Central Powers. (p. 531)

World War II (wûrld wôr) The war of 1939–1945 in which the Allies defeated the Axis powers. (p. 542)

z

ziggurat (zig′ū rat) A large temple located in the centers of ancient Sumerian cities. (p. 111)

Zionism (zī′ə niz əm) A movement to create a national homeland for the Jewish people. (p. 575)

---

pronunciation key

a **at**; ā **ape**; ä **far**; âr **care**; e **end**; ē **me**; i **it**; ī **ice**; îr **pierce**; o **hot**; ō **old**; ô **fork**; oi **oil**; ou **out**; u **up**; ū **use**; ü **rule**; ů **pull**; ûr **turn**; hw **white**; ng **song**; th **thin**; <u>th</u> **this**; zh measure; ə **about, taken, pencil, lemon, circus**

index

This Index lists many topics that appear in the book, along with the pages on which they are found. Page numbers after an m refer you to a map. Page numbers after a p indicate photographs, artwork, or charts.

CREDITS

Cover: Giraudon/Art Resource

Maps: Geosystems

Charts and Graphs: Eliot Bergman: pp 57, 290, 291, 319, 387, 425; Hima Pamoedjo: pp 357, 487, 513, 625

Chapter Opener Globes: Greg Wakabayashi

Illustrations: Richard Cowdrey: pp. 48-49; John Edens: pp. 564-565; Joseph Forte: pp. 42-43, 102-103, 284-285, 352-353; George Gaadt: pp. 68-69, 222-223; Theodore Glazer: pp. 106; Adam Hook: pp. 80, 314-315; Patricia Isaza: pp. 602, 611, 620, 628; Hrano Janto: pp. 73, 95; David McCall Johnston: pp. 128-129, 158-159, 260-261, 442, 454-455; W.B. Johnston: pp. 109, 166; Dave Joly: pp. 17, 37, 55, 91, 107, 114, 163, 206, 275, 289, 333, 375, 391, 459, 511, 531, 568, 603, 621, 627; Robert Korta: pp. 420-421; Rudy Lazlo: pp. 216-217; Angus McBride: pp. 140-141, 484-485; Peg McGovern: pp. 36; Hima Pamoedjo: pp. 18-19, 51, 75, 365, 395, 406-407, 503, 628; Roger Payne: pp. 207; Oliver Rennert: pp. 54; Steven Stankiewicz: pp. 88-89; Robert Van Nutt: pp. 323, 405, 382-383, 524-525 Cover: i. Lee Bolton Picture Library

PHOTOGRAPHY CREDITS: All photographs are by the McGraw-Hill School Division (MMSD)except as noted below.

i: Giraudon/Art Resource. iii: m. The Picture Cube; b. Gerald Champlong/The Image Bank. iv: b. P. Aventu Rier/Gamma Liaison; t. The Granger Collection. v: b. Art Resource, Inc.; t. Lee Boltin; m. Daemmrich/The Image Works. vi: t.l. Scala Art Resource; m., b. Lee Boltin. vii: b. Lee Boltin Picture Library; t. Woodfin Camp Picture Agency; b. Phillips Collection. viii: t. Robert Harding Picture Agency; m.l. Corbis/Bettmann Archives; b. Phillip Makanna/Ghost. ix: EPA Scala. x: vautier/Woodfin Camp. G2: b. Patrick Ward; t. Michael Yamashita. G23: Elizabeth Wolf. G3: t. David Ryan/Photo 20-20; t. Nicholas DeVore III; b. Gerald S. Cubitt; m. Susan Griggs Agency. **Chapter 1** 2: t. Suraj N. Sharma/Dinodia Picture Agency; b. Gerald Champlong/The Image Bank; m. The Picture Cube. 3: b. David L. Brill. 4: b. Grisewood & Dempsey, Ltd. 45: Adam Woolfitt. 5: b.l. Grisewood & Dempsey, Ltd.; t. Hugh Sitton/Tony Stone Images. 6: Frank Labua/Gamma Liaison. 7: t. Wang Fuchun/China Stock; m. Freeman Patterson/Masterfile; m. Thomas Kanzler/Viesti Associates; b. Thomas Mangelson/Images of Nature. 8: t.l. Earth Imaging/Tony Stone Images. 10: b.l. Less Stone/Sygma; b.r. D. Donne Bryant; m.l. D. Donne Bryant. 14: t.l. Pablo Bartholomew. 15: t.l. Dinodia. 16-17: Pablo Bartholomew. 18: t.r. courtesy Brian Lawlor; t.l. courtesy Rachel Dennis; b.l. courtesy Anna Patricia DeMartinez; b.r. courtesy Olanike Olakunki. 19: rtesy Harry Tan. **Chapter 2** 22: b. Frank La Bua/Gamma Liaison. 23: b. Gordon Gohan/National Geographic Society; m. Tom Bean/Tony Stone Worldwide; t. R. Ian llyod/Westlight. 25: m. Comstock; b. Ken Vinocur/The Picture Cube. 26: r. UPI/Corbis- Bettmann. 27: Authentic old ads. 28: l. Corbis/Bettmann; t. Uniphoto Picture Agency. 30: b.l. Robert Freck/Woodfin Camp, Inc.; m. The Granger Collection; b.r. William Kennedy/The Image Bank. 32: t.r. Uniphoto Picture Agency. 34: t.l. Paul Hanny/Gamma Liaison; t.r. Sygma. 35: b.r. Hinterleitner/Gamma Liaison; m. Rex U.S.A, Ltd. 38: t.l. Comstock. 39: t. courtesy Gustavo Araoz; m. courtesy Nancy Marzulla; b. courtesy Brenda Pavlic. **Chapter 3** 44: t.l. Pierre Boulot/Woodfin Camp. 45: b.r. Chris Johns/Tony Stone Images; b.l. AnthroPhoto File. 46: t.l. Ira Block. 47: b.l. George Holton/Photo Researchers; b.r. Erwin and Peggy Bauer/Bruce Coleman, Inc. 48: t.l. Steve Elmore/The Stock Market; t.r. Reunions des Musees Nationaux, Paris; b. Dr. Peter Beaumont/McGregor Museum, South Africa. 49: t.r., Institute of Vertebrate and Paleontholopy and Paleoanthropology, Beijing, China; b.r. Mark Newman/Photo Researchers. 5051: m. Gamma Liaison. 51: t.l. Boston Museum of Fine Arts/Explorer?; m. courtesy of The Trustees of the Victoria and Albert Museum; b.r. Image Bank. 52: t. Ed Malitsky/Liaison International. 53: b. Sonia Halliday Photography. 56: m., b. Dr. James Meelaart. 64: t.r. Israel Museum; t.l. The Granger Collection; m.r. The Metropolitan Museum of Art, Fletcher Fund, 1931 31.13.1; b. Gamma Liaison 65: m. Giraudon; b. Giraudon. 66: b.l. R. W. Nicholson. 66-67: Michael Yamashita, Woodfin Camp, Inc. 67: t.l. Brian Brake, Photo Researchers; m. Georg Gerster. **Chapter 4** 70: t.l. O.L. Mazzatesta/National Geographic Society. 72: b. Michael Holford/British Museum; m. Nino Mascardy/The Image Bank. 74: t.l. Superstock. 75: b. Wernher Krutein/Liaison International. 77: b. The Granger Collection; b. Louvre/Agence Photographique des Musees Nationale; l. source:Superstock/British Museum. 78: b.r. Lee Boltin; bkgnd. Brian Brake/Photo Researchers. 79: Bridgeman Art Library, British Museum/Art Resource. 82: m. Werner Forman Archive, The British Museum, London/Art Resource. 83: t.l. Giraudon; r. Paul Popper, Ltd.; b.l. Superstock. 84: t.r. Giraudon. 85: r. British Museum; t.l. Erich Lessing/PhotoEdit. 87: b. John G. Ross; t. Giraudon/Paris. 88: m. Kelvin Wilson. 89: b. Lee Boltin; t. Metropolitan Museum of Art. 90: t.l. Giraudon. 93: b. Mike Rothwell/FPG International. 94: t.r. The Granger Collection. 96: t.r. The Granger Collection. 97: b. Richard Steedman/The Stock Market. 98: l., r. The Granger Collection; m. Brian Brake/Photo Researchers. 99: b.l. Giraudon. **Chapter 5** 104: t.l. Nik Wheeler/Black Star. 108: t.l. Michael Holford/The British Museum. 111: m.r. Art Resource (Iraq Museum Baghdad); b. Nik Wheeler. 112: m.l. Baghdad Museum/Hirner Fotoarchive (Art Resource); b. Giraudon. 113: t.r. Musee du Louvre, Paris. 114-115:m. Comstock. 115: m. The Oriental Institute of Chicago. 116: m. Giraudon. 117: b.r. bicycles in Beijing, China; m. Bob Thomason/Tony Stone Images; t.r. Jerry & Sharon Austin/The Picture Cube. 118: b.l. Erich Lessing/Art Resource; b.r. British Museum. 120: t.l. The Bettmann Archive. 122: t. B.A. Stewart/National Geographic Society; b.m. Richard T. Nowitz. 123: b. The Jewish Museum. 124: t. Kay Chernush/The Image Bank; m. Zviki-Eshet/The Stock Market. 125: b. Miro Vintoniv/The Picture Cube. **Chapter 6** 130: t.l. Pramod Mistry/Dinodia. 131: b.l. Patrick Morrow. 132: t.r. Susan McCartney. 133: m.l. Ric Ergenbright; b. Charles Marden Fitch/Superstock. 135: b.r. Giraudon/Paris. 136: b. Harrison Forman; m. Jehangir Gazdar/Woodfin Camp, Inc. 137: t.r. Dilip Mehta/Contact Press. 138-139:b. George F. Mobley/National Geographic Society. 142: t.l. Lindsay Hebberd/Woodfin Camp, Inc. 142-143:b. Mike Yamashita. 144: t. Jeffrey Alford/Asia Access; m.r. Brian Vikander. 145: b. Robert Frerck/Odyssey Productions. 146: b. Arvind Garg/Gamma Liaison; m.l. Giraudon/New Dehli National Museum; m.r. Giraudon/Musee Guimet, Paris. 147: t.l. Galen Rowell. 148: m. EPA/Scala. 149: b. Ernt Jahn/Bruce Coleman, Inc.; t. Lindsay Hebberd/Woodfin Camp, Inc.; m. Scala/Art Resource, Inc. 151: t.r. The Granger Collection. 152: m.r. Hilarie Kavanagh/Tony Stone Worldwide; t. Everton/The Image Works. 153: b.r. Dinodia Picture Agency; b.l. Ric Ergenbright Photography. 154-155: Wolfgang Kaehler. 155: m. Pablo Bartholomew/Gamma Liaison. **Chapter 7** 160: t.l. Claus Meyer/Black Star. 161: (Background for Map) Wolfgang Kaehler. 162: m. Photographer Photos Co./Gamma Liaison; l. Forest Anderson/Gamma Liaison; r. Min Zhongjie/Sovphoto Eastphoto. 164: t.l. Smithsonian Institute. 165: b. James Burke/Life Magazine (c) 1961, Time Inc. 166: l. British Library/Werner Forman Archive/Art Resource, Inc. 167: t. ChinaStock Photo Library. 168: t.l. Wolfgang Kaehler. 169: b. Sovfoto/Eastfoto. 170: t.l. Xinhua News Agency; t.r. Gamma-Liaison. 171: m. Wolfgang Kaehler/Gamma-Liaison. 172-173:m. Rolan Lloyd/Westlight. 173: b.r. Wolfgang Kaehler. 174: t.l. Bibliotheque Nationale/Paris. 175: b. Bibliotheque Nationale/Superstock. 176: t.l. Anderson/Gamma Liaison. 177: b. Michael Holford. 178: b.l. Asian Art & Archaeology/Art Resource. 179: Wu Qing. 180: m. Bibliotheque Nationale/Giraudon; t.l. Xinxua/Gamma Liaison. 181: m.l. Sovfoto/Eastfoto; t. Minneapolis Institute of Arts; b.l. Sovfoto/Eastfoto. **Chapter 8** 185: b. Monica Stevenson for MMSD. 186: t.l. Werner Forman/Art Resource; t.r. Lee Boltin/Boltin Picture Library; b.l. Daemmrich/The Image Works. 186-187:b.r. Alan Beckey/The Image Bank. 187: r. Lauros-Giraudon/Art Resource. 188: b. James M. Gurney. 188-189: O. Louis Mazzatenta. 192: t.l. Rick Falco/Black Star. 194: t.l. Dimaggio/Kalish/The Stock Market; t.r. Calvin Larsen/Photo Researchers. 194-195:m. Art Resource, Inc. 195: b.r. Trireme Trust/Cambridge University, UK. 196: t.l. Robert Frerck/Woodfin Camp & Associates. 197: b. J. Pavlovsky/Sygma. 199: m.r. Michael Holford; b. Eric Lessing/Art Resource. 200: t.r. Art Resource. 201: b.l. FPG International. 202: t. Paul J. Sutton/Duomo. 202-203: Paul J. Sutton/Duomo. 203: t. Kathleen Kliskey/The Picture Cube; b. Al Tielemaus/Duomo. 204: t.l. Nimatallah/Art Resource. 205: t. David Lees; b. Harold Sund/The Image Bank. 209: t.l. Erich Lessing/Art Resource, Inc.; m. Art Resource. 210: Giraudon. 211: b. Culver Pictures. 212: t.l. Giraudon. 213: m.l. Art Resource; b.r. National Geographic Society. 215: m. Boltin Picture Library; t. Gilda Alberto Rossi/The Image Bank. 219: t.r., courtesy Robert Anderson; m. courtesy Martin Krause; b. courtesy Greek Tourist Board. **Chapter 9** 224: t.l. Mike Mazzaschi/Stock Boston. 226: Amanda Merullo/Stock Boston. 227: m.l. Michael Salas/The Image Bank. 230: t.l. Ronald Sheridan Photo Library. 231: b. John G. Ross/Art Resource. 233: b. Scala/Art Resource. 234-235: The Granger Collection. 236: t.r. Scala/Art Resource. 237: i. Ronald Sheridan/Ancient Art & Architecture Historical Museum of Vienna; r. Art Resource. 238-239:t. Randy Wells/Tony Stone Images. 239: m. Louis Goldman/Photo Researchers. 240-241: Elaine Harrington/The Stock Market. 240: m. Art Resource. 242: t.r. Scala/Art Resource; t.l. Erich Lessing/Art Resource; b.l. Alinari/Giraudon; b. D.L. Mazzatenta/National Geographic Society Image Collection. 243: t. Leonard Von Matt; b. Cauros/Giraudon. 244-245:m. Tone Stone Images. 245: m.r. Emory Kristof/National Geographic Society; b. David Ball/The Picture Cube; t. F.H.C. Birch/Sonia Halliday Photography. 246: t.l. Scala/Art Resource. (Sistine Chapel). 248: b. (Fra Angelico) Giraudon. 249: t. Superstock; b. Dean Conger/National Geographic Society. 250-251:b. UPI/Bettmann. 250: b. Jeff Greenberg/Photo Edit. 252: t.r. Erich Lessing/Art Resource. 253: b. Giraudon. 255: b. Giraudon; t. Allan Oddie/Photo Edit. 256: b. Marco Cristofori/The Stock Market. **Chapter 10** 262: b. The Stock Market; t.l. Robert Azzi/Woodfin Camp, Inc. 264-265:t. Superstock. 264: t. Tom Hollyman/Photo Researchers. 266: b. Eric Millette; t.l. Giraudon/Musee des Arts Africains et Doceanie, Paris. 268: t.r. Nabeel Turner/Tony Stone Images; t.l. Nicholas Devore/Tony Stone Images. 270: m. Superstock; t. Chip Hires/Gamma Liaison. 270-271:b. P. Manoukian/Sygma. 272: t.l. Michael Holford. 274: b.r. Michael Howell/Stock Boston, Inc.; l. Giraudon/Cairo National Library. 276: t.l. David Ball/The Stock Market; b. Art Resource, Inc. 276-277:m. Art Resource, Inc. 277: b. E.R. Degginger/Bruce Coleman, Inc.; t.r. Superstock. 278-279:m. The Granger Collection. 279: b. Tom Van Sant/Geosphere Project; t. Bibliotheque Nationale, Paris, France/Art Resource, Inc.; m. Giraudon. **Chapter 11** 286: t.r. Charles Hennechieu/Bruce Coleman, Inc. 288: t.l. Cindy Karp/National Geographic Society; t.r. Masterfile; b. Klaus Meyer/Black Star. 292: b. D. Donne Bryant Stock Photography; t.l. Rick Strange/The Picture Cube. 294: m. National Geographic Society. 294-295:m. National Geographic Society. 295: b. Kenneth Garrett/National Geographic Society. 296: t.l. Everton/The Image Works. 297: courtesy Nancy L. Hinchler Zuñiga. 298: t.l. Kathleen Campbell/Gamma Liaison; b. Hiro Matsumoto/Black Star. 300: b. Everton/The Image Works; m. Carolyn Schaefer/Gamma Liaison. 301: b.r. Kenneth Garrett/Woodfin Camp, Inc.; b.l. Kathleen Campbell/Gamma Liaison. 302: m. Vautier/Woodfin Camp, Inc. 303: t. Robert Freck/Woodfin Camp, Inc. 304: t. Markova/The Stock Market. 304-305:m. Ted Kaufman/The Stock Market. 305: t.r. Gamma-Liaison; m. Julian Baum/Photo Researchers. **Chapter 12** 309: b. Mager Photo for MMSD. 310: b.r. Christopher Liu/ChinaStock; t.r. Lee Boltin; t. Adam Woolfit/Woodfin Camp Inc.; b.l. Scala/Art Resource. 311: m.r. National Portrait Gallery, London/Superstock; b.r. Lee Boltin. 312-313: David Louis Olson. 312: l. Christopher A. Klein. 313: b. E. C. Erdis, Peabody Museum of Natural History; t. Robert S. Sacha. 316: t.l. Uniphoto 318: l. Bob Llewellyn/Superstock; b.r. Phyllis Greenberg/Comstock 320: t.l. Superstock 321: m. Superstock 322: m. Erich Lessing/Art Resource; b. Pascal Lebrun/Gamma Liaison 324: t.l. Zefo-Hans Adam/The Stock Market; r. Superstock 325: t. Jonathan Blair/Woodfin Camp and Assoc. 326: t.r. Michael Holford 326-327:b. Bridgeman/Giraudon 328-329:b. Giraudon 330: t.l. Evan Agostini/Gamma Liaison Int'l; m. Art Resource. 330-331:m. The Pierpont Morgan Library/Art Resource 331: b.r. Topham/The Image Works 332: l. Superstock 332-333:t. Adam Woolfit/Woodfin Camp 333: t.r. Adam Woolfitt/Woodfin Camp. 334: m. Howard Hughes/Superstock 335: t. The Granger Collection. 336: t.l. Evan Agostini/Gamma Liaison International. 337: b.l. Jim Zuckerman/Westlight; m. Scala/Art Resource, Inc. 338: b.r. Art Resource (Louvre) 339: m.r. Art Resource; t.l. Giraudon. 340: m.l. Time Museum, Rockford, Illinois; b.l. Metropolitan Museum of Art, H.O. Havemeyer Collection, bequest of Mrs. H.O. Havemeyer, 1929; m. The Granger Collection. 341: t.r. Kunstmuseum, Basel; b.r. Art Resource. 342: t.l. Photo Researchers. 343: m. Art Resource 344: b.l. Giraudon 346: t.l. Superstock. 346-347:t. Michael Holford. 348: m. The Granger Collection 349: t.l. The Kobal Collection; t.r. Martha Swope/Time Picture Syndication; b. The Granger Collection **Chapter 13** 354: t. Robert Caputo/Aurora. 356: l. Robert Caputo/Aurora; r. Alon Reininger/Contact Press Images. 358: l. Robert Caputo/Aurora; b.r. Georg Gerster/Comstock. 360: l. Wendy Stone/The Gamma Liaison Network; t.r. Robert Caputo/Aurora. 361: b. Kal Muller/Woodfin Camp & Associates. 362: t. Lee Boltin. 363: t.l. Volkmar Wentzel/National Geographic Society Image Collection; t.r. Aldo Tutino/Art Resource, Inc. 365: t.r. John Elk III/Bruce Coleman; m., m.l. The Granger Collection; b. Norman Myers/Bruce Coleman, Inc.; t. John Elk III/Bruce Coleman, Inc. 366: b.l. The Granger Collection. 367: t. Jeffrey Ploskonka/National Museum of African Art. 368: m. Marc and Evelyne Bernheim/Woodfin Camp 369: t.l., b.l. Jack Vartoogian; t.r. Jeffrey Salter. 370: l. Bruno De Hogues/Tony Stone Images. 371: m. Guido Alberto Rossi/The Image Bank. 372: t. Marc and Evelyne Bernheim/Woodfin Camp; b. Werner Forman Archive 374: b. Anne Martens/The Image Bank 376: t. Wendy Stone/ Gamma Liaison 378-379:t. James L. Stansfield/Nat'l Geographic Society. 378: b. Guido Alberto Rossi/The Image Bank. **Chapter 14** 384: t.l. Barbara Rowell. 386: l. Gamma Liaison; r. Galen Rowell 388: m. Giraudon 389: b. Superstock. 392: t.l. Superstock. 393: b.r. Superstock. 394: t.l. Christina Dameyer/Photo 20-20. 395: m. Courtesy of the Trustees of the Victoria and Albert Museum. 396: l. Air India Library; r. Dallas and John Heaton/Westlight. 397: m. Boltin Picture Library. 398: t.l. Kevin R. Morris/Tony Stone Images. 400: m. R.Ian LLoyd/Westlight. 400-401:m. Ernest Manewal/Photo 20-20. 402: m. Allan Seiden/The Image Bank. 406: b.l. SIPA Press/Art Resource; b.l. Giraudon. 407: b. Guido Alberto Ross/The Image Bank; t.r. The Granger Collection. 408: t.l. National Portrait Gallery,

London/Superstock; r. The Granger Collection 410: l. Ronald R. Johnson/Stockphotos, Inc 412: b.l. Boltin Picture Library 413: l. Fujifotos/The Image Works 414: l. Fukuhara, Inc./Westlight 414-415:m. Bridgeman/Art Resource 416: m. Superstock 417: r. Superstock **Chapter 15** 422: t.l. The Stock Market. 424: l. Aaron Strong/ Liaison International; r. Walter Leonardi/Gamma-Liaison. 426: t.l. Boltin Picture Library. 428: t. H. Tom Hall/ National Geographic Society. 428-429:t. Erich Lessing/Art Resource. 429: b. Boltin Picture Library. 430: b.l. Ned M. Seidler/National Geographic Society; t. Giraudon. 431: t. Art Resource, Inc. 434: t. Ric Ergenbright; b. Dallas Museum of Fine Art/Werner Forman Archive/Art Resource. 436: l. Ric Ergenbright; r. Nick Saunders/Barbara Heller/Art Resource. 437: t. Museum Fur Volkerkunde, Berlin/Werner Forman Archive/Art Resource; b. Wolfgang Kaehler. 438: t. Ric Ergenbright; b. Boltin Picture Library. 439: t.l. Bruce Coleman, Inc. 440: m. David Meunch 443: b. Greenlar/The Image Works 444: t.l. Peabody Museum/Harvard University, photo by Hille Burger; b.r. Lee Boltin; m.r. National Museum of the American Indian. 445: t.r. David Perdew/Stock South **Chapter 16** 449: b. Monica Stevenson for MMSD. 450: b. Superstock; t.r. Jonathan Blair/Woodfin Camp, Inc.; t.l. Lee Boltin; m. The Phillips Collection. 451: t.r. Eric Lessing/Art Resource; b.r. Michael Holford. 452-453: Gordon W. Gahan. 452: t. Don Kincaid. 453: t. National Maritime Museum, London; b.l. Jean-Leon Huens. 456: t.l. Museo Della Scienza, Scala/Art Resource. 457: l. Erich Lessing/Art Resource; r. The Granger Collection. 458: m.r. Erich Lessing/Art Resource; r. The Granger Collection. 460: b.l. Michael Holford. 461: b.r. European Space Agency. 462: t.l. Michael Holford. 463: m.r. The Granger Collection; b.r. Michael Holford. 465: t.l. Giraudon/Art Resource. 468: t. The Granger Collection. 468: l. Superstock; r. Giraudon. 469: t.r. Nick Saunders/Barbara Heller/Art Resource. 470: l. Nick Nicholson/The Image Bank; r. Alon Reininger/Woodfin Camp & Associates. 471: b.l. M. Timothy O'Keefe/Bruce Coleman, Inc. 472: b. The Granger Collection. 473: b.r. Roswell Museum and Art Center; Roswell Museum. 474: t.l. The Granger Collection. 476: t. Bridgeman/Giraudon. 478: t. Doug Armand/Tony Stone Images. 479: b. Image Works; t. Art Resource. 480: b. Image Works. 481: l. Image Works. **Chapter 17** 486: t.l. Superstock. 487: b. Giraudon. 489-492: Giraudon. 494: m. Giraudon. 495: m. Byron Augustin/DDB Stock Photo. 497: t. Super Stock. 498: m. Michael Evans/Sygma. 499: t. Gamma Liaison; m. Cindy Karp/Black Star; b. AP/Wide World Photos. 500: t.l. The Granger Collection. 501: t. Michael Holford; b. Victoria and albert Museum/Superstock. 502: t.l. Superstock 503: Josepa Szkoidinski/The Image Bank. 504: l. Bridgeman/Giraudon; r. Granger Collection. 505: t. Superstock. 508: t.l. Robert Harding Picture Library. 509: m. The Granger Collection; b. National Portrait Gallery, Smithsonian Institution/Art Resource. 510: l. Jack Fields/Photo Researchers, Inc.; r. Lauros-Giraudon. 512: b. Wernher Krutein/Liaison International. 514: t.m. Robert Harding. 514-515: Robert Harding. **Chapter 18** 520: m. Gamma-Liaison International; b. Bettmann Archives.; t.l. r. Philip Makanna/Ghosts. 521: m. Robert Harding; The Bettmann Archives. 522: b. Sygma. 522-523: NASA. 526: t.l. Bettmann Archive. 527: b.r. Roger-Violet. 529: Archive Photos. 530: m.r. Archive Photo; t.r. Roger-Violet; b.l. Roger Violet. 531: Bettmann Archive. 532: Art Resource, Inc. 534: l. PopperFoto/Archive Photos; r. Gamma-Liaison. 535: b. Roger-Violett. 536: t.l. UPI/Bettmann. 537: l. Scala/Art Resource; r. Sovfoto/Eastfoto. 538: l. Archive Photos; b. Roger Violett. 540: l. Hans Wild/Time Life 541: Roger-Violett/Sygma; r. Roger-Violett 545: m. Archive Photos 546-547: Gamma Liaison 549: m. Etienne De Malglaive/Liaison International 550: m. Sovfoto/Eastfoto 551552: Roger-Violett 553: m. Archive Photos 554: m. Sovfoto/Eastfoto 556558: UPI/Bettman 559: t.l. Sygma 560: t.r. The Bettman Archive; t.l. Werner Wolff/Black Star 560-561:m. UPI/Bettman **Chapter 19** 567: l. Owen Franken/Stock Boston; t.l. Carrion/Sygma. 569: The Bettmann Archive. 571: t.r. Archive Photos. 574: Superstock. 575: b.r. The Bettmann Archive. 577: b.r. Sygma. 578: t.r. Allen Tannenbaum/Sygma. 579: m. Karen Wald Cohen/Interns for Peace 580: t.l. Bettmann. 581: b.r. Popperfoto. 584: l. Sygma. 584-585:m. J.Martin/Popperfoto. 586: t.l. Gamma Liaison/Wolfgang Kaehler. 588: t.r. Bettman; l. Charles Bonnay/Black Star. 589: t. Ray Cranbourne/Black Star 590: t.l. Bettman; m. Hain Edvard/Gamma Liaison International **Chapter 20** 595-596: P.Piel/Gamma-Liaison. 597: l. Peter Turnley/Black Star; r. Bouvet/Gamma Liaison. 598: m. Paul O'Driscoll/Gamma Liaison; l. Peter Turnley/Black Star. 600: Igmor Zamur/Gamma Liaison. 602: t.r. Vlastinir Shone/Gamma Liaison; r. Archive Photos. 605: courtesy Zlato Filipovic. 606: t.l. Peter Turnley/Black Star. 608: b.l. S. Balic/Sygma. 610: Reuters/Bettman. 611: t.r. Tibor Bognar/The Stock Market. 612: t.l. Roy Franco/Panos. 613: courtesy Ashwell Zwane and Bernent Lekalakala. 614: t.l. Francis Li/Liaison International. 615: b.l. Tom Wagner/SABA; r. Ken Straiton/Stock Market. 617: t.r. Hirokuyi Matsumoto/Black Star. 618: m.r. P. Durand/Sygma; b.r. J. Langevin/Sygma; m.l. Bill Pierce/Sygma. 619: t.r. Liu Hueng Shing/Contact. 620: t.r. Mark Harris/Tony Stone Worlwide. 624: b.l. Richard Melloul/Sygma. 626: t. Jeff Titcomb/Liaison International; t.r. Stephen Derr/Image Bank. 628: t.r. Stephanie Maze/National Geographic Society. 631: t. courtesy Joanne Cheng; m. Georgey Kadar; b. Kassim Yahya. 635: b. Monica Stevenson for MMSD. Endpapers: Bridgeman/Art Library.

(continued from page ii)

Acknowledgments

Extract from **Children of the World** by E. Blauer; D.K. Wright, G. Holland, B.R. Rogers. Published by Gareth Stevens, Inc., Milwaukee, WI. Reprinted by permission.

From **The Sumerians: Their History, Culture and Character** by Samuel Noah Kramer. Copyright 1963 by The University of Chicago. Reprinted by permission of the publisher.

From **Pharaoh's People** by T.G.H. James. Copyright 1984 by T.G.H. James. Reprinted by permission of The University of Chicago Press.

From **God's Country: America in the Fifties** by J. Ronald Oakley. Copyright 1986 by J. Ronald Oakley. Red Dembner Enterprises Corp., New York.

From **Television** by Michael Winship. Copyright 1988 by Educational Broadcasting Corporation and Michael Winship. Random House, New York.

From **Monsoons,** edited by Jay S. Fein, Pamela L. Stephens. Copyright 1987 by John Wiley & Sons, Inc. A Wiley-Interscience Publication, John Wiley & Sons, Inc.

From **The Ancient Civilization of Angkor** by Christopher Pym. Copyright 1968 by Christopher Pym. A Mentor Book published by The New American Library, N.Y. & Toronto.

From **Angkor Heart of an Asian Empire** by Bruno Dagens. English translation copyright 1995 by Harry N. Abrams, Inc., N.Y. and Thames and Hudson Ltd., London. Harry N. Abrams, Inc., Publishers.

From **The Travels of Marco Polo,** a modern translation by Teresa Waugh from the Italian by Maria Bellonci. Translation copyright 1984 by Sadgwick and Jackson Limited. Facts on File Publications, N.Y.

From **The Longest Walk: An Odyssey of the Human Spirit** by George Meegan. Copyright 1988 by George Meegan. Dodd, Mead & Company, N.Y.

From **The Way of the Earth: Encounters with Nature in Ancient and Contemporary Thought** by T.C. McLuhan. Copyright 1994 by T.C. McLuhan. Simon & Schuster, N.Y.

From "The land is everything." quote printed in **Native Peoples Magazine** Vol. 6, Number 3, Spring 1993, quote from Gerald Vizenor. Copyright 1993 by Media Concepts Group, Inc. Media Concepts Group, Inc., AZ.

From **Coming of Age in the Milky Way** by Timothy Ferris. Copyright 1988 by Timothy Ferris. An Anchor Book published by Doubleday, a division of Bantam Doubleday Dell Publishing Group, Inc., N.Y. The Anchor Books Edition was published by arrangement with William Morrow and Company.

From **The Diary of a Young Girl: The Definitive Edition** by Anne Frank. Otto H. Frank & Mirjam Pressler, Editors, translated by Susan Massotty. Translation copyright © 1995 by Doubleday, a division of Bantam Doubleday Dell Publishing Group, Inc. Used by permission of Doubleday, a division of Bantam Doubleday Dell Publishing Group, Inc.

From **Red Azalea** by Anchee Min. Copyright 1994 by Anchee Min. Pantheon Books, a division of Random House, Inc.

From **China: The Long March** by Anthony Lawrence. Copyright 1986 by Intercontinental Publishing Corp., China National Publishing Industry Trading Corp. and China Photographic Publishing House. Heinemann Publishing House, London.

From **Mme Sun Yat-sen** by Jung Chang with Jon Halliday. Copyright 1986 by Jung Chang and Jon Halliday. Penguin Books.

From **The Cold War** by Martin Walker. Copyright 1993 by Walker & Watson Ltd. A John Macrae Book, Henry Holt and Company, N.Y.

From **The Africans** by David Lamb. Copyright 1983 by David Lamb. Vintage Books, a division of Random House, N.Y.

From **Holy War: The Crusades and Their Impact on Today's World** by Karen Armstrong. Copyright 1988, 1991 by Karen Armstrong. Papermac, a division of Macmillan Publishers Limited, London.

From **Long Walk to Freedom: The Autobiography of Nelson Mandela** by Nelson Mandela. Copyright 1994 by Nelson Rolihlahla Mandela. Little, Brown and Company.

From **Zlata's Diary: A Child's Life in Sarajevo** translated with notes by Christina Pribichevich-Zoric. Translation Copyright by Fixot et editions Robert Laffont, 1994. Viking, published by the Penguin Group, Penguin Books USA Inc., N.Y.

From **Self-Made Man: Human Evolution from Eden to Extinction** by Jonathan Kingdon. Copyright 1993 by Jonathan Kingdon. John Wiley & Sons, Inc.

From **Mesopotamian Myths** by Henrietta McCall. Copyright by The Trustees of the British Museum. British Museum Publications, Ltd.

From **Legacy of the Indus: A Discovery of Pakistan** by Samina Quraeshi. Copyright 1974 by Samina Quraeshi. Poem on pg. 8 Copyright 1974 by Salman Tarik Kureshi. John Weatherhill, Inc.

From **The Vedic Experience Mantramanjari,** edited and translated with introductions and notes by Raimundo Panikkar. Copyright 1977 by Raimundo Panikkar. University of California Press.

From **Four-Dimensional Man: Meditations Through the Rg Veda** by Antonio T. de Nicolas. Copyright 1976 by Nicolas Hays, Ltd. Nicolas Hays Ltd.

From **The Wisdom of the Buddha,** by Jean Boisselier. Copyright 1993 by Gallimard. English translation Copyright 1994 Harry N. Abrams, Inc., N.Y. Harry N. Abrams, Inc., New York.

From **The Odyssey of Homer** a new verse translation by Allen Mandelbaum. Copyright 1990 by Allen Mandelbaum. University of California Press.

From **God's Bits of Wood,** Sembene Ousmane translated by Francis Price. Copyright 1962 Doubleday & Company Inc. Heinemann Educational Books Ltd.

From **Serowe Village of the Rain Wind** by Bessie Head. Copyright 1981 by Bessie Head. Heinemann Educational Books Ltd.

From **The Search for Africa,** by Basil Davidson. Copyright 1994 by Basil Davidson. Times Books/Random House.

From **Corpus of early Arabic sources for West African history,** translated by J.F.P. Hopkins, edited and annotated by N. Levtzion & J.F.P. Hopkins. Copyright 1981 by University of Ghana, International Academic Union, Cambridge University Press. Cambridge University Press.

From "China-the End of an Era" from *The Nation Magazine* by Orville Schell. The Nation Magazine, July 17/24, 1995.

The Princeton Review
Handbook of
Test-Taking Strategies

DEDUCTION AND OUTSIDE KNOWLEDGE

Most of the multiple-choice exams you take will include charts, graphs, maps, time lines, and political cartoons. For some questions, you will need to look at this data to find the answer. The process of looking at the information provided, finding the answer to the question, and choosing the correct answer from among the answer choices is called DEDUCTION.

Not all the answers to the questions will be in the data, however. Sometimes, multiple-choice tests ask you to remember a fact that you learned in social studies class. You won't be able to find the correct answer on a map, chart, graph, or drawing; the correct answer will be in your memory. We call these OUTSIDE KNOWLEDGE questions.

Look at the map below, and then answer questions 1 and 2.

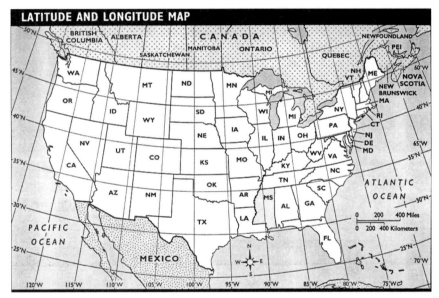

LATITUDE AND LONGITUDE MAP

1 Which state is closest to 40°N latitude?

- **A** Florida
- **B** West Virginia
- **C** Maine
- **D** North Carolina

2 The weather in Texas is warmer than the weather in Wisconsin because Texas is

- **F** closer to the equator
- **G** a larger state
- **H** closer to a body of water
- **J** west of Wisconsin

PROCESS OF ELIMINATION

When you take a multiple-choice test, you have an advantage that you don't have on other tests. On most tests, you must come up with the answers to the questions all on your own. For example, a test might ask "What is the capital of the United States?" You would then have to write the name "Washington D.C." on your answer sheet.

On a multiple-choice test, however, the correct answer is already written down for you; it is among the answer choices! All you have to do is figure out which of the answer choices is the correct one.

This is good news for you! It means that you can still answer a question correctly *even if you can't come up with the correct answer on your own*. That's because you can ELIMINATE choices that you know are *incorrect*. Eliminating answers this way will be especially helpful on OUTSIDE KNOWLEDGE questions. Sometimes you will be able to eliminate all of the choices except one. When that happens, it means that you have found the best answer by the PROCESS OF ELIMINATION.

Try using the process of elimination to answer this question:

1   The Pan American Highway extends from the northern tip of Mexico to the southern tip of—

   A   Italy
   B   Cuba
   C   Egypt
   D   Chile

Were you able to eliminate any *incorrect* answers? How many?

Now try using process of elimination To answer this question:

2   Which religion originated in India?

   F   Christianity
   G   Islam
   H   Buddhism
   J   Judaism

Sometimes process of elimination will help you eliminate ALL the incorrect answers. Sometimes it will only help you eliminate one or two. On a multiple-choice exam, it ALWAYS helps to use the process of elimination when you are unsure about which answer is correct, no matter what type of question you are working on.

Remember: Do not write in your textbook.

CRITICAL THINKING SKILLS

Some multiple-choice questions require you to use critical thinking skills to find the answer. These critical thinking skills may include:

- drawing conclusions
- evaluating information
- making generalizations

Read the quotation, then answer question 1.

"The good person is satisfied and calm; the mean person is always full of distress."
    —Confucius, Chinese scholar and teacher, 500 B.C.

1 Confucius would probably have agreed with which of the following statements?

A Justice is its own reward.

B Might makes right.

C A little white lie never hurt anyone.

D There's a sucker born every minute.

Study the graph. Then answer question 2.

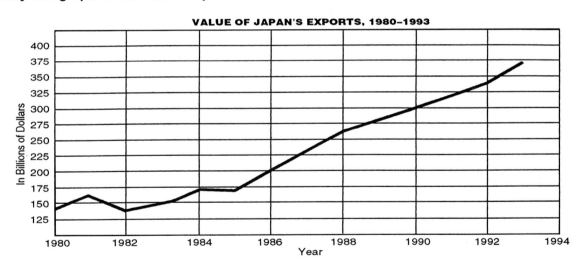

VALUE OF JAPAN'S EXPORTS, 1980–1993

2 Which of the following most likely caused the increase in the value of Japanese exports in 1987 and 1988?

F Japanese companies stopped advertising their products overseas in 1987.

G Japanese factories reduced production of goods in 1987.

H Prosperous nations like the United States increased the amount of Japanese goods they imported in 1987.

J Many Japanese factories closed in 1987.

READING COMPREHENSION

Some test questions specifically test your ability to read and understand what you have read. These questions may also require you to compare and contrast the people or things you read about.

Read about the four famous people. Then answer questions 1 and 2.

I was a great Chilean poet in the twentieth century. I won the Nobel Prize for Literature in 1971. I also served as a diplomat for my country.

Pablo Neruda

I was a great Russian composer of the nineteenth century. I wrote symphonies, concertos, and operas, but I am best known for my ballets *Swan Lake* and *The Nutcracker*.

Peter Ilyich Tchaikovsky

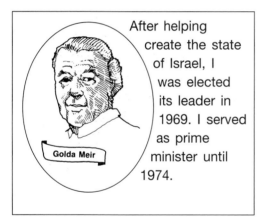

After helping create the state of Israel, I was elected its leader in 1969. I served as prime minister until 1974.

Golda Meir

I was the Mongol emperor who ruled Mongolia and China in the thirteenth century. I built the city of Beijing and greeted Marco Polo on his first visit to China.

Kublai Khan

1 Which of these people was probably LEAST involved in politics and government?

- **A** Pablo Neruda
- **B** Golda Meir
- **C** Peter Ilyich Tchaikovsky
- **D** Kublai Khan

2 Which two people were probably MOST interested in the arts?

- **F** Pablo Neruda and Peter Ilyich Tchaikovsky
- **G** Golda Meir and Pablo Neruda
- **H** Kublai Khan and Peter Ilyich Tchaikovsky
- **J** Peter Ilyich Tchaikovsky and Kublai Khan

Remember: Do not write in your textbook.

MAPS

The ability to read and understand maps is an important skill in social studies. Many of the multiple-choice tests you take will require you to read a map.

Look carefully at all the parts of a map. Maps contain a lot of information. Whenever you see a map, you should ask yourself questions like these:

- What do the titles of the maps tell you?
- Where are the map keys?
- What symbols are on the map keys? What do they stand for?
- Where is the compass rose on each map?
- Is there a map scale?

Study the two maps of Alberta, Canada. Then do questions 1 and 2.

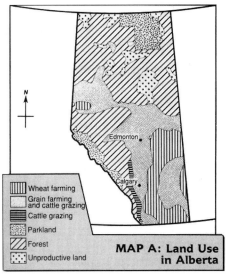

MAP A: Land Use in Alberta

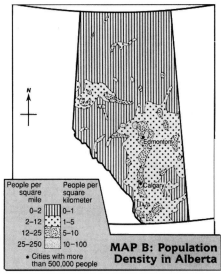

MAP B: Population Density in Alberta

1 The land surrounding both of Alberta's major cities is primarily used as

   A wheat farms

   B grain farms and cattle ranches

   C forests

   D parkland

2 Which of the following best explains the population density of northern Alberta?

   F The weather in northern Alberta is too cold to support a large population.

   G Alberta's biggest cities are in its northern section.

   H Wheat farming in northern Alberta attracts a large number of workers to the region.

   J Most residents of Alberta prefer to live in the forest.

GRAPHS

Different types of graphs are used to present numerical information. A **line graph** shows how something changes over time. A line graph might be used to show how the population of the United States has grown over the years. A **bar graph** compares amounts. A **bar graph** might show the population of different United States cities. A **circle graph** shows how a whole is divided into smaller parts. For example, a circle graph might show how the government divides its budget to pay for roads, defense, education, and other services.

On some multiple-choice tests, you will see a set of questions accompanied by more than one graph. Each question will contain clues to tell you which graph you should read to find the answer. Take the extra time to make sure you are looking at the correct graph. This will help you avoid careless errors.

Use the graphs and your own knowledge to do questions 1 through 3.

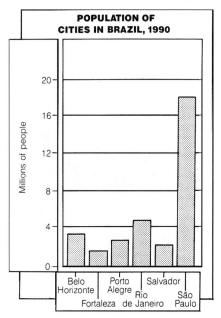

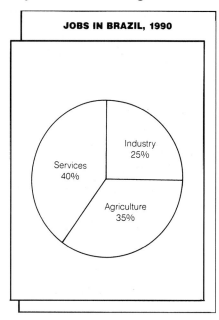

1 According to the graph, which city in Brazil had a population closest to 4,000,000 in 1990?

   A Fortaleza   **C** Rio de Janiero

   B Salvador   **D** Sao Paulo

2 In 1990, what part of the economy provided the greatest number of jobs to Brazilians?

   F Industry   **H** Agriculture

   G Services   **J** Arts and Entertainment

3 Which of the following jobs would fall under the category of "services"?

   A Factory worker   **C** Cattle rancher

   B Farmer   **D** Waitress

                                                 Remember: Do not write in your textbook.

POLITICAL CARTOONS

Some tests will ask you to look at and interpret a political cartoon. A political cartoon is an illustration or drawing that expresses a political point of view.

When you look at a political cartoon, ask yourself the following questions:

- What do the images in the cartoon represent? Are they *symbols* for something else? Uncle Sam is an example of a symbol. When he appears in a cartoon, he is being used as a symbol of the United States.
- What is the cartoonist's *point of view*? Is the cartoonist for or against the political issue that is the subject of the drawing? Look carefully at the details of the drawing. Do they provide hints about the artist's point of view?

Study the cartoon. Then do Numbers 1 through 3.

1 In the cartoon, the people under the umbrella represent

    A members of the United States Congress

    B citizens of the United States

    C Europeans who would like to move to the United States

    D foreign nations asking for financial assistance from the United States

2 The cartoonist would probably agree that the United States Constitution is

    F foolish   **H** important

    G difficult to understand   **J** outdated

3 Which of these would provide the most factual information about the United States Constitution?

    A a textbook about the United States government

    B a campaign poster for a Presidential candidate

    C a fictional movie about the American space program

    D an advertisement for a trip to Washington DC

Remember: Do not write in your textbook.

TIME LINES

Historical information is sometimes presented in a time line. A time line shows events in the order in which they occurred. It should be read from left to right, like a sentence. Sometimes a time line is presented vertically, in which case it should be read from top to bottom.

Some questions may ask you to find information on a time line. They may also ask you to remember outside knowledge about the subject of the time line.

Look at the time line below. Then answer questions 1 and 2.

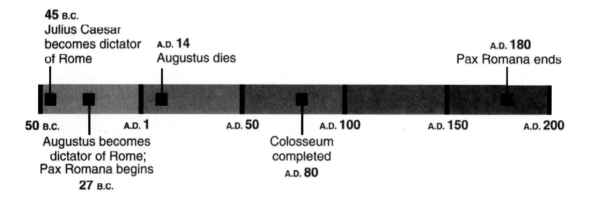

1 The best title for this time line would be:

A The Building of the Colosseum
B The Rule of Julius Caesar
C The Pax Romana
D The Rule of Augustus

2 In what year did Augustus die?

F 45 B.C.
G 27 B.C.
H A.D. 14
J A.D. 80

Remember: Do not write in your textbook.

ENCYCLOPEDIA OF MEDIA AND COMMUNICATION

The first comprehensive encyclopedia for the growing fields of media and communication studies, the *Encyclopedia of Media and Communication* is an essential resource for beginners and seasoned academics alike. Contributions from over fifty experts and practitioners provide an accessible introduction to these disciplines' most important concepts, figures, and schools of thought – from Jean Baudrillard to Tim Berners-Lee, and podcasting to Peircean semiotics.

Detailed and up to date, the *Encyclopedia of Media and Communication* synthesizes a wide array of works and perspectives on the making of meaning. The appendix includes timelines covering the historical record for each medium, from either antiquity or their inception to the present day. Each entry also features a bibliography linking readers to relevant resources for further reading. The most coherent treatment yet of these fields, the *Encyclopedia of Media and Communication* promises to be the standard reference text for the next generation of media and communication students and scholars.

MARCEL DANESI is the director of and a professor in the Program in Semiotics and Communication Theory at Victoria College, University of Toronto.

Encyclopedia
of Media and
Communication

Edited by Marcel Danesi

UNIVERSITY OF TORONTO PRESS
Toronto Buffalo London

ISBN 978-1-4426-4314-7 (cloth)
ISBN 978-1-4426-1169-6 (paper)

Printed on acid-free paper

Toronto Studies in Semiotics and Communication
Editors: Marcel Danesi, Umberto Eco, Paul Perron, Peter Schultz, and Roland Posner

Library and Archives Canada Cataloguing in Publication

Encyclopedia of media and communication / edited by Marcel Danesi.

(Toronto studies in semiotics and communication)
Includes bibliographical references.
ISBN 978-1-4426-4314-7 (bound) – ISBN 978-1-4426-1169-6 (pbk.)

1. Communication – Encyclopedias.   2. Mass media – Encyclopedias.
3. Semiotics – Encyclopedias.   I. Danesi, Marcel, 1946–   II. Series: Toronto studies in
semiotics and communication.

P87.5.E55 2013   302.203   C2012-905452-6

University of Toronto Press acknowledges the financial assistance to its publishing
program of the Canada Council for the Arts and the Ontario Arts Council.

  Canada Council   Conseil des Arts
for the Arts   du Canada

University of Toronto Press acknowledges the financial support of the Government of
Canada through the Canada Book Fund for its publishing activities.

Contents

Introduction

In the late 1990s, at the threshold of the age of the internet in which we now live, two blockbuster movies provided remarkable insight into the state of the contemporary world. The first one was the 1997 James Bond movie titled *Tomorrow Never Dies*; the other one was the now cult 1999 movie *The Matrix*. In the former, unlike the villains of previous Bond movies, an evil, deranged personage, a man called Elliot Carver, seeks control over the world through the manipulation of mass communications media. Carver has a 'geek criminal mind' and knows that by controlling what people see and hear he will be able to gain dominion over their minds. Elliot Carver personifies the danger of mind control by media moguls in an age when the media literally run the show. Indeed, we live in a world that is being increasingly threatened by those who, like the fictitious Elliot Carver, hold the levers of 'mass communications power,' that is, by those who control television networks, movie production studios, and computer media.

The ability of mass communications technologies to shape cognition and cultural evolution defines the dynamic of the modern world. Never before in the history of human civilization has the study of this dynamic become so critical. *The Matrix* illuminates this dynamic. Like the main protagonist of that movie, Neo, we now live 'on' and 'through' the computer screen. Our engagement with reality is largely shaped by that screen, whose technical name is the *matrix*, as the network of circuits that defines computer technology is called. But the same word also means 'womb,' etymologically speaking. The movie's transparent subtext is that, with the advent of the digital universe, new generations are now being born in two kinds of wombs – the biological and the technological.

Many studies published after these two movies were released have decried the serious dangers that the media and the new mass communications technologies pose to the human race. Some of these studies criticize the individuals and groups who control media institutions. But many more see the current state of affairs as an evolutionary rather than revolutionary state. Since prehistoric times, humans have used technology to improve their control over the world and the unknown. However, the question that the two movies beg is whether or not the technologies we have created are now starting to control us – a theme that has always been a staple of science fiction (*2001: A Space Odyssey* is a case in point). As the late Canadian communications guru Marshall McLuhan (1911–80) observed throughout his career, the media we make are unconscious extensions of our physical, sensory, and cognitive forms and processes. Thus we evolve through them, not independently of them. For example, with the invention of the telescope and the microscope (at about the same time in history), not only have we gained the capacity to see 'farther out' and 'farther in' respectively, but we have also changed dramatically and permanently. These 'vision-enhancing' devices have made possible the exploration of space and the human body, leading to the modern sciences of astronomy, biology, medicine, and forensics, and these, in turn, have guided (in part at least) how society has evolved and how human cognition (understanding of the world) has changed.

Studying the Media and Mass Communications

Separate university courses (and even departments) for studying the media, and especially the relationship of the mass media to all facets of human communication and culture, are proliferating at the speed of digital communication itself. The study has become so widespread that it has generated its own technical vocabulary, theoretical apparatus, and set of 'facts on file.' More important, it has provided different angles from which to view all forms of human communication (from vocal language and traditional writing to body language and new forms of writing) and culture (from narratives to video games). This implies that such study now has its own 'encyclopedia' structure. The word *encyclopedia* derives from a phrase signifying 'coming to grips with the contents of knowledge.' A comprehensive encyclopedia of media and communications – that is, a work for a general readership that presents the main aspects of a field of knowledge – is a basic tool that virtually everyone should have at his or her disposal, especially since we all live in the world of the matrix. That is the purpose of the present encyclopedia.

The fear that representations of reality, such as theatrical ones, have significant effects on people is an ancient one. It was espoused, for example, by the philosopher Plato. In 1922, the American journalist Walter Lippmann came forward to make the explicit claim that the modern-day mass media had a direct effect on people's minds. The American scholar Harold Lass-

well extended Lippmann's view in 1927, arguing that mass-mediated propaganda affected people's behaviours and overall world view. But these critiques remained mere opinions (albeit persuasively argued ones) until 1939. That was the year after the radio adaptation of H.G. Wells's novel about alien invasion, *The War of the Worlds*, led to the first true scientific study of the relation between media representations and mass psychology. The program was created by the famous actor and director Orson Welles as a drama in which a typical music radio broadcast was interrupted by a series of fake 'on-the-spot' news reports describing the landing of Martian spaceships. The radio audience was reminded, from time to time, that the program was fictional. But thousands nevertheless believed that Martians were actually invading the Earth. A number of people called the police and the army; others ran onto the streets. A year later, psychologist Hadley Cantril and a team of researchers at Princeton University decided to study the reasons why a fictional radio program would have the power to bring about such hysteria, focusing on why some people believed the fake reports and others did not. After interviewing 135 subjects, Cantril and his team concluded that the main factor distinguishing the two groups was critical thinking – educated listeners were more capable of recognizing the broadcast as a fake than less-educated ones. The Cantril report laid the foundation for a systematic study of the media in universities, leading eventually to a new field – media studies. Since the 1940s, the size and scope of this field has skyrocketed, becoming an area of interest, not only on the part of academics and researchers, but also on the part of virtually everyone.

A decade after the Cantril study, the late American engineer Claude Shannon laid the scientific foundations for investigating the relation between mass communication (in all its forms) and technology. Known as the 'bull's-eye model,' Shannon's approach aimed to identify the main components of communications systems and describe in precise mathematical terms how they functioned in the transmission and reception of information. The model consisted of a *sender* aiming a *message* at a *receiver* as if in a target range – hence the designation bull's-eye model. Shannon introduced terms such as *feedback* and *noise* permanently into the vocabulary of media and communications study. By the 1950s, the study of media was starting to take on its modern-day shape. Influential in that regard was Marshall McLuhan, whose books made it obvious that human cognition, culture, social evolution, and technology are intrinsically intertwined. McLuhan claimed that each major historical era took its overall cognitive style from the medium used most widely at the time. He designated the period from 1700 to the mid-1900s the 'Age of Print' because printed books were the chief media through which mass communications took place. That age changed the state of the world because print literacy became a desired and necessary social skill. As a consequence, legislation started cropping up in many places making the acquisition of literacy in school mandatory. Literacy encourages individualism and the growth of nationalism. It has even been claimed that literacy-produced cognitive states have been responsible for such events as the Enlightenment and Protestantism. Because electronic technology has increased both the breadth and speed of mass communications, it has come forward today to produce a second major paradigm shift in cognitive style. Cellphones, computers, and instant-messaging devices have influenced the lives of everyone alive today, even those who do not use them. The current age may be leading, as McLuhan suspected, to the end of individualism and literacy-inspired notions of knowledge associated with the previous age of print.

In the same era, media study was expanded to incorporate the investigation of the contents or meanings of media products. Leading the way in this regard was the French semiotician Roland Barthes, who showed for the first time, in his 1957 book *Mythologies*, that such products are modern-day reflexes of hidden mythic structures. *Mythologies* brought out the significance of studying media products in terms of how they recycle and embody meaning structures. A photograph in a newspaper, for instance, does more than just capture a fact or event literally. At one level, a photograph shows something in reality, of course; but at a secondary level, which Barthes called *mythological,* the photo evokes a series of subconscious meanings that bear upon how it is interpreted. A photo of a dog might, for example, evoke the subconscious features we associate socially with dogs (as pets or companions). This is emphasized (if desired) by anchoring the meaning of the photo in some way, such as by using a caption (for example, 'Man's Best Friend').

Since the 1960s, the study of media and mass communications has developed its own set of theories, facts, and analytical methodologies. The appeal of such study is that it leaves the interpretation of the modes and forms of social interaction used in a certain era flexible and open. There is, in fact, no one theory of media, but many. Media analysts today use a combination of ideas and techniques for diverse purposes. The study of media has thus, logically, developed into a highly 'interdisciplinary' mode of inquiry, drawing from disciplines such as anthropology, semiotics, linguistics, psychology, sociology, literary theory, aesthetics, and the like.

The Goal of This Encyclopedia

As fascinating and relevant to understanding the contemporary world as the work in these fields is, the writing is often too technical, laden with jargon, and highly abstruse. To unlock the relevance and significance of the work within these fields, a terminological key is required, especially by those who are new to them. The purpose of this encyclopedia is to provide such a key. It constitutes a collection of basic concepts, personages, schools of thought, historical movements, and cognate disciplines that make up the current field of media and communications study. The bibliography at the end of each entry contains not only references cited in the entry, or used as the basis for its contents, but also works that can be consulted for further reading.

The choice of entries has not been an easy one. As an instructor of media and communications courses at the University of Toronto for nearly four decades, I have had to trust my instincts. I have included what I feel is absolutely essential knowledge within the field itself, embracing entries from the primary interdisciplinary domains which inform the study of media – anthropology, psychology, linguistics, philosophy, sociology, and semiotics. For example, in choosing entries related to various genres (adventure stories, spy fiction, etc.), I have used the following criterion: if the genre is popular across various media, then it merits treatment here; otherwise it is left as the subject matter of other encyclopedias (such as literary ones). Nevertheless, there are many other entries that I could have included, but simply could not because of length considerations. I have had to limit my choices to the main items that recur in the relevant literature. Nevertheless, I have tried to cast as broad a net as possible, so as to gather within the pages of this encyclopedia – written by experts and practitioners of media studies – the bulk of the ideas that the media student or the interested general reader will need to know in order to understand what is going on in the field

Needless to say, there exist all kinds of handbooks and websites in this field: discourse analysis, introductions to media studies, and communication theory in text form. But the main thrust of this particular encyclopedia is to provide additional perspectives that one will not normally find in these other places and texts. The underlying thematic vision is based on semiotics, which is often missing from these kinds of works. In other words, many of the entries provided here are scattered in different places and forms, whereas the attempt in this volume is to unite them under the rubric of theories of meaning in media and communications. So, in some ways the whole encyclopedia can be read as a coherent treatment of the field with a specific emphasis – meaning.

I wish to express my sincere gratitude to James Leahy, who copy-edited this work, and Wayne Herrington, my editor at University of Toronto Press. I could not have done it without them.

Marcel Danesi

ENCYCLOPEDIA OF MEDIA AND COMMUNICATION

A

ADORNO, THEODOR (1903–69)

[See also: *Frankfurt School; Hegemony Theory; Habermas, Jürgen; Ideology Theory; Marcuse, Herbert; Marxism*]

Theodor Ludwig Wiesengrund Adorno was a social critic, musicologist, and composer whose critiques of twentieth-century popular culture became (and continue to be) a point of reference in media studies. Adorno was an original member of the Frankfurt School – a school of social inquiry founded at the University of Frankfurt in 1922 that applied Marxist philosophy to the critical analysis of modern capitalist societies. The School produced some of the best-known thinkers of the twentieth century, including Max Horkheimer, Walter Benjamin, Jürgen Habermas, and Herbert Marcuse. Influenced by German sociologist Max Weber's view that there was a direct relationship between the Protestant work ethic and the rise of materialistic capitalism, Adorno argued that this had brought about the end of true philosophical inquiry and a loss of the ability for people to think critically.

Adorno was the only child of a wine merchant of Jewish descent, Oscar Alexander Wiesengrund, who had converted to Protestantism, and a Catholic singer, Maria Barbara Calvelli-Adorno. He adopted Adorno as his surname (abbreviating Wiesengrund to the initial W) upon becoming a naturalized American citizen in the 1930s.

He studied philosophy with Hans Cornelius, a follower of Immanuel Kant, and music composition with the famous atonalist composer Alban Berg in Vienna. He was also influenced greatly by the writings of the playwright Karl Kraus and the literary critic Georg Lukács (*Theory of the Novel, History and Class Consciousness*). Adorno became a music critic early in his life, writing monographs on Mahler and Wagner. His 1949 book, *Philosophie der neuen Musik* (written while he was in exile in the United States), became an influential work in musicological circles. He established close intellectual relations with fellow Frankfurt School members Walter Benjamin and Max Horkheimer, as well as with Swiss-born American composer Ernst Bloch. He took on his first teaching position at Frankfurt University in 1928, after defending his thesis on Søren Kierkegaard's aesthetics.

In 1933 Adorno's professional titles were revoked by the Nazis, along with those of all professors of 'non-Aryan descent.' A year later he emigrated to England, and shortly after to the United States. While in America, he wrote the *Dialectic of Enlightenment* (*Dialektik der Aufklärung*, 1947), with Max Horkeimer, which laid the foundations for developing modern critical social theory. Shortly after the Second World War, he returned to Frankfurt University, teaching philosophy and sociology and becoming director of its Institute for Social Research (Institut für Sozialforschung). He was highly critical of the counterculture movement that took shape at the end of 1960s in both America and Europe. He apparently even got the local police to remove a group of students who had occupied the Frankfurt Institute from the campus. As a result, he became a target of student protest. In 1969, a group of bare-breasted female students took over his class as a sign of defiance. Adorno criticized the counterculture movement as being fundamentally anti-intellectual, seeing in it the kind of cultural arrogance that he believed was the spark for totalitarianism. He died of a heart attack on 6 August of that same year in Switzerland during a vacation there with his wife.

Adorno saw capitalism as a system that produced nothing but robotic 'worker-consumers.' It did so by manipulating the media to constantly promote its consumerist social agenda. As a result, capitalism, in the modern era, had led to an amorphous mass culture that reproduces itself constantly, remaining essentially the same throughout the course of its evolution, exploiting human resources for the profit of a few. He also blamed the modern social sciences for helping to bring this about, since he believed that they contributed unwittingly to the status quo by claiming to produce scientific and objective facts about the modern world. But all they ended up doing was admiring the very 'facts' they produced (as if there existed such things as raw facts without human interpretations of them), not critiquing their self-serving motivation. For Adorno (and other Frankfurt School members), culture in capitalist societies was tantamount to an 'industry.' The arts that this industry produces, therefore, are designed to have a short lifespan in the same way that manufactured products are. Despite the many polemical counter-arguments that Adorno's culture industry theory has elicited over the years, it is still referenced today, indicating that its core critical apparatus has always had some intellectual appeal.

The *Dialectic of Enlightenment* (with Horkheimer) is, arguably, Adorno's masterpiece. It was published in 1944 (in New York) with the title *Philosophische Fragmente*. A revised version came out in 1947 (in Amsterdam) with the title *Dialektik der Aufklärung*, and then again in 1969. The book argues that it is the arrogance of Enlightenment reason that has brought about the modern-day idolatry of progress, science, and technology and exalted the power of human beings over nature while at the same time keeping silent over the unscrupulous power exerted by a few human beings over others. It is this very exaltation of Enlightenment reason that has led to totalitarianism, war, and criminality, as well as to the transformation of true culture into an industry of products.

Adorno also took on the 'dialecticism' of Georg Wilhelm Friedrich Hegel, namely the belief that truth is reached by engaging in reasoning through a constant interplay of contrasting ideas. In *Negative Dialectics* (1966) he proposed a different type of dialecticism, one that does not lay claim to resolving all contradictions, or require an absolute negation of things, and consequently does not reduce 'difference' to unity, to the totality of the world. The Hegelian dialectic method is founded on differences and contradictions, and aims to unmask the desire of individuals to absorb differences in order to understand themselves. Adorno saw this philosophy as being slavishly dependent on dogmatic reason. A more critical dialectic method, he claimed, was required in order to allow for recognition of the importance of alterity (Otherness) as part of the construction of our own identities.

Perhaps Adorno's most crucial insight was that in an age of rampant materialism the commercially produced artistic products, the artistic expressions of the imagination, continue to be humanity's assurance that life is meaningful. True art cannot be reproduced, as it is by the contemporary culture industries. Beethoven's music, for instance, transcends political and cultural boundaries; the music of pop musicians is instead much more limited in its reach.

True art is based on the imagination, creativity, and a utopian perspective of human existence, not on marketplace economics. It is the manifest expression of an unconscious 'antithesis to reality' and a vehicle for escaping from that reality – a view that is similar to Martin Heidegger's aesthetics. This is the basic message to be found in Adorno's posthumously published book *Aesthetic Theory* (1970).

Augusto Ponzio

Bibliography

Adorno, Theodor. *Kierkegaard: Construction of the Aesthetic*. Minneapolis: University of Minnesota Press, 1933/1989.
– *Philosophy of New Music*. Minneapolis: University of Minnesota Press, 1949/2006.
– *The Authoritarian Personality*. New York: Harper and Brothers, 1950.
– *In Search of Wagner*. London: Versus, 1952/2005.
– *Prisms*. Cambridge: MIT Press, 1955/1981.
– *Against Epistemology: A Metacritique: Studies in Husserl and the Phenomenological Antinomies*. Cambridge: MIT Press, 1956/1982.
– *Kant's Critique of Pure Reason*. Stanford: Stanford University Press, 1959/2001.
– *Mahler: A Musical Physiognomy*. Chicago: University of Chicago Press, 1960/1988.
– *Critical Models: Interventions and Catchwords*. New York: Columbia University Press, 1963/1969/1998.
– *The Jargon of Authenticity*. London: Routledge and Kegan Paul, 1964/1973.
– *Negative Dialectics*. New York: Seabury Press, 1966/1973.
– *Alban Berg: Master of the Smallest Link*. New York: Cambridge University Press, 1968/1991.
– *Introduction to Sociology*. Stanford: Stanford University Press, 1968/2000.
– *The Positivist Dispute in German Sociology*. London: Heinemann, 1969/1976.
– *Aesthetic Theory*. Minneapolis: University of Minnesota Press, 1970/1999.
– *Gesammelte Schriften*. Frankfurt am Main: Surkamp, 1970–1986.
– *Notes to Literature*. 2 vols. New York: Columbia University Press, 1991/1992.
– *Nachgelassene Schriften*. Frankfurt am Main: Suhrkamp, 1993.
– *Beethoven: The Philosophy of Music; Fragments and Texts*. Cambridge: Polity Press, 1993/1998.
– *The Complete Correspondence with Walter Benjamin, 1928–1940*. Cambridge: Harvard University Press, 1999.
Adorno, Theodor, and Max Horkheimer. *Dialectic of Enlightenment: Philosophical Fragments*. Stanford: Stanford University Press, 1947/2002.
Cook, Deborah. *The Culture Industry Revisited: Theodor W. Adorno on Mass Culture*. Lanham, MD: Rowman and Littlefield, 1996.
Hammer, Espen. *Adorno and the Political*. New York: Routledge, 2005.
Jarvis, Simon, ed. *Theodor Adorno: Critical Evaluations in Cultural Theory*. 4 vols. London: Routledge, 2005.
O'Connor, Brian, ed. *The Adorno Reader*. Oxford: Blackwell, 2000.
Sherratt, Yvonne. *Adorno's Positive Dialectics*. Cambridge: Cambridge University Press, 2002.
Tiedemann, Rolf, ed. *Adorno, Habermas, and the Search for a Rational Society*. New York: Routledge, 2006.
Zuidervaart, Lambert. *Social Philosophy after Adorno*. Cambridge: Cambridge University Press, 2007.

ADVENTURE STORIES

[See also: *Cinema Genres; Mythology; Narrative; Print Culture; Pulp Fiction; Science Fiction; Spy Fiction; Thrillers; Video Games; Video Game Effects*]

Adventure stories (sometimes called *action stories*) are narratives involving heroes or heroines who defeat villains by using superhuman strength and intelligence, or other rare attributes. D'Ammassa (2008: vii–viii) defines such stories as narratives depicting events that 'happen outside the course of the protagonist's ordinary life, usually accompanied by danger, often by physical action.' Although this appears to be a simplistic definition, it actually captures the essence of the narrative formula that underlies the adventure story – a formula in which excitement, suspense, and cathartic resolution constitute its main ingredients, supporting the widely-held notion in psychoanalysis that this formula is a product of psychic Angst that is released through a fictional framework. While we cannot solve the world's problems ourselves, we allow our adventure heroes to do so in a make-believe way, thus restoring order to our chaotic experiences. The stories are as old as human history. From Homeric characters such as Achilles to modern-day fictional heroes such as Superman, Zorro, James Bond, Lara Croft, and agent Triple-X, the adventure story has been delivered in all forms and media, from oral narration to contemporary websites that cater to people's penchant for adventure on a daily basis. But while the media or modes of delivery may have changed, the basic 'adventure hero formula' has not, even though it has sometimes been deconstructed and then reassembled by writers and satirists for various purposes.

Historical Sketch

The adventure story has been a popular genre throughout time and across cultures, revealing its universal appeal and manifesting a universal structure of cognition embedded in the narrative. Many stories from the ancient world, which were based on actual historical events (or on how they were thought to have occurred), incorporated adventure in their narrative frameworks. The plot of many medieval romances was essentially an adventure story, with characters such as King Arthur, among many others, reflecting continuity with the heroes of mythic lore. More generally, the medieval adventure plot would typically involve romance between a hero and a lady, with the hero going through a series of adventures and challenges before meeting his paramour. The two would be separated by a second set of adventures, only to be reunited at the end in a felicitous reunion.

Starting in the fifteenth century, adventure novels gained popularity right after the invention of print technology made books cheaply available to anyone who wanted them. In the late eighteenth century the adventure plot started developing variations to the basic hero-and-his-lady formula, with writers such as Sir Walter Scott, Victor Hugo, and Robert Louis Stevenson. The latter's adventure stories *Treasure Island* and *Kidnapped* appealed to both children and adults. By the late 1800s (in America especially), print magazines and novels were being produced in bulk for mass consumption – the former were called *pulp fiction* magazines and the latter *dime novels*. The words *pulp* and *dime* refer to the fact that the magazines and the novels were produced cheaply, in contrast to those published on higher-quality paper, called *glossies* or *slicks*. The 'pulps,' as both magazines and novels came eventually to be called, revolved around the theme of a heroic figure out to seek justice, mixing in romance and sex in order to enhance their prurient appeal (Server 1993, Robinson and Davidson 2007). They were written in a sensationalistic style, attracting mass audiences. The first true fictional heroes of American popular culture come from the pulps – Doc Savage, The Shadow, the Phantom Detective, Buck Rogers, Fu Manchu, Hopalong Cassidy, Perry Mason, Nick Carter, Secret Agent X, Tarzan, Zorro. The popularity of the pulps was bolstered by sensationalistic cover designs, which copied the poster art style used by circuses and vaudeville theatres to attract audiences, with images of scantily dressed 'damsels in distress' and virile handsome heroes involved in fisticuffs with ugly and odious villains. Given their popularity, the pulps provided the scripts and style adopted by the early movie serials, such as those made by Republic Pictures in the 1930s and 1940s. These were designed to keep audiences in suspense as an episode typically ended with the hero or heroine 'suspended' (often literally) in some deadly situation from which escape seemed unlikely. The audience would eagerly come back the next week to find out how the 'cliffhanger' would be resolved. The same kind of formula is still evident in some of the James Bond movies and the *Raiders of the Lost Ark* films, among others, although the dangerous predicaments therein are resolved in a single movie sitting.

Adventure pulps (and the other pulp genres) were not devoid of literary merit. On the contrary, some of the greatest writers of the twentieth century – Isaac Asimov, Ray Bradbury, Edgar Rice Burroughs, Arthur C. Clarke, Philip K. Dick, Zane Grey, Robert A. Heinlein, Frank Herbert, Upton Sinclair – devoted their efforts to this popular narrative medium, and their stories are interesting and 'intellectual,' garnering a huge cadre of readers to this day. The writing of contemporary authors such as Stephen King and Anne Rice is cut from the same literary fabric as that used by such pulp writers. So, while the original pulps may have disappeared, the pulp genre endures as an instinctive mode of storytelling in contemporary fiction.

The adventure genre found a natural home in the comic book medium early in the twentieth century. While the Sunday newspaper comic strips were originally designed for children, the daily comic strips were intended to attract adult audiences. Harry Hershfield's *Abie the Agent*, originally published in 1914, was the first adult American comic strip, capitalizing on the popularity of the detective and mystery genres. The comic book adventure hero genre began with the publication in 1929 of *Tarzan* and *Buck Rogers* – the former adapted from the novels of writer Edgar Rice Burroughs. Both comics became instantly popular. The first comic superhero, Dr Mystic, was introduced in 1936 by Jerry Siegel and Joe Shuster. In 1938, *Action Comics* started publishing its *Superman* comic strip, co-created by the same Siegel and Shuster duo. So popular was the strip that, barely a year later, a series of comic book super-hero clones started cropping up across the American comic book landscape.

The 1940s saw the debuts of *Batman, The Flash, Green Lantern, Wonder Woman*, and *Captain America*.

Since the 1950s, the adventure story has been regularly recast for new audiences while maintaining the same basic formula; in some cases, it has been turned on its head with 'anti-heroes' or 'soft heroes' (such as the current *Spiderman* character). Steven Spielberg's Republic Pictures–style cliffhangers featuring Indiana Jones as the heroic figure (starting in 1981) are both a recasting and a revisioning of the 1940s adventure serial, and have spawned a multitude of imitators, from *The Mummy* and *Jason Bourne* films (based on the late Robert Ludlum's books), to movies such as *Romancing the Stone*, the *Pirates of the Caribbean* movies, and *National Treasure* (2004), to mention but a few. These are sometimes classified in media studies as 'thriller,' 'spy,' or 'detective' movies, although the boundary line between these genres and the adventure genre is often a blurry one. It could be claimed that the adventure story is a kind of *architext*, constituting the prototype from which subsequent texts or genres are derived – for example, the *Iliad* is the architext on which many adventure stories involving a valiant hero, a journey, and conquest have been subsequently based.

The Adventure Story Formula

The adventure story typically revolves around the exploits of a hero or heroine who fights in the name of justice; searches for a lost empire, city, or treasure; seeks to save someone; or engages in some other quest. Martin Green (1991) points out that there are seven main types of adventure tales, but that all of them share common elements. The story starts with a statement or portrayal of the situation that requires the intervention of a hero or heroine, who then sets out to accomplish the objective posed by the initial situation. The protagonist faces a series of physically and intellectually challenging trials, which he or she overcomes, often with the help of a partner or sidekick (which may also be an animal, such as a horse, or a machine, such as a car), triumphantly reaching the objective at the end. Modern-day adventure stories have often been modified to include anti-heroes, likeable villains (as in *Pirates of the Caribbean*), or 'dark heroes' (as in *The Dark Knight*). Such cases involve a modification to the traditional 'hero code,' not a radical departure from it. This suggests that the adventure hero or heroine is an archetype, as Carl Jung suggested, an idealized human being who rises above the world to lead it in some way out of its darkness. Incidentally, the concept of the anti-hero can be traced to Fyodor Dostoyevsky's novel *Notes from the Underground* (1864), which, for the first time in the history of literature, introduced the alienated anti-hero. Contemporary progeny can be seen in characters such as Arthur Miller's Willy Loman (*Death of a Salesman*, 1949) and J.D. Salinger's Holden Caulfield (*The Catcher in the Rye*, 1951), although the anti-hero concept can be traced back much further. Perhaps the most famous 'proto-anti-hero' of Western literature is Cervantes' Don Quixote (*Don Quixote de la Mancha*, 1605–15), a daydreaming vagabond who moves lackadaisically through a series of misadventures. A contemporary TV anti-hero is Dr Gregory House, a modern take on Sherlock Holmes. Unlike Holmes, however, House has not one faithful sidekick (Dr Watson), but several, including a longtime friend, the servile doctors who work under him at the hospital, and his female boss.

The traditional hero code was forged in the ancient myths. In bare outline form, it involves the exploits of imaginary or historically real heroic figures such as Achilles, Prometheus, Hercules, and others, who were courageous, noble, strong, and willing to sacrifice themselves for the good of others. The narratives composed about them consisted of several salient features – the hero might have come from another world or state of existence; he or she typically possessed superhuman or uncommon strength; he or she often had a flaw that rendered him or her vulnerable in certain situations; and he or she was on a quest to accomplish some goal. It is this code (or its variants) that surfaces in various guises and forms in modern adventure stories. Like the ancient heroes of myth and legend, the fictitious heroes of comic books, movies, and radio and television programs are normally strong, superhuman (to varying degrees), and flawed. The action hero Superman, for instance, comes from another world (the planet Krypton); has superhuman qualities (he can fly and cannot be killed by mere human means); helps weaker humans; defeats villains; and has a tragic flaw (exposure to kryptonite takes away his power).

Adventure stories have always played a crucial role in cultural traditions, depicting virtues that are rare, attainable by only a 'chosen few.' The hero is an archetypal embodiment of people's concept of virtue. In mythology, he or she was typically an individual, often of divine ancestry, who was endowed with great courage and strength, celebrated for his or her bold exploits, and who played a positive role in human affairs. Modern-day audiences feel the need for the hero archetype as intuitively as did the ancient ones who watched stage performances of the plays of such Greek dramatists as Aeschylus, Sophocles, or Euripides. The modern comic book superhero, thus, is an updated heroic persona suitable for the times in which we live. Superman is an urban hero who stands for 'truth,' 'justice,' and 'the American way,' as the 1950s TV series based on the comic book character proclaimed. And like the ancient heroes, Superman is devoted to saving humanity from itself. Rather than being sent by the gods from the afterworld, as were many of the ancient heroes, Superman came to Earth from a planet in another galaxy; he leads a 'double life' as a superhero and as Clark Kent, a 'mild-mannered' reporter for a daily newspaper; he is adored by Lois Lane, a reporter for the same newspaper who suspects (from time to time) that Clark Kent may be Superman; he wears a distinctive costume, battles villains, and so forth. Superman embodies all the heroic virtues that human beings, in their weakness, aspire to possess.

The same archetypal code manifests itself in other adventure heroes, albeit in varying forms and with different emphases. In the *Batman* stories (launched by DC Comics in 1939; artist Bob Kane) the code is characterized by other features – the hero has a helper, Robin; the opponent manifests himself or herself in various characters, depending on actual story, from the Riddler to the Penguin; Batman wears a mask; he employs an arsenal of weapons and gadgets to fight crime, including a Batmobile and a Batplane, as well as an all-purpose utility belt. *The Dark Knight* (2008) is also based on the same code, but it blends different genre styles, from film noir to gothic occultism and postmodernism. It is a filmic essay on the dark regions of the human psyche, and on evil as part of the human condition, not an external force.

Two thematic elements that have entered the modern-day adventure narrative are occultism and conspiracy. Adventure stories such as *Hellboy* involve occult forces as ingredients in the adventure formula, while stories such as *National Treasure* add a conspiratorial subplot to the adventure frame. They are not departures from the basic adventure formula; they simply extend it. In the conspiratorial narratives, the hero attempts to unmask some conspiracy or plot against a nation, group, or person. Conspiracy was also an element in ancient stories as well, but it has come to prominence today in an age where assassinations (the JFK and Martin Luther King assassinations), UFO sightings, and the like are perceived to be part of larger conspiratorial government agendas. This would explain, in part at least, the popularity of such novels as *The Da Vinci Code* and its various imitators.

Of the more contemporary adventure superhero narratives, *Watchmen* (released in 1986 as a graphic novel) is particularly interesting. In this case the hero, Rorschach, is a demented vigilante with a morphing inkblot mask (hence his name, which refers to the Rorschach technique in psychology) and the villain is someone called the Comedian. Both Rorschach and the Comedian are strange characters, seeming parodies of the ancient heroic and villainous archetypes. Richard Reynolds (1992: 107) states: 'While the Comedian is in part a satirical reworking of the state-sponsored, nationalistic breed of superhero most notably exemplified by Captain America or Nick Fury, Rorschach is a version of the night-shrouded hero embodied by characters from Batman through Daredevil.' In the 2009 *Watchmen* movie, the Comedian is killed and Rorschach appears with a host of seemingly zany characters, from a new superhero, Ozymandias, to neo-Watchmen who have emerged to replace older, retired ones. The bad guy does a very evil thing but escapes punishment by persuading people that his deed was actually beneficial. The movie, as with many other postmodern narratives, reverberates with moral ambiguity rather than certainty (as in the traditional adventure stories). Rorschach is an idealist who insists on moral absolutes in black and white terms; Ozymandias, on the other hand, is a pragmatist, accepting life as it presents itself. The choice of what is right or wrong is left to the audience to resolve.

As the *Watchmen* example illustrates, adventure stories have changed in step with the times. Batwoman, who was introduced in 1956, has become a lesbian in one of her new incarnations. There is now also a Black Panther, a hero figure for a fictitious African nation; the Great Ten, a team of Chinese heroes; an aboriginal girl hero; an Eskimo man; and an HIV-positive gay man. The 'European-based hero story' has finally become more inclusive.

Video Game Adventure

Video games provide both a new format for adventure and a source for creating movie narratives, with many movies now being based on video game themes or characters. In the early 1970s the electronic tennis game Pong introduced the video-game industry to the world. After the industry nearly collapsed in the mid-1980s, Japanese companies, especially the Nintendo Corporation, assumed leadership, improving game technology and introducing popular adventure games such as Donkey Kong and the Super Mario Brothers, thus spawning a video game culture that is now blossoming into one of the most influential of all contemporary recreational trends.

There are now different genres of video games and various formats in which they can be played. One of the most relevant ones is the so-called 'role-playing' genre, which gained popularity with the Dungeons and Dragons game, invented by E. Gary Gygax in the early 1980s. The game provides a framework for simulating the mythic and fantasy worlds of the traditional adventure story, but leaves the script up to the game players, who can imagine themselves to be knights and wizards and to possess enormous physical and moral strength. The game quickly migrated to the big screen, when Tom Hanks made his debut in the movie *Mazes and Monsters* (1982), which was based on the game. Players pretend to be in an adventure situation or environment, such as a battle or newly discovered place; each situation has its own rules, and each participant plays a specific role or character in the scenario. Occult and horror themes are amalgamated with adventure-fantasy themes, allowing players to engage in the same kind of fascination with the macabre and the grotesque that has always informed the spirit of pulp fiction. However, rather than writers and filmmakers creating the horror and adventure, the games allow users to do so. The increase in the popularity of online gaming of this type has resulted in the formation of subgenres, such as multiplayer online role-playing games. Participants create a character, known as an avatar, by inputting descriptions of appearance and behaviour into a communal online space for the game.

Other characters have no way of knowing whether the character corresponds to the real physical appearance or personality of the player. In this way realism and fantasy mesh completely.

Video gaming provides a new format for the adventure story, in which the make-believe element is put into the hands of the player. The player thus becomes the scriptwriter, actor, and director at once. The game enables players to participate in the outcome of a story, to explore its variables, and to take charge of the overall narrative script. The spectator is no longer a passive receiver of the story, but a participant in it. Video games give players the feeling of being immersed in a simulated world that resembles the real world. The division between the imaginary and the real is thus blurred, producing what the social critic Jean Baudrillard called the *simulacrum effect*, whereby the modern-day individual can no longer distinguish between reality and fantasy. Indeed, the latter, which he calls *hyperreality*, is more interesting than reality to the modern-day individual, and is starting to replace reality in society generally. Baudrillard may have a point, but then fantasy worlds were also created, albeit in a different way, by ancient theatre and other narrative traditions. The video game and other modern technologies simply extend the possibility of fantasizing; they do not make it the only form of cognition.

Like other forms of media and pop culture, video games have been the target of criticism from scholars, and have been subject to censorship, especially those that involve macabre themes or sex and violence. To a pop culture analyst this comes as no surprise, for these are the elements of pop culture that have always created moral panic in different eras. Those who oppose this new form of story-making are the usual suspects: politicians, organized special interest groups, and the like. Interestingly, recent surveys have shown that video games are attracting more diversified groups than the typical male teenager, appealing also to female players and older individuals.

The adventure story continues to find expression in contemporary popular media. As the ancients were certainly aware, we are a species that seeks to set things right in the world, to bring order to the chaos; the hero (whether fictional, real, or participatory), symbolizes this quest. As the poet W.H. Auden commented in a 1955 essay, 'The Shield of Achilles,' the adventure story is a format humans have used from time immemorial to secure moral balance in the world. It reassures us that we live in such a world. The hero (whether a superhero, a detective, a spy, or even an anti-hero) is our imaginary agent of justice. Of course, sometimes the wrongdoer gets away with the crime – a fact that seems to tap into our darker sense of reality. For example, Edgar Allan Poe's story 'The Cask of Amontillado' (1846), which portrays a horrific murder (enclosing the victim in a cellar), is narrated by the perpetrator himself. The *Saw* series of movies is a contemporary example of this kind of approach. Such stories terrify us because they acknowledge that evil-doers often get away with their deeds in real life. But whether the villain is punished or not, adventure stories are clearly part of an ongoing moral discourse in which humans have engaged from the beginning of time.

Marcel Danesi

Bibliography

Baudrillard, Jean. *Simulations*. New York: Semiotexte, 1983.

Cook, Michael L., and Stephen T. Miller. *Mystery, Detective, and Espionage Fiction: A Checklist of Fiction in U.S. Pulp Magazines, 1915–1974*. New York: Garland, 1998.

D'Ammassa, Don. *Encyclopedia of Adventure Fiction*. New York: Facts on File, 2008.

Fingeroth, Danny. *Superman on the Couch: What Superheroes Really Tell Us about Ourselves and Our Society*. New York: Continuum, 2004.

Green, Martin Burgess. *Seven Types of Adventure Tale: An Etiology of a Major Genre*. University Park: Pennsylvania State University Press, 1991.

Jensen, Jan, and Henk M.J. Maier, eds. *Epic Adventures: Heroic Narrative in the Oral Performance Traditions of Four Continents*. Münster: Lit, 2004.

Jung, Carl G. *The Essential Jung*. Princeton: Princeton University Press, 1999.

Kane, Michael. *Game Boys: Professional Videogaming's Rise from the Basement to the Big Time*. London: Penguin, 2008.

McCracken, Scott. *Pulp: Reading Popular Fiction*. Manchester: Manchester University Press, 1998.

Reynolds, Richard. *Super Heroes: A Modern Mythology*. Jackson: University of Mississippi Press, 1992.

Robinson, Frank M., and Lawrence Davidson. *Pulp Culture: The Art of Fiction Magazines*. Portland: Collectors Press, 2007.

Robinson, Lillian S. *Wonderwomen: Feminisms and Superheroes*. London: Routledge, 2004.

Server, Lee. *Danger is My Business: An Illustrated History of the Fabulous Pulp Magazines*. San Francisco: Chronical Books, 1993.

Taylor, T.L. *Play between Worlds: Exploring Online Game Culture*. Cambridge, MA: MIT Press, 2006.

ADVERTISING

[See also: *Brand Names; Branding; Culture Jamming; Logos; Radio; Television*]

The term *advertising* comes from the medieval Latin verb *advertere*, 'to direct one's attention to.' It refers to any type of public announcement intended to direct people's attention to the availability, qualities, and/or cost of specific commodities or services. The craft of advertising has, however, progressed considerably beyond the use of simple declarations of product availability. Since the middle part of the nineteenth century, it has ventured successfully into the domain of unconscious persuasion. Given its apparent effectiveness, advertising has been used with increasing regularity since the early 1960s as a vehicle to promote social issues and causes and as an important strategy in political campaigning. Anti-smoking and anti-drug advertising campaigns are cases in point. Advertising strategy is also used commonly in propaganda, publicity, and public relations. Propaganda is the craft of spreading and entrenching doctrines, views, and beliefs reflecting specific interests and ideologies (political, social, philosophical, and so on) by attempting to persuade people through various forms of appeal. Publicity is the technique of disseminating any information about a person, group, event, or product through some public medium so as to garner favourable attention. Public relations (PR) employs activities and techniques to establish positive attitudes and responses towards organizations, institutions, and/or individuals.

Advertising is a blend of art and science that combines aesthetic, rhetorical, and marketing statistical techniques in order to get people to perceive goods and services favourably and then to assess the effects of such techniques on consumer behaviour. Marketing is a term that does not have a single definition. In the area of advertising, it involves assessments of the effects that the specific advertising of products will have on individuals, taking into account social variables such as age, class, education, and lifestyle. In a word, marketing is the 'science' part of advertising, while creating ads and inventing brand names and logos constitutes its 'artistic' side.

The success of newspaper advertising in enhancing the sales of goods and services since the seventeenth century gave birth in 1914 to the Audit Bureau of Circulations in the United States, an independent organization founded and supported by newspaper and magazine publishers that provided them with circulation statistics. In 1936, the Advertising Research Foundation was established to integrate advertising and marketing research into a unitary enterprise. Today, the increasing sophistication with information-gathering and data-processing techniques makes it possible for marketers

and advertisers to direct their campaigns at specific 'market segments' (people classified according to various socio-economic, sociocultural, or psychosocial variables) with greater efficacy. The internet makes it possible today for advertisers to obtain critical information on people's reactions to certain ad texts almost instantly.

History

Outdoor signs displayed above shop doors indicating the types of goods and services available within them have been found by archaeologists in cities across the ancient world. As early as 3000 BCE, the Babylonians used such signs to identify trades. The ancient Greeks and Romans also hung signs outside their shops. Since few people could read, the merchants used pictures of the goods. These were, literally, the first 'signs' or 'marks' of the 'trades' (trademarks). In the late medieval period, tradespeople and guild members posted similar trademarks outside their shops. Medieval swords and ancient Chinese pottery, for instance, were marked with identifiable trade symbols so that buyers could trace their origin and determine their quality. Among the best-known trademarks surviving from those times are the striped pole of the barbershop and the three-ball sign of the pawnbroker shop.

Posters and wall inscriptions promoting goods and services are also ancient. A poster found in Thebes, and dated back to 1000 BCE, is now considered to be one of the world's first advertisements. It offered a slave in exchange for money. An outdoor poster found among the ruins of ancient Rome offered property for rent; an announcement found painted on a wall in Pompeii called the attention of travellers to a tavern located in a different town. Town criers – individuals hired to walk through streets to announce the availability of goods arriving by ship – were also common in port cities of the ancient world. The modern period of advertising may be said to begin after the invention of the modern printing press by Johannes Gutenberg in the late 1400s. Fliers and posters could, as a result, be printed quickly and cheaply and thus displayed in public places or inserted in books and pamphlets far and wide. Advertising was fast becoming an intrinsic part of the 'Gutenberg Galaxy,' as the Canadian communications theorist Marshall McLuhan (1962) named the new social order that ensued from the arrival of mass print technology. By the latter part of the seventeenth century, when newspapers started circulating widely, print advertisements started appearing regularly. The *London Gazette* became the first newspaper to reserve a section exclusively for advertising purposes for a fee. So successful was this venture that by the end of the seventeenth century several businesses came into existence in England for the specific purpose of creating newspaper ads for merchants and artisans. In general, these 'proto-ad agencies' designed the ad texts in the style of modern classifieds, without illustrative support. The ads did, however, show some of the same rhetorical flavour of their contemporary descendants, tailoring the language style to suit the wealthy clients who bought and read newspapers – a style that promoted the sale of such items as tea, coffee, wigs, books, and theatre tickets as part of an affluent and pleasure-based lifestyle.

The earliest classified ads in the United States could be found in the pages of the Boston *News-Letter* in 1704. Print advertising spread rapidly throughout the eighteenth century in both Europe and America, proliferating to the point that the writer and lexicographer Samuel Johnson felt impelled to make the following statement in *The Idler* (the name used for the essays he published in the London weekly called the *Universal Chronicle* between 1758 and 1760): 'Advertisements are now so numerous that they are very negligently perused, and it is therefore become necessary to gain attention by magnificence of promise and by eloquence sometimes sublime and sometimes pathetic.'

As print advertising became a fixture of the emerging industrialist society, ad creators throughout Europe and in some American cities began paying more and more attention to the design and layout of the ad text. Ads using words set in eye-catching blocks and contrasting type fonts became common. Also, slogans, catchy taglines, and other rhetorical devices were inserted regularly into the ad text in order to get people to associate a product with some aspect of lifestyle, personal amelioration, need, or significant life event (for example, romance) rather than just with what it was capable of doing. By the early decades of the twentieth century, advertising had become a large business enterprise on its own, and its textuality (forms of presenting and structuring information) spilled over into society at large, as familiarity with slogans, product characters, and themes in ads started to spread rapidly and broadly through print media and radio advertising. As a consequence, advertising was starting to change the perception of the role of goods and services in human life, transforming them from simple goods to objects of value beyond their functions and uses. In his 1922 book *Public Opinion*, the American journalist Walter Lippmann argued that the growth of a mass media culture and its attendant use of advertising had a powerful psychological effect on people's minds, changing human behaviour for the worse, and suggested that mass advertising had affected people's politics, familial relations, and general world view. The ads in the 1920s began to use techniques to persuade people that by buying a product they would fulfil certain desires, or avoid certain censures, not just acquire something practical. The growing awareness of the importance of advertising to product sales enhancement had already led to the establishment of the first true advertising agency in 1842 by Philadelphia entrepreneur Volney B. Palmer. By 1849, Palmer had offices in New York, Boston, and Baltimore in addition to his Philadelphia office. In 1875, N.W. Ayer and Son, another Philadelphia advertising agency, became a rival. In time, the firm hired writers and artists to create increasingly creative and persuasive print ads and marketing specialists to design advertising campaigns for clients. By 1900, most agencies in the United States were assuming responsibility for advertising. By the 1920s, such agencies had themselves become large business enterprises, constantly developing new techniques and methods that would, as Lippmann and others like him certainly thought, be capable of influencing the typical consumer to buy things that he or she may not necessarily need. The rise of consumerism in the 1920s was due to a mix of socio-economic factors, but one cannot underestimate the role of advertising in that mix. In the same decade, the growth of electrical technologies, such as electric billboards and new lithographic techniques for producing posters, along with the arrival of radio as a mass communications medium, provided advertising with new powerful channels for conveying its messages. Electricity made possible the illuminated outdoor poster, and photoengraving helped both the editorial and advertising departments of magazines create truly effective illustrative material that could be incorporated into ad texts. The advent of radio led to the invention and widespread use of a new form of advertising, known as the *commercial* – a mini-narrative or musical jingle revolving around a product or service and its uses. The commercial became quickly popular, with some of the jingles becoming hits in their own right. And since it could reach masses of potential customers, print-literate or not, it became even more influential than print ads as a vehicle for disseminating advertising messages. With the arrival of television after the Second World War, the advertising industry adapted the idea of the radio commercial to the new visual medium. In the 1950s, TV commercials, such as Pepsodent toothpaste's animations with snappy jingles, became so familiar to mass TV audiences that the perception of the products themselves became inextricably intertwined with the styles of the commercials created to promote them.

Fictitious cartoon product characters, from Mr Clean (representing a detergent product of the same name) to Speedy (a personified Alka-Seltzer tablet), had a high recognition factor and were as well known as Hollywood celebrities.

The internet has emerged to complement and supplement the print, radio, and TV media as a channel for persuasive advertising. Because the internet allows users to access businesses effectively through websites, it is becoming a dominant and ever-evolving advertising medium, even though it has not altered the basic psychology behind offline advertising methods. The internet provides graphics, audio, and various visual techniques to enhance the effectiveness of ad texts cheaply. It also has become ipso facto its own ad agency. Google is threatening the survival of the traditional ad agency because it collects money from advertisers not on the basis of promise, but on the basis of performance. Moreover, it sells directly to advertisers and provides free services, such as templates for creating ads, for which agencies have traditionally charged. The same kinds of advantages are offered by mobile device advertising. In effect, the new technologies are changing the ways in which advertising has been delivered, although they have not changed its basic persuasive strategies.

Basic Techniques

Advertisers today use many sophisticated presentation and text-making techniques. The most basic one is to create a 'personality' for the product with which a particular type of consumer can identify emotionally and/or socially. Take beer as an example. What kinds of people drink Budweiser? What kinds drink Stella Artois? The answers are provided by the advertisers themselves – the Budweiser drinker is portrayed as being a down-to-earth (male) personality who simply wants to 'hang out with the guys'; the Stella Artois drinker is represented as a smooth, sophisticated type (male or female) who appreciates the 'finer things' of life. The idea behind associating a product with a personality category is to capture the attention of particular types of individuals who identify with that type, so that they can see their own personalities or aspirations represented in the ad.

To create a personality for a product (as for any human being) it is necessary to assign it a name. This is the first act of turning a simple product into a 'brand.' So important is the brand name as an identifier that, on several occasions, it has itself become the metonymic moniker for the entire product line. Examples of this include *aspirin, xerox, cellophane, escalator,* and, more recently, *iPod*. Made-up names for everyday household products were first used towards the end of the nineteenth century in Europe and the United States. Previously, everyday products were sold in neighbourhood stores from large bulk containers, with no names attached to them. Around 1880, soap manufacturers started naming their products with labels such as Ivory, Pears, Sapolio, and Colgate because the market was starting to be flooded by uniform, mass-produced, and, thus, indistinguishable products. The strategy succeeded beyond expectations – consumption of the 'named products' went up astronomically. By the early 1920s, it became obvious that brand-naming was not just a simple strategy for product differentiation, but a symbolic gambit that propelled corporate identity and product recognition, ensconcing products into cultural group-think. Names such as Nike, Apple, Coca-Cola, McDonald's, Calvin Klein, and Levi's, have, in fact, become 'cultural symbols' recognized by virtually everyone living in a modern, consumerist society.

At a practical level, naming a product allows consumers to identify what product they wish to purchase (or not). But at a deeper psychological level, the product's name generates images that go well beyond this simple identifier function. Consider Armani shoes as a specific case in point. At a simple descriptive level, the name allows us to identify the shoes. However, this is not all it does. The use of the manufacturer's name assigns an aura of craftsmanship and superior quality to the product. The shoes are thus perceived to be the 'work' of an artist (Giorgio Armani). They constitute, in effect, a 'work of shoe art,' not just an assembly-line product for everyone to wear. In the world of fashion, designer names such as Gucci, Armani, and Calvin Klein evoke images of objets d'art, rather than of mere clothes, shoes, or jewellery; so too do names such as Ferrari, Lamborghini, and Maserati in the world of automobiles. The manufacturer's name, in such cases, extends the aesthetic and lifestyle symbolism of the product considerably. When people buy an Armani or a Gucci product, they tend to feel that they are buying a work of art to be displayed on the body; when they buy Poison, by Christian Dior, they might sense that they are buying a dangerous, but alluring, love potion; when they buy Moondrops, Natural Wonder, Rainflower, Sunsilk, or Skin Dew cosmetics they might feel that they are acquiring some of nature's beauty resources; and when they buy Eterna 27, Clinique, Endocil, or Equalia beauty products they might believe that they are getting products made with scientific precision. The name is the key that unlocks the unconscious psychic door to such symbolic worlds. As a recent ad for Ferrari claims, when buying something (like the car), one is buying a lifestyle: *Ferrari. It's Not Just a Car. It's a Lifestyle.*

Another way in which advertisers transform a product into a brand is through *logo* design. A logo is really a modern-day version of the trademark – the difference being that the modern logo goes far beyond a simple identifier function. For example, the McDonald's logo represents both the 'M' in the company name and 'golden arches' at the same time. Arches reverberate with mythic and even religious symbolism. They beckon people to march through them into a congenial environment that will 'do it all for you,' as one of the company's slogans so aptly phrases it. In addition, the meaning of 'golden' as something precious is also evoked at some psychological level.

Yet another basic technique is the *ad campaign.* At the turn of the twentieth century advertisers realized that a single ad put into a magazine or newspaper would hardly be capable of spreading product recognition broadly. So they devised the ad campaign, which can be defined simply as the use of diverse media to spread the same message using variations on the same theme. A recent example is the Mac computer campaign that pitted a cool 'Mac Guy' against a lifestyle dinosaur 'PC Guy,' which morphed into various skits shown on television and the internet. Some campaigns have been so well designed that they have become part of pop culture lore – 'Mmm, mm, good' (Campbell's Soup); 'Think small' (Volkswagen); 'Just do it' (Nike); 'A diamond is forever' (DeBeers); 'You deserve a break today' and 'I'm lovin it' (McDonald's); 'This Bud's for you' (Budweiser); 'It's the real thing' (Coca-Cola).

The internet has generated new ways to get a message across, complementing and expanding traditional ad campaign strategies. For example, in 2001 BMW hired several famous movie directors to make short 'online films' featuring its cars, which clearly blurred the line between art and advertising. Each film was only six minutes long, but it featured a prominent actor driving the car in an adventure-style way. Other advertising techniques made available by the internet are:

- banner advertising, or the use of ads that stretch across the top of a web page
- click-through advertising, whereby a user can click on a link on a banner ad or other onscreen ad to get through to the manufacturer of a product
- contextual advertising, by which ads automatically intrude into a web session, whether wanted or not
- email advertising, or the use of email to deliver pitches for a product or service
- pop-up ads that pop up on the screen when a user visits a particular website

- run-of-network banner advertising, which involves placing ads across a network of websites
- run-of-site banner advertising, whereby ads are placed on a specific website
- extramercial advertising, consisting in the use of ads that slide down a web page
- interactive advertising, which involves seeking input from the audience through the internet
- direct-response advertising, which makes an immediate response to a television commercial possible by providing an on-screen phone number, email address, or website
- interstitial advertising, consisting of images that appear and disappear on a screen as users click from one web page to the next
- shoshkeles, or floating ads, whereby animated objects, such as a car, are projected across the screen

Arguably, the most successful campaigns have been those that have co-opted themes, trends, and fads present in popular culture generally, or else made use of well-known personalities or celebrities. *Co-option* is defined as the strategy of adopting pop culture themes, trends, styles, emphases, and celebrities and adapting them to advertising objectives, creating a dynamic interplay between advertising and popular culture, whereby one influences the other through a constant synergy. The concept of *emergent code* is sometimes used to explain why the co-option strategy is effective and is an idea inspired by the work of the late culture critic Raymond Williams (1962). According to Williams, cultural behaviours and codes can be subdivided into dominant, residual, and emergent. The *dominant* code is the set of ideas, values, and lifestyles that define current or middle-of-the road norms in cultural behaviour; *residual* codes are those that were dominant in the past but are still in circulation in minor ways; and *emergent* codes are those that dictate future norms, revealing their elements in bits and pieces at the present time. Some of the more effective ad campaigns are those that tap into the emergent codes of a culture (in lifestyle, music trends, and so on).

Another technique is to create entertaining ads or commercials that involve socially and psychologically relevant themes. Among the various strategies used to do so are the following:

- the 'bandwagon' strategy, which consists of exaggerated claims that 'everyone' is using a particular product/service, inviting the viewer to jump on the bandwagon
- the 'disparaging copy' technique, whereby one brand is overtly critical of another company's products or campaigns
- the 'educational' strategy, which is designed to educate or inform consumers about a product/service, especially if it has only recently been introduced into the market
- the 'nostalgia' technique, which consists in using images from previous times when, purportedly, life was more serene and less dangerous
- the 'plain-folks' pitch, whereby a product/service is associated with common people who use it for practical purposes
- the 'something-for-nothing' lure, also known as 'incentive marketing,' which consists in giving away free gifts in order to give a favourable image to the product/service or company ('Buy one and get a second one free!' 'Send for free sample!' 'Trial offer at half price!' 'No money down!')
- the 'help your child' tactic, whereby parents are induced into believing that giving their children certain products will secure them a better life and future
- the 'ask mommy or daddy' technique, whereby children are exhorted to ask their parents to purchase some product for them
- the 'scare copy' or 'hidden fear' tactic, which is designed to promote such goods and services as insurance, fire alarms, cosmetics, and vitamin capsules by evoking the fear of poverty, sickness, loss of social standing, impending disaster, and so forth
- the use of 'jingles' and 'slogans' in order to enhance recognition of a product/service through music and rhetorical language
- 'satisfied customer testimonials,' which are statements made by satisfied customers who endorse a product/service
- the 'formula' tactic, which consists in the use of formulaic or trivial statements that sound truthful or authoritative ('A Volkswagen is a Volkswagen!' 'Coke is it!')
- the 'history' technique, whereby a significant historical event is incorporated into the ad, either by allusion or by direct reference
- the use of humour to make a product appealing and friendly, as is the case in many beer ads, which associate drinking beer with a recreational and youthful lifestyle
- the 'imperative web' technique, consisting in the use of the imperative form of verbs in order to create the effect that an unseen authoritative source is giving advice ('Join the Pepsi Generation!' 'Have a great day, at McDonald's!')
- the 'benefits' ploy, which emphasizes the advantages that may accrue from purchasing a product/service, such as the nutritional value of some food, or the performance of some car
- the 'mystery ingredient' technique, whereby a mystery ingredient in a drink, detergent, and so on is identified as being the source behind the product's appeal
- the 'alliteration' technique, whereby the initial consonant sound of a brand name is repeated ('The Superfree Sensation,' 'Marlboro Man')
- the 'positive appeal' strategy, intended to demonstrate why a product is attractive or important to possess
- the 'prestige' advertising tactic, whereby a product/service is placed and advertised in high-quality magazines or media programs so as to enhance the company's reputation

- the 'rational appeal' technique, consisting of logical arguments that demonstrate how the product/service might fulfil some need
- the 'reminder' technique, whereby an ad or commercial is designed to recall an advertisement that viewers are familiar with
- the 'secretive statement' strategy, consisting in the use of statements designed to create the effect that something secretive is being communicated, thus capturing people's attention by stimulating curiosity ('Don't tell your friends about …' 'Do you know what she's wearing?')
- the 'snob-appeal' approach, which aims to convince consumers that using a product/service will enable them to maintain or elevate their social status
- the 'soft sell' method, which uses subtle, rather than blatant, forms of persuasion (for example, the type of TV commercial that tells you what a product can do, in comparison to some other product in the same line)
- the 'teaser' technique, whereby little information about a product is given, thus making people curious to know more about it
- the 'viral advertising' technique, which consists of statements that attempt to capture people's attention by encouraging them to 'pass it on' (like a virus) to others
- the 'absence-of-language' tactic, consisting in the intentional omission of language, suggesting, by implication, that the product 'speaks for itself'; many perfume ads are constructed in this way
- the 'self-criticizing' or 'post-advertising' approach, which involves a brand's critique of its own advertising, pretending to be on the consumer's side but actually promoting itself in a clever way
- the 'retro-advertising' strategy, whereby a previous ad campaign, or the style of a previous ad campaign, is recalled to promote the same product/service or something similar to it
- the 'shock effect' technique, which consists in constructing ads that are designed to shock, thus garnering attention (for example, a Benetton ad of the 1990s that showed a priest and nun kissing)

There are various other techniques that require separate and more extended treatment here because of their widespread use. One technique, called *mythologization*, consists in the use of imagery and language designed to evoke ancient mythic themes and symbolism at a subconscious level. The use of animals such as snakes to promote cosmetics or clothing suggests a chain of mythic meanings that are associated with snakes, including fear, darkness, and evil. Since ancient times, snakes have been feared in many cultures because of their deadly venom. They have thus been used as symbols to evoke this pattern of meaning in narratives of all kinds. They also evoke phallic symbolism. These two patterns of meanings seem to be intertwined in many ads for high-quality products. Take, as an example, an ad used by Gucci in the early 2000s for one of its purses. The image in the ad was suggestive of slithering snakes caught in an embrace, which is indicative of copulation in the snake world. Male snakes will come into close proximity with a female snake only to form a 'mating ball.' The chainlike handle of the purse and the metal handcuff-like clasp in its centre also suggest this kind of sexual bondage, or, conversely, the image of the female protecting herself from the slithery males. These latent meanings are what give the ad powerful mythic nuances. There is, however, no empirical way to demonstrate that these nuances are really present in such ads. But the suggestion is there, and thus it is more accurate to say that mythologization is really a form of 'suggestology' or suggestive communication.

The second technique can be called *aestheticization*. This is the use of the same kinds of methods employed by visual artists to enhance the aesthetic appeal of ads. Perfume ads that show women surrounded by a dark void, or appearing mysteriously 'out of nothingness,' as in a dream, are created according to the principles of surrealist art – the art form that expresses the workings of the subconscious through fantastic imagery and the incongruous juxtaposition of subject matter. Many ads for perfumes, such as those for Chanel, are essentially 'surrealist canvases.'

The third technique is really a type of co-option technique. It can be called *real-life advertising*. Dove's Self-Esteem or Real Women campaign involves using 'real women, 'with 'real curves,' rather than professional models, in print ads and TV and internet commercials. The connection with reality TV culture is unmistakable. Real people are more interesting to consumers nowadays in a world where reality and fantasy have coalesced through the mass media. In contrast to professional models, who are attractive, sexy, ultra-thin, and have a flawless complexion, the Dove models are seemingly closer in body image to 'real women.' Dove claims to celebrate women's real curves. But real-life advertising is nonetheless a well-known ploy in advertising. The subtext is a transparent one – anyone can become beautiful, sexy, and young-looking with a little help from the 'appearance management experts.' The Dove strategy connects with consumers in the same way that reality TV does. It tells females that they, too, can be beautiful, with a little dab of its soap, of course.

The fourth technique is called *simulative advertising*. It can be defined as the use of styles and techniques present in various domains of popular culture to create advertising texts. A classic example goes back to 2002, when Mazda commercials simulated the surrealistic feeling of looking at a computer screen – a sensation captured by the 1999 movie *The Matrix*. The suggestion is that cars are toys that can be manipulated on a screen, permitting an 'escape from reality' into a fantasy world of 'total control.' In the commercial, a young boy was shown looking at cars as if they were on a screen, turning to his audience with the childish exclamation 'Zoom, zoom.' The idea in

simulative advertising is to look at what is going on in pop culture and then incorporate it into ad textuality. The strategy is to retell the ongoing cultural stories, or to create revisions of them, on the advertiser's own terms.

As mentioned above, choosing an effective brand name for a product is a fundamental advertising technique that falls under the rubric of *language-based techniques* (LBTs). A wrong name can be a disaster for a brand, as illustrated in the classic example of the Edsel car – manufactured by Ford in 1957 to meet the demand for a moderately expensive model. The car was a failure and was discontinued after 1959. One of the reasons for its failure was the fact that its name – after Edsel Ford, a son of Henry Ford – did not resonate with buyers. Surveys showed that people associated the name either with a tractor (Edson) or with the word 'weasel.' Among other LBTs, one can mention the coinage of appropriate slogans for a product and the creation of persuasive taglines for specific ad texts.

Another widespread technique is the use of testimonials by people endorsing a product. The endorser may be a 'person off the street' or a celebrity (a movie star or popular athlete). Celebrity testimonials started back in the 1920s, coinciding with the rise of celebrity culture. The endorser could also be a fictional character (for example, a cartoon character such as Bugs Bunny, or a comic book superhero).

Another strategy is the use of product characters, which are fictional people or cartoon characters (known as mascots) that are associated with a product. Among the best-known product characters of advertising history are: Betty Crocker, Aunt Jemima, Mr Clean, Ronald McDonald, Tony the Tiger, Snap, Crackle, Pop, Cap'n Crunch, the Energizer Bunny, the Gerber Baby, the Pillsbury Doughboy, Uncle Ben, Charlie the Tuna, Twinkie the Kid, and the Michelin Man. Many of these characters have become ersatz cultural celebrities themselves, independent of the products they represent. The Energizer Bunny, for instance, has been on programs such as *Cheers, ABC Wide World of Sports,* the Emmy Awards telecast, and the *Tonight Show.*

Perhaps the most common technique used today is called *blending* – tapping into pop culture trends and using them to blend in with them. The Budweiser ad campaigns, for example, have always tapped into the sitcom-style humour characteristic of young male congregations (the beer's target segment). This tactic is best exemplified by its 'Whassup?' campaign, which was joked about on TV talk shows, satirized on websites, mimicked by other advertisers, and used in conversations in society at large in the early to mid-2000s. The makers of Budweiser had perfectly tapped into the contemporary urban male psyche. The phrase, taken from hip-hop culture, caught on instantly with young people, who started greeting each other comically like the actors in the Budweiser commercials. The subtext of Budweiser's overall approach is transparent – in America today, beer, moronic humour, and young males go hand in hand. It is significant to note that director Charles Stone III brought the 'Whassup?' campaign back to promote Barack Obama for president in 2008. Budweiser also tapped into 'dude culture' in the mid-2000s with its commercials for Bud Light. The original Dude commercial has been viewed by millions on YouTube.

The above techniques have become so common and widespread that they are hardly ever recognized as strategies. Their effectiveness is governed only by the ingenuity of the advertiser, the limits of the various channels of communications used, legal restrictions in place where the advertising messages are delivered, and the self-imposed standards of the advertising industry. Many ads are now viewed as works of art, and awards, such as the Gold Lion, Bronze Lion, Clio, and Palme D'Or, are given out annually at the Cannes International Advertising Festival. Some ads have become historically iconic, for example: Apple Computer's *1984 Apple Macintosh* (1984), Wendy's *Where's the Beef?* (1984),

Duracell's original *Energizer Bunny* (1989), California Raisin Advisory Board's *Heard It through the Grapevine* (1986), Chevrolet's *Like a Rock* (1991), and Pets.com's *Because Pet's Can't Drive* (1999), among others.

Advertisers have sometimes been accused of using *subliminal advertising* – a technique designed to communicate a hidden meaning below the viewer's threshold of consciousness or apprehension (Key 1972). The most common type of subliminal technique is the embedding of images in an advertisement that are invisible to conscious awareness. Subtle sexual images, for instance, can be worked into the shape of spaghetti on a plate or into the puff of exhaled cigarette smoke. The theory behind such a technique is that the unconscious mind will pick up the image and make an association between eating the spaghetti or smoking a cigarette and sexuality, hence creating a false need for the product. However, no clear evidence has emerged to show that subliminal advertising is effective. Nonetheless, like the use of mythologization, it has been used in the past and probably still is used to a limited extent (it is illegal in many areas of the world).

The theory of subliminal advertising was first enunciated by a market researcher named James Vicary in a 1957 study that he admitted to be fraudulent a few years later. Vicary had apparently flashed the phrases 'Eat Popcorn' or 'Coca-Cola' on a New Jersey movie theatre screen every five seconds as the movies played. The phrases lasted barely three-thousandths of a second so that the audience would not consciously be aware that they had seen them. Sales of popcorn and Coca-Cola, Vicary claimed, soared in the theatre at intermission. Vicary's claims were discussed by Vance Packard in his 1957 book *The Hidden Persuaders,* which led to a public outcry against the use of brainwashing techniques by advertisers. However, when broadcasters and researchers attempted to repeat Vicary's experiment, they met with little or no success. Vicary admitted in 1962 that he had fabricated the findings in order to generate business for his market-research business.

Testing Advertising Efficacy

To gain a sense of the efficacy of an ad, commercial, or ad campaign, advertisers and marketers have developed a series of techniques, ranging from questionnaires to the use of devices such as the galvanometer (an instrument for detecting and measuring people's physiological responses to ad stimuli). These techniques include the following:

- values and lifestyles questionnaires (abbreviated commonly to VALS), which assess how categories of consumers feel about a product and how the ad campaign successfully represents their specific lifestyle aspirations
- copy testing techniques for measuring the effectiveness of advertising messages by showing ads to specific types of consumers and assessing how they react to them either with devices such as the galvanometer or with follow-up interview sessions
- recognition tests to check how well someone can recall an advertisement with or without prompting
- benchmark measuring, which involves measuring a target audience's response to the early stages of an advertising campaign in order to test the efficacy of the campaign
- evaluation questionnaires to ascertain how well an ad campaign has met its original aims
- commutation tests, which consist in changing an image or word in an ad and replacing it with another one in order to see what kind of reaction the change generates
- consumer juries, which are asked to compare, rank, and otherwise evaluate advertisements in a campaign
- consumer panel groups, which report on products they have used so that manufacturers can improve them on the basis of what they report

- day-after-recall tests, which are designed to determine how much someone can remember of an advertisement or commercial the day after it was broadcast
- the diary method, whereby respondents are asked to keep a written account of the advertising they have been asked to observe, the purchases they have made, and the products they have actually used
- eye tracking, which involves recording subjects' eye movements in order to determine which parts of the brain are activated while they are viewing an ad or commercial
- the technique of following the eye movements of internet users in order to determine what they look at and for how long so that webpage designers can improve the effectiveness of their sites
- the galvanometer test, which measures physiological changes in consumers when asked a question or shown some stimulus material (such as a print ad)
- the keyed ad technique, which asks subjects to write down a specially coded address that will indicate where they saw an ad, thus helping advertisers gauge the effectiveness of advertising in some particular newspaper or magazine
- the response method, whereby the efficacy of internet advertising is evaluated by the way people respond to it through such mechanisms as direct clicking
- tachistoscope testing, which measures a person's recognition and perception of various elements within an ad as it is altered in some way or as the environment in which it is viewed is changed (through lighting and various other modifications); the tachistoscope is a device that projects an image at a fraction of a second
- voice-pitch analysis, in which a subject's voice is analysed during his or her responses, so as to assess the subject's emotional reaction to an ad
- behavioural targeting, which is achieved by inserting data files on personal computers that keep track of surfing patterns

The segmentation or classification of people according to demographic (age, gender, class, economic level, and so on) and geographic variables is implicit in many of the above techniques. In addition, advertisers and marketers have come up with a series of psychographic or personality profiles which allow them to better target consumers as individuals. These include the following:

- the chief shopper: the individual who does the shopping for the household
- the enthusiast: any individual who loves ads and commercials for their own sake
- the reformer: the person who wants products that will improve the quality of his or her life, rather than products that appeal to his or her sense of lifestyle
- the succeeder: the person who wants products that will enhance his or her success in life
- the acquiescent: the person with an easygoing attitude towards advertising who is more likely to be impressed by humorous, clever, or eye-catching ads
- the aspirer: the individual who wants products that improve his or her ability to present a better social persona
- the impresser: the person who buys certain products to impress or keep up with neighbours

Critiques of Advertising

Ever since the appearance of Vance Packard's widely read *The Hidden Persuaders* (1957), an indictment of advertising as a hidden form of brainwashing, the entire industry has been under constant attack. Product advertising is attacked by both right-wing groups, who criticize it for promoting secular humanism and promiscuity, and by left-wing groups, who attack it instead for deceitfully influencing and promoting stereotypes and unabashed consumerism. Some of the critiques have an element of truth. Since the end of the nineteenth century, advertising has suc-

ceeded more than any economic process or socio-political movement in promoting consumerism as a way of life in the modern world. It has done so primarily by proposing marketplace solutions to virtually all emotional and social problems. Ads and commercials offer the same kinds of promises and hopes to which religions and social philosophies once held exclusive rights – security against the hazards of aging, a better position in life, popularity, personal prestige, social advancement, better health, happiness, and so forth.

To counteract the 'branding of society,' as it is often called, a movement consisting of anti-advertising activists called culture jammers (Lasn 2000) has gained considerable momentum since the early 2000s. Through their own website and magazine (*Adbusters*), culture jammers provide critiques of advertising, with clever parodies of advertising campaigns (called *subvertisements*), along with articles and forums on how to recognize media manipulation, information on lawsuits and legislation on consumer issues, links for sending emails to big businesses to contest their marketing strategies, and so on. But many people like advertising and may resent others telling them that such enjoyment is victimization (Heath and Potter 2004). Moreover, advertising is not in itself disruptive of the value systems of the cultural mainstream; rather, it reflects shifts already present.

It is now estimated that the average person today sees between 254 and 5,000 commercial messages each day. For this reason, the call for even more strict regulation will increase, given the ability of advertisers to adapt to new media: 'The cumulative effect of the new and increasingly savvy ways that advertisers will reach billions of global consumers is bound to amplify calls for a curb on the prevalence of visual and mental pollution' (Lenderman 2009: 157). But what constitutes 'mental pollution' is a matter of opinion. If advertising is indeed psychologically effective, as many claim, then it is primarily because it provides the kinds of messages that people want, consciously or unconsciously.

Marcel Danesi

Bibliography

Beasley, Ron, and Marcel Danesi. *Persuasive Signs: The Semiotics of Advertising.* Berlin: Mouton de Gruyter, 2002.

Berger, Arthur A. *Ads, Fads, and Consumer Culture: Advertising's Impact on American Character and Society.* Lanham: Rowman and Littlefield, 2000.

Danesi, Marcel. *Brands.* London: Routledge, 2006.

– *Why It Sells: Decoding the Meanings of Brand Names, Logos, Ads, and Other Marketing and Advertising Ploys.* Lanham: Rowman and Littlefield, 2008.

Dyer, Gillian. *Advertising as Communication.* London: Routledge, 1982.

Frank, Thomas. *The Conquest of Cool: Business Culture, Counterculture, and the Rise of Hip Consumerism.* Chicago: University of Chicago Press, 1997.

Goldman, Robert, and Stephen Papson. *Sign Wars: The Cluttered Landscape of Advertising.* New York: Guilford, 1996.

Heath, Joseph, and Andrew Potter. *The Rebel Sell: Why Culture Can't Be Jammed.* New York: HarperCollins, 2004.

Hoffman, Barry. *The Fine Art of Advertising.* New York: Stewart, Tabori and Chang, 2002.

Key, Brian Wilson. *Subliminal Seduction.* New York: Signet, 1972.

– *The Age of Manipulation.* New York: Holt, 1989.

Kilbourne, Jean. *Can't Buy My Love: How Advertising Changes the Way I Feel.* New York: Simon and Schuster, 1999.

Klein, Naomi. *No Logo.* New York: Knopf, 2000.

Lasn, Kalle. *Culture Jam: The Uncooling of America.* New York: Morrow, 2000.

Leiss, William, Stephen Kline, Sut Jhally, and Jacqueline Botterill. *Social Communication in Advertising: Consumption in the Mediated Marketplace.* London: Routledge, 2005.

Lenderman, Max. *Brand New World: How Paupers, Pirates, and Oligarchs Are Reshaping Business.* Toronto: Collins, 2009.

Lippmann, Walter. *Public Opinion.* New York: Macmillan, 1922.

McLuhan, Marshall. *The Gutenberg Galaxy: The Making of Typographic Man.* Toronto: University of Toronto Press, 1962.

Twitchell, James B. *Twenty Ads That Shook the World.* New York: Crown, 2000.

Williams, Raymond. *Communications.* London: Penguin, 1962.

Williamson, Judith. *Consuming Passions.* London: Marion Boyars, 1985.

AGENDA-SETTING

[See also: *Media Effects; Newspapers; Television*]

In media theory, the term *agenda-setting* refers to the view that the mass news media influence audience reception of the news by virtue of the fact that they choose which stories are worthy of broadcasting and how much significance and time are given to them. This emphasis on certain items as newsworthy then gets transferred to public and political agendas. The transfer of mass media agendas to public agendas is called *salience transfer*.

Agenda-setting theory was introduced by Maxwell McCombs and Donald Shaw in 1972 in their pioneering study of the effects of media coverage on the 1968 American presidential campaign, in which they showed that there was a definite correlation between the rate and extent of media coverage and people's opinions. The two researchers interviewed one hundred voters during the campaign about what they considered to be the key issues, ranking the responses against actual media coverage of the issues. Only randomly chosen voters who were undecided about whom to vote for were chosen for the study. The rankings of the interviewees and the media turned out to be virtually identical, leading the researchers to hypothesize that there existed a cause-and-effect correlation between the two. As the researchers put it, 'Although the evidence that mass media deeply change attitudes in a campaign is far from conclusive, the evidence is much stronger that voters learn from the immense quantity of information available during each campaign' (McCombs and Shaw 1972: 176). Thus, the media set the agenda for a political campaign, influencing people's attitudes towards the issues.

This finding has been corroborated by hundreds of follow-up studies. The key notion in agenda-setting is salience transfer (or transference), since it predicts that media emphasis on a particular issue translates into public emphasis on that same issue, while others that may be just as socially significant, or even more so, are ignored by and large because they have not been brought into public prominence through media exposure. In other words, the theory suggests that events that are showcased on major TV channels or internet sites are felt as being more significant and historically meaningful to viewers and, by transference, to public officials, than those that are not. A demonstration that gets airtime becomes a socially meaningful event; one that does not is generally ignored. This is why groups with their own political agendas will dramatically stage demonstrations in front of the cameras. In so doing they ensure public salience for their cause. Agenda-setting theory suggests that people experience historical significance through the mass media. Televised events such as the John F. Kennedy and Lee Harvey Oswald assassinations, the O.J. Simpson trial, the death of Princess Diana, the Bill Clinton sex scandal, the 9/11 attacks, and so on are perceived as portentous events through the filter of TV coverage. The 'salience transfer effect' of the media became obvious in the 1950s, when TV was beginning to come into its own. In a 1954 segment of his *See It Now* documentary program, announcer Edward R. Murrow of CBS News stood up to fanatical senator Joseph McCarthy's trumped-up campaign against the supposed Communist subversion of the media. Murrow used footage of McCarthy's own press conferences to expose the excesses and falsehoods of McCarthy's campaign. This led to the Senate

reprimanding McCarthy and divesting him of his ability to take further political action.

TV has set the agenda for social change since it entered the scene as a mass communications medium in the early 1950s, forcing changes on several occasions. For example: without TV coverage of the demonstrations against racism in the 1950s, the civil rights legislation that followed might never have been implemented; without TV's everyday coverage of the Vietnam war protests, that war might not have come to an end as early as it did; without TV coverage of the Watergate scandal, President Richard Nixon would probably not have resigned from office.

Today, agenda-setting seems to originate more often than not in the internet, with sites such as Facebook and Twitter becoming increasingly prominent in the salience transfer process. The synergy that now exists between online and offline media seems to be the force that is setting agenda-setting processes into motion. The presidential campaigns of George W. Bush and Barack Obama were influenced by this synergy, in which blogs and various social networking sites influenced the outcomes of both campaigns. This means that the traditional form of agenda-setting theory will have to be revised to account for the greater participation of the general public in the agenda-setting process. As Klaus Bruhn Jensen (2010: 136) puts it: 'Compared with the relatively familiar terrain of national political issues, and with the delimited set of print and broadcast media that McCombs and Shaw (1972) selected from, digital media complicate the question of how public agendas are to be defined and understood, and how they may be set.' Clearly, as media change, so do social behaviours and power alignments.

Marcel Danesi

Bibliography

Bruhn Jensen, Klaus. *Media Convergence*. London: Routledge, 2010.

McCombs, Maxwell E., and Donald L. Shaw. The Agenda-Setting Function of Mass Media. *Public Opinion Quarterly* 36 (1972): 176–87.

– The Evolution of Agenda-Setting Research: Twenty-Five Years in the Marketplace of Ideas. *Journal of Communication* 43 (1993): 58–67.

Weaver, David H. Thoughts on Agenda Setting, Framing, and Priming. *Journal of Communication* 57 (2007): 142–7.

ALPHABETS

[See also: *Communication; Language; Medium; Text-Messaging; Writing; Zipf's Law*]

The word *alphabet* is a combination of the first two letters of the Greek alphabet (**a** 'alpha' and **b** 'beta'). The alphabet is a system of standardized signs, called letters or characters, that represent the sounds of a language. In this sense, alphabets differ significantly from earlier writing systems, or scripts, such as pictographs, which represent objects, actions, or events pictorially. Ideographs, on the other hand, represent a word but provide no indication of its pronunciation, for example, @ = 'at,' and + = 'plus.' Syllabaries, likewise, specify the syllables of a language and thus provide some information about pronunciation.

In the second millennium BCE, the Semitic languages used signs to indicate only the consonants since the vowels were normally predictable by virtue of their position within a word. When the Greeks subsequently borrowed and modified the Phoenician (1700–1000 BCE) version of the Semitic alphabet, they added symbols for vowels to it. The Etruscans developed a version of the Greek alphabet, which was ultimately adopted by the Romans by the seventh century BCE, and then adapted it to the Latin language. The symbols employed in an alphabet are known technically as *graphemes* (Greek *graphein* 'to write').

The consistent use of punctuation dates back to the ancient Greeks in the fifth century BCE. The purposes of punctuation marks include disambiguating meaning, facilitating the oral reading of documents, and allowing people who read texts to understand the meaning of a passage clearly. A few punctuation marks directly affect the oral reading of a text, for example, the question mark (?) and the exclamation point (!) to indicate question intonation and emphatic intonation, respectively.

Most alphabets are not completely phonetic, as shown by the presence of homophones in English – that is, two words spelled differently but with identical pronunciations, for example, 'sun' and 'son.' The International Phonetic Alphabet (IPA), established in 1888 by the French organization *Association Phonétique Internationale* (International Phonetic Association), is an alphabet with a sufficient number of symbols and diacritics (accent and other kinds of marks) to allow linguists (and others) to transcribe the sounds of the languages and dialects of the world in a standardized and consistent manner, providing exact specifications of how a word, phrase, or sentence in a given language is pronounced.

It is also a known fact now that alphabet characters are derivatives of previous pictographs or picture symbols. For example, the letter A of our alphabet is an adaptation of the picture symbol for an ox – in effect, it is an ox standing on its horns. The Semites named it *aleph*, meaning *ox*, adapting the Egyptian hieroglyph (picture symbol) for an ox. The ancient Greeks later adopted this symbol and called it *alpha*. The Romans gave the letter its present form. The same kind of derivational story can be told for most of the alphabet characters.

Selected Uses of a Conventional Alphabet

The traditional alphabetic symbols may be used in various creative ways, for example, as 'eye dialect' and in abbreviations. The former is the creative or imaginative use of the alphabet of a language so as to provide a distinctive representation of differences in variant pronunciation. In other words, it is the use of conventional orthography to convey dialect differences. Thus, the sentence 'What does he want?' may be rendered in eye dialect as 'Wuzzee wan?' in order to convey that the person is speaking in a casual or non-standard register.

Abbreviations constitute a use of conventional orthographic symbols to convey messages and meaning in a succinct fashion. George K. Zipf (1902–50), a Harvard linguist, developed a theory which states that frequently used words and expressions tend to be reduced or compressed in form to facilitate ease of production in written or oral communication. This has become a veritable law of alphabetic writing. The rapid expansion of abbreviation style, especially in chat rooms, text messages (brief messages written on hand-held electronic devices), and netspeak (the abbreviated language used on the internet) are in line with this law. The following are a few examples of netspeak: ASAP (*as soon as possible*); LOL (*laughing out loud*); 2 (*to, too, two*); C, c (*see*).

Frank Nuessel

Bibliography

Baron, Naomi S. *Alphabet to Email: How Written English Evolved and Where It's Heading*. London: Routledge, 2000.
– *Always On*. Oxford: Oxford University Press, 2008.
Coulmas, Florian. *The Writing Systems of the World*. Oxford: Blackwell, 1989.
Crystal, David. *Language and the Internet*, 2nd ed. Cambridge: Cambridge University Press, 2006.
– *txtng: the gr8 db8*. Oxford: Oxford University Press, 2008.
Daniels, Peter T., and William Bright, eds. *The World's Writing Systems*. Oxford: Oxford University Press, 1995.
DeFrancis, John. *Visible Speech: The Diverse Oneness of Writing Systems*. Honolulu: The University of Hawaii Press, 1989.
Zipf, George K. *Human Behavior and the Principle of the Least Effort*. Reading, MA: Addison-Wesley, 1949.

ALTHUSSER, LOUIS (1918–90)

[See also: *Gramsci, Antonio; Hegemony Theory; Ideology Theory; Marxism; Structuralism*]

Louis Pierre Althusser was an Algerian-born Marxist philosopher who studied with Gaston Bachelard at the École Normale Supérieure in Paris, where he subsequently held a professorship in philosophy. He was a member of the French Communist party, but a strong critic of the various humanist and reformist socialist movements and trends that he saw misrepresenting the theoretical foundations of Marxism, invalidating the scientific socialism that it espoused and mixing science and ideology. As a 'structuralist Marxist,' he was critical of many aspects of structuralism itself, feeling that structuralism had become simply an intellectual fashion in the 1960s in France, manifesting itself in linguistics, literary criticism, and anthropology. Like the structuralism of French anthropologist Maurice Godelier, Althusser's was based on a close reading of Marx's original works, not secondary references to it.

After the fall of France in the Second World War, Althusser was interned in a German prisoner-of-war camp, where he remained for the remainder of the war. This experience further contributed to his periodic bouts with mental illness for the rest of his life (in 1947 he was even subjected to electroconvulsive therapy). In 1946, Althusser met Hélène Rytman, who became his companion. Eight years older than he, she was a revolutionary of Lithuanian-Jewish ethnic origin. In 1948, Althusser started his teaching career at the École Normale. Several of his students became eminent intellectuals in philosophy, literary criticism, sociology, and psychoanalysis, including Alain Badiou, Étienne Balibar, Jacques Rancière, Jacques Derrida, Michel Foucault, Pierre Macherey, Nicos Poulantzas, Jacques-Alain Miller, and Régis Debray.

During a bout with mental instability, on 16 November 1980, Althusser killed his wife. It was never established if his act was deliberate or accidental. Althusser claimed not to have had any memory of the event. Diagnosed as suffering from mental illness, he was never tried for the act and assigned in Sainte-Anne to a psychiatric hospital, being transferred subsequently to various criminal hospitals, psychiatric wards, nursing homes, and hospices. It was during this period that he wrote *L'Avenir dure longtemps*, his autobiography. He died of a heart attack on 22 October 1990 at the age of 72.

In contrast to popular humanistic interpretations of Marxism (for example, by Roger Garaudy and Jean-Paul Sartre) and to the official position of the French Communist party in the period following the so-called 'de-stalinization' of Marxist politics, Althusser maintained that Marx's theory was theoretically 'anti-humanistic.' He expressed his views in several key books: *Reading Capital*, co-authored with Étienne Balibar (1965), *For Marx* (1969), and *Lenin and Philosophy and Other Essays* (1971). In the introduction to *For Marx*, Althusser saw a radical 'epistemological break' between Marx's early writings (1840–5) and his later ones. In his view, this corresponded to a separation between 'scientific' Marxist theory and 'official ideology' – a separation generally misunderstood and underestimated by standard interpretations of Marx's thought, which revolve around notions of historical materialism, idealism, and economics. Marx's revolutionary view, as expressed in *The German Ideology* (written in 1845 with Friedrich Engels), consists in an abandonment of the categories of traditional German philosophy and classical political economy and the proposal of a new, original, and extraordinary theory constituting a new 'continent of knowledge.' Marxism for Althusser consists fundamentally in a critique of the traditional philosophical distinction between *subject* and *object*. Marx's theory is, thus, a theory of knowledge according to which information or facts (*the object*) cannot be accepted in the absolute, but as inseparable from larger social structures and personal involvement in them (*the subject*). Knowledge is, thus, 'theoretical practice.' In contrast to the idea of a *homo economicus* of classical political economy (an 'economic man') and to conception that the needs of individuals are independent of economic systems, based on specific modes of production, Marx saw knowledge schemas as inseparable from social processes of production. Humanism and historicism are also present in Marxist philosophy starting in 1845.

Althusser also espoused the psychoanalytic concept of *overdetermination*, which rejects the conception of a mechanical causality between 'structure,' in its economic social form, and 'superstructure,' or ideologically based state apparatuses, replacing it with a more complex model of 'multiple causality,' which implicates a conception of social contradictions that come near to Antonio Gramsci's concept of *hegemony*, or control of people through indirect means. Althusser thus sees individuals not as self-conscious and responsible agents, but as people who are unaware that the subjective roles they play have been imposed upon them by their specific upbringing. Views, values, desires, and preferences are inculcated in individuals by ideological (hegemonic) practices, which are imparted unconsciously by what Althusser called *ideological state apparatuses*, such as the family, the media, education, religious institutions, and so forth. Identities are thus (over)determined by means of simple and misleading binary notions such as 'us' versus 'them.'

Althusser's ideas have obvious implications for the study of media. Above all else, they suggest that media practices are themselves reflective of ideological practices and thus enter into a synergistic dynamism with them – one reflecting and reinforcing the other. Although different from some of the other Marxist-based theories of the media, such as culture industry theory, Althusserian analysis is still ensconced in the basic Marxist tenet that the ideological forms that dominate a society are ultimately reinforced by media institutions.

Augusto Ponzio

Bibliography

Althusser, Louis. *For Marx*. London: Verso, 1969.
- *Lenin and Philosophy and Other Essays*. London: Monthly Review Press, 1969.
- *Éléments d'autocritique*. Paris: Hachette, 1974.
- *Essays in Self-Criticism*. London: New Left Books, 1976.
- *Ce qui ne peut plus durer dans le parti communiste*. Paris: Maspero, 1978.
- *Journal de captivité*. Paris: Stock, 1992.
- *L'Avenir dure longtemps*. Paris: Stock, 1994.
Althusser, Louis, and Étienne Balibar. *Reading Capital*. London: New Left Books, 1965.
Balibar, Étienne. *Écrits pour Althusser*. Paris: La Découverte, 1991.
Callinicos, Alex, ed. *Althusser's Marxism*. London: Pluto Press, 1976.
Heartfield, James. *The 'Death of the Subject' Explained*. Sheffield: Hallam University Press, 2002.
Lewis, William. *Louis Althusser and the Traditions of French Marxism*. New York: Lexington Books, 2005.
McInerney, David, ed. *Althusser and Us*, special issue of *Borderlands e-Journal*, October 2005.
Montag, Warren. *Louis Althusser*. New York: Palgrave-Macmillan, 2003.
Schaff, Adam. *Structuralism and Marxism*. New York: Pergamon Press, 1978.

ANALOGUE MEDIA

[See also: *Digital Media; Medium; Transmission Modes*]

Analogue media are the media used for storing and transmitting communication data by recording and reproducing a physical quality used to represent a resemblance of the original source material such as a sound or an image. The notion of *media* (plural of the noun *medium*) refers to the enlisted means of giving thoughts or ideas originating in the mind of a message sender a physical form that can be encoded in some way and subsequently communicated to a message receiver.

The medium is, in other words, the material means of communicating some message that can be received in some way (for example, accessed through sense perception) and transmitted in some way (with words, sounds, images, and so on). For example, the voice of a speaker produces sounds that actually exist in a material form so that a listener can hear them. The sound is a material trace to the invisible thoughts or ideas of a speaker that would otherwise be imperceptible to a message receiver. Speech is a medium of communication that organizes sounds that are produced according to existing linguistic codes and understood by members of a cultural group that share an understanding of the language. Thus, sound is a physical aspect of speech, and a communication medium capable of transmitting verbal messages through the vocal-audible channel.

Analogue media can be used to record and reproduce the physical aspects of speech or sound. Written language is a mode of encoding speech that uses visual signs (known as pictographs, alphabet characters, and so on) to communicate ideas. The analogue dimensions of written language and print technology are embodied in the physical nature of ink and paper used to produce a visible medium.

The term *analogue* refers, thus, to the physical nature of media transmissions. It implies a physical record of some form of communication used to preserve or reproduce the original material encoded at the source. So, for example, the analogue waveforms of sound can be transformed by specially designed technological equipment in order to be preserved as a physical imprint on recording tape and then played back on compatible equipment designed to reproduce the original sound. Print media are those that inscribe words and images from the mind of a communicator so they can be physically preserved and transmitted.

Analogue media are 'indexical' in the sense that they provide physical evidence that points to the natural source of something like a sound or image that originally existed in another form. Like a footprint on the ground that indicates that someone must have been present to make that physical impression at some time in the past, an indexical sign is a representation that refers to an actual physical existence of something even when it is not currently present. The bones of a dinosaur point to its existence even if one has not been seen alive. A fingerprint similarly is an impression made by someone who touched something and subsequently left a visible physical sign as a record of the event. The physical imprint of sound waves on recording tape indicates that those sounds were produced somehow and recorded in the past. Print media suggest that someone had the thoughts or ideas expressed on the page. Photographic technology originally produced an image because a chemical reaction was caused when a specially prepared film technology was exposed to light. A photograph, film, or television image of a person, for example, indicates that the person appeared in front of a camera at some time.

Original recorded source material must have actually existed in some form, at some time, but the physical aspects of analogue media can be edited and manipulated. Photos and sound recordings can be altered. Hand-drawn illustrations can be used to create an illusion of motion using analogue media. Cartoon animation is a case in point, and adding recorded speech and other natural sound to it can enhance the illusion of realism and live action.

Special effects have been developed and used to enhance the entertainment value of film; alter perceptions of time and space; and create images of monsters, giants, and other visual and sound illusions. The same techniques can be used for deception by manipulating photographs or film of real people and situations. Thus analogue media can be used to create false representations or illusions.

Newer technologies based on *digital media* that convert analogue sound and images into numerical codes to be stored on and manipulated with computers are quickly replacing many of the previous analogue forms of media. Digital media offer even greater potential for manipulation and creativity than analogue media because computer technologies are designed to allow users to manipulate data stored as numerical codes. Still, digital data must in many contexts be converted back to an analogue form because users need the physical qualities that distinguish analogue media in order to see and hear the final product.

Elliot Gaines

Bibliography

Dizard, Wilson. *Old Media, New Media*. New York: Longman, 1997.
Hanson, Ralph E. *Mass Communication: Living in a Media World*. New York: McGraw-Hill, 2005.

ANG, IEN (b. 1954)

[See also: *Audience; Audience Research;, Culture and Media; Globalization; Race and Gender Diversity*]

Ien Ang is an internationally acclaimed scholar of cultural studies. She is especially known for her work on media audiences and the representation of race and gender in media texts. She was born in Java, Indonesia, and received her doctorate in social and cultural studies from the University of Amsterdam in 1990. She is the founding director of the Centre of Cultural Research (CCR) at the University of Western Sydney (UWS), where she is currently professor of cultural studies. The CCR has gained an international reputation for its interdisciplinary research on the cultural challenges facing the modern globalized world. Recently, Ang has been looking at the evolution of culture in Asian countries along with a team of scholars as part of the Australian Research Council's Cultural Research Network. As a result of her prominent reputation and research accomplishments, Ang was the first person to receive the title of Distinguished Professor at UWS.

Ang's interdisciplinary work pertains to patterns of cultural flow and exchange, and, more specifically, to the politics of identity, media and cultural consumption, globalization, popular culture, lifestyle of urban cultures, and migration and ethnicity in Australia and Asia. Although not trained as a historian, Ang has been actively engaged in exploring the historical roots of multicultural Australia, including how migration from Asia influences the country's groupthink. Some of Ang's books, including *Watching Dallas: Soap Opera and the Melodramatic Imagination* (1985), *Desperately Seeking the Audience* (1991), and *On Not Speaking Chinese: Living between Asia and the West* (2001), are considered points of reference in the cultural studies field.

Ang's research on the worldwide spread of the American soap opera *Dallas* has shown how popular culture throughout parts of the world has undergone 'Americanization.' In *Desperately Seeking the Audience*, she contrasts American television with European television, suggesting that the former 'segments' the audience into market niches, while the latter 'serves' it instead. Throughout her writings on the medium of television, Ang adopts the notion that television audiences are 'taxonomic collectives' (a term coined by philosopher and psychologist Rom Harré), that is, organized according to sociological background and catered to accordingly. Another one of her major works, *Living Room Wars: Rethinking Media Audiences for a Postmodern World*, focuses on gendered audiences, audiences for new global media, and the impacts of postmodernism on audiences across the globe. In that book, Ang points out that representations of audiences have historically been assumed by Western media scholars to be primarily homogeneous white ones. The real goal of contemporary media studies should be, instead, to expand the constituency of audiences so that the use of media

in the contemporary global village can be studied more realistically.

Alexandra Birk-Urovitz and Elizabeth Birk-Urovitz

Bibliography

Ang, Ien. *Watching Dallas: Soap Opera and the Melodramatic Imagination*. London: Methuen, 1985.
– *Desperately Seeking the Audience*. London: Routledge, 1991.
– *Living Room Wars: Rethinking Media Audiences for a Postmodern World*. London and New York: Routledge, 1995.
– *On Not Speaking Chinese: Living between Asia and the West*. London: Routledge, 2001.
Juluri, Vamsee. Globalizing Audience Studies: The Audience and Its Landscape and Living Room Wars. *Critical Studies in Mass Communication* 15 (1998): 85–90.

ANTHROPOLOGY OF THE MEDIA

[See also: *Linguistics; Culture and Communication; Culture and Media; Media Studies*]

Most approaches to the study of the media are based on some integrated use of different, but cognate, disciplines. Some of the disciplines enlisted by media scholars, such as linguistics or semiotics, focus on specific aspects or components of the media-culture nexus, such as language or non-verbal communication. The findings and insights garnered in such disciplines are applied directly to the study of specific media products (such as TV programs, advertising texts, and so on). Since their inception in the late 1930s, media studies have, in point of fact, been characterized by the adoption and integration of findings and ideas from various disciplines to the study of media texts and products.

One of the disciplines that figures prominently in media studies is anthropology, the study of human beings from biological, archaeological, sociocultural, and linguistic perspectives. Physical anthropology deals with human evolution, sociocultural anthropology with the ways in which people live in society, archaeological anthropology with the reconstruction of previous cultures through a study of artefacts, and linguistic anthropology with the role of language in the constitution of human groups. Anthropology emerged as an autonomous mode of study in the middle part of the nineteenth century. In North America the founder is considered to be Lewis Henry Morgan (1818–81), who conducted early pioneering research on Iroquois societies. In Europe, the founding figure was British scholar Edward B. Tylor (1832–1917), who developed a theory of human cultural evolution through a consideration of diverse religious practices. In the same era, Danish archaeologists at the Museum of Northern Antiquities in Copenhagen started systematic excavations of sites, discovering a sequential pattern in tool use from the Stone Age to the Bronze and Iron Ages that has become the basis for understanding human cultural development. Anthropology is, thus, less than 150 years old. Arguably, it was Tylor who, in 1871, came up with the first true anthropological analysis of culture, based on an investigation of the religious rituals and symbol systems of the indigenous peoples of Mexico. In 1884, Tylor established the first chair in anthropology at the University of Oxford, which he himself held from 1896 to 1909. Shortly thereafter, in 1888, similar chairs and departments were founded at Harvard and Clark universities in the United States. Their purpose was to give the scientific study of cultures an autonomous academic status.

Highly influential in shaping the early anthropological theories of culture was the notion of *cultural evolutionism* (Danesi and Perron 1999). Its source can be traced to Charles Darwin's (1809–82) theory of natural selection, elaborated in *On the Origin of Species* (1858) – namely, the idea that each generation of a species improves adaptively over preceding generations and

that this gradual and continuous process is the source of the evolution of the species as a whole. Natural selection was only part of Darwin's theoretical proposals; he also introduced the concept that all organisms are descended from common ancestors. His ideas posed a serious challenge to orthodox religion when they were first published.

While the purely biological aspects of Darwin's theory gained a foothold in the scientific community, and now seem unlikely to be challenged by any counter-proposals or alternatives, the extension of the theory to explain human nature and cultural evolution has always been fraught with difficulties. Soon after the publication of *On the Origin of Species*, a group of early anthropologists came to see culture ultimately as an extension of natural selection forces, enhancing the survivability and progress of the human species in non-genetic ways. The British philosopher Herbert Spencer (1820–1903), for instance, saw cultural institutions as explainable and as classifiable as living things. The idea that gained prominence in early anthropological theories, therefore, was that all cultures, no matter how diverse they may seem on the surface, developed according to a regular series of predictable adaptive stages reflecting a predetermined pattern built into the genetic blueprint of the human species. Morgan epitomized this view by arguing in his 1877 book *Ancient Society* that humanity had progressed by force of physical impulse from savagery, to barbarism, to civilization.

An early attack on cultural evolutionism came from the German social theorist Karl Marx (1818–83), who argued that cultures evolved not from adaptive tendencies in the human species, but as a result of individuals struggling to gain control over their lives. Cultural evolutionism could also not answer the question of why certain biologically risky tendencies are characteristic of people living in diverse cultures across the world, including such rites as sacrifice and brutal coming-of-age tests. While culture may have enhanced human survivability and reproductive success in some ways, in many others it had, curiously, put human survival at risk: humans must be nurtured for a prolonged period of time prior to sexual maturity, they cannot run as fast on average as other primates, they commit suicide for emotional and social reasons, and they do many other things that would seem to put their very survival in jeopardy. And yet, without culture, modern human beings would have great difficulty surviving. This is sometimes called the paradox of the human condition.

At the turn of the twentieth century, attacks on cultural evolutionism from anthropological quarters were gaining momentum. The American Franz Boas (1858–1942) argued against a biological theory of culture. If anything, he suggested, the reverse was true – culture had become a primary 'reshaper' of the biological paradigm. The view espoused by Boas has come to be known as *cultural relativism*. While evolutionists see humans as 'adaptors' to the environment, relativists see them as 'makers' of their own worlds. Among Boas's students at Columbia University, Edward Sapir (1884–1939), Margaret Mead (1901–78), and Ruth Benedict (1887–1948) became well-known cultural relativists. Sapir devoted his career to determining the extent to which the language of a culture shaped the thought patterns of its users, Mead to unravelling how childrearing practices influenced the behaviour and temperament of the maturing individual, and Benedict to understanding how each culture develops its own particular canons of morality and ethics that largely determine the choices individuals make throughout their lives.

The use of ethnographic methods in some media research comes from the anthropological domain. Ethnography is the study of some cultural phenomenon through systematic observation. It consists primarily in gathering empirical data on some media phenomenon, such as audience reaction to a particular kind of media product, through observing that audience with interviews, questionnaires, and so

forth. Other anthropologically based or anthropologically inspired ideas and techniques prevalent in media studies today are the following:

- *Cultural capital* is an idea traceable to the French social scientist Pierre Bourdieu (1930–2002), which suggests that it is the particular knowledge and background possessed by media audiences that shape their interpretation of media texts. Like monetary capital, people use cultural capital to identify with others and to differentiate themselves culturally.
- *Cultural criticism* is the analysis of how texts and representations influence individuals on the basis of the cultures in which they live.
- *Cultural imperialism* is the belief that the cultural artefacts of a politically dominant country enter into another country and eventually dominate it, thereby spreading the values of the dominant country to the exclusion of indigenous values.
- *Cultural memory* is the set of symbols and rituals that are acquired from being immersed in a culture and which, over time, become shapers of memory; the set is sometimes called a *memorate* (a 'memory template').
- *Cultural proximity* refers to the desire of people to experience media products in terms of their own cultural backgrounds.
- *Cultural contextualization* refers to the concept that in order to understand media it is essential to locate them in specific cultural contexts.
- *Culture industry theory* is the view that contemporary culture has been debased by being turned into a commodity controlled by profit-making enterprises, known as culture industries. In this view, the function of the media is not to enrich or enlighten, but to manipulate and indoctrinate. This idea comes from the Frankfurt School, which was founded at the University of Frankfurt in 1922 to carry out social research on culture texts and representations. Its aim was to

understand how human groups create meaning collectively under the impact of modern technologies and political systems. The school's main contention was that typical media fare in the contemporary world was vulgar and functioned primarily to pacify ordinary people.

Marcel Danesi

Bibliography

Danesi, Marcel. *Language, Society, and Culture: Introducing Anthropological Linguistics*. Toronto: Canadian Scholars' Press, 2008.

Danesi, Marcel, and Paul Perron. *Analyzing Cultures*. Bloomington: Indiana University Press, 1999.

Kuper, Adam. *The Chosen Primate: Human Nature and Cultural Diversity*. Cambridge, MA: Harvard University Press, 1994.

Levinson, David, and Melvin Ember, eds. *Encyclopedia of Cultural Anthropology*. 4 vols. New York: Henry Holt, 1996.

ARCHETYPE THEORY AND THE MEDIA

[See also: *Psychoanalytic Theory; Psychology of the Media*]

As used by the Swiss psychologist Carl Jung (1875–1961), *archetypes* are universal, unconscious figures that enable people to react to and comprehend situations, other people, rituals, and symbols in ways that are identical to their ancestors. Jung's studies of mythology convinced him that archetypes are deeply rooted in the psyche. Archetypal characters like the Joker, the Shadow, the Hero, and others, thus appear in different narratives, art forms, and discourses throughout history and across cultures but are understood in the same way. Modern-day representations, embodiments, or characterizations of these three archetypes include stand-up comedians, Dracula, and Superman, respectively. Each one symbolizes a different psychic need –

the need for laughter, the need to attenuate the power of fear, and the need to ensure the presence of valour in human affairs.

Archetype theory is of great value, therefore, in understanding the popularity of fictitious characters and certain texts and spectacles. In the Renaissance *Commedia dell'Arte* (a type of comedy characterized by improvisation on a standard plot outline) the characters were highly popular because they were embodiments of Jungian archetypes. The same actor always played the same role. There was Harlequin, the clownish valet; the Doctor, who was a quack with fraudulent solutions to human problems; the lustful Pulcinella, who concocted schemes to satisfy his desires; and so on. Similar archetypes are found in contemporary television sitcoms. For instance, the Sage archetype, who comments on a situation in which others have put themselves, can be seen in the character of Wilson on *Home Improvement*; the Clown archetype can be seen in the role of Cosmo Kramer on *Seinfeld*. Other stock characters of sitcoms, such as the ladies' man who is involved in sexual exploits, the meddler who spreads gossip, the grouch who continuously grumbles about life, among others, are similarly modern-day versions of archetypal figures. They strike a responsive chord in us because they represent real people. Masks worn at Carnival time are based on archetypal figures, as are the figures on Tarot cards, depicting vices, virtues, and elemental forces.

Although the notion of archetype is traced back to the Greek philosopher Plato's notion of an 'ideal form' imprinted into the human mind at birth, it is actually an intuitive one. When we speak of 'mother figures' or 'father figures' we are really alluding to archetypes that require no further elaboration. The main Jungian archetypes are: the Self, the facilitator of self-identity construction; the Shadow, representing fear and qualities obscured by the Self; the Anima, the feminine principle in all of us; the Animus, the corresponding masculine principle; and the Persona, representing the face or role we present to the world. Other archetypes, such as the Trickster, the Hero, the Mentor, the Sage, and so on, are psychic derivatives of these. Archetype theory is frequently enlisted by literary theorists, media analysts, and others to understand popular texts, events, spectacles, and various fads.

Marcel Danesi

Bibliography

Danesi, Marcel. *Popular Culture: Introductory Perspectives*. Lanham: Rowman and Littlefield, 2007.
Jung, Carl G. *The Essential Jung*. Princeton: Princeton University Press, 1983.

AUDIENCE

[See also: *Audience Research; Hall, Stuart; Hypodermic Needle Theory; Reception Theory; Two-Step Flow Model; Uses and Gratifications Theory*]

As used in media studies, the term *audience* refers to the receivers of various conventional types of media products or spectacles which have been designed for them on purpose. In the popular but fundamentally inadequate transactional model of communication that asks 'who says what to whom (?),' the audience is the receiver *to whom* messages are sent while the sender is an individual or group that creates messages intended for distribution to large numbers of recipients.

An audience generally has some shared characteristics that explain the uses and gratifications associated with consuming particular kinds of media. The types of media that people select, such as various genres of books, films, or television programs (which can be further classified as information or entertainment, or as mysteries, romances, comedies, or adventures) can help to identify audiences. Groups of people attracted to particular media demonstrate shared characteristics or a demographic structure that describes the audience by age, gender, ethnicity, or other special interests. For example, it has been documented that men tend to consume more sports media, while women more frequently watch soap operas or read romance novels, and young men actively engage in playing electronic video games. The study of why people choose certain media and the effects of media on society are clearly important on many levels.

Media producers themselves, along with special interest groups such as advertisers, governments, social scientists, and citizen groups, all have particular concerns about the social and moral impacts of media products on audiences. Still, while audiences are understood as groups of people, to some extent each member of the collective group will experience the medium as an individual, as some theoretical models explain.

The concept of the audience draws its raison d'être from considerations about the nature of the media, the identity of individuals and groups, and the 'space' where a given media product is received (radio, television, and so on). The active participation and agency, or independence, of people suggests that individual audience members have the potential to accept, reject, or negotiate alternative interpretations of media content that are different from the meanings intended by media producers. An audience may interpret a story intended as a serious and sincere commentary about society from a different point of view as comic or ironic at a later time and place. Various kinds of authoritative representatives like government officials, journalists, scientists, or corporate spokespeople may be doubted or questioned by audiences, who commonly demonstrate a tendency to negotiate the meaning of media on their own terms.

In spite of the media producers' intentions to inform, entertain, or persuade individuals who are collectively understood to constitute a particular audience in a specific way, invariably different audiences are affected by different conditions. The time, locus, and social conditions in which a media event takes place will affect the way a group or individual understands it. Individual audience members will thus understand intended meanings from their own diverse points of view. Audiences tend to consume mass media products either alone as individuals or in various groups when watching television or film, listening to recorded music or the radio, reading a book, magazine, newspaper, or using the internet. The nature of the medium in question, where and when an audience receives communication, and whether the audience members are alone or with a group in a public space like a theatre will affect experience of the media product and influence interpretations. In spite of their association with others who selectively use the same media, the situated conditions of audience members are significant because each person will interpret the meanings of messages actively because of his or her distinct personal history and cultural beliefs, practices, and values.

While there may be exceptions, it is also true that the particular medium involved will restrict or encourage specific audience reactions and interpretive tendencies. The audience for traditional print media can choose when to read individualistically – at home, in a library, or on a commuter train or bus. In contrast, audiences typically assemble as groups at designated times for traditional theatre performances and class lectures and discussions. In these types of spaces and situations there is potential for spontaneous interactivity that is not possible when the medium transmits through a one-way channel to the receiver. Film and television writers are absent or behind the scenes and remain inaccessible to individual audience members, or allow for slow, controlled interactions at best. Print media such as newspapers have always afforded an opportunity to engage journalists, editors, and commentators through traditional written modes of representation. The internet, on the other hand, allows audiences to respond more spontaneously and communicate individualistically because of the nature of the shared virtual space.

The concept of an audience is, clearly, a dynamic one in communication and media studies. The changing nature of the media alters the conditions for reception of media messages. Even the most basic notions of speech and reading assume certain shared cultural values that influence how an audience receives a communication. New media will continue to affect this process even more, as people throughout the globe will have to adapt to sophisticated emerging communications technologies that combine and develop innovations in television, radio, film, telephony, and so on.

Elliot Gaines

Bibliography

Hall, Stuart, ed. *Cultural Representations and Signifying Practice*. London: Open University Press, 1977.

Staiger, Janet. *Media Reception Studies*. New York: New York University Press, 2005.

AUDIENCE RESEARCH

[See also: *Audience; Hall, Stuart; Hypodermic Needle Theory; Katz, Elihu; Media Effects; Narrowcasting; Ratings; Reception Theory; Two-Step Flow Model; Uses and Gratifications Theory*]

Audience research (AR), or *audience analysis*, aims to identify and study the various aspects of the interpretation and reception of media texts that characterize specific types of audiences. *Audience* is defined as the group exposed to a media text or event (readers, spectators, listeners, viewers, internet surfers, and so on). Some audiences (such as those for sporting events in stadiums, rinks, movies in movie theatres, concerts in locales) are physically present at the event; other audiences (such as those for novels, television, radio, webcasts) are not.

The idea of AR entered media studies through the psychological research on how people respond to certain kinds of mass-produced messages. Audiences are divisible into segments or categories distinguished by specific psychosocial, socio-economic, and lifestyle characteristics. In general, AR has found that specific audiences tend to perceive a specific media text or event positively or negatively in accordance with their own life experiences and beliefs. For example, a secular viewer of a televangelism TV program will tend to interpret it critically and sceptically, whereas a faithful viewer will perceive it as directly relevant to his or her everyday life.

A fundamental goal of AR is to determine how audiences respond to media texts. It starts by classifying members of audiences according to geographic, demographic, and psychographic categories (age, class, gender, education, world view, region, ideology) and then assesses reactions according to the classifications. The main techniques used in determining audience constituency and their reactions to media are as follows:

- *Diaries* constitute the oldest form of AR. Chosen subjects are asked to record their listening or viewing preferences in a diary. A main weakness of this approach is that people are prone to forget to record their habits. Diaries were first used in 1936, when the BBC wanted to gauge audience opinion on programming. The BBC asked sample groups of people to keep diaries of their listening and viewing habits.
- *Interviews* conducted by researchers allow them to ascertain people's preferences and to map them against their demographic and psychographic characteristics.
- *Audience ethnography* is the method whereby the researcher joins a specific audience group and observes their reactions to media from within the group.
- *Electronic devices* such as the Portable People Meter (installed on television

sets, radios) allow researchers to keep track of viewing habits. Appropriate software can now track channel use. Known as *audience flow*, it is defined as the particular pattern shown by audiences changing radio or television channels within a given period of time.
- *New technologies* such as Nielsen's 'NetRatings' (among others) provide valuable information such as internet usage habits, attention span rates, and the like, while at the same time providing real-time audience data. Webcasting also provides opportunities for audiences to discuss programs on relevant websites or blogs, thus enriching the nature of the AR data that can be collected.

Once relevant data are gathered, the goal of AR shifts to sifting out any relevant statistical patterns present in the data. For example, the concept of *ratings point* (percentage of an audience viewing or listening to a particular program) is used to quantify the data. Closely related is the concept of *share point*, which indicates the percentage of all audiences that watched (or listened to) a certain program. The so-called Appreciation Index (used primarily in Great Britain) is a number between 0 and 100 that assesses the approval rating for a particular program. A score of 85 or above is considered to be excellent, while a score of 60 or lower is considered poor. The best-known AR companies are Arbitron, founded in 1949, which publishes regular reports for selected markets (www.arbitron.com), and A.C. Nielsen, which is well known for its sampling of television viewing in homes, especially for its development of the People Meter (attached to television sets), allowing researchers to record the channels being watched and sending the data to a computer centre for statistical analysis (www.nielsenmedia.com/ratings101.htm).

Another basic aim of AR is to help develop theories of audience behaviours. Among the many theories developed in this domain are the following:

- *Hypodermic needle theory*, or *one-step flow theory*, maintains that the program is received uncritically by audiences, producing a conditioning effect on them. For example, the theory would claim that violence on TV raises the level of violence in audiences who view violent programs, leading to a higher tolerance of violent behaviour in society at large.
- Unlike one-step flow theory, which sees the emission of a media text as a unidirectional process from the maker of the text to a passive receptive audience, *two-step flow theory* posits that audiences tend to accept the interpretations of those whom they see as 'leaders' in their respective communities, hence a 'second step' in the process. For example, religious audiences tend to accept the views of their church leaders on the acceptability or unsuitability of certain movies, TV programs, and the like.
- *Uses and gratifications theory* argues that audiences are not influenced directly by the media, but choose their media products to meet their needs or to get satisfaction or gratification from them.
- *Reception theory* maintains that audiences negotiate the interpretation of a media text according to their backgrounds and life experiences, not passively or robotically (as does one-step flow theory).
- *Obstinate audience theory* suggests that there is a two-way dynamic established between audiences and the media, whereby audience reactions influence how a program is ultimately accepted or received by society at large.

One of the more influential scholars in the field of AR is Elihu Katz (b. 1926). In a 1993 study (co-authored with Tamar Liebes), *The Export of Meaning: Cross-Cultural Readings of 'Dallas,'* Katz linked the patterns shown by audience reception to different cultural expectations, which induce the audience's 're-negotiation' of the meanings of a soap opera such as *Dallas*. The book is also important for having introduced a convergent approach to audience research that integrates different methods (qualitative versus quantitative), disciplines (linguistics, sociology), and communication features (text, context). In effect, Katz has shown that audiences around the world are active, not passive, participants.

With the advent of digital technologies, it has never been easier for audiences around the world to access programs. As a consequence, the traditional, localized (nationalistic) audience has become a more global, intercultural audience. As a result, AR research is changing, since it is becoming more and more obvious that the forms of media culture to which audiences are exposed today will be determined not only by those living in a specific area of the world, but increasingly by people in different regions of the globe. For example, YouTube has obliterated the distinction between target and global audiences, and between media producers and consumers.

Marcel Danesi

Bibliography

Berger, Arthur A. *Media and Society: A Critical Perspective*. Lanham, MD: Rowan and Littlefield, 2007.

Gauntlet, David. *Creative Explorations: New Approaches to Identities and Audiences*. London: Routledge, 2007.

Katz, Elihu, and Tamar Liebes. *The Export of Meaning: Cross-Cultural Readings of 'Dallas.'* Cambridge: Polity, 1993.

Moores, Shaun. *Interpreting Audiences: The Ethnography of Media Consumption*. London: Sage, 1993.

B

BAKHTIN, MIKHAIL MIKHAILOVICH (1895–1975)

[See also: *Discourse Theory; Popular Culture; Semiotics; Youth Culture*]

Mikhail M. Bakhtin was born in Orel, Russia, in November 1895, the son of a bank clerk and déclassé aristocrat. He grew up in Odessa, in the Crimea. Although Bakhtin claimed to have studied philology and classics at the University of Novorossisk in Odessa, transferred to the University of Petrograd, and graduated from the latter in 1918, there is no evidence he was ever registered formally at either of these institutions. (Indeed, it seems that Bakhtin's brother Nikolai was the person with these qualifications.) Regardless, Bakhtin taught elementary school in several provincial towns in Russia, ending up in the Russian town of Nevel'. Here, a group of like-minded intellectuals, the so-called 'Bakhtin Circle,' coalesced around him, first in Nevel' and later Vitebsk. Some members of the Circle were influenced strongly by neo-Kantian philosophy; others were more overtly Marxist. Although Bakhtin was the leading intellectual force, there were a number of other important participants, including Matvei I. Kagan (philosopher), Pavel N. Medvedev (literary critic and essayist), Lev V. Pumpianskii (literary theorist), and Valentin N. Voloshinov (poet, musicologist, linguist). The key theoretical assumption for the Circle was that the production of spoken or written language is *dialogical* in nature, wherein divergent sociocultural values are registered and re-accented continuously in the context of 'living speech,' according to extant social interactions and relations of power. Such dialogical properties of language use, and the cultural forms through which they were expressed (pre-eminently in the novel), were to be analysed and fostered so as to counteract the tendency on the part of dominant groups and institutions to strive for a kind of semantic and ideological closure (or 'monologism') vis-à-vis the construction of socially relevant signs and meanings.

During this Nevel'/Vitebsk period (roughly 1918–24), Bakhtin wrote a series of fragmentary texts, unpublished in his lifetime, in which he sought to develop a theory of 'alterity.' This concerns a phenomenological exploration of how individuals and their subjectivities are constituted, especially in an ethical sense, through their interpersonal relations. Bakhtin combined this project with a general aesthetics of artistic creation. This orientation owed a considerable debt to such European philosophers as Martin Buber, Søren Kierkegaard, and Immanuel Kant, but especially the existential phenomenologists, which would include Edmund Husserl, Heinrich Rickert, and Max Scheler. Unfortunately, in this period Bakhtin contracted osteomyelitis, a serious bone disease, which eventually led to the amputation of most of his right leg in 1938. Bakhtin was plagued by chronic ill health throughout his later life and owed much to the caregiving skills of Elena Aleksandrovna Okolovich, whom he married in 1921.

Bakhtin's fragmentary texts were eventually published in English under the titles *Toward a Philosophy of the Act* (1993) and *Art and Answerability: Early Philosophical Essays by M.M. Bakhtin* (1990). In the former, Bakhtin meditates on the implications of the disjuncture between immediate experience and *a posteriori* symbolic representations of it. This everyday sphere is crucial for Bakhtin, because it is where the unique character of our actions and deeds, and indeed our very selfhood, is constituted. However, the mentality of scientific rationalism and of modernity generally has encouraged the transcription of what Bakhtin calls 'Being-as-event' into a series of universalistic abstractions, reflected in the unabashedly utilitarian character of contemporary science and technology, which stifles our potential for continual growth or 'becoming.' What Bakhtin terms 'theoreticism' denigrates the sensuous and tangible character of the lived event, perpetrating a 'fundamental split between the content or sense of a given act/activity and the historical actuality of its being' (Bakhtin 1993: 2). In order to counteract this theoreticist drift, he argues that we must grasp the nature of the concrete deed or 'act' as it constitutes the essential 'value-centre' for human existence.

Although there is much about moral philosophy in *Towards a Philosophy of the Act*, the work contains relatively little about the phenomenon of intersubjectivity. This oversight was redressed in the later essays, eventually anthologized in *Art and Answerability*. Here, Bakhtin argues that Being is properly understood as an 'open process of axiological accomplishment,' a continuous activity of creating existential meaning, or what he terms the 'yet-to-be.' But since our ability to conceptualize ourselves as relatively cohesive and meaningful wholes, which is fundamental to the process of self-understanding and moral awareness,

cannot occur solely through our own thoughts, deeds, and perceptions, Bakhtin places singular emphasis on our relation of 'exotopy' vis-à-vis ourselves, which transcends our own perceptual and existential horizon. Invoking a visual metaphor, he contends that we can only exist through the 'borrowed axiological light of *otherness*' (Bakhtin 1990: 134). Genuinely participative thinking and acting require an engaged and embodied – or what he would later call a *dialogical* – relation to the other, and to the world at large. And because we are ultimately responsible for any 'answer' given to others and to the world in the course of (co-)authoring our life, alterity necessarily involves a normative dimension as well. Sharing is not simply an economic or abstractly ethical imperative, but rather an ontological condition of being human.

In 1924, the Bakhtin Circle moved to Leningrad, where it entered its most productive phase. This included the publication of Voloshinov's *Freudianism: A Marxist Critique* (1927 [1976]) and *Marxism and the Philosophy of Language* (1929 [1973]), as well as Medvedev's *The Formal Method in Literary Scholarship* (1928 [1978]). A distinguishing feature of these texts is the notion that the process by which dialogical meaning is shaped cannot be accounted for by the existing precepts of linguistic science or literary theory, but only through a broader sociological approach that conceptualizes actual language use in relation to the continuous struggle over scarce forms of economic, political, and cultural capital (for a fuller exposition, see Brandist 2002). There is considerable debate about who actually wrote many texts attributed, variously, either to other members of the Bakhtin Circle, especially Voloshinov and Medvedev, or entirely to Bakhtin. On this, see Ivanov (1974), Clark and Holquist (1984), and Morson and Emerson (1990).

For Bakhtin the year 1929 saw the publication of his first book, *Problems of Dostoevsky's Poetics* (1984a). What made Dostoevsky's novels special for Bakhtin was their 'polyphonic' quality, a 'plurality of independent and unmerged voices and consciousnesses, a genuine polyphony of fully valid voices' (1984a: 6). Dostoevsky's utilization of a polyphonic method that incorporated multiple and independent consciousnesses into the text was a pivotal artistic device, and the centrepiece of a dialogical principle that managed to subvert the *monologic* point of view of 'official' thought, language, and culture. *Problems of Dostoevsky's Poetics* received a hostile response from the cultural organizations of the Communist Party of the Soviet Union (CPSU), which were beginning to adopt the official aesthetic of socialist realism after the termination of the relative political openness and cultural experimentation that marked the New Economic Policy of the 1920s. Not surprisingly, Bakhtin was arrested in 1929 by the GPU (forerunner of the KGB), ostensibly for his affiliation with the Russian Orthodox Church. He was sentenced to five years in a labour camp in the Russian far north, which would have certainly resulted in his demise, given the fragile state of his health. Fortunately, this was reduced to exile in Kazakhstan, but only due to the personal intervention of Anatoly Lunacharsky, who was then Soviet commissar for culture.

Bakhtin's exile effectively signalled the dissolution of the Circle. An even worse fate, however, was to meet most of the other members. Although Medvedev eventually became full professor at the Historico-Philological Institute in Leningrad, he fell victim to the sweeping arrests and purges at the height of the Stalinist terror and disappeared in 1938. Voloshinov died of tuberculosis in 1935, and by 1944 all the other major figures within the Circle – except Bakhtin himself – had expired. While in exile, Bakhtin worked in various clerical jobs in different institutions in Siberia and Kazakhstan. When his sentence was completed, he was allowed to teach at a teacher's college in Saransk. During this period, he wrote some of his most important works, including a series of essays on the nature of language in literature and society in the context of European cultural history, and a lengthy treatise on what he called the 'chronotope,' concerning how temporal and spatial relationships connect and interact in both the social world and literary texts. These essays were collected and published in English in 1981 under the title *The Dialogic Imagination: Four Essays by M.M. Bakhtin*. Perhaps the most influential of these texts is 'Discourse in the Novel,' a book-length text that criticizes theoretical and aesthetic positions which serve to buttress and legitimize the centralization and hierarchization of what he terms the 'verbal-ideological' sphere. In particular, he dismisses the notion that the individual author is the epicentre of meaning and responsible for all aesthetic creativity, a position Bakhtin regards as a vestige of egological idealism. Indeed, the fetishization of the authorial voice has other, more ominous ramifications: for Bakhtin, it is nothing less than an expression of forces that strive to unify ideologically the social world and smother the concrete particularity of everyday life. The official language takes its cue from the rarefied conversational and literary generic forms characteristic of the educated elites, and it defines itself in contradistinction to the myriad 'low' or profane speech types found in the street, in the marketplace, and the public square (what he refers to as 'heteroglossia'). Nevertheless, this drive to unify the verbal-ideological world is never completely successful. Accompanying this centripetal tendency towards integration are (more or less powerful) centrifugal processes that continue unabated. The latter – which Bakhtin identifies increasingly with the 'folk-festive' genres of ordinary people – operate to subvert the officially sanctioned language system from within and ensure an impetus towards movement, change, and diversification.

Bakhtin's evocation of a ceaseless 'battle' between official (monologizing, centralizing) and unofficial (dialogizing, multiform) sociocultural forces represents a radical populism that reaches its apotheosis in what is arguably his most influential and politically charged text: namely, *Rabelais and His World* (1984b). Here he turns his attention towards the boisterous, disruptive, and libidinous qualities of popular cultural forms and the collective body, within a historical period marked by the collapse of medievalism and the emergence of a more open and humanistic Renaissance culture. Bakhtin celebrates the sixteenth-century writer François Rabelais and his novel *Gargantua and Pantagruel* for many reasons, but primarily because this work of fiction managed to incorporate the lived, everyday culture of the 'common folk [that] was to a great extent a culture of the loud word spoken in the open, in the street and marketplace' (Bakhtin 1984b: 182). The characteristic images and tropes of a 'thousand year-old popular culture' (symbolic inversions, ritualized parodies, and so forth) were capable of deflating the pompous idealism of the self-appointed scholastic guardians of order, propriety, and respectability, thereby undermining the ideological foundations of a gloomy and moribund medieval system. In repudiating the asceticism and other-worldly spirituality of medievalism, this folk-festive culture underscored the utopian promise embedded within the context of an everyday, informal sociality. Bakhtin's decision to focus on Rabelais and the folk-festive culture of this period is clearly not an arbitrary one. He consciously sets out to identify a historical conjuncture of great significance, marked by the breakdown of feudalism (with its denial and mortification of the flesh), but before the consolidation of Cartesian dualism and, eventually, the 'abstract rationalism and anti-historicism' of the Enlightenment.

Bakhtin completed *Rabelais and His World* in 1941 and submitted it as a PhD dissertation, but it was initially rejected. It was eventually published in the USSR in 1965 and translated into many languages. It should be noted, however, that recent scholarship has raised many questions about the originality of Bakhtin's argument in this book. For it appears that he relied

rather heavily on Ernst Cassirer's 1927 treatise *The Individual and the Cosmos in Renaissance Philosophy*, which Bakhtin seems to have plundered in verbatim chunks without attribution. See Poole (1998) and Lock (1999), for more details. After the dissertation fiasco, and despite the chaos that followed in the wake of the German invasion of Russia in 1941, Bakhtin managed to write a lengthy work on Goethe's aesthetics. Due to wartime paper shortages, and being an inveterate chain-smoker, Bakhtin systematically tore it up and used it for cigarette paper. Or so the story goes. What we do know is that a number of manuscripts were left to rot in a shed at his wartime residence; some were eventually recovered by some younger students who rediscovered his works in the 1960s.

After the end of the war, Bakhtin moved back and forth between a small town near Moscow and Saransk until the early 1960s, when he retired and was allowed to move to Moscow, where he died in 1975. Some of his final projects included an extensive re-working of his Dostoevsky book, published as a second edition in Russia in 1963, which incorporated much material on the carnivalesque prompted by his study of Rabelais, and a series of brief notes and fragments, including some programmatic essays on the human sciences, which returned to the more philosophical themes of his early period. The latter were collected and published in English as *Speech Genres and Other Late Essays* in 1986. Here, Bakhtin argues that interpretive understanding is certainly a textual process, but it is also historical and 'inter-contextual,' involving the active translation of meaning. Insofar as this process cannot avoid an entanglement with signs, which are constitutively polysemic (multi-meaningful) and unstable, the interpreter must reflexively enter the 'stream of language' as an active participant. Only then can the full 'semantic potential' of a text or utterance be revealed and ourselves enriched through a continuous dialogical encounter with other practices and traditions across different contexts which may be temporally and geographically remote, involving what Bakhtin calls 'great time.'

Although the more extravagant, even hagiographic claims made for Bakhtin's uniqueness have come in for major questioning and revision in recent years, and the so-called 'authorship debate' moulders away, his work (and that of the Circle) still enjoys widespread popularity. This includes such disciplines as anthropology, history, geography, linguistics, literary studies, media and communications studies, philosophy, political science, psychology, and sociology – and even in the natural sciences – as well as different and competing scholarly and ideological positions within each of these approaches, such as Marxism, deconstructionism, postmodernism, pragmatism, and so forth. Indeed, Bakhtin's writings have acquired virtually canonical status in such intrinsically multidisciplinary projects as cultural studies or feminism, to the point where Bakhtinian concepts like 'carnival,' 'heteroglossia,' and 'polyphony' have become part of their standard critical lexicon. This wide interest is not surprising, in part because of Bakhtin's own repeated insistence that his project, variously dubbed 'translinguistics' or 'dialogism,' is an inclusive and open-ended one, with broad relevance for all the human sciences. As such, the influence and importance of the key ideas developed, or at least popularized, by Bakhtin seem secure at the beginning of the twenty-first century.

Michael E. Gardiner

Bibliography

Bakhtin, Mikhail M. *The Dialogic Imagination: Four Essays by M.M. Bakhtin*. Ed. M. Holquist. Trans. C. Emerson and M. Holquist. Austin: Texas University Press, 1981.
– *Problems of Dostoevsky's Poetics*. Ed. and trans. C. Emerson. Manchester: Manchester University Press, 1984a.
– *Rabelais and His World*. Trans. H. Isowolsky. Cambridge: The MIT Press, 1984b.
– *Speech Genres and Other Late Essays*. Ed. C. Emerson and M. Holquist. Trans. V.W. McGee. Austin: Texas University Press, 1986.
– *Art and Answerability: Early Philosophical Essays by M.M. Bakhtin*. Ed. M. Holquist and V. Liapunov. Trans. and notes V. Liapunov, supplement trans. K. Brostrom. Austin: Texas University Press, 1990.
– *Toward a Philosophy of the Act*. Austin: Texas University Press, 1993.
Bakhtin, Mikhail M., and Pavel N. Medvedev. *The Formal Method in Literary Scholarship: A Critical Introduction to Sociological Poetics*. Trans. A.J. Wehrle. Cambridge, MA: Harvard University Press, 1985.
Brandist, Craig. *The Bakhtin Circle: Philosophy, Culture and Politics*. London: The Pluto Press, 2002.
Clark, Katerina, and Michael Holquist. *Mikhail Bakhtin*. Cambridge, MA: Harvard University Press, 1984.
Ivanov, Vyacheslav V. The Significance of M.M. Bakhtin's Ideas on Sign, Utterance, and Dialogue for Modern Semiotics. In *Semiotics and Structuralism: Readings from the Soviet Union*, ed. H. Baran, 310–67. White Plains: International Arts and Sciences Press, 1974.
Lock, Charles. The Bakhtin Scandal. *Literary Research* 31 (1999): 13–19.
Medvedev, Pavel N. *The Formal Method in Literary Scholarship: A Critical Introduction to Sociological Poetics*. Trans. Albert J. Wehrle. Baltimore: Johns Hopkins University Press, 1978.
Morson, Gary Saul, and Caryl Emerson. *Mikhail Bakhtin: Creation of a Prosaics*. Stanford, CA: Stanford University Press, 1990.
Poole, Brian. Bakhtin and Cassirer: The Philosophical Origins of Bakhtin's Carnival Messianism. In *Bakhtin: Studies in the Archive and Beyond*, ed. Peter Hitchcock. Durham, NC: Duke University Press, 1998.
Voloshinov, Valentin N. *Marxism and the Philosophy of Language*. Trans. L. Matejka and I.R. Titunik. Cambridge, MA: Harvard University Press, 1973.
– *Freudianism: A Marxist Critique*. Ed. I.R. Titunik and N. Bruss. Trans. I.R. Titunik. New York: The Academic Press, 1976.

BARTHES, ROLAND (1915–80)

[See also: *Myth; Mythology; Semiotics; Structuralism*]

Apart from Umberto Eco, Roland Barthes is probably the best-known semiotician outside academic circles. Barthes's version of sign theory is distributed across a number of works on literary theory and communications but is mainly to be found in his *Éléments de sémiologie* (1964). His influence in English-speaking academia is probably most directly traceable to the publication of Annette Lavers's and Colin Smith's 1967 translation of the book as well as Lavers's 1973 translation of the essays from the 1950s, originally published in French magazines and then collected by Barthes as *Mythologies* in 1957. *Mythologies* is still one of the chief reference points for many studies of 'media semiotics,' but Barthes's range of interests in 'modern society' also created the demand for a further, influential popular collection of essays which has been a fairly constant reference point for media studies: *Image-Music-Text* (1977), translated and edited by Stephen Heath. What made Barthes's work groundbreaking was his exposure of hitherto unconsidered elements of (initially French) popular culture. Each 'mythology' in the former volume – wrestling, the haircuts of the Roman characters in Joseph L. Mankiewicz's film of *Julius Caesar*, the face of Garbo, *steak frites*, striptease, the New Citroën, and the brain of Einstein, for example – provided evidence for Barthes that 'myth is a language' (Barthes 1973: 11). Indeed, Barthes claims to have actually initiated semiology in this work (Barthes 1973: 9), instituting the general science of signs that Saussure had first called for (in print) forty-one years earlier.

Barthes suggested that the media traded in popular cultural 'myths.' As a type of speech (as Barthes insisted it was) the myth that creates full-blown mythologies produces two levels of signification. The first level of this system Barthes calls the *language-object*: 'It is the language which myth gets hold of in order to build its own system' (Barthes 1973: 115). This level is the domain of the *signifiant* (sound pattern) and *signifié* (mental concept), which Saussure envisaged as being connected in the brain to produce a (linguistic) sign. For Barthes, this level is where straightforward indicating takes place: denotation. The second level, on the other hand, is *metalanguage*: a language that speaks about the first level. The level of metalanguage is constituted by connotation, and Barthes suggests that connotation is *cynical* because it relies on the level of denotation to naturalize any ideological proposition which it embodies. This is a key point, and although many texts in media studies wilfully and erroneously misread it (for example, Bignell 1997: 16–17), suggesting that connotation is the ideological villain, the analysis has had some mileage.

If it was not clear from the analysis of 'myth' offered by Barthes in *Mythologies*, then *Elements of Semiology* makes it apparent that central to his theory of the sign is that it not only is an ideological *vehicle* but, in fact, is ideological through and through. For Barthes and those who use his semiological analysis in media study, there is an analytic unity in his theory of both verbal and non-verbal signs. The ravages of ideology, when exposed, would be less convincing if they were distributed unevenly across different kinds of signifying systems. Indeed, Barthes's justly famous essays on photography (see Barthes 1977 and 1980) are important in this respect since they indicate that the denotative sign enacts a motivated relationship often as if it were in the service of 'validating' the injustice of the connotative sign, establishing its literalness and helping to *ground* ideology.

Undoubtedly, the possibilities offered for exposing and critiquing ideology by Barthes's sign theory were attractive to the post-1968 generation of academics teaching communications, media, and cultural studies in the 1970s and 1980s. Students might be set exercises in which the task was to unmask the mythologizing excesses of advertising, for example, in a way which would empower them against the myths perpetrated by the media in general, and empower them in a way which, supposedly, was unavailable to the 'masses' who did not go to university and learn the methods of semiology. In the 1990s and into the twenty-first century, as European governments' policies changed to encourage a massive expansion of student numbers, and as the barriers between high and low culture suffered some stress, teaching Barthes in this way was far less tenable.

Ironically, years before Barthes's initial conception of myth was being taken up by cultural critics and media theorists in Britain and North America, he had already shifted the emphasis of his analyses. In his 1971 retrospective on *Mythologies*, Barthes argued that the identification and uncovering of myths was no longer sufficient in the post-1968 world. Myths had become easily recognizable and their exposure a routine exercise. For Barthes, 'denunciation, demystification (demythification)' (1977: 166) of the bourgeois and the petit bourgeois had become, itself, a mythological *doxa*. 'Mythoclasm' was succeeded by 'semioclasm,' he claimed, and what was needed was a far-reaching interrogation of *all* sign systems and a *challenge* to their very basis. This is the project of Barthes which, arguably, was closest to the concerns of diverse media studies. The call for *semioclasm* came, not coincidentally, shortly after the formation of the International Association for Semiotic Studies in 1969, in which semioticians such as Thomas A. Sebeok broadened the entire agenda of sign study by encouraging its application to the whole of life. However, in the 1970s Barthes's project was sidetracked by the kinds of ideological critiques of 'realism' in the media that came to characterize the journal *Screen*.

At present, Barthes's basic approach to analysing media – a kind of close reading with Saussurean overtones – is still taught in media and communications courses and has much to recommend it. However, where Barthes's work interrogated media

texts to reveal how they worked (ideologically), there is now an increasing demand, met by approaches such as modelling systems theory, to additionally identify how texts implicate the feelings and emotions of their users.

Paul Cobley

Bibliography

Barthes, Roland. *Éléments de sémiologie*. Paris: Seuil, 1964.
– *Elements of Semiology*. Trans. A. Lavers and C. Smith. London: Cape, 1967.
– *Mythologies*. Trans. A. Lavers. London: Paladin, 1973.
– *Image-Music-Text*. Ed. and trans. S. Heath. London: Fontana, 1977.
– *La chambre claire*. Paris: Seuil, 1980.
Bignell, John. *Media Semiotics: An Introduction*. Manchester: Manchester University Press, 1997.

BATESON, GREGORY (1904–80)

[See also: *Constructivism; Cybernetics*]

Gregory Bateson was a British anthropologist who made significant contributions to various disciplines, including biology, psychology, cybernetics, and communication theory. He studied natural history at Cambridge University, graduating in 1926. Bateson was one of the first exponents of what came to be known as British social anthropology, studying under A.R. Radcliffe-Brown (1881–1955), a founder of modern-day anthropology. He met the American anthropologist Margaret Mead (1901–78) while conducting fieldwork on cultural practices in New Guinea in the 1930s. They were married from 1935 to 1950, each influencing the other's view of the relation between mind and culture. Bateson held academic positions at many institutions, including Stanford and the University of California. His major books are *Steps to an Ecology of Mind* (1972) and *Mind and Nature:*

A Necessary Unity (1979). Interestingly, along with Mead he may have been the first fieldworker to document his ethnographic observations with the use of photography, co-authoring with her a study based on the many photographs he took of the Balinese in their natural habitat (Bateson and Mead 1942).

Bateson's main works focus on the relation between mind, culture, and nature, contributing to the development of the field known as *cybernetics*, the study of communication in all species and in machines (especially computers). His best-known, and widely referenced, theory, put forward along with psychiatrists Donald Jackson, Jay Haley, and John H. Weakland, is *double-blind theory*, which he developed after studying various non-Western cultures and their rearing practices. He characterized such practices as leading children to instabilities in their thinking. Bateson suggested that this was brought about by repeated, conflicting messages of love and rejection from emotionally unstable parents. Double-blind theory is still a staple of clinical practice. The main tenet of the theory is that communication between clinician and patient must be balanced, equal, and based on mutual trust, not one in which the clinician assumes a role of control or dominance ('I suggest this is the best way for you') (Ruesch and Bateson 1951). This model of communication has often been extended by theorists to encompass an overall theory of communicative success.

Double-blind theory traces its roots to Bateson's fieldwork among the Balinese, a native society of Indonesia, where he noticed that mothers ignored their children's emotional outbursts of love or anger. In the West, Bateson pointed out, these would evoke a response in kind. Not so in the Balinese world. The mother is inclined, by cultural conditioning, simply to ignore even the child's affective behaviours. This approach to rearing injects social stability in the child that he called *stasis*, which diminishes the likelihood of emotional disturbances arising in adulthood. On the other hand, in societies where stasis is not part of rearing patterns, such as in the West, and where a dominance-based relation is encouraged between mother and child, the risk of developing unstable emotional behaviours in adulthood increases considerably. He called this *schismogenesis*. It is the source of schizophrenia in extreme cases. Avoiding contradictory emotional messages is thus the central premise of clinical practice based on double-blind theory, a practice that should instil a sense of balance between interlocutors, so that the mind can adapt harmoniously to the surrounding environment.

Bateson also understood that any form of human interaction operates in terms of contrasting levels above and beyond the exchange of information; he called those levels *metacommunicative*. Metacommunication occurs all the time and is a hidden agent in determining communicative success. Ultimately it is subjective-based information, indicating that what we say to each other implies how we relate to each other. This approach to communication has been echoed by others, whereby the sender and receiver of information are involved in the shaping of the communicative flow, employing a dynamic integrated system of metacommunicative inferences.

Perhaps the Batesonian idea that resonates most with anthropologists and clinicians today is that the human mind is shaped by emotional stresses. The less systemic stress in the environment, the more harmonious the world view. Like nature itself, human organisms seek *homeostasis*, or the ability to maintain a stable set of conditions inside the body and the mind. The more homeostatic the cultural system, the less aberrant mental behaviours. The Western tendency on control, rather than harmony, has led to the spate of mental diseases that are now recognized as being the result of upbringing practices. The vicious circle of a 'control and dependency pattern' that is typical of how Western cultures view the relation between humans and nature, and between humans themselves, is ultimately a destructive force in both nature and human life.

Marcel Danesi

Bibliography

Bateson, Gregory. *Naven: A Survey of the Problems Suggested by a Composite Picture of the Culture of a New Guinea Tribe Drawn from Three Points of View.* Stanford, CA: Stanford University Press, 1936.

— *Steps to an Ecology of Mind: Collected Essays on Anthropology, Psychiatry, Evolution, and Epistemology.* Chicago: University of Chicago Press, 1972.

— *Mind and Nature: A Necessary Unity.* New York: Hampton Press, 1979.

Bateson, Gregory, and Margaret Mead. *Balinese Character: A Photographic Analysis.* New York: New York Academy of Sciences, 1942.

Ruesch, Jurgen, and Gregory Bateson. *Communication: The Social Matrix of Psychiatry.* New York: Norton, 1951.

BAUDRILLARD, JEAN (1929–2007)

[See also: *Althusser, Louis; Frankfurt School; Marxism; McLuhan, Marshall; Postmodernism; Representation; Semiotics; Simulacrum Theory*]

The late French theorist Jean Baudrillard was one of the foremost critics of contemporary society and culture and is often seen as a representative of French postmodern theory, whose reflections on media and communication have been significant in various domains of academia. A prolific author of over thirty books, Baudrillard has commented on the most salient sociological and cultural phenomena of the contemporary era, including the erasure of the distinctions of gender, race, and class that structured modern societies in a new postmodern consumer, media, and high-tech society; the mutating roles of art and aesthetics in an era of media and communication; fundamental changes in politics and culture in the media society; and the impact of new media, information, and cybernetic technologies in the creation of a qualitatively different social order. For some years a cult figure of postmodern theory, Baudrillard moved beyond the problematic of the postmodern from the early 1980s to the present and developed a highly idiosyncratic mode of social and cultural analysis.

Among Baudrillard's most provocative theses are his reflections on the role of the media in constituting the postmodern world. Indeed, he provides paradigmatic models of the media as all-powerful and autonomous social forces that produce a wide range of effects, although his take on the media is ultimately idiosyncratic and surprising and goes beyond the parameters of contemporary academic media and communication theory. The links between Baudrillard and McLuhan on media and communication, and Baudrillard's characteristic analyses of the media and how his positions are connected with a postmodern break in history, in which media and new technologies are important forces, are critical themes in his work.

Baudrillard's Postmodern Media Theory: Signs, Simulations, and Implosion

A professor of sociology at the University of Nanterre from 1966 to 1987, Baudrillard took the postmodern turn in the mid-1970s, developing a new kind of social and cultural analysis that went beyond the confines of modern theory. He is ultimately important as a critic of modern society and theory who claims that the era of modernity and the tradition of classical theory is obsolete and that we need a novel mode of social analysis adequate to the emerging era of postmodernity.

In 1967, Baudrillard wrote a review of Marshall McLuhan's *Understanding Media* in which he claimed that McLuhan's dictum that the 'medium is the message' is 'the very formula of alienation in a technical society,' and he criticized McLuhan for naturalizing that alienation (Baudrillard 1967: 227ff.). At this time, he shared the neo-Marxist critique of McLuhan as a technological reductionist and determinist. By the 1970s and 1980s, however, McLuhan's formula that 'the medium is the message' eventually became the guiding principle of his own thought.

Baudrillard begins developing his theory of the media in an article 'Requiem for the Media' in *For a Critique of the Political Economy of the Sign* (1981). The title is somewhat ironic for Baudrillard is really only beginning to develop theoretical perspectives in which the media will play crucial roles in constituting a new type of postmodern society where individuals spend much time in and are deeply shaped by the media. Thus Baudrillard is writing a requiem here for a Marxist theory of the media, arguing:

> McLuhan has said, with his usual Canadian-Texan brutalness, that Marx, the spiritual contemporary of the steam engine and railroads, was already obsolete in his lifetime with the appearance of the telegraph. In his candid fashion, he is saying that Marx, in his materialist analysis of production, had virtually circumscribed productive forces as a privileged domain from which language, signs and communication in general found themselves excluded. (Baudrillard 1981: 164)

Baudrillard's critique of Marx begins a radical interrogation of and eventual break with Marxism that would culminate in *The Mirror of Production* (1975). Baudrillard begins to distance himself from Marxism in 'Requiem for the Media,' and in particular attacks Marx's alleged economic reductionism, or 'productivism,' and the alleged inability of Marxist theory to conceptualize language, signs, and communication.

As an example of the failure of Marxist categories to provide an adequate theory of the media, Baudrillard criticizes the German activist and writer Hans Magnus Enzensberger's media theory and his attempts to develop a socialist strategy for the media. Baudrillard dismisses this effort as a typical Marxist attempt to liberate productive forces from the fetters of productive relations, which fails to see that in their very form the mass media of communication

are anti-mediatory and intransitive. They fabricate non communication – this is what characterizes them, if one agrees to define communication as an exchange, as a reciprocal space of a speech and a response, and thus of a responsibility (not a psychological or moral responsibility, but a personal, mutual correlation in exchange) … they are what always prevents response, making all processes of exchange impossible (except in the various forms of response simulation, themselves integrated in the transmission process, thus leaving the unilateral nature of the communication intact). This is the real abstraction of the media. And the system of social control and power is rooted in it. (Baudrillard, 1981: 169–70)

It is curious that Baudrillard, interpreted by many of his followers as an avant-garde, postmodern media theorist, manifests in this passage both technophobia and a nostalgia for face-to-face conversation, which he privileges (as authentic communication) over degraded and abstract media communication. Such a position creates a binary dichotomy between 'good' face-to-face communication and 'bad' media communication, and occludes the fact that interpersonal communication can be just as manipulative, distorted, reified, and so on, as media communication (as Ionesco and Habermas, among others, were aware). Denouncing the media tout court in a Baudrillardian fashion rules out in advance the possibility of 'responsible' or 'emancipatory' media communication, and indeed Baudrillard frequently argues that there can be no good use of media.

Baudrillard presents a rather extreme variant of a negative model of the media that sees mass media and culture simply as instruments of domination, manipulation, and social control in which radical intervention and radical media or cultural politics are impossible. He shares a certain theoretical terrain on theories of the media with the Frankfurt School, many French Marxists like Louis Althusser, and those who see electronic media, broadcasting, and mass culture simply as a terrain of domination.

Hence, Baudrillard's generally negative and dismissive attitude towards the media could be contrasted with McLuhan's more 'neutral,' or even affirmative, stance. Yet following McLuhan's analysis of the centrality of television in contemporary culture, Baudrillard noted how the 'TV Object' was becoming the centre of the household and was serving an essential 'proof function' that the owner was a genuine member of the consumer society (Baudrillard 1981: 53ff.). The accelerating role of the media in contemporary society becomes for Baudrillard equivalent to the fall from the modern universe of production into the postmodern society of simulations. Modernity for Baudrillard is the era of production characterized by the rise of industrial capitalism and the hegemony of the bourgeoisie, while postmodern society is an era of simulation dominated by signs, codes, and models. Modernity thus centred on the production of things – commodities and products – while postmodernity in his optic is characterized by radical semiurgy, by a proliferation of signs, spectacle, information, and new media.

Furthermore, Baudrillard interprets modernity as a process of explosion of commodification, mechanization, media, technology, and market relations, while postmodern society is the site of an implosion of all boundaries, regions, and distinctions between high and low culture, appearance and reality, and just about every other binary opposition maintained by traditional philosophy and social theory. Furthermore, while modernity could be characterized as a process of increasing differentiation of spheres of life, postmodernity could be interpreted as a process of de-differentiation and attendant implosion.

The rise of the broadcast media, especially television, is an important constituent of postmodernity for Baudrillard, along with the rapid dissemination of signs and simulacra in every realm of social and everyday life. By the late 1970s, Baudrillard interprets the media as key simulation machines which reproduce images, signs, and codes, constituting an autonomous realm of (hyper)reality that plays a key role in everyday life and the obliteration of the social. 'Simulation' for Baudrillard denotes a situation in which codes, models, and signs are the organizing forms of a new social order where simulation rules. In the society of simulation, identities are constructed by the appropriation of images, and codes and models determine how individuals perceive themselves and relate to other people. Economics, politics, social life, and culture are all governed by the mode of simulation, whereby codes and models determine how goods are consumed and used, politics unfold, culture is produced and consumed, and everyday life is lived.

In addition, his postmodern universe is one of 'hyperreality' in which entertainment, information, and communication technologies provide experiences more intense and involving than the scenes of banal everyday life, as well as the codes and models that structure social interaction. The realm of the hyperreal (that is, media simulations of reality, Disneyland and amusement parks, malls and consumer fantasylands, TV sports, reality television, and other excursions into ideal worlds) is more real than real, and the models, images, and codes of the hyperreal come to control thought and behaviour. Yet determination itself is aleatory in a non-linear world, where it is impossible to chart causal mechanisms in a situation in which individuals are confronted with an overwhelming flux of images, codes, and models, any of which may shape an individual's thought or behaviour.

In this postmodern world, individuals flee from the 'desert of the real' for the ecstasies of hyperreality and the new realm of computer, media, and technological experience. Baudrillard's analyses of simulations and hyperreality constitute major contributions to media theory and critique. During an era when movie actors and toxic politicians simulate politics and charlatans simulate TV religion, the category of simulation provides an essential instrument of radical social critique, while the concept of hyperreality is also an extremely useful instrument of social analysis for a media, cybernetic, and information society.

Baudrillard's analyses point to a significant reversal of the relation between representation and reality. Previously, the media were believed to mirror, reflect, or represent reality, whereas now the media are coming to constitute a hyperreality, a new media reality – 'more real than real' – where 'the real' is subordinate to representation, leading to an ultimate dissolving of the real. Interestingly, the concept of reversal is also a major notion in McLuhan's theoretical arsenal that Baudrillard makes his own. For McLuhan, in a discussion of 'Reversal of the Overheated Medium,' 'the stepping-up of speed from the mechanical to the instant electric form reverses explosion into implosion' (McLuhan 1964: 35). This is, of course, the very formula that Baudrillard adopts to describe the contemporary situation of the implosion of culture in the media.

In his article 'The Implosion of Meaning in the Media,' Baudrillard claims that the proliferation of signs and information in the media obliterates meaning through neutralizing and dissolving all content – a process which leads both to a collapse of meaning and to the destruction of distinctions between media and reality. In a society supposedly saturated with media messages, information and meaning 'implode,' collapsing into meaningless 'noise,' pure effect without content or meaning. Thus, for Baudrillard, 'information is directly destructive of meaning and signification, or neutralizes it. The loss of meaning is directly linked to the dissolving and dissuasive action of information, the media, and the mass media ... Information devours its own contents; it devours communication and the social ... information dissolves meaning and the social into a sort of nebulous state leading not at all to a surfeit of innovation but to the very contrary, to total entropy' (Baudrillard 1983a: 96–100).

Baudrillard thus follows McLuhan in making 'implosion' a key constituent of contemporary postmodern society, in which social class, gender, political differences, and once-autonomous realms of society and culture collapse into each other, erasing previously defined boundaries and differences. In Baudrillard's society of simulation, the realms of economics, politics, the media, culture, sexuality, and the social all implode into each other. In this implosive mix, economics is fundamentally shaped by culture, politics, media, and other spheres, while art, once a sphere of potential difference and opposition, is absorbed into the economic and political, while sexuality is everywhere. In this situation, differences between individuals and groups implode in a rapidly mutating dissolution of the social and the previous boundaries and structures which social theory had once articulated and critically interpreted.

The Ecstasy of Communication

In 'The Ecstasy of Communication' Baudrillard describes the media as instruments of obscenity, transparency, and ecstasy – in his special sense of these terms (Baudrillard 1983b). He claims that in the postmodern mediascape, the domestic scene – or the private sphere per se – with its rules, rituals, and privacy, is exteriorized, or made explicit and transparent, 'in a sort of obscenity where the most intimate processes of our life become the virtual feeding ground of the media (the Loud family [on a PBS 'reality' series] in the United States, the innumerable slices of peasant or patriarchal life on French television). Inversely, the entire universe comes to unfold arbitrarily on your domestic screen (all the useless information that comes to you from the entire world, like a microscopic pornography of the universe, useless, excessive, just like the sexual close-up in a porno film): all this explodes the scene formerly preserved by the minimal separation of public and private, the scene that was played out in a restricted space' (Baudrillard 1983b: 130).

In addition, the spectacles of the consumer society and the dramas of the public sphere are also being replaced by media events that replace public life and scenes with a screen that shows us everything and without scruple or hesitation: 'Obscenity begins precisely when there is no more spectacle, no more scene, when all becomes transparence and immediate visibility, when everything is exposed to the harsh and inexorable light of information and communication' (Baudrillard 1983b: 130). In the ecstasy of communication, everything is explicit, ecstatic (out of or beyond itself), and obscene in its transparency, detail, and visibility: 'It is no longer the traditional obscenity of what is hidden, repressed, forbidden or obscure; on the contrary, it is the obscenity of the visible, of the all-too-visible, of the more-visible-than-visible. It is the obscenity of what no longer has any secret, of what dissolves completely in information and communication' (Baudrillard 1983b: 131). One thinks here of such 1980s U.S. media events as the trials and tribulations of Gary Hart and Donna Rice, of Jim Bakker and Jimmy Swaggart, of Ronald and Nancy Reagan's cancer operations and astrology games, or the sleazy business deals of his associates, and the dirty transactions of Iran/Contra – all of which have been exposed to the glaring scrutiny of the media in which what used to be private, hidden, and invisible suddenly becomes (almost) fully explicit and visible.

The 1990s saw an intensification of the ecstasy of communication with the Clinton sex scandals, which displayed intimate details of his private life, the O.J. Simpson trial, which depicted the minutiae of his tormented relation with his murdered wife Nicole, and countless other revelations of private affairs of the powerful and infamous in an increasingly tabloid infotainment culture. In the 'ecstasy of communication,' everything becomes transparent, and there are no more secrets, privacy, depth, or hidden meaning. Instead, a promiscuity of information and communication unfolds in which the media circulate and disseminate a teeming network of cool, seductive, and fascinating sights and sounds to be played on one's own screen and terminal. With the disappearance of exciting scenes (in the home, in the public sphere), passion evaporates in personal and social relations, yet a new fascination emerges ('the scene excites us, the obscene fascinates us') with the very universe of media and communication. In this universe we enter a new form of subjectivity where we become saturated with information, images, events, and ecstasies. Without defence or distance, we become 'a pure screen, a switching center for all the networks of influence' (Baudrillard 1983b: 133). In the media society, the era of interiority, subjectivity, meaning, privacy, and the inner life is over; a new era of obscenity, fascination, vertigo, instantaneity, transparency, and overexposure begins in which the media absorb and re-present all aspects of social life.

Baudrillard's Media Formalism

Baudrillard has many insights into the ways in which the media erode meaning, the social, communication, and politics. Going against models of the media as key forms of communication, in his analysis the media foster non-communication, generating pseudo-events, empty spectacle, and excess of meaning and information that implode into a black hole of noise and distraction. Denying specific manipulative effects of the media, Baudrillard privileges the form of media technology over what might be called the media apparatus, and thus subordinates content, meaning, and the use of media to its purely formal structure and effects. Baudrillard tends to abstract media form and effects from the media environment and thus erases political economy, media production, and media environment (that is, society as large) from his theory. Against abstracting media form and effects from context, some of Baudrillard's critics argue that the use and effects of media should be carefully examined and evaluated in terms of specific contexts. Distinctions between context and use, form and content, media and reality, all dissolve, however, in Baudrillard's theory, where global theses and apocalyptic pronouncements replace careful analysis and critique.

Baudrillard might retort that it is the media themselves which abstract from the concreteness of everyday, social, and political life and provide simulacra of actual events, which themselves become more real than 'the real' that they supposedly represent. Yet even if this is so, critics argue media analysis should attempt to recontextualize media images and simulacra rather than merely focusing on the surface of media form. Furthermore, instead of operating with a model of (formal) media effects, some claim it is preferable to operate with a dialectical perspective that posits multiple roles and functions to television and other media.

Furthermore, Baudrillard also rigorously avoids cultural and media politics. There is nothing in his theorizing concerning alternative media practices, for instance, which he seems to rule out in advance because in his view all media are mere producers of noise, non-communication, the extermination of meaning, implosion, and so on. In 'Requiem for the Media,' Baudrillard explicitly argues that all mass media communication falls prey to 'mass mediatization,' that is, 'the imposition of models': 'In fact, the essential Medium is the Model. What is mediatized is not what comes off the daily press, out of the tube, or on the radio: it is what is reinterpreted by the sign form, articulated into models, and administered by the code (just as the commodity is not

what is produced industrially, but what is mediatized by the exchange value system of abstraction)' (Baudrillard 1981: 175–6).

All 'subversive communication,' then, for Baudrillard has to surpass the codes and models of media communication – and thus of the mass media themselves, which invariably translate all contents and messages into their codes. Consequently, not only general elections but also general strikes have 'become a schematic reducing agent' (Baudrillard 1973: 176). In this (original) situation:

> The real revolutionary media during May (1968) were the walls and their speech, the silk-screen posters and the hand-painted notices, the street where speech began and was exchanged – everything that was an immediate inscription, given and returned, spoken and answered, mobile in the same space and time, reciprocal and antagonistic. The street is, in this sense, the alternative and subversive form of the mass media, since it isn't, like the latter, an objectified support for answerless messages, a transmission system at a distance. It is the frayed space of the symbolic exchange of speech – ephemeral, mortal: a speech that is not reflected on the Platonic screen of the media. Institutionalized by reproduction, reduced to a spectacle, this speech is expiring. (Baudrillard 1973: 176–7)

In this text, Baudrillard conflates all previously revolutionary strategies and models of 'subversive communication' to 'schematic reducing agents' and manifests here once again nostalgia for direct, unmediated, and reciprocal speech ('symbolic exchange'), which is denied in the media society. Haunted by a disappearing metaphysics of presence, Baudrillard valorizes immediate communication over mediated communication, thus forgetting that all communication is mediated (through language, signs, codes, and so on). Furthermore, he romanticizes a certain form of communication (speech in the streets) as the only genuinely subversive or revolutionary communication and media. Consistently with this theory, he thus calls for a (neo-Luddite) 'deconstruction' of the media 'as systems of non-communication,' and thus for the 'liquidation of the existing functional and technical structure of the media' (Baudrillard 1973: 177).

Douglas Kellner

Bibliography

Baudrillard, Jean. Review of *Understanding Media*. *L'Homme et la Société* 5 (1967): 227ff.
— *The Mirror of Production*. St Louis, MO: Telos Press, 1975 [1973].
— *For a Critique of the Political Economy of the Sign*. St Louis, MO: Telos Press, 1981 [1973].
— *Simulations*. New York: Semiotext(e), 1983a.
— The Ecstasy of Communication. In *The Anti-Aesthetic: Essays on Modern Culture*, ed. Hal Foster, 127–43. Washington: Bay Press, 1983b.
Enzensberger, Hans Magnus. Constituents of a Theory of the Media. In *The Consciousness Industry*. New York: Seabury, 1974.
Kellner, Douglas. *Jean Baudrillard: From Marxism to Postmodernism and Beyond*. Cambridge and Palo Alto: Polity Press and Stanford University Press, 1989.
McLuhan, Marshall. *Understanding Media*. New York: Bantam, 1964.

BEHAVIOURISM

[See also: *Cognitivism; Hypodermic Needle Theory; Media Effects; Psychology of the Media*]

Behaviourism is a school of psychology that is based on the belief that psychological research should be based on observable behaviours, not on inferring inner experiences. Behaviourism was introduced into psychology in 1913 by the American psychologist James B. Watson, who believed that changes in behaviour result from *conditioning*, a process whereby a new response is associated with a certain stimulus and becomes part of habitual thought.

The basic method in behaviourism for investigating complex forms of behaviour, from perception to language, is by observing, measuring, and then analysing the responses of human subjects to various stimuli under controlled conditions. While behaviourism never did deny the existence of inner experiences such as emotions and intuitions, it has always maintained that, since these cannot be studied in and of themselves apart from the conditions in which they occur, the only true scientific approach to the study of mentality is to vary those conditions in order to see what they produce. Behaviourism has had fertile applications to the study of media effects and has led to the technique of commutation, whereby a variable in a media text or event is changed and then the response that this produces in audiences or individual subjects is observed. For example, a viewer might be shown a TV commercial of a beautiful woman wearing red lipstick and then shown the same commercial without the lipstick. Follow-up interviews are then designed to see if the subject responds differently to the two commercials.

The key notion in behaviourism is that of the *conditioned response*, which was developed initially by the Russian psychologist Ivan Pavlov in 1902 in his work with dogs. Pavlov's original experiment showed how minds are conditioned by environmental flux. He presented a piece of meat to a hungry dog, producing in the dog the expected response of salivation. Pavlov called this the dog's *unconditioned response*; it is part of instinctual behaviour, not learned behaviour. Then Pavlov rang a bell at the same time that he presented the meat stimulus a number of times. He discovered that the dog eventually salivated only to the ringing of the bell, without the presence of meat. Clearly, the bell ringing, which would not have triggered the salivation instinctively, had brought about a *conditioned response* in the dog. For behaviourists this is essentially how learning unfolds in all species.

Watson proposed that human conditioning could be studied with virtually the same type of laboratory procedure, since all complex forms of behaviour are ultimately broken down into simple muscular and glandular processes and can thus be observed and measured directly. In one of his well-known studies, he struck a metal bar loudly each time a child touched a furry animal. The sound scared the infant, who gradually became frightened just at the sight of the animal. Watson maintained that any response in a child could be evoked if the environment could be controlled. In the mid-1900s, the American psychologist B.F. Skinner became famous for his studies on how rewards (positive conditioning) and punishments (negative conditioning) can influence behaviour. His work has had significant impacts on learning theories, even though behaviourism has fallen into disfavour. It is nonetheless present in latent form in many pedagogical and even clinical practices. Behaviour modification theory, for instance, is based on Skinner's ideas. It is used, for example, to help children who are facing mental challenges to learn school subjects. The children receive smiles, hugs, and other forms of positive reinforcement for doing their schoolwork. The same model of clinical practice has proved to be effective with juvenile delinquents.

Starting in the late 1960s, behaviourism became highly unpopular within mainstream psychology, but was still used (tacitly) in the so-called media effects studies, showing that exposure to media, such as simulated violence, leads to conditioned responses in certain audiences. Today, such theories are considered to be largely inconclusive, but they nevertheless persist in the common imagination, and in specific pedagogical and clinical practices (such as those mentioned above), since they seem to have intuitive appeal and to produce concrete results. The emergence of *cognitivism* in psychology in the 1960s led to the study of how someone's unique view of the environment determines his or her response to it. Today, psychologists focus on how

biological, psychological, and social factors may intermingle in complex behaviours, shaping the development of thoughts, feelings, and social behaviours.

Marcel Danesi

Bibliography

Pavlov, Ivan. *The Work of Digestive Glands.* London: Griffin, 1902.

Watson, John B. *Behaviorism.* New York: Norton, 1925.

– *Psychology from the Standpoint of a Behaviorist.* Philadelphia: Lippincott, 1929.

BELL, DANIEL (1919–2011)

[See also: *Internet; Media Studies*]

Daniel Bell (born Daniel Bolotsky) is an internationally acclaimed sociologist best known for his ideas on post-industrialism. Born on 10 May 1919 in New York to Jewish immigrant parents, his meagre upbringing was due to the untimely passing of his father at a young age, forcing Bell to be placed in a day orphanage in the Lower East Side of New York. At thirteen, he joined the Young People's Socialist League, which is said to have influenced his outlook greatly. In 1939, after graduating with a degree in ancient history from City College of New York, Bell pursued a career as a journalist, writing about social issues. He became managing editor of *The New Leader Magazine* from 1941 to 1945 and labour editor of *Fortune* from 1948 to 1958. Bell went to Paris in 1956–7 to serve as director of the Congress for Culture Freedom. Upon his return to the U.S., he received his PhD from Columbia University in 1960. In 1969, four years after co-founding the *Public Interest Magazine* with Irving Kristol, Bell left Columbia to teach at Harvard University, receiving the Henry Ford II endowed chair in 1980.

Throughout his career, Bell produced many books on the effects of capitalism on society, and how it finds a fertile terrain in the developments of science and technology. These works include: *Marxian Socialism in America* (1952), *The End of Ideology: On the Exhaustion of Political Ideas in the 1950s* (1960), *The Radical Right* (1963), *The Reforming of General Education* (1966), *The Coming of Post-Industrial Society* (1973), *The Cultural Contradictions of Capitalism* (1976), and *The Winding Passage* (1980). For his writings he received the Lifetime Achievement Award from the American Sociological Association in 1992, the Talcott Parsons Prize for the Social Sciences from the American Academy of Arts and Sciences one year later, and the Tocqueville Award from the French Government in 1995. He also received seventeen honorary degrees, including one from Harvard University and one from Keio University in Japan. Bell is perhaps best known for *The End of Ideology*, a collection of essays where he claims that new ideologies rise up from the ashes of spent ones (capitalism, scientism, industrialism, and so on) that characterized social evolution in the nineteenth and twentieth centuries. Bell saw a paradigm shift in the constitution of modern economies and societies as moving away from industrial bases, such as manufacturing, towards knowledge and information-based economies. Bell's concept has blurred into various derivative notions such as 'post-Fordism' and 'flexible specialization,' but it is his original model that still holds across the theoretical spectrum.

Through his post-industrial model, Bell predicted that the end of communism would bring about ethnic and religious conflicts throughout the world, and that the media would exacerbate the situation by simply highlighting the conflicts. In other works, Bell provided a blueprint for the new post-industrial society, a society that would be based on open access to information, the use of sophisticated technologies to conduct economic activities and politics, and the growth of the role of the media in setting social agendas. Interestingly, many of his predictions have revealed to be true in the current internet age. Indeed, we are now living in the kind of post-industrialist society that he envisioned decades ago.

Mariana Bockarova

Bibliography

Bell, Daniel. *The End of Ideology: On the Exhaustion of Political Ideas in the Fifties*. Glencoe, IL: Free Press, 1960.

Brick, Howard. *Daniel Bell and the Decline of Intellectual Radicalism: Social Theory and Political Reconciliation in the 1940s*. Madison: University of Wisconsin Press, 1986.

Elwell, Frank. Major Works by Daniel Bell. Rogers State University. faculty.rsu.edu/~felwell/ Theorists/Bell/MajorWorks.html (accessed 12 February 2009.

Jost, John T. The End of the End of Ideology. *The American Psychologist* 61 (2006): 651–70.

BENJAMIN, WALTER (1892–1940)

[See also: *Adorno, Theodor; Catharsis Hypothesis; Culture Industry Theory; Frankfurt School; Marcuse, Herbert*]

Walter Bendix Schönflies Benjamin, born in Berlin, was a renowned philosopher and literary critic who contributed significantly to Frankfurt School critical theory. He collaborated especially with Theodor Adorno and Max Horkheimer of the School. He was particularly influenced by writers such as Bertolt Brecht and Gerhom Scholem.

In 1917 Benjamin married Dora Sophie Pollak (née Kellner), with whom he had a son, Stefan Rafael. In 1919 he earned his PhD cum laude at the University of Bern with the essay 'Begriff der Kunstkritik in der Deutschen Romantik' ['The Concept of Criticism in German Romanticism']. He returned with his wife to Berlin to live with his parents and published *Kritik der Gewalt* [*Critique of Violence*] in 1921. He also translated Charles Baudelaire's *Tableaux Paris-iens* (1923) and the first volume of Marcel Proust's *À la Recherche du temps perdu* [*In Search of Lost Time*]. His critical reflections on translation are expressed in his essay 'The Task of the Translator.' In 1923 he started a life-long collaboration with Theodor Adorno at the Frankfurt School. His habilitation thesis on *The Origin of German Tragic Drama* (1924), however, was rejected by Frankfurt University, closing the door to an academic career there.

In 1926 Benjamin travelled to Moscow to join up with his paramour, Asja Lacis, a Bolshevik Latvian actress (whom he had met in Capri in 1924) living in Moscow, and to give to Anatolij Lunacharskij, the education commissar, his entry on the German writer Goethe for *Literaturnaja Enciclopedija*, which Lunacharskij rejected. (In 1924, Benjamin's entry, 'Goethes Wahlverwandt-schaften' ['Goethe's Elective Affinities'] was published by Hugo von Hoffmansthal in the magazine *Neue Deutsche Beiträge*.) While in Russia, he began writing his *Moscow Diary*. In 1927, he started work on *Das Passagen-Werk*. In 1928, the year of his separation from his wife (they were divorced two years later), he published *Einbahnstraße* [*One-Way Street*] and *Ursprung des Deutschen Trauerspiels* [*The Origin of German Tragic Drama*]. The following year, in Berlin, Asja Lacis, who at the time was Bertolt Brecht's assistant, introduced Benjamin to Brecht. Also in that year, Benjamin briefly embarked on a short-lived academic career as instructor at the University of Heidelberg. Because of Hitler's rise to power and his subsequent persecution of Jews, Benjamin, a German Jew, moved to the Spanish island of Ibiza, then on to Nice, Svendborg, Sanremo, and Paris. In the latter city, he met other German refugee artists and intellectuals and befriended intellectuals, artists, and writers such as Hannah Arendt, Hermann Hesse, and Kurt Weill. In 1936 he published 'L'Oeuvre d'art à l'époque de sa reproductibilité technique' ['The Work of Art in the Age of Mechanical Reproduction'] in the journal of the Frankfurt School, *Zeitschrift für Sozialforschung*. In 1937 he started work on *Das Paris des Second Empire bei Baudelaire* [*The Paris of the Second Empire in Baudelaire*, 1938]. Because Hitler took German citizenship away from Jews, Benjamin (left without a nationality) was incarcerated by the French authorities for three months in a camp near Nevers. Returning to Paris in January, he wrote *Über den Begriff der Geschichte* [*Theses on the Philosophy of History*, 1939–40], published posthumously. In that same year, he obtained a visa, negotiated by Max Horkheimer, for the United States, planning to depart for America from Portugal to escape the Nazis. On 27 September 1940, in Portbou, a French-Spanish border town in the Pyrenees, Benjamin, aged 48, was intercepted by the Spanish police. According to official reports, he committed suicide with an overdose of morphine. But the fact that he was buried in the consecrated section of a Roman Catholic cemetery in Portbou indicates that his death may not have been a suicide.

'The Task of the Translator' (1992 [1923]) is one of Benjamin's most important works. In it, he starts by asking the question of to whom the translation of a work of literature is addressed. His seemingly simplistic reply to his own question – 'For readers who do not understand the original' – is actually a rather insightful one. A translation, thus, says the 'same thing' as the source language, but in a more familiar language to the new reader. This 'same thing' is what the translation intends to 'communicate.' But, in the translation process, it does much more. The implication is obvious – translation mediates and transmits new content. The problem is not what a text intends to communicate, but rather how it does so and why. As Benjamin put it: 'It's essential quality is not statement or the imparting of information' (71). The original text is written with a specific readership in mind. On the other hand, the translated text is supposed to reach a readership for whom the text was not originally meant. The text 'resists translation,' so to speak, not because it cannot be rendered in a different language, but because it was not constructed to be translated. The problem of translatability is, thus, a problem of 'otherness' or alterity. In this way, Benjamin raised the broader question of whether a natural language can be adequately translated into other natural languages, given the different cultural-historical realities of speakers.

Benjamin then asks if translatability varies according to genre. Can poetry be translated? This question brings us full circle back to the relation between translation and communication: if a translation is expected to transmit what is communicated by the text, then a poetic work has very little to communicate. By mediating communication, translation thus mediates something inessential, and if the translator recomposes the poetry of one language into the poetry of a different language, what we end up getting 'is the inaccurate transmission of an inessential content' (72). Thus, the reader, the original author, the translator, a given historical-natural language, and a specific literary genre all affect the translation process. It is a question of who the addressee is: that is, to whom or to what is the text directed? At one level, the text is addressed to whoever can read it, that is, to whoever knows the same language. But this ignores the author's intentions and the limits imposed upon the author by the language itself as well as by the genre of the text. Here 'language' is used in the sense of a modelling device, capable of producing an 'infinite number of possible worlds' (as the philosopher Leibniz put it), and the 'play of musement' (as American philosopher Charles Peirce emphasized). Benjamin also stressed the relation between writing and translation, claiming that when pictographic forms of writing are involved the translation process becomes even more problematic. Pictographs are 'image' signs or icons that are used specifically to bring out visual qualities (Benjamin 1963/1998: 176ff.). This non-linguistic aspect of the original text is invariably lost in the translation.

Ultimately, translatability concerns the relation between *text* and *language*. The more a text reflects what Benjamin calls 'pure language,' the more it is translatable, and the more it *calls for* translation: 'If translation is a mode, translatability must be an essential feature of certain words' (Benjamin 1992: 73). Thanks to its relation with 'pure language,' a text is not only translatable, but is also bound to be translated. Furthermore: 'It is plausible that no translation, however good it may be,' says Benjamin, 'can have any significance as regards the original. Yet, by virtue of its translatability the original is closely connected with the translation' (73). The original text and its translation are thus vitally connected: the work survives in translation, just as life forms survive in descendancy. Translation does not add anything to the life of texts, but ensures their 'survival.' They thus have a life 'which finds its highest testimony in translation' (77). The idea of *life* and of the *survival* of artworks 'should be regarded with an entirely unmetaphorical objectivity' (72). In both cases there is a 'generator,' that is, an 'interpreted sign' and an 'engendered sign,' or 'interpretant sign,' which are connected by the 'translation mode' (72). There is thus an 'absolute alterity' between the two texts: the engendered text is another life form which flourishes in another time, and actually does not belong to the 'life' but the 'afterlife' of the original. As Benjamin (1992) puts it:

If the kinship of languages manifests itself in translations, this is not accomplished through a vague alikeness between adaptation and original. Wherein resides the relatedness of two languages, apart from historical considerations? All suprahistorical kinship of languages rests in the intention underlying each language as a whole – an intention, however, which no single language can attain by itself but which is realized only by the totality of their intentions supplementing each other: pure language. (75)

In the shift from historical-natural language to 'pure language,' one language is viewed with the eyes of another (as Bakhtin also pointed out). Here translation is more than communication; it 'goes beyond transmittal of subject matter,' as is obvious in the translation of literary works where communication is inessential. Benjamin (1992) elaborates this viewpoint as follows:

> Fragments of a vessel which are to be glued together must match one another in the smallest details, although they need not be like one another. In the same way a translation, instead of resembling the meaning of the original, must lovingly and in detail incorporate the original's mode of signification, thus making both the original and the translation recognizable as fragments of a greater language, just as fragments are part of a vessel. For this very reason translation must in large measure refrain from wanting to communicate something, from rendering the sense, and in this the original is important to it only insofar as it has already relieved the translator and his translation of the effort of assembling and expressing what is to be conveyed. A real translation is transparent; it does not cover the original, does not block its light, but allows the pure language, as though reinforced by its own medium, to shine upon the original all the more fully. It is the task of the translator to release in his own language that pure language which is under the spell of another, to liberate the language imprisoned in a work in his re-creation of that work. (80–1)

Translation does not represent the original text, but depicts it. The effect of a translation is to re-veil, not un-veil, the original. Translation goes from the said to saying, from the sayable to the unsayable. This is why Benjamin proclaims that 'the interlinear version of the Scriptures is the prototype or ideal of all translation' (82).

In other works, Benjamin critiques the capitalist-based mass media as existing primarily for their own reproduction (by all necessary means possible, including the use of deception). However, because of the pervasiveness of media images, deception strategies have changed. In a culture aspiring to be transparent – 'glass things do not have an 'aura'; glass is the special enemy of secrets' (Benjamin 1933/1977) – the use of images to deceive has become ineffectual. 'The destructive character' (an expression used by Benjamin in 1931 to describe the capitalist socio-economic system at the dawn of Nazism) of the present (meaning present-day society characterized by material production for the sake of production, by communication for the sake of communication) has its own constitutive obscenity. Destructive work needs a public as witness. The rapid succession and stratification of information in the name of 'transparency' becomes a sort of widespread 'voyeurism,' where appearance is everything, thus inhibiting control by common folk of their own situations. Attentivenes is replaced by confusion, a sense of scandal by accommodation and habitualization, and understanding by misunderstanding.

Another critical insight to be gleaned from Benjamin's writings is that of 'general indifferent labour,' which is a notion of fundamental importance for preserving capitalist societies. Even when planning alternative social systems, the dominant formula is 'work for all.' This mystification can be traced, says Benjamin, to the German labourer's *Gotha Programme*, where labour is defined as the source of all wealth and culture, unwittingly becoming a bridge from socialism to Nazism. Benjamin observes that Marx in his *Critique of the Gotha Programme* clarifies that labour is not the source of all wealth, adding that the bourgeoisie had its good reasons for investing in labour. Marx fought against the entrenched belief that labour is the source of wealth.

Augusto Ponzio

Bibliography

Adorno, Theodor. *Prisms (Studies in Contemporary German Social Thought)*. London: Neville Spearman, 1967. Reprint Cambridge, MA: MIT Press, 1981.

Benjamin, Andrew, and Peter Osborne, eds. *Walter Benjamin's Philosophy: Destruction and Experience*. London: Routledge, 1993.

Benjamin, Walter. Der destruktive Charakter. In W. Benjamin, *Gesammelte Schriften*, ed. R. Tiedermann and H. Schweppenhäuser, IV, 1, 396–401. Frankfurt am Main, 1931/1972. English translation, 'The Destructive Character,' in Benjamin, *Reflections*, 301–3.

– *Schriften*. Frankfurt am Main: Suhrkamp Verlag, 1955.

– *Illuminations. Walter Benjamin. Essays and Reflections*. Ed. and Intro. H. Arendt. New York: Schocken Books, 1986.

– *Moscow Diary*. Trans. R. Sieburth, ed. G. Smith, Preface by G. Scholem. Cambridge, MA: Harvard University Press, 1986.

– *Reflections. Walter Benjamin. Essays, Aphorisms, Autobiographical Writings*. Ed. and Intro. P. Demetz. New York: Schocken Books, 1986.

– *The Correspondence of Walter Benjamin and Gershom Scholem*. New York: Schocken, 1989.

– The Task of the Translator (1923). In *Theories of Translation. An Anthology of Essays from Dryden to Derrida*, ed. R. Schulte and J. Biguenet, 207–33. Chicago: University of Chicago Press, 1992.

– *The Correspondence of Walter Benjamin, 1910–1940*. Chicago: University of Chicago Press, 1994.

– *One Way Street and Other Writings*. Intro. S. Sontag, trans. E. Jephcott and K. Shorter. London: Verso, 1997.

– *Ursprung des deutschen Trauerspiels*. Frankfurt am Main: Suhrkamp Verlag, 1963. English translation, *The Origin of German Tragic Drama*, trans. J. Osborne. London: Verso, 1998.

– *Understanding Brecht*. London: Verso, 2003.

– *On Hashish*. Intro. by Marcus Boon. Cambridge: Harvard University Press, 2006.

– *Berlin Childhood around 1900*. Cambridge, MA: Harvard University Press, 2006.

Betancourt, Alex. *Walter Benjamin and Sigmund Freud: Between Theory and Politics*. Saarbrucken, Germany: VDM Verlag, 2008.

Buck-Morss, Susan. *The Dialectics of Seeing: Walter Benjamin and the Arcades Project*. Cambridge: MIT Press, 1991.

Leslie, Esther. *Walter Benjamin, Overpowering Conformism*. London: Pluto Press, 2000.

Malsey, Victor, Uwe Raseh, Peter Rautmann, Nicolas Schalz, and Rosi Huhn. *Passages. D'après Walter Benjamin / Passagen. Nach Walter Benjamin*. Mainz: Herman Schmidt, 1992.

Petrilli, Susan, ed. *Approaches to Communication: Trends in Global Communication Studies*. Madison: Atwood, 2008.

– Traducción como doctrina de comunicación inter-géneros y trans-géneros: una perspectiva semio-ética. *Signa. Revista de la asociación española de semiótica* 16 (2007): 463–92.

– Translation and Semiosis. In *Translation*, ed. and intro. Susan Petrilli, 17–37. Amsterdam: Rodopi, 2003.

Plate, S. Brent. *Walter Benjamin: Religion and Aesthetics*. London: Routledge, 2004.

Ponzio, Augusto. *The Dialogic Nature of the Sign*. Ottawa: Legas, 2006.

– Hypertext and Translation. In *Translation and the Machine: Technology, Meaning, Praxis*, ed. Steve Berneking and Scott S. Elliott, 95–102. Rome: Edizioni di Storia e Letteratura, 2007.

– Translation and the Literary Text. *TTR. Études sur le texte et ses transformations* 20, no. 2 (2007): 89–119.

– A Global Approach to Communication, Modeling and Dialogism. In S. Petrilli, ed., *Approaches to Communication*, 83–100.

– Communication with the Other and Moral Answerability in Mikhail M. Bakhtin. *Russian Journal of Communication* 1 (2008): 291–306.

Ponzio, Augusto, and Susan Petrilli. *Semiotics Unbounded: Interpretive Routes through the Open Network of Signs*. Toronto: University of Toronto Press, 2005.

– Translation as Listening and Encounter with the Other in Migration and Globalization Processes Today. *TTR. Traduction, Terminologie, Rédaction* 20, no. 2 (2006): 191–224.

Wizisla, Erdmut. *Walter Benjamin and Bertolt Brecht – The Story of a Friendship*. Trans. C. Shuttleworth. New Haven, CT: Yale University Press, 2009.

BERNERS-LEE, TIM (b. 1955)

[See also: *Googling; Hypertext; Internet; World Wide Web*]

As the inventor of the World Wide Web (WWW) and director of the World Wide Web Consortium, which oversees the development of the Web, Tim Berners-Lee is one of the most influential people in the world today – a world that has become highly dependent on the WWW for all kinds of activities, from information retrieval to social networking. As a computer scientist at the European Organization for Nuclear Research (CERN) physics laboratory near Geneva, Berners-Lee wrote the first Web software in 1990, which became part of the internet in 1991. It was the introduction of the Web that helped make the internet popular and easier to use, an event that has dramatically changed how people communicate, interact, and conduct business.

While at CERN in the early 1980s, Berners-Lee put forward a project that would use hypertext for the sharing and updating of information among researchers in a user-friendly fashion. Hypertext is a system that enables a computer user to go from one document to another by clicking underlined words or phrases, even if the documents are located on different parts of the internet. For example, on a website for *linguistics*, the word p̲h̲o̲n̲e̲m̲e̲ might appear as underlined. Clicking on the word will bring information about it to the screen (information contained either on the same site or elsewhere on the internet). Images, too, can be used as hyperlinks (hypertext links) to other documents, called *hot spots*. Berners-Lee built Enquire as a prototype system to show how all this could be accomplished easily. By 1989, CERN had evolved into the largest internet node in Europe. This allowed Berners-Lee the opportunity to connect hypertext to the internet via the Transmission Control Protocol (TCP) and domain name system. In 1990, with the help of Robert Cailliau, he

came up with another prototype, using ideas he had developed for the Enquire project. This one was deemed acceptable by CERN. Berners-Lee then went on to design and build the first web browser, editor, and server – called HTTPd (HyperText Transfer Protocol daemon). The first website at CERN went online in August 1991. A browser is a software package which locates and displays information on the Web easily through the use of a graphical user interface – a way of interacting with a computer using pictures as well as words. For example, the icon of a printer represents the command to print a document. By clicking the icon, the user gives the computer the command represented by that icon.

Berners-Lee's invention was the culmination of a paradigm shift that was set in motion after the Second World War. As computer technology improved steadily after the war, smaller and more affordable computers could be built for the science and business worlds. By 1975, it even became possible and economically feasible to produce personal computers (PCs) for the mass marketplace. The first PCs were introduced to the world in that year as word processors, which were essentially highly sophisticated typewriters. Nevertheless, PCs had the power of mainframe computers and could fit onto a desktop. The first commercial software for PCs appeared in 1978.

The idea of connecting PCs through telephony emerged by the end of the 1970s. Already in the 1960s, the Advanced Research Projects Agency (ARPA) of the U.S. Department of Defense was built to allow researchers working on military projects at research centres and universities across the country to develop a network called *Arpanet*. Arpanet made it possible to transfer data over specially equipped phone lines and satellite links. When the National Science Foundation connected universities and various research sites to Arpanet, the first functional electronic mail network was born. By 1981, a few hundred computers joined Arpanet, which gradually developed into an advanced network that came to be known as the *internet*.

The internet was very complicated to use at first – to access it, one had to learn a complicated series of commands. The breakthrough occurred in 1991, when Berners-Lee invented the World Wide Web, which facilitated internet access and use. The arrival of browsers in 1993 made internet use even easier. No other technology in the history of human communications has made it possible for so many people to interact with each other as routinely, cheaply, and easily as has the internet. Advances in WWW technologies have also led to a convergence of communications systems, which have led, in turn, to the crystallization of new internet-based lifestyles, careers, and institutions.

Today, the Web contains all types of documents, databases, and publications in all media forms (print, audio-oral, visual). The agglomeration of information it encompasses and the speed and facility at which it can be accessed have turned the internet into the primary source of knowledge engineering, information storage, and information retrieval, replacing traditional institutions such as reference libraries and print encyclopedias. Through sites such as Facebook and YouTube, the Web has also reshaped human social interaction. It has made 'indie culture' a reality, since anyone can post his or her own art, music, writing, videos, movies, or photography on websites, blogs, and so forth. Ultimately, Berners-Lee's invention has democratized the world in ways that could only have been achieved through political, philosophical, or military means in previous eras. As early as 1971, the so-called Project Gutenberg was founded by volunteers to digitize and disseminate the full texts of public domain books in online versions. Thanks to the WWW, a more comprehensive project today is under way to make classic works of human civilization as free and as accessible as possible.

Marcel Danesi

Bibliography

Alesso, Peter, and Craig F. Smith. *Thinking on the Web: Berners-Lee, Gödel and Turing*. Hoboken, NJ: John Wiley, 2009.

Berners-Lee, Tim, and Mark Fischetti. *Weaving the Web: Origins and Future of the World Wide Web*. London: Orion Business, 1999.

Cailliau, Robert, and James Gillies. *How the Web Was Born: The Story of the World Wide Web*. Oxford: Oxford University Press, 2000.

Hafner, Katie, and Matthew Lyon. *Where Wizards Stay Up Late: The Origins of the Internet*. New York: Simon and Schuster, 1996.

Herman, Andrew, and Thomas Swiss, eds. *The World Wide Web and Contemporary Cultural Theory*. London: Routledge, 2000.

Slevin, James. *The Internet and Society*. London: Polity, 2000.

Van Dijk, Jan. *The Network Society*. London: Sage, 1999.

Wise, Richard. *Multimedia: A Critical Introduction*. London: Routledge, 2000.

BIRDWHISTELL, RAY L. (1918–94)

[See also: *Body Language; Kinesics; Non-verbal Communication*]

American anthropologist Ray L. Birdwhistell is the founder of *kinesics,* the study of body language during communicative interaction, especially as its complements or accompanies vocal speech. Kinesics includes the study of gestures, facial expressions, eye movements, and posture. It is also frequently called the study of body language. But the latter term is really more the study of how one uses the body as a communication system in and of itself, separately from verbal language. Face-to-face communication between people is carried out primarily through vocal language. But, invariably, the meaning of the message being exchanged is found not solely in the meanings of the words used, but also in the subtle information that is conveyed through non-verbal signals, which are often more revealing of what is truly going on.

Kinesics (from the Greek *kinēsis*, 'movement') is now a branch of both anthropology and semiotics.

Birdwhistell became interested in analysing the way people interact by watching films; he noticed that people transmitted information unconsciously through their eye movements, facial expressions, hand gestures, and postures. For this reason he came to view body language as complementary to verbal language in face-to-face interaction. His first book on the topic, *Introduction to Kinesics*, published in 1952, discusses the role of body movements and gesture. As he states (Birdwhistell 1952: 157): 'The first premise in developing a notational system for body language is to assume that all movements of the body have meaning. None are accidental.' He called such movements *kinemes*. The kineme is the model for a set of movements that are not identical, 'but which may be used interchangeably without affecting social meaning' (Knapp 1978: 94–5) and thus 'can be construed as having a definite organization or structure, just as language is understood in terms of its grammar' (Duncan and Fiske 1977: xi).

Kinesic signs can be inborn (unwitting), learned (witting), or a mixture of the two. Blinking the eyes, clearing the throat, and facial flushing are innate (inborn). These are often involuntary, as are, for example, facial expressions of happiness, surprise, anger, disgust, and other basic emotions. Laughing, crying, and shrugging the shoulders are examples of mixed kinesic signals. They may originate as innate actions, but cultural rules shape their timing and use. Gestures such as a wink of the eye, a thumbs up, or a military salute are learned kinemes. Their meanings vary cross-culturally. Kinesic messages can give a look and feel to a conversation remembered long after spoken words fade away. They can also be structured to lie or conceal something. For example, pressing the lips together may indicate disagreement or doubt, even if the person's verbal statements convey agreement. When verbal and kinesic state-ments conflict, listeners will likely believe the latter more.

The main areas of research within kinesics are eye contact, posture, touch, gesture, and facial expression. Clothing is often included within the kinesic purview of research. Birdwhistell used slow-motion films of conversations to analyse kinesic behaviour. He also borrowed extensively from the science of linguistics to identify and catalogue the basic kinemes. Birdwhistell was influenced by the ideas of Margaret Mead and David Efron, especially the view that verbal and non-verbal communication formed a seamless system during face-to-face interaction, with one influencing the other, words suggesting or triggering body movements and, vice versa, body signals triggering lexical notions.

Marcel Danesi

Bibliography

Birdwhistell, Ray L. *Introduction to Kinesics*. Ann Arbor, MI: University of Ann Arbor, 1952.

– Background to Kinesics. *ETC* 13 (1955): 10–18.

– Kinesics and Communication. In *Explorations in Communication*, ed. E. Carpenter and M. McLuhan, 54–64. New York: Beacon, 1960.

– Paralanguage 25 Years after Sapir. In *Communication in Face to Face Interaction*, ed. J. Laver and S. Hutcheson, 82–100. Harmondsworth: Penguin, 1961.

– The Kinesic Level in the Investigation of the Emotions. In *Symposium on Expressions of the Emotions in Man*, ed. P. Knapp, 123–39. New York: International University Press, 1963.

– Kinesics. *International Encyclopedia of the Social Sciences*, vol. 8: 379–85. New York: Macmillan, 1979.

Duncan, Sharkey, and Donald W. Fiske. *Face-to-Face Interaction*. Hillsdale, NJ: Erlbaum, 1977.

Knapp, Mark L. *Nonverbal Communication in Human Interaction*. New York: Holt, 1978.

BLOCKBUSTERS

[See also: *Cinema; Cinema Genres; Cinema History*]

The blockbuster film functions much in the same frustratingly complex yet simple way that film genres work. The blockbuster film is easy to recognize, has obvious hallmarks, and yet, when attempts are made to define it, has proven consistently slippery and amorphous. It describes the very highest pinnacles of filmmaking achievement, while it has simultaneously been accused of representing the debased core of a capitalist filmmaking industry bent on annihilating the small and the aesthetically different with its media-saturating presence. *Blockbuster*, therefore, is never a neutral term. It is constantly bound up in debates about political and cultural power, in arguments about technology and the meanings of cinema; all the while, the blockbuster has become a concurrently uncontested, simple term used to describe the hit films produced by Hollywood. This entry will try to unpack some of these debates, to show how the blockbuster has gained cultural resonance and acceptance while also being mobilized as a pejorative phrase.

The dissonance inherent in the concept of the blockbuster has been recognized by film theorists. Thomas Schatz was one of the earliest academic critics to attempt to outline its meanings and significance, in an influential article titled 'The New Hollywood' (1993). Schatz claims that 'blockbuster hits are, for better or worse, what the New Hollywood is all about' (10), stating that the single most significant shift between classical Hollywood and the post-classical era has been the emergence of a new system of production based around the blockbuster film. He calls for a reconsideration of Hollywood as linked to a set of blockbuster film texts that marked industrial, economic, and cultural shifts that had taken place in the wake of America's rapidly changing postwar cinema. Citing Steven Spielberg's *Jaws* (1975), George Lucas's *Star Wars* (1977), and, perhaps

less obviously, *Saturday Night Fever* (1978) as exemplars of this new trend, Schatz proposes several kinds of newly emerging Hollywood films. First, he cites the 'prestige' film of the classical period of Hollywood cinema, paying due diligence to the many massive hit films of that period, which, adjusted for inflation, still represent some of Hollywood's biggest successes. However, Schatz then moves on to consider the 'calculated blockbuster,' films produced by studios in the post-classical era using the package unit system, with the intent to create phenomenal hits. Schatz then talks of *Jaws* and *Star Wars* as 'super-blockbusters' backed by newly emerging star directors. In 'The New Hollywood,' then, Schatz begins to create a hierarchical language of the blockbuster, one which delineates patterns within blockbuster film production and reception, and which attempts to form an elastic vocabulary with which to describe the blockbuster and related contemporary film phenomena. Such an elastic vocabulary is vital because not every calculated blockbuster succeeds: for every *Titanic* (1997) there are several films like *Cutthroat Island* (1995).

More recently, several theorists have attempted to outline and discuss the ramifications of blockbuster culture. Among them are two diverging conceptualizations that provide a sense of the breadth of blockbuster film studies. Julian Stringer tackled the work of defining the blockbuster in his edited collection titled *Movie Blockbusters* (2003). In his detailed introduction to the subject, and indeed to the difficulties of defining the blockbuster, Stringer proposes a new, genre-based method for thinking about these 'event movies' (1), based on James Naremore's work on film noir (1998). He states that the blockbuster can be thought of as 'a loose, evolving system of claims and counterclaims – or an influential multifaceted idea – the blockbuster circulates diverse kinds of knowledge concerning titles deemed to be social events' (3). Despite his resistance to an absolute definition, however, Stringer does outline what he feels to be the key terms of the debate. He cites 'size' – the blockbuster's relative enormity of scale – as its defining feature, with associated arguments in relation to spectacle and money providing the basis for what he perceives to be many of the theories that rage around the success and failure of these massive films (3–8).

Stringer's insistence on spectacle's role in the creation of blockbusters ties into another theorist's work on the subject. Geoff King has produced two books on the subject of the blockbuster (King 2000, 2002). His first, *Spectacular Narratives: Hollywood in the Age of the Blockbuster*, deals exclusively with the debate around spectacle as it relates to or negates film narratives, while in his second book, *New Hollywood Cinema: An Introduction,* King posits two separate versions of the 'new' Hollywood, one concerned with the language and commerce of authorship and art cinema, and another related to the production of blockbuster films. King makes a list in this second publication, providing another, more extended, set of key blockbuster features. He cites size, spectacle, expense, heavy promotion and advertising, large numbers of film prints, large numbers of simultaneous exhibition venues, and the use of 'pre-sold' products like books that provide a pre-existing audience for blockbuster films as integral to their status and calculated success (King 2002: 50). In contrast to Stringer's call for a genre-studies-based approach to the study of the blockbuster and its meanings, both King and Schatz take a more economic and historical approach.

Stringer's approach, if applied using newer theories of genre like Rick Altman's (1999) and Steve Neale's (1993), may actually provide a more holistic set of understandings about what the blockbuster is and means at any one time. For example, if the blockbuster is analysed using Altman's conceptualization of genres as processes, then it would be possible to trace the nature of the blockbuster in a given period through the traces that it leaves behind. Using the promotional, marketing, and

reception materials heavily produced and circulated around the release of blockbuster films, it becomes possible to concretize some of the claims being made for how they impact on culture. This closely relates to the work of political economists and reception theorists. For instance, in *Global Hollywood* (2002), Toby Miller et al. offer a version of screen theory with close ties to political economy, and argue, surprisingly, that Hollywood is not located in California, but has become a sprawling global monolith. They say that 'Hollywood's "real" location lies in its division of labour' (Miller et al. 2001: 3), thereby explaining the existence of 'Hollywood' blockbuster productions in, among other places, Australia, New Zealand, Prague, and England. By arguing that blockbuster filmmaking is a global concern, and tracking the traces of Hollywood's productions to prove their point, Miller et al. are able to explain some of the reasons why blockbuster films have become a naturalized part of so many cultures around the globe.

Likewise, Eileen Meehan (1991) and Marsha Kinder (1991) have provided excellent methodologies for understanding blockbuster films through their trace materials. Meehan and Kinder both argue for an understanding of films that sees them not as simple texts, but as central concepts in sprawling intertexts: a network of disparate texts connected along an interconnected relay that projects back to a central idea. As Meehan so neatly illustrates, blockbuster films are usually the product of multinational conglomerate companies looking to maximize the exposure and profit-making potential of their products. Thus there are usually tens if not hundreds of ancillary products related to the release of any blockbuster film, from things closely linked to the original film text like DVDs or novelizations, to more abstractly branded goods like *Lord of the Rings* (2001–3) lunchboxes and *Batman: The Dark Knight Rises* (2012) lava lamps. This situation has been complicated by the emergence of the internet and DVD in recent years, making the borders between sales regions for ancillary products increasingly porous. Likewise, Hollywood's responses to the challenges presented by the internet have been discussed by Miller et al. (2001). In reference to *Star Wars: The Phantom Menace* (1999), they report that 'digital piracy's shadow politics of distribution honoured *The Phantom Menace* as the first feature to be downloaded illegally in the UK from servers in Eastern Europe' and further that illicit 'versions of the film were available in Malaysia two days after its 19 May 1999 release in America' (136). As geo-linguistic boundaries become ever easier to cross, more and more blockbuster-related goods are being made available to the global audience, legally and otherwise. This border crossing has serious implications for the contemporary blockbuster, making it more legitimate to discuss them as global phenomena, while simultaneously signalling attempts by Hollywood to control the circulation of its products as negative or culturally imperialistic.

Contemporary blockbusters are, then, much more than film texts; they are often global phenomena. But being vastly profitable and consumed globally does not mean that blockbusters are risk-free ventures, or that they are somehow culturally neutral. Many calculated blockbusters are reported to have 'disappointing' box office results, or to be 'underperforming' films. With the average budget for blockbusters, before marketing costs, creeping above $100–$200 million in the past several years alone, the stakes for blockbuster productions are incredibly high. To offset such risks, studios tend to do one of several things. First, there is franchising, a phenomenon which has massively increased since 2000. The summer of 2007 alone might be termed the summer of trilogies, with the *Pirates of the Caribbean*, *Spiderman*, *Shrek*, and *Bourne* franchises receiving third episodes at cinemas. I use the term 'episodes' advisedly, as recent years have seen not just the release of sequels, but of planned triple (or more) film story arcs being released and filmed. Examples of this include not only the *Lord of the Rings* trilogy, but also the *Harry Potter* series of films and the *Matrix* trilogy, which all proclaim themselves as planned series of films, not as afterthought sequels produced in the wake of initial success. These sequels help studios not only to offset the massive budgets for the contemporary blockbuster, but also to capitalize on and extend the phenomenal status that such films garner.

Many of these franchises also have what Thomas Austin (2002) and others refer to as 'urtexts,' or pre-sold products attached to their releases. While such urtexts have typically been books and earlier versions of the same film, as in the case of *Bram Stoker's Dracula* (1992), the urtext would seem to have been expanding since the mid-1980s. It now encompasses video games (though these have not, on the whole, been very successful; examples include *Lara Croft Tomb Raider* [2001] and *Doom* [2005]), comic book adaptations (the *X-Men*, *Batman*, and *Superman* franchises, for example), and other pre-existing multimedia franchises that started not as films, but as other textual forms. A good example of an urtext that falls somewhere between the traditional and contemporary categories would be the *Harry Potter* franchise. Famously beginning as a series of novels by J.K. Rowling, the *Harry Potter* intertext now boasts not just blockbuster films produced in its likeness, but also multiple studio 'tours' and theme park rides, in addition to copious merchandising based both on the books and the films, making *Harry Potter* an iconic intertext and a massive global phenomenon.

Unlike *Harry Potter*, some films mask their blockbuster status. Steve Neale writes that 'largely unnoted, meanwhile, at least in film studies, the animated blockbuster feature has, in its own specific and particular way, helped revive not just the biblical epic … but, in films such as *Beauty and the Beast* (1991) … the traditions of the Broadway-oriented musical as well' (Neale 2003: 54). In the promotional materials for Disney's animated features, references to them as blockbusters are rare, despite the fact that some of the largest box office successes of the past twenty-plus years have been generated by Disney and its corporate partner Pixar (Wasko 2001). It is here that the negative readings of the label blockbuster can be most readily seen. After all, if the term was positive or even neutral, then why would Disney, itself a multimedia conglomerate with profit margins at stake, try to avoid the label? The commercial implications of the term, its links to size, money, and acquisitive commercialism, are all, potentially at least, at odds with the family market for these films, whose child audiences then tend to be served by films seeking association with innocence and 'magic' (Bazalgette and Buckingham 1995). It is not, therefore, just film studies that has failed to note the animated blockbuster: the label has been actively shunned by the industry itself (at least until the arrival of DreamWorks' star-laden *Shrek* in 2001). The animated blockbuster is a good example of how many, from the film industry through to its commentators, avoid the concept, even when making or reporting on some of Hollywood's most successful films.

Mobile, contested, disavowed, and yet easily understood and applied, the blockbuster continues to provide fruitful ground for attempts to understand the work of Hollywood. However, this globally understood phenomenon reaches further than Hollywood's films. In recent years, national cinemas have begun to produce their own answers to the Hollywood blockbuster phenomenon, creating what might be thought of as domestic blockbusters (Berry 2003). In Japan, for instance, Studio Ghibli's films regularly match Hollywood's films dollar for dollar in their home market. Moreover, there are some countries where Hollywood's movies have failed to penetrate, such as in India, where the most popular films by far remain those produced domestically in the Hindi language. The blockbuster is not just a contested term, then; it is a contested set of phenomena that the global market for film is attempting to answer. As Hollywood has been seeking

newness in franchising, other cinema industries have been responding. Therefore, while we are currently seeing the age of what might be termed the serialized blockbuster – the multi-film blockbuster that spans its stories across multiple releases and years, basically pricing other nations out of the blockbuster film market – we are also seeing the rise of the domestic blockbuster, especially in geo-linguistic markets where English is not the first language. While the blockbuster is a globally contested phenomenon, then, and while Hollywood retains a massive lead in the global markets for film, the domestic blockbuster may well be offering a new kind of grand film experience for audiences and a potential future challenge that Hollywood's blockbuster films will have to meet.

Rayna Denison

Bibliography

Altman, Rick. *Film/Genre*. London: BFI Publishing, 1999.

Austin, Thomas. *Hollywood, Hype and Audiences: Selling and Watching Popular Film in the 1990s*. Manchester: Manchester University Press, 2002.

Bazalgette, Cary, and David Buckingham, eds. *In Front of the Children: Screen Entertainment and Young Audiences*. London: BFI Publishing, 1995.

Berry, Chris. What's Big about the Big Film?: 'De-Westernising' the Blockbuster in Korea and China. In *Movie Blockbusters*, ed. Julian Stringer. London: Routledge, 2003.

Kinder, Marsha. *Playing with Power in Movies, Television and Video Games: From Muppet Babies to Teenage Mutant Ninja Turtles*. Berkeley: University of California Press, 1991.

King, Geoff. *Spectacular Narratives: Hollywood in the Age of the Blockbuster*. London: I.B. Tauris, 2000.

– *New Hollywood: An Introduction*. London: I.B. Tauris, 2002.

Meehan, Eileen. Holy Commodity Fetish, Batman!: The Political Economy of a Commercial Intertext. In *The Many Lives of the Batman*, ed.

Roberta E. Pearson and William Uricchio, 47–65. New York: BFI-Routledge, 1991.

Miller, Toby, et al., eds., *Global Hollywood*. Berkeley: University of California Press, 2002.

Naremore, James. *More than Night: Film Noir in Its Contexts*. Berkeley: University of California Press, 1998.

Neale, Steve. Melo Talk: On the Meaning and Use of the Term 'Melodrama' in the American Trade Press. *Velvet Light Trap* 32 (Fall 1993): 66–89.

– Hollywood Blockbusters: Historical Dimensions. In *Movie Blockbusters*, ed. Julian Stringer. London: Routledge, 2003.

Schatz, Thomas. The New Hollywood. In *Film Theory Goes to the Movies*, ed. Jim Collins, Hilary Radner, and Ava Preacher Collins, 8–36. New York: Routledge, 1993.

Shone, Tom. *Blockbuster*. London: Simon and Schuster, 2004.

Stringer, Julian, ed. *Movie Blockbusters*. London: Routledge, 2003.

Wasko, Janet. *Understanding Disney: The Manufacture of Fantasy*. Cambridge: Polity Press, 2001.

BLOG

[See also: *Blogging and the Blogosphere; Internet; World Wide Web*]

The term *blog* refers to a category of interactive texting that takes place using a website on the internet. A blog might include a personal diary or the written comments of an individual focused on a particular area of interest, and responses from readers expressing opinions or ideas about any of a great variety of topics such as current events, politics, or other specialized areas of interest. The term 'weblog' was first used in 1997 and later shortened to *blog* (Ryssdal 2007). It was derived from an association with the World Wide Web combined with the conventional meaning of the word *log*, referring to a detailed record of events like those originally written by the captain of a ship to chronicle the progress and significant events occurring during a journey at sea.

Blogs are a popular form of expression, but unlike conventional media that distribute news or circulate information and opinions, the people who create and maintain blogs generally have no systematic institutional oversight. Although some sites represent a political or ideologically oriented group, bloggers are generally independent of commercial interests and consider their efforts to communicate freely to be a part of a democratic exchange of ideas. Independence from corporate and other institutional controls is a reoccurring theme that is valued among bloggers. Authors and respondents can express any ideas or beliefs without necessarily substantiating what they say or providing evidence of any kind. Because of the nature of the internet, bloggers have a potential to exploit the interactive capacities and intimate qualities of communication made possible with multiple individual computer users. It is as if there was a large anonymous group assembled in a hall with a principle moderator and no immediate time constraints. As Landow (2007: 77–8) writes:

> The Weblog, or blog, as it is commonly known, is another new kind of discursive prose in digital form that makes us rethink a genre that originally arose when writing took the form of physical marks on physical surfaces … Blogs take the form of an online journal or diary most commonly written by a single person, and, like paper journals and diaries, they present the author's words in dated segments.

Eventually cashing in on the popularity of the *blogosphere*, journalists and large mainstream media outlets began to imitate blogs, and formerly independent bloggers saw the potential for profit through associations with mainstream media and other commercial interests. The nature of the medium provides a sense of intimacy, a feeling of immediacy, and encourages freedom of expression. Thus, others in the blogosphere, including entrepreneurs with profit motives, share the notion of an independent discursive space where internet users can freely exchange ideas and opinions.

Even with the emerging presence of profiteers in the blogosphere, there is still a perception that blogs maintain an environment that supports free expression and innovation. *Time* magazine chose 'You,' the internet user, as 'Person of the Year' in 2006 for 'seizing the reins of the global media, for founding and framing the new digital democracy, for working for nothing and beating the pros at their own game' (Poniewozik 2007: 174). *Time* was acknowledging the popularity and significance of the internet, its many interactive modes of mass communication phenomena, and the large number of people participating in 'Youtubing, Facebooking, Twittering, chronicling Your life and community, scrutinizing the candidates and the media, videotaping Yourself getting upset on behalf of Britney Spears' (174).

The term *blogs* is used inclusively to refer to internet sites, weblinks, all of the writers, and the discursive community that consider themselves an alternative to mainstream media and conventional authorities. Even as a forum for negotiation and argument, blogs generally appeal to audiences who share special interests, values, and beliefs. Rather than requiring empirical evidence or demonstrable expertise, popular consensus is effectively more authoritative than verification of data confirmed by experts. Links to other blogs or internet sites can be referenced to reinforce ideas circulated within the blogosphere without independent observation or verification. Like other cultural groups that share opinions and beliefs, popular consensus about an idea can be taken for its correctness according to the internal logic of the blogosphere. Discussions and arguments circulate among bloggers who negotiate and draw conclusions about the meanings of issues, events, and ideas.

Elliot Gaines

Bibliography

Herman, Andrew, and Thomas Swiss, eds. *The World Wide Web and Contemporary Cultural Theory*. London: Routledge, 2000.

Keren, Michael. *Blogosphere: The New Political Arena*. Lanham: Rowman and Littlefield, 2006.

Landow, George P. *Hypertext*. Baltimore: Johns Hopkins University Press, 2007.

Poniewozik, James. The Year of Them. Essay. *Time*, 31 December 2007, 174.

Ryssdal, Kai. *Marketplace*. Radio commentary. National Public Radio, 17 December 2007.

Slevin, James. *The Internet and Society*. London: Polity, 2000.

BLOGGING AND THE BLOGOSPHERE

[See also: *Blogs; Internet; World Wide Web*]

Blogging is a term, coined between 1997 and 1999, that refers to involvement with blogs, especially writing and using them for various purposes on a website. Blogging is now a major form of writing, replacing, in some cases, the traditional print article. The earliest blogs originated in the online discussion or chat groups of the early internet, some of which reach as far back as the 1970s (including such online services as bulletin board systems). Some blogs resemble magazines, complete with graphics, photos, audiovisual supports, and so on. Others are simple textual compositions. It is estimated that today there are more than 100 million bogs worldwide. They cover the entire gamut of human interest, from politics to cartoons.

Blogs have several advantages over print articles. First and foremost, they reach a broad (and potentially international) audience instantaneously and cheaply, whereas print articles take more time to release and entail many more costs to publish. Second, blogs can be edited online and thus can be updated continuously, while print articles need to be revised and republished over a period of time. Third, blogs can be maintained permanently on websites and indexed in any way one wishes (in the order in which they were written, according to themes, and so on). Fourth, blogs can easily include visual and audio material. Fifth, feedback on blogs is rapid and far-reaching, since most blogs allow for readers to respond and leave comments on the site, to which the blogger can reply. This has led to the formation of blogging communities, constituting what is called the *blogosphere*. A collection of 'local blogs' is sometimes called a *bloghood*. Comments are the basis for the so-called *trackback* feature, which transmits alerts to previous commentators. In addition, *permalinks* allow users to comment on specific posts rather than on entire blogs, and this, in turn, allows the blog to create an archive of past posts.

Blogs have impacted significantly on the conduct of journalism and on writing traditions generally, since they have democratized the process of publication. The internet has made it possible for anyone to establish a blog website and promote his or her views freely. One no longer has to submit a piece of writing to an editorial process based on selection and preference variables, as is typically the case in the world of traditional print culture. This means that there is likely to be very little prepublication quality control. The value of a blog is assessed by the inhabitants of the blogosphere, not by some editor or evaluator in advance. In other words, it is up to the user, not a filtering agent or agency, to decide if a blog has merit or not. In a way, this has put the onus on writers to write honestly and accurately, since their opinions and facts can easily be checked on the internet and discussed throughout the blogoshpere. The blogosphere has also introduced a new lexicon into everyday language (online and offline). Words like 'anyhoo,' 'dudely,' 'sexbot,' among others, originated on various blogs (Rodzvilla 2009).

Types of Blogs

Blogs are now divided into two main cat-

egories – according to theme and according to content. A blog categorized according to theme is often named accordingly; for example, a blog focusing on art is called an *artlog*, on videos *vlog*, on music *MP3 blog*, on photography *photoblog*, and so on. The main blogs classified according to content include:

- *Personal blogs*, which contain commentaries from individuals. These are essentially personal diaries, and it is from these that the blog concept originally evolved. Although most have a low readership, some have risen to fame especially during political campaigns.
- *Corporate blogs*, which are blogs used for corporate or business purposes, such as the marketing of products and services.
- *Question blogs*, which are websites (often maintained by experts, such as medical doctors) to which questions can be submitted.
- *Technical blogs*, which are maintained by researchers, scientists, and the like, and usually sponsored by an institution (such as university) or a publisher (such as a scholarly journal).
- *Genre blogs*, which include writings on the whole range of topics previously covered by magazines, journals, and other print publications. These include political blogs, travel blogs, education blogs, music blogs, legal blogs, among many others.

The Blogosphere

There is little doubt that blogging has expanded the range of, and accessibility to, purposeful writing. Many print journalists and radio and TV commentators now have blogs that both reproduce their original print texts and allow for updating and immediate reader commentary. The rise of the political blog to social importance is evidenced by various events in the early 2000s. In one 2002 case, bloggers critiqued comments made by U.S. Senate majority leader Trent Lott at a party in honour of Senator Strom Thurmond. Lott suggested that Thurmond would have made the ideal president. The bloggers portrayed this as implicit approval of racial segregation, since Thurmond had seemingly promoted segregation in his 1948 presidential campaign, as documents recovered by the bloggers showed. The mainstream media never reported on this story until after the bloggers broke it. The end result was that Lott stepped down as majority leader.

Given the increasing power of the blogosphere, it should come as no surprise to find that by 2004 politicians, governments, and other social groups joined the blogosphere. Many claim that U.S. President Barack Obama's 2008 victory was largely fuelled by enthusiastic bloggers constantly putting forward his message about the need for change.

Blogging has also made it possible for those who previously would not have been noticed by the mainstream media to garner attention. It is a form of Freudian 'id presentation,' a way of being noticed. Authors of books now have blogs to inform their readership about various aspects of their writing. A novelist, for example, might maintain a blog to inform readers about the background to the novel as well as to field questions from readers. Some have even used the blog format to publish their books, without going through a traditional publishing house. There are now prizes for the best blog-based book. In a phrase, the blogosphere is fast replacing what Marshall McLuhan called the 'Gutenberg Galaxy.' The latter had made writing the basis on which societies evolved socially and culturally, leading to the Enlightenment and other critical print-based movements; the evolutionary impulse associated with writing is now being transferred more and more to the blogosphere.

Marcel Danesi

Bibliography

Bruns, Axel, and Joanne Jacobs, eds. *Uses of Blogs*. New York: Peter Lang, 2006.

Keren, Michael. *Blogosphere: The New Political Arena*. Lanham: Rowman and Littlefield, 2006.

Landow, George P. *Hypertext*. Baltimore: Johns Hopkins University Press, 2007.

Perlmutter, David D. *Blogwars*. Oxford: Oxford University Press, 2009.

Ringmar, Erik. *A Blogger's Manifesto: Free Speech and Censorship in the Age of the Internet*. London: Anthem Press, 2007.

Rodzvilla, John, ed. *We've Got Blog: How Weblogs Are Changing Our Culture*. New York: Basic Books, 2009.

BODY LANGUAGE

[See also: *Birdwhistell, Ray L.; Gesture; Kinesics; Non-Verbal Communication; Proxemics*]

Body language is often used as a synonym for *non-verbal communication*. However, unlike the latter designation, body language refers more specifically to the movements of the body or of bodily organs as communicating agents in themselves, independent of the bodily movements accompanying vocal speech; non-verbal communication is the more general term covering both autonomous and complementary (to vocal speech) bodily communication. The study of the latter comes more specifically under the rubric of *kinesics*. There is, however, much overlap in the use of these terms. Kinesics is more a branch of anthropology and semiotics, focusing on social aspects of complementary non-verbal communication, while body language study is considered to be a branch of psychology that focuses on the relation between the body and unconscious systems of thought.

Body language is an intrinsic part of face-to-face communication. Human beings communicate over two-thirds of their messages through the body, producing up to 700,000 body-based signs, of which 1,000 are postures, 5,000 hand gestures, and 250,000 facial expressions (Morris et al. 1979). The body is clearly a primary system of human communication. Body signals can be innate and involuntary (flushing), acquired in cultural settings (the thumbs-up gesture), or a mixture of the two (winking).

Eye Contact

Psychological research on eye contact patterns has found considerable variation across cultures. The duration and pattern (looking into the eyes, looking down or up, and so on) of the contact convey what kinds of social relationships people have to each other and provide more general information on the nature of human relations in a specific culture. Southern Europeans tend to look into each other's eyes during conversation more than North Americans; males do not look into female eyes unless they are married or members of the same family in various non-European cultures. Some patterns convey specific cultural meanings. For example, gazing indicates sexual wonder, fascination, awe, or admiration depending on culture; staring communicates sexual curiosity, boldness, insolence, or stupidity, again depending on social context and culture. Some patterns appear to be universal: for example, across cultures staring is interpreted as a challenge; 'making eyes' at someone is perceived as flirtation or sexual interest; narrowing the eyelids communicates pensiveness, while bringing the eyebrows closer to each other conveys thoughtfulness; raising them communicates surprise; and so on.

Interestingly, it has been shown that men are sexually attracted to women with large pupils, which signal unconsciously a strong and sexually tinged interest, as well as making females look younger (Sebeok 1994). This would explain the cosmetic vogue in central Europe during the 1920s and 1930s of using a crystalline alkaloid eyedrop liquid derived from the chemical known colloquially as *belladonna* ('beautiful woman' in Italian). The women of the day bought the liquid because they believed that it would enhance their facial appearance and sexual attractiveness by dilating their pupils.

Posture

Across the world, posture (mainly unconscious) communicates a large amount of information about identity, gender, class, and moods, and plays a critical role in interpersonal relationships. Posture can be broken down into a series of specific movements and poses. As in the case of eye contact, there appear to be both universal postures as well as culture-based differences. Below is a list of some universal posture forms.

(1) Slumped posture = low spirits
(2) Erect posture = high spirits, energy, and confidence
(3) Leaning forward posture = open and interested behaviour
(4) Leaning away posture = defensive or disinterested behaviour
(5) Crossed arms = defensive behaviour
(6) Uncrossed arms = willingness to listen

Posture is a prominent feature in courtship displays, which may look comical or absurd to outsiders, but which constitute crucial modes of communication at key stages in the symbolic expression of sexual maturation to the members of a society or group. 'Sexual posing' makes sense only if the appropriate physical and social symbols and practices are present during courtship or flirtation. While such posing may be residues of ancient animal mechanisms, as some suggest, the great diversity that is evident in courtship across cultures implies that it is not a mere contemporary version of instinctual mating behaviour. Rather, sexual postures are shaped in large part by human notions of gender and romance and are, therefore, constantly inclined to change (Synnot 1993). In the human species, courtship is not only a reflex of biology, but also a product of history and tradition. It is the outcome of nature and culture cooperating in a type of partnership that is found nowhere else in the animal realm.

Touch

The study of touch constitutes its own sub-field of body language study called *haptics*. A common haptic pattern is 'handshaking.' The zoologist Desmond Morris (1969) claims that the Western form may have started as a way to show that neither person was holding a weapon. It thus was constructed as a 'tie sign' because of the bond of trust it was designed to create. Throughout the centuries, it morphed into a symbol of equality and fairness, being used to seal agreements of all kinds. Indeed, refusing to shake someone's outstretched hand is still interpreted as a 'counter-sign' indicating a challenge or an act of defiance. Handshaking reveals a high degree of cross-cultural variation. People squeeze the hand (as Europeans and North Americans do), shake the other's hand with both hands, shake the hand and then pat each other's back, lean forward or stand straight while shaking, and so on. Other haptic patterns include patting someone on the arm, shoulder, or back to indicate agreement or to give a compliment; linking arms to indicate companionship; putting one's arm around the shoulder to indicate friendship or intimacy; holding hands with family members or a lover to express intimacy; hugging to convey happiness at seeing a friend or a family member.

Such variation may have a basis in culture-specific perceptions of the body and the skin. Some people perceive the skin to be a surface 'sheath.' Others perceive the body as a 'container' of the human soul and thus think of themselves as being 'contained' behind their skin. The zones of privacy that define self-space in these cultures, therefore, include the clothes that cover the skin. Others feel instead that the self is located down within the body shell, resulting in a totally different perception of haptic behaviours. People in such cultures are in general more tolerant of crowds, of noise levels, of touching, of eye contact, and of body odours than are most North Americans.

One haptic behaviour that is shrouded in evolutionary mystery is osculation, known more commonly as kissing. When the lips of adult people touch, the kissing act is perceived normally as a romantic and/or erotic one. But not all kissing is sexual. Kissing other parts of the face, such as the forehead, the head, and the cheeks can be a way of showing affection to children, friends, or pets. Sexual kissing, however, is particularly interesting as an evolutionary and cultural phenomenon. Although it is not universal, it seems to be based on a common experience – the breast-sucking action of infants, implying vulnerability, closeness, and sensuality. Kissing is not common in traditional courtship within China or Japan; and it is completely unknown in many traditional African societies. Inuit and Laplander societies are more inclined to rub noses than to kiss to engage in sexual foreplay.

Gesture

Gesture is the use of the hands, the arms, and to a lesser extent, the head for communicative purposes. Although there are cross-cultural similarities in gesture, substantial culture-specific differences also exist both in the extent to which gesture is used and in the interpretations given to its uses. The head gestures for 'yes' and 'no' used in the Balkans seem inverted to other Europeans. In 1979, Desmond Morris and several colleagues at Oxford University examined twenty gesture forms in forty different areas of Europe, discovering that many of these had variable meanings, depending on culture – a tap on the side of the head could indicate completely opposite things, such as 'stupidity' or 'intelligence,' depending on where it is used.

Gesture is also found in non-human primates. Chimpanzees raise their arms in the air to signal that they want to be groomed; they stretch out their arms to beg or invite courtship (Beaken 1996: 51). These are purposeful signals and are intended to be regulatory of the actions of other chimps. But

the number of gestural forms that chimpanzees use is limited. Human gesturing,
on the other hand, is productive and varied. It can even be used as a substitute for
vocal language, as is the case with the sign
languages used by the hearing-impaired.
And it can be used as an alternate mode
of communication, as is the case with the
hand languages used by religious groups
during periods of imposed silence, with the
gestures used by traffic officers, and with
the hand and arm code used by conductors
of orchestras.

Using the index finger to indicate where
things are in a place constitutes a universal
gesture. Many simulation gestures to represent the shape of objects are also universal. People around the world tend to use
both hands together moving in opposite
directions – clockwise (the right hand) and
counter-clockwise (the left hand) – to refer
to a round object.

Gestures accompanying vocal speech are
called *gesticulants*. In 1992, David McNeill
videotaped a large number of people as
they spoke, gathering a substantial amount
of video data on gesticulant structure and
use. His findings suggest that gesticulants
are unconscious manual forms that convey
important images that cannot be shown
overtly in the substance of vocal speech, as
well as images of what the speaker is thinking about. Vocal speech and gesticulation,
thus, constitute a single integrated communication system in which both cooperate to express the person's intentions and
thoughts. Some gesticulants bear a close
resemblance to the referent or referential
domain of an utterance: for example, when
describing a scene from a story in which a
character bends a tree back to the ground,
a speaker might pretend to grip something
and pull it back. Some resemble the beating
of musical tempos, with the hand moving along with the rhythmic pulsation of
speech in the form of a simple flick of the
hand or fingers up and down, or back and
forth. McNeill's work gives us a good idea
as to how gesture and language complement each other in human communication.

As Frutiger (1989: 112) has also observed,
accompanying gesture forms reveal an
inner need to support what one is saying
orally: 'If on a beach, for example, we can
hardly resist drawing with the finger on the
smooth surface of the sand as a means of
clarifying what we are talking about.'

McNeill's gesticulant categories are actually subtypes of the more generic category
of gesture called an *illustrator* by researchers (Ekman and Friesen 1975):

1. *Illustrators*: These literally illustrate vocal utterances. Examples are the circular
   hand movements when talking of a
   circle; moving the hands far apart when
   talking of something large; moving both
   the head and hands in an upward direction when saying *Let's go up*.
2. *Emblems*: These directly translate words
   or phrases. Examples are the *Okay* sign,
   the *Come here* sign, the hitchhiking sign,
   waving, and obscene gestures.
3. *Affect displays*: These communicate emotional meaning. Examples are the typical
   hand movements that accompany states
   and expressions of happiness, surprise,
   fear, anger, sadness, contempt, disgust,
   and so on
4. *Regulators*: These monitor, maintain, or
   control the speech of someone else. Examples include the hand movements for
   Keep going, Slow down, What else happened?
5. *Adaptors*: These are used to satisfy some
   need. Examples include scratching one's
   head when puzzled, rubbing one's forehead when worried, and so on.

Some societies have developed complementary 'gesture languages,' which share
many features with vocal languages. A
well-known example is the one used by the
Plains people of North America as a means
of communication between tribes with different vocal languages. In inter-tribal communication, specifically developed manual
gestures are used to represent things in
nature, ideas, emotions, and sensations,
along with other referents of mutual importance to the tribes in contact. For example,

the gesture for a white person is made by drawing the fingers across the forehead, indicating a hat; the sensation of cold is indicated by a shivering motion of the hands in front of the body; and the same sign is used for 'winter' and for 'year.' The gesture language is so elaborate that a detailed conversation is possible using the gestures alone (Mallery 1972).

Gestures may also be used for symbolic and ritualistic purposes. In Christianity the 'sign of the cross' aims to recreate the crucifixion; in Buddhism, the *Mudras* are used during ceremonies involving meditation. The 'devil's hand,' with the index and little finger raised belongs to the domain of superstition, symbolizing, in some cultures, a horned figure intended to ward off the evil eye and in others a sign of 'cuckoldry.'

Facial Expression

In 1963, psychologist Paul Ekman founded the Human Interaction Laboratory in the Department of Psychiatry at the University of California at San Francisco for the purpose of studying facial expression. Over the years, Ekman and his team have identified certain facial expressions as universal signs of specific emotions (Ekman 1980, 1982, 1985, 2003; Ekman and Friesen 1975), breaking them down into characteristic components – eyebrow position, mouth movement or shape, and so on – which in various combinations determine the meaning of the expression. Many expressions, however, are culture-specific and thus part of learned behaviour. For example, staring into the eyes during face-to-face conversation is common in some cultures, but not in others. In Western culture, staring into someone's eyes during normal (neutral) conversation would be interpreted negatively or in non-neutral terms, since it is perceived as being connected with certain emotional states (romance, anger, for instance).

The Body as a 'Lie Detector' System

Unconscious or unwitting body signals reveal what a person is thinking: it is impossible for the body to lie (in a sense). The reason for this is that an incongruence would result in the use of body signals as one speaks, alerting an interlocutor that something suspicious is going on. For example, open palms are associated with honesty, but when a faker holds the palms out and smiles as he/she tells a lie, the incongruence of the gesture gives him/her away instantly. The pupils may contract, one eyebrow may lift, and the corner of the mouth may twitch. These signals combine to give a sense of contradiction with what the person is saying. The result is that one tends not to believe what is being said. Our brains seem to register a kind of 'tilt' when they perceive incongruence between vocal and body language.

Nevertheless, there are many people, such as actors, who train their bodies to give the impression that they are telling the truth, counteracting its natural instincts. Such people use their faces more often than other parts of the body, with smiles, nods, and winks as strategies to cover up lies. But even in the case of expert liars, the body signals ultimately tell the truth, even though the incongruence is harder to detect. A simple confirmation of this is to tell a deliberate lie, making a conscious effort to suppress body gestures while in full view of another person. It is practically impossible to stop the body from sending out contradictory signals. It is easier to lie in writing or on the phone.

Hand-to-Face Gestures

When a child tells a lie, he or she will instinctively cover the mouth with one or both hands immediately afterwards. This gesture is used, unwittingly, later in life in various forms and to various degrees. Often the adult pulls the hand away at the last moment, touching the nose instead. The latter gesture is more sophisticated and less obvious, but it still reveals mendacity.

Another common gesture is the 'mouth guard,' with the hand concealing the mouth and the thumb pressing against the cheek as the brain instructs the hands to suppress the deceitful words that are being said. Sometimes the gesture may involve only several fingers over the mouth or even a closed fist. Some people try to disguise this gesture with a false cough. Sophisticated versions of this gesture are the nose, eye, and ear touch gestures. The first consists of several light rubs below the nose, the second of a rubbing motion just below the eye, and the third of putting the hand over the ear. Similar signals of deceit are the neck scratch, with the index finger scratching below the earlobe or on the side of the neck, and the collar pull, whereby the collar of a shirt is pulled away from the neck by a finger or the entire hand.

Not all hand-to-face gestures imply deceit. For example:

- The 'fingers in the mouth' gesture, whereby the fingers are placed in the mouth, indicates that the person is under pressure.
- The 'hand on the cheek' gesture, involving the hand to support the head, is a sign that the person is bored.
- The 'evaluation' gesture, whereby a closed hand is made to rest on the cheek, often with the index finger pointing upwards, signals that the person is losing interest but nevertheless wants to appear interested for the sake of courtesy.
- The 'chin-stroking' gesture, whereby one hand moves to the chin and strokes it, is a sign that the person is making a decision.

Palm and Handshaking Gestures

The open palm is associated universally with truth, honesty, allegiance, and submission. This is why the right palm is held in the air when someone is giving evidence in a court of law as he/she holds the Bible in the left hand.

Body language research has shown that when people wish to be totally honest or open they will hold one or both palms out to the other person, saying something like 'to be perfectly honest' or 'to be open with you.' When someone hides his/her palms (usually behind the back), as children do conspicuously when they are lying, the person is trying to hide something or is not being open about something. If one tries to lie and hold the palms out, the body's lie detector system kicks in and an incongruence becomes visible. Most people find it difficult, if not impossible, to lie with their palms exposed.

Handshaking is a form of 'palm gesturing.' It can also be read to understand various cues during interaction: (1) taking control, (2) surrendering control, and (3) establishing equality. The first one can be seen when someone turns his/her hand so that the palm faces down in relation to the other person's palm. It conveys the need of the handshaker to take control of the encounter. The second one is the reverse gesture, manifesting itself when someone offers his/her hand with the palm facing upwards. This signals that he/she wants to give the other person control or make him/her feel that he/she should have control of the situation. The third pattern arises when two dominant people vie for control of the situation. It unfolds as a vice-like tug with both palms remaining in a vertical position as each person transmits a feeling of respect and rapport to the other.

There are various versions and subtypes of the above handshakes, known with such self-explanatory names as the 'knuckle grinder,' the 'stiff-arm thrust,' the 'fingertip grab,' and the 'arm pull.' These convey attitude at different stages of an interaction.

Hand and Arm Gestures

Rubbing the palms together is a way of communicating positive expectation. This is why someone who throws a pair of dice in gambling rubs his or her hands first in expectation. It is also the reason why a master of ceremonies tends to rub his/her palms as he/she says to the audience 'We have been looking forward to our next speaker.' The speed at which a person rubs the hands signals the degree of expectation he/she brings to the situation – the greater the rubbing the more the expectation. Incidentally, rubbing the thumb against the fingertips, palm, or index finger commonly signals money expectancy. Salespeople use it with their customers when they say 'I can save you some money today.'

Clenching the hands together in a central, raised, or lowered position (depending on whether the person is standing or sitting) is a confidence gesture. But it can also be a frustration gesture if the clenching is robust to the point of turning the knuckles white.

'Steepling' is the term used by Birdwhistell (1952) to indicate touching the fingers together to form a 'steeple.' The steeple form can be raised or lowered depending on the body's orientation, but it invariably communicates confidence and authority. It is a kind of 'know-it-all' gesture used commonly by people in authority or who wish to convey control. The raised steeple is used when the steepler is doing the talking and the lowered one when he/she is listening.

Gripping the hands, arms, and wrists behind the body often conveys a desire to establish superiority with respect to an interlocutor or gain confidence in a difficult situation. The palm-in-palm gesture (behind the back) is the most common of the gripping gestures and should not be confused with the wrist-gripping gesture, which is a signal of frustration or an attempt at self-control. One hand grips the other wrist or arm as if to prevent it from striking out. The further the hand is moved up the arm, the angrier the person is likely to be.

Thumb displays – with the other fingers in a pocket or under a jacket lapel, and the thumbs protruding out – are used typically to communicate confidence, domination, superiority, and even aggression. These become most obvious when the person sends out a contradictory verbal message. When a lawyer turns to a jury and says 'In my humble opinion …' as he/she displays the thumbs, tilting back the head, the effect on the jury attends to be counteractive one – making the jury feel that the lawyer may be insincere or pompous. To appear sincere, the lawyer might approach the jury with one foot forward, an open palm display, and a slight stoop. These are felt typically as conveying humility and honesty.

Folding the arms generally implies that the person has negative thoughts about the speaker and is thus paying less attention to what he/she is saying. Folding both arms together typically undergirds an attempt to hide from an unfavourable situation. It is also a negative sign in some situations, indicating that the person disagrees with what an interlocutor is saying. If the arms are gripped tightly it reveals a negative but restrained attitude. A variant of this sign is the partial arm gesture, with one hand holding the other near or at the elbow. This is perceived to show lack of self-confidence or humility. It is used typically by someone about to receive an award.

Head and Eye Signals

The two most common head movements are the nod and the shake. In Western culture, the former is a positive gesture indicating agreement and the latter a negative one indicating disagreement. The head position is also indicative of specific meanings:

- The 'head up' position (with the head remaining still) is assumed by the person who has a neutral attitude about what he/she is hearing.
- The 'head tilt' position reveals, instead, that the person is interested in what is being said and/or in who is speaking.
- The 'head down' position signals a negative or judgmental attitude.
- The 'hands behind the head' position conveys confidence and authority.

Other Kinds of Signals

Eye signals are among the most revealing

of all body signals because the eyes are a focal point on the face and because the pupils work independently of all other communication systems operating during interaction. The dilated pupil indicates erotic or sexual interest, and also enhances attractiveness. When a person is being dishonest or is holding back information, his/her eyes meet the other's eyes less than one-third of the time. When they meet more than two-thirds, the underlying message is either that he/she finds the other attractive (with the pupils dilating) or that he/she is hostile to him/her (with the pupils constricting). A good rapport with another person, therefore, entails a gaze that lasts a period between these two extremes.

Body language is a complex system of signals with a multitude of forms and meanings. Many are universal; but just as many are culture-specific. The sounds made by the body (sneezing, coughing, burping, and so on), the fluids that issue forth from it, the eye patterns that are used when speaking, the kinds of touching routines humans utilize during discourse, the facial expressions used to convey feelings, and the kinds of gestures and gesticulations that are found throughout the world are all interpreted as signifiers of specific meanings.

Discoveries in neuroscience have shown that non-verbal signs are produced and processed differently from words. Spoken language is processed in the cerebral cortex, a more developed area of the brain that is unique to human beings. In contrast, non-verbal cues are processed in lower, more primitive areas such as the limbic system. This is perhaps why we often produce and receive non-verbal cues without being consciously aware of doing so.

Marcel Danesi

Bibliography

Argyle, Michael. *Bodily Communication*. London: Methuen, 1975.

Armstrong, David F., William C. Stokoe, and Sherman E. Wilcox. *Gesture and the Nature of Language*. Cambridge: Cambridge University Press, 1995.

Beaken, Michael. *The Making of Language*. Edinburgh: Edinburgh University Press, 1996.

Birdwhistell, Ray L. *Introduction to Kinesics*. Ann Arbor, MI: University of Ann Arbor, 1952.

Borg, John. *Body Language: 7 Easy Lessons to Master the Silent Language*. Toronto: Prentice-Hall, 2008.

Bremer, Jan, and Herman Roodenburg, eds. *A Cultural History of Gesture*. Ithaca, NY: Cornell University Press, 1991.

Duncan, Starkey. Non-verbal Communication. *Psychological Bulletin* 72 (1969): 118–37.

Duncan, Starkey, and Donald W. Fiske. *Face-to-Face Interaction*. Hillsdale, NJ: Erlbaum, 1977.

Eco, Umberto. *Einführung in die Semiotik*. München: Fink, 1968.

Efron, David. *Gesture, Race, and Culture*. The Hague: Mouton, 1941.

Ekman, Paul. Movements with Precise Meanings. *Journal of Communication* 26 (1976): 14–26.

– The Classes of Non-verbal Behaviour. In *Aspects of Non-verbal Communication*, ed. W. Raffler-Engel, 89–102. Lisse: Swets and Zeitlinger, 1980.

– Methods for Measuring Facial Action. In *Handbook of Methods in Non-verbal Behaviour*, ed. K.R. Scherer and P. Ekman, 45–90. Cambridge: Cambridge University Press, 1982.

– *Telling Lies*. New York: Norton, 1985.

– *Emotions Revealed*. New York: Holt, 2003.

Ekman, Paul, and Walter Friesen. *Unmasking the Face*. Englewood Cliffs, NJ: Prentice-Hall, 1975.

Foucault, Michel. *The History of Sexuality*, vol. 1. London: Allen Lane, 1976.

Frutiger, Adrian. *Signs and Symbols*. New York: Van Nostrand, 1989.

Harper, Robert G., et al. *Non-verbal Communication: The State of the Art*. New York: John Wiley, 1978.

Key, Mary R. *Paralanguage and Kinesics*. Metuchen, NJ: Scarecrow, 1975.

Knapp, Mark L. *Non-verbal Communication in Human Interaction*. New York: Holt, 1978.

Mallery, Garrick. *Sign Language among North American Indians Compared with That among*

Other Peoples and Deaf-Mutes. The Hague: Mouton, 1972.

McNeill, David. *Hand and Mind: What Gestures Reveal about Thought.* Chicago: University of Chicago Press, 1992.

Morris, Desmond. *The Human Zoo.* London: Cape, 1969.

Morris, Desmond, et al. *Gestures: Their Origins and Distributions.* London: Cape, 1979.

Peck, Stephen R. *Atlas of Facial Expression.* Oxford: Oxford University Press, 1987.

Raffler-Engel, Walburga von, ed. *Aspects of Nonverbal Communication.* Lisse: Swets, 1980.

Scherer, Klaus R., and Paul Ekman. *Handbook of Methods in Non-verbal Behaviour Research.* Cambridge: Cambridge University Press, 1982.

Scherer, Klaus R., Harald G. Wallbott, and Ursula Scherer. Methoden zur Klassifikation von Bewegungsverhalten: Ein funktionaler Ansatz. *Zeitschrift für Semiotik* 1 (1979): 177–92.

Sebeok, Thomas A. *Signs: An Introduction to Semiotics.* Toronto: University of Toronto Press, 1994.

Sebeok, Thomas A., et al., eds. *Approaches to Semiotics.* The Hague: Mouton, 1964.

Synnott, Andrew. *The Body Social: Symbolism, Self and Society.* London: Routledge, 1993.

BOOK

[See also: *Books, History of; e-Book; Gutenberg Galaxy; Print Culture*]

The word *book* derives from the Old English *boc*, which comes from the Germanic root **bok*. What we now recognize as a book has evolved over the past five millennia into its present form through various events and processes. Precursors of the modern book include such cultural artefacts as the clay tablets of Mesopotamia and the papyrus scrolls of China, Egypt, Greece, Rome, and other cultures. The latter were documents copied by scribes, or produced via dictation. The paper scrolls used to produce books, however, were subject to environmental deterioration including decay, water damage, and so forth. By the fourth century CE, the process of producing 'books' had

become more sophisticated. At the time, the *codex* (Latin for wooden tablet for writing) became the medium for the production of these forerunners of books. A *codex* had a format much more similar to the modern book because it consisted of sheets bounded with rings, and with text on both sides of a sheet. Few people were literate, and the ability to read the *codices* was largely confined to monks in monasteries, where copying these documents took place. Monasteries were also the repositories for collections of books called libraries.

The Chinese developed the process of woodblock printing in the sixth century CE. Five centuries later, they would develop movable type for the printing of books. In Europe in 1440, Johannes Gutenberg (ca 1400–68) invented the printing press with movable metal type, an invention that would revolutionize the production of books and facilitate their mass production. The first such book was the Bible, published in 1456. The ability to produce books in mass quantity helped to increase literacy by providing low-cost books to the public.

Book Form

The book as we know it today is an assemblage of printed sheets consisting most often of paper or parchment. It has a cover that may be soft or hard. It has a spine, which joins the front and back covers where the pages are hinged with glue, or with a type of string. In the case of hardback books, there may be an additional cover called a dust jacket that contains the title and author on the front and some information about the content on the back with statements of approval, called blurbs, by well-known people (or institutions such as newspapers) on the back. Inside the book, there is often front matter that includes the frontispiece, which is a decorative page that may appear opposite the title page. Next, there is a copyright page, and in some types of books a table of contents, list of figures, list of tables, dedication, acknowledgments, foreword, preface, introduction, the body of the text, and back matter, which may include an appendix, glossary, index, notes, bibliography, and a colophon, or inscription at the back of the book that describes production notes related to the specific text including a designer, printing method, and so forth. Books may vary in size. They may be *quarto*, which means the book measures 11 to 13 inches in height. The *octavo*, the size of most hard covers today, may be as much as 9¾ inches tall. The *duodecimo* may be up to 7¾ inches tall.

Electronic Books

In the late twentieth century, books took on a new format, namely, the *e-book*, which consists of digitalized characters that may be transmitted electronically from a publisher via the internet (or some other digital medium) to the consumer. This new format requires the downloading of the virtual book onto a computer. Recently, however, a new electronic device for reading e-books, called a reader, with the dimensions of a book, and with clear and legible characters, is available for purchase. This device can store up to hundreds of books.

Whatever form they take, and in whatever medium they are produced, books have served vital functions in human history. They preserve knowledge, functioning as artificial memory systems, present new ideas, provide recreation, and so on. Their use of the written word and the manner in which words are placed on pages has conditioned human cognitive evolution considerably. Reading leads to reflection and a sense of objectivity. Literacy is essentially the ability to use books for various purposes.

Frank Nuessel

Bibliography

Avrin, Leila. *Scribes, Scripts and Books: The Book Arts from Antiquity to the Renaissance*. Chicago: American Library Association, 1991.

Eisenstein, Elizabeth L. *The Printing Press as an Agent of Change: Communications and Cultural Transformations in Early-Modern Europe*. Cambridge: Cambridge University Press, 1979.

Epstein, Jason. *Book Business: Publishing Past, Present, and Future*. New York: Norton, 2001.

McLuhan, Marshall. *The Gutenberg Galaxy: The Making of Typographic Man*. Toronto: University of Toronto Press, 1962.

Schifrin, André. *The Business of Books*. New York: Verso, 2000.

BOOKS, HISTORY OF

[See also: *Book; e-Book; Gutenberg Galaxy; Print Culture*]

A *book* is a collection of sheets containing verbal text, sometimes complemented with illustrations, bound together. The forerunners of books were the ancient Mesopotamian clay tablets and scrolls of ancient Egypt, Greece, and Rome. The Sumerians and Egyptians introduced many of the practices and conventions that are still used today in book layout and production, such as the use of a cover page with a title and the author's name placed on it. The Egyptian books were made typically of strips of papyrus that could be unrolled. Papyrus disintegrated in less than one hundred years. So, by the fourth century CE, the rectangular *codex* was used in its place. This was a ringed book consisting of wooden tablets covered with wax. Papyrus books were also gradually replaced by parchment books, a longer-lasting material that also cost less than papyrus. Until the invention of movable print technology, books were reproduced by professional scribes who copied a work manually. The scribes developed modes of writing that are still in use today – capital and small letters, a system for punctuation, and spaces between words.

Types of Books

Although there seem to be many types of

books, they are traditionally classified into three categories:

- *Trade books* are books written for the general public. These include novels, biographies, current affairs books, do-it-yourself books, cookbooks, travel guides, and the like. They are distributed through bookstores, book clubs, and on-line by sites such as Amazon.com.
- *Educational books* are the textbooks used for instruction in schools. Educational publishing houses often employ educators, professors, scholars, and other experts to write the books. The books are sold directly to buyers in school systems or else are distributed mainly through school and college bookstores. These are also available online.
- *Reference books* include information-based books such as dictionaries, encyclopedias, almanacs, and similar books. Most reference book publishers use specialists to write them. These books are also sold primarily to libraries and to individuals who want to have sources of information available to them. Today, most reference material is being published in electronic form and is available on websites such as Wikipedia, where the entries can be written by virtually anyone, not just experts.

Historical Sketch

There were very few books in the ancient and medieval worlds. They were commissioned primarily by the literate aristocratic and clerical minorities of society. This meant, in essence, that books were produced chiefly by scholars and/or clerics for other scholars or clerics and for rulers. In the medieval period, books were reproduced by monks working in the *scriptoria* (Latin for 'writing rooms') of monasteries mainly for religious purposes. They were made either with wooden covers fastened with clasps or else bound in leather. Often they were adorned with gems. Other kinds of books were commissioned by a very small part of the population that could

afford them and that knew how to read. Books thus remained mainly the privilege of the few until the late 1400s.

In the fifteenth century, two developments came forward that made it possible to break away from this pattern. One was the cheap production of paper and the other was the invention of the modern printing press. The Chinese had already invented a mechanical printing system from carved wood blocks in the sixth century CE; they also invented movable type technology in the eleventh. The first printed book, called the *Diamond Sutra*, was produced in 868 CE. Ink was spread on a block of wood, and an impression created on paper. The Koreans had invented metal movable type in the fourteenth century. It was the movable type technology that migrated to Europe in the fifteenth century. By the middle part of that century the German printer Johannes Gutenberg (ca 1400–68) developed the first modern movable type system for printing books cheaply en masse. Each alphabet letter was made with a separate piece of metal, which could then be used in any combination to produce words mechanically and quickly. The first book printed using such technology was the Bible in 1456, known appropriately as the Gutenberg Bible. As a consequence of making books cheap and broadly available, the new print technology created the conditions for literacy to spread among the general public, especially since it was believed that every believer should read the Bible. The first mass-produced books were known as *incunabula* (Latin for 'cradle'), printed with large type resembling the handwritten letters of the scribes.

Books became products of consumption for a new mass market; and the emergence of such a market led to the conceptualization of modern capitalism as a socio-economic model. New books emerged, written not only for religious or scientific purposes, but also more and more for public edification and for diversion. By the time of the Industrial Revolution vast numbers could be published at a low cost, as printing and paper technologies became more efficient. The book had become an item of mass consumption. Venice became the first centre for producing and trading books in the late 1400s. Aldus Manutius founded the first modern publishing house, called Aldine Press, in that city, a house that became widely known for its beautiful editions of Greek and Roman works published in small, cheap volumes.

Books have always been perceived as materials for storing knowledge. In fact, shortly after the advent of papyrus-produced books libraries started sprouting up everywhere in the ancient Middle East. One of the largest and most important was built in the third century BCE by the Greeks in Alexandria. By the second century CE libraries started cropping up in many parts of the world, leading to an upsurge in the desire of all people to gain literacy and to institutionalize advanced forms of learning. This led to the emergence of modern universities in the late eleventh century. With the spread of literacy came a concurrent need to organize knowledge – leading to the invention of the *encyclopedia*. The oldest encyclopedia is, actually, the *Natural History* (79 CE) by Roman writer Pliny the Elder (23–79 CE); the modern encyclopedia, however, was largely the result of the Enlightenment. Book-producing technology also provided the conditions for the creation of a mass market for books, leading to the rise of 'recreational reading' in the form of novels and other kinds of popular books, such as almanacs. To this day, books remain primary media for the preservation and dissemination of knowledge, as well as media for artistic expression and entertainment.

In America the first printing press was established by an English locksmith named Stephen Daye in Cambridge, Massachusetts. Daye's first published book was the *Bay Psalm Book*, in 1640. By the early nineteenth century, the market for books began increasing enormously. Book production expanded accordingly, especially after the invention of Linotype, a process for setting type mechanically, steam-powered printing machines, and efficient papermaking and bookbinding technologies. Paperback books became popular in that era. By 1885, a third of the paperback books published were called *dime novels*, because they cost 10 cents. Penguin Books, founded in 1935, became a world leader in paperback publishing, followed by Pocket Books, one of the largest American publishers, in 1939. Today, computers are used to set type for books, radically changing the way books are now being produced. Actually, computers themselves function as books, because text and illustrations may be read on their screens. Two novels by Stephen King, *Riding the Bullet* and *The Plant* were published in 2000 on the internet, rather than in traditional print paper format. The internet now also serves as a system for the sale of *e-books* (electronic books). When a user downloads an e-book to a special hand-held device, or to a computer with special software, the text appears as it would on a printed page. Many social commentators suggest, correctly, that the e-book is changing the way we are reading, writing, and selling books in radical and permanent ways. For one thing, more and more authors will likely be writing for Google than for a traditional publisher. Cellphone novels are also becoming popular, as authors circumvent the usual process of submitting a manuscript to a publisher and simply put out their works on a cellphone. The gatekeepers of literary quality are no longer the publishers, but the marketplace of readers themselves.

The Book in the Age of the Internet

The book will no longer be perceived by subsequent generations as an intrinsic documenter of history. This is because the e-book can be modified at any point in time and thus be perceived as being literally 'timeless.' Although an e-book's timeline can be tracked by computers, there will likely be little interest in doing so. As a result, we are starting to lose the traditional sense of 'textualized' (book-based) history. As writers and historians put out their works on Facebook, Twitter, and other online venues, traditional notions of historical documentation will continue to change radically. In early 2008, Smashwords allowed anyone to publish their work online, making the work available through online sites such as Amazon and iBookstore. Smashwords keeps a percentage of the selling price, negotiated with the author, who keeps the rest. Without a publisher's trademark, a book has to attract readers on its own, and may not sell until the online world decides that it is worth reading. But then, who is reading online-produced books? With millions of books available why would a reader choose any one of them, without the traditional gatekeeping guarantee that traditional book publishing offered? Questions such as these will be playing themselves out in the near future as book publishing migrates more to the online world.

Human communication history seems to be governed by three basic principles, which can, for the sake of argument, be called E-principles: *economy, efficiency, effort.* Communication systems seem to develop, first and foremost, in economical ways. If the grammar of a language is complex, as Old English grammar was, then people start to reduce its complexity to make it more 'economical.' Modern English has a much simpler grammar than Old English, relying more on syntax than on case structure, for example, to deliver meaning. Economy is the tendency of communication systems to compress forms so as to save time and energy in creating texts and delivering messages. Efficiency is how languages make use of few resources to cover large areas of meaning. For example, languages have a handful of terms to refer to the many shades of colour that Nature presents to the human eye. There are potentially 13 million shades that could be named by a language. But to make the task more efficient, languages have developed from two to around thirteen terms to

encompass basic colour meanings. Without such efficiency, remembering colour concepts would be an impracticable task. Efficiency is related to memory capacity. Economy and efficiency entail effort reduction, both in how we encode meanings and how we communicate them.

It is obvious that all three principles are operative on the internet. Books can be stored economically and efficiently through digitization. A lover of Shakespeare can download all his works and read them in any sequence desired – chronologically, thematically, and so on – by simply clicking appropriate icons on a screen. Google's massive text-digitization project, which aims to transfer library collections to the online format, is another way to economize on physical space storage of books and to make access to them more efficient. The world's massive print knowledge is now available simply by clicking on one's computer or other digital-downloading device.

Still, people are social beings. Going to a bookstore seems to satisfy various social needs. Bookstores now provide a social environment for books, including the sale of coffee and other social accoutrements. Thus, like the movie theatre, which continues to thrive despite YouTube, DVDs, and other film-carrying devices, so too the bookstore and print books will likely continue to exist, at least in the immediate future, because of their social value.

Marcel Danesi

Bibliography

Basbanes, Nicholas A. *A Splendor of Letters: The Permanence of Books in an Impermanent World.* New York: HarperCollins, 2003.

Eisenstein, Elizabeth L. *The Printing Press as an Agent of Change: Communications and Cultural Transformations in Early-Modern Europe.* Cambridge: Cambridge University Press, 1979.

Epstein, Jason. *Book Business: Publishing Past, Present, and Future.* New York: Norton, 2001.

Howard, Nicole. *The Book: The Life Story of a Technology.* New York: Greenwood, 2005.

Schifrin, André. *The Business of Books.* New York: Verso, 2000.

Thompson, John B. *Merchants of Culture: The Publishing Business in the Twenty-First Century.* New York: Polity, 2010.

BRAND NAMES

[See also: *Advertising; Branding; Logos*]

A pivotal strategy in the process of communicating brand identity and placing it successfully in the marketplace is the coinage of appropriate names for products. *Brand-naming* is a stratagem designed to convey conceptual images associated with products through a suggestive name. The practice emerged around 1880, when some soap manufacturers started naming their products so that they could be distinguished from similar ones in stores. Among the first brand names used were Ivory, Pears, Sapolio, and Colgate. It is not known which of these was first. The Ivory brand name goes back to 1882 and is considered to be the oldest by most advertising historians. The modern concept of brand was thus born. By simply coining descriptive or colourful names for products, manufacturers quickly discovered that sales increased significantly. As social critic Naomi Klein (2000: 6) aptly observes, brand-naming became 'a necessity of the machine age.' In some cases, the trademark itself was used as the brand name for the product. Such was the case with the Parker Pen – one of the first trademarks to be converted into a brand name, in 1888.

A name turns a product into a symbol. Brand names such as McDonald's, Nike, Apple, Body Shop, Calvin Klein, Levi's, and so forth have become symbols recognized by anyone living in a modern consumerist society. Such recognition would have been impossible if they were simply called hamburgers, running shoes, computers, and so on. The coinage of an appropriate brand name is thus the first crucial step in embedding a product into social consciousness as something larger than itself. At a practical level, naming a product has an identifier function, allowing consumers to identify what particular brand they may wish to purchase (or not). But the name, being a word, generates images that go well beyond this simple function. Consider Gucci shoes. The name of the manufacturer allows us to identify the shoes as different from other shoe brands. But it also assigns an aura of craftsmanship and superior quality to the shoe product, inducing us to grasp it unconsciously as the 'work' of a shoe artist (Giorgio Armani), not just an assembly-line product for everyone to wear. Designer names evoke images of clothes and shoes as objets d'art, rather than mere clothing or footwear. But the name must have pleasing qualities, otherwise it will work against such a perception. For example, the New York designer Ralph Lifshitz changed his name to Ralph Lauren, because it was more pleasant-sounding than his birth name. Similarly, Pietro Cardino altered his Italian name to Pierre Cardin in order to give it a more appealing 'French sound.'

Brand-naming strategies fall into several generic categories – *manufacturer names, fictitious character names, descriptors,* and *suggestive names* (Danesi 2008). The manufacturer, or *heritage*, name, as just discussed, imbues the product with connotations of tradition and artistry, whereas products named after a fictitious character (Mr Clean, Barbie, Betty Crocker) suggest specific qualities, such as cleanliness or idealized American womanhood. The descriptor name is a word or phrase, such as Easy On, Drip-Dry, Bug Off, Lestoil, Close-Up, or Wet 'N Wash, that describes the product in some way (for example, what the product allows users to accomplish with it). It can also be a toponym, identifying the geographical location of a product or of a company (American Bell, Western Union, etc.). Some descriptor names relate to lifestyle or some psychosocial trait. For example, General Mills introduced a yogurt category called Go-Gurt in 1998 for the 'tween' market. With names such as Berry Blue Blast and Rad Raspberry, the brand was an instant hit with that market. To quote Spiegel, Coffey, and Livingston (2004: 185): 'The name, Go-Gurt, focuses on the idea that this is yogurt you can eat "on the go," and "on the go" is expressed as tween activities – playing sports, skateboarding, and playing music. The characters used on the packaging are obviously tweens, not kids, not teens, and not adults.' Research shows that the more meanings a name evokes for the product's target audience, the more psychologically effective it is and the more possibilities it offers to the advertiser for creating truly effective advertising campaigns (Frankel 2004).

Suggestive names are those that symbolically evoke lifestyle and psychological meanings. Consider the name of the Acura car. It is, at a phonetic level, suggestive of the word 'accuracy.' But its form is also suggestive of how both Italian and Japanese words are constructed. The feminine nouns in the former language end in -a and certain Japanese words end in the suffix -ura (tempura). The brand name thus suggests, by extension, the stereotypically perceived qualities of both cultures at once – artistry and scientific precision.

The suggestion strategy can take many forms. For example, using certain word parts (such as suffixes) might convey scientific soundness. The brand names Androgel and Viramax for Viagra products are two examples. In both names, the first part (Andro- and Vir-) refers to various gender attributes (androgyny and virility respectively), while the suffixes evoke scientific connotations. Some names are suggestive of the qualities of nature – Aqua Velva, Cascade, Irish Spring, Mountain Dew, Surf, Tide, and so on. Others suggest lifestyle preferences or needs. For example, car models are often named to suggest countryside escape, wild west living, back-to-nature feelings, and so on – Dodge Durango, Ford Escape, Ford Explorer, Jeep Grand Cherokee, Jeep Renegade, Jeep Wrangler, Mercury Mountaineer, and so on.

Names constructed as hyperboles imply superiority, excellence, the big picture, a forward-looking attitude, and so on – Future Now, MaxiLight, Multicorp, PowerAde, SuperFresh, Superpower, UltraLite. Some names intimate generalities or superiority – Advantage Plus, General Electric, General Foods, General Mills, Okay Plus, People's Choice, Viewer's Choice, etc. The technique of combining parts of words is also very common. For example, the endings -tastic (as in fantastic), -tacular (as spectacular), -licious (as in delicious), -rama (as in panorama), among others, are common (Cook 2004: 68): Kid-Tastic, Snack-Tastic, Pet-tacular, Sports-tacular, Ice-A-Licious, Carb-O-licious, Beef-a-rama, Stretch-O-Rama, and so forth.

Suggestive names are mnemonically effective, because they link products to cultural symbolism and lifestyle. Cars named after animals (Mustang, Jaguar, Cougar, etc.) imply that automobiles have desirable qualities – a Jaguar brings to mind a large and powerful creature, a Cougar a fast and exotic animal, and so on. A car model named Park Avenue, on the other hand, suggests an upscale lifestyle, one named Cavalier nobility, Yukon exploration, Sonata classical sophistication, and so on. Brand names reveal the essence of what brand psychology is all about – creating effective symbolism for the product. The names given to video games fit in perfectly with the appetite for adventure (Final Fantasy X), play (PlayStation), intrigue and excitement (Grand Theft Auto), free-for-alls (Melee), and so on. These provide an actual profile of the prototypical (or stereotypical) gamer.

Brands named with alphabet and number symbols, or with acronyms, are now common: X-Factor, Toyota XR Matrix, iPod, X-Stick, XBox, PS3, Wii, and so on. These suggest 'techno-savvy,' tapping into a 'text-messaging' style of writing words that is in step with the time. Examples include: 2BFree (clothes), 4 Ever Nails, XM4Home (radio system), C-Thru-U Beautifying Sheer Tint, E Z Taxi, Spex Appeal, Xylocaine, Glam Gurlz, Hotpak, Minds@

Work (digital equipment) (Frankel 2004: 106–7; Cook 2004). Actually, this strategy was used long before the advent of the internet. Products such as Cheez Whiz, Spic 'N Span, Wheetabix, Kool cigarettes, and others were named in a similar way. Brand names such as Pret-O-Lite, U All Kno After Dinner Mints, Phiteezi Shoes, and U-Rub-IN actually go back to the 1920s (Cook 2004: 44). It seems to have always been a pattern within modern culture. Rock and rap musicians, for example, have typically used it to name themselves – Guns N Roses, Snoop Dogg, Salt N Pepa, etc.

The integration between brand-naming style and pop culture is part of the larger phenomenon known as *branding*. It is a phenomenon that came into full force in the 1920s. In 1929, for instance, the Disney Corporation permitted Mickey Mouse to be reproduced on school slates, knowing full well that this simple strategy would integrate the symbol of the Disney Corporation, and thus the corporation itself, into children's consciousness. In the 1930s, the Mickey Mouse brand name and logo were licensed with huge success. In 1955 *The Mickey Mouse Club* premiered on U.S. network television, further transforming the corporate brand into a symbol of childhood. As this example shows, the idea is to get a brand to become integrated with spectacles (movies, TV programs, etc.) and trends generally.

Marcel Danesi

Bibliography

Cook, Vivian. *Why Can't Anybody Spell?* New York: Touchstone, 2004.

Danesi, Marcel. *Why It Sells: Decoding the Meanings of Brand Names, Logos, Ads, and Other Marketing and Advertising Ploys*. Lanham: Rowman and Littlefield, 2008.

Frankel, Alex. *Word Craft: The Art of Turning Little Words into Big Business*. New York: Three Rivers Press, 2004.

Klein, Naomi. *No Logo: Taking Aim at the Brand Bullies*. Toronto: Alfred A. Knopf, 2000.

Nuessel, Frank. A Note on Names for Energy Drink Brands and Products. *Names* 58 (2010): 102–10.

Spiegel, David L., Timothy J. Coffey, and Gregory Livingston. *The Great Tween Buying Machine*. Chicago: Dearborn Trade Publishing, 2004.

BRANDING

[See also: *Advertising; Brand Names; Logos*]

Branding is a term used to refer to the marketing strategy of integrating brands into mainstream popular culture, by featuring them conspicuously in entertainment spectacles, sports events, movies, and so on. In 1982, for instance, Reese's Pieces were shown clearly in the movie *E.T.* – the first time any product could be identified as a specific brand in the script of a film. A year later, in 1983, Tom Cruise was seen donning a pair of Wayfarers (Rayburn sunglasses) in *Risky Business*. Sales for both products exceeded all expectations. Since then, products can be seen prominently in movies and TV programs, from recognizable car makes in James Bond movies to Macintosh computers in TV crime dramas. The Revlon Company paid for close-up shots of its products in the TV soap opera, *All My Children* in the early 2000s.

The showcasing of brands in different media is known more specifically as *placement*. The aim of this strategy is not just to get the product to be noticed by a large audience, but more importantly, to get it to become part of the script. To get a sense of how common (and extensive) this practice has become, the list below is a minimal list of movies and TV programs in which the Macintosh computer has been showcased in the 2000s:

- *Queer as Folk* (2000–5) – The iMac G4 appears frequently.
- *Legally Blonde* (2001) – Elle is the only student in her class who owns a tangerine clamshell iBook.

- *The Princess Diaries* (2001) – Jeremiah owns a graphite clamshell iBook.
- *George Lopez* (2002–7) – The family owns an iMac G4.
- *How to Lose a Guy in 10 Days* (2002) – Many iMac G4s can be seen in Benjamin Barry's office.
- *School of Rock* (2003) – Two iMac G4s are featured in the classroom.
- *Love Actually* (2003) – An advertisement for 'The All New iMac' appears in airport scenes.
- *Confessions of a Teenage Drama Queen* (2004) – The school band uses iBooks instead of musical instruments.
- *Mean Girls* (2004) – An iMac is seen on Ms Norbury's and Damian's desks.
- *The Pacifier* (2005) – Seth has an iMac in his room.
- *The Devil Wears Prada* (2006) – The computers in the office are Macs.
- *Californication* (2007) – In an early episode, a scene is filmed in an Apple Store.
- *Nim's Island* (2008) – Jack and Nim use an iMac to connect to the rest of the world.
- *Being Erica* (2009) – An iMac G5 can be seen in Erica's apartment.
- *Confessions of a Shopaholic* (2009) – Rebecca owns a MacBook.
- *The Proposal* (2009) – There are many iMacs in the office.

It is interesting to note that before the age of modern placement, a number of Hollywood movies from the late 1940s to the early 1960s focused on the psychological dangers posed by branding. Below is a list of relevant movies:

- *The Hucksters* (1947). Clarke Gable portrays a New York adman. His duties take him to Hollywood, where he creates a radio commercial for 'Beautee Soap,' which mimics the jingle style of the era. The objective of the movie is to show how ad agencies controlled what people saw on networks.
- *Mr. Blandings Builds His Dream House* (1948). Cary Grant (also a New York adman) seeks to create a blockbuster campaign for the ham product called 'Wham.' The movie is a spoof of the advertising culture that was shaping social values more and more.
- *A Letter to Three Wives* (1949). Ann Sothern is a writer of radio soap operas. Her husband is a critic of the media and advertising, which he sees as vulgarizing American culture. In one scene, the husband (George) states: 'The purpose of radio writing, as far as I can see, is to prove to the masses that a deodorant can bring happiness, a mouthwash guarantee success and a laxative attract romance.'
- *Callaway Went Thataway* (1951). Fred MacMurray and Dorothy McGuire are partners in an agency that creates a successful TV program based on old western movies, a program sponsored by a cereal called 'Corkies.' The movie is a satire of early television and its dependence on cinematic clichés.
- *A Face in the Crowd* (1957). Andy Griffith plays a hobo who is hired to act in commercials because of his ability to charm consumers by poking fun at the sponsors of programs. The movie constitutes a black parody of advertising culture.
- *Lover Come Back* (1961). Rock Hudson and Doris Day portray executives of rival ad agencies. Hudson lands clients by providing them with sex and alcohol.

A glance at a TV programming schedule mapped against advertising content reveals that placement is now a sophisticated 'contextualization' technique of marketing science. For example, commercials for food are placed commonly around dinner time on family channels, whereas commercials for beer are placed in prime time on channels that tend to attract a beer-drinking audience (such as the comedy channel).

Another major branding strategy is what the social critic Thomas Frank (1997) calls *co-option* (also called *co-optation*), which he characterizes as the 'conquest of cool' by the brands. Co-option is really a type of placement. It was evident as early as the 1920s, when a company like Coca-Cola co-

opted 'diner culture' with a simple placement strategy – it imprinted its distinctive
letter logo on drinking glasses, providing
them to diners and other eateries. As a
result, Coca-Cola became America's most
popular soft drink. Coca-Cola has always
used the co-option strategy effectively, as
is evident in its brotherly love and peace
campaigns of the counterculture era ('I'd
like to teach the world to sing in perfect
harmony') and its authenticity campaigns
of the sceptical 1970s and 1980s ('It's the
real thing').

As Frank points out, co-option is meant
to communicate unconsciously that brand
manufacturers are 'cool' and participants
in cultural changes and shifts. In the 1960s,
he claims, marketers realized that it was
in their best interest not to fight the anti-
consumerism philosophy of the hippies,
but rather to embrace it. The salient characteristic of this 'if-you-can't-beat-them-
join-them' strategy was the utilization of an
advertising style that mocked consumerism. The subtext was obvious – being anti-
establishment meant wearing 'hip clothes'
and buying products that claimed to stand
against tradition. Pepsi professed to be
the drink of the 'new generation.' Other
brands followed suit. Trends in pop culture
started to cross over to advertising, and
advertising styles reflected what was going on in culture or society generally. Take,
for example, a 2008 ad campaign mounted
by Diesel. It shows a young woman on the
right side of the ad who seems to be escaping from an unrecognizable fetter, with a
look of utter despair on her face. On the left
side, there is the face of a woman with graffiti of all kinds on her face. The messages
are not readable in their entirety. They are
suggestive of bits and pieces of ideas that
make up the cluttered urban landscape –
physical and psychological. The ad thus
seems to be decrying the modern world,
with its mixed, cluttered, and ultimately
meaningless languages. Today, we wear
this meaninglessness on our very faces, as
the ad suggests. Diesel has, by implication,
become our moral philosopher and abstract

artist, co-opting the same style and goals of
philosophy and modern art.

Another modern-day branding strategy
is called *co-branding*. It involves cooperation
among the brands – a truly singular event
in the history of marketing and advertising.
For example, in 2005, the Maytag repair-
man was featured in a commercial for the
Chevrolet Impala; in the same year the Taco
Bell chihuahua was seen in a commercial
for Geico. Co-branding between Starbucks
and the big bookstore chains has perhaps
become the most emblematic example of
this new partnership. Sipping coffee in
such an intellectual atmosphere conjures
up images of the chic cafés frequented by
the intellectuals of the late eighteenth and
early nineteenth centuries (as depicted
in paintings of the era). With new media,
co-branding is becoming easier and easier
to realize, producing a new form of branding, which can be called 'embedding.' The
website www.neopet.com is a case in point.
The site offers recreational and educational
activities for children. But at the site they
can also find links to other products associated with childhood – a McDonald's link, a
Lucky Charms game, and other such 'child-
based' brand embeds.

A long-standing branding strategy is
to sponsor events such as soccer matches,
golf tournaments, arts events, and the like,
associating the brand with the event historically. Sponsorship of the arts goes back
to the times when either the Church or
the nobility would sponsor artists. Known
as 'patrons' of the arts, these institutions
gained legitimacy beyond the political
sphere because of the sponsorship. This
kind of patronage was adopted by brands
in the 1920s, when radio programs such
as *Texaco Theater*, *General Electric Theater*, and
Kraft Theater were sponsored by certain
companies (as the names of the programs
indicate). The sponsor would be part of
the program, usually introducing it. As a
consequence, theatre in the early twentieth
century was perceived unconsciously as
being under the patronage of a new institution – the brand corporation.

Supporting worthy causes publicly is another common branding strategy. The Ronald McDonald House Charities is an example. Promoting an image of itself as a family-oriented company, McDonald's sponsors Ronald McDonald House Charities worldwide in which the families of critically ill children may lodge when the children have to undergo medical treatment away from their homes. The Ronald McDonald clown fits in perfectly with this image. The corporation's first mascot was a friendly, winking chef named Speedee, whose head was the shape of a hamburger. Speedee was later renamed Archie McDonald. In 1960 a local Washington, DC, TV show for children, called *Bozo's Circus*, featured Bozo the clown, who always drew large crowds during public appearances. After the show was cancelled, McDonald's hired the actor to make restaurant appearances, redesigning his outfit and giving him the rhyming name of Ronald McDonald. In this way, a childhood archetypal figure (the clown), associated with charity work for needy families, transformed the Golden Arches into a symbol of kindness, charity, and family values.

Another way to communicate that a brand is sensitive to world issues is to show support for a specific cause. The fashion industry now commonly embraces environmentalism by using organic fabrics, supporting an environmental lifestyle, and thus demonstrating a commitment to improving the health of the planet.

Perhaps the oldest branding strategy of all is the *ad campaign*. This can be defined as the use of a series of ads and commercials based on the same theme, characters, and jingles over a specified (or in some cases unspecified) time period and spread broadly through the use of various media (print, electronic, digital). Ad campaigns are also designed to allow brands to keep in step with changing socio-political trends. In the 1990s, Budweiser ad campaigns showed young urban males hanging around together and greeting each other with 'Whassup,' a catch phrase that became so popular that it was parodied on late-night talk shows, and used by people in daily conversations. The phrase, which originated in hip-hop culture, caught on with young people, who started greeting one another comically like the actors in the ads. By employing pop culture lingo, Budweiser increased recognition of its brand name. 'Whassup!' became a trademark of Budweiser.

The overall objective of branding is to tap into cultural spaces and events that govern lifestyle, values, and beliefs, turning the product into a symbolic key for gaining access to those spaces. As Alex Frankel (2004: 81) puts it: 'The most common marketing definition of a brand is that it is a *promise* – an unspoken pact between a company and a consumer to deliver a particular experience.'

Marcel Danesi

Bibliography

Altman, Lynn. *Brand It Yourself: The Fast, Focused Way to Marketplace Magic*. New York: Portfolio, 2006.

Atkin, Douglas. *The Culting of Brands*. New York: Portfolio, 2004.

Danesi, Marcel. *Brands*. London: Routledge, 2006.

Frank, Thomas. *The Conquest of Cool: Business Culture, Counterculture, and the Rise of Hip Consumerism*. Chicago: University of Chicago Press, 1997.

Frankel, Alex. *Word Craft: The Art of Turning Little Words into Big Business*. New York: Three Rivers Press, 2004.

Holt, Douglas B. *How Brands Become Icons: The Principles of Cultural Branding*. Boston: Harvard Business School Press, 2004.

Kornberger, Martin. *Brand Society: How Brands Transform Management and Lifestyle*. Cambridge: Cambridge University Press, 2010.

McLuhan, Marshall. *The Mechanical Bride: Folklore of Industrial Man*. New York: Vanguard, 1951.

– *The Gutenberg Galaxy*. Toronto: University of Toronto Press, 1962.

– *Understanding Media*. London: Routledge and Kegan Paul, 1964.

Twitchell, James B. *Twenty Ads that Shook the World.* New York: Crown, 2000.
– *Branded Nation.* New York: Simon and Schuster, 2004.

BRICOLAGE

[See also: *Popular Culture; Youth Culture*]

The term *bricolage* is used in various disciplines, prominent among which are popular and youth culture studies. It is a French term that means 'fiddling, tinkering' and thus, by extension, refers to a type of text, spectacle, lifestyle, or performance based on a 'do-it-yourself' creative pastiche with given symbolic materials. The term has been of particular importance in understanding the appeal of pop culture trends, which typically seem to have no unifying structure, just a random mixture of elements. From early vaudeville to the TV series *The Simpsons*, bricolage does in fact appear to accurately describe the admixture of styles, ideas, and levels of culture that are brought together in some programs and spectacles. Vaudeville was made up of a bricolage of acts, ranging from skits to acrobatic acts and classical music performances; *The Simpsons* brings together diverse elements from contrasting levels of culture in the same episode, creating effects similar to collage paintings.

Why is this appealing? The term was first used in anthropology by Claude Lévi-Strauss (1962) to designate the style used in many myths and tribal rituals that in themselves are meaningless but which, when assembled into texts and rites, evoke magical symbolism. It would seem that disparate elements become unified in the combinatory act itself, each contributing a part of the meaning to the whole. Of course, bricolage is the essence of many parodic spectacles – for example, when a clown dresses up with different types of clothes (a tuxedo, running shoes, a top hat, etc.). This bricolage of clothing makes sense on the clown but not on the average person.

Youth analyst Dick Hebdige (1979: 102) adopted Lévi-Strauss's term to describe youth subcultures such as the punks:

> In particular, the concept of bricolage can be used to explain how subcultural styles are constructed. In *The Savage Mind* Lévi-Strauss shows how the magical modes utilized by primitive peoples (superstition, sorcery, myth) can be seen as implicitly coherent, though explicitly bewildering systems of connection between things which perfectly equip their users to 'think' their own world. These magical systems of connection have a common feature: they are capable of infinite extension because basic elements can be used in a variety of improvised combinations to generate new meanings within them. Bricolage has thus been described as a 'science of the concrete' in a recent definition which clarifies the original anthropological meaning of the term.

In effect, such subcultures take elements of the mainstream culture and blend them together in pertinent spectacles in order to assail them and thus subvert their meanings.

Marcel Danesi

Bibliography

Lévi-Strauss, Claude. *La pensée sauvage.* Paris: Plon, 1962
Hebdige, Dick. *Subculture: The Meaning of Style.* London: Routledge, 1979.

BRITISH CULTURAL THEORY

[See also: *Centre for Contemporary Cultural Studies; Culture Industry Theory; Gramsci, Antonio; Hall, Stuart; Hegemony Theory*]

British cultural theory (or British cultural studies) refers to the scholars and the work they conducted at the University of Birmingham (UK), Centre for Contemporary Cultural Studies (CCCS), also called the Birmingham School. The roots of the school are in the courses given at the university by cultural critics Raymond Williams, Richard Hoggart, and Stuart Hall from the 1950s to the early 1960s. Their focus was transversal and interdisciplinary, bringing together literary and historical theories, text analysis, cultural anthropology, ethnic studies, popular culture and urban subculture studies, mass-media studies, and women's studies. The presence of Nikholaj Bakhtin, brother of famous Russian philosopher Mikhail M. Bakhtin, at the University of Birmingham from 1939 to 1946 was not un-coincidental to the birth and development of the Birmingham School. Nikholaj founded the Department of Linguistic Studies at the university, which still preserves his archives. In the novel *Saints and Scholars* by Terry Eagleton (1987), Nikolaj Bakhtin is one of the protagonists, along with philosopher Ludwig Wittgenstein, his friend at Cambridge, who was influenced by Nikolaj in his intellectual evolution as documented by the difference between Wittgenstein's early *Tractatus Logico-Philosophicus* and his later *Philosophical Investigations*.

The eclectic, many-sided, and 'synechist' approach of British cultural theory is best represented by Stuart Hall (b. 1932), a central figure in cultural studies generally. Synechism is the term used in cultural studies to refer to the tendency to regard such concepts as time, space, and the law as continuous. Among other things, Hall's approach combines trends and theoretical models such as Marxism, post-structuralism, critical race theory, and feminism, blending within it ideas from disciplines such as history, sociology, anthropology, and media studies. Hall's work concerns the problem of *hegemony*, a notion developed by Italian Marxist Antonio Gramsci, which refers to the cultural production of *consent* as opposed to *coercion*. Hall analyses language use as operating within a hegemonic framework of power – a framework under the control of public and corporate institutions, governments, and economic forces.

Cultural theory as conceived by the Birmingham School has greatly contributed to the analysis and critique of mainstream ideological practices in Western society and to the development of critical post-Marxism approaches to Western media. Books by Jorge Larrain are especially important to many media theorists. These include: *Concept of Ideology* (1979), *Identity and Modernity in Latin America* (2000), and *Identidad Chile* (2001).

Associated with British cultural theory is political dissent. This is especially evident in the work of people like Raymond Williams, Dick Hebdige, and Angela McRobbie. Hebdige's widely cited book, *Subculture: The Meaning of Style*, which was originally published in 1979, has become a crucial point of reference in the study of youth culture generally. Angela McRobbie, currently professor of communications at Goldsmiths College, University of London, is one of the most sophisticated and thoughtful analysts of gender and popular culture today. Her most recent book is *The Aftermath of Feminism: Gender, Culture and Social Change* (2008).

Williams's most renowned works are *Culture and Society, 1780–1950* (1958), and *The Long Revolution* (1961). In them, he analyses the relationship between culture and ideology. His interest in ideology was fuelled by his friendship with Italian culture critic Ferruccio Rossi-Landi (1921–85). Rossi-Landi is well known for his deconstruction of the Marxist relation between base structure (the actual social institutions) and superstructure (the overarching conceptual systems keeping sintitutions in place) from a semiotic perspective. So impressed was Williams by it that he promoted the posthumous publication of a book by Rossi-Landi, *Ideologia* (1982), in English translation with the title *Marxism and Ideology* (1990).

British cultural theory greatly influenced American cultural studies in the late 1980s and early 1990s. The two are different, however, in many ways. The latter is more concerned with notions of social class and how these interact with culture and media; the former has been primarily concerned with media representations of ethnicity, gender, and sexuality. British cultural theory has been influential, therefore, in bringing into existence an autonomous discipline that not only espouses a critical perspective of the study of media, but has also, in general, shown an interest in supporting marginalized social groups.

Susan Petrilli

Bibliography

Bakhtin, Mikhail M. *Lectures and Essays.* Birmingham: Birmingham University Press, 1963.

Bennett, Tony, et al., eds. *Culture and Social Process: A Reader.* London: Open University Press, 1981.

Carby, Hazel. *Reconstructing Womanhood: The Emergence of the Afro-American Woman Novelist.* Oxford: Oxford, University Press, 1987.

Denning, Michael. *Mechanic Accents: Dime Novels and Working Class Culture in America.* London: Verso, 1987.

Dent, Gina, and Michele Wallace, eds. *Black Popular Culture.* Seattle: Bay Press, 1992.

Eagleton, Terry. *Saints and Scholars.* London: Verso, 1987.

Gilroy, Paul. *Their Ain't No Black in the Union Jack.* Chicago: University of Chicago Press, 1990.

Grossberg, Lawrence, Cary Nelson, and Paula Treichler, eds. *Cultural Studies.* London: Routledge, 1991.

Hall, Stuart. *Encoding and Decoding in the Television Discourse.* London: The Seminar Press, 1973.

– Cultural Studies: Two Paradigms. *Media, Culture, and Society* 2 (1980): 57–72.

Hall, Stuart, et al., eds. *Culture, Media, Language.* London: Hutchison, 1980.

Hall, Stuart, and Padel Whannel. *The Popular Arts.* London: Beacon Press, 1964.

Hall, Stuart, and Phil Scraton. Law, Class and Control. In *Crime and Society,* ed. M. Fitzgerald, G. McLennan, and J. Pawson, eds. London: RKP, 1981.

Haraway, Donna. *Primate Visions.* London: Routledge, 1989.

Hebdige, Dick. *Subculture: The Meaning of Style.* London: Methuen, 1979.

Kellner, Douglas. *Media Matters: Cultural Studies, Identity and Politics between the Modern and the Postmodern.* London: Routledge, 1995.

McRobbie, Angela, and Mica Nava, eds. *Gender and Generation.* London: Macmillan, 1984.

Morley, David, and Kuan-Hsing Chen, eds. *Stuart Hall: Critical Dialogues in Cultural Studies.* London: Routledge, 1996.

Prendergast, Christopher, ed. *Cultural Materialism: On Raymond Williams.* Minneapolis: University of Minnesota Press, 1995.

Radway, Janice. *Reading the Romance: Women, Patriarchy and Popular Literature.* Chapel Hill: University of North Carolina Press, [1984], 1991.

Reed, T.V. *Fifteen Jugglers, Five Believers: Literary Politics and the Poetics of American Social Movements.* Berkeley: University of California Press, 1992.

Rose, Tricia. *Black Noise: Rap Music and Black Culture in Contemporary America.* Hanover: Wesleyan University Press, 1994.

Storey, John. *An Introduction to Cultural Theory and Popular Culture.* Athens: University of Georgia Press, 1998.

Turner, Graeme. *British Cultural Studies: An Introduction.* London: Unwin-Hyman, 1990.

Williams, Raymond. *Marxism and Literature.* London: New Left Books, 1977.

– *The Sociology of Culture.* New York: Schocken, 1982.

BROADCASTING

[See also: *Cable Television; Communication; Independent Production; Narrowcasting; Radio, Television; Television, History of; Webcasting*]

Broadcasting is the term used to refer to the transmission of a program (radio, television, web-based, and so on) for public use. The first commercially owned radio station to offer broadcasting to the general public after the First World War was built and sponsored by the Westinghouse Electric

Corporation. Known as KDKA, it broadcast mainly variety and entertainment shows. KDKA was followed by a station run by the American Telephone and Telegraph Company (AT&T), which started in 1922. It charged fees in return for airing commercials on its stations. Shortly thereafter a full-fledged radio broadcasting industry crystallized in the United States. Radio broadcasting was at first dominated by adaptations of stage dramas, vaudeville acts, and dramatizations of pulp fiction stories redesigned for the radio medium in the form of action serials, radio dramas, situation comedies, and soap operas. Broadcasting today is divided into commercial (or private) and public domains. The former runs primarily on the basis of advertising revenues, the latter on contributions from viewers, corporations, and government grants. With the advent of the internet and satellite technologies, broadcast systems – and broadcasting generally – continue to evolve.

Background

In 1895 Italian inventor Guglielmo Marconi (1874–1937) transmitted a message electronically that was picked up almost three kilometres away by a device that had not been connected to his transmitting device by means of a wire. Marconi had thus invented the first radiotelegraph (later shortened to radio), so called because its transmitted signals moved radially (outward) in all directions. It came to be known colloquially as the 'wireless.' Early radio broadcasting was dominated by experimenters and hobbyists who built their own transmitters for the purposes of making speeches, reciting something, or playing music (putting a microphone near a gramophone as it played a record on the turntable) to each other. Only with the success of KDKA and AT&T was the groundwork laid for professional radio broadcasting to emerge. In Great Britain, radio owners were charged yearly licence fees, collected by the government, which were passed on to an independent system, the British

Broadcasting Corporation (BBC). The BBC then produced news and entertainment programming for its network of stations – a *network* is an organization of affiliated stations that share common programming (although not exclusively so). Today, networks send signals to the affiliates via communications satellites.

Radio broadcasting reached the peak of its influence during the Second World War, carrying war news live from the battle-front into the homes of listeners. American president Franklin D. Roosevelt also used radio to address the American people with his so-called 'fireside chats.' The success of radio broadcasting spurred technology enterprises to develop a new medium of broadcasting, called television. The earliest patent for an all-electronic television broadcasting system was actually granted in 1927 to American engineer Philo T. Farnsworth (1906–71). By 1930 General Electric, Westinghouse, and the Radio Corporation of America (RCA) combined their efforts, under the research direction of Russian-born American physicist Vladimir Zworykin (1889–1982), to develop the first television cameras (called *iconoscopes*) in order to make television a viable commercial venture. Farnsworth and Zworykin are thus credited as the co-inventors of television. In 1935, the BBC broadcast experimental television programming in London for several hours each day. Then, at the 1939 New York World's Fair, RCA unveiled television to America with live coverage of the opening ceremonies of the fair.

Right after the Second World War four companies made network television broadcasting a practical reality by getting local stations covering different regions to transmit the same signal at the same time. Two of these, the National Broadcasting Company (NBC) and the Columbia Broadcasting System (CBS), had previously been successful in the radio broadcasting field. The other two – the American Broadcasting Company (ABC) and the DuMont Television Network – were new to the broadcasting business (DuMont left the business in

1955). By the mid-1950s, NBC, CBS, and ABC came to be known as the 'Big Three,' successfully appropriating American network television as their exclusive right. Only in the mid-1980s did this monopoly of the airwaves start to change with the emergence of a fourth network, Fox, owned by Rupert Murdoch. At the same time, cable television entered the broadcasting arena, ending channel scarcity once and for all. By the 1990s, and certainly by the early 2000s, broadcasting systems migrated to the world of emerging digital technologies. Today, it is accurate to say that there has been a convergence of all broadcasting systems, known as *digitization*, whereby traditional forms of broadcasting (radio and television) are now either complementing their broadcasts with internet sites or yielding completely over to them. This has led to such new forms of broadcasting as webcasts, podcasts, and the like. The simultaneous use of various broadcasting systems is called *multicasting*. The term *broadcast network* today has gained a larger meaning given that it can refer to over-the-air radio or television broadcasting, cable broadcasting, satellite transmission, or some other form of broadcasting.

Public and Commercial Broadcasting

The first radio stations and networks were the first successful commercial broadcasting systems in the United States, supported exclusively by advertising revenues. In 1967, the Public Broadcasting Act created a source of funding for public (non-commercial) broadcasting systems, resulting in the establishment of the Public Broadcasting Service (PBS) and National Public Radio (NPR) shortly thereafter. These operate on contributions from listeners and viewers, corporations, charity foundations, and funding from the Corporation for Public Broadcasting. Similar systems exist in Britain, Canada, and other countries.

Since its inception, commercial broadcasting has been subject to regulation in most countries at the national level. The regulation of entertainment-based broadcasting started with the Washington Radio Conference of 1922. At the conference, rules pertaining to transmission, frequencies, station identification, and advertising were given legislative form. The Radio Act of 1927 established a government agency to carry out regulation matters, called the Federal Radio Commission (FRC). The Communications Act of 1934 restructured the FRC into the Federal Communications Commission (FCC), which continues to control broadcasting in the United States. The FCC has been altered drastically since the early 1980s, in line with federal policy favouring the deregulation of industries. Lessened regulation has also been brought about by the rise of new technologies, such as the internet and cable television, which reach large audiences and are harder to regulate.

New commercially based broadcast delivery systems have been developed in recent years. Direct Broadcast Satellite (DBS), for example, provides people with a personal antenna capable of bypassing closed-circuit systems to capture satellite signals. Receivers now vary from radio and television devices to mobile devices such as cellphones and iPods. The internet has introduced a new form of broadcasting known, generally, as *webcasting*. Webcasting is used by both 'indie broadcasters' and the traditional radio and TV networks, who typically use it to simulcast some transmission or to allow for further content to be accessed by viewers. Webcasts are also used for business and educational purposes.

Broadcasting and Social Effects

Broadcasting has changed life permanently wherever it has been installed. It has brought the performances of artists, comedians, actors, singers, musicians, and others to large numbers of people who would have had no access to them otherwise. And it created continuity among media that now comes generally under the rubric of *convergence*. This occurs both at the technological level and at the content level. Radio broadcasting, for instance, was shaped by adaptations of previous media. Popular stage dramas were adapted to action serials, situation comedies, and soap operas; vaudeville provided the stars and the artistic material for comedy-variety programming; the daily newspapers were read on the air, leading to the establishment of the 'daily news' as a radio genre. Early television programming genres took over the radio menu of offerings and adapted it to the new visual medium. In the formative years of television, the stars of radio made the jump over to television. Radio and television personalities became national celebrities, and advertised products were as popular, if not more so, than the celebrities. Television became especially powerful as a 'stage' for an ever-expanding mass popular culture. With the spread of documentary news programs, the trend started by *Reader's Digest* of compressing information into digestible morsels had become intrinsic to television. The previous 'reader's digest' world of print had evolved into a 'viewer's digest' culture.

In 1991 British computer scientist Tim Berners-Lee (b. 1955) invented the World Wide Web while working at the European Organization for Nuclear Research (CERN). This simplified access to and utilization of the internet considerably. The introduction of browsers in 1993 further simplified usage, bringing about the current 'internet galaxy,' and thus leading to a convergence of all broadcasting systems into one digital 'meta-system.' The telephone was the first medium to be digitized in 1962. The digitization of print media started in 1967. Today, most major print media (newspapers and magazines) are available in online versions. The Direct Broadcast Satellite industry started producing digital programming for home satellite dishes in 1995. High-definition television (HDTV) became commercially available in 1998. Digital audio broadcasting (DAB) is radio broadcasting's version of television's DBS system, becoming popular with stations such as XM and Sirius. Compression technologies, known as MP3, are further enhancing the digitization process.

At present, there is a considerable spread of the webcasting mode of broadcasting, given its flexibility. Webcasts have no fixed schedules, and they can be downloaded for later playback. Traditional radio and television broadcasting systems now stream their programs in real time so that these can be viewed over the Web. Some news organizations use the Web to post additional stories, constantly updating the news, or offering extended versions of them.

The main lesson to be learned from studying the history of broadcasting is that there is no 'turning back the clock.' Once a new broadcasting system is introduced that reaches broader audiences and is cheap, it will guide the future course of how people come to access and understand media products. As McLuhan so aptly put it in 1964, each new broadcasting medium shapes the nature of the message it is designed to deliver: 'The medium is the message. This is merely to say that the personal and social consequences of any medium – that is, of any extension of ourselves – result from the new scale that is introduced into our affairs by each extension of ourselves, or by any new technology' (23). Remarkably, however, this has not meant the elimination of previous systems and forms of broadcasting, but rather a convergence. For example, the market for print materials such as novels and newspapers continues to be strong, although online versions are generally available. The term *convergence* was introduced into broadcasting and media studies in the mid-1990s by Nicholas Negroponte (b. 1943), who used it to characterize the digitization process. The term is now used to refer to the more general phenomenon of the blending of media, technology, and cultural forms.

Marcel Danesi

Bibliography

Abercrombie, Nicholas. *Television and Society.* Cambridge: Polity Press. 1996.

Bernard, Stephen. *Studying Radio.* London: Arnold, 2000.

Briggs, Asa, and Peter Burke. *A Social History of the Media*. London: Polity, 2002.

Briggs, Anthony, and Paul Cobley, eds. *The Media: An Introduction*. Essex: Addison Wesley Longman, 1998.

Campbell, Richard, Chris R. Martin, and Bettina Fabos. *Media and Culture: An Introduction to Mass Communication*. Boston: Bedford/St Martin's, 2005.

Carey, John W. *Communication as Culture: Essays on Media and Society*. Boston: Unwin Hyman, 1989.

Danesi, Marcel. *Understanding Media Semiotics*. London: Arnold, 2002.

Dizard, Wilson. *Old Media, New Media*. New York: Longman, 1997.

Fiske, John. *Television Culture*. London: Methuen, 1987.

McLuhan, Marshall. *Understanding Media*. London: Routledge and Kegan Paul, 1964.

Miller, Mark C. *Boxed In: The Culture of TV*. Evanston, IL: Northwestern University Press, 1988.

BULL'S-EYE MODEL

[See also: *Communication; Communication Theory; Shannon, Claude E.*]

The term *bull's-eye model* comes from the field of telephonic communications. It is one of the earliest communication models adapted by culture theorists, who took it from the technical work of the late engineer Claude Shannon (1916–2001). Shannon had devised it in the late 1940s as part of a mathematical framework intended to improve the efficiency of telecommunication systems. It came to be known as the 'bull's-eye model' because it portrayed the main components of such systems as if they were in a bull's-eye target range. Shannon also described in precise mathematical terms how these components functioned in the transmission and reception of information. In bare outline form, the model consists of a *sender* aiming a *message* at a *receiver* as if in a target range (see Figure 1).

Four additional components complete the overall model: channel, noise, redundancy, and feedback. The *channel* is the physical medium carrying the transmitted signals. For language, the channel can be the air (vocal speech), paper (writing), the hands (gesture), some electronic channel (for example, through the radio), among other channels. *Noise* is any interfering factor (physical or psychological) in the channel that distorts or impedes the reception of the message in some way. In radio and telephone transmissions, it is equivalent to electronic static; in face-to-face verbal interaction, the concept of noise can vary from an exterior sound (physical noise) to lapses of memory (psychological noise). Communication systems also have *redundancy* features built into them that allow for messages to be understood, or recovered, even if noise is present. The high predictability of certain words in some utterances ('Hi, how are …') and the patterned repetition of elements ('Yes, yes, I'll do it; yes, I will') are redundant features of conversation that greatly enhance successful information transfer. Finally, *feedback* refers to the fact that senders have the capacity to monitor the very messages they construct and send, modifying them according to the situation. Feedback includes, for instance, the physical reactions observable in receivers (facial expressions, bodily movements, etc.), which reveal how a message is being received.

The bull's-eye model provides a minimal technical language and theoretical framework for describing communication and its relation to human interaction and cultural behaviour. As such it continues to have widespread utility within both media and popular culture studies. The application of this model to the study of media culture can probably be traced back to 1954, when the American communication theorist Wilbur Schramm (1907–87) used it in this way, adding two other components to the original model: the *encoder*, the component (human or electronic) which converts a message into a form that can be transmitted through an appropriate channel, and the *decoder*, which reverses the encoding process so that the message can be received successfully. It has come to be called the *sender*

Figure 1

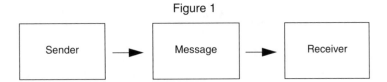

(or *source*)-*message-channel-receiver* model,
or SMCR for short. The SMCR continues
to be used because of its plainness and applicability to all types of mass communications systems.

A further elaboration of the SMCR was
put forward by George Gerbner (1919–
2005) in 1956. Encoding and decoding, according to Gerbner, involve knowledge of
all the relevant *codes* used in constructing
the message, including social codes such as
those that exist to define gender relations
in, say, a sitcom, or the features that make
an adventure hero superhuman. The code
is the 'message-constructing' system that is
subject to noise and other factors in the act
of communication.

The bull's-eye model has often been
critiqued for not taking into account meaning in the flow of information that occurs
between senders and receivers. But without
it, such discussions would probably never
have been contemplated in the first place.
Moreover, the advent of this model, springing from the work of Claude E. Shannon,
instantaneously founded the field of information studies, which has reshaped various
fields, from biology to economics to media
studies. Although it does not tell us anything about how information leads to belief
and knowledge systems, it still provides a
useful framework for understanding how
it occurs in a physical sense. Without this
framework, debates about the relevance
and meaning of information would be spu-
rious at best and solipsistic at worst.

Marcel Danesi

Bibliography

Baran, Stanley B. *Introduction to Mass Communication, Media Literacy, and Culture.* New York:
McGraw-Hill, 2004.

Berger, Arthur Asa. *Media and Communication
Research Methods.* London: Sage, 2000.
– *50 Ways to Understand Communication.* Lan-
ham: Rowman and Littlefield, 2006.
McQuail, Denis. *Mass Communication Theory: An
Introduction.* London: Sage, 2000.
Shannon, Claude E., and Warren Weaver. *The
Mathematical Theory of Communication.* Urbana:
The University of Illinois Press, 1949.

C

CABLE TELEVISION

[See also: *Broadcasting; Narrowcasting; Television; Television, History of*]

Cable television is television transmitted through coaxial cables. These consist of an inner conductor, an insulating layer, a metallic shield (the outer conductor), and a plastic jacket (the outer insulator). In an ideal coaxial cable, the signal (internal electromagnetic fields) exists between the inner and the outer conductor. The outer insulator prevents interference from external electromagnetic fields. The inner insulator is often made of polyethylene or teflon, while the outer insulator is often made of PVC (polyvinyl chloride). Coaxial cables allow for bidirectional communication, and since the television signal uses only a fraction of the bandwidth of the cables, cable television is now often coupled with broadband internet and telephony. This combination is called triple play. Cable television has two advantages over the traditional (antenna) forms of television: it came forward en masse in the 1980s to provide better reception and a greater variety of programming.

Cable television originated in 1948 in North America in order to make it possible to broadcast television signals to locations that either could not receive them through the airwaves or could only receive them but with significant interference. Cable and satellite television are now the two most common systems, arriving late in some areas of the world. In Indonesia, for example, cable television was not available until 1995. In Europe about 30 per cent of television households now have cable television; but in Macedonia, this number is much higher (67 per cent of all households). These numbers are, however, increasing daily. Today cable systems carry hundreds of channels, specializing in news, movies, comedy, science, music, sports, history, health, religion, weather, and so on. Certain channels charge a fee that a customer pays in addition to the monthly fee for basic cable service. Most cable services offer one or more channels that make movies or special events available on a pay-per-view basis.

Cable television gave birth to the concept of narrowcasting, or specialized broadcasting. In the past television was a unifier of audiences; cable television has instead become a separator or fragmentor of audiences. Here's what a perceptive internet blogger wrote about this:

> A group of coworkers was sitting in our company's break room. Someone walked in and mentioned that he had just gotten cable TV. 35 channels! Better reception! We all oohed and ahed. Then the discussion returned to the latest developments on *Dallas*, *The Cosby Show*, or *Star Search*. Our cable TV guy did not participate. He had watched channels none of us had even heard of. Within a few years, we all had at least basic cable with about 60 channels. The break room

discussions were more narrow. Few people watched the same shows. Those that did share that experience tended to cluster near one another for their essentially private talks. The encroaching isolation and lack of common interest was very evident. (http://bitteranalysis. blogspot.com/2008/09/how-chubby-checker-and-cable-tv_26.html [26 September 2008])

The internet has further fostered fragmentation, but whether this is a gain or a loss for society remains a matter of dispute. Narrowcasting provides programs that appeal to particular people according to age, racial background, interest group, and so forth. Cable has thus permanently changed the way people view television, heralding the evolution from broadcasting to narrowcasting.

Anders Søgaard

Bibliography

Fiske, John. *Television Culture*. London: Methuen, 1987.
Holland, Patricia. *The Television Handbook*. London: Routledge, 2000.
McQueen, David. *Television: A Media Student's Guide*. London: Arnold, 1998.
Newcomb, Horace. *Television: The Critical View*. New York: Oxford University Press, 2000.

CARTOONS, ANIMATED

[See also: *Cartoons, History of*]

Cartoons are texts based on drawing, usually depicting a humorous situation and often accompanied by a caption. The main types of cartoons are *editorial cartoons*, which provide commentary, usually satirical, on events or personages; *gag cartoons*, which make fun of groups in magazines and on greeting cards; *illustrative cartoons*, which are used with advertising or learning materials to reinforce certain points or special aspects of something; and *animated cartoons*, which are used to tell stories.

The earliest attempt made at mass communication came via cartoons. As long ago as 40,000 BCE, prehistoric humans were painting figures of animals on the walls of caves; while the reason for such paintings remains unknown, it is difficult to ignore the ancient symbolic power of cartoons. In the middle part of the nineteenth century, the political cartoons of Thomas Nast were powerful enough to undo the political machinery of New York political kingmaker Boss Tweed and encouraged northerners to support and enlist for the Union during the Civil War (Vinson 1957); in the late nineteenth century the comic strip *Yellow Kid* helped to shape the news media (Harrison 1981). Cartoons can be in print form or animated. Some of the most famous and notorious animated cartoons are adult-themed prime-time television shows (e.g., *South Park*, *The Simpsons*, *Family Guy*) or for adult viewing only (*Fritz the Cat*, Japanese hentai).

Similar to the technology used to fool the eye in motion pictures, animation uses a series of still pictures, though slightly different, to impose the sensation of screen movement in viewers. The difference with animation is that instead of stringing together a sequence of photographs to impart the effect, hand-drawn images, stop motion, or computer graphics are used (Harrison 1981). The first attempts to use hand-drawn images to simulate movement go back to the shadow theatre of China and the work of the German Renaissance scholar Athanasius Kircher in the seventeenth century. His 'magic lantern' and its ability to mimic movement was originally thought to be the work of witchcraft; fortunately, cooler heads prevailed and his device was accepted as a tool to entertain and educate (Solomon 1989). The French cartoonist Emile Cohl is recognized as the original animator with his work *Fantasmagorie* (1908), which was the first attempt to utilize systematic drawings to simulate movement (Crafton 1982). However, the first filmmaker to popularize the medium was Winsor McKay, whose *Gertie the Dinosaur* (1914) was an enormous success and produced a favourable result whereby others could profitably produce cartoons (Harrison 1981; Solomon 1989).

These pioneers paved the way for the animated media we see today. From Walt Disney's cinematic classic *Snow White* to the choppy Saturday morning cereal cartoons featuring Cap'n Crunch, child-themed animation has become a media institution. It is difficult to separate what childhood means in American culture without considering the part cartoons have played in defining it. Cartoons and their respective characters entertain children, and more importantly appear to sell to them.

Cartoons as Entertainment

Since the middle part of the 1960s, children's entertainment has become virtually synonymous with the animated cartoon (Mittel 2003). Whether it is on Saturday morning television, after school weekday television, Nickelodeon, the Cartoon Network, the Disney Channel, or at the local Cineplex, the preponderance of entertainment offerings for children are animated. In terms of television exposure, children up to twelve years of age are much more likely to view cartoon programming than any other type of programming (Wright et al. 2002). What is the impact, then, of exposure to cartoons? How does the consumption of this media genre influence children?

Concern with the content of children's television goes back to the early days, if not inception, of the medium (Kunkel and Wilcox 2001). In 1954, the U.S. Congress held hearings on the influence of television related to violence, and attempts were made to regulate the industry, but to no avail. Cartoons became the specific focus of the parent advocacy groups in the late 1960s because of their hypothesized ability to produce stereotypes and their apparent glorification of violent and anti-social behaviour (Kunkel 1991); and media research-

ers are continuing to investigate these outcomes to the present day.

In reviews of content, the evidence indicates that cartoons depict a great deal of violence (Williams et al. 1982; Calvert 1999; Potter 1999). Gerbner, Morgan, and Signorielli (1993) found that the violence in cartoons was five times greater than the amount found on prime-time television. Cartoon violence is especially vexing because the violence is not shown with any sense of realism. In cartoons, the characters are able to hit each other with shovels, drop anvils on their enemies, and electrocute themselves with few or no repercussions. Parents and researchers have always been fearful that children would emulate this behaviour or learn that violence had no real consequences.

Research on outcomes of exposure related to violent cartoons has been extensive, and the empirical evidence tends to indicate that a child's exposure to violent content may lead to some real-life aggression and violence. Paik and Comstock's wide-ranging meta-analysis (1994), for instance, found that there was a modest relationship between television violence and real-life violent behaviour over a number of studies, even though the correlation found was similar, if not larger, than the relationship between smoking and lung cancer. The effect of exposure to television violence has profound long-term implications as well. Heusmann et al.'s (2003) longitudinal study of exposure to violent content found that increased exposure was related to real-life violent and aggressive behaviour, even when controlling for socio-economic status, intellectual ability, and parenting.

Animated entertainment, and children's entertainment in general, has also affected the way children view the world via stereotypes. Content analyses examining the portrayals of female and minority characters have consistently shown an under-representation of these groups, in addition to skewed portrayals (Greenberg and Brand 1993; Aubrey and Harrison 2004). The portrayal of female characters suggests, by and large, that they are passive and interested in domestic affairs, while minority groups are portrayed as marginal and largely unimportant. By showing the world in a certain way, the theorized effect is that these inaccurate portrayals of the 'real' world then contribute to the child's perception of the world. This situation has been changing, as cartoons increasingly come to reflect shifts in social models. Contemporary cartoons show women as being just as violent as men. Still, there seems to be a double standard in all this. For example, the research conducted by Thompson and Zerbinos (1997) found that children perceived male characters as violent and active while they perceived female characters as domestic, interested in boys, and concerned with appearances. In addition, the more the children noticed the portrayals the more likely they were to hold traditional expectations for careers for both themselves and others. In the racial stereotyping research, Graves's (1999) review of effects revealed that racial and ethnic portrayals on television consistently affect children.

Cartoons as Salesperson

Animated characters and cartoons have also played a prominent role in marketing to children (Van Auken and Lonial 1985; Gunter et al. 2002). One way this is done is through the use of brand characters (Tony the Tiger, Charlie the Tuna, and the like) or through advertising on animated television series. The use of brand (cartoon) characters is a well-established practice in advertising, going back to early television (Kirkpatrick 1952). At one level, they are the face of a brand, giving it a visual cartoon form. At another level, though, they generate product awareness, contribute to brand image, and act as perpetual promotional tools (Phillips 1996). In the early 1990s there was a protracted debate regarding the character 'Joe Camel' (Henke 1995); critics of the tobacco industry claimed that the Camel's brand was using the cartoon character to entice children to smoke. Research by vari-

ous scholars indicated that children were able to recognize the character; however, the direct impact on attitudes related to smoking is undetermined (Fischer et al. 1991; Henke 1995; Arnett and Terhanian 1998; Pierce et al. 1999).

In some instances, cartoon characters become well-defined elements of popular culture and take on a life of their own (Kirkpatrick 1952). In the documentary *Super Size Me* (Spurlock 2003), the director showed schoolchildren pictures of a cartoon Ronald McDonald and President George W. Bush. The children appeared to have no problem recognizing the former figure, but were unable to identify the latter. While this is an anecdotal example, there is empirical evidence suggesting what types of qualities children respond to in a brand character. Children like characters they can relate to, seek to be like, or model (Guber and Berry 1993). Brand characters also provide a consistent identifier for children (Diamond 1977), who may become confused between different elements of a brand or have undeveloped literacy skills (Acuff and Reiher 1997). Brand characters help to make that connection for them (Henke 1995; Mizerski 1995).

The number of studies looking at brand characters and their effects on children are limited, though more have surfaced in recent years (Mizerski 1995; Henke 1995; Lapierre et al. forthcoming; Neeley and Schumann 2004). Yet even with this surge, the academic community is undecided about their effects. Neeley and Schumann (2004) conducted two studies which concluded that there were uncertain links between a brand character and a child's preference, intention, and choice of products. On the other hand, Mizerski (1995) found that character recognition (of age-appropriate products) had a direct effect on the preference of a product. In addition, Lapierre et al. (forthcoming) found that the more children liked a specific brand character, the more likely they were to ask for the associated product and engage in conflict with parents when their requests were denied.

Historically, another popular way to sell to children via cartoon characters is through host selling. Host selling is the practice of showing ads for products that use the same characters, which are featured in an adjoining television program (Kunkel et al. 2004). This type of programming can be effective, since children are unlikely to differentiate between the product and the show (Atkin 1975; Kunkel 1988). In a similar vein, advertisers have used popular toys as characters within programs. Many popular cartoon programs have been, in essence, half-hour-long commercials for the product (for example, *G.I. Joe*, *The Transformers*, and *My Little Pony*) in which the toy was created in tandem with the cartoon program (Greenfield et al. 1990). In the mid-1970s governments regulated such practices, yet due to the steady deregulation of the television and advertising industries, these practices have re-emerged (Kunkel et al. 2004).

Cartoons as Educators

As mention previously, television has often been perceived as a medium that acts in opposition to the educational process. Media scholar Neil Postman hypothesized in his book *The Disappearance of Childhood* (1982) that television was a major threat to educational development because of the passivity it engendered in people. Others have put forth the idea that television would affect learning via displacement from intellectual pursuits (Singer and Singer 1990). Because of these concerns, television broadcasters in the United States are mandated as part of their broadcasting licence to show educational and informational children's television programs as part of The Children's Television Act of 1990 (Calvert and Kotler 2003). However, due to controversy regarding compliance with the law, broadcasters make the claim that programs are ersatz educators. *The Flintstones*, it is claimed, provided children with a history lesson (Kunkel and Canepa 1994). Despite this defence, lawmakers strengthened the statute in 1996.

Animated cartoons have played an integral role in educating children (although live-action and puppet shows, such as *Sesame Street* and *Mr Rogers' Neighborhood*, are the relative stars in the field). Yet cartoons have been used to teach all manner of academic skills: problem solving (*Blue's Clues*), language development (*Dora the Explorer*), mathematics (*Cyberchase*), science and technology (*Cro*), and civics (*School House Rock*). One particular focus of educational television has been on the pre-social behaviours of children, with shows like *Hey Arnold!*, *Doug*, and *Winnie the Pooh* providing lessons to children on appropriate relations with peers and adults (Jordan et al. 2001). Research on outcomes has shown that cartoons, designed with the intention of providing a quality educational experience, can have all kinds of effects on children that are profound and long-lasting (Fisch 1998; Anderson et al. 2001).

Matthew Lapierre

Bibliography

Acuff, Dan S., and Robert H. Reiher. *What Kids Buy and Why: The Psychology of Marketing to Kids*. New York: Free Press, 1997.

Anderson, Daniel R., Aletha C. Huston, and Kelly L. Schmitt, eds. Early Childhood Television Viewing and Adolescent Behavior: The Recontact Study. *Monographs of the Society for Research in Child Development* 264 (2001): complete volume 4.

Arnetta, Jeffrey J., and George Terhanian. Adolescents' Responses to Cigarette Advertisements: Links between Exposure, Liking, and the Appeal of Smoking. *Tobacco Control* 7 (1998): 129–33.

Atkin, Charles K. *Effects of Television Advertising on Children: Survey of Children's and Mothers' Responses to Television Programs* (Report No. 8). East Lansing: Michigan State University, Department of Communication, 1975.

Aubrey, Jennifer S., and Kristen Harrison. The Gender-Role Content of Children's Favorite Television Programs and Its Links to Their

Gender-Related Perceptions. *Media Psychology* 6 (2004): 111–46.

Calvert, Sandra L. *Children's Journeys through the Information Age*. New York: McGraw-Hill, 1999.

Calvert, Sandra L., and Jennifer A. Cotler. Lessons from Children's Television: The Impact of the Children's Television Act on Children's Learning. *Applied Developmental Psychology* 24 (2003): 275–335.

Crafton, Donald. *Before Mickey: The Animated Film 1898–1928*. Cambridge, MA: MIT Press, 1982.

Diamond, Steven Leonard. The Development of Brand-Related Attitudes, Skills, and Knowledge in Children. PhD diss., Harvard University, 1977.

Fisch, Shalom M. The Children's Television Workshop: The Experiment Continues. In *A Communications Cornucopia: The Markle Foundation Essays on Information Policy*, ed. Monroe Edwin Price and Roger G. Noll, 297–336. Washington, DC: Brookings Institution, 1998.

Fischer, Paul M., Meyer P. Schwartz, and John W. Richards, Jr. Brand Logo Recognition by Children Aged Three to Six Years: Mickey Mouse and Old Joe Camel. *Journal of the American Medical Association* 266 (1991): 3145–8.

Gerbner, George, Michael Morgan, and Nancy Signorielli. Television Violence Profile No. 16: The Turning Point from Research to Action. Unpublished manuscript, Annenberg School for Communications, University of Pennsylvania, Philadelphia, 1993.

Graves, Sherryl B. Television and Prejudice Reduction: When Does Television as a Vicarious Experience Make a Difference? *Journal of Social Issues* 55 (1999): 707–27.

Greenberg, Bradley S., and Jeffrey E. Brand. Cultural Diversity on Saturday Morning Television. In *Children and Television: Images in a Changing Sociocultural World*, ed. Gordon L. Berry and Joy Keiko, 132–42. Thousand Oaks, CA: Sage, 1993.

Greenfield, Paticia M., Emily Yut, and Mabel Chung, eds. The Program-Length Commercial: A Study of the Effects of Television/Toy Tie-ins on Imaginative Play. *Psychology and Marketing* 7 (1990): 237–55.

Guber, Selinia, and Jon Berry. *Marketing To and Through Kids*. New York: McGraw Hill, 1993.

Gunter, Barrie, Bahman Baluch, and Linda J. Duffy. Children's Memory for Television Advertising: Effects of Programme-Advertisement Congruency. *Applied Cognitive Psychology* 16 (2002): 171–90.

Harrison, Randall. *The Cartoon: Communication to the Quick*. Beverly Hills: Sage, 1981.

Henke, Lucy L. Young Children's Perceptions of Cigarette Brand Advertising Symbols: Awareness, Affect, and Target Market Identification. *Journal of Advertising* 24 (1995): 13–28.

Huesmann, L. Rowell, Jessica Moise-Titus, and Cheryl-Lynn Podolski. Longitudinal Relations between Children's Exposure to TV Violence and Their Aggressive and Violent Behavior in Young Adulthood: 1977–1992. *Developmental Psychology* 39 (2003): 201–21.

Jordan, Amy B., Kelly L. Schmitt, and Emory H. Woodward, IV. Developmental Implications of Commercial Broadcasters' Educational Offerings. *Applied Developmental Psychology* 22 (2001): 87–101.

Kirkpatrick, C.A. Trade Characters in Promotion Programs. *Journal of Marketing* 17 (1952): 366–72.

Kunkel, Dale. Children and Host-selling Television Commercials. *Communication Research* 15 (1988): 71–92.

– Crafting Media Policy: The Genesis and Implications of the Children's Television Act of 1990. *American Behavioral Scientist* 35, no. 2 (1991): 181–202.

Kunkel, Dale, and Julie Canepa. Broadcasters' License Renewal Claims Regarding Children's Educational Programming. *Journal of Broadcasting and Electronic Media* 38 (1994): 397–416.

Kunkel, Dale, and Brian Wilcox. Children and Media Policy In *Handbook of Children and the Media*, ed. Dorothy G. Singer and Jerome L. Singer, 589–604. Thousand Oaks, CA: Sage, 2001.

Kunkel, Dale, Brian Wilcox, and Joanne Cantor eds. *Report of the APA Task Force on Advertising and Children*. American Psychological Association, 2004.

Lapierre, Matthew A., Leslie B. Snyder, and Nicole M. D'Alessandro. *Children and Trade Characters: Recall, Liking and Behavioral Outcomes*. Forthcoming.

Mittell, Jason. The Great Saturday Morning Exile: Scheduling Cartoons on Television's Periphery in the 1960s. In *Prime Time Animation: Television Animation and American Culture*, ed. Carol A. Stabile and Mark Harrison, 33–54. New York: Routledge, 2003.

Mizerski, Richard. The Relationship between Cartoon Trade Character Recognition and Attitude Toward Product Category in Young Children. *Journal of Marketing* 59 (October 1995): 58–70.

Neeley, Sabrina M., and David W. Schumann. Using Animated Spokes-Characters in Advertising to Young Children: Does Increasing Attention to Advertising Necessarily Lead to Product Preference? *Journal of Advertising* 33 (2004): 7–223.

Paik, Haejung, and George Comstock. The Effects of Television Violence on Antisocial Behavior: A Meta-analysis. *Communication Research* 21 (1994): 516–46.

Phillips, Barbara J. Defining Trade Characters and Their Role in American Pop Culture. *Journal of Popular Culture* 29 (1996): 143–58.

Pierce, John P., Elizabeth A. Gilpin, and Won S. Choi. Sharing the Blame: Smoking Experimentation and Future Smoking-Attributable Mortality Due to Joe Camel and Marlboro Advertising and Promotions. *Tobacco Control* 8 (1999): 37–44.

Postman, Neil. *The Disappearance of Childhood*. New York: Dell, 1982.

Potter, W. James. *On Media Violence*. Thousand Oaks, CA: Sage, 1999.

Singer, Dorothy G., and Jerome L. Singer. *The House of Make-Believe: Children's Play and the Developing Imagination*. Cambridge, MA: Harvard University Press, 1990.

Solomon, Charles. *Enchanted Drawings: The History of Animation*. New York: Knopf, 1989.

Spurlock, Morgan, producer/director. *Super Size Me* [Motion picture]. United States: Samuel Goldwyn Films, 2003.

Stabile, Carol A., and Mark Harrison. Prime Time Animation: An Overview. In *Prime Time Animation: Television Animation and American Culture*, ed. Carol A. Stabile and Mark Harrison, 1–11. New York: Routledge. 2003.

Van Auken, Stuart, and Subhash C. Lonial. Children's Perceptions of Characters: Human Versus Animate, Assessing Implications for Children's Advertising. *Journal of Advertising* 14 (1985): 13–22.

Vinson, J. Chal. Thomas Nast and the American Political Scene. *American Quarterly* 9, no. 3 (Autumn, 1957): 337–44.

Thompson, Teresa L., and Eugenia Zerbinos. Television Cartoons: Do Children Notice It's a Boy's World? *Sex Roles* 39 (1997): 415–32.

Williams, Tannis M., Merle L. Zabrack, and Lesley A. Joy. The Portrayal of Aggression on North American Television. *Journal of Applied Social Psychology* 12 (1982): 360–80.

Wright, John C., Aletha C. Huston, and Kimberlee C. Murphy. The Relations of Early Television Viewing to School Readiness and Vocabulary of Children from Low-Income Families: The Early Window Project. *Child Development* 72 (5 September 1995): 1347–66.

Wright, John C., Aletha C. Huston, and Elizabeth A. Vandewater, eds. American Children's Use of Electronic Media in 1997: A National Survey. In *Children in the Digital Age: Influences of Electronic Media on Development*, ed. Sandra L. Calvert, Amy B. Jordan, and Rodney R. Cocking, 35–54. Westport, CT: Praeger, 2002.

CARTOONS, HISTORY OF

[See also: *Cartoons, Animated; Comics; Comics, History of*]

Although people have been drawing pictures since prehistoric times, the origin of the modern cartoon can probably be traced to sixteenth-century German *broadsheets*, which were single pictures printed on large pieces of paper and used for mainly political purposes to sway people's opinions. The actual term *cartoon,* however, was first used by *Punch* magazine in 1843 to refer to the satirical drawings it published in its pages; the term comes from the Italian word *cartone* ('heavy paper' or 'carton'). Its meaning was extended in the twentieth century to describe the art of animated films. The latter are often called simply cartoons. Many pop culture figures were born as cartoon characters – Bugs Bunny, Woody Woodpecker, Tom and Jerry, Mickey

Mouse, among many others. Comic-strip art (including comic books) is really an extension of the cartoon concept. The Peanuts strip, by the late Charles Schulz, is in fact defined as either a comic strip or a cartoon.

Some of the sketches and drawings by Leonardo da Vinci are cartoon prototypes. But their intent was different from that of the modern cartoon, whose main intention is to satirize or provide some form of humour in a (usually) derisive way, although the cartoon concept has been extended to encompass other themes, topics, and styles.

The cartoon is an evolutionary derivative of caricature art – a drawing style that exaggerates or distorts the physical features of an individual or an object. The main intent of caricatures is to poke fun at certain subjects, from famous people to groups such as politicians, lawyers, or academics. The first caricatures surfaced in Europe in the 1500s. They attacked some aspect of Protestantism or Roman Catholicism during the Reformation. Caricature art blossomed during the 1700s and 1800s in Britain. William Hogarth's work, for instance, satirized different classes of English society. But perhaps the most famous caricaturist of the era was the Frenchman Honoré Daumier. His caricature of the obese King Louis Philippe as a giant pear has become a classic in the genre. As a result, Philippe had Daumier imprisoned. After his release, Daumier drew caricatures of the emerging middle class in France, satirizing bourgeois fashions, manners, language, and the like. In the United States, most caricatures have appeared as political cartoons in newspapers. Thomas Nast, for example, gained fame for caricatures published from 1869 to 1872 that attacked political corruption in New York City. Caricature art continues to this day. Leading American caricaturists include Patrick Oliphant and David Levine.

There are three main types of cartoons: *editorial cartoons*, which provide visual commentary, usually of a satirical nature, on current events in newspapers, magazines, and on websites; *gag cartoons*, which poke fun at groups rather than individuals and are typically found in magazines and on greeting cards; and *illustrative cartoons*, which are used with advertising or learning materials to illustrate important points or highlight special aspects of a product or educational topic.

The editorial cartoon was born in the eighteenth century, when the English painter and engraver William Hogarth launched the idea of using caricatures in a new satirical way. After *Punch* put out the first one, editorial cartoons began appearing regularly in British and U.S. magazines to lobby for causes. Thomas Nast became famous because of his use of cartoons to support political causes. His best-known works were the cartoons he drew about the American Civil War in *Harper's Weekly*, in which he severely criticized the concept and practice of slavery. Nast also introduced the elephant as the symbol of the Republican Party and the donkey as the symbol of the Democrats. By the late 1800s, editorial cartoons became regular features in daily newspapers, achieving in picture form what editorials realized with words. Most appeared as single panels (sometimes with captions) on editorial pages.

Like editorial cartoons, humorous gag cartoons have been around since the mid-1800s, remaining popular in newspapers, magazines and, today, on websites. They are also created as single panels and are often accompanied by a caption or by a bubble containing the words spoken by a character in the panel. In *The New Yorker* magazine, cartoonists such as James Thurber turned the gag cartoon into a powerful weapon of social commentary; others, such as Saul Steinberg, treated cartooning as an art form.

Illustrative cartoons were first used as supportive book illustrations for adult audiences, found generally in collections of jokes or humorous texts. They quickly migrated to instructional manuals and children's books. Advertising also makes frequent use of the cartoon to clarify and reinforce the sales pitch. Many companies even use cartoon characters as product logos (Mr Clean, Tony the Tiger, Michelin Man, Charlie the Tuna, and so forth).

Comic strips are not, strictly speaking, cartoons. They are narrative texts mixing verbal and pictorial elements. One of the first American works with the features of a comic strip was created by Richard Felton Outcault. Known as *Yellow Kid*, it was published on 5 May 1895 in the *New York Sunday World*. It depicted squalid city tenements and backyards filled with roaming pets, tough-looking men, urchins, and ragamuffins. One urchin was a flap-eared, bald-headed child, who always seemed to bear a quizzical, yet shrewd, smile. He was dressed in a long, dirty nightshirt, on which Outcault placed comments. Other early comic strips were the *Little Bears* by James Guilford Swinnerton, which appeared in the *San Francisco Examiner* in 1892, *The Katzenjammer Kids* by Rudolph Dirks, appearing in *The American Humorist* in 1897, and *Mutt and Jeff*, which appeared as *Mr A. Mutt* in a November 1907 issue of the *San Francisco Chronicle*.

Comic books are book-length narratives based on comic strips. These were first produced in 1933, when advertisers reprinted comic strips in magazine form to give away with certain merchandise. Comic books with original stories emerged a little later. *Superman*, first published in 1938, is the most famous early comic book. In the 1960s, the radical counterculture of the period spawned a genre known as *underground comics* (or *comix*), which aimed to explore forbidden subjects (drugs, sexual freedom, and radical politics) in comic-book ways.

The history of cartoons overlaps considerably with that of comics. Like other print materials, cartoons have found the cyberspace medium a perfect locus in which to thrive and evolve. Online e-toons now have substantial global audiences. Not only are traditional newspaper cartoons making their way to online venues, but a new cadre of online cartoonists is creating a new digital cartoon culture with its own style and audiences. In many ways, however, this new platform for the cartoon has revived its original parodic and satiric functions. For example, in the early 2000s, the e-toons called *Gary the Rat* (www.mediatrip.com) caricaturized a callous New York lawyer who morphs into huge rat, in obvious parody of Franz Kafka's *Metamorphosis*. The parodic function of cartoons, which had become somewhat diffuse in the print medium, seems to have reacquired its force online. *Queer Duck* (www.icebox.com) satirizes the ever-burgeoning profession of self-help psychology, the *God and Devil Show* (www.entertaindom.com) fake evangelism, *The Critic* (www.shockwave.com), celebrity culture, the *Star Wars Network* (www.atomfilms.com), the subculture spawned by the original 1970s movie series, and so on. Clearly, online cartoons have restored the medium's caricaturizing function.

E-toons, however, come and go much more quickly than printed cartoons. Online culture is adaptive, constantly changing with the times, making it more and more difficult to establish historical lineages and evolutionary tendencies, especially within specific media.

Marcel Danesi

Bibliography

Berger, Arthur Asa. *The Comic-Stripped American: What Dick Tracy, Blondie, Daddy Warbucks and Charlie Brown Tell Us about Ourselves*. New York: Walker and Company, 1978.

Couperie, Pierre, and Maurice C. Horn. *A History of the Comic Strip*. New York: Crown, 1968.

Gonick, Larry. *The Cartoon History of the Universe*. New York: Quill, 1982.

Weiss, Harvey. *Cartoons and Cartooning*. Boston: Houghton, 1990.

CASSIRER, ERNST (1874–1945)

[See also: *Language*]

Ernst Cassirer was one of the major philosophers of the twentieth century, whose work on the relation between language and myth remains central to this day in several fields, including linguistics, mythology, and media studies. He studied philosophy and literature at the University of Berlin, and he taught for many years at the Friedrich Wilhelm University in Berlin. He was elected chair of philosophy at the University of Hamburg until 1933, when, as a German Jew, he had to escape from Nazi Germany. After leaving Germany, he took the position of lecturer at Oxford University from 1933 to 1935, then of professor at Gothenburg University from 1935 to 1941, visiting professor at Yale from 1941 to 1943, and professor at Columbia University from 1943 until his death.

Many aspects of Cassirer's writing fall into the domain of the philosophy of language. For example, he developed the notion of the existence in the human psyche of an 'unconscious grammar' of experience whose canons are not those of logical (syntactic) thought, but of an archaic mythic-imaginative-experiential mode of cognition that still has power over the way we think. Contrary to generative linguistics, which claims that there is a 'deep structure' to language consisting of a small rudimentary and universal set of sentence-making rules, Cassirer's unconscious grammar consists of mental schemas or forms of the world fashioned from experiencing that world which, over time, are expressed as words, phrases, and larger syntactic structures, starting with mythic narratives, all of which mirror the structure of the forms and thus of the unconscious grammar.

He is also well known for defining humans as 'symbolic animals,' that is, as a species that relies not primarily on its instincts for conducting its life schemes, but on symbolism, which allows humans to reflect upon the world, record history and also guide human destiny. He referred to his own philosophy as the philosophy of symbolic forms (Cassirer 1998), its goal being to study how symbolism manifested itself as a guiding force in shaping human life and its psychic evolution.

Especially significant is Cassirer's idea that language structure and myth share a common ground and, thus, origin. The first nouns referred to animals, human beings, plants, and other natural phenomena that in the myths stood as symbols for meaningful and metaphysical ideas and events. He thus saw mythic symbolism as the original source for the development of conceptual thinking and grammar. This form of consciousness is imaginative and guided by conscious bodily experiences that are transformed into generalized ideas. He argued that, in its primitive form, myth was not merely a story, but the expression of a lived and imagined reality. It was not at all fictional, but experienced (imagined) as real, much like dreams were considered to be real experiences that occurred during the sleeping state. The mythic form of knowledge lives on in our rituals, governing our modes of perception and controlling our conduct in an unconscious fashion. It arose from communal emotional responses to nature – awe of thunder, fear of lightning, and so forth. In myth, the identity and basic values of the group were thus given symbolic meaning. These were then expressed as nouns, verbs, and other speech forms. Their organization into phrases mirrored the occurrence of their referents in time and space. Subjects (for example, people or gods) act on objects in real life, producing active sentences; when the forces of agency are unknown, then the objects become the subjects themselves (as in passive sentences). A similar mythic source can be found in all types of sentences and in the constitution of all grammatical categories.

Marcel Danesi

Bibliography

Cassirer, Ernst. *An Essay on Man*. New Haven: Yale University Press, 1944.
– *Language and Myth*. New York: Harper and Brothers, 1946.
– *Symbol, Myth, and Culture: Essays and Lectures*

of Ernst Cassirer 1935–1945, ed. D.P. Verene. New Haven: Yale University Press, 1979.
- *The Philosophy of Symbolic Forms*. 4 vols. New Haven: Yale University Press, 1998.

CASTELLS, MANUEL (b. 1942)

[See also: *Communication Theory; Cyberculture; Globalization; Internet; Mass Communication*]

Manuel Castells is a well-known sociologist and global media theorist known for his work on the 'information society.' He holds the Wallis Annenberg Chair in Communication Technology and Society at the University of Southern California's Annenberg School for Communication, as well as additional academic posts, including professor of international relations and professor of sociology. He has also been a research professor at the Open University of Catalonia in Barcelona and an adviser to UNESCO, the United Nations Development Program, as well as to numerous national government consultation agencies, including those of the governments of Mexico and Portugal.

Castells was born in Spain, and studied law and economics at the University of Barcelona. He received a political refugee fellowship in Paris as a result of his activism against Franco's dictatorship and eventually obtained his PhD in sociology from the Sorbonne in Paris in 1967, after having written his dissertation on a statistical analysis of location strategies of French industrial firms. His first book, *La Question urbaine* (1972), was published while he was teaching social research methodology and urban sociology at the University of Paris. It is now considered a classic work in the field, leading to the foundation of so-called 'new urban sociology.' Also important is his *Informational City: Information Technology, Economic Restructuring, and the Urban Regional Process* (1989), in which he examines how information technology influenced urban and regional changes in the United States. In

that book, Castells introduced the concept of 'space of flows,' a notion that defines the dynamic interaction between space (which, according to his definition, allows for real-time interaction over long distances), time, and society in the contemporary digital age.

His trilogy, titled *The Information Age: Economy, Society, and Culture*, was published between 1996 and 1998 and has been translated into more than a dozen languages. This work features his long-term research on the economic and social transformations associated with the information technology revolution – something that he examines cross-culturally. Castells's main argument is that a new type of capitalism emerged at the end of the twentieth century which was more variable and more global than ever before in human history, repeatedly facing worldwide (rather than nationalistic) challenges as a result of social movements that have sprung up from people's desire to gain personal control over their livelihoods. These challenges, he argues, are what fuel the information age. In his assessment, a basic dichotomy characterizes this age, which he labels as the net-versus-the self. The 'net' is defined as the organizational structures that have emerged as a result of the continued use of network communication media. These exist within highly developed economic sectors and corporations and even within communities and social sectors. Castells explains the 'self,' on the other hand, as representing all activities through which individuals attempt to establish their identities (which can be religious, ethnic, sexual, territorial, or national and are interpreted as being essentially fixed), despite the constant changes and instability that the information world presents. In Castells's view, the interactions between the net and the self can dramatically alter human experiences of all kinds (from the sensory to the cognitive and social).

Alexandra Birk-Urovitz and Elizabeth Birk-Urovitz

Bibliography

Castells, Manuel. *La Question urbaine*. Paris: Maspéro, 1972.

– *The Informational City: Information Technology, Economic Restructuring, and the Urban Regional Process*. Blackwell: Oxford: 1989.

– *The Information Age: Economy, Society, and Culture*, vol. 1: *The Rise of the Network Society*; vol. 2: *The Power of Identity*; vol. 3: *End of Millennium*. Oxford: Blackwell, 1996, 1997, 1998 (rev. ed. 2000).

– *The Internet Galaxy*. Oxford: Oxford University Press, 2001.

– An Introduction to the Information Age. In *The Information Society Reader*, ed. Frank Webster, Raimo Blom, Erkki Karvonen, Harri Melin, Kaarle Nordenstreng, and Ensio Puoskari, 138–49. London: Routledge, 2004.

Ince, Martin. *Conversations with Manuel Castells*. Oxford: Polity Press, 2003.

Stalder, Felix. *Manuel Castells and the Theory of the Network Society*. Oxford: Polity Press, 2006.

Susser, Ida. *The Castells Reader on Cities and Social Theory*. Oxford: Blackwell. 2002.

Webster, Frank, and Basil Dimitrou, eds. *Manuel Castells*. 3 vols. London: Sage, 2004.

CATHARSIS HYPOTHESIS

[See also: *Hypodermic Needle Theory; Media Effects; Two-Step Flow Theory*]

The term *catharsis* was used by Aristotle to explain the effect that tragic dramas have on an audience. Aristotle saw the original function of tragedy as allowing for the release of pent-up emotions. As a result of the tragic performance, the audience's emotions are cleansed and purified. This same term is now used by psychiatrists to refer to the purging effect that talking about fears and problems purportedly has during therapy sessions.

The term has surfaced frequently in media studies. Known as the *catharsis hypothesis*, it claims that representations of violence and aggression in media have a preventive purging effect, since an involvement in fantasy aggression provides a release from hostile impulses that otherwise might be acted out in real life. Research in the 1960s appeared to show that children's exposure to violence on television increased the likelihood that they would engage in violent acts. In 1972, the U.S. Surgeon General claimed that the evidence was overwhelming on this point. Recent research orientations have revisited this line of inquiry, producing more ambiguous results. It would seem that those who espouse the catharsis hypothesis come up with data supporting it; those who do not appear to find data to reject it (see Meyrowitz 1985; Liebert and Sprafkin 1988; Croteau and Hoynes 1997; Dutton 1997; Ryan 1999). The latter type of research studies concludes that media content not only mirrors cultural values but also shapes them. The former type of research finds that there does indeed exist a correlation between exposure to violence and violent behaviour, but that it is a negative one, thus lending credence to the catharsis hypothesis. The main extrapolation to be derived from the research is that the degree to which people are affected by media is not a simple matter of a statistical correlation derived from analysing specific subjects exposed to specific stimuli. It depends on many factors, such as social background, level of education, and so on.

The idea that the media are capable of directly swaying minds with the same kind of impact a hypodermic needle has on the body is known as hypodermic needle theory (HNT). But supporters of the catharsis hypothesis argue that the HNT view of media-induced violence ignores history. The ravages of violence and war are not just contemporary phenomena brought about by television or other modern-day media. They have always been symptomatic of the human condition. Indeed, one can argue that there was much more violence in earlier civilizations because people did not have the same kinds of outlets for catharsis that we have today. In the end, it is probably more accurate to say that media impacts are indirect and that children and adults select from a media text that to which they are already predisposed – a selection pattern guided by the families and communities in which children are reared.

Marcel Danesi

Bibliography

Croteau, David, and William Hoynes. *Media/ Society: Industries, Images, Audiences*. Thousand Oaks, CA: Pine Forge Press, 1997.
Dutton, Brian. *The Media*. London: Longman, 1997.
Liebert, Robert M., and Joyce M. Sprafkin. *The Early Window: Effects of Television on Children and Youth*. New York: Pergamon, 1988.
Meyrowitz, Joshua. *No Sense of Place: The Impact of Electronic Media on Social Behavior*. New York: Oxford University Press, 1985.
Ryan, John. *Media and Society*. Boston: Allyn and Bacon, 1999.

CELEBRITIES AND MEDIA ICONS

[See also: *Celebrity Culture*]

Celebrities are people who have become famous during their lifetimes because of their appearance in media (movies, radio, television, newspapers, and so on). Celebrity is a blemished term in academia, ever since Daniel Boorstin defined it in his 1961 book, *The Image*, as 'a person who is known for his well-knownness.' Much of the general public, however, has a different take on celebrities, seeing them as larger-than-life players in the drama of everyday human life. *Media icons* are celebrities who go beyond simple celebrity status, symbolizing some aspect of human life for a particular generation of people and, like religious icons, becoming part of pop culture history, even after death. Marilyn Monroe, for instance, came to symbolize American womanhood during her lifetime, and remains an icon to this day.

Although celebrities have existed throughout history, they were hardly the

kinds of people we recognize today as celebrities. One can argue that the ancient heroes were celebrities, as were saints, great artists, and others in different periods and in different places. But the association of media actors, singers, sports figures, and so on with celebrity status is a modern phenomenon. Especially critical in the creation of modern-day celebrities and icons were the early movies at the start of the twentieth century. By the 1910s, the first movie celebrities appeared on the American pop culture scene. Actors like Rudolph Valentino and Charlie Chaplin became household names because of the recognition afforded them by the movies. Another early medium that led to the rise of celebrity culture was the so-called 'yellow journalism' of the early twentieth century, which led to the tabloid genre in the 1920s. The tabloid, with its condensed and sensationalistic style, focused on the private lives of movie stars, recording artists, and the like, as the burgeoning entertainment culture of the 1920s generated interest in the private lives of the stars. This generated a new celebrity culture revolving around the media. To this day, magazines (in print or in television or online form, such as *Entertainment Weekly*) are channels of celebrity culture. Many celebrity and lifestyle magazines today offer readers a pastiche of stories and features on celebrities. Each issue features a celebrity on the cover, together with an article about that person inside the magazine.

In the 1920s, the names of radio and movie personalities became as recognizable and culturally important to Americans as those of politicians, scientists, artists, and writers. Celebrity status became a state of mind for virtually everyone. The late pop artist Andy Warhol summed up this situation when he stated that every person sought to have his or her 'fifteen minutes of fame.' Warhol was among the first to realize the intrinsic link between celebrity culture, pop culture, and group psychology. This is why he derived his artistic subjects from both consumerist and celebrity culture. Using a mechanical stencil process called *silkscreen*, he showed how such a culture generates a stilted world view. He repeated the images of icons, such as Marilyn Monroe, Elizabeth Taylor, and Chinese leader Mao Zedong, many times in a single canvas to bring out a singular fact – the modern world is based on the constant repetition of images, creating a an unconscious belief that mass production is the guiding principle of daily life. Warhol also realized that a celebrity need not necessarily be a real person; it could also be a product, such as a Campbell's soup can, or a fictional character as, for example, a cartoon character or a comic book superhero. If the masses knew about it, it was, ipso facto, a celebrity.

There is a difference between a celebrity and someone who is *famous*. Writers, politicians, artists, or scientists may be famous, but they are not necessarily celebrities, unless interest in them is spread by the mass media. The classic example is scientist Albert Einstein, who was initially famous among scientists, but who also became a celebrity through the attention paid to him by the media, with stories about his personal life, his political travails, and so on. As a consequence, Einstein was featured in comic strips, on T-shirts, on greeting cards, and many other forms associated with celebrity culture. However, by and large, it is mass entertainment personalities, such as movie actors, pop music stars, television actors, and the like who are the ones most likely to become celebrities, even if they deliberately attempt to avoid media attention. The case of Princess Diana is an example of someone who shied away from the media, but who nonetheless became a media target and, thus, an unwitting celebrity and now an icon.

Celebrities who become broadly popular and symbolic are more appropriately known as *icons*. The actress Marilyn Monroe is the classic example of a media icon. Her beauty and sensuality in movies made her a sex symbol. But in spite of her cinematic success, she led a tragic life, dying at the early age of 36 from an overdose of sleeping pills. Her death became instantly symbolic of the victimization of women, transforming her into an icon. Elvis Presley is another example of 'iconization,' as the process of becoming an icon can be called. Presley was the leading figure of the birth and rise of rock 'n' roll music and teenage culture in the mid-1950s. His records constantly hit the top of the charts, and many remain highly popular to this day. Like Monroe, Elvis became even more popular after his death in 1977. Movies by him and about him and reissues of his music continue to be produced. His home Graceland has become a kind of shrine to his memory.

The use of the term 'icon' has religious overtones and has entered popular culture to describe such personalities as the pop singer Madonna. At first, people were aware of the sacrilegious irony that her name (which in Christianity refers to the Mother of Christ) implied, given the sexual nature of her songs and performances. Hence the term 'icon' was applied to Madonna ironically. Media icons are in fact imbued with a quasi-religious aura. Like religious martyrs, their death is experienced as something otherworldly. Consequently, they are idolized like religious figures. The iconization process is similar to the canonization of saints. Like any type of sacred space that is designed to impart focus and significance to someone, a media stage creates larger-than-life personages by simply 'showcasing' them. This is why the early radio, and later television, was called a 'magic box.' Media personages become infused with a deified quality because they occupy a place in that magic box. Meeting movie actors causes great enthusiasm and excitement in many people because the celebrities are experienced subconsciously as otherworldly figures who have 'stepped out' of their magic box, or stepped down from the 'silver screen,' to interact with mere mortals, in the same way that, say, Prometheus came into the human world to help mortals out of their ignorance. Early or tragic death helps a celebrity gain iconic status. Monroe and Presley both died young and under tragic circumstances. Similarly, James Dean, Jimi Hendrix, Jim Morrison, Janice Joplin, Bruce Lee, Tupac Shakur, Kurt Cobain, and Heath Ledger have achieved iconic status under similar circumstances. The tragic assassination of John F. Kennedy transformed the president into an icon as well.

Icon status can also be achieved through longevity or pure charisma. Many celebrities attain iconic status if they are able to continue being popular across generations. Contemporary examples are Paul McCartney, the Rolling Stones, and Sean Connery. Fictional characters, such as Bugs Bunny, Superman, Batman, as well as products such as Campbell's soup, Coca-Cola, and Pepsi, have also achieved iconic status through longevity. Their fame stands in contrast to overnight celebrities, or *pop idols*, whose fame tends to be brief. Current examples are the many winners of the *American Idol* competition, who tend to disappear as quickly as they appeared on the media stage. The icon, on the other hand, is perceived to have lasting value. This is why stamps with Elvis Presley and the Beatles can be found alongside those featuring presidents and scientists. However, it is often difficult to draw the line between an idol, a celebrity, and an icon. Some names are perceived as being celebrities to some, icons to others, and unrecognizable to others today.

Celebrities created by the internet are called 'cybercelebrities.' More and more celebrity status is being gained through the online medium. YouTube in particular has become extremely influential in this domain. Becoming famous on YouTube often allows the cybercelebrity to cross over to other media. This 'across-media movement' is one of the many manifestations of convergence – the phenomenon of media converging into one overarching system. To become a celebrity today, one must be showcased by all media, but especially (more and more) by the online one. The internet is increasingly becoming the key for gaining access to other media.

Media icons and celebrities have a significant influence on society. Their clothing styles and speech mannerisms are imitated unconsciously. During the 1920s, young men wore slicked-down patent leather hair in imitation of the movie star Rudolph Valentino. In the 1950s, many sported a ducktail and sideburns like teen stars such as Elvis Presley and James Dean. During the 1960s, they copied the haircuts of the Beatles, consisting of long bangs that covered the forehead. In the 1990s, the fashions and mannerisms of rap stars and of 'girl power' bands influenced the fashions and body styles of many youths.

Each country has its own celebrity culture, consisting of its own film, radio, television, and sports stars. But in the internet age, the celebrity-making stage has become a truly global one, with the celebrities of one culture quickly crossing over to star status in another. The global system has even made it possible for individuals outside of the usual media stage to gain celebrity status. Two well-known examples are the late Mother Teresa and Pope John Paul II. In the global village the celebrity spotlight is cast on anyone who is deemed to be newsworthy. That same spotlight, however, canonizes saints and sinners indiscriminately. The exploits of 'dark celebrities,' such as serial killers and ruthless businessmen, are also part of celebrity culture. The names of Jeffrey Dahmer, Ted Bundy, the Zodiac killer, Son of Sam, and BTK are probably better known than those of the actors who portray them in movies and docudramas. The need for celebrities is, as Warhol suspected, a symptom of the modern world. History now references names like Marilyn Monroe, Elvis Presley, and Jeffrey Dahmer alongside names such as John F. Kennedy and Albert Einstein. Magazines like *People*, talk shows, and entire TV channels and websites are now devoted to celebrities and their lives. Celebrities are alternately portrayed as shining examples of saintly perfection when they win Grammy awards, Nobel prizes, or Oscars, or as decadent sinners if they become entangled in sex scandals or criminal behaviour.

Marcel Danesi

Bibliography

Boorstin, Daniel. *The Image*. New York: Vintage, 1961.

Braudy, Leo. *The Frenzy of Renown: Fame and Its History*. New York: Vintage, 1997.

Cashmore, Ellis. *Celebrity Culture*. London: Routledge, 2006.

Danesi, Marcel. *Popular Culture: Introductory Perspectives*. Lanham: Rowman and Littlefield, 2008.

Marshall, P. David. *Celebrity and Power: Fame in Contemporary Culture*. Minneapolis: University of Minnesota Press, 1997.

Turner, Graeme. *Understanding Celebrity*. London: Sage, 2004.

CELEBRITY CULTURE

[See also: *Celebrities and Media Icons; Popular Culture*]

Celebrity culture is one that values media celebrities as much as, if not more than, other personages traditionally esteemed as valuable members of society (philosophers, scientists, and so on). Such a culture is prevalent in societies where the ideas and beliefs of the masses are influenced by various forms of mass media. In societies such as these, a celebrity's success may in fact have little to do with talent, but is brought about almost exclusively by the media attention he or she receives. For example, Paris Hilton and William Hung received large amounts of attention in the media in the first decade of the twenty-first century, leading to society's adulation or disparagement of them – in celebrity culture both kinds of reactions often occur in tandem. Celebrities have become god-like figures, as the media display their sense of self-importance and often scandalous behaviour gratuitously. Celebrity culture is, according

to many critics, ultimately guided by the logic of consumerism. A celebrity is a brand that can be consumed publicly like any material product.

The Advent of Celebrity Culture

In the past, fame was assigned mainly to royal, religious, or mythical figures. But the advent of celebrity culture has enlarged the domain of fame considerably. Already in the post-industrialist era, the domain included military heroes, romantic fictional heroes, and political leaders. By the mid-twentieth century, professional athletes and movie stars became new denizens of this domain. This was due to a vast cultural change brought about by the communications revolution, which changed the face of fame from that of traditional heroes to media-generated pop culture icons. As a result of his aviation feats, Charles Lindbergh was an early media-created celebrity in America. Unfortunately, Lindbergh's success resulted in the tragic kidnapping and murder of his son. Since then the media-entertainment conglomerate has created a state of constant excitement about the personages it enlists, becoming a cultural cauldron for forging celebrity culture.

Famous people in the past were represented typically as majestic, dignified, graceful, and attractive usually because of their accomplishments. In today's media culture celebrities are represented in many diverse ways. Why are people so fascinated by a mere actor such as Tom Cruise? Is it because of his dramatic performances or his strange affiliation with Scientology? Television has brought intimacy with actors into our homes, and the audience quickly develops a close friendship with such actors (in an imaginary sense at least). This familiarity is what transforms actors into icons. It does not even matter if these are real actors. Contestants on reality television shows gain similar celebrity status, even if for a short period of time. It is the medium itself that magically constructs the iconography. For this reason anyone can become famous in a celebrity culture.

Celebrity culture has had various negative consequences, including the virtual elimination of privacy for the celebrities themselves, given society's extreme media-generated desire for stories about them. These crazes have destroyed many celebrity lives. Fans develop a self-defining relationship with celebrities and seek to become part of their scene. Fans often seek to be in the presence of celebrities, and often recreate their own lifestyles to reflect those of the people they admire, even if the celebrity is dead. The classic example of this is the reverence for Elvis Presley, which continues to this day, creating an 'Elvis culture' that is sustained (although in a diminishing way) by the media.

Social Functions of Celebrities

There is little doubt that media, such as the movies and television, have spawned the current celebrity culture. Like the heroes of ancient myths, the celebrities can be both exalted or condemned. The latter has become epidemic. Many celebrities are portrayed as having fallen from their pedestals, shown to be 'normal human beings' with their faults and fantasies, strengths and weaknesses. But the current media world can also take common folk and transform them into celebrity heroes. Reality television provides an outlet for this transformation, as do various internet sites such as YouTube. Today, fame is within the reach of anyone, as long as he or she can achieve significant 'media time,' so to speak.

The fame achieved by someone within celebrity culture does not necessarily involve any true accomplishment or even talent. Often, just appearing in the media in fashionable and expensive clothes, driving fancy cars, and dating other celebrities will do the trick. And celebrity culture no longer distinguishes between actors, politicians, scientists, and others. John F. Kennedy, who was attractive and whose parents were themselves famous, died very young and provides a striking example of a politician achieving true celebrity status. Academics, television hosts, and others are also candidates for celebrity status if they make it in a significant way to the media podium. An academic and politician can acquire celebrity status simply by publicly exposing his or her ideas in the right magazines, books, television shows, and the like. This was the case of Canadian communications theorist Marshall McLuhan, who achieved celebrity status after a cameo appearance in Woody Allen's movie *Annie Hall* (1977). And only in a celebrity culture can actors be transformed into political figures – one can mention Ronald Reagan and Arnold Schwarzenegger as two examples. Charismatic star athletes who are showcased in the media also acquire celebrity status easily. The function of all such media-created celebrities is to provide the same kinds of role models as mythic heroes of the past. And like the heroes, the celebrities can be both good and evil, strong or weak, and so on.

Celebrities thus exercise an important function in a secular and consumerist society. A competitive market requires consumers to keep the system moving. The rapid consumption of culture became a part of everyday life already in the Roaring Twenties. That is when the first true celebrities (mainly movie stars and radio personalities) came onto the scene. They become commodities like real products – a critique levelled at consumerist cultures from Marxist scholars, such as the members of the so-called Frankfurt School. Celebrities thus are perceived to be public property, tradable commodities, and objects for consumption. The celebrity's primary roles are to be part of a commercial and promotional world, even if the celebrities attempt to stay away from that world. In the 1930s, rich and famous celebrities such as Howard Hughes and Greta Garbo avoided being in the public eye, but they were still perceived to be public property and, thus, were the targets of newspaper and magazine stories. In a phrase, celebrities are walking advertisements for a consumerist culture in which human beings are expected to fulfil their dreams through consumption – no wonder that celebrities are typically hired by marketing agencies to promote products.

Needless to say, celebrity culture is a part of the overall entertainment culture promoted by the media. This is why the personal lives of celebrities are perceived as part of entertainment – exposed in the tabloid press, television talk shows, internet websites, and so forth. The sex scandals of celebrities are thus considered to be as much a part of the world of social meaning as were the sexual exploits of ancient mythic heroes. Such expositions actually render celebrities much more empathic with the public, since they showcase the celebrity's flaws or Achilles' heel (to utilize an appropriate mythic metaphor). Villain celebrities, like O.J. Simpson, are also part of this mythic world, as are serial killers and rogue politicians. Fame covers a broad range of functions in celebrity culture. Like commodities, the celebrities can be liked or disliked; the only criterion for success is if they are successful in the marketplace. Today's celebrities have become fixtures of social life assisted by the media-entertainment conglomerate. Celebrities must put their personal life on display to the world and be constantly in the media's line of sight; otherwise they will lose their status. The media consumer thus becomes an important agent in celebrity culture, deriving great pleasure from his or her participation in it. As long as consumers maintain an interest in them, celebrities will remain; otherwise they will disappear.

Barbara Dumanski

Bibliography

Braudy, Leo. *The Frenzy of Renown: Fame and Its History*. New York: Vintage, 1997.

Cashmore, Ellis. *Celebrity Culture*. London: Routledge, 2006.

Hesmondhalgh, David. Producing Celebrity. In *Understanding Media: Inside Celebrity*, ed. Jessica Evans and David Hesmondhalgh, 97–134. Maidenhead: Open University Press, 2005.

Marshall, P. David. *Celebrity and Power: Fame in Contemporary Culture*. Minneapolis: University of Minnesota Press, 1997.

Murray, Susan, and Laurie Ouellette, eds. *Reality TV: Remaking Television Culture*. New York: New York University Press, 2004.

Turner, Graeme. *Understanding Celebrity*. London: Sage, 2004.

CENSORSHIP

[See also: *Freedom of Speech; Intellectual Property; Pornography*]

Censorship is an institutional system set up to control what people may say, write, read, perform on stage, and so forth. Typically the control comes from a government or from institutions set up by the government. Censorship historically seems to have arisen whenever a government or a community feels threatened by free expression. The strictest form of censorship occurs typically in dictatorships and during wartime. The difference between censorship in modern-day democracies and in dictatorships is that the former generally limit censorship and are responsive to social input; the latter are not responsive at all. In the United States, the Bill of Rights and the Supreme Court serve as safeguards against unlimited censorship.

The history of censorship can be traced back to ancient societies, where it was considered to be a tool to regulate the moral and political behaviour of common people. It was recommended by philosophers such as Plato. Often the rules and regulations were seen as benevolent and in the interest of the people. This mindset still continues today, even though the legitimacy of censorship is often challenged by those who are censored.

In more recent times, two nations that have used censorship as a regulatory tool of expression in a widespread way are China and the former Soviet Union. Theocratic nations, such as Saudi Arabia, Iran, and Syria, also censor public forms of expression that go counter to their ideological systems of belief in order to maintain religious and political stability, which, they claim, is threatened by the 'immorality' of the modern media. As such examples show, censorship and ideology go hand in hand. And in some cases, censorship is part of the overall propaganda machine of the people in power. In most modern-day societies, however, censorship is viewed as inappropriate for adults, but necessary to protect children. Media products that are deemed unsuitable for children are thus controlled or supervised in some way so as to ensure that children have little or no access to them.

Types of Censorship

The most common type of censorship is the one that aims to preserve so-called standards of morality. In any democratic society even this form is viewed as questionable because it is an imposition of the values of some on the society as a whole. Many countries have developed obscenity laws, but the definition of obscenity seems to change from generation to generation, place to place. A second type is military. Military leaders often withhold information from the media for security reasons. In some countries, the media voluntarily censor themselves during wartime. A third type is political censorship, which is used by governments afraid of ideas that are in opposition with their own. Democracies do not officially allow such censorship. But they often block radical ideas from gaining wide diffusion. In the United States, for example, laws prohibit the expression of ideas that might lead to violence. Finally, there is religious censorship, which occurs in countries where religion plays a major role in governance.

Censorship Methods

There are two main methods of censor-

ship, called *formal* and *informal*. The former involves government officials who apply laws to control free expression; the latter occurs if no specific laws exist to cover an offensive mode of expression. Informal censorship often occurs when groups apply pressure to various companies by threatening to boycott their products.

Early Media Censorship

In the early age of radio, music was often censored (informally) for various reasons. Sometimes it was censored by the radio station itself. The task of censorship fell to the Federal Communications Commission (FCC) after it was established in 1934. The main criterion used in radio censorship was 'community standards' or 'audience reactions.' For instance, small-town radio stations were more likely to censor songs with prurient lyrics than big-city stations. The most common reasons for songs to be censored were strong sexual and drug lyrics. Here is a sample of songs that have been censored over the years:

- 1956: Billie Holiday: 'Love For Sale' (reason: it dealt with prostitution)
- 1956: Frank Sinatra: 'I Get a Kick Out of You' (reason: use of the word 'cocaine')
- 1977: Sex Pistols: 'God Save the Queen' (reason: the Queen is referred to as a fascist)
- 1984: Frankie Goes to Hollywood: 'Relax' (reason: it refers to sexual climaxing)
- 1987: Beastie Boys: 'Fight for Your Right to Party' (reason: it encourages loutish behaviour)

At one time, songs were simply banned from the radio. Now, some record labels make an effort to censor them ahead of time so as to preclude negative publicity, often offering 'radio-friendly' versions of the song so that it will get airtime. As it has turned out, many songs that ended up getting censored actually sold better as people wanted to hear the lyrics for themselves. In the 'censored' versions, sometimes the label offered alternative lyrics. At other times, the lyrics were censored by blanking, bleeping, or skipping to remove the offensive part of the song but keep the rest of the song intact.

Some examples of artists whose songs have been censored (and even banned) in the United States are as follows:

- Eminem: blacklisted by a number of radio stations and self-censored
- NWA: blacklisted by a number of radio stations, especially after the release of 'Fuck Tha Police'
- Marilyn Manson: blacklisted by a number of radio stations; several videos banned, especially after the Columbine shootings in April 1999, which some attributed to the possibility that his music influenced the shooters
- Slayer: blacklisted by a number of radio stations because of graphic satanic imagery
- Madonna: several videos banned for inappropriate sexual and religious imagery

Film Censorship

The moviemaking business was a self-censoring industry until 31 March 1930, when 'the Code' – the Motion Picture Production Code – was established by William Hays, the first president of the Motion Picture Producers and Distributors of America. The Code consisted of rules that the community later called, 'don'ts and be carefuls.' The three general principles of the Code were:

(1) No picture shall be produced that will lower the moral standards of those who see it.
(2) Correct standards of life, subject only to the requirements of drama and entertainment, shall be presented.
(3) Law, natural or human, shall not be ridiculed, nor shall sympathy be created for its violation.

Guidelines for directors were developed which included what was and was not appropriate in a motion picture. Some of these things included: respect for the American flag and prohibition of nakedness, suggestive dances, drug use, homosexuality, childbirth, and interracial relationships, to name just a few. The Code lasted until the late 1960s, when gay and civil rights groups challenged its legitimacy. As directors and actors pushed the envelope, upholding the Code became nearly impossible. The MPAA still needed some sort of mechanism to censor movies and ensure that objectionable material was not easily accessible to children, so the rating system was established, originally G, M, R, and X; then G, PG, R, and X; then (in 1984 after movies like *Gremlins* and *Indiana Jones: Temple of Doom*) G, PG, PG-13, R, and X; and finally after some trademark issues G, PG, PG-13, R, and NC-17. Today, sexual material and coarse language are more often censored than violent material for general public viewing. In Europe, the opposite seems to be the case, with violence being seen as more objectionable than sexuality and verbal profanity.

Krystle Dillard

Bibliography

Blecha, Peter. *Taboo Tunes: A History of Banned and Censored Songs*. San Francisco: Backbeat, 2004.
Day, Nancy. *Censorship, or Freedom of Expression?* New York: Lerner, 2000.
Heins, Marjorie. *Not in Front of the Children: Indecency, Censorship and the Innocence of Youth*. New York: Hill and Wang, 2001.
Hull, Mary E. *Censorship in America*. New York: ABC-Clio, 1999.

CENTRE FOR CONTEMPORARY CULTURAL STUDIES

[See also: *British Cultural Theory; Culture Industry Theory; Frankfurt School; Hall, Stuart; Marxism; Propaganda Theory*]

The Centre for Contemporary Cultural

Studies (CCCS) was an important school of media and popular culture of a Marxist orientation which developed several frameworks including *culture industry theory* (which originated in the Frankfurt School), or the view that the arts of contemporary capitalist cultures are promoted and experienced like manufactured 'products' rather than unique works, and their aesthetic value is appraised according to their market value. According to the theory, capitalist societies view culture as they do any economic process, as a product industry with monetary value.

The CCCS was founded in 1964 at the University of Birmingham by Richard Hoggart, who became its first director. It was established to investigate how bourgeois interests are served by the spread of popular culture. The scholars at the Centre took the view that modern-day capitalism had debased all forms of culture by turning the process of creating artistic works into a process of making 'commodities' that was controlled by profit-making enterprises. Though not affiliated institutionally with the Centre, some American social critics have drawn (and continue to draw) heavily upon the general arguments made by the CCCS. The Centre thus has had a considerable impact on contemporary culture theory in Britain and America. On the other hand, it has often been criticized for ignoring a basic question: Why has capitalist-based popular culture brought about more favourable changes to the social status of average people than any other sociocultural and socio-economic experiment in history, including (and especially) Marxism? The emotional appeal of popular culture, moreover, cannot be logically dismissed in a cavalier fashion as a mere instrument of commodification. On the contrary, popular culture has actually provided the means for common people to resist those in power, not be controlled by them, since it has allowed them access to the marketplace, no matter what media form it takes.

One of the best-known theorists of the CCCS is Stuart Hall, who has always em-

phasized the bidirectional nature of the audience interpretation of media texts, that is, the fact that audiences read texts not passively but actively, either accepting them as they are, negotiating their meanings, or else rejecting them outright. This approach has been a major break from the other Marxist frameworks of the CCCS. Hall questioned the dichotomy made in previous studies between the 'producers' of media texts and their 'consumers,' suggesting that the texts cannot be considered solely as homogeneous products consumed passively in the same way by everyone.

The members of the CCCS used a primarily interdisciplinary approach to media and textual criticism, incorporating insights from theoretical frameworks and fields such as semiotics, women's studies, sociology, and ethnography. They were particularly concerned with depictions of alterity, from representations (or lack thereof) of different races to different sexual orientations. The CCCS was a socially sensitive and crusading institute fighting for basic human rights. For example, under the leadership of Stuart Hall, the CCCS conducted an important research project that led in 1978 to the publication of *Policing the Crisis*, which showed how blacks were misrepresented in the media. Other leading researchers of the Centre (or associated with it ideologically) were Richard Johnson, David Morley, Charlotte Brunsden, Dorothy Hobson, Dick Hebdige, Sadie Plant, Frank Webster, Angela McRobbie, Raymond Williams, Tricia Rose, and Jorge Larrain. They examined specific facets of contemporary media in terms of the inequalities they produced and the misrepresentations they perpetrated by tacit agreement with those in power, as well as the ideological structures behind popular and youth culture.

The general thrust of the CCCS influenced the development of so-called 'propaganda theory' in the United States, a framework associated primarily with Noam Chomsky (Herman and Chomsky 1988). Essentially, the theory maintains that those in power, such as the government of the day, influence how the media present news coverage for the simple reason that the power brokers control the funding and (in many cases) ownership of the media. As a consequence, the media tend to be nothing more than a propaganda arm of those in power or those who wield great financial clout. The mainstream media are set up to 'manufacture consent.' They do this by selecting the topics to be showcased, establishing the tone of the issues that are discussed, and filtering out any contradictory information. Contrary to the common belief that the press is adversarial to those in power, propaganda theorists and theorists at the CCCS have consistently argued that it unwittingly (or sometimes wittingly) supports them because it is dependent on them for subsistence. However, propaganda and CCCS theorists have been severely criticized because they do not seem to accept the possibility that the average citizen can tell the difference between truth and manipulation. Moreover, because of the internet, the media are increasingly being taken to task. If consent was really manufactured, why is there so much online critique against those in power?

The CCCS was closed in 2002, with only four of its fourteen members retained to teach in other departments. A campaign was instantly initiated to save the CCCS. Many saw the closing as politically motivated, since the CCCS had always espoused radical views. Perhaps the shutting down of the Centre was a sign that cultural studies had taken a radical turn in a non-Marxist direction. In any case, the work of the CCCS remains as influential and extremely insightful today as it was in its heyday during the 1970s, 80s, and 90s.

Marcel Danesi

Bibliography

Bennett, Tony, et al., eds. *Culture and Social Process: A Reader.* London: Open University Press, 1981.

Eagleton, Terry. *Saints and Scholars.* London: Verso, 1987.

Gilroy, Paul. *Their Ain't No Black in the Union Jack.* Chicago: University of Chicago Press, 1990.

Grossberg, Lawrence, Cary Nelson, and Paula Treichler, eds. *Cultural Studies.* London: Routledge, 1991.

Hall, Stuart. *Encoding and Decoding in the Television Discourse.* London: The Seminar Press, 1973.

Hall, Stuart, and Padel Whannel. *The Popular Arts.* London: Beacon Press, 1964.

Hall, Stuart, et al., eds. *Culture, Media, Language.* London: Hutchison, 1980.

Haraway, Donna. *Primate Visions.* London: Routledge, 1989.

Hebdige, Dick. *Subculture: The Meaning of Style.* London: Methuen, 1979.

Herman, Edward S., and Noam Chomsky. *Manufacturing Consent: The Political Economy of the Mass Media.* New York: Pantheon, 1988.

Kellner, Douglas. *Media Matters: Cultural Studies, Identity and Politics between the Modern and the Postmodern.* London: Routledge, 1995.

McRobbie, Angela, and Mica Nava, eds. *Gender and Generation.* London: Macmillan, 1984.

Morley, David, and Kuan-Hsing Chen, eds. *Stuart Hall: Critical Dialogues in Cultural Studies.* London: Routledge, 1996.

Rose, Tricia. *Black Noise: Rap Music and Black Culture in Contemporary America.* Hanover: Wesleyan University Press, 1994.

Storey, John. *An Introduction to Cultural Theory and Popular Culture.* Athens: University of Georgia Press, 1998.

Turner, Graeme. *British Cultural Studies: An Introduction.* London: Unwin-Hyman, 1990.

Williams, Raymond. *Marxism and Literature.* London: New Left Books, 1977.

– *The Sociology of Culture.* New York: Schocken, 1982.

CHANNEL

[See also: *Bull's-Eye Model; Communication; Communication Theory; Feedback; Medium; Message; Noise; Shannon, Claude E.*]

In communication theory, the *channel* is the physical system, environment, or device that carries a transmitted signal. For example, speech is carried through the channel of air waves; a radio signal is carried through a certain frequency band.

The term comes from the information model of communication developed by the American telecommunications engineer Claude Shannon (1916–2001), who devised it in order to provide a theoretical framework for improving the efficiency of telecommunications systems. In the model, Shannon depicted information transfer between a sender and a receiver as a unidirectional process dependent on probability factors, that is, on the degree to which a message is to be expected in a given situation. It is termed the *bull's-eye model* because it portrays a sender (a person or a device such as a radio, for example) aiming a message at a receiver as if the latter were in a bull's-eye target range. The channel is the conduit that connects the sender and the receiver, carrying the transmitted signal. Vocally produced sound waves, for example, are transmitted through the air or through an electronic channel (such as the radio).

In the area of broadcasting, the term *channel* is used to refer to an assigned frequency. This is what keeps radio and television stations from interfering with each other's broadcasts. Frequency is defined in terms of units called hertz. AM radio stations transmit within a medium-wave frequency band, and FM stations within a very high frequency band. There are also *short-wave* bands and, now, *L-bands*, within which most DAB (digital audio broadcasting) signals now broadcast.

The technology of channel frequencies is becoming highly sophisticated, as television and radio stations become digitized and use satellite technologies. For example, *XM satellite radio*, founded in 1992 as American Mobile Radio Corporation, is a satellite service providing pay-for-service radio programming. Most of the channels are available via internet, and XM also offers music downloads.

Cable television, which actually emerged in the late 1940s, has greatly increased channel access and options. Some cable systems carry hundreds of channels. This has made *narrowcasting* an everyday reality. Unlike broadcasting, which has always attempted to reach the largest possible audience, narrowcasting is a term used to characterize programs that appeal to audiences with particular interests. These are the TV versions of common hobbies. Cable channels may specialize in news programs, movies (of all kinds and from different eras), comedy, science programs, documentaries, music (of different genres), health, religion, weather, and so on. Some channels allow a customer to pay for additional programming in addition to the monthly fee for basic cable service – called 'television on demand.' Most cable services offer one or more channels that make movies or special events available on a pay-per-view basis.

Marcel Danesi

Bibliography

Briggs, Asa, and Peter Burke. *A Social History of the Media: From Gutenberg to the Internet*, 2nd ed. Cambridge: Polity Press, 2005.

Shannon, Claude E. A Mathematical Theory of Communication. *Bell Systems Technical Journal* 27 (1948): 379–423.

Shannon, Claude E., and Warren Weaver. *The Mathematical Theory of Communication*. Urbana: University of Illinois Press, 1949.

CHOMSKY, NOAM (b. 1928)

[See also: *Cognitive Language Studies; Generativism; Propaganda Theory*]

Noam Chomsky is a distinguished figure, both in academia and in the area of social activism. He is a prolific author engaged in the fields of linguistics, radical politics, and philosophy, and a teacher at the Massachusetts Institute of Technology since 1955. Chomsky has been recognized as a leading political thinker and activist, whose critical perspective of contemporary socio-political reality goes hand in hand with the praxis of dissent.

His work on theoretical linguistics and psycholinguistics in the mid-1950s challenged the prevailing empiricist tradition in the language sciences of the times, and more specifically that of structuralism in linguistics and behaviourism in psychology. By shifting the interest of linguists to the explanation of the creative and innovative aspects of the use of language, Chomsky's approach came forward to challenge the study of language beyond simple functionalist explanations of its forms and away from the restrictive framework of the stimulus-response-based theories of language acquisition (Chomsky 1959). It is the syntax of sentences, their deep and surface structure – constituting a formal grammar – that accounts for the generation of language (Chomsky 1957). Additionally, the process of acquiring grammatical structures is for Chomsky an innate, genetically determined capacity ('language faculty') that endows the subject with linguistic competence. The realization of the language faculty takes place along a 'set of principles and parameters,' in terms of a 'universal grammar' that underlies all languages and determines their variation in accordance to various parameter settings and values (Chomsky 1981). From this perspective, Chomsky has advanced the scientific study of the grammar of natural language considerably, despite various critiques and even rejections of his work in recent approaches. It is to Chomsky that we owe the theory-based psycholinguistic focus that now guides linguistic inquiry in general.

Chomsky's theory is known broadly as transformational-generative grammar; it is a framework that evaluates the process of the constitution of language in terms of two levels, called 'deep' structure and 'surface' structure I-grammar, which characterizes the ways in which sentences are constructed mentally and communicated physically. The dialectic relationship between deep and surface structure is present in every natural human language and is mediated by language-specific transformational rules that relate the deep structure to surface structure, or the phonetic representations of the former (Chomsky 1965). According to Chomsky, it is the underlying logical form of language – its structure, and not the actual forms languages take – that is the true research object of linguistics; it constitutes an approach that acknowledges the fact that there are innate propensities in human cognition, rather than just experiences of the environment (Chomsky 1986). Characteristic here is the distinction Chomsky introduced between language in general and languages in particular, where the former ('I-language') indicates the internal functioning of language, as it is reflected in the generative quality of grammar that is innately and individually registered, as an 'E-language.' Chomsky's evaluation of the ontological and epistemological status of 'I-languages,' contrary to the epiphenomenal contextualization of 'E-languages,' questions the scientific foundation of any social identification of 'language' with a 'community' – which was characteristic of previous structuralist accounts. Such a position reverses the conceptualization of the relationship between language and communication: communication does not come in the wake of a common language shared by a people (E-language), but it is subjected to specifications of the 'universal grammar' across various individual languages ('I-languages'). Overall, Chomsky's evaluation of human language as a cognitive system, which acknowledges the language faculty in relation to individual human minds, has been highly controversial and stimulating and has guided a large portion of research in linguistics.

Although communication, viewed in its instrumental dimension, is not subjected, as Chomsky argues, to the function of a common language, when its mediated form comes into discussion, it is determined by the conventional framework in which mass media run – a doctrinal framework which reflects the position of media institutions within the nexus of a power system, satisfying the relevant ideology that supports it, revealing in this way 'what makes mainstream media mainstream' (Z Magazine, 1997a). Prominent here is Chomsky's attempt to address the synergistic constitution of a framework that takes place both structurally, in relation to a media institutional setting, when interacting with, and being related to, other power structures; and virtually, in terms of the socialization of the roles of the people working in media, not through any methods of purposeful censorship but along an axis of the internalization of beliefs and attitudes of the surrounding power system. This kind of synergy affects the nature of the product, reflecting the interests of the institutional structure, as well as exposing the audience to the market, and especially to the advertisers. Under these circumstances there is no place in the institutionally mediated world for true 'participants,' just for 'spectators,' who are treated as 'meddlesome outsiders,' incapable of actually being engaged in public affairs, whose choices and attitudes can be then moulded towards the maintenance of the status quo. This process of 'manufacturing consent' has been the primary concern for Chomsky throughout his critical evaluation of the role of the mass media in the modern world.

Known as the propaganda model, which Chomsky elaborated with Edward Herman (1988), it provides a systematic critical analysis of the function of corporate news media, elucidating the ways in which the latter serve to defend and support dominant government and private interests and requirements. Herman and Chomsky draw on a set of five news filtering processes, interacting and reinforcing one another, which account for the 'pattern of manipulation and systemic bias' spread through media operations. These filters – namely the concentration of media ownership among a few profit-orientated corporations, the central role of advertising for the competitive viability of mass media, the 'symbiotic relationship' of media with powerful sources and their agendas, the compromising policy that media follow in response to 'flak' producers, and finally, the 'ideology of anticommunism' as reproducing a dichotomized ('we' versus the 'enemy') frame of reality in favour of Western political culture

– have promoted the ends of the dominant privileged groups in society. The propaganda model has thus been used to describe media content: its exclusion of news stories critical of corporate interests; its commercialization, according to standards set by parameters of audience demographics; its devaluation of the investigative character of journalism, due to its heavy reliance on the agendas of corporate and government agencies and the mediation of its practices by the relevant public relations bureaucracies; its censoring of controversial material from the perspective of the corporate world, which might jeopardize media legitimacy; and its practice of using the same yardstick, journalistic standards, and so on to judge both sides of an issue (oppositional and supportive), thus reinforcing the very character of propaganda. However, Herman and Chomsky do not develop the propaganda model in terms of a conspiracy theory framework; rather, they base their analysis on the concept of a synergistic (and largely unconscious) adaptation on the part of media employees to the systemic demands set by the news-filtering agencies. From this point of view, media bias is not attributed to a totalitarian control imposed from above, but to the actual processes of recruiting, socializing, and consequently self-censoring tendencies of media personnel. Moreover, the political vehicle of opinions articulated within Western media shows a discrepancy, since it appears to involve (on the surface) a systematic debate and discussion on various issues, as long as it does not challenge the general consensus, the 'system of presuppositions and principles that constitute it.' In this context the very notion of 'free press' performing a watchdog role is negated through actual media practice.

Chomsky has been consistently and rigorously critical of 'consent manufacturing' by the mass media in the United States – the 'new art in democracy' in Lippmann's words – needed to 'tame the bewildered herd.' Propaganda works for democratic societies in the same way that state censorship works for a totalitarian system,

as the title of another book of his declares
– *Necessary Illusions: Thought Control in
Democratic Societies* (1989). The difference is
that democracies incorporate more subtle
methods of control, which, in the case of
the United States, are intertwined globally
and domestically; characteristic of this
is the use of a rhetorical paradigm based
on a 'containment of the enemy' perspective. Moreover, Chomsky has traced the
techniques of propaganda that form public
opinion both historically – exemplified by
propaganda agencies like the British Ministry of Information and the U.S. Committee
on Public Information (Creel Commission)
that initiated current techniques of opinion
engineering during the First World War –
and normatively, applying the propaganda
model to case studies of news coverage by
U.S. media across the world – the Vietnam
war (challenging the prevalent supposi-
tion that media were opposed to the war),
elections in Central America, Middle East
politics, the protests against the World
Trade Organization, issues surrounding
the objectives of the World Bank and the
International Monetary Fund, national terrorism, and domestic politics.

Overall, Chomsky relates the current mediation of information to the very practice
of democracy. The exercise of propaganda
practices accounts for the prevalence of the
concept of 'spectator democracy,' a state of
existence whereby the means of information are rigidly controlled and distorted, so
that the public does not participate actively
in the democratic process – it just 'watches'
it unfold. In this framework, the media perform a double role – serving those in power
and marginalizing any dissent (Chomsky
1997b). Implicit here is Chomsky's profound concern over the politics of power
(Chomsky 2002). He has always been
committed to the deconstruction of such
politics through his leftist critique of U.S.
foreign policy and its drive for domination, linking U.S. multinational interests
with super-national economic structures
(Chomsky 1999). He criticizes the military
responses to 11 September by pointing out
that the media have reinforced the specta-

tor democracy syndrome through a clever
use of rhetorical propaganda (the so-called
'war on terror') (Chomsky 2001). The real
motivation, Chomsky claims, behind this
war is an 'imperial grand strategy,' grounded on the threat or the use of military force,
through which the United States maintains
its hegemony (Chomsky 2003, 2005). By
identifying the abuse of power in normative terms (government corruption, violation of international laws) Chomsky clearly
hopes to address the supposed real threats
to democracy, tackling issues of 'democratic deficit' from within (Chomsky 2006).

Chomsky's propaganda model is useful,
therefore, in articulating an overall account
of the structural and ideological affiliations
among dominant institutions – government, business corporations, and media
– in the Western world, institutions that
serve elite interests. Such an interrelation
is strongly reflected, in the case of media
performance, in how the media practise an
agenda of public discussion ('selection of
topics,' 'framing of issues,' 'filtering of information,' and 'distribution of concerns')
– a practice which, in an ever-evolving
media milieu, is more and more interlinked
to the 'politics of power.' The mainstream
media hardly give significant space to real
investigative journalism, confining instead
any meaningful debate to the 'bounds of
acceptable premises.' The objective of journalists to transcend these boundaries, remaining independent – feasible, according
to Chomsky, along with the professional
qualities of impartiality, balance, and objectivity – is a matter of resistance. Chomsky
himself, a 'public intellectual,' has been
constantly on the frontlines of the struggle
against any oppressive structure, deploying
critical intervention in various arenas of the
public sphere, from university lecture halls,
to the media forum itself. 'It is the responsibility of intellectuals to speak the truth and
to expose lies' ('Responsibility of Intellectuals,' Chomsky 1967). However, 'to speak
the truth is not a particularly honourable
vocation. One should seek out an audience
that matters – and furthermore (another
important qualification), it should not be

seen as an audience, but as a community of common concern in which one hopes to participate constructively. We should not be speaking to, but with' ('Intellectuals and the Responsibility of Public Life,' 2001).

Pantelis Vatikiotis

Bibliography

Chomsky, Noam. *Syntactic Structures*. The Hague: Mouton, 1957.
– Review of Skinner's *Verbal Behavior*. *Language* 35 (1959): 26–58.
– *Aspects of the Theory of Syntax*. Cambridge, MA: MIT Press, 1965.
– *Lectures on Government and Binding*. Cambridge, MA: MIT Press, 1981.
– *Knowledge of Language: Its Nature, Origin, and Use*. New York: Praeger, 1986.
– *Necessary Illusions: Thought Control in Democratic Societies*. Boston: South End Press, 1989.
– What Makes Mainstream Media Mainstream. In *Z Magazine*, October 1997a. http://www.zcommunications.org/what-makes-mainstream-media-mainstream-by-noam-chomsky.
– *Media Control: The Spectacular Achievements of Propaganda*. New York: Seven Stories Press, 1997b.
– *Profit Over People: Neoliberalism and Global Order*. New York: Seven Stories Press, 1999.
– *9/11*. New York: Seven Stories Press, 2001.
– *Understanding Power: The Indispensable Chomsky*, ed. Peter R. Mitchell and John Schoeffel. New York: The New Press, 2002.
– *Hegemony or Survival: America's Quest for Global Dominance*. New York: Metropolitan Books, 2003.
– The Manipulation of Fear. In *Tehelka*, 16 July 2005.
– *Failed States: The Abuse of Power and the Assault on Democracy*. New York: Metropolitan Books/Henry Holt, 2006.
Herman, Edward, and Noam Chomsky. *Manufacturing Consent: The Political Economy of the Mass Media*. New York: Pantheon, 1988.
Intellectuals and the Responsibility of Public Life. Interview with Robert Borofsky. *Public Anthropology*, 27 May 2001.
The Responsibility of Intellectuals. *The New York Review of Books*, 23 February 1967.

CINEMA

[See also: *Cinema Genres; Cinema, History of*]

Cinema is, at a purely technological level, a mechanical optical-projection system that makes it possible to create moving images and to show them on some surface or screen. At an aesthetic level, cinema is the use of this system to create texts that can be put on display (for entertainment, information, and so on) before audiences. The technology is based on the 'persistence of vision,' by which the human eye sees twenty-four images per second and merges them together in a fluid motion at an unconscious level. Therefore, one does not see the actual moving images, but rather images that convey the illusion of movement – hence the illusory nature of the medium.

The goal of cinema production, since its very inception, has been to create a sense of admiration and wonder in the audience, a goal that emphasizes its entertainment function. This is the reason why cinema was transformed, early on, from a generic tool for expression and enunciation of narrative ideas and concepts into a medium with a very strong narrative textuality, leading to an industry with its own production and distribution patterns as well as its strategies aimed at the maximization of profit.

The manifold functions associated with cinema have been the topic of heated theoretical and critical debates since the birth of the medium, which started with the screening of *L'arrivée d'un train en gare de La Ciotat* by the Lumière Brothers in December 1895. In 1896 the French magician Georges Méliès produced a series of films that explored the potential of the new medium. In 1899, in a studio on the Parisian outskirts, Méliès made a ten-part version of the trial of French army officer Alfred Dreyfus and then produced *Cinderella* (1900). His short films were a hit with the public, being shown across the world. They were the first important examples of an art form that was in its infancy. The history of cinema has also run in parallel with the history of patents, as well as the history of marketing strategies aimed at attracting the widest possible market share, and at creating huge profits, unknown – in terms of amount and speed of profit-making – to other industrial sectors. Because of its potential to reach any audience, together with its function as an entertaining and artistic medium, cinema has radically altered world-view and global social structure in a relatively short span of time. The claim could be made that cinema is the first expression, both in terms of importance and in chronological terms, of a true planetary civilization.

The interest in optical phenomena showing moving images dates back to the seventeenth century. Inventions deriving from such interest evolved over subsequent years. But it was only after the invention of photography and its ability to produce snapshots that the technical groundwork for true cinema was laid. Since the outset, the technology was designed to be used in a public place where the 'moving pictures' (or movies, for short) could be shown to an audience on a relatively large screen, so as to create a shared experience. Cinema's success would depend, in fact, on the creation of a standard format and a relatively easy system for reproducing and projecting the movies. Paradoxically and ironically, the most recent devices (laptop computers, iPhones) have brought moving images back to the times when spectators gazed at them through a peephole in the prototype to the movie theatre, known as the nickelodeon, thus regenerating a more individual and private experience of cinema.

The history of cinema consists of two basic chapters – the pre-sound and the sound eras. The transition from silent (pre-sound) to sound films (films with a sound track) was a rapid one. Many films released between 1928 and 1929 had begun production as silent films but were hastily turned into

'talkies,' as they were called, to meet the growing demand. Added to these chapters are subsidiary ones on the development of colour technology, the amalgamation of discontinuous images (rearranged through editing), and more recently, the use of digital technologies. However, a major issue behind the 'turning point' mentioned above is the commercial nature of the medium as opposed to its aesthetic and purely artistic potential. The dominance of production strategies aimed at the maximization of profit has typically relegated to the fringes the use of cinema as a discursive medium for philosophical, scientific, or historical purposes. The advent of cinema as a major technological mass medium coincides with the overall cultural history of the twentieth century itself and its evolution into an era of major technological and medium-based social revolutions. Along with psychoanalysis, the new scientific theories that upset the certainties of previous centuries (such as quantum mechanics), and the upheavals caused by the multifaceted political ideologies of the 1900s, cinema became a major force in the century, in many ways guiding the evolution of modern society as a visually based one, thanks to its emotional immediacy and to its ability to set forth its own types of answers to the most important and widely felt issues of the times. It accomplished this through the use of visual imagery, which allowed it to project a unique perspective on anything deemed to be of value to society, from politics to lifestyle. As such, cinema formed a fundamental dynamic with social changes throughout the world.

Cinema was born in France and developed rapidly in several European countries at the turn of the twentieth century. But it was in the United States that cinema developed into an industry of mass entertainment. As far as the distribution of films and their exhibition in public halls was concerned, the kinetoscope device of Thomas A. Edison was at first the only patented system with the legal right to screen films, developing into a monopoly located mainly in New York and Chicago. Its audiences were primarily middle and upper class ones. In what was perceived as an unfair advantage, independent exhibitors soon started using their own projection devices in small theatres attended by increasingly large numbers of spectators. The war between Edison and the nickelodeons characterizes the first years of cinema growth in the United States. The reaction of some film producers to the dictates of the Edison trust that was controlling the richer eastern states is of utmost importance to understanding the development of cinema. In order to achieve total independence and to be able to produce enough film materials to satisfy the growing demand, some of the most entrepreneurial producers and investors moved to California, settling into a little-known suburb of Los Angeles called Hollywood, where they started building facilities for filmmaking at a low cost and high profit, thanks in no small part to the more favourable weather conditions for outdoor shooting. Hollywood has ever since been equated with cinema for the masses, having become an efficient and mass production and distribution system, and creating the first 'studio system,' with its pre-built structures and equipment for the mass serial production of movies (sets, props, complex three-dimensional settings for different films) with the aim of maximizing efficiency and profits. The studio system also became a way of relating a major production company with a particular style of filmmaking or with a particular film genre, deemed as characteristic of a given production company. For example, during the 1930s and 1940s, the Republic Pictures Studio came to be associated with the so-called 'cliff-hanger' serials that were hugely popular at the time. The increasing control over each phase of the moviemaking process and the increasing budget capacity for film production also contributed to making Hollywood the leader of film production in both the United States and abroad.

Various other countries – from France, the United Kingdom, and Germany, to Italy, Scandinavia, Russia, Japan, India,

and South America – developed their own movie industries in tandem with Hollywood, although there was much reciprocal influence between the countries and Hollywood. The term cinema took on a different meaning, even though the rules of film production and its commercial nature were basically the same. Cinema was seen as an art form, capable of performing cultural and educational functions of high social profile and interest – not just as a medium of mass entertainment. To many producers and directors in these countries, the main menu of Hollywood offerings was seen as crass and solely of mass-entertainment value, and (with few exceptions) devoid of intellectual or aesthetic involvement. Needless to say, this was understandable in the context of the times when it surfaced. The situation has changed drastically today. Both Hollywood and other production systems are engaged in both entertainment and aesthetics. Cinema has literally gone global, along with other media forms.

It was after the First World War that Hollywood became influential as a cinema-producing engine – a fact that could in part be explained by the fact that Europe had just come out of a highly destructive war. European cineastes saw the postwar era as a period to come to an understanding with the new social realities of the times. In Germany, postwar anxieties gave birth to expressionism; in France to surrealism and Dadaism; in the Soviet Union to politico-ideological commentary, since it was understood that cinema could be used as a powerful propaganda instrument. This was the case of cinematic trends during the Nazi period in Germany and the Soviet period in Russia. The influence of cinematic material on large audiences became a topic of great concern during the era, and studies on its influence became common. The idea that cinema and mass culture evolved in tandem remains to this day. Even in America, cinema was often used as a propaganda tool, promoting the 'American way of life' after the Second World War. When the European Reconstruction Plan (ERP) started, several representatives of the Motion Pictures Association of America (MPAA) participated actively in the negotiations on the aid plan that the U.S. administration had with European governments, requesting, as a precondition, a facilitated and wide distribution of American films in Europe, asserting once more the paramount importance of cinema not only as a profit-making industry, but also as an ideological instrument.

The twenty-first century has witnessed a veritable revolution in the delivery of cinema, with the advent of digital technologies such as DVDs and downloadable movies, making the viewing of movies a more individual experience (akin to reading). This development, combined with the arrival of cable and satellite television, which provide access to current films on special channels, seemed to threaten the survival of movie theatres. But it has not turned out to be that way. It seems that the communal experience of watching movies in a theatre is as part of the psychology of cinema as is extracting meaning or diversion from a film. So despite the challenge from the new 'digital universe,' the movie theatre seems to be as popular as ever, which is a testament to the power of the cinematic medium as an art form tailored perfectly for the modern imagination.

Carlo Coen

Bibliography

Abrams, Nathan, Ian Bell, and Jan Udris. *Studying Film*. London: Arnold, 2001.

Balio, Tino. *The American Film Industry*. Madison: University of Wisconsin Press, 1979.

Ellis, John. *Visible Fictions: Cinema, Television, Video*. London: Routledge, 1992.

Sklar, Robert. *Movie-Made America: A Cultural History of American Movies*. New York: Vintage, 1994.

CINEMA GENRES

[See also: *Blockbusters; Cinema; Cinema, History of; Genres*]

The term *cinema genres* is used to cover the whole range of movie offerings – a term coming initially out of the field of literary criticism. The term is now used in all the arts as a way of classifying works together according to common subject, theme, and style. Examples of literary genres are *poetry, prose, drama, fiction, mystery*; examples of classical musical genres are *sonata, symphony, concerto, string quartet.*

Cinema did not start out as a way of telling 'genre stories.' It grew out of a simple scientific experiment that was conducted to show that 'moving pictures' – such as a series of photographs of a running horse – were perceived by the human eye to represent the 'natural' movement of running. This very experiment was conducted in 1877 by Eadweard Muybridge (1830–1904), a British photographer working in California who used a row of photographic cameras with strings attached to their shutters to record the horse's movements. When the horse ran by, a string broke in succession, tripping the shutters. Then in 1888, Thomas Edison (1847–1931) invented the first practical motion picture camera, which he used to film fifteen seconds of one of his assistants sneezing. The 'movies' (short for 'moving pictures') had arrived. In 1895, Auguste Marie Louis Nicolas Lumière (1862–1954) and his brother Louis Jean Lumière (1864–1948) presented the first moving picture film in a Paris café.

The emergence of cinema as an art form began in earnest in 1899, when French magician Georges Méliès reconstructed on film the trial of French army officer Alfred Dreyfus and then produced the film *Cinderella* in 1900 and his sci-fi masterpiece *A Trip to the Moon* (1902). Méliès's films were an instant hit with the public. In 1903, Edwin S. Porter produced the first major American film, *The Great Train Robbery*. Moviemaking in America was soon to become a major, economically profitable industry. With the production of D.W. Griffith's *The Birth of a Nation* (1915), cinema had become a major form of mass entertainment across the United States.

Between 1915 and 1920, the American

movie industry established itself in Hollywood, which adapted vaudeville, comedic, and pulp fiction genres to satisfy the diverse tastes of an ever-burgeoning movie-going public. The first silent picture genres were thus born, consisting mainly of westerns, slapstick comedies, romantic melodramas, adventure movies, horror flicks, and sci-fi extravaganzas. Gangster movies and musicals dominated the subsequent 'talking screen' starting in the early 1930s. By the end of that decade, the blockbuster movie had arrived, exemplified by *Gone with the Wind* (1939). Fantasy and horror genres continued to be highly popular, with films such as *Dracula* (1931), *Frankenstein* (1931), *The Mummy* (1932), and *The Wizard of Oz* (1939). The 1940s saw an expansion of cinema genres, with the increasing turnover of popular novels and classic stories into filmic texts, exemplified by movies such as *Citizen Kane* (1941) and *The Magnificent Ambersons* (1942). In Europe, moviemakers were experimenting en masse with the filmic medium as a self-contained art form – an experimentation that dominated the European cinema scene in the 1950s, 1960s, and 1970s. Examples of this are Roberto Rossellini's *Open City* (1945) and Vittorio De Sica's *The Bicycle Thief* (1949) in Italy, and Ingmar Bergman's *The Seventh Seal* (1956), *Wild Strawberries* (1957), *Persona* (1966), *Cries and Whispers* (1972), *Scenes from a Marriage* (1973), and *Autumn Sonata* (1978) in Sweden – to mention just two examples. In Britain and the United States movies by Alfred Hitchcock (*Psycho* 1960), Peter Bogdanovich (*The Last Picture Show* 1971), Martin Scorsese (*Raging Bull* 1980), and Woody Allen (*Zelig* 1983, *Shadows and Fog* 1992) also fell outside the Hollywood mould of moviemaking.

As mentioned, early moviemakers drew on bestselling novels, pulp fiction, vaudeville, and other popular entertainment sources to create the first cinema genres. Among these, the following stand out:

Crime drama: *Little Caesar* (1930)
Sci-fi: *A Trip to the Moon* (1902)

Animation: *Snow White and the Seven Dwarfs* (1937)
Comedy: *It Happened One Night* (1934)
Character drama: *Citizen Kane* (1941)
Historical drama: *Intolerance* (1916)
Documentaries: *Nanook of the North* (1921)
Detective: *The Maltese Falcon* (1941)
Suspense: *M* (1931)
Monster: *King Kong* (1933)
Horror: *Nosferatu* (1922) and *Dracula* (1931)
Musicals: *Flying Down to Rio* (1933) and *The Wizard of Oz* (1939)
War: *Birth of a Nation* (1915) and *Wings* (1931)
Action-Adventure: *Thief of Baghdad* (1921)
Film noir: *Double Indemnity* (1944)
Westerns: *The Great Train Robbery* (1903) and the Republic serials
Romances: *The Sheik* (1921)
Melodrama: *The Perils of Pauline* (1914)

Starting in the 1950s, Hollywood updated its repertoire of genres by appropriating social themes that were becoming relevant at the time, some of which have remained intrinsic to moviemaking. From the adolescent-oriented 'beach party' movies to current 'slasher,' 'jackass,' and 'chick' flicks, the movies have shown an uncanny ability to create new genres to suit current tastes based on social trends and patterns. Slasher movies, like the *Friday the Thirteenth* series of movies, reveal a modern-day fascination with serial killers and with crime in general; jackass movies (comedies that portray individuals, especially young males, as idiotic) show a current fascination with moronic humour; and chick flicks (such as the *Bridget Jones's Diary* and *Sex and the City* movies), which deal with the plight of modern women, tap into a general social trend that highlights the consequences of women having achieved liberation. The latter genre constitutes a new filmic locus for women to come to grips with their new sense of freedom. In contrast to the fantasy world of the feminine-directed romance films, the chick flick assails the traditional view of women as passive beings.

Among the cinema genres that are now popular, the following can be mentioned:

Youth rebellion: *The Wild One* (1954), *Rebel Without a Cause* (1955)

Adventure/spy: the James Bond movies

Intrigue: the *Mission Impossible* movies, *The Da Vinci Code* (2006)

Romantic comedies: *Pillow Talk* (1959), *You've Got Mail* (1998)

New Science Fiction: *The Matrix* (1999)

Slasher: *Friday the Thirteenth* (1980), *I Know What You Did Last Summer* (1997), the *Saw* movies

Pop music: *Jailhouse Rock* (1957), *A Hard Day's Night* (1964), *Spice World* (1998), rap/hip-hop-based movies

Martial arts: the Bruce Lee movies

Rap/hip-hop: *8 Mile Road* (2002), *Barbershop* (2004)

African American: *Superfly* (1972)

Hispanic: *El Mariachi* (1992)

Coming-of-age: *The Breakfast Club* (1985)

Anti-war: *Apocalypse Now* (1979)

Sword and sorcery: *Conan the Barbarian* (1982), *Lord of the Rings* movies (2001–3), the *Harry Potter* movies (2000–7)

Disaster: *The Towering Inferno* (1974), *The Perfect Storm* (2000)

Apocalyptic: *Lost Souls* (2000), *Left Behind* (2001)

Fear: *Jaws* (1975), *Jurassic Park* (1993)

Dumb-jackass: *Dumb and Dumber* (1994) and *Jackass II* (2006)

Chick flicks: the *Bridget Jones's Diary* movies

Girl power: *Lara Croft* (2001)

Superhero movies: *Superman* movies, *Batman* movies

UFO and Alien: *X-Files* movies

Some of these genres recycle previous ones, but many are new. Added to the above are children's movies (such as the Disney movies), many of which are animated, and, more recently, movies based on graphic novels (such as *V for Vendetta*, 2006) and 'simulated reality' style movies, such as *The Blair Witch Project* (1999). The serial genre has always been popular. In the 1930s and 1940s, Republic Pictures made many so-called 'cliff-hanger' movies, which were seen on consecutive weeks in movie theatres, thus enticing audiences to come back regularly to see the outcome of the episodes. In recent times, the same concept has taken on different forms, either as sequels or as series of movies (*Star Wars, Indiana Jones, James Bond*, and so on).

A genre that has always been particularly popular is the 'thriller.' Among the early directors most closely associated with this genre is Alfred Hitchcock (1899–1980), whose movies reveal a complex psychology behind them – that is, they are not just movies for thrill-seeking audiences; they also engender reflection on the human condition. Starting with *Blackmail* (1929), Hitchcock's first talking film, the British-born director became famous for his imaginative use of sound in evoking suspense and a feeling of 'creepiness.' The term 'spine-chiller' was applied to the movie by critics, entering the language shortly thereafter. During the 1930s and 1940s Hitchcock gained international fame with *The Man Who Knew Too Much* (1934), *The 39 Steps* (1935), *The Lady Vanishes* (1938), *Suspicion* (1941), *Shadow of a Doubt* (1943), and *Notorious* (1946). His most creative period, however, was the 1950s and early 1960s, during which he produced such highly popular movies as *Strangers on a Train* (1951), *Rear Window* (1954), *The Man Who Knew Too Much* (1956), *Vertigo* (1958), *North by Northwest* (1959), *Psycho* (1960), and *The Birds* (1963). Today the thriller can take any form, from the detective story to the apocalyptic thriller, which focuses on the end of times or on some doomsday scenario.

Two other genres that continue to have staying power are horror and monster films. From early silent movies based on vampires to the zombie films of the 1950s and 1960s to current movies like the *Hostel* and the *Saw* films, the horror genre seems to be popular because, arguably, it provides a catharsis from unconscious psychic fear.

Monster movies, on the other hand, like *King Kong* (1933) and its contemporary derivatives, exploit our need to juxtapose grotesqueness against beauty – a formula that can be encapsulated as a 'beauty and the beast' aesthetics. Horror and monster movies are, in effect, dark psychic fantasies taking material form in ghosts, vampires, zombies, serial killers, slashers, and so on. In the same 'psychic ballpark,' so to speak, is the alien and UFO genre, which, since the 1950s, has been highly popular. In Ridley Scott's *Alien* movies (1978, 1986, 1992, 1997), John Carpenter's *The Thing* (1982), and the various *X-Files* movies (and their clones) the aliens seem to stand out as metaphors for our fear of the unknown, as well as a growing awareness that 'we are (probably) not alone' in the universe.

Science fiction is another genre that has shown itself to have staying power. Starting with Méliès's *A Trip to the Moon* (1902), the sci-fi movie has always been popular, as it was in print pulp fiction. Because of the ability of cinema technology to produce special effects, the sci-fi movie has always been ahead of the genre lineup in using new technologies, even though some of the 1950s sci-fi movies seem rather quaint to the modern eye – an eye that has become accustomed to sophisticated technologies in cinema production, starting with *Star Wars* in 1977.

One genre that emerged spontaneously in the cinema world itself in the 1980s can simply be called *postmodern* – a style of filmmaking that privileges images over narrative. The classic example of this technique is Godfrey Reggio's 1983 film *Koyaanisqatsi*. There are neither words nor a storyline in the movie, which unfolds as a series of seemingly discontinuous images. The film literally shows how destructive and meaningless a world based on the technological exploitation of the environment has become. Reggio cuts and pastes seemingly random images of cars on freeways; litter on streets; atomic blasts; people walking aimlessly, working robotically, or shopping mechanically in malls; deteriorat-

ing housing complexes; buildings being demolished; and so on, into a visual pastiche. The minimalist music of Philip Glass acts as a sonorous guide to decoding the interconnection among the images, interpreting them tonally. Glass's slow rhythms enervate and exhaust us, while his fast tempi – accompanying a frenzied chorus of singers chanting frenetically away – assault us and make us restless. When the filmic-musical collage finally ends, we feel an enormous sense of relief. This style of music contrasts with the style used to portray a vastly different world at the beginning and end of the movie – the world of the Hopi peoples of the U.S. southwest, a culture that does not pit humans against nature through the use technology. Glass's solemn choral music and Reggio's slow-moving camera depict the Hopi world as sacred and meaningful, contrasting it to the modern world and its frantic, insane rhythms. At the end, a warning is projected onto the screen: '*koyaanisqatsi* (from the Hopi language) crazy life, life in turmoil, life out of balance, life disintegrating, a state of life that calls for another way of living.'

Reggio's postmodern technique took cinema to a visual extreme. But it was successful, as audiences, conditioned by television and other visual media, understood its subtext emotionally. The use of imagery to carry the subtext is now a common technique. Recent examples of this legacy are *The Matrix* (1999) and *The Dark Knight* (2008). Although these movies use traditional narrative, dialogue, and progression, they nevertheless also use images as carriers of the filmic subtext.

As one final genre defining current trends, the *blockbuster* certainly stands out – a term coming out of theatre slang referring to a highly successful play. In cinema, the term refers to a movie that earns a large amount of revenue or one that is seen as sensationalistic, given its use of famous stars and elaborate movie sets. The two directors who respectively gave the blockbuster its birth and ensured its development are Cecil B. De Mille (1881–1959) and

Steven Spielberg (b. 1947). De Mille introduced the filmic blockbuster with his spectacular historical and biblical epics like *Joan the Woman* (1916), *The Ten Commandments* (1923), *The Sign of the Cross* (1932), *Cleopatra* (1934), and *Samson and Delilah* (1949). Spielberg's movie *Jaws* (1975), a thriller based on Peter Benchley's novel of the same name, has come to define the contemporary blockbuster. The movie showed Hollywood that an important segment of movie audiences was made up of young people. The same formula, albeit in a different narrative domain, was exploited by George Lucas with *Star Wars* (1977), a sci-fi blockbuster movie that further showed how important special effects were becoming to the modern eye.

Blockbusters are now common, from the *Harry Potter* and *Lord of the Ring* movies to the James Bond series of movies. Blockbuster style has become an unconscious pattern in major movie production. Pitting itself against this trend is the 'indie' movie: any film that is not produced by a major studio, but by an 'independent' producer or company.

An important influence on contemporary moviemaking style is the video game, with characters and plots taken from the games, showing that there is a convergence of media occurring in cinema. This can also be seen in movies that have a 'reality TV' style, such as *The Blair Witch Project*, in which we are projected into the action, in the same way as TV documentaries and realty shows do, whereby the spectator sees the action through the trembling hands of the camera operator. As these examples indicate, cinema's appeal and lasting power lie in its adaptability, flexibility, and creative use of new technologies.

Marcel Danesi

Bibliography

Abrams, Nathan, Ian Bell, and Jan Udris. *Studying Film*. London: Arnold, 2001.

Altman, Rick. *Film/Genre*. London: BFI, 1999.

Austin, Thomas. *Hollywood, Hype and Audiences: Selling and Watching Popular Film in the 1990s*. Manchester: Manchester University Press, 2002.

Balio, Tino. *The American Film Industry*. Madison: University of Wisconsin Press, 1979.

Ellis, John. *Visible Fictions: Cinema, Television, Video*. London: Routledge, 1992.

King, Geoff. *Spectacular Narratives: Hollywood in the Age of the Blockbuster*. London: IB Tauris, 2000.

– *New Hollywood: An Introduction*. London: IB Tauris, 2002.

Sklar, Robert. *Movie-Made America: A Cultural History of American Movies*. New York: Vintage, 1994.

Stringer, Julian, ed. *Movie Blockbusters*. London: Routledge, 2003.

CINEMA, HISTORY OF

[See also: *Blockbusters; Cinema; Cinema Genres*]

Compared with other major art forms, such as music or painting, cinema has a relatively brief history. The starting point of that history is the late 1800s, when the appropriate technology had been established to make the movies a reality. In 1826 the French physicist Joseph Nicéphore Niépce produced the first modern photographic camera, developed a little later by Niépce's partner, the painter Louis J.M. Daguerre, and the British scientist William Henry Fox Talbot. In 1877, the British photographer Eadweard Muybridge, while working in California, created the first successful 'moving photographs' of a running horse. He did this by setting up a row of cameras with strings attached to the shutters. Each time the horse ran by, it broke a string in succession, thus tripping the shutters. In 1888, the stage was set for Thomas Edison to invent the first functional motion picture camera, which he called the *kinetoscope*. He showed how it worked at the World's Columbian Exposition in 1893, with a fifteen-second film of one of his assistants sneezing. 'Kinetoscope parlours' were opened in a few American cities a few years later.

These were soon replaced by machines that could project images on a screen, allowing many people to view a film at the same time. In 1895, Auguste Marie Louis Nicolas Lumière and his brother Louis Jean Lumière used the developing technology to stage the first public showing of a 'moving picture' film in a Paris café. Film screenings in the United States came to be known as *movies*, becoming a popular form of entertainment virtually overnight. Travelling projectionists brought the movies to smaller cities and towns. They were without sound. Thus, the projectionists often used live actors to provide dialogue, and a little later titles were inserted within the films.

Historians trace the origin of modern cinema to 1896, when the French magician Georges Méliès produced a few films that explored the narrative potential of the new medium. In 1899, he made a ten-part movie of the trial of French army officer Alfred Dreyfus and in 1900 he produced *Cinderella* in 20 scenes. Méliès is primarily remembered, however, for his 1902 film *A Trip to the Moon*, in which he showed how the movie camera could capture the emotional subtleties of the human face through close-ups and angle shots. Although considered little more than curiosities today, Méliès's films are significant precursors of an art form that was in its infancy.

In 1903, the American inventor Edwin S. Porter produced the first major American silent film, *The Great Train Robbery*. Only eight minutes long, it influenced the subsequent development of motion pictures because it showed how it was possible to construct a unified visual narrative by interspersing scenes shot at different times and in different places. The suspenseful chase in the movie caught the imagination of early movie-goers. As a result, so-called *nickelodeon theatres* were opened up in major U.S. cities around 1905, located mainly in small stores that were easily convertible into 'theatres' by simply adding a screen and chairs. Admission was only five cents – hence the name *nickelodeon*. Small theatres (no longer called nickelodeons) started

springing up throughout the United States. Most of the films were short comedies, adventure stories, or performances by the leading vaudeville actors of the day. They were produced in New York City, New Jersey, Chicago, Florida, and a few other locations. However, as cinema culture expanded, filmmakers were drawn to Hollywood in California, primarily because its climate made outdoor shooting possible all year round. The first modern-style director was D.W. Griffith, who made hundreds of films between 1908 and 1913. His most successful and controversial movie was *The Birth of a Nation* in 1915. It was America's proto-blockbuster. Between 1915 and 1920, grandiose 'movie palaces' were built throughout the country. Hundreds of films per year came out of the Hollywood studios to satisfy a constantly expanding and fanatic movie-going public. The vast majority were westerns, slapstick comedies, and romantic melodramas such as Cecil B. De Mille's 1919 movie *Male and Female*. By the 1920s, motion-picture production had become a major business enterprise. The first Hollywood movie studios came onto the scene, including Columbia, Fox, Metro-Goldwyn-Mayer, Paramount, RKO, United Artists, Universal, and Warner Brothers.

The transition from silent to sound films – known at first as the *talkies* – occurred in the late 1920s. The first talking film to become a nationwide hit was *The Jazz Singer* (1927). Although silent for much of its duration, it featured the popular American entertainer Al Jolson, who sang and spoke in synchronous sound. In 1928, Walt Disney produced *Steamboat Willie*, the first ever talking animated film. The era of modern cinema had arrived, leading to the so-called *classic era* of the 1930s, a period dominated by gangster movies, horror films, comedies, musicals, animations, and love stories, including *The Public Enemy* (1931), *Dracula* (1931), *Frankenstein* (1931), *Scarface* (1932), *The Mummy* (1932), *Gold Diggers* (1933), *It Happened One Night* (1934), *Bringing Up Baby* (1938), *The Wizard of Oz* (1939), and one of the most popular films in motion-picture history, *Gone with the Wind* (1939). The era also saw the emergence of the thriller as a popular genre. British director Alfred Hitchcock led the way with *The Thirty-Nine Steps* (1935) and *The Lady Vanishes* (1938).

By the 1940s, cinema had become one of the largest and most profitable industries in the United States. It attracted artists from various other media. One American director who crossed over successfully from radio to cinema in 1940 was Orson Welles. He experimented with new camera angles and sound effects, greatly expanding the emotional reach of film. His *Citizen Kane* (1941) and *The Magnificent Ambersons* (1942) showed that cinema was evolving into an art form of its own. In the same decade, Hollywood became an ersatz historian with movies such as *Casablanca* (1942), which dramatized the struggles and emotional turmoil produced by international conflict. The movie became an instant hit and one of the most popular films in American cinematic history. Directors such as John Ford, Frank Capra, William Wyler, John Huston, and George Stevens followed suit, making important documentary films about the war.

After the war, filmmakers turned their attention to the reality of the new world order. Directors became more and more concerned with portraying the daily life of ordinary people, filming on location rather than on a studio set. In Italy, Roberto Rossellini (*Open City*, 1945) and Vittorio De Sica (*The Bicycle Thief*, 1949), among others, achieved a depth of real-life emotion that has since become associated with the cinematic medium generally. Sweden's Ingmar Bergman brought philosophical and intellectual depth to moviemaking, treating topics such as personal isolation, sexual conflict, and religious obsession in visually powerful ways (*The Seventh Seal*, 1956; *Wild Strawberries*, 1957). In effect, filmmakers who were previously little known outside their own countries gained international recognition. Japan achieved recognition with movies such as Akira Kurosawa's

Rashomon (1950) and Latin America with *Los Olvidados* (1950), directed in Mexico by Spanish director Luis Buñuel.

In 1948, the U.S. Supreme Court brought about a new chapter in movie history by requiring studios to rid themselves of their theatres. This eliminated studio control of movie projections. The studios never again regained the power they once had. In the 1950s Hollywood started losing ground to television. Its production declined from 550 films per year before the war to around 250 in that decade. Independent producers started springing up, and international co-productions became common. A number of theatres in the United States even started specializing in films by foreign directors, such as those of Federico Fellini and Ingmar Bergman. Both became as well known in America as home-grown directors. Fellini's *La Strada* (1954) and *Nights of Cabiria* (1957) became hits throughout the United States. Such movies showcased the artistic possibilities of movies during an era when Hollywood was seen primarily as a producer of gimmicks and overworked formulas. However, one area of the world where the Hollywood formulas remained appreciated was in France, where the movies of John Ford, Howard Hawks, and a few other studio directors became highly regarded. This led to the so-called French *New Wave* which had a substantial impact on moviemaking in the 1960s with the popularity of films such as *Le Beau Serge* (1958), directed by Claude Chabrol, *The Lovers* (1958), directed by Louis Malle, *The 400 Blows* (1959), directed by Francois Truffaut, and *Breathless* (1960), directed by Jean-Luc Godard. Throughout the 1960s, the names of foreign directors came to be as well known, if not more so, than those of American ones, including the Japanese director Nagisa Oshima, Italian director Bernardo Bertolucci, American-born director Stanley Kubrick, Polish director Roman Polanski, Czech director Milos Forman, among many others. Some of these crossed over to Hollywood, becoming extremely successful in their own right.

In the early 1970s, a new system of movie distribution made it possible to write a new chapter in movie history. Aware that they could gain greater financial returns by releasing a film in many cities at the same time, supported by television advertising, this new form of distribution remains predominant to this day. It was used at first to promote *The Godfather* (1972), directed by Francis Ford Coppola. The results far exceeded expectations, with the movie becoming the most commercially successful film produced to that time. A new generation of filmmakers surfaced, including Steven Spielberg and George Lucas, whose films *Jaws* (1975) and *Star Wars* (1977), respectively, introduced spectacular visual effects into filmmaking – effects that defined the new type of blockbuster. Lucas then produced and Spielberg directed the adventure movies *Raiders of the Lost Ark* (1981), *Indiana Jones and the Temple of Doom* (1984), *Indiana Jones and the Last Crusade* (1989), and *Indiana Jones and the Kingdom of the Crystal Skull* (2008), which were intended to recall the thrill of the cliff-hangers of the 1930s and 1940s. Spielberg made one of the most successful films in history, *E.T.: The Extra-Terrestrial* (1982).

By the 1980s and the 1990s, the international platform for movies was constantly expanding, with movies from Asia, Africa, the Middle East, Australia, and elsewhere gaining larger and larger American audiences. Perhaps the most important American director of the era was Woody Allen, whose satirical, pungent, and penetrating social comedies became unexpected hits, especially *Annie Hall* (1977) and *Hannah and Her Sisters* (1986). In the same era, Spike Lee became an important African-American voice in the cinema world with *School Daze* (1988), *Do the Right Thing* (1989), *Jungle Fever* (1991), and *Malcolm X* (1992). Other significant independent directors included Quentin Tarantino, who directed *Pulp Fiction* (1994); the Coen brothers, who directed *Fargo* (1996); and John Sayles, who directed *Lone Star* (1996). New means of distribution (cable television, video, mobile devices) further helped foster interest in all kinds of filmmaking, resulting in an increased variety of films from across the globe, from the Indian Bollywood movies to various kinds of movies coming from China and Russia. Although Hollywood has maintained its domination, filmmaking has never before had such an internationally based platform for audiences as it has today. Films such as *Crouching Tiger, Hidden Dragon* (2000), a United States-Taiwan co-production, directed by Ang Lee, and Chinese director Zhang Yimou's *Hero* (2002) and *House of Flying Daggers* (2004) are two examples of how that platform has expanded.

Digital technologies also introduced new types of cinematic styles in the 1990s and early 2000s. Many movies started to feature characters from video games and to use filming techniques simulating both reality television (using a roving camera following, for example, fugitives on foot) and a generic video style. The first such movie to do so was *The Blair Witch Project* (1999). In 2000, the British director Mike Figgis shot *Timecode* completely with digital cameras. In 2004, *The Aviator* used a technique to re-create the look of 1930s films. And today people even make movies for the online community. YouTube, for example, allows anyone to upload his or her movie and gain an instant international audience. This allows the online filmmaker a chance to get the attention of Hollywood and other studio systems if his or her movie becomes a hit. This 'across-media flow,' as it can be called, is a manifestation of convergence – the phenomenon of media blending into one overall mediated system. The online medium is becoming increasingly the audition locus for aspiring artists, directors, actors, scriptwriters, and the like to gain access to the cinematic world, diminishing somewhat the role of traditional gatekeepers to that world, such as agents or producers.

Will the movie theatre survive in an era when the internet and mobile technological devices have made it easier and more convenient to view movies in different ways and in different locales? Throughout the first century of its existence, the movie was experienced as a communal event, inside a movie theatre, with intermissions, food fare, and other social rituals. The movie theatre was the centre of attraction of cities and towns from the 1930s to the 1970s. But all that seemed to change when VCR technology threatened to transform the movie-watching experience into a more individualistic activity in the 1980s. With the advent of cable television and movie-rental stores, which feature relatively current films, the survival of movie theatres seemed to be doomed. But it did not come to pass. The traditional movie theatre has remained as popular as ever. The new technologies have actually stimulated even more interest in going to the movies. This suggests that movies are still perceived to be communal art forms, even though all kinds of films, past and present, are now available in different media and formats. Today's megaplexes feature not only movies and the usual fast food fare, but video game sections, restaurants, and various recreational outlets and devices. The movie theatre has become a self-contained entertainment locale. And moviemakers are also ensuring the continuity of the movie theatre by adopting and adapting technologies. For example, ever since the success of *Avatar* (2010), the advent of new 3-D technology is starting to change how audiences may wish to view movies, paving the way for a 'revolution' in movies, even though 3-D movies go back to the 1950s, when the technology was used primarily as a crude special effects gimmick in horror and sci-fi movies. Newer technologies are making 3-D more sophisticated and less dependent on external devices (such as cumbersome 3D glasses). In sum, cinema-going has survived as a social event because of advances in technology and the need for people to experience a film as a communal event.

Marcel Danesi

Bibliography

Abrams, Nathan, Ian Bell, and Jan Udris. *Studying Film*. London: Arnold, 2001.
Balio, Tino. *The American Film Industry*. Madison: University of Wisconsin Press, 1979.
Ellis, John. *Visible Fictions: Cinema, Television, Video*. London: Routledge, 1992.
Sklar, Robert. *Movie-Made America: A Cultural History of American Movies*. New York: Vintage, 1994.

CLOSED VERSUS OPEN TEXT

[See also: *Eco, Umberto; Text Theory*]

The distinction between *open* and *closed* texts was introduced into semiotics and literary theory by Italian semiotician Umberto Eco. The relation between the structure of a text and its interpretation has become a primary area of interest in various fields, including media studies. Especially crucial is the 'location' of a text's meaning. Does it lie in the intentions of the maker of the text – the novelist, the composer, the scriptwriter? Is successful interpretation of the text on the part of the 'reader' a simple matter of trying to determine the maker's intentions? Or does the text's meaning reside instead in the reader, regardless of the maker's intentions? Eco addressed such questions, suggesting that although infinite interpretations of the same text are possible according to reader variables, in reality the nature of the text itself and the author's intentions constrain the range of interpretations. When a given interpretation falls outside this range, other people tend to see it as erroneous, extreme, far-fetched, or implausible.

The two main kinds of texts, according to Eco, are closed and open. Simply put, a closed text is one that leads to a singular or fairly limited range of interpretations. Most 'whodunit' mystery stories are closed works because typically only one solution to a crime eventually surfaces, closing all other avenues of interpretation. An open work, on the other hand, allows readers to make up their own minds as to what it means. It requires a particular kind of reader. For instance, reading Joyce's *Finnegans Wake*, which is an open work, requires a reader who can make up his or her own mind as to its meaning. In effect, a closed text sets clear limitations on the reader's potential range of interpretations; it constitutes a kind of fixed structure – a map is a map, unless it is part of a treasure hunt with shifting meanings, in which case it can become an open work of sorts. An open work, on the other hand, is typical of various literary traditions of opening up the meaning to the reader. Poetic texts are generally open, since they are suggestive of an interrelated array of meanings based on the sense of words.

To convey what he means by textual openness Eco makes reference to the musical compositions of modern-day atonal composers like Luciano Berio and Karlheinz Stockhausen, who gave musical artists complete freedom to play them (or sing them) as they wished to do, without textual markings or forms restricting the range of interpretation. This openness was also characteristic of Baroque music, he claimed, and it certainly continues on in improvised forms of music, such as jazz. The key terms used by Eco to define openness are 'discontinuity,' 'ambiguity,' 'connotation,' 'possibility,' 'plurivocality,' and 'indeterminacy.' Every interpretation may give a particular reading to a text, but it does not exhaust its interpretive potential. Openness is, for Eco, the textual condition that leads to a free play of associations and, thus, to an aesthetic appreciation of it.

Marcel Danesi

Bibliography

Eco, Umberto. *The Role of the Reader. Explorations in the Semiotics of Texts*. Bloomington: Indiana University Press, 1979.
– *The Open Work*. Cambridge, MA: Harvard University Press, 1989.
– *The Limits of Interpretation*. Bloomington: Indiana University Press, 1990.
– *Interpretation and Overinterpretation*. Cambridge: Cambridge University Press, 1992.

CODE

[See also: *Codes, Types of; Non-verbal Communication; Semiotics*]

The origin of the word *code* is from the Latin *codex*, which is a wooden tablet intended for writing. A code may be a systematic set of rules designed to convert information from one format into another by means of letters, signs, and symbols through a systematic procedure; or it may be a self-contained system of signs that can be used to represent something (an example is the alphabet code of letters from which letter signs are selected to spell words).

The process of transmitting a message from a source to a goal (receiver) involves a twofold procedure of encoding and decoding a message by means of a specific code. First, the sender encodes a comprehensible message and conveys it to the receiver, who, in turn, decodes it, and subsequently understands its meaning. In order for there to be a successful transmission of a message, the sender and the receiver must be conversant in the code, for example, a human language, an encrypted communication, or other code.

Roman Jakobson (1896–1982) developed a model for the description of human speech acts which consists of a process of encoding and decoding language that involves a sender (addresser) and receiver (addressee) who collaborate to send and receive messages modified by a context (social interaction), a mode of contact (physical, psychological, and social connections that permit communication), and a code (language, symbols). This description of an act of communication may involve a linguistic code, or any other type of meaningful systematic symbols.

Selected Examples of Codes

Many examples of codes exist. There are verbal codes that involve the use of symbols for encoding speech. The alphabet, as mentioned, is one example of this sort of code because the alphabetic symbols, or graphemes, represent the sounds of a language in a written format. Non-verbal codes are those that do not involve language. This section will present examples of some well-known codes, including the Morse code, gesture codes, cryptography, and colour codes.

The Morse code was perhaps the first to facilitate long-distance communication in a truly global context. It was developed in the nineteenth century by Samuel F.B. Morse (1791–1872), who elaborated this system with co-inventor Alfred Vail (1807–52). The code consisted of a series of dots (short symbols) and dashes (long symbols) transmitted by sound, light flashes, electronic impulses via a telegraph wire, or in written format. Thus, the English letter 'a' was represented by '• –', the English letter 'b' by '– • • •', and so forth.

Gesture is a form of non-verbal communication that is co-present with all human languages. It is part of a kinesic code, popularly known as body language. It results from the fact that humans use parts of their bodies (fingers, hands, arms, face, and so forth) to convey certain messages. There may be a one-to-one correspondence between a word and a gesture. The 'victory sign' consists of the extension of the index finger and middle finger with the rest of the digits clasped tightly beneath to form the shape of the letter 'V.' Other kinesic, or bodily gestures, may involve the movement of certain body parts, for example, the rotation of the index fingers near the temple to signify 'crazy' or 'mad.' The meaning of these kinesic gestures may vary from one culture to another. Thus, a gesture used in one linguistic group may have an entirely different meaning in another.

The word *cryptography* derives from two Greek words, *kryptos* 'hidden' and *graphein* 'to write.' Cryptography is a special type of code which allows a sender to transmit information secretly to a recipient. In this system, a sender employs a methodical procedure for transmitting information by means of a 'key' that converts normal text into a secret code so that the message conveyed will only be known to a receiver who is also familiar with the key for unlocking the secret code. This type of code is associated with the military, governmental spy agencies, and more recently with commercial enterprises that develop codes to protect a person's identity and credit information in business transactions. This encoding process is known as encryption.

There are various procedures for encrypting messages. One involves the substitution of the twenty-six letters of the English alphabet with corresponding numbers, for example, '8-5-12-16' = 'help.' Another method of encryption is the transposition of letters in mirror image fashion, for example, 'evol' = 'love.' In the Second World War, the so-called German 'enigma machine' encrypted messages, though, ultimately, its secret code was deciphered, and this linguistic coup played an important role in the Allied victory. In that same war, the United States used speakers of Navajo, called code talkers, to encrypt secret messages in that language. Modern cryptography involves sophisticated computational procedures designed to thwart code breakers who continue to become ever more adept at decoding new encryption systems.

The use of colours to signify specific messages is common. Two examples of colour codes are those employed for national security purposes and to express interpersonal messages. One well-known manifestation of colour codes is the use of colour codes by the U.S. Homeland Security Office to indicate threat levels: (1) Green = 'low'; (2) blue = 'guarded'; (3) yellow = 'elevated'; (4) orange = 'high'; and (5) red = 'severe.' In the United States, flower colours may connote various meanings; for example, red roses symbolize love, white ones mean purity and secrecy, yellow ones mean friendship, and so forth.

In sum, codes are procedures or mechanisms designed to transmit messages from a sender to a receiver. They involve a set of symbols, signs, words, phrases, and so forth understood by both the sender and the receiver. Each culture has developed its own set of codes designed to express specific meanings within that culture. In addition to the four codes (Morse code, gesture codes, cryptography, and colour codes) discussed in this entry, there are many others, for example, in the non-verbal domain such as dress, music, dance, architecture codes, and so forth.

Frank Nuessel

Bibliography

Ekman, Paul, and Wallace V. Friesen. The Repertoire of Nonverbal Behavior: Categories, Origins, Usage, and Coding. *Semiotica* 1 (1969): 49–98.

Jakobson, Roman. The Speech Event and the Functions of Language. In *On Language*, ed. Linda R. Waugh and Monique Monville-Burston, 69–79. Cambridge: Harvard University Press, 1990.

Shannon, Claude E., and Warren Weaver. *The Mathematical Theory of Communication*. Urbana: The University of Illinois Press, 1949.

CODES, TYPES OF

[See also: *Code; Semiotics; Structuralism*]

The term *code* derives from the Latin word *codex* ('wooden book'), an etymology which reveals that, like a book, a code is anything that has structure, coherence, predictability, and, above all else, meaning-making potential. The term has been used in cryptography from ancient times to mean a system of making messages in secretive ways. In order for someone to read the original text, which is said to be *encoded*, he or she must know the *code* and use it to *decode* it. The use of the term *code* today in semiotics, linguistics, psychology, and communication science as a sign system that provides the means for constructing and interpreting words, texts, and so forth was introduced by Ferdinand de Saussure, a modern-day founder of semiotics, in his *Cours de linguistique générale* (Saussure 1916: 31). For Saussure the code was a generic form of *langue* (the abstract knowledge of how signs such as words, grammatical structures, and their relations can be used and interpreted). The texts, forms, and messages that it allows people to encode (construct) and decode (understand) was a form of *parole* (the concrete utilization of the code to represent something). For instance, if a verbal text is written in Swahili, the decoder must know the Swahili language and its grammar (*langue*) in order to extract any meaning from it *(parole)*. A code, of course, need not be only verbal. To understand punk dress, for example, one needs to know the 'hidden' political-ideological code behind it, which in this case consists of clothing items or style details. The leather collars with sharp spikes protruding from them that punks wore prominently were designed originally for dog training. The training spikes protruded inwards. The reason for this was negative conditioning – if a command was disobeyed, the dog's leash, attached to its collar, would be pulled, thus hurting the dog by driving the spikes into its neck. Being against all forms of authority and social conditioning, the punks reversed the dog collar in parody of such obedience training. The protruding spikes, therefore, symbolized a reversal of power alignments, signalling that the wearer would never be controlled by society. Like a word or phrase in a language the collar in the code of punk dress was imbued with a specific meaning and used to communicate such meaning in a non-verbal way.

Codes are found in all domains of human aesthetic, intellectual, and social life, from the juridical (for example, the *legal code*) to the lifestyle sphere (for example, *dress codes*). They provide the resources for constructing messages, carrying out actions, enacting rituals, and so on. Stories, fashion styles, musical trends, and so on are all code-based phenomena. The term has become particularly applicable to the study of advertising and modern media representations, which use codes of all kinds to create texts and spectacles. It would thus be a futile task to classify codes according to each art, mode of communication, ritual, or tradition present in human societies. This would be tantamount to documenting the entire meaning-making resources of societies. So a more generic approach must be used. A basic way to classify codes is to say that they can be *natural* or *conventional*. The former are those that are produced by nature (for example, the *genetic code*). Natural codes are decoded by humans in various ways, leading to knowledge codes (science, for example). These change over time as they become falsified by ongoing exploration and research. Conventional codes are those that are produced by people to represent, organize, explore, and record meaningful culture-specific events, practices, and traditions. These govern all aspects of human life. In order to make contact with someone successfully we must know the appropriate body and verbal language codes. These provide the meaningful forms and actions (words, expressions, how the hands are to be used in the contact ritual, the length of the contact, and so on) and rules for combining them that make contact rituals successful or meaning-bearing. Similarly, writing, music, painting, and other kinds of codes provide and specify the ways in which tones, harmonies, colours, figures, and so on can be selected and combined to produce symphonies, portraits, and so forth. These ways are not invented on the spot. They are shaped by historical processes and, thus, are subject to change, although they retain an intrinsic essence across time. Pop music today, for instance, is based on the same harmonic code that was established over 250 years ago in Europe. The musicians of that era, in turn, came to fashion their own harmonic practices on the basis of previous codes used in the music of earlier centuries.

Codes are directive of discovery. Take, as an example, the use of exponents in arithmetic. Initially, exponential notation had a simple purpose – it allowed people to represent the multiplication of identical digits with a new, condensed, and thus more practical notation (Danesi 2008). But as mathematicians started using the new notation they also started discovering novel and unexpected things, such as, for example, the fact that n^0 is equal to 1. This property of 0 would never have been discovered without the new notation. Exponential notation has also led to the discovery of other laws of arithmetic. In effect, a simple notational change in the arithmetic code has led to discoveries and an ongoing dynamic expansion of the original code. This is a virtual law of 'code dynamics.'

The relation between knowledge and codes has been debated since antiquity. St Augustine, for example, wrote that language gave form to knowledge: 'But how is it that a word which is not yet formed in the vision of the thought? How will it be like the knowledge of which it is born, if it has not the form of that knowledge, and is only now called a word because it can have it?' (cited in Perron and Danesi 2003: 34). Saussure, too, claimed that the 'real world' cannot be known directly by the human mind, since that very world is filtered by language and other codes. The classic example of how codes affect perception is shown in Figure 1, where two lines of equal length actually appear unequal to the visual perception of people living in Western societies (and possibly others).

The lower line appears to be longer because of the outward orientation of the arrowheads. In Western perception (and artistic representational) codes, outward means 'away' and thus 'longer,' while 'inward' means 'getting closer.' In other areas of the world, where this opposition is not part of pictorial codes, psychologists have found that people are not duped by the above illusion. Optical illusions provide

Figure 1

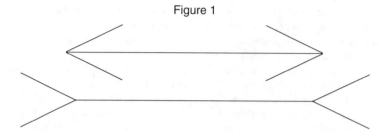

strong evidence to support the notion that codes mediate perception.

Above all else, codes furnish insights into how the human mind works. One of these seems to be the notion of *opposition*. For instance, *light* vs. *dark*, *good* vs. *evil*, and *masculine* vs. *feminine* are oppositions that are found universally and thus seem to reveal a basic cognitive structure in the human brain. They suggest that we think in terms of opposites. If there is *day* then there must be *night*; if there is a *positive* then there must be a *negative*; if there is a *ying* then there must be a *yang*; if there is a *left* then there must also be a *right*; and so on. There are, however, gradations in between these opposites. In the *night* vs. *day* opposition the cognitive space in between is covered by words such as *morning, noon, evening, afternoon*, and so on. But the mind seems initially to seek out 'poles' that are opposed to each other in some intuitive way. Filling in the conceptual space between these poles is generally a culture-specific process.

The psychological importance of opposition was noticed first by the psychologists (such as Wilhelm Wundt and Edward B. Titchener in the late nineteenth century). Saussure (1916) used the term *différence* ('difference'), claiming that the structures of a language do not take on meaning and function in isolation, but rather in differential (oppositional) relation to each other. For example, the meaning and grammatical function of a word such as *cat* in English can only be determined psychologically by opposing it to a word such as *rat* or some other minimal form (*bat, hat, pat, sat*). This will show, among other things, that the initial consonants in the words are cues for es-

tablishing the differential meanings of the words. From such oppositions we can see, one or two differential features at a time, what makes words unique in English, allowing us to pinpoint what each one means by virtue of how it is different from other words. At this micro-level of structure (known as phonemic), opposition allows us to sift out meaningful elementary signals from the phonic stream that constitutes the chain of speech.

Opposition theory was elaborated by a number of linguists who constituted the Prague circle in the early 1920s. They extended the Saussurean notion to the analysis of higher-level units. Opposition could be used, they claimed, to examine semantic relations such as synonymy (*close-near*), antonymy (*tall-short*), taxonomy (*apple-fruit*), part-whole relations (*handle-cup*), and so on. The Prague scholars soon realized, however, that the theory also produced anomalous results. When the opposition *male* vs. *female* is applied to the canine domain, for example, the term *bitch* surfaces as part of the opposition, a word that still exists in English to refer denotatively to a 'female dog.' But that opposition would crumble in actual fact because the word is rarely, if ever, used because of the social connotations it has taken on. Thus, an opposition such as *(male) dog* versus *bitch* could hardly be used to differentiate gender in canines. Clearly, the use of opposition needed elaboration to encompass social meanings, metaphor, and other creative devices.

As a consequence of the Prague Circle research, the theory of opposition underwent many modifications. But the basic idea behind it has remained intact. Its validity seems to lie in the psychological fact that signs have value only in relation to other signs and that the primary or default relation seems to be one of opposition. The validity of this idea works even at a practical level. How do we distinguish between a left and a right shoe? The technique of opposition will reveal that it is the shoe's orientation, designed to fit the structure of feet. In effect, opposition is what makes codes possible, and, in turn, codes reveal how the human mind classifies the raw information it receives through the senses, from experience, and so on.

There are countless conventional codes, each with specific psychological and social functions. The salient feature of each code is that it contains elements that signify something when they are organized or utilized in some oppositional way. For example, the fundamental way in which we conceive of number in modern mathematics is through a set of specific oppositions: for example, *positive* vs. *negative*, *even* vs. *odd*, *prime* vs. *composite*, *integer* vs. *fraction*, and so forth. These bring out conceptual differences that are meaningful in mathematics. In some areas, the opposing poles are reversals: *addition* vs. *subtraction*, *multiplication* vs. *division*, and so on.

Social codes underlie communication, interaction, rituals, lifestyle, notions of gender, and so on. They undergird behaviours that range from facial expression to the kind of walk used in fashion modelling. Consider, as a practical example, the zones that people maintain between each other during contact and greeting rituals. The closer people stand to each other, the more they are on familiar or intimate terms. In other words, the zones between people are used to encode and decode social meaning. The anthropologist Edward T. Hall started measuring these zones starting in the 1950s (Hall 1966, 1973). Hall discovered that in American culture a distance of under 6 inches was experienced as an intimate zone reserved for lovemaking, comforting, and protecting; a 6–18 in. zone was experienced instead as a zone where family members

and close friends should interact; a 1.5–4 ft. zone is felt to be the minimum comfortable zone that non-touching individuals tend to maintain; a 4–12 ft. zone is perceived as non-involving and non-threatening by most individuals; and a 12 ft. and beyond zone constitutes a formalized zone used for public communication (lectures, speeches, and so on). The zone dimensions vary, as might be expected, from culture to culture. So, while the basic code is universal, the various oppositions it encompasses will vary. The zones maintained by people during interaction are governed by a social code that informs them how to experience nearness and farness in emotional and social ways.

Knowledge codes allow for the classification and communication of knowledge of various kinds – mathematical, scientific, philosophical, and so forth. Take, for example, the decimal number system in mathematics. It is based on a small set of elements (signs), the digits from 0 to 9. A distinguishing feature of this code is that the value (actual magnitude) of any digit depends on the position it occupies in the numeral. The digit 2 has different values in the numbers 82 and 28 because it occurs in different positions in each. The value of a digit is thus determined by a rule – each digit in the numeral is 10 times greater than the value of the digit just to its right, and the total value that the numeral represents is determined by adding up the individual values of the digits that make it up. Another distinguishing feature of the code is that it organizes the numbers into oppositional classes, from *even* vs. *odd* to *real* vs. *imaginary*. As this code developed over the centuries it was applied to the study of mathematical relations, as well as to nature and human behaviours. It is such uses that have led to discoveries and the expansion of knowledge that would have otherwise been (literally) unthinkable. Take the case of the *prime* vs. *composite* number opposition. A prime number is a whole number that is not divisible without a remainder by any whole number other than itself and one; a composite number is any other integer, namely, a number that is exactly divisible by at least a number other than itself or the number one. This distinction has led to many discoveries and to the appearance of a whole set of problems and conundrums that would have otherwise been unimaginable. For example, Euclid showed that the number of primes is infinite, which seems to contradict common sense, since primes appear to become scarce as the numbers grow larger: 25 per cent of the numbers between 1 and 100, 17 per cent of the numbers between 1 and 1000, and 7 per cent of the numbers between 1 and 1,000,000 are primes. In the eighteenth century, Christian Goldbach found that he could write every even integer greater than 2 as the sum of two primes: $4 = 2 + 2, 6 = 3 + 3, 8 = 7 + 1$ or $3 + 5$, and so on. So far, no one has been able to prove what has come to be known as Goldbach's conjecture. Nor has anyone found a formula for generating prime numbers.

A third major type of code is the narrative one. It is a code that allows us to connect events as meaningful in temporal terms. The 'time frame' may be the past (as in historical narratives) or the future (as in science fiction stories); or else it may be an unspecified period of time, as in fables (*Once upon a time* ...). The narrative may be fact-based, as in a history book, newspaper report, a psychoanalytic session, or fictional, as in a fictitious novel, a comic strip, or a feature film. It is often difficult, if not impossible, to determine the boundary line between narrative fact and fiction. Indeed the *fact* vs. *fiction* opposition is a basic one in determining the value of narratives. Other oppositions that the narrative code encompasses include *self* vs. *other*, *hero* vs. *villain*, *good* vs. *evil*, *love* vs. *hate*. The ancient myths were mainly about the gods, the origins of things, and the foibles of human beings. Narratives about common people became popular only in the early Middle Ages, after the Italian Giovanni Boccaccio wrote the *Decameron* (1351–3), a collection of one hundred made-up tales set against

the background of the Black Death. The *Decameron* is the first real example of fiction in the modern sense of the word – the telling of stories for the sake of the telling. To escape the plague, ten friends take refuge in a country villa outside Florence. They entertain each other over ten days with a series of ten stories told by each member of the group in turn. As a result, the *Decameron* is the first work of fiction to provide a penetrating analysis of human character.

There are various other ways to classify codes, such as in terms of modality (*verbal* vs. *non-verbal*), structure (*simple* vs. *complex*), and so on. Changes to codes reflect significant changes in human life and in human societies.

Marcel Danesi

Bibliography

Andrews, Edna. *Markedness Theory*. Durham: Duke University Press, 1990.

Arnheim, Rudolf. *Visual Thinking*. Berkeley: University of California Press, 1969.

Battistella, Edwin L. *Markedness: The Evaluative Superstructure of Language*. Albany: State University of New York Press, 1990.

Danesi, Marcel. *The Quest for Meaning: A Guide to Semiotics Theory and Practice*. Toronto: University of Toronto Press, 2007.

– *Problem-Solving in Mathematics: A Semiotic Perspective for Teachers and Educators*. New York: Peter Lang, 2008.

Eco, Umberto. *A Theory of Semiotics*. Bloomington: Indiana University Press, 1976.

– *Semiotics and the Philosophy of Language*. Bloomington: Indiana University Press, 1984.

Frye, Northrop. *The Great Code: The Bible and Literature*. Toronto: Academic Press, 1981.

Hall, Edward T. *The Hidden Dimension*. New York: Doubleday, 1966.

– *The Silent Language*. New York: Anchor, 1973.

Lévi-Strauss, Claude. *Myth and Meaning: Cracking the Code of Culture*. Toronto: University of Toronto Press, 1978.

Perron, Paul, and Marcel Danesi, eds. *Classic*

Readings in Semiotics. Ottawa: Legas Press, 2003.

Saussure, Ferdinand de. *Cours de linguistique générale*. Ed. C. Bally and A. Sechehaye. Paris: Payot, 1916. Trans. W. Baskin, *Course in General Linguistics*. New York: McGraw-Hill, 1958.

Whorf, Benjamin Lee. *Language, Thought, and Reality*. Ed. J.B. Carroll. Cambridge, MA: MIT Press, 1956.

COGNITIVE DISSONANCE THEORY

[See also: *Audience Research; Media Effects*]

Cognitive dissonance, a term coined by the American psychologist Leon Festinger (1957), refers to the condition of conflict or anxiety resulting from an inconsistency between one's beliefs and one's actions, such as opposing the slaughter of animals while eating meat. People will seek out information that confirms their own attitudes and views of the world or that reinforces aspects of conditioned behaviour, avoiding information that is likely to be in conflict with their world view and that will thus bring about cognitive dissonance.

Festinger initially conceived of cognitive dissonance after reading an item in his local newspaper which bore the headline 'Prophecy from Planet Clarion Call to City: Flee that Flood,' referring to a UFO doomsday cult which had been told by the leader that the end of the world would come to pass on a certain date. The prediction, however, did not come about on that date. With several colleagues, Festinger and his colleagues saw this as a case that would induce dissonance in cult members, who would try to assuage it by some explanation that made sense to them. To test this hypothesis, Festinger and his team infiltrated the group, reporting results that confirmed it. The prediction, supposedly communicated by aliens to the leader, turned into a disconfirmed expectancy that caused dissonance in all group members.

Some members abandoned the group when the prophecy failed, but most of them attempted to downplay the event by accepting a new belief, namely that the planet was spared because of the group's resolve and faith. Festinger thus claimed that when people become uneasy after facing information that conflicts with their belief systems, they develop strategies to attenuate the dissonance they feel and often turn the contrasting information on its head, so as to make sense of it in terms of their belief system.

Cognitive dissonance theory has been used occasionally in audience research, which shows typically that audiences will tend to avoid TV programs that cause cognitive dissonance, choosing instead programs that are in consonance with their views. Cognitive dissonance sometimes leads to moral panic. As Stan Cohen (1972) observed in his insightful study of mods and rockers, whether it is a panicked reaction to Elvis's swinging hips or to the gross antics performed by rockers, many people typically react negatively at first to such behaviours. They do so in order to avoid a dissonance between their expectations of performance spectacles and the actual spectacles themselves. As it turns out, however, as these spectacles lose their impact, blending silently into the cultural mainstream or disappearing, the moral panic also dissipates. The members of Festinger's UFO cult can be seen to have initially suffered a form of moral panic, which they eventually resolved by rationalizing the failed prophecy on their own terms.

Marcel Danesi

Bibliography

Cohen, Stan. *Folk Devils and Moral Panics: The Creation of Mods and Rockers* London: MacGibbon and Kee, 1972.

Cooper, Joel M. *Cognitive Dissonance: 50 Years of a Classic Theory*. London: Sage, 2007.

Festinger, Leon. *A Theory of Cognitive Dissonance*. Evanston, IL: Row, Peterson, 1957.

COGNITIVE LANGUAGE STUDIES

[See also: *Chomsky, Noam; Cognitivism; Conceptual Metaphor Theory; Generativism; Post-Structuralism; Semiotics; Structuralism*]

The rise of cognitive studies in the second half of the twentieth century has transformed our ideas about communication, signs, language, and thought, introducing new perspectives and priorities in linguistics, rhetoric, poetics, and literary criticism. Noam Chomsky's innovative and influential linguistic theories represent a major contribution to early cognitivism. Research in experimental psychology associated with the cognitive paradigm has rekindled empirical studies in the processing, understanding, and production of discourse. Since the 1980s, a new generation of researchers has emphasized that human cognition is profoundly shaped by its bases in the body and by interactions with the environment. Contemporary studies have begun to take into account emotions, context, and socio-historical factors, perspectives generally bracketed by earlier cognitivism more exclusively focused on knowledge, information processing, universals, and the millenary evolution of the species. Book-length essays that present a broad spectrum of cognitive studies relevant to communication, linguistics, and text studies include Turner (1996), Richardson and Steen (2002), Stockwell (2002), Hogan (2003a, 2003b), and Croft and Cruse (2004).

Postwar Cognitivism, Artificial Intelligence, and Chomskyan Linguistics

Since its beginnings, modern cognitive science has privileged research in artificial intelligence, employing the computer as a key technology for linguistic inquiry and often as a model for thought and language as well (Flanagan 1992; Gardner 1987; Johnson-Laird 1988; Pylyshyn 1986; Schank 1982; Schank and Colby eds. 1973). The first generation of cognitivists created the applied linguistic subfield of computational (computer-assisted) linguistics, including natural language processing, machine translation, and speech recognition and synthesis. Noam Chomsky's critical 1959 review of behavioural psychologist B.F. Skinner's *Verbal Behavior* served as one of the most important manifestos of the nascent cognitive theory and its postulation of powerful mental structures. The generative grammar theory that Chomsky and his followers developed depicts language activity as the rule-governed manipulation of symbols, adopts a formal approach based on logic and mathematics, and formulates its descriptions as a sequence of explicit, computer-like instructions to analyse a sentence, expression, or sound (Chomsky 1957, 1965, 1981, 1995; Chomsky and Halle 1968). On the theoretical plane, positioning linguistics as a branch of cognitive psychology, the Chomskyan approach postulates complex mental processes and representations underpinning its formal model of language. It posits an innate 'universal grammar' and attributes to the mind a 'modular' architecture subsuming distinct, specialized faculties that function with a significant measure of autonomy, including separate linguistic components such as syntax, morphology, and phonology (Chomsky 1966, 1981; Jackendoff 1997; Pinker 1994; Fodor 1983).

The papers and publications that launched the 'Chomskyan revolution' define universal syntactic structures as formal mechanisms independent from meaning, the latter located instead in vocabulary items and in the non-linguistic speech situations or contexts (Chomsky 1957, 1965). This move parallels the manner in which the formalist wing of the philosophy dominant in English-language regions, the analytic tradition, establishes a universal logical predicate calculus independent from the propositions' reference to actual or possible objects, persons, and states of affairs in the world (Frege 1879; Carnap 1937, 1967; Russell 1940). Chomsky has always argued that the heart of linguistics is the study of core sentence syntax defined as a universal, innate, mental language faculty fully instantiated in normal individuals and unique to

Homo sapiens. He has advocated a focus on this 'I-language' (Internal-language) or linguistic competence and disparaged the study of 'E-language' (External-language) or performance, the actual utterances proffered by speakers, replete with 'errors,' poetic licence, and regional and individual 'accent.' In the course of his long and extraordinarily productive career, the MIT linguist has proposed significantly different overall 'architectures' defining how sentence syntax, sound, vocabulary, and meaning are interrelated (Chomsky 1965, 1981, 1995, 2000; Cook and Newson 2007), the changes coming in part in response to critiques. Throughout the various configurations, however, generative grammar has maintained its focus on formally articulated universal syntactic structures. Chomsky's theories dominated linguistics in certain English-language regions from the 1960s through the 1980s and have enjoyed significant influence throughout the globe.

Linguists who study meaning from a framework related to the Chomskyan paradigm work at the intersection of syntax and logic, using so-called 'Montague grammar' to extend truth-conditional semantics to linguistic expressions of quantity (for example, *some, any, a* in given constructions) for which analytic philosophy and symbolic logic cannot assign unambiguous definitions (Montague 1973; Bach 1989; Chierchia and McConnell-Ginet 1990; Heim and Kratzer 1998). Generative grammar and the formal analytic tradition share the goal of defining a universal symbolic calculus that accounts for core features of sentence grammar and logical propositions and that stands independent of contingent factors such as culture, historical conditions, and the idiosyncrasies of given natural languages. Chomskyan cognitivism has reaffirmed significant principles of philosophical rationalism, including the 'Cartesian linguistics' of general grammar (1966), and has promoted certain Enlightenment values such as the autonomy of the individual. Since the 1980s, a number of linguists have argued that modified versions of Chomsky's grammar possess significant psycho-

logical plausibility (for example, Berwick and Weinberg 1985; Bresnan 1982, 2001). While there have been few direct applications of Chomsky-inspired models to texts, Richard Ohmann has explored how literary stylistics can draw from generative grammar (1964), Thomas Pavel has studied narrative using generative principles (1976), and Fred Lerdahl and Ray Jackendoff have proposed a generative theory of tonal music (1983).

Cognitive research in fields adjacent to linguistics has also impacted on communication studies. Artificial intelligence has developed computer programs intended to model the cognitive processes entailed in reading, storytelling, and recall, and to effect virtual experimental studies of those activities. Aiming to simulate higher-order mental processes, 'symbolic' approaches bring together models of elementary contents (called 'data structures') such as logical propositions, rules, schemas, concepts, plans, images, and analogies, with models of mental procedures that select and combine, alter and create those contents, such as search and find, deduction and induction, matching, zooming, rotating, and retrieval. Artificial intelligence concepts and tools such as frames, scripts, and stacking have been used to represent how the mind develops and understands narratives, including how it defines and recalls characters and their situations and how it processes framing and metafictional discourse; such narrative structures play a powerful role in cognitive activities as varied as acquiring knowledge, accessing memory, communicating, and interacting socially (Schank and Abelson 1977; Schank 1995; Johnson-Laird 1983; Hobbs 1990; Ryan 1991; Emmott 1997; Bruner 2002; Fireman, McVay, and Flanagan 2003; Hogan 2003a, 2003b). Evolutionary psychology suggests that mechanisms central to communication including storytelling, role reversal, and counter-factual thinking may represent species-specific functional adaptations that have evolved to enhance survival and reproduction (Barkow, Cosmides, and Tooby 1992).

Experimental Psychology and Empirical Language Research

The cognitive paradigm that displaced behaviourism in psychology has reshaped experimental psychology and with it empirical studies of language, communication, and texts. Research today incorporates neurobiological observations, neuroscientific brain-imaging techniques such as functional magnetic resonance imaging and electroencephalography, and behavioural experiments that document psychophysical responses, reaction time, and eye movements (Edelman 1993; Kosslyn and Koening 1992; Damasio 1994). Eleanor Rosch's behavioural experiments identified a new kind of category defined by a prototype and members' degree of typicality (Rosch 1973a, 1973b, 1975, 1978). Prototype theory has changed how lexical semantics conceptualizes certain fields such as colour or furniture, how it defines the hierarchical levels within vocabulary, and how it accounts for the related meanings of an individual word, considered as a category (Lakoff 1987; Kleiber 1990; Taylor 1995). Together with Wittgenstein's notion of family resemblance, Rosch's radial categories have pointed to new strategies for defining genre and aesthetic movements (Wittgenstein 1973; Mancing 2000; Richardson 1997).

Other experimental psychological research on perception, attention, recall, and reading informs empirical analyses of how subjects process narrative and how they recognize and experience a host of poetic effects ranging from rhythm and rhyme to metaphor and description (Barney 1996; Bortolussi and Dixon 2003; Gerrig 1993; Kreuz and MacNealy 1996; Miall 2006; Tsur 1983, 1992; Turner 1985: 61–108). Going beyond the focus on information processing that characterized early cognitivism, these studies systematically investigate curiosity, emotional responses, and aesthetic pleasure (Feagin 1996; Spolsky 2007). Neuroscientific research on short- and long-term memory, on declarative (fact and experience focused) and procedural (skill- and process-oriented) forms of recall and knowledge informs studies on how fiction and autobiography depend on and represent memory (Nalbantian 2003; Schacter and Scarry 2000; Steen 1998). Experimental and textual research feed each other when one explores the relation between memory and oral literary forms: contemporary neuroscience proposes psychological explanations for prosodic and structural mechanisms, while mnemonic devices used at the micro- and macro-textual levels can provide critical insights into the psychophysics of recall (Leverage 2010; Rubin 1995).

Embodied Contextual Cognitive Research

Retreating from the use of the computer as a model for the human mind while still employing it extensively as a research instrument, the new generation of cognitive scientists argues that conceptualizing abilities including language develop together interdependently, over time, and through an interaction between the biological organism and its environment. Researchers adopt what George Lakoff has called the fundamental 'cognitive commitment': rather than espouse a particular a priori formalism, they endeavour to design their theories, structures, and models to reflect 'convergent evidence' about the mind-brain supplied by the various cognitive sciences including psychology, neuroscience, linguistics, artificial intelligence, and philosophy (Lakoff 1987; Lamb 1999). Thought and language are defined first and foremost not as formal calculi but as embodied practices shaped by the peculiarities of human physiology and its contact with the world, including sense organs, manner of locomotion and gesture, size and orientation (Gibbs 2006). Abstract thinking and verbal expression emerge as extensions and metaphorical applications of fundamental perceptual and sensory-motor processes developed in accomplishing everyday tasks. In this perspective, reality and world correspond above all to our species-specific 'construal' mediated by the body and by experience.

On the time scales of both the individual organism and the species, this new cognitive paradigm emphasizes that life forms increase their capacities by adapting existing structures to new ends, transferring and transposing such skills as spatial orienting, temporal planning, pattern recognition, and part-whole judgments across applications, including from nonverbal to verbal modes. In developmental and evolutionary psychology and in psycholinguistics, this holistic, anthropological perspective that Lakoff (1987) labels the 'generalization commitment' runs directly counter to Chomsky's and Fodor's emphasis on separate mental modules comprising largely innate structures. In the realm of computer modelling, while electronic blueprints that would reproduce cerebral functions remain out of reach, and while neuroscience remains in its infancy, researchers associated with embodied cognitivism adopt the 'reductionist' requirement of biological and psychological plausibility: rather than simply manipulating formal symbols and algorithms, their simulations aim to mimic features of the structured networks of neurons in the brain.

The theories that make up what is today called cognitive linguistics, rhetoric, and poetics originated as alternatives to the Chomskyan paradigm and stem from nuts-and-bolts problems linguists encountered in the latter's strategies, especially its initial construction of a firewall between core syntactic mechanisms and meaning. Positioning semantics at the heart of its investigations, the new cognitive approach describes meaning as emerging from a continuous interaction between language, general conceptualization, the particular communicative situation or discursive context, and encyclopedic knowledge. Charles Fillmore (1982) studies grammatical case relations as elementary meaningful structures and represents speakers' long-term general knowledge as organized in semantic 'frames' that schematize experience and that underpin and fill out the sense of particular utterances (Fillmore 1975, 1977). Ronald Langacker defines his 'cognitive grammar' as

embedded in conceptual schemas through which humans represent space, time, movement, awareness, and interaction: 'My central theoretical claim is that all grammatical structure is inherently symbolic and that all valid grammatical constructs have some kind of conceptual import' (Langacker 1991: 282; 1987, 2002). Discarding the concept of syntactic form advanced in Chomsky's standard theory, Fillmore's 'construction grammar' and Langacker's cognitive grammar adopt the continental structuralist view of symbolic expressions and constructions as meaningful forms, as entailing what Langacker calls a 'phonological pole' and a 'semantic pole' (Fillmore 1988; Langacker 1987: 76–7, 93–4; Saussure 1916 [1966]: 65–70). Leonard Talmy similarly argues that grammatical and lexical structures express cognitive frameworks developed in negotiating everyday force dynamics, figure-ground relations, causation, and the modulation of attention (Talmy 2000; Lakoff and Thompson 1975). The principle of 'iconicity' draws attention to how such aural or graphic dynamics as word order or the relative proximity or distance between units in an utterance, far from representing mere asemantic 'surface' phenomena, express conceptual relations such as sequence, grouping, and degree of relatedness (JohnQPublik n.d.: section 2.2).

Cognitive linguists explore how utterances and expressions which remain semantically 'undetermined' out of context prompt the hearer's construction of a richer, more specific meaning that incorporates more detailed background knowledge and contextual information in actual communicative events (Clark 1996; Sperber and Wilson 1995; Toolan 1996). The interpretation and even the acceptability of an utterance depend on how it is construed by a hearer in a particular context. The importance of context and language use in contemporary cognitive linguistics dovetails with their centrality in mainstream analytic philosophy and speech act theory (Austin 1962; Searle 1969). Pragmatic philosophers such as John Austin and John Searle have explicitly critiqued early cognitivism and its formalism, functionalism, and reliance on computers to model human thought (Austin 1961; Searle 1980, 1990, 1992).

Contemporary cognitive semantics spotlights rhetoric, viewed not so much as an art promising enhanced persuasiveness or aesthetic pleasure, but as a fundamental tactic by which the embodied mind solves problems, envisions alternatives, and creates new ideas within a given cultural environment (Gibbs 1994; Stockwell 2002). Indeed, in presenting the semantic phenomena, the theories themselves typically employ spatial models or metaphors – Langacker's initial term for his approach was 'spatial grammar.' George Lakoff and Mark Johnson show that much of our vocabulary and implicit long-term knowledge are built on conventional 'conceptual metaphors' that use a familiar phenomenon as a comparison for another topic, especially by mapping a source concrete spatial or sensori-motor domain to a target abstract domain such as time, quantity, or emotion (Lakoff and Johnson 1980; conceptual metonymies in Lakoff and Turner 1989). Johnson (1987) further analyses 'image schemas' such as contact, container, and balance notions grounded in embodied, pre-conceptual experience that function as building blocks for more elaborate reasoning, and Lakoff (1987) discusses 'idealized cognitive models' that structure fairly constant background knowledge. Mark Turner proposes that humans initially elaborate 'narrative imagining' as a way to track the movements of objects through space, then extend it to clarify and judge events, to give shape to projects and struggles, and to construct an individual and collective memory (1996: 4–5; 1991). Through the process of 'parable,' a kind of temporal and dynamic correlate to conceptual metaphor, we use concrete 'action-stories' to map out abstract processes: one narrative (for example, a *journey*) is projected onto, or blended with, another (for example, *life*) in order to shape and characterize the latter in a specific and striking manner (Turner 1996).

Adapting possible worlds' problematics including modality and multiple minds to

cognitive semantics, Gilles Fauconnier's mental spaces theory shows how discourse posits a particular configuration of factual, fictional, or hypothetical places and entities attributed to given perspectives or points of view, linking them together in lattices or matrices (Fauconnier 1985, 1997). Fauconnier and Turner (2002) study 'conceptual blending' in which two or more such mental spaces combine to form a novel idea through a combination of analogy and counterfactual thinking, creative metaphor, metonymy, or some other rhetorical figure. Conceptual metaphors, parable, and blending play a key role in 'binding,' in developing concepts that integrate perceptual impressions from a variety of senses. Avoiding a simplistic, unilateral focus on nature at the expense of nurture, or on universality to the detriment of historical and cultural specificity, recent comparative studies show how each natural language constructs significantly different grammatical and vocabulary structures upon the common base in perceptual and motor functions, and can indeed reorganize the mental schemas built on the latter (Feldman et al. 1996: 11–12, 16; Janda 2000: 5, 15).

Associated research in developmental psychology and evolutionary psychology has supported the cognitive principles of embodiment and generalization. Psycholinguistic findings depict the acquisition of first-language skills as intimately linked to and conditioned by the child's development of general perceptual, operational, and cognitive abilities (Mandler 1996; Tomasello and Bates eds. 2001; Tomasello and Slobin eds. 2005). This trans-modal view focused on experiential learning challenges the Chomskyan theory founded on modularity and nativism, which posits a separate, autonomous language faculty comprising powerful structures hardwired in the mind. Similarly, on a phylogenetic scale, researchers look for evolutionary antecedents of linguistic mechanisms, viewing language skills as applications and transpositions of other capabilities and strategies which Homo sapiens developed in earlier millennia in order to survive and thrive (Barkow, Cosmides, and Tooby eds. 1992).

Contemporary cognitive linguistics thus contrasts with Chomsky's theories on a number of key points. Whereas Chomsky-inspired theories portray language in action as the implementation of complex rules, the newer cognitive linguistics foregrounds imaginative uses of language. While Chomsky highlights core syntax defined as a distinct, universal mental faculty, today's cognitive linguists grant great attention to semantics and emphasize multi-modal, embodied, and contextual dynamics in learning and behaviour. Where Chomskyan models draw a clear and principled distinction between immanent linguistic meaning and the study of pragmatic, situational factors, the more recent cognitive current explores their interaction and even continuity. While generative grammar focuses on I-language and on a native speaker's intuitions of grammatical acceptability, today's cognitive linguistics devotes significant attention to varied samples of actual language use, and to language variation and change.

The computer-modelling techniques preferred in studies of embodied cognition highlight 'subsymbolic' approaches that mimic lower-order operations of the brain, viewed as biological underpinnings of the higher-order 'symbolic' processes of the mind such as concept formation, logical reasoning, problem solving, and thinking in images. Prominent since the 1980s but drawing from earlier psychological associationism and linguistic distributionalism, connectionist approaches represent cognitive activity as modifications affecting relational patterns among simple units, their clusters, and systems, depicting a radically decentralized thinking process. In connectionist computer simulations of the brain, thinking activates (artificial) neurons and propagates the excitement throughout a given local network, while learning from experience changes the strength of the links among the nodes (Rumelhart and McClelland 1986). Connectionism vaunts the plasticity of its networks and the importance of aiming for at least a measure of biological

realism. The parallel (that is, simultaneous rather than sequential) and distributed functioning of connectionist models enhances their ability to mimic aspects of vision, linguistic meaning, decision making, and choosing among rival explanations.

Two prominent proponents of the rival, formal cognivist approach co-authored a devastating critique of early connectionist research. In their critical review of Paul Smolensky (1988), Jerry Fodor and Zenon Pylyshyn (1988) charge that connectionism's adoption of associationism renders it incapable of elaborating any of the complex structures that form the heart of thought and language processes. If connectionist models possess any validity at all, they describe processes that merely 'implement' or physically realize symbolic structures, rather than altering, complementing, or supplanting them. Fodor and Pylyshyn (1988) observe that connectionism in fact represents a step backwards and not forwards inasmuch as it promotes a highly simplified view of thinking akin to vulgar behaviourism.

Responding to Fodor and Pylyshyn's critique, researchers have developed 'structured' neo-connectionist models that incorporate simulations of dynamical systems and such higher-order configurations as elementary schemas and rules, metaphors and narrative (Marcus 2001; Narayanan 1997; Regier 1996; Sharkey and Reilly eds. 1992; Shastri and Ajjanagadde 1993; Shastri, Gannes, Narayanan, and Feldman 1999). Dynamical models describe cognition using the physics and mathematics of systems such as planetary orbits, engine fuel flows, and wildlife populations, representing neural activity as a continuous process of forming and breaking interconnected patterns and forms (Chang, Gildea, and Narayanan 1998; Petitot 1991, 1994, 2004; Petitot and Barbaras 2002; Port and van Gelder 1995). Other computational simulations use probability models to mimic distributed subsymbolic processes (Feldman et al. 1996: 2–6, 21).

Jean Petitot (1994) illustrates a sample defence of neo-connectionism that develops two central arguments in response to Fodor and Pylyshyn (Petitot 1991). First, it emphasizes that the formal, logical structures preferred by Fodor, Pylyshyn, and Chomsky represent only one version of structure among many, and that dynamical structures derived from René Thom's catastrophe theory provide a better alternative since the actual mathematics has extensive applications in physics and can thus model actual physical, biological processes. Second, whereas the symbolic, functionalist approach disdains 'implementation,' exactly as generative grammar spurns E-language (performance) in favour of I-language (competence), neo-connectionism instead proposes an integrated theory that includes structures and I-language but defines subsymbolic forms and E-language as autonomous instances possessing their own processes. In this view, an autonomous but not independent or self-sufficient symbolic level 'emerges' from a dynamical subsymbolic level: symbolic superstructures possess associationist infrastructures. Petitot (1994) argues that with respect to explanatory power, the shoe is thus on the other foot: the symbolic approach defended by Chomsky, Fodor, and Pylyshyn will never be able to do anything but *describe* structurality, whereas the connectionist approach has the potential to *explain* it (Petitot 1994: 206).

The greater the advances achieved by neuroscience, the more it becomes reasonable to argue that computational simulations should establish parallel symbolic and subsymbolic models and chart their precise interrelations within a unified theory of cognition. The Berkeley Neural Theory of Language project thus defines symbolic and distributed dynamics as distinct but complementary superimposed levels at which cognitive activity can be grasped and analysed (Feldman et al. 2007). On the symbolic level, the project uses computational components including data structures and algorithms to model the functions of such cognitive and linguistic categories as spatial relations, metaphor, aspect, and frames, while on the

underlying subsymbolic level it employs computer simulations of neuronal processes and hippocampal systems to mime the functioning of structured connectionist mechanisms including temporal binding and recruitment learning. These successive layers of cognitive dynamics and computer simulations are then grounded in biological and physiological structures and processes studied by experimental neuroscience (Feldman 2006; Petitot 1991).

The new models of rhetoric, categories, emotions, and embodiment, and the new perspectives in evolutionary biology and in empirical language studies have fostered a growing interest in exploring literature through the lens of cognitive studies (Crane 2001; Esrock 1994; Herman 2003; Holland 1988; Keen 2007; Palmer 2004; Richardson and Spolsky 2004; Scarry 1999; Zunshine 2006). The relation between cognitive textual studies and earlier text theory remains a complex and evolving issue. One of the most important results of cognitive studies' prominence has been to give new lustre to such mainstream text-theoretic explorations as linguistics, psycholinguistics, the philosophy of language, and reader response theory, and to direct other disciplines' attention to perennial text-theoretic concepts such as metaphor, metonymy, narrative, and poetics. The behaviourist approach against which early cognitive science reacted and defined itself never reigned in text studies, although Skinnerian anti-mentalism and focus on observable phenomena foster the study of the 'text in itself' that characterized both New Criticism and continental structuralism. One can identify contrasts but also certain parallels between contemporary cognitive text studies and post-structuralism and postmodernism. Cognitive scholars evince respect rather than suspicion for scientific method and knowledge, reassert the claims of nature alongside those of nurture and culture, and propose a new pantheon of master thinkers and subfields, typically North American rather than continental – experimental psychology and neuroscience thus displace psychoanalysis, as generative or cognitive linguistics takes precedence over continental structural linguistics (Carroll 1995; Mancing 2003; Bordwell and Carroll 1996). On the other hand, contemporary research in both overall families of approaches typically foregrounds rhetorical and semantic processes, emphasizes the role of the addressee, articulates a contextual and experiential construction of reality, and maintains a keen interest in theoretical issues, including aspects of traditional speculative philosophy.

Amid enormous diversity, if cognitive studies today evinces affinities with a particular philosophical tradition, it would seem to be with the phenomenology that Edmund Husserl elaborated in the first half of the last century in an effort to provide a solid basis for modern science (1936). Husserl grounds his system in the relation between man and world: mathematics, logic, and science are ultimately rooted in human experience modulated by active perception and by a dynamic engagement with the natural and social environment. Maurice Merleau-Ponty worked closely with Gestalt research in experimental psychology in order to develop Husserl's ideas in the realm of perception (Merleau-Ponty 1945). More recently, phenomenologist Hubert Dreyfus has systematically critiqued the use of the digital computer and its symbol processing as a model for human cognition, emphasizing instead the critical role of the body, of human interest and experience, and the changing interaction of self, other subjects, and the perceived world (Dreyfus 1979, 1992; Searle 1990).

Contemporary cognitive studies effectively brings to the fore issues and concepts, methods and traditions that have been forgotten or relegated to the wings in recent times. Researchers have redirected attention to social variation in language (Labov 1972) and rekindled Karl Bühler's focus on communication, expressivity, and pragmatics (Bühler 1934). Studies have revived the nineteenth-century's use of natural science as a model for language and thought, as well as that era's close attention to lexical structures and their

semantic dynamics (for example, Darmesteter 1887). Contemporary cognitive linguistics resonates with earlier theories that foreground language as an instrument of thought (Bréal 1897; Guillaume 1973) and reassert Ferdinand de Saussure's theory of the sign as a bipolar phonological-semantic construction (Saussure 1916 [1966]). While features of 'Chomsky's revolution' remain firmly in place today, its strong versions of formalism and innateness, as well as its exclusive focus on core universal grammar, appear more and more as a brief North American excursus within the development of broad-based modern language sciences encompassing the perspectives of general grammar, rhetoric, comparative and historical linguistics, descriptive linguistics, pragmatics, sociolinguistics, and poetics.

Thomas F. Broden

Bibliography

Austin, John. The Meaning of a Word. In *Philosophical Papers*, ed. J.O. Urmson and G.J. Warnock, 23–43. Oxford: Oxford University Press, 1961.

– *How to Do Things with Words*. Cambridge: Harvard University Press, 1962.

Bach, Emmon. *Informal Lectures on Formal Semantics*. Albany: SUNY Press, 1989.

Barney, Tom. Phonetics and the Empirical Study of Poetry. In *Empirical Approaches to Literature and Aesthetics*, ed. Kreuz and MacNealy, 309–28. Norwood, NJ: Ablex, 1996.

Barkow, Jerome H., Leda Cosmides, and John Tooby, eds. *The Adapted Mind: Evolutionary Psychology and the Generation of Culture*. New York: Oxford University Press, 1992.

Berwick, Robert, and Amy Weinberg. The Psychological Relevance of Transformational Grammar: A Reply to Stabler. *Cognition* 19 (1985): 193–204.

Bloom, Paul. *How Pleasure Works: The New Science of Why We Like What We Like*. New York: W.W. Norton, 2010.

Bordwell, David, and Noël Carroll, eds. *Posttheory: Reconstructing Film Studies*. Madison: University of Wisconsin Press, 1996.

Bortolussi, Marisa, and Peter Dixon. *Psychonarratology: Foundations for the Empirical Study of Literary Response*. New York: Routledge, 2003.

Boyd, Brian. *On the Origin of Stories: Evolution, Cognition, and Fiction*. Cambridge: Belknap Press of Harvard University Press, 2009.

Boyd, Brian, Joseph Carroll, and Jonathan Gottschall, eds. *Evolution, Literature, and Film: A Reader*. New York: Columbia University Press, 2010.

Bréal, Michel. *Essai de sémantique: science des significations*. Paris: Hachette, 1897.

Bresnan, Joan. *Lexical-functional Syntax*. Malden: Blackwell, 2001.

Bresnan, Joan, ed. *The Mental Representation of Grammatical Relations*. Cambridge: MIT Press, 1982.

Bruner, Jerome. *Making Stories: Law, Literature, Life*. New York: Farrar, Straus and Giroux, 2002.

Bühler, Karl. *Sprachtheorie*. Stuttgart: Fischer, 1934. Translated by Donald Fraser Goodwin, *Theory of Language: The Representational Function of Language*. Philadelphia: Benjamins, 1990.

Carnap, Rudolf. *The Logical Syntax of Language*. New York: Harcourt Brace, 1937.

– *Meaning and Necessity*. Chicago: University of Chicago Press, 1967.

Carroll, Joseph. *Evolution and Literary Theory*. Columbia: University of Missouri Press, 1995.

Chang, Nancy, Daniel Gildea, and Srini Narayanan. A Dynamic Model of Aspectual Composition (1998). http://www.icsi.berkeley.edu/NTL/papers/asp.pdf (accessed 26 April 2007).

Chierchia, Gennaro, and Sally McConnell-Ginet. *Meaning and Grammar. An Introduction to Semantics*. Cambridge: MIT Press, 1990.

Chomsky, Noam. *Syntactic Structures*. The Hague: Mouton, 1957.

– Review of *Verbal Behavior* by B.F. Skinner. *Language* 35 (1959): 26–57.

– *Aspects of the Theory of Syntax*. Cambridge: MIT Press, 1965.

– *Cartesian Linguistics: A Chapter in the History of Rationalist Thought*. New York: Harper and Row, 1966.

– *Lectures on Government and Binding: The Pisa Lectures*. Holland: Foris, 1981.

– *The Minimalist Program*. Cambridge: MIT Press, 1995.

– *New Horizons in the Study of Language and Mind*. New York: Cambridge University Press, 2000.

Chomsky, Noam, and Morris Halle. *The Sound Pattern of English*. New York: Harper and Row, 1968.

Clark, Herbert H. *Using Language*. New York: Cambridge University Press, 1996.

Cook, Vivian, and Mark Newson. *Chomsky's Universal Grammar. An Introduction*. 3rd ed. Cambridge: Blackwell, 2007.

Crane, Mary Thomas. *Shakespeare's Brain: Reading with Cognitive Theory*. Princeton, NJ: Princeton University Press, 2001.

Croft, William, and D. Alan Cruse. *Cognitive Linguistics*. New York: Cambridge University Press, 2004.

Damasio, Antonio R. *Descartes' Error: Emotion, Reason, and the Human Brain*. New York: Grosset/Putnam, 1994.

Darmesteter, Arsène. *La Vie des mots étudiée dans leurs significations* (1887). New edition Paris: Champ Libre, 1979.

Donald, Merlin. *Origins of the Modern Mind: Three Stages in the Evolution of Culture and Cognition*. Harvard University Press, 1991.

– *A Mind So Rare: The Evolution of Human Consciousness*. New York: W.W. Norton, 2001.

Dreyfus, Hubert L. *What Computers Can't Do: A Critique of Artificial Reason*. Rev. ed. New York: Harper, 1979.

– *What Computers Still Can't Do. A Critique of Artificial Reason*. Cambridge: MIT Press, 1992.

Edelman, Gerald. *Bright Air, Brilliant Fire: On the Matter of Mind*. New York: Basic Books, 1993.

Emmott, Catherine. *Narrative Comprehension: A Discourse Perspective*. Oxford: Clarendon, Oxford University Press, 1997.

Esrock, Ellen J. *The Reader's Eye: Visual Imaging as Reader Response*. Baltimore: Johns Hopkins University Press, 1994.

Fauconnier, Gilles. *Mental Spaces: Aspects of Meaning Construction in Natural Language*. Cambridge: MIT Press, 1985.

– *Mappings in Thought and Language*. New York: Cambridge University Press, 1997.

Fauconnier, Gilles, and Mark Turner. *The Way We Think: Conceptual Blending and the Mind's Hidden Complexities*. New York: Basic Books, 2002.

Feagin, Susan L. *Reading with Feeling: The Aesthetics of Appreciation.* Ithaca, NY: Cornell University Press, 1996.

Feldman, Jerome A. *From Molecule to Metaphor. A Neural Theory of Language.* Cambridge: MIT Press, 2006.

Feldman, Jerome, George Lakoff, David Bailey, Srini Narayanan, Terry Regier, and Andreas Stolcke. L_0 – The First 5 Years of an Automated Language Acquisition Project. *Integration of Natural Language and Vision Processing: Grounding Representations,* special issue of *Artificial Intelligence Review* 10 (1996): 103–29. http://www.icsi.berkeley.edu/NTL/papers/first_five_years.pdf (accessed 27–8 April 2007).

Feldman, Jerome, George Lakoff, Srini Narayanan, Lokendra Shastri, and Eve Sweetser. The Neural Theory of Language. 2007. The University of California at Berkeley and the International Computer Science Institute. http://www.icsi.berkeley.edu/NTL/ (accessed 27–9 April 2007).

Fillmore, Charles. *Santa Cruz Lectures on Deixis, 1971.* Bloomington: Indiana University Linguistics Club, 1975.

– The Case for Case Reopened. In *Grammatical Relations,* ed. P. Cole and J.M. Sadock, 59–81. New York: Academic, 1977.

– Frame Semantics. In *Linguistics in the Morning Calm,* selected papers from SICOL-1981, edited by the Linguistic Society of Korea, 111–37. Seoul: Hanshin, 1982.

– The Mechanisms of Construction Grammar. *Proceedings of the Annual Meeting of the Berkeley Linguistics Society* 14 (1988): 35–55.

Fireman, Gary D., Ted E. McVay, Jr., and Owen J. Flanagan, eds. *Narrative and Consciousness: Literature, Psychology, and the Brain.* New York: Oxford University Press, 2003.

Flanagan, Owen. *Consciousness Reconsidered.* Cambridge: MIT Press, 1992.

Fodor, Jerry. *The Modularity of Mind. An Essay on Faculty Psychology.* Cambridge: MIT Press, 1983.

Fodor, Jerry, and Zenon Pylyshyn. Connectionism and Cognitive Architecture: A Critical Analysis. *Cognition* 28 (1988): 3–71.

Frege, Gottlob. *Begriffsschrift: eine der arithmetischen nachgebildete Formelsprache des reinen Denkens.* Halle-on-the-Saale: L. Nebert, 1879.

Edited and translated by Terrell Ward Bynum, *Begriffsschrift: A Formula Language, Modeled upon That of Arithmetic, for Pure Thought* in *Conceptual Notation and Related Articles.* New York: Clarendon, Oxford University Press, 1972.

Gardner, Howard. *The Mind's New Science: A History of the Cognitive Revolution.* 2nd ed. New York: Basic Books, 1987.

Geeraerts, Dirk, and Hubert Cuyckens, eds. *The Oxford Handbook of Cognitive Linguistics.* Oxford: Oxford University Press, 2007.

Gerrig, Richard. *Experiencing Narrative Worlds: On the Psychological Activities of Reading.* New Haven, CT: Yale University Press, 1993.

Gibbs, Raymond W. *The Poetics of Mind: Figurative Thought, Language, and Understanding.* New York: Cambridge University Press, 1994.

– *Embodiment and Cognitive Science.* New York: Cambridge University Press, 2006.

Guillaume, Gustave. *Principes de linguistique théorique de Gustave Guillaume.* Recueil de textes préparé en collaboration sous la direction de Roch Valin. Quebec: Presses de l'Université Laval, and Paris: Klincksieck, 1973.

Heim, Irene, and Angelika Kratzer. *Semantics and Generative Grammar.* Malden, MA: Blackwell, 1998.

Herman, David, ed. *Narrative Theory and the Cognitive Sciences.* Stanford, CA: Center for the Study of Language and Information, 2003.

Hobbs, Jerry. *Literature and Cognition.* Stanford, CA: Center for the Study of Language and Information, 1990.

Hogan, Patrick Colm. *Cognitive Science, Literature, and the Arts: A Guide for Humanists.* New York: Routledge, 2003a.

– *The Mind and Its Stories: Narrative Universals and Human Emotion.* New York: Cambridge University Press, 2003b.

Holland, Norman. *The Brain of Robert Frost: A Cognitive Approach to Literature.* New York: Routledge, 1988.

Husserl, Edmund. *Die Krisis der europäischen Wissenschaften und die transcendentale Phänomenologie: eine Einleitung in die phänomenologische Philosophie.* Belgrade, 1936. Translated by David Carr, *The Crisis of European Sciences and Transcendental Phenomenology: An Introduction to Phenomenological Philosophy.* Evansville, IL: Northwestern University Press, series Studies in Phenomenology and Existential Philosophy, 1970.

Jackendoff, Ray. *The Architecture of the Language Faculty*. Cambridge: MIT Press, 1997.

Janda, Laura. Cognitive Linguistics. Text for the 2000 Indiana University Summer Linguistics Workshop. http://www.indiana.edu/~slavconf/SLING2K/pospapers/janda.pdf (accessed 2 April 2007).

JohnQPublik (pseudonym). N.d. Cognitive Linguistics. http://www.chrisdb.me.uk/wiki/doku.php?id=cognitive_linguistics (accessed 13–14 April 2007).

Johnson, Mark. *The Body in the Mind*. Chicago: Chicago University Press, 1987.

Johnson-Laird, Philip Nicholas. *Mental Models: Towards a Cognitive Science of Language, Inference, and Consciousness*. New York: Cambridge University Press, 1983.

– *The Computer and the Mind: An Introduction to Cognitive Science*. Cambridge: Harvard University Press, 1988.

Keen, Suzanne. *Empathy and the Novel*. Oxford: Oxford University Press, 2007.

Kleiber, Georges. *La Sémantique du prototype. Catégories et sens lexical*. Paris: Presses Universitaires de France, série Linguistique Nouvelle, 1990.

Kosslyn, Stephen, and Olivier Koenig. *Wet Mind: The New Cognitive Neuroscience*. New York: Free Press, 1992.

Kreuz, Roger J., and Mary Sue MacNealy, eds. *Empirical Approaches to Literature and Aesthetics*. Norwood, NJ: Ablex, 1996.

Labov, William. *Sociolinguistic Patterns*. Philadelphia: University of Pennsylvania Press, 1972.

Lakoff, George. *Women, Fire, and Dangerous Things: What Categories Reveal about the Mind*. Chicago: University of Chicago Press, 1987.

Lakoff, George, and Mark Johnson. *Metaphors We Live By*. Chicago: University of Chicago Press, 1980.

Lakoff, George, and Henry Thompson. Introduction to Cognitive Grammar. *Berkeley Linguistic Society* 1 (1975): 295–313.

Lakoff, George, and Mark Turner. *More Than Cool Reason: A Field Guide to Poetic Metaphor*. Chicago: University of Chicago Press, 1989.

Lamb, Sydney M. *Pathways of the Brain. The Neurocognitive Basis of Language*. Philadelphia: Benjamins, 1999.

Langacker, Ronald W. *Foundations of Cognitive Grammar*, vol. 1: *Theoretical Prerequisites*; vol. 2: *Descriptive Application*. Stanford: Stanford University Press, 1987–91.

– *Concept, Image, and Symbol. The Cognitive Basis of Grammar*. 2nd ed. Berlin: Mouton de Gruyter, 2002.

Lerdahl, Fred, and Ray Jackendoff. *A Generative Theory of Tonal Music*. Cambridge: MIT Press, 1983.

Leverage, Paula. *Reception and Memory: A Cognitive Approach to the Chanson de Geste*. Amsterdam: Rodopi, 2010.

– Memory. In *Handbook of Medieval Studies: Terms, Methods, Trends*, ed. Albrecht Classen, 1530–7. New York: De Gruyter, 2010.

– Memory and Mnemonic Imagery in Some Chanson de Geste Prologues. *RLA: Romance Languages Annual* 11 (1999): 63–7.

Leverage, Paula, Howard Mancing, Richard Schweickert, and Jennifer Marston William, eds. *Theory of Mind and Literature*. West Lafayette: Purdue University Press, 2011.

Mancing, Howard. Prototypes of Genre in Cervantes' *Novelas ejemplares*. *Cervantes* 20 (2000): 127–50.

– Paradigms in Conflict. *Semiotica* 145 (2003): 139–49.

Mandler, Jean. Preverbal Representation and Language. In *Language and Space*, ed. P. Bloom, M.A. Peterson, L. Nadel, and M.F. Garret, 365–84. Cambridge: MIT Press, 1996.

Marcus, Gary F. *The Algebraic Mind: Integrating Connectionism and Cognitive Science*. Cambridge: MIT Press, 2001.

Merleau-Ponty, Maurice. *Phénoménologie de la perception*. Paris: Gallimard, 1945. Translated by Colin Smith, *Phenomenology of Perception*. New York: Routledge, 1986.

Miall, David S. *Literary Reading: Empirical and Theoretical Studies*. New York: Peter Lang, 2006.

Montague, Richard. The Proper Treatment of Quantification in Ordinary English. In *Approaches to Natural Language*, ed. J. Hintikka, J. Moravcsik, and P. Suppes, 221–42. Dordrecht: Reidel, 1973.

Nalbantian, Suzanne. *Memory in Literature: From Rousseau to Neuroscience*. New York: Palgrave Macmillan, 2003.

Narayanan, Srini. Knowledge-Based Action Representations for Metaphor and Aspect. PhD thesis, University of California, Berkeley, 1997.

Noë, Alva. *Out of Our Heads: Why You Are Not Your Brain, and Other Lessons from the Biology of Consciousness*. New York: Hill and Wang, 2009.

Ohmann, Richard M. Generative Grammars and the Concept of Literary Style. *Word* 20 (1964): 423–39.

Palmer, Alan. *Fictional Minds*. Lincoln: University of Nebraska Press, 2004.

Pavel, Thomas G. *La Syntaxe narrative des tragédies de Corneille: recherches et propositions*. Paris: Klincksieck, 1976.

Petitot, Jean. Why Connectionism Is Such a Good Thing. A Criticism of Fodor's and Pylyshyn's Criticism of Smolensky. *Philosophica* 47 (1991): 49–79.

– Dynamical Constituency: An Epistemological Analysis. *Sémiotiques* 6–7 (December 1994): 187–225. http://www.revue-texto.net/ Parutions/Semiotiques/SEM_n6-7_11.pdf (accessed 22–3 April 2007).

– *Morphologie et esthétique: la forme et le sens chez Goethe, Lessing, Lévi-Strauss, Kant, Valéry, Husserl, Eco, Proust, Stendhal*. Paris: Maisonneuve et Larose, 2004.

Petitot, Jean, ed. *Linguistique cognitive et modèles dynamiques*, special issue of *Sémiotiques* (Paris) 6-7 (1994). http://www.revue-texto.net/ Parutions/Semiotiques/Semiotiques.html.

Petitot, Jean, and Renaud Barbaras. *Naturaliser la phénoménologie: essais sur la phénoménologie contemporaine et les sciences cognitives*. Paris: CNRS, 2002.

Pinker, Steven. *The Language Instinct: How the Mind Creates Language*. New York: Harper, 1994.

Port, Robert F., and Timothy van Gelder, eds. *Mind as Motion: Explorations in the Dynamics of Cognition*. Cambridge: MIT Press, 1995. http://www2.lib.purdue.edu:3649/library/ books/view?isbn=0262161508 (accessed 3–4 May 2007).

Pylyshyn, Zenon W. *Computation and Cognition: Toward a Foundation for Cognitive Science*. Cambridge: MIT Press, 1986.

Regier, Terry. *The Human Semantic Potential. Spatial Language and Constrained Connectionism*. Cambridge: MIT Press, 1996.

Richardson, Alan. British Romanticism as a Cognitive Category. *Romanticism on the Net* 8 (November 1997). http://www.erudit.org/ revue/ron/1997/v/n8/005767ar.html (accessed 7 May 2007).

Richardson, Alan, and Ellen Spolsky, eds. *The Work of Fiction: Cognition, Culture and Complexity*. Aldershot, UK: Ashgate, 2004.

Richardson, Alan, and Francis Steen, eds. *Literature and the Cognitive Revolution*, special issue of *Poetics Today* 23.1 (Spring 2002).

Rosch, Eleanor. Natural Categories. *Cognitive Psychology* 4 (1973a): 328–50.

– On the Internal Structure of Perceptual and Semantic Categories. In *Cognitive Development and the Acquisition of Language*, ed. Timothy E. Moore, 111–44. New York: Academic, 1973b.

– Cognitive Reference Points. *Cognitive Psychology* 7 (1975): 532–47.

– Principles of Categorization. In *Cognition and Categorization*, ed. E. Rosch and Barbara B. Loyd, 28–48. Hillsdale, NJ: Lawrence Erlbaum, 1978.

Rubin, David. *Memory in Oral Traditions: The Cognitive Psychology of Epic, Ballads and Counting-Out Rhymes*. New York: Oxford University Press, 1995.

Rumelhart, David E., and James L. McClelland. *Parallel Distributed Processing: Explorations in the Microstructure of Cognition*. 2 vols. Cambridge: MIT Press, 1986.

Russell, Bertand. *An Inquiry into Meaning and Truth*. London: G. Allen and Unwin, 1940.

Ryan, Marie-Laure. *Possible Worlds, Artificial Intelligence, and Narrative Theory*. Bloomington: Indiana University Press, 1991.

Saussure, Ferdinand de. *Cours de linguistique générale*. 1916. Translated by Wade Baskins, *Course in General Linguistics*. New York: McGraw-Hill, 1966.

Scarry, Elaine. *Dreaming by the Book*. New York: Farrar, Straus, Giroux, 1999.

Schacter, Daniel, and Elaine Scarry, eds. *Memory, Brain, and Belief*. Cambridge: Harvard University Press, 2000.

Schank, Roger C. *Dynamic Memory: A Theory of Reminding and Learning in Computers and People*. New York: Cambridge University Press, 1982.

– *Tell Me a Story: Narrative and Intelligence*. Evanston, IL: Northwestern University Press, 1995.

Schank, Roger C., and Robert P. Abelson. *Scripts, Plans, Goals, and Understanding: An Inquiry into*

Human Knowledge Structures. Hillsdale, NJ: Lawrence Erlbaum, 1977.

Schank, Roger C., and Kenneth Mark Colby, eds. *Computer Models of Thought and Language*. San Francisco: W.H. Freeman, 1973.

Searle, John. *Speech Acts. An Essay in the Philosophy of Language*. New York: Cambridge University Press, 1969.

– Minds, Brains, and Programs. *The Behavioral and Brain Sciences* 3 (1980): 417–57.

– *The Rediscovery of the Mind*. Cambridge: MIT Press, 1992.

– Is the Brain's Mind a Computer Program? *Scientific American* (January 1990). Rpt. in *Readings in Language and Mind*, ed. Heimir Geirsson and Michael Losonsky, 264–73. Cambridge: Blackwell, 1996.

Sharkey, Noel E., and Ronan G. Reilly, eds. *Connectionist Natural Language Processing*. Hillsdale, NJ: Lawrence Erlbaum, 1992.

Shastri, Lokendra, and Venkat Ajjanagadde. From Simple Associations to Systematic Reasoning: A Connectionist Representation of Rules, Variables, and Dynamic Bindings Using Temporal Synchrony. *Behavioral and Brain Sciences* 16 (1993): 417–94. http://www.icsi.berkeley.edu/NTL/papers/bbs.shastri/text.pdf, http://www.icsi.berkeley.edu/NTL/papers/bbs.shastri/bhfigs1.pdf, and http://www.icsi.berkeley.edu/NTL/papers/bbs.shastri/bhfigs2.pdf (accessed 24 April 2007).

Shastri, Lokendra, D. Gannes, Srini Narayanan, and Jerome Feldman. A Connectionist Encoding of Parameterized Schemas and Reactive Plans. In *Hybrid Information Processing in Adaptive Autonomous Vehicles*, Lecture Notes in Computer Science, Lecture Notes in Artificial Intelligence, ed. G. Kraetzschmar and G. Palm, 29–38. Berlin: Springer, 1999.

Skinner, Burrhus Frederic. *Verbal Behavior*. New York: Appleton-Century-Crofts, 1957.

Smolensky, Paul. On the Proper Treatment of Connectionism. *Behavioral and Brain Sciences* 11 (1988): 1–23.

Sperber, Dan, and Deirdre Wilson. *Relevance: Communication and Cognition*. 2nd ed. Cambridge: Blackwell, 1995.

Spolsky, Ellen. *Word vs. Image: Cognitive Hunger in Shakespeare's England*. New York: Palgrave Macmillan, 2007.

Steen, Francis. 'The Time of Unrememberable Being': Wordsworth's Autobiography of the Imagination. *a/b: Auto/Biography Studies* 13 (1998): 7–38.

Stenning, Keith, Alex Lascarides, and Jo Calder. *Introduction to Cognition and Communication*. Cambridge: MIT Press, 2006.

Stockwell, Peter. *Cognitive Poetics: An Introduction*. New York: Routledge, 2002.

Talmy, Leonard. *Toward a Cognitive Semantics*. 2 vols. Cambridge: MIT Press, 2000.

Taylor, John R. *Linguistic Categorization. Prototypes in Linguistic Theory*. 2nd ed. New York: Clarendon, Oxford University Press, 1995.

Tomasello, Michael, and Elizabeth Bates, eds. *Language Development: The Essential Readings*. Malden, MA: Blackwell, 2001.

Tomasello, Michael, and Dan Isaac Slobin, eds. *Beyond Nature-Nurture Essays in Honor of Elizabeth Bates*. Hillsdale, NJ: Lawrence Erlbaum, 2005.

Toolan, Michael. *Total Speech: An Integrational Linguistic Approach to Language*. Durham, NC: Duke University Press, 1996.

Tsur, Reuven. *What Is Cognitive Poetics?* The Katz Research Institute for Hebrew Literature: Tel Aviv University, 1983.

– *Toward a Theory of Cognitive Poetics*. Amsterdam: North Holland, 1992.

Turner, Frederick. *Natural Classicism: Essays on Literature and Science*. New York: Paragon, 1985.

Turner, Mark. *Reading Minds: The Study of English in the Age of Cognitive Science*. Princeton: Princeton University Press, 1991.

– *The Literary Mind*. New York: Oxford University Press, 1996.

Vermeule, Blakey. *Why Do We Care about Literary Characters?* Baltimore: Johns Hopkins University Press, 2010.

Wittgenstein, Ludwig. *Philosophische Untersuchungen*. Translated by G.E.M. Anscombe *Philosophical investigations*. 3rd ed. New York: McMillan, 1973.

Zunshine, Lisa. *Why We Read Fiction: Theory of Mind and the Novel*. Columbus: Ohio State University Press, 2006.

Zunshine, Lisa, ed. *Introduction to Cognitive Cultural Studies*. Baltimore: Johns Hopkins University Press, 2010.

COGNITIVISM

[See also: *Behaviourism; Cognitive Language Studies; Psychology of the Media*]

The term *cognitivism* is used in several disciplines, including linguistics and psychology, in opposition to behaviourism. It is a movement which maintains that the emphasis of behaviourists on observable response phenomena to given stimuli is a dubious one, since most mental phenomena cannot be associated with simple bodily responses to specific stimuli. The initial approach of cognitivists was to 'get to' the 'unobservable' mental phenomena through modelling on computers. The underlying assumption was that the functions of the mind could be understood by inference if they were modelled by software designed to simulate them. Ulrich Neisser (1967: 6) put it as follows at the dawn of the movement:

> The task of the psychologist in trying to understand human cognition is analogous to that of a man trying to discover how a computer has been programmed. In particular, if the program seems to store and reuse information, he would like to know by what 'routines' or 'procedures' this is done. Given this purpose, he will not care much whether his particular computer stores information in magnetic cores or in thin films; he wants to understand the program, not the 'hardware.' By the same token, it would not help the psychologist to know that memory is carried by RNA as opposed to some other medium. He wants to understand its utilization, not its incarnation.

Neisser realized, however, that the computer metaphor, if brought to an extreme, would actually lead psychological science astray. So, only a few pages later he issued the following warning (Neisser 1967: 9): 'Unlike men, artificially intelligent programs tend to be single-minded, undistractable, and unemotional ... in my opin-

ion, none does even remote justice to the complexity of mental processes.'

In the twentieth century, mainstream psychology was defined by two primary movements – behaviourism and cognitivism. Based on Pavlov's discovery that a hungry dog could be conditioned to respond to a ringing bell – by simply associating the bell with a piece of meat and by eventually removing the meat stimulus – behaviourism became the main school of psychology from the early part of the twentieth century to the 1960s. The movement was bolstered by the ideas of John B. Watson (1929) and developed by B.F. Skinner (1938). Watson maintained that all complex forms of behaviour could be observed, measured, and explained by observing the simple motor and glandular processes that they purportedly brought about. These constituted the organism's response patterns to specific input stimuli. Skinner took stimulus-response theory further by adding the individual's interactions with the environment as crucial determinants of behaviour. He also showed that certain behaviours could be retained if they were reinforced in one of two ways – positively and negatively.

In the late 1960s, cognitivism emerged to replace behaviourism as the mainstream psychological method. The term *cognition*, rather than 'mind' or 'behaviour,' was employed widely in that decade in order to eliminate the artificial distinction maintained by behaviourists between inner (mental) and observable (behavioural) processes. Indeed, this word has now come to characterize all mental faculties and processes, from perception to language. Adopting insights and terms from the science of artificial intelligence, many cognitivists aimed initially to study the mind by seeking parallels between the functions of the human brain and computer concepts such as the 'coding,' 'storing,' 'retrieving,' and 'buffering' of information. Although cognitivism's goals are now much broader and include experientialist approaches to the mind such as cognitive linguistics that have nothing to do with simplistic artificial intelligence models of mind, there are still 'computationalist' residues in the movement. As Gardner (1985: 6) has put it, the guiding assumption of mainstream cognitivism has always been that there exists 'a level of analysis wholly separate from the biological or neurological, on the one hand, and the sociological or cultural, on the other' and that 'central to any understanding of the human mind is the electronic computer.' Cognitivism has, in effect, rekindled the mind-body problem: Is thought a derivative of individual experience, or is it inherent in mental structures independently of bodily processes and individual feelings?

Gardner's (1985: 6) formulation of the goals of cognitivism indicates how it envisions its approach in answering these questions:

> First of all, there is the belief that, in talking about human cognitive activities, it is necessary to speak about mental representations and to posit a level of analysis wholly separate from the biological or neurological, on the one hand, and the sociological or cultural, on the other. Second, there is the faith that central to any understanding of the human mind is the electronic computer. Not only are computers indispensable for carrying out studies of various sorts, but, more crucially, the computer also serves as the most viable model of how the mind functions ... The third feature of cognitive science is the deliberate decision to de-emphasize certain factors which may be important for cognitive functioning but whose inclusion at this point would unnecessarily complicate the cognitive-scientific enterprise. These factors include the influence of affective factors or emotions, the contribution of historical and cultural factors, and the role of background context on which particular actions of thought occur.

To grasp how early cognitivism approached mental phenomena, consider the highly acclaimed research on human vision by David Marr (1982). Marr simulated in a computer the essential features of vision (perception, recognition, and so on). He then specified the 'algorithms' that vision is purported to entail. Marr sought to explain visual perception, not by working directly with the visual nervous system, but by designing programs to be consistent with the processes known, observed, or suspected to underlie visual perception. Such work has been valuable in having forced psychologists to reconsider many of their assumptions about perception and to seek out much more clearly formulated explanations of visual processes. But which portions of Marr's program are indeed like those of human visual perception? Does the computer, following Marr's instructions, really 'recognize' objects, people, and events in the same ways that people do? These questions remain unanswered. In a similar critique to cognitive approaches to problem solving, Sheehan (1991: 262) suggests that the 'fact that both humans and machines can learn to play chess may suggest a number of interesting things about the human brain and mechanical intelligence, but it does not suggest that the two are necessarily alike in any other ways.'

While the view that human thought can best be studied separately from the sensory, emotional, and social fabric of human experience seems to be a modern premise, it is really a contemporary version of an age-old idea known as dualism, or the belief that the body and the mind are separate entities. It started with Plato, who claimed that ideas were innate and thus separable from experiential factors, and was later taken up by Thomas Hobbes and René Descartes. Hobbes defined mentality bluntly as arithmetical computation: that is, as a process akin to the addition and subtraction of numbers. He claimed that thinking was essentially a rule-governed mechanical process and that, in principle, machines capable of thought could be built. His solution to the mind-body problem was a blunt reduction of mental operations, including value and judgment, to the internal activities of the body. For Descartes mentality inhered exclusively in the manipulation of abstract symbols according to the rules of logic and mathematical proof. He refused to accept any belief, even the belief in his own existence, unless he could 'prove' it to be necessarily true. The Cartesian 'project' ushered in the modern era of modern science. Cognitive science is its contemporary descendant. In their book *Descartes' Dream*, Davis and Hersh (1986: 7) describe the Cartesian project as follows:

> The vision of Descartes became the new spirit. Two generations later, the mathematician and philosopher Leibnitz talked about the 'characteristica universalis.' This was the dream of a universal method whereby all human problems, whether of science, law, or politics, could be worked out rationally, systematically, by logical computation.

In contrast to Hobbes and Descartes, Immanuel Kant associated knowledge with bodily structures, positing that we participate mentally in the way we come to experience the world, but that the ways in which we perceive nature are largely determined by our concepts about it. He maintained that the world we know is largely invented by us on the basis of sense categories. Kantian strains in modern-day cognitivism now abound, as psychologists and linguists discover that modelling and sensing are different not only in degree but in essential quality.

Prefiguring contemporary cognitivism is the work of philosopher Ludwig Wittgenstein. In his influential *Tractatus Logico-Philosophicus* of 1921, Wittgenstein was interested in understanding how language captured information about the world. He saw sentences as propositions (inferences) about simple world facts. He thus developed a 'picture theory' of meaning by which propositions were purported to represent features of the world in the same

way that pictures did. Wittgenstein argued that the lines and shapes of drawings, for instance, showed how things were related to each other in physical space. So when the world is represented as a proposition 'pictures' it, then the proposition is 'true.' It is interesting to note that Wittgenstein had serious misgivings about his theory after it was published. In *Philosophical Investigations* (1953), he was perplexed by the fact that language could do much more than just construct propositions about the world. So he introduced the idea of 'language games,' by which he claimed that there existed a variety of linguistic games (describing, reporting, guessing riddles, making jokes, and so on) that went beyond simple picturing.

Early cognitivism was inspired not only by Wittgenstein's ideas, but also by clever computer notions such as the Turing machine, a concept developed by the mathematician Alan Turing (1936). To quote Garnham (1991: 20), such a machine is

> a mathematical abstraction that has the following property: if something can be worked out by mathematical calculation, in the broadest sense of that term, then there is a Turing machine that can do each specific calculation, and there is a General Turing machine that can do all of them. The way it works is that you pick the calculation you want done and tell the General Turing machine about the ordinary Turing machine that does that calculation. The general Turing machine then simulates the operation of the more specific one.

Turing's work on finite-state automata showed that the simple architecture of a four-operation machine – move right, move left, write a slash, erase a slash – could in principle carry out any recursive function. In 1950, shortly before his death, Turing suggested that one could program a computer in such a way that it would be virtually impossible to discriminate between its answers and those contrived by a human being. This notion has become immortalized as the 'Turing test.' Suppose you are an observer in a room which hides on one side a programmed computer and, on the other, a human being. The computer and the human being can only respond to your questions in writing – say, on pieces of paper which both pass on to you through slits in the wall. If you cannot identify, on the basis of the written responses, who is the computer and who the human being, then you must conclude that the machine is 'intelligent.' It has passed the 'Turing test.' For Turing, every intelligent response could be described in computational terms; that is, in terms of basic building blocks that can be carried out mechanically.

A rebuttal to 'Turing test' was put forward by John Searle (1984), who argued that a machine does not 'know' what it is doing when it processes symbols because it lacks intentionality. For example, a human being who translates Chinese symbols in the form of little pieces of paper by using a set of rules for matching them with other symbols or little pieces of paper knows nothing about the 'story' contained in the Chinese pieces of paper. Likewise, a computer does not have access to the 'story' that inheres in human symbols. Searle's is a clever argument. The human mind can process symbols at a rational surface level in the same way that a computer does. But only at a deep level of consciousness does it put them together into a meaningful whole. This is beyond the capacities of a machine whose operations are defined completely by formal syntactic structure.

By the late 1960s, cognitivism had become a major force in developmental psychology, following the work of Jean Piaget (Piaget 1969; Piaget and Inhelder 1969). The three cognitive stages of development that Piaget posited – sensory-motor, concrete operations, formal-logical thinking – had become widely accepted as the primary biological milestones of cognitive development. Piaget had shown, in a phrase, that humans progress from a sensory and concrete stage of mind to a reflective and abstract one. According to Piaget's observations, around the age of two, children start to develop symbolic abilities derived from mental images. As these become more dynamic, they prepare the child for more abstract thinking. Knowledge in the child emerges in terms of a direct relation to events in the immediate environment. Self-knowledge arises later.

Reactions to Piaget's theory have criticized it for its determinism and its overemphasis on cognitive processes at the expense of affect and emotion. The work of both Vygotsky (1961) and Bruner (1986, 1990) has thus been adopted by modern-day cognitivists to supplement and balance Piagetian psychology. Vygotsky proposed developmental stages that go from external (physical and social) actions to internal cognitive constructions and interior speech via the mind's ability to construct images of external reality. His definition of speech as a 'microcosm of consciousness' is particularly characteristic of his approach. Bruner suggested that the construction of the intellect starts with an 'enactive' stage, passes through an 'iconic' stage, and finally reaches a 'symbolic' stage. Action, imagination, and abstract thought are the chronologically related stages through which each child passes on the way to mature thinking: that is, the child first employs non-verbal symbols (action, play, drawing, painting, music, and so on), then imaginative constructs (narratives, fables, dramatizations, and so on), and finally oral expression and creative writing on the way to the development of abstract thought.

Cognitivists today also employ notions from neuroscience to guide their theories and provide empirical data on how the brain functions under certain conditions involving cognitive tasks. Modern imaging equipment such as PET scans and fMRI technologies are replacing the computer as devices for exploring how humans process information and develop thought patterns.

Cognitivism has rekindled interest in gestalt psychology, which flourished between

1910 and the mid-1940s, since the emphasis in that movement was also on studying the mind indirectly by trying to understand the relation between perception of form and knowledge. Gestalt psychologists believe that form-perception is the most important part of experience. This notion is also the basis of sub-movements within cognitivism, such as cognitive linguistics (mentioned above). Two gestalt principles in particular, known as closure and figure-ground perception, are now basic ones within cognitivism generally. The former explains why we perceive a fragmented circle as a complete circle and the latter why we tend to regard any kind of pattern as a figure against a background (such as words on a page).

In sum, cognitivism, which emerged as a reaction to behaviourism, has expanded its theoretical horizons, focusing on the outcomes of mental processes in human activities, from problem solving to the reading of media texts. Blending insights from linguistics, neuroscience, psychology, and anthropology, cognitive analysis has made it clear that not all thought processes can be understood as simple stimulus-response categories.

Marcel Danesi

Bibliography

Bruner, Jerome S. *Actual Minds, Possible Worlds.* Cambridge, MA: Harvard University Press, 1986.
– *Acts of Meaning.* Cambridge, MA: Harvard University Press, 1990.
Davis, Philip J., and Reuben Hersh. *Descartes' Dream: The World according to Mathematics.* Boston: Houghton Mifflin, 1986.
Gardner, Howard. *The Mind's New Science: A History of the Cognitive Revolution.* New York: Basic Books, 1985.
Garnham, Alan. *The Mind in Action: A Personal View of Cognitive Science.* London: Routledge, 1991.
Marr, David. *Vision: A Computational Investigation into the Human Representation and Processing of Visual Information.* New York: W.H. Freeman, 1982.
Neisser, Ulrich. *Cognitive Psychology.* Englewood Cliffs, NJ: Prentice–Hall, 1967.
Piaget Jean. *The Child's Conception of the World.* Totowa, NJ: Littlefield, Adams, 1969.
Piaget, Jean, and Barbel Inhelder. *The Psychology of the Child.* New York: Basic Books, 1969.
Searle, John R. *Minds, Brain, and Science.* Cambridge, MA: Harvard University Press, 1984.
Sheehan, James J. Coda. In *The Boundaries of Humanity,* ed. James J. Sheehan and Morton Sosna, 259–65. Berkeley: University of California Press, 1991.
Skinner, B.F. *The Behavior of Organisms.* New York: Appleton-Century-Crofts, 1938.
Turing, Alan. On Computable Numbers with an Application to the Entscheidungs Problem. *Proceedings of the London Mathematical Society* 41 (1936): 230–65.
– Computing Machinery and Intelligence. In *Computers and Thought,* ed. E.A. Feigenbaum and J. Feldman, 123–34. New York: McGraw-Hill, 1950.
Vygotsky, Lev. *Thought and Language.* Cambridge, MA: MIT Press, 1961.
Watson, John B. *Psychology from the Standpoint of a Behaviorist.* Philadelphia: Lippincott, 1929.
Wittgenstein, Ludwig. *Tractatus Logico-Philosophicus.* London: Routledge and Kegan Paul, 1921.
– *Philosophical Investigations.* New York: Macmillan, 1953.

COMEDY

[See also: *Genres; Situation Comedy*]

The term 'comedy' comes from *kómos*, the Greek word for revel. Comedies can be described as humorous narratives that are, as Aristotle (1952: 6) put it, 'imitations of men worse than average,' of men who are 'ridiculous' and have numerous other failings. The philosopher Henri Bergson (1900) described comic characters as 'rigid' and lacking in self-knowledge. Characters in comedies tend to be certain types of individuals, stock figures who are eccentric and often have obsessions and strange passions of one kind or another.

Comedies can be contrasted with tragedies, which tell the story of the fall of great men and women, usually because of some deficiencies in their character or other weakness. Comedies typically end in weddings, feasts, and other celebrations, while tragedies end with dead bodies on the stage. It can be suggested that tragedies release forces of pity and anguish, ending in a catharsis for audiences, while comedies, which move audiences to laughter, facilitate the release of libidinal forces, ending in a cathexis. Laughter generates endorphins in people, which create pleasurable feelings and other physical and psychological benefits. Comedies also give their audiences new insights into human nature and generate a feeling of optimism. It is much easier to make people cry in a tragedy than to make them laugh in a comedy.

Literary theorists have debated for centuries whether tragedy is a higher art from than comedy. Usually they argue that tragedy is more important and more 'high-level' than comedy. Tragedies unfold rather directly and everything leads to the conclusion, involving the death of the protagonist and often many others as well. Comedies are full of miscues, tangents, mistakes, misunderstandings, and other comic devices, but its heroes survive. With the development of postmodern thought, the debate about the status of comedy and tragedy was abandoned, since postmodern theory is based, among other things, on de-differentiation and does not distinguish between elite culture and popular culture or comedy and tragedy. In addition, many writers now combine comedy and tragedy and create works that are best described as tragicomedies. These works are either tragedies with comic elements in them or comedies with tragic elements.

Aristotle's *Poetics* dealt with comedic theatrical works, but now the term has been broadened and is used to deal with situation comedies and other kinds of humorous texts on television, screwball comedies and other genres of comedy in film, and, broadly speaking, any narrative text in any medium that is humorous and generates mirthful laughter. Many of the conventions found in ancient Greek comedies are still alive and well in contemporary comedies, since comedy exploits human frailties and foolishness. People are still as foolish and ridiculous as they were in the times of Aristophanes, whose play *The Birds* was produced in 414 BCE. This play combined satire, insults, wordplay, allusions, comic catalogues and many of the techniques found in contemporary comedies. Plautus, who died in 184 BCE, wrote *Miles Gloriosus*, about a braggart captain, and used many comic techniques that can be found in contemporary comic films and television shows, such as eccentricity, the revelation of ignorance, impersonations, irony, and far-fetched analogies. Had they been alive in contemporary times, Aristophanes and Plautus might well have been on the writing staff of a situation comedy like *Frasier*, which employed more than a dozen writers to create each twenty-two-minute episode.

Although there are a number of techniques found in all comedy, the focus on certain techniques varies from country to country and reflects aspects of each country's national character and history. For example, English comedies stress understatement and often ridicule 'upper-class twits,' churchmen, and other aspects of English culture, which most Americans cannot understand or appreciate. That is why comedy, unless it is physical or focused on broadly eccentric characters, does not travel. People in other countries often do not 'get' the allusions. The kind of comedy we like is also connected to our socioeconomic class, educational level, ethnicity, and other demographic matters.

Making people laugh is not easy, which explains why the maxim 'Death is easy, comedy is hard' is so truthful. Standup comedians often use graphic terms to describe their performances, saying that they 'killed' their audiences, making them laugh a great deal, or 'bombed,' and couldn't get a laugh out of their audiences. In recent years, comedians have moved from telling jokes, which are stories with punch lines, to observational humour, which deals with the absurdities of people and everyday life.

The subject of humour, which is the basic ingredient of comedies, is of great interest to the academic community, and many scholars in the humanities, social sciences, and other fields are investigating various aspects of the subject, trying to understand how humour is created and what role it plays in comedic texts, in our everyday lives, and in society at large. Comedy remains one of the few things about which we can say it is both pleasurable and good for us.

Arthur Asa Berger

Bibliography

Aristotle. Poetics. W. D. Ross, ed., *The Works of Aristotle*, Vol. 11. Oxford: Clarendon Press.

Berger, Arthur Asa. *The Art of Comedy Writing.* New Brunswick, NJ: Transaction, 1997.

Bergson, Henri. *Le rire: Essai sur la signification du comique.* Paris: Éditions Alcan, 1900.

Charney, Maurice. *Comedy: High and Low.* New York: Oxford University Press, 1978.

Felheim, Marvin. *Comedy: Plays, Theory, and Criticism.* New York: Harcourt, Brace, and World, 1962.

Fry, William F., Jr. *Sweet Madness: A Study of Humor.* Palo Alto, CA: Pacific Books, 1968.

Fry, William F., Jr., and Melanie Allen. *Make 'Em Laugh: A Study of Comedy Writers.* Palo Alto, CA: Science and Behavior Books, 1975.

Stott, Andrew. *Comedy.* London: Routledge, 2005.

Sypher, Wylie, ed. *Comedy.* New York: Doubleday Books, 1956.

COMICS

[See also: *Cartoons, Animated; Comics, History of*]

The term *comics* is used, generally speaking, to refer to both newspaper comics, comic books (which are actually maga-zines), and all other kinds of narrative texts or art forms which have the following characteristics:

- They employ drawings to tell the story.
- The drawings usually are in frames.
- There are recurring characters.
- The dialogue is in balloons.
- Other information is found in panels, usually at the bottom of frames.

All of these conventions are sometimes violated, but, generally speaking, comic strips and comic books follow them. Comics have been called 'an American idiom,' not because they were invented in the United States, but because they achieved their greatest early flowering in America.

The French term for comics, *bande dessinée*, which can be translated as 'designed (drawn) band,' is more accurate because many comic strips (often called 'the funnies') and comic books are not humorous by any means. In his book, *Understanding Comics: The Invisible Art*, which is itself a comic book, Scott McCloud suggests the best way to characterize comics is to use comics artist Will Eisner's characterization of them as 'sequential art.' After making a number of modifications of Eisner's definition, McCloud finally ended up with the following definition (1994: 9):

com-ics (kom-iks) n. plural in form used with a singular verb. 1. juxtaposed pictorial and other images in deliberate sequence, intended to convey information and/or to produce an aesthetic response in the viewer.

This definition, while not elegant, captures the most important elements of comics in general, but it does not deal with such matters as the characters typically found in them or the aesthetic and literary conventions typically followed by comics artists and writers.

Comics differ from cartoons in that cartoons generally are found in a single frame, do not have recurrent characters or a narrative line, and generally do not have dialogue in balloons. Cartoons conventionally have text in captions underneath the frame of the cartoon. Not all cartoons are humorous, either. There are funny cartoons, but there are also cartoons that comment on social and political matters of importance that are typically found in newspapers and magazines.

In recent years the comic strip art form has evolved into what might be described as pictorial or graphic novels, which often take on serious themes. For example, one of the most important of these graphic novels, Art Spiegelman's *Maus,* deals with the Holocaust. In addition, the comic strip has migrated to film and electronic media, and there are now many animated films, which we now realize are an art form with incredible possibilities. The Japanese animated film *Spirited Away* by Hayao Miyazaki shows that the aesthetic possibilities of animated films are enormous. Characters from the comics have also been used for serious films, musical comedies, and ballets, so it is an art form that lends itself to adoption by other art forms, in part because of the strong narrative line found in comics. The fact that McCloud uses the comic strip as a means of teaching us about comics is a good example of the didactic possibilities of the art form.

The earliest comics in the United States were thought of as children's sub-literature, so for many years social scientists and scholars in the humanities in America paid relatively little attention to them. European scholars, on the other hand, have long been interested in comics and what they reflect about culture. In recent years, there has been a good deal of interest shown by American scholars in the comics in many disciplines since they are now seen as an important means to determine values and beliefs that are found in cultures and subcultures. The University of Mississippi Press now has a large list of scholarly books on the comics.

Because of their distinct quality, and because the images reinforce the language

used, comics are also used as a means of teaching various subjects. Larry Gonick's *The Cartoon History of the Universe (Book 1)* is a good example of the way comic strip artists use the art form to teach and entertain. There have also been comic book treatments of Marxist theory, *Marx for Beginners,* and Freudian theory, *Freud for Beginners,* Johannes H. Loubser's *Archaeology: The Comic* is a comic book introduction to archaeology.

Comics also have been the subject of what we might call 'elite' art forms, such as oil painting; the pop art movement featured oil paintings of various comic strip and comic book characters. Painters such as Andy Warhol and Roy Lichtenstein are considered pop artists. Pop art raises a question about the nature of comics. If a comic strip frame is painted in oil on canvas, enlarged, and put in a frame, does it suddenly become 'elite' art? The question is being continuously debated. Comic book heroes have also been turned into movie heroes, and important films have been made in recent years in which Superman, Batman, The Fantastic Four, and other comic strip heroes are the stars.

In his book *The Art of the Funnies: An Aesthetic History,* Robert C. Harvey (1994: 8) makes an important point about how to deal with comics:

Comics use speech balloons and narrative breakdown to tell stories, but the art of the comics is not altogether the same as other narrative arts – despite seeming similarities. Comics can be (and too often are) evaluated on purely literary grounds, the critic concentrating on such things as character portrayal, tone and style of language, verisimilitude of personality and incident, plot, resolution of conflict, unity and themes. While such literary analysis contributes to an understanding of a strip or book, to employ this method exclusively ignores the essential character of the medium by overlooking its visual elements. Similarly, analysis that focuses on the graphics (discussing composition, layout, style, and the like) ignores the purpose served by the visuals – the story or joke that is being told. Comics employ the technique of both the literary and graphic arts, yet they are neither wholly verbal in their function nor exclusively pictorial.

With Harvey's comment in mind, one might suggest that in analysing comics, three basic components should be considered: the art style, the narrative line, and the dialogue. In this entry the focus is on American comics, but it must be understood that comics are a global art form and that there are important and interesting comics in most countries. Those interested in the global aspects of comics should consult the *International Journal of Comic Art*, an academic quarterly edited by John Lent, which has been published since 1999.

The art style of comic strip artists can vary from realistic portrayals, such as Alex Raymond's *Flash Gordon* and Harold R. Foster's *Prince Valiant*, to highly stylized ones such as Walt Kelly's *Pogo*, Al Capp's *Li'l Abner*, Charles Schulz's *Peanuts*, and Chester Gould's *Dick Tracy*. Gould's use of grotesque villains such as 'the mole' and 'flathead' and his use of strong blacks and whites made his strip a very powerful one. It was one of the first to show murders and graphic violence. Comics artists also use boldface lettering to emphasize certain words and make use of certain graphic conventions such as having thoughts appear in little clouds.

In addition to the art style found in a comic, we must also consider the narrative line. Humorous comics generally have a narrative that ends with some kind of resolution each day, while serious or dramatic comic strips have episodes that continue for weeks or months. Once one episode is resolved another one immediately begins. In *Dick Tracy*, as soon as the detective hero has captured or killed one villain, another one appears on the scene, and so the adventure continues. Some historically classic comic strips, such as *Dick Tracy, Little*

Orphan Annie, Blondie, and *Peanuts*, went on for many decades.

Finally, we must consider the way language is used in comics. We see quite remarkable language in George Herriman's *Krazy Kat*, which many scholars of the comics consider the greatest achievement in American comics. The plot of this strip was always the same: Ignatz Mouse, a malevolent mouse, spends all his time and energy figuring out how to 'Krease that Kat's bean with a brick.' Defending Krazy is Offissa B. Pupp, who loves Krazy and struggles valiantly and usually unsuccessfully to prevent Ignatz from hitting Krazy. In the first frame Pupp sees Ignatz hitting Krazy with a brick. He says 'Transgression.' In the next frame he grabs Ignatz and says 'Apprehension.' In the third frame he takes him under his arm and heads toward jail. He says 'Retribution.' In the final frame, the jail has not been drawn, so Pupp says 'WA-A-L … Finish it!!! Y'got Kartoonist's Kramp?' and Krazy says 'Ah. Sweet Procrastination.'

Al Capp was a satirist whose *Li'l Abner* poked fun at many aspects of American culture. The following description by one of his characters, Marryin' Sam, of an eight-dollar wedding shows Capp's skill with words:

Fust – Ah strips t' th' wait, and r assles th' four biggest guests!

Next – a fast demon-stray-shun of how t' cheat yore friends at cards!! – follyed by four snappy jokes – guaranteed to embarrass man or beast – an' – then, after ah dances a jig wif a pig, Ah yanks out two o' mah teeth and presents'em t' th' bride and groom as memetos o' th' occasion!! – then – Ah really gits goin!! Ah offers t' remove any weddin' guest's appendix, wif may bare hands – free!!

Capp uses dialect in this passage and mimics certain aspects of southwestern humour.

An early and influential analysis of violence and other forms of anti-social behaviour in the comics was psychiatrist Frederic

Wertham's *Seduction of the Innocent* (1954), which suggested that the reading of comics fostered juvenile delinquency. This claim was highly exaggerated and is not accepted as credible by most scholars. But the matter of violence in the comics, in both humorous and non-humorous forms, is a subject of considerable debate by contemporary social scientists. There is an enormous amount of comic violence in animated television shows for children, and most child development scholars believe it is harmful. And now, with the development of video games, violence continues to be a problem.

Another topic of interest for scholars involves the portrayal of women in comics. It is possible to study the way women are drawn, to examine what they say, and to count the number of images of women in frames in contrast to those of men in selected comics to see how women are represented, or under-represented, in various comics.

In Japan, where comics, known as *manga*, are very popular, there has been an interesting development in the way women are portrayed. In the sixties, there was a phenomenon known as *kawaii* or cuteness. Women were shown with large, round, non-Asian eyes and with hardly any breast development. In recent years, since the nineties, women have kept their round eyes but now they are shown in *manga* with highly developed bodies and are often featured in violent and sexually explicit scenarios involving bondage and rape. It has been suggested that these comics help middle-aged Japanese males deal with various kinds of repression in Japanese culture. Since there is very little violence in Japanese culture, it seems that we cannot draw a connection between violence in comics and in everyday life.

A number of 'erotic' comics have achieved popularity in America and elsewhere, such as *Barbarella* in France and *Jodelle* in Italy. This is to be expected for the comic strip lends itself to fantasy and artists have used the comic strip to portray women in various states of dress and un-dress. There was also a movement in the United States called 'underground' comics that were satirical and sexually explicit. Some of these comics had titles such as *Subvert Comics, The Fabulous Furry Freak Brothers, Mr. Natural, Feel Good Funnies,* and *Young Lust.*

Comics can be analysed from a number of perspectives:

- Artwork or text. For example, an issue of Superman comics.
- Artists and writers. They create the text.
- Medium. A comic strip or comic book or animated film.
- America (or any other country). Where the comics are produced.
- Audience. The fans and readers of the text.

All of these focal points can be connected with one another. Thus, for example, comics artists and writers are affected by the values and beliefs of the societies in which they work, by their target audiences, and by the limitations of the medium in which they are working.

Arthur Asa Berger

Bibliography

Appignanesi, Richard, and Oscar Zarate. *Freud for Beginners.* New York: Pantheon Books, 1979.

Benayoun, Robert. *Le Ballon dans La bande dessinée: Vroom, tchakc, zowie.* Paris: Éditions André Balland, 1968.

Berger, Arthur Asa. *Li'l Abner: A Study in American Satire.* New York: Twayne, 1964.

– *The Comic-Stripped American: What Dick Tracy, Blondie, Daddy Warbucks and Charlie Brown Tell Us about Ourselves.* New York: Walker and Company, 1978.

Couperie, Pierre, and Maurice C. Horn. *A History of the Comic Strip.* New York: Crown, 1968.

Gonick, Larry. *The Cartoon History of the Universe.* New York: Quill, 1982.

Harvey, Robert C. *The Art of the Funnies: An*

Aesthetic History. Jackson: University Press of Mississippi, 1994.

Inge, M. Thomas. *Comics as Culture.* Jackson: University Press of Mississippi, 1990.

Lippard, Lucy R. *Pop Art.* New York: Praeger, 1966.

Loubser, Johannes H.N. *Archaeology: The Comic.* Walnut Creek: AltaMira Press, 2003.

Lupoff, Dick, and Don Thompson, eds. *All in Color for a Dime.* New Rochelle, NY: Arlington House, 1970.

McCloud, Scott. *Understanding Comics: The Invisible Art.* New York: Harper, 1994.

McLuhan, Marshall. *The Mechanical Bride: Folklore of Industrial Man.* Boston: Beacon Press, 1967.

Reitberger, Reinhold, and Wolfgang Fuchs. *Comics: Anatomy of a Mass Medium.* Boston: Little, Brown, 1972.

Rius (Edoardo del Rio). *Marx for Beginners.* New York: Pantheon Books, 1976.

Sabin, Roger. *Adult Comics: An Introduction.* London: Routledge, 1993.

Silbermann, Alphons, and H.-D. Dyroff, eds. *Comics and Visual Culture: Research Studies from Ten Countries.* Munich: K.G. Saur, 1986.

Werthan, Fredric. *Seduction of the Innocent.* New York: Rinehart, 1954.

COMICS, HISTORY OF

[See also: *Cartoons, Animated; Cartoons, History of; Comics*]

Comics (strips and books) grew out of cartooning art, which originated in the sixteenth century in the form of the German *broadsheets*, or single drawings printed on large pieces of paper and used for political satire. An early comic strip *(Hogan's Alley)* was created in 1895 for *The New York World* by Richard Felton Outcault. Other newspapers followed suit with comic strips such as *Little Bears* by James Guilford Swinnerton, which was first published in the *San Francisco Examiner* a few years earlier in 1892, *The Katzenjammer Kids* by Rudolph Dirks, appearing for the first time in *The American Humorist* in 1897, and *Mutt and Jeff*, which

appeared as *Mr A. Mutt* in a November 1907 issue of the *San Francisco Chronicle*.

Newspaper syndicates introduced *Mutt and Jeff* to wider audiences, making it the first successful daily comic strip. To satisfy growing demand, newspapers started to publish collections of the individual strips in 1911, leading to the birth of the *comic book*. By 1933, comic books, such as *Joe Palooka* and *Connie*, which were based on well-known newspaper comic strips, became highly popular.

The Sunday comic strips were designed primarily for children. The daily ones, on the other hand, were intended for adults. Harry Hershfield's *Abie the Agent*, published in 1914, was the first adult comic book and capitalized on the popularity of the pulp detective genre of the era. An early influential contributor to the genre was Roy Crane, who created *Wash Tubbs* in 1924. The adventure comic emerged in 1929 with the publication of *Tarzan* and *Buck Rogers*. These have remained popular, arguably because their characters never age. There have been a few exceptions to this pattern – for example, in *Gasoline Alley* by Frank O. King the characters age day by day.

Comic books are, as their name implies, book-length or magazine-length comic strips. They are narratives told by means of cartoon drawings arranged in horizontal lines, strips, or rectangles, called *panels*. They are read like a verbal text from left to right. Dialogue is presented as words encircled by a *balloon*, which issues from the mouth or head of the character speaking. Movement is shown by means of lines of different sizes. For example, long thin lines trailing a running individual are designed to show speed; short broken lines indicate jumping. The first comic books were collections of popular newspaper strips. But the breakthrough for the comic book format came in 1938, following the phenomenal success in 1938 of *Action Comics*, of which the principal attraction was the *Superman* comic strip, created by Jerry Siegel and Joe Shuster. A year later, *Superman* spawned a series of comic-book superhero clones. By the 1940s the super-hero adventure comic, with its superhe-roes (Batman, Captain Marvel, The Flash, Green Lantern, Wonder Woman, Captain America), became a staple of popular cul-ture. In the 1950s Harvey Kurtzman, artist and editor of *Mad*, revived broad interest in the humour comic book genre, which had started with the *Famous Funnies* in the early 1930s but was eclipsed by the adventure comic by the end of the decade. At the same time, there was a growth of gruesome horror comics, which garnered a negative public reaction, and led several comic book publishers to establish a self-censorship program called the Comics Code Authority, which reviewed comic books before publication, removing mate-rial it found to be offensive.

Superhero comics enjoyed a revitalized success in the 1960s, after Jack Kirby and Stan Lee created four superheroes called *The Fantastic Four*, who, unlike the previous superheroes, had down-to-earth problems. In the same decade, counterculture youths used the comic book format as a vehicle for protest as well as for publishing previ-ously forbidden topics. The genre came to be known as *underground comics* (or *comix*), because the books were distributed outside of regular channels in order to bypass the Comics Code Authority.

Comics are both a form of recreation and an art form. *Krazy Kat*, for instance, has been regarded by many academics as one of the most amusing and imaginative works ever produced in America. The *Pea-nuts* comic strip by the late Charles Schultz, originally titled *Li'l Folks* and debuting in 1950, is one of the most popular comic strips in the history of comics, and its char-acters, from Charlie Brown to Lucy, have become icons of pop culture. The characters are all children who provide more insight into life than adults, who are relegated to the margins of the strip. The subtle sad-ness of the strip veils a deep search for the answers to the great questions of religion and philosophy – Who are we? What is life all about?

Starting in the 1970s, some smaller publishers began experimenting with new styles, sophisticated formats, and new storylines, leading to the birth of the so-called *graphic novel* – a comic book for adults, dealing with adult themes such as alienation, sexual relations, and terror-ism. Two celebrated examples are *Maus: A Survivor's Tale* (1986) and *Maus II* (1991) by Art Spiegelman. They recount the artist's relationship with his father and the experi-ences of his father and mother during the Holocaust. Graphic novels are much longer than typical comic books, and are often bound like paperback books. They became the fastest-growing segment of the publish-ing field in the early 2000s, providing vari-ous scripts to filmmakers, including *The Road to Perdition* (2002) and *Sin City* (2005). Actually, comic book heroes have always crossed over to the movies and television. *Superman, Batman, Watchmen, V for Vendetta, From Hell*, and *The League of Extraordinary Gentlemen*, among many others, have all led to movie versions.

Before the advent of television, comics set the tone for displaying new trends in clothing. They have inspired not only mov-ies, radio and TV programs, but also plays, musicals, ballets, popular songs, books, and toys. The word for the Allied Forces on D-Day was 'Mickey Mouse,' and the password for the Norwegian Underground was 'The Phantom.' Painters and sculptors have incorporated comic-book characters into their artworks, leading to the pop art movement. Film directors have adapted techniques of the comics into their films; and of course, Bugs Bunny, Homer Simp-son, Rocky and Bullwinkle, the Grinch, the Flintstones, Fat Albert, Popeye, Scooby-Doo, Arthur, Winnie the Pooh, Mr. Magoo, Felix the Cat, Yogi Bear, Mighty Mouse, Batman, Woody Woodpecker, Tom and Jerry, to mention just a few, have become veritable icons of popular culture.

A study of the style and content of some comic books also gives insight into the cultural world view of the historical pe-riod in which they were created. As Frank

Nuessel (2009) has recently written, even the names assigned to characters in a comic strip like *Dick Tracy* (1931), created by Chester Gould, reveal an ingenious historical use of onomastics, with villains being given names that reflect deviance in some way, and heroes' names reflecting positive traits. The villains are 'literally ripped from the headlines, representing gangsters and mobsters of the era' (Nuessel 2009: 64). Examples include: Cut Famoni, Lips Manlius, Alphonse Big Boy Caprice, Mamma, Breathless Mahoney, and Dan the Squealer Mucelli. Comic books are thus archaeological documents that show in their images and language what an era was all about.

Today, the comic book has made its way to online culture, where it continues to thrive in the form of online e-toons and webcomics, such as *Smoking Lion* (www.icebox.com) and *Mortal Kombat* (www.the-threshold.com). Regardless of the medium (print, electronic, and so on) in which they have appeared, and continue to appear, comics have broad appeal. The original print comics have even become popular memorabilia items for collectors. Comics have also shown themselves to be adaptable – Batwoman has been portrayed as a lesbian in one of her incarnations; Black Panther is the heroic king of a fictitious African nation; the Great Ten are a team of Chinese heroes. Moreover, comic book culture has gone truly global. For years, Japanese *manga* comic books and *anime* animated features, along with characters like Pokémon and Hello Kitty, have become popular among young people throughout the world. In effect, comics reflect who we are today probably better than any other textual genre. *South Park*, for instance, has become America's parodist and (im)moral conscience, dealing with current events in ways that parallel the comic genre's predecessors – the caricature and the gag cartoon. Comics seem to have a primal quality to them – a fact that was brought out by the movie *Unbreakable* (2002), directed by M. Night Shyamalan. Comic books, the movie claims, are modern-day manifestations of something universal, mirroring the kinds of pictorial stories imprinted in cave paintings and in writing systems such as the Egyptian hieroglyphs.

Marcel Danesi

Bibliography

Chute, Hilary. Comics as Literature? Reading Graphic Narrative. *PMLA* 123 (2008): 452–65.

Fingeroth, David. *Superman on the Couch: What Superheroes Really Tell Us about Ourselves and Our Society*. New York: Continuum, 2004.

Klaehu, Jeffery, ed. *Inside the World of Comic Books*. Montreal: Black Rose, 2007.

McCloud, Scott. *Understanding Comics*. Northampton: Kitchen Sink Press, 1993.

– *Making Comics: Storytelling Secrets of Comics, Manga and Graphic Novels*. New York: Harper, 2006.

Nuessel, Frank. A Note on the Names of Selected Characters and Villains in *Dick Tracy*. *Names* 57 (2009): 63–8.

Reynolds, Richard. *Superheroes: A Modern Mythology*. Jackson: University of Mississippi Press, 1992.

Robinson, Lillian S. *Wonderwomen: Feminisms and Superheroes*. London: Routledge, 2004.

Spiegelman, Art. *Maus: A Survivor's Tale*. New York: Pantheon, 1986.

– *Maus: A Survivor's Tale II*. New York: Pantheon, 1991.

Wright, Bradford W. *Comic Book Nation: The Transformation of Youth Culture in America*. Baltimore: Johns Hopkins University Press, 2001.

COMMUNICATION

[See also: *Cinema; Communication Theory; Channel; Feedback; Internet; Mass Communication; Medium; Message; Noise; Non-verbal Communication; Photography; Radio; Shannon, Claude E.; Telephony; Television; Writing; Zipf's Law*]

Strictly defined, *communication* is the exchange of messages between members of the same species. Of course, some interspecies communication occurs, but the signals exchanged will not have the same function, impact, or content as they do within a species and thus will either be interpreted differently or not at all (constituting simple noise). In the human species, the exchange can be *interpersonal* (between human beings), *group-based* (between some individual or media outlet and audiences), and *mass-based* (involving communication systems that encompass entire societies). Communication occurs by means of three main forms of transmission – some natural biological system (the voice, touch, etc.), some device (a book, a painting, etc.), or technology (a radio, a television set, etc.). The first type can be called *natural*, the second *artefactual*, and the third *technological*.

All organisms are equipped by their particular biological constitution with the means to transmit signals with their body. In humans, this includes the use of the voice, the face, the eyes, and the hands. Messages transmitted naturally fade rapidly and cannot be preserved without some 'preserving media'; books, paintings, sculptures are examples of such media. A technological medium is one that allows messages to be transmitted widely by means of some invention such as the telephone, the radio, the television set, the computer, and so on. Early societies used drums, fire and smoke signals, and lantern beacons to transmit messages over short distances. Messages were also attached to the legs of carrier pigeons trained to navigate their way to a destination and back home. In later societies, so-called semaphore systems based on flags or flashing lights were employed to send messages over relatively short but difficult-to-cross distances, such as from hilltop to hilltop or from one ship at sea to another. Today, communication systems involve sophisticated technologies such as satellites and the World Wide Web.

Writing

Before the advent of alphabets, people communicated and passed on knowledge through the spoken word – that is, through oral stories, wise sayings, and so on. However, *oral communication* does not produce stable knowledge – each time a story is told it is changed in detail by the storyteller, and, more importantly, it evanesces once it has been told, depending only on the memory of the hearers for its preservation. Even in early oral cultures, tools had been invented for recording and preserving knowledge and ideas in more durable and invariant forms. These were typically pictographic. A *pictograph* is a picture sign made on some surface (a cave wall, a tree trunk, etc.) with appropriate instruments (a carving tool, a stylus) to represent some object in the real world (a rock, the sun, the moon). Pictography is the most ancient writing system known. Despite its antiquity, it has not disappeared from the modern world, even though most written forms of communication are based on the alphabet. The figures designating male and female on washrooms and the no-smoking signs found in public buildings, to mention two common examples, are modern-day pictographs; so too are the icons on computer screens.

One of the first civilizations to adopt pictographic writing as an official means of recording ideas, keeping track of business transactions, and transmitting knowledge was ancient China. According to some archaeological estimates, Chinese writing may date as far as back the fifteenth century BCE. Another ancient civilization to use pictography regularly for a variety of practical social functions was ancient Sumeria around 3500 BCE. The Sumerian system was called *cuneiform*, because it was based on a set of wedge-shaped characters that were inscribed on clay tablets with a stylus (the word comes from Latin *cuneus*, 'wedge'). Cuneiform was versatile because it had pictographs for both concrete things and abstract notions – the concept of *sleeping*, for example, was represented by a picture of a person in a supine position. Abstract pictographs are called, more precisely, *ideographs*. To facilitate the speed of writing, the Sumerians eventually started using a few symbols, known as *phonographs*, standing for various sounds in pictographic words.

By about 3000 BCE the ancient Egyptians also started using a writing system, known as *hieroglyphic*, to record hymns and prayers, to annotate various community activities, and to register the names and titles of individuals and deities (*hieroglyphic* derives from Greek *hieros*, 'holy,' and *glyphein*, 'to carve'). Egyptian hieroglyphs were of all three varieties – pictographic, ideographic, and phonographic. With the development of papyrus around 2700 BCE, the Egyptians replaced hieroglyphic writing with a form known as *hieratic*, which was executed with blunt reed pens and ink. Hieratic was cursive and ligatured, allowing scribes to write more rapidly. It was used initially just for sacred writing, but eventually came to be used for all kinds of writing. Given the greater availability and affordability of papyrus, literacy came to be highly valued among the common people, although it continued to be used mainly by privileged members of Egyptian society (priests, aristocrats, merchants, etc.).

Once writing became widespread, it gradually began to evolve into a phonographic system so that it could be used more efficiently and rapidly. A complete phonographic system for representing single sounds is called *alphabetic*. The first alphabetic system emerged in the Middle East around 1000 BCE and was transported by the Phoenicians (a people from a territory on the eastern coast of the Mediterranean, located largely in modern-day Lebanon) to Greece. It contained symbols for consonant sounds only. When it reached Greece, symbols for vowel sounds were added to it, making the Greek system the first full-fledged alphabet in history. The Greeks also named each symbol (*alpha*, *beta*, *gamma*, etc.) in imitation of Phoenician words (*aleph*, 'ox'; *beth*, 'house'; *gimel*, 'camel,' etc.). From the first two names (*alpha* and *beta*) comes the word *alphabet*. Although many societies adopted the technique of alphabetic writing shortly thereafter, pictography continued to flourish in many areas. Pictographic writing systems are still used in many parts of the world.

Print Communication

Alphabet-based written communication altered the way people transmitted and recorded knowledge in those parts of the world where it was adopted. Whether they are produced on parchment, papyrus, paper, or a computer screen, written materials (such as books) have been the basis for recording, spreading, and preserving knowledge since the Greeks started using alphabetic writing. As the late Canadian communications theorist Marshall McLuhan often remarked, alphabetic print literacy brought about the first true 'cognitive revolution' in human history. It also brought about the first true 'communications revolution,' as the use of print materials started growing rapidly. The ancient Romans, for instance, transmitted the news with a handwritten sheet called *Acta Diurna* (Daily Events), which was the first newspaper.

With the growth of written communications came the need for more writing materials. In the first centuries of the Common Era the chief ones were papyrus and parchment. Parchment (made from the skin of a sheep or goat) was not as light as papyrus (made from the pith or the stems of sedge), but it was more durable. In the early medieval period, the rectangular *codex* became the standard book form. It was a small, ringed book consisting of two or more wooden tablets covered with wax, which could be marked with a stylus, smoothed over, and reused many times. Codices were used primarily to record texts related to the observance of the Christian liturgy. Paper was actually invented in the second century CE by the Chinese, who developed it from silk fibres. The Arabs took the Chinese technology to Europe in the eleventh century. Paper was lighter than all other materials used for writing up to that time, and thus more portable. It was also relatively inexpensive and thus spread throughout Europe. Until the 1400s, all paper materials were written by hand. Copyists called *scribes*, many of whom were monks, made duplicates of manuscripts and books. But they were very expensive, because the scribes decorated them with pictures and designs.

Although a Chinese printer named Bi Sheng had invented movable type in the 1000s, it was not until 1447 that a German printer named Johannes Gutenberg (ca 1400–68) perfected movable metal type technology, developing the first printing press capable of producing numerous copies of paper documents quickly and cheaply. The event was monumental in the history of communications. Printing shops sprung up all over Europe, publishing books, newspapers, pamphlets, and many other kinds of paper documents inexpensively. As a result, more books became available and more people gained literacy because it became an increasingly useful and necessary skill. With more and more people able to read, ideas could be spread more broadly than ever before. This situation is cited by historians as the basis for the revolutions of a religious, political, social, and scientific nature that led eventually to the so-called Renaissance, the period marking the transition from medieval to modern times. Books could be sent all over the world, and ideas started crossing political borders much more easily, uniting the world more and more into a worldwide 'communications system.' Standardized ways of doing things in the scientific and business domains emerged. In a phrase, the invention of the printing press was the technological event that paved the way for the establishment of a global civilization. McLuhan called this new world order the 'Gutenberg Galaxy.'

In the 1600s, printed news sheets called *corantos* appeared in the Netherlands, England, and other European nations. The coranto differed from newspapers before it in format, including a title on the upper first page of the publication and adopting a two-column format, unlike previous single-column formats. They reported mostly business news, and introduced a new feature in print communications – advertising. With the advent of the Industrial Revolution in the 1700s, print literacy became even more widespread, as books, magazines, and newspapers made information available to more and more readers. As a result, a new type of communications problem surfaced – plagiarism and illegal copying. In 1709, the British parliament passed the first true copyright law. Literary property became commercially valuable. Publishing surged during the late 1700s. Letter writing became increasingly popular. Also near the end of the century the French engineer Claude Chappe developed an early telegraph system for transmitting print, which consisted of a series of towers between Paris and other European cities. An operator in each tower moved a crossbar and two arms on the roof to spell out messages, which an observer on the next tower read and passed on.

In the twentieth century, printed documents became even more inexpensive and available en masse. Photocopying made duplication easier and more rapid. By the mid-1980s, desktop publishing (the design and production of publications of all kinds using microcomputers with graphics capability) became widespread, largely replacing all previous typesetting technologies. Sophisticated word-processing and graphics software are used today to produce all kinds of print materials. They can also be transmitted instantly via computer communication systems to other locations for editing, redesigning, and printing.

The new digital technologies have had a definite impact on human communication generally. It is now becoming possible to publish books directly on websites and to make traditional paper books available in various non-paper forms. Digital documents have also altered the nature of reading and researching via print, allowing readers to link directly different texts and images within the main text. This feature is known as *hypertextuality*. Thus, for example, an online encyclopedia allows a user to go from one to topic to another within a page of text by simply providing links that a reader can access by simply clicking them as they occur on some software such as a CD-ROM or website. If a reader wants to check, say, the meaning of a word on a page in a traditional book, he or she would have to physically consult another print source (such as a dictionary). Hypertextuality has made such a task much more practicable and efficient.

Hypertextuality is also leading to a redefinition of the roles of the author and the reader of a text. Hypertext novels, for instance, allow for multiple plot twists to be built into a story. They also enable readers to observe the story unfold from the perspective of different characters. Readers may also change the story themselves to suit their interpretive fancies. In such novels, the author sets a framework for the narrative, but the actual narrative is realized by the reader. The same kind of 'editing power' is now applicable to many (if not most) kinds of internet documents, from Web-based encyclopedias and dictionaries to online textbooks. In effect, electronic documents can always be updated and thus never be out of date.

Such documents can also store the equivalent information of myriad paper books. As a consequence, cyber-libraries have already sprung up and may eventually replace traditional libraries. Already in 1971, a project called (rather ironically) Project Gutenberg was established as a volunteer effort to digitize, archive, and distribute online the full texts of public domain books. The project continues to make these as free as possible, in formats that can be used on almost any computer. As of 2006, the project had over 19,000 items in its collection, with an average of over fifty new e-books being added each week. Most are in English, but there are also growing numbers in other languages, as similar projects are established in non-English-speaking countries. Similar projects are posting public domain materials on websites of their own, including the Google Library Project

and the World Digital Library Project of the Library of Congress, which intends to make available on the internet, free of charge and in multilingual format, significant materials from cultures around the world, including manuscripts, maps, rare books, musical scores, recordings, films, prints, photographs, architectural drawings, and the like.

Since anyone can download documents directly online, the purchase of electronic documents is also extremely easy and convenient. For this reason, many culture theorists predict that e-books will gradually replace traditional paper-based books. However, for the time being the paper book is still highly popular. People display books in their homes and offices as they would sculptures or paintings. They are comparatively convenient to hold and carry. For such reasons, traditional paper books continue to have a market value, as long as paper remains cheap and available. Nevertheless, the lesson to be learned from studying the development of communications technologies is that there is never a 'turning back the clock' once an innovation makes communication more rapid, cheap, and efficient. For the present, an audience for traditional books will continue to exist because people simply continue to enjoy reading and buying them. Purchasing books at a bookstore today, moreover, is a diverting and distracting experience in itself – something that bookstore chains have come to realize, as witnessed by the fact that they have joined forces with coffee chains. The market for paper-based print materials such as magazines and newspapers thus continues to be strong, even though online versions are springing up constantly and may eventually replace the paper versions in the not too distant future.

Telegraphy and Telephony

The first electronic apparatus for the transmission of written messages was the *telegraph*, which could send and receive electrical signals over long-distance wires.

The first commercial telegraph system was developed in Great Britain in the 1830s. A little later, in 1844, the American inventor Samuel F.B. Morse refined and patented the telegraph and developed the telegraphic code that bears his name (the Morse code). The code utilized 'on' and 'off' signals to represent individual letters of the alphabet. The telegrapher at one end of the line would tap on an electrical key, and the telegrapher at the other end would decode the tapping signals (on and off) as they came in, write down the message they contained, and send it to the recipient by messenger.

Telegraph cable was laid under the Atlantic Ocean in 1858, and regular transatlantic service began in 1866. It was the first interconnected global communications system in human history. Telegraphy was gradually replaced by telex systems in the early twentieth century, eliminating the need to use a code. Such systems consisted of teletypewriters connected to a phone network that sent and received signals. Users could type in a message in normal language, and the identical message would appear at the recipient's end, carried over telephone lines to telex machines anywhere in the world. As early as the 1930s these lines were also used to transmit pictures, a feature that led to the development of so-called Wirephoto service in international communications. In most countries, Wirephoto service was used mainly by banks, railroads, newspaper publishers, and merchants. High service rates barred more general use.

In 1876, the Scottish-born American inventor Alexander Graham Bell patented the first telephone, a device with the capacity to transmit sound over wires. Bell originally believed the telephone would be used to transmit musical concerts, lectures, and sermons. But after founding his own company, he quickly discovered that its appeal lay much more in the simple fact that it allowed ordinary people to talk to each other. In 1878 he founded the Bell Telephone Company as the first telephone exchange – a switchboard connecting any member of a group of subscribers to any other member. By 1894, roughly 260,000 Bell telephones were in use in the United States, about one for every 250 people. By the 1960s the telephone was perceived in many parts of the world as an essential service. With improvements in satellite technologies near the end of the twentieth century, the phone played a critical role in ushering in the 'internet galaxy,' providing subscribers with access to the internet and the World Wide Web by means of devices called modems. Today satellite and wireless mobile phone technologies have greatly enhanced the functionality of telephones. Since mobile phone devices, such as the iPhone, are capable of carrying visual, digital, and other kinds of signals, telephony can now send and receive all kinds of mass communications, from television reception to instant messaging and internet access services.

Photography and Cinema

Photography and cinema surfaced as forms of mass communication in the latter part of the nineteenth century. Photography actually goes back to the Renaissance, when the first crude camera, called a *camera obscura* (dark chamber), consisting of a box with a tiny opening in one side that allowed light to come in, was used mainly by painters as a sketching aid. In 1826 the French physicist Joseph Nicéphore Niépce produced the first modern camera. Photographic technology was developed shortly thereafter by French painter Louis J.M. Daguerre, who worked as Niépce's partner for several years, and the British inventor William Henry Fox Talbot. With Fox Talbot's method, film could be moved through the camera and used to take a series of pictures. Almost instantly, photography started to play an important role in science and mass communications, used by scientists, for instance, to record experiments and by newspapers to emphasize news coverage visually. To this day, it is used in advertising, in news reporting (photojournalism), for military reconnaissance, and so on. All major art museums hold exhibitions of photographs, and a number even specialize in photographic art.

The first successful 'moving photographs' were made in 1877 by Eadweard Muybridge, a British photographer working in California. Muybridge took a series of photographs of a running horse, setting up a row of cameras with strings attached to their shutters. When the horse ran by, it broke each string in succession, tripping the shutters. Muybridge's procedure influenced inventors in several countries to work toward developing devices for recording moving images. Among them was Thomas Edison, who invented the first functional motion picture camera in 1888 when he filmed fifteen seconds of one of his assistants sneezing. Shortly thereafter, Auguste Marie Louis Nicolas Lumière (1862–1954) and his brother Louis Jean Lumière gave the first public showing of a cinematic film in a Paris café in 1895.

Thus was born the technology of 'moving pictures,' or 'movies' for short, which became one of the most influential mass communications medium of the last one hundred years. Movies brought about a new way of communicating through visual images and a new conception of authorship. Whereas in print fiction the author(s) can be easily identified as the creator(s) of the text, in films the question of authorship is much more complex, since a screenwriter and a director are involved in a partnership (although many times the two are one and the same person). The function of screenwriters varies greatly with the type of film being produced. The screenwriter may be called upon to develop an idea or to adapt a novel, stage play, or musical to the special requirements of the screen. But the writer is not the key individual in the production of the film – that person is the director, the individual who visualizes the script and guides the production crew and actors in carrying out that vision. In theory, the director has artistic control over everything from the script itself to the final

cut of the film, although in reality various circumstances compromise this ideal of the director's absolute artistic authority. Nonetheless, it is the director's sense of the dramatic, along with his or her creative visualization of the script, that transforms it into a motion picture.

The late 1980s saw a revolution in film culture, with major releases being made available for home video viewing. That technological development, combined with the advent of cable television featuring relatively current films on special channels, seemed to threaten the long-term survival of movie theatres and created a climate of uneasiness in movie studios throughout the world similar to that of the early 1950s, when the advent of television as a mass communications medium challenged movie-going culture for the first time in the century. As a result, film companies started increasingly favouring large spectacle movies with fantastic special effects in the hope of luring the public away from home videos and back to the big screen. But their fears turned out to be unfounded. As in the early days of cinema, going to the movies remained a cultural ritual. Going to a movie theatre is a social act: it involves people coming together (even if anonymously) to participate at an event and reacting to the movie on the screen as a group, rather than in a solitary fashion.

Today, the threat to the traditional movie theatre is coming from the same sources that are threatening traditional paper book culture – cyberspace and new electronic devices such as DVDs, iPods, mobile phones, and the like. It remains to be seen, however, if the social function of movie theatres will be transferred to other locales (if indeed it can or will be replaced). As it has turned out, the advent of new media for delivering movies has actually fostered a much wider audience for movies. All kinds of films, past and present, are now available in different media and formats; rentals and sales of movie-carrying devices are providing new revenue for motion-picture companies (in some cases, more than their theatrical releases); and advance sales of video and other media rights enable small production companies to finance the creation of low-budget films. With television cable networks as additional sources of revenue, and functioning in some cases as producers themselves, a substantial increase in independent feature-film production has ensued. Digital video discs (DVDs), invented in the 1990s, in particular, have stimulated even more interest in movies. Making it possible to enjoy movies in the home with all the technological splendour offered by movie theatres (given the right equipment), DVDs (and other digital devices) have further entrenched movies in mass culture.

Sound Recordings

Sound recording technology emerged in the late nineteenth century. Thomas Edison invented the first phonograph (record player) in 1877. Edison recorded his version of 'Mary Had a Little Lamb' using a mouthpiece (Milner 2009). A decade later, the German-born American inventor Emile Berliner improved Edison's model, producing the flat-disk phonograph, or *gramophone*, which was used shortly thereafter for recording and playing back music. Around 1920, Berliner's mechanical technology began to be replaced by electrical recording and reproduction, in which the vibrations of the phonograph needle were amplified by electromagnetic devices.

By the 1920s, the cheapness and availability of mass-produced vinyl records led to a true paradigm shift in musical art – the entrenchment of pop music as mainstream music. New musical styles and idioms such as jazz, swing, country and western, soul, and rock are among the best-known genres that recording technology helped to spread throughout society. Since the 1920s, in fact, music has been perceived as a source of entertainment and distraction for mass audiences. Inevitably, as pop music styles proliferated throughout the century, so too did the tendency for audience fragmentation – that is, for niche audiences according

to music style or subgenre. Today, with so much music available through recordings and in different digital formats, music artists and producers are well aware that their music will appeal primarily to specific audiences.

Radio

Another mass communications electronic device that was invented in the late nineteenth century was the radio, at first called the *wireless*. The background scientific principles for its development were elaborated by various scientists, but it was the Italian-born American electrical engineer Guglielmo Marconi who applied them to the invention of the world's first true wireless radio device in 1895. His device could send and receive a signal at a distance of close to 3 km. In 1901, Marconi developed an appliance that could send signals much farther and with much less background noise. This led, about two decades later, to the development of commercial technology that established the radio as the first electronic mass communications medium, shaping trends in music, culture, and mass communications generally. Radio could reach many more people than print, not only because it could span great distances instantly, but also because its audiences did not necessarily have to be print literate. Programming could thus be designed with mass appeal. As a consequence, radio was pivotal in spreading popular culture – a culture for all, not just for the cognoscenti.

Evidence of a plan for radio broadcasting to the general public can be found in a 1916 memorandum written by David Sarnoff, an employee of Marconi's U.S. branch, American Marconi, which would eventually become the Radio Corporation of America (RCA). Sarnoff recommended that radio become a household 'utility.' His memo at first was not given any serious consideration by management. After the end of the First World War in 1918, however, several manufacturing companies began to seriously explore Sarnoff's idea for the mass-marketing of home radio receivers.

In an effort to boost radio sales in peace-time, the Westinghouse Electric Corporation of Pittsburgh established what many culture historians consider to be the first commercially owned radio station to offer a regular schedule of programming to the general public. It came to be known by the call letters KDKA, after it received its licence from the Department of Commerce (which held regulatory power following the end of the war) in October of 1920. KDKA aired various kinds of entertainment programs, including recorded music, which was generated by a phonograph placed within the range of a microphone. The station did not charge user fees to listeners, nor did it carry paid advertisements. Westinghouse used KDKA simply as an enticement for people to purchase home radio receivers.

Other radio manufacturers soon followed Westinghouse's example. The General Electric Company, for example, broadcast its own programs on station WGY in Schenectady, New York. RCA eventually gave Sarnoff permission to develop radio programming for home entertainment. Sarnoff opened stations in New York City a..d Washington, DC, and in 1926 he founded the National Broadcasting Company (NBC), an RCA subsidiary created for the specific purpose of broadcasting programs via a cross-country network of stations. The Columbia Broadcasting System (CBS) radio service was established shortly thereafter in 1928, becoming a dominant force in the American broadcasting industry over the subsequent fifty years. Already in 1922, the American Telephone and Telegraph Company (AT&T) began exploring the possibilities of toll broadcasting, that is, charging fees in return for the airing of commercial advertisements on its stations. Fearing legal action, however, the telephone company sold its stations to RCA and left the broadcasting business. In return, AT&T was granted the exclusive right to provide the connec-

tions that would link local stations to the NBC network.

The sale of radios more than justified the expense to manufacturers of operating broadcasting services. According to estimates by the National Association of Broadcasters, in 1922 there were 60,000 households in the United States with radios; by 1929 the number had topped 10 million. But increases in sales of radio receivers could not continue forever. The sale of advertising time loomed, consequently, as the only viable solution for the financial support of American radio broadcasting. The merger of advertising with radio programming was the event that, arguably, transformed the nature of mass communications. Non-commercial broadcasting would play only a minor role in the United States, and, in fact, there would not be a coast-to-coast non-commercial radio network until the formation of National Public Radio (NPR) in 1970. In Great Britain, on the other hand, radio owners have always paid yearly licence fees, collected by the government, which are turned over directly to the British Broadcasting Corporation (BBC).

During the Second World War, American commentator Edward R. Murrow changed the nature of news reporting radically with his sensational descriptions of street scenes during the German bombing raids of London, which he delivered as an eyewitness from the rooftop of the CBS news bureau there. American president Franklin D. Roosevelt utilized radio to bypass the press and directly address the American people with his 'fireside chats,' aware that the emotional power of the voice would be much more persuasive than would any logical argument he might put into print. The chats continue to this day as part of the American presidency. Adolf Hitler, too, saw the radio as a propaganda medium, using it to persuade millions to follow him. And the radio appeal from Japanese emperor Hirohito to his nation for unconditional surrender in August 1945 helped end the Second World

War following the atomic bombings of Hiroshima and Nagasaki.

Radio broadcasting dramatically changed social life wherever it was introduced. It brought news, information, and the arts directly into homes. Historically a privilege of the elite, the arts could be enjoyed by members of the general public, most of whom would otherwise not have access to venues such as the concert hall and the theatre. It helped engender an unprecedented mass culture for people of all social classes and educational backgrounds. The 'democratization process' started by the Gutenberg revolution in the domain of print, and by the gramophone in the field of music, was extended by the radio medium considerably.

At first, radio was no more than a new audio medium for print and theatrical forms. For example, it adapted the various genres of traditional stage drama, transforming them into radio dramas, action serials, situation comedies (or sitcoms), and so-called soap operas. It looked to vaudeville to garner and adapt material for its comedy-variety programming. And it modelled its news coverage on the format of daily newspapers – early announcers would, in fact, often simply read articles from the local newspaper over the air. Nevertheless, because of its capacity to reach large numbers of people, from the 1920s to the early 1950s radio broadcasting evolved into society's primary medium of information, arts appreciation, and, above all else, entertainment. Only after the advent of television in the 1950s did radio's hegemony in this domain begin to erode, as its audiences split into smaller, distinct segments. Today, radio is primarily a medium for automobile and office use. People listen to it mainly in their cars as they drive from location to location, or in their offices (or other places of work). Aware of this, radio stations typically present news and traffic information in a regular interspersed fashion throughout their broadcasts, or else present uninterrupted stretches of music during certain periods of the working day.

Many radio stations offer programming for niche audiences (sports stations, talk stations, etc.).

Today, radio has shown itself to have staying power and to be an adaptive medium. It is estimated that there are about two billion radio sets in use worldwide, with more than half concentrated in North America, the European Union countries, and Japan. In developing societies, too, nearly all citizens own or have access to a radio. All-digital stations are springing up all over. Programs and commercials are being transferred to digital databases for broadcasting. Some advertising agencies send in commercials on digital formats; other companies send their commercials to the stations' computer via high-speed internet links. Satellite stations such as XM and Sirius are also making inroads. In sum, the radio is not yet a relic and continues to be an integral part of mass communications.

Television

The scientific principles underlying the technology that led to the invention of television were established by the British electrical engineer John Logie Baird. A transmission tube was developed by the Russian-born American engineer Vladimir K. Zworykin in 1923 and the American inventor Philo T. Farnsworth in 1927. The first home television receiver was demonstrated in Schenectady, New York, in 1928, by American inventor Ernst F.W. Alexanderson. The images were small and unsteady, but the set was shown to have potential use in homes. The first television sets for mass utilization became commercially available in England in 1936 and in the United States in 1938. After the Second World War, technical improvements and prosperity led to a growing demand for these sets. In the United States, six television stations were established at first, each one broadcasting for only a few hours each day. By 1948, thirty-four all-day stations were in operation in twenty-one major cities, and about one million television sets had been sold. By the end of the 1950s national television networks were established in most industrialized countries. TV had emerged, in effect, to replace radio as the primary source of mass communications virtually across the world. As the twentieth century came to a close, TV went digital as broadcasters started transmitting TV signals in a digital (computer-based) format and integrating with online technology by offering additional programming or information on websites. Google and television have also merged to make television a kind of access device to the internet, and this will change how programming will be scripted in the future.

With the widespread growth of cable television, starting in the 1960s, and then of direct broadcast satellite (DBS) services (a term used to refer to satellite television broadcasts intended for home reception) in the 1990s, many new channels and types of programming are now available to people across the globe. As a consequence, previous debates about TV's impact on children, world culture, politics, and community life became even more widespread. On the one side, critics say that television feeds a constant stream of simplified ideas and sensationalistic images to unwitting viewers, that it negatively influences politics and voting patterns, that it destroys local cultures in favour of a bland 'Hollywood-oriented' distraction culture, and that it encourages passivity. On the other side, defenders say that television provides high-quality educational and cultural programming, and that it is the major source of local, national, and international news for many citizens who would otherwise remain uninformed. Whatever the truth, one thing is certain – TV has had an influence simply by making the same pattern and kind of programming (the same TV sitcoms, adventure programs, and variety shows) available across the globe.

As is the case with radio, advertising is the fuel that propels TV broadcasting. In the United States and Europe advertising agencies underwrite network and cable programming. Only in the area of public broadcasting is this not the case. Public TV services are generally supported by government funding, contributions from viewers, corporate gifts, and foundation grants. Direct broadcast satellite now provides viewers with a system capable of capturing satellite signals. But most channels available from satellites require subscription fees and licences.

Online programming has also become routine. Services such as Replay TV and America Online TV, among others, offer interactive formats that permit viewers to have more of a choice in what they watch at a certain time. But interactive TV is not new. In the winter of 1953, in the infancy of television broadcasting, a kid's show called *Winky Dink* was the first program to feature an interactive component. To interact with the show, viewers bought a kit that included a piece of plastic to cover the TV screen and a Magic Crayon. Kids could then assist the hapless Winky character out of jams. Prompted by the show's announcer, they could draw a bridge for him, for example, so that he could cross over a ravine and then erase the bridge, as instructed by the announcer, so that the bad guys would plunge into the ravine. The show ran for four years, and was revived in 1970.

The next step in interactive TV occurred in Columbus, Ohio, on 1 December 1977, where cable companies made a 'relay box' available to customers so that they could order movies whenever they wished. The system also showed city council meetings during which viewers got to express their opinions through the box. Such 'boxes' are still around today, but with many more interactive functions and sophisticated new features added to them. By the early 1990s, specialty channels provided by cable companies allowed viewers to watch shows whenever they chose to do so. Today, channels and programs have websites, which viewers can visit during, before, or after traditional broadcasts of shows. With new cable technologies, moreover, viewers can pause live TV and record shows onto low-cost hard drives with the click of a button. Microsoft's WebTV and AOLTV (America Online TV) allow users to pull up detailed information while they are watching a news or documentary broadcast. And, as mentioned, Google has made internet access and television programming one integrated system, by offering convergent technologies that will alter the future of television.

Digitization

Digitization is the process of converting traditional communications technologies into digital (computer-based) ones. The first telecommunications medium to be digitized was the telephone in 1962, with the installation of high-speed lines in phone networks capable of carrying dozens of conversations simultaneously. Phone equipment of all kinds is now fully digitized. A new high-speed phone technology, called digital subscriber line (DSL), has been installed across the globe. It has the capacity to transmit audio, video, and computer data over both conventional phone lines and satellite.

Similar or parallel 'digitization stories' can be told with regard to other media of mass communications. Today, most major newspapers are produced by means of digital technology and are available in online versions. The special effects created for the movie *Star Wars* in 1977 introduced digital technology into filmmaking. The first computer-generated movie, *Toy Story*, debuted in 1995. Such movies are now common. In the domain of home video technology, the DVD has supplanted the VHS tape. The digitally produced compact disc (CD) started replacing vinyl records and audiocassette tapes in the mid-1980s, shortly after its introduction in 1982. Further 'compressing technologies,' such as MP3, are cropping up regularly. Cable TV went digital in 1998, allowing broadcasters to increase the number of channel offerings. This technology was introduced primarily to meet competition from the direct broadcast satellite

(DBS) industry, which started producing digital multi-channel programming for reception by home satellite dishes in 1995. High-definition television (HDTV), which consists of transmitters and receivers using digital formats, became commercially available in 1998. Digital audio broadcasting (DAB) is the corresponding technology in radio broadcasting. Radio stations now use digital technology to create their programs.

The Internet

As computer technology improved steadily after the Second World War, smaller and cheaper computers could be built for all kinds of purposes. By the late 1970s, it became economically feasible to manufacture personal computers (PCs) for mass consumption. The first PCs were mainly word processors; that is, they simply added computer-based capacities to typewriters in order to make writing and changing printed text significantly easier and more sophisticated. The first microcomputers had the power of older, larger machines, but could fit onto a desktop. This was accomplished because of new miniaturization technologies that allowed manufacturers to compress the memory and processing power of thousands of circuits onto tiny chips of materials called semiconductors.

At the same time that computers were becoming faster, more powerful, and smaller, networks were being developed for interconnecting them. In the 1960s, the Advanced Research Projects Agency (ARPA) of the U.S. Department of Defense, along with researchers working on military projects at research centres and universities across the country, developed a network called the ARPANET for sharing data and mainframe computer processing time over specially equipped telephone lines and satellite links. Used at first for military purposes, the ARPANET became the first functional major electronic-mail network right after the National Science Foundation connected universities and non-military research sites to it. By 1981, around 200 computers were connected to ARPANET. The military then divided the network into two organizations – ARPANET and a purely military network. During the 1980s, the former was absorbed by NSFNET, a more advanced network developed by the National Science Foundation. It was that system that came to be known simply as the internet shortly after.

One of the main reasons for the slow growth of the early internet was the difficulty of using the network. To access the internet, users had to learn a complex series of programming commands. The internet's breakthrough occurred in the late 1980s with the arrival of the World Wide Web (WWW), developed by Tim Berners-Lee, a British computer scientist at the European Organization for Nuclear Research (CERN). The WWW is a system of computers and files that users may view and with which they can interact. The WWW provides access to a variety of information, including magazine archives, public and university library resources, current world and business news, computer programs, and so on. It can be accessed by a computer connected to the internet, which is itself a global consortium of interconnected computer networks. The WWW is organized so that users can move easily between documents called web pages. Users generally navigate the WWW using an application known as a browser, which presents text, images, sound, or other programs. As the internet incorporates new technologies that add such features as spoken-word commands, instantaneous translation, and increased availability of material, it will continue its rapid growth.

People can use computers to design graphics and full-motion video, send electronic mail, make airline or hotel reservations, search for all kinds of information, play games, listen to radio, watch television programs, and even visit 'electronic rooms' to chat with other people over the World Wide Web. In the history of human communications, no other device has made it possible for so many people to interact with each other, irrespective of the distance between them. Moreover, it is no longer appropriate to talk about 'competing' media. Advances in digital technologies and in telecommunications networks have led to a convergence of communications systems alongside traditional ones. This has led, in turn, to the emergence of new lifestyles and careers, to the creation of new institutions, and to radical changes in all domains of mass communications.

As mentioned, the World Wide Web was devised in 1989 by English computer scientist Timothy Berners-Lee to aid communication between physicists working in different parts of the world for the European Laboratory for Particle Physics. As it grew, however, the WWW revolutionized the use of the internet because, during the early 1990s, increasingly large numbers of users who were not part of the scientific or academic communities began to use the internet, due in large part to the WWW.

Until the early 1990s, most information on the internet consisted only of printed text. The introduction of the WWW made it possible to include graphics, animation, video, and sound. Today, the WWW contains tens of millions of documents, databases, bulletin boards, and electronic publications, such as newspapers, books, and magazines in all media forms (print, visual, etc.). The miasma of information it contains made it immediately obvious to internet users that appropriate technology was needed for them to be able to locate specific types of information. This led to the development of uniform resource locator (URL) technology. Using software that connects to the internet – called navigation or browser software – a computer operator can select a URL that contains information he or she wishes to access. The computer then contacts that address, making the information available to the operator. With millions of separate URLs, classification and indexing have clearly become critical internet functions. Indexing services – located on the internet itself – enable users to search for specific information by entering the topic that interests them.

The transfer of large databases onto the internet has created a new way of viewing and organizing the classification of information. People can post their own messages, opinions, commentaries, and ideas on any subject imaginable on websites, on personal blogs, and so forth. It has also become a primary reference tool with online dictionaries and encyclopedias becoming more and more common and acceptable to scholars and researchers. Unlike printed texts, internet pages can be updated constantly and, thus, are never out of date. Cyberspace is fast becoming a place for social and intellectual interaction.

Email has made regular mail appear cumbersome and inefficient. And because of listservs – electronic mailing lists that make it possible to send email to special-interest groups – it has truly created a worldwide system of time-efficient communications. With the arrival of instant messaging (IM) technologies, this is being enhanced further. IM is instantaneous, thus bypassing the lag time inherent in sending and receiving email. IM is a 'visual walkie-talkie' system that is leading to the employment of a new 'language code' online that is becoming increasingly compressed to meet the needs of instant written communications.

Clearly, the advent of the internet has had, and continues to have, enormous implications for how we carry out interpersonal, group, and mass communications. Email has largely replaced the written letter in most areas of social communications. Media and entertainment companies use the internet to broadcast audio and video, including live radio and television programs; to offer online chat rooms, in which people carry on discussions using written text; and to provide online news and weather programs. Scientists and scholars use the internet to communicate with colleagues, to conduct research, to distribute lecture notes and course materials to students, and to publish papers and articles.

The internet galaxy is expanding literally at the speed of light.

The internet has also become a highly effective medium of advertising, making it possible for all kinds of businesses around the world to communicate effectively and inexpensively. The feature of the internet that makes it attractive to the advertiser is the fact that the product or service can be ordered directly from the web page. Not only does an online ad about a specific product or service reach millions of potential customers through the WWW, but its users can acquire or request it on the spot, by simply clicking the appropriate icons.

Computers can now be put on top of TV sets so that people can interface with the internet as well as the new digital TV services. More and more computer boxes are being built into digital sets. Personal data assistants (PDAs), pocket-sized information devices that accept handwriting, keep people in contact with the internet and other media as well. In the near future, computers will be in charge of most communication channels, turning the world into a true digital global village.

Push technology, also known as webcasting or netcasting, is fast taking over the previous forms of mass communications. Push technology programs have no fixed schedules. A producer can offer audio or video presentations to anyone who subscribes to them. The user might either download the entire video for later playback or play it in real time over the internet. Real-time play is possible through a technology called streaming. Many radio stations stream their programming in real time so that people throughout the world may listen over the Web. Many also offer downloads of previous programming. Television networks and movie producers often use push technology to promote their products and to present clips from programs and motion pictures. Some television producers have created programming specifically for the Web. Such programs are often called webisodes. Some television news organizations use the Web to post

Figure 1

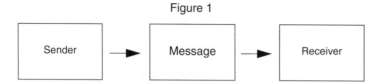

additional stories, constantly updating the news. They also offer extended versions of interviews and other features. Popular offerings include weather reports, global financial information, sports scores, and breaking news.

Finally, the creation of personal web pages is a particularly popular use of the WWW. Some people use them to share personal information or to promote particular ideas and theories. One type of page, called a *weblog* or *blog*, is a personal journal of thoughts and ideas for other users to read. A blog may also contain links to an individual's favourite websites. Most online services provide space on a resource computer called a server, or host, for hosting (storing) web pages and blogs for individuals. Never before in the history of communications have individuals had so much power of control over the means of communications as today. The alphabet brought about the first true paradigm shift in human culture; the internet is bringing about the second such shift.

The Study of Communication

The study of communication is conducted through separate subfields in universities across the world – primarily in linguistics, semiotics, psychology, anthropology, media studies, and communication studies. Among the myriad research approaches and findings accumulated over the last century, three types shed light upon the general nature of communication systems and the role they play in human life: studies that examine the overall structure of communication models; studies that investigate the effects of mass communications on people; and studies that investigate how communication systems change.

Scholars who made contributions to the first area have always focused principally on developing models that captured the main components of all its forms. One of these was the late Claude Shannon (1916–2001), who devised a model intended originally to improve the efficiency of telecommunication systems. Known as the 'bull's-eye model,' it essentially depicted communication as a system constituted by three main components – a *sender* aiming a *message* at a *receiver* as in a target range (see Figure 1).

Shannon's model included four other main components: *channel, noise, redundancy,* and *feedback*. The channel is the physical system carrying the transmitted signal. Vocally produced sound waves, for instance, can be transmitted through the air or through an electronic channel (for example, the radio). Noise refers to some interfering element (physical or psychological) in the channel that distorts or partially effaces a message. In radio and telephone transmissions, noise is equivalent to electronic static; in vocal linguistic transmissions, it can vary from any interfering exterior sound (physical noise) to lapses of memory (psychological noise). Communication systems have redundancy features built into them that allow for a message to be understood even if noise is present. For instance, in verbal communication the high predictability of certain words in many utterances ('Roses are red, violets are ...') is a redundant feature of verbal communication. Finally, Shannon used the term feedback to refer to the fact that senders have the capacity to monitor the messages they transmit and modify them to enhance their decodability. A more detailed diagram of the model, which also shows other components is shown in Figure 2.

Figure 2

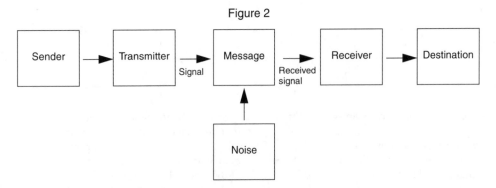

The main components of this model are the sender or source (S) of the communication; a message (M) and its information content; a channel (C) through which the message is transmitted from one place to another; and a receiver (R) to whom the message is directed. Logically, it has come to be known as the *source-message-channel-receiver* model, or SMCR model for short. The model was elaborated in 1954 by American communication theorist Wilbur Schramm (1907–87), who added two other components to the original bull's-eye model: the *encoder*, the organism or mechanism which converts the message into a form that can be transmitted through an appropriate channel; and a decoder, which reverses the encoding process so that the message can be received successfully. The SMCR model has been used extensively in media studies because of its simplicity and generalizability to all types of mass communications systems. It can, for instance, be used to portray the physical components of TV broadcasting simply, yet revealingly (see Figure 3).

Feedback (Ratings)

A further elaboration of the SMCR model was put forward by George Gerbner in 1956. In the case of oral verbal communication, the source and receiver are also the encoder and decoder respectively. Encoding and decoding in this case involve knowledge of the language used, as well as facial expression, gesture, and other non-verbal codes. The channel is the vocal apparatus that transmits the message through the medium of air. The message is adjusted according to the feedback behaviour observable in a receiver; noise in this case can be of both a physical and psychological nature.

The second type of research paradigm is the one that investigates the effects of mass communications and mass media on *audiences*, defined as the readers, spectators, listeners, or viewers receiving a message in print or electronic form. Early studies in this area seemed to demonstrate that mass communications media directly influenced audiences of all types, especially children and adolescents. Known as the *media effects studies*, they appeared to suggest, moreover, that media content does not just mirror cultural values but, rather, shapes them. The relevant studies are now classified under the rubric of hypodermic needle theory (HNT) because they claim that media are capable of directly swaying minds with the same kind of impact a hypodermic needle has on the body. A moderate version of HNT is called two-step flow theory. This asserts that media effects are indirect and are mediated by group leaders. These are people, such as clerics, media personalities, and so forth, who are identified within communities as representing the views of that community. This view is in fact partially verifiable, since people within different social classes come up with very different interpretations of media messages. They tend to perceive them as interpretive com-

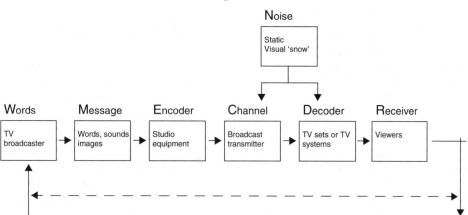

Figure 3

munities, which are inclined to coincide with real communities such as families, unions, neighbourhoods, and churches.

Another theoretical stance, called *cultivation and reception* theory, claims that media do not affect people – people use media for their own uses and gratifications. Associated with the work of American sociologist Elihu Katz, the basic claim of 'uses and gratifications' theory is that people are not passive consumers of media representations – they are opportunistic users of the media. Another theory has been put forward by British cultural theorist Stuart Hall (1973), who argues that people do not absorb texts passively, but rather *read* them (interpret them) in one of three ways, known as preferred, negotiated, and oppositional readings. The *preferred* reading is the one that the makers of texts have built into them and which, they hope, audiences will take from them. The *negotiated* reading is the one that results when audiences agree with, or respond in part, to the meanings built into texts. And an *oppositional* reading is one that is in opposition to what the maker of the text had intended. A simple way to understand the difference between the three types is to consider a comedian who has just told a joke on stage. If the audience laughs wholeheartedly, then the joke has produced the preferred reading. If only some of the audience laughs

wholeheartedly, while others chuckle or sneer, then the joke has brought about a negotiated reading. Finally, if the audience reacts negatively to the joke, with resentment, then it has produced an oppositional reading.

A third set of models falls under the general rubric of *selective perception theory*, which claims that audiences select from a media text what they are predisposed to do. Anti-pornography individuals who watch a TV debate on the relation of pornography to freedom of expression have been shown to take away from the debate only the views that are consistent with their particular viewpoint – namely, to restrict pornography under any and all circumstances. Libertarian individuals, on the other hand, tend to take away from it a sense of triumph by virtue of the fact that the debate occurred in the first place (thus legitimizing the topic). This suggests that the mass communications media have limited impacts on most individuals and that the communities in which they are reared have more of an influence on their world view than do media messages and images.

The study of mass communications has also been approached from political and ideological angles. The first to do this were so-called Frankfurt School theoreticians such as Theodor W. Adorno, Max Horkheimer, and Herbert Marcuse, who saw mass communications as serving a hidden 'culture industry' and obeying only the logic of consumer capitalism. Using Antonio Gramsci's concept of *hegemony*, the Frankfurt theorists claimed that the domination of society by the group in power occurs in large part by the group's control of mass communications. More recently, this view has been developed by Noam Chomsky and his followers. Known as the *propaganda model*, it asserts that those in power use the mass media to propagate their particular political messages in subtle yet effective ways. They do this by 'manufacturing consent' through the ways in which the news are reported and which aspects of the news are emphasized.

Another main type of research focus is the one that investigates questions of how communication systems change over time and how the changes correlate with larger social forces. One of the best-known scholars to consider these questions was the late Canadian communications theorist Marshall McLuhan. McLuhan (1951, 1962, 1964) claimed that the form of mass communication used is tied to technological innovations, affecting people's ways of thinking as well as the constitution and evolution of their social institutions. Each major period in history takes its character from the medium of communication used most widely at the time. McLuhan called the period from 1700 to the mid-1900s the 'age of print,' because in that era mass-produced printed materials were the chief means through which people gained and shared knowledge. Books encouraged reflection and individualism of thought, bringing about movements such as the Protestan Reformation and the Enlightenment. Changes in electronics technology brought forth the 'electronic age' starting in the early twentieth century. Because electronic communication speeds communication greatly, people in all parts of the world gradually became deeply immersed in the lives of everyone else through electronic media such as radio, television, and the internet. As a result, individualism and even

traditional notions of nationalism changed and continue to change. New international communities surfaced forming part of what McLuhan called the 'electronic global village.'

A related question that arises with regard to change in communication systems is the following: Are there any inherent biological or psychological principles or laws governing such change? This question was examined by the Harvard linguist George Kingsley Zipf for the first time in the early 1930s. Zipf (1949) claimed that many phenomena in language could be explained as the result of an inborn tendency in the human species to make the most of its communicative resources with the least expenditure of effort (physical, cognitive, and social). This tendency, he claimed, is independent of social and cultural factors. It is the product of a 'principle of least effort' (PLE) in the constitution of human communicative intent. The PLE is the reason why speakers minimize articulatory effort by 'compressing' the length of words and utterances. At the same time, people want to be able to interpret the meaning of words and utterances unambiguously and with least effort. Zipf demonstrated that there exists a constant correlation between the length of a specific word (in number of phonemes) and its rank order in the language (its position in order of its frequency of occurrence in texts of all kinds). The higher the rank order of a word (the more frequent it is in actual usage), the more it tends to be 'shorter' (made up with fewer phonemes). For example, articles (*a, the*), conjunctions (*and, or*), and other function words (*to, it*), which have a high rank order in English (and in any other language for that matter), are typically monosyllabic, consisting of one to three phonemes. Interestingly, this 'compression' force does not stop at the level of function words, as Zipf and others subsequently found. It can be seen to manifest itself, above all else, in the tendency for phrases that come into popular use to become abbreviated (*FYI, UNESCO, Hi, Bye, ad, photo, Mr, Mrs, Dr,*

24/7, etc.) or changed into acronyms (*aka, VCR, DNA, laser, GNP, IQ, VIP*, etc.).

Communication is constantly evolving. McLuhan's basic claim was that communication systems influence not only the way people exchange ideas but ultimately how they will evolve socially and culturally. Electronic gadgets, internet communications, and the like are creating new jobs, new ways of making contact, and new ways of storing and using information, as well as affecting the evolution of language, discourse, and the arts. In the human species, communication systems, knowledge, culture, society, cognition, and human behaviour are intrinsically linked.

Marcel Danesi

Bibliography

Baran, Stanley J. *Introduction to Mass Communication, Media Literacy, and Culture* New York: McGraw-Hill, 2004.

Berger, Arthur A. *Media and Communication Research Methods*. London: Sage, 2000.

– *Making Sense of Media: Key Texts in Media and Cultural Studies*. Oxford: Blackwell, 2005.

– *50 Ways to Understand Communication*. Lanham: Rowman and Littlefield, 2006.

Biagi, Shirley. *Media/Impact: An Introduction to Mass Media*. Belmont, CA: Wadsworth/Thomson Learning, 2001.

Briggs, Adam, and Paul Cobley, eds. *The Media: An Introduction*. Essex: Addison Wesley Longman, 1998.

Campbell, Richard, Christopher R. Martin, and Bettina Fabos. *Media and Culture: An Introduction to Mass Communication*. Boston: Bedford/St Martin's, 2005.

Crystal, David. *Language and the Internet*. Cambridge: Cambridge University Press, 2001.

Hall, Stuart. *Encoding and Decoding in the Television Discourse*. London: The Seminar Press, 1973.

Hanson, Ralph E., *Mass Communication: Living in a Media World*. New York: McGraw-Hill, 2005.

Herman, Andrew, and Thomas Swiss, eds. *The World Wide Web and Contemporary Cultural Theory*. London: Routledge, 2000.

Innis, Harold A. *Empire and Communication*. Toronto: University of Toronto Press, 1972.

McLuhan, Marshall. *The Mechanical Bride: Folklore of Industrial Man*. New York: Vanguard, 1951.

– *The Gutenberg Galaxy*. Toronto: University of Toronto Press, 1962.

– *Understanding Media*. London: Routledge and Kegan Paul, 1964.

McQuail, Denis. *Mass Communication Theory: An Introduction*. London: Sage, 2000.

Milner, Greg. *Perfecting Sound Forever: An Aural History of Recorded Music*. New York: Faber and Faber, 2009.

Slevin, James. *The Internet and Society*. London: Polity, 2000.

Straubhaar, Joseph, and Robert LaRose. *Media Now: Communications Media in the Information Age*. Belmont, CA: Wadsworth/Thomson Learning, 2002.

Zipf, George K. *Human Behavior and the Principle of Least Effort*. Boston: Addison-Wesley, 1949.

COMMUNICATION THEORY

[See also: *Communication; Discourse; Interactivity; Internet; Media Studies*]

The development of theories of communication in the human sciences has been variously shaped by divergent traditions in media and communication studies in Europe, North America, and Asia. 'Communications research,' which succeeded the study of rhetoric and linguistic communication in the early twentieth century, was interested in the relationship between a range of communicative technologies and the content of the messages they conveyed. What became the primary focus of such research in North America from the 1930s to the 1960s was the power of mass media, exemplified by 'effects analysis' and the 'uses and gratifications' approach. In the UK and Australia, media studies largely turned to the cultural analysis of texts and audiences, while Canadian scholarship became known for the political economy of mass media and the study of media environments. But the transformations in the telecommunications, information technology, and media industries in the decades either side of the millennia has given rise to several dramatic changes in communication theory.

First, these latter changes have broadened the field in which communication and media studies applies itself in both its theoretical and empirical pursuits. The first notable change is that 'mass communication' or 'media studies' is frequently resolved into the generic 'communication studies' to denote a more general field of study which can examine information, communication, and media and the convergence between them. This is reflected in the restructuring of university departments in the 1990s. In the United States, 'mass communication' has often been exchanged for 'communication' or 'communications,' while in the UK and Australia many older 'media studies' departments have added 'communication.'

Second, the above changes can be attributed to the fact that the study of centralized broadcast media, which includes the mass circulation of newsprint, radio, television, and cinema, has been joined by research into distributed networks of communication, made possible by the internet and the enhanced interactivity made possible by mobile telephony. These distributed networks formalized as 'new media' or 'cyberspace' have become distinct fields in their own right but have also spawned a revision of traditional analysis of mass media. Thus, for example, these changes have been accompanied by a renewed interest in architectures of communication and how new media have usurped the technological aspects of mass media.

But new media have had far less impact on the production of content as they have on the means of distribution of content. Being able to receive television on a mobile phone or download videos on the internet are two such examples.

Traditional media studies continue to offer core analysis of texts, audiences, and industry. The object of study with which it first emerged in Britain in the 1960s was overwhelmingly the semiotic study of media texts, which coincided with new methods for studying texts (print, film, television, radio) – structuralism (Roman Jakobson, Claude Lévi-Strauss, Roland Barthes) and the emerging 'post-structuralism' (Jacques Derrida, Michel Foucault, Jean Baudrillard, and the later Barthes). At the same time, the emergence of 'cultural studies' went on to explore the interrelationship between these texts and subcultures as well as practices of consumption.

In the United States, communication studies have largely been occupied with more empirical studies, which concentrate on the relationship between media forms and the messages they convey. The study of media and processes of communication should be further distinguished from 'mass communication theory,' which, like media studies of the 1970s onwards, was interested in the role of the audience in broadcast communication (or what was coming to be called 'mass media'). However, the relationship between the producers and receivers of messages in the mass communication model was predominantly one of 'effects analysis,' where the audience was conceived of as passive.

The effects tradition itself derives from transmission models of communication, which could be found in the information theory of 1950s America. Transmission models take communication events and intersubjectivity as their building blocks. Successful communication occurs when information is understood by sender and receiver in exact duplication. In the late 1940s this definition was advanced by Claude E. Shannon and Warren Weaver before it was successively revised by George Gerbner and applied to mass communication by Harold Lasswell. Lasswell insisted that mass communication needed a different methodological approach from personal communication, making his work useful for analysing broadcast. Lasswell was interested in the influence of communication structures on society as a whole. His most general set of questions were: *Who says what, in which channel, to whom and with what effect?* Lasswell's framing up of communication theory in this way proliferated into an array of sub-branches that looked at content, control, audience, and impact.

However, by the 1970s the application of transmission models to the study of audiences was challenged by members of the Centre for Contemporary Cultural Studies at the University of Birmingham. In a key essay, 'Encoding/Decoding,' Stuart Hall examined how every media text offered oppositional, negotiated, and dominant readings at the same time. Later, this analysis of negotiated meaning was taken up in the work of Dave Morley, Ien Ang, and Virginia Nightingale.

Notwithstanding, the transmission model of communication survives today in much of the literature on computer-mediated communication, but it is further challenged by the analysis of interactivity made possible by new media.

Leading this challenge is the work of 'second-media-age' thinkers like Howard Rheingold, George Gilder, and Mark Poster, who argue for the emancipatory qualities of new 'interactive' media. For them, traditional media of newspapers, radio, television, and cinema are viewed as repressive and controlling, whereas new media are seen to place the control of meaning making back into the hands of the individual to the extent that they enable interactivity. For some theorists, like Castells in *The Internet Galaxy* (2001: 374), these new media have inaugurated the 'interactive society,' 'a digitized, networked integration of multiple communication modes.' For the second media age thinkers, only computer-mediated or tele-mediated *interaction* is significant, and communication outside such networks, be it broadcast or face-to-face, becomes marginalized.

Holmes (2005) has argued that the second-media-age perspective has become an orthodoxy in contemporary communication theory, an alternative to which is

provided by John B. Thompson's typology of 'interaction' (Thompson 1995). Thompson distinguishes between three types of interaction: face-to-face, mediated interaction, and mediated quasi-interaction, which are analytically distinguishable by their spatio-temporal potential. The face-to-face occurs in a context of mutual presence and is interpersonal and dialogical. Mediated interaction (writing, telephoning) is also dialogical but is extended rather than mutual. Lastly, mediated quasi-interaction (books, radio, newspapers) is also extended in space and time, but is monological or 'one-way.' However, Thompson points out that senders and receivers within this kind of interaction nevertheless form bonds which transcend the fact of interaction.

What runs through all of these form-types is the progressive filtering-out of communication cues, where the face-to-face provides a high degree of contextual information (like body language and gestures), while the mediated forms substitute such information with narrower contexts (letterhead, signature, time announcement on the radio, station promotion, and so on).

Thompson's insights about 'interaction' provide some restraint to the fortunes of 'interactivity' in recent literature on the internet. In Thompson's model it follows that broadcast media are as capable of 'interactivity' as the internet and that its various sub-media are also capable of broadcast communication, such as bulk email and bulletin board postings. In turn, it needs to be asked why technologically extended 'interactivity' is so closely associated with the internet but not with, say, the entire history of telephony. In fact, the internet is not an appropriate model for such a blanket characterization, as it provides a platform for an array of communication functions: information retrieval, advertising, browsing, commerce, and many forms of anonymous communication. The only sub-media of the internet which uniquely provides a communication form that cannot be found in other media is Usenet or WWW-hosted discussion groups, which are capable of scales of participation that are not possible in embodied forums. But even with these, interactivity cannot be so easily heralded as some kind of special property.

An alternative approach to studying interactivity is to turn to sociological accounts of communicative integration. Interaction is still important but also needs to be viewed in terms of the fact that all concrete interactions occur in the context of dominant frames of communicative integration. The integration thesis rejects the idea that the study of communication is reducible to documenting empirically observable kinds of *interaction*, be these interpersonal or extended (Calhoun 1986, 1992). A person formed within a level of integration – for example, face-to-face or media-extended – does not have to engage in constant interactions within that frame (i.e., embodied dialogue or watching television) in order to be enveloped by the set of relations that are bound up in it. The integration thesis has also found continuation in the recent turn to ritual theories of communication (Carey 1989; Couldry 2003; Holmes 2005). Media provide us not only with important information about the world, but also, argue the ritual theorists, with confirmation of our relationship to the world. Seen in this way, tuning in or logging on are in fact a ceremony by which we renew this relationship. Couldry (2003: 7) argues: 'The exceptional sense of togetherness we may feel in media events is just a more explicit (ritualised) concentration of togetherness, which in a routine way, we act out when we switch on the television or radio, or check a news website, to find out what's going on.' It matters little from which kind of media individuals draw their sense of connection; what is significant is the extraordinary intimacy with which they engage with media, whether this involves 'curling up' in front of our favourite television program, or enjoying the personalized privacy of SMS communication with a friend. We become very attached to media, old and new. It is necessary to look beyond the functional explanations of media as 'entertainment' or 'information' and see media as central to modern identity.

David Holmes

Bibliography

Calhoun, Craig. Computer Technology, Large Scale Social Integration and the Local Community. *Urban Affairs Quarterly* 22 (1986): 329–49.
– The Infrastructure of Modernity: Indirect Social Relationships, Information Technology, and Social Integration. In *Social Change and Modernity*, ed. H. Haferkampf and N. Smelser, 205–36. Berkeley, CA: UCLA Press, 1992.
Carey, John. *Communication as Culture*. Boston: Unwin Hyman, 1989.
Castells, Manuel. *The Internet Galaxy*. London: Oxford, 2001.
Couldry, Nick. *Media Rituals: A Critical Approach*. London: Routledge, 2003.
Hall, Stuart. Encoding/Decoding. In *Culture, Media, Language: Working Papers in Cultural Studies, 1972–79*, ed. Stuart Hall et al. London: Hutchinson, 1980.
Holmes, David. *Communication Theory: Media, Technology, Society*. London: Sage, 2005.
Poster, Mark. *The Second Media Age*. London: Polity, 1995.
Thompson, John. *The Media and Modernity: A Social Theory of the Media*. Stanford: Stanford University Press, 1995.

CONCEPTUAL METAPHOR THEORY

[See also: *Chomsky, Noam; Cognitive Language Studies; Generativism*]

The approach to language as a system of concepts grounded in figurative language is known as *conceptual metaphor theory* (CMT). Although the term surfaced in the early 1980s, the theoretical notions that it embodies have a long history behind them, starting in the ancient world and elaborated more concretely throughout the twentieth century in psychology, semiotics, and linguistics. The theory has also had significant implications for the study of popular media, such as TV programs, pulp fiction literature, and the like (Danesi 2002).

Background

It was Aristotle (1952a, 1952b) who coined the term *metaphor* – itself as a metaphor (from Greek *meta* 'beyond' and *pherein* 'to carry') – in order to explain how people conceptualized abstractions in concrete ways. Unlike concepts referring to visible things, such as animals (*cat*), objects (*table*), and plants (*tree*), an abstract concept such as *life* cannot be perceived or shown concretely. However, by comparing it to something concrete, such as a *stage*, Aristotle suggested, we gain a good understanding of what this concept entails (at least in an imaginary way). With its characters, settings, and plots, the stage is felt to be an appropriate analogue for life. The theatre remains, to this day, an overarching metaphor for *life*. This is why we commonly use theatre terms to talk about life. For instance, if we ask someone *What is your life like?* we might get a response such as *My life is a comedy* or *My life is a farce*, from which we can draw real inferences about that person's life.

Although he recognized the knowledge-making power of metaphor, Aristotle ultimately dismissed it as a flight of fancy, a device of poets and orators, not a cognitive system for understanding the world. It was exceptional or idiomatic language, not systematic language. CMT has shown, however, that metaphor is the backbone of semantics. Take the metaphorical statement *Your friend is a snake*. Clearly, we know that a human being is not a reptile. So, why do we extract a meaning from a statement that links human personality to the perceived characteristics of snakes as dangerous animals? The answer is that we sense that humans and animals are interconnected in the natural scheme of things. It is this intuitive 'sense' that underlies how

we understand such statements. The late seventeenth- and early eighteenth-century Neapolitan philosopher Giambattista Vico emphasized that metaphor was evidence of how knowledge of the world originates from this such 'sense-making.' He called the capacity for such sense-making *poetic logic*: 'It is another property of the human mind that whenever men can form no idea of distant and unknown things, they judge them by what is familiar and at hand' (in Bergin and Fisch 1984: 122). The two parts of the metaphor suggest each other in specific, concrete ways. By saying that *life is a stage* we are also implying that *stages are life*. They imply each other – what happens on a stage is indicative of what happens in real life and what happens in real life is easily representable in theatrical ways.

Vico's view of metaphor was largely ignored by philosophers of his era, such as G.W.F. Hegel and John Stuart Mill, who, like Aristotle, insisted that metaphor was no more than a decorative accessory to literal language. Exceptions to this pattern were Immanuel Kant and Friedrich Nietzsche. Nietzsche divided human thought into two domains – perception, consisting of impressions and sensations, and conception, consisting of the ideas that the mind makes from perception. Conception results by linking impressions together. This linkage is imprinted in metaphor, which, however, has the effect of distorting the true perception of things. Metaphor is, thus, the source of our superstitions and of our illusory belief systems. Nietzsche saw it as a kind of self-fulfilling prophecy. Any attempt to create a universal system of knowledge based on language, therefore, would be a vacuous enterprise. Kant saw language as a modelling system of sensory experience. His approach led to the emergence 'phenomenology' in philosophy and psychology, or the view that thought is based in experiential phenomena.

Early psychologists, such as Gustav Theodor Fechner and Wilhelm Wundt, conducted the first experiments on how people processed figurative language (Wundt

1901). The linguist Karl Bühler (1908), too, collected data on how subjects paraphrased and recalled proverbs. He found that the recall of a given proverb was excellent if it was linked to a second proverb; otherwise it was easily forgotten. Bühler concluded that metaphorical thinking was based on associative memory and was, therefore, something to be investigated further. In a groundbreaking 1936 book, *The Philosophy of Rhetoric*, Ivor A. Richards then argued that metaphor created new sense, which was an amalgam of the two parts of a metapor. He called this amalgam the 'ground' of the metapor, and the other two parts the 'tenor' and the 'vehicle.' In the 1950s, the gestalt psychologists started to investiage the cognitive and emotional properties of metaphorical language (Osgood and Suci 1953; Brown, Leiter, and Hildum 1957; Asch 1950, 1958; Werner and Kaplan 1963). The philosopher Max Black (1962) then introduced a distinction that was to become fundamental in subsequent work, namely that a specific metaphor, such as *Your friend is a snake,* is really an exemplar of the more general conceptual category that links *people* and *animals*. The former is now called a *linguistic metaphor* and the latter a *conceptual metaphor.* A watershed 1977 study then showed that conceptual metaphors pervaded common everyday speech. Titled *Psychology and the Poetics of Growth: Figurative Language in Psychology, Psychotherapy, and Education,* it found that speakers of English uttered, on average, a surprising 3,000 novel metaphors and 7,000 idioms per week (Pollio, Barlow, Fine, and Pollio 1977). It became saliently obvious that metaphorical discourse could hardly be characterized as a deviation from literal semantics, or a mere stylistic accessory to literal conversation. Two collections of studies published shortly thereafter, *Metaphor and Thought* (Ortony 1979) and *Cognition and Figurative Language* (Honeck and Hoffman 1980), and a groundbreaking book by George Lakoff and Mark Johnson, *Metaphors We Live By* (1980), set the stage for CMT.

Among the many pivotal things about language and thought that subsequent research in CMT has uncovered, perhaps the most important one is that metaphor can no longer be construed as a stylistic option to literal meaning. Two studies (Pollio and Burns 1977; Pollio and Smith 1979) showed that even *anomalous strings*, as Chomsky (1957) called them, are not resistant to metaphorical interpretation. These are sentences made up of legitimate words that have syntactic structure but no meaning. Chomsky's example was *Colourless green ideas sleep furiously.* When subjects were asked simply if the words in such strings meant anything, they invariably came up with metaphorical meanings for them. The findings suggested, therefore, that literal meaning may be a limiting form of meaning, required for specific cognitive and communicative tasks, whereas metaphorical meaning may be the default form of abstract cognition.

Conceptual versus Linguistic Metaphors

Lakoff and Johnson's *Metaphors We Live By* is now considered to be the pivotal text of CMT, since it laid out the notions upon which the theory was subsequently elaborated, researched, expanded, and applied. Recall the example above of *Your friend is a snake.* The *friend* could have been conceptualized as any other animal or insect, such as a *gorilla*, a *pig*, a *puppy*, and so forth. The result would have been a different evaluation of his or her personality. In other words, each *linguistic metaphor* instantiates a more general concept: *people are animals.* *People* is termed the target domain and *animals* the source domain. The source domain is the lexical field of concrete animal concepts that allow us to grasp the target domain of human personality. The source for understanding the latter is not, however, limited to our experience of animals; it can be anything from a substance (*Your friend is a softie*) to electricity (*Your friend is always wired*). Each linguistic metaphor implies a different 'psychology' behind our evaluation of human personality. Portraying a *friend* as a *monkey*, for instance, forces us to imagine a human person in simian terms. The gist of CMT is, thus, that the mind grasps abstract concepts in sense-based ways. This suggests that language itself is a product of basic sense-making or bodily based experiences.

The Psychology of Metaphor

The bulk of the research in CMT has shown that metaphorical language is a product of systematic associative thinking. Consider the following sample of conceptual metaphors and the linguistic metaphors they permit in everyday discourse:

happiness is up/sadness is down
  (1) After the wonderful news, I am feeling really *up*.
  (2) My friend is always *down* after the weekend.

knowledge is light/ignorance is darkness
  (3) It is not quite *clear* to me what you mean by that.
  (4) Her comment left me in the *dark*.

ideas are food
  (5) There were a lot of ideas to *swallow* from his lecture.
  (6) I am trying to *digest* all that information.

ideas are people
  (7) Ancient ideas *live* on to this day.
  (8) That theory is still in its *infancy*.

ideas are fashion
  (9) That way of thinking is old *fashioned*.
  (10) Aristotle's ideas are back in *style*.

Lakoff and Johnson trace the source of such concepts to what they call *image schemas* (Lakoff 1987; Johnson 1987; Lakoff and Johnson 1999). These are 'mental outlines' that convert our concrete experiences (like perceived animal behaviours) into source domains for understanding abstractions

(like human personality). Whatever their neural substrate, they are capacities of the human brain that not only permit people to recognize experiential patterns, but also to anticipate new ones and to draw inferences from them. These are all imprinted in metaphor. For example, the experience of orientation – *up vs. down, back vs. front, near vs. far*, and so on – underlies how we conceptualize such concepts as *happiness* ('Lately my spirits are *up*'), *responsibility* ('You have to face *up* to your problems'), among many others. The common experience of how containers work and what they allow us to do, on the other hand, underlies such concepts as *mind* ('My mind is *full* of good memories'), *emotions* ('My heart is *filled* with hope'), and so on.

Conceptual metaphors also reveal a process that can be called *sense implication* (Danesi 2004). This is the ability of the brain to transform sensory, affective, or bodily experiences into conceptual forms. Traditionally, the results of this process are called *root metaphors*. The number of root metaphors in the core vocabularies of languages throughout the world is immense. Here are a few examples in English:

- Vision metaphors: *flash* of insight, *spark* of genius, a *bright* mind, a *brilliant* idea, a *flicker* of intelligence, a *luminous* achievement, a *shining* mind, a *bright* fire in his eyes, *sparking* interest in a subject, words *glowing* with meaning
- Touch metaphors: *seize* the opportunity, *grasp* an idea, *touch* a raw nerve, *pick through* those thoughts, *take* my advice, *give* me a hand
- Taste metaphors: I can *taste* victory, *savor* the moment, a *bitter* thought, *sweet* love, their *spicy* affair, a *palatable* proposition
- Hearing metaphors: to *hear* one out, to be all *ears*, to keep one's *ears* open, to be *deaf* to advice, out of *earshot*
- Olfactory metaphors: to *smell* a rat, that idea *stinks*, your proposal *reeks*

Edie (1976: 165) offers the following explanation of how these arise in the mind:

A word which primarily designates a perceptual phenomenon – for example the perception of light – once constituted is available for a new purpose and can be used with a new intention – for example to denote the process of intellectual understanding, and we speak of (mental) illumination. Once established, the metaphorical use of the original word is no longer noticed; its essential ambiguity tends to fall below the level of awareness from the moment that it is taken as designating another, now distinguishable, experience.

Idealized Cognitive Models

The systematicity of metaphorical thinking unfolds not only through the creation of conceptual metaphors, but also by a kind of higher-order metaphorical thinking. As abstract target domains are linked to source domains, the concepts become increasingly more interrelated and abstract, leading to what Lakoff and Johnson call *idealized cognitive models* (ICMs). Consider the target domain of *ideas* and *theories*. The source domains below, among others, reveal how we conceptualize that domain in English-speaking culture:

sight
  (1) Do you *see* what I am saying?
  (2) *Seeing* is believing.

geometry
  (3) The philosophies of Plato and Descartes are *parallel* in many ways.
  (4) Your theory is *diametrically* opposite to the one we learned last year.

plants
  (5) The concept of dualism has deep *roots* in philosophy.
  (6) The theory of quantum physics is a *budding* new one.

buildings
  (7) That argument is well *constructed*.

  (8) That is the *cornerstone* of relativity theory.

food
  (9) I cannot *digest* everything you said easily.
  (10) That is an *appetizing* idea.

fashion
  (11) That theory went *out of style* years ago.
  (12) Dualism is back in *fashion* these days.

commodities
  (13) I don't quite *buy* those new ideas.
  (14) You must *package* your ideas differently.

The constant 'mental navigation' through such source domains in common conversations and in cultural texts of all kinds produces an ICM of the target domain. The following utterances contain various combinations of the above source domains, showing how mental navigation might occur:

> I can't *see* what you want to do with that idea, even though it has *deep roots* in philosophy. Today, you will never be able to *sell* it to anyone. It is *diametrically* opposed to mainstream ideology.

An ICM can be defined as the sum of the source domains that a culture makes available for understanding, and thus talking about, a particular abstract concept. Research has shown that source domains overlap, intersect, and constantly piggyback on each other in the production of concepts. Before CMT, the study of metaphor fell within the field of rhetoric, where it was viewed as one of several figures of speech. But in cognitive linguistics today, the practice is to consider most as particular kinds of metaphor – for example, *personification* ('My cat speaks Italian') is seen as a particular kind of metaphor, one in which the target domain is an animal or inanimate object and the source domain a set of vehicles that are normally associated with human beings.

Metonymy and Irony

There are two other figures of speech that are considered to be cognitively different from metaphor in CMT – metonymy and irony. *Metonymy* is the process of representing a concept with something that is associated with it. In CMT no distinction is usually made between metonymy and synecdoche. Here are some examples:

(1) She loves *Hemingway* (= the writings of Hemingway).
(2) I saw many new *faces* in class today (= students).
(3) They always buy a *Saab* (= the car named Saab).
(4) The *buses* seem to be always on strike (= bus drivers).
(5) The *Church* does not condone that behaviour (= theologians, priests, and so on).
(6) The *White House* must lead by example (= the president, the American government).
(7) The *automobile* is destroying our health (= the collection of automobiles).
(8) He just got a new *set of wheels* (= car).
(9) We need *new blood* in this company (= new people).

In parallel with the notion of *conceptual metaphor*, the term *conceptual metonym* can be adopted to refer to generalized concepts based on metonymy rather than metaphor (Danesi 2004). Here are some examples:

the face for the person
  (1) He's nothing more than another pretty *face*.
  (2) Look at all those happy *faces* in the audience.
  (3) We sure need new *faces* around here.
  (4) Let's discuss this *face* to face.

a body part for the person
  (5) Get your *butt* over here!

(6) The Yankees need a *stronger arm* in centre field.
(7) We don't like *wagging tongues*.

the producer for the product
  (8) I'll have a *Miller Light*.
  (9) We bought a *Cadillac*.
  (10) He's got a *Picasso* in his office.

the object used for the user
  (11) My *violin* is squeaky today.
  (12) The *filet mignon* is a lousy tipper.
  (13) The *schools* are on strike.

the institution for the people in it
  (14) *Shell* has lowered its prices.
  (15) The *Church* must lead by example.
  (16) I don't approve of *government's* policies.

Conceptual metonyms reveal that we evaluate certain things as representative of larger things or processes. There are various reasons for this, but their discussion is beyond the purposes of this entry. Suffice it to say that experience, context, and other factors play a role. For example, the use of specific brand names such as *Kleenex* and *Xerox* to represent all similar products is an example of how it is much more efficient, or cognitively easier, to use metonymy in such cases than the literal terms (sanitary napkins, photocopies, and so on). The use of *butt* in 'Get your *butt* over here' reveals, instead, an indirect assessment of the person as being lazy, since the butt is the part of the anatomy involved in sitting down.

Irony is constrained in CMT to designate a strategy whereby words are used to convey a meaning contrary to their literal sense – for example 'I love being tortured' would be interpreted as ironic if it were uttered by someone experiencing unwelcome pain. The intent of the speaker, including his or her prosody (tone of voice, accent, and so on), the speaker's relation to the listener, and the context are all factors that establish the ironic meaning of an utterance. If the above sentence were uttered by a masochist, then it would hardly have an ironic meaning. Irony is often used as a means of criticizing human habits, ideas, and vacuous rituals. It is the basis for satire and parody.

Cultural Symbolism

Another important discovery of CMT is that a large portion of cultural symbolism and ritual is interconnected with metaphor, metonymy, and irony. Take, for instance, the *love is a sweet taste* conceptual metaphor, which is imprinted in expressions such as 'She's my *sweetheart*,' 'They went on a *honeymoon*,' and so on. The same imprint can be seen in the giving of sweets to a loved one on St Valentine's Day, the eating of cake at a wedding ceremony. These are all symbolic-ritualistic manifestations of the same concept. In effect, CMT has shown how language and culture are intrinsically intertwined. Take, as another example, the *justice is blind* conceptual metaphor in English. Its cultural crystallization is evidenced, for example, in the practice of using images of justice as a woman with a blindfold on. The *justice is a balance scale* conceptual metaphor is symbolized instead by images of a woman holding scales.

Scientific reasoning too is based on metaphor. Phenomena such as atoms, gravitational forces, or magnetic fields cannot be seen with the eyes. So, scientists use metaphor to take a look, so to speak, at them (Black 1962; Leatherdale 1974; MacCormac 1976; Gentner 1982). This is why atoms are described as *leaping* from one quantum state to another, electrons as *travelling in circles* around an atomic nucleus, and so on. Physicist Robert Jones (1982: 4) points out that for the scientist metaphor serves as 'an evocation of the inner connection among things.' Science is a search for connections, linkages, associations of some kind or other, and when these are established they are encoded in metaphorical models. The physicist K.C. Cole (1984: 156) puts it eloquently as follows:

The words we use are metaphors; they

are models fashioned from familiar ingredients and nurtured with the help of fertile imaginations. 'When a physicist says an electron is like a particle,' writes physics professor Douglas Giancoli, 'he is making a metaphorical comparison like the poet who says love is like a rose.' In both images a concrete object, a rose or a particle, is used to illuminate an abstract idea, love or electron.

Overall, CMT has shown that language is not separable from sensory and other corporeal processes, suggesting that it arises from neural networks or circuits that link many areas of the brain, not language-specific ones. In effect, language cannot be studied separately from the brain, the body, and culture. This is now called 'blending theory' – a theory articulated in a detailed way by Lakoff and Nuñez in their 2000 study of how mathematics originates in the mind. Basically, blending is the neural process which amalgamates experiences with cognition, producing largely metaphors and other blended phenomena such as diagrams, analogies, and the like.

As a final word, it should be mentioned that CMT has also been applied to media studies. For instance, the narrative content of TV programs can best be examined in terms of specific conceptual metaphors. The 1950s TV sitcoms *The Adventures of Ozzie and Harriet* and *Father Knows Best* were based on the metaphorical model of the *family* as a patriarchal institution. As a consequence, the father was portrayed as being an 'all-knowing' and reliable 'provider.' On the other hand, the main theme of the 1980s–1990s sitcom *Married with Children* was based on a different metaphorical model of *fatherhood*. The father was portrayed as a 'selfish boor' and a 'moronic adolescent.' In effect, CMT has revealed its usefulness in uncovering the conceptual systems on which programs and other media texts are based.

Marcel Danesi

Bibliography

Aristotle. *Rhetoric*. In *The Works of Aristotle*. Vol. 11. Ed. W.D. Ross. Oxford: Clarendon Press, 1952a.

– *Poetics*. In *The Works of Aristotle*. Vol. 11. Ed. W.D. Ross. Oxford: Clarendon Press, 1952b.

Asch, Solomon. On the Use of Metaphor in the Description of Persons. In *On Expressive Language*, ed. H. Werner, 86–94. Worcester: Clark University Press, 1950.

– The Metaphor: A Psychological Inquiry. In *Person Perception and Interpersonal Behavior*, ed. R. Tagiuri and L. Petrullo, 28–42. Stanford: Stanford University Press, 1958.

Bergin, Thomas G., and Max Fisch. *The New Science of Giambattista Vico*. Ithaca, NY: Cornell University Press, 1984.

Black, Max. *Models and Metaphors*. Ithaca, NY: Cornell University Press, 1962.

Brown, Roger W., Raymond A. Leiter, and Donald C. Hildum. Metaphors from Music Criticism. *Journal of Abnormal and Social Psychology* 54 (1957): 347–52.

Bühler, Karl. On Thought Connection. In *Organization and Pathology of Thought*, ed. D. Rapaport, 81–92. New York: Columbia University Press, 1951 [1908].

Chomsky, Noam. *Syntactic Structures*. The Hague: Mouton, 1957.

Cole, K.C. *Sympathetic Vibrations*. New York: Bantam, 1984.

Danesi, Marcel. *Understanding Media Semiotics*. London: Arnold, 2002.

– *Poetic Logic: The Role of Metaphor in Thought, Language, and Culture*. Madison: Atwood, 2004.

Dirven, Rene, and Marina Verspoor. *Cognitive Exploration of Language and Linguistics*. Amsterdam: John Benjamins.

Edie, James M. *Speaking and Meaning: The Phenomenology of Language*. Bloomington: Indiana University Press, 1976.

Geeraerts, Dirk, ed. *Cognitive Linguistics*. Berlin: Mouton de Gruyter.

Gentner, Dedre. Are Scientific Analogies Metaphors? In *Metaphor: Problems and Perspectives*, ed. D.S. Miall, 106–32. Atlantic Highlands, NJ: Humanities Press, 1982.

Gibbs, Raymond W. *The Poetics of Mind: Figurative Thought, Language, and Understanding*. Cambridge: Cambridge University Press, 1994.

Gill, Ann. *Rhetoric and Human Understanding*. Prospect Heights, IL: Waveland, 1994.

Honeck, Richard P., and Robert R. Hoffman, eds. *Cognition and Figurative Language*. Hillsdale, NJ: Lawrence Erlbaum Associates, 1980.

Johnson, Mark. *The Body in the Mind: The Bodily Basis of Meaning, Imagination and Reason*. Chicago: University of Chicago Press, 1987.

Jones, Robert. *Physics as Metaphor*. New York: New American Library, 1982.

Kövecses. Zoltan. *Metaphor: A Practical Introduction*. Oxford: Oxford University Press, 2002.

Lakoff, George. *Women, Fire, and Dangerous Things: What Categories Reveal about the Mind*. Chicago: University of Chicago Press, 1987.

Lakoff, George, and Mark Johnson. *Metaphors We Live By*. Chicago: Chicago University Press, 1980.

– *Philosophy in the Flesh: The Embodied Mind and Its Challenge to Western Thought*. New York: Basic, 1999.

Lakoff, George, and Rafael Núñez. *Where Mathematics Comes From: How the Embodied Mind Brings Mathematics into Being*. New York: Basic Books, 2000.

Leatherdale, W.H. *The Role of Analogy, Model and Metaphor in Science*. New York: New Holland, 1974.

Lee, David. *Cognitive Linguistics: An Introduction*. Oxford: Oxford University Press, 2001.

MacCormac, E. *Metaphor and Myth in Science and Religion*. Durham, NC: Duke University Press, 1976.

Ortony, Anthony, ed. *Metaphor and Thought*. Cambridge: Cambridge University Press, 1979.

Osgood, Charles E., and George J. Suci. Factor Analysis of Meaning. *Journal of Experimental Psychology* 49 (1953): 325–8.

Pollio, Howard R., and Barbara C. Burns. The Anomaly of Anomaly. *Journal of Psycholinguistic Research* 6 (1977): 247–60.

Pollio, Howard R., and Michael K. Smith. Sense and Nonsense in Thinking about Anomaly and Metaphor. *Bulletin of the Psychonomic Society* 13 (1979): 323–6.

Pollio, Howard R., Jack M. Barlow, Harold J. Fine, and Marilyn R. Pollio. *The Poetics of*

Growth: Figurative Language in Psychology, Psychotherapy, and Education. Hillsdale, NJ: Lawrence Erlbaum, 1977.

Richards, Ivor A. *The Philosophy of Rhetoric*. Oxford: Oxford University Press, 1936.

Tilley, Christopher. *Metaphor and Material Culture*. Oxford: Blackwell, 1999.

Werner, Heinz, and Bernard Kaplan. *Symbol Formation: An Organismic-Developmental Approach to the Psychology of Language and the Expression of Thought*. New York: John Wiley, 1963.

Wundt, Wilhelm. *Sprachgeschichte und Sprachpsychologie*. Leipzig: Eugelmann, 1901.

CONSTRUCTIVISM

[See also: *Deconstruction; Functionalist Theories*]

Constructivism is a theory of knowledge that draws from a wide variety of disciplinary domains, such as philosophy, education, psychology, and the physical sciences. According to Ernst von Glaserfield (1995), constructivism pivots on the notion that knowledge is not passively acquired through sensorial transmission, or through communication, but is actively constructed by the knowing subject. Moreover, rather than assisting the subject on a quest to discover an objective ontological reality, the role of cognition is adaptive and assists the subject as he/she organizes the data of his/her own experiential world. We find the essential tenets of constructivism in a philosopher such as Giambattista Vico (1688–1744), according to whom the only possible knowledge we can achieve is about what we construe. The general constructive view is that knowledge and reality do not possess or share an objective or absolute value. Traditional realists counter this idea by claiming that there is a reality that we can discover as a form of knowledge; moreover, what we know and external reality are in a relation of coherent correspondence. On the other hand, constructivists argue that knowledge emerges from the dynamics and interplay of personally adapted reality.

Michael J. Mahoney (2003) identifies four central notions that are shared by the different paradigms of knowledge expressing constructivism: (1) the experiential domain of humans is characterized by an ongoing active agency, and thus humans are passive figures dominated by greater forces; (2) humans dedicate a considerable amount of energy to ordering and organizing the data that result from world experience; (3) the ordering of personal activity pivots on the idea of self-reference, thus the centrality of the body in the organization of knowledge; (4) individuals can only be understood from within the context of the social and symbolic networks to which they belong.

The constructivist paradigm has produced a considerable body of research in the area of education. Some important figures here include John Dewey, Lev Vygotsky, and Jerome Bruner. The emphasis is on the learner more than on the teacher, and the key notion is that learning is the consequence of individual mental constructions, whereby the subject acquires knowledge by correlating newly acquired information with given data and thus producing decisive connections. Learning is conditioned by the context, values, and attitudes of the subject.

Constructivism is not a monolithic epistemology; it unfolds within a large variety of theories and approaches. The leading figure behind the philosophical and epistemological approach to constructivism is von Glasersfeld. Heinz von Foerster is well known for having developed the notion of a 'cybernetics of observing systems.' In the field of cognitive sciences, the fundamental works include those of Jean Piaget, according to whom we order and organize our world as we organize ourselves. In the area of biology, Humberto R. Maturana and Francisco J. Varela formulated the notion of the organizational closure of the nervous system. As well, there is also the constructivist theory of literature (also referred to as the empirical science of literature), which was cultivated in Germany during the 1980s. The basis for this theoretical framework and methodology is to be found in the sociology of literature, communication theories, and philosophical constructivism. And, of course, much use of the notion of constructivism has been made within media studies. The main claim in this domain is that the media construct, not just mirror, reality through representation and simulation. The dynamism between the media and reality is often called the 'simulacrum' in media studies.

Constructivism also refers to a literary movement established in Russia in 1923, where culture was perceived as encompassing all constellations of human life and production. Some of the key figures included Ilia Sel'vinski, Kornelii Zelinski, and Valentin Asmus.

Paul Colilli

Bibliography

Glasersfeld, E. von. *Radical Constructivism. A Way of Knowing and Learning*. London: Falmer Press, 1995.

Mahoney, Michael J. *Constructive Psychotherapy*. New York: Guilford, 2003.

CONSUMER CULTURE

[See also: *British Cultural Theory; Centre for Contemporary Cultural Studies; Culture Jamming; Frankfurt School; Mass Communication*]

The term *consumer culture* comes up frequently in studies of the mass media, being associated closely with capitalism and the spread of a purported banal form of popular culture. The term is almost invariably used in this negative way in critical theories of the mass media, starting with the writings of economist Thorstein Veblen (1899), who excoriated against the tendency of capitalist cultures to promote marketplace values and solutions to everything, including ethical and moral dilemmas.

The term abounds in the first systematic critiques of capitalist culture from the scholars at the so-called Frankfurt School, a department of social theory established at the University of Frankfurt right after the First World War. In one way or another, the members of the School took a highly negative view of the culture produced in consumerist societies such as that of the United States. They maintained that culture in such societies was made to conform to the same economic laws as those associated with goods and services; essentially, it was designed to be ephemeral and without lasting value, being sold and consumed in the marketplace. The Frankfurt School theorists were highly pessimistic about the possibility of genuine art and high culture under modern capitalism, condemning most forms of popular culture as vulgar, repetitive, formulaic, and concerned about making a profit (Bottomore 1984). A similar view was adopted a few decades later by semiotician Roland Barthes (1957), who called consumer culture a 'bastard' culture that induced 'neomania,' or the desire to consume new products incessantly. A little later, the Centre for Contemporary Cultural Studies at the University of Birmingham furthered the anti-consumerist cause by investigating how bourgeois interests were served by 'cultural products' such as pop music trends. They held the view that capitalist culture had debased all forms of culture by turning art into a 'commodity' controlled by profit-making enterprises. See Turner (1992) for an overview of the theories expounded by the Centre.

As early as the nineteenth century, British social critic Matthew Arnold (1822–83) saw the forms of mass culture that had emerged in industrialist society as tasteless and homogenized. He considered crass materialism to be a threat to civilized society. His attack was taken up by F.R. Leavis (1895–1978) in the 1930s and 1940s. Leavis excoriated American pop culture even more pungently, seeing in it evidence of the decline of human civilization.

Recently, the attack on consumer culture has taken various forms, such as the culture jamming movement, whereby advertisements and various trends are critiqued and satirized by turning them on their head, so to speak, to reveal how crass and meaningless they are (Lasn 2000). However, there has also been a growing reaction against negative portrayals of consumer culture. The main basis of the counter-attack is the question: Who decides what is 'good' culture and what is 'tasteless' or 'bastard' culture? Those who claim to know (at least implicitly) are really elitists since they seem to know exclusively what good culture is and thus what is to be done about eliminating bad culture. The masses are assumed to be zombies, unaware of the vulgarity to which they are subjected on a daily basis. Another counterargument presented by defenders of consumer culture is that it has brought about more favourable changes to the happiness and overall well-being of common folk than any other cultural experiment in history, including (and especially) Marxism. The emotional appeal of pop culture cannot be dismissed as a mere instrument of pacification, since it has actually provided the means for ordinary people to resist those in power, giving them a voice to articulate their resistance through marketplace democracy. Anyone can become a musician or writer if the marketplace deems them to be worthwhile. With the advent of websites such as YouTube and Facebook this empowerment has become even more conspicuous.

Among the first to endorse consumer culture as it presented itself were the so-called pop artists, who emerged in the 1950s. Many of those artists' works were satirical or playful, but they also validated the everyday experiences of ordinary people. The pop artists depicted scenes and objects from mass culture, sometimes with actual consumer products incorporated into their works. Perhaps the best-known exponent of the pop art movement was the American artist Andy Warhol (1928–87), whose depictions of Campbell's soup cans, Elvis Presley, and Marilyn Monroe embody the essence of the pop art movement.

Marcel Danesi

Bibliography

Barthes, Roland. *Mythologies*. Paris: Seuil, 1957.
Bottomore, Tom. *The Frankfurt School*. London: Routledge, 1984.
Danesi, Marcel. *Popular Culture: Introductory Perspectives*. Lanham: Rowman and Littlefield, 2008.
Lasn, Kalle. *Culture Jam: The Uncooling of America*. New York: Morrow, 2000.
Turner, Graeme. *British Cultural Studies*. London: Routledge, 1992.
Veblen, Thorstein. *The Theory of the Leisure Class: An Economic Study of Institutions*. Mineola: Dover, 1899.

CONTENT ANALYSIS

[See also: *Representation; Semiotics*]

Content analysis (CA) is a term with multiple meanings, depending on the discipline that employs it. It is used, for instance, to refer to a research approach in psychology and anthropology that aims to identify, classify, and analyse the content (meaning or interpretation) of media messages. It is also used in social science generally to indicate a quantitative approach to media content based on counting the number of times some item appears in a text and the reasons for this. The term is also sometimes used to indicate a technique for analysing transcripts of interviews. And in literary analysis, it refers to a study of the authorship and authenticity of texts, based on their stylistic and other features.

In media studies, the basic idea of CA is to discover the content of a text through its form. One way to do so is by using opposition theory, a basic psychological and semiotic method based on the assumption that we understand content through the relational (oppositional) features it encompasses. For example, we understand the meaning of *day* through consideration its opposite, *night*, at the same time. This allows us to compare and contrast conceptual differences between the two notions. This simple technique fleshes out the hidden meanings built texts, codes, and the like. For example, the *white-black* opposition (indicating unconsciously a *good-evil* dichotomy in Western conceptual tradition) appears often in media representations. The colour white suggests 'purity,' 'goodness,' and so on, while black suggests 'impurity,' 'evil,' and the like. In early Hollywood cowboy movies, this opposition could be seen often in the fact that heroes generally wore white hats and the villains black ones. However, since *black* also suggests 'mystery' and 'dauntlessness,' the opposition was sometimes reversed – the Zorro character of narrative, television, and movie fame, for instance, wore black, as did other fictional western heroes.

Another technique for determining content involves *semiotic* or *semiological* analysis. This is based in large part in fleshing out hidden or implicit meanings in texts. This approach to CA was put forward in the mid-1950s by the French semiotician Roland Barthes (1915–80), who claimed that the emotional allure of popular media texts and spectacles was due to the recycling of unconscious mythic content. In superhero comics, for instance, the heroes are (or at least were) honest, attractive, strong, albeit somewhat vulnerable. The villains, on the other hand, are portrayed as dishonest, cowardly, ugly, and cunning. The comics were actually recycling ancient mythic codes of the hero. Sports events, too, suggest mythic dramas, with the home team being 'the good side' and the visiting team 'the evil marauder.' The game is thus perceived to constitute a battle of mythic proportions. It is the unconscious mythological structure of media texts that gives them their appeal. A third technique of media-based CA involves *representation theory*, which is based on the notion that any text *represents* something in a particular way. In 1950s American TV sitcoms, the father was represented typically as a sage man who took charge of his family (as was the case with the sitcom *Father Knows Best*). Beginning in the 1970s, representations of the father changed. He was depicted as a character who was losing control of the family or who had lost interest in the traditional family (as for example in the sitcoms *All in the Family* or *Married with Children*). These different representations of fatherhood on television reflected changing views of the family in society along with the deconstruction of patriarchy.

A common CA technique used in literary studies is analysing texts statistically. Using frequency counts of words, syntactic structures, and the like, one can infer what emphases are present in text, what word collocations signify, and so on. Such analysis can also be used to determine authorship, if one knows that a certain writer has a predisposition for certain words, turns of phrase, and so on. This technique can also be extended to the study of non-verbal texts. For example in the analysis of radio and television programs, time counts, rather than word counts, are used.

Marcel Danesi

Bibliography

Barthes, Roland. *Mythologies*. Paris: Seuil, 1957.
– *The Pleasure of the Text*. New York: Hill and Wang, 1975.
Berelson, Bernard. *Content Analysis in Communication Research*. Glencoe: Free Press, 1971.
Holsti, Ole R. *Content Analysis for the Social Sciences and Humanities*. Reading, MA: Addison-Wesley, 1969.
Krippendorff, Klaus. *Content Analysis: An Introduction to Its Methodology*. 2nd ed. Thousand Oaks, CA: Sage, 2004.
Neuendorf, Kimberly A. *The Content Analysis Guidebook*. Thousand Oaks, CA: Sage, 2002.

CONTEXTUALISM

[See also: *Discourse; Discourse Theory; Jakobson's Model of Communication; Meaning*]

The term *context* is used in various disciplines, from psychology and linguistics to anthropology and media studies, to indicate that the meaning of something – a word, a text, and so on – can only be inferred or applied in a specific context. In its most extreme form, contextualism is the view that context (situation, place, culture, interlocutors, time frame, and so on) is determinative of all meaning and, thus, that there exist virtually no universals in how humans create and understand meanings through language, art, and all the other expressive forms of behaviour. A founder of the contextualist movement, Polish-born British anthropologist Bronislaw Malinowski (1922, 1923, 1929), argued that all cultures share the need to solve similar physical and moral problems, but the specific kinds of solutions they develop are determined by contextual factors — where the culture is located, what experiences it considers relevant, and so on. Similarly, the British anthropologist Alfred Radcliffe-Brown (1922) maintained that even a universal physical response like weeping had a context-specific fnction and meaning. Among the Andaman Islanders in the east Bay of Bengal he discovered that weeping was not primarily an expression of joy or sorrow, as one would expect in Western culture, but rather a ritualistic response to social events such as peace-making, marriage, and the reunion of long-separated intimates. In weeping together, the people renewed their ties of solidarity.

The branch in linguistics that aims to study the role of context on conversation is called *pragmatics*, a term coined by the American philosopher Charles S. Peirce (1839–1914) and developed in the 1930s by another American philosopher, Charles Morris (1901–79). The term *pragmatics* is now used to indicate the study of the meanings of language forms in their contexts of use, as opposed to meanings that can be established semantically by considering the linguistic forms in themselves (as in a dictionary). Take a sentence such as *The pig is ready to eat*. If uttered by a farmer during feeding time, then the utterance has literal meaning: 'There is an animal called a

pig and that animal is ready to eat.' If spoken by a cook announcing that pork meat is available for consumption, then the utterance has a different interpretation: 'The cooked pig is ready for people to eat.' Finally, if spoken by a person in a restaurant to describe someone who looks gluttonous and who shows a ravenous appetite, then the statement has metaphorical meaning: 'The person who appears to have the manners and appetite of a pig is ready to eat.' As work on the pragmatics of conversation has shown since the 1970s, it is virtually impossible to separate traditionally established semantic meaning from knowledge of how such meaning varies according to context of use. Language is, in a phrase, a context-sensitive instrument shaped by situational forces that are largely external to it. Language forms are not only intertwined with each other structurally, but are also highly sensitive to the subtle influences that usage situations have on them. The internal structures of language are pliable entities that are responsive to external social situations.

Among the first linguists to claim that context was a critical component in language was Roman Jakobson (1960). Jakobson maintained that meaning cannot be pinned down as in dictionaries because it is susceptible to the influences of situational factors. Consider how we interpret, say, a discarded soup can. If we come across it on the street, then we would interpret it is as garbage. However, if we see it on a pedestal in an art gallery, then the situation changes. Psychologically, we are disposed to interpret objects in an art gallery as artworks; the art gallery projects us into a social situation where this is a requirement. If we label the can as garbage, we are literally talking out of context.

In an era of 'mobile communications,' the notion of context will need to be expanded. The concept of 'contextual mobility,' for example, has emerged to capture the idea of how, literally, entire sets of social relations 'move about' during interaction on mobile devices. This leads to the notion of shifting contexts and their effects on communicative and social processes. As Bruhn Jensen (2010: 109) puts it: 'Communication transports contexts of meaningful interaction across space and time, and communicators bring contexts with them from place to place, as virtually present in their minds.'

Marcel Danesi

Bibliography

Bruhn Jensen, Klaus. *Media Convergence*. London: Routledge, 2010.

Duranti, Alessandro, and Charles Goodwin, eds. *Rethinking Context: Language as an Interactive Phenomenon*. Cambridge: Cambridge University Press, 1992.

Jakobson, Roman. Linguistics and Poetics. In *Style and Language*, ed. Thomas A. Sebeok, 34–45. Cambridge, MA: MIT Press, 1960.

Kay, Paul. *Words and the Grammar of Context*. Cambridge: Cambridge University Press, 1997.

Malinowski, Bronislaw. *Argonauts of the Western Pacific*. New York: Dutton, 1922.

– The Problem of Meaning in Primitive Languages. In *The Meaning of Meaning*, ed. Charles K. Ogden and Ivor A. Richards, 296–336. New York: Harcourt, Brace and World, 1923.

– *The Sexual Life of Savages in North-Western Melanesia*. New York: Harcourt, Brace, and World, 1929.

Radcliffe-Brown, Alfred Reginald. *The Andaman Islanders*. Cambridge: Cambridge University Press, 1922.

CONVERGENCE

[See also: *Globalization; Mass Communication; Media Literacy*]

The content of one medium is always another medium, or so Marshall McLuhan famously quipped in the 1960s. In the years since then – as we have increasingly evolved into a Web 2.0 world – we have come to see that media interaction is a two-way conversation. Old media capture and transform new media and new media adapt to speak with older media; this is a process that Jay Bolter and Richard Grusin have dubbed *Remediation* (1999). Other media historians theorize that the contact zone between digital media and society is a site of mutual convergence for technologies of communication, a site where all interconnections are in a state of flux and transformation (Briggs and Burke 2005). However, as our world has increasingly become one of media immersion, the distinctiveness of different technological devices has begun to blur. For some, this is an indicator that technological convergence is at hand and that all devices will eventually coalesce into a single all-purpose device. To be sure, there are what Mark Deuze calls 'structural trends' towards 'portable, customizable, interconnected, and converged devices and uses, which lends credence to the argument that media are increasingly embedded in (and recombinant with) all aspects of everyday life' (Deuze 2010). But even the closest signs of such a physical convergence of individual devices – for example, the iPod – need to solve considerable bandwidth and exorbitant user fee problems before they become ubiquitous. So far, a variety of devices proliferate and their uses overlap. On the upside, the barriers between such devices conversing *with each other* are slowly coming down.

But despite this embeddedness, or even because of it, the process of media convergence is difficult to map or to locate, remaining always a fluid and uncontainable event. Convergence is a complex mechanism that spans technologies, economics, social organizations, cultural frameworks, global networks, and property configurations. In 'Convergence? I Diverge' Henry Jenkins (2001, 2006) categorized the first five of these states as follows:

- *Technological convergence*, or the shift from analogue forms to the digitization of all content. Crossing modal borders fertilizes relationships and helps generate new applications across new platforms. Digital technologies also allow a single technology to perform multiple functions, as in the much-celebrated iPod (with myriad apps which includes everything from a camera to GPS technologies) or the Crossover Camera. The Crossover Camera is known as 'Scarlet' and is produced by Red Digital Cinema Camera. It is celebrated as a 'pocket professional' camera that unites the video and still features in super-high-definition and that was initially heralded as the end to the conventional camera (Borland 2008). More realistically, many devices now contain a camera function, and more and more devices take both still and digital images; the end result of this seems to be to make all kinds of cameras more popular, not less so.

- *Economic convergence*, or media conglomeration, where supermedia companies buy up media from the whole spectrum to profit from multimodal merchandising, franchise economics, and property violations.
- *Social convergence*, which includes channel switching, multimodal navigation or multitasking of all kinds.
- *Cultural convergence*, or participatory culture. Social networking and new levels of interactivity transform users into co-creators and foster transmediality or media that exist across multiple genres and/or channels.
- *Global convergence*, or hybrid cultural products arising from global cross-pollinations and exchange.

To those five states could be added *property monopoly convergence*, or the increasing trend among lawmakers to fail to distinguish between legitimate ownership or authorship (which builds on the past to produce something new) and piracy (which replicates or counterfeits media objects created by others for commercial or personal gain). The end result is that existing corporate creators' works are being privileged

above the new and control favoured over the freedom to create.

Convergence also affects the different states of media: media as artefact, media-generated activities, commons-based peer production, and user-generated social networking configurations in a world that is increasingly wired (Deuze 2010). Even President Barack Obama's administration – which wrought a revolution in government by using social networking strategies to mobilize an army of Twitter-, YouTube-, and Facebook-connected donors and supporters – has been making progress at integrating open-door, Web 2.0 approaches into that previously closed and secretive office.

Carolyn Guertin

Bibliography

Bolter, Jay David, and Richard Grusin. *Remediation: Understanding New Media.* New York and London: MIT, 1999.

Borland, John. Crossover Camera. *Technology Review* (22 April 2008). http://www.technologyreview.com/computing/20657/?a=f.

Briggs, Asa, and Peter Burke. *A Social History of the Media: From Gutenberg to the Internet.* 2nd ed. Cambridge, UK: Polity Press, 2005.

Deuze, Mark. *Media Life.* Cambridge, UK: Polity Press, 2010.

Jenkins, Henry. Convergence? I Diverge. *Technology Review* (June 2001). http://www.technologyreview.com/business/12434/.

– *Convergence Culture: Where Old and New Media Collide.* New York and London: MIT, 2006.

Jensen, Klaus Beuhn. *Media Convergence: The Three Degrees of Network, Mass, and Interpersonal Communication.* London: Routledge, 2010.

CONVERSATION ANALYSIS

[See also: *Discourse; Discourse Theory*]

Conversation analysis (CA) surfaced in the 1980s and 1990s out of a broad movement in linguistics to bring more focus on studying how people talk and how this influences not only talking itself but also language as a system of rules. Hutchby and Wooffitt (1998: 14) define CA as follows:

> CA is the study of recorded, naturally occurring talk-in-interaction. Principally, it is to discover how participants understand and respond to one another in their turns at talk, with a central focus being on how sequences of interaction are generated. To put it another way, the objective of CA is to uncover the tacit reasoning procedures and sociolinguistic competencies underlying the production and interpretation of talk in organized sequences of interaction.

The 'tacit reasoning procedures,' as Hutchby and Wooffitt call them, are part of what is known as *communicative competence* – a notion introduced into linguistics by Dell Hymes in 1971, which implies that knowing how to use language during conversation is as systematic as knowing the grammar of the language. Generally, the study of communicative competence falls under the rubric of *pragmatics*, the branch of linguistics that deals with how form and meaning vary according to situational and contextual factors. CA focuses specifically on such phenomena as turn-taking (who speaks at specific points in the conversation) and the kinds of strategies and tactics used to initiate, continue, or end conversations. In CA, sentences are studied as units within larger conversation or discourse units. Personal pronouns, for instance, are seen as trace and indentification devices serving conversational needs, not as pure grammatical structures. When someone uses 'I', he/she is the speaker; if he/she uses 'you,' then he/she is referring to someone to whom the talk is directed; and so on. One device that CA theorists especially look for is called a *gambit*, a word or phrase used to open a conversation ('May I say something?'), to keep it going (the use of 'like' to obviate interruption), to make it smooth, to repair any anomaly within it, and so on.

Although there is much leeway in the grammatical and lexical choices that can be made to carry out a conversation successfully, these choices are nonetheless constrained by factors such as situation, social rules, and style. For example, the utterances below convey anger, but in different socially-sensitive ways:

Don't say that, idiot!
It is best that you not say that!

The first one is uttered usually by someone who is on close or intimate terms with an interlocutor; the second one is uttered instead by someone who is on formal terms with an interlocutor, or else is intended to be ironic. The two choices are constrained by situation and social relationship. Conversations can be aggressive or subdued, competitive or cooperative, and so on, depending on situation. Identifying the linguistic features that make them so is the primary objection of CA. Erving Goffman (1959, 1978) referred to these phenomena as part of the *social framing* of conversation, whereby language is made to fit a situation strategically. Framing imparts a sense of togetherness among interlocutors as well as a sense of security. Politeness, for example, is the result of framing. As Robin Lakoff (1975) has discussed, speakers will refrain from saying what they mean in some situations in the service of the higher goal of politeness.

The works of sociologists Sacks, Jefferson, and Schegloff (for example, 1995) have given CA many of the concepts and techniques used for carrying out analyses. A primary one is that of *sequence* – conversations are understood as a sequence of actions and events. The occurrence of certain signals in conversation, such as asking a questions, elicits matching utterances, known as answers, in the follow-up turn in a conversation. The two utterances are said to form an *adjacency pair* in the sequence. Today, CA research encompasses not only purely verbal exchanges and what they mean but also non-verbal cues used during conversations. Called 'multimodality research,' the goal of this type of work is to understand how gesture, facial expression, posture, and the zones people keep during conversation shape the language used in conversation and vice versa.

Marcel Danesi

Bibliography

Andersch, Elizabeth G., Lorin C. Staats, and Robert N. Bostrom. *Communication in Everyday Use*. New York: Holt, Rinehart and Winston, 1969.

Cutting, Joan. *Pragmatics and Discourse*. London: Routledge, 2002.

Goffman, Erving. *The Presentation of Self in Everyday Life*. Garden City: Doubleday, 1959.

– Response Cries. *Language* 54 (1978): 787–815.

Sacks, Harvey, Gail Jefferson, and Emmanuel A. Schegloff. *Lectures on Conversation*. Oxford: Blackwell, 1995.

Hutchby, Ian, and Robin Wooffitt. *Conversation Analysis*. Cambridge: Polity Press, 1998.

Hymes, Dell. *On Communicative Competence*. Philadelphia: University of Pennsylvania Press, 1971.

Lakoff, Robin. *Language and Woman's Place*. New York: Harper and Row, 1975.

CRIME GENRE

[See also: *Adventure Stories; Detective Stories; Pulp Fiction*]

As their name suggests, *crime* stories, also known as *whodunits* or *mystery* stories, deal with crimes, usually murder, and how they are solved by a detective (or detectives) who puts together clues at a crime scene and gradually develops a profile of the criminal. The distinction between crime and detective stories is a thin one, but the difference lies in the fact that the crime story need not always involve detective heroes, nor do they have to be fictional. Thus, documentaries about crime are included under the crime genre rubric. The appeal of this genre is probably due to the fact that it constitutes a kind of mystery jigsaw puzzle, with the pieces being put together little by little so that the reader or viewer can participate intellectually in solving the case.

Although crime has existed since time immemorial, the origin of crime fiction is traced generally to Edgar Allan Poe's story *The Murders in the Rue Morgue* (1841). That story set the formula for crime stories in general. The components of the formula include: (1) clues needed to figure out who committed the crime; (2) the use of human logic and imagination to solve the crime; (3) a subplot, often of an amorous nature, that adds romantic or sexual interest to the story; (4) an unexpected twist or turn of events that lead to the denouement and the solution. The crime story is a mystery that is solved by human ingenuity. The great fictional detectives all excelled at deductive and inferential reasoning. They have been replaced today by crime scene investigation teams who use technology to help them logically figure out who committed the crime. Edgar Allan Poe's Auguste Dupin, Sir Arthur Conan Doyle's Sherlock Holmes, G.K. Chesterton's Father Brown, and Agatha Christie's Hercule Poirot, are now eclipsed by CSI teams on television and in movies, but the basic formula has not changed. By solving crimes, the audience (readers, viewers, and so on) is engaging in puzzle solving along with the fictional or real crimes solver(s), drawing inferences from the available evidence, and reaching a conclusion from the given facts. In most stories, however, there is a twist that is meant to lead the audience astray so that the final solution comes as a surprise. In a fundamental way, the crime genre is the first truly interactive form of literature.

Stories and legends have been written about criminals and villains throughout history. In American lore, outlaws such as Jesse James and Billy the Kid are as well known as heroes such as Davy Crockett and Jim Bowie. The fascination with crime and criminals probably reveals an engagement with fear and the lure of the unusual and the non-normal. Criminals evoke panic and admiration at once. The spread of the crime story as a genre started right after Poe's story in the nineteenth century with the rise of pulp fiction, much of which dealt with lurid crime plots and handsome heroes who solved them with a combination of wit, brawn, and sexual appeal.

By the 1920s crime novels and magazines (both fictional and factual) were being produced in bulk for mass consumption. Many critics at the time pointed to this garish fascination with crime as a result of the rise of actual crime rates in large urban centres and the belief that crime agencies and police authorities were the unsung heroes of society. The first pulp magazine is considered to be Frank Munsey's *Argosy Magazine* of 1896. The word *pulp* was used to indicate that the texts were produced with cheap paper. Fictional pulp detectives and crime fighters such as Doc Savage, The Shadow, and the Phantom Detective became instant household names. Crime had become an obsession and a growing cultural industry. Media effects scholars started arguing in the late 1930s that the increase in crime rates correlated with the fascination with crime fiction. Copycats, they claimed, wanted to enact in real life what they read in stories or saw in movies. Fictional villains such as the Joker and the Riddler of Batman comic fame became celebrities and points of reference in actual forensic science.

The popularity of the early crime novels and movies was bolstered by the sensationalistic covers and movie posters that emphasized garishness, with their scantily dressed 'damsels in distress' and virile heroes shown in fisticuffs with villains. The original crime stories were made into radio serials and movie serials (the latter by Republic Pictures) in the 1930s and 1940s. Audiences loved them because they were designed to keep them in suspense as an episode ended with the hero or heroine, or his or her paramour, caught in a cliff-hanger situation. The audience would come back or tune in the next week to find out how the situation would be resolved. The same cliffhanger formula is still evident in the James Bond movies and the *Raiders of the Lost Ark* films, with the situation being resolved within the same movie at various 'cliffhanger points.' Some of the fictional characters of the serials, from Fu Manchu, Perry Mason, Nick Carter, and Secret Agent X, to Dick Tracy and The Shadow, among many others, have become an enduring part of pop culture lore.

The crime genre continues to be highly popular, from movies such as *The Godfather* and *The Untouchables* to CSI (Crime Scene Investigation) TV programs such as *CSI: Miami* and *CSI: NY*. Two subgenres that have shown themselves to be particularly popular are *film noir* and *serial killer* films. The former is a crime story where the action usually takes place at night and in dingy settings, such as seedy hotels and rundown buildings. The use of edgy music and camera angles that focus on shadows lurking in the dark bring out the suspenseful horror of the genre even more – hence the term *noir* (French for 'black'). The genre flourished during the 1940s and 1950s, but it has recently made a comeback in movies such as *The Dark Knight* (2008). Unlike other crime fighters, the film noir protagonists are likely to be disillusioned and cynical, ending up destroyed themselves, at least morally. The classic examples of early film noir were the crime novels written by Dashiell Hammett, Raymond Chandler, and James M. Cain and many of the early movies directed by Alfred Hitchcock, of which *Psycho* (1960) is perhaps the most iconic example. Other movies in the film noir style include *The Maltese Falcon* (1941), *Double Indemnity* (1944), *The Naked City* (1948), *The Asphalt Jungle* (1950), *Point Blank* (1967), *Chinatown* (1974), *Taxi Driver* (1976), *The Grifters* (1990), *L.A. Confidential* (1997), *Memento* (2001), and *The Dark Knight* (2008).

The serial killer genre is a type of film noir. Although the genre can be traced to Alfred Hitchcock's silent 1926 film *The Lodger*, it did not reach widespread popularity until the 1970s when real serial killers started proliferating in society. Fiction and real life seemed to have become mirrors of each other. For example, the case of the Zodiac killer, as he was called in the 1960s, spawned a series of fictional portrayals. One of these was *Dirty Harry* (1971), in which a killer named Scorpio is captured and killed by Dirty Harry Callaghan, a cowboy-style cop played by Clint Eastwood. Another one is David Fincher's 2007 *Zodiac*, with its unsettling subtext of serial killers as symbols of the times, tapping into our fear of the unknowable. By the 1980s, the genre had become one of the most popular of all crime genres when Hannibal Lecter made his screen debut in *Manhunter*. *Silence of the Lambs* hit the screen in 1991, followed by Fincher's *Se7en* in 1995. Since then serial killers are everywhere, in movies and in documentaries, a fact that has blurred the lines between fantasy and fact. Channels such as the Discovery Channel feature real serial killers in various programs. One of the key questions that this genre raises is whether or not the proliferation of real serial killers is a result of pop culture's fascination with them. Serial killers have become celebrities, even admitting in public to committing crimes because they crave attention.

Media specialists have devoted considerable research to studying the crime genre. One relevant theory, called *cultivation theory*, developed by American theorists George Gerbner and Larry Gross (1976) provides a framework for understanding the popularity of crime stories and their effects on audiences. The theory asserts that individuals who spend a lot of time watching violent television programs, such as crime dramas, develop a belief that the world is a much more dangerous place than it really is. This causes them to be more anxious and mistrusting. This phenomenon has been termed the 'mean world syndrome.' At the same time, such programs enforce existing norms. The reason is that they generally communicate the theme that crime does not pay, leading viewers

to have a greater respect for law and order and thus to be more supportive of harsh police measures.

Marcel Danesi

Bibliography

Danesi, Marcel. *Popular Culture: Introductory Perspectives.* Lanham, MD: Rowman and Littlefield, 2008.

Gerbner, George, and Larry Gross. Living with Television: The Violence Profile. *Journal of Communication* 26 (1976): 76.

Gerbner, George, Larry Gross, Michael Morgan, and Nancy Signorielli. Living with Television: The Dynamics of the Cultivation Process. In *Perspectives on Media Effects*, ed. Jennings Bryant and Dolf Zillman, 17–40. Hillsdale, NJ: Lawrence Erlbaum Associates, 1986.

Miller, K. *Communications Theories: Perspectives, Processes, and Contexts.* New York: McGraw-Hill, 2005.

CULTIVATION THEORY

[See also: *Content Analysis; Gerbner, George; Media Effects; Television*]

Cultivation theory is a media and communications explanatory framework developed by American theorists George Gerbner and Larry Gross, who worked on it with various colleagues. The theory posits two interrelated things: (1) that certain media, especially television, 'cultivate' people's perceptions of reality and (2) that the media have a conservative social function – to cultivate existing norms.

Using comparisons of occasional to frequent television viewers, Gerbner and his team found that those who spent more time watching television (so-called 'heavy television viewers') tended to develop beliefs and attitudes about reality that were consistent with the messages in television programs, rather than the real world. Heavy television viewers ended up perceiving the world as a much more dangerous, gloomy, and frightening place than it actually is, which causes them to develop a greater sense of anxiety, vulnerability, alienation, and interpersonal mistrust. This phenomenon is termed the 'mean world syndrome' (Gerbner and Gross 1976).

Gerbner also found that television had a hidden normative structure – namely to enforce existing norms. Violence on TV and in movies does not lead to more crime in society, because the programs and movies usually show that violence does not pay, having the same type of effect of a morality play. TV violence is intended to caution people about the dangers of such violence and, consequently, to bring about its condemnation. This is, of course, related to the mean world syndrome, since those who believe that the world is a dangerous place tend to have a greater respect for law and order and to support drastic police measures to bring such order about. The syndrome thus concomitantly creates a fascination with violence itself. This explains why sensationalistic news programs dealing with real-life violence (such as the O.J. Simpson case) are so popular. They are seen symbolically as examples of 'what the world is coming to.'

Cultivation theory is an example of a sociological theory of the media. It is a view that takes into account the relation between media, culture, and social values and norms.

Alexandra Birk-Urovitz and Elizabeth Birk-Urovitz

Bibliography

Gerbner, George, and Larry Gross. Living with Television: The Violence Profile. *Journal of Communication* 26 (1976): 76.

Gerbner, George, Larry Gross, Michael Morgan, and Nancy Signorielli. Living with Television: The Dynamics of the Cultivation Process. In *Perspectives on Media Effects*, ed. J. Bryant and D. Zillman, 17–40. Hillsdale, NJ: Lawrence Erlbaum Associates, 1986.

Miller, Katharine. *Communications Theories: Perspectives, Processes, and Contexts*. New York: McGraw-Hill, 2005.

CULTURE AND COMMUNICATION

[See also: *Communication; Culture and Media*]

The juxtaposition of the notions of culture and communication requires a brief discussion and definition of both terms. The word 'culture' comes from the past participle *cultus* of the Latin verb *colere*, which means 'to till.' In its broadest sense, the term refers to recurrent patterns of human behaviour and associated artefacts that reflect the beliefs, customs, traditions, and values of a particular society or group of people. This behaviour includes oral and written symbols such as language (folk tales, proverbs) as well as other traditions including dress, religion, rituals (dance, music, and other culture-specific rites), and so forth. Artefacts may include the representational arts such as paintings, pottery, sculpture, written literature, architecture, and the tools necessary to create them – all of which are transmitted from one generation to another.

Communication (Latin *communis* 'common'), on the other hand, refers to the transmission of messages through diverse means including language, gestures, writing, codes, and so forth. Communication may be viewed as both a process and a product. In the former case, communication involves the creation, transmission, circulation, and reception of messages, while in the latter it means the material system employed to transmit the message, for example, computer, telephone, various types of mail including email.

The notions of culture and communication go hand in-hand because the various manifestations of culture – that is, the symbolic presentation of observable artefacts (costumes, dress, food, tools, housing, representational art, and so forth) and the reproducible linguistic aspects (oral history, folk tales, and so forth) of a society – may be communicated in a wide variety of print and non-print means. In essence, culture constitutes a set of meaning systems used by the members of a specific community for the purpose of significant shared interactions and interchanges that reflect the core values of that society.

Human communication most likely originated first through gestures and subsequently by means of primitive utterances that signified basic information (location, danger, and so forth) necessary for survival. The systematic graphic representation of human language developed around the fifth millennium BCE with pictographs, and, subsequently, ideographs, syllabaries, and finally alphabets.

The process of communication may be individual-to-individual, or it may involve larger audiences. The ability to communicate with larger audiences was facilitated by the development of systems of writing (pictographs, ideograms, syllabaries, alphabets) as well as the development of the printing press in fifteenth-century Europe by Johannes Gutenberg (ca 1400–68), though a printing process, known as woodblock printing, had already been developed in China in the sixth century CE.

The European development of the printing press with movable type facilitated the dissemination of written culture, and depictions of the representational arts. As a result, various manifestations of literature (novels, short stories, poetry, and so forth) were made available to a burgeoning literate public. Subsequently, newspapers and magazines provided additional venues for the reading public.

The transmission of verbal culture (tales, poetry, proverbs) through communication may involve only personal contact with individuals or groups of people in oral cultures. Culture may be transmitted from one individual to another through time by means of cultural artefacts such as books, paintings, sculpture, and other tangible manifestations of culture.

A process for the communication of culture exists. First, a society selects what is significant from its environment. Next, those elements deemed to be meaningful are consolidated into the signs of a culture (language, icons, symbols, and so forth). Third, these representations of expressive behaviour are then categorized into social codes (language, music, dance, painting, and so forth) which allow individuals in a society, or the entire community, to encode and decode the texts (literature, music, painting, and so forth) produced by that population. Finally, context (anthropological, historical, psychological, social, and so forth) determines the format of culture and how it is communicated. As a specific society develops, it chooses what is meaningful, and, over time, this becomes the collective culture of that group.

In the nineteenth century, various electronic means became available for the transmission of messages (telegraph, telephone), though these tended to involve ephemeral personal communication rather than lasting cultural artefacts. In the twentieth century, various means for communicating cultural knowledge became widespread, for example, film, photography, radio, television, recordings, and the internet. Each one of these media provided diverse mechanisms for the universal dissemination of culture in all of its manifestations.

Frank Nuessel

Bibliography

Berger, Arthur Asa. *50 Ways to Understand Communication*. Lanham, MD: Rowman and Littlefield, 2006.

Danesi, Marcel, and Paul Perron. *Analyzing Cultures: An Introduction and Handbook*. Bloomington: Indiana University Press, 1999.

Kroeber, Alfred L., and Clyde Kluckhohn. *Culture: A Critical Review of Concepts and Definitions*. New York: Vintage Books, 1960.

CULTURE AND MEDIA

[See also: *Culture and Communication; Medium*]

The relation of culture and media is intimate, necessarily, because culture, in many definitions, requires a medium. Yet, since at least the nineteenth century, culture has become one of the most difficult, richly connotative concepts to define. The most definite assertion one can make of 'culture' is that it is widely accepted that its roots are to be found in the Latin verb *colere*, among whose associated meanings is 'to cultivate' – although in quotidian uses of culture this root is all but forgotten. As a rich concept in social life or a web of meaning in which social life is suspended, culture is most commonly unnoticed or, alternatively, to be encountered as the object of what the anthropologist Geertz (borrowing from the philosopher, Ryle) calls 'thick description.' To explicate the matter, Geertz uses Ryle's example of two boys in a room, rapidly contracting their right eyelids: is this a wink, a twitch, a deliberate message, to someone in particular, coded, without cognizance of the rest of the company? These and other questions have to be addressed before any analysis can reach an understanding of the 'piled-up structures of inferences and implications' (Geertz 1993: 7) which characterize communications in any culture.

Culture in this broad sense, then, consists of all structures of meaning in which communication takes place. In the nineteenth century and in the early part of the twentieth century, ethnography provided a template and inspiration for understanding not only the specific cultures of so-called primitive peoples but also the broader concept of culture itself, especially as experienced in the industrialized, communication-perfused West. In modernity, the definition of culture is made more difficult than in 'primitive' societies because the global proliferation of media and messages has problematized the identification of a common core. Indeed, anthropology in the second half of the twentieth century had to transform its methodology: thick description could only be achieved through a melange of interpretive approaches from the humanities rather than through the methodological prescriptions of the social sciences.

Assessing culture from a perspective which straddles the humanities and social sciences, Jenks (2003: 8–9) offers a four-fold typology which cuts across many conceptions of culture. First, he suggests that culture is a 'cerebral' or cognitive capacity. This carries with it the notion of culture as a product of uniquely human consciousness, the pinnacle of achievement on Earth, and feeds into ideas of false consciousness (as found in some varieties of Marxism), Romanticism, Matthew Arnold, and the Frankfurt School. Culture is thus an exemplification of humans' status as 'chosen.' Second, he suggests that culture is embodied and collective. This conception of culture sees it as evidence of moral development, and an evolutionary feature of humans that, ultimately, is instrumental in the imperialist civilizing process foisted onto 'savage' or so-called primitive societies in the late nineteenth century. Third, Jenks outlines culture as descriptive: it refers to a body of work, the best that has been thought and written, special knowledge, training, and socialization whose products are commemorated in museums and archives. Fourth, Jenks argues that culture has been seen as a social category. This is the idea that culture is to be considered, in fact, as the whole way of life of humans generally and in specific cultures.

Where, in previous epochs, culture may have evinced a limited number of coordinates and may have indeed been allocated to specific kinds of communications, it has become increasingly difficult to suggest where the boundaries of culture lie. Mass communication has meant not just the proliferation of the texts of culture but also, in the process of extending the availability of texts, a blurring of the boundaries between those texts intended for the elite and those for the 'masses.' Jenks (2005), proceeding from reports of the collapse of the high culture/low culture distinction, suggests that modern understandings of culture take place within the tension of *absolutist* and *relativist* tendencies. In the former, attempts are made to establish and maintain a given culture while eschewing traces of other cultures; in the latter, there is an inclination towards seeing cultures and cultural artefacts as equivalent and even, sometimes, equal. Similarly, one could argue that culture is played out across a slightly different tension which is related to the previous one without mapping onto it directly. This is the tension between *elitism* and *egalitarianism*, where culture is either considered to be the preserve of a few or is, alternatively, posited as the possession of all. Within each tension the fate of culture can be played out in a number of different ways.

Within the parameters of absolutism/relativism and elitism/egalitarianism, culture presupposes a series of connotations derived from the conceptual root of culture in 'cultivation' and, especially, the extended metaphor of 'horticulture.' In use as early as 1837, when it was employed by Coleridge, the notion of culture as 'horticulture,' the enhancement of gardens or natural environments, can be seen to be absolutist (in that it suggests that there is the category of cultivation against one of non-cultivation); relativist (there are different kinds of cultivation); elitist (only some should have the power of cultivation); egalitarian (everyone can, potentially, cultivate).

Most frequently, culture is seen as opposite to 'nature.' The root of the latter in the Latin verb 'to be born' suggests that the contrast lies in qualities of innateness distinct from the process of cultivation. Elitist understandings of culture, in particular, have utilized this distinction in the attempt to delineate culture as a pinnacle of achievement. Such an elitist/absolutist conception of culture appears, in some ways curiously, in the work of the neo-Marxist analysis of media conducted by the Frankfurt School from the 1920s to the 1970s (see Swingewood 1977). Here, culture is given an elitist definition in order that it might exclude popularly consumed artefacts produced by the industries of mass communication. In general, much Marxist work on defining culture, and especially associated concepts regarding 'high culture,' has

tended to adopt an elitist stance despite the expectation that it might support egalitarianism (the culture of the proletariat).

The most significant work on the elitist complicity with culture's role in social stratification has come from outside the Marxist tradition and has been largely focused on media. Pierre Bourdieu (1986) equates culture with a specific 'habitus' accruing to groups in societies. The habitus is a social space which comprises 'both the generative principle of objectively classifiable judgments and the system of classification … of these practices' (1986: 170). The relationship of these practices and products of culture, argues Bourdieu, generates 'taste' in a range of cultural spheres such that culture can be redefined as a social space for groups pursuing different versions of language, art, and style. The difference, of course, will be determined by stratification, including such obvious sociological factors as income, occupation, and education in a given habitus. The other key concept in Bourdieu's contribution to understanding culture is taken directly from Marx. It demonstrates that culture relies on its own form of capital in the same manner as the economy does, allowing and preventing group members to traverse the spaces of different stratifications according to the amount of 'cultural capital' that they accumulate and the kinds of media they use. Above all, Bourdieu's work shows how even supposedly egalitarian conceptions of culture, such as making museums accessible to all classes, nevertheless have the tendency to reproduce the elitism inherent in social stratification.

The idea of culture as a whole way of life, beyond the media relation, is associated primarily with the work of Raymond Williams, but it has also been taken up by sociologists and anthropologists as the most appropriate means of investigating the bewildering variegation of communications in modernity. Indeed, Williams (1981) envisaged culture as precisely an object of sociology rather than, say, art theory, in his understanding of culture as a product of formations, institutions, forms, means of production, reproduction, organizations, and ideology. Williams's work (see, especially 1985), stresses that culture is a *process* whose continual movement is checked only by the vicissitudes and conflicts between those factors of which it is a product. As such, Williams posits a radically egalitarian way of conceiving the matter: unlike those egalitarian conceptions of culture with an absolutist tinge that suggest fine art should be a province of all, regardless of habitus, Williams's conception proceeds from the assumption that the practices of all people in society are eligible to be considered as parts of culture. Any relativist overtones in this understanding are vitiated by the fact that Williams repeatedly attempts to erase the line between elite and popular culture, stressing not their relativity but their commonality.

The pinnacle of attempts to dismantle cultural hierarchies and to analyse media in a cultural frame has been the 'semiotics of culture.' Semiotics, commonly concerned with interpersonal and, sometimes, interspecies or 'interorganism' communication, recognizes that culture must be sought in a conception derived from the manifold nature of communicative acts. Principally, this conception is based on a reorientation of the putative culture/nature division. Thomas A. Sebeok sums up the matter succinctly when he refers to culture as that 'minuscule part of nature compartmentalized by some anthropologists' (Sebeok 1986: 60). Contemporary semiotics is concerned with communication across nature and culture, comprising both the verbal and the non-verbal, and sees the action of signs as continuous across both realms. That is, the signs that occur in the known universe are predominantly non-verbal, but a small number of them are verbal (based on language). Culture, however, the preserve of humans (which, in turn, are natural phenomena, animals), is based predominantly on the uniquely human capacity for language. Contemporary semiotics investigates language as a 'modelling system' characterized by verbal and non-verbal signs and, following the work of the Moscow-Tartu school and Sebeok, understands culture as the product of three distinct processes of modelling in humans. The primary modelling system is language as a cognitive capacity for differentiation, ontogenetically and phylogenetically manifested in non-verbal communication. The secondary modelling system is the capacity for verbal communication, manifested in speech and writing. The tertiary modelling system is the realm of culture in which complex connective and metaphorical manifestations of the primary and secondary modelling systems are circulated (see Sebeok and Danesi 2000).

The benefits of the semiotic understanding of culture are to be found in its avoidance, in consonance with Williams's conception, of many of the pratfalls of egalitarianism/elitism and absolutism/relativism, as well as in its renegotiation of the fallacious culture/nature dichotomy which has impeded the investigation of culture and which, in 1959, famously, led C.P. Snow to lament the seemingly unstoppable divergence of the humanities and the sciences. For media and communications, the semiotic understanding of culture offers the opportunity to rethink the ways and means by which culture is 'mediated.'

Paul Cobley

Bibliography

Bourdieu, Pierre. *Distinction: A Social Critique of the Judgment of Taste*. Trans. R. Nice. London: Routledge, 1986.

Geertz, Clifford. Thick Description. In *The Interpretation of Cultures*. London: HarperCollins, 1993.

Jenks, Chris. Introduction. In *Culture: Critical Concepts in Sociology*. 4 vols. London: Routledge, 2003.

– *Culture*. 2nd ed. London: Routledge, 2005.

Sebeok, Thomas A. Vital Signs. In *'I Think I Am a Verb': More Contributions to the Doctrine of Signs*. New York and London: Plenum Press, 1986.

– In What Sense Is Language a 'Primary Modeling System'? In *Semiotics of Culture*, ed. H. Broms and R. Kaufmann. Helsinki: Arator, 1991.

Sebeok, Thomas A., and Marcel Danesi. *The Forms of Meaning: Modeling Systems Theory and Semiotic Analysis*. Berlin and New York: Mouton de Gruyter, 2000.

Swingewood, Alan. *The Myth of Mass Culture*. London: Macmillan, 1977.

Williams, Raymond. *Culture*. Glasgow: Fontana, 1981.

– *The Long Revolution*. London: Chatto and Windus, 1985.

CULTURE INDUSTRY THEORY

[See also: *Adorno, Theodor; British Cultural Theory, Frankfurt School, Hegemony Theory, Marcuse, Herbert; Marxism; Media Studies*]

Culture industry theory is associated with the Frankfurt School (Germany), where a cadre of critical theorists was affiliated with the Institut für Sozialforschung (Institute for Social Research). It was originally located at the University of Frankfurt (1923–33). However, due to the rise of the Nazi party, it relocated first to Geneva, Switzerland (1933–5), and then to New York (Columbia University, 1935–49), before returning to the University of Frankfurt in 1949. The influential members of the Frankfurt School included Max Horkheimer (1895–1973), Theodor Adorno (Wiesengrund, 1903–69), Herbert Marcuse (1898–1979), Walter Benjamin (1892–1940), Erich Fromm (1900–80), Lee Lowenthal (1900–93), and Friedrich Pollock (1894–1970). The members of this school were primarily Marxist (Karl Marx, 1818–83) in their interpretation of economic and social issues.

Because of the rise of Hitler and the Nazi party in Germany, Theodor Adorno lost his academic position in Germany, and was forced to leave that country for the United Kingdom (1934–8). Ultimately, he moved to the United States to work on the Princeton Radio Research Project. For Adorno, mass cultural products were a debasement of the original work. While in the United States, Adorno became shocked at the degree of commercialization of culture in his new country. Ultimately, Max Horkheimer and then Adorno moved to California, where they co-authored an important treatise in 1947 entitled *Dialektik der Aufklärung: Philosophische Fragmente*, and subsequently translated into English in 1972, and again in 2002, as *Dialectic of Enlightenment: Philosophical Fragments*. This work is significant because one part of this volume dealt with what the authors labelled the 'culture industry.' According to them, the corporations that produce popular culture ('pop culture') function as factories of popular cultural products. At the time of the original publication of this classic work (1947), radio and film were the prevailing exemplars of mass culture. These cultural products became formulaic and consumers were said to crave such entertainment with an ever-increasing fervour. In general, it was asserted, the public failed to question the ideological purposes of these cultural creations. In fact, communal consumption of these products had the effect of diverting attention from real economic, political, and social problems. Because of the overwhelming controlling effect of the cultural industry, those under its spell were unaware of its manipulative power.

The very use of the term 'industry' in the phrase 'culture industry' is pejorative. It suggests that it is a capitalist enterprise designed to employ formulaic procedures with the intention of manipulating the public. The use of mechanical reproduction of cultural products ensures that the systemic hierarchy and centralization will endure. It is this mechanization of culture that guarantees that culture will be reduced to its lowest possible common denominator. It should be noted that at least one member of the Frankfurt School, Walter Benjamin, held less pessimistic views about the effects of mass culture.

Predating the Frankfurt School, English writer Matthew Arnold (1822–83) was critical of the mass popularization of culture when he advanced his culture versus civilization viewpoint. Subsequently, Frank R. Leavis (1895–1978) also condemned popular culture, especially U.S. popular culture, as a clear indication of the degradation of civilization. In 1964, Richard Hoggart (b. 1918) established the Centre for Contemporary Cultural Studies at the University of Birmingham, where he was its director until 1973. The theoretical underpinnings of the Centre were essentially Marxist. The faculty studied popular culture and took the position that it had become 'commoditized' – that is, its mass production had debased an essentially pristine culture.

Culture industry theory is not without its critics. Even Herbert Marcuse, a member of the Frankfurt School, pointed out that certain African-American and 'hippie' popular cultural manifestations had demonstrated a certain Romantic idealism. Furthermore, Danesi (2008) argues that popular culture has been a means by which the people have engaged in resistance to the power elite rather than being controlled by it. Likewise, Edward Palmer Thomson (1924–93) espoused a similar view. Peter Hohendahl has taken a similar position. These criticisms include the fact that 'high culture' may also be used as a justification for capitalism.

Frank Nuessel

Bibliography

Danesi, Marcel. *Popular Culture: Introductory Perspectives*. Lanham, MD: Rowman and Littlefield, 2008.
– *X-Rated: The Power of Mythic Symbolism in Popular Culture*. New York: Palgrave Macmillan, 2009.
Hohendahl, Peter U. *Prismatic Thought: Theodor W. Adorno*. Lincoln: University of Nebraska Press, 1995.
Horkheimer, Max, and Theodore W. Adorno. *Dialectic of Enlightenment*. Trans. John Cumming. New York: Herder and Herder, 1972.
[*Dialektik der Aufklärung: Philosophische Fragmente*, Amsterdam: Querido, 1947].
– *Dialectic of Enlightenment: Philosophical Fragments*. Trans. Edmond Jephcott. Stanford, CA: Stanford University Press, 2002.
Thomson, Edward Palmer. *The Making of the English Working Class*. 3rd ed. Pelican, 1980.

CULTURE JAMMING

[See also: *Advertising; Branding; Consumer Culture*]

Culture jamming (CJ) is a technique by which a group or individual subverts a commercial or advertising message, either by altering it (such as defacing a poster) or by creating new texts that publicly challenge well-acknowledged concepts that exist in society, most commonly, the marketplace. The medium in which CJ is supposed to take place is not fixed, but predominantly culture jammers have preferred print, especially billboards, which are in the public realm, such as those advertising for cigarettes, women's clothing, and political parties, and are common and easily accessible to the jammers and easily viewable by the public. CJ may be achieved by simply changing the text of an advertisement to say something shocking to alarm the public, or by painting or creating a new image so that it sends an entirely different message that will catch the public eye. In this sense, CJ can be considered first and foremost an act of anti-consumerism. However, with the powerful works of art by individuals such as Banksy (a pseudonymous London-based artist and activist), whose messages of subversion take the form of thoughtfully executed images ranging from comments on consumerism, to his more abstract comments on war, peace, and the nature of humanity, it is readily turning into a stand-alone art that is not necessarily dependent on some existing text. Essentially, CJ has become a kind of public 'tagging art,' based on creating images and messages using spray paint on a building, street, or sidewalk, regardless of the intended purpose of CJ. Whatever the case, the public will recognize it as a culture jam and thus be affected by it as a reminder of the kinds of manipulative messages that bombard us in daily life.

Accordingly, it is very easy to take this highly malleable and polarized concept and turn it into a vehicle for consumerism. If Banksy appears to express the ebb and flow of everyday life, with a highly satirical twist, then *Adbusters*, under the editorship of Estonian-born activist Kalle Lasn, might be considered the highest form of CJ. The once highly esteemed and controversial magazine offered 'subvertisements' (ads making fun of ads) for the masses in large colour print accompanied by witty articles, but has now turned into what many less affectionately call a 'sell-out' magazine.

Impressive global events that originated with *Adbusters*, such as the 'Buy Nothing Day,' have had some effect. For instance, their promotion of so-called eco-friendly 'Blackspot' shoes sold quite well, leading *The New York Times Magazine*'s special 'Year in Ideas' to remark unabashedly that it is was one of the 'best ideas of 2003.' Even though CJ emerged in the hope of challenging marketplace capitalism by using simple techniques, such as blacking out the logo of a Nike shoe in an ad or poster, it has unwittingly become itself a part of the same consumerist universe. Advertising companies seeking to gain the same amount of success can now appeal to the consumers of *Adbusters* with similar shock tactics. The line between real subversion and put-on style is a thin one indeed.

While the culture and mindset of CJ are constantly changing, its supporters continue to use small-scale acts of culture jamming. Today, CJ is not confined solely to consumer advertising; it covers public relations ploys and political propaganda. It also has taken up social causes.

Siobhan MacLean

Bibliography

Barnard, Adam. The Anger Management Is Not Working. *Capital $ Class* 84 (2004): 125–8.
Boivie, Illana. Buy Nothing Improve Everything. *The Humanist* 63, no. 6 (November/December 2003): 7–9.
Harold, Chrstine. Pranking Rhetoric: Culture Jamming as Media Activism. *Critical Studies in Media Communication* 21, no. 3 (2004): 189–211.
Heath, Joseph, and Andrew Potter. *The Rebel Sell: Why Culture Can't Be Jammed.* New York: HarperCollins, 2004.
Lasn, Kalle. *Culture Jam: The Uncooling of America.* New York: Morrow, 2000.

CURRAN, JAMES (b. 1945)

[See also: *Media Literacy; Media Products*]

James Curran, professor of communications at Goldsmiths College, University of London, since 1989, is a distinguished academic and a prolific author and editor whose works on media and communication have been translated in many languages – works that probe a vast range of theoretical and empirical issues, including media history, the political economy of media, media and politics, media policy, and journalism. Curran has shown why various cultural issues are intertwined with, and reflected in, conceptualizations of media theory in general. It is this dialectic that runs through his work.

In media history, Curran's reappraisal of the conventional interpretation of the emergence of a 'free' press in Britain (the Whig thesis) and his further critical account of its development around the middle of the nineteenth century onwards has become a pivotal one. Curran re-examines press history by challenging the exclusive evaluation of press independence of the mainstream commercial newspapers, bringing to the foreground the crucial role played by the largely neglected radical press, which in the late eighteenth century emblematized press autonomy (Curran 1977). The 'low publishing costs' at that time, as well as the 'self-sufficient' nature of the radical press, established a link between working-class movements and press-based radical consciousness. The increasing retreat of the committed radical press in the second half of the nineteenth century followed soon after the repeal of the 'taxes on knowledge' (Boyce, Curran, and Wingate 1978a). As Curran argues, this cannot be fully explained without considering the structural changes in the press industry itself, including the dominant role of advertising in the emergence of the modern press system, along with its economic and political repercussions, and the industrialization of the press (Curran 1978b), which resulted in the loss of control of the radical press by working-class interests, subsequently transforming the nature of ideological 'struggles' from conflict to consensus.

The interpretation of 'media making' from a 'historical political economy perspective' is the subject of an in-depth sociological analysis of the role of the press by Curran in collaboration with J. Seaton (Curran and Seaton 2003). From their perspective, the emergence of press barons and the creation of press empires in the late nineteenth and early twentieth centuries marked a paradigm shift away from the dependence of the press on political structures to its dependence on market factors. This led to the press becoming more and more interested in covering entertainment news rather than constituting a source of critique of political and other socially important matters. State regulation and economic control of the press during wartime, however, unintentionally rekindled radical journalism, 'liberating' the press from the pressures exerted by the advertising industry. This was followed by the 'revival of proprietary control,' caused by the increasing concentration of media ownership and its 'integration into core sectors of financial and industrial capital' (conglomerates).

Curran identifies numerous influences,

pressures, and constraints on press and broadcasting organizational structure – including media concentration, corporate ownership, mass market pressures, state censorship, and the growing role of advertising (Curran 1986) – as influencing the media to support dominant power interests. However, it is not a predetermined process in support of the status quo; on the contrary, there are several countervailing influences – political, cultural, and so on – to which media are subjected that need to be investigated (Collins, Curran, Garnham, and Scannell 1996). Thus, Curran acknowledges the fact that media content is shaped by pressures from above and below, being present in the very context in which the content operates. He demonstrates this by examining the crisis of public service broadcasting in a British setting (Liebes and Curran 1998), pointing out the relevant forces that rendered it under attack – i.e., political changes (the right-wing shift in British politics and the rise of liberal corporatism), social changes (the growing pluralization of British society along with the cultural revolution of the 1960s), which, through the conflict between traditionalists and liberals, resulted in the challenge to established values (Curran, Gaber, and Petley 2005), and subsequent challenges to the institutional legitimacy and revenue base (the emergence of lobbies opposed to public service broadcasting, and of new communications technologies [cable and satellite television]).

Within this framework, Curran looks at diverse aspects of media policy in relation to different conceptualizations of the democratic role of the media. He critically reviews different approaches and proposals that have been put forward to reform media, focusing on two rival ideologies regarding the organization of the press (market competition) and of the control of broadcasting (state intervention). His critique of the neoliberal and socialist approaches to the media consists in showing that the choice of the political values that legitimatize the organization of media are at stake here. At a time when the underlying rationale of free market competition seems to prevail as a principle for broadcasting organization, Curran stresses instead that both the press and broadcasting media gain social accountability through the public forum. In this regard, the media should always, by default, serve the interests of the public rather than of those in power. By probing alternative strategies of reforming the media, Curran actually provides a framework for liberal theories to gain a concrete form; if this does not occur, Curran claims, 'the New Right will continue to dominate – partly by default' (Curran 1986).

Accordingly, from a radical democratic approach, articulated in the context of a pluralistic conceptualization of the public sphere that acknowledges the collective, self-organized tradition of civil society, Curran (Curran and Gurevitch 2005) goes on to sketch the relevant principles behind a 'democratic media system.' One of these concerns the equitable representation of different social groups both within and through the media. Namely, a democratic media system should provide a locus for the voices of all groups in society to be heard, not just the voices of the dominant group. This not only gives space to different interests, promoting competing definitions of the common good; it also encompasses the possibility of engendering a mutual understanding of others that facilitates the attainment of the collective good. Such a conception of democracy reveals an attempt to establish a functional relation between the individual and the common good that will be able to maintain equilibrium between conflict and conciliation, and between fragmentation and unity. From this perspective, by re-evaluating the media as major forces in democratic functioning, Curran suggests that any meaningful media model should be as representative as possible of the society it serves with respect to structure and organization. The model consists of: 'core public sector' media (public service television channels that reach a mass audience); 'civic sector' media (media linked to organized groups and social networks); 'professional sector' media (media through which professional communicators relate to the public on their own terms); 'social market sector' media (minority media, operating within the market, supported by the state); and 'private enterprise sector' media (media related to the public as consumers). In this way, the overall media system will gain independence from both state and market control.

By taking into account a vast range of media production activity which is realized in the realm of everyday life, Curran then looks at the constitution of media power, since media power is part of what is at stake. From this point of view, Curran pays attention to new media practices, drawing specifically on the internet's potential of opening new and powerful spaces for democratic engagement, and assessing the challenges and limits of the possible new ways of doing journalism (as is the case of the net magazine openDemocracy). In regards to the actual realm of the communication process, Curran consistently locates media in the wider social context of their implementation, evaluating the interplay of diverse forces that determine the character and the course of media influence in different situations: whether deconstructively, undermining the provision of information (as in the case of the prevalence of human interest stories over public affairs in the coverage of British press in late 1970s) (Curran, Douglas, and Whannel 1980), or reactively, setting constraints on the media's ability to generate moral panic in society at large (Curran 1987).

Overall, Curran's work runs extensively and intensively through diverse aspects of the interplay between media and power – the relationship of the mass media to power in society, how control is exercised over media, and the nature of the power exerted by the media. These concerns are reflected in his various works directed at revitalizing media study in various disciplines. By critically reviewing competing approaches to media history (liberal, feminist, populist, libertarian, anthropological, and radical), in the framework of the development of British media with respect to wider trends in society in different periods, Curran (2002) points out the need to look at media in broader non-partisan ways. He constructs a new synthesis of media history by 'folding the history of the British media into a narrative of British society,' and revealing that how media shape – and are shaped by – the development of modern society. Besides, Curran's contextualization of media history (in national terms) weaves together the various approaches, including the technological deterministic view of media, which, though highly polemical, nevertheless sheds light on the kinds of challenges new media practices encompass for the established patterns of communication and power.

Curran's work has gradually advanced the need to interconnect cultural and media/communication studies, addressing in this way the entire system from production to consumption. In a reappraisal of the new revisionism in mass communication research of the 1980s and early 1990s (Curran 1990), Curran traces the main developments in media research and theory, from the initial polarization between liberal and Marxist perspectives of the media and revisionist accounts of power, to revisionist assessments of audience reception, media influence, and cultural value. Correspondingly, when considering 'media-making' itself, Curran has identified basic issues related to both media production (internal organization, ownership and control, the functioning of the market, and public policy issues) and media-based cultural products, including discursive spaces in media content, intertextual and multiple interpretations of media content, and the representation of fragmented identities. Curran's interest in transcending the boundaries of the dichotomy between media-centred approaches, which view media primarily as organizations, and socio-centric ap-

proaches, which explain media according to audience patterns, promotes what he calls a widescreen approach to the study of media (Curran 2000a).

Curran has also analysed revisionist attempts undertaken during the 1990s which have focused on the role of globalization. This has taken away from the hegemony of the Western media, bringing about a 'decentred process' that is transforming and interconnecting the whole world, diversifying communications systems as well as the social spaces of identity formation. However, Curran points out, such a view says little about the redistribution of power in the new global context. It fails especially to acknowledge the central role of nations as definers of power structures and what he calls markers of the difference (Park and Curran 2000b). Curran makes one more call for a critical response to new challenges for media theory and research, by turning to radical history, economics, and political studies.

Pantelis Vatikiotis

Bibliography

Boyce, George, James Curran, and Pauline Wingate, eds. *Newspaper History: From Seventeenth Century to Present Day*. London: Constable, 1978a.

Collins, G. Richard, James Curran, Nicholas Garnham, and Paddy Scannell, eds. *Media, Culture, and Society: A Critical Reader*. London: Sage, 1996.

Couldry, Nick, and James Curran, eds. *Contesting Media Power: Alternative Media in a Networked World*. Lanham: Rowman and Littlefield, 2003.

Curran, James. *Mass Communication and Society*. London: Sage, 1977.

– *The British Press: A Manifesto*. London: Macmillan, 1978b.

– *Bending Reality: The State of the Media*. London: Pluto Press, 1986.

– *Impacts and Influences: Essays on Media Power in the Twentieth Century*. New York: Methuen, 1987.

- Reappraisal of the New Revisionism in Mass Communication Research. *European Journal of Communication* 5, no. 2/3 (1990): 135–64.
- ed. *Media Organizations in Society*. London: Arnold, 2000a.
- *Media and Power*. London: Routledge, 2002.

Curran, James, and Michael Gurevitch. *Mass Media and Society*. 4th ed. London: Arnold, 2005.

Curran, James, and Jean Seaton. *Power without Responsibility*. 6th ed. London: Routledge, 2003.

Curran, James, Angus Douglas, and Garry Whannel. The Political Economy of the Human-Interest Story. In *Newspapers and Democracy*, ed. Anthony Smith, 51–69. Cambridge, MA: MIT Press, 1980.

Curran, James, Ivor Gaber, and Julian Petley. *Culture Wars: The Media and the British Left*. Edinburgh: Edinburgh University Press, 2005.

Curran, James, David Morley, and Valerie Walkerdine, eds. *Cultural Studies and Communications*. London: Hodder Arnold, 1996.

Curran, James, Anthony Smith, and Valerie Walkerdine, eds. *Impacts and Influences: Essays on Media Power in the Twentieth Century*. New York: Methuen, 1987.

Liebes, Tamar, and James Curran. *Media, Ritual and Identity*. London: Routledge, 1998.

Park, Myung-Jin, and James Curran. *De-Westernizing Media Studies*. London: Routledge, 2000b.

CYBERCULTURE

[See also: *Castells, Manuel; Cyberspace; Global Village; Gutenberg Galaxy; Haraway, Donna; Online Culture*]

Cyberculture refers to the interrelationship between culture and the new technologies. The study of cyberculture involves investigating how culture is shaped by technology, but also how culture affects technology. In a 'tech-savvy' era, with sophisticated computer-based devices and tools such as the cellphone, the BlackBerry, and the internet, the concept of a 'physical humanity' that lives in a material culture is being reassessed in terms of the concept of a 'post-humanity' that now lives (at least in part) in cyberculture. Anthropologist Arturo Escobar (1994: 212–13) appropriately notes that 'the spread of the written word, the preeminence of the machine, the control of time and space, and the biological and biochemical revolutions of the past 100 years produced unprecedented biotechnical arrangements which today find new forms of expression in cybercultural terms.' Escobar further remarks that 'new technologies in two areas: artificial intelligence (particularly computer and information technologies) and biotechnology … embody the realization that we increasingly live and make ourselves in techno-biocultural environments structured by novel forms of science and technology.' This is why the modern world is often referred to as a 'wired world.'

The idea of a cyberculture existing in cyberspace can be traced back to science-fiction writer William Gibson (b. 1948), who, in his first novel *Neuromancer* (1984), coined the term *cyberspace* to describe the beginnings of a dehumanized, high-tech world. For Gibson cyberspace constituted a computer-simulated world that appears more real to people (or at least more interesting) because they can interact with it through devices. The concept of cyberspace was Gibson's reaction to the advent of technologies and sciences such as cybernetics, computer science, and informatics that were starting at that time to bring about a true paradigm shift in human social evolution, leading eventually to the notion of modern humans as cyborgs living in a cyberculture (Macek 2005). Intel's invention of the microprocessor and developments by Apple Computer set the stage for computers to move permanently into everyone's daily life. This led to an ever-burgeoning popular interest in technology, computers, and electronic communications among the general population From the 1990s to today, cyberculture has become an unconscious pattern of life, radically changing institutions and even human cognition.

Perhaps one of the best-known works in popular culture which first dealt with the theme of cyberculture was Stanley Kubrick's 1968 movie *2001: A Space Odyssey*, based on the novel by science-fiction writer Arthur C. Clarke. The power of artificial intelligence, represented by HAL in the movie, made it a prophetic movie.

Today, the term cyberculture is often synonymous with online culture, since a significant part of cyberculture emerges on the internet. However, cyberculture is not just limited to the internet. In fact, with devices such as the BlackBerry, text messaging on mobile phones, computer or video games, and the like have coalesced with the internet to produce contemporary versions of cyberculture. Together, these devices are now used routinely for communication, information-gathering, learning, and so on.

Perhaps the two scholars best known for theorizing about cyberculture are Manuel Castells and Donna Haraway. Among the key topics they helped introduce into cyberculture study are 'life on the screen,' meaning how people project their identities onto cyberspace; 'network society,' or the idea that the world is no longer a linear bidirectional one of senders and receivers, but a 'networked' one of multiple senders and receivers located on a diverse platform of information sources; 'space of flows,' which describes the fact that in cyberspace the relation between interlocutors is in a constant flow; and 'cyborg theory,' or the idea that with technology humans can now enhance their abilities mechanically and that this is having a profound influence on how we view ourselves.

Alexander Lim

Bibliography

Bell, David. *Cyberculture Theorists: Manuel Castells and Donna Haraway.* London: Routledge, 2007.

Escobar, Arturo. Welcome to Cyberia: Notes on the Anthropology of Cyberculture. *Current Anthropology* 35 (1994): 211–31.

Macek, Jakub. Defining Cyberculture. July 2005. http://macek.czechian.net/defining_cyberculture.htm (accessed 28 January 2009).

CYBERNETICS

[See also: *Communication; Feedback; Information; Shannon, Claude E.*]

Cybernetics is the science aiming to study regulation and control in humans, animals, organizations, and machines. It was conceived by mathematician Norbert Wiener (1894–1964), who coined the term in 1948 in his book *Cybernetics, or Control and Communication in the Animal and Machine.* Wiener may not have been aware at the time that the same word was used in 1834 by the physicist André-Marie Ampère to denote the study of government in his classification system of human knowledge. Ampère, in turn, had probably taken it from Plato, who used it to signify the governance of people. Wiener popularized the social implications of cybernetics, drawing analogies between machines (robots and computers) and humans in his best-selling 1950 book *The Human Use of Human Beings: Cybernetics and Society.*

Cybernetics views communication in all self-contained complex systems as analogous. It is not interested in the material forms of such systems, but in the ways in which such forms are organized to constitute the system. Because of the increasing sophistication of computers and the efforts to make them behave in humanlike ways, cybernetics today is closely allied with artificial intelligence and robotics, drawing as well on ideas developed in information theory.

As used in communication studies, the term applies primarily to the analysis of systems in which the feedback and error-correction signals control the operation of the systems. Such signals (or signal systems) are called *servomechanisms*. Servomechanisms were first used in military and marine navigation equipment. Today they are used in automatic machine tools, satellite-tracking antennas, celestial-tracking systems, automatic navigation systems, and anti-aircraft control systems. A primary task of cybernetics is to understand the guidance and control servomechanisms that govern the operation of social interaction and then to devise better ways of harnessing them.

The cybernetic approach to communication involves developing a taxonomy of notions, principles, and procedures for understanding the phenomenon of communication. In many ways, the late Canadian communication theorist Marshall McLuhan (1911–80) could be characterized as an ersatz cybernetician, since he shared many of the same interests of the early cyberneticians. For example, McLuhan believed that the type of technology developed to record and transmit messages determines how people process and remember them. The term *information* invariably comes up in any cybernetic discussion of communication. Cyberneticians define it simply as any form of data that can be received by humans, animals, or machines. In one cybernetic model, information is seen as something probabilistic – a ringing alarm signal carries more information than one that is silent, because the latter is the 'expected state' of the alarm system and the former its 'alerting state.' The mathematical aspects of information theory were developed by the American telecommunications engineer Claude Shannon (1916–2001). He showed, essentially, that the information contained in a signal is inversely proportional to its probability. The more probable a signal, the less information 'load' it carries with it; the less likely it is, the more load it carries.

Shannon devised his mathematical model in order to improve the efficiency of telecommunications systems. His model essentially depicted information flow as a unidirectional process dependent on probability factors, that is, on the degree to which a message is to be expected or not in a given situation. It is called the 'bull's-eye model' because a sender of information is defined as someone or something aiming a message at a receiver of the information as if he, she, or it were in a bull's-eye target range. Shannon also introduced several key terms into the general study of communication: channel, noise, redundancy, and feedback. Shannon's model has, over the years, been useful in providing a terminology for describing cybernetic aspects of communication systems.

Marcel Danesi

Bibliography

Brier, Søren. *Cybersemiotics*. Toronto: University of Toronto Press, 2007.

Cherry, Colin. *On Human Communication*. Cambridge, MA: MIT Press, 1957.

Wiener, Norbert. *Cybernetics, or Control and Communication in the Animal and the Machine*. Cambridge, MA: MIT Press, 1949.

CYBERSPACE

[See also: *Castells, Manuel; Cyberculture; Global Village; Gutenberg Galaxy; Haraway, Donna; Online Culture*]

Cyberspace is the term coined by American novelist William Gibson in his 1984 novel *Neuromancer*, a novel that was the inspiration for the emergence of cyberpunk science fiction writing. Cyberpunk narratives take place typically in a bleak, dehumanized future world dominated by technology and robotic humans. Gibson's description of cyberspace is worth repeating here (Gibson 1984: 67):

> *Cyberspace.* A consensual hallucination experienced daily by millions of legitimate operators. A graphic representation of data abstracted from the banks of every computer in the human system. Unthinkable complexity. Lines of Light ranged in the nonspace of the mind, clusters of constellations of data. Like city lights, receding.

Cyberspace is an interactive and immersive virtual electronic space. The internet is its primary environment. Cyberspace now has its own communities (Facebook communities, Second Life, Multiple User Domains, and so on) and its own set of conventions for communicating and interacting. Movement and interaction in cyberspace are, of course, virtual. This makes it 'hyperreal,' to use Jean Baudrillard's (1983) widely used term. Hyperreality exists on or through the screen. As Mikael Benedikt (1991: 1) notes, in cyberspace 'the tablet becomes a page becomes a screen becomes a world, a virtual world. Everywhere and nowhere, a place where nothing is forgotten yet everything changes.' The modern human lives in two universes, that of physical reality and that of hyperreality, blurring the distinction between biological humanity and technological humanity. Feminist critic Donna Haraway (1991) introduced the term *cyborg* to characterize this new form of consciousness. In cyborg theory boundaries such as human and non-human, organism and machine, and physical and non-physical are obliterated.

The advent of cyberspace has led to many reassessments of, and debates on, traditional notions of life itself. The internet promises a type of immortality that only religions in the past could have ensured. Although the form of immortality is devoid of consciousness (which religions pledge), it is nonetheless a real possibility that most people would never have been able to contemplate previously. What is online about ourselves will define us well beyond our mortal lives. In the past, only artists, writers, musicians, and other 'important' individuals would have been able to leave behind their 'selves' for posterity through their work; now virtually anyone can do something similar. Our Facebook pages and our tweets define us, remaining in cyberspace well beyond our physical lives. In cyberspace we can leave a record of ourselves for future generations to read. This is affecting not only how we remember and grieve, but also how we view mortality.

There are now cases of people grieving for those whom they have met only online. Websites now reveal outpourings of grief, memorial-making, and the like on the part of people who made contact with the deceased only online. The digital afterlife is something tangible, something that people can grasp in a practical way. A group of online businesses have sprung up to allow people to control their afterlife selves and to manage the details of one's real and digital death. Cyberspace, as Gibson claimed, is indeed an infinite one, in both the physical and spiritual senses – it is a virtual universe without physical boundaries and provides a bizarre sense of reassurance that life will go on even after we are dead in the real world.

Marcel Danesi

Bibliography

Baudrillard, Jean. *Simulations*. New York: Semiotexte, 1983.

Bell, David. *Cyberculture Theorists: Manuel Castells and Donna Haraway*. London: Routledge, 2007.

Benedikt, Michael. *Cyberspace: First Steps*. Cambridge, MA: MIT Press, 1991.

Gibson, William. *Neuromancer*. London: Grafton, 1984.

Haraway, Donna. *Simians, Cyborgs and Women: The Reinvention of Nature*. London: Routledge, 1991.

D

DATA MINING

[See also: *Information; Information Society*]

Data mining is the term used by computer scientists to refer to the techniques of extracting relevant information from a set of raw data. The techniques include the automatic grouping of documents or files, categorizing them into directories, and analysing patterns and interrelationships within them. One particular technique, called *filtering*, involves making profiles of people's interests and then comparing these against related information from various sources. Marketers can then use the profiles for producing ads or service alerts to those identified as having an interest in something specific. Data mining has had many other important applications in diverse fields, from marketing to psychology.

Data mining using computers started in the 1960s, but manual data mining systems can be traced back to antiquity. The Greek scholar Callimachus devised a catalogue for the library in Alexandria, Egypt, in the 200s BCE, subdividing the library's holdings into fields such as jurisprudence, poetry, philosophy, history, oratory, and miscellaneous. In the early medieval period, monks developed concordances for the Bible – alphabetical lists of the principal words in the Bible with references to the passages in which they occur. And the American librarian Melvil Dewey developed his widely used 'Dewey Decimal Classification System' in 1876 for organizing materials in a library. Dewey divided books into ten main categories, each represented by numbers, and each of these into more specialized fields. For example, the category of *Technology* is numbered with the digits from 600–699; it is then broken up into ten subclasses: 630–639 represents works in agriculture, which are then further subdivided into field crops, garden crops, and so on.

Today, data mining software extracts patterns and relationships from all kinds of digitally-produced data. The process is called Discovery in Databases. A number of World Wide Web search engines, such as Google, use data mining techniques to analyse information across the billions of links connecting Web pages in order to determine which pages are the most popular or what relevance they have to various fields. This information is then used to rank search results.

Given the widespread use of data mining by marketers, government agencies, and others, some social critics have charged that it is leading to an information society in which personal data can be used nefariously. This might, as Bell (2007: 13) observes, eventually transform human beings 'into data and lodged in databases thanks to the manifold technologies of data collection that monitor our habits and routines (from our shopping practices to our workplace productivity.' The answer to stopping the mining of personal information is, according to some, to 'stay offline.'

But even those who do not go online leave 'data trails' through the use of credit cards, social security numbers, and so forth. The world of Big Brother seems to have arrived, claim many. As Landow (2006: 376) puts it, the greatest danger today is that 'the newest versions of data-mining and computer-based surveillance will permit those with control of the machines total control over all information and the people who read, write, and exchange it. Manuel Castells (1996) calls the social process of turning everything and everyone into data sets 'informationalism.' The debate brought about by informationalism is taking various forms, from post-humanism, the philosophy that humans are no longer at the centre of things, just more advanced forms of biological information, to cyborg theory, which claims that humans will be merging with technologies to enhance their biological and psychological abilities.

Clearly, the advent of data mining has had social and psychological consequences. Every detail of our lives (what we buy, where we go, what romantic interests we have, and so on) is now extractable from the internet, and the personal information can be bundled and bartered by data-mining companies. Needless to say, data-mining media and techniques of the past, from telemarketing to phone surveys, posed the same dangers. But the breadth and scope of the data-mining techniques available with the new technologies are mind-boggling, since it is now possible to collate disparate facts about individuals and generate profiles of various kinds about them (psychographic, sociographic, and so on) in a matter of seconds.

The psychologist Carl Jung feared that modern societies were losing the view of the individual as a unique human being, turning the person into a convenient 'unit' that can be easily categorized, manipulated, and exploited. Some now see data mining as a panopticon, the circular prison envisaged by philosopher Jeremy Bentham in the eighteenth century in which the prisoners cannot tell if they are being observed, so they must assume that they always are. In the panopticon, as in cyberspace, there is a loss of control of one's identity. It is in the hands of others. Together with social media, such as Facebook, where people post intimate details about their lives, it is becoming obvious that the new world of computer-mediated-communications is drastically changing traditional concepts of identity, privacy, and individualism as we become more and more inured to practices such as data mining.

Marcel Danesi

Bibliography

Bell, David. *Cyberculture Theorists: Manuel Castells and Donna Haraway*. London: Routledge, 2007.

Castells, Manuel. *The Information Age: Economy, Society, and Culture*. Oxford: Blackwell, 1996.

Jung, Carl. *The Undiscovered Self*. New York: Mentor, 1957.

Landow, George P. *Hypertext 3.0: Critical Theory and New Media in an Era of Globalization*. Baltimore: Johns Hopkins University Press, 2006.

DECODING VERSUS ENCODING

[See also: *Bull's-Eye Model; Code; Code, Types of; Communication Theory*]

The terms *decoding* and *encoding* refer respectively to the construction and deciphering of signals in a communication system on the basis of a *code* – a set of signs (such as alphabet characters) which are used for messaging making. The two terms were introduced into communication theory in 1954 by the American theorist Wilbur Schramm (1907–87), who added them to the emerging technical lexicon developed by Claude Shannon, a contemporary theorist of communication systems. The *encoder* is the organism or machine that converts elements in a code into a message in such a way that it can be transmitted through an appropriate channel; the *decoder* reverses the process so that the message can be received and deciphered successfully. Schramm's model has come to be known as the *sender* (or *source*)-*message-channel-receiver* model, or SMCR for short. The SMCR continues to be used to this day in the study of mass communications systems. The model was further refined in 1956 by George Gerbner (1919–2005), who expanded the concept of codes to encompass social codes such as those that define relations such as gender and class. A similar use of the terms was employed by Roman Jakobson in his classic 1960 essay on communication.

Culture theorist Stuart Hall (1973) utilized the terms in reference to discourse practices and the decoding processes they revealed. In theory, those who control the levers of the media have power over those who receive media messages. But, Hall noted, this does not mean that the encoder's message will necessarily be interpreted as desired. He argued that decoders do not absorb media messages passively, but decode them in one of three ways, which he termed *preferred*, *negotiated*, and *oppositional*. The preferred reading is the message that media encoders hope audiences will take from their communications. The negotiated reading results when audiences accept only part of the intended message. And an oppositional reading is one that is in opposition to the intended message. A concrete way to understand the difference between the three types is to consider a comedian who has just told a joke before an audience. If most audience members laugh, then the joke has produced the preferred reading. If only half of the audience laughs, then the joke has triggered a negotiated reading. Finally, if most of the audience reacts negatively to the joke, then it has produced an oppositional reading.

Marcel Danesi

Bibliography

Hall, Stuart. Encoding/Decoding. *Working Papers in Cultural Studies, 1972–79*. Centre for Con-

temporary Cultural Studies, 128–38. London: Hutchinson, 1973.

Jakobson, Roman. Linguistics and Poetics. In *Style and Language*, ed. T.A. Sebeok, 34–45. Cambridge, MA: MIT Press, 1960.

Schramm, Wilbur. *Men, Women, Messages and Media*. New York: Harper and Row, 1982.

Shannon, Claude E. A Mathematical Theory of Communication. *Bell Systems Technical Journal* 27 (1948): 379–423.

DECONSTRUCTION

[See also: *Derrida, Jacques; Post-Structuralism; Semiotics; Structuralism*]

Deconstruction is an approach to textual analysis introduced by the late French philosopher Jacques Derrida (1930–2004). The fundamental idea in deconstruction is the contention that the meaning of a text cannot be determined in any absolute way because it shifts according to who analyses it, when it is analysed, how it is analysed, and so on. Moreover, every text has inbuilt world views that come from historical traditions; these are imprinted in the words and themes used. Deconstruction challenges traditional assumptions about texts as mirrors of reality because words, Derrida claimed, refer only to other words. And they carry with them historically based biases and prejudices. He rejected the traditional way scholars interpreted literary fiction as a means of portraying life and the view that the author of a work is the source of its meaning. A narrative text has no unchanging, unified meaning, because the author's intentions cannot be unconditionally accepted or even identified. There are an infinite number of legitimate interpretations of a text that are beyond what the author intends. Hence, the text deconstructs itself over time.

Deconstruction can be located as a textual analytic technique under the more general rubric of *post-structuralism*, associated not only with Derrida but also with another French philosopher Michel Foucault (1926–

84) (Derrida 1976; Foucault 1972). The main intent of the movement was to show that signs (such as words) do not encode reality, but rather construct it and even obfuscate it. By their very nature, sign systems are self-referential – signs refer to other signs, which refer to still other signs, and so on. Thus, what appears logical and real in a text turns out to be mere verbal invention when deconstructed. Derrida was fixated with *logocentrism* –the view that knowledge is constructed by linguistic categories, rendering even science virtually useless because it requires language. Language encodes 'ideologies,' not 'reality,' and because language is the indispensable tool of knowledge-producing enterprises such as science, these end up communicating nothing more than the self-referential meanings of the words themselves. For Derrida, words are empty structures, devoid of true reference to the world and, thus, can stand on their own for virtually anything. They can also become dangerous if they encode prejudices.

Although not a deconstructionist, Roland Barthes (1957) also saw texts in a similar way. He divided their meaning structure into two levels: the linguistic and the mythical. The former has informational or referential meaning. For example, a word such as *lion*, at this level, refers to 'a large, carnivorous, feline mammal of Africa.' But, the instant the word is used in a text, it invariably triggers a mythical sense – namely, a 'very brave person, generally regarded as fierce or ferocious.' The meaning of texts thus oscillates back and forth between the linguistic and mythic levels.

Deconstruction is today one of the options available to the literary critic. In the end, the deconstruction movement envisioned by Derrida was, arguably, nothing more than an overreaction to structuralism in its most radical forms. One of its most fruitful applications was (and perhaps continues to be) in the domain of media studies, anticipating reader-response theory, or the view that audiences play a role in shaping the experience of texts. Feminist deconstructionists, for instance, examine the ways in which the gender of the writer or the reader affects the textual experience.

Marcel Danesi

Bibliography

Barthes, Roland. *Mythologies*. Paris: Seuil, 1957.
Belsey, Catharine. *Poststructuralism*. Oxford: Oxford University Press, 2002.
Derrida, Jacques. *Of Grammatology*. Trans. G.C. Spivak. Baltimore: Johns Hopkins University Press, 1976.
Foucault, Michel. *The Archeology of Knowledge*. Trans. A.M. Sheridan Smith. New York: Pantheon, 1972.
Norris, Christopher. *Deconstruction: Theory and Practice*. London: Routledge, 1991.

DEFAMATION

[See also: *Freedom of Speech; Internet*]

This entry provides an analysis based primarily on United States law with some reference being made to Canadian law and the law in other common law jurisdictions. The following should not be interpreted as providing legal advice in any manner whatsoever.

Libel refers to the publication of a defamatory written statement, whereas *slander* refers to defamatory statements that are spoken. Traditionally the distinction was probably made because of the fact that written statements were potentially more persistent and likely to be more widely circulated than spoken statements. However, with the advent of, first, radio then television and now the internet such distinctions are less clear cut. The initial response in many jurisdictions to new broadcast media was to consider that potentially defamatory statements made on radio or television should be classified as libel. More recently we have seen some jurisdictions essentially do away with the distinction between slander and libel, seeking to determine the potential seriousness of the defamatory statements in the light of a variety of factors such as the potential number of individuals who have access to the statements in question, the length of time that the statements are likely to be accessible, and so on.

A defamatory statement is one which is likely to have a negative impact on an individual's reputation. Clearly this covers a very wide range of possible statements and recognizes, as the common law, that an individual's reputation clearly has value. Under common law the publication of a false statement concerning an individual is the defining fact underlying an action with respect to libel or slander. The onus is generally on the defendant to prove the truth of the statement rather than on the plaintiff to provide proof that it is false. Further, in common law there is no need for the plaintiff to prove that the defendant had any intention of harming the plaintiff's reputation – proving that the statement in question had been published – that it is overheard or accessible by a third party or third parties is sufficient.

In order to win a libel case generally speaking the plaintiff has to prove each of the following: (1) defamation; (2) identification; (3) publication; (4) in cases relating to issues of public interest, *fault* on the part of the publisher or broadcaster. Identification requires that the statement is sufficiently specific as to be understood as referring to a single individual or a small group of individuals. Publication generally has been taken to mean that the statement in question is made known to a third party – that is, a party other than the source of the defamatory statement and the individual allegedly defamed.

If judgment in a libel or slander action favours the plaintiff then a remedy is likely to include the assessment of damages, in some instances the publication of a retraction of the relevant statements and, in certain circumstances, the granting of an injunction barring any further publication of the defamatory statements.

The treatment of the legal actions relating to libel, in particular, has become more nuanced than the traditional approach based on the common law. In the first place, in the United States, a distinction has evolved concerning the status of the plaintiff. If the plaintiff is a 'public figure' then the plaintiff has to demonstrate that the defendant acted with malice or with reckless disregard for the truth of the statement. There is some conflict between the courts as to the defining characteristics of a 'public figure.' Further, in the United States, the plaintiff has to prove malice on the part of the defendant in making the defamatory statement. 'Actual malice' has been explained by Justice Kennedy of the United States Supreme Court in the court's opinion rendered in *Masson* (Masson v. New Yorker Magazine, 85 F.3rd 1394) as a 'falsehood knowingly published or published with reckless disregard for the truth.' It is worth noting that United States courts are often influenced by concerns relating to the upholding of the First Amendment when considering defamation suits particularly when they involve issues of public interest or involve individuals who have catapulted themselves into the vortex of public concern. Canadian law has generally not recognized such a clear distinction between libel actions brought by public individuals and private individuals. However, a recent ruling by the Supreme Court of Canada in the case of *WIC Radio Ltd. and Raif Mair v. Kari Simpson* (WIC Radio Ltd. v. Simpson, 2008 SCC 40) has begun to tread this path. A British case which came before the House of Lords under appeal in 2006 also established a fairly strong defence for the media in defamation suits when the allegedly defamatory statement(s) concern issues in the public interest.

A variety of potential defences are available to a defendant when a libel or slander action is brought against them. The first, and perhaps most obvious, is that the allegedly defamatory statements were true. As we have noted, under common law, the onus is on the defendant to prove that the statements are true. However, it should be noted that there may be a cause of action even when true statements are published about an individual, but the cause of action will not be libel or slander but may relate to such causes of action as *invasion of privacy*.

If a statement is defamatory, common law has also historically recognized that on a limited number of occasions such statements are privileged even if they are motivated by malice. In these cases complete immunity from being subject to a lawsuit is provided. Absolute privilege is provided to members of parliament with respect to statements made on the floor of the relevant debating chamber and to statements, whether written or oral, made during judicial or quasi-judicial proceedings. It is important to note that it is often the case that the scope of absolute privilege has been extended by statute in many common law jurisdictions. In addition to absolute privilege the defence of qualified privilege has evolved allowing the media to report on government proceedings as long as their reporting is fair and accurate.

A distinctly different defence is the defence of fair comment. To the extent that statements are expressions of opinion rather than fact, they are not actionable. It is important to note that courts have been sensitive to situations where statements of fact essentially masquerade as statements of opinion. In a recent ruling of the Canadian Supreme Court (WIC Radio Ltd. v. Simpson, 2008 SCC 40) it was noted that in order to satisfy the fair comment defence a defendant is only required to prove that: (a) the statement at issue constituted comment; (b) it had a basis in true facts; and (c) it concerned a matter of public interest. The court further noted that the fair comment defence may be trumped by the existence of malice, which must be proved by the plaintiff.

In the United States some defendants in libel cases have sought the *neutral reportage* defence. This defence has been recognized by the second circuit Court of Appeals and relates to situations where media attempt to report neutrally both sides of a controversial issue. However, this defence has not

been generally accepted by courts in the United States.

Two technical defences which may be available arise out of consent by the individual defamed or the operation of the statute of limitations. In this context consent refers to a situation where it can be shown that the plaintiff gave consent to the libellous publication.

If the plaintiff wins a libel case damages are assessed by the court. The plaintiff does not have to present evidence of actual damages. However, in the case of slander it is typically necessary for the plaintiff to provide such evidence.

With respect to responsibility for a defamatory statement, and hence exposure to potential libel or slander suits, it should be noted that, in addition to the author of the allegedly defamatory statements, any individual or organization that republished the allegedly defamatory statement may find themselves the target of a defamation suit. However, distributors such as bookstores are not considered to be liable. As noted below, in the United States internet service providers (ISPs) may be able to seek immunity from prosecution under the safe harbour provisions of the Communications Decency Act.

It is important to observe that differences between countries with respect to the difficulty of winning a defamation suit may result in what is termed 'forum shopping.' The term refers to the attempt to select a forum for hearing a defamation suit which will be most amenable to the plaintiff's case. It has often been considered that defamation suits are 'easier' to win before the Canadian and British courts than before the United States courts though the United States courts often award far higher damages.

Defamation and New Media

As we have noted above the invention of radio and television and, more recently, the internet, has had a significant impact on the potential for media organizations and, indeed, individuals to be exposed to libel suits. As material created by individuals and organizations is more widely disseminated increased attention needs to be paid to the statements that are made in podcasts, internet radio and television, chat rooms, websites, and so forth.

With respect to radio and television, many jurisdictions have enacted laws to extend and refine the common law treatment of defamation. However, generally speaking statutes have not been enacted to refine and extend common law, or, indeed existing statutes, into the domain of defamation and the internet. It seems reasonably clear that making statement available on the internet constitutes publication and that providing access to the statements of others available on the internet amounts to republication. More problematic is whether the same standards of reportage should apply to all individuals and organizations that make potentially defamatory statements concerning issues of public interest. Indeed, the very notion of what constitutes a reporter has become very fluid with the advent of the internet and such reportage as that represented by blogs.

It is important to note that in the United States, until recently, internet service providers considered that they could avail themselves of safe harbour provisions in the Communications Decency Act and thus be immune to defamation suits relating to websites maintained for customers as long as they adopted a 'hands-off' policy with respect to the contents of these websites. However, some recent cases have led to the suggestion that such 'safe harbour' provisions may not be as bulletproof as had been assumed.

One particular area of concern with respect to defamation and the internet relates to the exercise of jurisdiction by the courts. In an earlier time considerable control could be exercise over the distribution of print and television, such that organizations could be fairly confident that they would not face defamation suits brought by individuals or organizations not resi-

dent in geographical areas where content was distributed. The internet potentially allowed for the distribution of content to any user having access to the internet wherever in the world they might be located. This leads to two notable cases. In *Gutnick v. Dow Jones & Jones Inc.* a resident of the State of Victoria, Australia, brought suit against Dow Jones claiming that a defamatory statement had been published in *The Wall Street Journal* and also made available on the Web to subscribers to an online news service. Although the article containing the statements was not directed towards the residents of the State of Victoria and only a trivially small number of individuals accessed the relevant website from Australia, the High Court of Australia (Gutnick v. Dow Jones & Co. Inc. [2001] VSC 305 (28 August 2001)) supported the exercise of jurisdiction by the State of Victoria. The case was settled out of court. A more disturbing case, reversed on appeal, was *Bangoura v. The Washington Post* (Bangora v. Washington Post 2005, 202 O.A.C. 76), which was heard in Ontario, Canada. The facts of the case were that the *Washington Post* published and made available on the Web allegedly defamatory statements concerning the plaintiff when he was resident in Kenya in 1997. Bangora's suit before the Ontario court commenced in April 2003 when he was resident in Ontario. The Ontario court concluded that it had jurisdiction, raising the possibility that media making use of the internet might find themselves facing suits from anywhere in the world. The potential assertion of jurisdiction by the Ontario court sent a shiver through the media industry. However, the ruling was overturned by the Supreme Court of Ontario.

Recent Canadian Jurisprudence

In a recent judgment (Grant v. Torstar Corp., 2009 SCC 61) the Supreme Court of Canada recognized a new defence that can potentially be available to plaintiffs in defamation cases – namely 'public interest responsible communication.' The Supreme

Court indicated that the determination of the public interest would be the responsibility of the judge in a particular proceeding whereas the determination of whether the actions of the individual or media organization constituted responsible communication would be the responsibility of the jury. It is important to note that in reaching this judgment the Supreme Court of Canada essentially introduced a defence that might otherwise be referred to as responsible journalism. Further, the Supreme Court of Canada, in choosing the more general term 'communication' rather than 'journalism,' explicitly recognized that the defence was available to bloggers and other new media communicators.

Anthony Wesley

Bibliography

Collins, Matthew. *The Law of Defamation and the Internet*. Oxford: Oxford University Press, 2001.

Davidson. Alan. *The Law of Electronic Commerce*. Cambridge: Cambridge University Press, 2009.

Internet and Online Law. New York: Law Journal Press, 2010.

Overbeck, Wayne. *Major Principles of Media Law*. Boston: Wadsworth, 2009.

DENOTATION VERSUS CONNOTATION

[See also: *Meaning; Semiotics*]

The terms *denotation* and *connotation* are used in various disciplines, from semiotics and linguistics to media studies. The former indicates a kind of 'core' meaning that can be extracted from a sign (word, symbol, etc.), the latter the additional meanings that the same sign evokes. The core meaning of the word *cat*, for example, is 'creature with four legs, whiskers, retractile claws,' and so forth. This allows us to distinguish a *cat* from some other mammal. The word *denotation* is derived from the compound Latin verb *de-noto*, 'to mark out, point out, specify, indicate.' The word *nota* ('mark, sign, note') itself derives from the verb *nosco*, 'to come to know,' 'to become acquainted with,' 'to recognize.' The denotative meaning is called the *denotatum* (plural *denotata*).

When we call a human being a 'cool cat,' or when we tell someone that his or her statement has let 'the cat out of the bag,' the word is being used connotatively, that is, with meanings that have been added to it over time. A connotative meaning is called the *connotatum* (plural *connotata*). Consider the exclamation *oh*. In addition to being a sign of surprise (denotatum), it can have various other expressive senses (connotata), depending on the tone of voice with which it is uttered. If one says it with a raised tone, as in a question ('Oh?'), then it would convey doubt or incredulity. If articulated emphatically, with a lowered tone ('Oh!'), then it would connote disappointment. Connotation, as its name implies, is meaning that goes along with the *nota*.

There is a looping pattern between the two modes of meaning. Take, for example, the word *house*. Denotatively, the word refers to a 'structure for human habitation,' no matter what its dimensions are, what specific shape it has, and so on. Now, the same word has acquired various connotata over time, such as the following:

The *house* is not in session =
  'legislative assembly, quorum'
The *house* roared with laughter =
  'audience in a theatre'
He's in one of the *houses* at Harvard =
  'dormitory'

Connotata are in theory infinite, since anything that assumes the basic denotatum of 'structure for human habitation' which 'humans' can be seen to 'inhabit' in some way is a candidate for connotation. This is why that word can even be applied to new technologies: 'The internet *houses* a lot of information,' 'It is a *storehouse* of knowledge,' and so on.

Connotation is the operative meaning-making and meaning-extracting mode in the production and decipherment of creative texts such as poems, novels, musical compositions, artworks, advertising materials, and all kinds of media texts. It is not an option in interpretation; it is something we are inclined to extract from a text or form. For example, the numbers 7 and 13 in Western culture invariably connote 'fortune,' 'destiny,' 'bad luck,' and so on, in addition to their denotata as signs for specific quantities. Connotata are hardly secondary and dismissible interpretations. They have real-world consequences. This is evidenced, for instance, by the fact that high-rise buildings in our society typically do not label the 'thirteenth floor' as such, but rather as the 'fourteenth,' in order to avoid the possibility of inviting the bad fortune associated connotatively with the number 13 to the building and its residents.

Abstract concepts are particularly high in connotative content. In 1957, the psychologists Osgood, Suci, and Tannenbaum showed this by developing an investigative technique they called the *semantic differential*, which allowed them to flesh out the connotative (culture-specific) meanings that abstract concepts elicit. Subjects are posed a series of questions related to a particular concept – *Is X good or bad? Should Y be weak or strong?* etc. – which they rate on seven-point scales. Their ratings are then analysed statistically. Suppose that subjects are asked to rate the concept 'ideal father' in terms of the following: *Should the ideal father be flexible or stern in raising his children? Should the ideal father be modern or traditional in his approach to the family?* And so on. A subject who feels that fathers should be more 'stern' than 'flexible' would place a mark towards the *stern* end of the *flexible-stern* scale; one who feels that a president should be 'traditional' would place a mark towards the *traditional* end of the *modern-traditional* scale; and so on. By asking a large number of subjects to rate the father figure in this way, we would get a 'connotative profile' of fatherhood in terms of the

statistically significant variations in actual ratings that it evokes. Research utilizing the semantic differential has shown that the range of variations forms a culture-specific pattern. For example, the word *noise* turns out to be a highly emotional concept in Japanese culture, since Japanese subjects tend to rate it consistently at the ends of the scales presented to them; on the other hand, for Americans, who rate it in the mid-ranges of the same scales, it is a fairly neutral concept. Connotation is constrained by a series of factors, including cultural agreements as to what signs mean in certain situations. All signification (whether it is denotative or connotative) is a relational and associative process – that is, signs acquire their meanings not in isolation, but in relation to other signs and to the contexts in which they occur.

The terms denotation and connotation are somewhat analogous to philosopher Gottlob Frege's (1879) distinction between *reference* and *sense* and philosopher Rudolf Carnap's (1942) terms *intension* and *extension*. While there are subtle differences among these various terms, they are virtually synonymous:

reference = denotation = intension
sense   = connotation = extension

The first use of the denotation vs. connotation dichotomy is often credited to philosopher John Stuart Mill (1806–73), but it can be dated back to the medieval Scholastics, and in particular to William of Ockham (ca 1284–1347). Such scholars use the term connotation to mean the sum of the referents that a word bears. The American linguist Leonard Bloomfield introduced the distinction in linguistics in his influential 1933 book called *Language*, a distinction elaborated a little later by the Danish linguist Louis Hjelmslev (1961). Although Hjelmslev's elaboration is rather abstruse, it nevertheless had the practical effect of putting this basic distinction on the agenda of linguists and semioticians once and for all. Especially relevant is his characterization of connotation as a 'secondary semiotic system' for expressing subjective meanings and as an inbuilt feature of signs, not just a matter of individual choice.

Marcel Danesi

Bibliography

Bloomfield, Leonard. *Language*. New York: Holt, Rinehart, and Winston, 1933.

Carnap, Rudolf. *Introduction to Semantics*. Cambridge, MA: Harvard University Press, 1942.

Danesi, Marcel. *The Quest for Meaning: A Guide to Semiotic Theory and Practice*. Toronto: University of Toronto Press, 2007.

Eco, Umberto. *Semiotics and the Philosophy of Language*. Bloomington: Indiana University Press, 1984.

Frege, Gottlob. *Begiffsschrift eine der Aritmetischen nachgebildete Formelsprache des reinen Denkens*. Halle: Nebert, 1879.

Hjelmslev, Louis. *Prolegomena to a Theory of Language*. Madison: University of Wisconsin Press, 1961.

Osgood, Charles E., George J. Suci, and Percy H. Tannenbaum. *The Measurement of Meaning*. Urbana: University of Illinois Press, 1957.

Rigotti, Eddo, and Andrea Rocci. Denotation versus Connotation. *Encyclopedia of Languages and Linguistics*. 2nd ed. Oxford: Elsevier, 2006.

DERRIDA, JACQUES (1930–2004)

[See also: *Deconstruction*]

Jacques Derrida was a French philosopher, born in Algiers, Algeria, known mainly as the founder of the deconstruction movement, which has been influential in literary criticism and media studies. For Derrida, traditional philosophy has always been misguided in attempting to answer profound existential questions by assuming that language encodes ideas without distortion. Derrida saw philosophical discourse as entangled, circular, and serving the particular interests of the philosopher. It was hardly a tool for gaining truth about

reality, which is elusive by its very nature. Deconstruction was his way of showing how actual words become entangled and deconstruct themselves in the process, producing meaningless garble.

Derrida was also critical of the concept of opposition in linguistics and semiotics, termed *différence* by Saussure (1916). He coined the term *différance* (spelled with an 'a') to indicate that the whole process of showing minimal differences between signs in order to glean meaning from them as itself a deconstructive process, because *différence* was a logocentric theoretical concoction, which rendered it useless. In pairs such as *day/night*, opposition theory would posit that *day* as the default concept, called 'unmarked,' and *night* as the 'marked' one, or the one that is defined in terms of *day*. Thus, we can say that *night* is an absence of *day*, but not vice versa. Problems emerge, however, with oppositions such as *male/female* and *self/other*, which encode biases, not just neutral *différences*. But Derrida has been criticized for missing, or ignoring, the fact that the choice of one or the other as the default concept would actually identify, not construct, the bias. Derrida (1977: 237) claimed that our oppositions deconstruct themselves; that is, they fall apart, revealing their biased 'exigencies' as he calls them:

In idealization, to an origin or to a 'priority' seen as simple, intact, normal, pure, standard, self-identical, in order *then* to conceive of derivation, complication, deterioration, accident, etc. All metaphysicians have proceeded thus: good before evil, the positive before the negative, the simple before the complex, the essential before the accidental, the imitated before the imitation, etc. This is not just *one* metaphysical gesture among others; it is *the* metaphysical exigency.

Derrida failed to see that oppositions can be, and often are, reversed. This has happened, for example, to the *young/old* opposition in Western society. In the nineteenth and early twentieth centuries, *old* was seen as the unmarked form in terms of social status. By the 1920s a marketplace youth culture emerged to make *young* the unmarked one. Today, being young and staying young for longer and longer periods is the accepted norm (Danesi 2002). Such reversals exist across the domain of cultural oppositions. They certainly do deconstruct themselves, as Derrida claimed, but in so doing they are reversing the social factors that led to their emergence in the first place.

Marcel Danesi

Bibliography

Danesi, Marcel. *Forever Young: The 'Teen-Aging' of Modern Culture.* Toronto: University of Toronto Press, 2002.

Derrida, Jacques. *Of Grammatology.* Trans. Gayatri Chakravorty Spivak. Baltimore: Johns Hopkins University Press, 1977.

– *Writing and Difference.* Chicago: University of Chicago Press, 1978.

Kamuff, Peggy, ed. *A Derrida Reader: Between the Blinds.* New York: Columbia University Press, 1991.

Saussure, Ferdinand de. *Cours de linguistique générale.* Paris: Payot, 1916.

DETECTIVE STORIES

[See also: *Adventure Stories; Crime Genre; Pulp Fiction*]

The detective story is an important fiction genre that is formulaic and follows certain conventions, though there are endless variations and permutations of the basic formula. There are two kinds of detectives: the 'tough-guy' detective, as exemplified by Sam Spade, the hero of Dashiell Hammet's *The Maltese Falcon,* and the 'classical' detective, as exemplified by Sherlock Holmes and more recently by Hercule Poirot, the hero of Agatha Christie's *Murder on the Orient Express.* In both kinds of detective stories, a fictional detective solves a mystery, usually involving one or more murders, through the use of deductive and inductive reasoning. According to the conventions of the genre, readers of detective stories are supposed to be given all the information needed to solve the crime but they do not recognize important clues, which are usually found in descriptions of characters and events and dialogue. So it is up to the detective, at the denouement of the story, to identify the criminal and show how he or she solved the crime.

Readers of mysteries usually compete with the detective in attempting to solve the mystery and figure out who the murderer is but usually are unable to do so, in part because they are given false leads (red herrings). That is why mysteries are also called 'whodunits.' Once the detective explains the solution, readers can then see that they missed important clues or made faulty inferences.

It is generally held that Edgar Allan Poe's story 'The Murders in the Rue Morgue,' featuring C. August Dupin, was the first fictional mystery story. This story, published in 1841, was followed by two other stories by Poe, 'The Mystery of Marie Roget' and 'The Purloined Letter,' which set the stage for the development of the modern detective story. Poe's Dupin was somewhat eccentric and following Poe's lead, many detectives, especially in the classical genre, have had curious interests and unusual personalities and lifestyles. We see these characteristics to an extreme in Arthur Conan Doyle's detective Sherlock Holmes, the first consulting detective, who is given a sidekick, Dr Watson, who lacks Holmes's brilliant mind and ability to unravel mysteries. It is usually Watson who recounts the stories, describing in considerable detail how Holmes used his incredible abilities of deduction and insight to understand the meaning of events that transpire in the story and solve the mystery.

There are any number of subgenres of the detective story, such as police procedurals and closed-door mysteries, and many other fictional genres often involve detection such as spy stories and science fiction stories. Another convention that mystery writers follow is that the murderer has to be one of the main characters, all of whom must have a sufficient motivation to kill the victim and thus be suspect. The psychiatrist Martin Grotjahn has suggested, in his book *Beyond Laughter: Humor and the Subconscious*, that mystery readers are reactivating repressed interest in matters that preoccupied them when they were children, such as sexual intercourse, menstruation, defloration, pregnancy, and birth. Mysteries, he adds, transform our earlier interest in sexuality and transform it into an interest in justice in the persona of the great detective.

A trip to any public library reveals that a relatively large percentage of its fiction section is devoted to detective stories. The detective story is also popular in other countries; detective novels have been translated from Russian, German, Dutch, Italian, Hebrew, and many other languages. The detective story has also been adopted to teach various subjects: Arthur Asa Berger's *Durkheim Is Dead: Sherlock Holmes Is Introduced to Sociological Theory*, about sociological theory, and Adrian Praetzellis's *Death by Theory: A Tale of Mystery and Archaeological Theory*, on archaeological theory, are used in courses on these subjects in colleges and universities.

Arthur Asa Berger

Bibliography

Berger, Arthur Asa. *Postmortem for a Postmodernist*. Walnut Creek: AltaMira Press, 1997.
– *Durkheim Is Dead: Sherlock Holmes Is Introduced to Sociological Theory*. Walnut Creek, CA: AltaMira Press, 2003.
Grotjahn, Martin. *Beyond Laughter: Humor and the Subconscious*. New York: McGraw-Hill, 1966.
Nevins, Jr., Francis M., ed. *The Mystery Writer's Art*. Bowling Green, OH: Bowling Green University Popular Press, 1970.
Praetzellis, Adrian. *Death by Theory: A Tale of Mystery and Archaeological Theory*. Walnut Creek, CA: AltaMira Press, 2000.

DIALECT

[See also: *Language; Media and Communication*]

The term *dialect*, as used in linguistics, refers to any variant of a language as it manifests itself in different regions where the language is spoken or along social lines or registers. If the variation is regional, then the dialect is called *geographical*; if it is social, then it is called *social* or sometimes *sociolectal*. Many dialects develop because of divisions within a society, such as those related to economic class and religion. For example, the inhabitants of Martha's Vineyard, in Massachusetts, adopted particular vowel pronunciations to distinguish themselves from people vacationing on the island.

The dividing line between *dialect* and *language* is a thin one. The Romance languages – French, Spanish, Portuguese, Romanian, Friulian, Sardinian, Rumansh – were dialectal variants of Latin, spoken in regions that gradually achieved nationhood at some point after the demise of the Roman Empire. The dialects of Latin spoken in the regions were raised to the status of *national languages*, because they were used in territories that achieved political autonomy. Subsequent variations within each new speech community arose from geographic factors, that is, from the physical separation of speakers from the centre or centres where the 'prestige dialect' was spoken.

The term *dialect* derives from Greek *dialektos* meaning 'speech,' referring to the actual ways in which people commonly used the Greek language for everyday communication. These typically varied from a linguistic 'norm' or 'standard' that was set up for official use to variants forms that characterized certain situations or were used in certain regions. So, in a fundamental way, dialects are 'natural' forms of language, while standard or national languages are forms that have been refined to produce communal usage norms. For example, the French spoken in Paris is considered the standard form of French. Those who do not speak Parisian French are perceived to be speaking a dialect. But originally, Parisian French was itself a dialect of spoken Latin. The reasons why it achieved 'norm status' have a long history behind them that has nothing to do with any intrinsic quality in the dialect. This is true of all other language situations. In Italy, the emergence of Florentine Tuscan as the basis for the standard language was tied to its use by great medieval writers (Dante, Petrarch, Boccaccio) who happened to live in Florence and thus who used Florentine in their writings because it was their native tongue. People from all over Italy wanted to read the works of the Florentine writers. Tuscan was thus guaranteed a wide reading audience and, consequently, spread throughout the peninsula, gradually becoming the norm for developing a standard language.

Linguists determine if two languages are related dialectally by using what they call, loosely, *mutual intelligibility*. If the differential types of speech used by two speakers are not intelligible to both, then the types are classified as different languages; if they are intelligible, then they are considered to be dialects of the same language. As Chambers and Trudgill (1998: 3) aptly put it, this 'has the benefit of characterizing dialects as subparts of a language and of providing a criterion for distinguishing between one language and another.' There are, however, problems with this criterion, because many levels of mutual intelligibility exist (even among unrelated languages), and linguists must decide at what level speech differences are mutually intelligible or not. However, in practice most can tell whether or not two speech forms are related.

To study dialects, linguists have developed a number of specific tools. One is the *dialect atlas*. As its name indicates, it is a collection of maps of specific regions, each one showing the actual form a word or phrase takes on in the regions surveyed.

The first to construct such maps was a German schoolteacher named Georg Wenker in 1876. He mailed a list of sentences written in standard German to other schoolteachers in northern Germany, asking them to transcribe them into their local dialects. In this way, Wenker compiled over 45,000 questionnaires, each containing 40 sentences, allowing him to produce two sets of maps highlighting different linguistic features. He bound the maps together under the title *Sprachatlas des Deutschen Reichs*. Wenker's questionnaire method remains the basis for conducting dialect surveys to this day, even though the technology and sophistication for gathering the data have, of course, evolved considerably. Dialectologists now send observers into the designated region(s) to conduct and record interviews, or else they conduct the interviews through online sites. This fieldwork approach started with the Swiss linguist Jules Gilliéron (1854–1926) in the latter part of the nineteenth century. Gilliéron devised a questionnaire consisting of 1,500 common vocabulary items that his primary fieldworker, Edmond Edmont (1848–1926), used to compile the relevant data from various parts of France. From 1896 to 1900, Edmont was able to collect and transcribe 700 interviews at 639 locations. The results were published as the *Atlas linguistique de la France* between 1902 and in 1910. Today, in addition to questionnaire techniques, dialectologists have at their disposal software that allows them to analyse large amounts of data quickly and to produce linguistic maps with a great degree of accuracy.

Not all linguistic variants are considered to be dialects. The terms *pidgin* and *creole*, for instance, refer to different kinds of variant languages (Holm 1989). A pidgin emerges to make communication possible between two or more groups that speak different languages, one of which is the dominant language and thus the basis for the pidgin. Pidgins, such as the Pidgin English of the Solomon Islands of New Guinea, typically simplify the grammar of the dominant language. This is evident in such patterns as the use of infinitives in place of conjugated verbs and the reduction or elimination of various determiners (articles, demonstratives, and so on). If the language of a pidgin-using community spreads and becomes part of the society, then it is called a *creole*, from the Spanish word *criollo*, meaning 'native to the place.' The children of such people are then its first true native speakers. Creole speakers develop their own identities and cultural forms, through the new language. The creole music of Louisiana, for instance, is now viewed as an important artistic musical idiom. Creoles are testimony to the powerful instinct in humans to create language on the basis of need and then to use it creatively.

Dialects that encode social differentiation are called social dialects or sociolects. If they are associated with educated and high-class speakers, they are considered to be part of 'good language'; if not, they are viewed as 'slang.' A slang expression may be a new word, or it may be an old word with a new meaning. People use slang more often in speaking than in writing, and more often with friends than with strangers. But this is changing in the world of text messages and online communications, where sociolectal differences are breaking down. In fact, the use of 'high' language is being restricted more and more to specific registers and social domains. Many slang expressions become colloquialisms, expressions used in everyday conversation, and which quickly become part of the norm. Words and expressions such as *jock, cool, loony, chick, dude, sloshed, chill out, 24/7*, among many others, originated as slang forms.

Typically, social dialects reflect different emphases and roles in diverse societies. In traditional Japanese culture, for example, the word for 'stomach' is *hara* among men, but *onaka* among women, probably alluding to the fact that, biologically, the two stomachs are different. Similarly, in Koasati (an indigenous language spoken in Louisiana), men say *lawawhol* to refer to 'lifting,' while women say *lakawhos*, perhaps imply-

ing that the lifting abilities of the two genders are different. People are highly sensitive to such differential details in speech. A classic study by American linguist William Labov (1967) brings this out. Labov made tape recordings of the conversations of New York City residents of different ethnic backgrounds and social classes. One of the features that stood out in the recordings was the use of /r/ after vowels in such words as *bird, tired, beer,* and *car*. He found that an '/r/-less' pronunciation was perceived to be old-fashioned and, thus, of low prestige. The highest occurrence of the pronunciation of /r/ was in young people aged 8 to 19. In a subsequent study (1972), he was able to link this pronunciation pattern of /r/ in New York City to social mobility. Simply put, those aspiring to move from a lower class to a higher one attached great prestige to the way (or style) in which the /r/ was pronounced.

A decade before Labov's work, John Fischer interviewed a group of elementary schoolchildren in 1958, finding that the children often alternated between two pronunciations of the present participle verb suffix -*ing*: *reading* vs. *readin'*. The choice was related to the gender, social background, personality, and mood of the children. If the girls came from families with an above-average income, and had dominating or assertive personalities, they used the *reading* pronunciation. However, as the children became more relaxed, all of them, regardless of background, were more likely to use the *readin'* pronunciation.

Marcel Danesi

Bibliography

Chambers, Jack K., and Peter Trudgill. *Dialectology*. Cambridge: Cambridge University Press, 1998.

Fischer, John L. Social Influences in the Choice of a Linguistic Variant. *Word* 14 (1958): 47–57.

Holm, John A. *Pidgins and Creoles*. Cambridge: Cambridge University Press, 1989.

Labov, William. The Effect of Social Mobility on a

Linguistic Variable. In *Explorations in Sociolinguistics*, ed. S. Lieberson, 23–45. Bloomington: Indiana University Research Center in Anthropology, Linguistics and Folklore, 1967.
– *Language in the Inner City*. Philadelphia: University of Pennsylvania Press, 1972.

DIALOGUE

[See also: *Bakhtin, Mikhail Mikhailovich; Discourse; Discourse Theory*]

The term *dialogue* has a long history in several disciplines, from philosophy and education to modern-day cultural theory. Basically, it means an exchange of information, ideas, or opinions in some structured and object-oriented way between interlocutors.

The link between dialogue and knowledge was established in antiquity by teachers and philosophers. The dialogue format, as a question-and-answer exchange, was first introduced into Western philosophy by Socrates. He believed in the superiority of the dialogue over writing, spending hours in the public places of Athens, engaging in dialogical exchanges with anyone who would comply. The so-called 'Socratic method' is still as valid today as it was then. Socrates claimed that only through dialogue do we come to understand our own ignorance, because by its very nature it entices us to investigate truth further. Socrates inveigled his partner to consider certain beliefs until a contradiction was reached with the disputed belief indirectly. In this way, the interlocutor was made to accept the untenability of his or her initial belief or hypothesis and to consider other hypotheses, which are then, in turn, also subjected to the same process of dispute. Most of the dialogues, therefore, are not resolved – as in real life.

Dialogue goes on all the time in human life, manifesting itself in conversations, chats, and even silently within ourselves. The Russian psychologist Lev Vygotsky (1962, 1978) showed that 'internal dialogue' surfaces early in life as a spontaneous means for grasping the meaning of the information in the world. When children speak to themselves during play, they are engaging in true investigative dialogue, testing out ideas as they are imprinted in the phonic substance of words.

It was Plato, Socrates' pupil, who introduced the use of dialogue as a form of philosophical inquiry. Except for the *Apology*, all of Plato's writings are constructed in dialogical form (to greater or lesser degrees). After Plato, the dialogue was relegated primarily to the literary domain, although it is said that Aristotle (Plato's pupil) wrote several philosophical dialogues in Plato's style, none of which, however, have survived. The dialogue was revived by early Christian writers, such as St Augustine, Boethius, and somewhat later Peter Abelard. However, under the powerful influence of Scholasticism, it was replaced by the more formal and concise genre of the *summa*, or synthetic treatise, of which the most widely known is the one by St Thomas Aquinas.

The dialogue was reintroduced into philosophical inquiry by various European philosophers in the late seventeenth century. For example, in 1688, the French philosopher Nicolas Malebranche published his *Dialogues on Metaphysics and Religion*, contributing to the genre's revival. The Irish prelate George Berkeley employed it as well in his 1713 work *Three Dialogues between Hylas and Philonous*. Perhaps the most important use of the dialogue in scientific writing was by Galileo in his *Dialogue Concerning the Two Chief World Systems* of 1632. Such uses of the dialogue have been abandoned since the Enlightenment. The dialogue has given way in the sciences to the treatise, the essay, and similar prose forms of writing.

The modern-day intellectual who expanded the concept of dialogue to encompass social interaction was the late Russian philosopher and literary scholar Mikhail Bakhtin (1895–1975). For a long period of time his ideas remained virtually unknown outside of Russia. Through English translations of his works in the 1980s and 1990s (Bakhtin 1981, 1986, 1990, 1993a, 1993b), Bakhtin's ideas are now being applied to all kinds of fields (for example, Clark and Holquist 1984; Ponzio 1986, 1993, 2006; Ponzio and Petrilli 2005; Holquist 1990; Morson and Emerson 1990; Vice 1997; Farmer 1998; Hirschkop 1999).

For Bakhtin the dialogue allows people to give voice to their consciousness and to understand that there exist three main forms of self-awareness and identity – 'I-for-myself,' 'I-for-the-Other,' and 'Other-for-me.' The first one is an unreliable source of identity. It is through the 'I-for-the-Other' form that we develop a true sense of who we are, because it incorporates the views of others into our models of ourselves. Conversely, the 'Other-for-me' perspective is the way in which others construct their own self-identity. Identity, in this Bakhtinian framework, is a shared form of consciousness; it can never be 'finalized,' that is, completely understood, known, or labelled, as is the tendency of social scientists to do. People change and never really fully reveal themselves as they truly are.

Marcel Danesi

Bibliography

Bakhtin, Mikhail M. *The Dialogic Imagination: Four Essays*. Austin: University of Texas Press, 1981.
– *Speech Genres and Other Late Essays*. Austin: University of Texas Press, 1986.
– *Art and Answerability*. Austin: University of Texas Press, 1990.
– *Rabelais and His World*. Bloomington: Indiana University Press, 1993a.
– *Toward a Philosophy of the Act*. Austin: University of Texas Press, 1993b.
Clark, Katerina, and Michael Holquist. *Mikhail Bakhtin*. Cambridge: Harvard University Press, 1984.
Farmer, Frank, ed. *Landmark Essays on Bakhtin, Rhetoric, and Writing*. Mahwah, NJ: Hermagoras Press, 1998.
Hirschkop, Ken. *Mikhail Bakhtin: An Aesthetic for Democracy*. Oxford: Oxford University Press, 1999.
Holquist, Michael. *Dialogism: Bakhtin and His World*. London: Routledge, 1990.
Morson, Gary Saul, and Caryl Emerson. *Mikhail Bakhtin: Creation of a Prosaics*. Stanford, CA: Stanford University Press, 1990.
Ponzio, Augusto. *Dialogo sui dialoghi*. Ravenna: Longo, 1986.
– *Signs, Dialogue and Ideology*. Amsterdam: John Benjamins, 1993.
– *The Dialogic Nature of Sign*. Ottawa: Legas, 2006.
Ponzio, Augusto, and Susan Petrilli. *Semiotics Unbounded: Interpretive Routes in the Open Network of Signs*. Toronto: University of Toronto Press, 2005.
Vice, Sue. *Introducing Bakhtin*. Manchester: Manchester University Press, 1997.
Vygotsky, Lev S. *Thought and Language*. Cambridge, MA: MIT Press, 1962.
– *Mind in Society*. Cambridge, MA: Cambridge University Press, 1978.

DIGITAL DIVIDE

[See also: *Convergence; Internet; Media Literacy*]

With the onset of the internet age beginning in the mid-1990s, many national governments and international organizations started viewing the new information and communication technology (ICT) as a vehicle for achieving wider socio-economic development, believing that it could be used to address problems in the fields of education, health, rural development, poverty alleviation, and employment equity. According to the G7/G8 Summit in 2000 (Okinawa): 'ICT may be applied to almost every problem in probably all sectors … the highest social application of ICT is *poverty alleviation*.' Similarly, the Millennium Declaration, adopted by the United Nations in 2000, stated: 'ICTs can help alleviate poverty, improve the delivery of education and health care, make government services more accessible, and much more.' The United Nations Development Program

(UNDP), the World Bank, and the International Telecommunications Union (ITU) have since been promoting the spread of ICT, particularly in developing countries.

While acknowledging the benefits of ICT, governments and international organizations soon came to fear that ICT could actually widen the gap between 'information-rich' and 'information-poor' peoples, creating a new division called the 'digital divide.' It is argued that this could have serious consequences and result in new forms of socio-economic inequalities if governments fail to take appropriate policy measures. Many nations in both the developing and developed world have since formulated ICT policies to inhibit this digital divide from becoming a reality and to ensure that ICT benefits one and all. Some examples are: Bermuda's 'Information Island of the 21st century'; Singapore's 'Intelligent Island'; the UK's 'IT for All' and 'Closing the Digital Divide: Information and Communication Technology in Deprived Areas'; India's 'Information Technology for Masses'; Denmark's 'dk21' and 'IT Universities'; and South Africa's 'Electronic Government: The Digital Future.'

The Digital Future of ICT for Development (ICT4D) has been used for e-governance to improve the quality of citizen participation, accountability, and transparency. The IDRC- (International Development Research Centre) funded project on local e-governance has undertaken work in ten African countries and has found better modalities for staff efficiency, user information, and rapid accommodation and service delivery and provisions. ICT can promote e-governance to rectify the inequities from human governance, or h-governance. This provides a compelling reason to bridge the digital divide rather than retain or sustain it.

Angathevar Baskaran and Mammo Muchie

Bibliography

Baskaran, Angathevar, and Mammo Muchie, eds. *Bridging the Digital Divide: Innovation Systems for ICT in Brazil, China, India, Thailand and Southern Africa.* London: Adonis-Abbey, 2006.

Flor, Alexander G. *ICT and Poverty: The Indisputable Link.* Paper presented to Third Asia Development Forum on Regional Economic Cooperation in Asia and the Pacific. Bangkok: Asian Development Bank, 11–14 June 2001.

Mansell, Robin. From Digital Divides to Digital Entitlements in Knowledge Societies. *Current Sociology* 50, no. 3 (2002): 407–26.

Selwyn, Neil, and Keri Facer. *Beyond the Digital Divide: Rethinking Digital Inclusion for the 21st Century.* Futurelab, 2007. www.futurelab.org.uk/openingeducation.

DIGITAL MEDIA

[See also: *Analogue Media; Medium; Transmission Modes*]

Digital media generally refers to developments in electronic technologies used for the production, storage, distribution, and reception of specific forms of mass communication. As an extension of computer technology that uses binary numeric codes to operate programs and represent data, the term *digital* refers to the numeric methods of processing, representing, and transmitting numerical data that will be converted to more accessible communication and information.

To the extent that media consumers cannot directly receive and interpret the rapid electronic processing of numerically coded data, digital media depend on the technological conversion of digital data to physical or analogue media. The term *analogue* refers to the physical nature of visible and audible *media* representations. The notion of analogue media then refers to a physical record of some form of communication used to preserve or reproduce a representation that is similar to the original presence of the perceptible source material such as words, sounds, and images. Limited to sense perceptions such as the capacities to hear and see the actual physical world, humans are dependent on technologies to convert digital media data back into an analogue form in order to be effectively usable. Examples of digital media include the internet, World Wide Web, global positioning systems, compact discs, cellphones, digital video, digital audio, and digital animation. Each of these digital technologies functions as a communication medium.

Media (plural of the noun *medium*) generally refers to the necessary means of representing thoughts or ideas originating in the mind of a message sender in a physical form so that they can be perceived and subsequently used to communicate to a message receiver. The medium is the material means of communicating that can be used for storing or transmitting words, sounds, images, and ideas to be received through sense perception. The capacities to hear, feel, smell, taste, and see are necessary for apprehending the world and surviving, but media primarily exploit sight and sound to create communicative representations. Analogue media use the actual physical nature of sound and images to record, store, and transmit messages, ideas, information, and entertainment. Digital media specifically involve electronic media and have radically changed the overall processes of recording, storing, and transmitting communication data, but still must deliver an audible or visible form of communication.

Digital media have significant advantages over analogue media because they can be reproduced and transmitted with coded data rather than masses of physical materials. Digital media are faster and more economical to store, reproduce, and transmit. An entire newspaper or musical performance can be sent from one computer to another without cutting a tree to make paper, or producing ink to print, or producing plastic or vinyl polymer materials. Besides the expense of materials and manufacturing, multiple generations of copies of analogue media may lose quality while digital media are reproduced by copying coded numerical data that are unaffected by the process.

Technologies continue to be developed so that digital media can be transferred extremely rapidly over great distances, making global communication fast and economically available to more people. Cellphones, the internet and World Wide Web, global positioning systems, digital radio and television, and other new developments are affecting business, politics, and everyday life. Digital technologies have helped countries that lacked traditional analogue communication infrastructures to modernize quickly and take advantage of the newest innovations. Scientists, engineers, and business entrepreneurs are motivated to explore new innovations and encourage global use of digital communication systems. Digital media will continue developing and exploiting the speed and adaptability of electronic technologies using numerical codes for every kind of individual and mass communication.

Elliot Gaines

Bibliography

Hafner, Katie, and Matthew Lyon. *Where Wizards Stay Up Late: The Origins of the Internet.* New York: Simon and Schuster, 1996.

Montgomery, Katherine C. *Generation Digital: Politics, Commerce, and Childhood in the Age of the Internet.* Cambridge, MA: MIT Press, 2007.

Slevin, James. *The Internet and Society.* London: Polity, 2000.

DIGLOSSIA

[See also: *Dialect*]

Speakers of all languages perceive some forms of speech as being 'higher' socially and culturally, and others as being 'lower.' These entail differences in pronunciation, grammar, and vocabulary which are perceived by people as differences in class, upbringing, education, and the like. Language, like dress, is a conveyor of identity and character. Different linguistic forms

Table 1

	High	Low
Greek	Katharévousa	Dhimotiki (Demotic)
Arabic	'al-fush (Classical)	'al-'ammiyah (Colloquial)
Swiss German	Hochdeutsch (High German)	Schweizerdeutsch (Low German)

and registers are tied to social perceptions and even to the ways in which some societies organize themselves. For example, at the top of the social ladder in Javanese society are the aristocrats, in the middle the townsfolk, and at the bottom the farmers. Appurtenance to any one of these levels brings along with it a distinct style of speech that identifies the speaker's location on the ladder. The top, or highest, register is used not only by aristocrats who do not know one another very well, but also by members of the townsfolk if they are addressing a high government official. The middle register is used by townsfolk who are strangers to each other (or who do not know each other very well), and by peasants when addressing their social superiors. The lowest register, or style of speech, is used by peasants, or by an aristocrat or townsperson talking to peasants, and among friends. The latter is also the form of language used to speak to children.

The study of how language variation is perceived socially and what it means in terms of the speaker's identity is one of the central topics of modern-day dialectology. Within this field, the study of the relation between the socially perceived higher and lower forms of language comes under the rubric of *diglossia* – a term introduced into linguistics by the American linguist Charles Ferguson in 1959. Ferguson observed that societies tended to evaluate forms of speech, like forms of culture, as being of *high* or *low* prestige. The former is used for official, formal, religious, and scholarly purposes, and the latter for colloquial and various vernacular purposes. Ferguson noted, moreover, that the high form always had a strong literary tradition and that it

was never acquired as a native dialect, but introduced through formal education.

Ferguson studied situations in which there existed two markedly divergent varieties of a language, each employed in specific social ways. One of the varieties was the basis for ordinary conversations and interactions; the other was the basis for formal communication and writing. He called the former Low (L) and the latter High (H). Together, the two constitute a diglossic system. Diglossia turns out to be a widespread phenomenon. Some widely known examples are found in modern Greek, Arabic, and Swiss German as shown in Table 1.

In these societies, the functional distinction between H and L forms of speech is clear-cut and socially significant; in others it is not. H forms are used typically for writing, sermons, lectures, newscasts on television, poetry, science, and so on; these are learned in school. L forms are used instead in routine talk and communicative behaviour and in various informal contexts (including humour, cartoons, etc.). The H and L forms of language reveal differences in phonology, grammar, and vocabulary. For instance, there is a marked difference in the pronunciation of *Hochdeutsch* and *Schweizerdeutsch*, with each one evoking specific social perceptions associated with it. Some communities actually use only the H form, while others the L one, thus demarcating themselves linguistically and socially. There are three noun cases in classical Arabic, whereas colloquial Arabic does not have any. In Greece, there are many word pairs marked as either H or L, such as *ínos* (H) and *krasí* (L) for referring to 'wine.' In restaurants, only the H form is written on menus, while diners would ask for wine with the L word (see Trudgill 1983).

The H and L dichotomy is a functional one even in areas where situations such as those described above do not exist. It constitutes an index of identity and social solidarity. The H dialects are often believed by their speakers (and others) to be more beautiful and logical and thus more appropriate for aesthetic and various other social purposes. But diglossic situations tend to become unstable in the face of movements towards the adoption of a single standard. To quote Crystal (2010: 43):

> In such circumstances, there are arguments in favour of either H or L varieties becoming the standard. Supporters of H stress its link with the past, and its claimed excellence, and they contrast its unifying function with the diversity of local dialects. Supporters of L stress the need to have a standard which is close to the everyday thoughts and feelings of the people, and which is a more effective tool of communication at all levels. 'Mixed' positions, setting up a modified H or L, are also supported; and the steady emergence of L-based standards has been noted in China, Haiti, and several other areas. In Greece, the diglossic era came to an end in 1976, when the government banned Katharévousa in schools and promoted Dhimotiki in official texts.

Diglossia is found throughout the world. Today, it is connected to identity and differentiation. In England, the pronunciation of /h/, as in *hat*, conveys social information. Members of certain social groups often adopt a particular pronunciation of /h/ as a way of distinguishing themselves from other social groups. Similarly, the inhabitants of Martha's Vineyard, in Massachusetts, have adopted particular vowel pronunciations to distinguish themselves from people vacationing on the island.

Sara Maida-Nicol

Bibliography

Crystal, Davis. *The Cambridge Encyclopedia of Language*. 3rd ed. Cambridge: Cambridge University Press, 2010.

Ferguson, Charles. 'Diglossia.' *Word* 15 (1959): 325–40.

Fishman, Joshua A., Robert L. Cooper, and Roxana Ma. *Bilingualism in the Barrio*. Bloomington: Indiana University Press, 1971.

Haugen, Einar. The Stigmata of Bilingualism. In *The Ecology of Language: Essays by Einar Haugen*, ed. S.A. Dil, 307–24. Stanford: Stanford University Press, 1972.

Hudson, Alan, and Joshua Fishman. Focus on Diglossia. *International Journal of the Sociology of Language* 157 (2002): entire issue.

Trudgill, Peter. *Sociolinguistics*. Harmondsworth: Penguin, 1983.

DISCOURSE

[See also: *Cognitive Language Studies; Conversation Analysis; Discourse Theory; Narrative; Speech Act Theory*]

Discourse is the use of language for social reasons. The study of discourse comes under various rubrics, including *pragmatics, discourse analysis,* or *discourse theory*. The basic idea in all of them is to study the meanings of linguistic forms in their contexts of use, as opposed to the study of the meanings contained within the linguistic forms themselves. Although the informal study of discourse existed already in late nineteenth-century linguistics, its systematic study started in the 1970s, when British philosopher Paul Grice (1975) introduced the notion that interlocutors make the assumption that anything spoken in a specific social context is intended to be relevant (whether it is true or not), and the American linguist Dell Hymes (1971, 1972) introduced the notion of *communicative competence* to describe a speaker's ability to use language meaningfully in communicative settings.

The notion of *register* is central in all models of discourse. Register refers to language forms that relate to degree of formality of usage. These identify the communicative purpose, the social context, and the status of the speakers. As the linguist Martin Joos argued in a 1967 book titled *The Five Clocks of English*, we unconsciously use different kinds of registers at specific times because of the social conditions associated with them. For example, in the morning our speech is informal when interacting with family members, while at work the register varies from formal (with a superior) to informal (with a work companion), and so on.

Another common notion in discourse analysis is that of *speech act* (Austin 1962). A speech act is a verbal form (word, expression, etc.) that replaces or elicits a physical (or other kind of) action in a socially appropriate fashion. 'Be careful!' for instance, has the same kind of effect as putting a hand in front of someone to block him or her from doing something carelessly (among other things). The statement 'Get out of here!' has the same effect as marching someone out the door. The central idea in speech act theory is that language structures are sensitive to situational variables and entail agency relations (actors, actions, and so on):

(1) Don't do that, you clown!
(2) It is best that you not do that!

Generally, (1) would be spoken by someone who is on intimate terms with an interlocutor; while (2) would be uttered by someone who is on formal terms – (1) is abrasive and emotionally charged; (2) is evasive and emotionally neutral. The act inherent in both is the same one (not doing something), but the speech form used also provides social information. However, if (1) involves conflict or emotional clash, then it might occur in formal contexts; (2) could also be construed ironically and thus be used in informal contexts.

As Robin Lakoff (1975) has observed, speakers regularly refrain from saying what they mean in many situations in the service of a hidden goal of politeness in its broadest sense, that is, to fulfil what has been called a *phatic* function. The following snippet of conversation is typical of how this function often manifests itself in English discourse:

Speaker A:	Hi, how are you?
Speaker B:	Great. See ya' later.
Speaker A:	OK!

Speaker A's question is not intended literally. It is used as a formulaic mode of contact, albeit with a well-wishing subtext built into it. This is understood by B, whose answer ignores the literal meaning. If B had said something such as 'I am not well,' then the conversation would have taken a completely different turn, since its structure was not perceived as phatic by B or else B wanted to provide information of a certain kind.

As the foregoing discussion suggests, the rules of language are intertwined with the rules of discourse. In his ground-breaking study of communicative competence, Dell Hymes (1971) identified eight basic factors that shape the language-communication interface in discourse. He named each one so that its initial letter would be a letter in the word *speaking*:

S = *setting* and *scene*: the time, place, and psychological setting
P = *participants*: the speaker, listener, audience involved in a speech act
E = *ends*: the desired or expected outcome
A = *act sequence*: how form and content are delivered
K = *key*: the mood or spirit (serious, ironic, jocular, etc.) of the speech act
I = *instrumentalities*: the dialect or linguistic variety used by the speech community
N = *norms*: conventions or expectations about volume, tone, rate of delivery, etc.
G = *genres*: different types of performance (joke, formal speech, sermon, etc.)

Work on discourse has proliferated since Hymes's model. The list below includes some of the main categories used today in the study of discourse:

(1) *Instrumental*: discourse used to satisfy various needs: 'May I have some sugar please?'
(2) *Regulatory*: discourse intended to control others: 'Please shut the window!'
(3) *Interactional*: discourse with no actual meanings as such, but aiming simply to maintain social ties and relations, filling in blanks or gaps in a conversation, making contact, and so on: 'Hi, how's it going?' This has also been termed *phatic* (as discussed above).
(4) *Personal*: discourse used as a channel of emotional release or intentionality: 'Ouch!' 'Hey, what are you doing?'
(5) *Heuristic*: discourse intended to gain information: 'What's that called?' 'Can you explain that notion to me?'
(6) *Imaginative*: discourse intended to convey unique ideas creatively: 'Time flies as they say.'
(7) *Representational*: language aiming to represent or classify things – 'animals' vs. 'objects,' 'liquids' vs. 'solids,' and so on.
(8) *Performative*: discourse used in rituals and performances (magic, prayers, etc.).
(9) *Socialization*: discourse used to indicate connection to a society, community, or group (jargon, slang, colloquialisms, etc.). Speaking in certain ways, according to a certain style, etc. is intended to provide access to groups or communities. Belonging implies knowledge of how to utilize specific linguistic cues.

A particularly interesting example of discourse is oath taking. The judicial oath, for instance, is taken by a witness in a court of law who swears that all of his or her statements will be true. Often the witness must lay a hand on a religious text while taking the oath, connecting the linguistic function to the sacred dimension. This means, in effect, that the person is making a declara-tion through God. Oaths reveal a deeply entrenched belief that language has magical or sacred origins. Any infringement of this belief is seen as a dishonest act. A person who takes an oath in court and then makes a dishonest statement while under oath will be declared guilty of perjury, a crime that is punishable by a fine or a jail sentence.

Marcel Danesi

Bibliography

Andersch, Elizabeth G., Lorin C. Staats, and Robert N. Bostrom. *Communication in Everyday Use*. New York: Holt, Rinehart and Winston, 1969.

Austin, John L. *How to Do Things with Words*. Cambridge, MA: Harvard University Press, 1962.

Bonvillain, Nancy. *Language, Culture, and Communication: The Meaning of Messages*. Upper Saddle River, NJ: Prentice-Hall, 2003.

Brown, Penelope, and Steven C. Levinson. *Politeness: Some Universals in Language Usage*. Cambridge: Cambridge University Press, 1989.

Bühler, Karl. *Sprachtheorie: Die Darstellungsfunktion der Sprache*. Jena: Fischer, 1934.

Cherwitz, Richard, and James Hikins. *Communication and Knowledge: An Investigation in Rhetorical Epistemology*. Columbia: University of South Carolina Press, 1986.

Cutting, Joan. *Pragmatics and Discourse*. London: Routledge, 2002.

Dance, Frank. *Human Communication Theory*. New York: Holt, Rinehart and Winston, 1967.

Edwards, Derek. *Discourse and Cognition*. London: Sage, 1997.

Fairclough, Norman. *Discourse and Social Change*. London: Blackwell, 1992.

– *Critical Discourse Analysis: The Critical Study of Language*. London: Longman, 1995.

Firth, J.R. *Papers in Linguistics: 1934–1951*. Oxford: Oxford University Press, 1957.

Gill, Ann. *Rhetoric and Human Understanding*. Prospect Heights, IL: Waveland, 1994.

Goffman, Erving. *The Presentation of Self in Everyday Life*. Garden City, NY: Doubleday, 1959.

Grice, Paul. Logic and Conversation. In *Syntax*

and Semantics, ed. P. Cole and J. Morgan, vol. 3: 41–58. New York: Academic, 1975.

Halliday, M.A.K. *Introduction to Functional Grammar.* London: Arnold, 1985.

Hymes, Dell. *On Communicative Competence.* Philadelphia: University of Pennsylvania Press, 1971.

– Models in the Interaction of Language and Social Life. In *Directions in Sociolinguistics: The Ethnography of Communication*, ed. J. Gumperz and D. Hymes. New York: Holt, Rinehart and Winston, 1972.

Joos, Martin. *The Five Clocks of English.* New York: Harcourt, Brace and World, 1967.

Malinowski, Bronislaw. The Problem of Meaning in Primitive Languages. In *The Meaning of Meaning*, ed. C.K. Ogden and I.A. Richards. New York: Harcourt, Brace and World, 1923.

Saussure, Ferdinand de. *Cours de linguistique générale.* Paris: Payot, 1916.

Searle, John R. *Speech Acts: An Essay in the Philosophy of Language.* Cambridge: Cambridge University Press, 1969.

– A Classification of Illocutionary Acts. *Language in Society* 5 (1976): 1–23.

Tannen, Deborah. *Talking Voices.* Cambridge: Cambridge University Press, 1989.

– *Framing in Discourse.* Oxford: Oxford University Press, 1993.

Van Dijk, Teun., ed. *Discourse as Social Interaction.* London: Sage, 1997.

DISCOURSE THEORY

[See also: *Bakhtin, Mikhail Mikhailovich; Discourse; Speech Act Theory*]

The term *discourse*, as used in *discourse theory*, refers to language use in a social context. There are, however, two different ways of using the term. Both are important in order to understand the nature of the discourse theories that are developed and applied in various areas of the communication sciences today. In its basic meaning *discourse* can refer to a *speech* or to a *text*, that is, to an instance of language use spoken or written. In linguistics, where the term originates, discourse is used in particular to refer to the organization of whole texts or utterances as well as to intermediate, relatively autonomous verbal communicative units larger than a sentence or clause. Therefore the study of discourse is the study of language beyond the sentence.

In linguistics, the importance of studying discourse was advocated as early as the 1920s by the Russian linguist and literary scholar Mikhail M. Bakhtin, who anticipated many key concepts of current discourse theories, in particular in the works he wrote with his associate Valentin N. Voloshinov. In contrast to Ferdinand de Saussure's focus on language as a stable system of signs (Saussure being the founder of modern linguistic method), abstracted from the concrete instances of language use, Bakhtin saw the social event of verbal interaction through dialogue as the essence of language and how it has evolved. Bakhtin's ideas remained all but forgotten for several decades, and despite the work of other important precursors, such as Phillip Wegener (1885/1991), Leo Spitzer (1922), Karl Bühler (1934), Emile Benveniste (1966), Bronislaw Malinowski (1922), Zellig Harris (1960), and Kenneth Pike (1971), the study of discourse remained stagnant until the late 1960s. In tandem with a 'pragmatic turn' in linguistics, inspired by the work of philosophers such as John L. Austin (1960), Paul Grice (1975), and John R. Searle (1969), discourse analysis emerged as a proper subfield of linguistics. Most discourse theories share with pragmatics the idea that the use of language is a social action designed to bring about changes in institutional social realities as well as in interpersonal relationships.

As used today, *discourse* can also refer to the particular way in which language is used by a certain social group, community, institution, class, ethnic group, subculture, ideology, age generation, and so on. This is why one can refer to 'the discourse of economists,' 'the discourse of the liberals/conservatives,' 'corporate discourse,' or the 'discourse of baby boomers' versus 'the discourse of generation X,' and so forth.

Such uses of the word imply something that is typical, recurrent, and characteristic (both at the level of content and at the level of form) in the speech of certain people or communities. In turn, the various 'discourses' reveal the values, practices, and social rules of the speakers. Such discourses are typically characterized by *keywords* (and *key phrases*) understood as words (and phrases) that appear with significant frequency in the speech acts of the discourse users (Stubbs 2010). It is this meaning of the term that has become popular in the social sciences, a trend that started with the work of French historian and philosopher Michel Foucault (1971). But it was Bakhtin who foreshadowed this trend, especially with his notions of *speech genre* and *intertextuality* (see below). Following Scollon and Scollon (2001), it is perhaps more appropriate to use the term *discourse system* rather than just *discourse* in this case. According to Scollon and Scollon (2001) discourse systems are characterized by a *jargon* shared by the members of the group, by specific ways of behaving, by the adoption of a particular ideology, and by peculiar forms of interpersonal relationships.

Three kinds of *discourse theories* can now be identified:

(1) theories that explain how discourse works, focusing on how people use language in social interaction, in general, or within specific social contexts (families, schools, private corporations, universities, the media);

(2) theories that use textual or conversational data to determine how the *discourse system* is used in its social contexts, and how stable repeated instances of language use contributes, maintains, or defines the relevant social realities (interpersonal relationships, behaviours within enterprises and other organizations, media, cultural communities, ethnic groups, etc.); and

(3) theories that use the notion of discourse as a vehicle to get to the basis of social forms, behaviours, ideologies, etc. –

gender as discourse, race as discourse, corporate strategy as discourse, linguistic theory as discourse, epidemiology as discourse, displacement as discourse, etc. The recurring phrase 'X *as discourse*' is meant to stress the fact that a certain speech phenomenon is the product of unconscious processes of social construction and ideological reproduction influenced by power relations. Typically these processes are 'invisible' (in part) to the social actors involved, who tend to perceive them as more 'natural' than they really are.

Type (1) theories focus mostly on discourse as understood within pragmatic linguistics; type (2) theories also focus on this type of discourse but also look at the broader uses of speech patterns within groups; type (3) theories fall outside the domain of linguistics proper, belonging more to cultural analysis. The distinction between types (1) and (2) is hard to establish at times, being mainly a matter of degree. Both aim to provide an account of the social characteristics of speech, rather than giving an in-depth consideration to the workings of discourse in any of its meanings.

Core Concepts

While discourse studies today are extremely diverse, there are some concepts that are shared by virtually all approaches to the phenomenon. Interestingly, these were all prefigured or originated in Bakhtin's work.

Context

The use of language in human interaction depends crucially on contextual factors. Bakhtin expresses this idea by saying that each utterance is made of two parts: the verbal part and a non-verbal, implicit, part. The latter has to be 'recovered' inferentially – through an *enthymeme*, as he calls it – starting from the non-verbal context of the utterance. This includes: (1) a spatial purview common to the participants; (2) a common knowledge and understanding of the circumstances, and (3) a shared *evaluation* of these circumstances (Voloshinov 1983). In modern discourse theory, the notion of *common ground* (Clark 1996) provides a sophisticated version of Bakhtin's idea of a shared context for understanding. The common ground notably includes some representation of what Grice (1975) calls the accepted common purpose or direction of the communicative interaction. Such an assumption of a shared purpose provides, in the Gricean framework, an essential guidance in working out the implied meanings conveyed by the non-verbal component of discourse. As argued convincingly by Levinson (1992), discourse is embedded in human activities that belong to recurrent and recognizable *activity types*, which assign precise roles to participants and greatly constrain the kind of utterances that may be exchanged. The textual correlate of these activity types is represented by discourse genres.

Discourse Genres

In Bakhtin's (1986) original conception, verbal communication cannot be explained outside of its connection with the immediate speech situation and the broader social context, and linguistics should consider the *forms of organization of whole utterances* as its primary object. This organization is based on forms called *genres*. Genres are typical patterns corresponding to recurring communication needs arising in a given sphere of human activity. Discourse genres can be written or spoken, dialogic or monologic. Some randomly chosen examples of discourse genres are: the encyclopedia entry, the research paper, the sermon, the news interview, the job interview, the editorial, the press conference, the university lecture, the medical consultation, the court sentence, a personal advertisement in a newspaper. All these have a compositional structure of their own that speakers use to

guide their expectations. Different genres are also characterized by specific stylistic choices. The term *register* is sometimes used to refer to these choices. *Genre analysis* is currently an important and flourishing area of modern discourse studies.

Intertextuality/Interdiscursivity

Contemporary discourses derive from previous ones. This means that discourses are *intertextual* or *interdiscursive*, since they invariably cite (directly or indirectly) previous speech through some strategy (mention, imitation, presupposition, rejoinder, explanation, critique, parody, etc.). Some texts, of religious, political, or aesthetic significance, can become *canonical* for a certain cultural community: the Bible, Shakespeare's plays, the Declaration of Independence, and Martin Luther King's 'I have a dream' speech are canonical texts. At another level, the notion of intertextuality is essential for understanding the functioning of discursive production in the media and popular culture in general, from television to comics (think of the importance of *seriality*, or of phenomena such as the *remake*, the *cross-over* or the *cameo*). The study of *intertextuality* is nowadays a burgeoning field of research within discourse studies in particular among anthropologically oriented discourse scholars.

Dialogism

A third principle informing Bakhtin's (1982) view of discourse is the *dialogical principle* (*dialogism*), which extends and complements the notion of intertextuality. According to this influential view, dialogue is fundamental for understanding any form of discourse. In fact, all kinds of discourse, monologic or dialogic, are always oriented towards an addressee and his/her explicit and implicit response. This is particularly apparent in *rhetorical discourse*, which is aimed at securing the consent of an addressee and is constructed to anticipate the addressee's reactions and objections. In modern discourse studies dialogism finds a counterpart in the principle of *sequentiality*, which is at the base of *conversation analysis* (CA) initiated by sociologists Sacks, Jefferson, and Schegloff (for example, 1995). According to this principle, the occurrence of certain actions in conversation (for instance, *questions*) entails matching utterances (*answers*) in the subsequent turn in a conversation. The two sequentially related utterances are said to form an *adjacency pair*. Dialogism is as important in the study of mediated communication as it is for the study of face-to-face dialogue. Traditional mass media texts (from advertisements to televised news) are essentially monological: yet they are rife with dialogical pretence and attempts to partially overcome this limitation (for example, *call-in shows*). The new electronic media, on the other hand, exploit hypertext and other interactive means, thus fostering novel forms of dialogue and leading to an even greater intertextuality.

Coherence

Besides strictly dialogical relations such as *question-answer*, Bakhtin used the dialogical principle also to explain how paragraphs in a monological discourse are linked to one another: a paragraph can be linked to the preceding one by answering a question, by anticipating possible objections, by clarifying seeming incongruencies, and so on (Voloshinov 1986). This notion anticipated current theories of *discourse coherence* which deal with the issue of how discourse segments cohere into meaningful wholes. A prominent approach to coherence, espoused by Mann and Thompson (1988), describes the internal structure of discourse in terms of *rhetorical relations* holding between sentences and between paragraphs. A discourse is coherent when relations of this kind can be congruously established between its units. These are typically pragmatic in nature and can be described in terms of the effects they evoke in the addressee by linking the discourse units

involved. Argumentation is a paramount example of such a rhetorical relation. It can be described as a complex speech act presenting one statement (argument) as supporting the credibility or acceptability of another statement (thesis or standpoint) in front of a real or imagined discussant.

Discourse Analysis

Another important characteristic shared by discourse theories is their close connection with the practice of discourse analysis, which, in turn, is based on the analysis of discourse data. It is particularly important to stress the use of data, since discourse theory is commonly seen as a highly abstract, 'philosophical' trend within the field of communication science. The role of data in the evolution of discourse theory has been enhanced by technological developments that have made it possible to access and store new kinds of speech data. These include the use of reliable and inexpensive recording technologies, which have made it possible to conduct in-depth analyses of spoken discourse, and the availability of digitally processed corpora of authentic spoken and written languages. This has allowed discourse analysts to use the quantitative techniques that help them determine the relationship between frequency of usage of certain forms (for instance, keywords), and the types of notions and social patterns these reveal.

Approaches to discourse also include a theoretically motivated set of analytical concepts dealing with the definitions of the basic units of discourse and providing theoretically based constraints on their sequencing and integration into higher-level communicative units. In fact, the names of major frameworks like *conversation analysis* (Sacks, Jefferson, and Schegloff 1995), *ethnography of communication* (Hymes 1974), *interactional socio-linguistics* (Gumperz 1982), and *systemic functional linguistics* (Halliday 1985; Martin 1992) indicate both a methodological approach to analysing discourse and a theoretical view of language use that informs it. Notwithstanding the great diversity of approaches, it seems that the reliance on the analysis of samples of actual discourse is a defining feature of current discourse analysis. At the same time, no simple analysis that relies on samples of actual discourse can count as true discourse analysis. This should always be based on theoretically valid categories.

Andrea Rocci

Bibliography

Austin, John L. *How to Do Things with Words.* Cambridge, MA: Harvard University Press, 1960.

Bakhtin, Mikhail M. *The Dialogic Imagination.* Trans. C. Emerson and M. Holquist. Austin: University of Texas Press, 1982.

– *Speech Genres and Other Late Essays.* Trans. Vern W. McGee. Ed. C. Emerson and M. Holquist. Austin: University of Texas Press, 1986.

Benveniste, Emile. *Problèmes de linguistique générale I.* Paris: Gallimard, 1966.

Bühler, Karl. *Sprachtheorie. Die Darstellungsfunktion der Sprache.* Stuttgart/New York: Gustav Fischer, 1934.

Clark, Herbert H. *Using Language.* Cambridge: Cambridge University Press, 1996.

Foucault, Michel. *The Archeology of Knowledge.* Trans. A.M. Sheridan Smith. New York: Pantheon, 1971.

Grice, Paul H. Logic and Conversation. In *Syntax & Semantics*, vol. 3: *Speech Acts*, ed. Peter Cole and Jerry L. Morgan, 41–58. New York: Academic Press, 1975.

Gumperz, John J. *Discourse Strategies.* Cambridge: Cambridge University Press, 1982.

Halliday, M.A.K. *Introduction to Functional Grammar.* London: Arnold, 1985.

Harris, Zellig. *Structural Linguistics.* Chicago: University of Chicago Press, 1960.

Hymes, Dell. *Foundation of Sociolinguistics: An Ethnographic Approach.* Philadelphia: University of Pennsylvania Press, 1974.

Levinson, Steven C. Activity Types and Language. In *Talk at Work*, ed. Paul Drew and John Heritage, 66–100. Cambridge: Cambridge University Press, 1992.

Malinowski, Bronislaw. *Argonauts of the Western Pacific.* New York: Dutton, 1922.

Mann, William C., and Sandra A. Thompson. Rhetorical Structure Theory: Toward a Functional Theory of Text Organization. *Text* 8 (1988): 243–81.

Martin, James R. *English Text: System and Structure.* Amsterdam: John Benjamins, 1992.

Pike, Kenneth. *Language in Relation to a Unified Theory of the Structure of Human Behavior.* The Hague: Mouton, 1971.

Sacks, Harvey, Gail Jefferson, and Emmanuel A. Schegloff. *Lectures on Conversation.* Oxford: Blackwell, 1995.

Scollon, Ron, and Suzanne Wong Scollon. *Intercultural Communication.* 2nd ed. Oxford: Blackwell, 2001.

Searle, John R. *Speech Acts: An Essay in the Philosophy of Language.* Cambridge: Cambridge University Press, 1969.

Spitzer, Leo. *Italienische Umgangssprache.* Leipzig: K. Schroeder, 1922.

Stubbs, Michael. Three Concepts of Keywords. In *Keyness in Texts*, ed. Marina Bondi and Mike Scott, 21–42. Amsterdam: John Benjamins, 2010.

Voloshinov, Valentin. Discourse in Life and Discourse in Poetry: Questions of Sociological Poetics. In *Russian Poetics in Translation*, ed. A. Shukman. Bakhtin School Papers 10 (1983): 5–30.

– *Marxism and the Philosophy of Language.* Trans. L. Matejka and I.R. Titunik. Cambridge, MA: Harvard University Press, 1986.

Wegener, Phillip. *Untersuchungen über die Grundfragen des Sprachlebens.* Halle: Max Niemeyer, 1885.

E

e-BOOK

[See also: *Book; Book, History of*]

The term *e-book* (short for 'electronic book'), also known as a *digital book*, refers to an electronic version of a book that can be read on a screen, usually via a hand-held device designed especially for this purpose. Easy access to numerous books in online venues, the facility with which e-books can be downloaded, and the storage capacity of e-book are the main factors that are catapulting e-books to the front of the line in book production, formatting, and distribution. Although the printed (paper) book still exists and continues to have a large audience, e-books are starting to garner more and more of the book-reading market. A reading device can store the same amount of material that in the past would have required significant bookshelf space and special classification systems for accessing the print materials.

E-books were made available in 1971 by the so-called Gutenberg Project, which digitized books in libraries and made them available electronically for special groups, such as professionals and scientists. Various formats for e-books have emerged since then for a more general public, such as the PDF version adopted by Adobe. There are now numerous formats for acquiring and reading e-books. Today, publishing houses are increasingly moving to the e-book format, as are authors, who can now publish themselves easily by simply making their texts available on specific websites. E-publishing has several advantages over print publishing. An e-book can include animations, videos, and sounds; it can also be updated quickly and distributed instantaneously. In e-publishing, space is much less limited than it is in print publishing. A standard CD-ROM or e-reader can hold the equivalent of hundreds of thousands of pages of text. With internet distribution, the length is a minor concern; more important is the size of sound and visual files, which can take considerable time to transmit to a computer

E-books and e-publishing have their critics, who claim that the technology is opening up the floodgates to the production of useless textual materials without gatekeepers (the traditional publishers) to guarantee quality in book publication and to ensure appropriate compensation to authors. Authorship became intertwined with publishing houses, as well as with the marketplace itself, which ultimately decided which books would rise above the chaff. The 'indie' movement, abetted by online technologies, has changed this situation drastically.

The first e-books were put on CD-ROMS between 1985 and 1992. In the latter year, Charles Stack's Book Unlimited began the practice of selling downloadable books online. By the mid-1990s digital books, without previous print versions, started appearing throughout the internet. By the late 1990s the first online publishers came into existence, as e-book reader technologies started to emerge to meet the needs of the new world of e-publishing. In the first years of the twenty-first century, print publishers started offering online versions of their books, and reference and school textbooks became available in the e-book format. In 2008, e-books were being made available for use with iPhones and similar mobile devices.

A Google search of the word *e-book* generates millions of sites offering books for downloading. This is evidence that the internet galaxy has replaced the Gutenberg galaxy – Marshall McLuhan's term for the social order brought into existence by mass-production print (paper) technologies. However, as McLuhan (McLuhan 1962; McLuhan and Fiore 1967) warned, this change in medium – from paper to screen – is never without repercussions of a psychological and social nature. Electronic media are extensions of the human nervous system, he claimed. The electronic book mirrors brain processes much more simulatively than does the printed book. The brain stores information and processes it holistically (literally, in whole chunks). The format of e-books simulates this process, since it contains the information in one locale, as does the brain. The paper book, on the other hand, fragments these processes by separating them into different locales and organizes them in a linear (non-holistic) fashion. It would seem, as McLuhan suggested, that the objects we create are, in the end, reproductions of ourselves.

The e-book has radically changed the social meaning of books. The printed book, with its cover, allowed others to ascertain what we were reading and what kinds of books we preferred. This information was often used as part of one's identity. With an e-book this possibility is diminished, unless someone looks over the shoulder of the reader. The book can no longer be construed as a sign of one's intellectual or aesthetic pursuits, since it is now easier to keep one's reading habits secret. Paralleling the shift in music consumption from discs to downloads, e-reading is disrupting the world of print publishing in the same way. This does not imply that reading printed

books is coming to an end. On the contrary, the ready availability of e-books is likely to lead to an increase in reading. But 'book culture' is changing and evolving along a different path.

Marcel Danesi

Bibliography

Howard, Nicole. *The Book: The Life Story of a Technology*. New York: Greenwood, 2005.

McLuhan, Marshall. *The Gutenberg Galaxy: The Making of Typographic Man*. Toronto: University of Toronto Press, 1962.

McLuhan, Marshall, and Quentin Fiore. *The Medium Is the Massage: An Inventory of Effects*. New York: Bantam, 1967.

ECO, UMBERTO (b. 1932)

[See also: *Closed versus Open Text; Peircean Semiotics; Semiotics; Structuralism; Text Theory*]

Umberto Eco was born in Alessandria (in northern Italy) in 1932. Philosopher, media critic, novelist, he is above all else a semiotician who introduced semiotics as an autonomous discipline into Italian academia. His theory of signs, and especially of language, has had a number of implications for the study of media. As a writer he achieved fame for his first novel *The Name of the Rose* (1980), which became a worldwide bestseller and then a movie. The novel was followed by *Foucault's Pendulum* (1988), *The Island of the Day Before* (1994), *Baudolino* (2002), *The Mysterious Flame of Queen Loana* (2004), and *The Prague Cemetery* (2010). The mind of the semiotician is evident in all these works of fiction, which involve the use of symbolism and its relation to cultural evolution.

Eco's overall view of what the form of semiotic theory should involve includes the following three components:

- the nature of the constitution of signs
- the role of interpretation in understanding the meaning of signs

- the role of inferential thinking in such interpretation

Eco examines the epistemological nature of signs in his 1975 book *Trattato di semiotica generale* (*Theory of Semiotics*), then again in 1981 (in his entry on signs for an encyclopedia and now in *Semiotics and the Philosophy of Language*), and in 1997 in *Kant and the Platypus*. In these works, Eco also argues for the centrality of the science of semiotics, stressing the fact that signs should be viewed independently from the limited views of sign structure that linguists tend to have.

He starts by observing the different meanings of the term 'sign' (word, gesture, etc. ...), and faced with these multiple meanings, he first of all distinguishes the theoretic questions that the issue of the sign makes it necessary to deal with, such as:

- the relationship between the laws of sign structure and the laws of thought
- the relationship between signs and concepts
- the relationship between enunciations (forms such as utterances that utilize signs) and facts
- the relationship between objects and signs
- the relationship between denotation and connotation in sign interpretation

Eco then re-examines the models of sign constitution by great thinkers, such as Plato, Aristotle, the Stoics, Augustine, the Medieval Scholastics, to name but a few. Through this 'archaeology of sign study,' Eco was among the first to identify two main models of the sign within semiotics: a *binary model* and a *triadic model*. But he has never seen these necessarily as contrastive. Rather, all Eco's semiotics is (also) an attempt to make these two models converge, relating the lesson of linguistics to the second paradigm, which is more strictly philosophical. The former is useful as a template for studying sign constitution in itself, and the latter for relating sign structure to the interpretative modalities of sign users.

At the base of the sign's linguistic conception lies the category of meaning and value and the principle of binarism. The sign is the result of a correlation of two components: expression and content, called technically *signifier* and *signified*. The linkage of these two components is seen to be arbitrary. From this, it follows that language has no motivated (sense-based) relationship with reality. Thus, the same object (say, *paper*) can be encoded by different signifiers according to language: *papier* in French, *carta* in Italian, and so on. Such a model plays down the role of subjectivity in sign use, highlighting the conventional and socially normative dimension of signs. The creation and use of a sign occurs within a certain community, at a certain point in time, and according to the conventions of that community and its language. The identity of the sign – its value – is, from this perspective, differentiative; the sign *paper* assumes a value based on the relationships it has with other signs (*paper* is different from *tablets*, for example).

As Eco points out (after Ferdinand de Saussure, one of the modern-day founders of semiotics), it was Louis Hjelmslev who took up and developed these suppositions, projecting the signifier-signified structure of the sign onto two distinct levels – expression and content respectively. These two levels are concurrent (an expression is such only in relationship to a certain content, and, likewise, a content is such only with respect to a certain expression); they subdivide the *forms* of meaning, cutting out the 'continuum' of sense, thus categorizing the world and rendering it discrete. In 1976, Eco came to realize the value of Hjelmslev's contribution, as 'de-materializing' the sign and transforming it into a *function*, that is, into a relation between two interchangeable 'functives' (specific types of function). The link between the form of expression and the form of the content is always cultural and conventional, and the relationship between these two levels of the sign's function is never given once and for all on the basis of a bond of logical implications (like 'if A then B' or 'if smoke, then fire'), but is always to be defined or re-definable (depending on the culture, epoch, social context). As Eco argues, it behooves semioticians to look more closely at the processes that produce signs and at the relationships that bind a certain expression (be it a sequence of letters, a facial expression, a gesture, or the colours of a flag) to a certain content. This linkage is, clearly, the outcome of a cultural and social process. Eco (1976: 49) concludes by asserting that:

- a sign is not a physical entity, the physical entity being at most the concrete occurrence of a pertinent expressive form;
- a sign is not a fixed semiotic entity, but rather a variable entity where expression and content converge.

The sign, therefore, cannot be described as a simple binary structure ('something standing for something else'), but rather as an inferential structure whose potential for infinite meaning is constrained only by context, which requires that it be given a specific interpretation only in a specific context. This view is, clearly, in line with that of the Stoics and with that of Charles S. Peirce, another modern-day founder of semiotics. According to Peirce, all thought takes place through signs. And this process is potentially infinite. One sign refers to another one (as in a dictionary definition) in an unlimited chain of interpretations. But context restrains this process. Interpretations in certain contexts morph into interpretative habits, conventions, and codes, which then re-enter the circle of sign production, remaining potentially open to new interpretations.

According to this conception, the sign is essentially a *renvoi* (a referral) *of* something *to* something else, and is interpreted every time as something which stands for something else in some way or from some point of view. In this perspective everything can become a sign, under certain conditions. So signs do not have definite referents or fixed meanings but procedural, contextual, and interpretative functions. They model

the world through *interpretants*. The interpretant may be of various kinds. It can have a dictionary-like form (similar to the dictionary definition for a word such as *zebra*). It can assume a visual form, such as a drawing of a zebra. It can have the form of a behaviour that, even without having a direct connection with the sign from which it started, is nevertheless the consequence – the 'effect' – of it. There is no limited or fixed number of interpretants. They are infinite, because every interpretant is, in turn, a sign itself and may thus produce other signs (if one draws a picture of a zebra, one might have to explain it in words, for example). For Peirce, this process is limitless.

In *Kant and the Platypus* Eco goes further into Peirce's inferential model of the sign, insisting on the *contractual* nature of signs. The equivalences established by the codes are in fact only sclerotizations of semiosis where the 'stands for' of an expression is negotiated every time through processes of trial and error and perceptive judgments that gradually adjust. Signs thus have three dimensions for Eco. First, they involve individual cognitive activity (the Cognitive Type) by which a sign user recognizes something as a sign (for example a photo of a certain type of dog). Then there is the set of interpretants associated conventionally with the sign (the Nuclear Content) by which its potential limitless content is constrained by context and various conventions of usage. Finally, the complex knowledge associated with a specific occurrence of the sign (the Molar Content) involves a type of encyclopedic knowledge that comes with sign utilization. As claimed by Peirce, this whole process is inferential, proceeding by means of hunches, associations, adjustments, and the like.

The implications of this view are far-reaching. First, there cannot be any specific sign system that can adequately capture reality, because the sign systems of every culture are always partial and dynamic, continuously in a state of reorganization. Thus, any dictionary model of meaning is useless because it aims for a-temporality and universality. Culture is not a dictionary made up of equivalences, but a network that can be crossed in different directions according to different interpretative paths. This is why an encyclopedic semantic model is more useful, where meanings are given not through decodification but abduction. Thus, it is impossible to conceive of a stable network of meanings encoded in signs and sign systems. Every part or portion of the encyclopedia can be connected to any portion of the network, on the basis of a subjective inference. That means that every entry of the encyclopedia is open and can produce new contents, among the ones authorized by the context; it is up to the subject.

Eco has also been instrumental in developing text theory. In *Opera aperta* (1962), he reflects on contemporary serial art style, such as the music of Stockhausen and abstract expressionist painting, both of which can only be assigned a meaning through the particular aesthetic responses of individual listeners or viewers. In *Lector in fabula* (1979) Eco compares a text to a 'lazy machine,' with gaps in it that are filled in by the user or reader who engages with it. Without the reader's input, there is no meaning. Every text, thus, has an 'ideal reader,' because every text, on account of its particular form and function, demands particular competencies, dispositions, and choices on the part of the reader. This is the '*intentio opera*' – namely, what the text requires of its readers, and this is what semiotics has to focus on as its proper object (studying not the pragmatic reactions of readers but the text's strategy). But texts are not completely open-ended. Obviously, we can interpret a text in any way we want, even claiming that Dante's *Divine Comedy* is an adventure story. But this, Eco says, would not be an *honest* interpretation of the text. And such honesty is what we require in the first place for interpretation to occur.

Eco's ideas of the ideal reader and the strategy of texts have had various applications in media studies. He was probably the initiator of the concept of text as embracing anything that involves an interactive relationship between the author, the reader, and the text itself.

Anna Maria Lorusso

Bibliography

Eco, Umberto. *A Theory of Semiotics*. Bloomington: Indiana University Press, 1976.
– *The Role of the Reader: Explorations in the Semiotics of Texts*. Bloomington: Indiana University Press, 1979.
– *Semiotics and the Philosophy of Language*. Bloomington: Indiana University Press, 1984.
– *Interpretation and Overinterpretation*. Cambridge: Cambridge University Press, 1992.
– *Kant and the Platypus: Essays on Language and Cognition*. New York: Mariner Books, 1997.
Peirce, Charles S. *Collected Papers of Charles Sanders Peirce*. Vols. 1–8. Ed. C. Hartshorne and P. Weiss. Cambridge, MA: Harvard University Press, 1931–58.
Saussure, Ferdinand de. *Cours de linguistique générale*. Ed. C. Bally and A. Sechehaye. Paris: Payot, 1916; trans. W. Baskin, *Course in General Linguistics*. New York: McGraw-Hill, 1958.
Scholes, Robert. *Semiotics and Interpretation*. New Haven: Yale University Press, 1982.

EDUCATIONAL TECHNOLOGY

[See also: *Electronic Media; Multimedia*]

Educational technology (ET) refers to the use of technology (from overheads to internet-assisted learning sites) to carry out some educational process whose primary purpose is to improve learning. Thus, educational technology covers a broad range of meanings, from the use of audio-visual media to the modelling of educational processes via technological concepts (such as hypertext) and the use of new technologies to deliver educational content. The main question involving the use of modern technologies (or any technologies for that matter) for delivering educational content is whether it makes a substantive difference over more traditional methodologies (Prendes 1998).

The first uses of what today we call hypertext goes back to 1945, when the American engineer Vannevar Bush (1890–1974) introduced it as a kind of proto-concept in his article 'As We May Think.' The concept of how things are interconnected (which is what hypertextuality essentially implies) was in line with the educational ideas of John Dewey in the United States, Maria Montessori in Italy, and Paolo Freire in Brazil. The concept of hypertextuality opens the door to understanding the psychology of concept formation in humans and the role of the individual in autonomous learning. It is in this light that current forms of educational technology have come to play a potentially major role in education.

Words, arguments, tools, and software are, as McLuhan and McLuhan wrote in *Laws of Media* (1988), types of media that are interconnected with different cultural levels of understanding in different societies. They are also the media used to carry out educational practices throughout the world. Contemporary ET extends such media, offering new interactive environments in which to work, teach, and learn, at the same time that it breaks down the traditional walls between people in different cultures by allowing people across the globe to interrelate freely through the World Wide Web. Although there are multiple culture-specific factors in how ET is used, ultimately it is its capacity to connect the world in a hypertextual fashion that makes it a harbinger of the future. Its range is truly remarkable. Since August 1995, for example, sixty photographs of Yosuke Yamahata can be seen on the server of the Exploratorium, of the North American Museum of Sciences. It has become a site used throughout the world for various educational purposes. Analogously, in France the Ligue de l'Enseignement offers cinematic productions made in small areas to schools and secondary schools. And in Spain, ET has made it possible for teacher-training

programs to take place virtually, becoming the basis for such programs at, for example, the Faculty of Education of the University of Murcia.

The field of ET is evolving along two paths, as a complementary facet of traditional education – ET *in* education – and as part of a process of the technologization *of* education. An amalgamation of both these paths is opening up a third one, namely the possibility of researching educational trends through digital technologies – a possibility that is line with an overall global STS trend – involving the ever-growing relationship between science (S), technology (T), and society (S).

The use of ET in education has always had a practical objective – the use of technological media in the classroom to assist the teacher in carrying out educational tasks more efficiently and even more effectively. In the audio-visual era of the 1960s, 1970s, and 1980s, teachers would bring tape recorders, overheads, slides, movie projectors, along with print media (newspapers, magazines, etc.) to class in order to enhance learning outcomes. It was already obvious that the use of ET had a practical learning objective. In a phrase, teachers have from time immemorial been using all kinds of devices and materials as supports for delivering education.

In the current age, the computer has emerged to give teachers even more flexibility and breadth for using technology as a supportive teaching resource. Microsoft makes a software program called Pint, for example, in which the mouse is used like an artificial pencil. But unlike a simple pencil, the mouse and the screen interact with the student to allow him/her to reflect upon what the hands are capable of doing. According with Gimeno (1995), critics of ET tend to see such media forms as falling outside the perimeter of true education. However, the situation is not much different from past use of blackboards. All materials fall into the domain of ET. Given the versatility of educational software today, teachers are even more capable of using technologiy in personal and specialized ways. And the new ET allows teachers to reach a global audience, so that they can share their pedagogy with people outside their classrooms.

The traditional environment where education has taken place is, of course, the classroom, which is an actual room inside a building. This traditional locus can now easily be expanded and even transformed with the addition of the new possibilities of ET. These can bring the classroom to the world, so to speak, since the classroom itself does not even have to be a real space; it can even be an online (virtual) one. A classroom can be transformed into a medium itself through electronic devices. As a consequence the whole concept of classroom and of teacher-learner interactions is changing. ET can go beyond simply transforming a classroom into a broadcast studio; it can itself become an integral component of the teaching process. The classroom is beginning to look more and more like an environment in which sophisticated electronic media are gradually becoming the primary ones through which educational content is being delivered.

ET is evolving dynamically, keeping pace with overall shifts in the ever-changing online world. One use of ET is the so-called MOODLE (Modular Object-Oriented Dynamic Learning Environment) project, which is an online repertoire of materials that makes it possible for teachers and students to interact virtually. Like any learning-mediated system (LMS), MOODLE has the capacity to customize interfaces with menus, links, and content spaces. In 2004 MOODLE had more than 1,160 sites in 81 countries. It is now used in schools, universities, training centres, businesses, hospitals, and libraries. Contributing to the development of MOODLE, and its derivatives, are the Open University (United Kingdom), the Istituto Superiore di Sanità (ISS) in Italy, Microsoft, Google, and the Open Polytechnic (New Zealand), which provides statistical information on its results and PostgreSQL software. MOO-DLE has made possible a veritable global learning community

MOODLE can deliver education in both direct and mediated formats (De Kerckhove 1997; Prendes 1995). The power of such ET was already recognized in 1969 by the National Council for Educational Technology (NCET) and in 1970 by the Commission on Instructional Technology (CIT). By the early 1980s, the use of ET in education became a major theme in professional educational circles. In 1977, the Council for Educational Technology (CET, before NCET) in the United Kingdom introduced the concept of global knowledge made possible by emerging developments in ET. In the same year, the AECT started to debate the idea that ET could not only complement learning but enhance it considerably, basing its premises on the research of various educators at the end of 1970s.

ET not only has facilitated the delivery of education, both within traditional and new online environments; it has also become a medium itself for envisioning new forms of education. SUPERCOMET-2, for example, was a project sponsored by the European Union in the 1990s, under the auspices of its Leonardo da Vinci Program. It was designed to facilitate the connectivity among sixteen countries by providing materials for the teaching of high school physics that can be easily customized to local interests. Among its resources were a teacher's guide and a CD-ROM, which was tested by educators to guarantee flexibility for local educational purposes. The teacher's guide and CD-ROM were used in various high school classrooms via content modules and computer simulations. More sophisticated projects are now available throughout the global village.

According to Cabero (2001) ET is becoming a major force in the delivery of education and is now shaping curriculm and learning theories across the world. Among the many advantages that it encompasses are the following:

- ET makes the delivery of global forms

of teacher training possible, at the same time providing each teacher ample opportunities to develop his or her specific talents.

- Since it is not limited by locale and teachers' time limitations, it can go on 24 hours a day and all over the world and make life-long learning a practical reality.
- It is a source for imparting e-literacy skills.
- It makes it possible for educators across the globe to interact.
- Although it has a global reach, ET also provides the software for local educational needs, making it adaptable to culture-specific concerns.

Lucía Amorós-Poveda

Bibliography

Amorós, Lucía. MOODLE como recurso didáctico. *Congreso Internacional EDUTEC*, 23–6 October 2007. Buenos Aires (Argentina).

Bush, Vannevar. As We May Think (1945). http://www.theatlantic.com/unbound/flashbks/computer/bushf.htm.

Cabero, Julio. *Tecnología educativa. Diseño y utilización de medios en la enseñanza*. Barcelona: Paidós, 2001.

De Kerckhove, Derrick. *Connected Intelligence: The Arrival of the Web Society*. Toronto: Somerville House, 1997.

Gimeno, Sacristán J. *El Curriculum: una reflexión sobre la práctica*. 5th ed. Madrid: Morata, 1995.

Martínez, Francisco, and Maria Prendes. *Nuevas Tecnologías y educación*. Madrid: Pearson, 2004.

McLuhan, Marshall, and Eric McLuhan. *Laws of Media: The New Science*. Toronto: University of Toronto Press, 1988.

Prendes, Maria. Redes de cable y enseñanza. In *Nuevos canales de comunicación en la enseñanza*, ed. J. Cabero and F. Martínez Sánchez. Madrid: Centro de Estudios Ramón Areces, 1995.

– *Proyecto docente de tecnología educativa*. Universidad de Murcia: Inédito, 1998.

WSIS. *Declaration of Principles. Building the Information Society: A Global Challenge in the New Millennium*. Geneva, 2003. http://www.itu.int/wsis/documents/doc_multi-en-1161 | 1160.asp.

e-GOVERNMENT

[See also: *Digital Divide; Internet*]

The term *e-government* (also spelled as *egovernment*, *eGovernment*, *eGov*, *e-Gov*) refers to 'the use of information and communication technologies, and particularly the Internet, as a tool to achieve better government' (OECD 2003: 23). This definition integrates the three main categories into which the many definitions of e-government can be grouped: as (1) the use of the internet for public administration activities, (2) (more generally) the use of information and communication technologies (ICT) in public administration, and (3) a capacity to transform public administration itself through the use of ICT and the internet. E-government activities can be distinguished – as it is done for e-commerce – according to the different entities involved, as follows: government to government (G2G), government to businesses (G2B), and government to citizens (G2C).

The use of ICT and the internet in public administration has various important aspects, in addition to its impacts on different levels of government. In general, e-government can be seen as a 'solar system' with four 'planets' revolving around it, representing: (1) legal and political issues, (2) technological issues, (3) stakeholders' issues, and (4) economic issues. Many of these overlap with the evolution of modern-day media, especially the internet.

First of all, every e-government activity is likely to have an impact on rights and duties, and must thus be structured to meet all laws and regulations. In many cases, new laws and regulations have had to be implemented in order to cope with new contexts, as, for instance, in e-voting, electronic signatures, and legal requirements related to privacy and document archiving. ICT and the internet are make a space possible in which people expect to have a more direct access to public administration, be it through a higher transparency of its procedures (authorizations, certifications, tenders, evaluation procedures, and so on) or a reduction of time needed to interact with the administration itself: paying taxes, getting documents, reserving for health-care services (part of e-health or other services). A different view has also emerged in the political arena, involving the relationships between candidates and elected politicians and citizens. There is a demand for more interaction, and the internet – besides the mass media – has started to play an important role during elections in maintaining the reputation of politicians and public organizations.

Technologies continue to evolve, challenging public administrations at different levels. One is the security and privacy issue: Should governments adopt open-source pieces of software or proprietary ones? A second relevant issue in this field is that of compatibility – many public administrations in the same country should be able to dialogue (at the G2G level) so as to ensure that businesses and citizens get the maximum advantages from e-government. Joining the technological sphere could mean offering very advanced services, but only to few people, hence producing or enlarging a so-called digital divide, that is, 'the inequalities that exist in Internet access based on income, age, education, race/ethnicity, and … between rural and metropolitan areas, through such factors as pricing and infrastructure' (Hill 2004: 27).

E-government activities and services require that people in the public administration and citizens/businesses acquire new competencies and adopt new procedures. E-government must be accepted and adopted (or possibly rejected) by the relevant stakeholders. Here again the issue of the digital divide is a pivotal one and usually involves calls for maintaining different procedures at the same time in order not to bring any disadvantage to any citizen, especially those who – due to economic,

cultural, or physical reasons – could be left behind.

The above situation applies as well to G2C relationships, which means usually an increase in costs. In addition, activities needed to equip public administrations for e-government (technologies, know-how, a consistent legal framework, and related procedures) are quite expensive and require major investments. Such investments are made even more risky by the nature of the technologies themselves, which change all the time. It is worth mentioning that public administration has been shaped for millennia by writing processes, which for centuries have given enormous power to the printed word, whereby documents, bulletins, requests, forms, authorizations, taxes, and so on have been, and are still conceived as, occurring primarily in printed form. In the digital age, there is the promise of significant reductions in the use of paper, more efficient writing styles, higher system competitiveness (simplified procedures, which is attractive to new business enterprises), and a reduction in the number of public employees required. All this will lead to lower administrative costs.

According to the UN Global E-Government Readiness Index, five different stages can be distinguished in e-government implementation: *emerging presence*, or basic information offered online; *enhanced presence*, or information which is still one-way, but with enhanced capabilities, such as search functions; *interactive presence*, or the realization of basic interactions between government and people; *transactional presence*, the enhancement of completing transactions, such as paying taxes or getting certificates; and *networked presence*, in which 'the government is willing and able to involve the society in a two-way dialogue. Through employing the use of web comment forms, and innovative online consultation mechanisms, the government actively solicits the views of people acting in their capacities as consumers of public services and as citizens. Implicit in this stage of the model is the integration of consultation and collective decision making' (UNDESA 2004: 14).

Lorenzo Cantoni

Bibliography

Cantoni, Lorenzo, and Stefano Tardini. *Internet.* London: Routledge, 2006.

Hill, Evan. Some Thoughts on E-Democracy as an Evolving Concept. *Journal of E-Government* 1 (2004): 23–39.

OECD. *The E-Government Imperative.* Paris: OECD E-Government Studies, 2003.

UNDESA. *UN Global E-Government Readiness Report 2004. Towards Access for Opportunity.* United Nations Department of Economic and Social Affairs, 2004.

ELECTRONIC MEDIA

[See also: *McLuhan, Marshall; Media Studies; Medium; Multimedia*]

Electronic media is a general term for technologies that require electricity in order to function and transmit communication. A more specific usage of the term refers to all media that require electronics or electro-mechanical energy to access the content of the communication. The primary electronic media sources include radio, telephone, television, fax, DVDs, CD-ROMs, the internet, and kiosks. The term excludes printed, paper-based media (such as books, newspapers, magazines, catalogues, letters, or outdoor billboards), which may be produced electronically but do not need electricity to be accessed, as well as oral, visual, and performance media that involve sounds, images, gestures, or hand tools (such as the human voice, theatre, painting, or photography). In a world where technologies are increasingly converging, electronic media encompass an ever-widening range of possibilities that herald a new era in human communication. The significance of electronic media is that new technologies make it possible for any human being in the world to connect with any other human being, producing one of the great transformations in the history of communication, and holding the potential to transform human consciousness itself.

Marshall McLuhan, Electronic Technologies, and Media Theory

One of the more influential theories concerning the importance of the advent of electronic (or electric) media was offered by Marshall McLuhan (1911–80), who called this transformation the *electronic revolution.* The revolution in electric media began with the invention of the telegraph in 1844, and continued with radio, films, telephone, and, finally, the computer. The electronic revolution is an intensification, acceleration, and implosion of expansive forces unleashed in two previous revolutions in communication media: the *Gutenberg revolution* that came in the wake of the introduction of the movable-type printing press in the fifteenth century, and the *literate revolution*, which started with the adoption of the phonetic alphabet by the ancient Greeks in the fifth century BCE. The literate revolution was the catalyst that shifted humans out of oral patterns of speech and thought and made way for the ascendancy of rational and linear thought processes associated with literate forms of communication. The Gutenberg revolution accelerated and intensified these processes of change and reinforced fragmentary and mechanistic modes of mentality. The rise of electronic media, McLuhan argued, represents a break with fragmentary and mechanistic forms of mentality produced by print technologies, just as phonetic alphabetic literacy was a break with the mythic and tribal mentality associated with orality. Along with a change in mentality, the electronic revolution will reconfigure societies and cultures. Whereas the force of change in the literate and Gutenberg revolutions was directed outward, the move from print to electric media entails a reversal to implosion. The contracting energies initiated by the arrival of electronic media run counter to patterns of organization characteristic of the two previous revolutions, producing tensions and interactions that will ultimately reconfigure all aspects of mental, social, political, economic, religious, and cultural life.

Electronic Media as Extensions of the Human Central Nervous System

All technologies are extensions of the human physical body or psyche, argued McLuhan, and electric circuitry is an extension of the central nervous system. With the advent of electronic media, human beings have been able to extend our physical and mental capacities around the world, setting ourselves outside of our bodies, creating an external central nervous system. Under electric conditions, the world is within our grasp and perception achieves a global reach. When communication moves around the globe at the speed of nerve impulses in the human body, human awareness is not limited to a single level of information movement, but, rather, instantly takes in the total situation or field. Putting our physical bodies inside our extended nervous systems by means of electric media establishes a dynamic whereby previous technologies that expand human capacities are translated into information systems, rewiring people into organisms that wear our brains outside our skull and our nerves outside our skin, creating total and inclusive awareness in a mediated extension of consciousness. Through electronic media in the age of global information, 'we wear all mankind as our skin' (McLuhan 1964: 47). For McLuhan, electronic media have the potential to unite all human beings in a new form of collective and connected consciousness.

On the negative side, McLuhan argued, in his *Understanding Media*, that extending the human central nervous system around the world under electronic media conditions creates a violent and hyper-stimulated experience that threatens to overwhelm the exposed nerves. An effect of this intense experience is profound anxiety, apathy, and anomie. In order to bear the heightened sensory experience, people have to anaesthetize themselves, which leads to feelings of numbness, alienation, and depersonalization. Like the body under conditions of shock or the mind in a state of repression, the nervous system under electronic conditions is susceptible to a numbing self-hypnosis that keeps us unaware of the mental and social effects of new technology by rendering them invisible. Thus, electronic media have both positive and negative effects and create problems of human involvement and organization for which there is no precedent in previous eras.

McLuhan's arguments concerning the import of electronic media provoked sharply polarized reactions. While many dismissed his views, others regarded his vision as prescient. Though he wrote his major works prior to the widespread adoption of the computer and before the introduction of the World Wide Web, a growing number of scholars today maintain that his arguments concerning electronic media presaged the arrival of the internet and the age of information, along with their negative effects and repercussions. McLuhan's views of electronic media are seen by many scholars as having set the stage for the post-humanist turn toward studies in communication, media, and culture. Whether his views are rejected or accepted, no contemporary theory of electronic media can be considered comprehensive if it fails to engage with McLuhan's theses.

Twyla Gibson

Bibliography

de Kerckhove, Derrick. *The Skin of Culture.* Toronto: Somerville House, 1995.

McLuhan, Marshall. *The Gutenberg Galaxy: The Making of Typographic Man.* Toronto: University of Toronto Press, 1962.

– *Understanding Media: The Extensions of Man.* Cambridge, MA: MIT Press, 1964.

– *Understanding Me: Lectures and Interviews.* Edited by Stephanie McLuhan and David Staines. Toronto: McClelland and Stewart, 2003.

McLuhan, Marshall, and Quentin Fiore. *The Medium Is the Massage: An Inventory of Effects*. New York: Bantam, 1967.

EMAIL

[See also: *Instant Messaging; Internet; Mass Communication*]

Email (otherwise known as *electronic mail*) is a form of digital communication associated with the internet. In its most primitive form, it involves the electronic transmission of textual messages from one computer user to another. With the increasing speed of the internet, however, email today can often contain file attachments and/or multimedia content such as photos and graphics.

The benefits of email are apparent – it facilitates rapid information exchange, the ability to communicate across vast distances, inexpensively and flexibly in terms of when and what one reads. According to the Radicati Group's Q3 2007 *Market Numbers Update*, the total number of email users in 2007 was estimated at 1.2 billion (Tekrati 2007). Consequently, email has been adopted universally for personal and business letter–based communication (known as 'snail mail'). For the individual, email has provided a quick and easy way for him/her to keep in touch and correspond at his/her convenience. For businesses, email has bridged time and distance gaps, allowing for a greater level of connectedness and collaboration between companies and clients. Along with social media of various kinds, email is one of the most common modes of communication in the world today.

The beginnings of email can be traced back to the mid-1960s with the compatible time-sharing system (CTSS). Developments with computer terminals such as the Q-32 or the IBM 7094 at the Massachusetts Institute of Technology allowed users to exchange text messages over the system (Van Vleck 2004). As computers and computer networks continued to develop, the concept of exchanging messages between users soon expanded to allow for the sending of messages between different computers. In 1971, Ray Tomlinson, who worked with the programs SNDMSG and READMAIL, developed a version of SNDMSG which was compatible with ARPANET (an early form of the internet) (Crocker 2000). Using the '@' symbol to separate the user name and the host name, Tomlinson created the standard email address notation which we still use today. Over the course of the decade, improvements continued to be made with regard to the technology of mail reading, transmission, and header capabilities (allowing for sorting of messages by subject and date).

During the 1980s, further technological advancements with regard to the transmission of email continued to develop. The late 1980s saw the emergence of user-friendly technology within the commercial realm, and by the mid-1990s, such technology made universal access to email a reality, with companies such as America Online linking their email systems to the internet. Since then, email has become one of the primary channels through which people interact on a daily basis.

There are two main protocols used for email retrieval: IMAP4 (Internet Message Access Protocol) and POP3 (Post Office Protocol). The IMAP protocol allows users to access email on a server; emails are stored remotely and synchronized with a user's local computer. This protocol is more commonly used by large institutions such as universities, and is more complex than the POP protocol. POP3, which is more typically used by internet service providers, facilitates message retrieval by downloading all emails to the user's local computer. While it is possible to leave messages on the server in a POP environment, generally users need not stay connected to the server while working with their messages. This is due to the fact that downloaded messages are deleted remotely (unless otherwise specified) and stored locally on the user's computer. Generally, most email retrieval clients can support both these formats.

The SMTP protocol, otherwise known as Simple Mail Transfer Protocol, is used for sending out emails. Typically, over an unsecured connection, the SMTP protocol uses the TCP/IP connection over port 25 to 'push' out messages. In institutional settings, proprietary email servers can be set up for the purposes of sending and receiving email. Some of these include the Microsoft Exchange Server, Novell Groupwise, Lotus Notes, and the Research in Motion's BlackBerry.

The format of an email can be divided into two main parts: the header and the body. Every email message contains a header, which provides specific information such as sender, date, subject, and intended receiver:

From– the name and/or email address of the sender;
To – the name and/or email address of the recipient(s);
Subject – a user-defined title pertaining to the topic of the email;
Date – the date and time at which the original message was written.

Email messages may sometimes contain other information such as server and/or routing information, carbon copy recipients, blind carbon copy recipients, content type, reply-to address formats, and other reference information. The body of the email contains the content or text. This can be in either plain text format, or HTML format. With the HTML format, users can customize an email's layout and style by defining the font, adding embedded images and graphics, and utilizing other functions associated with rich-text editors. In addition to the main content, emails can sometimes include a user-defined signature line with information about the sender, such as name, title, and place of employment. Finally, emails may also contain file attachments, allowing users to send files of almost any type to another user.

There are numerous client-side software applications available for sending and receiving emails on an end user's computer. These email clients, which can be set up to connect to various types of servers (POP, IMAP, or Exchange server), offer certain benefits to the end user – the ability to download and view messages on a computer, better integration with other applications, search and indexing capabilities, better message organization tools, and built-in address books and calendar.

Web companies now offer free email addresses to its users. Currently, Yahoo Mail, Google Mail, and Hotmail are among the most popular free email providers, based on total number of registered users. While certain providers such as Yahoo and Google do offer POP and IMAP capabilities, most users of free email services rely on Web-based email. In other words, users access their email through the company's website via a Web-based client. Thus, there is no need for a software client on the user's local computer to download messages. There are certain advantages and disadvantages to this. The main benefit is that users can access their email anywhere in the world from a computer. The main drawback stems from the fact that there are more limited features with Web-based interfaces, alongside the fact that users have to be connected to the internet to access messages. Many institutional or corporately provided email accounts offer both a Web-based and a server-based option to its users for convenience.

Despite the benefits of email, there are many issues and problems associated with its use. First, as with any medium of communication, email is not devoid of unwanted correspondence, known as spam. Every day, billions of spam messages, such as junk mail and unsolicited advertisements, are sent to users. Furthermore, the ease of sending and forwarding messages has allowed for the propagation of chain mail, otherwise known as 'forwards.' These are essentially messages which users pass on to other users in their address books through mass mailings to multiple senders.

From a security perspective, there are numerous privacy issues Emails are typically sent in an unsecured environment. In other words, they can be intercepted by others, or compromised when either inadvertently sent to the wrong user, or deliberately and maliciously accessed through hacking. Consequently, this has forced institutions and corporations working with sensitive information to employ stricter security standards (stronger passwords and the use of secured network connections), in addition to placing a disclaimer at the end of outgoing messages. Despite this, there are still ongoing risks posed by fake emails which pretend to originate from legitimate senders. These seemingly legitimate messages trick users into giving up personal information (such as banking information and passwords) in a process known as 'phishing.' There are also problems posed by virus transmission via email. Since computer viruses can often take over a person's email account and use it to send out virus-infected emails, unsuspecting users can often be victims.

With the advent of BlackBerries, iPods, smartphones, and other sophisticated mobile devices, people are now able to access their email anywhere. All this implies that the nature of correspondence has changed drastically since the advent of electronic technologies. As a consequence, it has led to new models of writing, new forms of language, and the like. The implications of these shifts in communication have become targets of study and research since at least the late 1990s (Baron 2000).

Alexander Lim

Bibliography

Baron, Naomi S. *Alphabet to Email: How Written English Evolved and Where It's Heading*. London: Routledge, 2000.

Crocker, Dave. Email History, How Email Was Invented. Living Internet (7 January 2000). http://www.livinginternet.com/e/ei.htm (accessed 11 January 2009).

Freeman, John. *The Tyranny of E-Mail: The Four-Thousand-Year Journey to Your Inbox*. New York: Scribner, 2009.

Tekrati Inc. *The Industry Analyst Reporter* (16 October 2007). http://software.tekrati.com/research/9512/ (accessed 9 January 2009).

Van Vleck, Tom. The IBM7094 and CTSS (10 September 2004). http://www.multicians.org/thvv/7094.html (accessed 10 January 2009).

ETHNOGRAPHY

[See also: *Anthropology of the Media; Media Studies*]

Ethnography is a research technique practised primarily by anthropologists whereby the researcher lives among groups of people, interacting with them and interviewing them in a systematic way, in order to gain insights about them as collectivities and then to write up such insights as a set of observations. In some ways, it can be said that ethnography has always been implicit in the written testimonials of ancient travellers, who made annotations in their notebooks on the behavioural diversity they saw among the peoples they visited, thus chronicling first-hand the characteristics of other people's cultures. The Greek historian Herodotus (ca 484–425 BCE), who spent a large part of his life travelling through the ancient world, was probably the first to record cultural differences he noticed (with respect to Athenian culture) in the people he came across. The result was his *Historia*, which can be considered the first true ethnography of human culture (Danesi and Perron 1999). Inspired by Herodotus, other ancient historians, like the Roman Tacitus (ca 55–117 CE), also described the languages, character, manners, and geographical distribution of the peoples they visited.

Modern ethnographic method consists not only in visiting others, but in living among them and interacting with them in some way. This mode of ethnographic research started with the American anthropologist Franz Boas (1858–1942), who claimed that in order to understand others, the researcher had to become like them. Among Boas's students at Columbia University in the 1920s and 1930s, Edward Sapir (1884–1939), Margaret Mead (1901–78), and Ruth Benedict (1887–1948) became well-known ethnographers.

By the early 1930s, it became obvious that a standard repertoire of notions and techniques was required for conducting ethnographic analyses. This was provided by Leonard Bloomfield (1887–1949) in his 1933 textbook *Language*. For two decades afterwards, linguists and anthropologists went about the painstaking work of collecting information on the different indigenous languages and cultures of America. The approach came to be known as *descriptive*, since the goal was to describe languages as a means towards understanding the cultures that used them. Linguistics was construed to be, ipso facto, an ethnographic science. Although this changed in some quarters already by the late 1950s, in the contemporary field known as linguistic anthropology, it continues to be the main modus operandi.

The actual activity of gathering information while living among a group is known more specifically as *fieldwork*. Two classic ethnographies based on fieldwork are *Argonauts of the Western Pacific* (1922), by the Polish-born anthropologist Bronislaw Malinowski, and *The Nuer* (1940), by the British anthropologist E.E. Evans-Pritchard.

Marcel Danesi

Bibliography

Agar, Michael. *The Professional Stranger: An Informal Introduction to Ethnography*. New York: Academic Press, 1996.

Danesi, Marcel, and Paul Perron. *Analyzing Cultures*. Bloomington: Indiana University Press, 1999.

Erickson, Ken C., and Donald D. Stull. *Doing Team Ethnography: Warnings and Advice*. London: Sage, 1997.

EYE CONTACT

[See also: *Body Language; Kinesics; Non-Verbal Communication*]

Eye contact, or the looking patterns exhibited by people as they communicate in face-to-face, and now screen-to-screen, interactions, is a form of non-verbal communication that is largely instinctive, rather than learned in specific contexts. Eye contact is not unique to the human species. Dogs and other mammals construe a direct stare as a threat or challenge; breaking eye contact is a signal of surrender to a more dominant (powerful) dog.

Although eye contact schemas are largely unconscious, cultural upbringing conditions the actual form of the schemas, reflecting culture-specific meanings and social functions:

- Across cultures, the duration of the eye contact indicates what kinds of social and personal relationships people have with each other.
- Staring is interpreted as a challenge across the world, although some cultures tolerate it much more than do others.
- Making eyes at someone – looking into someone's eyes to reveal sexual interest – is normally interpreted as flirtation.
- In many cultures, looking at someone with malicious intent is viewed as a curse or an ominous sign. Known as the 'evil eye,' it is perceived to be a stare that is purported to have the power to harm or bewitch someone.
- Making eye contact early or late during a communicative interaction indicates the kind of relationship one wishes to have with the communicant; this varies considerably across cultures.
- When the pupils dilate during excited states, they tend to elicit a sexual response in an observer.
- Narrowing the eyelids indicates pensiveness across cultures.
- Bringing the eyebrows together communicates thoughtfulness; raising them conveys surprise.
- Southern Europeans and Latin Americans, among others, tend to look more into each other's eyes during conversation than do North Americans; in some cultures males do not look into female

eyes unless they are married or are members of the same family.

- In Western culture, gazing is interpreted as sexual wonder, fascination, awe, or admiration; staring is perceived as sexual curiosity, boldness, insolence, or stupidity; peering is construed as looking narrowly, searchingly, and seemingly with difficulty; ogling is interpreted as staring in an amorous, usually impertinent manner.

Marcel Danesi

Bibliography

Ellsberg, Michael. *The Power of Eye Contact*. New York: Harper, 2010.

F

FACEBOOK

[See also: *MySpace; Social Networking*]

Facebook is the name of one of the most frequented and social networking sites, having evolved into an intrinsic part of digital culture and life in cyberspace. Facebook asks members to create a personal profile that includes biographical information, audio-visual supports (photos, videos, music, etc.), and a listing of preferences (hobbies, aesthetic tastes, etc.).

The earliest social networking sites were developed in the mid-1990s but did not become popular until the development of Friendster in 2002. Facebook was introduced in 2004 at Harvard University by student Mark Zuckerberg for use by the students there. By 2005, Facebook had eclipsed Friendster. It then migrated to other Ivy League schools and by 2006 to universities and colleges across the globe. In that same year, Facebook opened its membership to anyone thirteen years of age or older. Microsoft Corporation bought a share in Facebook a year later, making it available to anyone. It is now one of the most lucrative digital businesses, collecting revenue mainly from banner advertising (since membership is free).

Facebook has since expanded considerably, with scientific and professional groups, justice courtrooms, the police, and other organizations opening up sites to carry out intragroup discussions and exchanges of information, to keep up to date, and so on. Television networks, artists, and musicians also have Facebook sites for communicating with fans, followers, and audiences generally. Facebook and other social networking sites have quickly developed into primary social media for people to communicate and to carry out their life routines, even more than they did in the age of the telephone. And this has changed the nature of how individuals now experience social life, altering the ways in which identity is created and managed, and how the sense of self is constructed. Screen-to-screen communication is thus now as much a part of life as face-to-face communication, leading to writing as a complement of orality, not an option to it. Some social critics are pointing out that Facebook is leading to a superficial form of interaction. Others claim instead that Facebook is actually allowing people to feel more comfortable about themselves, giving them the opportunity to construct their own profiles and to prepare them emotionally to negotiate face-to-face contact more successfully.

Why people expose themselves online through profiles, photos, and other private artefacts is a question in the social sciences, especially given the fact that the 'fad effect' of Facebook, as it can be called, has subsided. Is Facebook replacing the confessional or psychoanalyst's couch, allowing people to confess in public? Why do people desire to construct their identities through Facebook? Perhaps, as some social media critics suggest, everyone has found a means for obtaining those fifteen minutes of fame, as Andy Warhol aptly put it. Being popular or famous is a spreading obsession, perhaps spurred on by the presence of the 'like' button on sites throughout the internet.

When the internet came into wide use, it was heralded as bringing about a liberation from conformity and a channel for expressing one's opinions freely. But this view of the internet is fast becoming an anachronism. Counting the number of 'friends' on Facebook is seemingly more crucial than venting one's philosophical or aesthetic viewpoints. The internet is being used more and more to construct a popular persona, a process tied to rudimentary human needs – the need to present oneself in a favourable light to others, the need to confess in public, the need to gossip, the need to stay connected to others, and so on. For this reason it has become 'addictive' for many users, as they seek out other people's reactions to their daily updated diaries (Lanier 2010; Kirkpatrick 2010). Marshall McLuhan constantly argued that our most significant mass communications technologies shaped the ways in which we evolved, cognitively, culturally, and socially. Facebook is such a technology. Echoing what the Frankfurt School scholars said about the Fordist world of mass production culture in the pre-internet era, it can be said that Facebook culture is built on the same promise of the attainment of temporary happiness. But, as individuals become more and more accustomed to the passing joys or spasms of relief offered by Facebook, they will start to realize how recurring, formulaic, and infantile most of Facebook's possibilities really are, even if they continue to be active in it. The main reason for this may be that, having grown up in a Facebook universe, they may feel it is the only option available to them, being unable to imagine doing anything else. The triumph of Facebook lies in its promise to allow human needs to be expressed individualistically, even though most users soon start to realize that its true force lies in the compulsive attachment it instils in them.

In the past, social relations, enduring cultural traditions, and stable patterns of work, life, and leisure kept people united in real space. The internet has shattered this assurance, forcing individuals to develop new strategies to manage the shocks of everyday life. Facebook has offered a broad range of utopian options for gaining control over meaning and experience, emancipating people from the bonds of traditional patterns of meaning making. Yet under the spell of the new medium, these options have become strangely similar to those of the past at best, or degenerated into fetishized practices of self-enhancement. On the other hand, as the Frankfurt scholars predicted, perhaps Facebook is the revolutionary tool, as they called it, that will finally jolt humans out of their intellectual and artistic lethargy and awaken in them the sense of individual power that is crucial for true creativity to occur in the first place.

Marcel Danesi

Bibliography

Atwan, Gregory. *The Facebook Book*. New York: Abrams, 2008.

Kirkpatrick, David. *The Facebook Effect: The Inside Story of the Company That Is Connecting the World*. New York: Simon and Schuster, 2010.

Lanier, Jaron. *You Are Not a Gadget: A Manifesto*. New York: Knopf, 2010.

McLuhan, Marshall. *Understanding Media: The Extensions of Man*. Cambridge, MA: MIT Press, 1964.

Vander Veer, Emily A. *Facebook: The Missing Manual*. New York: Pogue, 2008.

FACIAL EXPRESSION

[See also: *Body Language; Eye Contact; Kinesics; Non-Verbal Communication*]

Facial expressions are sources of signalling and message making in human interaction. They can be unconscious or witting, depending on the situation and user.

Unconscious expressions are types of instinctive signals; witting expressions are learned responses to specific situations. In 1963, psychologist Paul Ekman established the Human Interaction Laboratory in the Department of Psychiatry at the University of California at San Francisco to systematically study all forms of facial expressions. He was joined by Wallace V. Friesen in 1965 and Maureen O'Sullivan in 1974. Over the years, the Laboratory has documented and researched the nature and range of facial expressions, establishing a taxonomy that has been used extensively in the social sciences. By breaking down an expression into its characteristic components – eyebrow position, eye shape, mouth shape, nostril size, etc. – one can determine the meaning of the expression. It has been found that of all signalling systems, there is less cross-cultural variation in facial expression than in other modes of communication.

The team has identified forty-six basic facial movements that produce more than 10,000 microexpressions. Their classification system is called the Facial Action Coding System (FACS). FACS has been adopted as a screening tool in dozens of airports and also by various police departments. As Ken Adler (2006) has shown, throughout history people have attempted to develop precise techniques to help them detect liars, from the Chinese practice of making a suspect chew rice (since a dry mouth was believed to expose a liar) to the belief in India that lying makes the toes curl up. Modern techniques, such as FACS, Adler argues, are nothing more than contemporary attempts to do similar things. Detecting lies remains largely an intuitive, not a scientific, skill.

Of particular interest to semiotics and psychology are the looking patterns that define social relations.

Moreover, psychologists have found that specific individuals are responsive to particular kinds of facial expressions and not to others from puberty onwards. This means that culture plays a significant role in the interpretation of facial expressions. For example, as psychologist John Money

(1986) has argued, at puberty individuals start reacting to specific kinds of expressions in romantic ways. These are developed during childhood in response to specific contextual experiences and influences. At adolescence, they unconsciously guide the individual in differentiating between a romantic expression and any other. Clearly, the role of facial expressions in human communication is constrained by both biology and upbringing. The two coalesce at puberty to generate interpretive models of what an expression means.

Marcel Danesi

Bibliography

Adler, Ken. *The Lie Detectors*. New York: The Free Press, 2006.

Ekman, Paul. Movements with Precise Meanings. *Journal of Communication* 26 (1976): 14–26.

– The Classes of Nonverbal Behavior. In *Aspects of Nonverbal Communication*, ed. W. Raffler-Engel, 89–102. Lisse: Swets and Zeitlinger, 1980.

– Methods for Measuring Facial Action. In *Handbook of Methods in Nonverbal Behavior*, ed. K.R. Scherer and P. Ekman, 45–90. Cambridge: Cambridge University Press, 1982.

– *Telling Lies*. New York: Norton, 1985.

– *Emotions Revealed*. New York: Holt, 2003.

Ekman, Paul, and Wallace Friesen. *Unmasking the Face*. Englewood Cliffs, NJ: Prentice-Hall, 1975.

Fridlund, Alan J. *Human Facial Expression: An Evolutionary View*. New York: Academic, 1994.

Money, John. *Lovemaps: Clinical Concepts of Sexual/Erotic Health and Pathology, Paraphilia, and Gender Identity from Conception to Maturity*. Baltimore: Johns Hopkins University Press, 1986.

Peck, Stephen Rogers. *Atlas of Facial Expression*. Oxford: Oxford University Press, 1987.

FANZINES

[See also: *Celebrity Culture; Magazines*]

The word *fanzine* was coined by Russ Chauvenet, editor of *Detours* and U.S. amateur chess champion, in 1940. A fanzine, unlike a regular magazine, is a magazine for and by fans and devoted to the coverage of some person (such as a rock star) or activity (such as rock music, skateboarding, and the like). Traditional fan magazines are commercial magazines published by a producer to promote certain celebrities; fanzines, on the other hand, have their origin in the amateur press. The term is also used to refer to magazines produced by fans for other fans of a celebrity or a hobby (such as a particular video game). The early fanzines of this type were created around punk bands in the mid-1970s, spreading to other domains of popular culture, such as sports, where teams would publish fanzines for their fans.

One of the significant events in the history of fanzines is the publication of Hugo Gernsback's magazine *Amazing Stories* in 1926. The letters column of the magazine in a few years turned into a forum for readers who wanted to discuss or add to the stories presented in the magazine. The first true fanzine, however, was *The Comet*, established in 1930, and edited by Raymond Palmer and Walter Dennis for sci-fi fans. The magazine was published for the Science Correspondence Club in Chicago.

A TV show that has inspired the greatest variety of fanzines is *Star Trek*. The first Star Trek fanzine was called *Spockanalia* and its early issues were published while the show was still on the air. Fanzines based on movies and TV shows are called 'media fanzines.' Other subgenres include punk fanzines (for example, *Sniffin' Glue*) and horror movie fanzines.

The writing found in fanzines is in many respects similar to that found in online media today such as Facebook or blogs. Fan opinions are commented on by others, and the style is informal and full of coded language that is understood mainly by fan insiders. Internet fanzines are known as efanzines.

The Hugo Awards honour the best fanzine every year. In 2008, the winner was *File 770* edited by Mike Glyer. *File 770* also won the award in 1984, 1985, 1989, 2000 and 2001.

The sustaining practice of fanzines and efanzines is witness to the emotional power of pop culture. Whether it be Elvis Presley, skateboarding, Beatles albums, videogames, or punk culture, fanzines reveal that people living in an entertainment society react emotionally (and nostalgically) to the people and events that populate the world of entertainment. Fanzines are a product of this mindset. But this does not mean that such culture is incapable of producing meritorious forms of art. Indeed, *Star Trek* is an example of a TV program that dealt with some of the most profound philosophical themes of human history.

Anders Søgaard

Bibliography

Schelly, Bill. *The Golden Age of Comic Fandom.* Seattle, WA: Hamster Press, 1995.

FEDERAL COMMUNICATIONS COMMISSION

[See also: *Broadcasting; Censorship; Freedom of Speech; Media Literacy*]

In February 1934, President Franklin D. Roosevelt asked the U.S. Congress to create a new agency to be called the Federal Communications Commission (FCC). The new FCC was to regulate common carrier communications (telegraph and telephone) and broadcast communications (radio and later television). Congress responded by passing the Communications Act of 1934, and the U.S. Federal Communications Commission open its doors for business on 11 July of that year. The Federal Communications Commission is an agency that is tasked with regulating some of the most important and complicated industries in the United States. It is an agency that affects almost every American, but is known by very few.

Prior to the formation of the Commission, the telephone and telegraph industries were regulated by the Interstate Commerce Commission (ICC) and radio was regulated by the Federal Radio Commission (FRC). The styles of regulation practised at these two agencies could not have been more different. The ICC believed the telephone and telegraph industries were public utilities that should be viewed as natural monopolies. A public utility is any industry, like the railroad, that is considered so central to the economic well-being of society that it must be provided to the public without discrimination and at a reasonable rate. A natural monopoly is when it is believed that goods and services can be most efficiently provided by a single firm. So the ICC regulated the telephone and telegraph industries by regulating the rates they could charge the public and by creating entry barriers to protect the industries from competitors.

Radio, on the other hand, was regulated not because it was a natural monopoly, but because of the characteristics of the physical world. The electromagnetic spectrum over which radio waves travel is a finite resource. There is only space for a certain number of transmitters to operate, otherwise the whole broadcasting system would be subject to interference. Thus, the government had to figure out how it would decide who got to have a radio station and who did not. Furthermore, radio was more than just electromagnetic signals – it was also a content source. Content providers, like newspapers, traditionally were not regulated by the government under the restrictions set by the First Amendment. But following the advent of radio broadcasting, it quickly became clear that there were more people who wanted to provide radio programming than there was space for it on the spectrum. While anyone can start a newspaper, not everyone can start a radio station. Thus the concept of the regulation of broadcasting in the public interest for convenience and necessity evolved. The very nature of the industry required that

the government choose one over another. Thus it would choose those who it believed would best serve the listening public.

Commissioners

The FCC today is headed by five commissioners who are nominated by the president and confirmed by the Senate. The commissioners serve staggered five-year terms. Only three of the five commissioners can be from the same political party. The president designates one commissioner to be the chair. The chair acts as the chief executive officer and coordinates much of the administration of the agency.

The demographic characteristics of the FCC commissioners have varied over the years. Eighty-four people have served since 1934, including sixty-nine men and fifteen women. There have been eleven commissioners from ethnic minority groups, including two Asian Americans, three Hispanic Americans, and six African Americans. At the time of their appointment, commissioners have ranged in age from thirty-two to sixty-four, with the average age nearly forty-eight. There have been forty-two Democrats, forty Republicans, and two Independents.

Law has been the most common background of the commissioners, with fifty-five commissioners having had some type of legal education. There have been three commissioners with PhDs in fields like history and economics. Sixty-four of the eighty-four commissioners had no prior experience at the Commission. But fifty-four of them had been serving in some form of local, state, or federal government position immediately prior to being appointed, including two governors and three members of the U.S. House of Representatives. The majority of those who came from outside of government service were lawyers in private practice before joining the Commission.

Organizational Structure

Below the political appointees level are

a variety of staff offices, including seven policymaking bureaus. The bureaus run almost as separate entities, making and enforcing their own rules and policies. The bureaus are staffed by civil servants who are pegged as experts in their particular areas. Thus the power of the bureaus to set the agenda for the Commission cannot be overestimated. The bureaus are the Public Safety and Homeland Security Bureau (which oversees public safety issues including 911 and infrastructure protection), the Wireline Competition Bureau (which regulates landline telephone), the Wireless Bureau (which regulates cellphones, two-way radios, pagers, etc.), the Media Bureau (which regulates radio, television, cable television, and satellite television), the International Bureau (which deals with all international activity including international telephone rates, satellite issues, and trade negotiations), the Consumer and Governmental Affairs Bureau (which collects and analyses consumer complaints and inquiries, developing and distributing material to inform the public, and also handling all matters pertaining to the telecommunications industry and the disabled community), and the Enforcement Bureau (which enforces all communication laws and FCC rules).

There are also ten offices that handle a variety of duties at the FCC separate from the work of the bureaus.

- Office of the Managing Director
- Office of the General Counsel
- Office of the Administrative Law Judges
- Office of the Inspector General
- Office of Engineering and Technology
- Office of Strategic Planning and Policy Analysis
- Office of Legislative Affairs
- Office of Media Relations
- Office of Workplace Diversity
- Office of Communications Business Opportunities

Decision Making

As an 'expert' agency, the FCC was created to delve into the details of regulating complicated industries. Congress hands down general laws and broad policies for the communications industries, but it is the FCC that must develop the specific rules to enforce Congressional mandates. The FCC is obligated to follow all the guidelines set down by the Administrative Procedures Act; thus an important part of any FCC rule-making procedure is gathering public comments. The FCC asks for comments from any and all interested parties with two different processes: Notices of Inquiry (NOIs) and Notices of Proposed Rulemaking (NPRMs). NOIs solicit comments on broad topics without formally proposing any rules. NPRMs seek comments on specific rules that the Commission is considering. These public comments can play an important role in shaping government policy because they can bring to light new facts or unintended consequences of a particular rule. If there is still a lack of clarity or new issues develop, the Commission can issue a Further Notice of Proposed Rulemaking. Once the comment period has passed, the Commission will issue a Report and Order (R&O), making the final decision known.

Any decision made by the FCC is subject to judicial review in the federal court system. Most challenges to FCC rules go to the U.S. Court of Appeals for the District of Columbia Circuit. The FCC has been involved in well over 1,700 appellate and Supreme Court decisions in the last seven decades. Most appeals hinge on whether the FCC acted in a manner that was arbitrary and capricious. That means either that the Commission's decision was not based on the evidence or that a rule was not fairly applied to the party in question. If a rule is judged arbitrary and capricious by the courts, the FCC then often has to rewrite the rule in question or drop it completely.

Political Environment

Independent regulatory commissions like the FCC were designed as expert agencies specifically to remove politics from the regulatory process. But the FCC does not operate in a vacuum. The reality is that it is vulnerable to pressure from outside forces. There are, in fact, six major political actors involved in communications policy, according to the definitive work on the matter, *The Politics of Broadcast Regulation* by Erwin G. Krasnow, Lawrence D. Longley, and Herbert A. Terry (1982). The FCC is, of course, the most important actor in the regulatory environment. But Congress, the regulated industries, the White House, the courts, and interest groups/members of the public are also powerful forces in crafting policy.

Congress holds sway over the FCC in many ways. The Senate must approve all nominations to the Commission. It holds hearings on each nomination and often uses those hearings to push a particular agenda. Both the House and the Senate maintain oversight over all agency activities and often call commissioners to testify about policies to which they object. Congress also controls the FCC's budget and can pass legislation ordering the Commission to do (or not do) something. Indicative of Congress' influence is a statement once made by Speaker of the House Sam Rayburn. He famously put his arm around the shoulder of newly appointed FCC Chair Newton Minow and said, 'Just remember one thing, son. Your agency is an arm of the Congress; you belong to us. Remember that and you'll be all right' (cited in Krasnow, Longley, and Terry 1982: 89). Commissioners are well aware of the power of Congress and often make decisions that they believe follow the intent of those powerful people.

The industries that are regulated by the FCC also hold a great deal of sway over agency decision making. The commissioners and staff spend a significant amount of time interacting with members of the regulated industries. That can lead to what is called 'regulatory capture,' when the regulators overly sympathize with the concerns of the regulated. In addition, there is much movement of people between the regulated industries and the FCC. Staff and commissioners often join the regulated industries when their time at the agency is through. Former commissioners often become powerful lobbyists and the prospect of future employment can be a powerful persuasive device. The regulated industries can also influence the FCC indirectly by lobbying Congress. When a regulated industry persuades a member of Congress to put pressure on the FCC, the Commission can be overwhelmed. But the regulated industries do not speak with a unified voice, and thus their power can be diluted when different industries or companies work at cross-purposes.

The White House has some influence over FCC policy based on the fact that nominations to the Commission are made by the president. The personal relationship between the president and the individual commissioners can impact the White House's influence on policy. For example, Chairman Reed Hundt was a close personal friend of both President Bill Clinton and Vice President Al Gore. That relationship led to the White House having enormous sway over the activities of the FCC. Some have said that the Commission's agenda was set by the vice president's office throughout Hundt's tenure. On the other hand, when a president is disinterested in the Commission, that too can influence FCC actions. President George W. Bush failed to nominate two new commissioners when Republican seats came open. With two seats unfilled, the work at the Commission ground to a halt on many controversial issues because Chair Kevin Martin was unable to get a majority, being the only Republican member of a three-person Commission.

The federal courts get involved with the FCC in three basic ways. They can rule on the process by which a rule or decision was made, the constitutionality of the results, or whether the FCC had the statutory authority to take a particular action. There have been a number of issues in which the courts have been deeply involved, such as media ownership or the Equal Employment Opportunity rules. In those cases, the courts have monitored the Commission's decisions closely and repeatedly overturned rules supported by both the FCC and

Congress on constitutional or procedural grounds.

Interest groups and concerned individuals do have some influence over FCC policy. But those groups usually only succeed when they are allied with another, more powerful actor. For example, following the infamous 'wardrobe malfunction' at the 2004 Super Bowl, about 542,000 people complained to the Commission about seeing Janet Jackson's breast for less than two seconds. The FCC fined CBS $550,000 and Chairman Kevin Martin cited the 'record' number of complaints as a major reason behind the FCC's actions. Around the same time, about 1.5 million people complained about the concentration of media ownership and the Commission ignored those concerns. An anti-indecency group known as the Parents Television Council was hailed as the force behind the CBS fine. But the fact of the matter is that Chairman Martin, members of Congress, and President George W. Bush were all pushing for increased regulation of indecency. At the same time, even though Democratic commissioners Jonathan Adelstein and Michael Copps were also concerned about media concentration, none of the other, more powerful groups had gotten involved. Thus it is safe to say that interest groups are only as powerful as their friends in high places.

Telephone Regulation

As was discussed earlier, telephone regulation began with two concerns: setting affordable rates and maintaining the status quo of the natural monopoly. Over the years, the FCC has deregulated the telephone industry in a number of ways. It created policies to foster competition between telephone companies and data communications service providers. It also facilitated the transition to competition in long-distance telephone service. More recently, the Commission has attempted to facilitate competition in local telephone service as mandated by the Telecommunications Act of 1996. The Commission also licenses cellphones, pagers, and other personal communications devices.

Broadcasting Regulation

The history of broadcast regulation is complicated by the fact that broadcasting is both a delivery system and a content provider. The Commission, therefore, had always had to walk a fine line between the First Amendment rights of the broadcasters and listeners and the finite limits of the broadcast spectrum. Congress mandated in the Radio Act of 1927 (and later in the Communications Act of 1934) that broadcasting be regulated in the public interest, convenience, and necessity, language borrowed from public utility regulation. But exactly what was meant by serving the public interest has been a source of controversy for nearly 80 years.

At first, acting in the public interest seemed to mean only that stations would follow the technical requirements set by the FCC and avoid causing unnecessary interference with other stations. But the standard quickly evolved to include content guidelines. For example, the Federal Radio Commission revoked the licence of 'Doctor' John R. Brinkley in 1930 for using his station solely as a means for prescribing his patent medicines to listeners who wrote in with medical problems. Brinkley was also known for using his station to encourage men with impotence to come to his Kansas facility for his famous 'goat gland' operation. The U.S. Court of Appeals later upheld the FRC's actions by stating that evaluating the past performance of a station was not censorship.

The public interest standard went through many other incarnations, including limiting network programming and requiring the 'opportunity for local self-expression, the development and use of local talent, programs for children, religious programs, educational programs, public affairs programs, editorialization by licensees, political broadcasts, agricultural programs, news programs, weather and market reports, service to minority groups, and entertainment programs' (1960 *En Banc Programming Inquiry*, 44 F.C.C. 2303 at 2314). Since the late 1970s, however, the FCC has backed away from formal definitions of the public interest, instead choosing to allow the marketplace to determine the public interest in broadcast programming.

A second important historical component to the regulation of broadcasting is the notion of scarcity and a need to provide a diversity of voices. Spectrum scarcity was recognized as a rationale for content and ownership regulation as early as 1943. In 1969, the U.S. Supreme Court ruled that the First Amendment rights of the listeners were more important than the First Amendment rights of the broadcasters. Thus station owners had to serve the needs of the listening public rather than simply saying whatever they wanted over the public airways. This notion of scarcity was also used to justify strict ownership limits on broadcast stations.

Recent Republican FCC chairs like Michael Powell and Kevin Martin have maintained that in the age of the internet and the ever-expanding cable universe, scarcity is no longer an issue and thus all ownership regulations should be lifted. The Telecommunications Act of 1996 drastically altered the long-standing ownership limits and the FCC's new rules have been debated by the FCC, Congress, and the courts for a decade. Most recently, the FCC has been holding public hearings around the country on the issue of ownership limits. These hearings have been filled with people complaining of poor programming from media giants like Clear Channel Communications, which owns more than 10 per cent of all radio stations in the United States. But Chairman Martin remained firm that there is a diversity of voices available to the public.

The issue of scarcity and the need to define the public interest resulted in many rules governing broadcast content over the decades. Everything changed, however, with the massive deregulation that oc-

curred during the Reagan administration. Almost every content rule and guideline was thrown out in the belief that the market would determine the best programming. President Reagan's first FCC chair was Mark Fowler, whose faith in the market was demonstrated when he described television as just a 'toaster with pictures' ('The FCC: Compete or Die,' 34).

One area of regulation that has survived the deregulation of the 1980s is indecency. Since the beginning of radio communication, it has been illegal to broadcast obscene, indecent, or profane speech. Obscenity is not protected by the First Amendment and is completely banned from the broadcast airways. But the Commission rarely gets involved with obscenity cases, preferring to leave it to the FBI. Indecency, however, has been a major issue at the Commission for decades.

Currently, indecent speech is defined as 'language or material that, in context, depicts or describes, in terms patently offensive as measured by contemporary community broadcast standards for the broadcast medium, sexual or excretory organs or activities' (FCC, 'Obscene, Profane, and Indecent Broadcasts'). Indecent broadcast speech is illegal only when there is a reasonable risk that unsupervised children will be in the audience. FCC rules state that broadcast stations can air indecent material after 10 p.m. and before 6 a.m. This time is known as the safe harbour, and stations can air indecent speech without fear of a fine.

While indecency has been an issue of concern since the beginning of radio, it was the rise of the shock jocks like Howard Stern that made the regulation of indecency a major concern for the Commission. Beginning in late 1980s and ending with his departure to satellite radio, Stern was the point man on indecency. He personally racked up a majority of the fines issued prior to Janet Jackson's wardrobe malfunction at the 2004 Super Bowl.

Since the Super Bowl incident, the Commission has focused more on television programming and singular incidences of profanity than it has on shock jocks like Stern. The Commission has issued fines for things like a teen orgy scene in an episode of the CBS drama *Without a Trace*, a rape scene in a Spanish-language movie aired on a Telemundo station, and some explicit language in the PBS documentary, *The Blues: Godfathers and Sons*. The Commission has also stated that they will begin fining stations for fleeting profanity, such as when Cher said 'fuck 'em' during a live broadcast of the 2002 Billboard Music Awards or when a former *Survivor* contestant referred to another cast member as a 'bullshitter' on the CBS news program *The Early Show*.

While radio stations have paid or settled most of the indecency fines issued prior to 2004, the television networks have not been so quick to open their chequebooks. The major networks challenged the FCC's evolving definition of indecency in a case that went to the U.S. Supreme Court twice. In the end, the networks were found not liable but the Court upheld the underlying definition of indecency as constitutionally sound.

Cable Regulation

Cable television began roughly at the same time as broadcast television. Towns without stations put up large antennas to pull in distant signals and ran cables from the antennas into subscribers' homes. At first, the FCC did not want to be in charge of regulating cable. In 1956, the Commission stated officially that it did not have any authority over cable. By the early 1960s, however, the broadcast industry was demanding that the Commission protect television stations from the burgeoning cable industry. The FCC issued the first cable rules in 1965, calling it an ancillary service to broadcasting. The Commission got the statutory authority to regulate cable from Congress with the Cable Act of 1984. The FCC has regulated cable rates and programming offerings off and on ever since.

Kimberly A. Zarkin

Bibliography

FCC. Obscene, Indecent, and Profane Broadcasts. http://www.fcc.gov/cgb/consumerfacts/ obscene.html (accessed on 18 December 2006).

The FCC: Compete or Die. *The Economist*, 31 January 1987, 34.

Krasnow, Erwin G., Lawrence D. Longley, and Herbert A. Terry. *The Politics of Broadcast Regulation*. 3rd ed. New York: St Martin's Press, 1982.

FEEDBACK

[See also: *Bull's-Eye Model; Channel; Communication; Communication Theory; Cybernetics; Medium; Redundancy; Shannon, Claude E.*]

In media studies, communication theory, and information theory, *feedback* is defined as the capability of a sender in a communication system of detecting signals or cues issuing back from the intended receiver of the sender's message, or from the system itself, so that the performance or control of the communication system (or the contents of a message) can be maintained, adapted, modified, or improved. Technically, feedback is the return of a segment of the output of a system to the input, especially when used to maintain performance or to control the system. In human communication systems this means that senders have the ability to monitor the messages they transmit and to alter them to enhance their understandability. This includes, for instance, detecting physical reactions during conversations such as facial expressions or verbal cues in the receiver that signal the effect that the message is having on him or her.

The term was coined in 1948 by American mathematician Norbert Wiener (1894–1964), the founder of cybernetics. For Wiener, mechanisms for self-correction in machines serve the same purpose that the nervous system in humans serves in coordinating information to determine which actions will be performed. Feedback is the fundamental concept of cybernetic theory. When an event or state is part of a chain of cause-and-effect processes within a system, then the event or state is said to 'feed back' into itself. In an electronic-mechanical heating system, for example, the feedback mechanism is the thermostat which controls the system or keeps it in balance – when a certain temperature is reached, a mechanism in the thermostat sends information to the temperature-regulating system to shut down or start up. This self-correcting process is an example of what cyberneticians call 'negative feedback,' whereby changes in output are fed back to the input source so that the change is reversed. In 'positive feedback,' an increase in output is fed back to the source, expanding the output, thus creating a snowballing effect. An example is the screeching sound that occurs when a microphone is brought too close to its loudspeaker.

Generally, the feedback process depends on certain information being present or programmed into a system. Information is defined in this case as data that can be received by humans or machines, and as something that is mathematically probabilistic – a ringing alarm signal carries more information than one that is silent because the latter is the 'expected state' of the alarm system and the former its 'alerting state.' When an alarm is tripped in some way, the feedback process is started and the information load of the system increases (indeed, reaches its maximum). The one who developed the mathematical aspects of information and feedback theory was the American telecommunications engineer Claude Shannon (1916–2001), who showed that the information contained in a signal is inversely proportional to its probability of occurrence – the more likely a signal, the less information load it carries; the less likely, the more. Weiner's and Shannon's model is extremely useful in providing a terminology for describing aspects of communication systems, such as feedback, but it tells us little about how messages take on meaning in specific contexts.

In media studies, the term is used generally to refer to audience reactions to a program or, in advertising, to an ad or ad campaign. Such feedback is used to help producers of programs and creators of ads to tailor them to audience tastes and expectations.

Marcel Danesi

Bibliography

Hailman, Jack. *Coding and Redundancy*. Cambridge, MA: Harvard University Press, 2008.
Shannon, Claude E. A Mathematical Theory of Communication. *Bell Systems Technical Journal* 27 (1948): 379–423.
Wiener, Norbert. *Cybernetics, or Control and Communication in the Animal and the Machine*. Cambridge, MA: MIT Press, 1949.

FEMINISM

[See also: *Ang, Ien; Ferguson, Marjorie; Media Studies; Pornography*]

As an interdisciplinary field, communication is home to a number of feminist theories, issues, and practitioners. These are widely different, connected centrally only by the belief that oppression of women exists in some form and that this must end. In communication, a concern with feminism may be directed at any number of media or forms of interaction, and may focus on aspects including some but not necessarily all of the following: the gendered nature of interpersonal communication, inclusion in the production process, representation of women and girls in media content, the intrinsic inequality of a media industry built around capitalism, and the contradictory implications for females in a supposedly liberational digital environment.

However, feminism itself emerged long before communication was officially recognized as a discipline. The first cohesive feminist movement, often classified as the first wave, emerged in the mid-nineteenth century, coalescing around issues such as improvements in the education of girls and women, women's suffrage, property, divorce and custody rights, and greater access to certain professions. This was largely a middle-class movement originally based in Britain, and many of its adherents would not have described themselves as feminist at the time.

By the time the second wave rolled in, the term feminism had been in existence for a number of decades, and was embraced by a variety of women. The second wave of feminism is perhaps the one best recognized, though not necessarily understood, by the majority of North Americans and Europeans. Eventually coming into its own against the backdrop of an America whose political and social landscape was being challenged and transformed by the civil rights, anti-war, and environmental movements in the 1960s, feminism positioned itself in the mainstream, with the help of a few iconic figures who used the media to their advantage. Perhaps the best known of these are Gloria Steinem, founder of *Ms.* Magazine, and Betty Friedan, founder of NOW (National Organization for Women) and author of *The Feminine Mystique*, the book that spoke to many middle-class suburban women of a 'problem that had no name,' a lack of fulfilment experienced by women whose status as housewives and mothers overshadowed their identity. More activist figures claimed to be sidelined by the power of the press, written off as 'bra burners' or man haters following a number of publicity stunts captured on national television that depicted these women as extremists.

In their glory days, both *Ms.* and NOW commanded a large and loyal following, and some of the gains made for women in the 1960s and 1970s can be credited to initiatives such as NOW's sit-ins – complete with newspaper and television crews called in by the media-savvy Friedan, a former magazine writer – at hotels or clubs that had excluded women. On these social questions, as well as some political ones around issues such as affirmative action or abortion rights, the second wave made great inroads. However, the second wave also came to be seen as outdated and irrelevant by some women who felt that the forms of feminism it encompassed did not speak sufficiently to their issues. In particular, second-wave feminism, which had emerged as an essentially white, middle-class North American movement, was criticized for its lack of ethnic diversity, its inattention to all classes, and its neglect of problems of global significance, including various forms of colonialism and imperialism.

This kind of critique intersected with a larger move from modernism to postmodernism, with the emphasis switching from broad social and political questions to a host of problems centred on difference and discourse. Accordingly, the concerns of third-wave feminists, coming to particular prominence in the 1990s, have been diverse and difficult to summarize. Problems of social justice and inequity are central to the third wave, yet its attention to the analysis and production of aesthetics, for instance, as well as a broad acceptance of cultures, classes, and traditions, sometimes leads to criticisms that the third wave is insufficiently united, with too much emphasis on frivolity and not enough on true activism.

While the waves metaphor may satisfy those who prefer general or chronological categorizations, in actual fact feminists, including those tagged with the second-wave label, demonstrate considerable diversity. Second-wave feminism encompassed liberal, socialist, Marxist, and radical activists, among others, and at times the differences among these groups have seemed greater than their similarities.

The liberal paradigm is perhaps the one that even casual observers would be able to identify as feminism, and it is one of the oldest, dating back at least to Mary Wollstonecraft and her eighteenth-century text, *A Vindication of the Rights of Woman*. Liberal feminism seeks to correct inadequate gender representation in a variety of forms and places, a mission that often takes the form of lobbying to alter laws, regulations, and common practices. While affirmative action, for instance, is not embraced by all liberal feminists, some have endorsed it as a measure needed to balance the number of women in the workplace, as well as certain public institutions. Other measures may be less sweeping, but they would advocate the insertion of women into spaces otherwise dominated by a masculine presence, with the hope that greater egalitarianism would eventually become accepted and a matter of form. After all, according to such a view, men and women are not nearly as different in their talents and abilities as socialization processes would have us believe.

A number of other perspectives would criticize such a view for its inadequacy in attacking patriarchy at its roots. As a system based on unequal power relations, patriarchy extends into every aspect of society, oppressing women in ways that go beyond policy and legalities. A radical feminist, as the name implies, would advocate more extreme solutions than a liberal one, demonstrating limited or no interest in fitting into an existing patriarchal structure. One central area of oppression that some radical feminists target is female biology, which can subjugate women in a society that encourages reproduction without supporting it financially or psychologically. Other areas of concern include the pressure to exhibit so-called feminine characteristics and to conform to heterosexual norms even when these may simply increase male domination of women. Examples of thinkers who could be classified as radical include Kate Millett, Shulamith Firestone, Adrienne Rich, and Andrea Dworkin.

Radical feminists are concerned with numerous ways in which patriarchy manifests itself, and thus some may also be Marxist feminists, placing emphasis not only on patriarchy, but on capitalism. Socialist feminism is likewise occupied with questions about the intersection of patriarchy and capitalism, but for Marxists, capitalism is ultimately the structure that contributes most substantially to women's oppression. Marxist feminists consider that different classes of women will not experience oppression in entirely the same way. A working-class woman may experience pressures utterly foreign to the middle-class woman, who may – however inadvertently – contribute to the oppression of her less privileged sisters. While Marxism originally offered limited commentary on the unique challenges faced by women, Marxist and socialist feminists have built upon the work of Marx and Engels in highlighting women's working conditions, the inequality of their wages compared with those of men, and the need to acknowledge their unpaid labour, which allows for the continued functioning of an economic system aimed at extracting maximum profit at the expense of the lower classes. Many of these ideas also form the basis of a related school of thought, feminist political economy, which maintains a focus on power relations, production, and labour.

Post-colonial feminism may also take some of these factors into account, but it is concerned with other aspects of power, questioning the ethnocentrism of theories that do not acknowledge the legacies of colonialism and imperialism. Under the rubric of either or both, women in the developed world could be seen as contributing to the oppression of those in the developing world, or they may simply fail to understand the same, due to cultural difference and relative privilege. A feminist such as bell hooks combines more than one approach, highlighting multiple levels of discrimination that could be faced by women of colour on the basis of race, class, and gender. With her consistent criticism of what she calls 'white supremacist capitalist patriarchy,' hooks has brought particular attention to the intersection of these traits, while Chandra Talpade Mohanty was one of the first feminists to articulate clearly the question of oppression among women of different races, cultures, and perspectives.

Postmodern feminism is also concerned with difference of another kind. Unlike most of the other streams, postmodern feminism does not look to one or two forms of patriarchal oppression. Rather, it turns a critical eye on all notions of truth, identity, and values, noting that there is no universal form of woman or self. Postmodern feminists vary widely in their approaches, which may at times be labelled post-structuralist due to great emphasis on language and on the deconstruction of prevailing categories of gender. At one point, postmodern feminism was considered a largely French phenomenon due to the towering presence of practitioners such as Hélène Cixous, Luce Irigaray, and Julia Kristeva, but it may also be linked to the work of North American theorists such as Judith Butler, who helped analyse gender and the gendered body as artificial constructs. Her ideas have been applied in looking at many individuals who cross gender boundaries, including notable performers such as Madonna.

Psychoanalytic feminism looks at gender and self in a decidedly different manner, addressing many of Sigmund Freud's pronouncements on the childhood development of identity and sexuality. While most psychoanalytic feminists reject Freud's apparent sexism and essentialism, nonetheless many, including Karen Horney, Clara Thompson, Nancy Chodorow, Carol Gilligan, and Juliet Mitchell, have spoken to certain Freudian concepts in their examinations of psychosexual development, and these concepts are found repeatedly in analyses of media content, particularly film. These ideas regarding development and gendered differences may also be applied to studies of interpersonal communication and how interpersonal skills may vary between men and women.

These different forms of feminist thought have applied themselves in varied ways and settings. One of the first scholars to combine a feminist approach with communication analysis was Gertrude J. Robinson, who offered a number of pioneering studies around gender and media and was perhaps most influential in her commentaries on news content and the production of news. Drawing upon aspects of political economy, she offered statistical determinations of female underrepresentation in positions of power as well as a broader study of the symbols and ideologies found in media narratives. Her work remains some of the best known in this area and helped pave the way for subsequent discussions of biased content and production in the newsroom, such as Barbara Freeman's discussion of the unwritten rules and pressures that affected female reporters in 1960s Canada.

The news is generally characterized as a serious and worthwhile object of study, but 'women's magazines' or 'women's books' have often been dismissed as softer, frivolous, and the instrument of corporations that impose their patriarchal capitalist ideology upon a passive audience. While there may be some truth to this interpretation, writers such as Angela McRobbie, Ann Barr Snitow, and Janice Radway offered new approaches to women's reading, providing the possibility that these genres may be more complex than imagined, that they offered employment opportunities to women who are still excluded from more highbrow corners of the publishing industry, and that women may not be entirely passive or deluded when they consume such literature.

Similarly, discussions of film and television have addressed a host of issues. Feminist research on the portrayal of film covers its history, such as early, contradictory portrayals of women as plucky heroines who could only be saved by marriage, or depictions of suffragettes that alternately furthered and hindered the campaign for expanded voting rights. In the 1970s, Laura Mulvey's commentaries on film helped move attention towards a psychoanalytic framework and towards the key concept of the male gaze as the presumed spectator of many cinematic classics. Psychoanalysis still informs much of the feminist research on cinema, and to a certain extent may influence critiques of television.

Television, however, has always been a somewhat different medium from film, particularly given its location in the home – a space that is still more commonly associated with feminine domesticity than with masculine pursuits – and the longtime success of daytime serials aimed largely at a female audience. Groundbreaking work by authors such as Tania Modleski, Mary Ellen Brown, Christine Geraghty, Dorothy Hobson, and John Fiske on the ways that daytime television may simultaneously appear to empower women and confirm dominant ideologies of women's position in the private sphere operates in tandem with research by theorists such as Michèle Mattelart, who investigates the ways in which such programs naturalize a consumerist, domestic existence for women. Theorists such as Andrea L. Press have added commentaries on class as a key component of interpretation for female audiences of prime-time television, while Ellen Seiter has looked at representations of gender and race in television and advertising. The latter plays a large role in the television industry but can be analysed in a number of settings, including magazines, newspapers, and the internet.

The internet, in particular, has given rise to new interpretations of feminist theory. Over time, the question of technology – how can it and should it be used, what are the implications, what is the potential for increasing or decreasing inequity – has come to occupy the minds of many feminist communication scholars. From Michèle Martin's work on the telephone and the ways in which it has been adopted and adapted by women, to the data collected by scholars such as Ellen Balka, Leslie Regan Shade, Dale Spender, and Sherry Turkle in their observations of the ways women use technology in domestic or professional settings, research has indicated unintended side effects when new technologies are introduced into society.

Some theorists have suggested that the prevalence of digital technology, in particular, is indicative of a seismic shift in our very way of being, and that women are uniquely positioned to exercise dominance in the world of cyberspace, given their assumed competencies in areas of interpersonal communication. While this stance can assume a relatively liberal form, it can also assume a more radical appearance, as evidenced by Sadie Plant and Donna Haraway, who note that human beings are already moving towards a cyborg existence. The most optimistic of these perspectives is often referred to as cyberfeminism. Cyberspace is seen in these utopian formulations as a space where markers of gender, race, class, and age are all masked and thus can no longer be used to discriminate; others note that anonymity can also protect those who carry out sexual harassment, stalking, the production and distribution of pornography, and so forth.

In other words, no matter how new a technology, medium, or other form of communication may seem, similar questions assert themselves repeatedly regarding gender and equality. There is no one branch of feminist theory that answers all of these, and at times theories may operate in conjunction or they may demonstrate considerable overlap. Regardless of which perspective(s) one may endorse, feminist theory and practice are integral to the study of communication.

Faiza Hirji

Bibliography

Babe, Robert E. *Canadian Communication Thought: Ten Foundational Writers*. Toronto: University of Toronto Press, 2000.

Barrett, Michele. *Women's Oppression Today: Problems in Marxist Feminist Analysis*. London: Verso, 1980.

Bradley, Patricia. Mass Communication and the Shaping of US Feminism. In *News, Gender and Power*, ed. Cynthia Carter, Gill Branston, and Stuart Allan, 160–73. New York: Routledge, 1998.

Butler, Judith. *Gender Trouble: Feminism and the Subversion of Identity*. New York: Routledge, 1990.

Chodorow, Nancy. *The Reproduction of Mothering:*

Psychoanalysis and the Sociology of Gender. Berkeley: University of California Press, 1978.

Cixous, Hélène. The Laugh of the Medusa. *Signs* 1 (1976): 245–64.

Firestone, Shulamith. *The Dialectic of Sex: The Case for Feminist Revolution*. New York: Morrow, 1970.

Freeman, Barbara M. *The Satellite Sex: The Media and Women's Issues in English Canada, 1966–1971*. Waterloo, ON: Wilfrid Laurier University Press, 2001.

Friedan, Betty. *The Feminine Mystique*. London: Victor Gollancz, 1963.

Gilligan, Carol. *In a Different Voice: Psychological Theory and Women's Development*. Cambridge, MA: Harvard University Press, 1982.

Haraway, Donna. *Simians, Cyborgs and Women: The Reinvention of Nature*. London: Free Association Books, 1991.

hooks, b. *Feminist Theory from Margin to Center*. Boston: South End Press, 1984.

Irigaray, Luce. *This Sex Which Is Not One*. Ithaca, NY: Cornell University Press, 1985.

Kristeva, Julia. *Desire in Language: A Semiotic Approach to Literature and Art*. Oxford: Basil Blackwell, 1981.

Martin, Martin M. *'Hello Central?': Gender, Technology and Culture in the Formation of Telephone Systems*. Montreal: McGill-Queen's University Press, 1991.

McRobbie, Angela. *Feminism and Youth Culture: From 'Jackie' to 'Just Seventeen.'* Boston: Unwin Hyman, 1991.

Millett, Kate. *Sexual Politics*. Garden City, NY: Doubleday, 1980.

Mitchell, Juliet. *Psychoanalysis and Feminism*. London: Lane, 1974.

Modleski, Tania. *Loving with a Vengeance: Mass-Produced Fantasies for Women*. Hamden, CT: Archon, 1982.

Mohanty, Chandra Talpade. *Feminism without Borders: Decolonizing Theory, Practicing Solidarity*. Durham, NC: Duke University Press, 2003.

Mulvey, Laura. *Visual and Other Pleasures*. Bloomington: Indiana University Press, 1989.

Plant, Sadie. *Zeroes and Ones: Digital Women and the New Technoculture*. New York: Doubleday, 1987.

Radway, Janice. *Reading the Romance: Women,*

Patriarchy, and Popular Literature. Chapel Hill: University of North Carolina Press, 1984.

Rich, Adrienne. *Of Woman Born: Motherhood as Experience and Institution*. London: Virago, 1977.

Spender, Dale. *Nattering on the Net: Women, Power and Cyberspace*. Toronto: Garamond, 1996.

Steeves, H.L., and J. Wasko. Feminist Theory and Political Economy: Toward a Friendly Alliance. In *Sex and Money: Feminism and Political Economy in the Media*, ed. E.R. Meehan and E. Riordan, 16–29. Boston: Northeastern University Press, 2002.

Tong, Rosemarie. *Feminist Thought: A Comprehensive Introduction*. Boulder, CO: Westview Press, 1989.

Turkle, Sherry. *Life on the Screen: Identity in the Age of the Internet*. New York: Simon and Schuster, 1995.

Wollstonecraft, Mary. *A Vindication of the Rights of Woman, with Strictures on Political and Moral Subjects*. Ed. C.W. Hagelman, Jr. New York: Norton, 1967.

FERGUSON, MARJORIE (1929–99)

[See also: *Feminism; Globalization; Magazines; Mass Communication*]

Marjorie Ruth Ferguson was a renowned media scholar who worked especially on the social implications of communications technologies and global communications, as well as on the role of women in the media around the world. Ferguson was born in Victoria, British Columbia. She attended the University of British Columbia and moved to London, England, in 1949. Her first career was in women's journalism. In the 1950s, with no formal qualifications, she joined the staff of Odhams' (later IPC) *Woman* magazine, the most widely circulated women's magazine in Britain, and quickly became the publication's associate editor.

Ferguson obtained her PhD in sociology from the London School of Economics (LSE) in 1979 and taught there from 1978 to 1988. Her first major publication was

Forever Feminine: Women's Magazines and the Cult of Femininity (1985). The book, which was based on her doctoral thesis, was one of the first major works to seriously examine women's magazines and their implications for female readers. During the 1980s, she was very active in alerting people to the repercussions of new communication technologies, leading to two influential books that she edited: *New Communication Technologies and the Public Interest* (1986) and *Public Communication: The New Imperatives* (1990).

During her time at LSE, Ferguson encouraged the institution to broaden its curriculum to include media and communication studies. She had little success with this endeavour and decided to move to the United States, where media studies had gained broader acceptance at universities. In 1988, she began working at the College of Journalism at the University of Maryland and eventually became the director of its doctoral program. She taught at the college for more than ten years on media and politics, media systems of different countries, and political communications.

As the term 'globalization' entered the academic jargon, Ferguson emphasized the restraining power of nationality and 'sense of place' as expressed through language, religion, and tradition. She predicted that national ties would become increasingly stronger in a period of globalization, influencing people's ideas and behaviours; consequently, she was often critical of McLuhan's 'global village' theory.

During her career, Ferguson was a consultant to both the British Broadcasting Corporation and various publishers. She was also on the Board of Editorial Advisors of *American Journalism Review* (published by Maryland's College of Journalism), and was involved with such publications as the *Journal of Communication; Culture and Communication;* the *European Journal of Communication;* and *Media, Culture, and Society.*

Alexandra Birk-Urovitz and Elizabeth Birk-Urovitz

Bibliography

Ferguson, Marjorie. *Forever Feminine: Women's Magazines and the Cult of Femininity.* London: Sage, 1985.
– *New Communication Technologies and the Public Interest.* London: Sage, 1986.
– *Public Communication: The New Imperatives.* London: Sage, 1990.
– *Cultural Studies in Question.* London: Sage, 1997.
Schlesinger, Philip. In Memoriam – Marjorie Ferguson, 1929–99. *Media, Culture, and Society* 22 (2000): 117–19.

FISKE, JOHN (b. 1939)

[See also: *Communication Theory; Media Studies; Popular Culture; Television*]

John Fiske, theorist of communication and culture studies, and critic of mass media culture, has focused on sign theory in the mass media, mass culture, and the interaction of meaning systems with media portrayals.

Born, raised, and formally educated in Britain, Fiske is best known for his work conducted at the University of Wisconsin-Madison, where he was Professor of Communication Arts for a number of years. Among his most important works are *Power Plays, Power Works* (1993), *Understanding Popular Culture* (1989), *Reading the Popular* (1989), and *Television Culture* (1987). Fiske is currently retired and residing in Massachusetts.

Fiske, a proponent of the importance of popular culture, writes: 'Popular culture is made by the people, not imposed on them' (Fiske 1989: 65). The cultural meanings assigned by individuals to popular culture texts differ not only in terms of socio-economic status, ethnicity, or gender, but also in subjective ways. Thus, it is irrelevant to categorize any text as more or less meaningful or not meaningful at all. It all depends on the individual user or interpreter of the text. Fiske uses the term 'productive pleasures' to emphasize this. There are three such pleasures: hegemonic, whereby the audience does not participate in negotiating textual meaning because the text's meaning is transparent; popular pleasures, which are the most common (whereby the text is perceived as relevant to one's daily life); and evasive pleasures, whereby the text provides a vehicle for evasion or escape from daily life. Fiske also maintains, however, that popular culture involves the negotiation of meaning based on unequal power structures. In this sense, popular culture is a 'micropolitical' phenomenon since 'the politics of popular culture can play the greater part in the tactics of everyday life' (Fiske 1984: 69). Thus, while supporting popular culture, he also notes that its inequalities must be disclosed in order to bring about equality in society.

Mariana Bockarova

Bibliography

Fiske, John. *Television Culture*. London: Methuen, 1987.
– *Understanding Popular Culture*. Boston: Unwin Hyman, 1989.
– *Media Matters: Race and Gender in U.S. Politics*. Minneapolis: University of Minnesota Press, 1996.

FOUCAULT, MICHEL (1926–84)

[See also: *Althusser, Louis; Deconstruction; Postmodernism; Post-Structuralism*]

A French interdisciplinary academic, Michel Foucault was a leading late-twentieth-century intellectual and for the last fifteen years of his life professor of the History of Systems of Thought at the prestigious Collège de France. Foucault reconstructed the systems of the period-specific practices of past disciplines whose objects of analysis or manipulation were particular aspects of the human being. He had one

foot in the historical archive, piecing together aspects of past disciplines, and the other in the present, putting in perspective various features of what we have become. Playing original and radical reconstructions of the past against apparently indispensable presuppositions of the present, Foucault generated controversial critical 'histories of the present' and contributed to the political advocacy of marginalized groups. His work resulted in a large following throughout the arts and social sciences, but also considerable criticism.

While the young Foucault was studying at the celebrated École normale supérieure, the French intellectual world experienced the zenith of phenomenology and existentialism, the central figure of which was Jean-Paul Sartre (1905–80), philosopher, author, and critic of bourgeois conformism, oppression, and capitalism. Sartre, who quit the academy and became an internationally recognized public intellectual, argued that humans are essentially free to choose what they will be, famously claiming that humans make nothing but what they make of themselves. This radical account of human agency amounted to a philosophical humanism in which each individual is and ought to be fully responsible for his or her life. Eventually, Sartre would weave into his humanism the threads of Marxism, according to which humans are indeed agents who make their history through their practices but whose practices are significantly conditioned by the existing dominant social relations. However, Sartre argued that the conditions of the present, which limit the agency of human practice, are themselves the inertial residue of past practices – ossified past actions that have become customary, unintended patterns of social behaviour, the 'practico-inert.' By reducing the limiting conditions of human practice to the practices of past humans, Sartre generated a Marxism in which the agency of human history was entirely reduced to human practice in the last instance – that is, a

Marxism fully compatible with philosophical humanism. One of the most important features of Foucault's work is that it stands altogether outside the domain of philosophical humanism. In an interview first published in *Les lettres françaises* on 31 March 1966, Foucault pointed out that he did not try to explain disciplines in terms of the practico-inert, but rather in terms of what he called the 'theoretico-active.'

Each of us has to learn the practice of the discipline we eventually find ourselves pursuing. We admit that the set of essential characteristics that constitutes the discipline – its rules, customs, and nomenclature – precedes existing subjects who have yet to learn the discipline. Thus we must admit that the agency of the practitioner as such is determined by the pre-existing discipline's essential characteristics. From the philosophical humanist's perspective, such determination would limit the agency of the free subject (at least in the first instance). However, since only particular, limited subjects seem to exist in reality, perhaps the fully free existential and phenomenological subject is a fiction. Because each discipline, not unlike each individual, has irreducible characteristics peculiar to itself, and because the condition of existence of the practitioner of a discipline is that he or she espouse and enact the discipline's relevant characteristics, the practitioner's agency is not limited by but rather produced by the relevant determinations. Thus, in the history and philosophy of disciplines one will find theoretically rich disciplinary practices that must be said to actively produce agency by producing the practitioners who categorize, manipulate, and order the relevant objects. Piecing together the 'regularity' – that is, the systematicity – of the practice of a historically specific discipline would be to analyse phenomena in a theoretico-active fashion. This is the sense in which the rules of regularity of a 'discursive formation' or an 'apparatus' are 'not negative,' but rather 'positive' or 'productive.' Often misunderstood, Foucault did not argue that discursive formations and apparatuses were positive in the sense of being good; he argued that they were positive in that they did not negate or limit agency, practices, and objects, but rather produced them.

What we may call Foucault's philosophical anti-humanism did not originate merely as a critical stand against the philosophical humanism of Sartre. Rather, it originated largely in the structuralist movement – a cauldron of French intellectual activity that had been warming for some time and would boil over and largely displace philosophical humanism after the 1950s. The humanist paradigm of the subject was to be swept away in a flood of approaches for which the generality or universality of language became paradigmatic. Some of the roots of the structuralist movement are actually to be found in phenomenology and existentialism broadly understood. Most notable with respect to Foucault was the incredible influence in France of the German philosophers Edmund Husserl (1859–1938) and Martin Heidegger (1889–1976), as well as the French philosopher Maurice Merleau-Ponty (1908–61). Husserl and Heidegger were the fathers of phenomenology, to whom Sartre owed a great deal, but whose works also contained important theoretical horizons and pathways that led beyond the centrality of the subject, as Heidegger made clear in his 1947 'Letter on Humanism,' largely a critical response to Sartre. Merleau-Ponty moved from positions close to Sartre to positions close to structuralism over the course of his career, becoming one of the first French academics to take seriously the work of the Swiss grandfather of structural linguistics Ferdinand de Saussure (1857–1913), which influenced those who were to become the leading figures of structuralism. The influences of Heidegger, Merleau-Ponty, and others are evident in both Foucault's first book, the short *Mental Illness and Personality* (1954), and his long 'Introduction' (of the same year) to the French translation of

Dream and Existence by the phenomenological psychiatrist Ludwig Binswanger (1881–1966). Foucault sought to understand the world as experienced in imagination and dream, and he argued that imagination and dream co-constitute non-imaginative waking experience, for we must admit that often almost all of what is meaningful about an object of experience is not perceivable – it is imagined, as it were. Using this approach, Foucault sought to understand the world as experienced by the mentally ill. He also argued that it was crucial to situate each experienced world of mental illness in the antagonistic social conditions out of which it arose, providing a largely Marxist analysis of social conditions. Although he was to continue to study psychology and mental illness for seven more years, he would leave behind phenomenology and Marxism.

For the 1962 reissue of his first book, the title was changed to *Mental Illness and Psychology*, and the concluding third of the text was overhauled to reflect the new approach evident in what is generally considered Foucault's first major work, *History of Madness* (1961). This massive book was his doctoral thesis, submitted to Georges Canguilhem (1904–95), a historian and philosopher of science who had a major influence on structuralism and on Foucault. Most of *History of Madness* was not translated and published in English for 45 years, but it was abridged by Foucault and reissued in French in 1964, and the abridged version was translated into English and published in 1965 as *Madness and Civilization*. *History of Madness* provides us with an analysis of the disciplines that dealt with madness during the European 'classical age' (roughly the period from the middle of the seventeenth century to the end of the eighteenth century). According to Foucault, those disciplines were radically different from the relevant disciplines of both the Renaissance and the nineteenth century, and they have been misunderstood by traditional historians, who have seen in them little

more than a general brutality that libratory nineteenth-century practitioners would reform. In fact, the classical disciplines of madness consisted of rational and regular practices, and the disciplines of mental illness that succeeded them and stand at the beginning of our own practices consisted of social and political measures to enforce conformity to bourgeois norms. Actually, both the classical and the nineteenth-century disciplines are rational, regular, social, and political, but since we espouse and enact the characteristics of our own epoch's disciplines, significantly different past practices are identified as irrational, brutal, and standing on the other side of the libratory reform that has resulted in our apparently enlightened present. The German philosopher Friedrich Nietzsche (1844–1900), who was for Foucault both a major influence and a harbinger of philosophical antihumanism, put the general point quite nicely in *Thus Spoke Zarathustra*: 'This is my pity for all that is past: I see how all of it is abandoned … to the pleasure, the spirit, the madness of every generation, which comes along and reinterprets all that has been as a bridge to itself' (Nietzsche 1984: 26).

This kind of approach to past and present practices was taken by Foucault throughout his career. The goal was not to argue that the past was better, or that we should go back to it, but to open much less anachronistic pathways to the study of past disciplines, to bracket the presupposition that current disciplines must be progressively reformed past disciplines, and to show that past and present disciplines are sets of regular, rational, social, and political practices.

Two years after *History of Madness*, Foucault published *The Birth of the Clinic* (1963), which provided analyses of both the classical and the nineteenth-century disciplines that dealt with physical illness. Not unlike in *History of Madness*, Foucault argued that the nineteenth-century clinical gaze was a misunderstood regular, rational, social, and political practice that supplanted the relevant classical disciplines. Three years later, *The Order of Things* (1966) appeared, Foucault's most challenging book. *The Order of Things* provided an analysis of three distinct disciplines during the classical age, those that dealt with life, labour, and language. Foucault argued that the regularities between the three disciplines of natural history, analysis of wealth, and general grammar radically exceeded regularities between any one of the disciplines and the versions of itself that either preceded it in the renaissance or followed it in the nineteenth century. The classical disciplines exhibit a regularity of practice that operates within the presuppositional space of epistemological taxonomy. That is, the dominant mode of analysis espoused and enacted by practitioners in these particular classical disciplines was the representation of objects in what amounted to complex tables of classification. In the nineteenth century, the dominant mode of analysis shifted. The taxonomical representation of objects was succeeded by analysis rooted in the human subject. The discursive concept of 'man' as the very ground of knowledge and action was born, inaugurating the philosophical humanism that the structuralists, Foucault, and others would challenge in the twentieth century. In an interview first published in *Magazine Littéraire* in April–May 1969, Foucault argued that structuralism should focus less on the analysis of structures and more on the role of the subject in the whole process. In the end, Foucault is generally thought to have exceeded the structuralist movement, and is commonly called a leading 'post-structuralist' or 'postmodernist.'

In 1969 Foucault published *The Archaeology of Knowledge*, in which he elaborated the details of the complete 'archaeological' method he developed in the production of his first three major books. What Foucault meant by archaeology was an approach to the past that reconstructed the regular functioning of actual disciplines. This work was not done either by digging up and interpreting ancient shards or by postulating an original principle (an '*arch*' in ancient

Greek) of historical continuity. Rather, it was done in the 'archive' of the past texts and statements of the relevant practitioners.

After *The Archaeology of Knowledge*, it took six years for Foucault to publish another major work, *Discipline and Punish*, and then a year later in 1976 *The History of Sexuality, Volume I* appeared, probably his two most influential books. Between *The Archaeology of Knowledge* and *Discipline and Punish*, Foucault's general term for his method shifted from 'archaeology' to 'genealogy.' Although this shift elicited many pages of commentary, it amounted to a new emphasis, not a substantial methodological change. If the objects of archaeological analysis were the regular functioning patterns of discursive formations (for example, the classical discipline of the analysis of wealth), the objects of genealogical analysis would be the regular functioning patterns of relations of power that constitute particular social and political apparatuses (for example, incarceration after the eighteenth century). Certainly relations of power come to the fore in *Discipline and Punish* and *History of Sexuality I*, but similar relations are in the earlier books (if less explicitly so), the analysis of discursive formations continues in the later books, and the overall approach of writing critical histories of the present continues throughout.

Along with the two-volume *Capitalism and Schizophrenia* by Gilles Deleuze (1925–95) and Félix Guattari (1930–92), the preface for which was written by Foucault, *Discipline and Punish* and *History of Sexuality I* can be read as a formidable challenge to what were during the middle decades of the twentieth century influential articulations of Marxism and psychoanalysis. Louis Althusser (1918–90), one of the leading figures of structuralism who had been influenced by Merleau-Ponty and Canguilhem, combined psychoanalysis and structuralism within a Marxism that certainly influenced Foucault, especially with respect to the analysis of the productive determination of the agency of subjects. However, in the first chapter of *Discipline and Punish* Foucault distinguished himself from Althusser, for whom capitalism is maintained in large part by two apparatuses that produce 'good subjects': the repressive state apparatus (for example, the police), and the ideological state apparatus (most importantly the education system and the institution of the family). For Foucault, however, agency after the classical age is the product neither of repressive violence nor of ideological indoctrination, and its determinations are not to be found exclusively within a few institutions such as the police or the school. Taking the modern birth of the prison as his point of departure, Foucault argued that penal practices before the nineteenth century, which often involved torture, were misunderstood by traditional historians, who saw in them nothing but a brutality that was criticized by late eighteenth-century reformers, resulting in progress to the much more humane penalty of generalized imprisonment. However, Foucault argues, seventeenth- and eighteenth-century torture consisted of rational and regular practices. Furthermore, it was not its brutality that was the chief target of criticism for the reformers. And finally, the models endorsed by the reformers excluded generalized imprisonment. To explain the rapid proliferation of generalized imprisonment as the standard penalty of Western Europe and North America in the nineteenth century, Foucault argued that these regions underwent a basic social and political transformation between the mid-eighteenth and mid-nineteenth centuries in which a new political technology emerged in education, patient care, military training, the organization of work, and the reform of criminals. This transformation and these political techniques, not a narrative of reform, account for the prison. The new political techniques consisted in isolating each individual within its population, collecting knowledge about the individual, and turning that knowledge to good use with respect to the relations of power by which the individual's circumstances and

options might be modified, with the goal of re-forming the individual according to a graded hierarchy of achievement. These techniques were applied to bodies – for example, exercises imposed on the isolated and monitored inmate or student, in his cell or at her desk respectively. The techniques were applied to bodies via carefully organized spaces and times, from the prison's cellular architecture and the duration of the inmate's sentence to the school's dispersion of desks and classrooms, its student records, and its graduated terms of study. And the techniques were applied in order to render the bodies both docile and useful, producing the reformed criminal, the good student, the cured patient, the trained soldier, or the productive worker. Neither repressive violence nor ideological indoctrination, but rather relations of knowledge and relations of power applied to the body, are what distinguish the determination of modern agency.

History of Sexuality I turns the above analysis toward aspects of the wider population as an object. In the middle of the twentieth century the sexual liberation movement often sought intellectual credentials in fusions of Marxism and psychoanalysis, in authors such as the Frankfurt school's Herbert Marcuse (1898–1979). Apparently a response to Victorian sexual repression, sexual liberation was actually, Foucault argued, much more of a process in which sex had been made an object of knowledge. The resulting knowledge had been turned to good use with respect to the relations of power by which populations are reproduced and maintained. Foucault began with historians' claims about Victorian repression – that there was a general interdiction against expressions of sexuality – but, he argued, in fact there was a proliferation of discourse about sexuality at the time. The analysis here is roughly analogous to that in *The Order of Things*, according to which the discursive concept of 'man' became the very ground of knowledge and action in the nineteenth century. According to *History of Sexuality I* it is 'sex' that becomes a ground of libratory expression. Of course, humans and sex have been around for a long time, but not as the presupposed grounds of knowledge, action, liberation, or expression. Although humans have always had sex, the view that there is something called 'the sex drive' or 'the truth of sex,' that it has been repressed, and that it ought to be liberated is both something new and something that has been a perfect mechanism of incitement to generate knowledge about sex. In the hands of appropriate practitioners such knowledge enables the manipulation of behaviours and the reproduction of healthy populations. This even involves such issues as eugenics, racial purity, and the like, which became more than mere possibilities in the nineteenth and twentieth centuries. The deployment of sexuality was a set of strategic practices, but it could not be reduced to the intentions of subjects – it was 'intentional but non-subjective,' roughly analogous to what Foucault called the 'theoretico-active' ten years earlier.

After *History of Sexuality I*, it was not until 1984 that Foucault published his last two major works, two parts of the large project he would be unable to finish because of his failing health and eventual death that year: *The Use of Pleasure: The History of Sexuality, Volume II* and *The Care of the Self: The History of Sexuality, Volume III*. Between *History of Sexuality I* and these final books another change in emphasis occurred, this time toward the analysis of how subjects are constituted and how they might manage their own liberty. Clearly, this issue, though previously not explicit in Foucault's analyses, was always present. Foucault began from the material in *History of Sexuality I*, but he turned back to Western classical antiquity to analyse the transformation from Greco-Roman polymorphic pleasures of the body, including sexual relations between men and boys, to Christian sexual desire. The Greco-Romans enjoyed the pleasures of the body as one might enjoy the pleasures of fine dining today. There was no postulation of desire as one's deep and morally reveal-

ing truth, but rather an aesthetic and moderate use of pleasure. The Christians problematized desire as a fundamental moral concern and a force to be strictly regulated, something to which Foucault would have drawn lines of connection from his analysis in *History of Sexuality I*, but the project was stopped short by his death.

In addition to eight major works, Foucault wrote and published a great deal of other items during his life. Many of his essays and interviews have been collected in various volumes, and his lecture courses at the Collège de France continue to be edited, translated, and published.

John Duncan

Bibliography

Althusser, Louis. Ideology and Ideological State Apparatuses. In *Mapping Ideology,* ed. Slavoj Zizek, 100–39. New York: Verso, 1994.

Deleuze, Gilles, and Félix Guattari. *Anti-Oedipus: Capitalism and Schizophrenia.* Trans. Robert Hurley, Mark Seem, and Helen R. Lane. Minneapolis: University of Minnesota Press, 1983.

– *A Thousand Plateaus: Capitalism and Schizophrenia.* Trans. Brian Massumi. Minneapolis: University of Minnesota Press, 1987.

Foucault, Michel. *The Order of Things: An Archaeology of the Human Sciences.* Unidentified collective translation. New York: Pantheon, 1971.

– *The Birth of the Clinic: An Archaeology of Medical Perception.* Trans. Alan Sheridan-Smith. New York: Pantheon, 1973.

– *The Archaeology of Knowledge.* Trans. A.M. Sheridan-Smith. New York: Harper Colophon, 1976.

– *Discipline and Punish: The Birth of the Prison.* Trans. Alan Sheridan. New York: Pantheon, 1977.

– *The History of Sexuality I: An Introduction.* Trans. Robert Hurley. New York: Pantheon, 1978.

– Dream, Imagination, and Existence. Trans. Forest Williams. *Review of Existential Psychology and Psychiatry* 19 (1984–5): 29–78.

– *The Use of Pleasure: The History of Sexuality,*

Volume II. Trans. Robert Hurley. New York: Pantheon, 1985.

– *The Care of the Self: The History of Sexuality, Volume III.* Trans. Robert Hurley. New York: Pantheon, 1986.

– *Mental Illness and Psychology.* Trans. Alan Sheridan. Berkeley and Los Angeles: University of California Press, 1987.

– *Foucault Live (Interviews, 1966–84).* Trans. John Johnston. New York: Semiotext(e), 1989.

– *History of Madness.* Trans. Jonathan Murphy and Jean Khalfa. London and New York: Routledge, 2006.

Heidegger, Martin. *Basic Writings.* New York: Harper and Row, 1977.

Nietzsche, Friedrich. *The Portable Nietzsche.* Trans. Walter Kaufmann. New York: Penguin, 1984.

Sartre, Jean-Paul. *Critique of Dialectical Reason.* Trans. Alan Sheridan-Smith. London: NLB, 1976.

FRANKFURT SCHOOL

[See also: *Adorno, Benjamin; Culture Industry Theory; Habermas, Jürgen; Hegemony Theory; Marcuse, Herbert; Marxism; Media Effects*]

The Frankfurt School (complete title, The Frankfurt Institute for Social Research) was an institute founded at the University of Frankfurt in 1922. It was the world's first Marxist school of social criticism and research, and its aim was to understand the ways in which human societies constructed meaning collectively under the impact of modern technologies and capitalist modes of economic production. Its members became extremely famous over time and are still quoted often in the areas of media, culture, and communication studies. Among them were: Friedrich Pollock (1894–1970), Theodor W. Adorno (1903–69), Walter Benjamin (1892–1940), Max Horkheimer (1895–1973), Herbert Marcuse (1898–1979), Erich Fromm (1900–80), Leo Lowenthal (1900–93), and Jürgen Habermas (b. 1929). The school's main view was that modern capitalist cultures were vulgar, produc-ing 'cultural products' intended mainly to placate ordinary people. Representative works of Frankfurt School scholars include: Horkheimer and Adorno, *The Dialectic of Enlightenment*; Horkheimer, *The Eclipse of Reason, Critical Theory*; Adorno, *Minima Moralia, The Authoritarian Personality, Negative Dialectics*; Benjamin, *The Work of Art in the Age of Its Mechanical Reproduction, Theses on the Philosophy of History*; Marcuse, *Reason and Revolution, Eros and Civilization, One-Dimensional Man, Essay on Liberation, Negations, Soviet Marxism, Studies in Critical Philosophy, Counterrevolution and Revolt, Hegel's Ontology*; Lowenthal, *Literature, Popular Culture, and Society*; and Fromm, *Escape from Freedom*.

The two main events that left their mark on the Frankfurt School were the failure of working-class revolutionary movements in Western Europe after the First World War and the rise of Nazism. Common interests shared by members of the school included philosophy, social research, Hegelian-Marxist dialectics, and Marx's critiques of capitalism. But the Frankfurt School scholars differed with respect to the dogmatism of orthodox communism, condemning what they saw as the lethal illusions of liberalism and the arrogance and hypocrisy of the social-democratic political parties.

By contrast with dominant philosophical trends such as positivism, materialism, and phenomenology, the Frankfurt School scholars proposed a return to the basic ideas found in Kant, Hegel, Marx (the publication in the 1930s of Marx's *Economic-Philosophical Manuscripts* and *The German Ideology* exerted a strong influence on them), and Freud (see particularly Herbert Marcuse's book of 1954 *Eros and Civilization*) – all writers whom they read voraciously.

In contrast to scientism and dogmatism, the Frankfurt School scholars adopted the critical philosophy of Immanuel Kant, who used the term *critique* to attack the limits of Western reason – see especially Horkheimer's and Adorno's *Dialectic of Enlightenment* (1944). The latter uses the *Odyssey* as a paradigm for the analysis of bourgeois consciousness and of Western reason in general. But the concept of critique as elaborated by the Frankfurt School must also be understood in an epistemological sense, following Marx, who characterized his analyses as 'critiques of political economy.' In this sense, the Frankfurt School scholars elaborated the Marxist critique of bourgeois ideology and critiqued alienated labour and the exploitation of labour by means of a dominant mode of communication, mass culture, negation of contradiction, suppression of dissent, and repressive intolerance. The scholars saw the cultural 'products' of capitalist society as analogous to manufactured products. These were not meant to last, as were the great works of art, but rather to be turned over quickly. The whole of mass capitalist culture was thus seen as a 'culture industry' producing music, spectacles, and the like that were meant to be ephemeral and of little value. The only logic they served was that of the marketplace, not of any aesthetic sense.

Augusto Ponzio

Bibliography

Adorno, Theodor W. *The Culture Industry*. London: Routledge, 1999.

Habermas, Jürgen. *Structural Transformation of the Public Sphere*. Cambridge, MA: MIT Press, 1989.

Horkheimer, Max, and Theodor W. Adorno. *Dialectic of Enlightenment*. New York: Herder and Herder, 1972.

Jay, Martin. *The Dialectical Imagination: A History of the Frankfurt School and the Institute for Social Research 1923–1950*. Berkeley: University of California Press, 1996.

Lowenthal, Leo. *Literature, Popular Culture and Society*. Englewood Cliffs, NJ: Prentice-Hall, 1961.

Marcuse, Herbert. *Studies in Philosophy and Social Science* 9, no. 1 (1941): 414–39.

Shapiro, Jeremy J. The Critical Theory of Frankfurt. *Times Literary Supplement*, 4 October 1974.

Wiggershaus, Rolf. *The Frankfurt School: Its History, Theories and Political Significance*. Cambridge, MA: The MIT Press, 1995.

FRANKFURT SCHOOL AND CRITICAL THEORY

[See also: *Frankfurt School; Marxism*]

The term 'Frankfurt School' refers to a group of German-Jewish intellectuals associated with the Institut für Sozialforschung, a private research foundation established in Frankfurt in 1922 to study the structures and practices of society from a Marxist perspective. In 1931, Max Horkheimer became the Institute's director and broadened its initial emphasis upon history and political economy to include an explicitly interdisciplinary and holistic investigation into the social, economic, political, cultural, moral, psychological, and philosophical foundations of modern social life. Over the next four decades, those scholars now described as part of the Institute's 'first generation' – including, most famously, Horkheimer, Theodor Adorno, Herbert Marcuse, Walter Benjamin, Erich Fromm, and Leo Lowenthal – undertook an extraordinary variety of research ranging from detailed empirical studies of phenomena such as the family and social values to more speculative theoretical meditations on philosophical, historical, and aesthetic themes. In 1933 the Institute was moved to Geneva to escape Nazi persecution; the following year, some of its operations were relocated to the United States, where the majority of its associates spent the war years. Intrigued by the prospect of participating in the democratic reconstruction of West Germany, Horkheimer and Adorno returned the Institute to Frankfurt in 1950.

Although it is impossible to distil a common theoretical framework or research program from the diverse array of thinkers and texts we now associate with the Frankfurt School (and it is a label they never used themselves), it is fair to say that the basic question which guided their work was why modern societies had largely failed to realize the enormous potential for human freedom, individual autonomy, and material prosperity enabled by advances in their technological and productive capacities. Inspired by a tradition of philosophical and social critique from Kant through Hegel to Marx, they sought to confront modern societies with the broken promise of the bourgeois revolutions to achieve genuine, universal human emancipation. Critical theory, in other words, was conceived as a form of *immanent critique* which, as Marcuse noted in *One-Dimensional Man*, 'analyzes society in the light of its used and unused or abused capabilities for improving the human condition' (1964: x).

For the most part, this analysis consisted of an extremely bleak portrait of mass society in which the vast majority of individuals were successfully integrated into systems of economic, political, and cultural domination, leaving little opportunity for resistance or social change. In significant ways, such a gloomy outlook may be traced to the historical conditions in which critical theory took shape and which it was trying to explain between the 1930s and 1950s. First, the working class had not become the 'gravedigger' of capitalism as Marx had prophesied, but instead had been largely co-opted through a combination of consumer culture and nationalistic ideology. Second, the emergence of fascism, culminating in world war, the Holocaust, and the use of atomic weapons testified to the frightening capacity of human beings to use technological rationality for the most barbaric of ends. Third, the Stalinization of the Soviet Union and emergence of the Cold War left little hope for the prospect of any radical global alternatives to the one-dimensional societies presided over by these superpowers and their client states. The Frankfurt School has often been condemned on the basis of its relentless and totalizing pessimism, which some have suggested is not only reflective of this specific historical period (and thus of limited contemporary relevance) but also symptomatic of the personal experience of exile. Others, though, insist that critical theory's analysis of capitalism, technology, instrumental rationality, and mass culture identi-fied important structures and trends within human society that have grown more rather than less pervasive and intense over time. As such, its principle insights remain useful in making sense of our world today.

Among the most influential, controversial, and often misunderstood elements of critical theory in media studies is the role it assigns to mass culture in reducing the human capacity for critical thought as well as sustaining the legitimacy of capitalist socioeconomic structures. Writing in the early 1940s, Horkheimer and Adorno coined the term *Kulturindustrie* to denote the systematic application of the principles, procedures, and values of industrial capitalism to the creating and marketing of mass culture. Entertainment corporations, they argued, were churning out a never-ending supply of films, magazines, books, and newspapers following the same Fordist logic that governed the production of other consumer commodities such as automobiles or clothing. Contrary to those who claimed that the use of private market mechanisms to regulate the exchange of culture and communication promoted the freedom and independence of the media (as compared to state censorship), Horkheimer and Adorno suggested that the growth of a capitalist culture industry had actually transformed culture into a staunch ally of existing structures of power and domination. Unlike some relatively crude Marxist criticisms, however, their argument was not based upon an instrumental conception of media as a propaganda tool deployed by ruling elites to inject or impose a passive form of 'false consciousness' upon the helpless and duped masses. Instead, they focused upon how culture and communication had been transformed by their integration within and subordination to the logic of a capitalist economy.

What properties do cultural objects acquire when they are conceived, produced, and promoted, first and foremost, as commodities for profit? They must be efficiently produced to minimize costs, effectively promoted to stimulate demand, and easily consumed to maximize sales. These priorities elevate a particular dialectic of sameness and difference as *the* governing principle for all cultural products. On the one hand, cultural commodities must be standardized: first, it is faster, cheaper, and more efficient to produce multiple commodities according to the same formula; and, second, such commodities can be easily consumed because they conform to the existing cultural habits, expectations, and stereotypes of the audience. On the other hand, marketability demands that repetition be hidden beneath the illusion of individuality, difference, and novelty. The trivial differences of a cultural product must be deliberately foregrounded and exaggerated to market it as something 'new' or 'different.' Mass culture becomes a form of pseudo-individualization in which trivial differences disguise an underlying sameness and homogeneity. For Horkheimer and Adorno, the triumph of this basic logic was ensured by three complementary developments: first, all cultural production was increasingly rationalized, coordinated, and centralized in the hands of large media corporations; second, each corporation shared the same objective of maximizing the extraction of profit from culture; third, culture and communication were increasingly organized as a promotional arm for other commodities of consumer capitalism.

Horkheimer and Adorno feared that a cultural environment dominated by these principles would fatally compromise the capacity of individuals to engage in critical thought. The essence of critical thought, they believed, was the use of culture and language to open up a conceptual and/or aesthetic distance between subject and object, between people and their social and material environment. Great works of art, for instance, do not simply reflect the world but defamiliarize it, forcing us to conceptualize and experience the world around us in new ways (as well as reflect upon the deficiencies of all forms of representation). Culture should challenge and destabilize prevailing ideas, values, and assumptions through which we make sense of our world. Above all, it ought to enable the imagination of alternative forms of social life and thus keep faith with the utopian but immanent potential of society to become something other than it is today. Mass culture, they argued, had precisely the opposite effect, betraying culture's potential by leaving humanity stranded in the desert of the real. 'It is not because they turn their backs on washed-out existence that escape films are so repugnant,' wrote Adorno, 'but because they do not do so energetically enough, because they are themselves just as washed-out, because the satisfactions they fake coincide with the ignominy of reality, of denial. The dreams have no dream' (1996: 222). The ideological effect of the culture industry was not to distract consumers from reality with escapist fantasy but instead to confirm that reality as inescapable. 'There are no more ideologies in the authentic sense of false consciousness, only advertisements for the world through its duplication' (Adorno 1981: 34). In other words, the Frankfurt School did not attack the culture industry for being too powerful or manipulative but rather for being too weak and ineffective to sustain critical reflection or energize the imagination of utopian alternatives to existing ways of life.

Furthermore, they believed that mass culture could only be properly understood if conceptualized in relation to the changes that capitalism had brought to other spheres of social life including, most notably, the workplace and the family. The techniques of mass production coupled with the widespread application of scientific management had systematically stripped autonomy, creativity, and independence from the labour process, forcing most workers to numb their critical faculties as they performed simplistic and repetitive tasks. Bored and exhausted by the drudgery of the assembly line or the sales counter, most people craved 'mindless' entertainment which could be consumed without too much thought or concentration. In order to satisfy this need, however,

cultural commodities had to secretly reproduce the patterns of cognition, experience,
and feeling that dominated everyday life.
'They want standardized goods and pseu-
do-individuation, because their leisure time
is an escape from work and at the same
time is molded after those psychological
attitudes to which their workaday attitudes
exclusively habituates them' (Adorno and
Simpson 1941: 38). The culture industry
did not single-handedly 'inject' ideological
support for capitalist society into helpless
individuals. Instead, it organized, reinforced, and intensified patterns of thought,
action, feeling, and pleasure that had become socially dominant because of their
embodiment in a wide range of similarly
commodified structures and practices such
as a dehumanizing work life.

Equally as important, early empirical
studies conducted by Frankfurt School researchers on the family suggested that the
psychological processes of identity formation had been badly damaged in modern
society, leaving many individuals with
undeveloped egos that were incapable of
imposing any real discipline over more
primitive desires. Lacking any real sense
of self-identity, such individuals were ripe
for exploitation by the culture industry's
pledge to provide instinctual gratification,
thereby intensifying psychological dependence upon the cheap pleasures of mass
culture. Above all, a lack of self-confidence
and personal autonomy left many highly
vulnerable to the promise that social status,
acceptance, and belonging could be easily
secured by imitative assimilation to the
practices and values of consumer culture.
Such promises, though, were infinitely and
openly postponed by a culture industry
that appeared to have successfully locked
consumers into an endless Sisyphyean
cycle of expectation and disappointment.
'The promissory note of pleasure issued
by plot and packaging is indefinitely
prolonged: the promise, which actually
comprises the entire show, disdainfully
intimates that there is nothing more to
come, that the diner must be satisfied with

reading the menu' (Horkheimer and Adorno 2002: 111). As individuals became accustomed to this pattern, the culture industry
acquired a certain immunity from critique:
at some level, people knew how repetitive,
formulaic, and infantile most of its offerings were, yet continued to consume them
because it was the only option available
to them and they could no longer imagine
doing anything else. 'The triumph of advertising in the culture industry [consists
in] the compulsive imitation by consumers
of cultural commodities which, at the same
time, they recognize as false' (Horkheimer
and Adorno 2002: 136).

The work on mass culture was only
one aspect of the much broader critique of
human reason and social evolution undertaken by critical theory. Jointly composed
by Horkheimer and Adorno during their
U.S. exile in the early 1940s, *Dialectic of
Enlightenment* sketched out a sweeping
portrayal of human history in which our
eventual success in using reason to dominate nature has betrayed the original aim
of the Enlightenment to bring freedom and
happiness to all individuals. The origins of
human reason, they argue, can be traced
to a primal fear of the unknown, a hostile,
dangerous, and terrifying natural world.
Born out of the desperate attempt to manage and repress this fear, human beings
developed forms of thought and belief
that enclose the world in representative
systems of growing complexity. Myth, for
instance, was propelled by the desire to
conceptualize and explain phenomena in
a symbolic and often anthropomorphized
form that human beings could understand,
to render the unknown into the known.
The Enlightenment developed new forms
of scientific inquiry and instrumental reason that ridiculed and condemned myth
yet were motivated by a similar desire to
predict, manipulate, and control the natural
world. In philosophical terms, the subject
conceives of the object only in terms of
how it can serve the needs or desires of the
subject. Over time this instrumental form
of reasoning had proven remarkably adept

at increasing humanity's power over nature and had been embedded within a wide range of social institutions, practices, and technologies. However, it also marginalized or displaced other forms of non-instrumental reason and understanding that could not similarly justify themselves as enhancing human productive capacities. The rationality of means trumped the rationality of ends: strengthening instrumental reason had become an end in itself rather than subordinated to the satisfaction of real human needs. For the Frankfurt School, capitalism represented the perfection of this logic insofar as the production of wealth was organized to increase profit and the accumulation of capital rather than maximize human freedom and happiness. The erosion of critical thought coupled with the systematic alienation that commodity fetishism imposed upon experience had made it virtually impossible for atomized and isolated individuals to exercise any rational authority over their environment. Although the collective power of humanity over nature had grown exponentially, it had also been matched by the emergence of a reified social world that appeared as inscrutable, unpredictable, and dangerous as nature must once have seemed to humanity's distant ancestors. Enlightenment dissolved back into myth as human beings, once again, had little choice but to submit to forces seemingly beyond their control or understanding, making a mockery of Kant's famous rallying cry *'sapere aude!'* (dare to know).

Following Adorno's death in 1969 – he had taken over as the Institute's director after Horkheimer's retirement in the mid-1960s – intellectual leadership of Frankfurt School critical theory passed to a 'second generation' of thinkers. Foremost among these was Jürgen Habermas and his ongoing attempt to renovate critical theory by foregrounding the emancipatory potential embedded within inter-subjective social relations and communication. Horkheimer and Adorno had originally conceived *Dialectic of Enlightenment* as a means of rescu-

ing the Enlightenment from itself by distinguishing between its positive and negative dimensions. But the grand, sweeping nature of their indictment of human reason as inaugurating self-destructive forms of social and natural domination was interpreted by many, including Habermas, as marking the project of modernity beyond redemption: at its outset, the Enlightenment for Horkheimer and Adorno 'is the result of a drive to self-preservation that mutilates reason, because it lays claim to it only in the form of purpose-rational mastery of nature and instinct – precisely as instrumental reason' (Habermas 1987a: 111). If reason itself was so deeply flawed, then the very possibility of critical theory, and the social and political praxis it was to inspire, fades before a hermetic (and bourgeois) retreat into the contemplation of aesthetics and philosophy. Habermas rejected these conclusions on the grounds that they failed to identify both the positive, critical dimensions of rationality as well as the many progressive accomplishments of modernity, including democracy, the rule of law, aesthetic and cultural diversity, fundamental human rights and freedoms, and so on.

In *The Structural Transformation of the Public Sphere*, initially published in German in 1962 but not translated into English until three decades later, Habermas developed an immanent critique of capitalist modernity through a historically grounded investigation into the emergence and erosion of the public sphere between the eighteenth and twentieth centuries. Originating initially in the coffee houses of London and then gradually spreading to other urban centres in Europe, the public sphere represented the formation of public spaces (and, later, printed media) in which individuals could gather to discuss and debate matters of commerce, culture, and politics. Although the actual practices of discussion were often restrictive and exclusionary (on the basis of gender, education, class, race, and religion), the philosophical principles which regulated the exchange of ideas in these places were drawn from the Enlightenment's basic precept that all human beings have the capacity to use reason to participate in their own self-government. This right to personal autonomy, suggested Habermas, was best exercised in a deliberative fashion: 'in regard to enlightenment, therefore, thinking for oneself seemed to coincide with thinking aloud and the use of reason with its public use' (1989: 104). Four key features of the public sphere can be identified which, though not always fully adhered to, constituted its normative foundations (Calhoun 1992: 12–13). First, all participants are to be regarded as formally equal: social or other distinctions are irrelevant for the purposes of discussion. Second, the quality of discourse and argument is to be assessed and adjudicated strictly on the basis of reason alone. Third, subject matters are not to be restricted or shaped by external authorities but are to be entirely dependent upon the autonomous decisions of the participants. Fourth, any individual should have the right to participate. As an ideal if not always in practice, the public sphere created a protected space of freedom and autonomy in which people could debate and discuss the important social, cultural, and political questions of the day. However, the expansion of the public sphere in the form of mass communication has come at the expense of the quality and autonomy of political discourse. In a critique of the perversion of mass communication that shares much with Horkheimer and Adorno's culture industry thesis, Habermas lamented the 'structural transformation' (and erosion) of the public sphere under the influence of powerful economic and political forces. Active participation by engaged individuals in rational debate is displaced by the passive consumption of media spectacle engineered by states and corporations in the interests of profit and ideological legitimation. Despite his far more enthusiastic reception of the Enlightenment, Habermas ultimately ended up unable to ground the principles of the public sphere in the historical conditions and

social institutions of contemporary society. Instead, the concept of the public sphere served primarily as a tool for criticizing the failures and shortcomings of existing forms of communication.

In later work such as *The Theory of Communicative Action* (1984) he shifted away from this historical mode of investigation and critique to explore the transhistorical foundations of reason embedded within all forms of human communication. Habermas faults Marxist and non-Marxist critics alike for failing to adequately distinguish between an instrumental, strategic, or technological rationality oriented towards the subject's mastery, control, and domination of objects and the communicative rationality that governs and coordinates linguistically mediated interaction between subjects. One of the properties shared by all acts of speech is an underlying normative commitment to reaching a shared understanding between individual subjects. While this may not always occur and speech may also be used to pursue other ends, this commitment is a necessary precondition for human communication. In order for people to reach such an understanding, the legitimacy of each speech act is dependent upon three validity claims. First, statements are *true* insofar as their representation of objective reality is as accurate as possible; second, statements are *right* insofar as any moral or ethical claims they offer are legitimate and defensible according to prevailing social, cultural, and legal norms; and, third, statements are *sincere* insofar as they genuinely reflect the will, understanding, and feeling of the speaker. The universal (though implicit) presence of such criteria enables the use of reason to facilitate debate, discussion, and the achievement of consensus as a means of coordinating social action. Habermas argues that the rationality of communicative action takes shape and is sustained within the *lifeworld* of human society, the dense but informal network of shared meanings, cultural traditions, and social interaction that constitute everyday life. In contrast, instrumental forms of rationality are rooted in the *system*, which is composed of structures, institutions, technologies, and patterns of action that organize the material reproduction of society: in particular, *money* (the capitalist economy) and *power* (the welfare state) are identified as the two dominant 'steering media' which coordinate human action in accord with their own systemic objectives. Problems arise when the fragile balance between these two spheres is disturbed by the expansionary tendency of the system to colonize the lifeworld and thereby erode the basis for human thought and action based upon communicative rationality. But unlike the much deeper and more radical critique of capitalist modernization offered by first-generation scholars, Habermas constructs a vigorous defence of the Enlightenment and modernity, arguing that the principles of reason immanent to many of the institutions and practices of contemporary society continue to furnish ample grounds for critical theory.

Although Walter Benjamin was never a formal member of the Institute for Social Research (but did receive a small stipend in the late 1930s), his work is often identified as part of Frankfurt School critical theory. In media studies, Benjamin is best known for his 1936 essay 'The Work of Art in the Age of Mechanical Reproduction,' a deceptively simple set of observations on the effect of new media such as film and photography on the social and political significance of art and culture. On the one hand, he was hopeful that increasing accessibility to culture through reproduction would empower the masses to grapple with an exploitative economic and political reality in new ways and thereby mobilize previously repressed desires for social transformation. On the other hand, he also recognized the danger that in the absence of such mobilization, these desires could also be harnessed to more destructive ends. Horrified by how the spectacular pleasures offered by films such as Leni Riefenstahl's *Triumph of the Will* and *Olympiad* could sabotage critical thought, he concluded his essay by noting that mankind's 'self-

alienation has reached such a degree that it can experience its own destruction as an aesthetic pleasure of the first order' (1969: 242). Benjamin's occasional and often cryptic optimism about new cultural technologies has often been used to position him as a foil to Adorno's far more hostile reception of mass culture, even as an intellectual progenitor to work in cultural studies. Yet the aesthetic, intellectual, and normative commitments shared by these two thinkers on issues of culture, history, and philosophy far outweigh their differences: most importantly, both shared a desire to rescue the possibilities for critical thought and experience in a world where such possibilities are increasingly eviscerated by instrumental reason and capitalist social relations. While Benjamin was far more willing to speculate about the irrepressible utopian energies for revolution scattered throughout the spaces of everyday life, he was equally liable to reflect apocalyptically upon the catastrophic history of so-called human progress.

In the final decade of his life (which ended in his suicide in 1940 during a flight from Nazi occupied France), Benjamin devoted himself to exploring the transformation of urban experience in the posthumously published *Arcades Project* (1999). Consisting of a massive collection of quotations, aphorisms, and a few schematic essays, this unconventional text has exercised a powerful influence across traditional academic disciplines. While Benjamin's investigations ostensibly focused upon Paris, his ambition was a critical history of how capitalist urbanization, and its associated technologies and cultural forms, had irrevocably revolutionized the means through which people experienced, understood, and engaged with social reality. In the past, dense networks of social relations, enduring cultural traditions, and recurring patterns of work, life, and leisure had anchored generation after generation within stable patterns of meaning and experience. The disruptions of modernity had shattered these patterns, forcing individuals to develop new social, cultural, and psychological strategies to manage the perpetual shocks that were now part of everyday life. In the wake of such changes, an intoxicating range of utopian impulses for happiness, freedom, and autonomy were emancipated from the traditional cultural forms that had contained them. Yet under the spell of the commodity form, these possibilities were routinely petrified into fetishized objects, practices, and spaces which constituted a mythic dreamworld for humanity. Mass consumption of these commodities perversely ensured that the collective wish for a better world they expressed would never be satisfied. Benjamin's provocative vision of capitalist modernity as a hellish fate in which human beings were bound to infinite cycles of expectation and disappointment planted the conceptual seed which would later ripen into Horkheimer and Adorno's *Dialectic of Enlightenment*. But unlike their relentlessly negative exposition, Benjamin insisted that a revolutionary pedagogical tool described as the 'dialectical image' could jolt humanity out of its slumbers and awaken it to its collective social and political power to finally make good on the utopian vision it has possessed for so long in the form of a dream.

Critical theory has itself attracted many critics who have attacked the work of the Frankfurt School for a wide range of faults from the perceived mandarin elitism of its principle exponents and the totalizing character of its indictment of capitalist society to the historical specificity (and limitations) of its analysis and its refusal (with the possible exception of Habermas) to offer any pragmatic program for social and political reform. Many of these criticisms have substantial merit and there is little question that as a comprehensive or systematic theorization of contemporary social and cultural life, critical theory fails on many counts. That being said, however, there are few scholarly traditions that can match the Frankfurt School's rigour, complexity, and critical force in exploring the social, cultural, and intellectual foundations and implications of the Enlightenment, moder-

nity, and capitalism. Beyond the interdisciplinary tour de force contained in some of their best-known work, critical theorists of the first and second generation also offer us a wealth of insights in the form of aesthetic, literary, and cultural criticism that addressed the most important intellectual debates of their day. Finally, the Frankfurt School has influenced a wide range of scholars across many disciplines, who continue to apply, refine, and renovate the key concepts and ideas of the original scholars.

Shane Gunster

Bibliography

Adorno, Theodor. Cultural Criticism and Society. In *Prisms*. Trans. Samuel Weber and Shierry Weber. Cambridge: MIT Press, 1981.

– *M. Inima Moralia: Reflections from a Damaged Life*. Trans. E.F.N. Jephcott. New York: Verso, 1996.

Adorno, Theodor, with the assistance of George Simpson. On Popular Music. In *Studies in Philosophy and Social Science* 9 (1941): 17–48.

Benjamin, Walter. The Work of Art in the Age of Mechanical Reproduction. In *Illuminations*. Ed. Hannah Arendt. Trans. Harry Zohn. New York: Schocken Books, 1969.

– *The Arcades Project*. Prepared on the basis of the German volume edited by Rolf Tiedemann. Trans. Howard Eiland and Kevin McLaughlin. Cambridge: Belknap Press of Harvard University Press, 1999.

Calhoun, Craig. Introduction: Habermas and the Public Sphere. In *Habermas and the Public Sphere*, ed. Craig Calhoun. Cambridge: MIT Press, 1992.

Habermas, Jürgen. *The Theory of Communicative Action, Volume 1*. Trans. Thomas McCarthy. Boston: Beacon Press, 1984.

– The Entwinement of Myth and Enlightenment: Max Horkheimer and Theodor Adorno. In *The Philosophical Discourse of Modernity*. Trans. Frederick G. Lawrence. Cambridge: MIT Press, 1987a.

– *The Structural Transformation of the Public Sphere: An Inquiry into a Category of Bourgeois Society*. Trans. Thomas Burger with the assistance of Frederick Lawrence. Cambridge, MA: MIT Press, 1989.

Horkheimer, Max, and Theodor Adorno. *Dialectic of Enlightenment: Philosphical Fragments*. Ed. Gunzelin Schmid Noerr. Trans. Edmund Jephcott. Stanford: Stanford University Press, 2002.

Marcuse, Herbert. *One-Dimensional Man: Studies in the Ideology of Advanced Industrial Society*. Boston: Beacon Press, 1964.

FREEDOM OF SPEECH

[See also: *Censorship; Defamation; Pornography*]

Freedom of speech is the right to express ideas and opinions in a democratic society without fear of censorship or punishment. Although freedom of speech is enforced by law, the development of new technologies over the last decade, particularly the internet, has brought the concept under scrutiny. With increased diversity and anonymity more people are expressing their ideas through cyberspace. These ideas sometimes include pornography and hate speech.

The guarantee of free speech in the United States began in 1783, when America became independent from Britain and the monarchy was replaced with a representative system of government. As a concept, freedom of speech originally surfaced from the seventeenth-century English context of political activitism, known as the freedom of the press movement. The First Amendment to the American Constitution states that Congress shall make no law prohibiting or abridging the free exercise to freedom of speech or of the press.

The responsibility of the free press is to discuss or dispute information. Journalism's purpose is to search out what is true. However, in a democratic society, truth is considered diversely and, hence, is difficult to pin down and debate. The goal is to protect freedom of the press by ensuring diversity and avoiding intimidation from powerful public or private interests. The freedom guaranteed by the Constitution is a freedom to express and communicate ideas without restraint, whether orally, in print, or by other means of communication.

In the First Amendment, the primary purpose of the courts is to protect speech that promotes a robust public debate. For example, in the late nineteenth century, Congress had passed laws against obscenity. But court decisions eased such restrictions right after they were passed, lifting bans on such books as *Ulysses* by James Joyce in 1933 and *Lady Chatterley's Lover* by D.H. Lawrence in 1960. In 1989, the Supreme Court proclaimed that the government cannot punish someone for burning the American flag as a form of political protest, and in 2000 it ruled that the government has no right to require cable systems to limit sexually explicit channels to late-night hours.

In the twenty-first century, technologies have emerged to challenge the spirit of the First Amendment. The internet in particular poses a serious problem. The term anonymity refers to the ability to conceal one's identity while communicating one's own political and religious ideas, without fear of government intimidation or public retaliation. Anonymity is especially appealing to internet users who engage in unpopular, controversial, or embarrassing forms of communication without sacrificing their privacy or reputations. Since 1998, plaintiffs allegedly harmed by anonymous internet postings have filed many civil defamation lawsuits against 'John Doe' defendants. In the digital age the notion of freedom speech is taking on a broader definition.

Freedom of speech and of the press has always been heralded as a vital component of the political, social, and cultural systems of democracies. Ironically, it is in the United States that censorship forces have frequently surfaced. Nevertheless, the First Amendment to the Constitution still serves as a safeguard for the freedom of the news media. In a democratic society, everyone is allowed to have freedom of thought, belief, opinion, and expression.

Barbara Dumanski

Bibliography

Cohen-Almagor, Rafael. *The Boundaries of Liberty and Tolerance*. Gainsville: The University Press of Florida, 1994.

Steffens, Bradley. *The Free Speech Movement*. New York: Greenhaven Press, 2004.

Trager, Robert, and Donna Lee Dickerson. *Freedom of Expression in the Twenty-First Century*. Thousand Oaks: Pine Forge Press, 1999.

FUNCTIONALIST THEORIES OF THE MEDIA

[See also: *Media Effects; Sociology of the Media; Uses and Gratifications Theory*]

Functionalist theories attempt to explain the media as a collective means to satisfy individual needs. Cognitive-functionalist research in media theory is focused on what media do to subjects, from bodily arousal to intellectual stimulation, while sociological functionalism is interested in how media are involved in bringing about changes in society. The latter approach is traced to both Herbert Spencer (1820–1903), the English sociologist who sought to apply Darwinian evolutionary theory to human societies, and French sociologist Émile Durkheim (1858–1917), who saw modern culture as an alienating system. The theory typically views the media as effecting social change, at the same time that they mirror such change. The main challenge for functionalists is to explain how change is initiated. Unable to provide any viable psychological theory, early functionalism has often been associated with conservatism. Contemporary versions, known as neofunctionalism, attempt to meet the challenge of explaining change by emphasizing the role of uncertainty and creativity in media systems. A different, but related, objection to functionalism, raised by Niklas Luhmann (1964), is its inability to explain self-reference and the changes initiated by self-reference.

What do these two objections mean? First, it is conceivable that the media constitute a system of collective means to fulfil individual needs. And it is possible that this system might stabilize itself in an equilibrium for satisfying them. One objection would be that functionalist theories of the media may explain how the system restabilizes itself once it has been destabilized, but they have nothing to say about how it got destabilized in the first place. In fact it seems to follow from functionalist theories that the media should not change at all. Neofunctionalism counters that change in the media is initiated by free will and creativity, to which someone like Luhmann would reply that self-corrective action is also important and not covered by this explanation. It is also claimed that functionalism presumes a 'subjectless history' that is driven by forces outside the existence of social agents. The continuity and reproducibility of society are supposedly seen as something that happens with mechanical inevitability through processes of which people are unaware. Functionalism is thus critiqued for being nothing more that a version of radical materialism, even though few contemporary functionalists would subscribe to such a viewpoint in this extreme form.

Cognitive-functionalist research has a different notion of functions, focusing on how media shape cognition. Sports shows, for example, are intended to evoke a certain form of bodily arousal. A more radical version of cognitive functionalism is the kind that can be traced to the Turing test or to Daniel Dennett's (1978) evolutionary-based philosophy of mind, which reduces cognition to its observable functions and leaves no room for unobservable conscious activity. This type of functionalism is a derivative of Cartesian dualism. Its roots can be traced back to the work of psychologist William James (1842–1910) and educator John Dewey (1859–1952). The notion of functions in their work refers to cognitive functions not only in individuals, but also in the human species as a whole. Behaviourism, on the other hand, had insisted that only observable reactions to external stimuli could be studied scientifically. While the empirical domain has been expanded by modern technology (for example, brain scanners), experimental design, and a better understanding of unconscious processing, cognitive functionalists still cite early twentieth-century theorists as sources of inspiration. Others have traced functionalism back to Aristotle's theory of the soul or to the mechanistic philosophy of British philosopher Thomas Hobbes.

A third kind of functionalism relevant to media and communication studies is linguistic functionalism – that is, the view that linguistic structure is determined by its communicative functions. Linguistic functionalism is often opposed to a brand of linguistic formalism that sees linguistic structure as autonomous and constrained only by our biological paradigm. Do grammatical structures serve a function? Or are they present in the brain because of the way language evolved? Linguistic functionalism would favour the former perspective. Today, the use of both perspectives in tandem seems to be the rule in explanatory frameworks. If one wanted to explain why a rose is red, there is both a functionalist answer (to attract animals) and a formalist answer (biochemistry). If language is something that evolved by mere chance, like the universe, functional explanations will lead us down the wrong path; but if, on the other hand, language is the result of a conscious effort to communicate, functional explanations will have more relevance. Language may of course, like roses, lie somewhere in between.

Common to all kinds of functionalism is the belief that the objects of study – societies, cognitive capacities, or languages – exist because they serve a function and must serve that function to continue to exist. Underneath this belief lurks naive Darwinism: that is, the idea that organisms must serve a function to pass the test of evolution; or even that they must serve a function to emerge in the first place. But the test of evolution does not imply a priori functions. Cognitive capacities, including linguistic ones, may arise as by-products of something else. Consequently, not everything needs to serve a purpose. Language or consciousness may be just a by-product of complex problem solving. The usefulness of complex problem solving does not mean that language and consciousness are useful on their own. Second, evolution takes time. Social changes occur in historical time, not in biological time. They are simply too rapid to meet the test of evolution. Many functionalists believe that societies can be viewed as organisms, but the analogy does not seem to go very far, when viewed critically.

Anders Søgaard

Bibliography

Dennett, Daniel. *Brainstorms*. Montgomery, VT: Bradford Books, 1978.

Dik, Simon. *Functional Grammar*. Amsterdam: North-Holland, 1978.

Durkheim, Émile. *The Division of Labor in Society*. London: Macmillan, 1984.

Fodor, Jerry. *Psychological Explanation*. New York: Random House, 1968.

Holmwood, John. Functionalism and Its Critics. In *Modern Social Theory: An Introduction*, ed. A. Harrington, 87–109. Oxford: Oxford University Press, 2005.

Luhmann, Niklas. *Funktionen und Folgen formaler Organisation*. Berlin: Duncker and Humblot, 1964.

Putnam, Hillary. *Mind, Language, and Reality*. Cambridge: Cambridge University Press, 1975.

Spencer, Herbert. *The Study of Sociology*. New York: Appleton, 1891.

G

GENERATIVISM

[See also: *Chomsky, Noam; Cognitive Language Studies; Cognitivism; Conceptual Metaphor Theory; Lakoff, George*]

Generativism is the term referring to a model of language and a school of linguistics that emerged in the late 1950s, following Noam Chomsky's groundbreaking 1957 book *Syntactic Structures*. Generativism aims to find a blueprint of linguistic competence that aims to explain how we learn and use languages without any special training. Chomsky posits that the human brain is equipped at birth with rule-making principles that allow the infant to acquire any language. He calls this the 'I-language' (Internal-language). The I-language is subjected to culture-specific factors that operate on it to produce the grammar of the language to which the child is exposed, which he calls 'E-language' (External-language).

Chomsky's view of language has its roots in the ideas of the seventeenth-century Port Royal Circle, which had put forward the idea of a 'universal grammar.' For example, the members of the Circle would analyse a sentence such as *An all-knowing God created the visible world* as being made up of simpler constituent sentences:

(1) God is all-knowing.
(2) God created the world.
(3) The world is visible.

These were elemental sentences that could not be broken down further. Through the rules of grammar, they are combined to produce the complex sequence, *An all-knowing God created the visible world*. The Port Royal grammarians claimed that we are born with sentence-making principles, and that these allow speakers of different languages to figure out how complex sentences are formed. Chomsky has always acknowledged his debt to the Port Royal grammarians, admitting that it was strikingly similar to his own framework for describing language competence. Like the Port Royal linguists, Chomsky focused on certain sentence forms as constituting minimal units of the I-language, and others as transformations of these units into complex sentences of an E-language (Chomsky 1957):

(1) John is eager to please.
(2) John is easy to please.

Both of these sentences, Chomsky observed, would seem to be built from the same structural plan on the 'surface,' each consisting of a proper noun followed by a copula verb and predicate complement. However, despite the same apparent linear structure, the two sentences mean very different things: (1) can be paraphrased as 'John is eager to please someone' and (2) as 'It is easy for someone to please John.' These paraphrases are, in fact, the different 'deep structure' forms that we detect in the two sentences. Why do we detect them? Because, as Chomsky concluded, we have access to the I-language in the 'deep structure' that we can turn into specific sentences, which sometimes have identical 'surface structures' in the E-language.

Many arguments have come forward to challenge this model. One objection is that sentences are not the basic units of language. According to Michael Halliday (1985), sentences are 'text-governed' structures. Consider, for example, the following stretch of conversation (Danesi 2008), which does not contain pronouns. Although it is understandable, we nevertheless perceive it as awkward grammatically:

Speaker A: Chloe is a good person.
Speaker B: Yes, Chloe is a good person.
Speaker A: However, Chloe always likes to talk about Chloe.
Speaker B: Yes, Chloe does indeed always talk about Chloe.

The more appropriate version of the conversation would contain pronouns instead:

Speaker A: Chloe is a good person.
Speaker B: Yes, she is a good person.
Speaker A: However, she always likes to talk about herself.
Speaker B: Yes, Chloe does indeed always talk about herself.

The use of the pronoun is 'systemic,' that is, pronouns connect the various parts of the conversation logically like trace devices. The choice of pronouns is hardly due to I-language or E-language structural requirements; rather, it is motivated by text conventions. In other words, the forms of language are sensitive to, and dependent on, cultural devices, rather than sentence structure in itself.

Another approach to language that has emerged to challenge the validity of the generativist paradigm started in the early 1980s, coming gradually to be known as *cognitive linguistics*. The most prominent figure in the movement is the American lin-

guist George Lakoff (1987), who, ironically, was a student and follower of Chomsky. Lakoff has shown that syntactic rules themselves are products of a meaning-making process that is highly metaphorical and imaginative. Syntax is dependent on meaning, not the other way around, as Chomsky had assumed.

But perhaps the most convincing counterarguments to generativism come from the study of language development. Generativists claim that we are all born with a language faculty or 'organ' and that exposure to speech in social contexts simply triggers various 'parameters' of that faculty to generate the specific languages to which children are exposed. Chomsky put forward the notion of a Universal Grammar (UG) to explain the I-language, explicating why children learn to speak so naturally, without training – when the child learns one fact about a language, the child can easily infer other facts without having to learn them one by one. Differences in language grammars are thus explainable as choices of rule types, or parameters, from the UG.

There are several problems with this theory. First, the it is essentially restricted to accounting for the development of syntax in the child, ignoring a much more fundamental creative force in early infancy: the ability to apply words creatively to situations so as to fill in conceptual gaps. Second, it ascribes primacy to language, ignoring other faculties such as gesture and facial expression (or assigning them a secondary status). Since these develop in tandem with language during infancy, also without any training, does the brain possess 'universal non-verbal grammars'? Third, Chomsky completely disregarded the role of imitation in early language. As Crystal (1987: 232) remarks:

It has also been recognized that imitation is a distinct skill in language acquisition – many children spend a great deal of time imitating what their parents have just said. This is most noticeable when new sounds or vocabulary are being learned, but it has been shown that imitation may be important in the development of grammar too. Often, children imitate sentence patterns that they are unable to produce spontaneously, and they stop imitating these structures when they start to use them in speech – suggesting that imitation is a kind of 'bridge' between comprehension and spontaneous production.

Today, generativism is on the wane as a mainstream model of language. But it has left some significant residues, especially the tendency to associate language with cognitive and neural processes. The generative model has also been useful in the development of programming languages for automatic translation. Such languages however cannot handle meaning processes very well, which, as Chomsky has always claimed, lie outside of the language faculty proper.

Marcel Danesi

Bibliography

Chomsky, Noam. *Syntactic Structures*. The Hague: Mouton, 1957.

– *Aspects of the Theory of Syntax*. Cambridge, MA: MIT Press, 1965.

– *Reflections on Language*. New York: Pantheon, 1975.

– *Some Concepts and Consequences of the Theory of Government and Binding*. Cambridge, MA: MIT Press, 1982.

– *Knowledge of Language: Its Nature, Origin, and Use*. New York: Praeger, 1986.

– Language and Mind. In *Ways of Communicating*, ed. D.H. Mellor, 56–80. Cambridge: Cambridge University Press, 1990.

– *The Minimalist Program*. Cambridge, MA: MIT Press, 1995.

– *New Horizons in the Study of Language and Mind*. Cambridge: Cambridge University Press, 2000.

– *On Nature and Language*. Cambridge: Cambridge University Press, 2002.

Crystal, David. *The Cambridge Encyclopedia of Language*. Cambridge: Cambridge University Press, 1987.

Danesi, Marcel. *Language, Society, and Culture: Introducing Anthropological Linguistics*. Toronto: Canadian Scholars' Press, 2008.

Halliday, Michael A.K. *Introduction to Functional Grammar*. London: Arnold, 1985.

Lakoff, George. *Women, Fire, and Dangerous Things: What Categories Reveal about the Mind*. Chicago: University of Chicago Press, 1987.

GENRES

[See also: *Popular Culture; Media Studies; Narrative; Uses and Gratifications Theory*]

Aristotle was the earliest important theoretician of genres. He starts his *Poetics* by discussing two literary forms, similar in nature to what we now call *genres*. He writes: 'Our subject being Poetry, I propose to speak not only of the art in general but also of its species and their respective capacities … Epic poetry and Tragedy, as also Comedy … are all viewed as a whole, modes of imitation.' Comedy, Aristotle suggests, is 'an imitation of men worse than average' and tragedy is 'essentially an imitation not of persons but of action and life, of happiness and misery.' There is one other important form or meta-genre, histories, and within each of these meta-genres there are endless variations.

The term 'genre,' from the French, is used to describe a kind or type of narrative, regardless of the medium carrying the text. We find genre texts in books, on television, in films, on television, in songs, and in many other media. Among the most popular genres are hard-boiled and classical detective stories, romances, spy stories, westerns, and science fiction stories, with some texts mixing elements from one or more genres. I might add that the term genre can also be applied to texts that are not traditionally seen as fictional narratives, such as quiz shows and news shows, since they all tend to follow certain patterns or models.

Table 1

Uses and Gratifications	Genres
To satisfy curiosity and be informed	documentaries, news shows, talk shows, quiz shows
To identify with the divine	religious shows
To be entertained and amused	situation comedies, domestic comedies, musical comedies
To reinforce belief in justice	police shows, law shows
To reinforce belief in romantic love	romance novels, soap operas
To participate vicariously in history	media events, sports shows
To see villains in action	police shows, action-adventure shows
To obtain outlets for sexual drives in a guilt-free context	pornography, fashion shows, soft core commercials, soap operas
To experience the ugly	horror shows
To find models to imitate	talk shows, action shows, award shows, sports shows, commercials
To experience the beautiful	travel shows, art shows, culture shows, symphony concerts, operas, ballet

Genre stories tend to be formulaic and rely upon widely known and accepted conventions and plot structures. These conventions help audiences understand what happens in texts and allow writers to create these texts, since they can rely on expectations on the part of audiences and can use formulas to satisfy these expectations. In essence, we classify texts according to their genres. At the opposite pole to genres are texts that are highly inventive and follow no formulas, such as James Joyce's novels *Ulysses* and *Finnegan's Wake*.

When we write about genre texts, it is useful to consider their genres to help us make sense of the text and better understand the role that a genre plays in creating a given text. There is a philosophical problem that we face when considering genres: do classes of things exist? Are kinds of things or classes of things, such as the genre 'comedies,' as 'real' as an example of something, such as an episode of *Seinfeld*? Some philosophers, realists, argue that only particular things are real and a concept or abstraction such as genre is unreal or has a secondary status as far as reality is concerned.

Gratifications from Genres

We might ask ourselves why genres are

so popular. Aside from making it easy for people to understand what events in a text mean, genres also provide a number of gratifications for readers, viewers, or listeners of generic texts. The focus here is upon the psychological payoff genres provide and on the uses people make of generic fictions. Some of the research on the uses and gratifications approach deal with listening to soap operas, reading comic books, and reading romance fiction novels. It is possible to suggest that certain genres provide specific uses and gratifications, which are considered in Table 1.

One of the difficulties of the uses and gratifications approach is that it is very difficult to quantify the uses people make of genres and to tie events in a given text to this or that gratification. Nevertheless, it is quite obvious that people listen to radio soap operas, watch soap operas on television, read comic books and other kinds of 'pulp literature,' and listen to country and western songs because they provide a number of gratifications.

Formulas in Popular Narratives

Popular genres consist of certain formulaic elements. That is, genre fictions generally follow a number of conventions regard-

Table 2

Genre	Romance	Western	Science fiction	Spy
Time	early 1900s	1800s	future	present
Location	rural England	edge of civilization	outer space	world
Hero	lords, upper-class types	cowboy	space man	agent
Heroine	damsel in distress	schoolmarm	space gal	woman spy
Secondary	friends of heroine	townspeople, indians	technicians	assistant agents
Villains	seeming friends who lie	outlaws	aliens	moles
Plot	find love	restore law and order	repel aliens	find moles
Theme	love conquers all	justice and progress	save humanity	save free world
Costume	gorgeous dresses	cowboy hat	space gear	trench coat
Locomotion	cars, horses, carriages	horse	rocket ship	sports car
Weaponry	fists	six-gun	ray gun, laser gun	pistol with silencer

ing where they take place, what kinds of heroes and villains are found in them, and what their themes and plots are like. These elements are spelled out in Table 2, which deals with romance novels, westerns, science fiction stories, and spy stories.

Not all texts in a given genre follow every convention, but this chart lists some of the more common formulaic elements found in these particular genres. Within each genre, scholars have elaborated subgenres. Thus Will Wright, in his book *Six-Guns and Society,* argues that there are four variations on the western: the classical western, the vengeance western, the transition western, and the professional western, and that each of these variations reflects a stage in the development of capitalism in the United States.

The Fairy Tale as Ur-Genre

In *Popular Culture Genres: Theories and Texts,* Berger suggests that the fairy tale can be thought of as an ur-genre, from which all the other genres have evolved. Thus, science fiction draws upon fights with monsters, aliens, magic carpets, and magical beings who help the heroes of fairy tales in their adventures. The detective story has evolved out of the fairy-tale hero's search for a kidnapped heroine, and soap operas are a literary – some would say sub-literary

– variation of the conflicts and problems found in families in many fairy tales. The fairy tale, in turn, seems to have evolved out of our dreams, which are the most personal narratives we experience and in which we are the heroes and heroines who become transformed into others.

Are Genres Sub-Literary?

Genre fiction, like detective, spy, and science fiction novels, are sometimes described as 'sub-literary,' meaning they have a lesser literary status than non-genre works, but many critics suggest that some genre texts are significant and important works of art. It does not make sense to categorically dismiss all genre works as little more than trash, even though a great number of formulaic texts have no literary value. That is because most 'serious' non-genre novels have little literary value as well, so it seems most useful to look at particular texts to see whether they have merit and not dismiss them all. One can argue, in fact, that many of our best novels and films are genre texts – for example, *The Maltese Falcon, 2001: A Space Odyssey, Blade Runner,* and *The Third Man.* Since genre texts make up a large portion of our reading, viewing, and listening, it makes sense for scholars to examine these texts to consider their aesthetic merits and demerits and to see what light they shed on the cultures in which they are created and consumed.

Arthur Asa Berger

Bibliography

Berger, Arthur Asa. *Popular Culture Genres: Theories and Texts*. Newbury Park, CA: Sage, 1992.

Cawelti, John. *The Six-Gun Mystique*. Bowling Green, OH: Bowling Green University Popular Press, 1971.

Todorov, Tzvetan. *The Fantastic: A Structural Approach to a Literary Genre*. Cleveland, OH: Press of Case Western Reserve University, 1973.

Wright, Will. *Six-Guns and Society*. Berkeley: University of California Press, 1975.

GERBNER, GEORGE (1919–2005)

[See also: *Cultivation Theory; Media Effects; Television*]

George Gerbner was a leading theorist and critic who emphasized the vast power of the media over human attitudes, thought patterns, and behaviour. He is recognized internationally for his research on the effects of the media on society – specifically, the long-term impacts of television violence on viewers' perceptions of reality. Gerbner's research projects were supported by numerous organizations, including the National Institute of Mental Health, the National Science Foundation, the Administration on Aging, the President's Commission on the Causes and Prevention of Violence, the Surgeon General's Scientific Advisory Committee on Television and Social Behavior, the U.S. Commission on Civil Rights, and the Screen Actors Guild.

Born and raised in Budapest, Gerbner was of half-Jewish descent who had intended to study folklore at the University of Budapest, but was forced to migrate to the United States in 1939 to escape the Hungarian regime. He earned a degree in journalism from the University of California, Berkeley, and after graduation worked briefly as a writer for the *San Francisco Chronicle*. He enlisted in the U.S. Army during the Second World War and served in the 541st Parachute Infantry (101st Airborne) and the Office of Strategic Services (OSS), earning a Bronze Star for his service behind enemy lines. After the war, he worked for a short time as a journalist and received his master's degree after writing the first-ever master's thesis on the subject of education and television at the University of Southern California, where he also obtained his PhD.

In 1956, Gerbner was hired as a professor at the University of Illinois' Institute for Communications Research. By the beginning of the 1960s, his work included various subject areas such as: the portrayal of pscyhiatric illness and teachers in mainstream media, the meanings of magazine covers, and the content analysis of ideological principles in American and foreign newspapers. Gerber became dean of the Annenberg School of Communication at the University of Pennsylvania in 1964 and maintained this position until 1989. He played an influential role in expanding that university's involvement with communication theory.

After retiring from his position as dean, he became an independent researcher and educator and took up the following positions: visiting lecturer at the University of Athens; visiting professor at the University of Budapest, Salesian University, and Villanova University; Bell Atlantic Professor of Telecommunication at Temple University; and distinguished visiting professor at the American University in Washington and the American University in Cairo. He served as editor of the *Journal of Communication* from 1974 to 1991 and was also the chair of the editorial board of the *International Encyclopedia of Communications* for a number of years.

Gerbner's views of the media were influenced by his fascination with European folklore. Partly because of his lifelong interest in folklore, Gerbner claimed that television held a prominent role in American culture because of its folkloristic qualities, broadcasting stories that were an amalgam of truth and fiction (as in folklore). Television, according to Gerbner, was the country's main storyteller: 'The television set has become a key member of the family; the one who tells most of the stories most of the time … television dominates the symbolic environment of modern life' (Gerbner, Gross, Morgan, and Signorielli 1980: 14). As such, the TV narrative promulgated a set of broad, biased assumptions about the 'facts of life' that probably influenced young people's beliefs and perceptions of their world. The effects of television, Gerbner claimed, should not be analysed in terms of individual television programs or genres, but rather as a medium that transmits a pattern of messages in a particular way. This concept led to the establishment of a three-pronged, integrated research strategy for media and communications research that he carried out with a team of researchers:

(1) 'institutional process analysis,' investigating the influences that affect the patterns of media messages (for example, how media messages are selected, produced, and distributed);
(2) 'message system analysis,' exploring the characteristics of these patterns (the recurring elements/images in media content);
(3) 'cultivation analysis,' studying the influence of the patterns on viewers' conceptions about reality.

In 1968, the National Commission on the Causes and Prevention of Violence, created at the request of President Lyndon Johnson, appointed Gerbner and his colleagues to analyse the effects of TV violence on people. Known as the 'Cultural Indicators Project,' the research catalogued trends in television content and examined how watching television influenced viewers' attitudes and world views. To this day, this project is still considered to be the most extensive and authoritative study of media effects. Previous research had examined whether view-

ing television violence correlated with more aggression in society. Gerbner and his team, on the other hand, were more concerned with how television violence influenced world view. With Larry Gross (1976), he used his findings to develop 'cultivation theory' – the view that television viewing, over time, subtly 'cultivates' audience members' perceptions of reality. Gerbner found, in fact, that those who spent more time watching television ('heavy television viewers') tended to have beliefs and values about reality that were more in line with the tenor of the programs they watched, rather than with other models of the real world. Heavy viewers seemed to believe that the world was a much more dangerous, gloomy, and frightening place than it actually was, thus developing a greater sense of anxiety, vulnerability, alienation, and mistrust of others. This phenomenon was termed the 'mean world syndrome' (Gerbner and Gross 1976).

The implications, Gerbner warned, were obvious: television violence is a model of 'who can get away with what against whom,' with women, the young, the elderly, as well as some minorities being victimized the most (Signorielli and Gerbner 1988: xi). Television conveys a strong, symbolic message about social relationships and the structure of power in society, tending to encourage and reinforce the acceptance of violence as a fact of life, and this has enormous implications: 'Fearful people are more dependent, more easily manipulated and controlled, more susceptible to deceptively simple, strong, tough measures and hard-line postures. They may accept and even welcome repression if it promises to relieve their insecurities' (Signorielli and Gerbner 1988: xxi).

Gerbner also critiqued the representations that TV promoted. Most programs involved stories about young, wealthy, idealized Caucasian men involved in professional settings like a law firm, a doctor's office, and the like. On the contrary, female, young, old, and minority characters were involved in a narrower range of activities.

These subtle messages, he argued, cultivated viewers to believe that Caucasian males were the leaders of society and that all others were in some way subsidiary to them. This has changed, of course. But many claim that the change was in part motivated by studies such as those by Gerbner and his team.

Gerbner portrayed television as a 'cultural environment' into which children were born and from which they received their primary modes of information: 'For the first time in human history, most of the stories about people, life and values are told not by parents, schools, churches, or others in the community who have something to tell, but by a group of distant conglomerates that have something to sell. This is a radical change in the way we employ creative talent and the way we cast the cultural environment. The roles we grow into and the ways others see us are no longer home-made, hand-crafted, community-inspired. They are products of a complex manufacturing and marketing process. Television is the mainstream of the process' (Gerbner 1995: 72).

In the early 1990s, Gerbner founded the Cultural Environment Movement (CEM), an international advocacy group composed of organizations and individuals working for greater diversity in mass media representation, ownership, and employment: 'CEM is working for freedom from stereotyped formulas; for respecting the integrity of cultures and opposing the homogenisation; for investing in a freer and more diverse cultural environment; and for citizen participation in cultural decisions that shape our lives and the lives of our children' (Gerbner 1995: 76).

Alexandra Birk-Urovitz and Elizabeth Birk-Urovitz

Bibliography

Gerbner, George, and Larry Gross. Living with Television: The Violence Profile. *Journal of Communication* 26 (1976): 172–99.

Gerbner, George, Larry Gross, Michael Morgan, and Nancy Signorelli. The 'Mainstreaming' of America: Violence Profile no. 11. *Journal of Communication* 30 (1980): 10–29.

Gerbner, George, Larry Gross, Michael Morgan, and Nancy Signorielli. Growing Up with Television: Cultivation Processes. In *Media Effects: Advances in Theory and Research*, ed. Jennings Bryant and Dolf Zillmann, 43–67. Mahwah, NJ: Lawrence Erlbaum Associates, 2002.

Signorielli, Nancy, and George Gerbner. Violence and Terror in the Mass Media: An Annotated Bibliography. Westport, CT: Greenwood, 1988.

GESTURE

[See also: *Kinesics; Non-Verbal Communication; Proxemics*]

Humans communicate their messages over two-thirds of the time through the body, producing around 700,000 signs, including around 1,000 bodily postures, 5,000 hand gestures, and 250,000 facial expressions (Morris et al. 1979). Gesture is an instinctive form of communication, defined as the use of the hands (and sometimes other body parts) to communicate something. Although the term is often used more broadly, in this entry it will be restricted to hand (manual) gesturing.

The ability to use the hands for grasping and pointing was achieved by our hominid ancestors after they developed the ability to walk upright. The upright posture liberated the hands for use in various ways, allowing early humans to make tools, to use fire, and to make gestural forms. Although many gestures seem to be universal, some can be quite culture-specific. In 1979, Desmond Morris and a research team at Oxford University looked at twenty gesture forms in forty different European societies or communities. They discovered that many of these had different meanings – for example, a tap on the side of the head could indicate completely opposite things, 'stupidity' or 'intelligence,' depending on cultural context. The overall conclusion reached by the study was that many gestures, like words, have culture-specific meanings.

Gesture is also found in various primate species. Chimpanzees, for example, raise their arms to signal that they want to be groomed; they stretch their arms to beg or invite; and they point to things to locate them (Beaken 1996: 51). These gestures are, evidently, purposeful and regulatory of the actions of other chimps. But the number of gestural forms of which primates are capable is rather limited when compared with the domain of human gesturing, which encompasses not only the common hand gestures accompanying vocal speech, but also the sign languages used by the hearing-impaired, the sign languages used by religious groups for various sacred reasons, the hand signals used by traffic personnel, the gestural movements used by orchestra conductors, and so on.

Phylogenetically, gesture is a more fundamental and instinctive form of communication than vocal language. As such, it has left its residues in common communication behaviours such as the fact that when one does not speak the language of an interlocutor, one instinctively resorts to gesture in order to get a message across or to negotiate some meaning. If one were to describe an automobile, not knowing the appropriate word, one would tend to use the hands to portray a steering wheel and the motion used to steer a car, accompanying this gesture, perhaps, with an imitative motor sound. This common occurrence suggests that gesture is not only a fundamental mode of communication, but also that it is a much more universal, and less culture-dependent, mode than vocal language. For example, across the world, using the index finger to point to things is an instinctive gesture. Representing the shape of objects with the hands also seems to be universal: to represent a round object people typically use both hands moving in opposite – clockwise (the right hand) and counter-clockwise (the left hand) – directions. Fingers are used across the world to represent number concepts. However, some gestures (known as symbolic) are often different, especially if they are used for social functions or for carrying out interactional protocols such as greeting, affirmation, and the like. The child developmental literature has documented that the use of gesture appears before the advent of vocal language, since children show an instinctive ability to point and use other simple hand movements for practical purposes. And, of course, in individuals with impaired vocal organs, gesture and writing constitute the main modes of communication.

Gesture accompanies vocal speech. As the psycholinguist David McNeill (1992, 2005) has documented in various important studies, the gestures used by people commonly as they speak are hardly random; rather, they reinforce meaning. McNeill videotaped a large sample of people as they spoke, and found that the gestures they used, which he called *gesticulants*, exhibited imagery that cannot be shown through vocal words. This suggested to him that vocal speech and gesture constituted a single integrated communication system that allows speakers to get messages across effectively through both modalities.

McNeill classifies gesticulants fall into five main categories. First, there are *iconic* gesticulants, which are hand movements that the speaker uses to allow interlocutors to picture what is being said. For example, when someone was describing a scene in which a character bent a tree back to the ground, the speaker appeared to grip something in the air and pull it back. This action was, in effect, a manual depiction of the action being described verbally, revealing the speaker's point of view (he could have taken the part of the tree instead). Second, there are *metaphoric* gesticulants, which are also pictorial, but more abstract. For example, McNeill observed a speaker who was talking about a cartoon raise up his hands as if he were offering a kind of object to his listener. The action represented the cartoon as if it were an object that he offered to the listener. This type of gesticulant is the counterpart of metaphors such as *pre-*

senting an idea, putting forth an idea, offering advice, and so on, which instantiate the conceptual metaphor *ideas are conduits*. Third, there are *beat* gesticulants, which are hand actions that resemble the beating of musical tempo, whereby speakers flick a hand or fingers up and down, or back and forth, to accompany the rhythmic pulsation of speech. Beats mark the introduction of new concepts in an utterance. Fourth are *cohesive* gesticulants, which are used to show that separate parts of an utterance are supposed to hold together, through a repetition of the same gesticulant. The repetition is meant to convey cohesiveness. Fifth, *deictic* gesticulants are hand actions that indicate something that had been mentioned earlier in the conversation, such as waving a hand near the ear and shoulder to indicate that something has passed.

McNeill's gesticulant categories are actually subtypes of the more generic category known as an *illustrators*, which are used literally to illustrate the content of vocal utterances. Other categories are emblems, affect displays, regulators, and adaptors. *Emblems* are gestures that are used in place of words or phrases, such as the 'Okay' sign, the 'Come here' sign, the hitchhiking sign, waving, obscene gestures, and so forth. *Affect displays* are hand gestures that aim to communicate emotional meaning. Examples include the hand movements that accompany expressions of happiness, anger, surprise, sadness, fear, contempt, disgust, and so on. *Regulators* are hand movements that allow an interlocutor to modify or affect the speaker's utterance or his or her rate of delivery. Examples include the gestures for 'Keep going,' 'Slow down,' and 'What else happened?' *Adaptors* communicate some state of mind. Examples include scratching the head when puzzled, rubbing the forehead when worried, and so on.

Gesture is also used as a replacement for vocal language in some communities. In the case of hearing-impaired individuals, it is a primary means of communication along with writing. The hand signs used (as in American Sign Language) corre-

spond to the word units of vocal language. As Goldin-Meadow (2003: 94) has aptly observed, 'sign languages assume the structural properties characteristic of spoken languages.' Sign languages are used as well by some cultures to complement vocal speech. One of the best-known examples is the system used by the Plains people of North America, in which the sign language functions as a means of communication between tribes with different verbal languages. The gestures used represent things in nature, ideas, emotions, and sensations. For instance, the sign for a white person is formed by drawing the index and third fingers across the forehead, indicating a hat. Special signs also exist for each tribe and for particular topological referents (rivers, mountains, etc.). The sensation of cold is communicated by means of a shivering gesture in front of the body; the same sign is used for 'winter' and 'year,' because the Plains peoples count years in terms of winters. Turning the hand in a slow relaxed fashion means vacillation, doubt, or possibility; a quicker movement is the question sign (Mallery 1972).

Gestures are also used commonly for sacred symbolic purposes. In Christianity the 'sign of the cross' is a gesture that aims to symbolize the Crucifixion. In Buddhism, the *mudras* are gestures used during ceremonies to represent various sacred concepts (meditation, reasoning, doctrine, protection, enlightenment, unification of matter, and spirit). The 'devil's hand,' with the index and little finger raised to form a horned figure belongs to the domain of superstition, symbolizing, in some cultures, a sign to ward off the evil eye and in others to indicate cuckoldry.

Gesture has been used to attempt the teaching of human language to primates – who lack the requisite anatomical organs for vocal speech – to determine if they are capable of language. In 1966, for instance, a chimpanzee named Washoe was adopted by the Gardners, a husband and wife team who taught her to use American Sign Language at almost one year of age (Gardner and Gardner 1969). The Gardners reported that Washoe learned to use 150 ASL signs in just over four years, and that she began to put hand signs together to express concepts resembling the early sentences of children, such as 'Go in,' 'Hug hurry,' and 'Out open please hurry.' Apparently when Washoe once saw a duck, an animal for which she had not learned a word, she devised the expression *water bird*. Washoe was later given an infant chimpanzee to raise, and, according to the Gardners, she tried to teach him how to use ASL, which the baby chimp learned to do, albeit to a limited extent.

In the 1970s, Herbert S. Terrace of Columbia University also used ASL to train a chimp named Nim Chimpsky (Terrace 1979, 1983; Terrace, Petitto, Sanders, and Bever 1979). Nim learned to use 125 signs and seemed to understand basic notions of syntax: for example, the chimp put the word *more* before another word (*chocolate, tickle*) consistently to indicate quantity. However, analysis of the videotapes also shows the chimp using aberrant sentences such as 'Give orange me give eat orange me eat orange give me eat orange give me you.' Francine Patterson of Stanford University used ASL to teach language to a gorilla named Koko (Patterson 1978; Patterson and Linden 1981; Ward 1999) claiming that Koko could form various kinds of sentences and, amazingly, could understand and produce puns, jokes, and even tell lies.

Another husband and wife team, David and Ann Premack (1976, 1983), who actually started experimentation back in the 1960s, took a different approach, training a chimp named Sarah to communicate with them by placing metal-backed chips on a magnetic board. The chips stood for concepts arbitrarily: for example, a pink square = 'banana'; a blue triangle = 'apple'; and so forth. Sarah developed the ability to respond to and even construct sentences made with combinations of such symbols.

In yet another set of primate experiments, Duane and Sue Rumbaugh taught common chimpanzees and bonobos to associate symbols to everyday referents (Rumbaugh 1977; Savage-Rumbaugh 1986; Savage-Rumbaugh, Rumbaugh, and Boysen 1978; Savage-Rumbaugh, Romski, Sevcik, and Pate 1983). In one case study, a chimp observed a trainer hide a food item in a container. The chimp knew how to press a key on a computer keyboard with the symbol for the food item in question, and did so. This was seen by a second chimp, who was then able, on the basis of the keyboard signal, to locate the food item. This result might seem remarkable, but Epstein, Lanza, and Skinner (1980) were able to get the same behaviour from two pigeons, named Jack and Jill, who were put in adjoining cages with a transparent wall between them. Jack pecked a key labelled 'What colour?' as a cue for Jill to look behind a curtain with red, green, and yellow lights that were not visible to Jack. After seeing which light was illuminated, Jill pecked one of three keys, which Jack could see. Jack responded by pecking a key labelled 'Thank you,' whereupon Jill was given a food reward. All this demonstrates that animals of different species can easily figure out signals in their environment and use this knowledge to obtain needs. It does not show that they possess the signals as part of a more general faculty of communication.

Recently, some experimenters have tried to teach chimps to articulate actual words. Keith and Cathy Hayes seem to have been successful in teaching a chimp named Vicki how to utter a few words (Urban 2002). Others, such as Mary Lee Jensvold and Allan Gardner, have taught chimpanzees to apply what they learn from humans to new situations (Jensvold and Gardner 2000). For instance, a researcher would raise a specific topic, and then ask a chimpanzee a relevant question on it. The chimps were apparently able to understand and elaborate upon simple questions, in ways that are similar to children.

Despite all the enthusiasm and the extraordinary claims, conditioning cannot be ruled out as a factor in the experiments.

This does not imply that animals do not possess sophisticated communication systems. But whether the animals described in the above experiments actually learned to speak human language is really an unresolved question. Moreover, the primate trainers may have read much more in the behaviours of their animals than was really there. The Gardners had even hired a hearing-impaired ASL user to help train Washoe. Later on he made the following relevant comment (cited in Pinker 1994: 37):

Every time the chimp made a sign, we were supposed to write it down in the log. They [the Gardners] were always complaining because my log didn't show enough signs. I watched really carefully. The chimp's hands were moving constantly. Maybe I missed something, but I don't think so. The hearing people were logging every movement the chimp made as a sign. Every time the chimp put his hand in his mouth, they'd say 'Oh, he's making the sign for drink,' and they'd give him some milk. When the chip scratched himself, they'd record it as the sign for scratch. Sometimes the trainers would say, 'Oh, amazing, look at that, it's exactly like the ASL sign for give!' It wasn't.

Marcel Danesi

Bibliography

Armstrong, David F., William C. Stokoe, and Sherman E. Wilcox. *Gesture and the Nature of Language*. Cambridge: Cambridge University Press, 1995.

Beaken, Mike. *The Making of Language*. Edinburgh: Edinburgh University Press, 1996.

Emmorey, Karen, and Judy Reilly, eds. *Language, Gesture, and Space*. Hillsdale, NJ: Lawrence Erlbaum Associates, 1995.

Epstein, Robert, Robert P. Lanza, and Burrhus F. Skinner. Symbolic Communication between Two Pigeons. *Science* 207 (1980): 543–5.

Gardner R. Allen, and Beatrice T. Gardner. Teaching Sign Language to a Chimpanzee. *Science* 165 (1969): 664–72.

Goldin-Meadow, Susan. *Hearing Gesture: How Our Hands Help Us Think*. Cambridge, MA: Belknap Press, 2003.

Jensvold, Mary Lee, and R. Allen Gardner. Interactive Use of Sign Language by Cross-Fostered Chimpanzees (*Pan troglodytes*). *Journal of Comparative Psychology* 114 (2000): 335–46.

Kendon, Adam. *Gesture: Visible Action as Utterance*. Cambridge: Cambridge University Press, 2004.

Mallery, Garrick. *Sign Language among North American Indians Compared with That among Other Peoples and Deaf-Mutes*. The Hague: Mouton, 1972.

McNeill, David. *Hand and Mind: What Gestures Reveal about Thought*. Chicago: University of Chicago Press, 1992.

– *Gesture and Thought*. Chicago: University of Chicago Press, 2005.

Morris, Desmond, et al. *Gestures: Their Origins and Distributions*. London: Cape, 1979.

Patterson, Francine G. The Gesture of a Gorilla: Language Acquisition in Another Pongid. *Brain and Language* 5 (1977): 72–9.

Patterson, Francine G., and Eugene Linden. *The Education of Koko*. New York: Holt, Rinehart and Winston, 1981.

Pinker, Stephen. *The Language Instinct: How the Mind Creates Language*. New York: William Morrow, 1994.

Premack, Ann James. *Why Chimps Can Read*. New York: Harper and Row, 1976.

Premack David, and Ann James Premack. *The Mind of an Ape*. New York: Norton, 1983.

Rumbaugh, Duane M. *Language Learning by Chimpanzee: The Lana Project*. New York: Academic, 1977.

Savage-Rumbaugh, E. Sue. *Ape Language: From Conditioned Response to Symbol*. New York: Columbia University Press, 1986.

Savage-Rumbaugh, E. Sue, Duane M. Rumbaugh, and Sally Boysen. Symbolic Communication between Two Chimpanzees. *Science* 201 (1978): 641–4.

Savage-Rumbaugh, E. Sue, Mary A. Romski, Rose Sevcik, and James L. Pate. Assessing Symbol Usage versus Symbol Competency.

Journal of Experimental Psychology: General 112 (1983): 508–12.

Terrace, Herbert S. *Nim*. New York: Knopf, 1979.

– Apes Who Talk: Language or Projection of Language by Their Teachers? In *Language in Primates: Perspectives and Implications*, ed. J. de Luce and H.T. Wilder, 22–39. New York: Springer-Verlag, 1983.

Terrace, Herbert S., Laura-Ann Petitto, Robert J. Sanders, and Tom G. Bever. Can an Ape Create a Sentence? *Science* 206 (1979): 891–902.

Urban, Greg. Metasignaling and Language Origins. *American Anthropologist* 104 (2002): 233–46.

GLOBAL VILLAGE

[See also: *Electronic Media; Internet; McLuhan, Marshall*]

The term *global village* was coined in the 1960s by media theorist Marshall McLuhan (1911–80) to describe how human beings are increasingly connected by electric (or electronic) technologies, which virtually eliminate the effects of space and time so that the globe contracts into one interconnected, metaphorical 'village.' According to McLuhan, technologies are extensions of human physical and mental capacities; the wheel is an extension of the foot, the book an extension of the eye, and electric circuitry an extension of the central nervous system. When the central nervous system is distributed in a global embrace through electronic technologies, awareness of others is heightened and humans return to tribal conditions. The term 'global village' has entered the language as a popular idiom. Scholars point out that the notion is significant for having anticipated some of the conditions and effects of the wired world in an era of globalization and the World Wide Web.

Electronic Extension, Secondary Orality, and the Retrieval of Tribal Culture

The advent of electronic media in the *electric revolution* is the third major technologi-cal milestone in the history of communication technology that began with the *literate revolution* in the fifth century BCE, which moved humans out of the mindset of oral and tribal culture and into a literate mentality. The *Gutenberg revolution* accelerated the millennia-long expansionist forces of change and shifted people out of the culture of the manuscript, producing mechanization, specialization, and alienation. The effects of the two previous revolutions were reversed when human capacities achieved a global reach. Whereas the ancient Greeks went from primary orality and tribalism to literacy – and the Gutenberg revolution hastened these processes of change – the electric revolution has touched off an implosion that retrieves tribal culture in an era of 'secondary orality.'

McLuhan's concept of the global village was likely influenced by Catholic theologian Teilhard de Chardin's notion of the 'noosphere' (from the Greek *nous* meaning 'mind' and *sphaira* meaning 'sphere' or 'globe'), a form of global consciousness emerging from the interaction of human minds in increasingly complex forms of organization and integration, a process which is fostered and accelerated by widely distributed communication connections leading ultimately to the unified mind of the Omega Point, conceived as evidence of the 'body of Christ.' Teilhard's interpretation was censured by the Catholic Church, and his writings circulated underground for years, influencing a generation of Catholic scholars. McLuhan appears to have borrowed and adapted Teilhard's vision, arguing that electric technologies make it possible to instantly translate any code or language into any other code or language. Extending our senses and nerves around the world creates a state of unified collective awareness that may have been similar to the condition of human beings before the fall at the Tower of Babel.

While McLuhan's retribalized global village has most often been portrayed as a peaceful and harmoniously functioning community – and this was indeed McLuhan's hope for the future – his vision was not as straightforwardly optimistic as much popular use of the term would suggest. Life in the global village has a shadow side that is hostile. As McLuhan stated in his final television interview, 'tribal people, one of their main kinds of sport is butchering each other.' The negative effect of the shift to global communication is that being linked to everyone leaves many people feeling overwhelmed and without a personal identity. The response is violence. War, torture, terrorism, and other violent acts are 'quests for identity' in the global village. To many, McLuhan's observations concerning the global village were prescient. Understanding both the positive potential and the negative effects of life in the global village has become one of the pressing challenges in today's increasingly interconnected world of communication.

Twyla Gibson and Stuart J. Murray

Bibliography

McLuhan, Marshall. *Understanding Media: The Extensions of Man.* Cambridge, MA: MIT Press, 1964.
– *Understanding Me: Lectures and Interviews.* Edited by Stephanie McLuhan and David Staines. Toronto: McClelland and Stewart, 2003.
McLuhan, Marshall, and Quentin Fiore. *The Medium Is the Massage: An Inventory of Effects.* New York: Bantam, 1967.

GLOBALIZATION

[See also: *Global Village; Mass Communication; McLuhan, Marshall*]

The term *globalization* refers to the process whereby the lives and destinies of people across the world are increasingly linked economically, politically, and culturally. Simply put, it is the awareness of the world as a single place. Such planetary consciousness is necessary, some argue, because the results of global warming, environmental erosion, the AIDS pandemic, global terrorism, and nuclear proliferation are likely to affect all humans, regardless of their geographical location or material conditions. But the adjective *global* functions to signify less catastrophic scenarios as well. A new vocabulary has emerged in which the *global* attaches to a range of phenomena that either reflect or shape the ceaseless traffic of people, images, and ideas at the present time. References are being made to global fashion, global youth, global tourism, global cities, global community, and so on, both in newspaper reports and in academic research. Globalization suggests both the benefits and the costs of an interdependence that has become the hallmark of the contemporary era.

Indeed, globalization informs every aspect of life, as events or trends in one part of the world, such as those of fashion or modelling, can get adopted in another, affecting standards of beauty, health, and self-esteem of a significant part of the population. Such interchanges are numerous, but complex to analyse or even explain. Thus, in the social sciences, globalization is 'poorly defined and difficult to research systematically' (Crane 2002: 1) and 'there are as many conceptualizations of globalization as there are disciplines' (Pieterse 1995: 45). The most common understandings stem from economics, in which globalization is the system generated by the movement towards integrated world markets in production and finance. In the fields of political science and sociology, international relations and history, communications, cultural studies and urban studies, attempts have been under way since the late 1980s to reorganize modes of analysis to accommodate the global into local and national frameworks. New terms such as 'glocalization' served to emphasize continuities and changes in the 1990s. And what is new in the way the contemporary world works is itself a matter for definition. For example: 'What is new about the modern global system is the chronic intensification of patterns of interconnectedness mediated by such phenomena as the modern communications industry and new informational technology and the spread of globalization in and through new dimensions of interconnectedness: technological, organizational, administrative and legal, among others, each with their own logic and dynamic of change' (quoted in Altman 2001: 15). In his preface to an influential collection on the topic, cultural theorist Fredric Jameson writes: 'Globalization falls outside the established academic disciplines, as a sign of the emergence of a new kind of social phenomenon, fully as much as an index of the origins of those disciplines in nineteenth-century realities that are no longer ours' (Jameson and Miyoshi 1998: xi). A general sense among scholars is that a major historical shift calls for a paradigm shift in scholarship as well.

The idea of globalization, especially with respect to media, was first popularized by the Canadian thinker Marshall McLuhan in his provocative phrase, the 'global village.' In the early 1960s, McLuhan embraced the then-new technology of television as capable of bringing the world's peoples closer together. Television would function as an electronic hearth or fireplace and recreate the tribal communities that had been supplanted by the individualizing tendencies of the print medium. Taking cues from his mentor, the economic historian Harold Innis, McLuhan argued that the culture of print had fostered the era of nationalism and the destructive conflicts of the twentieth century. With the spread of television, however, national xenophobia would gradually disappear, giving way to the 'retribalization' of humankind.

Although the utopian cast of McLuhan's thinking about globalization, and his optimism regarding the potential for harmony of television and other new media made many people question the validity of his claims, many of his ideas survive in the globalizing tendencies noted in the economic and political realities of the present time.

Globalization is commonly understood as having three characteristics:

(1) It is driven by the economic doctrine of neoliberalism, favouring the workings of the free market, competition in terms of labour and production, and Western-style consumerism.
(2) It has resulted in the weakening of nation-states and the creation of a 'borderless world.'
(3) New technologies of information and communication have compressed space and time through the instantaneous transfer of messages and images across the world.

Given the scope of the changes taking place, not everyone regards the discourse of globalization as addressing all players equally. Many anti-globalization activists see it as a synonym for 'Americanization' or the forcible imposition of American values, commodities, and business practices on the rest of the world. Thus globalization is a highly charged topic and viewed in contradictory ways by people of different backgrounds or ideological persuasions.

The post-9/11 world has brought to the fore some of the fissures and ambiguities surrounding globalization. The attacks on the twin towers in New York transfixed television audiences around the world, and the coverage that followed elicited global sympathy for the United States. But America's subsequent 'war on terror,' its invasion of Iraq, and prolonged occupation of that country have reawakened fears of American dominance. Internet images of the hanging of Saddam Hussein circulated worldwide have only added to the sense of power inequities haunting visions of global justice and shared principles of peace and democracy.

Genealogies of Globalization

Although globalization is generally regarded as concerned with the present, it did not arise unexpectedly, but has a genealogy (or several) and historical antecedents. Indeed, many scholars have decried the lack of a historical sense that informs many discussions of economic as well as cultural globalization. Four genealogical narratives can be identified; they are intertwined, and separated here only for purposes of convenience. Primary among them from the perspective of media is the story of how technologies of communication have historically played a central role in epochal change, or in the rise and fall of centres of power. Another view traces continuities between the industrial revolutions of the past and the post-industrial or information age of the present. A third complex of overlapping accounts includes the relationship of globalization to modernity and postmodernity; to colonialism and neo- or post-colonialism; and to the origins and development of nationalism and the nation-state. Finally, a fourth relates to genealogies of new media that aim to highlight changes in human perception brought about by each new invention, and the consequences for the global public sphere. Each of these genealogies and their related terms are described below.

Ronald Deibert, an international affairs scholar, uses communications technologies as a lens to explain 'world order transformation' (1997). By this he means those large-scale changes in societies that replace one political and cultural system with another, such as the shift from the medieval to the modern era in Europe, and the era of the nation-state to that of transnational corporations, global financial markets, and non-governmental organizations of the present day. These particular shifts, he demonstrates, were brought about by the printing press and the culture of literacy in the first instance, by hypermedia or the new digital-telecommunication technologies in the current era. Drawing on Innis (1950, 1951) and McLuhan (1964), Deibert proposes 'medium theory' as a persuasive explanatory framework to understand global shifts in power. Innis had advanced the idea that forms of media embody either a space or a time 'bias': they tend to favour

extension over vast spaces (for example, the medium of print and paper) or duration in time (for example, the media of stone, clay, or parchment used in ancient times). He observed that the dominance of a particular medium leads to 'monopolies of knowledge,' the concentration of political and social power in particular groups, such as the clergy in medieval times, the urban bourgeoisie in the modern era, and (one might add) the high-technology sectors of today. Deibert argues that the media must be seen as 'environments' in which certain forces are less or more likely to 'fit in' and function. The hypermedia environment of computer networks, digital data flows, and telecommunication links creates a strong incentive for transnational firms to operate.

Deibert's emphasis on communication technologies in 'world' history (he focuses primarily on the West) provides a link to views that explain globalization as the transition from industrial to post-industrial society, or what Manuel Castells (1997) has called the 'information age.' Brought on by the technological revolution of the 1970s, the information society is governed by the core techno-economic process of knowledge generation: 'For the first time in history, the human mind is a direct productive force, not just a decisive element of the production system … What we think, and how we think, become expressed in goods, services, material and intellectual output, be it food, shelter, transportation and communication systems, computers, missiles, health, education, or images' (Castells 2000: 31). The path back leads to the two previous industrial revolutions, of the mid-eighteenth century and the mid-nineteenth century, and even further back to the spirit of discovery of the European Renaissance. Scholars note that earlier technological revolutions took place only in a few societies, and diffused in a limited geographic area. Europeans borrowed some of the discoveries that took place in China, but China and Japan remained closed to European technology for many centuries. The current revolution is global, however, in that financial markets are integrated through the infrastructure of communications networks. Thus we have a genealogy that focuses on technologically driven changes in the economy and resultant social formations.

A third genealogical argument links globalization to the five-hundred-year history of 'modernity' in the West (beginning in 1492), a history that continues into the present, according to some, or has been superseded by the condition of postmodernity, according to others. The concept of modernity provides the linchpin, so to speak, of several related themes. Characterized by individualism, scientific rationality, and technological progress, it is seen as the driving force behind the earlier phases of globalization that resulted from the European voyages of discovery, slavery, imperial conquest and settlement, capitalism, and the age of nationalism. Modern ideas about society and social institutions that were transforming the West were later also introduced into colonized countries, while the latter's customs were treated as pre-modern and hence backward. Capitalist development, of which Marx wrote passionately in the nineteenth century, depended on the colonies for its raw materials. The historian Eric Hobsbawm calls the period between 1875 and 1914 the Age of Empire, and notes: 'A world economy whose pace was set by its developed or developing capitalist core was extremely likely to turn into a world in which the "advanced" dominated the "backward"; in short into a world of empire' (1989: 56). Keeping this background in mind, Stuart Hall points out that today's globalization is not a new phenomenon and, particularly in the context of Britain, emerges out of its history of colonialism (1991: 20).

This history intersects with modern media's development in crucial ways. The railways and transatlantic cables were laid to provide the infrastructure for imperial communications, and these eventually benefited Third World countries as well. Benedict Anderson (1983) has shown how print capitalism created the imagined community of the nation, shaping the course of events for nationalist movements of independence throughout the twentieth century. The culture of empire, according to Ella Shohat and Robert Stam (1994), was underpinned by cinema, especially the images of the non-white 'primitive' that were circulated worldwide by Hollywood films.

Globalization's history, then, is located in the triumph of Western modernity and its spread through colonization. An interesting critique of this prevailing view is put forth by Enrique Dussel (see Jameson 1998), who calls a paradigm that associates the rise of modernity exclusively with the West as Eurocentric. He proposes, instead, that an interregional system that goes back 4,500 years was in place *before* Europe's conquest of Amerindia in 1492. India, China, and the Muslim world were at the centre of this interregional system, and Columbus could only imagine that he had reached India when he accidentally arrived at the Caribbean. Europe's modernity was not a spontaneous development but rather a form of reaction to the power dynamics of the interregional system.

Many scholars, however, see globalization as marking a break from the troubled legacies of modernity, and as linked to postmodernity. They associate the latter with openness to difference and multiculturalism, fluid identities, and negotiable borders. According to Morley: 'Globalization is about the compression of time and space horizons and the creation of a world of simultaneity and depthlessness. Global space is a space of flows, an electronic space, a decentered space, a space in which frontiers and boundaries have become permeable' (1995: 115).

Finally, a genealogy of the media themselves, when connected to the above perspectives, points to its own narrative of globally shared aesthetic awareness. Many have argued that media must be studied in relation to major shifts in perception. In his famous essay 'The Work of Art in the Age of Mechanical Reproduction' (1934), Walter Benjamin claimed that the arrival of photography and motion pictures had forever redefined 'aura' that was predicated on the uniqueness of an object. Wolfgang Schivelbusch (1986) demonstrated how the railways as mode of transportation forever changed the intimate relationship to space that slower modes of travel, such as by foot or by carriage, had made possible. Susan Sontag and Roland Barthes have discussed the medium of photography and its relationship to personal memory or the collective memory of global events. But it is in the analysis of digital technologies, video games, and the online environment that notions of humanity, cyberworlds, virtual reality, and so forth are likely to have the most direct relevance to everyday practices of global interchange. The 1990s saw a surge in the formation of virtual communities and their promise of new forms of sociality.

Major Themes and Debates

While the intersections of media and globalization are numerous, a few themes stand out. These are:

(1) media and identity in the global era
(2) homogenization and hybridization of cultures
(3) the globalization of media industries

Media and Identity in the Global Era

Issues of identity have long been at the heart of media and cultural studies, with media representations of race, class, and gender shaping identities of individuals and groups. 'Tell me what you see, and I will tell you why you live and what you think,' was advanced as the slogan appropriate for the primacy of the visual in the postmodern era (Debray 1995). Globalization fit in well with postmodernism's rejection of identity as fixed and inviolate. Globalization processes are generally held to be plural, uneven, and overlapping. In an influential formulation, the anthropologist Arjun Appadurai explains globalization in

terms of the 'disjuncture' and 'difference' of cultural flows. By this he means that the flows of money, people, images, machinery, and ideas do not happen in a planned and coordinated fashion, but crisscross along an infinite and unpredictable variety of paths. He states that 'the sheer speed, scale, and volume of each of these flows are now so great that the disjunctures have become central to the politics of global culture' (1996: 37). In a similar vein, the work of British media scholar David Morley foregrounds the heightened practice of mobility, both physical and symbolic, as electronic landscapes proliferate via communications and transport technologies (1995). These and other theorists seek to study the implications of such movement for notions of belonging, citizenship, and identity. They question whether the framework of globalization renders moot the social sites of identity formation such as the family, the locality, or the nation. However, as Dennis Altman (2001) reminds us, the literature on globalization is often based on individual authors' own sense of familiarity with certain places and not with others, so that the general is inevitably filtered through the particular, the world evoked through one's experiences of it. Thus Appadurai finds it relevant to cite examples of family visits to Indian cities in order to make a larger point about transnational anthropology and the shifting terrain of ethnographic practice (1996: 48–65). And Morley considers what immigration from Britain's former colonies has meant for that country's sense of national identity.

   The model of consensus versus conflict structures views of the impact of globalization on local identities. Grim predictions of a 'clash of civilizations' (Huntington 1993) that would mark the twenty-first century as non-Western cultures initiate violent clashes with the advanced capitalist West have been countered by analyses of a 'civilization of clashes' (Appadurai 2006) in which globalization breeds dissatisfaction for the world's dispossessed and feeds nationalist passions. A sense of ethnic particularity or 'cultural closure' (Bayart 2005) accompanies the interconnections that globalization spawns, in a dialectic of proximity and heterogeneity. Where identity is not under threat, global/local dynamics result in a process of accommodation and change (Wilson and Dissanayake 2000; Skelton and Allen 1999). Through empirical case studies, researchers critically examine how local contexts and cultural patterns determine attitudes to, and the effects of, globalization processes in Brazil and India, Thailand and Japan, Mexico and the Caribbean. The impact of 'Third World' cultures on the United States and the UK, such as through the absorption of minority or immigrant populations and their music or cuisine, points to transformations in the industrialized world as well.

Globalization and Culture: Homogenization versus Hybridization

Jan Nederveen Pieterse notes: 'The most common interpretations of globalization are the ideas that the world is becoming more uniform and standardized, through a technological, commercial and cultural synchronization emanating from the West' (in Featherstone 1995). An early response to cultural globalization, it continues to have currency. Globalization is often seen as a threat to the survival of specific ways of life in traditional societies through what is variously termed 'McDonaldization' or 'Coca-Colonization.' One author states: 'In the villages of Lower Bavaria, just as in Calcutta, Singapore or the "favelas" of Rio de Janeiro, people watch Dallas on TV, wear blue jeans and smoke Marlboro as a sign of "free, untouched nature"' (quoted in Beynon and Dunkerley 2000: 22). Fears of a widespread commodification of culture following patterns of media consumption and lifestyles familiar in the United States are frequently voiced. The charge of media imperialism (see below) against dominant U.S. media corporations was made by critics like Ariel Dorfman and Armand Mattelart (1975) and Herbert Schiller (1969), who pointed to the transfer of American values and ideologies as insidious and dangerous to the vitality of other ways of life. More recently, the rise of ethnic nationalisms, fundamentalist Islam, and terrorism in many parts of the world are seen as enraged responses to America's military might and the hegemony of its media and popular culture.

Opponents of the homogenization argument point out the many instances of hybridization in the contemporary world, such as Latino rock, Mandarin pop, the influence of Korean television stars in Japan, and numerous other examples of cultural synthesis and combinations. Further, hybridity is not a new phenomenon but has always been present, and reflects observable social realities. Cultures have always borrowed from one another and new mixed elements have emerged. But the general phenomenon of cultural mixing has increased with the advance of globalization. Authors caution, however, that hybridity can only be understood within the context of power relations and the functions of capital. A celebratory attitude to hybridity is likely to overlook the workings of transnational capitalism itself. 'For it is the claim of IBM, CNN, etc. that they are indeed the harbingers of a culture of global productivities, knowledges, pleasures' (quoted in Tomlinson 1999: 145).

The Globalization of Media Industries

Nowhere are the workings of capitalism more evident than in the functioning of the culture industries. The transnationalization of media companies is not only the source of huge profits but of cultural domination as well. Concentration of ownership and control of the media in a handful of corporations has long been documented by researchers (Guback, Schiller, Herman and Chomsky, Bagdikian, and others). With economic globalization, they argue that these corporations are now dominant players on the global stage. Time-Warner, Disney, Viacom, Bertelsmann, the News Corporation, and General Electric are the parent companies responsible for many of the media programs and artefacts circulated around the world. Bagdikian notes that thanks to the internet and interactive cable, the lines separating traditional forms of media, such as newspapers, television programs, and movies, have become blurred. 'By owning all these media, a few large corporations have mass communications power that far exceeds the capabilities of smaller firms, social action organizations, and individuals' (2000: xv). Moreover, he notes that the media companies function as a cartel and not as competitors in the capitalist marketplace. 'Global Hollywood' provides a particularly salient example of media corporate power (Miller et al. 2001). Building on its historical dominance in film distribution going back to the 1920s, contemporary Hollywood is the undisputed leader in the global market. Its earnings through television programs, video, and theatrical screenings showed astonishing growth in nearly all regions of the world between the 1970s and 1991 (Miller et al. 2001: 8). Its power resides in the way it is able to exploit the market in cultural labour that has emerged in the global era.

The business practices of global Hollywood do not, however, guarantee standardized modes of reception on the part of audiences. Stokes and Maltby provide accounts of the reception of Hollywood films, television, and video by non-American audiences to demonstrate a history 'very different from the conventional, unidirectional process articulated in theories of cultural and media imperialism, in which commercial hegemony leads to ideological dominance' (2004: 7). They argue that these theories need to be rethought in relation to the viewing habits of actual (and active) audiences. They note that 'the 'Americanization of the world' has actually involved the circulation across national boundaries of a multinational popular culture which recognizes no frontiers' (2004: 4). It was in Hollywood's interests to see that its films were smoothly adaptable to various cultures. Audiences in such diverse settings

as Central Africa, Japan, India, Australia, Turkey, Belgium, France, and England testify to the social experience of movie-going and its relationship to time and context. For example, Nezih Erdogan describes how, in the 1940s, with Europe in ruins, Turkey's model of westernization shifted from Europe to America. Popular film magazines exploited this interest by presenting stories and photos of Hollywood stars. A 'Turkish' star in Hollywood – Turhan Bey – became a vehicle for projected longings as well as national feelings on the part of Turkish audiences. Another instance of the complex dynamics of reception concerns the 'Copperbelt cowboys' of colonial northern Rhodesia (Zambia). In that case censored and disjointed images of Hollywood films (especially cowboy films) became the means to engage with notions of modernity. And young viewers in a Flemish town who were surveyed in 2001 overwhelmingly preferred Hollywood films over European or local Flemish films because of the former's perceived high-tech sophistication and pleasing exoticism.

Reversing the flow from West to East, it is important to note the popularity of Japanese animated films and other cultural products such as computer games in the United States (Iwabuchi in Crane 2002: 268). Devoted fans of Japanese animations in Western countries express a yearning for Japan and the desire to be born there. The source of origin of a cultural product becomes less important than the fact of its circulation and appropriation.

'Not a global village but customized cottages'

The literature on globalization, then, like the phenomenon itself, is not an organic whole but rather a series of overlapping theories and debates, reflecting the complexity of the interactions taking place. What is evident is that the discourse of globalization has taken off in several directions and is here to stay. At once an economic and political process, a form of consciousness, and an emergent theoretical paradigm, globalization must be understood in multiple ways. As the world becomes more integrated, as the scale and intensity of human contact grow even further, and as innovations in media technologies continue to create new publics, the need to make sense of these developments can only accelerate.

Sumita S. Chakravarty

Bibliography

Altman, Dennis. *Global Sex*. Chicago: University of Chicago Press, 2001.

Anderson, Benedict. *Imagined Communities: Reflections on the Origin and Spread of Nationalism*. Rev. ed. London, New York: Verso, 1991; originally 1983.

Appadurai, Arjun. *Modernity at Large: Cultural Dimensions of Globalization*. Minneapolis: University of Minnesota Press, 1996.

– *Fear of Small Numbers: An Essay on the Geography of Anger*. Durham, NC, and London: Duke University Press, 2006.

Bagdikian, Ben. *The Media Monopoly*. 6th ed. Boston: Beacon Press, 2000.

Bayart, Jean-François. *The Illusion of Cultural Identity*. Chicago: University of Chicago Press, 2005.

Benjamin, Walter. *Gesammelte Shriften*. Ed. R. Tidermann and H. Schweppenhäuser. Frankfurt am Main: Suhrkamp Verlag, 1934.

Beynon, John, and David Dunkerley, eds. *Globalization: The Reader*. New York: Routledge, 2000.

Berger, Peter, and Samuel Huntington, eds. *Many Globalizations: Cultural Diversity in the Contemporary World*. New York: Oxford University Press, 2002.

Castells, Manuel. *The Rise of the Network Society*. Berkeley: University of California Press, 1997.

Crane, Diana, ed. *Global Culture: Media, Arts, Policy, and Globalization*. London and New York: Routledge, 2002.

Debray, Regis. The Three Ages of Looking. *Critical Inquiry* 21 (1995): 529–55.

Deibert, Ronald. *Parchment, Printing and Hypermedia: Communication in World Order Transformation*. New York: Columbia University Press, 1997.

Denning, Michael. *Culture in the Age of Three Worlds*. London, New York: Verso, 2004.

Dorfman, Ariel, and Armand Mattelart. *How to Read Donald Duck: Imperialist Ideology in the Disney Comic*. New York: International General, 1975.

Featherstone, Mike, ed. *Global Culture: Nationalism, Globalization and Modernity*. London: Sage, 1995.

Guback, Thomas. *The International Film Industry: Western Europe and America since 1945*. Bloomington: Indiana University Press, 1969.

Hall, Stuart. The Local and the Global, Globalization and Ethnicity. In *Culture, Globalization and the World-System: Contemporary Conditions for the Representation of Identity*. Binghamton, NY: SUNY Dept. of Art and Art History, 1991.

Herman, Edward, and Noam Chomsky. *Manufacturing Consent: The Political Economy of the Mass Media*. New York: Pantheon Books, 1988.

Herman, Edward, and Robert McChesney. *The Global Media: The New Missionaries of Corporate Capitalism*. London: Cassell, 1997.

Hobsbawm, Eric. *The Age of Empire 1875–1914*. New York: Vintage Books, 1989.

Huntington, Samuel. The Clash of Civilizations? *Foreign Affairs* (1993): 22–49.

Innis, Harold. *Empire and Communications*. Oxford: Oxford University Press, 1950.

– *The Bias of Communication*. Toronto: University of Toronto Press, 1951.

Jameson, Fredric, and Masao Miyoshi, eds. *The Cultures of Globalization*. Durham, NC, and London: Duke University Press, 1998.

McLuhan, Marshall. *Understanding Media: The Extensions of Man*. New York: McGraw Hill, 1964.

Miller, Toby, et al. *Global Hollywood*. London: BFI, 2001.

Morley, David. *Spaces of Identity: Global Media, Electronic Landscapes and Cultural Boundaries*. London and New York: Routledge, 1995.

Pieterse, Jan Nederveen. Globalization as Hybridization. In *Global Modernities*, ed. Mike Featherstone, S. Lash, and R. Robertson, 24–45. London: Sage, 1995.

Sakr, Naomi. *Satellite Realms: Transnational Television, Globalization and the Middle East*. London: I.B. Tauris, 2001.

Schiller, Herbert. *Mass Communications and American Empire*. 2nd ed. Boulder, CO: Westview Press, 1992; originally 1969.

Schivelbusch, Wolfgang. *The Railway Journey: The Industrialization of Time and Space in the Nineteenth Century*. Berkeley: University of California Press, 1986.

Shohat, Ella, and Robert Stam. *Unthinking Eurocentrism: Multiculturalism and the Media*. London: Routledge, 1994.

Skelton, Tracey, and Tim Allen, eds. *Culture and Global Change*. London and New York: Routledge, 1999.

Stokes, Melvyn, and Richard Maltby. *Hollywood Abroad: Audiences and Cultural Exchange*. London: BFI, 2004.

Tomlinson, John. *Globalization and Culture*. Chicago: University of Chicago Press, 1999.

Wilson, Rob, and Wimal Dissanayake, eds. *Global/Local: Cultural Production and the Transnational Imaginary*. Durham, NC, and London: Duke University Press, 1996.

GOFFMAN, ERVING (1922–82)

[See also: *Bateson, Gregory; Conversation Analysis; Discourse; Ethnography*]

Canadian sociologist Erving Goffman was a pioneer in promoting qualitative (observational or ethnographic) research methods in the study of human interaction. He originated the concept of *frame analysis* – the technique of dividing human interaction into separate schemas or frames of behaviour that can then be analysed in terms of constituent units of selfhood-portrayal, recognizable by others intuitively as part of personality. Taking his cue from Gregory Bateson (1936; Ruesch and Bateson 1951), he called the sequence of actions that identify a person's behavioural characteristics a 'strip' (an obvious reference to the comic strip as conspicuously exemplifying a structured sequence of actions). The method of frame analysis consists in: (1) describing the strip (the actual behavioural scene), (2) reducing it to a psychological typology, and (3) interpreting the social code deployed by the characters in the strip. In effect, Goffman drew attention to the implicit fact that everyday life unfolds very much like a cartoon theatrical performance, because people feel as if they are on a stage and thus seek to skilfully stage their character according to social context. People are 'character actors' who employ gestures, props, and conversation to impress each other for specific reasons. The Latin term for 'cast of characters' is *dramatis personae*, literally, 'the persons of the drama,' a term betraying the theatrical origin of our concept of personhood. *Persona* was the 'mask' in Greek theatre. We seem, in a phrase, to perceive life as a stage.

Goffman was born in Manville, Alberta, and raised in nearby Dauphin. He graduated from the University of Manitoba with a degree in chemistry. Goffman subsequently enrolled at the University of Toronto, graduating with a degree in sociology and anthropology, and then moved on to the University of Chicago, where he received his doctorate in sociology in 1953. Goffman's work has been critical in showing that our sense of selfhood emerges through symbolic interaction, and this, like the theatre, unfolds systematically in terms of frames of behaviour, much like theatre scripts, which he called the social codes by which people live. Goffman actually defined the frame space as if it were a theatre, with a front region in which the 'actors' perform their scripts, and the background of others is described as if it constituted an audience situation. Goffman introduced such notions as 'context,' 'situational effects,' and 'role-playing' as basic sociological concepts. These have been adopted and adapted by communication theorists to describe how face-to-face verbal communication unfolds.

Marcel Danesi

Bibliography

Bateson, Gregory. *Naven: A Survey of the Problems Suggested by a Composite Picture of the Culture of a New Guinea Tribe Drawn from Three Points of View*. Stanford, CA: Stanford University Press, 1936.

Goffman, Erving. *The Presentation of Self in Everyday Life*. New York: Anchor, 1959.

– *Encounters*. Indianapolis: Bobbs-Merrill, 1961.

– *Asylums*. New York: Doubleday, 1961.

– *Stigma*. Englewood Cliffs, NJ: Prentice-Hall, 1963.

– *Strategic Interaction*. Philadelphia: University of Pennsylvania Press, 1969.

– *Frame Analysis*. New York: Harper and Row, 1974.

– *Gender Advertisements*. New York: Macmillan, 1978.

Ruesch, Jurgen, and Gregory Bateson. *Communication: The Social Matrix of Psychiatry*. New York: Norton, 1951.

GOOGLING

[See also: *Internet; World Wide Web*]

The term *googling* has come into broad use to designate the use of the Google search engine (and now other engines) to search for something on the internet. The term reflects both the paradigm shift that has occurred in information systems and an acknowledgment of the social power that Google itself has attained over a relatively short period of time. Indeed the company's declared goal is to organize information from around the world and make it accessible to anyone through the World Wide Web. Google services include email, advertising services, text translation, personalized Web pages, and video sharing through YouTube, among others.

Google was established in 1995 by Larry Page and Sergey Brin, graduate students in computer science at Stanford University. At first they created a search engine that they called BackRub, running the business from their dormitories. The name they finally chose, *Google*, is derived from the mathematical term *googol* (the number represented by 1 followed by 100 zeros), which itself was coined by mathematicians Kasner and Newman in a 1940 book, *Mathematics and the Imagination*. The term was seen by Page and Brin as appropriate because it was representative of the vast amount of information that is available on the World Wide Web. Google was launched officially in 1998, becoming a publicly traded company in 2004. The word *googling* was added to the Oxford and Merriam-Webster dictionaries in 2006, despite the company's efforts to prohibit uses of the word as a common English word. Like the use of *kleenex* to represent all tissues, this happens periodically when a particular brand or service is seen to represent or symbolize the entire class of similar products or services (and their related activities, events, etc.). Google's opposition came as somewhat of a surprise, given Page and Brin's stated mission of making all kinds of information available and usable by anyone for any reason. It seems that they wanted to make an exception – their own service – to their stated goal.

The advent and utilization of googling reverberates with many philosophical and sociological nuances and concerns. One of these involves copyright, authorship, and the public domain. The latter term refers to a legal category that covers creative works (books, musical scores, etc.) that the public may use freely. The works are called intellectual property. When works fall into the public domain, anyone can use them as they wish without having to pay royalties and without being subject to any liability. Copyrighted material enters the public domain when the copyright expires. In the United States, the copyright is valid for the copyright holder's lifetime plus 70 years. This law was passed in 1998 for books copyrighted after 1 January 1923. The law was called the Sonny Bono Copyright Term Extension Act or, more colloquially, the 'Mickey Mouse Protection Act,' since at the time it was feared that Mickey Mouse was about to enter the public domain.

The advent of Google has led to a debate about what constitutes public domain, given the agreements made by Google with copyright holders. Already in 1971, a venture called 'Project Gutenberg' was initiated by early volunteers to digitize, archive, and distribute online the full texts of public domain books. As of 2006, the project had over 19,000 items in its collection, with an average of over fifty new books being added each week. There are now similar projects posting various public domain materials on websites. Literally millions of books are now available online. This has had a profound effect on the book publishing world and on print culture generally. The noble idea of opening up all books and libraries to everyone via Google is highly idealistic, but it remains to be seen if it is practicable. In the United States, copyright was included in the Constitution (Article 1, Section 8) for 'limited times' and only to promote 'the progress of science and useful arts.' In effect, the Constitution put the public's right to access information before private profit.

Google has always seen its mission as putting library collections online as a means of encouraging universal literacy – the ultimate goal of enlightened democracies, as it has constantly asserted. In October 2005, Google faced a class action suit by authors and publishers. The suit was resolved in 2009. The settlement created a Book Rights registry that represents the copyright holders. In return, Google is allowed to sell access to copyrighted books, which are mainly out of print. Users can print out digitized versions of the books by purchasing Google's 'consumer license.' Google keeps 37 per cent of the revenues, giving 63 per cent to the copyright holders. As of early 2010, Google has digitized some 10 million books. And given various recent settlements over copyright lawsuits, Google has emerged as a major player in how books will be distributed and made available in the future. Changes in any copyright laws must now take Google into account.

There are unseen dangers in this 'googlization' phenomenon. For one thing, it would turn the internet into a vehicle for 'privatizing' knowledge through individualized user access – knowledge that has traditionally been part of the public sphere. Second, the knowledge system is put into the hands of the digitizers, who will choose what to make available, even though Google has claimed that it will try to make 'everything possible' available. Third, Google is creating the largest reference library in the history of humanity. While the goal is a laudable one – making information as widely accessible as possible – there is also the danger of giving one particular company, Google, enormous power.

Another major issue with respect to the Google universe is the effects it might have on cognition, identity, socializing, and communication (among other things). Does Google make us more intelligent than in the past (since it purportedly entices more people to read) or more stupid, since it seems to stress the use of information without reflection (Bauerlein 2008)? It is beyond the purpose of the present entry to enter into the debate that this question has generated. Suffice it to say that the reading and writing tools and rules we use to understand the world contribute to shaping how we form out thoughts and how we perceive the world. And thus googling will unquestionably have effects on all of us – what these are still remain to be seen.

The question of identity also constantly comes up in academic discussions of the Google universe. Once a profile on a social networking site like Facebook is uploaded onto the internet along with various other information about an individual, then the identity of that individual takes on (literally) a life of its own. Cyberspace personalities emerge and are subject to a global assessment. The risks are obvious. First and foremost, the whole issue begs the question of what identity is real in today's world – the online or the offline one? – and whether online portrayals or representations of someone will have an effect on that individual in the offline world. The question of privacy also comes up, since Google (and other search engines) will allow virtually anything to be uploaded. Well-known media-reported cases have given us partial glimpses into the implications this might have. One example occurred in 2005 when a young woman was riding on the subway in South Korea with a small dog. The dog urinated in the subway, and a minor argument ensued between the woman and various passengers. Upset, the woman exited without cleaning up the mess. Before she could exit, however, a passenger on the train snapped a photo of her and her dog, subsequently posting it on an online discussion board. The story spread quickly, and local news outlets picked it up right after. Within days, the woman was identified and her name and other identifying information were posted online. Unable to escape the notoriety and public humiliation that she suffered online, the woman became depressed and, after offering a public apology, dropped out of university.

Another example of online behaviour affecting offline behaviour is that of a thirteen-year-old American girl who met someone on MySpace whom she thought was a sixteen-year-old boy named Josh Evans. They entered into an online friendship. The girl's family claims that her spirits were lifted after forming this friendship. In 2006, however, the tone of Josh's messages changed ominously. He no longer desired the girl's friendship. After vicious online arguments, the girl ended up committing suicide. Six weeks after her death, the parents discovered that 'Josh' was actually a fictitious character created by the mother of one of the girl's former friends, who used the fake profile to exact revenge on the girl for having 'wronged' her own daughter. By and large, such tragic cases remain infrequent. They gain media attention, and they are really no different than tragic cases that occurred in the past when only an offline world existed. Nevertheless these cases beg new questions about how we make information available through the new social modeia.

Googling provides an increased capacity for people to do what they used to do offline, but in a more efficient way. However, it also encourages ephemerality and extreme faddishness. It does so by spreading so-called 'viral events' – events that are spread on the Web from person to person. A new rock band, for instance, can be discovered and become a celebrity over night after appearing on YouTube. But, as it all too often turns out, it then quickly fades from public favour, the YouTube video remaining a sad memento of the band's fifteen minutes of fame. Wasik (2009) coined the term *nano-celebrity* to describe this pattern of celebrity making. The Web is one huge system for perpetrating 'nano-phenomena,' as they can be called. As Harkin (2009: 6) puts it, such phenomena are not part of a business conglomerate conspiracy. Indeed, they would not have come about in the first place without the complicity of common people seeking to peer into each other's lives: 'In doing so we volunteered ourselves to act as human nodes ferrying information back and forth on a vast information loop – and, at least for the time we spent there, we would find ourselves behaving as such.'

Critical studies are beginning to show that googling is bringing about a new form of culture and a new form of consciousness (Auletta 2008; Carr 2008). With services such as Google Chat, Google Voice, Google Maps, Google Documents, Google Buzz, Google Calendar, Google Earth, Google Reader, Google News, Google Profiles, YouTube, Blogspot, Google Profiles, Google Alerts, Google Translate, Google Book Search, Google Groups, among many others, the whole world is now, literally, at one's fingertips on the screen. But what kind of world is it, decry the critics? Statistics and popularity rule the Google universe. Using the algorithm called PageRank, Google can easily determine the relevancy of sites and thus, by implication, assign value to information through measurement. Rather than just ranking sites according to the number of times a particular searchword is used, Google ranks them on the basis of the number of links the sites have. If a popular site is linked to a page, then that link is given even greater relevancy. Relevancy is thus tied to statistically determined popularity. As Carr (2008) argues, this meaning of relevancy is based on a science of measurement, not around any assessment of the intrinsic value of information. As a result, Carr believes, Google has conditioned us to process information efficiently and statistically, not in terms of understanding. So, rather than encourage reading in the reflective sense of the word, Google is leading to selective and superficial browsing, guided by the criterion of popularity.

Google has evolved into what many critics call a 'world brain' that we use to think together (Levy 2001; Vaidyanatan 2011). It is where everyone goes for information, answers, advice, and to present oneself to the world through social media. Google defines its mission as organizing the world's information, leaving it up to individuals to make of it what they want. But unwittingly Google has created the 'information society.' Google is one huge 'ratings medium' that ranks even users of its information as they use the engine. As Vaid (2011: 89) puts it, 'We are not Google's customers: we are its product. We – our fancies, fetishes, predilections, and preferences – are what Google sells to advertisers. The questions raised by the advent of Google are now the substance of great debates across the social sciences and philosophy. Do we want to be considered as individuals or do we want to be unit cells in the ever-expanding world brain of Google?' The paradox lies in the fact that, for the first time in history, these questions can be contemplated and debated by virtually anyone, on Google.

Marcel Danesi

Bibliography

Auletta, Ken. *Googled: The End of the World as We Know It.* New York: Penguin, 2009.

Bauerlein, Mark. *The Dumbest Generation: How the Digital Age Stupefies Young Americans and Jeopardizes Our Future or, Don't Trust Anyone under 30.* New York: Penguin, 2008.

Carr, Nicolas. *The Shallows: What the Internet Is Doing to Our Brains.* New York: Norton, 2008.

Cleland, Scott, and Ira Brodsky. *Search and Destroy: Why You Can't Trust Google Inc.* New York: Telescope, 2011.

Edwards, Douglas. *I'm Feeling Lucky: The Confessions of Google Employee Number 59.* Boston: Houghton Mifflin Harcourt, 2011.

Epstein, Jason. *Book Business: Publishing Past, Present, and Future.* New York: Norton, 2001.

Hafner, Katie, and Matthew Lyon. *Where Wizards Stay Up Late: The Origins of the Internet.* New York: Simon and Schuster, 1996.

Harkin, James. *Lost in Cyburbia: How Life on the Net Has Created a Life of Its Own.* Toronto: Knopf, 2009.

Herman, Andrew, and Thomas Swiss, eds. *The World Wide Web and Contemporary Cultural Theory.* London: Routledge, 2000.

Jarvis, Jeff. *What Would Google Do?* New York: Collins Business, 2009.

Kasner, Edward, and James R. Newman. *Mathematics and the Imagination.* New York: Simon and Schuster, 1940.

Levy, Steven. *In the Plex: How Google Thinks, Works, and Shapes Our Lives.* New York: Simon and Schuster, 2011.

Nakhimovsky, Alexander, and Tom Myers. *Google, Amazon, and Beyond: Creating and Consuming Web Services.* New York: Apress, 2003.

Slevin, James. *The Internet and Society.* London: Polity, 2000.

Vaidhyanathan, Siva. *The Googlization of Everything (and Why We Should Worry).* Berkeley: University of California Press, 2011.

Van Dijk, Teun. *The Network Society.* London: Sage, 1999.

Wasik, Bill. *And Then There's This: How Stories Live and Die in Viral Culture.* New York: Viking, 2009.

GRAMSCI, ANTONIO (1891–1937)

[See also: *Culture Industry Theory; Hegemony Theory; Ideology Theory; Marxism; Media Effects*]

Antonio Gramsci was an Italian philosopher, political theorist, and politician. He was a founding member and leader of the Communist Party of Italy, until he was imprisoned under Mussolini's regime. In spite of difficult life conditions for his family, he obtained his secondary school diploma, and in 1911, thanks to a study grant, he enrolled at the Faculty of Arts at the University of Turin, where he focused on linguistics and language-related subjects, studying under Matteo Bartoli. As demonstrated in particular by Franco Lo Piparo (1974, 2008), there is a close connection between Gramsci's linguistic background and his originality in politics. He gave up his university education in early 1915 without finishing his degree, but not without acquiring an extensive knowledge of history and philosophy. During his university courses, he became familiar with the writings of Antonio Labriola, Rodolfo Mondolfo, Giovanni Gentile, Benedetto Croce, and with Hegelian Marxism, which was denominated by Labriola as 'philosophy of praxis.' In Turin (a city which at the time was going through a process of industrialization, with the Fiat and Lancia factories recruiting workers from the poorer regions of Italy), Gramsci became friends with Palmiro Togliatti, Angelo Tasca, and Umberto Terracini. In April 1919, Gramsci and his friends collaborated in setting up the weekly newspaper *L'Ordine Nuovo: Rassegna Settimanale di Cultura Socialista* (The New Order: A Weekly Review of Socialist Culture) after writing for the socialist newspaper *Il Grido del Popolo* and for the Piedmont edition of *Avanti!* (the official organ of the Italian Socialist Party), for which he also was a co-editor. On 1 January 1921, *L'Ordine Nuovo* became a daily newspaper.

The Communist Party of Italy (*Partito Comunista d'Italia* or *PCI*) was founded on 21 January 1921, in the town of Livorno. In 1922 Gramsci travelled to Russia as a representative of the new party. Here, he met Julka Schucht (1896–1980), a young violinist, whom he later married and with whom he had two sons, Delio (1924–81) and Giuliano (born in 1926). The year 1922 also witnessed the rise of fascism in Italy. In late 1922 and early 1923, Mussolini's government started a campaign of repression against the opposition parties, arresting most of the PCI leadership. Consequently, at the end of 1923, Gramsci travelled from Moscow to Vienna, were he had been sent to establish links with the Italian communist party and the other European parties. In 1924 Gramsci was elected as a deputy of the PCI for the Veneto region and became general secretary of the PCI. Thanks to parliamentary immunity, he lived in Rome while his family stayed in Moscow. The official newspaper of the communist party, *L'Unità*, was published for the first time on 12 February. At the Lyons Congress of the PCI in January 1926, Gramsci called for a united front to restore democracy to Italy. On 9 November 1926 as a result of a new wave of emergency laws enforced by the Fascist government, Gramsci was arrested by the police, despite parliamentary immunity, and brought to Regina Coeli, the infamous prison in Rome. The immediate sentence was for five years' confinement on the island of Ustica, but subsequently, in 1928, he was sentenced to twenty years' imprisonment (in Turi, near Bari). While he was in prison he wrote *Quaderni dal carcere* (*Prison Notebooks*), consisting of more than 30 notebooks and 3,000 pages. He also wrote his extraordinary letters from prison to friends and especially to family members, the most important of whom was not his wife Julka but rather a sister-in-law, Tania Schucht. His best friend, the economist Piero Sraffa, used his personal funds and contacts in order to obtain the books and periodicals that Gramsci wanted while in prison. We have the *Prison Notebooks* in its current form thanks to Sraffa's assistance and to the intermediary role played by Tania, since without their help these writings would never have come to public knowledge. By 1934 Gramsci's health had deteriorated, and as a consequence he gained conditional freedom. He was transferred to hospitals in Civitavecchia, Formia, and then Rome, where he died at the age of 46.

Marx had claimed that the dominant ideas of a society are those held and imposed by the dominant class. Gramsci's concept of *hegemony* draws on this claim. In the capitalist system of production, the dominant class tends to maintain control over the masses, not just through force and coercion, but through the imposition of ideology – that is to say, through cultural hegemony by which the values of the dominant class are made to pass and circulate as natural or common values and are presented as a common heritage of ideas, constituting the expression of a sort of 'common sense' value system. The dominant class aims to obtain consensus, manipulating public opinion in such a way that the people identify their own well-being with the well-being of the dominant class, and consequently they end up unwittingly helping the dominant class maintain its power and reproduce the conditions of its domination. The function of the intellectual is to help the dominated classes demystify this situation and describe it for what it is. This is possible through an adequate critique of the dominant ideology as simply a play on logic using ordinary language and ordinary behaviour. Hegemony by the dominant class is obtained not only through control of verbal and non-verbal behaviours, but also by control over the language system itself, given that all linguistic dialogue, according to Gramsci, is political in nature. In Gramsci's view, any class aiming to dominate a society thus has to obtain cultural hegemony and broad social consensus over the whole nexus of institutions, social relations, and ideas present in it.

This led Gramsci to develop a theory that emphasized the importance of the social *superstructure*, but not in purely Marxist terms, but as a mere level above basic social *structure*, defined as the economic base of a society. Instead, Gramsci subdivides superstructure into (1) *civil society*, consisting of schools, newspapers, associations, churches, common ideas, and the mass media (this is the sphere of ideology where hegemony is based on so-called 'free consensus,' and (2) *political society*, consisting of the government, police, armed forces, law courts, and other hegemonic structures (this is the sphere of the *state* where dominance is directly exercised when 'free consensus' fails). As Ferruccio Rossi-Landi (1990: 65) observed, the relevance today of this approach for media and communication studies, and the ideological structures that guide the use of the media, is that sign systems (like language) serve the interests of the power elite primarily by producing consensus. Consequently, says Rossi-Landi, the dominant class is the class that controls communication and interpretation processes in a given society: 'In the light of the critical edition of his work and of certain letters of fairly recent publication, it can be said that Gramsci had at least an inkling of all this' (1990: 65–6). Gramsci's notion of civil society confers upon languages and signs the role of mediation between base and superstructure. This implies a *dialectical trichotomy* mediated by sign systems. This approach also makes it obvious that the so-called 'natural order of things' must be questioned by each and every one of us. In today's society, mass communication is such an important factor in social processes that we can conceive of it in terms of 'communication-production,' as proposed by Augusto Ponzio (1991). In the communication-production system, ideology and common sense are so closely linked that they converge. In this way, the idea of the 'end of ideologies' has asserted itself and become widespread. In such a situation, the Gramscian point of view comes forward as being as relevant as it ever was. Gramsci's writings provide the media analyst with an important source of theoretical instruments for an insightful understanding of hegemony in the modern world.

Susan Petrilli

328   Gramsci, Antonio (1891–1937)

Bibliography

Gramsci. Antonio. *Lettere dal carcere*. New ed. by S. Caproglio and E. Fubini. 4 Vols. Turin: Einaudi, 1965.

– *Quaderni del carcere. Selections from the Prison Notebooks of Antonio Gramsci*. London: Lawrence and Wishart, 1971.

– *Quaderni del carcere*. Critical edition by Istituto Gramsci. Ed. V. Gerratana. Turin: Einaudi, 1975.

Joll, James. *Antonio Gramsci*. New York: Viking, 1977.

Leone De Castris, Arcangelo. *Egemonia e fascismo: Il problema degli intellettuali negli anni trenta*. Bologna: Il Mulino, 1981.

– *Estetica e politica: Croce e Gramsci*. Milan: Franco Angeli, 1989.

– *Sulle ceneri di Gramsci: Pasolini, i comunisti e il '68*. Rome: Datanews, 1997.

– *Gramsci rimosso*. Rome: Datanews 1997.

Lo Piparo, Franco. *Lingua, intellettuali, egemonia in Gramsci*. Bari-Rome: Laterza, 1979.

– *Comunista? La chiave linguistica dell'originalità di Gramsci*. Palermo: Gea Schirò, 2008.

Ponzio, Augusto. *Dialogo e narrazione*. Lecce: Milella, 1991.

Rossi-Landi, Ferruccio. *Marxism and Ideology* (1982). Trans. R. Griffin. Oxford: Clarendon, 1990.

GRICE'S MAXIMS

[See also: *Conversational Analysis; Discourse Theory*]

Herbert Paul Grice (1926–85) was an American philosopher who studied the logical structure of argumentation during conversations and the implications this had for human interaction. He is especially known for what have come to be called his *maxims* for how successful conversations unfold (or, more accurately, should unfold). They are as follows:

(1) *Maxim of quantity*: (a) make your contribution as informative as required for the purposes of the exchange; (b) do not make it more informative than required

(2) *Maxim of quality*: make it true, so (a) do not say what you believe to be false, (b) do not say something for which you lack adequate evidence

(3) *Maxim of relation or relevance*: be relevant

(4) *Maxim of manner*: be perspicuous; thus (a) avoid obscurity of expression, (b) avoid ambiguity, (c) be brief, (d) be orderly

It is not clear why these maxims have become so widely cited, since they are really common-sense recommendations. Perhaps they remind people that communication is part of ethical behaviour, or at least should be. Grice also pointed out that most of the meanings that are built into utterances are implicit, rather than explicit. He called the process *conversational implication*. He illustrated it as follows (Grice 1991: 306):

A: How is John getting on his new job at the bank?
B: Oh, quite well I think; he likes his colleagues, and he hasn't been in prison yet.

B's answer seems to contain an irrelevant remark about John having not been in prison yet. A, however, likely infers that B was implying something more, such as, for instance, that John 'is the sort of person likely to yield to the temptation provided by his occupation' (Grice 1991: 306). How does A arrive at this conclusion? Grice proposed that it occurred through a cooperation on the part of the interlocutors that reflects a 'common purpose, or set of purposes' upholding the reason behind the conversation. The interlocutors want to be cooperative, contributing meaningfully to the purpose of the exchange. So, A extracts from B's utterance that B wanted to communicate more than what he actually said. It is this pattern of inferential reasoning that characterizes utterance meaning and which, obviously, can be a source of misunderstanding in many conversations.

Marcel Danesi

Bibliography

Grice, Herbert Paul. *Studies in the Way of Words*. Cambridge, MA: Harvard University Press, 1989.

– Logic and conversation. In S. Davis, ed., *Pragmatics: a Reader*. Oxford: Oxford University Press, 1991. (Reprint of the paper originally presented in the William James Lectures at Harvard University in 1967 and circulated as a typescript.)

GUTENBERG GALAXY

[See also: *Communication; McLuhan, Marshall*]

The term *Gutenberg Galaxy*, after Johannes Gutenberg (ca 1400–68), the German printer who invented the modern printing press, was coined by the late communications theorist Marshall McLuhan (1911–80) to describe the social order that resulted from the availability of cheap books as a result of print technology and the spread of literacy that this technological event brought about.

Starting in 1951, McLuhan claimed that there existed an intrinsic interconnection between developments in mass communications technologies and culture. The concept of *technology* in McLuhan included artefacts, tools, and mental concepts or 'tools' such as the alphabet. Each major period in history takes its character, McLuhan suggested, from the technology used most widely at the time to encode and store information. For this reason, McLuhan called the period from 1700 to the mid-1900s the 'Age of Print,' constituting the 'Gutenberg Galaxy.' In that age printed books were the chief means of mass communications. The consequences of print technology were felt throughout the world and changed cultures by making print materials available broadly and, thus, leading to a rise in print literacy, individualism (since reading is done alone), and the growth of nationalism (since printed books encourage thinking in a specific language). As Harkin (2009: 53) has put it, McLuhan's term captures much more than a technological innovation that brought about job losses to a few monks who earned their living as manuscript copyists. The advent of cheap print technology had precipitated the demise of the oral tradition of storytelling and helped to develop languages; it had fostered individualism by making millions of books available to large numbers of people to read on their own; it had even imposed a level of standardization in the use of language. The clearly sequenced and ordered way in which books were produced and then read had gone on to reconfigure almost everything. The growth of bureaucracy, the linear sequence of industrial processes that characterize the modern factory and industrial life, even the nation-state – all these, according to McLuhan, had been thrown forward like a roll of dominoes by the book.

The 'Electronic Age' displaced the 'Age of Print' by the middle part of the twentieth century, leading to what some have called the 'Electronic Galaxy.' Again, the consequences of this have been monumental. Because electronic communications increase the speed and reach of interactions, they have brought about a 'global village' with, paradoxically, the same kinds of characteristics of the early tribes, such as the need to belong to a specific group. The Electronic Age may be leading, as McLuhan suspected, to the end of individualism and print-based notions of literacy and nationhood.

The modern-day media can best be understood in terms of McLuhan's framework of integrating media, technology, and culture into an overall system of social evolution. Convergence, in one of its basic meanings today, embraces the utilization of all media, from traditional print (magazines, newspaper) to online forms – a situation that could only arise in the Electronic Galaxy, leading to its redesignation as the 'Digital Galaxy.' Any media system or product in this galaxy will survive and become self-perpetuating only if it develops the ability to adapt to changes in mass communications technologies.

Marcel Danesi

Bibliography

Harkin, James. *Lost in Cyburbia: How Life on the Net Has Created a Life of Its Own.* Toronto: Knopf, 2009.

McLuhan, Marshall. *The Mechanical Bride: Folklore of Industrial Man.* New York: Vanguard, 1951.

– *The Gutenberg Galaxy.* Toronto: University of Toronto Press, 1962.

– *Understanding Media.* London: Routledge and Kegan Paul, 1964.

H

HABERMAS, JÜRGEN (b. 1929)

[See also: *Frankfurt School; Postmodernism; Speech Act Theory*]

Jürgen Habermas is a German philosopher and an important member of the second generation of the Frankfurt School of Marxist social critics who has written highly influential works in areas that include social-political theory, aesthetics, epistemology, and philosophy of religion. Habermas received his doctorate in philosophy in 1954 at the University of Bonn with a dissertation on German philosopher Friedrich Wilhelm Schelling. His first work to gain recognition was *The Structural Transformation of the Public Sphere* (1962). This work documents the growth of the bourgeois sphere and identifies the development of a communicative ideal that pivots on the possibility of an inclusive critical dialogue unencumbered by social and economic forces. The participants in such a public sphere regard each other as equals with the common objective of achieving an understanding on issues that concern everyone. Other fundamental works by Habermas include *The Philosophical Discourses of Modernity* (1985), where, in opposition to Jean-François Lyotard's idea of postmodernity, he contends that modernity constitutes for us a task that is not yet fulfilled. For Habermas, the way of dealing with the project of modernity is offered by intersubjectivity; rather than proceeding from the isolated subject as it faces external reality, Habermas posits a paradigm that involves subjects sharing a dialogue as the basis for social thought. Habermas distinguishes between instrumental reason and communicative reason, which is capable of bringing societies on the path to democracy.

In *The Theory of Communicative Action* (1981), Habermas achieves an announced objective, that of integrating philosophy with the social sciences and the empirical disciplines. He constructs a theory that involves an analysis of communicative rationality, namely, the rational element inherent in everyday speech. In Habermas's mind, rationality is not the acquisition of any given knowledge, but instead the manner in which a speaking and acting subject is able to possess and employ knowledge. Habermas makes reference to a 'performative attitude,' which entails the idea that language is an instrument for coordinating human activity. 'Communicative action,' according to Habermas, refers to the fact that speaking subjects organize their actions and quest for personal or shared objectives on the strength of a common understanding that the objectives are essentially sound. For Habermas, the illocutionary (promissory) potential of the speech act is crucial for the realization of communicative action, and he links the significance of speech acts to the activity of providing reason. To be sure, speech acts necessarily entail utterances that require reasons, that is, utterances that are open to critique and further substantiation. In essence, Habermas's idea of communicative action is founded on the belief that social order relies on the ability of subjects to accept the intersubjective value of the various and differing claims upon which social order constructs itself.

Habermas's preoccupation with communicative rationality and political thought merge in his discourse theory of deliberative democracy. His goal is to illustrate the manner in which his communicative action theory lends its applicability in society. More recently, Habermas has given much consideration to the link between religion and philosophy and has encouraged a dialogue in which secular and religious thought interact with each other with the objective of acquiring a mutual understanding. He has also been enlisted frequently in the domain of media studies, especially his idea of communicative rationality, whereby the media are seen as essentially lacking such rationality, appealing mainly to the emotional part of human cognition.

Paul Colilli

Bibliography

Habermas, Jürgen. *The Theory of Communicative Action*. Trans. Thomas McCarthy. 2 vols. Cambridge: Polity Press, 1986–9.
– *The Philosophical Discourses of Modernity*. Trans. Frederick G. Lawrence. Cambridge, MA: MIT Press, 1987.
– *The Structural Transformation of the Public Sphere*. Trans. Thomas Burger. Cambridge, MA: MIT Press, 1991.
– *Between Naturalism and Religion*. Trans. Ciaran Cronin. Cambridge: Polity Press, 2008.

HACKING

[See also: *Internet; World Wide Web*]

Hacking is defined as the use of a computer to gain unauthorized access to another computer or data system. More specifically, it is the act of programming 'enthusiastically,' according to the online Jargon File (Raymond 2003). The term has almost lost its original meaning ('the making of furniture with an axe'), being today understood mainly in terms of computer and internet culture. The same Jargon File gives a series of definitions for the word *hacker* (the person who performs the act of hacking). For a hacker, programming enthusiastically is only the first step: he or she 'enjoys exploring the details of programmable systems and how to stretch their capabilities, as opposed to most users, who prefer to learn only the minimum necessary'; furthermore, the hacker likes to have 'an intimate understanding of the internal workings of a system, computers and computer networks in particular' (Malkin and Parker 1993).

The first who called themselves hackers, back in the 1960s, were programmers at the Massachusetts Institute of Technology (MIT) and the University of California, Berkeley. Those programmers wrote operating systems, built up the internet, ran Usenet (a popular forum-like sector of the internet), and contributed (indirectly) to the eventual development of the World Wide Web. But, most importantly, they shared a common culture and code of ethics that could be encapsulated as 'the belief that information-sharing is a powerful positive good, and that it is an ethical duty of hackers to share their expertise by writing open-source code and facilitating access to information and to computing resources wherever possible' (Raymond 2003). The idea of sharing solutions and ideas, and of making the source code available for anyone to use it, learn it, and modify it, was driven by the academic spirit that pervaded the groups who established the first network protocols and technical standards.

A famous hacker was Linus Torvalds, who in the 1990s created the Linux operating system, a widely used open-source software. Linux was based on the GNU operating system, written in 1983 by Rich-

ard Stallman (Artificial Intelligence Laboratory, MIT), and on BSD Unix, created by
Bill Joy in 1977, an open-source version of
the Unix operating system (by hackers Ken
Thompson and Dennis Ritchie). Stallman
claimed that hacking activities are marked
by 'playfulness, cleverness, and exploration' (Stallman 2002). Other notable hackers
were Tim Berners-Lee (CERN), who invented the World Wide Web; Marc Andrees-
sen (National Center for Supercomputing
Applications), the author of the first Web
surfing program (Mosaic, later known as
Netscape Navigator); and Steve Wozniak, a
member of the Bay Area Homebrew Computer Club, who in 1976 built the Apple I,
the first user-friendly personal computer.
The MIT hackers also wrote the first computer games.

In the last few years, the term *hacker* and
its derivatives have been used by mainstream press with a negative connotation.
Newspapers often call hacking the activity
of breaking computer systems to steal data,
information, passwords, or to cause some
kind of malfunction. The hacker community prefers to define those people as *crackers*,
emphasizing the concepts of breaching and
law infringement.

Marco Faré

Bibliography

Cantoni, Lorenzo, and Stefano Tardini. *Internet*.
London: Routledge, 2006.
Malkin, Group G., and T. LaQuey Parker.
RFC1392 – Internet Users' Glossary (1993).
http://www.faqs.org/rfcs/rfc1392.html
(accessed 20 January 2009).
Raymond, Eric, ed. *The On-Line Hacker Jargon
File*, version 4.4.7 (2003). http://www.catb
.org/jargon/ (accessed 20 January 2009).
Stallman, Richard. *On Hacking* (2002). http://
www.stallman.org/articles/on-hacking.html
(accessed 20 January 2009).
Torvalds, Linus, Pekka Himanen, and Manuel
Castells. *The Hacker Ethic: And the Spirit of the
Information Age*. London: Secker and Warburg,
2001.

HALL, EDWARD T. (1914–2009)

[See also: *Intercultural Communication; Non-Verbal
Communication; Proxemics*]

The American anthropologist Edward T.
Hall developed the branch of anthropology and semiotics called *proxemics*, which
studies how people in different cultures
use interpersonal zones and space to communicate socially. Hall was born in Webster
Groves, Missouri, and received his doctorate from Columbia University in 1942. He
taught at various universities, including
the University of Denver and Northwestern. The foundations for his interest in
proxemic behaviour were laid during the
Second World War, when he served in the
U.S. military in both Europe and the Philippines. From 1933 to 1937 he also lived
among the Navajo and Hopi people in Arizona. His interest in the ways people from
different cultures interact makes him the
founder of the contemporary field of intercultural communication.

His lasting contribution to the field of
both non-verbal and intercultural communication is his work on 'interpersonal
zones,' which are fashioned from the distances people feel they should maintain
between each other on the basis of social
and personal relations and the orientation
that their bodies should assume during interaction. These then become institutionalized unconsciously as part of social contact
code, regulating the 'zones,' that people
maintain between each other. For instance,
when strangers in Western society are introduced to each other, each one knows not
only to extend the right hand to initiate a
handshake, but also how far away to stand
from the other. They would also know not
to touch any other part of the body – arms,
face, etc. In other cultures, even hand contact may not be allowed and the zone between the two may be greater. The greater
the distance between bodies during interaction the greater the formality implied.

As Hall discussed, zones are the product of the intersection between biological

mechanisms and cultural traditions. This is why they vary across the world but are substantially derived from the same universal sense of territoriality, or the cross-species needed to secure and organize space for shelter and survival. In human life, territoriality translates into social codes that guide how people sense zones and orientation as meaningful.

Marcel Danesi

Bibliography

Hall, Edward T. *The Silent Language*. Greenwich, CT: Fawcett, 1959.
- *The Hidden Dimension*. Garden City, NY: Anchor Books, 1966.
- *Handbook for Proxemic Research*. Washington, DC: Society for the Anthropology of Visual Communication, 1974.
- *Beyond Culture*. Garden City, NY: Anchor Books, 1976.
- *The Dance of Life*. Garden City, NY: Anchor Books, 1983.

HALL, STUART (b. 1932)

[See also: *British Cultural Theory; Centre for Contemporary Cultural Studies; Media Effects*]

Stuart Hall is a Jamaican-born cultural theorist and major figure in 'British cultural theory' whose work on the representations of race and gender in the media has been widely influential. Hall attended Merton College at Oxford University for an MA after winning a Rhodes scholarship. Thereafter, he became an active socialist, founding the *New Left Review*, a political journal, which espoused Marxist ideas and socialist beliefs, and leaving his PhD studies in 1958. One year later, Hall started teaching media studies at Chelsea College while working as a supply teacher in Bristol and editing the *New Left Review*. By 1964, along with Paddy Whannel, he co-wrote *The Popular Arts*, in which he argued that the mass media should be studied autonomously,

and not as vehicles for traditional cultural forms. Hall was asked by Richard Hoggart to join the first Cultural Studies program at the Centre for Contemporary Cultural Studies at Birmingham University. Four years later, he took over Hoggart's position as the director of the Centre, remaining so until 1979. He accepted the position of professor of sociology at Open University in Buckinghamshire in the same year, retiring in 1997.

Hall has been on the Runnymede Trust's commission on the future of multi-ethnic Britain, and acted as chair of INIVA, the Institute of International Visual Arts, and Autograph ABP. Among his many significant works are: *Situating Marx: Evaluations and Departures* (1972), *Encoding and Decoding in the Television Discourse* (1973), *Reading of Marx's 1857 Introduction to the Grundrise* (1973), *Policing the Crisis* (1978), *The Hard Road to Renewal* (1988), *Resistance through Rituals* (1989), *Modernity and Its Future* (1992), *The Formation of Modernity* (1992), *Questions of Cultural Identity* (1996), *Cultural Representations and Signifying Practices* (1997), and *Visual Culture* (1999).

In *Policing the Crisis: Mugging, the State and Law and Order* (1978), Hall suggests that the media's reportage of muggings and other crime-based stories is part of a game of social control as practised in capitalist systems, where crime statistics are manipulated in order to cause moral panic, which in turn induces the public to support repressive measures on the part of those in power. On the other side of this theoretical stance, Hall also understood that audiences are not robotic receivers of media content. Rather, they decode media texts differently. They may decode it *preferentially*, that is as the media producers prefer them to do so, in a *negotiated* fashion, whereby they accept only part of the content as relevant to them, or even *oppositionally*, reacting negatively to it. The final interpretation of the text is dependent on the cultural background of the audience members. The margin of understanding, Hall claimed, occurs when the producer of a text encodes it in a way that the audience will decode differently.

Mariana Bockarova

Bibliography

Adams, Tim. Cultural Hallmark. Guardian.co.uk (23 September 2007). http://www.guardian.co.uk/society/2007/sep/23/communities.politicsphilosophyandsociety.

Davis, Helen. *Understanding Stuart Hall: An Introduction*. London: Sage, 2004.

Hall, Stuart. Cultural Studies: Two Paradigms. *Media, Culture, and Society* 2 (1980): 57–72.

– *Encoding and Decoding in the Television Discourse*. London: The Seminar Press, 1973.

– *Policing the Crisis*. New York: Palgrave, 1978.

Hall, Stuart, and Paddy Whannel. *The Popular Arts*. London: Beacon Press, 1964.

Hall, Stuart, et al., eds. *Culture, Media, Language*. London: Hutchison, 1980.

HARAWAY, DONNA (b. 1944)

[See also: *Castells, Manuel; Cyberculture*]

Donna Haraway is a feminist scholar whose ideas about the impact of technology on our perception of the body (especially the female body) have become widely quoted in media, culture, and communication studies. Haraway was born in Denver, Colorado, She earned her doctorate in biology at Yale in 1972. She is currently professor in the History of Consciousness Program at the University of California at Santa Cruz. She was awarded the prestigious J.D. Bernal Award for lifetime contributions for her work on the role of women in science and the role of machines in human life.

Among her many ideas, Haraway has shown that in scientific writing there is a tendency to 'masculinize' the relevant narratives, whereby males are seen as dominant and females as passive throughout the scientific narration. As she suggests, this is an unconscious bias that tells us more about the sociology of science than it does about science itself. As she puts it (Haraway 1989: 377): 'My hope has been that the always oblique and sometimes perverse focusing would facilitate revisionings of fundamental, persistent western narratives about difference, especially racial and sexual difference.'

Haraway is also well known for her work on 'cyborg theory,' or the view that the machines humans create are extensions of ourselves, replacing in many cases functions of the human body and mind. A cyborg is a hybrid, merging human and machine parts and systems into an integrated whole. Although it has always been a creature of science fiction, the advanced technologies of today are making it more and more likely that the merger will become reality. Haraway sees the cyborg as a metaphor for eliminating biased gender and racial arguments based on purely organic evolutionary narratives. This is because the cyborg can have both masculine and feminine traits, thus completely effacing the artificial sexual dichotomy that has been maintained in science and philosophy generally. Cyborg theory is thus a deconstructionist theory, aimed at injecting balance into science and its masculinist bias.

Haraway introduced the notion of multiple subjectivities as part of cyborg theory. She defines it as the split self of cyborg consciousness, who is 'the one who can interrogate positionings and be accountable, the one who can construct and join rational conversations and fantastic imaginings that change history. Splitting, in this context should be about *heterogeneous multiplicities* that are simultaneously necessary and incapable of being squashed into isomorphic slots or cumulative lists' (Haraway 1991: 193).

Haraway's split refers to the merging of human and machine, and posits that human consciousness unfolds in terms of 'multiple agents' operating within a combination of competing forces within the body. She calls this the post-human condition: 'the posthuman subject is an amalgam, a collection of heterogeneous components, a material-informational entity whose boundaries undergo continuous construction and reconstruction' (Haraway 1989: 3).

Marcel Danesi

Bibliography

Haraway, Donna. *Primate Visions: Gender, Race, and Nature in the World of Modern Science.* London: Routledge, 1989.
- *Simians, Cyborgs, and Women: The Reinvention of Nature.* London: Free Association Books, 1991.
- ed. *The Haraway Reader.* London: Routledge, 2004.

HEGEMONY THEORY

[See also: *Culture Industry Theory; Gramsci, Antonio; Marxism*]

Media hegemony occurs when a particular political economic structure of media institutions and associated production, distribution, and ideological practices are dominant because they are preferred by producers, regulators, and the public, and become the social norm. The key ingredient in any hegemony is consent: hegemony cannot be reduced to domination or manipulation; rather hegemony indicates consensual relationships among groups or classes whereby one sector represents and leads others. Subordinate and allied groups and classes receive material, political, and/or cultural benefits as they adhere to the hegemonic relationship (Artz and Murphy 2000). Hegemonic leaders succeed, in part, because alternative relations appear undesirable, unachievable, or untenable to most supporters and followers. Thus, groups become hegemonic not through coercion or domination but due to their leadership: their ability to articulate and meet the needs of subordinate or allied groups and classes. Media hegemony does not necessarily indicate monopoly or dominance by one or a few media corporations or groupings; rather certain media structures and practices become dominant as acceptance, preference, and implementation of those structures and practices become the norm.

As a concept, media hegemony applies the insights of Antonio Gramsci (1965, 1971, 1975), an Italian communist theoretician who modernized the concept of hegemony in the 1930s. Gramsci explained hegemony as a form of political, social, and ideological leadership. He recognized the ability of capitalist classes in the industrialized West to win consent of the working and middle classes, and other social formations. Gramsci also noted that hegemony remains in flux, must continually be renegotiated among social classes, and if challenged by an emerging political or social power will be 'armored with coercion' by dominant groups unwilling to relinquish power. Gramsci was primarily concerned with historic blocs of contending social forces and their political agencies. While he accorded language, ideology, and communication significant instrumentality in establishing any hegemonic leadership, Gramsci did not specifically identify media as institutions of hegemony. After his writings were translated to English in the 1970s, an array of scholars, including Christine Buci-Glucksmann, Anne Showstack Sassoon (1987), Stuart Hall (1986), Kate Crehan (1988), James Lull, and others have interpreted, revised, and extended hegemony to many phenomena, including media (Artz and Kamalipour 2004).

Media – understood as the combination and coordination of technology, production and distribution practices, programming content, the social context of reception, and the institutional and regulatory structures that organize the dominant forms – appear in communities, nation-states, internationally, and globally. Throughout the history of media development and use, a variety of technologies, production practices and norms, programming contents and genre, social uses, and institutional and regulatory structures have appeared. Occasionally, one technology dominates the mass communication system, but its social and cultural use depends on ownership and control of the technology.

Media hegemony expresses relations and practices whereby a particular system of media production, distribution, and use becomes dominant because existing and emerging media outlets follow the lead, the model, the norm of that particular media system. For example, Hollywood – understood as movie production characterized as studio-dominated, celebrity-driven, stylistically 'narrative realism' scripted and imaged, and mass-marketed for profits from audience revenue – has hegemonic position in the global film industry. From India's Bollywood, Korea, and an emerging 'blockbuster' Chinese cinema, to European and Latin American movies, filmmakers around the world emulate the Hollywood model, and (absent viable, available alternatives) public audiences often 'prefer' Hollywood-style movies, whether action-adventure, dramatic thriller, or romance. The French government's attempt to regulate Hollywood imports is an indication of the dominance of U.S. production studios in global production and export; it also indicates the hegemony of Hollywood for mass audiences in Europe.

Corporate media hegemony also characterizes contemporary global radio and television structures and practices. Nation-states and their government agencies (following the hegemonic lead and coercive imperatives of market capitalism) are facilitating the promotion of radio and television media that are deregulated, privatized, and commercialized. Government policies frequently reflect the coercive arming of hegemony, as international capitalist agencies (such as the International Monetary Fund and the World Bank) often determine the policies of developing countries in need of financial assistance or trade deals. Yet, as government-run and public service media are rapidly being replaced by private ownership, the model of advertising-driven entertainment for narrowcast, market-targeted media audiences has achieved hegemonic status. Political parties and government officials in developing and developed nation-states have energetically moved to institute media in the image of market-based, corporate-run media. Neoliberal reforms now permit foreign ownership, subsidiary operations, and joint ventures of domestic media around the globe. More importantly, the developing transnational media corporations have established hegemony in global media practices – even domestically owned and operated media in every geographic region are opting for the market model, as they compete for audience share and advertising revenue.

Hegemony depends on consent; consent depends on benefit. The material benefits for those who own and operate privatized media are obvious: profits from media advertising are plentiful. Political rewards likewise are significant for private media owners who can set national public agendas by controlling information flow within their broadcast area. From Berlusconi in Italy and Azcarrago in Mexico to Murdoch in Australia, the United Kingdom, and the United States, the political power attached to privately held media is demonstrable. The corporate media model wins consent around the globe because for-profit domestic and regional media companies aspire to such influence and their respective governments facilitate the commercial terrain. Cultural benefits accruing to private media may be more difficult to concretize, but certainly private media are well positioned to influence social communication within any heavily mediated society. Whether or not they recognize hegemonic relations, media scholars have provided ample evidence that entertainment and information media impact social values and beliefs and cultural norms.

From the perspective of media hegemony, the spectre of cultural imperialism has been subsumed by the recruitment of national and regional media enterprises which have adopted and refined the corporate media model to meet the cultural preferences of local markets (Artz 2006). The nationality of owners of various global media institutions is less relevant for hegemony than the development of private media operations which follow the production, financing, and distribution of the corporate media model of advertising-driven programming for audience share. The geographic identifiers of West or North in describing media operations have lost some purchase, as nation-states and media in the developing South now champion the neoliberal free market model of mass communication: the consumer market, the advertising market, the marketplace of ideas.

Corporate media hegemony best describes contemporary international media structures and practices, but other non-global structures and practices have appeared and continue to represent alternative means and methods for mass communication. In Nicaragua from 1980 to 1990, publicly funded, community-based, public access media flourished and became hegemonic – leading the resurrection of media in a country devastated by forty years of dictatorship. Private media continued to exist, but those media no longer represented the needs and interests of the majority of the population. The Corporación de Radiodifusión del Pueblo (CORADEP) led the development of a democratic, participatory media system in Nicaragua under the leadership of the Frente Sandinista Liberación Nacional (FSLN) government. A model of independent journalism, partisan objectivity, community correspondents, locally produced news, and open media access by entire communities predominated in the country for over ten years, not due to government coercion, but because laws and structures were established which provided citizens opportunities to produce their own media messages, programs, and practices. The hegemony of democratic, participatory media was interrupted and overturned as a result of the U.S. counter-insurgency campaign against the government of Nicaragua during the 1980s.

In 2005, another more ambitious media model developed which challenges corporate media hegemony. Telesur (Televisora del Sur – Television of the South) was launched as a pan-Latin American satellite network jointly financed by Venezuela, Argentina, Uruguay, and Cuba. Bolivia joined the following year. A coordinating board of professional journalists and over forty journalists from countries throughout Latin America produce news, documentaries, and entertainment programs that emphasize the perspectives and voices of the Latin American working people and indigenous populations. Meanwhile, the Venezuelan government has promoted community-based radio broadcast – over 200 local stations, operated and directed by community organizations, now have licences and minimum financing. Together, Telesur and the community radio movement in Venezuela represent a counter-hegemonic bloc contesting but not displacing the commercial media (Venevisión, Globovisión, RCTV), which remain dominant in audience share. Under these conditions, the mediascape in Venezuela has no hegemonic leader. Media hegemony may be recovered by the corporate media and its entertainment-based, commercially organized norms, or a new media hegemony may be assembled if more community operators and citizen groups are successful in demonstrating the political and cultural advantages of a public-access, locally produced, nationally coordinated media system. As Gramsci would have it, media hegemony in Venezuela and elsewhere is the outcome of the political, social, and ideological battle for leadership – which is ongoing and always being renegotiated as social groups and classes vie for leadership and seek to advance their interests.

Whether local, national, or global, corporate or democratic and participatory, media hegemony only occurs as a leadership successfully represents the interests of many by producing and distributing programming and messages articulating the images, interests, and needs of allies and subordinate groups.

Lee Artz

Bibliography

Artz, Lee. The Corporate Model from National to Transnational. In *The Media Globe: Trends in International Communication*, ed. Lee Artz and Yahya Kamalipour, 24–56. Lanham, MD: Rowman and Littlefield, 2006.

Artz, Lee, and Yahya Kamalipour, eds. *The Globalization of Corporate Media Hegemony*. Albany: State University of New York Press, 2004.

Artz, Lee, and Bren Murphy. *Cultural Hegemony in the United States*. Beverly Hills: Sage, 2000.

Crehan, Kate. *Gramsci, Culture and Anthropology*. London: Pluto Press, 1988.

Gramsci. Antonio. *Lettere dal carcere*. New ed. by S. Caproglio and E. Fubini. 4 vols. Turin: Einaudi, 1965.

– *Quaderni del carcere. Selections from the Prison Notebooks of Antonio Gramsci*. London: Lawrence and Wishart, 1971.

– *Quaderni del carcere*. Critical edition by Istituto Gramsci. Ed. V. Gerratana. Turin: Einaudi, 1975.

Hall, Stuart. Gramsci's Relevance for the Study of Race and Ethnicity. *Journal of Communication Inquiry* 10 (1986): 5–27.

Sassoon, Anne Showstack. *Gramsci's Politics*. 2nd ed. Minneapolis: University of Minnesota Press, 1987.

HERMENEUTICS

[See also: *Text Theory*]

Hermeneutics is the term used in philosophy, semiotics, and literary theory to refer to the systematic study of written texts (from Greek *hermeneuo* 'translate' 'interpret'). Hermeneutics can be traced back to Plato and Aristotle, and it was implicit in the writings of St Augustine (354–430 CE), who emphasized that texts served a fundamental psychological need – the need felt by humans to encode and, thus, remember the world. St Augustine also emphasized that the whole process of understanding what texts, such as the Bible, mean is partly based on social conventions and partly on individual reactions. This idea was consistent with the textual traditions that had been established by the ancient philosophers and expanded by Clement of Alexandria (ca 150–215 CE), the Greek theologian and early Father of the Church. Hermeneutics was (and continues to be) the study of texts by taking into account their linguistic features and the historical contexts in which they were written.

In the Middle Ages and the Renaissance, the study of texts was expanded considerably, paving the way for the emergence of philology as a discipline a few centuries later. Philology is the study of change in language as it is reflected in texts. Hermeneutics was developed considerably in the nineteenth century by theologian Friedrich Schleiermacher (1768–1834) and philosopher Wilhelm Dilthey (1833–1911) into a systematic study of textual structure and authorial style. In the twentieth century, hermeneutics became a main technique of semiotics and literary criticism, developed by scholars such as Hans-Georg Gadamer (1994), who saw texts as based on the world views and the subjectivity of interpreters, not on authorial intent.

The main techniques of hermeneutics, loosely defined and applied are: (1) a determination of the historical relevance of the text; (2) a compilation of its peculiar linguistic features and the role they play in the text's construction and interpretation; (3) the intent of the text in the period in which it was written through an etymological-philological analysis (that is, determining what certain word forms tell us about the period in which it was written); and (4) an overall assessment of its value to history.

Marcel Danesi

Bibliography

Bruns, Gerald L. *Hermeneutics: Ancient and Modern*. New Haven, CT: Yale University Press, 1992.

Gadamer, Hans-Georg. *Truth and Method*. New York: Continuum, 1994.

HORROR FICTION

[See also: *Cinema Genres; Pulp Fiction*]

Horror stories are narratives that are designed to evoke fear through the use of frightening characters (monsters, vampires, etc.), dark settings (haunted castles, dark forests, etc.), or blood and gore (body parts crawling around, entrails taking on lives of their own, etc.). There is considerable overlap between horror fiction and mystery fiction and science fiction. But the horror narrative is distinct in how it engages the audience in fear-eliciting tactics and techniques thus exploiting our seemingly deep-rooted fascination with terror.

The origin of the horror story is traced to the Gothic novel, of which the first known example is *The Castle of Otranto* (1764), written by Horace Walpole. It is a tale of supernatural terror that caught on with the public instantly. The stories were called Gothic because they typically took place in gloomy castles built in the Gothic style. These had secret passageways, dungeons, and towers that provided ideal settings for strange happenings to occur unexpectedly. Most were set in Italy or Spain because these countries in that era seemed remote and mysterious to English readers. In the 1800s, the Gothic novel gave birth to the horror novel genre proper, starting with *Frankenstein* (1818) by Mary Shelley. The new genre influenced American writers such as Nathaniel Hawthorne, Herman Melville, and Edgar Allan Poe.

The popular interest in the horror narrative and its many subgenres, which range today from slasher movies to traditional haunted house and vampire stories, really started with pulp fiction. The appeal of the horror pulp magazines was bolstered by sensationalistic cover designs, with monsters, vampires, and scantily dressed women shown in dark, foreboding settings. Horror programs on early radio were also highly popular. The deep voices that introduced horror programs such as *Inner Sanctum* were designed to frighten listeners, as was the eerie signature music used to announce the program.

Why are we so attracted to horror stories? The Greek philosopher Aristotle saw the theatre form itself as a spectacle that allowed people to come to grips with their inbuilt fears through catharsis. The anticipation of evil, the anxiety of impending doom that a horror story creates in us, is resolved by the horror narrative itself, safely and conclusively. The narrative thus allows us to 'release' inner fear through catharsis. However, when the release does not occur, then the horror remains. This is the technique used by some film directors, such as Alfred Hitchcock. Catharsis is suspended because of the lack of any real resolution at the end of the story or because there are no monsters, alien creatures, vampires, or the like to help channel fear into the open through screaming, shouting, screeching, or crying.

The horror genre creates fear in several ways – through the use of dark settings, haunted places, monsters and eerie creatures (werewolves, vampires, etc.), repugnant images (showing body parts), and various audio-visual effects (unexpected appearances, banging doors, etc.) intended to startle and surprise audiences. In some ways, horror fiction has the same function as the carnival freakshows, where 'monsters' of nature evoke an unconscious fear of the grotesque. Fictional monsters like Frankenstein and King Kong stir up a similar kind of fear.

The horror genre has always been a staple of movie fare. From the zombie movies of the 1950s and 1960s to current gore and slasher movies like the *Hostel* and *Saw* series, the horror movie seems to provide a cathartic relief from the horrors of real life. There are other explanations of the meaning of horror movies, from psychoanalytic theories to feminist critiques (Willis 1997; Jones 2002). It seems plausible, however, to interpret horror stories as a means to escape to a fantasy world – a dark, horrific place where we can confront our inner nightmares in a safe way. The director who has shown a deep understanding of horror is the Canadian David Cronenberg. In his classic *Videodrome* (1983), he makes it obvious that the real horror is the video medium itself, having become a metaphor for modern life. A video virus emits infectious rays that induce hallucinations in viewers – for example, a television screen becomes a huge pair of lips, a videocassette is inserted forcibly into a woman's genitals. At the end the protagonist mutates into a video-cassette, ready to induce hallucinations in others. *Videodrome* is both a warning and a parody about modern-day critiques of horror as well as a metaphor for the horrors of technology. As Cronenberg himself put it: 'Censors tend to do what only psychotics do: they confuse reality with illusion' (Cronenberg 1992: 134).

The ghosts, vampires, zombies, undead, serial killers, slashers of horror stories are archetypes that populate this 'dead zone,' as master horror writer Stephen King has labelled it in one of his stories. In *Dawn of the Dead* (1978), the *Alien* movies (1978, 1986, 1992, 1997), and *The Thing* (1982), the fictional alien characters are perfect examples of such archetypes. They invade our private spaces, imposing themselves more and more indelibly on us. The subtext is an obvious one: the ultimate fear comes from within the human mind itself. In *The Texas Chainsaw Massacre* (1974), the character Hitchhiker slits his hand open just for the thrill of it. Onlookers recoil in horror, except for Franklin, who (as an invalid) realizes that only a small membrane of skin lies between the inner organs of the body and the outside world. Breaking that skin is protected only by social taboos. The gap between the inner and outer worlds is liter-ally a thin one. When the inner body 'spills out' into the world, as it does in many horror stories, it becomes nothing but matter devoid of life. In Tod Browning's 1932 movie *Freaks*, the horror comes from its shots of an armless, legless man crawling with a knife between his teeth, and then emerging from under a circus wagon like a gigantic worm. At the end, a high-wire artist is transformed into a chicken with the head of a woman. This fascination with 'freakishness' has always been evident in horror movies. In *Attack of the 50 Foot Woman* (1958) we witness a woman grow to be nearly fifty feet tall; in *The Fly* (1958) we see a scientist experimenting with matter transference and accidentally exchanging his arm and his head with those of the fly in the transfer chamber; and in *The Blob* (1958), *The Crawling Eye* (1958), and *Creature from the Black Lagoon* (1954), we encounter various slithering, slimy, and horrific creatures. Fear of the body is a frequent theme in the horror genre; otherwise such movies would not be as popular as they are. The same fascination with the body and freakishness is evident in current TV shows such as *Fear Factor* and the CSI programs, which regularly show the body parts of victims openly, from human organs to tissues found on blood-soaked floors or furniture.

There has been a considerable psychological debate about why horror is such a popular genre. One view is that it taps into emotions that would otherwise be repressed. Another is that it allows for the cathartic release of darker feelings. A third theory posits that the interest in horror is simply a part of human curiosity about mysterious and scary aspects of existence – the horror is anchored in the unknown, and it is this that we wish to understand. Horror stories often revolve around the mystery of monsters and what they tell us about ourselves. The repulsive nature of monsters is precisely what makes them appealing. Horror brings out our need for beauty, since it constitutes its counterpart. The spectacle of horror reminds us that there is a good side to life that we must strive for. It is part of the profane, the carnivalesque. As a consequence, it validates the sacred, as the social critic Mikhail Bakhtin argued in his writings on the nature of carnivals (Bakhtin 1981). In the end, though, we will probably never really understand why horror stories are so alluring. It is unlikely that any one theory will fully explain its appeal. Fear of the dark and of mysterious events seems to be an innate response of childhood. Paradoxically, getting scared was one of the first pleasures we experienced as children. Perhaps horror stories are nothing more than reminders of this.

Marcel Danesi

Bibliography

Cronenberg, David. *Cronenberg on Cronenberg*. London: Faber and Faber, 1992.

Jones, Darryl. *Horror: A Thematic History in Fiction and Film*. London: Arnold, 2002.

McLelland, Bruce A. *Slayers and Their Vampires: A Cultural History of Killing the Dead*. Ann Arbor: University of Michigan Press, 2006.

Sklar, Robert. *Movie-Made America: A Cultural History of American Movies*. New York: Vintage, 1994.

Willis, Donald C. *Horror and Science Fiction Films*. Lanham, MD: Scarecrow Press, 1997.

Wright, Angela. *Gothic Fiction*. New York: Palgrave Macmillan, 2007.

HYPERMEDIA AND HYPERTEXT

[See also: *Berners-Lee, Tim; Multimedia; Text Theory*]

The term *hypermedia* is used to describe any media that involve links of various kinds – musical, graphic, video, audio, and so forth. In contrast to *multimedia*, which refers to the amalgamation of various media into a singular text, hypermedia refers to the linkage of media in a digital way with various texts that are external to the one at hand. Both terms hypermedia and hypertext were coined in 1965 by graphics designer Ted Nelson. The best example of hypermedia is the World Wide Web, where sites are found that provide multimedial hyperlinks (hypertext links). By clicking on the hyperlink, the user is immediately connected to the document specified by the link. Web pages are written in a simple computer language called HTML (hypertext markup language). A series of instruction 'tags' are inserted into pieces of ordinary text to control the way the page looks and can be manipulated when viewed with a Web browser. Tags determine the typeface and act as instructions to display images. They can be used to link with other web pages.

Hypertext is a system of storing written text, images, and other kinds of files that allow for links to related texts, images, and the like. Hypertext makes it easy for users to browse through related topics, regardless of their presented order. In internet browsers, hypertext links (hotlinks) are usually indicated by a word or phrase with a different font or colour or by an underline. These create a branching structure that permits direct, unmediated jumps to related information.

The first hypertext system was introduced by Apple Computer with its HyperCard software in 1987, providing users with a processing system consisting of 'cards' collected together in a 'stack,' with each card containing text, graphics, and sound. This was the first program to provide a linking function permitting navigation among files of computer print text and graphics by clicking keywords or icons. By 1988 compact disc players were built into computers, introducing hypertext-capable CD-ROMs onto the computer market. It was Tim Berners-Lee who introduced hypertextuality to the internet in 1991, as a system that enables a user to go from one document to another by clicking words or phrases, even if the documents are found on different parts of the internet. Clicking the word brings information to the screen (information contained either on the same site or elsewhere on the internet).

There are two main kinds of hyperlinks (Petroni 2011: 98–100). Visual hyperlinks utilize icons, pictures, and other visual forms (videos, animations, and so on); generally, these are called 'procedural links' because they are highly standardized and conventional. Second, verbal hyperlinks utilize words or sequences of words or numbers embedded into texts or standing alone.

Hyperlinks can be divided in two ways (Petroni 2011: 94–5):

(1) *static links*, which are point-to-point connections that are embedded in a written text;
(2) *dynamic links*, which are built into databases occurring separately from the documents to which they refer.

Hypertextuality may actually mirror how the brain processes written texts. Reading a printed page is a one-dimensional process which consists in decoding the individual words and their combinations in sentences in the framework of a specific textual system (a novel, a dictionary, etc.) and then assigning a holistic interpretation to it. Information on any specific sign in the text must be sought out physically: for example, if one wants to follow up a reference in the text, one has to do it by consulting other printed texts. This is what we do when we want to look up the meaning in a print dictionary of a word found in a print text. As opposed to the linear textuality of paper books, hypertextuality permits the user to browse through related topics on the same screen, without having physically to search them out in other books or textual materials.

Interpreting a text involves three processes. First is the ability to access the actual contents of the text at the level of the signs in it. Only someone possessing knowledge of the sign codes with which the text has been assembled can accomplish this. If it is in Russian, then in order to derive a meaning from it, the decoder must first know the Russian language. The second process entails knowledge of how the text generates its meanings through a series of internal and external signification processes. This requires some knowledge on the part of the decoder of cultural codes other than the strictly verbal and non-verbal ones used to physically create the text. Finally, various contextual factors enter into the entire process to constrain the interpretation; for example, what the individual reader will get from the text or what the intent of the maker of the text was. The integration of these dimensions makes possible the extraction of a meaning from the text. This triadic process mirrors computer hypertextuality. The physical structure of hypertextuality on the computer screen may thus constitute a kind of mirror model of how we process texts in the brain.

Marcel Danesi

Bibliography

Danesi, Marcel. *Understanding Media Semiotics.* London: Arnold, 2002.

Landow, George P. *Hypertext 3.0: Critical Theory and New Media in an Era of Globalization.* Baltimore: Johns Hopkins University Press, 2006.

Petroni, Sandra. *Language on the Multimodal Web Domain.* Rome: Aracne, 2011.

HYPODERMIC NEEDLE THEORY

[See also: *Media Effects; Two-Step Flow Theory*]

Hypodermic needle theory (HNT) claims that the mass media can directly influence the human mind, with the same kind of impact that a hypodermic needle has on the body. The theory has been a topic of debate within both psychology and media studies.

The starting point for the investigation of HNT was the 1938 radio broadcast of Orson Welles's adaptation of the H.G. Wells novel *War of the Worlds*. It was designed as a radio docudrama simulating the style of a news broadcast. Welles made it sound very realistic. As a consequence, many listeners believed that the broadcast was real, despite periodic announcements that it was fiction. Some people in the New Jersey area (where the invasion was reported to have occurred) left their homes and phoned the local authorities. The event became a topic of media attention and led to the first psychological study of the effects of media on people, called the Cantril Study, after Hadley Cantril who headed a team of researchers at Princeton University. After interviewing 135 subjects, the team concluded, however, that better-educated and thus more critical listeners were more capable of recognizing the broadcast as fiction than were less-educated listeners. They also concluded that the panic was real, even though many subjects did not admit to believing the fake broadcast, lying about it to hide their shame.

The Cantril Study seemed to demonstrate that the media did indeed produce negative impacts, but since its methodology was subsequently found to be flawed, it really did not establish a verifiable causal link between the radio broadcast and the degree of panic reported. Actually, the panic was not as widespread as was reported by the media, which produced screaming headlines such as: 'Radio Fake Scares Nation' (*Chicago Herald Tribune*, 31 October 1938); 'Radio Listeners in Panic' (*New York Times*, 31 October 1938); 'Fake "War" on Radio Spreads Panic over U.S.' (*New York Daily News*, 31 October 1938).

Titled *The Invasion from Mars: A Study in the Psychology of Panic* (1940), the Cantril Study is perhaps the first study to put forward a version of what soon came to be called HNT. The theory was instantly debated, starting with sociologist Paul Lazarsfeld (1901–76), who suggested that audiences got out of media content what they were already inclined to get from it. In his 1950 study *The People's Choice*, he and his team of researchers found that the media had little power to change people's opinions about how to vote in a presidential election. People simply extracted from newspapers or radio broadcasts those views that matched their preconceptions, ignoring the others.

Together with Elihu Katz (b. 1926), Lazarsfeld subsequently found that the perception of media content was filtered by 'leaders' of the communities to which audiences belonged. Audiences are, in other words, interpretive communities, since the people in them are part of influential social structures such as families, unions, neighbourhoods, and churches. In such communities, some members take on the role of 'opinion leaders' and thus arbitrate how other members will interpret media content. So, in contrast to HNT, in which media are seen to have a direct impact on a homogeneous audience, Lazarsfeld and Katz saw it as a two-step process, in which opinion leaders interpret media content and then pass it on to group members.

The power of media to affect people's opinions, however, cannot always be dismissed. This was evident in the 1960 Kennedy-Nixon TV debate. People who listened to the debate on radio proclaimed that Nixon had won it and that they would vote for him. Those who saw it on television proclaimed the opposite: Nixon looked unkempt and worried. He also sweated noticeably. Kennedy looked confident, coming across as a young and idealistic 'president of the future.' Kennedy went on to win the election.

Marcel Danesi

Bibliography

Berger, Arthur A. *Media and Communication Research Methods*. London: Sage, 2000.

Biagi, Shirley. *Media/Impact: An Introduction to Mass Media*. Belmont, CA: Wadsworth/Thomson Learning, 2001.

Cantril, Hadley, *The Invasion from Mars: A Study in the Psychology of Panic*. Princeton: Princeton University Press, 1940.

Heins, Marjorie. *Not in Front of the Children: Indecency, Censorship and the Innocence of Youth*. New York: Hill and Wang, 2001.

Lazarsfeld, Paul, et al., *The People's Choice*. New York: Columbia University Press, 1950.

McQuail, Denis, *Mass Communication Theory: An Introduction*. London: Sage, 2000.

Staiger, Janet. *Media Reception Studies*. New York: New York University Press, 2005.

I

IDEOLOGY THEORY

[See also: *Hegemony Theory; Marxism*]

The term *ideology* was coined by Antoine-L.-C. Destutt de Tracy (1754–1836) in his 1796 book, *Mémoire sur la faculté de penser*. He then wrote a five-volume work on the topic of ideology called *Éléments d'idéologie* (1801–15), in which he conceives of ideology as a sort of 'primary philosophy,' a basic way of understanding human mental faculties. Destutt de Tracy belonged to a heterogeneous group of thinkers known as the *Ideologues*. This meaning of ideology as the 'science of ideas' has in modern times been substituted by a more negative sense of ideology as 'false consciousness' or 'false thought' – a meaning associated with the work of Marx and Engels, but which can be traced back to Napoleon, who used it in a disparaging sense against the French, calling them 'doctrinaires.' This meaning occurs (albeit to a limited extent) in Destutt de Tracy and later in Vilfredo Pareto (1848–1923) from the school of Lausanne (*Systèmes socialistes*, 1902–3, *Trattato di sociologia generale*, 1916). Another meaning of *ideology*, coming essentially from a book by Karl Mannheim (1893–1947), *Ideology and Utopia* (1929), is the equating of ideology with 'world view.'

In the twentieth century, it was the Russian social critic Mikhail M. Bakhtin who theorized Mannheim's conception by relating ideology to sign systems, seeing it as world view with a social basis. Bakhtin emphasized the inseparability of signs and ideology. He maintained that an adequate interpretation of Marxist ideology theory based on structure and superstructure is not possible without including signs in the theory. The question of the signs-ideology relation undergirds most of Bakhtin's works, including his books on Dostoevsky and Rabelais, and those he authored with (or using the name of) Valentin N. Voloshinov (1894–1937) and Pavel N. Medvedev (1891–1938). The distinction he made in *Freudianism* (Voloshinov 1927) between official ideology and unofficial ideology is applied in *Rabelais* to the literature of the humanist and Renaissance periods, which he sees as being linked to the 'low genres' of medieval comico-popular culture. In *Marxism and Philosophy of Language* (1929, under the name of Voloshinov), Bakhtin looks at how carnivalesque genres also undergird high European literature. Bakhtin uses the term 'carnival' to refer to the complex phenomenon, present in all cultures, of attitudes, conceptions, and verbal and non-verbal signs based on comedy and on a satirizing of the 'sacred' form of culture. In his revision of his book on Dostoevsky in 1963, Bakhtin inserts a chapter on the genesis of Dostoevsky's 'polyphonic' style (a style where many voices are given legitimacy) as emanating in the comical genres of popular culture. He sees the polyphonic form of writing as the epitome of 'carnivalized literature.'

In *Rabelais* (1965), Bakhtin describes the sign as a plurivocal form, the expression of centrifugal forces in linguistic life, unfolding in public places where vulgarity and decorum blend into a polyphony of discourse genres. In contrast to oversimplified and suffocating interpretations of Marxism, Bakhtin thus developed Marx's idea that the human spirit is fully realized when the dictates of necessity end. Consequently, a social system that is effectively alternative to capitalism is one which considers 'free time' as real social capital, and not 'working time,' since the former is what made possible the 'great era' of literature.

Today, ideology theory has taken a different turn because of the advent of global communications and the concurrent stress on improving the means of production and productivity and on non-corporeal communication. This view contrasts sharply with Bakhtin's carnivalesque view of ideology, based on a conception of intercorporeity (bodies interacting with each other), rather than on the abstract virtuality of modern communications. Though dominant, the logic of production, individualism, and efficiency cannot suppress the constitutive human inclination towards non-functionality (free time and intercorporeal communication), Bakhtin would claim. The properly 'human' is the properly 'non-functional.' This is why the carnivalesque endures as a state of mind even in the current age of cybercommunications. Art, Bakhtin would claim, is our portal into non-functionality. Orwell's *1984*, for instance, has for decades been used by many as a moral tale inspiring resistance against production-based and efficiency-based social systems.

One of the first journals devoted to the study of ideology was founded in the spring of 1967 by the Italian philosopher and semiotician Ferruccio Rossi-Landi, who called the quarterly journal *Ideologie* (Ideologies). In his 1972 paper written for that journal, 'Ideologia come progettazione sociale' (in Rossi-Landi 1972a) (Ideology as Social Programming), Rossi-Landi brings ideology theory in line with the modern world by, first, rejecting its definition as 'false conscience,' replacing it with the notion of 'social programming,' which he pursued subsequently in *Il linguaggio come lavoro e come mercato* (Language as Work and Trade) (1968) and *Semiotica e ideologia* (Semiotics and Ideology) (1972b), where he shows that ideology is a result of specific sign systems (language, art forms, etc.) acquired in specific social contexts. Rossi-Landi's semiotic approach to ideology is being used today to explain a host of cultural phenomena, including the media domination of cultural forms. In line with Marxist theory, Rossi-Landi defined the dominant class as the class that controls the production and spread of the messages and discourses constituting a given society (Rossi-Landi 1972a: 203–4). Then, in *Linguistics and Economics* (1975), *Ideologia* (1978), and *Metodica filosofica e scienza dei segni* (Philosophical Methods and the Science of Signs) (1985), he equates his view of social programming to the view of hegemony expressed by Antonio (see Ponzio 2008).

The scholar Adam Schaff (1913–2007) also saw the need to eradicate the view of ideology as false consciousness, connecting it to language and sign systems (as did Bakhtin). Schaff saw the need for an approach to ideology theory as a 'semantic' theory of human language and socialization. For Schaff, the concepts of 'choice,' 'responsibility,' and 'individual freedom' are affected by a 'tyranny of words' and ultimately by 'linguistic alienation.' Schaff provides a three-pronged approach to the study of ideology: (1) a genetic approach, which would examine the physical conditions from which any ideology is seen to emerge; (2) the structural approach, which will define the specific forms of ideology (establishing differences in logical terms between the structure of ideological discourse and the structure of scientific discourse); and (3) the functional approach, which will examine the functions fulfilled by ideology in relation to social group, class interests, and so forth.

In the end, however, one cannot escape

the definition given to ideology by Marx and Engels as false consciousness, since this is the meaning still being used (implicitly or explicitly) in various contemporary media theories. In the Marxist tradition, expressions such as 'bourgeois ideology' and 'ideological science' actually reveal a functionalist view of ideology, as Schaff pointed out. In this framework, ideology is understood as a system of opinions related to social tendencies which are, in turn, founded on a system of values that undergird typical social behaviours and world views.

Susan Petrilli

Bibliography

Bakhtin, Mikhail M. *Problemy poetiki Dostoevskogo*. Moscow: Sovetskij pisatel, 1963. Eng. trans. and ed. C. Emerson, *Problems of Dostoevsky's Poetics*. Minneapolis: University of Minnesota Press, 1984.

– *Tvorchestvo Fransua Rable*. Moscow: Khudozhestvennia literature, 1965. Eng. trans. H. Iswolsky, ed. K. Pomorska, *Rabelais and His World*. Cambridge: Massachusetts Institute of Technology, 1968.

Destutt de Tracy, Antoine-L.-C. *Éléments d'idéologie* (1801–15). Ed. Henri Gouhier. Paris: Vrin, 1970.

– *Mémoire sur la faculté de penser* (1796). Ed. Anne Deneys. Paris: Fayard, 1992.

Mannheim, Karl. *Ideologie und Utopie*. 4 vols. Bonn: Cohen, 1929. Auflage Frankfurt a. M.: Schulte-Bulmke, 1965.

Medvedev, Pavel N. *The Formal Method in Literary Scholarship: A Critical Introduction to Sociological Poetics* (Russian orig. 1928). Eng. trans. A.J. Wehrle. Baltimore: Johns Hopkins University Press, 1978.

Petrilli, Susan. Linguistic Production, Ideology and Otherness: Augusto Ponzio's Contribution to the Philosophy of Language. *Semiotica* 112 (1996): 263–87.

– ed. *Ideology, Logic, and Dialogue in Semioethic Perspective*. Special issue of *Semiotica* 148 (2004).

Ponzio, Augusto. *Individuo umano, linguaggio e globalizzazione nella filosofia di Adam Schaff. Con una intervista ad Adam Schaff*. Milan: Mimesis, 2002.

– *Il linguaggio e le lingue. Introduzione alla linguistica generale*. Bari: Graphis, 2002.

– *Semiotica e dialettica*. Bari: Edizioni dal Sud, 2004.

– *Produzione linguistica e ideologia sociale*. New enlarged ed. Bari: Graphis, 2006.

– *Linguaggio, lavoro e mercato globale. Rileggendo Rossi-Landi*. Milan: Mimesis, 2008.

Rossi-Landi, Ferruccio. *Significato, comunicazione e parlare comune*. Padua: Marsilio, 1961, 1998.

– *Il linguaggio come lavoro e come mercato*. Milan: Bompiani, 1968. New edition by A. Ponzio, 1992. Eng. trans. M. Adams et al., *Language as Work and Trade*. South Hadley, MA: Bergin and Garvey, 1983.

– *Scritti programmatici di Ideologie*. Rome: Edizioni di Ideologie, 1972a.

– *Semiotica e ideologia*. Milan: Bompiani, 1972b.

– *Linguistics and Economics*. The Hague: Mouton, 1975, 1977.

– *Ideologia*. Milan: ISEDI, 1978. New expanded edition, Milan: Mondadori, 1982. Eng. trans. R. Griffin, *Marxism and Ideology*. Oxford: Clarendon, 1990.

– *Metodica filosofica e scienza dei segni*. Milan: Bompiani, 1985.

– *Between Signs and Non-signs*. Ed. and Intro. S. Petrilli. Amsterdam: John Benjamins, 1992.

Schaff, Adam. *Strukturalismus und Marxismus*. Vienna: Europa Verlag, 1974. Eng. trans. *Structuralism and Marxism*, Oxford: Pergamon Press.

– *Humanismus, Sprachphilosophie, Erkenntnistheorie des Marxismus*. Vienna: Europa Verlag, 1975.

Vilfredo Pareto. *Les Systèmes socialistes*. Paris: Giard and Brière, 1902–3.

– *Trattato di sociologia generale*. Florence: Barbera, 1916.

Voloshinov, Valentin N. *Frejdizm* (orig. Russian ed. 1927). Moscow-Leningrad. Eng. trans. I.R. Titunik, *Freudianism: A Critical Sketch.*, ed. I.R. Titunik with N.H. Bruss. Bloomington: Indiana University Press, 1987.

– *Marksizm i filosofija jazyca* (orig. Russian ed. 1929). Leningrad. Eng. trans. L. Matejka and I.R. Titunik, *Marxism and the Philosophy of Lan-*

guage. Cambridge, MA: Harvard University Press, 1973.

INDEPENDENT PRODUCTION

[See also: *Cinema, History of; Internet; Narrow-casting*]

Independent production, also known as 'indie' production, is work financed and prepared outside of major conglomerate media industries. Independent productions are now common in the film and music domains.

The term 'indie' was coined by movie producers who resisted being controlled by the Motion Picture Patents Company, also known as the Edison Trust. The trust, made in 1908, involved eight American film companies (Edison, Biograph, Vitagraph, Essanay, Selig, Lubin, Kalem, American Star) along with one foreign company, American Pathe, a distributor, George Kleine, and a film supplier, Eastman Kodak. The trust covered sixteen patents on almost all American-produced films. It was originally put in place in order to create cooperation among film companies, but it instead became a monopoly of the production and distribution of movies. The trust required that all producers, distributors, and exhibitors pay licensing fees and set standard fees for film. Eastman Kodak was the executive supplier, only supplying film to licensed companies. The trust also began cooperating with the National Board of Censorship. While the deadline to pay licensing fees was set for January 1909, many 'independents' protested: Fox in New York and Carl Laemmle (today known as Universal) in Chicago were leaders in the 'independent movement,' illegally distributing foreign films and producing movies by importing raw film and using cameras not covered in the patents.

In 1910, members of the Edison Trust made efforts to control the 'independents' by creating a distribution company, General Film. Although in 1912 General Film dominated the market, both General Film and the Motion Picture Patent's Company were charged by the Attorney General with violating the Sherman Anti-Trust Act (which limits monopolies). A court decision allowed the 'independents' to use standard cameras. As a result, many 'indie' films were licensed. The eventual demise of the Motion Picture Patents Company came in October 1915, when a federal court ordered its dissolution. So, ironically, long before today's so-called indie revolution, the establishment of Hollywood as a major locus for moviemaking (chosen by producers to get away from the previous eastern monopolizing companies) was an act of revolution.

The definition of indie production today has changed, however. It entails a form of filmmaking that goes contrary to Hollywood's expensive and often sensationalistic mode of moviemaking. Instead, the indie producers use low-budget film sets, cast, and crew to create films typically with a more aesthetic or artistic focus, rather than pure entertainment value. Indie productions, ironically, have themselves become profitable, even having their own festivals (the Sundance Film Festival being the most notable). 'Sundance,' as it is widely known, was founded in 1978 by filmmakers Sterling Van Wagenen and Charles Gary Allison in an attempt to attract filmmakers to Utah. Now, the film festival has grown into the leading site for showcasing both American and international independent feature-length and short films. It has introduced now-famous directors to the world of cinema, including Quentin Tarantino and Robert Rodriguez.

Similarly, in an attempt to distinguish themselves from mainstream music producers, 'indie' musicians have become an integral part of the contemporary music scene. Indie music started as part of an 'underground music scene,' where it developed cult-like followings. Because of the internet, indie music is now a pattern, rather than an exception. Indie rock musicians are unsigned artists who prefer to make music for its own sake or to showcase themselves to audiences on their own, not a record label's terms. The indie music scene originated in the late 1980s in the United Kingdom, and has since evolved into a parallel music universe to the mainstream music scene, with its own genres, among which Britpop (British guitar pop music) and Riot Grrrl, a feminist punk rock movement are the best-known ones to have sprung up from the indie music scene. In the indie universe, trends seem to come and go very rapidly. Those indie musicians who become popular online generally tend to migrate towards the mainstream.

Mariana Bockarova

Bibliography

Aberdeen, J.A. The Edison Movie Monopoly. Cobblestone Entertainment. http://www .cobbles.com/simpp_archive/edison_trust .htm (accessed 11 February 2009).
Sarr, Paul. *The Creation of the Media: Political Origins of Modern Communications.* New York: Basic, 2005.

INFORMATION

[See also: *Information Society; McLuhan, Marshall; Media Literacy*]

Information is a concept with ancient roots that translates across multiple fields of inquiry. Use of a general model of information allows scholars to share ideas and employ words with the same meaning to describe information phenomena across the spectrum of academic disciplines.

Information has often been defined in relation to four distinct but related concepts: data, facts, knowledge, and intelligence. Information is organized data presented in context, a coherent collection of messages or cues structured in a way that has meaning or use for human beings. Data may be described as a set of discrete, objective facts about events that become information when assigned meaning or value. Facts involve information that is true, that actually exists, or that can be verified according to an established standard of evaluation. Knowledge can be seen as information in context, together with an understanding of how to use that information; it is a mix of information, experience, and values that provides a framework for assessing and incorporating new information. Knowledge can be either explicit (a person is able to make this information available for introspection) or tacit (the person is not able to make this information available for introspection). Intelligence refers to the quality of the information (e.g., information concerning crucial facts, military intelligence, a secret) or to the capacity of a sentient being to combine data, facts, information, and knowledge with insight and acuity. Intelligence is derived from information as information is derived from facts and data. Information may therefore be defined as facts and data organized to describe a particular situation or problem and information is what people share with each other when they communicate.

Information and Media

Information is conveyed through a medium, such as language, dance, music, architecture, databases, or electronic documents. In organizations, information becomes embedded in documents and repositories as well as in organizational routines, processes, practices, and norms. In societies and cultures, information is transmitted through numerous cues and in contemporary societies, via mass media such as newspapers, television, radio, or Web 2.0.

Information (and the study of its transmission, processing, and principles) was initially a branch of statistics and probability theory overlapping with cybernetics and systems theory. Information is a significant notion that has been adopted in the arts (languages, fine art, music), sciences (biology, physics), and social sciences (particularly economics and psychology) as a construct that holds across disciplinary boundaries and divisions. Studies of information in the arts emphasize the meaning and interpretation of information; the sciences typically stress the engineering principles of transmission and perception; studies in the social sciences usually consider how people are able or unable to communicate accurately due to different experiences and attitudes. Whereas in mathematics and other statistical applications, 'information' is considered separate from meaning and is used to refer only to data accurately sent and received, in humanities and social science disciplines, information and meaning are not considered separate.

In a number of disciplines, the principles of information theory have been applied to systems wherein a message can be sent from one place to another. There are many different systems including ordinary language, visual images, textual genres, and musical recordings. The important distinction between information theory and media theory is that information is a theory of transportation, whereas media is a theory of translation and transformation. Whereas information theory built on the mathematical model of communication proposed by Claude Shannon and Warren Weaver, so that the theory is grounded in mathematical principles of how information is encoded, moved through a channel, and decoded by a recipient, the study of media focuses on the nature of the mediation, examining the effects of the medium through which that information is conveyed. In information theory, the model is of information being transported between encoder and decoder; media theory, by contrast, views the communication transaction as encompassing the encoder, medium, and decoder in a translation of information that somehow has a transformative impact on that information. So, for example, when a person attempts to describe the image on a vase in words on a page, or translate a book to a movie, or adapt a short story for a radio program, the information is transformed when it is converted from one medium to another.

Information in Historic Language

The word 'information' has its origins in the Latin word *informare*, which means 'to give form, to shape, to form an idea of something, or to describe,' so the root of the modern meaning can be discerned in the use of *informare*, meaning the shaping of an idea in one's mind, that is, to inform. Though the word information comes down to us from the Latin, the Romans had borrowed the concept from the ancient Greek *eidos* (form, shape, pattern). For the Greeks, the *eidos* represented the fundamental shaping forces of the universe that unfolded in regular patterns. The ancients held that the form manifest in an object, image, or text was prior to the content. The table, for example, participates in the idea of a table and both have the same name, the idea of the table and the table. The table takes its place in a complex system of sequences of dichotomous classifications arranged in hierarchies and used to classify all the phenomena in the physical world. The content is *informed* by being organized into various shapes and patterns based on classifications that arrange information in sequences of topics (*topoi*, places) and ideas. Whereas we think of ideas as things occurring in the mind or brain or as things that are transmitted by culture or history, the Greeks thought of forms and ideas as occupying a radically different place or space. We consider topics as occurring in different paragraphs in a text; in the Greeks' system, topics were thought to occupy a particular mental place. In this mental place system, the interwoven sequences of classifications that formed the framework of the different places were called the forms, and ideas were ordered and arranged within this system of places. The forms and ideas were thought to occupy a different world, but one that our world matches in the sense that the order on our planet is a reflection of certain fundamental mathematical principles that govern the order of the cosmos. Thus, in the ancient Greek system, information was organized into topics and ideas which were grouped with other like notions and stored in a particular mental place relative to other ideas in a complex mental architecture organized by way of various taxonomies of classifications.

Having come down through the Latin, these connotations associated with information entered the English language through the earliest uses of the verb 'inform' (to give form or character, or to imbue with ...), which date from the fourteenth century, and from which our noun derives. 'Inform' survived as a seldom-used word in the language until it re-emerged in information theory in the twentieth century.

History of the Field

Information theory was pioneered in the 1940s by Claude Shannon, an electrical engineer at Bell Telephone Laboratories, who was primarily concerned with the efficiency and clarity of radio, telephone, and telegraphic transmissions during the Second World War. Shannon worked with Warren Weaver on the classic book *The Mathematical Theory of Communication* (1947), which developed a model of the communication process. The significance of this book was immediately recognized by scholars in a range of disciplines and became the basis for many later studies in information theory.

Shannon's investigations considered the effects of factors such as entropy (the randomness or disorder of the information or its source), interference ('noise' or distortion), data redundancy, channel capacity, and transmission speed on the rate of errors in transmission – that is, how these factors affected the probability of an error-free transmission – and developed principles concerning the construction of binary codes that would minimize errors and maximize efficiency. In information theory, the concept of 'coding' refers to the translation of data into a stream of binary 'on/off' messages representing 'bits' of information (the principle of the computer chip), and is

similar to the view of language in semiotics or structuralism as a series of 'signs' or 'signals' with conventional connotations.

Shannon's work on 'information theory' built on research in Harry Nyquist's 1924 article 'Certain Factors Affecting Telegraph Speed,' published in the *Bell System Technical Journal*, which referred to what was transmitted over the telephone wire as 'information.' There are two basic factors governing the maximum speed of data transmission: first, the shape of a signal; and second, the choice of code used to represent the intelligence. Nyquist was able to measure the amount of intelligence that can be transmitted using an ideal code. Four years later and in the same journal, R.V.L. Hartley, also an engineer, published *The Measurement of Information*, addressing the 'precision of the information' and the 'amount of information' in the transmission. Hartley argued that information exists in the transmission of symbols that convey 'certain meanings to the parties communicating.' When receiving information, the receipt of each symbol allows for the 'elimination' of other possible symbols and their associated meanings.

The precision of information depends on the other symbol sequences that might have been chosen. The measure of these other sequences provides an indication of the amount of information transmitted. Hartley suggested taking 'as our practical measure of information the logarithm of the number of possible symbol sequences.' Thus, if we receive four different symbols occurring with equal frequency, this represents two *bits* of information. Hartley was aware that there was a relationship between the amount of energy in an information system and the amount of information that could be transmitted. Energy serves as a component of the transmission process; applying energy to an information transmitting system increases the ease with which the recipient receives or hears the transmitted signal in order to decode its message. Increasing the signal-to-noise ratio increases the probability that the information will be received correctly. Thus, information does not carry energy; energy carries information.

Information Theory

Entropy is for information theorists the measure of the disorder in a system: the idea is that natural processes tend to move from relative order toward disorder. The term was borrowed from the Greek word (*entropē*) for 'transformation' or 'turning towards' by the German physicist Rudolf Julius Emmanuel Clausius in 1850 in his articulation of the second law of thermodynamics, which states, in part, that 'the entropy of the universe tends to a maximum.' The principle of entropy entails that the disorder in a closed system always increases, and as the entropy of a system increases, there is less energy available and the system becomes progressively less ordered. Entropy can also be defined in terms of complexity based on the number of ways the parts of a system can be organized; the greater the number of possible arrangements, the greater the entropy. (Some information theorists take issue with this definition, arguing that the growing complexity of information distribution and consumption leads to greater social and technological organization, not less.) In the mid-nineteenth century, the German physicist Hermann von Helmholtz and others predicted that the universe (considered a closed system) will eventually 'run down,' ultimately reaching maximum entropy and suffering a 'heat death' when all temperature differences have disappeared.

A system of low entropy and a high degree of order provides relatively clear, unambiguous information and 'sends a message' about where all the elements are and how they are ordered in a coherent arrangement. 'Noise,' in information theory, is what is produced in a high-entropy, disordered system. As a system moves toward higher entropy, order decreases and noise increases, causing interference. The system provides less detail and sends less infor-

mation about the system as a whole until gradually it disperses into undifferentiated parts, a homogenized mixture wherein it is hard to identify the components and harder to receive, decode, and understand the message.

Repetition (or redundancy) is a fundamental mechanism for distinguishing messages from noise, and order from disorder, in a communications system and is therefore a crucial principle enabling communication. Verbal and visual messages are expressed through codes – languages – and messages conform to the rules of the code. Repetition is the reproduction of information as verified by objective observation. Verbatim repetition involves precisely the same words, or exactly the same visual form, but allows for some differences in style. Duplication is a repetition that is an identical copy of the original. To reduplicate is to repeat again and again, to double in order to produce an inflectional or derivational form. Reiteration refers to a process of achieving a result by repeating a sequence of steps to get successively closer to the desired outcome. In linguistic or visual codes, synonymy is created by reiteration that involves not exact repetition, but the substitution of a related item that has equivalence of meaning. Antonymy refers to instances where words or visual elements are presented as polarities, as with day and night. Ellipsis entails instances where something is left unsaid or not depicted that the listener or viewer must fill in themselves. In synonymy, something with equivalent meaning is substituted, while in ellipsis, the place is left blank or there is a silence, or in a visual representation, that place is left empty. Observers or receivers must know the language or visual code well enough to know when something is missing, and to go on and fill in the missing elements themselves.

Redundancy is the term in information theory for repetition of parts or all of a message to provide alternative functional channels in case of a transmission failure. In nearly all forms of communication, more messages are sent than are strictly necessary to convey the information intended by the sender. Such additional messages diminish the unexpectedness, the surprise effect of the information, making it more predictable. This extra ration of predictability is redundancy, and it is one of the major concepts in information theory. With each repetition, redundancy eliminates alternative inaccurate interpretations, so that clarity increases gradually over a number of iterations.

Social anthropologists have analysed the function of repetition in cultural systems, and their understanding is derived from the principles of structural linguistics. The way they explain redundancy as a cultural phenomenon has a great deal in common with that of information theorists. For example, if a person is trying to communicate a message to a friend who is just out of earshot, he will typically shout the message several times, giving slightly different wordings each time, and supplement these with visual cues or signals. The friend at the receiving end may not get the meaning of individual messages, but when she puts the information together, the redundancies and the mutual consistencies and inconsistencies will make readily apparent what her friend is attempting to communicate. In this way, repetition is an enabler of communication because it reinforces precision and reduces errors in the transmission and decoding of information. Just as Hartley argued that information exists in the transmission of signs that communicate certain meanings to the people communicating, when receiving information, the receipt of each symbol makes it possible to eliminate other possible symbols and their associated meanings so that clarity increases with each repetition.

Based on the premise that information theory can be applied to different systems, scholars such as Ann Steiner, in her 2007 work *Reading Greek Vases*, have applied information theory to comparative analyses of verbal repetition in texts such as Homer's *Iliad* and *Odyssey* and repetition

of visual images and motifs on material artefacts, specifically Greek vases of the late Archaic period. Since verbal and visual messages are expressed through language codes, and Athenian vase imagery is varied but still highly repetitive, the hypothesis is that vase painting is a redundant system producing vital cultural information. The principle of redundancy suggests that the great variety of scenes on Athenian vases send a finite set of key cultural messages.

Shannon and Weaver's model of a communication system describes how information is encoded, transmitted via a channel, and then decoded. The Shannon and Weaver communication model may be understood in functional terms so that the model can be translated to other systems and applied to different media and even abstract notions, including perception, observation, belief, and knowledge.

Critics have argued that the model of information transmission proposed by Shannon has been applied in theoretical domains distant from the electrical communication environment in which it was developed and that the theory has been frequently used to characterize situations that do not meet the assumptions and constraints of the original paradigm. Others counter that while the underlying principles of information theory are based on mathematics, it does not necessarily follow that applications of its principles to other domains is inaccurate. While information may be considered separate from meaning in mathematics and used only with regard to data accurately transmitted, in other disciplines, information and meaning are not considered distinct.

Semiotics, the science of signs, which is integrated with structural linguistics both in origin and in application, provides an explanation as to why theoretical models developed for information theory can be applied to verbal and visual languages. Semiotics informs us that the visual imagery on Athenian vases, for example, is a unified language with its own rules of grammar and syntax, where information is encoded through visual symbols much as experience and objects are encoded through words in ordinary language. The principle of repetition confirms that the language of imagery on vases is in fact a code. Individual images belong to a wider set of contexts in the culture beyond what is represented on a single vase. Thus, every image resonates with a number of related images in the cultural code (the language in which the images are expressed). To recognize these connotations, we must look at a range of images from the same time period which allows us to contextualize the information presented on any one vessel. Thus, the repertories of images in the cultural code are all interconnected. Images on any one vase participate in a language that, through repetition over many instances, builds up a cumulative meaning that exceeds that particular representation. The image on any one vase is *informed* by the entire culture.

Fields of Inquiry

Information is a concept that has increasing relevance in the arts and sciences. Since information can be applied to any system in which a message can be sent from one place to another, information theory has been applied to diverse systems in the humanities including everyday language, genres, visual images, and music. Information has also become a useful concept in the sciences. Cellular biologists, for example, think of deoxyribonucleic acid (DNA) as a code that contains information; genes contain information that is communicated to a new cell through mitosis. Economists discuss money as information that is increasingly transmitted across the internet as electronic commerce. Computer scientists consider bits on a hard disk to be the smallest quantity of data. In cognitive psychology, information-processing theory likens the human brain to a computer, considering mental processes in terms of the input, storage, manipulation, and retrieval of data. In this perspective, incoming sense impressions are encoded according to established patterns – as images, symbols, concepts, and so on, or, in the connectionist view, as separate but interconnected 'bits' of information. They are then stored in memory, where they are available for future retrieval and for comparison with other information in learning and problem-solving applications. Each of these disciplines has advanced by applying the idea of information to the problems in its field of inquiry.

Twyla Gibson

Bibliography

Davenport, Thomas H., and Laurence Prusak. *Working Knowledge.* Cambridge, MA: Harvard Business School Press, 1998.
Hartley, R.V.L. The Transmission of Information. *Bell System Technical Journal* 7 (1928): 535–63.
Nyquist, Harry. Certain Factors Affecting Telegraph Speed. *Bell System Technical Journal* 3 (1924): 324–46.
Shannon, Claude E., and Warren Weaver. *The Mathematical Theory of Communication.* Urbana: University of Illinois Press, 1949.
Steiner, Ann. *Reading Greek Vases.* Cambridge: Cambridge University Press, 2007.

INFORMATION SOCIETY

[See also: *Globalization; Information; Internet; Mass Communication; McLuhan, Marshall*]

The term *information society* (IS) is used in cyberculture and media studies to refer to an economic system based primarily on the retrieval, processing, and management of information, in opposition to an economic system based on the production of material goods. The latter is known as an *industrial society*. By extension, IS refers to the fact that in the age of the internet information, in all its forms and uses, is the basis of both the economic system and a prized target of cultural and knowledge-making activities. Other terms that are used to mean more or less the same thing, but with subtle differences, are *post-industrial society, post-Fordism* (referring to the role of the automobile and, thus, of Henry Ford, in the establishment of an industrial society), *postmodern society, knowledge society,* and *network society.*

The advent of an information society lends support to Marshal McLuhan's contention that any major change in mass communications technologies invariably leads to a paradigm shift in the social order. The invention of cheap print technologies led to the diffusion of literacy and thus to the emergence of literacy-based social structures and values, from obligatory schooling to industrialist workplaces that required the ability to read and reason. With the advent of the computer and the internet, information-based activities have come to the forefront. From this, knowledge industries have risen to the top as the most important ones. This does not mean the disappearance of a material-goods economy, but its convergence with the new one, since computer media are now used for the design, production, and distribution of material goods.

As a consequence, the way people come to understand the world has changed, especially the ways in which work is understood and valued. In the industrial world, working at specific hours (nine to five, for example) and on specific days of the week (Monday to Friday) were considered to be 'natural' ways of working. In the information world, where work can be done around the clock through portable computing devices, and where family members are not necessarily tied to the same locale, the concept of work, workplace, and family are in flux. This has raised worldwide debates on the role of traditional social institutions in human life. Political systems too are adapting to the new world order. In an IS, totalitarian models of political control are becoming increasingly less effective because people can exchange information almost instantly through digital media and thus look beyond the confines imposed by the totalitarian system to garner support

for political change. In fact, where such regimes exist, control of the information media is seen as the most important aspect of political control.

But in the IS debates several myths have arisen. The first one is that print books are dead. Books still exist, and even though they may become more and more available in e-book form, the concept and function of the book as a container of knowledge, creative writing, and so on, are alive and well. A second myth is that this is an 'information age.' Every age is such an age. The media for delivering information have changed, but the need for and use of information have been present in all eras. Perhaps it is more accurate to say that information is more available now than ever before, because of the internet. More troubling to many is the purported decline in the deep, reflective reading of texts, given an age where digesting snippets of information (such as tweets) seems to be the rule. But there is no reason to believe that reading discontinuously is a characteristic only of the digital age. People have always 'consulted' books for information for various reasons; reading texts from cover to cover still exists in the domain of fiction, for example.

Perhaps the most important question concerns the relation of information to knowledge and meaning in an IS. Information is unstructured, raw data until it is given a form and a meaning, and transformed into usable knowledge. The founder of information theory was Claude E. Shannon, who defined it as an abstract 'quantity' present in some communication system. In 1945, Shannon published a paper entitled 'A Mathematical Theory of Cryptography,' which was stamped as a secret document and thus never made public. He published an expurgated version in 1948, called 'A Mathematical Theory of Communication,' which became the founding work for information theory. Decoding what the 'message' in any amount of information is, claimed Shannon, should be separated from measuring the information itself. One can always decipher the content, if one wants. But information can and should be considered on its own.

Before Shannon, no one thought of envisioning information as a quantifiable entity. And no one thought that there may be a mathematical relation between information and the devices that carried it. In the mid-1960s, Gordon Moore, the electrical engineer and founder of Intel Corporation, put forth a law which showed that there is such a relation. The law, known as 'Moore's law,' states that the price of electronic devices would decrease as their numbers increased by a factor of two every month and by a factor of one hundred every decade. The prediction turned out to be remarkably accurate. The law applies as well to the information that the devices carry. The storage of information is called 'memory,' and its processing 'computing.' The law in this case states that the price of memory and computing increases by a factor of a hundred every decade.

Shannon's idea of information as a quantifiable entity was based on how computers and various other devices carry and store information. The information is stored in electric charges. One level of charges represents the digit 0, and the other 1. A 0 or a 1 by itself is called a *bit*, which is an abbreviation of *binary digit*. The computer uses combinations of eight bits, called *bytes*, which may be one of 256 distinct values, or patterns of 0 and 1 bits. Millions of transistors process bit charges by switching them from circuit to circuit. When a circuit is off, it corresponds to 0; when it is on, it corresponds to 1. Computer information is measured in multiples of bytes – a kilobyte equals 1,024 bytes; a megabyte, 1,048,576 bytes; a gigabyte, 1,073,741,824 bytes; and a terabyte, 1,099,511,627,776 bytes.

The U.S. Library of Congress is estimated to contain 100 trillion bits of information. A memory disc drive storing the same amount of information today weighs only a few pounds and costs less than a thousand dollars (Gleick 2011) – a fact that shows

how Moore's law operates. But, as Gleick (2011) and other social critics suggest, this conceptualization of information is the cause of the sense of meaninglessness that people feel today with respect to the flood of information that bombards us constantly. This has implications for an IS. For such a society to evolve and even survive, it must bring back meaning into the flood so that it will not drown us.

Marcel Danesi

Bibliography

Castells, Manuel. *The Rise of the Network Society.* Oxford: Blackwell, 2000.

Gleick, James. *The Information: A History, a Theory, a Flood.* New York: Pantheon, 2011.

Fuchs, Christian. *Internet and Society: Social Theory in the Information Age.* London: Routledge, 2008.

McLuhan, Marshall. *The Gutenberg Galaxy: The Making of Typographic Man.* Toronto: University of Toronto Press, 1962.

– *Understanding Media: The Extensions of Man.* Cambridge, MA: MIT Press, 1964.

Shannon, Claude E. A Mathematical Theory of Communication. *Bell Systems Technical Journal* 27 (1948): 379–423.

Shannon, Claude E., and Warren Weaver. *Mathematical Theory of Communication.* Chicago: University of Illinois Press, 1949.

Webster, Frank. *Theories of the Information Society.* London: Routledge, 2006.

INNIS, HAROLD (1894–1952)

[See also: *Communication; McLuhan, McLuhan*]

Harold Innis occupies a unique place in the history of Canadian thought for his work as an economic historian and as one of the pioneers in communication theory. His contributions to the understanding of the development of Canada led him to a leadership role, not only in his profession, but also in the growth of Canadian universities and society. His studies also formed the basis of what is called the 'staples theory' of economic development and, later in his career, a wide-ranging theory on Western civilization and the role that media and communications played in creating that civilization. It is his later analysis of the tensions between space- and time-bound societies that led Innis to a rather bleak view of our future but that makes him one of the twentieth century's pre-eminent thinkers on civilizations. His emphasis on the role of communications and media also makes Innis a central figure in communication theory.

Innis was born on 5 November 1894 near the small southwestern Ontario town of Otterville, a name that is ironic given Innis's later studies of fur-bearing animals. He lived on a farm and, as Alexander John Watson's biography *Marginal Man: The Dark Vision of Harold Innis* suggests, this provided Innis 'a rich practical background for a future economic historian' (2006: 30). Innis grew up in a predominately Scottish environment, where the attendant values of hard work and respect for education played a role in his development. In addition, living in a farming district where one's livelihood is dependent on the fluctuations of markets and the difficulties of getting products to market influenced Innis in his formulation of the staples theory. The theory places the exploitation of natural resources such as wheat, grain, timber, furs, fish, and minerals at the centre of economic activity. It was a short step for Innis in his later years to expand the notion of staples to include ideas and values as central to civilization itself.

North American societies, from the beginning, were dependent on the cod fisheries, especially in New England and Atlantic Canada. Innis devoted his 1940 study *The Cod Fisheries* to European demand for fish and its impact on North American societies. The link between the fisheries and the nature of government is signalled in the book's section headings, such as 'The Mackerel and Confederation,' 'Trawls and

Responsible Government,' 'The End of Sail,' and 'The End of Responsible Government.' The book is a plea for responsible public institutions – a plea that would become even more pronounced in Innis's later writings.

Innis, however, did not begin forming his staple theory model with the cod but rather with a central symbol for Canada – the beaver – in *The Fur Trade in Canada*, which appeared in 1930. On the one hand, *The Fur Trade* is a detailed study of the facts of the trading pelt industry. On the other hand, it is a guide to understanding how economies work, how colonialism operated, how Canada developed differently from the then-emerging United States, how geography shapes and is shaped by human activity, how technology rises, and how interconnected communication systems became integral to North American society. It also details the contributions of the aboriginal population to the success of the fur trade and the creation of Canadian society.

Innis pursued his graduate work in the United States at the University of Chicago and was undoubtedly influenced by the Chicago School of Social Thought. Nonetheless, as Watson (2006: 114) has concluded, in the end he did not fit in there. However, Innis was able to separate his thought from the prevailing mainstream European models derived from Adam Smith and David Ricardo, which, in his view, did not fit the circumstances of the New World. Innis's rejection of the European economics of 'production' led him towards other aspects of economic theory, especially the one that places distribution at its centre.

Innis was also resistant to other theories such as the frontier thesis, prevalent in many American schools, and to Marxism, which could not easily be applied to a country without a factory system or a proletariat. While Innis was quite capable of exposing many of the negative aspects of emerging capitalism, he remained insensitive to the suffering imposed on the working class, as can be seen in *History of*

the Canadian Pacific Railroad (1923), a study
that focuses mainly on finance capitalism,
but does not mention the many labourers
who lost their lives in the construction of
the railroad.

The Fur Trade is an explanation of how
Canada came into being and why it resisted becoming part of the United States.
It is about colonization seen through the
analysis of a centre and its margins or
hinterlands. Innis viewed North America
from the perspective of how it incorporated
European culture into the new frontier. The
centre-margin thesis was adopted by other
economic historians after Innis's death, for
example, Tom Easterbrook and S.D. Clark
both at the University of Toronto. From the
perspective of the emerging trade in the
New World, the fashion habits of the centre, especially England's desire for beaver
hats and furs, translated into an increasing
demand that fed into an exchange with
North America for manufactured goods
that would transform the continent.

Nonetheless, the demand for beaver
soon outstripped the easily accessed source
of pelts. From the beginning, the European
colonists were dependent on the aboriginal
inhabitants for securing the pelts. Innis's
description of how the indigenous peoples
not only allowed for the survival of the
European settlers but also advanced the
trading interest is a story that later commentators have built on. While Innis had
little concern for indigenous culture per
se, he was one of the first commentators
to recognize the immense contribution
the indigenous nations made to Canada's
development. Their involvement in the fur
trade was also one of the chief differences
in approach from the American exploitation of the fur trade. In part, this related to
the differences in geography and climate.
Unlike the cod that preferred warmer
waters, beavers were more sought after
in regions with a more severe winter. The
cold weather thickens the pelt. Accessing
the beaver involved, especially after the
early years, the use of the river system,
where mastery of canoeing was critical.
The indigenous peoples of Canada were
more proficient than their counterparts to
the south. Innis's narrative then follows the
massacre of the beaver, as hunting made
an ever-deeper penetration into the west.
This penetration required the development
of forts and trading posts to establish a network dependent initially on the canoe but
soon requiring different forms of transport.
Hence the symbiosis between expansion
and forms of transportation, as flat-bottom
boats replaced canoes, steam power replaced manual power, and the railway replaced water forms of transit.

In these economic history studies, Innis
rarely lifts his sights above the descriptive
only to issue the occasional sweeping statement, as he does in the concluding chapter
of *The Fur Trade*: 'The economic history of
Canada has been dominated by the discrepancy between the centre and the margin of
Western civilization' (2001: 385). His economic histories were recognized by a few
for their potential. It was only when Innis's
focus changed to the question of Western
civilization that Innis the theorist emerged
and his work became more recognized.

Innis's biographer, Alexander John
Watson, tells the story of Innis's involvement in the First World War. Innis was
wounded and returned home, having experienced the horror of the war that Watson
believed marked him for the rest of his
life, creating in his words 'the dark vision.'
Whatever personal wounds came from the
war it undoubtedly started Innis down
the path to thinking about culture and the
values held by society. Out of the historical
research on Canada grew a larger template
that views civilizations from the tension of
space and time and the values that are created by emphases on one or the other. Out
of this also came the larger theories upon
which Innis's reputation as a communication theorist rests.

Innis faced a dilemma when he embarked on studies of the history of Western civilization. Although he was able to

research many original documents and indeed could voyage, as he did to learn about the fur trade and northern communities, for the larger theoretical canvas he had to rely on the work of others. Some of this expertise was readily at hand in the Classics department of the University of Toronto. Eric Havelock's studies of the transition from oral to written societies or the important work of C.N. Cochrane on Christianity and classical culture, to name just two, were sources of ideas and of academic legitimacy. At other times, Innis drew from his earlier teachers or from scholars as he sensed a need for further information. While this gives his later works a type of 'cut-and-paste style' and, from time to time, it may be hard to discern what is authentically Innis and what is not, his overall thesis emerges in his view of empire as arising from space- and time-binding communications.

The return to the past encompassed a number of articles that concerned the civilizations in Egypt, Babylonia, Greece, and Rome. In an overall sense, Innis was advancing the thesis, captured in the titles of two of his later collections of essays – *The Bias of Communication* (1968) and *Empire and Communications* (1972) – that there exists a bias in every mode of communication that contributes to the type and structure of each empire. Empires are thus seen through the perspective of continuity in time and extension in space, each facilitated or enhanced by the specific dominant technology that underlies communication itself. Within the empire there is a struggle between these two aspects with a preponderance of one over the other that always threatens the 'equilibrium' of the empire. Spatial emphasis tends to support the 'political' structure, whereas a concern for time tends to reinforce the 'religious' aspects of any empire.

Take, for example, Innis's analysis of the tensions in ancient Greece between the oral tradition and the emergent writing-based culture. This gave rise to increased commerce, favouring, as it did, the spatial as-

pects that would later develop into the Roman Empire. It also spawned monopolies of power vested in those who could read and write. This is ground also traversed by Eric Havelock and later reworked by Marshall McLuhan, but it is interesting that Innis saw, even in Plato, a balance of the oral tradition, with its epics and poems, and his written dialogic approach. For Innis, the oral tradition does not in the end die out but becomes dominated by the written and the spatial. Even in his time he felt that the oral tradition of British common law and the unwritten constitution were preferred to the written Roman law or the written American Constitution. Universities were another venue where the oral tradition survived (through dialogue), even though it was threatened by the rise of social science and the power of vested interests in the university.

The march toward empire followed the shift to the use of materials to write on. Innis connects the use of stone, papyrus, and paper with the attendant quasi-monopolies that each conferred on those best able to use these media. In some cases, the use of paper was tied to the use of uniform alphabets and the use of the vernacular. This allowed for a resistance to the control exercised by religion or large-scale political organizations that only writing can afford. At other times, the improvement in communications created the possibility of empire by allowing for the creation of interconnected large administrations. Once embarked on the centrality of the media, it is a short distance for Innis to look at the newspaper, itself a wonderful product of the staples system, and then the radio as the emergent communication technologies of his time. Each of these communications innovations would have profound implications for the social evolution of North America in particular.

It is interesting that Innis used the notion of empire to describe the great political organizations in the past and continued to use it to describe the United States of his time, which he viewed as increasingly imperialistic. Again, the margins, in this case the United States in reference to Europe, become important as the site of innovation and challenge along with new modes of communication. These, he claimed, destabilize the 'equilibrium' between space and time. The relentless expansion of the United States in the nineteenth century was pushed by the railroad and the telegraph, which furthered western settlement and destabilized the older power structure of the eastern seaboard. Similarly, the growth of the south through the cotton industry was aided by technological improvements in both the harvesting and transport of the cotton. Innis pointed to a number of incidents where the conflicts engendered by competing modes of communication were resolved by force. In his last publication, *The Changing Concepts of Time* (2004), Innis details the large number of American presidents who had a military career before entering politics and how this career often was the springboard to electoral success. Coupled with the new modes of communication such as the newspaper, Teddy Roosevelt became a paradigm of foreign military adventurism feeding the domestic market skewed ideas especially through the 'yellow journalism' of the Hearst publications. Later, President Franklin Roosevelt used a new mode of communication, the radio, to speak directly to the people in an attempt to circumvent the Congress. Innis's 'conclusion' can be easily seen in this quotation from his essay entitled 'The Strategy of Culture': 'The overwhelming pressure of mechanization evident in the newspaper and the magazine has led to the creation of vast monopolies of communication. Their entrenched positions involve a continuous, systematic, ruthless destruction of elements of permanence essential to cultural activity. The emphasis on change is the only permanent characteristic' (2004: 11).

Innis, as he approached his death in 1952, became more pessimistic about a resolution of the dominance of spatial organization fuelled both by imperialisms and by the new technologies over the time-bound institutions that would preserve and enhance a sense of continuity and permanence. Two essays that he wrote for *The Bias of Communication* ('A Plea for Time' and 'The Problem of Space') (1968) capture his struggle to readjust the imbalance of Western civilization. The plea was based, in part, on the Canadian experience at the margins set against American spatial imperialism. Innis the economist is never far from the surface in these essays as he is more concerned with the 'market' that will balance space and time without providing an indication of the content of this new balance. Arthur Kroker's judgment in *Technology and the Canadian Mind* (1984) that Innis advocated a pragmatic liberalism based on a technological realism is accurate. In this realism Innis has articulated one of the first substantive theories of the relation of power, culture, and communication.

In many ways Innis was too exceptional to be the centre of a school of thought. In Toronto and branching out across Canada are many thinkers who have been influenced by Innis even while disagreeing with him, including Marshall McLuhan, Tom Easterbrook, S.D. Clark, Danny Drache, Derrick de Kerkove, Marcel Danesi, and perhaps most influential in developing aspects of Innis's thought, Arthur and Marilouise Kroker. All contribute to our understanding of empire and communications.

David Cook

Bibliography

Innis, Harold. *History of the Canadian Pacific Railroad*. London: P.S. King, 1923.
- *The Bias of Communication*. Toronto: University of Toronto Press, 1968.
- *Empire and Communications*. Toronto: University of Toronto Press, 1972.
- *The Cod Fisheries: The History of an International Economy*. Toronto: University of Toronto Press, 1978.
- *The Fur Trade in Canada*. Toronto: University of Toronto Press, 2001.

– *The Changing Concepts of Time.* Lanham: Rowman and Littlefield, 2004.

Kroker, Arthur. *Technology and the Canadian Mind.* Montreal: New World Perspectives, 1984.

Watson, Alexander John. *Marginal Man: The Dark Vision of Harold Innis.* Toronto: University of Toronto Press, 2006.

INSTANT MESSAGING

[See also: *Email; Internet; Text Messaging*]

Instant messaging (IM) is an ever-expanding form of interpersonal communication that allows for immediate response between two or more people via a variety of devices connected through a digital network. It differs from electronic mail (email) in that it allows for real-time conversation at speeds that are virtually equal to face-to-face speech delivery. IM occurs in real time, thus allowing users to conduct a back-and-forth communication act. Examples of IM services on the internet are: AOL Instant Messenger, Google Talk, iChat, Windows Live Messenger, and Yahoo! Messenger. IM services allow users to create 'buddy lists' of other users – a service that notifies a user when someone on the buddy list is online.

History

Long before the internet was established in its current state, messages were being exchanged from computer to computer through the Compatible Time Sharing System (CTSS) as early as the mid-1960s (Van Vleck 2004). The subsequent two decades saw the establishment of the Internet Message Access Protocol (IMAP4) and Post Office Protocol (POP3) for the retrieval and transmission of messages on dedicated servers. The most important development which would subsequently lead towards instant messaging was the introduction of the Quantum Link, offered on the Commodore 64 and Amiga lines of personal computers. Launched on 5 November 1985, Quantum Link was developed by Quantum Computer Services, based in Vienna, Virginia. It allowed connected customers to send online messages (OLM) from one user to another (Evans 2002). Using the Commodore's PET Standard Code of Information Interchange (PETSCII) character set, users were able to view rudimentary OLMs that listed the name of the sender. The early 1990s saw the advent of the online chat room, designed to accommodate the increasing number of users on the internet. The chat room worked as a bulletin board of sorts, where multiple users were able to type in messages that would be seen by everyone in a given 'room' (Tyson and Cooper 2001). The popularity of chat rooms and Quantum Link would later inspire rapid developments in the IM field. Quantum Computer Services later renamed itself America On-Line (AOL) in 1991.

ICQ

The Israeli development house Mirabilis released the IM program ICQ (a homophonic acronym for 'I Seek You') in November 1996. ICQ was the first free IM application to be made available to the public. At the time, the Windows operating system did not have a service similar to Quantum Link. Consequently, Mirabilis took it upon itself to deliver a program that retained the accessibility and tools of Quantum Link, while also incorporating the Channel system of organized multi-user groups created by Mark Jenks (De Hoyos 2009). Not wanting the real-time market to be cornered by Mirabilis, AOL released AOL Instant Messenger (AIM) in May 1997, while also acquiring Mirabilis for $407 million in 1998. With user bases rapidly ballooning into the millions, it was inevitable that new competitors would enter the market: Yahoo Messenger by Yahoo! in 1998 and MSN Messenger by Microsoft in 1999. In 2000, open-source applications Jabber and Trillian were introduced, giving users simultaneous access to the ICQ, AIM, Yahoo, and MSN IM protocols. By the year 2007, Yahoo Messenger alone had 248 million users (Baker 2008).

Mobiles

Short Message Service (SMS) developed as a means to send short text-based messages through telecommunication devices for those who were away from a computer. Originally introduced in the early part of the 1990s, the service allowed cellphone users to send SMS messages of 160 characters or less through the Global System for Mobile Communication (GSM) cellular network. The relative accessibility and low cost of SMS encouraged users to flock to the service, and hundreds of billions of texts are now sent out annually (Ahmed 2002). SMS currently has the same capabilities as IM, especially on smart phones, allowing mobile phone users to have real-time conversations between other SMS-capable devices and even computers.

Today, IM has evolved into a medium that allows for more than just real-time conversation to occur between users. Most of the major IM applications now offer file sharing capabilities, multi-player gaming, integration between IM and standard emails, communication between IM applications and SMS devices, weather updates, and local news, among numerous other options. In addition, the built-in audio and video capabilities of IM applications such as Skype, MSN, and Yahoo messenger allows users to see each other face to face and hear each other's voices. As a result, billions of people around the world are now able to have fully fledged conversations without physical limitations. Because of IM, device-to-device communication has become a kind of default register of informal communication, with email having morphed into a more formal register, and voice-to-voice phoning a mode that implies a certain level of urgency that is not present in the SMS register.

Alexander Lim

Bibliography

Ahmed, Rashmee Z. UK Hails 10th birthday of SMS. *The Times of India*. Bennett Coleman and Co. Ltd. (4 December 2002). http://timesofindia.indiatimes.com/articleshow/30216466.cms (accessed 14 January 2009).

Baker, Loren. Yahoo to Support OpenID for its 248 Million Users, OpenID to Support Yahoo ID's. Search Engine Journal (17 January 2008). http://www.searchenginejournal.com/yahoo-to-support-openid-for-its-248-million-users-openid-to-support-yahoo-ids/6258/ (accessed 14 January 2009).

De Hoyos, Brandon. The World's First IMs. *Instant Messaging*. About.com. http://im.about.com/od/imbasics/a/imhistory_2.htm (accessed 14 January 2009).

Evans, Al. Remember Q-Link. (July 2002). http://www.qlinklives.org/qlink-new/html/remember_q-link.html (accessed 14 January 2009).

Tyson, Jeff, and Alison Cooper. How Instant Messaging Works. HowStuffWorks, Inc. (28 March 2001). http://communication.howstuffworks.com/instant-messaging1.htm (accessed 14 January 2009).

Van Dijk, Jan. *The Network Society*. London: Sage, 1999.

Van Vleck, Tom. The IBM7094 and CTSS (10 September 2004). http://www.multicians.org/thvv/7094.html (accessed 14 January 2009).

Wise, Richard. *Multimedia: A Critical Introduction*. London: Routledge, 2000.

INTELLECTUAL PROPERTY

[See also: *Defamation*]

The term *intellectual property* (IP) refers to the property on a non-material good, connected to a creation of the mind. Abstract creation implies an intellectual effort. Commonly, IP comprises four types of rights. One is that of *author* or *authorship rights*: usually known as 'copyrights' in common-law systems, they are specific to artistic creations. The second is *patents*, protective rights granted for technological inventions. The third is *trademarks*, protected symbols (or logos) which distinguish goods or services as belonging to different companies or individuals. The fourth type is *designs*, the shapes of a two- or three-dimensional object. IP rights may also be categorized as 'registered rights' and other rights which do not need registration, like copyrights or neighbouring rights protecting performers, interpreters, producers, and broadcasters. Registered rights (for example, patents, trademarks, designs) usually depend on an entry in a public register, which in principle guarantees the holder exclusive use and control of the work, creation, or product. In these cases, the territorial principle applies, and IP protection is assured by a country only if it is registered in that country. Registered rights are usually limited in time or need and must thus be renewed.

Economically, without rules on IP, the exploitation of non-material works that are publicly accessible (for example, a song) is easily circumvented, which discourages the production of new ideas or concepts. One function of IP is therefore to protect the work from piracy and encourage individual creativity. IP also has a social function, because IP protection stimulates economic trade and fosters the development and growth of a society through innovation.

The original concept of IP was intended to protect the economic well-being of authors and their literary works. It evolved with the support of and by means of communication and technology as well as through various social events. Historically, the first actual copyright act was issued in England in 1709 with the 'Statute of Anne'; the copyright issue was extended to the United States with the Constitution of 1787 and the Patent Act of 1790. The following international legal sources (the list is not exhaustive) are worth mentioning: the Madrid system for the international registration of marks (the agreement of 1891 and the protocol of 1989); the Paris Convention for the Protection of Industrial Property of 1883; the Bern Convention for the protection of Literary and Artistic works of 1886; the Hague Agreement concerning the International Registration of Industrial Designs of 1925; the Strasbourg Agreement concern-

ing the International Patent Classification; the Nice Agreement concerning the International Classification of Goods and Services for the Purposes of the Registration of Marks; the Locarno Agreement establishing the International Classification for Industrial Designs; the Vienna Agreement establishing the International Classification of the Figurative Elements of Marks.

Modern international IP is managed by the World Intellectual Property Organization (WIPO). Founded in 1967, it became a specific agency of the United Nations in 1974. The modern IP conventions and laws had to be amended after the rise of the internet and the new legal challenges it posed.

Marcello Baggi

Bibliography

Overbeck, Wayne. *Major Principles of Media Law.* Boston: Wadsworth, 2009.

INTERACTIVITY

[See also: *Educational Technology; Multimedia*]

The term *interactivity* refers to a system of communication in which there is the possibility of responding to, participating in, or affecting the information delivered or contained in the system. An *interactive program*, for instance, is a computer program that has the capacity to modify its outcome or formatting in response to input from a user. A computer game is an interactive program. Many educational software programs are similarly interactive.

There are three main levels of interactivity: (1) *non-interactive*, which refers to any system in which a message cannot be related (or relatable) to previous messages; (2) *reactive*, which refers to any system in which a message can be related (or relatable) only to an immediately previous message; and (3) *interactive*, which refers to any system in which a message can be related (or relatable) to a number of previous messages and to the relationship between them.

Human-to-human communication involves both verbal and non-verbal exchanges that are interrelated both to the immediate context in which the communication takes place (reactive communication) and to a system of implicit references, such as previous conversations, social patterns, and so forth (interactive communication). Essentially, interactivity in human-to-human systems involves a sense of collaboration between the interlocutors in the interest of guaranteeing a successful outcome to the communication. Human-to-machine interaction (sometimes called wiki communication) involves the exchange of information or instructions between a human individual and a computer (or some other device). To be interactive, a computer system must be responsive to users' actions.

The notion of interactivity has also been extended to embrace consumer-to-user and user-to-user interactions in the marketing, media, and advertising worlds. In this framework, the media are seen as channels for commercial messages to consumers or audiences that the latter can interact with, in contrast to the non-interactive media of the past (Hoffman and Novak 1996). With the advent of email and instant messaging technologies, along with social media, consumers are now able to communicate directly and instantly with different companies. This type of communication helps both the company and the consumer. Consumers can pass on their opinions on the different products to companies, and the company is able to identify which of their products has captured the interest of consumers (and why it has done so).

Angela Palangi

Bibliography

Hoffman, Donna L., and Thomas P. Novak. Marketing in Hypermedia Computer-Mediated Environments: Conceptual Foundations. *Journal of Marketing* 60 (1996): 50-68.

Liu, Yuping, and L.J. Shrum. What Is Interactivity and Is It Always Such a Good Thing? Implications of Definition, Person, and Situation for the Influence of Interactivity on Advertising Effectiveness. *Journal of Advertising* 31 (2002): 53–64.

INTERCULTURAL COMMUNICATION

[See also: *Conversation Analysis; Culture and Communication; Discourse; Hall, Edward T.*]

Human communication is a social ritual that involves implicit rules of conduct and verbal devices that guide how it unfolds (Goffman 1959). When interlocutors who speak the same language and who belong to the same culture enter into a conversation they automatically know how to utilize these rules and devices. When the speakers belong instead to different speech communities, yet engage in conversation through a common language, which may or may not be spoken by either one of them as a native language, then problems of miscommunication may emerge.

The problems that characterize such *intercultural communication* (IC) are characteristic of life in a global society. For this reason, IC has become an area of study in several fields, from psychology and sociology (Klyukanov 2005) to linguistics (Danesi and Rocci 2009). It is now assigned an autonomous disciplinary status in various academies throughout the world.

Research on conversations reveals that human interaction is marked by verbal devices that allow people to connect with each other, to get something specific out of an interaction that is beneficial to them, and so forth. Clearly, these are used and interpreted in IC in different ways, since people from different cultures and language backgrounds tend to 'define their collective identities by drawing boundary lines between themselves, looking for a mutually acceptable boundary fit' (Klyukanov 2005: 21). Lack of knowledge of the appropriate conversational devices will entail a 'meaning asymmetry' whereby only a 'set formula' is used or a wrong one applied to the situation. Misunderstandings are often traceable to this asymmetry.

As Klyukanov (2005: 36) observes, human interaction is coloured by uncertainty. The implication of this for IC study is rather profound, since it suggests that interlocutors tend to bring specific expectations to the speech situation and that these are hardly ever objectively determinable. Most of the time, the 'objectives' that are latent in a conversation involve regulation, and thus are uncertain. The two main objectives are, arguably: (1) the formation or maintenance of close bonds, and (2) the linkage of the conversation to perceptions of solidarity and empathy. Of course, these objectives can be enacted in a fairly straightforward fashion by speakers with a common linguistic-cultural background, although many failures to do so also characterize such interactions. But in the case of IC, they are perhaps the most difficult ones to accomplish.

Another aspect of IC is what Klyukanov (2005: 60) calls the 'performativity principle':

When people communicate with one another, they try to reach their goals by using various language means. Every act of communication is a performance whereby people face each other (either literally or in a mediated fashion, such as via telephone or the Internet) and, as if on stage, present themselves – their very identities – dramatically to each other.

The concept of communication as a self-presenting strategy through performativity can be traced to the work of the late Erving Goffman (1959). Every time we speak we are exposing who we are, or purport to be. We are in effect playing an imaginary role in the imaginary theatre of life each time we engage others in conversation. This role entails knowledge of the script (or frames) that a specific speech community makes available. That is where the problem lies in IC – there tend to be different (and often contrasting) cultural scripts or frames being acted out in many situations. The strategies used in the delivery of a personal agenda or in the construction of persona in conversation, even in highly ritualized situations, are not predictable to anyone who does not have access to the source scripts (which Goffman called codes) as fashioned by historical cultural forces. In normal intracultural conversation, words ensure that there is a predictability to relations; that is, they ensure that the ways in which people interact in their cultural spheres, and in society generally, are regular and fluid. They are, in other words, regulatory strategies designed to maintain cooperation and harmony, even if, paradoxically, the actual act of conversation is conflictual. But in IC the predictability might be lacking, leading to misunderstanding and even conflict.

Another problematic feature of IC is the contact of potentially divergent world views in the interactional setting. Klyukanov (2005: 93) characterizes this as the 'positionality principle':

Intercultural communication is a matter of positionality. As cultures occupy different positions and interact, their cultural gaze makes it possible for them to see the world and their own place in it. In this process, cultural meanings are generated, or – to put it another way – each culture is grounded.

The notion that language, culture, and world view are interlinked generally falls under the rubric of the *Whorfian hypothesis* (WH), after the American anthropological linguist Benjamin Lee Whorf (1897–1941). The WH posits, basically, that languages predispose speakers to attend to certain concepts as being necessary. But, as Whorf (1956) emphasized, this does not mean that understanding between speakers of different languages is blocked. On the contrary, through translation and various modes of cooperation people are always attempting to understand each other. Moreover, Whorf claimed, the resources of any language allow its speakers to invent new categories any time they want. When we name something anew, we are putting forth something anew and thus expanding cognition. All this raises some interesting questions about expectations during IC, because a specific language predisposes its users to view certain social roles in culture-specific terms. This may trigger unanticipated reactions and may be the most typical source of arguments in encounters between people of radically different cultural backgrounds.

Marcel Danesi

Bibliography

Danesi, Marcel, and Andrea Rocci. *Global Linguistics: An Introduction*. Berlin: Mouton de Gruyter, 2009.

Goffman, Erving. *The Presentation of Self in Everyday Life*. Garden City, NY: Doubleday, 1959.

Klyukanov, Igor E. *Principles of Intercultural Communication*. Boston: Allyn and Bacon, 2005.

Whorf, Benjamin Lee. *Language, Thought, and Reality*. Ed. J.B. Carroll. Cambridge, MA: MIT Press, 1956.

INTERNET

[See also: *Broadcasting; Communication; Convergence; Digital Divide; Mass Communication; Webcasting; World Wide Web*]

The internet has become a buzzword that signals the technological achievements of the late twentieth and early twenty-first century in digital networks. What makes the internet so appealing to millions of users is its versatility, speed, economic potential, and connectivity. The internet has not only changed many aspects of daily life for those users for whom internet is a daily activity, it has also created new opportunities for the creation of virtual spaces, e-commerce, digital publishing, and the like. On the one hand, early writings on the internet characterized it as a utopian place, where new communities of solidarity could be formed without constraints of space and time. On the other hand, sceptics saw the internet as another technology that would draw people away from family and friends and alienate them from society. These dystopian and utopian views are slowly becoming obsolete, as the evidence suggests that the internet has blended into the rhythms of everyday life and is used for a wide variety of purposes, such as surfing for information, playing online games, communicating, and making important life decisions, without necessarily revolutionizing the fabric of society. This entry provides a brief overview of the history of the internet and discusses key theories, approaches, debates, and challenges in the field of internet studies.

The Historical Context of the Internet

The development of the internet needs to be understood in the historical context of the Cold War. There was not only an arms race taking place between the Union of Soviet Socialist Republics (USSR) and the United States, but also a race for technological developments. With an impending nuclear war, there was a sense in the United States that resources needed to be allocated to both armament and communications. On 4 October 1957 the USSR launched Sputnik I, the world's first artificial satellite to orbit the Earth. In the context of the Cold War, this was perceived in the United States as a technological and scientific advantage of the Communist bloc. To counteract this supremacy, a number of measures were taken. In 1958 the U.S. Department of Defense (DoD) created the Defense Advanced Research Projects Agency (DARPA) with the mandate of developing new and strategic forms of communication. The agency worked in conjunction with scientists to create new forms of diffusing information through data networks that would allow the United States to have an advantage over the USSR. An important scientific achievement of DARPA was the Advanced Research Projects Agency Network, or ARPANET. ARPANET was unique in that it allowed data to move swiftly and flexibly through a network without being burdened by specific physical constraints. For example, information could continue to be delivered to its destination even if one of the routes along the way was no longer in operation. This made ARPANET the first network based on packet switching technology and set a benchmark for the development of what is known today as the internet.

Pioneers in Internet History

The history of the internet is marked by a number of internet pioneers who made breakthrough innovations that led to the internet we are familiar with today. These pioneers seldom worked alone, forming tightly interconnected networks linking academia, government, the military, and business. The first glimpse of what the internet would become can be found in a series of documents from August 1962 in which J.C.R. Licklider of the Massachusetts Institute of Technology (MIT) discussed the concept of the 'Galactic Network.' The Galactic Network was envisioned as a set of globally interconnected computers that would enable people to access data and programs from a distance. At the time, the sharing of computer resources through access to supercomputers hosted at a few locations in the United States and Europe was a primary research goal.

Three developments can be identified as central to the materialization of the Galactic Network. A first central development was packet switching, pioneered by Leonard Kleinrock, another professor at MIT, who published a seminal paper in 1961. Packet switching theory maintains that information can be broken down into pieces (or packets) and then sent from one destination to another. The packets travel through any open route available without necessarily sticking together and maintaining a certain

order. However, the packets rearrange themselves once they reach their final destination. It became clear that information could travel more efficiently using packets rather than circuits, and this became the basis for ARPANET. A final breakthrough in the practical application of packet switching technology occurred when the computers at the University of California, Los Angeles (UCLA) and Stanford got connected through telephone lines for the first time. When Charles Kleine, one of the researchers at UCLA, tried to connect to a computer at Stanford by typing 'L-O,' the computer crashed as he typed the next letter, 'G.' Nonetheless, Stanford received the 'LO,' making the first communication between computers possible. By 1 December 1969, two other computers were connected to the grid – Santa Barbara and Utah – constituting the first four nodes of ARPANET. The theoretical developments and practical applications of packet switching were the first milestone in the development of the internet.

A second major breakthrough occurred when Vinton Cerf and Robert E. Kahn wrote a paper outlining an internet protocol and system architecture, called TCP/IP, that regulated transport and forwarding services of data. The Transmission Control Protocol (TCP) allowed different machines to route and assemble data packets, while the Internet Protocol (IP) provided a global addressing mechanism that organized the transfer of data packets to their destination. This protocol continued to be developed to allow for the swift transfer of data across networks. A third major turning point in the history of the internet was the development and implementation of the World Wide Web, WWW, or just the Web. Sir Tim Berners-Lee, while working at the Conseil Européen pour la Recherche Nucléaire (CERN) in Switzerland in 1989, developed a system of interlinked text – hypertext – that can be accessed via the internet through a Web browser. A Web browser is the interface that allows users to access Web pages containing text, image, video, and sound and allows them to navigate from one Web page to another via hyperlinks. Hypertext radically changed the nature of the internet by facilitating access to information as well as the ability to locate and interconnect that information, making the Web an easy-to-use interface for less technically adept users.

The transition from the military/scientific to the civilian fields came in 1987, when the National Science Foundation (NSF) started funding and maintaining the civilian nodes of ARPANET. The NSF then worked with DARPA to expand ARPANET to provide connectivity for the wider scientific and academic community, relying on the TCP/IP standard. The NSF had built a T1 supercomputer backbone capable of bringing together the five supercomputers in America. NSFnet, as these new networks came to be known, proved to be much faster and efficient than the older ARPANET. Commercial conglomerates soon became interested in the financial implications of this new technology. In 1990, ARPANET was formally decommissioned and NSFnet became the main network of networks. Finally, in 1991 the NSF allowed commercial enterprises to use NSFnet, marking the beginning of our modern-day internet. The military nodes of ARPANET developed in parallel to the internet and were no longer directly connected to the internet.

The Nature of the Internet

The internet is a flexible tool that supports a wide range of capabilities based on information; it allows for worldwide broadcasting, the dissemination of information, and collaboration and interaction among individuals and their computers without time and space constraints. The internet consists of interconnected computer networks that constantly exchange data; these interconnections between households, academic institutions, businesses, and government agencies are often referred to as 'a network of networks' which together form the infrastructure of the internet. It is important to distinguish between the internet, which can be thought of as the infrastructure carrying the information, and the various services and software that can be accessed through the internet, such as the World Wide Web, email, File Transfer Protocol (FTP), instant messaging, and many other applications. These applications function on top of the internet and help with the transmission and display of data.

The Digital Divide

The term digital divide refers to the situation in which some people have access to the internet while others do not. These differences in access point toward inequalities that are grounded in such characteristics as: (1) class, (2) gender, (3) urban or rural address, and (4) race/ethnicity. Early adopters of the internet were characterized as primarily white males with higher socio-economic status living in urban areas. While the gap in internet access has considerably narrowed since the mid-1990s, scholars have identified variations between users in terms of the types of access they have to the Web (dial-up, broadband, and wireless), their knowledge and skills when online, and the variety of activities performed. Hence, equality of internet access may be less of a concern today, but differences between internet users continue to be an important component of the digital divide. In addition, the term global digital divide describes the gap that exists in access to the internet between developed and developing countries. Developing countries continue to struggle in their effort to become digital, having to overcome numerous barriers, including (1) lack of infrastructure in terms of hardware, software, and internet connectivity; (2) low levels of literacy; and (3) lack of computers and internet skills. Nonetheless, the composition of internet users has changed considerably since the early inception of the Web, with a large proportion of Asians, Europeans, and South Americans using it. Statistical data on users around the world and information on programs of digital literacy can be obtained from the United Nations (UN) website as well as through the World Internet Project (WIP), an international collaboration of scholars.

Social Impact of the Internet

As Canadian communication scholar Marshall McLuhan stated, technologies shape our society, and at the same time, society shapes how technologies are developed, implemented, and used. The internet has grown dramatically in terms of the content offered, the services available, and the number of global users. Thus, the internet has had a revolutionary impact on all aspects of life – including work, play, communication, politics, and education – on a global scale. Through its communication capabilities, the internet can overcome constraints of time and space, creating the notion of a smaller planet.

Utopian-Dystopian Debate

Many analysts have suggested that the internet will bring positive change to people's lives due to its rapid diffusion among the world's population, its relatively low cost for getting online, its ease of use, and its diversity of information sources and communication tools. The internet will bring about a digital revolution in which a sense of community will be restored by connecting friends and family near and far, providing information resources on a wide variety of topics, and stimulating various groups of individuals to engage in political and organizational participation. The digital realm will foster new forms of community by providing a space in which people with common interests can meet. Online communities will flourish because people will be able to choose communities of shared interests regardless of their physical location. Howard Rheingold describes in his classic book *The Virtual Community* how one of the earliest online communities, THE WELL (Whole Earth Electronic 'Link'),

became a close-knit social network providing members social support, friendship, information, and a forum for discussion. Through the internet, people are maintaining far-flung ties with virtual communities as well as local relationships with friends and family. The utopian perspective expands to other social effects including e-learning, e-democracy, and e-commerce. While the internet has had a strong impact on social life, it has not always had the long-lasting and revolutionary effects predicted by early analysts.

On the other hand, scholars see a parallel between the effects of television and the internet because both technologies draw people away from their immediate environments, potentially alienating them from social interactions and civic engagement. Social contact online can be immersive, drawing people away from face-to-face and phone contact. Moreover, the global nature of the internet can have negative consequences for local community. Even those activities that are social can lead to domestic conflict. Maintaining many far-reaching ties may result in less time for interactions with household members. In addition, if people are spending more time online, public spaces become less relevant for interaction and socializing. The addictive component of the internet has also been identified as potentially harmful, with people spending many hours, for example, playing online games, becoming involved in online sex, and engaging in virtual environments. While both utopian and dystopian perspectives pinpoint important aspects of the internet, the impact of the internet on society has been less pronounced than predicted by these perspectives. The internet has become a part of most people's everyday life, presenting some advantages and some challenges.

Asynchronous and Synchronous Forms of Communication

A key distinction about the internet is made between asynchronous and synchronous forms of communication. Asynchronous forms of communication do not require communication partners to be simultaneously available to exchange messages, allowing for flexible communication across time and space. The most common forms of asynchronous communication are email, social network sites, newsgroups, and listservs. Social network sites (SNSs) are defined as online services where users create a profile – consisting of information about their birthdates, music preferences, reading preferences, and so on – with the intention of connecting that profile to other profiles to create a social network. Some of the most popular social network sites include MySpace, Facebook, Bebo, and BlackPlanet. Although all age groups use social network sites, young people and university students are by far the largest group of adopters. What makes social network sites particularly attractive to this group of individuals is the ability to converse with their friends and peers, share digital cultural artefacts and ideas, and connect to vast networks of interest.

Synchronous forms of communication have had a strong impact on society because they embody the promises of the information age and the networked society and allow for instant or real-time communication with multiple individuals across the globe. A wide range of internet applications support synchronous forms of exchange: instant messaging, Internet Relay Chat (IRC), and cyberworlds. Instant messaging (IM) systems are defined as applications that provide text-based, near-synchronous communication between two or more users who are usually known to one another. Some of the most popular IM platforms include AOL Instant Messenger (AIM), Google Talk, ICQ, Tencent QQ, Skype, Windows Live Messenger (WLM), and Yahoo! Messenger. Instant messaging is one of the largest-growing internet applications – estimates suggest that approximately 510 million users worldwide send nearly 12 billion messages each day. Although all age groups in society use instant messaging, the Pew Internet and American Life project has identified young people as the largest group of adopters. What makes it appealing for this group of users is its speed, display of availability information, and support for multiple conversations.

Studying and Researching the Internet

Not only is the internet an evolving technology that constantly recreates itself, it is also a social technology. The internet does not simply drive social trends; it also resonates with and responds to social trends. Hence, there are a number of challenges that researchers need to take into consideration. First, the internet has chameleon-like properties that are constantly changing. The most prominent changes include the large expansion of content, the increase in bandwidth, the ubiquity of access, and the commercialization of the internet. Second, the composition of internet users has also changed from users who were predominantly young, white, North American, and male to a more diverse set of users. Third, many of the changes associated with the internet are specific to a particular user group. For example, women seek health information on the internet more frequently than men. Thus, the particulars of a group have to be examined to understand how they are appropriating the internet and how the internet fits into their everyday routines. Finally, there has been an implicit assumption that as the internet diffuses around the world, it will increasingly resemble the North American internet. That is, email will be a principal use, complemented by Web surfing. Yet, with time and research, two things are becoming clear. First, internet use varies around the world. For example, Catalans use email less frequently than North Americans, and Japanese, Chinese, and Europeans often use short message texting (SMS) or instant messaging instead of email. Second, cultural norms and practices influence how the internet is used on a daily basis. Culture plays an important role in determining who adopts the internet and the role the internet plays in the daily life of these cultures.

Internet research is an interdisciplinary area of study. Of great importance to internet scholars and policymakers is the Association of Internet Researchers (AoIR), founded in 1996. AoIR organizes an annual conference and promotes a listserv for discussion. The International Communication Association (ICA) presents an international forum for researchers to get together and discuss current research, curriculum innovations, and challenges, as well as key concerns of media professionals. While internet studies cross disciplines, some universities have started to offer programs specifically geared toward internet studies, such as the Oxford Internet Institute.

Anabel Quan-Haase

Useful Websites

Association of Internet Researchers (AoIR). http://aoir.org/
AoIR brings together international researchers, practitioners, and policymakers with an interest in the design, uses, social consequences, and developments of the internet. The website also incorporates a mailing list, a wiki, workgroups, newsletters, and publications.

International Communication Association (ICA). http://www-rcf.usc.edu/~ica/
The ICA is an organization linking communications researchers and includes mass communication as one of its seventeen principal divisions. This group also publishes several journals, such as the *Journal of Communication*.

'Internet.' Wikipedia.org. http://en.wikipedia .org/wiki/internet
This entry offers a brief overview of the development and significance of the internet.

Internet Corporation for Assigned Names and Numbers (ICANN). http://www.icann.org/
ICANN is an international non-profit partnership whose aim is to keep the internet secure, stable, and interoperable. The website contains information on the history, mission, and current challenges of managing unique internet identifiers or addresses.

NASA History on Sputnik. http://history.nasa .gov/sputnik/
This site provides historical background on the launch of Sputnik I and its social, political, and international significance.

National Communication Association (NCA). http://www.natcom.org
The NCA is a non-profit organization dedicated to researching communication and publicizing scholarship within communications. The NCA is responsible for publishing nine academic journals.

Oxford Internet Institute (OII). http://www.oii .ox.ac.uk/
The OII is a department of the University of Oxford dedicated to researching the societal implications of the internet. The website contains publications and press releases in the areas of the internet in everyday life, internet governance and democracy, e-learning, and the social shaping of the internet.

Pew Internet and American Life Project (PEW). http://www.pewinternet.org/
PEW is a non-profit 'fact tank' focused on examining the impact on the internet. The website contains reports, presentations, data sets, and press releases on the internet's impact on children, families, communities, the workplace, health care, and civic and political life.

United Nations Information and Communication Technology Web site. http://stdev.unctad .org/themes/ict/docs.html/
This website contains reports from around the world about the current state of the digital divide. Information is available on recent conferences that address concerns around the global digital divide.

World Internet Project (WIP). http://www .worldinternetproject.net/
WIP is a major international, collaborative project founded in 1999 by the University of Southern California Annenberg School Center for the Digital Future, and is focused on examining the social, political, and economic influence of the internet and other new technologies. The website contains publications on household and nation adoption and use of the internet.

Bibliography

Abbate, Janet. *Inventing the Internet*. Cambridge, MA: MIT Press, 1999.

Castells, Manuel. *The Internet Galaxy: Reflections on the Internet, Business, and Society*. Oxford: Oxford University Press, 2001.

Cerf, Vinton G., and Robert E. Kahn. A Protocol for Packet Network Intercommunication. *IEEE Transactions on Communications* 22 (1974): 637–48.

Internet. *Encyclopaedia Britannica* (Online). 2008. http://www.search.eb.com/eb/article-218353 (accessed 24 April 2008).

Leiner, Barry M., Vinton G. Cerf, David D. Clark, Robert E. Kahn, Leonard Kleinrock, Daniel C. Lynch, John Postel, Lawrence G. Roberts, and Stephen S. Wolff. The Past and Future History of the Internet. *Communications of the ACM* 40 (1997): 102–8.

Markoff, John. *What the Dormouse Said: How the Sixties Counterculture Shaped the Personal Computer Industry*. New York: Viking, 2005.

Putnam, Robert D. *Bowling Alone: The Collapse and Revival of American Community*. New York: Simon and Schuster, 2000.

Rheingold, Howard. *The Virtual Community: Homesteading on the Electronic Frontier*. Rev. ed. Cambridge, MA: MIT Press, 2000.

Wellman, Barry, and Caroline Haythornthwaite, eds. *The Internet in Everyday Life*. Oxford: Blackwell, 2002.

INTERNET AND SOCIAL INTERACTION

[See also: *Internet; Social Networking*]

The internet today has become more than just a source of information. It is now a major point of reference for social interaction. The previously labelled 'information highway' has morphed into a 'social roadway.' The internet has become a social space in which many interactions now take place: from online dating (e-dating) – a form of dating that allows people to meet others through the use of social network sites, which provide the medium for computer-mediated communication (CMC) – to everyday communicative activities on sites such as Facebook and Twitter. Finding a romantic or sexual partner is no longer just part of a 'real-world' ritual, but also of a 'hyperreal' one, to use Baudrillard's (1983) epithet for the imaginary world of reality created by engagement with computer-generated spaces. The initial stages and contact techniques often take place in hyperreal space with real-world contact coming at a later point in time. The possibility of constructing personas for romantic purposes is now seemingly part of the social game. Users can sign into the site with minimal information using pseudonyms (such as a nickname), a purported age, and email address. Or they can go through a lengthy process of filling out information about themselves, including likes/dislikes, hobbies, music preferences, and so on, to give a more detailed representation of themselves.

After going through the initial process in hyperspace, individuals are then in a position to sift through all eligible mates who match their expectations. The process of matching is narrowed down when individuals seek specific traits in their partners – a search bolstered by the site's social script and analyses of the user's needs and wants. For example, one can seek a partner within a certain age range, of a specific nationality, and/or of a certain religious background. Initially, many people will often browse through photos to get an idea of what their options are before actually interacting with someone online. The internet is taking the role of courtship tutors and/or romantic locales of various kinds. And it would seem that hyperspace is viewed as much more reliable than any other locus for such interaction, as studies continually show (for example, Romm-Livermore and Setzekom 2008).

Many social networking sites have an IM (instant message) option. If a contactee does not respond, the feeling of rejection that usually coincides with face-to-face encounters is reduced because of the many other options available to the contactor. From this point forward, discourse unfolds in ways that are similar to those in a face-to-face encounter but are often more direct and personal, with the computer screen acting as a kind of emotive filter. In effect, using Jakobson's (1961) notion of emotivity, the online world is allowing for the emotional aspects of oral speech to become attenuated and thus repackaged through the writing medium in more controlled ways.

Many online friendships and relationships carry on for months or, in some cases, years before a face-to-face encounter is negotiated. This is due, paradoxically, to various 'real-world' restrictions such as geographical barriers. Those who choose to continue the interaction then utilize other CMC modes of contact, from email to webcams and Skype. These allow for individuals to communicate while viewing each other in real time. This brings intimate conversation closer to real-space interaction. When communicating through typed text there is more opportunity for misunderstanding. Without facial expressions and intonation the communication becomes disjointed and must be inferred delicately. The proliferation of webcams and the use of video-conferencing applications like Skype have made it easier to maintain a long-distance relationship.

Initially, social interactions through Facebook and online dating rituals through various sites were looked at negatively by society at large. People who used it were often considered desperate and lacking real social skills. In a short time, and certainly by the mid-2000s, the stigma vanished. There are websites now specifically designed to introduce people to others who are like-minded or of the same ethnicity, race, or religion such as JDate, Love from India, or Manhunt for gay men. In fact, the world has become a digital global village, and the social interaction aspect of the internet is bringing this out more and more.

Lorraine Bryers

Bibliography

Baudrillard, Jean. *Simulations*. New York: Semiotext(e), 1983.
Goffman, Erving. *The Presentation of Self in Everyday Life*. Garden City, NY: Doubleday, 1959.
Romm-Livermore, Celia, and Kristina Setzekom, eds. *Social Networking Communities and EDating Services: Concepts and Implications*. New York: IGI Global, 2008.

INTERTEXTUALITY

[See also: *Hypermedia and Hypertext; Text Theory*]

The term *intertextuality* is used in several disciplines, especially literary studies and media studies, to refer to how texts generate meaning. Intertextuality is the connection between one text and other texts by allusion, inference, implication, or suggestion. Extracting a meaning from, say, John Bunyan's novel *Pilgrim's Progress* (1678, 1684) depends upon knowing the relevant Bible narrative and the theological concept of a journey from the City of Destruction to the Celestial City. James Joyce's novel *Ulysses*, which takes its title from Homer's Ulysses (Odysseus in Greek), interconnects the adventures of the main character, Leopold Bloom, to those of the Homeric Ulysses. Bloom, an advertising salesman, his wife Molly, and young Stephen Dedalus are the Joycean counterparts of Ulysses, his wife Penelope, and their son Telemachus in the Greek epic. Bloom's one-day adventures in Dublin mirror the many years of wanderings Ulysses endures as he tries to return home to Ithaca after fighting in the Trojan War. *Ulysses* is also filled with intertextual references to many areas of knowledge, including theology, mythology, astronomy, Irish legends, history, and languages such as Hebrew, Latin, and Gaelic.

The notion of intertext was introduced into semiotics by Roland Barthes and elaborated subsequently by Julia Kristeva. As Barthes pointed out, a text is constituted by bits of codes, various conventional formulas, and specific kinds of discourses, all of which pass into the text and are reconfigured within it. For Barthes the text is, thus, a blend of unconscious quotations, without quotation marks. For Kristeva a text is more than the result of a single author's efforts – it is the result of other texts converging on it through the author's own unconscious memory. Any text is, thus, the result of an author absorbing and transforming other texts. It is an intertextual creation.

Marcel Danesi

Bibliography

Barthes, Roland. Theory of the Text. In *Untying The Text*, ed. Robert Young, 31–47. London: Routledge, 1981.

Kristeva, Julia. *Séméiotiké: Recherches pour un sémanalyse.* Paris: Seuil, 1969.

J

JAKOBSON'S MODEL OF COMMUNICATION

[See also: *Bull's-Eye Model; Communication; Discourse*]

The communication model developed by the Moscow-born American linguist and semiotician Roman Jakobson (1896–1982), has become influential in communication studies and other social sciences. The model, which was based on linguist Karl Bühler's *Organon* model (Bühler 1934), identifies the main functions and constituents of human communication in a comprehensive way. Jakobson (1960) posited six constituents that make up verbal communication:

(1) an *addresser* who starts (or addresses) a communication; the addresser can be a single person, an organization, or any other entity capable of communicating something;
(2) a *message* that he or she constructs for some reason or in response to something;
(3) an *addressee* to whom the message is addressed; the addressee can be a single person (as in a conversation), an audience, and so on;
(4) a *context* in which the message is constructed and which gives it its overall meaning; for example, the utterance 'Help me' would have a different meaning depending on whether it was spoken by someone lying motionless on the ground or by a student in a classroom working on a difficult math problem;
(5) a mode of *contact* by which a message is delivered; this involves the social and psychological connections that exist or are established between the addresser and addressee; it could be face to face, through a chatroom, on Facebook, and so on; the mode can thus be synchronous, occurring at the same time (as in oral conversation or through devices such as instant-messaging devices;
(6) a *code* providing the expressive forms or resources (language, gesture, facial expressions, etc.) for constructing and deciphering messages meaningfully and efficiently.

Each of these constituents determines or involves a different communicative function:

(1) *emotive*, which comprises the addresser's emotions, attitudes, social status, etc.; emotivity here refers to the addresser's intent, which, no matter how literal his or her message might be, will invariably involve the latent presence of emotions;
(2) *conative*, which is the effect (physical, psychological, social) that the message has or is expected to have on the addressee;
(3) *referential*, which is a message constructed to carry information unambiguously; it is also the term that indicates that

any message is perceived as referring to something other than itself;

(4) *poetic*, which is a message constructed with poetic style;

(5) *phatic*, which is a message designed to establish or ensure continuous social contact;

(6) *metalingual*, which is a message referring to the code being used ('The word *noun* is a *noun*').

Jakobson's model suggests that ordinary discourse goes well beyond a situation of simple information transfer. It involves determining and comprehending *who* says *what* to *whom*; *where* and *when* it is said; and *how* and *why* it is said. Jakobson was among the first to point out that human discourse is shaped by the setting, the message, the expressive resources used (verbal and non-verbal), and the participants, making an emotional claim on everyone involved.

The notions of phatic function and context require further elaboration here. At a pure contact level, the phatic function ensures fluid social continuity. So, for example, when two office workers pass each other in the morning and say, 'Hi, how's it going?' 'Not bad, and you?' they are not literally inquiring about each other's health. The formulas used are part of phatic speech and are intended solely for making contact and keeping the social relation going. All kinds of rituals and social practices are based on phatic communication, which is not intended to create new meanings but to reinforce ritualistic ones and, thus, to ensure social cohesion. The term context is not a synonym for setting. Taking his cue from Otto Jespersen (1922), Jakobson saw the words used in communication as 'shifters,' pointing to the cause and context of an utterance – place (*here*, *there*), time (*now*, *then*), and specificity (*this*, *that*). In other words, language use is a shifter process, whereby cues are constantly referring to spatio-temporal aspects of the communication act.

Finally, Jakobson claimed that one of the functions in the model becomes dominant depending on message and context. In poetry, the poetic function dominates, as it does in some formulaic contexts (as in greeting cards and love letters).

Marcel Danesi

Bibliography

Bühler, Karl. *Sprachtheorie: Die Darstellungsfunktion der Sprache*. Jena: Fischer, 1934.

Eco, Umberto. The Influence of Roman Jakobson on the Development of Semiotics. In *Roman Jakobson: Echoes of His Scholarship*, ed. D. Armstrong and C.H. van Schoonefeld, 39–58. Lisse: The Peter de Ridder Press, 1977.

Jakobson, Roman. Linguistics and Poetics. In *Style and Language*, ed. T.A. Sebeok, 34–45. Cambridge, MA: MIT Press, 1960.

– *Six Lectures on Sound and Meaning*. Trans. John Mepham. Cambridge, MA: MIT Press, 1978.

– *The Framework of Language*. Ann Arbor: Michigan Studies in the Humanities, 1980.

Jespersen, Otto. *Language: Its Nature, Development and Origin*. London: Allen and Unwin, 1922.

Waugh, Linda R. *Roman Jakobson's Science of Language*. Lisse: Peter de Ridder, 1976.

JAMESON, FREDRIC (b. 1934)

[See also: *Postmodernism; Marxism*]

Fredric Jameson is considered to be one of the foremost contemporary Marxist literary critics writing in English. He has published a wide range of works analysing literary and cultural texts and developing his own neo-Marxist theoretical position. A prolific writer, he has assimilated a large number of theoretical discourses into his project and has intervened in many contemporary debates while analysing a diversity of cultural texts, ranging from the novel to video, from architecture to postmodern film.

Jameson's early work was mainly on literature, but in the 1980s he turned to media and popular cultural criticism as well. Over the past decades, Jameson has published a diverse and complex series of theoretical inquiries and cultural studies. One begins to encounter the characteristic range of interests and depth of penetration in his studies of science fiction, film, magical narratives, painting, and both realist and modernist literature. Although Jameson has never developed a specific media theory, he has analysed many forms of media and popular culture, including film, video, and popular literature. Thus, his work can be seen as part of the movement toward cultural studies as a replacement for canonical literary studies. Yet cultural studies for Jameson are part of a broader project of developing interdisciplinary theory of culture, politics, and society.

Jameson has characteristically appropriated into his theory a wide range of positions, from structuralism to post-structuralism and from psychoanalysis to postmodernism, producing a highly eclectic and original brand of Marxist literary and cultural theory. Marxism remains the master narrative of Jameson's corpus, a theoretical apparatus and method that utilizes a dual hermeneutic of ideology and utopia to criticize the ideological components of cultural texts, while setting forth their utopian dimension, and that helps produce criticism of existing society and visions of a better world. Influenced by Marxist theorist Ernst Bloch, Jameson thus has developed a hermeneutical and utopian version of Marxist cultural and social theory.

Drawing on Bloch, Marcuse, and other neo-Marxist theories, Jameson has suggested that mass cultural texts, such as films, often have utopian moments and proposes that radical cultural criticism should analyse both the social hopes and fantasies in the films as well as the ideological ways in which fantasies are presented, conflicts are resolved, and potentially disruptive hopes and anxieties are managed (Jameson 1979, 1981). In his reading of *Jaws*, for instance, the shark stands in for a variety of fears (uncontrolled organic nature threatening the artificial society, big business corrupting and endangering community, disruptive sexuality threatening the disintegration of the family and traditional values, and so

on) which the film tries to contain through the reassuring defeat of evil by representatives of the current class structure. Yet *Jaws* also contains utopian images of family, male bonding, and adventure, as well as socially critical visions of capitalism that articulate fears that unrestrained big business will inexorably destroy the environment and community.

In Jameson's view, mass culture thus articulates social conflicts, contemporary fears and utopian hopes, and attempts at ideological containment and reassurance. According to Jameson (1979: 144),

works of mass culture cannot be ideological without at one and the same time being implicitly or explicitly Utopian as well: they cannot manipulate unless they offer some genuine shred of content as a fantasy bribe to the public about to be so manipulated. Even the 'false consciousness' of so monstrous a phenomenon of Nazism was nourished by collective fantasies of a Utopian type, in 'socialist' as well as in nationalist guises. Our proposition about the drawing power of the works of mass culture has implied that such works cannot manage anxieties about the social order unless they have first revived them and given them some rudimentary expression; we will now suggest that anxiety and hope are two faces of the same collective consciousness, so that the works of mass culture, even if their function lies in the legitimation of the existing order – or some worse one – cannot do their job without deflecting in the latter's service the deepest and most fundamental hopes and fantasies of the collectivity, to which they can therefore, no matter in how distorted a fashion, be found to have given voice.

Jameson's hermeneutic of media culture contains a mode of dialectical criticism that involves thinking which reflexively analyses categories and methods, while carrying out concrete analyses and inquiries. Categories articulate historical content and thus must be read in terms of the historical environment out of which they emerge. For Jameson, dialectical criticism thus involves: thinking that reflects on categories and procedures while engaging in specific concrete studies; relational and historical thinking, which contextualizes the object of study in its historical environment; utopian thinking, which compares the existing reality with possible alternatives and finds utopian hope in literature, philosophy, and other cultural texts; and totalizing, synthesizing thinking, which provides a systematic framework for cultural studies and a theory of history within which dialectical criticism can operate. All these aspects are operative throughout Jameson's work, the totalizing element coming more prominently (and controversially) to the fore as his work evolved.

Jameson has published two collections of essays on film, *Signatures of the Visible* (1990) and *The Geopolitical Aesthetic* (1992), consisting of characteristically astute readings of individual films as well as major statements on contemporary film theory, 'The Existence of Italy' and 'Totality as Conspiracy'; his work remains outside the mainstream of contemporary film studies. Slavoj Zizek, a figure who has himself written extensively about film but remains intransigently outside of any mainstream critical position, took up Jameson's intervention at a conference on Krzysztof Kieślowski to present his reflections of Jameson, Kieślowski, Lars von Trier, and revolutionary politics. In a different register Michael Chanan interviewed Jameson on film. In this wide-ranging discussion, Jameson reflects upon Cuban and Latin American cinema, the politics of *Screen* in the 1970s, documentary film-making, and the role of music in film. In particular Chanan and Jameson explore the crucial role music and sound play for our sense of temporality in film and how this connects to the familiar Jamesonian concerns of narrative, realism, and form.

In general, Jameson is perhaps best known on a global scale as one of the major theorists of the postmodern. The important essay 'The Existence of Italy' (in *Signatures of the Visible*) develops this problematic, as do the studies in *Postmodernism* (1991), *The Cultural Turn* (1998), *A Singular Modernity* (2002), and *Archaeologies of the Future: The Desire Called Utopia and Other Science Fictions* (2007). Indeed, Jameson's studies on postmodernism are a logical consequence of his theoretical project. Within his analysis, Jameson situates postmodern culture in the framework of a theory of stages of society – based on a neo-Marxist model of stages of capitalist development – and argues that postmodernism is part of a new stage of capitalism. Every theory of postmodernism, he claims, contains an implicit periodization of history and 'an implicitly or explicitly political stance on the nature of multinational capitalism today' (1991: 3). Following Ernest Mandel's periodization in his book *Late Capitalism* (1975), Jameson claims that 'there have been three fundamental moments in capitalism, each one marking a dialectical expansion over the previous stage. These are market capitalism, the monopoly stage or the stage of imperialism, and our own, wrongly called postindustrial, but what might better be termed multinational, capital' (1991: 35). To these forms of society correspond the cultural forms realism, modernism, and postmodernism.

Jameson emerges as a synthetic and eclectic Marxist cultural theorist who attempts to preserve and develop the Marxist theory while analysing the politics and utopian moments of a diversity of cultural texts. His work expands literary analysis to include popular culture, architecture, theory, and other texts and thus can be seen as part of the movement toward cultural studies as a replacement for canonical literary studies.

Douglas Kellner

Bibliography

Homer, Sean. *Fredric Jameson, Marxism, Hermeneutics, Postmodernism*. New York and London: Routledge.

Homer, Sean, and Douglas Kellner, eds. *Fredric Jameson: A Critical Reader*. London: Palgrave Macmillan, 2004.

Jameson, Fredric. *Marxism and Form*. Princeton: Princeton University Press, 1971.

- *Fables of Aggression: Wyndham Lewis, the Modernist as Fascist*. Berkeley: University of California Press, 1979.

- *The Political Unconscious*. Ithaca, NY: Cornell University Press, 1981.

- *Late Marxism: Adorno, or, the Persistance of the Dialectic*. London: Verso, 1990.

- *Signatures of the Visible*. New York and London: Routledge, 1990.

- *Postmodernism, or the Cultural Logic of Late Capitalism*. Durham, NC: Duke University Press, 1991.

- *The Geopolitical Aesthetic*. Bloomington: Indiana University Press, 1992.

- *The Cultural Turn. Selected Writings on the Postmodern, 1983–1998*. London: Verso, 1998.

- *A Singular Modernity*. London: Verso, 2002.

- *Archaeologies of the Future: The Desire Called Utopia and Other Science Fictions*. London: Verso, 2007.

Kellner, Douglas, ed. *Postmodernism/Jameson/Critique*. Washington, DC: Maisonneuve Press, 1989.

JOURNALISM

[See also: *Newspapers; Print Culture*]

What is journalism? And how does it fit into the context of media and communication studies? The most prototypical representation of journalism, in both the media and in the scholarly literature, is that of the enthusiastic and righteous reporter investigating the secret or illegal affairs of corrupt and powerful politicians. This is the image that comes across in movies such as *All the President's Men*, with Robert Redford as the prototypical investigative reporter. The only difference between a reporter and a criminal investigator in this scenario is that (1) the affairs that are of interest to the reporter need not be strictly illegal (as long as they involve a cover-up), and (2) the reporter needs to sell his or her story. Of course,

this scenario is not restricted to political intrigue, as long as the stories are about people or organizations that have some direct or indirect influence on the readers' daily lives. Watergate-style journalism is often referred to as *watchdog journalism*. Murrey Marder (an ex-reporter at *The Washington Post*) puts it as follows (Marder 2010): 'For me the watchdog reporter is always in a struggle, because he is always trying to extract time to think.' A more neutral term for this kind of journalism is perhaps *investigative journalism*. As Tony Burman (2006: 2) of CBC News observes: 'There is no more important contribution that we can make to society than strong, publicly-spirited investigative journalism.' As these two citations bring out, the tradition of Watergate-style journalism is a highly celebrated. Other, less celebrated, traditions include Gonzo journalism (Johnny Depp in *Fear and Loathing in Las Vegas*), new journalism (Philip Seymour Hoffman in *Capote*), and sports journalism (Josh Hartnett in *Resurrecting the Champ*). Finally, there is paparazzi journalism. In the words of Phil Graham, also an ex-reporter at the *Washington Post*, all forms of journalism constitute 'a first rough draft of history' (cited in Easton 2004: 31).

Journalism is typically defined as the collecting, writing, and editing of news and information for media, such as newspapers, television, websites, and the like. Local reporters cover stories of local community interest such as fires, sports events, and other local stories. National reporters, on the other hand, cover stories of broader national interest, such as presidential campaigns and international events. Freedom of the press in democratic countries encourages the exchange of ideas freely through the media, while in government-controlled societies, the media are expected to present mainly news that supports the philosophy and policies of the government. Developments in technology are shrinking audiences for traditional journalistic media (newspapers and broadcast television). Today, many (if not most) people use the internet for journalistic purposes. Advertisers also have been shifting their spending from mass media to niche media. Most newspapers and television outlets now have online news sites. ABC News, for instance, can be viewed on cable television or on a cellular telephone (among other media).

So, what role should journalism play today? Controversy over the role of journalism is best represented by the debate between Walter Lippman and John Dewey in the 1920s. Lippman saw journalism as a mediator between politicians or institutions and the public. Reporters, he thought, were supposed to explain, sum up, and criticize what the politicians do, or what is decided within society's institutions. Dewey saw journalism as vastly different, since, in his view, the public does not need mediators. The goal of journalism is, rather, to engage the public and politicians in dialogue and debate.

If one of the roles of journalism is, for example, to investigate the secret affairs of influential people and institutions, journalism can be said to involve moral or ethical dimensions. For that reason, reporters are expected to follow a strict code of conduct, such as using multiple sources, declining gifts from interviewees, and avoiding conflict-of-interest situations. Another expectation is encapsulated in the so-called *harm limitation principle*, from the Code of the Society of Professional Journalists: 'Show compassion for those who may be affected adversely by news coverage,' and 'Balance a criminal suspect's fair trial rights with the public's right to be informed.' Gonzo journalism, however, suspends many of the tenets of this code of conduct. Traced back to Hunter S. Thompson (author of and main character in *Fear and Loathing in Las Vegas*), this constitutes a style of journalism that deliberately blurs the distinction between fact and fiction. Gonzo stories also typically involve the reporter himself/herself as the main character: 'Unlike Tom Wolfe or Gay Talese, I almost never try to reconstruct a story; they're both much better reporters than I am, but then, I don't think of myself as a reporter,' Thompson once said (cited in Thompson 2009: 57).

Codes of conduct are also balanced with a more concrete goal of journalism, hinted at in (2) above; namely, to sell newspapers, TV ads, internet banners, and so on – in other words, to make money. Codes of conduct and the need to earn money are often in conflict, as seen in extreme cases of paparazzi journalism. The somewhat disparate goals of being society's watchdog and earning money may also be in conflict. There have been some concerns in recent years about the fact that reporters no longer investigate complex political issues because the public is not interested in them and that politicians deliberately obfuscate their decisions in order to avoid difficult press questions. All this seems to support Lippman's view of journalism. On the other hand, in Denmark, a best-selling novel written by an ex-reporter led to the reopening of a criminal case from the eighties, in part because of the public interest in best-selling novels, but also because of the political pressure that ensued from the ex-reporter's treatment of the case.

The many dilemmas of modern reporters are illustrated by quotes such as the following: 'Trying to be a first-rate reporter on the average American newspaper is like trying to play Bach's "St Matthew's Passion" on a ukulele' (anonymous). On the other hand, the value of a free press in society cannot be underestimated. To honour outstanding achievements in journalism that meet the goal of journalism and satisfy the code of conduct, the Pulitzer Prize, named after Joseph Pulitzer, is awarded each April. The first prize was announced in 1917. In 2007, the prize in the category for investigative journalism was given to Brett Blackledge of *The Birmingham News* 'for his exposure of cronyism and corruption in the state's two-year college system, resulting in the dismissal of the chancellor and other corrective action' (Pulitzer Prize website 2011). The long list of Pulitzer Prize winners informs us that journalism can make the world a better place if it takes seriously its obligation to investigate people and institutions. It is for this reason that the story of the lonesome reporter has become a modern legend, as evidenced by the Hollywood movies cited above.

Anders Søgaard

Bibliography

Burman, Tony. Thoughts on Journalism. Quoted in *Canadian Association of Journalists Newsletter*, May 2006, 2–3.

Carey, James. *Communication as Culture*. Boston: Unwin Hyman, 1989.

Dewey, John. *The Public and Its Problems*. New York: Holt, 1927.

Graham, Phil. 1998. Quoted in Eric B. Easton, *Who Owns the 'First Rough Draft of History'? Reconsidering Copyright in News*. Paper 134. Berkeley: Electronic Press, 2004.

Lippmann, Walter. *Public Opinion*. New York: Harcourt, Brace, 1922.

Marder, Murrey. 1998: This Is Watchdog Journalism. http://www.nieman.harvard.edu/reportsitem.aspx?id=100536 (accessed 10 March 2010).

Pulitzer Prize. Investigative Reporting. http://www.pulitzer.org/bycat/Investigative-Reporting (accessed March 2010).

Thompson, Anita S. *Ancient Gonzo Wisdom: Interviews with Humter S. Thompson.* New York: Da Capo Press, 2009.

K

KATZ, ELIHU (b. 1926)

[See also: *Audience Research; Lazarsfeld, Paul; Media Effects; Uses and Gratifications Theory*]

Elihu Katz is a sociologist whose main research interest is the nature of human communication and the role of media in human life. Throughout his career, Katz made significant contributions to the field of media research through his numerous and widely respected theories. He also established novel methodological models for conducting media effects research and advanced audience research. For his accomplishments, he was appointed Distinguished Trustee Professor of Communication at the University of Pennsylvania's Annenberg School of Communication – a position he has held since 1992 – and was elected a member of the American Academy of Arts and Sciences. He is also the former director of the Israel Institute of Applied Social Research and is an Emeritus Professor within the Department of Sociology and Anthropology at the Hebrew University of Jerusalem.

During the 1940s and 1950s, social psychology and sociology were heavily involved in mass communications research. In 1955, Katz's first book, written with his Columbia University mentor Paul Lazarsfeld, and entitled *Personal Influence: The Part Played by People in the Flow of Mass Communications*, was published. The work claimed that the social psychology of the group accounts for the diffusion of media effects, and carefully examined the relationship between interpersonal communication and mass communication. Despite the fact that mass communication has become a field in its own right since then, Katz has routinely drawn upon social psychology and sociology to analyse its processes and effects.

Some of Katz's subsequent books, including *Medical Innovation: A Diffusion Study* (1966) and *The Politics of Community Conflict: The Fluoridation Decision* (1969), co-authored with James Coleman and Herbert Menzel, and Robert Crain and Donald Rosenthal respectively, also focus on the relation between mass and interpersonal communication, but concentrate on specific events (for example, the dissemination of medical innovations and fluoride use). Katz explores how mass media processes are anchored in their various contexts (political, social, and psychological) yet still allow for the manoeuvrability of the 'active audience.' His works generally reflect French psychologist Gabriel Tardé's view of the public sphere as consisting of interactions among mass media (institutional contexts), public opinion (democratic processes), and conversation (interpersonal networks).

In the 1960s, Katz's research focus shifted to the acculturation of immigrants in Israel. Later in the decade, after founding the Hebrew University's Communications Institute in Jerusalem, he accepted the Israeli government's request to lead the task force responsible for introducing television broadcasting. Katz subsequently worked with E.C. Wedell to introduce broadcasting in developing countries and collaborated with a team of scholars to assess the impact of television on Israeli culture and communication.

In 1993, Katz's book, co-authored with Tamar Liebes, *The Export of Meaning: Cross-Cultural Readings of 'Dallas,'* integrated his work on uses and gratifications theory with that on social networks and diffusion, examining the underlying social structures associated with television. He links these to audience reception in different cultures and explores the effects of cultural imperialism and how it induces a 're-negotiation' of *Dallas*'s (the American TV soap opera) themes. *The Export of Meaning* is also important for using a convergent approach to audience research, since it integrates different methods (qualitative versus quantitative, textual analysis), disciplines (linguistics, sociology, and mass communications), and communication components (audience, text, context) in order to draw a portrait of the 'active viewer.' To this day, Katz and Liebes's work on *Dallas* is one of only a handful of studies that have examined the relationship between cultural context, media imperialism, and audience reception.

Alexandra Birk-Urovitz and Elizabeth Birk-Urovitz

Bibliography

Katz, Elihu, and Tamar Liebes. *The Export of Meaning: Cross-Cultural Readings of 'Dallas.'* Cambridge: Polity, 1993.
Katz, Elihu, and Yael Warshel, eds. *Election Studies: What's Their Use?* Boulder, CO: Westview Press, 2000.
Elihu, Katz, et al., eds. *Canonic Texts in Media Research: Are There Any? Should There Be? How About These?* New York: Polity Press, 2002.
Livingstone, Sonia. The Work of Elihu Katz: Conceptualizing Media Effects in Context. In *International Media Research: A Critical Survey*, ed. J. Corner, P. Schlesinger, and R. Silverstone, 18-47. London: Routledge, 1997.

KINESICS

[See also: *Non-Verbal Communication; Proxemics*]

Kinesics is the scientific study of the body movements involved in communication, especially as they accompany speech. These include gestures, facial expressions, eye contact, and posture. Kinesic communication is studied both as a complementary and as a substitutive mode to verbal (vocal) language. The founder of the discipline was the American anthropologist Ray L. Birdwhistell (1918–94). Influenced by his teacher, the anthropologist Margaret Mead (1901–78), and the research of David Efron (1941), Birdwhistell started analysing the way people interacted by watching films in the late 1940s, documenting how people communicated information through eye movements, facial expressions, postures, and other bodily schemas. His first book on his findings, *Introduction to Kinesics*, came out in 1952. In a series of subsequent studies (1955, 1960, 1961, 1963, 1974, 1979), Birdwhistell established and institutionalized kinesics within anthropology. His method of analysing non-verbal behaviour was based on American structural linguistics: 'The first premise in developing a notational system for body language is to assume that all movements of the body have meaning. None are accidental' (Birdwhistell 1970: 157). In analogy with the concept of *phoneme*, he designated such movements *kinemes*, which are defined as body schemas that 'may be used interchangeably without affecting social meaning' (Knapp 1978: 94–5) and thus 'can be construed as having a definite organization or structure, just as language is understood in terms of its grammar' (Duncan and Fiske 1977: xi).

Birdwhistell divided the study of kinesic communication into four main methodological procedures:

(1) *prekinesics*, the actual description the relevant movements, called *kines* (in analogy with *phones*), which constitute the raw data of kinesic research, includ-

ing movements of the head, face, trunk, shoulder, hands, legs, feet, and neck;

(2) *microkinesics*, the organization of the kines into kinemes and their variants, called *allokines* (in analogy with *allophones*);

(3) *social kinesics*, the analysis of the social meanings of each kineme;

(4) *parakinesics*, the analysis of qualifiers such as intensity, range, velocity of movement associated with the kinemes.

Kinesics has been applied to the study of various communicative situations, from lying to the ordinary uses of gesture in daily interactions. Discoveries in psychology and especially the neurosciences indicate that non-verbal communication is processed in different parts of the brain than verbal communication. The latter is processed primarily in the cerebral cortex, a highly evolved area that is unique to the human species. In contrast, non-verbal cues are processed in lower areas such as the limbic system, connecting us to our animal heritage. They are thus laden with emotional meaning.

Marcel Danesi

Bibliography

Birdwhistell, Ray L. *Introduction to Kinesics*. Louisville: University of Ann Arbor, 1952.

– Background to Kinesics. *ETC* 13 (1955): 10–18.

– Kinesics and Communication. In *Explorations in Communication*, ed. E. Carpenter and M. McLuhan, 54–64. New York: Beacon, 1960.

– Paralanguage 25 Years after Sapir. In *Communication in Face to Face Interaction*, ed. J. Laver and S. Hutcheson, 82–100. Harmondsworth: Penguin, 1961.

– The Kinesic Level in the Investigation of the Emotions. In *Symposium on Expressions of the Emotions in Man*, ed. P. Knapp, 123–39. New York: International University Press, 1963.

– *Kinesics and Context*. Philadelphia: University of Pennsylvania Press, 1970.

– The Language of the Body. In *Human Communication*, ed. A. Silverstein, 203–11. Hillsdale, NJ: Erlbaum, 1974.

– Kinesics. In *International Encyclopedia of the Social Sciences*, vol. 8: 379–85. New York: Macmillan, 1979.

Duncan, Starkey. Nonbverbal Communication. *Psychological Bulletin* 72 (1969): 118–37.

Duncan, Starkey, and Donald W. Fiske. *Face-to-Face Interaction*. Hillsdale, NJ: Erlbaum, 1977.

Efron, David. *Gesture, Race, and Culture*. The Hague: Mouton, 1941.

Ekman, Paul. *Telling Lies*. New York: Norton, 1985.

– *Emotions Revealed*. New York: Holt, 2003.

Key, Mary Ritchie. *Paralanguage and Kinesics*. Metuchen, NJ: Scarecrow, 1975.

Knapp, Mark L. *Nonverbal Communication in Human Interaction*. New York: Holt, 1978.

Raffler-Engel, Walburga von, ed. *Aspects of Nonverbal Communication*. Lisse: Swets, 1980.

L

LACAN, JACQUES (1901–81)

[See also: *Popular Culture; Psychoanalysis; Semiotics*]

Jacques Lacan was a French psychoanalyst whose theories on language and the unconscious have been adopted broadly within various subfields of media, literary, and pop culture studies. Lacan was born in Paris and attended the Jesuit College Stanislas. But by the mid-1920s he became disillusioned with religion, entering medical school and specializing in psychiatry in 1926 at the Sainte-Anne Hospital in Paris. His interests broadened to encompass the role of language and the unconscious mind in art and human interaction. Throughout his career he remained a fervent Freudian, holding seminars on the structure of the unconscious that were open to the public throughout the 1950s. From these seminars and the writings connected to them came the notions that have become highly admired among some scholars, especially the one that everything we do, even in art, is guided by the 'language of the unconscious mind,' which itself mirrors actual language. Using the Freudian notions of id, ego, and super-ego, he mapped linguistic structures to the origin and formation of these three psychic levels. Thus, language that is emotional and evocative is id-based, whereas language that is self-serving is ego-based; finally, language that is conventional and formulaic is super-ego-based. The interesting thing in this Lacanian framework is that the unconscious part of the mind already possesses these three levels as if they were built into the very structure of the brain. In other words, language and the unconscious mirror each other, being replicas of a deep psychic force that seeks to understand itself. This comes out in psychotherapy as it does in conversation and, more broadly, in human cultural activities. This is why we 'understand' all these. We already possess the 'understanding structures' inside of us.

These three dimensions correspond to three orders of cognition. First, there is the imaginary, which is the area through which the ego 'navigates' to make sense of the world. This distorts perceptions of others since it is inward-focused. It is, for Lacan, part of human biology. Essentially, we imagine who we are by a kind of internal imaginary instinct. Second, there is the symbolic, which is where awareness of others emerges and interacts or interferes with the imaginary in the process of understanding the world. This is part of cultural rearing. Finally, the 'real' is the sense we have of the external world, a sense that is 'cut through' by the symbolic, as Lacan put it. It is what is outside language.

Despite the abstruse views that Lacan put forward in his writings, he nonetheless has attracted a significant following of scholars. His legacy rests on the notion that language, cognition, and culture are a product of the three-level interaction between the imaginary, the symbolic, and the real.

Marcel Danesi

Bibliography

Lacan, Jacques. *The Language of the Self: The Function of Language in Psychoanalysis.* Baltimore: Johns Hopkins University Press, 1968.
– *Television: A Challenge to the Psychoanalytic Establishment.* New York: Norton, 1990.
– *Écrits: A Selection.* New York: Norton, 2002.

LAKOFF, GEORGE (b. 1941)

[See also: *Cognitive Language Studies; Conceptual Metaphor Theory; Generativism*]

American linguist George Lakoff is the leading figure in cognitive linguistics, an approach to language study that has come forward since the early 1980s to compete against the generativist model of language, associated with Noam Chomsky. Lakoff taught linguistics at UCLA at Berkeley for most of his career. He is now retired. In recent years, he has garnered international attention with his writings in the realm of politics and the metaphorical structure of political discourse. Interestingly, Lakoff started off his career as a student of generativism under Chomsky. In most of its versions, generativism holds that syntax (sentence structure) is independent of meaning. Lakoff and Chomsky engaged in a debate that became rather fierce in the 1980s and 1990s, but which has subsided since the 2000s, given that Lakoff's ideas have finally penetrated the mainstream with generativism gradually receding.

Of particular importance to linguistics is Lakoff's notion of *conceptual metaphor*, which he developed initially with philosopher Mark Johnson in their now-classic 1980 book *Metaphors We Live By*. Consider the metaphorical statement 'That person is a snake.' In it there are two referents:

(1) 'that person,' called the *topic*; and (2) 'a snake,' termed the *vehicle*. The linkage of the two creates a new form of meaning, called the *ground*, that is much more than the simple sum of the meanings of the two referents. It engenders a perspective of personality that literal language cannot possibly convey – a perspective that is sensory and based on cultural experience of snakes as dangerous reptiles. The reason why we speak this way, claims Lakoff, is because we unconsciously perceive qualities in one domain (the animal kingdom) as coexistent in another domain (human personality). The brain 'blends' these two domains into what Lakoff and Johnson called a 'conceptual metaphor,' namely 'humans are animals.' Utterances of this type – 'John is a gorilla,' 'Mary is a snail,' and so on – are not, therefore, isolated examples of poetic fancy. Rather, they are specific *linguistic metaphors* manifesting the unconscious conceptual metaphor.

Lakoff and Johnson termed each of the two domains the *target domain* (human personality) and the *source domain* (animals). Conceptual metaphors form the basis of how we grasp abstractions. Take, for example, linguistic metaphors such as the ones below:

(1) Your ideas are *circular*, leading us nowhere.
(2) I never saw the *point* of that idea.
(3) Those are *central* to the entire discussion.
(4) Our ideas are *diametrically* opposite.

The target domain in these linguistic metaphors is 'ideas,' and the source domain is 'geometrical figures/relations.' The conceptual metaphor is, therefore: *ideas are geometrical figures/relations*. The origin of this conceptual metaphor is traceable in all likelihood to the tradition of using geometry in mathematics and education to generate ideas and to train the mind to think logically. Such conceptual metaphors permeate everyday language. Lakoff and Johnson trace their cognitive source to *im-*

age schemas – mental outlines or images that are produced by our sensory experiences of locations, movements, shapes, substances, and so forth, as well as our experiences of social events in general. They are 'thought mediators' that allow us to articulate our sensations and experiences with words in systematic ways.

With Rafaél Núñez (Lakoff and Núñez 2000), Lakoff has shown how blending occurs in mathematics, constituting the source of mathematical ideas. At the foundation of mathematical thought are four different yet related image schemas that underlie the blended mathematical concepts: object collection, object construction, measurement with sticks, and movement along a path. These common human activities and experiences are the basis of our arithmetical concepts. The theory is controversial among mathematicians and philosophers, but Lakoff has never backed down, claiming that the same cognitive processes involved in language are also involved in mathematics. Whether verifiable or not, his idea provides a fertile intellectual ground for connecting different disciplines in systematic and fruitful ways.

Marcel Danesi

Bibliography

Lakoff, George. *Women, Fire, and Dangerous Things.* Chicago: University of Chicago Press, 1987.

– *The Political Mind: Why You Can't Understand 21st-Century American Politics with an 18th-Century Brain.* New York: Viking, 2008.

Lakoff, George, and Mark Johnson. *Metaphors We Live By.* Chicago: University of Chicago Press, 1980.

– *Philosophy in the Flesh: The Embodied Mind and Its Challenge to Western Thought.* New York: Basic, 1999.

Lakoff, George, and Rafaél Núñez. *Where Mathematics Comes From: How the Embodied Mind Brings Mathematics into Being.* New York: Basic, 2000.

LANGUAGE AND THE MEDIA

[See also: *Chomsky, Noam; Communication; Jakobson's Model of Communication; Linguistics; Media Studies; Medium*]

Language is the primary means through which humans communicate, encode knowledge, pass it on to subsequent generations, investigate reality, and entertain themselves. Language constitutes an overarching knowledge and memory system. The ancient Greeks characterized language as part of *lógos*, meaning both word and thought, implying that the two are inseparable.

All languages serve humans in similar ways – they allow people to classify the things in their world (simply by naming them), and thus to understand them as abstractions. To accomplish this basic task languages have five basic things in common: (1) a system of distinctive sounds and (typically) symbol signs (pictographs, alphabet characters, etc.); (2) meaning-bearing forms known as words; (3) grammatical structure (a way of combining words to make messages); (4) rules and protocols for using language for various functions; and (5) resources for making new linguistic structures (words, phrases, etc.).

Linguists differentiate between *language* and *speech*. The former is a mental sign system, consisting of principles for making, understanding, and using words, phrases, and so forth. Speech, on the other hand, is the physical use of language to create and transmit actual messages. Speech can be vocal, as in spoken communication, or nonvocal, as in writing or gesturing. No particular effort is required in infancy to learn how to speak and, ultimately, to develop full-blown language. By simply being in regular contact with speakers of a language, children gradually learn whatever language they are exposed to. By the age of five or six, they show an extraordinary control of their native language (or languages). This has led some linguists, notably Noam Chomsky (b. 1928), to argue that our brain is equipped at birth to acquire language on the basis of speech samples. He calls the 'equipment' a 'universal grammar' (UG), defining it as a set of innate principles that inform, or unconsciously guide, each child in acquiring the particular grammar of a language from the bits and pieces of that language to which she or he is exposed.

The idea of an innate predisposition towards language is not a modern one. It goes back to the ideas of the Greek philosopher Plato (ca 427–347 BCE), who asked: How it is that children, whose contacts with the world are brief and limited, are able to know as much as they do know? Plato's answer to his own question was that much of what we know is innate. Knowledge of a particular language, therefore, is a matter of setting in motion the innate mechanisms and allowing them to do their work of language creation. Plato's theory is called the 'poverty of stimulus' theory, since it claims that we would otherwise have to explain why children develop full language on the basis of simple exposure to fragments of it in a very short time. The opposing idea that the mind is an empty slate is illogical. But, as many linguists have countered, is it not also possible that children come endowed with a creative capacity to process incoming information by trial and error, extrapolating from it whatever they need, changing their guesses only when corrected (by others or by the force of experience). The Russian psychologist Lev S. Vygotsky (1962) called children 'little poets' because he noticed that they used the resources of the language to which they are exposed to make inferences about the world and to construct verbal forms that are quite similar to those created by poets.

Studying the relationship between language and the media is a growing field of linguistics. The media have a clear effect on language and verbal communication generally. Take the word *cool* as an example. This word came out of early jazz culture, referring to a type of musical jazz style.

In the mid-1950s it was appropriated by the media to describe a lifestyle trend associated with adolescence. It meant (and continues to mean) knowing how to look, walk, and talk in socially attractive and youthful ways. It was the media, thus, that brought this word (with that meaning) into common usage (even if traces of this meaning go back further in time). This is not an isolated example. The words, phrases, and mannerisms initiating in the media that gain general currency were called part of *pop language* by journalist Leslie Savan in 2005. Pop language allows people to 'talk the talk.' Pop language actually traces its source to the American showman P.T. Barnum (1810–91). To promote his attractions, Barnum relied on colourful language, using hyperbole to create interest in his shows and exhibits. Barnum introduced expressions such as the following into colloquial American English:

'Don't miss this once-in-a-lifetime opportunity!'
'Limited edition at an unbelievably low price!'
'All items must go!'
'Not to be missed!'

The style and vocabulary used in early pulp fiction magazines and novels were similarly part of an emerging pop language style. With the rise and spread of the media, pop language style has become more and more prevalent. Savan notes that people from all walks of life, from adolescents to doctors and lawyers, are using a media-sitcom conversational style, which appears to carry with it a built-in applause or laugh sign. Expressions such as 'That is so last year,' 'Don't go there,' 'Get a life,' 'I hate it when that happens,' 'It doesn't get any better than this,' all come from television sitcoms or popular movies. Pop language, claims Savan, is light, self-conscious, and highly ironic, replete with put-downs and exaggerated inflections. Savan compares the 1953 Disney cartoon *Peter Pan* with the

2002 sequel *Return to Never Land* and points out how the former film was free of pop and trendy phrases. The sequel, however, is replete with them, including such mannerisms as 'In your dreams, Hook,' 'Put a cork in it,' 'Tell me about it,' 'You've got that right,' and 'Don't even think about it.'

Savan's point seems to be that in the past, the primary conduits of such language were great writers. Shakespeare, for instance, brought into common usage such slang terms as *hubbub*, *to bump*, and *to dwindle*. But since the advent of media culture, the sources of pop language are the media, not great writers. Although there seems to be an elitist subtext to Savan's overall assessment of pop language, her main point that the media are powerful conduits of linguistic innovation is well-taken. *Animal House* (1978) introduced *wimp*, a commonly used term for someone who is fearful or has no courage, and *brew*, which means getting a beer; *Clueless* (1995) introduced *As if*, an exclamation of disbelief, and *whatever* to convey disinterest in what another person is saying; and *Mean Girls* (2004) introduced *plastic*, meaning fake girls who look like Barbie dolls, and *fetch*, which is an abbreviation of 'fetching' to describe something cool and trendy.

As the platform for pop language trends shifts to cyberspace, or at least converges with it, online verbal trends are now mirroring and guiding language evolution across the globe. In sum, the synergy between language change and the mass media is undeniable. In addition to its study in the fledgling branch called media linguistics, this synergy is becoming more and more a target of interest within various branches of linguistics (from psycholinguistics to sociolinguistics).

Marcel Danesi

Bibliography

Chomsky, Noam. *Syntactic Structures.* The Hague: Mouton, 1957.

– *On Nature and Language.* Cambridge: Cambridge University Press, 2002.

Crystal, David. *Language and the Internet.* 2nd ed. Cambridge: Cambridge University Press, 2006.

Savan, Leslie. *Slam Dunks and No-Brainers: Language in Your Life, the Media, Business, Politics, and, Like, Whatever.* New York: Alfred A. Knopf, 2005.

Vygotsky, Lev S. *Thought and Language.* Cambridge, MA: MIT Press, 1962.

LAZARSFELD, PAUL (1901–76)

[See also: *Hypodermic Needle Theory; Media Effects; Two-Step Flow Theory*]

Paul Felix Lazarsfeld was an influential sociologist who pioneered various methodologies based on quantitative analysis that came to be used to conduct research in the areas of mass communication, public opinion, voting behaviour, and popular culture. Born on 13 February 1901 in Vienna, Austria, Lazarsfeld graduated in 1924 with a doctoral degree in mathematics from the University of Vienna. There, he remained as a mathematics instructor for the next five years. In 1929, he took on an instructorship in social psychology at the Psychological Institute of the University of Vienna and eventually served as the director of its Division of Applied Psychology. In Vienna, Lazarsfeld turned his attention to analysing the unemployment rate in a nearby town, Marienthal. In 1933, he published his findings in *Marienthal: The Sociography of an Unemployed Community*. The work was immediately considered to be groundbreaking for its use of quantitative analysis. That same year, Lazarsfeld was offered a grant from the Rockefeller Foundation in the United States. Four years after arriving, he became the director of the foundation's Office of Radio Research and in 1940 became the director of the Columbia Bureau of Applied Social Research.

Lazarsfeld became particularly famous for his analysis of voting behaviour, based on two studies of presidential elections in the United States in Erie County, Ohio, in 1940 and Elmira, New York, in 1948. He discovered that people tended to vote for the party they (or their immediate community) would have voted for traditionally, no matter how the candidates were portrayed in the media. A change in voting pattern would occur only if leaders in a community brought forward conflicting opinions. This led Lazarsfeld to develop his influential model of media, known as the 'two-step flow of information.' The model claims that the information relayed by the media reaches its audience in two stages: (1) the community leaders first interpret the information from the media directly and then (2) pass it on to community members. The notion of 'personal influence' was coined as a result of this transitional step from the media's communication of a message to the audience's response. The model helped explain how the mass media influence an audience's decisions and could be used to help shape future outcomes.

In 1950, Lazarsfeld became chair of Columbia University's sociology department, and thirteen years later he was named Quetelet Professor of Social Science, eventually moving to the University of Pittsburgh until his death in 1976. Among his many influential works, *The People's Choice: How a Voter Makes Up His Mind in a Presidential Campaign* (with Bernard Berelson and Hazel Gaudet; 1944) and *Personal Influence: The Part Played by People in the Flow of Mass Communications* (1955; with Elihu Katz) have become classics in the field and are still widely referenced.

Mariana Bockarova

Bibliography

Jerabek, Hynek. Paul Lazarsfeld – The Founder of Modern Empirical Sociology: A Research Biography. *International Journal of Public Opinion Research* 13 (2001): 229–44.

Lazarsfeld, Paul F., and Elihu Katz. *Personal Influence: The Part Played by People in the Flow of Mass Communications*. Glencoe, IL: Free Press, 1955.

Lazarsfeld, Paul F., Bernard Berelson, and Hazel Gaudet. *The People's Choice*. New York: Columbia University Press, 1950.

LÉVI-STRAUSS, CLAUDE
(1908–2009)

[See also: *Myth; Structuralism*]

Claude Lévi-Strauss was a Belgian-born French anthropologist and is considered the founder of structuralism in anthropology. He expanded the basic notion of opposition within structuralism, which posits that signs have value only in relation to other signs. The relation can be binary, as are phonemic oppositions (*cat* vs *rat*); it can be four-part, as in some semantic distinctions (*rich-not rich-poor-not poor*); it can be 'graduated,' since in between an opposition such as *night* vs *day*, there are gradations (*morning, noon, afternoon, evening*); or it can be cohesive (set-based) as Lévi-Strauss argued. These are not mutually exclusive. The specific type of opposition that applies to a situation depends on what system (language, kinship, etc.) or subsystem (phonemic, semantic, etc.) is involved. In some systems, pairs of oppositions seem to cohere into sets forming recognizable units. Lévi-Strauss found that the elementary unit of kinship is made up of a set of four oppositions: *brother* vs *sister*, *husband* vs *wife*, *father* vs *son*, and *mother's brother* vs *sister's son*. He went on to suggest that similar sets characterized other cultural systems and, thus, that their study would provide key insights into the fundamental structure of human societies.

Crucial to Lévi-Strauss's anthropology is the Saussurean notion of *value* (*valeur*). Rather than carrying intrinsic meaning, Saussure argued that signs had *valeur* in differential relation to other signs. He called this *différence*. It is through *différence* that the meaning of something is determined. To understand the value of an American dollar, for instance, one must know that the dollar can be exchanged for a certain quantity of various coins – for example, four quarters, ten dimes, and so forth. Similarly, a mythic concept such as 'hero' has *valeur* because it can be exchanged with, say, the concept of 'villain' or with another concept such as 'father' in an associative chain of reasoning. It can also be compared to other concepts, such as 'good,' which has the same *valeur*.

Overall, Lévi-Strauss's contribution to anthropology and various other disciplines was leaving behind the instinctual quest to find what he often called 'unsuspected harmonies' across the spectrum of human culture. His proposal was to look for pairs of opposites common to all human societies. His fieldwork among Amerindian tribes in the 1930s impressed upon him that those harmonies were present in myths (Lévi-Strauss 1978). The purpose of a myth, he suggested, was to provide a logical theory that could explain inherent opposites or contradictions. The human brain, he thought, structured cognition in terms of binary opposites. Throughout cultures, humans have attempted to resolve the tension between them through myth making.

One of these attempts was to resolve the tension between raw and cooked food, which he saw as a primordial opposition between nature and culture (Lévi-Strauss 1964). Cooked food allows humans to leave the world of nature behind and to focus on their own adaptations. Culture emerges the instant that cooked food does. Another primordial opposition is found in the difference he made between the 'savage mind' and the mind of the 'thinker' (Lévi-Strauss 1962). The former has a 'tinkler' approach to the world, working with the hands to extract from it what is necessary for survival. The thinker is an engineer who has a more abstract approach to solving practical problems of existence. The engineer invents tools and materials that transcend the limitations imposed on humans by the immediate environment. The tinkler and the engineer face similar problems of survival,

but they solve them in dissimilar ways. The tinkler's mind is spontaneous, the engineer's methodical.

Other primordial oppositions discussed by Lévi-Strauss in various works are 'I versus we' and 'language versus word.' In kinship patterns among the Amerindian societies, Lévi-Strauss found that the Western ideal of individual self-expression was not valued at all. He concluded, therefore, that it was simply part of Western tradition. This ideal favours the 'I.' In the tribes he visited the 'we' or communal approach to life was instead the dominant one. This experience showed him that what we often call 'common sense' is really nothing more than 'communal sense.' From Ferdinand de Saussure (1916), the founder of modern linguistics, he took the distinction between *langue*, or the system of language itself, and *parole*, or the use of words for specific purposes. Lévi-Strauss extended this distinction to other codes. Thus, for instance, in music there is a *langue* that inheres in the harmonic, rhythmic, and various other possibilities that it makes available to composers and performers. When someone plays an actual piece of piano music, on the other hand, then the performer is engaging in *parole*, using *langue* for a specific reason.

Although today anthropology, linguistics, and semiotics are not bound to opposition theory as Lévi-Strauss envisioned it, these disciplines have nevertheless been influenced by it. Lévi-Strauss's influence is still conspicuous.

Marcel Danesi

Bibliography

Lévi-Strauss, Claude. *Structural Anthropology.* New York: Basic, 1958.
– *La pensée sauvage.* Paris: Plon, 1962.
– *The Raw and the Cooked.* London: Cape, 1964.
– *Myth and Meaning: Cracking the Code of Culture.* Toronto: University of Toronto Press, 1978.
Saussure, Ferdinand de. *Cours de linguistique générale.* Paris: Payot, 1916.

LINGUISTICS

[See also: *Chomsky, Noam; Communication and Media; Conceptual Metaphor Theory; Discourse; Language and the Media; Media Studies*]

The origins and nature of language have fascinated humans since the dawn of civilization. The motivation for establishing a 'science of language,' however, can be traced only as far back as 1786, when the English scholar Sir William Jones (1746–94) suggested that Sanskrit, Persian, Greek, and Latin sprang from the same linguistic source and thus belonged to the same 'language family.' Shortly thereafter, the systematic study of languages started in earnest, leading in the subsequent century to the emergence of *linguistics* as a science of language.

One of the first attempts to describe a language scientifically occurred in the fifth century BCE, when the Indian scholar Panini compiled a grammar of the Sanskrit language. Grammars are the equivalents of scientific theories in physics or chemistry. They show how words are constructed from smaller structures or units and how they cohere into the construction of sentences and larger forms (such as texts and discourses). Grammar is a theoretical construct. The Greek philosopher Aristotle (384–22 BCE) put forward the first division of sentences into *subject* and *predicate* – a division that has remained fundamental to this day. The Greek scholar Dionysius Thrax, who lived between 170 and 90 BCE, then showed how the parts of speech relate to each other in the formation of sentences. He identified *nouns, verbs, articles, pronouns, prepositions, conjunctions, adverbs,* and *participles* as the main parts. Thrax's grammar was adopted and elaborated by Roman grammarian Priscian, who lived in the sixth century CE.

In the seventeenth and eighteenth centuries, the first surveys of languages were attempted, in order to determine which features of grammar were universal and which were specific to various languages.

In the latter century, a group of French scholars, known as the Port Royal Circle, put forward the idea of a 'universal' grammar, showing how certain sentences are derivatives of others, and thus part of the brain's innate grammar. Operating in the mind, they claimed, was a set of principles of sentence formation that speakers used unconsciously. The linguist Noam Chomsky has always acknowledged his debt to the Port Royal grammarians, admitting that it was strikingly similar to his 1957 framework for describing linguistic competence.

The German scholar Wilhelm von Humboldt (1767–1835) also espoused a universalist view of language, but his take on the issue was quite different from that taken by the Port Royal grammarians and later by Chomsky. He viewed the particular sentence structure of the language spoken, which he called the *innere Sprachform* (internal structure), as conditioning how people came to view reality. In effect, each language has a different *innere Sprachform* that conditions how people view the world. Von Humboldt's work was, thus, the precursor of a view of language known as 'linguistic relativity,' which nonetheless has roots in the ancient Greek philosophy of *correspondence* whereby words and meanings are seen to mirror each other. Humboldt (1836 [1988]: 43) put it as follows:

> The central fact of language is that speakers can make infinite use of the finite resources provided by their language. Though the capacity for language is universal, the individuality of each language is a property of the people who speak it. Every language has its *innere Sprachform*, or internal structure, which determines its outer form and which is a reflection of its speakers' minds. The language and the thought of a people are thus inseparable.

It was the Swiss philologist Ferdinand de Saussure (1857–1913) who put the finishing touches on the blueprint for the emerging science of language by proposing that the new science should focus on *langue* ('language'), the system of rules that members of a speech community recognize as their 'language,' rather than on *parole* ('word'), or the ability to use the rules in conversations, writing, and so forth (Saussure 1916). Basic to Saussure's plan for the scientific study of *langue* was the notion of *différence* ('difference, opposition'). This is the view that the structures of a language (such as its single words) do not take on meaning and function in isolation but rather in differential relation to each other. For example, the linguist determines the meaning and grammatical function of the word *red* by opposing it to a word such as *bed*. This shows, among other things, that the initial consonants /r/ and /b/ are important in English for establishing the meaning of both words. These are designated *phonemes*. From such *différences* we can see, one or two differential features at a time, what makes the word *red* unique in English, not just phonemically but also at other levels of language, allowing us to pinpoint what *red* means by virtue of how it is different from other words.

Saussure's approach came to be known as *structuralism*. In Europe, it was adopted and elaborated by a number of linguists who congregated in the Czech city of Prague, coming to be known as the Prague Circle in 1920. In America, the structuralist approach was adopted in the early twentieth century by the anthropologist Franz Boas and his student Edward Sapir. However, unlike Saussure, Boas and Sapir did not see the goal of linguistics as a study of *langue*, but rather as the description of how a speech community uses a language for its specific cognitive, social, and cultural purposes.

The first major rupture from the structuralist tradition came in 1957, when Chomsky argued that any truly scientific understanding of language could never be developed from a piecemeal description of sounds, word forms, and so on, through simple differential techniques. Like the Port Royal grammarians, Chomsky argued that

a true theory of language would have to explain, for instance, why all languages seem to reveal a similar pattern for constructing complex sentences from more simple ones. He thus suggested that all languages are built on the same blueprint, present in the brain at birth, and that individual languages are context-specific derivatives of this blueprint. Since the late 1960s, various arguments have come forward to challenge the Chomskyan paradigm. It has been pointed out, for instance, that abstract rule-making principles do not explain the semantic richness of languages. Moreover, there are other kinds of universals that Chomskyan theory ignores

One major argument against the Chomskyan paradigm is that sentences are not the basic units of language – discourse *texts* are (stretches of speech consisting of logically concatenated sentences). British linguist Michael Halliday (b. 1925), for instance, showed that some parts of speech are 'text-governed' structures, not sentence-based elements (Halliday 1985). Consider, for example, the following stretch of conversation, which has no pronouns in it. Even though it is completely understandable, we nevertheless perceive it as being awkward:

Speaker A: Alex is a great guy.
Speaker B: Yes, Alex is a great guy.
Speaker A: But Alex always likes to talk about Alex.
Speaker B: Yes, Alex does indeed always talk about Alex.

The more appropriate version of the conversation is one in which pronouns are used instead:

Speaker A: Alex is a great guy.
Speaker B: Yes, *he* is.
Speaker A: But *he* always likes to talk about *himself*.
Speaker B: Yes, *he* does indeed always talk about *himself*.

The use of pronouns is 'systemic'; that

is, it connects the various parts of the conversation, linking them logically like a trace device. In effect, the choice of pronouns is hardly due to sentence structure in itself; it is motivated by text structure.

Another approach to language that has emerged to challenge Chomskyan theory started in the early 1980s, and is known as *cognitive linguistics*. This approach focuses on the relation between language, cognition, and culture. The most prominent figure in the movement is the American linguist George Lakoff (b. 1941). In his influential book, *Women, Fire, and Dangerous Things* (1987), Lakoff looked at an interesting property of the Australian language Dyirbal to show the inadequacies of Chomskyan theory and the need for linguistics to focus on the semantic properties of words, rather than on sentence-formation principles. Like other languages, Dyirbal has grammatical gender – each of its nouns must be assigned to one of the available genders. In European languages, the gender of abstract (non-biological) nouns is, arguably, unpredictable from its meaning. For example, the word for 'table' is masculine in German (*der Tisch*), feminine in French (*la table*), and neuter in Greek (*to trapézi*). Dyirbal has four genders, each of which is determined by meaning. One of the four includes all nouns referring to *women*, to *fire*, and to things that are *dangerous* (snakes, stinging nettles, and the like). Clearly, the words and the grammatical categories used in Dyirbal reflect a view of the world that is vastly different from that implicit in the grammars of European languages.

Many ideas originating in linguistics are commonly used in media analysis. One of these is the notion of opposition. Originally this referred to the view that words are kept recognizably distinct by the presence of minimal differences between them. The forms *pin* and *bin* are recognizably distinct word units because the difference between initial /p/ and /b/ cues a difference in meaning. This minimal, or *binary*, difference cue is what keeps the two words perceptibly distinct from each other.

The theory was extended by the Prague School linguists to encompass larger forms and structures of language. Their claim was that many aspects of language are structured in terms of opposites, including semantic ones – *good* vs *evil*, *night* vs *day*, and so on. An opposition often leads to a connected set of derived oppositions. So, for example, in a narrative the *good* characters are opposed to the *evil* ones in terms of derived oppositions such as *us* vs *them*, *right* vs *wrong*, and *truth* vs *falsity*. These manifest themselves in actions, dialogues, plot twists, and the like. Oppositions have been found to occur in all kinds of media portrayals. The *hero* vs *villain* opposition can be seen in adventure comics in the persona of Batman, for example, on the hero side of the opposition, and the Riddler on the villain side (along with other evil characters).

Marcel Danesi

Bibliography

Boas, Franz. *Race, Language, and Culture.* New York: Free Press, 1940.

Chomsky, Noam. *Syntactic Structures.* The Hague: Mouton, 1957.

– *On Nature and Language.* Cambridge: Cambridge University Press, 2002.

Halliday, Michael A.K. *Introduction to Functional Grammar.* London: Arnold, 1985.

Humboldt, Wilhelm von [1836]. *On Language: The Diversity of Human Language Structure and Its Influence on the Mental Development of Mankind.* Trans. P. Heath. Cambridge: Cambridge University Press, 1988.

Sapir, Edward. *Language.* New York: Harcourt, Brace, and World, 1921.

Saussure, Ferdinand de. *Cours de linguistique générale.* Paris: Payot, 1916.

LITERACY

[See also: *Media Literacy; Orality; Writing*]

Literacy is the ability to read and write, or to manipulate symbols in specific knowledge domains such as mathematics (where literacy is called *numeracy*), computers (*computer literacy*), and so on. It also refers to the possession of enough knowledge and skill to function intellectually in a society. This is called *functional literacy*.

Before the fifteenth century and the advent of cheap print technology, most people in Europe were illiterate, never having had the opportunity to learn to read and write. Not only were there few schools, and books scarce and expensive, but literacy was not required to carry out work in farming villages and in the trades of the medieval towns. Most literate people belonged to the nobility, the upper classes, or the clergy. But the printing press changed this. The late Marshall McLuhan (1962, 1964) characterized the new world order brought about by the advent of the printing press as the 'Gutenberg galaxy,' after the European inventor of the printing press, the German printer Johannes Gutenberg. Through cheap books and other materials, the printed word became the chief means for the propagation and recording of knowledge and ideas. And because books could cross national boundaries, the printing press set in motion the globalization of knowledge and science, thus encouraging literacy across the globe and paving the way for such events and movements as the European Renaissance, the Protestant Reformation, and the Enlightenment. With the spread of literacy and with industry becoming a dominant part of economic life during the eighteenth and nineteenth centuries, great numbers of people started migrating to cities. In order to find employment they had to learn how to read instructions and perform other tasks that required literacy. Governments began to value education more, and systems of public schooling cropped up everywhere. By the late 1800s, formal elementary education had become a virtual necessity.

Today, literacy is considered to be the chief means for gaining prestige and economic well-being. In the 1960s, the United States government set up a federal program called Adult Basic Education to provide basic instruction in reading and writing for illiterate or undereducated adults. In 1970, the Office of Education (now the Department of Education) initiated the 'Right to Read' movement in order to improve how literacy is imparted in schools and to encourage private organizations to offer instruction to illiterate adults. Countries across the world have similar literacy programs and legislation. In the 1960s, the People's Republic of China hired 30 million volunteer teachers with the slogan 'You Who Can Read, Teach an Illiterate.' In 1961, Cuba sent many of its teachers to rural areas to instruct illiterate people, increasing the country's literacy rate from 75 to 96 per cent. However, functional illiteracy remains a major problem in developed countries. A 2003 U.S. Department of Education survey discovered that many Americans lacked functional literacy skills – for example, about 15 per cent of Americans aged sixteen and older were unable to find and understand information in short texts. As a consequence, some states now require students to pass standardized reading and writing tests before they graduate from high school.

The world literacy rate has risen since the late nineteenth century. By 2000, 79 per cent of people were literate, although there continues to be a high level of functional illiteracy. Today, there are new forms of literacy that have emerged because of the digital revolution. *Digital* and *media literacy* have entered the common lexicon to characterize this new situation. Literacy is changing, but its basic form has not, since most media texts, digital and otherwise, still require the ability to read and write a language.

Marcel Danesi

Bibliography

Grimond, Joseph. *Literacy*. Oxford: Oxford University Press, 1972.

Jackson, Margaret. *Literacy*. London: David Fulton, 1993.

McLuhan, Marshall. *The Gutenberg Galaxy*. Toronto: University of Toronto Press, 1962.
– *Understanding Media*. London: Routledge and Kegan Paul, 1964.

LOGO

[See also: *Advertising; Branding*]

A *logo* is a picture that stands for for a brand. The NBC peacock, the Macintosh apple, the Playboy bunny, Ralph Lauren's polo horseman, and Lacoste's alligator are just a few examples of memorable logos. These logos have become as much a part of the modern cultural landscape as national flags and sports team symbols.

Historically, a *trademark* was any symbol that distinguished the products of one company from those of another. But a modern-day logo does much more than identify products differentially. Consider the McDonald's golden arches logo. At a purely visual level, they form the letter 'M,' the first letter in the brand name. But at an unconscious level, arches reverberate with mythic symbolism – they are portals or gates beckoning people to go through them to a better world on the other side. The arches thus beckon people unconsciously to go through them into a place that 'will do it all for you,' as one of the company's previous slogans put it.

There are various types of logos. A classic example of a *letter logo* is the one used by Coca-Cola, which consists of the brand name written in a distinctive calligraphic style. The letter logo is a visual rendering of the brand name that stylizes the letters of that name in some distinctive way. Another famous letter logo is the one for Campbell's soup. As mentioned, the McDonald's arches suggest the first letter of the eatery's name. So the McDonald's logo is considered both a letter and a symbolic logo. The letter logo in this case can be called alphabetic, since it represents only the initial letter of the brand name, not the whole name. Another example of this type of letter logo

is Volkswagen, where the V and W refer to Volks (people) and Wagen (vehicle).

Another subtype of the letter logo is *acronymic*, consisting of the initial letters of the brand name. An example is the IBM logo, whose letters stand for International Business Machines. The parallel-line design of the acronym is also symbolic since it conveys a sense of something accurate, methodical, and scientific. The Adidas logo suggests both the letter 'A' (the first letter of the brand name) and the shape of a running shoe. It is thus an example of an alphabetic logo as well as a descriptor logo. *Portrait logos* are pictures of real or fictitious persons – for example, Uncle Ben, Wendy's, Betty Crocker, or Mr Clean. A well-known portrait logo (sometimes called a *mascot*) is the cartoon character Mickey Mouse, which came into being in 1929. Like a mascot in sports, it is perceived as something that brings good luck and humour. Two other well-known cartoon portrait logos are the Michelin Man, which is a kind of toy made up of tires (rather than toy blocks), and Charlie the Tuna, the product logo for Star-Kist tuna, whose friendly and humorous appearance is clearly designed to impart joyfulness.

A subtype of the portrait logo is the *effigy*. The Betty Crocker products, for instance, bear the effigy of a fictitious female. The logo was first created in 1921 by Gold Medal, and Betty's physical appearance – that of an idealized stay-at-home wife – was fixed in 1936. By the mid-1940s Betty had become the second most popular woman in America after Eleanor Roosevelt. Decades later a new image was fashioned for Betty – older and friendlier. Today, the effigy has been updated to reflect a new perception of American womanhood: Betty now resembles an independent 'woman of the world' who still maintains family values. The Betty Crocker logo 'makeover' is a perfect example of how brands attempt to keep in step with the times through symbolic means.

Some portrait logos are based on real people. These include Duncan Hines, a highly popular newspaper columnist who was born in Bowling Green, Kentucky, in 1880, and whose image can be found on cake and brownie mix boxes.

Descriptor logos are trademarks that literally show the product (service) or what the product (service) is about. An example is that of a phone company, such as Bell, which uses the picture of a bell as its logo. Well-known descriptor logos include animal figures such as the jaguar and the cougar that stand for cars called Jaguar and Cougar, and the yellow tail kangaroo logo for Yellow Tail wine.

Suggestive logos are visual signs that suggest something about the product. For example, the apple logo for the Mac computer is suggestive of the biblical narrative of temptation. The Playboy bunny logo suggests both the playfulness and the prolific sexual activities associated with rabbits. The Ferrari logo, which is a black, powerful horse, evokes the qualities associated historically with horses – nobility, status, power, and beauty. The horse is shown in a shield, which suggests heraldry and the fact that in medieval times it was carried by a knight so that he could be recognized from a distance. The Cadillac car also uses a shield-like crest figure as its logo. Its upper-class heraldic style conveys nuances of nobility blended with distinctiveness. In feudal times upper-class families passed their coats of arms down from one generation to the next. By heraldic law, no two families could use the same coat of arms.

Symbolic logos consist of letter or numerical symbols. For example, the small 'i' used by Apple for its iMac, iPod, iPhone, and iTunes products is an alphabet logo with symbolic qualities. It refers not to the brand or company name, as does the VW logo (above), but to something else. It symbolizes internet and text-messaging style, which frequently uses lower-case letters, as well as individuality, imagination, and many other concepts that begin with the letter *i*.

Another symbolic alphabet logo is the letter X as in the XBox video game system. This letter has many built-in meanings –

mystery (*X-Files*), the forbidden (X-rated movies), danger (the sign used on poison containers), adventure and excitement (Agent Triple X), and so on. Neumeier (2007) uses the term *icon* to refer to a logo that both stands for the brand name (or part thereof) and serves as a visual symbol. Icons are effective because they 'respond to the new reality by jumping off the printed page and interacting with people' (Neumeier 2007: 87). Neumeier claims that the most effective icon is the *avatar*, which is a logo 'that can move, morph, or otherwise operate freely as the brand's alter ego.'

Geometric logos are based on geometric figures. Many of today's most successful logos are based on geometrical forms. A well-known example is the Mercedes-Benz three-pointed star, which is supposed to suggest the company's domination of the land, the sea, and the air (Daimler, the founder, had a strong desire to produce not only cars, but also ships and aircraft). The placement of the star in a circle suggests perfection and eternity (qualities that one would desire in an expensive automobile). A large number of carmakers have adopted geometrical forms for their logo designs. The Audi logo, for example, consists of four interlocking rings, symbolizing the 1932 merger of four independent motor-vehicle manufacturers. It thus symbolizes partnership and stability. The Toyota logo consists of three ovals. The two centre ones suggest a relationship of mutual trust between the driver and Toyota. They also combine to form the letter 'T' for Toyota. Walsh, Winterich, and Mittal (2010) found that logo designs that were circular or smooth, in contrast to angular, have a broad appeal, especially in countries like China and India.

The histories of logo design and product marketing overlap considerably. It is impossible to advertise and promote 'logoless' products with any degree of success. Modern-day logos are not just trademarks; they are visual forms that influence people's unconscious perception of products. Arguably, the goal of marketing is to get people to react to logos in ways that parallel how people once responded to sacred or mythical pictures etched onto cave walls.

Marcel Danesi

Bibliography

Holt, Douglas B. *How Brands Become Icons: The Principles of Cultural Branding.* Boston: Harvard Business School Press, 2004.

Jhally, Sut. *The Codes of Advertising.* New York: St Martin's Press, 1987.

Neumeier, Marty. *The Brand Gap.* Berkeley: New Riders, 2006.

Walsh, Michael F., Karen Page Winterich, and Vikas Mital. Do Logo Redesigns Help or Hurt Your Brand? The Role of Brand Commitment. *Journal of Product and Brand Management* 19 (2010): 76–84.

LOTMAN, YURI (1922–93)

[See also: *Culture and Media; Semiotics; Structuralism*]

Yuri M. Lotman (also Jurij) was a prominent Russian-born semiotician and cultural scholar, whose work was conducted within the framework of the Tartu School (at the University of Tartu in Estonia) of culture analysis. Lotman was, early on in his career, a composer and instructor of music and music theory. Unable to find permanent work in Russia, he went to Estonia in the early 1950s teaching Russian literature at the University of Tartu, eventually setting up his own school of culture and sign analysis.

Of particular importance to the study of media and communications is Lotman's concept of the *semiosphere*. This is the notion that signs, symbols, texts, and any other expressive or representational human artefacts inform and sustain cultural life. In biology, life is sustained by the *biosphere*. By analogy, cognitive life is sustained by the semiosphere. The semiosphere forms a kind of intrinsic partnership with the biosphere to regulate human behaviour and to shape psychic and cultural evolution. But it is not a deterministic system, like the biosphere. Humans have the capacity to redesign the semiosphere or parts of it that they deem necessary to their cognitive and emotional survival or interests. On the one hand, the semiosphere is restrictive because it imposes on those born and reared into a specific culture its historically transmitted system of meanings (signs, symbols, texts, etc.), largely determining how individuals come to perceive the world. On the other hand, this system is also liberating because it provides the expressive resources for individuals to create new texts and encode new meanings whenever they wish to do so. New expressive forms are thus constantly being added to the semiosphere by new generations of people. New generations of artists, scientists, philosophers, and others create forms (texts, theories, artworks, and so on) that allow for discovery and innovation, without losing the vital continuity with the past.

Marcel Danesi

Bibliography

Andrews, Edna. *Conversations with Lotman: Cultural Semiotics in Language, Literature, and Cognition.* Toronto: University of Toronto Press, 2003.

Lotman, Jurij M. *Analysis of the Poetic Text.* Ann Arbor, MI: Ardis, 1975.

– *Semiotics of Cinema.* Ann Arbor: University of Michigan Press, 1976.

– *The Structure of the Artistic Text.* Ann Arbor: University of Michigan Press, 1977.

– *Universe of the Mind: A Semiotic Theory of Culture.* Bloomington: Indiana University Press, 1991.

– On the Semiosphere. *Sign System Studies* 33 (2005): 205–29.

M

MAGAZINES

[See also: *Fanzines; Print Culture; Pulp Fiction*]

Magazines, otherwise known as periodicals or serials, are regularly produced publications consisting of articles, features, and often photographs and illustrations on various topics, and sponsored generally by advertising revenues and subscriptions. Historically, magazines were more book-like in structure and had low circulation numbers. Since the turn of the twentieth century, magazines have evolved in format and style. Similar to newspapers, most magazines are 'popular' publications written for the masses. However, they generally have a stronger in-depth focus on topics, and feature more detail than typical newspapers. Unlike academic journals, magazines are written in an accessible, easy-to-read style, without citations and bibliographies.

Magazines cater to a broad spectrum of interests:

Art – *Art and Antiques*
Business – *Business Week, Forbes, Fortune, The Economist*
Cars – *Car and Driver, Motor Trend*
Current affairs – *Newsweek, Time Magazine*
Entertainment – *Entertainment Weekly, People Magazine*
Fashion – *InStyle*
Health and Fitness – *Your Health Now*
History – *History Today*
Hobbies – *In-Fisherman Magazine, Games*
Humour – *MAD Magazine*
Literary – *The New York Review of Books*
Music – *Rolling Stone*
Politics – *Harper's Magazine, The Atlantic Monthly, National Review*
Science – *National Geographic, Popular Science*
Sports – *Sports Illustrated*
Teen – *Teen Beat*

Magazines are typically produced under the guidance and control of an editor-in-chief, who is responsible for all aspects of operations and policies. An editorial board, consisting of various editors (such as features, section, news, opinions, senior, and/or managing editors), is responsible for the specific contents of the publication. Other important staff roles include: publisher, production manager, photographers, columnists, commentators, journalists, and reporters. Occasionally, an advisory board may be present to provide further guidance, especially for non-profit publications.

A significant portion of a magazine's operational budget stems from expenditures relating to staff salaries, marketing and promotions, along with printing and production. Magazines are generally funded through subscriptions, advertising, and off-the-rack sales. Non-profit magazines can sometimes also be funded through sponsorships. With overall readership of print publications declining in recent years due to the impact of the internet, many traditional magazine publishers are now beginning to see declining profits and are struggling to maintain operational capacity. Most of these now have online versions to bolster readership.

Commercial-quality magazines are typically printed using an offset press. Pages can be printed in black-and-white, full colour, or multi-toned colour, depending on the style of the magazine. These pages are then bound together either through a process known as 'saddle-stitching' (folded and stapled) or 'perfect binding' (glued spine, often for thicker magazines). The sizes of magazines can vary, but often are 8.5 by 11 inches. Most retail magazines today feature glossy full-colour covers, printed on slightly thicker glossy paper.

Depending on the type of magazine, and the timeliness of its content, the production schedule of a magazine may vary. For magazines with more time-sensitive content such as politics or business, production schedules will typically be weekly or bi-weekly. Magazines which are more specialized, such as literary magazines or hobby-based magazines, may be published on a quarterly or monthly basis. Publication dates found on the covers of released magazines can sometimes be up to a month in advance, allowing ample time for distribution and mailing.

The earliest magazines were the German *Erbauliche Monaths-Unterredungen* (1663–8), the French *Journal des Sçavans* (1665), and the *Philosophical Transactions* (1665) of the Royal Society of London, which were collections of essays on trends and research in the arts, literature, philosophy, and science. These were followed by 'essay periodicals' in the early eighteenth century, such as the British publications *The Tatler* (1709–11), *The Spectator* (1711–14), *The Rambler* (1750–2), and *The Idler* (1758–60), the latter founded by the British lexicographer, writer, and critic Samuel Johnson (1709–84). Later in the century, general-purpose magazines emerged, starting with *The Gentleman's Magazine* (1731–1907) in England, an event that marked the first use of the word *maga-*

zine, which meant 'storehouse,' alluding to the fact that the magazine was a 'storehouse' of political reports, essays, stories, and poems.

By the middle part of the nineteenth century, magazine publication expanded considerably, mirroring and guiding social trends at the same time. *Godey's Lady's Book* (1830–98) set the style in women's clothing and manners; the *Illustrated London News* (1842), the *Fortnightly Review* (1865–1954), *Punch* (1841) in England, *L'Illustration* in France (1843–1944), *Die Woche* (1899–1940) in Germany, and *Leslie's Illustrated Newspaper* (1855–1922) and *Harper's Weekly* (1857–1916) in the United States catered to a new affluent middle class of readers; *Youth's Companion* (1827–1929) and *St. Nicholas* (1873–1940) were among the first children's magazines published in the century, considered useful not only for entertaining children, but for imparting literacy to them; and family magazines such as the *Saturday Evening Post* (1821–) started to proliferate.

With the advent of *Cosmopolitan* (1886–), fashion magazines for women came into the picture, becoming and remaining to this day among the most popular of all magazines. Also catering to a female readership were *Ladies'* (later *Woman's*) *Home Companion* (1873–1957), *McCall's Magazine* (1876–), *Ladies' Home Journal* (1883–), *Good Housekeeping* (1885–), and *Vogue* (1892–). *Reader's Digest* began publication in 1922, an event that revealed that people had increasingly little time to read entire books. Weekly newsmagazines such as *Time* (1923) and *Newsweek* (1933), and weekly and biweekly magazines, such as *Life* (1936–72, revived as a monthly in 1978), *Look* (1937–71), and *Ebony* (1946–), came onto the market in the same and subsequent decades.

Today, magazine publishing continues to cater to specialized tastes. *Consumer Reports* (1936–), for example, evaluates consumer products; *GQ* (1957–) focuses on issues of concern to urban males; *Rolling Stone* (1967–) is devoted to the promulgation and assessment of pop music trends; *Ms.* (1970–) deals with topics of concern to women; *People* (1974–) features items on celebrities; *National Geographic World* (1975–) provides non-technical information from the worlds of science, history, and travel to a broad audience; *Discover* (1980–) is a science magazine catering to a general public; and *Wired* (1993–) looks at issues pertaining to computer technology and digital culture generally.

Today, e-zines (magazines published on the internet) are proliferating, having various advantages over paper-based magazines – they can be updated regularly, they can incorporate reader comments instantly, they can be linked with other sources of information, and so forth. The internet now also has 'magazine chat rooms,' where readers can click to get the latest gossip or information about their areas of interest.

Most magazines are really 'thematic' readers, since users take from them what they want to get, thus reading the magazine for practical information or entertainment. Magazines are intended to be kept much longer than newspapers, and thus are manufactured with a smaller page size and printed on better paper. They are also less concerned with daily changing events than are newspapers, covering topics of broader interest to readers (within the area of interest). Writing ranges from factual or practical reporting to a more literate and effusive style. Writers have contributed either occasionally or regularly to magazines. And many well-known writers published their early works in them.

Despite being a predominantly print-medium product, many magazines now have either an electronic version/website, or are strictly Web-based. This has allowed magazines to expand their audience through an inexpensive and highly adaptive platform. The benefits of publishing online are numerous: more responsive reporting (outside of regular publication schedules), greater reader interaction (through blogs, comment sites, and sharing), and the ability to use dynamic content (videos, audio, and other media). As a result, magazines such as *The Economist* and *People* now have websites which provide rich content above and beyond that which is found within their printed publications. Feeling the squeeze from declining print readership, many publications are now beginning to turn their focus more towards the internet and online magazine development.

Alexander Lim

Bibliography

Gough-Yates, Anna. *Understanding Women's Magazines*. London: Routledge, 2003.

Harris, Michael, and Tom O'Malley. *Studies in Newspaper and Periodical History*, Westport, CT: Greenwood Press, 1997.

Janello, Amy, and Brennon Jones. *The American Magazine*. New York: Abrams, 1991.

Winship, Janice. *Inside Women's Magazines*. London: Pandora, 1987.

MARCONI, GUGLIELMO
(1874–1937)

[See also: *Broadcasting; Communication; Radio*]

Italian-born scientist Guglielmo Marconi is known as the inventor of wireless telecommunications. He called his invention a *radiotelegraph* (shortened to *radio*), because its signal moved outward in all directions, that is, *radially*, from the point of transmission. For his invention, Marconi shared the 1909 Nobel Prize in physics with Karl Ferdinand Braun of Germany, who had developed the technical means of increasing the range of radio transmissions.

As with other inventions, pegging the invention of a device such as the radio on one person does not tell the whole story. Wireless transmission technology grew out of the theories and experiments of many people. Joseph Henry of the United States and Michael Faraday of Britain had experimented with electromagnets in the 1830s, developing the theory that the electric current in one wire produced a current in another wire, even though the wires were not connected physically. This came to be known as induction theory. Then, in 1864, another British physicist, James Clerk Maxwell, used induction theory to put forward the idea that electromagnetic waves travelled at the speed of light. In the 1880s, Maxwell's theory was corroborated by experiments conducted by the German physicist Heinrich Hertz. In 1891, the Austria-Hungary-born American inventor Nikola Tesla invented a high-frequency transformer called the *Tesla coil*, which became a vital component of electronic transmitters, thus setting the stage for Marconi to send the first radio signals through the air, using electromagnetic waves to transmit telegraph signals a distance of more than 1.6 kilometres. Shortly thereafter, engineers developed devices called 'vacuum tubes' that could be used to detect and amplify transmitted radio signals. The first commercial vacuum tube was patented by American inventor Lee De Forest in 1907. It was called a *triode* or *audion*, constituting the key element in radio reception. Incidentally, Tesla had developed high-voltage, high-frequency equipment, which he used to send signals between his laboratory and a hotel in New York City. In 1943, the Supreme Court of the United States invalidated many of Marconi's radio equipment patents, recognizing that Tesla had patented similar inventions prior to Marconi.

Marconi had read about Hertz's work and began experimenting with wireless telegraphy as far back as 1894 in his hometown of Bologna, but the Italian government showed no interest in the work. So, Marconi went to London, England, where, in 1896, he received the first patent on his so-called wireless telegraphy system. He then obtained financial support in 1897, forming the Wireless Telegraph and Signal Company. In 1899, three British warships were the first to be equipped with the wireless telegraph, and, in the same year, Marconi sent a wireless message across the English Channel to France. The first transatlantic signal was sent on 12 December 1901, when the Morse code letter *S* from Poldhu,

Cornwall, was transmitted to St John's, Newfoundland. Marconi's fame expanded considerably after his wireless equipment helped rescue ships and locate the sinking ocean liners *Republic* in 1909 and *Titanic* in 1912, saving the lives of many people. The first demonstrations of wireless telegraphy in the United States took place in 1899, after Marconi had been invited by the *New York Herald* newspaper to cover the America's Cup races in New Jersey.

Already in 1900, Marconi had established the American Marconi Co., which would eventually become the Radio Corporation of America (RCA), to broadcast radio transmissions. It is difficult to pinpoint when the first radio broadcast took place. However, it is unlikely that it took place in any concrete form until 1918. That was the year when the American inventor Edwin H. Armstrong improved the technology of radio receivers considerably, although a plan for radio broadcasting to the general public can be traced back to a 1916 memorandum written by David Sarnoff (1891–1971), an employee of American Marconi. In it Sarnoff recommended that radios be promoted as household 'utilities.' After the First World War ended in 1918, several manufacturing companies began seriously to explore the idea of mass-marketing radio receivers. It was probably the Westinghouse Electric Corporation of Pittsburgh which established the first commercially owned radio station, called KDKA, which offered a regular schedule of programmed broadcasting to the general public. KDKA received its licence in October of 1920 from the Department of Commerce, which at the time held regulatory power after the end of the war. KDKA aired various kinds of programs, including recorded music, using a phonograph with a microphone placed before it. The station did not charge user fees, nor carry paid advertisements. It appears that Westinghouse used KDKA as an enticement for people to buy home radio receivers.

Marconi's wireless had transformed the world by the 1920s, ushering in the age of radio broadcasting. In 1926 Sarnoff himself founded the National Broadcasting Company (NBC), an RCA subsidiary that broadcast programs through a cross-country network of stations. The Columbia Broadcasting System (CBS) radio service followed suit in 1928. The AT&T Company had already begun exploring the possibilities of 'network broadcasting' in 1922, charging fees in return for the airing of commercial advertisements on its stations. However, fearing legal action, it sold its stations to RCA. In return, AT&T was given the exclusive right to provide the connections linking local stations to the NBC network.

Marcel Danesi

Bibliography

Ahern, Steve, ed. *Making Radio*. Sydney: Allen and Unwin, 2006.

Hong, Sungook. *Wireless: From Marconi's Black-Box to the Audio*. Cambridge, MA: MIT Press, 2001.

MARCUSE, HERBERT (1898–1979)

[See also: *Adorno, Theodor; Frankfurt School; Habermas, Jürgen; Hegemony Theory, Ideology Theory; Marxism*]

Herbert Marcuse was a German-born Marxist philosopher and social theorist. He was widely known for his criticisms of capitalism, and was especially influential to the counterculture movement of the 1960s. He is called the 'father of the New Left' because, unlike Marx, he did not believe that it would be workers who would overthrow capitalism, but students, intellectuals, and minority groups.

Marcuse served with the German army in the First World War and after the war became a member of a Soldiers' Council that participated in the failed socialist Spartacist uprising. After completing his PhD thesis at the University of Freiberg in 1922, on the German *Künstlerroman*, he went to work as

a bookseller in Berlin, returning to Freiberg in 1929 to study philosophy with Martin Heidegger (1889–1976).

With Heidegger, Marcuse wrote his Habilitation thesis, which was published in 1932 as *Hegel's Ontology and Theory of Historicity*, in spite of Heidegger's rejection of the work. In 1933, Marcuse joined the Frankfurt Institute for Social Research, becoming closely aligned with Max Horkheimer (1895–1973), Theodor W. Adorno (1903–69), and others in the institute's inner circle. To flee from Nazism, Marcuse, a German Jew, emigrated from Germany, going first to Switzerland, and then, in 1934, to the United States, where he became a naturalized citizen in 1940, living there for the rest of his life.

During the 1930s and early 1940s Marcuse worked at Columbia University, which provided offices and academic affiliation to refugees like him. In 1941 he published *Reason and Revolution*, an introduction to Hegelian-Marxist dialectical thinking and social analysis. In that work it is obvious that, besides Georg Wilhelm Friedrich Hegel, Karl Marx, and Martin Heidegger, Marcuse was influenced by Immanuel Kant, Søren Kierkegaard, Friedrich Wilhelm Nietzsche, Sigmund Freud, Edmund Husserl, and György Lukács. In 1955 he published *Eros and Civilization*, a synthesis of Marx and Freud that put forward an outline for the foundation of a non-repressive civilization. Marcuse's libertarian perspective anticipated many of the counterculture values of the 1960s, helping to influence the intellectual and political thought of that decade. Marcuse argued that the capitalist system, as a social system organized around profit and exploitation, produces a 'surplus of repression' by imposing unnecessary labour, restrictions on sexuality, and limitations on the individual's capacity for creativity and innovation.

In 1952 Marcuse began a teaching career as a political theorist, first at Columbia University and Harvard University, then, from 1958 to 1965, at Brandeis University, where he taught philosophy and politics, and finally (when he was past the usual retirement age) at the University of California, San Diego. In 1958 he published *Soviet Marxism*, a critical study of the Soviet Union, focusing his critique on the Soviet bureaucracy and outlining the differences between authentic Marxist theory and Soviet Marxism.

Perhaps his most influential work was his 1964 book *One-Dimensional Man*, which aroused a great deal of interest in the student movement of the 1960s. This book significantly influenced the emergence of the so-called New Left cadre of critics. *One-Dimensional Man* is a wide-ranging critique of 'advanced industrial society' and its techniques of stabilization, consensus-making, and social control. By engendering false needs in individuals, such societies create the conditions by which people are absorbed mindlessly into the existing system of production and consumption, thus ensuring the continuity of that very system. This, according to Marcuse, is why the working classes lose their revolutionary zeal in capitalist systems. It is through the mass media and popular culture that the 'one-dimensional' human being is forged and shaped – an individual who 'reproduces' the existing system and thus lacks any desire to critique or oppose the system. In his 1965 essay 'Repressive Tolerance,' Marcuse characterizes capitalist democracies as enfolding a subtle form of totalitarianism by seeming, on the surface, to be highly tolerant while in effect being highly repressive.

Marcuse married three times. His first wife was the mathematician Sophie Wertman (1901–51), with whom he had a son, Peter (born 1928). His second marriage was to Inge Neumann (1913–72), the widow of his close friend Franz Neumann (1900–54). In 1976 he married his third wife, Erica Sherover (1938–88), a former graduate student and forty years his junior. His son Peter is currently professor emeritus of Urban Planning at Columbia University. Marcuse died on 29 July 1979, after suffering a stroke during a visit to Germany. He had just spoken at the Frankfurt Römerberggespräche, and was about to go to the Max Planck Institute for the Study of the Scientific-Technical World in Starnberg, having been invited to go there by the second-generation Frankfurt School theorist Jürgen Habermas.

Augusto Ponzio

Bibliography

Alford, C. Fred. *Science and the Revenge of Nature: Marcuse and Habermas.* Gainesville: University of Florida Press, 1985.

Bokina, John, and Timothy J. Lukes, eds. *Marcuse: New Perspectives.* Lawrence: University of Kansas Press, 1994.

Lukes, Timothy J. *The Flight into Inwardness: An Exposition and Critique of Herbert Marcuse's Theory of Liberative Aesthetics.* London: Associated University Presses, 1986.

Marcuse, Herbert. *Reason and Revolution.* New York: Oxford University Press, 1941

– *Eros and Civilization.* Boston: Beacon Press, 1955.

– *Soviet Marxism.* New York: Columbia University Press 1958.

– *One-Dimensional Man.* Boston: Beacon Press, 1964.

– *Negations.* Boston: Beacon Press, 1968.

– *An Essay on Liberation.* Boston: Beacon Press, 1969.

– *Counterrevolution and Revolt.* Boston: Beacon Press, 1972.

– *Studies in Critical Philosophy.* Boston: Beacon Press, 1973.

– *The Aesthetic Dimension.* Boston: Beacon Press, 1978.

Pippin, Robert, et al., eds. *Marcuse: Critical Theory and the Promise of Utopia.* South Hadley, MA: Bergin and Garvey, 1988.

MARKEDNESS THEORY

[See also: *Content Analysis; Structuralism*]

A foundational principle in structuralism as it is practised in fields such as semiotics, linguistics, psychology, and anthropology is called *opposition*. It constitutes a model of cognition that can be traced back to antiquity, when it was called dualism (Ogden 1932; Hjelmslev 1939, 1959; Babin 1940; Benveniste 1946; Bochénski 1961; Deely 2001; Anfindsen 2006). The modern-day version was formalized for the first time by the so-called Prague School of linguists (Jakobson, Karcevski, and Trubetzkoy 1928; Jakobson 1932, 1936, 1939; Trubetzkoy 1936, 1939; Pos 1938, 1964) and gestalt psychologists (Ogden and Richards 1923; Ogden 1932). A pivotal derivative of this principle was called *markedness theory* by the Prague School linguists, becoming a major framework for studying language in the 1950s and 1960s, and a little later the mass media. Markedness theory was attacked by poststructuralism in the late 1960s (Derrida 1967). But it was a temporary setback (Andrews 1990; Andrews and Tobin 1996; Battistella 1990, 1996), since it continues to be used profitably as a framework in several fields, from linguistics to media analysis.

The basic idea behind opposition theory is that the mind grasps the meanings of objects and concepts not in isolated singular ways, but in terms of relations. Among the first to understand this were the early founders of psychology (Wundt 1880; Titchener 1910). Ferdinand de Saussure (1916) called it *différence*. When we hear the word *cat* we recognize it as distinct because it is differentiated from other words such as *rat* or *fat* through a sound cue in initial position. In the late 1920s, the Prague School (known formally as the Prague Linguistic Circle) expanded upon Saussure's notion, establishing it as the primary approach to the study of sign systems across disciplines (Wallon 1945; Parsons and Bales 1955; Lévi-Strauss 1958, 1971; Blanché 1966; Chomsky and Halle 1968; Belardi 1970; Ivanov 1974; Needham 1973; Fox 1974, 1975; Lorrain 1975; Jakobson and Waugh 1979).

The essence of the theory is that there exists a small universal set of 'binary' concepts, such as *yes/no* and *right/left*. Research in various disciplines has found, in fact,

that these occur across cultures. The two parts of such 'oppositions' are called *poles*. Other kinds of concepts can be located between the two poles, implying a kind of 'gradience' in conceptual systems. For instance, in the *white/black* polar opposition, colour concepts such as *yellow, red*, and so on are gradient ones since they fall between the *white* and *black* poles. This resonates with validity both in nature and in culture – gradient colours are found distributed on the light spectrum, while *white* and *black* are polar. Words for polar concepts are found in all languages; gradient ones, on the other hand, show great variation across the world's languages. In like manner, between the polar concepts *day/night*, which are found universally, gradient concepts such as *twilight, dawn, noon, afternoon*, and so on, show culture-specific variations. Polar concepts form binary oppositions; gradient concepts do not. In English, it is difficult to put, say, *yellow* into a binary opposition with another colour. But, as Ogden (1932) pointed out, some oppositions, such as *town/country*, are binary and not universal; they are clearly culture-specific. Part of the research in this field is, thus, to determine which concepts are universal and which are not.

Like Saussure, the Prague School theorists first applied opposition theory to the study of sound systems, identifying various types and tokens of oppositional structure within them. They also came up with a typology of oppositions – for example, a *multidimensional opposition* is one in which the differential features that are common to both sounds also occur in other sounds; a *one-dimensional* or *bilateral* opposition is one in which the features common to both sounds do not occur in other sounds; and so on. In a phonemic opposition, such as the one between /p/ and /b/ (for example, *pin* vs. *bin*), one of the two is considered to be more basic, and the other is connected to it in some way. In this case, the /p/ is assigned 'basic' status, called unmarked, and the /b/ is assigned a 'marked' status, standing out for several reasons – it is less frequent as an initial constituent of words; it has a different feature (voiced, meaning that the vocal cords vibrate) that makes it more noticeable; and so on.

This theory can be applied to all levels of language. Many polar concepts, for instance, seem to be formed on the basis of an overriding 'meta-opposition,' as it can be called: *presence/absence*. In the *day/night* opposition, for example, *night* is conceived as being 'absence of daylight,' while *day* is not normally conceived as being 'absence of night time.' Clearly, polar concepts relate to each other in terms of 'markedness' – *night* is marked with respect to *day*. The pole *day* is perceived to be the 'present' concept in the opposition. It is the 'unmarked' pole, while the other one, *night*, is related to it through 'absence' and is the 'marked' pole. Not all oppositions show such clear-cut markedness, however. They may be equipollent, as in the *give/accept* opposition, since either pole in it could be assigned unmarked status, depending on the situation or on the viewpoint of those using the opposition (Tiersma 1982; Eckman 1983). Markedness has many implications. First and foremost, it constitutes an unconscious conceptual reflex that guides language use. When an opposition such as *tall/short* is involved, we ask instinctively 'How *tall* is he?' not 'How *short* is he?' because, unless there is a specific reason to do so, we assume *tallness* to be the unmarked pole, and *shortness* to be 'absence of tallness' and thus the marked one. This likely shows that tallness is a culture-specific attribute rather than a natural one.

Despite its obvious utility, markedness theory became a target of criticism within the post-structuralism movement in semiotics (Foucault 1972; Derrida 1967; Belsey 2002; Mitchell and Davidson 2007). The post-structuralists did not view markedness theory as a tool for investigating structure; they saw it, instead, as validating that very structure. Derrida in particular pointed out that it was a logocentric concoction, and that it was ultimately perilous because of the inequalities it encoded. In a binary

opposition such as *day/night* there are no problems accepting *day* as the unmarked form and *night* as its marked counterpart. Problems arise, however, with oppositions such as *male/female* and *self/other*. But Derrida missed the fact that markedness can be used diagnostically to identify social inequities, not validate them. Moreover, it is a useful analytical device for understanding oppositional structure and its ramifications in cultural terms. Consider the *right/left* opposition (Needham 1973). This polarity comes from the fact that we have a right and left hand (foot, leg, ear, and eye). The *right* pole is the unmarked one simply because most people are right-handed. If the reverse were ever to happen, whereby left-handedness became the norm, then the markedness relation would be reversed. As this simple example shows, markedness theory can be used to relate forms (words, symbols, and so on) to cultural emphases. It is for this reason that it continues to be used in various disciplines, from linguistics and semiotics to anthropology and psychology.

Marcel Danesi

Bibliography

Andrews, Edna. *Markedness Theory*. Durham, NC: Duke University Press, 1990.

Andrews, Edna, and Yishai Tobin, eds. *Toward a Calculus of Meaning: Studies in Markedness, Distinctive Features and Deixis*. Amsterdam: John Benjamins, 1996.

Anfindsen, Jens. Aristotle on Contrariety as a Principle of First Philosophy. Thesis, Uppsala University, 2006.

Babin, A. Eugene. The Theory of Opposition in Aristotle. Doctoral thesis, University of Notre Dame, 1940.

Battistella, Edwin L. *Markedness: The Evaluative Superstructure of Language*. Albany: State University of New York Press, 1990.

– *The Logic of Markedness*. Oxford: Oxford University Press, 1996.

Belardi, Walter. *L'opposizione privativa*. Napoli: Istituto Universitario Orientale di Napoli, 1970.

Belsey, Catharine. *Poststructuralism: A Very Short Introduction*. Oxford: Oxford University Press, 2002.

Benveniste, Emile. Structure des relations de personne dans le verbe. *Bulletin de la Société de Linguistique de Paris* 43 (1946): 225–36.

Blanché, Robert. *Structures intellectuelles*. Paris: Vrin, 1966.

Bochénski, Innocentius M. *A History of Formal Logic*. Notre Dame: University of Notre Dame Press, 1961.

Chomsky, Noam, and Morris Halle. *The Sound Pattern of English*. New York: Harper and Row, 1968.

Deely, John. *Four Ages of Understanding: The First Postmodern Survey of Philosophy from Ancient Times to the Turn of the Twentieth Century*. Toronto: University of Toronto Press, 2001.

Derrida, Jacques. *De la grammatologie*. Paris: Minuit, 1967.

Eckman, Fred R., et al., eds. *Markedness*. New York: Plenum, 1983.

Foucault, Michel. *The Archeology of Knowledge*, trans. by Alan M. Sheridan Smith. New York: Pantheon, 1972.

Fox, James J. Our Ancestors Spoke in Pairs: Rotinese Views of Language, Dialect and Code. In *Explorations in the Ethnography of Speaking*, ed. Richard Bauman and Joel Scherzer, 65–88. Cambridge: Cambridge University Press, 1974.

– On Binary Categories and Primary Symbols. In *The Interpretation of Symbolism*, ed. R. Willis, 99–132. London: Malaby, 1975.

Hjelmslev, Louis. Note sur les oppositions supprimables. *Travaux de Cercle Linguistique de Prague* 8 (1939): 51–7.

– *Essais linguistique*. Copenhagen: Munksgaard, 1959.

Ivanov, V.V. On Antisymmetrical and Asymmetrical Relations in Natural Languages and Other Semiotic Systems. *Linguistics* 119 (1974): 35–40.

Jakobson, Roman. Zur Struktur des russischen Verbum. In *Charisteria Guilelma Mathesio Quinquagenario a Discipulis et Circuli Linguistici Pragensis Sodalibus Oblata*, 74–84. Prague: Prazsky lingvistick, 1932.

– Beitrag zur allgemeinen Kasuslehre: Gesamtbedeutungen der russischen Kasus. *Travaux du Cercle Linguistique de Prague* 6 (1936): 244–88.

– Observations sur le classement phonologique des consonnes. *Proceedings of the Fourth International Congress of Phonetic Sciences* (1939): 34–41.

– *Kindersprache, Aphasie und algemeine Lautgesetze*. Uppsala: Almqvist and Wiksell, 1942.

– The Role of Phonic Elements in Speech Perception. *Zeitschrift fuer Phonetik, Sprachwissenschaft und Kommunikationsforschung* 21 (1968): 9–20.

Jakobson, Roman, and Morris Halle. *Fundamentals of Language*. The Hague: Mouton, 1956.

Jakobson, Roman, and Linda Waugh. *Six Lectures on Sound and Meaning*. Cambridge, MA: MIT Press, 1979.

Jakobson, Roman, Gunnar Fant, and Morris Halle. *Preliminaries to Speech Analysis*. Cambridge: MIT Press, 1952.

Jakobson, Roman, Serge J. Karcevskij, and Nicolas Trubetzkoy. Proposition au premier congrès international des linguistes: Quelles sont les méthodes les mieux appropriées à un exposé complet et pratique de la phonologie d'une langue quelconque? *Premier Congrès International des Linguistes, Propositions* (1928): 36–9.

Lévi-Strauss, Claude. *Anthropologie structurale*. Paris: Plon, 1958.

– *L'Homme nu*. Paris: Plon, 1971.

Lorrain, François. *Réseaux sociaux et classifications sociales*. Paris: Hermann, 1975.

Mitchell, W.J.T., and Arnold I. Davidson, eds. *The Late Derrida*. Chicago: University of Chicago Press, 2007.

Needham, Rodney. *Right and Left*. Chicago: University of Chicago Press, 1973.

Ogden, Charles K. *Opposition: A Linguistic and Psychological Analysis*. London: Paul, Trench, and Trubner, 1932.

Ogden, Charles K., and Ivor A. Richards. *The Meaning of Meaning*. London: Routledge and Kegan Paul, 1923.

Parsons, Talcott, and Robert F. Bales. *Family, Socialization, and Interaction Process*. Glencoe, IL: Free Press, 1955.

Pos, H.J. La notion d'opposition en linguistique. *Xle Congrès International de Psychologie* (1938): 246–7.

– Perspectives du structuralisme. In *Études pho-nologiques dediées à la mémoire de M. le Prince K. S. Trubetzkoy*, 71–8. Prague: Jednota Ceskych Mathematiku Fysiku, 1964.

Saussure, Ferdinand de. *Cours de linguistique générale.* Ed. C. Bally and A. Sechehaye. Paris: Payot, 1916.

Tiersma, Peter M. Local and General Marked-ness. *Language* 58 (1982): 832–49.

Titchener, Edward B. *A Textbook of Psychology.* Delmar: Scholars' Facsimile Reprints, 1910.

Trubetzkoy, Nicolas S. Essaie d'une théorie des oppositions phonologiques. *Journal de Psy-chologie* 33 (1936): 5–18.

– Grundzüge der Phonologie. *Travaux du Cercle Linguistique de Prague* 7 (1939): entire issue.

Wallon, Henri. *Les origines de la pensée chez l'enfant.* Vol. 1. Paris: Presses Universitaires de France, 1945.

Waugh, Linda. Markedness and Phonological Systems. *LACUS Linguistic Association of Can-ada and the United States Proceedings* 5 (1979): 155–65.

Wundt, Wilhelm. 1880. *Grundzüge der physiolo-gischen Psychologie.* Leipzig: Englemann.

MARKETING AND THE MEDIA

[See also: *Advertising; Audience Research; Branding*]

Marketing is the business of finding buy-ers for company products, or audiences for media products. Marketing is so vital today that about half the cost of production or manufacturing goes to marketing expenses. There are five basic marketing activities: market research, product development, distribution, pricing, and promotion. The United States has the largest marketing in-dustry in the world, with its centre in New York City.

Marketers determine the demand for products and services, describe the profiles of probable customers or media audiences, and measure potential sales or reactions to products. They also ascertain how price influences demand. And they test the ef-fectiveness of advertising. A market study begins with the statement of a problem that the business or media client wants to solve. This leads to a thorough description of the information or data to be gathered. The data can be obtained through such means as questionnaires, interviews, sales audits, electronic scanners, direct observation, and ratings. They can also be obtained through sources such as government agencies and universities.

The primary objective of marketing research is to identify the individuals or groups who are most inclined to react positively to a certain product on the ba-sis of age, sex, education, class, income, occupation, and other demographic and psychographic variables. Marketers also measure the size and makeup of radio, TV, and internet audiences at different periods of time, using this information in selecting media in which to place ads or in preparing a 'media plan' that will provide *reach* – the number of people who will be exposed to a product – and *frequency* – the number of occasions to which they will be exposed to the product.

Among the strategies and devices used by marketers in the areas of media and ad-vertising, the following are now standard:

- *VALS* (the values and lifestyles) question-naires, which indicate how consumers feel about or react to a product;
- *copy testing*, which measures the efficacy of media programs and advertising mes-sages by showing programs or ads to sample audiences;
- *recognition testing*, which indicates how well someone can recall a program, an advertisement, etc., with or without prompting;
- *benchmark measuring*, which assesses a target audience's response to the early stages of an advertising campaign or pilot program;
- *evaluation questionnaires*, which assess how well a program or an ad campaign has met its original aims and reached its target audience;
- *commutation testing*, which involves

changing an image or word in an ad, 'commuting' it with another one, in order to see what kinds of reactions the change produces in subjects;

- *consumer jury testing*, which consists of asking consumers to compare, rank, and evaluate advertisements or media products;
- *consumer panel groups*, in which subjects report back to the marketers on products they have used, or programs they have watched, thus providing vital feedback;
- *DAGMAR* (defining advertising goals for measured advertising results), which is used to identify the effects of an ad campaign or a program in its various stages, from awareness of the product or program to action (purchasing, viewing);
- *day-after-recall testing*, which indicates how much someone can recall about an advertisement or program the day after it was broadcast;
- *diary method*, in which subjects keep a written account of the advertising or programs they have been exposed to, the purchases they have actually made, etc.;
- *eye tracking*, which records the eye movement of subjects in order to determine which parts of the brain are being activated while they are viewing some ad or program; in the case of the internet the technique is employed to determine what users look at and for how long;
- *forced exposure*, whereby subjects are asked to view an ad or a TV program and provide commentary on it;
- *galvanometer testing*, which is the use of a galvanometer to measure physiological changes in audiences or consumers when asked a question or shown some stimulus;
- *motivational research*, which involves the use of questionnaires and other materials investigating the reasons why people watch certain TV programs or buy specific types of merchandise;
- *response testing*, which evaluates the efficacy of internet ads by how users respond to them through direct clicking;
- *tachistoscope testing*, which determines

a person's recognition or perception of various elements within an ad or program by changing lighting and exposure or embedding images in some text;

- *voice-pitch analysis*, which assess a subject's emotional reaction to an ad or program by recording the subject's voice during commentary and analysing its tonal patterns.

Marcel Danesi

Bibliography

Jacobson, Michael F., and Laurie Ann Mazur. *Marketing Madness: A Survival Guide for a Consumer Society.* Boulder, CO: Westview, 1995.

Kotler, Philip, and Gary Armstrong. *Principles of Marketing.* Englewood Cliffs, NJ: Prentice-Hall, 1993.

Seabrook, John. *Nobrow: The Culture of Marketing – The Marketing of Culture.* New York: Knopf, 2000.

MARXISM

[See also: *Culture Industry Theory; Frankfurt School; Hegemony Theory; Ideology Theory*]

Based on the work of German philosopher Karl Marx, the term *Marxism* is used in various fields to apply any use of Marx's ideas to a specific theoretical task at hand – be it literary criticism or media analysis. Essentially, Marx claimed that capitalism would collapse and that communism would eventually take its place. The end of capitalism would be brought about by a workers' revolution against the owners of the means of production. The workers would subsequently gain control of society's economic resources and of the reins of government. Marx's main political theory is found in a book he co-wrote with the German journalist Friedrich Engels – the *Communist Manifesto* (1848).

Marx claimed that material forces (nature and human economic production) determined ideas and the evolutionary paths that societies take. His philosophy can be summed up in terms of four ideas: (1) history progresses through a series of conflicts; (2) the physical world accounts for everything real (materialism); (3) public ownership of property should be the basis for economic production (socialism); and (4) market forces determine economic activity. Marx believed that all civilizations had experienced class conflict between workers and the owners of the means of production. In ancient societies, these two classes were the slaves and their masters; in the Middle Ages, they were the vassals and the lords; and in industrialized capitalist societies, they were the workers and the bourgeois factory owners.

Marxism today entails an array of philosophical and political conceptions which, rightly or wrongly, refer to Marx's original ideas. As Hans Magnus Enzensberger quips in *Gespräche mit Marx und Engels* (1970), Marx himself had stated: 'The only thing I can say is that I'm not a Marxist!' Many of Marx's ideas continue to be used in one form or another, even if the users are probably not aware of their source. One of these is the concept of alienation, which is used in sociology and psychology. His ideas surface, in fact, in a broad range of disciplines, from philosophy, sociology, and economics to anthropology, history, media studies, aesthetics education, and literary criticism. Unfortunately, as Ferruccio Rossi-Landi (1978: 16) observes, 'Marx's greatness as the founder of scientific socialism has obscured his greatness as a thinker.'

'Marxism' and 'Marxist' are abstractions which in Marx's own framework would hardly be perceived as being 'determining,' especially when used as simple labels. Marxism was, and still is, frequently conceived of as a mere ideological theory. Antoine Meillet (1950) was right when he observed that scientific research cannot take place under such a banner. Marx said that he was not Marxist if Marxism, as was often the case, was to be conceived of as a speculative (Hegelian) type of philosophy – a deductive system of thought based on fixed principles. Marx and Engels would have rejected such a philosophy outright. For Marx any framework must be empirically verifiable, not speculative, and thus subject to being falsified or, at the very least, revised (Schaff 1975).

Marxist theory has been highly productive in the area of media and mass communications studies. For Marxists, media products in capitalist systems are essentially 'commodities' which, like material commodities, can be sold in the marketplace of ideas, where they have a short life. Marx did not see commodities as given and natural, but as signs of how the social system was organized. In a Marxist framework, commodities are thus studied not only at the level of exchange, but also at the level of production and consumption. A commodity is more than a mere product because it functions as a message. Marx's demystification of bourgeois economies and in particular his analysis of commodities as messages are really in line with basic semiotic method. Commodities are part of social reproduction cycles in capitalist systems, constituting messages of a particular kind. All this suggests that economics should be viewed as a branch of the communication sciences, especially semiotics (see Ponzio 1986, 1989). A major contribution coming from the Marxist perspective for a better understanding of culture and society consists, therefore, in showing the relationship of commodities to their social significations. 'Civil society,' as defined by Antonio Gramsci (1891–1937), is the social zone where consensus is produced, and it is that zone that is the most proper place for the study of sign systems, whether verbal or non-verbal. Following Adam Schaff (1913–2006) in *Introduction to Semantics* and what he called the 'fetishism of signs' (referring to Marx's critique of the 'fetishism of goods'), signs and messages should be viewed in their connection to human individuals and to social relations.

Among the different Marxist approaches to media and culture, the best-known are the Frankfurt School; structural Marxism (influential in France during the late 1960s and 1970s), associated with the work of the French theorists Louis Althusser (1918–90) and Maurice Godelier; British cultural theory, associated with the Centre for Cultural Studies of the University of Birmingham, which boasts such well-known media scholars as Stuart Hall (1932–) and Raymond Williams (1921–88); and the Communist Party Historians Group of Great Britain, which was founded in 1946 with Edward Palmer Thompson (1924–93), Eric Hobsbawm (b. 1917), Christopher Hill (1912–2003), and Raphael Samuel (1934–96). Prominent Marxist authors include: the Hungarian philosopher Georg Lukács (1885–1971); the Italian writer, politician, and political theorist Antonio Gramsci; the German philosopher Karl Korsch (1886–1961); the German-American philosopher Herbert Marcuse (1898-1979); the existentialist philosopher and writer Jean-Paul Sartre (1905–80); the German pragmatist philosopher George Klaus (1912–74); the American economist Paul Marlor Sweezy (1910–2004), founding editor of the magazine *Monthly Review*; and the Polish philosopher Adam Schaff. In contrast to the 'anti-humanist Marxism' of Louis Althusser, who qualified Marxist humanism as revisionism, Schaff maintained the humanistic character of Marx's original conception and as a member of the Communist Polish Party showed evidence of social alienation even in countries where 'real socialism' had been installed, that is, where socialism had been realized.

Susan Petrilli

Bibliography

Enzensberger, Hans Magnus. *Gespräche mit Marx und Engels*. Italian translation by A. Casalegno, *Colloqui con Marx ed Engels*. Turin: Einaudi, 1977.

Klaus, Georg. *Die Macht des Wortes*. Berlin: Veb Deutscher Verlag der Wissenchaften, 1964 and 1969. Italian translation, *Il potere della parola. Raffigurazione e teoria pragmatica del discorso*.

Introduced and edited by Arianna De Luca. Bari: Graphis, 2006.

Marcellesi, Jean-Baptiste, et al. *Linguaggi e classi sociali: marxismo e stalinismo*. Papers collected by Augusto Ponzio. Bari: Dedalo, 1978.

Marx, Karl. *Matematische Manuskripte*. German/Russian bilingual text. Moskva: Nauka, 1986. Italian translation and critical edition by A. Ponzio, *Manoscritti matematici*. Milan: Spirali, 2005.

Ponzio, Augusto. Economics. In *Encyclopedic Dictionary of Semiotics*, ed. Thomas A. Sebeok, 215–17. Berlin: Mouton de Gruyter, 1986.

– Semiotics and Marxism. In *The Semiotic Web 1988*, ed. T. Sebeok and J. Umiker-Sebeok, 387–416. Berlin: Mouton de Gruyter, 1989.

– *Individuo umano, linguaggio e globalizzazione nella filosofia di Adam Schaff*. Con una intervista ad Adam Schaff. Milan: Mimesis, 2002.

– *Linguaggio, lavoro e mercato globale. Rileggendo Rossi-Landi*. Milan: Mimesis, 2008.

Rossi-Landi, Ferruccio. *Ideologia*. Milan: Mondadori, 1978 and 1982. English translation by R. Griffin, *Marxism and Ideology*. Oxford: Clarendon, 1990.

Schaff, Adam. *Introduction to Semantics* (Polish original 1960). English translation by O. Wojtasiewics. London: Pergamon Press, 1962.

– *Structuralismus und Marxismus*. Vienna: Europa Verlag, 1974.

– *Humanismus Sprachphilosophie Erkenntnistheorie des Marxismus*. Vienna: Europa Verlag, 1975.

– *Stereotypen und das menschliche Handeln*. Vienna: Europa Verlag, 1980.

Voloshinov, Valentin N. *Marksizm i filosofija jazyca*. Leningrad, 1929. English translation by L. Matejka and I.R. Titunik, *Marxism and the Philosophy of Language*. Cambridge, MA: Harvard University Press, 1973.

MASS COMMUNICATION

[See also: *Broadcasting; Communication; Frankfurt School; Internet; Media Effects; World Wide Web*]

What role does mass communication play in our lives? What are the effects of creating and distributing cultural goods on a mass scale for individuals and society?

How does the audience make sense of the unlimited stream of content being produced by the media industry? While the nature of mass communication has drastically changed since the inception of the discipline of mass communication in the early twentieth century, understanding the role mass media play in people's everyday lives is still of utmost importance. The role of the mass media in people's lives also changes continually as society develops and new forms of mass media emerge. For example, since the 1990s the internet and cellphones have radically transformed how media content is produced, accessed, and distributed. This shift in mass communication raises many questions about how new forms of mass media are used, the nature of the audience in producing and consuming content, and the effects it has on society. Scholars and policymakers will have to develop different frameworks and approaches to address these questions. This entry provides a brief overview of the history of mass communication and discusses key theories, approaches, debates, and challenges in the field.

Defining Mass Communication

In the past, definitions of mass communication focused on the distribution of content on a large scale through traditional mass media including print, cinema, photography, and radio and television broadcasting – forms of communication that are mass distributed and centrally produced. With the introduction of digital technologies and the enormous popularity of the internet in many parts of the world, traditional definitions of mass media have expanded to include forms of information diffusion that are decentralized in the production and distribution of content. These are often referred to as the *new mass media*, or *new media* for short. New media comprise a wide range of applications such as file exchange programs (e.g., file transfer protocol, or FTP), websites, and weblogs (or blogs). The internet has not only created different types

of communication, but also has provided traditional media with distinct forms of production and distribution. Print sources, such as newspapers, often have an online version mirroring content from the print counterpart, but also including additional information and distinct forms of content production and distribution unique to the internet. In this way, new media have enhanced how content produced for traditional media is packaged, accessed, and used.

Recent developments in communication technologies, such as cellphones, personal organizers, email, and instant messaging, have begun to blur the distinction between the mass media and person-to-person communication. Some theorists consider person-to-person forms of computer-mediated communication (CMC), such as interpersonal communication transmitted over the internet or via cellphones, as instances of mass communication because of their volume, their capacity to diffuse information on a mass scale, and their employment of publicly accessible communication channels (Lorimer and Gasher 2004). Moreover, person-to-person forms of communication can now include internet applications and other forms of information production and dissemination (Rheingold 2002). For example, BlackBerries allow users to make phone calls, read and write email, and browse and edit the Web. A BlackBerry is a wireless personal digital assistance (PDA) which supports receiving and sending email, cellphone, text messaging, web browsing, and other services. BlackBerries were introduced in 1999 by the Canadian company Research In Motion (RIM). The use of an ever-increasing array of technologies and applications to create, diffuse, and access information has challenged our understanding of mass communication and mass media, and created new areas of research for mass communication studies.

Early Beginnings of Mass Communication

The origin of the mass media is often traced to the mid-fifteenth century, when Johannes Gutenberg invented printing in Mainz, Germany. Before Gutenberg's invention, the reproduction of texts was cumbersome because each copy needed to be handwritten. What made Gutenberg's invention unique was the design of a movable type that allowed for the mass reproduction of texts. The printing press rapidly spread throughout Europe, leading to major social, cultural, religious, and political change. Hand in hand with the diffusion of the printing press and the availability of more print materials came an increase in literacy. In Italy during the Renaissance, printing helped primarily in the reproduction and dissemination of texts from classical antiquity (Greece and Rome). Particularly well known are the carefully crafted prints by Aldus Manutius in Venice, his collection consisting of a wide range of preserved first editions. In Germany, the Protestant Reformation took advantage of the possibilities afforded by text reproduction and disseminated ideas in the form of manuscripts, cheap prints, and woodcuts that challenged the doctrines and practices of the Catholic Church. As the printing press became more established, there was an increase throughout Europe in the production of original content with writers expressing their ideas and using printing as a means of dissemination. Concerns about copyright, freedom of expression, and rights of access to distributing printed material first began to emerge in this period, as reflected in the *Aeropagitica*, Milton's well-known essay against censorship as outlined in the 1643 Licensing Order proposed by the English Parliament. Despite the changes that have occurred in the production of texts since Gutenberg's invention of movable type, these concerns continue to be of great relevance to current debates about mass communication.

Mass Society Theory

Even though the invention of the printing press is considered a milestone in the history of mass communication, the notion of a mass society formed and influenced by the mass media emerged only in the late nineteenth and early twentieth centuries in the writings of European thinkers such as Émile Durkheim, Ferdinand Tönnies, and Max Weber. These authors were the first to outline the changes and challenges of modern society, although it was not until the formation of the Frankfurt School that the link between mass media production and consumption and the emergence of a mass audience was examined in more detail. The Frankfurt School was a part of the Institute for Social Research at the University of Frankfurt, and members based their writings on Karl Marx's analysis of the exploitation of workers through capitalist means of production. Max Horkheimer, Theodor Adorno, and Herbert Marcuse, all key members of the Frankfurt School, critically examined the impact on cultural life of the production of cultural goods through capitalist means. For them, mass-produced cultural goods led to standardization and uniformity in content, destroying individuality and multiplicity of choice. In their view, exposure to standardized cultural goods – e.g., movies produced in Hollywood – caused members of society to become homogeneous, uncritical, and passive masses with little will power to resist the appeal and influence of the mass media. Although today's conception of the *mass audience* and the effects of mass media on the audience have changed dramatically since the early writings of the Frankfurt School, their notion of the mass audience remains a key concept in studies of mass communication.

Effects Theory

Early influential thinkers also include a number of American writers. Walter Lippman, a journalist and writer, in his 1922 book *Public Opinion*, portrayed a view, similar to the Frankfurt School, of mass media as having a strong and direct effect on audiences. Lippman saw the world as represented through 'pictures in our heads' (1922: 3); the mass media shaped our understanding of the world by providing us with pictures of things we had not experienced ourselves. Yale scholar Harold Lasswell, who was influenced by Lippman's work, also saw the media as shaping public opinion. In *Propaganda Techniques in World War I* (1927), he argued that propaganda had a powerful effect on people's views and behaviours. His ideas stemmed from observations he made during the First World War of people's attitudes and beliefs shaped through a bombardment of war slogans. Lippman, Lasswell, and others saw the mass media as having a uniform and immediate impact on individuals, whom they perceived as vulnerable and unable to form their own opinions. Theories such as these, that portray the media as an all-pervasive power, are often referred to as 'magic bullet theories' or 'hypodermic needle theories' because they emphasize the media's targeted ability to incite particular thoughts or reactions. Underlying these approaches to media effects was an assumption that audiences were homogeneous and that individuals would express identical reactions regardless of their differences in demographic variables, such as age, gender, and socio-economic status. Such views were consonant with contemporary behavioural learning theories that maintained that people's behaviour was largely shaped by the aspects of the outside world such as the media environment (Lowery and DeFleur, 1995).

The Model of Limited Effects

The writings of mass society scholars and effects theorists led to a series of investigations about the influence of the mass media on society. Of particular importance is the work of Paul Lazarsfeld, Bernard R. Berelson, Elihu Katz, and Hazel Gaudet at the Bureau for Applied Social Research at Columbia University in New York, where they used survey polling and interviews to investigate the extent to which the mass media influenced a wide range of behav-

iours, including voting and consumption decisions. The conclusion drawn from a series of panel studies was that the mass media did not have a strong, direct impact on people's everyday decisions. Instead, other factors, including selective attention, retention, age, gender, and political affiliation, appeared to mitigate the effect of the mass media. These findings led to the formulation of the *model of limited effects*. Paul Lazarsfeld and Elihu Katz proposed an alternative model focusing on social processes that influenced how information flowed from the mass media to the audience. In their book *Personal Influence* (1955), they identified opinion leaders as a pivotal linkage between the mass media and the public, and argued that not all individuals are equally exposed and influenced by the mass media. Opinion leaders take the role of gatekeepers of information because they receive messages from the mass media, interpret these, and diffuse them through their personal networks. Based on these findings, they proposed the *two-step flow theory of communication*, where the audience is not conceived as atomized, vulnerable individuals, but rather as members of complex social networks through which information flows. Similarly, in *The Effects of Mass Communication* (1960), Joseph Klapper argued that the mass media only play a limited role in changing beliefs and decisions, and that social relations are the critical factor in opinion formation.

Revisiting Effects Theory

In the 1970s and 1980s theorists began to revisit the assumptions of effects theory by acknowledging that while the effects of mass media were limited, they were nevertheless profound and long-term. Bernard Cohen (1963), for example, argued that while the media cannot change people's opinions about issues, it can influence which topics people consider relevant. Related to Cohen's ideas, Maxwell McCombs and Donald Shaw proposed *agenda-setting theory* in 1972 based on their 1968 study of the presidential campaign in Chapel Hill, North Carolina. In that study, they found that the media were instrumental in shaping the topics that were the focus of public debate. From this perspective, the media exert their influence by directing public attention and shaping what people care about (Griffin 2006). A second line of theorizing similar to agenda-setting theory was shaped by George Gerbner in the 1960s. Gerbner was head of the Cultural Indicators research project and dean of the Annenberg School of Communications at the University of Pennsylvania when he undertook a series of studies investigating the impact of television on the audiences' attitudes, behaviours, and ideas of the world. In a 1976 study, Gerbner compared the beliefs of television viewers with that of non-viewers and found that perceptions of violence of those who watched frequently were higher than the perceptions of infrequent television watchers. He proposed *cultivation theory* based on the idea that television had small but cumulative long-term effects on attitudes. The main problem he saw with television viewing, in particular heavy watching, was that it 'cultivated' specific images and attitudes. For example, people watching television may believe that there is more violence in society based on the images represented on television. As McQuail and Windahl (1993) note, cultivation theory does not see television as providing a direct reflection of the world, but rather as representing a world in itself. A third perspective was formulated by German scholar Elisabeth Noelle-Neumann (1984), who saw the media as having powerful long-term effects on public opinion formation and expression. Her work is most known for the *spiral of silence framework*, where she argues that individuals who perceive their opinion to be in the minority tend to remain silent because of fear of confrontation, ridicule, or isolation. In her view, the role of the media is to reflect the majority opinion and 'silence' other voices. Hence, the media do not have a direct effect on individuals' opinions, but rather have an effect on what individuals perceive the majority opinion to be.

Political Economy

Like their predecessors in the Frankfurt School, *political economy of media* theorists draw heavily on Marx's analysis of capitalist means of production and study how ownership and control influence power dynamics. Political economists of media examine the structure of ownership underlying media production and the social, political, and cultural consequences of ownership and control. In their classic work *Manufacturing Consent*, Edward Herman and Noam Chomsky (1988) discuss five ways in which in North America media content is used to keep control over the masses: (1) Ownership of media is concentrated in the hands of a few powerful and wealthy people (the elite). The elite's views, which are often conservative, are presented in the media. (2) Because media depend on advertisers for their revenues, they will focus on simple and light-hearted topics that support a consumer mood in audiences. (3) The experts used in news sources are likely to be members of the elite themselves representing the elite's viewpoint on key issues. (4) If news stories contradict or dismiss the elite's viewpoint, the elite uses various forms of discipline or 'flak' to keep the media in line. (5) Ideologies are formulated in people's minds in the form of enemies or alliances that help justify the elite's political strategy – for example, the threat of communism during the Cold War.

The Mass Audience

Research on audiences is undertaken from three different perspectives: media research, public media research, and academic research. Media research examines audiences from a commercial standpoint and attempts to determine audience size and composition in order to target content and advertisements accordingly. From a commercial point of view, audiences are a commodity that can be sold to advertisers. Therefore, a good understanding of the audience helps to attract advertisers and improve product placement. Public media research examines the audiences' habits and preferences in order to improve the services it provides to the public. Public media need to be in tune with their audiences and be able to provide relevant programming. By contrast, academic research is independent from commercial and public interests and its main aim is to increase knowledge about audiences and their relation to the mass media by elaborating on existing theories and proposing alternative ones. Questions of interest include: (1) how audiences use the mass media in their everyday lives; (2) how the mass media affect their audiences; (3) how audiences make sense of the information received through the mass media; and (4) how cultural, historical, political, and other contextual factors affect how audiences use and respond to the mass media. Each of these perspectives provides different views and understandings of the mass audience.

In our current media landscape, two trends intersect to shape the nature of the mass audience. First, the audience is fragmented because of an increase in the number of specialty channels in radio and television broadcasting. Not only are more channels available through cable, but for many programs content on demand is now offered via the internet. Moreover, with the increasing popularity of computer-mediated communication (e.g., email, instant messaging, and chat) and internet applications (e.g., YouTube, Google, and Facebook) the audience is divided into silos by a wide range of media types. There is no longer a uniform audience exposed to the same type of media and content, but instead different groups form with unique media preferences and habits. A second trend influencing the nature of the mass audience is the shift from audiences as consumers to audiences as producers of what Philippe Aigrain terms the *creative commons* – that is, the sum

of all original works produced. New media are more likely to facilitate and promote content production because it is decentralized and easily accessible with an internet connection. For example, on YouTube, a video sharing site, people upload videos and comment on videos, creating a blur between consumers and producers of content as well as experts and novices. Moreover, as content production becomes more accessible to the audience, the audience will be more fragmented and more likely to be a blend of producer and consumer.

Studying and Researching Mass Communication

Courses on mass communication are offered in journalism, mass communication, and media studies programs. The curriculum prepares students for careers in journalism, photojournalism, advertising, public relations, and radio and television broadcasting. Generally speaking, journalism programs combine theory and practice with a focus on teaching key practical skills for journalistic jobs. Mass communication programs tend to focus on issues around media institutions and processes, such as production and diffusion of information, media effects, and consumption. These programs tend to focus on quantitative research, for example survey research, public opinion polling, and content analysis. By contrast, media studies programs often draw from the field of cultural studies, relying less on quantitative methods. In recent years, the study and research of mass communication have been broadened to include questions and concerns about new media and computer-mediated communication. David Gauntlett has outlined in a recent article entitled 'Media Studies 2.0' a series of challenges and changes in the way media, content, and audiences are investigated as a result of digital technologies.

In the United States, programs in journalism and mass communication offered at colleges and universities are evaluated by the Accrediting Council on Education in Journalism and Mass Communications, or ACEJMC. These evaluations guarantee high standards by assessing the curriculum offered and the professional values and competencies across programs. Of great interest to researchers, students, teachers, and professionals is the Association for Education in Journalism and Mass Communication (AEJMC). The mandate of the AEJMC is to provide a forum for educators, scholars, and professionals to discuss curriculum issues arising in journalism, mass communication, and media studies programs, to promote research in communication, and debate concerns around freedom of expression in our society. The International Communication Association (ICA) presents an international forum for researchers to get together and discuss current research, curriculum innovations, and challenges, as well as key concerns of media professionals. National associations of importance in North America are the National Communication Association (NCA) in the United States and the Canadian Communications Association (CCA).

Anabel Quan-Haase

Online Resources

Accrediting Council on Education in Journalism and Mass Communication (ACEJMC). http://www2.ku.edu/~acejmc/
This council evaluates university and college journalism and mass communication programs, providing resources and information to students and to university faculty and administration.
Association for Education in Journalism and Mass Communication (AEJMC). http://www.aejmc.org/
The AEJMC in an educational organization directed to faculty in mass communications and journalism, administrators, professionals, and students.
Canadian Communications Association (CCA). http://www.acc-cca.ca/

The CCA links and disseminates research by scholars and professionals working in communications, as well as journalism, media studies, and art.
International Communication Association (ICA). http://www-rcf.usc.edu/~ica/
The ICA is an organization linking communications researchers and includes mass communication as one of its seventeen principal divisions. This group also publishes several journals, such as the *Journal of Communication*.
John Milton's Areopagitica. http://www.uoregon.edu/~rbear/areopagitica.html
This site provides the text of English writer John Milton's 1664 anti-censorship essay, *Areopagitica*.
Mass Communication entry, Wikipedia.org. http://en.wikipedia.org/wiki/Mass_communication
This entry offers a brief overview of mass communication.
National Communication Association (NCA). http://www.natcom.org
The NCA is a non-profit organization dedicated to researching communication and publicizing scholarship within communications. The NCA is responsible for publishing nine academic journals.

Bibliography

Aigrain, Philippe. Diversity, Attention and Symmetry in a Many-to-Many Information Society. *First Monday* 11, no. 6 (2006). http://firstmonday.org/issues/issue11_6/aigrain/index.html.
Anderson, James A. *Communication Theory: Epistemological Foundations*. New York: The Guilford Press, 1996.
Baldwin, John R., Stephen D. Perry, and Mary Anne Moffitt, eds. *Communication Theories for Everyday Life*. Boston: Pearson, 2004.
Cohen, Bernard C. *The Press and Foreign Policy*. Princeton: Princeton University Press, 1963.
Gauntlett, David. Media Studies 2.0 (February 2007). http://www.theory.org.uk/mediastudies2.htm (accessed 23 February 2007).

Gerbner, George, and Larry Gross. Living with Television: The Violence Profile. *Journal of Communication* 26, no. 2 (1976): 172–99.

Griffin, Em. *A First Look at Communication Theory.* 6th ed. Boston: McGraw Hill. 2006.

Herman, Edward S., and Noam Chomsky. *Manufacturing Consent: The Political Economy of the Mass Media.* New York: Pantheon Books, 1988.

Klapper, Joseph T. *The Effects of Mass Communication.* New York: Free Press, 1960.

Lasswell, Harold D. *Propaganda Techniques in World War I.* Cambridge, MA: MIT Press, 1927 [1971].

Lazarsfeld, Paul F., and Elihu Katz. *Personal Influence: The Part Played by People in the Flow of Mass Communications.* Glencoe, IL: Free Press, 1955.

Lazarsfeld, Paul F., Bernard Berelson, and Hazel Gaudet. *The People's Choice.* New York: Columbia University Press, 1968.

Lippman, Walter. *Public Opinion.* New York: Macmillan, 1922.

Lorimer, Rowland, and Mike Gasher. *Mass Communication in Canada.* 5th ed. Don Mills, ON: Oxford University Press, 2004.

Lowery, Shearon A., and Melvin L. DeFleur. *Milestones in Mass Communication Research: Media Effects.* 3rd ed. White Plains, NY: Longman, 1995.

McCombs, Maxwell. News Influence on Our Pictures of the World. In *Media Effects: Advances in Theory and Research*, ed. Jennings Bryant and Dolf Zillmann, 34–56. Hillsdale, NJ: Lawrence Erlbaum, 1994.

McQuail, Denis, and Sven Windahl. *Communication Models for the Study of Mass Communication.* London: Longman, 1993.

Miller, Katharine. *Communication Theories: Perspectives, Processes, and Contexts.* New York: McGraw-Hill, 2005.

Noelle-Neumann, Elisabeth. *The Spiral of Silence: Public Opinion – Our Social Skin.* Chicago: University of Chicago Press, 1984.

Rheingold, Howard. *Smart Mobs: The Next Social Revolution.* Cambridge, MA: Perseus, 2002.

Scheufele, Dietram A., and Patricia Moy. Twenty-Five Years of the Spiral of Silence: A Conceptual Review and Empirical Outlook. *International Journal of Public Opinion Research* (1999): 954–82.

McLUHAN, HERBERT MARSHALL (1911–80)

[See also: *Communication; Electronic Media; Global Village; Gutenberg Galaxy; Information; Innis, Harold; Media Effects*]

Marshall McLuhan was a communications and media philosopher best known for studying the media in relation to cultural evolution and technological change. He was born on 21 July 1911 in Edmonton, Alberta. The family moved to Winnipeg, Manitoba, where McLuhan earned both his bachelor of arts and master of arts degree at the University of Manitoba. He then went to study at the University of Cambridge in England. In 1936, McLuhan took a job as a teaching assistant at the University of Wisconsin, before joining the faculty at the University of Saint Louis. His decision to join that Roman Catholic institution came after his conversion to Catholicism in 1937. In fact, he taught at Roman Catholic institutions for the rest of his career by choice. Upon receiving his PhD degree in 1943 from Cambridge, while still working at Saint Louis University, McLuhan returned to Canada to teach at Assumption College in Windsor, Ontario, before becoming a faculty member of St Michael's College, a Catholic college at the University of Toronto. In Toronto, McLuhan met Harold Innis, a political economist who profoundly influenced McLuhan's ideas of the media as 'extensions' of the human body and brain. In 1957, McLuhan, along with others who belonged to the Toronto School of Communication, as it is now known, began a periodical, *Explorations.* With funding from the Ford Foundation, the University of Toronto created the Centre for Culture and Technology in 1963, which McLuhan headed. In 1970, McLuhan was made a Companion of the Order of Canada, having received six honorary degrees. McLuhan was appointed the McDermott Chair at the University of Dallas. He received the Gold Medal Award from the President of the Italian Republic at Rimini, the Christian Culture Award at

Assumption University, and the President's Cabinet Award at the University of Detroit. He passed away on 31 December 1980.

McLuhan's many books include: *The Mechanical Bride: Folklore and Industrial Man* (1951), *Understanding Media: The Gutenberg Galaxy* (1962), *The Extensions of Man* (1964), *The Medium Is the Massage* (1967), *War and Peace in the Global Village* (1968, with Quentin Fiore and Jerome Angel), *Through the Vanishing Point* (1968, with Harley Parker), *Counter-Blast* (1970, with Harley Parker), *From Cliché to Archetype* (1970), *Culture Is Our Business* (1970), *The Global Village* (1988, with B.R. Powers), *Laws of Media* (1988, with Eric McLuhan), and *Essential McLuhan* (1995).

McLuhan's best-known work is, arguably, *Understanding Media: The Extensions of Man,* in which he coined the phrase 'the medium is the message,' meaning that a 'medium shapes and controls the scale and form of human association and action' (1962: 9) and is therefore the message. In the book, he also developed the concept of 'hot' and 'cool' media, which are terms referring to the different degrees of participation someone experiences with respect to a specific medium. A medium that requires more effort to extract meaning from it is said to be 'cool' and to have 'low definition,' while one which requires very little effort is 'hot' and has 'high definition.' As McLuhan wrote, 'any hot medium allows of less participation than a cool one, as a lecture makes for less participation than a seminar, and a book for less than a dialogue' (1962: 25).

McLuhan put forward four 'laws' to which all human artefacts (including media) are subject: amplification, obsolescence, reversal, and retrieval. These laws, also known as the 'lifecycle' of a medium, imply that a new invention or technology will at first enhance some sensory, intellectual, or other faculty of the user; then, while one area is amplified, another is lessened or eventually rendered obsolete, until the artefact is used to maximum capacity and must reverse its characteristics

until it is retrieved in another medium. An example given by McLuhan is that of print, which initially enhanced the concept of 'individualism,' rendering group identity obsolete until it changed from a single printed text to mass production, whereby mutual reading allowed for the retrieval of group identity.

In *The Medium Is the Massage*, we find another of his famous remarks (now a cliché), namely that we now live in a 'global village,' with no limits of time and space, since anyone around the world can communicate with anyone else at any time. It is through electronic media, therefore, that we are recapturing our innate sense of tribalism, from which we were separated especially in the age of print.

The idea of a global village was not an original one. Lewis Mumford had expressed a similar idea in *Technics and Civilization* (1934). And in 1948, Wyndham Lewis had observed that the 'earth has become one big village, with telephones laid from one end to the other' (Lewis 1948: 21). It was the way in which McLuhan articulated his idea rather than the actual idea that caught people's attention. Moreover, in seeing the electronic village as interconnected by electrons as extensions of neurons he provided a framework for understanding how we merge with our media products cognitively. His colleague at the University of Toronto, Harold Innis, was also discussing the effects of communication systems on society in his *Bias of Communication*, published in 1951, the same year in which McLuhan published *Mechanical Bride*. In both, we can discern an interest in different kinds of media for the evolution of knowledge.

McLuhan actually hated the modern world and its intrusive technology. He saw the allure of a fictitious comic book hero such as Superman as a 'symptom' of what happens when philosophy and traditional ethics vanish from everyday thought (Coupland 2010). He was an expert in Renaissance literature and an avid reader of James Joyce, both of which put him in a frame of mind to look critically at the world, especially at how changes in language reflect changes in cognition, and how these result in changes in mass communications technologies. His fear was that Big Brother, in the form of mass communications technologies, would take over the world and that people would acquiesce because it was convenient for them to do so.

McLuhan is often critiqued for not having a theory about anything, just a series of aphorisms and sound bytes. Again, it was more the manner in which he put forth his ideas rather than the content of his ideas that is important. Inspired by reading Giambattista Vico (McLuhan and McLuhan 1992), the Neapolitan philosopher who wrote in a similar way, McLuhan used a style that was poetic and aphoristic, for only in this way, he thought, could deep ideas be articulated concretely without losing them in the prosaic train of thought.

As electronic media proliferate and become more sophisticated, McLuhan's work continues to be relevant. His concepts of the global village, his laws of media, and his view of the media as extensions of human abilities continue to form a large fund of ideas in media studies today.

Mariana Bockarova

Bibliography

Coupland, Douglas. *Marshall McLuhan: You Know Nothing of My Work!* New York: Atlas, 2010.

Lewis, Wyndham. *America and Cosmic Man.* New York: Doubleday, 1948.

McLuhan, Marshall. *The Mechanical Bride: Folklore of Industrial Man.* New York: Vanguard Press, 1951.

– *The Gutenberg Galaxy: The Making of Typographic Man.* Toronto: University of Toronto Press, 1962.

– *Understanding Media: The Extensions of Man.* Cambridge, MA: MIT Press, 1964.

– *Understanding Me: Lectures and Interviews.* Edited by Stephanie McLuhan and David Staines. Toronto: McClelland and Stewart, 2003.

McLuhan, Marshall, and Quentin Fiore. *The Medium Is the Massage: An Inventory of Effects.* New York: Bantam, 1967.

McLuhan, Marshall, and Eric McLuhan. *The Laws of Media: The New Science.* Toronto: University of Toronto Press, 1992.

Mumford, Lewis. *Technics and Civilization.* New York: Harcourt, Brace, 1934.

McQUAIL, DENIS (b. 1938)

[See also: *Media Effects; Media Studies*]

Denis McQuail is a leading expert in media and communication studies, best known for his widely quoted book *Mass Communication Theory*. After receiving his PhD from the University of Leeds, he began teaching at the University of Southampton and at the University of Leeds. He is now an emeritus professor of sociology and mass communication at the School of Communication Research (ASCOR) at the University of Amsterdam.

In *Mass Communication Theory*, McQuail argues that the media constantly offer people models of behaviour, thus imparting or reinforcing norms and values to society. The internet, according to McQuail, is changing the role of the audience through its interactivity functions and its capacity to overcome the traditional barriers of space and time. Its easy accessibility interconnects information and knowledge content to the global community. Knowledge of the world is thus becoming less and less culture-specific. But despite these features, the internet is nonetheless being exploited for the traditional reasons – selling, advertising, propaganda, and persuasion. McQuail claims the uses of media, the internet or otherwise, remain the same.

Mariana Bockarova

Bibliography

McQuail, Dennis. *Mass Communication Theory: An Introduction.* London: Sage, 2000.
– *Media Accountability and Freedom of Publication.* Oxford: Oxford University Press, 2003.

MEANING

[See also: *Communication and the Media; Conceptual Metaphor Theory; Denotation versus Connotation; Language; Markedness Theory; Semiotics, Structuralism*]

How do humans determine the meanings of symbols, words, sentences, and texts? There probably is no definitive answer to this question. This is compounded by the fact that the word *meaning* in English (and its equivalent in other languages) has many meanings, as Ogden and Richards showed in their 1923 work *The Meaning of Meaning.* The word had at least twenty-three meanings in English, including the following:

She *means* to go there.	= 'intends'
A red light *means* stop.	= 'indicates'
Family *means* everything to him.	= 'has importance'
Her look was full of *meaning.*	= 'special import'
Life must have a *meaning.*	= 'purpose'
What does that word *mean* to you?	= 'signify'
etc.	

The terms *reference, sense,* and *definition* are used in linguistics and semiotics in place of 'meaning.' Reference is the process of pointing out and encoding something in words or symbols; sense is what the encoded thing (known as the *referent*) entails psychologically, culturally, historically, and socially; and definition is a formal statement about the referent. Words may have the same *referents,* but they have different *senses.* For instance, both the words *rabbit* and *hare* refer to a 'long-eared, short-tailed, burrowing mammal of the family Leporidae.' But the two have different senses: a *hare* refers to a larger mammal, with longer ears and legs; *rabbit* is viewed as a 'pet,' while a *hare* is not. The German philosopher Gottlob Frege (1879) stressed the importance of this distinction, using the example of how we named the 'fourth smallest planet and the second planet from the Sun.' Both *Venus* and *Morning Star* are used, but they have different senses – *Venus* refers to the planet itself (even if it embodies implicit references to the goddess of the same name), while *Morning Star* brings out the fact that Venus is visible in the east before sunrise. Willard O. Quine (1961) used the example of a situation in which someone overhears the word *Gavagai* during a conversation between two speakers of a different language when a rabbit is sighted. The non-native speaker, however, cannot determine if the word means 'rabbit,' 'undetached rabbit parts,' or 'rabbit stage' because, as he has discovered from studying the language, these are all senses evoked by the word *Gavagai.* The meaning, therefore, remains indeterminate unless it can be inferred from the *context* in which it is used.

Definition is a statement about what a form means. As useful as it is, it is something that leads inevitably to circularity. Consider the dictionary definition of *cat* as 'a small carnivorous mammal domesticated since early times as a catcher of rats and mice and as a pet and existing in several distinctive breeds and varieties.' A problem that immediately surfaces is the use of *mammal* to define *cat.* In effect, one concept has been replaced by another. So, what is the meaning of *mammal*? The dictionary states that it is 'any of various warm-blooded vertebrate animals of the class Mammalia.' But this definition too entails the question, What is an *animal*? The dictionary goes on to define an *animal* as an *organism,* which it defines, in turn, as an individual form of *life.* It then goes into a loop by defining *life* as the property possessed by *organisms.* Looping patterns surface in all domains of human knowledge, suggesting that forms can never be understood in the absolute, only in relation to other signs and forms. In a definition, looping is caused by the fact that words are used to define other words. What this shows, in effect, is that there is no such thing as an 'absolute meaning.'

The words *denotation* and *connotation* are preferred to *reference* and *sense* within both linguistics and semiotics. The meaning of *cat* as a 'creature with four legs, whiskers, retractile claws' is its *denotative* meaning. This is the meaning used to distinguish a *cat* – a mammal with 'retractile claws,' 'long tail' – from some other mammal. All other senses associated with the word *cat* are *connotative*: *He's a cool cat* (an attractive and suave person); *She let the cat out of the bag* (a secret). Connotation results from the accretion of senses added to words and symbols through usage. By naming something a *cat*, speakers of English have necessarily differentiated it conceptually from other animals. The world is ipso facto divided conceptually into a basic ontological opposition – animals that are perceived to be *cats* and all the other animals, perceived as *non-cats*. This bears cognitive consequences – by having the word *cat* in our mental lexicon we are inclined to attend to the presence of this creature in the world as unique. We can then turn our attention to the world of *non-cats*. In that larger cognitive domain, we detect creatures that seem to have physical affinities to *cats* (whiskers, tails, retractile claws, etc.). This suggests a larger conceptual category. In English, the name for that category is *feline*. As soon as that larger domain is named, we have again divided the world into an opposition – *felines* and *non-felines*. In the feline part of the opposition, we can devise further conceptual differentiations, naming them *lions, tigers, cougars, jaguars,* and so forth. We might then consider further distinctions as being useful – *Siamese* and *Persian* (indicating the origin of the cat) are two such distinctions. We eventually stop such opposition-based naming when we see it as being no longer useful or necessary.

In psychology, the word *feline* is said to encode a *superordinate* concept – a concept with a general classificatory function; the word *cat* encodes a *basic* or *prototypical* concept (type of feline); and *Siamese* a subordinate one (indicating a type of *cat*). The reason for making such fine distinctions is based in social or cultural practices or needs. In a world where felines are prominent, people develop a sophisticated terminology to refer to them; in a world where they do not exist, there are no words for them; and in others where they have a low frequency, there are only a few words for them. In the latter worlds, what we call *cats* may not even have been identified as distinctive, and thus, apportioned to some other domain, along with what we call *dogs* and *horses*, given that they are all four-legged creatures.

The notions developed within conceptual metaphor theory are now used widely to show how abstract concepts are built from concrete ones through figuration (metaphor, metonymy, and other associative processes) (Lakoff and Johnson 1980, 1999). Consider the sentence *That colleague is a snake.* The linkage of two seemingly diverse definitional categories creates a meaning that is much more than the simple sum of the meanings of the two categories (Richards 1936). Utterances such as *John is a gorilla* or *Mary is a snail* are not isolated metaphors (called *linguistic metaphors*). Rather, they are specific instantiations of a mental blend – *people are animals.* Lakoff and Johnson (1980) called this a *conceptual metaphor* – human personality is the *target domain* and animal behaviours the *source domain*, representing the concrete concepts that deliver the metaphor (the 'source' of the metaphorical concept).

Figurative meaning manifests itself in two other main ways, through metonymy (and its counterpart synecdoche) and irony. *Metonymy* is the process of using an attribute of something to stand for the thing itself, as when 'brass' stands for 'military officers'; *synecdoche* is a figure of speech in which the word for part of something is used to mean the whole: for example, 'sail' for 'boat.' *Irony* results from a use of words to convey a meaning contrary to their literal sense: for instance, *I love being tortured* uttered by someone writhing in pain will normally be interpreted as an ironic, not a denotative, utterance. In other words, irony creates a discrepancy between appearance and reality, thus engendering a kind of 'meaning tension by contrast.'

Marcel Danesi

Bibliography

Frege, Gottlob. *Begiffsschrift eine der Aritmetischen nachgebildete Formelsprache des reinen Denkens.* Halle: Nebert, 1879.

Lakoff, George, and Mark Johnson. *Metaphors We Live By.* Chicago: University of Chicago Press, 1980.

Lakoff, George, and Mark Johnson. *Philosophy in the Flesh: The Embodied Mind and Its Challenge to Western Thought.* New York: Basic, 1999.

Ogden, Charles K. *Opposition: A Linguistic and Psychological Analysis.* London: Paul, Trench, and Trubner, 1932.

Ogden, Charles K., and Ivor A. Richards. *The Meaning of Meaning.* London: Routledge and Kegan Paul, 1923.

Quine, Willard. *From a Logical Point of View.* Cambridge: Harvard University Press, 1961.

Richards, Ivor A. *The Philosophy of Rhetoric.* Oxford: Oxford University Press, 1936.

Saussure, Ferdinand de. *Cours de linguistique générale.* Ed. C. Bally and A. Sechehaye. Paris: Payot, 1916.

MEDIA CITIES

[See also: *Globalization; Global Village*]

'Media city' is a term currently used to describe urban media industry centres operating at quite different geographical levels. They range from small-scale local urban clusters of media industry firms to the large-scale regional clustering of media industry activities in the cultural metropolises of the global urban system. Today, the economy of large cities and metropolitan regions is developing towards an increasingly knowledge-intensive and innovation-driven economy, and the media industry is playing a prominent role in this development trend. The media industry is characterized by a strong concentration in the large cities and metropolitan regions. Within these cities and urban regions, the media industry tends to the formation of local clusters (in terms of the spatial concentration of interacting firms), particularly in those inner urban districts where the media firms can find the best creativity impulses. At the same time, the global media firms locate their subsidiary firms and branch offices in the outstanding urban media industry clusters, thereby extending the global connectivity of the large cities and metropolitan regions. In metropolitan regions, which are classified as prominent media cities, the media industry clusters perform a quite strong contribution to urban economic growth. This entry will focus on the geographical organization and institutional order of the media industry as part of the creative economy of cities.

Media Cities and the Institutional Order of the Media Industry

A main characteristic of the geographical organization of the media industry is the selective concentration of media firms in a limited number of large cities and metropolises within the urban system – the most prominent media cities of North America are Los Angeles, New York, and Toronto; the leading media cities in Europe are London, Paris, Berlin, Munich, Milan, and Amsterdam (Krätke and Taylor 2004). The second important characteristic of the media industry is the formation of 'clusters' within the area of large cities, that is, the local concentration of interacting media firms from which dense inter-firm transaction and communication networks emerge. This clustering of specialized firms predominantly occurs in particular urban districts, preferably located in the inner-city area. The locational patterns of the culture and media industry in large cities such as Los Angeles and London reveal that the media industry and cultural production tend to the formation of local agglomerations of specialized firms (Scott 2000; in his comprehensive publication Scott also presents detailed case studies of the media cities Los Angeles, San Francisco, New York, and Paris). The third most important feature of the present-day media industry's institutional order is the globalization of large cultural enterprises, which enables global media firms with their worldwide network of subsidiaries and branch offices to forge links between the urban clusters of media production activities. This supra-regional and international linkage of urban media industry clusters lies at the heart of an emerging network of global media cities within the worldwide urban system.

Today's media industry is a highly differentiated business incorporating diverse sub-sectors that range from creative content production (e.g., in the film and music industry) to technology-intensive branches of the media industry like multimedia production and the internet economy. The major sub-sectors of this industry are audio-visual media (music industry, film- and TV-industry, publishing and printing), the advertising industry, and new cross-sectional activities like the multimedia industry and the internet economy. The products of these activities are of the utmost cultural importance in that they function as agents of information, influence, and persuasion, or as vehicles of entertainment or social self-portrayal. The 'image production' activities of the cultural economy (Scott 2000) in today's marketing society include not merely the product images created by advertising and design agencies, but also the lifestyle images communicated via the program formats of the entertainment and media industries. There is considerable overlapping between the cities' culture industry and the media sector, since a large part of urban cultural production is being organized as a particular activity branch within the media industry. Together they contribute to an increasing mediatization of social communication and entertainment. The media industry is a driving force in the process of commercialization of urban cultural production and lies at the heart of the trend towards a 'culturalization of the urban economy,' given that its market success is founded on the construction of images and extensive marketing activities that are being produced and filled with content by the media industry.

There are further characteristics of the media industry which are linked to the specific features of media cities. Media firms are functioning as main providers of content for the growth sectors of new information and communication technologies and the increasing number of private TV channels. At the same time, the media industry is subject to frequently changing styles and fashions. Thus there is demand for media products with continuously renewed content (Ryan 1992). Fuelled by this dynamic, the media industry clusters in large cities are contributing to the urban economic growth quite positively in terms of job creation and formation of new start-up firms. Second, creative knowledge and continuous innovation of products are most important in the media business. At the same time, the media industry is characterized by a pronounced institutional diversity of its economic actors. The media industry of large cities usually contains a very large number of small, specialized media firms and creative 'freelancers' as well as large customer firms like TV channels and global media firms with a diversified range of activities. Within this institutional setting, the interaction of firms and particularly their cooperation on a project basis (e.g., a particular film production or TV series) in flexibly organized inter-firm networks is widespread. The need for continuous and flexible interaction of specialized media industry firms strongly encourages the formation of local media industry clusters within large urban regions (Krätke 2002).

Media Cities as Centres of Creativity and the Production of Lifestyle Images

Local cluster formation of media firms (as mentioned) regularly occurs in particular urban districts: within large cities and metropolitan regions the media industry clusters are frequently concentrating in culturally attractive inner urban districts or in the districts which are preferred by the city's 'creative scenes' and subcultures. First, the locational preferences of media industry actors are geared towards a spatial combination of working, living, and leisure/cultural life. Second, media firms are seeking locations in proximity to other media firms, since local clustering offers a variety of opportunities for flexible inter-firm cooperation and communication networks (Krätke 2002). Local clustering of media firms in the inner urban districts of a metropolitan region offers easy access to a variety of creativity impulses and to specific (creative) knowledge resources. Furthermore, local clustering is supportive for the creation of a sense of community among start-up firms (which might be helpful for lowering start-up risks). Third, local clustering in culturally attractive inner urban districts offers direct access to urban scenes and (sub-) cultural milieux which are being perceived by the media industry actors as a major source of inspiration and a particular resource of creativity (Florida 2005).

As regards the relationship between urban cultures and the media industry, the prominent media cities are functioning as 'lifestyle producers.' This includes the production of lifestyle images, on which many lifestyle groups are based in recent times. The lifestyle image production activity is a part of the culture and media industry activities. This image production activity is concentrated in the prominent media cities, from which lifestyle images are being spread in the worldwide urban system. In conjunction with the increasing mediatiza-

tion of social communication and entertainment, the culture and media industry functions as a 'trend machine' that picks up on the trends which are developing primarily in the leading metropolises and media cities, exploits them commercially (Ryan 1992), and transmits them worldwide as part of the phenomenon of globalization. This global export of symbolic messages by the culture and media industries has a growing impact on everyday cultures, i.e., value systems and ways of life.

The locations of lifestyle image production activities are the urban media industry clusters that are established primarily in prominent media cities. However, the local concentration of the media industry activity in particular urban districts, which tend to be situated in culturally attractive inner-city areas, is not solely determined by the economic driving forces of cluster formation. It also has much to do with urban lifestyle: in cities such as New York, London, and Berlin, culture and media firms prefer inner-city locations in which living and working environments merge with leisure-time culture. The specific quality of urban life clearly becomes a factor of attraction here. Since this factor of attraction is constituted by the culture and media industry actors themselves, we can speak of a socially produced location advantage of the inner-urban areas of large cities and metropolitan regions. For the firm owners and employees in the media industry the local connection between working, living, and leisure time activities is a factor of attraction that is in harmony with their lifestyle. These people often prefer to live in a 'subcultural' urban district that they can use as a creativity-stimulating social environment which enhances the productivity and innovative capacity of their media content production activity. In the local media industry clusters of prominent media cities there is a direct link between certain lifestyle forms and specific urban forms of creative production activity and thus a clear overlapping of the geographies of production and consumption (Krätke 2003).

The growth of culture and media industry clusters in selected large cities and metropolitan regions is related to the fact that these cities have the sociocultural properties to become a prime location of the 'creative class,' in terms of Richard Florida's concept (2002 and 2005). A concentration of the creative class, in which particularly the human actors of the culture and media scene have a high share, attracts such firms as the music industry as well as the firms of other branches of the media industry. Furthermore, this attraction power also applies to a whole range of other knowledge-intensive industrial activities (the software industry, the life sciences sector, etc.). Florida emphasizes the sociocultural properties which make a city like London, New York, or Berlin particularly attractive as a place of living and working for the creative class: 'Creative people ... don't just cluster where the jobs are. They cluster in places that are centers of creativity and also where they like to live' (Florida 2002: 7). Thus lifestyle attributes of the creative class and a supportive sociocultural milieu are at the centre of a city's attractiveness to the creative economy. At the same time, attractiveness to the creative economy is a major development factor of media cities.

Florida highlights the role of a 'social milieu that is open to all forms of creativity – artistic and cultural as well as technological and economic' (Florida 2002: 55). In an urban sociocultural milieu which is characterized by openness to a diversity of cultures and lifestyles, the many different forms of creativity can take root and flourish. In urban districts where subcultural scenes like a cutting-edge music scene or vibrant artistic community are flourishing, the actors of different activity branches of the creative economy are attracted and stimulated, and a cross-fertilization between different sub-sectors of the culture and media industry is being facilitated (e.g., the combination of creative-content-producing activities and technology-centred media industry activities in today's multimedia industry). A supportive sociocultural milieu as well as the local clustering of media firms and institutions is facilitating the rapid transmission and diffusion of knowledge and ideas (creativity impulses) and thus enhances the innovative capacity of urban media industry clusters.

Moreover, in particular cases the city as a whole can become an attraction factor for the media business in that the symbolic quality of the specific location is being incorporated into the products of the culture and media industry (Scott 2000). Hence production locations such as New York, Hollywood (Los Angeles), Paris, and Berlin are perceived in the sphere of the media as being 'brand names' that draw attention to the attractive social and cultural qualities of the cities concerned. This includes, in particular, the perception of the city as a social space in which there is a pronounced variety of different social and cultural milieux. As regards the content and 'design' of their products, media firms have to contend with rapidly changing trends (Ryan 1992). For that reason the media firms wish to be near the source of new trends that develop in certain metropolises such as New York, Los Angeles, London, Paris, and Berlin.

Metropolises of this kind as well as the upcoming media cities in the urban system are being perceived as a living space with a sociocultural milieu that is marked by great 'openness' and an atmosphere of tolerance. This is turn enhances their attractiveness for creative talents and makes them a source of inspiration for cultural producers. Marked social and cultural variety and openness, therefore, represent a specific 'cultural capital' of a city, which is highly attractive for the actors of the creative economy and particularly the media industry (Krätke 2003). On a local level, this cultural capital of a city might also be characterized as a specific 'subcultural' capital of particular districts within the city. The development of media industry clusters in selected large cities and metropolitan regions and hence the formation of media cities is to a large extent being driven by the location choices of creative people, who 'prefer places that are diverse, tolerant and open to new ideas' (Florida 2002: 223).

The knowledge-intensive activities and the creative economy are an important resource of future urban economic development. However, a flourishing creative and knowledge economy is based on place-specific sociocultural milieux which positively combine with the dynamics of cluster formation within the urban economic space. The formation of media cities thus depends on the dynamic interplay of economic, sociocultural, and spatial factors.

Globalization and Global Media Cities

Today's media industry is characterized by a marked trend towards the globalization of corporate organization. The formation of huge media groups is accompanied by the creation of an increasingly global network of branch offices and subsidiaries. This global network of firms linked under the roof of a media group (i.e., the global media firm) has its local anchoring points in those centres of the worldwide urban system that function as cultural metropolises and centres of the media industry. Thus the media industry is also a prime mover for globalization processes in the urban system, in which urban media industry clusters act as the major local nodes in the globally extended organizational networks of the large media groups (Krätke 2003). The globalization strategy of media firms is geared towards using the different media cities' creative potential, knowledge, and innovation resources on a global scale. The setting up of a subsidiary firm or a branch office in the leading centres of the media industry offers the opportunity to incorporate the latest fashion trends in the sphere of culture and media as quickly as possible and, at the same time, to exploit the latest technological developments in the media sector (e.g., in digital image processing and internet applications). At the local level, the global players in the media industry are networking with the small, specialized producers and service providers of the media indus-

try, thereby establishing a global network of their branch offices and subsidiary firms which links the geographically widespread urban centres of media production with one another. In this way the global media firms are creating a global connectivity of the world's prominent media cities.

A 'global media city' is characterized by the overlapping of the locational networks of a variety of global media firms. This applies, for example, to New York, Los Angeles, Toronto, London, Paris, Milan, Berlin, and Munich. Here, the local and the global firms of the media industry are linked in a development context that fosters the formation of a large urban media cluster whose international business relations are handled primarily via the global media firms that are present. The local media cluster in Potsdam, which is part of the Berlin metropolitan region, might be taken as an example (Krätke 2002) to show that the media cluster firms are not only closely networked within the local business area but are also integrated into the supra-regional location networks of global media firms: in the case of Potsdam the local cluster firms are directly linked with the resident establishments of global media firms from Paris, London, and New York. The global media groups are organizing the worldwide marketing and distribution of their respective media products and are thus contributing to the global spread of media content and formats which are generated in the major production centres of the global media industry, in particular in Los Angeles, New York, Paris, London, Munich, and Berlin (Krätke and Taylor 2004).

Most research on today's world city network has been concentrated on the formation of global cities as the prime locational centres of global firms of advanced producer services. The intra-firm flows of information, knowledge, instruction, and other business between enterprise units of advanced producer service firms has created a world city network based upon the organizational patterns of global firms (Taylor 2004). Research on the media industry's world geography and the network of 'global media cities' in particular started by identifying the most important urban nodes of the global media firms' locational network (Krätke 2003). The locational pattern of the global media firms' organizational units reveals a highly selective geographic concentration on a global scale: in 2001, more than 50 per cent out of nearly 3,000 branch offices and subsidiary firms of global media groups were concentrated in only 22 cities within the global urban system. The leading group of 'alpha' world media cities contained the cities of New York, Los Angeles, London, and Paris, which are ranked as genuine global cities in virtually every analysis of the global urban system. Thus it has to be stressed that today's global cities are to be characterized not only as centres of global corporate services, but also as major centres of the media industry. However, among the other cities that qualify as major global media cities there are interesting deviations from the widely employed global city system: the 'alpha' group of global media cities also includes Berlin, Munich, and Amsterdam, three cities that in global city research which focuses on corporate services were ranked as 'third-rank' world cities. In the system of global media cities, by contrast, these cities are included in the top group, since they have achieved a degree of integration into the location networks of global media firms that qualifies them as internationally outstanding centres of the media industry.

Whereas the global city network constituted by advanced producer services has major nodes which are quite evenly represented in all the major regions of the world (Taylor 2004) – with the exception of Africa – the network of global media cities reveals a rather uneven distribution in favour of the European economic territory (Krätke 2003). In North America, the prime nodes of global locational networks of the media industry are concentrated on just three outstanding centres – New York, Los Angeles,

and Toronto. Europe, on the other hand, has the largest number of media cities with a high global connectivity. The main reason for this is cultural diversity, since the European economic territory has a large number of different nation-states and a multitude of distinct 'regional' markets and cultures. This cultural market differentiation is at the same time a driving force for the organization of global production networks in the media industry with local anchoring points in different nation-states. The above-described network of global media cities as a whole is a reflection of the locational system run by the Western world's media industry, which concentrates primarily on North America and Europe. Large media groups with a transnational impact also exist in Asia (particularly in the metropolitan regions of Mumbai, Taipai, Hong Kong, and Shanghai), but the outstanding media cities of Asia are to be characterized as large urban media industry centres which for the most part serve the various national markets within the world region of Asia.

The formation of media cities has great influence on the developmental dynamics of the media industry. The selective concentration of media industry firms in large cities and metropolitan regions is a component of the overall structural change of the economy of large cities and metropolitan regions towards an increasingly knowledge-intensive and creative economy. In metropolitan regions which are classified as prominent media cities, the media industry activities strongly contribute to urban economic growth. Media cities are characterized by the formation of large clusters of interacting media firms. This clustering is accompanied by dense inter-firm cooperation and flows of knowledge, ideas, and creativity impulses which are strengthening the innovative capacity and development dynamics of urban media industry clusters. In other words, agglomeration economies are of particular significance in the organization and development of the media industry. At the same time, the development of media cities is related to the locational preferences of the 'creative class' and thus dependent on specific socio-cultural properties like diversity, tolerance, and cultural and subcultural capital, which are most important for a city's attractiveness to the creative economy. Within the framework of a globalizing media industry, the prime media cities of the urban system are functioning as major geographic nodes of the organizational networks of global media firms, which in turn leads to an accelerated growth dynamic of global media cities. Contemporary globalization processes in the spheres of culture and the media are to a large extent proceeding from these prime locational centres of the media industry.

Stefan Krätke

Bibliography

Florida, Richard. *The Rise of the Creative Class: And How It's Transforming Work, Leisure, Community and Everyday Life.* New York: Basic, 2002.

– *Cities and the Creative Class.* New York: Routledge, 2005.

Krätke, Stefan. Network Analysis of Production Clusters, The Potsdam/Babelsberg Film Industry as an Example. *European Planning Studies* 10 (2002): 27–54.

– Global Media Cities in a Worldwide Urban Network. *European Planning Studies* 11 (2003): 605–28.

Krätke, Stefan, and Peter J. Taylor. A World Geography of Global Media Cities. *European Planning Studies* 12 (2004): 459–77.

Ryan, Bill. *Making Capital from Culture: The Corporate Form of Capitalist Cultural Production.* Berlin and New York: Walter de Gruyter, 1992.

Scott, Allen J. *The Cultural Economy of Cities: Essays on the Geography of Image-Producing Industries.* London: Sage, 2000.

Taylor, Peter J. *World City Network: A Global Urban Analysis.* London, New York: Routledge, 2004.

MEDIA EFFECTS

[See also: *Bull's-Eye Model; Catharsis Hypothesis; Cognitive Dissonance Theory; Cultivation Theory; Culture Industry Theory; Data Mining; Functionalist Theories; Hegemony Theory; Hypodermic Needle Theory; Psychology of the Media; Reception Theory; Simulacrum Theory; Two-Step Flow Theory; Uses and Gratifications Theory*]

Does the portrayal of violence on television or in movies lead to real-life violence? Does exposure to frivolous sitcom humour weaken serious dialogue? These questions underlie the rationale behind a line of inquiry that attempts to assay the effects of media on people. Known generally as *media effects (ME) studies*, the goal of research in this field of inquiry is to answer questions such as these. The earliest scientific ME studies go back to the late 1930s. Although this strong claim that media directly influence people is now largely abandoned or at least questioned, the weaker claim that media impacts are indirect does seem to hold some validity. Given the obvious importance of such questions, it should come as little surprise to find that research on the purported effects of the mass media has been a target of great interest to psychologists and other social scientists.

Long before the use of psychological surveys and experimental techniques for investigating MEs, a number of scholars saw the advent of mass media culture as spawning a form of 'commodity culture' that was consumed by people in the same way that they consumed manufactured products. The starting point for such critique can be found in the writings of the British social critic Matthew Arnold (1822–83) who, already in the nineteenth century, saw mass culture as being tasteless and homogenized. Arnold initiated a 'culture versus civilization' argument, warning that mass culture was a threat to civilized society. Arnold's attack was taken up by Frank R. Leavis (1895–1978) in the 1930s and 1940s. Leavis saw the spread of American pop culture through mass communications technologies as evidence of the decline of civilization. Although these are now seen as elitist critiques, they are still reference points in the ME debate.

In between Arnold and Leavis, a group of scholars known as the Frankfurt School philosophers also approached the question of MEs from a specific ideological angle – that of Marxism. The Frankfurt School (in full: The Frankfurt Institute for Social Research) was founded at the University of Frankfurt in 1922 as a school of social research aiming to understand how human groups evolved collectively under the impact of modern technology and capitalism. Scholars like Theodor W. Adorno (1903–69), Walter Benjamin (1892–1940), Max Horkheimer (1895–1973), Herbert Marcuse (1898–1979), Erich Fromm (1900–80), and Leo Lowenthal (1900-93) took a highly negative view of mass culture, seeing its emergence as part of a hidden 'culture industry' controlled by power brokers who aligned cultural productions with the logic of marketplace capitalism. Adorno and Horkheimer traced the source of this to the Enlightenment and the subsequent Industrial Revolution. Breaking somewhat from this mould was Walter Benjamin, who put forward a 'catharsis hypothesis,' by which he suggested that the vulgar aspects of mass culture allowed common people to release pent-up energies and, thus, ended up having the effect of pacifying them.

In his 1922 book *Public Opinion*, the American journalist Walter Lippmann argued that the growth of mass media culture had a powerful direct effect on people's minds and behaviour. Although he did not use any empirical evidence to back up his argument, Lippmann's claim is the earliest version of what has come to be called hypodermic needle theory (HNT) – namely, the view that the mass media can directly influence behaviour in the same way that a hypodermic needle can directly affect the body. The American scholar Harold Lasswell took up Lippmann's basic argument in *Propaganda Technique in World War I*

(1927), also suggesting that mass-mediated propaganda affected people's politics, family relations, and general outlooks and behaviours.

But HNT remained at the level of speculation until a truly remarkable event took place in 1938 – the radio broadcast of *War of the Worlds*, Orson Welles's radio adaptation of the H.G. Wells novel about the invasion of Earth by aliens. Many listeners appeared to mistake the broadcast for the real thing, despite regular announcements that it was fiction. Apparently, people left their homes in panic and contacted the local authorities. The event led to the first psychological study of MEs, called the Cantril Study, after Princeton University professor Hadley Cantril, who, with a team of researchers, decided to interview 135 subjects after the event. Titled *The Invasion from Mars: A Study in the Psychology of Panic* (1940), Cantril's study seemed to lend empirical support to HNT when he concluded that the panic caused by the broadcast was real, even though many subjects did not admit to believing it, lying in order to hide their shame.

The Cantril Study was quickly criticized by psychologists and sociologists as being flawed. Among other things, it did not establish a true statistical correlation between the radio broadcast and the degree of reported panic. Moreover, the panic may have been caused by subsequent media reports that intentionally exaggerated the story. In actual fact, no deaths or serious injuries were ever linked to the radio broadcast, and the streets were never crowded with hysterical citizens running around in panic as the media claimed. The reported panic was itself a media fiction.

However, to many observers the Cantril Study seemed to demonstrate that the media did indeed produce effects on people, opening the door to a host of follow-up studies aiming to determine the extent to which media impacts were real. Already in the 1940s scholars started to find different kinds of results, showing, in contrast to the Cantril Study, that people got out of media content what they were already inclined to get. For example, in an influential 1948 study, *The People's Choice*, the American sociologist Paul Lazarsfeld (1901–76) and a team of researchers found that the media had very little (if any) ability to change people's minds about how they would vote in an election. People simply took out of media content only the views that fitted their preconceptions, paying no attention to the others.

Follow-up research has largely corroborated Lazarsfeld's findings. Known generally as *selective perception theory*, it has demonstrated, cumulatively, that the perception of media content is context-bound and often mediated by so-called 'leaders' of the communities in which people live. Lazarsfeld and Elihu Katz (1955) showed that people's interpretations of media content were consistent with the values of the social class or group to which they belonged. Individuals reacted typically to media as members of interpretive communities – families, unions, neighbourhoods, churches, and so forth. In such communities, 'opinion leaders' (for example, union leaders, church ministers) tend to influence how other members will interpret media content. So, in contrast to HNT, which portrays media impact as a one-step flow reaching a homogeneous audience directly, selective perception theory sees it as a two-step flow, in which the first step is through the opinion leader(s) who interpret media content and then, in the second step, pass on their opinions to group members.

In partnership with George Gerbner (1919–2005), Lazarsfeld also argued that the media actually had a conservative social function, rather than a supposed disruptive one. For example, the representation of violence and deviancy on TV crime programs and in movies will hardly lead to more violent crime in society, because such representation has a moral subtext to it – it warns people about the dangers of violence and crime. This is known as *cultivation theory* because it claims that the media 'cultivate,' not threaten, the status

quo. The over-representation of violence in the media, therefore, is intended to reinforce a respect for law and order, since the 'bad guys' will ultimately have to pay for their sins. There is a catch here, however. In the 1960s and 1970s, Gerbner undertook studies investigating the effects television violence had on audiences, finding that the beliefs of 'heavy television viewers' had a heightened sense that the world was a more violent place. He called this phenomenon the 'mean world syndrome.' German scholar Elisabeth Noelle-Neumann (1984) saw the media as having lasting effects. Her *spiral of silence theory* claims that people will tend to remain silent about what they believe, thinking that they are in the minority and thus fearing confrontation or ridicule. They perceive the media as reflecting the majority opinion, and, thus, they tend to remain silent.

In a series of studies, Elihu Katz argued that audiences are not passive consumers of media representations. On the contrary, he claimed, they use the media for their own purposes and gratifications. In his *uses and gratifications theory*, he maintained that media do nothing to people; rather, people use the media for their own desires. British cultural theorist Stuart Hall (b. 1932) also suggested that people do not absorb media passively but rather *read* them in one of three ways – the *preferred* reading is the one that the media hope people will take from their representations (but this is not a guarantee). In the *negotiated* form of reading, people are affected only partially by media content. In an *oppositional* reading, people take away the opposite meaning from what the makers had intended.

In 1972 Maxwell McCombs and Donald Shaw proposed *agenda setting theory*, based on a study in which they found that the media exerted considerable influence by shaping what people are supposed to care about. In other words, what makes it to the media gets attention. At about the same time, feminist critics started attacking the mainstream media for misrepresenting women and catering to the desires of patriarchal institutions and viewers. The early feminists argued that representations of women in the media were essentially degrading and played a role in promoting violence against women. Although no empirical evidence was ever presented to back up the latter claim, some of the critiques were well founded. The images of women in the media as either 'sexual creatures' or 'subservient homemakers' were common, even though there were notable exceptions. But the tide in feminism veered drastically in the opposite direction in the late 1980s. By the 1990s feminist critics saw the media as a critical means through which women had gained liberation, allowing them to assume a sexual persona openly. Called *postfeminism*, the new feminism claimed that the display of female sexuality in media should not be viewed as exploitation, but rather as a subversive form of representation against previous and largely religious representations of women.

Of interest to the whole ME debate are lines of investigation that have been pursued in different domains and by scholars in different disciplines. The *catharsis hypothesis* claims that the function of the media is to provide a vehicle for people to vent their pent-up emotions. Thus, overrepresentations of violence and aggression in the media end up having a preventive effect, since by engaging in a fantasy form of aggression, some people are released from hostile impulses that they would otherwise act out in real life. However, the relevant research on this subject has turned out to be ambiguous. The main finding that can be extrapolated from the research is that the degree to which people are affected by media content depends on background factors such as level of education, which Cantril had originally found in his study.

Also of interest is *propaganda theory*, which claims that the media tend to serve the interests of those in power by manufacturing consent on important issues. The theory is associated with the American linguist Noam Chomsky (Herman and Chomsky 1988), who claims that those in charge of the media determine what news coverage to select and how to present it, making them nothing more than a propaganda arm of the government in power. Examples mentioned as evidence include TV coverage of the Vietnam War and the war on terror (in Afghanistan and Iraq). Propaganda theorists, like other ME supporters, do not seem to believe that ordinary people can tell the difference between truth and manipulation. They claim that the only way the media can be held accountable is by making them broadly accessible. Such access is now becoming a reality because of the internet.

There is one more line of inquiry that merits discussion here – namely the ideas of Canadian communications theorist Marshall McLuhan (1911–80) – since it takes the ME hypothesis and projects it onto a broader psychological and socio-evolutionary terrain. McLuhan claimed that there existed an unconscious synergy between technology, media, and cultural evolution. Each major period in history takes its character from the medium used most widely at the time. From 1700 to the mid-1900s, print technology gave prominence to the print medium. McLuhan called this the 'age of print' and the 'Gutenberg galaxy' – after the inventor of modern print technology, Johannes Gutenberg (ca 1395–1468). In that period, printed books were the chief tools through which mass communications and cultural changes took place. The 'electronic age' displaced the Gutenberg galaxy in the twentieth century. Since electronic modes of communication increase the speed at which people can interact and the number of people who can be reached, they have influenced the lives of everyone, even of those who do not use them.

In McLuhan's view, the reason why media evolution and human evolution now coincide is that media are extensions of sensory, affective, and cognitive processes. Media are thus tools, not only in the literal sense of the word, but also in the sense of intellectual artefacts. An axe extends the ability of the human hand to break wood;

the wheel allows the human foot to cover great distances; the computer allows the human mind to extend its computational prowess; and so on. As the media change, so do our sensory and thus our knowing prowess. The result is sociocultural change.

Today, ME studies have been directed increasingly at the effects of the internet and other digital technologies on individuals and societies. Some researchers claim that the merger of machines and brains is on the verge of becoming a reality (Chlorost 2011). Cyborg theory maintains that through the use of chips and other devices we will evolve into a new species. Implanting a BlackBerry in the brain would be, according to the theory, a logical and inevitable outcome of how technology and human life have been merging since antiquity. Critics counter that this is really a naive wish and that most people want to use technology, not merge with it.

The effects of the internet cannot be denied. As Pariser (2009) has documented in his research, Google is now able to contour every search to match the profile of the individual making the search. The search process is thus 'personalized.' This means that Google can inform a user what is best for him or her. Google can in this way direct a user to information that reinforces the person's supposed world view, ideological inclinations, and beliefs. This cuts people off from different viewpoints and dissenting opinions. The internet is thus generating 'mind bubbles' in which individuals remain imprisoned. Pariser (2009: 24) puts it as follows: 'Democracy requires citizens to see things from one another's point of view, but instead we're more and more enclosed in our own bubbles' (2009: 24).

Another negative effect of the new media is that we might be losing our sense of self as we interconnect with others through the internet. Echoing Marshall McLuhan, Lanier (2010: 12) suggests:

> We [engineers] make up extensions to your being, like remote eyes and ears (webcams and mobile phones) and expanded memory (the world of details you can search for online). These become the structures by which you connect to the world and other people ... We tinker with your philosophy by direct manipulation of your cognitive experience ... It takes only a tiny group of engineers to create technology that can shape the entire future of human experience with incredible speed.

ME study is probably more important today than it ever was, as it focuses on the ways in which new media change people and societies. It is evolving into an investigation that looks not only at how individuals are affected by media, but at how technology, media, and the human brain interact.

Marcel Danesi

Bibliography

Adorno, Theodor W. *The Culture Industry*. London: Routledge, 1999.

Cantril, Hadley, *The Invasion from Mars: A Study in the Psychology of Panic*. Edison, NJ: Transaction Publishers, 1940.

Chorost, Michael. *World Wide Mind: The Coming Integration of Humanity, Machines, and the Internet*. New York: Free Press, 2011.

Cook, Deborah. *The Culture Industry Revisited: Theodor W. Adorno on Mass Culture*. Lanham, MD: Rowman and Littlefield, 1996.

Gerbner, George, and Larry Gross. Living with Television: The Violence Profile. *Journal of Communication* 26 (1976): 172–99.

Grossberg, Lawrence, Cary Nelson, and Paula Treichler, eds. *Cultural Studies*. London and New York: Routledge, 1991.

Hall, Stuart. *Encoding and Decoding in the Television Discourse*. London: The Seminar Press, 1973.

Herman, Edward S., and Noam Chomsky. *Manufacturing Consent: The Political Economy of the Mass Media*. New York: Pantheon, 1988.

Horkheimer, Max, and Theodor W. Adorno. *Dialectic of Enlightenment*. New York: Herder and Herder, 1972.

Jay, Martin. *The Dialectical Imagination: A History of the Frankfurt School and the Institute for Social Research 1923–1950*. Berkeley: University of California Press, 1996.

Jenkins, Henry. *Convergence Culture: Where Old and New Media Collide*. New York and London: MIT, 2006.

Katz, Elihu. *Election Studies: What's Their Use?* Boulder, CO: Westview Press, 2000.

Klapper, Joseph T. *The Effects of Mass Communication*. New York: Free Press, 1960.

Lanier, Jaron. *You Are Not a Gadget*. New York: Vintage, 2010.

Lasswell, Harold D. *Propaganda Techniques in World War I*. Cambridge: MIT Press, 1927.

Lazarsfeld, Paul F., and Elihu Katz. *Personal Influence: The Part Played by People in the Flow of Mass Communications*. Glencoe, IL: Free Press, 1955.

Lazarsfeld, Paul F., Bernard Berelson, and Hazel Gaudet. *The People's Choice*. New York: Columbia University Press, 1950.

Lippmann, Walter. *Public Opinion*. New York: Macmillan, 1922.

Lowenthal, Leo. *Literature, Popular Culture and Society*. Englewood Cliffs, NJ: Prentice-Hall, 1961.

Lowery, Shearon A., and Melvin L. DeFleur. *Milestones in Mass Communication Research: Media Effects*. 3rd ed. White Plains, NY: Longman, 1995.

Marcuse, Herbert. *One Dimensional Man*. Boston: Beacon Press, 1964.

– *An Essay on Liberation*. Boston: Beacon Press, 1969.

McCombs, Maxwell. News Influence on Our Pictures of the World. In *Media Effects: Advances in Theory and Research*, ed. Jennings Bryant and Dolf Zillmann, 23–34. Hillsdale, NJ: Lawrence Erlbaum, 1994.

McLuhan, Marshall. *The Mechanical Bride: Folklore of Industrial Man*. New York: Vanguard, 1951.

– *The Gutenberg Galaxy*. Toronto: University of Toronto Press, 1962.

– *Understanding Media*. London: Routledge and Kegan Paul, 1964.

McQuail, Denis. *Mass Communication Theory: An Introduction*. London: Sage, 2000.

McRobbie, Angela, and Mica Nava, eds. *Gender and Generation*. London: Macmillan, 1984.

Noelle-Neumann, Elisabeth. *The Spiral of Silence: Public Opinion – Our Social Skin*. Chicago: University of Chicago Press, 1984.

Pariser, Eli. *The Filter Bubble: What the Internet Is Hiding from You*. Harmondsworth: Penguin, 2009.

Tong, R. *Feminist Thought: A Comprehensive Introduction*. Boulder, CO: Westview Press, 1989.

Wiggershaus, Rolf. *The Frankfurt School: Its History, Theories and Political Significance*. Cambridge, MA: MIT Press, 1995.

Williams, Raymond. *Marxism and Literature*. London: New Left Books, 1977.

– *The Sociology of Culture*. New York: Schocken, 1982.

MEDIA LITERACY

[See also: *Electronic Media; Globalization; Literacy; McLuhan, Marshall; Media Effects*]

Western culture is currently obsessed with notions of literacy. The concept of literacy, as a result, gets awkwardly mapped onto all manner of media, learning, and forms of engagement, creating bastard hybrids like 'social literacy,' 'cultural literacy,' 'visual literacy,' and 'media literacy.' We now clumsily use the word as a means of discussing our facility in navigating a vast array of cultural and social differences and environments. Unfortunately, literacy does not translate very well across cultures in an age of globalization because it is a concept that exists only in English (Kress 2003: 22). Other languages do not even have a word for it, although they do for the concept of alphabetic writing or of being 'lettered,' as in *alphabetisme* in French. Over two decades ago, classicist Eric Havelock (1986) observed that this preoccupation with literacy in contemporary culture existed alongside our newly rediscovered awareness of the earlier 'crisis in communication' that was the historical shift from orality to alphabetic culture, and that this obsession has arisen to such prevalence precisely because we are perched at the moment where literacy is ceasing to be the guiding light of cultural navigation.

The noun *literacy* is a late arrival in the linguistic world. Just as the word and concept of being *literate* was born roughly contemporaneous with the need for printing press technology (circa 1432 for the word, 1436 for the machine), *illiterate* did not exist until more than a century later in 1556 when books had become widely available (if not affordable) commodities (OED Online). *Literacy,* by contrast, as a word and a concept only sprung into being in 1883 in the context of universal education (OED Online) and at a time when photography was just beginning to be animated by the early moving picture technologies that pre-dated film's arrival in 1895. As the spread of media choices expanded, a word was needed to privilege text as the signature badge of an education, and to designate it as unique in its properties. We continue to use the term literacy now among and for our escalating wealth of increasingly visual media precisely because it is such a powerful metaphor to describe a particular means of engagement with our technologies.

As screen-based media gain greater cultural importance and relevance over print-based ones, the traditional monocular focal point of visual perspective (credited with birthing the Renaissance) is similarly starting to wane as a useful tool for making sense of our time and world. It is the monomodal nature of literacy and perspective that has relegated these tools that have ruled Western culture for so long to the backseat in the immersive spaces of multi-media culture. As the current generation of technologies of media creation and distribution become increasingly powerful and accessible, discursive practice in our multimodal cultural environment now includes the ability to pick and choose between media of expression, which might involve alphabetic text as well as image, sound, and animation. So-called 'media literacy' is this new ability to navigate multimodally using social software and participatory media, and to combine them with the navi-gation of new mnemonic technologies and methods. Media convergence through the combined forces of digitization and globalization is transforming these phenomena into a new hybrid altogether as mode and media separate, as literacy is superseded by multimodality, and perspective is replaced by multidimensional orientation in a post-literate world.

Post-literacy does not mean that literacy is dead, but that the essence of what it means to be literate in our digital culture has so altered our world that the old rules no longer apply. Post-literacy is a revolutionary new way of engaging with cultural information. Our world is in a massive state of transition as we undergo a paradigm shift, a sea change in the way we perceive and interact with culture and media. From their own unique viewpoints, Marshall McLuhan, Walter Ong, and Vilém Flusser have all documented these visual and discursive revolutions that Western civilization is experiencing as a result of unprecedented technological change. In another age, literacy and the printed book in particular marked a similar transition from oral to written culture that wholly transformed human consciousness. The alphabet, McLuhan argued, splintered the senses, privileging the eye above all others and superseding the ear that had ruled the oral world. Printing and the printing press gave birth to nationalism and eventually to the private self and to private expression (2004: 58–60). The book imposed temporality on the word, Ong (1988) argues, making it appear to be finite and making words seem to be authoritative. The author within such a technological framework of information dissemination became a monolithic authority, a construct, whose power was indisputable within the concrete space of the printed page. This shift away from orality led to the birth of history and the sciences, codification, classification, hierarchies and other linear methods of ordering knowledge.

In the last two centuries, we have undergone a sensory re-alignment again with the arrival of electricity as communication technologies have been replaced by information technologies:

> With the advent of a world environment of simultaneous and instantaneous information, Western man shifted from visual to acoustic space, for acoustic space is a sphere whose center is everywhere and whose boundaries are nowhere. Such is the space created by electric information which arrives simultaneously from all quarters of the globe. It is a space which phases us out of the world of logical continuity and connected stability into the space-time world of the new physics, in which the mechanical bond is the resonant interval of touch where there are no connections, but only interfaces. (McLuhan 2004: 194)

As immersion becomes the norm for interfacing with our information and ubiquitous computing increasingly prevalent, we take for granted being plugged in. Where the mechanical media had functioned as an extension of our bodies, electric – and later electronic – media become virtual extensions of our nervous systems and our interface with the world. The significance of this lies in the fact that the new media are information systems with 'a completely different set of effects on psyche and society from any effects that the old mechanical technologies had' (McLuhan 2004: 62–3). The electronic media birthed this acoustic space with public interfaces, moving us out of the private mind frame that contained our thoughts, bursting the bindings on the monolithic book and other binary logics, and allowing us to experience a new structuring of our attention: a new kind of participation. This new attention is an embodiment of McLuhan's view of media as the 'extensions of man': an externalization of the senses that the electronic media have wrought on us and on our bodies.

Theorist Gregory Ulmer has extended the concept of (post)literacy into the digital age by coining the neologism *electracy*.

What literacy is to print, electracy is to digital media. It seeks to describe the skill or facility required to create born-digital media, including hypermedia, social software, and virtual worlds. Combining the word 'electricity' with a Derridean 'trace' (the spatial abilities exhibited by all communications media), it is a 'prosthesis that enhances and augments a natural or organic human potential': 'What literacy is to the analytical mind, electracy is to the affective body,' Ulmer says. 'If literacy focused on universally valid methodologies of knowledge (sciences), electracy focuses on the individual state of mind within which knowing takes place (arts)' (Ulmer 2003: xi). Functioning as a rhetoric for electronic media, electracy ultimately is a grammatological extension of the history of literacy. Our contemporary shift from print literacy to electronic interactivity propagated by the electronic media troubles these temporal and spatial logics anew. We are shifting again to a new dispersed logic that is in a perpetual state of flux. The interconnected networks of systems theory have rewoven the visual back into the fabric of language, and have intertwined them with the new condition of speed – movement being the new dynamic in the linguistic system.

All of these communications models – from McLuhan's to Ong's to Ulmer's – unfortunately embody an innate flaw. These theories all use literacies – from oral to print to digital media – as their governing paradigm, and, as a result, all have an inherent print bias built into them. The same is true of Alan Liu's *Transliteracies Project* (2005) at the University of California at Santa Barbara, which seeks to study all kinds of literacy, particularly online reading and the code switching between different forms that occurs in online reading and different disciplines. By definition therefore in a post-literate world, they cannot span the full complexity of embodied human communications. Our communications networks, f2f and virtual alike, are clearly interfaces that we use to navigate a matrix of gestures, signs, words, images, and electronic signals. German communications theorist Vilém Flusser (2002) puts forward a different model that will be useful to us here. He sees the primary media – that is our first mode of communication – not as a less evolved form of communication like orality, but instead sees the foundational form as *gesture*. By design under the literacy models orality is always already a poor relation of print culture. To apprehend is to seize or to grasp – etymologically it means literally to lay hold of – and so this act of grasping and abstracting information is central in Flusser's thinking to how we make sense of the world. This is still an incomplete model. For one thing, writing in all cultures was born of the need to keep inventories, accountings, and genealogies. Numeracy, therefore, must have an integral place in this model that has never been addressed. As well, the photograph in the nineteenth century enacted a transformation on how we comprehend the world that was as earthshaking and as transformative as the alphabet in its day. To speak of visual literacy, however, is semantically nonsensical and again demotes another form to a lower rung on the literacy ladder. Images are best understood in terms of semiotics or more exactly visual semiosis. The electronic media have wrought another transformation on how we communicate and it is once more concerned with the numerical. The need to crunch numbers and store information gives birth to the computer. It is the addition of mathematics to the model though – in the form of conceptual modelling – that births yet another new visual interface of communication: interactivity or what we might call gestural semiosis. Flusser dubs this latest paradigm shift the 'end' of history. More tempered in his views than McLuhan, Flusser believes that, as children of the digital age, we are entering an era of what he calls 'post-history' – for, history as a science was born of writing. This new visual – and highly self-conscious – form of history is what he calls 'unimaginable' in 1983 and what we might call 'multimedia' or 'participatory' or even 'spatialized' three

decades later. Where print is a time-based mode (like speech, dance, and music), the new screen-based technologies are spatial, existing in three or more dimensions.

Literacy and perspective are similar in their ability to seamlessly unite mode and medium. Literacy links the temporal mode of writing with the book, and visual perspective unites the mode of the image with painting, photography, and other visual media. Perspective is a technology or tool for mapping an idealized relationship between our vision, our perception, and an object in the distance. Where traditional, linear perspective required a stationary viewer (as positioned by technologies like Alberti's window), the immersive perspective of the network assumes a spectator who looks everywhere at once, assumes a spectator both situated and in motion. This is, of course, a more realistic reading of our place and situation in the world than quattrocento perspective artists ever imagined. Our perception of our world is dynamic, with change presupposing a situation, and time presupposing perspective (Merleau-Ponty 2002: 411). In the matrices of the digital realm, time too has shifted to become part of spatialized perspective, foregrounding a constantly changing temporal structure and contingency as the defining qualities of the electronic media.

Back in the 1960s, McLuhan argued that this transition to an acoustic world exhibited all the growing pains of a metamorphosis: our entrance into a third age of historical comprehension. Drawing on German historian Jean Gebser's (1986) vision of three mutative stages of historical development, McLuhan saw the first age as the unperspective world, that of the pre-Socratic philosophers with their belief in the holistic unity of all things. The second age was the perspective world of the Renaissance, where linearity and trajective lines of sight were born through the written and, particularly, the printed word. Gebser's third age, McLuhan argued, is what we are living now: an aperspective world birthed from the spark of electricity and come of age in the computer. In the current age, transformed first by the visual semiotic, then with the gestural mathematics of conceptual modelling into the haptic semiotic, post-literacy (McLuhan's acoustic interface or Gregory Ulmer's electracy) dominates and the analogue is replaced by the digital. This transformation has shifted our perception of our senses and the way in which we interact with our environment. What is clear is that a new multiple perspective, not an aperspective that Gebser posits but instead a pan-perspective or, more exactly, an *orientation,* is emerging in our methods of engagement with digital texts and the world at large. This new perspective is a systemic way of thinking or an ecosystem that blends the notion of community or the performative with that of the network. Renaissance art used a single focal point as a means of depicting perspective, ultimately thereby fixing a moment in time and space, and negating movement on the part of the viewer. The new media take this further and do not use perspective as a simple orientation, but privilege instead *dis*orientation. The science of the body in motion in the spaces of a digital object creates splintered perspectives, which, by definition, cannot be fixed except in time – that is, in the real time of the present moment. This shift in perspective to multiple viewpoints is a trademark of the paradigm shift of the information revolution itself, altering not just how we see, but transforming our vision and the nature of our gaze into dynamic, multidimensional abilities.

The concept of an artistic medium also has roots in visual perspective. Rosalind Krauss questions whether the term 'medium' continues to be of any use, reduced as it is since the advent of the aperspectival and multiperspectival schools known as Minimalisms. She ultimately decides that contemporary works of art exist as recursive structures in a 'post-medium condition,' and, since the nature of a medium is the sum of its 'manifest physical properties,' it ultimately, therefore, must 'specify

itself' or speak its own shape (Krauss 1999: 7). For Friedrich Kittler, too, a medium is technologically dependent, being a discourse network, that is being a domain of cultural exchange (Wellbery 1990: xiii), and mediality is the inherent condition wherein an art form can speak itself. It is no accident, for instance, that the most celebrated graphic designer of the 1990s, David Carson, who is credited with bridging the gap in the design aesthetic from print culture to the Web, titled his 1995 monograph *The End of Print.* Carson shifted the horizon of the page, rupturing it visually and typographically in his work for skateboarding and surfer magazines. His most radical contribution was taking print design and layout to the point of illegibility. He performed spatial typographic dances, inverted text and images, applied irregular margins (including ones that lay beyond the edge of the page and splayed type in the gutter), and generally bent or broke every print design rule. What his work addressed was the absence of emotional engagement the print medium held for the MTV-saturated GenXers. It failed to speak to them on any level. Carson is generally credited with taking print as far as it could go. Web designers would pick up where his work in the 90s leaves off to develop a new born-digital aesthetic that was both more legible and more participatory.

In the virtual spaces of the electronic network, this dynamic interplay of spatial relationships between modes of speaking and shifting constellations or configurations of ideas makes for fluid or variable architectures that proliferate:

Branching options multiply, menus reproduce, windows open on other windows, and screens display other screens in a literal dispersal that disseminates rather than integrates. Hierarchy unravels in a web where top and bottom, up and down, lose consistent meaning. Everything – everywhere is middle. Instead of an organic whole, a hypertext is a rent texture whose meaning is unstable and whose boundaries are constantly changing. (Taylor and Saarinen 1994: 6)

Hypermedia revel in this pan-perspectival disorder, and the media-literate, particularly feminist theorists, have sought to reclaim the chaotic state that has traditionally been gendered female as a politicized form.

This shift in the visual horizon was foretold by one of the great twentieth-century prophets, Albert Einstein. He prophesied the coming of the 'second bomb' in the wake of the atomic one; he warned that a destructive force called 'unlimited information' would follow in the footsteps of wartime industrialism: 'A bomb whereby real-time interaction would be to information what radioactivity is to energy. The disintegration then will not merely affect the particles of matter, but also the very people of which our societies consist' (Virilio 1995: n.p.). This explosion is the creation of new subjectivities for 'real-time' perspectives. Once global time (as opposed to local time, which, Virilio argues, the media and supersonic travel have eliminated) is implemented as a mediated event, all history will come to a standstill, teleology will be at an end, and only the present moment will have substance. Once real time is accepted as the norm for temporal navigation, then new kinds of fractured subjectivities will inevitably arise from the dust of that detonation. Mark Taylor and Esa Saarinen see this structural shift to a virtual architecture of the future as something they call 'electrotecture' (1994: 4). Electrotecture is a participatory medium. It blends the artistic and architectural task of the re-presentation of essential structure in aesthetic form in virtual space. The foundation is fractured or digitized by nature, incorporating the 'endless construction, deconstruction and reconstruction' (6) of data from information pools – whether online or stored on a computer's hard drive. Moving into the field of topological – geometric – space, even the coordinates charted here are constantly shifting. Freed from considerations of linear time and Cartesian space, the new media nevertheless continue to render time and space, but in subjective and non-referential ways.

Cybercultures and virtual worlds undermine the stability of the print aesthetic and call notions of situatedness into question (Virilio 2000: 130). The rise of the virtual realm has erased the natural horizon, as there can be no sense of depth or distance beyond the illusory in electronic space. Without a horizon by which to orient ourselves, our own embodied knowledge becomes our compass point and a body to steer by – our sole means of orienting ourselves in the digital world. The boundary, circle, sphere, and limit of our vision, thought, and action become the horizon of the media itself, as with touch interfaces of the Apple iPhone, the transparent, interactive screens of the type seen in the film *Minority Report* (a technology released commercially in 2008), or the permeable 3D spaces of James Cameron's film *Avatar*. A region bounded by limited knowledge or experience has a false horizon, the imagined outer limits of a text's discourse network, or its own textual frame. This represents not the end of perspective but the end of a hegemonic construction of a virtual world. As a result, the horizon of the digital is like the event horizon of a black hole. It is not something that we steer towards, but something that we are immersed in, interpolated by, something subject to forces and trajectories of incredible magnitude, even as we try to steer out of it.

Our level of media literacy can be judged by how easily we move through information space. This is what defines its meanings, connections, and dimensions, for connectivity and context are what make information valuable once it fulfils its role as a medium of exchange and is applied as (embodied) knowledge, or transcoded into data. It is especially significant how radically our conception of information alters once it becomes something that we can visualize, something aestheticized, something that we can move through and navigate via links in electronic spaces, rather than something whose arrival we passively await. Mathematician Claude Shannon's (and later Warren Weaver's) idea of information was an attempt to quantify a scientific theory and lay the foundation for a new technology of communication. Sidestepping the complexities of quantifying information through its internal differences to other possible messages, rather than through its external context, he worked from the assumption that the information content was constant (Hayles 1987: 25). Shannon separated text from context (and from all ties to situatedness or historicity) by defining it as a probability function, and over time information has come to be measured in bits (Hayles 1987: 24–5). A bit is like a particle: it is the smallest unit of information possible – even its name is foreshortened, from binary digit – and the mode of its storage. While the speedy bit's ontology may always be in a state of flux, its instantaneous transmission is independent of the content of the message. This separation of meaning and content in the informational landscape is the trademark of the latest information revolution. I say latest because each time a technology or new media has transformed Western society it has wrought a paradigm shift of immense proportions.

According to media theorist Derrick de Kerckhove in *Connected Intelligence*, this last revolution is the fifth Western culture has undergone. The first – alphabetic writing – marked the separation of speech from print. The second was the invention of the printing press with its movable type; an assembly line of sorts, it was the first use of automation in the production of culture. The third revolution came about with the advent of the mass media – radio and television – in the wake of an urban population shift. The fourth revolution, de Kerckhove says, came with the computer. The fifth – the emergence of the information age – is under way now: the rise of interactive media in an ongoing transition from an analogue to a participatory, image-mapped network. It brings with it the concept of

choice and creative engagement. It generates personalized media: faxes, cellphones, email, chat, the internet, e-commerce, the World Wide Web, multi- and hypermedia, Web art, teleconferencing, TiVo, virtual and augmented realities, texting, blogs, vlogs, wikis, podcasting, and wearable computing. With the fifth revolution, information and the media are becoming increasingly fragmented, modular, and dense, and the information/content divide continues to widen. Communication is a complicated web of networked relations. In conversation, most of what we communicate is non-verbal. Similarly, in the new media most information is dynamic, sensory, extra-textual, and visual. This shift to an increasingly visual culture and visual mode of speaking is a part of the transformation apparent in the matrices of virtuality.

The vanishing point that stretches towards infinity that we have seen in the visual perspective of art becomes a temporal rendition of the infinite in the interiorities of virtual space. This virtual horizon is therefore a false or man-made horizon subject to subjective interpretation in which the *'frame of the screen,'* our perspective on the text, has superseded the 'distant horizon *line'* (original emphasis; Virilio 2000: 119) of our traditional perspective on the real world. Paul Virilio argues that a third dimension of matter in real space has sprung up to supplement 'mass' and 'energy'; that dimension is 'information' and that real-time perspective has resulted in a blending of this virtual with actual matter (119). A new temporal perspective on and in information space is this commingling of the actual and the virtual, and in such a space only our bodies, our sensory experiences, can be a reliable measure of our orientation. They become our interface between the two domains, creating a discursive space in the electronic text for the browser to insert herself into. This threshold between states opens a site and place for art that is mathematically infinite, multiperspectival, dynamic, networked, fluid and is in a perpetual state of flow. Since perception is movement by definition, perspective is naturally thrown into motion once the interactor in media culture defines her own lines of sight. There can be no unitary experience of a world or text in such a space. This is not the blurred image of the matrix in motion, but an endless series of arches of sliced, still images constellated in space and time. A fixed shape for the fluid matrix as it spins across the cosmos is visible only in each individual instant of freeze-framed blinks, in each instantaneous moment.

The new media continue this process of perspectival fragmentation that Albert Einstein sees in information, Walter Benjamin and Gilles Deleuze in film, Marshall McLuhan in television, and Paul Virilio in time. The materials of the arts have changed, losing their substance (not their materiality) as celluloid and the airwaves have been displaced by code, but this transition and trajectory was audible throughout the last century to those who did listen. Friedrich Kittler, for instance, reassessed the nineteenth and twentieth centuries to uncover the shattering effects of education, communication, psychophysics, and psychoanalysis as the forces that splintered language and perception into bits, into the technologies of the senses, including optics, acoustics, motor impulses, etc., and from there into Saussure's linguistic components, signifier, signified, and referent (Kittler 1990: 216). Lev Manovich in *The Language of New Media* looks at the further fracturing of language and art (particularly film) that has occurred in the postwar period, producing the ultimate modular form: digital computing. The language of the new media is the grammar and syntax in the structuring of electronic objects – and not just original ones. New art forms that recycle culture like fanzines, remixing, digital sampling, skinning, and modding are commonplace in electronic culture.

We are, of course, as Kittler, Michel Foucault, and Jacques Derrida have argued, never entirely separate from the machineries of the system we are a part of. There can be no doubt as to how completely this marks a shift in our consciousness from the analogue to the digital, and from perspective to opticality. This is not to say that the analogue has ceased to exist. The digital and the analogue continue to co-exist side by side, just as oral and literate cultures did for hundreds of years. The mind is also no longer considered to be a part of the brain, but is emergent from the biological neural net. Emergence is a property of chaos theory. It is something that arises unexpectedly from the random soup of the system, the microbe in the primordial goo, and is wholly contextual, grounded in its own organic architecture. If mind is an emergent property of the system as a whole, then the biology of the brain, like the hardware – and wetware – of the net, is the engine that generates it. Mind is the interface between the body (including the brain) and the intelligence, and it is the mind, not the brain, that we interact with as the skin of our engagement between our body's ideas and our own – our self's. This is not so much a point of view as a 'point of being,' or so media theorist Derrick de Kerckhove (1997: 84) argues. If our point of view is constantly in flux, if our point of view is multiple, then it is simultaneously all points of view and none of them. Therefore, our perspective is clearly ontological, more about being – or becoming – than about a fixed point in space. A point of becoming is multiperspectival, acting as the control centre for an interface to track the speed of human cultural evolution. The speed of the interface is what we deem intelligence, just as computers networked together have not simply more but exponentially greater computing power. This is not a hegemonic system; there is no direct or predetermined route, no single, correct path, in the entropy of a topological network. This is the direction of the digital citizen situated in place and time of information space. This gesture is the obsessive overload, drawing everything into it, and our disorientation is not just spatial. It is temporal as well.

Media literacy rejects linear and temporal constructions in favour of spatial and associational ones. The shift from the book (print) to the screen (image) privileges this movement from the primacy of time to the ascendance of space. Greg Ulmer, Jay Bolter, and others argue that indexical print and associational media have competing logics (Ulmer 1994: 34–6) guided as they are by different modes. In the age of the book, we were accustomed to the linkage of medium (book) and mode (writing) with no separation between the two. In the digital age, all modes – writing, sound, image, etc. – are digital and so modality has become unhinged from its material instantiation (Kress 2003: 5). This is not to say that modes lack materiality (sound in speech, for instance, or light in image), but that our sensory engagement with them is irremediably altered. Kress defines mode as 'the name for a culturally and socially fash-ioned resource for communication' (45). Modes are culturally framed, and each has its own grammar and syntax in terms of usage, but they are most important for their abilities to link different logics of commu-nication and disparate dimensions (45–6). Gesture, for instance, links the logic of both space and time, and writing is being trans-formed by screen-based media into new in-carnations that are more spatially oriented with the use of spacing, mixed fonts, blocks of text, bullet points, etc. (46). 'But mixed logics are, above all, a feature of multimo-dal texts, that is texts made up of elements of modes which are based on different log-ics' (46), and it is the new social softwares and participatory forms of engagement that competing logics really comes to the fore.

In 'The History of Communication Me-dia,' Friedrich Kittler highlights the differ-ence and distinctiveness (defined by McLu-han) between *information* systems, methods of flow, storage, and retrieval, and *commu-nications* systems, which include everything from networks of roads to language itself. The first paradigm shift that followed the printing press, he says, disconnected inter-action from communication. Our second shift, to the electronic media, he argues, has separated communication and information

(1996: n.p.). He identifies the uncoupling of communication from knowledge as the hallmark feature of our system, just as Shannon separated text from context, and cybernetics isolated the organizational pat-tern of a system from its physical structure. The contemporary separation of media and mode follows this trend. Writing unites methods of storage with methods of trans-mission, and the speed of the new media links communication with the synaptic matrix of the relational gestures of informa-tion sorting. In fact, in the communication media, speed is arguably becoming more important than the message, for, just as information theory separated text from context, so the digital media severed com-munication from the information medium of its transmission (Kittler 1996: n.p.). The logic of the mode of writing shaped the book as a tool for accessing knowledge. As the shift to screen-based technologies makes the image the new dominant mode, so the configuration of knowledge changes in its wake. It shifts the focus from the medium being the message to the mode as something multiple in space and time.

Print culture was time-bound, situated in the sequence, and this hierarchical im-portance of time in our culture is apparent in our everyday language. We can live on 'borrowed time,' make the most of our 'free time,' and even suffer from 'jet lag.' Computers both run on time – driven by their CPU clocks – and undermine the constants of the temporal dimension – 'se-quence, duration and rhythm' – manipulat-ing them into 'multiple times' or multiple temporal dimensions across information space (McLuhan and McLuhan 1988: 53). The subjective or experiential dimension that we might call computer time, the time of our browsing, however, is a different mode of measure; time, for us, in virtual-ity is unhinged, affixed to motion, vision, and shifting perspectives rather than to the computer's finite, experienced space in time or space in place. Our movement in the simulated time of the computer's world blends with the sensory experience of real-time navigation to produce a new kind of time. Sensory time, the space of the old, familiar world of the body, is immediate and is freeze-framed in the experiential realm: the here and the now. But this new time, called 'real time,' is what Paul Virilio dubs a new perspective born of the electronic age. Real time is a mediated experience of the present moment where we are made conscious of *spatialized time* as an experiential dimension. Like Vilém Flusser's vision of post-history, Virilio sees this as a kind of post-time, a global time system that replaces the simultaneity of photography with the instantaneity of electronic communications (1995: n.p.) This new foregrounding of temporal space as a sensory environment for the communication of aesthetic information results in a privileging of the sensory interface of the body: 'Word, image and sound intersect in the machine and are projected so that one must read, look, hear simultaneously' (Taylor and Saarinen 1994: 6). This multiplication, intertwining, and periscoping of interlocking layers of sensory environments create an urban landscape, like William Gibson's cyberspatial vista, that mingles perceptual and literal discourses and modes of engagement. The act of creation and design thereby blend, becoming a single motion and moment (Taylor and Saarinen 1994: 11): 'interiority and exteriority fold into each other to create surfaces that know no depth and yet are not merely superficial' (2). This interplay of folded space is a dynamic one, like a Möbius strip that we must navigate to perform these multidimensional layers with a mouse, revealing the interiorities of structures within structures. These are not just text or images (or sound or animation, etc.), but spatial relationships among ideas.

These spatial relations are more than simply perceptual; they involve perspective as well. McLuhan argues that the 'effects of technology do not occur at the level of opinions or concepts, but alter sense ratios or patterns of perception steadily and without any resistance' (1964: 33). Artists, unlike other people, see this clearly, he argues,

and there is certainly more than a grain of truth to it. According to him, they are the only people who master the technological transitions because they have an innate understanding of the mechanics of sensory perception (33). For McLuhan, it was the medium of print – not the content – that produced a split sense of auditory and visual experiences, a sense of individuation and a sense of continuity between space and time (86–7). For Gertrude Stein, the only thing that changed from one generation to another was our sensory perception, what she called our 'time-sense.' She defined vision as the dynamic in the creative system that transformed our sense of time and produced new schools of thought and art (1926: 513). We would say that they generate new modes once our interfaces have become as dynamic as us. We must remain in motion as we keep trying alternate paths. Point of view has always been by definition fixed in time, but the dynamic nature of digital disorientation invites in the transformative spatial, unfolding intrinsic dimensions out into limitless moments in space. Motion is disoriented perspective in the new media. The science of the body in motion in the spaces of the text creates multiple, shifting points of view, trajectories of the subject, which, by definition, cannot be fixed except in place in time, that is in the 'now.' According to Andrew Benjamin, motion throws the subject into a state of flux, for the subject can only exist in the present moment (Keller 1995: 1.3). This shift in perspective to multiple viewpoints is a trademark of the paradigm shift of the information revolution as new technologies permit a new 'deployment' of subjectivities (1.3), ultimately altering not just how we see, but transforming our vision itself. Text becomes behavioural rather than static and reading becomes browsing, a different way of interacting. This is what Gebser and McLuhan were referring to when they called our contemporary age of historical comprehension an aperspective world.

The early switch from predominantly oral forms of literacy to predominantly written forms wrought a transformation from incorporating practices to inscribing practices, a shift from listening to writing and reading (Connerton 1989). The new media are shifting this balance once more and introducing a kind of contextualized and embodied knowledge in real time that is more participatory than print culture can ever be. We can see 'multiple orderings of reality' in different kinds of cultures: 'different cultural frameworks of knowledge and experience that build, in essence, different kinds of worlds. [Anthropologist Stanley Jeyaraja] Tambiah compares and contrasts two basic frameworks found in human culture, one based on *causality* and the other on *participation*' (Davis 1998: 174). Causality is linear logic, derived from print culture, whereas participatory culture is the more holistic approach of oral culture that plugs the human back into their environment, but super-charges them with a very contemporary self-awareness. McLuhan argues that the new media have introduced a new kind of participatory culture – acoustic culture – that is not so much a return to oral forms, as it is a blending of causal and participatory ones. More and more, we see the inclusion of poetry, song, story, image, even animation within theoretical and mass media contexts. That would have been inconceivable even a few years ago. This new emphasis on participation in media is supported by a decline in television viewing among our young people and an increased interest in interactive media forms, like blogging, computer games, and virtual worlds like *Second Life*. What is clear is that the new interaction technologies are reintroducing a kind of *tantra* into our *techne*. *Tanta* is Sanskrit for weaving and *tantra* is traditional Buddhist practice where one lives one's beliefs rather than talking about them (Zukav 1979: 312), just as we have always experienced the present moment as a spatial rather than a temporal dimension (McLuhan and McLuhan 1988: 47). More and more digital culture seems to point towards the creation of media

which are spaces of becoming or sites for the inscription of subjectivity.

We are now suffering the growing pains of the reintegration of René Descartes's two spheres, along with the switch from the classical binary system to Gebser and McLuhan's aperspective world, the tectonic shift from linear, logical, and sequential information theory to the simultaneous, discontinuous, and resonant networked new media (McLuhan and McLuhan 1988: 90). We are entering the mediated age of the multiple. Situated subjectivity is inherent in the interactor's role as a material and metaphorical counterpoint to the metaphors and materialities of science in the visual virtuality of art. Situatedness is of course a quality of print as well, but from an assumed single, focalized perspective. It is network culture and the mass media that further fragment time and vision, shattering notions of a single viewer and multiple viewers seeing the same thing. The introduction of perspective as a dynamic component of the present introduces 'trajectivity,' what Paul Virilio calls in *Open Sky* a subject in perpetual motion, into our first-person engagement with place, space, and time (1997: 24). The trajective point of view engenders multiperspectival looking or multiple perspectives, the notion of all things being simultaneously possible and intrinsically interconnected in a digital environment.

The twentieth century was witness to the violence of the shift from mechanistic to systems thinking on a global scale, and birthed a new organizational paradigm with which to understand the structure of the natural, social, and technological worlds. More and more, systems have become aggregate structures, incorporating greater and greater complexity (the notion of networks nesting within networks, for instance) as this shape becomes native to our ways of thinking, and of classifying and storing data. The focus in systems thinking has therefore become situated and contextual as a means of understanding the nature of internal patterns that connect.

In the relational web of our engagement with new media texts, the digital world is an enfolded discourse network that determines where we as browsers can journey and, to a lesser extent, what we will find there. It also ensures that our experience of the Möbius flow of the text as a whole is greater than the sum of its parts and that the journey, not the meaning, is our reason for plugging ourselves into the form.

This capacity for interconnectedness is a shift in the logic of our engagement with media too. It is what we would otherwise call promiscuity, or the dynamic desire of wanderlust. It is an attraction and a quest for union and a kind of spiritual transcendence of individuation. Cyber-feminist theorist Rosi Braidotti argues that 'the "transitional space" [of our virtual journeys] … must be understood as an interface, marking both the distance and the proximity between the spatial surface of bodies. "Something that both forms a boundary and opens up into endless possibility"' (Braidotti 1994: 201). The gap between our bodies as interfaces and sites of linkages in the new media therefore is not only a space of desire, but also one that acknowledges difference within ourselves and with(in) others. In a textual environment, it calls for a cross-pollination of ideas between text, browser, embodied now-time, and occupied space. It calls for trajective perspectives.

Subjectivities too have complex dimensions, being composed of many self-similar components like gender, age, class, race, sexual preference, and abilities. Theories of subjectivity over the last one hundred years have also become increasingly fragmented, from Sigmund Freud's subconscious to Henri Bergson's five sensory facets of subjectivity to Gilles Deleuze and Felix Guattari's schizophrenic subject. Subjectivity can now more accurately be seen as a dynamic *process* of embodied knowledge that inhabits the fractal domain. We all have an infinite number of self-similar selves. This is a paradigm shift from the unified self to the plural, from the individual to the mob,

from the eye to full-bodied engagement. We are being reborn, not with re-unified senses, but with a meta-awareness of ourselves as multi-sensory beings at a distance from our bodies and in them at the same time. This state is constantly in the process of redefining its own place and complexity according to a network of power formations. It follows that this embodied materialism is a manifestation of what Teresa de Lauretis, after Michel Foucault, called the 'technology of the self' (qtd in Braidotti 1994: 99). The technology of the self is the material dimension of the subject that measures how genderings (i.e., personal situation) structure subjectivity as a variable of its own complexity; in short, the technology of subjectivity is a redefinition of genderings in the matrix of a collectivity of post-human differences (Braidotti 1994: 99) where the subject is an emergent property of the whole.

When place and perspective emerge as a vantage point for complex subjectivities, we acquire added dimensions in our engagement with the world. We move from a two-dimensional topography into a multidimensional topology, something that feminist theorists have long argued was desirable to avoid binary constructs. Donna Haraway called this notion of multiple subjectivities the split self or cyborg consciousness. She says:

> The split and contradictory self is the one who can interrogate positionings and be accountable, the one who can construct and join rational conversations and fantastic imaginings that change history. Splitting, not being, is the privileged image for feminist epistemologies of scientific knowledge. 'Splitting' in this context should be about *heterogeneous multiplicities* that are simultaneously necessary and incapable of being squashed into isomorphic slots or cumulative lists. (Haraway 1991: 193)

These multiplicities are not reducible either to (gendered) human or machine or to simplex dimensionality, but instead exist in topological space. 'This geometry,' Haraway says,

> pertains within and among subjects. The topography of subjectivity is multidimensional, so, therefore, is vision. The knowing self is partial in all its guises, never finished, whole, simply there and original; it is always constructed and stitched together imperfectly, and therefore able to join with another, to see together without claiming to be another. (193)

While Haraway's split specifically refers to the merging of human and machine, doubled visions have long inhabited theoretical spaces. N. Katherine Hayles, for instance, takes Haraway's cyborg consciousness to a new level. Hayles posits human subjectivities as multiple agents operating from a matrix of competing desires, motives, and forces with the body acting as the steersman between shifting states of being. She calls this the post-human. Uniting consciousness and the body, 'the post-human subject is an amalgam, a collection of heterogeneous components, a material-informational entity whose boundaries undergo continuous construction and reconstruction' (1999: 3). This subjectivity is fractal, modelled on the complexity of the network and mapping the malleable relations between self, vision, consciousness, discourse, and environment. But while Hayles's network subjectivity is emergent and distributed (291), it is still locked within a framework of human-computer interactivity. Shifting subjectivities more completely draw in the motion of the body in space. Like the shifts in perspective that have marked the great ages of Western civilization, the 'trajective' maps 'movement from here to there,' which we require to understand shifts in ways of seeing (Virilio 2000: 24), as a dynamic kind of post-human subjectivity. This evokes Elizabeth Grosz's (1994) Möbius strip as a dynamic form of embodied transformation in the subjective

selves. The subject is not in the system, but is born of the interaction of interior and exterior, in the twisting and intertwining of the components therein. This is the monstrous multiplicity of the *mestizo*, the in/visible, irreducible hybrid, who is always in a state of flux. In the same way, browsing by way of participatory culture is a portal to alternative perspectives and models, bringing the post-human environment into the orientation of the trajective, topological domain.

We are multiple. 'I' has become a subject position of the multitude. Participatory culture (a term coined by Henry Jenkins to describe cult fan behaviour in response to mass media) is the cultural framework that has superseded literacy. It has some very specific attributes, according to Jenkins: it has 'low barriers to artistic expression and civic engagement'; 'strong support for creating and sharing one's creations with others'; an 'informal mentorship' system where skills are passed from more experienced members to novices; a burning belief in the 'cause' (members' 'contributions matter'); and strong ties within the community (Jenkins 2006: n.p.). Participatory culture, rather than interactivity (the latter being a property of technology, not of cultural behaviour), is the current prevailing means of engagement and embodied citizenship in the world (Jenkins 2006: n.p.). The death of the nation-state and unitary nationality comes with this, just as the younger generation chooses texting, Facebooking, and tweeting as ways of being and inhabiting their own skins. Likewise when the new modal media meet perspective, multimodal orientation is born. Multimodality is as revolutionary a means of engagement with our environment as quattrocentro perspective was once for the eye and world view. Just as the new logics of wandering and browsing have replaced navigation, literacy with all of its colonialist baggage (Johnson-Eilola 1998: 27), bound up as it is by notions of ownership, nation, and a single, unified self, has evolved into a multimodal orientation. Like navigation as a reality and metaphor of new media interaction, engagement has moved from notions of frontierism, screen real estate, and linear constructs like the 'information superhighway' to new logics of media production, shared space, and discourse communities.

The next great revolution in the time of post-literacy is already well under way. The twenty-first century shake-up is not a new kind of publishing or broadcasting, but both of those things combined. As technology is removing barriers previously posed by geography, the connectivity of participatory culture is driven through a major shift in access to the means of media production (commonly referred to as an offshoot of Web 2.0 technologies). The leading edge of participatory culture is the email, texting, blogging, teleconferencing, and webcam revolution that broke down traditional networks, created discourse communities, and accelerated the speed of information circulation until virtually simultaneous or 'real-time' communication was possible. Blogging and vlogging and other kinds of participatory journalism revolutionized Web publishing, adding hyperlinks and introducing subscription (RSS feeds) and broadcast (podcasting) into the exploding arena of personal opinion. Blogging is infamous for having brought down governments in the Philippines and elsewhere, and changing the ways elections are fought. Open-source software (like Linux or Mozilla's Firefox browser), wikis (collaboratively authored online encyclopedias), and game-mods (like Minh Le's multi-million copy blockbuster *Counter-Strike*, which was a modified version of *Half-Life*) have made collaboratory authorship readily accessible to millions. Social bookmarking and phototagging (like at the popular sites del.icio.us and Flickr) have enabled collective, associational knowledge creation in the field of classification, thereby altering the science of classification altogether, according to Howard Rheingold (2002). Where sharing tags have produced massive new public resources, they have

also eliminated specialists and classification hierarchies from the equations, and produced new kinds of organizational structures (Rheingold 2002). The common thread in all of these computer-mediated forms of communication is people and the personalization of technologies. All of these manifestations of social software are revolutionary because they use multiple modes to communicate, set out to form discourse communities – or, more accurately, what we call social networks – as a primary aim, and do so cooperatively at a grassroots level. This very grassroots organizational structure is undercut by the fact that the means of access and online server space are still ominously owned by multinational corporate conglomerates. Cellphone culture (*keitai* culture it is called in Japan) – there are now in excess of three billion cellphone users worldwide – is one such networked community that stands out as both exemplary and having unique properties. Mobile technologies have resulted in an evolutionary shift for a whole new generation who use their thumbs differently, serve to create private spaces in public, and have spawned a particular kind of spontaneous political gathering called flash mobs. These human networks are extremely powerful forces for change, especially in terms of transforming the act of reading into a more creative process.

Sun Wu's NUWeb Project at Taiwan's Chung Cheng University is also motivated by the fear of the corporate ownership of personal information and the need to create a medium for the personalization of interfaces. The first incarnation of the Web was generated by large media conglomerates (content service providers) who addressed users as consumers; Web 2.0 saw the arrival of social software and personal media like Facebook, MySpace, Blogger, digg, and YouTube, which allowed individuals to participate as content creators. Web 3.0, Wu promises, will take us to the next level (Lovink 2007: n.p.) by shifting us away from colonialist tendencies and corporate power. His invention, NUWeb, which he believes to be the next stage in Web interfaces, is an open-source 'user-centric software. It is a decentralized portal and information system aiming at providing … more efficient and effective information sharing, community service, and information management' (qtd in Lovink 2007: n.p.). NUWeb shifts the server onto the user's own system, giving her ownership and control over her own information and its access. The customizable system interconnects with the larger network, which, like YouTube or Flickr, fosters participation and information sharing without size constraints, corporate meddling, or other restrictions. Whether this incarnation of Web 3.0 lives up to its promises is open to debate, but its guiding philosophy as a blueprint for where we and our media are going seems inevitable. It might already be here in the iPod app and other personalizable software and interfaces.

What is coming is not the inability to read or the end of literacy, but the emergence of a new kind of dynamic, embodied navigation of text, image, sound, and so forth. We already carry a bit of this in our individualized iPods and MP3 players, customizing our media to our own liking. Multimodal orientation is not replacing literacy, but is in fact a new way of reading, looking, listening, and moving. Concerned experts who study and measure the erosion of literacy in university graduates, for instance, miss the point that this generation has a whole new and different set of skills that their forbearers lacked *in addition to* the old literacy skills, which are no longer so important. The new kinds of media literacies that are emerging now are difficult to classify unless we look at them as requiring multimodal orientation as a means of navigating their spaces. More important, this new form of learning and engaging is not just about movement, but about embodiment and the creation of a new kind of physical knowledge (Gershenfeld 2005: 7). Neil Gershenfeld, director of MIT's Center for Bits and Atoms, dubs the next logical step in this transformation 'personal fabrication.' It goes beyond taking or classifying photos to a point where we will create our own personal, one-of-a-kind technologies. Reuniting design and production with individual need, Gershenfeld says this shift to personalization is not for entertainment or purely creative purposes, but in order 'to put control of the creation of technology back in the hands of its users' (8). This sounds like the heady Cold War mainframe days again when the concept of a 'personal' computer was unimaginable. Gershenfeld's lab does not involve a *Star Trek*–style replicator, but instead a new kind of social knowledge and physical interaction in the design and creation process. User-centric softwares and personalized technology surely are the leading indication that the end of the era of mass culture is immanent. A few decades ago what sold restaurant meals was uniqueness, not sameness, and water cooler culture revolved around the discussion of a single, shared television experience. Now we have come full circle. We expect identical meals globally and program our individual viewing experience from our airplane seat as we sit a world apart from each other watching different films in different languages.

Carolyn Guertin

Bibliography

Blackwell, Lewis, and David Carson. *The End of Print: The Grafik Design of David Carson*. San Francisco: Chronicle Books, 2000.

Braidotti, Rosi. *Nomadic Subjects*. New York: Columbia University Press, 1994.

Capra, Fritjof. *The Web of Life*. New York: Anchor, 1997.

Carson, David (with Lewis Blackwell). *The End of Print: The Graphic Design of David Carson*. San Francisco: Chronicle Books, 1995.

Connerton, Paul. *How Societies Remember*. Cambridge: University of Cambridge Press, 1989.

Davis, Eric. *Techgnosis: Myth, Magic + Mysticism in the Age of Information*. New York: Three Rivers Press, 1998.

de Kerckhove, Derrick. *Connected Intelligence.* Toronto: Somerville House, 1997.

Electracy entry. Wikipedia. http://en.wikipedia .org/wiki/Electracy (accessed 7 January 2007).

Flusser, Vilém. *Writings.* Trans. Erik Eisel. Minneapolis and London: University of Minnesota Press, 2002.

Foucault, Michel. *The Order of Things.* New York: Vintage, 1994.

Gebser, Jean. *The Ever-Present Origin: Foundations of the Aperspectival World.* Trans. Noel Barstad with Algis Mickunas. Athens: Ohio University Press, 1986.

Gershenfeld, Neil. *FAB: The Coming Revolution on Your Desktop – From Personal Computers to Personal Fabrication.* New York: Basic, 2005.

Grosz, Elizabeth. *Volatile Bodies: Toward a Corporeal Feminism.* Bloomington: Indiana University Press, 1994.

Guertin, Carolyn. Wanderlust: The Kinesthetic Browser in Cyberfeminist Space. *Extensions Journal.* Vol 2. UCLA. (February 2007). http:// www.wac.ucla.edu/extensionsjournal/.

Haraway, Donna. *Simians, Cyborgs and Women.* New York: Routledge, 1991.

Havelock, Eric. *The Muse Learns to Write: Reflections on Orality and Literacy from Antiquity to the Present.* New Haven, CT: Yale University Press, 1986.

Hayles, N. Katherine. Text Out of Context: Situating Postmodernism within an Information Society. *Discourse* 9 (spring-summer 1987): 24–36.

– *How We Became Posthuman.* Chicago: University of Chicago Press, 1999.

Jenkins, Henry. *Textual Poachers: Television Fans and Participatory Culture.* New York and London: Routledge, 1992.

Jenkins, Henry. Confronting the Challenges of Participatory Culture: Media Education for the 21st Century (Part One) *Confessions of an Aca/Fan: The Weblog of Henry Jenkins.* 19 October 2006. http://www.henryjenkins .org/2006/10/confronting_the_challenges_ of.html (accessed 7 November 2007).

Johnson-Eilola, Johndan. Negative Spaces. In *Literary Theory in the Age of the Internet*, ed. Todd Taylor and Irene Ward, 17–33. New York: Columbia University Press, 1998.

Keller, Ed. Cinematic Thresholds: Instrumentality, Time and Memory in the Virtual. 1995. http://www.basilisk.com/C/CineThressH_ 966.html (accessed 10 January 2007).

Kittler, Friedrich A. *Discourse Networks 1800/1900.* Trans. Michael Metteer with Chris Cullens. Stanford, CA: Stanford University Press, 1990.

– The History of Communication Media. Online posting. 30 July 1996. *Ctheory.* http://www .ctheory.net/articles.aspx?id=45 (accessed 10 January 2007).

Krauss, Rosalind. *A Voyage on the North Sea: Art in the Age of the Post-Medium Condition.* New York: Thames and Hudson, 1999.

Kress, Gunther. *Literacy in the New Media Age.* London and New York: Routledge, 2003.

Kress, Gunther, and Theo van Leeuwen. *Multimodal Discourse: The Modes and Media of Contemporary Communication.* London: Oxford University Press, 2001.

Liu, Alan. *Transliteracies Project.* 17–18 June 2005. http://transliteracies.english.ucsb.edu/ category/research-project/ (accessed 13 January 2007).

Lovink, Geert. Web 3.0: For the User, by the User, of the User. Posting to the nettime-l mailing list. 14 January 2007. http://www.nettime.org (accessed March 2009).

McLuhan, Marshall. *Understanding Media: The Extensions of Man.* Toronto: Signet, 1964.

– *Understanding Me: Lectures and Interviews.* Ed. Stephanie McLuhan and David Staines. Toronto: McClelland and Stewart, 2004.

McLuhan, Marshall, and Eric McLuhan. *Laws of Media: The New Science.* Toronto: University of Toronto Press, 1988.

Manovich, Lev. *The Language of New Media.* Cambridge: MIT Press, 2001.

Merleau-Ponty, Maurice. *Phenomenology of Perception.* London: Routledge, 2002.

Ong, Walter J. *Orality and Literacy: The Technologizing of the Word.* London and New York: Routledge, 1988.

Rheingold, Howard. *Smart Mobs: The Next Social Revolution.* Cambridge, MA: Basic, 2002.

– Social Bookmarking. 23 October 2006. http:// www.socialtext.net/medialiteracy/index .cgi?social_bookmarking.

Shannon, Claude E., and Warren Weaver. *The*

Mathematical Theory of Communication. Urbana: University of Illinois Press, 1998 [1949].

Stein, Gertrude. Composition as Explanation. *Selections: Writings 1903–1932.* New York: The Library of America, 1926, 520–9.

Taylor, Mark, and Esa Saarinen. *Imagologies: Media Philosophy.* London and New York: Routledge, 1994.

Ulmer, Gregory L. *Heuretics: The Logic of Invention.* Baltimore: Johns Hopkins University Press, 1994.

– *Internet Invention: From Literacy to Electracy.* New York: Longman, 2003.

Virilio, Paul. Speed and Information: Cyberspace Alarm! Trans. Patrice Riemans. 27 August 1995. *Ctheory.* http://www.ctheory.net/printer.asp?id=72 (accessed 20 March 2006).

– *Open Sky.* Trans. Julie Rose. London: Verso, 1997.

– *Information Bomb.* Trans. Chris Turner. London: Verso, 2000.

Wellbery, David E. Foreword. Discourse Networks 1800/1900. Trans. Michael Metteer, with Chris Cullens. Stanford, CA: Stanford University Press, 1990, vii–xxxiii.

Wu, Sun. NUWeb. Taiwan. http://www.nuweb.cc/tw/index-c1.htm (accessed 13 January 2007).

Zukav, Gary. *The Dancing Wu Li Masters.* New York: Bantam, 1979.

MEDIA PRODUCTS

[See also: *Consumer Culture; Mass Communication*]

In general, products can be defined as goods offered to a market for attention, acquisition, use, or consumption and that might satisfy a want or need (Kotler, Armstrong, Saunders, and Wong 2001). A definition of media products depends to some extent on the perspective taken. Fundamentally, there are two different perspectives on media 'offerings.'

From a cultural perspective, it is commonly claimed that media content cannot be treated as (other) products (Croteau and Hoynes 2001). Media do not supply consumers with products in demand according to the rules of market and competition as practised in other industries. Instead, they are assumed to be cultural goods with informational, educational, and social functions, thus serving the public interest. Success is then measured by the extent to which this public interest is served through diverse, substantial, and innovative content. In opposition to the business perspective, it is argued that media serve societal needs and should be a primary source of information and education for citizens as well as public deliberations. Media are at the core of what is referred as to the public sphere, where democratic processes take place in the form of a public dialogue of citizens. To ensure this public dialogue, it is contended that media should be citizen resources, helping both members of majorities and minorities to be informed and active participants in social and political life (Croteau and Hoynes 2001). Mass media have a social integration function by providing access and platforms of dialogue for people across social, cultural, and geographical boundaries.

From a business perspective, media products are subject to the same basic economic, financial, and managerial laws and forces to which standard business theories and analysis methods can be applied (Picard 2005). This can be exemplified for marketing by changing the word consumer to audience and recognizing purchase behaviour as similar to watching, listening, or reading (McDowell 2006).

These two perspectives correspond with the twofold role of media content and its conflicting logics: a profit-orientated logic with the goal of customer satisfaction on the one hand, and a sociocultural logic with the goal of serving the public interest on the other hand.

When referring to media, both the cultural and the business perspective explicitly or implicitly refer to *mass media* as that media section addressed to mass audiences. Common mass media are generally said to include at least (1) broadcasting media such as television and radio, (2) motion pictures and documentaries, (3) printed media such as newspapers and magazines, (4) online media, (5) computer games, and (6) music. In the following, the underlying premise is that media products are offers supplied by mass media for attention to the public and/or to consumer markets and/or for acquisition on advertising markets. However, even if we assume that the media offer products, on closer examination it is evident that media offerings display certain specific characteristics. These characteristics cause them to differ significantly not only from other kinds of products but also among themselves (Picard 2005).

Media products consist of material and immaterial components. Immaterial content is bundled and often transported on a material carrier such as paper or a CD. Both from a cultural and a business perspective it is the *content* that forms the pivotal core of the product, because it is the content that constitutes the reason for customer demand, on audience markets as well as on advertising markets. Consumers seek to satisfy their information and entertainment needs, while advertisers seek access to consumers through placing their promotional content close to or even within content (as in the case of product placements or other forms of so-called advertiser branded content).

According to the *cultural* perspective, media products offered to audiences are not (or at least not merely) commercial goods designed to serve certain consumption benefits but must be viewed mainly for the ways they contribute to their sociocultural environment (Doyle 2002). The sociocultural importance of the mass media is therefore closely linked to goals such as education and information of the public, whom artistic and/or journalistic content should serve. Unlike other businesses, media content is also more visible and disputed in the public (Picard 2005). Media products make up much of people's daily free-time budgets and provide them with topics for discussion before and after consumption, thereby having an integrative

function for society. Due to the social, political, and sociocultural importance of the mass media, media content is granted special protection from copyrights and related rights (Picard 2005) and even constitutional laws (Reca 2006). At the same time, even though many media markets have been liberalized in the past two decades, especially radio and television products remain to a high extent subject to regulation and public policymaking.

From an *economic* perspective, the cultural importance of media products can be described as the effects caused by (the consumption of) media product. Often referred to as externalities, the consumption of media content – for example, a political article in a newspaper – has effects on third parties. The politicians portrayed by the journalist might be affected by a change in public opinion caused by the article. Whereas in other business fields externalities are often undesired by-products such as environmental pollution, (positive) externalities are frequently an explicit goal in the production and distribution of media content. However, a distinction needs to be made between positive and negative externalities. For example, negative externalities describe the consequences of pornographic and/or violent content, especially when consumed by children. An example for positive externalities would be influencing public opinion during pre-election by broadcasting information content about the candidates. These positive externalities of media products can be ascribed especially to *merit goods*. This term describes goods which should be consumed from a normative perspective by as many people as possible in a society (as the content in the example above), but which do not always meet sufficient demand by the public. It can be argued that it is basically the merit good character of public service content which explains their financing through taxes or licence fees. It is therefore public service broadcasters' explicitly or implicitly defined mission to produce and distribute (also) content with merit good characteristics.

Furthermore, many media products exhibit key features of public goods on the audience market (Doyle 2002; Reca 2006). Public goods are different from private goods in that they are not used up by consumption as private goods are – while a bottle of lemonade is empty once drunk, television or radio shows can very well be consumed by other readers or listeners. Another criterion supporting the classification of many forms of media content as public goods is the non-exclusivity of ownership. Exclusivity of consumption can only be put into effect when offering pay TV and other non-free content. In these cases only those consumers who have purchased the products can consume them.

From a *management* perspective, the specific features of media products on audience markets provide a challenge to the management of its production and marketing. In the case of media content the product quality is difficult not only to forecast (Picard 2005) but also to define, because quality criteria can differ greatly. In general, quality criteria can be distinguished as follows, depending on their focus (Reca 2006):

- supply-focused quality criteria, as mostly defined by the professionals themselves;
- demand-focused quality criteria, based on audience needs and expectations;
- society-focused quality criteria, based on the ability to fulfil sociocultural or political goals in democratic societies.

Furthermore, defining the quality level of a media product and then being able to consistently produce content on this level is challenging due to the fact that media products, for example news shows, have to be reproduced constantly. Another specific feature of media products is that many decisions regarding their creation are based on other than economic criteria (Picard 2005). Unlike in other businesses, journalists and/or entertainment editors are in charge of content development, not product or brand managers. This is often a source of conflict within media organizations, when inspiration-driven content developers, consumer-insight-driven marketers, and profit-driven controllers dispute on content creation and success criteria (Aris and Bughin 2005).

Other challenges to the management of media products are consumer-related. First, consumer research and pre-testing often prove to be not very effective, which makes the success of new product launches highly uncertain (Picard 2005). Second, switching costs and the risks involved in media choices are low for consumers. For example, in the case of television, all it takes to switch from one media offer to another is to use the remote control (McDowell 2006). The risk of choosing the 'wrong' channel is very low compared with choosing a new car. Third, related to the low risk is the fact that audiences' media choice and consumption behaviour is generally characterized by low involvement and habitual decision making. McDowell (2006) sums up this challenge to media management by stating that consumers are not motivated to invest substantial cognitive effort in media product decision making. Another general feature of media products is the fact that media products are especially vulnerable to piracy and counterfeiting (Picard 2005). Because of the ongoing digitization of the media, it has become easier and easier to create and distribute counterfeit copies of DVDs, CDs, and so forth.

So far, media products on audience markets have been discussed collectively in order to point out some shared specifics. However, there are also great differences among them, some of which fundamentally affect their management. Media products can, for instance, be differentiated along aspects such as their frequency of creation (single versus continuous creation). *Single-creation* products such as books, feature films, and games are based on unique creative ideas as opposed to *continuous-creation* products such as television and internet content provision and newspapers, which involve ongoing content generation (Picard 2005). These two different kinds of content have several implications with regard to their management (Picard 2005):

- The management of single-creation products is largely project management, while continuous creation products are characterized by process management.
- The generation of single-creation products often involves 'hit' strategies in the sense that the rarer cases of successful products must cover the losses of the more frequent flops; once successfully introduced, continuous-creation products are much less risky and can be modified and optimized even after product launch, to adjust to changing competitive environments and/or consumer preferences.
- Single-creation products are characterized by high marketing costs to create attention and are highly dependent on the audience's familiarity with, and the creative/journalistic capabilities of, the involved professionals. Continuous-creation products can build brands in order to lower marketing costs, lower dependency on talent, and enhance habitual media use through consistent promotion, placement, and packaging/formatting of branded content.

Many profit-oriented media companies offer products both on consumer and advertising markets. This situation of serving a dual market causes commercial media products to have a combined product nature which makes them complex: while the media content itself has to appeal to audiences as a first step, the audience contacts generated through (past) consumption have to be packaged, priced, and sold to advertisers as a second step (Doyle 2002). The extent of audience reach, as measured in ratings, is important for most commercial media companies as most of them gain their main revues from advertising. Thus, from a commercial media company's perspective, generating non-advertising

content is an important goal but only in the endeavour to sell advertising space or airtime to advertisers. It serves mainly as an incentive for the audience to also consume promotional content.

The importance of generating audiences is not restricted to profit-oriented media companies. Non-profit media firms such as public service broadcasters pay attention to ratings, too (Doyle 2002). To them, the (demographic) profile of their audience becomes important against the background of having to demonstrate public utility in terms of sufficient reach. By proving sufficient public acceptance, non-profit media companies are in a better position to negotiate their funding through the public, for example through taxes or licence fees in the case of public service broadcasters.

Per-Erik Wolff

Bibliography

Aris, Annet, and Jacques Bughin. *Managing Media Companies: Harnessing Creative Value.* Chichester: John Wiley and Sons, 2005.

Croteau, David, and William Hoynes. *The Business of Media: Corporate Media and the Public Interest.* Thousand Oaks, CA: Pine Forge Press, 2001.

Doyle, Gillian. *Understanding Media Economics.* London: Sage, 2002.

Kotler, Philip, Gary Armstrong, John Saunders, and Veronica Wong. *Principles of Marketing: Third European Edition.* Harlow: Prentice Hall, 2001.

McDowell, Walter S. Issues in Marketing and Branding. In *Handbook of Media Management and Economics*, ed. Alan B. Albarran, Sylvia M. Chan-Olmsted, and Michael O. Wirth, 229–50. Mahwah: Lawrence Erlbaum Associates, 2006.

Picard, Robert G. Unique Characteristics and Business Dynamics of Media Products. *Journal of Media Business Studies* 2 (2005): 61–9.

Reca, Ángel A. Issues in Media Product Management. In *Handbook of Media Management and Economics*, ed. Alan B. Albarran, Sylvia M. Chan-Olmsted, and Michael O. Wirth,

181–201. Mahwah: Lawrence Erlbaum Associates, 2006.

MEDIA STUDIES

[See also: *Anthropology of the Media; Linguistics and the Media; Media Effects; Sociology of the Media*]

The systematic study of the media started in the late 1930s after Orson Welles's radio broadcast of *War of the Worlds*. That incident showed how media had the power to blur the line between fantasy and reality and, thus, affect people's behaviours. The broadcast informed radio listeners that Martians had landed and invaded New Jersey. From time to time, an announcer reminded the audience that the broadcast was fictional. But many believed the reports. Concerned citizens called the police and the army. Mass hysteria was reported by the papers the next day.

The event caught the attention of Hadley Cantril of Princeton University, since it appeared to show that media representations have real effects on people. Cantril and a team of researchers conducted the first true study of media effects, titled *The Invasion from Mars: A Study in the Psychology of Panic* (1940). After interviewing 135 subjects, the team concluded that the panic was real, although many subjects did not admit to it, apparently lying about it to hide their shame. Although the study's methodology was subsequently questioned as being flawed, it had one concrete outcome – it introduced the disciplinary study of media in universities. In a study titled *The People's Choice* American sociologist Paul Lazarsfeld (1948) followed up on Cantril's study, claiming that the media had few if any real impacts, since people took from media content what they were predisposed to take. For example, he found that media coverage did not change people's minds about how they would vote in elections – all they got out of newspapers or radio broadcasts were validations of their preconceived views, ignoring all others. In 1956, Lazarsfeld and

Katz found, moreover, that audiences were not monolithic entities but constituted interpretive communities guided by opinion leaders (directly or indirectly). The latter filtered media content, interpreted it, and then passed it on to their communities.

It was obvious by the mid-1950s that the study of the media could generate interesting findings that had broader implications than people could have previously imagined. At first, such study was considered to be part of more general disciplinary approaches such as psychology, sociology, or anthropology. Courses thus started cropping up throughout the United States dealing with the effects of the media, their evolution and structure, within traditional social science departments. The findings and insights garnered in the human and social sciences soon caught the attention of other kinds of scholars – those concerned with the relation between the media, society, and culture. By the mid-1950s, the media became a target of interest among literary scholars, cinema professors, philosophers, linguists, and semioticians. The approach taken by such scholars to media has always been characterized by 'interdisciplinarity,' that is, by an integration of findings and ideas emanating from different disciplines. By the early 1960s departments of 'media studies' started cropping up on campuses across America, Europe, and a few other countries – countries where the media played a critical role in daily life.

The academic study of media began branching out in several new directions in the 1950s. One involved investigating the relation of media to various domains – mass communications technologies, genre theory, narrative, and sociocultural evolution. The leader of this new approach was the Canadian communications theorist Marshall McLuhan (1911–80), who claimed that these were all interconnected. McLuhan never really coined a term for his theory. However, the term *convergence theory* is used today to refer to the integration of technologies with cultural forms and socio-evolutionary tendencies (Negroponte

1995). McLuhan also originated the idea of mediation, or the notion that media influence how people understand the world. This is why the mediasphere (as it is called in media studies) has largely replaced the traditional spheres (religious, political, etc.) in shaping how people come to understand the world. McLuhan also realized that changes in media lead to changes in knowledge-storing and knowledge-making systems. This was so because media are extensions of human beings – they extend sensory, physical, or intellectual capacities. The axe has extended the ability of hands to break wood; the wheel of feet to cover distances; the computer of the brain to process information. Media have extended the ability of humans to communicate and interact with each other more efficiently and across great distances. The study of the interconnection between media and communications became a major focus of media studies in the 1950s and 1960s.

A full-fledged media study academic enterprise followed the publication of French semiotician Roland Barthes's 1957 book *Mythologies*. Barthes saw mediated culture as a 'bastard form of mass culture' plagued by 'humiliated repetition' and generating a constant need for 'new books, new programs, new films, news items, but always the same meaning' (Barthes 1975: 24). For Barthes, media forms of all kinds (blockbuster movies, spectacles) were nothing more than recyclings of previous forms. Since the mid-1960s, Barthes's approach to media has been a constant point of reference. Departments, journals, book series, and associations flourished in the 1970s and 1980s. By the 1990s, media studies had carved a niche for itself not only on many campuses, but also in the broader academic terrain. Today, media studies is a flourishing autonomous discipline across the world, encompassing a broad range of emphases and interests, from the development of theoretical models and methodological tools, to the examination of the relationship between media and the political, cultural, social, and economic spheres of human life.

Media studies has branched out to include 'area-specific' studies – for example, television, radio, internet, and video games.

Two factors influencing the evolution and content of media studies today are technology and globalization. In his online article 'Media Studies 2.0,' David Gauntlett argues for a new approach to the study of media – an approach that should no longer focus on the traditional division between audiences and producers, but on the effects of the new technologies on the collapse of such traditional dichotomies. It is more accurate to say that there is a close relation between technology, social evolution, and the media. Today, media analysts continue to identify and dissect the various genres that make up the menu of offerings in media, including internet media, as well as explore the nature of audiences for each genre. Internet audiences exist as communities in the same way that audiences existed for everything from vaudeville spectacles to television sitcoms.

Marcel Danesi

Bibliography

Baran, Stanley J. *Introduction to Mass Communication, Media Literacy, and Culture.* New York: McGraw-Hill, 2004.

Barthes, Roland. *Mythologies.* Paris: Seuil, 1957.

– *The Pleasure of the Text.* New York: Hill and Wang, 1975.

Cantril, Hadley. *The Invasion from Mars: A Study in the Psychology of Panic.* Edison, NJ: Transaction Publishers, 1940.

Katz, Elihu, and Paul F. Lazarsfeld. *Personal Influence: The Part Played by People in the Flow of Mass Communications.* Glencoe, IL: Free Press, 1956.

Lazarsfeld, Paul F., et al. *The People's Choice.* New York: Columbia University Press, 1948.

McLuhan, Marshall. *The Mechanical Bride: Folklore of Industrial Man.* New York: Vanguard, 1951.

– *The Gutenberg Galaxy.* Toronto: University of Toronto Press, 1962.

– *Understanding Media.* London: Routledge and Kegan Paul, 1964.

McLuhan, Marshall, and Eric McLuhan. *Laws of Media: The New Science*. Toronto: University of Toronto Press, 1988.

Negroponte, Nicholas. *Being Digital*. New York: Knopf, 1995.

MEDIATED COMMUNICATION

[See also: *Broadcasting; Communication; Instant Messaging; McLuhan, Marshall; Media Effects; Media Literacy*]

Mediated communication consists of the transmission of information via a signal, representation, tool, or technology overcoming constraints of space and time associated with in-person communication. The twentieth century has seen the diffusion of a large number of innovations in mediated communication, from the telephone to the widespread adoption of the internet and mobile technologies.

Early Beginnings of Mediated Communication

The earliest forms expression from 26,000 to 28,000 years ago found in Namibia are abstract paintings that depict predominantly animals. Another example is the Lascaux Grotto in Dordogne, France, whose paintings are estimated to have been produced about 17,000 years ago. In the cave, there are approximately 600 paintings and drawings and almost 1,500 engravings of animals and other symbols. Mediated communication became more elaborate with the introduction of writing. Early hieroglyphs were ideographic or illustrative of actual objects, while later hieroglyphs were phonetic characters, representing sounds. Another early system of writing was cuneiform, used in the Middle East in the last three millennia BCE; languages employing this style of writing included Sumerian, Hurrian, Hittie, and Urartian. North Semitic is considered one of the earliest complete alphabets, originating in Syria around the eleventh century BCE and later influencing Phoenician and Aramaic, from which many of today's alphabets stem, including the European, Hebrew, Arabic, and Indian alphabets. Maya hieroglyphs, which are composed primarily in Classic Maya of about 300 to 500 logograms, were the earliest form of writing in the Americas, dating from 300 to 200 BCE. With respect to the materials employed in early forms of writing, clay, stone, animal bones, bark, cloth, and metal were initially popular, but eventually other more durable materials were preferred, including, papyrus, palm leaves, bamboo strips, parchment (made from animal skin), and wax tablets. While paper was invented in China around 105 CE, it only became more regularly used in Europe by the fourteenth century. Early books consisting of written pages stitched together on one side, called codex, can be traced to the fourth and fifth century, when they were commonly used to record the Gospels. In different periods intentions for writing varied and are associated with different materials. In some instances, such as with Egyptian tombs, written texts were meant to be permanent and often inscribed in stone. In other situations, writing was meant to preserve records, as in the case of banking archives from ancient Crete. The practice of religious rituals and prayers was also described in many texts. The study of the history and social circumstances of written information that have been preserved on hard or durable materials is referred to as *epigraphy*. A further category of ancient written inscriptions can be classified as impermanent, not intended to be preserved, and can offer valuable insights into the everyday life of ancient cultures.

The Toronto School of Communication

Understanding how mediated communication impacts society has a long tradition in communication studies, starting with the early investigations of scholars from the Toronto School of Communication. Its key intellectuals were Edmund Carpenter, Eric A. Havelock, Harold A. Innis, Marshall

McLuhan, and Walter J. Ong. Havelock originally trained in Britain, then taught at the University of Toronto in the 1930s, and later was appointed at Harvard and Yale. Havelock's thinking was instrumental in highlighting the social changes brought about by the move from oral to literate society. In his book *Preface to Plato* (1963), he described two fundamental shifts resulting from the move to literacy in Greek culture at the end of the fifth century: (1) the content of thought and (2) the organization of thought. His thinking has been instrumental in the fields of literacy studies and in recent theorizing about the social changes brought about by digital communication. Nonetheless, his work has remained controversial among academics because of its lack of rigorous methodology. Walter Ong continued with Havelock's theorizing around the pervasive shift the Greeks underwent from an oral to a literate society. In *Orality and Literacy* (1982), Ong contrasts oral and literate societies in terms of the expression of culture and norms. He introduces in his book the concept of second orality to describe how electronic media (television and telephones) create a culture that integrates elements from both oral and literate societies. A parallel line of thinking developed in Innis and McLuhan. Innis was a professor of political economy at the University of Toronto with an interest in the economic, structural, and social changes resulting from literacy. In *Empire and Communications*, he introduced the concept of media bias and distinguished between forms of communication that have a 'space bias' versus those that have a 'time bias.' For him, ancient Greek was an example of an oral society with a time bias that supported community and metaphysics. By contrast, the Roman Empire had a space bias favouring imperialism and commerce. Other space-binding media include print, radio, television, and digital media because they overcome space constraints to reach a wide range of people. McLuhan's analysis focused in *The Gutenberg Galaxy: The Making of Typographic Man* (1962) on the impact of print on culture, but went further to include electronic media in his books *Understanding Media* (1964) and *The Global Village: Transformations in World Life and Media in the 21st Century* (1989). McLuhan's well-known aphorism 'the medium is the message' underlined the need to examine the impact of media on people instead of focusing only on content. For him, the characteristics of media had a much more pervasive influence on society than content alone in terms of social structure and how individuals processed information and engaged with the material. He studied in detail the impact of television on society and concluded that it not only compressed time and space, but also radically transformed an individual's information processing. McLuhan is often seen as a visionary because many of his aphorisms, such as the 'global village,' continue to resonate with the way the internet is bringing people together from across the globe in virtual communities.

Early Developments in Mediated Communication

The late nineteenth/early twentieth centuries saw a proliferation of innovations in transportation, electric lighting, the radio, and the telephone. A common form of communication predating electrical transmission of messages was the use of smoke signals, flags, or beacons as a form of distant communication, sometimes described as an optical telegraph or semaphore. Napoleon made use of a system developed in France in 1794 by Claude Chappe which was very effective in transmitting messages via towers spaced five to ten miles apart and stretching a total of 4,800 kilometres. Because of the speed of communication it granted over long distances, the system was promptly employed in other parts of Europe. A series of inventions followed, leading to the introduction of the telegraph, a device that was developed in the mid-nineteenth century and until the first half of the twentieth century was the main form of transmitting printed information by wire or radio wave over long distances. The invention of the telegraph was followed by the telephone, which slowly revolutionized the way people communicated with one another. What was unprecedented about the telephone was its mass adoption and widespread impact on society. The first telephone invented by Alexander Graham Bell allowed only for the transmission of sounds and speech could not be discerned. Around the First World War I the party (or shared) line was introduced, making the phone much more affordable. It was not until the 1920s that automatic dialling was introduced and there was no longer the necessity for operators. While today telephones are normalized in society, the adoption was difficult and encountered large resistance from users. In his seminal book *America Calling*, Claude Fischer writes about the resistance the telephone encountered from diverse groups and the ways in which the telephone changed American society. Moreover, Fischer saw that 'as much as people adapt their lives to the changed circumstances created by a new technology, they also adapt that technology to their lives' (1992: 5). Hence, the impact of the telephone was not radical, but rather the technology was embedded in existing norms and practices and functioned as an additional form of communication.

The Rise of the Internet and Computer-Mediated Communication

We have seen a dramatic increase in internet use since the 1990s, affecting the way people live, work, and play in the developed world. For a large proportion of the population of internet users, internet access is a daily activity as Lee Rainie and Scott Keeter of the Pew Internet and American Life Project (2006) have shown. Communication via the internet is referred to as computer-mediated communication (CMC). Generally, the distinction is made between asynchronous and synchronous forms of communication, where the former refers to

exchanges where communication partners do not need to be present at the same time, while in the latter communication occurs in real time. With the proliferation of the internet a number of debates emerged around its impact on society. Utopians see the internet as stimulating positive change in people's lives because of its rapid diffusion to all strata of the population, its diminishing costs for getting online, its ease of use, and its variety of information and communication tools. These analysts foresee a digital revolution that is restoring a sense of community by connecting friends and kin near and far, providing information resources on a wide variety of topics and engaging various groups in political and organizational participation. They hope that the digital realm will lead to new forms of community by providing a meeting space for people with common interests, overcoming limitations of space and time. They expect online communities to flourish as people choose communities of shared interests regardless of their physical location. Howard Rheingold (1993) has described how the WELL, a text-based message board, developed into a community of friendship, support, entertainment, and information. On the other hand, sceptics claim that the internet, with its entertainment and information capabilities, draws people away from family and friends. Further, by facilitating global communication and involvement, it reduces interest in the local community and its politics. Both perspectives – the utopians and dystopians – see the internet as a major force of social transformation. What if the internet has neither radically transformed the nature of community nor markedly diminished it? Evidence is showing that the internet adds to existing patterns of communication. As Andrew Flanagan and Miriam Metzger argue, it is 'used in a manner similar to other, more traditional technologies' (2001: 153). Quan-Haase and Wellman (2004) state that the internet primarily supports communication with friends and family and provides opportunities to fill communication gaps. Perhaps the most revolutionizing part of the internet is its compression of time and space. In *No Sense of Place*, Joshua Meyrowitz concludes that 'when we communicate through telephone, radio, television, or computer, where we are physically no longer determines where and who we are socially' (1985: 15). While the impact of the internet on social relationships, communication, and community continues to spark debate, there is no doubt that radically different forms of interaction and social structure are emerging.

The Instant Connect Culture of IM and Social Network Sites

Instant messaging (IM), similar to email in the 1990s, has had a strong impact on communication. IM facilitates text-based, near-synchronous communication between two or more users. IM embodies the promises of the information age and the networked society because it allows for instant communication with multiple individuals who can be located across the globe. The core features of IM applications are: (1) a display of messages through a pop-up mechanism the moment they are received; (2) a visible list of contacts (buddies) compiled by the user; and (3) a method for indicating when buddies are online and available to receive a message. Some of the most popular IM platforms include AOL Instant Messenger (AIM), Google Talk, ICQ, Skype, Windows Live Messenger (WLM), and Yahoo! Messenger. IM is one of the largest-growing internet applications; in 2005 Business Wire reported that about half a million users worldwide were sending nearly 12 billion messages each day. What makes IM appealing for users is its speed, display of availability information, and support for multiple conversations. An important question that emerges from the use of IM for maintaining social ties is the medium's ability to support meaningful and intimate interactions. While IM consists of text-based interactions, it is often compared to 'live' conversations in terms of its interactivity and display of presence information. IM's synchronicity gives it a feel of live conversation because messages can be exchanged almost in real time. As Quan-Haase (2008) argues, the presence and availability of information provided in IM allows communication partners to monitor when others are online and to initiate spontaneous conversations.

Another form of mediated communication that has gained enormous popularity worldwide is the social network sites. Social network sites (SNSs) are websites devoted to socializing, reconnecting with old friends, and making new friendships. Examples of social network sites are Friendster, hi5, Facebook, YouTube, and MySpace. On social network sites participants create a self-descriptive profile, often including information about their preferences and habits. Then links are established between profiles, creating a complex web of connections between friends and friends of friends. In this way, one can not only find out what friends are up to, but also see who their friends are. Social network sites vary in terms of their focus. For example, Friendster is primarily devoted to dating: users can see their friends' profiles, creating opportunities to date people they did not know before. By contrast, Classmates.com helps people get back in touch with friends from high school. Classmates.com is geographically based and organized by country, region, and school. The most popular college-based social network site is Facebook, with over 42 million active members worldwide in 2007. In Facebook, users are organized around college and university campuses, high schools, employers, and geographic regions. In this way, people are grouped by their previous affiliations, allowing them to reconnect with people from their past. The popularity of these websites is greatest with teenagers and university students, who update their profiles regularly.

Studying and Researching Mediated Communication

The study of mediated communication is interdisciplinary in nature, with courses being offered in linguistics, mass communication, media studies, psychology, and sociology. The area of mediated communication has been broadened extensively with the rise in computer-mediate communication and mobile phones and includes questions about the use of new media and their social consequences. Similarly, the methodologies employed are diverse, ranging from large-scale survey research to in-depth case studies of particular innovations, uses, and effects of communication technologies. As with all research that focuses on new technologies, there are also a number of challenges involved in the inquiry. Communication technologies are constantly evolving, with old features being dropped or modified and new features continually being added. As new technologies emerge and old ones continually change, it is important to examine the spectrum of communication technologies and their role in relation to each other. Research on mediated communication is presented and discussed in a number of different forums. The International Communication Association (ICA) is an international forum where presentations are given on both historical and current research on mediated communication. With a specific focus on CMC, the Association of Internet Researchers (AoIR) brings together international academics with an interest in the uses and effects of communication technologies.

Anabel Quan-Haase

Online Resources

Association of Internet Researchers (AoIR). http://www.aoir.org/
AoIR is an international, interdisciplinary, scholarly association consisting of researchers with an interest in the advancement of internet studies. The association hosts an open-access mailing list, has a website with extensive resources, and organizes an annual conference.

Canadian Communications Association (CCA). http://www.acc-cca.ca
The CCA links and disseminates research by scholars and professionals working in communications, as well as journalism, media studies, and art.

Electronic Frontier Foundation (EFF). http://www.eff.org
The EFF is concerned with freedom of expression on the Web.

International Communication Association (ICA) http://www-rcf.usc.edu/~ica/
The ICA is an organization that links communications researchers and includes mass communication as one of its seventeen principal divisions. This group also publishes several journals, such as the *Journal of Communication*.

McLuhan Program in Culture and Technology. http://www.mcluhan.utoronto.ca/
The McLuhan Program offers a wide range of resources on the life and work of Marshall McLuhan. It also offers courses on the digital age.

Bibliography

Business Wire. With Nearly 12 Billion Instant Messages Each Day, IM is Growing into a Serious Business Collaboration Tool, IDC Finds. Business Wire, 5 October 2005. http://www.findarticles.com/p/articles/mi_m0EIN/is_2005_Oct_5/ai_n15661786.

Carpenter, Edmund, and Marshall McLuhan, eds. *Explorations in Communication*. Boston: Beacon Press, 1960.

Fischer, Claude S. *America Calling: A Social History of the Telephone to 1940*. Berkeley, CA: University of California Press, 1992.

Flanagin, Andrew J., and Miriam J. Metzger. Internet Use in the Contemporary Media Environment. *Human Communication Research* 27, no. 1 (2001): 153–81.

Goldsmith, Jack, and Tim Wu. *Who Controls the Internet? Illusions of a Borderless World*. New York: Oxford University Press, 2006.

Havelock, Eric A. *Preface to Plato*. Cambridge, MA: Harvard University Press, 1963.

Innis, Harold A. *The Bias of Communication*. Toronto: University of Toronto Press, 1951.

Innis, Harold A., and David Godfrey. *Empire and Communications*. Rev. ed. Victoria, BC: Press Porcepic, 1986.

Jacobs, Gloria. Complicating Contexts: Issues of Methodology in Researching the Language and Literacies of Instant Messaging. *Reading Research Quarterly* 39, no. 4 (2004): 394–406.

Katz, James, and Mark Aakhus, eds. *Perpetual Contact: Mobile Communication, Private Talk, Public Performance*. Cambridge: Cambridge University Press, 2002.

Lewis, Cynthia, and Bettina Fabos. Instant Messaging, Literacies, and Social Identities. *Reading Research Quarterly* 40, no. 4 (2005): 470–501.

Ling, Rich. *The Mobile Connection: The Cell Phone's Impact on Society*. San Francisco: Elsevier, 2004.

McLuhan, Marshall. *The Gutenberg Galaxy: The Making of Typographic Man*. Toronto: University of Toronto Press, 1962.

– *Understanding Media: The Extension of Man*. New York: McGraw-Hill, 1964.

McLuhan, Marshall, and Bruce R. Powers. *The Global Village: Transformations in World Life and Media in the 21st Century*. Oxford: Oxford University Press, 1989.

Meyrowitz, Joshua. No Sense of Place: *The Impact of Electronic Media on Social Behavior*. New York: Oxford University Press, 1985.

Nissen, Hans J., Peter Damerow, and Robert K. Englund. Archaic Bookkeeping: Early Writing and Techniques of Economic Administration in the Ancient Near East. Trans. Paul Larsen. Chicago: University of Chicago Press, 1993.

Ong, Walter. *Orality and Literacy: The Technologizing of the Word*. 2nd ed. New York: Routledge, 2002 [1982].

Pew Internet and American Life Project. Social Networking Websites and Teens: An Overview. Online report (2007). http://www.pewinternet.org/pdfs/PIP_SNS_Data_Memo_Jan_2007.pdf.

Quan-Haase, Anabel. Instant Messaging on Campus: Use and Integration in Students' Everyday Communication. *The Information Society* 25, no. 1 (2008).

Quan-Haase, Anabel, and Barry Wellman. How Does the Internet Affect Social Capital? In *Social Capital and Information Technology*, ed.

Marlene Huysman and Volker Wulf, 151–76. Cambridge, MA: MIT Press, 2004.

Rainie, Lee, and Scott Keeter. Pew Internet Project Data Memo. Pew Internet & American Life Project: 1–13. Online report (2006). http://www.pewinternet.org/pdfs/PIP_Cell_phone_study.pdf.

Rheingold, Howard. *The Virtual Community: Homesteading on the Electronic Frontier*. Reading, MA: Addison-Wesley, 1993.

Thurlow, Crispin. Generation txt? Exposing the Sociolinguistics of Young People's Text-Messaging. *Discourse Analysis Online* (2002). http://www.shu.ac.uk/daol/articles/open/2002/003/thurlow2002003-01.html.

Whittaker, Steve. Theories and Methods in Mediated Communication. In *The Handbook of Discourse Processes*, ed. Arthur C. Graesser, Morton A. Gernsbacher, and Susan R. Goldman, 243–86. Mahwah, NJ: Lawrence Erlbaum Associates, 2003.

MEDIUM

[See also: *Communication; Information; Mass Communication; McLuhan, Marshall; Message; Writing*]

The etymology of the word 'medium' is from the Latin word *medium* = 'middle,' with the plural form *media*. With respect to communication, medium refers to any means, or instrument, employed for the purpose of transmitting a message, or other form of communication.

Prior to the development of the alphabet as well as other writing systems, and the printing press, there existed three communicative modes: (1) gesture, (2) vocal speech (oral-auditory mode), and (3) pictography (graphic symbols that represent a concept or object). With the invention of the alphabet by the Phoenicians in the second millennium BCE, and the European invention of the printing press with movable type by Johannes Gutenberg (1400?–1468) in the fifteenth century (though a form of printing called woodblock printing had been introduced in China much earlier), the ability to mass produce books became a reality.

The latter was instrumental in producing a means to increase literacy through public education. It also provided an instrument for popular entertainment (novels, short stories, poetry, essays, and so forth) for the literate public.

Mass media refers to the various ways in which messages may be transmitted in contemporary society to a very large audience. There is a basic division in media between the print media (books, newspapers, magazines, photography) and non-print, or electronic media (film, radio, television, CDs, and the internet). Each medium provides entertainment and instruction intended for a mass audience. The print media, for example, provide instruction (facts, information, and interpretation) and entertainment (novels, short stories, poetry, essays), some of which may be accompanied by illustrations including photographs and artwork. The non-print media, likewise, provide instruction and entertainment for the public. Non-print media include those with visual and auditory capability (CD-ROMs, DVDs, film, internet, television). Other non-print media include those with auditory capacity only (radio programming, recordings of various sorts).

The internet, a global system of interconnecting networks that permit public access by various means including the telephone, radio waves, fibre optic systems, and so forth, is the most recent medium available for widespread communal usage. Thus, an individual may connect to the internet anywhere at any time. Within the internet, the World Wide Web consists of interconnected documents, and other materials linked by URLs (uniform resource locators). Originally designed to provide communication links between colleges and universities in the 1960s and 1970s, the internet has revolutionized the mass media. Its multiple functions include email, file sharing, instant messaging, voice over IP (internet protocol), and so forth. More recently, an individual may download other media formats such as music to an iPod or similar music device. A person may also watch previously broadcast television and radio programs, view films, enrol in and take classes at various levels, to name but a few options. This all-in-one broadcast medium has had a profound effect on the traditional print and non-print media. In the twenty-first century, all of these media may be accessed via the internet through the procedure known as 'downloading' (film, music, radio, television shows). Moreover, newspapers are now readily available on the internet, which has contributed to the demise of afternoon newspapers and a reduction in sales of the remaining ones. There is an ongoing convergence of the established media into the new medium of the internet. Furthermore, the advent of the cellular telephone has provided yet another means of access to the internet.

The renowned Canadian scholar Marshall McLuhan (1911–80) hypothesized that the electronic media had converted the world into a global village. Moreover, for McLuhan, the form in which information and communication are encoded and transmitted is responsible for determining the nature of a given culture. Oral, literate, and electronic cultures differ significantly from each other. McLuhan argued that in the modern electronic era people worldwide had interconnectivity because they could all tune into events as they unfolded in any part of the world. He dubbed this aspect of the electronic media 'the global village.' In this global village, all people have an 'electronic interdependence.' Another of his well-known mantras is the statement 'the medium is the message,' by which he meant that the format of the code (written, oral, visual) will determine the type of message transmitted. An oral message means that an individual knows the phonemic code of a language, a written message means that an individual knows the alphabetic code, a visual message means that an individual knows the pictographic and gestural codes, and so forth. Furthermore, McLuhan classified media as 'hot' or 'cool.' A 'hot' medium is one that focuses on a single sense and is information-laden, for example, film, which emphasizes the sense of sight. A 'cool' medium, on the other hand, is one that contains less information, and thus requires the audience to 'fill in' the missing information, for example, a comic book.

Frank Nuessel

Bibliography

Berger, Arthur A. *Making Sense of Media: Key Texts in Media and Cultural Studies*. Oxford: Blackwell, 2005.

McLuhan, Marshall. *The Gutenberg Galaxy: The Making of Typographic Man*. Toronto: University of Toronto Press, 1962.

– *Understanding Media: The Extensions of Man*. New York: McGraw-Hill, 1964.

Noll, A. Michael. *The Evolution of Media*. Lanham: Rowman and Littlefield, 2006.

MESSAGE

[See also: *Bull's-Eye Model; Communication Theory; Feedback; Noise; Meaning*]

In communication theory, a *message* is what is passed on or transmitted through the channel by or through a sender and aimed at a receiver. In human communication, a message is constructed by talking, writing, and so forth; in computer software, a message is a piece of information passed from the application or operating system to the user. In human communication a message can be verbal (based on an exchange of words) or non-verbal (as in facial expressions or body language).

The terms *message* and *meaning* are often used interchangeably. But this is inaccurate. Consider a simple greeting such as 'Hi, great day, isn't it?' It is, of course, a simple *message*, an oral transmission from one person to another. But the *meaning* of the message can be literal, whereby the speaker is acknowledging the kind of day it is in order to make social contact. On the other hand, its meaning could be ironic,

if uttered on a cold, snowy, and miserable day. Clearly, the notion of *message* is not coincident with that of *meaning*. A message can have more than one meaning, or several messages can have the same meaning. In the mass media, it is often the case that many layers of meanings are built into the same message.

A message can contain blocks of text as well as various types of complementary information (such as to whom or what it is destined, what the nature of its content is, and so on). It can be aimed directly from a sender to a receiver through a physical link or channel, or it can be passed, either in whole or in part, through electronic, mechanical, or digital-computer media – instant messaging and email are examples of the latter.

Marcel Danesi

Bibliography

Shannon, Claude E. A Mathematical Theory of Communication. *Bell Systems Technical Journal* 27 (1948): 379–423.

Wiener, Norbert. *Cybernetics, or Control and Communication in the Animal and the Machine*. Cambridge, MA: MIT Press, 1949.

MODERN CONTINENTAL THEORIES OF COMMUNICATION, DISCOURSE, AND LANGUAGE

[See also: *Cognitive Language Studies; Conceptual Metaphor Theory; Discourse; Discourse Theory; Jakobson's Model of Communication; Post-Structuralism; Semiotics; Structuralism*]

Concepts in twentieth-century European linguistics and semiotics have found considerable applications worldwide in communication studies, narrative theory, poetics, and film and media studies. The following short discussions and definitions can provide a first entry into the area, for which excellent specialized dictionaries and encyclopedias are available (Ablali and

Ducard 2009; Crystal 1992; Dubois et al. 1972; Ducrot and Todorov 1972; Ducrot and Schaeffer 1999; Greimas and Courtés 1993; Martin and Ringham 2000, 2006; Sebeok 1986; and Taylor and Winquist 2001).

Communication

Roman Jakobson identifies six key components enabling communication: *addresser, addressee, message, code, channel,* and *context* (1990: 69–79). To each component corresponds a linguistic function: a set toward the addresser (e.g., speaker, writer) brings the *emotive* or *expressive* function into salience, as evidenced notably in interjections, intonation, and dramatic interpretation. An orientation toward the addressee (e.g., listener, reader) mobilizes the field of the *conative* function crucial to imperatives, vocatives, performatives, and to the rhetoric of persuasion. The *poetic* function highlights the message in and of itself, particularly its structure, design, and musicality, while the *metalingual* function emphasizes the code, as do conversational queries like 'What do you mean by that remark?' or 'Do you see what I mean?' and as do grammars and linguistics in a more general way. Focused on the psychological bond and physical channel linking addresser and addressee, the *phatic* function comes to the fore when interlocutors concentrate on initiating, maintaining, discontinuing, or re-establishing communication, and when issues of connectivity, sound quality, technical infrastructure, and different media become critical. Involving the speech context, the *referential* (*denotative, cognitive*) function is put in play most directly by demonstrative pronouns, designation, deixis, or indexicality, and by correlations between language and the physical and cultural world.

Jakobson's metalingual function adapts Alfred Tarski's distinction between *metalanguage* and *object language*: the former designates a specialized, artificial code devised by logicians, philosophers, and linguists to describe the latter, a natural language in its customary communicative uses (Tarski

1946). Critical theorists such as Roland Barthes, Jacques Derrida, and Julia Kristeva argue that any metalanguage inextricably interacts with a natural language in such a way as to sap the hierarchy or segregation between the two. Greimas (1966 [1983: 82–98]) studies the mechanisms by which speakers engaged in normal discourse coin new expressions, formulate partial definitions of words and objects, and summarize each other's remarks, thereby elaborating fragments of metalanguages and models of discourse.

Continental theory typically distances itself from the notion of 'communication' conceived as the mere transmission of information, from 'representation' understood as the verbal recreation of a stable external world not dependent on experience and culture, and from 'expression' viewed as a simple linguistic exteriorization of a subject's prior articulated thought. Whereas its technological bent leads information theory to describe discourse as a factual 'message' that one individual transmits to another like a discrete object, continental theorists tend to view verbal interaction through the lenses of politics and poetry, and thus highlight persuasion, indirection, irony, (self-)censorship, metaphorical language, and interpretation. Their research on signs and language aims not just at the purposeful communication of data or knowledge but at 'signification' more generally, at any meaningful interaction among subjects. Animadverting upon a mechanistic version of *communication,* Derrida emphasizes that when discourse is produced it is subjected to *dissemination,* to being excerpted, (mis)quoted, de- and recontextualized, 'clarified' and explained, summarized and amplified, forgotten or ignored – processes that alter the initial text in ways that escape the speaker's control (Derrida 1980).

Paris semiotics proposes a theory of communication that embraces multiple media including natural language, gesture, body language, advertising images, and film. The theory emphasizes the intersubjective dynamics that undergird interaction and highlights relations between expression and action (Greimas and Courtés 1993 [1982: 'Communication']). The semiotic notion of communication is inscribed within the broader contexts of economic exchanges, psychological interactions among individuals and groups, and the interface between humans and the natural and cultural environment. A 'sender-subject' initiates an exchange in order to manipulate, intimidate, seduce, or tempt a 'receiver-subject,' who in turn exercises scepticism, prevarication, resistance, and strategy to achieve objectives (Greimas and Courtés 1993 [1982: 'Manipulation']). Exchanges typically happen within the framework of an implicit 'contract,' convention, or understanding that regulates the kind of interaction that takes place and that impinges on how initiatives are interpreted (Greimas and Courtés 1993 [1982: 'Contract,' 'Polemic']). This contractual dynamic between subjects incorporates measures of cooperation and conflict, confidence and mistrust, shared values and conflicts of belief. Whether individual or collective subjects are involved, communication puts in play power relations that alternately favour free, constrained, veiled, or even censored expression, potentially involving provocation, intimidation, liberation, or extortion.

Paris semiotics emphasizes that communication requires appropriate 'competences' on the part of the participants, such as pragmatic, linguistic, narrative, and psychological competences (Greimas and Courtés 1993 [1982: 'Competence']). At the same time, communicative exchanges produce meaning and transform the participants, enlightening or confusing them, instilling or altering attitudes and intentions, fostering cohesion or discord, creating utterly new 'messages' and novel components within pre-existing 'codes.' Given forms of exchange may entail particular conditions: rituals may exclude the presence of non participants, 'personal' or confidential communications may require exclusivity, and negotiations may call for

intermediaries. Eric Landowski proposes a phenomenological view of communication as a spontaneous and sensate, holistic and mutual 'contagion' between interactants (2004: 105–37).

Utterance and Enunciation

Developing the distinction between code and message, Émile Benveniste identifies two modes of language: a *semiotic* mode in which expressions are constituted as oppositional and combinatorial entities within a language system, and a *semantic* mode in which actual sentences and their components uttered by participants in the linguistic interaction 'refer to the world of objects … relate to specific and concrete situations' (1966: 128; 1974: 63–5). Benveniste further distinguishes between the *utterance* (*énoncé*) or product of speaking/writing and the *enunciation* (*énonciation*) or production of discourse.

Utterance serves as the neutral linguistic term for a message of any length, which may or may not respect normative grammar or other constraints, and may involve one or more addressers and addressees. By extension, continental theoreticians and critics speak of the filmic utterance, the musical utterance, the pictorial utterance, and so forth, to designate expressions in other media. From a semantic perspective, one can distinguish between two types of simple utterances, one whose predicate 'qualifies' the subject by attributing one or more qualities to it, using an adjective or a noun, for example, and one whose predicate attributes a function to the subject, by means of an action verb, for example (Greimas 1966 [1983: 138–9, 176–9]). The French linguist Lucien Tesnière (1959) proposes that the sentence can be viewed as a simple 'show' or drama whose action (verb) entails a configuration of central players (subject, object, indirect object) and secondary participants such as certain adverbs (cf. 'dependency grammars,' e.g., Robinson 1970). Complex sentences can be described as 'transformations' of more basic structures. Emphasizing 'localist' theories, the Danish linguist Louis Hjelmslev describes a language's cases and prepositions as forming a system of interrelated semantic arrays (1935–7, cf. Viggo Brøndal 1940). Drawing from Tesnière, Hjelmslev, and Brøndal, A.J. Greimas presents the sentence as a show or drama comprising a core action articulated by three oriented signifying relations that link subject and object (transitivity, teleology, desire or phobia), sender and receiver (etiology, communication, transfer), and helper and opponent (power, 1966 [1983: 146–52, 176–9]). Hjelmslev's and Greimas's models can be compared to case grammars developed in North American linguistics (e.g., Anderson 1971, Fillmore 1977).

Enunciation designates the process by which a particular utterance is realized, including the act by which the addresser produces it, the event in which the addressee experiences it, and the dynamic between addresser and addressee that makes the message possible and that the utterance institutes or transforms (Benveniste 1966 [1971: 217–30], 1974: 67–88). An initial linguistic study of enunciative mechanisms can focus on their traces and representations observable in such utterances as 'Now hear this' and 'I'm not really sure I can answer that question.' Jakobson thus identifies units of the code whose referential value depends directly on the message and parameters of its context: these *shifters* include for example personal pronouns (e.g., *I, you*) and certain adverbs of time and place (e.g., *here, now*; 1990: 386–9). Among addressers and addressees, one can distinguish between the *enunciator* and *enunciatee* corresponding to the (observed or presupposed) real participants in the interaction, on the one hand, and the *narrator* and *narratee* designating representations of the latter found within a text (e.g., 'the author would like to thank …'; 'the impatient reader may wonder …'; Greimas and Courtés 1993 [1982: 'Enunciator/Enunciatee']). Benveniste labels *discourse* the enunciative mode he considers standard in which individuals engage

in conversation within a real-life situation, reversibly employing such expressions as 'I' and 'you,' 'here' and 'there' with each other; he terms *history* an enunciative mode he considers less typical which minimizes the use of signs designating the immediate communicative situation in favour of an objectified, didactic style (e.g., 'The senator told a reporter that on the designated site …'; 1966 [1971: 205–17]).

More broadly, studying the enunciation can entail investigating the psychological and social conditions of the generation and perception of the utterance, as do psycholinguistics, sociolinguistics, and, for literature, reception theory (cf. genetic criticism). Julia Kristeva terms the text perceived as a phenomenon (cf. utterance) in the form of published material, familiar grammatical structures, and known phonetic or graphic articulations the *pheno-text*, and she labels the processes that generate the discourse the *geno-text* (cf. enunciation), which she investigates using psychoanalytic and Marxist methods (1969: 278–89).

Paris semiotics designates *enunciative praxis* the processes by which speakers judge, transform, and take responsibility for utterances and discursive forms, from words and expressions to motifs, topoi, and genres (Fontanille 2003 [2006: 195–207]). Arguing that each language, culture, and even text establishes its own intersubjective personal field and thus its particular enunciative schema, Jacques Fontanille notes that whereas the Indo-European idioms that Benveniste uses as a model constitute personal pronouns as deictics and derive them from an originary 'I,' Asian languages such as Japanese define such pronouns as descriptive values and found them instead on impersonal social rank (Fontanille 2003 [2006: 189–91], cf. 1999: 106–15).

Positioning his research in relation to speech act theory, Oswald Ducrot investigates enunciative structures specific to presupposition and to argumentation in discourse, including mechanisms particular to inferences, to interrogatives, and to polyphony or multiple speakers (Ducrot 1984,

1991; Ducrot and Anscombre 1983; Ducrot and Zagar 1996; cf. List 1985). Analysing enunciative phenomena in conversations, Catherine Kerbrat-Orrecchioni identifies basic components, rhythms, and structural organizations, examines politeness strategies, and studies the ritualization of speech in fixed types of exchanges (Kerbrat-Orrecchioni 1990, 1992, 1994). Her research has explored the role of verbal interaction in the development of interpersonal relations and has delineated both universal and culturally specific aspects of linguistic exchanges. Related studies examine dynamics specific to questions and to 'trialogues' or conversations among three speakers (Kerbrat-Orrecchioni 1991; Kerbrat-Orrecchioni and Plantin 1995; cf. Kerbrat-Orrecchioni 2004). Herman Parret's explorations of pragmatics and enunciation bring together philosophical, linguistic, and semiotic perspectives (1983, 1995, 2006).

Saussurean Linguistics

Ferdinand de Saussure's 1916 *Course in General Linguistics* (*CGL*) remains a foundational text for continental language theory. Although linguists have critiqued features of the *CGL* ever since it appeared, the power and generality of its concepts as well as the clarity of its exposition have assured it significant and ongoing influence in linguistics and in other fields. In order to account for a wide variety of languages, and to synthesize features of philosophically oriented French grammars and German comparative and historical linguistics, the *CGL* focuses on a small set of elementary principles that underlie language rather than on more specific phenomena such as parts of speech (e.g., noun, adjective, verb), tense, or types of phonological transformations.

CGL's attention to meaning, to social perspectives, and to language variation and change gives it resonance with trends in contemporary cognitive linguistics. From the 1950s to the 1980s, Saussure's ideas nourished interdisciplinary research in continental structuralism and post-structuralism.

Temporal Perspectives

A *synchronic* perspective studies a particular state of an idiom at a given moment in time; synchronic phenomena function simultaneously in the same system (Saussure 1916 [1966: 101–39]). A *diachronic* perspective examines change over time; diachronic phenomena are in a state of change, belonging to different stages of development (Saussure 1916 [1966: 140–82]). The *panchronic* perspective emphasizes permanent features of a linguistic structure; panchronic mechanisms remain unchanged over a long period, as have the syntactic functions associated with word order in English.

Saussure's principles of synchronic analysis illustrate his vision of a natural language as a network of interrelations: 'language is a system of interdependent terms in which the value of each term results solely from the simultaneous presence of the others' (1916 [1966: 114]). At the same time, the Swiss linguist emphasizes that all languages are in continual flux, whether evolutionary or revolutionary, and that speakers constantly reinterpret and refigure linguistic units even as phonological transformations restructure sound and initiate changes in grammar and vocabulary (1916 [1966: 140, 169–82, 153–61]). In cases of conquest, colonization, and nomadism, different languages coexist without forming an organic whole (1916 [1966: 193–5]). These views jibe with the perspective of the pragmatic philosopher Ludwig Wittgenstein, who similarly stresses that as practices evolve in a society, so too do their myriad corresponding linguistic forms: 'New types of language, new language-games, as we may say, come into existence, and others become obsolete and get forgotten … the *speaking* of language is part of an activity, or of a form of life.' (1973: §23, p. 11).

The Linguistic Sign

In order to underline the specificity of each language, the *CGL* defines the sign as the relation between a *signifier* (its distinctive sound) and a *signified* (its distinctive meaning) within a given idiom. In a language, signifiers are diacritically constituted as differences among signifiers, as signifieds are instituted as differences among signifieds, while the relation between signifier and signified creates linguistic value, a triadic scheme, and founds the sign as a positive historical entity (Saussure 1916 [1966: 65–7, 102–22]). Iconic relations between signifier and signified illustrated by onomatopoeia ('cockle-doodle-do,' 'quack quack') and by significant word order and grouping in lists are called *motivated* relations (Saussure 1916 [1966: 67–70]; cf. Genette 1976). More specifically, Saussure terms systematic relations among signifiers and signifieds illustrated by regular word formation, grammatical agreement, conjugations, and declensions 'the *mechanism* of language' (1916 [1966: 127–31]). Following the American linguist William Dwight Whitney and in opposition to Adamic theories of language popular in early nineteenth-century comparative grammar, the *CGL* highlights the conventional, institutional relation between signifier and signified that characterizes the greater part of a natural language's vocabulary and that accounts for its idiosyncratic networks of polysemy, synonymy, and homonymy. Saussure (somewhat unfortunately) terms such an unmotivated, non-systematic relation *arbitrary* (1916 [1966: 131–4]). Saussurean discussions of the sign emphasize socio-psychological perspectives, formal semiotic structure, and the cultural specificity of each language.

The didactic *CGL* gives words and short phrases as examples of signs, and multiplies simple metaphors, comparing the sign to a sheet of paper whose recto figures the signifier and whose verso represents the signified, for example (1916 [1966: 113]). His posthumously published notebooks explore more complex views, such as the hypothesis that the anagram functions as a key compositional device in Latin poetry: layered over the conventional unfolding of the verse, a second reading stitches together fragments of words to form additional 'hidden' signs disseminated throughout the poem (Saussure 1971). Developing the Saussurean tradition, Hjelmslev defines a sign in a natural language or in any comparably complex semiotic system as the relation between one or more *expression* planes that compose its distinctive outward form and one or more *content* planes that constitute its distinctive sense (1943 [1961: 47–60]). Reacting against Chomsky's concept of syntactic transformations that do not affect meaning, the cognitive linguist Ronald Langacker adopts the Saussurean sign model, identifying a 'phonological pole' and a 'conceptual pole' for every symbolic expression or structure (1987: 76–86).

Types of Relations among Units

Syntagmatic relations obtain among units in a string (e.g., word, phrase, sentence), while *paradigmatic* relations associate a unit to others that could take its place in the string. Employing the term 'associative' for paradigmatic, Saussure contrasts the pair: 'The syntagmatic relation is *in praesentia*. It is based on two or more terms that occur in an effective series. Against this, the associative relation unites terms *in absentia* in a potential mnemonic series' (1916: [1966: 123]). 'Horizontal,' syntagmatic relations involve combination (the work of the addresser) and segmentation (the task of the addressee); 'vertical' paradigmatic relations entail substitutability, selection, and similarity. Calling the latter the 'axis of selection,' Jakobson compares it to the rhetorical figure of metaphor, relating the 'axis of combination' (cf. syntagmatic relations) to metonymy (1990: 119–20). Emphasizing the importance of phonetic, rhythmic, grammatical, and semantic parallelisms and contrasts for poetry, he defines the genre: 'The poetic function projects the principle of equivalence from the axis of selection into the axis of combination' (1990: 78). The notions of paradigmatic and syntagmatic relations show up in cognitive science (e.g., Feldman, Lakoff, Bailey, Narayanan, Regier, and Stolcke 1996: 5–6; Langacker 1987: 74–5, 94–6, 472–4).

Norms and Usage

Saussure divides the phenomena of *speech* (French *langage*) within a given idiom between those belonging to *language* (*langue*) that are common to the speech community and must be learned by its members and phenomena termed *speaking* (*parole*) that are specific to particular uses of the idiom and which its members initiate. Saussure (1916) highlights the advantages of focusing on *language* as a system, while Saussure (2002) outlines a linguistics of *speaking*. Calling the virtual system *language* (*langue*) and instances of its use in actual sentences *discourse* (*discours*), Benveniste (1966, 1974) explores how communicative discourse fosters (inter)subjectivity and refers to objects and cultural concepts. A.J. Greimas (1976), François Rastier (1989), and Jacques Fontanille (2003) develop Benveniste's concepts to elaborate a linguistics and poetics that identifies organizing principles underlying extensive stretches of discourse and entire texts.

Thomas F. Broden

Bibliography

Ablali, Driss, and Dominique Ducard, eds. *Vocabulaire des études sémiotiques et sémiologiques*. Paris: Honoré Champion and Besançon; Presses Universitaires de Franches-Comté, 2009.

Anderson, John M. *The Grammar of Case*. New York: Cambridge University Press, 1971.

Barthes, Roland. *Le système de la mode*. Paris: Seuil, 1967. Translated by Matthew Ward and Richard Howard, *The Fashion System*. New York: Hill and Wang, 1983.

Benveniste, Émile. *Problèmes de linguistique générale*. 2 vols. Paris: Gallimard, 1966 and 1974. Vol. 1 translated by Mary Elizabeth Meek, *Problems in General Linguistics*. Coral Gables, FL: University of Miami Press, 1971.

Brøndal, Viggo. *Præpositionernes theori indledning til en rationel betydningslære*. Copenhagen: B. Lunos bogtrykkeri, 1940. Translated by Pierre Naert, *Théorie des Prépositions: introduction à une sémantique rationnelle*. Copenhagen: Munksgaard, 1950.

Crystal, David. *An Encyclopedic Dictionary of Languages and Linguistics*. Cambridge: Blackwell, 1992.

Derrida, Jacques. *La carte postale de Socrate à Freud et au-delà*. Paris: Flammarion, 1980. Translated by Alan Bass, *The Post Card: From Socrates to Freud and Beyond*. Chicago: University of Chicago Press, 1987.

Dubois, Jean, et al. *Dictionnaire de linguistique*. Paris: Larousse, 1972.

Ducrot, Oswald. *Le dire et le dit*. Paris: Minuit, 1984.

– *Dire et ne pas dire. Principes de sémantique linguistique*. Paris: Hermann, 1991.

Ducrot, Oswald, and Jean-Claude Anscombre. *L'argumentation dans la langue*. Brussels: Mardaga, 1983.

Ducrot, Oswald, and Jean-Marie Schaeffer. *Nouveau dictionnaire encyclopédique des sciences du langage*. 2nd ed. Paris: Seuil, 1999.

Ducrot, Oswald, and Tzvetan Todorov. *Dictionnaire encyclopédique des sciences du langage*. Paris: Seuil, 1972. Translated by Catherine Porter, *Encyclopedic Dictionary of the Sciences of Language*. Baltimore: Johns Hopkins University Press, 1979.

Ducrot, Oswald, and Igor Z. Zagar. *Slovenian Lectures: Argumentative Semantics*. Ljubljana: ISH, 1996.

Feldman, Jerome, George Lakoff, David Bailey, Srini Narayanan, Terry Regier, and Andreas Stolcke. L_0 – The First 5 Years of an Automated Language Acquisition Project. In *Integration of Natural Language and Vision Processing: Grounding Representations*, special issue of *Artificial Intelligence Review* 10, no. 1–2 (April 1996): 103–29. Pages refer to the pdf file available online at http://www.icsi.berkeley.edu/NTL/papers/first_five_years.pdf (accessed 27–8 April 2007).

Fillmore, Charles. The Case for Case Reopened. In *Grammatical Relations*, ed. P. Cole and J.M. Sadock, 59–81. New York: Academic, series Syntax and Semantics no. 8, 1977.

Fontanille, Jacques. *Sémiotique et littérature. Essais de méthode*. Paris: Presses Universitaires de France, 1999.

– *Sémiotique du discours*. 2nd ed. Limoges: PULIM, 2003. Translated by Heidi Bostic, *The Semiotics of Discourse*. New York: Peter Lang, 2006.

Genette, Gérard. *Mimologiques: voyage en Craty-lie*. Paris: Seuil, 1976. Translated by Thaïs E. Morgan *Mimologics*. Lincoln: University of Nebraska Press, 1995.

Greimas, Algirdas J. *Sémantique structurale: recherche de méthode*. Paris: Larousse. Rpt. Paris: Presses Universitaires de France, 1986. Translated by Daniele McDowell, Ronald Schleifer, and Alan Velie, *Structural Semantics: An Attempt at a Method*. Lincoln: University of Nebraska Press, 1983.

– *Maupassant: la sémiotique du texte: exercices pratiques*. Paris: Seuil, 1976. Translated by Paul Perron, *Maupassant. The Semiotics of the Text; Practical Exercises*. Philadelphia: Benjamin, 1988.

Greimas, Algirdas J., and Joseph Courtés. *Sémio-tique: dictionnaire raisonné de la théorie du lan-gage*. Paris: Hachette, 1979, new edition with bibliography 1993. Translated by Larry Crist and Daniel Patte et al., with a bibliography by Edward McMahon, *Semiotics and Language: An Analytical Dictionary*. Bloomington: Indiana University Press, 1982.

Hjelmslev, Louis. *La catégorie des cas. Étude de grammaire générale*. 2 vols. Aarhus, Denmark: Universitetsforlaget Aarhus, series Acta Jut-landica 7.1 and 9.1, 1935 and 1937. Rpt. in one volume, Munich: Wilhelm Fink, series International Library of General Linguistics no. 25, 1972.

– *Omkring Sprogteoriens Grundlaeggelse*. Co-penhagen: Munksgaard, 1943. Translated by Francis J. Whitfield, *Prolegomena to a Theory of Language*. Rev. ed. Madison: University of Wisconsin Press, 1961.

Jakobson, Roman. *On Language*. Ed. Linda R. Waugh and Monique Monville-Burston. Cambridge, MA: Harvard University Press, 1990.

Kerbrat-Orrecchioni, Catherine. *Les interactions verbales*. 3 vols. Paris: Armand Colin, 1990, 1992, 1994.

– ed. *La question*. Lyon: Presses Universitaires de Lyon, 1991.

– ed. *Polylogue*, special issue of *Journal of Prag-matics* 36, no. 1 (2004).

Kerbrat-Orrecchioni, Catherine, and Christian Plantin, eds. *Le trilogue*. Lyons: Presses Uni-versitaires de Lyon, 1995.

Kristeva, Julia. *Séméiotikè, recherches pour une sémanalyse*. Paris: Seuil, 1969.

Landowski, Eric. *Passions sans nom: essais de socio-sémiotique III*. Paris: Presses Universitaires de France, 2004.

Langacker, Ronald W. *Foundations of Cognitive Grammar*. Vol. 1: *Theoretical Prerequisites*. Vol. 2: *Descriptive Application*. Stanford: Stanford University Press, 1987–91.

List, Kathleen Louise. Coherence and Cohe-sion: Contextualization of Oswald Ducrot's General Theory of Linguistic Semantics. PhD dissertation, University of Michigan, 1985 [includes English translations of lectures by Ducrot].

Martin, Bronwen, and Felizitas Ringham. *Dic-tionary of Semiotics*. London and New York: Cassel, 2000.

– *Key Terms in Semiotics*. London: Continuum, 2006.

Parret, Herman. *Semiotics and Pragmatics. An Evaluative Comparison of Conceptual Frame-works*. Philadelphia: Benjamins, 1983.

– *La communauté en paroles*. Brussels: Mardaga, 1995.

– *Epiphanie de la présence*. Limoges: PULIM, series Nouveaux Actes Sémiotiques, 2006.

Rastier, François. *Sens et textualité*. Paris: Ha-chette, 1989. Translated by Frank Collins and Paul Perron, *Meaning and Textuality*. Toronto: University of Toronto Press, 1997.

Robinson, Jane J. Dependency Structures and Transformational Rules. *Language* 46 (1970): 259–85.

Saussure, Ferdinand de. *Cours de linguistique générale*, 1916. Translated by Wade Baskins, *Course in General Linguistics*. New York: Philosophical Library, 1959, rpt. New York: McGraw-Hill, 1966.

– *Les mots sous les mots. Les anagrammes de Ferdi-nand de Saussure*. Ed. Jean Starobinski. Paris: Gallimard, 1971. Translated by Olivia Emmet, *Words upon Words: The Anagrams of Ferdinand de Saussure*. New Haven, CT: Yale University Press, 1979.

– *Écrits de linguistique générale*. Ed. Simon Bou-quet and Rudolf Engler. Paris: Gallimard, 2002. Translated by Carol Sanders and Mat-thew Pires with the assistance of Peter Figueroa, *Writings in General Linguistics*. New York: Oxford University Press, 2006.

Sebeok, Thomas A., ed. *Encyclopedic Dictionary of Semiotics*. 3 vols. New York: Mouton de Gruyter, 1986.

Tarski, Alfred. *O logice matematycznej i metodzie dedukcyjne*. Translated by O. Helmer, *Introduction to Logic and to the Methodology of Deductive Sciences*. New York: Oxford University Press, 1946, new edition 1994.

Taylor, Victor E., and Charles E. Winquist, eds. *Encyclopedia of Postmodernism*. New York: Routledge, 2001.

Tesnière, Lucien. *Éléments d'une syntaxe structurale*. Paris: Klincksieck, 1959, rev. ed. 1966.

Whitney, William Dwight. *The Life and Growth of Language: An Outline of Linguistic Science*. New York: D. Appleton, 1896.

Wittgenstein, Ludwig. *Philosophische Untersuchungen*. Translated by G.E.M. Anscombe, *Philosophical Investigations*. 3rd ed. New York: Macmillan, 1973.

MP3

[See also: *Instant Messaging; Internet; World Wide Web*]

MP3, which stands for MPEG (Motion Pictures Expert Group) Audio Layer III, is a method of audio compression which allows any music file to be made smaller with little or no loss in sound quality. A typical digital signal takes a 16-bit (stereo quality) sample and records it at an audio bandwidth around 44.1 KHZ (the standard for compact discs or CDs) (Brandenburg and Bosi 1997). MP3 coding allows for a raw audio sample to be reprogrammed in a manner which uses replacement sounds of a lower bit rate while disregarding sounds on bandwidths not auditory to the human ear. This streamlines the remaining data within the file, which results in a file faithful to the original recording but only a fraction in size. MP3 has quickly become the industry standard in usage and has revolutionized the way music is created and delivered to mass audiences.

While many were involved developing the technology which would lead to the creation of MP3, Dieter Seitzer and Karlheinz Brandenburg of the Fraunhofer Institut Integrierte Schaltungen (Fraunhofer IIS) are the people most associated with the MP3 format. Fraunhofer IIS is a division within the Fraunhofer Society, which is a collection of state-funded groups within Germany that specialize in various fields of applied science (Fraunhofer IIS 2007). Seitzer, a professor at the University of Erlangen, worked on retaining the quality of music that was being transferred over a phone line. With the advent of the internet, and the standard connection speed of 28.8 Kbps, it was necessary to find a way to send high-fidelity sound files in a practical and efficient way. Brandenburg, dubbed 'the father of MP3,' applied his expertise in electronics and mathematics to refining the compression algorithm which would form the basis of MP3. Upon the completion of MP3, Brandenburg ensured that the technology was marketed as shareware, copywritten commercial software that is distributed freely on a trial basis with the option of paying to obtain a licence and full usage of the software (Ford 2000). In 1992, the International Organization for Standardization (ISO) integrated the compression algorithm created by Brandenburg and his team into the MPEG-1 video format. It beat out stiff competition from rival groups within Germany and from the United States of America, who had created the Layer-1 and Layer-2 methods of compression. Despite this, all three algorithms were ultimately approved by the ISO and integrated into MPEG-1 (Fraunhofer IIS 2008). In 1995, the .mp3 file name extension was adopted for MPEG Layer 3, replacing the former .bit extension.

In 1996, Fraunhofer IIS and its French-based partner Thomson Consumer Electronics obtained an American patent for MP3 (mp3licensing.com). It was not until the following year that MP3 would become part of the 1990s tech explosion, when Brandenburg took the technology to

Silicon Valley (the tech sector of San Jose, California). Fraunhofer IIS began enforcing their patent rights on MP3 in 1998. Consequently, any firm that created a program pertaining to MP3 encoding/decoding and the ripping of audio data would have to pay royalties to Fraunhofer IIS. This led other developers to create MP3 alternatives such AAC, Ogg Vorbis, WMA, and RealAudio in order to avoid paying licensing fees to the Fraunhofer/Thomson conglomerate. MP3 would eventually retain its market share, as by the time other formats were created, there was already widespread familiarity with MP3 encoding programs. Furthermore, there were thousands of MP3 files already in circulation by that point. Eventually, even large companies such as Microsoft were forced to pay Fraunhofer/Thomson a sizeable licensing fee to release media in the MP3 format (BBC News 2007).

One such beneficiary of the initial technological exchange with Silicon Valley was Justin Frankel, founder of a small company called Nullsoft. Nullsoft would go on to create the MP3 audio player Winamp, which would be the first free mainstream MP3 player. In combination with the website mp3.com, which was providing thousands of free MP3 format songs at the time, the MP3 craze started among consumers (Schubert 1999). AOL (a subsidiary of Time Warner Inc. and a major internet provider) paid nearly $100 million in 1999 to acquire Nullsoft and its team of programmers (Mook 2004). However, the strict corporate culture of a multimillion-dollar company such as AOL was too much for the free-spirited members of Nullsoft, and soon Nullsoft began development on various projects in secret. The Gnutella peer-to-peer (P2P) network was the result of one such project and led to the development of other P2P programs such as Napster. These file-sharing networks provided avenues for consumers to share data directly from one computer to another without regulation. This ultimately led to hundreds of licences and patents being circumvented through file sharing. In quick succession, there were aggressive campaigns launched by the Recording Industry Association of America (RIAA) and Motion Picture Association of America (MPAA), which sought to quell the growing movement of illegal downloading and copyright infringement. The RIAA argued that allowing consumers to freely transfer unlicensed MP3 files over P2P networks would cause sales of CDs to decrease (Schubert 1999). Additionally, such activity infringed on the intellectual properties created by the music industry and its artists. Hundreds of developers, including those of Napster, were involved in massive lawsuits with the RIAA and ultimately were shut down or purchased by RIAA members. Eventually, the music industry realized that the acceptance and integration of licensed MP3 downloading services would be vital to the survival of the industry. As a result, the launch of online MP3 stores such as Rhapsody and iTunes (both established in 2001) were supported by the RIAA, alongside the sales of CDs.

MP3 remains an important technological advance in today's digital world. With CD sales continuing to decline annually, and downloads of individual MP3 tracks now reaching into the millions, it is only a matter of time before MP3 is recognized as the pre-eminent method for creating and sharing audio recordings. This has had radical implications for the recording industry, given that virtually anyone can use the technology to record music and make it available online.

Alexander Lim

Bibliography

BBC News. Microsoft Faces $1.5bn MP3 Payout. British Broadcasting Company. 22 February 2007. http://news.bbc.co.uk/2/hi/business/6388273.stm (accessed 13 January 2009).

Brandenburg, Karlheinz, and Marina Bosi. Overview of MPEG Audio: Current and Future Standards for Low Bit-Rate Audio Coding.

Journal of the Audio Engineering Society 45 (1997): 4–21.

Ford, Nelson. The History of Shareware and PsL. *History of Shareware*. 2000. Association of Shareware Professionals. http://www.asp-shareware.org/users/history-of-shareware.asp (accessed 13 January 2009).

Fraunhofer IISa. Profile. The Fraunhofer Institute for Integrated Circuits IIS. October 2007. http://www.iis.fraunhofer.de/EN/profil/index.jsp (accessed 13 January 2009).

Fraunhofer IISb. The mp3 History 02. The Fraunhofer Institute for Integrated Circuits IIS. October 2008. http://www.iis.fraunhofer.de/EN/bf/amm/mp3history/mp3history02.jsp (accessed 13 January 2009).

Mook, Nate. Death Knell Sounds for Nullsoft, Winamp. *Betanews*. Betanews Inc. 10 November 2004. http://www.betanews.com/article/Death_Knell_Sounds_for_Nullsoft_Winamp/1100111204 (accessed 13 January 2009).

mp3licensing.com. Patents. http://mp3licensing.com/patents/index.html (accessed 13 January 2009).

Schubert, Ruth. Tech-Savvy Getting Music for a Song Industry Frustrated that Internet Makes Free Music Simple. *Seattle Post-Intelligencer*, 10 February 1999, B1.

MULTIMEDIA

[See also: *Educational Technology; Hypermedia and Hypertext; Text Theory; World Wide Web*]

Multimedia design and multimedia computer systems are now everywhere, from cellular phone MMS (multimedia messaging system) to video webcasts. At the same time, less technologically sophisticated multimedia materials coexist with these, such as a printed book accompanied by a CD. *Multimedia* is the use of *different media* to construct texts. The most important feature of digital multimediality is its *hypertexuality*, which refers to the use of a software system that links topics on the screen to other information and graphics, which are accessed by clicking on them. A hypertext is thus a kind of 'superior text' involving the use of many codes (verbal and non-verbal).

The word *hypertext* was coined by Theodor Holm Nelson in the 1960s in reference to how certain words are immediately linked to other words. This definition was expanded with the advent of hypercard and hypermedia technology to include any text that could be 'stretched' to include 'links' to other texts. Today, it refers mainly to websites and pages created with HyperText Markup Language (HTML) that have the capacity to link their particular information to other sites on the Web. This enables users to move directly from a site-specific link (usually a highlighted word, phrase, or picture) to related links at the same site or on a different site. A mouse or other input device is used to click on the link.

Such linkage strategies involve various representational processes. Tolhurst (1995) has, in fact, made a difference between a functional hypertextuality and a semantic one. The former refers to the practical use of text, diagrams, pictures, and tables within a text. This type of hypertext simply turns a traditional 'book page' into a multimedia one, with non-linear structure. The latter refers to the kind of hypertext whereby it is possible to make specific decisions with regard to the kind of information to be accessed. It is not simply added to a regular text; rather, it is part and parcel of the text itself, providing semantic links that the user may not have even considered. It is this kind of hypertext that can be more specifically labelled 'open-ended' since it involves interconnecting information, taking particular decisions according to the possibilities offered by the hypertext maker, and so on.

Multimedia hypertextuality is now often used as a model of creating knowledge systems, which include capacities for data storage, administration, linkage, and retrieval. This model has been extended to describe human knowledge systems generally (including those of individuals). Multimedia-hypertextual knowledge systems are powerful because they offer suggestions for interconnecting what would otherwise seem to be separate forms of knowledge. They offer visible links between subjects.

De Kerckhove (1997) describes hypertextuality as a means for tracking and storing interconnected information through the establishment of nodes and links between one type of information (say verbal) information and another (say visual). The concept of multimedia is, thus, refined to mean interconnectivity among modes of information stored in specific ways. The World Wide Web is, in this model, the first true hypertextual system allowing for such interconnectivity to unfold in a practical way. In the past, separate modes of information were distributed in different media, from library buildings to archives and the like. With the Web such physical distribution has been replaced by the instantaneity of virtual distribution.

Multimedia is a term that initially had a host of meanings. Today, it is used primarily to refer to web pages using different media to generate their texts (print, images, sounds, video). With advanced technologies emerging on a daily basis, it is obvious that the design and engineering aspects of multimediality offer expanding possibilities all the time. Essentially, though, the term multimedia entails thinking in more than one medium (as was the case in the era of print literacy without the incorporation of non-verbal media in text production). It also entails such notions as interactivity, distributed information, differential text formats, and the like. As a result of the WWW revolution in mass communications, there now exist multimedia corporations whose function is integrating books, newspapers, radio, television, and other media into integrated hypertextual (multimedia) networks.

A perfect example of the strategic use of multimediality is Channel 13, in Chile, which started broadcasting in 1959. In 1968 it delivered its broadcasting by satellite, and then by cable in 1995. In 1999, it opened up its website (www.canal13.cl) to attract younger viewers, integrating as well with the newspaper *El Mercurio*. The channel now uses the robotic system LMS (Learning Mediated System) and FLEXI-CART, creating the establishment of a Livelong Learning Centre that allows users to gain access to actual information about advanced technologies. There are many other similar examples throughout the world. In effect, the world of traditional media is rapidly morphing into an integrated world of multimedia. Many businesses are also transforming themselves into multimedia companies. Salient Marketing, for example, is an Ottawa-based internet marketing firm, with experience in Web design and e-commerce. It also has experience in public sector, retail, telecommunications, e-business, legal, high-tech, travel, and other enterprises, working together with national and multinational organizations like Nortel, Canada Post, the Department of Foreign Affairs and International Trade, Industry Canada, and the Department of National Defence, among others.

Perhaps in no other field has multimediality become so intrinsic as in education. Educational software, self-learning computer packages, hypertextual learning websites, and the like are proliferating everywhere. Even some academies are now transforming themselves into multimedial institutions. One example is the CCRTVU (China Central Radio and TV University), which started as far back as 1978. It constitutes an open and distance education institution, under the direct supervision of the Ministry of Education, which offers, on a nationwide basis, multimedia courses through radio, TV, print, audio-visual materials, and computer networks. Antonio R. Bartolomé (1994) has pointed out that such materials are unusual in that they also require knowledge of how to use multimedia, in addition to knowledge of how to extract information from them. In fact, most users see the various media in the software as offering support to print textuality. Thus, it is probably more accurate to call such materials *multisupport* ones.

Other uses of multimedia technology include *multimedia shows*. A multimedia show integrates various audio-visual and sensory technologies. It can project images, digital sounds, lighting variations, relays, dimmers, smoke machines, ventilators, introduce actual scents, and so on. The aim is to offer a multisensory experience to audiences.

Multimedia documents can be defined simply as multisensory documents involving the integrated use of various media texts. Such documents allow users to literally see interconnections among various items, no matter in what medium such items exist. Thus, in an online advertisement, one can show how the visual ad itself alludes to some classic painting or how it may make allusions to some piece of music. It allows the user to gain different insights into the contents of the text (Prendes and Solano 2000).

Multimediality is also characteristic of the online job configurations, which now include teleworking, e-learning, and e-commerce. The biggest configuration, or distributed multimedia system, is of course the World Wide Web. It has promoted in a short time what can be called 'thinking in networks' and has introduced new textualities such as weblogs, photoblogs, wiki pages, and the like. In this new multimedia virtual world we can now find integrated computer systems (Hypersession, BSCW, MOODLE), communicative systems (Open Business Club 'Open BC,' Hi5, del.icio.us, Google, Gmail, Yahoo), and audio-visual and interactive video (Flickr, Pandora, YouTube, Camfrog). These are changing how we have traditionally viewed documents and texts.

In sum, multimedia refers generally to a computer-controlled combination of text, graphics, sound, visual text, motion pictures, and other types of media, having a variety of applications in education, entertainment, job training, and other areas. Unlike traditional print textuality, the hypertextuality that multimedia technology makes available allows users to become active participants rather than passive observers. A multimedia encyclopedia, for example, uses hypermedia technology to create its texts. It is a collection of text, photographs, diagrams, videos, animations, interactive features, sound clips, and other content presented in part or in whole or in various combinations. The content of hypermedia texts allows possibilities that were not previously feasible. For example, a music student can listen to a sound clip of a composer that he or she is learning about, while reading about the piece being performed. The student can also link to other articles through the Web. This expands the information-gathering process involved in knowledge making considerably (Landow 1995). For Lévy (1995) this process models learning adequately, since thinking in various media allows for a subject to be literally viewed from different sensory-perspectival angles, a modality made possible by the integrated use of verbal text, diagrams, maps, simulations, and the like.

Although multimedia involves the use of various media, it does not follow that it presents information in a fragmented way. On the contrary, because it integrates the various media into a single hypertext, it is actually a more unitary way to encode knowledge, showing its interconnectivity to various codes (visual, verbal, auditory, tactile, etc.). In this sense, it is perhaps more accurate to label it *multicodality*, reserving the term *multimediality* to refer to the actual physical software used to create hypertexts.

Lucía Amorós Poveda

Bibliography

Adell, Jordi, and Charles Belvver. Hipermedia distribuido en el Mac: el proyecto World Wide Web. *Actas del I Congreso Universidad y Macintosh*. UNED, Madrid, September 1994. Available in CD ROM Unimac 94. Madrid: Dpto. de Informática y Automática, Sciences Faculty, UNED, 1994.

Amorós, Lucía. *Evaluación de hipermedia en la enseñanza*. Doctoral thesis, Universidad de Murcia (España), 2004.

Bartomolé, Antonio R. Sistemas multimedia. In *Para una tecnología educativa*, coord. J.M. Sancho. Barcelona: Horsori, 1994.

Canal 13. http://canal13.com.

China Central Radio and TV University. http://www.edu.cn/20010101/21803.shtml.

De Kerckhove, Derrick. *Connected Intelligence. The Arrival of the Web Society*. Somerville House, 1997.

Landow, George P. *Hypertext. The Convergence of Contemporary Critical Theory and Technology*. Baltimore: Johns Hopkins University Press, 1995.

Levy, Pierre. *Qu'est-ce que le virtuel?* Paris: La Découverte, 1995.

Ottawakiosk.com. http://www.ottawakiosk.com/multimedia.html.

Prendes, Maria P. *El lenguaje de la imagen*. Murcia: DM, 1998.

– 2001: una odisea en el ciberespaci. In *Nuevas Tecnologías y Educación*, ed. F. Martínez and Maria P. Prendes, 171–94. Madrid: Pearson, 2004.

Prendes, Maria P., and Isabel M. Solano. Multimedia. In *Redes multimedia y diseños virtuales*, ed. R. Pérez, 25–43. Oviedo: Publishing Services at the Universidad of Oviedo, 2000.

Prosa, S.A. http://www.prosa.es.

Tolhurst, Denise. Hypertext, Hypermedia, Multimedia Defined? *Educational Technology* 35, no. 2 (1995): 21–6.

MUTIMODALITY

[See also: *Body Language; Gesture; Multimedia*]

Multimodality is a term used broadly in media and communications studies today to refer to the amalgamation of various 'modalities' of communication, from audio-oral to gestural. It refers to the use of body language during face-to-face communication and to the use of complementary audio-visual and graphic supports in digital texts.

The main sensory modes of communication are as follows:

- *auditory-vocal* (vocal speech, singing, whistling, crying, etc.)
- *visual* (pictography, sign languages for the hearing-impaired, drawings, etc.)
- *tactile* (touch languages for the visually impaired; alphabetic toy blocks used to impart familiarity with letter shapes through touch, etc.)
- *olfactory* (perfumes and colognes, religious incense, etc.)
- *gustatory* (chemical ingredients in food that attempt to reproduce certain natural tastes, etc.)

Marshall McLuhan (1962, 1964) claimed that modality varies according to culture. Human beings are endowed by nature to decipher information with all the senses. Our *sense ratios*, as he called them, are equally calibrated at birth to receive information in a balanced fashion. However, in social settings, it is unlikely that all the senses will operate at the same ratio. One sense ratio or the other increases according to the modality emphasized in a culture. In an oral culture, the *auditory sense ratio* is the one that largely shapes information processing and knowledge interpretation; in a print culture, on the other hand, the *visual sense ratio* is the influential one. This raising or lowering of sense ratios is not, however, preclusive. Indeed, we can have various sense ratios activated in tandem. For example, if one were to hear the word *dog* uttered, the auditory sense ratio would process the meaning of the word. If, however, one were to see the word written on a sheet of paper, then the visual sense ratio would be activated instead. A visual depiction of the *dog* accompanied by an utterance of the word would activate the auditory and visual sense ratios in tandem.

Marcel Danesi

Bibliography

McLuhan, Marshall. *The Mechanical Bride: Folklore of Industrial Man*. New York: Vanguard, 1951.
– *The Gutenberg Galaxy*. Toronto: University of Toronto Press, 1962.
– *Understanding Media*. London: Routledge and Kegan Paul, 1964.
McLuhan, Marshall, and Eric McLuhan. *Laws of Media: The New Science*. Toronto: University of Toronto Press, 1988.

MYSPACE

[See also: *Facebook; Social Networking*]

Along with Facebook, MySpace is one of the most popular social networking sites. It was founded in 2003 by University of California graduates Tom Anderson and Chris De Wolfe, although there is some dispute about this. The site was acquired by News Ciro in July 2005 for $580 million (US). It became the most popular site in 2006, being eclipsed by Facebook only a few years later. MySpace offers users the chance to communicate regularly and continuously. It is an online social networking community in which people are encouraged to make contact, interact, and share personal information and pictures. The user homepage features status updates, applications, subscriptions, game alerts, and many other features that have become part of digital communications generally. 'MySpace' is a space for people to indulge themselves. This is reflected especially in the MySpace feature called 'Moods.' Moods are emoticons that convey the mood the user. It is also visible in the kinds of profiles that the site features, which contain two basic subsections: 'About Me' and 'Who I'd Like to Meet.' There is also a 'Comments' section where comments are left to be read by the user.

MySpace, like Facebook, is now also a platform for artists and others to showcase their talents. MySpace also has a service similar to YouTube where people can post performances, lectures, lessons, and the like for anyone to see. Through MySpace everyone can put themselves in the limelight. MySpace is part of what can be called an emerging digital gossip culture, as some analysts have argued (Kelsey 2007). A perusal of bulletins on MySpace sites shows that people do indeed use MySpace to gossip about others or to defend themselves against gossip. MySpace, Facebook, and YouTube have become discursive channels. As Kelsey (2007: xiv) aruges, MySpace is comparable to 'the speakeasies of the '30s, the soda shops of the '50s, and even the scandalous impact of Elvis Presley.' Like all other social networks, MySpace harvests private information from users (including one's likes and dislikes), using it to target people for commercial purposes. Along with other social network venues, MySpace is redefining the nature of interaction, demographics, and relations.

Marcel Danesi

Bibliography

Boyd, Danah M., and Nicole Ellison. Social Network Sites: Definition, History, and Scholarship. *Journal of Computer-Mediated Communication* 13 (2007). http://jcmc.indiana.edu/vol13/issue1/boyd.ellison.html.
Kelsey, Candice M. *Generation MySpace*. New York: Marlowe, 2007.
Van Dijk, Jan. *The Network Society*. London: Sage, 1999.

MYTH

[See also: *Barthes, Roland; Mythology*]

Myth is commonly assumed to designate the primal stories shared by members of a society or community. It is often thought to consist of fictional narratives which, at root, reveal the most deep-seated beliefs, attitudes, and desires of a group of people. At the very least, it usually contains semi-fictional stories. As such, myth is frequently contrasted with 'history' and the real, as well as to the deliberate confections of 'literary' fictions. In the context of media and communications, then, myth is one important means of inculcating established discussions of 'objectivity,' on the one hand, and fictional 'veracity' or 'persuasiveness' on the other. Media forms such as news, putatively committed to truth and objectivity, can be seen to replay myths in various forms; avowedly fictional forms such as soap opera, alternatively, can be seen to embody a specific kind of verisimilitude.

Myth is derived from the Greek word 'muthos,' meaning 'anything that is spoken,' and is hence often taken to mean simply 'speech.' However, 'muthos' refers also to 'story' which, in the origins of narrative, was always spoken (prior to the invention of writing) and was told by a storyteller who was not necessarily the author. After Aristotle especially, 'muthos' became associated with the kind of binding in narratives that adds up to a 'plot' or, as Ricoeur (1984) would say, 'emplotment.' It is hardly surprising, given myth's grounding in speech, in narrative, and in signs, that myths became an important focus for a linguistically based semiotics of media and communications. Semiotic treatments of myth have identified a split in 'the mythological' between that which is at the deepest, most profound roots of human consciousness and that which is commonplace and everywhere on the surface. Two approaches have had an important influence on the course of semiotics. They are associated with the anthropologist Claude Lévi-Strauss (1908–2009) and the literary/cultural critic, Roland Barthes (1915–80).

Lévi-Strauss took it as given that myths were stories which gave sense to the society in which they flourished; but he also sought to analyse myth's very basis to reveal that its deep-rooted patterns were responsible for the complex surface patterns of the stories themselves. Moreover, he sought to demonstrate that the uniform 'deep' patterns were able to generate a

considerable diversity of 'surface' myths. Broadly, then, Lévi-Strauss considered myth's roots to be fairly consistent, despite the many shifts of narrative that took place across cultures on the surface, and devised a method which enabled him to break down all myths to allow the identification of a basic substrate. The most famous example of this is his 1955 interpretation of the Oedipus myth in which he treats it 'as an orchestra score would be if it were unwittingly considered as a unilinear series' (1977: 213):

Say, for instance, we were confronted with a sequence of the type: 1, 2, 4, 7, 8, 2, 3, 4, 6, 8, 1, 4, 5, 7, 8, 1, 2, 5, 7, 3, 4, 5, 6, 8 … the assignment being to put all the 1's together, all the 2's, the 3's, the result is a chart:

1	2		4			7	8
	2	3	4		6		8
1			4	5		7	8
1	2			5		7	
		3	4	5	6		8

He then goes on to break down the features of the Oedipus myth – for example, 'Oedipus marries his mother, Jocasta' and 'Antigone buries her brother, Polynices, despite prohibition' (1977: 214) – which he re-orders in a similar way. Summing up his view of myth in general, Lévi-Strauss concludes that 'the kind of logic in mythical thought is as rigorous as modern science, and that the difference lies not in the quality of the intellectual process, but in the nature of things to which it is applied' (1977: 230). He suggests, then, that myth has a kind of 'fictional veracity.'

Where Lévi-Strauss proposes that an analysis of 'mythical thought' can reveal the deep structure of the human mind, Barthes's notion of myth, while attempting to be equally revelatory, prefers to stay at the surface level. Famously, in *Mythologies* (1957; English translation 1973), Barthes drew together a series of brief articles he had written for magazines in the period 1954 to 1956 to demonstrate different aspects of the myth of French life and society. These included media artefacts such as the haircuts of the Roman characters in Joseph L. Mankiewicz's film of *Julius Caesar* and the face of Garbo, all of which were shown to embody a myth. From the outset, Barthes insists that 'myth is a language' (1973: 11), but he also adds that

- it is a collective representation;
- it involves credibility, which is sustained by 'inversion' (the element of the fictional but not the fanciful);
- it is expressed in all places in the contemporary world;
- it is susceptible to semiological analysis. (Barthes 1977a: 165–6)

For Barthes, 'nothing can be safe from myth' (1973: 131); it is everywhere in communications. It can take almost anything and transform its cultural bearing into a seemingly natural one. Like Lévi-Strauss, Barthes sees myth as a process of thought which enables the conceptualization of pressing matters in human existence. But it is also the medium of ideology and the profane, the domain of stereotypes and other means of fixing limits to representation.

The form that the 'speech' of myth takes for Barthes involves systems of 'denotation' and 'connotation.' As Barthes suggests in his analysis of an advertising photograph (1977b: 36–7), there is a tendency for connotation to be foregrounded in representations. Embodied in connotation will also be an ideological travesty of the truth. Despite the foregrounding of connotation, myth uses 'denotation' (straightforward indicating), at the level of the *language-object*, to 'naturalize' what is expressed: 'it is the language which myth gets hold of in order to build its own system' (1973: 115). So, for Barthes, myth is a two-level process: popular culture and everyday life are 'mythical' because they are 'spoken' through a naturalization. What is 'hidden' in Barthes's

version of myth, and what needs to be revealed by semiology, is the *inversion* of real relations that has taken place to transform an ideological proposition into common sense.

This concept of myth has been persuasive in the study of media and communications. It has redrawn the relation of communications to ideology and has encouraged strenuous interrogation of the very act of representation, lest media consumers forget the entrenched stories and political coordinates that are repeatedly played out in representations.

Paul Cobley

Bibliography

Barthes, Roland. *Mythologies*. Trans. A. Lavers. London: Paladin, 1973.
– Change the Object Itself. In *Image – Music – Text*, ed. and trans. S. Heath. London: Fontana, 1977a.
– The Rhetoric of the Image. In *Image – Music – Text*, ed. and trans. S. Heath. London: Fontana, 1977b.
Lévi-Strauss, Claude. *Structural Anthropology 1*. Trans. C. Jacobson and B. Grundfest Schoepf. Harmondsworth: Penguin, 1977.
Ricoeur, Paul. *Time and Narrative*. Vol. 1. Baltimore and London: Johns Hopkins University Press, 1984.

MYTHOLOGY

[See also: *Barthes, Roland; Myth*]

The term *mythology* was used by the French semiotician Roland Barthes in 1957 to explain why the spectacles and entertainment forms of pop culture have such emotional appeal. Barthes explains the appeal in terms of mythology, that is, in terms of the recycling of ancient mythic themes by the industry of popular culture. The implication is that the industry speaks an unconscious 'mythic language' which gives it great appeal, since mythic language is powerful at a psychic level. The study of cultural mythologies has become a major target of interest within semiotics and media studies (Holbrook and Hirschman 1993; Docker 1994; Gottdiener 1995; Bignell 1997).

As John Storey (2003) argues, the idea of pop culture came forward to replace that of 'folk' culture, becoming a target of autonomous academic study in the late 1950s when Barthes showed the importance of studying such things as wrestling and blockbuster movies to understand how they play on largely unconscious mythical meanings. As Jean Baudrillard (1998) has emphasized, pop culture engages the masses, rather than the cognoscenti, because it takes the material of everyday life and gives it expression and significance. Everything from comic books to fashion shows have mass appeal because they emanate from within the culture, not from authority figures. Pop culture makes little or no distinction between art and recreation, distraction and engagement.

To distinguish between the original myths and their pop culture versions, Barthes designated the latter *mythologies*. In early Hollywood westerns, for instance, the mythic struggle of good vs evil manifested itself in various symbolic and representational ways. The cowboy hero has many of the traits of various ancient mythic heroes – strength, physical beauty, honesty, and vulnerability. The cowboy villain has all the opposite traits – cowardice, physical ugliness, dishonesty, and cunning. The hero is beaten up at some critical stage, but against long odds he becomes a champion of ethics and justice. This 'narrative structure' is fundamentally mythical in origin. Because of the power of the mythological system underlying the western, it is little wonder to find that cowboy heroes such as Roy Rogers, John Wayne, Hopalong Cassidy, and the Lone Ranger became cultural icons, symbolizing virtue, heroism, and righteousness. Although Hollywood has also showcased female characters, most of the women portrayed in the early westerns played a subsidiary supporting role to the male hero.

The Superman character of comic book and cinematic fame is another example of a recycled mythic hero. He too possesses the same characteristics of his mythic predecessors – he comes from another world (the planet Krypton) in order to help humanity overcome its weaknesses; he has superhuman powers; but he has a tragic flaw (exposure to the substance known as kryptonite takes away his power). Because it constitutes a mythological system, Barthes argued that pop culture has had a profound impact on modern-day ethics. In the historical development of ethics, three principal standards of conduct have been proposed as the highest good: happiness or pleasure; duty, virtue, or obligation; and perfection, the fullest harmonious development of human potential. In traditional cultures, these standards were established through religious and philosophical traditions. In pop culture, they are established through mythological language as it manifests itself in popular spectacles. Ethical issues that are showcased on TV, for example, are felt as being more significant and historically meaningful to society today than those that are not.

Marcel Danesi

Bibliography

Barthes, Roland. *Mythologies*. Paris: Seuil, 1957.

Baudrillard, Jean. *Toward a Critique of the Political Economy of the Sign*. St Louis: Telos, 1978.

– *The Consumer Society*. London: Sage, 1998.

Bignell, Jonathan. *Media Semiotics: An Introduction*. Manchester: Manchester University Press, 1997.

Danto, Arthur C. *Andy Warhol*. New Hampshire: Yale University Press, 2009.

Docker, John. *Postmodernism and Popular Culture: A Cultural History*. Cambridge: Cambridge University Press, 1994.

Gottdiener, Mark. *Postmodern Semiotics: Material Culture and the Forms of Postmodern Life*. London: Blackwell, 1995.

Holbrook, Morris B., and Elizabeth C. Hirschman. *The Semiotics of Consumption: Interpreting Symbolic Consumer Behavior in Popular Culture and Works of Art*. Berlin: Mouton de Gruyter. 1993.

Richards, Barry. *Disciplines of Delight: The Psychoanalysis of Popular Culture*. London: Free Association, 1994.

Shuker, Roy. *Understanding Popular Culture*. London: Routledge, 1994.

Storey, John. *Inventing Popular Culture*. London: Blackwell, 2003.

N

NARRATIVE

[See also: *Adventure Stories; Books, History of; Crime Genre; Horror Fiction; Pulp Fiction; Romance Fiction; Science Fiction; Text Theory*]

Narrative is a universal expressive form based on connected events (known as the plot), people (known as characters), locations (known as the setting), over a time period by a teller (also known as sender, author, or narrator). In effect, a narrative is any text – verbal (a story, a novel, and so on) or non-verbal (a cartoon, and so on) – that has been constructed to model a sequence of events or actions that are experienced as being logically connected to each other or causally intertwined in some fashion. The sequence may be fact-based, as in a newspaper report, a historical treatise, or a psychoanalytic session, or fictional, as in a novel or a fairy tale. It is often difficult to determine the boundary line between fact and fiction in narration.

Making sense of a narrative text is not a simple process of analysing the meanings of the individual words with which it is constructed and adding them together semantically; rather, it entails interpreting the whole text at various levels. One of these is the level of the *subtext*. This is the underlying theme, premise, or intent of the narrative. It is not announced explicitly by the characters or the narrator. It is implicit in the plot, setting, or characterization, and thus is extractable from cues within the main text. Some of these cues may be provided in the form of *intertexts*, which are allusions, citations, or references within the narrative text to other texts external to it, but upon which the text is constructed. For example, the main text of a movie such as *Blade Runner* unfolds as a sci-fi detective story, but its subtext is, seemingly, a religious one – the search for a creator and thus a quest for the meaning of life. This interpretation is bolstered by the many intertextual cues to Biblical themes and symbols in the movie, such as a dove and an apparent 'crucifixion' of a robotic character at the end of the movie.

In the main text, the *plot* is basically what the narrative is all about. It is a telling of events that are connected logically (chronologically, historically, and so on) to each other. It is this interconnection that makes readers perceive them as mirroring real-life events. *Character* refers to the personages or beings (animals, for example) that make up the plot. Each one is a sign or archetype standing for a personality type – the hero, the villain, the lover, the friend, and so on. The *setting* is the location where, and the time when, the plot is supposed to take place. The *narrator* is usually a character in the text or the author of the text. Each provides a different perspective on the story for the reader. The reader can thus feel a part of the narrative, looking at the action as if he or she were in it, or aloof from it, looking at the action as if from the outside.

Fictional narratives (from Latin *fingere* 'to form, make, put together') did not become a popular until the Middle Ages, although they may have ancient roots. Egyptian papyri indicate that King Cheops (2590–2567 BCE) revelled in the fictional stories that his sons purportedly told him. The Greek statesman Aristides (ca 530–468 BCE) wrote a collection of short stories about his hometown, Miletus. The *Golden Ass* of Apuleius (ca 125–200 CE) was also a fictional text designed to provide social and moral commentary. Fiction became a standard writing craft in the Middle Ages, after Giovanni Boccaccio (1313–75) published the *Decameron* (1351–3), a collection of 100 tales set against the background of the Black Death in Florence (Fiesole). It is the first example of fiction in the modern sense. Novels have always constituted the most popular use of the narrative. At the turn of the century, and certainly by the 1920s, novels were being produced in bulk for mass markets, as part of a *pulp fiction* trend. They were the successors of the *dime novels* of the nineteenth century. The main themes of these novels revolved on sensationalistic crime, sex, adventure, horror, and so forth. The characters of these novels have become part of pop culture lore. They include The Shadow, the Phantom Detective, Mickey Spillane, Dick Tracy, Perry Mason, Tarzan, among many others. The twentieth century also saw the rise and spread of the so-called 'best-seller,' the counterpart to the movie blockbuster. As White (1980: 5) puts it, 'to raise the question of narrative is to invite reflection on the very nature of culture and, possibly, even on the nature of humanity itself.'

The systematic study of narrative is called *narratology*. It can probably be traced to a famous 1928 work by the Russian critic Vladimir Propp (1895–1970), who argued that a relatively small number of innate, unconscious archetypal units make up narratives of all kinds. Thus, certain characters (the hero, the villain, and so on) are really signs or symbols for personality types. Moreover, plots are structured around universal images (journeys, trials, and so on) that also go into the 'narrative grammar.' Propp's theory would explain why narratives are similar the world over. These allow humans across cultures to make sense of the real world. For semiotician Roland Barthes (1966: 1), the narratives of the world cover a vast number of genres and are constructed in various modes and media: oral, written, images, gesture, painting, news items, conversation, and so on: 'Narrative couldn't care less about good or bad literature: international, transhistorical narrative is simply there, like life itself.'

Narratological theory owes much to the so-called Russian Formalists, through a careful examination of what linguist Roman Jakobson called *literaturnost*, 'literarity,' the features of literature that distinguish it from other types of discourse. The Formalists started by comparing poetic language with spoken language, using linguistic theories that enabled them to examine relationships between forms of language and discourse, and to investigate the structures that made poetic language unique, or at least different from other kinds of literature. A year after Propp's work, the critic Shklovsky (1929) demonstrated the presence of universal stylistic processes in text composition, no matter how heterogeneous the texts seemed to be. Thus, a narrative or poetic work of art was not an isolated phenomenon – its value could be understood in relation to other works. The identification of basic techniques or devices regarded mainly those that went into plot construction: circular construction, composition by steps, decomposition of the plot into episodes, the use of frames, and rhetorical procedures (parallelism, enumeration, oxymoron, and so on). This led to a distinction between the construction of a work (subject) and the materials used to do so (fable).

The Prague Linguistic School (1926–48) continued and elaborated the tradition handed down to them by the Russian Formalists. For example, they claimed that Saussure's (1916) distinction between language as a system *(langue)* and individual uses of that system *(parole)* could also be applied to literature. Essentially, the Prague School linguists showed that *parole* is not only as important as *langue*, but that it often influenced its historical evolution. In effect, literature and literary genres were not only similar to common discourse, but also had an effect on the language system used to construct them. Change came through usage, not through some internal evolutionary propensity in language.

Many of the ideas of the Russian Formalists and the Prague School linguists were mirrored by Anglo-American narrative analysis, even though the latter was not at first influenced in a direct way by the two European trends. Simply put, the Anglo-American narratologists propounded ideas that were similar to those of their European counterparts but with a more informal approach. For example, Henry James (1934) wrote about 'dramatic scenes,' 'form,' 'character,' and 'first-person narrative.' Similarly, Lubbock (1921) and Forster (1927) used simple concepts such as 'telling and showing,' 'voice,' and 'flat and round characters.' As insightful as these were, they lacked the systematicity brought to the task at hand by the Formalists and the Prague linguists. A second generation of critics attempted to classify literary works in terms of 'conventions' (Frye 1957) or 'forms of plot' (Friedman 1955a). It is in the concepts of 'point of view' (Friedman 1955b) and 'time' (Mendilow 1952), or 'temporal distance and point of view' (Booth 1961a), that the Anglo-American contribution to narrative stands out – a contribution crowned by Wayne Booth's now-classic *The Rhetoric of Fiction* (1961b).

In France, narratology developed along the theoretical lines established by Roman Jakobson (Russian Formalism) and Claude Lévi-Strauss (structuralism). Lévi-Strauss advocated the use of the methods of the social sciences, especially anthropology and linguistics, in narrative analysis. In his analysis of myth (1963: 62, 71, 33) he outlined why he thought structural linguistics was particularly useful:

First, structural linguistics shifts from the study of *conscious* linguistic phenomena to the study of their unconscious infrastructure; second, it does not treat *terms* as independent entities, taking instead as its basis of analysis the relations between terms; third, it introduces the concept of *system*; finally, structural linguistics aims at discovering *general laws*, either by induction or by logical deduction, which would give them an absolute character.

This led to a 'Parisian School' led by Roland Barthes (1966). The School based its approach to narrative on the deductive procedures of structural linguistics, and especially the level-by-level approach of this school of thought. Each level bears a hierarchical relationship to other levels, and narrative elements are both distributed on each level in a systematic way and form integrative relations at each level. Barthes distinguished three main levels – 'functions,' 'actions,' and 'narration' – linked together cohesively. A function has meaning only within the 'field of action' of an *actant* (a narrative element such as a character or a setting), and action is meaningful only when narrated through a specific code. He then divides functional units into 'kernels' (or 'cardinals') and 'indices' (or 'catalysts'), which allows readers to understand the units by referring them to the levels on which they exist through the syntax of the language used and by logical presupposition. Whether labelled *dramatis personae* or *actants*, characters constitute a level of description rendering 'actions' intelligible. They are the *agents* defined by their participation in a limited number of classifiable plots. Although this might seem somewhat abstruse, it actually is a formalization of common notions. Using Propp's ideas, the Parisian semioticians, led by Algirdas Greimas (for example, 1987), showed that actants (character profiles) occurred in oppositional pairs (Subject/Object, Addresser/Addressee, Helper/Opponent) projected along the entire narrative and become meaningful only on the third level of description – narration.

In line with such ideas, Tzvetlan Todorov (1969) put forward a 'text grammar' of narrative based on the notions of *proper name*, which corresponds to the agent, the *adjective*, which corresponds to the qualification of the agent (adjectives are divided into three groups – *state, property,* and *status*), and *verb*, which represents the predicate of an action. In other words, Todorov formalized the relation between language grammar and text (narrative) grammar, with the latter being essentially a magnification of the former – an idea that bore great fruit among many scholars in the 1970s and 1980s. Genette (1988), for example, distinguished three levels of analysis: the story *(histoire)*; the narrative *(récit)*; and narration *(narration)* – the real or imaginary setting in which the *récit* takes place. Crucial to Genette's model is the notion of *time*, which he subdivides into order, duration, and frequency; *mood*, in which he links point of view and distance (showing and telling); and *voice* (the tone of the narration itself). In a key work, Umberto Eco (1979) focused attention not on the process of making narratives, but on the interpretive frames used by readers of narratives – an angle that has now become a dominant one. Eco examines the sociocultural contexts in which a narrative is forged and what makes it meaningful to its readers. Shortly thereafter, Paul Ricoeur (for example, 1983) sketched a general theory of narrative discourse based on understanding the historiography behind a work, its place in literary practices, and its claims to presenting 'truth.'

Already in the late 1950s and certainly by the 1970s, narratological structuralism started to be questioned. The attack on structuralist principles of the narrative have come to be classified under the rubric of post-structuralism – a movement associated initially with the late French philosophers Michel Foucault (1926–84) (for example, 1972) and Jacques Derrida (1930–2004) (for example, 1976). The central idea that set off this movement was that narratives are logocentric and thus specific to the biases inherent in the language used to carry out the narration. According to Derrida narrative texts were self-referential forms – texts referring to other texts, which referred to still other texts, and so on ad infinitum. Thus, what appears to be meaningful upon reading a plot turns out to be circular and convoluted. Many narratologists have severely criticized this radical stance of Derrida. It has nevertheless had an impact on narratology and literary studies generally. Derrida saw human knowledge as subject to linguistic categories. These characterized semiotic and narratological practices themselves, rendering them useless. Because written language is the tool of knowledge-producing enterprises, these practices end up mirroring nothing more than the linguistic categories used to produce them.

Even before the emergence of post-structuralism, narratology was undergoing a serious re-evaluation. Its alliance with structural linguistics was questioned by various scholars, some of whom opted for generative models, pragmatic models, and others of language. Perhaps the most promising line of inquiry in this regard is the advent of the cognitive linguistic movement, a movement that is based on the notion that linguistic grammar does not exist independently of cognition and culture and that it has a poetic basis (Lakoff and Johnson 1980, 1999). Today, the use of notions such as *conceptual metaphors* in literature (life is a journey, life presents obstacles, and so on) is still in its infancy, but it is starting to produce new and interesting ideas. The objective of all narratological theories remains, however, the quest for understanding why stories exist in the human species and why they are so powerful.

Paul Perron

Bibliography

Bal, Mieke. *Narratology: Introduction to the Theory of the Narrative.* Toronto: University of Toronto Press, 1985.

Barthes, Roland. Introduction à l'analyse structural du récit. *Communications* 8 (1966): 1–27.

Belsey, Catharine. *Poststructuralism*. Oxford: Oxford University Press, 2002.

Booth, Wayne C. Distance and Point of View: An
Essay in Classification. *Essays in Criticism* 11
(1961a): 60–79.

– *The Rhetoric of Fiction*. Chicago, London: University of Chicago Press, 1961b.

Derrida, Jacques. *Of Grammatology*. Trans. Gayatri Chakravorty Spivak. Baltimore: Johns
Hopkins University Press, 1976.

Dirven, René, and Marina Verspoor. *Cognitive
Exploration of Language and Linguistics*. Amsterdam: John Benjamins, 1998.

Eco, Umberto. *The Role of the Reader. Explorations
in the Semiotics of Texts*. Bloomington: Indiana
University Press, 1979.

– *Interpretation and Overinterpretation*. Cambridge: Cambridge University Press, 1992.

Forster, E. M. *Aspects of the Novel*. London: Arnold, 1927.

Foucault, Michel. *The Archeology of Knowledge*.
Trans. Alan M. Sheridan Smith. New York:
Pantheon, 1972.

Friedman, Norman. Forms of Plot. *Journal of General Education* 8 (1955a): 241–53.

– Point of View in Fiction. *Publications of the Modern Language Association* 70 (1955b): 1160–84.

Frye, Northrop. *Anatomy of Criticism*. Princeton:
Princeton University Press, 1957.

Genette, Gérard. *Narrative Discourse Revisited*.
Ithaca, NY: Cornell University Press, 1988.

Greimas, Algirdas J. *On Meaning: Selected Essays
in Semiotic Theory*. Trans. Paul Perron and
Frank Collins. Minneapolis: University of
Minnesota Press, 1987.

Lakoff, George, and Mark Johnson. *Metaphors We
Live By*. Chicago: University of Chicago Press,
1980.

– *Philosophy in Flesh: The Embodied Mind and Its
Challenge to Western Thought*. New York: Basic,
1999.

Leitch, Thomas M. *What Stories Are: Narrative
Theory and Interpretation*. University Park:
Pennsylvania State University Press, 1986.

Lévi-Strauss, Claude. *Structural Anthropology*.
New York: Basic, 1963.

Lubbock, Percy. *The Craft of Fiction*. London: J.
Cape, 1921.

Mendilow, Adam Abraham. *Time and the Novel*.
London, New York: Routledge and Paul, 1952.

Nash, Christopher. *Narrative in Culture*. London:
Routledge, 1994.

Norris, Christopher. *Deconstruction: Theory and
Practice*. London: Routledge, 1991.

Prince, Gerald. *Narratology: The Form and Functioning of Narrative*. Berlin: Mouton, 1982.

Propp, Vladimir J. *Morphology of the Folktale*. Austin: University of Texas Press, 1928.

Ricoeur, Paul. *Time and Narrative*. Chicago: University of Chicago Press, 1983.

Saussure, Ferdinand de. *Cours de linguistique
générale*. Paris: Payot, 1916.

Shklovsky, Viktor O. *Teorii Prozy*. Moscow:
Nauka, 1929.

Todorov, Tzevetlan. *Grammaire du Décameron*.
The Hague: Mouton, 1969.

White, Hayden C. The Value of Narrativity in
the Representation of Reality. *Critical Inquiry* 7
(1980): 5–12.

NARROWCASTING

[See also: *Broadcasting; Cable Television*]

Narrowcasting refers to broadcasting that
is aimed at specific, or niche, audiences, in
contrast to general *broadcasting*. Broadcasting transmissions can be received by anyone with standard reception equipment,
whereas narrowcasting transmissions are
received by someone with special equipment (a cable system equipped to carry
them, a satellite dish, and so on). Narrowcasting services are subject to special fees.

Narrowcasting for cable television involves encrypted signals running through
a cable company's descrambling services
before being viewed by the consumer, thus
allowing for a monthly charge to be implemented on viewable material. Because cable television is now present in most households in North America, 'narrowcasting' is
now a term loosely used to describe most
cable television services. Certain channels
are, however, special subscription channels,
whose contents are only available to those
who will pay for them. In the area of radio,

satellite radio (also known as subscription radio) is an example of a narrowcasting source, since it provides listeners with commercial-free channels (news, weather, sports, music channels, and so on) for a fee. And, of course, internet websites which require user registration now constitute a popular source of narrowcasting materials. Mailing lists and podcasts are classifiable, in fact, as 'narrowcasting services,' because they often require a subscription and are highly niche-oriented.

Narrowcasting originated in the late 1960s in response to the stance taken by the three major television networks – NBC (National Broadcasting Company), CBS (Columbia Broadcasting System), and ABC (American Broadcasting Company) – of avoiding the broadcasting of content that would offend viewers. As a result, independent networks, videocassette viewing, and other forms of new media began to proliferate, seeking out specific groups of people who would acquire their specialized programs (not available through the networks). With the growth of digital and satellite technologies, such specialized programs and products have become the norm, not the exception. In fact, today, most specialized channels are supported by advertising in the same way as are traditional network channels.

The techniques and forms of narrowcasting have proved both socially and economically powerful, as those who subscribe to certain media may tend to associate with others of the same group, and advertisers may be able to more easily reach their target audiences through narrowcasting.

Mariana Bockarova

Bibliography

Barnard, Stephen. *Studying Radio*. London: Arnold, 2000.

Briggs, Asa, and Peter Burke. *A Social History of the Media*. London: Polity, 2002.

Campbell, Richard, Christopher R. Martin, and Bettina Fabos. *Media and Culture: An Introduc-*
tion to Mass Communication. Boston: Bedford/St Martin's, 2005.

Dizard, Wilson P. *Old Media, New Media*. New York: Longman, 1997.

Massey, Kimberly. Narrowcasting. The Museum of Broadcast Communications. http://www.museum.tv/archives/etv/N/htmlN/narrowcasting/narrowcasting.htm (accessed 11 February 2009).

NETWORK

[See also: *Broadcasting; Communication*]

The term *network* refers to a group of radio or television stations with a core set of programs that they broadcast at the same time, with local or regional programs inserted at other times. Network programming began with the advent of radio as a mass communications medium around 1921, when WJZ in New York City and WGY in Schenectady, New York, broadcast the World Series simultaneously, using a simple network connected by telephone lines. This type of broadcasting, called 'chain broadcasting,' soon became popular across the United States. The Radio Corporation of America (RCA) formed the National Broadcasting Company (NBC) in 1926 as the first permanent national network.

The term network was then applied to television and, more recently, to internet programming. The internet is, in fact, a de facto network, connecting computers to share and process information. Today's computer networks enable information to be transferred rapidly from one computer to another, and users can share information or even work together on the same document at the same time in cyberspace. Local area networks (LANs) connect computers in a single location, such as an office. A central computer called the 'server' holds common files and allows for interconnectivity. The computers connected to the server are called 'clients.' Wide area networks (WANs) can spread across the globe. Secure links known as 'firewalls' prevent users of a WAN from getting unauthorized access to resources on a LAN.

The World Wide Web is a worldwide network of interconnected computer files connected to each other on the internet. The Web was originally created for linking words in text files to those in other text files via hypertext, a software system that links topics on a computer screen to connected information and graphics by a clicking method. Today, much of the information on the Web has been converted from print into digital form, and even more information has been created specifically for the Web. The information resides at websites, which are identified by a unique address known as a uniform resource locator (URL). Using a software package called a web browser, a computer user can select a URL and go to a website connected to that address.

Marcel Danesi

Bibliography

Van Dijk, Jan. *The Network Society*. London: Sage, 1999.

NEWS WEBSITES

[See also: *Journalism; Newspapers*]

A *news site* is a website with the primary purpose of reporting news. It may be general or subject-specific – a general news site reports all or most of the news in sections as one would ordinarily see them in a print newspaper, including local, national, and international news as well as segments on sport, business, lifestyle, and classified advertising; a subject-specific news site is one which reports only certain news for niche audiences. Popular subject-specific sites (also known as 'niche websites') are those dealing with entertainment news.

The first general news site was the *News and Observer*, from Raleigh, North Carolina, which began using computers in 1973 and eventually created NandO.net in 1994. It began with editors feeding stories from the newspaper's main newsroom onto the website. Using Java-powered animated photo display, NandO soon began posting accompanying news photos on its site, integrating them with the stories. Shortly before both the newspaper and NandO. net were sold to the McClatchy newspaper conglomerate, growing popularity and a faithful readership induced NandO and its online counterpart to become autonomous operations. Reprocessing almost all of the incoming feeds from Associated Press, Reuters, the *New York Times*, the *Wall Street Journal*, the *Los Angeles Times*, Bloomberg, and others, NandO editors selected stories, wrote new headlines for them, and sorted feeds into category pages – National, World, Political, Sports, Business, and Topic, which included dozens of links for developing stories. After being sold, NandO New Media became McClatchy New Media, and NandO news became the '24 Hour News' section of all McClatchy newspaper websites.

While other news sites soon followed the NandO pattern, including the *New York Times*, CNN, and the BBC, a new type of news site emerged in 1996 – a more personalized one available through My Yahoo which allowed registered users to personalize their own pages with sections of the news that interested them, including weather, stock portfolios, and the like. In 2004, the service allowed users not only to personalize the news, but also to add other features such as blogs and fan sites onto their home pages, further popularizing the site.

In order to stay competitive, many sites have added multimedia features. In 2000, when the stock market crashed, many sites experienced financial difficulties. NBC Internet News shut down its online project, but MSNBC survived due to its partnership with Microsoft. With enormous losses, the Rupert Murdoch News Corp, a media conglomerate, closed its online division as well. As bigger news corporations began to shut down, a sudden surge of news blogs emerged, controlled by columnists who were free from former editorial and advertising restraints. This led to the spread of the blogosphere and to a new impetus in constructing news sites that now combine traditional news sources with respected blogger sources. This new amalgamation seems to have congealed and become the main form of news reporting online.

Mariana Bockarova

Bibliography

Glaser, Mark. Digging Deeper: Your Guide to Personalized News Sites. PBS Media Shift. http://www.pbs.org/mediashift/2006/03/digging-deeperyour-guide-to-personalized-news-sites080.html (accessed 7 January 2009).

Ritchie, Donald A. *Reporting from Washington: The History of Washington Press Corps*. Oxford: Oxford University Press, 2005.

Schonfeld, Erick. Survey Confirms What We All Know: Net Beats Newspapers as a Source for News. Tech Crunch. http://www.techcrunch.com/2008/12/25/pew-survey-confirms-what-we-all-know-net-beats-newspapers-as-a-source-for-news/ (accessed 7 January 2009).

NEWSPAPERS

[See also: *Communication; Journalism; News Websites; Print Culture*]

Newspapers are print (and online) publications devoted to presenting and commenting on news, current events, and special features (such as sports and entertainment). There are two newspaper formats: standard and tabloid. The former is larger than the latter. There are three kinds of newspapers: daily, weekly, and special-interest. Dailies print the news (national, local, international), carry editorials, special columns, feature articles, and the like. Some dailies publish both a morning and an evening edition. A few large cities have more than one daily newspaper and may also have a so-called 'Sunday' or 'weekend' edition, which has additional features, more advertising, special sections, and supplementary materials (a magazine, for example). Notable dailies in the United States are: the *Christian Science Monitor*, the *New York Times*, *USA Today*, the *Wall Street Journal*, the *Boston Globe*, the *Chicago Tribune*, the *Dallas Morning News*, the *Detroit News*, the *Los Angeles Times*, the *Miami Herald*, the *Philadelphia Inquirer*, and the *Washington Post*. Weekly newspapers reach a smaller readership and publish news of a more individualized nature related to local interests (weddings, births, and so on). Special-interest newspapers cover news of interest to specific groups (business associations, labour unions). They may also focus on specific topics, such as entertainment, sports, or the arts.

Historians trace the origins of newspapers to the handwritten news sheets distributed in public places in ancient times. One of these was the Roman *Acta Diurna* (Daily Events), starting in 59 BCE. The first print newspaper is generally believed to be the Chinese circular called *Dibao*, which was produced on carved wooden blocks around 700 CE. The first regularly published paper newspaper can be traced to Germany in 1609. By the late 1800s, newspapers had become popular in Europe, with competing newspapers reporting crimes, disasters, and scandals, along with political and socially relevant news. Few reported international news.

The *Publick Occurrences, Both Foreign and Domestick*, a three-page paper, was published in 1690 in Boston, becoming the first newspaper published in the United States. It was suppressed by the government after the first issue because it was believed to contain doubtful information. The most probable reason was that the government feared the power of print to sway citizens against it. In 1704, the *Boston News-Letter* was established. It reported local and foreign news and included births, deaths, and social events sections. In 1721, the *New England Courant* was founded by James Franklin in Boston. In 1723, his younger brother,

Benjamin Franklin, founded the *Pennsyl-vania Gazette* and the *General Magazine*. The first New York City newspaper, called the *Gazette*, began printing in 1725. It was followed by the *New York Weekly Journal*, founded by John Peter Zenger, whose critiques of the British colonial governor led to his arrest and imprisonment on charges of libel. Zenger was found not guilty and his trial became the precedent for the notion of a free press in America. It became evident that the press had become a powerful forum for dissent, leading the way to the development of modern journalism as a critical practice in democratic societies.

In 1783, the first regularly published daily newspaper was launched in Philadelphia. It was called the *Pennsylvania Evening Post and Daily Advertiser*. Its integration of news and advertisements became a model for newspapers in general. Advertising had become integral to the newspaper business, supporting it financially more than subscriptions or individual purchases. In 1833, Benjamin Henry Day published the *New York Sun*, bringing about a 'penny press' trend in newspaper publishing. The *Sun* included sensationalistic reports of crime and entertainment in the same issue and cost a penny. After the first telegraph line was built in 1844, news could now be transmitted quickly across the country, leading to an amalgamation of newspapers in 1848 called the Associated Press (AP). The AP was formed because of the advent of the penny press and other cheap newspaper formats which catered to sensationalistic tastes through the use of exciting and shocking stories or language at the expense of accuracy and reflection. The AP was formed to restore objectivity and seriousness to newspaper reporting – a standard that is still pursued today in schools of journalism.

Newspapers became highly popular during the Civil War, with their graphic accounts of battlefront events.

As newspapers competed more and more for circulation audiences, a new populist form of journalism surfaced, developed by Joseph Pulitzer and William Randolph Hearst, that focused on sensationalistic coverage, catchy art design, and the incorporation of comic strips, such as *The Yellow Kid*, for entertainment. The term 'yellow journalism' (in reference to the strip) emerged to describe the new form of journalism.

Yellow journalism led to the tabloid genre shortly thereafter, gaining wide popularity in the 1920s. The tabloid was smaller, more condensed, and sensationalistic, focusing on stories concerning the occult, the bizarre (from alien creatures to miraculous cures), and media celebrities. Tabloids to this day continue to embody these features and are considered to be part of recreational culture rather than serious forms of journalism.

Despite the newspaper's popularity in the twentieth century, high operating costs and the internet have driven many out of business. In 1980, *The Columbus (Ohio) Dispatch* became the first electronic newspaper in the United States. In addition to its regular edition, the *Dispatch* began making its editorial content available to the computers of a small number of subscribers. Today, newspapers have online versions of their print editions and even entire issues are available online. In an era of convergence, people still purchase print newspapers to read on public transport or in coffee shops.

Some online newspapers include many of the same stories that appear in the printed version; others might include extended stories that have been omitted in the printed version because of space limitations. Online versions might also include certain information that is available only by subscription. Online newspapers have several advantages over print versions. They can present breaking news in a timely manner (since websites can be updated constantly), thus allowing them to compete with radio and television.

Newspapers have traditionally been powerful shapers of public opinion. The *Washington Post*'s revelations about the Watergate scandal helped bring about the resignation of U.S. President Richard Nixon in 1974. Newspapers have always provided a platform for debating, showcasing, and critiquing public figures and issues. But they are also entertainment, advertising, and pure information texts. With their comics sections, puzzle pages, sports sections, classified information, entertainment news, book and movie reviews, they constitute what can be called 'collage texts' that are read not as narratives, but as collages, that is, as assemblages of items that nonetheless create a whole. Some newspapers have blurred the stylistic and content lines between tabloid and serious journalism, intentionally mixing elements of both. *USA Today*, which began publication in 1982, modelled itself after TV and is quickly becoming the default newspaper style, especially in online versions.

Newspapers depend for their survival on advertising revenue, not circulation. This is why, on average, most newspapers allocate half of their space to advertising. More than three hundred years ago, the *London Gazette* was the first newspaper to apportion a section exclusively to advertising. By the end of the seventeenth century, various agencies had been set up with the specific role of creating newspaper ads. It can thus be argued that newspapers brought the modern age of advertising into existence. Layouts with big words and contrasting fonts became widespread. Language forms (words and phrases) were coined to make the ad text persuasive. Strategic repetitions of a product's name, taglines set in eye-catching patterns (vertically, horizontally, diagonally), supporting illustrations, and the creation of slogans, were just some of the advertising techniques introduced by newspaper ad makers.

Today it is claimed that newspaper reading is declining and that people are not turning to websites in place of print newspapers. As Harkin (2009: 181) observes:

The result, in many industries, has been to throw up a ready alternative to many hierarchies based on information and expertise, and subject everything possible to a new kind of peer-review system based on the opinion of masses of ordinary pundits. The precipitous collapse of the habit of newspaper reading among young adults, for example, has not thus far been compensated for by their gravitation towards newspaper websites.

It remains to be seen, however, if the newspaper (in whatever format) has outlived its function. People still seek entertainment and information in the newspaper format. If the newspaper does indeed disappear, it will be because the functions of reading will have changed drastically.

Marcel Danesi

Bibliography

Barnhurst, Kevin G., and John C. Nerone. *The Form of News: A History*. New York: Guilford, 2001.

Douglas, George H. *The Golden Age of the Newspaper*. Westport, CT: Greenwood, 1999.

Eisenstein, Elizabeth L. *The Printing Press as an Agent of Change: Communications and Cultural Transformations in Early-Modern Europe*. Cambridge: Cambridge University Press, 1979.

Epstein, Jason. *Book Business: Publishing Past, Present, and Future*. New York: Norton, 2001.

Harkin, James. *Lost in Cyburbia: How the Net Has Created a Life of Its Own*. Toronto: Knopf, 2009.

Harris, Michael, and Tom O'Malley. *Studies in Newspaper and Periodical History*. Westport, CT: Greenwood, 1997.

Martin, Shannon E., and David A. Copeland, eds. *The Function of Newspapers in Society: A Global Perspective*. Westport, CT: Praeger, 2003.

Tancer, Bill. *Click*. New York: Hyperion, 2008.

NOISE

[See also: *Bull's-Eye Model; Channel; Communication; Communication Theory; Cybernetics; Feedback; Information; Medium; Redundancy; Shannon, Claude E.*]

In communication theory, *noise* is anything that interferes with the transmission or reception of a signal or a message. In electronic transmissions, noise is equivalent to static (in radio systems) or 'snow' (in television systems). In human verbal communication, noise is any physical (sneezing, chatter, and so on) or cognitive (memory lapses) interference. In computing systems, it is data without meaning (produced as an unwanted by-product of computing activities), or unwanted data (such as spam). In a phrase, noise is random and unwanted interference in a communication system. However, noise is still considered information, since it can tell a sender or receiver what is aberrant in a situation.

In communication theory, *information* is considered to be something mathematically probabilistic – a ringing alarm signal carries more information than one that is silent, because the silent state is the 'default state' of the alarm system and the former its 'alerting state.' The mathematical aspects of information theory were developed by the American telecommunications engineer Claude Shannon (1916–2001), who showed that the information contained in a signal is inversely proportional to its probability. The more probable a signal, the less information 'load' it carries with it, and vice versa. Noise is anything that upsets this probabilistic status.

Shannon devised his model in order to improve the efficiency of telecommunication systems. It depicts communication as a unidirectional information transfer dependent on probability factors, that is, on the degree to which a message is expected or not in a given system. Noise is why communication systems have redundancy features built into them. These allow for a signal or message (depending on the system) to be decoded even if noise is present. For instance, in verbal communication the high predictability of certain words in many utterances ('Roses are red, violets are …') and the patterned repetition of elements ('Yes, yes, I'll do it; yes, I will') are redundant features that greatly increase the likelihood that a verbal message will get decoded successfully.

Shannon's model is useful in providing a terminology for describing aspects of communication and media systems, but it tells us little about how messages and meanings shape and ultimately determine the nature of human communication events and how some types of noise may have a cultural basis. Indeed, it could be claimed that by 'making noise' people can bring about change to existing systems of communication.

A common use of the term *noise* in media studies is in reference to sounds or images that are added to a text to supplement or enhance its meaning or to create mood and atmosphere. For example, cartoons use 'audio noise' to create 'sound effects.' 'Visual noise' refers instead to both aberrations in image reception ('snow') and to an intentional use of unexpected or 'noisy images' to enhance meaning. Sometimes noisy images are used to hide transitions in the digital representation of colour – a technique known as *banding*.

Marcel Danesi

Bibliography

Hailman, Jack. *Coding and Redundancy*. Cambridge, MA: Harvard University Press, 2008.
Shannon, Claude E. A Mathematical Theory of Communication. *Bell Systems Technical Journal* 27 (1948): 379–423.
Wiener, Norbert. *Cybernetics, or Control and Communication in the Animal and the Machine*. Cambridge, MA: MIT Press, 1949.

NON-VERBAL COMMUNICATION

[See also: *Birdwhistell, Ray L.*; *Body Language*; *Kinesics*; *Proxemics*]

Non-verbal communication is communication by means of facial expressions, gestures, postures, and other non-verbal modes. It sometimes includes grooming habits, clothing styles, and such cosmetic practices as tattooing and piercing. It has been estimated that humans convey over two-thirds of their ideas and feelings through the body, producing up to 700,000 physical signs, including 1,000 bodily postures, 5,000 hand gestures, and 250,000 facial expressions (Morris et al. 1979). Across cultures, non-verbal forms of communication are perceived as representing something culturally relevant in particular social situations. These include such communication modes as posture, eye contact, touch, gesture, and the like. These are usually studied under the general rubric of *kinesics*, and their investigation is carried out primarily within specific disciplines – anthropology, psychology, linguistics, and semiotics, for example.

Commonly called 'body language,' *kinesic communication* can be defined simply as the use of the body to form and transmit messages of various kinds. Developed by the American anthropologist Ray L. Birdwhistell (1918–94) in the mid-1950s, the systematic study of such communication has since become a major branch of various disciplines. Birdwhistell found that much of body language during conversation reinforced vocal communication. For this reason, within linguistics it is often called *paralanguage*, that is, 'language on top of language.' Birdwhistell conducted kinesic research and formulated his analyses on the basis of the general methods and concepts of American descriptive linguistics of the 1950s. He collected his data by filming people during conversations and then analysing the postures, facial expressions, and gestures during interaction with notions derived from linguistics. Birdwhistell maintained that it was possible to write a 'kinesic grammar' in the same way that linguists write a grammar of language.

Kinesic patterns can be inborn (unwitting), learned (witting), or a mixture of the two. Blinking the eyes and facial flushing, for instance, are involuntary (inborn) kinesic signals. These include facial expressions of happiness, surprise, anger, disgust, and other basic emotions. Laughing, crying, and shoulder shrugging, on the other hand, are examples of mixed kinesic signals, which may originate as involuntary

actions, but are shaped by cultural rules in their timing, use, and overall intensity. Winking of the eye, raising a thumb, or giving a military salute are learned kinemes. Like language, kinesic actions can be structured to lie or conceal something. For example, pressing the lips together may be used to indicate disagreement or doubt, even if the individual's verbal statements convey agreement. When linguistic and kinesic statements conflict, listeners tend to pay more attention to the latter.

In 1963, psychologist Paul Ekman established the Human Interaction Laboratory in the Department of Psychiatry at the University of California at San Francisco for the purpose of studying facial expressions and eye contact. He was joined by Wallace V. Friesen in 1965 and Maureen O'Sullivan in 1974. Over the years, the research team has identified certain facial expressions as universal and others as culture-specific, although they have found relatively little variation across cultures in the nature of the components – eyebrow position, eye shape, mouth shape, nostril size – and in their combinations (Ekman 1980, 1982, 1985, 2003; Ekman and Friesen 1975).

Research on eye contact has found that the length of time involved in eye contact, along with the pattern of contact (looking into the eyes, looking askance, and so on), are culturally conditioned, conveying the kinds of social relationship people have with each other during conversation. Some, however, appear to be universal: for example, staring is interpreted as a challenge across cultures; 'making eyes' is normally interpreted as flirtation; narrowing the eyelids communicates pensiveness, and getting the eyebrows to come nearer together conveys thoughtfulness; raising the eyebrows is usually interpreted as expressing surprise. However, even such kinemes are shaped in their detail by culture. Southern Europeans tend to look more into each other's eyes during conversation than do North Americans; in some societies males are not expected to look into female eyes unless they are married or members of the same family. Some convey specific meanings. For example, gazing is interpreted as indicative of sexual wonder, fascination, awe, or admiration, depending on culture; staring is perceived as sexual curiosity, boldness, insolence, or stupidity, again depending on social context and culture.

A large amount of eye-based communication unfolds in the form of unwitting signals. Research (Sebeok 1990) has shown that men are sexually attracted to women with large pupils, since these unconsciously convey a strong sexual interest, as well as making females look younger. This would explain the popularity of the cosmetic called *belladonna* ('beautiful woman' in Italian) in the 1920s and 1930s, which was a crystalline alkaloid eye-drop liquid. As the linguist Karl Bühler (1934: 28) has aptly pointed out, such signals act like regulators, eliciting or inhibiting some action or reaction.

Posture kinemes communicate social information, playing a critical role in interpersonal relationships. These can be defined as specific body movements or poses conveying social meanings. As in the case of eye contact, there are both universals and culture-based differences in posture kinemes. Below is a list of some purportedly universal posture kinemes:

- Slumped posture usually indicates low spirits.
- Erect posture indicates high spirits, energy, and confidence.
- Leaning forward suggests open and interested behaviour.
- Leaning away typically means defensive or disinterested behaviour.
- Crossed arms also convey defensive behaviour.
- Uncrossed arms suggest a willingness to listen.

Posture and posing are prominent in courtship. While posing may be a residue of ancient animal mechanisms within humans, as some suggest, the great diversity that is evident in poses across cultures implies that it is hardly just instinctual mating behaviour. Rather, sexual postures and poses are shaped by culture-specific notions of gender and romance and are, therefore, subject to change. In the human species, sexual posing is not only a reflex of biology, but also a product of history and tradition.

Touch is another area of non-verbal communication research. The study of tactile communication has its own subfield, called *haptics*. Handshaking, for example, is a haptic form of communication. The anthropologist Desmond Morris claims that the Western form of handshaking started as a way to show that neither person was holding a weapon. It became a 'tie sign,' because it was intended to establish a bond between people. Throughout the centuries, this sign developed into a symbol of equality and fairness, being used to seal agreements of all kinds. Refusing to shake someone's outstretched hand is perceived as a 'counter-sign' of aggressiveness or as a challenge. Predictably, this form of tactile greeting reveals cross-cultural variation. People might squeeze each other's hands (as Europeans and North Americans do), shake the other's hand with both hands, lean forward or stand straight while shaking, and so on. Haptic greeting is not limited to manual touch patterns. It might include patting someone on the arm, shoulder, or back; linking arms to indicate companionship; encircling the other's shoulder to indicate friendship or intimacy; hugging to express happiness at seeing a friend or a family member.

One aspect of touch behaviour that is shrouded in evolutionary mystery is osculation (kissing). When the lips of adult people touch, the act is perceived as a romantic or an erotic one. Kissing other parts of the face (the forehead, the head, the cheeks) is a way of showing affection to children, friends, or pets. Erotic kissing seems to be a kind of mock-suckling action, suggesting closeness and sensuality. But it is not universal. It is not common in China or Japan; and it is completely unknown in various African societies. Inuit and Laplander societies rub noses, rather than kiss, to engage in sexual foreplay.

Gesture is another major area of kinesic research. Gesture can be defined simply as the use of the hands, the arms, and (to a lesser extent) the head to communicate. Although there are cross-cultural similarities in gesture, there are also many differences. For example, the head gestures for 'yes' and 'no' used in the Balkans are the inverse of the ones used by Europeans. The latter shake the head up and down to mean 'yes,' while the former use the same one to indicate 'no,' and vice versa. In 1979, Desmond Morris and a research team at Oxford University examined twenty gesture forms in forty different regions of Europe. They discovered that many of the same gesture forms had different meanings, depending on culture – a tap on the side of the head might indicate completely opposite things, 'stupidity' or 'intelligence,' according to social context.

Gesture is also found in primate communication behaviour. Chimpanzees, for example, will raise their arms to signal that they want to be groomed; they will stretch out their arms to beg or invite; and they can point to things. The number of gestural forms of which chimpanzees is capable is limited when compared with human gesturing, which is productive and varied. Moreover, human gesturing can be used as a substitute for vocal language, as is the case with the sign languages used by the speech-impaired. It can also be used as an alternate mode of communication, as is the case with the gesture-sign languages used by religious groups, traffic personnel, conductors of orchestras, and so on.

Using the index finger is the most common form of gesture (indicating where things are in space and time), although any body part that can be moved directionally (lips, nose, tongue) can be used to point out referents in the immediate environment, to give directions, and so forth. Simulative gestures are employed commonly to represent the shape of objects while people speak: for example, to refer to a round object we tend to use both hands together moving in opposite – clockwise (the right hand) and counter-clockwise (the left hand) – directions. Such a gesture is a kind of 'spatial drawing movement.' If the movements of the hands during gesture are transferred by some drawing instrument onto some surface, the referent of the gesture will be transferred to the surface as a visual figure. Fingers are also used to represent symbols (by portraying the outline of the symbol), such as the V-sign indicating victory, peace, and other referents.

Research by David McNeill (1992, 2005) has shown that gesture is commonly a complementary communicative feature of vocal conversation. McNeill videotaped people as they spoke, and concluded that accompanying gestures, which he called *gesticulants*, are unconscious movements which convey images during speech, as well as indications of what the speaker is thinking about. Vocal speech and gesticulation constitute a single integrated system of communication. A speaker who, while describing a scene from a story in which a character bends a tree back to the ground, was observed by McNeill as appearing to grip something and pull it back. His gesture was a visual representation of the action talked about. He also observed a speaker announcing that he had just seen a cartoon, simultaneously raising up his hands as if offering his listener a kind of object.

McNeill's gesticulant categories are subtypes of the more generic category of gesture called an *illustrator*. They are used unconsciously to illustrate vocal messages. Other categories include the following:

- *Emblems*. These are gestures that translate words or phrases. Examples include the *Okay* sign, the *Come here* sign, the hitchhiking sign, and so on.
- *Affect displays*. These are gestures used to communicate emotional meaning. Examples include the hand movements that accompany states and expressions of happiness, surprise, fear, anger, sadness, contempt, or disgust.

- *Regulators.* These are gestures used to monitor, maintain, or control the speech of someone else. Examples include the hand gestures for *Keep going, Slow down, What else happened?*
- *Adaptors.* These are gestures used to satisfy some need. Examples include scratching one's head when puzzled, rubbing one's forehead when worried, and so on.

Gestures may also be used for sacred symbolic purposes. For example, in Christianity the sign of the cross aims to recreate the central event of Christianity – the Crucifixion. In Buddhism, the mudras are used during ceremonies to represent meditation, reasoning, enlightenment, unification of matter, and spirit. The 'devil's hand,' with the index and little finger raised, on the other hand, belongs to the realm of superstition, symbolizing, in some societies, a horned figure intended to ward off the evil eye and in others, a sign of 'cuckoldry.'

The role of non-verbal communication in human interaction cannot be overemphasized. In theatre and in all media spectacles, knowing how to use appropriate body language is part of dramatic art. The eye contact patterns that are used when speaking, the kinds of touching routines utilized during discourse, the kinds of gestures and postures that accompany speech are all part of the script, both in fiction and in real life. Because kinesics has produced a substantial and substantive database and theoretical literature, it is now common to separate the various areas mentioned in this entry into separate subfields. For instance, gesture is now studied separately across various disciplines (linguistics, semiotics, psychology, and so on).

Marcel Danesi

Bibliography

Argyle, Michael. *Bodily Communication.* New York: Methuen, 1988.

Armstrong, David F., William C. Stokoe, and Sherman E. Wilcox. *Gesture and the Nature of Language.* Cambridge: Cambridge University Press, 1995.

Bellack, Leopold, and Samm Sinclair Baker. *Reading Faces.* New York: Bantam, 1983.

Birdwhistell, Ray L. *Introduction to Kinesics.* Louisville: University of Ann Arbor, 1952.

– Background to Kinesics. *ETC* 13 (1955): 10–18.

– Kinesics and Communication. In *Explorations in Communication*, ed. Edmund Carpenter and Marshall McLuhan, 54–64. New York: Beacon, 1960.

– Paralanguage 25 Years after Sapir. In *Communication in Face to Face Interaction*, ed. John Laver and Sandy Hutcheson, 82–100. Harmondsworth: Penguin, 1961.

– The Kinesic Level in the Investigation of the Emotions. In *Symposium on Expressions of the Emotions in Man*, ed. Peter H. Knapp, 123–39. New York: International University Press, 1963.

– *Kinesics and Context: Essays on Body Motion Communication.* Harmondsworth: Penguin, 1970.

– The Language of the Body. In *Human Communication*, ed. Albert Silverstein, 203–11. Hillsdale, NJ: Erlbaum, 1974.

– Kinesics. In *International Encyclopedia of the Social Sciences*, vol. 8: 379–85. New York: Macmillan, 1979.

Bremer, Jan, and Herman Roodenburg, eds. *A Cultural History of Gesture.* Ithaca, NY: Cornell University Press, 1991.

Bühler, Karl. *Sprachtheorie: Die Darstellungsfunktion der Sprache.* Jena: Fischer, 1934.

Davies, Rodney. *How to Read Faces.* Woolnough: Aquarian, 1989.

Duncan, Sharkey. Non-Verbal Communication. *Psychological Bulletin* 72 (1969): 118–37.

Duncan, Sharkey, and Donald W. Fiske. *Face-to-Face Interaction.* Hillsdale, NJ: Erlbaum, 1977.

Efron, David. *Gesture, Race, and Culture.* The Hague: Mouton, 1941.

Ekman, Paul. Movements with Precise Meanings. *Journal of Communication* 26 (1976): 14–26.

Ekman, Paul. The Classes of Non-Verbal Behavior. In *Aspects of Non-Verbal Communication*, ed. Walburga von Raffler-Engel, 89–102. Lisse: Swets and Zeitlinger, 1980.

– Methods for Measuring Facial Action. In

Handbook of Methods in Non-verbal Behavior,
ed. Klaus R. Scherer and Paul Ekman, 45–90.
Cambridge: Cambridge University Press,
1982.
– *Telling Lies.* New York: Norton, 1985.
– *Emotions Revealed.* New York: Holt, 2003.
Ekman, Paul, and Wallace Friesen. *Unmasking
the Face.* Englewood Cliffs, NJ: Prentice-Hall,
1975.
Emmorey, Karen, and Judy Reilly, eds. *Language,
Gesture, and Space.* Hillsdale, NJ: Lawrence
Erlbaum Associates, 1995.
Fridlund, Alan J. *Human Facial Expression: An
Evolutionary View.* New York: Academic, 1994.
Goldin-Meadow, Susan. *Hearing Gesture: How
Our Hands Help Us Think.* Cambridge, MA:
Belknap, 2003.
Kendon, Adam. *Gesture: Visible Action as Utter-
ance.* Cambridge: Cambridge University Press,
2004.
Key, Mary Ritchie. *Paralanguage and Kinesics.*
Metuchen, NJ: Scarecrow.
Knapp, Mark L. *Non-Verbal Communication in Hu-
man Interaction.* New York: Holt, 1978.
Landau, Terry. *About Faces: The Evolution of the
Human Face.* New York: Anchor, 1989.
McCracken, Grant. *Big Hair: A Journey into the
Transformation of Self.* Toronto: Penguin, 1985.
McNeill, David. *Hand and Mind: What Gestures
Reveal about Thought.* Chicago: University of
Chicago Press, 1992.
– *Gesture and Thought.* Chicago: University of
Chicago Press, 2005.
Montagu, Ashley. *Touching: The Human Signifi-
cance of the Skin.* New York: Harper and Row,
1986.
Morris, Desmond, et al. *Gestures: Their Origins
and Distributions.* London: Cape, 1979.
Peck, Stephen Rogers. *Atlas of Facial Expression.*
Oxford: Oxford University Press, 1987.
Raffler-Engel, Walburga von, ed. *Aspects of Non-
Verbal Communication.* Lisse: Swets, 1980.
Rush, John A. *Spiritual Tattoo: A Cultural History
of Tattooing, Piercing, Scarification, Branding,
and Implants.* Berkeley: Frog, 2005.
Scherer, Klaus R., and Paul Ekman, eds. *Hand-
book of Methods in Non-Verbal Behavior Research.*
Cambridge: Cambridge University Press,
1982.

O

ONLINE CULTURE

[See also: *Cyberculture; Instant Message; Internet; Media Literacy; Social Networking; World Wide Web*]

Online culture, an offshoot of cyberculture, refers to the behavioural and social patterns that have arisen from the use of the internet. Today, the internet has become an increasingly popular venue for people to congregate (virtually), resulting in the crystallization of a new form of culture based on online modes of communicating and interacting. *Time* magazine summarizes this trend as follows: 'The unchallenged colossus of adolescent communication works like the telephone, the back fence, the class bulletin board (and, at times, the locker room), all rolled into one virtual mosh pit' (Duffy 2006).

Since 2000, activities such as online social networking have soared (Hempel and Lehman 2005). As of 2009, sites such as Facebook had more than 150 million active users (Facebook 2009). It is clear that social networking is providing the conditions for new cultural forms in areas of human rituals (from courtship to gossip), which are evolving into collages of information, entertainment, and communication (Rosenbush 2005). With the advent of face-to-face communication over the internet (as for example with Skype technology) practices of social contact and of verbal interaction are changing how people see themselves and others (Kappas and Krämer 2011; Ben Ze'ev 2011). Age, gender, and political and cultural barriers are crumbling as the user base widens. Other than statistics relating to number of clicks on certain sites, email usage, blog subscriptions, and the like, surprisingly little is known empirically about the effects of the changes taking place. New branches of cognitive science and various social sciences have started to assess what has been learned regarding how people communicate online and how online culture is laying the foundations for a new world civilization with few boundaries and barriers (if any). Using new computer-based experimental techniques, this line of inquiry is looking into such issues as how visual cues in computer-mediated communication are interpreted and how they influence the flow of communication, how video- and avatar-based communication is affecting human interaction, how nonverbal communication unfolds over the internet, and so on.

In the early days of the internet, Web-savvy individuals tended to congregate in online chat rooms and/or discussion boards that were sometimes organized according to topical or recreational interests. These forums allowed users from around the world to meet new people and interact in a non-face-to-face mode of contact. As well, they provided an additional channel through which individuals could 'find' others who shared common interests. Many of these popular discussion boards would later develop into Web communities, or e-communities, as users began to spend an increasing amount of time interacting in this new way.

With the advent of instant messaging (such as Microsoft MSN, Yahoo! Messenger, and AOL Instant Messenger), online users were then provided with a new form of real-time contact, which today also includes audio and video features. The use of instant messaging has led to the rise of internet slang (sometimes called Netlingo). In an effort to simplify and shorten the amount of typing involved in Web communications via instant messaging, users began to use abbreviated forms or acronyms in order to express common phrases or feelings. Some of these include: LOL for 'laugh out loud,' BRB for 'be right back,' and TTYL for 'talk to you later.'

Social networking websites allow users to create an online presence for themselves through online profiles, which contain anything from contact information to photos, videos, and other personal details, and are thus a powerful and efficient means by which users can interact, keep in touch, and meet new people. Two of the most popular social networking websites are currently Facebook and MySpace. Facebook was launched in 2004 by Harvard University student Mark Zuckerberg; it began initially as 'a digital version of those little photo guides of incoming college freshmen and quickly expanded to include the student bodies of more than 2,100 colleges' (Duffy 2006). The idea was to provide a networking tool that would allow people to communicate more efficiently. Today, there are more than 150 million active users, with the fastest-growing demographic being those thirty years and older (Facebook 2009). In contrast, MySpace was initially started as a site for musicians to promote their music. From this base, founders Tom Anderson and Chris DeWolfe were able to create a social networking website which allowed numerous bands to post their music, photos, tour dates, and songs. Today, it is a website with home pages, photos, music,

and other features of social networking sites (Rosenbush 2005).

Such sites have become successful for a simple psychological reason. In an age of alienation, as many sociologists and psychologists have claimed, they give the individual free reign to make contact with others and to reveal his or her persona publicly. The other reason why they continue to succeed is that they are adaptive to change. By always 'playing to the norm' and keeping their image 'cool,' they keep up with their audiences and with social trends generally. By stressing the user-based nature of the sites, Facebook and MySpace have allowed people to present themselves as they wish. Numerous dating websites, such as PerfectMatch.com, Lavalife, and Match. com, help connect people who are looking for romance. These sites, which utilize profiles in a similar manner to Facebook and MySpace, allow users to browse, search, and get in touch with potential matches. Built with advanced screening features, these sites provide an opportunity for individuals to meet people outside of their typical social circles. Dating websites have a substantial following, and online dating is just as entrenched in online culture as are typical social networking sites. Online culture is changing courtship practices. Falling in love, flirting, cheating, even having sex online have all become part of everyday life. Research on this aspect of online culture is focusing on questions such as: How is an online affair possible when the two people involved may never meet each other in the real world? Why do we tell complete strangers our most intimate secrets? Is online romance changing the monogamous nature of romance?

Also part of online culture is 'blog culture.' The popularity and accessibility of blogs (such as www.blogger.com) have presented an opportunity for individuals to easily write and publish their ideas to the masses via the internet. Furthermore, sites such as YouTube (www.youtube.com) and Photobucket (www.photobucket.com) have allowed people to make their own videos and photos available online. As a result, this has prompted a new era of online activism and citizen journalism, since this medium of communication once again ascribes power to the individual, rather than to an organization (such as a newspaper). Blogs and e-publishing sites are now employed to promote causes, debate issues, lobby governments, report on current events, and infuse new perspectives into the global forum.

Local reporters and citizens have played an increasingly valuable role in adding to the reporting carried out by traditional mainstream media, especially in war zones, disaster zones, or regions of infighting, where communications and logistical access are often poor or non-existent. It is often difficult to get traditional reporters and journalists 'on the ground' immediately, especially when there are high levels of violence, civil war, curfews, and travel restrictions. The use of devices such as cellphones and digital cameras to capture live events by people on the scene has changed the nature of reporting and the overall modality in which political pressure is exerted. Clearly, it is now the average citizen who has emerged as a major player in news awareness, leading to a new and powerful form of 'citizen' or 'participatory' journalism. Through the internet, participants are effectively able to bypass the filters of traditional media and get their independent accounts into the public sphere, thus making it possible like never before to hold the media accountable by checking their facts, reporting on their biases, and fleshing out inaccuracies from their reports. To wit: it was the prominent role of bloggers and citizen reporters which led *Time Magazine* to select 'You' as their 2006 Person of the Year.

The rise of online culture can be linked to rise of the 'global village.' But there are new dangers within this village. Often, users enter their phone numbers, email addresses, mailing addresses, and online messager screen names into their profiles, which double as address books. This has provided a conduit through which friends can check up on one another and stay in touch. However, it also opens up people's lives to public dissection and can even lead to dangerous situations: for example, as has been reported, someone who is dishonoured in an online site may seek revenge in the offline world; some impressionable young people have even committed suicide because of comments passed around in 'Facebook cliques.' The other danger is that of 'identity role-playing,' whereby the individual's imaginary profile can become his or her real-life one. This leads to anomalous situations of various kinds. For instance, some employers today will now check a potential job applicant's Facebook or MySpace profile in order to gain a broader insight into the applicant and their personality. In this sense, individuals are accountable for whatever they post online. There have been numerous reported instances of individuals getting fired over postings on their Facebook page. Within the school community, students have also received suspensions for inappropriate content posted regarding course material, study groups, and school staff (Sharplin 2009).

Above all else, the new online culture is redefining the concept of *identity* (Hlebec et al. 2006; Putnam 2006). MySpace's CEO Chris DeWolfe has acknowledged that 'the idea was to create this community where people could create accurate representations of themselves and put their lives online.' Assuming or creating online identities is known as the formation of 'digi-selves' (Federman 2002). Sites such as Second Life – a virtual reality world where individuals can literally create a 'second life' – are making the enactment of the digi-self more and more of a daily reality. In virtual worlds, individuals are able to escape from everyday life and interact with a whole new online community. The can 'tell their characters' to do whatever they like, and assume whatever sort of personality they wish. There have been several documented instances where individuals have taken their second life so seriously that it has drastically affected their 'first life' in the real world. Clearly, online culture is no longer part of a mindscape, it is fast becoming part of the real-worldscape.

Alexander Lim

Bibliography

ABC News. Parents: Cyber Bullying Led to Teen's Suicide. Accessed: http://abcnews .go.com/GMA/Story?id=3882520&page=1 (accessed 26 January 2009).

Ben Ze'ev. *Love Online: Emotions on the Internet.* Cambridge: Cambridge University Press, 2011.

Duffy, M. A Dad's Encounter with the Vortex of Facebook. Time Inc. (19 March 2006). http://www.time.com/time/magazine/ article/0,9171,1174704,00.html (accessed 13 January 2009).

Facebook. Statistics. http://www.facebook.com/ home.php#/press/info.php?statistics (accessed 26 January 2009).

Federman, Mark. Cultural Paradox of the Global Village. *The McLuhan Program in Culture and Technology.* http://www.mcluhan.utoronto .ca/article_culturalparadox.htm (accessed 26 January 2009).

Hempel, Jessi, and Paula Lehman. The MySpace Generation. *Business Week,* 12 December 2005, 88–93.

Hlebec, Katja, Lozar Manfreda, and Valentina Vehovar. The Social Support Networks of Internet Users. *New Media and Society* 8 (2006): 9–32.

Kappas, Arvid, and Nicole C. Krämer, eds. *Face-to-Face Communication over the Internet: Emotions in a Web of Culture, Language, and Technology.* Cambridge: Cambridge University Press, 2011.

Rosenbush, Steve. Hey, Come to This Site Often? *Business Week,* 19 July 2006, 66.

Sharplin, Scott. Facebook Casebook 2009. SEE Magazine. http://www.seemagazine.com/ article/city-life/city/facebook0115/ (accessed 26 January 2009).

ORALITY

[See also: *Communication; Electronic Media; Literacy; McLuhan, Marshall*]

Orality (competence in communicating by speech and gesture) has typically been conceived in contrast to literacy (competence in writing and reading). This 'great divide' between oral and literate communication was initially related to two radically different modes of expression, representing different cognitive styles and kinds of societies. Oral expression was poetic, circular, and imitative; its cognitive style concrete, mythical, and emotional; and its societies primitive and uncivilized. Literate expression was philosophical, linear, and original; its modes of cognition abstract and rational; its societies advanced and civilized. In recent decades, new research has contributed to an understanding of orality and oral traditions as complex technologies for storing, retrieving, and transmitting information. Findings from studies of living oral societies along with research from ancient, medieval, and contemporary traditions has challenged the assumption of a 'divide' between orality and literacy. Today, orality is conceived as a continuum, ranging from ongoing oral traditions, to living oral traditions that persist alongside and in interaction with written traditions, to literate cultures that still manifest traces of oral origins, through to new sorts of orality mediated by electronic media (cellular telephone, radio). Orality is now considered to encompass primary orality (cultures with no knowledge of writing); oral tradition (communication stored in memory and transmitted through time via the spoken word) involving verbal art (epic, poetry) or narrative (in either performance language or everyday speech styles); oral literature (an oxymoron referring to compositions created without writing and then later documented); oral history (events that happened in the speaker's lifetime); and secondary orality (oral/aural and visual communication preserved by electronic media). Orality is a significant field of inquiry in religion, classics, archaeology, and history; the basis of research in the study of media ecology, cultural studies, and information and communication technology; a focus in literary studies, linguistics, education, and music; and a major topic in anthropology, ethnography, folklore, and performance studies.

The study of orality and literacy was inaugurated by the research of American classicist Milman Parry (1902–35), whose analysis of Homer's *Iliad* and *Odyssey* showed that these epic poems were too complex to have been created by one poet; the language rules governing repeating formulaic patterns in the verse could only be the cumulative product of an entire tradition of poetry making to which generations of poets contributed over centuries (Parry 1971). Theorizing that the epics were too long to have been memorized verbatim in the absence of writing, Parry argued that formulaic patterns were mnemonic devices used by poets living in a wholly oral culture prior to the advent of the technology of the phonetic alphabet. He proposed that oral poets – *rhapsodes* (meaning sewers of songs) – stitched together the epics during a performance by selecting ready-made formulas from a stock inventory of expressions, each of which was tailored to fit into a section of the hexameter verse and to dovetail with the formulas that came before and after (Parry 1971: 268). The stock expressions, together with the methods for organizing them into lines and then episodes and then entire plot patterns, constituted a completely unified 'technology for verse making.' To test the veracity of his hypotheses concerning the ancient Homeric tradition, Parry, along with his assistant Albert B. Lord (1912–91), conducted fieldwork with the then-living South Slavic oral tradition. Their research became the single most important critical perspective on Homer and the basis for numerous other studies of orality in ancient, medieval, and contemporary literatures. Today, more than one hundred national literatures are involved in the study of orality and literacy, including Arabic, Chinese, English, French, German, Greek, Japanese, Russian, Spanish, as well as African language families and North American Aboriginal traditions.

Twyla Gibson

Bibliography

Foley, John Miles. *Homer's Traditional Art*. University Park: Pennsylvania State University Press, 1999.

Goody, Jack. *The Interface between the Written and the Oral*. Cambridge: Cambridge University Press, 1987.

Havelock, Eric A. *Preface to Plato*. Cambridge, MA: The Belknap Press of Harvard University Press, 1963.

Lord, Albert Bates. *The Singer of Tales*. Cambridge, MA: Harvard University Press, 1964.

McLuhan, Marshall. *The Gutenberg Galaxy: The Making of Typographic Man*. Toronto: University Press, 1962.

Ong, Walter J. *Orality and Literacy: The Technologizing of the Word*. New York: Routledge, 1991. (Original work published 1982.)

Parry, Milman. *The Making of Homeric Verse: The Collected Papers of Milman Parry*. Edited and translated by Adam Parry. Oxford: Clarendon Press, 1971.

Thomas, Rosalind. *Literacy and Orality in Ancient Greece*. Cambridge: Cambridge University Press, 1992.

Vansina, Jan. *Oral Tradition as History*. Madison: University of Wisconsin Press, 1964.

P

PEIRCEAN SEMIOTICS AND CULTURAL PRODUCTIONS

[See also: *Saussurean Semiotics; Semiotics*]

The American philosopher and semiotician Charles Sanders Peirce (1839–1914) depicts a universe permeated by signs that ceaselessly migrate, change, and develop as they circulate among subjects, organisms, and other sites: 'All this universe is perfused with signs, if it is not composed exclusively of signs' (Peirce 1905, in 1960: 5.448n, cf. 2.302). Peirce's emphasis on signs forms part of his attempt to think together the processes of 'inner' and 'outer' worlds, to identify synergies, syncretisms, and tensions between the actions of mind and body, spirit and matter. Rather than focusing on language as has the analytic tradition that currently enjoys pre-eminence in English-language philosophy, Peirce explores the fundamental semiotic conditions for all perception, for individual and collective acts, for the elaboration of habits and laws, and indeed for the growth of natural processes in general. In contrast to the formal analytical tradition (Carnap 1937; Frege 1879; Russell 1956; Whitehead and Russell 1910), Peirce grants at least as much attention to humanistic perspectives as to logic and mathematics, and studies closely not only how events get defined in the exact sciences but also how they impact on experience, human endeavours, and the lived environment. 'Sign' represents

Peirce's general term that corresponds to what structuralist and post-structuralist theory has called (verbal and non-verbal) 'text' or 'discourse,' and notably embraces both familiar, conventional symbols (e.g., traffic signals, advertising jingles, common gestures, vocabulary words) and new, singular productions of any temporal duration or spatial expanse, such as a movie, a song, a political demonstration, or a website.

Peirce's Doctrine of Signs

While Charles S. Peirce enjoyed a number of interests throughout his life, his major contributions to scholarship lay in philosophy. This entry sketches Peirce's semiotic ideas and the developments they have inspired beyond philosophy, in the study of cultural productions such as film, photography, literature, and historiography.

Peirce offers the definition: 'A sign, or *representamen*, is something which stands to somebody for something in some respect or capacity. It addresses somebody, that is, creates in the mind of that person an equivalent sign, or perhaps a more developed sign. That sign which it creates I call the *interpretant* of the first sign. The sign stands for something, its *object*. It stands for that object, not in all respects, but in reference to a sort of idea, which I have sometimes called the *ground* of the representamen' (1897 fragment, in 1960: 2.228, cf. 2.274; Nöth 1990: 42–4; Sebeok 1985: 5–10). The formulation of the interpretant defines the sign as a temporal and dynamic phenomenon open onto communication, while the parallel inclusion of the object and its ground establishes a framework able to address issues which Frege (1892) investigates as the relation between sense and reference.

Teresa De Lauretis adopts Peirce's explicit emphasis on the role of the subject who experiences the sign in order to assert the agency of the film viewer in the face of social constraints, and to critique deterministic formulations of *suture* which theorists developed from the works of Jacques Lacan and Louis Althusser (De Lauretis 1984: 178–9; cf. Metz 1977, Mulvey 1975). In theorizing the viewer's cinematic experience, De Lauretis incorporates Peirce's open-ended notion of the interpretant as any 'more developed sign' and rejects the limits that theorists such as Umberto Eco place on interpretation (Eco 1979). She invokes Peirce's emphasis on agency as well as his all-inclusive definition of signs in order to extend notions of creativity and cultural production from a focus on an artist's oeuvre to a broader conception that also emphasizes consciousness-raising projects (De Lauretis 1984: 178).

Peirce identifies 'three categories of elements' among 'phenomena': *firsts* designate 'qualities' or 'likenesses,' *seconds* 'actual facts,' while *thirds* comprise 'laws' (1896, in 1960: 1.418–20). As firsts, Peirce gives the examples of 'red, bitter, tedious, hard, heartrending, noble,' considered as pure qualities, as potential sensations: 'What the world was to Adam on the day he opened his eyes to it, before he had drawn any distinctions, or had become conscious of his own existence – that is first, present, immediate, fresh, new initiative, original, spontaneous, free, vivid, conscious, and evanescent' (1890, in 1960: 1.357). Key for inquiry into perception, *firstness* entails *vagueness,* fluid boundaries, and volatility. Firsts functioning as signs appear imprecise but poignant, an evanescent but pure presence, 'a purely monadic state of feeling' that short-circuits any precise connections or memories, as do the qualities

that characterize intuitions of 'happy' or 'sad' colours or musical sounds: 'tones are signs of visceral qualities of feelings. But the best example is that of odors … odors have a remarkable tendency to *presentmentate* themselves, that is to occupy the entire field of consciousness, so that one almost lives for the moment in a world of odor' (Peirce 1894, in 1960: 1.303, and 1905, in 1960: 1.313).

Peircean *secondness* incorporates firstness while adding the dimension of events and singularity, of perception and experience. Seconds are 'the actual facts'; 'It is the matter that resists' (1896, in 1960: 1.419). Secondness entails self and other, effort and impedance: 'as the consciousness *itself* is two-sided, so it also has two varieties; namely, action, where our modification of other things is more prominent than their reaction on us, and perception, where their effort on us is overwhelmingly greater than our effect on them … The idea of other, of *not,* becomes a very pivot of thought. To this element I give the name of Secondness' (1903, in 1960: 1.324). The 'indeterminacy' of firsts contrasts with the 'haeccity' of seconds: 'The qualities, in so far as they are general, are somewhat vague and potential. But an occurrence is perfectly individual … We feel facts resist our will … mere qualities do not resist' (Peirce 1896, in 1960: 1.419, cf. 1890, in 1960: 1.405).

Cumulating the traits of all three modes of existence, *thirdness* comprises habits, regulation, and conceptualization. 'The third category of elements of phenomena consists of what we call laws when we contemplate them from the outside only, but which when we see both sides of the shield we call thoughts' (Peirce 1896, in 1960: 1.420). Thirdness concerns exchange and consensus, meaning and value, purpose and ideal. Peirce enumerates features of thirdness and secondness when he obliquely defines the mode which he considers the most difficult of the three modes to comprehend, firstness: 'Firstness … precedes all synthesis and differentiation; it has no unity and no parts. It cannot be articulately thought: assert it, and it has already lost its character-istic innocence; for assertion always implies a denial of something else. Stop to think of it, and it has flown!' (1890, in 1960: 1.357).

Gilles Deleuze observes that the em-phasis on action, suspense, and character found in mainstream movies foregrounds secondness, whereas innovative filmic sequences at least momentarily displace the viewer's attention toward thirdness or firstness (1983: 197, 220–3; cf. Bogue 2003). Complex psychological dramas such as Hitchcock's highlight intellectual processes associated with thirdness (Deleuze 1983: 274–6), while unusual close-ups, illogical cuts, and asynchronous image and sound can break narrative continuity and elicit images experienced as free-floating sense impressions unrelated to plot, character, and reference, producing flashes of first-ness (Deleuze 1983: 142).

Peirce applies his three categories of phenomena to the components he identi-fies in semiosis, distinguishing for example among immediate, dynamical, and final interpretants (Peirce and Welby 1977: 110–11; cf. Nöth 1995: 43–4). The immediate interpretant (cf. firstness) designates 'the effect the sign produces or may produce upon a mind, without any reflection on it,' the dynamical interpretant (cf. secondness) the 'direct effect actually produced by a Sign upon an Interpreter of it ... that which is experienced in each act of Interpretation and is different in each from that of any other,' while the final interpretant (cf. third-ness) denotes that which would be deemed the 'true interpretation' of a sign if an 'ul-timate opinion were reached' (Peirce and Welby 1977: 110–11).

Peirce's reflections on thirdness as medi-ation, translation, and communication rep-resent one of the hallmarks of his semiotics, providing an antidote to the binarism high-lighted by a number of postwar method-ologies. Exploring approaches to mediation found in sociology and psychology, Mertz and Parmentier (1985) compare Peircean thirdness with other triadic models, includ-ing Pythagoras, Hegel, and Lévi-Strauss.

In his study of the relation between the self and democracy throughout American his-tory, Norbert Wiley (1994) plays Peirce off the American psychologist and philosopher George Herbert Mead, arguing that the self can be construed as a 'trialogue' in which the present self 'I' talks to the future self 'you' about the past self 'me.'

Peirce also applies the primitive trio of *firstness, secondness,* and *thirdness* recur-sively as an elementary schema to generate three further triads (Peirce 1960: 2.234–63; cf. Nöth 1995: 44–5, Theleffsen 2000): 'Signs are divisible by three trichotomies; first, according as the sign in itself is a mere quality, is an actual existent, or is a general law; secondly, according as the relation of the sign to its object consists in the sign's having some character in itself, or in some existential relation to that object, or in its relation to an interpretant; thirdly, accord-ing as its Interpretant represents it as a sign of possibility or as a sign of fact or a sign of reason' (Peirce 1960: 2.243). As before, the second and third classes entail their predecessor(s).

'Triadic relations of comparison' define a first set of three types of signs considered as logical possibilities (cf. firstness): the *qualisign,* 'a quality which is a sign' (1960: 2.244), the *sinsign,* 'an actual existent thing or event which is a sign,' and the *legisign,* 'a law that is a sign' (1960: 2.244–6). Writing to Lady Welby in 1904, Peirce summarizes: 'As it is in itself, a sign is either of the na-ture of an appearance, when I call it a *quali-sign;* or secondly, it is an individual object or event, when I call it a *sinsign* ... or third-ly, it is of the nature of a general type, when I call it a *legisign'* (cited in Sebeok 1985: 8). Reading texts typically entails focusing on the legisign function of language, but at-tending primarily to the sound or concrete shape and layout of a sonnet means experi-encing the work as a qualisign, while focus-ing on the designative character of on-stage theatrical gestures and dialogues engages a play as a sinsign (cf. Nöth 1990: 46).

'Triadic relations of performance' or actual facts produce the most widely discussed and applied Peircean trichotomy of signs, that based on their respective type of ground (cf. secondness). The *icon* refers to an object by virtue of its inherent characters, the *index* designates 'a sign which refers to the object that it denotes by virtue of being really affected by that object,' while the *symbol* is 'a sign which refers to the object that it denotes by virtue of a law, usually an association of general ideas' (1960: 2.247–9; cf. Feibleman 1946: 90). Contemporary cognitive linguistics uses the principle of iconicity to show that aural or graphic dynamics such as word order or the relative proximity or distance between units in an utterance, far from representing mere asemantic 'surface' phenomena as in early generative grammar, express fundamental conceptual relations such as sequence, grouping, and degree of relatedness (JohnQPublik n.d., section 2.2). Comparing the Peircean doctrine of the diagram to the Husserlian concept of categorical intuition, Frederik Stjernfelt (2007) outlines a realist semiotics of pictorial art and literature based on the American theorist's discussions of ideal schemas. For Barry King (2001), a photograph functions as an icon insofar as it represents practices and forms in the world, and as a symbol to the extent that it is created and perceived through the frameworks of varied and changing aesthetic norms. Inversely, Eduardo Neiva (2001) argues that secondness plays a more important role in photography because events, history, chance, and nature play a more important role in specifying images' signification than do conventions, rules, and cultural associations. Literary realism and naturalism depend on indexicality through their evocation of specific historical events, individuals, and material objects (Nöth 1995: 47), and Vladimir Karbusicky studies music as an indexical sign whose object is the emotions evoked by a given piece (1986: 39–107, cf. Hatten in Hénault 2002: 557 and Tarasti 1994: 54–7).

'Triadic relations of thought' determine a last ternary set of sign types representing intellectual processes (thirdness) differentiated by their object class. The *rheme* or term designates a possible object; the *dicent* or *dicisign*, a proposition, is an actual object; and the *argument*, 'a legal sign' such as a conclusion or inference based on premises, constitutes a legal object (Peirce 1960: 2.250–2; Feibleman 1946: 92). A lie told to someone can imply a rheme, communicating a possible (but not actual) object. Blanking out one of the terms in a logical proposition produces a rheme: the open slot created suggests a potential but not an actual object. The logical premise itself is an example of a dicent, an articulated thought that asserts or denies something. In the same vein, the relations of implication among coordinated terms, predicates, and propositions within a syllogism can produce an argument as a sign.

The above discussion represents a mere sketch of some of C.S. Peirce's most celebrated proposals for semiotics, which in turn form only a part of his wider writings on philosophy and science. For didactic purposes, the preceding exposition attempts to simplify and present clearly in one panorama a host of complex ideas which Pierce changed in ways both small and considerable from one time and venue to another. Curious minds may deepen their understanding of the American philosopher and semiotician by exploring compact anthologies of his writings (Peirce 1956, 1992, 1998; Peirce and Welby 1977), by perusing his biography (Brent 1998), or by sampling essays from one of the two near-comprehensive editions of his work (1934, 1982–).

Applications, Explorations, Developments

Rather than delving further into purely philosophical reflections on semiotics, the rest of this article briefly examines Peirce's doctrine of signs in relation to other disciplines. The thinker's early philosophical ideas developed in part through his conversations in the 1870s Harvard University satellite group The Metaphysical Club, which in its first phase included a number of lawyers and jurists, especially Oliver Wendell Holmes, Jr and Nicholas St John Green. The pragmatism formulated in this forum and in further exchanges among Peirce, William James, and John Dewey helped shape the movement of legal realism in North America. Peirce's writings directly inspired the work of the jurist Jerome Frank and continue to stand against renewed conceptions of natural law. Arguing against the notion that written tomes such as Napoléon's *Code civil* state eternal truths and unchanging objective realities, the legal scholar François Gény used Peirce to show that the meaning of a statute comprises the deductions that it makes possible and the social consequences that its potential interpretations introduce (Kevelson 1987: 71). In this perspective, a body of laws represents 'a continuous, evolving system of thought … for each successive instance in the continuing, vital process of legal reasoning' (71–2).

After Peirce's lifetime, and most particularly after the Second World War, his semiotics inspired research in a wide array of fields. Two illustrative domains include literature and history, on which the subsequent exposition is concentrated. This choice of fields owes more to the present author's inclinations than to Peirce's, and another essay could just as easily highlight different areas, such as law, education, art, music, or the pure sciences.

Peircean Literary Criticism

Many literary critics today have based their theory of literature on C.S. Peirce's semiotics, drawing attention to the way it integrates signs into the natural and cultural environment and how it foregrounds the subjects who experience signs and are changed by them. Iris Smith's (1985) essay on Antonin Artaud's theory of theatre provides an illustrative application of Peirce's sign doctrine to a literary topic (cf. Sebeok and Umiker-Sebeok 1980). Both the early twentieth-century French playwright and

the semiotician endeavour to overcome Cartesian dualism, delineating continuities between material, corporeal processes and immaterial force and values. Similarly, both Artaud the modernist and Peirce the pragmatist underline the kinetic character of artistic creation and experience, in direct opposition to the classical ideal of contemplative stasis (Winckelmann 1764). The 'Theatre of Cruelty' (Artaud 1938) includes a distinctive insistence on the indexicality of dramatic action: dismissing pure fiction, Artaud calls for a plot anchored in actual public events, as his 1935 drama *Les Cenci* revisits the calamitous misdeeds of a Renaissance Roman family.

On the other hand, Smith (1985) argues that the Theatre of Cruelty simplifies and truncates dramatic processes in crucial ways. *The Theater and Its Double* advises against staging masterpieces, claiming that the consecration of canonicity paralyses the performance, freezing the creativity of artists and audience. Smith invokes the Peircean interpretant and the growth of signs to contend instead that semiosis always remains dynamic and open, that director, actors, and spectators can craft novel dimensions of the canonical repertoire (and a masterpiece is often defined as a work for which each generation discovers new significance). For Smith, features of Artaud's aesthetics belie an idealism that distorts actual theatrical hermeneutics and that at times collapses the dynamic triadic sign into a simpler, static dyad in which the theatrical representamen is paired with an interpretant in one-to-one fashion. In a utopian mode, the Theatre of Cruelty thus envisions an audience melded into a unified body, whereas Smith asserts that Peirce's more realistic view of semiosis can account for the diversity of spectators' responses to a performance. Similarly, while Artaud optimistically envisions that the meaning of his performance will be one and immediately obvious to the public, Smith calls on the distinction between dynamical and final interpretants to point out that theatregoers' interpretations of a work typically change and develop over time. Artaud's desire for absolute iconicity, for the public to accede to pure dramatic sensation, betrays a Platonic overvaluation of the object at the expense of the sign (Smith 1985).

Peirce and History

Explicitly focused on 'the growth of signs,' Peirce's semiotics is founded on models of historical processes. Moreover, the same 'facts' that ground so many historiographies constitute a quintessential example of Peirce's key category of secondness: 'We feel facts resist our will. That is why facts are proverbially called brutal' (Peirce 1960: 1.418–19; Langlois and Seignobos 1897). It can be interesting to peek into Peirce's own forays in historical inquiry, to identify the principles for research in history which his semiotics proposes, to offer samples of his influence on scholars and professionals in the field, and most importantly, to define contemporary strategies for research and practice in history that are informed by the doctrine of signs.

The semiotician and scholar of American history William Pencak has explored the relation between C.S. Peirce and the field of history. In his essay 'Charles S. Peirce, Historian and Semiotician,' Pencak notes that the American philosopher took a keen interest in Napoleon Bonaparte late in life: he read prodigiously on the French emperor and drafted an immense manuscript which, like many of his writings, remained unpublished during his lifetime (Pencak 1993: 66–71). In keeping with the historiographic conventions of his day, C.S. Peirce also devised macro-chronologies of modern Western history, calibrating critical changes on two successive temporal scales, every half-millennium and every generation or thirty-three years (Pencak 1993: 77–9). The seismic generational events often point to an implicit, additional intermediate-term rhythm of historical processes: thus the seven turning points that a Peirce manuscript identifies as punctuating the span from the early sixteenth century to the later

seventeenth century all directly concern the struggle between Protestants and Catholics in France and Germany: '1519 Luther's theses, 1547 Battle of Muhlenberg, 1572 St. Bartholomew's Massacre, 1598 Edict of Nantes, 1618 Thirty Years' Wars, 1648 Peace of Westphalia, 1685 Revocation of the Edict of Nantes' (Peirce 1893, in 1960: 6.314, quoted in Pencak 1993: 77–8).

Peirce's theoretical reflections on history and the writing of history may provide more food for thought today than his actual assays in the field. Firmly asserting humanistic principles and opposing deterministic theories, his philosophy of history seems to combat most vociferously then-common Darwinist versions of social evolutionism. Pencak summarizes the key components of the semiotician's perspective: 'First, history does not "evolve," it erupts – suddenly transforming itself under the pressure of surprising events. Second, at such conjunctures, great men do make a difference, men who cannot possibly be considered "products" of "forces." And third, these men do in fact shape history, *to the extent that* they wholeheartedly and unselfishly dedicate themselves to a higher ideal' (Pencak 1993: 53). A key facet of Peirce's thought, the first point emphasizes that if the philosopher affirms the importance of 'the formation of habits,' he attributes equal weight to 'the violent breaking up of habits' in explaining human behaviour and the unfolding of beliefs and ideas over time. Lecturing on the history of science, Peirce argued that rather than evolving through the gradual accumulation of modest gains, fields proceed by 'leaps,' 'by new observations and reflections' (Peirce ca 1896, in 1960: 1.101–9, quoted in Pencak 1993: 55). His emphasis on 'cataclysmic' transmutation over progressive evolution presages the 'epistemological break' of a later philosopher similarly convinced of the importance of both discontinuous change and the socio-psychological conditions of scientific advances and blockages, Gaston Bachelard (Bachelard 1938, 1940; cf. Kuhn 1962). The second point noted by Pencak underlines the inalienable agency which Peirce ascribes to human beings, especially to exceptional individuals, while the third point asserts the force of an idea that can inspire men to unselfishly dedicate themselves to bringing it to realization. The historian and semiotician Brooke Williams emphasizes that a semiotic perspective in historiography underlines that 'human beings are not merely products but also agents of culture or "meaning," and hence creative producers of signs and sign systems' (1991: 390).

Williams and Pencak show that Peirce's views on the modes of scientific thinking in the realms of philosophy and science possess relevance for research in history (Williams 1991: 410–12; Pencak 1993: 55). Whereas methodological pronouncements on historiography often draw attention to the importance of *induction* and *deduction*, emphasizing the role of logical inferences drawn from documented particular events and from general laws and premises (e.g., Hempel 1942), Peirce foregrounds as well the critical part played by what he considers a third form of reasoning called *abduction*. Exemplified by the conjecture 'If Socrates is mortal, perhaps all men are mortal,' Peircean abduction assumes the forms of educated guess, hypothesis formation, and probable argument, somewhere in between mere random trial and error (Popper 1972), on the one hand, and necessary inference or simple observation, on the other (Peirce 1960: 7.219, 5.189, 5.196). In Peirce's conception of the scientific method, abductive reasoning represents the first of three stages, in which the investigator forms and selects 'explanatory hypotheses,' after remarking mould on neglected Petri dishes, for example. The scientist then employs deduction to infer what else must be the case if a given hypothesis is true, based on known general principles, and finally uses induction to test the hypothesis by drawing general conclusions from particular instances, including findings gleaned from controlled experiments (Peirce 1960: 4.541, 2.777, 5.171). Considered a subset of induction prior to Peirce, abduction not only allows

the American philosopher to transform one more dyad into a triad, it also highlights mental processes which can create new rules based on novel observations rather than merely establish relations among existing notions, thus foregrounding a key characteristic of modern science.

As an inchoative, heuristic form of reasoning, abduction is closely associated with questioning and with curiosity, and with the mental 'Pure Play' that Peirce calls 'musement' and which plays such an essential role in coming up with original, creative ideas (1908, in 1960: 6.458–9). Abduction and non-linear, undirected 'contemplation' are triggered by the 'surprising fact' which 'either disappoints an expectation, or breaks in upon some habit of expectation of the inquisitor,' thereby encouraging the latter into a more original, unexpected investigative path (Peirce 1908, in 1960: 6.469). The striking, isolated, and inexplicable fact can engender aching doubt, which in turn fosters the creative thinking that brings 'the fixation of belief,' completing the cycle. Peirce's account of scientific method grants special recognition to neglected initial processes that indirectly prompt discovery, alongside the commonly cited procedures used to develop, check, and present those discoveries. His depiction of scientific activity diverges from the Darwinism of his day, but also paints a picture different from Carl Hempel's later view of history as a science dedicated to identifying and applying the general laws that explain processes in time.

More generally, contemporary scholars with a historical bent whose research is informed by C.S. Peirce and by the thinkers that inspired his doctrine of signs argue that semiotics overcomes the dichotomy that still exists in historiography between objective 'realism' and subjective 'idealism.' By emphasizing the defining role of the sign and the constitutive function of the observer, the semiotic paradigm mediates between the nineteenth-century historiographic 'model in which "document" refers to a prejacent given reality, which a rigorously applied "objectivity" can directly access as history,' on the one hand, and an 'idealist or glottocentric model' that encloses the historian within her own cognitive framework or in a 'prisonhouse of language,' cut off from real contact with the past (Williams 1991: 409; Toews 1987: 882; cf. Jameson 1972). Semiotics instead proposes to define 'objectivity' through the 'object' of the observing subject's attention and experience, which entail signs: 'In contrast to philosophical idealism and realism alike, th[e semiotic] perspective presupposes an interaction whereby the environment and the social interactions it sustains ... come to exist as "objects" within observation. Whereas physical aspects of the surroundings may exist in nature prior to the observer, the point at hand is that they further exist precisely *as* objects of awareness only through signs and precisely in relation to the observer' (Williams 1991: 395; Deely 1990; and Merrell 1987).

Defining the modes by which signs effect mediation between subject and object, between nature, culture, and mind, semiotics thus proposes a ground for the philosophies of history formulated by such figures as Carl Becker and Benedetto Croce, who underline the observer's participation in constituting knowledge of the past. Becker thus uses such terms as 'affirmations,' 'representations,' and 'symbols' in place of 'facts,' and emphasizes that they 'do not really exist until the historian, at the very least, selects and affirms them *in relation* to one another,' depicting the past in view of advancing some purpose for the future (Becker 1926, quoted in Pencak 1993: 86). Rather than propose new models or methods, semiotics can aid in clarifying the parameters that define the community of historians' work (Williams 1991: 392).

Alongside this emphasis on the interpretative role played by the subject as writer of history, semiotic-minded historians also draw attention to how signs inform the actions of historical subjects. Pencak thus contends: 'Although he did not use the word, Becker was developing a semiotics of history,' in that, in Becker's own words, he

'endeavored to convey to the reader, not a record of what men did, but a sense of how they thought and felt about what they did,' sometimes using 'a rather free paraphrase of what some imagined spectator or participant might have thought,' in order to 'enable[] the reader to enter into such states of mind' (1921: vii–viii, quoted in Pencak 1993: 85; cf. Williams 1985). The Austrian-American historian Eric Voegelin published on some of C.S. Peirce's most important essays in the 1920s and incorporated significant elements of his and his fellow Metaphysics Club members' pragmatics into his work. For Pencak, 'Voegelin's lifelong concern with the symbols through which societies have understood themselves and through which thinkers have sought to interpret human experience foreshadowed semiotics' (1993: 109). This interest in the signs and signifying systems through which cultures represent themselves and their world points to semiotics as an inquiry ultimately into how individuals and communities develop and circulate knowledge (Anderson et al. 1984; Deely 1986; Sless 1986: 1).

Just as they affirm the importance of semiotics for history, so too do semioticians informed by C.S. Peirce assert the significance of the historical perspective for semiotics. John Deely notes that the transdisciplinary semiotic perspective brings 'a restoration of historical thought to its properly central place in humanistic inquiry,' 'revealing the centrality of history to the enterprise of understanding in its totality' (1984: 407, 1990: 81). Similarly, the postwar American semiotician Thomas A. Sebeok asserts that the doctrine's critical task is to explore the processes that effect changes in sign systems, to analyse how they develop or come undone in the context of the cultural practices of a given environment, '*how* a code is made and unmade in relation to functioning in an *Umwelt*-become-*Lebenswelt*' (1977: 36).

Other Fields

Peirce's doctrine joins with John Poinsot's scholastic philosophy in forming the foundations of John Deely's semiotics that foregrounds a theory of textuality and otherness (1994). Colapietro (1989) analyses Peirce's conception of the individual self and investigates the relation of his semiotics to experimental psychology. On the other hand, incorporating the broad, non-anthropomorphic perspectives at work in contemporary astronomy and physics, Corrington (1994, 2000) draws on Peirce and a host of twentieth-century semioticians in an endeavour to shift theology and philosophy away from a 'narcissistic' focus on human consciousness and the individual self and toward a comprehensive grasp of nature, cosmology, and unconscious processes. An outgrowth of an earlier attempt to articulate the (non-) foundations of written texts, Merrell (1991) argues that Peirce's semiotics effectively foresees many of the critical concepts subsequently investigated by twentieth-century mathematics, physics, and philosophy, from quantum mechanics and the theory of relativity to post-structuralism and chaos theory (Merrell 1982). In addition to the semiotic categories sketched above, the essay discusses Peirce's concepts of semiosis, process, evolution, and the growth of signs, contrasts his continuous view of space and time with his notion of discontinuous 'cuts,' and highlights Peirce's ideas about community, his pragmatic approach to truth and meaning, and his 'convergence' theory of knowledge. In a monograph intended for undergraduates and graduate students, Everaerrt-Desmedt (2006) sketches nuanced applications of Peircean concepts to contemporary art, studying the iconoclastic surrealist Magritte (icon and hypoicon), the French postwar avant-garde painter Yves Klein, the Mexican photographer Humberto Chavez Mayol (deduction, induction, abduction), the writer Marguerite Duras, and the filmmaker Wim Wenders.

Thomas F. Broden

Bibliography

Anderson, Myrdene, John Deely, Martin Krampen, Joseph Randsell, Thomas A. Sebeok, and Thure von Uexküll. *A Semiotic Perspective on the Sciences: Steps toward a New Paradigm.* Victoria College of the University of Toronto: Toronto Semiotic Series, no. 5, 1984. Rpt. in *Semiotica* 52.1–2 (1984): 7–47.

Artaud, Antonin. *Le théâtre et son double.* Paris: Gallimard, 1938. Translated by Mary Caroline Richards, *The Theater and Its Double.* New York: Grove, 1958.

– *Oeuvres complètes.* Vol. 4. Paris: Gallimard, 1987 [contains *Le théâtre et son double, Le théâtre de Séraphin,* and *Les Cenci*].

Bachelard, Gaston. *La formation de l'esprit scientifique. Contribution à une psychanalyse de la connaissance objective.* Paris: Vrin, 1938. Translated by Mary McAllester Jones, *The Formation of the Scientific Mind: A Contribution to a Psychoanalysis of Objective Knowledge.* Manchester: Clinamen, 2002.

– *La philosophie du non: essai d'une philosophie du nouvel esprit scientifique.* Paris: Presses Universitaires de France, 1940. Translated by G.C. Waterstone, *The Philosophy of No: A Philosophy of the New Scientific Mind.* New York: Orion Press, 1968.

Becker, Carl Lotus. *The Eve of the Revolution. A Chronicle of the Breach with England.* New Haven, CT: Yale University Press, 1921.

– What Are Historical Facts? *Western Political Quarterly* (1955): 327–40 [initially a 1926 public address].

Bogue, Ronald. *Deleuze on Cinema.* New York: Routledge, 2003.

Brent, Joseph. *Charles Sanders Peirce: A Life.* Revised and enlarged ed. Bloomington: Indiana University Press, 1998.

Carnap, Rudolf. *The Logical Syntax of Language.* New York: Harcourt Brace, 1937.

Colapietro, Vincent M. *Peirce's Approach to the Self. A Semiotic Perspective on Human Subjectivity.* Albany: State University of New York Press, 1989.

Corrington, Robert S. *Ecstatic Naturalism: Signs of the World.* Bloomington: Indiana University Press, 1994.

– *A Semiotic Theory of Theology and Philosophy.* Cambridge: Cambridge University Press, 2000.

Croce, Benedetto. Teoria e storia della storiografia. *Rassegna* 25.6 (1917), rpt. Bari: G. Laterza & Figli, 1920. Translated by Douglas Ainslie,

History: Its Theory and Practice. New York: Russell and Russell, 1960.

Deely, John. A Context for Narrative Universals, or Semiology as a *Pars Semeiotica. The American Journal of Semiotics* 4.3–4 (1986): 53–68.

– *Basics of Semiotics.* Bloomington: Indiana University Press, 1990.

– *The Human Use of Signs, or: Elements of Anthroposemiosis.* Lanham, MD: Rowman and Littlefield, 1994.

De Lauretis, Teresa. *Alice Doesn't: Feminism, Semiotics, Cinema.* Bloomington: Indiana University Press, 1984.

Deleuze, Gilles. *Cinéma 1. L'image-mouvement.* Paris: Minuit, 1983. Translated by Hugh Tomlinson and Barbara Habberjam, *Cinema 1: The Movement Image.* Minneapolis: University of Minnesota Press, 1986.

– *Cinéma 2. L'image-temps.* Paris: Minuit, 1985. Translated by Hugh Tomlinson and Robert Galeta, *Cinema 2: The Time-Image.* Minneapolis: University of Minnesota Press, 1989.

Dewey, John. Logical Method and Law. *Philosophical Review* 33 (November 1924): 560–72.

Eco, Umberto. *A Theory of Semiotics.* Bloomington: Indiana University Press, 1979.

Everaert-Desmedt, Nicole. *Interpréter l'art contemporain. La sémiotique peircienne appliquée.* Brussels: De Boeck and Larcier, series *Culture et communication,* 2006.

Frank, Jerome. *Law and the Modern Mind.* 1930. New edition New York: Coward-McCann, 1949.

Frege, Gottlob. *Begriffsschrift: eine der arithmetischen nachgebildete Formelsprache des reinen Denkens.* Halle-on-the-Saale: L. Nebert, 1879. Edited and translated by Terrell Ward Bynum, *Begriffsschrift: A Formula Language, Modeled upon That of Arithmetic, for Pure Thought,* in *Conceptual Notation and Related Articles.* Oxford: Clarendon Press, 1972.

– Über Sinn und Bedeutung. *Zeitschrift für Philosophie und philosophische Kritik* 100 (1892): 25–50. Translated as On Sense and Reference. In *Translations from the Philosophical Writings of Gottlob Frege,* ed. Peter Geach and Max Black, 56–78. New York: Philosophical Library, 1952.

Gény, François. *Méthode d'interprétation et sources en droit privé positif: essai critique.* Paris: A. Chevalier-Marescq, 1899. Translated by Jaro

Mayda, *Method of Interpretation and Sources of Private Law.* 2nd ed. St Paul, MN: West Publishing, 1963.

Green, Nicholas St John. *Essays and Notes on the Law of Tort and Crime.* Edited by Frederick Green. Menasha, WI: George Banta, 1933.

Hatten, Robert S. Music Theory and General Semiotics: A Creative Interaction. In *Hi-Fives. A Trip to Semiotics,* ed. Roberta Kevelson, 71–84. New York: Peter Lang, 1998. Expanded, revised, and translated into French as Théorie de la musique et sémiotique générale: une interaction créative. In *Questions de sémiotique,* ed. Anne Hénault, 563–83. Paris: Presses Universitaires de France, 2002.

Hempel, Carl G. The Function of General Laws in History. *The Journal of Philosophy* 39 (1942): 35–48. Rpt. in *Theories of History. Readings from Classical and Contemporary Sources,* ed. Patrick L. Gardiner, 344–56. New York: Free Press, 1959.

Holmes, Oliver Wendell, Jr. *The Common Law.* 1881. New edition, Cambridge: Belknap Press of Harvard University Press, 1963.

Jameson, Fredric. *The Prison-House of Language: A Critical Account of Structuralism and Russian Formalism.* Princeton NJ: Princeton University Press, 1972.

JohnQPublik (pseudonym). Cognitive Linguistics. Online text from the ZBB. http://www.chrisdb.me.uk/wiki/doku.php?id=cognitive_linguistics (accessed 13–14 April 2007).

Karbusicky, Vladimir. *Grundriss der musikalischen Semantik.* Darmstadt: Wissenschaftliche Buchgesellschaft, 1986.

Kevelson, Roberta. *Charles S. Peirce's Method of Methods.* Philadelphia: Benjamins, 1987.

King, Barry. On Semiotic Determinism and the Visual Sign. *The American Journal of Semiotics* 17.3 (Fall 2001): 47–68.

Kuhn, Thomas. *The Structure of Scientific Revolutions.* Chicago: University of Chicago Press, 1962; revised edition 1970.

Langlois, Charles-Victor, and Charles Seignobos. *Introduction aux études historiques.* Paris: Hachette, 1897. Translated by G.G. Berry, *Introduction to the Study of History.* New York: Holt, 1912.

Merrell, Floyd. *Semiotic Foundations: Steps toward*

an Epistemology of Written Texts. Bloomington: Indiana University Press, 1982.

– Of Position Papers, Paradigms, and Paradoxes. *Semiotica* 65.3–4 (1987): 191–223.

– *Signs Becoming Signs. Our Perfusive Pervasive Universe.* Bloomington: Indiana University Press, 1991.

Mertz, Elizabeth, and Richard Parmentier, eds. *Semiotic Mediation: Sociocultural and Psychological Perspectives.* Orlando: Academic, 1985.

Metz, Christian. *Le signifiant imaginaire.* Paris: UGE, 1977; rpt. Paris: Christian Bourgois, 1993, 2002. Translated by Celia Britton, Anwyl Williams, and Alfred Guzzett, *The Imaginary Signifier: Psychoanalysis and the Cinema.* Bloomington: Indiana University Press, 1977.

Mulvey, Laura. Visual Pleasure and Narrative Cinema (1975). Rpt. in *Feminism and Film Theory,* ed. Constance Penley, 57–68. London and New York: Routledge, 1988.

Neiva, Eduardo. An Argument against the Conventionalist Interpretation of Images. *The American Journal of Semiotics* 17.3 (Fall 2001): 69–90.

Nöth, Winfried. *Handbook of Semiotics.* Bloomington: Indiana University Press, 1995.

Peirce, Charles Sanders. *Collected Papers of Charles Sanders Peirce.* Vols. 1–6 edited by Charles Hartshorne and Paul Weiss, 1931–5, vols. 7–8 edited by Arthur W. Borks, 1958. Cambridge: Harvard University Press, rpt. 8 vols., Belknap Press, Harvard University Press, 1960. [Per convention, references are to the publication or composition date of the piece, when available, then to the volume and paragraph number.]

– *The Philosophy of Peirce: Selected Writings.* Edited by Justus Buchler. London: Routledge and Kegan Paul, 1956.

– *Writings of Charles S. Peirce: A Chronological Edition.* Edited by Max Frisch, Christian Kloesel, and the Peirce Edition Project. 6 vols. to date. Bloomington: Indiana University Press, 1982–.

– *The Essential Peirce. Selected Philosophical Writings.* Volume 1 (1867–1893) and Volume 2 (1893–1913). Edited by Nathan Houser and Christian Kloesel. Bloomington and Indianapolis: Indiana University Press, 1992, 1998.

Peirce, Charles Sanders, and Victoria Welby. *Semiotics and Significs: The Correspondence between Charles S. Peirce and Victoria Lady Welby.* Edited by Charles S. Hardwick. Bloomington: Indiana University Press, 1977.

Pencak, William. *History, Signing In: Essays in History and Semiotics.* New York: Peter Lang, 1993.

Popper, Karl. *Objective Knowledge: An Evolutionary Approach.* Oxford: Clarendon Press, 1972.

Ranke, Leopold von. *Geschichten der romanischen und germanischen Völker von 1494 bis 1535.* Leipzig and Berlin: Bey G. Reimer, 1824. Introduction edited and translated by Roger Wines in L. von Ranke, *The Secret of World History: Selected Writings on the Art and Science of History,* 55–9. New York: Fordham University Press, 1981.

Russell, Bertrand. *Logic and Knowledge: Essays, 1901–1950.* Edited by Robert Charles Marsh. New York: Capricorn Books, 1956, 1971.

Russo, Elena. *Skeptical Selves. Empiricism and Modernity in the French Novel.* Stanford, CA: Stanford University Press, 1996.

Sebeok, Thomas A. *Contributions to the Doctrine of Signs.* New edition with a preface by Brooke Williams. Lanham, MD: University Press of America, series Sources in Semiotics 4, 1985 [1st ed. 1976].

Sebeok, Thomas A. *The Sign and Its Masters.* Revised edition Lanham MD: University Press of America, 1977.

Sebeok, Thomas A., and Jean Umiker-Sebeok. *You Know My Method: A Juxtaposition of Charles S. Peirce and Sherlock Holmes.* Bloomington, IN: Gaslight, 1980.

Sless, David. *In Search of Semiotics.* Totowa, NJ: Barnes and Noble, 1986.

Smith, Iris. The Semiotics of the Theater of Cruelty. *Semiotica* 56.3–4 (1985): 291–307.

Stjernfelt, Frederik. *Diagrammatology. An Investigation on the Borderlines of Phenomenology, Ontology, and Semiotics.* New York and Berlin: Springer, Series Synthese Library no. 336, 2007.

Tarasti, Eero. *A Theory of Musical Semiotics.* Bloomington: Indiana University Press, 1994.

Theleffsen, Thorkild. Firstness and Thirdness Displacement: Epistemology of Peirce's Sign Trichotomies. *Applied Semiotics / Sémiotique appliqué* 10 (2000). http://www.chass.utoronto.ca/french/as-sa/ASSA-No10/No10-A2.html (accessed 8 January 2009).

Toews, John E. Intellectual History after the Linguistic Turn. The Autonomy of Meaning and the Irreducibility of Experience. *American Historical Review* 82.4 (1987): 879–907.

Whitehead, Alfred North, and Bertrand Russell. *Principia mathematica.* New York: Cambridge University Press, 1910.

Wiley, Norbert. *The Semiotic Self.* Chicago: University of Chicago Press, 1994.

Williams, Brooke. History and Semiotics in the 1990s. In *History and Semiotics,* ed. Brooke Williams and William Pencak, special issue of *Semiotica* 83.3–4 (1991): 385–417.

Williams, Brooke. What Has History to Do with Semiotics? *Semiotica* 54.3–4 (1985): 267–333.

Winckelmann, Jean-Joachim. *Geschichte der Kunst des Alterthums.* 2 vols. Dresden, 1764.

PHENOMENOLOGY

[See also: *Behaviourism; Cognitivism*]

Phenomenology is an approach to the study of cognition as influenced by experience, and has been adopted by various schools of psychology and communication science. It was originally developed by the German philosopher Edmund Husserl in the early 1900s, to emphasize the importance of conscious experience in the development of cognitive and perceptual categories. Husserl wanted to understand how consciousness – awareness of sensations and emotions – works in order to better understand how experience shapes the human brain.

Phenomenologists define experiential *phenomena*, and the processes involved in consciousness, such as perception and desiring, as *acts*. The intrinsic relationship between phenomena and conscious acts is called *intentionality*. Phenomenologists maintain that past experiences limit people's ability to understand phenomena, providing them with presuppositions that restrict the range of understanding. One way to counteract this is through 'fantasy variations,' that is, by imagining how the same experience would change under

varying circumstances. The features of the experience that remain constant, despite the variations, are seen to constitute its essence. Famous phenomenologists include the French psychologist Maurice Merleau-Ponty (1942, 1945) and the German philosopher Martin Heidegger (1967). Both argued that phenomenology should not be limited to an analysis of consciousness. Phenomenology has had an impact on the study of intentionality across several disciplines, emphasizing the role of the subject in acts of consciousness. Phenomenology has made it clear that humans are not machines and, thus, that they cannot be studied as 'units' in a random population.

Marcel Danesi

Bibliography

Heidegger, Martin. *Phaenomenologie und Theologie.* Frankfurt: Klostermann, 1967.

Husserl, Edmund. *Philosophie der Arithmetik.* The Hague: Nijhoff, 1890.

Lanigan, Richard L. *Speaking and Semiology: Maurice Merleau-Ponty's Phenomenological Theory of Existential Communication.* The Hague: Mouton, 1972.

Merleau-Ponty, Maurice. *La structure du comportement.* Paris: Presses Universitaires de France, 1942.

– *Phénomenologie de la perception.* Paris: Gallimard, 1945.

PHOTOGRAPHY

[See also: *Cinema; Cinema, History of*]

Photography is the art and science of taking photographs. The ancient Greek philosopher Aristotle discovered that when light is passed through a small hole an upside-down image of an object would result. This discovery was not used to construct a camera until about the sixteenth century, when the first crude camera, called a *camera obscura* (dark chamber), was made in Italy. It consisted of a huge box with a tiny opening in one side that allowed light to pass through. On the opposite side, the light formed an inverted image. The camera obscura was large enough for a person to go in it. Thus, it was used chiefly by artists as a sketching aid.

A camera obscura could only project images onto a surface. In 1727, a German physicist named Johann H. Schulze discovered silver salts, which turned dark when exposed to light. Shortly thereafter, Swedish chemist Carl Scheele discovered that the changes in the salts caused by light could be rendered permanent by chemical treatment. In 1826 French inventor Joseph Nicéphore Niepce (1765–1833) found a way to produce a permanent image in the camera obscura device – a view from Niepce's window, which is the world's first photograph. In 1831 the French painter Louis Daguerre (1789–1851) succeeded in developing the first positive image. In 1889, the American entrepreneur George Eastman (1854–1932) manufactured the first camera for public use.

One of the most important technical advances in photography was the instant processing of film. The instant camera was introduced in 1947, becoming popular throughout the world. The original camera was large and expensive. But by the 1990s, instant cameras were hand-sized, and many studio cameras could be adapted for instant photography by means of specific kinds of attachments.

During the 1950s, new manufacturing processes increased the speed, or light sensitivity, of both black and white and colour film. In the same decade, electronic devices called light amplifiers, which intensify dim illumination, made possible the photographing of even the faint light of distant stars. Such technological advances made both amateur and professional photography a reality. Today, digital cameras, which were introduced in the early 1990s, can produce images instantly. They have a light-sensitive mechanism called a 'charge-coupled device' (CCD). The lens focuses light on the device, which changes it into electronic signals. The images can thus be viewed immediately on cameras equipped with a liquid crystal display (LCD) screen.

Photography became an art form from the time it first came onto the scene. From the 1860s through the 1890s it was seen as an alternative to painting, permitting greater representational fidelity. It was viewed, in other words, as a kind of shortcut to traditional visual artistic representation. For instance, Swedish photographer Oscar Gustave Rejlander (1813–75) and English photographer Henry Peach Robinson (1834–1901) attempted to reproduce painting forms with their cameras. In the same period, Robinson) pioneered the method of creating one print from several different negatives. Portraits made by Julia Margaret Cameron (1815–79) were designed to emulate the painting styles of her era. English-American photographer Eadweard Muybridge (1830–1904) captured images of animals and people in motion. Like painters, these early photographic artists made a selection of what was to be photographed and how it was to be photographed. This could be planned ahead of time or carried out on the spot. They manipulated lighting, focus, and camera angles to alter the appearance of the image. Developing and printing processes could be modified as well to produce desired results, or else the photograph could be combined with other media to produce a composite art text.

The use of photography as a substitute for the visual arts was challenged early on by English photographer Peter Henry Emerson (1856–1936), who saw photography as an art unto itself. In 1902, American photographer Alfred Stieglitz (1864-1946) put into practice Emerson's views. He founded the Photo-Secession movement, which heralded photography as an autonomous art form. Stieglitz organized important photo exhibitions at his gallery, 291, in New York City. László Moholy-Nagy (1895–1946) in Hungary and Man Ray (1890–1976) in the United States used photography to capture absurd events, like the Dada movement. In the 1930s, several California photographers formed the Group f/64 (f/64 is the lens aperture that gives great depth of field), whose goal it was to produce realistic images of natural objects, people, and landscapes. In the 1950s a tendency toward subjectivity characterized the work of Americans Minor White (1908–76) and Aaron Siskind (1903–91). Beginning in the 1960s the making of composite prints, retouching, and painting over photographs became common. The best-known exemplar of this style is William Wegman (b. 1943).

Photography today is both an art form and a tool in media and science. Major art museums hold regular exhibitions of photographs. Among outstanding art photographers are Donald McCullin of Britain and Lee Friedlander of the United States, whose photography is intended to document the social life of their countries. Another 're-alistic photographer' worthy of mention is Harry Callahan of the United States, whose photos include detailed, sharply focused images that are the equivalents of expressionist paintings. The American photographer Jerry Uelsmann also uses photography as a 'surrealist art form,' producing dreamlike photos by combining several negatives into a single print. Eileen Cowin, another American photographer, portrays her own family life, suggesting a type of ongoing soap opera in the routines of modern-day life.

The four most common uses of photography today, outside of the artistic domain, are: commercial photography, portraiture, photojournalism, and scientific photography. Commercial photographers take photos (of food, clothing, and so on) for ads or illustrations that appear in magazines and other publications. Portrait photographers take photos of people (fashion models, celebrities) and of special events in the lives of people (weddings, graduations, and so on). Photojournalists take photos for newspapers or magazines, providing visual text for reports. Scientific photography includes forensic, medical, and engineering uses of photography. Forensic photographers take pictures of crime scenes so that details that might be missed by the naked eye can be gleaned by observing the photos. Medical photos provide visual information used by physicians to detect and treat illnesses. Medical photographers may use such equipment as microscopes, X-ray machines, and scanning machines. Engineering photos allow engineers to make more accurate designs of structural materials.

Angela Palangi

Bibliography

Dubois, Philippe. *L'acte photographique.* Brussels: Labor, 1988.

Rosenblum, Naomi. *A World History of Photography.* New York: Abbeville Press, 1997.

PICTOGRAPHY

[See also: *Alphabets; Communication; Writing*]

The word *pictography* is a compound word that derives from the Latin *pictus* (the past participle of the verb *pingere* 'to paint') and the Greek verb *graphein* 'to write.' Thus, the word pictography means to write through painting. A pictograph, sometimes called a pictogram, is a visual representation of an object or a word that represents that object. These icons are images that resemble their referent. Historically, visual symbols have been associated with various writing systems, including the Sumerian cuneiform writing with its partial pictographic and partial symbolic forms, or the Egyptian hieroglyphic system with an admixture of ideograms which are visual representations of objects, and phonograms or representations of sounds. Pictography has sometimes been labelled as idea writing.

The literal meaning of pictograph, 'to write with painting,' corresponds to its historical development. More precisely, in the nineteenth century in the small Spanish town of Altamira, in 1879, an amateur archaeologist and his young daughter discovered a cave that contains primitive graphic depictions of bison, boars, horses, and some anthropomorphic figures etched in stone with charcoal about 15,000 years ago. Likewise, a cave in southern France in the town of Lascaux contains similar prehistoric sketches that date from 13,000 BCE. These cave paintings represent a one-to-one correspondence with the animals in that locale and, occasionally, the inhabitants. These prehistoric drawings may be considered to be among the earliest manifestations of the pictogram.

Around 3200 BCE, the Sumerians, who inhabited the southern Mesopotamia region, developed a writing system in which the wedge-shaped strokes were combined to represent the form of the object to which they refer, for example, bird, fish, head, plow, and so forth. The development of writing systems slowly evolved from pictographs to more sophisticated procedures that included ideograms, or ideographs, that is, symbols that represent meaning without pronunciation, logograms or logographs, symbols that correspond exactly to real words without an indication of their pronunciation, and, finally, alphabets, which represent the sounds of a language.

The use of visual symbols to represent various verbal meanings became common in the twentieth century, even though such icons had existed for millennia. Four contemporary examples of pictographs include traffic signs and symbols, emoticons, logos, and comic strips.

Traffic Signs

The mass production and proliferation of the automobile in the early twentieth century led to the development of traffic signs, graphic depictions of traffic regulations meant to indicate visually what a driver must do in certain circumstances. These sign shapes include: (1) octagon (eight sides) for 'stop'; (2) inverted triangle for 'yield'; (3) circle for 'railroad crossing,' and so forth. Moreover, these signs have colour codes associated with them – for example,

red means that a driver must obey certain rules ('STOP,' 'do not enter'); yellow is a warning ('ICE'), while green indicates directions and distances. Many of these traffic pictograms are uniform throughout the United States so that drivers may recognize instantly the traffic regulation or warning specified.

Emoticons

The word *emoticon* derives from the combination of the words 'emotion' and 'icon' (*emot* + *icon*). Emoticons are formed by the juxtaposition or combination of symbols found on computer keyboards to represent emotional states, people, animals, or objects as did the primitive pictographs. Scott Fahlman, a professor at Carnegie Mellon University in Pittsburgh, is credited with popularizing the emoticon. These forms are now a staple of the electronic media and the ubiquitous email. Table 1 illustrates selected examples of emoticons that indicate a psychological state and a concept or object in the real world.

Table 1

Emoticon	Meaning
:)	Smile
: (	Frown
>:o)	Devil
_/	Glass

Logos

Companies devote a great deal of time and effort to the development of a brand name to provide a unique identity for a product or service so that it will have instant visual recognition. Many company *logos* – an abbreviation of the word logotype (derived from the Greek word *logos*, 'word') – are immediately recognizable without an identifying name. Examples are the 'swoosh' of Nike (a sort of stylized check mark), the golden arches of McDonald's, and the multicoloured apple (with a bite missing from the right side) of Apple. Such brand identification requires no text, but only the icon, to identify the brand name and its product.

Comic Strips

Comic strips may be single panels or a series of panels of sequential art that appear in daily and Sunday newspapers. These popular pictographs most often contain a mixture of text and drawings. Some feature action-adventure, while others contain humour. A few newspaper comic strips are 'speechless'; that is, none of the characters ever speaks. Typical of this type of strip was the humorous *Henry*, created by Carl Anderson (1865–1948) in 1932, that features a bald youth who never talks. A more recent 'speechless' newspaper comic strip is *Lio* by Mark Tatulli, which features the sometimes dark adventures of a young boy with a vivid imagination. Both of these strips are examples of modern-day serial pictographs.

Pictographs serve various functions. First, they permit those with print illiteracy to identify certain public places by means of icons, as for example when certain urban subway systems utilize pictographic icons as a way to recognize stops. Second, they serve a safety or warning function because they allow drivers to recognize them immediately and react to specific 'rules of the road' (danger, caution, and so forth). Third, they may provide individuals with a creative outlet with electronic communication systems through the use of emoticons. Fourth, commercial logos provide instant recognition of a product or service. This sort of product identification allows the pre-literate to recognize commercial enterprises such as restaurants, amusement parks, and so forth. Visual product identification allows commercial enterprises to imprint early brand loyalty on children when a pictograph is associated with a product or service such as food or entertainment. Finally, in this same fashion, certain comic strips allow non-literate people to enjoy an adventure with serial pictographs that communicate a narrative non-verbally. Many additional types of pictographs exist in all societies.

Frank Nuessel

Bibliography

Crystal, David. *A Glossary of Netspeak and Text-speak*. Edinburgh: Edinburgh Press, 2004.
DeFrancis, John. *Visible Speech: The Diverse Oneness of Writing Systems*. Honolulu: University of Hawaii Press, 1989.
Horn, Maurice, ed. *The World Encyclopedia of Comics*. Philadelphia: Chelsea House Publishers, 1999.
Jensen, Hans. *Sign, Symbol and Script: An Account of Man's Efforts to Write*. 3rd rev. ed. New York: G.P. Putnam's Sons, 1969.

PIRACY

[See also: *Intellectual Property*]

In recent years, the word *piracy* has been used in contexts typically related to software, music, intellectual propriety, or patents. Nevertheless, it still has not completely lost its original meaning ('an act of robbery on the high seas'; Merriam-Webster Online 2009): 'old-style' pirates once terrified the seas off Africa's east coast, stopping commercial vessels and hijacking the crews.

However, in its most common contemporary meaning, piracy is the 'unauthorized copying of original works and performances which are protected under copyright or related rights,' according to the Swiss Anti-Counterfeiting and Piracy Platform. Copyright and related rights protect intellectual works such as music, verbal texts, movies, software, and inventions. The copying of these kinds of works could be authorized by the owner of the rights, with the use (mostly the selling) of licences. For instance, users of software applications, such as a text editor or a spreadsheet, are allowed to use them because the publisher gives them a licence that says under which conditions users can use and install the applications on their computers. Although this kind of piracy is a less physical and violent version of piracy on the high seas, it still constitutes theft – namely, the theft of the intellectual efforts of other people (*The Economist* 2008) and causes damage to the relevant industry in terms of loss of income. According to many associations of software, music, and movie industries, every unauthorized copy is a licence that is not sold; others do not agree, arguing that pirates would not buy it in any case for cultural, economic, or other reasons.

The problem of piracy acquired particular importance with the mass spread of digitalized information and digital devices. Years ago, when most information was not digital, illegal copying was an expensive, time-consuming activity that gave outcomes of poor quality. For instance, music was sold on physical supports such as vinyl disks or tapes, where it was analogically recorded. Unauthorized copies were usually recorded on tapes. Even with high-end devices, the copies were never of the same quality as the originals. Furthermore, every copy entailed a cost in terms of time (normal tape recorders could copy only in real time) and money (the blank tape also had a cost). When CDs and CD players hit the market, this situation did not change significantly: although music was digitally recorded and released, digital recorders were not for sale. Music piracy was not considered a major problem by the CD-manufacturing industry, although many countries enacted further laws to protect intellectual property. For the same reasons, text (book) and movie piracy has never really become a serious problem: books are still sold in analogical form (paper), movies on DVD are digitalized, and the current technology does not allow an easy way to copy them.

The spread of digital information (mainly software and music) changed this situation drastically. The copying of digitalized information is fast and cheap, with the copy and original having the exact same quality. Moreover, it does not require any physical support, since it can be carried out over computer networks (including the internet), and needs only minimal support devices, such as a USB key to transfer files from one digital device to another. Such piracy is fast becoming a major infringement problem. According to some estimates, 90 per cent of installed copies of Windows operating systems in some emerging markets are pirated; unofficially, Microsoft admits that 'tolerating piracy of its products has given it huge market share and will boost revenues in the long term, because users stick with Microsoft's products when they go legit' (*The Economist* 2008).

Marco Faré

Bibliography

Economist. Piracy: Look for the Silver Lining. *The Economist*, 19 July 2008 23. http://www.economist.com/opinion/displaystory.cfm?story_id=11750492, (accessed 23 January 2009).

Gay, Joshua, ed. *Free Software Free Society: Selected Essays of Richard M. Stallman.* Boston: GNU Press, 2002. http://www.gnu.org/philosophy/words-to-avoid.html#Piracy (accessed 23 January 2009).

Hunt, Ken. Don't Fear the Pirates. GlobeandMail.com (2007). http://www.theglobeandmail.com/servlet/story/RTGAM.20071127.wtq-1107pirates/BNStory/GlobeTQ/?pageRequested=all (accessed 23 January 2009).

Merriam-Webster Online. http://www.merriam-webster.com/dictionary/piracy (accessed 23 January 2009).

SIIA (Software and Information Industry Association). *What Is Piracy?* (2009) http://www.siia.net/piracy/whatis.asp (accessed 23 January 2009).

Swiss Anti-Counterfeiting and Piracy Platform. What Is Counterfeiting and Piracy? http://www.stop-piracy.ch/en/candp/cap10.shtm, 2009 (accessed 23 January 2009).

PODCASTING

[See also: *Internet; Online Culture*]

A podcast is an audio file containing information and music which is available for downloading through the internet on media players or devices. Podcasts are generally pre-recorded, or, in some cases, can be streamed 'live.' The word *podcast* is an amalgam of 'broadcast,' the distribution of audio information, and 'iPod,' a portable image, video, and music player produced by Apple Inc. While podcasts may seem similar to regular radio shows, podcasts can be conveniently downloaded at any time, and users often subscribe to their preferred podcasts at the iTunes Store (Apple's online shopping facility which sells music, games, and podcasts). Once the podcast has been recorded, the show is then distributed through RSS – Really Simple Syndication – to the iTunes Music Store Podcast Directory or individual websites. The podcast is then available for downloading or subscription, by which one can receive alerts of programming automatically.

The theory of podcasting, as a framework for automatic downloading and synchronization, began in 2001 with Adam Curry, a former employee of the youth-targeted Music Television (MTV) network, and Dave Winer, the developer of RSS (Really Simple Syndication, which allows for updates to be quickly put on the internet). With the 'Daily Source Code' podcast, listeners were made aware that they could create and host their own radio shows. As a result, podcasting soared. Podcasts specific to certain niche audiences were posted for downloading on popular blogs, and soon blogs became pivotal in the popularization of podcasting.

While podcasting has become popular mainly as a vehicle for broadcasting programming and informational text of all kinds, it also has practical applications. Many podcasts are being made by the business world, given that podcasting is a cheap medium for delivering advertising in a seemingly personalized fashion. School materials are now also being delivered as podcasts, allowing students to download recorded lessons and exercise materials. Podcasts of language lessons, museum tours, and conference meeting minutes are now also part of the podcasting galaxy, one that promises to expand and thus characterize the future of all kinds of broadcasting.

Mariana Bockarova

Bibliography

Geoghegan, Michael, and Dan Klass. *Podcast Solutions*. Berkeley, CA: Apress, 2005.

Watson, Stephanie. How Podcasting Works. How Stuff Works. http://computer.howstuffworks.com/podcasting1.htm (accessed 23 December 2008).

POPULAR CULTURE

[See also: *Frankfurt School*]

Popular culture, as well as being sustained by media and communications, has many different sources and definitions. Popular culture is commonly thought to consist of the texts found in television, films, the internet, radio, books, magazines, and all media that reach a great many people. Yet the varied definitions of popular culture suggest that it is more than what is disseminated by media.

One prevalent definition suggests that popular culture is, simply, a form of everyday life culture. This broad view, taken to a sociological limit, includes such practices as washing and cooking, which are not necessarily implicated with media. Another view of popular culture, which has been particularly influential with respect to media and communications, is its association with an urban existence and capitalism, especially the latter's complicity in a 'culture industry' as an opiate for the populace. This view is usually associated with (a caricature of) the Frankfurt School, yet the metropolitan aspect of the definition is certainly not denigrated by all (see, for example, Chambers 1986). Yet another view sees popular culture as an outgrowth of pre-capitalist practices. In the days before the nineteenth century, such practices were generally untrammelled by capitalism. The largely disorganized holiday football matches in rural British communities are an example of this. So, too, are pastimes such as fishing and hunting. Yet, these are unaffected by media, too. Nevertheless, the culture of pastimes is important for post–Frankfurt School arguments in which it might be argued that contemporary popular culture is a debased version of pre-capitalist pastimes as much as it is a continuation of the traditions that prevailed before capitalism.

For the Frankfurt School and for others, popular culture is also defined by the extent to which it is opposed to high culture. This has more than one sense, however: the popular is opposed to the high brow in that it is different and sometimes supposedly inferior; yet what is popular is also opposed to high culture in that it is deliberately antagonistic. The latter sense is synonymous with 'populism,' which itself has its own subdivisions (positive: identification with the common people and their culture; opportunistic: siding with the common people for cynical purposes). There is a general belief that the barriers that were maintained between high and low culture during the period of capitalism and mass society were dismantled or at least eroded with the onset of postmodernism (Huyssen 1987).

Where oppositional forces are concerned, it has become clear, partly through sociological investigation, that mainstream culture (which might include popular culture at various moments) as well as elite culture frequently have to bow to internal and external demands. In the second part of the twentieth century, it became increasingly evident that diversity within Western culture was one factor in producing 'subcultures.' 'Subcultures' are generally thought to consist of communities of people who come together to pursue practices and observe (sometimes recently developed) customs that are somehow divorced from or in opposition to 'mainstream culture.' The relation of 'subcultures' to culture in general is problematic insofar as it involves a putative separation of one from the other but also involves a kind of symbiosis in which mainstream culture may attempt to co-opt subculture (often in an ultimately elitist fashion), while subcultures may force mainstream culture to accept subcultures or to transform by way of the naturalization of specially developed subcultural vocabulary, expression, styles, and other forms of communication.

Frequently, though not exclusively, 'subcultures' have been associated with youth tastes and pastimes. Youth culture has therefore existed close to the core of popular culture since the former's emergence after the Second World War and has spawned a massive industry of youth media (see Osgerby 2004). For those critical of youth culture, it is self-evident that its pivotal role in popular culture is simply a part of the capitalist process of targeting a specific audience (the much-vaunted sixteen to twenty-five age group) in order to sell goods and services. For those who celebrate it, youth culture is sometimes opposed to popular culture (viewed as the mainstream, 'the man,' parents, and the older generation) and at other times is seen as its vanguard (for example, the spread of popular dissent in the West in the 1960s). For yet another critical perspective, youth culture, as a key part of popular culture, has been constantly co-opted and incorporated by capitalism to reinvigorate the mainstream (see Danesi 2003).

What cannot be denied is that a phenomenon as diverse as popular culture cannot be reduced to simple definitions or pleas to arguments such as 'the lowest common denominator.' On the contrary, popular culture must negotiate a set of complex ideological, cultural, and economic relationships in order to sustain itself and in order to make the category of the 'popular' meaningful. Popular culture cannot simply be any media output that is considered to have a substantial base of adherents. Arguably, pornography and classical music have very strong followings in contemporary Western society, although, for a number of reasons, they are seldom considered in discussions of popular culture.

Paul Cobley

Bibliography

Chambers, Iain. *Popular Culture: The Metropolitan Experience.* London: Methuen, 1986.

Danesi, Marcel. *Forever Young: The Teen-aging of Modern Culture.* Toronto: University of Toronto Press, 2003.

Huyssen, Andreas. *After the Great Divide: Modernism, Mass Culture, Postmodernism.* London: Macmillan, 1987.

Osgerby, Bill. *Youth Media.* London: Routledge, 2004.

PORNOGRAPHY

[See also: *Censorship; Freedom of Speech*]

Pornography, or porn, is the representation of sexual behaviour that is intended to sexually excite audiences. A distinction is commonly made between pornography and erotica. The objective of the former is the graphic depiction of sexual activities with no further purpose than that, while erotica is sexual representation that uses explicit imagery for narrative or aesthetic purposes. The word pornography is derived from the Greek words *porni* ('prostitute') and *graphein* ('to write'), and was originally defined as any work of art or literature that depicted the life of prostitutes. Pornography can be used in any medium – in books, drawings, animation, sculpture, painting, film, and so on. Excluded from the purview of pornography are live sexual acts, such as stripteases.

Defining what is pornographic or erotic is a delicate and difficult issue. Are the ancient statuettes of naked women por-

nographic or erotic? Are the Greek and Roman nude sculptures and intaglios similarly pornographic or erotic? In the area of narrative, are the plays of fifteenth-century Pietro Aretino pornographic (as many claimed they were), or the novel *Lady Chatterley's Lover* by D.H. Lawrence? Most countries have taken a legal approach to pornography. For example, in the United States, the so-called Comstock law, which prohibited the mailing of indecent materials, was passed in 1873 (named for Anthony Comstock, a crusading reformer against sexual depictions of any kind). The law was used to set up a system of censorship by postal officials without going to court. If they decided a book, picture, or other item was indecent, they seized it and refused to deliver it. Since the mid-1900s, the U.S. Supreme Court has narrowed the legal definition of pornography, basing it on the First Amendment to the Constitution, thus placing constitutional limits on censorship. Ironically, the Comstock law is still in force, although the U.S. Postal Service almost never uses the law to seize mail.

The terms *obscenity* and *pornography* are often used interchangeably. Both have been used to claim that they can corrupt public morals. Most American states have laws against selling obscene materials. There are also federal laws against the interstate sale of obscene materials or its transmission on radio or television. But such laws have always been hard to enforce, mainly because it is difficult to determine what is obscene or pornographic according to law. Congress actually passed the first federal law against obscenity as part of the Tariff Act of 1842. In the 1957 case of *Roth versus the United States*, the Supreme Court ruled that freedom of speech and the First Amendment were important aspects of the whole controversy and thus that only those materials that a court had determined to be legally obscene could be seized. But the Supreme Court provided loose guidelines for defining obscene material. In the 1973 case of *Miller versus California*, it held that material could be considered legally obscene only if:

(1) contemporary community standards would find that the material appeals only to prurient (sexually arousing) interests;
(2) the material is demonstrably offensive;
(3) the material lacks serious literary, artistic, political, or scientific value.

In the 1974 case of *Jenkins versus Georgia*, the Supreme Court unanimously determined that local standards play a limited role in assessing what is obscene. A national Commission on Obscenity and Pornography had reported in 1970 that there was no reliable evidence that pornography caused crime or violence against women. The commission recommended repeal of all anti-pornography laws for consenting adults. It also recommended that each state adopt laws to protect young people. In 1986, however, another Commission on Pornography determined that there was a correlation between sexually violent or degrading materials and the amount of sexual violence in society. Today, the only truly strictly controlled form of pornography involves children. Child pornography laws exist throughout the world.

With the advent of the internet, adult pornography has proliferated. Early studies of internet porn have supported the 1970 commission's findings – namely that pornography is self-contained and does not lead to derivative behaviours, despite continuing attempts by some to argue to the contrary with their own set of facts and arguments (see, for example, Sarracino and Scott 2008). Some feminist critics even see pornography as liberating common women from the patriarchal view of them as homely and non-sexual beings. They see it as a subversive form of representation and, thus, as a crucial part of the ongoing sexual revolution in women's liberation (Phoca and Wright 1999; Smith 2007; Sabo 2009). As an extreme form of sexual explicitness, pornography has in fact influenced sexual mores since the 1970s, being seen by religious leaders as a serious threat to the political and social order. The subtext

in these attacks, however, seems to be that women appear to accept it as much as men, contrary to what patriarchal models have embodied in the past. The same kind of blatant sexual style has become common, spreading among musical and video artists. Pornography for some is a form of social criticism against authoritarianism, albeit much less so in the age of the internet, with women themselves becoming more and more the producers and distributors of porn. It would appear that those who take pornography seriously are its opponents.

The spread of pornography to the online medium and its proliferation there seem to herald the fact that it has evolved simply into an erotic genre of representation. In fact, there has been a significant decline in visits to pornographic websites recently, due, in all probability, to the fact that pornography no longer has a deep emotional hold on people living in a largely secular world and, perhaps, because there are new and more participatory ways of seeking online sex. As Tancer (2008: 26) aptly observes: 'Who needs porn when Facebook gives you the opportunity to hook up in the flesh?' And as Harkin (2009: 109) observes, referring to a recent survey, young people today have migrated away from traditional pornographic art to 'a vast virtual menagerie full of ordinary people exposing themselves either for their lover or everyone else to see.'

Angela Palangi

Bibliography

Dennis, Donna. *Licentious Gotham: Erotic Publishing and Its Prosecution in Nineteenth Century New York.* Cambridge, MA: Harvard University Press, 2009.

Fraterrigo, Elizabeth. *Playboy and the Making of the Good Life in America.* Oxford: Oxford University Press, 2009.

Harkin, James. *Lost in Cyburbia: How Life on the Net Has Created a Life of Its Own.* Toronto: Knopf, 2009.

Long, Kat. *The Forbidden Apple: A Century of Sex*

and Sin in New York City. New York: Ig Publishing, 2009.

Phoca, Sophia, and Rebecca Wright. *Introducing Postfeminism.* Cambridge: Icon, 1999.

Sabo, Anne G. Highbrow and Lowbrow Pornography: Prejudice Prevails against Popular Culture: A Case Study. *Journal of Popular Culture* 42 (2009): 147–61.

Sarracino, Carmine, and Kevin M. Scott. *The Porning of America: The Rise of Porn Culture, What It Means, and Where We Go from Here.* New York: Beacon, 2008.

Smith, Clarissa. *One for the Girls! The Pleasures and Practices of Reading Women's Porn.* Chicago: University of Chicago Press, 2007.

Tancer, Bill. *Click.* New York: Hyperion, 2008.

POST-HUMANISM

[See also: *Cyberculture; Cyberspace; Postmodernism; Post-Structuralism*]

The term *post-humanism* is used broadly to refer to an era in which humans no longer dominate the world but instead have merged with their machines and with animals to create a new world order that puts humans not at the centre of the world but as equal partners with other intelligences (artificial and animal). It now has five generally accepted meanings:

- Post-humanism is a philosophy in opposition to traditional humanism, or the view that humans are makers of their own world, not subject to external metaphysical forces, and thus at the centre of the universe. In post-humanism, humans are just small organic particles in the overall scheme of things.
- Post-humanism shows the need for modern humans to move beyond archaic concepts of human nature and to establish a society that includes other species and machines.
- Post-humanism is a reaction to the world of virtual communications in cyberspace, where relations between humans can unfold totally in such a space. Therefore,

a new definition of reality is required.

- Post-humanism is a philosophical movement aiming to obliterate all traditional distinctions through technology – for example, eliminating age-based differences through cosmetic and medical anti-aging technologies.
- Post-humanism is a critical strain of philosophy aiming to attack all traditional notions of religiosity and spirituality.

Post-humanism is often equated with both postmodernism and post-stucturalism, which are now viewed as complementary theoretical stances. Post-humanism is also embraced by ecologists and environmentalists as a philosophy that aims to counteract the destruction of nature by economic forces.

Marcel Danesi

Bibliography

Bell, David. *Cyberculture Theorists: Manuel Castells and Donna Haraway.* London: Routledge, 2007.

Benedikt, Michael. *Cyberspace: First Steps.* Cambridge, MA: MIT Press, 1991.

Gibson, William. *Neuromancer.* London: Grafton, 1984.

Haraway, Donna. *Simians, Cyborgs and Women: The Reinvention of Nature.* London: Routledge, 1991.

POSTMAN, NEIL (1931–2003)

[See also: *Media Effects*]

Neil Postman was an American media critic, author, and professor. He is best known for his arguments about the dangers of the entertainment industry in education and his insistence that the efficiency and rapidity that come from technology cannot be substituted for human values.

Postman was born and raised in New York City. After receiving his bachelor of science degree in 1953 from the State University of New York at Fredonia, he went on to earn his MA and EdD (in 1958) from Columbia University. One year later, he began working as an English teacher-educator at NYU, writing books on educational reform, including *Television and the Teaching of English* (1961), *The Uses of Language* (1962), *Language and Reality* (1967), *Teaching as a Subversive Activity* (1969), co-authored with Charles Weingartner, and *Teaching as a Conserving Activity* (1979). He remained a faculty member at NYU for thirty-nine years. In 1971, Postman founded NYU's Steinhardt School of Education's program in Media Ecology and was chair of the Department of Culture and Communication until 2002. In 1986, Postman was given the George Orwell Award for Clarity in Language by the National Council of Teachers of English, as well as the Christian Lindback Award for excellence in teaching. In 1988, he was given NYU's Distinguished Teacher Award and by 1993, Postman was appointed a University Professor at NYU, an honour held by only sixteen others. In 1998, he was named the Paulette Goddard Professor of Media Ecology. Postman wrote twenty books and over two hundred articles for various reviews such as *New York Times Magazine*, the *Atlantic*, the *Saturday Review*, the *Washington Post*, the *Los Angeles Times*, and *Le Monde*.

Postman, who often worked with, and was inspired by, Marshall McLuhan, was perhaps best known for his book *Amusing Ourselves to Death: Public Discourse in the Age of Show Business* (1985). In this book, he compares George Orwell's vision of the future with Aldous Huxley's. Orwell offered his vision in his novel *Nineteen Eighty-Four*, in which a society's individual rights were seized by an authoritarian government, while Huxley wrote about his particular vision in *Brave New World*, where society would end up medicating people with 'soma,' after which they gladly exchanged their rights for entertainment. Explaining that 'form excludes the content,' which means that a certain medium can only present a limited number of ideas, Postman feared that certain media would become

society's 'soma,' and that everything of any importance would be devalued to a commodity of entertainment through the media. He altered McLuhan's phrase 'the medium is the message' to 'the medium is the metaphor,' insisting that the nature and effects of the information presented will differ according to medium. Postman pointed out that reading requires intense intellectual involvement, whereas the same story told on television involves only passive processing of content. Politically, the eighteenth century, or the Age of Reason, was based on the power of the written word. Language had great value and the achievements of American presidents, for instance, were often assessed in terms of the kind of language they used. Today, visual media dominate, and these transform political discourse into entertainment, making arguments that would once have been appraised as meaningful now seem insignificant. The 'visual image' is all that seems to count, not the content of the discourse. *Amusing Ourselves to Death* has been translated into eight languages and has sold over 200,000 copies worldwide.

Postman was particularly concerned with children's upbringing in a media-saturated world. In *The Disappearance of Childhood* (1994), he explains how childhood developed throughout history; while children were once seen as small adults, the Enlightenment brought broader knowledge of children's issues to public light, leading gradually to today's concept of 'childhood' as a meaningful period of development. While this has led to a marked differentiation in appearance – children and adults dress, speak, and behave differently – the new media technologies have come forward to blur the boundaries of this very differentiation. Since children now have easy access to information intended for adults, the result is a diminishment of their developmental potential.

Postman put forward the concept of a 'technopoly,' a society which believes 'the primary, if not the only, goal of human labor and thought is efficiency, that technical calculation is in all respects superior to human judgment.' Postman warned of the growth of 'technophiles,' those who could not see the downside of technology and would constantly demand more innovation and therefore more information, which would itself become a form of pollution. The only way to improve the situation, as Postman saw it, would be to get students to use technology smartly by being educated in the history, social effects, and psychological biases of technology.

Postman's ideas of how media technologies shape the lives of people have become widely publicized, influencing educators, writers, and media critics.

Mariana Bockarova

Bibliography

Postman, Neil. *Amusing Ourselves to Death: Public Discourse in the Age of Show Business.* New York: Viking Penguin, 1984.
– *Technopoly: The Surrender of Culture to Technology.* New York: Alfred A. Knopf, 1992.
– *The Disappearance of Childhood.* New York: Random House, 1982/1994.
Rosen, Jay. Neil Postman: Some Recollections. PressThink, Ghost of Democracy in the Media Machine (7 October 2003). http://journalism.nyu.edu/pubzone/weblogs/pressthink/2003/10/07/postman_life.html (accessed 20 January 2009).
Saxon, Wolfgang. Neil Postman, 72, Mass Media Critic, Dies. *The New York Times* (9 October 2003). http://query.nytimes.com/gst/fullpage.html?res=9403E4D81F3CF93AA357 53C1A9659C8B63&sec=&spon=&pagewant ed=1 (accessed 18 January 2009).
Sowin, Joshua. The Neil Postman Information Page. http://www.neilpostman.org/#articles. (accessed 20 January 2009).

POSTMODERNISM

[See also: *Jameson, Fredric; Post-Structuralism*]

The term *postmodernism* means, literally, 'after modernism.' It can also mean 'moving beyond' or 'opposing' modernism. To understand what postmodernism is we must understand how it differs from modernism, the period that came before it. In 1924 the writer Virginia Woolf wrote: 'In or about December, 1910, human character changed … All human relations have shifted – those between masters and servants, husbands and wives, parents and children. And when human relationships change there is at the same time a change in religion, conduct, politics and literature' (cited in Light 2007: 23). She was discussing what we can characterize as the development of the modernist sensibility.

The term 'modern' comes from the fifth-century Latin word *modernus*, which was used by historians and others to differentiate the pagan era from the Christian era. As Bryan S. Turner explains in his book *Theories of Modernity and Postmodernity* (1990), modernism involves a rejection of history and the notion of differentiation. We can see this in modernist architecture, which tends to be stylistically pure, while postmodernist architecture often blends many different styles in a building. We can compare the modernist work of the Dutch architect Mies van der Rohe, with his 'glass curtain walls,' and the work of the postmodernist architect Philip Johnson, whose AT&T skyscraper has a Roman colonnade on the street level, a neoclassical midsection, and a Chippendale pediment on its top. This means that postmodernism involves a kind of cultural eclecticism and de-differentiation.

After 1960, postmodernism became what might be described as a 'cultural dominant.' This is the term that Fredric Jameson uses to characterize postmodernism. He argues that postmodernism is actually an advanced form of modernism and is characterized by the capitalism that flourished during that period. This is made clear in the title of his book *Postmodernism or, The Cultural Logic of Late Capitalism.* As he explains, postmodernism involves a 'break' from modernism (1991: 2):

[There is] one fundamental feature of

all the postmodernisms … namely the effacement in them of the older (essentially high-modernist) frontier between high culture and so-called mass or commercial culture … The postmodernisms have, in fact, been fascinated precisely by this whole 'degraded' landscape of schlock and kitsch, of TV series and *Reader's Digest* culture, of advertising and motels, of the late show and the grade-B Hollywood film, of so-called paraliterature, with its airport paperback categories of the gothic and the romance, the popular biography, the murder mystery, and the science fiction or fantasy novel.

Postmodernism, he adds, is the culture of figures such as Andy Warhol, Philip Glass, Thomas Pynchon, and Ishmael Reed and movements such as pop art, photorealism, and the nouveau roman.

Some theorists argue that postmodernism is not just an 'advanced' or different form of modernism but is considerably different from it in important ways and has an identity of its own. Postmodernism, these theorists assert, helps explain what has been going on in American culture and in many other cultures since approximately 1960, when the influence of modernism started fading. The argument that Virginia Woolf made about the changes brought on by modernism can also be made about postmodernism. Postmodernist theorists argue that around 1960 another important change occurred in our sensibilities, as we moved beyond modernism into a postmodern era. There are some scholars who argue that postmodernism is passé and that we now live in a post-postmodernism period, but none of them has been able to think up a suitable name for this period.

There is a considerable amount of debate about modernism and postmodernism in our universities, and some critics of postmodernism suggest it was nothing more than a fad popularized by French and continental intellectuals; defenders of postmodernism argue that postmodernist theory is necessary to explain the world we now live in. Postmodern theorists believe that postmodernism represents an important 'cultural mutation' in beliefs, attitudes, philosophies, and aesthetic sensibilities that occurred after 1960.

Postmodernism also developed around the same time as capitalism became dominant not only as an economic system, but as a culture-producing system, associated with mass consumption, which dominates fashion and shapes people's lifestyles. The Marxist concept of products as 'cultural forms' was a motivating factor in raising awareness of the power of 'forms' or 'signs' to guide social evolution. According to postmodern theorists, we now live in a world dominated by signs, by simulations, by media, and by images. As a result, our sense of reality has been undermined and our modernist attitudes about elite culture and popular culture have been discarded. In postmodernist culture the pastiche becomes a dominant mode and eclecticism rules. Jean-François Lyotard expresses this sensibility in *The Postmodern Condition: A Report on Knowledge* (1984: 76):

Eclecticism is the degree zero of contemporary general culture: one listens to reggae, watches a western, eats McDonald's food for lunch and local cuisine for dinner, wears Paris perfume in Tokyo and 'retro' clothes in Hong Kong; knowledge is a matter for TV games. It is easy to find a public for eclectic works. By becoming kitsch, art panders to the confusions which reign in the 'taste' of patrons. Artists, gallery owners, critics and the public wallow together in the 'anything goes,' and the epoch is one of slackening. But this realism of the 'anything goes' is in fact that of money; in the absence of aesthetic criteria, it remains possible and useful to assess the works of art according to the profit they yield. Such realism accommodates all tendencies, just as capital accommodates all 'needs,' providing that the tendencies and needs have purchasing power. As for taste, there is no need to be delicate when one speculates or entertains oneself.

Lyotard points out that there is, in fact, a unifying factor beneath the seeming randomness and eclecticism of postmodern culture, namely that of money. The question that arises is whether there can ever be an end to the eclecticism and experimentation in lifestyles that it reflects.

If modernism involves making distinctions between the elite arts and popular culture, postmodernism breaks down the distinctions between the elite arts and popular culture, proposing models of culture grounded in experimentation. Modernism involved an attitude of 'high seriousness' towards life, while postmodernism adopts a more playful, ironic attitude. In postmodernist societies, people 'play' with their identities, changing them when they feel bored with their old ones. Postmodernism also involves stylistic eclecticism with the pastiche as a dominating metaphor.

Unlike modernists, postmodernists believe we can never know reality, that we are always being misled by illusions, simulacra, and hyperreality, the term the French sociologist Jean Baudrillard uses for the world of images and simulations that pervade everyday life. Postmodernism is a reaction to the power of consumer culture, in contrast to what we might call the production culture of modernism. The heroes of postmodernism tend to be celebrities and entertainment figures, whose tastes and consumption habits are held up as models to us all.

The British historian Arnold Toynbee is credited with being one of the first writers to use the term *postmodern* in his multi-volume work *A Study of History*, the first volume of which appeared in 1934. The term started becoming more popular in the 1960s. Bernard Rosenberg (1957), a sociologist, used the term in an introduction he wrote to *Mass Culture*. He writes: 'First besieged with commodities, postmodern man himself becomes an interchangeable part in the whole cultural process' (1957: 4). In this passage, Rosenberg ties postmodernism to the mass media and the rise of consumer culture and suggests a process of dehumanization at work in postmodernist cultures. Rosenberg connects postmodernism with what has been called 'cultural homogenization' on a global level, which differs from the view of many postmodern theorists that it leads to the opposite, a kind of anarchic hyper-differentiation.

Charles Jencks (1977), an architect known for his postmodern buildings, sees postmodernism as inherently democratic and as a reflection of the multicultural, multi-ethnic societies in which we now live. He uses the term 'double-coding' to refer to the use of different aesthetic styles in a building. Thus, in one building you can find styles connected both to modernism and postmodernism that relate to the different socio-economic classes and ethnic groups who will use the building, groups with different levels of taste and sophistication. Postmodern architects such as Robert Venturi, Robert Stern, and Michael Graves use both popular and elitist styles in their buildings to appeal to the varying tastes of the people who see and use their buildings.

One of the most useful characterizations of postmodernism appears in Ellis Cashmore and Christ Rojek's anthology, *Dictionary of Cultural Theorists*. They suggest that the fixed and universal categories and certainty found in modernism has been replaced by an inability to accept any agreed-upon cultural boundaries or certainties in postmodernism, which has abandoned a belief in scientific rationality and all-embracing theories of truth and progress (1999: 6).

This notion is echoed by Lyotard in *The Postmodern Condition* (1984: xxiv):

> Simplifying to the extreme, I define *postmodern* as incredulity toward metanarratives. This incredulity is undoubtedly a product of progress in the sciences: but that progress in turn presupposes it. To the obsolescence of the metanarrative apparatus of legitimation corresponds, most notably, the crisis of metaphysical

philosophy and of the university institution which in the past relied on it. The narrative function is losing its functors, its great hero, its great dangers, its great voyages, its great goal.

According to Lyotard, we no longer have faith in the great, all-encompassing, narratives or systems of thought (as manifested in philosophy, political ideologies, and religions) that have provided us with ways of behaving and apprehending the world. In a postmodern world, many different narratives are fighting for our acceptance, and this has led to a crisis of legitimation. Whose ideas are correct? How do we distinguish between right and wrong? Our incredulity toward these metanarratives has made it difficult to answer these questions.

Postmodernism may seem, at first sight, to be relativistic but that assessment may not be correct. That is one of the controversies about postmodernism. Many postmodernist theorists argue that just because it is not correct to accept one 'universal' standard does not mean there are no standards at all. Postmodernists may not believe in metanarratives but that does not mean they do not believe in any narratives. The question then arises – how does one decide which narratives are valid?

Friedrich Nietzsche faced this problem in his book *The Will to Power*. In this book he wrote that he had an aversion to any 'one total view of the world.' He added that there are only interpretations, not facts. This notion is basic to postmodern thought, which argues that there are 'countless meanings' or ways of looking at things, which is what Nietzsche called 'perspectivism.' The more perspectives you have on something, he suggested, the closer you get to apprehending it as it really is.

Postmodernism raises the question of whether we can establish just societies without universally accepted beliefs in notions such as equality, democracy, and the rule of law. Many postmodernist theorists, with their focus on cultural phenomena,

do not answer such questions, but it is inherent in the logic of postmodernist thought that just and democratic societies can coexist with postmodernist culture. For example, the United States and Japan are often held up as exemplars of postmodern democratic societies.

Some theorists argue that there are two kinds of postmodernism – 'conservative' and 'critical' postmodernism. Conservative postmodernist thought tends towards relativism and an 'anything goes' attitude, while critical postmodernist thought attempts to deal with the limitations and the failures of modernism and to find ways of creating societies that are more just and democratic.

A Google search for 'modernism' will yield 9,370,000 websites that deal with the subject. A search for 'postmodernism' will turn up 5,580,000 sites. Google also offers a program called the 'postmodern essay generator' that creates different parodies of postmodernist thought each time you click on it. These parodies use the names of well-known postmodernist thinkers such as Baudrillard and Lyotard and the language of postmodernist thought, such as *simulacra*, *hyperreality*, and *eclecticism*, to ridicule the subject. They also include titles of make-believe books by make-believe authors. In addition, Google reveals that there 18,100 websites dealing with post-postmodernism.

What the Google searches reveal is that modernism and postmodernism (and, if it actually exists, post-postmodernism) remain as subjects of considerable interest, contention, conflict, and perhaps confusion, to contemporary cultural theorists. We may not be able to define postmodernism precisely or to everyone's satisfaction and we may not be able to distinguish it from modernism, but as we look around the world we live in, with its remarkable and 'strange' new buildings, with its shopping malls and its Disneylands, with films such as *Rashomon* and *Blue Velvet*, and with our media-saturated societies, we cannot help but think that whatever postmodernism may be, it certainly has led to profound changes in our societies.

Arthur Asa Berger

Bibliography

Baudrillard, Jean. *Le système des objets*. Paris: Denoel-Gonthier, 1968.
– *The Mirror of Production*. St Louis, MO: Telos Press, 1975.
– *Simulations*. New York: Semiotext(e), 1983.
Berger, Arthur Asa. *Postmortem for a Postmodernist*. Walnut Creek, CA: AltaMira Press, 1997.
– *The Postmodern Presence: Readings on Postmodernism in American Culture and Society*. Walnut Creek, CA: AltaMira Press, 1998.
– *The Portable Postmodernist*. Walnut Creek, CA: AltaMira Press, 2003.
Best, Steven, and Douglas Kellner. *Postmodern Theory: Critical Interrogations*. New York: Guilford Press, 1991.
Cashmore, Ellis, and Christ Rojek, eds. *Dictionary of Cultural Theorists*. London: Arnold, 1999.
Featherstone, Mike, ed. *Theory, Culture and Society: Special Issue on Postmodernism* 5, no. 2–3 (June). London: Sage, 1988.
– *Consumer Culture and Postmodernism*. London: Sage, 1991.
Foster, Hal, ed. *The Anti-Aesthetic: Essays on Postmodern Culture*. Port Townsend, WA: Bay Press, 1983.
Gottdiener, Mark. *Postmodern Semiotics: Material Culture and the Forms of Postmodern Life*. Oxford: Blackwell, 1995.
Jameson, Fredric. *Postmodernism, or The Cultural Logic of Late Capitalism*. Durham, NC: Duke University Press, 1991.
Jencks, Charles. *The Language of Post-Modern Architecture*. New York: Rizzoli, 1977.
Kellner, Douglas. *Jean Baudrillard: From Marxism to Postmodernism and Beyond*. Stanford, CA: Stanford University Press, 1989.
Light, Alison, *Mrs Woolf and the Servants: The Hidden Heart of Domestic Service*. London: Fig Tree, 2007.
Lyotard, Jean-François. *The Postmodern Condition: A Report on Knowledge*. Minneapolis: University of Minnesota Press, 1984.
McQuire, Scott. *Visions of Modernity*. London: Sage, 1998.
Nietzsche, Friedrich. *The Will to Power*. New York: Random House, 1987.
Rosenberg, Bernard. *Mass Culture: The Popular Arts in America*. New York: The Free Press, 1957.
Toynbee, Arnold. *A Study of History*. Oxford: Oxford Unversity Press, 1934–61.
Turner, Bryan S., ed. *Theories of Modernity and Postmodernity*. London: Sage, 1990.

POST-STRUCTURALISM

[See also: *Barthes, Roland; Deconstruction; Derrida, Jacques; Foucault, Michel; Semiotics; Structuralism*]

Post-structuralism refers to a variety of different theoretical principles (the most important models being deconstruction, semiotics, and discourse analysis) that share a similar objective, that of critiquing structuralism and, in particular, its purported universalism. Structuralism is rooted in the notion that human culture can be understood by means of identifying and interpreting the universal and unaltering structures that are reproduced in the wide variety of cultural products such as artworks, rituals, verbal language, and other vehicles of communication and culture. Ferdinand de Saussure's linguistics constitutes a major theoretical source for the principles inherent in the post-structuralist refutation of structuralism. In the *Course in General Linguistics* (1916) Saussure insisted on the arbitrary nature of the linguistic sign and proposed partitioning the sign into signifier (form) and signified (meaning). Saussure argued that language is based not so much on nomenclature and correspondence as it is in 'difference.' Precisely because the sign is arbitrary in nature, there can be no unchanging and universal pretext for communicating and understanding a given idea through a given word. Consequently, the meanings that a verbal sign produces are basically arbitrary and ensconced by convention and usage.

Jacques Derrida borrowed the Sausserean notion of linguistic difference and developed the idea of 'différance.' This term is intended to expose Saussure's concept of non-coincidence as unfounded and points to the notion of spatial and temporal differing. On this idea Derrida builds the notion that there exists nothing 'outside' a text or any other product of human culture, and that signification is structured from within a communicative system as an operation of difference. Thus, the representation constructed by any mode or variety of textuality is not a mimetic representation of the world but instead a self-representation. That in turn produces an empty image of referentiality that hides a bottomless pit of signs.

Another aspect of structuralism that Derrida critiques is what he calls the 'structurality of structure,' namely, the centre. In 'Structure, Sign and Play in the Discourse of the Human Sciences' (1966), Derrida argues that the major property attributed to the centre is to give balance and organize the overall structure. In the post-structuralist paradigm the centre is revealed as incoherent and contradictory, and constitutes a 'mythology of presence.' Thus, if there is no guarantee of a stable authority or 'centre,' and if signification is essentially arbitrary and forever in a state of flux, then, according to post-structuralism, there is no absolute foundation for evaluating the truth. Consequently, the models of knowledge rooted in the structuralist formulation of truth lack legitimacy. Moreover, the post-structuralist paradigm critiques what Derrida, following Martin Heidegger, terms 'onto-theology': that is, a manner of perceiving the world where meaning and value are posited in the transcendent nature (*onto* being) of an eternally unaltered entity or idea. As well, post-structuralism rejects 'phallogocentrism,' a mode of perceiving the world where cultural and social energies are posited in an image of abstract presence (*phallus*) and expressed in the immobile categories of reason (*logos*).

The post-structuralist paradigm was propagated by Roland Barthes, who, like Derrida, argued that verbal language is essentially an interplay of differences of signification operating within a sign-producing network. Julia Kristeva, through what she terms 'semanalysis,' seeks to direct the return of the speaking body, with its drives and impulses, into verbal language. Kristeva, who critiques the unity of the subject, follows the insights of Jacques Lacan, who theorizes about a subject who acknowledges the fact that the signifier is what governs the operations of the signified.

Michel Foucault's contribution to the post-structuralist paradigm consists of, among other things, the concepts of 'archaeology' and 'genealogy,' which could be categorized as anti-historicist paradigms of discourse analysis. They are concerned not so much with chronological order or succession, or with causality. Rather, the emphasis is on the emergence of power, as well as its role in the disjunctures that occur in discursive formations.

Paul Colilli

Bibliography

Barthes, Roland. *The Rustle of Language*. Trans. Richard Howard. Berkeley: University of California Press, 1989.

Derrida, Jacques. *Of Grammatology*. Trans. Gayatri Chakravorty Spivak. Baltimore and London: Johns Hopkins University Press, 1976.

Foucault, Michel. *The Archaeology of Knowledge and the Discourse on Language*. Trans. A.M. Sheridan Smith. New York: Pantheon, 1972.

Kristeva, Julia. *Desire in Language: A Semiotic Approach to Literature and Art*. Ed. Leon Roudiez. Trans. Tomas Gora, Alice Jardine, and Leon S. Roudiez. New York: Columbia University Press, 1980.

Lacan, Jacques. *Écrits: A Selection*. Trans. Bruce Fink. New York: Norton, 2002.

PRIMING

[See also: *Media Effects*]

The term *priming* is used in both media and psychology. In media, priming refers to the practice of bringing certain aspects of media to the forefront in order to influence public opinion. In psychology, priming occurs when exposure to a stimulus or concept leads to enhanced processing of the same or a related stimulus or concept. Although these uses of priming are based on different areas of research, they are related: priming in media is possible because underlying psychological mechanisms support such practices; these underlying mechanisms are the focus here.

Priming occurs at multiple levels of analysis, including social, semantic, lexical, and perceptual levels. Watching a frightening movie may increase the accessibility of *danger schemata* that influence how an individual interprets shadows and ambiguous noises. Reading the word 'nurse' may increase the accessibility of *medical schemata* that influence the speed with which a person recognizes the written word 'doctor.' Deciding whether the sequence of letters v-e-r-b-a-l spells an English word is accomplished faster if the word was recently displayed than if it was not, a phenomenon known as *repetition priming*.

A body of cognitive and neuroscientific evidence suggests that priming can operate outside of conscious awareness. Priming is one of two key components of the *implicit memory* system (the other is 'procedural learning,' responsible for acquisition of habits and skills). Implicit memory is especially intriguing because it can occur automatically and in the absence of conscious control, and there is abundant evidence that it is functionally and anatomically independent from *explicit memory* (conscious or declarative memory). In contrast to explicit memory, implicit memory is observed across the lifespan and across species, is largely unrelated to IQ or other measures of intellectual functioning, and is robust in the face of disorders and dysfunctions that compromise explicit memory. For example, whereas implicit memory remains fairly stable between the ages of three and eighty, performance on explicit memory tasks initially improves with age (in children), reaches a peak during adulthood, but then declines with advancing age (in the eld-

erly). Such differences in developmental trajectories imply that there are distinct systems underlying implicit and explicit memory.

Phenomena related to unconscious memory received considerable attention in studies of Freud and Janet, but implicit memory was largely overlooked within psychology in the first half of the twentieth century. During this time, experimental psychology was influenced by behaviourism (e.g., Ivan Pavlov, B.F. Skinner), a movement that urged researchers to focus on the identification of laws connecting stimulus inputs to behavioural outputs without reference to internal processes. Research on memory expanded as behaviourism was gradually superseded by the 'cognitive revolution,' but unconscious forms of memory were late to become part of mainstream research.

Initially, researchers drew inferences about memory by examining responses to tasks such as free recall and recognition, which make explicit reference to the circumstances of encoding. By relying on such tasks, researchers were inadvertently restricting their investigations to conscious forms of memory. It soon became clear, however, that information encoded during learning episodes is often expressed without conscious recollection. These effects were revealed through indirect or *implicit* tests of memory. Instead of being asked directly to remember information that had been encoded in a prior learning episode, participants are merely asked to perform a task such as completing a word fragment such as d_ct_r. The choices used to complete word fragments and the speed of fragment completion are influenced by prior exposure to the same or related words.

It may be argued that implicit (unconscious) and explicit (conscious) memory can be differentiated by the tasks that elicit them: explicit memory tasks make reference to the encoding episode, which leads to a conscious awareness of the act of remembering; implicit memory tasks make no reference to the initial encoding episode and such tasks may not evoke an awareness of the act of remembering. Effects of memory demonstrated through the latter (implicit) tasks reflect *priming* (or procedural memory), but this does not preclude the contribution of explicit memory to performance. Indeed, it is rare that tasks are 'process pure' and elicit only implicit memory processes. In order to confirm that participants completed an implicit memory task without consciously or intentionally accessing the information acquired in the learning episode, researchers typically include two tests of memory, one explicit and one implicit. The aim is to demonstrate dissociated performance between the two tests, with memory for the learning episode revealed on the implicit test, but no recollection of the episode displayed on the explicit one.

Although such effects implicate a form of memory that bypasses conscious awareness, researchers generally avoid the label 'unconscious memory' because the term *unconscious* has historical, philosophical, and medical connotations that may potentially confound the phenomena of interest. Nonetheless, questions in contemporary studies of implicit memory are part of a long-standing fascination with unconscious influences on behaviour (for a review, see Schacter 1989). In 'The Passion of the Soul' Descartes (1649) wrote about how aversive experiences may become imprinted on the brain without any memory of the experience (cf. Schacter 1989). Leibnitz (1916) wrote about how people often have a 'facility for conceiving certain things, because we formerly conceived them, without remembering them' (1916: 106). British physiologist William Carpenter investigated the phenomenon of 'automatic writing' (writing that occurs involuntarily while a subject is hypnotized) and concluded that 'ideas which have passed out of the conscious memory, sometimes express themselves in involuntary muscular movements' (1874: 524–5). Within the field of psychiatry, Freud and Janet are well known for their discussions of hysterical amnesia following emotional trauma.

Finally, nineteenth-century neurologists identified cases of amnesia following brain trauma in which patients showed clear evidence of learning, but without an accompanying awareness that learning had taken place. One of the first and most famous investigators to document implicit memory in neurological cases was Sergei Korsakoff (1889). Investigating an amnesic syndrome that follows prolonged alcoholism, Korsakoff described one patient whom he had given an electric shock. The patient had no conscious memory that he had been given an electric shock, but when shown the case that contained the electric shock apparatus, he speculated that Korsakoff had probably come to electrify him. Korsakoff's interpretation of such effects was that amnesic patients retained traces of memory that were too faint to reach consciousness but that were still powerful enough to influence behaviour. Later, Claparède (1911: 51) reported what was to become one of the most famous cases of implicit memory in amnesia. Once while shaking hands with an amnesic woman, Claparède hid a pin in his hand and pricked her. Although the woman had no conscious memory of the event, she refused subsequently to shake hands with Claparède, stating 'sometimes pins are hidden in hands.'

One of the striking differences between early and contemporary discussions of implicit memory is methodology. Until the latter half of the twentieth century, most of the observations about implicit memory were anecdotal or were reported under poorly controlled clinical or experimental conditions. This lack of experimental control made it impossible to refine theoretical explanations of implicit memory effects. For example, controlled experiments have cast doubt on Korsakoff's hypothesis that implicit memory effects are produced by traces that are too weak to exceed the threshold of consciousness. Instead, effects of implicit and explicit memory appear to arise from independent memory systems.

Several lines of evidence suggest that implicit memory is a separate system from explicit memory. Priming is conceived as 'spreading activation' whereby exposure to a word, percept, or concept causes its temporary activation in the brain, providing facilitated access to it and to other words (or percepts or concepts) in the same semantic or perceptual network; the middle and superior temporal lobes, particularly the left side, have been associated with lexical and semantic priming (Wible et al. 2006; Matsumoto et al. 2005). Procedural learning, the other main branch of implicit memory, is thought to be associated with subcortical structures in the brain, including the basal ganglia and cerebellum. Both priming and procedural learning operate independently of the hippocampal and parahippocampal structures in the medial temporal lobe and the diencephalic structures (including thalamus and mamillary bodies), whereas the creation of explicit memories is critically dependent upon these structures (for review see Green and Kopelman 1997).

As mentioned, behavioural studies have revealed that performance on implicit and explicit memory tasks follow different developmental trajectories, which would not be expected if they arose from the same memory system. Implicit and explicit memory effects are also dissociated in terms of 'surface-structure' information (e.g., typescript), which has a much bigger impact on the former than the latter. For example, on a repetition priming task, if the word 'doctor' were written in one font and then re-presented later in a different font, the magnitude of priming of the word would be smaller although recognition of it would be unaffected (Graf and Mandler 1984). Conversely, the 'depth of processing' at encoding (i.e., whether information is processed superficially or more meaningfully) typically affects explicit memory – the more deeply encoded the better the recollection – but has little impact on the performance of implicit memory (Jacoby and Dallas 1981). More generally, implicit memory effects are remarkably robust – an observation that has led some researchers to reason that im-

plicit memory is part of an evolutionarily old system (Reber 1993).

Arguably the strongest evidence that priming effects can occur in the absence of explicit memory comes from clinical studies of organic amnesia. The amnesic syndrome is produced by damage to the medial temporal and diencephalic regions of the brain, most commonly through viral infection (e.g., herpes encephalitis), chronic alcoholism (in which case the amnesia produced is called 'Korsakoff's syndrome'), or stroke. The syndrome is characterized by severe impairment on explicit memory tests measuring the recollection of newly learned information (much greater impairment than that observed on tests of intellectual function) along with preserved performance on tests of implicit memory, including both priming and procedural learning. (Note that the ability to recollect information from a person's pre-amnesic past is variable from patient to patient in organic amnesia.) A seminal finding illustrating the independence of implicit and explicit memory systems was obtained by Johnson, Kim, and Risse (1985). Here, amnesic patients were played a series of novel melodies, and later that day they were replayed the same melodies along with some new ones. While patients reported no explicit recognition of any of the melodies, they nonetheless reported much greater preference for the ones they had been exposed to earlier.

The real-world application of priming and implicit memory is now ubiquitous. In the rehabilitation of people with disorders of explicit memory, for example, an increased understanding of implicit and explicit memory systems has led to an intervention called 'errorless learning' (Baddeley and Wilson 1994). Normally, the explicit system enables us to remember any errors that we make during learning, thereby allowing us to eliminate them voluntarily on the next execution of the task. When the explicit system is compromised, errors made while learning (e.g., turning the wrong way while learning a route) are subsequently repeated (Anderson and Craik 2006). When teaching skills to people with impaired explicit memory, it is therefore essential to avoid errors in learning. Thus, in contrast to trial-and-error learning, people with explicit memory disorders are taught in a way that avoids potential errors, giving rise to 'errorless learning.'

In the 1960s, with the rise of television came the folklore of subliminal advertising. Subliminal messages were designed to pass beneath the normal limits of conscious awareness while still affecting behaviour unconsciously. James Vicary coined the term *subliminal advertising* and formed the Subliminal Projection Company. In 1957, Vicary reported that he was able to increase sales of Coca-Cola by tachistoscopically flashing the message 'drink Coca-Cola' on a movie screen for 1/3000 of a second at five-second intervals. The idea of subliminal messages was soon popularized in the media and became a public concern, with conspiracy theories of governments and cults using the technique for sinister purposes. Advertising companies were led to believe that if they tachistoscopically flashed images of a product on television and cinema screens, audience members would be left with an inexplicable urge to run out and purchase the product. Subliminal advertising was even banned in the United Kingdom and Australia, but in 1962, Vicary admitted that he fabricated his claims, and the efficacy of subliminal advertising remains controversial (Boese 2006; Dixon 1971).

There is little doubt that advertising is a powerful form of priming, whether accomplished through association (feeling masculine while smoking a cigarette) or through the repetition of key concepts in images and jingles. The effects of repetition are surprisingly potent, as illustrated by the so-called 'mere exposure effect' (Kunst-Wilson and Zajonc 1980) whereby strong preferences for any type of stimulus (e.g., random dot patterns) can be developed merely through repeated exposure, even when the exposure occurs in the back-ground or in a degraded form. Again, such preferences appear to emerge automatically and unconsciously, giving credence to the idea of subliminal advertising. The implications of priming and implicit memory for media are clear and powerful: we do not need to consciously *remember* the words and images we see and hear in order to be influenced by them.

William Forde Thompson and Robin Green

Bibliography

Anderson, Nicole D., and Fergus I. Craik. The Mnemonic Mechanisms of Errorless Learning. *Neuropsychologia* 44 (2006): 2806–13.

Baddeley, Alana D., and Barbara A. Wilson. When Implicit Learning Fails: Amnesia and the Problem of Error Elimination. *Neuropsychologia* 32, no. 1 (1994): 53–68.

Boese, Alex. *Hippo Eats Dwarf: A Field Guide to Hoaxes and Other B.S.* New York: Harcourt, 2006.

Carpenter, William B. *Principles of Mental Physiology.* London: John Churchill, 1874.

Claparède, Edouard. Recognition and 'Me-ness.' In *Organization and Pathology of Thought,* ed. David Rapaport, 58–75. New York: Columbia University Press, 1951. Reprinted from *Archives de Psychologie* 11 (1911): 79–90.

Descartes, René. *Les passions de l'âme.* Paris: Henry Le Gras, 1649.

Dixon, Norman F. *Subliminal Perception: The Nature of a Controversy.* New York: McGraw-Hill, 1971.

Graf, Peter, and George Mandler. Activation Makes Words More Accessible, but Not Necessarily More Retrievable. *Journal of Verbal Learning and Verbal Behavior* 23 (1984): 55, 553–68.

Green, Robin E.A., and Michael D. Kopelman. Neural Organization of Memory and of Memory Impairments. In *Behavioral Neurology,* ed. Michael Trimble and Jeffrey Cummings, 139–57. Oxford: Butterworth Heinemann, 1997.

Jacoby, L.L., and M. Dallas. On the Relationship between Autobiographical Memory and Perceptual Learning. *Journal of Experimental Psychology General* 110, no. 3 (1981): 306–40.

Johnson, Marcia K., Jung K. Kim, and Gail Risse. Do Alcoholic Korsakoff's Syndrome Patients Acquire Affective Reactions? *Journal of Experimental Psychology: Learning, Memory, and Cognition* 11, no. 1 (1985): 22–36.

Korsakoff, Sergei S. Étude medico-psychologique sur une forme des maladies de la mémoire. *Revue Philosophique* 28 (1889): 501–30.

Kunst-Wilson, William Raft, and Robert B. Zajonc. Affective Discrimination of Stimuli That Cannot Be Recognized. *Science* 207 (1980): 557–8.

Leibnitz, Gottfried Wilhelm. *New Essays Concerning Human Understanding.* Chicago: Open Court, 1916.

Matsumoto, Atsushi, et al. Linking Semantic Priming Effect in Functional MRI and Event-Related Potentials. *Neuroimage* 24, no. 3 (2005): 624–34.

Reber, Arthur S. *Implicit Learning and Tacit Knowledge: An Essay on the Cognitive Unconscious.* New York: Oxford University Press, 1993.

Schacter, Daniel L. Implicit Memory: History and Current Status. *Journal of Experimental Psychology: Learning, Memory and Cognition* 13, no. 3 (1989): 501–18.

Wible, Cynthia G., et al. Connectivity among Semantic Associates: An fMRI Study of Semantic Priming. *Brain and Language* 97, no. 3 (2006): 294–305.

PRINT CULTURE

[See also: *Books; Books, History of; Comics; Magazines; Newspapers; Pulp Fiction*]

Print culture refers to a wide variety of published materials including books, newspapers, magazines, and comics. Johannes Gutenberg (ca 1400–68) is credited with producing the first European movable type technology. This process facilitated the mass production of books and print materials such as posters. Subsequently, hot metal typesetting appeared in the nineteenth century. In the twentieth century, cold typesetting became the dominant mode of printing through the use of phototypesetting by which today's printed materials are produced.

The word 'book' derives from the Old English *boc* from the Germanic root *bok*. The concept of the book has evolved over five millennia into its current format. The antecedents of today's books are to be found in the handwritten works of Sumerian and Egyptian scribes as early as the third millennium BCE. These primitive forms feature many of the elements found in modern books (cover page with title and author's name). In the Roman period, the codex with bound parchment paper (350 CE) became the standard 'book' design. By 1000 CE, technological innovations began to appear: movable clay typesetting in China, movable metal typesetting in Korea (1234), and Gutenberg's printing press (1453). Gutenberg's printing press led to the production of inexpensive books of all sorts. Books became objects of knowledge and entertainment, making them desirable and leading to a general desire to gain literacy. Subsequent innovations included the development of the rotary press in the United States (1846), linotype and offset lithography (1880s), computer typesetting (1960s), desktop publishing (1980s), and the e-book, an electronic form of the printed book (2000s). All of these technical advances enhanced the production of books and reduced the associated expenses of making them.

By the eighteenth and nineteenth centuries, writers were becoming cultural icons, as their novels and poems gained wide audiences.

Since the late 1990s, the traditional 'book' has been supplemented by electronic books, or e-books. E-book reading devices are now available for readers. A wide variety of books may now be downloaded onto these devices for a fee. Brand names include Kindle by Amazon.com and Sony Reader by Sony. Another electronic book format is the audiobook. This format was originally developed to make texts available to visually impaired or illiterate readers. Previously available on audiocassettes and CDs, they are now downloadable on various digital formats (MP3, Windows Media Audio, and so forth).

A similar story can be written for other

print genres, including newspapers, magazines, and comics. These may have ancient roots, but their popularity would never have been possible without the advent of cheap print technology.

Interestingly, print culture has converged with electronic culture, producing hybrid forms of writing. Some film and television characters have produced comics; for example, *Buffy, The Vampire Slayer* first appeared as a film (1992), then a television series (1997–2003), and ultimately a comic book – *Buffy the Vampire Slayer Season Eight* (2007–). Spin-offs of this franchise, including novels, electronic games, and a card game, have also been successful.

Like the other print media (books, newspapers, magazines), comics are now available in an online format. Webcomics include cartoon strips and graphic novels. Their financial viability has yet been proven. Scott McCloud (2000: 222) advocated this format for comics in his book *Reinventing Comics*. In fact, his notion of the '*infinite canvas*' refers to digital comics with an unlimited length on one page. This format allows the comic artist and comic narrator much more freedom than does the conventional print comic format (time shift, indefinite length, special effects, greater artistic detail, and so forth).

While conventional print culture (books, newspapers, magazines, comics) is a staple, new and emerging technologies are having a decided influence on the more traditional forms of print culture distribution. This trend is likely to continue, though its total replacement by electronic formats is unlikely. Finally, significant legal and ethical issues are related to the print media and print culture, for example, copyright laws, freedom of the press, censorship, new forms of literacy, what constitutes a text, and so forth.

Frank Nuessel

Bibliography

Avrin, Leila. *Scribes, Scripts and Books: The Book Arts from Antiquity to the Renaissance*. Chicago: American Library Association, 1991.

Eisenstein, Elizabeth L. *The Printing Press as an Agent of Change: Communications and Cultural Transformations in Early-Modern Europe*. Cambridge: Cambridge University Press, 1979.

Finkelstein, David, and Alistair McLeery. *A History of the Book*. London: Routledge, 2005.

McCloud, Scott. *Understanding Comics*. New York: HarperCollins, 1993.

– *Reinventing Comics*. New York: Harper, 2000.

– *Making Comics*. New York: Harper, 2006.

PROPAGANDA THEORY

[See also: *Chomsky, Noam; Media Effects*]

The word *propaganda* comes the Latin verb *propagare* 'to propagate,' and refers to an organized dissemination of a canon or set of beliefs that reflect a particular viewpoint. Propaganda theory specifically alludes to a model proposed by Edward S. Herman (b. 1925) and Noam Chomsky (b. 1928) in their book *Manufacturing Consent: The Political Economy of the Mass Media*. The propaganda model of the media asserts that the entrepreneurial media businesses engage in the selling of a product (readers, viewers, listeners) to other industries.

Propaganda theory has five distinct elements, or filters, which affect the way in which news appears in the media. The first is the 'ownership filter,' which refers to the domination by corporate conglomerates of information and news presented to mass audiences. The presentation of the news contains an inherent bias intended to favour the financial interests of these organizations. Thus, the more harmful a piece of news is to that interest, the greater are the chances that it will be subject to bias or suppression. The second is the 'funding filter,' whereby media corporations have a specific product to offer to advertisers; namely, their prosperous readers and decision makers. As a result, any news item that runs counter to the profit motive of the large media organizations will be rejected or marginalized. In fact, it is the audience that is the product being sold by the media, and not the news itself. The third filter is 'sourcing,' which includes the government and its various arms as well as major corporations – at the national level in the United States, this includes the White House, the Pentagon, and the State Department. Furthermore, corporations of all types as well as trade groups supply 'news' to the corporate media in a predigested fashion (copies of speeches, press releases written in simple language) designed to reflect an official point of view that serves the best interests of these groups. Moreover, these vested interests provide comfortable space, schedule press conferences at times that allow news deadlines to be met, and provide photo opportunities to ensure that a favourable slant is offered in the media. The fourth filter is 'flak.' This constitutes negative reactions to news items and news programs (for example, letters to the editor, email messages, telephone calls, lawsuits, petitions, boycotts, enactment of new laws). Flak may be costly to the media in economic terms, or in terms of their power and authority. Sometimes flak may be produced by conservative groups in an effort to fight what they consider to be liberal bias in the media, although the reverse may also be true. The fifth and final filter is what Herman and Chomsky called 'anti-communism.' At the time their book was published (1988), the Cold War was still raging. Today, this filter might better be labelled 'anti-ideology' – that is, ideas or notions that support movements unfriendly to the profit motive of the corporate media. The anti-communism filter and, more recently, the anti-ideology filter constitute a means of repressing dissidents by branding them as traitors who are against basic freedoms (speech, religion, press, and so forth). The best example of this is 'McCarthyism,' a reference to Senator Joseph McCarthy (1908–57) of Wisconsin who waged a campaign against communists in the public sector, especially those who worked in the entertainment industry.

Not everyone has accepted the Herman-Chomsky theory of propaganda. *The Anti-Chomsky Reader* (Collier and Horowitz 2004), for example, is replete with essays that argue against this model. Likewise, Jeffery Klaehn (2002) has written an essay critical of the Herman-Chomsky propaganda theory and questioning its basic tenets. According to Klaehn, while propaganda theory asserts that ordinary people are incapable of distinguishing between truth and deception, many people are able to evaluate news critically.

Frank Nuessel

Bibliography

Danesi, Marcel. *Popular Culture: Introductory Perspectives*. Lanham, MD: Rowman and Littlefield, 2008.

Collier, Peter, and David Horowitz, eds. *The Anti-Chomsky Reader*. San Francisco: Encounter, 2004.

Herman, Edward S., and Noam Chomsky. *Manufacturing Consent: The Political Economy of the Mass Media*. New York: Pantheon, 1988.

Klaehn, Jeffery. A Critical Review and Assessment of Herman and Chomsky's 'Propaganda Model.' *European Journal of Communication* 17 (2002): 147–82.

PROXEMICS

[See also: *Body Language; Hall, Edward T.; Kinesics; Non-Verbal Communication*]

Proxemics (from Latin *proximus*, 'near') is defined as the study of how individuals and groups perceive and organize the zones and distances they maintain between each other as they interact. The discipline has applications in the fields of anthropology, social psychology, and semiotics. The study of proxemics was founded by the American anthropologist Edward T. Hall in the late 1950s and early 1960s. As a soldier during the Second World War, Hall observed the zones people maintain during conversations, coming soon to realize that many (if not most) breakdowns in communication were attributable to unconscious differences in the ways that interlocutors of different cultures perceived interpersonal zones and in the ways they behaved within them. Hall developed proxemic methods and theory throughout the 1960s and 1970s (Hall 1959, 1963a, 1963b, 1964, 1966, 1968, 1974, 1976, 1983). Using American culture as his point of reference, he showed how to measure and assess critical interpersonal zones accurately and meaningfully.

Hall defined proxemics in 1963 as 'the study of how man unconsciously structures microspace – the distance between men in conduct of daily transactions, the organization of space in his houses and buildings, and ultimately the layout of his towns' (1963b: 1003). A year later, he restricted the term to mean 'the study of the ways in which man gains knowledge of the content of other men's minds through judgments of behavior patterns associated with varying degrees of proximity to them' (1964: 41), which he restricted two years later to the investigation of 'the interrelated observations and theories of man's use of space as a specialized elaboration of culture' (1966: 1).

Hall's proposal to study interpersonal zones has led to a large body of data on this aspect of social behaviour. Most of it shows that such zones can be measured with great accuracy, varying according to age, gender, and other social variables (Segaud 1973; Loof 1976; Pinxten et al. 1983; Watson and Anderson 1987). Hall did not explicitly claim that proxemics was a branch of any existing science, such as semiotics, even though the very idea of proxemics is de facto semiotic in nature. The classification of proxemics as a branch of semiotics started with Eco (1968: 344–9) and Watson (1970, 1974). It is now an area of study within several disciplines, including psychology and anthropology.

The study of proxemic behaviour involves investigating (1) spatial dimensions, (2) the levels of interpretation of these dimensions, and (3) the physical features of spaces. Each one of these can be subdivided into three subcomponents, called *micro, meso* and *macro. Microspace* is the immediate physical zone around a human being, constituting a sphere of privacy; *mesospace* is the next zone, which is within the person's reach, but falls outside the privacy sphere; and *macrospace* refers to the larger spheres around a person, including public spaces, settlements, cities, and beyond. The three levels of analysis of these spaces are called *infra, pre,* and *micro*. The infra level is rooted in our 'biological past' (Hall 1966: 95) and is thus based on our innate sense of territoriality, which involves establishing boundaries. The pre level is rooted instead in sensory reactions (tactile, visual) to space and people in physical contexts that are given specific meanings in a culture. These are interpreted at a micro level. The physical features are called *fixed, semi-fixed*, and *dynamic*. Fixed features include such things as walls and territorial boundaries; semi-fixed features include mobile elements such as curtains and screens; and dynamic features are those that can move about in certain spaces, for example, vehicles.

Animals (including humans) reside in territories that they appropriate either by force or in some negotiated arrangement with other animals. These make it possible for animals to procure shelter, food, and habitation safely. Biologists define *territoriality* as: (1) an innate survival mechanism that permits an animal to gain access to, and defend control of, critical resources (food, nesting sites, and so on); and (2) the instinctive need of an animal to procure a safe boundary around itself. The zoologist Konrad Lorenz (1903–89) was among the first to identify and document territorial patterns, which, he claimed, were as important to an animal's survival as were its physiological attributes. Lorenz also suggested that human aggression was explainable as a residual mechanism of territoriality – a controversial theory that became popularized through Robert Ardrey's 1966 book *The Territorial Imperative*, leading to a debate in academia and society at large on the nature and origin of human aggression. The main implication to be derived from territoriality theory is that we all need to maintain a spatial boundary around ourselves for our protection and sanity. Hall clearly saw the relevant social implications of this, discovering that the boundaries or zones we maintain can be measured very accurately, allowing for statistical variation, and that the dimensions varied from society to society. In North American society, he found that a zone of under six inches between two people was perceived as an 'intimate' distance; while 1.5 to 4 feet was considered the minimum safety zone. Intrusions into the intimate zone by strangers cause considerable discomfort. If the 'safe' distance were breached by some acquaintance, on the other hand, it would be interpreted as a sexual advance or as a normal intrusion by a family member or child. It all depends on who the 'intruder' is.

Hall posited eight factors as shaping proxemic behaviour:

(1) postural-sex identifiers (standing vs. sitting, male vs. female)
(2) sociofugal-sociopetal orientation factors (face-to-face, back-to-back)
(3) kinesthetic factors (distances of body parts, from reaching to contact)
(4) touching factors (from caressing and holding to no contact)
(5) visual factors (gazing, looking away, looking directly into the eyes)
(6) thermal factors (whether radiated heat is detected or not)
(7) olfaction factors (detection of odour or breath)
(8) vocal factors (loudness of voice, tone of voice)

The actual description of the factors used in situ is called *proxetic* description (in analogy with *phonetic* description in linguistics), and the analysis of how these relate to each other structurally is called *proxemic* analysis (in analogy with *phonemic* analysis in linguistics). The relevant *proxemes* (meaningful zone units) are determined by comparing them with one another within the broader framework of an interaction.

Overall, Hall found that there are four main zones: *intimate*, *personal*, *social*, and *public*. Hall further subdivided these into 'far' and 'close' phases. For American culture he found these to be as follows: (1) intimate distance (0–18 in.), (2) personal distance (1.5–4 ft.), (3) social distance (4–12 ft.), and (4) public distance (12 ft. and beyond). At intimate distance, the senses are activated and the presence of the other is unmistakable. The close phase (0–6 in.) is emotionally charged and is typically reserved for lovemaking, comforting, and protecting; the far phase (6–18 in.) is the zone in which family members and close friends interact under normal conditions. Personal distance is the minimum comfort zone between individuals who do not know each other or who have a formal relationship to each other. In the close phase (1.5–2.5 ft.), one can grasp the other by extending the arms, allowing for hand-shaking. The far phase (2.5–4 ft.) is anywhere from one arm's length to the distance required for both individuals to touch hands for greeting purposes. This zone is considered non-involving and non-threatening by most people. The close phase (4–7 ft.) is typical of impersonal transactions and casual gatherings. Formal language and behaviour are characteristic of the far phase (7–12 ft.). Public distance is the distance at which one can take either evasive or defensive action if physically threatened. Hall noticed that people tend to keep at this distance from important public figures or from anyone participating at a public function. Discourse at this distance tends to be highly structured and formalized (for example, lectures, speeches).

The study of proxemic behaviour has made it obvious that physical spaces and the features within them are perceived as meaningful. Very little work has been conducted in the area of 'media zones,' defined as the virtual zones felt by people according to the type of medium involved (radio seems to be more intimate because of its audio-oral nature, while television is felt as being more removed). As online culture spreads, this is starting to be a main topic for research.

Marcel Danesi

Bibliography

Ardrey, Robert. *The Territorial Imperative*. New York: Atheneum, 1966.

Eco, Umberto. *Einführung in die Semiotik*. München: Fink, 1968.

Hall, Edward T. *The Silent Language*. Greenwich: Fawcett, 1959.

– Proxemics: The Study of Man's Spatial Relations. In *Man's Image in Anthropology*, ed. I. Galdston, 442–5. New York: International University Press, 1963a.

– A System for the Notation of Proxemic Behavior. *American Anthropologist* 65 (1963b): 1003–26.

– Silent Assumptions in Social Communication. *Disorders of Communication* 42 (1964): 41–55.

– *The Hidden Dimension*. Garden City: Anchor, 1966.

– Proxemics. *Current Anthropology* 9 (1968): 83–108.

– *Handbook for Proxemic Research*. Washington, DC: Society for the Anthropology of Visual Communication, 1974.

– *Beyond Culture*. Garden City: Anchor, 1976.

– *The Dance of Life*. Garden City: Anchor, 1983.

Lawrence, Denise L., and Setha M. Low. The Built Environment and Spatial Form. *Annual Review of Anthropology* 19 (1990): 453–505.

Loof, D. de. Some American and German Customs Compared. *Le Langage et l'Homme* 30 (1976): 37–46.

Moles, Abraham, and Elisabeth Rohmer. *Psychologie de l'espace*. Tournai: Casterman, 1978.

Nöth, Winfried. *Handbook of Semiotics*. Bloomington: Indiana University Press, 1990.

Pinxten, Rik, Ingrid van Dooren, and Frank Harvey. *Anthropology of Space*. Philadelphia: University of Pennsylvania Press, 1983.

Segaud, Marion. Anthropologie de l'espace. *Espaces et Sociétés* 9 (1973): 29–38.

Sundstrom, Eric, and Irwin Altman. Interpersonal Relationships and Personal Space: Research Review and Theoretical Model. *Human Ecology* 4 (1976): 47–67.

Watson, O. Michael. *Proxemic Behavior*. The Hague: Mouton, 1970.

– Proxemics. In *Current Trends in Linguistics* 12, ed. Thomas A. Sebeok, 311–44. The Hague: Mouton, 1974.

Watson, O. Michael, and Myrdene Anderson. The Quest for Coordinates in Space and Time. *Reviews in Anthropology* 14 (1987): 78–89.

PSYCHOANALYTIC THEORY

[See also: *Feminism; Marcuse, Herbert; Psychology of the Media*]

Psychoanalytic theory starts with Freud's notion that the psyche has a number of different levels, one of which, the unconscious, is not ordinarily accessible to us. As he wrote in his essay 'Psychoanalysis' (1963: 235–6):

> It was a triumph for the interpretative art of psychoanalysis when it succeeded in demonstrating that certain mental acts of normal people, for which no one had hitherto attempted to put forward a psychological explanation, were to be regarded in the same light as the symptoms of neurotics: that is to say that had a *meaning*, which was unknown to the subject but which could easily be discovered by analytic means … A class of material was brought to light which is calculated better than any other to stimulate a belief in the existence of unconscious mental acts even in people to whom the hypothesis of something at once mental and unconscious seems strange and even absurd.

Although we may think we are aware of everything that is going on in our minds, we are mistaken, for, as Freud explained, there are 'unconscious mental acts' that we do not recognize.

A convenient way to understand the human psyche is to imagine it as being like an iceberg. The part of the iceberg that we can see, which floats above the water, is what psychoanalytic theorists call consciousness. Just below the water line are a few feet of the iceberg we can dimly make out – that is what we call the pre-conscious. We do not ordinarily think about the contents of the pre-conscious, but if we want to, we can become aware of what lies there. Then there is the part of the iceberg, the largest part, that we cannot see, which Freud called the unconscious.

The iceberg analogy suggests that most of what is in our minds is not accessible to us, but the unconscious is important because in many ways it shapes our behaviour. We are not in complete control of our behaviour and are vulnerable to various emotional and irrational appeals that often shape our actions. Freud called this approach to the human psyche his *topographic* hypothesis.

He later elaborated another hypothesis about the human mind, his *structural* hypothesis. In this hypothesis, there is a continual battle going on in our minds between its three elements – the id, the ego, and the superego. Freud described the id in his *New Introductory Lectures in Psychoanalysis* as follows (quoted in Hinsie and Campbell, 1970: 372):

We can come nearer to the id with images, and call it chaos, a cauldron of seething excitement. We suppose that is somewhere in direct contact with somatic processes, and takes over from them instinctual needs and gives them mental expression … These instincts fill it with energy but it has no organization and no unified will, only an impulse to obtain satisfaction for the instinctual needs, in accordance with the pleasure-principle.

If this 'cauldron of seething excitement' dominates us, we have a great deal of energy but cannot use it effectively because we are always being drawn by a desire to take care of our instinctual needs.

Opposing the id is the superego, which can be described as conscience and the way our personality functions morally. In *An El-ementary Textbook of Psychoanalysis,* Charles Brenner describes the superego as follows (1974: 111–12):

1. the approval or disapproval of actions and wishes on the grounds of rectitude. 2. critical self-observation. 3. self-punishment. 4. the demand for reparation or repentance of wrong-doing. 5. self-praise or self-love as a reward for virtuous or desirable thoughts and actions. Contrary to the ordinary meaning of 'conscience,' however, we understand that the functions of the superego are often largely or completely unconscious.

Thus we find two opposing elements in the human psyche. The id seeks gratification and has great energy, but it cannot be allowed to dominate our behaviour because we are social animals and must submit to the demands of civilization – demands which often cause us considerable mental anguish. On the other hand, if the superego dominates, we become paralysed by guilt and doubt.

This is where the ego comes in. The ego is that element of our psyches that mediates between the conflicting demands of the id and the superego. The ego tests reality and stores up experiences in memory, in an effort to find a way to balance the demands of the id and superego and allow people to be free of neurotic compulsions based on overly powerful id or superego elements in the psyche. It seeks to harness the energy of the id in socially constructive ways by using the superego to moderate id behaviour. Many psychological problems people face are caused by either an overly powerful id or superego.

The ego uses a number of different defence mechanisms to find ways to control id-based impulses and superego-based anxieties and guilt. These defence mechanisms operate at the unconscious level. Some of the more important defence mechanisms are:

• *Ambivalence.* A feeling of both love and

hatred toward some person at the same time.

- *Avoidance.* A refusal to pay attention to subjects that are disturbing because they are connected to unconscious aggressive or sexual impulses.
- *Denial.* A refusal to accept the reality of something by blocking it from consciousness.
- *Fixation.* An obsessive preoccupation with or attachment to something or someone.
- *Projection.* A denial of negative and hostile feelings in oneself by attributing them to someone else.
- *Rationalization.* A means of excusing one's behaviour by offering reasons or excuses.
- *Reaction formation.* A situation which occurs when ambivalent feelings create problems and which is dealt with by suppressing one element and overemphasizing the other, its opposite.
- *Regression.* An individual's return to an earlier stage in development when confronted with stressful or anxiety-provoking situations.
- *Repression.* A barring of consciousness of wishes, memories, desires that are derived from the unconscious. Repression is considered the most basic defence mechanism.
- *Sublimation.* A transferring of sexual impulses and other desires and impulses into other kinds of behaviour, such as writing, painting, and other kinds of creative arts.
- *Suppression.* A voluntary attempt to put out of mind and consciousness something we find upsetting and distasteful. Suppression is voluntary, unlike repression, which works at the unconscious level. Suppression is considered the second most important defence mechanism.

These defence mechanisms are of interest to media and communication scholars, as well as therapists, since they can be found in so many narratives and other texts found in the media. They appear in these works because they are in the unconscious of the people who create them.

We must recall that Freud called psychoanalysis an 'interpretative art.' One of the ways it can be applied is by using psychoanalytic theories to deal with symbolic behaviour. A symbol is something that stands for something else. A symbol can stand for institutions, ideas, beliefs, values, and wishes. In psychoanalytic theory, symbols are important because they are often used to disguise aggressive wishes and sexual desires, and, in the case of dreams, prevent our dream censors from waking us if the sexual content of our dreams becomes too evident.

As Freud points out in *The Interpretation of Dreams*, symbolism is all pervasive in human life. As he writes (1901/1965: 386):

> Symbolism is not peculiar to dreams, but is characteristic of unconscious ideation, in particular, among people, and is to be found in folklore, and in popular myths, legends, linguistic idioms, proverbial wisdom and current jokes, to a more complete extent than in dreams.

In his discussion of dreams, he offers some typical examples of the symbolism found in dreams (1900/1965: 389):

> The Emperor and Empress (or the King and Queen) as a rule really represent the dreamer himself or herself … All elongated objects, such as sticks, tree-trunks and umbrellas may stand for the male organ – as well as all long, sharp weapons such as knives, daggers and pikes … Boxes, cases, chests, cupboards and ovens represent the uterus, and also hollow objects, ships, and vessels of all kinds. Rooms in dreams are usually women.

From this list we can see that many objects have a hidden, symbolic and often sexual significance. In the pages that follow Freud deals with other symbols, mentioning that snakes are an important phallic symbol. This notion of objects having a sexually symbolic nature often strikes people as ridiculous and absurd. We must recognize that these symbols are operating at the unconscious level and are often tied to myths and legends. Freud himself said 'sometimes a cigar is only a cigar,' in reference to the notion that symbolic objects have a sexual dimension, but this quotation suggests, also, that sometimes a cigar isn't only a cigar.

There are two ways that the sexual content in dreams is disguised, according to Freud. The first way is by condensation, in which parts of different sexual symbols are combined into one that disguises the dream's sexual content and thus fools the dream censor. The other, displacement, involves the substitution of one image for another which is associated with it but which is not explicitly sexual, thus evading the dream censor, which wakes us if there is too overtly a sexual dimension to our dreams.

Dreams are a very controversial subject and one about which theorists continually argue. The Freudian position is described by the psychoanalytic writer Erich Fromm in his book *The Forgotten Language: An Introduction to the Understanding of Dreams, Fairy Tales and Myths* (1957: 67):

> Dreams are understood to be the hallucinatory fulfillment of irrational wishes and particularly sexual wishes which have originated in our early childhood and have not been fully transformed into reaction formations or sublimations. These wishes are expressed as being fulfilled when our conscious control is weakened, as is the case in sleep.

The notion that dreams are a means of satisfying frustrated desires and thus a form of wish-fulfilment is at the heat of the controversy over the Freudian theory of dreams.

Another Freudian theory that many people find difficult to accept involves his theory of infant sexuality and, in particular, his notion of the Oedipus complex, which

was named after the myth of Oedipus. In this myth, an oracle prophesizes that Laius, the king of Thebes, will be killed by his son. When Laius's wife Jocasta gives birth to a son, Oedipus, Laius arranges to have the son left on a mountain peak to die. He is unaware that Oedipus has been rescued and taken to a king, Polybus, in Corinth, who raises him as his son.

When Oedipus hears that a prophecy says he will kill his father, Oedipus leaves Corinth to spare Polybus. On the road to Thebes he meets Laius at a crossroads, they get into a fight, and Oedipus kills Laius. He then goes to Thebes, which is under a plague from a monster, the Sphynx, which has the face of a woman and the body of a lion. The Sphynx devours anyone who cannot answer this riddle: 'What creature goes on four feet in the morning, two feet at noon, and three feet in the evening?' Oedipus answers 'A man, who crawls as a child, walks on two feet in the prime of his life, and needs a cane to walk in old age.' When he answers the riddle correctly, the Sphynx kills itself and Oedipus is welcomed into Thebes as its saviour. He is made king, marries Jocasta, the wife of the former king (not knowing that she is his mother), and they have two children. Later Thebes is visited by another plague. Tiresias, a blind prophet, is sent to an oracle, which says that the murderer of Laius must be punished for Thebes to be rid of the plague. When Oedipus discovers that he is the one who killed Laius, his real father, and that he has married his mother, he blinds himself and Jocasta commits suicide.

This myth is a paradigmatic one that Freud believed explained the process of development in all children. There is, in this story and Freud believed in the lives of all children, hostility toward the parent of the same sex and an attraction to the parent of the opposite sex that eventually manifests itself. As a rule, children overcome their Oedipus complex and can lead normal lives, but those who cannot become neurotic. Freud argued that the Oedipus complex is the core of all neuroses.

Freud wrote about his discovery of the Oedipus complex in a letter to a friend, Wilhelm Fleiss, on 15 October 1897 (quoted in Martin Grotjahn 1966: 84):

Being entirely honest with oneself if a good exercise. Only one idea of general value has occurred to me. I have found love of the mother and jealousy of the father in my own case too, and now believe it to be a general phenomenon of early childhood ... If that is the case, the gripping power of *Oedipus Rex*, in spite of all the rational objections to the inexorable fate that the story presupposes, becomes intelligible ... Our feelings rise against any arbitrary individual fate ... but the Greek myth seizes on a compulsion which everyone recognizes because he has felt traces of it in himself. Every member of the audience was once a budding Oedipus in fantasy, and this dream-fulfillment played out in reality causes everyone to recoil in horror, with the full measure of repression which separates his infantile from his present state.

In this letter Freud adds that he thinks that there is a strong Oedipal component to *Hamlet*, though he is talking not about Shakespeare's conscious intentions but his unconscious feelings of kinship with his tragic hero.

This brings us to our final consideration, the role that psychoanalytic theory plays in the study of mass-mediated and other kinds of texts. The English critic Simon Lesser points out that psychoanalysis investigates the same themes that our greatest fiction writers deal with, namely 'the emotional, unconscious or only partly comprehended bases of our behavior' (1957: 15). Psychoanalytic theory, according to Lesser, offers us systematic and well-validated knowledge about the non-rational and in some cases irrational forces that shape our behaviour, areas which before the development of psychoanalytic theory were not accessible to criticism.

Psychoanalytic theory has been used by Bruno Bettelheim to investigate fairy tales, by Erich Fromm to study myths and dreams, by Ernest Jones to analyse *Hamlet*, and by many other writers to interpret novels, films, humour, television shows, and other forms of the elite arts and popular culture. Other theorists, such as Carl Jung and Alfred Adler, offer different insights into the human psyche and personality, but it is Sigmund Freud and his followers who have defined psychoanalytic theory as we commonly know it.

Arthur Asa Berger

Bibliography

Berger, Arthur Asa. *The Hamlet Case: The Murders at the MLA.* New York: Xlibris, 2000.

Bettelheim, Bruno. *The Uses of Enchantment: The Meaning and Importance of Fairly Tales.* New York: Vintage, 1977.

Brenner, Charles. *An Elementary Textbook of Psychoanalysis.* Garden City, NY: Doubleday, 1974.

Freud, Sigmund. *The Interpretation of Dreams.* New York: Avon, 1901/1965.

– *Civilization and Its Discontents.* London: Hogarth, 1963.

Fromm, Erich. *The Forgotten Language: An Introduction to the Understanding of Dreams, Fairy Tales and Myths.* New York: Grove, 1957.

Grotjahn, Martin. *Beyond Laughter: Humor and the Subconscious.* New York: McGraw-Hill, 1966.

Hinsie, Leland E., and Robert Jean Campbell. *Psychiatric Dictionary.* New York: Oxford University Press, 1970.

Jones, Ernest. *Hamlet and Oedipus.* New York: W.W. Norton, 1949.

Lesser, Simon O. *Fiction and the Unconscious.* Boston: Beacon, 1957.

PSYCHOLOGY OF THE MEDIA

[See also: *Media Effects; Psychoanalytic Theory*]

Psychology is the discipline that studies the human mind and human behaviour. Its modern-day origins are usually traced to Wilhelm Wundt (1832–1920), who founded the first laboratory of experimental psychology in 1879 in Leipzig, laying the groundwork for a new scientific discipline of the mind, separate from philosophy, which he claimed would allow researchers using experimental techniques to discover the 'laws of mind.' Actually, Wundt was preceded a few decades earlier by two German scientists – the physiologist Johannes P. Muller and the physicist Hermann L.F. von Helmholtz – who introduced the first systematic techniques for investigating sensation and perception. The American philosopher William James opened his own psychology laboratory in the United States a little after Wundt. His 1890 book, *Principles of Psychology*, is considered to be the first textbook in the field.

Psychologists have consistently shown interest in investigating the effects the media have on people. Known as *media effects studies* the relevant findings coming out of this line of inquiry can be divided into two broad categories – those that show significant effects and those that do not. The former come under the rubric of hypodermic needle theory (HNT), which claims to show that the mass media can directly influence behaviour, swaying minds with the same kind of impact a hypodermic needle has on the body. The second line of thought claims that media impacts are indirect and are mediated by a host of social factors. The latter view claims that people within different social classes typically come up with very different interpretations of media products. This is because they constitute *interpretive communities*, which coincide with real communities such as families, unions, neighbourhoods, and churches.

An interesting notion within media psychology is that of *association*, which posits that people's views of media content are formed on the basis of how it can be associated with existing cultural concepts. From the 1920s to the late 1960s, psychologists used association theory as a framework for explaining how human beings make sense of things. Radio sitcom programs, for instance, are felt by listeners to be meaningful

(not just entertainment) because they are associated with real-life situations. The theory has resurfaced to explain how certain media products are received and linked both to each other and to social life.

Another commonly used psychological notion in media studies is that of Carl Jung's *collective unconscious*, which refers to the view that humans across cultures share a deeper level of symbolism present in the unconscious part of the mind. This includes symbols called *archetypes*, such as the trickster, which enable people to react to situations in ways similar to their ancestors. This is why all cultures have clowns, comedians, or similar trickster characters. Archetypes surface in media representations, explaining why such representations become so popular.

Behaviourist studies of the media involve assessing how the media condition human behaviour and actions. The term *behaviourism* was coined in 1913 by John B. Watson (1878–1958). It is based on the view that observable and quantifiable behaviour provides the only valid data for psychologists to study. The key notion is that of the *conditioned response*, which was developed initially by the Russian psychologist Ivan Pavlov (1849–1936) in 1904. When Pavlov presented a piece of meat to a hungry dog, the animal would salivate spontaneously, as Pavlov expected. He called this the dog's *unconditioned response*. After ringing a bell while presenting the meat stimulus a number of times, Pavlov soon found that the dog would salivate only to the ringing bell, without the meat stimulus. The ringing, which would not have triggered the salivation initially, had brought about a *conditioned response* in the dog. This scenario was extended to encompass all forms of learning, including human learning. Starting in the late 1960s, behaviourism fell into disfavour among most psychologists. However, in the field of media studies, some of its principles are still used to establish if there is any relationship between certain media products and the responses they evoke. The question this line of research begs is: Do the media habituate people to behave in specific ways? The concept of *desensitization* also comes up within this line of inquiry. This is the claim that by viewing portrayals of violence or sexuality in the media, people tend to become insensitive to violence and sexual degradation in real life. No real evidence, however, has ever come forward to substantiate this claim. A sub-claim is called *early window theory*, which maintains that media provide children with a 'window on the world' before they have developed the critical ability to judge what they are exposed to, thus influencing their world view as they grow up. Again, there is little evidence to support this claim.

Another psychological notion that is relevant to the study of media is *contagion effect theory*, or the view that the media have the power to bring about hysteria. A classic example of this can be seen in the Cabbage Patch doll craze of 1983. Hordes of parents were prepared to pay almost anything to get one of those dolls for their children during the Christmas season. Scalpers offered the suddenly and inexplicably out-of-stock dolls for hundreds of dollars through the classified ads. Such mass hysteria was an extreme manifestation of the contagion effect, created by an effective media-based marketing campaign.

Marcel Danesi

Bibliography

Bühler, Karl. *Sprachtheorie: Die Darstellungsfunktion der Sprache*. Jena: Fischer, 1934.

Klapper, Joseph T. *The Effects of Mass Communication*. New York: Free Press, 1960.

Lazarsfeld, Paul F., and Elihu Katz. *Personal Influence: The Part Played by People in the Flow of Mass Communications*. Glencoe, IL: Free Press, 1955.

Lowery, Shearon A., and Melvin L. DeFleur. *Milestones in Mass Communication Research: Media Effects*. 3rd ed. White Plains, NY: Longman, 1995.

McQuail, Denis. *Mass Communication Theory: An Introduction*. London: Sage, 2000.

Staiger, Janet. *Media Reception Studies*. New York: New York University Press, 2005.

Watson, John B. *Behaviorism*. New York: Norton, 1925.

Wundt, Wilhelm. *Sprachgeschichte und Sprachpsychologie*. Leipzig: Eugelmann, 1901.

PUBLIC BROADCASTING

[See also: *Broadcasting; Federal Communications Commission; Radio; Television*]

Public broadcasting is the distribution of television and radio programs that are supported predominantly by public funding, generally in the form of tax revenues or licensing fees. It is different from commercial broadcasting, which is mainly supported by funding from corporations. Many public stations do on-air underwriting spots, which are similar to advertisements seen on commercial broadcasting stations, in order to raise money from viewers and potential business sponsors.

Public broadcasting varies in its range of operation, from local to national, depending on the station and country. American public broadcasting stations, for example, offer programs from national networks (such as the Public Broadcasting Service), while others offer programs produced locally. In the United States, public broadcasting is seen as an important contributor to the nation's media culture and is generally regarded as having a positive effect on society. This is mainly because of its educational, news, and cultural programming for both children and adults. Such programming is generally less palatable to the mass market than programs offered by commercial broadcasting networks, although a number of public broadcasting programs, such as *Nova, Mister Rogers' Neighborhood*, and *Evening at the Pops* became popular years ago, and remain so in many instances.

In Canada, a similar tradition of national public broadcasting exists. The Canadian Broadcasting Corporation (CBC), known

as Société Radio-Canada in French, operates radio, television, and an online website
(www.cbc.ca). It was created by the Canadian Parliament in 1936. Its headquarters
are in Ottawa, Ontario. It owns around one
hundred television and radio stations, providing programming to more than twenty-
five affiliate stations. The CBC owns most
of 1,400 rebroadcasters, which are low-
power stations that receive and retransmit
programming. The CBC provides special
radio service to northern Canada in eight
languages and in dialects of the indigenous
cultures there. Radio Canada International,
a short-wave radio service of the CBC,
broadcasts in seven languages. The Canadian government finances the majority of
the CBC's programming. Unlike its American counterparts, the CBC gets other funds
primarily from advertising.

In commercial broadcasting, radio stations offer a narrower range of programs
than television stations. The same holds
true for public radio and television stations.
Most often, public radio offers musical genres that are less popular among the mainstream audience, such as jazz and classical
music. In recent years, however, some
radio public broadcasting networks such as
National Public Radio (NPR) in the United
States have expanded their programming
to include more esoteric music, talk shows,
and foreign news broadcasts.

Broadcasting first emerged in the 1920s.
American broadcasting, from the outset,
was envisaged as being commercial. Public
broadcasting was not seriously considered
at the time since it was thought that commercial broadcasting could provide a sufficient range of services to satisfy radio and,
eventually, television audiences.

In the 1920s and 1930s, public broadcasting in the United States was formed on a
small-scale basis, and its programming was
primarily educational. Institutions such as
colleges and schools were provided with licences for a small number of non-commercial radio stations that were not supported
by government. It was only in the 1950s,
with the advent of television, that interest

in public broadcasting was heightened,
especially among community and national
organizations, which desired to produce
cultural and educational programming for
general audiences. On 25 May 1953, the
first non-commercial educational television station (KUHT) was established at the
University of Houston. For the subsequent
decade, public television broadcasting's
main focus was on formal instruction (ITV)
and education (ETV).

The Educational Television Facilities Act was signed by President John F.
Kennedy on 1 May 1962. This provided
'pub-casting' (the precursor of the Public
Telecommunications Facilities Program,
PTFP) with significant federal funding.
By the middle of the 1960s, there was a
surge in the number of ETV stations and
non-commercial radio stations, as approximately 100 ETV and 400 non-commercial
radio stations were formed. This surge was
mainly the result of financial support from
the Ford Foundation, which offered grants
to community organizations throughout
the United States and encouraged educational institutions and state agencies
to expand their ETV offerings. The Ford
Foundation also contributed to the establishment of a national production network,
the National Educational Television and
Radio Center (NETRC). The NETRC eventually became the NET as it came to focus
entirely on television programming. It created and broadcasted culture and public
affairs programs, but the programs were
only small in number and delivered by
videotape. On 5 November 1967, the *Public
Broadcasting Laboratory (PBL)*, a Sunday-
night magazine program, was introduced
by the Ford Foundation.

The growing number of public broadcasting television networks eventually
resulted in their division by region. Networks such as the Eastern Educational
Network (EEN), the Southern Educational
Communications Association (SECA),
and the Pacific Mountain Network (PMN)
were created. Just as the number of non-
commercial stations began to expand, so

too did the audience numbers. Expanded audiences meant increased public support; funding for public broadcasting was boosted and the planning that went into national program production and networking increased.

The Carnegie Commission passed the Public Broadcasting Act of 1967 in response to increased audience interest and the lack of national funding that was being provided for public television. The act recommended public broadcasting's expansion from a limited entity that provided mainly educational programming to a model that would suit more general purposes. It also provided an action plan, suggesting how the transformation might be accomplished.

The Public Broadcasting Act was successful in bringing about significant changes. A national structure for public broadcasting was created, as was a foundation for the future of public broadcasting in the United States for the rest of the twentieth century. The act also established the national Corporation for Public Broadcasting (CPB) and dictated that the governing board for CPB was to be appointed by the President of the United States and by the national Senate. In turn for CPB offering a greater amount of national programming and fostering support for American non-commercial stations, the act authorized CPB to receive national government funds. Since Congress refused to endow a long-term funding source, however, it was decided that CBP funding decisions would be made on a yearly basis.

In 1969, CPB was incorporated, and shortly thereafter it produced two new organizations by collaborating with pre-existing public broadcasting stations and groups. The new organizations, the Public Broadcasting Service (PBS) and National Public Radio (NPR), were established to manage the interconnected systems that were previously under the jurisdiction of CPB. PBS started its operations in 1970 with a total of 128 member stations, and telephone lines were used to provide its services. *Sesame Street*, a widely acclaimed educational program for children, debuted in 1969. This program was produced by the Children's Television Workshop (CTW) and ultimately shown on public broadcasting networks throughout the world (including PBS in the United States). Hartford Gunn was selected as the first president of PBS in February 1970.

During the 1970s, the main organizational structure of American public broadcasting coalesced, although small modifications are still being made. The CPB was regarded by some to have had too much dominance over public broadcasting – something that was not present in other countries. The programming and board appointments that were made exacerbated these concerns. Public broadcasting was not without its successes at this time, however. *Masterpiece Theatre*, which became a widely popular and long-running drama series, premiered on PBS in 1971. Also in 1971, NPR broadcasted Senate hearings on ending the war in Vietnam. This broadcast marked the beginning of NPR's service. In 1978, PBS became the first television network in the United States to broadcast programs across the country using satellite technology.

In the 1980s, PBS and NPR experienced significant organizational problems, and their relationship with CPB became somewhat fractured. PBS and NPR began to have more exclusive ownership of stations and independence from CPB. Over time, however, American Public Radio, which was established from a part of Minnesota Public Radio (MPR) and eventually became Public Radio International (PRI), was providing competition to NPR. In 1980, closed captioning, which was developed by PBS, was offered for the first time. It appeared on three networks, including PBS for *Masterpiece Theatre*. During February 1983, a variety of public television stations in the United States broadcast open-heart surgery, which was covered by KAET, a PBS station in Phoenix. This was not the only important contribution that PBS made to television technology; the network has used video for the blind, stereo sound, dubbing, and the internet to provide its programming to a wider audience.

As the distribution capacities of satellite and cable broadcasting increased, and as greater demand was created for more diversified services, public broadcasting stations were established more frequently in urban centres, allowing a greater number of audience members to have access to more than one broadcasting signal. In the mid-1990s, approximately half of the American population had access to at least three public radio stations and at least two public television stations.

Even with the further expansion of public broadcasting, some previous concerns about its funding and structure still existed. Its organizational structure also seemed unnecessarily complex. A lack of commitment to public broadcasting became apparent when the Telecommunications Act of 1996 failed to even mention public broadcasting. This was despite the fact that, overall, it was still considered an important contributor to the public and social good.

Non-commercial broadcasting continued to be transformed with the momentous changes that telecommunications technology brought about during the last quarter of the twentieth century. Throughout the 1980s and 1990s, digital technologies were progressing at a brisk pace, and media forms (both commercial and public) were being reconfigured. Public and other broadcasting systems were challenged near the end of the century, when digital transmission, via the internet and World Wide Web, with its greater data transmission and multimedia capabilities, was converging with, and even replacing, traditional broadcasting. Public broadcasting was given new opportunities when the Federal Communications Commission (FCC) decided to convert all broadcasting to digital technology. The growth of internet users facilitated public broadcasting's new ability to supplement, and, in some cases, compete with its traditional services.

In the twenty-first century, public broadcasting still comprises a relatively small portion of the media industry in the United States, but it is still considered by many to be an essential component.

Alexandra Birk-Urovitz and Elizabeth Birk-Urovitz

Bibliography

Ickes, L.R. *Public Broadcasting in America*. New York: Nova, 2006.

McCauley, Michael P., Lee Artz, and DeeDee Halleck. *Public Broadcasting and the Public Interest*. Armonk, NY: M.E. Sharpe, 2003.

PULP FICTION

[See also: *Adventure Stories; Books, History of; Crime Genre; Horror Fiction; Narrative; Romance Fiction; Science Fiction; Text Theory*]

Pulp fiction refers to cheaply produced and highly sensationalistic, serialized fiction magazines that were highly popular from the 1920s to the 1950s. They were produced in bulk for mass entertainment. The word *pulp* refers to the fact that the magazines were produced on cheap wood pulp paper, in contrast to those that used higher-quality paper, called *glossies* or *slicks*. The first true pulp is considered to be Frank Munsey's *Argosy Magazine* of 1896.

The pulps were written in a sensationalistic and lurid way, attracting a large readership. As a consequence, pulp detectives and crime fighters such as Doc Savage, The Shadow, and the Phantom Detective became household names. Titles of the early pulp magazines included: *Dime Detective, Planet Stories, Adventure, Black Mask, Startling Stories, Flying Aces, Amazing Stories, Black Mask, Spicy Detective, Horror Stories, Unknown and Weird Tales, Marvel Tales, Oriental Stories,* and *Thrilling Wonder Stories.* Their popularity was augmented by their cover designs, which resembled the poster art used by circuses and vaudeville theatres to attract audiences, with scantily dressed 'damsels in distress' or handsome, virile heroes involved in fisticuffs with villains. The pulp genre was adapted early on for radio and the cinema, in the form of radio and movie serials, such as those made by Republic Pictures in the 1930s and 1940s. The serials kept audiences in suspense because an episode ended typically when the hero or heroine was seen entangled in some dangerous situation from which he or she could not possible emerge alive. The audience would come back the following week to find out how the cliffhanger would be resolved. The term *cliffhanger* is often used synonymously with *pulp fiction*.

The main pulp genres were horror, sword and sorcery, science fiction, adventure, westerns, crime (especially of the *noir* variety), romance, gangster, war, sports, mystery, and the occult. Although many featured different characters, plots, and settings, the most popular ones featured a single character. These came to be known more specifically as *hero pulps*. Popular pulp heroes included: Buck Rogers, Flash Gordon, Dick Tracy, Perry Mason, Zorro, Fu Manchu, Captain Future, Conan the Barbarian, Doc Savage, The Phantom Detective, The Shadow, Domino Lady, Hopalong Cassidy, Nick Carter, Secret Agent X, Tarzan, The Avenger, and The Spider.

With rising paper costs and competition from other media, the pulps (and their radio and cinema derivatives) started losing market supremacy by the late 1950s. The bankruptcy in 1957 of the American News Company, which was the main distributor of pulp magazines, marked the end of the pulp fiction era. But the cliffhanger formula is still evident in current movies, such as the James Bond movies, the *Raiders of the Lost Ark* films, and others. Pulp fiction also engaged some of the greatest writers of the twentieth century, including Isaac Asimov, Ray Bradbury, Edgar Rice Burroughs, Arthur C. Clarke, Philip K. Dick, Zane Grey, Robert A. Heinlein, Raymond Chandler, Arthur Conan Doyle, Erle Stanley Gardner, Frank Herbert, H.P. Lovecraft, O. Henry, and Upton Sinclair. Contemporary writers such as Stephen King and Anne

Rice work in the same tradition as the pulp fiction writers. So, while the original pulps may have disappeared, the pulp format and style remain. Pulp fiction conventions are held every year in the United States. In the early 2000s there was also an attempt to bring the pulps back with the publication of magazines such as *Blood N' Thunder, High Adventure*, and *Secret of the Amazon Queen*. Moonstone Books revived some of the old pulps with its new editions of *The Phantom, Zorro, The Spider, Domino Lady*, and *The Avenger* in 2001. Although not as successful as was anticipated, the revival has nonetheless occurred in online venues, where pulp has a considerable following.

Marcel Danesi

Bibliography

Haining, Peter. *The Classic Era of the American Pulp Magazines*. Chicago: Chicago Review Press, 2001.

McCracken, Scott. *Pulp: Reading Popular Fiction*. New York: St Martin's, 1998.

Robinson, Frank M., and Lawrence Davidson. *Pulp Culture: The Art of Fiction Magazines*. Portland, OR: Collectors Press, 1998.

Q

[See also: *Advertising; Anthropology of the Media; Media Studies*]

QUALITATIVE AND QUANTITA-
TIVE RESEARCH

Qualitative and quantitative research are used in the study of media. The former focuses on observation and ethnographic research, the latter on statistical methods. Traditionally, qualitative research has been cast as the method that gives greater depth to an understanding of the effects of media and advertising, but is less often used by decision makers as substantiation for important decisions. Quantitative research is usually seen as helping to validate hunches, to give statistical weight to opinions, and to endorse points of view. It is considered to bring a more rigorous and credible form of research to the table, but is also seen to lack the imagination and compelling insight of qualitative research. Qualitative research has been viewed as responsible for the 'how' and 'why' questions and quantitative research for the 'what,' 'when,' where,' and 'how often' questions.

Quantitative research does work to quantify the numbers of people who hold beliefs and carry out certain types of behaviour, and allows us to know more exact proportions through percentages or indices of sympathy towards a particular view. It is used for instance by pollsters to predict the results of an election or to canvass a large number of people on the image of services and products. What this type of research does not really allow a company to do is to dig beneath and better grasp the reasoning and human factors behind this. So quantitative research could, for instance, highlight a divergence in preference in a usage and attitude study of a brand conducted in India between pork and beef that correlates with part of a city but could completely miss the religious issues involved. Qualitative research is more eclectic and more flexible for investigating more complex, sensitive areas of culture.

Qualitative research has its roots in Freudian psychoanalytic practice and works within a model in which individuals report on their behaviour through discussion led by a skilled moderator, who is able to tease out further insights. Qualitative research is essentially a means of understanding people's needs and responses through dialogue and group methods, known as focus groups, where discussion and interaction are encouraged. Qualitative research as a tool in marketing came to prominence in the United States in the 1950s as advertisers sought to use the tools of psychology and social science to better understand their customers. Pioneers of so-called 'motivational research' such as Ernst Dichter predicated their consultancies, which convened panels of individuals segmented by their psychological make-up, on the basis that emotional appeals were the most important selling points. Probing motivations and unlocking the purchase triggers in 'depth interview' sessions was the key to this. At the time, Dichter's work was seen as scandalous. The insidious techniques of motivational researchers were summed up by Vance Packard (1957: 37) in his seminal work *The Hidden Persuaders* as follows: 'People's subsurface desires, needs, and drives were probed in order to find their points of vulnerability … for example … the drive to conformity, need for oral stimulation, yearning for security. Once these points of vulnerability were isolated, the psychological hooks were fashioned and baited and placed deep in the merchandising sea for unwary prospective customers.' In the 1970s, qualitative research gained a wider recognition, and 'respectability' through the 1980s, growing rapidly as a mainstream approach through the 1990s. Today, it is seen as an integral part of how media corporations set their strategic vision.

The origins of quantitative research predate qualitative research. Quantitative research grew up as a technique of measurement in the physical sciences. It was pioneered by Gustav Fechner in his work on psychophysics, which built on the work of Ernst Heinrich Weber. From there, it was adopted by media researchers. One of the first to do so was George Gallup. Working at Northwestern University, Gallup developed some of the earliest techniques to measure advertising and copy effectiveness, media, and audience profiles. He also conducted one of the first opinion polls for the 1936 U.S. election. Despite the inroads made by qualitative research, alluded to above, its more established cousin, quantitative research, is still the dominant form of market research. The latest topical data (from global trade association ESOMAR based on 2006 data) show that of the total spent on global research 86 per cent is allocated to quantitative research.

Global quantitative research firms are numerous, with companies such as Ipsos-Mori, Synovate, A.C. Nielsen, Kantar (which includes Millward Brown, BMRB, and Research International), and Taylor Nelson Sofres offering a range of products from usage and attitude studies to advertising tracking and other more sophisticated techniques. Online research has grown in popularity as a means of combining the range and sample sizes of quantitative research with the ability to canvass opinion in real time.

The structure of qualitative research involves a number of phases. The first is briefing from the client on objectives. The researcher then determines who the study should target and in what format contact should take place. The drafting of a screener questionnaire is geared to ask a combination of open and closed questions in order to ascertain that the right individuals are being asked to take part in the study. Once groups or individual depths have been scheduled, fieldworkers canvass people's attitudes in a variety of forums. After fieldwork and data gathering have been completed, a period of analysis occurs which involves sifting through the data, which include interview transcripts and more informal inputs, such as scribbled notes. Finally, there is a debriefing phase in which the study results are delivered in a presentational format. A qualitative research project typically takes six weeks or so from commissioning to the final debriefing.

Qualitative research is mainly used to gather evidence, to test out theories, and provide more nuance to the research study.

Qualitative research can work in three main ways:

- *Diagnosis*, which provides a depth of understanding of a present state of affairs, for instance, why a brand launch has failed or why people lapse from using a brand after a certain age.
- *Prognosis*, in which audiences or customers provide responses to options, plans, and proposals.
- *Creativity* where respondents are used as sources of ideas, innovation, and inspiration. This is often the case where the client wants to make a more radical change, either by inventing new prod-

ucts, carving out new categories, or revamping their products or programs.

Quantitative research generally has a longer 'turnaround' time than its qualitative counterpart. Quantitative research can take from four to twelve weeks from the point of commissioning to the final debriefing phase. Quantitative teams are around the same size as those used for qualitative, though the interviewing itself may often be outsourced to logistics companies for great efficiency.

Most commercial research can be categorized into either tracking, ad hoc (custom), or syndicated research. Tracking quantitative research (whether conducted continuously, monthly, quarterly) allows a company to follow the progress of initiatives from measuring sales after product launch to tracking recently released advertising and other communication. This will typically involve measuring the same metrics at regular intervals, often every quarter. This allows manufacturing organizations to check on the uptake of the product or the susceptibility of prospects to communication. This type of tracking allows managers to keep an eye on the performance of a brand or levels of esteem in which a company is held. This allows the company decision makers to take appropriate actions to correct suboptimal behaviours and ensure key performance indicators.

A quantitative researcher typically employs several specialist techniques derived from applied mathematics, such as regression analysis to understand what factors are driving response or cluster analysis to help with segmentation of a sample and other techniques. Cluster analysis identifies segments of people who tend to respond in a broadly similar way, similar enough to be targeted with the same message or product proposition. Correlation analysis helps researchers understand which variables are related and how to know the strength of the relationship. Regression analysis shows the relative contributions of different issues to particular outcomes. This, in turn, helps

clients to prioritize investments – such as allocation of media spending or where to invest to maximize customer satisfaction – and addresses other aspects of the marketer's problem-solving brief. Quantitative research can be utilized to address a diverse range of topics such as advertising awareness, brand choice, product purchase, customer satisfaction, and employee motivation.

Quantitative research is not immune to criticism. Its reliance on statistics as a silver bullet or panacea has come under attack. For example, David Boyle in his book *Tyranny of Numbers: Why Counting Can't Make Us Happy* argues that an obsession with numbers now blights modern society and makes grappling with real issues more difficult. He suggests that there are things that cannot be measured and cites examples such as Jeremy Bentham's experiments in utilitarianism as cases that make nonsense of the notion of measurability improving our welfare or understanding. Nassim Nicholas Taleb in his 2007 book *The Black Swan: Fooled by Randomness* argues that the world is changed most by highly improbable events (e.g., 9/11 or the success of Google) and yet the statistics discipline excludes these 'outliers.' The upshot of this is that we are lured into giving too much credence to extrapolating constructs such as 'bull market' that do not always have sound empirical or predictive basis. In short, numbers can fool us into thinking we know more than we do.

Quantitative research uses the unit as the basic means of counting. This could be an individual but could equally be a couple or a household. Questions must be exactly the same for everyone. Questions are mostly structured or semi-structured in format (but can also be open). Sample sizes must be big enough to be meaningful (i.e., quantifiable). Broadly speaking, qualitative research is good for uncovering the factors underlying a topic and quantitative research for ranking those factors. In sum, quantitative and qualitative approaches are two aspects or modalities of the same instinct and meet the same need – to find out what is going on in an area of human activity or marketplace and to better understand the relevant context. Both in their own way keep actors and entities in touch with their constituencies and contexts.

Chris Arning

Bibliography

Boyle, David. *Tyranny of Numbers: Why Counting Can't Make Us Happy.* New York: HarperCollins, 2001.

Packard, Vance. *The Hidden Persuaders.* New York: McKay, 1957.

Taleb, Nassim Nicholas. *The Black Swan: Fooled by Randomness.* London: Routledge, 2007.

R

RACE AND GENDER DIVERSITY IN THE MEDIA

[See also: *Feminism; Representation*]

Diversity, as it concerns race and gender in the media, typically refers to the inclusion of women and people of colour in news and other media content, and to the equitable representation of these groups within the media professions. Diversity in media content and employment arose as a demand of popular liberation movements led by women and various groups composed of non-white persons, beginning in the 1960s and continuing to the present time. These movements have sought to remove discriminatory structures blocking women and people of colour from achieving full equality and social participation within their societies. Structures of concern have included not only legal, political, economic, educational, and religious mechanisms, but also the media, which are widely understood to be powerful tools for purveying information, educating, shaping public opinion, and setting agendas for public discourse and policy.

Women and people of colour formulated their media-related critiques around sexist and racist practices in the media. In relation to media content, the focus was on persistent stereotyping, omission, marginalization and misrepresentation in both news and entertainment genres. In the United States, where there was a particularly vigorous movement to stop racist and sexist media practices, civil rights and women's organizations focused on specific issues like inadequate news reporting of race and gender relations, harmful stereotypes in television programming, and the general omission of Black, Latino, Native American, Asian, and feminist perspectives. In relation to numbers of professionals, both women and racial minorities were few in number before passage of the Equal Opportunities Act in 1972. Advocacy groups like the National Association for the Advancement of Colored People (NAACP) and National Organization for Women (NOW) led campaigns to expand progressive race and gender perspectives in both news and television programming over the ensuing decades. In addition, lawyers for these (and other) groups worked together with labour unions to legally challenge discrimination based on sex and race.

The results have been mixed. All struggles by marginalized people against oppressive institutional practices bring about a dialectical process that is typically long in time frame and characterized by uneven progress. In other words, at any given moment, one finds both signs of positive change and stubborn resistance (including backlash). As a result of women's and civil rights movements, however, gender and racial diversity in the media is greater today in several ways. In news, women presently constitute about a fourth of the subjects in major newspaper stories, and about a third of both print and broadcast reporters, according to the 2005 Global Media Monitoring Project. U.S. television programs today feature women in major roles of many dramas, and increasing numbers of women are writing scripts, directing, and producing prime-time programs. Racial diversity has also increased, particularly for African Americans in dramatic television program roles, and as actors and filmmakers. The downside is that neither women nor people of colour have achieved parity in terms of representation in these professions, and, more troubling, stereotypes persist in several ways. Women's victimization has become a staple of both news reporting and prime-time dramas, without accompanying analyses (to explain why) or indications of women's long-standing efforts to stem violence against them by men. African-American men and other men of colour are more likely to be depicted as criminals in television dramas than white men, and they are treated more harshly by reporters in newscasts about crime than are white men, according to numerous academic studies. These are only a few examples of problems that remain.

The situation is similar in other nations. Racism and sexism in the media (at content, professional, and ownership levels) are long-standing cross-cultural problems that have been the focus of social movements for self-determination by women and indigenous people within as well as among nations. The internationality of these problems came to light in the 1970s, in relation to both the New World Information Order debates, led by developing nations, and at a series of meetings held by women during the UN Decade for Women (1976–85). In the first case, leaders from Africa and other nations of the global South charged the United States and European news agencies with dominating global news flow and flooding their nations with Western images, values, and products, thereby extending a system of neocolonialism and cultural imperialism. Women's complaints were

that females appeared in less than 4 per cent of world news (in the 1970s) and that female stereotypes abounded in all media genres. Remedies emerged that included the creation of alternative media structures, including news agencies like Pan African News Agency (PANA), Caribbean Area News Agency (CANA), and several Women's Feature Service programs to provide coverage of issues from non-Western, non-male perspectives. Within individual nations, monitoring and advocacy groups have set about creating more indigenous media and increasing gender-sensitive news and other media content. South Africa since the early 1990s – that is, after apartheid – represents a particularly good example of women organizing across racial and class lines to monitor news and other media, to train journalists and news producers, and to establish new media.

Diversity initiatives led by women and people of colour are presently shifting to the macro levels of media ownership and media policy. Since the 1990s, media ownership has become concentrated in fewer and fewer hands in both industrialized and developing nations. Powerful wealthy media moguls, most of whom are Western males of European heritage, oversee media empires that include movie studios, book publishing, newspapers, magazines, television stations, theatres, theme parks, and many other products and services. These corporate bastions present new challenges by feminists and people of colour to gain access to storytelling, image-making, and jobs, the last of which are diminishing in number. Media Reform Conferences, held biannually since 2003 in the United States, and the United Nations' World Summit for the Information Society meetings, held in Geneva and Tunis in 2003 and 2005 respectively, are some of the events at which diversity concerns associated with sexism and racism in the media are being considered in relation to ownership and other media governance policies.

Carolyn M. Byerly

Bibliography

Courtenoy, Alice E., and Thomas W. Whipple. *Sex Stereotyping in Advertising*. Lexington, MA: Lexington Books, 1983.

Van Zoonen, Liesbet. *Feminist Media Studies*. London: Sage, 1994.

RADIO

[See also: *Broadcasting; Communication; Marconi, Guglielmo; Television*]

Technologically, the term *radio* refers to the transmission of sounds converted into electromagnetic waves directly through space to a receiving device, which converts them back into sounds. The invention of the radio is traced to the work of Nikola Tesla, an American inventor from Austria-Hungary who, in 1891, invented the Tesla coil, a type of high-frequency transformer. In 1895, the Italian-born engineer Guglielmo Marconi (1874–1937) transmitted an electronic signal successfully to a receiving device without any wired connection. He called his invention a *radiotelegraph* (later shortened to *radio*), because its signal moved outward radially (in all directions). In 1901, Marconi invented an alternator appliance that could send signals farther and with less background noise. Between 1906 and 1910, inventor Lee De Forest devised the vacuum tube, called the Audion tube, improving radio reception; Reginald Fessenden made the first radio broadcast from the Metropolitan Opera House in New York City shortly thereafter. This new technology opened up the path for the radio, known at first as the *wireless*, to emerge as a powerful electronic mass medium, shaping trends in society generally. Radio could reach many more people than could print, not only because its reach spanned great distances, but also because its listeners did not have to be print literate.

In 1912, the U.S. Congress passed the first licensing legislation (the Radio Act of 1912) intended to address the problems of amateur radio operators jamming the airwaves. Fifteen years later, it revised the legislation (Radio Act of 1927), creating a Federal Radio Commission to supervise radio operators in order to ensure that they served the public interest and to standardize frequency designations. It was clear that the era of radio broadcasting had arrived in full force.

Radio Broadcasting

Evidence of a plan for radio broadcasting to the general public is found in a 1916 memorandum (*The Radio Box Memo*) written by David Sarnoff (1891–1971), who was an employee of American Marconi, the company that would become the Radio Corporation of America (RCA). In the memo, Sarnoff recommended that radio be made into a 'household utility.' Several companies took up Sarnoff's idea of mass-marketing home radios very seriously. Frank Conrad of the Westinghouse Electric Corporation of Pittsburgh founded KDKA as the first experimental radio station in 1916. The station's broadcast of the 1920 presidential election results on 2 November 1920 is considered to be the beginning of professional broadcasting. KDKA offered a regular schedule of programming to the general public, including entertainment programs and recorded music using a phonograph placed within the range of a radio microphone. The station did not charge user fees, nor did it carry advertising. Westinghouse saw KDKA simply as an enticement for people to purchase radios.

Other radio manufacturers followed suit. Sarnoff himself opened stations in New York City and Washington, DC, and in 1926 he founded the National Broadcasting Company (NBC) with a cross-country network of local stations. The Columbia Broadcasting System (CBS) radio service was established shortly thereafter in 1928, becoming a leader in the broadcasting industry over the subsequent fifty years.

According to estimates by the National Association of Broadcasters, in 1922 60,000 households in America had radios; by 1929 the number had topped 10 million. But the sale of radio receivers could not cover the costs of broadcasting. The only viable solution for the economic survival of radio broadcasting was advertising. The confluence of advertising with radio programming was the event that transformed mass the evolving media culture. There would be no national non-commercial radio network until the establishment of National Public Radio (NPR) in 1971, well after the golden age of radio. In Great Britain, on the other hand, radio owners paid yearly licence fees, collected by the government, which were turned over (and continue to be turned over) directly to the publicly run British Broadcasting Corporation (BBC).

Radio broadcasting reached the pinnacle of its popularity and influence during the Second World War, when American reporter Edward R. Murrow (1908–65) changed the nature of news reporting with his eyewitness descriptions of street scenes during the German bombing raids of London, which he delivered live from the rooftop of the CBS news bureau there. The immediacy of such reporting was powerful. Aware of radio's emotional power, American president Franklin D. Roosevelt was the first politician to use radio as a propaganda tool, bypassing the press and directly addressing the American people with his 'fireside chats' during the Great Depression. Radio broadcasting started losing its mass audiences to television by the late 1940s, morphing into an information- and music-based medium. In 1948, the DJ radio era took off, with Top 40 radio becoming the most popular type of radio format in 1955.

Today, radio broadcasting consists mainly of the news, music, sports, and talk genres, thus catering to niche audiences. In 1996, Congress passed the Telecommunications Act, allowing for consolidation in radio ownership across the United States. Satellite and Web-based radio programs emerged in 2002. File sharing and online radio programs have now become highly popular, revitalizing radio somewhat.

Overall, radio is a medium for specialized purposes – people listen to it in their cars or in their offices (or other places), as they do something else. Radio stations thus typically present traffic information regularly interspersed throughout their broadcasts or present music of various styles.

Radio Genres

Because it reached large numbers of people, from the 1920s to the early 1950s radio became the first electronic mass medium. At first, radio programming simply adapted the traditional stage, vaudeville, and pulp fiction genres, modifying them to its particular audio-oral characteristics and producing the first widely popular dramas, action serials, situation comedies, soap operas, and comedy-variety programs that defined American pop culture. It modelled its news coverage on the format of daily newspapers. Radio announcers would simply read articles from the local newspaper over the air. As people became bored with this, editing the news for oral delivery started occurring. As a result, newscasting became its own genre.

The sitcom is often pegged as being the first radio-created genre. But this is not completely accurate. The sitcom ('situation comedy') was an adaptation of an improvised form of vaudevillian comedy skit routine that, itself, traced its roots to the Commedia dell'Arte – a type of improvised comedy that arose in Italy in the sixteenth and seventeenth centuries characterized by a recurring comedic plots and stock characters. It was a highly popular form of 'street theatre,' as opposed to the more serious theatre of the court. Common folk came out in flocks to see Commedia performances because they dealt with common situations, such as love affairs, betrayal, friendship, and the like, in a farcical and often hilarious way. The actors used makeshift stages in piazzas. The script was called a *scenario* (an outline of a basic plot), and the characters wore masks to bring out their personalities visually. The same actors played the same roles, improvising as they went along according to audience reactions. Some of the characters, like Harlequin the clown and Pantaloon the old man, became so popular that many people wore their particular masks at carnival time.

Radio sitcoms had many of the same features of the Commedia, except that the scripts were fixed. They explored love and romance in the home, the workplace, and other common locations in a comedic and often farcical manner. They took the script of everyday life and turned it into a fictional radio comedy. The first widely popular sitcom, which premiered in 1928 on NBC, was *Amos 'n' Andy*, in which actors performed the roles of African-American characters in outrageous caricature. *The Goldbergs* (1929–50), *Life with Luigi* (1948–53), and other sitcoms based on family life dealt with another social situation of the era – immigration. Lucille Ball's *My Favorite Husband* (1948–51) was an exception to the standard sitcom fare, developing the artistry of the genre considerably, by injecting into it Commedia elements such as the battle between the sexes, neighbour conflicts, and other mundane situational themes.

Variety shows, taken directly from stage vaudeville, were also popular adaptations of early radio. Radio stars such as Jack Benny, Fred Allen, and Edgar Bergen were, in fact, vaudeville actors and comedians who made the transition over to radio. A variety hour consisted typically of short monologues and skits, alternating with musical acts.

Radio drama also became highly popular, using one of two formats – *anthology* and *serial*. The former consisted of stage-type plays. It included *Mercury Theater on the Air* (1938–41), created by Orson Welles, and *Theatre Guild of the Air* (1945–54). The serials, on the other hand, consisted of the same characters, situations, and settings involved in similar plots week after week. These included urban police dramas, such as *Gangbusters* (1935–57), private eye mysteries, such as *The Shadow* (1930–54), and

westerns, such as *The Lone Ranger* (1933–55). A highly popular type of serial, called soap opera, was broadcast on a daily basis during the afternoon, being aimed at a female audience. It was so named because soap and detergent manufacturers sponsored many of the programs. Consisting of continuing episodes (seemingly without end), the soaps explored romance, friendship, and familial relations in emotionally involving ways. People felt as if they were listening in to an ongoing situation in other people's lives, becoming intimately familiar with the characters of the soaps. The invention of the soap opera is credited to Irna Phillips in Chicago during the 1920s. The first true soap opera is generally considered to be *Painted Dreams*, which premiered in 1930. It flopped, but its successors, such as *The Guiding Light*, *Backstage Wife*, and *The Romance of Helen Trent*, became popular across the nation. Much has been written about the relationship between soap operas and gender stereotyping. Suffice it to say here that the soap opera was aimed at women because they were the ones who typically stayed at home in the radio era. The fact that the soaps dealt primarily with romance, however, should come as no surprise and should not be attributed to a gender bias. Romance has always been a part of popular culture, aimed at mixed (not gendered) audiences, from the medieval romances to the great romance novels of the nineteenth century.

In the area of news reporting, radio offered not only simple readings of printed news, but also live coverage of some events – something that newspapers could not do. As a consequence, print journalism became a supplemental medium to radio, focusing on in-depth coverage and editorial opinion. Today, radio continues to be a primary source of the news. So-called 'drive time' (7–9 a.m. and 4–7 p.m.) – when many people drive to and from work – has become radio's prime time. Programming during this time consists mainly of traffic bulletins, weather reports, breaking and current news items, time checks, and the like. Some stations have 'news-only formats,' reflecting the radio's evolution into a medium for niche audiences. National Public Radio's *All Things Considered* (1971–) and *Morning Edition* (1979–) were developed as morning and evening 'on-air newspapers' for sophisticated audiences.

Radio has always been a promoter of trends in pop music. The jazz, swing, rock, and hip-hop movements spread originally through radio, spurring consumers to buy records. And, last but not least, radio has always been a perfect medium for 'talk.' The early talk shows were really no more than commentaries on current affairs. But they soon evolved into gossip programs. The talk show is now one of the most popular of all radio genres.

Radio and Advertising

The newspaper was the first medium to rely on advertising in the late eighteenth century. The same kind of pattern occurred with radio. Even an entire genre – the soap opera – was named for the type of advertiser that sponsored it. However, at first, there was resistance to the use of the radio for commercial purposes. In fact, in 1922, when the first radio commercial advertisements (known simply as *commercials*) were aired on station WEAF, there was an uproar. But the uproar quickly subsided, as people became accustomed to the commercials. Stations often sold advertising agencies full sponsorship, which included placing the product name in a program's title, as for example *Palmolive Beauty Box Theater* (1927–37) or *The Texaco Star Theater* (1948–53). The ratings system came into being from the sponsors' desire to know how many people they were reaching. In 1929 Archibald Crossley launched *Crossley's Cooperative Analysis of Broadcasting*, using telephone surveys to assay daily estimates of audience sizes for radio networks. The A.C. Nielsen Company was founded shortly thereafter in the mid-1930s, becoming the main radio ratings service. The ratings were used to help set the price of commercials and, ultimately, to determine whether the program would stay on the air. Only public radio stations have remained exempt from the 'ratings game,' since they are financed by government subsidies, individual donations, and various corporate grants.

As mentioned, radio introduced the *commercial* into advertising – a mini-narrative revolving around a product or service. Early commercials consisted of pseudo-scientific sales pitches, satires of movies, and memorable jingles. They became so familiar that they helped create the first fictitious advertising personalities, from *Mr Clean* (representing a detergent product of the same name) to *Speedy* (a personified Alka-Seltzer indigestion tablet). The jingle became a source of recognizable tunes throughout society, from *Mr Clean in a just a minute* (for the Mr Clean detergent product) to *Plop, plop, fizz, fizz oh what a relief it is* (for the Alka-Seltzer stomach product). Various jingles, in fact, became hit tunes on their own.

At first the commercials were delivered at the beginning of a show and often at the end. Gradually, they were interspersed throughout a program, usually prefaced with an announcer telling the listeners 'We pause for a brief commercial announcement.' It was from this standard statement that the term *commercial* comes. Radio advertising can reach people as they do other things, such as driving a car or working. Advertisers can also stylize their commercials according to audience demographics. By selecting the station in this way, advertisers can reach the people most likely to buy their products directly, creating commercials suited to them in terms of content and style.

Even in today's TV and online world, radio remains a widely-used medium, converging with the other media in a complementary manner. When it was the main mass medium, people sat around it at various times of the day in their homes. The voices that introduced programs and the voices of the actors on the programs were recognized throughout society. In a phrase, radio revived a kind of (tribalistic) 'orality' (based on the human voice) as a mode of mass communication. Orality has great emotional appeal. When we listen to the modulations of the human voice, without a visual component, we are greatly affected by its emotional qualities. Reading and writing activate linear thinking processes in the brain because printed ideas are laid out one at a time and can thus be connected to each other sequentially; orality, on the other hand, is inextricable from the people speaking.

Radio broadcasting has influenced and even changed social life wherever it was introduced. By bringing the arts directly into homes it democratized aesthetics. Historically a privilege of the aristocracy (or the cognoscenti), the arts could be enjoyed by anyone, without having to go to the concert hall or the theatre. The parallel growth of network radio and Hollywood cinema, both of which were launched as mass commercial enterprises in 1927, created an unprecedented mass culture for people of all socio-economic classes and educational backgrounds. In the internet age, radio has shown itself to have great resilience. Digital satellite radio stations, such as XM and Sirius, are showing that the radio is not yet a relic. It may have come down from its top perch, but it continues, nevertheless, to be an integral part of mass culture.

Marcel Danesi

Bibliography

Barnard, Stephen. *Studying Radio*. London: Arnold, 2000.

Heyer, Paul. *The Medium and the Magician: Orson Welles, the Radio Years, 1934–1952*. Lanham, MD: Rowman and Littlefield, 2005.

Neer, Richard. *FM: The Rise and Fall of Rock Radio*. New York: Villard, 2001.

Rudel, Anthony. *Hello Everybody! The Dawn of American Radio*. New York: Harcourt, 2009.

RADWAY, JANICE (b. 1949)

[See also: *Feminism; Race and Gender Diversity; Romance Fiction*]

Janice Radway is a professor in Duke University's literary studies program. She is acclaimed as a leader of post-feminist thought (a school that sees women's sexuality and romantic ideologies as part of the process of gaining liberation, not as part of a patriarchal system), studying women's textual preferences, and the power of female-directed texts to give women assertiveness. Among her most influential works are: *Interpretive Communities and Variable Literacies* (1984) and *Reading the Romance: Women, Patriarchy, and Popular Literature* (1987/1991).

Radway received her BA from Michigan State University in 1971, her MA from the State University of New York at Stony Brook in 1972, and her PhD from Michigan State University in 1977. Before going to Duke, she taught in the American Civilization Department at the University of Pennsylvania, where she also served as editor of the *American Quarterly*. Her research interests include the history of literacy, particularly as it bears, and has borne, on the lives of women.

Radway's reputation lies primarily on her widely cited book on women's literature, *Reading the Romance*. Her analysis of women's romantic literature is an example of what has come to be known as 'reception theory' in media studies. This emphasizes the reader's reception of a text – which can be negotiated or even oppositional. In this framework, the reader is not viewed as a passive absorber of textual content, but rather an active contributor to its meaning. The sum total of meanings produced in this way lead to the text's overall reception in a culture. In reading romances, Radway found that women readers found the act of reading pleasurable in itself, above and beyond what society had to say about such works. The romantic narrative, she claims, has appeal because of its predictable structure, which somehow taps into women's imaginations. This consists of the following three main features:

- an opening section that presents a tense situation;
- an intermediate intervention section that brings about and explains the final situation;
- a final resolution of the initial tension.

The traditional romance narrative unfolds as follows. The heroine rejects her comfortable background to follow a man whom she thinks has romantic and sexual interests in her. At first, she reacts antagonistically to his advances and a 'tense situation' is established. Intervention then follows, as the heroine and her lover become separated, leading to her rejection of her own antagonism, especially after the lover shows kindness and tenderness towards her. Eventually, he declares his love for her and they are happily reunited.

At first, it would seem that such narratives are designed to maintain existing patriarchal views of love and romance. However, Radway emphasizes that one must differentiate between any purported ideological formatting of text, the meaning of the narrative as it is received by women readers, and the significance itself of this reception. Radway suggests that there really is no ideology behind such texts, since women themselves have always read them as forms of 'escapism' from domestic pressures, even if they might feel guilty about it. In effect, women readers form 'interpretive communities.' The fictional text encourages women to think that marriage and motherhood, for example, do not lead to a loss of their identity. The promise of romance provides them with the escape they need and an opportunity to give vent to their sexual and romantic feelings. This kind of reading activity is compensatory, Radway claims, because it allows women to focus on themselves and to establish their sexual identity through imaginary means. In sum, women do not read ro-

mances passively; they develop their own readings of them. Such reading constitutes empowerment, allowing women to actually change their lives if they so wish.

Angela Palangi

Bibliography

Radway, Janice. *Reading the Romance: Women, Patriarchy, and Popular Literature*. London: Verso, 1987/1991.

Staiger, Janet. *Media Reception Studies*. New York: New York University Press, 2005.

RATINGS

[See also: *Audience Research*]

The term *ratings* has two meanings in media studies. It refers to: (1) the system of identifying programs and movies according to content with recommendations for appropriate audience (G rating, PG rating, and so forth); and (2) the science of estimating the size of a radio or TV audience for a program of series, the results of which are used by broadcasters and sponsors to determine how many people they are reaching.

Traditionally ratings have been used for movies and television programs (although they have also been occasionally used for other media). In the United States, the Motion Picture Association of America (MPAA), founded in 1922, is responsible for movie rating system currently in use. As can be seen in Figure 1, it is based on age.

TV broadcasters generally oppose government-legislated regulations, claiming that these interfere with their right to freedom of expression. The U.S. Congress and citizens' groups, however, claim that the airwaves are public property, and thus that the government does have the right to create appropriate regulations. As a compromise, in 1997 television and cable networks adopted a voluntary ratings system, much like the MPAA system for movies, which

Figure 1

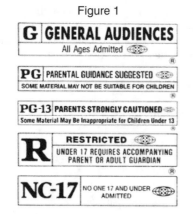

received FCC (Federal Communications Commission) approval in 1998. The purpose of the system is to inform viewers of the suitable audience for a certain program based on its content – for example, G (suitable for all audiences), Y7 (inappropriate for children under age 7), and MA (for mature audiences only). The rating may also indicate the nature of the content, such as V for violence or L for indecent language.

The second use of the term *ratings* applies to the use of scintific methods for measuring the success of a TV program or series. This is typically done by measuring the percentage of all households that are tuned to a particular program – known as the *share*. Nielsen Media Research has traditionally ranked as the main national audience measurement service in the United States, providing television stations and advertisers with information about share and with data about viewing audiences, such as their age, income, education, sex, and so on. Today, the Arbitron Ratings Company is the leading service at the local level. It uses techniques similar to those of Nielsen. A national audience survey typically consists of 5,000 households. The households are paid a small fee for their availability. The premise is that this is a sufficient sample to indicate the viewing habits of the entire country. The primary method of collecting data is that of viewer diaries, in which viewers annotate their viewing hab-

its. The ratings researchers may also use a device to measure a TV audience, known as the People Meter, which resembles a remote-control unit. Household members are asked to press an assigned key on the meter. This indicates who is watching a TV program. The meter thus makes it possible to register the age and gender of a viewer.

Historically, market researcher Arthur Nielsen (after whom the Nielsen ratings are named) developed the ratings system during the 1930s for radio programming. In 1950, he used the same system to rate television viewing habits. Today, with new technologies, the Nielsen system has been updated to provide 'streams' of data in order to take into account delayed viewing patterns.

Since viewers are aware of being part of a survey, it is claimed that the ratings system used by Nielsen can lead to 'experimenter bias' whereby the viewers will try to adjust their habits in ways that they think are appropriate to the research itself. Another criticism of the Nielsen ratings system is that it does not usually measure viewing habits outside of the household environment – in dormitories, at airport terminals, and so forth – which may have significance in determining program popularity. Since the advent of internet TV, Nielsen has expanded its research methodology to include digital media. For this reason, Nielson developed NetRatings in 2007.

Today, a new type of rating has emerged. Rating scales (from one star to five stars) are used commonly to provide indications of consumer opinions of products on various sites, such as Amazon.com, TV.com, Ratings.net, and Criticker, which uses a rating scale from 0 to 100. Ratings.net also allows users to rate products in terms of different qualities and performances (such as those on YouTube). Such ratings are not as 'scientific' as Nielsen ratings, since they provide no demographic data. Nevertheless, they constitute a basis upon which people can present their opinions to others. The greatest weakness of online ratings is that they represent the opinions mainly of those inclined to submit ratings in the first place. Thus, they may not be representative.

Marcel Danesi

Bibliography

D'Andrea, William L. *Killed in the Ratings*. New York: Harcourt, 1986.

REALITY TV

[See also: *Television; Television Genres; Television, History of*]

Factual programming is arguably the area of television culture which has seen the most significant changes in recent years. The emergence of new terms such as the 'docusoap,' 'popular factual programming,' and reality TV indicates this shift, and these changes have attracted much comment from critics, academics, broadcasters, and viewers. With new forms of programming jostling for space within the category of factual programming – a category which once meant television news, current affairs, or documentary – it is true to say that not everyone has seen this as a welcome development in television culture. As Richard Kilborn (2003: 1) explains:

> In the eyes of some, much of what has occurred in the domain of factual television is indicative of a more general cultural malaise. Programming that allegedly makes few demands on its audience is now seen to dominate the schedules of mainstream broadcasters, while programmes that stimulate debate or provide some form of cultural enlightenment are, it is claimed, a much less visible presence.

With changes in factual programming cast as evidence of a wider 'dumbing down' of cultural life, many critics have pointed to the significance of the contemporary television environment in explaining these shifts. In the multi-channel landscape, the commercial pressures on broadcasters have become increasingly intense, with a much larger number of channels competing for their audience share. The commercialization of television has also seen the gradual erosion of public service broadcasting as the dominant framework in many national contexts. Within this environment, the pressure to attract audiences with popular formats has placed a premium on audience accessibility – and the importance of programs explicitly designed to entertain, rather than educate and inform. At least in terms of 'event' formats such as *Big Brother, Survivor, Pop Idol, American Idol*, or *The Apprentice*, reality TV also speaks more widely to how broadcasters are trying to capture audiences in the multi-channel universe. 'Event' programs are not only a way to help a 'channel stand out from the crowd' (Bazalgette 2001: 20). Reality TV has also been a key site upon which television has aimed to encourage the development of the interactive audience. This is equally a strategy to hold onto the viewer in a climate where channel – or even program – loyalty can no longer be assured.

Defining Reality TV

From the perspective of television, media, and communication studies, reality TV has represented a visible site for exploring and debating many aspects of contemporary television, ranging from the economic significance of the format, the global circulation in format trade, television interactivity, television celebrity, to the politics of representation (gender, class, ethnicity, and sexuality). But genre is equally pertinent here as there is always some difficulty in defining exactly what is meant by the term 'reality TV.' As Graham Barnfield (2002: 49) commented: 'Over the last decade, such a wide range of productions have been categorised as reality TV that one wonders if the term is too general to be helpful.' In the 1980s and 1990s, attention was focused on 'real crime' television, and in the United

States, NBC's *Unsolved Mysteries* (1987) is seen to have led the way. This was followed by a number of programs focusing on the work of the police and emergency services (which offered fast-moving, action-packed sequences as a key appeal). A similar history has also been reported in the UK (see Dovey 2000). In Britain, real-crime programs such as *Airport* (1996), *The Cruise* (1997), *Driving School* (1997), *Vets in Practice* (1997–2002) and *Airline* (1998–) combine an interest in an 'observational' perspective on everyday life with the narrative structures and characterizations of soap operas. In the 'game-doc' phase, factual programming increasingly incorporated elements of the game or talent show (e.g., *Big Brother, Survivor, The Amazing Race, The Apprentice, Joe Millionaire, I'm a Celebrity … Get Me Out of Here! Dancing with the Stars, American Idol*). In the period 1999–2001, with the success of *Big Brother* and *Survivor*, the term reality TV gained a wider currency in the press, television viewing guides, and everyday conversation.

But it is still quite difficult to isolate the attributes that link the range of programs associated with the 'reality' label. Some consist of self-enclosed episodes, while others adopt an ongoing serial structure. Not all employ a similar low-grade 'reality' aesthetic, and some make greater use of the hand-held camera, montage sequences, and musical cues. Not all shows pivot on the spectacle of placing the self under pressure in a television environment (real crime TV aims to follow rather than directly precipitate action and retains a distance from its subjects), and not all shows involve a relationship between interactivity and eviction, fostering a combination of cooperation and competition between contestants and handing part of the narrative control to the audience. Furthermore, given the rise of interest in 'celebrity' reality TV, not all shows are based around the claim to display the experiences of 'ordinary' people. Finally, it is useful to note that the term 'reality' is used in different ways in different national contexts. For example, in the United States, a program such as *Who Wants to Be a Millionaire* could be classed as 'reality'; in Britain, where the show was devised, it would be called a quiz show.

This points to the fact that genres are not only defined at the level of the program text. Recent work on television genre has emphasized how generic categories need to be understood as intertextual, operating at the level of relations *between* texts, as well as in the material which circulates *around* them. Genres also operate within the reviewing practices of critics, the opinions of audiences, and the production and marketing strategies of the television industry (see Mittell 2004). Thus, we might look at how programs are promoted and reviewed, as well as how they are discussed by audiences and contestants. For example, given that reality programming has often been condemned by critics for lowering television standards (and for having a low cultural value), it is notable that the term is often used to judge and *evaluate* programs. A British critic in *The Observer* discussed the program *Wife Swap* (which began in the UK in 2003 on Channel 4), in which two women swap homes and families for two weeks and the viewers watch what transpires:

'Channel Four argues that *Wife Swap* is serious factual programming that examines social issues,' says one industry source. 'In fact, it's "Reality" – salacious tabloid crap.' But even here, opinions may vary. *The New Statesman* described *Wife Swap* as 'the most important documentary series of the decade.' (Robinson 2004: 18)

As we can see, the program is categorized as a 'documentary' or as reality TV depending on the perspective and intentions of the categorizer. While it might be suggested that all programs labelled as reality TV at least make a claim to being 'unscripted,' the nature of what we mean by 'unscripted' has been perhaps the key point of contestation and debate where reality TV is concerned. Deciphering what appears to be 'unscripted,' spontaneous, or 'real' is central to the framework of viewing that is encouraged by reality TV. Perhaps the most that can be said in aiming to define reality TV is that it represents, in the words of Susan Murray and Laurie Ouellette, 'an unabashedly commercial genre united less by aesthetic rules or certainties than by the fusion of popular entertainment with a *self-conscious claim to the discourse of the real'* (2004: 2; my emphasis).

Factual Programming in a 'Post-Documentary' Context

The difficulties of definition here point to what the documentary theorist John Corner (2001) referred to as our 'post-documentary' context. He does not use the term to indicate that documentary is now finished; rather, he uses the term to signal the 'scale of [documentary's] relocation as a set of practices, forms and functions.' Elements of a post-documentary context include a borrowing of a 'documentary look' across different types of programming – something which complicates the rules for recognizing a documentary. Second, a performative, playful element has emerged within popular factual programming. Program contexts encourage a self-conscious emphasis on performance and self-display. Corner positions these shifts under the umbrella of the 'documentary as diversion,' where the main aim is to deliver entertainment. Indeed, one of the reasons reality TV has generated such heated debate about the current 'state' and future of television is because documentary has traditionally been positioned as a 'serious' genre and (in the European context) a key form of public service broadcasting. Even though fiction has historically examined many serious social, political, and cultural issues, we tend to associate fiction with 'entertainment' and the factual moving image with something more instructive. The rise of reality TV has challenged these assumptions – to controversial effect.

The rise of popular factual programming has often been discussed in the terms of television's wider retreat from engaging with the 'public sphere.' While the docusoap did aim to take the viewer to real social relations which existed before the recording of the program, the later game-doc formats have unfolded within arenas constructed solely *for* television, taking an acute interest in the performance of personal identity. While *Big Brother*, for example, is still constructed as an opportunity for observation, it is also understood (by program makers, contestants, and viewers) as a performative opportunity in its own right. But with programs such as *Big Brother*, it seems increasingly problematic to criticize them for failing to live up to a documentary remit when they are not claiming or aiming to *be* 'documentaries.' In this respect, while we can certainly consider whether the rise of popular factual programming has limited opportunities for the commissioning of more 'serious' documentary programs, it is also important to judge these newer programs on their *own* terms – as hybrid texts which clearly attract and appeal to audiences in new ways.

Case Study: *Wife Swap*

The format of *Wife Swap* was initially created by RDF Media for British television before being sold to the United States and other national territories. It involves, as the opening voice-over to one edition explains, 'two wives swapping lives, families and lifestyles for two weeks to see what they can learn about themselves. What is it like [for a career woman to live] … with a traditional man? How will a stay-at-home Mum find the business life?' (TX, 11 April, 2004, Channel 4, UK). In this sense, the program partly sets itself up as a form of social experiment and a learning process for the participants taking part. At the same time, it is over-determined by the framework of the format, with the swap, and thus the narrative, planned and constructed in such a way as to create explosive conflicts and clashes. In terms of class identity and gender roles, the families are explicitly 'cast' as polar opposites, and the editing, which cuts between the two households, deliberately sets up and exploits these differences while inviting the viewer to judge each set-up. (In the U.S. version, clashes are also cast at the level of religion, sexuality, and ethnicity, while gender and class remain more prominent frames in the UK version.) The women spend the first week living by their new family's rules, while after 'Rule Change Day,' they can alter the organization and running of the household, making decisions about child discipline, decor, and household chores. In the edition introduced above, Margaret from Wolverhampton, a 'stay-at-home Mum who has been raising her eight children for 22 years,' swaps with 'self-made businesswoman and workaholic Deirdre,' whose three-year-old son Frankie attends a nursery full time. Margaret is married to Phil, a grumpy, penny-scrimping, 'traditional man,' while Deirdre's partner Brian, a soft-spoken Canadian man, is open to a more equal and modern division of gender roles.

Fictional genres such as the soap opera and the sitcom have certainly focused attention on the family and the organization of gender roles within the domestic sphere. But when compared to *Wife Swap,* they have not trained such attention on domestic responsibilities and the division of labour within the home. As Helen Piper observes of the program: '[A] [fictional] treatment that took seriously the domestic everyday conflicts of two nuclear families, would [n]ever make it further than a commissioning executive's wastepaper bin' (2005: 285). The fact that in the different context of reality TV we are only too willing to watch this narrative indicates its investment in, and appeal to, the 'real.'

For those concerned about shifts in factual programming, the idea of the format has often been seen as a somewhat negative force – associated with overt producer intervention in the name of entertainment and the manipulation of the participants on screen. For example, John Corner (2006a: 73) observes that by 'deliberately intervening in the world in order to encourage an entertaining drama of personal contrasts, *Wife Swap* departs from conventional documentary practice and aligns itself with the game show and with sitcom.' At the same time, he also acknowledges that 'by using real domestic settings and routines it exposes some of the rhythms, tensions and contradictions of everyday living and indeed the structures of [gender], *wealth, class and culture, in ways not open to more conventional documentary treatments*' (73; my italics). We are certainly aware of the deliberate oppositional 'casting' of the families and may also be suspicious about the degree of agency really exercised by the participants. Although the program involves many 'confessional' moments from the participants, it also claims to adopt a fly-on-the-wall observational style where overt intervention on the part of the producers is played down. Indeed, the production crew are rarely seen or heard in the program. This may lead us to question what role the producers have in shaping the unfolding narrative of decisions, changes, and conflicts.

But Corner's comments also indicate how the program, by virtue of its format, may actually offer us access to images, experiences, and perspectives not available in either fiction or traditional documentary forms. By the end of an episode of *Wife Swap,* it is common for the program to apparently offer a perspective which supports the 'middle-ground': working women admit they need to spend more time with their children, while house-husbands emerge aiming to be more 'manly' and look forward to a more 'egalitarian' division of gender roles. But along the way, the pressure of the format produces some fascinating insights. For example, when Margaret has to deliver a business presentation for Deirdre's company to a packed conference room, she is quite clearly overwhelmed by her own sense of personal satisfaction: 'You really are somebody here, whereas at home,

I've always felt a bit forgotten,' she says. She goes on to explain how she would like a part-time job to balance with her role as a housewife and mother, but in a confession to the camera she realizes, 'But I need [husband] Phil's support for that, and I haven't got that.' Similarly, while the edition sees working Mum Deirdre reduced to the brink of tears as she realizes that she often puts her job before her son, we also see her admit, 'I play with Frankie infrequently, because if I'm brutally honest, I find it boring ... I don't really know what to do with [children].'

Rather than a necessary sign of trivialization and manipulation, it is also possible to see the *Wife Swap* format as productive in enabling these moments. With real women voicing their dissatisfaction with traditional gender roles, this arguably has a power which it would not have in fiction. Furthermore, a more traditional documentary treatment would be interested in extracting the 'typical' from the particular here – using the families to examine wider social shifts or issues. Yet it is precisely the experience of the 'pressure-cooker' format, isolating individuals in confined situations, which gives these moments their impact and power. It also seems problematic to suggest that because the format is focusing on *individual* families it has nothing to say about the world 'out there' beyond the boundaries of the television screen. After all, feminist critics made clear many years ago that the 'personal is political.' This in itself draws attention to the *gendered* nature of the debate surrounding documentary and reality TV, and relies on the argument that we have seen a shift from public to private, from education to entertainment, and from the weighty to the trivial. The implication here is that reality TV represents a negative 'feminization' of documentary.

Viewing Reality TV: Selfhood and Surveillance

The emphasis on reality TV as being more contrived and constructed than traditional factual programming tends to imply that documentaries once simply observed and recorded life 'as it happened.' This is clearly not the case, and there is a rich heritage of debate which has interrogated documentary's claim to reflect reality (see Winston 2000). From this point of view, it might be suggested that the highly performative context of reality TV has at least drawn attention to the constructed nature of the real, offering a 'refreshing change from the more conventional kind of play-acting, that of pretending that the camera is not there and that the space of action is purely naturalistic' (Corner 2006b: 95). In fact, and particularly in the UK context, it has been suggested that the rise of the later reality formats was in part a response to viewers' rising scepticism about the 'truth' value of both the documentary and the docusoap. There was a heated debate in the late 1990s about fakery and deceit in a limited number of British documentaries and docusoaps (see Winston 2000), and it has been argued more widely that postmodern thinking has encouraged us to reject the assertion that there can be any such thing as 'truth' through the eye of the camera lens.

Reality TV is certainly explicit about its staging of reality. It incarcerates participants in a house, or drops celebrities, stripped of mobile phones and other comforts, into the middle of the jungle, with the clear intention to create conflict and tension. But as the term reality TV evidently suggests, this is far from implying, as the postmodern position may indicate, that such programming has abandoned a claim to the real. Indeed, it has intensified it, shifting the locus of authenticity onto the performance of self. (It seems to say, 'yes the environment is constructed and the characters are "cast," but let's leave "reality" to unfold and *capture* what happens.') In this sense, in playing to a potentially more sceptical and media-aware audience, programs such as *Big Brother* and *I'm a Celebrity ... Get Me Out of Here!* involve constant discussion of performance itself: 'Does this look good on the camera?' 'Who is simply performing to get votes?' At the same time, these programs involve us in the process of trying to decipher the 'real' within this space. As Annette Hill's (2002: 324) audience research on reality TV has explained, reality TV engages a

> particular viewing practice: audiences look for the moment of authenticity when real people are 'really' themselves in an unreal environment … [Capitalizing] on the tension between performance and authenticity, [the programs] ask contestants and viewers to look for the 'moment of truth' in a highly constructed and controlled television environment.

As this suggests, reality TV can be seen as combining a postmodern scepticism of the real, with a more modernist investment in the real as both identifiable and desirable. In fact, across formats, the contestant most likely to win a reality show is often the one who is seen as most having been 'themselves' on screen (and never the contestant who has been seen to 'play' a good 'game'). The fact that we seem to want to reward people who appear to maintain an authentic identity in a highly mediated and 'close watch' context may speak to the contemporary experience of surveillance.

In 1978 Christopher Lasch famously described our 'culture of narcissism' in which social identity is constructed and affirmed by the ubiquitous presence of mediation. As he argued (1978: 47):

> Modern life is so thoroughly mediated by electronic images that we cannot help responding to others as if their actions – and our own – were being recorded and simultaneously transmitted to an unseen audience or stored up for close scrutiny at some later time … This all seeing eye no longer takes us by surprise or catches us with our defences down. We need no reminder to smile. A smile is permanently graven on our features, and we already know from which of several angles it photographs to best advantage.

This quote clearly anticipates the continued spread of surveillance culture, a framework which has structured a number of analyses of reality TV – especially *Big Brother* (e.g., Wong 2001; Palmer 2002). With the housemates surveilled twenty-four hours a day, seven days a week, *Big Brother* has been read as a microcosm of our surveillance society. And just as society has put up remarkably little resistance to the increasing surveillance of everyday life, so we might note that reality TV has done much to normalize and naturalize the practice of surveillance. In fact, the concept of entering the *Big Brother* house is generally understood as a special and privileged space which people are eager to enter. Upon leaving, many contestants claim it was the 'best' experience of their lives.

Celebrity and Reality TV

Reality TV plays out the contemporary sense that celebrity is the ultimate way of validating one's own identity, and reality TV has represented a key site for debates about the status and future of modern fame. Reality TV contestants have often been constructed as epitomizing a celebrity culture in which an ethos of 'famous for being famous' has regrettably triumphed over the concepts of talent and hard work (see Holmes 2004a). It would be an understatement to suggest that public voices have expressed their disapproval for people who have achieved public visibility and wealth, without drawing upon entrepreneurial skills, education, or obvious 'talent.'

Reality TV might be seen as opening up a wider range of roles for 'ordinary' people on television, and it is true that members of the public are no longer simply cast to play the social 'victim' (in a documentary, for example), or the 'straight' man/woman to a dominant host (the quiz/game show). But the extent to which reality TV fame is necessarily new, or more 'democratic,' is a more complex question. First, it is useful to observe differences between programs. The reality-pop programs, such as *America's Got*

Talent, Fame Academy, American Idol, and *The X-Factor,* have launched music careers for many contestants – with varying degrees of success around the globe. On one level, these shows are produced for a media-aware audience which understands that celebrity images are produced and manu-factured to some degree. In the UK, the programs make constant references to the packaging and selling of the contestants. But this is always accompanied by an em-phasis on 'specialness.' In terms of insisting upon an indefinable sense of 'specialness' and charisma, the use of such phrases 'you've got the X factor' or 'star quality' have become something of a convention, with the implication being that, in viewing the show, *we* should look for these quali-ties too (see Holmes 2004b). The programs seem to suggest that manufacture is a necessary component in the fame-building process, but that there must be the indefin-able magic of 'star quality' upon which to build. The concept of grooming raw talent has a long history in the construction of stardom, and many of the myths used by these programs are very traditional, dating back to the construction of stars in the Hol-lywood star system (see Dyer 1998). In this respect, the programs combine both 'new' and 'old' explanations of fame.

Big Brother may certainly seem less tradi-tional in this respect. It appears to lack any emphasis on the importance of work or 'tal-ent' (Holmes 2004a). Overall, it is perhaps more honest about the fact that obtaining fame can simply be about being *media*ted – being on TV. But the fact that a number of contestants have gone on to jobs in the field of light entertainment (i.e., as presenters, actors) questions the idea of a truly radical break with the past. Furthermore, while reality TV may appear to have promised a more 'democratic' form of celebrity which is open to 'all,' television producers clearly retain their status as the gatekeepers of fame. It is comparatively hard to get on *Big Brother* (thousands of people apply), and on a broader level, celebrity is by nature a hierarchical system, separating out the few

from the 'rest.' Much like power, fame can never receive equal distribution. As Paul McDonald (1995: 66) has observed, if we were all famous, then no one would be fa-mous, and this fact is worth some thought in the face of arguments which insist on the democratic nature of reality TV celebrity.

Global Formats

Finally, reality TV has done much to fore-ground the contemporary significance of format adaptation in contemporary tel-evision. Although the trading of formats between different countries has occurred since the earliest days of television (and radio), the importance of the format has undoubtedly increased. There are a number of reasons for this, which include the in-creasing transnationalization of television as well as the more competitive context in which the medium now exists. Formats are a 'cost-effective way of filling schedules with local productions rather than expen-sively produced locally produced drama' (Steemers 2004: 174). Broadcasters are more likely to be risk-averse in the multi-channel environment – keen to capitalize on and repeat successes which have been 'proven' elsewhere. Many countries have recognized the success of formats such as *Big Brother* or *American Idol,* and aimed to replicate their popularity within different national contexts.

Reality TV may be an example of the increasing globalization of television – which many regard as evidence of cultural homogenization. As Silvio Waisbord (2004: 360) has asked: 'What better evidence of cultural homogenization than format television? A dozen media companies are able to do business worldwide by selling the same idea, and audiences seem to be watching national variations of the same show.' Yet he also goes on to argue that at 'a deeper level … formats attest to the fact that television still remains tied to local and national cultures' (360). Waisbord is emphasizing here how formats are attrac-tive to broadcasters because they offer an idea 'tried and tested' elsewhere, with the possibility for 'local' inflection and adaptation. Scholars of format circulation are thus interested in the processes of textual adaptation: what can be learned about national and cultural identity through 'the national colouring acquired by the translation' (Moran 1998: 165). So, while a reality game show may be structured by a format which includes a written description of the game and its rules, information about the prize, set design, and visual style, as well as information about software for graphics (Moran 1998: 65), there is still scope for broadcasters to adapt a format to suit the different cultural mores (or television systems) of different national cultures. For example, in certain Middle-Eastern versions of *Big Brother* participants were segregated by sex. Aspects of adaptation can also come from the reactions of the contestants themselves. In the first Spanish *Big Brother* the housemates all united against Big Brother, nominating each other equally so that they were all up for eviction at once. The documentary *Big Brother around the World* (TX 20 June, 2004, Channel 4, UK), explains:

> In a country still recovering from thirty years of fascist rule under Franco, the housemates refused to obey the dictates of Big Brother ... The Spanish [were] ... different with their reaction to authoritarianism. [There has been] this long period of the Franco government and Right wing dictatorship and now the young people are very much anti-authoritarianism.

Equally, differences can be more subtle in nature. The British version of the U.S. program *The Apprentice,* in which candidates compete to win a high-powered job with a business mogul, is less openly ruthless and capitalist in nature when compared with the U.S. version. The British show dispenses with the U.S. catchphrase, 'It's not personal, it's just business,' and it is less aggressive in encouraging the contestants to pursue a form of ruthless, unbridled

individualism. While the CEO in charge, Alan Sugar, is certainly respected by the contestants, he is not 'idolized' in the manner of the U.S. CEO, Donald Trump, and the British program is more cautious about celebrating evidence of Sugar's extravagant consumption (which in any case does not exist on the same level as that of Donald Trump). While the opening title sequence of the American version sings about 'Money, Money, Money' and having 'it all,' the British version has no title sequence as such, and the American version makes a much greater use of dramatic music and slow-motion footage to mediate tense moments. The differences here are complex: after all, both the United States and Britain are advanced capitalist nations, structured by the values of capitalism and individualism. But the idea of working hard, being the 'best,' rising to the top, and enjoying the fruits of one's achievements clearly speaks to a version of the American Dream, suggesting that *The Apprentice* might connect more closely with American cultural values than British.

But while the U.S. version of *The Apprentice* may launch images of business dominance and the United States as a world power, the quiz show has also been a site upon which changing trends in format trade have emerged. The global success of *Who Wants to be a Millionaire* (beginning in 1998 in the UK) and *Big Brother* (beginning in 1999 in Holland) began a trend which, to some degree, has broken the American dominance of the format market, with Western Europe, Australia, and New Zealand all gaining a foothold here. This is not to downplay the inequalities which still exist in the global trade of formats and other audio-visual products (Waisbord 2004: 361), but only to suggest that reality TV provides an interesting case study to re-examine how formats are being bought and sold in world television markets. As *Format News* commented, 'these days a hit international format is just as likely to have originated in the UK, Holland, or even Israel as it is in the US' (Schreiber 2002: 2).

The Future of Reality TV

When it first emerged, many critics prophesied that reality TV would be a temporary
'fad,' but this essay has aimed to demonstrate how it is the result of wider shifts in
factual programming on television (which
are unlikely to be reversed). The form is continuing to evolve, with formats hybridizing,
combing, and innovating in new ways.

Given that reality television has prompted cultural debate about 'taste,' ethics, and
integrity in television programming, commentators have repeatedly forecast that
boundaries will be pushed more and more
in the pursuit of ratings. The BBC drama-
documentary *If TV Goes Down the Tube*
(TX, 21 March 2005, BBC2, UK) imagined a
situation in which a distraught teenage girl
hangs herself in a (fictitious) reality show
called *The Cage*. The production team were
pictured looking on – wary about intervening lest they lose audience ratings – and not
assisting the girl until it was too late. While
it is the case that reality TV cultivates an
ever-increasing appetite for, and expectation of, escalating conflict and emotion on
screen, there is little evidence that these
grim prophecies have been, or will be, fulfilled.

Su Holmes

Bibliography

Barnfield, Graham. From Direct Cinema to Car-
Wreck Video: Reality TV and the Crisis of
Content. In *Reality TV: How Real Is Reality TV?*
ed. Dolan Cummings, 22–34. Oxford: Hodder
and Stoughton, 2002.

Bazalgette, Peter. *Big Brother* and Beyond. *Television,* October 2001, 20–3.

Corner, John. Documentary in a Post-Documentary Culture? A Note on Forms and Their
Functions (2001). http://www.1boro.ac.uk/
research/changing.media/John%20Corner
%20paper.htm.

– Analysing Factual TV. In *Tele-Visions*, ed. Glen
Creeber, 69–73. London and New York: BFI,
2006a.

– A Fiction (Un)like Any Other? *Critical Studies
in Television* 1, no. 1 (2006b): 89–96.

Dovey, Jon. *Freakshow: First Person Media and
Factual Television.* London: Pluto, 2000.

Dyer, Richard. *Stars.* London: BFI, 1998.

Hill, Annette. Big Brother: The Real Audience.
Television and New Media 3, no. 3 (2002):
323–41.

Holmes, Su. All You've Got to Worry about Is
the Task, Having a Cup of Tea, and What
You're Going to Eat for Dinner: Approaching Celebrity in *Big Brother.* In *Understanding
Reality Television*, ed. Su Holmes and Deborah Jermyn, 111–35. London and New York:
Routledge, 2004a.

– Reality Goes Pop! Reality TV, Popular Music
and Narratives of Stardom in *Pop Idol* (UK).
Television and New Media 5, no. 2 (2004b):
147–72.

Kilborn, Richard. *Staging the Real: Factual TV Programming in the Age of Big Brother.* Manchester:
Manchester University Press, 2003.

Lasch, Christopher. *The Culture of Narcissism.*
New York: W.W. Norton, 1978.

McDonald, Paul. I'm Winning on a Star: The
Extraordinary Ordinary World of *Stars in
Their Eyes. Critical Survey* 7, no. 1 (1995):
59–66.

Mittell, Jason. *Genre and Television: From Cop
Shows to Cartoons.* London and New York:
Routledge, 2004.

Moran, Albert. *Copycat TV: Globalisation, Programme Formats and Cultural Identity.* Luton:
Luton University Press, 1998.

Murray, Susan, and Laurie Ouellette, eds. *Reality
TV: Re-making Television Culture.* New York:
New York University Press, 2004.

Palmer, Gareth. Big Brother: An Experiment in
Governance. *Television and New Media* 3, no. 3
(2002): 295–310.

Piper, Helen. Reality TV, *Wife Swap* and the
Drama of Banality. *Screen* 45, no. 4 (winter
2005): 273–86.

Robinson, James. Pap – or Porn with a Purpose?
The Observer, 18 July 2004, 18.

Schrieber, Dominic. Formats – Now the Networks are Taking Notice. *Format News,* October 2002 (supplement to *Broadcast,* 4 November 2002).

Steemers, Jeanette. *Selling Television: British Tel-*

evision in the Global Marketplace: London and
New York: BFI, 2004.

Waisbord, Silvio. McTV: Understanding the Global Popularity of Television Formats. *Television and New Media* 5, no. 4 (2004): 359–83.

Winston, Brian. *Lies, Damn Lies and Documentary.*
London: BFI, 2000.

Wong, James. Here's Looking at You: Reality TV,
Big Brother and Foucault. *Canadian Journal of
Communication* 26 (2001): 33–45.

RECEIVER VERSUS SENDER

[See also: *Bull's-Eye Model; Communication;
Communication Theory; Jakobson's Model of
Communication*]

In communication theory the terms *receiver*
and *sender* are used to indicate the source
and destination of a transmission of information. The receiver is the destination and
the sender is the source of the transmission.
Either one can be inanimate (radios and
radio stations) or animate (human beings).

In models of human communication,
such as the one by Roman Jakobson (1960),
the sender and receiver are renamed *addresser* and *addressee* to bring out the fact
that the communication event is bidirectional and interactive. In media theory, the
sender is generally understood to be the
maker of a media text (a TV program or an
advertisement) and the receiver the audience or consuming public. Between the
sender and the receiver is the code, or system of meanings imprinted in words and
symbols that determines the outcome of the
sending and the reception. One of the characteristics of any code is called redundancy,
a built-in 'predictability feature' that guarantees successful transmission even in the
presence of interferences of various types,
known cumulatively as noise. Redundancy
features ensure that a message has a high
probability of being received and deciphered even if noise is present. One such
feature is the high predictability of certain
sounds, like vowels, in words. For example,
the sentence *My brthr stds mthmtcs*, which is
lacking the vowels in its words, can easily

be reconstructed by a speaker of English
as *My brother studies mathematics.* Also the
high predictability of certain words in
many utterances is an inbuilt redundancy
feature of human communication: for example, *Roses are red, violets are …*

Marcel Danesi

Bibliography

Jakobson, Roman. Linguistics and Poetics. In
Style and Language, ed. T.A. Sebeok, 34–45.
Cambridge, MA: MIT Press, 1960.

Shannon, Claude E. A Mathematical Theory of
Communication. *Bell Systems Technical Journal*
27 (1948): 379–423.

RECEPTION THEORY

[See also: *Audience Research; Media Effects*]

Reception theory, promoted mainly by Stuart Hall (for instance, Hall 1973), emphasizes the role of the reader or audience in
the reception of media texts, not the author
or the process itself. It is also known as
reader response theory. Its main tenet is that
a media text is successfully communicated
or not depending on audience reception,
not on any intrinsic merit it is deemed to
have by people other than the audience.
The audience reception can be *preferred,
negotiated,* or *oppositional*. The former is
the interpretation that the makers of a text
have attempted to build into it. Reception
in this case overlaps with the objectives
of the text maker. A negotiated meaning
is one in which the text is received only
in part as the makers intended it to be
received. Other parts are 'negotiated' by
the audience, who add or subtract meanings from it. In this case reception does
not coincide, but rather intersects, with
construction. Finally, audiences may read
a text in an oppositional fashion, rejecting
it or coming up with an interpretation that
is diametrically opposed from its intended
one. In this case reception diverges from
construction.

Reception theory has shifted the focus from authors to interpreters. The role of audiences in this model is to add to the overall meanings of texts. Those that accrue over time are then worked into the text in its cultural setting. In effect, the text's meaning is the result of authorship and reception; that is, the meaning of a text is not inherent within the text itself, but, rather, crystallizes from the relation that is formed between the text and its readers. Unlike traditional literary theory, which assigns some 'grand interpretation' to texts, reception theory radicalizes the role of common people, giving them the power to decide what a text entails in both interpretive and aesthetic terms.

Reception theorists identify various types of readers: the imagined reader, who is the reader imagined by the author; the ideal reader, who is the one considered to be the most competent one for the text; and the actual reader. Reception theory also enlists psychology, in that it is concerned with how meaning is created by, or in, the reader through the process of reading.

Angela Palangi

Bibliography

Hall, Stuart, and Padel Whannel. *The Popular Arts*. London: Beacon Press, 1964.
- *Encoding and Decoding in the Television Discourse*. London: The Seminar Press, 1973.
- Cultural Studies: Two Paradigms. *Media, Culture, and Society* 2 (1980): 57–72.
Hall, Stuart, et al., eds. *Culture, Media, Language.* London: Hutchison, 1980.
Staiger, Janet. *Media Reception Studies.* New York: New York University Press, 2005.

RECORDINGS

[See also: *Broadcasting; Communication; MP3*]

Recording describes the process of copying mechanically or electronically some input (vocal, musical, and so on). Recordings include print, images, and sound reproduction. The *Penguin New English Dictionary* defines recording as 'a permanent account of something that serves as evidence of it.' Recordings have become important storage and reproduction systems. Because they can be kept and archived beyond the moment of capture, recordings enable us to retrieve information and relive experiences many generations after the instance of creation.

The development of human recording capacity has certainly been a determining influence on the development of media and communications. The right to record and entitlement to control the archives of recordings have always been contested. The history of recordings has been a story of societal development and power relations.

In the earliest documented human societies spoken language emerged as a means of revering ancestors and of extending and perpetuating group life. The first cave paintings or engravings were created during the Upper Paleolithic period (40,000 to 10,000 BCE); at this stage pictographic recording was a crude representation of reality rather than an interpretive account of it. Writing inscription is the oldest form of human recording. The earliest writing using character codes for meaning dates back earlier than 3000 BCE. Peoples in Egypt, Sumeria, and Pakistan recorded symbols on clay tablets. Writing at this stage consisted of indentations made using a blunt stylus and in its earliest stage of development was a vehicle for recording important cultural concepts and events. Egyptians chronicled the glories of successive pharaohs. Mayans recorded their cosmic belief system. Mandarins in ancient China used ideograms to record their laws.

The gradual consolidation of monotheistic religions helped elevate the importance of writing. The medieval Church guarded access to literacy and books. In the Islamic caliphates, state calligraphers were commissioned to reproduce texts that promoted orthodoxy. Islam in particular forbids depictions of prophets, so calligraphy flourished as a means of glorifying important figures through ornate text.

Writing has undergone two principal paradigm shifts. The first was the development of the alphabet that abstracted words as sound sequences from the concepts or objects to which they referred. The second was the invention of the printing press in the late fifteenth century century. This enabled a massive proliferation of printed texts, augmenting the power of the word but making orthodoxy more difficult to maintain. The Reformation in Europe was brought about by dissent over alternative textual interpretations and disputes over ecclesiastical monopoly over scripture. Ultimately the emergence of a literate public caused massive social change, political upheaval, and ultimately led to the age of revolution.

Sound and image recording technologies developed in fits and starts through the latter half of the nineteenth century. In 1833 Nicholas Daguerre produced the first recognizable photograph by allowing light to form an image on a copper plate coated with iodine and sensitized silver. By the mid-1840s the ability to freeze-frame accurate reproductions of buildings led to the diffusion of this technology across France. In 1881 the American inventor George Eastman stumbled upon a technique for inserting a flexible spool that enabled multiple exposures. The burgeoning popularity of the photo went hand in hand with the rise of the bourgeoisie and construction of the private sphere. The home became the province of family remembrance with souvenirs and photographs of ancestors rapidly eclipsing portrait paintings as the media of choice. The end of the nineteenth century was a watershed. For the first time, industrial production turned towards household consumer markets that until then had not been exploited. This fed the development of household goods that adorned or enlivened home life. The appearance and profusion of sound recording and reproduction at the turn of the twentieth century were due to a combination of entrepreneurial impulse and social forces. Impresario-inventers like Thomas Edison,

Emile Berliner, and Guglielmo Marconi dedicated themselves to fathoming the potential of mechanical communication technologies. Initially, the quest was the novelty of recording traces of sounds and to represent them visually – phonograph means 'voice writer.' It was some time before it occurred to anyone to reverse the process to reproduce sound. Early attempts used techniques borrowed from photo-etching technology by using acid to make undulations on a metal plate.

The earliest proper recording machine, the phonograph, was invented by Edison. It used a rotating foil-covered cylinder and a stylus attached to a flexible diaphragm. The recorder spoke or sang into the horn, causing the stylus to vibrate, thus inscribing a modulated groove into the surface of the soft tin foil 'phonograph' cylinder. On replay the modulated groove would cause the stylus and diaphragm to vibrate, resulting in a sound wave being emitted from the horn. Alexander Bell, Chichester Bell, and Charles Sumner Tainter used a wax-coated cardboard cylinder. Emile Berliner superseded both of these with his gramophone. The sound tracing was first etched side-to-side in a spiral on a zinc disc, then this master was electroplated to create a negative which could then be used to imprint copies in vulcanized rubber (and later shellac) – a process better suited to mass reproduction of musical entertainment. The new equipment was originally conceived as dictation office equipment but was a commercial failure in this guise. Rethinking the new invention and repositioning it as an entertainment item through jukeboxes and phonograph arcades established a market for private recordings. Berliner's gramophone company, headquartered in Montreal, began an intense promotion of the gramophone that highlighted the volume, endurance, and space-saving size of discs as opposed to cylinders.

In North America and Europe the piano had established music as one of the main sources of family entertainment. The popularity of music hall and folk music that this stimulated also fuelled the popularity and growth of the phonograph and gramophone. The gramophone spread a taste for operatic and symphonic music to those who could never have afforded to hear live performance. It also spread different sorts of jazz, blues, country, and a variety of ethnic musical styles to a large number of groups who would not otherwise have been interested in them. Writers such as William Howland Kenney argue that recordings of this era constitute collective memories which when replayed conjure up certain events, moods, and feelings. 'Inevitably, then, the phonograph, not unlike the slide projector, moving picture projector, and VCR, offered a technological aid to remembering. Phonograph records "froze" past performances as engraved sound pictures: 78 rpm records offered Americans memories of memories' (Kenney 1999: xvii).

The gramophone's period of greatest influence was from 1890 to 1940. From then on, radio gained the upper hand though the two technologies were complementary. Recordings became the staple of radio broadcasting while the radio became a primary medium of publicity for the gramophone record. A major breakthrough in recording quality came in the 1930s with the invention of the magnetic recording. This was based on the principle of using a current flowing through a coil to create a magnetic field that would in turn magnetize a moving metal wire or tape endowed with magnetic properties. On replay, the magnetized tape moves across the head gap of a similar head to that used in recording, inducing a current in the coil and providing an electrical output. In the 1970s BASF of Germany developed a chromium dioxide formulation with better signal-to-noise ratios. This meant that magnetic taping technology became the industry standard. Vinyl discs, however, remained the principal commercial playback medium. Vinyl became the prime vehicle for recording, though this was due to capacity for fast reproduction, which boosted revenues of

the recording industry, more than because of its improved sound quality.

The most important repercussion of mechanical recording has been the gradual separation of music from its live performance. Initially, recordings were seen as an ingenious means of reproducing an event to which the listener might not otherwise have access. The performance thus became de-contextualized and disembodied and its replication became transportable into any setting. This meant that anyone could enjoy a Verdi aria or a Bach fugue – not just those with the resources to afford a box at the opera or a seat at the concert hall. As soon as recordings came onto the scene a new conception of 'past' and 'present' arose which homogenized time and space. This ushered in a shift whereby music became less the preserve of a certain social class – as it would have been when classical music and folk music played to distinct audiences – and more determined by generation. If Beethoven and popular forms like ragtime were both available on the same format, this meant a levelling of status between and across music genres. Theodor Adorno, a critical theorist writing in the 1940s, resisted this trend, lamenting the vulgarity of popular music that, through recordings, had been accorded the same nominal status as classical music. Adorno believed that what he dubbed the 'culture industry' was a capitalist ploy designed to propagate a false consciousness in modern society. The recording industry, he charged, churned out prefabricated products that each deviated only superficially from a formula designed to appeal to the lowest common denominator. Adorno argued that commercial ethics compromised the aesthetic purity of music by recycling pre-digested musical themes that reflected social norms. Adorno's powerful critique has been rehearsed many times since, though it downplays the improvisational brilliance of jazz, which arguably restored for a time the primacy of the performer.

The growing popularity of recordings throughout the twentieth century changed the way people listened to music and what they expected from it. On the one hand the aura of the musician lessened in importance and it became more difficult to be idiosyncratically brilliant without any reference point. Listeners started to anticipate certain notes and phrases, and recorded music gradually became paraphrases of previous recordings by a different set of musicians. Recordings also changed the nature of musicianship such that musicians could listen to themselves for the first time, which would change the nature of interpretation. Musicians today are radically different from those of the previous century whose vocal or instrumental utterances were able to seem totally idiosyncratic without a corpus of previous recordings against which to judge them. Recordings also brought about an individualization of listening patterns, shifting the locus from the public space of the concert hall to the private space of the parlour and living room. This individualization has continued into the digital age with the headphoned sound bubbles of the Walkman and the iPod.

Recordings are one of the defining attributes of the digital age. The internet, which is emblematic of the digital, is itself one vast knot of media recordings. Any contemporary account of recordings must take into account the shift in technology that has installed recording capability as a default feature of all sorts of appliances. This means that present-day recordings are no longer purposeful but routine and procedural. Recording is simply what digital 'does' in its normal mode of operation. Recording is often now an indiscriminate, unwitting by-product of simply using a particular digital function.

Digital refers to media whereby information is encoded as binary language, as opposed to analogue representation of data in variable, but continuous, wave forms. Analogue is recorded as continuous variations in sound pressure. Digital on the other hand registers the amplitude of sound only at specific points but many thousands of times a second, slicing it into a multitude of tiny segments. On reproduction the digital system then makes use of an error correction device that compares these recorded segments with a time binary structure which enables 're-clocking' of uneven pulse and elimination of distorted signals. This digital data format makes for high-fidelity reproduction with minimal degradation with each successive replication and enables durable storage. The paradigm shift to digital was partly the result of the inherent limitations of the analogue format. The narrow dynamic range of analogue recording and the problem of sound distortion eventually became a bottleneck that could not be overcome. The level of compression required in order to reduce distortion at a particular amplification did not allow any further increase in sound quality. Digital recording involves using a channel coding system that converts a pattern of binary data in the bumps on an optical surface of a CD or magnetic flux on a DAT tape to equivalent outputs in the transmission medium.

The digital interface has altered the way music is made and tracks are put together. Audio workstations such as Apple's Pro Tools allow immense flexibility and control over how and what the user can record. The creation of aliases and different storage regions allow multiple sessions to be recorded. Features such as grabbers, scrubbers, trimmers, zoomers, and selectors allow sound to be manipulated like paint on a palette or canvas. Snatches of audio can be cut and pasted into new positions, and vocal passages grafted on top of each other on a timeline to create harmonic variation. Timelines can be duplicated countless times and customized to create a range of mixes or overdubbed to create a more perfect version of a track. Creative scope has also increased due to boosted storage capacity. Audio compression standards such as MPEG have increased the capacity of minidisk and hard drive storage. They do this by using powerful algorithms to distil 'signal traffic' down by up to twelve times. The algorithms exploit flaws in human hearing such that redundant sounds – those that pass beneath our sensitivity thresholds and are thus undetectable anyway – can be stripped out to lose data.

The upshot of this is that music producers have few limitations on their art. They can produce tracks extremely quickly or spend weeks creating as many reiterations as their creative vision or commissioning client demands. On the other hand, the formidable array of sound design tools at their disposal has forced the development of special skills and disciplines. First, to be fast and efficient, producers need to be able to see sound as well as hear it. A talent for synthesis and composition has become a most precious skill, and knowing what goes together is as respected as singular invention in the digital realm. The power of digital manipulation has ushered in a need for parsimony in what is recorded. Because there is no limit to the number of sound elements to be added, knowing when to stop adding layers and limit the clutter has become a vital part of the producer's repertoire.

Chris Cutler writes about sampling in his article 'Plunderphonia.' In it he argues that musical technology made sampling inevitable and turned the computer into a musical instrument. 'What brought plundering to the centre of mass consumption low art music was a new technology that made sound piracy so easy that it didn't make sense not to do it' (1994: 21). Technologically, sampling allows unprecedented control, enabling recorded sounds to be visualized as waveforms and stretched, sliced in half, and shifted to order. Artistically, sampling transforms the act of production into an act of critical consumption. For Cutler, the rise of sampling simply brought music into line with other art forms where importation of ready-made materials into artwork had long been common practice through citation in pop art and modernist literature. Sampling as we know it started in the 1970s with rock artists such as Frank Zappa, Brian Eno, and The Residents and classical music figures like Stockhausen. The type of sampling involved has varied from tiny untraceable snippets contorted

beyond recognition to whole sections lifted and resituated in new works with minimal adjustment. Sampling has since been taken to a new level of complexity through the predominant influence of the hip-hop scene on popular musical practice. Tricia Rose suggests that whereas before hip-hop the sample was a shortcut to live instrumentation or as deliberate protest, hip-hop gave tactical priority to the cut and paste ethos. Samples were used to build new musical structures rather than to flesh out existing ones and recorded materials included everyday sounds and morphed sections of songs. Because the backbone of a hip-hop record is a looped break rather than a progressive flow of music, finding the perfect sound excerpt to constitute it became a critical quest. Indeed, the notion of 'digging in the crates' for rare records became the touchstone of the hip-hop producer's art. In this sense hip hop is both deconstructive and recuperative in that it retrieves sounds long forgotten and recontextualizes them in surprising new ways. Hip-hop music has established a culture of revivalism rehabilitating and reinterpreting old genres. Recordings enable us to loop back to relive these epochs anew, and arguably the nostalgia lag is shortening every year. Indeed hip-hop artists pay homage to their heroes by sampling breaks and lyrical passages for their tracks. An original hip-hop lyrics archive (www.ohhla.com) is an example of this obsession with chronicling even a relatively young art form.

Rose, quoting Snead and Small, traces the prevalence of sampling, scratching, and looped rhythmic lines to the repetition inherent in African oral traditions. She suggests that the suspension of time that this looping entails is about equilibrium and certainty rather than perpetual progress. In this sense it is an important rupture with the tradition of Western classical music rooted in the notion of the Enlightenment project. Hip-hop music is in this sense the apotheosis of recordings in that it is in itself composed of miniature recordings – recordings eating themselves. Sampling, like recordings before it, has had its detractors who bemoan the lack of originality. Many artists have been accused of theft and for violating copyright. But this has come up against the ambiguity of work that crosses what John Oswald called the 'threshold of recognizability,' where plagiarism is difficult to prove. After a few high-profile legal cases in the 1990s things seem to have calmed down with artists gaining prior clearance for use of recordings and a more accepting attitude on the part of the sampled party.

Recordings have changed our interaction with the media by shifting consumption habits. From podcasts to personal video recorders, it has never been easier to access media content. The accessibility of sound and video files on the internet that can be clicked on at any time has enabled people to defer their enjoyment of content till the most convenient time. This has posed a challenge to radio stations and TV channels who used to trade on the topicality of their minute-to-minute programming. They must work harder to sharpen the appeal, vim, and topicality of live shows in order to attract a real-time audience and differentiate them from an archived version. With the growing proliferation of DVRs (digital video recorders) users are now equipped to preset programming and screen out unwanted content. Recent studies suggest that the new devices lead people to increase the quality rather than the quantity of what they watch. Time shifting of selected shows varies from watching them later the same day to stockpiling several episodes of a favourite program for viewing all at once on a weekend or when the user has more time to catch up. There are some items such as news broadcasts that viewers still want to watch live. While there is some skipping through ads, DVRs mean that viewers can be more discerning about which ads they watch.

What best exemplifies the present-day fetish for recordings is the prevalence of what has been called 'life caching.' Life caching has caught on across the world among youth cultures and involves recording aspects of one's life online or on portable hard drives. Life caching includes,

but is not limited to, blogs (online diaries) scrapbooking, mobile blogging, and posting home videos on the internet. Blogs can be political or personal. Most often though they are forums for individual hobbyists with a desire to record and publicize their everyday lives to whoever might stumble upon them.

There are a number of theories as to why human beings are so driven to record. Recordings can be fuelled by vanity, by a need to raise self-worth, a desire for validation, for control, or to keep track of one's existential development; but many of those who keep blogs would suggest they do so just for fun and because the technology enables them to do so. Jacques Derrida linked the mania for recording with what he called the death drive. Derrida came to his conclusions by examining the history of Freudian psychoanalysis and various attempts to reveal the truth about Freud and in particular the psychoanalytic approach to understanding hidden memories. He suggests that we create recordings or archives not to record the past but to cheat our own extinction and to consort with the future. This is a poignant view in light of the current mania for life caching in uncertain times. 'There would be no archive drive without the radical finitude, without the possibility of a forgetfulness – there is no archive fever without the threat of this death drive, this aggression and destruction drive' (1995: 19). But Derrida shows the paradox of the archive by deconstructing the word to reveal a term he argues is contaminated with connotations of command and effacement. In fact, according to Derrida, it is precisely because archiving supplements memory that it incites forgetfulness and amnesia. He speculates on the effects of email – incipient technology at the time of his writing – and other memory prostheses on human memory and how we record for posterity.

One of the consequences of the prevalence of recordings is the attendant exteriorization of memory. Computers and other recording machines mean that we need to know not facts but how to access those facts. Marshall McLuhan believed that every medium eventually shapes its shapers. He argued that every technology moulds our minds, warping humanity while we are oblivious to its effects because we are fixated on media content and not the impact of the medium itself. A logical extension of this argument is that the proliferation of recordings and archiving, while initially aiding recall, could eventually be responsible for stunting it. Could our dependence on recordings stultify our ability to retain information and eventually, after hundreds of years, reverse and atrophy brain development?

Recordings started off as a means of capturing and perpetuating the rare, precious, and expensive – they were about salvaging scarcity. Recordings are now a way of diffusing a glut or surfeit of information and experience. George Bataille, the founder of surrealism, wrote a tract on political economy entitled *The Accursed Share*, which postulates that human ventures are invariably prompted by the need to destroy a natural surplus of energy. To record is to indulge in an experience twice over. So are recordings simply about luxury? The changing nature of recordings is thus very much in keeping with the hegemony of consumerism in North American societies. Social theorists such as Jean Baudrillard believe that the primary logic of the consumerist system is a relentless encouragement to consume. Following his argument, it is possible to argue that recordings are a means of feasting on experience in parallel to our penchant for shopping and the purchase of superfluous goods.

Chris Arning

Bibliography

Adorno, Theodor. *Philosophy of New Music.* Minneapolis: University of Minnesota Press, 1949/2006.

Bataille, George. *The Accursed Share.* Volume 1. Cambridge, MA: Zone Books, 1991.

Baudrillard, Jean. *Consumer Society: Myths and Structures.* London: Sage, 1998.

British Library Board. *Aural History: Essays on Recorded Sound.* London: British Library, 2001.

Channon, Michael. *Repeated Takes: A Short History of Recording and Its Effects on Music.* London: Verso, 1996.

Clichy, Patrice. *Dynamics of Modern Communication: The Shaping and Impact of New Communication Technologies.* London: Sage, 1995.

Cutler, Chris. Plunderphonia. In *Audio Cultures: Readings in Modern Music*, ed. Christoph Cox and Daniel Warner, 138–56. New York: Continuum, 1994.

Derrida, Jacques. *Archive Fever: A Freudian Impression.* Trans. Eric Prenowitz. Baltimore: Johns Hopkins University Press, 1995.

Eisenberg, Even. *The Recording Angel: Music Records and Culture from Aristotle to Zappa.* New Haven, CT: Yale University Press, 2005.

Gould, Glenn. The Prospects of Recording. In *Audio Cultures: Readings in Modern Music*, ed. Christoph Cox and Daniel Warner, 115–26. New York: Continuum.

Grayson, Kent, with David Shulman. Indexicality and the Verification Function of Irreplaceable Possessions: A Semiotic Analysis. *Journal of Consumer Research* 27 (June 2000): 17.

Keenan, M. Kevin. *Invasion of Privacy: A Reference Handbook.* Santa Barbara: ABE-CLIO, 2005.

Kenney, William Howard. *Recorded Music in American Life: The Phonograph and Popular Memory, 1890–1945.* Oxford: Oxford University Press, 1999.

Leathers, David. *Pro Tools Bible – Pro Tools and Beyond.* New York: Melner Hill, 2004.

Solomon, Michael, Diane Barrett, and Neil Broom. *Computer Forensics Jumpstart.* New Jersey: Sybex, 2004.

Sony Service Centre Europe. *Digital Audio and Compact Disc Technology.* Oxford: Butterworth Heinemann, 2001.

REDUNDANCY

[See also: *Bull's-Eye Model; Channel; Communication; Communication Theory; Cybernetics; Feedback; Information; Medium; Noise; Shannon, Claude E.*]

As used in information theory, *redundancy* is the number of bits (binary digits) required to transmit a message less the number of bits of information in the message. More generally, it is the term used to refer to the mechanisms or devices in a communication system that are involved in combating noise (any interference in the transmission that affects the decipherment of a message). It is also used, occasionally, to refer to the expected or default state of a system. For example, in an 'alarm system,' it is obvious that a ringing alarm signal carries distinct information; a silent one, on the other hand, is the 'expected,' 'default,' or even 'redundant' state of the system. The term redundancy comes out of the communications model developed by the American telecommunications engineer Claude Shannon (1916–2001).

In Shannon's model, the term *noise* refers to an interfering element (physical or psychological) in the channel of communication that distorts or partially effaces a message. In broadcast transmissions, this is equivalent to electronic static (radio) or visual snow (television); in speech, it can be an interfering exterior sound (physical noise) or a speaker's lapses of memory (psychological noise). Noise is the reason why communications systems have redundancy features built into them. These ensure that a message has a high probability of being decoded even if noise is present at the time of transmission or speech. The high predictability of certain sounds or words in many utterances is an inbuilt redundancy feature. For example, a speaker of English will easily decode the following sentence, even if it is missing elements: *I wll cme tmro to yr plce* ('I will come tomorrow to your place'). This means that our sense of structure and predictable pattern is itself part of how humans construct their communication systems.

Computing redundancy involves *entropy*, defined as the measure of random errors occurring in a system. To put it another way, it is the measure of the amount of disorder or randomness in a system. Because there are many more random than organized ways in which things occur, disorder has a higher probability than does order. It

follows that ordering things requires effort. Shuffling a deck of cards produces a jumbled distribution of cards. Ordering them, of course, requires effort. The measures of entropy and effort are thus intertwined, as is the measure of redundancy.

In media studies, the term redundancy is sometimes used to refer to the overuse of some element (or elements) so that it becomes familiar through saturation. Many advertising campaigns work on this principle. The constant repetition of themes in a campaign, the use of slogans, and so forth, are all manifestations of saturation.

Marcel Danesi

Bibliography

Hailman, Jack. *Coding and Redundancy*. Cambridge, MA: Harvard University Press, 2008.

Shannon, Claude E. A Mathematical Theory of Communication. *Bell Systems Technical Journal* 27 (1948): 379–423.

Wiener, Norbert. *Cybernetics, or Control and Communication in the Animal and the Machine*. Cambridge, MA: MIT Press, 1949.

REPRESENTATION

[See also: *Content Analysis; Semiotics*]

Representation is the process of depicting or recounting some event or concept in some specific way – with words, visual images, or musical sounds (separately or in various combinations). The intent of the representer, the historical, cultural, and social contexts in which the representation is made, the purpose for which it is made, and what it is designed to depict all play a role in how it is interpreted by its intended receivers.

For example, representing 'fatherhood' in a television sitcom involves telling family stories with the father as a prototypical 'father character.' In the 1950s, the father figure was portrayed as someone who was all-knowing and in charge of the family. The sitcom that best represented this view was *Father Knows Best*. In the 1980s and 1990s, however, the same figure was depicted in sitcoms such as *Married with Children* and *The Simpsons* as someone who was just the opposite. The process of deriving meaning from any such representation, known more specifically as *reading* in media theory, was (and continues to be) a variable one, influenced by social concepts of the father popular at the time the text is made and viewed, by individual and communal experiences vis-à-vis fatherhood, and by many other contextual factors that put limits on the range of meanings a specific representation will evoke.

Among the first to consider the connection between representation and real life were the ancient Greek philosophers Plato and Aristotle. Aristotle considered representation – verbal, visual, or musical – as the primary means through which human beings come to perceive reality, identifying *mimesis* (imitation or simulation) as the most basic and natural form for representing the world. Nonetheless, Aristotle also warned that representations create illusory worlds and, thus, can easily lead people astray. Plato believed that representations never really tell the truth but instead 'mediate' it, creating nothing but illusions that lead us away from contemplating life as it really is. He thus suggested that representations need to be monitored because they can foster antisocial reactions or encourage the imitation of evil things. The reason why we accept such things as movie ratings and other restrictions on our freedom to interpret representations individually highlights society's 'Platonic attempt' to restrict or modify representations to protect people (especially children) from exposure to them.

But this does not mean that people are passive consumers of representations. On the contrary, they are involved directly in giving the representations specific kinds of interpretations. Moreover, people belong to 'interpretive communities.' If the community to which audiences belong is predisposed to be in agreement with a representation's intended meaning, then the interpretation is said to be a preferred one. For example, anyone belonging to an evangelical community where public sexual portrayals are denounced will tend to interpret a television documentary denouncing internet sex as a warning about moral corruption in the world. On the other hand, a member of a civil rights group who sees the exact same documentary would react critically to it, seeing it as containing a potentially dangerous subtext that could lead to unnecessary restrictions on people's rights to decide for themselves what to see. That person is said to give the same representation an oppositional reading. Other groups and individuals (non-evangelicals and non–civil libertarians) will likely react to the same documentary in a 'mixed interpretive' fashion. This is known as a negotiated reading, because the individuals are essentially negotiating the representation as being partially true (in their view). Clearly, the 'truth of the matter' – whether or not internet sex is leading to moral corruption – is a matter of interpretation, not fact.

Two American researchers, Paul Lazarsfeld and Elihu Katz (1955), put forward a similar view to that of Plato and Aristotle in their study of media, claiming that the world views that the media construct, whether true or not, become the accepted realities at a specific point in time. However, as they also argue, people show that they are not passive consumers of media representations, but, rather, use the media for their own purposes and are thus in the main immune from the potentially conditioning factors that may issue forth from being exposed to the media. This is because representations are not stable, changing rapidly to conform with shifts in social mores, ethics, and world views.

Marcel Danesi

Bibliography

Hall, Stuart, ed. *Cultural Representations and Signifying Practice*. London: Open University Press, 1977.

Lazarsfeld, Paul F., and Elihu Katz. *Personal Influence: The Part Played by People in the Flow of Mass Communications.* Glencoe, IL: Free Press, 1955.

Merrell, Floyd. *Peirce, Signs, and Meaning.* Toronto: University of Toronto Press, 1997.

Staiger, Janet. *Media Reception Studies.* New York: New York University Press, 2005.

ROMANCE FICTION

[See also: *Narrative; Radway, Janice*]

Romance fiction is, as its name implies, fiction dealing with romance. Perhaps its best-known modern manifestations are the so-called Harlequin novels. Romance stories are universal, appearing throughout the ancient and medieval worlds. From that tradition we have inherited the lore surrounding famous love partners, such as Daphnis and Chloe, Romeo and Juliet, Tristan and Isolde, and Lancelot and Guinevere. From the 1100s to the 1400s the romance started to proliferate, gaining wide popularity. The medieval romances dealt with knightly combat, adventure, and courtship. The legends and stories about King Arthur and the knights of the Round Table were among the most popular of all the romances, remaining so to this day. So too were the stories about Alexander the Great, the Spanish hero El Cid, and the emperor Charlemagne and his faithful knight Roland. Horace Walpole's *The Castle of Otranto* (1764) was the first Gothic romance, a genre that revolved around mystery, terror, and the supernatural. Elements of the Gothic romance continue to be used in popular novels, movies, and programs about courtship.

The romance focuses typically on an amorous relationship between two people. In the nineteenth century Jane Austen expanded the genre with her novel *Pride and Prejudice*, highlighting the emotional psychology of the female in the love partnership and not the exploits of a male hero. The expansion of the genre to include more partners in the romantic situation came to characterize the twentieth-century romance, which found its main expression in radio and television soap operas. The origin of the 'sexy romance' can be traced back to Avon Books' publication of Kathleen Woodiwiss' *The Flame and the Flower* (1972). This type of romance is highly erotic and sexual, rather than purely romantic. Since then the genre has remained enormously successful, comprising over half of the paperback books sold in the mid-2000s.

Despite the popularity of romance novels, the genre has attracted significant criticism, especially on the part of the early feminist scholars, who saw it as a palliative to keep women enslaved to men. But the tide has changed, with post-feminism emphasizing the role that romance plays in female psychology. Present-day 'chick lit' is a post-feminist creation. The first example of chick lit is the 1997 novel *Bridget Jones's Diary* by Helen Fielding. The plots revolve around twenty- and thirty-year-old women starting out on a career track in big cities and in search for the 'perfect guy.' The general subtext is that 'It's OK to be an unmarried woman or even not have a romantic partner.' The genre constitutes a condemnation of traditional courtship practices, but not of romance per se. TV programs such as *Sex and the City* are also products of the genre.

Romance novels are divided into *category* or *series* romances and *single title* romances. The former are short books published regularly with sequels, corresponding to the TV soaps. The latter are individual novels that are not followed by sequels, although some authors have written them as part of a set, such as a trilogy. Thematically, the romance can also be subdivided into historical or epic romances (*Gone with the Wind*) and adventure and suspense romances, such as the ones typical of pulp fiction. Examples are the recent James Bond movies in which Bond falls in love with a woman, unlike previous Bond movies where he was only interested in engaging in sexual relations with women.

Janice Radway analyses romantic fiction in *Reading the Romance* (1987) and argues that women find the act of reading love stories pleasurable in itself, above and beyond what critics have to say about them. The romance, she claims, has appeal because it taps into women's particular psychology and deals with their real emotional lives. The structure of the romance is as follows: the opening presents a tense or difficult situation; an intermediate section presages and explains the final outcome; the ending provides a resolution of the initial tension.

In the typical romance, the heroine at first rejects her life to follow a man who she thinks is interested romantically in her. But she reacts in a hostile way to his advances, bringing about a tense situation. The heroine and her lover are then separated for unexpected reasons, leading her to declare her love after the man has shown kindness and tenderness towards her. Eventually, they declare their love passionately, overcome obstacles, and are happily united at the end. This format does not, of course, unfold in all romances, but it is a pattern within most of them, even if the romance deals with rejection of that pattern (as in chick lit). And, of course, there are romances where the story does not end happily ever after, of which the Romeo and Juliet legend is a classic example. Star-crossed lovers, evil lovers, and the like are all part of the genre as it has manifested itself throughout its history.

Radway emphasizes that women readers understand the various formats of the romance and gladly become engaged with them. There really is no agenda or stereotyping of women in such texts. Women read them for escape from the pressures of their daily lives. The romance allows women to think reflectively about love, sexuality, marriage, and motherhood. This kind of reading thus allows women to focus on themselves and their desires and worries. Such reading constitutes female empowerment, not victimization.

Marcel Danesi

Bibliography

Radway, Janice. *Reading the Romance: Women, Patriarchy, and Popular Literature.* London: Verso, 1987/1991.

Ramsdell, Kristin. *Romance Fiction: A Guide to the Genre.* Englewood, CO: Libraries Unlimited, 1999.

Regis, Pamela. *A Natural History of the Romance Novel.* Philadelphia: University of Pennsylvania Press, 2003.

Staiger, Janet. *Media Reception Studies.* New York: New York University Press, 2005.

S

SAUSSUREAN SEMIOTICS

[See also: *Peircean Semiotics; Semiotics; Structuralism*]

The Swiss linguist Ferdinand de Saussure (1857–1913) is considered to be the modern-era founder of both linguistics and semiotics as autonomous disciplines through his *Cours de linguistique générale* (1916), a textbook compiled after his death by two of his own university students at the University of Geneva. Saussure used the term *sémiologie* (*semiology*), which he had been using in his personal correspondence as far back as 1894, to designate the new discipline of sign study. The term *semiotics*, adopted by the International Association of Semiotic Study in 1969, comes out of a different tradition associated primarily with the American philosopher Charles S. Peirce, reaching back to the physician Hippocrates in the ancient world and to English philosopher John Locke in the seventeenth century.

Saussure (1916: 15–16) proposed that the main objective of semiology (should it ever come into existence) was to understand the social function of signs:

> It is possible to conceive of a science which studies the role of signs as part of social life. It would form part of social psychology, and hence of general psychology. We shall call it *semiology* (from the Greek *semeion*, 'sign'). It would investigate the nature of signs and the laws governing them. Since it does not yet exist, one cannot say for certain that it will exist. But it has a right to exist, a place ready for it in advance. Linguistics is only one branch of this general science. The laws which semiology will discover will be laws applicable in linguistics, and linguistics will thus be assigned to a clearly defined place in the field of human knowledge.

Saussure was born in 1857 in Geneva. He specialized in science at the University of Geneva before turning his interests to language studies at the University of Leipzig in 1876. He published his only book, *Mémoire sur le système primitif des voyelles dans les langues indo-européennes* [Memoir on the Original Vowel System in the Indo-European Languages], as a student in 1879. The work is an important one on the vowel system of Proto-Indo-European, the parent language from which the Indo-European languages have descended. From 1881 to 1891, Saussure taught at the École des Hautes Études in Paris. He then became professor of Sanskrit and Comparative Grammar at the University of Geneva. Although he never wrote another book, two of his students, C. Bally and A. Sechehaye, collected the lecture notes they had taken during his classes and, along with other materials, wrote *Cours de linguistique générale* (1916), which bears their teacher's name.

Saussure separated the historical study of language change from its purely descrip-

Figure 1

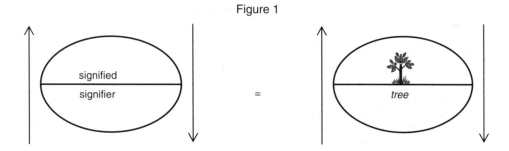

tive study, calling the former *diachronic* and the latter *synchronic* – a distinction that remains to this day. He put forward a model of the sign that has come to be known as 'binary,' that is, composed of two parts. He called the physical part of the sign, such as the actual sounds that make up a word such as *dog*, the *signifier*, and the concept or mental image that the sign elicits, the *signified* (literally 'that which is signified by the sign'). The signifier is recognizable as such because it has a *structure*. This can be determined by a native speaker because it is different from other meaning-bearing words such as *log* or *bog*, standing in a minimal relation of difference to them. The differential cue is the initial 'd,' of course, but its meaning-bearing distinctiveness is due to the fact that it combines with the other sounds in a structured way. Now, once a form or structure is associated with a meaning (a mental image), the relation between the two is bidirectional or binary – that is, one necessarily implies the other. The word *tree* is a word in English because it has a recognizable phonetic structure that generates a mental concept (an arboreal plant). (See Figure 1.)

So, when we utter or hear the word *tree* the image of an arboreal plant inevitably comes to mind, and, in fact, we cannot block that image from occurring; vice versa, when we see an arboreal plant the word *tree* comes automatically to mind. This is anecdotal evidence that both components of the sign exist in tandem, not separately. This model of the sign traces its origin back to the medieval Scholastics,

who also viewed the sign (*signum*) as an identifiable form composed of two parts – a *signans* ('that which does the signifying') and a *signatum* ('that which is signified'). The intrinsic relation that inheres between signs and the concepts they evoke is called *signification* or *semiosis* today.

Saussure claimed, moreover, that there is no necessary reason for creating the word *dog* other than the social need to do so. Any other form would have served the same purpose just as effectively. For this reason, Saussure's model of the sign is called 'arbitrary.' There is no evident reason for using, say, *tree* or *arbre* (French) to designate 'an arboreal plant.' Any other well-formed structure would do in either language. Saussure did admit, however, that some signs were motivated by the imitation of some sensory or perceivable property detectable in their referents. Onomatopoeic words (*drip*, *whack*, and so on), he conceded, were created to imitate real physical sounds. But such words were the exception, not the rule. Moreover, onomatopoeia is highly variable, not systemic. For example, the expression used to refer to the sounds made by a rooster is *cock-a-doodle-do* in English, but *chicchirichì* (pronounced 'keekkeereekee') in Italian. Obviously, simulating what a rooster sounds like when it crows is largely an arbitrary process, depending on culture. But this part of Saussurean theory has been highly problematic and thus a target of criticism. The reason is a simple one – such words are highly suggestive of actual crowing, no matter how different they may seem phonetically. And any other signifier would be perceived as anomalous. Moreover, many core words in a language possess a latent sound-imitative quality built into their structure. Consider the word *duck* (Danesi 2007). The sounds in its make-up are, to be sure, part of a large number of permissible assemblages that can be envisioned in English word construction, as Saussure would have it. But the final /k/ of that word clearly suggests the kind of sound the animal in question is perceived to make. It is an unconscious model of that sound. The model is called a *sound symbol* in linguistics. Saussure was obviously unaware of, or uninterested in, the role of sound symbolism in the formation of the core vocabularies of languages; nor could he be, because its discovery as a primary force in language origins was made several decades after his death by the linguist Morris Swadesh in the 1950s (see Swadesh 1971).

Semioticians today use a blend of Saussurean and Peircean ideas and techniques at various stages of analysis and for diverse purposes. Saussure himself suggested that semiology take on an interdisciplinary orientation, connecting itself to both linguistics and psychology. This suggestion has remained a basic one to this day.

Marcel Danesi

Bibliography

Danesi, Marcel. *The Quest for Meaning: A Guide to Semiotic Theory and Practice*. Toronto: University of Toronto Press, 2007.

Eco, Umberto. *A Theory of Semiotics*. Bloomington: Indiana University Press, 1976.

– *Semiotics and the Philosophy of Language*. Bloomington: Indiana University Press, 1984.

Saussure, Ferdinand de. *Cours de linguistique générale*. Ed. Charles Bally and Albert Sechehaye. Paris: Payot, 1916. Trans. Wade Baskin, *Course in General Linguistics*. New York: McGraw-Hill, 1958.

Swadesh, Morris. *The Origins and Diversification of Language*. Chicago: Aldine-Atherton, 1971.

SCIENCE FICTION

[See also: *Adventure Stories; Books, History of; Crime Genre; Horror Fiction; Narrative; Romance Fiction; Text Theory*]

Science fiction is so named because it is fiction that deals with the potential effects of science and technology (real or imagined) on human beings. Common themes in the genre include time travel, space exploration, incredible inventions or discoveries, life in other universes or dimensions, invasions of the Earth by aliens, ideal societies called *utopias* and their opposite called *dystopias*.

Science fiction has ancient roots. In his *True History* (160 CE) Lucian of Samosata described a trip to the moon; the seventeenth-century British prelate and historian Francis Godwin similarly wrote about travel to the moon; Sir Thomas More described a futuristic world in *Utopia* (1516); the French author Cyrano de Bergerac wrote *Other Worlds* (1657), which is about trips to the moon and the sun; English writer Jonathan Swift's *Gulliver's Travels* (1726) is about a series of fantastic sea voyages; and Voltaire's *Micromegas* (1752) is the first fictional story that dealt with visitors from other planets. However, science fiction as we know it today traces its roots to the period after the Industrial Revolution when, in her novel *Frankenstein or the Modern Prometheus* (1818), the British novelist Mary Shelley explored the potential of science and technology for destruction and evil. After the publication of her novel, the genre emerged as a new form of popular fiction. The first writer to specialize in it first was the Frenchman Jules Verne (1828–1905), whose highly successful novels included *Journey to the Center of the Earth* (1864) and *Around the World in Eighty Days* (1873). The first major English writer of science fiction was H.G. Wells (1866–1946), whose *Time Machine* (1895), *The Island of Dr Moreau* (1896), and *The War of the Worlds* (1898) became, and continue to be, cult classics.

In the twentieth century the popularity of science fiction grew with the rising importance of science and the astounding growth of technology. George Méliès's 1902 film *A Trip to the Moon* is one of the first works of cinematic art. The novel *We* (1924) by the Russian writer Yevgeny Zamyatin provided a dystopic portrait of a nightmarish world shaped by technology. The Czech writer Karel Capek introduced the term *robot* in his play *R.U.R.* (1921) and foreshadowed the horrors of the atomic bomb in his novel *Krakatit* (1924). British writer Olaf Stapledon dealt with the eventual extinction of humanity in his novel *Last and First Men* (1930). *Brave New World* (1932) by Aldous Huxley and *1984* (1949) by George Orwell, as well as *Fahrenheit 451* (1953) by the American author Ray Bradbury, dealt with the theme of a society enslaved by science and technology, open to accepting totalitarianism as a political way of life.

Science fiction also became a favourite genre of pulp fiction. The first pulp fiction magazine, called *Amazing Stories*, began publishing in 1926. It was founded by Hugo Gernsback, who was also the first to use the term *science fiction*. Various science fiction pulps followed suit shortly thereafter dealing primarily with scientific marvels and becoming more and more conscious of social concerns as the years went by. Writers such as Robert A. Heinlein, Isaac Asimov, and Theodore Sturgeon became influential first and foremost as science-fiction writers, exploring notions of morality, religion, sex, and the nature of existence in their writings. The genre also crossed over to radio and the movies, becoming extremely poplar in both media.

Science fiction gained wider audiences in the 1950s and 1960s through the movies and TV, coinciding with the advent of nuclear energy and space exploration. Fiction and reality started to mirror each other. The genre became more and more critical of science and technology. One of the best-known TV science fiction programs was *Star Trek* (originally 1966–9). Other popular programs included *The Twilight Zone* (1959–64, revived 1985–7), *Lost in Space* (1965–8), *Dr Who* (1963–89; 2005–present), and *The X-Files* (1993–2002). Today there is even a SyFy Channel that caters to a large fan base for the genre. And, of course, there are many online venues where fans can indulge their passion for science fiction.

A new type of science fiction writing appeared in the 1960s and 1970s called *new wave*, featuring anti-heroes and post-human scenarios. Key authors in the style included Brian Aldiss, J.G. Ballard, Michael Moorcock, Harlan Ellison, Roger Zelazny, Samuel R. Delany, and Octavia E. Butler. In the 1980s, yet another new category of science fiction, called *cyberpunk*, appeared. The genre dealt with the ways the new computer systems and modes of communication shaped our perceptions of the world and our relationships with others. One of the best-known examples of cyberpunk is *Neuromancer* (1984) by William Gibson, the novel which introduced the term *cyberspace* to the world. The main thematic thrust of cyberpunk is that our daily interactions in cyberspace have led surreptitiously to the entrenchment of a bizarre modern form of consciousness. Computers allow users to move and react in simulated environments, manipulating virtual objects in place of real objects. Constant engagement with such environments is conditioning people more and more to perceive the world as a simulacrum – a world where fiction and reality have fused completely. The modern-day human being, as the 1999 movie *The Matrix* brought out, is born first through a real womb and then through an artificial one – the computer screen. The word *matrix* meant womb in Latin; today it means computer screen.

Science fiction has always attracted young audiences. With the popularity of the British writer J.K. Rowling's *Harry Potter* fantasy novels and movie versions in the 2000s, the genre started to produce new works for such audiences. Most of them are designed to address issues of identity and social acceptance. Examples include *Feed* (2002) by M.T. Anderson and *Messenger*

(2004) by Lois Lowry. But many science fiction works continue to stress the dangers of scientific discoveries or else explore the new vistas that science is opening up to human consciousness. They deal with topics such as androids, black holes, imaginary worlds, mad scientists, lost worlds, and alien creatures. The latter topic is especially popular. Since the 1960s, movies, TV programs, documentaries, best-seller books, websites, and magazines that deal with UFOs and aliens, either as fiction or scientific fact, have proliferated. On TV the UFO theme is the key one in programs such *ALF* (1986–90), *X-Files* (1993–2002), *Third Rock from the Sun* (1996–2001), *Roswell* (1999–2007), and many others. This is also a staple of movies: *The Day the Earth Stood Still* (1951), *The Thing* (1951), *It Came from Outer Space* (1953), *Invasion of the Body Snatchers* (1956), *Not of This Earth* (1957), *UFO Incident* (1975), *Close Encounters of the Third Kind* (1977), *Alien* (1979), *E.T.* (1982), *Predator* (1987), *Mars Attacks* (1996), *Independence Day* (1996), *K-Pax* (2001), *Signs* (2002).

Marcel Danesi

Bibliography

Luckhurst, Roger. *Science Fiction*. Cambridge: Polity, 2005.

Scholes, Robert, and Eric S. Rabkin. *Science Fiction: History, Science, Vision*. Oxford: Oxford University Press, 1977.

Westphal, Gary, ed. *The Greenwood Encyclopedia of Science Fiction and Fantasy: Themes, Works, and Wonders*. Westport, CT: Greenwood, 2005.

SEMIOTICS

[See also: *Barthes, Roland; Mythology; Peircean Semiotics and Cultural Productions; Post-Structuralism; Structuralism*]

Semiotics is the study of the meanings of human intellectual and artistic products, from words, symbols, narratives, symphonies, paintings and comic books, to scientific theories and mathematical theorems. This might seem to be a daunting task, encompassing virtually all the creative and knowledge-making activities that make up human life. But semiotics focuses more narrowly on the meaning of the *signs* – symbols, words, images – used in such activities and their connection to history. The word *sign* is used in semiotics to encompass anything that stands for something other than itself. So a word is not simply a combination of sounds that stand for the sounds themselves but a unitary structure that stands for something else. Similarly a symbol such as a cross figure is not a visual representation that stands not for two lines crossing at right angles, but for a series of meanings such as 'plus' (in arithmetic) or Christianity (in religion).

Let's look at an example more closely. The sign formed by raising the index and middle fingers of the hand in the shape of a 'V' is normally interpreted to stand for 'victory' or 'peace' by people living in North America or Europe. The link to victory was established at the end of the Second World War by British Prime Minister Winston Churchill after he used it publicly to emphasize the victorious outcome for the Allied forces. The sign has more ancient origins, however; it was used by the Romans, for example, for various purposes (to indicate victory, to greet someone). Shortly thereafter, the V-sign became a symbol against war and human conflict among counterculture youths, turning Churchill's meaning on its head. But the semiotic story of the V-sign does not stop there. It can also be used much more practically to indicate the number '2' or the letter 'V' itself. In some cultures, moreover, it is used as a greeting sign. In others it stands for 'femininity' and 'fertility.' Explaining meanings such as '2' or 'victory' is a fairly simple task. On the other hand, explaining a meaning such as 'femininity' is not. In such a case, the semiotician becomes a 'detective' and, like a true detective, would start by considering the shape of the sign itself as a clue for unravelling the reason for such meanings, looking for corroborating evidence among the symbolic and representational traditions in cultures across the world that use the sign with this meaning, as well as in current manifestations.

The foregoing discussion encapsulates what semiotics is essentially all about. It is about investigating, deciphering, documenting, and explaining the what, how, and why of 'signs,' no matter how simple or complex they may be. Since the middle part of the twentieth century, semiotics has grown into a truly broad field of inquiry. It has been applied to the study of body language, art forms, discourses of all kinds, visual communication, media, advertising, narratives, language, objects, gestures, facial expressions, eye contact, clothing, space, cuisine, rituals – in a phrase, to anything that human beings produce and use to communicate and represent something in some meaningful way.

History

The term *semeiotics* (spelled now as *semiotics*) – from Greek *sêmeiotikos*, 'observant of signs' – was coined by Hippocrates (ca 460–370 BCE), the founder of Western medicine, to designate the study of the warning signs produced by the human body, known more commonly today as symptoms. Hippocrates argued that the particular physical form that a symptom takes – a *semeion* ('mark') – constitutes a vital clue for finding its source. It is something with recurrent visible features that stand for 'something invisible' – a disease, malady, or ailment. With this simple concept, Hippocrates established medicine as a diagnostic 'semeiotic' science – that is, as a science based on the detection and interpretation of bodily signs. Semeiotic method was entrenched into medical practice by the physician Galen of Pergamum (ca 130–200 CE) a few centuries later.

The concept of *semeion* was expanded in antiquity to include human-made signs (such as words) that stood for psychological or emotional states. Among the first to

differentiate between *natural* (physical) and *conventional* (human-made) signs was the Greek philosopher Plato (ca 427–347 BCE). Plato was intrigued by the fact that a single word had the capacity to refer not to specific objects, but to all objects that resemble each other in some identifiable way. For example, the word *circle* does not refer to a singular thing (although it can if need be), but to anything that has the property 'circularity.' For this reason, Plato argued that words are not simple replacements for things – a particular circle can be altered in size, but it will still be called a *circle*. The ideas that we capture with words could not be part of the everyday world, which is changing and imperfect. They made reference to recurrent properties in objects. Plato's illustrious pupil Aristotle (384–322 BCE) took issue with his teacher, arguing that words start out as practical devices that do indeed allow us to name singular things, rather than refer to properties (circularity, roundness) in them. We discover that certain things have such properties as we go along naming them. It is at such points of discovery that we create abstract words (indicating 'categories') that allow us to refer to the similar properties: plants, animals, objects, for example. In contrast to Plato's 'mentalist' theory of the sign, Aristotle's theory is called 'empirical.'

Eventually, the question arose as to whether or not there is any connection between natural and conventional signs. Among the first to discuss a possible relationship were the Stoics (around 308 BCE), who argued that we create conventional signs (words and symbols) in response to what we perceive as significant. They are 'responses' to the world. It was St Augustine (354–430 CE), the early Christian church father and philosopher, who was among the first to argue persuasively for a fundamental difference between the two in his *De doctrina christiana* ('On Christian Doctrine'). For St Augustine, natural signs *(signa naturalia)* are qualitatively distinct from conventional ones because they lack intentionality. These included not only bodily symptoms, but also the rustling of leaves, the colours of plants, the signals that animals emit, and so on. Conventional signs *(signa data)*, on the other hand, are the product of human intentionality. These include not only words, but gestures and the symbols that humans invent to serve their psychological, social, and communicative needs. Finally, St Augustine considered miracles to be messages from God and, thus, sacred signs. These can only be understood on faith, although such understanding is partly based on specific religious interpretations of them.

Interest in signs seems to have faded shortly thereafter. It was only in the eleventh century that it was rekindled as a result of the translation of the works of Plato, Aristotle, and other key Greek philosophers. The outcome was the movement known as *Scholasticism*. The Scholastics were Christian thinkers who sought to solve general philosophical and theological problems, such as the provability of the existence of God. Using Aristotelian theory as their basic frame of reference, they asserted that signs captured real truths. So a word such as *tree* meant exactly what it stood for – an arboreal plant. Similarly, the word *love* captures a human sentiment that we all know is real. But within this movement there were some – the so-called *nominalists* – who argued that 'truth' was a matter of opinion and that signs captured, at best, only variable human versions of it. John Duns Scotus (ca 1266–1308) and William of Ockham (ca 1285–1349), for instance, stressed that signs referred only to other signs rather than to actual things – a perspective that is strikingly akin to some modern theories of the sign. So, for example, *tree* is meaningful because its inventor decided that a particular plant required identification rather than being considered a plant in general. So, too, the words *arm* and *hand* capture two different 'realities,' but in Russian one word *(ruká)* suffices, including both parts of the body. In effect, there is no truth, just our interpretation of it. And interpretations vary considerably,

as the world's languages show. The theologian St Thomas Aquinas countered, however, that although signs vary in how they represent the world, it still cannot be denied that they refer to real things. At about the same time, the English philosopher and scientist Roger Bacon developed one of the first comprehensive typologies of signs, claiming that, without a firm understanding of the role of signs in the construction of knowledge, discussing what truth is or is not would end up being a trivial matter of subjective opinion.

It was John Locke who put forward the specific proposal of incorporating semiotics into philosophy in his *Essay Concerning Human Understanding* (1690). Locke saw semiotics as an investigative instrument for philosophers, not as a distinct discipline or method of inquiry. The idea of fashioning an autonomous discipline of sign study did not crystallize until the late nineteenth century, when the Swiss linguist Ferdinand de Saussure put such an idea forward in his *Cours de linguistique générale* (1916), a textbook compiled after his death by two of his university students. Saussure used the term *sémiologie* (English *semiology*) – which he had used in personal correspondence as far back as 1894 – to designate the new discipline. He suggested that the main goal of semiology (should it ever come into being) was to understand the social function of signs – that is, how signs allow people to refer to things in their social environments in specific ways and how they allow people to interact.

Today, Locke's term *(semeiotics)*, spelled *semiotics*, is the preferred one. It is the one that was adopted by the International Association of Semiotic Studies in 1969. The term *significs*, coined by Victoria Lady Welby (1837–1912) in 1896, is also used occasionally in the technical literature, but with a specific sense – the study of the relation of signs to the senses and the emotions. It was the American philosopher Charles S. Peirce who put Locke's term into wide circulation. Along with Saussure, Peirce is a founder of modern semiotics. Although his writing style is rather dense and his ideas not easily understood, Peirce's basic theory of the sign has become central. Perhaps his greatest insight is that signs are 'informed hunches' as to what something means in human terms. Our experience of the world, therefore, influences how a sign is constituted and why it is brought into existence in the first place. Simply put, we construct a *semeion* not because we simply want to refer to something or classify it, but because we sense a relation between the sign and the thing it names. This can be seen clearly in imitative or onomatopoeic words such as such as *plop* or *zip*, which are intended to resemble the sounds associated with the objects or actions to which they refer. The very same kind of inferential process occurs across levels of conceptualization.

Following on the coattails of Saussure and Peirce, a number of key people developed semiotics into the discipline that it has become today. The philosopher Ludwig Wittgenstein suggested that signs were pictures of reality, presenting it as if it were a series of images. Each time we utter a word such as *tree*, the image of the plant comes to mind. When we combine it with *apple*, the image is rendered more precise (in contrast to, say, a *fig tree*). And so on. This view continues to inform a large part of semiotic theory and practice. The American semiotician Charles Morris (1901–79) divided semiotic method into: (1) the study of sign assemblages, which he called *syntactics*; (2) the study of the relations between signs and their meanings, which he called *semantics*; and (3) the study of the relations between signs and their users, which he called *pragmatics*. The Russian-born American semiotician Roman Jakobson (1896–1982) studied various facets of sign construction but is probably best known for his model of communication, which suggests that sign exchanges are hardly ever neutral but involve subjectivity and goal attainment of some kind – that is, when we speak we intend to get something out of it, and the nature of the signs used bear this out. The French semiotician Roland

Barthes illustrated the power of using semiotics for decoding the hidden meanings in pop culture spectacles such as wrestling matches and Hollywood blockbuster movies. French semiotician Algirdas J. Greimas developed the branch of semiotics known as *narratology*, which studies how human beings in different cultures invent similar kinds of narratives (myths, tales, etc.) with virtually the same stock of characters, motifs, themes, and plots. The Hungarian-born American semiotician Thomas A. Sebeok was influential in expanding the semiotic paradigm to include the comparative study of animal signalling systems, which he termed *zoosemiotics*, and the study of *semiosis* in all living things, which has come to be called *biosemiotics*. Semiosis is the innate ability to produce and comprehend signs in a species-specific way. The interweaving and blending of ideas, findings, and scientific discourses from different disciplinary domains was, Sebeok claimed, the distinguishing feature of biosemiotics. Finally, Italian semiotician Umberto Eco has contributed significantly to our understanding of how we interpret things such as signs and texts, claiming that we read a novel, for instance, not just for its content, but also to get insight from it or to relate it to our life schemes.

The Study of Meaning

The object of semiotic inquiry is 'meaning' and how it manifests itself in human activities. A little reflection will reveal, however, that this is a confusing word indeed. As the psychologists Charles Ogden and I.A. Richards showed in their 1923 work *The Meaning of Meaning*, there are at least twenty-three meanings of the word *meaning* in English, adding to the confusion. Here are some of them:

He *means* to study math.	= 'intends'
A red light *means* stop.	= 'indicates'
Happiness *means* everything.	= 'has importance'

Her look was full of *meaning*.	= 'special import'
Does life have a *meaning*?	= 'purpose'
What does love *mean* to you?	= 'convey'

To avoid such built-in vagueness and ambivalence, the terms *reference, sense*, and *definition* are used instead in semiotics. Reference is the process of pointing out or identifying something; sense is what that something elicits psychologically, historically, and socially; and definition is a statement about what that something means by convention. Words may refer to the same (or similar) things, known as *referents,* but they have different senses. For example, the 'long-eared, short-tailed, burrowing mammal of the family Leporidae' can be called *rabbit* or *hare* in English. Both words *refer* essentially to the same kind of mammal. But there is a difference of sense – *hare* is the more appropriate term for describing the mammal if it is larger, has longer ears and legs, and does not burrow. Another difference is that a *rabbit* can be perceived as a 'pet,' while a *hare* is unlikely to be recognized as such. The German philosopher Gottlob Frege was among the first to point out the role of sense in theories of meaning. Frege's famous example was that of the 'fourth smallest planet and the second planet from the Sun' as being named both *Venus* and the *Morning Star*. The two terms referred to the same thing, he observed, but they have different senses – *Venus* refers to the planet in a straightforward referential way (nevertheless with implicit references to the goddess of sexual love and physical beauty of Roman mythology), while *Morning Star* brings out the fact that the planet is visible in the east just before sunrise. Knowledge of signs, clearly, includes awareness of the senses that they bear in social and historical context – a fact emphasized further by philosopher Willard O. Quine. In his classic example, Quine portrayed a linguist who overhears the word *Gavagai* from the mouth of a native inform-

ant when a rabbit is sighted scurrying through the bushes. But the linguist cannot determine if the word means 'rabbit,' 'undetached rabbit parts,' or 'rabbit stage,' all of which are senses of that word. The sense, therefore, will remain indeterminate unless it can be inferred from the context in which *Gavagai* occurs.

Definition is a statement about what something means by using words and other signs (for example, pictures). As useful as it is, the act of defining leads inevitably to circularity. Take the dictionary definition of *cat* as 'a small carnivorous mammal domesticated since early times as a catcher of rats and mice and as a pet and existing in several distinctive breeds and varieties.' One of the problems that emerges from this definition is the use of *mammal* to define *cat*. In effect, one term has been replaced by another. So, what is the meaning of *mammal*? A *mammal*, it states, is 'any of various warm-blooded vertebrate animals of the class Mammalia.' But this definition is hardly a viable solution. What is an *animal*? The dictionary defines *animal* as an *organism*, which it defines, in turn, as an individual form of *life*, which it then defines as the property that distinguishes living *organisms*. At that point the dictionary has gone into a referential loop, since it has employed an already-used concept, *organism*, to define *life*. This looping pattern surfaces in all domains of human knowledge. It suggests that signs can never be understood in the absolute, only in relation to other signs.

In contemporary semiotics, the terms *denotation* and *connotation* are preferred to reference and sense. Consider, again, the word *cat*. The word elicits an image of a 'creature with four legs, whiskers, retractile claws,' and so forth. This is its *denotative* meaning, which is really a mental picture of *cat* in terms of specific features that are perceived to define cats in general – 'retractile claws,' 'long tail.' The denotative meaning allows users of signs to determine if something real or imaginary under consideration is an exemplar of a 'cat.' Similarly, the word *square* elicits a mental image characterized by the distinctive features 'four equal straight lines' and 'meeting at right angles.' It is irrelevant if the lines are thick, dotted, 2 metres long, or 80 feet long. If the figure has 'four equal straight lines meeting at right angles,' it is denotatively a square. The word *denotation*, incidentally, is derived from the compound Latin verb *de-noto*, 'to mark out, point out, specify, indicate.' The noun *nota* ('mark, sign, note') itself derives from the verb *nosco* ('to come to know,' 'to become acquainted with,' and 'to recognize').

All other associations with the words *cat* and *square* are connotative – that is, they are derivational or extensional and thus culture-specific. Some connotative senses of *square* can be seen in expressions such as the following:

She's so *square*.	= 'old fashioned'
He has a *square* disposition.	= 'forthright,' 'honourable'
Put it *squarely* on the table.	= 'evenly,' 'precisely'

The concept of *square* is an ancient one and, thus, probably known by everyone (hence 'old-fashioned'); it is also a figure with every part equal (hence 'forthright'); and it certainly is an even-sided figure (hence 'evenly'). Connotation encompasses all kinds of senses, including emotional ones. Consider the word *yes*. In addition to being a sign of affirmation, it can have various emotional senses, depending on the tone of voice with which it is uttered. If one says it with a raised tone, as in a question, 'Yes?' then it would convey doubt or incredulity. If articulated emphatically, 'Yes!' then it would connote triumph, achievement, or victory.

Connotation is the operative sense-making and sense-extracting mode in the production and decipherment of creative texts such as poems, novels, musical compositions, or artworks – in effect, of most of the non-technical texts that people create. But this does not imply that meaning in technical (information-based) domains

unfolds only denotatively. On the contrary, many (if not all) scientific theories and models are constructed connotatively, even though they end up being interpreted denotatively over time. Portraying an atom as a miniature solar system is an example of this. While it may be incorrect denotatively, it nonetheless provides initial insights into atomic structure. Connotation is not an option, as some traditional philosophical and linguistic theories of meaning continue to sustain to this day; it is something we are inclined to extract from a sign. The V-sign discussed above, for example, has a denotative meaning, as we saw – it can be used to represent the number 2 – but only in response to a question such as: 'How many dollars do you have in your pocket?' This denotative meaning – two fingers representing the number 2 directly – is established by a very restricted context. However, in most other contexts the V-sign hardly ever elicits a denotative interpretation. This applies to all kinds of signs – even to digits. The numbers 7 and 13 in our culture invariably reverberate with connotative meanings such as 'fortune,' 'destiny,' 'bad luck,' and so on.

Abstract concepts such as *motherhood, masculinity, friendship,* and *justice* are particularly high in connotative content. In 1957, the psychologists Charles Osgood, G.J. Suci, and P.H. Tannenbaum showed this empirically by using a technique they called the *semantic differential*. The technique allows investigators to flesh out the connotative (culture-specific) meanings that abstract concepts elicit. It consists in posing a series of questions to subjects about a particular concept – *Is X good or bad? Should Y be weak or strong?* The subjects are then asked to rate the concept on seven-point scales. The ratings are collected and analysed statistically in order to sift out any general pattern they might bear.

Suppose that subjects are asked to rate the concept 'ideal American president' in terms of the following scales: for example, *Should the president be young or old? Should the president be practical or idealistic? Should the president be modern or traditional?*

young	—	—	—	—	—	—	—	old
	1	2	3	4	5	6	7	
practical	—	—	—	—	—	—	—	idealistic
	1	2	3	4	5	6	7	
modern	—	—	—	—	—	—	—	traditional
	1	2	3	4	5	6	7	
attractive	—	—	—	—	—	—	—	bland
	1	2	3	4	5	6	7	
friendly	—	—	—	—	—	—	—	stern
	1	2	3	4	5	6	7	

A subject who feels that the president should be more 'youngish' than 'oldish' would place a mark towards the *young* end of the top scale; one who feels that a president should be 'bland' would place a mark towards the *bland* end of the *attractive-bland* scale; and so on. If we were to ask a large number of subjects to rate the president in this way, we would get a 'connotative view' of the American presidency in terms of the statistically significant variations in sense that it evokes. Interestingly, research utilizing the semantic differential has shown that the range of variations is not a matter of pure subjectivity but, rather, forms a socially based pattern. In other words, the connotations of many (if not all) abstract concepts are constrained by culture: for example, the word *noise* turns out to be a highly emotional concept for the Japanese, who rate it consistently at the ends of the scales presented to them, whereas it is a fairly neutral concept for Americans, who tend to rate it on average in the mid-ranges of the same scales. Connotation is not, therefore, open-ended; it is constrained by a series of factors, including conventional agreements as to what signs mean in certain situations. Without such constraints, our systems of meaning, known as *signification* systems, would be virtually unusable. All signification (whether it is denotative or connotative) is a relational and associative process – that is, signs acquire their meanings not in isolation, but in relation to other signs and to the contexts in which they occur.

The distinction between denotation and connotation is analogous to Frege's distinction between reference and sense. And indeed these terms are used interchangeably in the relevant semiotic literature, as are Rudolf Carnap's (1891–1970) terms *intension* (= denotation) and *extension* (= connotation). While there are subtle differences among these terms, it is beyond the present purposes to compare them. Suffice it to say that in current semiotic practice they are virtually synonymous. The distinction between denotation and connotation as we understand it today was used for the first time by the American linguist Leonard Bloomfield in his seminal 1933 book called *Language*, a distinction elaborated by the Danish linguist Louis Hjelmslev a little later. Although Hjelmslev's treatment is a highly abstruse and largely confusing one, it nevertheless had the effect of putting this basic distinction on the semiotic agenda once and for all. Especially relevant is Hjelmslev's characterization of connotation as a 'secondary semiotic system' for expressing subjective meanings.

Semiotics also makes an important distinction between the terms *image* and *concept*. The former is the mental picture of a referent that is evoked when a sign is used; the latter is the culture-specific interpretation that is assigned to that picture. There are two types of concepts – concrete and abstract. The former is the concept that is formed when the sign refers to something that can be seen, heard, smelled, touched, tasted – that is, observed in some direct sensory way. The latter is the concept formed when the sign refers to something that cannot be perceived in a direct sensory fashion. A 'cat' constitutes a concrete concept because the existence of a real cat in the physical world can be perceived and thus easily pictured in the mind. On the other hand, 'love' is an abstract concept because, although it can be experienced emotionally, it cannot be observed directly – that is, the emotion itself cannot be separated from the behaviours or states of mind it produces. The mental image that it evokes is, thus, hardly a clear-cut one.

The distinction between concrete and abstract concepts is a general one. In actual fact, there are many degrees and layers of concreteness and abstraction in mental imagery and concept formation that are influenced by social, historical, and other kinds of external or contextual factors. In the middle part of the twentieth century, psychologists started classifying concepts in terms of a three-tiered hierarchical system to bring out their 'degree-ness.' At the highest level, called the *superordinate* level, concepts are considered to have a highly general classificatory (abstract) function. So, for example, in the dictionary definition of *cat*, the related concept of *mammal* would be viewed as a superordinate concept because it refers to the general category of animals to which a cat belongs. Then there is the *basic* or *prototypical* level, which is where the word *cat* itself would fit in. This is the level where basic types of mammals are classified – cats, dogs, goats, hogs, horses, and so forth. The third level, called the *subordinate* level, is where more detailed ways of referring to something occur. There are, in fact, many types (breeds) of cat – *Siamese, Persian, Abyssinian, Korat*, for example – which allow us to refer to culturally meaningful differences in detail. However, such notions as levels and hierarchies

are problematic, as Umberto Eco pointed out in his 1984 book *Semiotics and the Philosophy of Language*. The main difficulty, he suggested, is that decisions as to where a term belongs in a hierarchy invariably end up being a matter of subjective choice.

Ultimately, signs allow people to recognize certain patterns in the world over and over again, thus acting as directive guides for taking action in the world. Signs are thus closely tied to social needs and aspirations – a fact emphasized by many semioticians, especially the Russian theorist Mikhail Bakhtin. Bakhtin went so far as to claim that signs gain meaning only as they are exchanged by people in social dialogue or discourse. In effect, he maintained that all human meaning is constructed dialogically (socially).

Two Models of the Sign

Semiotic inquiry is guided by two fundamental models of the sign – the one put forward by Saussure and the one elaborated by Peirce. Saussure posited a 'binary' model of the sign – a structure with two components. He termed the physical part of the sign, such as the sounds that make up the word *cat*, the *signifier*, and the concept that the sign elicits, the *signified* (literally 'that which is signified by the sign'). Saussure claimed, moreover, there is no necessary motivation or reason for creating the word *cat* other than the social need to do so. Any other signifier would have done the job just as effectively. This is why his model of the sign is also called 'arbitrary.' Peirce, on the other hand, saw signs as possessing 'triadic' structure – the actual physical sign, the thing to which it refers, and the interpretation that it elicits in real-world situations. He called the sign itself a *representamen* (literally 'something that does the representing') and the concept that it encodes the *object* (literally 'something cast outside for observation'). He termed the meaning that we get from a sign the *interpretant*. This constitutes a 'derived' sign because it entails the further production of meanings arising from the context in which a sign is used. In our culture, a *cat* is considered to be a domestic companion, among other things; in others it is viewed primarily as a sacred animal (akin to a sacred cow in some societies); and in others still it is considered to be a source of food (cat meat). Thus, while the sign refers to virtually the same mammal in different cultures (no matter what name is used), its interpretant varies considerably, constituting a source of supplementary sense making.

Peirce also developed a comprehensive typology of signs. He identified sixty-six types in total. Newcomers to semiotics often react with perplexity to his typology, which consists of seemingly obscure and unfathomable notions such as *qualisigns*, *sinsigns*, and *legisigns*. But it is quite straightforward. As its name implies, a *qualisign* is a representamen that draws attention to some *quality* of its referent (the object it represents). In language, an adjective is a qualisign since it draws attention to the qualities (colour, shape, size) of things – *a blue sweater*. In other sign systems, qualisigns include colours (painting), harmonies, and tones (music). A *sinsign* is a representamen that *singles* out a particular object – a pointing finger and the words *here* and *there* are examples of sinsigns. A *legisign* is a representamen that designates something by convention (literally 'by law'). Legisigns include various kinds of symbols and emblems such as those used on flags and logos.

Unlike Saussure, Peirce viewed sign creation as originating in the perception of some property in an object. For this reason, he called the initial act of sign construction a 'firstness' event. Firstness is, more technically, a tendency to forge signs as simulations of objects. The outcome is a sign that resembles what it stands for in some way. Peirce called such a sign an *icon*. When the 'V' sign discussed above is made to stand for the letter V, it is defined as an icon. Since icons are fashioned in culture-specific contexts, their manifestations across cultures are not exactly alike, even though they spring from the same firstness tendency. Peirce used the term *hypoicon* to acknowledge this culture-constrained dimension of firstness. Nevertheless, because it is a firstness (sensory-based) sign, its referent can be figured out even by those who are not a part of the culture, if they are told how it simulates, resembles, or substitutes it. A 'secondness' tendency in sign-creation consists in relating objects in some way. He called signs that result from this tendency *indexes*. The pointing finger is a basic example of an index. When we point to something, we are in fact relating it to our location as pointers. If it is close by we refer to it as *near* or *here*. If not, we refer to it as *far* or *there*. Finally, Pierce claimed that a 'thirdness' tendency consists in creating signs in historically based or conventional ways. He called signs that result from this tendency *symbols*. The cross figure used to stand for Christianity is a perfect example of a symbol. Although it represents the figure of a cross on which Christ was crucified, it is interpreted historically and conventionally as a sign standing for the religion that was founded after Christ's death.

Despite the obvious richness and breadth of Peircean sign theory, the Saussurean model continues to have a wide use among semioticians because it is a much more expedient one to apply, especially in the initial phases of analysis. Signifiers can easily be separated from contexts of occurrence and studied abstractly in relation to signifieds, albeit somewhat artificially. Peirce's model, however, has proven to be a more insightful and all-encompassing one in the development of a comprehensive theory of meaning.

The Semiotic Study of Media and Communications

It is accurate to say that semioticians today use a blend of Saussurean and Peircean concepts and techniques at various stages of analysis and for diverse purposes. They also frequently use ideas and findings from related or cognate disciplines, especially linguistics, philosophy, psychology, and anthropology. It should be noted, however, that this 'interdisciplinary' mode of inquiry is a two-way street, since many ideas developed within semiotics proper are now found scattered in cognate fields. Today semiotics is playing a prominent role in the study of media and mass communications. It was the French semiotician Roland Barthes who drew attention in the 1950s to the value of doing so with the theoretical tools of semiotics. After the publication of his pivotal book *Mythologies* in 1957, semiotic theory became widely used within the fields of *critical analysis*, a branch of cultural studies that examines the relationship between audiences and media genres, and *functional analysis*, a branch of sociology that studies media institutions and their effects on group behaviour. Scholars from both these fields were attracted particularly by Barthes's thesis that the meaning structures built into media products and genres are derived from the ancient myths, bestowing upon them the same kind of significance that is traditionally reserved for religious rituals. They also tended to side with Barthes's trenchant critique of this ploy as a duplicitous and morally vacuous one that was ultimately subversive of true cultural evolution.

As early as the 1960s, another well-known French semiotician, Jean Baudrillard, continued from where Barthes left off. Baudrillard scathingly attacked the entire media-based consumerist pop culture industry as one large distraction-producing factory intent on blurring the lines between media and reality. That industry has produced a 'simulacrum' – the effect that leads contemporary people to the inability to no longer distinguish, nor want to distinguish, between reality and fantasy. Baudrillard claimed that the borderline between representation and reality has utterly vanished in today's media-based world, collapsing into a mindset where the distinction between media texts and reality has broken down completely.

As a simple example of how semiosis works in pop culture, consider the comic book figure of Superman, who was introduced in 1938 by *Action Comics* and published separately in *Superman Comic Books*. What or who does Superman represent? The answer is, of course, that he stands for 'a hero' in the tradition of mythic superhuman heroes, such as Prometheus and Hercules. As a heroic figure Superman has, of course, been updated and adapted culturally – he is an 'American' hero who stands for 'truth,' 'justice,' and 'the American way.' Like the ancient heroes, Superman is indestructible, morally upright, and devoted to saving humanity from itself. Moreover, like all mythic heroes, he has a 'tragic flaw' – exposure to 'kryptonite,' a substance that is found on the planet where he was born, renders him devoid of his awesome powers.

Answering the question of why Superman (or any comic book action hero for that matter) appeals to modern-day audiences requires us to delve into the origin and history of the hero sign. In mythology and legend, a hero is an individual, often of divine ancestry, who is endowed with great courage and strength, celebrated for his bold exploits, and sent by the gods to Earth to play a crucial role in human affairs. Heroes are signs, character abstractions who embody lofty human ideals for all to admire – truth, honesty, justice, fairness, moral strength, and so on. Modern-day audiences feel this as intuitively as did the ancient ones who watched stage performances of Aeschylus's (ca 525–456 BCE) *Prometheus Bound, Prometheus Unbound,* and *Prometheus the Fire-Bringer* in Greece. Rather than being sent by the gods to help humanity (something that would hardly be appropriate in a secular society), Superman came to Earth from a planet in another galaxy; he leads a 'double life,' as hero and as Clarke Kent, a 'mild-mannered' reporter for a daily newspaper; he is adored by Lois Lane, a reporter for the same newspaper who suspects (from time to time) that Clark Kent may be Superman; and he wears a distinctive costume. This 'Superman code' was used from one issue to the next by the creators, making Superman extremely popular. The character continues, in fact, to be a favourite one in contemporary pop culture, having appeared on radio and television, as well as in motion pictures.

The colours of the costume Superman wears are signs in the code. His red cape suggests 'noble blood' and his blue tights the 'hope' he brings to humanity. Of course, the red and blue combination is also indicative of 'American patriotism' – these are, after all, colours of the American flag. How Superman acts, how he behaves, how he looks, and what he does are, in effect, all predictable aspects of the 'Superman code,' no matter who tells it or in what medium it is told. Codes are 'organizational systems or grids' of structures (signs) that are used to generate stories or to make representations of something. They can be highly formal as, for example, the code of arithmetic in which all the structures (numerals) and rules (addition, subtraction) are firmly established. Or they can be highly flexible as, for example, the code for greeting people, which varies according to who the participants in the greeting ritual are.

The 'Superman code' can be used in various ways to generate a 'Superman story.' The actual story is called a *text*. Conversations, letters, speeches, poems, television programs, paintings, scientific theories, and musical compositions are other examples of texts. A text constitutes a specific 'weaving together' of elements from a code (or codes) in order to represent something. A novel, for instance, is a verbal text constructed with a set of codes, including the language code, the narrative code, and many other codes and subcodes. Note, however, that the novel is interpreted not in terms of its constituent parts, but rather holistically as a single form. This is why when we ask someone what a novel means, he or she does not refer to the novel's actual words used in the sequence in which they occur, but rather to the overall meaning that he or she has extracted from it: for example, 'The novel *Crime and Pun-*

ishment paints a grim portrait of the human condition.'

The different stories that are written about Superman's adventures are texts based on the same 'Superman code.' So, in any specific Superman story we can expect to find that our hero will be fighting some villain; that he may flirt at some point with Lois Lane as Clark Kent; that he will come across a crisis that he must resolve with his extraordinary powers; and so on. The meaning of the text is conditioned by *context*. The context is the situation – physical, psychological, and social – in which the text is constructed or to which it refers. If read in its comic book format, a Superman text will be interpreted as an adventure story. However, if a satirist such as the American filmmaker Woody Allen were to portray Superman in a movie, then the movie text would hardly be construed as an adventure, but rather as a satire or parody of the Superman figure, of its media representations, or of some other aspect related to the 'Superman code.'

A technique also used in media semiotics to flesh out the meanings built into characters such as Superman is that of *opposition*. Take, as a simple example, the differences that are associated with the *white-dark* dichotomy in Western culture. The colour *white* connotes 'cleanliness,' 'purity,' and 'innocence,' while its antonymic counterpart *dark* connotes 'uncleanness,' 'impurity,' and 'corruption.' This dichotomy is used with such regularity by the mass media that it generally goes unnoticed. From early cowboy movies, in which the heroes wore white hats and the villains black ones, to contemporary advertisements, in which such items as 'dark leather gloves' evoke impressions of sadomasochism, the set of oppositions associated with the *white-dark* dichotomy are being constantly recycled in various media representations.

On the other hand, this same dichotomy could be utilized for the reverse purpose: that is, to link the connotations associated with darkness to heroes so that they can be perceived as mysterious and dauntless, fighting evil on its own symbolic terms. This is why the Zorro character of cinema fame wears black, as did several Hollywood western characters of the past (such as Lash Larue).

The use of semiotics in the study of media allows us to show how meaning is built into media texts of all kinds. Since these lie generally just below the threshold of awareness, the process of interpreting media texts is called, logically enough, 'decoding.'

Marcel Danesi

Bibliography

Barthes, Roland. *Elements of Semiology*. London: Cape, 1968.

Bloomfield, Leonard. *Language*. New York: Holt, Rinehart, and Winston, 1933.

Danesi, Marcel. *The Quest for Meaning: A Guide to Semiotic Theory and Practice*. Toronto: University of Toronto Press, 2007.

Deely, John. *Four Ages of Understanding: The First Postmodern Survey of Philosophy from Ancient Times to the Turn of the Twentieth Century*. Toronto: University of Toronto Press, 2001.

Eco, Umberto. *A Theory of Semiotics*. Bloomington: Indiana University Press, 1976.

– *Semiotics and the Philosophy of Language*. Bloomington: Indiana University Press, 1984.

Nöth, Winfried. *Handbook of Semiotics*. Bloomington: Indiana University Press, 1990.

Ogden, Charles K., and Ivor A. Richards. *The Meaning of Meaning*. London: Routledge and Kegan Paul, 1923.

Osgood, Charles E., George J. Suci, and Percy H. Tannenbaum. *The Measurement of Meaning*. Urbana: University of Illinois Press, 1957.

Posner, Roland, Klaus Robering, and Thomas A. Sebeok, eds. *Semiotik/Semiotics. Ein Handbuch zu den zeichentheoretischen Grundlagen von Natur und Kultur / A Handbook on the Sign – Theoretic Foundations of Nature and Culture*. 4 vols. Berlin: Mouton de Gruyter, 1997–2004.

Saussure, Ferdinand de. *Cours de linguistique générale*. Ed. Charles Bally and Albert Sechehaye. Paris: Payot, 1916. Trans. Wade Baskin, *Course in General Linguistics*. New York: McGraw-Hill, 1958.

Sebeok, Thomas A. *Global Semiotics*. Bloomington: Indiana University Press, 2002.

SENSATIONALISM IN THE MEDIA

[See also: *Journalism; Newspapers*]

Never in the history of humankind has it been easier to have instant access to news, sports, entertainment, and information than it is today. We do not wait for the morning paper or the nightly news on television any more than we flip the dial on our radios waiting for the music to be interrupted by a bulletin. With the advent of RSS (Really Simple Syndication) readers – offering a constant flow of news, sports, or any other user-defined alerts – which are available for almost all internet Web browsers and portable electronics, including cellular telephones that can alert us the moment a breaking news happens, we can literally get our news within seconds. This access has not only changed the way we get our news, but how fast we get it, and from whom. A myriad of choices has contributed to our ever-growing sense of awareness of the world around us. In some way, in some form, access to mass media has impacted our lives. And it has also shaped the way we think because some of the sources of the information that are most important to us may not be entirely objective or without bias. It can be objective, presenting all the facts, and it can be sensationalized, which results in constant exposure and aggressive reporting efforts that can sometimes be used by the broadcast source as a tool for achieving success or recognition in their respective media discipline.

The number of news, sports, and entertainment stories that continuously bombard us is staggering. It seems a week does not pass without something being sensationalized by the media, which includes print, radio, television, and other electronic sources. But when does a 'story' make the transition from an objective presentation of the facts, without distortion, embellishment, or concealment, and become sensationalized? When does a story or an event dominate the headlines for so long that one can be easily motivated to change the channel, tune to another station, surf to another website, choose another topic of interest on their electronic alerts or RSS readers, avoid reading the morning paper, or looking at the gossip publications that greet you when you check out at your favourite grocer?

The answer lies within all of us. All of us have reached that point at one time or another. We see news and events become so sensationalized – so blown out of proportion – that our collective, inner emotions will have had enough, and we will move on to another channel, another station, or another page. It is then that you can be fairly certain that the transition from objective and relevant reporting to sensationalism has been completed and that it will continue as long as there are people who yearn for it and strive to make it an integral part of their news reporting. It should be noted that there are legitimate news stories that continually develop, and are worthy of being separated from the word 'sensationalism' by facts that surface as it unfolds – revelations that add relevance and importance to the subject matter. In these cases, we must be the ones who decide what is most important to us in terms of quality and quantity.

Therefore, to discuss sensationalism in the media, we must focus at the *news* media. For it is most often a legitimate news operation that propagates and disseminates these stories. The format, or the way it is delivered, is irrelevant. It can quickly flow from video, to print, to audio, to text message alerts on an iPod. Sometimes within seconds. We must also be careful not to label a major news event or disaster as being sensationalized, such as the terrorist attacks against the United States in 2001. The attacks at the World Trade Center and the Pentagon were obvious, legitimate news stories with new details that emerged

by the hour. Given the enormous gravity of the importance and historical significance of that tragic day, 11 September 2001, nothing needed to be sensationalized. The United States was attacked by a terrorist group. Innocent people were killed. It was the first attack on American soil since Pearl Harbor. And it was a bona fide, albeit horrid, news story that kept billions of people around the world glued to their televisions and radios, staring at magazines and newspapers with disbelief and anger, or clicking their mouse as they scanned for the latest news, streaming video, or grisly photo on the internet.

The terrorist attacks of that day eventually did become sensationalized when it came time to point fingers at those who were to blame for such a tragedy. A commission was created. Hearings were held on Capitol Hill, and a parade of people from all branches of government were brought before the microphones and cameras. The inquisition became front-page news even as rubble and human remains were still being excavated and removed from ground zero.

But, however careful we must be to separate true, authentic journalism from reporting that is blown out of proportion, we must also be able to distinguish what really qualifies as sensationalism in the media. A good example are the tabloids that dominate the racks at newsstands and retail stores with headlines (and photos) that announce the discovery of three-legged tigers with a human head, or pictures of an alien autopsy, or the latest gossip about a high-profile Hollywood couple who file for divorce. These tabloids take 'sensationalism' and turn it into an art form of sorts. A very profitable art form.

Why? Because those tabloids, for the most part, are *in the business* of sensationalism. And because there are millions of people around the world who purchase those tabloids, there is a willing audience – a dedicated *market* for those publications that either sensationalize factual news or offer subject matter that is so profoundly ridiculous that our own natural curiosity forces us to just take a peek inside the cover while we wait for the grocery line to finally reach the cashier station. We could actually be the ones who help promulgate the spread of rumours, gossip, and sensationalized news simply by being active (and paying) participants, even if we look at it with a grain of salt or with the clear intent of being amused by the outright absurdity of the subject matter being headlined.

And while some of these tabloids publicly insist that they do practise 'real' journalism, the 'real' evaluation must be left to those who read them. In this case, one must be alert to the presentation, and whether or not *all* the facts or all sides of the story are reported and, more importantly, verified.

From the first symbols etched into clay tablets by ancient Sumerians to today's massive global media machine, sensationalism has been a part of mass communication. In ancient Rome, Caesar and Nero (and others) used military force to gain compliance and command worship. But they also made use of the media of the day. In ancient Rome, they used the printed word – handbills, symbols, and graffiti displayed in public areas – to serve as their personal messenger of edicts and threats as long as they reigned. It was not news. It was propaganda. Napoleon, Lenin, and Hitler also controlled the media and access to the media in their respective lands. In this context, we cannot make the connection between sensationalism and journalism because you cannot have both unless the media is totally unrestrained by governmental control, such control as found today in Iran, North Korea, Cuba, and China, to name a few. Sensationalism and true journalism require that you *must* have a free press. Anything else is propaganda.

In colonial times, the free press in the United States was under control of private individuals or small partnerships. Spared from government censorship, sensationalism took on a new role. Long prevented by the prospect of imprisonment or even death for expressing dissenting views

against the government of their former country, or even their new country, colonists were exposed to everything from daily, scathing rebukes of British leaders to the embellishment of the trials following the Boston Massacre that killed five Boston citizens.

As politics became an integral part of the fabric of the new country, newspapers were the only source of information about government, its representatives, and those who campaigned to represent their constituents. Political advertising could be very influential. Eventually, as even private standards relaxed, politicians and untested challengers alike engaged in smear campaigns not unlike some of the rhetoric we see today before election time.

As journalists and their outlets became more courageous, the term 'investigative journalism' came forth, and sensationalism took on a new meaning. And since newspapers and a few periodicals (up until the time that radio became the primary source for news and entertainment in the late 1920s) were the only source of information available in those days, people had to formulate their opinions based solely on what they read or heard from barkers in the town square or by word of mouth from visitors. In time, it became very easy for unscrupulous editors to lace a legitimate news story with their own personal opinion without identifying it as such. Bias soon became a part of the media, especially editorial content.

In more modern times, as radio and television began to compete for the eyes and ears of willing recipients around the globe in the early to mid-twentieth century, gossip and sensationalism became almost intertwined. Even then, newspaper editors, television and radio programmers, and news directors knew that gossip and sensationalism translated into readers, listeners, and viewers, which, in turn, translated into advertising dollars.

Gossip columnists from newspapers and radio, and later, television, took sensationalism to great heights. In the early twentieth century, Louella Parsons gained fame and notoriety by exposing the excesses and tribulations of high-profile celebrities and prominent members of high society. Parsons paved the way for people like Hedda Hopper, Walter Winchell, and – in more recent times – Rona Barrett and Ana Marie Cox (aka 'Wonkette'), who became sure bets to catch the eyes and ears of those looking for a good scandal or the latest gossip about steamy relationships.

Gossip columnists were often the catalysts for news. Any discussion of the bridge between journalism and sensationalism in the media cannot be complete unless we acknowledge the influence of rumours and gossip on the news media. Knowing that the public craves any tidbit of dubious information that could become chatter at the dinner table or the corner lunch counter, news directors, editors, and journalists combined gossip and factual news in their offerings, sometimes leading to tragic results that tarnished the name of good journalism and even defamed those who were their targets.

In 1921, silent film star and comedian Roscoe 'Fatty' Arbuckle was accused of sexually assaulting and eventually murdering Virginia Rappe, a developing Hollywood star, who died from complications after Arbuckle allegedly smothered her with his massive body during the accused rape. The media, which at that time was dominated by newspapers and magazines, spared no expense at printing all of the gory details, describing the 'injury' and embellishing and exploiting aspects of the story that kept people paying to read the next day's headlines about this sensational story. Rarely were there any inclusions of evidence that may have exonerated Arbuckle until dispatches and transcripts of the trial that followed were published, giving the public its first look at the other side of the story. In the end, after three separate trials, Roscoe Arbuckle not only was found innocent, but the jury even sent him a letter of apology that was published around the world.

But the damage had been done. It was too late. Although Arbuckle did not murder or even contribute to the murder of Virginia Rappe, the negative press generated by the trial made studio executives wary about employing him. After the trial, Arbuckle was able to secure only sporadic work and died in his sleep at the age of 46.

Some historians agree that Arbuckle's trial was first conducted in the media, which heavily influenced public opinion at the time. Certainly, sensationalism in the media had became an ugly word, and an even uglier harbinger of things to come as the formats of mass media and the way they were used became more widespread. Arbuckle was just the first of many others to fall victim to sensationalism in the media.

Even consumers (and one angry automaker) can be unwitting victims of sensationalism. In 1992, *Dateline*, a weekly NBC news program, targeted a fatal truck crash when the fuel tank – called a 'sidesaddle' tank – exploded from a direct impact. Since there was no video of the actual event, *Dateline* decided to 'dramatize' the crash and how it might have happened. They rigged a 'sidesaddle' tank vehicle with pyrotechnics that would cause a fire if any gasoline from the ruptured fuel tank escaped, causing a spectacular fire. The problem was that *Dateline* did not tell viewers that the vehicle was rigged to ignite gasoline and explode on impact. Every owner of a vehicle with a 'sidesaddle' fuel tank became concerned. Dealerships were inundated with phone calls from frightened owners. And an innocent automaker was cast as an evil villain by 'allowing such vehicles to be built and sold.' The negative coverage had the effect of convincing people that they shouldn't buy any vehicle with 'sidesaddle' fuel tanks, which included many pickup trucks. The financial implications for the automaker could have been disastrous had nobody questioned the story. Fortunately, an investigation into that *Dateline* broadcast confirmed the deliberate use of pyrotechnics, and found that, despite those explosives detonating under the vehicle in the *Dateline* story, the actual gasoline tank from that vehicle didn't even rupture at all. As a result, an attempt to draw ratings (the program was heavily promoted immediately following the previous week's program) by NBC forever tarnished the reputation of *Dateline* and the entire NBC news operation, and resulted in scepticism about professional journalism as a whole by the general public. NBC executives and the program's hosts did publicly apologize, but only after irrefutable evidence of their 'staged' explosion was exposed. Several producers were also forced to resign.

A word even uglier than 'sensationalism' is 'bias' when discussing any current state of the media. In his book, *Bias*, veteran CBS news correspondent Bernard Goldberg exposed the political bias that permeates the media and results in any news story becoming sensationalized and one-sided. An example Goldberg cited was a report from the conservative Media Research Center that monitored the nightly television news during broadcasts on CNN, NBC, ABC, and CBS during the presidency of George H.W. Bush. During his four-year term in office, these networks aired seventy-one stories about the homeless across America. In 1995, almost three years into the Clinton administration, only nine stories about the plight of the homeless made the evening news on those networks. Did the homeless problem in America suddenly disappear while a Democrat was president?

Goldberg also cited another example of political bias in 2003, just weeks after President George W. Bush took the oath of office, when Bob Jamieson, reporting for the Sunday edition of *ABC World News Tonight*, told his viewers that 'in New York City the number of homeless in the shelter system has risen above twenty five thousand a night for the first time since the late 1980s' (cited in Goldberg 2001). The context of that statement immediately raised suspicions. Clearly, political bias and sensationalism in the media work in tandem. Bias is constantly being craftily and sometimes stealthily weaved into the context of news, sports, and entertainment programming. Any discussion of sensationalism in the media must include the influence of biased reporting.

Just about any major media source, be it a newspaper, magazine, daily newspaper, or regularly scheduled television or radio news program, can serve as the outlet for presentations that can be very one-sided and blatantly biased, to say nothing of being sensationalized. Today, news organizations such as the *New York Times, NBC, CBS, MSNBC,* and *CNN* have been accused of having a left-wing political bias that distorts or sensationalizes their content. Conversely, the Rupert Murdoch (who has contributed millions to republican political campaigns) –owned *Fox News Network* and the *New York Daily News*, and the corporate-controlled *Washington Times* and even the *Wall Street Journal* have been branded or accused by liberals as the mouthpieces of conservatives. Is it because they present both sides of a story, or subscribe to higher journalistic standards?

Sensationalism will always be a part of the media, regardless of the format. Every news, sports, and entertainment organization that is a part of or uses mass media as a delivery system for their programming stands ready to capitalize on any event that will bring more viewers, more readers, more subscribers, or more listeners in their direction. And with more and more formats of media available to us, sensationalism is bound to expand. But the new digital media have given access to many individual voices, preparing the ground for sensationalism to be grounded more and more in the public sphere and thus more open to being exposed for what it is.

Jeff Cutsail

Bibliography

Arbucklemania. http://www.silent-movies
.com/Arbucklemania.

Bird, S. Elizabeth. *For Enquiring Minds: A Cultural*

Study of Supermarket Tabloids. Knoxville: University of Tennessee Press, 1992.

Campbell, W. Joseph. *Yellow Journalism: Puncturing the Myths, Defining the Legacies*. Westport, CT: Praeger, 2003.

Cohen, Daniel. *Yellow Journalism; Scandal, Sensationalism and Gossip in the Media*. New York: Twenty-First Century Books, 2000.

Cushman, Thomas. *A Matter of Principle: Humanitarian Arguments for War in Iraq*. Berkeley: University of California Press, 2005.

Goldberg, Bernard. *Bias*. Washington, DC: Regnery Publishing, 2001.

Goodman, Amy, and Michael Goodman. *The Exceptions to the Rulers*. New York: Hyperion, 2005.

Jackson, Jessica E. Sensationalism in the Newsroom: Its Yellow Beginnings, the Nineteenth Century Legal Transformation, and the Current Seizure of the American Press. *Notre Dame Journal of Law, Ethics, & Public Policy* 789 (2005): 790–3.

Keller, Morton. *American Media and the Collapse of Standards*. http://www.hoover.org.

Parsons, Louella. *Tell It to Louella*. New York: Putnam's, 1961.

West, Darrell W. *The Rise and Fall of the Media Establishment*. Palgrave Macmillan, 2001.

SENSORY COMMUNICATION

[See also: *Communication; Non-Verbal Communication*]

Sensory communication is, as its name implies, communication through and by use of the senses. The use of the senses to communicate something is called a *mode*. The main modes are as follows:

Sensory Mode	Features
Auditory-vocal	This characterizes speech, physiological vocal signals and symptoms (for example, coughing and snoring), musical effects (for example, whistling), and voice modulation (the use of vocal tones to communicate identity and feeling-states).
Visual	This is the relevant mode in sign languages, writing, visual representation (drawing, sculpting, and so on).
Tactile	This is characteristic of communication unfolding by means of touch (handshaking, patting, hugging, slapping, and so on).
Olfactory	This involves communication through the channel of smell (using perfumes to communicate a sensuous feeling, using aromas for various effects).
Gustatory	This involves communication by means of taste (food spices, and so on).

Sensory communication between humans and other species will occur in some modes, but not in all. If the mode or modes of the species in question are vastly different, then virtually no message exchange is possible. It is unlikely that humans and ants will ever enter into a communicative exchange such as the one that has evolved over the years between humans and cats or dogs.

The imprinting of sensory modes into language (usually unconsciously) is called *iconicity*. Photographs, portraits, and Roman numerals such as I, II, and III are iconic forms designed to stand for their referents in a visual way. Onomatopoeic words (*drip, plop, bang, screech*) are words simulating the sounds that certain things, actions, or movements are perceived to make and thus stand for their referents in an auditory-oral way. A block with a letter of the alphabet carved into it is a tactile form that allows the user to figure out the letter's shape by touch. Iconicity is evidence that sensory communication is a more basic and ancient form of communication than is language. This is borne out by the first inscriptions, cave drawings, and pictographic signs of humanity, indicating the important role that visual communication has played in our species. Iconicity is also evident in childhood development. Children instinctively make scribbles and elemental drawings at about the same time that they utter their first words. If one gives a child some drawing utensil at around the age of two or three, he or she will instinctively start scribbling on a drawing surface. As time passes, the scribbles become more and more controlled, with recognizable forms emerging. Although children, with adult prompting, may learn to label their forms as 'suns' or 'faces,' they do not seem inclined at first to draw anything in particular, since the act of making shapes appears to be instinctive and pleasurable in itself. Of course, the visual forms eventually suggest 'things' to the child as his or her ability to use language for naming purposes develops; but initially, the child seems content to engage in drawing solely for the pleasure of it, without attaching explicit associations of meaning to it.

Marcel Danesi

Bibliography

Classen, Claire. *Worlds of Sense: Exploring the Senses in History and across Cultures.* London: Routledge, 1993.

Classen, Claire, David Howes, and Anthony Synnott. *Aroma: The Cultural History of Smell.* London: Routledge, 1994.

SERIALS

[See also: *Adventure Stories; Books, History of; Cinema Genres; Crime Genre; Horror Fiction; Narrative*]

The serial is a fictional narrative consisting of a set of episodes (also known as *chapters*). The episodes are designed to keep audiences waiting to see, hear, or read the next episode because of the ending of the previous episode, which is desgned typically to keep the audience in suspense in some way. Another use of this term is in reference to any set of episodes on radio or television that tell an entire story but are separated into episodes on account of time constraints. It is the former use of the term that is the focus of this entry.

The film serial genre traces its origins to the pulp fiction 'cliffhanger' magazine serials of the early part of the twentieth century which kept readers in suspense because an episode would typically end when the hero or heroine would get caught up in some dangerous situation – such as being trapped in a car that was about to fall over a hill into the abyss below – from which escape seemed unlikely. The serial crossed over to early silent cinema in the first decade of the twentieth century. The audience would come back enthusiastically to the movie theatre the week after to see how the cliffhanger situation would be resolved. The genre was an instant hit with early movie-goers. A typical serial had from twelve to fifteen chapters. In addition to the hero or heroine and villain there was the sidekick or partner of the hero or heroine, who typically provided comic relief, and the sidekick or partner of the villain who provided the brawns for the bad side. Romance always played a part in the script, as did the occasional betrayal subplot.

Movie historians identify the first movie serial as the 1910 production of *Arsene Lupin Contra Sherlock Holmes* (in five episodes). The same decade saw the rise of popularity of the genre with Edison's *What Happened to Mary?* (1912), *The Adventures of Kathlyn* (1913), the *Perils of Pauline* (1914), *The Ventures of Marguerite* (1915), and *The Hazards of Helen* (1917). Interestingly, the earliest heroes in the movies were primarily women. The studios that produced most of the serials were the Weiss Brothers, Mascot, Universal, Columbia, Victory, and Republic Pictures, the latter becoming the leader in serial production starting in 1937. Serials were especially popular with children and that is why most of them involved action-packed plots with adventure heroes or heroines battling villains who would be responsible for the cliffhanger endings of a chapter before finally being caught in the final episode. A typical Saturday afternoon at the movies from the 1920s to the 1950s included a chapter of a serial, along with two feature films and animated cartoons. Serials were also part of regular fare on radio in the 1920s, 1930s, and 1940s, and on early TV in the late 1940s and throughout the 1950s. Among the most popular are the following: *The Crimson Ghost*; *Zorro Rides Again*; *The Real Adventures of Wild Bill Hickok*; *The Lone Ranger*; *Flash Gordon*; *Buck Rogers*; *Dick Tracy*; *The Green Hornet*; *The New Adventures of Tarzan*; *The Lost City*; *The Phantom Rider*; *Jungle Jim*; *Undersea Kingdom*; *Radar Men from the Moon*.

The serial style was adopted by Walt Disney with his early TV series featuring heroes such as Davy Crockett and Zorro. And it was revived by contemporary movies such as the Indiana Jones set, the difference being that cliffhanger situations were distributed throughout a single movie text and not 'to be continued next week,' as the original serials. The original movie serials disappeared in the 1950s – the last one was the 1956 serial produced by Columbia called *Blazing the Overland Trail*. They were replaced by the concept of the sequel and by television series, both of which incorporated elements of the serial formula. There have also been many serial-style series that emerged on television, including *Doctor Who* and *Danger Island*. There were also attempts to revive the original movie serial. In the 2000s, Cliffhanger Productions produced several serial formats for the video market. These can now be seen on YouTube. Although the serial may have disappeared from the screen, its descendants are noticeable nonetheless, with movie series such as the Indiana Jones, Jason Bourne, and James Bond films in which there is considerable crossover material from movie to movie.

Marcel Danesi

Bibliography

Barbour, Alan G. *Days of Thrills and Adventure*. New York: Macmillan, 1970.

Lahue, Kalton C. *Continued Next Week: A History of the Moving Picture Serial*. Norman: University of Oklahoma Press, 1969.

SHANNON, CLAUDE E. (1916–2001)

[See also: *Bull's-Eye Model; Channel; Communication; Communication Theory; Cybernetics; Feedback; Information; Medium; Noise; Redundancy*]

Claude Elwood Shannon was an American mathematician and engineer whose ideas and research laid the groundwork for the study of all kinds of communications systems. Shannon was born in Petoskey, Michigan, growing up in nearby Gaylord. He received his BA in electrical engineering and mathematics from the University of Michigan in 1936 and his MA and PhD in mathematics from the Massachusetts Institute of Technology. His master's thesis showed how binary digits could be used in the design of computers. In 1941, Shannon was hired by Bell Laboratories in New Jersey to conduct research on the efficiency of telecommunications systems. His paper 'A Mathematical Theory of Communication' was published in Bell's technical journal in 1948, becoming the basis upon which modern information theory was founded. In 1956, he joined MIT, where he taught until his retirement in 1978.

Shannon's groundbreaking paper aimed to solve the problem of how best to encode information, using notions from probability theory. He developed in it the key concept of information *entropy* as a measure for the randomness or uncertainty in a signal or message. With Warren Weaver, he wrote *The Mathematical Theory of Communication* in 1949, which made his model of information accessible to non-specialists. It is that book that spread his model broadly, influencing various fields of inquiry. Shannon's model attempts to show how information is encoded and decoded by humans, animals, or machines. Information is considered to be something mathematically probabilistic. For example, a ringing alarm system carries more information when it is 'on' than when it is 'off' because the latter is the 'expected state' of the alarm system and the former its 'alerting state.' The information contained in a signal, thus, is inversely proportional to its probability. The more probable a signal, the less information load it carries; the less likely, the more. Shannon used this notion to improve the efficiency of telecommunication systems. But it quickly spread to other domains and is commonly called the *bull's-eye model* because it defines a communications system as one in which a sender aims a message at a receiver as if the latter were in a bull's-eye target range.

Shannon introduced several key notions to the general study of communication – concepts that continue to be used to this day:

- *Channel* is the physical system carrying any transmitted signal or message. In human speech vocally produced sound waves can be transmitted through the channel of air or through an electronic channel such as the radio.
- *Noise* is any interfering element (physical or psychological) in the channel that distorts or partially wipes out a signal or message. In radio transmissions, noise is called static; in TV transmission, visual interference is called 'snow'; in speech, it can be lapses of memory (psychological noise).
- To counteract noise, communication systems have *redundancy* features built into them which guarantee that a message is likely to be decoded even if noise is present. In speech the high predictability of certain sounds or words and the patterned repetition of elements are redundant elements. For example, English speakers will easily decode the following sentence even though it has no vowels in it: *Thy wll drp by tmrrw* (They will drop by tomorrow).
- *Feedback* refers to the fact that senders have the capacity to monitor signals or messages and alter them to enhance their reception on the basis of informa-

tion coming back from receivers. In verbal communication this includes, for instance, the reactions observable in receivers (facial expressions, for example), which indicate the effect that a message is having as it is being communicated.

Shannon's model has provided a rich vocabulary for describing communication systems, even though it might not tell us anything about how messages take on the meanings that they do in human interaction.

Marcel Danesi

Bibliography

Shannon, Claude E. A Mathematical Theory of Communication. *Bell Systems Technical Journal* 27 (1948): 379–423.

Shannon, Claude E., and Warren Weaver. *Mathematical Theory of Communication.* Chicago: University of Illinois Press, 1949.

Wiener, Norbert. *Cybernetics, or Control and Communication in the Animal and the Machine.* Cambridge, MA: MIT Press, 1949.

SIMULACRUM THEORY

[See also: *Baudrillard, Jean; Media Effects*]

In media studies the term *simulacrum* is associated with the late Jean Baudrillard, who used it to claim that contemporary people can no longer distinguish, or want to distinguish, between reality and fantasy, having become so accustomed to watching television and going to the movies. Baudrillard maintained that the borderline between representation and reality has utterly vanished in today's image-based world of media, collapsing into a mindset where the distinction between fiction and reality has broken down completely. The content produced by the media is perceived as *hyperreal*, that is, as more real than real.

The term *simulacrum* comes from Latin where it means 'likeness' or 'similarity,' and was used in the nineteenth century by painters to describe drawings that were seen merely to be copies of other paintings rather than emulations of them. Aware of this designation of the term, Baudrillard (1983, 1987) insisted that a simulacrum effect is not the result of a simple copying or imitation, but a form of consciousness, which he called *hyperreal*, that emerges on its own after long exposure to the media through four stages: (1) a basic reflection of reality (the normal state of consciousness); (2) a perversion of reality; (3) a pretence of reality; and (4) the simulacrum, which bears no relation whatsoever to reality. Gilles Deleuze (1968: 69), on the other hand, saw the emergence of simulacra effects as emerging on their own, without reference to the media. They are part of the human imagination and thus are inevitable.

Baudrillard extended the notion to include fictional or cultural ideas, events, and spectacles. An example he liked to use was that of Disney's Fantasyland and Magic Kingdom, which are copies of other fictional worlds. They are copies of copies and, yet, people appear to experience them as more real than real, indicating that simulated worlds are more desirable than real ones. They are 'simulation machines' which reproduce past images to create a new cognitive and social environment for them. One thus constructs his or her identity in this simulated world, perceiving himself or herself on its own terms and relating to others accordingly. Disneyworld, malls, sports events, and social media sites are more meaningful than real worlds, which are perceived as banal and boring. Eventually, as people engage constantly with the hyperreal, everything – from politics to art – becomes governed by simulation. Only in such a world is it possible for advertising – the maximum producer of simulation – to become so powerful. This is why, according to Baudrillard, people are easily duped by TV-religion charlatans and infomercial hucksters. Simply put, they make promises related to life in the hyperreal.

The simulacrum effect would explain the rise in popularity of so-called reality TV programs. Sometimes labelled 'popular factual television,' this genre produces the simulacrum effect because it blends information, entertainment, documentary, and drama into one form. Reality television dates back to 1948, when Allen Funt's *Candid Camera* first aired, a program that was itself based on a previous radio show. The program showed everyday people in contrived situations, tricking them into doing or saying things unknowingly. The idea was to show how funny people could be in the world of the simulacrum. A radio series called *Nightwatch* in the early 1950s, which followed California police officers in Culver City, was also very popular. In 1973, a twelve-part series called *An American Family* put the Loud family's private lives on display. The program drew more than 10 million viewers and became a pop culture landmark. In 1992, MTV's *The Real World* debuted. It took place in a house where seven strangers from different backgrounds were supposed to live together for several months. Their daily lives were captured on film. The program thus demonstrated what happened when the characters on screen were not acting, but being themselves. The term reality TV came into use in 2000, when CBS's *Survivor* first aired, becoming an instant hit. In that show contestants living in an isolated setting face challenges in order to win prizes. Since then, the number of reality TV shows and websites has proliferated, from real-life cop investigations (as in *The First 48*) to job interview sessions conducted by Donald Trump.

The popularity of the genre, which blurs the distinction between the real and the imaginary, seems to validate the notion of simulacrum theory. As people become accustomed to looking at all kinds of screens, from television to computer screens, it is really a small cognitive step into the world beyond the looking glass (to use a Lewis Carroll metaphor) to believe that it is as real as the world outside the screen. The 1999 movie *The Matrix* portrayed a world in which life is shaped by the screen. Like the main protagonist, Neo, we now experience reality 'on' and 'through' the computer screen, and our consciousness is largely shaped by that screen. It is instructive to note that the producers had approached Baudrillard to be a consultant for the movie. Apparently, he turned them down.

Marcel Danesi

Bibliography

Baudrillard, Jean. *The Mirror of Production*. St Louis: Telos, 1975.
– *For a Critique of the Political Economy of the Sign*. St Louis: Telos, 1981.
– *Simulations*. New York: Semiotexte, 1983.
– *The Ecstasy of Communication*. St Louis: Telos, 1987.
Bignell, Jonathan. *Big Brother: Reality TV in the Twenty-First Century*. New York: Palgrave Macmillan, 2005.
Deleuze, Gilles. *Difference and Repetition*. New York: Columbia University Press, 1968.
Essany, Michael. *Reality Check: The Business and Art of Producing Reality TV*. Oxford: Elsevier, 2008.
Genosko, Gary. *McLuhan and Baudrillard*. London: Routledge, 1999.
Hill, Annette. *Reality TV: Audiences and Popular Factual Television*. New York: Routledge, 2005.
Huff, Richard M. *Reality Television*. Westport, CT: Praeger, 2006.
Schlesinger, Phillip. *Putting 'Reality' Together*. London: Constable, 1993.

SITUATION COMEDY

[See also: *Comedy; Television Genres*]

A *situation comedy*, also referred to as a *sitcom*, is a popular type of humorous episodic program that is most commonly associated with television. Using established characters with predictable personalities, relationships, and problems, sitcoms generally provide unsophisticated entertainment intended to amuse its audiences without

challenging them too much. Historically originating as a genre on radio, many of the earliest television sitcoms were evolved from characters and programs that were first developed and broadcast on radio during the early part of the twentieth century and later adapted for television. Still earlier antecedents came from vaudeville and other live stage and musical variety shows that included sketch comedy and predictable character types.

As the name suggests, a situation comedy depends on a problematic state of affairs introduced early in the story as a premise for a humorous interactive play. Sitcoms generally depend on a consistent cast of characters in relationships that share situations like those that might occur in a family, neighbourhood, workplace, or other shared environment. Situation comedies are generally short formulaic programs presented as a series that repeatedly uses the same locations, established premises, and characters that are predictable as far as their relationships, settings, values, and behaviours are concerned, and the kinds of comic situations they will face and ultimately resolve.

With an expectation that resolution and closure will occur by the end of each episode, sitcoms are generally presented as a *series*. The notion of a series depends on the repeated use of an established premise, familiar characters, and a narrative closure at the end of each episode. This type of regular ending is in contrast to a *serial*, which continues the narrative from one episode to the next. More like a soap opera or a novel that follows developing characters and situations from chapter to chapter, a serial does not necessarily resolve situations in a single episode and tends to persist in introducing new problems and complications that carry over from episode to episode.

While there are always exceptions to the rules, variations to established themes, and new concepts always being developed, part of the appeal of sitcoms is familiarity and repetition. The use of the same familiar characters, settings, and relationships from episode to episode, the easy-to-watch half-hour format, and a simple yet humorous story that is set up by a problem that is resolved within the time constraints of the show are aspects of the typical sitcom.

Characters drive most of the plots with their strategies to solve problems and to deal with relationships. Occasionally a situation comedy might develop a plot over the course of several episodes, but more commonly the characters and subsequent episodes do not suggest any memory of past events from earlier stories. The regular players are forced to live within or to challenge the defining characteristics of their situations and status that correspond to their fictitious constructed narrative communities.

As with any particular media genre or other systems of representation, situation comedies should not be dismissed as mere entertainment. Media producers create programs with the intention of appealing to audiences and aim to fulfil emotional needs for pleasure through an ideology of mass culture. Part of the appeal of popular media is that people like to talk with others about their own reactions to a program, its characters, and situations, after experiencing it. Programs are generally produced as products and the audiences are considered recipients and consumers. A situation comedy will tell stories that normalize lifestyles and consumer choices while presenting problems and offering solutions that reflect existing values, beliefs, and strategies for dealing with everyday situations. Whether the stories rely on family members, a community or neighbourhood, a group of friends, an occupational workplace, or institutional setting, narrative structures necessarily integrate cultural assumptions and a range of ideological perspectives that reflect social values and power structures that are defined and restricted through the storytelling processes and by resolutions that satisfy the audiences' expectations for normal, acceptable life choices.

Situation comedies have successfully represented a variety of contexts for situational humour and social commentary depicting lifestyles from the homes of ordinary or exceptional families or individuals, schools, hospitals, police stations, offices, and businesses. They have represented various perspectives about age, race, class, political affiliation, and sexual orientation. Sitcoms have also been animated and extended to science fiction and other combinations of genres. While situation comedies rely on familiar situations and social conventions, they also provide an acceptable space to negotiate social values and norms. Exaggerated representations of stereotypes of age, race, class, and gender may be intended to be humorous and entertaining, but are perpetually negotiated, and the plot resolution to most sitcom problems generally reaffirms mainstream social group, family, and community values.

Elliot Gaines

Bibliography

Abercrombie, Nicholas. *Television and Society*. Cambridge: Polity, 1996.

Fiske, John. *Television Culture*. London: Methuen, 1997.

Levine, Elana. *Wallowing in Sex: The New Sexual Culture of 1970s American Television*. Durham, NC: Duke University Press, 2007.

Mills, Brett. *Television Sitcom*. London: British Film Institute, 2005.

SOCIAL NETWORKING

[See also: *Online Culture; YouTube Culture*]

Social networking refers to the process of interacting through online websites such as Twitter, LinkedIn, Facebook, Googlet, MySpace, FriendWise, FriendFinder, Orkut, Classmates, Webkinz, and Bebo. On these sites it is assumed that individuals share common interests and interact in a patterned way. Entry to a networking site involves constructing a 'public profile' (a selected synthesis of one's autobiography) and interacting with other individuals using the online site.

The first true social network site, Six-Degrees (sixdegrees.com), was launched in 1997. Users were able to create profiles, as well as to list and view 'Friend lists.' But SixDegrees closed down in 2000, for the reason that most users did not have an extensive list of friends online at that time. From 1997 to 2001, AsianAvenue, BlackPlanet, and MiGente emerged, allowing combinations of profiles and viewable materials, while LiveJournal allowed more control over viewable profiles. In 2000, LunarStorm, a Swedish networking site, added guestbooks and diary pages, which have become common features of today's social networking sites.

From 2001 to 2002, four social networking sites were launched: Ryze, Tribe.net, LinkedIn, and Friendster. While Ryze.com was popular in San Francisco, Ryze and Tribe.net did not really catch on. LinkedIn continues as a business service, and Friendster was transformed, initially, into a dating site, designed to help 'friends of friends' meet each other through viewable profiles. As a consequence, Friendster surged in growth. In fact, because Friendster's database and servers were unable to handle the exponential growth, the site would often crash. Combined with frequent 'Fakesters,' people who would include massive Friends texts in order to view more profile, and the company's response of deleting all users with fake photos, many users lost trust in the site and abandoned it en masse.

From 2003 onward, new sites were launched, including Visible Path and Xing. Niche-audience social networking sites were also created, including many with an ethic or cultural focus – for instance, Care2 for activists, MyChurch for Christian churches, Flickr for photo sharing, and YouTube for video sharing. While corporations reactivated social networking sites (even if they had previously failed),

Google's Orkut became a national social networking site in Brazil and Microsoft's Windows Live Spaces became extremely popular in Mexico, Italy, and Spain.

MySpace's launch in 2003 came at a propitious time, since Friendster was losing users. Indie rock bands were among the first to create MySpace profiles in order to advertise themselves and to connect with their fans. Many teenagers joined MySpace in 2004, forcing the site to change its policy to allow minors. With its ability to personalize profile pages and to use colour and music, MySpace succeeded, catering to three distinct populations of users: musicians, teenagers, and college students. In 2005, MySpace was purchased by News Corporation for $580 million (U.S.). Shortly afterward, a series of media-exposed sexual encounters between adult predators and minors who had met on MySpace caused legal action to be taken against the site, with general mistrust of it ensuing.

In 2004, Mark E. Zuckerberg started Facebook, which originally catered to a Harvard student niche community. It quickly began expanding, allowing at first only users with a university email address to join. By September 2005, Facebook began to allow high school students, corporate networks, and regional networks to sign up for a Facebook account. A distinct feature of Facebook was that users' profiles could not be made public to all users but only to the designated groups themselves. Applications were soon added, allowing users to personalize their profiles based on their application (that is, allowing users to post what they desired or to play games attached to their profile with appropriate applications). For all these reasons, Facebook soon attracted more users than MySpace and is now one of the most popular of all such sites, with Twitter and LinkedIn quickly gaining momentum. While social networking sites continue to grow, Ning has recently launched a new kind of hosting service that encourages users to create their own networking sites. This pattern of 'individualization,' which has seemingly been encouraged by the advent of the internet, is fast becoming a major feature of all Web-based communication.

The socio-philosophical implications of social networking are immense. Suffice it to say that at no other time in history has it been possible for individuals to enter into a public forum to be observed by anyone else and to interact with anyone one wishes. But the massive amount of personalized information that is now available and distributed is exceptional and may, in the end, be shifting the focus from using information for knowledge purposes to using it for its own sake.

Statistics bear out that a paradigm shift is imminent. Social networking sites have accumulated a massive global popularity, causing many corporations to invest in these sites, where a single company may easily reach a certain target audience of millions. While there are social advantages to being a part of social networking sites, such as keeping in touch with old friends and meeting new people, information from one social networking site user to the next in some cases can be considered classified to the public, which has prompted many companies to block their employees from accessing such sites.

While it is still too early to tell what the overall psychological and social impact of online networking will be, there is little doubt that networking sites will continue to expand for the simple reason that they make interpersonal communication rapid and efficient. They also provide virtual 'hang-out spaces' in which to indulge our ever-present urge for gregariousness.

Mariana Bockarova

Bibliography

Boyd, Danah M., and Nicole Ellison. Social Network Sites: Definition, History, and Scholarship. *Journal of Computer-Mediated Communication* 13 (2007). http://jcmc.indiana.edu/vol13/issue1/boyd.ellison.html.

Van Dijk, Jan. *The Network Society*. London: Sage, 1999.

SOCIOLOGY OF THE MEDIA

[See also: *Anthropology of the Media; Digital Divide; Propaganda Theory*]

Various contemporary studies and investigations of the relation between the mass media and people's attitudes and world views come under the general rubric of the *sociology of the media*. This term refers primarily to the main theories and methods used by sociologists rather than to the use of sociological theory, in itself, to analyse the mass media.

Sociology is the study of the people and institutions that make up human society and how they interrelate. One of the most commonly used tools of sociologists is *demographic analysis*, which is a systematic, statistically based study of the size, make-up, and distribution of human groups. The analysis is based on collecting information such as people's ages, birth and mortality rates, marriage rates, ethnic backgrounds, migration patterns, and the like. Demographics now also include data on roles and status of individuals. Two common techniques for gathering such information are the *survey* and the *interview*. These are intended to measure people's attitudes on various subjects. Most of these are conducted with the use of prepared questionnaires consisting of questions about the interviewee's background and his or her opinions on the subject under investigation.

A term coming out of sociological theory that often crops up in media study is *habitus* – a term coined by Marcel Mauss (1872–1950) and used later on by Pierre Bourdieu to refer to the ways in which society's dominant classes talk, act, and behave. Noting that social success depends largely on the individual's ability to absorb the habitus of the dominant class, Bourdieu suggested that it is similar to, but more fundamental than, knowing a language. But the study of internet language, text messaging, and the like, for example, shows that the spread of an evolving common code is emerging in offline communication as well, thus leading to a diminution of the role of habitus in society.

An important sociological concept that has commonly been adopted by media scholars is that of *alienation* – a term coined by Karl Marx to describe a sensed estrangement from other people, society, or work. Sociologists define alienation as a blocking or dissociation of a person's feelings. Some believe that alienation is produced by a shallow and depersonalized society. French social theorist Émile Durkheim (1858–1917) suggested that alienation stemmed from a loss of religious traditions. He used the term *anomie* to refer to the sense of alienation and purposelessness experienced by a person or a class as a result of a lack of moral standards and values (Durkheim 1912). The term is often used in the literature by those who believe that anomie makes some people more susceptible to the effects of mass media. Some media analysts also talk of 'alienation effects,' which are the effects produced by using alienating techniques such as unsettling lighting effects or bizarre soundtracks that force an audience to develop a critical attitude towards what they are exposed to.

Another sociologically oriented view to have arisen in the last few decades is that of *Americanization*, or the purported influence the United States has on the culture of other nations through the over-representation of its popular culture in the global mass media. The term has a negative connotation if the influence is imposed unwillingly; it has a positive connotation if the influence is sought voluntarily.

Other sociological concepts that have been enlisted in media studies include the following:

- From Marxist theory, the term *articulation* is used to refer to a purported linkage that is established between seemingly disparate forms of culture or media products (for example, rap music linking with previous rock and jazz styles). In sociological theory it means the joining together of social forces in a hierarchical way (with one being dominant over the other).

- Also from sociological theory is the so-called 'Bass double action model of internal news flow' (Bass 1969) model that describes news as being processed in two stages before release: first, by those who gathered the information (reporters, researchers, photographers), and second, by those who are concerned with making the information consistent with the values and norms of the news organization (writers, editors).

- British sociologist Basil Bernstein's (1924–2004) concept of social code as a means of understanding how people in a society are treated by others is also used often in the discussion of media products.

- Durkheim's notion of *collective representation* is often used to refer to the creation of media texts or products by a community that reveal something crucial about it (history, beliefs, values, shared experiences).

- The concept of *digital divide* also comes from the sociological domain. It is the view that digital technology and its attendant culture contribute to the exacerbation of social inequalities because not everyone has equal access to such technology, and even among those who do, not everyone is equally competent in using it.

- Herman and Chomsky's propaganda model of news reporting articulated in *Manufacturing Consent: The Political Economy of the Mass Media* (1988) is yet another sociologically based concept. The two scholars claim that the overriding consideration of news agencies is supporting the views of those in power and, thus, essentially producing a form of propaganda rather than impartial news commentary.

Marcel Danesi

Bibliography

Bass, A.Z. Redefining the Gatekeeper Concept: A U.N. Radio Case Study. *Journalism Quarterly* 46 (1969): 59–72.

Bernstein, Basil. *Class, Codes, and Control: Applied Studies Towards a Sociology of Language*. London: Routledge, 1973.

Durkheim, Émile. *The Elementary Forms of Religious Life*. New York: Collier, 1912.

Herman, Edward S., and Noam Chomsky. *Manufacturing Consent: The Political Economy of the Mass Media*. New York: Pantheon, 1988.

SPEECH

[See also: *Conversation Analysis; Linguistics and the Media; Speech Act Theory*]

In linguistics, a differentiation is made between *language* and *speech*. Language is a mental code, consisting of certain specific types of signs (words, grammatical forms, and so on) and of the structural principles or rules for creating, understanding, and using them to communicate something. Speech, on the other hand, is the use of language to form and transmit messages, that is, to communicate something. Speech can be vocal, involving the use of the vocal organs (tongue, teeth, lungs), also known as articulate or vocal speech, or non-vocal, as in writing or in gesturing. One can have language without speech; but one cannot have speech without language because speech is dependent on the language system. It is its expression. Children construct their language systems by simple exposure to speech samples of it, suggesting that they have the capacity to extract linguistic pattern from, and relate it to, the expressions they hear. They do this by listening

to older people, gradually acquiring the sounds and words used by them, by associating them with objects, ideas, and actions in their environment.

Vocal speech is made possible by the lowering of the larynx (the muscle and cartilage at the upper end of the throat containing the vocal cords). This phenomenon is unique to the human species. In the first months of life, infants breathe, swallow, and vocalize in ways that are similar to other primates (gorillas and chimpanzees) because, like the primates, they are born with the larynx high in the neck. Around the third month of life, however, the larynx starts to descend, gradually altering how the child will use the throat, the mouth, and the tongue from then on. The larynx's low position means that the respiratory and digestive tracts will cross above it, which entails a few risks – food can easily get lodged in the entrance of the larynx; drinking and breathing simultaneously can lead to choking. In compensation, however, the lowered larynx permits the articulation of speech sounds, since a chamber above the vocal folds that can modify sound is produced. In turn, this prepares the child for the acquisition of language as a vocal system of signs.

The distinction between language and speech has been given different names, even though they are associated with differential theoretical frameworks. The most famous ones are those used by the founder of modern-day linguistics, Ferdinand de Saussure (1916), who used the terms *langue* (language) and *parole* (speech), and Noam Chomsky (1957), who used the terms *linguistic competence* and *performance* respectively.

Marcel Danesi

Bibliography

Aitchison, Jean. *The Articulate Mammal: An Introduction to Psycholinguistics*. London: Hutchison, 1983.

Aitchison, Jean. *The Seeds of Speech: Language*

Origin and Evolution. Cambridge: Cambridge University Press, 1996.

Chomsky, Noam. *Syntactic Structures*. The Hague: Mouton, 1957.

Saussure, Ferdinand de. *Cours de linguistique générale*. Ed. Charles Bally and Albert Seche-haye. Paris: Payot, 1916.

SPEECH ACT THEORY

[See also: *Discourse; Discourse Theory*]

Speech act theory proposes a philosophical inquiry into the ways in which speaking effects action in the world. This predominantly anglophone current in the philosophy of language illustrates the 'linguistic turn' of the twentieth century and carries forward more particularly the later Wittgenstein's and ordinary language philosophers' pragmatic alternative (Wittgenstein 1953; Ryle 1949) to the earlier formal analytic method (e.g., Carnap 1937; Frege 1879, 1892; Russell 1931, 1956). While continuing the latter's close scrutiny of linguistic expressions, speech act theorists investigate the practical functions of everyday language rather than the truth-conditional properties of logical propositions and their relation to the kind of statements formulated by the natural sciences. Lectures at Harvard and Oxford by John Austin published in 1962 as *How to Do Things with Words* launched the main avenues of inquiry, which John Searle developed in systematic fashion and integrated more fully into the analytic tradition.

Noting that analytic philosophers were treating all linguistic utterances as statements, in the process neglecting questions and exclamations, commands, wishes, and concessions, Austin (1962) starts out by distinguishing between two types of sentences: *constatives*, which describe a state of affairs in the world and may be true or false, and *performatives*, which when uttered can perform the action they evoke provided certain conditions are met (1962: 1–11). Examples of performatives include the 'I do' stated in a marriage ceremony, 'I leave my watch to my brother' written in a will, and 'I bet you a dollar it will rain tomorrow.' Describing a performative entails foregrounding the utterance itself as an act while showing how it is related to the verbal and non-verbal context in which it is spoken. Austin studies a host of *felicities* and *infelicities*, which determine whether saying something effects the action evoked or not: whether or not a convention exists for saying *x*; whether or not the persons, place, and time are appropriate for the utterance within the convention; whether there are flaws or hitches in performing the act; whether the speaker is serious and sincere; and whether subsequent acts jibe with the act considered (1962: 12–45). In Austin's essay, lawyerly terms and thinking enjoy a place of prominence, whereas jokes and theatre, fiction and poetry represent chaff that needs to be winnowed from the inquiry in order to leave discourse in which a man's word is his bond.

When closer investigation fails to yield either a finite list of performatives or satisfactory criteria by which to differentiate them from constatives, Austin strikes out in a new direction, identifying three senses in which proffering an utterance effects an act (1962: 91–132). First, with respect to the linguistic code or structure, and without regard for any particular context or speech situation, uttering a sentence with a certain meaning constitutes a *locutionary* act, comprising phonetic, phatic (grammatical), and rhetic (semantic; sense and reference) acts. Second, within a given communicative situation, in saying something we can perform an *illocutionary* act: by virtue of its conventional force, and provided the proper felicity conditions are met, the utterance itself undertakes an action, asks or answers a question, or informs, orders, or warns someone of something. Third and more generally, by saying something we accomplish a *perlocutionary* act any time our words result in a change of behaviour, attitude, or belief. The essay focuses on defining illocution with precision and on distinguishing it from locution and especially perlocution.

In the case of an illocutionary act, to *say* something is to *do* that which one says, such that act and utterance are simultaneous and 'identical' by virtue of a specific convention. On the other hand, the perlocutionary force of an utterance designates all that the addresser actually brings about by uttering the sentence, such as persuading, convincing, deterring, but also surprising, deceiving, or leading into error. For Austin, illocutionary acts engage the addresser's intentionality, while perlocutionary consequences embrace both intended and unintended effects. In a perlocutionary act the consequence is posterior and remains an effect: such results can be unpredictable, indefinite, and infinite in scope. Illocutionary acts take such forms as 'I order you to' and 'I warn you that,' whereas 'I convince you that' or 'I dissuade you from' designate perlocutionary acts; similarly, 'I threaten you with' is illocutionary while 'I intimidate you by' is perlocutionary (1962: 131). Austin concludes that this distinction between three aspects of an utterance or between three types of utterances effectively replaces the initially proposed contrast between constatives and performatives.

Developing Austin's ideas, John Searle's 1969 *Speech Acts: An Essay in the Philosophy of Language* formulates an explicit philosophical analysis of the illocutionary act, fleshes out its relation to central concepts of the analytic tradition, including reference and predication, and outlines a contemporary philosophy of language in which 'speech act theory' plays a leading role. Searle defines any illocutionary act as the set of semantic rules that account for its use in speech, extracting the rules from the conditions that are necessary and sufficient for the act to be successfully performed (1969: 54–5). He thus identifies nine such conditions for 'promising,' then formulates the use of promise illocutions as governed by five rules, which require for example that the utterance predicate a future act of the speaker and that the speaker undertake

the obligation to effect the act (1969: 57–64). Extending the example, Searle studies eight other types of illocutionary acts ranging from 'request' and 'question' to 'thank' and 'congratulate,' defining each act as a set of four types of rules bearing on the propositional content, the preparation, the sincerity, and the function of the act, respectively (1969: 64–7). The analyses specify speaker and hearer psychological states, beliefs, and intentions (cf. Grice 1989).

Searle (1969) outlines how the sample studies can point to a general and systematic theory of illocutionary acts. A number of rules are interrelated: certain kinds of illocutionary acts represent subsets of other illocutions for example, as posing questions figures as a form of request (1969: 69). Illocutionary force ultimately rests on a core set of seven principles, including the point or purpose of the act, the propositional content of the utterance, the degree of strength of the illocutionary point, and the degree of strength of the sincerity conditions (Searle 1969: 70; cf. Searle and Vanderveken 1985). The essay emphasizes that no simple one-to-one correspondence between an utterance and an act obtains: on the one hand, polite formulations containing no literal performative can in context carry illocutionary force and thus serve as indirect or implicit illocutions. A guest's remark 'It's getting a bit late' at a party can thus function as a suggestion to revellers that they should go home. Inversely, a single utterance can simultaneously perform multiple illocutionary acts: the guest's remark can also represent an order to a partner to go get the coats, and an amiable objection to the host's preceding claim that 'The night is still young' (Searle 1969: 70–1).

Searle's wide-ranging 1969 essay further integrates speech acts into a philosophy of language that includes carefully argued views on predication, sense and reference, use and mention, and meaning and intention. The book continues Wittgenstein's and Austin's work of drawing philosophy closer to language as used by speakers in the everyday social arena and away from statements formulated by the natural sciences. Searle thus distinguishes between 'brute' and 'institutional' facts: the former concern such physical (or mental) data as sense experience and the findings of natural science, while the latter depend on social institutions such as government, law, and marriage (1969: 50–3). Whereas logical positivism construed language as if it concerned knowledge about brute facts, language including illocutionary acts produces institutional facts and must be studied in that perspective. Similarly, arguing that 'speaking a language is engaging in a rule-governed form of behavior,' Searle distinguishes between *regulative* and *constitutive* rules: whereas the former constrain, organize, or normalize activities that exist independently of the rules, such as eating, socializing, or wearing clothes, the latter institute activities, including games like chess, tennis, or volleyball (1969: 22, 33–42). *Speech Acts* describes the semantic structure of a language and speakers' illocutions as conventional realizations of underlying constitutive rules (1969: 37).

Speech act theory's significant accomplishment was not to reveal that speaking can effect action – two and a half millennia of rhetorical studies, Sigmund Freud's theory and methodology of the 'talking cure,' and Jean-Paul Sartre's 'existential psychoanalysis' got there first – but rather to do so persuasively within the tradition of analytic philosophy. While maintaining the latter's emphasis on rigour, lucidity, and argument, and while continuing to address issues brought into prominence by earlier formal analytic philosophers, Austin and Searle broadened the perspective beyond language as truth-conditional statements about the natural world. Studies such as Searle and Vanderveken (1985), Recanati (1990), and Vanderveken (1990–1) develop Austin's and Searle's early pioneering essays. Berlin et al. (1973), Lepore and Gulick (1991), and Grewendorf and Meggle (2002) provide appraisals and responses to the project. Smith (2003) brings

together essays at once introducing and critiquing Searle's work.

Speech act theory focuses on isolated utterances made by a single speaker rather than on longer texts or sustained verbal interaction among several speakers as do linguists working on the pragmatics of conversational analysis or text grammars (Levinson 1983: 284–370). For the latter, and for most studies in communication and literature, few utterances meet speech act theory's felicity conditions: Austin's and Searle's extensive discussions of infelicities represent a treasure trove of real communicative dynamics to be analysed. Unlike a field such as modal logic (Wright 1951), speech act theorists have not developed a calculus that would define the logical relations among illocutionary acts (implication, contradiction, tautology, absurdity). Jerrold Katz (1977) argues that speech act theory does not merit the term theory at all, that Austin and Searle (and Ludwig Wittgenstein, Gilbert Ryle, and P.F. Strawson) wrongly equate (linguistic) meaning with (language) use, whereas sentences comprise both inherent and contextual meanings. According to Jerrold Katz, Austin and Searle confusedly amalgamate phenomena pertaining to at least two distinct theories: one that would study how grammatical structures inherently determine sentence types, including constatives and performatives (cf. I-language, competence), and another that would examine how subjects apply grammatical, contextual, and non-linguistic knowledge in producing and understanding illocutionary acts (cf. E-language, performance).

Both Austin and Searle have critiqued aspects of contemporary formal approaches to language and mind, including those found in artificial intelligence, cognitivism, and psychological functionalism (Putnam 1975; Pylyshyn 1984). Austin (1961) objects to the use of the digital computer and its symbol processing as a model for human cognition. Searle's celebrated 'Chinese Room' article argues against functionalism, the cognitivist notion that language use can be modelled as the manipulation of abstract symbols (1980, cf. 1990). While crediting Noam Chomsky with effecting a paradigm shift in linguistics, Searle argues that his syntax-oriented grammar does not justify suppositions about innate mental faculties, and that generative grammar has been superseded by subsequent theories that devote due attention to semantics and pragmatics.

While making reference to literary works, Austin and Searle systematically exclude literature from the contexts that meet the felicity conditions under which utterances can accomplish actions in the world. Literary theoreticians and critics have welcomed the exclusion as an invitation to pose fundamental questions about the status of literature, and have demonstrated the relevance of speech act concepts for fiction, theatre, and poetry. Richard Ohmann and Mary Louise Pratt investigate rhetorical strategies that writers employ and cultural conventions that readers mobilize when they engage literature as discourse which can accomplish goals and bring about cognitive and affective consequences (Ohmann 1971; Pratt 1977). Sandy Petrey picks up on Austin's characterization of context as collective in order to develop a socio-political theory of literary speech acts (1990). In a celebrated series of exchanges, Jacques Derrida challenged Austin's use of intentionality and debated Searle on sign theory, the nature of communication, and the relation of the subject to language and action (Derrida 1977; Searle 1977). J. Hillis Miller's analyses of novels by Marcel Proust and Henry James question the distinctions between constatives and performatives, between literary and non-literary language, and between poetry and essay (Miller 2001).

Thomas F. Broden

Bibliography

Anscombe, G.E.M. [Gertrude Elizabeth Margaret]. *Intention*. Ithaca, NY: Cornell University Press, 1957.

Austin, John L. The Meaning of a Word. In *Philosophical Papers*, ed. J.O. Urmson and G.J. Warnock, 23–43. Oxford: Oxford University Press, 1961.

– *How to Do Things with Words*. Cambridge, MA: Harvard University Press, 1962.

Barthes, Roland. L'ancienne rhétorique. Aide-mémoire. In *Communications* 16 (1970). Translated by Richard Howard, The Old Rhetoric: An Aide-mémoire. In *The Semiotic Challenge*, 11–94. New York: Hill and Wang, 1988.

Berlin, Isaiah, et al. *Essays on J.L. Austin*. Oxford: Clarendon Press, 1973.

Carnap, Rudolf. *The Logical Syntax of Language*. New York: Harcourt Brace, 1937.

– *Meaning and Necessity*. Chicago: University of Chicago Press, 1967.

Derrida, Jacques. *Limited Inc., a b c …* Baltimore: Johns Hopkins University Press, 1977.

Frege, Gottlob. *Begriffsschrift: eine der arithmetischen nachgebildete Formelsprache des reinen Denkens*. Halle-on-the-Saale: L. Nebert, 1879. Edited and translated by Terrell Ward Bynum, *Begriffsschrift: A Formula Language, Modeled Upon That of Arithmetic, for Pure Thought*. In *Conceptual Notation and Related Articles*. Oxford: Clarendon Press, 1972.

– Über Sinn und Bedeutung. In *Zeitschrift für Philosophie und philosophische Kritik* 100 (1892): 25–50. Translated as On Sense and Reference. In *Translations from the Philosophical Writings of Gottlob Frege*, ed. Peter Geach and Max Black, 56–78. New York: Philosophical Library, 1952.

Freud, Sigmund. *Vorlesungen zur Einführung in die Psychoanalyse*. Leipzig, 1916. Translated by Joan Riviere, *A General Introduction to Psychoanalysis*. Garden City, NY: Garden City, 1935.

Grewendorf, Günther, and Georg Meggle, eds. *Speech Acts, Mind, and Social Reality*. Dordrecht: Kluwer, 2002.

Grice, Paul. *Studies in the Way of Words*. Cambridge, MA: Harvard University Press, 1989.

Katz, Jerrold. *Propositional Structure and Illocutionary Force: A Study of the Contribution of Sentence Meaning to Speech Acts*. New York: Crowell, Language and Thought series, 1977.

Lepore, Ernest, and Robert van Gulick, eds. *John Searle and His Critics*. Oxford: Blackwell, 1991.

Levinson, Stephen C. *Pragmatics*. New York: Cambridge University Press, Cambridge Textbooks in Linguistics series, 1983.

Miller, Joseph Hillis. *Speech Acts in Literature.* Stanford, CA: Stanford University Press, 2001.

Ohmann, Richard. Speech Acts and the Definition of Literature. *Philosophy and Rhetoric* 4 (1971): 1–19.

Petrey, Sandy. *Speech Acts and Literary Theory.* New York: Routledge, 1990.

Pratt, Mary Louise. *Toward a Speech Act Theory of Literary Discourse.* Bloomington: Indiana University Press, 1977.

Putnam, Hilary. *Mind, Language, and Reality.* New York: Cambridge University Press, 1975.

Pylyshyn, Zenon W. *Computation and Cognition: Toward a Foundation for Cognitive Science.* Cambridge, MA: MIT Press, 1984.

Recanati, François. *Les énoncés performatifs: contribution à la pragmatique.* Paris: Minuit, 1981. Translated *Meaning and Force: The Pragmatics of Speech Acts.* New York: Cambridge University Press, 1987.

Russell, Bertrand. *The Scientific Outlook.* New York: W.W. Norton, 1931.

– *Logic and Knowledge: Essays, 1901–1950.* Ed. Robert Charles Marsh. New York: Capricorn, 1956.

Ryle, Gilbert. *The Concept of Mind.* Chicago: University of Chicago Press, 1949.

Sartre, Jean-Paul. *Saint Genet, comédien et martyr.* Paris: Gallimard, 1952. Translated by Bernard Frechtman, *Saint Genet, Actor and Martyr.* New York: New American Library, 1964.

Searle, John. *Speech Acts. An Essay in the Philosophy of Language.* New York: Cambridge University Press, 1969.

– Reiterating the Differences: A Reply to Derrida. *Glyph* I (1977): 198–208.

– Minds, Brains, and Programs. *The Behavioral and Brain Sciences* 3 (1980): 417–57.

– Is the Brain's Mind a Computer Program? *Scientific American* (January 1990). Rpt. in *Readings in Language and Mind,* ed. Heimir Geirsson and Michael Losonsky, 264–73. Cambridge, MA: Blackwell, 1996.

Searle, John, and Daniel Vanderveken. *Foundations of Illocutionary Logic.* New York: Cambridge University Press, 1985.

Smith, Barry, ed. *John Searle.* New York: Cambridge University Press, Contemporary Philosophy in Focus series, 2003.

Strawson, Peter F. *Individuals: An Essay in Descriptive Metaphysics.* London: Methuen, 1959.

Vanderveken, Daniel. *Meaning and Speech Acts.* 2 vols. New York: Cambridge University Press, 1990–1.

Wittgenstein, Ludwig. *Philosophische Untersuchungen / Philosophical Investigations.* Bilingual text edited and translated by G.E.M. Anscombe. New York: Macmillan, 1953.

Wright, Georg Heinrich von. *An Essay on Modal Logic.* Amsterdam: North Holland, 1951.

SPY FICTION

[See also: *Adventure Stories; Science Fiction; Thrillers*]

Spy fiction refers to narratives that involve action, adventure, and intrigue, revolving around the exploits and romantic interests of a government spy or secret agent who must fight against terrorists or assassins. The classic example of spy fiction is found in the novels and movies featuring James Bond, the fictional English secret agent created by British novelist Ian Fleming. Bond is a debonair, sophisticated agent who attracts beautiful women and is the nemesis of villains. His code name is 007 – the double-0 means that he is licensed to kill at his own discretion. Fleming introduced Bond in *Casino Royale* (1953). He appeared in eleven other novels and two collections of short stories. The first Bond motion picture produced was *Dr No* (1962). The subsequent (and still ongoing) film series has made stars out of actors Sean Connery, Roger Moore, Timothy Dalton, Pierce Brosnan, and most recently Daniel Craig.

The genre traces its origins to James Fenimore Cooper's *The Spy* (1821) and *The Bravo* (1831). Notable early novels in the genre include Rudyard Kipling's *Kim* (1901), Baroness Emmuska Orczy's *The Scarlet Pimpernel* (1905), Robert Erskine Childers's *The Riddle of the Sands* (1903), Joseph Conrad's *The Secret Agent* (1907), and the over 100 novels of William Le Queux and E. Phillips Oppenheim published between 1900 and 1914. Also prominent in the genre was John Buchan, whose novel *The Thirty-Nine Steps*

(1915) was adapted by Alfred Hitchcock into a popular movie.

The spy genre was a staple of pulp fiction magazines and movie serials. By the 1930s and 1940s it became one of the more popular genres in several media (print, radio, and cinema). In that decade Eric Ambler wrote *Epitaph for a Spy* (1938) and *Journey into Fear* (1940), which became best-sellers. Ambler used the genre to put forward liberal political views. Several of his villainous Soviet agents were portrayed as heroic characters, going against the grain of the times. Helen MacInnes's *Above Suspicion* (1939) also became a best-seller and was subsequently made into a movie. She also wrote several other spy novels, including *Assignment in Brittany* (1942), *Decision at Delphi* (1961), and *Ride a Pale Horse* (1984). Manning Coles's *Drink to Yesterday* (1940) introduced the spy hero Thomas Hambledon, a forerunner to James Bond.

Throughout the 1950s and 1960s the spy genre became popular in both print and movie form. Desmond Cory introduced the 'licensed to kill' agent concept; Graham Greene wrote popular anti-imperialist novels such as *Our Man in Havana* (1959); Ian Fleming introduced James Bond into pop culture with *Casino Royale* (1953); and authors John Le Carré and Frederick Forsyth used the genre to explore the constitution of politics in the modern world. Starting with *The Spy Who Came in from the Cold* (1963), Le Carré (the pen name of David John Moore Cornwell) introduced the anti-hero secret agent, an individual who was typically a low-level civil servant involved with the routine affairs in a government bureaucracy as well as with cloak-and-dagger espionage and intrigue. Le Carré's characters are manipulated by their superiors and thus are destined to partly fail in their espionage ventures.

The 1970s marked the entrance of Robert Ludlum into the spy genre field, starting with *The Scarlatti Inheritance* (1971). His trilogy of novels about a spy named Jason Bourne – *The Bourne Identity* (1980), *The Bourne Supremacy* (1986), and *The Bourne Ultimatum* (1990) – became major motion pictures. The spy novel has continued to enjoy broad success to the present day, with the publication of best-sellers such as *The Hunt for Red October* (1984) by Tom Clancy, *Harlot's Ghost* (1991) by Norman Mailer, *A Spy By Nature* (2001) by Charles Cumming, and *Dead Line* (2008) by Stella Rimington. The genre has also created several popular films, from the James Bond, Jason Bourne, and *Mission Impossible* movies, to blockbusters such as *Munich* (2005), *Syriana* (2005), and *The Constant Gardener* (2005); television series such as *La Femme Nikita* (1997–2001), *Alias* (2001–6), and *24* (2001–10); as well as many websites catering to the genre. The genre also crossed over successfully to the video game universe, of which the *Metal Gear* set of games is the most representative. Spy fiction has spawned several subgenres, including *spy-fi*, which combines elements of the traditional spy genre with those of science fiction, especially the use of sophisticated gadgets, fast vehicles, and high-tech weaponry, *spy comedy*, which spoofs the traditional spy stories, and *spy horror*, which combines elements of supernatural thrillers with those of spy fiction.

The critical response to the spy genre has been ambivalent. Some critics simply see it as a form of escapism from the real world of political intrigue. In spy novels, movies, and TV programs, the villain is vanquished and the dangers of the real world are vanquished (at least temporarily). The genre thus has a communal cathartic effect. Other critics see the genre as a vehicle for critiquing the world, especially such institutions as the CIA, in order to provide a better model of how human affairs should be run.

Marcel Danesi

Bibliography

Britton, Wesley. *Beyond Bond: Spies in Fiction and Film*. Westport, CT: Praeger, 2005.
– *Onscreen and Undercover: The Ultimate Book of Movie Espionage*. Westport, CT: Praeger, 2006.

STRUCTURALISM

[See also: *Semiotics; Post-Structuralism*]

Structuralism is the general term used in various disciplines, including media studies, to designate an approach to human artefacts that sees them as products of relations. In music, for example, the arrangement of tones into structures known as melodies is felt to be 'musically correct' only if this arrangement is consistent with harmonic structure, that is, with relations among the tones. In order to recognize something as a melody, one must: (1) be able to differentiate it from other melodies; and (2) know how its component parts fit together. More technically, the former is called *paradigmatic* (differential) and the latter *syntagmatic* (combinatory) structure.

The notion of structure is central to both linguistics and semiotics. The term *structuralism* is, in fact, sometimes used as a synonym for these disciplines. For the sake of historical accuracy, it should be mentioned that structuralism grew out of the work and ideas of the early founders of psychology, who attempted to give a scientific analysis of conscious experience by breaking it down into its specific structures.

One of the main tenets of structuralist analysis is that of *opposition*. What keeps two words such as *cat* and *rat* distinct? A structuralist would say that it is, in part, the fact that the phonic difference between initial *c* and *r* is perceived as distinctive. This constitutes a paradigmatic feature of the two words. Similarly, a major and minor chord in the same key will be perceived as significantly distinct on account of a half-tone difference in the middle note of the chords. These examples show that forms are recognized as meaning-bearing structures in part through a perceivable difference built into some aspect of their physical constitution – a minimal difference in sound or tone, for example. The psychological importance of this structural feature was noticed by the early psychologists, especially Wilhelm Wundt

(1832–1920) and Edward B. Titchener (1867–1927), who termed it *opposition*. In his *Cours de linguistique générale* (1916), the linguistic Ferdinand de Saussure saw opposition, which he called *différence*, as an intrinsic property of language. The linguist determines the meaning and grammatical function of a word such as *cat* by opposing it to another word such as *rat*. This will show not only that the initial consonants *c* and *r* are distinctive in English, but also what makes the word *cat* unique, pinpointing what *cat* means by virtue of how it is different from other words such as *rat*, *hat*, and so on.

Paradigmatic structure is one part of how we recognize meaning-bearing structures. The other part is syntagmatic structure. Consider the words *cat* and *rat* once again. These are perceived as being structurally appropriate English words, not only because they are recognizable as distinct through a simple binary opposition of initial sound cues, but also because the combination of sounds with which they are constructed is consistent with English word structure. On the other hand, *rtat* would not be recognizable as a legitimate word because it violates a specific aspect of such structure – namely, English words cannot start with the cluster *rt*. This is an example of syntagmatic structure. In music, a melody is recognizable as appropriate only if the notes follow each other according to the rules of harmony.

Differentiation co-occurs with combination. When putting together a simple sentence, for example, we do not choose the words in a random fashion, but rather according to their paradigmatic and syntagmatic properties. The choice of the noun *brother* in the subject slot of a sentence such as *My brother loves school* is a paradigmatic one, because other nouns of the same kind – *girl*, *man*, *woman*, and so on – could have been chosen instead. But the choice of any one of these for that sentence slot constrains the type – *love* vs. *drink* – and form – *loves* vs. *loving* – of the verb that can be chosen and combined with it. Co-occurrence is a structural feature of all meaning-bearing systems.

As a technique, opposition was elaborated by a number of linguists who met regularly in Prague in the early 1920s. The linguist Nicolas Trubetzkoy (1936, 1968), for example, called word pairs such as *cat-rat* that differed by only one sound in the same position *minimal pairs*. Opposition was also used to examine higher-level oppositions such as synonymy (*big-large*), antonymy (*big-little*), taxonomy (*rose-flower*), part-whole relations (*handle-cup*), and so on. As C.K. Ogden (1932: 18) claimed, 'the theory of opposition offers a new method of approach not only in the case of all those words which can best be defined in terms of their opposites, or of the oppositional scale on which they appear, but also to *any* word.' In the 1930s and 1940s, structuralists started noticing that opposition was not confined to language. It cropped up in the analysis of non-verbal systems as well. In the integer system of numbers, oppositions include *positive-versus-negative*, *odd-versus-even*, and *prime-versus-composite*; in music, basic oppositions include *major-versus-minor* and *consonant-versus-dissonant*.

The Prague School linguists also argued that there were levels or orders of oppositions. In arithmetic, the *addition-versus-subtraction* opposition is the basic one, while the *multiplication-versus-division* opposition is a derived one – since multiplication is repeated addition and division repeated subtraction. The *addition-versus-subtraction* opposition is thus a first-order, or binary, opposition, and the derived multiplication-versus-division opposition a second-order opposition; it is part of a *quartic* opposition: *addition-versus-subtraction-versus-multiplication-versus-division*. In an analogous vein, French semiotician Algirdas J. Greimas introduced the notion of the 'semiotic square' to connect sets of oppositions (Greimas 1987). Given a concept (for example, *rich*), Greimas claimed that we determine its overall meaning by opposing it to its contradictory (*not rich*), its contrary (*poor*), and its contradictory (*not poor*) in tandem. Also,

as work with binary oppositions showed in the 1950s, there are gradations within the binary oppositions themselves, which are due to culture-specific connotative processes. So, for example, between *night* and *day* there is *dawn, noon, twilight,* and other gradations. Thus, *night* and *day* would seem to be limiting poles in a continuum of meaning that can be segmented in any way a language (and culture) desires or needs. Anthropologist Claude Lévi-Strauss also entered the debate on opposition theory in the 1950s by showing that pairs of oppositions often cohere into sets forming recognizable units. In analysing kinship systems, Lévi-Strauss (1958) found that the elementary unit of kinship was made up of a set of four oppositions: *brother* vs. *sister, husband* vs. *wife, father* vs. *son,* and *mother's brother* vs. *sister's son*. Lévi-Strauss suspected that similar sets characterized units in other cultural systems and, thus, that their study would provide fundamental insights into the overall nature of human social organization.

Since its inception, structuralism has been criticized as being artificial. However, the Prague School linguist Roman Jakobson (1942) argued that the notion of opposition could actually be used to explain the psychology of language ontogenesis. He showed that sound oppositions that occur frequently are among the first ones learned by children. Nasal consonants – /n/ and /m/ – exist in all languages; significantly, they are also among the earliest sounds acquired by children. On the other hand, consonants pronounced near the back of the throat are relatively rare and, seemingly, are among the last sounds to be acquired by children. In other words, the theory of opposition predicts the sequence of sound acquisition in children.

Another critique of opposition theory has been that it does not take into account associative meaning and structure. The study of such structure came to the forefront in the 1970s within linguistics itself (Pollio, Barlow, Fine, and Pollio 1977; Lakoff and Johnson 1980, 1999; Fauconnier and Turner 2002). The American linguist George Lakoff and philosopher Mark Johnson are primarily responsible for this paradigm shift, claiming in 1980 that a simple linguistic metaphor such as 'My brother is a tiger' cannot be viewed as an idiomatic replacement for some literal form, but, rather, that it revealed a conceptual systematicity. It is, more specifically, a token of an associative structure that they called a *conceptual metaphor*. This is why we can also say that *Sam* or *Sarah* or whoever we want is an animal – a *gorilla, snake, pig, puppy,* and so on – in attempting to portray his or her personality. Each specific linguistic metaphor ('Sam is a gorilla,' 'Sarah is a puppy,' and so on) is an instantiation of an abstract metaphorical formula – *people are animals*. Now, does the existence of such formulas in cognitive activity lead to an invalidation of opposition theory? Conceptual metaphors are formed through *image schemata*, as Lakoff and Johnson have argued (Lakoff 1987; Johnson 1987). The image schematic source for the *people are animals* conceptual metaphor seems to be an unconscious perception that human personalities and animal behaviours are linked in some way. In other words, it is the output of an ontological opposition: *humans-as-animals*. It constitutes, in other words, an example of how opposition manifests itself as an associative, not just a binary or multi-order, phenomenon. In this case, the two poles in the opposition are not contrasted (as in *night-versus-day*), but equated: *humans-as-animals*. This suggests that oppositional structure operates in a non-contrastive way at the level of figurative meaning.

The most severe critiques of opposition theory have revolved around the relative notion of *markedness* (Tiersma 1982; Eckman et al. 1983; Andrews 1990; Battistella 1990). In oppositions such as *night-versus-day*, it can easily be claimed that the 'default' pole is *day* – that is, the notion in the opposition that we perceive as culturally or psychologically more fundamental. This pole is called the *unmarked* pole, and the other

pole, the *marked* one (since it is the one that stands out). This analysis can be justified, arguably, because it has a source in human biology – we sleep at night and carry out conscious activities in the day. Now, the problem is deciding which pole is marked and unmarked in a socially problematic opposition such as the *male-versus-female* one. The answer seems to vary according to the social context to which the opposition is applied. In patrilineal societies the unmarked form is *male*, but in matrilineal ones, such as the Iroquois (Alpher 1987), it appears to be *female*. Markedness, thus, seems to mirror social realities. Thus, its dismissal by various philosophers and semioticians, such as Michel Foucault (1972) and Jacques Derrida (1976), seems unwarranted. Their critiques led to the movement known as *post-structuralism*, which started in the late 1950s and gained prominence in the 1970s. In post-structuralism, oppositions are to be 'deconstructed' (as Derrida put it) and exposed as resulting from an endemic logocentrism on the part of the analyst, not the result of some tendency present in the human brain. In contrast to Saussure's idea of *différence*, Derrida coined the word *différance* (spelled with an 'a' but pronounced in the same way) to intentionally satirize Saussurean theory. With this term Derrida wanted to show that Saussure's so-called discoveries could be deconstructed into the implicit biases that he brought to the analytical task at hand, because a science of language can never succeed since it must be carried out through language itself and thus will partake of the slippage (as he called it) it discovers.

Post-structuralism has had a profound impact on many fields of knowledge. Because written language is the basis of knowledge-producing enterprises, such as science and philosophy, post-structuralists claim that these end up reflecting nothing more than the writing practices used to articulate them. But in hindsight, there was (and is) nothing particularly radical in this diatribe against structuralism. Already in the 1920s, Jakobson and Trubetzkoy started probing the 'relativity' of oppositions in the light of their social and psychological functions. Basing their ideas in part on the work of German psychologist Karl Bühler (1879–1963), they claimed that language categories mirrored social ones. The goal of a true structuralist science, therefore, was to investigate the isomorphism that manifested itself between oppositions and social systems. In other words, opposition theory was the very technique that identified social inequalities, not masked them.

Opposition theory has found special fertile ground in the study of media. Essentially, it allows media analysts to flesh out the hidden meanings built into texts. Take, for example, the differences that are associated with the *white-versus-black* opposition. The former connotes positive values, while the latter connotes negative ones in Western culture. This opposition manifests itself symbolically in all kinds of media texts. In early Hollywood cowboy movies, for example, heroes wore mainly white hats and villains black ones. Interestingly, Hollywood also turned the poles of an opposition around every once in a while in order to bring out the same pattern of connotative nuances even more forcefully. This is why the television and movie character Zorro wears black, as did several Hollywood western heroes of the past (such as Lash Larue).

Marcel Danesi

Bibliography

Alpher, Barry. Feminine as the Unmarked Grammatical Gender: Buffalo Girls Are No Fools. *Australian Journal of Linguistics* 7 (1987): 169–87.

Andrews, Edna. *Markedness Theory*. Durham, NC: Duke University Press, 1990.

Battistella, Edward L. *Markedness: The Evaluative Superstructure of Language*. Albany: State University of New York Press, 1990.

Bühler, Karl. *Sprachtheorie: Die Darstellungsfunktion der Sprache*. Jena: Fischer, 1934.

Derrida, Jacques. *Of Grammatology*. Trans. Gay-atri Chakravorty Spivak. Baltimore: Johns Hopkins University Press, 1976.

Eckman, Fred R., et al., eds. *Markedness*. New York: Plenum, 1983.

Fauconnier, Gilles, and Mark Turner. *The Way We Think: Conceptual Blending and the Mind's Hidden Complexities*. New York: Basic, 2002.

Foucault, Michel. *The Archeology of Knowledge*. Trans. A.M. Sheridan Smith. New York: Pantheon, 1972.

Greimas, Algirdas J. *On Meaning: Selected Essays in Semiotic Theory*. Trans. P. Perron and F. Collins. Minneapolis: University of Minnesota Press, 1987.

Jakobson, Roman. Observations sur le classement phonologique des consonnes. *Proceedings of the Fourth International Congress of Phonetic Sciences*, 1939, 34–41.

– *Kindersprache, Aphasie und algemeine Lautgesetze*. Uppsala: Almqvist and Wiksell, 1942.

Johnson, Mark. *The Body in the Mind: The Bodily Basis of Meaning, Imagination and Reason*. Chicago: University of Chicago Press, 1987.

Lakoff, George. *Women, Fire, and Dangerous Things: What Categories Reveal about the Mind*. Chicago: University of Chicago Press, 1987.

Lakoff, George, and Mark Johnson. *Metaphors We Live By*. Chicago: University of Chicago Press, 1980.

– *Philosophy in the Flesh: The Embodied Mind and Its Challenge to Western Thought*. New York: Basic, 1999.

Lévi-Strauss, Claude. *Structural Anthropology*. New York: Basic, 1958.

Ogden, Charles K. *Opposition: A Linguistic and Psychological Analysis*. London: Paul, Trench, and Trubner, 1932.

Osgood, Charles E., George J. Suci, and Percy H. Tannenbaum. *The Measurement of Meaning*. Urbana: University of Illinois Press, 1957.

Pollio, Howard R., Jack M. Barlow, Harald J. Fine, and Marilyn R. Pollio. *The Poetics of Growth: Figurative Language in Psychology, Psychotherapy, and Education*. Hillsdale, NJ: Lawrence Erlbaum Associates, 1977.

Saussure, Ferdinand de. *Cours de linguistique générale*. Ed. C. Bally and A. Sechehaye. Trans. W. Baskin, *Course in General Linguistics*. New York: McGraw-Hill, 1916/1958.

Tiersma, Peter M. Local and General Markedness. *Language* 58 (1982): 832–49.

Trubetzkoy, Nicolas S. Essaie d'une théorie des
oppositions phonologiques. *Journal de Psychologie* 33 (1936): 5–18.

– *Introduction to the Principles of Phonological Description*. The Hague: Martinus Nijhoff, 1968.

T

TABLOIDS

[See also: *Newspapers*]

The term 'tabloid' refers to a small-format newspaper, approximately half the size of a broadsheet newspaper. It was originally designed for easier reading on crowded public transport. Tabloid newspapers have acquired pejorative connotations in contrast to the more serious, higher-quality journalism traditionally associated with broadsheet newspapers. However, the distinction based on format alone does not indicate content or tone as many 'quality' newspapers around the world use a smaller format, often preferring to use the term 'compact' rather than 'tabloid' to refer to their layout. In the UK and many other European countries, the major tabloid newspapers are dailies and compete in the same marketplace as the more prestigious papers. In the United States, tabloids tend to be weekly publications and are distributed mostly in supermarkets.

Tabloid newspapers offer their readers entertainment rather than hard news. Their approach is emotional, sensational, and provocative, using pictures and large, punchy headlines to attract their readers. Their stories are shorter than those in the 'quality' press and their use of language is more informal, colloquial, and populist in approach, and more accessible for their readership. In Britain, they are sometimes referred to as 'red-tops' in reference to the colour of their mastheads. They focus on crime, sex, celebrity, and sports and are frequently accused of over-simplifying complex issues, muckraking, and making personal attacks on well-known figures. Tabloids have borne the brunt of arguments about declining journalistic standards to the extent that 'tabloidization,' or the use of tabloid values (including an emphasis on sensationalism, confrontation, and personalization), is used beyond newspapers to refer to charges of 'dumbing down' the content in the mass media more generally.

Debates about tabloidization centre on its effects on the quality of public discourse and on the erosion of investigative news journalism especially on politics and economics, and its replacement with 'softer' stories based on human interest and personal experience, creating a tension between the provision of entertainment and the dissemination of information. Indeed, the term 'infotainment' is often used in conjunction with these accusations. News and current affairs programs have been criticized for their increasing emphasis on the personal lives, experiences, and opinions of both celebrities and ordinary people, their focus on the human-interest angle, and their adoption of a more informal conversational style of addressing their audiences. In the manner of tabloid newspapers, some women's magazines feature 'scoops' on celebrity gossip and scandal which seem to be based on speculation, and long-range camera shots. Radio and television talk shows can take on tabloid values, too, through their emphasis on celebrity and personality, especially when their aim is to orchestrate confrontation as a means of entertaining their audiences. On the other hand, tabloid media are often defended as engaging new audiences and enabling a populist critique of authority which is not possible in more elite media forms.

Susan McKay

Bibliography

Biressi, Anita, and Heather Nunn, eds. *The Tabloid Culture Reader*. Maidenhead: Open University Press, 2008.

Conboy, Martin. *Tabloid Britain: Constructing a Community through Language*. Abingdon, UK: Routledge, 2006.

Glynn, Kevin. *Tabloid Culture: Trash Taste, Popular Power, and the Transformation of American Television*. Durham, NC: Duke University Press, 2000.

Langer, John. *Tabloid Television: Popular Journalism and the 'Other News.'* London: Routledge, 1998.

Sparks, Colin, and John Tulloch, eds. *Tabloid Tales: Global Debates over Media Standards*. Lanham, MD: Rowman and Littlefield, 2000.

TACTILE COMMUNICATION

[See also: *Non-Verbal Communication; Sensory Communication*]

Tactile communication is communication by means of touch. The study of tactile communication comes under the rubric of *haptics* and is incorporated within fields such as psychology, anthropology, and semiotics. An example of tactile communication is handshaking. The anthropologist Desmond Morris (1969) suggests that the Western form of handshaking may have begun as a means to indicate that neither person in a greeting ritual was holding a weapon. It thus started out as a 'tie sign' because of the bond of trust it was de-signed to establish. Subsequently, the sign became a symbol of equality among individuals, being employed to seal agreements and eventually as a simple greeting protocol. But even in the latter case, the original meaning is still resonant – refusing to shake someone's outstretched hand is interpreted as a 'counter-sign' of aggressiveness or as a challenge. Predictably, the form of the ritual varies considerably across cultures, and each variant form (duration of the handshake, the manner in which the hands touch) bears subtle meaning differences. Haptic communication is not limited, of course, to handshake greetings. Other forms include patting someone on the arm, shoulder, or back to convey agreement or as a complimentary gesture; linking arms to indicate companionship; putting one's arm around the shoulder to indicate friendship or intimacy; holding hands to express intimacy; hugging to convey happiness.

Anthropologists are unclear as to why tactile communication varies so much across cultures. Maybe it is a matter of culture-based perceptions. Some people think of themselves as being 'contained' in their skin; others feel instead that the self is located within the body shell, resulting in a totally different perception of how haptic behaviours are to be enacted.

One aspect of tactile communication that is shrouded in evolutionary mystery is kissing. When the lips of both people touch, the kissing act is perceived normally as erotic, sensual, or romantic. But not all kissing is erotic. Kissing the head, for example, can be a way of showing affection to children and pets. Kissing someone's feet can be a sign of servility or deference. But erotic kissing is particularly interesting as a cultural phenomenon because it seems to be a kind of mock-suckling of the sexual partner, implying vulnerability, closeness, and thus sensuality. This is perhaps why prostitutes may be willing to perform a variety of sexual acts, but generally draw the line at kissing. Nonetheless, lip kissing, known more technically as osculation, is not universal. It is not common in the traditional cultures of China or Japan, for instance; and it is completely unknown in many African societies. Traditional Inuit and Laplander societies are more inclined to rub noses than to kiss during courtship.

Marcel Danesi

Bibliography

Montagu, Ashley. *Touching: The Human Signifi-cance of the Skin.* New York: Harper and Row, 1986.
Morris, Desmond. *The Human Zoo.* London: Cape, 1969.

TALK SHOWS

[See also: *Radio; Television*]

A *talk show* is a radio or television program, moderated by a host or hosts, in which an individual or group of people speak on a variety of topics. The talk show may represent a specialist or a group of experts that discuss their area of work in relation to the show's agenda. Talk shows come out of early twentieth-century radio broadcasting, evolving from the audience-performer type of talk of popular theatre and vaudeville and reshaped and adapted for radio and later television. The term *talk show* emerged in the mid-1960s.

Talk radio can consist of a host talking through the whole program or involve listener participation, usually through live broadcasts, with a host and listeners who call in by telephone to the show. The callers are usually screened by a show's producer to maximize audience interest and, in the case of commercial talk radio, attract advertisers. Generally, the shows are organized into segments in public or non-commercial radio, and music is sometimes played in place of commercials. Variations of talk radio include conservative talk, progressive talk, hot talk, and sports talk.

Talk radio became a national pastime when radio lost its mass media hegemony to television in the 1950s and began to serve niche audiences. Radio talk shows must abide by Federal Communications Commission (FCC) community service requirements and the Fairness Doctrine, which is designed to serve the public interest. In the 1970s and 1980s, many listeners abandoned AM music formats for the high-fidelity sound of FM radio. The talk radio format began to catch on in such places as Cincinnati, Ohio, and Rochester, New York, where AM radio had low ratings. In the 1990s, talk radio experienced dramatic growth.

Conservative talk radio emerged in America in 1926, when Catholic priest Father Charles E. Coughlin attracted 45 million listeners for his weekly radio talks. His show ended in the 1940s. A generation later, new conservative talk shows emerged, such as the one hosted by Rush Limbaugh, an articulate talk-show host out of Sacramento. Limbaugh replaced Joe Pyne, a staunch conservative. Limbaugh rose to national status by offering his program free of charge to stations across the nation. He now has over 20 million listeners. Limbaugh imitators have spread from state to state.

Progressive or *liberal talk shows* are devoted to providing a channel for progressive and liberal viewpoints. These programs have existed for many decades as well. In the 1960s, free-form rock stations WMCA in New York and WERE in Cleveland featured outspoken hosts Alan Berg and Alex Bennett, who espoused liberal views of controversial events such as the Vietnam War and the civil rights movement. One of the most notable liberal talk-show hosts was Michael Jackson, who had a show for thirty-five years at KABC in Los Angeles, often commenting on both political and national issues.

During the 1990s, radio stations found that a schedule of all-conservative talk developed stronger listener loyalty than liberal talk programs. Today, there are around 100 liberal talk programs compared with over 600 conservative stations. The former have moved largely to the internet and to digital formats. For example, Air America Radio's webstream has consistently ranked in the top ten of the most-listened-to webcast stations and networks. When podcasts became available through iTunes, the liberal commentator Al Franken's show became very popular.

Hot talk attracts mainly an audience of males between the ages of eighteen to forty-nine. It intersperses rock music. Hot talk shows include programs such as those run by hosts Howard Stern, Don Imus, Opie and Anthony, Ron and Fez, and others who are frequently called 'shock jocks' because of the rawness (and even vulgarity) of their commentaries. Hot talk is found mainly on FM and satellite radio. The subject matter generally consists of pop culture issues rather than politics or social issues, as is typical on AM talk shows.

Sports radio or *sports talk radio* is devoted entirely to discussions of sporting events. Again, such radio attracts mainly males and is, thus, generally conducted in a boisterous fashion, featuring debates among the hosts and callers. Sports talk is available in both local and syndicated forms, and is carried on the North American satellite radio networks from ESPN Radio, Sporting News Radio, and Fox Sports Radio.

Around 2005, internet-based talk radio shows became cost-effective. Now it is possible for a listener to access a variety of services and even to host his or her own internet-based talk radio show without investing significant capital in the enterprise.

From its emergence as a mainstream mass medium in the late 1940s, television has always spotlighted the talk show genre. The TV talk show is always participatory – between a host and an audience, between a host and a guest, or between a host, a guest, and callers. The host is the 'star' who becomes associated with the show – for example, Oprah Winfrey and Jerry Springer. The most popular format for the TV talk show is the one conducted in front of a studio audience. This allows for the host to interact with audience members and in-

vited guests. Often, the show involves the 'subsidiary' crew, including the technicians who help televise the program.

The first cycle of TV talk shows spans the years 1948 to 1962, also known as the golden age of TV talk, with famous hosts such as Arthur Godfrey, Edward R. Murrow, Dave Garroway, Steve Allen, Arlene Francis, Mike Wallace, and Jack Paar. These hosts had extensive radio experience before coming to television. The second cycle spanned the years 1962 to 1974, when the networks took over from sponsors and advertising agencies, which were the dominant forces in talk programming. Three new hosts in particular became society-wide pop icons – Johnny Carson, Barbara Walters, and Mike Wallace – showing the growing power of television as a mass medium. The third cycle started in 1974 and ended in 1980, when syndicated talk programming reigned supreme. Television talk shows grew from five to over twenty, with late-night, daytime, and early-morning shows. For example, Phil Donahue expanded his daytime talk show nationally in 1979, becoming the nation's number one syndicated television talk show host. The fourth cycle spanned the years 1980 to 1990, defined as the post-network era of TV in which traditional news and entertainment programming changed drastically with the advent of cable and specialized channels. Talk shows became almost pure entertainment. With cable came a steady stream of reality-based programming and infotainment and carnivalesque shows (Ricki Lake and Jerry Springer). The fifth cycle, from 1990 to 2000, was renowned for late-night talk shows, such as *The Late Show with David Letterman* and Ted Koppel's *Nightline*. Both Koppel and Letterman gained increased ratings over time, becoming television stars in their own right. In the first decade of the 2000s, late-night talk shows continued to be popular. Among them were shows hosted by Jay Leno and Conan O'Brien.

The late-night entertainment talk show has remained a staple of TV programming fare. This features a host who performs comedic monologues and introduces celebrity guests. This chat format is the heart of the show, which may also include additional comic and even musical acts. This type of programming became popular with *The Tonight Show* starting in the late 1950s and continuing to this day. *The Tonight Show* became one of the most popular programs for NBC.

Daytime talk show hosts, on the other hand, are not typically comedians. They play the role of mediator, teacher, preacher, counsellor, confessor, or even ombudsperson. It was Phil Donahue, from 1963 to1967, who established the basic format of daytime talk, with his direct dialogue with guest experts and celebrities and with audience participation. Donahue's airing of issues raised by the women's movement helped turn what were formerly considered private issues into public ones.

The early-morning news talk magazine show presents news and entertainment, rather than comedy or social issues. Many hosts who began in morning talk later went on to anchor evening news and entertainment shows: for example, John Chancellor, Barbara Walters, Tom Brokaw, and Jane Pauley. Such shows reached (and continue to reach) a more limited number of households.

Barbara Dumanski

Bibliography

Barker, David C. *Rushed to Judgment: Talk Radio, Persuasion, and American Political Behavior.* New York: Columbia University Press, 2002.

Carter, Bill. *The Late Shift: Letterman, Leno, and the Network Battle for the Night.* New York: Hyperion, 1994.

Douglas, Susan J. *Listening In: Radio and the American Imagination, from Amos 'n' Andy and Edward R. Murrow to Wolfman Jack and Howard Stern.* New York: Times Books Random House, 1999.

Hirsch, Alan. *Talking Heads: Political Talk Shows and Their Star Pundits.* New York: St Martin's, 1991.

Livingstone, Sonia, and Peter Lunt. *Talk On Television: Audience Participation and Public Debate.* London: Routledge, 1994.

Metz, Robert. *The Today Show.* Chicago: Playboy, 1977.

Mitchell, Jack W. *Listener Supported: The Culture and History of Public Radio.* Westport, CT: Praeger, 2005.

Munson, Wayne. *All Talk: The Talkshow in Media Culture.* Philadelphia: Temple University Press, 1993.

Priest, Patricia Joyner. *Public Intimacies: Talk Show Participants and Tell-All TV.* Creskill, NJ: Hampton, 1995.

Timberg, Bernard. The Unspoken Rules of Television Talk. In *Television: The Critical View*, ed. Horace Newcomb, 24–38. New York: Oxford University Press, 1994.

– *Television Talk: A History of the TV Talk Show.* Austin: University of Texas Press, 2002.

Walker, Jesse. *Rebels on the Air: An Alternative History of Radio in America.* New York: University Press, 2001.

TELEPHONY

[See also: *Communication*]

The term *telephony* comes from the Greek *tele* (distance) and *phonè* (voice) and indicates the process of sending voice messages through space. In contemporary common usage it means the practice of talking to other people using a tool invented in the late nineteenth century called the telephone.

According to this definition, the acoustic signals used by Darius the Great (549–485 BCE), Alexander the Great (356–323 BCE), and Gaius Julius Caesar (100–44 BCE) to transmit military orders could be considered an early form of telephony. But the invention of what is still considered the *telephone* was completed only in the second half of the nineteenth century. As often seen in the history of technology, it was developed in the wake of a series of discoveries in physics and was claimed by many inventors such as Alexander Graham Bell, Elisha Gray, Antonio Meucci, and Philippe Reis.

The event that made history was on 10 March 1876, when Bell succeeded in speaking words over a telephone. In June 1876, Bell exhibited his telephone device at the Centennial Exposition in Philadelphia. The first telephones did not have switchboards. A simple pair of iron wires connected the phones. As more telephones came into use, connections were required to link them. Switchboards solved this problem. The first switchboard was established in 1877 in Boston. Telephone services soon began operating in the United States and other parts of the world. The first international telephone connection was established in 1891, between London and Paris.

Even in the United States, where it early became part of everyday life, the diffusion of the telephone was slower than that of other media for three main reasons. First, the telephone had to compete against an older and apparently similar communication technology, the electrical telegraph. In Europe, telegraphy was a state monopoly protected by governments, while in the United States Western Union considered the new medium 'an electrical toy.' Second, the high cost of building and providing this technology for both the users and companies wanting to expand the network also limited its expansion. Finally, until the First World War in the United States and the Second World War in Europe, the telephone was considered an expensive commercial tool which had very little to do with society's basic needs.

After the Second World War telephony was the subject of social studies that aimed to establish its main impacts. The most significant result was the discovery of what Ithiel de Sola Pool in *The Social Impact of the Telephone* (1977) called 'effects in diametrically opposite directions': the telephone was responsible for both the compression *and* expansion of distances, the increase *and* reduction of privacy, the intensification *and* reduction of social contacts.

The U.S. FCC issued the first licence for commercial cellular systems in 1983. At the beginning of the 1990s, mobile or cellphones started appearing – a new wireless medium that allows people to make phone calls virtually from anywhere. Wireless telephony has dramatically increased the use of the telephone throughout the world. Now, in the first decades of the new millennium, the meaning of the word 'telephony' is about to change again; indeed, the possibility of calling through the internet using VoIP (Voice Internet Protocol) presages a totally free service.

Gabriele Balbi

Bibliography

Baker, Burton H. *The Gray Matter: The Forgotten Story of the Telephone*. St Joseph, MI: Telepress, 2000.

Huurdeman, Anton A. *The Worldwide History of Telecommunications*. Hoboken, NJ: John Wiley, 2003.

TELEVISION

[See also: *Broadcasting; Communication; Television Genres; Television, History of*]

Television is a medium that transmits pictures and sound by electromagnetic means. The signals are broadcast from a station to television sets (designed to receive the signals and convert them into sound and audio) in homes or various mobile devices. TV is most commonly used as a source of information and entertainment and continues to be a major medium, although it is increasingly converging with the internet and, in some instances, giving way to the latter medium.

There are various ways in which TV is delivered. *Commercial television* stations sell advertising time in order to pay for their operating costs and to make a profit. Most commercial broadcasts are designed to appeal broadly for this reason. These include sitcoms, soap operas, action-packed dramas, news and newsmagazine programs, sports, game shows, talk shows, children's programs, documentaries, travel shows, and reality programs

Public television stations are non-profit channels. They collect money for their operations from various sources, including viewer donations, business and government contributions, and (in some countries) licence fees. Public TV usually provides more educational and cultural programming because it is not dependent on advertising and does not need to attract huge audiences. Viewers can also earn school credits through public television in some countries. Some public television stations produce current events programs that deal critically with contemporary issues. In some programs viewers and studio audiences are invited to join in discussion.

Cable television delivers TV to sets through cables. It can thus offer improved reception and a greater variety of programming. Cable television was first used in the late 1940s in order to bring network broadcasting to isolated areas that could not receive TV signals. Since the 1960s, cable systems have gained broad popularity, leading to narrowcasting, which unlike network broadcasting, offers programming that appeals to a specific group. Cable channels offer programming such as movies, news, sports, music, comedy, health, religion, weather, documentaries, science and technology, and erotica. Some cable services offer adult education classes. Certain channels charge a fee that a customer pays in addition to the monthly fee for basic cable service. In addition, cable services offer movies and sports events on a pay-per-view basis.

Satellite television offers an even greater number of channels and can transmit them virtually anywhere on the globe. A satellite operating over Europe, for example, can transmit programs to viewers in France, Italy, Spain, Germany, the Netherlands, the United Kingdom, and other countries. Subscribers use dish-shaped antennas to receive DBS (direct broadcast satellite) signals. Most DBS programming provides the same kinds of services as cable companies do.

Many of the commercial television stations in the United States are affiliates of one of four national networks: ABC, CBS, FOX, or NBC. An affiliate agrees to carry programs provided by a network. Smaller networks, such as the United Paramount Network (UPN), supply programming in a number of cities. Most non-network programming consists of old movies, talk shows, game shows, and reruns. These programs are called *syndicated*, because they are sold to the individual stations individually by independent organizations called *syndicators*. The success of a commercial TV program is measured in ratings and share. Ratings are used to measure the percentage of households equipped with television that are tuned to a particular program; share measures the percentage of households that are tuned to a particular program. The leading ratings analyst at the national level is Nielsen Media Research. The Arbitron Ratings Company is the leading audience measurement service at the local level. The Federal Communications Commission (FCC) regulates television (and radio) broadcasting in the United States. It issues broadcasting licences to stations, assigns broadcast frequencies, sets standards for broadcasters, and evaluates truthfulness in advertising.

TV has been instrumental in bringing about significant and important changes. The images of the Vietnam War broadcast daily in the 1960s and early 1970s brought about public protest and an end to the war. The treatments of controversial issues on shows such as *All in the Family* and *The Smothers Brothers Comedy Hour* were instrumental in bringing about a change in various areas of society, from sexual mores to human rights. On the negative side, many critics and social scientists claim that TV may have brought about cognitive impoverishment, since it feeds a constant stream of simplified ideas, thus negatively influencing politics, destroying local cultures in favour of a bland entertainment culture, and encouraging passivity in people. Despite these criticisms, TV has been a powerful force in the world since it came onto the international stage in the late 1940s. With online television becoming more and more widespread, television will continue to be an influential mass communications medium.

Television has had a noticeable effect on electoral politics. The classic example is the 1960 presidential campaign when candidates Richard M. Nixon and John F. Kennedy agreed to participate in a series of debates, which were broadcast simultaneously on television and radio. According to surveys, radio listeners felt that Nixon had won the debates and were predisposed to vote for him; television viewers, on the other hand, picked Kennedy, who went on to win the election. When asked why they voted for Kennedy, people stated that he simply 'looked' better (more honest, young, and attractive), while Nixon came across as looking confused and rigid. This event showed that TV had become the dominant medium in the United States and that the visual image had more emotional power than media, print, or audio.

TV has always functioned as a documenter of modern history. Events that are shown on TV are felt as being more historically meaningful than those that are not. Events such as the Kennedy assassinations, the Vietnam War, the Watergate hearings, the Rodney King beating, the O.J. Simpson trial, the death of Princess Diana, the Bill Clinton sex scandal, the 9/11 attack, the Iraq war, and Barack Obama's presidential campaign are perceived as important historical events. Without the TV camera to document them, it is unlikely that they would be ensconced in communal memory. People make up their minds about the guilt or innocence of someone by watching news and interview programs. The TV medium has become our historian and our courtroom at once. Edward R. Murrow of CBS News became a hero when he stood

up to Senator Joseph McCarthy on his *See It Now* documentary program. The images of the Vietnam War that were transmitted into people's homes brought about an end to the war by mobilizing social protest. An MTV flag was hoisted over the Berlin Wall as it crumbled in 1989.

When asked about the collapse of communism in Eastern Europe, the Polish leader Lech Walesa was reported as having said that it 'all came from the television set.' Television had undermined the stability of the communist regime when satellite images of Western programs and commercials were received by people living in communist countries. TV had shrunk the world into a global village.

Marcel Danesi

Bibliography

Abercrombie, Nicholas. *Television and Society*. Cambridge: Polity Press, 1996.

Dovey, Jon. *Freakshow: First Person Media and Factual Television*. London: Pluto, 2000.

Fiske, John. *Television Culture*. London: Methuen, 1987.

Meehan, Eileen R. *Why TV Is Not Our Fault: Television Programming, Viewers, and Who's Really in Control*. Lanham: Rowman and Littlefield, 2005.

Newcomb, Horace. *Television: The Critical View*. New York: Oxford University Press, 2000.

TELEVISION GENRES

[See also: *Genres; Television; Television, History of*]

Television is an electronic medium that broadcasts many different kinds of programs, each of which can be classified as belonging to a genre or, in some cases, mixed genres. The term 'genre' comes from the French language and means 'type' or 'kind.' Media theorist Douglas Kellner (2001: 4) offers a useful definition of genre:

A genre refers to a coded set of formulas

and conventions which indicate a culturally accepted way or organizing material into distinct patterns. Once established, genres dictate the basic conditions of a cultural production and reception. For example, crime dramas invariably have a violent crime, a search for its perpetrators, and often a chase, fight, or bloody elimination of the criminal, communicating the message 'crime does not pay.'

When we watch television we do not actually watch the medium of television, per se, but specific television programs – or, to use the term popular in academic circles, *texts*. All media are based on texts, which all fall into various categories or genres. The scholarly interest in genres has developed in recent years because of interest in how genres affect the creation of television programs; what the social, cultural, and political implications of different genres may be; how genres begin and evolve; and why some genres, such as the western, died out after years of great popularity.

Tim Bywater and Thomas Sobschak's *An Introduction to Film Criticism: Major Critical Approaches to Narrative Film* (1989: 90) explores how we 'discover' genres:

> Essentially the problem is the question of which came first, the chicken or the egg. One has to select a group of films prior to identifying them as a genre; however, the very selection process is shaped by a definition of the genre supposedly not yet arrived at. What makes a critic talk about musicals as a group is some prior notion of what a musical is.

They point out that we identify genres by looking for similarities in texts relating to common themes, subject matter, settings, characters, conventions, plots, and important material objects. One thing we must recognize is that television is essentially a dramatic medium. As Martin Esslin writes (1982: 6–7),

the language of television is none other than that of *drama:* television – as indeed the cinema with which it has much in common – is, in its essence, *a dramatic medium;* and looking at TV from the point of view and with the analytic tools of dramatic criticism and theory might contribute to a better understanding of its nature and many aspects of its psychological, social, and cultural impact, both in the short term and on a long term, macroscopic time scale.

It is difficult, in many cases, to place a particular show in a category, since some of them could fit in several genres. Nevertheless, it is reasonable to assign many shows to a particular television genre. Some of the more important formulaic broadcast television genres, and programs that can be placed in each genre, are:

- *Commercials.* The television commercial is the most important genre found on television in the United States since our system of paying for television is based on money made by stations broadcasting commercials and, in effect, selling their audiences to corporations. The Macintosh '1984' commercial by Ridley Scott is one of the most celebrated television commercials.
- *News shows.* Television broadcasts many hours of local news and usually a half-hour of national network news, plus weekly news programs such as *60 Minutes, 20/20*, and Sunday news interview shows such as *Meet the Press.* News was originally seen as a public service but in recent years has become an important source of revenue for television stations and networks. Documentaries are an important category of news programs and deal with political, social, cultural, economic, and other topics of interest. The number of documentaries on commercial television stations has dropped considerably over the years, but documentaries can still be found on public television and occasionally on the networks.
- *Situation comedies.* The payoff from a

good situation comedy, in terms of audience size, is considerable. Among the most important situation comedies of recent years are *Seinfeld, Frasier,* and *Friends,* each of which has gone into syndication and made enormous amounts of money for the creators and producers. Most situation comedies, which are full of eccentric characters involved in humorous relationships, do not last very long and many are taken off the air after only a few weeks.

- *Sports broadcasts.* Sports have a dramatic quality because in many cases we do not know what the outcome of the contest will be until it is over. Many games are decided in the final seconds of the game. Sports programs are one way that advertisers can reach male viewers aged 18 to 45, who are important target audiences for products like beer, automobiles, and sports equipment.

- *Crime shows.* These shows deal with the battle between the police and criminals of one kind or another and are generally extremely violent. Some of the more popular crime shows of recent years are *Crime Scene Investigation, CSI Miami,* and *Cold Case.* The classical detective show involves crime but generally is not violent and features a detective who solves a mystery by exhibiting superior powers of observation and intellect.

- *Soap operas.* This genre is characterized by complicated love relationships and family problems, generally with physically attractive romantic leads. Some soaps have young protagonists, such as those featured on youth channels, whose target audience is adolescents, while others, like *Desperate Housewives,* focus on older audiences. Some programs, such as *Grey's Anatomy,* do not present themselves as soaps but are considered to be soap operas by many critics.

- *Game shows.* In these shows participants guess the price of some object or answer questions on some subject, with those who are successful having the chance to win prizes and sometimes large sums

of money. These programs are cheap to produce and attract large audiences.

- *Children's programs.* These programs are designed specifically to entertain and/or educate young children. Some children's programs feature cartoons that are humorous but full of violence, leading many psychologists to urge parents not to allow their children to view this material. Some of the more important children's shows are *Sesame Street, Barney,* and *The Teletubbies.*

- *Religious programs.* These programs deal with religious themes and feature various television evangelists and other figures who talk about the Bible and other religious texts and various topics relating to religion. Some of these shows are broadcasts of religious services.

- *Talk shows.* These shows, such as *Dr Phil,* involve troubled individuals and families, who are given advice by a host. An important subcategory of these shows are the late-night comedy talk shows, hosted by comedians such as David Letterman, who interview show business celebrities.

- *Reality shows.* These shows represent a new genre and in recent years have become very popular. They are relatively inexpensive to produce since they are not scripted. But they are highly edited and so are not as 'real' as many viewers think. They combine a number of other genres and have elements of game shows, travel shows, and action-adventure shows.

- *Science and education shows.* These shows have an educational content and find ways of instructing viewers and entertaining them at the same time. *Nova,* which is broadcast on public television, is an example of a science show that also has dramatic qualities.

- *Cooking shows.* In these shows chefs (many of whom have become celebrities) teach viewers how to make various dishes from a number of different cuisines.

- *Action-adventure shows.* This category covers a wide range of dramas, some of which have elements of horror or the supernatural. In the fall 2006 season, programs with a supernatural theme, such as *Lost*, *Heroes*, and *Jericho* were popular, but the rate at which shows are taken off the air, when audiences stop watching them in the desired numbers, means that they may not be around for very long.

Arthur Asa Berger

Bibliography

Aristotle. *The Basic Works of Aristotle*. Ed. and trans. R. McKeon. New York: Random House, 1941.

Berger, Arthur Asa. *The TV-Guided American*. New York: Walker, 1975.

– *Popular Culture Genres*. Thousand Oaks, CA: Sage, 1992.

Bywater, Tim, and Thomas Sobchack. *An Introduction to Film Criticism: Major Critical Approaches to Narrative Film*. New York: Longman, 1989.

Esslin, Martin. *The Age of Television*. San Francisco: W.H. Freeman, 1982.

Kellner, Douglas. Television Images, Codes and Messages. *Illuminations* 7, no. 4 (2001): 2–19.

TELEVISION, HISTORY OF

[See also: *Broadcasting; Reality TV; Television; Television Genres*]

A practical nationwide television broadcasting system began operating in the United States in the late 1940s. But the prototype for television was devised as early as 1884 by the German inventor Paul Gottlieb Nipkow, who invented a scanning device that sent pictures over short distances. The scanner became the basis for the first television camera, developed by the Russian-born American engineer Vladimir K. Zworykin in 1923 and perfected a little later by the American inventors Philo T. Farnsworth and Allen B. DuMont. The first television receiver was exhibited in Schenectady, New York, in 1928, by the American inventor Ernst F.W. Alexanderson. Few knew what to do with it, and TV remained in the media background until after the Second World War. It was only by the late 1940s that television became an affordable commodity for most people, taking over as the major mass medium.

The first television sets were actually sold in England and the United States in 1936. In that year, the Radio Corporation of America (RCA) installed television receivers in 150 homes in the New York City area. NBC (which was owned by RCA) began experimental telecasts to these homes, starting with a cartoon episode of *Felix the Cat*. By 1939, NBC produced regular TV broadcasts, which were suspended when the United States entered the Second World War. After the war, a surge in demand for TV sets materialized. As a result, six television stations were built, each broadcasting for only a few hours a day. As early as 1941 the FCC (Federal Communications Commission) turned its attention to setting standards for television broadcasting.

The 1950s

By 1948, thirty-four stations were installed in twenty-one cities and were broadcasting all day. Over 1 million television sets were sold in that year. That year marks the beginning of the so-called golden age of television, with the premier of the first successful variety shows. The first community antenna television (CATV) was also established. In 1950 sales of TV sets soared to about 6 million. Television had become big business. In that year the A.C. Nielsen Market Research Company started tracking TV audience behaviours. By the end of the 1950s the National Broadcasting Company (NBC), the Columbia Broadcasting System (CBS), the American Broadcasting Company (ABC), and the DuMont Television Network (which went out of business in 1955) had become powerful media institutions. Aware of the fact that TV was replacing radio as the primary source of mass entertainment, manufacturers started producing

TV sets en masse and introduced colour television technology in 1954, though it did not become marketable until the late 1960s. The U.S. Senate even began hearings on the purported effects of television violence on children.

The early TV programs were direct adaptations from radio genres (and often simple crossovers). These included comedy and variety shows (*Toast of the Town* hosted by Ed Sullivan, *Your Show of Shows*, starring Sid Caesar); westerns (*Gunsmoke, Have Gun Will Travel, The Lone Ranger, Roy Rogers, Wagon Train, Bonanza*); children's programs (cartoons, *Howdy Doody, Mickey Mouse Club, Captain Kangaroo*); soap operas (*The Guiding Light, The Edge of Night*); sitcoms (*I Love Lucy, Father Knows Best, My Three Sons, The Adventures of Ozzie and Harriet, The Jack Benny Program*); professional wrestling matches; news telecasts; quiz shows; anthology dramas (*Goodyear-Philco Playhouse, Studio One*); talk shows (*Jack Paar*); and police, private-eye, and lawyer programs (*Dragnet, Perry Mason, 77 Sunset Strip*).

TV was, at first, little more than 'visual radio.' Coverage of special events was common. For example, the 1951 broadcast of the Kefauver hearings on organized crime and the 1954 coverage of the Army-McCarthy hearings (over alleged communist infiltration in U.S. institutions) brought the real world into everyone's homes. TV's influence became even more noticeable in 1960, when presidential candidates John F. Kennedy and Richard M. Nixon faced off against each other in a series of nationally-televised debates. Many believe that the debates contributed to Kennedy's victory in the election, since it highlighted his youth and attractiveness, which were becoming advantages in the political arena in that era.

Despite differences between radio and television, most media historians see the development of genres in both broadcast media as constituting a single history. For example, *I Love Lucy* (1951–7), starring Lucille Ball, was adapted from her radio show *My Favorite Husband* (1948–51). The comedy-variety genre, a hybrid of vaude-

ville and nightclub entertainment, was also a cross-over from radio. In the early years, many of the stars were comedy-variety performers in both vaudeville and radio, including Milton Berle, Sid Caesar, Jackie Gleason, Martha Raye, and Red Skelton. Similarly, the radio soap opera crossed over to TV. At first, the soaps were no more than afternoon 'romance interludes' for stay-at-home women. But their appeal spread quickly, attracting larger audiences. TV did, however, elaborate some radio fare considerably. For example, like radio, the earliest years of television news coverage offered little other than simple reports. But in 1956, NBC introduced *The Huntley-Brinkley Report*, a half-hour national telecast which not only presented the news but also provided commentary on news events.

The 1960s

In the 1960s television became a mainstream entertainment and information medium across the world, as well as a historical documenter. The assassination of President Kennedy on 22 November 1963 united the country in grief, and the killing of Lee Harvey Oswald live, in full view of TV cameras, showed the dramatic impact that television had on people's emotions. News programming expanded. TV brought scenes of the Vietnam war to viewers on a nightly basis. The war became the first war 'fought on television,' as many commented. In the same decade, TV brought war protests, civil rights marches, the assassinations of Robert F. Kennedy and Martin Luther King, and other socially relevant events before the eyes the world. It is unlikely that the social changes that ensued in that decade would have materialized without TV. Even variety shows, such as *The Smothers Brothers Comedy Hour*, dealt openly with controversial issues such as abortion, divorce, racism, sexism, alcoholism, and drug abuse. *Rowan and Martin's Laugh-In* became the top-rated show of the late 1960s because it regularly dealt with the same issues in a satirical and comedic vein. *It's a Man's World*, a sitcom that premiered on NBC in 1962, brought the reality of everyday life to the little screen. It followed the daily lives of four young men dealing with controversial issues such as premarital sex, feminism, and the generation gap.

This kind of programming, however, blended with lighter fare such as the sitcoms *The Beverly Hillbillies* (1962–71), *Bewitched* (1964–72), and *I Dream of Jeannie* (1965–9) to keep audiences watching the tube. These were accompanied by police and private-eye dramas such as *The Mod Squad*, *Hawaii Five-O*, *The Rockford Files*, and *Magnum, P.I.*; war and spy programs such as *Rat Patrol* and *The Man from U.N.C.L.E.*; and medical dramas such as *Ben Casey* and *Marcus Welby, M.D.* It became obvious that television was blurring the lines between entertainment and intellectual engagement, indicating that pastiche was the distinguishing characteristic (and appeal) of popular culture.

Worry about television content became widespread. The U.S. Senate hearings on television violence took place, ironically, on television.

In 1966 colour broadcasting began, and in 1967 Congress created the Corporation for Public Broadcasting, leading to the establishment of public television channels. With the broadcast of *60 Minutes* in 1968, it was becoming more and more obvious that television was taking over from print journalism as the major source of information and social criticism. In that same decade *Star Trek* debuted, creating the first fan club for a television or radio program in history.

The 1970s

Under pressure from the Federal Communications Commission (FCC), the networks adopted a 'family hour' format in the early 1970s to provide 'wholesome' early-evening family programming. But prime time sitcoms such as *All in the Family* and *The Mary Tyler Moore Show*, and the first made-for-TV movies, explored and showcased controversial social, moral, and political issues. The 1977 eight-part miniseries *Roots*, which probed the African-American experience, showed dramatically that TV could even help in a reinterpretation of history. Public television also emerged to provide not only social criticism and exposure to the arts, but also children's education, with programs such as *Sesame Street*.

In 1972 early cable television was made available to cities by the FCC. By 1976, Ted Turner's WTBS in Atlanta, which had the capacity to uplink with emerging satellite technology, became the first 'superstation.' In 1975 HBO (Home Box Office) also began broadcasting via satellite. VCRs were also introduced in that decade. But perhaps the most significant, yet hardly known, phenomenon was the appearance of interactive TV in Columbus, Ohio, on 1 December 1977, when cable companies made a 'relay box' available to customers. This allowed them to order movies on demand. The system also broadcast city council meetings, allowing viewers to express their opinions via the box. There was also a Your Call Football service that made it possible for viewers to anticipate the plays in football games.

The 1980s and 1990s

The 1980s and the 1990s is sometimes called the age of the sitcom, with programs such as *M*A*S*H*, *The Cosby Show*, *The Simpsons*, *Seinfeld*, and *Friends* being the most popular of all genres. Along with sitcoms, science fiction, lawyer, doctor, and other series formats dominated prime time. Quiz shows (*Wheel of Fortune*, *Jeopardy*, *Who Wants to Be a Millionaire*) rated highly as well. In 1980 CNN premiered as a twenty-four-hour cable news network, owned originally by Ted Turner, putting the first true chink in the network television system's armour. Narrowcasting was just around the corner. Cable also gave pop music its own television venue with the establishment of MTV in 1981. In 1987, Rupert Murdoch founded Fox Television to rival the Big

Three networks – NBC, CBS, ABC. New channels and networks started cropping up, including UPN (United Paramount Network) and WB (Warner Brothers). Specialty cable channels emerged, from A&E and Discovery to the Movie and the Disney Channel. The 1980s also saw the rise in popularity of the hour-long drama format with programs such as *Hill Street Blues* and *St Elsewhere*, whose plots featured different characters from week to week. The decade also saw an increase in the degree of sexuality, violence, and coarse language used in programs. Many people believed that TV had gone too far. Studies of television started to proliferate.

As cable attracted more and more audiences in the 1990s, the networks struggled to find new ways to win them back. They did so with moderate success, holding back viewer erosion with successful programs such as *Seinfeld*, *CSI*, *ER*, reality shows such as *Dateline NBC*, *Prime Time Live*, *Cops*, *America's Most Wanted*, and *America's Funniest Home Videos*. In 1994 the direct broadcast satellite (DBS) industry debuted, providing even more challenges to the networks' hegemony. In 1996 the Telecommunications Act abolished most TV ownership restrictions, further threatening the networks. Given the rise in adult content through the new broadcasting venues, parental advisories were mandated for TV programs in 1997, and a year later the V-chip – a computer chip installed in a television set that could be programmed to block or scramble material containing a special code in its signal indicating that the material was violent or sexually explicit – was introduced.

The 2000s

By the early 2000s narrowcasting had become a reality, with all kinds of specialty channels available through cable or satellite. Television and the internet also merged to create a co-broadcasting system whereby television channels established internet websites to deliver the same or comple-

mentary content of their programming. Sitcoms such as *Everybody Loves Raymond* (2000) and *Will and Grace* (2000) continued to be popular on the networks, as did *CSI*, *ER*, and reality programming. Talk shows (*David Letterman, Oprah*) continued to enjoy broad popularity.

In 2003, VOD (video on demand) was introduced. By the middle part of the 2000s, television's hegemony was starting to erode, as it started to compete with popular websites such as YouTube. Not only do all network (and most cable) channels and programs have websites today, which viewers can visit during, before, or after traditional broadcasts of shows, but also various features such as interactive games and delayed viewing are now becoming available in various technological formats, including webcasting and podcasting. Microsoft's WebTV and AOLTV (America Online TV) now allow users to pull up detailed information while they are watching a news or documentary broadcast.

TV may have lost some of its primacy to new online media, but it is still a dominant medium of entertainment, social criticism, and information. Will traditional television remain? It will, in the same way that radio has remained, converging with new technologies. As long as TV mirrors trends and preoccupations, it will survive.

Marcel Danesi

Bibliography

Abercrombie, Nicholas. *Television and Society*. Cambridge: Polity Press, 1996.

Danesi, Marcel. *Popular Culture: Introductory Perspectives*. Lanham, MD: Rowman and Littlefield, 2008.

Fiske, John. *Television Culture*. London: Methuen, 1987.

Meehan, Eileen R. *Why TV Is Not Our Fault: Television Programming, Viewers, and Who's Really in Control*. Lanham, MD: Rowman and Littlefield, 2005.

Newcomb, Horace. *Television: The Critical View*. New York: Oxford University Press, 2000.

TEXT MESSAGING

[See also: *Email; Instant Messaging; Podcasting*]

Text messaging (TM) is the term used to describe the act of transmitting and receiving an electronic message by cellular phone or other mobile device. The message is sent over the internet or some other computer network. It occurs in real time, since both users can conduct a back-and-forth exchange. Text messages involving mobile phones and personal digital assistants are said to use short message service (SMS). The actual texts are called both *text messages* and *SMS*.

TM has influenced how people interact and communicate. Perhaps the most interesting phenomenon from a purely communicative standpoint is *text speak*. Essentially, this is a form of shorthand (based on abbreviations, acronyms, alphanumeric symbols, and so on) that makes real-time communication unfold quickly and effectively. Even the term *text messaging* is now written as *txt msg*. Text speak developed originally in bulletin board systems and chatrooms so that users could type more quickly, relying on the redundancy features built into language: vowels, for example, are largely predictable in written words and thus can be eliminated. Text speak occurs across languages. In Mandarin Chinese, for example, numbers that sound like words are used in place of the words.

There is now software that attempts to infer what words are being typed so that TM can occur even more quickly. Websites such as *transl8it* ('translate it') standardize text speak so that it can be used more systematically and broadly for communication, like the Morse code and other telegraphic writing systems before it. As a consequence, there are now standard dictionaries and glossaries of text speak available online.

The basic pattern in constructing text speak (TS) words involves shortening a word in some linguistically logical way. For example, *I love you*, is shortened to *i*

luv u or even *ilu*. Deciphering the TS form is dependent on user familiarity. Words and expressions that are used frequently in communication get shortened systematically. During face-to-face interaction our goal is to get messages across as quickly, efficiently, and clearly as possible. Text speak has projected this principle onto the text messaging medium. It is relevant to note that TM is now used by professionals such as doctors and lawyers to interact with colleagues. In the absence of face-to-face communication, TM has made it much easier for professionals to collaborate with colleagues. In the past, doctors would mail letters to colleagues seeking advice; now a text message can do the job virtually in an instant.

Some observers are decrying text speak as a product of modern-day versions of inertia and ennui. Helprin (2009), for instance, cautions that the new digital forms of communication, and the internet generally, produce an addictive effect on people and how they process information, rendering them much less reflective and less inclined to appreciate artistic and literary greatness. Others (Crystal 2006, 2008) respond that text messaging is no more than an efficient way to create written messages for informal communication. People use text speak, not to generate thoughtfulness and literary communication, but to keep in contact and to facilitate communication. In no way does this imply that people have lost the desire to read and reflect upon the world.

Among the controversial items that are brought up during the debate are sexting and cyberbullying. The former is the sending of sexually explicit text messages or photographs via mobile phone; the latter is the use of text messages to intimidate or threaten someone. But these kinds of messages have always existed, in different media. It is not the TM medium that encourages them; actually, because these message can easily be transported to other media (such as Facebook), TM may actually discourage prurient and threatening communication for fear of being exposed publicly.

TM has become the preferred medium of communication especially among adolescents, as studies such as the one by Lenhart (2010) make clear. She found that in 2009, teens (twelve to seventeen years of age) used the following methods to contact their friends:

- text messaging: 54 per cent
- cellphone: 38 per cent
- face to face: 33 per cent
- landline phone: 30 per cent
- social network site: 25 per cent
- instant messaging: 24 per cent
- email: 11 per cent

It is relevant to note that no less an authority on language trends than the *Oxford English Dictionary* has inducted many items from text speak into its lexicon. This is an affirmation of the plasticity and adaptiveness of language.

Marcel Danesi

Bibliography

Baron, Naomi S. *Alphabet to Email: How Written English Evolved and Where It's Heading.* London: Routledge, 2000.
– *Always On.* Oxford: Oxford University Press, 2008.
Crystal, David. *Language and the Internet.* 2nd ed. Cambridge: Cambridge University Press, 2006.
– *txtng: the gr8 db8.* Oxford: Oxford University Press, 2008.
Helprin, Mark. *Digital Barbarism: A Writer's Manifesto.* New York: HarperCollins, 2009.
Lenhart, Amanda. More and More Teens on Cell Phones. Pew Internet and American Life Project. http://pewresearch.org/pubs/1315/teens-use-of-cell-phones (accessed 1 September 2011).
Sebba, Mark. *Spelling and Society: The Culture and Politics of Orthography around the World.* Cambridge: Cambridge University Press, 2007.

TEXT THEORY

[See also: *Discourse; Narrative; Semiotics; Speech Act Theory*]

Text theory studies literature, scientific discourse, journalism, and everyday speech using concepts adapted from linguistics, philosophy, anthropology, aesthetics, and other fields. Within communication studies, it represents a qualitative alternative to content analysis' quantitative approach. Originating in continental Europe in the context of structuralism and post-structuralism, text theory has encompassed both a scientific, academic project and a cultural critique. Employing methods that break with key features of traditional humanism, theorists study texts' internal organization, social context, and strategies for guiding interpretation and influencing behaviour. Almost from the outset, text theorists engaged non-verbal cultural productions, investigating photography, visual advertising, film, and performance genres. Text theory represents one of the major paradigms through which media studies established itself as a scholarly enterprise distinct from commercial journalism in the last third of the twentieth century.

While its concerns reach back to the ancients, 'text theory' is the expression coined around 1973 by Julia Kristeva and Roland Barthes to designate the approach they and other collaborators to the French review *Tel Quel* were elaborating (Barthes 1973, 1973 [1994]; Kristeva 1969; Ducrot and Todorov 1972 [1979: 356–61]). The term was soon extended to comprise related methods grounded in linguistics, structuralism, and semiotics which had adopted 'text' as the term for their object of study since the mid-1960s, influenced in part by Russian figures such as Mikhail Bakhtin. In a celebrated essay entitled 'From Work to Text,' Barthes announces: 'In the face of the *work* – a traditional notion … the need for a new object is emerging, one obtained by sliding or reversing previous categories. This object is the *Text*' (1981: 70; my translation; published translations are generally indicated by a second date within brackets). Reacting against historical perspectives inherited from the nineteenth century, text theorists de-emphasize the relation between author and work and highlight instead the text itself and the dynamic between text and reader. Barthes's article 'The Death of the Author' famously proclaims, 'the true locus of writing is reading … the birth of the reader must be ransomed by the death of the Author' (1967). The hermeneutics shifts from that defined by Friedrich Schleiermacher and Wilhelm Dilthey, which founds interpretation in the psychological and linguistic genesis of the work, to that proposed in the twentieth century by Heinrich Georg Gadamer and Paul Ricoeur, which locates the basis of understanding as much in the present as in the past: each subject's encounter with a document or artwork can uncover a novel aspect of the text and reveal its insights into today's critical problems. The increased role attributed to the addressee dovetails with contemporaneous experimental music, literature, and visual art that highlights the agency of the listener, reader, and viewer (e.g., Group 63 in Italy, Oulipo and the *Nouveau roman* in France).

Evincing the 'linguistic turn' to inquiry that marks its era, text theory entails a set toward language and the language sciences, an orientation that infuses it with at least a measure of formalism and leads it to investigate internal discursive dynamics, their immanent play and structure. Yet the theorists describe the textual practices as unmaking and remaking existing linguistic habits, and construct discourse as a dialogue and debate among different perspectives, interests, cultures, and eras. Emphasizing that experimental literature employs language but violates its norms, Kristeva proposes the following definition: 'I define *the text* as a translinguistic apparatus that redistributes the order of language … the text is thus a *productivity*' (1969: 113). More broadly, text theory provides conceptual tools for critical investigations of socie-

ties and history. Barthes (1957) proposes to demystify the 'mythologies' of everyday French life in order to expose the underlying rhetoric of middle-class ideology, especially the strategy of presenting its petit-bourgeois practices and beliefs as founded on transcendent principles rather than on historically circumscribed interests.

Theorists emphasize that in spite of its phenomenal appearance as a bounded and finite artefact, the text exists above all as process rather than as product: it reveals creative events, engenders multifarious reactions and interpretations, and promises unpredictable readings to come. Reviving the dead metaphor concealed in the Latin origin of the word *text*, 'that which is woven' (cf. textile), Barthes emphasizes that 'Text means *Fabric*, but whereas until now we have always taken this fabric as a product, a ready-made veil behind which meaning (truth) lurks more or less hidden, we are now accentuating, in the fabric, the generative idea that the text makes itself, works itself out through a perpetual intertwining … If I liked neologisms, I would define text theory as a *hyphology* (*hyphos* is fabric and spider's web)' (Barthes 1973: 100–1 [1975: 64]). Emphasizing the 'thickness' of language and the 'productivity' of the text, theorists critique perspectives that reduce discourse, films, or photographs to a static and transparent lens that would serve only to reveal the real world or the true person beyond, strategies they see at work in Realist and Naturalist aesthetics and in the commercial film industry (Ducrot and Todorov 1972 [1979: 357]).

Distancing themselves from certain psychological and historical explanations for creative and interpretative processes, theorists emphasize that texts circulate and infiltrate other texts through the medium of writers and readers. In a study that synthesizes Bakhtin's research on 'dialogism' and 'polyphony' in the novel, Kristeva introduces the concept of *intertextuality*: 'Every text is constructed as a mosaic of quotations, every text is the absorption and transformation of another text. In place of the notion of intersubjectivity, that of *intertextuality* takes shape' (1969: 146). In addition to the 'horizontal, linear' relations that link linguistic units in discourse, the initiated reader attends as well as to 'vertical, translinear' connections with other texts in a dynamic that mimes the interlacing warp and weft evoked in the etymology of *text* (Ricardou 1978: 245). In a belletristic context, the resultant references, resistances, and responses engender the literary value of the text, raising it above the level of utilitarian communication (Genette 1979: 87; Riffaterre 1978). Systematically examining varieties of intertextuality, Genette (1982) studies the mechanisms of quotation, allusion, and summary; compares pastiche to parody; and explores the communicative dynamics of sequel, supplement, translation, adaptation, and generic transposition. Returning to Bakhtin's studies of fiction as intra- and intercultural dialogue, Jacques Fontanille envisions intertextuality as a form of 'intersemioticity' and investigates what an author writing in one social, intellectual, and aesthetic context looks for and thinks to find in the work of an author from a different context (1999: 129–58). The approach seeks to specify how the 'target' text selects and appropriates, transforms and deforms elements of the 'source' discourse as a function of the convergences and divergences between the two writers and their natural and cultural environments. Offering his own 'anxiety of influence' toward Jorge Luis Borges as an example, Umberto Eco describes intertextuality as a triangular dynamic in which the vast 'universe of the encyclopedia' interacts with two authors (2002).

Intertextuality revises conventional philological and literary doctrines of imitation to the extent that it substitutes textual analysis for a psychology of the person, posits a pluralistic enunciation in place of a homogeneous Cartesian subject, and defines a heterogeneous discourse instead of the Romantic notion of the work as an organic whole. Whereas traditional criticism emphasizes the identification of influences

on an author and sources for a work, looking especially among other literati, Barthes emphasizes that the intertext typically appears anonymous and unconscious, its origins remaining imprecise, lost, or forgotten. Every text incorporates and reworks shards of ambient and former cultures, 'bits of codes, formulae, rhythmic models, fragments of social languages' (Barthes 1973 [1994: 1683]). The concept of intertextuality develops Saussure's principle of immanence and the Russian Formalists' emphasis on the autonomy of art in critical ways: the dialogic character of literature establishes it as an exchange among speaking subjects and among societies. Thus, while discourse neither simply reflects the world nor expresses the person as such, it does effect interactions among concrete historical subjects and groups. Entering fully into the perspectives of dialogism and polyphony means abandoning the notion of the closed, objective 'text in itself': whether literary, legal, or scientific, every text exists only as a praxis among plural instances.

Envisioning intertextual relations among cultures across history, Yuri Lotman proposes a canonical cyclical narrative (1966 [1990: 143–7]). When a culture imports (verbal, visual, musical) texts from a more prestigious foreign culture, it initially maintains their air of 'foreignness' – indeed, natural language works are often read in the foreign tongue. In time, however, the host culture and the imported texts restructure each other such that the codes informing the foreign artefacts become integrated into the discursive fabric of the receiving group. The foreigners progressively lose their aura of prestige, while the new forms elaborated by the host milieu incorporate and transform the imported models – whereupon the dynamic comes full circle and can begin again, with the erstwhile importing culture now positioned in the centre of the 'semiosphere,' exporting its productions to the periphery.

Emerging at a time of ever-increasing specialization in research and intellectual inquiry, text theory proceeds from a desire to break down barriers among fields, to make connections among related projects, and to foster interdisciplinary collaborations and the exchange of concepts and methods. Rooted in the language sciences, text theory explores how its outlook and central concepts could lead to new ways of analysing non-verbal cultural practices and productions. Barthes's lively magazine articles collected in book form as *Mythologies* (1957) use text-theoretic notions to examine critically the social image and function of the new Citroën DS sedan, traditional culinary dishes such as steak and fries, advertisements for household cleaning fluids and abrasive cleansers, popular movies and electoral posters, and performances such as World Wrestling Association–style wrangling. In more developed essays of the late 1950s and early 1960s, Barthes outlined and illustrated elements of a 'rhetoric of the image' that adapts principles in continental structural linguistics to the analysis and ideological critique of visual artefacts such as photographs, billboard and magazine advertisements, and film (Barthes 1957 [1972: 107–59], 1962 and 1964 [both in 1977: 15–51]). Umberto Eco emphasizes that text theory focuses on the multiple specific 'codes' that inform the production, perception, and interpretation of artefacts, and which include modes of expression conveying ideologies at a given point in history, practices and forms particular to given media such as painting or music, and aesthetic conventions governing the treatment of perspective, themes, lighting, colour, verisimilitude, and so forth (1968). Defining architecture as a rhetoric, Eco (1968) proposes that the utilitarian features of a space constitute its denotative meaning, while the multiple symbolic codes that inform the structure comprise its connotative senses. Greimas envisions a semiotic model of the 'urban life style' comprising a 'spatial signifier and a cultural signified': an ideological deep structure generates a surface spatial grammar that accounts for the interrelations and interactions among the individual or collective subjects and the

objects making up the built environment (1974, in 1990: 139–59).

Barthes's studies inspired Christian Metz's investigation of cinema, which blossomed into the first thoroughgoing and sustained extension of text theory into non-verbal media. Metz explains the path he chose: 'The only principle of relevance capable of defining the semiology of film today is … the will to treat films like *texts*, like units of discourse, thereby forcing oneself to search for the different *systems* (whether they be codes or not) that inform those texts' (Metz 1971: 14). Fernande Saint-Martin and Jean-Marie Floch have elaborated ambitious methods for analysing fixed images, while Robert Hatten and Eero Tarasti have adapted text-theoretic concepts to the study of music. Studying non-verbal phenomena as 'texts' (or 'discourse') entails attending to cultural productions more than to purely physical entities, to perceptions more than to quantitative data, and to meaning at least as much to being; it involves methodically investigating the organization of processes and artefacts rather than focusing on isolated events or acts, units or facts (e.g., Branigan 1984; Buckland 2000; Buckland ed. 1995; Casetti 1986; Colin 1992; Deleuze 1983, 1985; Eco 1968: 105–88; Groupe Mu 1992; Heath 1981; Odin 1990; Rose 1986; Uspenskii 1971; Wollen 1969).

In a broad, generational impetus, text theorists voice scepticism toward a host of traditional concepts and methods used in philosophy, psychology, history, grammar, and literary criticism, deemed tributary of a bygone era, and call for fresh reflection and systematic investigation using contemporary approaches. Nonetheless, text theorists at times reach back to earlier paradigms: many thus turned their backs on the behaviourism that dominated psychology in the 1950s and 1960s and drew instead from the wide-ranging psychoanalytic theses of Sigmund Freud, Melanie Klein, and Jacques Lacan, as many tempered the logico-mathematical bent of analytical philosophy with healthy doses of the speculative tradition exemplified by Georg Wilhelm Friedrich

Hegel, Friedrich Nietzsche, Charles Sanders Peirce, and Martin Heidegger. Rather than confining themselves to the formal models of sound and sentence structures elaborated in Chomskyan linguistics, many text theorists continued to explore continental structural linguistics, following up the links that Roman Jakobson, Émile Benveniste, and A.J. Greimas established between linguistics and poetry, narrative, visual image, psychology, and philosophy. Instead of espousing free-market neoclassical microeconomic theory and its developments in general equilibrium analysis, game theory, and oligopoly theory, figures such as Barthes and Kristeva invoked Marxist perspectives that conjoin issues in economics, politics, and history. For text theorists, Marxism, psychoanalysis, anthropology, and modern linguistics have effected a Copernican revolution that 'decentres' the subject, shifting agency from the individual person to unconscious and collective processes, casting suspicion on the contents of consciousness, and demanding the mediation that systematic analysis, explanation, and critical thinking can bring (Foucault 1969 [1995: 12–13]; cf. Ricoeur 1969 [1974: 236–66]). At the same time, accepting the twentieth-century scientific proposition that the observer's point of view plays an essential role in constituting the object, theorists dismiss the positivists' faith in objective facts and qualify the pristine distance the subject would like to keep from the phenomenon under study.

In crucial ways, text theory reverses the reigning North American model for the social sciences today: it remains resolutely qualitative instead of quantitative, values theoretical inquiry as much as empirical research, and maintains an affinity for philosophy even while duelling with antecedent metaphysics. While incorporating rigorous methods, text theorists typically highlight the irreducible importance of interpretation and emphasize that studying an object changes it; some openly critique society and its mainstream productions rather than cultivating the detached stance of the specialist or the objective scientist.

Text theory has played an important role in Western intellectual life, including in English-language cultures, in part because it has gone beyond specialized disciplinary perspectives to link its investigations to fundamental issues of human values, social organization, and history. Proposing a broad vision of the 'human sciences' and the 'sciences of culture,' theorists strive notably to overcome the dichotomy between the sciences and the humanities, to federate the many fields that study man and society, and to bring together researchers who investigate discourse or other comparable cultural artefacts (Greimas 1966; Lévi-Strauss 1950; Rastier ed. 2003). Drawing from generative and structural linguistics, from Peircean and Saussurean semiotics, and from mathematics and logic, Yuri Lotman positions his and related Soviet text-theoretical research within 'the trend proper to contemporary science to overcome the opposition between the exact sciences and the humanistic sciences considered unshakable by nineteenth-century scholars' (1967: 107). Bakhtin asserted in the early 1970s that 'the text (written and oral) is the primary given … of all thought in the human sciences and philosophy in general … The text is the unmediated reality (reality of thought and experience), the only one from which these disciplines and this thought can emerge. Where there is no text, there is no object of study, and no object of thought either' (in 1986: 103). Text theorists aim to identify or forge core common principles and procedures for research, and incorporate social-science postulates when examining literature and art, phenomena heretofore generally considered the exclusive province of humanistic perspectives.

Text theory subsumes a great variety of currents, individuals, and distinctive contributions, bringing together methods originating in France, Switzerland, and Italy, in Eastern Europe and the former Soviet Union, in Great Britain and North America, and beyond. In one commonly recognized partition, such figures as Mikhail Bakhtin, (the early) Roland Barthes, Umberto Eco, Jacques Fontanille, Gérard Genette, Algirdas Julien Greimas, Yuri Lotman, François Rastier, Cesare Segre, and Tzvetan Todorov have sought to secure a scholarly, scientific status for their projects; have constructed models of signification that incorporate constraints that society and communication commonly place on individual interpretations; and have considered literature and art as integral to the normal functioning of language and visual imagery. Inversely, theorists such as (the later) Barthes, Jacques Derrida, Michel Foucault, and Julia Kristeva have sharply and systematically critiqued the founding tenets of science and academia, and have combated limits and habits that institutional discourses strive to impose on the subject's experience of the text. Barthes and Kristeva have argued that experimental art and literature require approaches separate, at times opposite, from those used to analyse everyday cultural expressions. In general, the scholars mentioned first have drawn attention to schemata that organize content and communicative exchanges, while the second set of thinkers have highlighted the role that the material 'letter' (signifier, representamen, sign-vehicle) plays in signification; the first group privileges the 'view from afar' of the objective scholar, whereas the second foregrounds the dynamic entangling of subject and object that remakes both instances. The divide parallels the rough distinction made in the 1980s between structuralism and post-structuralism.

Yet this and any other attempt to draw grand partitions within text theory remain approximate and imprecise, and can never do justice to the complexity and nuances of each thinker's work and its variations across time. Other tensions cut across the (post-)structuralist contrast, and few individual projects carry forward the breadth of the revolution that early text theory proclaimed. The closer a study tacks to contemporary Western scientific norms, the less it enters into a critical questioning of the subject and subjectivity, while the more a method highlights socio-political or psychoanalytical components, the less it distances itself from a traditional focus on the genesis of the work. In spite of the imperfect character of the distinction, the rest of this article first examines research that develops text theory as a scientific project and academic discipline, then sketches critical text theory defined in part as oppositional practices, and concludes by comparing text-theoretical research to English-language approaches.

Text Theory as Scientific Project

Important currents in text theory have founded a general semantics; developed a linguistics of discourse; elaborated new rhetorics, stylistics, and poetics; and launched rigorous methods for analysing visual images, architecture, design, and music. Straddling the social sciences and the humanities, the researchers aim to participate in building the 'human sciences.' They have defined their method above all in relation to linguistics and cultural anthropology, even as they have foregrounded interpretation and drawn from the philosophy of language and from continental systematic philosophers. Initially part of the structuralist revolution, these efforts cultivate scientific methods, scholarly discourse, clarity, and terminological precision – orientations that ran counter to a number of influential post-1968 currents in the humanities, but which today find themselves in tune with cognitive studies. Indeed, much of scientific text-theoretic research represents a continental correlate to contemporary directions in cognitive linguistics, poetics, and visual studies. The labels which these text theorists have devised for their projects include semantics, semiotics, semiology, rhetoric, poetics, and narratology.

In the 1950s, Algirdas Julien Greimas and Roland Barthes studied cultures by analysing their vocabularies and how their structures evolved and shifted over the generations. Greimas published an influential manifesto for an interdisciplinary project inspired by Saussurean principles and by new trends in historiography (Greimas 1956; cf. Broden 1995). A series of articles by Barthes outlines approaches to fashion informed by structural linguistics, while his books show how concepts drawn from the language sciences can characterize an author's style and opus, illuminate literary periods and trends, and dissect consumer society (1953, 1954, 1957). Paralleling Roman Jakobson's linguistics and poetics, Claude Lévi-Strauss's cultural anthropology, and Jacques Lacan's psychoanalysis, the research led to the broader, widespread 1960s development of structuralist methods throughout the human sciences. In this decade, Barthes's semiology and Greimas's semantics and semiotics renovated rhetorical studies and discourse analysis; analysed the narrative organization of fiction, drama, film, and essays; and commenced related explorations of photography, film, fashion, and visual advertising (e.g., in Barthes 1985, 1967; Greimas 1966, 1970). Barthes and Greimas attracted dynamic students, collaborators, and fellow travellers to their project, including Michel Arrivé, Jean-Claude Coquet, Gérard Genette, Julia Kristeva, Christian Metz, François Rastier, and Tzvetan Todorov.

The text theory initiated by Barthes and Greimas owes a considerable debt to continental structural linguistics. In Ferdinand de Saussure's *Course in General Linguistics*, researchers found an outline of the most general features of language as a signifying activity, as well as the invitation to found a broader but related 'semiology,' '*A science that studies the life of signs within society*' (1916 [1959: 16]). Roman Jakobson paints a comprehensive view of language that embraces rhetoric and poetics alongside phonology, morphology, and semantics, and positions the study of non-verbal cultural artefacts including film and painting within a general semiotic rather than a linguistic perspective (1990; cf. Eco in Krampen et al. eds. 1987: 109–27). Pioneering French research on linguistic pragmatics, Émile

Benveniste investigates how the speaking subject constructs itself in language and how discourse effects reference and communication (1966, 1974). A.J. Greimas and his collaborators have drawn extensively from Louis Hjelmslev, who emphasizes the systematic character of linguistic processes, including semantics, and extends key Saussurean concepts to the rest of science, rethinking them in the light of symbolic logic and the philosophy of language (1935–7, 1943, 1959).

Text theory has also drawn considerably from anthropology, folklore, and mythology, which accentuates its proximity to qualitative methods in the social sciences. Lévi-Strauss showed how the principles of phonology could be applied to aspects of social organization such as kinship and totem, and to myths and their cultural context (1950, 1955, 1962, 1964–71). Georges Dumézil extended historical Indo-European linguistics by developing a comparative mythology that traces the dissemination and evolution of social structures, ideologies, and individual characters throughout ancient myths, epics, legends, and histories (1940–5, 1968–73, 1969). In folklore, Vladimir Propp distilled the plots of Russian fairy tales into an elegant narrative model comprising fixed action sequences and roles (1928). Propp's 'morphology' specifies the incidence of variants and cultural contents, identifies global mechanisms that shape 'the tale as a whole,' and illustrates how procedures such as omission, repetition, and nesting condition how the matrix is realized in actual tales. Text theory has found considerable inspiration in other sources as well, from aesthetics (Souriau 1950) to Russian formalism (Lemon and Reis 1965; Todorov ed. 1966), from logic (Tarski 1936) to the philosophy of language (Austin 1962; Searle 1969).

While the events of May 1968 and the relative snub reserved for *The Fashion System* (1967) encouraged Barthes and others to explore a text theory that distanced itself from linguistics and from conventional scholarly discourse, figures including Eco,

Genette, Greimas, and Todorov maintained their initial scientific orientation. Greimas recruited new collaborators who developed the project in fresh directions, including Denis Bertrand, Ivan Darrault, Paolo Fabbri, Jean-Marie Floch, Jacques Fontanille, Jacques Geninasca, Anne Hénault, Eric Landowski, Jean Petitot, and Claude Zilberberg.

Natural Language Texts

Contemporary text theory studies natural language discourse as comprising multiple interrelated levels and components. Theorists examine global, text-whole phenomena, sentence mechanisms, and local, micro-semantic processes focused on word, context, and vocabulary. Text-whole dynamics include genre, narrative, and rhetorical strategies. Theorists study genres and discourse types as cultural norms, as prototypes of wholes that guide how speakers combine and interpret local units, and as schemata that prompt the rhetorical shifts of words from one semantic domain to another in context (Fontanille 1999: 159–68; Genette 1979; Rastier 1989 [1997: 20–8]). If broad terms like drama and poetry appear widespread and perennial, a genre or discursive type often corresponds to a specific practice in society, as do the résumé and the want ad, the press release, the editorial, and the obituary. Like social practices, genres and discourse types can form, change, and disappear in connection with historical transformations and exchanges with other cultures. A genre may prescribe the ways in which subjects participate in the speech act and its representation in discourse: a typical play presents actors speaking on stage, a scholarly essay generally cites other writers as authorities, and a lyric love poem often constructs the addressee as the object of desire. Genre may also specify a standard of grammatical and lexical acceptability (cf. homily vs radio ad), distinctive interpretative conventions, and length, theme, and temporal orientation.

Generic constraints intersect with other cultural 'codes' that mediate experience and provide conventions for producing and perceiving discourse (Eco 1976). Comprising practices, their cultural meanings, and the customs governing their use, such codes include the pragmatics of conversation and public addresses, and the proxemics regulating intersubjective space among speakers, for example. Expression codes define such variables as type styles, layout norms, and audio mixing standards, while ideological codes establish conventions of verisimilitude and propriety (Casetti and Di Chio 1997: 262–3). Eco defines the 'idiolect' as 'the individual and private code of a single speaker' expressed in iterative fashion throughout a particular subject's discourse (1968: 68, cf. sociolect).

The earliest and most lasting achievements in text theory include methods for analysing narrative. Numerous studies of fiction, theatre, film, traditional stories, and historical and philosophical works have identified models of fundamental action sequences, agent roles, contractual and polemical interactions, and thematic transformations (e.g., Bal 1985; Barthes et al. 1966; Chatman 1978; Fontanille 1998 [2006: 90–142]; Greimas 1966 [1983: 197–256], 1970 [1987: 63–120], 1976; Prince 1982; Rastier 1989 [1997: 41–52, 132–50]; Todorov 1969, 1971). Narrative structures give shape and rhythm to an extensive discourse, and include processes strategically combined to achieve an ultimate goal. Animate and inanimate textual actors move in and out of roles such as Subject and Anti-subject (cf. protagonist and antagonist), Sender (cf. addresser, benefactor, authority), and Receiver (addressee, beneficiary, subordinate), pursuing their ends, forging alliances, and engaging enemies. Textual actors desire or fear objects and other subjects, and are united with or separated from them through acquisition or loss, gift, or theft. Coming up against rivals' efforts, actors develop simulacra of these counterprograms and elaborate strategies that include struggle and deception in order to vanquish or circumvent adversaries. The triadic 'test' represents a common action sequence, consisting of confrontation, conflict, and resolution in an agonistic mode, and comprising contract, transmission, and consequence in a collaborative mode. On the cognitive dimension, a similar string progresses from question to assumption, then interpretation.

Studying myths, folktales, and action movies, text theory has identified a popular narrative schema comprising four major stages which together present the 'meaning of life' as a quest (Greimas 1966 [1983: 233–43]; Greimas and Courtés 1993 [1982: 'Narrative Schema']; Fontanille 1999 [2006: 73–5]; Rastier 1989 [1997: 132–50]; cf. Propp 1928). In a first segment, in order to remedy a dire predicament brought about by the enemy, an authority figure appeals to a (often unlikely) hero, who in a second sequence successfully negotiates an initial set of adventures, thereby obtaining the means to redress the calamity. In a third moment, the champion journeys to face the adversary and in a determining struggle achieves victory or meets defeat. In a final sequence, the arbiters of right and wrong mete out reward and punishment to the authors of the central deeds and misdeeds. The initial and final segments entail cognitive interactions that frame and give sense to the central sequences focused on action. The stages reveal a common internal formal articulation, progress through a canonical spatial cycle (e.g., here → there → elsewhere → here), and carry forward global thematic transformations that allow the text to reaffirm the existing social order or to contest the status quo and propose new existential and collective values. Alongside the quest schema, other narrative forms privilege surprise, unpredictability, risk, or vacuousness (Fontanille 1999 [2006: 76–80]; Zilberberg 1993). Landowski argues that genuine *becoming* takes place not through 'programmed' action but rather through the subject's 'availability' and openness to 'adventure' and the 'largely accidental path of *discovery*' (2004: 67–9).

Parallel to the study of narrative action, the analysis of enunciation examines discourse as a communicative process engaging speaking subjects situated in an environment at a particular time (Eco 1990; Fontanille 1998 [2006: 57–8]; Greimas and Courtés 1993 [1982: 'Enunciation,' 'Disengagement,' 'Engagement']; Groupe Mu 1970; Johansen 1993, 2002; Rastier 1989 [1997: 58–61]). Emphasizing that the text is realized as a dialogue between author and reader, Eco argues that text theory must analyse both systems of signification and of communication (1976). Even an individual subject produces a polyglot discourse by rhetorically shaping utterances in order to obtain a desired effect in the addressee(s). Many texts construct internal, linguistic representations of author and reader, attributing particular strategies and dispositions to each, and painting distinctive pictures of their give and take throughout the unfolding of discourse (Eco 1979). Stories also elaborate successive enunciative frames which conjure up 'paper' speakers and listeners within the text, inserting remarks or letters from other subjects, generating a play within a play or stories within a story. Genette (1972) systematically lays out the extensive plotting resources temporal mechanisms offer, and compares different strategies for positioning the narrator within or without the nested layers of stories and conversations that make up fiction. He analyses modes of quoting, reporting, or summarizing a speaker within the text and specifies their relevance for defining genres (cf. Hamburger 1957). Rastier's 'dialogics' classifies modal expressions which colour utterances through such lenses as obligation, (im)possibility, and desire, and which set up differentiated but interrelated 'universes of discourse' or linguistic possible worlds within a text (1989 [1997: 54–8], cf. Fauconnier 1985). Oswald Ducrot has studied the mechanisms of argumentation in everyday language (Ducrot and Zagar 1996), while Catherine Kerbrat-Orrecchioni analyses the structure, pragmatics, and cultural context of conversation (1990, 1992,

1994). A published poet and celebrated novelist, Eco emphasizes that textuality involves a cooperation between writer and reader and not just a solipsistic erotic reader, thus pointing to a dialogic hermeneutic ethics. Labelling deconstructionism a 'dangerous critical heresy,' he has consistently objected to post-structuralism's 'aberrant decoding' and its 'cancer of uncontrolled interpretation' (1968, 1990, 1992).

Initially focused on action-oriented popular stories, text theory developed more elaborate methods to study cognitive and emotional phenomena when it turned its attention to complex literary and scientific works (Barthes 1970; Coquet 1985–6; Fontanille 1999; Greimas 1976, 1990: 11–138). Theorists have explored how texts restrict the distribution of knowledge in calculated fashion, posing enigmas which can be deepened and shared before being solved, setting up secrets, disguises, and ruses, staging mistaken identities and misinterpretations, deploying misunderstandings and cognitive dissonances. The basis of murder mysteries, psychological thrillers, baroque drama, and theatrical recognition scenes, the mechanisms generate narrative tension, suspense, and surprises, propelling the plot forward toward revelations and resolutions. They also help lay out the text's key belief systems, position the actors among those options, and resolve the central conflicts of the work, dynamics particularly evident in the *Bildungsroman*, the drama of ideas, and the thesis novel (Suleiman 1983: 80–118). Discursive subjects' performances presuppose cognitive competences: key modalities such as wanting, being able, knowing, and believing govern their doing and being. The acquisition and loss of such modal values trace the development of a discursive actor's competence, while the coexistence of conflicting modalizations such as *having-to-do* and *not-being-able-to-do* can engender critical tensions in the actor and in the text. These modalities also define fundamental levels of argumentation in essays, including scientific and political discourse, and delineate basic clas-

sifications of cultural objects. Jean-Claude Coquet formulates a sophisticated typology of modal configurations that identify such discursive agents as the non-subject, the subject according to law, and the subject according to will (1985–6, cf. Fontanille 1999 [2006: 111–12, 120–2]). Greimas and Fontanille (1991) outline a method for studying the discursive semantics of emotions using modal values and also aspectual categories such as perfective-imperfective and inchoative-terminative.

Whereas linguists from Saussure to Chomsky mainly use the dictionary as their model for word meaning, foregrounding existing signs with established meanings, text theorists frame their investigation within global and contextual frameworks and show how discourse forges new cognitive constructs such as ideas, actions, and characters, and how speakers transform familiar words to give them new senses specific to a given text. While Chomsky and other recent American linguists have concentrated on developing a complex and powerful sentence syntax, text theorists work from a set toward meaning and seek approaches that integrate linguistic and textual analysis. Theorists focus on devising relatively simple semantic representations of grammar that can point to how sentence structures contribute to elaborating text-whole narrative and communicative dynamics, to shaping the content, connotations, and cohesion of words in context at the lexical, micro-semantic level. Grammatical classes such as noun and verb can thus be compared to the narrative concepts of actor and action, as sentence-level case grammar categories such as subject and patient can be related to plot roles such as protagonist and antagonist. Sentences are interpreted as semantic propositions of action and predication which cumulatively construct global textual actors, objects, and processes, and which articulate collective identities, formulate social values, and communicate, sustain, or challenge stereotypes (Galatanu 1994, 2000).

For analysing theme and connotations,

and for studying words and their relation to the sentence and to longer strings, text theory defines semantic units such as the word in context (*sememe*), the dictionary word (*lexeme*), and differential semantic features (*semes*) (Greimas 1966; Hébert 2001; Pottier 1974, 1992; Rastier 1987, 1989 [1997: 33–40, 75–83]). Obtained by componential analyses somewhat comparable to phonological methods, the semes or semantic features comprise basic qualities of the cultural world, perceptual traits, and grammatical categories. Common pairs such as nature-culture and life-death often play a key role in organizing texts. Other traits correspond to dictionary classifiers that locate expressions within semantic fields defined by social practices, such as 'culinary,' 'maritime,' and 'botany.'

The recurrence of semantic features and their compounds along the spoken or written chain defines isotopy, a central concept that opens onto analyses of theme and topic, cohesion and coherence in discourse. Introduced by A.J. Greimas and developed by a host of continental scholars, the notion of isotopy plays a central role in Rastier's methodology (1987, 1989 [1997: 33–40, 101–31, 150–63, 168–84]; cf. Eco 1986: 189–201). Text theory investigates how to identify isotopies in short and in extensive discourses, how to define the relations among multiple isotopies in a work, and how to specify the interaction between isotopies and individual words in context. By identifying links among successive sentences and connections among units in different sentences, isotopic analysis helps account for discursive cohesion, one of the main concerns of 'text linguistics' (Adam 2005; Petöfi ed. 1979; Petöfi and Reiser eds. 1972; Schmidt 1976). Eco emphasizes that texts such as literary works possess sufficient complexity to allow for multiple isotopies and interpretations by different readers and analysts (1968).

Alongside studies of literature and popular culture, text theorists have applied and developed their methodologies in analyses of scientific discourse, exploring the linguistic and rhetorical procedures used to report experiments carried out, to characterize their results, to evoke or contest evidence, and to assess rival explanations (Bastide 2001; Greimas and Landowski eds. 1979; Greimas 1990: 11–91). Theorists investigate the mechanisms used to marshal critical passages of other scholars' publications within one's own argument and to integrate past research into a coherent narrative that launches a new inquiry. Descriptive studies show how scientific discourse expresses, combines, and at times suppresses modalities (e.g., certainty, uncertainty, necessity) in assessing the credibility of earlier conclusions and in formulating fresh hypotheses. Constructing themselves as anthropologists, Bruno Latour and Steve Woolgar examine a biochemical research lab, delineating the spatial design and movement entailed in its collective enunciations, establishing its division of labour and its technical support, and defining the key temporal variables and rhythms of the lab's activities (1986). The analysis reveals that each of the group's discursive venues (lab, article, textbook) privileges modalizations of a characteristic 'level,' producing statement types ranging from highly modalized hypotheses (lab), to qualified suppositions (article), and to fact (textbook, cf. Latour 1999).

While most scientific text theory has analysed verbal and non-verbal representations of communication, action, ideas, and emotions as rational processes engaging stabilized forms, since the 1980s research has also investigated phenomena that precede or elude such mechanisms, exploring descriptions of momentary breaks with familiar signs and routines, scrutinizing intuitions of novel emergent forms and significations. Studies examine the perceptual dynamics entailed in processing artefacts as novel or familiar signs and signifying schemata. Often returning to the philosophical phenomenology that undergirded some of the earliest text-theoretic research (e.g., Greimas 1966; cf. Holenstein 1975; Husserl 1936; Merleau-Ponty 1945), the new explorations dovetail with text-theoretic work in non-verbal media, especially music, visual images, and industrial design objects. In these media, sensible forms appear less closely tied to conventional meanings, even as they remain salient and elicit significant emotional responses. Research also engages and at times incorporates elements of contemporaneous cognitive linguistics that emphasizes embodied cognition, grounds discursive activity in perceptual and motor processes, and works closely with experimental psychology (e.g., Lakoff 1987; Lakoff and Johnson 1980; Langacker 1987–91; cf. Gibbs 2006). Emphasizing the new and widened perspectives, text theorists analyse aesthetics and the dynamics of the sensible, exploring the relations between the aesthetic and the ethical, between the sensible and the intelligible – and not only the relations between stable signs and signifying schemata representable as signifier and signified, as expression and content planes. Like Maurice Merleau-Ponty (1945) and James J. Gibson (1966, 1979), text theorists often emphasize the fusion of the senses in experience rather than their separation into distinct sense channels, foregrounding the rhythms and relations that combine and transcend data from the component 'modes' or 'modalities.'

Alongside earlier models of discrete, discontinuous states and their transformations, newer studies elaborate models of continuous and gradual phenomena and processes of becoming (e.g., Coquet 1997; Fontanille ed. 1995; Fontanille and Zilberberg 1998). Whereas earlier text theory often referenced logico-mathematical concepts and methods in the early twentieth-century tradition of Nicolas Bourbaki and David Hilbert, newer research highlights spatial and temporal schemata and the point of view of the observer (e.g., Fontanille 1999; Petitot 2004). While many earlier studies concentrate on defining textual dynamics as architectural mechanisms, identifying constituent units and specifying their relation to other components, some recent studies endeavour to describe experience, to depict the qualities that give impressions

their 'lived' effect (e.g., Landowski 2004). Whereas most earlier text theory adopts a retrospective vantage which crisply maps out all possibilities within a finite framework, the new research privileges an '*in act*' perspective that espouses the unfolding outlook of the subject who with limited, uncertain knowledge negotiates situations whose outcomes remain unknown or unforeseeable (Fontanille and Zilberberg 1998; Fontanille 1999; Landowski 2004: 66–9; cf. Bremond 1973).

The new topics examined do not fundamentally alter the core methodological steps that have always characterized text-theoretic approaches. For a given topic, researchers still gather an appropriate corpus, analyse it looking for appropriate models, check the hypotheses and schemata devised, define new concepts and procedures in relation to the existing theory, and organize and present findings according to didactic strategies. The resultant product still frequently takes the form of a close description invoking systematic schemata – but may also entail a more philosophical style.

Exploring aesthetic experience, A.J. Greimas's *De l'imperfection*('On Imperfection') focuses on exceptional, intense experiences that stand out against the backdrop of habitual sensations. The essay pays special attention to temporal and aspectual features of the phenomena and highlights synaesthesia and syncretism of different senses. Greimas (1987) proposes to investigate such moments of 'aesthesia' by attending first to those in which the most-studied sensory channel, vision, dominates, then forging into lesser-known senses including touch and hearing (cf. Landowski, Dorra, and de Oliveira eds. 1999). Landowski and Fiorin eds. (1997) develop Greimas's aesthetic concepts in wide-ranging explorations of 'good taste' and bad. A number of studies examine verbal renditions of gustatory experiences found in literature, journalism, historical essays, and dictionaries, such as drinking coffee and smoking Havana cigars, tasting wine and tippling beer. A gourmet's account of savouring freshly fried food highlights the anticipation that occupies the subject's entire body and mind and describes the simultaneous, synaesthetic bursts of flavour and aroma, of audible crackling and tactile crunchiness. The essays analyse the component perceptions and the overall sense impressions they compose, chart temporal dynamics such as successive unfolding in stages and isolated instants of sensation, and investigate the socialization and ritualization of gastronomic, oenological, and other hedonistic practices.

Non-Verbal Media

In the 1970s, text-theoretic semiotics began to develop methods for exploring non-verbal phenomena, beginning with architecture and visual images (in Floch 1990, 1995; Renier ed. 1984; Uspenskii 1971; Saint-Martin 1980, 1990; Thürlemann 1982; Zeitoun ed. 1979). Musical semiotics pursues postwar musicologists' efforts to go beyond purely formal analyses, to reclaim values associated with structures, and to delineate systematic relations between the two orders (Hatten 1998; cf. Meyer 1956). Drawing from both continental and North American semiotics, Eero Tarasti (1994) effects systematic transpositions of Greimas's generative model and of Peirce's sign typology that reinterpret each component in a profoundly musical sense. Tarasti applies his complex and flexible method in descriptive studies of works by Beethoven, Chopin, Debussy, and others (cf. 2002). Robert Hatten (1994, 2004) develops the concept of markedness or asymmetrical oppositions (Roman Jakobson, Michael Shapiro) to describe the connections between formal and expressive structures. Allusions to recognizable cultural and affective style types engender a complex texture, the juxtapositions and sequences forging each piece as a unique and unpredictable emergent synthesis. Close investigations of compositions in the Viennese classical tradition (Mozart, Shubert, and Beethoven) illustrate and elaborate the theory (cf. also Karbusicky 1986; Lerdahl and Jackendoff 1983; Monelle 2000; Nattiez 1975).

To date, however, the visual image, film, and design have emerged as the most vigorous arenas for non-verbal text theory and semiotics. Analyses of individual advertisements, photographs, and company logos examine the sensible qualities and organization of the image and their relation to its thematics. Jean-Marie Floch's studies investigate the socio-historical significations of representational and stylistic components and illustrate strategies for defining the 'visual identity' of a product or group (1990, 1995). His 'plastic semiotics' shows how such images as magazine advertisements and art photographs often select and correlate a limited number of perceptual and semantic categories in order to develop a characterized look and a clear message (e.g., 1990 [2001: 79–90]). The visual categories include contrasts of colour and tone, of topological axes and types of lines, and contrasts between eidetic types, especially abstract geometric forms. Fernande Saint-Martin's theoretical essays and close descriptions of paintings develop a 'toplogical semiology' inspired by gestalt psychology's work on vision, studying the role perceptually salient axes and points play in an image (1990). Groupe Mu has elaborated and illustrated a contemporary 'rhetoric of the image' that integrates research in the psychology and physics of perception. Their 1992 manual provides an introduction to issues and methods in early text-theoretic visual studies, while Göran Sonesson critically surveys foundational works in pictorial semiotics, including those of Floch, Groupe Mu, and Saint-Martin (1989).

Visual research inspired by these first steps has represented a particularly dynamic arena within text theory over the last three decades. The studies of photographs, modern and contemporary paintings, graphic conventions, and public spaces identify salient sensible contrasts in an image, construct broader systems of perceptual categories, describe the thematic and narrative content and its relation to the plastic dimension, and explore the visual rhetoric which the enunciative strategies elaborate. Parallel to the semantic concept of isotopy, Omar Calabrese (1985) proposes and illustrates visual *isography*, the integration of the image's sensible components, including visual and tactile. The essay studies the relations among several isographies in an image ('pluri-isography') and salient sensible rhythms set in relief against a dominant pattern ('allography'). Lucia Corrain and Mario Valenti (1991) analyse the plastic schemata of light and shadow found in early seventeenth-century paintings of nocturnal scenes and explores the unique relation the intimate religious or secular situations establish with the viewer. Articles in Dondero and Novello-Paglianti eds. (2006) examine the role syncretism among the senses plays in perceiving gardens and similar spaces (159–318), and explore the relation between image and text in alphabets and other forms of writing, in monogrammatic signatures, in painting, and in public gardens (9–158). Studying the contemporary stained glass windows that Pierre Soualges created for the twelfth-century Romanesque church in Conques, France, Marie Renoue (2001) analyses light as intensity, diffusion, and colour, and proposes classifications of types of lines and of surfaces in relief. Recent research analyses the resources, tactics, and values that condition specific kinds of photography today. Fontanille (2006) shows that the presentation techniques employed by a gourmet French chef serve as a visual rhetoric that communicates gustatory and tactile contrasts and suggests how each dish is to be eaten – occasionally venturing to amuse or even trick the client (in Beyaert-Geslin and Novello-Paglianti eds. 2005: 195–216). Inversely, in the case of print news photos studied by Beyaert-Geslin (2009), issues of truth and representation trump aesthetics: photojournalist, editor, and viewer are called above all to negotiate the proper distance between elucidation and discretion and to respect competing and complementary frameworks for evaluating the veracity of the image, which variously foreground the didactic, the contingent, or the unusual. Similarly, didactics generally takes precedence over aesthetics in the scientific uses

of photographic images examined by Dondero and Fontanille (2012). The book compares how researchers employ the visuals in their lab experiments, in their articles and conference papers (in conjunction with mathematics), and in textbooks. At times, photographs play a critical constitutive role in constructing the very object under investigation. Ethics and aesthetics come together in Dondero (2007), which analyses in detail work by a half dozen contemporary photographers who mobilize religious imagery. After sketching a theoretical definition of sacred photograhy, the study shows how certain artists use and transform iconographic traditions in the plastic arts, while others focus on developing new visual strategies to evoke fundamental human themes such as dignity, destiny, sickness, and death. Basso Fossali and Dondero (2006) retrace the evolution of text-theoretical approaches to visual images and outline novel proposals for employing C.S. Peirce's semiotics to explore photography. Sebeok and Umiker-Sebeok eds. (1995) and Lanigan ed. (2001) offer worldwide panoramas of related visual research, while Nöth ed. (1997) collects studies on the media, including graphic design and pictorial art, film, television and video, and computers. Corrain ed. (1999), Corrain and Valenti eds. (1991), Corrain ed. (2004), Hénault and Beyaert eds. (2004), and Parouty-David and Zilberberg eds. (2003) provide samples of (post-)Greimassian visual research, as do issues of the journals *Signata*, *Visio*, and *Visible* (Beyaert-Geslin and Novello-Paglianti eds. 2005; Dondero and Novello-Paglianti eds. 2006; Badir and Roelens eds. 2008; Gigante ed. 2008; cf. Carani 1994).

Casetti (1986) and Casetti and Di Chio (1997) outline methods for analysing film and television that combine text theory with the study of social context, technology, and the entertainment industry. Casetti (1986) identifies four fundamental cinematic points of view that can operate in a film: (1) objective camera, (2) unreal objective camera, and (3) subjective camera, which position the spectator respectively as witness, as movie camera, and as character.

The fourth point of view, interpellation, functions in the mode of an aside, directly addressing the audience (1986: 77–84, cf. 51–3). Outlining a multi-layered text-theoretic model that incorporates a significant pragmatic component, Roger Odin (2000) shows how cultural signifying practices define different types of films, and examines social factors that impinge on cinematic production (cf. Chateau 1986). Michel Colin (1992) and Warren Buckland (2000) propose to renovate cinematic text theory by bringing it into the cognitive paradigm, adapting Noam Chomsky's generative model and founding their models of comprehension in experimental psychology. Furthering new research on perception, Laura Marks (2000) analyses the effects generated by 'haptic visuality,' or tactile impressions conveyed by images, found in experimental 'intercultural' cinema made by exile and minority filmmakers who straddle at least two cultures. Desiderio Blanco (2003) illustrates and develops seven key recent Paris semiotic concepts by using each one to analyse a particular film, investigating such problematics as the phenomenology of presence, the veri-dictional contract that links the cinematic addresser and addressee, affective dynamics, aesthetic perception, and enunciative mechanisms. Paolo Peverini (2004) studies rhythm and editing strategies that construct the body and identity in that prime youth-culture medium, the music video, including the David Bowie production *Outside*. In a tour de force, Basso Fossali (2008a) studies the entire corpus of David Lynch's features, shorts, and television series in chronological order. Two visual strategies recur throughout the works: Lynch fragments the images into multiple parallel domains, each possessing its own autonomous set of representations and themes, and he uses the enunciative contract between cameraman and viewer to formulate metafilmic commentaries that take the onscreen images as their object.

Jean-Marie Floch's research derived from his work as a consultant has given impetus to text-theoretic studies in marketing and design (1990, 1995). Applying the methods he developed for visual images as well as a panoply of text-theoretic concepts, Floch and fellow theorists have established applied semiotic studies as an alternative to established multivariate methods. Focused on pronounced contrasts, the semiotic method has proven particularly effective in new or particularly complex markets lacking well-defined architectures, whereas the multivariate approach produces richer, more nuanced results useful for established contexts (Martial Pasquier, in Fontanille and Barrier eds. 1999: 107–14). Whereas multivariate analyses process from quantifiable verbal responses to a large volume of questionnaires, the qualitative semiotic study can analyse a multi-media corpus, examining actual products, open-ended interviews with users, on-site observations, verbal and visual advertisements, promotional materials, and logos. Requiring less time, cost, and personnel hours, the text-theoretic approach can also be used as a preliminary tactic, followed up by a multivariate study where appropriate.

Floch employs his plastic semiotics and the socio-historical interpretation of cultural forms to define the visual identity of a product or service (1990, 1995). Coco Chanel's pre-war daytime fashions for women thus counterpoise classical control, stability, and duration to baroque freedom, movement, and flash: sober, practical designs executed in natural colours and time-honoured cuts are enlivened by multicoloured embroidery, gaudy jewellery, and glittering chains (1995 [2000: 85–115]). By borrowing styles from labourers' uniforms and menswear, Chanel composed an image of the modern affluent female as an active woman who works, plays sports, and gets involved in public life. Comparative studies map a product or company vis-à-vis its rivals: Floch thus contrasts the strategies of rival European home-products companies Habitat and Ikea, and specifies material, mythical, and economic differences between the French Opinel penknife and the Swiss Army knife. Studies emphasize how the physical, spatial configuration of products, stores, and other sites favour or hinder various behaviours: office furniture configures intersubjective relations among workers, communicating relations of hierarchy and equality, facilitating or limiting collaborations. Essays on the Paris subway and on hypermarkets describe and categorize users based on how they interact with the layout and what they are looking for: some subjects go on autopilot, aiming to attain their goal with minimal output; others almost turn the outing into a game, staying attentive to every opportunity to be more effective; still others prefer a richer experience and remain open to distractions, surprises, and new discoveries.

Floch proposes a general 'grid of consumption values' that identifies key principles guiding subjects' aspirations and purchases. The schema transforms the fundamental design opposition between utility and aesthetics (e.g., Baudrillard 1968) into a four-point sequence and array. Use-oriented functionality subdivides into *critical* values, which highlight the subjects' strategic thinking, and *practical* values, which emphasize properties of the object itself, both axiologies focusing on usefulness and de-emphasizing higher-order desiderata. The contrasting aesthetic attitude subdivides into *ludic* values that entail acting on impulse, catering to a whim, or seeking out products with specific sensible qualities, while *utopian* values express a subject's ideal self-image. In a temporal mode, Floch's grid traces a household's successful progression throughout the years, while in a classificatory mode, it can categorize such images as the types of car ads that air on TV (Floch 1990 [2001: 108–37], 1995 [2000: 116–25]).

Studies by Jean-Marie Floch and others (e.g., Umiker-Sebeok ed. 1987) have inspired considerable text-theoretic work in marketing, which also draws from research in visual images, space and architecture, the natural world, social discourse, and everyday practices (Basso Fossali 2008b; Ceriani 1997; Ceriani ed. 1998; Deni ed. 2002; Fontanille and Barrier eds. 1999; Fontanille and Zinna eds. 2005; Landowski

and Marrone eds. 2001; Semprini ed. 1990). Rather than limiting their role to that of the critic positioned outside of and after the creative process, contemporary studies follow Floch in emphasizing the contribution that text theorists can play in developing, presenting, and distributing products. Andrea Semprini (1993) uses Floch's quaternary schema of consumer values to explore how marketing strategies can construct, protect, dilute, and transform commercial brand names. Pezzini and Cervelli eds. (2006) investigate the interaction between subjects and two main sites, retail outlets and museums, focusing on practices performed, qualitative experience, and cultural context. Attentive to social perspectives, Nicolas Couégnas and Erik Bertin eds. (2005) study packaging, strategic planning, and other marketing issues in an endeavour to further Floch's 'concrete semiotics' that aims to rejuvenate theoretical perspectives through descriptive case studies. Marc Monjou (2007) examines a recently inaugurated municipal swimming pool in Bordeaux, France, identifying dysfunctional design aspects, confusing layout, and poor communication and signage. Fabienne Plegat-Soutjis emphasizes that each series in a publishing house must define an identity at once visual and thematic, then establish the necessary communicative structures so that the various services that select, produce, and promote the books work together, yielding harmonious graphic and verbal content and style throughout the series' books and in all the material put out by the commercial, advertising, and press divisions (in Fontanille and Barrier eds. 1999: 115–22). Basso Fossali (2008b) outlines theses for the study of cultural practices and communication, then develops the ideas in studying contemporary consumer habits, brand strategies, packaging designs, lifestyles and their relation to product identity, and print, television, and radio advertising.

Denis Bertrand analyses the biochemical paradigm that has played such a prominent role in advertisements for food, dietary supplements, and personal care products since the early 1990s (in Couégnas and Bertin eds. 2005: 37–48). In addition to liberally sprinkling its images and discourse with the statistics and terminology of organic chemistry, the new framework displaces the focus from the external world to the individual's internal body, from the relation between self and others to that between the self and itself. Fragmenting both product and user, the new rhetoric personifies the commodity, which speaks and acts independently, and metonymically transforms corporeal part into whole: finger nails and hair must eat well in order to grow strong and healthy. The global, enveloping body becomes transparent, revealing its inner components as autonomous sensing and deciding agents.

The semiotics of design studies decorative or instrumental industrial objects mass-produced as commodities but incorporating aesthetic refinements that position them in between engineering and art. A particular designer's distinctive touch imparts a look that raises the object above the level of simple use and exchange value. Text-theoretic design research concentrates on communication issues, on the customer's overall experience, and on the user's interaction with the object, rather than on its physics, technology, electronics, or manufacturing. Recent studies make use of André Leroi-Gourhan's work on how tools guide and constrain their use by humans, and employ James Gibson's concept of *affordance* as applied to everyday objects by Donald Norman (Leroi-Gourhan 1943–5; Gibson 1966, 1979; Norman 1988, 2002). Integrating cultural theory, Andrea Semprini (1995) shows that far from functioning as an inert passive substance, the quotidian object of material culture exerts its agency as an implement that transforms other products in characterized ways, that configures spaces and interactions, and that contributes to defining the practices of daily life. Gianfranco Marrone (1999) describes the communicative processes and intersubjective experience that the traditional corded telephone constructs for its users. Alessandro Zinna (2004) examines

perceptual and communicative dynamics specific to new electronic media, investigating the Mac interface as a perceptual and symbolic interaction between human and machine. Michela Deni (2002) defines the effectiveness and the *user-friendliness* of contemporary commodities as a relation between their operational and communicative functionality. The shape and the contrastive materials and colours used in new ergonomic toothbrushes represent cognitive enhancements that help convey to the user where they are to be grasped and how they should be used, while recent swivel-head razors function in a more purely 'factitive' manner, since even without such a preliminary perceptual 'apprenticeship,' their mobility renders them more effective. Such design issues are all the more fundamentally semiotic in that whatever the reality, the item's appearance must convince potential buyers of its usability, judged according to the parameters commonly applied to its particular commodity category (cf. Beyaert-Geslin 2012).

New theoretical perspectives prepare, complement, and take account of the research in visuality, marketing, and design. Methods initially focused on action and interaction have reversed their perspectives to highlight perception and the object. Just as intersubjectivity refers to associations and interactions among subjects, 'interobjectivity' designates connections and interdependencies among objects: paradigmatic interobjective relations include classifications, hierarchies, circulation within narratives, and transformations and cycles of an object, while syntagmatic relations include arrangements, combinations, and interplay of objects co-present within a concrete or virtual space-time continuum (Deni 2002; Landowski and Marrone eds. 2002). Jean-François Bordron (1991, 2011) draws from phenomenology and semiotics to define the object from an eidetic perspective, considering it as a possible object of perception (cf. Ouellet 1992). Focusing on the categories of part-whole, genus-species, and rank, the essay identifies twelve types of 'wholes' defined by the kinds of parts each comprises, its relation between parts and whole, and the relations among parts, which results in distinctions between composition, configuration, architecture, agglomeration, chain, fusion, figure, aggregate, atom, and extension. Jean Petitot follows René Thom (1975) in using catastrophe theory to renovate the concept of organic morphology developed by Goethe and Cuvier. His analyses of Proust's and Stendhal's fiction demonstrate how simple topological forms generate more complex narrative schemata and discursive configurations (2004). Exemplifying structured neo-connectionist research, Petitot's approach incorporates simulations of dynamical systems and higher-order symbolic schemata to model neural activity as a continuous process of forming and breaking interconnected patterns and forms (Petitot ed. 1994; Petitot and Barbaras 2002).

As Petitot (2004) revises the classic generative semiotic model, other recent research also integrates the new theories of perception, visuality, and the object within established continental theories of signification, narrative, and the subject. Jacques Fontanille demonstrates how models of thinking, feeling, and interacting can be used to study cultural practices central to design and marketing: his essay on luxury sketches its distinctive anthropological structures of exchange, identifies its characteristic emotional dynamics, and traces the defining interactions of its constituent agent roles (in Couégnas and Berin eds. 2005: 103–27). In addition to the 'transformational actants' engaged in narrative action, Fontanille identifies 'positional actants' that model subjects' perception and enunciation (cf. 1999 [2006: 103–10]). Elsewhere, Fontanille proposes that alongside the content models that text theory has defined, such as narrative, modal, and enunciative schemata, the sensible world is articulated at the successively more comprehensive levels of sign, text, object, situation, and 'form of life' (in Fontanille and Zinna eds. 2005: 193–203). Fontanille (2012) and Coquet (1997, 2007) outline complementary theoretical frameworks that found

text theory in phenomenology. Conjoining an attention to social practices and a phenomenological perspective, Eric Landowski argues that subjects do not experience fashion trends as constraints imposed from without so much as opportunities to attune themselves to the ever-novel present, to adhere more fully to the becoming in which they find themselves engaged (1997: 115–16). From the vantage of a 'cultural semiotics,' François Rastier (2004) analyses money as a social object at the intersection of ethics and economics, defining it in a typology of things, in action sequences (e.g., bodies → objects → waste), and in interpretative paths that construct tools and signs (e.g., works, myths, rituals). Objects such as money are constituted differently in three successively wider zones of perception: subjective, intersubjective, and impersonal (I, 'identitary'; thou, 'proximate'; he and she, 'distal').

Critical French Text Theory

Roland Barthes, Jacques Derrida, Michel Foucault, Julia Kristeva, and other critical French theorists investigate convergences of language and power, animadvert upon the erosion of communication, promote experimental cultural productions, and advocate alternative social practices. Foucault turns against central features of the linguistic and semiotic paradigm that informed his first books when he envisages a renovated Enlightenment project in which 'criticism is no longer going to be practiced in the search for formal structures with universal value … it is not seeking to make possible a metaphysics that has finally become a science; it is seeking to give new impetus, as far and wide as possible, to the undefined work of freedom' (1984: 45–6). In this pursuit, historiography must model itself not on signification or communication but on conflict: 'The history which bears and determines us has the form of a war rather than that of a language: relations of power, not relations of meaning' (Foucault 1977, in 1984: 56). Emphasizing the historical character of cultural beliefs, the North American theorist Joan Wallach Scott (1988) asserts that the malleability of a social category like gender can encourage a committed, idealist scholar to endeavour to 'make a difference' and not just study one: 'It is precisely by exposing the illusion of the permanence or enduring truth of any particular knowledge of sexual difference that feminism necessarily historicizes history and politics and opens the way for change' (1988: 10–11). A number of text theorists emphasize that the critical stance must extend to the researcher's own subject position, methodology, and findings. Kristeva defines the semiotics she proposes as 'a constant critique that refers back to itself, that is, that critiques itself … Thus any semiotics can only be practiced as a critique of semiotics' (1969: 30–1; cf. Scott 1988: 8). Accepting the heritage of the existentialist problematic of the Other (subject), critical text theory questions the hierarchical relation that has traditionally positioned the analyst on a plane above the analysand, the (typically Western) anthropologist over the (usually non-Western) indigenous subject studied (Deleuze and Guattari 1972; Geertz 1975; cf. De Beauvoir 1949).

Contesting the binarism they see prevalent in culture and enshrined in cybernetics, linguistics, and structuralism, critical text theorists search for alternatives in at times a utopian spirit. Derrida thus refuses 'the binary difference that governs the decorum of all codes,' the 'implacable destiny which immures everything for life in the figure 2' (1982 [1991: 455]). His deconstructionism contends that the essays that found modern philosophy and science set up core dichotomies of mind vs matter, form vs substance, and speech vs writing, such that they privilege the first term over the second in each instance, purporting to retain and promote the first while rejecting the second. Derrida's readings show that instead, at key junctures in the foundational essays, the paired terms substitute for each other, exchange values, or become inextricably linked. In the deconstructionist view, far from pointing up mere foibles in the writers' prose or formal aporias in

language, the works thereby illustrate key mechanisms of Western thought and society: pervasive and ultimately repressive 'logocentrism' idealizes speech and reason, erroneously presenting material and symbolic procedures as purely mental, spiritual processes. The authors purvey the view that philosophical, social-scientific, and moral issues can be worked out with the rigour and universality of algebra or geometry that transcend metaphor and neutralize the idiosyncrasies of particular cultures and languages. Derrida began applying his approach to explore questions in tune with topical issues in the 1980s, speaking and writing in support of then-imprisoned Nelson Mandela, and investigating key principles at stake in debates on immigration, such as fraternity, hospitality, and democracy (Derrida and Mandela 1986; Derrida 1994; Derrida and Dufourmantelle 1997).

For Joan Wallach Scott, the forces of social change wield a deconstructionist logic: 'Contests about meaning involve the introduction of new oppositions, the reversal of hierarchies, the attempt to expose repressed terms, to challenge the natural status of seemingly dichotomous pairs, and to expose their interdependence and their internal instability' (1988: 7, cf. 41). The feminist scholar armed with text-theoretic concepts is no longer relegated to circumscribed empirical research that incrementally adds new information about women's condition at a given place and time, but can critically examine the changing overall framework of a society's conceptions about gender (Scott 1988: 2–5).

Rejecting exclusionist 'either-or' logics as well as linear and narrative triadic dialectics (Hegel, Marx), critical text theorists privilege instead 'neither-nor' (circumvention), 'both-and' (neutralization), in-between logics (gradualism), and dispersed multiplicities (decentralization) that elude dichotomies and fracture totalities. Barthes thus argues that literature given over to negating art in its current vitiated state only leads to irrelevance or recuperation, whereas the *pleasurable* text succeeds by a *subtle subversion* through which it 'evades the paradigm, and seeks some *other* term: a third term, which is not, however, a synthesizing term but an eccentric, extraordinary term' (1973 [1975: 55]). Sceptical of teleological narratives and their overly ambitious syntheses, Foucault opposes efforts to import 'the categories of cultural totalities (whether world-views, ideal types, the particular spirit of an age)' (1969 [1995: 15, cf. 16]). He gives prominence instead to methods that emphasize the complexity and heterogeneity of societies and the coexistence of parallel, superimposed processes that operate on different chronological scales (e.g., Fernand Braudel's three durations) to trace the 'space of a dispersion' rather than a single movement, whole, or crystalline structure (Foucault 1969 [1995: 10, 15–16]). Against the injunction to desire *either* men *or* women, Hélène Cixous calls for a bisexuality that embraces instances of both genders within each individual (1975 [1986: 85]). Similarly, for Derrida, the response to the question 'What is poetry?' 'is lost in anonymity, between city and nature, an imparted secret, at once public and private, *absolutely* one and the other, absolved from within and from without, neither one nor the other' (1991: 223). Viewing the elementary building blocks of language such as sentence structure and vocabulary as ideological frameworks, feminist text theorists formulate key terms such as 'woman' as critical notions that necessarily defy positive definitions. Kristeva asserts: 'In "woman" I see something that cannot be represented, something that is not said, something above and beyond nomenclatures and ideologies' (1974, in Marks and de Courtivron eds. 1980: 137). Such strategies for escaping binary injunctions while circumventing the totalizing schemata of productive negation and dialectics develop Lévi-Strauss' critique of Sartre's Marxist theory of praxis (Lévi-Strauss 1962 [1966: 245–69]; Sartre 1960).

Critiquing the model of the 'branching tree diagram' in which roots and limbs sprout from a main trunk in orderly fashion, a schema widely used in historical linguistics, in continental structuralism, and in Chomsky's grammar, Gilles Deleuze and Félix Guattari propose the alternative of the rhizome: 'In contrast to centered (even polycentric) systems with hierarchical modes of communication and preestablished paths, the rhizome is an acentered, nonhierarchical, nonsignifying system without a General and without an organizing memory or central automaton, defined solely by a circulation of states' (Deleuze and Guattari 1980, in Deleuze 1993: 36). Whereas for Derrida, Deleuze, and Lacan, the centred subject largely represents an illusion, an interested or delusional fiction, Foucault and Fredric Jameson at times argue that contemporary society has transformed the genuinely centred subject of modernity into a decentred, fragmented postmodern subject deprived of agency and bereft of aesthetic intensity. Jean-François Lyotard defines the late twentieth-century postmodern era as 'incredulity toward metanarratives,' as a disbelief in the unifying religious and political, artistic and philosophical frameworks from which industrial societies drew their values and judged events (1979 [1984: 31–7]). In the absence of such grand, transcendent schemes, contemporary populations deploy 'little narratives,' or multifarious local, occasional, and circumstantial strategies that inform their planning and decision making (1979 [1984: 37–49]).

Paul Ricoeur notes that 'the parallelism between text theory, action theory, and the theory of history is immediately suggested by the *narrative* genre of discourse' (1977 [1986: 183]). Exploring the '"content of the form" of narrative discourse in historical thought,' the historian Hayden White (1973) uses text theory to show that 'narrative, far from being merely a form of discourse that can be filled with different contents, real or imaginary as the case may be, already possesses a content prior to any actualization of it in speech or writing' (1987: xi). White notes that in the most radical text-theoretic formulations, narrative structures themselves represent 'semiological apparatuses that produce meanings' that can function as social myths affording subjects 'imaginary relations to their real conditions of existence' and advancing the political ends of particular groups (1987: x). The Middle-Eastern historian Edward Said argues that Western discourse has constructed myths of the 'Orient' which enjoy the social force of reality: Europeans' and North Americans' travel logs, exotic novels, and pictorial art, as well as their scholarship, curricula, and institutes devoted to training colonial administrators cumulatively generate an image of the East as an inverted, partly wished-for and partly feared picture of the West (1978). Similarly, Benedict Anderson demonstrates how nineteenth-century Latin American nationalist discourse, institutions, and state practices developed 'imagined communities' possessing very real, substantive effect (1991).

Arguing that Western societies' attitudes toward their signs have changed fundamentally over time, text theorists have proposed macro-chronologies that identify successive eras or 'epistemes,' including medieval, classical, modernist, and postmodernist, defining each epoch by its semiotic economy (Baudrillard 1983; Foucault 1966: 11–16; Kristeva 1969: 116–19). Jean Baudrillard thus describes the classical period as characterized by a metaphysics of depth in which the signifier is tied to a signified grounded in a univocal, fixed referent. This transcendent regime contrasts with that of the modern industrial age transformed by democratization in which the relation between signifier and signified becomes indirect. In the ensuing contemporary postmodern era, depth and reference disappear altogether, leaving signifiers to evoke signifieds freely in a play of mere surfaces (Baudrillard 1983: 7–9). Efrat Tseëlon (1992) illustrates Baudrillard's corresponding three 'orders of simulacra' in the domain of clothing: classical dress functions in the counterfeit mode, imitating and reflecting the natural and divine social order, while modernist apparel works in a productive mode, its subtle signifier nuances evoking social distinctions defined through moral values of taste and elegance. Postmodernist styles illustrate the mode

of simulation, in which sartorial signifiers from Third World saris and jellabas to black mourning crepe and military camouflage circulate among Westerners today as purely aesthetic forms divorced from reference to history or external reality (Tseëlon 1992).

The attention that such figures as Michel Foucault, Judith Butler, Edward Said, and Joan Wallach Scott devote to discourse, culture, and identity differentiates their analyses from earlier critical methodologies more focused on technology, geography, and economics. The Nietzschean 'genealogy' which Foucault formulated in the early 1980s adopts the *Annales* and structuralist embrace of a wealth of materials, not just archival but also literary, architectural, artistic, and corporeal – even though the method rejects the concepts of 'total history' and functional wholes. In one sense, the importance that critical text theorists attribute to discourse and the media, including advertising and the entertainment business, updates Marxism, complementing the latter's socio-economic analysis of the industrial West with a cultural critique of post-industrial consumerism.

Critical Literary Theory

After 1968, Roland Barthes distanced himself from the approaches informed by linguistics and the social sciences that had inspired his research on semiology, literature, fashion, film, and advertising for nearly two decades. Giving freer rein to more subjective, intuitive, and Nietzschean perspectives, *S/Z* (1970) and more decisively still *The Pleasure of the Text* (1973) value the reader's private pleasure over objective truth or scientific knowledge, highlight indefinable and ineffable qualities rather than concepts, terminology, and methodology, and celebrate unlimited polysemy over finite ambiguities and prioritized levels of interpretation. Whereas the critiques of petit-bourgeois culture in his earlier *Writing Degree Zero* and *Mythologies* evince the committed, pro–working class perspectives of Bertolt Brecht's theatre project and of Jean-Paul Sartre's existential Marxism, *The*

Pleasure of the Text adds significant aristocratic, sybaritic notes in evoking a refined experience of individual jubilation and ecstasy inaccessible to hoi polloi and to mass media: 'No significance (no bliss) can occur, I am convinced, in a mass culture … for the model of this culture is middle-class … The asocial character of bliss: it is the abrupt loss of sociality' (1973 [1975: 38–9]).

Mindful of philosophical, psychoanalytical, and symbolic interpretations as much as of linguistic definitions, Barthes's later work presents the order of the signified as static, closed, conventional, and intolerant, promoting the signifier as the sphere of movement, openness, and plurality. His Text is the realm of 'the signifier's infinite' (1971: 72), of the 'unpredictable flashes of language's infinites' (1973 [1994: 1685]). Asserting ludic and artistic values, the later Barthes declares that 'textual analysis refuses the idea of a final signified: the work doesn't stop, doesn't close itself off; it is less a question of explaining or even of describing, than of entering into the play of signifiers … textual analysis is pluralistic' (1973 [1994: 1688]). For Barthes, the commonality of the linguistic signifier-signified circuit that defines communication and founds language as a collective process inevitably ties meaning to orthodoxy (Saussure 1916 [1959: 11–15]). He foregrounds an organic and innocent 'letter' tied to the imaginary (cf. Lacan 1966) at the expense of shared semantic structures instituted by social law and prohibition. Privileging the kinetic corporeality of the signifier, the sensuous texture of the 'writerly' text resembles cinematic dialogues when we hear 'their materiality, their sensuality, the breath, the gutturals, the fleshiness of the lips, a whole presence of the human muzzle' (1973 [1975: 67]). Barthes's visceral distaste for commercial and institutional control over art and ideas leads him to proclaim hermeneutic anarchy: 'As the Order of the signifier, the Text participates in its fashion in a social utopia … it is the space in which no way of speaking has an edge over another' (1971: 77). Systematically contesting methodologies that use their scientific bases to limit or deny the individual reader's agency and subjectivity, Barthes invites reading a work through the lens of literature with which the reader but not the writer is familiar, and welcomes interpretations that run counter to a work's original socio-historical context and to its author's intention (1971).

Barthes's post-1968 work describes the ideal artistic experience as 'erotic,' thereby designating not only the sensual pleasure it can stir, but also more specifically a subjective dynamic common to aesthetic and sexual experience: 'Text theory … is a science of *bliss*, for every "textual" text (implicated in the field of significance) ultimately tends to induce or to experience the *loss of consciousness* (the nullification) which the subject fully assumes in erotic bliss' (1973 [1994: 1689]). The supreme textual encounter defines the contemporary historical subject as a 'living contradiction,' a tension between the constitution and the dissolution of the self, a 'split subject, who simultaneously enjoys, through the text, the consistency of his selfhood and its collapse, its fall' (1973 [1975: 21]).

Julia Kristeva analyses modernistic and avant-garde literature as radically different from the everyday communication described by mainstream contemporary linguistics such as Chomsky's generative grammar. The patterned violations of norms found in the artistic texts are attributed to traumas in the writer's youth or later experience and to social disruptions tied to historical crises. Kristeva terms the text perceived as a *phenomenon* in the form of published material, familiar grammatical structures, and known phonetic or graphic articulations the 'pheno-text'; she labels the processes that *generate* the experimental effects the 'geno-text' (1969: 278–89). Like Deleuze and Guattari's rhizome – and Jacques-Alain Miller's Lacanian mechanism of suture – Kristeva's geno-text comprises a purely differential, indexical, and materialist 'logic of the signifier' which, conjoined to historical, ideological forces as well as to grammar, occupies the place of pride which Greimas's generative model reserves for deep, universal semantic structures (Kristeva 1969: 287; Miller 1966; cf. Greimas and Courtés 1993 [1982: 'Generative Trajectory']). Emphasizing the psychoanalytic component of her approach, Kristeva distinguishes two parallel fundamental signifying modes whose interactions define corresponding types of textual practices (1974: 17–30). 'Semiotic' processes linked to early childhood when the infant lives in a dyadic relation with the mother manifest themselves as rhythmic impulses and expressive sounds; they redirect the individual's energy and drives through condensation and displacement. 'Symbolic' processes associated with later, post-Oedipal developments structure the subject's action on the world, govern communicative interaction with others, and inform the transformations these dynamics bring about in the person and in history. Selective research in expressive phonetics, speech pathologies, psychoanalytic treatments, poetics, and aesthetics investigates semiotic phenomena; while semantics, modal logic, pragmatics, speech act theory, and the linguistics of the enunciation analyse symbolic processes. Kristeva has concentrated on exploring the interface between the two signifying orders and on defining the characterized types of productions their conjunctions engender.

The text theory inspired by Barthes and Kristeva evinces a preference for literature that cultivates multiple meanings, connotations, and intertextual resonances, for artistic writing that features striking cadences and sonorities, for works that overwhelm, defy, or subvert generic boundaries, common interpretive conventions, and middle-class standards of taste. Tzvetan Todorov emphasizes that for Kristeva, 'the text has always functioned as a *transgressive* field with regard to the system according to which our perception, our grammar, our metaphysics, and even our scientific knowledge are organized' (1966: 357). Receiving special attention are authors largely ignored or marginalized in their time but retrospectively considered precursors of modernism and postmodernism, such as François Rabelais, Laurence Sterne, the

marquis de Sade, the comte de Lautréamont, and Franz Kafka. Also enjoying particular consideration are writers whose difficult language denied them a widespread readership in their day, like Stéphane Mallarmé, the later James Joyce, and practitioners of such postwar experimental narrative currents as the *nouveau roman* in France, the *Nuevo Narrativo* and novel of the 'boom' in Latin America, and the Spanish neo-baroque. At the same time, Barthes famously found rich 'textual' phenomena in works by the most canonical of authors, from the duc de La Rochefoulcauld and Montesquieu to Chateaubriand and that paragon of Realism, Honoré de Balzac (e.g., Barthes 1970).

Critical Film Theory

Roland Barthes's rhetoric of the image inspired Christian Metz to investigate how text-theoretical concepts can effectively explore 'the cinematic apparatus' (1968–73, 1970, 1977, 1991). Metz's theoretical essays and his analyses of films by Sergei Eisenstein, Alfred Hitchcock, Jean-Luc Godard, and other directors emphasize that cinema differs greatly from language (and also from the fixed image) (1968 [1974: 108–16, cf. 60–91]). Live-action movies typically display representations more than signs: the relation between cinematic signifier and signified is largely motivated rather than primarily arbitrary, the filmic images are not doubly articulated as are linguistic signs, nor are they systematically organized by any schema comparable to sentence structure, phonology, or morphology. Furthermore, unlike speech, a film functions more as (one-way) expression than as (two-way) communication. Yet within specific cinematic traditions and genres, Metz identifies units and combinatorial patterns which depend on techniques that function as conventional codes, including aspects of framing, depth of field, camera movement, and shot combinations. His seminal study of the 'large syntagmatic category' thus defines the immediate visual constituents of the fictional narrative film as a paradigm of eight terms, each one defined by its distinctive syntagmatic organization of images, especially shots, such as chronological or achronological, simultaneous vs consecutive, alternating (i.e., ABABAB …) vs linear (AAAA …), and continuous vs discontinuous (1968 [1974: 119–37, 145–6]). Chase scenes typically align alternating shots, switching back and forth from pursuer to pursued, whereas the most straightforward narratives adopt a linear arrangement, for example. Metz and Michèle Lacoste illustrate, refine, and extend the model in analyses of Jacques Rozier's 1962 film *Adieu Philippine* (in Metz 1968 [1974: 149–82]). Beginning in the early 1970s, a number of theorists following Metz or striking out in new directions have developed an array of approaches to film inspired by text theory (Andrew 1984; Bellour 1979; Dusi 2003; Ivanov, Lotman, Zholkovsky 1981; Kälberer 2000–5; Lotman 1973; Miller and Stam eds. 1999: 45–63, 84–104, 123-145; Möller-Nass 1986; Silverman 1983; Simon and Vernet eds. 1983; Zizek 2001).

On the enunciative plane, as personal pronouns and other shifters explicitly insert subjects into verbal discourse, the viewing subject is 'sutured' into film through such devices as the shot-reverse-angle-shot sequence commonly used to shoot face-to-face conversations: a shot of character A implicitly situates the spectator as a second, off-screen character B looking at the first character on-screen, while the next image, shot from the reverse angle, shows the second character B from the vantage of the first character A now off-screen, and so forth, thus 'stitching' the viewer and her off-screen site into the cinematic space (Oudart 1969; Heath 1977–8; cf. Hayward 2000: 382–5). A film can orchestrate such techniques in order to construct a particular subject position from which the work becomes intelligible – a tactic which can advance the goal of enticing the viewer to enter into and reproduce the industry's ideology. Drawing on Lacan, Metz argues that the spectator identifies with the addressee thus constructed: the viewer fetishizes the film images, entertaining a partial 'suspension of disbelief' even while recognizing their illusory status (1975 in Hollows, Hutchings, and Jancovich, eds. 2000: 213–18, cf. 194–5). The entertainment industry can attempt to utilize such subject-position devices as part of an effort to encourage spectators to consume filmic fantasies – enjoyed, like dreams, in the dark – which promise happy endings to every conflict. More generally, cinematic devices suture together in an apparently seamless whole the viewer's infantile pleasurable identification with eye candy and action stars, on the one hand, and his critical observations of techniques and codes, on the other. Metz's last book examines enunciation, studying traces or representations of the movie's productive process, including shots of equipment and crew, 'camera-look' shots, the device of the film within the film, certain types of off-screen voices, cinematic point of view, and distinctive directorial styles (1991, cf. Casetti 1986).

Other film theorists have developed Metz's work by placing it in dialogue with parallel contemporary approaches. Led by the journal *Camera Obscura*, British and North American theorists have confronted the textual perspective with feminist projects (e.g., De Lauretis 1987; Silverman 1983). Laura Mulvey (in Penley ed. 1988: 57–68) argues that the ways commercial movies conjugate the eyes of camera, spectator, and actors cater to male viewers by objectifying and devaluing female characters, and by using fetishism, voyeurism, and sadism to defuse the threat posed by strong women in films. Critics have subsequently argued that spectators fluidly espouse an array or sequence of different perspectives within a single film, including masculine and feminine personas (Hollows et al. eds. 2000: 229–32).

Text Theory and English-Language Approaches

Initiated and led today by continental figures, text theory can be compared to certain English-language approaches, including currents in sociolinguistics and sociology, discourse analysis and critical linguistics, literary criticism informed by linguistics and by philosophy, and qualitative marketing research attuned to communication and cultural symbolisms. Text theorists' fundamental choices also resonate with recent work in cultural anthropology and in postmodern studies. Indeed, viewed from a North American vantage, text theory's overall project resembles an anthropology that develops its models of behaviour and belief systems not through data gathered in field research but through an analysis of lived experience as constructed in discourse and other cultural productions. The continental approach rejoins more empirical Anglo-American sensibilities through its emphasis on textual description and on methodology, on the close analysis of artefacts using explicitly-defined procedures and terms.

Text theory has affinities with Erving Goffman's research on the ritualization of social behaviour and interaction, including discourse, non-verbal communication, and visual advertising (1967, 1979). It evinces parallels with John Gumperz's interactional sociolinguistics focused on intercultural communication and on the crucial role social context and power relations play in determining linguistic variation and conversational interpretations and inferences (1981). Greimas's and Rastier's linguistic analyses of 'isotopy' can be compared to anglophone research on cohesion in discourse beyond the limits of the sentence (Brown and Yule 1983; Stubbs 1983; van Dijk and Kintsch 1983; van Dijk ed. 1997). In literary studies, the continental approaches resemble English-language theory and criticism oriented toward formal, structural, and stylistic analysis and away from traditional historical perspectives, such as the new rhetorics aimed at textual analysis developed by Kenneth Burke (1945) and Wayne Booth (1961), and the poetics of the Chicago School and the New Criticism. A double cultural and cognitive turn has drawn research akin to continental narratology away from a concern for universals and typologies and toward realism in both

the outer social and natural world and in the inner, psychological sphere. The result includes a variegated patchwork of local narratologies focused on a specific region, gender, ethnicity, or political practice, informed by poetics, rhetoric, phenomenology, and empirical psychological research (e.g., Fludernik 1996; Genette 2004; Grünzweig and Solbach eds. 1999; Herman ed. 1999, 2002, 2003).

Continental textual and discursive semantics (e.g., Greimas 1966; Groupe Mu 1970; Rastier 1987, 1989) shares significant features with the contemporary cognitive linguistics and poetics developed by such scholars as Gilles Fauconnier, Mark Johnson, George Lakoff, and Mark Turner (Fauconnier and Turner 2002; Johnson 1987; Lakoff and Johnson 1980; Lakoff 1987; Turner 1996). Turning against the formal, asemantic syntax defined by Chomsky's standard theory, today's cognitive grammar reclaims the continental structuralist model of the sign as a signifier-signified dyad, the schema which runs throughout text theory: Ronald Langacker thus defines linguistic expressions and constructions as comprising a 'phonological pole' and a 'semantic pole' (Langacker 1987: 76–7, 93–4; Saussure 1916 [1959: 65–70]). Greimas's analyses of enunciative 'engagement' and 'disengagement' (or 'shifting-in' and 'shifting out') can be compared to Gilles Fauconnier's cognitive studies of 'space builders,' as Paris semiotic narrative models parallel Leonard Talmy's outline of a 'Cognitive Framework for Narrative Structure' (Fauconnier 1985; Greimas and Courtés 1993 [1982: 'Engagement,' 'Disengagement']; Talmy 2000: vol. 2, 417–82).

Like text theory, M.A.K. Halliday's systemic and functional linguistics analyses discourse beyond the sentence, examines connections between verbal interactions and social relations and purposes (Halliday's 'interpersonal function'), and investigates the role ideology plays in speech (Halliday 1978; Halliday and Hassan 1985; Hodge and Kress 1988; Kress 1989; Martin and Rose 2003; Wodak and Chilton eds. 2005; Young and Harrison eds. 2004).

Halliday-inspired 'critical linguistics' has studied narrative fiction, exploring point of view and its implications for modals and truth conditions in discourse (Simpson 1993; cf. Thibault 1991). Like text theorists, practitioners of the approach have extended its purview to visual communication, including television (Hodge and Tripp 1986; Kress and Van Leeuwen 1996).

Text theorists view each of their separate studies as part of an evolving project to develop an overall theory of language in relation to cognition and to society. This objective remains less common in the more practical world of the language sciences in English. However, Jerome Bruner (1986, 1990), Noam Chomsky (1966, 1968, 1988), Jerry Fodor (1983), George Lakoff (1987), and Kenneth Pike (1967) have proposed similarly ambitious, wide-reaching theories that attempt to specify in some detail the architecture of language and its interconnections to thought, the human organism, and society.

In the field of marketing, text-theoretical approaches are akin to research on lifestyles, which complements basic socio-demographic data by devising more detailed and nuanced profiles of consumer types that highlight their personality and mood (e.g., Mitchell 1983). Similarly, research by Jean-Marie Floch and fellow continental theorists rejoin essential features of qualitative North American marketing research that highlights the symbolic dimension and aims to analyse and shape consumers' experience with products and services (e.g., Mick 1995).

Like many critical text theorists such as Barthes and Kristeva, Clifford Geertz's cultural anthropology argues for cultural pluralism and questions universalism, draws attention to the interpretative activity integral to research, and analyses the effect that the scientist has on the milieu studied and on the data generated (Geertz 1975). Like text theory, postmodern studies foregrounds language and other social codes, decentres the subject, critiques claims to objective knowledge, and makes use of the language arts to analyse new cultural forms (e.g., Charles Jencks's *double-coding*; Bertens and Natoli 2002). English-language theorists influential in defining postmodern studies have drawn liberally from essays by Barthes and Kristeva, and experimental writers privileged by the latter two figure prominently in the pantheon of postmodern world literature.

Critiques and Further Reading

Although this venue cannot do them justice, the critics of text theory are as numerous, as varied, and as significant as its proponents. Vladimir Propp (1966 [1984]) has censured the abstract appropriation and alteration to which French theorists have subjected his narrative model of Russian fairy tales. Fredric Jameson argues that concepts formulated to analyse the modern era and its dichotomy between appearances and underlying being no longer hold in the emerging postmodern age: text-theoretic oppositions between signifier and signified and between surface and deep structures dissolve in today's uniform flat play of simulacra, as do comparable hermeneutic contrasts like Marxist reality vs ideology, Freudian latent vs manifest content, and existentialist authenticity vs bad faith (Jameson 1991: 12). Carroll (1988), Bordwell and Carroll eds. (1996), and Branigan (2006) criticize psychoanalytic film theory and its portrayal of viewer as victim, instead promoting empirical and cognitive psychology and other methods for exploring the subject's perception and interpretation of moving pictures. Antoine Compagnon (1998) claims that features of text-theoretic literary criticism defy common sense, while Thomas Pavel (2001) objects to the generalized extension of concepts developed in linguistics to literature and other cultural productions (cf. Reiss 1988). Reaffirming traditional humanism and the Enlightenment project, Jules Ferry and Alain Renaut (1985) denounce the entire enterprise of decentring the subject as a facet of 1960s waywardness.

Further explorations of text theory in English could begin with the appropriate sections of handbooks and anthologies of theory (Leitch ed. 2001; Richter ed. 1998) or film theory (Hollows, Hutchings, and Jancovich eds. 2000; Mast, Cohen, and Baudry eds. 1992). Succinct introductions to major text theorists can be found in Bertens and Natoli eds. (2002) and Groden and Kreiswirth (1994), and one-volume selected readings from each of the major continental figures and currents are available. English-language dictionaries and concise encyclopedias of specialized terms include Taylor and Winquist (2001), Ducrot and Todorov (1972 [1979]), and Greimas and Courtés (1993 [1982]), as well as Martin and Ringham (2005), Sebeok ed. (1994), and, for film studies, Hayward (2000). Dosse (1994) and Pavel (1989) recount the unfolding of structuralist text theory, while Silverman (1983) surveys developments in film studies. The English translations of Rastier (1989) and Fontanille (1998) together outline central directions in contemporary text theory, while Floch (1990, 1995) and Perron (1996, 2003) offer good illustrations. Ablali and Ducard eds. (2009, in French) provide good introductions and a glossary of key terms for both classical and recent Romance-language text theory.

Thomas F. Broden

Bibliography

Ablali, Driss, and Dominique Ducard, eds. *Vocabulaire des études sémiotiques et sémiologiques*. Paris: Honoré Champion and Besançon: Presses universitaires de Franche-Comté, 2009.

Adam, Jean-Michel. *La linguistique textuelle: introduction à l'analyse textuelle des discours*. Paris: Armand Colin, 2005.

Anderson, Benedict. *Imagined Communities: Reflections on the Origin and Spread of Nationalism*. Rev. ed. London and New York: Verso, 1991.

Andrew, Dudley. *Concepts in Film Theory*. New York: Oxford University Press, 1984.

Austin, John L. *How to Do Things with Words*. Cambridge, MA: Harvard University Press, 1962.

Badir, Sémir, and Nathalie Roelens, eds. *Intermédialité visuelle*, special issue of *Visible* (Limoges) 3 (2008).

Bakhtin, Mikhail M. *The Dialogic Imagination: Four Essays*. Ed. Michael Holquist. Austin: University of Texas Press, 1981.

– *Speech Genres and Other Late Essays*. Ed. Caryl Emerson and Michael Holquist. Translated from the Russian by Vern W. McGee. Austin: University of Texas Press, Slavic series no. 8, 1986.

Bal, Mieke. *Introduction to the Theory of Narrative*. Toronto: University of Toronto Press, 1985, 2nd ed., 1997.

Barthes, Roland. *Le degré zéro de l'écriture*. Paris: Seuil, 1953. Trans. Annette Lavers and Colin Smith, *Writing Degree Zero*. New York: Hill and Wang, 1968.

– *Michelet*. Paris: Seuil, 1954.

– *Mythologies*. Paris: Seuil, 1957. Ed. and trans. Annette Lavers, *Mythologies*. New York: Farrar, Straus and Giroux, 1972.

– Eléments de sémiologie. *Communications* 4 (1964): 91–135. Trans. Annette Lavers and Colin Smith, *Elements of Semiology*. New York: Hill and Wang, 1968.

– The Death of the Author. Trans. Richard Howard. In *The Minimalism Issue*, ed. Brian O'Doherty, special issue of *Aspen* 5–6 (1967), http://www.ubu.com/aspen/aspen5and6/index.html (accessed 5 February 2007).

– *Le système de la mode*. Paris: Seuil, 1967. Trans. Matthew Ward and Richard Howard, *The Fashion System*. New York: Hill and Wang, 1983.

– *S/Z*. Paris: Seuil, 1970. Trans. Richard Miller, *S/Z*. New York: Hill and Wang, 1974.

– De l'oeuvre au texte, *Revue esthétique* (1971). Rpt. in *Le Bruissement de la langue. Essais critiques IV*, 69–77. Paris: Seuil, 1984. Trans. Stephen Heath, From Work to Text, in *Image, Music, Text*, 155–64. New York: Hill and Wang, 1977.

– Texte (théorie du), *Encyclopaedia universalis*, 1973. Rpt. in *Oeuvres complètes*, vol. 2, 1966–73. Ed. Éric Marty, 1677–89. Paris: Seuil, 1994.

– *Le plaisir du texte*. Paris: Seuil, 1973. Trans.

Richard Miller *The Pleasure of the Text*. New York: Farrar, Straus, and Giroux, 1975.

– *Image, Music, Text*. Selected texts translated by Stephen Heath. New York: Hill and Wang, 1977.

– *A Barthes Reader*. Ed. Susan Sontag. New York: Hill and Wang, 1982.

– *L'aventure sémiologique*. Paris: Seuil, 1985. Trans. Richard Howard, *The Semiological Challenge*. New York: Hill and Wang, 1988.

Barthes, Roland, et al., eds. *Recherches sémiologiques. L'analyse structurale du récit*, special issue of *Communications* 8 (1966).

Basso Fossali, Pierluigi. *Interpretazione tra mondi. Il pensiero figurale di David Lynch*. Rev. ed. Pisa: Edizioni ETS, 2008a [1st edition 2006].

– *La Promozione dei valori. Semiotica della communicazione e dei consumi*. Milan: Franco Angeli, 2008b.

Basso Fossali, Pierluigi, and Maria Giulia Dondero. *Semiotica della fotografia*. Rimini: Guaraldi, 2006. French translation by Nathalie Roelens, Sabrina D'Arconso, and Clément Lévy. *Sémiotique de la photographie*. Limoges: Pulim, 2001.

Bastide, Françoise. *Una notte con Saturno. Scritti semiotici sul discorso scientifico*. Ed. Bruno Latour. Rome: Meltemi, series Segnature, 2001.

Baudrillard, Jean. *Le système des objets. La consommation des signes*. Paris: Gallimard, 1968, rpt. Denoël/Gonthier, 1981, series Méditations. Trans. James Benedict, *The System of Objects*. London and New York: Verso, 1996.

– *Simulations*. Trans. Paul Foss, Paul Patton, and Philip Beitchman. New York: Semiotext(e), 1983.

Beauvoir, Simone de. *Le deuxième sexe*. Paris: Gallimard, 1949. Trans. and ed. H.M. Parshley, *The Second Sex*. New York: Knopf, 1952.

Bell, Philip, and Marko Milic. Goffman's *Gender Advertisements* Revisited: Combining Content Analysis with Semiotic Analysis. *Visual Communication* 1, no. 2 (June 2002): 203–22.

Bellour, Raymond. *L'analyse du film*. Paris: Albatros, 1979. Ed. and trans. Constance Penley, *The Analysis of Film*. Bloomington: Indiana University Press, 2000.

Benveniste, Emile. *Problèmes de linguistique générale*. 2 vols. Paris: Gallimard, 1966, 1974. Vol. 1 translated by Mary Elizabeth Meek, *Problems in General Linguistics*. Coral Gables, FL: University of Miami Press, 1971.

Bertens, Hans, and Joseph Natoli, eds. *Postmodernism: The Key Figures*. Oxford: Blackwell, 2002.

Beyaert-Geslin, Anne. *L'image préoccupée*. Paris: Hermès Lavoisier, 2009.

– *Sémiotique du design*. Paris: Presses Universitaires de France, 2012.

Beyaert-Geslin, Anne, and Nanta Novello-Paglianti, eds. *La diversité sensible*, special issue of *Visible* 1. Limoges: Pulim, 2005.

Blanco, Desiderio. *Semiótica del texto fílmico*. Lima: Universidad de Lima, 2003.

Booth, Wayne C. *The Rhetoric of Fiction*. Chicago: University of Chicago Press, 1961.

Bordron, Jean-François. Les objets en parties (esquisse d'ontologie matérielle). *Langages* 103 (September 1991): 51–65.

– *L'iconicité et ses images. Études sémiotiques*. Paris: Presses Universitaires de France, 2011.

Bordwell, David, and Noël Carroll, eds. *Post-Theory: Reconstructing Film Studies*. Madison: University of Wisconsin Press, 1996.

Branigan, Edward. *Point of View in the Cinema*. Amsterdam and New York: Mouton, 1984.

– *Projecting a Camera: Language Games in Film Theory*. New York: Routledge, 2006.

Braudel, Fernand. Histoire et sciences sociales: la longue durée, *Annales* 13.4 (Oct.–Dec. 1958): 725–53. Trans. Sarah Matthews, History and the Social Sciences: The Longue Durée. In *On History*, 25–54. Chicago: University of Chicago Press, 1980.

Bremond, Claude. *La logique du récit*. Paris: Seuil, 1973.

Broden, Thomas F. A.J. Greimas (1917–1992): Commemorative Essay. *Semiotica* 105, no. 3–4 (1995): 207–42.

– Linguistic Semantics for Literature and the Human Sciences Today. *Semiotica* 124, no. 1–2 (April 1999): 81–127.

– Image, Sign, Identity: Jean-Marie Floch and Visual Semiotics. *The American Journal of Semiotics* 18, no. 1–4 (2002): 237–58.

– In Memoriam: Jean-Marie Floch (1947–2001), Visual Semiotician. *The American Journal of Semiotics* 18, no. 1–4 (2002): 193–208.

Brown, Gillian, and George Yule. *Discourse Analysis*. Cambridge: Cambridge University Press, 1983.

Bruner, Jerome. *Actual Minds, Possible Worlds.* Cambridge: Harvard University Press, 1986.

– *Acts of Meaning.* Cambridge: Harvard University Press, 1990.

Buckland, Warren, ed. *The Film Spectator: From Sign to Mind.* Amsterdam: Amsterdam University Press, 1995.

– *The Cognitive Semiotics of Film.* Cambridge: Cambridge University Press, 2000.

Burke, Kenneth. *A Grammar of Motives.* New York: Prentice-Hall, 1945.

Calabrese, Omar. *La macchina della pittura.* Bari: Laterza, 1985.

Carani, Marie. Perspective, Point of View, and Symbolism. In *Advances in Visual Semiotics. The Semiotic Web 1992–93,* ed. Thomas A. Sebeok and Jean Umiker–Sebeok, 283–317. Berlin and New York: Mouton de Gruyter, 1994.

Carnap, Rudolf. *The Logical Syntax of Language.* New York: Harcourt Brace, 1937.

Carroll, Noël. *Mystifying Movies: Fads and Fallacies in Contemporary Film Theory.* New York: Columbia University Press, 1988.

Casetti, Francesco. *Dentro lo sguardo: il film e il suo spettatore.* Milan: Bompiani, 1986. Trans. Nell Andrew with Charles O'Brien, *Inside the Gaze: The Fiction Film and Its Spectator.* Bloomington: Indiana University Press, 1998.

Casetti, Francesco, and Federico Di Chio. *Analisi della televisione: strumenti, metodi e pratiche di ricerca.* Milan: Bompiani, 1997. Spanish translation by Charo Lacalle Zalduendo, *Análisis de la televisión: instrumentos, métodos y prácticas de investigación.* Barcelona, Mexico City, and Buenos Aires: Paidós, 1999.

Ceriani, Giulia. Invitation to Travel: The Window-Shop Relationship in the Communication of Fashion. In *Semiotics of the Media. State of the Art, Projects, and Perspectives,* ed. Winfried Nöth, 841–50. New York and Berlin: Mouton de Gruyter, 1997.

– ed. *L'image réfléchie. Sémiotique et marketing,* special issue of *EIDOS* (Étude de l'Image dans une Orientation Sémiologique), 1998.

Certeau, Michel de. *Heterologies: Discourse on the Other.* Trans. Brian Massumi. Minneapolis: University of Minnesota Press, 1986.

Chateau, Dominique. *Le cinéma comme langage.* Brussels: Association Internationale Sémiologique du Spectacle and Paris: Publications de la Sorbonne, Atelier de création et d'études vidéographiques, 1986.

Chatman, Seymour. *Story and Discourse: Narrative Structure in Fiction and Film.* Ithaca, NY: Cornell University Press, 1978.

Chomsky, Noam. *Syntactic Structures.* The Hague: Mouton, 1957.

– *Aspects of the Theory of Syntax.* Cambridge: MIT Press, 1965.

– *Cartesian Linguistics: A Chapter in the History of Rationalist Thought.* New York: Harper and Row, 1966.

– *Language and Mind.* New York: Harcourt, Brace and World, 1968.

– *Language and Politics.* Ed. C.P. Otero. Montreal and New York: Black Rose, 1988.

– *New Horizons in the Study of Language and Mind.* New York: Cambridge University Press, 2002.

Cixous Hélène. Sorties. In Cixous and Catherine Clément, *La jeune née.* Paris: Union Générale d'Éditions, 1975. Trans. Betsy Wing, Sorties: Out and Out: Attacks/Ways Out/Forays. In *The Newly Born Woman,* 63–132. Minneapolis: University of Minnesota Press, 1986.

– *The Hélène Cixous Reader.* Ed. Susan Sellers. New York: Routledge, 1994.

Colin, Michel. *Cinéma, télévision, cognition.* Nancy: Presses de l'Université de Nancy, 1992.

Compagnon, Antoine. *Le démon de la théorie. Littérature et sens commun.* Paris: Seuil, 1998. Trans. Carol Cosman, *Literature, Theory, and Common Sense.* Princeton: Princeton University Press, series New French Thought, 2004.

Coquet, Jean-Claude. *Le discours et son sujet.* 2 vols. Paris: Klincksieck, 1985–6.

– *La quête du sens.* Paris: Presses Universitaires de France, series Formes sémiotiques, 1997.

– *Phusis et logos. Une phénoménologie du langage.* Saint-Denis: Presses Universitaires de Vincennes, 2008.

Corrain, Lucia. *Semiotica dell'invisibile. Il quadro a lume di notte.* Bologna: Esculapio, 1996.

– ed. *Leggere l'opera d'arte II. Dal figurativo all'astratto.* Bologna: Esculapio, series Progetto Leonardo, 1999.

– ed. *Semiotiche della pittura. I classici. Le ricerche.* Rome: Meltemi, series Segnature, 2004.

Corrain, Lucia, and M. Valenti, eds. *Leggere l'ope-*

ra d'arte. Dal figurativo all'astratto. Bologna: Esculapio, 1991.

Couégnas, Nicolas, and Erik Bertin eds. *Solutions sémiotiques*. Paris: Lambert Lucas, 2005.

D'haen, Theo, ed. *Linguistics and the Study of Literature*. Amsterdam: Rodopi, 1986.

De Lauretis, Teresa. *Technologies of Gender: Essays on Theory, Film, and Fiction*. Bloomington: Indiana University Press, 1987.

Deleuze, Gilles. *Cinéma 1. L'image-mouvement*. Paris: Minuit, 1983. Trans. Hugh Tomlinson and Barbara Habberjam, *Cinema 1: The Mouvement Image*. Minneapolis: University of Minnesota Press, 1986.

– *Cinéma 2. L'image–temps*. Paris: Minuit, 1985. Trans. Hugh Tomlinson and Robert Galeta, *Cinema 2: The Time-Image*. Minneapolis: University of Minnesota Press, 1989.

– *The Deleuze Reader*. Ed. C.V. Boundas. New York: Columbia University Press, 1993.

Deleuze, Gilles, and Félix Guattari. *Anti-Oedipe. Capitalisme et schizophrénie*. Paris: Minuit, 1972. Trans. Robert Hurley, Mark Seem, and Helen R. Lane, *Anti-Oedipus: Capitalism and Schizophrenia*. Minneapolis: University of Minnesota Press, 1983.

– *Mille plateaux: capitalisme et schizophrénie*. Paris: Minuit, 1980. Trans. Brian Massumi, *A Thousand Plateaus: Capitalism and Schizophrenia*. Minneapolis: University of Minnesota Press, 1987.

Deni, Michela. *Oggetti in azione. Semiotica degli oggetti: dalla teoria all'analisi*. Milan: Franco Angeli, 2002.

– ed. *La semiotica degli oggetti*, special issue of *VS Quaderni di studi semiotici* (Bologna, Italy) 91–2 (January–August 2002).

Derrida, Jacques. *De la grammatologie*. Paris: Minuit, 1967. Trans. Gayatri Cakravorty Spivak, *Of Grammatology*. Baltimore: Johns Hopkins University Press, 1976.

– *A Derrida Reader: Between the Blinds*. Ed. Peggy Kamuf. New York: Columbia University Press, 1991.

– *Politiques de l'amitié*. Paris: Galilée, 1994. Trans. George Collins, *Politics of Friendship*. London and New York: Verso, 1997.

Derrida, Jacques, and Anne Dufourmantelle. *De l'hospitalité*. Paris: Calmann-Lévy, 1997. Trans. Rachel Bowlby, *Of Hospitality. Anne Dufourm-*

antelle Invites Jacques Derrida to Respond. Stanford: Stanford University Press, 2000.

Derrida, Jacques, and Nelson Mandela. *Pour Nelson Mandela*. Paris: Gallimard, 1986. Trans. Mustapha Tlili, *For Nelson Mandela*. New York: Seaver, 1987.

Dijk, Teun A. van, ed. *Discourse Studies: A Multidisciplinary Introduction*. 2 vols. London: Sage, 1997.

Dijk, Teun A. van, and Walter Kintsch. *Strategies of Discourse Comprehension*. New York: Academic Press, 1983.

Dilthey, Wilhelm. Die Entstehung der Hermeneutik. In *Gesammelte Schriften*, vol. 5, 317–38. Stuttgart: B.G. Teubner, 1957. Translated in *The Hermeneutics Reader: Texts of the German Tradition from the Enlightenment to the Present*, ed. Kurt Mueller-Vollmer. New York: Continuum, 1985.

Dondero, Maria Giulia. *Fotografare il sacro. Indagini semiotiche*. Roma: Meltemi, 2007. French trans. François Provenzano, *Le sacré dans l'image photographique. Etudes sémiotiques*. Paris: Hermès Lavoisier, 2009.

Dondero, Maria Giulia, and Jacques Fontanille. *Des images à problèmes. Le sens du visuel à l'épreuve de l'image scientifique*. Limoges: Pulim, 2012.

Dondero, Maria Giulia, and Nanta Novello-Paglianti, eds. *Syncrétismes*, special issue of *Visible* 2. Limoges: Pulim, 2006.

Dosse, François. *Histoire du structuralisme*. 2 vols. Paris: La Découverte, 1994. Trans. Deborah Glassman, *History of Structuralism*. 2 vols. Minneapolis: University of Minnesota Press, 1997.

Ducrot, Oswald, and Jean-Marie Schaeffer. *Nouveau dictionnaire encyclopédique des sciences du langage*. Paris: Seuil, 1995.

Ducrot, Oswald, and Tzvetan Todorov. *Dictionnaire encyclopédique des sciences du langage*. Paris: Seuil, 1972. Trans. Catherine Porter *Encyclopedic Dictionary of the Sciences of Language*. Baltimore: Johns Hopkins University Press, 1979.

Ducrot, Oswald, and Igor Z. Zagar. *Slovenian Lectures: Argumentative Semantics*. Ljubljana: ISH, 1996.

Dumézil, Georges. *Jupiter, Mars, Quirinus*. 3 vols. Paris: Gallimard, 1940–5.

- *Heur et malheur du guerrier. Aspects mythiques de la fonction du guerrier chez les Indo-européens.* Presses Universitaires de France, 1969. Trans. Alf Hiltebeitel, *The Destiny of the Warrior.* Chicago: University of Chicago Press, 1970.
- *Mythe et épopée.* 3 vols. Paris: Gallimard, 1968, 1970, 1973. Vol. 2 translated as *The Destiny of a King, The Plight of a Sorcerer,* and *The Stakes of the Warrior.* Berkeley: University of California Press, 1973, 1983, 1986. Vol. 3 translated as *Camillus: A Study of Indo-European Religion as Roman History.* Berkeley: University of California Press, 1980.

Dusi, Nicola. *Il cinema come traduzione. Da un medium all'altro: letteratura, cinema, pittura.* Torino: UTET, 2003.

Eco, Umberto. *Opera aperta: forma e indeterminazione nelle poetiche contemporanee.* Milan: Bompiani, 1962. Trans. Anna Cancogni and Bruce Merry in *The Open Work.* Cambridge, MA: Harvard University Press, 1989.
- *La struttura assente. Introduzione alla ricerca semiologia.* Milan: Bompiani, 1968, new ed. 1994. French translation by Uccio Esposito–Torrigiani, *La structure absente. Introduction à la recherche sémiotique.* Paris: Mercure de France, 1972, new ed. 1984.
- *A Theory of Semiotics.* Bloomington: Indiana University Press, 1976.
- *The Role of the Reader: Explorations in the Semiotics of Texts.* Bloomington: Indiana University Press, 1979.
- *Lector in fabula: la cooperazione interpretativa nei testi narrativi.* Milan: Bompiani, 1979.
- *Semiotics and the Philosophy of Language.* Bloomington: Indiana University Press, 1986.
- The Influence of Roman Jakobson on the Development of Semiotics. In *Classics of Semiotics,* ed. Martin Krampen, Klaus Oehler, Roland Posner, Thomas A. Sebeok, and Thure von Uexküll, 109–27. New York: Plenum, series Topics in Contemporary Semiotics, 1987.
- *I limiti dell'interpretazione.* Milan: Fabbri, Bompiani, Sonzogno. *The Limits of Interpretation.* Bloomington: Indiana University Press, 1990.
- Overinterpreting Texts. In U. Eco, Richard Rorty, Jonathan Culler, and Christine Brooke-Rose, *Interpretation and Overinterpretation,* ed. Stefan Collini, 45–66. Cambridge and New York: Cambridge University Press, 1992.
- *Sulla letteratura.* Milan: Bompiani, 2002. Trans. Martin McLaughlin, *On Literature.* Orlando, FL: Harcourt, 2004.

Fauconnier, Gilles. *Mental Spaces: Aspects of Meaning Construction in Natural Language.* Cambridge: MIT Press, 1985.

Fauconnier, Gilles, and Mark Turner. *The Way We Think: Conceptual Blending and the Mind's Hidden Complexities.* New York: Basic, 2002.

Ferry, Luc, and Alain Renaut. *La pensée 68: essai sur l'anti-humanisme contemporain.* Paris: Gallimard, 1985. Trans. Mary H.S. Cattani, *French Philosophy of the Sixties: An Essay on Anti-Humanism.* Amherst: University of Massachusetts Press, 1990.

Floch, Jean-Marie. *Sémiotique, marketing et communication: sous les signes, les stratégies.* Paris: Presses Universitaires de France, 1990. Trans. Robin Orr Bodkin, *Semiotics, Marketing, and Communication. Beneath the Signs, the Strategies.* New York: Palgrave, St Martin's Press, 2001.
- *Identités visuelles.* Paris: Presses Universitaires de France, 1995. Trans. Pierre Van Osselaer and Alec McHoul, *Visual Identities.* New York: Continuum, 2000.
- *Bricolage. Lettere ai semiologi della terra ferma.* Ed. M. Agnello and Gianfranco Marrone, translated from the French by Elisabetta Gigante. Rome: Meltemi, series Segnature, 2006.

Fludernik, Monika. *Towards a 'Natural' Narratology.* New York: Routledge, 1996.

Fodor, Jerry. *The Modularity of Mind. An Essay on Faculty Psychology.* Cambridge: MIT Press, 1983.

Fontanille, Jacques, ed. *Le devenir.* Proceedings of the Conference Linguistique et Sémiotique III held at the Université de Limoges. Limoges: Pulim, series Nouveaux Actes Sémiotiques, 1995.
- *Sémiotique et littérature. Essais de méthode.* Paris: Presses Universitaires de France, 1999.
- *Sémiotique du discours.* Limoges: Pulim, 1999. 2nd ed. 2003. English translation of the 2003 edition by Heidi Bostic, *The Semiotics of Discourse.* New York: Peter Lang, 2006.
- *Corps et sens.* Paris: Presses Universitaires de France, 2011.

Fontanille, Jacques, and Guy Barrier, eds. *Les métiers de la sémiotique.* Limoges: Pulim, 1999.

Fontanille, Jacques, and Claude Zilberberg.

Tension et signification. Brussels: Mardaga, 1998.

Fontanille, Jacques, and Alessandro Zinna, eds. *Les objets au quotidien*. Limoges: Presses Universitaires de Limoges, series Nouveaux Actes Sémiotiques, 2005.

Foucault, Michel. *Les mots et les choses. Une archéologie des sciences humaines*. Paris: Gallimard, 1966, rpt. 1992. Translated *The Order of Things. An Archeology of the Human Sciences*. New York: Pantheon, 1970.

– *L'archéologie du savoir*. Paris: Gallimard, 1969. Trans. A.M. Sheridan Smith, *The Archeology of Knowledge,* 1972, new edition New York: Pantheon, 1995.

– *The Foucault Reader*. Ed. Paul Rabinow. New York: Pantheon, 1984.

Gadamer, Hans-Georg. *Wahrheit und Methode. Grundzüge einer philosophischen Hermeneutik*. Tübingen: J.C.B. Mohr, 1960. Trans. Garrett Barden and John Cumming, *Truth and Method*. New York: Seabury, 1975.

Galatanu, Olga. Convocation et reconstruction des stéréotypes dans les argumentations de la presse écrite. In *Le lieu commun,* special issue of *Protée* (Quebec) 22, no. 2 (1994): 75–9.

– La reconstruction du système de valeurs convoquées et évoquées dans le discours médiatique. In *Actes du XXIIe Congrès International de Linguistique et Philologie Romanes, Brusells, 23–29 July 1998,* 251–8. Tübingen: Max Niemeyer, 2000.

– Signification, sens et construction discursive du monde et de soi. In *Signification, sens et formation,* ed. J.M. Barbier and O. Galtanu, 25–43. Paris: Presses Universitaires de France, 2000.

Geertz, Clifford. *The Interpretation of Cultures: Selected Essays*. London: Hutchinson, 1975.

Genette, Gérard. *Figures*. Vol. 3. Paris: Seuil, 1972. Trans. Jane E. Levin, *Narrative Discourse: An Essay in Method*. Ithaca, NY: Cornell University Press, 1980.

– *Introduction à l'architexte*. Paris: Seuil, 1979. Trans. Jane E. Lewin, *The Architext: An Introduction*. Berkeley: University of California Press, 1992.

– *Palimpsestes. La littérature au second degré*. Paris: Seuil, 1982. Trans. Channa Newman and Claude Doubinsky, *Palimpsests. Literature in the Second Degree*. Lincoln: University of Nebraska Press, 1997.

– *Métalepse. De la figure à la fiction*. Paris: Seuil, 2004.

Gibbs, Raymond W. *Embodiment and Cognitive Science*. New York: Cambridge University Press, 2006.

Gibson, James Jerome. *The Senses Considered as Perceptual Systems*. Boston: Houghton Mifflin, 1966.

– *The Ecological Approach to Visual Perception*. Boston: Houghton Mifflin, 1979.

Gigante, Elisabetta, ed. *Diagrammes, cartes, schémas graphiques,* special issue of *Visible* (Limoges: Pulim) 4 (2008).

Goffman, Erving. *Interaction Rituals. Essays in Face-to-Face Behavior*. Chicago: Aldine, 1967.

– *Gender Advertisements*. Cambridge: Harvard University Press, 1979.

Greimas, Algirdas J. *Sémantique structurale: recherche de méthode*. Paris: Larousse, 1966. Trans. Daniele McDowell, Ronald Schleifer, and Alan Velie, *Structural Semantics: An Attempt at a Method*. Lincoln: University of Nebraska Press, 1983.

– *Du sens*. 2 vols. Paris: Seuil, 1970, 1983. Partial English translation in 1987 and 1990.

– *Maupassant: la sémiotique du texte: exercices pratiques*. Paris: Seuil, 1976. Trans. Paul Perron, *Maupassant. The Semiotics of the Text: Practical Exercises*. Amsterdam and Philadelphia: Benjamin, 1988.

– *Sémiotique et sciences sociales*. Paris: Seuil, 1976. Partial translation in 1990.

– *On Meaning: Selected Writings in Semiotic Theory*. Trans. Paul Perron. Minneapolis: University of Minnesota Press, 1987.

– *The Social Sciences, a Semiotic View*. Trans. Paul Perron and Frank Collins. Minneapolis: University of Minnesota Press, 1990.

Greimas, Algirdas J., and Joseph Courtés. *Sémiotique. Dictionnaire raisonné de la théorie du langage*. Paris: Hachette, 1979, new edition with bibliography 1993. Trans. Larry Crist, Daniel Patte, et al., *Semiotics and Language: An Analytical Dictionary*. Bloomington: Indiana University Press, 1982.

Greimas, Algirdas J., and Jacques Fontanille. *La sémiotique des passions. Des états de choses aux états d'âme*. Paris: Seuil, 1991. Trans. Paul Perron and Frank Collins, *The Semiotics of Passions: From States of Affairs to States of Feeling*. Minneapolis: University of Minnesota Press, 1993.

Greimas, Algirdas J., and Eric Landowski, eds. *Introduction à l'analyse du discours en sciences sociales*. Paris: Hachette, 1979.

Groden, Michael, and Martin Kreiswirth. *The Johns Hopkins Guide to Literary Theory and Criticism*. Baltimore: Johns Hopkins University Press, 1994.

Groupe Mu [Jean Dubois, Francis Édeline, Jean-Marie Klinkenberg, Philippe Minguet, F. Pire, H. Trinon]. *Rhétorique générale*. Paris: Seuil, 1970, new ed. 1982. Trans. Paul B. Burrell and Edgar M. Slotkin, *A General Rhetoric*. Baltimore: Johns Hopkins University Press, 1981.

– [Francis Edeline, Jean-Marie Klinkenberg, and Phillipe Minguet]. *Traité du signe visuel. Pour une rhétorique de l'image*. Paris: Seuil, 1992.

Grünzweig, Walter, and Andreas Solbach, eds. *Grenzüberschreitungen: Narratologie im Kontext / Transcending Boundaries: Narratology in Context*. Tübingen: Narr, 1999.

Halliday, Michael Alexander Kirkwood. *Language as Social Semiotic*. London: Arnold, 1978.

Halliday, Michael, Alexander Kirkwood, and Ruqaiya Hasan. *Language. Context and Text: Aspects of Language in a Social-Semiotic Perspective*. Deakin: Deakin University Press, 1985.

Hamburger, Käte. *Die Logik der Dichtung*. Stuttgart: E. Klett, 1957. Trans. Marilynn J. Rose, *The Logic of Literature*. Bloomington: Indiana University Press, rev. ed. 1973.

Hatten, Robert S. *Musical Meaning in Beethoven: Markedness, Correlation, and Interpretation*. Bloomington: Indiana University Press, 1994.

– Music Theory and General Semiotics: A Creative Interaction. In *Hi-Fives. A Trip to Semiotics*, ed. Roberta Kevelson, 71–84. New York: Peter Lang, 1998. Expanded, revised, and translated as Théorie de la musique et sémiotique générale: une interaction créative, in *Questions de sémiotique*, ed. Anne Hénault, 563–83. Paris: Presses Universitaires de France, 2002.

– *Interpreting Musical Gestures, Topics, and Tropes: Mozart, Beethoven, Schubert*. Bloomington: Indiana University Press, 2004.

Hayward, Susan. *Cinema Studies. The Key Concepts*. 2nd ed. London and New York: Routledge, 2000.

Heath, Stephen. Notes on Suture. *Screen* 18, no. 4 (winter 1977–8): 48–76. Rpt. in Heath, *Questions of Cinema*. Bloomington: Indiana University Press, 1981.

Heath, Stephen. *Questions of Cinema*. Bloomington: Indiana University Press, 1981.

Hébert, Louis. *Introduction à la sémantique des textes*. Paris: Honoré Champion, series Bibliothèque de Grammaire et de Linguistique No. 9, 2001.

Hénault, Anne, and Anne Beyaert, eds. *Ateliers de sémiotique visuelle*. Paris: Presses Universitaires de France, 2004.

Herman, David, ed. *New Perspectives on Narrative Analysis*. Columbus: Ohio State University Press, 1999.

– ed. *Story Logic. Problems and Possibilities of Narrative*. Lincoln: University of Nebraska Press, 2002.

– ed. *Narrative Theory and the Cognitive Sciences*. Stanford: CSLI Publications, 2003.

Hjelmslev, Louis. *La catégorie des cas. Étude de grammaire générale*. 2 vols. Aarhus: Universitetsforlaget Aarhus, series Acta Jutlandica 7.1 and 9.1, 1935 and 1937. Rpt. in one volume, Munich: Wilhelm Fink, series International Library of General Linguistics vol. 25, 1972.

– *Omkring Sprogteoriens Grundlaeggelse*. Copenhagen: Munksgaard, 1943. Trans. Francis J. Whitfield, *Prolegomena to a Theory of Language*. Baltimore: Waverly, 1953; rev. ed. Madison: University of Wisconsin Press, 1961.

– *Essais linguistiques*. Copenhagen: Nordisk Sprog-og Kulturforlag, series Travaux du Cercle Linguistique de Copenhague no. 12, 1959. New edition by François Rastier, Paris: Minuit, 1971.

Hodge, Robert, and D. Tripp. *Children and Television. A Semiotic Approach*. Cambridge: Polity, 1986.

Hodge, Robert, and Gunther Kress. *Social Semiotics*. Ithaca, NY: Cornell University Press, 1988.

Holenstein, Elmar. *Roman Jakobsons phänomenologischer Strukturalismus*. Frankfurt am Main: Suhrkamp, series Taschenbuch Wissenschaft no. 116, 1975. Trans. Catherine Schelbert and Tarcisius Schelbert, *Roman Jakobson's Approach to Language: Phenomenological Structuralism*. Bloomington: Indiana University Press, 1976.

Hollows, Joanne, Peter Hutchings, and Mark Jancovich, eds. *The Film Studies Reader*. New York: Oxford University Press, 2000.

Husserl, Edmund. *Die Krisis der europäischen*

Wissenschaften und die transcendentale Phänomenologie: eine Einleitung in die phänomenologische Philosophie. Belgrade, 1936. Trans. David Carr, *The Crisis of European Sciences and Transcendental Phenomenology: An Introduction to Phenomenological Philosophy.* Evansville, IL: Northwestern University Press, series Studies in Phenomenology and Existential Philosophy, 1970.

Hymes, Dell. *Foundations in Sociolinguistics: An Ethnographic Approach.* Philadelphia: University of Pennsylvania Press, 1974.

Ivanov, Vyacheslav, Yuri Lotman, and Alexander Zholkovsky. *Film Theory and General Semiotics.* Ed. L.M. O'Toole. Trans. L.M. O'Toole, Stephen Rudy, and Ruth Sobel. Vol. 8 of *Russian Poetics in Translation.* Oxford: Holdan, 1981.

Jakobson, Roman. *Language in Literature.* Ed. Krystyna Pomorska and Stephen Rudy. Cambridge: Belknap Press, Harvard University Press, 1987.

– *On Language.* Ed. Linda R. Waugh and Monique Monville-Burston. Cambridge: Harvard University Press, 1990.

Jameson, Fredric. *Postmodernism, or, the Cultural Logic of Late Capitalism.* Durham, NC: Duke University Press, 1991.

Jencks Charles. *The Language of Post-Modern Architecture.* London: Academy, 1977; 4th rev. ed. 1984.

Johansen, Jørgen Dines. *Dialogic Semiosis: An Essay on Signs and Meaning.* Bloomington: Indiana University Press, 1993.

– *Literary Discourse: A Semiotic-Pragmatic Approach to Literature.* Toronto: University of Toronto Press, 2002.

Johnson, Mark. *The Body in the Mind: The Bodily Basis of Meaning, Imagination, and Reason.* Chicago: University of Chicago Press, 1987.

Kälberer, Daniel. *Film Bibliography. Overview: Text Theory.* 2000–5, http://www.fachinformation–filmwissenschaft.de/stichwort/t/texttheorie.html (accessed 8 February 2007).

Karbusicky, Vladimir. *Grundriss der musikalischen Semantik.* Darmstadt: Wissenschaftliche Buchgesellschaft, 1986.

Kerbrat-Orrecchioni, Catherine. *Les interactions verbales.* 3 vols. Paris: Armand Colin, 1990, 1992, 1994.

Klein, Melanie. *Die Psychoanalyse des Kindes.* Vienna: Internationaler Psychoanalytischer, 1932. Trans. Alix Strachey, *The Psycho-analysis of Children.* London: Leonard and Virginia Woolf at the Hogarth Pr. and the Institute of Psycho-Analysis, series International psychoanalytical library no. 22, 1937.

Krampen, Martin, Klaus Oehler, Roland Posner, Thomas A. Sebeok, and Thure von Uexküll, eds. *Classics of Semiotics.* New York: Plenum, series Topics in Contemporary Semiotics, 1987.

Kress, Gunther. *Linguistic Processes in Sociocultural Practice.* Oxford: Oxford University Press, 1989.

Kress, Gunther, and Theo Van Leeuwen. *Reading Images: The Grammar of Visual Design.* London: Routledge, 1996.

Krippendorff, Klaus. *Content Analysis. An Introduction to First Methodology.* London: Sage, 1980.

Kristeva, Julia. *Séméiotikè, recherches pour une sémanalyse.* Paris: Seuil, 1969.

– *La révolution du langage poétique.* Paris: Seuil, 1974.

– *Polylogue.* Paris: Seuil, 1977.

– *The Portable Kristeva.* Ed. Kelly Oliver. New York: Columbia University Press, 1997.

Lacan, Jacques. *Écrits.* Paris: Seuil, 1966. Trans. Bruce Fink in collaboration with Héloïse Fink and Russell Grigg, *Écrits: The First Complete Edition in English.* New York: W.W. Norton, 2006.

Lakoff, George. *Women, Fire, and Dangerous Things: What Categories Reveal about the Mind.* Chicago: University of Chicago Press, 1987.

Lakoff, George, and Mark Johnson. *Metaphors We Live By.* Chicago: University of Chicago Press, 1980.

Landowski, Eric. *Présences de l'autre: essais de socio-sémiotique II.* Paris: Presses Universitaires de France, 1997.

– *Passions sans nom: essais de socio-sémiotique III.* Paris: Presses Universitaires de France, 2004.

Landowski, Eric, and José Luiz Fiorin, eds. *O gosto da gente, o gosto das coisas. Abordagem semiótica.* São Paulo: EDUC, 1997. Italian translation by Maria Spina and Roberto Marro, *Gusti e disgusti. Sociosemiotica del quotidiano.* Torino: Testo and Immagine, series Controsegni, 2000.

Landowski, Eric, and Gianfranco Marrone, eds. *La société des objets. Problèmes d'interobjectivité*, special issue of *Protée* (Chicoutimi, Quebec) 29, no. 1 (2001). Italian translation by Antonio Perri, *La società degli oggetti. Problemi di interoggettività*. Rome: Meltemi, series Segnature, 2002.

Landowski, Eric, Raúl Dorra, and Ana Claudia de Oliveira, eds. *Semiótica, estesis, estética*. Sao Paulo: EDUC, Puebla, Mexico: Universidad Autónoma de Puebla, 1999.

Langacker, Ronald W. *Foundations of Cognitive Grammar*. Vol. 1: *Theoretical Prerequisites*. Vol. 2: *Descriptive Application*. Stanford: Stanford University Press, 1987–91.

Lanigan, Richard L., ed. *The Semiotics of the Image*, special issue of the *American Journal of Semiotics* 17, no. 3 (fall 2001).

Latour, Bruno. *Pandora's Hope. Essays on the Reality of Science Studies*. Cambridge, MA: Harvard University Press, 1999.

Latour, Bruno, and Steve Woolgar. *Laboratory Life. The Construction of Scientific Facts*. 2nd ed. Princeton: Princeton University Press, 1986.

Leitch, Vincent, ed. *The Norton Anthology of Theory and Criticism*. New York: Norton, 2001.

Lemon, Lee T., and Marion J. Reis, eds. *Russian Formalist Criticism: Four Essays*. Trans. and with an Introduction by L.T. Lemon and M.R. Reis. Lincoln: University of Nebraska Press, 1965.

Lerdahl, Fred, and Ray Jackendoff. *A Generative Theory of Tonal Music*. Cambridge: MIT Press, 1983.

Leroi-Gourhan, André. *Évolution et techniques*. Vol. 1: *L'homme et la matière*. Paris: Albin Michel, 1943. Vol. 2: *Milieu et techniques*. Paris: Albin Michel, 1945.

Leroi-Gourhan, André. *Le geste et la parole*. 2 vols. Trans. Anna Bostock Berger, *Gesture and Speech*. Cambridge: MIT Press, 1993.

Lévi-Strauss, Claude. Introduction à l'oeuvre de Marcel Mauss. In Marcel Mauss, *Sociologie et anthropologie*, ed. Georges Gurvitch, ix–lii. Paris: Presses Universitaires de France, 1950; new ed. 1973.

– The Structural Study of Myth. In *Myth: A Symposium*, special issue of *Journal of American Folklore* 270 (1955): 428–44.

– *Anthropologie structurale*. 2 vols. Paris: Plon, 1958, 1973. Vol. 1 translated by Claire Jacobson and Brooke Grundfest Schoepf, vol. 2 by Monique Layton, *Structural Anthropology*. New York: Basic Books, 1963, 1976.

– *La pensée sauvage*. Paris: Plon, 1962. Trans. George Weidenfeld, *The Savage Mind*. Chicago: University of Chicago Press, 1966.

– *Le totémisme aujourd'hui*. Paris: Presses Universitaires de France, 1962. Trans. Rodney Needham, *Totemism*. Boston: Beacon, 1964.

– *Mythologiques*. 4 vols. Paris: Plon, 1964–1971. Trans. John and Doreen Weightman, *Introduction to a Science of Mythology*. 4 vols. New York: Harper and Row, 1964–81.

Lotman, Yuri M. Moscow: Tartu University Press, series The Languages of Russian Culture, 1966. Trans. Ann Shukman, *Universe of the Mind. A Semiotic Theory of Culture*. London and New York: I.B. Tauris, 1990, rpt. 2001.

– *Metodi esatti nella scienza letteraria sovietica*. Trans. Vittorio Strada, *Strumenti Critici* 1, no. 2 (February 1967): 107–29.

– *Semiotika kino I problemy kinoestetiki*, 1973. Trans. Mark E. Suino, *Semiotics of the Cinema*. Ann Arbor: Department of Slavic Languages and Literature, University of Michigan Press, 1976.

Lucid, Daniel P., ed. *Soviet Semiotics: An Anthology*. Trans. and with an Introduction by D.P. Lucid. Baltimore and London: Johns Hopkins University Press, 1977.

Lyotard, Jean-François. *La condition postmoderne: rapport sur le savoir*. Paris: Éditions de Minuit, 1979. Trans. Geoff Bennington and Brian Massumi, *The Postmodern Condition: A Report on Knowledge*. Minneapolis: University of Minnesota Press, 1984.

Marks, Elaine, and Isabelle de Courtivron, eds. *New French Feminisms: An Anthology*. New York: Schocken, 1980.

Marks, Laura. *The Skin of the Film: Intercultural Cinema, Embodiment, and the Senses*. Durham, NC: Duke University Press, 2000.

Marrone, Gianfranco. *C'era una volta il telefonino. Un indagine sociosemiotica*. Rome: Meltemi, series Segnature, 1999.

Martin, Bronwen, and Felizitas Ringham. *Key Terms in Semiotics*. London: Continuum, 2005.

Martin, J.R., and David Rose. *Working with Discourse. *Meaning beyond the Clause*. New York: Continuum, 2003.

Mast, Gerald, Marshall Cohen, and Leo Baudry, eds. *Film Theory and Criticism: Introductory Readings*. New York: Oxford University Press, 1992.

Merleau-Ponty, Maurice. *Phénoménologie de la perception*. Paris: Gallimard, 1945. Trans. Colin Smith, *Phenomenology of Perception*. New York: Routledge, 1976.

Metz, Christian. *Essais sur la signification au cinéma*. 2 vols. Paris: Klincksieck, 1968, 1973. Vol. 1 translated by Michael Taylor as *Film Language: A Semiotics of the Cinema*. New York, Oxford University Press, 1974.

– *Langage et cinéma*. Paris: Larousse, 1970. Trans. Donna Jean Umiker-Sebeok, *Language and Cinema*. The Hague: Mouton, 1974.

– *Film Language: A Semiotics of Cinema*. Chicago: University of Chicago Press, 1971 [1990].

– *Le signifiant imaginaire*. Paris: UGE, 1977. Trans. Celia Britton, Anwyl Williams, and Alfred Guzzett, *The Imaginary Signifier: Psychoanalysis and the Cinema*. Bloomington: Indiana University Press, 1977.

– *L'énonciation impersonnelle, ou le site du film*. Paris: Méridiens Klincksieck, 1991. Partial translation, The Impersonal Enunciation, or the Site of Film (In the Margin of Recent Works on Enunciation in Cinema). *New Literary History* 22 (Summer 1991): 747–72.

Meyer, Leonard B. *Emotion and Meaning in Music*. Chicago: University of Chicago Press, 1956.

Mick, David Glen. *Technological Consumer Products in Everyday Life: Ownership, Meaning, and Satisfaction*. Cambridge, MA: Marketing Science Institute, 1995.

Miller, Jacques-Alain. La suture: éléments de la logique du signifiant. *Cahiers pour l'analyse* 1 (winter 1966): 39–51. Trans. Jacqueline Rose Suture (Elements of the Logic of the Signifier), *Screen* 18, no. 4 (winter 1977–8): 24–34.

Miller, Toby, and Robert Stam, eds. *A Companion to Film Theory*. Oxford: Blackwell, 1999.

Mitchell, Arnold. *The Nine American Lifestyles. Who We Are and Where We Are Going*. New York: Macmillan, 1983.

Möller-Nass, Karl-Dietmar. *Filmsprache. Eine kritische Theoriegeschichte*. Münster: MAks, 1986.

Monelle, Raymond. *The Sense of Music: Semiotic Essays*. Princeton: Princeton University Press, 2000.

Monjou, Marc. Dispositional Properties of the Objects. Design Semiotics in Use. Paper presented at the Ninth Conference of the International Association for Semiotic Studies, Helsinki and Imatra, Finland, 11–17 June 2007. Working paper version available online at http://www2.uiah.fi/sefun/DSIU_papers/DSIU%20_%20Monjou%20_%20Dispositional%20Properties.pdf.

Nattiez, Jean-Jacques. *Fondements d'une sémiologie de la musique*. Paris: Union Générale, 1975. Trans. Carolyn Abbate, *Music and Discourse: Towards a Semiology of Music*. Princeton: Princeton University Press, 1990.

Norman, Donald A. *The Psychology of Everyday Things*. New York: Basic, 1988.

– *The Design of Everyday Things*. New York: Basic, 2002.

Norris Christopher. *The Truth about Postmodernism*. Oxford: Blackwell, 1993.

Nöth, Winfried, ed. *Semiotics of the Media. State of the Art, Projects, and Perspectives*. New York: Mouton de Gruyter, series Approaches to Semiotics no. 127, 1997.

Nöth, Winfried. *A Handbook of Semiotics*. Bloomington and Indianapolis: Indiana University Press, 1990.

Odin, Roger. *Cinéma et production de sens*. Paris: Armand Colin, 1990.

– *De la fiction*. Brussels: De Boeck, 2000.

Oudart, Jean-Pierre. La suture. *Cahiers du cinema* 211 (April 1969): 36–39 and 212 (May 1969): 50–5. Translated Cinema and Suture, *Screen* 18, no. 4 (Winter 1977–8): 35–47. Rpt. in *Cahiers du Cinema: The Politics of Representation*, ed. Nick Browne, 45–57. Cambridge: Harvard University Press, 1990.

Ouellet, Pierre. *Voir et savoir. La perception des univers du discours. Essais littéraires*. Candiac, Quebec: Balzac, 1992.

Parouty-David, Françoise, and Claude Zilberberg, eds. *Sémiotique et esthétique*. Proceedings of the Sémio 2001 conference in Limoges, France. Limoges: Pulim, 2003.

Pavel, Thomas G. *The Feud of Language. A History of Structuralist Thought*. Oxford: Blackwell, 1989.

– *The Spell of Language. Poststructuralism and Speculation.* English version by Linda Jordan and Thomas G. Pavel. Chicago: University of Chicago Press, 2001.

Peirce, Charles Sanders. *Collected Papers of Charles Sanders Peirce.* Ed. Charles Hartshorne and Paul Weiss. 6 vols. Cambridge: Harvard University Press, 1960.

Penley, Constance, ed. *Feminism and Film Theory.* London and New York: Routledge, 1988.

Perron, Paul. *Semiotics and the Modern Quebec Novel: A Greimassian Analysis of Thériault's Agaguk.* Toronto: University of Toronto Press, 1996.

– *Narratology and Text. Subjectivity and Identity in New France and Québécois Literature.* Toronto: University of Toronto Press, 2003.

Perron, Paul, and Frank Collins, eds. *Paris School Semiotics.* 2 vols. Philadelphia: John Benjamins, 1989.

Petitot, Jean, ed. *Lingustique cognitive et modèles dynamiques,* special issue of *Sémiotiques* (Paris: Didier Érudition) 6–7 (1994). Available online at http://www.revue–texto.net/Parutions/Semiotiques/Semiotiques.html (accessed April 2006).

Petitot, Jean, and Renaud Barbaras. *Naturaliser la phénoménologie: essais sur la phénoménologie contemporaine et les sciences cognitives.* Paris: CNRS, 2002.

Petitot, Jean. *Morphologie et esthétique: la forme et le sens chez Goethe, Lessing, Lévi-Strauss, Kant, Valéry, Husserl, Eco, Proust, Stendhal.* Paris: Maisonneuve et Larose, 2004.

Petitot-Cocorda, Jean. *Morphogenèse du sens I. Pour un schématisme de la structure.* Preface by René Thom. Paris: Presses Universitaires de France, series Formes Sémiotiques, 1985. Trans. Franson Manjali, *Morphogenesis of Meaning.* Bern and New York: Peter Lang, series European Semiotics, vol. 3, 2004.

Petöfi, János S., ed. *Text vs Sentence. Basic Questions of Text Linguistics.* Hamburg: Helmut Buske, 1979.

Petöfi, János S., and H. Reiser, eds. *Studies in Text Grammar.* Dordrecht: Reidel, 1972.

Peverini, Paolo. *Il videoclip. Strategie e figure di une forma breve.* Rome: Meltemi, series Segnature, 2004.

Pezzini, Isabella, and Pierluigi Cervelli, eds. *Scene del consumo: dallo shopping al museo.* Rome: Meltemi, series Segnature no. 35, 2006.

Pike, Kenneth. *Language in Relation to a Unified Theory of Structure of Human Behavior.* The Hague: Mouton, 1967.

Poster, Mark. *The Mode of Interpretation: Poststructuralism and Social Context.* Chicago: University of Chicago Press, 1990.

Pottier, Bernard. *Linguistique générale: théorie et description.* Paris: Klincksieck, 1974.

– *Sémantique générale.* Presses Universitaires de France, 1992.

Prince, Gerald. *Narratology: The Form and Functioning of Narrative.* Berlin: Mouton, 1982.

Propp, Vladimir. *Morfologiia skazki.* Saint-Petersburg: Nauka and Academia, 1928. 1958 English translation by Laurence Scott revised by Louis A. Wagner, *Morphology of the Folktale.* Austin: University of Texas Press, rev. ed. 1968.

– Struttura e storia nello studio della favola. In *Morfologia della fiaba. Con un intervento di Claude Lévi-Strauss e una replica dell'autore,* edited and translated by Gian Luigi Bravo, 201–29. Torino: Enaudi, 1966. English translation, Study of the Folktale: Structure and History, *Dispositio* 1 (1976): 277–92. Also available as The Structural and Historical Study of the Wondertale in *Theory and History of Folklore,* ed. Anatoly Liberman, 67–81. Minneapolis: University of Minnesota Press, 1984.

Rastier, François. *Sémantique interprétative.* Paris: Presses Universitaires de France, 1987.

– *Sens et textualité.* Paris: Hachette, 1989. Trans. Frank Collins and Paul Perron, *Meaning and Textuality.* Toronto: University of Toronto Press, 1997.

– ed. *Introduction à une science des cultures.* Paris: Presses Universitaires de France, 2003.

– Deniers et veau d'or: des fétiches à l'idole, *Texto!* (March 2004), http://www.revue–texto.net/Inedits/Rastier/Rastier_Deniers.html (accessed 3 August 2007).

Reiss, Timothy. *The Uncertainty of Analysis.* Ithaca, NY: Cornell University Press, 1988.

Renier, Alain, ed. *Espace: construction et signification.* Paris: Éditions de la Villette, 1984.

Renoue, Marie. *Sémiotique et perception esthétique: Pierre Soulages et Sainte-Foy de Conques.* Limoges: Pulim, 2001.

Ricardou, Jean. *Nouveaux problèmes du roman.* Paris: Seuil, 1978.

Richter, David H., ed. *The Critical Tradition: Classic Texts and Contemporary Trends.* 2nd ed. Boston and New York: Bedford/St Martin's, 1998.

Ricoeur, Paul. *Le conflit des interprétations.* Paris: Seuil, 1969. Ed. Don Ihde and trans. Kathleen M. Laughlin, *The Conflict of Interpretations: Essays on Hermeneutics.* Evanston IL: Northwestern University Press, 1974.

– Expliquer et comprendre. Sur quelques connexions remarquables entre la théorie du texte, la théorie de l'action et la théorie de l'histoire, *Revue philosophique de Louvain* 75 (February 1977): 126–47. Rpt. in P. Ricoeur, *Du texte à l'action. Essais d'herméneutique II,* 179–203. Paris: Seuil, 1986.

– On Interpretation. Trans. Kathleen McLaughlin. In *Philosophy in France Today,* ed. Alan Montefiore, 175–97. Cambridge and New York: Cambridge University Press, 1983. Shorter French version, De l'interprétation. In *Du texte à l'action. Essais d'herméneutique II,* 14–39. Paris: Seuil, 1986.

Riffaterre, Michael. *Semiotics of Poetry.* Bloomington: Indiana University Press, 1978.

Rose, Jacqueline. *Sexuality in the Field of Vision.* New York: Verso, 1986.

Said, Edward. *Orientalism.* New York: Vintage, 1978.

Saint-Martin, Fernande. *Les fondements topologiques de la peinture.* Montreal: HMH–Hurtubise, 1980.

– *The Semiotics of Visual Language.* Bloomington: Indiana University Press, 1990.

Sartre, Jean-Paul. *Critique de la raison dialectique, précédé de Questions de méthode.* Paris: Gallimard, 1960. Trans. Alan Sheridan-Smith and Quintin Hoare, *Critique of Dialectical Reason,* ed. Jonathan Rée and Arlette Elkaïm–Sartre. 2 vols. Corrected edition London and New York: Verso, 1991.

Saussure, Ferdinand de. *Cours de linguistique générale.* Ed. Tullio de Mauro. Paris: Payot, 1985 [1st ed. 1916]. Trans. Wade Baskins, *Course in General Linguistics.* New York: Philosophical Library, 1959, rpt. in paperback 1964, 1966 with same pagination.

Schleiermacher, Friedrich. *Hermeneutik.* Heidelberg: C. Winter, 1974. Trans. and ed. Andrew Bowie, *Hermeneutics and Criticism and Other Writings.* Cambridge and New York: Cambridge University Press, 1998.

Schmidt, Siegfried J. *Texttheorie. Probleme einer Linguistik der sprachlichen Kommunikation.* Munich: Fink, rev. ed. 1976.

Searle, John. *Speech Acts: An Essay in the Philosophy of Language.* Cambridge: Cambridge University Press, 1969.

Sebeok, Thomas A., ed. *Encyclopedic Dictionary of Semiotics.* 3 vols. Berlin and New York: Mouton de Gruyter, rev. ed. 1994.

Sebeok, Thomas A., and Donna Jean Umiker-Sebeok, eds. *Advances in Visual Semiotics: The Semiotic Web 1992–93.* Berlin and New York: Mouton de Gruyter, 1995.

Semprini Andrea, ed. *Lo sguardo sociosemiotico: comunicazione, marche, media, pubblicità.* Milan: Franco Angeli, series Impresa, comunicazione, mercato no. 3, 1990, 5th ed., 2003.

– *Marche e mondi possibili. Un approccio semiotico al marketing della marca.* Milan: Franco Angeli, series Impresa, Comunicazione, Mercato, 1993, 6th ed., 2004. Spanish translation, *El marketing de la marca: una aproximación semiótica.* Barcelona: Paidós, 1995.

– *L'objet comme procès et comme action. De la nature et de l'usage des objets dans la vie quotidienne.* Paris: L'Harmattan, 1995. Italian translation, *L'oggetto come processo e come azione. Per una sociosemiotica della vita quotidiana.* Bologna: Progetto Leonardo, Esculapio, series Teoria della Cultura, 1996.

Shapiro, Michael. *The Sense of Grammar: Language as Semeiotic.* Bloomington: Indiana University Press, 1983.

Silverman, Kaja. *The Subject of Semiotics.* New York and Oxford: Oxford University Press, 1983.

Simon, Jean-Paul, and Marc Vernet, eds. *Énonciation et cinéma,* special issue of *Communications* 38 (1983).

Simpson, Paul. *Language, Ideology, and Point of View.* New York: Routledge, series Interface, 1993.

Sonesson, Göran. *Pictorial Concepts: Inquiries into the Semiotic Heritage and Its Relevance to the Interpretation of the Visual World.* Lund, Sweden: Lund University Press, 1989.

Souriau, Paul. *The Aesthetics of Movement.* New York: Oxford University Press, 1950.

Stubbs, Michael. *Discourse Analysis: The Sociological Analysis of Natural Language.* Oxford: Basil Blackwell, 1983.

Suleiman, Susan Rubin. *Authoritarian Fictions. The Ideology of the Novel as a Literary Genre.* New York: Columbia University Press, 1983.

Talmy, Leonard. *Toward a Cognitive Semantics.* 2 vols. Cambridge, MA: MIT Press, 2000.

Tarasti, Eero. *A Theory of Musical Semiotics.* Bloomington: Indiana University Press, 1994.

– *Existential Semiotics.* Bloomington: Indiana University Press, 2000.

– *Signs of Music: A Guide to Musical Semiotics.* New York and Berlin: Mouton de Gruyter, 2002.

Tarski, Alfred. *O logice matematycznej i metodzie dedukcyjne.* Lywów, series Bibljoteczka matematyczna, nos. 3–5, 1936. Trans. O. Helmer, *Introduction to Logic and to the Methodology of Deductive Sciences.* New York: Oxford University Press, 1946, new edition 1994.

Taylor, Victor E., and Charles E. Winquist. *Encyclopedia of Postmodernism.* London: Routledge, 2001.

Tel Quel collective. *Théorie d'ensemble.* Paris: Seuil, 1968.

Thibault, Paul J. *Social Semiotics as Praxis: Text, Social Meaning Making, and Nabokov's Ada.* Minneapolis: University of Minnesota Press, series Theory and History of Literature No. 74, 1991.

Thom, René. *Structural Stability and Morphogenesis: An Outline of a General Theory of Models.* Reading: Benjamin, 1975.

Thürlemann, Felix. *Paul Klee: analyse sémiotique de trois peintures.* Lausanne: L'Age d'homme, 1982.

Todorov, Tzvetan, ed. *Théorie de la littérature. Textes des formalistes russes.* Translated from the Russian by T. Todorov. Paris: Seuil, 1966.

– *Grammaire du 'Décaméron.'* The Hague: Mouton, 1969.

– *La poétique de la prose.* Paris: Seuil, 1971. Trans. Richard Howard, *Introduction to Poetics.* Minneapolis: University of Minnesota Press, 1981.

Tseëlon, Efrat. Fashion and the Signification of Social Order. *Semiotica* 91, no. 1–2 (1992): 1–14.

Turner, Mark. *The Literary Mind.* New York: Oxford University Press, 1996.

Umiker-Sebeok, Donna Jean, ed. *Marketing and Semiotics: New Directions in the Study of Signs for Sale.* Berlin and New York: Mouton de Gruyter, 1987.

Uspenskii, Boris Andreevich. Special issue of *Trudy po znakonym sistenam* (Tartu) 5 (1971). Trans. P.A. Reed, *The Semiotics of the Russian Icon,* ed. Stephen Rudy. Lisse: Peter de Ridder Press, series Semiotics of art, no. 3, 1976.

Wallach Scott, Joan. *Gender and the Politics of History.* New York: Columbia University Press, 1988.

White, Hayden V. *Metahistory: The Historical Imagination in Nineteenth-Century Europe.* Baltimore: Johns Hopkins University Press, 1973.

Wodak, Ruth, and Paul Chilton, eds. *A New Agenda in (Critical) Discourse Analysis. Theory, Methodology, and Interdisciplinarity.* Amsterdam and Philadelphia: John Benjamins, 2005.

Wollen, Peter. *Signs and Meaning in the Cinema.* Bloomington: Indiana University Press, 1969, 2nd ed. 1972.

Young, Lynne, and Claire Harrison, eds. *Systemic Functional Linguistics and Critical Discourse Analysis. Studies in Language Change.* New York: Continuum, 2004.

Zeitoun, Jean, ed. *Sémiotique de l'espace. Architecture, urbanisme, sortir de l'impasse.* Paris: Denoël/Gonthier, 1979.

Zilberberg, Claude. Le Schéma narratif à l'épreuve. *Protée* (Chicoutimi, Quebec) 21, no. 1 (Winter 1993): 65–88.

– *De la forme de vie aux valeurs.* Paris: Universitaires de France, 2011.

Zizek, Slavoj. *Enjoy Your Symptom! Jacques Lacan in Hollywood and Out.* New York: Routledge, 1992.

THRILLERS

[See also: *Adventure Stories; Crime Genre; Horror Fiction; Science Fiction; Spy Fiction*]

Thriller is the term used to refer to fiction that has an exciting, thrilling, spine-tingling plot involving crime, espionage, the supernatural, or some other suspense-creating aspect. The thriller genre traces its origins to the pulp 'cliffhanger' serials of the 1920s and 1930s. These kept readers and movie audiences in suspense because an episode would end when the hero or heroine would get entangled in some dangerous situation, such as being trapped in a room that was on fire with seemingly no escape route. The audience would come back eagerly to the movie theatre the week after, or buy the next issue of the magazine, to find out how the situation would be resolved. Thrillers often overlap with crime or mystery stories. The difference lies in the fact that the hero of a thriller must thwart the villain's plans, rather than uncover the perpetrator of a crime. In a thriller we know who the criminal is; in a whodunit we do not usually know until the end.

Among the various thriller subgenres, the following are the most popular:

- The *action thriller,* which features a protagonist in a race against time to save someone or to stop a villain from destroying the world or killing a group of people. There is plenty of action and the focus is on the physical prowess of the hero or heroine, who is typically an expert in the martial arts or weaponry. Examples include the James Bond, Jason Bourne, and *Transporter* films.
- The *conspiracy thriller,* which revolves around a protagonist facing some conspiracy and thus struggling to expose the people behind it. Examples include: *The Da Vinci Code, The Chancellor Manuscript, JFK,* and *Three Days of the Condor.*
- The *crime thriller,* which involves a crime fighter going after an evil villain, or the police chasing members of gangs or organized crime syndicates. The story revolves around killings, chases, shootouts, and betrayals. Examples include: *The Godfather, Seven, Reservoir Dogs,* and *The Asphalt Jungle.*
- The *disaster thriller,* which features some sort of disaster, human-made or natural, such as a flood, an earthquake, a volcano eruption, a contagious viral outbreak,

a nuclear power plant explosion, or a breakdown in computer networks. Examples include *Earthquake,* the *Poseidon Adventure,* and *Mars Trilogy.*
- The *erotic thriller,* in which a dangerous erotic situation leads to a thrilling resolution or outcome. Examples include: *Basic Instinct, Dressed to Kill, Fatal Attraction,* and *In the Cut.*
- The *horror thriller,* where villains evoke suspense or a feeling of fear or unease. The classic example is Hitchcock's *Psycho,* which not only keeps us in suspense to the end but also evokes fear. Other examples include the Hannibal Lecter, *Hostel, Orphan,* and *Saw* films.
- The *legal thriller,* involving lawyers as protagonists who are often in danger of losing both their legal cases and their lives. Examples include the John Grisham stories and the Perry Mason novels and TV programs.
- The *political* and/or *spy thriller,* in which the protagonist must fight against terrorists or assassins who are trying to bring down the government for which he or she works, and thus the stability of the world. Examples include: the James Bond and Jason Bourne movies, *Seven Days in May, The Day of the Jackal, The Manchurian Candidate, Agency.*
- The *psychological thriller,* which features a conflict between the main protagonist(s) and/or within the minds of the characters. The master of this genre was Alfred Hitchcock with movies such as *Psycho* and *Suspicion* and *Shadow of a Doubt* (these can be categorized in other subgenres as well). Other examples include: *Blue Velvet, The Talented Mr Ripley,* and *The Sixth Sense.*
- The *supernatural thriller,* which combines features of all thrillers (adventure, conflict, chases, etc.) with elements of the occult and the supernatural. Examples include *Carrie* and *Unbreakable.*
- The *techno thriller,* which features the usual ingredients of thrillers in the context of technology, which is described or illustrated dramatically so that the

audience can understand the plot. *Blade Runner* and *The Hunt for Red October* are classic examples of this genre.

Marcel Danesi

Bibliography

Cobley, Paul. *The American Thriller.* New York: Palgrave, 2000.

Derry, Charles. *The Suspense Thriller: Films in the Shadow of Alfred Hitchcock.* Jefferson: McFarland, 1988.

Indick, William. *Psycho Thrillers: Cinematic Explorations of the Mysteries of the Mind.* Jefferson: McFarland, 2006.

Palmer, Jerry. *Thrillers: Genesis and Structure of a Popular Genre.* London: Arnold, 1978.

Rubin, Martin. *Thrillers.* Cambridge: Cambridge University Press, 1999.

TRANSMISSION MODES

[See also: *Analogue Media; Communication; Digital Media*]

There are two main modes in which messages, images, and other forms can be transmitted – *digital* and *analogue*.

Digital modes involve electronic equipment that uses information in the form of the digital numerical binary code – the code consisting of 0 and 1. Devices that are based on digital information include personal computers, calculators, traffic light controllers, compact and video disc players, cellular telephones, text-messaging devices, communications satellites, and high-definition television sets. Unlike digital coding, analogue coding is variable and subject to an infinite number of values. They are electronic systems that have a constantly variable signal. Today, the two modes can be converted into each other. For example, the sound stored on a compact disc (CD) as digital information can be broken down into over 65,000 levels. A CD player then translates this information back into analogue information so that a sound

system can convert it into sound waves.

In sum, analogue refers to any device or signal that has continuously varying qualities, such as voltage or audio; digital refers to the transfer of information encoded as a series of bits (binary digits) rather than as a fluctuating signal in a communications channel. The terms have also been used by extension in fields such as psychology and linguistics. An analogue message, for example, is one that has various interpretations assigned to it; a digital one is limited to its literal meaning.

Marcel Danesi

Bibliography

Dizard, Wilson. *Old Media, New Media.* New York: Longman, 1997.

Hanson, Ralph E. *Mass Communication: Living in a Media World.* New York: McGraw-Hill, 2005.

TWITTER

[See also: *Facebook; MySpace; Social Networking Sites*]

Twitter is a social networking site that has become highly popular throughout the world since it was launched in 2006 by Jack Dorsey. The messages on Twitter are known as *tweets* – a terminology that is intended to suggest the sounds made by birds and thus, by association, the role of aviary communication both in terms of its perceived 'gentleness' and its previous role in human communication (carrier pigeons). Tweets are inserted on a user's profile page and delivered to subscribers known as *followers* – suggesting a kind of 'bird-pet' relation between people. Twitter is essentially an SMS (short message service) service on the Internet, since it allows for text messaging to take place without text-messaging devices. As the site claims, Twitter sees itself more as an 'information network' than a social networking site, although it incorporates both functions.

The term tweeting suggests, as the company itself admits, the feeling of buzzing a friend, similar to the way a bird chirps or tweets to capture attention. Twitter became broadly popular after the 2007 South by Southwest Festival, during which over 60,000 tweets were exchanged by the participants daily on plasma screens in the hallways of the conference. In this way, the conference-goers were able to keep in touch constantly throughout the event. The enthusiasm of the conference-goers soon spread across cyberspace, leading to the emergence of Twitter as a major internet site and tweeting as a common communicative activity. Like all other such sites, Twitter is now delivered on mobile devices and is now largely financed by advertising.

Most tweets are purely conversational – exchanges between friends, associates, colleagues, and acquaintances. Despite what the company says, information is not the main attraction of Twitter – indeed, only around 10 per cent of its contents can be considered to be purely informational. It is psychological and social. Some have designated such sites as venues for 'social grooming,' that is, for presenting oneself in a favourable way to others in order to gain attention and to gather 'followers.' Institutions of various kinds, from NASA to universities, now use tweeting as a source of contact with clients and colleagues.

Some critics claim that the 'twitterization' of culture has changed how we think and react to information, as well as how we perceive interpersonal relations. It is suggested that the limited length of each tweet, the desire for followers, and the constant flow of tweets are all leading to a withdrawal from reflective communication and to an engagement in superficial exchanges. While this may be true, the critics may be missing the historical point that informal daily interaction has probably always been this way. Twitter has simply made it possible for people to enlarge the range of the informal communication, not introduce it into social life.

Marcel Danesi

Bibliography

Bearman, David, and Jennifer Trant, eds. MW2010: Museums and the Web 2010. www .conference.archimuse.com/conferences/ mw/mw2010 (accessed April 2010).
Calore, Michael. Twitter Cloning: Tiny Blogs Bloom Everywhere. *Wired*. *www.wired.com/ software/webservices/news/2007/05/twitter_ clones* (accessed June 2009).

TWO-STEP FLOW OF COMMUNICATION

[See also: *Hypodermic Needle Theory; Lazarsfeld, Paul; Media Effects*]

What information do people use to make decisions? How strong is the influence of the mass media on the formation of public opinion? These were pressing questions in the first half of the twentieth century and continue to be of great relevance today in the information society, where we have seen a massive expansion of information sources and forms of diffusing information through digital networks. The formation of public opinion and individuals' decision-making processes are complex phenomena that have been examined from a wide range of scientific approaches. The two-step flow model of communication represents a scientific breakthrough in the field and a departure from previous work in the area. The model was first proposed and further developed by researchers at the Bureau for Applied Social Research (BASR) at Columbia University in New York who were conducting a series of studies to better understand how public opinion is formed in specific social situations, for example, voting during an electoral campaign.

Historical Background

To understand the importance of the two-step flow of communication model, the historical context in which it was developed has to be reviewed first. Most research on public opinion preceding the model focused on the impact of mass media and postulated that mass media had a strong and direct effect on how people made decisions. This view was often summarized under 'magic bullet theories' or 'hypodermic needle theories' because they emphasized the media's targeted ability to incite particular thoughts or reactions. These theories on media effects assumed that audiences consisted of atomized, homogeneous individuals who reacted in prescribed forms to the messages conveyed in the media without being able to reflect on their behaviour. Researchers probably gave mass media – e.g., film and television – such a prominent role because they were relatively new at the time. Moreover, researchers were often influenced by behaviourist theories that were prevalent in psychology at the time. In this historical context, the researchers at the Bureau for Applied Social Research demonstrated through a series of studies that interpersonal relationships are a central factor in determining changes in public opinion and that mass media play a secondary role. These results led to the development of a new framework, one where interpersonal relations need to be examined in more detail to understand how information diffuses within social systems and influences public opinion.

The Key Assumptions of the Two-Step Flow of Communication Model

Paul F. Lazarsfeld, Bernard Berelson, and Hazel Gaudet documented in their book *The People's Choice* (1968) the results and conclusions of their study of the influence of mass media on political behaviour during the 1940 U.S. election campaign. This was the first panel study to investigate how and why people decide for whom to vote in an election and the changes that occur in their attitudes over time. The study took place in Erie County, Ohio, located on Lake Erie between Cleveland and Toledo. To trace how individuals' voting decisions changed over time and what factors affected these changes, participants were surveyed over a seven-month period about

once a month. The most striking finding from their panel was the low impact of the mass media in comparison to the impact of personal influence on an individual's decision-making process. Two reasons were identified for the strong influence of personal relationships. First, personal relationships reach a greater number of individuals than do the mass media as many people were not exposed to either radio or print. People reported being engaged in discussions with others about who they were going to vote for and why, much more than exposure to radio or print. The findings suggest that political debate with friends and family was an important component in the decision-making process. In particular, personal influence was of relevance for those who had not made a decision about which candidate they would vote for and for those who changed their vote during the campaign. Second, individuals who were less interested in political matters were more likely to discuss the electoral campaign with personal ties than obtain information from formal sources, such as newspapers or the radio.

Furthermore, Lazarsfeld, Berelson, and Gaudet found that information did not flow equally through the social network. They identified certain key individuals, whom they termed 'opinion leaders,' as playing an important role in how information diffuses. Opinion leaders differed from non-leaders in that they reported that formal sources of information were more effective than personal relationships as sources of influence. In addition, opinion leaders were more likely to engage in political debate than non-leaders. Based on these findings, the authors postulated the two-step flow of communication hypothesis, which stated that information often flows from the mass media to opinion leaders and from them to the non-leaders. These findings led the authors to revise the assumptions previously made about the mass audience and its relationship to the mass media. No longer could the notion prevail of an isolated, homogeneous mass audience solely influenced by the mass media. What emerged, however, was the image of a connected audience embedded in a complex social system, through which information flows in a flexible and dynamic manner. Moreover, the study pointed toward complex forms of information diffusion through people's connections, often with key individuals in the centre of the information flow. This study represented a turning point in terms of how mass media and information flow were conceptualized.

Limitations in the Conceptualization of the Two-Step Flow of Communication Model

Despite the importance of the two-step flow of communication model for understanding how information diffuses in society and what the role of mass media is, the model also has some limitations. One problem is that the conceptualization of opinion leaders is based primarily on respondents' self-reported data. Nevertheless, this is not a sufficient source of data to identify opinion leaders because people may be biased in terms of their influence on others' opinions and their role in the social system. Another problem is that follow-up studies found that opinion leaders were not exposed randomly to any type of information, but to information that was related to the area in which they exerted their influence. The patterns of information seeking thus seem to be determined by the area of interest of the opinion leader. At the same time, opinion leadership will only occur in this area, making the phenomenon specific to subjects or domains of opinion leadership.

Further Developments of the Two-Step Flow of Communication Model

Intensive debate followed the publication of *The People's Choice* in the field of public opinion, social theory, and communication. Two key developments resulting from the two-step flow of communication hypothesis were the refinement of the model itself and the introduction of formal methods to study the influence of social relationships on information flow. In terms of the refinement of the model, in a study on how medical innovations diffuse, James S. Coleman, Elihu Katz, and Herbert Menzel (1966) found that influential doctors, in comparison to non-influential ones, not only show higher readership of medical journals, but also have the tendency to more frequently attend out-of-town meetings. Opinion leaders' outward orientation was described as *cosmopolitanism*, an interest in happenings outside of the immediate environment. Similarly, Merton's study of influentials examined those individuals who are at the centre of their advice-giving network and their patterns of media use. To identify influentials in a small town, Merton interviewed eighty-six informants in Rovere and asked them whom they would turn to for help or advice. Merton realized that the distinction between influentials and non-influentials did not fully explain different patterns of media use. He therefore introduced a second dimension, namely influentials' foci of attention, that distinguishes between two types of influentials. The *locals* focused on local issues, while the *cosmopolitans* focused on issues of importance that lay outside the town. This distinction turned out to be fruitful in terms of understanding patterns of media use. Cosmopolitans read more, but, more important, they read other types of information sources. Locals were more inclined to read tabloids because these informed them about local developments and gossip. Similarly, the two types of influentials also showed different patterns of socializing. Cosmopolitans had friends who shared similar interests and were concerned with culture and politics, while locals tended to know many people. Thus, distinctive patterns and functions of information sources and socializing could be observed for distinctive social roles.

In terms of the methodology, better approaches have been proposed to the measurement of opinion leaders and how information flows to them and from them. For example, social network analysis (SNA) developed as an interdisciplinary area of study that focuses on the theory and methodology of how individuals in society are connected and how information and other resources flow through these connections or ties. SNA is a compilation of concepts and methods that can be used to analyse the relational aspects of social structure. It focuses on observable interactions between individual persons and patterns of relationships among groups of individuals. In addition, the foundation of the International Network for Social Network Analysis (INSNA) in 1978 by Professor Barry Wellman has increased the popularity of SNA. The association unites researchers from many countries, publishes *Connections*, a bi-annual bulletin featuring news, scholarly articles, abstracts, and book reviews, and also maintains a website. Lastly, it sponsors the annual International Social Networks conference and leads a discussion forum called SOCNET.

Anabel Quan-Haase

Online Resource

INSNA (International Network for Social Network Analysis): http://www.insna.org/. INSNA is an association that brings together parties interested in methods and theory of social network analysis. The website contains a wide range of resources for scholars.

Bibliography

Berelson, Bernard R., Paul F. Lazarsfeld, and William N. McFee. *Voting: A Study of Opinion Formation in a Presidential Campaign*. Chicago: University of Chicago Press, 1954.

Cohen, Bernard C. *The Press and Foreign Policy*. Princeton: Princeton University Press, 1963.

Coleman, James S., Elihu Katz, and Herbert Menzel. *Medical Innovation: A Diffusion Study*. New York: Bobbs Merrill, 1966.

Katz, Elihu. The Two-Step Flow of Communication: An Up-to-Date Report on a Hypothesis. *Opinion Quarterly* 21, no. 1 (1957): 61–78.

Katz, Elihu, and Paul F. Lazarsfeld. *Personal Influence: The Part Played by People in the Flow of Mass Communications*. Glencoe, IL: Free Press, 1955.

Klapper, Joseph T. *The Effects of Mass Communication*. New York: Free Press, 1960.

Lippmann, Walter. *Public Opinion*. New York: Macmillan, 1922.

McQuail, Denis, and Sven Windahl. *Communication Models for the Study of Mass Communication*. London: Longman, 1993.

Merton, Robert K. Patterns of Influence: Cosmopolitans and Locals. In *Social Theory and Social Structure*, ed. Robert K. Merton, 387–420. Glencoe, IL: The Free Press, 1999.

Miller, Katherine. *Communication Theories: Perspectives, Processes, and Contexts*. 2nd ed. New York: McGraw-Hill, 2005.

Rogers, Everett M. *Diffusion of Innovations*. New York: Free Press, 1962.

– *A History of Communication Study: A Biographical Approach*. New York: Free Press, 1994.

Ryan, Bryce, and Neil C. Gross. The Diffusion of Hybrid Seed Corn in Two Iowa Communities. *Rural Sociology* 8, no. 1 (1943): 15–24.

Valente, Thomas W. *Network Models of the Diffusion Innovations*. Cresskill, NJ: Hampton Press, 1995.

Wellman, Barry, and S.D. Berkowitz, eds. *Social Structures: A Network Approach*. Cambridge: Cambridge University Press, 1988.

U

USES AND GRATIFICATIONS

[See also: *Hypodermic Needle Theory; Katz, Elihu; Media Effects*]

One of the more enduring theoretical frameworks from which to examine questions of 'how' and 'why' individuals make use of a diverse array of media has been the uses and gratifications theory to media behaviour. Uses and gratifications theory and its particular methodological approach have provoked rigorous academic debate regarding its strengths, weaknesses, and, most important, its continued relevance to new media technologies. The personal computer, the internet, mobile phones, and the wide range of applications available online have all necessitated changes to, and new applications of, the uses and gratifications paradigm. Throughout the various shifts and updates to the theoretical paradigm that have taken place, however, there has remained a consistent list of overarching research questions that have guided scholars, including: Why do people use one type of medium or technology instead of another? Are the gratifications individuals obtain through the use of one medium rather than another an accurate predictor of repeated use?

The Role of the Audience

One of the central presuppositions of uses and gratifications theory is that the audience is not passive, inert, or submissively duped by the messages originating from media sources. Early theories on mass communication conceived of the audience as homogeneous and proposed that individual audience members would express identical reactions to media communications regardless of their individual differences. In uses and gratifications theory, the audience is characterized as active, discerning, and motivated in their media use. The goal-directedness of the mass audience is what distinguishes uses and gratifications theory from previous approaches in communication theory, such as the hypodermic needle model. In this model, the link between the media and the audience is seen as unidirectional, with the media injecting a passive audience member with a message that is uncritically accepted by the individual. In opposition to this model, Elihu Katz, a pioneer of uses and gratifications research, argues that more attention needs to be devoted to what people do with the media rather than the influence or impact of the media on the individual. According to Katz, people's individual values, interests, social roles, and life circumstances are important factors in shaping how and which media are consumed. Moreover, people make sense of the messages originating from the media based on these idiosyncratic factors, and therefore media use needs to be understood as an individual choice instead of being examined from the perspective of media influence or impact.

When we conceive of the audience as actively choosing and using media in response to specific needs or goals, the foundations for examining the identifiable gratifications that the media provide are in place. When an audience has a need for escape, for instance, there are specific media that may gratify this need in a more satisfactory manner than others. If audience members are unsatisfied with the level of gratification provided by one medium, they will look to a different medium to obtain the gratifications initially sought yet withheld. In the uses and gratifications paradigm, repeated use of a particular medium indicates that the individual is gratifying an identifiable need in a satisfactory fashion. Therefore, identifying the particular needs or goals of the individual in his or her use of a particular medium is the first step in identifying the reciprocal gratifications obtained through specific media use.

Understanding Needs

In a defining article entitled 'On the Use of Mass Media for Important Things,' Elihu Katz, Michael Gurevitch, and Hadassah Haas (1973) identified five categories that conceptually grouped an audience member's needs. The first category is cognitive need. These needs are related to strengthening the individual's knowledge and understanding of current and past events as they are portrayed in the media. The second category is affective needs. These needs are related to creating aesthetic, pleasurable, and emotional experiences that result from exposure to the various media. The third category is integrative needs. With integrative needs the individual's desire to augment his or her credibility, confidence, stability, and status through the ownership and use of media is identified. The fourth category is needs related to strengthening contact with family, friends, and the social world in general. These needs can also sometimes perform an integrative function. Finally, needs related to escape or tension release are de-fined in terms of distancing oneself from one's traditional or habitual social roles. Katz, Gurevitch, and Haas drew up these five categories to serve as general umbrella groupings that encompass the specific needs that could potentially be satisfied by various media.

Media Gratifications

In addition to examining the types of needs that motivate individual audience members, it is equally important to examine in more detail the actual gratifications that media use provides. For Elihu Katz, Jay G. Blumler, and Michael Gurevitch (1974), the source of these gratifications originates in three central attributes and/or situations of media use: (1) gratifications can be obtained through the particular content to which the individual is exposed by the various media; (2) gratifications can be obtained through simply being exposed to the media; and (3) gratifications can be obtained from the social context in which media consumption takes place. Further analysing the sources of gratifications that audience members obtain from the media, Katz, Blumler, and Gurevitch argue that each medium offers a unique blend of characteristics that distinguish its gratifications from other media. In terms of content, each medium will provide content that is characteristic of its format. Additionally, media diverge in the kinds of attributes they naturally embody. For instance, some media provide only printed text, while other media provide only sound. And still other media offer a multiplicity of blended formats. Finally, each medium provides different settings where exposure to the media takes place, which also affect the gratifications obtained. Television is usually watched in the privacy of the home, whereas movies are often seen in public theatres. There exists a wide range of media, and the different characteristics of each will lead to different types and levels of gratifications. With all of these variances taken into consideration, there are nonetheless gratifications received from the media that can generally be classified into four different categories, as will be discussed next.

Media theorists Denis McQuail, Jay G. Blumler, and J.R. Brown (1972) have divided gratifications into four distinct categories. *Diversion* is the first gratification and refers to the pleasure of escaping from the constraints of routine and the problems associated with everyday life. Media also serve as places of emotional release enabling the individual to overcome stress, dysphoria, and other negative affect. The second gratification is linked to *personal relationships* and shows the role of the media as a venue for socialization with friends and family. It also sees the media as a potential substitute for companionship when people feel isolated. The third gratification consists of *personal identity* and describes how media allow individuals to explore reality from different perspectives that reinforce or challenge their social norms, mores, and values. Finally, the media offer a form of gratification that has been called a *surveillance* or a *watchdog* function. The media provide members of society with information on socio-political and cultural events of personal and/or social importance. In this way, gratifications are obtained by 'keeping an eye on' current news and allowing citizens to be informed. The four types of gratifications proposed by McQuail, Blumler, and Brown have been influential in understanding what motivates people to use different media. Research has demonstrated that other types of gratifications are also possible, and a number of disparate typologies have been developed that account for the specifics of different media and the various social situations in which they are consumed.

In uses and gratifications theory a key distinction is made between gratifications obtained and gratifications sought. Gratifications obtained refer to those gratifications that audience members actually experience through their use of the media. In contrast, gratifications sought refer to those gratifications that audience members expect to

obtain from a medium before they have actually come into contact with it. What is central is that gratifications obtained may dovetail or differ in a significant fashion from the gratifications sought, and the resulting gap can predict the level of satisfaction/dissatisfaction that individual audience members have with a particular medium. When a medium provides or surpasses the expected gratifications initially sought, this leads to recurrent use of the medium and ultimately to predictable consumption habits. In cases where a medium does not fulfil the sought-after gratifications, audience members will be disappointed and will predictably no longer continue utilizing the specific medium. This will lead audience members to seek out a different medium that can provide the kinds of gratifications they are seeking. Therefore, understanding the gap between gratifications obtained and gratifications sought is important for analysing how different audience members utilize various kinds of media, the expectations that they bring to their media habits, and the gratifications they actually obtain from their exposure to a diverse array of media products. This kind of analysis also helps to explain the development of media habits and the role of media in the individual audience member's everyday life.

Limitations of Uses and Gratifications Theory

Despite being highly influential in the field of communications, the uses and gratifications theory has also been pointedly criticized for being simplistically functional and lacking sophistication and nuance. Thomas E. Ruggiero (2000), in an article entitled 'Uses and Gratifications Theory in the 21st Century,' lists a number of arguments that summarize much of the historical criticism of uses and gratifications theory. The first criticism is that uses and gratifications theory is too focused on the individual and does not consider in enough detail the social context of media use. This narrow focus on individuals and their use of media makes it difficult to examine the broader societal implications of media use. Second, core conceptual categories, such as motives, needs, uses, and gratifications, have been ill-defined and used inconsistently across a number of studies. This has created a climate of confusion regarding the precise meaning and definition of these core concepts, which has led to inconsistent use and opaque theorizing when clarity and precision are required. Third, individual studies, such as Robert Abelman's (1987), have focused on distinct media or genres within a medium and have identified a wide range of uses and gratifications unique to the various media and/or genres. This has led to excessively narrow typological distinctions, making it difficult to compare results across media and/or genres and resulting in a lack of internal theoretical coherence. Finally, the foundational presupposition of an active audience that autonomously controls the choices made regarding their patterns of media consumption, and just as significantly an audience that is able to accurately report on their personal motivations for using a particular medium after the fact, has been called into question because it may be simplistic, naive, or simply incorrect. Overall, the approach focuses on an individual's use of media and the gratifications accrued without examining macro-level phenomena linked to the role of ownership and control in mass media and the social, political, and economic consequences of media consumption. Thereby it has a rather limited scope and is only applicable to a limited number of phenomena and research questions. While it is important to be aware of these limitations, uses and gratifications theory has made an important contribution to answering questions about how media use changes over time, how an individual's choices are influenced by the degree of gratification obtained through use, the influence of the contexts in which media are consumed, and what role audience choice plays in the individuated uses of media. The approach continues to have relevance

to the field of communication theory today due in part to its applicability across a wide range of media products and genres.

Uses and Gratifications Theory in New Media

New media, such as videogames, instant messaging (IM), and blogging, are in many ways fundamentally distinct from old media, such as newspapers, radio, and television. One of the distinguishing features of new media is interactivity, which describes the potential of users to provide content as a response to a source or communication partner. Moreover, in new media, the distinction between consumer and producer tends to blur, which has led to the introduction of the term 'prosumer' to describe how users can take control over the production and distribution of content. Interactivity becomes central in the uses and gratifications theory because it directly addresses the notion of the active audience member who has control over the communication process and makes choices about media use. The internet through digitization provides users great flexibility. They can store, duplicate, or print texts and images, or diffuse information through websites, blogs, online communities, and different types of computer-mediated communication. This provides audience members with more control over content, its distribution, and use than traditional media.

The uses and gratifications theory has provided some insight into what gratifications interactive media are providing. Louisa Ha and E. Lincoln James in their article 'Interactivity Re-examined' (1998) suggest that four user types exist on the internet, each of them fulfilling different kinds of needs online. For 'self-indulgers' and 'Web surfers,' the playfulness of interactive media fulfils a need for entertainment. For this group, interactive media also allow them to make choices, giving them more control over their communication experience. By contrast, for task-oriented users, the internet provides a wide array of sources allowing them to be well-informed. For expressive users, computer-mediated communication allows for exchanges around the globe in real time with people who share common interests. A series of studies has also emerged around the uses and gratifications of specific types of new media. For example, studies looking at the use of instant messaging and the gratifications obtained from users found that IM is used primarily for social entertainment purposes followed by social attention, task accomplishment, and meeting new people. Some differences have been found in motivations between males and females, with the former indicating use of IM primarily for reasons of sociability and the latter for entertainment and relaxation. Taken together, IM users see it as a key catalyst for forming and maintaining social relationships, providing entertainment, and diversion. Important new research from the uses and gratifications theory is emerging in the area of new media and shedding light on what motivates individuals, in particular young people, to switch from traditional media to new media and what kinds of gratifications new media are providing to its users.

Anabel Quan-Haase and Brian A. Brown

Bibliography

Abelman, Robert. Why Do People Watch Religious TV? A Uses and Gratifications Approach. *Review of Religious Research* 29, no. 2 (December 1987): 199–210.

Blumler, Jay G., and Elihu Katz, eds. *The Uses of Mass Communications: Current Perspectives on Gratifications Research.* Beverly Hills, CA: Sage, 1974.

Flanagin, Andrew J. IM Online: Instant Messaging Use among College Students in Communication Research Reports 22, no. 3 (August 2005): 175–87.

Ha, Louisa, and E. Lincoln James. Interactivity Re-Examined: A Baseline Analysis of Early Business Web Sites. *Journal of Broadcasting and Electronic Media*, 42, no. 4 (1998): 457–74.

Katz, Elihu, Michael Gurevitch, and Hadassah Haas. On the Use of Mass Media for Important Things. *American Sociological Review* 38 (April 1973): 164–81.

Katz, Elihu, Jay G. Blumer, and Michael Gurevitch. Utilization of Mass Communication by the Individual. In *The Uses of Mass Communications: Current Perspectives on Gratifications Research,* ed. Jay G. Blumler and Elihu Katz, 19–32. London: Sage Annual Reviews of Communication Research Volume 3, 1974.

LaRose, Robert, Dana Mastro, and Matthew S. Eastin. Understanding Internet Usage: A Social-Cognitive Approach to Uses and Gratifications. In *Social Science Review* 19, no. 4 (winter 2001): 395–413.

Leung, Louis. College Student Motives for Chatting on ICQ. *New Media and Society* 3, no. 4 (2001): 483–500.

McQuail, Denis. With the Benefit of Hindsight: Reflections on the Uses and Gratification Paradigm. *Critical Studies in Mass Communication* 1, no. 1984 (1984): 177–93.

McQuail, Denis, Jay G. Blumler, and J.R. Brown. The Television Audience: A Revised Perspective. In *Sociology of Mass Communication,* ed. Denis McQuail, 135–65. London: Longman, 1972.

O'Donohow, Stephanie. Advertising Uses and Gratifications. *European Journal of Marketing* 28, no. 8/9 (1994): 52–75.

Ruggiero, Thomas E. Uses and Gratifications Theory in the 21st Century. *Mass Communication and Society* 3, no. 1 (2000): 3–37.

V

VAUDEVILLE

[See also: *Radio; Television, History of*]

Vaudeville is a form of theatrical presentation that developed in late nineteenth-century America. The main element of the form was variety; rather than attempting large-scale, unified artistic works, vaudeville houses presented a series of short pieces by different performers in a range of styles. These could include operatic arias, Shakespearean monologues, scientific lecture-demonstrations, animal acts, slapstick comedy, and 'song and dance numbers.'

Vaudeville was innovative in its accessibility. Many urban vaudeville houses were open from morning until night; after paying their entry fees to a 'continuous vaudeville,' patrons could stay, if they liked, until the house closed. Small-town vaudeville, presented by travelling companies, made cultural highlights accessible to many rural people.

High-risk new commissioned works, and long, expensive rehearsals are part of traditional theatre, opera, and ballet. Vaudeville's simpler form meant these could be made available broadly. These lower overhead costs meant lower ticket prices, which put vaudeville shows within the means of a broad public. Low costs and popular pricing made vaudeville a commercially successful form.

Vaudeville producers often firmly guided the tone of their productions, giving strict guidelines to performers about acceptable material, and hiring ushers who could double as bouncers if necessary. Some vaudevilles were closely related to the flamboyant burlesque shows, while others avoided 'the use of a single word, expression or situation that will offend the intelligent, refined and cultured classes' (1902 ad for 'Polite Vaudeville').

With their crowd-pleasing, commercial emphasis, vaudevilles were often criticized as debased by lovers of the arts. However, for famous performing artists, a season in vaudeville could mean a well-paying contract and recognition from wider audiences. Many notable actors, singers, and dancers of the era chose to perform with vaudeville and sometimes returned to their traditional venues with new audiences, thanks to their vaudeville exposure.

Between these famous acts, other performers would present the lighter, folksier fare for which vaudeville is most remembered. The flexible variety format meant that 'small-time' producers could sometimes risk presenting unknown acts to fill out a program. If the unknowns were booed off the stage, they could be fired immediately; if they were entertaining, they could perhaps rise to fame and the 'big time.'

Vaudeville shows had no set format, but certain positions were considered the 'best in the bill.' Acts that did not require sound, such as acrobats or mimes, were often used as 'warm-up acts' to quiet down new audiences, and deliberately terrible acts were used as 'chasers' to empty the house.

After decades of popularity, vaudeville was eventually superseded by film. Although there were attempts to combine vaudeville and cinema, mixing short films and live performance, film soon replaced vaudeville as popular, cheap entertainment. The vaudevillians most remembered today are those who, like Charlie Chaplin, the Marx Brothers, Mae West, and W.C. Fields, successfully translated their vaudeville acts into this new medium.

Tricia Postle

Bibliography

Vaudeville, Old and New: An Encyclopedia of Variety Performers in America. London: Routledge, 2007.

VIDEO

[See also: *Cinema, History of; Photography; Video Games; Video Games, History of*]

The term *video* refers to any system of recording or broadcasting visual images electronically. Originating from Latin for 'I see,' video can refer to a movie recorded on videotape or disk; a short movie made by a musical group to accompany a song; or any visual text that contains some artistic or narrative form. Today, with the efficiency, practicality, and affordability of digital cameras, it is possible for amateurs to make videos and to distribute them broadly via the internet with appropriate software. Digital recording devices installed in cellular telephones or digital photo cameras are extremely portable, making it easy to record and transmit video almost instantly. In a sense, we now live in a 'video-verse' ('video universe').

Videos have had an immense impact on modern soceity. The music video, a performance of a song accompanied by a dramatic or narrative text, became popularized through the Music Television (MTV) network in the 1980s. While MTV is now known as a youth network, its music videos strongly influenced and continue to influence popular culture as well as advertising in their style and general texture. With the advent of the music video, a video jockey (VJ) who introduces and comments on the videos has also become common. In 2005, the video website YouTube was introduced, defining the form, content, and aesthetic patterns that make up the contemporary video scene. YouTube was one of the first websites that allowed for the easy uploading of videos. With video recorders found on simple handheld devices, one can quickly upload a video that has the potential to be viewed by millions.

Mariana Bockarova

Bibliography

Mellor, David. *A Sound Person's Guide to Video.* Woburn, MA: Focal Press, 2000.

Music Video. Columbia Encyclopedia, Sixth Edition. 2008. http://www.encyclopedia.com/doc/1E1-musicvide.html (accessed 6 January 2009).

Video Jockey. Oxford Pocket Dictionary of Current English. Encyclopedia.com. http://www.encyclopedia.com/doc/1O999-videojockey.html (accessed 6 January 2009).

VIDEO GAMES

[See also: *Video; Video Games, Effects of; Virtual Reality*]

The terms video game, computer game, and digital game have increasingly become conflated. What have traditionally been called video games – that is, games played via a monitor and controller through a console with interchangeable games (e.g., XBox, Playstation2, Nintendo, Atari) – are included with games designed for play on personal computers (CD-ROM games, massively multiplayer online games [MMOGS], simple Flash-based games), handheld game machines (e.g., GameBoy, GameGear, Playstation Portable, NintendoDS), and, more recently, mobile phones and personal data assistants. While this plethora of platforms is of academic interest, for the sake of specificity the issues discussed here will focus on console-based video games, which make up 57 per cent of the software sales market (Kerr 2006).

History of Video Games

There is some debate as to what the 'first' video game was. Candidates range from a cathode ray tube game developed in 1947 by Thomas T. Goldsmith Jr and Estle Ray Mann, to a tic-tac-toe game created by Alexander Douglas in 1952, to the more oft-cited 1958 tennis simulation created by William Higginbotham. It was not until 1972 that the Magnavox Odyssey became the first commercially sold home video gaming system. That same year Atari produced *Pong*, one of the most widely recognized early video games. The Atari 2600, which came out in 1977, proved much more popular than the Odyssey, becoming the first console to achieve wide commercial success. This success, however, did not last long. The video game 'crash' of 1983 marked a point of decline in the U.S. video game industry and the rise of the Japanese gaming industry. Nintendo released its Entertainment System (NES) in 1983, followed by SEGA with its Master System (1985) and Genesis (1989). Both companies' success was highly related to their use of character branding: the *Mario Brothers* (Ocean Software, 1987) for Nintendo and *Sonic the Hedgehog* (SEGA, 1991) for SEGA.

Video game history following this early period becomes a story of one-upmanship. In 1991, Nintendo responded to SEGA's presence with the SuperNES. Atari attempted, and failed, to re-enter the market with the 64-bit Jaguar console in 1993. Sony entered the console wars in 1994, with its PlayStation. The introduction of the PlayStation limited the impact of SEGA's Saturn (1995), the first system to allow internet access. The Nintendo64, released in 1996, was also unsuccessful in comparison to the Playstation, but still a highly marketed and reasonably successful system. The 1998 SEGA Dreamcast struggled due to a lack of games that made use of its online gaming capabilities, as well as a lack of overall investment on the part of game developers. This marked the end of SEGA's participation in the console wars as they shifted their focus from hardware to game software from that point on. The new millennium was defined by the struggles between three consoles: Sony's Playstation2, Nintendo's GameCube, and relative newcomer Microsoft's Xbox. The modern console war is defined by these systems' successors: Sony's Playstation3, Nintendo's Wii, and Microsoft's Xbox360.

Genres of Games

There are many different types of video games (Kerr 2006). The most noted genres include the following (though these categories are not mutually exclusive):

- *Platform:* Characters in these games climb up and down or jump to and from platforms while progressing through obstacles and achieving game goals (*Mario Brothers*, *Donkey Kong*).
- *Adventure:* These games involve puzzle-solving, exploration, and interaction with non-player characters (NPCs), and are narratively focused (*Myst* and *The Secret of Monkey Island*).
- *Roleplaying (RPGs):* These games allow for the development of characters and teams via use of statistics, available characteristics, and success in the game. These games often have quests aside from the main game objective that allow for character development and non-linear game play (the *Final Fantasy* series and *Fallout: Brotherhood of Steal*).
- *Sports:* These games simulate various traditional sports (football, basketball, hockey) and are consistently among the

top-selling games. More often than not, these games are produced under licensing agreements with professional sports organizations, but some are also fantasy-based (the *Madden* series of NFL games and *Backyard Football*).

- *Racing:* As with sports games above, these are also simulation games. These games involve racing a variety of vehicles around tracks of varying complexity and character (*Live for Speed* and the *NASCAR Racing* series).
- *Action:* These are typically marked by the presence of violence as the main feature. They rarely have deep narratives or character interaction and rely on 'twitch' (or fast reaction) game play (*Mortal Kombat* and *Street Fighter*).
- *First Person Shooters (FPS):* These are a subgenre of action games that are exemplified by a point of view allowing players to see what is in front of their avatar and their hand/gun. Other characteristics of play are the increasing deadliness of weapons available as one progresses through the game and an emphasis on 'twitch' play (*Doom* and *Duke Nukem*).
- *Puzzle:* These are among the more addictive types of games, as they are characterized by short rounds and easy accessibility. Players rely on logic, pattern recognition, and strategy (*Tetris* and *Lemmings*).
- *Simulation:* Simulations encompass a wide variety of games ranging from flight simulators to city planning games. The main characteristic of this genre is the emphasis on realistic situations, though in some cases this is a very simplified version of reality (*The Sims* and *Nintendogs*).
- *Strategy:* These games are broadly described as ones in which the player's decisions have high significance in determining game outcomes. They require logical thinking, often occur in real time (or speeded up real time), and have more abstract forms of success than other game genres (*Civilization* and *Age of Empires*).

Demographics

In 2005, video games made $6.1 billion in sales (Entertainment Software Association 2006). A major concern for both the video game industry and academic game research is who plays these games. According to the latest market data, 69 per cent of American heads of household played video games in 2005 (ibid.). Forty-four per cent of video game players are between eighteen and forty-nine years of age with the average age of video game purchasers around forty. Twenty-five per cent of gamers were over the age of fifty in 2005; 38 per cent of gamers were female. Although there are no market demographics that analyse the racial/ethnic breakdown of gamers specifically, one article notes a study by the Kaiser Family Foundation that found African Americans between eight and eighteen years old are more dedicated gamers, in terms of time and monetary investment, than their white counterparts (Wilburn 2005).

Themes in the Literature

Since their inception, video games have been the target of academic scrutiny. Four main themes are found in the game studies literature: the effects of violent game content on the audience, the social effects of game play, the impact of group representation in games (gender, race, and so on), and the relationship between video games and learning.

Violence

Video game violence, particularly in the aftermath of the Columbine High School shootings of 1999, has been the source of much concern for academics, legislators, and parents. Many studies have attempted to quantify the amount of violence in video games, but differences in numbers arise when different definitions of violence are used. One study, analysing the top 78 games in 1999, found that 25 per cent included extreme violence and 30 per cent had some violence (Walsh 1999). A 2001 review of the top seventy video games determined that 89 per cent contained violence of some kind; 49 per cent had serious violence; 40 per cent comic violence; 41 per cent required violence to complete game goals; and 17 per cent used violence as the main focus of the game (Glaubke and Children Now 2002).

Several authors have argued that because video games require active engagement by the audience they are actually more harmful and likely to induce players to violence when compared with traditional media (Anderson and Bushman 2002; Dill and Dill 1998; Grossman and DeGaetano 1999). Research on the matter is uncertain as survey data cannot prove causation; experimental data cannot prove long-term effects; violence and aggression are often defined in very different manners; sample sizes are small; and the relationship between experimental and everyday settings is questionable. Bryce and Rutter's (2006) review of the video game violence literature concludes that due to the above methodological problems 'the proposed consequences of exposure to game violence [are] inconclusive and often contradictory.' However, Anderson (2003) has argued that the wealth of studies across these various methodologies does support a link between violent video game play and aggression. Further, Gentile and Anderson (2006) propose that the effects of violent video game content can be mitigated or enhanced by various child-specific factors, including possessing a hostile attribution bias (risk is higher), being a boy (risk is higher), having parents involved in media-related decisions (risk is lower), or a prior history of fighting (risk is higher).

Social Impact

Since the earliest days of video game play concerns have been raised about the socially isolating qualities of gaming. Most research has found, however, that video game play is much more socially active than it is socially secluding. Much of the literature studying this topic has focused on computer-based MMOG playing and not on console play. Generally speaking, industry statistics claim that 51 per cent of gamers play 'in-person with other players at least one hour a week' and a quarter 'play games with others online for at least an hour per week' (ESA 2006). With the presence of online play capabilities in all of the next-generation consoles, this number will probably rise.

Representation

Most of the video game representation literature has focused on the representation of women in games; however, racial representations and, to a lesser extent, sexual minority representations are beginning to receive attention (Barton 2004; Huntemann and Media Education Foundation 2002; Delp 1997; Glaubke and Children Now 2002; Cassell and Jenkins 2000; Leonard 2006; Beasley and Collins Standley 2002). There are two separate types of concerns regarding in-game representation. The first is the impact of negative or stereotypical portrayals of minority groups on perceptions of that group. The second is the impact of 'symbolic annihilation' (discussed in Tuchman 1978; Gerbner and Gross 1976) of minority groups on members of those groups becoming gamers. For instance, Cassell and Jenkins (2000) note that the oversexualized and objectified representations of women in games make gaming an unwelcoming environment for female gamers.

Learning

A large body of research suggests that video games as a medium are well suited for learning. Some researchers believe that games can encourage problem-solving skills and logical thinking (Inkpen et al. 1995; Higgins 2000; Whitebread 1997). Kirriemuir and McFarlane (2004) point out that much of this research has been based primarily on extrapolating from psychological theory rather than empirical research: 'Recent studies at NESTA Futurelab have raised some questions as to whether children are in fact able to move from intuitive problem solving in the game to an understanding of effective processes for identifying problems and generating hypotheses and solutions in other context.'

Along similar lines, a review of literature by Sandford and Williamson (2005) states that 'computer games are designed "to be learned" and therefore provide models of goods learning principles.' Studies on learning through games in informal settings (i.e., outside of school) find that game research increasingly focuses on how game structure encourages learning, rather than what content children are learning from particular games. These researchers point to the theories of Seymour Papert (1980), Thomas Malone (1980), Steven Johnson (2005), and James Paul Gee (2003) as evidence for the learning-supportive quality of video and computer games. Moreover, the social and collaborative aspects of games (both online and off) allow opportunities for children to teach one another how to play games more effectively. These studies are balanced with the acknowledgment that games used outside of school are tied to issues of childhood obesity, are often violent, and lack adequate representations of women and minorities.

Video game consoles have existed for three and a half decades. While industry forerunners like *Pong* used only simple graphics, many modern video games possess increasingly realistic (or at least high-resolution) visual imagery. Early video games relied on simple control systems, while the newer systems rely on more complex input schemes. Some systems have moved to motion-sensitive controllers or even full-body movements. Not all video games require complex movements or have true-to-life realistic graphics. Because of their varying quality, complexity, cost, and reach, it is difficult to make many wide-sweeping claims about video games. What can be said, however, is that video games have made a significant impact on popular culture around the world.

Adrienne Shaw

Bibliography

Andersen, Craig A. An Update on the Effects of Playing Violent Video Games. *Journal of Adolescence* 27 (2003): 113–22.

Anderson, Craig A., and Brad J. Bushman. Human Aggression. *Annual Review of Psychology* 53 (2002): 27–51.

Barton, Matthew D. Gay Characters in Video Games, 17 March 2004. http://www .armchairarcade.com/aamain/content. php?article.27 (accessed 1 April 2006).

Beasley, Berrin, and Tracy Collins Standley. Shirts vs Skins: Clothing as an Indicator of Gender Role Stereotyping in Video Games. *Mass Communication and Society* 5, no. 3 (2002): 279–93.

Bryce, Jo, and Jason Rutter. Digital Games and the Violence Debate. In *Understanding Digital Games*. London: Sage, 2006.

Cassell, Justine, and Henry Jenkins, eds. *From Barbie to Mortal Kombat: Gender and Computer Games*. Cambridge, MA: MIT Press, 2000.

Delp, Christopher A. *Boy Toys: The Construction of Gendered and Racialized Identities in Video Games*. Greenville, NC: East Carolina University, 1997.

Dill, Karen E., and Jody C. Dill. 1998. Video Game Violence: A Review of the Empirical Literature. *Aggression and Violent Behavior* 3, no. 4 (1998): 407–28.

Entertainment Software Association (ESA). *Essential Facts about the Computer and Video Game Industry* (2006). http://www.theesa.com/ archives/files/Essential%20Facts%202006.pdf (accessed March 2007).

Gee, James Paul. *What Video Games Have to Teach Us about Learning and Literacy*. New York: Palgrave Macmillan, 2003.

Gentile, Douglas A., and Craig A. Andersen. Violent Video Games: Effects on Youth and Public Policy Implications. In *Handbook of Children, Culture, and Violence*, ed. N.E. Dowd, D.G.

Singer, and R.F. Wilson, 225–46. Thousand Oaks, CA: Sage, 2006.

Gerbner, George, and Larry Gross. Living with Television: The Violence Profile. *Journal of Communication* 26 (1976): 172–99.

Glaubke, Christina R., et al. *Fair Play? Violence, Gender and Race in Video Games*. Oakland, CA: Children Now, 2002.

Grossman, Dave, and Gloria DeGaetano. *Stop Teaching Our Kids to Kill: A Call to Action against TV, Movie and Video Game Violence*. New York: Crown, 1999.

Higgins, Steve. The Logical Zoombinis. *Teaching Thinking* 1, no. 1 (2000): entire issue.

Huntemann, Nina, and Media Education Foundation. *Game Over: Gender, Race and Violence in Video Games*. Northhampton, MA: Media Education Foundation, 2002.

Inkpen, Kori M., Kellogg S. Booth, Steven D. Gribble, and Maria M. Klawe. Give and Take: Children Collaborating on One Computer. Paper read at CHI 95: Human Factors in Computing Systems, Denver, CO, 1995.

Johnson, Steven. *Everything Bad Is Good for You: How Popular Culture Is Making Us Smarter*. London: Allen Lane/Penguin, 2005.

Kerr, Aphra. *The Business and Culture of Digital Games: Gamework/Gameplay*. London: Sage, 2006.

Kirriemuir, John. A History of Digital Games. In *Understanding Digital Games*, ed. Jo Bryce and Jason Rutter. London: Sage, 2006.

Kirriemuir, John, and Angela McFarlane. *Literature Review in Games and Learning*, NESTA Futurelab Series. Bristol: NESTA Futurelab, 2004.

Leonard, David J. Not a Hater, Just Keepin' It Real: The Importance of Race- and Gender-Based Game Studies. *Games and Culture* 1, no. 1 (2006): 83–8.

Malone, Thomas. *What Makes Things Fun to Learn? A Study of Intrinsically Motivating Computer Games*. Palo Alto: Xerox, 1980.

Papert, Seymour. *Mindstorms: Children, Computers and Powerful Ideas*. New York: Basic Books, 1980.

Sandford, Richard, and Ben Williamson. *Games and Learning: A Handbook from Futurelab*. Bristol, UK: Futurelab, 2005.

Tuchman, Gaye. The Symbolic Annihilation of Women by the Mass Media. In *Hearth and Home: Images of Women in the Mass Media*, ed. Gaye Tuchman, Arlene Kaplan Daniels, and James Benet, 3–38. New York: Oxford University Press, 1978.

Walsh, David. *1999 Video and Computer Game Report Card* (1999) http://mediaandthefamily.org/1999vgrc2.html (accessed March 2007).

Whitebread, David. Developing Children's Problem Solving: The Educational Uses of Adventure Games. In *Information Technology and Authentic Learning*, ed. Angela McFarlane, 29–48. London: Routledge, 1997.

Wilburn, Thomas. Guns, Gangs and Greed: Gaming's Hip Hop Diversity Gap. *The Escapist* (2005). http://www.escapistmagazine.com/issue/15/4 (accessed March 2007).

VIDEO GAMES, EFFECTS OF

[See also: *Video Games*]

Video games played on a video console started out as arcade games as far back as the 1920s. Although the technology has changed, the basic idea behind their popularity has not – video games are a form of escapism. A modern video game is really an arcade game with expanded technical capabilities. In the early 1970s an electronic tennis game named *Pong* introduced the video-game industry to the United States. After this industry nearly collapsed in the mid-1980s, Japanese companies, such as the Nintendo Corporation, assumed leadership, improving game technology and introducing popular adventure games such as *Donkey Kong* and the *Super Mario Brothers*. Since then video game culture has blossomed into one of the most profitable of all media ventures. As a result, concerns over the effects of video games on behaviour have cropped up across the social landscape.

The term *video game* is now used to refer to any electronic game, whether it is played on a computer with appropriate software, on a console, on some portable device (such as a cellphone), or online. There are now genres of video games, and various formats in which they can be played. One of the most significant games is the so-called role-playing game (RPG), which gained popularity with *Dungeons and Dragons* in the 1980s. Players pretend to be in a situation or environment, such as a battle or newly discovered place; each simulated situation has its own rules and each participant is expected to play a specific role or character in the scenario. Occult and horror themes, along with related fantasy themes, are also common. In effect, video games are taking over many of the functions of cinema and television in the domain of escapism. Rather than allow filmmakers or TV producers to create the horror, fantasy, and adventure, the video games allow users to do so themselves. The increase in the popularity of online gaming has resulted in the appearance of subgenres, such as multiplayer online role-playing games, which, as L. Taylor (2006) has recently remarked, are designed for sociability and interaction.

The question of the effects of video games on its users is now a common one in media effects studies. First, there is the question of socialization. Are video games changing how people socialize? The game structure of RPGs is fully multi-user. Participants create a character, known as an avatar, by inputting descriptions of appearance and behaviour into an online space for the game. Other characters have no way of knowing if the avatar's appearance is the real physical appearance of the player or not. In this way reality and fantasy overlap. As Gary Fine (1983: 4) observed in the early 1980s, for many players such games constitute their main reality. For the game to work as an aesthetic experience, the 'players must be willing to bracket their natural selves and enact a fantasy self.' Thus, video games provide 'a structure for making friends and finding a sense of community' (59). When players enter into the RPG world they assume a fantasy identity, abandoning their real-life one. It allows players to 'endow themselves with attributes that in reality they do not possess: strength, so-

cial poise, rugged good looks, wisdom, and chivalric skills' (60).

For many, the video game is replacing the traditional media and genres – adventure, spy, war, sports – making the escapism more powerful by taking the make-believe element from the author and putting it directly into the hands of the player. In RPGs, the player is the scriptwriter, actor, and director at once. It is virtual cinema that now has its own culture, with attendant websites, blogs, and magazines. Video games give players the feeling of being immersed in a simulated world that resembles the real world. Games such Nintendo 3 and Wii also record and send the speech and movements of the participant to the simulation program. As Taylor (2006) has argued, however, video games do not alienate gamers, as many critics of video game culture contend. On the contrary, they actually serve a socializing function. He also points out that while video games may have started out as the solitary pursuit of male teenagers, they have morphed into a degendered form of social activity. Similarly, the studies collected by Adams and Smith (2008) show that gaming culture is really a digital village culture, providing numerous possibilities for people who share common interests and fantasies to engage in them collectively, as if they were in 'electronic tribes.'

Video games have been the target of opposition and censorship, especially those that involve macabre themes, sex, or violence. This comes as no surprise, for these are the elements that have always created moral panic in different eras. The research in this domain and in others continues to be ambiguous. Recent surveys have shown, moreover, that video games are attracting more diversified groups than the typical male teenager, including almost as many female players as males and older individuals, especially for casual online and mobile phone games.

Perhaps the question that comes up most frequently is whether video games affect intelligence. Some say that it does

(Kutner and Olson 2009). Others, such as Steven Johnson (2005), argue video games may actually be producing powerful new forms of consciousness and intelligence, since they provide a channel for the same kind of rigorous mental workout that mathematical theorems and puzzles do. As a consequence, they can improve the problem-solving skills of players. The complex plots and intricacies of video games are making people sharper today because of a 'Sleeper curve' – Johnson took the term from Woody Allen's 1973 movie *Sleeper*, in which a granola-eating New Yorker falls asleep and wakes up in the future, where junk foods actually prolong life, rather than shorten it. According to Johnson, the most apparently debasing forms of mass culture, such as video games, are turning out to be 'nutritional' after all.

This may or may not be true. Will our next scientists, artists, and geniuses be addicted video game players? It is quite a stretch of the imagination to say that video games enhance problem-solving skills and that these are helping our species evolve. At present, there exists no solid evidence to suggest that video games affect intelligence any more or less than, say, watching television or reading an adventure narrative.

Marcel Danesi

Bibliography

Adams, Tyrone L., and Stephen A. Smith, eds. *Electronic Tribes: The Virtual Worlds of Geeks, Gamers, Shamans, and Scammers*. Austin: University of Texas Press, 2008.

Bissell, Tom. *Extra Lives: Why Video Games Matter*. New York: Pantheon, 2010.

Fine, Gary Alan. *Shared Fantasy: Role-Playing Games as Social Worlds*. Chicago: University of Chicago Press, 1983.

Gelder, Ken. *Subcultures: Cultural Histories and Social Practice*. London: Routledge, 2007.

Johnson, Steven. *Everything Bad Is Good for You: How Today's Popular Culture Is Actually Making Us Smarter*. New York: Riverside, 2005.

Kane, Michael. *Game Boys: Professional Videogaming's Rise from the Basement to the Big Time*. London: Penguin, 2008.

Kutner, Lawrence, and Cheryl K. Olson. *Grand Theft Childhood: The Surprising Truth about Violent Video Games*. New York: Simon and Schuster, 2009.

Taylor, T.L. *Play between Worlds: Exploring Online Culture*. Cambridge, MA: MIT Press, 2006.

VIRTUAL REALITY

[See also: *Simulacrum Theory, Video*]

Virtual reality (VR) – a term coined in the late 1980s by artist and scientist Jaron Lanier – is a computer-simulated, three-dimensional environment designed to appear and feel like a real environment. Although the term 'virtual environment' is similarly used, the two terms share definitions and are used interchangeably.

In a virtual environment, one typically experiences a sense of immersion. The user's ability to explore this environment and to change perspectives within it creates a 'simulacrum' of reality. The term simulacrum is generally traced to the ideas of the late philosopher Jean Baudrillard (for example, Baudrillard 1983). Latency, referring to the time a user moves his eyes to the change of view, can also deeply affect the sense of immersion – if the latency period lasts too long, one may become aware of the simulated environment, thus losing the overall VR effect. There are two components of immersion: depth of information refers to the quality and amount of data a user receives; breadth of information refers to the number of senses simulated. While most virtual environments concentrate on visual and audio components, touch simulation in virtual environments is expanding.

One's interaction within the virtual environment is crucial to experiencing the simulacrum effect. A successful interaction is dependent on a user's navigation within the environment, which relies on speed (the rate one's actions are incorporated in reality), range (the results from a user's actions), and mapping (natural responses which make sense to respond to the user's actions).

VR began in the mid-1950s. The cinematographer Morton Heilig wanted to stimulate all senses in order to enrich the overall movie experience, eventually building the 'Sensorama' machine in 1960 – a chair which was able to tilt, allowing the viewer to stare at a wide-angle television which showed three-dimensional films accompanied by sound, fans, and odour emitters. Although Heilig was unable to obtain funding for the Sensorama, his work stimulated further research into creating VR in the subsequent digital age. In 1961, the Philco Corporation developed the 'Headsight' – a head mount with a video screen and tracking system, linked to cameras, allowing an adjusted camera angle when a user turned his or her head.

By 1965, Ivan Sutherland, a computer scientist, began using a graphics accelerator instead of a camera for his 'Ultimate Display' device, through which users could look into environments that appeared as real as physical reality. The device was connected to a computer, which provided all the graphics displayed and allowed head movements to change the view. By 1979, the United States military quickly adopted similar strategies for flight simulation, as it was much cheaper and safer than training in the air. With better technologies in the 1980s, pilots were able to navigate through highly detailed virtual worlds. In 1989, the sensory glove was invented to explore the different possibilities of real hand movements, whereby one movement of a finger would signal an action.

While vast technological changes were being implemented in the military, the entertainment industry began to produce movies using computer graphic technology used in virtual environments, such as *Star Wars, Terminator*, and *Jurassic Park*. Video games, a direct spin-off of VR used by the military, gained popularity in the 1980s in large part because of the incorporation of

VR techniques and formats. For example, expanding on the technologies of the sensory glove, the toy company Mattel produced a mitt for children to help them confront challenges in a popular Nintendo game.

VR has now branched out into other domains, such as architecture, where virtual models of building plans are made so that potential residents can walk through a structure before it is even built, allowing clients to suggest alterations. The automobile industry now also uses VR technology to build prototypes, allowing designers to make alterations. In effect, VR technologies have been changing not only the way we interact with computers, but also the way we experience reality. Nintendo's Wii is the latest example of VR research that is changing how people experience simulations and, thus, where the entertainment industry may ultimately be evolving. While the ability to track in devices with a minimal latency period is rare in previous VR technologies, the Wii controller is able to accomplish this successfully. Wii has thus made it possible for individuals with limited motion abilities to play golf or tennis, or to engage in boxing. With further research and innovation, VR systems will surely become cheaper and more accessible, allowing more people to benefit from them.

Mariana Bockarova

Bibliography

Baudrillard, Jean. *Simulations*. New York: Semiotexte, 1983.
Cambourne, Keeli. Wiihabilitation. http://www.theage.com.au/news/technology/wiihabilitation/2008/06/22/1214073021865 (accessed 28 December 2008).
Durlach, Nathaniel, and Anne Mavor. Virtual Reality: Scientific and Technological Challenges. Washington, DC: National Academies Press, 1995.
Lumsden, Joanna. *Handbook of Research on User Interface Design and Evaluation for Mobile Technology*. Idea Group Inc., 2008.

Strickland, Jonathan. How Virtual Reality Works. http://electronics.howstuffworks.com/virtual-reality9.htm (accessed 28 December 2008).

Tate, Scott. Virtual Reality: A Historical Perspective. Virtual Reality website. http://ei.cs.vt.edu/~history/Tate.VR.html (accessed 28 December 2008).

VISUAL COMMUNICATION

[See also: *Semiotics; Sensory Communication*]

The study of visual communication is a major branch of anthropology, art theory, psychology, and semiotics. It became a major field after the publication of two influential books: Rudolf Arnheim's *Visual Thinking* (1969) and Jonathan Berger's *Ways of Seeing* (1972). Visual communication is defined as the use of visual forms (drawings, shapes, pictures) to construct and transmit some message.

Psychological studies have shown that images vary along cultural lines. When asked to visualize a triangle, for example, people living in Western cultures will come up with the equilateral triangle as the primary image or form, seeing other kinds of triangles as sub types of this form. The equilateral triangle is called a 'cultural prototype' (Rosch, 1973, 1975, 1981; Rosch and Mervis 1975; Taylor 1995). It is the triangle that is perceived to be exemplary or representative of all triangles. Obtuse-angled, right-angled, and acute-angled triangles are perceived to be 'deviations' from this 'triangle mean.'

Ferdinand de Saussure (1857–1913), one of the modern-day founders of linguistics and semiotics, used the word *image* in two senses (Saussure 1916: 16). He defined a signifier (such as a word) as a 'sound image' and its signified (meaning) as the 'conceptual image' that the signifier calls to mind. Recent work on conceptual imagery has shown that Saussurean images are 'schematic' in form (Lakoff and Johnson 1980, 1999; Lakoff 1987; Johnson 1987).

This has led to the emergence of *image schema* theory within linguistics and other disciplines. The image schema is defined as an unconscious mental outline of recurrent shapes, actions, dimensions, orientations, and objects that underlie common concepts. For example, an impediment is anything, such as a wall, a boulder, another person, that blocks forward movement. Experience informs us that we can go *around* the impediment, *over* it, *under* it, *through* it, or else *remove* it and continue on. On the other hand, the impediment could impede us, so that we would have to *stop* and *turn back*. All of these actions can be easily visualized in the mind. Lakoff and Johnson argue that this very same image schema is the psychological reason why we say such things as: 'They *got through* that difficult time'; 'He felt better after he *got over* his cold'; 'You want to *steer clear of* financial debt'; 'With the bulk of the work *out of the way*, I was able to call it a day'; 'The rain *stopped* us from enjoying our outing'; 'You cannot *go* any *further* with that proposal; you'll just have to *turn back*.' Image schemata are crucial in abstract concept formation, linking bodily and perceptual experiences.

Drawing pictures, making charts, sketching diagrams, and the like are part of *visual representation*. These result from the use of elemental signifiers (forms) such as *points*, *lines*, and *shapes* combined in various ways to represent figures (Dondis 1986). Consider what figures can be made with three straight lines. Among other things, they can be joined up to represent by resemblance a triangle, the letter 'H,' or a picnic table. If chevrons or arrowheads are adjoined to lines, they can be used as signifiers to represent movement and direction. Shapes are visual signifiers that can be used to represent the outline of something. For example, to show the shape of the sun, one could draw a circle; to represent the surface of a table one can draw a rectangle.

Other visual elements include value, colour, and texture. *Value* refers to the darkness or lightness of a line or shape. It represents dark and light contrasts, especially in conveying mood changes. *Colour* also conveys mood and feeling in a visual text such as a painting. This is why we refer to colours as 'warm,' 'soft,' 'cold,' or 'harsh.' Colour has culture-specific meanings: e.g., in American culture *yellow* connotes cowardice; in China it means royalty. Texture refers to the phenomenon that some visual forms (lines, shapes, and so on) evoke tactile and other sensory modalities. Wavy lines, for example, tend to produce a much more pleasant sensation than angular ones. By increasing the number of edges on angular lines, the unpleasant sensation tends to increase. The term that is used to characterize this phenomenon is *synesthesia*.

Today, elemental visual forms have found a new medium – the digital one (Horn 1998; Darley 2000). Digital visual signs, such as the computer icon and the emoticon (an icon that conveys emotional information) are part of digital communications. Emoticons are strings of text characters that, when viewed sideways, form a face expressing a particular emotion. Common emoticons include the smiley :-) or :) (meaning 'I'm smiling at the joke here'), the winkey ;-) (meaning 'I'm winking and grinning at the joke here'), :-(('I'm sad about this'), :-7 ('I'm speaking with tongue in cheek'), :D or :-D (big smile; 'I'm overjoyed'), and :-O (either a yawn of boredom or a mouth open in amazement). In an email message or other digital text, a letter, word, or phrase that is encased in angle brackets indicates the attitude the writer takes toward what he or she has written. This is called an *emotag*. Often emotags have opening and closing tags, similar to HTML tags, that enclose a phrase or one or more sentences. For example: <joke> 'You didn't think I was telling the truth, did you?' </joke>.

Although now considered a separate field of its own, both within semiotics and linguistics, *writing* is also often included under the visual communication rubric. The ancient Egyptians called their writing system *hieroglyphic* because they used it to record hymns and prayers, to register the names and titles of individuals and deities, and to record various community activities (Goldwasser 1995). In their origins most scripts were deemed to have sacred or mystical function – for example, the Sumerians attributed the origin of writing to Nabu and the Greeks to Hermes.

The earliest form of writing was *pictographic*, consisting of pictures to represent objects. For example, a circle can be used as a pictograph of the sun and a wavy line of a river. The figures designating *male* and *female* on washrooms and the *no-smoking* signs found in public buildings are modern-day pictographs. One of the first civilizations to use pictographic writing was ancient China, which may date as far back as the fifteenth century BCE. Another fully developed pictographic system was used by the Sumerian-Babylonian society nearly five thousand years ago. The Sumerians recorded their pictographic representations on clay tablets with wedge-shaped forms. This is why such writing is called *cuneiform*. Cuneiform writing was very expensive and impractical and, thus, was developed, learned, and used primarily by rulers and clerics. In Egypt, hieroglyphic pictography emerged around 2,700 to 2,500 BCE. The Egyptians inscribed hieroglyphs on walls and tablets, but also used papyrus to record their writings, making it more practicable for many more classes of people.

Abstract or complex forms of pictographs are called *ideographs*. Common symbols for such things as public telephones or washrooms are all ideographic. Ideographs represent things such as actions. For example, an ideograph of a student may show a young person reading a book. More abstract ideographs are known as *logographs*. A logographic system combines pictography and ideography. For example, the Chinese pictographs for *sun* and *tree* are combined to represent the Chinese spoken word for *east*. The first *syllabaries* – systems of visual characters standing for syllables – developed from such amalgamated systems. To facilitate the speed of writing, the Sumerians and the Egyptians eventually streamlined their pictographs, transforming them into symbols for the actual sounds of speech. This is called *phonographic* writing. A complete phonographic system for representing single sounds is called *alphabetic*. The first such system emerged in the Middle East around 1,000 BCE and was transported by the Phoenicians to Greece. It contained signs for consonant sounds only. In Greece, signs for vowel sounds were added to it, making the Greek system the first complete alphabetic system.

There is no culture without visual communication. Today, it is said that we live in a visual culture, where the image is much more predominant than the spoken word. But this is an oversimplification. Human cultural life has always involved visual representation, to larger and greater degrees.

Marcel Danesi

Bibliography

Arnheim, Rudolf. *Visual Thinking.* Berkeley: University of California Press, 1969.

Berger, John. *Ways of Seeing.* Harmondsworth: Penguin, 1972.

Darley, Andrew. *Visual Digital Culture: Surface Play and Spectacle in Media Genres.* London: Routledge, 2000.

Deregowski, Jan B. Pictorial Perception and Culture. *Scientific American* 227 (1982): 82–8.

Dondis, Donis A. *A Primer of Visual Literacy.* Cambridge, MA: MIT Press, 1986.

Dunning, William V. *Changing Images of Pictorial Space: A History of Visual Illusion in Painting.* Syracuse, NY: Syracuse University Press, 1991.

Goldwasser, Orly. *From Icon to Metaphor: Studies in the Semiotics of the Hieroglyphs.* Freiburg: Universtätsverlag, 1995.

Hatcher, Evelyn P. *Visual Metaphors: A Methodological Study in Visual Communication.* Albuquerque: University of New Mexico Press, 1974.

Horn, Robert E. *Visual Language: Global Communication for the 21st Century.* Bainbridge Island: MacroVU, 1998.

Johnson, Mark. *The Body in the Mind: The Bodily Basis of Meaning, Imagination and Reason.* Chicago: University of Chicago Press, 1987.

Kosslyn, Stephen M. *Ghosts in the Mind's Machine: Creating and Using Images in the Brain.* New York: W.W. Norton, 1983.

– *Image and Brain.* Cambridge, MA: MIT Press, 1984.

Lakoff, George. *Women, Fire and Dangerous Things: What Categories Reveal about the Mind.* Chicago: University of Chicago Press, 1987.

Lakoff, George, and Mark Johnson. *Metaphors We Live By.* Chicago: University of Chicago Press, 1980.

– *Philosophy in the Flesh: The Embodied Mind and Its Challenge to Western Thought.* New York: Basic, 1999.

Rosch, Eleanor. On the Internal Structure of Perceptual and Semantic Categories. In *Cognitive Development and Acquisition of Language*, ed. T.E. Moore, 111–44. New York: Academic, 1973.

– Cognitive Reference Points. *Cognitive Psychology* 7 (1975): 532–47.

– Prototype Classification and Logical Classification: The Two Systems. In *New Trends in Cognitive Representation: Challenges to Piaget's Theory*, ed. E. Scholnick, 73–86. Hillsdale, NJ: Lawrence Erlbaum Associates, 1981.

Rosch, Eleanor, and Carolyn B. Mervis. Family Resemblances. *Cognitive Psychology* 7 (1975): 573–605.

Saint-Martin, Fernande. *Semiotics of Visual Language.* Bloomington: Indiana University Press, 1990.

Saussure, Ferdinand de. *Cours de linguistique générale.* Paris: Payot, 1916.

Sebeok, Thomas A., and Jean Umiker-Sebeok, eds. *Advances in Visual Semiotics.* Berlin: Mouton de Gruyter, 1994.

Taylor, John R. *Linguistic Categorization: Prototypes in Linguistic Theory.* Oxford: Oxford University Press, 1995.

Tufte, Edward R. *Visual Explanations: Images and Quantities, Evidence and Narrative.* Cheshire: Graphics Press, 1997.

W

WEBCASTING

[See also: *Broadcasting; Podcasting*]

Webcasting refers to broadcasting online. A webcast may be live or on demand. The largest webcasters are radio and TV stations who use webcasting technology to simulcast their programs. Webcasting is also used in various other ways – for instance, for commercial purposes (video presentations of corporations), for e-Learning (to transmit lectures and seminars), by private individuals to create their own videos. The fact that webcasting technology is cheap and broadly accessible has led to the rise of independent media as significant players in the current 'mediaverse.'

The University of North Carolina radio station WXYC was the first station to broadcast over the internet, becoming, in effect, the first one to use webcasting in place of traditional broadcasting. Now, virtually all the major media outlets use webcasts in tandem with regular broadcasts. Webcasts have allowed events, such as local sports events, to gain a broad international audience. In the past, amateur sports would hardly ever be showcased on the broadcast media. Webcasting has allowed these events to garner a relatively large audience. The same pattern has emerged for such things as poker matches, chess games, and other recreational activities. Some have become so popular online that they have crossed over to the traditional media. The popularity of poker competitions is a case in point. Without webcasting, it is unlikely that poker would have become so popular in the traditional television medium.

Webcasting is evidence that the new technologies have been eroding the power held by previous media institutions. With the spread of webcams and other similar devices (cellphones, iPods, etc.) people throughout the globe can become producers and directors at once, using their own devices as cameras and their homes as studios. Their actors can be taken from real life and webcast with or without their knowledge. A growing number of people find the world of independently made webcasts more exciting than traditional broadcasts, since these are seen as more representative of real life. The boundaries between the private and the public, between fact and fiction, have thus become blurred. Webcasting technologies are creating the new celebrities, many of whom cross over (or back) to the traditional media.

Marcel Danesi

Bibliography

Herman, Andrew, and Thomas Swiss, eds. *The World Wide Web and Contemporary Cultural Theory*. London: Routledge, 2000.

Jarvis, Jeff. *What Would Google Do?* New York: Collins Business, 2009.

Nakhimovsky, Alexander, and Tom Myers. *Goog-*

le, *Amazon, and Beyond: Creating and Consuming Web Services*. New York: Apress, 2003.

Slevin, James. *The Internet and Society*. London: Polity, 2000.

WEBSITES

[See also: *Internet; World Wide Web*]

A *website* is an interconnected set of web pages – computer files displayed as pages on a computer screen, which are accessible through the World Wide Web (WWW) by means of a web browser. The first web page, created by Tim Berners-Lee, went online in 1991, turning the WWW into a cyberspace of information, with all kinds of documents, sounds, and videos stored on multiple computers that are connected by hypertext links.

The best way to describe how a website works is by an example. When someone types a web address on a computer that is connected to the internet the request goes to a server computer, which will respond by sending the requested document in an HTML (hypertext markup language) language format (which is the programming language of the WWW). When the computer receives the HTML document, the browser translates it to web pages. As mentioned, a website is a series of web pages that are accessible through the WWW, and specifically through the homepage, which is also called the 'index page' or 'universal root' (URL). Different pages of the website are connected to each other by links, which are usually underlined or have a different colour from that of the remainder of the text.

In the late 1980s, the internet was still very cumbersome, due to the numerical addresses that had to be remembered and used in order to reach websites. Moreover, every computer that was connected to the internet had its own unique password, and therefore users had to keep track of the password along with the list of websites. Berners-Lee wrote the first hypertext transfer protocol (HTTP), a programming language that connects web pages across the internet. He also developed the universal resource identifier (URL), which assigns a unique address to each website, and HTML, which formats the pages that contain hypertext links. By the winter of 1990 the program for the World Wide Web, with a point-and-click browser, was finished by Berners-Lee. The first web server installed outside Europe was the one by Paul Kunz in December 1991 at the Stanford Accelerator Center. By 1993 there were 130 sites on the Web. The proliferation of such sites began shortly thereafter. Today, the number of websites is literally countless and continues to grow.

Websites are formatted in two different styles – static and dynamic. The former has the same content every time the page is loaded unless a change is made by the web developer and the new version of that website is loaded onto the server. Dynamic websites can change themselves or can be changed by a user, for example, when he or she clicks on a link. Examples of dynamic websites are database-driven ones such as online banking sites.

The main types of websites are: commercial, personal, organizational, educational, entertainment, news, blog, and hybrid. Commercial websites are designed to sell products and services. A commercial website will allow a customer to shop online, verify credit card numbers, and process orders. Personal websites are used by individuals or small groups of people. They contain information about those individuals and groups. Organizational websites are intended to advocate the point of view of a group of people or for group members to communicate with each other through message boards or chatrooms. Educational websites provide information about educational institutions. Entertainment websites offer entertainment news items, while news websites provide news and commentary. Blogs (which may include chatrooms) enable users to post their viewpoints and commentaries online. Hybrid websites are designed eclectically – for example, a business website might provide additional documents or news for their visitors so as to attract more customers.

Maryam Rasti

Bibliography

Hafner, Katie, and Matthew Lyon. *Where Wizards Stay Up Late: The Origins of the Internet*. New York: Simon and Schuster, 1996.

Herman, Andrew, and Thomas Swiss, eds. *The World Wide Web and Contemporary Cultural Theory*. London: Routledge, 2000.

Slevin, James. *The Internet and Society*. London: Polity, 2000.

Van Dijk, Jan. *The Network Society*. London: Sage, 1999.

WESTERNS

[See also: *Adventure Stories, Pulp Fiction*]

Westerns are narratives about the American West and its powerful mythology in the foundations of general American culture. The West, with its rugged topography and dangers for settlement, brought about a cowboy culture that was imprinted into communal memory by writers and film-makers, making the cowboys the new heroes of America, strong men who challenged wild, rampant crime and sought to impose order on the West. Many of the early stories portrayed conflicts between cowboys, the U.S. cavalry, pioneers, and Native Americans. Writers such as Zane Grey (*Riders of the Purple Sage*, 1912), A.B. Guthrie, Jr (*The Big Sky*, 1947), Louis L'Amour (*Hondo*, 1953), and Larry McMurtry (*Lonesome Dove*, 1985) are especially known for their westerns as metaphors for the American psyche – a psyche that stresses individuality, freedom, open spaces, and a desire to conquer the wild.

The western was one of the most popular genres in pulp fiction and early movie serials, producing some of America's first fictional heroes, including Roy Rogers, The Lone Ranger, Hopalong Cassidy, and Kit Carson, among others. The plot formula of the genre consisted of a conflict between outlaws and defenders of law and order (sheriffs, marshals, rangers, cowboys, etc.), which would get resolved with the hero cowboy defeating the villain in a gun duel. A horse was typically the hero's partner. Sometimes it was a sidekick. The Lone Ranger had both – the horse Silver and the sidekick Tonto. The hero also branded a gun and was an expert marksman. Along with a gun and holster, the cowboy hero's attire included a Stetson hat, boots with spurs, and sometimes a bandana. A woman would faithfully fall in love and follow her hero, providing him with emotional solace. The settings included the deserts of the west (such as those in New Mexico and Arizona) and the various small isolated towns that dotted the landscape.

The first important silent motion picture in the United States was a western – *The Great Train Robbery* (1903). From the 1920s through the 1950s, hundreds of western movies were produced by Hollywood, especially in serial form. The cowboy heroes of these movies, such as Gene Autry and Tom Mix, became household names. A more serious treatment of westerns and of Native Americans started to appear in the 1950s with movies such as *High Noon* (1952) and *Shane* (1953) and much later with *Unforgiven* (1992) and *Dances with Wolves* (1990). Radio and television also contributed to the popularity of the western, adapting the pulp fiction and cinematic narratives to their specific media. Popular western programs included *The Lone Ranger, Roy Rogers, Hopalong Cassidy, Gunsmoke, Maverick, Have Gun Will Travel, Wagon Train, Bonanza*, and *The Wild Wild West*.

The various subgenres of the western include the following:

- The *classic western* features strong, handsome cowboy heroes fighting injustice wherever it occurs; these include the early movies with Roy Rogers, Hopalong Cassidy, and The Lone Ranger.

- The *spaghetti western*, a low-budget film made by an Italian film company, became a popular genre during the 1960s and 1970s through movies such as *The Good, the Bad, and the Ugly* starring Clint Eastwood and directed by Sergio Leone. These took place in barren landscapes in Italy that resembled similar landscapes in the American West and typically featured the high-noon gun duel, but did not feature conflicts with Native Americans.
- The *ostern*, as Eastern European westerns produced at about the same time were called, portrayed Native Americans much more favourably than the classic westerns.
- The *revisionist western* shows a greater sensitivity to the Native American plight than did the classic western, gives women a more substantive role to play, and deals with psychological issues more realistically. These include movies such as *Dances with Wolves*, *Hud*, and *Lonestar*.
- The *science fiction western* combines elements of science fiction in a western setting; examples include *The Wild Wild West*, *Serenity*, *Westworld*, and *Bravestar*.

The western genre has lost much of its popularity today, although some of its residue excitement can now be found in video games and in online sites. Its demise as a mainstream genre is undoubtedly due to the fact that the 'wild wild west' has little significance today. It is no longer an arid landscape to be conquered, geographically or psychically.

Marcel Danesi

Bibliography

Newman, Kim. *Wild West Movies*. New York: Bloomsbury, 1990.

Sklar, Robert. *Movie-Made America: A Cultural History of American Movies*. New York: Vintage, 1994.

WIENER, NORBERT (1894–1964)

[See also: *Communication; Cybernetics; Cyberspace; Feedback*]

Norbert Wiener was an American mathematician who developed techniques that were used to analyse data transmitted by radio – techniques that had the capacity to sift useful information from undesired interferences known technically as noise. He extended his investigative orientation to the study of similarities shared by the human nervous system and machines, such as computers. This led to the founding of the science of cybernetics.

Wiener was born in Columbia, Missouri, receiving a PhD from Harvard University at the age of eighteen. He went on to teach at the Massachusetts Institute of Technology from 1919 to 1960.

Wiener observed that people and machines carried out their functions in purposeful and orderly ways, seeking stability in the enactment of these methods. One of the most important characteristics shared by humans and machines was *feedback*, which involves the circling back of information to a control device (such as the human brain) to adjust behaviour or functioning. For instance, when a human being's body temperature is too high or too low, the body feeds this information back to the brain. The brain then reacts to correct the temperature or to suggest ways to seek a solution. A household thermostat functions in much the same way, using feedback to adjust the operation of a furnace to maintain a fixed temperature. Cybernetics has led to attempts to build machines that simulate human behaviour, including decision making and analysis of data. It has led to post-humanism and cyborg theories of human evolution. Some argue that cybernetics started a second revolution, called the information society, a revolution that has displaced the previous industrial age. Since the 1940s, cybernetics has influenced work in biochemistry, computer science, psychology, and communication science.

Marcel Danesi

Bibliography

Wiener, Norbert. *Cybernetics or Control and Communication in the Animal and the Machine.* New York: Wiley, 1921.
– *Extrapolation, Interpolation, and Smoothing of Stationary Time Series.* Cambridge, MA: MIT Press, 1949.

WIKIPEDIA

[See also: *Books, History of; World Wide Web*]

The term *wiki* is the name given to a website that allows visitors to edit and change its content, sometimes without the need for registration. The first software to be called a wiki was WikiWikiWeb, named by its maker, computer programmer Ward Cunningham. He apparently took it from the name of a Hawaiian airport shuttle.

Wikipedia (a blend of *wiki* and *encyclopedia*) is arguably the most popular of all the wikis. It is a free multilingual online encyclopedia that was launched on 15 January 2002 by Larry Sanger and Ben Kovitz. At first, they wanted to create an English-language encyclopedia project called *Nupedia*, to be written by qualified contributors, in line with a previous attempt to develop an internet-based encyclopedia project called the *Interpedia* (launched in 1993). The rapid growth of Nupedia soon led to the formation of Wikipedia, written and edited collaboratively by volunteers and visitors to the site. For this reason there has been controversy over Wikipedia's accuracy and overall validity, since it is susceptible to vandalism and to subjectivity. The encyclopedia has taken steps to remedy this situation, but it still remains a 'marketplace' reference source, where knowledge, like commercial products, can be negotiated, tailored, and discarded as the values of that marketplace change. The main idea behind Wikipedia is to bring the domain of knowledge within everyone's reach.

Wikipedia's founders describe it as 'an effort to create and distribute a multilingual free encyclopedia of the highest quality to every single person on the planet in his or her own language.' Like any online site, it makes research efficient by providing hyperlinks in each entry and other 'cross-referencing' tools that facilitate the search for specific information. The articles are now also linked to other digital forms (such as dictionaries provided by computer programs). Another important aspect of the Wikipedia concept is that it is not a rigidly created site, impervious to change without authoritative consent (as is the case in traditional encyclopedias). The idea is to involve all users in a continuing process of creation, reconstruction, and collaboration in the domain of knowledge, thus ensuring that the knowledge source is constantly evolving and up to date.

The Wikimedia Foundation, a not-for-profit organization, manages Wikipedia and other related projects: Wiktionary (a wiki dictionary) and Wikibooks (textbooks). The actual Wikipedia site is operated by a community of so-called Wikipedians under the supervision of Jimmy Wales. They attempt to ensure that a neutral approach is maintained on the part of visitors. Most of the available articles are under the GNU Free Documentation License, which means that they may be reproduced free of charge. Critiques of Wikipedia are that it is inaccurate and poorly edited. This may be true, but the Wikipedians have started to turn it more and more into a traditional, quality-controlled online reference tool. Moreover, it seems that its infelicities soon get noticed and eliminated. Wikipedia is a self-organizing reference system.

In 2004, Wikipedia doubled in size. The number of articles increased from under

500,000 to over 1 million. In 2005, Wikipedia introduced multilingual and subject portals. In 2007, Wikipedia contained 7.5 million articles in approximately 250 different languages. In April 2008, the 10 millionth Wikipedia article was posted on Hungarian Wikipedia. A few months later, the English Wikipedia reached 2.5 million articles.

Maryam Rasti

Bibliography

Ayers, Phoebe, Charles Matthews, and Ben Yates. *How Wikipedia Works*. San Francisco: No Starch Press, 2008.

Herman, Andrew, and Thomas Swiss, eds. *The World Wide Web and Contemporary Cultural Theory*. London: Routledge, 2000.

WIRELESS COMMUNICATION

[See also: *Marconi, Guglielmo; Radio*]

Wireless communication refers to the sending and receiving of information through air or space rather than through wires or cables. Common wireless devices include walkie-talkies and cellular telephones. More technically, it is transmission of information from a single source to a single destination by modulating a radio wave with message, where radio wave is referred to as a part of the electromagnetic waves, which can be generated by alternating current in an antenna.

Broadcasting is different from communications, because the former refers to information transmission from a single source to unknown multiple destinations, whereas the latter is a transmission from a single source to a single destination. However, both wireless communications and wireless broadcasting are mentioned in this article, because historically they developed in tandem.

In 1864, J.C. Maxwell predicted the existence of electromagnetic waves, and in 1888,

H.R. Hertz proved it. In 1896, G. Marconi took his 'wireless telegraph' to England and demonstrated his system in London. In 1901, he was successful in transmitting the first transoceanic wireless communication by sending the Morse code word of 's (…)' in frequency band of 850 kHz across the Atlantic from Poldhu, Cornwall, England, to St John's, Newfoundland, a distance of 3,200 km. The signal was generated based on spark-gap, so its spectrum occupied the entire bandwidth of the frequency spectrum. Nowadays, the type of the signal is called 'impulse radio,' which is known as a kind of UWB (ultra wide-band). It is interesting to see that wireless communication was born in the form of 'digital' communication, where transmitted messages were selected from a finite set of alphabets. Wireless telegraph was used in the LF (low-frequency) band, which ranges from 30 kHz to 300 kHz, until the 1930s and then the MF (medium frequency), which ranges from 300 kHz to 3 MHz until the 1990s internationally for ships and aircrafts. However, nowadays, wireless telegraph is not used as an international communication tool except by amateur radio enthusiasts.

R.A. Fessenden invented AM (amplitude modulation) radio, which modulates a carrier amplitude with analogue information such as music and voice. In 1906, he was successful in transmitting the first audio radio program broadcast to ships in Brant Rock, Massachusetts. The AM signal occupied a small portion of the frequency spectrum, so multiple stations were able to broadcast simultaneously by allocating a different carrier frequency to each station in a frequency division manner. In 1920, the first commercial audio radio broadcast station started on air with carrier frequency of 1020 kHz in Pittsburgh, Pennsylvania. Later in 1933, E.H. Armstrong invented FM (frequency modulation) radio, which modulates a carrier frequency with analogue information. The FM signal required a wider bandwidth of frequency spectrum than the AM signal but it improved the quality of information transmission. Nowadays, AM audio broadcast services are provided mainly in the MF, and FM audio broadcast services are provided mainly in the VHF (very high frequency) band, which ranges from 30 MHz to 300 MHz. In addition, international shortwave broadcasting uses the HF (high-frequency) band, which ranges from 3 MHz to 30 MHz, because the ionosphere reflects the HF signals well.

On the other hand, the idea of video broadcasting, namely, television, dates back to the 1870s, but the first electromechanical television system was invented in the UK in 1925 and the first all-electronic television system was invented in Japan in 1926. In 1928, the first regularly scheduled television service began with carrier frequency of 790 kHz in New York City. Today there are several analogue colour television standards over the world: NTSC (National Television Systems Committee), PAL (Phase Alternating Line), and SÉCAM (Séquentiel Couleur à Mémoire). NTSC, which was standardized in the United States in 1958, has now been adopted in North America, some countries in South America and Asia, and in other countries. It transmits sound signals as FM and video signals as AM in a frequency bandwidth of 6 MHz. PAL, which was developed in Germany in 1963, is now adopted in most Western European countries expect France, some countries in South America, and other countries. It also transmits sound signals as FM and video signals as AM in frequency bandwidth of 6 MHz. SÉCAM, which is the first European colour television standard developed in France in 1956, is now adopted in France, most Eastern European countries, and in most countries in Africa and the Middle East. It transmits both sound and video signals as FM in frequency bandwidth of 6 MHz. Most terrestrial video broadcasting services are provided mainly in the VHF band and the UHF (ultra high-frequency) band, which ranges from 300 MHz to 3 GHz.

In addition to the analogue broadcasting mentioned above, digital broadcasting is now available around the world. In Europe, based on the successful results from the DAB (digital audio broadcasting) field trials and measurements held between 1988 and 1992, DVB-T (terrestrial digital video broadcasting) was standardized in 1996, and the UK put it into commercial service in 1998. In the United States, ATSC (Advanced Television Systems Committee) was standardized in 1996 and was put into commercial service in 1998. On the other hand, in Japan, ISDB-T (terrestrial integrated services digital broadcasting) was standardized in 2000, and the commercial service was put in service in 2003. DVB-T is similar to ISDB-T in the sense that both standards use OFDM (orthogonal frequency division multiplexing) as modulation scheme, but the difference between them is that the former supports only stationary reception whereas the latter supports not only stationary but also mobile receptions. In 2004, DVB-H (handheld), also with the use of OFDM, was standardized for battery-powered handheld receivers.

Besides the terrestrial analogue/digital audio and video broadcasting, satellite has been playing an essential role in intercontinental delivery of video signals. For instance, Telstar 1, which was launched by the United States in 1962, was the first satellite which was equipped with transmitter and receiver onboard, where the frequencies were 6.390 GHz uplink (from earth station to satellite) and 4.170 GHz downlink (from satellite to earth station). With Telstar 1, the first trans-Atlantic delivery of television pictures between the United States and UK/France was successful in 1962. Then with Relay 1, which was a non-geostationary satellite, the first trans-Pacific delivery of television pictures was successful between the United States and Japan in 1963 with shocking news of the assassination of President John F. Kennedy. Today, geo-stationary satellites, which were proposed by A.C. Clarke as ideal telecommunications relays in 1945, are providing direct broadcast services in many countries with frequency of C (4–8 GHz) and Ku (10–18 GHz) bands.

After Marconi's successful demonstration of the transoceanic wireless telegraph, mobile radio communication systems were mainly based on Morse code until the 1910s. In the early 1920s, the first land mobile radio telephone system based on AM was developed for police cars in Detroit, Michigan, which was a kind of radio broadcast from an operator to policemen in cars. After the invention of FM in 1935, almost all police systems were converted to FM from AM by the 1940s.

The United States was the first country to introduce a land mobile telephone system, but it was restricted to police and emergency use until the 1940s. For instance, the FCC (Federal Communications Commission) was created in 1934, but it never opened the radio spectrum for private radio telephone channels until the Second World War. In 1946, the first American commercial mobile radio telephone service, called MTS (mobile telephone system), was introduced for private customers in St Louis, Missouri, which was connected to wired PSTN (public switched telephone network). It was a simplex manual system where only one-way communication was allowed at a time and mobile units called in to operators who manually placed the calls. The modulation type was analogue narrow-band FM operating on six channels in the 150 MHz band (VHF) with 60 kHz channel spacing, and the coverage radius of one base station was 20–30 km. In 1964, a new service called IMTS (improved mobile telephone service) was introduced, in which calls were automatically placed. The modulation type was still analogue narrow-band FM in the 150 MHz band (VHF), and a single base station covered a whole city.

The concept of cellular phones was invented for police car systems in the late 1940s, but the first analogue portable cellular phone was developed in 1973. Analogue cellular phone systems are called 'first-generation (1G) mobile communication systems.' The NTT (Nippon Telegraph and Telephone) system was introduced in Japan in 1979 as the first commercial 1G mobile communication system. Then, NMT (Nordic Mobile Telecommunication System) was introduced into Saudi Arabia and Nordic countries in 1981, and AMPS (Advanced Mobile Phone System) was introduced into the United States in the same year. All the 1G systems were based on FDD (frequency division duplex), where different carrier frequencies are assigned to down (forward) link (from base station to mobile) and up (reverse) link (from mobile to base station), respectively, FDMA (frequency division multiple access) where a different frequency channel is assigned to each mobile user, and narrow-band FM. The 1G cellular mobile phone services were provided mainly in the 800 MHz, 900 MHz, and 450 MHz (UHF) bands.

In the early 1990s, digital cellular phone systems, called the second generation (2G) mobile communication systems, were developed. GSM (Global System for Mobile Communications, original acronym of Groupe Spécial Mobile) was introduced into Germany in 1991 as the first commercial 2G mobile communication system. PDC (personal digital cellular) and D-AMPS (digital-AMPS, also known as IS-54) were introduced into Japan and the United States in 1993, respectively. The 2G systems were based on FDD and TDMA (time division multiple access), in which a different time slot is assigned to each mobile user. GSM and its variants today are really de facto standards, which are providing over 2 billion mobile connections in over two hundred countries in Europe, Asia (except Japan and Korea), North and Latin Americas, Africa, Oceania, and so on.

On the other hand, the CDMA (code division multiple access)-based 2G mobile communication system was developed as IS-95 in the United States and was introduced into Korea as the first commercial system in 1996. Unlike FDMA and TDMA, which assigned different frequency and time resources to mobile users, CDMA assigns spreading codes which occupy the same wider-frequency bandwidth but give much less interference to each other.

The 2G cellular phone services were and have been provided mainly in the UHF band. The data transmission rates supported are less than several tens of kilobits per seconds, which are high enough not for multimedia transmission but for low data transmission such as short message service. The 2G systems are supported with circuit-switched backbone network, and a 2G system supported with mixed circuit- and packet-switched backbone network is referred to as 2.5G system, such as GPRS (general packet radio services).

With remarkable advances in wireless communication, and battery and signal processing technologies, wireless communication networks among computers and devices which are not directly manipulated by humans have drawn much attention since the 1990s. One example is WPAN (wireless personal area network), which connects computer peripherals such as mouse, keyword, display, printer, USB memory, and so on by wireless with typical transmittable range of less than 10 m. For instance, Bluetooth was released as an industrial specification in 1999, with maximal data transmission rates of around 700 kbits/sec in the ISM band. It was approved as IEEE 802.15.1 in 2002 and its data transmission rate has been enhanced up to 3.0 Mbits/sec. In 2006, Wibree was also developed, which is similar to Bluetooth but has much less energy consumption.

Another example is WSN (wireless sensor network), which connects sensor devices by wireless. Replacement of batteries is difficult and often prohibitive in wireless sensor communication nodes, so energy saving is one of the most important issues in WSN as well as enhancement of throughput and latency. Because of the energy saving, high data transmission rate is not targeted in WSN. Besides the WPAN and WSN, a SG (Study Group) on WBAN (wireless body area network), which connects devices on the human body for entertainment and health care purposes, was established in the IEEE 802.15 working group in November 2006. It also supports wireless communications from, to, and between implanted devices. Much care is given to address health concerns from electromagnetic radiation from such devices, so not only transmission power but also SAR (specific absorption ratio) will be specified in the standard.

Shinsuke Hara

Bibliography

IEEE 802.11b. Wireless LAN Medium Access Control (MAC) and Physical Layer (PHY) Specifications: Higher Speed Physical Layer (PHY) Extension in the 2.4 GHz Band. IEEE, 1999.

IEEE Std. 802.11. Information Technology – Telecommunications and Information Exchange between Systems – Local and Metropolitan Area Networks – Specific Requirements – Part 11: Wireless Lan Medium Access Control (MAC) and Physical Layer (PHY) Specifications. IEEE, 1997.

IEEE Std. 802.11a. Wireless Medium Access Control (MAC) and Physical Layer (PHY) Specifications: High-Speed Physical Layer Extension in the 5 GHz Band. IEEE, 1999.

IEEE Std. 802.11g. Wireless LAN Medium Access Control (MAC) and Physical Layer (PHY) Specifications. IEEE, 2003.

IEEE Std. 802.16e. Air Interface for Fixed and Mobile Broadband Wireless Access Systems Amendment for Physical and Medium Access Control Layers for Combined Fixed and Mobile Operation in Licensed Bands. IEEE, 2006.

Sarker, Tapan K., Robert J. Mailloux, Arthur A. Oliner, Magdalena Salazar-Palma, and Dipak L. Senguputa. *History of Wireless*. Hoboken, NJ: John Wiley & Sons, 2006.

WORLD WIDE WEB

[See also: *Berners-Lee, Tim; Internet*]

World Wide Web is defined as a system of computer files linked together on the internet. Tim Berners-Lee, an English computer scientist at the European Organization for Nuclear Research (CERN) physics laboratory near Geneva, Switzerland, is the individual who created the first Web software in 1990, which became part of the internet in 1991 and made the internet easy to use. The World Wide Web (WWW) is the term used to refer to the sum of all the web pages on the internet, encoded in specific languages (for example, HTML, or Hyper-Text Markup Language).

The Invention of the WWW

The World Wide Web was invented, as mentioned, by Tim Berners-Lee and his staff at CERN. Actually, Berners-Lee invented the Web in 1989 and implemented it in 1990, making the first successful Web communication between a server and a client. Berners-Lee is currently the director of the World Wide Web Consortium (W3C), the most important standard organization for the WWW, which aims at developing 'interoperable technologies (specifications, guidelines, software, and tools) to lead the Web to its full potential' (www.w3c.org). The invention of the Web was a milestone in the development of the internet, since it promoted its worldwide diffusion by allowing network applications to access the graphic level and the multimedia richness of offline computers, thus making the world of computers and that of the internet converge.

According to its inventor (Berners-Lee 2000: 37),

the fundamental principle behind the Web was that once someone somewhere made available a document, database, graphic, sound, video, or screen at some stage in an interactive dialogue, it should be accessible (subject to authorization, of course) by anyone, with any type of computer, in any country. And it should be possible to make a reference – a link – to that thing, so that others could find it. This was a philosophical change from the approach of previous computer systems. People were used to going to

find information, but they rarely made references to other computers, and when they did they typically had to quote a long and complex series of instructions to get it.

Conceptually, the invention of the WWW consisted in putting together *hypertext* and computer networks. Hypertexts are particular kinds of texts that allow different paths to fruition; basically, digital hypertexts are texts composed of nodes and links.

Nodes are the content units; since they can be made not only of texts, but also of images, graphics, video, and audio, some authors prefer to use the term 'hypermedia' (Nielsen 1995; Cantoni and Paolini 2001). Depending on how nodes are designed and produced, different kinds of hypertexts can be identified: in *static* hypertexts designers define the content of each and every node. In *dynamic* hypertexts, nodes (and links) are automatically produced starting from a database: in these cases designers define the rules for arranging the content of a hypertext, but this may change all the time; dynamic hypertexts are very commonly used in big websites that need to be updated very frequently, such as news websites or portals. A specific kind of hypertext is called *adaptive*, which tries to adapt its contents to the user's needs, taking into consideration, for instance, the user's profile, his or her previous interactions with the hypertext, the behaviour of other users in the hypertext, and so on; adaptive hypertexts are useful where the need for a highly tailored communication is strong, as, for instance, in e-commerce websites, where the system, recognizing the client, can offer him or her a more customized content.

Links are connections between nodes, that is, references 'from one document to another (external link) or from one location in the same document to another (internal link), that can be followed efficiently using a computer' (Berners-Lee 2000: 235). Links have a starting point (*anchor*), which is usually a piece of text or an image, and a destination point, which can be any kind of medium (a text, an image, a video, an animation, a sound); in hypermedia, anchors can be usually recognized because the mouse cursor changes its appearance when it passes over them, and, if the anchor is a piece of text, this is often different from normal text (e.g., it is coloured in blue and underlined). Links are not to be considered only as references to other parts of the hypertext; they are something more, since they show the possibility of interacting with the hypertext: links can be seen as actions which can be performed when reading a hypertext, from very basic actions (e.g., going to another hypertext node) to more complex ones (e.g., buying or selling a product, sending a message, subscribing to a service).

Websites and Search Engines

The most significant and diffused application of hypertexts are *websites*. A website is a 'site (location) on the World Wide Web. Each Web site contains a home page, which is the first document users see when they enter the site. The site might also contain additional documents and files. Each site is owned and managed by an individual, company or organization' (http://www. webopedia.com/TERM/w/Web_site. html).

Websites are usually made of files codified in *HTML*, the language most used in the WWW. HTML is a markup language that is able to represent connections between hypertexts and uses marking elements (tags). HTML tags have two main functions: they qualify the type of an element, such as the title, the head, and so on (*descriptive* function), and they give instructions to the browser on how elements must be represented on the web page, for instance in bold, italic, and so on (*prescriptive* function).

Browsers are software applications which allow Web users to surf the Web and to access web pages by interpreting HTML files and other languages used on the Web.

The first popular web browser was NCSA Mosaic, whose version 1.0 was released in September 1993 (its development was discontinued in 1997). Very soon a so-called *browser war* broke out, an intense competition to dominate the web browser marketplace. In particular, in the late 1990s, Internet Explorer – the browser developed by Microsoft – and Netscape Navigator struggled for dominance. In March 2008 the most used browsers were Internet Explorer (74.8 per cent market share), Firefox (17.8 per cent), and Safari (5.8 per cent) (http://marketshare.hitslink.com/report. aspx?qprid=0).

To access a web page, surfers have to input in the browser a URL (uniform resource locator), which is the address of the resource (e.g., www.webopedia.com). The URL is then translated by a service called DNS (domain name system) into the IP address, which is the unique number assigned to each computer connected to the internet (an IP address is, for instance, 195.176.176.173, which corresponds to the URL: www.unisi.ch). Thus, through the DNS a request is sent from the browser to the computer with that IP number; the request is then managed on that computer by a web server, which answers by sending to the user's browser the requested resource/file (or an error message, if the request could not be fulfilled).

After a first period when websites were mostly considered as new technological artefacts, the importance of approaching websites from a communicative point of view became clear: 'Increasingly, organizations find that the creation of Web sites is not merely a hobby of their Information Systems people, but an essential part of their internal and external communication. Thus the website and the communication policy it embodies becomes the responsibility of managers and communication people, as well as the creation and maintenance of the organization's flyers, catalogues, commercials, annual reports or helpdesk service. Those people will approach planning and producing a Web site as a communication design process, rather than a technical design process' (van der Geest 2001: 1).

Five dimensions have to be taken into consideration when approaching websites as communication events/activities:

(1) the addressers of the message, that is, the people who publish the website and perform all the related activities, such as designing, developing, maintaining, promoting, evaluating, and improving it, as well as interacting with the concerned publics;
(2) the addressees, that is, the visitors/users of a website;
(3) the message itself, that is, the contents and the services offered by the website: the information it transmits, the activities it allows, such as following a link, sending a message, making a payment, voting, subscribing, interacting, and so on;
(4) the channel through which the message is sent, that is, the technical tools which make contents and services available: hardware, software, network connection, visual interfaces, and so on;
(5) the context in which the website is inserted, that is, its relevant market.

Fundamental components of the WWW are *search engines*: these are particular Web services which allow surfers to search and retrieve information over the Web through full-text searches performed on the content of web pages. Technically, search engines are pieces of software that perform three main activities: (1) they fetch web pages through special software called *spiders* (or *crawls*, *bots*, etc.) and load them into their own database; (2) they *index* all the web pages gathered in the database by means of a ranking algorithm (i.e., a set of rules according to which different resources are put in order of relevance for given keywords); (3) they *answer* to the users' searches by presenting them the Web resources that best fit users' queries. Different search engines have developed different ranking algorithms and criteria in order to offer more relevant results to the users. The most popular search engine is Google, which in March 2008 had a market share of 77.7 per cent, followed by Yahoo (12.1 per cent), and MSN (3.3 per cent) (http://marketshare. hitslink.com/report.aspx?qprid=4).

Web 2.0

The term *Web 2.0* refers to the 'second generation of the World Wide Web that is focused on the ability for people to collaborate and share information online. Web 2.0 basically refers to the transition from static HTML Web pages to a more dynamic Web' (http://www.webopedia.com/ TERM/W/Web_2_point_0.html). The term was proposed for the first time in 2004 as a provocative suggestion, and has since then captured a great attention. The novelty brought by Web 2.0 is not so much technical, since it does not provide completely new technologies; the main technical innovation in Web 2.0 is Ajax (Asynchronous JavaScript and XML), which is not a technology itself but a new model that consists in using existing technologies so as to ease the way users can interact with online applications, allowing them to work asynchronously (that is offline) and to easily update their online spaces. Web 2.0 is a new way of using the Web itself, whose key component are *user-generated contents* (UGC): according to Kolbitsch and Maurer (2006: 187), Web 2.0 tools 'enable user participation on the Web and manage to recruit a large number of users as authors of new content,' thus obliterating 'the clear distinction between information providers and consumers.' As a matter of fact, Web 2.0 tools have lowered the publication threshold, enabling people with little technical competence to publish online.

Besides expanding the group of online publishers – hence moving from 'passive' / 'read only' competence to 'active' / 'read and write' competence – Web 2.0 also supports a different metaphor of the Web itself, not only conceived as an expanding library (where you can go and pull as much information as you like), but also as a public place, where people go to meet other people and have shared experiences. A further aspect of Web 2.0 worth considering is that it fulfils the multimedia promise of the Web. Thanks to a wider diffusion of large bandwidth internet access, more rich media contents can be published and enjoyed.

Web 2.0 includes many different applications, which have been classified in different typologies. A McKinsey research survey (2007), for instance, proposes a classification into nine different categories. The most popular Web 2.0 applications are blogs, folksonomies, social networks, and wikis.

Blogs (short for *Web logs*) are websites that offer a very easy publication interface, organize contents, as in diaries, according to a temporal axis, can allow for feedback by readers, and 'syndicate new items to make it easier to keep up without constant checking back' (Hall 2002). The rapid spread of blogs has given rise to the so-called *blogosphere*, a network of more or less loosely interconnected blogs in which the author of one blog can easily comment on other blogs. Strictly related to blogs is *RSS* (*Really Simple Syndication* or *RDF Site Syndication*, where RDF stands for resource description framework), which allows users to subscribe to automatic distribution of news (RSS) feeds; similar in nature is *podcasting*, the distribution of audios or videos over the internet, collecting them through aggregators, and playing them on portable devices like iPods, other MP3 players, and so on.

Collective intelligence tools or *folksonomies* are tools that collect and organize pieces of information coming from the members of a group in an attempt to represent the group knowledge. A folksonomy is defined by users who assign one or more tag (a label) to describe the web resource they want to classify. The websites del.icio.us and Flickr are two examples of successful folksonomies, where thousands of users store, tag (label), and share web pages and photos. Folksonomies are also commonly used as an alternative to traditional search engines, since the tags added to a web resource by a user make the resource searchable by other users.

Social networks are services that support social exchanges within given groups, allowing members to share data and knowledge or find the right people.

Wikis (from the Hawaiian word 'wiki wiki': 'quick') are websites that support collaborative document editing. The most famous wiki-based web service is Wikipedia, the 'free encyclopedia that anyone can edit' (http://en.wikipedia.org/wiki/Main_Page). As observed by Kolbitsch and Maurer (2006: 195), 'the success of Wikipedia builds on the tight involvement of the users, the sense of the community, and a dedication to developing a knowledge repository of unprecedented breadth and depth.'

Stefano Tardini and Lorenzo Cantoni

Bibliography

Battelle, John. *The Search: How Google and Its Rivals Rewrote the Rules of Business and Transformed Our Culture*. New York: Portfolio, 2005.

Berners-Lee, Tim. *Weaving the Web. The Original Design and Ultimate Destiny of the World Wide Web by Its Inventor*. New York: HarperCollins, 2000.

Cantoni, Lorenzo, and Paolo Paolini. Hypermedia Analysis. Some Insights from Semiotics and Ancient Rhetoric. *Studies in Communication Sciences* 1, no. 1 (January 2001): 33–53.

Cantoni, Lorenzo, and Stefano Tardini. *Internet*. Routledge Introductions to Media and Communications. London, New York: Routledge, 2006.

Hall, Michael. Give Your Users the Power of the Press with Weblogs and Wikis. *Intranet Journal*, 16 December 2002. http://www.intranetjournal.com/articles/200212/ij_12_16_02a.html (accessed 11 April 2008).

Kolbitsch, Josef, and Hermann Maurer. The Transformation of the Web: How Emerging Communities Shape the Information We Consume. *Journal of Universal Computer Science* 12, no. 2 (2006): 187–213.

McKinsey. How Businesses Are Using Web 2.0. A McKinsey Global Survey. *The McKinsey Quarterly*, 2007.

Nielsen, Jakob. *Multimedia and Hypertext. The Internet and Beyond*. Cambridge, MA: AP Professional, 1995.

O'Reilly, Tim. What Is Web 2.0? Design Patterns and Business Models for the Next Generation of Software, 30 September 2005. http://www.oreillynet.com/pub/a/oreilly/tim/news/2005/09/30/what-is-Web-20.html?page=1 (accessed 11 April 2008).

Surowiecki, James. *The Wisdom of Crowds: Why the Many Are Smarter Than the Few and How Collective Wisdom Shapes Business, Economies, Societies, and Nations*. New York: Doubleday, 2004.

van der Geest, Thea M. *Web Site Design Is Communication Design*. Amsterdam, Philadelphia: John Benjamins, 2001.

WRITING

[See also: *Alphabets; Zipf's Law*]

Writing is linguistic communication through the use of symbols that can be recorded in various media or materials. Writing emerges in the earliest cultures, alongside vocal language, in the form of pictures, called *pictographs*. Pictographic systems still exist, alongside alphabetic ones, in many languages. Moreover, pictography is still used for more general communication. The signs standing for men and women on public washrooms are examples of modern pictographs. Writing serves many functions. The books, magazines, and other materials that are based on writing allow us to gain information, derive entertainment, and so on. Some written texts, such as sacred texts, are the sources for the legal and ethical systems adopted by specific societies.

Pictography dates from the Neolithic era. One of the first civilizations to make pictography its official means of recording ideas, business transactions, and transmitting

knowledge was ancient China, dating as far as back as the fifteenth century BCE. The basic principle in early pictography is the use of images to stand directly for something. The degree of pictorial resemblance is higher for concrete things (*tree, bird, man, woman, child*) than it is for abstract referents (*evening, sleeping*). A *tree* can be shown with a simple drawing, whereas *the twilight* would have to be shown with several pictorial elements such as a sun crossing a horizontal line. The latter type of pictograph is called an *ideograph*. Ideographs assume knowledge of the relation between the pictorial elements and the referent. For example, the Chinese ideograph for *east* is a combination of the pictographs for *sun* and *tree* (Billeter 1990). Increasingly abstract pictographs are known as *logographs*. These combine elements of pictography and ideography.

A well-documented pictographic-logographic system, called *cuneiform*, was used by the ancient Sumerian culture 5,000 years ago. It consisted of wedge-shaped symbols recorded on clay tablets. Cuneiform was developed and used primarily by rulers and clerics. Another well-documented pictographic-logographic script, called *hieroglyphic*, was invented in Egypt around the same time for recording hymns and prayers, the names of deities, and various community activities (*hieroglyphic* derives from Greek *hieros* 'holy' and *glyphein* 'to carve'). The myths of many cultures attribute the origin of writing to deities – the Cretans to Zeus, the Sumerians to Nabu, the Egyptians to Toth, the Greeks to Hermes. The hieroglyphic system eventually developed sound-modelling elements within it called *phonographs*. These are signs standing for parts of words, such as syllables or individual sounds. The first true *phonographic-syllabic* systems were developed by the Semitic peoples of Palestine and Syria. They are still used in some cultures. Japanese, for example, is still written with two complete syllabaries – the *hiragana* and the *katakana*. A phonographic system for representing single sounds is called *alphabetic*. The first such system, consisting of phonographic symbols for consonant sounds only, emerged in the Middle East. It was transported by the Phoenicians to Greece, where symbols for vowel sounds were added to it. The Greek writing system thus became the first full-fledged alphabetic one.

The transition from pictography to alphabets was evolutionary, not revolutionary. Every alphabet character is a stylized version of a previous pictograph. The letter A, for instance, was originally the Egyptian pictograph of the head of an ox – a pictograph that spread to other parts of the Middle East. At some point, people started to draw the head in its bare outline. It was this kind of pictorial shorthand sign that came eventually to stand for the word for ox (*aleph*). Around 1,000 BCE Phoenician scribes started drawing the ox sign sideways, and the resulting symbol came to stand for the first sound in the word. As such 'abbreviated picture writing' became more common and letters stopped changing directions, the A assumed the upright position it has today in Roman script. The Greeks started the practice of naming each symbol – *alpha, beta, gamma*, and so on – which were imitations of Phoenician words (*aleph* 'ox,' *beth* 'house,' *gimel* 'camel,' and so on). The idea of an alphabetic order was derived from the fact that the sequence of letters was used to stand for the numbers in order – alpha stood for 1, beta for 2, and so on.

The tendency towards shorthand or abbreviation is as strong today as it was in the past. We commonly abbreviate the names of friends and family members (*Alex* for *Alexander, Cathy* for *Catharine, Chris* for *Christopher, Debbie* for *Deborah*), common phrases (*TGIF* for *Thank God it's Friday*), and of anything else that refers to something common or familiar (*ad* for *advertising, asap* for *as soon as possible*). Such writing is efficient, taking up less space, and is tied to social processes and perceptions of various kinds. Many institutions use abbreviations to represent themselves (*AP* for *Associated Pres, CIA* for *Central Intelligence Agency, IBM* for *International Business Machines Corporation*). These seem to imbue them with a unique symbolic status. And, indeed, abbreviations have always been used by people of authority or positions of social importance. These suggest a high level of literacy. They are used in scholarly and scientific writing (*e.g., etc., QED, laser*, and so on). Not all abbreviation is tied, of course, to high-register writing. It is often used simply to make writing rapid and efficient. And this is why it is used in *text speak* – the writing used to create messages in text-messaging programs. To increase the speed at which messages can be input and read in real time, a series of shorthand forms have emerged that are now part of text speak: for example, *2dA* (today), *2moro* (tomorrow), *b4* (before), *bf/gf* (boyfriend/girlfriend), *brb* (I'll be right back), *btw* (by the way), *cm* (call me), *lol* (laughing out loud/lots of love), *ruok* (Are you OK?). With few, if any, corrective forces at work in cyberspace, several questions emerge: Is text speak spreading to the offline world? Is it changing how people will write and even talk in the future? The use of abbreviation for communicative ease purposes is nothing new, but it has never been as widespread as it is in text speak. In today's cyber universe, not answering the many text messages that people receive on a daily basis is perceived negatively. Slowness in response is sometimes even penalized by ostracism or reprobation. Moreover, it seems the text speak style is now becoming more and more part of branding. Names with the small letter 'i' are now common: iCaps (eye care products), iCom (computer software), iMac (model of Mac computer), iMark (eye shadow), iZod (shoes), to name a few. Such brand names resonate with internet chic. The 'i' suggests 'imagination,' 'internet,' 'ingenuity,' and 'intelligence,' among other things.

Spelling has also been used for symbolic reasons. By flying in the face of orthographic traditions that bespeak of 'whiteness,' rap artists, for example, have used their own form of spelling in order to signal a break from the hegemony of white culture. The non-compliant attitude behind how rap artists spell their names (for example, 2Pac, Jay-Z, Salt 'N' Pepa) exudes linguistic empowerment. Rapper Chuck D articulated rap's anti-hegemonic stance in a 1992 interview with *XXL* magazine: 'This is our voice, this is the voice of our lifestyle, this is the voice of our people. We're not going to take the cookie cutter they give us let them mold us.' However, it should be mentioned that long before rap, a similar style was adopted by such groups as Guns N' Roses, Led Zeppelin, and The Monkees. The poet e.e. cummings (1894–1962) also went against orthographic conventions by writing only in lower case, adopting unusual punctuation, or eliminating spaces. Spelling differences are also one of the features that set American English apart from British English. Noah Webster proposed in 1828 the elimination of *u* in words such as *colour, harbour, favour,* and *odour*. His proposal was received enthusiastically, since it was perceived as a way for America to show its break symbolically from its British past. American English was, in fact, a language that was once considered to be subversive by the British. In effect, there is much more to writing than meets the eye.

Marcel Danesi

Bibliography

Billeter, Jean François. *The Chinese Art of Writing.* New York: Rizzoli, 1990.

Cook, Vivian. *Why Can't Anybody Spell?* New York: Touchstone, 2004.

Coulmas, Florian. *The Writing Systems of the World.* Oxford: Blackwell, 1989.

Daniels, Peter T., and William Bright, eds. *The World's Writing Systems.* Oxford: Oxford University Press, 1995.

Harris, Roy. *The Origin of Writing.* London: Duckworth, 1986.

Schmandt-Besserat, Denise. *Before Writing.* 2 vols. Austin: University of Texas Press, 1992.

Y

YOUTUBE

[See also: *Cyberculture; Facebook; Googling; Internet; Online Culture; Social Networking; Twitter*]

YouTube is a video-sharing website, founded in 2005 by Chad Hurley, Steve Chen, and Jawed Karim, that features videos posted by individuals as well as by musicians, artists, TV networks, and other professionals and institutions. It allows users to comment on and rate videos. YouTube members can also start a discussion about a video, transforming YouTube into a social networking site. They can also email YouTube video links to others. Today, YouTube also offers advertising, video diaries known as *vlogs*, 'made-for-YouTube' movies, and material created by professors for use in courses. YouTube was purchased by Google in 2006, with a consequent burgeoning of viewership, a fact that forced television networks to use YouTube to promote their programs. In 2007, YouTube joined the Cable News Network (CNN) for a series of presidential campaign debates in which users could post videos asking candidates questions.

As Strangelove (2010) has shown, the YouTube phenomenon cannot be easily categorized in terms of traditional theories of media and popular culture. One can see an anonymous musician playing classical music in a clip that has been viewed over 60 million times. An inebriated David Hasselhoff attempting to eat a hamburger also gets millions of views. A cat playing the piano goes 'viral.' It is difficult to say what this tells us about viewers and users of YouTube, other than it has opened up the 'performance stage' to virtually everyone and that anything captured on video and uploaded to YouTube will attract the interest of someone else somewhere in the world. Notwithstanding the typical comments by some critics that such sites are 'peeping tom' venues, it seems that the YouTube phenomenon is documenting a paradigm shift in how we view others and engage with them in the 'global village.'

Marcel Danesi

Bibliography

Strangelove, Michael. *Watching YouTube: Extraordinary Videos by Ordinary People*. Toronto: University of Toronto Press, 2010.

Tancer, Bill. *Click*. New York: Hyperion, 2008.

Z

ZIPF'S LAW

[See also: *Language; Communication; Media; Print Culture; Writing*]

In communication studies, Zipf's law, named after Harvard linguist George Kingsley Zipf, claims that there is a mathematical correlation between the frequency of a form (such as a word or sentence) and its size (as measured in number of phonemes, words, and so on). Practically, this means that there is a tendency in language towards efficiency and economy, which manifests itself in compressed forms (abbreviations of words and phrases, acronyms) in all domains of language use. Scholars and scientists have always used abbreviations and acronyms of various kinds to facilitate swift and precise technical communications. Abbreviations such as *etc., et al., op. cit.,* and *N.B.,* are still part of 'scholarspeak,' as it may be called. Similar reductive tendencies exist in everyday discourse and especially in internet-based communications (emails, text messages, and so on).

The Principle of Least Effort

Various theories have been fashioned to explain why languages change. One of the most interesting ones was articulated in the 1950s by the French linguist André Martinet, who claimed that languages change as a result of the operation of eco-nomic tendencies. Calling it the *principle of economic change*, Martinet posited that complex language forms and structures tended towards reduction, abbreviation, compression, levelling, or elimination over time. For example, the opposition between short and long vowels in Latin, which produced a relatively large inventory of distinct words in that language, was levelled in the emerging sound systems of the Romance languages and later eliminated. Latin had ten distinct vowel sounds, equivalent approximately to the vowel phones represented by the letters *a, e, i, o, u.* In addition, each vowel was pronounced as either long or short – for example, the pronunciation of the word spelled *os* could mean either 'mouth' or 'bone,' depending on whether the vowel was long or short (respectively). The ten-vowel phoneme system was, to a large extent, reduced or levelled in the Romance languages, in line with the principle of economic change. Distinctions of meaning were preserved nonetheless (as they are in modern Italian) but with less phonic material.

Although the interaction between economy and change comes under various names in the linguistic literature, it is commonly called the *principle of least effort* (PLE). The fact that such a principle may be operative in determining the actual constitution of linguistic systems was first identified in the 1930s by the Harvard linguist George Kingsley Zipf. Zipf claimed that many phenomena in language could be explained as the result of an inborn tendency in the human species to make the most of its communication resources with the least expenditure of effort (physical, cognitive, and social). This tendency was independent of individual and culture. As Van de Walle and Willems (2006: 756) write, Zipf saw language as a 'self-regulating structure' evolving 'independently from other social and cultural factors.' The PLE is, Zipf claimed, the reason why speakers minimize articulatory effort by shortening the length of words and utterances. At the same time, people want to be able to interpret the meaning of words and utterances unambiguously and with least effort. In one of his most famous studies (1932), Zipf demonstrated that there exists an intrinsic interdependence between the length of a specific word (in number of phonemes) and its rank order in the language (its position in order of its frequency of occurrence in texts of all kinds). The higher the rank order of a word (the more frequent it is in actual usage), the more it tends to be 'shorter' (made up with fewer phonemes). For example, articles *(a, the)*, conjunctions *(and, or)*, and other function words *(to, it)*, which have a high rank order in English (and in any other language for that matter), are typically monosyllabic, consisting of one to three phonemes. This 'compression' force does not stop at the level of function words, however, as Zipf and others subsequently found. It can be seen to manifest itself in the tendency for phrases that come into popular use to become abbreviated *(FYO, UNESCO, Hi, Bye, ad, photo, Mr, Mrs, Dr, 24/7,* and so on) or changed into acronyms *(aka, VCR, DNA, laser, GNP, IQ, VIP,* and so on). It can also be seen in the creation of tables, technical and scientific notation systems, indexes, footnotes, bibliographic traditions, and so on. In effect, the general version of Zipf's law proclaims that the more frequent or necessary a form for communicative purposes, the more likely it is to be rendered compressed or economical in physical structure. And the reason for this seems to be an inherent psychobiological tendency in the human species to expend the least effort possible in representation and communication.

The PLE involves not only abbreviation and acronymy, but also phenomena such as blending, or the creation of a new (shorter) word that combines two other words. *Sexpert*, for instance, is a blend of *sex* or *sexual* and *expert*. Similarly, *electrocute* is a blend of *electricity* and *execute*, *guestimate* of *guess* and *estimate*, *motel* of *motor* and *hotel*, and *brunch* of *breakfast* and *lunch*.

To grasp the essence of Zipf's law, all one has to do is take all the words in a substantial corpus of text, such as an issue of the *New York Times*, and count the number of times each word in it appears. If the frequencies of the words are then plotted on a histogram and sorted by rank, with the most frequently appearing words *(a, the, for, by, and)* first, then the resulting curve will be found to approach the shape of a straight line with a slope of –1. A study of Zipfian histograms has revealed certain tendencies: (1) the magnitude of words tends, on the whole, to stand in an inverse relationship to the number of occurrences (the more frequent the word the shorter it tends to be); and (2) the number of different words in a text seems to be ever larger as the frequency of occurrences becomes ever smaller.

Since the mid-1950s, Zipfian-inspired research has established empirically that there is a tendency in all aspects of language towards the compression of high-frequency forms. Zipf's law has been found to characterize many types of activities and behaviours, from numeration patterns (Raimi 1969) to the distribution of city populations (Hill 1998).

The relation of word frequency (p_n) to rank order (n) was formalized by Zipf as follows:

$$\log p_n = A - B \log_n \text{ (where A and B are constants and } B \approx 1)$$

For the sake of historical accuracy, it should be mentioned that this type of outcome was known long before Zipf. In the nineteenth century, it was found that if the digits used for a task (to enumerate, classify, and so on) are not entirely random but somehow socially or naturally based, the distribution of the first digit is not uniform – 1 tends to be the first digit in about 30 per cent of cases, 2 will come up in about 18 per cent of cases, 3 in 12 per cent, 4 in 9 per cent, 5 in 8 per cent, and so on This was discovered in 1881 by the American astronomer Simon Newcomb, who noticed that the first pages of books of logarithms were soiled much more than the remaining pages. In 1938, mathematician Frank Benford investigated listings of data, finding a similar pattern to that uncovered by Newcomb in income tax and population figures, as well as in the distribution of street addresses of people listed in phone books. Zipf's main contribution was in showing empirically that patterns of this type manifest themselves regularly and almost 'blindly' in human representational efforts, especially in language.

Shortly after the publication of Zipf's law, the mathematician Benoit Mandelbrot, who developed the modern-day branch of mathematics known as fractal geometry, became fascinated by it (Mandelbrot 1954), since he detected it as being a particular type of what is called a 'scaling' law in biology. As a mathematician, Mandelbrot also made appropriate modifications to Zipf's original law, and, generally speaking, it is Mandelbrot's version of the law that is used today to study frequency distribution phenomena in several branches of linguistics, such as corpus linguistics, lexicostatistics, glottometrics, textlinguistics, and quantitative linguistics generally.

Cyberlanguage

Nowhere is the operation of Zipf's law as apparent today as it is in the forms that are created in cyberspace. Emails, text messages, and the like are the media through which, and in which, such forms develop profusely and with rapidity. To increase the speed at which such messages can be input and received, a series of common abbreviations, acronyms, and other reduced structures have become part of a common cyberlanguage (Crystal 2001). Here are a few common English cyberforms:

b4	=	before
bf/gf	=	boyfriend/girlfriend
f2f	=	face-to-face
gr8	=	great
h2cus	=	hope to see you soon
idk	=	I don't know
j4f	=	just for fun
lol	=	laughing out loud
cm	=	call me
2dA	=	today
wan2	=	want to
ruok	=	Are you OK?
2moro	=	tomorrow
g2g	=	gotta go

Other economizing tendencies include the lack of distinction between upper and lower case, the elimination of apostrophes (*im, dont, isnt, didnt*), and reduced use of punctuation. By ignoring such stylistic devices, the user saves time by limiting the hand actions performed on the keyboard. Crystal (2001: 87) calls this the 'save a keystroke principle': 'Most of the Internet is not case-sensitive, which thus motivates the random use of capitals or no capitals at all. There is a strong tendency to use lowercase everywhere. The "save a keystroke" principle is widely found in e-mails, chat groups, where whole sentences can be produced without capitals (or punctuation).'

Formal writing takes time and effort. In today's cybernetic universe, both come at a premium. Not answering the barrage of emails or text messages that people receive on a daily basis is perceived negatively. Slowness in response is, at times, even penalized by social ostracism or various other forms of reprobation. Logically, reduction of forms helps counteract the situation by making it possible to respond to a sender quickly and rapidly. Various strategies of condensation have thus evolved within cyberlanguage that are consistent with the PLE. In addition to the traditional abbreviation and acronymic reductions, cyberforms are produced through various phonic and numeric replacements. For example, in the cyberform *How R U?* ('How are you?') the letters *R* and *U* are pronounced in the same way as are the words *are* and *you* but take less time to type. In the cyberform *B4* ('before') the *B* is pronounced like the morpheme *be-* and *4* like the morpheme *fore*. Such replacements are common, reflecting an economizing strategy that allows for rapid inputting of messages in email, chatroom, and text messaging forms of cyber communication.

Implications

The tendency towards economy has always been a factor in linguistic communication. Cyberspace has simply sped up the process. Where once it took decades for a change to penetrate the language, now it seems to take only days. Of course, many of the cyberforms will disappear. Only those that gain general currency will remain. So, although the PLE suggests a kind of 'blind operation' of economic forces in language, the social aspect is still an imperative in ultimately conditioning what forms remain and which ones will disappear. Logically, the nature of cybercommunications – their rapidity, their quantity, and so on – has implications for change in language. How will literacy be defined in, say, the year 2067? What form will writing take?

There are many more questions that a Zipfian analysis of communication elicits, especially in the relation of verbal to nonverbal communication. Is there a relation between gesture form and its utility and frequency? Are gestures that are more abrupt than others higher in frequency (of usage) than those that are more elaborate? How does one measure 'length' or 'size' in the non-verbal domain? Do non-verbal forms that are used with verbal ones – such as the gestures that accompany speech – match them in Zipfian terms? Zipfian analysis has the capacity to show that humans, in their apparent quest for economy, end up producing new systems that produce new ideas and serendipitous discoveries. Just why data conform to Zipfian distributions can be a matter of some controversy. The fact that Zipfian distributions arise in randomly generated texts suggests that in linguistic contexts, the law is a statistical artefact. That is, one starts with an alphabet of N letters, one of which is a blank space and thus acts as a word separator. By picking letters randomly, with a uniform distribution, one generates a random string; the string will consist of 'words' of various lengths. After ranking these words, and plotting their frequency, one obtains precisely Zipf's law. Thus, Zipf's law does not seem to shed any light on the linguistic structure of language, but is rather an artefact of using letters to spell words.

Whatever the case, what Zipf's law shows, or at least suggests, is that general conditions exist in communication systems that determine the equilibrium of the systems in terms of their forms and meanings. It is the specific conditions that shift with time and place, not the general tendencies.

Marcel Danesi

Bibliography

Crystal, David. *Language and the Internet*. Cambridge: Cambridge University Press, 2001.

Hill, Ted P. The First Digit Phenomenon. *American Scientist* 86 (1998): 358–63.

Kucera, Henry, and W. Nelson Francis. *Computational Analysis of Present-Day American English*. Providence, RI: Brown University Press, 1967.

Li, Wentian. Random Texts Exhibit Zipf's-Law-Like Word Frequency Distribution. *IEEE Transactions on Information Theory* 38 (1992): 1842–5.

Mandelbrot, Benoit. Structure formelle des textes et communication. *Word* 10 (1954): 1–27.

Martinet, André. *Économie des changements phonétiques*. Berne: Verlag, 1955.

Miller, George A., and Edwin B. Newman. Tests of a Statistical Explanation of the Rank-Frequency Relation for Words in Written English. *American Journal of Psychology* 71 (1958): 209–18.

Nowak, Martin A. The Basic Reproductive Ratio of a Word, the Maximum Size of a Lexicon. *Journal of Theoretical Biology* 204 (2000): 179–89.

Perline, Richard. Zipf's Law, the Central Limit Theorem, and the Random Division of the Unit Interval. *Physical Review* 54 (1996): 220–3.

Raimi, Ralph A. The Peculiar Distribution of First Digits. *Scientific American* 221 (1969): 109–19.

Ridley, Dennis R., and Emilia A. Gonzales. Zipf's Law Extended to Small Samples of Adult Speech. *Perception and Motor Skills* 79 (1994): 153–4.

Rousseau, Ronald, and Qiaoqiao Zhang. Zipf's Data on the Frequency of Chinese Words Revisited. *Scientometrics* 24 (1992): 201–20.

Vande Walle, Willy F., and Klaas Willems. Zipf, George Kingsley (1902–1950), in *Encyclopedia of Languages and Linguistics*, 2nd ed., ed. K. Brown, vol. 13: 756–7. Oxford: Elsevier Science, 2006.

Wyllys, Ronald E. Measuring Scientific Prose with Rank-Frequency ('Zipf') Curves: A New Use for an Old Phenomenon. *Proceedings of the American Society for Information Science* 12 (1975): 30–1.

Zipf, George Kingsley. Relative Frequency as a Determinant of Phonetic Change. *Harvard Studies in Classical Philology* 40 (1929): 1–95.

– *Selected Studies of the Principle of Relative Frequency in Language.* Cambridge, MA: Harvard University Press, 1932.

– *The Psycho-Biology of Language: An Introduction to Dynamic Philology.* Boston: Houghton-Mifflin, 1935.

– *Human Behavior and the Principle of Least Effort.* Boston: Addison-Wesley, 1949.

Timelines

Print Media

2400 BCE	Papyrus, based on reeds, is used along the Nile River for writing
350	The Romans produce the *codex* book made with parchment pages bound together
600	Illuminated manuscripts are produced by scribes (primarily monks), featuring decorative designs on each page
700	Arab traders introduce paper to the Western world
1000	Movable clay typesetting is invented in China
1234	Movable metal typesetting is invented in Korea
1453	Johannes Gutenberg transforms a wine press into a printing press, leading to the mass production of books
1455	The Gutenberg Bible is the first book published with the new printing technology
1602	The first public lending library, called the Bodley, is established
1620	Corantos, the first news sheets, are published in northern Europe
1640	The first book published in the American colonies is *The Bay Psalm Book*; it is printed in Boston
1640s	*Diurnos*, which are the forerunners of the first daily newspapers, are published in England
1644	English poet John Milton praises and defends freedom of speech in his pamphlet titled *Aeropagitica*
1690	Boston printer Benjamin Harris publishes the first American newspaper, *Publick Occurrences, Both Foreign and Domestick*
1721	The *New England Courant* begins publication
1731	The first popular magazine, called *Gentleman's Magazine*, is published in England
1732	Benjamin Franklin publishes his popular *Poor Richard's Almanack*
1735	Freedom of the press is debated after a jury rules in favour printer Peter John Zenger, who had criticized the government in print and was charged with libel
1751	The first modern encyclopedia is put together by French scholars
1776	The American Declaration of Independence is disseminated throughout the nation by newspapers
1783	The first American daily, the *Pennsylvania Evening Post and Daily Advertiser*, is published
1789	Freedom of the press is enshrined in the American Constitution by the First Amendment
1790	First American copyright law is passed, as publishing houses start to proliferate
1790	The Copyright Act is passed
1798–1800	The Alien and Sedition Acts attempt to curtail press criticism of the government
1821	The *Saturday Evening Post* is launched, appealing directly to female readership
1827	The first African American newspaper, *Freedom's Journal*, makes its appearance

1828	The first Native American newspaper, *The Cherokee,* makes its debut
1833	The *New York Sun* is founded as the first penny press newspaper
1833	The penny press era is ushered in after the *New York Sun* is published, costing only one cent and thus starting the trend of making newspapers affordable
1836	Sarah Josepha Hales creates Godey's *Lady's Book*, the first modern women's magazine
1846	The rotary press is invented in the U.S. and *Harper's Weekly* begins regular publication
1848	Six newspapers form the Associated Press, relaying news stories around the country via telegraphy
1860s	The dime novel is established as a mass paperback book; *New York Morning* reaches a circulation of 80,000, highlighting the fact that newspapers had become an integral part of mass communications
1878	Joseph Pulitzer starts a new journalism movement
1879	A Postal Act lowers the postal rate for magazines, allowing them to thrive
1880s	Linotype and offset lithography are used to lower the cost of book production
1883	Pulitzer buys the *New York World,* ushering in the era of yellow journalism
1895	William Randolph Hearst enters newspaper publishing with sensationalistic techniques
1896	Adolph Ochs buys the *New York Times*, making responsible journalism its primary objective
1909	An important Copyright Act is passed
1914	First Spanish-language paper in the United States, *El Diario-La Prensa*, is founded in New York
1917	The Pulitzer Prize is established at Columbia University
1920s	Newspaper chains spring up, marking a decline in the number of daily metropolitan newspapers
1922	*Reader's Digest* is launched
1923	Henry Luce founds *Time* magazine
1936	*Life* magazine starts publication
1939	Robert de Graaf establishes Pocket Books
1953	*TV Guide* is launched, indicating the start of modern media convergence
1955	The *Village Voice* is launched in Greenwich Village as the first underground newspaper
1960s	Computer-based typesetting begins
1969	The *Saturday Evening Post* is among the first magazines to succumb to specialized competition
1971	Borders bookstore opens up in Ann Arbor. Chain bookstores and superstores start springing up shortly thereafter
1972	Watergate scandal stimulates a new era of investigative journalism
1974	*People* magazine starts publication
1980	Ohio's *Columbus Dispatch* is the first newspaper to go online
1982	*USA Today* is launched, the first paper modelled after television
1995	Amazon.com is established
1998	The Digital Millennium Copyright Term Extension Act is passed
1998	The *Dallas Morning News* is the first newspaper to break a major story on its website instead of its front page. Increasing use of the internet leads to the development of blogs, discussion groups, and the like, which take on many functions of traditional newspapers
2000s	Microsoft and Adobe start making online books (e-books) available
2003	Thousands of newspapers offer some kind of online news service; blogs, websites, etc. appear to take on many of the traditional functions of print media
2008–	e-Books become widespread as devices known as e-readers (tablets that can contain electronic text) are mass marketed

Radio and Recordings

1877	Thomas Edison invents the wax cylinder phonograph
1887–8	Emile Berliner manufactures the gramophone to play mass-produced discs
1896	Guglielmo Marconi develops the first radio transmitter
1906–10	Lee De Forest invents the vacuum tube, called the Audion tube, and Reginald Fessenden broadcasts the first radio program from the Metropolitan Opera House in New York City
1910	Congress passes the Wireless Ship Act requiring ships to carry wireless radio
1912	Congress passes a Radio Act, licensing radio transmitters
1916	David Sarnoff, of American Marconi, writes a famous memo, *The Radio Box Memo*, in which he proposes to make radio a 'household utility'
1916–20	Frank Conrad founds KDKA in Pittsburgh as the first experimental radio station in 1916. The station's broadcast of the 1920 presidential election results on 2 November 1920 is generally considered the beginning of professional broadcasting
1922	The first uses of radio for commercial purposes begin with the airing of the first advertisements by AT&T on station WEAF. This causes an uproar
1926	The first radio broadcasting network, NBC, is created by RCA. AT&T abandons radio broadcasting
1927	Congress's Radio Act creates the Federal Radio Commission. Congress also passes the Federal Communications Act of 1934, allowing commercial interests to control the airwaves. AM stations are allocated
1933	FM radio is developed
1934	The Federal Communications Commission (FCC) is created
1938	Mercury Theater of the air broadcasts *War of the Worlds*, demonstrating how quickly a mass medium can cause public panic
1941	Chain broadcasting rules are developed
1947	Radio starts to lose audiences to television. Magnetic audiotape is developed by 3M
1948	33 1/3 records are introduced by Columbia Records and 45 rpm records are introduced by RCA Victor. The DJ radio era takes off
1955	Top 40 radio becomes the most popular type of radio format
1956	Stereo recordings are invented and mass-produced
1962	Cassette tapes are introduced
1970s	FM radio stations gain popularity, introducing narrowcasting
1971	National Public Radio starts broadcasting with *All Things Considered*
1979	Sony engineer Akio Morita invents the portable Walkman
1981	Music Television (MTV) is born, becoming an arm of the recording industry
1982	Compact discs are introduced
1987	WFAN is launched as the first all-sports radio station, further spreading the narrowcasting trend
1990s	Talk radio becomes popular. Old and new genres, from country to gospel and opera become popular with target audiences creating niche recording and radio markets
1996	Congress passes the Telecommunications Act, allowing for consolidation in radio ownership across the United States
1997	DVDs make their debut
1998	Music download sites proliferate on the internet
2000	MP3 technology shakes up the music industry, as internet users share music files on Napster. Napster is eventually ordered to stop unauthorized file sharing
2000s	Satellite and web-based radio programs emerge in 2002. File-sharing, online radio programs, etc. become highly popular. Rap and hip hop remain popular but lose their market domination
2001	Peer-to-peer internet services make music file-sharing popular
2003	Apple Computer's iTunes music store makes its debut

2008–on   Satellite radio makes its appearance, paralleling pay-per-view television, as radio increasingly converges with other media

Film and Video

1877   Eadweard Muybridge records motion on film for the first time
1888   Thomas Edison manufactures the first motion picture camera
1889   Hannibal Goodwin develops film technology, opening up the door to cinematography
1894   Thomas Edison opens up the first kinetoscope parlours with coin-operated projection machines
1895   The Lumière brothers show the first short films in Paris
1896   Thomas Edison invents the Vitascope, which is capable of large-screen projection
1903   Edwin S. Porter's *The Great Train Robbery* gains popularity, indicating that the era of cinema has arrived
1907   Storefront movie parlours, called nickelodeons, with a five-cent admission, begin to flourish
1910s   Silent films become popular. The first movie celebrities emerge in the late 1910s and early 1920s
1914   Movie palaces start opening up in New York City
1915   D.W. Griffith's *Birth of a Nation*, the first true feature film, gains great success
1920s   The Big Five studios (Paramount, MGM, Warner Brothers, Twentieth Century–Fox, RKO) and the Little Three studios (Columbia, Universal, United Artists) are established in the late 1920s
1922   The American movie industry establishes voluntary censorship
1927   Soundtrack technology produces the first talkie, *The Jazz Singer* (1927) starring Al Jolson
1930s   The 1930s is often called the Golden Age of Cinema
1947   The House Un-American Activities Committee starts holding hearings on communism in Hollywood
1957   In the *Roth vs. United States* case the Supreme Court sets community standards as the criteria for defining obscenity
1968   MPAA movie ratings are introduced
1976   VCRs are introduced
1990s   Independent films become popular
1995   The first megaplex movie theatre is built in 1995 in Dallas. *Toy Story* is the first completely computer-generated movie, starting a new trend in movie production
1997   DVDs come onto the scene
2000   Movies integrate with the internet, where trailers are shown and where full features can be seen; YouTube features snippets and even entire movies
2009–   Movie technology brings back 3-D and animation becomes more and more dominant as a mode of moviemaking

Television

Late 1800s   The cathode ray tube makes television technology possible
1884   In Germany, Paul Nipkow patents the electrical telescope, further developing TV technology
1927   Philo T. Farnsworth broadcasts the first TV picture electronically. He applies for a TV patent
1935   Farnsworth conducts the first public demonstration of TV in Philadelphia
1936   Television service debuts in Britain
1939   NBC starts regular television broadcasts from New York City
1941   The FCC sets standards for television broadcasting
1948   The first network TV variety shows usher in the golden age of television. The first community antenna television (CATV) is established

1950	The A.C. Nielsen Market Research Company starts tracking TV audience behaviours
1950s	Television becomes a dominant medium, with previous radio genres and radio personalities making the move over to TV
1954	Colour television technology is introduced. The U.S. Senate begins hearings on the purported effects of television violence on juvenile delinquency
1958–9	Quiz show scandals tarnish TV's image
1960	The first satellite system, called Telstar, is established. The Kennedy-Nixon presidential debates illustrate the power of television to influence public opinion
1961	A second round of Senate hearings on television violence takes place
1966	Prime-time programs are broadcast in colour
1967	Congress creates the Corporation for Public Broadcasting, leading to the establishment of public television
1968	The National Commission on the Causes of Violence concludes that TV violence encourages violent behaviour
1971	*All in the Family* introduces controversial social issues to prime-time programming
1972	The FCC makes cable available to cities. The U.S. Surgeon General releases a research report on the relation between television and social behaviour
1975	HBO (Home Box Office) begins broadcasting via satellite. VCRs are introduced. Under FCC pressure, broadcasters adopt a family-hour format
1976	Cable becomes popular with Ted Turner's WTBS in Atlanta
1980	CNN premieres as a 24-hour cable news network
1981	Cable also brings MTV onto the scene in 1981
1987	Rupert Murdoch's Fox television makes its debut
1990s	New channels and networks open up
1990	The Children's Television Act mandates children's programming
1994	The direct broadcast satellite (DBS) industry debuts
1996	The Telecommunications Act abolishes most TV ownership restrictions
1997	Parental advisories mandated for TV programs
1998	The V-chip is introduced. HDTV broadcasting begins
2000s	Narrowcasting becomes a reality, with all the specialty channels available along with network programming. Television and the internet merge to create a co-broadcasting system, whereby television channels and internet websites deliver the same or complementary content
2002	The FCC rules to end analogue broadcasting by 2007, transforming TV to a digital medium
2003	VOD (video on demand) is introduced
2008–on	Television merges more and more with the internet to produce simultaneous webcasts of programs and to provide more programming and information associated with networks

The Internet and the World Wide Web

1822	Charles Babbage develops a computer device that becomes a model for future technology
1844	Telegraphy constitutes a data network forerunner
1866	Transoceanic telegraph service begins
1876	The telephone is introduced
1915	The first transcontinental phone call is made possible with new technologies
1939	John Vincent Atanasoff of Iowa State University designs the first modern computer
1946	J. Presper Eckert and John Mauchly invent ENIAC, the first general-purpose computer, for military purposes
1951	Eckert and Mauchly introduce UNIVAC for civilian purposes
1962	The first communications satellite, the first digital phone networks, and the first pagers are introduced

1964	The first local area network (LAN) is put into service to support nuclear weapons research
1965	BASIC is developed
1969	Arpanet is the first communication network established by the American defence department
1971	Microprocessors are developed
1972	The first video game, Pong, is introduced. Email is developed for communications on Arpanet
1975	The first personal computer, Altair, is introduced
1977	The first fibre-optic network is created
1978	Cellular phone service begins
1980s	Fibre-optic cable is developed, making it possible to transmit digital messages. Hypertext is developed
1982	The National Science Foundation sponsors a high-speed communications network, leading to the internet
1983	Arpanet starts using TCP/IP, essentially launching the internet
1984	Apple Macintosh is the first PC with graphics
1989	Tim Berners-Lee develops concepts and techniques that form the basis of the World Wide Web. AOL (America Online) is formed, later becoming the first successful internet service provider
1990	The first internet search engine, Archie, is developed
1991	The internet opens to commercial uses, HTML is developed, and the World Wide Web is launched by Berners-Lee
1993	The first point-and-click Web browser, Mosaic, is introduced
1994	The first internet cafés open. Jeff Bezos launches Amazon.com
1995	Digital cellular phones are introduced on the market
1996	The Telecommunications Act and the Communications Decency Act are passed. Google is launched
2000	Cookies technology allows for information profiles to be created, enabling data-mining practices to burgeon
2001	Instant-messaging services appear
2002	Broadband technology is developed by South Korea
Mid–late 2000s	The internet converges with older media (radio, television, etc.) to produce online versions of previous broadcasting. It also becomes a source of new forms of communication, with websites such as MySpace, YouTube, and Twitter
2010	Google starts the process of digitizing books, as copyright issues become more and more pressing

Advertising

1625	The first true advertisement appears in an English newspaper
1735	Benjamin Franklin sells ad space in the *Pennsylvania Gazette*
1792	The first propaganda ministry is established in France
1804	The first classified ads in America run in the *Boston News-Letter*
1830s	The penny press becomes the first advertising-supported media outlet
1841	The first ad agency is established in Boston by Volney Palmer to represent newspaper publishers
1860s	Advertising is incorporated into magazines
1871	P.T. Barnum establishes his Greatest Show on Earth, using techniques that become the basis of sensationalistic advertising
1880s	Brands (products with names) appear
1887	*Ladies Home Journal* is designed to be a medium for consumer advertising
1914	The Federal Trade Commission is established in 1914 to help monitor advertising practices
1920s	Newspapers and magazines start depending heavily on advertising revenues

1922	Newspaper columnist Walter Lippmann publishes a controversial book, *Public Opinion*, in which he shows how advertising shapes public perception negatively. The first radio commercial is aired
1942	The systematic study of propaganda and advertising effects is started by the U.S. military
1950s–60s	30-second and 60-second TV commercials become routine
1957	Vance Packard's *The Hidden Persuaders* is published, warning people of the dangers of persuasive advertising
1971	Tobacco ads are banned from television
1984	Apple's Macintosh commercial at the Super Bowl halftime takes advertising to a new aesthetic level
Mid-1980s	Brand placement and a general partnership between advertising and pop culture solidify
1994	Internet banner advertising begins
1995	The internet advertising agency DoubleClick is founded
1998	Tobacco ads are banned from billboards
2000s	The internet and the World Wide Web become increasingly attractive as sites for advertising. New forms of advertising, such as pop-ups, appear
2010	Advertising styles adapt continuously to the world of cyberspace, and many brands increasingly become a part of popular culture

List of Contributors

Arning, Chris: Qualitative and Quantitative Research; Recordings
Artz, Lee: Hegemony Theory
Baggi, Marcello: Intellectual Property
Balbi, Gabriele: Telephony
Baskaran, Angathevar: Digital Divide
Berger, Arthur Asa: Comedy; Comics; Detective Stories; Genre; Postmodernism;
  Psychoanalytic Theory; Television Genres
Birk-Urovitz, Alexandra: Ang, Ien; Castells, Manuel; Cultivation Theory; Fergu-
  son, Margorie; Gerbner, George; Katz, Elihu; Public Broadcasting
Birk-Urovitz, Elizabeth: Ang, Ien; Castells, Manuel; Cultivation Theory; Fergu-
  son, Margorie; Gerbner, George; Katz, Elihu; Public Broadcasting
Bockarova, Mariana: Bell, Daniel; Fiske, John; Hall, Stuart; Independent Produc-
  tion; Lazarsfeld, Paul; McLuhan, Marshall; McQuail, Denis; Narrowcasting;
  News Websites; Podcasting; Postman, Neil; Social Networking; Video; Virtual
  Reality
Broden, Thomas F.: Cognitive Language Studies; Modern Continental Theories;
  Peircean Semiotics; Speech Act Theory; Text Theory
Bryers, Lorraine: Internet and Social Interaction
Byerly, Carolyn M.: Race and Gender Diversity
Cantoni, Lorenzo: e-Government; World Wide Web
Chakravarty, Sumita S.: Globalization
Cobley, Paul: Barthes, Roland; Culture and Media; Myth; Popular Culture
Coen, Carlo: Cinema
Colilli, Paul: Constructivism; Habermas, Jürgen; Post-Structuralism
Cook, David: Innis, Harold
Cutsail, Jeff: Sensationalism
Denison, Rayna: Blockbusters
Dillard, Krystle: Censorship
Dumanski, Barbara: Celebrity Culture; Freedom of Speech; Talk Shows
Duncan, John: Foucault, Michel
Faré, Marco: Hacking; Piracy
Gaines, Elliot: Analog Media; Audience; Blogs; Digital Media; Situation Comedy
Gardiner, Michael E.: Bakhtin, Mikhail Mikhailovich

Gibson, Twyla: Electronic Media; Global Village; Information; Orality
Green, R.: Priming
Guertin, Carolyn: Convergence; Media Literacy
Gunster, Shane: Frankfurt School and Critical Theory
Hara, Shinsuke: Wireless Communication
Holmes, David: Communication Theory
Holmes, Su: Reality TV
Kassam, Faiza Hirji: Feminism
Kellner, Douglas: Baudrillard, Jean; Jameson, Fredric
Krätke, Stefan: Media Cities
Lapierre, Matthew: Cartoons
Lim, Alexander: Cyberculture; Email; Instant Messaging; Magazines; MP3; On-
    line Culture
Lorusso, Anna Maria: Eco, Umberto
Maclean, Siobhan: Culture Jamming
McKay, Susan: Tabloids
Maida-Nicol, Sara: Diglossia
Muchie, Mammo: Digital Divide
Murray, S.J.: Global Village
Nuessel, Frank: Alphabets; Books; Code; Culture and Communication; Culture
    Industry Theory; Medium; Pictography; Print Culture; Propoganda Theory
Palangi, Angela: Interactivity; Photography; Pornography; Radway, Janice;
    Reception Theory
Perron, Paul: Narrative
Petrilli, Susan: British Cultural Theory; Gramsci, Antonio; Ideology Theory;
    Marxism
Ponzio, Augusto: Adorno, Theodor; Althusser, Louis; Benjamin, Walter; Frank-
    furt School; Marcuse, Herbert
Postle, Tricia: Vaudeville
Poveda, Lucía Amorós: Educational Technology; Multimedia
Quan-Haase, Anabel: Internet; Mass Communication; Mediated Communication;
    Two-Step Flow Model; Uses and Gratifications Theory
Rasti, Maryam: Websites; Wikipedia
Rocci, Andrea: Discourse Theory
Shaw, Adrienne: Video Games
Søgaard, Anders: Cable Television; Fanzines; Functionalist Theories; Journalism
Tardini, S.: World Wide Web
Thompson, William: Priming
Vatikiotis, Pantelis: Chomsky, Noam; Curran, James
Wensley, Anthony: Defamation
Wolff, Per-Erik: Media Products
Zarkin, Kimberly A.: Federal Communications Commission